Longman
Pocket
Roget's®
Thesaurus

Edited by
Susan M. Lloyd BA MPhil

VIKING

Contents

Preface

What is a thesaurus?

A thesaurus is an extensive collection of English words, expressions and phrases, ranging from the literary to the colloquial, from the technical and scientific to the theoretical. This collection is arranged under headings according to meaning and incorporates helpful cross-referencing.

What is it for?

A thesaurus brings together a wide range of ways to express the same idea, using synonyms, negatives, idioms, similes and different parts of speech. Whether you are using it to find a word you have temporarily forgotten, or to find a more specific or more formal term, a thesaurus helps you to express your thoughts more clearly and effectively, and at the same time to increase your vocabulary and knowledge of the language.

The Longman Pocket Roget's Thesaurus

This new version of the classic Roget's Thesaurus contains the most up-to-date vocabulary and a unique Word Finder. The Word Finder is much more than an index: it is the key to your search, noting and relating *every* appearance of a given word or phrase in the text. Slang is kept to a minimum; obsolete, rare, over-specialised and narrowly technical words have not been included. The aim has been to provide a broad general and easily accessible vocabulary of modern English.

How to use the thesaurus

The thesaurus consists of a Word Finder, arranged alphabetically, and the text, subdivided into Heads, which is arranged numerically. To find a range of expressions for your chosen idea, simply follow these steps:

easy 220 (4), 376 (4), 516
(2), 701 (3), 848 (6), 880
(6)

1 look up in the Word Finder a
word expressing your idea, or a
word for which you wish to find an
alternative: take 'easy' for
example.

2 You will find your word is
followed by one or more numbered
references. The number before the
brackets is the number of the Head
where that word appears, in this
case, 701.

701
Facility

Noun ... ...
(1) *facility*, ease, convenience,
comfort; capability, feasibility
469 *possibility*; easing, making
easy, smoothing, simplification, free hand, full play; clean
slate 744 *scope*; facilities, provision for 703 *aid*; leave 756
permission; simplicity, no difficulty; easy going, plain seen;
downhill 309 *descent*.

(2) *easy thing*, no trouble, a
pleasure, child's play; short
work, light work, sinecure; picnic, piece of cake 837 *amusement*; plain sailing, easy ride,
nothing to it, easy target, sitting duck, walkover 727 *victory*; cinch 473 *certainty*.

Adjective
(3) *easy*, effortless, undemanding, painless; frictionless 258
smooth; not hard, foolproof;
easily done, feasible 469 *possible*; facilitating, helpful 703
aiding; downhill, downstream,
with the current; convenient
376 *comfortable*; approachable,
289 *accessible*; comprehensible
516 *intelligible*.

3 Turn to Head 701 in the text.
Here there are a variety of ways of
expressing 'facility', arranged in
paragraphs according to whether
they are nouns, verbs, adjectives or
adverbs (not all parts of speech are
necessarily represented in each
Head).

4 The number in brackets tells
you which paragraph contains the
word you looked up in the Word
Finder. 'Easy' had the reference
701(3), so it appears in the third
paragraph, the first of two
paragraphs of adjectives. Here are
many alternatives for 'easy',
arranged according to shades of
meaning. Some of these may be
dealt with more fully under
another Head – this is then given
as a cross-reference, consisting of
the Head number and the word
printed in italics at the beginning
of the relevant paragraph.

5 If you cannot find a suitable word amongst the adjectives try looking at the nouns or verbs. Sometimes the use of an opposite expression can be more effective – most Heads are grouped in pairs of opposite meanings. The surrounding Heads may be helpful too – Heads of similar meaning are grouped together.

6 Many English words have several meanings, or shades of meaning. If you cannot find the exact meaning you require try looking up one of the other references. A glance at the Classification table (see below) may help you to choose the most likely references of those given.

Roget's Classification System

A general idea of how the various Heads are interconnected will help you to use the thesaurus most effectively. They follow a logical progression. The first part of the book deals with the world around us, from abstract ideas to the physical universe . The second part is concerned with human beings: the human mind, the human will, and the human spirit.

CLASS ONE
Abstract Relationships (Heads 1–182) abstract ideas such as order, number, quantity, time, cause and effect.

CLASS TWO
Spatial Relationships (Heads 183–318) size, shape, movement, presence, etc.

CLASS THREE
The Material Universe (Heads 319–446) the universe, life, the five senses.

CLASS FOUR
Human Beings

 i) *the mind* (Heads 447–594) intellectual activities; communication by means of art and language.

 ii) *the will* (Heads 595–816) planning, doing, opposition and conflict, authority, having and getting.

iii) *the spirit* (Heads 817–987) emotions; morality and the law; spirituality and religion.

Word Finder

A

a 88 (3)

A-bomb 723 (14)

A1 34 (5), 644 (6)

à la 18 (4)

à la carte 301 (12), 605 (9)

à la mode 848 (5)

a priori 5 (6), 848 (8)

A.B. 270 (1)

abacus 86 (6)

abandon 41 (6), 296 (4), 458 (5), 603 (5), 621 (3), 779 (4), 822 (2), 833 (2), 918 (3), 943 (1), 944 (1)

abandon hope 853 (4)

abandon oneself 835 (6)

abandoned 41 (4), 46 (5), 621 (2), 774 (3), 779 (3), 934 (4)

abandonment 621 (1), 779 (1), 822 (2), 824 (1), 835 (1)

abase 165 (9), 311 (7), 655 (8)

abasement 867 (1), 872 (1), 872 (2), 879 (1)

abash 872 (7)

abashed 872 (4)

abate 27 (5), 37 (4), 37 (5), 39 (3), 51 (5), 105 (4), 163 (10), 177 (6), 198 (7), 204 (5), 309 (3), 352 (10)

abatement 198 (1), 831 (1)

abattoir 362 (5)

abbess 986 (6)

abbey 192 (6), 986 (9), 990 (3)

abbot 986 (5)

abbreviate 39 (3), 204 (5), 569 (3), 592 (5)

abbreviated 204 (3), 569 (2)

abbreviation 33 (1), 198 (1), 204 (2), 559 (1), 569 (1), 592 (1)

abbreviator 592 (3)

ABC 68 (1), 524 (6), 534 (3), 558 (1)

ABC (guidebook) 87 (3)

abdicate 621 (3), 734 (5), 753 (3)

abdicating 753 (2)

abdication 753 (1), 916 (3)

abdication of authority 734 (1)

abdicator 753 (1)

abdomen 194 (3), 224 (2)

abdominal 194 (25)

abduct 786 (9), 788 (7)

abduction 786 (1), 788 (1)

abductor 786 (4), 789 (1)

abeam 239 (4)

aberrant 84 (5), 188 (2), 282 (2), 294 (2), 495 (4)

aberration 84 (2), 188 (1), 282 (1), 294 (1), 456 (1)

abet 181 (3), 703 (5)

abetment 156 (1), 706 (1)

abetting 181 (2), 703 (4)

abettor 156 (2), 612 (5)

abeyance 145 (4), 674 (1), 677 (1)

abhor 769 (3), 888 (7), 924 (9)

abhorrence 769 (1), 861 (1), 888 (1)

abhorrent 888 (4), 888 (5)

abhorring 861 (2)

abide 1 (6), 108 (7), 113 (6), 144 (3), 192 (21)

abide by 488 (7), 532 (5), 768 (3)

abiding 113 (4)

ability 5 (1), 160 (2), 178 (1), 469 (1), 498 (1), 629 (1), 640 (1), 694 (1)

abject 856 (3), 867 (4), 879 (3), 922 (4), 930 (5)

abject fear 854 (1), 856 (1)

abjuration 533 (1), 603 (2), 753 (1)

abjure 533 (3), 603 (7)

ablaze 379 (5), 417 (8)

able 160 (8), 469 (2), 498 (4), 640 (2), 694 (4)

able, be 28 (9), 160 (10), 629 (2)

able-bodied 162 (8), 678 (7)

able seaman 270 (1), 722 (12)

able to pay 800 (4)

able to speak 579 (6)

ablutionary 648 (8)

ablutions 339 (1), 341 (2), 383 (2), 648 (3)

abnormal 17 (2), 84 (7), 188 (3), 503 (7), 503 (8), 517 (3), 565 (2), 914 (3), 951 (9), 970 (7)

abnormality 17 (1), 84 (2), 188 (1), 246 (2), 503 (5), 951 (3)

aboard 189 (6), 275 (12)

abode 184 (3), 187 (2), 187 (3), 192 (1)

abolish 2 (8), 165 (6), 752 (4)

abolished 161 (5)

abolition 165 (1), 752 (1)

abominable 645 (4), 861 (3), 888 (5), 934 (6)

abominably 32 (18)

abominate 888 (7)

abomination 861 (1), 888 (1), 888 (3)

aboriginal 68 (6), 127 (5), 191 (3), 191 (6)

aborigine 135 (1)

aborigines 191 (3)

abort 167 (6), 172 (5), 728 (8)

aborted 728 (4)

abortion 84 (2), 670 (2), 728 (1)

abortive 172 (4), 509 (3), 641 (5), 670 (4), 728 (4)

abound 635 (7), 637 (5)

about 9 (10), 33 (12), 200 (8), 230 (4)

about, be 200 (5)

about face 286 (5), 603 (1)

about the size of it 18 (1)

about to 124 (7), 179 (2)

about to be 155 (2)

about to burst 330 (2)

about-turn 148 (1), 282 (4), 286 (2), 603 (1)

above 64 (5), 209 (14), 238 (6)

above all 34 (12), 638 (9)

above average 34 (4)

above-board 540 (2) 699 (3)

abundantly **32** (17)

abuse **176** (8), **616** (1), **634** (4), **645** (7), **655** (8), **675** (1), **675** (2), **735** (7), **867** (2), **885** (6), **899** (2), **899** (6), **899** (7), **921** (5), **924** (10), **924** (13), **926** (1), **951** (11)

abuse one's authority **735** (8)

abused **163** (5)

abusive **709** (6), **885** (5), **899** (4), **900** (2), **926** (5)

abut **200** (5)

abut on **202** (3)

abutment **202** (1), **218** (2), **713** (3)

abutting **202** (2)

abysmal **211** (2)

abyss **201** (2), **211** (1), **255** (2), **663** (1), **972** (1)

academic **10** (4), **492** (2), **512** (3), **512** (4), **534** (5), **536** (3)

academic circles **492** (1)

academic dress **228** (4)

academic honour **866** (4)

academic title **870** (2)

academician **492** (2)

academy **490** (2), **539** (1)

accede **758** (3)

accede to the throne **733** (11)

accelerate **36** (5), **135** (5), **174** (7), **277** (7), **279** (7), **285** (4), **680** (3), **821** (7)

acceleration **36** (1), **277** (2), **680** (1)

accent **398** (1), **532** (1), **532** (7), **547** (14), **560** (2), **577** (2), **577** (4), **580** (1), **593** (5)

accented **577** (3)

accents **577** (1), **579** (1)

accentuate **532** (7)

accentuated **577** (3)

accentuation **564** (1), **577** (2), **593** (5)

accept **299** (3), **485** (7), **487** (3), **488** (6), **488** (7), **721** (3), **758** (3), **782** (4), **786** (6), **923** (8)

accept an apology **909** (4)

accept battle **718** (12)

accept from **782** (4)

accept gracefully **907** (4)

accept payment **962** (4)

accept responsibility **917** (9)

accept the call **917** (9)

acceptable **299** (2), **642** (2), **826** (2), **828** (3), **859** (10)

acceptance **299** (1), **488** (1), **758** (1), **782** (1), **923** (1)

accepted on trust **485** (6)

access **68** (5), **263** (6), **289** (1), **297** (1), **297** (2), **299** (1), **305** (1), **318** (2), **624** (2)

accessibility **289** (1)

accessible **200** (4), **263** (13), **289** (3), **299** (2), **469** (2), **624** (8), **701** (3), **744** (5)

accession **38** (1), **289** (1), **295** (1), **733** (1)

accessories **228** (1)

accessory **6** (2), **40** (1), **89** (2), **637** (2), **639** (2), **703** (4), **707** (3)

accessory to, be **703** (5)

accidence **564** (1)

accident **6** (1), **154** (1), **159** (1), **279** (3), **616** (1), **618** (1), **731** (2)

accident-prone **731** (6)

accidental **6** (2), **154** (4), **159** (5), **410** (2), **618** (5)

accidentally **159** (8)

acclaim **488** (6), **866** (1), **866** (13), **923** (3), **923** (10)

acclaimed **866** (10)

acclamation **923** (3)

acclimatize **610** (8), **669** (11)

acclimatized **610** (7)

accolade **866** (4), **923** (2)

accommodate **24** (10), **28** (10), **78** (5), **187** (5), **703** (5), **719** (4), **784** (5)

accommodate oneself **83** (7)

accommodating **78** (2), **83** (4), **897** (4)

accommodation **24** (4), **78** (1), **83** (1), **183** (4), **192** (2), **719** (1)

accompaniment **80** (1), **89** (1), **89** (2), **123** (1)

accompanist **89** (2), **413** (2)

accompany **89** (4), **123** (4), **181** (3), **202** (3), **284** (4), **413** (9), **689** (5), **742** (8), **884** (7), **889** (7)

accompanying **89** (3), **181** (2)

accomplice **89** (2), **707** (3)

accomplish **676** (5), **725** (6), **727** (6)

accomplished **694** (4)

accomplishment **164** (1), **694** (1), **725** (2), **727** (1)

accomplishments **490** (3)

accord **13** (3), **16** (3), **24** (1), **24** (9), **28** (9), **50** (4), **60** (4), **83** (7), **158** (3), **181** (3), **410** (9), **488** (6), **710** (3), **758** (1), **758** (3), **781** (7)

accord an ovation **886** (3)

accordance **16** (1), **488** (1)

according as **8** (5)

according to **24** (5), **83** (10)

according to plan **83** (10)

according to rule **81** (3), **83** (6)

accordingly **8** (5)

accordion **414** (5)

accost **289** (4), **583** (3), **761** (5), **884** (7)

accosting **761** (1)

account **86** (11), **87** (1), **485** (8), **524** (2), **548** (8), **588** (1), **590** (1), **797** (2), **802** (1), **803** (1), **804** (4), **808** (1), **808** (5), **866** (2)

account book **87** (1), **548** (1), **808** (2)

account for **156** (9), **158** (4), **520** (8)

account owing **803** (1)

account rendered **808** (1)

accountability **180** (1)

accountable **808** (4), **917** (5)

accountancy 86 (1), 808 (1)

accountant 86 (7), 549 (1), 798 (1), 808 (3)

accounting 808 (1), 808 (4)

accounting for 158 (1)

accounts 86 (1), 548 (2), 802 (1), 808 (1)

accoutrements 228 (1)

accredit 751 (4)

accredited 485 (6), 751 (3)

accretion 38 (1), 40 (1), 59 (1)

accrue 6 (3), 38 (4), 157 (5), 782 (5)

accumulate 36 (4), 45 (9), 74 (11), 632 (5), 771 (7), 786 (6)

accumulation 32 (2), 36 (1), 43 (4), 62 (1), 74 (7), 632 (1), 632 (2), 632 (3), 771 (1)

accumulative 771 (4)

accumulator 74 (8), 160 (6)

accuracy 20 (2), 455 (1), 457 (1), 494 (3), 540 (1), 567 (1)

accurate 24 (8), 80 (6), 455 (2), 457 (3), 494 (6), 520 (6), 540 (2), 567 (2), 590 (6), 699 (3)

accurately 494 (8)

accursed 659 (5), 731 (6), 825 (6), 827 (4), 888 (5), 899 (5), 934 (6), 980 (5)

accusable 924 (8), 928 (7), 954 (5), 963 (7)

accusation 532 (1), 914 (1), 924 (2), 926 (1), 928 (1), 959 (1)

accuse 158 (3), 524 (9), 526 (5), 528 (10), 714 (3), 924 (10), 924 (12), 926 (7), 928 (8), 959 (7)

accuse oneself 939 (4)

accused 928 (6), 959 (4)

accused person 750 (1), 928 (4), 959 (4)

accused, the 928 (4)

accuser 524 (5), 926 (3), 928 (3), 959 (4)

accusing 466 (5), 924 (6), 928 (5), 959 (5)

accustom 534 (8), 610 (8)

accustom oneself 610 (8)

accustomed 610 (6), 865 (2)

accustomed to 610 (7)

ace 88 (2), 696 (1)

acerbic 393 (2)

acerbity 388 (1), 391 (1), 393 (1), 885 (2)

aces 629 (1)

acetic 393 (2)

ache 377 (2), 377 (5), 377 (6), 645 (1), 825 (7)

achievable 469 (2)

achieve 69 (6), 628 (4), 676 (5), 725 (6), 727 (6)

achieve liberty 667 (5), 738 (10), 746 (4)

achieve marvels 864 (7)

achieve one's aim 642 (3)

achieve victory 727 (11)

achieved 725 (4)

achievement 164 (1), 285 (1), 547 (11), 676 (2), 725 (1), 725 (2), 727 (1)

achiever 676 (3)

Achilles' heel 661 (2)

aching 377 (1), 377 (3), 377 (4), 684 (2), 825 (5), 827 (3)

aching heart 825 (2)

aching muscles 684 (1)

achromatism 426 (1)

acid 168 (1), 174 (6), 391 (2), 393 (1), 393 (2), 393 (3), 659 (3), 949 (4)

acid drops 301 (18)

acid-forming 393 (2)

acid test 461 (1)

acid yellow 433 (3)

acidity 388 (1), 393 (1)

acidulous 393 (2)

ack-ack 723 (11)

acknowledge 158 (3), 460 (5), 488 (6), 526 (6), 588 (4), 768 (3), 782 (4), 884 (7), 907 (5), 915 (2), 962 (3), 981 (11)

acknowledge a claim 915 (8)

acknowledged 526 (2), 807 (2)

acknowledgement 158 (1), 460 (1), 588 (1), 907 (2)

acknowledging 907 (3)

acme 213 (1), 845 (1)

acne 651 (12)

acolyte 707 (1), 986 (7), 988 (6)

acoustic 398 (3), 415 (5)

acoustician 398 (2)

acoustics 398 (2), 415 (1)

acquaint 524 (9)

acquaint oneself 490 (8)

acquaintance 490 (1), 524 (1), 880 (1), 880 (3)

acquainted 490 (5), 880 (6)

acquainted with, be 490 (8)

acquiesce 181 (3), 488 (7), 597 (6), 721 (3), 758 (3)

acquiescence 83 (1), 181 (1), 488 (1), 597 (1), 721 (1), 739 (1), 753 (1), 756 (1), 758 (1), 823 (2)

acquiescent 24 (5), 488 (4), 597 (4), 721 (2), 739 (3), 823 (3), 828 (2)

acquire 74 (11), 148 (3), 629 (2), 656 (13), 771 (7), 780 (5), 782 (4), 785 (2), 786 (6), 792 (5)

acquire knowledge 536 (4)

acquire the habit 610 (8)

acquired 6 (2), 771 (6)

acquirement 694 (1), 771 (1)

acquiring 771 (4), 786 (5), 816 (5)

acquisition 74 (1), 272 (1), 632 (1), 771 (1), 782 (1), 786 (1), 807 (1)

acquisitive 771 (4), 786 (5), 816 (5), 859 (8), 932 (3)

acquisitiveness 816 (2), 932 (1)

acquit 668 (3), 746 (3), 909 (4), 917 (10), 919 (3), 927 (6), 960 (3) acquit oneself **688** (4)

acquittal **667** (1), **668** (1), **746** (1), **768** (1), **905** (3), **909** (1), **917** (1), **919** (1), **927** (1), **960** (1), **988** (4)

acquitted **744** (5), **746** (2), **909** (3), **919** (2), **935** (4), **960** (2)

acreage **183** (2), **777** (3)

acres **183** (2)

acrid **388** (3), **391** (2), **397** (2)

acridity **388** (1), **391** (1)

acrimonious **885** (5), **891** (3)

acrimony **174** (3), **885** (2), **891** (1), **898** (1)

acrobat **162** (4), **594** (10)

acrobatic **162** (9), **327** (3)

acrobatics **162** (3)

acronym **558** (2)

across **220** (3), **220** (7), **222** (11)

across the counter **791** (7)

acrostic **518** (1), **530** (2), **558** (2)

acrostics **837** (8)

acrylic fibre **208** (2)

act **20** (5), **173** (3), **541** (2), **541** (6), **594** (2), **594** (4), **594** (17), **628** (4), **676** (2), **676** (5), **688** (4), **727** (7), **737** (2)

act a part **850** (5)

act foolishly **138** (6), **495** (8), **499** (6), **695** (8), **849** (4), **857** (4)

act for **755** (3)

act like a tonic **174** (8)

act of believing **485** (1)

act of choosing **605** (1)

act of courtesy **884** (2)

act of folly **499** (2)

act of God **165** (3), **596** (1), **740** (1)

act of inhumanity **898** (3)

act of judgment **480** (1)

act of submission **721** (1)

act of theft **788** (1)

act of will **595** (0)

act of worship **981** (3), **988** (5)

act out **69** (6)

act the role **594** (17)

act upon **612** (8), **676** (5), **739** (4)

acted **594** (15)

acted upon **173** (2)

acting **114** (4), **150** (4), **173** (2), **541** (2), **541** (4), **551** (1), **594** (8), **594** (15), **676** (4)

acting for **755** (2)

action **154** (1), **173** (1), **623** (2), **676** (1), **676** (2), **678** (1), **688** (1), **716** (7), **718** (7), **725** (2), **768** (1), **928** (1), **959** (1)

action painting **553** (3)

actionable **928** (7), **953** (5), **954** (5), **959** (6)

activate **174** (8)

activation **174** (2), **678** (1)

activator **143** (1), **174** (4)

active **154** (5), **174** (5), **265** (3), **318** (4), **597** (4), **622** (5), **676** (4), **678** (7), **682** (4), **821** (3)

active, be **173** (3), **174** (7), **678** (11), **680** (3), **682** (6), **688** (4), **704** (5), **897** (6)

active in, be **676** (5)

active interest **678** (1)

active service **718** (6)

actively **32** (17), **678** (14)

activeness **676** (1), **678** (1)

activism **678** (1)

activist **671** (2), **678** (5), **708** (2)

activity **174** (1), **174** (2), **265** (1), **622** (1), **622** (3), **628** (1), **676** (1), **678** (1), **680** (1), **687** (1), **818** (2)

actor **20** (3), **150** (2), **445** (3), **520** (4), **579** (5), **594** (9), **676** (3), **708** (1), **837** (14)

actor-manager **594** (9)

actress **594** (9)

actual **1** (5), **121** (2), **494** (4)

actuality **1** (2)

actually **1** (8), **3** (4)

actuarial **808** (4)

actuary **86** (7), **808** (3)

actuate **173** (3), **265** (5), **612** (8)

acuity **498** (2)

acumen **498** (2)

acupuncture **263** (2), **375** (2), **658** (10), **658** (12)

acupuncturist **658** (14)

acute **174** (6), **176** (5), **256** (7), **374** (3), **374** (4), **407** (2), **498** (4), **698** (4)

acute angle **247** (2)

acute ear **415** (1)

acutely **32** (17)

acuteness **256** (1), **498** (2)

AD **108** (12), **120** (2), **528** (3)

ad hoc **80** (9), **609** (3), **609** (5), **670** (3)

ad infinitum **107** (3)

ad-lib **579** (9), **594** (17), **595** (3), **609** (4), **670** (3)

ad-libbing **609** (1)

ad nauseam **106** (7), **570** (7), **838** (6)

adage **496** (1)

adagio **278** (7), **410** (4), **412** (8)

Adam and Eve **66** (1)

adamant **602** (4)

Adam's apple **253** (2)

adapt **24** (10), **143** (6), **520** (9)

adapt oneself **83** (7)

adaptability **327** (1), **640** (1), **694** (1)

adaptable **24** (7), **83** (4), **640** (2), **694** (4)

adaptation **24** (4), **83** (1), **143** (2), **494** (3), **520** (3), **589** (5)

adapted **83** (4)

adapter **143** (3), **589** (7)

add **36** (5), **38** (3), **45** (11), **48** (4), **50** (4), **54** (6), **54** (7), **64** (4), **65** (4), **86** (12), **197** (5), **303** (4), **546** (3)

add a flourish **546** (3)

add a meaning **521** (3)

add on **38** (3)

add to **38** (3), **45** (9)

add up **38** (3)

add up to **86** (11), **514** (5)

add water **339** (3), **341** (7)

added 38 (2), 303 (3)
added, be 38 (4)
added to 546 (2)
addenda 589 (5)
addendum 40 (1)
adder 365 (13)
addict 504 (3), 610 (4), 651 (18)
addicted 949 (10)
addicted to 610 (7)
addiction 610 (1), 943 (1)
addictive 949 (12)
adding 36 (1), 303 (1)
adding to 38 (1), 832 (1)
adding up 38 (1)
addition 36 (1), 36 (2), 38 (1), 40 (1), 43 (1), 45 (2), 52 (1), 59 (1), 85 (4), 86 (2), 197 (1), 303 (1), 546 (1)
additional 6 (2), 36 (3), 38 (2), 65 (2), 303 (3), 637 (4)
additionally 38 (5)
additive 38 (2), 40 (2), 301 (10)
address 185 (1), 186 (1), 187 (2), 192 (1), 272 (8), 579 (1), 579 (2), 579 (9), 583 (1), 583 (3), 624 (1), 694 (1)
address oneself to 68 (8), 672 (3)
addressee 191 (2), 588 (2), 782 (2)
adduce 466 (8)
adenoidal 580 (2)
adenoids 253 (2)
adept 696 (1)
adequacy 635 (1), 640 (1)
adequate 635 (3), 640 (2), 732 (2)
adequate income 635 (1)
adhere 38 (4), 48 (3), 202 (3)
adhere to 768 (3)
adherence 48 (1)
adherence to 768 (1)
adherent 48 (2), 284 (2), 707 (1), 765 (3), 973 (7), 978 (14)
adhering to 768 (2)
adhesion 48 (1), 202 (1)

adhesive 45 (5), 45 (6), 47 (9), 48 (1), 48 (2), 354 (3), 778 (3)
adhesive tape 47 (9)
adhesiveness 48 (1), 354 (3)
adieu 296 (7)
adieus 296 (2)
adjacency 200 (1)
adjacent 200 (4), 202 (2)
adjectival 564 (3)
adjective 564 (2)
adjoin 200 (5), 202 (3)
adjoining 200 (4), 202 (2)
adjourn 136 (7), 145 (8)
adjournment 108 (2), 136 (2)
adjudge 480 (5)
adjudicate 480 (5)
adjudication 480 (1)
adjudicator 480 (3)
adjunct 38 (1), 40 (1), 53 (1), 53 (4), 53 (5), 56 (1), 66 (1), 67 (1), 69 (2), 89 (2), 197 (1), 231 (4), 630 (4)
adjuration 532 (1), 532 (2), 761 (2)
adjure 532 (5), 761 (7)
adjust 24 (10), 28 (10), 60 (3), 62 (5), 83 (8), 117 (7), 123 (4), 143 (6), 177 (6), 410 (9), 623 (8), 654 (10), 669 (11), 719 (4)
adjust oneself 83 (7)
adjustable 83 (4)
adjusted 24 (8), 50 (3), 83 (4), 494 (6)
adjustment 24 (4), 28 (4), 83 (1), 143 (1), 719 (1), 770 (1)
adjutant 707 (1), 741 (8)
admass 544 (1)
administer 673 (3), 676 (5), 689 (4), 783 (3)
administer justice 955 (5)
administration 62 (1), 689 (1)
administrative 689 (3), 733 (9), 955 (4)
administrator 686 (1), 690 (3)

admirable 644 (4), 864 (5), 866 (8), 923 (6)
admirably 923 (13)
admiral 722 (12), 741 (7)
admiralty 722 (11)
Admiralty chart 551 (5)
admiration 864 (1), 887 (1), 920 (1), 923 (1)
admire 864 (6), 887 (13), 920 (5), 923 (8)
admire oneself 873 (5)
admired 920 (4)
admirer 887 (4), 923 (4)
admiring 887 (9), 920 (3), 923 (5)
admiringly 923 (12)
admissibility 24 (3), 78 (1)
admissible 24 (6), 78 (3), 299 (2)
admission 78 (1), 297 (1), 299 (1), 466 (2), 488 (1), 526 (1), 532 (1)
admit 38 (3), 56 (4), 78 (5), 231 (8), 263 (17), 299 (3), 466 (7), 475 (9), 488 (6), 526 (6), 532 (5), 782 (4), 786 (6)
admit defeat 721 (3), 728 (9), 834 (9)
admit of 469 (3)
admit one's a 121 (3)
admittance 297 (1), 299 (1), 782 (1)
admitted 58 (2), 78 (3), 488 (5)
admitting 299 (2)
admixture 43 (1), 43 (2)
admonish 664 (5), 691 (4), 924 (11)
admonisher 664 (2), 691 (2)
admonishment 664 (1)
admonition 613 (1), 924 (4)
admonitory 664 (3), 691 (3)
ado 678 (1)
adolescence 130 (1)
adolescent 130 (4), 132 (2), 670 (4)
adopt 11 (7), 605 (6), 673 (4)

adopted 38 (2), 170 (4), 605 (5), 979 (8)

adopted child 11 (3)

adoption 169 (1), 605 (1), 923 (1)

adoptive 170 (4)

adoptive father 169 (3)

adorable 841 (3), 887 (11)

adoration 979 (1), 981 (1)

adore 887 (13), 920 (5), 981 (11)

adoring 887 (9)

adorn 574 (6), 844 (12)

adorned 844 (10)

adornment 844 (1)

adrift 10 (3), 46 (5), 46 (15), 75 (2), 282 (7)

adroit 694 (4)

adroitness 694 (1)

adulation 546 (1), 923 (2), 925 (1)

adulator 925 (2)

adulatory 925 (3)

adult 134 (2), 134 (3), 669 (8)

adult education 534 (2)

adulterate 43 (7), 143 (6), 655 (9)

adulterated 43 (6), 163 (5)

adulteration 43 (1), 163 (1), 339 (1), 647 (1), 655 (3)

adulterer 952 (1)

adulteress 952 (2)

adulterous 951 (9)

adultery 887 (3), 951 (3)

adulthood 134 (1)

adultness 131 (2), 134 (1), 373 (1), 669 (4)

adumbrate 155 (4), 551 (8), 590 (7)

adumbration 524 (3)

advance 36 (1), 36 (4), 53 (1), 64 (4), 156 (10), 265 (1), 267 (11), 285 (1), 285 (3), 285 (4), 289 (1), 289 (4), 628 (4), 640 (4), 642 (3), 654 (1), 654 (8), 654 (9), 703 (5), 727 (6), 759 (1), 784 (1), 784 (5), 866 (14)

advance against 712 (10)

advance guard 237 (1)

advance notice 664 (1)

advance upon 289 (4)

advanced 126 (6), 135 (4), 285 (2)

advanced guard 664 (2)

advanced in years 131 (6)

advanced studies 534 (2)

advanced technology 630 (3)

advanced thinker 126 (3)

advanced years 131 (3)

advancement 36 (1), 285 (1), 654 (1), 866 (5)

advances 289 (1), 889 (1), 889 (2)

advancing 289 (2)

advantage 34 (2), 159 (3), 160 (1), 615 (2), 640 (1), 642 (1), 688 (2), 727 (1), 727 (2), 771 (3), 778 (1)

advantageous 615 (3), 640 (3), 642 (2), 644 (8), 771 (5)

advent 124 (1), 289 (1), 295 (1)

adventitious 6 (2), 38 (2), 159 (5)

adventure 154 (1), 672 (1), 855 (6)

adventurer 268 (1), 461 (3), 618 (4), 722 (3), 857 (2)

adventures 590 (3)

adventurous 618 (7), 672 (2), 855 (4), 857 (3)

adverb 564 (2)

adverbial 564 (3)

adversary 705 (1)

adverse 14 (3), 138 (3), 511 (7), 616 (2), 643 (2), 645 (3), 702 (6), 704 (3), 731 (4), 827 (5), 853 (3)

adversity 154 (2), 165 (3), 616 (1), 659 (1), 700 (1), 731 (1), 825 (1), 825 (2), 827 (1)

advert 528 (3)

advertise 455 (7), 511 (8), 524 (10), 528 (11), 638 (8), 877 (5), 923 (9)

advertisement 522 (2), 524 (1), 528 (3), 531 (4), 612 (2), 761 (1), 793 (1)

advertiser 522 (3), 524 (4), 528 (6), 612 (5), 923 (4)

advertising 528 (2), 612 (2)

advertising agent 528 (6)

advertising copy 528 (3)

advice 480 (2), 524 (1), 524 (3), 584 (3), 612 (2), 669 (1), 691 (1), 693 (1)

advice against 691 (1)

advisability 642 (1)

advisable 8 (3), 24 (7), 137 (5), 173 (2), 469 (2), 498 (5), 605 (5), 640 (2), 642 (2), 673 (2)

advise 524 (9), 524 (11), 612 (9), 664 (5), 691 (4)

advise against 613 (3), 664 (5), 691 (4), 762 (3)

advised, be 691 (5)

advisedly 617 (7)

adviser 480 (3), 500 (1), 524 (4), 537 (1), 612 (5), 664 (2), 678 (6), 691 (2), 696 (2), 703 (3), 720 (2), 754 (1)

advising 480 (4), 524 (7), 584 (5), 691 (3)

advising against 691 (3)

advisory 480 (4), 524 (7), 584 (5), 691 (3)

advisory board 692 (1)

advocacy 612 (2), 703 (1), 958 (5)

advocate 231 (3), 579 (5), 612 (5), 612 (9), 691 (2), 691 (4), 707 (4), 923 (4), 923 (8), 927 (2), 927 (5), 958 (1), 958 (2), 958 (7), 959 (7)

aegis 660 (2)

aeon 110 (2)

aerate 323 (5), 336 (4), 340 (6), 355 (5), 382 (6), 652 (6), 685 (4)

aerated 323 (3), 325 (2), 340 (5), 355 (3)

aeration 336 (1), 340 (1)

aerial 209 (8), 271 (6), 340 (5), 531 (3)

aerial warfare 718 (6)

aerobatic 271 (6)

aerobatics 271 (1)

aerodrome 271 (2)
aerodynamic 271 (6), 276 (5), 336 (3)
aerodynamics 271 (1), 336 (1), 340 (4), 352 (2)
aerofoil 271 (5), 276 (1)
aeronaut 268 (1), 271 (4)
aeronautical 271 (6), 276 (5)
aeronautics 271 (1), 276 (1), 308 (1), 313 (1), 837 (6)
aeroplane 276 (1)
aerosol 287 (3), 338 (2)
aerospace 271 (1), 271 (6), 276 (5), 340 (2)
aesthete 846 (2)
aesthetic 374 (3), 819 (3), 841 (3), 846 (3)
aesthetician 556 (1)
aestheticism 846 (1)
aesthetics 374 (1), 841 (1), 846 (1)
aetiological 156 (7)
aetiology 156 (1)
afar 199 (6)
affability 882 (2), 884 (1)
affable 882 (6), 884 (4)
affair 452 (1), 645 (1)
affair of honour 716 (6)
affairs 154 (2), 622 (1), 676 (2)
affect 9 (7), 178 (3), 179 (3), 522 (8), 541 (6), 614 (4), 638 (7), 821 (6), 821 (8), 850 (5)
affectation 20 (1), 491 (3), 497 (2), 519 (2), 542 (5), 543 (2), 560 (1), 574 (2), 576 (1), 688 (1), 839 (1), 848 (1), 850 (1), 871 (1), 873 (2), 922 (1), 950 (2)
affected 20 (4), 147 (5), 483 (2), 491 (7), 497 (3), 519 (3), 541 (4), 543 (4), 574 (4), 576 (2), 651 (22), 817 (2), 818 (4), 847 (4), 847 (5), 848 (5), 849 (2), 850 (4), 871 (4), 873 (4), 875 (4), 950 (6), 979 (7)
affected, be 522 (8), 541 (7), 688 (4), 850 (5), 873 (5), 875 (7)

affectedness 20 (1)
affecter 545 (3), 850 (3)
affecting 818 (6), 821 (4), 827 (6)
affection 819 (1), 887 (1), 923 (1)
affectionate 887 (9), 889 (4), 897 (4)
affectionately 887 (16)
affections 5 (4), 7 (1), 178 (1), 817 (1)
affidavit 466 (2), 532 (2), 959 (1)
affiliation 11 (1), 158 (1), 706 (2)
affinity 9 (1), 11 (1), 18 (1), 179 (1), 291 (1), 859 (3)
affirm 158 (3), 466 (7), 473 (8), 479 (3), 485 (7), 512 (6), 514 (4), 522 (7), 528 (10), 532 (5), 563 (3), 579 (8), 614 (4), 737 (7), 764 (4), 855 (6)
affirmation 160 (1), 466 (2), 488 (1), 522 (1), 532 (1), 571 (1), 579 (1), 614 (1), 638 (1), 764 (1), 959 (1)
affirmative 473 (5), 522 (5), 532 (3), 571 (2)
affirmatively 532 (8)
affirming 532 (3)
affix 38 (3), 40 (1), 45 (11), 48 (4), 67 (1), 564 (2)
affixture 38 (1)
afflict 827 (8), 963 (8)
afflicting 827 (6)
affliction 616 (1), 651 (2), 659 (1), 825 (1)
affluence 635 (2), 730 (1), 800 (1)
affluent 635 (4), 730 (4), 800 (3)
afford 633 (5), 635 (8), 781 (7), 800 (6), 806 (4)
afford sanctuary 299 (3)
affordable 812 (3)
afforest 366 (12)
afforestation 366 (3), 370 (1)
afforested 366 (10)
affray 61 (4), 716 (7)

affront 827 (2), 827 (8), 878 (2), 891 (8), 921 (2), 921 (5)
affronted 829 (3)
aficionado 504 (3), 707 (4)
afield 199 (6)
afire 379 (5)
aflame 417 (8)
aflame with 818 (4)
afloat 1 (4), 269 (6), 269 (7), 275 (12), 343 (4)
afoot 1 (4), 678 (8)
aforesaid 64 (2), 119 (2)
aforethought 608 (2), 617 (3)
afraid 854 (6)
afraid, be 854 (9)
afraid to touch 457 (3)
afresh 106 (8), 126 (9)
aft 238 (6)
after 65 (5), 120 (2), 120 (4), 238 (4), 238 (6), 284 (5), 619 (7)
after a fashion 33 (10)
after a time 120 (4)
after a while 120 (4)
after all 31 (7)
after Christ 120 (2)
after-dinner 120 (2), 301 (34)
after time 136 (8)
afterbirth 167 (2)
aftercare 658 (12)
aftereffect 67 (1)
afterglow 41 (1), 67 (1)
afterlife 67 (1), 124 (2), 971 (1)
aftermath 67 (1), 120 (1), 157 (1)
afternoon 129 (1), 129 (5)
afternoon tea 129 (1)
afters 67 (1)
aftershave 843 (3)
aftertaste 67 (1), 386 (1)
afterthought 67 (1), 136 (1)
afterwards 65 (5), 120 (4)
again 91 (4), 106 (8)
again and again 106 (7), 139 (4)
against 182 (4), 240 (4), 704 (3), 704 (6)
against custom 611 (2)

against nature 470 (2)
against one's will 598 (5)
against reason 499 (5)
against the grain 259 (10),
598 (5)
against the rules 84 (5),
914 (3)
agape 263 (13)
agate 437 (3), 844 (8)
age 108 (3), 108 (8), 110
(2), 117 (4), 127 (1), 127
(8), 131 (1), 131 (8), 161
(2), 655 (7), 842 (1), 842
(6)
age, an 113 (1)
age group 74 (3), 77 (1),
123 (2), 538 (4)
age-old 127 (6)
aged 131 (6)
ageing 32 (4), 127 (7), 131
(6), 161 (7), 163 (4), 499
(4), 655 (5), 842 (4)
ageism 481 (3)
ageless 115 (2), 130 (4)
agency 173 (1), 628 (1),
676 (1), 689 (1), 751 (1)
agenda 154 (2), 452 (1),
622 (1), 623 (2)
agent 150 (2), 156 (2), 164
(4), 231 (3), 628 (2), 630
(5), 676 (1), 686 (1), 690
(3), 720 (2), 754 (1), 755
(1), 793 (2), 923 (4)
agent, be the 156 (9)
agent provocateur 527
(2), 738 (5)
ages 113 (1)
agglomerate 48 (1)
agglutinate 45 (9), 45 (11),
48 (4), 778 (5)
aggrandize 197 (5), 866
(14)
aggravate 36 (5), 176 (9),
655 (7), 655 (9), 700 (6),
709 (8), 728 (8), 827 (8),
832 (3), 888 (8), 891 (9)
aggravated 655 (5), 832
(2)
aggravatedly 832 (4)
aggravating 827 (5)
aggravation 36 (1), 655
(3), 700 (1), 827 (1), 832
(1), 891 (1)

aggregate 52 (2), 74 (11),
324 (3)
aggregation 74 (7)
aggression 712 (1)
aggressive 174 (5), 176
(5), 678 (7), 709 (6), 712
(6), 716 (9), 718 (9), 881
(3)
aggressively 712 (13)
aggressiveness 718 (3)
aggressor 709 (5), 712 (5),
722 (1), 881 (2)
aggrieve 827 (11)
aghast 854 (6), 864 (4)
agile 277 (5), 694 (4)
agility 277 (1)
agitate 63 (3), 63 (4), 176
(8), 265 (5), 279 (7), 317
(6), 318 (6), 352 (10), 374
(6), 456 (8), 547 (21), 678
(11), 738 (10), 827 (10),
854 (12)
agitated 142 (2), 152 (4),
176 (5), 312 (3), 318 (4),
678 (7), 821 (3), 822 (3),
825 (5), 854 (7)
agitated, be 141 (6), 163
(9), 312 (4), 317 (4), 318
(5), 377 (6), 818 (8), 819
(5), 821 (9), 822 (4), 825
(7), 854 (9), 854 (11)
agitation 152 (1), 174 (2),
176 (2), 265 (1), 279 (1),
317 (1), 318 (1), 678 (1),
678 (2), 680 (1), 738 (2),
818 (1), 821 (1), 822 (1),
822 (2), 825 (3), 854 (1),
854 (2)
agitator 176 (4), 489 (2),
579 (5), 612 (5), 654 (5),
663 (2), 690 (2), 705 (1),
738 (5), 821 (2)
aglow 379 (5), 417 (8)
agnostic 474 (6), 486 (3),
974 (3), 974 (5)
agnosticism 449 (3), 486
(1), 486 (2), 974 (1)
ago 122 (3), 125 (12)
agog 453 (3), 507 (2), 821
(3), 859 (7)
agonize 377 (6), 825 (7)
agonizing 377 (3), 825 (5),
827 (3)

agony 377 (1), 825 (1)
agoraphobia 854 (3)
agrarian 344 (5), 370 (7)
agree 13 (3), 24 (9), 181
(3), 597 (6), 710 (3), 758
(3)
agree to 488 (6)
agree to differ 719 (5)
agree with 488 (6)
agree with one 652 (5)
agreeable 24 (5), 83 (4),
376 (3), 597 (4), 730 (5),
758 (2), 826 (2), 841 (6)
agreeableness 884 (1)
agreed 24 (5)
agreed to 765 (4)
agreeing 8 (3), 13 (2), 24
(5), 28 (7), 83 (4), 123 (3),
181 (2), 245 (2), 410 (7),
425 (7), 488 (4), 597 (4),
710 (2)
agreement 13 (1), 16 (1),
18 (1), 24 (1), 28 (1), 50
(1), 83 (1), 181 (1), 245
(1), 488 (1), 488 (2), 706
(1), 710 (1), 758 (1), 765
(1)
agribusiness 370 (1)
agricultural 344 (5), 370
(7)
agricultural college 539
(3)
agricultural labourer 686
(2)
agricultural worker 370
(4)
agriculturalist 164 (4)
agriculture 164 (1), 171
(2), 366 (4), 370 (1), 669
(3)
agriculturist 370 (4)
agronomic 370 (7)
agronomics 370 (1)
agronomist 370 (4)
aground 700 (5)
ague 318 (2)
ahead 34 (4), 64 (5), 124
(4), 199 (7), 237 (6), 283
(4), 285 (5)
ahead of its time 135 (4)
ahead of one's time, be 84
(8)

aid 38 (1), 156 (10), 162 (5), 167 (1), 173 (1), 178 (1), 218 (1), 218 (15), 285 (4), 310 (1), 310 (4), 471 (5), 488 (1), 612 (2), 612 (9), 628 (1), 628 (4), 640 (1), 640 (4), 642 (3), 658 (1), 658 (19), 660 (2), 701 (1), 701 (8), 703 (1), 703 (5), 706 (4), 756 (1), 781 (7), 880 (2), 884 (5), 897 (2), 897 (5), 901 (1), 923 (1)

aid and abet 612 (9)

aid to beauty 843 (3)

aid to memory 505 (3)

aide 703 (3)

aide-de-camp 707 (1), 741 (8)

aide-memoire 505 (3)

aided 701 (5)

aider 156 (2), 284 (2), 612 (5), 628 (2), 703 (3), 707 (1), 713 (6), 742 (1), 755 (1), 880 (2), 903 (1)

aider and abettor 612 (5)

aiding 35 (4), 181 (2), 628 (3), 640 (2), 701 (3), 703 (4), 706 (3), 742 (7), 756 (3), 758 (2), 781 (5), 897 (4), 901 (6)

aileron 271 (5), 276 (1)

ailing 651 (21)

ailment 651 (2)

aim 187 (5), 281 (1), 281 (7), 617 (2), 617 (6), 622 (1), 671 (4), 859 (5)

aim at 281 (7), 617 (6), 619 (5)

aim for 281 (5)

aim too high 306 (3)

aim well 187 (5)

aimed 281 (3)

aiming at 179 (2)

aimless 61 (7), 618 (6)

aimless activity 678 (2)

air 253 (2), 319 (4), 323 (1), 325 (1), 336 (2), 340 (1), 340 (6), 342 (6), 352 (1), 352 (6), 382 (6), 412 (3), 445 (5), 459 (13), 526 (5), 652 (1), 685 (4), 688 (1)

air arm 722 (14)

air commodore 741 (9)

air-condition 382 (6)

air-conditioning 340 (1), 382 (1)

air crew 271 (4)

air current 352 (1)

air duct 353 (1)

air fight 718 (7)

air-filter 340 (1), 648 (5)

air flow 352 (1)

air force 276 (1), 722 (14), 741 (9)

air freight 272 (2)

air-hole 263 (4), 353 (1)

air letter 588 (1)

air lock 231 (3)

air mail 531 (2)

air marshal 741 (9)

air officer 271 (4), 741 (9)

air-passage 353 (1)

air pipe 352 (6), 352 (7), 353 (1)

air pocket 190 (2), 340 (1)

air raid 712 (1)

air service 718 (6)

air shaft 353 (1)

air space 271 (2)

air stream 352 (1)

air terminal 271 (2)

air-to-air 271 (6)

air transport 271 (2)

air travel 265 (1), 271 (2), 276 (1), 295 (2)

air traveller 268 (1)

airbase 271 (2)

airborne 209 (8), 271 (6), 308 (3)

airborne, be 271 (7), 323 (4)

airborne division 722 (14)

airbus 276 (1)

aircraft 276 (1), 722 (14)

aircraft carrier 722 (13)

aircraftman 271 (4), 722 (14)

aircraftwoman 271 (4)

airdrop 272 (1)

aired 342 (4)

airer 217 (3)

airfield 271 (2)

airiness 325 (1)

airing 267 (1), 340 (1), 352 (6), 648 (2)

airless 266 (5), 397 (2), 653 (2)

airlift 271 (2), 272 (2), 272 (6)

airline 271 (2)

airliner 276 (1)

airman 271 (4)

airmanship 718 (4)

airplane 276 (1)

airport 271 (2), 276 (1), 295 (2)

airs 850 (1), 873 (2), 875 (1)

airs and graces 873 (2)

airship 276 (2), 722 (14)

airsick 271 (6), 300 (5)

airspace 184 (2)

airstrip 271 (2)

airtight 264 (5)

airway 271 (2), 353 (1)

airwoman 271 (4)

airworthy 271 (6), 272 (5), 276 (5), 660 (5)

airy 4 (3), 271 (6), 323 (3), 336 (3), 340 (5), 352 (8), 921 (3)

airy-fairy 513 (5)

aisle 263 (7), 990 (4)

ajar 263 (13)

akimbo 247 (5)

akin 9 (5), 11 (5), 200 (4), 360 (3)

akin, be 11 (7)

al fresco 223 (4)

alabaster 427 (2)

alacrity 277 (1), 597 (1), 678 (1), 833 (1)

alarm 400 (1), 547 (5), 664 (1), 665 (1), 854 (1), 854 (12)

alarm bell 414 (8)

alarm clock 665 (1)

alarmed 854 (6)

alarmism 854 (4)

alarmist 665 (2), 854 (5)

alas 905 (9)

albatross 365 (4)

albino 84 (3), 426 (1), 426 (3), 427 (1)

album 505 (3), 592 (2)

albumen 358 (1)

alchemic **984** (6)

alchemist **143** (3), **983** (5), **984** (4)

alchemy **147** (1), **984** (1)

alcohol **301** (28), **658** (6)

alcoholic **162** (6), **301** (32), **651** (18), **949** (5), **949** (11), **949** (12)

alcoholic drink **174** (4), **301** (28), **949** (1)

alcoholism **503** (4), **651** (3), **659** (3), **859** (2), **949** (3)

alcove **194** (23), **255** (2)

alderman **690** (4), **692** (3), **741** (6)

ale **301** (28)

alert **455** (2), **455** (7), **457** (4), **547** (22), **664** (5), **665** (1), **665** (3), **669** (7), **678** (7), **819** (4)

alertness **455** (1), **457** (1), **498** (2)

alfresco **340** (7)

algae **196** (5), **366** (6)

algebra **86** (3)

algebraic **85** (5), **86** (9)

algebraist **86** (7)

algorithm **86** (1), **86** (3)

alias **561** (4), **562** (1)

alibi **190** (1), **614** (1), **927** (1)

alien **6** (2), **10** (3), **46** (5), **59** (2), **59** (4), **84** (5), **883** (4)

alien element **10** (1), **59** (1)

alienate **46** (9), **881** (5), **888** (8)

alienated **881** (3)

alienation **881** (1), **888** (1)

alight **187** (8), **295** (5), **309** (3), **311** (8), **379** (5)

align **16** (4), **24** (10), **62** (4), **216** (7), **249** (4), **587** (7)

align oneself **708** (8)

aligned **16** (2)

aligned with **281** (3)

alignment **281** (1)

alike **18** (4)

alimentary **301** (33)

alimony **777** (4), **807** (1), **896** (1)

alive **1** (4), **360** (2), **498** (4), **819** (4)

alive and kicking **360** (2), **656** (6)

alive, be **1** (6), **360** (4)

alive to **374** (3), **490** (5), **819** (2)

alive with **104** (5)

all **26** (2), **52** (2), **54** (1), **79** (2), **79** (4)

all-ability **534** (5)

all aboard **269** (14)

all along **108** (10), **113** (11)

all and sundry **79** (2)

all anyhow **61** (12)

all at once **116** (4)

all at sea **474** (6)

all but **33** (11), **200** (8)

all change **151** (1)

all clear **547** (5), **660** (1), **756** (2)

all comers **705** (1)

all correct **60** (5)

all day **113** (11)

all day long **113** (11)

all ears **415** (5), **453** (3), **455** (2)

all ears, be **415** (6), **455** (4)

all-embracing **32** (5), **52** (7), **78** (2), **79** (3)

all-engulfing **786** (5)

all eyes **438** (6), **455** (2)

All Father **965** (3)

all feeling **819** (3)

all found **633** (4)

all hands **79** (2)

all-holy **965** (6)

All-holy, the **965** (3)

all-in **78** (2), **684** (2)

all in all **30** (6), **52** (9)

all in good time **137** (8)

all-in wrestling **716** (5)

all-inclusive **78** (2)

all-knowing **490** (5), **965** (6)

all manner of **15** (4), **82** (2)

all-merciful **965** (6)

All-merciful, the **965** (3)

all of a piece **16** (2)

all off **69** (4)

all one **28** (8)

all one's life **113** (10)

all out **277** (9)

all over **183** (8)

all over, be **69** (5), **889** (6)

all over one **925** (3)

all over with **361** (5)

all over with, be **165** (11)

all-powerful **162** (6), **965** (6)

all-purpose **640** (2)

all right **644** (9), **732** (2)

all round **54** (9), **230** (4)

all-rounder **162** (4), **696** (1), **837** (16)

all-seeing **965** (6)

all set **669** (7)

all shapes and sizes **17** (1)

all sorts **43** (4), **79** (2)

all-star **594** (15), **644** (4)

all-sufficing **633** (4), **635** (3)

all the best **730** (10)

all the more **34** (12), **36** (6)

all the rage **848** (5)

all the same **468** (5)

all the world **52** (2)

all there **502** (2)

all things considered **52** (9)

all thumbs **695** (5)

all to the good **615** (6)

all together **45** (15), **52** (10), **74** (12)

all together now **706** (6)

all told **54** (8)

all-wise **965** (6)

all wrong **616** (2)

Allah **965** (3)

allay **37** (4), **177** (7), **719** (4)

allegation **466** (2), **532** (1), **614** (1), **928** (1)

allege **532** (5), **614** (4)

alleged **512** (5), **614** (2)

alleged reason **475** (5)

allegiance **739** (2), **745** (1), **917** (1)

alleging **928** (5)

allegorical **462** (2), **519** (3), **523** (4)

allegorist **590** (5)

allegory 18 (2), 462 (1), 519 (1), 590 (2)

allegretto 412 (8)

allegro 412 (8), 833 (9)

alleluia 923 (2), 981 (13)

allergic 374 (3), 651 (22), 861 (2)

allergy 374 (1), 651 (1), 861 (1), 888 (1)

alleviate 37 (4), 177 (7), 701 (9), 831 (3)

alleviation 37 (2), 177 (1), 831 (1)

alleviative 177 (2), 177 (4)

alley 263 (7), 624 (6)

alleyway 624 (6)

alliance 9 (1), 11 (1), 45 (1), 50 (1), 181 (1), 706 (2), 708 (3), 765 (1)

allied 45 (5), 50 (3), 708 (6), 710 (2)

alligator 365 (13)

alliteration 18 (2), 106 (2), 574 (1), 593 (5)

alliterative 18 (4), 106 (3), 574 (4), 574 (1)

allocate 783 (3)

allocation 783 (1), 783 (2)

allocution 579 (1), 583 (1)

allopathic 658 (18)

allopathy 658 (10)

allot 26 (4), 62 (4), 673 (5), 777 (6), 783 (3)

allotment 53 (5), 370 (3), 777 (4), 783 (1), 783 (2)

allow 39 (3), 158 (3), 469 (3), 469 (4), 475 (9), 488 (6), 488 (7), 526 (6), 701 (8), 736 (3), 756 (5), 758 (3), 823 (6)

allow access 299 (3)

allow an appeal 960 (3)

allow credit 784 (5)

allow for 31 (5)

allow in 299 (3)

allow rest 685 (4)

allow to lapse 138 (6)

allow to leak 772 (4)

allowable 469 (2), 756 (4), 781 (6), 927 (4)

allowance 31 (2), 40 (2), 42 (1), 468 (1), 703 (2), 736 (1), 756 (1), 771 (2),

777 (4), 781 (2), 783 (2), 807 (1), 810 (1)

allowed 478 (3), 756 (4)

allowed in 297 (4)

allowing 8 (6), 488 (4)

allowing for 31 (7), 468 (2)

alloy 43 (3), 50 (2), 359 (1)

allude 519 (4), 523 (6), 524 (11)

allude to 9 (8), 514 (5)

alluding 9 (6)

allure 291 (1), 291 (4), 826 (4), 859 (13), 887 (15)

allurement 291 (1), 612 (2)

alluring 612 (6), 821 (4), 887 (11)

allusion 9 (4), 519 (1)

allusive 9 (6), 512 (4), 514 (3), 519 (3), 568 (2)

allusive, be 523 (6)

alluvial 344 (5)

alluvial plain 348 (1)

alluvium 344 (3)

ally 45 (9), 703 (3), 706 (4), 707 (1), 707 (3), 708 (8), 765 (5), 880 (3)

almanac 87 (3), 117 (4)

almightiness 965 (2)

almighty 160 (8), 965 (6)

almighty dollar 797 (3)

Almighty, the 965 (3)

almost 33 (11), 200 (8), 647 (5)

almost all 32 (3)

almost none 105 (1)

almost remember 506 (5)

almost unheard of 140 (2)

alms 781 (2), 897 (2)

alms-giving 781 (1), 781 (5)

almsgiving 981 (3)

almshouse 192 (17), 662 (2)

aloft 209 (11), 209 (14), 308 (4)

alone 10 (3), 46 (5), 88 (4), 88 (6), 883 (5), 883 (6)

along 203 (9)

along with 38 (5), 89 (5), 123 (5)

alongside 200 (7), 219 (4), 239 (4)

aloof 49 (2), 454 (2), 871 (4), 881 (3), 883 (5)

aloofness 456 (1), 820 (1), 883 (1)

aloud 400 (5), 577 (3)

alpenstock 218 (2)

alphabet 68 (1), 87 (1), 558 (1)

alphabetic 558 (5), 586 (7)

alphabetical order 60 (1)

alphabetically 558 (7)

alpine 209 (10)

already 119 (5)

also 38 (5)

also-ran 35 (2), 716 (8), 728 (3)

altar 990 (4)

alter 143 (5), 143 (6), 468 (3)

alter course 282 (3)

alter ego 13 (1), 18 (3), 707 (3), 880 (4)

alterable 152 (3), 152 (4)

alteration 15 (1), 143 (1), 147 (2)

altercation 709 (3), 716 (1)

altered 15 (4)

alterer 143 (3)

altering the case 468 (2)

alternate 12 (2), 12 (3), 65 (2), 65 (3), 72 (3), 141 (6), 152 (5), 317 (5)

alternately 12 (4), 141 (8)

alternating 12 (2), 65 (2), 72 (2), 141 (4)

alternating current 160 (5)

alternation 12 (1), 65 (1), 72 (1), 141 (1), 143 (1), 152 (1), 317 (2)

alternative 150 (2), 605 (1), 623 (3)

alternatively 150 (6), 605 (9)

alternator 160 (6)

although 31 (7), 182 (4), 468 (4)

altimeter 209 (7), 247 (3), 465 (6)

altimetry 209 (7), 247 (3), 465 (2)

altitude 209 (1)

altitudinal 209 (8)

alto 413 (4)
alto clef 410 (3)
altogether 52 (9), 54 (8)
altogether, the 229 (2)
altruism 901 (1), 931 (1), 933 (2)
altruist 897 (3), 901 (4)
altruistic 897 (4), 901 (6), 931 (2)
alumni 538 (3)
always 79 (7), 108 (10)
always the same 13 (2)
always with 89 (3)
a.m 117 (8), 128 (1)
amalgam 43 (3), 50 (2)
amalgamate 43 (7), 50 (4)
amalgamated 43 (6)
amalgamation 50 (1)
amanuensis 549 (1), 628 (2), 707 (1)
amass 45 (9), 74 (11), 632 (5)
amateur 491 (1), 538 (2), 556 (1), 695 (4), 697 (1), 846 (2), 859 (6)
amateur theatricals 594 (1)
amateurish 491 (4), 695 (4), 695 (6)
amatory 887 (12)
amaze 508 (5), 821 (8), 864 (7)
amazed 508 (3), 864 (4)
amazement 508 (1), 821 (1), 864 (1)
amazing 32 (7), 508 (2), 864 (5), 864 (9)
amazingly 32 (19)
amazon 162 (4), 176 (4), 373 (3), 722 (4)
amazonian 162 (10), 855 (4)
ambassador 529 (5), 754 (3)
ambassadorial 755 (2)
ambassadress 754 (3)
amber 357 (5), 430 (1), 432 (1), 433 (1), 844 (8)
ambergris 357 (5)
ambidexterity 241 (1)
ambidextrous 90 (2), 91 (2), 241 (2), 694 (4)
ambience 230 (1)

ambiguity 25 (1), 474 (1), 514 (2), 517 (1), 518 (1), 568 (1)
ambiguous 84 (5), 467 (2), 474 (4), 514 (4), 517 (3), 518 (2), 541 (3), 568 (2)
ambiguous, be 474 (8)
ambition 612 (1), 617 (1), 622 (1), 852 (2), 859 (1), 859 (5), 932 (1)
ambitious 617 (3), 671 (3), 672 (2), 852 (4), 859 (7)
ambitious person 859 (6)
ambivalence 518 (1)
ambivalent 14 (3), 518 (2)
amble 267 (3), 267 (13), 267 (15), 278 (1), 278 (4)
ambrosia 301 (9)
ambrosial 390 (2)
ambulance 274 (1)
ambush 508 (5), 523 (1), 525 (9), 527 (2), 527 (5), 542 (4), 542 (10), 661 (1), 663 (1), 698 (2), 698 (5)
ambushment 523 (1), 527 (2)
ameliorate 654 (9)
amelioration 654 (1)
amen 488 (11)
amen to that 488 (11)
amenable 487 (2), 597 (4), 739 (3)
amend 654 (10)
amendment 31 (1), 654 (2), 656 (1), 658 (1)
amends 31 (1), 658 (1), 787 (1), 941 (1)
Americanism 560 (2)
Americanize 147 (8)
amethyst 436 (1), 844 (8)
amiability 826 (1), 884 (1), 887 (2), 897 (1)
amiable 717 (3), 826 (2), 848 (6), 884 (4), 887 (11), 897 (4)
amicability 880 (2)
amicable 710 (2), 880 (6)
amicable relations 9 (1)
amicably 880 (9)
amid 43 (9), 231 (11)
amiss 616 (3), 645 (8)
amity 710 (1), 880 (1)
ammonite 125 (3), 251 (2)

ammunition 723 (12)
ammunition box 723 (2)
ammunition chest 194 (7), 723 (2)
amnesia 506 (1)
amnesic 506 (4)
amnestied 909 (3)
amnesty 506 (2), 550 (1), 668 (1), 719 (2), 905 (7), 909 (1), 909 (4), 919 (1), 919 (3)
amoeba 33 (5), 196 (5)
among 43 (9), 231 (11)
amoral 820 (5), 860 (2), 934 (3), 951 (7), 974 (5)
amoralism 974 (1)
amorality 860 (1), 934 (1), 951 (2)
amorous 499 (4), 887 (9)
amorous glance 889 (2)
amorphism 244 (1)
amorphous 17 (1), 55 (3), 244 (2), 246 (3), 335 (4), 842 (4)
amorphousness 244 (1)
amount 26 (1), 797 (2), 809 (1)
amount to 86 (11), 809 (6)
amp 160 (6)
ampere 160 (6)
amphibian 269 (7), 274 (1), 365 (2), 365 (12), 365 (18), 722 (13)
amphibious 84 (5), 90 (2), 91 (2), 365 (18)
amphitheatre 594 (7), 724 (1)
amphora 194 (13)
ample 32 (4), 104 (4), 183 (6), 195 (6), 195 (8), 205 (3), 635 (4), 813 (3)
amplification 197 (1), 520 (3)
amplifier 400 (2), 414 (10), 415 (4)
amplify 36 (5), 197 (5), 520 (9), 570 (6)
amplifying 516 (3)
amplitude 32 (1), 54 (2), 183 (3), 205 (1)
ampoule 194 (1)
amputate 39 (3), 46 (10), 658 (20)

13

amputation 39 (1), 658 (11)

amulet 844 (7), 983 (3)

amuse 826 (3), 837 (20), 839 (5), 849 (4)

amuse oneself 61 (11), 497 (4), 604 (4), 622 (7), 824 (6), 833 (7), 837 (21), 882 (8)

amused 824 (4), 833 (4), 837 (19)

amusement 531 (4), 594 (4), 622 (1), 701 (2), 824 (3), 826 (1), 833 (2), 837 (1), 882 (3)

amusement arcade 618 (3), 837 (5)

amusing 826 (2), 833 (4), 837 (18), 849 (3), 882 (6)

an 88 (3)

anachronism 118 (1), 138 (1), 495 (2)

anachronistic 118 (2), 122 (2), 127 (7)

anaemia 163 (1), 426 (1), 651 (10)

anaemic 163 (4), 426 (3), 651 (20), 651 (22)

anaesthesia 375 (1)

anaesthetic 177 (2), 375 (2), 375 (3), 658 (7), 658 (17), 679 (5), 831 (1)

anaesthetist 658 (14)

anaesthetize 375 (6), 658 (20), 831 (3)

anaesthetized 375 (3)

anagram 151 (1), 518 (1), 530 (2), 558 (2)

anagrammatic 558 (5)

anal 302 (5)

analgesia 375 (1)

analgesic 375 (2), 375 (3), 658 (4), 658 (7), 658 (17), 831 (1), 831 (2)

analogical 462 (2)

analogous 9 (5), 12 (2), 245 (2)

analogue 13 (1), 18 (3), 22 (1), 28 (6), 86 (10), 89 (2), 90 (1), 91 (1), 518 (1)

analogue computer 86 (6)

analogy 9 (2), 18 (1), 462 (1)

analyse 46 (10), 51 (5), 62 (6), 459 (13), 461 (7), 475 (11), 564 (4)

analysed 62 (3)

analysis 46 (2), 51 (1), 62 (1), 86 (2), 459 (1), 461 (1), 564 (1)

analyst 461 (1)

analytic 459 (11), 461 (6)

anarchic 61 (9), 734 (4), 738 (7), 738 (8), 744 (7), 769 (2), 954 (7)

anarchism 734 (2), 738 (3), 769 (1)

anarchist 61 (6), 149 (2), 168 (1), 176 (4), 708 (2), 738 (4), 904 (1)

anarchistic 149 (3), 176 (5), 734 (4)

anarchy 61 (1), 733 (4), 734 (2), 769 (1), 954 (3)

anathema 888 (3)

anathematize 899 (6), 977 (3), 988 (10)

anathematized 977 (2)

anatomical 331 (3)

anatomist 367 (2)

anatomy 331 (1), 358 (2), 367 (1)

ancestor 66 (1), 169 (3)

ancestors 361 (3)

ancestral 125 (7), 127 (6)

ancestress 169 (4)

ancestry 5 (5), 11 (1), 68 (4), 169 (2), 868 (1)

anchor 45 (11), 47 (6), 187 (5), 187 (8), 192 (21), 266 (8), 269 (4), 531 (5), 660 (2), 852 (1)

anchorage 187 (3), 295 (2)

anchored 153 (6), 187 (4)

anchoress 986 (6)

anchorite 883 (3), 945 (2), 979 (4)

ancient 32 (4), 125 (6), 125 (7), 127 (4), 866 (8)

ancient monument 125 (2), 548 (3)

ancient wisdom 127 (3)

ancient world 125 (2)

anciently 127 (9)

ancients, the 66 (1), 125 (2)

ancillary 35 (4), 703 (4)

and 38 (5), 342 (5)

and also 38 (5)

and no further 236 (4)

and so 8 (5), 157 (7)

and so forth 38 (5)

and so on 38 (5)

andante 278 (1), 410 (4), 412 (8)

androgynous 84 (7), 373 (5)

androgyny 84 (1)

anecdotal 10 (3), 505 (6)

anecdote 590 (2)

anecdotist 590 (5)

anemometer 352 (2), 465 (6)

anemometry 340 (4), 352 (2)

anew 106 (8), 126 (9)

angel 890 (1), 935 (2), 937 (1), 968 (1), 970 (5)

angel of death 168 (1), 361 (1)

angelic 887 (11), 933 (3), 935 (3), 968 (3)

angelize 968 (4)

anger 821 (1), 822 (2), 888 (1), 891 (2), 891 (9), 924 (1)

angered 891 (4)

angle 247 (2), 247 (7), 445 (1), 481 (5), 619 (6)

angle for 859 (11)

angle of vision 438 (5)

angled 247 (5)

angler 619 (3)

Anglican 976 (5), 976 (10), 978 (6)

anglicism 560 (2)

anglicize 147 (8)

angling 619 (2)

Anglo-Catholic 976 (4), 976 (10)

anglophone 579 (6)

angrily 891 (10)

angry 176 (6), 503 (9), 821 (3), 891 (4), 900 (2)

angry, be 176 (7), 438 (8), 547 (21), 891 (7), 924 (9)

angry with 891 (4)

angst 825 (1), 834 (2)

anguish 377 (1), 645 (1), 825 (1)

anguished 825 (5)

angular 247 (5), 248 (3)

angular figure 247 (4)

angular measure 247 (3), 465 (1)

angularity 45 (4), 220 (1), 247 (1), 248 (2), 261 (1), 267 (7), 294 (1)

angulated 247 (6)

anima 447 (2)

animal 125 (3), 132 (3), 365 (2), 365 (18), 448 (2), 943 (2)

animal charge 547 (11)

animal disease 651 (17)

animal fat 357 (3)

animal fibre 208 (2)

animal food 301 (8)

animal husbandry 164 (1), 167 (1), 348 (2), 369 (1), 370 (1)

animal kingdom 365 (1)

animal life 360 (1), 365 (1)

animal noise 409 (1)

animal physiology 367 (1)

animal spirits 162 (2), 360 (1), 833 (1)

animality 360 (1), 365 (1), 448 (1)

animate 162 (12), 174 (8), 612 (9), 821 (7), 833 (8), 855 (8)

animate matter 358 (1)

animated 360 (2), 678 (7), 819 (4), 833 (3)

animated cartoon 445 (4)

animation 360 (1), 445 (3), 678 (2), 821 (1), 833 (1)

animism 320 (1), 973 (2)

animist 320 (1)

animistic 973 (8)

animosity 861 (1), 881 (1), 888 (1), 891 (1)

animus 447 (2), 881 (1)

ankle 45 (4), 214 (2)

ankle-deep 211 (2), 212 (2)

ankle-length 203 (5)

anklet 844 (7)

annals 117 (4), 548 (1)

anneal 329 (3)

annex 38 (3), 40 (1), 45 (10), 745 (7), 771 (7), 786 (7)

annexation 38 (1), 45 (2)

annihilate 2 (8), 165 (6), 362 (11)

annihilation 2 (2), 165 (1)

anniversary 108 (3), 110 (1), 141 (3), 141 (5), 876 (2), 876 (3), 988 (7)

anno domini 108 (12), 131 (3)

annotate 520 (8), 547 (19), 591 (5)

annotation 520 (2)

annotative 520 (6)

annotator 520 (4)

announce 511 (8), 524 (10), 528 (10), 561 (6)

announce itself 154 (6)

announce oneself 189 (4)

announcement 511 (1), 524 (1), 528 (1)

announcer 524 (4), 528 (6), 529 (5), 531 (5), 561 (3), 579 (5)

annoy 377 (5), 827 (9), 834 (11), 891 (9)

annoyance 616 (1), 645 (1), 659 (1), 825 (3), 827 (2), 891 (1)

annoyed 825 (6), 891 (4)

annoying 645 (2), 645 (4), 827 (5), 829 (4)

annual 110 (3), 114 (4), 141 (5), 366 (7), 528 (5), 589 (4)

annuities 797 (2)

annuity 804 (2), 807 (1)

annul 165 (6), 752 (4), 954 (9)

annular 250 (6)

annulled 954 (5)

annulment 752 (1), 896 (1)

anode 160 (5)

anodyne 177 (4), 831 (2)

anoint 333 (3), 334 (4), 357 (9), 988 (10)

anointed 357 (7), 965 (6)

anointment 334 (1), 357 (1)

anomalistic 84 (7)

anomalous 61 (7), 84 (7)

anomalousness 61 (1), 84 (1)

anomaly 61 (1), 84 (1)

anon 562 (2)

anonymity 491 (2), 523 (1), 525 (1), 562 (2)

anonymous 88 (3), 491 (6), 525 (3), 525 (4), 562 (4)

anonymous, be 562 (5)

anonymously 525 (10)

anorak 228 (10)

anorexia 301 (1), 946 (1)

another 15 (4), 38 (2), 65 (2)

another light on 15 (3)

'another place' 692 (2)

another story 15 (3)

another time 122 (1)

another version 15 (3)

answer 24 (9), 85 (4), 151 (3), 156 (6), 157 (1), 460 (1), 460 (5), 467 (1), 475 (11), 479 (1), 520 (1), 584 (6), 588 (1), 588 (4), 623 (3), 635 (6), 640 (4), 642 (3), 658 (1), 714 (3), 727 (7), 839 (5), 878 (6)

answer back 460 (5), 475 (11), 714 (3), 878 (6)

answer for 180 (3), 755 (3)

answer the purpose 727 (7)

answer to 9 (7), 12 (3), 561 (7)

answerable 156 (7), 180 (2), 803 (4), 917 (5)

answerable, be 156 (9)

answerer 460 (3), 584 (4)

answering 24 (5), 460 (4), 467 (2)

answering back 460 (1), 714 (1), 878 (2), 878 (5)

answering to 9 (5), 12 (2)

ant 33 (5), 365 (16)

ant heap 171 (3)

antacid 658 (4)

antagonism 182 (1), 704 (1), 881 (1), 888 (1)

antagonist 705 (1), 881 (2)

antagonistic 25 (4), 182 (2), 704 (3), 888 (4)

antagonize 861 (5), 881 (5), 888 (8), 891 (8)

antagonizing 888 (5)
antarctic 240 (2)
Antarctic 380 (1)
ante 64 (5)
antecedent 64 (2), 66 (1),
119 (1), 119 (2)
antedate 64 (3), 118 (3)
antedated 118 (2)
antediluvian 119 (2), 127
(5), 127 (7)
antelope 365 (3)
antenatal 119 (2), 167 (5)
antenna 254 (3), 378 (3),
531 (3)
anterior 64 (2), 119 (2)
anteroom 194 (20), 237 (1)
anthem 412 (5), 981 (5),
981 (11)
anthill 192 (4), 209 (3)
anthologist 592 (2)
anthologize 592 (5)
anthology 74 (1), 589 (2),
592 (2), 593 (2)
anthracite 385 (2)
anthrax 651 (17)
anthropoid 365 (18), 371
(6)
anthropoid ape 365 (3)
anthropological 371 (6)
anthropology 371 (2)
anthropophagy 301 (1)
anti- 14 (3), 704 (3)
anti-Christian 980 (4)
anti-Church 974 (5)
anti-Semitism 481 (3), 888
(1)
antibiotic 658 (4), 658 (7)
antibody 658 (4)
antic 837 (3)
antichrist 974 (3)
antichristianity 974 (2)
anticipate 118 (3), 119 (4),
124 (6), 135 (5), 507 (4),
510 (3), 597 (6), 669 (10)
anticipated 127 (8), 507
(3)
anticipating 507 (2), 597
(4)
anticipation 66 (1), 118
(1), 124 (3), 135 (3), 507
(1), 510 (1), 669 (1)
anticipatory 64 (2), 507
(2), 510 (2)

anticlerical 974 (5), 980
(4)
anticlimax 497 (1), 508
(1), 509 (1), 572 (1), 849
(1)
anticlockwise 286 (3), 315
(6)
antics 497 (2)
anticyclone 340 (3)
anticyclonic 340 (5)
antidotal 14 (3), 182 (2),
658 (17)
antidote 14 (1), 182 (1),
658 (4)
antigen 658 (4)
antihistamine 658 (4)
antilogarithm 85 (2)
antipathetic 25 (4), 84 (5),
182 (2), 292 (2), 861 (2),
861 (3), 881 (3), 888 (4)
antipathy 182 (1), 861 (1),
881 (1), 888 (1)
antiperspirant 843 (3)
antiphon 460 (1), 981 (5)
antiphonal 460 (4)
antipodal 14 (3), 221 (3),
240 (2)
antipodean 14 (3), 199 (3),
240 (2)
antipodes 14 (1), 69 (2),
199 (2)
antiquarian 125 (5), 127
(4), 492 (3), 549 (2), 589
(8)
antiquarianism 125 (4)
antiquary 125 (5), 492 (3)
antiquated 118 (2), 122
(2), 125 (6), 127 (7), 641
(4), 674 (3)
antique 32 (4), 127 (2), 127
(4), 522 (2)
antiquities 125 (2), 127 (2)
antiquity 66 (1), 125 (1),
125 (2), 127 (1), 127 (2),
548 (2), 632 (3)
antiseptic 648 (7), 652 (4),
658 (3), 660 (6)
antisocial 883 (5), 902 (3)
antithesis 14 (1), 462 (1),
519 (2), 574 (1)
antithetical 14 (3), 574 (5)
antler 254 (3), 256 (2)

antonym 14 (1), 514 (2),
559 (1)
antonymous 14 (3), 514
(4), 559 (4)
anvil 218 (5), 279 (4)
anxiety 507 (1), 825 (3)
anxious 457 (3), 507 (2),
825 (5), 854 (7)
anxious, be 854 (11)
anxious to please 884 (3)
any 26 (3), 79 (4), 562 (2)
any how 458 (7)
any number 85 (1)
any time 122 (3)
any time now 122 (3)
anybody's 774 (3)
anyhow 61 (12)
anyone 79 (2)
anything but 15 (4)
apace 680 (2)
apart 46 (5), 46 (15), 199
(6)
apart from 57 (6)
apartheid 46 (2), 57 (1)
apartment 192 (9), 194
(19)
apartment block 192 (9)
apathetic 175 (2), 454 (2),
508 (3), 606 (2), 677 (2),
679 (7), 820 (4), 865 (2)
apathy 175 (1), 454 (1),
508 (1), 601 (1), 820 (1),
860 (1), 974 (1)
ape 20 (3), 20 (5), 365 (3)
aperient 263 (11), 263
(13), 300 (2), 302 (5), 648
(4), 658 (5)
aperitif 66 (2), 174 (4), 301
(28)
aperture 263 (1), 442 (6)
apex 213 (1), 213 (2)
aphasia 580 (1)
aphasic 580 (2)
aphid 365 (16)
aphorism 496 (1), 569 (1)
aphoristic 496 (3), 569 (2),
693 (2)
aphrodisiac 174 (4), 887
(12)
Aphrodite 967 (1)
apiary 192 (4), 369 (2)
apiece 80 (10)
aping 20 (4)

aplomb 153 (1), 599 (1)

apocalypse 165 (3), 975 (1)

apocalyptic 165 (4), 511 (6), 975 (3)

Apocrypha 975 (2)

apocryphal 474 (7)

apogee 199 (1), 213 (1)

Apollo 321 (8)

apologetic 614 (3), 830 (2), 939 (3), 941 (4), 967 (1)

apologetics 475 (4)

apologies 830 (1)

apologist 475 (6), 927 (2)

apologize 603 (7), 721 (4), 830 (4), 939 (4), 941 (5)

apology 603 (2), 614 (1), 939 (1), 941 (1)

apology for 22 (1), 851 (3)

apoplectic 891 (4)

apoplexy 161 (2), 651 (2)

apostasy 603 (1), 607 (1), 657 (1), 980 (1)

apostate 147 (4), 489 (3), 603 (3), 603 (4), 974 (4), 978 (5), 978 (7), 980 (3), 980 (4)

apostatize 489 (5), 601 (4), 603 (6), 657 (2), 930 (8), 974 (7), 978 (9), 980 (6)

apostle 529 (5), 537 (3), 973 (6)

apostleship 985 (2), 985 (3)

apostolic 975 (4), 985 (6), 985 (7)

apostrophe 547 (14), 579 (1), 583 (1), 585 (1)

apostrophize 579 (9), 583 (3), 585 (4), 761 (7)

apothecary 658 (15)

apotheosis 866 (5)

appal 827 (11), 854 (12)

appalled 854 (6)

appalling 827 (6), 854 (8)

apparatus 630 (1)

apparel 228 (2)

apparent 443 (2), 445 (7), 471 (3), 473 (4), 522 (4)

apparently 445 (9), 471 (7)

apparition 440 (2), 445 (1), 522 (1), 970 (3)

appeal 291 (1), 291 (4), 532 (1), 532 (5), 533 (1), 583 (1), 612 (8), 761 (1), 761 (2), 761 (7), 762 (3), 826 (1), 841 (1), 887 (2), 959 (3)

appeal against 762 (3)

appeal to 583 (3), 761 (5), 761 (7)

appeal to arms 716 (7), 716 (11)

appeal to reason 475 (4), 475 (9)

appealer 763 (1)

appealing 178 (2), 826 (2), 859 (10), 887 (11)

appear 68 (8), 295 (4), 443 (4), 445 (8), 522 (9), 526 (7)

appear for 755 (3)

appearance 7 (2), 8 (1), 18 (1), 68 (1), 223 (1), 243 (1), 295 (1), 438 (5), 443 (1), 445 (1), 513 (2), 522 (1), 614 (1)

appearances 445 (1), 848 (2)

appearing 443 (2), 445 (7), 466 (5), 471 (3), 522 (4), 542 (6)

appease 177 (7), 719 (4), 828 (5), 981 (12)

appeasement 177 (1), 719 (1), 719 (2)

appeasing 828 (3)

appellant 763 (1), 915 (1), 928 (3), 959 (4)

appellation 561 (1), 561 (2)

append 38 (3), 65 (4)

appendage 40 (1), 53 (2), 89 (2)

appendectomy 658 (11)

appendicitis 651 (7)

appendix 40 (1), 69 (2), 589 (5)

appertain to 9 (7), 58 (3), 78 (4)

appertaining to 9 (5)

appetite 301 (1), 386 (1), 859 (2), 859 (3)

appetizer 66 (2), 174 (4), 301 (14), 390 (1)

appetizing 386 (2), 390 (2)

applaud 488 (6), 547 (21), 835 (6), 866 (13), 886 (3), 923 (10)

applause 547 (4), 835 (1), 866 (1), 876 (1), 923 (3)

apple 301 (19)

apple-green 434 (3)

appliance 156 (5), 628 (2), 630 (1)

appliances 629 (1)

applicability 9 (3), 640 (1), 673 (1)

applicable 9 (6), 24 (6), 640 (2), 642 (2)

applicant 460 (3), 763 (1)

application 9 (4), 449 (2), 455 (1), 514 (2), 519 (1), 520 (1), 536 (2), 600 (1), 628 (1), 673 (1), 678 (3), 759 (1), 761 (1)

applied 628 (3), 640 (2), 673 (2)

applied mathematics 86 (3)

applied science 490 (4)

applique 844 (4)

apply 9 (8), 673 (3), 759 (4), 761 (5)

apply a match 381 (9)

apply for 627 (6), 756 (6)

apply oneself 536 (5), 682 (6)

apply oneself to 672 (3)

apply pressure 740 (3)

apply the closure 69 (6)

apply the mind 449 (7)

apply to 761 (5)

appoint 605 (7), 608 (3), 622 (6), 751 (4), 783 (3)

appointed 596 (6), 608 (2)

appointment 605 (1), 622 (3), 669 (2), 751 (2)

apportion 26 (4), 46 (10), 53 (7), 62 (4), 75 (4), 92 (5), 465 (14), 673 (5), 775 (5), 781 (7), 783 (3)

apportionment 46 (3), 62 (1), 75 (1), 783 (1)

apposite 9 (6)

appositeness 9 (3), 24 (3)

appraisal 463 (2), 465 (1), 480 (2)

17

appraise 463 (3), 465 (13), 480 (6)

appraiser 465 (8), 480 (3)

appreciate 36 (4), 447 (7), 465 (13), 490 (8), 811 (4), 824 (6), 846 (4), 887 (13), 907 (5), 923 (8)

appreciation 36 (1), 463 (1), 480 (2), 520 (1), 818 (1), 907 (1), 923 (1)

appreciative 480 (4), 846 (3), 907 (3), 923 (5)

apprehend 490 (8), 507 (4), 516 (5), 747 (8), 786 (6)

apprehended 507 (3)

apprehension 507 (1), 661 (1), 786 (1), 854 (2), 959 (2)

apprehensive 507 (2), 825 (5), 854 (7)

apprehensiveness 854 (2)

apprentice 538 (2), 670 (4), 686 (3), 742 (4)

apprentice oneself 536 (4)

apprenticeship 536 (1)

apprise 524 (9)

approach 68 (5), 124 (1), 124 (5), 155 (3), 179 (3), 200 (1), 200 (5), 200 (6), 263 (6), 265 (1), 269 (10), 289 (1), 289 (4), 293 (1), 295 (1), 583 (3), 623 (2), 624 (1), 624 (2), 759 (1), 759 (3), 761 (1), 761 (5), 880 (8), 884 (7)

approachable 289 (3), 701 (3)

approaches 289 (1)

approaching 9 (5), 124 (4), 155 (2), 200 (4), 289 (2), 295 (3)

approbation 488 (1), 756 (1), 866 (1), 920 (1), 923 (1), 976 (2)

approbatory 923 (5)

appropriate 8 (3), 9 (6), 24 (6), 80 (5), 306 (4), 771 (7), 786 (7), 915 (5)

appropriation 771 (1), 773 (1), 783 (1), 786 (1)

appropriator 786 (4)

approvable 923 (6)

approval 488 (1), 756 (1), 866 (1), 923 (1)

approve 605 (6), 605 (7), 756 (5), 824 (6), 923 (8)

approved 610 (6), 615 (3), 642 (2), 866 (7), 923 (7), 933 (3)

approving 605 (4), 824 (4), 835 (4), 923 (5)

approvingly 923 (12)

approximate 18 (4), 200 (4), 200 (6), 289 (4)

approximate to 18 (7)

approximately 33 (11), 200 (8)

approximating 9 (5)

approximation 9 (2), 18 (1), 86 (2), 289 (1)

appurtenances 777 (1)

appurtenant 9 (5)

apricot 432 (1)

April fool 544 (1), 851 (3)

April shower 114 (2)

April showers 152 (2)

apron 228 (15), 594 (6), 989 (1)

apron strings 745 (1)

apropos 9 (10), 24 (6), 137 (9)

apropos of 24 (11)

apse 990 (4)

apt 9 (6), 24 (6), 80 (5), 498 (4), 694 (4), 846 (3)

apt to 179 (2), 180 (2)

aptitude 24 (3), 152 (1), 160 (2), 179 (1), 498 (1), 597 (1), 694 (2)

aptly 24 (11)

aptness 24 (3), 179 (1), 494 (3), 694 (2)

aquamarine 435 (1), 435 (3)

aquanaut 313 (2)

aquaplaning 837 (6)

aquarium 369 (4)

Aquarius 321 (5)

aquatic 269 (7), 339 (2)

aquatic mammal 365 (3)

aquatics 269 (3), 837 (6)

aquatint 553 (5), 555 (1)

aqueduct 351 (1), 624 (3)

aqueous 339 (2)

aquiline 247 (5), 365 (18)

arabesque 222 (1), 844 (3)

arabesques 574 (1)

Arabic numerals 85 (1)

arable 370 (7)

arable farm 370 (2)

arable farming 370 (1)

arable land 344 (3), 370 (2)

arachnid 365 (2)

arbiter 691 (2), 957 (2)

arbiter of taste 846 (2)

arbitrariness 10 (1), 604 (1)

arbitrary 10 (3), 84 (5), 477 (5), 595 (1), 602 (5), 604 (3), 733 (7), 735 (5), 744 (8), 954 (7)

arbitrary power 735 (2)

arbitrate 480 (5), 720 (4), 770 (2)

arbitration 480 (1), 710 (1), 720 (1)

arbitrator 480 (3), 720 (2), 957 (2)

arboreal 366 (10)

arboretum 366 (2), 370 (3)

arbour 192 (16), 194 (23), 421 (1), 837 (4)

arc 248 (2), 250 (4)

arc light 420 (4)

arcade 248 (2), 624 (5), 796 (2)

Arcadian 699 (3), 935 (3)

arcane 517 (2), 523 (2), 525 (3)

arch 32 (13), 34 (5), 47 (1), 214 (2), 218 (2), 248 (2), 248 (4), 248 (5), 253 (6), 253 (9), 833 (4), 850 (4)

arch of heaven 253 (4)

arch over 248 (5)

archaeologist 125 (5), 255 (5), 484 (2), 549 (2)

archaeology 125 (4)

archaic 127 (4), 127 (7), 560 (4)

archaism 125 (2), 127 (2), 133 (2), 148 (1), 560 (1)

archaize 125 (11)

archangel 968 (1)

archangelic 968 (3)

archbishop 741 (5), 986 (4)

arouse suspicion **459** (16)

aroused **818** (4)

arpeggio **410** (2)

arraign **928** (9), **959** (7)

arraignment **928** (1)

arrange **24** (10), **56** (5), **60** (3), **62** (4), **143** (6), **164** (7), **187** (5), **413** (8), **608** (3), **623** (8), **648** (9), **669** (11)

arranged **9** (5), **60** (2), **62** (3), **74** (9), **412** (7), **605** (5)

arranged match **894** (2)

arrangement **9** (1), **12** (1), **24** (4), **56** (1), **60** (1), **62** (1), **71** (2), **74** (1), **77** (1), **81** (2), **164** (1), **187** (1), **243** (2), **412** (4), **669** (1), **765** (1)

arrant **32** (13), **522** (4), **930** (5)

array **60** (1), **62** (1), **62** (4), **71** (2), **104** (1), **187** (5), **228** (1), **228** (31), **669** (11), **718** (7), **722** (8), **844** (12)

arraying **62** (1)

arrears **803** (1)

arrest **145** (1), **702** (1), **747** (3), **747** (7), **747** (8), **786** (6), **821** (8), **959** (2)

arresting **821** (5)

arrival **68** (1), **286** (2), **289** (1), **295** (1), **309** (1)

arrive **38** (4), **154** (6), **189** (4), **269** (9), **289** (4), **295** (4), **445** (8), **615** (5), **725** (7), **730** (6)

arriving **289** (2), **295** (3)

arrogance **871** (1), **878** (1)

arrogant **735** (5), **871** (3), **878** (4), **878** (6)

arrogate **734** (6), **735** (8), **786** (7), **915** (5), **916** (8)

arrogated **916** (6)

arrogation **306** (1), **786** (1), **878** (1), **916** (2), **954** (3)

arrow **256** (2), **277** (4), **287** (2), **547** (6), **723** (4), **889** (3)

arrow case **194** (10)

arrowhead **247** (1), **256** (2)

arsenal **74** (7), **632** (2), **687** (1), **723** (2)

arsenic **659** (3)

arson **165** (1), **379** (2), **381** (3)

arsonist **168** (1), **381** (3), **904** (1)

art **56** (1), **164** (1), **243** (1), **551** (3), **622** (1), **694** (1), **698** (2), **844** (2)

art equipment **425** (4), **553** (6)

art form **243** (1)

art gallery **632** (3)

art historian **556** (1)

art nouveau **551** (3)

art of healing **658** (10)

art of management **689** (1)

art of memory **505** (4)

art of reasoning **475** (1)

art of war **718** (4)

art school **539** (1)

art style **551** (3), **553** (2)

art subject **553** (4)

artefact **164** (2)

Artemis **967** (1)

arterial **624** (8)

artery **351** (1), **624** (6)

artesian well **632** (1)

artful **498** (4), **542** (6), **698** (4), **930** (4)

artful dodger **698** (3)

artfully **698** (6)

artfulness **541** (2), **698** (1), **930** (1)

arthritic **651** (22)

arthritis **651** (15)

arthropod **365** (2)

article **164** (2), **319** (3), **528** (2), **564** (2), **589** (2), **591** (2), **795** (1)

article of clothing **228** (3)

article oneself **536** (4)

articled clerk **538** (2)

articles **485** (2)

articles of faith **485** (2), **973** (4)

articulacy **579** (4)

articulate **45** (9), **516** (2), **563** (3), **577** (3), **577** (4), **579** (6), **579** (8)

articulated **45** (5)

articulated lorry **274** (12)

articulation **577** (1), **577** (2), **579** (1)

artifice **623** (3), **698** (2), **850** (2)

artificial **18** (6), **164** (6), **542** (7), **543** (4), **576** (2), **694** (7), **850** (4)

artificial eye **439** (1)

artificial fibre **208** (2)

artificial insemination **167** (1)

artificial lake **346** (1)

artificial leg **267** (7)

artificial light **417** (1)

artificial limb **150** (2)

artificiality **543** (2), **575** (1), **576** (1), **850** (1)

artillery **400** (1), **723** (11)

artisan **164** (4), **556** (1), **630** (5), **676** (3), **686** (3), **696** (2)

artist **20** (3), **164** (4), **513** (4), **520** (4), **549** (1), **556** (1), **594** (10), **676** (3), **696** (2)

artiste **413** (1), **594** (10)

artistic **551** (6), **575** (3), **694** (7), **841** (3), **846** (3)

artistic composition **56** (1)

artistic effort **164** (1)

artistic licence **744** (1)

artistry **378** (1), **553** (1), **694** (1), **846** (1)

artless **244** (2), **491** (4), **540** (2), **573** (2), **576** (2), **609** (3), **670** (3), **670** (4), **695** (6), **699** (3), **842** (5), **847** (4), **847** (5), **869** (9), **929** (3), **935** (3)

artless, be **699** (4), **885** (6), **935** (5)

artlessly **699** (5)

artlessness **491** (1), **540** (1), **573** (1), **576** (1), **699** (1), **847** (1), **935** (1)

arts **557** (3)

arts, the **490** (3)

as **18** (9)

as ... as can be **54** (8)

as a consequence **157** (7)

as a preliminary **64** (5)

as a result **157** (7)

as a reward 962 (5)
as a start 68 (11)
as a whole 52 (8)
as an excuse 614 (5)
as before 144 (4)
as different as chalk from cheese 14 (3)
as directed 60 (5)
as friends 880 (9)
As God is my witness! 532 (9)
as good as 28 (8), 28 (11), 52 (9), 200 (8)
as good as one's word 929 (4)
As I stand here 532 (9)
as if 18 (9)
as it is 7 (5)
as it were 18 (9)
as much again 91 (4)
as one 45 (15), 74 (12), 706 (5), 708 (9)
as or so long as 112 (1)
as promised 764 (6)
as regards 9 (10)
as such 5 (10)
as the case may be 8 (5)
as the crow flies 249 (5), 281 (8)
as they say 496 (4)
as things are 7 (5)
as things go 154 (8)
as to 9 (10)
as usual 83 (10), 610 (9)
as well as 38 (5)
as you were 148 (4)
ascend 32 (15), 36 (4), 209 (12), 220 (5), 265 (4), 271 (7), 298 (5), 308 (4), 310 (5), 323 (4), 654 (8)
ascendancy 34 (1), 160 (1), 178 (1), 727 (2), 866 (2)
ascending 32 (4), 209 (8), 220 (4), 271 (6), 308 (3)
ascending order 71 (2)
ascension 186 (2), 308 (1)
ascent 27 (1), 36 (1), 71 (2), 218 (5), 220 (2), 265 (1), 296 (1), 308 (1), 310 (1), 323 (1), 624 (2), 654 (1), 837 (6)
ascertain 473 (9), 484 (4)

ascertained 473 (4), 490 (7), 494 (4)
ascetic 500 (1), 801 (2), 820 (3), 942 (2), 942 (3), 945 (2), 945 (3), 979 (4), 979 (7), 986 (5)
ascetic, be 942 (4), 945 (4), 981 (12)
ascetically 945 (5)
asceticism 636 (1), 801 (1), 823 (1), 941 (3), 942 (1), 945 (1), 946 (1), 979 (3), 981 (3), 985 (1)
ascribable 915 (2)
ascribe 158 (3), 915 (8)
ascription 158 (1)
aseptic 648 (7), 652 (4)
ash 332 (2), 366 (4), 381 (4), 385 (2), 649 (2)
ash-blond 427 (5)
ash-grey 429 (2)
ashamed 872 (4), 936 (3), 939 (3)
ashamed, be 872 (6)
ashen 426 (3)
ashen-faced 854 (6)
ashes 41 (1), 363 (1), 381 (4), 429 (1), 649 (2), 729 (1)
ashore 344 (8)
ashy 426 (3), 429 (2)
aside 239 (4), 401 (6), 523 (1), 524 (3), 583 (1), 585 (1)
asinine 365 (18), 499 (4)
asininity 499 (2)
ask 459 (13), 491 (8), 761 (5)
ask a boon 761 (5)
ask a price 809 (5)
ask for 459 (13), 859 (11)
ask for credit 785 (2)
ask for more 636 (8)
ask for quarter 905 (8)
ask for terms 721 (3)
ask for trouble 711 (3), 857 (4)
ask in 882 (10)
ask leave 756 (6)
ask mercy 721 (4), 762 (3), 905 (8), 909 (5)
ask questions 453 (4), 459 (14)

ask too much 811 (5)
askance 220 (7)
asker 763 (1)
askew 29 (2), 61 (7), 220 (3), 220 (7), 246 (3)
asking 459 (1), 761 (1), 761 (3)
asking about 459 (1)
asking for it 963 (7)
asking questions 459 (2)
aslant 220 (3), 220 (7)
asleep 266 (4), 679 (9)
aspect 7 (2), 8 (1), 186 (1), 438 (5), 445 (1)
aspects 5 (3)
aspen leaf 318 (1)
asperity 885 (2), 891 (2), 892 (1)
aspersion 341 (2), 867 (2)
asphalt 357 (5)
aspic 389 (1)
aspirant 763 (1), 852 (3), 859 (6)
aspirate 300 (8), 304 (4), 352 (11), 407 (1), 407 (4), 577 (4)
aspirated 577 (3)
aspiration 300 (3), 304 (1), 577 (2), 612 (1), 617 (2), 852 (2), 859 (1), 859 (5)
aspire 308 (4), 852 (6)
aspire to 617 (6), 859 (11)
aspiring 617 (3), 852 (4), 859 (7)
ass 501 (1), 697 (1)
assail 712 (7)
assailant 705 (1), 712 (5), 722 (1)
assailing 712 (6)
assassin 168 (1), 176 (4), 362 (7), 904 (2)
assassinate 362 (12)
assassination 362 (2)
assault 176 (2), 279 (2), 712 (1), 712 (7), 951 (11)
assay 461 (1), 461 (7)
assayer 461 (3)
assegai 723 (6)
assemblage 45 (2), 50 (1), 56 (1), 62 (1), 74 (1), 293 (1), 771 (1)

assemble 45 (9), 56 (5), 74 (10), 74 (11), 164 (7), 295 (6)

assembled 45 (5), 50 (3), 74 (9)

assembly 45 (1), 50 (1), 74 (2), 164 (1), 584 (3), 692 (1), 837 (1), 875 (3), 882 (3)

assembly line 71 (1), 164 (1)

assembly room 837 (5)

assembly rooms 192 (14)

assent 24 (1), 24 (9), 181 (1), 181 (3), 475 (9), 485 (7), 488 (1), 488 (6), 526 (6), 597 (1), 597 (6), 721 (1), 721 (3), 739 (4), 756 (5), 758 (1), 758 (3), 765 (1), 923 (1), 923 (8)

assented 153 (5), 488 (5), 512 (5)

assenter 488 (3), 765 (3), 879 (2), 925 (2), 979 (4)

assenting 24 (5), 181 (2), 488 (4), 597 (4), 721 (2)

assert 532 (5)

assert oneself 178 (3), 678 (11), 746 (4)

assert roundly 532 (5)

assertion 466 (2), 532 (1)

assertive 162 (6), 473 (5), 532 (4)

assertive, be 532 (5)

assertiveness 532 (1)

assess 465 (13), 809 (5)

assess for tax 809 (7)

assessable 465 (10), 809 (4)

assessed 809 (4)

assessment 465 (1), 480 (2), 809 (3)

assessment centre 748 (1)

assessor 465 (8), 480 (3), 957 (2)

asset-stripper 786 (4)

asset-stripping 786 (2)

assets 629 (1), 632 (1), 777 (2)

asseverate 532 (5)

asseveration 532 (1)

assiduity 455 (1), 457 (1), 600 (1), 678 (3), 682 (1)

assiduous 139 (2), 455 (2), 457 (3), 678 (9)

assign 62 (4), 187 (5), 272 (6), 621 (3), 673 (5), 751 (4), 753 (3), 777 (6), 779 (4), 780 (3), 780 (4), 781 (7), 783 (3), 915 (8)

assign a place 187 (5)

assign a role 594 (16)

assign to 673 (3)

assignable 158 (2), 915 (2)

assignation 882 (4)

assigned 158 (2)

assigned place 185 (1)

assignee 782 (2)

assignment 672 (1), 751 (2), 780 (1), 783 (1)

assimilate 16 (4), 50 (4), 83 (8), 147 (8), 299 (4)

assimilate to 18 (8)

assimilated 83 (4), 147 (5)

assimilation 18 (2), 24 (4), 44 (2), 50 (1), 78 (1), 83 (1), 147 (1), 299 (1)

assimilative 299 (2)

assist 628 (4), 703 (5)

assist at 189 (4)

assistance 628 (1), 633 (1), 703 (1)

assistant 35 (2), 628 (2), 703 (3), 703 (4), 707 (1), 742 (1)

assistant bishop 986 (4)

assistant to, be 703 (7)

assisting 703 (4)

assize 959 (3)

assizes 956 (2)

associate 45 (9), 50 (4), 74 (10), 89 (2), 686 (4), 706 (4), 707 (3), 708 (3), 708 (8)

associate with 89 (4)

associated 9 (5), 45 (5), 50 (3), 89 (3), 706 (3)

association 9 (1), 45 (1), 50 (1), 74 (3), 88 (1), 89 (1), 181 (1), 622 (1), 706 (2), 708 (3), 708 (5), 775 (2), 880 (1), 882 (1)

association, an 706 (2)

assonance 18 (2), 106 (2), 574 (1), 593 (5)

assonant 106 (3)

assorted 15 (4)

assortment 16 (1), 43 (4), 62 (1), 71 (2), 74 (6), 74 (7), 77 (2)

assuage 177 (7), 266 (9), 679 (13), 719 (4), 823 (7), 826 (3), 831 (3)

assuagement 177 (1)

assuaging 177 (4)

assume 158 (4), 228 (32), 471 (6), 475 (12), 485 (7), 485 (8), 507 (4), 541 (6), 735 (8), 850 (5), 852 (6)

assume a disguise 525 (9)

assume an alias 562 (5)

assume command 733 (11)

assume ownership 786 (7)

assumed 512 (5), 850 (4)

assuming 8 (6), 916 (6)

assumption 158 (1), 310 (1), 475 (2), 485 (3), 512 (1), 852 (1), 916 (2)

assurance 159 (4), 473 (2), 485 (1), 532 (1), 660 (1), 764 (1), 852 (1), 873 (1), 878 (1)

assure 473 (9), 485 (9), 764 (4), 767 (6)

assured 473 (5), 485 (4), 532 (4), 660 (4)

assuredness 473 (1)

asterisk 547 (14)

astern 238 (6), 286 (6)

asteroid 321 (6)

asthma 651 (8)

asthmatic 352 (9), 406 (2), 651 (18), 651 (22)

astigmatic 440 (3)

astigmatism 440 (1)

astir 678 (8)

astonish 508 (5), 864 (7)

astonished 508 (3), 864 (4)

astonishing 32 (7), 84 (6)

astonishingly 32 (19)

astonishment 508 (1), 864 (1)

astound 821 (8), 864 (7)

astounded 864 (4)

astounding 32 (7), 508 (2), 864 (5)

astrakhan 226 (6)

astral 321 (14)

at rest 175 (4), 266 (4), 683 (4)

at right angles 215 (5)

at sea 269 (6), 343 (4), 495 (5)

at sea level 210 (2)

at short notice 114 (5), 135 (8), 680 (4)

at sight 438 (10)

at sixes and sevens 61 (12)

at sunrise 128 (8)

at the back 238 (6)

at the beginning 68 (11)

at the bottom 35 (6), 214 (5)

at the bottom or the root of 156 (9)

at the breast 132 (5)

at the core 225 (5)

at the double 277 (9), 680 (5)

at the eleventh hour 136 (8)

at the foot of 210 (4)

at the front 718 (8)

at the heart of 225 (5)

at the helm 269 (13), 689 (3), 689 (6)

at the mercy of 180 (2), 661 (5), 745 (5)

at the midpoint 70 (3)

at the peak 34 (11)

at the ready 669 (7)

at the salute 920 (3)

at the same time 123 (5)

at the stake 963 (12)

at the top 213 (6)

at the top of one's voice 400 (5)

at the wheel 269 (13)

at this moment 121 (4)

at this time 121 (4)

at times 139 (6)

at variance 25 (4), 704 (3), 709 (6), 881 (3)

at variance with 489 (6)

at variance with, be 709 (7)

at war 716 (9), 718 (8)

at war with 881 (3)

at will 595 (3), 744 (11)

at work 173 (2), 676 (4), 678 (8)

at your service 739 (5)

atavism 5 (5), 106 (2), 148 (1)

atavistic 5 (7), 148 (2)

atheism 449 (3), 486 (1), 973 (1), 974 (1)

atheist 486 (3), 974 (3), 980 (3)

atheistic 974 (5)

Athena 967 (1)

athlete 162 (4), 716 (8), 722 (1)

athlete's foot 651 (12)

athletic 162 (9), 327 (3), 682 (4), 716 (9), 837 (19)

athletic honour 729 (2)

athleticism 162 (3)

athletics 162 (3), 265 (1), 682 (2), 716 (1), 716 (2), 837 (6)

athletics coach 537 (2)

athwart 220 (3), 222 (11)

atlas 87 (3), 321 (2), 551 (5)

atmosphere 178 (1), 209 (1), 230 (1), 340 (2)

atmospheric 340 (5)

atmospherics 318 (3), 411 (1)

atoll 349 (1)

atom 33 (3), 88 (2), 196 (2), 319 (4)

atom bomb 723 (14)

atomic 160 (9), 196 (11)

atomic bomb 160 (7)

atomic physics 319 (5)

atomic pile 160 (7)

atomic war 718 (1)

atomic warhead 723 (13)

atomization 51 (1), 338 (1)

atomize 51 (5), 338 (4)

atomizer 338 (2)

atonal 410 (8)

atonality 411 (1)

atone 787 (3), 909 (5), 939 (4), 941 (5)

atonement 31 (2), 658 (1), 787 (1), 939 (1), 941 (1), 963 (1), 981 (6)

atoning 787 (2), 939 (3), 941 (4)

atop 213 (6)

atrocious 898 (7), 934 (6)

atrocity 176 (1), 898 (3), 936 (2)

atrophy 161 (2), 651 (3), 651 (16)

attach 38 (3), 45 (10), 45 (11)

attach no importance to 639 (7)

attach strings 747 (9)

attaché 754 (3)

attaché case 194 (7)

attached 45 (8)

attached to 887 (9)

attachment 40 (1), 45 (2), 53 (1), 887 (1)

attack 68 (8), 174 (1), 176 (2), 279 (1), 279 (2), 279 (3), 289 (1), 289 (4), 297 (1), 297 (7), 306 (4), 318 (2), 475 (11), 577 (1), 599 (1), 624 (1), 651 (2), 702 (1), 712 (1), 712 (7), 714 (1), 716 (11), 718 (6), 718 (7), 718 (11), 723 (3), 727 (2), 727 (9), 788 (2), 924 (2), 924 (10), 928 (9)

attack of nerves 503 (2)

attacker 59 (3), 168 (1), 297 (3), 705 (1), 709 (5), 712 (5), 722 (1), 881 (2), 924 (5), 926 (3)

attacking 59 (4), 174 (5), 297 (4), 709 (6), 712 (6), 718 (8)

attain 295 (4)

attain one's majority 134 (4)

attain one's objective 727 (6)

attainable 289 (3), 469 (2)

attainment 694 (1)

attainments 536 (1)

attempt 461 (7), 597 (6), 600 (4), 617 (1), 617 (6), 671 (1), 671 (4), 672 (1), 672 (3), 676 (1), 676 (5), 678 (11), 682 (1), 682 (6), 716 (2)

attempt the impossible 470 (6)

attempting 461 (6), 597 (4), 671 (3)

attend 89 (4), 189 (4), 284 (4), 455 (4), 658 (20)

attend to 768 (3)

attend upon 742 (8)

attendance 89 (1), 189 (1)

attendant 89 (2), 89 (3), 189 (2), 284 (2), 742 (1), 742 (3)

attention 415 (2), 449 (1), 455 (1), 457 (1), 494 (3), 507 (1), 536 (2), 678 (3), 725 (1), 875 (2)

attention to 768 (1)

attention to detail 455 (1)

attentions 920 (1)

attentive 415 (5), 449 (5), 453 (3), 455 (2), 457 (3), 490 (5), 494 (6), 498 (4), 536 (3), 599 (2), 682 (4), 768 (2), 819 (4), 858 (2), 862 (3), 884 (3)

attentive, be 415 (6), 438 (8), 441 (3), 449 (7), 453 (4), 455 (4), 457 (5), 490 (8), 524 (12), 678 (11), 768 (3)

attentively 457 (8)

attentiveness 455 (1), 457 (1)

attenuate 206 (7), 325 (3)

attenuated 206 (4)

attenuation 198 (1), 325 (1)

attest 466 (7), 488 (8), 532 (6)

attestation 466 (2), 473 (1)

attested 466 (5), 473 (4)

attic 194 (22), 213 (2)

attire 228 (1), 228 (31)

attitude 7 (1), 8 (1), 451 (1), 485 (3), 512 (1), 688 (1), 817 (1)

attitudinize 850 (5)

attitudinizer 850 (3)

attorney 754 (1), 755 (1), 958 (2)

Attorney General 955 (2)

attract 74 (11), 156 (9), 178 (3), 288 (3), 291 (4), 612 (8), 826 (4), 859 (13), 887 (15)

attract notice 178 (3), 443 (4), 455 (7), 522 (9), 547

(21), 638 (7), 821 (8), 875 (7)

attracting 160 (9), 178 (2), 288 (2), 291 (3), 612 (6), 826 (2), 859 (10), 887 (11)

attraction 76 (1), 160 (3), 178 (1), 179 (1), 288 (1), 29' (1), 612 (2), 612 (4), 826 (1), 859 (5), 890 (2), 983 (2)

attractions 841 (1), 887 (2)

attractive 178 (2), 291 (3), 826 (2), 841 (6), 859 (10), 887 (11)

attractiveness 826 (1), 887 (2)

attributable 158 (2), 915 (2)

attribute 5 (2), 80 (1), 89 (2), 158 (3), 160 (2), 907 (5), 915 (8)

attributed 156 (7), 158 (2)

attributed to 157 (3)

attribution 156 (1), 158 (1), 915 (1)

attributive 564 (3)

attrition 332 (1), 333 (1), 718 (6)

attune 24 (10), 410 (9)

attuned to 24 (8)

attunement 24 (4)

atypical 17 (2), 19 (2), 21 (4), 84 (7)

au fait 694 (6)

au pair 151 (4), 191 (2), 742 (2)

au revoir 296 (7)

aubergine 436 (1)

auburn 430 (3), 431 (3)

auction 759 (3), 793 (1), 793 (4)

auction off 793 (4)

auction room 796 (1)

auctioneer 793 (2)

auctioneering 793 (1)

audacious 855 (4), 857 (3), 878 (4)

audacity 855 (1), 857 (1), 878 (1)

audibility 398 (1), 400 (1), 415 (1)

audible 398 (3), 400 (3), 415 (5), 516 (2), 579 (6)

audience 415 (2), 415 (3), 441 (2), 528 (2), 583 (1), 584 (3), 594 (14)

audio 398 (1), 398 (3)

audiometer 398 (2)

audiophile 415 (3)

audiotypist 586 (6)

audiovisual 398 (3), 415 (5), 534 (5)

audit 86 (11), 459 (13), 808 (1), 808 (5)

audition 415 (2), 459 (4), 461 (1), 584 (3)

auditions 594 (2)

auditor 808 (3)

auditorium 441 (2), 539 (4), 594 (7)

auditory 398 (3), 415 (5)

auger 263 (12)

augment 27 (5), 32 (15), 36 (5), 38 (3), 86 (12), 162 (12), 197 (5), 632 (5)

augmentation 36 (1), 36 (2), 197 (1)

augur 511 (8)

augur well 730 (8), 852 (7)

augury 511 (2), 511 (3)

august 32 (4), 638 (6), 866 (8)

aunt 11 (2), 373 (3)

Aunt Sally 851 (3)

aura 230 (1), 866 (2)

aural 415 (5)

aureole 250 (3), 417 (1)

aurora 128 (1), 967 (2)

auroral 128 (5), 239 (2)

auspicate 68 (10), 156 (9)

auspice 511 (3)

auspices 660 (2), 703 (1)

auspicious 137 (5), 511 (7), 642 (2), 730 (5), 852 (5)

auspicious, be 703 (6), 730 (8)

auspicious hour 137 (1)

Aussie 59 (2)

austere 573 (2), 945 (3), 979 (7)

austerely 945 (5)

austerity 391 (1), 636 (1), 945 (1), 979 (3)

authentic 21 (4), 466 (5), 494 (5)

authenticate 466 (7), 473 (9), 488 (8), 767 (6)

authentication 473 (1)

authenticity 13 (1), 21 (2), 494 (2)

author 150 (2), 156 (2), 164 (4), 529 (4), 586 (5), 589 (7), 590 (5), 591 (3), 593 (7), 623 (5)

authoritarian 595 (1), 689 (3), 733 (7), 735 (3), 735 (5)

authoritative 160 (8), 178 (2), 466 (5), 473 (4), 485 (6), 689 (3), 733 (7), 737 (5), 975 (4), 976 (8)

authoritatively 737 (9)

authorities, the 741 (1)

authority 27 (1), 32 (1), 34 (1), 64 (1), 160 (1), 466 (1), 466 (3), 480 (1), 500 (1), 524 (4), 638 (4), 689 (1), 696 (2), 733 (1), 735 (1), 743 (1), 747 (1), 751 (1), 756 (2), 866 (2), 868 (1), 868 (3), 955 (1), 985 (1)

authorization 160 (2), 737 (4), 756 (1)

authorize 160 (11), 751 (4), 756 (5), 915 (8)

authorship 156 (1), 586 (1)

autism 503 (1), 883 (1)

autistic 503 (7)

auto 274 (11)

autobiographer 590 (5)

autobiographical 590 (6)

autobiography 590 (3)

autocracy 733 (3), 735 (2)

autocrat 638 (4), 690 (2), 735 (3), 741 (2)

autocratic 595 (1), 733 (7), 735 (5)

autograph 21 (2), 505 (3), 547 (2), 547 (13), 547 (20), 586 (3)

autohypnosis 375 (1)

automate 86 (13), 160 (11), 164 (7)

automated 160 (9), 164 (5), 630 (6)

automatic 86 (10), 450 (2), 596 (5), 628 (3), 630 (6), 723 (10)

automatic pilot 271 (4)

automatic reflex 609 (1)

automatic writing 984 (3)

automatically 610 (9)

automation 160 (6), 164 (1), 628 (1), 630 (3)

automatism 450 (1), 984 (3)

automaton 551 (2), 630 (2)

automobile 274 (11), 274 (16)

autonomous 733 (9), 744 (7)

autonomy 744 (2)

autopsy 361 (1), 364 (6), 459 (1)

autumn 110 (1), 127 (1), 129 (3)

autumn colours 430 (1)

autumnal 129 (6)

autumnal equinox 129 (3)

auxiliary 35 (2), 35 (4), 38 (2), 40 (2), 150 (2), 218 (2), 628 (2), 703 (3), 703 (4), 707 (1), 722 (4), 722 (7), 880 (3)

avail oneself of 673 (4)

availability 189 (1), 605 (1), 640 (1), 779 (1)

available 189 (2), 289 (3), 628 (3), 632 (4), 633 (4), 640 (2), 673 (2), 759 (2), 779 (3), 793 (3)

avalanche 149 (1), 309 (1), 380 (3), 637 (1)

avant-garde 64 (2), 66 (1), 126 (3), 126 (6), 283 (1), 594 (15)

avant-propos 66 (2)

avarice 771 (1), 786 (3), 816 (2), 859 (1), 932 (1)

avaricious 771 (4), 816 (5), 859 (8), 932 (3)

avatar 965 (4), 975 (1)

avenge 714 (3), 735 (7), 906 (3), 910 (5), 963 (8)

avenge oneself 910 (5)

avenger 910 (3), 963 (5)

avenging 910 (4)

avenue 192 (8), 192 (15), 624 (6)

aver 532 (5)

average 23 (1), 26 (1), 30 (1), 30 (4), 30 (5), 70 (1), 79 (1), 79 (3), 83 (5), 86 (4), 625 (1), 647 (3), 732 (1), 732 (2)

average out 30 (5), 464 (4), 770 (2)

average specimen 30 (3)

averageness 30 (1), 30 (3), 33 (1), 35 (1), 79 (1), 177 (1), 732 (1), 869 (4)

averages 86 (4)

averse 861 (2), 888 (4)

averse to 598 (3)

aversion 598 (1), 861 (1), 888 (1)

aversion therapy 658 (12)

avert 282 (6), 713 (10)

avert one's eyes 438 (8), 439 (3), 872 (6)

averting 762 (2)

avian 365 (18)

aviary 192 (4), 369 (3), 369 (4)

aviation 271 (1)

aviational 276 (5)

aviator 271 (4)

avid 821 (3), 859 (7)

avid for 453 (3)

avidity 786 (3), 816 (2), 859 (1)

avocado 434 (3)

avoid 46 (7), 46 (9), 57 (5), 190 (6), 199 (5), 280 (3), 282 (3), 286 (5), 290 (3), 460 (5), 518 (3), 525 (9), 598 (4), 620 (5), 621 (3), 626 (3), 667 (6), 674 (4), 677 (3), 679 (11), 713 (10), 760 (4), 769 (3), 854 (10), 856 (4), 858 (3), 861 (4), 883 (8), 883 (9), 888 (7), 918 (3), 924 (9), 942 (4)

avoid bloodshed 717 (4)

avoid excess 732 (3), 942 (4)

avoid notice 523 (5)

avoid the issue 620 (5)

avoid the trap 698 (5)

avoidable 620 (4)

avoidance 57 (1), 190 (1), 598 (1), 620 (1), 621 (1), 660 (1), 667 (1), 674 (1), 677 (1), 702 (1), 861 (1), 883 (1), 918 (1)

avoided 861 (3), 883 (6)

avoider 620 (2), 918 (1)

avoiding 49 (2), 598 (3), 620 (3), 667 (4), 861 (2), 883 (5), 942 (3), 950 (5)

avoirdupois 195 (3)

avow 466 (7), 488 (6), 526 (6), 532 (5)

avowal 488 (1), 526 (1), 532 (1)

avowed 526 (2)

avuncular 11 (5)

await 124 (6), 136 (5), 474 (8), 507 (5)

awaiting 507 (2)

awaiting trial 928 (6)

awake 455 (2), 678 (7)

awake to 819 (2)

awaken 821 (6)

awaken to 524 (12)

award 480 (1), 480 (5), 729 (1), 781 (1), 781 (2), 781 (7), 866 (4), 962 (1), 962 (3)

awarded 782 (3)

awarder 781 (4)

aware 374 (3), 490 (5), 498 (4), 819 (2), 819 (4)

aware, be 490 (8)

awareness 374 (1), 447 (1), 490 (1), 498 (2)

awash 341 (5)

away 190 (4), 199 (3), 199 (6)

awe 821 (1), 854 (1), 854 (12), 864 (1), 864 (7), 920 (1), 920 (7), 981 (1)

awe-inspiring 821 (5), 854 (8), 864 (5)

awed 864 (4)

awesome 854 (8), 864 (5)

awestruck 818 (4), 854 (6), 864 (4), 920 (3)

awful 645 (2), 645 (4), 854 (8)

awfully 32 (18)

awkward 84 (5), 195 (9), 499 (4), 576 (2), 643 (2),

695 (5), 700 (4), 709 (6), 738 (7), 827 (5), 842 (5), 847 (5), 849 (2)

awkward age 130 (1)

awkward person 738 (4)

awkwardness 491 (1), 695 (1), 709 (2)

awl 263 (12)

awning 226 (3), 421 (1)

AWOL 190 (4)

awry 61 (7), 220 (3), 246 (3), 616 (2), 616 (3)

axe 165 (6), 204 (5), 256 (5), 300 (7), 311 (6), 723 (7), 964 (3)

axe-grinder 623 (5)

axe-grinding 932 (3)

axe to grind 617 (2)

axiom 473 (1), 475 (2), 494 (1), 496 (2)

axiomatic 473 (4), 475 (7), 496 (3)

axiomatics 86 (3)

axis 218 (11), 225 (2), 315 (3), 465 (5), 706 (2), 708 (3)

axle 218 (11), 315 (3)

axle grease 334 (2)

axle load 322 (2)

ayatollah 741 (5)

ayes, the 488 (3)

azimuth 216 (1), 281 (2)

azure 435 (1), 435 (3), 547 (16)

B

babble 350 (9), 401 (4), 477 (7), 503 (10), 515 (3), 515 (6), 581 (2)

babe 132 (1), 935 (2)

babe in arms 699 (2)

Babel 61 (2), 411 (1), 557 (1)

baboon 365 (3)

baby 132 (1), 132 (5), 163 (2), 196 (8), 856 (2)

baby boom 171 (1)

baby-sit 457 (6)

baby-sitter 660 (3), 749 (1)

baby-sitting 457 (2)

babyhood 68 (1), 130 (1)

babyish 132 (5), 163 (4), 499 (4), 856 (3)

baccalaureate 866 (4)

baccarat 837 (11)

Bacchanalia 61 (4)

Bacchanalian 944 (3)

Bacchus 967 (1)

bachelor 372 (1), 744 (7), 870 (2), 895 (2)

bachelor girl 373 (3), 895 (3)

bachelor-like 895 (4)

bachelorhood 895 (1)

bacillus 196 (5), 651 (5), 659 (3)

back 65 (2), 69 (4), 218 (2), 221 (4), 227 (2), 238 (1), 238 (4), 238 (5), 282 (3), 286 (4), 286 (6), 286 (7), 326 (5), 352 (10), 605 (6), 618 (8), 703 (6), 784 (5), 791 (4), 923 (8)

back and fill 269 (10)

back and forth 317 (7)

back away 290 (3), 598 (4), 620 (5)

back door 238 (1), 263 (6)

back down 148 (3), 286 (4), 603 (5), 621 (3), 760 (4)

back-end 129 (3), 238 (1)

back entrance 238 (1)

back-handed 518 (2)

back-handed compliment 924 (2)

back number 127 (2)

back of beyond 199 (2), 883 (2)

back on 238 (5)

back out 286 (4), 603 (5), 856 (4)

back seat 35 (1)

back-seat driver 268 (4), 678 (6)

back side 238 (1)

back slang 560 (3)

back-slapping 875 (1), 880 (6), 882 (6)

back street 624 (6), 655 (2)

back-to-back 192 (7), 192 (20), 238 (6), 240 (4)

back-to-front 221 (3), 221 (6)

back to normal 656 (6)

back to the beginning 148 (4)

back up 218 (15), 703 (5)

back water 286 (4)

back where one started 148 (1)

backache 377 (2)

backbencher 35 (2), 692 (3)

backbite 926 (7)

backbiter 926 (4)

backbiting 926 (1)

backbone 5 (2), 162 (2), 174 (1), 218 (10), 225 (2), 238 (1), 599 (1), 600 (2)

backbreaking 682 (5)

backchat 460 (1), 839 (2), 878 (2)

backcloth 594 (6)

backdrop 238 (1), 594 (6)

backer 594 (12), 618 (4), 707 (4)

backfire 402 (1)

backgammon 837 (9)

background 8 (1), 199 (1), 230 (1), 238 (1), 490 (1), 524 (1), 844 (1)

background music 412 (4)

background radiation 417 (4)

backing 227 (1), 286 (1), 286 (3), 326 (2), 703 (1)

backlash 148 (1), 157 (1), 280 (1), 714 (1), 715 (1), 762 (1)

backlog 632 (1)

backpacker 268 (1)

backpedal 278 (6), 286 (4), 603 (7)

backroom 523 (2)

backside 238 (2)

backslide 148 (3), 603 (5), 657 (2), 934 (7), 980 (6)

backslider 603 (3), 904 (3), 974 (4), 980 (3)

backsliding 148 (1), 286 (2), 603 (1), 657 (1), 934 (1), 974 (1), 974 (5), 980 (1), 980 (4)

backstage 238 (1), 594 (18)

backtrack 286 (4), 603 (7)

backward 136 (3), 238 (6), 286 (3), 491 (4), 499 (3), 598 (3), 620 (3), 655 (5), 670 (4), 699 (3)

backward-looking 125 (9), 286 (3)

backward motion 265 (1)

backward step 286 (1)

backwardness 491 (1), 499 (1), 598 (1), 861 (1)

backwards 286 (6)

backwash 350 (3), 350 (5)

backwoods 184 (3)

bacon 301 (16)

bacteria 196 (5), 651 (5), 659 (3)

bacterial disease 651 (3)

bad 35 (4), 51 (3), 616 (2), 639 (6), 641 (5), 645 (2), 647 (3), 653 (2), 655 (5), 731 (4), 898 (5), 914 (3), 922 (4), 924 (8), 930 (4), 934 (3), 934 (6)

bad air 653 (1)

bad apple 143 (3)

bad argument 475 (4)

bad art 847 (1)

bad at 645 (2)

bad bargain 811 (1)

bad behaviour 934 (1)

bad blood 881 (1), 888 (1)

bad books 924 (1)

bad case 477 (2)

bad character 867 (1)

bad climate 653 (1)

bad conscience 936 (1)

bad debt 803 (1)

bad deed 676 (2)

bad drains 653 (1)

bad dream 513 (3), 665 (2)

bad example 10 (2), 938 (1)

bad faith 541 (1), 769 (1), 930 (2)

bad fit 25 (3)

bad form 611 (2), 847 (2)

bad fortune 731 (2)

bad grammar 564 (1), 565 (1)

bad guy 938 (1)

bad habit 659 (1), 943 (1)

bad hand 697 (1)

bad health 651 (1)

bad influence 645 (1), 938 (1)

bad job 695 (2)

bad judgment 954 (1)

bad language 885 (2), 899 (2)

bad law 954 (1)

bad light 419 (2), 867 (1), 926 (1)

bad likeness 19 (1), 552 (1)

bad logic 477 (2)

bad lot 904 (1)

bad luck 159 (1), 509 (1), 616 (1), 731 (2)

bad-mannered 885 (4)

bad manners 688 (1), 847 (2), 885 (1)

bad match 25 (3)

bad name 867 (1)

bad news 509 (1), 529 (1)

bad odour 397 (1), 867 (1), 888 (2)

bad patch 700 (1), 731 (1)

bad person 147 (4), 738 (4), 867 (3), 904 (3), 914 (1), 938 (1), 940 (1), 980 (3)

bad policy 643 (1)

bad press 924 (2), 926 (1)

bad qualities 645 (1)

bad reputation 867 (1)

bad result 616 (1)

bad smell 394 (1), 397 (1)

bad taste 25 (2), 464 (1), 495 (3), 551 (3), 576 (1), 839 (1), 847 (1), 914 (1), 916 (1), 934 (2), 951 (1)

bad temper 892 (1), 893 (1)

bad-tempered 893 (2)

bad times 731 (1)

bad value 811 (1)

bad weather 340 (3)

badge 547 (9), 547 (11), 729 (1), 743 (3), 844 (5)

badge of loyalty 547 (9)

badge of mourning 547 (9)

badge of office 547 (9)

badge of rank 547 (9), 743 (3), 989 (2)

badge of rule 547 (9), 743 (2)

badger 365 (3), 459 (14), 827 (9)

badinage 584 (1), 839 (2)

badly 32 (20), 33 (9), 645 (8)

badly-acted 594 (15)

badly adjusted 495 (6)

badly brought up 847 (5)

badly done 645 (2), 695 (6)

badly dressed 842 (5)

badly made 842 (4)

badly off 731 (5)

badly served 509 (2)

badminton 837 (7)

badness 35 (1), 645 (1), 731 (2), 827 (1), 847 (1), 867 (3), 914 (1), 934 (1)

baffle 474 (9), 700 (6), 702 (10), 704 (4), 727 (10), 864 (7)

baffle comphrehension 517 (6)

baffle description 864 (7)

baffled 161 (7), 474 (6), 509 (2), 517 (5), 700 (5), 728 (5)

bafflement 474 (2), 509 (1), 728 (2)

baffling 829 (4)

bag 74 (6), 194 (9), 253 (9), 273 (1), 771 (7), 786 (6)

bag-snatcher 789 (1)

bag-snatching 788 (1)

bagful 26 (2)

baggage 194 (7), 272 (3), 702 (4), 777 (1), 878 (3)

bagginess 49 (1), 205 (1)

baggy 49 (2), 183 (6), 194 (24), 195 (6), 205 (3), 217 (4)

bagpipe 352 (5)

bagpipes 414 (6)

bags 32 (2), 228 (12)

Baha'ism 973 (3)

bail 746 (1), 767 (1), 959 (2)

bail one out 767 (5)

bail out 272 (7), 300 (8), 703 (5)

bailee 754 (1)

bailiff 300 (2), 370 (4), 690 (3), 741 (6), 742 (3), 955 (2)

bain-marie 194 (14)

bairn 132 (1)

bait 291 (1), 291 (4), 542 (2), 542 (4), 542 (10), 612 (4), 827 (9), 891 (9)

baize 222 (4)

bake 301 (40), 326 (5), 342 (6), 379 (7), 381 (8)

baked 342 (4)

baked beans 301 (20)

baker 633 (3)

baker's dozen 99 (2)

bakery 301 (5)

baking 301 (5), 379 (4), 381 (1)

baking-powder 323 (2)

balance 12 (3), 24 (10), 28 (1), 28 (3), 28 (10), 30 (1), 31 (2), 31 (5), 41 (1), 53 (1), 54 (1), 86 (11), 153 (1), 153 (8), 245 (1), 322 (3), 322 (5), 465 (5), 465 (11), 498 (2), 502 (1), 575 (1), 601 (4), 637 (2), 823 (1)

balance accounts 771 (7), 808 (5)

balance due 627 (1)

balance of forces 28 (3)

balance of nature 28 (3)

balance of power 28 (3)

balance sheet 808 (1)

balance to pay 803 (1)

balanced 24 (8), 28 (7), 245 (2), 498 (5), 502 (2)

balanced diet 301 (3)

balances 797 (2), 802 (1)

balancing 28 (4), 31 (3), 182 (2), 322 (2)

balancing act 770 (1)

balcony 254 (2), 594 (7)

bald 229 (5), 258 (3), 540 (2), 572 (2), 573 (2), 576 (2), 838 (3)

baldness 229 (2), 572 (1), 573 (1)

bale 74 (6), 187 (7), 370 (9)

bale out 271 (7), 298 (5)

baleful 898 (4)

balk 218 (9)

balk at 620 (5)

ball 252 (2), 287 (2), 723 (4), 837 (13), 837 (15)

ball and chain 748 (4)

ball game 837 (7)

ball-player 837 (16)

ball up 63 (5)

ballad 412 (5), 590 (2), 593 (2)

ballade 593 (4)

ballast 31 (2), 31 (5), 153 (3), 322 (1)

balled 252 (5)

balled up 61 (8)

ballerina 594 (9), 837 (14)

ballet 56 (1), 594 (5), 837 (13)

ballet dancer 594 (9)

ballet dancing 594 (5), 837 (13)

ballet school 539 (1)

ballet shoes 228 (27)

ballet skirt 228 (13)

balletic 594 (15)

ballistic 287 (6)

ballistic missile 723 (4)

ballistics 287 (1), 723 (1)

balloon 194 (2), 197 (4), 232 (1), 252 (2), 252 (6), 253 (9), 276 (2), 323 (1), 837 (15)

ballooning 253 (7), 271 (1)

balloonist 271 (4)

ballot 532 (1), 605 (2)

ballot box 605 (2)

ballroom 837 (5)

ballroom dancing 837 (13)

ballyhoo 528 (2)

balm 177 (2), 334 (2), 658 (2), 658 (8), 826 (1), 831 (1)

balminess 396 (1)

balmy 379 (6), 730 (5), 833 (6)

baluster 218 (10)

balustrade 218 (3), 235 (3)

bamboo 366 (8)

bamboozle 525 (8), 542 (8), 542 (9)

ban 57 (1), 57 (5), 702 (1), 702 (9), 747 (1), 747 (7),

757 (1), 757 (4), 899 (1), 988 (10)

banal 496 (3), 610 (6), 840 (2)

banality 496 (1), 840 (1)

banana 301 (19)

banana republic 639 (4), 733 (6)

band 47 (1), 47 (4), 47 (7), 74 (4), 77 (1), 208 (3), 250 (3), 413 (3), 437 (3), 538 (4), 686 (4), 708 (1), 722 (8)

band of heroes 855 (3)

band together 50 (4), 74 (10), 706 (4)

bandage 45 (12), 47 (4), 198 (3), 208 (3), 226 (5), 226 (13), 439 (4), 656 (11), 658 (9), 658 (20), 702 (9)

bandbox 194 (7)

bandeau 47 (7)

banded 62 (3), 437 (8), 708 (6)

banded together 181 (2)

bandit 738 (4), 789 (2), 883 (4)

banditry 738 (1), 788 (2)

bandmaster 413 (3)

bandolier 47 (7)

bands 989 (1)

bandsman 413 (3)

bandstand 192 (16)

bandy 246 (4)

bandy-legged 246 (4), 267 (10)

bandy words 151 (3), 584 (6)

bane 168 (1), 178 (1), 616 (1), 645 (1), 651 (4), 651 (5), 653 (1), 659 (1), 663 (1), 731 (1), 825 (1), 825 (3), 827 (1), 827 (2), 888 (3), 898 (1), 904 (5)

baneful 336 (3), 659 (5), 827 (3), 888 (5), 898 (5)

bang 174 (7), 264 (6), 279 (1), 279 (2), 279 (7), 279 (9), 398 (1), 400 (1), 400 (4), 402 (1), 402 (4)

banger 274 (11), 301 (16), 402 (1), 420 (7)

banging 400 (1), 402 (2)

bangle 844 (7)

banish 57 (5), 188 (4), 300 (6), 883 (9)

banishment 188 (1), 300 (1), 963 (4)

banister 218 (10)

banisters 218 (3)

banjo 414 (2)

banjoist 413 (2)

bank 209 (2), 218 (6), 220 (2), 220 (5), 239 (1), 344 (2), 632 (2), 632 (5), 784 (2), 798 (1), 799 (1)

bank account 800 (1)

Bank holiday 837 (1)

bank on 473 (7), 485 (7), 507 (4), 852 (6)

bank rate 803 (2)

banked 632 (4)

banker 784 (3), 794 (1), 798 (1)

banking on 507 (2)

banknote 797 (5)

bankroll 797 (5)

bankrupt 727 (10), 728 (3), 728 (6), 772 (2), 801 (2), 801 (3), 805 (3), 805 (4)

bankruptcy 728 (1), 769 (1), 772 (1), 805 (2)

banned 57 (3), 757 (3)

banner 547 (12)

banquet 301 (35), 635 (2), 837 (2), 837 (23), 882 (3)

banqueter 301 (6)

banqueting 301 (2)

banqueting hall 301 (2)

banshee 970 (4)

bantam 33 (5), 196 (4), 365 (6)

bantamweight 722 (2)

banter 584 (1), 839 (2), 839 (5), 851 (1), 851 (5)

baptism 299 (1), 303 (2), 341 (2), 988 (3), 988 (4)

baptism of fire 68 (2)

baptismal 299 (2), 988 (8)

Baptist 976 (5), 976 (11)

baptistry 990 (4)

baptize 68 (10), 299 (3), 303 (7), 561 (6), 979 (11), 988 (10)

baptizer 561 (3)

bar 39 (4), 57 (1), 57 (5), 57 (6), 192 (12), 194 (19), 203 (3), 218 (2), 235 (3), 264 (2), 264 (6), 349 (1), 410 (3), 437 (3), 702 (9), 747 (1), 747 (7), 748 (2), 757 (4), 797 (7), 924 (9), 956 (1), 956 (4), 958 (5), 961 (3)

bar graph 86 (4)

barb 256 (2), 256 (11)

barbarian 59 (4), 168 (1), 176 (4), 847 (3), 847 (4), 869 (7), 869 (9), 885 (3), 904 (2)

barbaric 244 (2), 847 (5), 869 (9)

barbarism 560 (1), 565 (1), 576 (1), 699 (1), 847 (1), 898 (2)

barbarity 176 (1), 898 (2), 898 (3)

barbarize 655 (8)

barbarous 176 (5), 576 (2), 869 (9), 898 (7)

barbecue 301 (12), 301 (40), 837 (2), 882 (3)

barbed 256 (7)

barbed wire 702 (2), 713 (2)

barber 648 (6), 843 (5)

barbered 648 (7)

barbican 713 (4)

barbiturate 658 (7)

bard 413 (1), 593 (6)

bardic 593 (8)

bare 44 (4), 172 (4), 190 (5), 229 (4), 229 (6), 342 (4), 522 (5), 526 (4), 636 (4)

bare-headed 920 (3)

bare minimum 635 (1)

bare neck 229 (2)

bare-necked 229 (4)

bare one's teeth 711 (3), 893 (3)

bare possibility 472 (1)

bare subsistence 636 (1)

bare the fangs 900 (3)

bared 229 (4)

barefaced lie 543 (1)

barefoot 229 (4), 801 (4)

bareheaded 229 (4)

barelegged 229 (4)

barely 33 (9)

barely audible 401 (3)

bareness 190 (2), 229 (2)

bargain 488 (2), 765 (1),
765 (5), 766 (4), 791 (2),
791 (6), 792 (1); 812 (1),
816 (6)

bargain basement 796 (3)

bargain price 810 (1), 812
(1)

bargain-rate 812 (3)

bargainer 792 (2)

bargaining 584 (3), 766
(1), 791 (1), 792 (4)

barge 273 (1), 275 (7)

barge in 297 (8), 306 (4)

barge pole 269 (5)

bargee 270 (4)

baritone 404 (1), 413 (4)

bark 226 (6), 333 (3), 409
(3)

bark at 827 (9)

bark one's shins 279 (8)

barker 528 (6)

barking 409 (1)

barley sugar 301 (18)

barley water 301 (27)

barm 323 (2)

barmaid 742 (1)

barmy 503 (8)

barn 370 (6), 632 (2)

barn dance 837 (14)

barnstorm 850 (5)

barnstormer 594 (9)

barnstorming 594 (8)

barograph 209 (7), 340 (4)

barometer 340 (3), 340
(4), 465 (6)

barometric 340 (5)

barometry 340 (4)

baron 638 (4), 868 (5)

baron of beef 301 (16)

baroness 868 (5)

baronet 868 (5)

baronetcy 868 (2)

baronial 868 (6)

Baroque 553 (3), 844 (1)

barque 275 (1), 275 (5)

barrack 702 (10)

barracker 702 (5), 926 (3)

barracks 192 (2)

barrage 403 (1), 712 (3),
713 (2)

barrage balloon 276 (2),
722 (14)

barred 57 (3), 264 (4), 437
(8), 757 (3)

barrel 194 (12), 252 (3)

barrel organ 414 (5)

barren 161 (7), 172 (4),
641 (5)

barren waste 172 (3)

barrenness 172 (1)

barricade 57 (1), 235 (3),
702 (9), 713 (2), 713 (9)

barricaded 713 (8)

barricades 738 (2)

barrier 57 (1), 233 (1), 235
(3), 713 (2)

barring 57 (6)

barrister 958 (1)

barristership 958 (5)

barrow 209 (3), 253 (5),
274 (4), 364 (5), 796 (3)

barrow boy 793 (2), 794
(3)

bartender 742 (1)

barter 12 (1), 12 (3), 28
(2), 151 (1), 151 (3), 272
(1), 766 (1), 780 (1), 780
(3), 791 (1), 791 (4), 804
(4)

bartered 151 (2)

bas-relief 554 (1)

basal 214 (3), 218 (14)

basalt 344 (4)

base 35 (1), 69 (2), 73 (1),
156 (3), 186 (1), 187 (3),
187 (5), 192 (1), 194 (21),
207 (1), 210 (1), 214 (1),
218 (4), 645 (2), 722 (7),
867 (4), 879 (3), 930 (5),
934 (6)

base metal 359 (1)

base troops 722 (7)

baseball 837 (7)

baseboard 214 (1)

based on 214 (3), 466 (5)

based on, be 218 (16)

baseless 495 (4)

basement 194 (21), 214 (1)

baseness 930 (1), 934 (1)

bashful 598 (3), 874 (2)

bashfulness 598 (1), 874
(1), 950 (1)

BASIC 86 (5)

basic 156 (8), 214 (3), 638
(5)

basic substance 319 (4)

basics 1 (2)

basilica 990 (3)

basilican 990 (6)

basilisk 84 (4)

basin 194 (16), 255 (2)

basis 66 (2), 156 (6), 214
(1), 218 (4), 669 (1)

basis of argument 475 (5)

bask 379 (7), 730 (6)

bask in 376 (6), 824 (6)

basket 194 (6)

basketball 837 (7)

basketwork 194 (6), 222
(3)

bass 404 (1), 413 (4)

bass baritone 413 (4)

bass clef 410 (3)

bassoon 414 (6)

bassoonist 413 (2)

bast 208 (2)

bastard 938 (3), 954 (4)

bastardy 170 (2), 170 (3)

baste 45 (12), 301 (40), 357
(9)

basted 357 (7)

basting 47 (5)

bastion 713 (3)

bat 279 (9)

batch 26 (2), 74 (3), 74 (6)

batch processing 86 (5)

bate 257 (3)

bated breath 578 (1)

bath 194 (13), 303 (2), 341
(2), 648 (3)

bath chair 274 (4)

bath water 339 (1)

bathe 269 (12), 303 (7),
313 (3), 341 (6), 341 (8),
648 (9), 837 (21)

bathed in tears 836 (4)

bathing 648 (9)

bathing belle 841 (2)

bathos 497 (1), 849 (1)

bathrobe 228 (6)

bathroom 194 (19)

bathysphere 211 (1), 313
(2)

batik 555 (2), 844 (2)

batman 742 (2)

baton 218 (2), 547 (9), 743 (2)

batsman 837 (16)

battalion 722 (8)

batten 208 (3)

batten down 264 (6)

batten on 301 (35), 879 (4)

batter 165 (7), 220 (1), 244 (3), 279 (8), 279 (9), 301 (22), 356 (1), 645 (7)

battered 655 (6)

battering ram 279 (5), 723 (5)

battery 74 (7), 160 (6), 192 (10), 369 (2), 459 (4), 722 (8), 723 (11)

battle 362 (4), 682 (6), 716 (7), 716 (10), 718 (7), 724 (2)

battle-axe 892 (2)

battle cruiser 722 (13)

battle cry 547 (8), 665 (1), 711 (1), 718 (1), 718 (6)

battle front 718 (7)

battle of wills 704 (1)

battle orders 718 (6)

battle royal 716 (7), 718 (7)

battle station 718 (7)

battledress 228 (5)

battlefield 362 (5), 724 (2)

battleground 362 (5), 716 (7), 718 (7), 724 (2)

battlement 713 (3)

battlemented 713 (8)

battlements 213 (1)

battler 716 (8)

battles 718 (6)

battleship 722 (13)

batty 503 (8)

bauble 4 (2), 639 (3), 837 (15), 844 (6)

bawd 952 (5)

bawdiness 951 (1)

bawdy 951 (6)

bawl 408 (1), 408 (4), 836 (1), 836 (6)

bawl out 924 (13)

bawling 400 (1), 408 (2)

bay 194 (4), 248 (2), 255 (2), 273 (4), 345 (1), 409 (3)

bay window 263 (5)

bayonet 712 (4), 712 (9), 723 (8)

bays 547 (9), 729 (1), 866 (4)

bazaar 793 (1), 796 (2), 796 (3)

bazooka 723 (4), 723 (11)

BC 108 (12), 119 (2)

be 1 (6), 121 (3), 186 (4), 189 (4), 360 (4), 494 (7)

bête-noire 861 (1), 888 (3)

beach 344 (2)

beachhead 724 (2), 778 (1)

beachwear 228 (19)

beacon 420 (6), 547 (5), 664 (1), 665 (1)

beacon fire 379 (2)

bead 252 (2), 844 (12)

beading 844 (2)

beadle 741 (6)

beadlike 252 (5)

beads 981 (4)

beads of sweat 302 (4)

beagle 365 (10)

beak 254 (3), 537 (1)

beaked 248 (3)

beaker 194 (15)

beam 47 (1), 218 (9), 222 (2), 226 (2), 239 (1), 281 (1), 417 (2), 417 (12), 631 (1), 833 (7), 835 (8)

beaming 417 (8), 824 (5), 833 (3)

bean 33 (4)

beanpole 206 (2)

beans 301 (20)

bear 167 (6), 171 (6), 198 (3), 218 (15), 273 (12), 281 (4), 365 (3), 793 (2), 818 (7), 823 (6), 825 (7), 892 (2), 902 (2)

bear a grudge 888 (7)

bear a resemblance 18 (7)

bear away 786 (9)

bear down on 176 (7), 289 (4), 712 (10)

bear fruit 167 (6), 640 (4), 727 (7)

bear hard on 735 (7)

bear hug 778 (1), 889 (1)

bear ill will 881 (4)

bear in mind 449 (7), 455 (5)

bear malice 881 (4), 888 (7), 891 (5), 898 (8), 910 (6)

bear no malice 909 (4)

bear no resemblance 19 (3)

bear on 218 (16)

bear one company 89 (4)

bear oneself 688 (4)

bear out 466 (8), 478 (4), 927 (5)

bear the blame 936 (4)

bear the brunt 715 (3)

bear the cost 804 (5), 806 (4)

bear the stamp 157 (5)

bear up 218 (15), 310 (4), 855 (6)

bear upon 9 (7)

bear with 909 (4)

bear with a sore head 834 (4)

bear witness 466 (7), 532 (5)

bear young 164 (7)

beard 259 (2), 711 (3)

bearded 259 (5)

beardless 130 (4), 229 (5)

bearer 273 (2), 742 (1)

bearing 9 (1), 218 (2), 218 (11), 273 (10), 281 (1), 445 (5), 514 (1), 547 (11), 688 (1), 818 (3)

bearing on 9 (10), 24 (6)

bearing rein 748 (4)

bearing upon 9 (5)

bearings 186 (2)

bearish 365 (18), 793 (3), 812 (3), 885 (5)

bearskin 228 (23), 713 (5)

beast 176 (4), 365 (2), 649 (5), 842 (2), 904 (2), 904 (5), 938 (3)

beast of burden 273 (3), 365 (2), 365 (3), 686 (2)

beast of prey 362 (6), 365 (2), 786 (4), 904 (5)

beastliness 645 (1), 827 (1)

beastly **645** (4), **842** (3), **888** (5), **944** (3)

beasts and fishes **365** (2)

beat **34** (7), **141** (1), **141** (6), **184** (2), **185** (1), **279** (9), **301** (40), **305** (5), **306** (5), **317** (1), **317** (4), **318** (6), **332** (5), **403** (3), **410** (4), **413** (9), **622** (4), **624** (4), **648** (9), **727** (10), **963** (9)

beat a retreat **286** (4)

beat a tattoo **403** (3)

beat about the bush **570** (6)

beat all comers **727** (11)

beat down **165** (7), **791** (6), **812** (6), **816** (6)

beat flat **216** (7)

beat hollow **727** (10)

beat in **255** (8)

beat off **292** (3)

beat one's brains **449** (7)

beat one's breast **836** (5)

beat out **253** (9)

beat swords into plough-shares **719** (5)

beat the air **279** (9)

beat the record **34** (7)

beat time **117** (7), **413** (9)

beat up **279** (9), **354** (6), **712** (9)

beaten **35** (4), **624** (8), **728** (5)

beaten down **216** (4)

beaten track **838** (2)

beater **619** (3)

beatific **615** (3), **971** (3)

beatification **866** (5), **979** (2), **988** (4)

beatified **979** (8)

beatify **968** (4), **979** (12)

beating **141** (4), **279** (1), **279** (2), **727** (2), **728** (2), **963** (2)

beating heart **360** (1)

beau **372** (1), **848** (4)

beau monde **846** (2), **848** (3)

beauteous **841** (3)

beautician **333** (1), **648** (6), **843** (5)

beauties **887** (2)

beautification **843** (1)

beautified **843** (6), **844** (11)

beautifier **843** (3)

beautiful **376** (3), **575** (3), **644** (4), **826** (2), **841** (3), **843** (6), **887** (11)

beautiful, be **841** (7)

beautiful people **848** (3)

beautify **654** (9), **841** (8), **843** (7), **844** (12)

beautifying **843** (1)

beauty **245** (1), **575** (1), **826** (1), **841** (1)

beauty, a **644** (3), **646** (2), **694** (3), **841** (2), **890** (2)

beauty parlour **843** (4)

beauty queen **841** (2)

beauty salon **843** (4)

beauty spot **841** (2)

beauty treatment **843** (1)

beaux arts **551** (3)

beaver **365** (3), **686** (2)

beaver away **678** (11)

bebop **837** (14)

becalmed **266** (4), **702** (7)

because **156** (11), **158** (5)

because of **157** (7)

beck **350** (1)

beckon **547** (21)

become **1** (7), **147** (6), **154** (6), **316** (3), **841** (8)

become a habit **610** (7)

become a martyr **361** (8)

become a member **708** (8)

become addicted **943** (3)

become airborne **308** (4)

become audible **415** (7)

become aware **374** (5)

become aware of **447** (7)

become complete **54** (5)

become extinct **2** (7), **37** (5), **69** (5), **361** (8)

become familiar **889** (7)

become insolvent **805** (5)

become invisible **444** (4)

become known **490** (9), **526** (7)

become large **195** (10)

become overcast **355** (6)

become pious **979** (10)

become public **528** (12)

become scarce **37** (5)

become small **33** (8), **37** (5), **196** (12), **198** (6), **206** (6)

become solid **324** (6)

become teetotal **948** (4)

become visible **443** (4)

becoming **1** (1), **24** (5), **147** (5), **445** (1), **841** (6), **846** (3)

bed **207** (1), **214** (1), **218** (4), **218** (7)

bed down **369** (10), **679** (12)

bed linen **226** (8)

bed of nails **825** (1)

bed of roses **730** (2)

bed of thorns **825** (1)

bedclothes **226** (8)

bedded **207** (4)

bedding **207** (3), **226** (8)

bedding-roll **194** (9)

bedeck **844** (12)

bedecked **228** (29), **844** (11)

bedevil **63** (5), **517** (6), **700** (6), **827** (10), **969** (6)

bedevilled **503** (8)

bedim **419** (7), **439** (4)

bedlam **61** (2), **61** (4), **400** (1), **503** (6)

bedouin **268** (2)

bedpan **194** (13), **649** (3)

bedraggled **61** (7), **649** (7)

bedridden **651** (21)

bedrock **1** (2), **144** (1), **153** (2), **156** (3), **214** (1), **218** (4)

bedroll **218** (7)

bedroom **194** (19)

bedside manner **658** (12)

bedside reading **590** (4)

bedsitter **192** (9)

bedspread **226** (8)

bedstead **218** (7)

bedtime **129** (1)

bee **365** (16)

bee in one's bonnet **604** (2)

bee-keeper **369** (5)

bee-keeping **369** (1)

beech **366** (4)

beef **301** (16)

beef cattle **365** (7)

beef farming 369 (1)

beef up 162 (12)

beefy 162 (8), 195 (8)

beehive 192 (4), 253 (4), 369 (2)

beeline 200 (2), 249 (1), 281 (1), 625 (1)

beer 301 (28)

beer cellar 192 (12)

beer garden 192 (12)

beery 949 (11), 949 (12)

beeswax 357 (3)

beetle 365 (16)

beetle-browed 254 (4)

beetling 209 (11)

beetroot-red 431 (3)

befit 24 (9), 642 (3), 915 (4), 917 (8)

befitting 24 (7)

befool 542 (9)

before 64 (5), 119 (5), 189 (6), 237 (6), 283 (4)

before and since 113 (11)

before, be 64 (3), 119 (3)

before Christ 108 (12)

before long 135 (6)

before now 119 (5)

before one's eyes 189 (2), 237 (6), 443 (2), 443 (5)

before one's time 135 (7)

before the Flood 127 (9)

before the house 452 (3)

before the mast 269 (13)

before the times 122 (2)

before then 119 (5)

before time 118 (2)

beforehand 119 (5), 135 (7), 283 (2)

befriend 24 (9), 89 (4), 703 (6), 880 (8), 882 (8)

befuddle 949 (16)

beg 629 (2), 761 (6), 816 (6), 879 (4)

beg a favour 761 (5)

beg, borrow or steal 629 (2), 771 (7), 785 (2)

beg for favours 879 (4)

beg for mercy 721 (4), 905 (8)

beg forgiveness 909 (5)

beg in vain 761 (6)

beg off 760 (4), 762 (3)

beg pardon 909 (5), 941 (5)

beg permission 756 (6)

beg the question 477 (7)

beg to differ 489 (5)

beget 156 (9), 167 (7), 360 (6)

begetter 156 (2), 169 (3)

beggar 679 (6), 763 (2), 801 (2), 801 (6), 869 (7)

beggarliness 801 (1)

beggarly 801 (4)

beggary 801 (1)

begging 761 (1)

begging letter 761 (1)

begin 64 (3), 68 (8), 106 (4), 148 (3), 156 (9), 296 (6), 360 (5), 445 (8), 669 (10), 672 (3), 682 (7)

begin again 68 (8)

begin from 157 (5)

beginner 68 (1), 297 (3), 461 (5), 493 (1), 501 (2), 538 (2), 544 (1), 697 (1), 699 (2)

beginner's luck 727 (1)

beginning 21 (1), 55 (4), 66 (2), 66 (3), 68 (1), 68 (6), 126 (5), 127 (1), 127 (5), 130 (1), 135 (1), 156 (3), 156 (7), 196 (10), 244 (2), 295 (1), 445 (1), 534 (3), 536 (1), 669 (1), 670 (4), 876 (1)

beginning again 106 (1)

beginnings 156 (3)

begotten 360 (3)

begrudge 598 (4), 816 (6)

begrudged 598 (3)

beguile 495 (9), 542 (8), 837 (20), 925 (4)

beguiling 542 (6), 925 (3)

begun 68 (6)

behave 688 (4), 933 (4)

behave badly 688 (4)

behave naturally 24 (9)

behave oneself 688 (4)

behave towards 688 (4)

behave well 688 (4), 929 (5)

behaving 688 (3)

behaviour 445 (5), 624 (1), 676 (1), 688 (1)

behavioural 688 (3)

behaviourism 447 (3)

behead 46 (10), 362 (10), 963 (12)

beheading 963 (3)

behind 238 (1), 238 (2), 238 (6), 284 (5)

behind bars 747 (6), 750 (2)

behind, be 238 (5), 284 (4)

behind closed doors 525 (10)

behind one 125 (6)

behind one's back 190 (9)

behind schedule 136 (3)

behind the scenes 238 (6), 444 (5), 523 (2), 525 (3)

behind the times 118 (2), 122 (2), 127 (7), 491 (4)

behind time 118 (2), 136 (3), 136 (8)

behind time, be 118 (3)

behindhand 136 (3), 307 (4), 670 (3), 805 (4)

behindhand, be 136 (4)

behold 438 (7)

beholden 907 (3), 917 (5)

beholder 441 (1)

behove 913 (5), 915 (4), 917 (8)

behoving 917 (6)

beige 430 (3)

being 1 (1), 1 (4), 80 (4), 817 (1)

being, a 1 (1)

being alive 360 (1)

being elsewhere 190 (1)

being everywhere 189 (1)

being exercised 173 (2)

being separated 46 (1)

belabour 279 (9), 963 (10)

belated 136 (3)

belatedness 670 (1)

belay 45 (12)

belay there 269 (14)

belch 300 (3), 300 (11), 352 (7), 352 (11)

belching 300 (3), 300 (5), 651 (7)

beleaguer 718 (11)

beleaguered 232 (2)

belfry 990 (5)

belie 704 (4)

belief 471 (1), 473 (2), 485 (1), 487 (1), 852 (1), 973 (3), 979 (1)
believable 471 (3), 485 (5)
believe 471 (6), 473 (7), 485 (7), 487 (3), 512 (6), 764 (5), 852 (6), 976 (12), 979 (9)
believe in 485 (7)
believed 485 (5), 976 (8)
believed, be 485 (10)
believer 973 (7), 976 (7), 979 (4)
believer, be a 485 (7)
believing 473 (5), 485 (4), 487 (2), 976 (8), 979 (6)
belittle 37 (4), 483 (4), 922 (6), 924 (10), 926 (6)
belittlement 37 (2)
belittling 483 (2)
bell 117 (3), 412 (2), 414 (8), 547 (5), 665 (1)
bell, book and candle 899 (1)
bell-bottomed 205 (3)
bell ringer 412 (2)
bell ringing 412 (2)
bell shape 252 (4)
bell-shaped 248 (3), 252 (5), 255 (6)
bell wether 365 (8)
belle 841 (2), 848 (4)
belles-lettres 591 (2)
belletrist 557 (4), 591 (3)
bellicose 709 (6), 716 (9), 718 (9), 877 (4)
bellicosity 709 (2), 712 (1), 718 (3), 892 (1)
belligerency 718 (2)
belligerent 709 (6), 716 (9), 718 (8), 881 (3)
bellow 400 (4), 408 (4), 409 (3), 577 (4), 891 (7), 900 (3)
bellowing 400 (3)
bellows 352 (5)
bells 414 (8)
belly 194 (3), 224 (2), 253 (2), 253 (9)
belly dancer 594 (10)
belly worship 947 (1)
bellyacher 829 (2)
bellyful 54 (2)

bellying 253 (7)
belong 9 (7), 24 (9), 58 (3), 78 (4), 89 (4), 773 (5)
belong to 56 (3), 58 (3), 708 (8), 773 (5)
belonging 58 (2), 78 (3), 89 (3), 773 (3), 880 (1), 882 (1)
belongings 777 (1)
beloved 887 (5), 887 (11), 890 (1)
below 65 (5), 210 (4)
below average 35 (6)
below par 29 (2), 35 (6), 307 (2), 647 (3), 651 (21)
below-stairs 869 (8)
below the belt 914 (4)
below the horizon 199 (7)
below the mark 307 (4)
below the salt 869 (8)
below the surface 210 (2), 523 (2)
below zero 380 (5)
belt 47 (7), 184 (1), 198 (3), 228 (24), 250 (3), 279 (9), 345 (1), 963 (9)
bemedal 866 (14)
bemedalled 844 (11)
bemoan 836 (5)
bemused 456 (4), 503 (8)
bench 218 (5), 218 (6), 956 (1), 956 (4), 957 (1)
bench mark 465 (5)
bench of bishops 985 (5)
bench of judges 956 (1)
benchmark 547 (7)
bend 46 (13), 47 (4), 63 (3), 83 (7), 83 (8), 143 (6), 220 (5), 220 (6), 246 (1), 246 (5), 247 (1), 248 (2), 248 (4), 248 (5), 282 (1), 282 (3), 282 (6), 311 (9), 327 (4), 612 (8)
bend backwards 238 (5)
bend down 248 (5), 311 (9)
bend one's steps 267 (11)
bend over 220 (5), 248 (5), 261 (3), 311 (9)
bend over backwards 682 (6)
bend round 314 (4)
bend the mind 449 (7)
bend to 179 (3)

bended knees 761 (2)
bending 210 (2), 248 (1)
bending down 248 (1)
beneath 210 (4)
beneath, be 210 (3)
beneath contempt 922 (4)
beneath one 867 (6)
benediction 615 (1), 897 (1), 907 (2), 981 (3), 981 (4), 988 (5)
benefaction 813 (1)
benefactor 703 (3), 707 (4), 781 (4), 813 (2), 903 (1), 937 (1)
benefactress 903 (1)
benefice 777 (2), 985 (3)
beneficed 986 (11)
beneficence 644 (1), 897 (1)
beneficent 897 (4)
beneficial 615 (3), 640 (3), 642 (2), 644 (8), 652 (4), 658 (17)
beneficiary 67 (3), 170 (2), 755 (1), 776 (3), 782 (2), 800 (2), 852 (3)
benefit 34 (2), 508 (1), 615 (2), 615 (4), 640 (1), 640 (4), 642 (1), 642 (3), 644 (11), 673 (1), 703 (2), 730 (8), 771 (1), 771 (3), 781 (2), 897 (5), 901 (2)
benefit by 615 (5)
benefit match 781 (2)
benevolence 597 (1), 615 (1), 617 (1), 644 (1), 703 (1), 736 (1), 756 (1), 880 (2), 884 (1), 887 (1), 897 (1), 901 (1), 905 (1), 931 (1)
benevolent 703 (4), 781 (5), 813 (3), 880 (6), 884 (3), 884 (4), 897 (4), 901 (6), 905 (4), 909 (2), 931 (2), 933 (3), 979 (6)
benevolent, be 644 (11), 703 (5), 736 (3), 859 (11), 897 (5), 909 (4), 979 (9)
benevolent despotism 733 (3)
benevolently 897 (7)
benighted 129 (5), 439 (2)

benign 652 (4), 660 (4), 897 (4)

benign climate 652 (1)

benign tumour 651 (11)

benignity 897 (1)

bent 84 (7), 179 (1), 220 (3), 248 (3), 248 (4), 481 (5), 597 (1), 817 (1), 930 (4)

bent line 203 (3)

bent upon 859 (7)

benumb 375 (6), 382 (6)

benumbed 375 (3), 679 (7)

bequeath 272 (6), 777 (6), 780 (4), 781 (7), 800 (5), 800 (8)

bequeathal 780 (1)

bequest 771 (1), 777 (4), 780 (1), 781 (2)

berate 924 (13)

bereave 786 (10), 834 (11), 896 (5)

bereaved 161 (6)

bereft 161 (6), 772 (2)

bereft of hope 853 (2)

beret 228 (23)

beri-beri 651 (6)

beribboned 844 (11)

berry 164 (2), 301 (19), 366 (7)

berserk 176 (6), 503 (9), 891 (4)

berth 187 (5), 192 (2), 192 (10), 192 (21), 295 (2), 295 (4), 622 (3)

beseech 761 (7), 981 (11)

beseeching 761 (2), 761 (4)

beset 230 (3), 232 (3), 284 (4), 761 (5), 827 (9)

besetting 79 (4), 610 (5)

beside 200 (7), 239 (4)

beside oneself 503 (9), 821 (3), 891 (4)

beside the point 10 (4)

besides 38 (5)

besiege 230 (3), 232 (3), 712 (8), 718 (11), 761 (5), 827 (9)

besieged 232 (2)

besieger 712 (5), 722 (1)

besieging 718 (6)

besotted 481 (6), 499 (4), 503 (8), 887 (10)

bespatter 341 (7)

bespeak 135 (5), 466 (6)

bespectacled 440 (3)

bespoke 80 (6), 228 (30)

best 32 (4), 34 (5), 34 (6), 34 (7), 644 (6), 727 (10)

best behaviour 848 (2), 884 (1)

best blood 868 (1)

best clothes 228 (2)

best ever 34 (6)

best friend 880 (4)

best man 707 (1)

best part 32 (3), 52 (3)

best-seller 589 (1), 590 (4), 644 (3), 793 (1)

best, the 615 (1)

bested 728 (5)

bestial 365 (18), 944 (3), 951 (8)

bestiality 944 (1), 951 (3)

bestir oneself 678 (11)

bestow 781 (7)

bestow a title 866 (14)

bestow alms 781 (7)

bestow upon 781 (7)

bestowal 781 (1)

bestowed 781 (6)

bestrew 75 (4)

bestride 183 (7), 205 (5), 226 (14), 305 (5)

bet 618 (2), 618 (8), 716 (2), 716 (10)

bet on 473 (7)

betimes 135 (6)

betoken 466 (6), 511 (8), 522 (7)

betray 509 (5), 526 (4), 541 (5), 542 (8), 603 (6), 930 (8)

betray itself 443 (4)

betray one 524 (9)

betray oneself 495 (8)

betrayal 526 (1), 542 (1), 930 (2)

betrayed 509 (2)

betrayer 938 (2)

betraying 526 (3)

betrothal 764 (1), 765 (1), 889 (2), 894 (3)

betrothed 764 (3), 887 (5), 894 (8)

better 34 (4), 34 (7), 605 (5), 618 (4), 644 (4), 654 (6), 654 (9), 656 (6)

better for 654 (6)

better not 643 (2)

better oneself 654 (8)

betterment 615 (2)

betting 618 (2)

betting shop 618 (3)

between 12 (4), 231 (11)

between ourselves 525 (10)

between the lines 523 (3)

between two fires 661 (6)

between whiles 108 (10)

bevel 46 (11), 220 (1), 220 (3), 220 (6)

beverage 301 (26)

bevy 74 (3), 104 (2)

bewail 836 (5)

beware 457 (5), 664 (6), 858 (3)

bewilder 456 (8), 474 (9), 864 (7)

bewildered 474 (6), 491 (4), 503 (8), 864 (4)

bewildering 474 (4)

bewilderment 474 (2), 491 (1), 728 (2)

bewitch 147 (7), 449 (11), 612 (8), 745 (7), 826 (4), 864 (7), 887 (15), 969 (6), 983 (11)

bewitched 503 (8), 596 (5), 612 (7), 887 (10), 899 (5), 983 (9)

bewitching 612 (6), 826 (2), 887 (11)

bewitchment 147 (1), 612 (2), 821 (1), 983 (2)

beyond 34 (11), 199 (4), 199 (7), 237 (6)

beyond compare 32 (18), 34 (5)

beyond doubt 473 (6)

beyond hope 853 (3)

beyond measure 32 (18)

beyond one 470 (3), 517 (3)

beyond one's means 811 (2)

beyond praise 646 (3), 923 (6)

beyond price 811 (3)

beyond recall 506 (3)

beyond reckoning 107 (2)

beyond seas 59 (5)

beyond, the 361 (1)

beyond the pale 57 (3), 847 (4)

bezique 837 (11)

bi- 90 (2)

bias 29 (1), 178 (3), 179 (1), 179 (3), 220 (1), 246 (1), 246 (5), 282 (6), 449 (10), 449 (11), 473 (2), 476 (1), 481 (3), 481 (5), 481 (11), 495 (1), 503 (5), 602 (2), 604 (1), 605 (1), 612 (8), 859 (3), 861 (1), 877 (1), 914 (2), 978 (1)

biased 29 (2), 220 (1), 246 (3), 473 (5), 481 (8), 485 (4), 495 (4), 602 (4), 708 (7), 914 (4)

biased, be 481 (12), 487 (3), 914 (6)

biased judgment 481 (3)

bib 228 (3), 228 (15)

Bible 975 (2)

Bible-worship 979 (3)

biblical 466 (5), 975 (4), 976 (8)

bibliographer 589 (6)

bibliographical 589 (8)

bibliography 87 (1), 589 (4), 589 (5)

bibliophile 492 (3), 504 (3), 589 (6)

bibliophilic 589 (8)

bicameral 90 (2), 692 (4)

bicentenary 99 (6), 141 (3), 876 (2)

bicentennial 876 (3)

biceps 162 (2)

bicker 475 (11), 709 (9)

bickering 25 (4), 709 (1)

bicycle 267 (6), 267 (15), 274 (3)

bicycle pedal 287 (3)

bicyclist 268 (4)

bid 618 (2), 671 (1), 671 (4), 737 (6), 759 (1), 759 (3), 761 (1), 792 (1)

bid against 704 (4)

bid fair 852 (7)

bid fair to 179 (3), 471 (4)

bid farewell 296 (4)

bid for 617 (1), 617 (6), 761 (5), 791 (6), 792 (5)

bid good morning 884 (7)

biddable 597 (4), 739 (3)

bidder 792 (2)

bidding 737 (1), 792 (4)

bidding prayer 981 (4)

bide one's time 136 (5), 507 (5), 677 (3)

bidet 648 (3)

biennial 110 (3), 141 (5), 366 (7)

bier 218 (7), 364 (2)

bifocal 90 (2)

bifocals 442 (2)

bifurcate 92 (4), 92 (6), 247 (5), 247 (7), 294 (3)

bifurcation 92 (2), 247 (1), 294 (1)

big 32 (4), 195 (6), 195 (10)

big bang theory 321 (1)

big battalions 638 (4), 722 (6), 735 (2)

Big Brother 735 (3), 741 (2)

big cat 365 (11)

Big City, the 184 (4)

big drum 414 (9), 875 (1)

big game 365 (2)

big-game hunt 619 (2)

big-game hunter 619 (3)

big gun 638 (4)

big letter 558 (1)

big-mouthed 400 (3), 877 (4)

big noise 178 (1), 638 (4)

big picture 445 (4)

big screen 445 (3)

big spender 815 (2)

big stick 612 (4), 740 (1), 900 (1)

big talk 546 (1)

big toe 214 (2), 378 (4)

big top 226 (3), 594 (7)

bigamist 894 (4)

bigamous 894 (7)

bigamy 894 (2)

bigger 197 (3)

biggest slice of the cake 52 (3)

biggish 32 (4)

bighead 873 (3)

bigheaded 873 (4)

bight 345 (1)

bigness 32 (1), 195 (2)

bigot 473 (3), 481 (4), 493 (1), 602 (3), 979 (5)

bigoted 473 (5), 481 (8), 602 (4), 735 (4)

bigotry 473 (2), 481 (4), 487 (1), 602 (2), 735 (1), 978 (1), 979 (3)

bigwig 34 (3), 178 (1), 371 (3), 638 (4), 644 (2), 690 (3), 741 (2), 866 (6), 868 (4), 871 (2)

bijou 196 (8)

bike 267 (15), 274 (3)

bikini 228 (19)

bilateral 12 (2), 90 (2), 239 (2), 765 (4)

bilateral deed 767 (2)

bile 912 (1)

bilingual 557 (4), 557 (5), 579 (6)

bilingualism 557 (2)

bilious 433 (3), 651 (20), 892 (3), 893 (2)

biliousness 433 (1), 651 (7)

bilk 805 (5)

bilker 805 (3)

bill 87 (1), 254 (3), 528 (3), 528 (11), 547 (13), 588 (1), 594 (16), 737 (8), 797 (5), 802 (1), 808 (1), 808 (5), 809 (1)

bill and coo 889 (6)

bill of exchange 797 (5)

bill of fare 87 (1), 301 (12)

bill of lading 87 (1)

bill of rights 915 (1)

billed 594 (15)

billet 185 (1), 187 (5), 192 (2)

billet doux 588 (1), 889 (2)

billet on 187 (5)

billiard room 837 (5)

billiards 837 (7)

billion 99 (5)

billionth 99 (6)

billow 209 (6), 253 (2), 350 (5)
billowing 253 (7)
billows 343 (1)
billowy 248 (3), 253 (7)
bills 803 (1)
billy goat 365 (7)
billycan 194 (14)
bin 194 (13)
binary 86 (10), 90 (2)
binary system 85 (1)
bind 45 (12), 50 (4), 74 (11), 153 (8), 198 (7), 226 (13), 264 (6), 324 (6), 370 (9), 656 (12), 702 (9), 745 (7), 747 (7), 747 (9), 766 (3), 838 (2), 917 (11)
bind by fate 596 (8)
bind oneself 764 (4)
bind up 656 (11)
binding 45 (2), 47 (4), 198 (5), 226 (5), 234 (3), 324 (5), 596 (4), 693 (2), 733 (7), 740 (2), 766 (2), 844 (5), 917 (6)
binding over 747 (1), 963 (4)
binge 949 (1)
bingo 618 (2), 837 (11)
bingo hall 837 (5)
binnacle 269 (4), 270 (2)
binocular 438 (6)
binoculars 442 (3)
binomial 90 (2)
biochemistry 358 (2)
biodegradable 46 (6), 51 (4), 114 (4)
biographer 589 (7), 590 (5)
biographical 590 (6)
biography 548 (1), 589 (2), 590 (3)
biological 358 (4), 360 (2)
biological weapon 659 (3)
biologist 358 (2)
biology 167 (1), 316 (1), 319 (5), 331 (1), 358 (2), 367 (1)
bionic man 864 (3)
biosphere 321 (2)
biotechnology 358 (2)
bipartisan 24 (5), 90 (2), 488 (5), 706 (3), 710 (2)

bipartite 92 (4)
bipartition 92 (1)
biped 90 (1), 365 (2)
biplane 276 (1)
birch 366 (4), 963 (9), 964 (1)
birching 963 (2)
bird 132 (3), 365 (2), 365 (4)
bird cage 369 (3)
bird catcher 619 (3)
bird-fancier 369 (5)
bird life 365 (1)
bird lore 367 (1)
bird of passage 114 (2), 268 (2), 365 (4)
bird of prey 365 (4)
bird sanctuary 666 (1)
bird watcher 441 (1)
bird watching 367 (1)
birdbrain 501 (1)
birdlike 365 (18)
birdlime 47 (9)
birds 365 (2)
bird's-eye view 438 (5), 592 (1)
birdsong 409 (1)
biretta 989 (1)
birth 68 (1), 68 (4), 167 (1), 167 (2), 169 (2), 360 (1), 868 (1)
birth control 172 (2), 702 (1)
birth rate 86 (4), 167 (1)
birthday 108 (3), 141 (3), 876 (2)
birthday suit 229 (2)
birthmark 651 (12), 845 (1)
birthplace 156 (3), 192 (5)
birthright 119 (1), 777 (4), 915 (1)
biscuit 430 (3)
biscuits 301 (23)
bisect 46 (10), 92 (5), 783 (3)
bisected 92 (4)
bisection 28 (4), 46 (3), 92 (1)
bisexual 84 (7), 91 (2), 167 (4)
bisexuality 84 (1)
bishop 986 (4)

bishopric 184 (3), 985 (3), 985 (4)
bistro 192 (13)
bit 26 (2), 33 (2), 53 (5), 58 (1), 86 (5), 748 (4)
bit, a 33 (10), 108 (1)
bit by bit 27 (6), 46 (14), 53 (9), 80 (10), 278 (8)
bit missing 647 (1)
bit part 594 (8)
bit player 594 (9)
bitch 365 (10), 904 (4), 938 (3)
bitchy 898 (4)
bite 33 (2), 46 (11), 53 (5), 174 (1), 176 (7), 301 (11), 301 (36), 377 (5), 388 (1), 655 (10), 659 (1), 829 (6), 892 (4), 893 (1)
bite one's tongue 830 (4)
bite the dust 165 (11), 309 (4), 728 (9)
bite to eat 301 (12)
biter bit 714 (1)
biting 174 (6), 301 (1), 377 (3), 380 (5), 388 (1), 827 (3), 827 (5), 839 (4), 885 (5)
biting tongue 924 (3)
biting wit 839 (1)
bits 641 (3)
bits and pieces 43 (4), 53 (5), 641 (3)
bitten 887 (10)
bitter 301 (28), 377 (3), 380 (5), 388 (3), 391 (2), 393 (2), 827 (4), 829 (3), 830 (2), 861 (3), 888 (4), 891 (3), 892 (3), 898 (4)
bitter cup 731 (1), 825 (1), 827 (1)
bitter end 69 (3)
bitter enemy 881 (2)
bitter pill 731 (1), 827 (1), 888 (3)
bitter struggle 716 (2)
bitterly 32 (17), 32 (18), 32 (20), 891 (10)
bitterness 393 (1), 645 (1), 659 (1), 825 (2), 827 (1), 829 (1), 861 (1), 881 (1), 888 (1), 891 (1), 898 (1)
bitters 393 (1)

bittersweet 14 (3), 377 (3)
bitty 53 (6), 55 (3), 72 (2), 196 (10)
bitumen 357 (5)
bivalve 90 (1), 365 (14)
bivouac 187 (3), 187 (8), 192 (1), 192 (21), 266 (3)
bizarre 84 (6), 513 (5), 849 (2)
blabber 581 (3)
black 46 (9), 57 (5), 228 (4), 364 (8), 418 (1), 418 (3), 418 (6), 425 (7), 428 (1), 428 (4), 428 (6), 547 (9), 616 (2), 757 (4), 934 (6)
black and blue 428 (5), 435 (3), 436 (2)
black and white 14 (2), 417 (6), 426 (1)
black art 983 (1)
black belt 696 (1)
black books 867 (1), 888 (2)
black box 549 (3)
black cat 983 (3)
black cloud 900 (1)
black comedy 594 (3), 839 (1)
Black Death 651 (4)
black economy 796 (1)
black eye 655 (4), 845 (1)
black-eyed 428 (4)
black-haired 428 (4)
black-hearted 898 (4), 934 (3)
black hole 321 (4)
black ice 380 (2)
black look 893 (1), 924 (3)
black magic 645 (1), 969 (3), 983 (1)
black mark 924 (4)
black market 791 (2), 796 (1), 954 (5)
black mood 834 (2)
black notes 410 (2)
black one's eye 655 (10)
black out 375 (5), 418 (6), 550 (3), 757 (4)
black person 428 (1)
black pigment 428 (3)
black sheep 904 (3), 938 (1)

black-skinned 428 (4)
black spot 661 (1)
black, the 802 (1)
black thing 428 (2)
black-tie 875 (6)
blackball 57 (5), 300 (6), 607 (3), 867 (11), 883 (9)
blackbird 365 (4)
blackboard 586 (4)
blacked 757 (3)
blacked out 418 (4), 757 (3)
blacken 418 (6), 425 (8), 428 (6), 547 (19), 655 (9), 867 (11), 924 (10), 926 (7)
blackened 428 (4)
blackening 418 (2), 428 (1)
blackguard 904 (1), 904 (2), 938 (2), 938 (3)
blackheads 651 (12)
blacking 428 (3), 702 (1)
blackish 428 (5)
blackleg 84 (3), 603 (3), 603 (6), 738 (4), 888 (3)
blacklegging 769 (2)
blacklist 46 (9), 87 (1), 561 (6), 883 (9), 924 (1), 924 (9), 961 (3)
blacklisted 883 (6), 924 (7)
blackmail 737 (3), 737 (8), 740 (1), 740 (3), 761 (1), 761 (5), 786 (3), 786 (11), 788 (4), 788 (9), 790 (1), 809 (3), 900 (1), 900 (3)
blackmailer 786 (4), 904 (3)
blackness 418 (1), 428 (1)
blackout 375 (1), 418 (2), 506 (1), 594 (2), 684 (1), 757 (1)
blacksmith 369 (1)
blackthorn 366 (4)
bladder 194 (2), 252 (2)
blade 256 (5), 257 (1), 269 (5), 287 (3), 366 (5), 723 (8)
blame 924 (2), 924 (12), 928 (1), 928 (8), 936 (1)
blame for 158 (3)
blame oneself 830 (4), 939 (4)
blamed 936 (3)

blameful 936 (3)
blameless 935 (4)
blamelessly 935 (6)
blamelessness 935 (1)
blameworthy 867 (5), 924 (8), 928 (7), 934 (6), 936 (3)
blaming 926 (5)
blanch 426 (4), 426 (5), 427 (6)
bland 177 (4), 258 (3), 840 (2), 884 (3), 925 (3)
blandishment 612 (2)
blandishments 889 (1), 925 (1)
blandness 884 (1)
blank 2 (1), 16 (2), 103 (1), 190 (2), 190 (5), 243 (1), 264 (4), 423 (2), 426 (3), 450 (2), 491 (4), 517 (2), 820 (3)
blank, be 450 (4)
blank cartridge 190 (2)
blank cheque 744 (3), 813 (1)
blank mind 450 (1)
blank paper 190 (2)
blank verse 593 (5)
blanket 78 (2), 79 (3), 226 (8), 226 (13), 464 (2)
blankness 506 (1)
blare 400 (1), 400 (4), 404 (1), 404 (3), 407 (5)
blaring 400 (3), 407 (2)
blarney 515 (3), 925 (4)
blase 454 (2), 865 (2)
blasé 838 (4), 860 (2)
blaspheme 899 (7), 974 (7), 980 (6)
blasphemer 980 (3)
blaspheming 980 (4)
blasphemous 980 (4)
blasphemy 980 (1)
blast 176 (2), 340 (1), 352 (1), 352 (4), 352 (10), 400 (1), 402 (1), 402 (4), 655 (9), 665 (1), 712 (11), 898 (8), 899 (7), 899 (8), 983 (11)
blast furnace 383 (1), 687 (1)
blast-off 271 (3), 271 (7), 296 (1)

blasted 172 (4), 645 (5), 983 (9)
blasting 899 (4), 983 (7)
blatancy 528 (2), 847 (1), 875 (1), 878 (1)
blatant 32 (10), 528 (8), 847 (4), 875 (5)
blatantly 32 (19)
blaze 260 (3), 379 (2), 379 (7), 417 (11), 427 (2), 547 (1), 547 (18), 547 (19)
blaze a trail 701 (8)
blaze of glory 866 (4)
blaze of light 417 (1)
blaze the trail 64 (3)
blazer 228 (10)
blazing 379 (5)
blazon 528 (10), 547 (11), 547 (19), 866 (13), 875 (7)
blazoned 547 (16)
blazonry 547 (11)
bleach 342 (6), 426 (2), 426 (4), 426 (5), 427 (6), 648 (9)
bleached 342 (4), 426 (3), 427 (4)
bleacher 426 (2)
bleaching 342 (2), 426 (1), 843 (2)
bleak 129 (7), 172 (4), 190 (5), 731 (4)
bleariness 440 (1)
bleary-eyed 440 (3)
bleat 409 (3), 829 (5)
bleater 829 (2)
bleed 298 (6), 300 (8), 300 (9), 341 (6), 658 (20), 786 (11), 811 (5)
bleed to death 361 (8)
bleeding 298 (2), 302 (2), 335 (5), 651 (10)
bleeding heart 887 (8)
bleep 407 (1)
bleeper 531 (1), 547 (5)
blemish 35 (1), 163 (1), 246 (2), 307 (1), 495 (3), 547 (1), 547 (2), 548 (4), 647 (2), 651 (12), 655 (4), 655 (9), 842 (1), 842 (2), 842 (7), 845 (1), 845 (3), 867 (2)
blemished 55 (3), 214 (4), 246 (4), 259 (4), 267 (10),

437 (8), 440 (3), 647 (3), 842 (4), 845 (2)
blench 818 (8), 854 (10)
blend 43 (3), 43 (7), 50 (2), 50 (4), 164 (7), 301 (40), 388 (2), 410 (9)
blended 43 (6), 50 (3)
blender 43 (1)
blending 43 (1), 50 (1)
bless 615 (4), 730 (8), 826 (3), 907 (5), 923 (8), 923 (9), 979 (12), 981 (11), 968 (10)
blessed 615 (3), 730 (5), 824 (5), 923 (7), 971 (3), 988 (8)
blessed virgin 968 (2)
blessed with 773 (2)
blessedness 824 (2), 979 (2)
blessing 615 (1), 615 (2), 756 (1), 897 (1), 907 (3), 923 (1), 981 (3), 981 (4)
blessings 730 (1)
blight 51 (2), 168 (1), 645 (1), 655 (2), 655 (9), 659 (2), 731 (1), 898 (8), 983 (11)
blight one's hopes 509 (5)
blighted 983 (9)
blighted hopes 509 (1)
blighting 983 (7)
blind 226 (4), 375 (3), 417 (11), 421 (2), 421 (3), 421 (4), 439 (2), 439 (4), 440 (3), 456 (3), 491 (4), 499 (5), 527 (3), 542 (2), 542 (4), 542 (8), 596 (5), 602 (4), 614 (1), 698 (2), 820 (3), 820 (7), 865 (2)
blind alley 145 (5), 624 (6), 641 (2), 702 (2)
blind as a bat 439 (2)
blind bargain 618 (2)
blind, be 439 (3), 456 (7), 458 (5), 481 (12), 820 (6)
blind belief 485 (1)
blind chance 159 (1)
blind corner 444 (1)
blind date 882 (4)
blind drunk 949 (8)
blind eye 439 (1)
blind faith 487 (1)

blind flying 271 (1),
blind ignorance 491 (1)
blind man's buff 837 (10)
blind oneself to 481 (12)
blind person 439 (1)
blind side 439 (1), 440 (1)
blind spot 439 (1), 440 (1), 444 (1), 456 (1), 481 (3)
blind to 820 (5), 865 (2)
blind to, be 439 (3), 820 (6), 865 (4)
blinded 439 (2), 440 (3)
blindfold 421 (4), 439 (2), 439 (4), 542 (8)
blindfolded 421 (3), 491 (4)
blinding 417 (8)
blindness 439 (1), 440 (1), 444 (1), 456 (1), 481 (3)
blink 438 (3), 438 (8), 439 (3), 440 (1), 440 (4)
blinker 421 (4), 439 (4), 440 (1), 542 (8)
blinkered 439 (2), 491 (4)
blinkers 421 (1)
blinking 440 (3)
bliss 824 (2)
blissful 730 (5), 824 (5), 826 (2), 971 (3)
blister 194 (2), 253 (2)
blistered 259 (4)
blistering 379 (4)
blithe 824 (5), 833 (3)
blitz 165 (2), 165 (7), 712 (1), 712 (3), 712 (11), 718 (7)
blitzkrieg 712 (1)
blizzard 176 (3), 352 (4), 380 (2)
bloated 195 (8), 197 (3), 246 (4), 253 (7), 637 (3), 842 (4)
bloc 708 (2)
block 192 (8), 195 (3), 218 (5), 264 (6), 324 (3), 326 (1), 555 (1), 586 (8), 702 (1), 713 (9), 713 (10), 757 (4), 805 (5), 820 (2), 964 (3)
block and tackle 310 (2)
block in 553 (8)
block letters 586 (2)

block out **233** (3), **243** (5), **554** (3), **669** (10)
block printing **587** (1)
block release **534** (2)
block up **702** (9)
blockade **230** (3), **232** (1), **232** (3), **264** (1), **264** (6), **702** (1), **702** (2), **702** (9), **712** (1), **712** (8), **718** (6), **718** (11), **747** (2)
blockader **712** (5)
blockading **718** (6)
blockage **145** (2), **702** (1), **702** (2)
blockbuster **590** (4)
blockhead **501** (3)
blockhouse **713** (4)
blocking **702** (6)
bloke **372** (1)
blond **426** (1), **426** (3), **427** (5), **433** (1), **841** (2)
blonde **373** (3)
blood **68** (10), **77** (3), **169** (2), **302** (2), **335** (3), **431** (1)
blood and thunder **594** (3)
blood bank **632** (2)
blood clot **335** (3)
blood count **335** (3)
blood-curdling **854** (8)
blood disease **651** (10)
blood donor **781** (4)
blood feud **709** (3)
blood group **77** (1), **335** (3)
blood-horse **273** (5)
blood-letting **362** (1)
blood lust **176** (1)
blood money **719** (2), **941** (1)
blood poisoning **659** (4)
blood pressure **651** (9)
blood-red **431** (4)
blood relation **11** (2)
blood relationship **11** (1)
blood sport **619** (2)
blood sports **362** (1)
blood-sucking **786** (3)
blood-thirsty **176** (6)
blood vessel **351** (1)
bloodbath **362** (4), **712** (2)
bloodhound **365** (10), **459** (8), **619** (3)
bloodiness **735** (2)

bloodless **4** (3), **163** (4), **426** (3), **651** (22), **717** (3)
bloodlessly **717** (5)
bloodlessness **426** (1)
bloodshed **362** (1), **362** (4), **718** (6), **898** (3)
bloodshot **431** (4)
bloodstained **335** (5), **362** (9), **431** (4)
bloodstock **273** (5), **868** (1), **868** (4)
bloodstream **335** (3)
bloodsucker **735** (3), **786** (4), **904** (3)
bloodthirstiness **898** (2)
bloodthirsty **362** (9), **645** (3), **718** (9), **898** (7)
bloody **176** (5), **335** (5), **362** (9), **431** (4), **735** (6), **898** (7)
bloody-minded **602** (4), **704** (3), **738** (7)
bloody one's nose **655** (10)
bloom **130** (3), **167** (6), **171** (6), **197** (4), **207** (1), **263** (17), **366** (7), **650** (1), **650** (3), **669** (3), **730** (6), **841** (7)
bloomer **495** (3)
bloomers **228** (12), **228** (17)
blooming **130** (4), **134** (3), **174** (5), **263** (13), **366** (1), **366** (9), **650** (2), **841** (6)
blossom **36** (4), **157** (2), **164** (2), **171** (6), **197** (4), **366** (7), **730** (6)
blossom-time **128** (3)
blot **252** (2), **299** (4), **342** (6), **428** (6), **495** (3), **547** (19), **649** (2), **649** (9), **695** (9), **842** (2), **842** (7), **845** (1), **845** (3), **867** (2)
blot out **165** (6), **525** (7), **550** (3)
blotch **437** (4), **845** (1)
blotted out **525** (4)
blotter **342** (3)
blotting out **165** (1)
blotting paper **342** (3)
blouse **228** (16)
blow **176** (7), **197** (4), **243** (5), **279** (2), **311** (6), **340**

(6), **352** (1), **352** (4), **352** (10), **401** (4), **413** (9), **508** (1), **509** (1), **616** (1), **676** (2), **684** (5), **731** (1), **825** (1), **963** (2)
blow a safe **788** (7)
blow along **352** (10)
blow away **165** (7), **287** (7)
blow down **165** (7), **311** (6)
blow hard **352** (10)
blow hot and cold **152** (5), **601** (4)
blow in **295** (4)
blow off **300** (11)
blow off steam **336** (4)
blow one's mind **503** (12)
blow one's money **815** (4)
blow one's own trumpet **873** (5), **877** (5)
blow open **176** (8)
blow out **165** (8), **382** (6), **418** (7)
blow over **145** (6)
blow sky-high **479** (3)
blow the whistle on **664** (5)
blow to bits **165** (7)
blow up **36** (5), **46** (13), **75** (3), **165** (7), **176** (2), **176** (7), **176** (8), **197** (5), **310** (4), **352** (10), **352** (12), **728** (8), **891** (6)
blow wave **843** (2)
blower **263** (4), **340** (1), **352** (6)
blowhole **263** (4), **353** (1)
blowing **197** (2), **352** (5), **352** (8)
blowing up **352** (5)
blowlamp **383** (1)
blown up **340** (5), **546** (2)
blowout **301** (2), **301** (12), **402** (1)
blowpipe **287** (3), **352** (5), **353** (1), **723** (4)
blows **716** (7), **891** (2)
blowy **352** (8)
blubber **357** (3), **836** (6)
blubber-lipped **205** (4)
blubbery **357** (6)
bludgeon **279** (9), **735** (8), **740** (3)
bludgeoning **735** (2)

blue 162 (4), 412 (7), 434
(3), 435 (1), 435 (3), 435
(4), 547 (9), 729 (2), 834
(6), 951 (6)
blue and red 436 (1)
blue-black 428 (4), 435 (3)
blue blood 169 (2), 335 (3),
868 (1)
blue-blooded 848 (6), 868
(6)
blue-chip 644 (7), 767 (2)
blue-collar worker 686 (2)
blue ensign 547 (12)
blue-eyed boy 890 (2)
blue jeans 228 (12)
blue joke 839 (2)
blue moon 109 (1)
blue pencil 550 (1), 550
(3), 654 (10), 757 (4)
blue pigment 435 (2)
blue sea 435 (1)
blue sky 435 (1)
blue-stocking 490 (6)
blue with cold 380 (6)
blueness 435 (1)
blueprint 23 (1), 551 (1),
551 (8), 592 (1), 623 (1),
623 (8), 669 (1)
blueprinted 623 (6)
blues 412 (1), 412 (5), 834
(2)
bluestocking 492 (2)
bluff 176 (5), 209 (2), 257
(2), 491 (3), 541 (2), 542
(2), 542 (8), 614 (1), 614
(4), 850 (5), 877 (2), 877
(5), 885 (5)
bluffer 545 (3), 850 (3),
877 (3)
bluffing 491 (7)
bluish-grey 429 (2)
bluishness 435 (1)
blunder 282 (5), 456 (7),
481 (9), 495 (3), 495 (8),
521 (3), 565 (3), 695 (7),
695 (8), 695 (9), 728 (7)
blunderbuss 723 (9)
blunderer 501 (1), 697 (1)
blundering 495 (5)
blunt 163 (10), 204 (3), 210
(2), 257 (2), 257 (3), 258
(3), 375 (6), 522 (5), 532

(4), 540 (2), 699 (3), 847
(5), 885 (5)
blunt, be 257 (3)
blunt edge 257 (1)
blunt instrument 257 (1)
blunt-nosed 257 (2)
blunted 257 (2)
bluntness 257 (1), 573 (1),
699 (1), 885 (2)
blur 419 (1), 419 (7), 440
(5)
blurb 528 (3)
blurb-writer 923 (4)
blurred 244 (2), 419 (4),
444 (3)
blurry 419 (5)
blurt 609 (4)
blurt out 524 (9), 526 (5),
579 (8)
blush 379 (1), 425 (3), 431
(1), 431 (5), 547 (1), 818
(1), 818 (8), 872 (2), 872
(6), 874 (1), 874 (3), 936
(1)
blush unseen 444 (4), 867
(8), 874 (3)
blushful 950 (5)
blushing 431 (3), 818 (3),
854 (2), 874 (1), 874 (2),
936 (3)
bluster 161 (4), 176 (1),
176 (7), 877 (1), 877 (2),
877 (5), 878 (1), 891 (7),
900 (1), 900 (3)
blusterer 877 (3), 878 (3)
blustering 176 (6), 854 (2),
877 (1), 878 (4), 900 (2)
blustery 176 (5), 352 (8)
BO 397 (1)
boa constrictor 198 (3),
365 (13)
boar 365 (9)
board 207 (2), 218 (5), 218
(12), 297 (5), 297 (7), 301
(7), 301 (35), 326 (1), 633
(5), 690 (1), 692 (1), 712
(7), 956 (1)
board and lodging 633 (1)
board game 837 (9)
board meeting 74 (2)
board out 192 (21)
board room 692 (1)

boarder 191 (2), 301 (6),
538 (1)
boarding 712 (1)
boarding house 192 (2)
boarding school 192 (2)
boards 226 (5), 594 (6)
boards, the 594 (1)
boast 78 (5), 482 (1), 546
(3), 727 (8), 850 (5), 866
(12), 871 (1), 871 (6), 873
(5), 875 (1), 875 (7), 877
(2), 877 (5), 878 (6), 890
(2), 900 (1), 900 (3), 923
(9)
boast of 773 (4), 871 (6),
877 (5)
boaster 176 (4), 545 (3),
722 (1), 850 (3), 856 (2),
871 (2), 877 (3), 878 (3)
boastful 543 (4), 546 (2),
871 (4), 873 (4), 877 (4),
878 (4), 900 (2)
boastfulness 877 (1)
boasting 482 (1), 515 (3),
543 (4), 546 (1), 574 (2),
854 (2), 856 (1), 871 (1),
873 (1), 877 (1), 877 (4),
923 (2)
boat 269 (1), 269 (8), 275
(1), 275 (7)
boat-builder 686 (3)
boat race 716 (3)
boat train 274 (13)
boater 228 (23)
boathouse 192 (10)
boating 269 (3), 837 (6)
boatman 270 (4)
boatswain 270 (1), 270 (2)
bob 117 (3), 217 (2), 217
(5), 311 (2), 312 (4), 317
(1), 317 (4), 322 (1), 843
(2)
bob up 308 (4)
bobbing 312 (3), 920 (3)
bobsleigh 274 (2)
bobsleighing 837 (6)
bode 511 (3)
bodice 228 (3)
bodily 3 (4), 52 (10), 176
(10), 319 (6), 376 (5), 944
(3)
bodily harm 616 (1)
bodily pain 377 (1)

bodily removal 786 (1)
bodily weakness 163 (1)
body 3 (2), 26 (1), 32 (3),
52 (3), 74 (4), 319 (2), 319
(3), 363 (1), 371 (3), 390
(1), 708 (4), 708 (5)
body and soul 52 (8)
body blow 279 (2)
body-building 162 (3), 301
(33), 652 (4)
body forth 6 (4), 223 (3),
319 (7)
body language 547 (4)
body odour 397 (1)
body of law 953 (3)
body politic 371 (5), 733
(6)
body stocking 228 (9)
bodyguard 89 (2), 660 (3),
713 (6), 722 (1), 742 (3)
boffin 686 (2)
bog 347 (1), 649 (2)
bogey 513 (3)
bogged down 136 (3)
boggy 347 (2)
bogus 541 (3), 542 (7), 543
(4)
bogy 938 (4), 970 (4)
Bohemian 84 (3), 84 (5),
744 (4)
boil 253 (2), 301 (40), 318
(5), 318 (7), 355 (5), 379
(7), 651 (14), 652 (6), 821
(9)
boil down 37 (4), 198 (7),
204 (5)
boil down to 514 (5)
boil over 176 (7), 298 (6),
891 (6)
boiled sweets 301 (18)
boiler 194 (14), 365 (6),
383 (2)
boiler suit 228 (9)
boiling 176 (6), 318 (3),
355 (1), 379 (4), 381 (1),
822 (3), 891 (4)
boiling point 379 (1)
boisterous 61 (9), 176 (5),
822 (3)
boisterousness 822 (1)
bold 254 (4), 522 (5), 571
(2), 855 (4), 855 (6), 857
(3)

bold as brass 878 (4)
bold front 711 (1), 855 (1)
bold move 623 (3)
bold stroke 855 (2)
boldface 587 (3)
boldness 855 (1), 878 (1)
bole 252 (3), 366 (4)
bollard 305 (3)
Bolshevism 733 (4)
bolshie 704 (3)
bolster 218 (8), 218 (15),
703 (5)
bolster up 833 (8), 855 (8)
bolt 45 (11), 47 (5), 74 (6),
222 (4), 235 (3), 264 (2),
264 (6), 277 (6), 296 (5),
301 (35), 620 (6), 947 (4)
bolt upright 215 (2)
bolted 264 (4)
bomb 160 (7), 165 (7), 168
(1), 402 (1), 712 (11), 723
(14)
bomb site 190 (2)
bombard 165 (7), 287 (8),
712 (11)
bombardier 722 (5)
bombardment 165 (2), 287
(1), 400 (1), 712 (3), 718
(6)
bombast 497 (1), 515 (3),
574 (2), 849 (1), 877 (2)
bombastic 546 (2), 570 (3),
574 (5), 849 (2), 877 (4)
bomber 276 (1), 722 (14)
bomber jacket 228 (10)
bombing 712 (3), 718 (6)
bombshell 508 (1)
bon appetit 301 (41)
bon mot 839 (2)
bon vivant 882 (5), 947 (2)
bon voyage 296 (7)
bona fide 494 (5), 540 (2)
bonanza 632 (1), 635 (2),
637 (1), 730 (1), 781 (2),
800 (1)
bond 9 (1), 45 (1), 45 (4),
47 (1), 218 (9), 231 (3),
702 (2), 745 (5), 748 (4),
764 (1), 765 (1), 767 (2),
778 (1), 797 (5), 915 (1),
917 (1)
bondage 745 (3), 747 (3)
bonded 708 (6)

bonding 45 (4)
bonds of friendship 880
(1)
bone 300 (8), 326 (1), 326
(5)
bone-breaking 259 (4)
bone china 381 (5)
bone-headed 499 (3)
bone-idle 679 (8)
bone-lazy 679 (8)
bone of contention 709
(4), 716 (1)
bone-setting 658 (12)
bone-weary 684 (2)
boned 326 (4)
bonehead 501 (3)
boneless 161 (7)
bones 41 (1), 363 (1), 414
(8)
bonfire 379 (2)
bonhomie 875 (1), 882 (2),
897 (1)
bonnet 228 (23)
bonny 650 (2), 833 (3), 841
(3)
bonsai 366 (4)
bonus 29 (1), 40 (2), 612
(4), 637 (2), 781 (2), 807
(1), 962 (1)
bony 206 (5), 326 (3)
boo 408 (3), 408 (4), 547
(4), 921 (2), 921 (5), 922
(5), 924 (1), 924 (9)
boobs 253 (3)
booby 501 (2), 697 (1)
booby prize 695 (1), 729
(1)
booby trap 542 (4), 663
(1), 713 (2), 723 (14)
booing 547 (4)
book 87 (5), 135 (5), 548
(1), 548 (8), 586 (3), 589
(1), 590 (4), 627 (6), 771
(7), 773 (4), 808 (5), 924
(11), 928 (9)
book a passage 269 (9)
book collector 589 (6)
book dealer 589 (6)
book-keeper 549 (1)
book-keeping 548 (2)
book-learned 490 (6)
book-learning 490 (2)
book list 87 (1)

book lover 589 (6)
book-loving 589 (8)
book of fate 596 (2)
book of psalms 988 (6)
book of words 594 (3)
book printer 587 (5)
book trade 528 (1)
bookbinder 589 (6)
bookcase 194 (5)
booked 548 (6), 627 (3), 778 (4)
booking 548 (2)
booking clerk 793 (2)
bookish 490 (6), 536 (3)
bookishness 490 (2)
bookkeeper 86 (7), 798 (1), 808 (3)
bookkeeping 808 (1), 808 (4)
booklet 589 (1)
bookmaker 618 (4)
bookmaking 159 (4)
bookperson 589 (6)
books 87 (1), 586 (1), 808 (2)
bookseller 589 (6)
bookworm 492 (1), 538 (1), 589 (6)
boom 36 (4), 171 (1), 218 (2), 400 (1), 400 (4), 402 (4), 403 (3), 404 (1), 656 (3), 713 (2), 730 (1), 730 (6), 793 (1)
boom and bust 317 (2)
boom town 36 (1)
boomerang 280 (1), 280 (3), 714 (1), 714 (3), 723 (4)
booming 400 (3), 403 (1), 403 (2), 404 (2), 730 (4)
booming economy 730 (1)
boon 615 (2), 781 (2)
boor 885 (3)
boorish 695 (5), 847 (5), 885 (4)
boorishness 847 (2), 885 (1)
boost 36 (1), 36 (5), 174 (2), 174 (8), 279 (1), 310 (1), 482 (4), 528 (11), 703 (1), 703 (5)
boost one's morale 703 (5)
booster 174 (4), 531 (3)

boot 194 (7), 279 (10), 300 (1)
boot-licking 920 (3)
boot out 300 (6)
boot polish 648 (4)
booth 192 (7), 194 (4), 796 (3)
bootlace 47 (4)
bootleg 788 (7)
bootless 634 (3), 728 (4)
boots 228 (27)
booty 729 (1), 771 (1), 786 (1), 790 (1)
booze 301 (28), 949 (14)
boozer 949 (5)
boozy 949 (7), 949 (11)
bop 837 (14)
border 68 (5), 200 (5), 202 (1), 230 (1), 232 (3), 234 (1), 234 (3), 234 (4), 234 (5), 236 (1), 236 (2), 236 (3), 239 (3), 370 (3), 844 (5), 844 (12)
border with 202 (3)
bordered 234 (4)
borderer 191 (1)
bordering on 200 (4)
borderline 474 (4)
borderline case 474 (1), 700 (3)
Borders 184 (3)
bore 197 (5), 205 (1), 255 (8), 263 (2), 263 (18), 309 (3), 350 (2), 350 (5), 581 (5), 684 (6), 825 (3), 827 (10), 834 (12), 838 (2), 838 (5), 840 (3), 863 (3)
bore into 297 (5)
bore stiff 838 (5)
bore to tears 838 (5)
bored 263 (14), 454 (2), 829 (3), 838 (4), 863 (2)
borehole 255 (4), 263 (2), 339 (1)
borer 263 (12)
boring 263 (8), 309 (1), 570 (4), 572 (2), 827 (5), 829 (4), 838 (3)
boring person 838 (2)
boring thing 838 (2)
boring work 838 (2)
boringly 838 (6)
born 360 (3)

born again 939 (3), 979 (8)
born-again Christian 976 (7)
born alive 360 (3)
born, be 1 (7), 68 (8), 167 (6), 360 (5)
born dead 361 (6)
born for 694 (5)
born loser 728 (3)
born of 157 (3)
borough 184 (3)
borrow 20 (6), 767 (6), 785 (2), 792 (5), 802 (3), 803 (6), 816 (6), 916 (8)
borrow from 785 (2)
borrowed 560 (4)
borrower 20 (3), 763 (2), 803 (3)
borrowing 560 (1), 785 (1), 788 (1), 792 (1), 803 (1), 805 (1)
Borstal 748 (1)
bosom 228 (3), 253 (3), 447 (2), 817 (1)
bosom friend 880 (4)
boss 34 (3)
bosun 270 (1)
bosun's mate 270 (2)
botanical 366 (9)
botanical garden 368 (1)
botanist 368 (1)
botany 358 (2), 368 (1)
botch 495 (8), 552 (1), 552 (3), 695 (2), 695 (9), 728 (7)
botched 647 (3), 695 (6)
botching 695 (2)
both 90 (2)
bother 318 (3), 455 (4), 456 (8), 678 (1), 678 (13), 700 (6), 702 (8), 825 (3), 827 (9), 891 (9)
botheration 827 (2)
bothersome 645 (5), 700 (4), 827 (5)
bothersome task 825 (3)
bottle 194 (13), 301 (26), 666 (5)
bottle-green 434 (3)
bottle opener 263 (11)
bottle up 505 (7), 747 (7)
bottled fruit 301 (19)
bottled up 747 (5)

bottleneck 198 (1), 206 (1), 702 (2)
bottling 632 (2)
bottling plant 666 (2)
bottom 69 (2), 210 (1), 211 (1), 214 (1), 214 (3), 238 (2)
bottom rung 73 (1)
bottom side up 221 (6)
bottom, the 35 (1)
bottom up 221 (3)
bottomless 211 (2), 972 (3)
bottomless pit 211 (1), 972 (1)
bottomless purse 797 (2), 800 (1)
bottommost 35 (3)
botulism 659 (4)
boudoir 194 (19), 843 (4)
bouffant 253 (7), 843 (6)
bough 53 (4), 366 (4)
bought 792 (3), 930 (6)
boulder 344 (4)
boulevard 192 (15)
bounce 280 (1), 308 (1), 308 (4), 312 (4), 317 (4), 328 (1), 328 (3), 877 (1)
bounce back 286 (4), 656 (8)
bounce up 310 (4)
bouncer 300 (2), 660 (3)
bouncing 174 (5), 312 (3), 650 (2), 833 (3), 878 (4)
bouncing cheque 805 (1)
bouncy 328 (2)
bound 45 (8), 236 (3), 277 (2), 277 (6), 312 (1), 312 (4), 589 (8), 596 (6), 745 (5), 747 (5), 764 (3), 778 (4), 803 (4)
bound for 281 (3)
bound for, be 281 (5)
bound to be 473 (4)
bound to happen 155 (2)
boundaries 184 (1)
boundary 46 (2), 69 (2), 234 (1), 236 (1), 236 (2)
boundary stone 236 (1)
bounder 847 (3), 938 (3)
boundless 107 (2), 183 (6)
boundlessness 32 (1), 107 (1)
bounds 185 (1), 233 (1)

bounteous 813 (3)
bounteousness 813 (1)
bountiful 781 (5), 813 (3), 897 (4)
bountifulness 813 (1)
bounty 703 (2), 781 (2), 813 (1)
bouquet 74 (6), 390 (1), 394 (1), 396 (1), 923 (2), 923 (3)
bouquet garni 301 (21)
bourgeois 869 (5), 869 (8)
bourgeois ethic 83 (1)
bourgeoisie 732 (1), 869 (1), 869 (4)
bourne 350 (1)
bout 110 (1), 716 (4)
bout of sickness 651 (2)
boutique 796 (3)
bovine 365 (18)
bow 248 (2), 248 (5), 250 (3), 253 (6), 253 (9), 287 (3), 311 (2), 311 (9), 414 (3), 721 (4), 723 (4), 844 (5), 879 (4), 884 (2), 884 (7), 920 (2), 988 (10)
bow and scrape 920 (6)
bow down 311 (9)
bow down before 981 (11)
bow down to 866 (13)
bow-legged 246 (4), 248 (3), 267 (10)
bow out 296 (4)
bow-string 963 (12)
bow-stringing 963 (3)
bow tie 228 (22)
bow to 35 (5), 721 (3)
bow to fate 596 (7)
bow wave 350 (5)
bowdlerize 648 (10), 655 (9)
bowdlerized 950 (5)
bowed 248 (3), 253 (8)
bowed down 872 (4)
bowel movement 302 (3)
bowels 224 (2)
bower 194 (23), 421 (1)
bowery 421 (3)
bowing 248 (1), 879 (3), 920 (3)
bowl 194 (16), 255 (2), 287 (2), 287 (7), 315 (5)
bowl a break 282 (6)

bowl along 258 (5), 277 (6)
bowl one over 508 (5)
bowl out 300 (7), 727 (10)
bowl over 161 (9), 311 (6), 864 (7)
bowled over 864 (4)
bowler 228 (23), 287 (5), 837 (16)
bowline 47 (3)
bowling 287 (1)
bowls 837 (7)
bowman 287 (4), 722 (5)
bows 237 (3)
bowsprit 237 (3), 254 (2)
box 192 (7), 194 (4), 194 (7), 226 (13), 232 (3), 235 (1), 235 (4), 279 (9), 594 (7), 632 (2), 716 (11)
box file 194 (10)
box girder 218 (9)
box of tricks 698 (2)
box office 594 (7), 799 (1)
box-office hit 594 (2)
box room 194 (19)
box up 747 (10)
boxed up 232 (2)
boxer 365 (10), 722 (2)
boxing 716 (4)
boxing glove 279 (4)
boxing match 716 (4)
boy 132 (2), 372 (1)
boycott 46 (9), 57 (1), 57 (5), 702 (1), 883 (9), 924 (1)
boyfriend 372 (1), 880 (3), 887 (4)
boyhood 130 (1)
boyish 130 (4), 132 (5), 499 (4), 670 (4)
boyishness 130 (1)
bra 228 (17)
brace 45 (13), 47 (5), 74 (3), 90 (1), 162 (12), 218 (2), 218 (15), 685 (4)
brace oneself 599 (3), 669 (13)
braced 326 (4)
bracelet 250 (3), 844 (7)
braces 47 (5), 217 (3), 228 (17)
bracing 174 (5), 652 (4), 685 (2), 833 (6)
bracken 366 (6)

bracket 28 (10), 45 (9), 47 (1), 77 (1), 90 (3), 218 (2), 218 (12), 231 (9)
bracket together 9 (8)
bracket with 18 (8)
bracketed 28 (7)
bracketed with 18 (4)
brackets 547 (14)
brackish 388 (4)
brae 209 (2)
brag 837 (11), 866 (12), 877 (2), 877 (3), 877 (5), 878 (6)
braggadocio 856 (1)
braggart 856 (2), 877 (3), 877 (4)
bragger 871 (2)
bragging 877 (1), 877 (4)
Brahma 965 (3)
Brahman 986 (8)
braid 47 (4), 208 (3), 222 (1), 222 (9), 844 (5)
braille 586 (1)
brain 213 (3), 362 (10), 447 (1), 492 (2)
brain-child 451 (1)
brain damage 448 (1), 503 (1)
brain-damaged 503 (7)
brain death 361 (2)
brain disease 651 (3)
brain haemorrhage 651 (16)
brain tumour 651 (16)
brain-twister 530 (2)
brain wave 451 (1)
brain worker 492 (2), 686 (2)
brainchild 164 (2)
braininess 498 (1)
brainless 448 (2), 499 (4)
brainlessness 448 (1), 499 (2)
brains 447 (1), 498 (1), 623 (5)
brainstorm 503 (2), 822 (2)
brainwash 147 (7), 178 (3), 534 (7), 535 (3), 610 (8), 655 (8)
brainwashed 147 (5)
brainwashing 534 (1)
brainwork 449 (1)

brainy 498 (4)
braise 301 (40)
brake 145 (7), 177 (2), 266 (9), 278 (1), 278 (6), 366 (2), 747 (1), 747 (7), 748 (4)
bramble 256 (3), 366 (6)
bran 301 (22)
branch 53 (4), 75 (3), 77 (1), 170 (2), 183 (7), 192 (4), 350 (1), 366 (4), 708 (3)
branch line 624 (7)
branch off 92 (6), 294 (3)
branch out 282 (3)
branching 75 (2), 92 (2), 183 (6), 245 (1), 282 (2)
branching off 282 (1)
branching out 75 (1), 294 (1)
brand 77 (2), 381 (2), 381 (10), 383 (1), 420 (3), 547 (2), 547 (13), 547 (19), 845 (3), 867 (2), 867 (11), 924 (2), 924 (10), 926 (1), 928 (8)
brand-new 126 (5)
branded 547 (17), 777 (5)
branding 381 (2)
brandish 317 (6), 318 (6), 522 (8), 673 (3), 875 (7), 877 (5)
brandished 318 (4), 522 (6)
brandy 301 (28)
brash 878 (4)
brashness 878 (1)
brass 43 (3), 352 (5), 400 (2), 404 (1), 413 (3), 414 (1), 414 (7), 433 (1), 548 (3), 797 (1), 800 (1)
brass band 74 (4), 413 (3)
brass rubbing 553 (5)
brass tacks 1 (2)
brasserie 192 (13)
brassiere 228 (17)
brassiness 407 (1)
brassy 400 (3), 407 (2), 432 (2)
brat 132 (1)
bravado 875 (1), 877 (1), 877 (2), 878 (1)

brave 711 (3), 722 (1), 722 (4), 855 (3), 855 (4), 855 (6), 875 (5)
brave face 711 (1), 855 (1)
brave person 676 (3), 855 (3)
bravely 855 (9)
bravery 855 (1)
bravo 722 (1), 857 (2), 923 (14)
bravura 413 (6), 694 (3), 711 (1)
brawl 61 (4), 709 (3), 709 (9), 716 (7)
brawler 705 (1), 738 (6)
brawn 162 (2)
brawny 162 (8), 195 (8)
bray 400 (1), 400 (4), 404 (3), 407 (4), 409 (3)
braying 407 (2)
brazen 407 (2), 522 (5), 871 (3), 878 (4), 934 (3), 940 (2), 980 (4)
brazen-faced 878 (4)
brazen it out 878 (6)
brazenness 711 (1), 875 (1), 878 (1)
brazier 383 (1)
breach 46 (1), 201 (2), 709 (1), 881 (1), 916 (1)
breach of faith 930 (2)
breach of law 954 (2)
breach of promise 543 (1), 769 (1), 930 (2)
breach of the peace 61 (4)
breach of trust 788 (4)
bread 301 (9), 301 (22)
bread and butter 301 (13)
bread and cheese 301 (13)
bread and water 391 (1), 636 (1), 946 (1)
breadth 26 (1), 32 (1), 183 (2), 195 (1), 205 (1), 465 (3)
breadth of mind 498 (3)
breadthways 205 (6)
breadwinner 686 (2)
breadwinning 771 (1)
break 46 (1), 46 (7), 46 (13), 55 (1), 71 (2), 72 (1), 72 (4), 137 (2), 145 (4), 146 (1), 165 (7), 176 (8), 201 (1), 201 (2), 244 (3),

282 (1), 282 (3), 330 (3), 332 (5), 350 (9), 655 (10), 681 (1), 685 (1), 727 (10), 730 (1)
break a habit 611 (4)
break a law 84 (8)
break away 46 (7), 75 (3), 667 (5), 709 (7), 738 (10), 918 (3), 978 (9)
break bounds 176 (7)
break camp 296 (5)
break down 44 (6), 46 (8), 51 (5), 165 (7), 307 (3), 728 (7), 836 (6), 854 (9)
break even 28 (9), 771 (7)
break faith 541 (5), 769 (3), 930 (8)
break in 297 (7), 297 (8), 369 (8), 534 (8), 610 (8), 735 (8), 745 (7)
break in on 63 (3)
break in pieces 46 (13)
break in two 46 (13)
break in upon 72 (4)
break into a smile 835 (8)
break it off 621 (3)
break loose 746 (4)
break new ground 68 (9)
break of 656 (11)
break of day 128 (1)
break off 55 (5), 72 (4), 145 (6), 330 (3)
break one's heart 834 (11)
break one's neck 361 (8)
break one's spirit 735 (8)
break one's word or one's promise 769 (3)
break out 68 (8), 176 (7), 298 (5), 667 (5), 712 (7)
break ranks 75 (3)
break silence 579 (8)
break the bank 771 (9)
break the flag 547 (22)
break the ice 68 (9), 880 (8)
break the law 738 (9), 914 (6), 954 (8)
break the peace 176 (7), 716 (11)
break the rules 914 (6)
break the seal 526 (4)
break the silence 400 (4)
break through 298 (5)

break up 46 (7), 46 (8), 46 (10), 46 (13), 51 (5), 75 (3), 75 (4), 165 (3), 165 (7), 165 (11), 641 (7)
break up with the past 149 (4)
break water 269 (10), 298 (5), 308 (4)
break wind 300 (11)
break with 709 (7)
break with custom 84 (8)
breakable 330 (2)
breakaway 738 (2), 744 (7), 978 (2), 978 (7)
breakdown 46 (2), 51 (1), 145 (2), 161 (2), 165 (3), 651 (2), 651 (16), 702 (3), 728 (1), 836 (1)
breaker 350 (5)
breaker-in 537 (2)
breakfast 301 (12), 301 (35)
breakfast room 194 (19)
breaking 46 (2), 578 (2)
breaking point 709 (4)
breaking surface 308 (1)
breaking up 165 (3)
breaking voice 578 (1)
breaking wind 300 (3)
breakneck 220 (4), 277 (5), 680 (2), 857 (3)
breakneck speed 277 (1)
breakout 298 (1), 667 (1), 712 (1)
breakthrough 484 (1), 712 (1), 727 (1)
breakup 46 (1), 51 (1), 69 (3), 75 (1)
breakwater 254 (2)
bream 365 (15)
breast 237 (5), 253 (3), 308 (5), 817 (1)
breast-feed 301 (39)
breast-high 209 (8)
breast milk 301 (30)
breast pocket 194 (11)
breast stroke 269 (3)
breast the current 269 (12)
breast the tide 704 (5)
breastplate 253 (3), 660 (2), 713 (5)
breasts 253 (3)

breath 33 (2), 394 (1), 401 (1)
breath of air 352 (3), 685 (1)
breath of life 360 (1)
breath-sweetener 396 (2)
breathalyser 461 (4)
breathe 1 (6), 298 (7), 317 (4), 340 (6), 352 (11), 360 (4), 394 (3), 524 (11), 577 (4), 579 (8), 818 (8)
breathe again 831 (4)
breathe freely 746 (4)
breathe hard 352 (11)
breathe heavily 352 (11)
breathe in 299 (4), 352 (11)
breathe into 821 (6)
breathe life into 360 (6)
breathe one's last 361 (7)
breathe out 300 (9), 352 (11)
breathed 578 (2)
breather 145 (4), 685 (1)
breathing 317 (1), 352 (7), 360 (1), 360 (2)
breathing out 302 (1)
breathing space 145 (4), 683 (1)
breathless 318 (4), 578 (2), 580 (2), 680 (2), 684 (3), 818 (5), 854 (7), 859 (7), 864 (4)
breathtaking 32 (7), 864 (5)
bred 164 (6), 369 (7)
bred to 490 (6)
breech delivery 167 (2)
breeches 228 (12)
breechloader 723 (9)
breed 5 (3), 11 (4), 36 (4), 36 (5), 74 (3), 77 (3), 164 (7), 166 (3), 167 (6), 167 (7), 369 (9), 669 (12)
breed stock 36 (5), 164 (7), 167 (7), 369 (9), 669 (12)
breed with 45 (14)
breeder 164 (4), 369 (5), 537 (2)
breeding 164 (1), 167 (1), 167 (5), 369 (1), 846 (1), 848 (2)
breeding ground 156 (4)

breeze 352 (3)
breeze block 631 (2)
breeze in 297 (5)
breeziness 352 (1), 833 (1)
breezy 340 (5), 352 (8), 833 (3), 921 (3)
breve 410 (3)
brevet 737 (4), 751 (2)
breviary 975 (2), 981 (4)
brevity 33 (1), 114 (2), 204 (1), 569 (1)
brew 301 (28), 623 (9), 669 (12)
brewery 687 (1)
brewing 155 (2), 164 (1)
briar 388 (2)
bribable 792 (3), 930 (6)
bribe 31 (4), 612 (4), 612 (12), 759 (1), 759 (3), 781 (2), 781 (7), 792 (5), 804 (2), 804 (4), 962 (3)
bribed 792 (3)
bribery 612 (2), 792 (1)
bric-a-brac 639 (3), 844 (1)
brick 192 (20), 381 (5), 890 (2), 929 (2), 937 (1)
brick wall 702 (2)
brickbat 287 (2)
bricklayer 686 (3)
bricks 837 (15)
bricks and mortar 164 (3), 192 (8), 631 (2)
brickwork 164 (3)
bridal 894 (3), 894 (9)
bride 373 (3), 894 (4)
bridegroom 372 (1), 894 (4)
bridesmaid 707 (1)
bridge 45 (10), 47 (1), 222 (1), 256 (4), 305 (1), 305 (5), 624 (3)
bridge over 305 (5), 719 (4), 770 (2)
bridge the gap 701 (8)
bridged 624 (8)
bridgehead 237 (1), 724 (2), 778 (1)
bridging loan 784 (1)
bridle 296 (6), 369 (8), 747 (1), 747 (7), 748 (4), 891 (6)
bridlepath 624 (5)

bridleway 624 (5)
brief 33 (6), 114 (5), 204 (3), 204 (4), 524 (9), 569 (2), 569 (3), 669 (11), 737 (6)
brief counsel 959 (7)
brief encounter 114 (2)
brief oneself 669 (13)
brief span 114 (2), 204 (1)
briefcase 194 (10)
briefed 490 (6), 524 (8), 669 (7)
briefing 524 (1), 669 (1), 691 (1)
briefly 114 (7), 569 (4)
briefness 33 (1), 114 (2), 204 (1)
briefs 228 (17)
brier 256 (3)
brig 275 (5)
brigade 74 (3), 722 (8)
brigadier 741 (8)
brigand 789 (2)
brigandage 712 (1), 738 (1), 788 (2)
bright 417 (8), 417 (9), 420 (8), 425 (6), 498 (4), 648 (7), 833 (3), 841 (3), 841 (4), 852 (5)
bright and early 135 (4)
bright, be 417 (15)
bright-eyed 841 (6)
bright-hued 425 (6)
bright idea 498 (1), 623 (3)
bright red 431 (3)
bright side 826 (1)
bright young thing 126 (3)
brighten 417 (13), 833 (7), 841 (8)
brightness 417 (1), 498 (1), 839 (1), 841 (1)
brilliance 417 (1), 425 (3), 498 (1), 841 (1), 866 (2), 875 (1)
brilliant 417 (8), 425 (6), 498 (4), 646 (3), 839 (4), 844 (8), 866 (9), 875 (4)
brim 54 (5), 234 (1), 635 (7)
brim over 306 (3), 637 (5)
brimful 54 (4)
brimming 54 (2), 54 (4), 863 (2)

brimstone 385 (4), 433 (1)
brindled 437 (8)
brine 339 (1), 343 (1), 666 (2)
bring 273 (12)
bring a charge 928 (9)
bring a suit 959 (7)
bring about 154 (6), 156 (9), 164 (7), 612 (10), 725 (6)
bring an action 928 (9)
bring back 668 (3), 787 (3)
bring comfort 831 (3)
bring down 311 (6), 712 (9), 712 (11)
bring forward 285 (4)
bring home to 485 (9), 821 (8)
bring in 299 (3), 771 (10), 809 (6)
bring in question 459 (13)
bring into disrepute 867 (11)
bring into focus 293 (3)
bring into play 173 (3)
bring it off 727 (6)
bring near 200 (6), 289 (4)
bring off 156 (9)
bring on 156 (9), 285 (4), 669 (12)
bring order into 62 (5)
bring out 522 (7), 587 (7)
bring religion to 979 (11)
bring round 485 (9), 502 (4), 612 (10)
bring shame upon 867 (11)
bring sorrow 834 (11)
bring to 36 (5), 38 (3), 266 (9)
bring to a head 36 (5), 669 (12)
bring to a standstill 145 (7)
bring to an end 69 (6)
bring to bear 673 (3)
bring to fruition 654 (9), 669 (12)
bring to God 979 (11)
bring to heel 745 (7)
bring to justice 959 (7)
bring to life 360 (6), 590 (7)

bring to light 522 (7)
bring to market 793 (4)
bring to mind 505 (7)
bring to notice 522 (7), 638 (8)
bring to one's notice 455 (7)
bring to rest 177 (7), 187 (5), 266 (9), 269 (10)
bring to their senses 502 (4)
bring together 38 (3), 45 (9), 50 (4), 56 (5), 74 (11), 462 (3), 592 (5), 632 (5), 669 (11), 719 (4), 720 (4), 737 (6), 771 (7), 786 (6)
bring up 164 (7), 300 (10), 534 (6)
bring up badly 535 (3)
bring up the rear 238 (5), 284 (4)
bring up to date 126 (8)
bring word 524 (10)
bringing back 787 (1)
bringing together 45 (2), 74 (1)
brink 69 (2), 200 (1), 234 (1)
brinkmanship 688 (2)
briny 343 (1), 388 (4)
brisk 114 (5), 174 (5), 277 (5), 569 (2), 678 (7)
bristle 215 (3), 256 (3), 259 (1), 259 (2), 259 (8), 310 (4), 891 (6), 900 (3)
bristle up 254 (5), 259 (8)
bristle with 104 (6), 256 (10), 635 (7), 637 (5)
bristling 256 (7), 259 (5)
bristly 256 (7), 259 (5)
bristols 253 (3)
brittle 53 (6), 163 (8), 326 (4), 330 (2), 542 (7)
brittle, be 330 (3)
brittleness 49 (1), 163 (1), 163 (3), 330 (1), 332 (1)
broach 68 (9), 156 (9), 300 (8), 350 (11), 528 (9)
broad 32 (4), 79 (3), 183 (6), 195 (6), 195 (8), 197 (3), 205 (3), 346 (1), 495 (6), 560 (5), 951 (6)
broad accent 577 (2)

broad-based 78 (2), 79 (3), 205 (3)
broad, be 36 (4), 197 (4), 205 (5), 226 (14)
broad-brimmed 205 (3)
broad-chested 205 (3)
Broad-Church 976 (10)
broad day 417 (1)
broad grin 835 (2)
broad hint 524 (3)
broad humour 839 (1)
broad-minded 498 (5)
broadcast 75 (2), 75 (4), 79 (6), 311 (5), 524 (10), 528 (1), 528 (7), 528 (9), 529 (1), 531 (4), 579 (2), 594 (3)
broadcaster 524 (4), 529 (4), 531 (5), 579 (5)
broadcasting 75 (1), 438 (4), 445 (2), 524 (1), 528 (1), 528 (2), 528 (3), 531 (3), 539 (5)
broadcloth 222 (4)
broaden 36 (5), 79 (6), 197 (4), 197 (5), 205 (5)
broadening 36 (1)
broadminded 744 (5)
broadmindedness 498 (3)
broadsheet 528 (4)
broadside 239 (1), 712 (3), 723 (11)
broadside on 239 (4)
broadsword 723 (8)
Broadway 594 (1)
broadways 205 (6)
brocade 222 (4)
brochure 528 (4), 589 (1)
brogue 560 (2), 577 (2), 580 (1)
brogues 228 (27)
broil 301 (40)
broiler 365 (6)
broiler house 369 (2)
broiling 379 (4)
broke 772 (2), 801 (3)
broken 46 (4), 53 (6), 72 (2), 163 (5), 259 (4), 369 (7), 647 (3), 655 (6)
broken bones 655 (4)
broken down 641 (4)
broken English 560 (2)
broken glass 259 (1)

broken ground 259 (1)
broken heart 825 (2), 887 (3)
broken in 369 (7)
broken marriage 896 (1)
broken promise 601 (1), 930 (2)
broken ranks 72 (1)
broken reed 161 (4)
broken resolve 601 (1)
broken romance 887 (3)
broken silence 400 (1)
broken up 165 (5)
broken-winded 651 (22), 684 (3)
broken word 543 (1), 930 (2)
broker 231 (3), 794 (1)
broker for, be 755 (3)
brolly 226 (4)
bromide 839 (2)
bronchial 651 (22)
bronchitic 651 (22)
bronchitis 651 (8)
bronco 273 (8)
bronze 43 (3), 430 (1), 430 (3), 430 (4)
bronzed 381 (6), 430 (3)
brooch 47 (5), 844 (7)
brood 74 (3), 132 (3), 170 (1), 449 (8), 834 (9)
brood mare 273 (4)
brood on 910 (6)
brooding 449 (2), 669 (6)
broody 167 (5)
brook 350 (1)
brook no denial 532 (5), 740 (3)
brook no rival 911 (3)
broom 648 (5)
broomstick 206 (2)
broth 301 (14)
brothel 951 (5)
brother 11 (2), 18 (3), 372 (1), 707 (3), 880 (3), 986 (5)
brother or sister to, be 11 (7)
brotherhood 11 (3), 74 (3), 708 (4), 880 (1), 986 (5)
brotherly 11 (5), 880 (6), 887 (9), 897 (4)

brotherly love 887 (1), 897 (1)

brothers and sisters 74 (4)

brought low 728 (5), 872 (4)

brought on 612 (7)

brought to heel 745 (4)

brought up to date 126 (7)

brouhaha 318 (3)

brow 213 (2), 213 (3), 237 (2), 253 (4), 254 (3)

browbeat 612 (10), 854 (12), 924 (11)

browbeaten 745 (4)

brown 418 (6), 430 (1), 430 (3), 430 (4), 431 (3)

brown pigment 430 (2)

brown sauce 389 (2)

brown study 449 (1), 456 (2)

browned 430 (3)

browned off 829 (3), 834 (5), 838 (4)

brownie 970 (2)

brownish 430 (3)

brownness 430 (1)

browse 301 (37), 536 (5)

bruise 176 (8), 377 (1), 378 (7), 616 (1), 645 (7), 655 (4), 655 (10), 845 (1)

bruiser 722 (2), 904 (2)

brunch 301 (12)

brunette 373 (3), 428 (4), 430 (1), 430 (3), 841 (2)

brunt 279 (3), 700 (1)

brush 184 (4), 200 (5), 202 (3), 238 (1), 258 (2), 333 (3), 378 (7), 648 (5), 648 (9), 716 (7)

brush aside 479 (3), 680 (3)

brush-off 292 (1), 292 (3), 300 (6)

brush up 536 (5)

brush with 718 (12)

brushed 259 (5)

brushing 202 (2), 333 (1)

brushwood 366 (2), 385 (1)

brushwork 553 (1)

brusque 176 (5), 569 (2), 582 (1), 582 (3), 885 (5), 893 (2)

brusqueness 582 (1)

brutal 176 (5), 735 (6), 885 (5), 898 (7), 906 (2), 934 (6)

brutality 176 (1), 898 (2), 898 (3)

brutalize 655 (8), 820 (7), 934 (8)

brutalized 898 (7), 934 (4)

brute 176 (4), 365 (2), 448 (2), 735 (3), 885 (3), 904 (2), 904 (5), 938 (4)

brute creation 448 (1)

brute force 162 (1), 176 (1), 733 (3), 735 (2), 740 (1), 954 (3)

brute matter 319 (2)

brutish 365 (18), 869 (9), 898 (7), 944 (3)

brutishness 847 (2)

bubble 4 (2), 194 (2), 252 (2), 253 (2), 318 (3), 318 (5), 323 (1), 341 (1), 350 (9), 355 (1), 355 (5)

bubble and squeak 301 (20)

bubble gum 301 (18)

bubble up 318 (7), 350 (9)

bubbles 355 (1)

bubbling 355 (1), 818 (5)

bubbly 301 (29), 336 (3), 355 (3), 821 (3)

bubo 253 (2)

buccaneer 722 (3), 788 (9), 789 (2)

buccaneering 788 (2), 788 (6)

buck 312 (4)

buck up 831 (3)

bucket 194 (13)

bucket down 350 (10)

bucking 312 (3)

bucking bronco 312 (2)

buckle 46 (13), 47 (5), 246 (1), 246 (5)

buckle to 599 (3), 672 (3), 678 (11)

buckled 246 (3), 251 (4)

buckler 713 (5)

buckshot 723 (12)

bucolic 370 (7)

bud 36 (4), 68 (4), 156 (3), 253 (2), 303 (6), 366 (7)

Buddha 973 (6)

Buddhism 449 (3), 973 (3)

Buddhist 973 (7)

budding 68 (6), 126 (5), 130 (4), 197 (3)

buddy 372 (1), 880 (5)

budge 265 (4), 265 (5)

budgerigar 365 (4)

budget 633 (5), 808 (1), 808 (5)

budget price 812 (1)

budgetary 797 (9), 808 (4)

budgeting 633 (1), 808 (1)

buff 258 (4), 333 (3), 430 (3), 504 (3), 648 (9)

buff, the 229 (2)

buffer 231 (3), 660 (2), 713 (1)

buffer state 202 (1), 231 (3), 733 (6)

buffet 192 (13), 194 (5), 279 (9), 645 (7)

buffoon 501 (1), 697 (1), 851 (3)

buffoonery 497 (2), 849 (1)

bug 365 (16), 415 (6), 651 (5)

buggery 951 (3)

bugging 415 (2)

buggy 274 (11)

bugle 414 (7), 718 (1)

bugle-call 547 (8)

bugler 413 (2)

build 56 (1), 56 (5), 164 (7), 243 (1), 243 (5), 310 (4), 331 (1)

build up 36 (5), 54 (6), 56 (1), 74 (11), 162 (12), 192 (22), 197 (5), 209 (13), 310 (4), 528 (11), 632 (5)

build up to 56 (3)

builder 164 (4), 310 (2), 686 (3)

building 164 (1), 164 (3), 192 (6)

building block 631 (2)

building material 164 (3), 631 (2)

building society 784 (2), 799 (1)

buildings 192 (8)

buildup 36 (1), 482 (1), 528 (3)

built-in 58 (2), 89 (3), 224 (3)

built on 214 (3)

built on sand 152 (4)

built-up 192 (18)

built-up area 184 (3), 192 (8)

bulb 252 (2), 253 (2), 366 (6), 420 (4)

bulbous 252 (5)

bulge 36 (2), 36 (4), 253 (1), 253 (2), 253 (9), 724 (2)

bulging 54 (4), 253 (7), 254 (4)

bulk 26 (1), 32 (3), 52 (3), 53 (5), 104 (3), 195 (1), 195 (3), 197 (5), 205 (2), 253 (2), 301 (10), 322 (1)

bulk-buy 632 (5)

bulk large 32 (15), 195 (10), 638 (7)

bulkhead 231 (2)

bulkiness 195 (3)

bulky 3 (3), 32 (4), 195 (6)

bull 365 (7), 737 (2), 792 (2)

bull market 811 (1)

bull-necked 205 (4)

bulldog 365 (10)

bulldog courage 855 (1)

bulldoze 165 (7), 279 (8), 740 (3)

bulldozer 168 (1), 216 (3), 279 (5), 332 (3)

bullet 252 (2), 277 (4), 287 (2), 723 (4), 723 (12)

bullet head 252 (2)

bullet-headed 252 (5)

bulletin 524 (2), 529 (1), 588 (1)

bulletproof 162 (7), 660 (5), 713 (8), 715 (2)

bullfighter 716 (8)

bullion 797 (7)

bullish 792 (4), 811 (2)

bullock 161 (3), 273 (3), 365 (7)

bullring 362 (5), 724 (1)

bull's-eye 225 (2)

bully 176 (4), 722 (1), 735 (3), 735 (8), 827 (9), 854 (12), 856 (2), 869 (7), 878 (3), 898 (8), 900 (3), 904 (2), 938 (1)

bully boy 176 (4)

bully into 612 (10), 740 (3)

bullying 854 (8), 878 (4), 898 (3), 900 (2)

bulwark 218 (2), 713 (1), 713 (3)

bumble 695 (9)

bumble bee 365 (16)

bumbler 697 (1)

bumbling 695 (5)

bump 253 (1), 253 (2), 254 (3), 259 (8), 279 (3), 318 (1), 405 (1), 405 (3), 655 (4)

bump into 279 (8), 295 (6)

bump up 36 (5)

bumper 54 (2), 231 (3), 301 (26)

bumper crop 635 (2)

bumpiness 259 (1), 318 (1)

bumpkin 869 (6)

bumptious 873 (4), 878 (4)

bumptiousness 873 (1), 878 (1)

bumpy 259 (4)

bun 259 (2), 301 (22)

bunch 48 (3), 74 (4), 74 (5), 74 (6), 74 (10), 74 (11), 708 (1)

bundle 74 (6), 74 (11), 194 (9), 632 (1)

bundle of joy 132 (1)

bundle of nerves 819 (1)

bundle off 680 (3)

bundle out 300 (6)

bung 264 (2)

bungalow 192 (6)

bungle 138 (6), 495 (3), 495 (8), 695 (2), 695 (9), 728 (1), 728 (7)

bungled 495 (6), 645 (2), 647 (3), 695 (6)

bungler 491 (1), 501 (1), 697 (1), 728 (3)

bungling 458 (1), 495 (3), 675 (1), 695 (2), 695 (5), 728 (1)

bungling idiot 697 (1)

bunion 253 (2)

bunk 218 (7)

bunker 194 (21), 632 (2), 702 (2), 713 (2)

bunny 365 (3)

bunsen burner 383 (1)

bunting 547 (12)

buoy 269 (4), 323 (1), 547 (7)

buoy up 218 (15), 310 (4)

buoyancy 323 (1), 328 (1), 852 (1)

buoyant 269 (7), 308 (3), 323 (3), 323 (4), 328 (2), 833 (3), 852 (4)

buoyed up 323 (3)

burden 322 (1), 322 (6), 593 (4), 645 (7), 659 (1), 700 (1), 702 (4), 702 (8), 731 (1), 735 (8), 825 (3), 827 (2)

burden with 193 (2)

burdened 273 (10), 322 (4)

burdened with, be 273 (12)

burdensome 645 (2), 682 (5), 700 (4), 702 (6), 827 (5)

bureau 194 (5)

bureaucracy 689 (1), 733 (4)

bureaucrat 690 (4), 741 (6)

bureaucratic 689 (3), 733 (9)

burgeon 36 (4), 167 (6), 171 (6)

burgeoning 130 (4)

burgher 191 (3)

burglar 789 (1)

burglar alarm 665 (1)

burglary 788 (1)

burgle 788 (7)

burgundy 431 (1)

burial 303 (2), 364 (1), 550 (1)

burial chamber 364 (5)

burial place 364 (4)

burial service 364 (2)

buried 211 (2), 364 (7)

burlesque 497 (2), 546 (1), 552 (3), 593 (3), 594 (3), 594 (15), 839 (5), 849 (1),

butt end 69 (2)

butt in 231 (10), 678 (13)

butter 327 (1), 334 (4), 357 (3), 357 (9)

butter fingers 695 (2)

butter up 925 (4)

buttercup 366 (6), 433 (1)

butterfingers 697 (1)

butterflies 318 (1), 854 (2)

butterfly 365 (16), 456 (1), 601 (2)

butterscotch 301 (18), 430 (1)

buttery 357 (6)

buttocks 238 (2)

button 47 (5), 196 (2), 250 (2), 253 (2)

button up 228 (32)

buttoned-up 525 (6)

buttonhole 289 (4), 396 (1), 581 (5), 583 (3), 778 (5), 844 (1)

buttonholing 583 (1)

buttress 153 (3), 162 (12), 218 (2), 218 (15), 254 (2), 713 (3), 990 (5)

butts 724 (1)

buxom 195 (8), 833 (3), 841 (5)

buy 771 (7), 792 (1), 792 (5), 806 (4)

buy a round 804 (5)

buy and sell 791 (4)

buy back 792 (5)

buy blind 618 (8)

buy in 792 (5)

buy in instalments 785 (2)

buy off 612 (12)

buy on account 792 (5)

buy on credit 792 (5)

buy out 792 (5)

buy outright 792 (5)

buy over 792 (5)

buy up 792 (5)

buyer 776 (2), 782 (2), 792 (2)

buyer's market 796 (1)

buying 771 (1), 780 (1), 792 (1), 792 (4)

buying off 668 (1)

buying over 792 (1)

buying price 809 (2)

buying up 792 (1)

buzz 271 (7), 401 (4), 403 (1), 404 (3), 406 (3), 409 (1), 409 (3), 529 (2)

buzz word 559 (1)

buzzer 547 (5)

by 11 (5), 119 (5), 360 (3), 629 (3), 639 (5)

by a head 201 (5)

by a length 201 (5)

by accident 159 (8)

by and by 124 (7)

by and large 52 (9), 79 (7)

by authority 733 (14)

by chance 159 (8)

by consent 488 (9)

by degrees 27 (6), 53 (9), 71 (7), 278 (8)

by dint of 160 (12), 629 (3)

by-election 605 (2)

by far 34 (12)

by favour 112 (1), 916 (5)

by favour of 756 (7)

by force 162 (13), 176 (10), 740 (4)

by force of habit 610 (9)

by God's will 965 (7)

by hand 272 (9), 682 (8)

by heart 505 (12)

by instinct 476 (4)

by-law 81 (1), 915 (9), 953 (8)

by leave 756 (7)

by letter 588 (5)

by letters 558 (7)

by mail 588 (5)

by main force 162 (13), 176 (10), 740 (4)

by means of 628 (5), 629 (3)

by means of a spell 983 (12)

by name 561 (8)

by night 129 (8), 418 (8)

by no means 33 (13)

by oneself 88 (4), 88 (6)

by order 953 (5), 953 (8)

by oversight 456 (10)

by-play 547 (4)

by post 588 (3)

by-product 40 (2), 67 (1), 89 (2), 157 (1), 164 (2)

by proxy 150 (6), 755 (4)

by rail 267 (16)

by reason of 156 (11)

by right 915 (9)

by road 267 (16)

by rote 106 (7)

by slow degrees 278 (8)

by stealth 525 (11)

by storm 176 (10)

by the book 60 (5), 81 (4), 83 (10)

by the clock 81 (4)

by the skin of one's teeth 33 (9)

by the way 9 (10), 10 (6), 137 (9), 305 (6)

by trial and error 461 (9)

by turns 12 (4), 141 (8), 151 (4)

by virtue of 160 (12)

by warrant of 733 (14)

by way of 281 (8), 624 (9)

by-word 851 (3)

bygone 125 (6), 127 (2)

bygone days 125 (1)

bypass 620 (5), 624 (4), 624 (6), 626 (3)

byre 192 (10), 369 (3)

bystander 189 (1), 441 (1)

byte 86 (5)

byway 624 (5)

byword 496 (1), 867 (3)

C

cab 194 (19), 274 (9), 274 (14)

cab driver 268 (5)

cabal 523 (1), 623 (4), 623 (9), 708 (1), 738 (3)

cabalism 984 (1)

cabalist 984 (4)

cabalistic 983 (7), 984 (6)

cabaret 594 (4), 594 (7), 837 (5)

cabbage 175 (1), 301 (20)

cabbalistic 523 (4)

cabby 268 (5)

caber 287 (2)

cabin 192 (7), 194 (19), 747 (10)

cabin boy 270 (1)

cabin cruiser 275 (7)

cabinet 194 (5), 194 (19), 218 (5), 632 (2), 689 (1), 690 (1), 692 (1)

cabinet minister 690 (4)

Cabinet seat 733 (5)

cable 47 (2), 208 (2), 217 (3), 524 (1), 529 (3), 531 (1)

cable railway 274 (13), 310 (2)

cablegram 531 (1)

cache 525 (1), 527 (1), 632 (1)

cachou 392 (2), 396 (2)

cackle 409 (3), 835 (2), 835 (7)

cacophonous 411 (2)

cacophony 407 (1), 411 (1), 576 (1)

cactus 256 (3), 366 (6)

cad 847 (3), 869 (7), 888 (3), 938 (3).

cadaver 363 (1)

cadaverous 206 (5), 363 (2), 426 (3)

caddy 194 (8), 273 (2)

cadence 309 (1), 398 (1), 410 (1), 593 (5)

cadenza 410 (2), 412 (4)

cadet 120 (2), 130 (4), 538 (2)

cadge 761 (6), 816 (6)

cadger 679 (6), 763 (2)

cadging 786 (1), 816 (5)

cadmium yellow 433 (2)

cadre 708 (1)

Caesarian 167 (2)

Caesarian birth 304 (1)

caesura 593 (5)

café 192 (13), 301 (5)

cafeteria 192 (13)

caffeine 658 (6)

caftan 228 (7)

cage 192 (10), 194 (1), 194 (4), 232 (3), 235 (1), 747 (10)

cagebird 365 (4)

caged 747 (6)

cagey 698 (4)

cairn 548 (3)

caisson 194 (7), 274 (7)

cajole 542 (9), 612 (10), 761 (5), 925 (4)

cajolery 612 (2), 925 (1)

cajoling 925 (3)

cake 48 (3), 301 (23), 324 (3), 324 (6), 392 (2), 649 (9)

caked 324 (4), 649 (7)

cakes and ale 301 (9)

calamitous 616 (2), 645 (3), 731 (4)

calamity 616 (1), 731 (2)

calcify 326 (5)

calculable 86 (8), 465 (10)

calculate 86 (12), 465 (11), 480 (6), 507 (4), 623 (8), 858 (3)

calculated 608 (2)

calculated risk 617 (1)

calculated to 179 (2)

calculated to, be 179 (3)

calculation 86 (1), 465 (1), 480 (2), 507 (1)

calculation of chance 159 (4)

calculator 86 (6), 86 (7)

calendar 87 (1), 87 (3), 108 (9), 117 (4), 117 (7), 589 (4)

calendar month 110 (1)

calendared 108 (6)

calends 108 (3)

calf 132 (3), 226 (6), 267 (7), 365 (7)

calf love 887 (1)

calibrate 27 (4)

calibrated 27 (2), 465 (10)

calibration 27 (1)

calibre 77 (2), 205 (1), 498 (1)

calico 222 (4)

caliph 741 (3)

caliphate 733 (5)

call 297 (5), 400 (1), 400 (4), 408 (1), 408 (3), 409 (1), 409 (3), 524 (10), 528 (1), 547 (8), 561 (6), 612 (2), 665 (1), 718 (1), 718 (6), 737 (6), 859 (11), 882 (4), 985 (2)

call a halt 145 (7), 747 (7)

call a spade a spade 573 (3), 699 (4)

call attention to 455 (7)

call by name 561 (6)

call down on 859 (11), 899 (6)

call for 627 (1), 627 (6), 761 (5)

call for enquiry 459 (16)

call forth 612 (9)

call girl 952 (4)

call in 74 (11), 299 (3), 673 (5), 691 (5), 882 (9)

call in question 486 (8), 533 (3)

call into being 68 (9), 167 (7)

call madam 884 (5)

call names 921 (5), 924 (10)

call of duty 917 (1)

call off 752 (4)

call on 691 (5), 761 (5), 761 (7), 981 (11)

call one's bluff 711 (3)

call one's own 773 (4)

call out 145 (7), 716 (11)

call over 86 (11)

call sir 884 (5)

call the tune 733 (12)

call to 583 (3)

call to arms 547 (8), 718 (1), 718 (5), 718 (10)

call to mind 505 (7)

call to order 60 (3)

call to prayer 981 (4)

call together 737 (6)

call-up 74 (1), 74 (11), 528 (1), 718 (5), 718 (10), 740 (1), 983 (10)

call upon 917 (11)

callboy 742 (1)

called 561 (4)

called for 627 (3), 793 (3)

called to the bar 958 (6)

called-up 74 (9)

caller 297 (3), 882 (5)

calligrapher 20 (3), 586 (5)

calligraphic 586 (7)

calligraphist 586 (5)

calligraphy 551 (3), 586 (2)

calling 612 (1), 622 (2)

calling for 627 (5)

calling names 924 (3)

callipers 465 (5)

callisthenics 682 (2)

callous 820 (5), 898 (7), 906 (2)

calloused 326 (3)

callousness 735 (1), 820 (1), 898 (2), 906 (1)

callow 130 (4), 670 (4), 699 (3)

callus 326 (1)

calm 177 (1), 177 (3), 177 (7), 258 (1), 258 (3), 266 (2), 266 (5), 399 (2), 613 (3), 820 (3), 823 (3), 823 (7), 831 (3), 860 (2)

calm down 266 (8), 266 (9)

calm seas 701 (1)

calmed down 823 (3)

calmness 820 (1), 823 (1), 865 (1)

calorie 160 (3), 379 (3)

calories 301 (10)

calorific 301 (33), 379 (6), 381 (7)

calumniate 926 (7), 928 (8)

calumniation 926 (1)

calumniator 926 (4), 928 (3)

calumny 524 (3), 529 (2), 867 (2), 899 (2), 926 (2), 928 (2)

calvary 990 (4)

calve 167 (6)

Calvinist 976 (11)

calypso 412 (5)

calyx 366 (7)

camaraderie 880 (2), 882 (1)

camber 220 (1), 220 (6), 248 (2), 248 (4), 253 (6), 253 (9)

cambered 253 (8)

Cambridge-blue 435 (3)

camel 273 (3), 365 (3)

cameo 554 (1), 590 (1)

camera 442 (6), 549 (3), 551 (4)

cameraman or - woman 551 (4)

camiknickers 228 (17)

camisole 228 (16)

camouflage 19 (1), 19 (4), 20 (2), 20 (5), 525 (1), 525 (7), 527 (3)

camouflaged 20 (4), 444 (2), 525 (4)

camp 187 (3), 187 (8), 192 (1), 192 (21), 708 (1), 837 (21), 850 (4)

camp bed 218 (7)

camp fire 882 (3)

camp follower 284 (2), 742 (4)

camp it up 594 (17), 850 (5)

camp up 839 (5)

campaign 267 (4), 672 (1), 676 (1), 676 (5), 682 (1), 682 (6), 688 (2), 716 (7), 716 (11), 718 (6), 718 (11), 901 (1)

campaign against 762 (3)

campaigner 676 (3), 722 (4)

campaigning 267 (4), 718 (6), 718 (8)

campanile 990 (5)

campanologist 412 (2)

campanology 400 (1), 403 (1), 412 (2)

camped up 594 (15)

camper 268 (1), 274 (11)

campestral 348 (3)

camphor 357 (5), 396 (2)

camping 187 (4), 837 (6)

campus 76 (1), 192 (14), 539 (1), 539 (4)

can 194 (8), 194 (13), 194 (15), 666 (5)

can opener 263 (11)

canal 272 (2), 351 (1)

canal boat 275 (7)

canal system 351 (1)

canalize 255 (8)

canalled 262 (2)

canapé 301 (14)

canard 529 (2)

canary 365 (4)

canary yellow 433 (3)

canasta 837 (11)

cancan 837 (14)

cancel 2 (8), 182 (3), 550 (3), 621 (3), 674 (5), 752

(4), 757 (4), 779 (4), 909 (4), 924 (9)

cancel out 14 (4), 182 (3), 467 (4)

cancellation 2 (2), 182 (1), 533 (1), 550 (1), 674 (1), 752 (1), 779 (1), 916 (3)

cancelled 2 (3), 69 (4), 752 (3), 909 (3)

cancelling out 467 (2)

Cancer 321 (5), 645 (1), 651 (3), 651 (11), 659 (2)

cancerous 651 (22)

cancerous growth 651 (11)

candelabra 420 (4)

candid 494 (4), 522 (5), 540 (2), 699 (3), 926 (5), 929 (4)

candid friend 926 (3)

candidate 460 (3), 461 (5), 716 (8), 763 (1), 852 (3), 859 (6)

candidate, be a 759 (4)

candidature 605 (2), 759 (1)

candidly 540 (4)

candied 392 (3)

candle 385 (3), 420 (3)

candle power 417 (1)

candlelight 419 (3)

candlepower 465 (3)

candlestick 420 (4)

candour 494 (1), 522 (1), 540 (1), 699 (1), 929 (1)

candy 301 (18), 392 (2), 392 (4)

candyfloss 355 (1)

cane 963 (9), 964 (1)

canine 365 (10), 365 (18)

caning 963 (2)

canister 194 (7), 194 (8)

canker 659 (2)

cannabis 949 (4)

canned goods 795 (1)

cannery 666 (2)

cannibal 301 (6), 362 (6), 904 (2)

cannibalism 301 (1)

cannibalistic 301 (31), 898 (7)

cannibalize 46 (10)

canning 666 (1)

cannon 723 (11)

cannon fodder 722 (5)

cannon into 279 (8)

cannon off 280 (3)

cannonade 287 (8), 403 (1), 712 (3), 712 (11)

cannonball 252 (2), 287 (2), 723 (12)

canny 498 (4), 698 (4), 814 (2), 858 (2)

canoe 269 (11), 275 (8)

canoeing 269 (3)

canoeist 270 (4)

canon 81 (1), 412 (4), 412 (5), 485 (2), 693 (1), 737 (2), 973 (4), 975 (2), 986 (4)

canon law 693 (1)

canonical 83 (6), 466 (5), 485 (6), 693 (2), 973 (9), 975 (4), 976 (8), 989 (3)

canonical books 975 (2)

canonical robes 989 (2)

canonicals 228 (5), 743 (2), 989 (1)

canonicity 466 (1), 976 (1)

canonization 866 (5), 979 (2), 988 (4)

canonize 866 (14), 979 (12), 985 (8)

canonized 979 (8)

canopy 226 (3)

cant 220 (1), 220 (5), 220 (6), 477 (8), 541 (1), 541 (7), 542 (8), 560 (3), 560 (6), 979 (3), 980 (6)

can't bear 888 (7)

can't stand 861 (4), 888 (7)

can't wait 859 (11)

cantankerous 709 (6), 892 (3), 893 (2)

cantata 412 (5), 981 (5)

canteen 192 (13), 194 (7), 194 (19)

canter 265 (2), 267 (15)

canticle 412 (5), 981 (5)

cantilever 218 (2)

canting 29 (2), 541 (4), 980 (4)

cantonment 192 (1)

canvas 222 (4), 226 (3), 269 (5), 553 (5)

canvass 459 (1), 528 (9), 584 (7), 605 (8), 676 (5), 793 (4)

canvass for 703 (6)

canvasser 459 (9), 475 (6), 676 (3), 763 (1), 793 (2)

canvassing 459 (1), 528 (2), 605 (4)

canyon 201 (2), 209 (2), 255 (3)

cap 34 (7), 213 (2), 213 (5), 226 (1), 226 (13), 228 (23), 264 (2), 547 (9), 714 (3), 723 (13), 725 (7)

cap and gown 228 (4)

cap in hand 761 (4), 879 (5)

capability 24 (3), 160 (2), 178 (1), 694 (1), 701 (1)

capable 24 (7), 160 (8), 469 (2), 498 (4)

capable of, be 160 (10)

capable of life 360 (2)

capable of proof 478 (3)

capacious 32 (4), 18° (6), 194 (24), 195 (6)

capacity 5 (2), 32 (1), 54 (2), 78 (1), 160 (2), 183 (4), 195 (1), 236 (1), 469 (1), 498 (1), 629 (1), 640 (1), 694 (1)

cape 228 (21)

caper 312 (1), 312 (4), 837 (21), 837 (22)

capillary 208 (1), 263 (16), 351 (1)

capital 34 (5), 213 (1), 213 (4), 362 (8), 558 (5), 629 (1), 632 (1), 638 (5), 644 (5), 777 (2), 797 (2), 800 (1)

capital city 184 (4)

capital gain 771 (3)

capital gains tax 809 (3)

capital-intensive 622 (5)

capital letter 558 (1)

capital murder 362 (2)

capital punishment 362 (1), 963 (3)

capital sin 934 (2)

capitalism 791 (2), 800 (1)

capitalist 741 (1), 797 (8), 800 (2)

capitalize on 137 (7), 673 (3)

capitation 86 (1), 86 (4)

capitation tax 809 (3)

capitulate 721 (3)

capitulation 721 (1)

capon 161 (3), 365 (6)

capping 34 (6), 226 (1)

caprice 152 (1), 412 (4), 474 (3), 513 (2), 595 (0), 601 (1), 603 (1), 603 (3), 604 (1), 604 (2), 850 (1), 859 (3), 887 (1)

capricious 17 (2), 82 (2), 84 (5), 114 (3), 152 (3), 456 (6), 474 (5), 601 (3), 603 (4), 604 (3), 822 (3), 839 (4), 849 (2), 887 (9)

capricious, be 143 (5), 152 (5), 604 (4), 609 (4)

capriciously 604 (5)

Capricorn 321 (5)

capsizal 221 (2)

capsize 29 (3), 221 (4), 221 (5), 269 (10)

capsized 221 (3)

capstan 310 (2), 315 (3)

capsular 255 (6)

capsule 194 (1), 366 (7)

captain 34 (9), 689 (5), 690 (1), 741 (7), 741 (8)

captaincy 64 (1), 689 (2)

caption 520 (2), 547 (1), 547 (13), 561 (2), 563 (1)

captious 477 (4), 604 (3), 892 (3), 924 (6)

captivate 612 (8), 745 (7), 887 (15)

captivated 824 (4)

captivating 826 (2), 887 (11)

captive 742 (6), 747 (6), 750 (1), 750 (2)

captivity 745 (3), 747 (3)

captor 741 (1), 776 (1), 786 (4)

capture 513 (7), 551 (8), 727 (9), 745 (7), 747 (8), 771 (7), 786 (1), 786 (6)

car 267 (6), 274 (11), 276 (2)

car driver 268 (5)

car park 235 (1), 305 (3)

car transporter 274 (12)
carafe 194 (13)
caramel 301 (18), 430 (1)
carapace 226 (1)
carat 322 (2)
caravan 192 (7), 274 (5)
carbohydrates 301 (10)
carbolic 648 (4)
carbon 381 (4)
carbon copy 22 (2)
carbon paper 631 (3)
carbonate 336 (4), 355 (5)
carbonated 336 (3)
carboniferous 385 (5)
carbonization 381 (2)
carbonize 381 (10)
carboy 194 (13)
carbuncle 253 (2)
carcass 363 (1)
carcinogen 659 (3)
carcinogenic 653 (2)
card 84 (3), 207 (2), 547 (13), 548 (1), 588 (1), 631 (3), 839 (3)
card-carrying member 708 (3)
card game 837 (11)
card index 62 (2)
card-player 837 (16)
card punch 86 (5), 263 (12)
card vote 605 (2)
cardboard 542 (7), 552 (2), 631 (3)
cardboard box 194 (8)
cardigan 228 (11)
cardinal 5 (6), 34 (5), 85 (5), 638 (5), 741 (5), 986 (4)
cardinal number 85 (1)
cardinal points 281 (2)
cardinal-red 431 (3)
cardinal virtues 933 (2)
cardinalship 985 (3)
cardiovascular disease 651 (9)
cards 618 (2), 837 (11), 837 (15)
cardsharp 545 (4)
cardsharping 542 (2)
care 457 (1), 622 (1), 622 (4), 751 (2), 825 (3), 827 (1), 897 (6)

care for 457 (6), 660 (8), 859 (11), 887 (13), 897 (5)
careen 220 (5)
career 71 (1), 265 (1), 277 (3), 277 (6), 285 (1), 622 (2), 688 (1)
career woman 373 (3)
careerist 623 (5), 678 (5), 859 (6), 932 (2), 932 (3)
carefree 683 (2), 833 (3)
carefree mind 833 (1)
careful 278 (3), 455 (2), 457 (3), 814 (2), 816 (4), 858 (2), 929 (4)
careful, be 455 (4), 457 (5), 507 (4), 664 (6), 678 (11), 858 (3)
careful of 768 (2)
careful steward 814 (1)
carefully 457 (8)
carefulness 455 (1), 457 (1), 498 (2), 673 (1), 814 (1), 858 (1), 862 (1)
careless 61 (7), 456 (3), 458 (2), 572 (2), 670 (3), 860 (2)
careless, be 634 (4)
carelessly 857 (5)
carelessness 458 (1), 495 (2)
cares 731 (1), 825 (3)
caress 200 (5), 235 (4), 333 (3), 378 (1), 378 (7), 547 (21), 826 (3), 831 (3), 884 (7), 887 (13), 889 (1), 889 (6), 925 (4)
caressing 887 (9), 889 (4)
caretaker 742 (1), 749 (1), 754 (1)
careworn 825 (5), 834 (6)
cargo 193 (1), 272 (3), 777 (1), 795 (1)
cargo boat 275 (3)
cargo vessel 273 (1)
caricature 19 (1), 19 (4), 20 (2), 20 (5), 497 (2), 521 (3), 546 (1), 546 (3), 552 (1), 552 (3), 553 (5), 839 (1), 839 (5), 851 (2), 851 (3), 851 (6), 926 (2), 926 (6)
caricaturist 20 (3), 556 (1), 839 (3)

caries 51 (2)
carillon 403 (1), 412 (2), 414 (8)
caring 897 (1)
carmine 431 (2), 431 (3)
carnage 362 (4)
carnage, shambles 165 (2)
carnal 319 (6), 944 (3), 951 (8)
carnality 944 (1)
carnation 366 (6)
carnival 837 (2), 875 (3)
carnivore 301 (6), 365 (2)
carnivorous 301 (31)
carol 412 (5), 413 (10), 835 (6)
carol singers 413 (5)
carousal 837 (2)
carouse 837 (2), 837 (23), 882 (8), 949 (14)
carouser 949 (5)
carp 365 (15), 829 (5), 893 (3), 924 (12)
carpe diem 837 (24)
carpenter 686 (3)
carpet 226 (9)
carpet sweeper 648 (5)
carpeted 226 (12)
carpeting 226 (9), 924 (4), 963 (1)
carping 924 (6)
carport 192 (10)
carriage 218 (2), 265 (2), 272 (2), 274 (6), 274 (13), 445 (5), 688 (1)
carriageway 624 (6)
carried 488 (5)
carried away 821 (3)
carrier 218 (2), 272 (4), 273 (1), 529 (6), 651 (5), 653 (1)
carrier bag 194 (9), 273 (1)
carrier pigeon 273 (2), 529 (6)
carrion 51 (2), 363 (1), 363 (2), 649 (2)
carrot 301 (20), 612 (4)
carroty 431 (3)
carry 167 (6), 183 (3), 199 (5), 218 (15), 228 (32), 272 (6), 273 (12), 638 (7), 727 (9)

carry across **305** (5)
carry away **165** (7)
carry conviction **485** (10)
carry no weight **639** (7)
carry off **786** (9)
carry on **146** (3), **146** (5),
622 (9), **676** (5), **688** (5),
689 (4), **889** (6)
carry on a conversation
584 (6)
carry on to **199** (5)
carry one's years **113** (6)
carry oneself **688** (4)
carry out **164** (7), **672** (3),
676 (5), **688** (5), **725** (6),
768 (3)
carry-over **40** (1), **41** (1),
86 (12), **273** (12), **305** (5),
808 (5)
carry the can **544** (3), **924**
(14)
carry the day **727** (11)
carry through **54** (6), **69**
(6), **174** (7), **273** (12), **599**
(3), **600** (4), **628** (4), **646**
(5), **669** (12), **676** (5), **725**
(5), **727** (6)
carry weight **178** (3), **466**
(6)
carry with one **612** (10)
carrying **167** (5), **400** (3),
404 (2)
carsick **300** (5)
cart **273** (1), **273** (12), **274**
(5)
cart away **188** (4)
cart horse **273** (6)
cart off **188** (4)
carte blanche **744** (3)
cartel **706** (2), **708** (5), **747**
(2), **765** (1)
carter **268** (5), **273** (1)
cartilage **324** (3), **329** (1)
cartilaginous **329** (2)
carting **272** (2)
cartographer **465** (7)
cartography **551** (5)
carton **194** (8)
cartoon **445** (4), **553** (5),
839 (1), **851** (2)
cartoonist **556** (1), **839** (3)
cartridge **723** (12)
cartridge paper **631** (3)

cartwheel **221** (2)
carve **46** (10), **46** (11), **164**
(7), **243** (5), **262** (3), **551**
(8), **554** (3), **844** (12)
carve up **783** (3)
carved **243** (3), **554** (2)
carver **556** (2)
carving **586** (1), **844** (2)
caryatid **218** (10)
cascade **309** (1), **309** (3),
350 (4), **350** (9)
case **7** (1), **83** (2), **154** (1),
194 (7), **194** (10), **235** (1),
452 (1), **475** (4), **475** (5),
524 (2), **564** (1), **622** (1),
651 (18), **959** (1)
case, be the **494** (7)
case dismissed **960** (1)
case-ending **564** (2)
case for **915** (1)
case-hardened **162** (6)
case history **466** (1), **548**
(1), **590** (1)
case in point **9** (3), **24** (3),
83 (2)
case law **959** (3)
case record **466** (2)
case to answer **475** (5), **928**
(1)
casement **263** (5)
cash **771** (7), **797** (1), **797**
(4), **797** (12)
cash a cheque **797** (12)
cash and carry **792** (4),
796 (3)
cash book **808** (2)
cash box **799** (1)
cash desk **799** (1)
cash down **804** (6)
cash flow **797** (2)
cash in on **615** (5), **673** (3)
cash nexus **797** (1)
cash on delivery **792** (4),
804 (6)
cash payment **804** (1)
cash register **86** (6), **549**
(3), **799** (1)
cash transaction **797** (3)
cashier **752** (5), **797** (8),
798 (1), **804** (2), **808** (3)
casino **618** (3), **837** (5)
cask **194** (12)
casket **194** (8), **364** (1)

casserole **194** (14), **301**
(13), **301** (40)
cassette **414** (10)
cassette recorder **414** (10)
cassock **228** (7), **989** (1),
989 (2)
cast **5** (3), **22** (1), **86** (11),
164 (7), **179** (1), **229** (7),
243 (1), **243** (5), **287** (1),
287 (7), **381** (8), **440** (1),
551 (8), **554** (1), **554** (3),
594 (9), **594** (15), **594** (16),
658 (9), **817** (2), **845** (1)
cast a gloom over **834** (12)
cast a horoscope **511** (9)
cast a shadow **418** (6), **834**
(12)
cast a spell on **983** (11)
cast a vote **605** (8)
cast about **459** (15), **474**
(8)
cast about for **619** (5)
cast anchor **187** (8), **266**
(8), **269** (10)
cast aspersions **926** (6)
cast away **779** (4)
cast down **311** (6)
cast horoscopes **983** (10)
cast-iron **326** (3)
cast its skin **229** (7)
cast lots **511** (9)
cast of mind **817** (1)
cast off **37** (5), **41** (4), **46**
(7), **269** (10), **296** (6), **621**
(3), **674** (3), **674** (5), **779**
(2), **779** (4)
cast-offs **641** (3)
cast one's net **619** (6)
cast up **86** (12), **300** (6),
310 (4)
castanets **414** (8)
castaway **883** (3)
caste **77** (1), **77** (3), **80** (3),
866 (2), **868** (1)
castellated **713** (8)
castigate **613** (3), **924** (11),
963 (8)
castigation **612** (2)
casting **594** (2)
casting lots **511** (2)
casting vote **29** (1), **178** (1)
castle **192** (6), **713** (4)

castrate 161 (10), 172 (6), 655 (9)

castrated 161 (7)

casual 6 (2), 61 (7), 159 (5), 458 (2), 618 (5), 683 (2), 744 (6)

casual clothes 228 (2)

casual labour 686 (4)

casual labourer 686 (2)

casualness 458 (1)

casuals 228 (27)

casualties 361 (4)

casualty 159 (1), 731 (2)

casualty station 658 (13)

casuist 475 (6), 477 (3)

casuistical 477 (4)

casuistry 477 (1), 541 (1)

casus belli 709 (4), 716 (1)

cat 365 (11), 619 (3), 964 (1)

cat and dog 704 (2)

cat burglar 789 (1)

cataclysm 165 (2), 176 (2)

cataclysmic 149 (3), 165 (4), 176 (5), 350 (7)

catacomb 211 (1)

catalepsy 375 (1)

cataleptic 375 (3)

catalogue 62 (1), 62 (6), 87 (1), 87 (5), 524 (6), 548 (7), 808 (5)

catalogued 87 (4)

catalysis 51 (1), 143 (1)

catalyst 143 (3), 174 (4), 628 (2)

catamaran 275 (9)

catapult 287 (3), 287 (7), 723 (4)

cataract 209 (6), 350 (4), 439 (1), 440 (1)

catarrh 302 (1), 302 (4), 651 (8)

catastrophe 69 (1), 149 (1), 154 (1), 165 (3), 616 (1), 731 (2)

catastrophic 149 (3), 616 (2), 731 (4)

catcall 400 (4), 547 (4), 851 (1), 921 (2), 924 (1)

catch 47 (5), 74 (11), 145 (7), 259 (8), 266 (7), 333 (3), 412 (5), 415 (6), 459 (3), 490 (8), 508 (5), 527

(2), 542 (4), 551 (8), 619 (6), 647 (2), 651 (23), 698 (2), 702 (3), 716 (5), 747 (8), 771 (7), 778 (5), 786 (1), 790 (1), 818 (7), 859 (5), 882 (5), 890 (2)

catch-22 702 (2)

catch-22 situation 700 (3)

catch a crab 269 (11)

catch a likeness 20 (6)

catch cold 380 (7)

catch fire 379 (7), 822 (4)

catch napping 508 (5)

catch off one's guard 508 (5)

catch on 178 (4), 610 (7), 848 (7)

catch one's breath 352 (11)

catch one's drift 516 (5)

catch one's eye 887 (15)

catch out 300 (7), 542 (9), 542 (10)

catch phrase 560 (1), 563 (1)

catch sight of 438 (7)

catch the eye 443 (4), 455 (7)

catch unawares 670 (7)

catch up 277 (8)

catch up with 289 (4)

catching 178 (2), 653 (3)

catching cold 380 (1)

catching sight 438 (4)

catchment area 184 (2)

catchword 496 (1), 547 (8), 559 (1)

catchy 410 (6)

catechism 459 (2), 485 (2), 976 (1)

catechist 537 (1), 973 (6)

catechization 534 (1)

catechize 459 (14)

catechizer 459 (10), 537 (1)

categorical 473 (5), 478 (2), 532 (4), 737 (5), 917 (6)

categorization 77 (1)

category 7 (1), 77 (1)

cater 301 (39), 633 (5)

cater for 759 (3), 882 (10)

caterer 301 (5), 633 (3), 793 (2), 794 (2)

catering 301 (5), 633 (1)

caterpillar 132 (3), 365 (17)

caterwaul 400 (4), 407 (5), 408 (3), 409 (3)

caterwauling 411 (1)

cathartic 300 (4), 594 (15), 658 (17)

cathedral 990 (3)

cathedral city 184 (4)

catherine wheel 315 (3), 420 (7)

catheter 351 (2)

cathode 160 (5)

catholic 79 (4), 976 (4), 976 (8), 976 (9)

catholicism 976 (3)

catholicity 79 (1), 976 (1)

catlike 365 (18)

catnap 679 (4), 679 (12)

cat's-eyes 305 (3), 547 (6)

cat's-paw 350 (5), 544 (1), 628 (2), 707 (1), 879 (2)

cattiness 926 (1)

cattle 273 (3), 365 (7), 869 (2)

cattle cake 301 (8)

cattle farm 369 (2)

cattle farmer 369 (5)

cattle farming 370 (1)

cattle pen 235 (1), 369 (3)

cattle-rustling 788 (1)

cattle thief 789 (1)

catty 898 (4), 926 (5)

catwalk 624 (3)

Caucasian 11 (6), 427 (4)

caucus 74 (1), 708 (1)

caudal 69 (4)

caught in the act 936 (3)

caught napping, be 458 (6)

caught out, be 456 (7), 508 (4)

caught unawares 670 (3)

cauldron 194 (14), 383 (2)

cauliflower 301 (20)

cauliflower ear 253 (2)

caulk 264 (6)

causal 156 (7), 178 (2), 628 (3)

causal means 156 (5)

causal relation 9 (2)

causality 156 (1)

causally 156 (11)

causation 68 (1), 156 (1), 173 (1), 612 (1)

causative 156 (7)

cause 9 (2), 68 (10), 143 (6), 154 (6), 156 (2), 156 (6), 156 (9), 164 (4), 164 (7), 173 (3), 178 (1), 285 (4), 475 (5), 523 (5), 595 (2), 612 (1), 612 (5), 612 (10), 628 (1), 628 (4), 901 (1), 959 (1)

cause a stoppage 702 (9)

cause and effect 9 (2), 156 (1)

cause celebre 864 (3)

cause desire 859 (13), 887 (15)

cause discontent 509 (5), 827 (11), 829 (6), 834 (11)

cause dislike 292 (3), 391 (3), 613 (3), 827 (11), 829 (6), 838 (5), 861 (5), 863 (3), 888 (8), 891 (8), 924 (14)

cause doubt 474 (9), 486 (8), 613 (3), 864 (7), 926 (7)

cause feeling 374 (6), 378 (8), 818 (7)

cause for shame 922 (2)

cause loathing 888 (8)

cause of action 612 (1)

cause of injury 659 (1)

cause offence 881 (5), 885 (6), 891 (8)

cause pain 827 (8)

cause resentment 829 (6), 891 (9)

cause thought 449 (10)

cause to smell 394 (3)

caused 65 (2), 154 (3), 157 (3), 158 (2), 180 (2), 612 (7)

causeless 159 (6), 618 (6)

causer 156 (2)

causeway 624 (3)

caustic 174 (6), 388 (3), 818 (6), 827 (3), 898 (5), 924 (6), 926 (5)

causticity 388 (2)

cauterization 381 (2), 658 (11)

cauterize 381 (10), 658 (20)

caution 84 (3), 136 (2), 278 (1), 455 (1), 457 (1), 510 (1), 524 (3), 524 (11), 598 (1), 613 (3), 660 (2), 664 (1), 664 (5), 691 (1), 711 (3), 767 (1), 854 (4), 856 (1), 858 (1), 900 (3), 924 (11)

cautionary 511 (6), 613 (2), 664 (3), 691 (3)

cautionary tale 590 (2)

cautious 278 (3), 457 (3), 457 (4), 474 (6), 510 (2), 582 (2), 598 (3), 664 (4), 854 (7), 858 (2)

cautious, be 278 (4), 457 (5), 498 (6), 510 (3), 601 (4), 660 (9), 854 (11), 856 (4), 858 (3)

cautiously 858 (4)

cautiousness 858 (1)

cavalcade 71 (3)

cavalier 456 (3), 885 (4), 921 (3)

cavalry 268 (4), 273 (7), 274 (7), 722 (10)

cavalry regiment 722 (8), 722 (10)

cavalryman 722 (10)

cave 192 (3), 211 (1), 255 (2), 263 (8)

cave-dweller 191 (1)

cave in 46 (13), 255 (7), 309 (3)

caveat 664 (1)

caved in 255 (6)

caveman 372 (1)

caver 309 (1)

cavern 255 (2), 418 (1)

cavernous 183 (6), 211 (2), 255 (6)

caviar 301 (15)

cavil 475 (11), 477 (8), 486 (7), 489 (1), 489 (5), 924 (1)

caviller 477 (3)

caving 309 (1), 837 (6)

cavity 194 (1), 201 (2), 211 (1), 255 (2), 262 (1), 263

(1), 263 (4), 263 (8), 311 (1)

cavort 312 (4), 837 (22)

caw 407 (4), 409 (3)

cayenne 389 (1)

cease 69 (5), 145 (6), 621 (3), 674 (5), 677 (3), 715 (3), 719 (5), 728 (7), 738 (10)

cease-fire 145 (4), 145 (6), 719 (1)

cease resistance 721 (3)

cease to be 361 (7)

cease to exist 2 (7)

cease to feel 375 (5)

ceaseless 71 (4), 115 (2)

ceaseless energy 678 (2)

ceasing 145 (1)

cede 621 (3), 779 (4), 781 (7)

cedilla 547 (14)

ceilidh 837 (13)

ceiling 26 (2), 209 (1), 226 (2), 236 (1), 443 (1)

celebrant 981 (8), 988 (6)

celebrate 61 (11), 505 (9), 528 (10), 727 (8), 833 (7), 835 (6), 837 (23), 866 (13), 876 (4), 884 (6), 884 (7), 886 (3), 920 (5), 923 (10), 981 (11), 981 (12), 988 (10)

celebrated 528 (8), 866 (10)

celebrating 833 (5), 876 (3), 981 (9)

celebration 74 (2), 295 (1), 301 (2), 505 (3), 727 (2), 729 (1), 833 (2), 835 (1), 837 (1), 866 (5), 875 (2), 875 (3), 876 (1), 886 (1), 907 (2), 923 (3), 988 (3), 988 (5)

celebratory 505 (6), 833 (5), 875 (6), 876 (3), 886 (2)

celebrity 730 (3), 866 (3), 866 (6)

celerity 277 (1)

celestial 321 (14), 965 (5), 968 (3), 971 (3)

celestial body 321 (4)

Celestial City 971 (1)

celibacy 88 (1), 172 (1), 744 (2), 895 (1), 950 (1), 985 (1)

celibate 88 (2), 88 (4), 895 (2), 895 (4), 950 (3), 986 (5), 986 (12)

cell 160 (6), 192 (17), 194 (4), 196 (2), 224 (2), 235 (1), 255 (2), 358 (1), 360 (1), 662 (1), 706 (2), 708 (1), 708 (3), 748 (2), 883 (2)

cellar 194 (21), 211 (1), 301 (7), 527 (1), 632 (2)

cellarage 194 (21)

cellist 413 (2)

cello 414 (3)

cellophane 631 (3)

cellular 194 (25), 255 (6), 358 (3)

cement 45 (9), 47 (9), 48 (4), 326 (1), 631 (2)

cement a union 708 (8)

cemented 45 (7)

cementing 48 (1)

cemetery 361 (1), 364 (4), 990 (2)

cenotaph 364 (5)

censor 39 (3), 57 (5), 480 (3), 550 (3), 747 (7), 757 (4), 924 (9), 950 (4)

censored 757 (9), 924 (7), 950 (5)

censorious 480 (4), 735 (4), 924 (6)

censorship 550 (1), 735 (1), 747 (1), 757 (1), 950 (2)

censurable 867 (5), 924 (8)

censure 480 (6), 851 (1), 867 (2), 924 (2), 924 (4), 924 (11), 928 (1), 936 (1)

censuring 924 (6)

census 86 (1), 86 (4), 87 (1), 459 (1)

census-taker 86 (7)

cent 33 (4), 797 (4)

centaur 84 (4), 970 (5)

centenarian 99 (4), 99 (6), 133 (1)

centenary 99 (4), 99 (6), 141 (3), 876 (2)

centennial 99 (6), 110 (3), 141 (5), 876 (3)

centering 74 (1), 187 (1), 293 (1), 293 (2)

centimetre 203 (4), 204 (1)

centipede 99 (4), 365 (17)

central 70 (2), 156 (8), 224 (3), 225 (3), 638 (5)

central heating 381 (1)

central position 30 (2), 225 (1), 625 (1)

centrality 224 (1), 225 (1)

centralize 50 (4), 62 (5), 76 (2), 225 (4), 293 (3)

centralized 50 (3), 733 (9)

centrally 225 (5)

centre 1 (3), 5 (2), 30 (2), 70 (1), 74 (11), 76 (1), 185 (1), 187 (5), 224 (1), 225 (2), 225 (4), 231 (2), 293 (3), 638 (3), 708 (2), 722 (7), 724 (1)

centre of attraction 76 (1)

centre of gravity 225 (2)

centre on 76 (2), 186 (4), 293 (3)

centre point 225 (2)

centre upon 225 (4)

centreboard 153 (3)

centrepiece 844 (1)

centrifugal 75 (2), 223 (2), 292 (2), 294 (2)

centrifugal force 292 (1)

centrifuge 294 (2)

centripetal 225 (3), 291 (3), 293 (2)

centrist 708 (2)

centro- 225 (3)

centurion 99 (4), 722 (4)

century 99 (4), 110 (1), 722 (8)

century, a 113 (1)

cephalic 213 (4)

ceramics 381 (5), 554 (1)

cereals 301 (22), 366 (8)

cerebral 447 (5)

cerebrate 449 (7)

cerebration 449 (1)

ceremonial 875 (2), 875 (6), 988 (1), 988 (8)

ceremonialism 988 (2)

ceremonialist 988 (6)

ceremonially 988 (12)

ceremonious 875 (6), 988 (9)

ceremoniousness 875 (2)

ceremony 875 (2), 876 (1), 988 (1), 988 (2), 988 (3)

cerise 431 (3)

certain 26 (3), 80 (6), 101 (2), 124 (4), 153 (4), 155 (2), 466 (5), 471 (2), 473 (4), 475 (7), 485 (4), 490 (7), 494 (4), 507 (2), 522 (4), 596 (4), 727 (4), 852 (4)

certain, a 88 (3)

certain age, a 131 (2)

certain, be 471 (6), 473 (7), 485 (7), 488 (6), 490 (8), 507 (4)

certain person 562 (2)

certain proportion 53 (1)

certain quantity 104 (2)

certainly 32 (16), 473 (10)

certainty 466 (1), 471 (1), 473 (1), 478 (1), 485 (1), 507 (1), 516 (1), 660 (1), 701 (2), 852 (1)

certifiable 503 (7)

certificate 466 (3), 548 (1), 767 (2), 797 (5), 866 (4)

certification 473 (1), 488 (1)

certified 473 (4), 503 (7)

certify 466 (7), 473 (9), 532 (5)

certitude 473 (1)

cervical 218 (14)

cervix 218 (10)

cessation 69 (1), 69 (3), 72 (1), 145 (1), 266 (1), 668 (1), 679 (1)

cesspit 649 (4)

cesspool 632 (2), 649 (4)

cetacean 365 (3)

cha-cha 837 (14)

chafe 333 (3), 377 (5), 377 (6), 655 (10), 738 (9), 822 (4), 827 (8), 891 (7)

chaff 366 (8), 839 (2), 839 (5), 851 (5)

chaffing 851 (4)

chafing 827 (1)

chagrin 825 (2), 829 (1)

chagrined 509 (2), 825 (6), 834 (5)

chain 47 (1), 47 (2), 48 (1), 71 (1), 71 (2), 203 (4), 209 (2), 702 (4), 747 (9), 748 (4)

chain gang 750 (1)

chain mail 713 (5)

chain of reasoning 9 (3)

chain reaction 71 (1)

chain-smoke 388 (7)

chain smoker 388 (2)

chain store 796 (3)

chair 218 (6), 310 (4), 690 (1), 741 (1), 866 (13), 876 (4), 884 (6), 923 (10)

chairman 690 (1)

chairmanship 689 (2), 733 (5)

chairperson 690 (1)

chairwoman 690 (1)

chaise longue 218 (6)

chalet 192 (7)

chalet-bungalow 192 (6)

chalice 194 (15)

chalk 333 (3), 344 (4), 553 (6), 553 (8), 586 (4)

chalk out 547 (19)

chalk up 547 (19), 548 (8)

chalky 332 (4), 344 (5), 427 (4)

challenge 459 (3), 459 (14), 489 (1), 489 (5), 532 (5), 533 (1), 533 (3), 547 (8), 612 (6), 704 (1), 704 (4), 709 (1), 709 (8), 711 (1), 711 (3), 712 (1), 712 (7), 715 (3), 716 (10), 900 (1), 928 (8)

challenger 702 (5), 705 (1), 716 (8)

challenging 452 (2), 489 (3), 532 (4), 612 (6), 711 (2), 738 (7)

chamber 192 (17), 194 (19)

chamber music 412 (1)

chamber of commerce 708 (5), 794 (1)

chamber orchestra 413 (3)

chamber pot 194 (13), 649 (3)

chamberlain 742 (3)

chambermaid 742 (2)

chambers 192 (2), 192 (9)

chameleon 152 (2), 601 (2)

champ 301 (36), 891 (7)

champagne 301 (29)

champion 34 (3), 34 (5), 644 (3), 644 (6), 660 (8), 696 (1), 703 (6), 707 (4), 713 (6), 713 (9), 727 (3), 866 (6), 901 (4), 903 (1), 927 (2), 927 (5)

championship 34 (1), 703 (1), 923 (1)

chance 6 (1), 89 (2), 137 (2), 152 (2), 154 (1), 154 (6), 159 (1), 159 (5), 159 (7), 469 (1), 471 (1), 474 (1), 596 (2), 618 (1), 618 (2), 730 (1), 731 (2)

chance discovery 159 (1), 484 (1)

chance it 159 (7), 618 (8)

chance upon 159 (7)

chancel 990 (4)

chancellor 690 (1), 741 (6)

Chancellor of the Exchequer 798 (1)

chancy 159 (5), 474 (4), 618 (7), 661 (3)

chandelier 217 (2), 420 (4)

chandler 794 (1)

change 15 (1), 15 (6), 19 (4), 29 (3), 142 (1), 143 (1), 143 (5), 147 (2), 147 (6), 152 (1), 152 (5), 178 (3), 228 (32), 229 (7), 265 (1), 797 (1), 797 (4)

change colour 818 (8), 854 (10)

change course 143 (5)

change direction 282 (3), 294 (3)

change for 150 (5)

change for the better 654 (1)

change for the worse 143 (1)

change hands 780 (5), 793 (5)

change hands for 809 (6)

change money 151 (3)

change of allegiance 603 (1)

change of direction 143 (1)

change of hands 780 (1)

change of heart 143 (1)

change of life 131 (2), 172 (1)

change of mind 603 (1)

change of mood 603 (1)

change of place 272 (1)

change of position 143 (1)

change of purpose 603 (1)

change one's mind 152 (5), 603 (5)

change one's tune 15 (6), 603 (5)

change out of recognition 147 (8)

change places 265 (4), 780 (5)

change round 143 (6)

change sides 601 (4), 603 (6)

change the face of 149 (4)

changeability 152 (1), 474 (3), 604 (1)

changeable 82 (2), 143 (4), 152 (3), 474 (5), 819 (4)

changeable thing 152 (2), 601 (2)

changeableness 17 (1), 82 (1), 114 (1), 143 (1), 152 (1), 819 (1)

changeably 152 (6)

changed 15 (4)

changed, be 143 (5)

changed person 147 (4), 603 (3)

changeful 8 (3), 17 (2), 82 (2), 114 (3), 143 (4), 152 (3), 265 (3), 474 (5), 601 (3), 822 (3), 893 (2)

changeful, be 152 (5)

changefulness 152 (1)

changeless 153 (4), 965 (6)

changeling 150 (2)

changeover 780 (1)

changes 412 (2)

changing 152 (3)

changing back 148 (1)

channel 297 (2), 305 (1), 345 (1), 351 (1), 524 (4), 624 (2), 628 (2)

channel steamer 275 (1)

channelled 262 (2)

chant 408 (1), 408 (4), 412 (5), 413 (10), 577 (4)

chanter 413 (4)

chanteuse 413 (4)

chanting 400 (1), 981 (3)

chantry 990 (3)

chaos 51 (1), 61 (1), 61 (2), 165 (2), 244 (1), 734 (2)

chaotic 61 (7)

chaotically 17 (3)

chap 201 (2), 259˙(1), 371 (3), 372 (1)

chapel 706 (2), 708 (3), 978 (3), 990 (3), 990 (4)

chapel-going 981 (7), 981 (9)

chapel of ease 990 (3)

chapel people 976 (6)

chaperon 89 (2), 89 (4), 457 (6), 660 (3), 749 (1)

chaperonage 457 (2)

chaplain 742 (2), 986 (3), 986 (7)

chaplaincy 985 (3)

chapped 259 (4)

chaps 239 (1)

chapter 53 (3)

chapter and verse 466 (1)

char 381 (10), 428 (6)

character 5 (3), 7 (2), 56 (1), 77 (2), 80 (1), 80 (4), 84 (3), 85 (1), 371 (3), 466 (3), 558 (1), 594 (8), 817 (1), 839 (3), 866 (1), 933 (1)

character actor 594 (9)

character assassination 926 (1)

characteristic 5 (4), 5 (8), 15 (5), 80 (1), 80 (5)

characterize 16 (4), 551 (8), 561 (6), 590 (7)

characterized 817 (2)

characterless 16 (2), 190 (5), 244 (2), 867 (4), 934 (4)

characters 586 (2), 594 (9)

charade 547 (4), 551 (1), 594 (1)

charades 837 (8)

charcoal 385 (1), 428 (2), 553 (6)

charge 54 (7), 160 (3), 160 (11), 176 (7), 193 (2), 277 (6), 279 (3), 322 (6), 547 (11), 574 (6), 619 (5), 622 (3), 660 (2), 689 (1), 691 (4), 693 (1), 712 (1), 712 (10), 718 (12), 737 (1), 737 (6), 742 (4), 751 (2), 751 (4), 803 (1), 808 (5), 809 (1), 809 (3), 809 (5), 914 (1), 917 (1), 924 (12), 928 (1), 928 (9), 959 (1), 959 (7)

charge falsely 928 (9)

charge in 297 (7)

charge nurse 658 (16)

charge to one's account 802 (3)

charge with 158 (3), 928 (8)

charge d'affaires 754 (3)

chargeable 803 (5), 809 (4), 928 (7)

charged 160 (9), 322 (4), 809 (4), 928 (6)

charger 273 (7), 722 (10)

charges 809 (1)

chariot 274 (6)

charioteer 268 (5)

charisma 160 (1), 178 (1)

charismatic 178 (2)

charitable 781 (5), 813 (3), 897 (4), 901 (6), 905 (4)

charitable, be 901 (8)

charitableness 897 (1)

charitably 897 (2)

charity 703 (1), 703 (2), 781 (1), 781 (2), 813 (1), 887 (1), 897 (1), 897 (2), 901 (1), 905 (1), 931 (1), 933 (2), 979 (1)

charlatan 493 (2), 545 (3), 658 (14), 695 (4), 850 (3), 877 (3)

charlatanism 491 (3), 541 (2), 695 (1), 850 (2)

Charleston 837 (14)

charm 291 (1), 291 (4), 612 (2), 612 (4), 612 (8), 666 (2), 826 (1), 826 (3), 826 (4), 841 (1), 844 (7), 887 (2), 887 (15), 983 (2), 983 (3), 983 (11)

charmed 597 (4), 824 (4), 887 (10), 983 (8), 983 (9)

charmed circle 74 (3), 644 (2)

charmed life 660 (1)

charmer 291 (1), 644 (3), 841 (2), 925 (2), 983 (5)

charming 291 (3), 826 (2), 841 (6), 887 (11)

charms 841 (1), 887 (2)

charnel house 364 (1)

charred 428 (4)

charring 381 (2)

chart 87 (1), 186 (1), 267 (8), 269 (4), 524 (6), 551 (5), 551 (8)

charter 548 (1), 744 (10), 746 (3), 751 (2), 751 (4), 756 (2), 767 (2), 785 (3), 915 (1), 919 (3), 953 (3)

charter flight 271 (2)

chartered 756 (4)

chartered accountant 808 (3)

charwoman 648 (6)

chary 816 (4)

chase 267 (3), 277 (6), 284 (1), 348 (2), 362 (1), 554 (3), 617 (2), 619 (2), 619 (5), 837 (4), 837 (6), 859 (11), 887 (14), 889 (7), 924 (9)

chase away 292 (3)

chaser 301 (26)

chasm 46 (1), 201 (2), 211 (1), 255 (2), 663 (1)

chassis 214 (1), 218 (2), 218 (13), 331 (1)

chaste 573 (2), 846 (3), 933 (3), 942 (3), 950 (5)

chasten 834 (12), 872 (7), 963 (8)

chastened 177 (3), 834 (5), 872 (4), 939 (3)

chastening 834 (7)

chastise 735 (7), 924 (11), 963 (8)

chastisement 963 (1)
chastiser 963 (5)
chastity 172 (2), 874 (1),
933 (1), 942 (1), 950 (1)
chasuble 989 (2)
chat 529 (2), 584 (2), 584
(6)
chat to 882 (8)
chatter 380 (7), 403 (1),
403 (3), 409 (3), 515 (3),
579 (8), 581 (2), 581 (5),
584 (2)
chatterbox 581 (3)
chatterer 524 (5), 529 (4),
579 (5), 581 (3), 584 (4)
chattering 318 (2), 380 (6),
581 (2)
chatty 524 (7), 529 (7), 581
(4), 584 (5), 882 (6)
chauffeur 268 (5), 742 (2)
chauvinism 80 (3), 371
(5), 481 (3), 718 (3), 877
(1), 901 (3)
chauvinist 481 (4), 722 (3),
877 (3), 901 (5)
chauvinistic 481 (8), 877
(4), 901 (7)
cheap 812 (3), 847 (4)
cheap and nasty 812 (3),
847 (4)
cheap, be 812 (5)
cheap rate 812 (1)
cheap to make 812 (3)
cheapen 641 (7), 655 (9),
793 (4), 810 (2), 812 (5),
812 (6), 847 (6)
cheapen oneself 867 (10)
cheaply 812 (7)
cheapness 37 (1), 639 (1),
809 (1), 810 (1), 812 (1)
cheat 541 (2), 542 (1), 542
(2), 542 (8), 545 (4), 698
(3), 698 (5), 786 (11), 788
(8), 789 (3), 930 (8), 938
(2)
cheating 541 (2), 541 (3),
542 (1), 542 (6), 698 (1),
788 (4), 930 (7)
check 86 (11), 136 (2), 145
(2), 145 (7), 177 (1), 177
(6), 182 (1), 204 (5), 278
(6), 437 (2), 457 (5), 459
(1), 459 (13), 461 (1), 461

(7), 462 (1), 473 (1), 473
(9), 547 (13), 702 (1), 702
(8), 702 (10), 727 (10), 728
(2), 731 (1), 747 (1), 747
(7), 772 (1), 844 (3)
check list 462 (1)
check on 459 (13), 461 (7)
check oneself 145 (7), 578
(3)
check the speed 465 (11)
check with 462 (3)
checker 459 (9)
checkers 837 (9)
checking 182 (2)
checklist 87 (1)
checkmate 145 (2), 145
(7), 727 (2), 727 (9), 728
(2)
checkout 549 (3)
checkup 459 (1)
cheek 239 (1), 878 (2), 878
(6), 885 (2), 899 (2)
cheek by jowl 89 (5), 200
(7), 202 (5)
cheeky 878 (5), 885 (4),
921 (3)
cheeky devil 878 (3)
cheep 409 (1), 409 (3)
cheer 174 (8), 301 (9), 408
(1), 408 (3), 408 (4), 547
(4), 821 (6), 826 (3), 828
(5), 831 (3), 833 (2), 833
(7), 833 (8), 835 (6), 837
(20), 852 (7), 855 (8), 876
(4), 905 (6), 920 (6), 923
(10)
cheer on 612 (9)
cheer up 831 (3), 833 (7)
cheerful 828 (2), 833 (3)
cheerful, be 824 (6), 831
(4), 833 (7), 835 (6), 837
(21)
cheerful giver 813 (2)
cheerfully 833 (9)
cheerfulness 162 (2), 833
(1), 852 (1)
cheeriness 833 (1)
cheering 824 (4), 826 (2),
833 (6), 876 (1), 923 (3)
cheerless 827 (4), 834 (8),
853 (3)
cheerlessness 827 (1), 834
(1)

cheers 301 (41), 835 (1),
835 (9)
cheery 833 (3)
cheese 301 (24)
cheese board 301 (17)
cheese-paring 814 (1), 816
(1)
cheesecloth 222 (4)
chef 301 (5), 633 (3)
chef d'oeuvre 164 (2), 644
(3), 646 (1), 676 (2), 694
(3)
chemical element 319 (4)
chemical warfare 723 (3)
chemical weapon 659 (3)
chemise 228 (8), 228 (17)
chemist 143 (3), 319 (5),
461 (3), 658 (15)
chemistry 147 (1), 319 (5)
chemotherapy 658 (12)
cheque 797 (5)
cheque book 808 (2)
chequer 437 (2), 437 (9),
844 (3)
chequered 437 (7)
cherish 457 (6), 505 (7),
660 (8), 666 (5), 703 (6),
821 (7), 887 (13), 889 (5)
cherish a grievance 829
(5)
cherish a grudge 891 (5),
898 (8)
cherish an opinion 485 (8)
cheroot 388 (2)
cherry-red 431 (3)
cherub 132 (1), 890 (1),
968 (1)
cherubic 968 (3)
cherubim 968 (1)
Cheshire cat 835 (3)
chess 837 (9)
chess piece 837 (15)
chess-player 837 (16)
chessboard 437 (2)
chest 194 (7), 224 (2), 253
(3)
chest of drawers 194 (5)
chesterfield 218 (6)
chestnut 273 (4), 430 (3),
839 (2)
chesty 352 (9)
chevron 220 (1), 247 (1),
743 (3), 844 (3)

chew 46 (12), 301 (36), 332 (5)
chew over 449 (8)
chew the cud 301 (37)
chew up 301 (36)
chewing 301 (1)
chewing gum 301 (18), 328 (1)
chewing the cud 301 (1)
chiaroscuro 417 (6), 553 (1)
chic 841 (5), 848 (1), 848 (5)
chicanery 477 (1), 542 (2), 698 (1), 930 (3)
chick 132 (3), 890 (1)
chicken 132 (3), 301 (16), 365 (6)
chicken feed 301 (8)
chicken-hearted 856 (3)
chicken liver 856 (1)
chicken out 856 (4)
chicken pox 651 (5)
chicken run 369 (2)
chide 899 (6), 924 (11)
chiding 924 (4), 924 (6)
chief 34 (3), 34 (5), 68 (7), 638 (4), 638 (5), 690 (1), 741 (4)
chief justice 957 (1)
chief magistrate 741 (6)
chief part 32 (3), 52 (3)
chief priest 986 (8)
chief thing 5 (2), 52 (3), 638 (3)
chieftain 741 (4)
chieftainship 733 (5)
chiffon 222 (4)
chiffonier 194 (5)
chignon 259 (2)
chilblain 651 (14)
chilblains 380 (1)
child 132 (1), 170 (1), 170 (2), 196 (4), 935 (2)
child-bearing 373 (5)
child-like 935 (3)
child of fortune 730 (3)
child of nature 699 (2)
childbirth 167 (2)
childhood 130 (1)
childish 130 (4), 132 (5), 499 (4), 572 (2), 639 (6)
childishness 499 (1)

childless 172 (4)
childlike 132 (5), 699 (3)
children 11 (2), 132 (1), 170 (1)
children's games 837 (10)
child's play 639 (2), 701 (2)
chill 177 (6), 380 (1), 380 (5), 382 (6), 613 (3), 731 (1), 854 (12)
chill to the marrow 382 (6)
chilled 382 (4)
chilliness 380 (1)
chilly 380 (5), 380 (6), 380 (7)
chime 401 (4), 403 (3), 404 (1), 412 (2)
chime in 24 (9)
chimera 513 (3)
chimerical 4 (3), 513 (6)
chimes 400 (1), 414 (8)
chiming 106 (3), 412 (2)
chimney 201 (2), 263 (10), 353 (1), 383 (1)
chimney corner 192 (5)
chimney stack 263 (10)
chimney sweep 648 (6)
chimpanzee 365 (3)
chin 232 (7), 254 (3)
china 381 (5)
china cabinet 194 (5)
china clay 631 (1)
chinaware 381 (5)
Chinese checkers 837 (9)
Chinese lantern 420 (4)
chink 201 (2), 206 (1), 262 (1), 401 (1), 404 (1)
chip 33 (3), 46 (11), 46 (13), 53 (5), 196 (7), 330 (3), 332 (5), 547 (13), 554 (3), 837 (15)
chip away 198 (7)
chip in 231 (10)
chip off the old block 18 (3)
chipboard 631 (1)
chips 301 (20)
chiromancy 511 (2)
chiropodist 658 (14), 843 (5)
chiropody 658 (11)
chiropractice 658 (11)

chirp 409 (3), 413 (10)
chirpy 833 (3)
chirrup 409 (3)
chisel 46 (11), 164 (7), 243 (5), 256 (5), 554 (1), 554 (3), 555 (1), 630 (1)
chit 196 (4), 547 (13)
chit-chat 584 (2)
chivalrous 372 (2), 855 (4), 868 (6), 884 (3), 897 (4), 929 (3)
chivalry 855 (1), 855 (2), 884 (1), 901 (1), 931 (1)
chlorinate 652 (6)
chlorinated 652 (4)
chlorination 652 (2)
chloroform 375 (2)
chlorophyll 434 (2)
chock 218 (2)
chock-a-block 54 (4)
chock-a-block, be 54 (7)
chock-full 54 (4), 635 (5)
chocolate 301 (18), 301 (30), 430 (1)
choice 46 (2), 64 (1), 84 (6), 390 (2), 463 (1), 595 (0), 597 (1), 605 (1), 605 (5), 644 (4), 744 (2), 826 (2), 841 (3), 846 (3), 859 (3), 887 (1)
choice of words 563 (1), 566 (1)
choiceless 606 (2)
choiceness 846 (1)
choir 413 (5), 986 (7), 990 (4)
choir-singing 412 (5)
choirboy 413 (5)
choirstall 218 (6), 990 (4)
choke 264 (2), 264 (6), 362 (10), 407 (4), 637 (5), 702 (8)
choke damp 659 (3)
choke on 578 (4)
choker 844 (7)
cholera 651 (6), 651 (7)
choleric 892 (3)
cholesterol 301 (10)
chomp 301 (36)
choose 595 (2), 597 (6), 605 (6), 859 (11), 862 (4)
choose freely 597 (6)
choosing 595 (1), 605 (4)

choosy 605 (4), 846 (3), 862 (3), 862 (4)

choosy, be 605 (6)

chop 46 (11), 53 (5), 301 (16)

chop and change 143 (5), 152 (5), 604 (4)

chop up 46 (11)

chopper 256 (5), 276 (1), 723 (7)

choppiness 318 (1)

choppy 259 (4), 350 (7)

chops 239 (1)

choral 412 (7), 413 (7)

chorale 412 (5)

chord 50 (1), 249 (1), 410 (2)

chore 682 (3), 838 (2)

choreographer 594 (13)

choreographic 594 (15)

choreography 56 (1)

chores 622 (3), 682 (3)

chorister 413 (5), 986 (7)

chortle 835 (2), 835 (7)

chorus 16 (3), 20 (7), 24 (9), 50 (1), 106 (1), 123 (4), 141 (1), 408 (4), 410 (9), 412 (5), 413 (5), 413 (10), 488 (2), 488 (6), 579 (5), 594 (9)

chorus girl 594 (10)

chosen 34 (4), 46 (5), 124 (4), 596 (6), 597 (5), 605 (5), 644 (4), 923 (7), 979 (8)

chosen few 80 (3), 644 (2)

chosen race 80 (3)

Christ 973 (6)

christen 68 (10), 561 (6), 988 (10)

Christendom 976 (3), 985 (1)

christened 561 (4)

christening 561 (1), 988 (4)

Christian 973 (7)

Christian fellowship 976 (3)

Christian name 561 (2)

Christian rite 303 (2), 939 (1), 988 (4)

Christianity 973 (3)

Christianize 979 (11)

Christmas 129 (4)

chromatic 410 (8), 425 (5)

chromatic scale 425 (1)

chromatics 425 (2)

chrome yellow 433 (2)

chromosome 5 (5), 358 (1)

chronic 113 (4), 651 (21)

chronic invalid 651 (18)

chronicle 117 (4), 117 (7), 548 (1), 548 (7), 590 (2)

chronicler 117 (5), 549 (2), 590 (5)

chronograph 117 (3)

chronographic 117 (6)

chronologer 117 (5)

chronological 117 (6)

chronological error 118 (1)

chronologist 117 (5)

chronologize 117 (7)

chronology 87 (3), 108 (3), 117 (4), 589 (4)

chronometer 117 (3), 269 (4)

chronometry 117 (1)

chrysalis 132 (3), 226 (5)

chubbiness 195 (3)

chubby 195 (8)

chubby-faced 195 (8)

chuck 287 (1), 287 (7)

chucker-out 300 (2)

chuckle 835 (2), 835 (7)

chuckling 835 (5)

chug 265 (4), 278 (4), 403 (3)

chum 372 (1), 707 (3), 880 (5)

chump 501 (3)

chunk 53 (5), 195 (3)

chunkiness 195 (3)

chunky 195 (8), 259 (4)

church 164 (3), 192 (14), 708 (1), 981 (7), 990 (3)

church bell 414 (8), 665 (1)

church exterior 990 (5)

church-goer 976 (6)

church-going 981 (7), 981 (9)

church interior 990 (4)

church member 976 (6), 979 (4), 981 (8), 987 (1)

Church Militant 976 (3)

church ministry 985 (2)

church office 985 (3)

church officer 741 (6), 986 (7)

Church on earth 976 (3)

church people 976 (6)

church service 981 (7), 988 (5)

church, the 976 (2), 976 (3), 985 (1), 988 (4)

churchlike 990 (6)

churchly 985 (6)

churchman or - woman 976 (6)

churchwarden 986 (7)

churchyard 364 (4), 990 (5)

churlish 816 (4), 847 (5), 885 (5), 898 (4)

churlishness 885 (1), 893 (1)

churn 194 (13), 315 (3), 315 (5), 318 (6)

churn out 164 (7)

chute 220 (1), 298 (3), 309 (1), 350 (4), 351 (1)

chutney 389 (2)

ci-devant 119 (2)

cicada 365 (16)

cider 301 (28)

cigar 388 (2)

cigar-shaped 252 (5)

cigarette 388 (2)

cigarette case 194 (10)

cinch 47 (7), 544 (1), 701 (2)

cinder 381 (4)

Cinderella 639 (4)

cinders 385 (2), 649 (2)

cinecamera 442 (6)

cinema 442 (1), 445 (3), 594 (1), 594 (3), 594 (7), 837 (5)

cinnamon 389 (1), 430 (1)

cipher 4 (2), 85 (1), 86 (12), 103 (1), 520 (9), 525 (2), 530 (2), 547 (1), 547 (3), 558 (2), 586 (1), 639 (4)

ciphered 86 (9), 558 (5)

circa 200 (8)

circle 71 (1), 71 (5), 74 (2), 74 (3), 207 (2), 230 (3),

232 (1), **233** (1), **250** (2), 250 (8), 267 (12), 269 (10), 314 (4), **315** (5), 441 (2), 524 (4), 594 (7), 626 (1), 626 (3), 708 (1)

circler 314 (2)

circlet 250 (3)

circling 141 (4), 314 (1), 315 (1), 315 (4)

circuit 71 (1), 71 (5), 160 (5), **233** (1), 250 (2), 250 (5), 267 (1), 282 (1), 314 (1), 314 (4), 624 (4), 626 (1), **626** (3)

circuit judge 957 (1)

circuition 71 (1), 250 (5), 314 (1), 626 (1)

circuitous 230 (2), 251 (5), 282 (2), 314 (3), 626 (2)

circuitous route 626 (1)

circuitously 626 (4)

circular 71 (4), 79 (1), 81 (3), 250 (6), 528 (1), 588 (1), 737 (2)

circular course 250 (2)

circular saw 315 (3)

circularity 71 (1), **250** (1), 252 (1)

circularize 528 (9), 737 (6)

circularized 528 (7)

circulate 75 (4), **305** (5), 314 (4), 528 (9), 528 (12), 780 (5), 797 (10)

circulation 75 (1), 250 (5), 305 (2), 314 (1), 335 (3), 528 (1), 626 (1)

circum- 230 (2)

circumcision 968 (3)

circumference 184 (1), 195 (1), 199 (1), **223** (1), 230 (1), **233** (1), 236 (1), 250 (2)

circumflex 314 (3)

circumjacent 230 (2)

circumlocution 563 (1)

circumnavigate 269 (10)

circumscribe 46 (9), 230 (3), **232** (3), **233** (3), 235 (4), **236** (3), 264 (6), 289 (4), 293 (3), 303 (4), 314 (4), 660 (8), 702 (9), 747 (7)

circumscribed 8 (3), 187 (4), **232** (2), 747 (5), 778 (4)

circumscription **232** (1)

circumspect 457 (4), 858 (2)

circumspection 858 (1)

circumstance 7 (1), 8 (1), 9 (1), 27 (1), 89 (2), 154 (1), 154 (2), 178 (1), 321 (2)

circumstanced 8 (3)

circumstances 8 (1), 80 (2), 777 (2)

circumstantial 8 (3), 466 (5)

circumvent 542 (8), 620 (5), 698 (5)

circus 250 (2), 369 (4), 594 (4), 594 (7), 724 (1), 837 (4)

circus horse 273 (4)

circus manager 690 (3)

circus rider 162 (4)

cirrus 355 (2)

cistern 194 (12), 632 (2)

citadel 662 (1), 713 (4)

citation 9 (4), 466 (1), 522 (2), 729 (2), 923 (2), 959 (2)

cite 80 (8), 83 (9), 106 (4)

cite the evidence 466 (8)

cited 106 (3)

citizen 191 (3), 742 (5), 744 (4), 869 (5)

citizenry 191 (5), 371 (4), 869 (1)

citizenship 745 (1)

citrus fruit 301 (19)

city 184 (4), 192 (1), 192 (8)

city-dweller 191 (1)

city slicker 191 (3)

city state 733 (6)

civic 371 (7)

civic centre 76 (1)

civil 371 (7), 848 (6), 884 (3)

civil bar 958 (5)

civil code 953 (3)

civil court 956 (2)

civil disobedience 715 (1), 738 (1)

civil engineer 686 (3)

civil engineering 164 (1)

civil law 953 (3)

civil rights 744 (1), 915 (1)

civil servant 690 (4), 741 (6)

civil service 733 (2), 751 (1)

civil war 718 (1), 738 (2)

civilian 717 (2), 717 (3)

civility 654 (3), 846 (1), 884 (1), 884 (2)

civilization 490 (3), 654 (3)

civilize 654 (9)

civilized 848 (6)

civilizing 654 (7)

civvies 228 (6)

clack 403 (1), 403 (3)

clad 228 (29)

cladding 226 (10)

claim 184 (2), 614 (1), 614 (4), 627 (1), 627 (6), 737 (3), 737 (8), 761 (1), 761 (5), 859 (1), 859 (11), 915 (1), 915 (5), 915 (6), 959 (1)

claim attention 455 (7), 821 (8)

claim unduly 915 (5)

claimable 915 (2)

claimant 763 (1), 859 (6), 915 (1), 959 (4)

claiming 761 (3)

clairvoyance 476 (1), 511 (2), 984 (2)

clairvoyant 476 (2), 510 (2), 511 (4), 511 (6), 984 (5), 984 (7)

clam 582 (1)

clamber 308 (5)

clammy 354 (5)

clamorous 400 (3), 408 (2), 761 (3)

clamour 400 (1), 408 (4), 761 (1), 924 (1)

clamour for 761 (5), 859 (11)

clamp 45 (11), 47 (5), 778 (2)

clamp down 264 (6)

clamp down on 735 (7), 747 (7)

clear out 296 (5), 298 (5), 300 (8), 648 (9)
clear-sighted 438 (6), 498 (4)
clear the air 395 (3)
clear the decks 669 (11)
clear the ground 701 (9)
clear the throat 300 (11)
clear the way 64 (3), 283 (3)
clear thinking 498 (2)
clear thought 498 (2)
clear up 145 (6), 417 (13)
clearance 44 (3), 183 (4), 201 (1), 300 (3), 756 (1), 756 (2), 793 (1), 927 (1)
clearance sale 793 (1)
cleared 960 (2)
clearing 263 (7), 366 (2)
clearly 443 (5)
clearness 422 (1), 443 (1), 516 (1), 567 (1)
clearway 624 (6)
cleave 46 (10), 46 (11), 46 (13), 92 (5)
cleave to 48 (3)
clef 410 (3), 410 (5)
cleft 46 (1), 46 (4), 92 (4), 201 (2)
cleft palate 580 (1), 845 (1)
cleft stick 700 (3)
clemency 736 (1), 905 (3)
clench 264 (6)
clench one's teeth 599 (3)
clench the fist 900 (3)
clenched fist 547 (4)
clergy 979 (4), 981 (8), 986 (1)
clergyman 986 (2)
cleric 986 (2)
clerical 985 (6), 986 (11)
clerical collar 989 (1)
clerical dress 989 (1)
clerical error 495 (3)
clerical worker 686 (2)
clerihew 569 (1), 593 (3), 839 (2)
clerk 492 (1), 549 (1), 586 (5), 690 (4), 707 (1), 793 (2), 986 (7)
clerk of the court 958 (3)

clever 498 (4), 694 (4), 839 (4)
clever dick 500 (2)
clever hands 694 (1)
cleverness 498 (1), 694 (1)
cliche 16 (1), 106 (1), 559 (1)
cliché 496 (1), 515 (1), 560 (1), 563 (1)
cliché-ridden 572 (2)
clichéd 496 (3)
click 47 (5), 401 (1), 402 (3), 405 (3)
client 610 (4), 707 (4), 792 (2)
clientele 791 (2), 792 (2)
cliff 209 (2), 215 (1), 344 (4)
cliff-hanging 821 (4)
climacteric 131 (2)
climactic 34 (6)
climate 178 (1), 179 (1), 184 (1), 340 (3)
climatic 340 (5)
climatology 340 (3)
climax 34 (1), 34 (10), 54 (5), 73 (1), 213 (5), 669 (12), 725 (1), 725 (7), 821 (1)
climb 36 (4), 209 (2), 220 (5), 271 (7), 285 (3), 308 (4), 308 (5)
climb down 309 (3)
climbable 308 (3)
climber 268 (1), 308 (2), 366 (6)
climbing 271 (6), 308 (1), 308 (3)
clime 184 (1), 340 (3), 344 (1)
clinch 45 (11), 45 (14), 48 (3), 716 (4), 725 (5), 778 (1), 778 (5)
clinch a deal 758 (3)
clincher 69 (1), 475 (5), 479 (1)
cling 48 (3), 889 (6)
cling to 200 (5), 778 (5), 887 (13)
clinging 48 (2), 778 (3), 889 (4)
clinging to 778 (1)
clinging vine 48 (1)

clinic 534 (1), 658 (13)
clinical 658 (18)
clinical death 361 (2)
clink 401 (1), 404 (1)
clink glasses 876 (5)
clinker 649 (2)
clinker-built 207 (4)
clip 37 (4), 39 (3), 45 (10), 46 (11), 47 (5), 198 (7), 204 (5), 279 (1), 843 (2)
clip one's wings 702 (8)
clip one's words 580 (3)
clip the wings 161 (9), 278 (6)
clip the wings of 641 (7)
clipper 275 (3), 275 (5)
clippers 256 (5)
clipping 33 (3), 843 (2)
clique 74 (4), 706 (2), 708 (1)
cliquey 708 (7)
cliquish 481 (8), 708 (7)
cliquishness 706 (1)
clitoris 167 (3)
cloak 226 (5), 228 (21), 421 (1), 614 (1), 660 (8), 713 (9)
cloak and dagger 525 (5)
cloaked 226 (12)
cloakroom 194 (19)
clobber 279 (9)
cloche 228 (23), 370 (3)
clock 117 (3), 117 (7)
clock in 68 (8), 117 (7)
clock out 117 (7), 296 (4)
clock time 108 (3), 117 (2)
clock-watcher 679 (6)
clockwise 315 (6)
clockwork 61 (3), 630 (2), 837 (15)
clod 53 (5), 324 (3), 344 (3), 501 (3)
clod-hopping 840 (2)
clog 228 (27), 649 (8), 649 (9), 747 (7)
clog dance 594 (5), 837 (14)
clog dancer 312 (2)
clogged up 264 (4)
cloister 235 (4), 662 (1), 883 (2), 986 (9)
cloistered 232 (2), 264 (5), 883 (7), 986 (12)

clone 18 (3), 22 (1)

close 18 (4), 45 (9), 69 (1), 69 (5), 69 (6), 145 (6), 185 (1), 192 (8), 198 (6), 200 (4), 202 (2), 202 (5), 206 (4), 235 (1), 264 (5), 264 (6), 279 (7), 289 (2), 324 (4), 350 (12), 379 (6), 421 (4), 494 (6), 525 (6), 582 (2), 656 (12), 702 (9), 747 (4), 816 (4), 986 (10), 990 (5)

close a gap 45 (9)

close at hand 124 (4), 200 (7)

close attention 455 (1)

close behind 200 (7), 238 (6)

close contact 202 (1)

close down 69 (6)

close fighting 716 (7)

close finish 200 (2), 716 (2)

close-fitting 48 (2)

close friend 880 (4), 887 (5)

close friendship 880 (1)

close grips 200 (2), 716 (7)

close in 232 (3), 293 (3)

close in on 289 (4)

close of day 129 (1)

close one's eyes 364 (9), 456 (7)

close-packed 324 (4)

close quarters 200 (2), 716 (7)

close range 200 (2)

close reading 536 (2)

close relation 9 (2)

close-run 200 (4), 716 (9)

close season 108 (2), 145 (4)

close secrecy 525 (2)

close-set 45 (7)

close shave 661 (1), 667 (1)

close study 449 (2)

close-textured 324 (4)

close the ranks 48 (3), 200 (5), 669 (11), 718 (12)

close to 200 (4), 200 (7)

close to tears 836 (4)

close up 198 (6), 200 (2), 551 (4)

close upon 120 (4)

close with 48 (3), 293 (3), 712 (9), 716 (10), 716 (11)

closed 198 (4), 264 (4), 481 (8), 778 (3)

closed door 57 (1)

closed mind 481 (4), 608 (1)

closed shop 57 (1), 708 (1), 747 (2)

closed to 820 (5)

closed vowel 577 (1)

closeness 200 (1), 887 (1)

closet 194 (5), 194 (19), 527 (1)

closing 69 (4), 264 (1)

closing down 145 (2)

closing in 289 (2), 293 (1)

closure 45 (2), 47 (5), 69 (1), 145 (2), 198 (1), 235 (3), 264 (1), 700 (1), 702 (1)

clot 324 (3), 324 (6), 335 (3), 354 (1), 354 (6), 501 (3), 651 (9)

cloth 164 (2), 222 (4), 631 (1)

cloth, the 986 (1), 989 (1)

clothe 228 (31), 633 (5)

clothe oneself 228 (32)

clothed 228 (29)

clothes 228 (2)

clothes brush 648 (5)

clothes-conscious 848 (5)

clotheshorse 217 (3)

clothesline 217 (3)

clothier 228 (28), 686 (3)

clothing 228 (1), 228 (2), 844 (6)

clotted 324 (4), 354 (4), 649 (7)

clotted cream 301 (24)

clotting 354 (2)

cloud 104 (2), 336 (2), 338 (1), 339 (1), 341 (1), 355 (2), 355 (6), 421 (4), 423 (1), 423 (3)

cloud-capped 209 (8)

cloud over 355 (6), 423 (3)

cloud-seeding 350 (6)

cloudbank 355 (2)

cloudburst 176 (3), 350 (6)

clouded 355 (4), 423 (2)

cloudiness 355 (2), 419 (1)

cloudless 342 (4), 417 (9), 730 (5)

cloudlet 355 (2)

cloudscape 355 (2)

cloudy 341 (4), 355 (4), 355 (6), 418 (4), 419 (4), 423 (2)

clout 178 (1), 279 (2), 279 (9), 963 (2), 963 (9)

clove 389 (1)

clove hitch 47 (4)

cloven 46 (4), 92 (4), 201 (3)

cloven hoof 969 (2)

cloven-hoofed 214 (4)

clover 730 (2)

cloverleaf 624 (6)

clown 497 (4), 501 (1), 594 (10), 697 (1), 839 (3), 851 (3)

clowning 497 (2), 839 (1), 849 (1)

clownish 695 (5), 837 (18), 849 (2), 849 (3)

cloy 637 (5), 820 (7), 838 (5), 863 (3)

cloyed 820 (4), 838 (4)

cloying 391 (2), 637 (3), 838 (3)

club 74 (3), 76 (1), 192 (14), 279 (4), 279 (9), 706 (2), 708 (1), 708 (3), 723 (5), 964 (1)

club-footed 246 (4)

club together 706 (4), 708 (8)

clubbable 708 (6)

clubhouse 192 (14)

cluck 409 (1), 409 (3)

clue 460 (1), 466 (1), 490 (1), 512 (1), 520 (1), 524 (3), 547 (1)

clueless 491 (4), 700 (5)

clump 74 (6), 267 (14), 324 (3), 366 (2)

clumsiness 576 (1), 695 (1), 842 (1)

clumsy 25 (5), 195 (9), 278 (3), 495 (5), 499 (3), 576 (2), 643 (2), 645 (2), 695

(5), 842 (5), 847 (5), 849 (2)

clumsy, be 495 (8), 655 (9), 695 (9)

clumsy clot 697 (1)

clumsy hand 586 (2)

clumsy style 566 (1)

cluster 74 (3), 74 (5), 74 (10)

cluster bomb 723 (14)

clutch 74 (3), 132 (3), 778 (5)

clutch at 786 (6)

clutched 778 (4)

clutches 778 (1)

clutter 61 (2), 63 (4), 104 (6)

co- 28 (7)

co-agency 173 (1)

co-director 707 (3)

co-opt 605 (6)

co-optation 605 (1)

co-optative 605 (4)

co-option 605 (1)

co-partner 775 (3)

co-religionist 976 (6)

co-sharing 775 (2)

co-star 594 (17)

co-tenant 775 (3)

co-worker 89 (2), 686 (4), 707 (2)

coach 274 (6), 274 (10), 274 (13), 534 (6), 534 (8), 537 (1), 537 (2), 669 (5), 669 (11)

coach and four 274 (6)

coach driver 268 (5)

coach-horse 273 (6)

coaching 534 (1)

coachman 268 (5)

coagulate 48 (3), 324 (6), 354 (6)

coagulated 354 (4)

coagulation 45 (1), 324 (2), 354 (2)

coal 160 (4), 383 (2), 385 (1), 385 (2), 385 (3), 420 (3), 428 (2)

coal-bearing 385 (5)

coal-black 428 (4)

coal-burning 381 (7)

coal deposit 385 (2)

coal fire 379 (2)

coal forest 125 (3)

coal measure 385 (2)

coal measures 359 (1)

coal-miner 255 (5)

coal scuttle 194 (13)

coal seam 385 (2)

coalesce 13 (3), 50 (4), 706 (4)

coalescence 13 (1), 45 (1), 50 (1), 324 (1)

coalescent 45 (5), 50 (3)

coalfield 385 (2)

coalhole 194 (21)

coalition 45 (1), 706 (2), 708 (2), 708 (3)

coarse 259 (4), 331 (4), 391 (2), 464 (3), 576 (2), 670 (4), 842 (5), 847 (4), 869 (8), 951 (6)

coarse fishing 619 (2)

coarse grain 259 (1)

coarse-grained 331 (4)

coarsen 655 (9), 820 (7), 847 (6)

coarseness 259 (1), 391 (1), 464 (1), 573 (1), 576 (1), 820 (1), 847 (1), 951 (1)

coast 239 (1), 239 (3), 258 (5), 267 (11), 305 (5), 344 (2), 677 (3)

coast home 701 (7)

coastal 234 (4), 344 (6)

coaster 218 (5), 275 (3)

coastguard 270 (3), 749 (1)

coastline 233 (1), 234 (1), 344 (2)

coat 207 (1), 207 (5), 226 (6), 226 (16), 228 (10), 228 (20), 258 (4), 423 (3), 425 (8), 553 (8), 844 (12), 875 (7)

coat of arms 547 (11)

coat of paint 226 (10)

coat-tails 217 (2), 228 (3)

coated 423 (3), 542 (6)

coating 207 (1), 226 (1), 226 (10), 227 (1)

coax 612 (11), 761 (5), 889 (5), 925 (4)

coaxing 612 (2)

cob 192 (20), 273 (9)

cobalt 435 (2)

cobble 226 (7), 631 (2)

cobbled 624 (8)

cobbled together 164 (6)

cobbler 228 (28), 656 (5)

cobblestone 226 (7)

cobbling 656 (2)

cobra 365 (13)

cobweb 163 (3), 208 (1), 222 (3), 649 (2)

cobwebby 649 (7)

cocaine 375 (2), 949 (4)

cochineal 425 (4), 431 (2)

cock 365 (6), 669 (11)

cock-a-hoop 833 (5), 877 (4)

cock a snook 921 (5)

cock a snook at 878 (6)

cock-and-bull story 543 (3)

cock-eye 440 (1)

cock-eyed 220 (3), 246 (3)

cock-shy 287 (1)

cock up 215 (3), 215 (4), 254 (5)

cockade 547 (10), 844 (5)

cockcrow 128 (1)

cockerel 365 (6)

cockiness 873 (1), 878 (1)

cockney 191 (3), 560 (2), 560 (5)

cockpit 194 (19), 276 (1)

cockroach 365 (16)

cocksure 485 (4), 878 (5)

cocktail 43 (3), 301 (28)

cocky 871 (4), 878 (5)

cocoa 301 (27), 301 (30)

coconut 301 (19)

cocoon 132 (3), 194 (1), 226 (5), 660 (8)

COD 792 (4)

cod-liver oil 357 (2)

coda 40 (1), 67 (1), 69 (1), 238 (1), 410 (1), 412 (4)

coddle 889 (5)

code 62 (1), 81 (1), 523 (1), 525 (2), 525 (7), 530 (2), 547 (3), 586 (1), 929 (1)

code-breaker 520 (4)

code of duty 917 (3)

code of honour 917 (3)

coded 523 (4), 525 (4)

codicil 40 (1), 67 (1)

codification 62 (1), 953 (2)
codify 62 (6)
codpiece 228 (3)
coeducation 534 (2)
coeducational 534 (5)
coefficient 85 (2)
coerce 733 (12), 740 (3)
coercion 735 (2), 740 (1)
coercive 735 (5), 740 (2), 747 (4)
coeval 123 (2), 123 (3)
coexist 1 (6), 89 (4), 123 (4), 202 (3), 823 (6)
coexistence 1 (1), 89 (1), 710 (1), 717 (1)
coexistent 123 (3), 710 (2)
coexisting 24 (5)
coextensive 28 (7), 219 (2), 245 (2)
coffee 301 (27), 430 (1)
coffee bar 192 (13)
coffee-coloured 430 (1)
coffee estate 370 (2)
coffee morning 882 (3)
coffee pot 194 (14)
coffer 194 (7), 632 (2)
coffers 799 (1)
coffin 194 (7), 364 (1)
coffin-nail 388 (2)
coffined 364 (7)
cog 256 (4), 260 (1), 260 (3)
cogency 160 (1)
cogent 160 (8), 475 (7), 571 (2), 740 (2)
cogiate 449 (7)
cogitation 449 (1)
cogitative 449 (5)
cognac 301 (28)
cognate 11 (5)
cognition 447 (1), 490 (1)
cognitive 447 (5), 490 (5)
cognize 447 (7), 490 (8)
cognoscente 696 (2), 846 (2)
cogwheel 260 (1)
cohabit 45 (14), 89 (4), 894 (11)
cohabitation 894 (1)
cohere 45 (14), 48 (3), 181 (3), 202 (3), 324 (6), 354 (6)

coherence 24 (2), 45 (1), 45 (2), 47 (9), 48 (1), 88 (1), 202 (1), 324 (1), 354 (3), 502 (1), 516 (1)
coherent 48 (2), 502 (2), 516 (2)
cohesion 45 (1), 48 (1)
cohesive 45 (5), 45 (6), 45 (7), 45 (8), 48 (2), 324 (4), 354 (5), 778 (3)
cohesively 48 (5)
cohesiveness 48 (1)
cohort 722 (8)
cohorts 722 (6)
coif 228 (23)
coiffeur 843 (5)
coiffure 843 (2)
coil 61 (3), 234 (3), 248 (5), 251 (2), 251 (10), 314 (1), 843 (2), 844 (3)
coil up 252 (6)
coiled 61 (8), 251 (8)
coin 164 (7), 243 (5), 250 (2), 513 (7), 541 (8), 797 (4), 797 (10)
coin money 800 (7)
coin-spinning 837 (12)
coin words 560 (6)
coinage 33 (4), 560 (1), 797 (4)
coincide 13 (3), 24 (9), 89 (4), 123 (4), 202 (3)
coincide with 28 (9)
coincidence 13 (1), 28 (1), 89 (1), 89 (2), 123 (1), 154 (1), 159 (1), 181 (1), 618 (1)
coincident 13 (2), 28 (7), 123 (3), 181 (2)
coincidental 89 (3), 159 (5), 618 (5)
coinciding 24 (5)
coined 797 (9)
coir 208 (2)
coital 45 (6)
coition 45 (3), 167 (1)
coke 385 (2)
col 47 (1), 206 (1), 209 (2)
colander 194 (16), 263 (3)
cold 129 (7), 302 (1), 361 (6), 375 (4), 380 (1), 380 (5), 382 (4), 651 (5), 651 (8), 659 (2), 670 (5), 685

(2), 731 (4), 820 (3), 823 (3), 860 (2), 881 (3)
cold, be 324 (6), 380 (7)
cold-blooded 365 (18), 858 (2), 898 (7)
cold climate 380 (1)
cold comfort 829 (1)
cold-eyed 898 (7)
cold feet 854 (2)
cold fish 820 (2)
cold front 380 (2)
cold heart 820 (1)
cold-hearted 820 (3), 932 (3)
cold meats 301 (14)
cold-shoulder 57 (5), 292 (3), 458 (5), 607 (1), 607 (3), 620 (5), 883 (9), 885 (6)
cold snap 380 (2)
cold steel 712 (4), 723 (8)
cold storage 136 (2), 382 (1), 384 (1), 666 (1)
cold sweat 854 (1)
cold-type 587 (6)
cold war 718 (1)
cold weather 340 (3), 380 (2)
cold wind 352 (1), 731 (1)
coldness 380 (1), 731 (1), 860 (1), 883 (1), 950 (1)
coleslaw 301 (14)
colic 377 (2), 651 (7)
collaborate 488 (6), 597 (6), 603 (6), 706 (4)
collaborating 488 (4), 706 (3)
collaboration 181 (1), 706 (1)
collaborator 89 (2), 488 (3), 603 (3), 703 (3), 707 (2)
collage 50 (1), 553 (5)
collapse 51 (1), 145 (6), 161 (2), 161 (8), 163 (1), 165 (3), 309 (1), 309 (3), 651 (2), 651 (23), 655 (2), 655 (7), 684 (1), 684 (5), 721 (4), 728 (1), 728 (2), 728 (7), 854 (9)
collapsed 651 (21)

collar 47 (7), 47 (8), 228 (22), 250 (3), 747 (8), 748 (4)

collate 462 (3)

collateral 9 (5), 11 (5), 31 (2), 89 (3), 170 (4), 219 (2), 239 (2), 767 (1)

collaterality 9 (2), 170 (3)

collation 301 (12), 462 (1)

colleague 89 (2), 686 (4), 707 (3), 775 (3), 837 (16), 880 (3), 880 (5)

collect 45 (9), 74 (10), 74 (11), 592 (5), 771 (7), 782 (4), 786 (6)

collect a toll 786 (8)

collect dust 649 (8)

collect funds 771 (7)

collect one's thoughts 449 (7)

collect oneself 823 (5)

collected 498 (5), 592 (4), 865 (2)

collected, be 823 (5)

collected poems 593 (2)

collection 62 (1), 74 (1), 74 (7), 522 (2), 589 (5), 592 (2), 632 (3), 771 (1), 781 (3), 782 (1), 804 (1), 981 (6)

collective 79 (3), 775 (1), 775 (4)

collective bargaining 766 (1)

collective farm 775 (1)

collective noun 74 (1)

collectively 52 (10), 74 (12), 89 (5), 708 (9), 775 (7)

collectivism 733 (4), 775 (1)

collectivist 775 (3)

collectivized 74 (9)

collector 74 (8), 492 (3), 504 (3), 782 (2), 859 (6)

collector's piece 522 (2), 694 (3)

college 164 (3), 539 (1)

College of Arms 547 (11)

college of further or higher education 539 (1)

collide 25 (6), 182 (3), 279 (8), 289 (4), 295 (6), 378

(7), 709 (7), 712 (9), 712 (10)

collide with 279 (8), 295 (6)

collie 365 (10)

colliery 255 (4), 687 (1)

collision 25 (1), 45 (1), 165 (3), 176 (1), 182 (1), 279 (3), 293 (1), 709 (3), 716 (7)

collision course 200 (1), 279 (3), 293 (1)

collocate 62 (4), 74 (11)

collocation 62 (1), 74 (1)

colloid 354 (1)

colloquial 519 (3), 557 (5), 560 (5)

colloquialism 519 (2), 560 (3)

colloquy 579 (1), 584 (1), 584 (3)

collude 181 (3), 706 (4)

colluding 181 (2)

collusion 181 (1), 541 (2), 542 (1), 706 (1)

collusive 541 (3), 542 (6)

colon 224 (2), 263 (9), 351 (2), 547 (14)

colonel 741 (8)

colonial 59 (2), 191 (4)

colonialism 371 (5), 733 (2), 745 (1)

colonist 191 (4), 297 (3)

colonization 187 (1)

colonize 187 (8), 189 (4), 192 (21), 745 (7), 786 (7)

colonized 745 (4)

colonnade 71 (2), 624 (5)

colony 74 (5), 170 (2), 184 (2), 187 (3), 191 (5), 733 (6), 742 (5)

coloration 417 (1), 425 (1), 425 (3)

colossal 32 (6), 195 (7), 209 (9)

colossus 195 (4), 209 (5), 554 (1)

colour 5 (3), 43 (2), 43 (7), 43 (8), 77 (2), 178 (3), 226 (16), 417 (1), 425 (1), 425 (8), 431 (5), 437 (1), 445 (1), 445 (5), 468 (3), 477 (8), 553 (1), 553 (8), 614

(1), 818 (8), 844 (12), 874 (3), 891 (6)

colour bar 57 (1)

colour-blind 440 (3), 464 (3)

colour blindness 439 (1)

colour in 425 (8)

colour prejudice 481 (3)

colour printing 555 (2)

colour scheme 425 (1)

colour sergeant 722 (4)

colour supplement 528 (4)

colour up 431 (5), 872 (6)

coloured 417 (8), 425 (5), 428 (4), 553 (7)

coloured person 428 (1)

colourful 417 (8), 425 (5), 425 (6), 437 (5), 590 (6)

colouring 425 (3), 547 (2), 553 (1)

colouring matter 425 (4)

colourless 163 (4), 163 (6), 426 (3), 427 (5), 572 (2), 651 (20), 840 (2)

colours 547 (9), 547 (12)

colourwash 425 (4)

colt 132 (3), 273 (4), 723 (10)

coltish 132 (5), 678 (7)

column 209 (4), 218 (10), 252 (3), 267 (4), 539 (5), 591 (2), 722 (8)

columnist 589 (7)

coma 375 (1), 651 (2), 679 (4)

comatose 375 (3), 679 (9), 820 (4)

comb 256 (4), 258 (2), 258 (4), 459 (15), 648 (5), 648 (9)

comb out 62 (7)

combat 716 (1), 716 (7), 716 (10), 716 (11), 718 (12)

combat fatigue 503 (2)

combat troops 722 (7)

combat zone 724 (2)

combatant 362 (6), 716 (8), 722 (1), 881 (2)

combative 709 (6), 712 (6), 716 (9), 718 (9)

combativeness 709 (2), 712 (1), 718 (3)

combed 258 (3)

comber 350 (5)

combination 24 (1), 43 (1), 43 (3), 45 (1), 45 (2), 50 (1), 56 (1), 74 (1), 86 (2), 88 (1), 708 (3)

combination lock 47 (5)

combination union 706 (2)

combinations 228 (17)

combine 38 (4), 43 (7), 45 (9), 48 (3), 50 (4), 56 (5), 88 (5), 164 (7), 706 (2), 706 (4), 708 (5)

combine harvester 370 (6)

combine with 50 (4)

combined 43 (6), 45 (5), 50 (3), 181 (2)

combined operations 718 (6)

combining 24 (5)

combustible 381 (7), 385 (5)

combustion 381 (2)

come 295 (4)

come about 1 (6), 154 (6)

come across 771 (7)

come after 65 (3), 71 (5), 120 (3), 284 (4)

come along 267 (17)

come amiss 25 (6)

come apropos 24 (9)

come back again 286 (5)

come back at 460 (5), 839 (5)

come before 57 (5), 64 (3), 68 (9), 119 (3), 119 (4), 135 (5), 156 (10), 283 (3), 299 (3), 511 (8), 638 (7), 669 (10), 689 (5), 701 (8), 959 (9)

come behind 284 (4)

come between 231 (7), 231 (10), 709 (8)

come by 771 (7)

come clean 526 (6), 540 (3)

come close 200 (5)

come closer 289 (4), 289 (5), 293 (3)

come down 309 (3), 350 (10), 812 (5)

come down in the world 801 (5)

come down on 735 (7)

come first 34 (9), 638 (7)

come forward 759 (4)

come full circle 314 (4)

come-hither look 438 (3), 889 (2)

come home 286 (5)

come home to 821 (8)

come in 78 (4), 289 (4), 297 (5), 782 (5)

come in contact 202 (3)

come in force 162 (11)

come in handy 640 (4)

come in last 728 (9)

come into 771 (8), 773 (4), 782 (4), 786 (7)

come into contact 378 (7)

come into existence 68 (8), 154 (6)

come into money 800 (7)

come into one's head 449 (9)

come into the world 360 (5)

come into view 289 (4), 443 (4)

come naturally to 24 (9)

come near 289 (4)

come next 65 (3)

come of 157 (5)

come of age 134 (4)

come off 145 (6), 154 (6), 948 (4)

come off best 727 (11)

come off on 48 (3)

come on 155 (3), 285 (3)

come out 68 (8), 145 (6), 298 (5), 528 (12), 679 (11), 715 (3), 762 (3)

come out for 605 (6)

come out on top 727 (6)

come out with 522 (7), 526 (5), 609 (4)

come over 516 (4)

come round 656 (8), 758 (3)

come round again 141 (6)

come round to 485 (9)

come short 307 (3), 636 (7)

come short of 35 (5)

come through 660 (7)

come to 86 (11), 656 (8), 685 (5), 809 (6)

come to a crisis or a head 725 (7)

come to a head 34 (10)

come to a point 293 (3)

come to an agreement 765 (5)

come to an end 69 (5), 145 (6)

come to an understanding 719 (5)

come to be 1 (7)

come to believe 485 (7)

come to blows 716 (11), 881 (4)

come to dust 361 (8)

come to fruition 725 (7)

come to grief 728 (8), 731 (7)

come to grips 716 (11)

come to hand 782 (5)

come to heel 284 (4), 739 (4)

come to know 490 (8), 524 (12)

come to life 360 (4)

come to light 526 (7)

come to mind 449 (9)

come to nothing 2 (7), 307 (3), 728 (8)

come to one's ears 415 (6)

come to one's knowledge 490 (9)

come to one's senses 374 (5), 502 (3)

come to pass 154 (6)

come to pieces 728 (7)

come to power 160 (10)

come to rest 187 (8), 192 (21), 266 (8), 679 (11)

come to stay 144 (3), 153 (7)

come to terms 24 (9)

come to the help of 703 (5)

come to the point 9 (7)

come to the rescue 668 (3)

come together 74 (10), 293 (3)

come under 78 (4)
come under fire 661 (8)
come undone 46 (7)
come unstuck 46 (7), 49
(4), 75 (3), 695 (7), 700 (7)
come up 417 (11)
come upon 295 (6), 484 (4)
come what may 599 (5)
come within range 289 (4)
comeback 656 (3)
comedian 594 (9), 839 (3)
comedienne 594 (9), 839
(3)
comedown 309 (1), 509
(1), 872 (2)
comedy 594 (3), 835 (2),
849 (1)
comedy of manners 594
(3)
comeliness 841 (1)
comely 841 (3)
comestibles 301 (9)
comet 321 (6)
cometary 321 (14)
comfort 177 (7), 376 (2),
701 (1), 703 (1), 703 (5),
800 (1), 824 (2), 826 (3),
828 (1), 828 (5), 831 (1),
831 (3), 833 (8), 852 (7),
905 (2), 905 (6)
comfortable 24 (8), 376
(4), 651 (21), 683 (2), 701
(3), 701 (5), 730 (5), 800
(3), 824 (5), 826 (2), 828
(2)
comfortably off 800 (3)
comforter 228 (22)
comforting 177 (4), 376
(4), 685 (2), 831 (2), 833
(6)
comfortless 827 (4), 834
(8), 853 (3)
comic 501 (1), 528 (4), 594
(10), 594 (15), 835 (5), 839
(3), 839 (4), 849 (3)
comic interlude 849 (1)
Comic Muse 594 (1)
comic opera 412 (5), 594
(3)
comic poet 594 (13)
comic relief 590 (2)
comic strip 839 (1)
comic turn 839 (1), 849 (1)

comic verse 849 (1)
comical 497 (3), 835 (5),
839 (4), 849 (3)
comicalness 839 (1)
coming 124 (4), 289 (1),
289 (2), 295 (1)
coming after 65 (1)
coming and going 317 (2),
678 (8)
coming before 64 (1)
coming events 124 (1), 155
(1)
coming out 68 (2)
coming together 45 (1),
706 (2)
coming towards 289 (1)
comma 547 (14)
command 34 (2), 178 (3),
547 (8), 595 (0), 595 (2),
627 (1), 673 (5), 689 (2),
689 (5), 691 (4), 693 (1),
718 (6), 733 (2), 733 (10),
733 (12), 737 (1), 737 (6),
740 (3), 751 (2), 773 (4),
859 (1), 859 (11), 917 (11)
command a view 209 (12)
command of words 579
(4)
command respect 638 (7),
866 (11), 920 (7)
commandant 741 (8)
commandeer 740 (3), 786
(7)
commandeering 786 (1),
786 (5)
commander 34 (3), 741
(7), 741 (8)
commander-in-chief 741
(8)
commanding 34 (4), 638
(6), 733 (7), 737 (5), 740
(2)
commandingly 737 (9)
commandment 693 (1),
737 (1)
commandoes 722 (7)
comme il faut 848 (5)
commemorate 505 (9),
876 (4)
commemoration 505 (2),
505 (3), 866 (5), 876 (1)
commemorative 505 (6),
876 (3)

commence 68 (8)
commencement 68 (1)
commend 691 (4), 923 (8),
923 (9)
commendable 615 (3), 923
(6), 933 (3)
commendably 923 (13)
commendation 923 (2)
commendatory 923 (5)
commended 923 (7)
commender 923 (4)
commensurable 85 (5), 86
(8)
commensurate 9 (5), 24
(5), 86 (8)
comment 480 (6), 520 (2),
532 (1), 532 (5), 579 (1),
591 (2)
comment on 520 (8)
comment upon 455 (6),
591 (5)
commentary 496 (1), 520
(2), 579 (2), 591 (1)
commentate 591 (5)
commentator 480 (3), 520
(4), 524 (4), 531 (5), 591
(3)
comments 480 (2)
commerce 584 (1), 622
(1), 791 (2)
commercial 528 (3), 531
(4), 622 (5), 791 (3)
commercial traveller 793
(2)
commercialism 847 (1)
commercialize 791 (4),
847 (6)
commercialized 847 (4)
commiserate 836 (5), 905
(6)
commiserating 905 (4)
commiseration 905 (2)
commissar 741 (2)
commissariat 301 (7), 633
(1)
commissary 633 (2), 754
(2)
commission 36 (2), 68
(10), 74 (4), 272 (6), 529
(3), 605 (1), 605 (7), 622
(2), 622 (3), 622 (6), 669
(2), 669 (11), 676 (1), 689
(1), 693 (1), 733 (1), 737

75

(1), 737 (4), 737 (6), 751 (1), 751 (2), 751 (4), 756 (2), 771 (2), 777 (6), 780 (1), 780 (3), 781 (7), 783 (2), 804 (2), 809 (1), 810 (1), 866 (14), 876 (1), 876 (4), 917 (1), 917 (11)

commissionaire 264 (3), 529 (6)

commissioned 751 (3)

commissioner 690 (4), 741 (6), 754 (2), 955 (3)

commissioner for oaths 958 (3)

commit 272 (6), 676 (5), 781 (7), 914 (6)

commit a crime 914 (6)

commit a foul 914 (6)

commit a solecism 565 (3)

commit adultery 951 (10)

commit an error 495 (7)

commit hara-kiri 362 (13)

commit murder 362 (12)

commit oneself 532 (5), 599 (3), 605 (6), 672 (3), 764 (4), 917 (9)

commit rape 951 (11)

commit sacrilege 980 (6)

commit suicide 361 (8), 362 (13)

commit suttee 362 (13)

commit to memory 505 (10)

commit to prison 747 (10)

commit to the flames 381 (10)

commitment 764 (1), 803 (1), 917 (1)

commitments 702 (4)

committal 959 (2)

committed 532 (3), 764 (3), 803 (4), 917 (5)

committee 74 (4), 708 (1), 733 (1), 754 (1)

commode 194 (5), 649 (3)

commodious 183 (6)

commodity 319 (3), 795 (1)

commodore 741 (7)

common 35 (4), 79 (3), 83 (5), 139 (2), 557 (5), 610 (6), 774 (3), 775 (1), 775

(4), 837 (4), 847 (4), 869 (8)

common cause 706 (1)

common cold 651 (5)

common consent 488 (2)

common denominator 85 (2)

common factor 85 (2)

common feature 18 (1)

common good 901 (1)

common knowledge 524 (1), 528 (2)

common land 775 (1), 777 (3)

common law 127 (3), 693 (1), 953 (3)

common-law marriage 894 (2)

common lot 732 (1)

common man 30 (3), 732 (1)

common or garden 83 (5)

common ownership 775 (1)

common people, the 869 (1)

common practice 610 (2)

common prayer 981 (7)

common reference 9 (1)

common sense 502 (1)

common soldier 722 (5)

common source 9 (1)

common speech 557 (1), 573 (1)

common stamp 16 (1)

common touch 882 (2), 884 (1)

commonalty 35 (1), 74 (3), 371 (4), 639 (4), 869 (1)

commoner 79 (2), 732 (1), 847 (3), 869 (5)

commonly 139 (4)

commonness 35 (1), 79 (1), 847 (2)

commonplace 30 (4), 79 (3), 83 (5), 490 (7), 496 (1), 563 (1), 610 (6), 639 (6), 732 (2), 840 (2)

commonplace book 592 (2)

commons 301 (7), 869 (1)

commonsense 498 (1)

commonwealth 733 (6)

commotion 61 (4), 176 (1), 318 (3), 546 (1), 678 (4), 709 (3), 818 (1), 821 (1), 822 (2)

communal 371 (7), 708 (6), 775 (4)

communalize 632 (5), 775 (6), 780 (3), 786 (7)

communally 775 (7)

commune 191 (5), 524 (10), 706 (2), 775 (1)

commune with 584 (6)

communicable 272 (5), 653 (3)

communicant 976 (6), 979 (4), 981 (8), 981 (9)

communicate 45 (10), 514 (5), 524 (10), 526 (5), 528 (9), 547 (22), 588 (4), 590 (7), 981 (12)

communicating 624 (8)

communication 272 (1), 524 (1), 529 (3), 584 (1), 588 (1)

communication, a 524 (1)

communication of knowledge 524 (1)

communicative 524 (7), 526 (3), 581 (4), 584 (5)

communicator 272 (4), 524 (4)

communion 584 (1), 981 (1)

communiqué 524 (2), 529 (1)

communism 733 (4), 775 (1), 901 (1)

communist 654 (5), 775 (3)

communist bloc 733 (6)

communistic 775 (4)

communists 708 (2)

community 371 (4), 706 (2), 708 (4), 978 (3)

community centre 76 (1), 192 (14)

community service 901 (2)

commutable 150 (4)

commutation 150 (1), 151 (1)

commutator 160 (6)

commute 141 (6), 150 (5), 151 (3), 267 (11)

commuter 191 (1), 268 (1)

commuting 267 (1)

compact 24 (1), 33 (6), 48 (2), 78 (1), 194 (10), 196 (8), 198 (4), 198 (7), 204 (3), 324 (4), 324 (6), 488 (2), 569 (2), 764 (1), 765 (1), 767 (2), 770 (1), 791 (2), 843 (3)

compacted 198 (4)

compaction 198 (2)

compactly 48 (5)

compactness 324 (1)

companion 18 (3), 89 (2), 707 (3), 742 (3), 880 (4)

companionable 882 (6)

companionship 89 (1), 880 (1), 882 (1)

companionway 263 (6), 308 (1)

company 74 (2), 74 (4), 89 (1), 594 (9), 686 (4), 706 (2), 708 (1), 708 (5), 722 (8)

comparability 18 (1), 462 (1)

comparable 9 (5), 28 (8), 462 (2)

comparative 27 (3), 34 (4), 462 (2), 564 (3)

comparative grammar 564 (1)

comparative philology 557 (2)

comparatively 33 (9), 462 (4)

compare 9 (8), 18 (8), 27 (4), 28 (10), 462 (3), 463 (3), 519 (4)

compare and contrast 462 (3)

compare notes 462 (3), 691 (5)

compare to or with 462 (3)

compare with 18 (7)

compared 9 (5), 31 (3), 462 (2), 519 (3)

comparing 462 (1), 480 (2)

comparison 9 (2), 18 (2), 27 (1), 462 (1), 480 (2), 519 (1), 519 (2)

compartment 46 (1), 53 (3), 77 (1), 185 (1), 194 (4), 274 (13)

compass 27 (1), 160 (2), 160 (10), 183 (3), 199 (1), 230 (3), 269 (4), 270 (2), 314 (4), 465 (5), 547 (7), 727 (7)

compass point 239 (1), 281 (2)

compass reading 269 (2), 281 (1)

compassion 905 (1), 931 (1)

compassionate 819 (2), 905 (4)

compatibility 24 (4), 710 (1), 880 (1), 882 (2), 887 (1)

compatible 24 (5), 710 (2), 880 (6)

compatriot 11 (2)

compeer 28 (6), 123 (2)

compel 83 (8), 160 (10), 178 (3), 596 (8), 612 (8), 612 (10), 627 (6), 733 (12), 735 (8), 737 (6), 740 (3)

compel to accept 740 (3)

compelled 596 (7)

compelling 156 (7), 160 (8), 162 (6), 178 (2), 571 (2), 596 (4), 610 (6), 627 (5), 733 (7), 735 (5), 737 (5), 740 (2), 747 (4)

compendious 204 (3), 592 (4)

compendium 33 (2), 50 (1), 62 (1), 87 (1), 196 (3), 198 (1), 204 (2), 520 (3), 569 (1), 589 (5), 590 (1), 591 (1), 592 (1)

compensate 12 (3), 24 (10), 28 (9), 28 (10), 31 (4), 54 (6), 322 (5), 787 (3), 804 (4), 941 (5), 962 (3)

compensating 31 (3)

compensation 28 (4), 31 (1), 31 (2), 150 (1), 150 (3), 719 (2), 753 (1), 771 (2), 787 (1), 804 (1), 915 (1), 941 (1), 963 (4)

compensatory 31 (3), 182 (2), 787 (2), 941 (4), 962 (2)

compere 531 (5), 690 (3)

compete 716 (10), 759 (4)

compete with 704 (4)

competence 160 (2), 635 (1), 694 (1), 800 (1)

competent 160 (8), 640 (2), 694 (4), 694 (6), 733 (7), 955 (4)

competing 716 (9), 911 (2)

competition 704 (1), 716 (1), 716 (2), 911 (1)

competitive 34 (4), 704 (3), 716 (9)

competitor 702 (5), 705 (1), 716 (8), 722 (1), 837 (16), 881 (2), 911 (1)

competitors 704 (2)

compilation 56 (1), 74 (1), 74 (7), 592 (2)

compile 56 (5), 74 (11), 592 (5)

complacency 828 (1)

complain 762 (3), 829 (5), 836 (5), 893 (3)

complain of 651 (23)

complainer 763 (1), 829 (2), 834 (4), 836 (1)

complaining 829 (3), 836 (4)

complaint 651 (2), 762 (1), 827 (2), 829 (1), 836 (2), 914 (1), 924 (1), 928 (1)

complaisance 736 (1)

complaisant 83 (4), 736 (2), 739 (3), 756 (3)

complement 18 (3), 40 (1), 54 (2), 54 (6), 58 (1), 74 (4), 78 (1), 89 (2), 270 (1)

complementary 12 (2), 54 (3), 85 (5)

complete 52 (4), 54 (3), 54 (6), 149 (3), 165 (4), 203 (5), 600 (4), 635 (3), 646 (3), 646 (5), 725 (4), 725 (5)

complete answer 479 (1)

complete, be 54 (5), 78 (5), 637 (5)

complete idiot 501 (1)

complete set 52 (2), 632 (3)

complete victory 727 (2)

complete works 589 (2), 589 (5)

completed 669 (8), 725 (4), 727 (4)

completely 32 (17), 52 (8), 54 (8)

completeness 32 (1), 52 (1), 54 (1), 69 (3), 74 (5), 89 (2), 236 (1), 725 (1)

completing 54 (3), 69 (4), 725 (3)

completion 54 (1), 54 (2), 67 (1), 69 (1), 157 (1), 165 (1), 165 (3), 635 (1), 654 (2), 669 (3), 676 (1), 725 (1), 727 (1)

completive 34 (6), 38 (2), 54 (3), 69 (4), 725 (3)

complex 43 (6), 52 (1), 61 (8), 222 (6), 251 (9), 331 (1), 474 (4), 503 (5), 517 (3), 568 (2), 700 (4)

complex number 85 (1)

complexion 5 (3), 7 (1), 7 (2), 425 (3), 445 (5)

complexity 43 (4), 61 (3), 222 (1), 251 (3), 530 (2), 568 (1), 700 (1)

compliance 181 (1), 597 (1), 721 (1), 739 (1), 758 (1), 768 (1)

compliant 597 (4), 739 (3), 758 (2), 768 (2), 879 (3)

complicate 63 (5), 700 (6), 832 (3)

complicated 61 (8), 251 (9), 700 (4), 832 (2)

complication 61 (3), 651 (2), 700 (1), 832 (1)

complicity 706 (1), 775 (2), 936 (1)

compliment 866 (4), 866 (13), 884 (2), 886 (3), 923 (2), 923 (9), 925 (1), 925 (4)

complimentary 812 (4), 886 (2), 923 (5), 925 (3)

complimenting 866 (5)

compliments 886 (1), 889 (1)

comply 597 (6), 739 (4), 758 (3), 768 (3), 879 (4)

comply with 83 (7)

complying 739 (3)

component 40 (1), 43 (2), 53 (1), 58 (1), 58 (2), 89 (3), 193 (1), 319 (4), 630 (2)

component part 58 (1)

components 58 (1)

comport oneself 688 (4)

compos mentis 502 (2)

compose 43 (7), 50 (4), 54 (6), 56 (3), 56 (5), 62 (4), 74 (11), 78 (4), 164 (7), 413 (8), 586 (8), 587 (7), 823 (7)

compose differences 720 (4), 770 (2)

compose music 56 (5), 410 (9), 413 (8)

compose oneself 669 (13), 823 (5)

composed 177 (3), 587 (6), 823 (3), 865 (2)

composed, be 823 (5)

composed of 56 (2)

composer 164 (4), 413 (1)

composing 56 (1), 56 (2), 58 (2), 78 (2), 78 (3)

composite 43 (6), 45 (5), 50 (4), 101 (2)

composition 43 (3), 50 (1), 50 (2), 56 (1), 62 (1), 74 (1), 74 (7), 78 (1), 164 (1), 164 (2), 331 (1), 412 (1), 412 (4), 553 (1), 586 (1), 587 (1), 844 (3)

compositor 587 (5)

composure 823 (1), 865 (1)

compote 301 (17)

compound 43 (3), 43 (7), 50 (2), 56 (5), 164 (2), 185 (1), 235 (1)

compound interest 803 (2)

comprehend 56 (4), 78 (5), 490 (8), 516 (5)

comprehensible 516 (2), 701 (3)

comprehension 78 (1), 490 (1)

comprehensive 32 (5), 52 (7), 54 (3), 78 (2), 79 (3), 534 (5)

comprehensive school 539 (2)

comprehensiveness 78 (1)

compress 37 (4), 45 (13), 198 (7), 204 (5), 206 (7), 324 (6), 569 (3), 658 (9)

compressed 198 (4), 204 (3)

compressible 198 (4), 325 (2), 327 (2)

compression 33 (1), 37 (2), 160 (3), 198 (2), 204 (2), 206 (3), 264 (1), 569 (1), 592 (1), 747 (2), 778 (1)

compressive 198 (5)

compressor 198 (3), 264 (2)

comprise 45 (9), 56 (4), 78 (5), 79 (5), 224 (5), 773 (4)

comprised in, be 78 (4)

comprising 78 (1), 78 (2)

compromise 12 (1), 24 (4), 30 (2), 30 (5), 31 (2), 31 (5), 150 (2), 151 (3), 177 (1), 601 (1), 601 (4), 625 (6), 661 (9), 706 (1), 719 (1), 719 (4), 734 (1), 734 (5), 758 (1), 765 (1), 765 (5), 766 (4), 770 (1), 770 (2), 823 (6), 926 (7), 941 (1)

compromising 601 (3), 867 (5), 926 (5)

Comptometer 86 (6)

compulsion 16 (1), 156 (2), 160 (1), 503 (2), 596 (1), 606 (1), 735 (2), 737 (1), 740 (1), 745 (2), 747 (1), 747 (2), 761 (1)

compulsive 596 (4), 735 (5), 737 (5), 740 (2)

compulsorily 740 (4)

compulsory 596 (4), 627 (5), 740 (2), 917 (6)

compunction 830 (1), 905 (1), 939 (1)

compunctious 905 (4)

computable 86 (8), 465 (10)

concubine 952 (3)

concur 24 (9), 89 (4), 123 (4), 181 (3), 219 (3), 488 (6)

concurrence 45 (1), 74 (2), 89 (1), 123 (1), 154 (1), 181 (1), 293 (1), 488 (1)

concurrent 24 (5), 181 (2), 219 (2)

concurrently 123 (5), 181 (4)

concurring 488 (4)

concuss 279 (9), 375 (6)

concussion 279 (1)

condemn 362 (10), 479 (3), 480 (5), 899 (6), 924 (10), 961 (3), 963 (8), 977 (3)

condemnable 914 (3)

condemnation 924 (2), 961 (1), 963 (1)

condemnatory 928 (5)

condemned 479 (2), 596 (6), 655 (6), 825 (6), 899 (5), 936 (3), 961 (2), 977 (2)

condemned cell 748 (2)

condemning 924 (6)

condensation 45 (1), 48 (1), 324 (2), 341 (1), 354 (2)

condense 36 (5), 198 (6), 198 (7), 324 (6), 569 (3), 592 (5)

condensed 198 (4), 324 (4), 569 (2)

condescend 758 (3), 867 (10), 871 (5), 872 (5), 884 (5)

condescending 871 (4), 872 (3), 884 (3)

condescension 871 (1), 872 (1)

condiment 301 (9), 301 (21), 388 (1), 389 (1)

condition 7 (1), 468 (1), 468 (3), 534 (7), 610 (8), 650 (1), 651 (2), 766 (1), 917 (11)

conditional 7 (3), 468 (2), 474 (4), 747 (4), 766 (2)

conditionally 7 (5), 8 (6), 468 (4), 766 (5)

conditioned 596 (5), 766 (2)

conditioned reflex 610 (3)

conditioning 534 (1), 610 (3)

conditions 8 (1), 110 (1), 468 (1), 627 (1), 751 (2), 766 (1)

condole 836 (5), 905 (6)

condolence 836 (2), 897 (1), 905 (2)

condom 172 (2)

condone 823 (6), 909 (4)

condoned 909 (3)

condoning 909 (2)

conduce 156 (10), 179 (3), 180 (3), 181 (3), 471 (5), 640 (4), 642 (3), 703 (5), 756 (5)

conducive 179 (2), 628 (3)

conduct 64 (3), 89 (4), 273 (12), 283 (3), 413 (9), 445 (5), 610 (2), 676 (1), 688 (1), 688 (5), 689 (1). 689 (4), 689 (5), 848 (2)

conduct oneself 688 (4)

conduction 160 (5)

conductivity 265 (1)

conductor 23 (2), 117 (3), 160 (5), 268 (5), 413 (3), 690 (2)

conduit 255 (2), 262 (1), 263 (9), 297 (2), 298 (3), 305 (1), 339 (1), 341 (3), 350 (2), 351 (1), 624 (2), 624 (4)

cone 252 (4), 366 (7)

confection 43 (3), 164 (2)

confectioner 633 (3)

confectionery 301 (18), 301 (23), 392 (2)

confederacy 706 (2), 708 (3)

confederate 706 (4), 707 (1), 707 (3), 708 (6)

confederation 706 (2), 708 (3), 733 (6)

confer 475 (11), 584 (7), 691 (5), 766 (4), 781 (7)

confer a right 915 (8)

confer an honour 866 (14)

confer ownership on 780 (3)

conference 74 (2), 415 (2), 459 (1), 538 (4), 584 (3), 691 (1), 692 (1), 706 (1), 720 (1)

conferring 584 (5)

confess 466 (7), 485 (7), 488 (6), 524 (9), 526 (6), 532 (5), 540 (3), 928 (8), 936 (4), 939 (4), 941 (6), 961 (3), 988 (10)

confess the truth 540 (3)

confessed 526 (2)

confession 466 (2), 485 (2), 488 (1), 526 (1), 532 (1), 936 (1), 939 (1), 941 (3), 985 (2)

confessional 485 (6), 990 (4)

confessions 590 (3)

confessor 939 (2), 979 (4), 986 (3)

confetti 33 (3)

confidant 537 (1)

confide 526 (5), 699 (4), 852 (6)

confide in 691 (5)

confidence 473 (2), 485 (1), 507 (1), 524 (1), 530 (1), 660 (1), 852 (1)

confidence man 545 (4)

confidence trick 542 (2), 788 (4)

confident 473 (5), 485 (4), 507 (2), 532 (4), 852 (4), 855 (5)

confidential 525 (3)

confiding 487 (2), 699 (3)

configuration 243 (1)

confine 234 (5), 236 (3), 525 (7), 747 (10), 883 (10)

confined 232 (2), 747 (4), 747 (6)

confinement 167 (2), 747 (3), 883 (2)

confines 184 (1), 185 (1)

confirm 153 (8), 162 (12), 466 (8), 473 (9), 480 (5), 488 (3), 532 (5), 758 (3), 764 (4), 915 (8), 927 (5), 988 (10)

confirmation 466 (1), 473 (1), 488 (1), 532 (1), 758 (1), 765 (1), 988 (4) confirmatory 466 (5)

confirmed 153 (5), 488 (5), 610 (7), 915 (2)

confirmed habit 610 (1)

confirmed liar 545 (2)

confiscate 786 (10), 963 (8)

confiscation 786 (2), 963 (4)

confiscator 786 (4)

conflagration 379 (2), 381 (2)

conflict 14 (1), 15 (6), 25 (1), 25 (6), 182 (1), 704 (1), 709 (3), 709 (7), 716 (1)

conflict with 14 (4), 182 (3)

conflicting 25 (4), 704 (3), 881 (3)

confluence 45 (1), 289 (1), 293 (1), 350 (2)

conform 16 (3), 20 (7), 24 (10), 83 (7), 143 (6), 488 (7), 739 (4), 768 (3), 848 (7)

conform to 83 (7)

conformable 20 (4), 24 (5), 81 (3), 83 (4), 768 (2), 976 (8)

conformably 83 (10)

conformance 24 (2), 181 (1)

conformation 24 (4), 83 (1), 243 (1)

conforming 81 (3), 83 (4), 181 (2), 739 (3), 979 (6)

conforming to 24 (5)

conformism 610 (2)

conformist 20 (3), 83 (3), 488 (3), 610 (4), 979 (4)

conformity 16 (1), 20 (1), 24 (2), 81 (2), 83 (1), 610 (1), 610 (2), 882 (2), 979 (1)

confound 63 (3), 63 (5), 479 (3), 727 (10), 854 (12), 864 (7)

confound it 899 (8)

confounded 645 (5)

confraternity 708 (4)

confront 189 (4), 237 (5), 240 (3), 462 (3), 704 (5), 715 (3)

confront with 759 (3)

confronting 240 (2)

Confucianism 973 (3)

confuse 63 (3), 63 (5), 440 (5), 456 (8), 464 (4), 474 (9), 517 (6)

confused 43 (6), 61 (7), 444 (3), 464 (2), 477 (6), 491 (4), 568 (2)

confusedly 17 (3), 61 (12)

confusing 474 (4)

confusion 43 (4), 61 (2), 165 (2), 503 (2), 557 (1), 645 (1), 872 (2)

confutation 460 (2), 467 (1), 479 (1), 533 (1), 927 (1)

confute 460 (5), 467 (4), 475 (11), 479 (3), 486 (8), 489 (5), 533 (3), 613 (3), 704 (4), 709 (7), 878 (6), 928 (8)

confuted 467 (3), 479 (2), 495 (4)

confuted, be 479 (4)

conga 837 (14)

congeal 324 (6), 354 (6), 382 (6)

congealing 324 (5)

congealment 48 (1), 324 (2)

congenial 24 (5), 376 (3), 880 (6), 887 (11)

congeniality 24 (4)

congenital 5 (7), 817 (2)

congenital idiocy 503 (1)

congenital idiot 504 (1)

congest 637 (5)

congested 637 (3)

congestion 74 (5), 637 (1)

conglomerate 74 (10), 74 (11), 324 (3), 708 (5)

congratulate 835 (6), 886 (3), 923 (10)

congratulate oneself 824 (6), 835 (6), 871 (6)

congratulation 876 (1), 886 (1)

congratulations 835 (1), 886 (1)

congratulatory 886 (2)

congregate 48 (3), 74 (10), 104 (6), 200 (5), 289 (4), 293 (3), 295 (6), 297 (7)

congregated 50 (3)

congregation 74 (2), 692 (1), 708 (4), 976 (6), 981 (8), 987 (1)

congress 692 (1), 692 (2)

congruent 13 (2), 28 (7), 245 (2)

congruent, be 13 (3)

congruity 18 (1), 245 (1)

congruous 24 (5), 245 (2)

conic 252 (5)

conic section 248 (2)

conical 252 (5), 256 (9), 293 (2)

conifer 366 (4)

conjectural 512 (4)

conjecture 461 (2), 471 (6), 474 (1), 480 (6), 485 (3), 512 (2), 512 (6), 524 (3)

conjoin 38 (3), 45 (9)

conjointly 45 (15)

conjugal 887 (9), 894 (9)

conjugality 894 (1)

conjugate 90 (2), 564 (4)

conjugation 564 (1)

conjunction 45 (1), 181 (1), 202 (1), 564 (2)

conjunctive 45 (6), 564 (3)

conjuncture 8 (2)

conjure 542 (8), 761 (7), 983 (10)

conjure up 505 (8)

conjuring 542 (3), 542 (6), 983 (7)

conjuror 545 (5), 594 (10), 983 (5)

connect 9 (8), 45 (10), 62 (4), 71 (6)

connect with 9 (8)

connected 9 (5), 45 (5), 50 (3)

connectedness 9 (1), 48 (1)

connection 9 (1), 11 (1), 45 (1), 47 (1), 48 (1), 706 (2)

connective 47 (1)

connivance 706 (1), 734 (1), 736 (1), 756 (1)

connive 181 (3), 706 (4), 736 (3), 756 (5), 758 (3), 909 (4)

connive at 458 (5), 703 (6), 734 (5), 914 (6)

conniving 181 (2), 736 (2), 756 (3), 758 (2)

connoisseur 74 (8), 301 (6), 492 (3), 504 (3), 696 (2), 846 (2)

connotation 514 (2), 518 (1), 547 (1)

connotative 547 (15)

connote 514 (5), 523 (6), 547 (18)

conquer 308 (5), 727 (9), 786 (6), 786 (7)

conquered, the 728 (3)

conquering hero 727 (3)

conqueror 727 (3), 776 (1)

conquest 727 (2), 728 (2), 745 (1), 887 (5)

conquistador 727 (3)

consanguineous 11 (5)

consanguinity 9 (1), 11 (1), 169 (2), 170 (3)

conscience 457 (1), 490 (1); 596 (1), 612 (1), 740 (1), 917 (2)

conscience-stricken 830 (2), 939 (3)

conscientious 457 (3), 768 (2), 862 (3), 917 (5), 929 (3), 929 (4)

conscientious objection 738 (1)

conscientious objector 705 (1), 717 (2)

Conscious 320 (2), 374 (3), 447 (5), 490 (5)

conscious of 819 (2)

conscious of, be 490 (8)

consciousness 374 (1), 447 (1), 490 (1)

conscript 718 (10), 722 (4), 740 (3)

conscript army 722 (6)

conscription 718 (5), 740 (1), 745 (2)

consecrate 759 (3), 781 (7), 979 (12), 981 (12), 985 (8), 988 (10)

consecrate to 673 (3)

consecrated 979 (8), 986 (11), 968 (8)

consecration 759 (1), 866 (5), 979 (2), 981 (6), 985 (2), 988 (4)

consecutive 9 (5), 65 (2), 71 (4)

consensus 181 (1), 488 (2), 710 (1)

consent 24 (1), 24 (9), 181 (1), 488 (1), 488 (6), 488 (8), 597 (1), 597 (6), 612 (13), 721 (1), 736 (3), 739 (4), 756 (1), 756 (5), 758 (1), 758 (3), 923 (1)

consenting 488 (4), 597 (4), 758 (2)

consenting party 488 (3), 765 (3)

consentingly 488 (9)

consequence 24 (2), 65 (1), 67 (1), 154 (1), 157 (1), 638 (1)

consequent 65 (2), 157 (1)

consequent upon 157 (3)

consequential 154 (3), 157 (3), 478 (2)

consequently 157 (7), 475 (13)

conservancy 666 (1)

conservation 144 (1), 366 (3), 660 (2), 666 (1), 814 (1)

conservationist 666 (2), 814 (1)

conservatism 144 (1), 610 (1)

conservative 127 (7), 144 (1), 144 (2), 483 (2), 666 (3), 708 (2), 708 (7), 858 (2)

conservative estimate 483 (1)

conservatoire 539 (1)

conservator 666 (2)

conservatory 194 (23), 370 (3)

conserve 46 (9), 632 (5), 660 (8), 666 (5)

conserved 666 (4)

conserving 666 (3)

consider 449 (8), 455 (6), 459 (13), 463 (3), 480 (6)

consider as 485 (8)

consider beneath one 922 (5)

considerable 3 (3), 32 (4), 104 (4), 195 (6), 638 (5)

considerably 32 (17)

considerate 455 (2), 457 (3), 848 (6), 884 (4), 897 (4), 931 (2)

consideration 449 (2), 455 (1), 480 (2), 638 (1), 781 (2), 846 (1), 884 (1), 897 (1), 920 (1), 931 (1)

considered 608 (2)

consign 272 (8), 751 (4), 781 (7)

consign to earth 364 (9)

consignee 690 (3), 754 (1), 755 (1), 782 (2), 792 (2), 798 (1)

consignment 272 (3), 780 (1)

consist in 1 (6)

consist of 56 (4), 78 (5)

consistency 16 (1), 24 (2), 81 (2), 324 (1), 494 (1)

consistent 16 (2), 24 (5), 475 (7), 494 (4)

consistent, be 24 (9), 494 (7)

consistent with 24 (5), 83 (4)

consisting of 78 (2)

consistory 985 (5)

consolation 831 (1), 905 (2)

consolation prize 729 (1)

consolatory 831 (2)

console 194 (5), 218 (12), 831 (3), 833 (8), 905 (6)

console oneself 831 (4)

consolidate 74 (11), 324 (6), 592 (5)

consolidation 45 (1), 48 (1)

consoling 831 (2)

consomme 301 (14)

consonant 24 (5), 558 (3), 577 (1)

consort 89 (2), 894 (4)

consort with 89 (4)

consortium 706 (2)

conspectus 50 (1), 52 (1), 592 (1)

conspicuous 443 (3), 522 (4), 638 (6), 866 (9)

conspicuous, be 522 (9)

conspicuous expenditure 815 (1)

conspicuously 32 (19)

conspicuousness 443 (1)

conspiracy 181 (1), 525 (2), 623 (4), 706 (1), 765 (1)

conspirator 545 (1), 623 (5)

conspiratorial 525 (5), 623 (7)

conspire 50 (4), 181 (3), 525 (9), 623 (9), 706 (4)

constable 741 (6), 955 (3)

constabulary 955 (3)

constancy 599 (1), 600 (1), 739 (2), 929 (1)

constant 13 (1), 13 (2), 16 (2), 81 (3), 85 (1), 113 (4), 115 (2), 139 (2), 153 (2), 153 (4), 494 (6), 599 (2), 600 (3), 739 (3), 929 (4)

constant loser 731 (3)

constant supply 632 (1)

constantly 139 (5)

constellation 74 (3), 321 (4), 866 (6)

consternation 854 (1), 864 (1)

constipate 324 (6)

constipating 198 (5), 324 (5)

constipation 264 (1), 302 (3), 324 (2), 651 (7)

constituency 184 (3), 605 (3)

constituent 53 (1), 58 (1), 58 (2), 78 (3)

constituents 193 (1)

constitute 56 (3), 58 (3), 78 (4)

constituting 56 (2)

constitution 5 (3), 56 (1), 68 (1), 78 (1), 331 (1), 693 (1), 733 (6), 953 (1)

constitutional 5 (8), 733 (9), 915 (2), 953 (5)

constitutional government 733 (4)

constitutionalism 953 (1)

constrain 740 (3)

constraining 740 (2)

constraint 745 (1), 747 (1)

constrict 45 (13), 198 (7)

constricted 198 (4)

constriction 198 (2), 206 (3), 747 (2)

constrictor 198 (3)

construct 56 (5), 164 (7), 243 (5)

construct a plot 590 (7)

construction 56 (1), 62 (1), 164 (1), 331 (1), 514 (2), 520 (1), 554 (1)

constructive 164 (5), 466 (5), 703 (4)

constructive criticism 691 (1)

constructor 164 (4)

construe 520 (8), 564 (4)

construing 564 (1)

consul 690 (4), 741 (6)

consulate 733 (5), 754 (3)

consulship 733 (5)

consult 449 (8), 584 (7), 691 (5)

consultant 500 (1), 511 (4), 537 (1), 658 (14), 691 (2), 696 (2)

consultation 459 (1), 584 (3), 691 (1), 706 (1)

consultative 584 (5), 691 (3)

consultative body 691 (2)

consumable 673 (2)

consume 51 (5), 165 (6), 165 (10), 333 (3), 627 (6), 634 (4), 655 (9), 673 (3), 673 (5), 806 (4)

consume time 108 (8)

consumed 634 (3), 673 (2)

consumed with 818 (4)

consumer 301 (6), 792 (2)

consumer demand 792 (1)

consumer goods 795 (1)

consuming 165 (4)

consummate 32 (13), 54 (3), 69 (6), 646 (3), 646 (5), 725 (6)

consummation 54 (1), 69 (1), 725 (1)

consumption 37 (1), 206 (2), 299 (1), 301 (1), 627 (1), 634 (1), 651 (8), 673 (1), 772 (1)

consumptive 198 (4), 206 (5), 651 (18), 651 (22)

contact 45 (1), 45 (10), 202 (1), 378 (1), 524 (4), 524 (10), 588 (2)

contact lens 442 (2)

contact print 22 (1)

contagion 178 (1), 272 (1), 651 (4), 651 (5), 653 (1)

contagious 178 (2), 272 (5), 651 (22), 653 (3)

contain 56 (4), 78 (5), 230 (3), 773 (4), 778 (5)

contained 232 (2), 778 (4)

contained in, be 78 (4)

container 194 (1), 272 (3), 273 (1), 632 (2)

containerize 193 (2), 272 (7)

containing 56 (2), 78 (2), 194 (24)

containing air 340 (5)

containment 230 (1), 232 (1)

contaminate 43 (8), 272 (6), 641 (7), 649 (9), 655 (9)

contaminated 651 (22)

contamination 43 (1), 272 (1), 645 (1), 649 (1), 655 (3)

contemplate 438 (9), 449 (8), 507 (4), 617 (5), 981 (11)

contemplation 438 (3), 449 (2), 455 (1), 507 (1), 979 (1), 981 (1), 981 (4)

contemplative 449 (5), 979 (4), 979 (6), 981 (8), 986 (12)

contemporary 89 (3), 121 (2), 123 (2), 123 (3), 126 (6)

contempt 871 (1), 878 (1), 899 (2), 921 (1), 921 (2), 922 (1), 926 (1), 980 (1)

contemptibility 922 (2)

contemptible 35 (4), 639 (6), 645 (2), 849 (2), 867 (4), 867 (5), 921 (4), 922 (4), 930 (5)

contemptuous 878 (4), 922 (3), 926 (5)

contemptuously 922 (7)

contend 532 (5), 704 (4), 716 (10), 718 (12), 759 (4)

contend with 715 (3)

contender 162 (4), 268 (4), 460 (3), 461 (5), 671 (2), 702 (5), 704 (2), 705 (1), 709 (5), 716 (8), 722 (1), 837 (16), 881 (2)

contending 200 (4), 704 (3), 716 (9)

content 376 (2), 376 (4), 597 (4), 635 (1), 635 (5), 635 (6), 683 (2), 719 (4), 823 (1), 824 (3), 824 (4), 826 (3), 828 (1), 828 (2), 828 (5), 833 (1), 833 (8), 923 (1), 923 (5)

content, be 635 (8), 828 (4)

contented 635 (5), 828 (2)

contentedly 828 (6)

contentedness 828 (1)

contenting 635 (3), 828 (3)

contention 459 (3), 704 (1), 709 (2), 709 (3), 716 (1), 912 (1)

contentious 709 (6), 716 (9)

contentiousness 709 (2)

contentment 828 (1)

contents 26 (2), 32 (2), 74 (6), 193 (1), 224 (2), 272 (3), 452 (1), 514 (1), 777 (1), 795 (1)

contest 162 (3), 267 (5), 716 (2), 716 (10), 837 (6)

contest at law 959 (7)

contestant 705 (1), 716 (8)

contested 959 (6)

contesting 959 (5)

context 8 (1), 9 (1), 89 (2), 514 (2)

contextual 8 (3), 9 (5)

contextually 9 (9)

contiguity 45 (1), 200 (1), 200 (3), 202 (1)

contiguous 200 (4), 202 (2)

contiguous, be 183 (7), 200 (5), 202 (3), 378 (7)

contiguously 202 (5)

continence 942 (1), 950 (1)

continent 184 (1), 344 (1), 950 (5)

continental 59 (2), 59 (4), 184 (5), 191 (1), 344 (7)

contingency 6 (1), 8 (2), 154 (1), 159 (1), 469 (1), 474 (1), 507 (1)

contingent 8 (3), 53 (1), 154 (3), 157 (3), 180 (2), 469 (2), 474 (4), 766 (2)

contingent, be 474 (8)

continual 71 (4), 115 (2), 139 (2), 146 (2)

continually 139 (5)

continuance 65 (1), 71 (1), 111 (1), 113 (2), 115 (1), 144 (1), 146 (1), 600 (1), 610 (1)

continuation 40 (1), 62 (1), 65 (1), 67 (1), 71 (1), 146 (1)

continue 71 (5), 71 (6), 108 (7), 113 (6), 146 (3), 146 (4), 154 (6), 203 (8), 600 (4)

continued 71 (4)

continuing 71 (4), 108 (4), 144 (2)

continuity 16 (1), 48 (1), 60 (1), 62 (1), 65 (1), 71 (1), 106 (2), 139 (1), 146 (1), 164 (1), 202 (1), 265 (1), 285 (1), 445 (3)

continuity girl 594 (11)

continuo 410 (1)

continuous 36 (3), 65 (2), 71 (4), 115 (2), 141 (4), 146 (2), 202 (2), 726 (2)

continuous tense 111 (1)

continuous time 71 (1)

continuously 71 (7), 115 (5), 139 (5)

continuum 71 (1), 183 (1)

contort 246 (5)

contorted 251 (4)

contortion 246 (1)

contortionist 162 (4)

contour 233 (1), 243 (1), 445 (6)

contra- 14 (3)

contraband 757 (3), 790 (1), 954 (5)

contraception 161 (1), 172 (2), 658 (7), 702 (1)

contraceptive 172 (2), 182 (2)

contraceptive pill 658 (7)

contract 37 (4), 37 (5), 196 (12), 198 (6), 198 (7), 204 (5), 206 (7), 488 (6), 569 (3), 651 (23), 672 (1), 764 (4), 765 (1), 765 (5), 766 (4), 791 (6)

contracted 33 (6), 196 (9), 198 (4), 204 (3), 206 (4), 264 (4), 569 (2)

contractile 198 (4)

contractility 198 (2)

contracting 198 (1)

contraction 33 (1), 37 (1), 37 (2), 198 (1), 204 (2), 206 (3), 264 (1), 559 (1), 592 (1)

contractional 198 (5)

contractions 167 (2)

contractor 671 (2), 676 (3), 765 (3)

contractual 24 (5), 765 (4)

contradict 14 (4), 25 (6), 460 (5), 467 (4), 479 (3), 489 (5), 533 (1), 704 (4)

contradicting 460 (4)

contradiction 14 (1), 25 (1), 294 (1), 460 (2), 479 (1), 489 (1), 533 (1), 704 (1)

contradictory 14 (3), 25 (4), 477 (5), 533 (2), 704 (3)

contradistinction 14 (1)

contralto 404 (1), 413 (4)

contraposition 240 (1)

contraption 623 (3), 630 (1)

contrapuntal 412 (7)

contraries 14 (2), 704 (2)

contrariety 14 (1), 15 (1), 17 (1), 19 (1), 25 (1), 84 (1), 182 (1), 294 (1), 317

converter 143 (3)

convertible 13 (2), 274 (11), 673 (2)

convex 195 (8), 197 (3), 252 (5), 253 (7)

convex, be 197 (4), 252 (6), 253 (9)

convexity 248 (1), 252 (1), 253 (1)

convey 265 (5), 272 (6), 273 (12), 514 (5), 524 (10), 780 (3)

convey a meaning 514 (5)

conveyance 267 (6), 272 (2), 274 (1), 289 (1), 780 (1), 781 (1)

conveyancer 958 (2)

conveyancing 780 (1)

conveying 289 (2)

conveyor 273 (1), 274 (15)

conveyor belt 272 (2), 274 (15)

convict 479 (3), 750 (1), 904 (3), 961 (3)

convicted 479 (2), 936 (3), 961 (2)

conviction 473 (2), 485 (1), 534 (1), 852 (1), 924 (2), 961 (1)

convince 147 (7), 473 (9), 478 (4), 485 (9), 612 (10), 979 (11)

convince oneself 473 (7), 485 (9)

convinced 473 (5), 485 (4)

convinced, be 485 (7)

convincing 471 (3), 473 (5), 478 (2), 485 (5), 590 (6)

convivial 833 (3), 882 (6)

conviviality 833 (1), 837 (2), 882 (2)

convocation 74 (2), 692 (1), 985 (5)

convoke 74 (11)

convoluted 246 (3), 251 (4)

convolution 61 (3), 222 (1), 246 (1), 248 (1), 248 (2), 250 (3), 251 (1)

convoy 89 (2), 89 (4), 273 (12), 660 (2), 660 (8), 749 (1)

convulse 63 (3)

convulsion 61 (1), 61 (4), 63 (1), 149 (1), 176 (2), 318 (2), 377 (2)

convulsive 176 (5), 318 (4)

coo 409 (3)

cook 301 (5), 301 (40), 381 (8), 633 (3), 669 (12), 742 (2)

cook for 633 (5)

cook the books 788 (8), 808 (5)

cook up 541 (8), 623 (9)

cooked 301 (34), 381 (6)

cooked meats 301 (14)

cooker 383 (1)

cookery 301 (5), 357 (3), 381 (1)

cookery book 301 (5)

cookhouse 194 (19), 301 (5)

cooking 155 (2), 301 (5)

cool 37 (4), 177 (3), 177 (6), 380 (1), 380 (5), 382 (6), 412 (7), 429 (2), 498 (5), 613 (3), 685 (2), 820 (3), 823 (3), 831 (3), 860 (2), 878 (5), 883 (5)

cool cheek 878 (2)

cool down 502 (3), 823 (7)

cool-headed 823 (3)

cool off 685 (4), 860 (4)

cool one down 685 (4)

cool one's heels 136 (5)

coolant 384 (1)

cooled 340 (5), 382 (4)

cooler 384 (1)

coolie 273 (2)

cooling 352 (6), 382 (1), 685 (2)

cooling off 860 (2)

coolness 380 (1), 820 (1), 823 (1), 860 (1), 881 (1)

coop 192 (10), 369 (3)

coop up 747 (10)

cooper 686 (3)

cooperate 24 (9), 50 (4), 89 (4), 181 (3), 488 (6), 597 (6), 703 (5), 706 (4), 708 (8), 710 (3), 765 (5), 775 (5)

cooperating 739 (3)

cooperation 24 (1), 54 (1), 151 (1), 156 (1), 173 (1), 181 (1), 597 (1), 628 (1), 703 (1), 706 (1), 710 (1), 765 (1), 775 (1), 880 (1)

cooperative 24 (5), 45 (5), 50 (3), 89 (3), 181 (2), 488 (4), 597 (4), 615 (3), 703 (4), 706 (2), 706 (3), 708 (3), 708 (6), 775 (1), 775 (4)

cooperatively 706 (5)

cooperator 707 (2)

coordinate 28 (7), 62 (5), 465 (4), 465 (5)

coordinates 228 (9)

coordination 28 (4)

coot 365 (4)

cope 989 (2)

cope with 28 (9), 688 (5), 704 (5)

copied 20 (4)

copier 20 (3)

coping 213 (1)

copingstone 213 (1)

copious 171 (4), 635 (4)

copper 194 (14), 383 (2), 430 (1), 432 (1)

copper-coloured 432 (2)

copper engraving 555 (1)

copperplate 586 (2), 586 (7)

coppers 797 (1)

coppery 432 (2)

coppice 366 (2)

copse 366 (2)

Coptic 976 (4)

copula 47 (1)

copulate 45 (14), 167 (7)

copulation 45 (3), 167 (1)

copulative 564 (3)

copulatory 45 (6)

copy 13 (1), 16 (1), 18 (3), 20 (1), 20 (6), 22 (1), 23 (1), 91 (1), 91 (3), 106 (4), 166 (3), 529 (1), 542 (5), 548 (1), 551 (4), 586 (1), 586 (3), 587 (2), 785 (2), 786 (7), 788 (7)

copy editor 589 (7)

copy from 20 (6)

copy out 20 (6), 586 (8)

copybook 23 (1), 23 (4), 83 (6), 586 (7)

copycat 20 (3), 83 (3)

copyhold 777 (3), 777 (5)

copyholder 776 (1)

copying 20 (1), 586 (1), 785 (1)

copyist 20 (3), 556 (1), 586 (5)

copyright 777 (2), 915 (1), 915 (5)

copywriter 528 (6), 589 (7)

coquetry 603 (1), 604 (2), 850 (1), 887 (2), 887 (3), 889 (2), 925 (1)

coquette 603 (3), 604 (4), 850 (3), 850 (5), 887 (4), 887 (15), 889 (7), 925 (2)

coquettish 604 (3), 850 (4), 887 (9), 889 (4)

cor Anglais 414 (6)

coral 125 (3), 365 (14), 431 (3), 844 (8)

coral reef 349 (1)

corbel 218 (12)

cord 47 (2), 47 (4), 208 (2)

cordage 47 (3)

corded 222 (6)

cordial 301 (27), 388 (1), 658 (6), 818 (3), 818 (6), 880 (6), 882 (6)

cordiality 597 (1), 818 (2), 880 (2), 882 (2)

cordon 230 (1), 233 (1), 235 (3), 264 (2)

cordon bleu 301 (5), 696 (1), 729 (2)

cordon off 232 (3), 235 (4)

cordon sanitaire 660 (2)

cords 228 (12)

corduroy 222 (4)

core 1 (3), 3 (2), 5 (2), 76 (1), 225 (2)

corer 263 (12)

cork 264 (2), 264 (6), 323 (1)

corkage 809 (1)

corkscrew 251 (2), 251 (10), 263 (11), 263 (12), 304 (2), 315 (5)

corm 366 (6)

corn 253 (2), 301 (22), 326 (1), 651 (14)

corn exchange 796 (1)

corn market 796 (1)

cornea 438 (2)

corner 8 (1), 185 (1), 247 (1), 247 (7), 255 (2), 314 (4), 527 (1), 727 (10), 773 (1), 792 (5), 964 (2)

corner shop 796 (3)

corner the market 135 (5), 773 (4)

cornered 247 (5), 700 (5)

cornered, be 596 (7)

cornering 314 (1), 792 (1)

cornerstone 218 (2), 638 (3)

cornet 252 (4), 414 (7), 722 (4), 741 (8)

cornetist 413 (2)

cornflakes 301 (22)

cornflower 435 (1)

cornice 213 (1), 844 (2)

cornucopia 171 (3), 632 (1), 635 (2), 813 (1)

corny 496 (3)

corny joke 839 (2)

corolla 366 (7)

corollary 40 (1), 89 (2), 157 (1), 475 (3), 480 (1)

corona 250 (3), 321 (8), 417 (1)

coronary 651 (9)

coronary thrombosis 651 (9)

coronation 751 (2), 866 (5), 876 (1)

coroner 957 (1)

coroner's court 956 (2)

coronet 228 (23), 743 (1)

corporal 319 (6), 741 (8)

corporal punishment 963 (2)

corporate 181 (2), 706 (3), 708 (6)

corporation 622 (1), 706 (2), 708 (5), 794 (1)

corporeal 319 (6)

corporeality 3 (1)

corps 74 (4), 722 (8)

corps de ballet 594 (9)

corpse 51 (2), 361 (3), 363 (1)

corpulence 195 (3), 205 (2)

corpulent 195 (8)

corpus 52 (1), 589 (2)

corpuscle 196 (2), 335 (3)

corpuscular 196 (11)

corral 74 (11), 232 (3), 235 (1), 369 (8)

corralled 747 (6)

correct 60 (2), 83 (6), 143 (6), 177 (6), 494 (4), 494 (6), 524 (9), 564 (3), 575 (3), 587 (7), 646 (5), 654 (10), 846 (3), 848 (5), 848 (6), 875 (6), 884 (3), 924 (11), 929 (3), 963 (8)

correct speech 557 (1)

correct time 117 (2)

correction 654 (2)

corrective 182 (2), 658 (1), 658 (17), 963 (6)

correctness 846 (1), 848 (2), 875 (2), 884 (1)

corrector 963 (5)

correlate 9 (7), 12 (3), 18 (3), 24 (10), 151 (3), 157 (6), 317 (5), 462 (3)

correlation 9 (2), 12 (1), 18 (1), 18 (3), 28 (4), 31 (1), 56 (1), 62 (2), 86 (4), 141 (1), 151 (1), 245 (1), 317 (2)

correlative 9 (5), 12 (2), 18 (3), 24 (5), 28 (8), 141 (4), 151 (2), 245 (2), 460 (4)

correlatively 12 (4)

correspond 9 (7), 12 (3), 24 (9), 83 (7), 219 (3), 524 (10), 586 (8), 588 (4), 882 (8)

correspond to 18 (7)

correspond with 588 (4)

correspondence 9 (2), 12 (1), 18 (1), 524 (2), 529 (3), 531 (2), 586 (3), 588 (1)

correspondence course 534 (2)

correspondent 460 (3), 524 (4), 529 (4), 588 (2), 589 (7), 754 (2), 782 (2) corresponding 12 (2), 24 (5), 28 (8), 219 (2)

corresponding to 9 (5), 18 (4), 460 (4)

correspondingly 18 (9)

corridor 68 (5), 194 (20), 624 (2)

corridor of time 113 (1)

corrie 255 (3)

corrigenda 589 (5)

corrigendum 495 (3)

corroborate 466 (8), 473 (9), 478 (4), 494 (7), 532 (5), 532 (6), 767 (6)

corroboration 466 (1), 488 (1), 532 (1)

corroborative 466 (5)

corrode 381 (10), 655 (9)

corrosion 655 (2)

corrosive 168 (1), 174 (6), 645 (3), 659 (3), 827 (3)

corrugate 259 (9), 262 (3)

corrugated 251 (7), 259 (4)

corrugation 251 (1), 259 (1), 262 (1)

corrupt 51 (5), 535 (3), 560 (4), 612 (12), 645 (6), 649 (6), 649 (9), 655 (5), 655 (8), 930 (6), 934 (4), 934 (8)

corrupted 51 (3)

corruptible 930 (6)

corruption 51 (2), 649 (1), 930 (1), 934 (1)

corsage 228 (3)

corsair 275 (2), 789 (2)

corset 198 (3), 198 (7), 228 (17), 748 (4)

cortege 71 (3), 278 (2), 364 (2)

cortex 226 (6), 447 (1)

cortisone 658 (7)

coruscate 417 (11)

corvette 722 (13)

cosh 279 (4), 279 (9), 723 (5)

cosine 85 (3)

cosmetic 339 (1), 357 (4), 396 (2), 425 (4), 431 (2), 843 (3)

cosmetic surgery 843 (1)

cosmetician 843 (5)

cosmic 32 (5), 321 (13), 417 (10)

cosmic dust 321 (4)

cosmogonic 321 (13)

cosmogony 321 (1)

cosmological 321 (13)

cosmology 321 (1)

cosmonaut 271 (4)

cosmopolitan 79 (4), 192 (18), 696 (2), 848 (3), 848 (6), 901 (4), 901 (6)

cosmos 52 (1), 321 (1)

cosset 889 (5)

cost 465 (13), 808 (5), 809 (2), 809 (5), 809 (6), 811 (1)

cost a fortune 811 (4)

cost a lot 811 (4)

cost-cutting 814 (2)

cost little 812 (5)

cost of living 86 (4), 806 (1), 809 (2)

cost one dear 811 (4)

costliness 811 (1)

costly 165 (4), 644 (7), 645 (3), 811 (2)

costs 31 (2), 806 (1), 963 (4)

costume 228 (9), 594 (6)

costumier 228 (28)

cosy 196 (8), 376 (4), 730 (5), 826 (2), 828 (2)

cosy chat 584 (2)

cot 218 (7)

cotangent 85 (3)

coterie 74 (3), 74 (4), 77 (1), 708 (1)

coterminous 69 (4)

cottage 192 (7)

cottage cheese 301 (24)

cottage industry 622 (1)

cottager 191 (2)

cotton 208 (2), 222 (4)

cotton wool 208 (2)

couch 216 (6), 218 (6), 218 (7)

cough 300 (11), 302 (1), 302 (6), 352 (7), 352 (11), 407 (4), 651 (8)

coughing 302 (1), 352 (7), 352 (9)

could be 469 (5)

couldn't care less 860 (4)

coulter 256 (5)

council 74 (2), 584 (3), 690 (1), 691 (2), 692 (1), 754 (1), 955 (1), 956 (1), 985 (5)

council chamber 692 (1)

councillor 690 (4), 692 (3), 741 (6)

counsel 664 (5), 691 (1), 691 (2), 691 (4), 754 (1), 958 (1)

counselling 691 (1)

counsellor 480 (3), 500 (1), 612 (5), 690 (4), 691 (2), 703 (3), 754 (1)

count 78 (5), 86 (1), 86 (11), 612 (8), 638 (7), 868 (5)

count as 150 (5)

count down 86 (11)

count for nothing 639 (7)

count heads 86 (11), 605 (8)

count on 485 (7), 852 (6)

count one's blessings 828 (4)

count one's steps 465 (11)

count out 57 (5), 919 (3)

count the cost 858 (3)

count the minutes 117 (7)

count up 86 (12)

count upon 471 (6)

count with 78 (6)

countable 86 (8)

countdown 68 (3), 86 (1)

counted 78 (3)

counted out 57 (3)

countenance 237 (2), 445 (5), 703 (6)

counter- 14 (3), 86 (7), 182 (2), 182 (3), 218 (5), 218 (12), 460 (4), 460 (5), 547 (13), 702 (10), 704 (4), 713 (10), 714 (3), 796 (3), 837 (15)

counter-espionage 459 (7)

counter-revolution 148 (1)

counter-revolutionary 705 (1), 738 (4)

counteract 14 (4), 31 (5), 161 (9), 163 (10), 177 (7),

182 (3), 280 (3), 467 (4), 702 (10), 704 (4)

counteracting 182 (2), 460 (4), 467 (2), 658 (17), 702 (6), 704 (3)

counteraction 14 (1), 157 (1), 182 (1), 713 (1), 762 (1)

counteractive 14 (3), 702 (6)

counterattack 712 (1), 712 (7), 714 (1)

counterblast 182 (1), 714 (1)

countercharge 927 (1)

counterclaim 761 (1), 762 (1)

counterevidence 467 (1)

counterfeit 20 (6), 22 (1), 150 (4), 541 (2), 541 (3), 541 (6), 541 (8), 542 (5), 542 (7), 542 (8), 543 (5), 797 (10)

counterfeit money 797 (6)

counterfeiter 20 (3), 545 (1), 789 (3)

counterfoil 547 (13)

countermand 737 (1), 737 (6), 752 (1), 752 (4), 757 (1), 757 (4)

countermarch 286 (5), 718 (11)

counterorder 737 (1), 752 (1)

counterpane 226 (8)

counterpart 13 (1), 18 (3), 28 (6)

counterpetition 762 (1)

counterpoint 14 (1), 410 (1)

counterpoise 28 (4), 28 (10), 29 (1), 31 (2), 31 (5), 322 (1), 322 (5)

counters 86 (6)

countersign 460 (1), 466 (7), 488 (8), 547 (8), 547 (20)

countersigned 765 (4)

countersigner 765 (3)

countertenor 407 (1), 413 (4)

countervail 466 (8)

countervailing 467 (2)

countess 868 (5)

counting 78 (2), 86 (1)

counting heads 86 (1)

counting house 799 (1)

counting instrument 86 (6)

counting the cost or the risk 858 (2)

counting the risk 858 (1)

countless 104 (5), 107 (2)

countrified 192 (19)

country 184 (1), 184 (5), 344 (1), 733 (6)

country and western 412 (1)

country bumpkin 869 (6)

country cousin 869 (6)

country dance 837 (14)

country dancing 837 (13)

country-dweller 191 (1), 191 (3), 370 (4), 869 (5), 869 (6)

country folk 191 (5)

country house 192 (6)

country seat 192 (1)

countryfolk 869 (1)

countryman or woman 869 (6)

countryside 184 (3)

counts 80 (2)

county 184 (3), 733 (6)

County Court 956 (2)

county set 868 (2)

coup 623 (2), 676 (2)

coup de grace 69 (1), 165 (3), 362 (1), 725 (1)

coup de main 712 (1)

coup de théâtre 594 (2), 864 (2)

coup d'état 149 (1), 738 (2), 954 (3)

coupé 274 (11)

couple 18 (3), 45 (9), 45 (14), 90 (1), 90 (3), 894 (11)

coupled 45 (5), 89 (3)

couplet 90 (1), 593 (4)

coupling 45 (2), 47 (6)

courage 174 (1), 599 (1), 600 (2), 660 (1), 711 (1), 855 (1), 931 (1)

courageous 162 (10), 855 (4), 866 (8), 871 (3), 931 (2)

courageous, be 661 (8), 672 (3), 855 (6)

courageously 855 (9)

courier 268 (1), 268 (4), 273 (2), 520 (5), 524 (6), 529 (6), 742 (1)

course 71 (1), 146 (1), 179 (1), 207 (1), 265 (1), 267 (8), 267 (11), 277 (3), 281 (1), 285 (1), 301 (3), 301 (13), 350 (9), 624 (4), 658 (12)

course of action 623 (2)

course of events 154 (2)

course of studies 536 (2)

course of study 534 (3)

course of time 108 (1), 111 (1), 154 (2), 285 (1)

courser 273 (7), 277 (4), 365 (10)

court 89 (2), 192 (8), 263 (7), 438 (8), 619 (5), 692 (1), 724 (1), 742 (3), 761 (5), 848 (3), 859 (11), 887 (14), 887 (15), 889 (7), 925 (4), 956 (2), 963 (5)

court disaster 661 (8), 857 (4)

court dress 875 (2)

court jester 839 (3)

court-martial 956 (2)

Court of Appeal 956 (2)

court of justice 956 (2)

court of law 956 (2)

court officer 955 (2)

court shoe 228 (27)

courteous 455 (2), 848 (6), 872 (3), 882 (6), 884 (3), 897 (4), 920 (3), 931 (2)

courteous act 295 (1), 311 (2), 880 (2), 882 (2), 884 (2), 920 (2)

courteous, be 758 (3), 872 (5), 884 (5)

courteously 884 (8)

courtesan 373 (3), 952 (4)

courtesy 311 (2), 688 (1), 823 (1), 846 (1), 848 (2), 872 (1), 880 (2), 882 (2),

cramp **163** (10), **198** (7), **318** (2), **377** (2), **655** (9), **702** (8), **747** (1), **747** (7)

cramp one's style **161** (9), **636** (7), **702** (8)

cramped **196** (8), **576** (2), **636** (4), **747** (5)

cramping **636** (3), **702** (6), **747** (4)

crane **217** (3), **274** (15), **310** (2), **365** (4)

crane fly **365** (16)

crane one's neck **438** (9)

cranial **213** (4)

cranium **213** (3), **253** (4)

crank **84** (3), **218** (3), **315** (5), **501** (1), **504** (2), **513** (4), **602** (3), **851** (3)

crank up **669** (11)

crankiness **481** (5), **503** (5), **604** (1)

cranky **251** (4), **503** (8), **892** (3)

cranny **194** (4), **255** (2), **527** (1)

crapulence **949** (2)

crapulous **949** (9)

crash **149** (1), **165** (3), **271** (7), **279** (3), **309** (1), **309** (4), **400** (1), **400** (4), **402** (1), **402** (4), **728** (8), **805** (5)

crash dive **271** (1), **313** (1)

crash helmet **228** (23), **662** (3)

crash in **176** (7), **297** (7)

crash into **279** (8)

crash-land **271** (7)

crash landing **271** (1)

crashing **400** (3)

crass **32** (13), **522** (4), **847** (4)

crassness **847** (1)

crate **194** (6)

crater **255** (2), **263** (4), **321** (9)

cravat **47** (4), **228** (22)

crave **627** (6), **761** (5), **761** (6), **859** (11), **912** (3)

craven **856** (2), **856** (3)

craving **627** (4), **859** (1), **859** (7)

crawl **111** (3), **265** (4), **269** (3), **278** (1), **278** (4), **378** (8), **603** (5), **721** (4), **879** (4)

crawl with **104** (6)

crawler **879** (2)

crawling **104** (5), **278** (3), **649** (6), **721** (2), **879** (1), **879** (3)

crawling with **54** (4), **635** (5)

crayon **425** (8), **553** (6), **553** (8), **586** (4)

craze **437** (3), **503** (5), **503** (12), **604** (2), **610** (2), **848** (1), **859** (3)

crazed **503** (8)

craziness **503** (5)

crazy **246** (3), **481** (6), **497** (3), **499** (4), **503** (8), **849** (2)

crazy about **887** (10)

crazy paving **17** (1), **226** (7), **437** (2)

creak **401** (1), **407** (1)

creaking **407** (2)

cream **301** (24), **301** (30), **354** (1), **357** (4), **605** (7), **638** (3), **644** (2), **658** (8), **843** (3)

cream cheese **301** (24)

cream-coloured **433** (3)

cream cracker **301** (22)

creamed **534** (5)

creamy **354** (4), **357** (6), **390** (2), **425** (7), **427** (5), **433** (3)

crease **261** (1), **261** (3)

creased **261** (2), **835** (5)

create **156** (9), **164** (7), **243** (5), **513** (7), **866** (14), **891** (7)

create a role **594** (17)

create an opening **137** (7)

create deadlock **700** (6)

create discord **709** (8)

created **164** (6), **243** (3)

created being **365** (2)

creation **1** (1), **21** (1), **68** (1), **156** (1), **164** (1), **164** (2), **228** (8), **243** (2), **321** (1), **551** (1)

creative **21** (3), **156** (7), **164** (5), **171** (4), **513** (5)

creative worker **164** (4), **513** (4), **676** (3)

creative writer **589** (7)

creative writing **557** (3), **586** (1)

creativeness **21** (1), **513** (1)

creativity **513** (1)

creator **156** (2), **164** (4), **965** (3)

Creator, the **164** (4)

creature **3** (2), **164** (2), **365** (2), **371** (3), **628** (2), **879** (2)

creature of habit **610** (4)

creaturely **371** (6)

creche **539** (2)

credence **485** (1)

credential **466** (3), **548** (1), **767** (2), **923** (1)

credibility **471** (1), **485** (1)

credibility gap **25** (1)

credible **469** (2), **471** (3), **473** (5), **485** (5), **976** (8)

credibly **485** (11)

credit **158** (1), **178** (1), **485** (1), **485** (7), **703** (2), **764** (1), **784** (1), **784** (5), **800** (1), **802** (1), **802** (3), **803** (1), **808** (5), **866** (1), **907** (2), **907** (5), **915** (1), **915** (8), **923** (1), **923** (2)

credit account **785** (1)

credit card **785** (1), **802** (1)

credit company **784** (2)

credit note **802** (1)

credit side **771** (3)

credit squeeze **747** (2), **814** (1)

credit title **907** (2)

credit with **158** (3)

credit-worthy **800** (4)

creditable **644** (4), **866** (7), **923** (6)

credited **158** (2)

credited with, be **782** (5)

crediting **907** (3)

creditor **633** (2), **784** (3), **802** (2)

credits **445** (3), **802** (1), **807** (1)

creditworthiness 802 (1)
creditworthy 866 (7)
credo 485 (2), 973 (4), 976 (1)
credulity 487 (1), 542 (1), 612 (3)
credulous 481 (6), 485 (4), 487 (2), 544 (2)
credulous, be 485 (7), 487 (3), 612 (13)
credulous person 487 (1)
credulousness 487 (1), 612 (3)
creed 485 (2), 973 (4), 976 (1)
creedal 473 (4), 485 (6), 532 (4), 973 (9), 976 (8)
creek 345 (1)
creel 194 (6)
creep 113 (9), 259 (8), 265 (4), 278 (1), 278 (4), 378 (8), 523 (5), 525 (9), 879 (2), 879 (4), 925 (2)
creep in 297 (5)
creep out 298 (5)
creep up on 508 (5)
creeper 366 (6)
creeping 278 (3)
creeping flesh 259 (1)
creeps 378 (2)
creepy 541 (4), 854 (8), 879 (3)
creepy-crawly 365 (17), 659 (1)
cremate 364 (9), 381 (10)
cremation 364 (1), 381 (2)
crematorium 364 (1), 383 (1)
crenellated 260 (2)
Creole 59 (2), 191 (4), 557 (1)
creosote 226 (16), 666 (5)
crepe 428 (2), 547 (9)
crepe paper 631 (3)
crepuscular 129 (5)
crescendo 36 (1), 36 (6), 308 (1), 400 (1), 400 (3), 400 (5), 412 (8)
crescent 36 (3), 192 (8), 248 (2), 248 (3), 250 (4)
crescent moon 321 (9)
crescent-shaped 250 (6)
Crescent, the 973 (3)

cress 301 (20)
crest 34 (1), 209 (2), 213 (1), 213 (5), 259 (3), 547 (11), 868 (1)
crested 547 (16)
crestfallen 509 (2), 834 (5), 872 (4)
cretin 504 (1)
cretinism 503 (1)
cretinous 503 (7)
crevasse 201 (2)
crevice 201 (2)
crew 58 (1), 74 (4), 173 (3), 191 (2), 269 (10), 270 (1), 669 (11), 686 (4), 708 (1)
crib 20 (6), 22 (1), 218 (7), 520 (3)
cribbing 20 (1)
crick 377 (2)
cricket 365 (16), 837 (7)
cricketer 837 (16)
crime 676 (2), 738 (1), 914 (1), 930 (1), 930 (3), 934 (1), 934 (2), 936 (2), 954 (2)
crime story 590 (4)
crime wave 954 (3)
criminal 84 (3), 84 (5), 869 (7), 904 (3), 930 (5), 934 (6), 936 (3), 938 (2), 954 (2), 954 (6)
criminal bar 958 (5)
criminal court 956 (2)
criminal intent 617 (1)
criminal investigation 459 (6)
criminal law 953 (3)
criminal offence 954 (2)
criminal world 904 (3), 934 (1)
criminality 930 (1), 934 (1), 936 (1), 954 (2)
criminologist 459 (8)
criminology 954 (2)
crimp 251 (11), 260 (3)
crimped 251 (7)
crimson 431 (1), 431 (3), 431 (5)
crimson lake 431 (2)
cringe 311 (9), 721 (4), 739 (4), 745 (6), 856 (4), 879 (4)

cringing 879 (1), 879 (3)
crinkle 247 (7), 248 (5), 251 (11), 259 (9), 261 (1), 261 (3)
crinkled 259 (4)
crinkly 251 (7)
crinoline 228 (13)
cripple 161 (9), 163 (10), 651 (18), 655 (9), 702 (8)
crippled 55 (3), 161 (7), 163 (7)
crippling 655 (3)
crisis 8 (2), 137 (3), 154 (1), 236 (1), 286 (2), 627 (2), 638 (2), 661 (1), 700 (3), 821 (1)
crisp 251 (11), 259 (4), 326 (4), 326 (5), 330 (2), 390 (2), 569 (2)
crispness 330 (1)
crispy 330 (2)
crisscross 222 (1), 222 (6)
criterion 23 (1); 461 (4), 462 (1), 465 (5)
critic 480 (3), 489 (2), 520 (4), 591 (3), 829 (2), 846 (2), 924 (5)
critical 8 (2), 137 (6), 154 (5), 463 (2), 480 (4), 591 (4), 638 (5), 651 (21), 661 (3), 661 (4), 700 (4), 829 (3), 846 (3), 862 (3), 924 (6)
critical, be 829 (5)
critical moment 8 (2)
critical time 137 (3)
criticism 480 (2), 520 (1), 532 (1), 557 (3), 591 (2), 691 (1), 924 (2), 926 (1)
criticize 463 (3), 480 (6), 591 (5), 829 (5), 846 (4), 924 (10), 926 (6)
criticized 924 (7)
critique 463 (1), 480 (2), 520 (1), 591 (2)
croak 407 (4), 409 (3)
croaking 578 (2)
crochet 222 (3), 222 (9), 844 (4)
crock 194 (13)
crockery 194 (1), 381 (5)
crocodile 71 (3), 203 (3), 365 (13)

crocodile tears 541 (2), 836 (2)
croft 192 (6), 370 (2)
crofter 191 (2), 370 (4)
crone 133 (3)
crony 707 (3), 880 (5)
crook 218 (2), 220 (6), 247 (1), 247 (7), 248 (5), 282 (6), 789 (1), 904 (3), 938 (2), 989 (2)
crooked 220 (3), 246 (3), 247 (5), 282 (2), 523 (4), 698 (4), 845 (2), 930 (4)
crooked lawyer 958 (1)
crookedness 220 (1), 246 (1), 788 (5), 930 (1)
croon 401 (4), 413 (10)
crooner 413 (4), 594 (10)
crop 157 (2), 164 (2), 194 (3), 204 (5), 301 (37), 370 (1), 632 (1), 771 (2), 771 (7), 843 (2)
crop-full 54 (4)
crop up 68 (8), 154 (6), 159 (7)
cropping 301 (1)
croquet 837 (7)
crore 99 (5)
crosier 743 (2), 989 (2)
cross 43 (5), 43 (7), 92 (2), 96 (1), 182 (3), 220 (5), 222 (2), 222 (8), 247 (1), 267 (12), 305 (5), 306 (3), 364 (2), 547 (9), 547 (13), 659 (1), 702 (4), 704 (3), 729 (2), 731 (1), 829 (3), 891 (4), 892 (3), 893 (2), 964 (3), 989 (2), 990 (4)
cross-bencher 744 (4)
cross benches 705 (1), 744 (1)
cross-bred 43 (6)
cross-breed 43 (5), 43 (7)
cross-country 281 (8)
cross-examination 459 (2), 959 (3)
cross-examine 459 (14)
cross-examiner 459 (10)
cross-eye 440 (1)
cross-eyed 440 (3)
cross-fertilization 43 (1)
cross-fire 712 (3)
cross-grained 259 (4)

cross-hatch 418 (6)
cross-hatching 418 (2)
cross-legged 222 (6)
cross one's fingers 487 (3)
cross one's heart 532 (6)
cross oneself 988 (10)
cross out 39 (3), 547 (19), 550 (3)
cross over 222 (8), 305 (5)
cross purposes 704 (1), 709 (1)
cross-question 459 (14)
cross-reference 9 (4), 62 (2), 62 (6)
cross-stitch 844 (4)
cross swords 279 (8), 475 (11), 716 (11)
cross swords with 704 (5), 709 (7)
Cross, the 973 (3)
cross the floor 603 (6)
cross the mind 449 (9)
cross the Rubicon 68 (9), 605 (6)
cross under 222 (8)
cross-vote 738 (9)
cross wind 731 (1)
cross with 45 (14)
crossbar 218 (9), 222 (2)
crossbones 222 (2)
crossbow 723 (4)
crosscurrent 182 (1), 240 (1), 350 (2), 663 (1), 702 (2), 704 (1)
crossed 220 (3), 222 (6), 331 (4), 437 (8), 624 (8)
crossed in love 888 (6)
crossed lines 521 (1)
crossing 43 (1), 45 (1), 45 (2), 45 (4), 222 (1), 222 (6), 269 (1), 294 (1), 305 (1); 305 (2), 305 (3), 305 (4), 624 (6)
crossing out 550 (1)
crossness 893 (1)
crosspatch 834 (4), 902 (2)
crossroads 8 (2), 76 (1), 222 (1), 294 (1), 624 (6)
crosswind 352 (1), 702 (2)
crosswise 220 (7), 222 (11)
crossword 530 (2)
crosswords 837 (8)
crotch 247 (1)

crotchet 410 (3)
crotchety 84 (5), 602 (5), 604 (3), 892 (3)
crouch 210 (3), 311 (9), 854 (10)
crouching 210 (2)
croup 238 (2)
croupier 798 (1)
croutons 301 (22)
crow 365 (4), 428 (2), 727 (8), 835 (2), 835 (6), 835 (7)
crow over 727 (8), 877 (5)
crowd 52 (2), 61 (2), 74 (5), 74 (10), 104 (1), 104 (6), 202 (3), 324 (6), 441 (2), 637 (1), 702 (9), 869 (2)
crowd in 297 (7)
crowd psychology 74 (5)
crowd together 198 (7)
crowded 45 (7), 74 (9), 104 (5)
crowds 32 (2)
crown 34 (10), 54 (1), 213 (1), 213 (2), 213 (3), 213 (5), 236 (3), 250 (3), 279 (9), 310 (4), 547 (9), 617 (2), 646 (5), 725 (7), 729 (1), 733 (1), 743 (1), 751 (4), 844 (12), 866 (4), 866 (14), 876 (4), 884 (6)
crown all 34 (10), 725 (7)
crown lands 777 (3)
crown one's wishes 826 (3)
crowned head 741 (3)
crowning 34 (6), 54 (3), 69 (4), 213 (4), 725 (3), 727 (4), 866 (5)
crow's nest 209 (4), 213 (2)
crucial 8 (3), 137 (6), 156 (8), 478 (2), 638 (5)
crucial moment 8 (2), 137 (3)
crucial question 459 (3)
crucible 147 (3), 194 (13)
crucifix 222 (2), 990 (4)
crucifixion 362 (1), 553 (4), 825 (1), 963 (3)
cruciform 222 (6)
crucify 377 (5), 645 (7), 963 (12)

crude 55 (3), 425 (6), 576
(2), 647 (3), 670 (4), 695
(6), 842 (5), 847 (5)
crude estimate 512 (2)
crudity 699 (1)
cruel 176 (5), 176 (6), 362
(9), 645 (3), 718 (9), 735
(6), 827 (3), 898 (7), 906
(2), 934 (4), 934 (6), 940
(2)
cruel act 176 (1), 898 (3),
936 (2)
cruel humour 839 (1)
cruelly 32 (20), 645 (8)
cruelty 645 (1), 735 (1),
898 (2), 898 (3)
cruise 265 (4), 269 (1), 269
(9)
cruise missile 723 (4)
cruiser 722 (13)
cruising 269 (1), 269 (3)
crumb 33 (3), 53 (5), 301
(22), 332 (5)
crumble 37 (4), 46 (13), 51
(5), 163 (9), 165 (11), 330
(3), 332 (5), 655 (7), 655
(9)
crumbliness 330 (1), 332
(1)
crumbling 37 (1), 127 (7),
163 (5), 165 (5)
crumbling power 734 (1)
crumbly 53 (6), 330 (2),
332 (4)
crumbs 41 (2), 641 (3)
crumpet 301 (22)
crumple 63 (4), 198 (1),
246 (5), 251 (11), 259 (9),
261 (3)
crumple up 165 (11)
crumpled 251 (4), 261 (2)
crunch 46 (12), 301 (36),
332 (5), 407 (4)
crupper 238 (2)
crusade 676 (1), 718 (1),
901 (1)
crusader 722 (3), 901 (4),
979 (5)
crusading 979 (7)
crusading spirit 901 (1)
cruse 194 (13)
crush 74 (5), 165 (7), 176
(8), 198 (7), 311 (4), 311

(7), 332 (5), 378 (7), 479
(3), 613 (3), 645 (7), 655
(10), 727 (9), 727 (10), 834
(11), 872 (7), 887 (1)
crush barrier 662 (3)
crushed 165 (5), 356 (2),
825 (5), 834 (5), 872 (4)
crushing 165 (1), 165 (4),
682 (5), 702 (6), 725 (3),
727 (4), 827 (6)
crushing blow 165 (3)
crust 53 (5), 223 (1), 226
(1), 226 (6), 301 (11), 301
(22), 321 (2), 324 (6), 326
(1), 344 (1)
crustacean 365 (2), 365
(14)
crusty 892 (3), 893 (2)
crutch 218 (2), 228 (3), 247
(1)
crux 222 (2), 530 (2), 638
(3)
cry 377 (6), 398 (1), 400
(1), 407 (5), 408 (1), 408
(3), 409 (1), 409 (3), 528
(1), 577 (1), 577 (4), 761
(1), 836 (1), 836 (6), 848
(1)
cry down 926 (6)
cry for joy 835 (6)
cry for mercy 762 (3)
cry for the moon 641 (8)
cry one's eyes out 836 (6)
cry out 408 (3), 408 (4)
cry out a 762 (3)
cry out against 613 (3)
cry out for 627 (6), 859
(11)
cry over 836 (5)
cry quits 721 (3)
cry shame 924 (10)
cry too soon 665 (3)
cry up 482 (4), 528 (11),
546 (3), 923 (9)
cry wolf 665 (3)
crybaby 163 (2), 836 (3)
crying 400 (3), 408 (2), 836
(1), 836 (4)
crying out for 627 (5)
crypt 194 (21), 211 (1), 364
(5), 527 (1), 990 (4)
cryptic 474 (4), 517 (2),
523 (4), 525 (3), 984 (6)

crypto- 523 (2), 525 (3)
cryptogram 525 (2), 530
(2)
cryptographer 520 (4)
cryptographic 523 (4), 525
(4)
cryptography 523 (1), 525
(2)
crystal 324 (3), 422 (1),
422 (2)
crystal ball 511 (4)
crystal-clear 422 (2), 443
(3)
crystal-gazer 511 (5), 984
(4)
crystal gazing 511 (2), 984
(1)
crystalline 245 (2), 326
(3), 422 (2)
crystallization 147 (1), 326
(2)
crystallize 324 (6), 326 (5),
392 (4)
crystallized 324 (4), 392
(3)
cub 132 (3), 167 (6)
cub reporter 529 (4)
cubbyhole 192 (17), 194
(4)
cube 36 (5), 86 (12), 93 (2),
94 (3), 247 (4)
cube root 85 (2)
cubic 183 (5), 465 (9)
cubic content 183 (1), 183
(2)
cubic contents 465 (3)
cubical 247 (6)
cubicle 194 (4), 194 (19)
cubing 36 (1)
Cubism 553 (3)
Cubist 556 (1)
cuckold 951 (3)
cuckoo 106 (1), 365 (4),
409 (1)
cuckoo in the nest 59 (3)
cucumber 301 (20)
cuddle 889 (1), 889 (6)
cuddlesome 889 (4)
cuddling 889 (1)
cuddly 887 (11)
cudgel 279 (4), 279 (9), 723
(5)
cue 505 (3), 524 (3)

cue in 594 (17)

cuff 228 (3), 261 (1), 279 (2), 963 (2), 963 (9)

cuff link 47 (5)

cuirass 253 (3), 713 (5)

cuisine 301 (5)

cul-de-sac 145 (5), 264 (1), 624 (6), 700 (1), 702 (2)

culinary 301 (34)

culinary herb 301 (21), 366 (6)

cull 362 (1), 605 (7), 786 (6)

culminate 34 (10), 54 (5), 213 (5), 725 (7)

culminating 32 (4), 34 (6), 213 (4), 725 (3)

culmination 54 (1), 213 (1), 308 (1), 725 (1)

culottes 228 (13)

culpability 914 (1), 936 (1)

culpable 914 (3), 924 (8), 936 (3)

culprit 904 (3), 928 (4)

cult 848 (1), 973 (1), 981 (2), 988 (3)

cult image 982 (3)

cultivate 36 (5), 156 (9), 164 (7), 167 (7), 171 (5), 174 (8), 366 (12), 370 (9), 534 (8), 632 (5), 654 (9), 669 (10), 669 (12), 925 (4)

cultivated 164 (6), 490 (6)

cultivation 156 (1), 370 (1), 490 (3), 536 (1), 654 (3), 669 (3), 846 (1)

cultivator 167 (1), 370 (4), 669 (5)

cultural 534 (5), 654 (7)

culture 369 (9), 490 (3), 534 (2), 536 (1), 654 (3), 846 (1)

culture shock 508 (1)

cultured 490 (6), 542 (7)

culvert 351 (2)

cumber 322 (5)

cumbersome 195 (9), 322 (4), 643 (2), 695 (5)

cummerbund 228 (24)

cumulative 36 (3), 466 (5)

cumulatively 71 (7)

cumulus 74 (7), 355 (2)

cuneiform 247 (6), 558 (1)

cunning 34 (1), 498 (2), 498 (4), 498 (5), 541 (2), 541 (3), 542 (1), 542 (6), 623 (7), 688 (2), 694 (1), 694 (4), 698 (1), 698 (4), 930 (4)

cunning, be 542 (8), 623 (9), 676 (5), 698 (5)

cunningly 698 (6)

cup 194 (15), 218 (15), 252 (4), 255 (2), 255 (7), 596 (2), 729 (1)

cup-holder 34 (3)

cupboard 194 (5), 632 (2)

cupboard love 541 (2)

cupful 26 (2), 33 (2)

Cupid 887 (7), 967 (1)

cupidity 816 (2), 859 (1)

cupola 226 (2), 253 (4)

cuppa 301 (26)

cupped 255 (6)

cupped hands 194 (18)

cur 365 (10), 938 (3)

curability 656 (4)

curable 656 (6), 658 (18)

curacy 985 (3)

curate 986 (3)

curate's egg 647 (1)

curative 656 (7), 658 (17), 831 (2)

curator 492 (3), 660 (3), 690 (3), 749 (1), 754 (1)

curb 177 (6), 278 (1), 278 (6), 747 (1), 747 (7), 748 (4)

curd 324 (3)

curdle 324 (6), 354 (6)

curdle the blood 827 (11)

curdled 324 (4), 354 (4)

curdled milk 301 (30)

curds 301 (24), 301 (30), 354 (1)

cure 182 (3), 342 (6), 611 (4), 629 (1), 654 (9), 656 (4), 656 (11), 658 (1), 658 (12), 658 (19), 666 (5), 669 (12), 719 (4), 831 (3)

cure-all 658 (1)

cure of 611 (4), 656 (11)

cured 656 (6)

curer 656 (5)

curettage 300 (3)

curette 300 (8)

curfew 129 (1), 665 (1), 747 (2), 757 (1)

Curia 956 (3)

curio 522 (2), 694 (3), 844 (1)

curiosity 84 (3), 453 (1), 455 (1), 459 (1), 821 (1), 864 (3)

curious 84 (6), 453 (3), 459 (11), 507 (2), 841 (3), 859 (7)

curious, be 453 (4), 459 (13)

curiously 32 (19)

curiousness 453 (1)

curl 208 (1), 248 (2), 248 (5), 251 (2), 251 (11), 261 (3), 843 (2), 843 (7)

curl one's lip 547 (21), 835 (8), 922 (5)

curl up 315 (5)

curl upwards 308 (4)

curled 251 (7), 843 (6)

curlers 843 (2)

curlicue 251 (2), 844 (3)

curling 837 (7)

curls 259 (2)

curly 251 (7), 259 (5)

curmudgeon 885 (3)

currency 79 (1), 528 (2), 797 (1)

current 79 (3), 121 (2), 154 (4), 265 (1), 281 (1), 285 (1), 350 (2), 352 (1), 490 (7), 528 (7), 557 (5), 640 (2), 663 (1)

current affairs 154 (2)

current date 121 (1)

current of thought 449 (1)

curriculum 534 (3)

curriculum vitae 548 (1)

curried 388 (2)

curry 301 (13), 388 (6)

curry favour 879 (4), 925 (4)

curry powder 389 (1)

currycomb 333 (3), 369 (10)

curse 178 (1), 302 (2), 616 (1), 645 (1), 659 (1), 731 (1), 827 (2), 829 (1), 859 (11), 885 (6), 888 (7), 899 (1), 899 (2), 899 (6), 899

(7), 899 (8), 900 (3), 914 (1), 921 (5), 924 (10), 924 (13), 961 (3), 980 (6), 983 (2), 983 (11)

curse on, a 899 (8)

curse one's folly 830 (4)

cursed 645 (5), 899 (5), 983 (9)

cursing 176 (6), 709 (6), 829 (3), 878 (4), 885 (5), 892 (3), 899 (3), 899 (4), 900 (2), 921 (3), 926 (5), 980 (4)

cursive 586 (7)

cursorily 458 (7)

cursory 33 (7), 114 (3), 456 (3), 680 (2)

curt 569 (2), 582 (2)

curtail 39 (3), 204 (5), 655 (9)

curtailed 39 (2), 204 (3)

curtailment 39 (1), 46 (3), 198 (1), 204 (2)

curtain 69 (1), 226 (4), 231 (2), 421 (2), 440 (1), 444 (1), 594 (2)

curtain call 106 (2), 594 (2), 923 (3)

curtain off 57 (5), 421 (4)

curtain rod 217 (3)

curtains 217 (2), 361 (2)

curtness 582 (1)

curtsy 311 (2), 311 (9), 884 (2), 884 (7), 920 (2), 920 (6)

curvaceous 248 (3), 253 (7), 841 (5)

curvature 203 (3), 220 (1), 247 (1), 248 (1), 253 (1), 282 (1)

curve 218 (2), 220 (1), 220 (6), 248 (2), 248 (4), 250 (4), 251 (1), 253 (6), 282 (3), 314 (4)

curved 220 (3), 247 (5), 248 (3), 250 (6), 253 (7), 253 (8), 255 (6), 257 (2), 258 (3), 314 (3), 841 (5)

curved, be 248 (4)

curves 257 (1)

curving 257 (2)

curvy 248 (3)

cushion 163 (10), 177 (2), 177 (6), 218 (8), 218 (15), 231 (9), 327 (1), 327 (4), 660 (2), 660 (8), 713 (9), 831 (1), 831 (3)

cushion of air 340 (1)

cushioned 683 (2)

cusp 69 (2), 213 (2), 256 (2)

cusped 256 (7)

cuss 709 (9), 885 (6), 899 (2), 899 (7)

cussed 704 (3), 898 (4)

cussedness 602 (1), 704 (1)

custard 392 (2)

custodial 660 (6), 747 (4)

custodian 660 (3), 749 (1)

custodianship 747 (3)

custody 660 (2), 747 (3)

custom 60 (1), 79 (1), 127 (3), 144 (1), 610 (1), 791 (2), 792 (1), 848 (2)

custom house 799 (1)

customary 79 (3), 81 (3), 610 (5), 865 (3)

customer 371 (3), 610 (4), 707 (4), 792 (2)

customs 807 (1), 809 (3)

cut 33 (6), 37 (2), 37 (4), 39 (3), 42 (1), 46 (4), 46 (11), 190 (6), 198 (7), 201 (2), 204 (2), 204 (3), 204 (5), 222 (8), 243 (1), 243 (5), 255 (4), 256 (10), 260 (1), 260 (3), 262 (3), 277 (6), 279 (2), 279 (9), 287 (7), 301 (16), 301 (36), 311 (6), 370 (9), 377 (1), 377 (5), 445 (6), 551 (8), 554 (3), 555 (3), 655 (4), 655 (10), 712 (4), 783 (2), 783 (3), 804 (2), 810 (1), 810 (2), 812 (6), 845 (1), 872 (7), 883 (1), 885 (6)

cut a dash 638 (7), 848 (7), 875 (7)

cut a figure 848 (7)

cut above, a 34 (4), 644 (6)

cut across 220 (5), 305 (5)

cut adrift 46 (7)

cut and dried 62 (3), 80 (6), 669 (9)

cut and run 296 (5), 620 (6)

cut and thrust 475 (4), 475 (11), 712 (4), 712 (9), 716 (7)

cut back 37 (4), 39 (3), 204 (5)

cut both ways 467 (4)

cut capers 312 (4)

cut corners 680 (3)

cut costs 814 (3)

cut dead 458 (5), 883 (9)

cut deep 46 (11)

cut down 39 (3), 46 (11), 165 (7), 204 (5), 311 (6), 362 (11), 712 (9)

cut glass 844 (2)

cut in two 92 (5)

cut into 46 (11)

cut loose 46 (7), 744 (9)

cut no ice 639 (7)

cut off 46 (9), 46 (11), 232 (3), 702 (8), 786 (10)

cut one short 578 (4)

cut one's throat 362 (11)

cut open 46 (11), 658 (20)

cut out 243 (5), 264 (2), 304 (4)

cut out for 24 (7), 642 (2), 694 (5)

cut price 810 (1), 812 (1), 812 (3)

cut rate 810 (1)

cut round 46 (11)

cut short 46 (11), 145 (7), 165 (8), 204 (5)

cut-throat 165 (4)

cut through 46 (11), 263 (18)

cut to pieces 362 (11)

cut up 46 (11)

cutback 204 (2)

cute 850 (4)

cuticle 226 (6)

cutlass 723 (8)

cutlery 256 (5)

cutlet 53 (5), 301 (16)

cuts 747 (2), 814 (1)

cutter 275 (5), 275 (7)

cutthroat 362 (7), 716 (9)

cutting 46 (3), 255 (4), 256 (7), 366 (6), 445 (3), 571 (2)

cutting away 46 (3)
cutting back 37 (2)
cutting down 946 (1)
cutting edge 256 (5)
cutting off 46 (3)
cutting open 46 (3)
cutting out 304 (1)
cuttings 548 (1)
cyanide 659 (3)
cybernetics 86 (5), 630 (3)
cycle 71 (1), 106 (2), 110
 (2), 141 (2), 250 (5), 267
 (15), 274 (3)
cycle lane 305 (3)
cycle race 716 (3)
cyclic 141 (4), 315 (4)
cycling 305 (2), 837 (6)
cycling cape 228 (21)
cyclist 268 (4)
cyclone 315 (2), 340 (3),
 352 (4)
cyclonic 315 (4), 340 (5)
cyclostyle 20 (6)
cygnet 132 (3), 365 (4)
cylinder 252 (3), 315 (3)
cylindrical 252 (5), 263
 (16)
cymbals 414 (8)
cynic 483 (1), 486 (3), 902
 (2), 926 (3)
cynical 486 (4), 820 (3),
 853 (2), 860 (2), 926 (5)
cynicism 820 (1), 834 (1),
 853 (1), 902 (1)
cynosure 866 (6), 890 (2)
cyst 651 (14)
cystic fibrosis 651 (8)
cytology 358 (2)
cytoplasm 358 (1)
cytoplasmic 358 (3)

D

D-day 68 (3), 108 (3)
dab 33 (3), 279 (2), 378 (7)
dab hand 696 (1)
dabble 341 (7), 461 (7)
dabble in 458 (4), 491 (8),
 837 (21)
dabble in shares 791 (5)

dabbled 341 (4)
dabbling 491 (3), 491 (7),
 678 (10)
dace 365 (15)
dad 169 (3)
daddy 169 (3)
daddy longlegs 365 (16)
dado 844 (2)
daffodil 366 (6), 547 (11)
daft 499 (4), 503 (8)
dagger 256 (2), 723 (8)
daily 139 (4), 141 (5), 141
 (7), 528 (4), 610 (6), 742
 (1)
daily bread 301 (9), 622
 (2)
daily market 796 (1)
daily round 16 (1), 71 (1),
 141 (2), 610 (1), 622 (1),
 838 (2)
dainties 301 (9)
daintiness 648 (1), 846 (1),
 862 (1)
dainty 163 (8), 196 (8), 390
 (1), 390 (2), 648 (7), 841
 (5), 846 (3), 862 (3)
dainty palate 301 (4)
dairy 194 (19), 687 (1)
dairy cattle 365 (7)
dairy farm 369 (2), 370 (2)
dairy farming 369 (1)
dairy product 301 (24)
dais 218 (5), 539 (5)
daisy 366 (6)
dalliance 889 (1)
dally 136 (4), 837 (21), 889
 (6)
Dalmatian 437 (4)
dam 264 (6), 341 (3)
dam up 350 (12), 702 (9)
damage 37 (1), 63 (3), 163
 (10), 467 (4), 616 (1), 634
 (1), 634 (4), 636 (9), 641
 (1), 645 (1), 645 (6), 655
 (3), 655 (9), 845 (3), 926
 (7)
damage the case 467 (4)
damaged 655 (5), 845 (2)
damages 31 (2), 787 (1),
 809 (2), 963 (4)
damaging 467 (2), 634 (2),
 645 (3), 867 (5), 898 (5),
 926 (5)

damascene 437 (9)
damask 222 (4)
dame 373 (4), 741 (1)
dammed 360 (3)
damn 899 (6), 899 (7), 899
 (8), 924 (10), 961 (3)
damnable 616 (2), 645 (5),
 827 (4)
damnably 32 (18)
damned 645 (5), 899 (5),
 972 (3)
damning 466 (5), 899 (4)
damp 339 (1), 341 (1), 341
 (4), 382 (6), 405 (3), 834
 (12)
damp course 214 (1)
damp down 37 (4), 747 (7)
damp one's ardour 613 (3)
damp squib 728 (1)
damped 405 (2)
dampen 177 (6), 341 (7),
 401 (5), 613 (3), 834 (12)
damper 177 (2), 264 (2),
 401 (2), 405 (1), 414 (11),
 613 (1), 702 (5), 834 (4),
 924 (5)
damping 341 (2), 613 (2),
 702 (6)
dampness 341 (1)
damsel 373 (3)
dance 265 (4), 312 (1), 312
 (2), 312 (4), 315 (1), 317
 (2), 317 (4), 412 (4), 417
 (11), 594 (5), 833 (7), 837
 (13), 837 (14), 837 (22)
dance attendance on 879
 (4)
dance for joy 835 (6)
dance hall 837 (5)
dance step 312 (1)
dance with fury 891 (7)
dancer 312 (2), 315 (3),
 594 (10), 837 (14)
dancing 265 (1), 312 (1),
 312 (3), 318 (1), 833 (4),
 837 (13)
dandelion 366 (6)
dandle 889 (6)
dandruff 649 (2)
dandy 848 (4), 850 (3)
dandyism 850 (1)
danger 160 (5), 471 (1),
 474 (3), 511 (3), 523 (1),

618 (2), 661 (1), 663 (1), 664 (1), 667 (1), 700 (3), 857 (1)

danger-loving 855 (5), 857 (3)

danger of 661 (2)

danger past 660 (1)

danger signal 400 (1), 414 (8), 420 (6), 511 (1), 547 (5), 661 (1), 664 (1), 665 (1)

dangerous 645 (3), 661 (3), 700 (4), 853 (3), 854 (8), 898 (4), 900 (2)

dangerous, be 661 (9)

dangerous course 661 (1)

dangerousness 892 (1)

dangle 49 (4), 217 (1), 217 (5), 317 (4), 522 (8)

dangler 217 (2)

dangling 49 (2), 217 (4), 317 (3)

dank 341 (4)

dankness 341 (1)

dapper 841 (6)

dapple 437 (9)

dapple grey 273 (4), 429 (2)

dappled 437 (7)

dappling 437 (4)

Darby and Joan 90 (1), 133 (4), 894 (4)

dare 599 (3), 661 (8), 672 (3), 704 (4), 711 (1), 711 (3), 855 (6), 900 (1)

dare swear 532 (5)

daredevil 855 (3), 857 (2), 857 (3)

daring 522 (5), 661 (1), 671 (3), 672 (2), 855 (1), 855 (4), 857 (3), 875 (5), 951 (7)

dark 129 (1), 129 (5), 418 (1), 418 (3), 425 (7), 428 (4), 428 (5), 430 (3), 491 (6), 523 (2), 834 (8), 930 (4)

Dark Ages 110 (2)

dark and handsome 841 (3)

dark, be 418 (5)

dark blue 435 (3)

dark brown 430 (3)

dark clouds 731 (1)

dark-coloured 418 (3)

dark colouring 428 (1)

Dark Continent 491 (1)

dark glasses 226 (4), 421 (1), 424 (1), 442 (2)

dark horse 491 (2), 523 (1), 530 (1)

dark purple 436 (2)

dark-skinned 428 (5)

darken 418 (6), 419 (7), 421 (4), 428 (6), 439 (4), 440 (5), 444 (4), 525 (7), 834 (12)

darken the doors 297 (1)

darkened 418 (3), 444 (2)

darkening 418 (2), 428 (1)

darkling 418 (8)

darkness 129 (1), 418 (1), 419 (1), 428 (1), 439 (1), 731 (1)

darling 887 (5), 887 (11), 890 (1), 890 (2)

darn 45 (9), 656 (12), 899 (8)

darned 645 (5)

darning 656 (2)

dart 152 (5), 265 (4), 277 (6), 287 (2), 287 (7), 723 (4)

darting 152 (1), 277 (5)

darts 837 (8)

dash 33 (2), 43 (2), 47 (1), 174 (1), 176 (7), 277 (2), 277 (6), 350 (9), 547 (14), 547 (19), 599 (1), 678 (11), 680 (1), 680 (3), 716 (3), 727 (10)

dash against 279 (8)

dash at 712 (10)

dash forward 277 (6)

dash off 551 (8), 586 (8)

dash one's hopes 509 (5), 728 (8), 834 (12)

dashed 728 (5), 872 (4)

dashed hopes 853 (1)

dashing 277 (5), 571 (2), 848 (5), 855 (4), 875 (5)

data 86 (5), 466 (1), 475 (2), 512 (1)

data bank 86 (5), 505 (4), 632 (2)

data processing 86 (5), 160 (6), 196 (7), 548 (1), 630 (2), 632 (2)

date 108 (3), 108 (9), 117 (2), 117 (4), 117 (7), 301 (19), 882 (4), 882 (8), 887 (4), 889 (7)

date line 92 (3), 117 (2)

date list 117 (4)

dated 108 (6), 127 (7)

dated, be 117 (7)

dateless 115 (2)

dating 117 (1), 117 (4)

daub 226 (16), 425 (8), 515 (1), 515 (6), 552 (1), 552 (3), 553 (8)

daubed 553 (7)

dauber 556 (1), 697 (1)

daubing 553 (1)

daughter 170 (2), 373 (3)

daughter church 990 (3)

daughterly 170 (4), 739 (3)

daunt 854 (12)

dauntless 855 (5)

davit 217 (3)

dawdle 113 (9), 136 (4), 267 (13), 267 (14), 278 (1), 278 (4), 679 (11)

dawdler 278 (2), 679 (6)

dawdling 679 (2), 679 (8)

dawn 66 (1), 68 (1), 68 (8), 127 (5), 128 (1), 417 (3), 417 (13)

dawn chorus 128 (1)

dawn upon 449 (9)

dawning 128 (1), 128 (5)

day 108 (3), 110 (1)

day after day 106 (7), 139 (5)

day and age 108 (3)

day and night 14 (2)

day before 66 (1), 119 (1)

day by day 106 (7), 108 (10), 113 (11)

day centre 192 (14)

day-dreamer 513 (4)

day of abstinence 946 (2)

Day of Judgment 69 (3)

day of obligation 988 (7)

day of observance 988 (7)

day of rest 683 (1), 988 (7)

day pupil 538 (1)

day release 534 (2)

day-star 321 (8)
day to remember 876 (2)
day trip 267 (1)
daybreak 128 (1)
daydream 513 (3), 513 (7), 859 (1), 859 (11)
daydreamer 456 (1)
daydreaming 456 (2), 456 (4)
daylight 128 (1), 201 (1), 417 (1)
days 108 (1), 110 (2)
day's march 199 (1)
days of grace 136 (2)
days of yore 125 (1)
days to come 120 (1)
daytime 128 (1), 128 (5)
daze 864 (7)
dazed 375 (3), 864 (4)
dazzle 417 (1), 417 (5), 417 (11), 439 (4), 440 (5), 542 (8), 821 (8), 841 (7), 864 (7), 866 (2), 875 (7), 887 (15), 920 (7)
dazzled 440 (3), 864 (4)
dazzler 841 (2)
dazzling 417 (8), 427 (4), 644 (4)
de jure 915 (9), 953 (5)
de luxe 376 (4), 875 (4)
de rigueur 917 (6)
deacon 986 (2), 986 (4), 986 (7)
deaconess 986 (2)
dead 2 (5), 125 (6), 175 (2), 361 (6), 401 (3), 405 (2)
dead and gone 361 (6)
dead, be 361 (7)
dead beat 684 (2)
dead body 361 (3), 363 (1)
dead calm 266 (2)
dead centre 225 (2), 494 (6)
dead certainty 473 (1)
dead drunk 375 (3), 949 (8)
dead end 145 (5), 264 (1), 264 (4), 700 (1), 702 (2)
dead heat 28 (5), 123 (1)
dead letter 161 (4)
dead level 216 (1)
dead loss 641 (2)

dead march 278 (1), 364 (2)
dead of night 129 (2)
dead-on 494 (6)
dead quiet 266 (2)
dead reckoning 86 (1), 269 (2), 465 (1)
Dead Sea 346 (1)
dead-set at 712 (1)
dead silence 399 (1)
dead sound 405 (1)
dead straight 249 (2)
dead, the 361 (3)
dead to 820 (5)
deaden 177 (7), 375 (6), 401 (5), 405 (3), 820 (7)
deadline 69 (3), 236 (1)
deadliness 840 (1)
deadlock 28 (3), 145 (2), 266 (1), 470 (1), 677 (1), 700 (1), 702 (2), 726 (1)
deadly 165 (4), 362 (8), 616 (2), 645 (3), 653 (4), 898 (4)
deadly dull 840 (2)
deadly sin 934 (2)
deadpan 266 (6), 820 (3), 834 (7)
deaf 375 (3), 416 (2), 456 (3), 602 (4), 820 (3)
deaf-aid 415 (4)
deaf and dumb 416 (2), 578 (2)
deaf, be 416 (3), 456 (7), 458 (5), 760 (4)
deaf ears 456 (1)
deaf-mute 416 (1), 416 (2), 578 (1)
deaf-mutism 416 (1), 578 (1)
deaf to 416 (2), 760 (2), 820 (5)
deaf to, be 292 (3)
deafen 400 (4), 416 (4)
deafened 416 (2)
deafening 400 (3)
deafness 416 (1), 456 (1)
deal 32 (2), 75 (4), 676 (2), 765 (1), 783 (1), 783 (2), 783 (3), 791 (2), 930 (3)
deal gently with 736 (3)

deal hardly with 735 (7)
deal in 791 (4)
deal in futures 791 (5)
deal out 75 (4), 781 (7), 783 (3)
deal with 9 (7), 591 (5), 622 (9), 688 (5), 766 (4), 791 (4)
dealer 686 (1), 793 (2), 794 (1)
dealing 791 (1)
dean 537 (1), 690 (1), 986 (4)
deanery 985 (3), 985 (4)
deanship 131 (4)
dear 165 (4), 490 (7), 645 (3), 811 (2), 875 (4), 887 (11), 890 (1)
dear, be 811 (4)
dear heart 890 (1)
dear one 890 (1)
dearest 890 (1)
dearly 32 (17), 811 (7)
dearly-bought 811 (2)
dearness 809 (1), 811 (1)
dearth 172 (1), 636 (2)
death 2 (2), 51 (2), 114 (1), 168 (1), 266 (2), 361 (1), 616 (1)
death blow 69 (1)
death certificate 361 (4)
death chamber 964 (3)
death-dealing 362 (9)
death duty 809 (3)
death knell 361 (1)
death mask 22 (1)
death notice 361 (4)
death of 827 (2)
death rate 86 (1), 361 (4)
death rattle 352 (7), 361 (2)
death ray 723 (3)
death roll 361 (4)
Death Row 748 (2)
death sentence 963 (3)
death song 836 (2)
death toll 361 (4)
death trap 661 (1)
death warrant 963 (3)
deathbed 136 (3), 361 (2), 651 (2)
deathblow 361 (1), 362 (1), 728 (2)

decimal system 85 (1), 86 (1)

decimalize 100 (3)

decimate 100 (3), 105 (4), 163 (10), 165 (6), 362 (11), 963 (12)

decimation 100 (1), 165 (1), 362 (4)

decipher 520 (10), 522 (7)

decipherable 516 (2)

deciphered 520 (7)

decipherment 520 (3)

decision 480 (1), 595 (0), 599 (1), 605 (1), 617 (1), 737 (2), 959 (3)

decision-making 689 (1)

decisive 137 (6), 156 (7), 178 (2), 466 (5), 478 (2), 599 (2)

decisive factor 156 (2)

deck 194 (4), 207 (1), 218 (4), 226 (7), 226 (15), 228 (31), 414 (10), 837 (15), 844 (12)

deck out 844 (12)

decked 207 (4)

decked out 844 (11)

deckhand 270 (1)

deckle edge 234 (3), 260 (1)

declaim 528 (10), 579 (9)

declaimer 579 (5)

declamation 574 (2), 579 (2), 579 (3)

declamatory 574 (5)

declaration 532 (1), 764 (1)

declaration of faith 485 (2)

declaratory 532 (3)

declare 514 (5), 526 (5), 528 (10), 532 (5), 579 (8), 737 (7), 753 (3)

declare black 757 (4)

declare forfeit 916 (9)

declare heretical 977 (3)

declare oneself 526 (4)

declare war 709 (7), 712 (7), 718 (10)

declared 522 (6)

declension 143 (1), 163 (1), 564 (1)

declination 186 (2)

decline 35 (1), 37 (1), 37 (5), 127 (1), 163 (1), 163 (9), 220 (5), 286 (1), 286 (4), 290 (3), 309 (1), 309 (3), 564 (4), 607 (3), 655 (1), 655 (7), 731 (1), 731 (7), 760 (4)

declined 607 (2)

declining 37 (3), 131 (6), 286 (3), 731 (5), 760 (1)

declining years 131 (3)

decoction 301 (26), 337 (2), 658 (2)

decode 520 (10)

decoded 520 (7)

decoder 520 (4)

decoding 520 (1), 520 (3)

decolletage 229 (2)

décolleté 229 (4)

decolorize 426 (5), 427 (6)

decomposable 46 (6), 51 (4)

decompose 44 (6), 46 (7), 46 (8), 46 (10), 46 (13), 51 (5), 62 (6), 75 (3), 75 (4), 127 (8), 361 (8), 397 (3), 649 (8), 655 (7), 655 (9)

decomposed 51 (3), 163 (5), 397 (2), 645 (2), 649 (6), 651 (22), 655 (5), 655 (6)

decomposition 44 (2), 46 (1), 46 (2), 51 (1), 62 (1), 165 (1), 332 (1), 649 (1)

deconsecrate 987 (3)

deconsecrated 980 (5), 987 (2)

decontaminate 648 (10)

decontrol 746 (1), 746 (3)

decor 445 (2), 594 (6)

decorate 38 (3), 147 (8), 226 (16), 437 (9), 546 (3), 574 (6), 654 (9), 841 (8), 843 (7), 844 (12), 866 (14)

decorated 17 (2), 844 (10)

decoration 547 (9), 574 (1), 729 (2), 743 (3), 844 (1), 866 (4), 962 (1)

decorations 876 (1)

decorative 553 (7), 844 (9)

decorative art 551 (3)

decorator 143 (3), 656 (5), 686 (3)

decorous 24 (7), 60 (2), 848 (6), 950 (5)

decorum 846 (1), 848 (2)

decoy 291 (1), 291 (4), 527 (2), 542 (4), 542 (10), 545 (4)

decrease 26 (2), 33 (1), 33 (8), 37 (1), 37 (4), 37 (5), 39 (1), 39 (3), 71 (2), 143 (5), 163 (9), 172 (1), 196 (12), 198 (1), 198 (6), 266 (7), 290 (3), 309 (1), 309 (3), 655 (1), 655 (7), 772 (1)

decreased 37 (3)

decreasing 33 (6), 35 (3), 37 (3), 105 (2), 163 (5), 198 (4), 655 (5)

decreasingly 37 (6)

decree 480 (1), 480 (5), 528 (1), 608 (1), 693 (1), 737 (2), 737 (7), 953 (2), 953 (7)

decree absolute 737 (2), 896 (1)

decree nisi 737 (2), 896 (1)

decreed 608 (2), 953 (5)

decrement 37 (1), 39 (1), 42 (1)

decrepit 131 (6), 163 (4), 651 (20), 655 (6)

decrepitude 163 (1), 655 (2)

decried 924 (7)

decry 922 (6), 926 (6)

decrying 926 (5)

dedicate 759 (3), 781 (7), 979 (12), 981 (12), 988 (10)

dedicate to 673 (3), 868 (13)

dedicated 597 (4), 599 (2), 739 (3), 901 (6), 931 (2), 979 (8)

dedication 597 (1), 599 (1), 759 (1), 866 (5), 901 (1), 931 (1), 979 (1), 979 (2), 981 (6), 988 (4)

deduce 471 (6), 475 (10), 478 (4), 480 (5), 520 (8)

deducible 466 (5), 478 (2)

deduct 39 (3), 46 (8), 786 (6), 810 (2)

deducted 39 (2)

deduction 37 (2), 39 (1), 42 (1), 475 (1), 478 (1), 480 (1), 805 (1), 810 (1)

deductive 475 (7)

deed 154 (2), 157 (1), 466 (2), 623 (2), 623 (3), 638 (2), 676 (2), 682 (3), 688 (1), 694 (3), 727 (1), 767 (2), 855 (2)

deed of agreement 765 (1)

deeds 688 (1)

deem 485 (8)

deep 32 (4), 183 (6), 210 (2), 211 (2), 343 (1), 343 (3), 400 (3), 407 (3), 425 (6), 498 (5), 517 (4), 523 (2), 525 (3), 818 (6), 972 (3)

deep, be 211 (3), 313 (4)

deep blue 435 (3)

deep down 211 (4), 224 (6)

deep feeling 818 (1)

deep-freeze 382 (6), 384 (1), 632 (2)

deep-frozen 382 (4)

deep in 211 (2), 211 (4), 455 (2)

deep-laid 669 (8), 698 (4)

deep-laid plot 623 (4)

deep litter 369 (2)

deep mourning 836 (1)

deep reflection 449 (2)

deep-rooted 5 (6), 113 (4), 153 (6), 162 (6), 610 (5), 817 (2)

deep-sea 211 (2), 269 (6), 343 (1)

deep-sea fishing 619 (2)

deep-seated 5 (6), 113 (4), 153 (6), 610 (5)

deep sense of 818 (1)

deep sleep 679 (4)

deep space 321 (1)

deep thought 449 (1)

deep-toned 404 (2)

deepen 36 (5), 197 (5), 211 (3), 428 (6), 832 (3)

deepening 832 (1)

deeply 32 (17), 211 (4), 224 (6)

deeply-felt 818 (6)

deepness 211 (1), 224 (1)

deeps 211 (1)

deer 365 (3)

deer stalker 619 (3)

deer stalking 619 (2)

deface 244 (3), 550 (3), 641 (7), 655 (9), 842 (7), 845 (3)

defaced 842 (4)

defacement 550 (1)

defacer 168 (1)

defamation 926 (1)

defamatory 924 (6), 926 (5), 928 (5)

defame 867 (11), 921 (5), 924 (10), 926 (7), 928 (8)

defamer 529 (4), 926 (4), 928 (3)

default 55 (5), 307 (1), 805 (1), 805 (5), 918 (1)

defaulter 789 (3), 803 (3), 805 (3), 918 (1)

defaulting 803 (4), 805 (4)

defeat 34 (7), 35 (1), 75 (4), 165 (3), 165 (6), 306 (5), 474 (9), 479 (3), 607 (1), 727 (2), 727 (10), 728 (2), 731 (1)

defeat easily 727 (10)

defeated 35 (4), 509 (2), 728 (5), 745 (4), 829 (3), 834 (5), 872 (4)

defeated, be 721 (3), 728 (9)

defeated, the 728 (3)

defeatism 834 (1), 853 (1), 856 (1)

defeatist 721 (1), 834 (5), 853 (1), 853 (2), 854 (5), 856 (3)

defecate 302 (6)

defecation 302 (3), 649 (3), 651 (7)

defect 35 (1), 55 (2), 163 (1), 307 (1), 603 (6), 616 (1), 636 (1), 647 (2), 934 (2)

defection 603 (1), 621 (1), 738 (1), 918 (1), 930 (2)

defective 35 (4), 55 (3), 246 (4), 503 (7), 647 (3), 845 (2)

defective, be 647 (4)

defective vision 438 (1), 440 (1)

defector 603 (3)

defence 182 (1), 292 (1), 460 (2), 467 (1), 475 (4), 614 (1), 660 (2), 713 (1), 715 (1), 718 (7), 723 (3), 837 (16), 927 (1), 959 (3)

defence, a 713 (1)

defenceless 161 (6), 161 (8), 163 (4), 163 (5), 661 (5)

defencelessness 161 (2)

defences 235 (1), 235 (2), 253 (5), 256 (2), 660 (2), 702 (2), 713 (2)

defend 475 (11), 660 (8), 703 (6), 713 (9), 927 (5)

defend oneself 614 (4)

defendant 460 (3), 750 (1), 928 (4), 959 (4)

defended 713 (8)

defender 660 (3), 713 (6), 722 (1), 749 (1), 903 (1)

defending 713 (7), 927 (3)

defensible 660 (5), 713 (8), 927 (4)

defensible space 184 (2)

defensive 713 (7), 854 (7)

defensive battle 718 (7)

defensive, the 713 (1)

defensively 713 (11)

defensiveness 854 (2), 877 (1)

defer 136 (7), 726 (3)

defer to 488 (6), 488 (7), 721 (3), 739 (4), 920 (5)

deference 721 (1), 739 (1), 739 (2), 884 (f), 920 (1)

deferential 739 (3), 879 (3), 884 (3), 920 (3)

deferment 136 (2)

deferred payment 803 (1), 805 (1)

defiance 489 (1), 532 (1), 533 (1), 547 (4), 704 (1), 709 (1), 709 (2), 711 (1), 718 (1), 738 (1), 855 (1), 878 (1), 900 (1)

defiance of time 113 (2)

defiant 84 (5), 489 (3), 522 (5), 532 (4), 711 (2), 738 (7), 855 (4), 878 (4), 878 (5)

defiantly 711 (4)

delete **39** (3), **165** (6), **550** (3)

deletion **39** (1), **550** (1)

deliberate **278** (3), **608** (2), **617** (3), **617** (4), **681** (2), **691** (5), **823** (3), **858** (2)

deliberate omission **57** (1)

deliberately **136** (9), **617** (7)

deliberation **278** (1), **449** (2), **691** (1), **858** (1)

deliberative **449** (5), **691** (3)

delicacies **301** (9)

delicacy **163** (1), **378** (1), **390** (1), **694** (1), **841** (1), **846** (1), **862** (1), **950** (1)

delicate **163** (6), **163** (8), **330** (2), **331** (4), **425** (7), **494** (6), **651** (20), **700** (4), **841** (5), **846** (3), **862** (3), **950** (5)

delicate distinction **15** (2)

delicate health **163** (1), **651** (1)

delicatessen **301** (9)

delicious **376** (3), **390** (2), **392** (3), **644** (5), **826** (2)

deliciousness **826** (1)

delight **821** (6), **824** (1), **826** (4), **833** (8), **837** (1), **837** (20)

delight, a **826** (1)

delight in **824** (6)

delighted **488** (4), **597** (4), **824** (4), **833** (5)

delightful **376** (3), **826** (2)

delightfulness **826** (1)

delimit **236** (3), **547** (19)

delineate **233** (3), **551** (8)

delineation **233** (1), **551** (1), **590** (1)

delineator **556** (1)

delinquency **738** (1), **934** (1), **936** (1)

delinquent **869** (7), **904** (3)

deliquesce **337** (4)

deliquescence **337** (1)

deliquescent **337** (3)

delirious **503** (9), **651** (22), **818** (5), **821** (3), **822** (3)

delirious, be **503** (10)

delirium **503** (4), **513** (3), **515** (1), **651** (2), **822** (2)

delirium tremens **503** (4), **949** (3)

deliver **272** (6), **287** (7), **633** (5), **656** (9), **666** (5), **668** (3), **701** (9), **703** (5), **713** (9), **746** (3), **780** (3), **781** (7), **787** (3), **792** (5)

deliver a speech **579** (9)

deliverable **668** (2)

deliverance **304** (1), **666** (1), **666** (2), **667** (1), **668** (1), **703** (1), **746** (1), **787** (1), **831** (1), **903** (1)

delivered **746** (2)

delivery **167** (2), **272** (1), **577** (1), **579** (1), **633** (1), **667** (1), **668** (1), **688** (1), **780** (1)

delivery van **273** (1), **274** (12)

dell **255** (3)

delousing **648** (2)

delta **344** (1), **348** (1)

delude **542** (8)

delude oneself **495** (7)

deluded **495** (5), **503** (8)

deluge **341** (2), **341** (8), **350** (4), **350** (6), **637** (5)

delusion **513** (3), **542** (1)

delusions **503** (2)

delusive **542** (6)

delve **255** (8), **370** (9)

delve into **459** (13)

demagnetize **182** (3)

demagogue **579** (5), **690** (2), **738** (5)

demagoguery **733** (4)

demagogy **733** (4)

demand **459** (13), **596** (8), **627** (1), **627** (6), **664** (1), **737** (3), **737** (8), **761** (1), **761** (5), **766** (3), **786** (7), **809** (1), **809** (3), **809** (5), **827** (9), **859** (11), **900** (1), **900** (3)

demand attention **455** (7)

demand obedience **917** (11)

demand payment **737** (8)

demand security **764** (5)

demand too much **684** (6)

demanding **55** (3), **627** (5), **684** (4), **700** (4), **737** (5), **761** (3), **859** (7), **862** (3)

demarcate **236** (3), **547** (19), **783** (3)

demarcation **236** (1)

demarcation line **236** (1)

demean oneself **867** (10), **872** (5), **879** (4)

demeaning **867** (6)

demeanour **445** (5), **547** (4), **688** (1)

demented **63** (2), **503** (7), **503** (8), **503** (9)

dementia **503** (1)

demesne **777** (3)

demi- **92** (4)

demigod **646** (2), **966** (1), **967** (2)

demijohn **194** (13)

demilitarize **161** (9), **719** (5)

demise **361** (2)

demobilization **75** (1), **717** (1), **719** (1)

demobilize **46** (8), **75** (4), **719** (5), **746** (3)

democracy **371** (5), **733** (4)

democratic **733** (9)

democrats **708** (2)

démodé **127** (7)

demographer **371** (2)

demography **86** (4), **371** (2)

demolish **46** (13), **51** (5), **149** (4), **163** (10), **165** (7), **176** (8), **279** (8), **311** (6), **479** (3), **550** (1), **718** (11)

demolisher **168** (1)

demolition **165** (1), **655** (3)

demon **176** (4), **854** (4), **938** (4), **969** (2), **970** (4), **970** (5)

demon for work **678** (5)

demonetize **797** (11)

demonetized **797** (9)

demoniac **969** (5)

demoniacal **969** (5)

demoniacal possession **983** (2)

demonic **678** (7), **969** (5), **970** (6)

demonize **969** (6)

demonology **969** (3)

demonstrable **473** (4), **478** (3)

demonstrate **475** (11), **478** (4), **485** (9), **494** (7), **520** (8), **522** (8), **532** (5), **540** (3), **678** (11), **711** (3), **738** (10), **762** (3), **875** (7), **927** (5)

demonstrated **473** (4), **478** (3), **494** (4), **540** (2)

demonstrated, be **478** (5)

demonstrating **466** (5), **478** (2)

demonstration **74** (1), **461** (1), **466** (1), **473** (1), **475** (3), **478** (1), **488** (1), **522** (1), **596** (1), **762** (1), **818** (1)

demonstrative **466** (5), **478** (2), **547** (15), **817** (2), **880** (6), **887** (9), **889** (4)

demonstrativeness **818** (1)

demonstrator **520** (5), **522** (3), **738** (4), **738** (5)

demoralize **655** (9), **854** (12), **934** (8)

demoralized **161** (7), **854** (6), **934** (4)

demoralizing **934** (6)

demote **37** (4), **311** (7), **752** (5), **867** (11), **963** (8)

demoted **867** (7)

demotic **557** (5)

demotion **37** (2), **309** (1), **311** (1), **752** (2), **867** (1)

demur **468** (1), **468** (3), **475** (11), **486** (2), **486** (7), **489** (1), **489** (5), **533** (3), **598** (1), **598** (4), **715** (1), **715** (3), **762** (3)

demure **823** (3), **834** (7), **850** (4), **874** (2)

demureness **823** (1), **834** (3), **850** (2), **874** (1), **950** (2)

demurring **598** (3), **760** (2), **874** (2)

demythologize **974** (7)

den **192** (3), **192** (17), **255** (2), **527** (1), **662** (1), **883** (2)

den of thieves **788** (5)

denationalize **786** (7)

denature **655** (8)

denial **467** (1), **479** (1), **486** (1), **489** (1), **533** (1), **603** (2), **760** (1), **769** (1)

denied **489** (4)

denier **208** (2), **331** (2), **486** (3)

denigrate **921** (5), **926** (7)

denigrated **921** (4)

denigration **926** (1)

denigrator **926** (4)

denigratory **921** (3), **926** (5)

denim **222** (4)

denims **228** (12)

denizen **191** (1)

denomination **77** (1), **708** (1)

denominational **77** (5)

denominator **85** (2)

denotation **514** (2)

denotative **547** (15)

denote **80** (8), **514** (5), **547** (18), **551** (8)

denouement **69** (1), **154** (1), **725** (1)

denounce **524** (9), **528** (10), **888** (7), **924** (10), **926** (7), **928** (8)

denounced **928** (6)

denouncer **926** (3)

dense **45** (7), **48** (2), **74** (9), **162** (7), **205** (4), **322** (4), **324** (4), **354** (4), **499** (3)

dense, be **36** (5), **48** (3), **198** (7), **324** (6), **354** (6)

densely arrayed **324** (4)

denseness **499** (1)

density **319** (1), **324** (1)

dent **255** (1), **255** (8), **260** (3), **279** (2), **279** (8), **311** (1), **311** (4)

dental **256** (8)

dental surgeon **658** (14)

dented **255** (6)

dentifrice **648** (4)

dentist **658** (14)

dentistry **658** (11)

dentures **256** (4)

denude **229** (6), **786** (10)

denuded **163** (5), **772** (2)

denunciation **479** (1), **899** (1), **928** (1)

deny **479** (3), **486** (6), **533** (3), **752** (4), **760** (4)

deny entry **57** (5)

deny firmly **760** (4)

deny God **974** (7)

deny in part **533** (3)

deny one's rights **914** (6)

deny oneself **621** (3), **942** (4), **981** (12)

denying **467** (2), **533** (2), **760** (2)

denyingly **760** (5)

deodorant **395** (1), **648** (4), **843** (3)

deodorization **395** (1), **648** (2)

deodorize **395** (3), **648** (10)

deodorized **395** (2)

deodorizer **395** (1)

depart **46** (7), **190** (7), **267** (11), **290** (3), **296** (4), **298** (5), **446** (3), **621** (3)

depart from **15** (6)

depart this life **296** (4), **361** (7)

departed **361** (6)

departed spirit **970** (3)

departing **296** (3)

departing from **15** (4)

department **53** (3), **77** (1), **622** (4)

department store **796** (3)

departure **68** (3), **290** (1), **296** (1), **298** (1), **308** (1), **446** (1), **621** (1), **667** (1), **753** (1)

departure from **15** (1)

depend **89** (4), **157** (6), **474** (8)

depend on **473** (7), **485** (7), **745** (6)

dependability **768** (1)

dependable **768** (2), **929** (4)

dependant **35** (2), **89** (2), **284** (2), **707** (1), **742** (4), **879** (2)

dependants **702** (4)
dependence **9** (2), **35** (1), **745** (1), **774** (1)
dependence on **485** (1)
dependency **733** (6), **742** (5)
dependent **35** (4), **217** (4), **745** (5), **774** (2), **879** (3)
dependent on **157** (3), **180** (2)
depending **157** (3)
depending on **8** (5), **474** (4)
depict **551** (8), **590** (7)
depicting **553** (1)
depiction **551** (1), **590** (1)
depilation **843** (2)
depilatory **843** (3)
deplete **634** (4), **636** (9)
depleted **634** (3)
depletion **634** (1)
deplorable **645** (2), **827** (6), **830** (3), **836** (4)
deplore **830** (4), **836** (5), **924** (9)
deploy **187** (5), **197** (4), **673** (5)
deployment **294** (1)
deponent **466** (4)
depopulate **165** (9), **300** (8)
depopulated **190** (5)
deport **57** (5), **272** (7), **300** (6)
deportation **57** (1), **272** (1), **300** (1), **963** (4)
deported **883** (6)
deportee **300** (1), **883** (4)
deportment **445** (5), **688** (1)
deposal **752** (2)
depose **188** (4), **734** (7), **752** (5), **786** (10), **916** (9)
deposed **161** (5), **916** (7)
deposit **41** (2), **53** (1), **187** (5), **324** (3), **324** (6), **344** (3), **632** (1), **632** (5), **649** (2), **767** (1), **804** (1)
deposit of faith **973** (4)
deposited **41** (4), **767** (3)
deposition **466** (2), **532** (2), **734** (2), **752** (2)
depositor **802** (2)

depository **632** (2)
depot **76** (1), **187** (3), **295** (2), **632** (2), **796** (2)
depravation **655** (1)
deprave **655** (8)
depraved **645** (2), **655** (5), **934** (4), **951** (8)
depravity **645** (1), **934** (1)
deprecate **468** (3), **489** (5), **598** (4), **613** (3), **664** (5), **678** (11), **704** (4), **715** (3), **738** (10), **762** (3), **829** (5), **830** (4), **861** (4), **924** (9)
deprecating **874** (2)
deprecation **489** (1), **532** (1), **533** (1), **598** (1), **613** (1), **664** (1), **691** (1), **702** (1), **715** (1), **760** (1), **761** (1), **762** (1), **769** (1), **829** (1), **924** (1), **924** (4), **981** (4)
deprecatory **489** (3), **533** (2), **598** (3), **613** (2), **664** (3), **760** (2), **762** (2), **829** (3), **924** (6)
depreciate **483** (4), **797** (11), **810** (2), **812** (5)
depreciated **797** (9)
depreciating **483** (2), **921** (3), **922** (3)
depreciation **37** (1), **42** (1), **483** (1), **772** (1), **797** (3), **805** (1), **812** (1), **926** (1)
depredation **165** (2)
depredations **788** (3)
depress **37** (4), **210** (3), **255** (8), **311** (4), **613** (3), **827** (10), **829** (6), **834** (12)
depressed **255** (6), **834** (5), **893** (2)
depressing **827** (4), **834** (8)
depression **210** (1), **211** (1), **255** (1), **255** (2), **255** (3), **311** (1), **340** (3), **503** (2), **655** (1), **731** (1), **801** (1), **834** (2)
depressive **503** (7)
deprivation **46** (2), **190** (1), **300** (1), **636** (2), **752** (2), **772** (1), **774** (1), **916** (3), **963** (4)

deprive **163** (10), **300** (6), **752** (5), **780** (3), **786** (10), **801** (6), **834** (11), **867** (11), **916** (9)
deprive of form **244** (3)
deprive of power **161** (9)
deprive of sight **439** (4)
deprived **772** (2), **801** (3), **916** (7)
deprived of **627** (4)
depth **26** (1), **32** (1), **183** (2), **195** (1), **201** (2), **203** (1), **210** (1), **211** (1), **224** (1), **255** (2), **465** (3)
depth charge **723** (14)
depth of mind **498** (3)
depth of space **183** (1)
depth required **211** (1)
depths **210** (1)
depths of misery **825** (2)
depths of space **199** (1)
deputation **751** (1)
depute **751** (4)
deputed **751** (3)
deputize **150** (5), **520** (8), **622** (8), **755** (3)
deputizing **755** (2)
deputy **35** (2), **150** (2), **231** (3), **686** (1), **754** (1), **755** (1)
deputy head **537** (1)
derail **63** (3), **188** (4)
derailment **188** (1)
derange **51** (5), **61** (10), **63** (3), **75** (4), **222** (10), **244** (3), **246** (5), **259** (9), **261** (3), **297** (8), **318** (6), **456** (8), **503** (12), **645** (6), **655** (9), **702** (8), **734** (5), **827** (10)
deranged **63** (2), **503** (7)
derangement **61** (1), **63** (1), **188** (1), **655** (3), **825** (3)
derby **228** (23)
derelict **41** (3), **774** (3), **779** (2), **883** (4)
dereliction of duty **918** (1)
derestrict **779** (4)
deride **835** (7), **851** (5)
deriding **980** (4)
derision **835** (2), **851** (1), **922** (1), **980** (1)

derisive 174 (6), 519 (3), 543 (4), 835 (5), 849 (3), 851 (4), 878 (5), 921 (3), 924 (6), 926 (5), 980 (4)

derisively 921 (6)

derisory 835 (5), 849 (2)

derivable 157 (3), 158 (2)

derivation 68 (4), 156 (3), 158 (1), 559 (1)

derivative 20 (4), 85 (2), 157 (3)

derive 771 (7)

derive from 157 (5), 158 (3)

dermatitis 651 (12)

dermis 226 (6)

derogatory 483 (2), 867 (6), 926 (5)

derrick 310 (2)

derv 385 (1)

dervish 945 (2), 986 (5)

desalinate 648 (10)

descant 412 (3), 413 (10), 570 (6), 591 (5), 981 (5)

descend 35 (5), 37 (5), 220 (5), 265 (4), 286 (4), 309 (3), 311 (8), 313 (3), 313 (4), 322 (5), 350 (9)

descend from 157 (5)

descendant 41 (3), 67 (3), 170 (2)

descendants 124 (1)

descended 157 (3), 170 (4)

descending 220 (4), 271 (6), 309 (2), 655 (5)

descending order 71 (2)

descent 11 (1), 37 (1), 65 (1), 71 (1), 120 (1), 169 (2), 170 (3), 211 (1), 220 (2), 265 (1), 271 (1), 309 (1), 313 (1), 655 (1), 701 (1), 728 (1), 868 (1)

descration 921 (1)

describe 505 (9), 524 (10), 548 (7), 551 (8), 586 (8), 590 (7)

describe a circle 232 (3), 233 (3), 250 (8)

description 18 (2), 20 (2), 547 (1), 551 (1), 557 (3), 561 (1), 561 (2), 589 (2), 590 (1)

descriptive 516 (3), 551 (6), 590 (6)

descry 438 (7)

desecrate 649 (9), 655 (9), 675 (2), 916 (8), 921 (5), 980 (6)

desecrating 980 (4)

desecration 980 (1)

desecrator 980 (3)

desert 165 (2), 172 (3), 172 (4), 183 (1), 190 (2), 342 (1), 342 (4), 344 (1), 458 (5), 603 (5), 603 (6), 620 (6), 621 (3), 644 (1), 769 (3), 856 (4), 883 (2), 896 (5), 918 (3), 933 (2)

desert sands 172 (3)

deserted 88 (4), 190 (5), 458 (3), 883 (7), 896 (3)

deserted village 779 (2)

deserter 603 (3), 620 (2), 856 (2), 918 (1)

desertification 172 (1)

desertion 603 (1), 621 (1), 738 (1), 856 (1), 896 (1), 918 (1), 930 (2)

deserts 688 (1), 714 (1), 913 (1), 915 (1), 962 (1)

deserve 644 (10), 915 (7)

deserve praise 923 (11)

deserve to lose 772 (4)

deserved 913 (4), 915 (2)

deserving 644 (4), 915 (3), 923 (6)

deserving pity 905 (5)

deshabille 228 (6), 229 (1)

desiccate 342 (6)

desiccated 342 (4)

desiccation 340 (1), 342 (2), 381 (1), 666 (1)

design 23 (1), 56 (1), 56 (5), 164 (1), 164 (7), 243 (1), 551 (1), 551 (8), 553 (1), 553 (5), 617 (1), 617 (5), 623 (1), 623 (8), 844 (3)

designate 80 (8), 120 (2), 124 (4), 547 (19), 605 (5), 605 (7)

designation 77 (1), 561 (1), 561 (2)

designed 192 (20), 608 (2), 617 (4)

designedly 617 (7)

designer 164 (4), 556 (1), 594 (12), 623 (5)

designing 243 (2), 541 (4), 930 (4), 932 (3)

designless 159 (5), 618 (6)

desirability 605 (1), 627 (2), 642 (1)

desirable 642 (2), 828 (3), 859 (10), 887 (11), 923 (6)

desire 291 (1), 507 (4), 513 (3), 595 (2), 597 (6), 612 (1), 617 (1), 617 (6), 627 (6), 761 (1), 761 (5), 816 (2), 825 (1), 830 (1), 830 (4), 834 (9), 859 (1), 859 (5), 859 (11), 887 (1), 887 (14), 912 (1), 912 (3)

desired 507 (3), 627 (3), 828 (3), 859 (10), 887 (11), 923 (6)

desired object 615 (2), 617 (2), 859 (5), 890 (2)

desirer 859 (6)

desiring 507 (2), 597 (4), 617 (3), 821 (3), 825 (6), 859 (7), 887 (9), 912 (2), 951 (8)

desirous 859 (7)

desirously 859 (14)

desist 72 (4), 145 (6)

desk 194 (5), 218 (5)

desk worker 686 (2)

desolate 165 (9), 172 (4), 190 (5), 853 (2), 883 (6), 883 (7)

desolation 165 (2)

despair 508 (4), 509 (4), 825 (2), 834 (1), 834 (9), 853 (1), 853 (4)

despair of, the 938 (1)

despaired of 361 (5), 853 (3)

despairing 483 (2), 825 (6), 834 (5), 853 (2)

desperado 162 (4), 176 (4), 362 (7), 855 (3), 857 (2), 904 (2)

desperate 32 (13), 176 (6), 853 (2), 853 (3), 853 (5), 855 (4), 857 (3)

desperate bid 618 (2)

desperate remedy 629 (1)

desperate situation 661 (1)

desperately 32 (18)

desperation 853 (1)

despicable 867 (4), 867 (5), 922 (4), 934 (6)

despise 483 (4), 547 (21), 862 (4), 871 (5), 878 (6), 888 (7), 921 (5), 922 (5), 924 (9), 926 (6)

despised 867 (4), 922 (4)

despising 871 (4), 878 (4), 899 (4), 921 (3), 922 (3), 926 (5)

despite 25 (7), 31 (7), 182 (4), 468 (5), 704 (6)

despoil 165 (9), 788 (9)

despoiler 168 (1), 789 (2)

despondency 834 (1), 853 (1)

despondent 825 (6), 834 (5)

despondent, be 825 (7)

despot 735 (3), 741 (2)

despotic 735 (5), 735 (6), 954 (7)

despotic, be 735 (8)

despotism 733 (3), 735 (2)

dessert 67 (1), 301 (13), 301 (17), 392 (2)

dessert wine 301 (29)

destination 145 (5), 617 (2)

destine 155 (4), 596 (8), 608 (3)

destine for 617 (5)

destined 124 (4), 155 (2), 596 (6)

destiny 69 (3), 124 (1), 124 (2), 155 (1), 156 (2), 178 (1), 507 (1), 596 (1), 596 (2), 608 (1)

destitute 627 (4), 774 (2), 801 (3)

destitution 801 (1)

destroy 2 (8), 46 (8), 46 (12), 165 (6), 188 (4), 300 (6), 304 (4), 362 (10), 362 (11), 467 (4), 479 (3), 645 (7), 655 (9), 727 (10), 801 (6)

destroy one's good name 926 (7)

destroyed 161 (5), 165 (5), 728 (6)

destroyed, be 51 (5), 165 (11), 361 (8), 655 (7), 718 (11), 728 (9), 731 (7)

destroyer 168 (1), 176 (4), 216 (3), 659 (1), 722 (13), 786 (4), 904 (1)

destroying 165 (4)

destruction 2 (2), 46 (2), 51 (1), 69 (3), 165 (1), 176 (1), 176 (2), 182 (1), 300 (1), 304 (1), 333 (1), 362 (1), 362 (4), 634 (1), 655 (2), 655 (3), 738 (2)

destructive 149 (3), 165 (4), 176 (5), 616 (2), 634 (2), 645 (3), 731 (4)

destructive, be 634 (4)

destructiveness 165 (1)

desuetude 611 (1), 621 (1), 674 (1), 779 (1)

desultory 61 (7), 152 (4), 456 (6)

detach 46 (8), 49 (3), 75 (4), 272 (7), 272 (8)

detachable 46 (6)

detached 10 (3), 49 (2), 192 (20), 744 (7), 820 (3), 913 (4)

detached house 192 (6)

detachment 46 (1), 46 (2), 53 (1), 456 (1), 722 (7), 722 (8), 820 (1), 823 (1), 913 (2)

detail 33 (2), 53 (1), 80 (8), 272 (7), 272 (8), 570 (6), 590 (7), 722 (7), 722 (8), 737 (6), 844 (3)

detailed 54 (3), 80 (6), 570 (3), 590 (6)

details 80 (2), 590 (1)

detain 747 (10), 778 (5)

detained 747 (6), 750 (2), 778 (4)

detainee 750 (1)

detect 394 (3), 438 (7), 484 (5), 516 (5)

detectable 443 (2)

detection 459 (6), 484 (1), 490 (1)

detective 441 (1), 453 (2), 459 (8), 524 (5), 955 (3)

detective story 590 (4)

detective work 459 (6)

detector 269 (4), 459 (9), 484 (2)

détente 177 (1), 710 (1), 719 (1)

detention 136 (2), 702 (1), 747 (3), 778 (1), 959 (2), 963 (4)

detention camp 748 (3)

deter 613 (3), 702 (8), 854 (12), 900 (3)

detergent 648 (4), 648 (8)

deteriorate 35 (5), 51 (5), 127 (8), 147 (6), 163 (9), 165 (11), 634 (4), 651 (23), 655 (7), 657 (1), 674 (5), 731 (7), 832 (3), 980 (6)

deteriorated 35 (4), 131 (6), 198 (4), 645 (2), 647 (3), 653 (2), 655 (5), 731 (5), 832 (2), 845 (2)

deteriorating 655 (5)

deterioration 35 (1), 37 (1), 131 (3), 143 (1), 147 (1), 161 (2), 163 (1), 165 (3), 198 (1), 611 (1), 616 (1), 634 (1), 645 (1), 655 (1), 657 (1), 731 (1), 772 (1), 801 (1), 832 (1)

determinant 85 (2), 156 (2)

determination 595 (0), 599 (1), 602 (1), 617 (1), 678 (3), 855 (1)

determine 62 (4), 69 (6), 80 (8), 156 (9), 595 (2), 599 (3), 617 (5)

determined 595 (1), 599 (2), 599 (3), 602 (4), 855 (4)

determinism 449 (3), 596 (1)

determinist 596 (3)

deterministic 596 (4)

deterrence 613 (1), 854 (4)

deterrent 182 (1), 660 (2), 664 (3), 713 (1), 723 (3), 854 (4), 900 (1), 900 (2)

detest 861 (4), 888 (7)

detestable 645 (4)

dethrone 734 (7), 752 (5), 916 (9)

dethroned 916 (7)

dethronement 734 (2), 752 (2)

detonate 176 (7)

detonation 176 (2), 402 (1)

detonator 385 (3), 723 (13)

detour 282 (1), 624 (4), 626 (1)

detract 483 (4), 851 (5), 898 (8), 922 (6), 924 (10), 926 (6)

detract from 37 (4), 39 (3)

detracting 483 (2), 829 (3), 851 (4), 878 (4), 885 (5), 898 (4), 924 (6), 926 (5), 928 (5)

detraction 483 (1), 851 (2), 867 (1), 878 (1), 921 (1), 924 (1), 926 (1)

detractor 483 (1), 486 (3), 489 (2), 835 (3), 839 (3), 904 (1), 924 (5), 926 (3), 980 (3)

detriment 641 (1), 643 (1), 655 (3)

detrimental 643 (2), 645 (3)

detritus 74 (7)

deuce 28 (5), 90 (1)

devaluation 797 (3), 805 (1)

devalue 641 (7), 655 (9), 797 (11)

devalued 797 (9)

devastate 165 (9)

devastation 165 (2), 712 (2)

develop 1 (7), 36 (4), 36 (5), 157 (5), 164 (7), 192 (22), 197 (5), 285 (3), 285 (4), 316 (3), 534 (6), 551 (9), 654 (8), 654 (9)

develop into 147 (6)

developed 164 (5)

developed from 157 (3)

developer 164 (4)

developing 130 (4)

development 36 (1), 134 (1), 147 (1), 157 (2), 164 (1), 167 (1), 197 (1), 285 (1), 316 (1), 654 (1)

deviant 84 (3), 84 (7)

deviate 15 (6), 46 (7), 143 (5), 152 (5), 220 (6), 239 (3), 265 (4), 278 (4), 282 (3), 290 (3), 294 (3), 570 (6), 620 (5), 626 (3), 728 (7)

deviating 10 (3), 15 (4), 46 (4), 84 (5), 152 (4), 188 (2), 220 (3), 223 (2), 265 (3), 267 (9), 282 (2), 294 (2), 456 (5), 495 (4), 495 (5), 570 (4)

deviation 10 (2), 15 (1), 17 (1), 84 (1), 84 (2), 86 (4), 143 (1), 188 (1), 220 (1), 239 (1), 251 (3), 265 (1), 272 (1), 282 (1), 294 (1), 305 (3), 306 (1), 307 (1), 626 (1)

deviationism 84 (1)

deviationist 84 (3), 738 (4)

device 451 (1), 547 (11), 623 (3), 628 (2), 629 (1), 630 (1)

devil 176 (4), 388 (6), 934 (1), 938 (4), 969 (2), 970 (4), 970 (5), 983 (5)

devil incarnate 904 (4), 938 (4)

devil-may-care 618 (6), 857 (3)

Devil, the 969 (1)

devil worship 934 (1), 969 (3), 982 (1)

devil-worshipper 969 (4), 982 (4)

devil-worshipping 982 (5)

devilish 645 (5), 898 (7), 934 (3), 969 (5), 970 (6)

devilishly 32 (18)

devilry 934 (1), 969 (3)

devil's advocate 477 (3)

devious 282 (2), 314 (3), 698 (4), 930 (4)

deviousness 930 (1)

devise 272 (6), 449 (7), 513 (7), 623 (8), 777 (6)

devised 608 (2)

devitalize 163 (10)

devoid 190 (5)

devoid of logic 476 (2)

devoid of taste 387 (2)

devoid of truth 495 (4)

devolution 51 (1), 751 (1), 780 (1)

devolve 780 (3)

devolve on 917 (8)

devote 781 (7), 979 (9)

devote oneself 931 (3)

devote thought to 449 (7)

devote to 673 (3)

devoted 599 (2), 739 (3), 880 (6), 887 (9), 931 (2), 979 (6), 981 (9)

devoted to 610 (7)

devotee 504 (3), 610 (4), 859 (6), 978 (4), 981 (8)

devotion 597 (1), 599 (1), 739 (2), 887 (1), 920 (1), 979 (1), 981 (1), 981 (6)

devotional 973 (8), 981 (10)

devotions 981 (4)

devour 165 (6), 165 (10), 299 (4), 301 (35), 634 (4), 786 (7), 786 (11), 947 (4)

devoured by 818 (4)

devourer 786 (4)

devouring 301 (1), 786 (5), 947 (3)

devout 973 (8), 976 (8), 979 (6), 981 (9)

devoutness 979 (1)

dew 341 (1)

dew point 341 (1)

dewiness 126 (1), 341 (1), 648 (1)

dewlap 217 (2)

dewpond 346 (1)

dewy 126 (5), 128 (5), 341 (4), 648 (7)

dexterity 694 (1)

dexterous 694 (4)

dextral 241 (2)

dextrality 239 (1), 241 (1)

dextro- 241 (2)

dextrous 241 (2)

dhoti 228 (14)

dhow 275 (5)

di- 90 (2)

diabetes 651 (3)

diabetic 651 (18), 651 (22)

diabolic 934 (3), 969 (5), 972 (3), 982 (5), 983 (7)

diabolical 645 (5), 898 (7), 969 (5)

diabolism 969 (3), 974 (2), 982 (1), 983 (1)

diabolist 969 (4), 982 (4)

diabolize 969 (6)

diadem 743 (1), 844 (8)

diaeresis 547 (14), 593 (5)

diagnosis 77 (1), 651 (19), 658 (10)

diagnostic 5 (8), 15 (5), 80 (5), 459 (11), 547 (2), 547 (15)

diagnostician 658 (14)

diagonal 92 (3), 220 (1), 220 (3), 222 (6), 281 (3)

diagonally 220 (7)

diagram 233 (1), 551 (1), 623 (1)

diagrammatic 547 (15), 551 (6)

dial 117 (3), 524 (10), 665 (3)

dial 999 665 (3)

dialect 80 (1), 517 (1), 557 (1), 560 (2), 565 (1), 577 (2), 580 (1)

dialectal 557 (5), 560 (5)

dialectic 459 (2), 475 (1), 475 (3), 475 (7)

dialectical materialism 449 (3)

dialectician 475 (6)

dialectics 475 (1)

dialogue 459 (2), 460 (1), 475 (3), 475 (4), 584 (1)

dialysis 658 (11)

diameter 92 (3), 205 (1)

diametrically opposite 14 (3)

diamond 247 (4), 844 (8)

diamond jubilee 141 (3)

diamond-studded 875 (4)

Diana 321 (9), 619 (3), 967 (1)

diaphanous 422 (2)

diarist 117 (5), 549 (2), 589 (7), 590 (5)

diarrhoea 302 (3), 651 (7)

diary 117 (4), 505 (3), 548 (1), 590 (3)

diaspora 75 (1)

diatonic 410 (8)

diatribe 579 (2), 924 (2)

dice 46 (11), 301 (40), 511 (4), 618 (2), 618 (8), 837 (12), 837 (21)

dice with death 661 (8), 857 (4)

dicer 837 (16)

dicey 661 (3)

dichotomy 46 (3), 92 (1)

dicing 837 (12)

dictaphone 549 (3)

dictate 579 (8), 596 (8), 689 (5), 691 (4), 733 (10), 733 (12), 737 (1), 737 (2), 737 (6), 740 (3)

dictated 577 (3), 596 (4)

dictated to, be 733 (13)

dictation 596 (1), 606 (1), 737 (1), 737 (2), 740 (1)

dictator 735 (3), 741 (2)

dictatorial 481 (7), 595 (1), 689 (3), 733 (7), 735 (5), 737 (5), 740 (2)

dictatorship 689 (2), 733 (3), 735 (2)

diction 563 (1), 566 (1)

dictionary 87 (2), 559 (2), 589 (4)

dictum 473 (1), 496 (1), 579 (1)

didactic 534 (5), 691 (3)

didacticism 691 (1)

die 2 (7), 23 (3), 296 (4), 361 (7), 555 (2)

die a natural death 361 (7)

die away 27 (5), 37 (5)

die down 37 (5), 266 (7), 352 (10), 382 (6)

die fighting 361 (8)

die for 931 (3)

die hard 361 (8), 602 (3)

die in harness 600 (4)

die in one's sleep 361 (7)

die out 2 (7), 37 (5), 69 (5), 361 (8)

die rich 800 (5)

die the death 963 (13)

die untimely 361 (8)

died out 2 (5)

diesel 274 (14)

diesel oil 385 (1)

diet 198 (7), 301 (1), 301 (3), 658 (12), 942 (4), 946 (4)

dietary 301 (33)

dieter 942 (2)

dietetic 301 (33)

dietetics 301 (3)

dieting 301 (3), 942 (1), 946 (1)

dietitian 301 (3)

differ 14 (4), 15 (6), 19 (3), 25 (6), 294 (3), 489 (5), 709 (7)

difference 10 (1), 14 (1), 15 (1), 17 (1), 19 (1), 25 (1), 29 (1), 41 (1), 46 (1), 80 (1), 85 (4), 143 (1), 294 (1), 463 (1)

differences 709 (1), 978 (2)

differencing 547 (11)

different 14 (3), 15 (4), 15 (6), 17 (2), 19 (2), 21 (4), 25 (4), 34 (4), 46 (5), 59 (4), 80 (5), 82 (2), 147 (5)

different kettle of fish 15 (3)

different thing 15 (3)

different time 122 (1)

differential 15 (1), 27 (1), 85 (2), 85 (5), 771 (2)

differential calculus 86 (3)

differentiate 15 (7), 19 (4), 46 (9), 80 (8), 86 (12), 462 (3), 463 (3)

differentiating 15 (5)

differentiation 15 (2), 463 (1)

differently 15 (8)

differing 15 (4), 489 (3), 977 (2)

difficult 459 (12), 470 (3), 517 (3), 568 (2), 682 (5), 700 (4), 702 (6), 738 (7), 862 (3), 885 (5), 893 (2)

difficult, be 643 (3), 700 (6), 702 (10), 731 (7)

difficult choice 605 (1)

difficult for, be 731 (7)

difficult person 700 (1)

difficulties 801 (1)

difficulty 61 (3), 517 (1), 530 (2), 568 (1), 700 (1), 702 (2), 731 (1), 738 (4), 825 (1), 832 (1)

diffidence 854 (2), 874 (1)
diffident 474 (6), 874 (2)
diffraction 417 (5)
diffuse 10 (4), 54 (3), 75 (4), 79 (6), 528 (9), 540 (2), 570 (3), 576 (2), 590 (6)
diffuse, be 10 (5), 80 (8), 106 (5), 570 (6), 579 (8), 581 (5)
diffused 75 (2)
diffusely 570 (7)
diffuseness 515 (3), 563 (1), 568 (1), 570 (1), 574 (2), 579 (1), 581 (1), 838 (1)
diffuser 272 (4)
diffusion 46 (1), 75 (1), 189 (1), 272 (1), 297 (1), 524 (1)
diffusive 570 (4)
dig 255 (4), 255 (8), 279 (2), 318 (1), 318 (6), 370 (9), 459 (5), 459 (15)
dig down 309 (3)
dig for 459 (15), 619 (5)
dig in 187 (8), 660 (9), 713 (9), 718 (12)
dig into 459 (13)
dig one's heels in 599 (4)
dig out 255 (8), 304 (4)
dig up 304 (4), 364 (10)
dig up the past 125 (11)
digest 62 (1), 143 (6), 299 (4), 301 (35), 449 (8), 455 (4), 592 (1), 721 (4), 823 (6)
digested 669 (8)
digestibility 301 (1)
digestible 301 (32)
digestion 62 (1), 299 (1), 301 (1)
digestive 299 (2), 658 (17)
digestive disorders 302 (3), 651 (7)
digger 255 (5)
digging 459 (5), 459 (11)
digging out 304 (1)
digit 85 (1), 378 (3)
digital 85 (5), 86 (9), 86 (10), 378 (6)
digital computer 86 (6)
digital watch 117 (3)

dignification 866 (5)
dignified 575 (3), 821 (5), 848 (6), 866 (8), 871 (3), 875 (6), 884 (3)
dignify 866 (14)
dignifying 866 (8)
dignitary 741 (6), 986 (4)
dignity 575 (1), 688 (1), 848 (2), 866 (4), 871 (1), 875 (1), 875 (2)
digress 282 (3), 570 (6)
digression 282 (1), 306 (1), 626 (1)
digressive 10 (3)
digs 192 (2)
dike 201 (2), 235 (2), 351 (1)
dilapidated 51 (3), 127 (7), 163 (5), 163 (8), 165 (5), 649 (7), 655 (6), 661 (4), 673 (2), 801 (4)
dilapidation 37 (1), 51 (2), 165 (1), 655 (2), 673 (1), 801 (1)
dilate 36 (4), 197 (4), 325 (3), 352 (12), 570 (6)
dilation 197 (2)
dilatory 136 (3), 278 (3), 679 (8)
dilemma 474 (2), 605 (1), 700 (3)
dilettante 491 (7), 492 (3), 493 (2), 846 (2), 859 (6)
dilettantism 490 (2), 491 (3), 846 (1)
diligence 274 (8), 455 (1), 457 (1), 678 (3), 768 (1)
diligent 455 (2), 457 (3), 536 (3), 768 (2)
dilute 37 (4), 163 (10), 325 (3), 339 (3), 341 (7)
diluted 163 (5), 339 (2), 387 (2)
dilution 163 (1), 339 (1)
dim 4 (3), 355 (4), 418 (3), 418 (6), 419 (4), 419 (7), 423 (2), 424 (2), 426 (3), 426 (5), 440 (4), 444 (3), 499 (3), 517 (3), 834 (5)
dim, be 418 (5), 419 (6), 426 (4), 440 (5), 444 (4)
dim memory 506 (1)

dim sight 438 (1), 439 (1), 440 (1)
dim-sighted 439 (2), 440 (3), 845 (2)
dim-sighted, be 439 (3), 440 (4)
dim the light 418 (6)
dim-witted 499 (3)
dime 33 (4), 797 (4)
dimension 183 (2)
dimensional 243 (3)
dimensions 26 (1), 195 (1), 465 (3)
diminish 37 (4), 39 (3), 105 (4), 177 (6), 204 (5)
diminished 35 (3), 163 (5)
diminishing 105 (2)
diminishing returns 772 (1)
diminuendo 37 (6), 412 (8)
diminution 33 (1), 37 (2), 39 (1), 42 (1), 51 (2), 198 (1), 204 (2)
diminutive 33 (6), 196 (8), 559 (1), 561 (2)
dimly 419 (8)
dimmed 418 (4)
dimness 418 (1), 418 (2), 419 (1), 444 (1), 523 (1), 655 (1)
dimple 255 (2)
dimpled 195 (8), 255 (6)
dimply 195 (8)
dimwit 501 (3)
din 318 (3), 400 (1), 411 (1)
dine 301 (35), 301 (39)
dine out 301 (35)
diner 192 (13), 301 (6)
diner-out 882 (5)
ding 404 (3)
dingdong 28 (7), 106 (3)
dinghy 275 (7), 275 (8)
dingle 255 (3)
dingy 425 (7), 426 (3), 649 (7), 655 (6), 842 (5)
dining 301 (1)
dining out 301 (1)
dining room 194 (19)
dinky 196 (8)
dinner 301 (12), 837 (2)
dinner jacket 228 (10)
dinosaur 125 (3), 127 (2), 195 (4), 365 (2)

dint **255** (1), **255** (8), **279** (2), **279** (8)

diocesan **985** (6), **986** (4)

diocesans **987** (1)

diocese **184** (3), **985** (4)

Dionysius **967** (1)

dip **220** (2), **220** (5), **255** (2), **255** (3), **269** (12), **303** (2), **303** (7), **309** (1), **311** (1), **311** (4), **313** (1), **313** (3), **341** (8), **418** (7), **419** (7), **420** (3), **425** (8), **547** (22), **648** (3)

dip down **309** (3)

dip into **536** (5)

dip slope **220** (2)

dip the flag **547** (22)

diphtheria **651** (8)

diphthong **577** (1)

diploma **466** (3), **548** (1), **751** (2), **866** (4)

diplomacy **698** (1), **720** (1), **766** (1), **884** (1)

diplomat **696** (2), **720** (2), **754** (3)

diplomatic **541** (4), **694** (4), **755** (2), **848** (6)

diplomatic bag **531** (2)

diplomatic corps **754** (3)

diplomatic immunity **919** (1)

diplomatist **696** (2), **698** (3), **720** (2)

dipped **311** (3), **418** (4)

dipper **194** (18), **313** (2)

dipping **220** (4)

dipsomania **859** (2), **949** (3)

dipsomaniac **949** (5), **949** (11)

diptych **553** (5)

dire **645** (3), **731** (4)

direct **34** (9), **44** (4), **83** (8), **178** (3), **249** (2), **269** (10), **272** (8), **281** (3), **281** (4), **281** (8), **283** (3), **466** (5), **494** (6), **534** (6), **547** (18), **567** (2), **594** (16), **612** (8), **625** (4), **676** (5), **689** (5), **733** (10)

direct action **738** (2)

direct course **625** (1)

direct current **160** (5)

direct line **170** (3)

direct one's gaze **438** (8)

direct opposite **14** (1)

direct taxation **809** (3)

directed **240** (2), **281** (3), **494** (6)

directed towards **281** (3)

directing **34** (4), **178** (2), **689** (3), **955** (4)

direction **9** (1), **179** (1), **240** (1), **267** (8), **281** (1), **445** (3), **534** (1), **594** (2), **624** (4), **688** (1), **689** (2), **693** (1), **733** (2), **733** (4)

direction finder **281** (1), **547** (6)

directive **281** (3), **737** (1)

directly **32** (16), **116** (4), **135** (8), **249** (5), **573** (4)

directness **249** (1), **567** (1)

director **520** (5), **594** (12), **676** (3), **690** (1), **733** (1), **741** (1)

directorial **689** (3)

directorship **34** (1), **269** (2), **689** (2), **733** (1), **733** (2), **733** (5), **741** (1)

directory **87** (3), **524** (6), **547** (1), **589** (4)

dirge **364** (2), **412** (4), **412** (5), **593** (2), **836** (2)

dirk **723** (8)

dirndl **228** (13)

dirt **41** (2), **226** (1), **332** (1), **397** (1), **423** (1), **641** (3), **649** (2), **845** (1), **951** (1)

dirt-encrusted **649** (7)

dirt-free **648** (7)

dirty **61** (7), **332** (4), **419** (7), **423** (2), **458** (2), **458** (3), **645** (2), **649** (7), **649** (8), **649** (9), **653** (3), **801** (4), **845** (2), **867** (4), **951** (6)

dirty habits **649** (1), **653** (1)

dirty joke **839** (2)

dirty look **438** (3)

dirty person **61** (5), **649** (5)

dirty trick **542** (2), **616** (1), **930** (3)

dirty weather **176** (3), **352** (4)

dirty work **930** (3)

disability **643** (1), **651** (2)

disable **37** (4), **161** (9), **163** (10), **165** (8), **641** (7), **655** (9), **702** (8)

disabled **161** (7), **163** (5), **163** (7), **266** (4)

disabled person **651** (18)

disablement **655** (3)

disabuse **524** (9), **526** (4), **534** (6)

disaccustom **611** (4), **674** (5)

disadvantage **35** (1), **616** (1), **643** (1)

disadvantageous **643** (2)

disaffect **613** (3)

disaffected **881** (3)

disaffection **489** (1), **888** (1)

disagree **14** (4), **15** (6), **25** (6), **411** (3), **486** (6), **489** (5), **533** (3), **598** (4), **709** (7)

disagree with **645** (6), **827** (11), **861** (5)

disagreeable **377** (3), **397** (2), **827** (4), **861** (3), **885** (4)

disagreeableness **827** (1)

disagreeing **10** (3), **14** (3), **15** (4), **17** (2), **25** (4), **84** (5), **411** (2), **861** (2)

disagreement **14** (1), **15** (1), **19** (1), **25** (1), **84** (1), **411** (1), **489** (1), **533** (1), **709** (1), **861** (1)

disallow **57** (5), **470** (5), **489** (5), **607** (3), **757** (4), **916** (9), **924** (9)

disallowance **752** (1)

disallowed **489** (4), **760** (3)

disappear **2** (7), **114** (6), **190** (7), **290** (3), **296** (5), **444** (4), **446** (3), **525** (9), **550** (3), **772** (5)

disappearance **114** (1), **190** (1), **444** (1), **446** (1)

disappeared **190** (4)

disappearing **114** (3), **190** (4), **444** (2), **446** (2), **772** (3)

discomposed 825 (5)

discomposure 61 (1), 825 (3)

disconcert 63 (3), 456 (8), 509 (5), 702 (8)

disconcerted 456 (5), 508 (3), 509 (2), 728 (5), 825 (5)

disconcerting 702 (6)

disconnect 46 (8), 72 (4)

disconnected 10 (3), 46 (4), 72 (2)

disconnectedness 46 (1)

disconnection 10 (1), 46 (1), 72 (1)

disconsolate 825 (6), 829 (3), 834 (6), 853 (2)

discontent 489 (1), 509 (1), 509 (5), 547 (4), 616 (1), 636 (1), 665 (1), 738 (1), 762 (1), 825 (2), 829 (1), 834 (2), 891 (1), 893 (1), 924 (1)

discontented 489 (3), 509 (2), 636 (4), 825 (6), 829 (3), 834 (5), 838 (4), 861 (2), 885 (5), 891 (3), 892 (3), 893 (2), 912 (2)

discontented, be 547 (21), 636 (8), 762 (3), 829 (5), 834 (9), 836 (5), 891 (5), 893 (3)

discontenting 509 (3), 636 (3), 827 (4), 829 (4)

discontinuance 752 (1)

discontinuation 72 (1), 145 (1)

discontinue 55 (5), 69 (6), 72 (4), 145 (6), 165 (8), 752 (4)

discontinued 72 (2)

discontinuity 10 (1), 46 (1), 49 (1), 55 (1), 72 (1), 108 (2), 138 (1), 140 (1), 142 (1), 145 (1), 145 (2), 201 (1), 231 (4)

discontinuous 10 (3), 46 (4), 55 (3), 72 (2), 140 (2), 142 (2)

discontinuous, be 72 (3)

discontinuously 72 (5), 142 (3), 201 (5)

discord 14 (1), 15 (1), 25 (1), 25 (3), 43 (4), 61 (1), 398 (1), 407 (1), 407 (4), 411 (1), 411 (3), 576 (1), 709 (1)

discordance 411 (1)

discordant 14 (3), 15 (4), 25 (4), 400 (3), 407 (2), 411 (2), 425 (6), 709 (6)

discotheque 837 (5)

discount 39 (1), 39 (3), 42 (1), 458 (5), 771 (2), 783 (2), 804 (2), 810 (1), 810 (2), 812 (1)

discounting 468 (2)

discourage 613 (3), 702 (8), 757 (4), 829 (6), 834 (12), 854 (12)

discouraged 834 (5)

discouragement 613 (1), 702 (1), 853 (1)

discouraging 613 (2), 702 (6), 829 (4)

discourse 534 (4), 534 (7), 570 (6), 579 (1), 579 (2), 591 (1)

discourse upon 591 (5)

discourteous 176 (5), 695 (5), 847 (5), 878 (5), 885 (4), 893 (2), 908 (2), 921 (3)

discourteously 885 (7)

discourtesy 688 (1), 769 (1), 847 (2), 878 (2), 883 (1), 885 (1), 893 (1), 921 (1), 922 (1)

discover 64 (3), 68 (9), 154 (7), 156 (9), 159 (7), 164 (7), 267 (11), 438 (7), 447 (7), 449 (7), 484 (4), 522 (7), 524 (12), 526 (4), 619 (5), 623 (8), 771 (7)

discoverable 490 (7)

discovered 490 (7)

discoverer 66 (1), 164 (4), 484 (2)

discovering 484 (3)

discovery 68 (1), 125 (2), 156 (1), 164 (1), 445 (1), 451 (1), 459 (1), 459 (6), 484 (1), 490 (1), 520 (1), 526 (1), 547 (1), 632 (1), 771 (1)

discredit 486 (6), 486 (8), 867 (1), 867 (3), 867 (11), 926 (7)

discreditable 32 (10), 645 (2), 867 (5), 924 (8)

discredited 486 (5), 495 (4), 867 (4), 867 (7), 888 (6), 924 (7)

discreet 525 (6), 582 (2), 858 (2)

discreet, be 525 (8)

discrepancy 15 (1), 25 (1)

discrepant 15 (4), 25 (4)

discrepant, be 25 (6)

discrete 46 (5), 72 (2)

discretion 498 (2), 525 (1), 605 (1), 694 (1), 856 (1), 858 (1)

discretionary 595 (1), 597 (5), 744 (8)

discriminate 15 (7), 462 (3), 463 (3), 498 (6), 561 (6), 605 (7), 846 (4), 862 (4), 914 (6)

discriminate against 481 (12)

discriminated 15 (4)

discriminating 463 (2), 605 (4), 819 (3), 846 (3), 862 (3)

discrimination 15 (2), 29 (1), 447 (1), 463 (1), 480 (1), 481 (3), 498 (2), 605 (1), 846 (1), 914 (2)

discriminatory 914 (4)

discursive 475 (7), 570 (4), 591 (4)

discus 250 (2), 287 (2)

discus-thrower 287 (5)

discuss 459 (13), 475 (11), 528 (9), 584 (7), 591 (5)

discussion 475 (4), 584 (3), 591 (1)

discussion group 74 (2)

disdain 607 (3), 871 (5), 878 (1), 921 (5), 922 (1), 922 (5)

disdainful 871 (4), 878 (4), 921 (3), 922 (3)

disdainfully 922 (7)

disease 79 (1), 161 (2), 301 (3), 361 (2), 379 (1), 636

(1), 645 (1), 651 (3), 659 (1)

diseased 229 (5), 645 (2), 651 (22)

diseased mind 447 (1)

disembark 269 (9), 269 (10), 295 (5)

disembodied 320 (3), 970 (7)

disembowel 300 (8)

disembroil 62 (7)

disenchant 148 (3), 613 (3), 827 (11)

disenchanted 148 (2), 860 (2), 861 (2)

disenchantment 148 (1), 827 (1)

disencumber 323 (5), 668 (3), 701 (9), 831 (3)

disencumbered 701 (5)

disendow 752 (5)

disendowment 752 (2)

disengage 46 (7), 46 (8), 286 (4), 746 (3)

disengagement 46 (1), 286 (1), 304 (1)

disentangle 44 (6), 46 (8), 62 (7), 316 (3), 701 (9), 746 (3)

disentangled 44 (4), 62 (3)

disentitle 161 (9), 786 (10), 916 (9)

disentitlement 916 (3)

disestablish 752 (5)

disfavour 888 (2), 924 (1)

disfigure 244 (3), 547 (19), 655 (9), 842 (7), 845 (3)

disfigured 525 (4), 842 (4)

disfigurement 842 (1), 845 (1)

disfranchise 745 (7), 916 (9)

disfranchised 606 (2), 745 (4), 916 (7)

disgorge 300 (8)

disgrace 867 (1), 867 (2), 867 (11), 872 (2), 914 (1), 921 (5), 922 (5), 930 (1), 951 (11)

disgrace oneself 867 (9), 867 (10)

disgraced 867 (4), 867 (7)

disgraceful 645 (2), 867 (5), 934 (6)

disgruntled 509 (2), 829 (3)

disguise 19 (1), 19 (4), 20 (2), 20 (5), 143 (6), 147 (8), 226 (1), 228 (21), 421 (1), 525 (1), 525 (7), 527 (3), 541 (6), 542 (5), 698 (1)

disguised 20 (4), 444 (2), 525 (4)

disguised war 718 (1)

disguisedly 542 (11)

disgust 827 (1), 827 (11), 829 (6), 834 (12), 838 (5), 861 (1), 861 (5), 888 (8)

disgusted 825 (6)

disgusting 391 (2), 645 (4), 827 (4), 838 (3), 861 (3), 888 (5)

dish 43 (3), 194 (16), 194 (17), 301 (13), 321 (11)

dish up 633 (5)

dish-washer 648 (6)

disharmony 15 (1), 25 (1), 61 (1), 411 (1)

dishearten 613 (3), 702 (8), 829 (6), 834 (12)

disheartened 834 (5)

disheartening 702 (6), 829 (4)

dishevel 63 (4)

dishevelled 61 (7)

dishonest 474 (5), 525 (5), 541 (3), 645 (2), 698 (4), 788 (6), 867 (5), 930 (4), 932 (3), 934 (3), 954 (6)

dishonest, be 509 (5), 541 (5), 542 (8), 603 (6), 769 (3), 805 (5), 930 (8)

dishonestly 930 (9)

dishonesty 788 (5), 914 (1), 930 (1), 934 (1), 954 (2)

dishonour 867 (1), 867 (11), 914 (1), 921 (5), 926 (7), 930 (1), 951 (11)

dishonourable 867 (5), 924 (8), 930 (4), 930 (8)

dishonoured 867 (7)

dishonouring 805 (1)

disillusion 509 (1), 509 (5), 524 (9), 526 (4), 613 (3), 827 (1), 827 (11), 830 (1), 834 (1), 888 (1)

disillusioned 830 (2), 834 (5), 860 (2), 861 (2), 888 (4)

disillusioned, be 516 (5)

disincentive 613 (1), 702 (1), 702 (6)

disinclination 598 (1), 861 (1)

disincline 613 (3)

disinclined 489 (3), 861 (2)

disinfect 172 (6), 648 (10), 652 (6)

disinfectant 648 (4), 648 (8), 658 (3)

disinfected 652 (4)

disinfection 648 (2), 652 (2)

disinfest 300 (8)

disingenuous 541 (3), 930 (4)

disingenuousness 543 (2)

disinherit 779 (4), 786 (10), 801 (6)

disinherited 779 (3)

disintegrate 46 (7), 46 (8), 46 (13), 51 (5), 75 (3), 655 (7)

disintegrated 51 (3)

disintegration 46 (2), 51 (1)

disinter 364 (10)

disinterested 813 (3), 872 (3), 897 (4), 901 (6), 913 (4), 931 (2), 933 (3)

disinterested, be 931 (3)

disinterestedness 597 (1), 901 (1), 931 (1)

disinterment 364 (6)

disjointed 572 (2)

disjointedly 46 (14)

disjunctive 46 (5)

dislike 598 (1), 598 (4), 704 (1), 715 (1), 838 (1), 860 (4), 861 (1), 861 (4), 881 (1), 888 (1), 888 (7), 924 (1), 924 (9)

disliked 25 (4), 292 (2), 391 (2), 645 (4), 827 (4),

829 (4), 842 (3), 860 (3), 861 (3), 867 (4), 888 (5), 888 (6), 914 (3), 924 (7)

disliking 598 (3), 825 (6), 838 (4), 861 (2), 881 (3), 888 (4)

dislocate 46 (8), 63 (3), 161 (9), 176 (8), 188 (4)

dislocation 46 (2), 63 (1), 188 (1)

dislodge 63 (3), 188 (4), 300 (6)

disloyal 603 (4), 769 (2), 881 (3), 918 (2), 930 (7)

disloyal, be 918 (3)

disloyalty 738 (1), 738 (3), 769 (1), 881 (1), 918 (1), 930 (2)

dismal 418 (3), 827 (4), 834 (6), 834 (8)

dismally 33 (9)

dismantle 46 (10), 163 (10), 165 (7), 641 (7), 655 (9), 674 (5)

dismantled 670 (6)

dismast 641 (7), 655 (9)

dismasted 670 (6)

dismay 727 (10), 825 (3), 834 (12), 853 (1), 854 (1), 854 (12)

dismayed 825 (5), 834 (5), 854 (6)

dismember 46 (10), 46 (11), 963 (12)

dismembered 46 (4)

dismemberment 51 (1)

dismiss 57 (5), 75 (4), 188 (4), 292 (3), 300 (7), 479 (3), 674 (5), 679 (13), 752 (5), 760 (4), 779 (4), 860 (4), 922 (6)

dismissal 57 (1), 292 (1), 296 (2), 300 (1), 752 (2), 916 (3), 981 (4)

dismount 295 (5), 309 (3)

dismounted 46 (4), 728 (6)

disobedience 61 (1), 489 (1), 533 (1), 734 (2), 738 (1), 760 (1), 769 (1), 829 (1), 918 (1), 930 (2), 934 (1), 978 (1)

disobedient 149 (3), 176 (5), 533 (2), 598 (3), 602

(5), 700 (4), 704 (3), 709 (6), 711 (2), 715 (2), 734 (4), 738 (7), 829 (3), 893 (2), 918 (2), 921 (3), 930 (7), 934 (3), 978 (7)

disobedient, be 738 (9)

disobey 61 (10), 533 (3), 704 (4), 734 (6), 738 (9), 769 (3), 918 (3)

disobey orders 738 (9), 918 (3)

disobeyed 921 (4)

disobeying 738 (7)

disobliging 898 (6)

disorder 10 (1), 17 (1), 51 (5), 61 (1), 61 (10), 63 (1), 63 (3), 72 (1), 75 (4), 142 (1), 244 (1), 244 (3), 458 (1), 645 (1), 649 (1), 651 (3), 702 (8), 734 (2), 738 (2), 847 (2)

disordered 61 (7), 63 (2)

disordered, be 61 (10), 649 (9)

disorderliness 61 (1)

disorderly 61 (9), 176 (5), 400 (3), 734 (4), 738 (8), 847 (5), 949 (6)

disorganize 63 (3)

disorganized 61 (7), 734 (3)

disorientate 63 (3), 188 (4)

disorientated 282 (2), 474 (6)

disorientation 282 (1)

disown 533 (3), 752 (4), 779 (4), 924 (9)

disowned 533 (2), 774 (3), 779 (3), 924 (7)

disparage 37 (4), 483 (4), 867 (11), 921 (5), 922 (6), 926 (6)

disparaged 921 (4)

disparagement 921 (1), 924 (1), 926 (1)

disparager 926 (3)

disparaging 851 (4), 924 (6), 926 (5)

disparate 10 (3), 15 (4), 19 (2), 29 (2)

disparity 10 (1), 15 (1), 19 (1), 25 (1), 29 (1)

dispassionate 480 (4), 820 (3), 823 (3), 913 (4)

dispassionateness 823 (1)

dispatch 135 (2), 188 (4), 265 (5), 272 (1), 272 (8), 277 (1), 301 (35), 362 (1), 362 (10), 529 (1), 588 (1), 678 (1), 678 (11), 680 (1), 680 (3), 725 (5)

dispatch box 194 (7), 531 (2)

dispatch clerk 272 (4)

dispatch news 524 (10)

dispatch rider 529 (6)

dispatcher 272 (4)

dispatches 524 (2)

dispel 46 (8), 75 (4), 165 (6), 292 (3)

dispensable 637 (4), 639 (5), 641 (4)

dispensary 658 (13)

dispensation 57 (1), 668 (1), 689 (1), 756 (1), 779 (1), 783 (1), 919 (1)

dispense 75 (4), 746 (3), 756 (5), 781 (7), 783 (3)

dispense from 668 (3)

dispense with 674 (4), 779 (4)

dispensed with 674 (2), 779 (3)

dispenser 658 (15)

dispensing 783 (1)

dispersal 37 (2), 46 (1), 46 (2), 75 (1), 272 (1)

disperse 37 (5), 46 (7), 46 (8), 51 (5), 61 (10), 63 (4), 75 (3), 75 (4), 79 (6), 165 (6), 188 (4), 203 (8), 265 (5), 292 (3), 311 (5), 446 (3), 634 (4), 727 (10)

dispersed 46 (4), 61 (7), 75 (2)

dispersed, be 75 (3), 197 (4), 263 (17), 267 (13), 294 (3)

dispersion 46 (1), 46 (2), 49 (1), 75 (1), 197 (1), 272 (1), 294 (1), 634 (1)

dispirit 613 (3), 834 (12)

dispirited 834 (5)

dispiritedness 834 (1)

dissentient 84 (3), 489 (2)

dissenting 17 (2), 25 (4), 84 (5), 489 (3), 709 (6), 744 (7), 829 (3), 861 (2), 977 (2), 978 (7), 980 (4)

dissertate 591 (5)

dissertation 520 (2), 570 (1), 579 (2), 589 (2), 591 (1)

dissertator 591 (3)

disservice 616 (1), 641 (1), 898 (3)

dissidence 25 (1), 84 (1), 489 (1)

dissident 25 (3), 84 (3), 84 (5), 489 (2), 489 (3), 705 (1), 738 (4), 829 (2), 829 (3), 978 (5)

dissimilar 15 (4), 17 (2), 19 (2), 19 (3). 29 (2)

dissimilarity 15 (1), 17 (1), 19 (1), 21 (1), 29 (1), 552 (1)

dissimulate 541 (6)

dissimulation 525 (1), 541 (2)

dissipate 75 (4), 165 (6), 446 (3), 634 (4), 815 (4)

dissipated 163 (5), 944 (3), 951 (8)

dissipated, be 951 (10)

dissipation 75 (1), 634 (1), 815 (1), 943 (1), 944 (1), 951 (2)

dissociate 46 (8)

dissociate oneself 598 (4)

dissociation 10 (1), 46 (1), 533 (1), 704 (1), 978 (2)

dissoluble 46 (6), 337 (3)

dissolute 951 (8)

dissoluteness 951 (2)

dissolution 37 (2), 46 (1), 46 (2), 51 (1), 69 (3), 165 (1), 752 (1)

dissolvable 46 (6)

dissolve 27 (5), 51 (5), 75 (3), 244 (3), 337 (4), 446 (3), 551 (4), 752 (4)

dissolve a marriage 896 (5)

dissolve in tears 836 (6)

dissolved 896 (3)

dissolving 51 (1), 165 (1)

dissonance 25 (1), 411 (1)

dissonant 411 (2)

dissuade 148 (3), 177 (6), 486 (8), 613 (3), 664 (5), 691 (4), 702 (8), 757 (4), 762 (3), 829 (6), 834 (12), 854 (12)

dissuasion 613 (1), 762 (1)

dissuasive 613 (2), 762 (2)

distaff 222 (5)

distaff side 11 (4), 373 (2)

distal 199 (3)

distance 15 (1), 70 (1), 183 (3), 199 (1), 203 (1), 285 (3)

distance between 201 (1)

distance of time 113 (1)

distant 59 (4), 88 (4), 199 (3), 223 (2), 401 (3), 444 (2), 454 (2), 871 (4), 881 (3), 883 (5)

distant, be 199 (5), 290 (3)

distant future 124 (1)

distant past 125 (1)

distant time 108 (1)

distaste 861 (1)

distasteful 827 (4)

distemper 651 (17)

distend 197 (4), 197 (5)

distended 197 (3)

distension 197 (2)

distil 44 (7), 298 (7), 304 (4), 338 (4), 648 (10)

distillation 5 (2), 44 (2), 304 (1), 338 (1)

distilled 301 (32)

distilled liquor 301 (28)

distiller 648 (6)

distillery 338 (2), 687 (1)

distinct 15 (4), 19 (2), 46 (5), 80 (6), 398 (3), 400 (3), 443 (3), 516 (2), 577 (3)

distinction 15 (2), 80 (1), 463 (1), 866 (2), 866 (4), 868 (1), 870 (1)

distinctive 15 (5), 46 (5), 80 (5)

distinctive feature 80 (1)

distinctness 15 (1), 398 (1), 400 (1), 443 (1), 577 (1)

distinguish 15 (7), 19 (4), 46 (9), 438 (7), 463 (3), 498 (6), 516 (5), 866 (14)

distinguished 15 (4), 32 (8), 34 (4), 575 (3), 638 (6), 866 (9)

distinguishing 15 (5)

distort 46 (13), 143 (6), 147 (8), 176 (8), 220 (6), 244 (3), 246 (5), 251 (11), 521 (3), 541 (5), 546 (3), 552 (3), 655 (8), 655 (9), 842 (7)

distorted 10 (3), 84 (7), 204 (3), 220 (3), 246 (3), 251 (4), 525 (4), 647 (3), 842 (4)

distorted image 552 (1)

distortion 25 (1), 29 (1), 220 (1), 244 (1), 246 (1), 521 (1), 535 (1), 541 (1), 543 (1), 546 (1), 552 (1), 675 (1), 842 (1), 845 (1)

distract 63 (3), 456 (8)

distracted 456 (5), 821 (3)

distracted, be 456 (7)

distraction 456 (2), 822 (2)

distrain 786 (10)

distraint 786 (2)

distraught 503 (9), 821 (3)

distress 377 (1), 377 (5), 616 (1), 645 (7), 684 (1), 684 (6), 731 (1), 801 (1), 821 (8), 825 (1), 825 (3), 827 (8)

distress call 547 (8)

distress oneself 825 (7)

distress signal 547 (5), 665 (1)

distressed 825 (5)

distressing 616 (2), 645 (2), 818 (6), 827 (6)

distribute 528 (9), 783 (3)

distributed 528 (7)

distribution 62 (1), 75 (1), 783 (1)

distribution list 588 (1)

district 53 (3), 184 (3), 184 (5), 185 (1), 187 (2), 192 (1), 192 (8), 344 (1), 733 (6)

district nurse 658 (16)

district officer 741 (6)

distrust 486 (2), 486 (7), 854 (11), 911 (1), 911 (3)

distrustful 486 (4), 854 (7), 911 (2)

disturb 51 (5), 63 (3), 138 (4), 188 (4), 318 (6), 374 (6), 456 (8), 827 (10), 854 (12)

disturb the peace 709 (9)

disturbance 61 (4), 63 (1), 318 (3), 738 (2)

disturbed 176 (5)

disunion 10 (1), 25 (1), 46 (1), 51 (1), 61 (1), 165 (1), 176 (2), 263 (1), 332 (1), 709 (1)

disunite 46 (8), 49 (3), 51 (5), 53 (7), 72 (4), 75 (4), 163 (10), 165 (7), 188 (4), 263 (17), 641 (7), 655 (10), 668 (3), 701 (9), 779 (4), 896 (5)

disunited 10 (3), 46 (4), 51 (3), 53 (6), 72 (2), 88 (4), 92 (4), 201 (3), 217 (4)

disunity 25 (1), 709 (1)

disuse 611 (1), 621 (1), 674 (1), 779 (1)

disused 127 (7), 161 (5), 172 (4), 607 (2), 611 (2), 674 (3), 679 (7)

ditch 201 (2), 231 (2), 235 (2), 255 (2), 271 (7), 346 (1), 351 (1), 351 (2), 370 (9), 603 (5), 607 (3), 660 (2), 674 (5), 713 (2), 779 (4)

dither 474 (8), 601 (4)

ditto 13 (5), 20 (7), 106 (4), 106 (8), 488 (6)

ditty 412 (5), 593 (3)

diuretic 302 (5), 658 (5)

diurnal 128 (5)

divan 218 (6), 218 (7)

dive 192 (12), 269 (10), 269 (12), 271 (7), 277 (2), 309 (1), 309 (3), 309 (4), 313 (1), 313 (3), 341 (6), 837 (21)

diver 211 (1), 309 (1), 313 (2)

diverge 25 (6), 46 (7), 75 (3), 75 (4), 92 (6), 220 (5), 282 (3), 294 (3)

diverge from 15 (6)

divergence 15 (1), 17 (1), 19 (1), 25 (1), 46 (1), 75 (1), 92 (2), 265 (1), 282 (1), 294 (1)

divergent 15 (4), 17 (2), 46 (4), 75 (2), 220 (3), 282 (2), 294 (2)

divers 15 (4), 82 (2), 104 (4)

diverse 15 (4), 17 (2), 82 (2)

diverseness 15 (1)

diversify 143 (6)

diversion 10 (2), 282 (1), 305 (3), 542 (2), 542 (4), 837 (1)

diversity 10 (1), 15 (1), 17 (1), 82 (1)

divert 220 (6), 282 (6), 456 (8), 675 (2), 837 (20)

diverted 456 (5)

divertimento 412 (4)

divest 621 (3), 752 (5), 786 (10)

divest of 229 (6)

divest oneself of 229 (7)

divested of 229 (4)

divestment 229 (1)

divide 46 (10), 53 (7), 62 (6), 86 (12), 92 (5), 213 (1), 231 (2), 709 (8), 783 (3)

divide by four 98 (2)

divide by three 95 (3)

divide by two 92 (5)

divide up 46 (10)

divided 46 (4), 53 (6), 709 (6)

divided skirt 228 (13)

dividend 53 (1), 85 (2), 771 (3), 775 (2), 783 (2)

dividers 465 (5)

dividing 46 (5)

dividing by two 92 (1)

dividing line 28 (4), 46 (2), 92 (3)

divination 321 (11), 476 (1), 511 (2), 984 (1)

divine 510 (3), 511 (9), 512 (6), 841 (3), 887 (11), 965 (5), 965 (6), 973 (5), 973 (8), 983 (10), 984 (9), 986 (2)

divine attribute 965 (2)

divine essence 965 (1)

divine function 668 (1), 941 (2)

divine hero 966 (1), 967 (2)

divine inspiration 975 (1)

divine king 966 (1)

divine message 975 (1)

divine nature 965 (1)

divine office 981 (7)

divine principle 965 (1)

divine revelation 975 (1)

divine right 733 (1)

divine service 981 (7)

divinely 965 (7)

divineness 965 (1)

diviner 511 (5), 513 (4), 664 (2), 983 (5), 983 (6), 984 (4)

diving 269 (3)

diving bell 211 (1)

diving bird 313 (2)

divining rod 484 (2)

divinity 965 (1)

divisible 46 (6), 85 (5)

division 46 (3), 51 (1), 53 (3), 62 (1), 77 (1), 86 (2), 231 (2), 605 (2), 692 (2), 708 (3), 722 (8), 783 (1), 883 (2), 978 (2)

divisor 85 (2)

divorce 46 (2), 46 (7), 46 (8), 169 (1), 896 (1), 896 (5)

divorce decree 896 (1)

divorced 46 (4), 779 (3), 896 (3)

divot 53 (5)

divulge 526 (5), 528 (9), 579 (8), 928 (8)

dixie 194 (14)

Dixieland 412 (1)

dizziness 315 (1), 440 (1), 651 (2)

dizzy 209 (8), 315 (4), 456 (6), 503 (8), 949 (9)

dizzy height 209 (1)

DNA 5 (5), 358 (1)

do 7 (4), 24 (9), 156 (9), 160 (10), 164 (7), 173 (3), 301 (2), 628 (4), 640 (4), 642 (3), 676 (5), 678 (11), 682 (6), 688 (4), 725 (6), 727 (7), 768 (3), 837 (1), 876 (4), 917 (10)

do a deal 765 (5), 766 (4), 791 (6)

do a favour 644 (11)

do a handstand 221 (4)

do a job 622 (7)

do a play 594 (16), 594 (17)

do a portrait 553 (8)

do a swap 791 (4)

do again 106 (4)

do an injury 914 (6)

do as asked 758 (3)

do as one is told 739 (4)

do as one will 595 (2)

do as others do 83 (7)

do away with 165 (6), 362 (10)

do away with oneself 362 (13)

do before 119 (4)

do business 622 (9), 676 (5), 791 (4)

do business with 622 (9), 791 (4)

do by halves 726 (3)

do chores 742 (8)

do credit to 866 (13)

do down 542 (8)

do duty for 622 (8)

do easily 701 (7), 727 (11)

do evil 645 (6)

do for 703 (7), 727 (10), 742 (8)

do good 615 (4), 640 (4), 642 (3), 644 (11), 654 (9), 730 (8), 897 (5), 897 (6)

do-gooder 597 (3), 901 (4)

do homage 721 (4)

do homage to 920 (5)

do honour to 876 (4)

do into 520 (9)

do its job 173 (3)

do justice 913 (6)

do justice to 591 (5), 927 (5)

do law 958 (7)

do likewise 20 (7)

do magic 983 (10)

do marvels 727 (7)

do no good 728 (8)

do no harm 644 (11)

do-nothing 677 (2), 677 (3), 679 (11)

do nothing but 139 (3)

do one proud 813 (4)

do one's best 597 (6), 671 (4), 678 (11)

do one's bidding 739 (4)

do one's bit 917 (10)

do one's duty 739 (4), 768 (4), 917 (10), 933 (4)

do one's own thing 84 (8)

do one's utmost 682 (6)

do one's worst 898 (8)

do oneself credit 866 (11)

do oneself proud 944 (4)

do-or-die 857 (3)

do out of 542 (8)

do penance 939 (4), 941 (6), 988 (10)

do repairs 656 (12)

do scales 413 (9)

do subtraction 39 (3)

do sums 38 (3), 86 (12)

do the groundwork 669 (10)

do the honours 882 (10)

do the job 727 (7)

do the pools 618 (8)

do the trick 727 (7)

do thoroughly 54 (6)

do to order 739 (4)

do twice over 637 (6)

do up 45 (9), 126 (8), 264 (6), 654 (9), 656 (12)

do violence to 176 (8), 675 (2), 769 (3)

do well 285 (3), 615 (5), 727 (6), 730 (6), 800 (7)

do without 620 (5), 674 (4), 779 (4)

do wonders 727 (7), 864 (7)

do wrong 645 (6), 645 (7), 735 (8), 914 (6), 934 (7), 954 (8)

do your worst 711 (5)

docile 369 (7), 597 (4), 739 (3)

docility 597 (1), 739 (1)

dock 46 (11), 187 (5), 192 (10), 192 (21), 204 (5), 269 (10), 295 (2), 295 (4), 632 (2), 655 (9), 748 (2), 956 (4)

docked 39 (2)

docker 270 (4)

docket 87 (5), 547 (13), 547 (19), 548 (7)

docking 271 (3), 295 (1)

dockyard 687 (1)

doctor 143 (6), 150 (2), 447 (4), 492 (1), 500 (1), 503 (1), 656 (5), 656 (11), 658 (14), 658 (20), 666 (5), 691 (2), 703 (7), 870 (2), 973 (5)

doctorate 866 (4)

doctrinaire 473 (3), 473 (5), 481 (4)

doctrinal 485 (6), 973 (9), 976 (8)

doctrine 485 (2), 973 (4)

document 466 (1), 466 (8), 478 (4), 548 (1), 548 (7)

documentary 445 (4), 466 (5), 524 (1), 524 (7), 531 (4), 590 (6)

documentation 466 (1), 478 (1), 548 (1)

documented 466 (5), 548 (6)

doddering 131 (6), 318 (4)

dodge 220 (5), 265 (4), 477 (8), 541 (6), 542 (2), 620 (1), 620 (5), 623 (3), 698 (2), 698 (5), 769 (3)

dodgy 661 (3)

dodo 127 (2), 365 (2)

doe 365 (3)

doer 676 (3), 678 (5), 686 (1), 690 (3), 708 (2)

doff 49 (3), 229 (7), 522 (9), 526 (4), 621 (3), 674 (5)

dog 89 (4), 284 (4), 365 (10), 619 (3), 619 (5)

dog collar 989 (1)

dog days 128 (4)

dog-eared 261 (2), 655 (6), 673 (2)
dog-end 388 (2)
dog fox 365 (3)
dog in the manger 932 (2)
dog racing 716 (3)
dog-tired 684 (2)
dog track 724 (1)
dog-watches 129 (1)
dogcart 274 (6)
dogfight 716 (7), 718 (7)
dogged 600 (3), 602 (4)
doggedness 600 (1), 602 (1)
doggerel 593 (3), 593 (8), 849 (1), 849 (3)
dogging 619 (1)
doggy 365 (18)
doghouse 192 (10)
dogma 473 (1), 485 (2), 973 (4)
dogmatic 473 (4), 473 (5), 481 (7), 485 (6), 532 (4), 602 (4), 973 (9)
dogmatism 473 (2), 481 (4), 602 (2)
dogmatist 473 (3), 602 (3)
dogmatize 473 (8), 532 (5)
dog's ear 261 (1)
dogsbody 678 (5), 686 (2), 707 (1), 742 (1)
dogtooth 260 (1)
doing 164 (1), 173 (1), 173 (2), 676 (1), 676 (4), 768 (2)
doing again 106 (1)
doing one's best 597 (4), 671 (3)
doing penance 939 (3), 941 (4)
doing time 747 (6)
doings 154 (2)
doldrums 834 (1)
dole 636 (1), 901 (2)
dole out 465 (14), 781 (7), 783 (3)
doleful 834 (6), 836 (4)
doll 196 (4), 837 (15)
doll up 843 (7)
dollar 797 (4)
dolled up 843 (6), 844 (11)
dollop 53 (5)
dolly 196 (8)

dolphin 365 (3)
dolt 501 (3)
doltish 499 (3)
domain 77 (1), 184 (2), 622 (4), 777 (3)
dome 209 (4), 213 (3), 226 (2), 248 (2), 252 (2), 253 (4)
Domesday Book 87 (1)
domestic 191 (6), 192 (19), 224 (3), 365 (18), 369 (7), 742 (2), 749 (1), 883 (5)
domestic animal 365 (2)
domestic drudge 742 (2)
domestic science 301 (5)
domestic servant 742 (2)
domestic service 745 (2)
domesticate 369 (8), 610 (8)
domesticated 187 (4), 369 (7), 745 (4)
domestication 369 (1)
domesticity 883 (2)
domicile 192 (1)
domiciled 189 (2), 191 (6)
domiciliary 191 (6)
dominant 34 (5), 178 (2), 410 (2), 733 (7)
dominate 160 (10), 178 (3), 178 (4), 209 (12), 733 (12), 745 (7)
dominating 209 (11)
domination 34 (1), 733 (2)
domineer 735 (8)
domineering 733 (7), 735 (5), 735 (6)
dominion 733 (2), 733 (6)
domino 228 (21), 837 (15)
domino theory 71 (1)
dominoes 837 (8)
don 228 (32), 492 (1), 537 (1), 868 (4)
donate 781 (7), 806 (4)
donation 612 (4), 703 (2), 781 (1), 781 (2)
done 157 (3), 610 (6), 725 (4), 848 (5)
done by hand 164 (6)
done for 165 (5), 361 (5)
done for effect 875 (4)
done in haste 680 (2)
done thing 610 (2), 848 (2)
donjon 713 (4)

donkey 273 (3), 365 (3), 501 (1)
donkey-grey 429 (2)
donkey jacket 228 (10)
donkey's years 113 (1)
donkeywork 682 (3)
donnish 481 (7), 490 (6)
donnishness 481 (4)
donor 167 (1), 633 (2), 781 (4)
don't-care 857 (3), 860 (2)
doodle 456 (7), 551 (8), 553 (5)
doodling 456 (2)
doom 69 (3), 155 (4), 165 (3), 361 (1), 596 (2), 596 (8), 963 (1)
doom merchant 854 (5)
doomed 114 (4), 165 (5), 361 (5), 596 (6), 731 (6), 825 (6)
doomsday 124 (2)
door 263 (6), 297 (2)
door jamb 218 (10), 263 (6)
door knocker 279 (4)
doorkeeper 264 (3), 742 (1)
doorknob 263 (11)
doorman 264 (3)
doormat 226 (9), 721 (1), 856 (2)
doorpost 218 (10)
doorstep 234 (2), 263 (6)
doorway 68 (5), 194 (20), 234 (2), 237 (1), 263 (6), 264 (2), 297 (2), 298 (3), 624 (2)
dope 375 (6), 501 (2), 658 (7), 949 (4)
dope addict 504 (1)
dope fiend 949 (4)
doped 375 (3), 949 (10)
dopey 499 (4), 679 (7), 679 (9)
dormancy 175 (1), 523 (1), 677 (1)
dormant 175 (2), 266 (4), 523 (2), 752 (3)
dormitory 192 (2), 194 (19)
dorsal 238 (4)
dorsal region 238 (2)

dosage 26 (2), 465 (1)

dose 26 (2), 53 (5), 465 (1), 658 (2), 658 (20), 783 (2)

doss down 192 (21)

doss-house 192 (11)

dossier 466 (2), 524 (1), 548 (1)

dot 33 (3), 185 (1), 437 (4), 547 (19)

dot with 437 (9)

dotage 131 (3), 487 (1), 503 (1)

dote 487 (3), 499 (6), 503 (10), 887 (14)

doting 487 (2), 499 (4), 887 (9)

dotted about 75 (2)

dotted line 72 (1)

dotty 503 (8)

double 13 (1), 18 (3), 36 (5), 90 (2), 91 (2), 91 (3), 106 (4), 150 (2), 197 (5), 261 (3), 265 (2)

double agent 459 (7), 545 (1)

double back 286 (5)

double bass 414 (3)

double bill 594 (3)

double-boiler 194 (14)

double-check 473 (9)

double chin 195 (3)

double-cross 542 (8), 698 (5), 930 (8)

double-crosser 545 (1)

double-crossing 930 (7)

double-dealer 603 (3)

double-dealing 541 (2), 930 (2)

double-decker 274 (10)

double dutch 515 (1), 517 (1)

double-dyed 32 (13)

double-edged 174 (5)

double entendre 518 (1), 951 (1)

double exposure 91 (1)

double figures 99 (2)

double file 90 (1)

double first 727 (3)

double glazing 227 (1), 401 (2)

double harness 706 (1)

double-jointed 327 (3)

double life 90 (1)

double meaning 518 (1)

double peg 301 (26)

double-quick 277 (5)

double take 438 (4)

double-talk 515 (1), 541 (1)

double think 477 (1)

double up 684 (6)

double vision 440 (1)

doubled 91 (2), 261 (2)

doubled up 835 (5)

doubleness 91 (1)

doublet 559 (1)

doubletalk 518 (1)

doublethink 495 (1), 543 (2)

doublets 90 (1)

doubling 36 (1), 91 (1), 106 (1), 261 (1)

doubly 32 (17), 91 (4)

doubly sure 660 (6)

doubt 449 (3), 472 (1), 474 (2), 474 (8), 486 (2), 486 (7), 489 (1), 491 (8), 598 (1), 854 (11), 858 (1), 911 (1), 911 (3), 974 (1)

doubter 486 (3)

doubtful 459 (12), 474 (4), 474 (6), 486 (4), 854 (7), 858 (2), 867 (4), 930 (4)

doubtfully 486 (10)

doubtfulness 474 (1), 489 (1)

doubting 474 (6), 486 (4), 601 (3), 700 (5), 854 (7), 911 (2), 974 (5)

doubting Thomas 486 (3)

douche 648 (3), 658 (5)

dough 301 (22), 327 (1), 356 (1), 797 (1)

doughnut 301 (23)

doughty 162 (8), 855 (4)

doughy 327 (2), 356 (2), 426 (3)

dour 735 (4), 834 (7)

dourness 820 (1)

douse 311 (4), 313 (3), 341 (8), 382 (6), 418 (7)

dove 365 (4), 717 (2), 720 (2), 935 (2)

dove-grey 429 (2)

dove-like 935 (3)

dovetail 24 (9), 45 (9), 222 (8), 231 (8)

dowager 133 (3), 373 (3), 896 (2)

dowdiness 847 (1)

dowdy 842 (5), 847 (5)

dower 67 (1), 777 (4), 777 (6), 781 (1), 781 (7), 807 (1), 915 (1)

dower house 192 (6)

down 210 (4), 215 (5), 259 (2), 309 (5), 311 (6), 327 (1), 548 (6), 772 (2), 834 (5), 893 (2)

down-and-out 731 (3), 801 (2), 801 (4), 869 (7)

down-and-outs 869 (3)

down at heel 655 (6), 801 (4)

down, be 772 (4)

down on one's luck 731 (6)

down payment 767 (1), 804 (1)

down rush 277 (2)

down stage 594 (6)

down tools 145 (6), 715 (3), 738 (10)

downbeat 410 (4), 834 (5)

downcast 834 (5)

downdraught 309 (1)

downfall 165 (3), 309 (1), 728 (2), 731 (1)

downgrade 963 (8)

downhearted 834 (5)

downhill 220 (2), 220 (4), 309 (5), 701 (1), 701 (3)

downing 301 (1)

downpour 309 (1), 350 (6)

downright 32 (13), 32 (16), 54 (1), 54 (8), 540 (2)

downrightness 540 (1)

downs 209 (2), 348 (1)

Down's syndrome 499 (1), 503 (1)

downstage 594 (18)

downstairs 210 (4), 309 (5)

downstream 281 (8), 309 (5), 701 (3)

downtown 184 (4)

downtrodden 745 (4)

downward course 655 (1)

downward motion 265 (1)

downward trend 37 (1), 309 (1)

downwards 210 (4), 309 (5)

downwind 281 (8)

downy 208 (4), 258 (3), 259 (6), 327 (2), 376 (4)

dowry 777 (4)

dowse 459 (15)

dowsing 476 (1), 484 (1)

dowsing rod 484 (2)

doyen 131 (4), 696 (2)

doze 679 (4), 679 (12)

dozen 99 (2)

dozer 679 (6)

doziness 679 (3)

dozing 679 (9)

dozy 679 (9)

drab 16 (2), 425 (7), 430 (3), 834 (8), 840 (2), 842 (5), 952 (2)

drabness 840 (1)

drachm 322 (2)

Draconian 735 (4)

Draconian laws 735 (1)

draft 22 (1), 23 (1), 56 (5), 75 (4), 272 (7), 551 (1), 586 (8), 623 (1), 623 (8), 722 (6), 740 (3), 797 (5)

draft off 75 (4)

drag 136 (6), 182 (1), 203 (7), 288 (3), 291 (1), 291 (4), 333 (1), 702 (1), 702 (4), 747 (1), 748 (4), 827 (2), 838 (2), 838 (5)

drag artist 594 (10)

drag artiste 20 (3)

drag down 288 (3)

drag for 459 (15)

drag from 304 (4), 740 (3)

drag-line 255 (5)

drag-net 222 (3)

drag on 108 (7), 111 (3), 113 (9), 136 (6), 203 (7)

drag one's feet 278 (4), 598 (4), 679 (11)

drag oneself 598 (4)

drag out 113 (8), 304 (4), 702 (10)

drag towards 291 (4)

drag up 310 (4)

dragging 278 (3), 598 (3), 838 (3)

dragging out 113 (3), 136 (2)

draggle 217 (5)

dragnet 288 (1), 619 (2)

dragon 84 (4), 420 (2)

dragonfly 365 (16)

dragoon 722 (10), 740 (3)

drain 194 (1), 201 (2), 263 (8), 298 (2), 300 (8), 342 (6), 346 (1), 351 (2), 370 (9), 632 (2), 634 (4), 649 (4), 673 (3), 684 (6), 772 (1), 786 (8)

drain away 37 (5)

drain into 350 (9)

drain off 300 (8)

drain one's glass 301 (38)

drain out 298 (6)

drainage 298 (2), 300 (3), 342 (2), 648 (2), 649 (2)

drained 342 (4)

drained of colour 426 (3)

draining 342 (2)

drainpipe 252 (3), 298 (3), 351 (2)

drake 365 (4)

dram 301 (26)

drama 56 (1), 531 (4), 557 (3), 593 (2), 594 (1), 594 (3), 676 (2), 678 (1), 821 (1)

dramatic 594 (15), 821 (4), 821 (5), 864 (5), 875 (5)

dramatic critic 594 (14)

dramatic irony 590 (2)

dramatic monologue 594 (3)

dramatic poem 593 (2)

dramatic poet 593 (6)

dramatics 594 (2)

dramatis personae 594 (9)

dramatist 589 (7), 594 (13)

dramatization 594 (2)

dramatize 522 (8), 546 (3), 551 (8), 594 (16)

dramatized 594 (15)

dramaturgy 20 (2), 594 (2)

drape 217 (1), 217 (5), 228 (31)

draper 228 (28)

draperies 217 (2)

drapery 228 (7)

drapes 217 (2)

drastic 174 (5), 735 (4)

drastically 32 (18)

drat 899 (8)

dratted 645 (5)

draught 211 (1), 288 (1), 301 (26), 322 (1), 335 (2), 352 (1), 352 (6), 388 (1), 658 (2), 731 (1), 837 (15)

draught animal 365 (2)

draught animals 273 (3)

draught horse 273 (6)

draughts 837 (9)

draughtsman or - woman 549 (1)

draughtsmanship 553 (1)

draughtsperson 556 (1)

draughty 352 (8)

draw 20 (6), 28 (5), 28 (9), 56 (5), 74 (11), 123 (1), 188 (4), 206 (7), 233 (3), 243 (5), 265 (5), 288 (3), 291 (1), 291 (4), 304 (4), 352 (10), 379 (7), 388 (7), 551 (8), 553 (8), 590 (7), 618 (2), 618 (8), 771 (7), 782 (4), 859 (5), 859 (13), 887 (15)

draw a blank 728 (7)

draw a circle 314 (4)

draw a comparison 462 (3)

draw a parallel 9 (8), 219 (3), 462 (3)

draw a salary 771 (7)

draw and quarter 963 (12)

draw aside 282 (6)

draw attention 455 (7)

draw attention to 522 (8)

draw back 266 (4), 288 (3), 290 (3), 620 (5)

draw blood 655 (10), 712 (7)

draw breath 360 (4), 360 (5)

draw forth 522 (7)

draw in 198 (6), 198 (7), 288 (3), 293 (3)

draw lots 618 (8)

draw money 797 (12)

draw near 200 (5), 289 (4)

draw off 39 (3), 300 (8), 304 (4), 786 (6)

draw on 633 (5), 673 (4)

draw one out **584** (6)
draw one's sword **900** (3)
draw out 113 (8), **188** (4), 197 (5), **203** (8), **304** (4)
draw tears **821** (6), **827** (8), **834** (11)
draw the line 57 (5), **236** (3), **463** (3), **605** (7)
draw the line at 757 (4), **924** (9)
draw the teeth 161 (9)
draw the teeth of 257 (3)
draw tight 45 (13)
draw to a close 69 (5)
draw together 45 (9), **198** (6), **198** (7)
draw towards 291 (4)
draw up 56 (5), **145** (6), **266** (8), **295** (4), **623** (8)
drawback **616** (1), **647** (2), **702** (2)
drawbridge **263** (6), **624** (3), **713** (4)
drawer **194** (4), **288** (1)
drawers **228** (17)
drawing **160** (9), **288** (1), **288** (2), **551** (1), **553** (1), **553** (5)
drawing board **623** (1)
drawing off **304** (1)
drawing out **304** (1)
drawing pin 47 (5)
drawing room **194** (19)
drawing round **232** (1)
drawing to **291** (1)
drawing together 45 (2), **198** (1)
drawl **203** (8), **278** (4), **577** (2), **577** (4), **580** (1), **580** (3)
drawn **28** (7), **206** (5), **288** (2), **551** (7)
drawn game **28** (5), **726** (1)
drawn out **838** (3)
drawn tight **198** (4)
drawn to, be **289** (4)
drawn together **264** (4)
drawstring 47 (4), 47 (5)
dray **274** (5)
dread **507** (1), **854** (1), **854** (9), **854** (11)
dreaded **507** (3)

dreadful **32** (7), **645** (3), **645** (4), **731** (4), **827** (6), **854** (8)
dreadfully **32** (18)
dreading **507** (2), **854** (7)
dreadlocks **259** (2)
dream 4 (2), **440** (2), **450** (4), **456** (7), **513** (3), **513** (7), **617** (2), **679** (12), **841** (2), **852** (6), **859** (5)
dream dreams **513** (7)
dream girl **864** (3)
dream of **617** (6), **852** (6), **859** (11)
dream up **513** (7)
dream world **513** (3)
dreamer **504** (2), **513** (4), **679** (6)
dreaming **449** (5), **456** (4), **513** (5), **679** (9)
dreaming of **852** (4)
dreamland **679** (4)
dreamlike **419** (5), **445** (7)
dreams **679** (4)
dreamy **456** (4), **513** (6)
dreariness **827** (1), **834** (1), **840** (1)
dreary **418** (3), **827** (4), **834** (5), **834** (8), **838** (3), **840** (2), **842** (5)
dredge **304** (4), **311** (5)
dredge up **304** (4), **310** (4)
dredger **255** (5), **275** (1), **304** (2), **310** (2)
dregs **35** (2), **41** (2), **649** (2), **938** (1)
dregs of society **869** (2)
dregs, the **867** (3)
drench **165** (6), **298** (6), **303** (7), **306** (4), **339** (3), **341** (8), **350** (9), **637** (5), **648** (9), **863** (3)
drenched **341** (5), **347** (2), **637** (3)
dress **28** (10), **228** (1), **228** (8), **228** (31), **301** (40), **547** (10), **630** (4), **658** (20), **669** (11), **844** (12)
dress circle **441** (2)
dress in **228** (32)
dress rehearsal **594** (2)
dress sense **841** (1), **848** (1)

dress uniform **228** (5)
dress up **228** (31), **228** (32), **541** (6), **541** (7), **843** (7), **875** (7)
dressage **267** (5)
dressed **228** (29), **669** (7)
dresser **194** (5), **218** (5), **218** (12)
dressiness **848** (1)
dressing **228** (1), **301** (5), **389** (1), **658** (9)
dressing down **924** (4)
dressing gown **228** (6)
dressing room **594** (7)
dressing station **658** (13)
dressing up **228** (1)
dressmaker **228** (28)
dressmaking **228** (1)
dressy **848** (5), **875** (5)
dribble **33** (2), **278** (4), **279** (10), **287** (1), **287** (7), **298** (6), **298** (7), **350** (9)
dribbling **298** (2)
dried fruit **301** (19)
dried out **342** (4), **948** (3)
dried up **172** (4), **342** (4)
dried vegetables **301** (20)
drift 74 (7), **179** (1), **265** (4), **271** (7), **278** (4), **281** (1), **282** (1), **282** (5), **307** (1), **323** (4), **458** (6), **514** (1), **677** (3), **744** (9)
drift apart 75 (3)
drift away 75 (3), **290** (3)
drift towards **289** (4)
drifter **268** (2), **275** (4), **679** (6)
drifting **161** (7)
driftwood 75 (1)
drill 16 (1), 16 (4), 81 (2), **222** (4), **263** (12), **263** (18), **400** (4), **534** (1), **534** (8), **610** (1), **610** (2), **610** (3), **630** (1), **669** (11), **682** (2), **718** (4), **875** (2)
drilled **263** (14)
drink **177** (7), **299** (4), **300** (8), **301** (26), **301** (38), **335** (2), **837** (23), **949** (14)
drink a health **876** (5)
drink and be merry **837** (24)
drink hard **949** (14)

drink in 455 (4), 536 (4)
drink moderately 948 (4)
drink one's fill 301 (38)
drink to 876 (5), 884 (6),
920 (6), 923 (10)
drink to excess 943 (3)
drink up 300 (8), 301 (38)
drinkable 301 (32)
drinker 301 (25), 837 (17),
949 (5)
drinking 299 (1), 301 (25),
833 (4), 949 (1)
drinking bout 949 (1)
drinking bowl 194 (16)
drinking cup 194 (15)
drinking horn 194 (15)
drinking water 339 (1)
drinks 882 (3)
drip 163 (2), 278 (4), 298
(6), 298 (7), 300 (9), 309
(3), 341 (1), 341 (6), 350
(9), 350 (10), 501 (2), 658
(2), 838 (2)
drip-dry 342 (6)
drip-feeding 301 (1)
dripping 341 (4), 357 (3)
dripping wet 341 (5)
drive 160 (3), 160 (11), 173
(3), 174 (1), 174 (7), 263
(6), 263 (18), 265 (5), 267
(1), 267 (15), 277 (2), 277
(6), 277 (7), 279 (2), 279
(7), 279 (9), 287 (1), 287
(7), 532 (1), 571 (1), 599
(1), 612 (9), 624 (2), 673
(3), 678 (2), 680 (3), 684
(6), 712 (1), 735 (8), 740
(3)
drive a bargain 791 (6)
drive apart 46 (9)
drive away 292 (3)
drive dangerously 661 (9)
drive forward 279 (7)
drive home 532 (7), 725
(5), 821 (8)
drive in 45 (11), 263 (6),
297 (5)
drive insane 503 (12)
drive into 279 (8)
drive mad 63 (3), 503 (12),
891 (9)
drive off 296 (6), 788 (7)

drive on 146 (3), 146 (5),
285 (3)
drive through 682 (6)
drive to despair 834 (11)
drive to one's death 362
(10)
drivel 298 (7), 499 (6), 503
(10), 515 (2), 515 (6), 570
(6)
drivelling 131 (6)
driver 268 (5), 305 (2), 630
(5), 742 (2)
driving 277 (3), 305 (2),
350 (7)
driving at, be 514 (5)
driving force 160 (1), 287
(3), 612 (1)
driving off 292 (1)
driving rain 350 (6)
drizzle 341 (1), 341 (6), 350
(6), 350 (10)
drizzling 341 (4)
drizzly 350 (8)
droll 839 (4), 849 (3)
drollery 497 (2), 839 (1),
849 (1)
dromedary 273 (3)
drone 16 (1), 365 (16), 401
(4), 403 (1), 403 (3), 407
(5), 409 (1), 409 (3), 577
(4), 580 (3), 679 (6)
drone on 840 (3)
droning 16 (2)
drool 298 (7), 301 (35), 515
(6)
droop 163 (9), 217 (5), 309
(3), 309 (4), 679 (11), 684
(5), 834 (9)
drooping 163 (4), 217 (4),
309 (2), 684 (2)
drop 33 (3), 37 (1), 37 (5),
43 (2), 69 (6), 161 (8), 163
(9), 196 (2), 211 (1), 211
(3), 217 (2), 229 (7), 252
(2), 253 (2), 265 (5), 286
(1), 286 (4), 298 (7), 300
(9), 309 (1), 309 (3), 311
(5), 311 (6), 341 (1), 350
(9), 350 (10), 352 (10), 594
(6), 621 (3), 674 (5), 695
(9), 721 (4), 779 (4)
drop a brick 695 (9)

drop a brick or a clanger
495 (8)
drop a hint 524 (11)
drop anchor 187 (8), 269
(10), 295 (4)
drop behind 238 (5), 284
(4)
drop bombs 712 (11)
drop by drop 27 (6), 53 (9)
drop curtain 594 (6)
drop down 309 (3)
drop down dead 361 (8)
drop in 295 (4), 297 (5),
303 (4), 882 (9)
drop in temperature 380
(1)
drop in the ocean 33 (2)
drop into place 73 (3)
drop off 679 (12)
drop one's guard 857 (4)
drop one's voice 401 (4),
578 (5)
drop out 84 (8), 621 (3),
726 (3), 744 (9)
drop the hem 203 (8)
drop the mask 540 (3)
drop too much 949 (1)
droplet 33 (3), 196 (2), 252
(2)
dropout 84 (3), 489 (2), 728
(3), 829 (2)
dropped 360 (3)
dropped catch 695 (2)
dropping 309 (1), 309 (2)
droppings 302 (4), 649 (2)
drops 658 (2)
dropsical 197 (3)
dross 41 (2), 649 (2)
drought 342 (1), 636 (2),
659 (2)
drove 74 (3)
drover 268 (5)
drown 54 (7), 165 (6), 165
(8), 311 (4), 313 (3), 313
(4), 361 (8), 362 (10), 550
(3)
drown one's voice 416 (4),
578 (4)
drown oneself 362 (13)
drowned 54 (4), 211 (2),
341 (5)
drowning 313 (1), 362 (1)

drowse 456 (7), 458 (6), 679 (4), 679 (12), 684 (5)
drowsiness 679 (3)
drowsy 679 (9), 838 (3)
drubbing 728 (2)
drudge 678 (5), 682 (7), 686 (2), 742 (1)
drudgery 678 (3), 682 (3)
drudging 682 (4)
drug 375 (2), 375 (6), 658 (7), 658 (20), 679 (13)
drug abuse 949 (4)
drug addict 504 (1), 610 (4), 944 (2), 949 (4)
drug addiction 651 (3), 949 (4)
drug dependence 949 (4)
drug oneself 949 (15)
drug-taking 388 (2), 504 (1), 610 (4), 658 (7), 659 (3), 821 (2), 944 (2), 949 (4)
drug traffic 791 (2)
drugged 161 (7), 375 (3), 679 (7), 949 (10)
drugget 226 (9)
druggist 658 (15)
Druid 983 (5), 986 (8)
Druidess 983 (5), 986 (8)
drum 194 (12), 252 (3), 279 (9), 317 (4), 403 (3), 413 (9), 414 (9)
drum major 690 (2)
drum out 300 (6)
drum-roll 547 (8)
drummer 413 (2)
drumming 106 (3), 279 (1), 317 (1), 403 (1)
drumming out 300 (1)
drums 413 (3), 718 (1)
drunk 499 (4), 949 (5), 949 (6)
drunk, be 949 (13)
drunkard 301 (25), 837 (17), 944 (2), 949 (5)
drunken 61 (9), 301 (31), 944 (3), 949 (7), 949 (11)
drunkenness 301 (25), 637 (1), 837 (2), 943 (1), 949 (1)
drupe 366 (7)
dry 49 (2), 172 (4), 299 (4), 332 (4), 340 (6), 342 (4),

342 (6), 350 (12), 379 (4), 381 (8), 393 (2), 407 (2), 506 (5), 572 (2), 573 (2), 594 (17), 648 (9), 666 (5), 669 (12), 838 (3), 839 (4), 859 (9), 942 (3)
dry area 948 (1)
dry, be 342 (5), 379 (7), 859 (12)
dry-clean 648 (9)
dry cleaner 648 (6)
dry climate 342 (1)
dry-eyed 906 (2)
dry eyes 820 (1)
dry goods 222 (4), 795 (1)
dry land 344 (1)
dry measure 465 (3)
dry off 342 (5)
dry one's eyes 831 (3), 831 (4)
dry out 342 (5), 948 (4)
dry-point 555 (1)
dry rot 649 (2)
dry run 461 (1)
dry season 342 (1)
dry spell 340 (3)
dry up 37 (5), 145 (6), 342 (5), 578 (3), 634 (4), 636 (7)
dry wine 301 (29)
dryad 967 (3)
dryer 304 (2), 342 (3)
drying 342 (2), 666 (1)
drying out 948 (3)
drying up 342 (2)
dryness 172 (3), 342 (1), 838 (1), 839 (1), 859 (2)
dt's 949 (3)
dual 90 (2), 91 (2)
dual carriageway 305 (3), 624 (6)
dual personality 90 (1)
dual-purpose 91 (2)
duality 18 (3), 74 (3), 90 (1)
dub 561 (6), 562 (5), 866 (14)
dubiety 474 (2), 486 (2), 601 (1), 605 (1), 606 (1), 700 (3)
dubious 472 (2), 474 (4), 474 (6), 867 (4)
dubiousness 474 (1)

ducal 868 (6)
duchess 741 (4), 868 (5)
duchy 733 (6)
duck 103 (1), 269 (12), 303 (7), 309 (3), 311 (2), 311 (4), 313 (3), 341 (8), 365 (4), 620 (1), 620 (5)
duckboards 226 (7), 624 (3)
ducking 311 (1), 313 (1), 341 (2)
ducking stool 964 (2)
duckling 132 (3), 365 (4)
ducks 890 (1)
ducky 890 (1)
duct 263 (9), 351 (1)
ductile 327 (3)
ductility 327 (1)
dud 161 (5), 728 (3)
dud cheque 797 (6)
dude 544 (1)
due 124 (4), 642 (2), 803 (5), 913 (4), 915 (2)
due, be 913 (5), 915 (4), 917 (8)
due order 60 (1)
due payment 804 (1)
due proportion 9 (3)
due respect 920 (1)
due to 157 (3)
due to, be 157 (5), 915 (4)
duel 90 (1), 716 (6), 716 (11)
duelling pistol 723 (10)
duellist 705 (1), 709 (5), 716 (8), 722 (1)
dueness 158 (1), 688 (1), 714 (1), 913 (1), 915 (1), 917 (1)
duenna 749 (1)
dues 782 (1), 807 (1), 809 (1), 809 (2), 915 (1)
duet 90 (1), 412 (6), 706 (1), 710 (1)
duffel bag 194 (9)
duffel coat 228 (20)
duffer 493 (1), 501 (3), 697 (1)
dug in 713 (8)
dug out 255 (6)
dugout 255 (4)
duke 741 (4), 868 (5)
dukedom 733 (6), 868 (2)

dynamic energy 174 (1)
dynamical 279 (6)
dynamics 162 (5), 265 (1)
dynamism 160 (3), 174
(1), 678 (2)
dynamite 165 (7), 168 (1),
174 (1), 287 (3), 663 (1),
723 (13)
dynamo 156 (5), 160 (6),
174 (1), 678 (5)
dynastic 733 (8)
dynasty 71 (1), 733 (2), 741
(3), 868 (1)
dysentery 651 (7)
dyspepsia 651 (7)
dyspeptic 893 (2)

E

each 12 (1), 79 (4), 80 (10)
each one 79 (2)
each other 12 (1), 12 (4)
eager 597 (4), 678 (7), 818
(5), 821 (3), 859 (7)
eager beaver 678 (5)
eagerly 859 (14)
eagerness 678 (2), 818 (2),
859 (1)
eagle 365 (4), 438 (2)
ear 157 (2), 415 (4)
ear plugs 401 (2)
ear-splitting 400 (3), 407
(2)
ear trumpet 400 (2), 415
(4)
earache 377 (2)
earl 868 (5)
earldom 868 (2)
earlier 64 (5), 119 (2), 119
(5), 122 (3)
earliest 119 (2)
earliness 128 (1), 135 (1),
670 (1)
early 68 (6), 116 (3), 118
(2), 125 (6), 127 (5), 128
(5), 135 (4), 135 (6), 137
(4), 138 (2), 277 (5)
early, be 117 (7), 118 (3),
119 (3), 124 (6), 135 (5),

283 (3), 495 (7), 510 (3),
542 (8), 670 (7)
early bird 135 (1)
early comer 135 (1)
early days 68 (1)
early hour 135 (1)
early humanity 371 (1)
early man 66 (1)
early matured 670 (4)
early riser 135 (1)
early stage 135 (1)
early stages 68 (1)
earmark 547 (2), 547 (19),
605 (7), 617 (5)
earmarked 547 (17)
earn 771 (7), 915 (7)
earn a dividend 771 (9)
earn a living 771 (7)
earn interest 36 (4)
earn one's living 622 (7)
earned 915 (2)
earned income 771 (2)
earner 686 (2)
earnest 455 (2), 532 (3),
599 (2), 767 (1), 768 (2),
804 (1), 818 (5), 979 (7)
earnest, be 532 (7)
earnestly 818 (9)
earnestness 455 (1), 599
(1), 678 (3), 834 (3)
earning 622 (5), 771 (1)
earnings 771 (2), 782 (1),
786 (1), 804 (2), 807 (1)
earphones 415 (4)
earring 217 (2), 844 (7)
earshot 415 (1)
earth 160 (5), 192 (3), 319
(4), 321 (2), 321 (6), 344
(1), 660 (8), 662 (1), 662
(3)
earth-dweller 191 (3)
earth goddess 966 (2)
Earth Mother 171 (2), 966
(2)
earth sciences 186 (1), 321
(12), 344 (1)
earth-shaking 317 (3), 638
(5)
earth up 702 (9)
earthbound 191 (6), 823
(3)
earthenware 164 (2), 381
(5)

earthiness 944 (1)
earthling 371 (1)
earthly 321 (15)
earthly Paradise 971 (1),
971 (2)
earthquake 168 (1), 317
(1)
earth's crust 344 (1), 359
(1)
earthwork 125 (2), 209
(3), 253 (5), 364 (5), 548
(3), 713 (2), 713 (4)
earthy 344 (5), 944 (3)
earwig 365 (17)
ease 37 (4), 37 (5), 177 (7),
323 (5), 376 (2), 683 (1),
685 (4), 694 (1), 701 (1),
701 (8), 701 (9), 703 (5),
800 (1), 824 (2), 831 (3)
ease into place 303 (4)
ease off 177 (5)
ease oneself 302 (6)
ease out 779 (4)
ease up 278 (5)
easeful 376 (4), 683 (2)
easel 218 (13)
easily 701 (10)
easily depressed 822 (3)
easily done 701 (3)
easily frightened 856 (3)
easily pleased 828 (2)
easily provoked 822 (3)
easily roused 892 (3)
easily taken in 487 (2)
easily tempted 934 (5)
easing 177 (1), 656 (4), 685
(1), 701 (1), 703 (1), 831
(1)
east 239 (1), 281 (2)
east and west 14 (2), 184
(1)
East End 184 (4)
East side 184 (4)
Easter sepulchre 990 (4)
easterly 239 (2)
eastern 239 (2), 281 (3)
Eastern Orthodoxy 976
(3)
Easterner 59 (2)
Eastertide 128 (3)
eastward 239 (2)

easy **220** (4), **376** (4), **516** (2), **701** (3), **848** (6), **880** (6)

easy, be **701** (6)

easy chair **218** (6)

easy come, easy go **114** (7), **815** (6)

easy-going **266** (5), **701** (1), **701** (4), **717** (3), **736** (2), **823** (3), **860** (2)

easy in mind **828** (2)

easy manners **882** (2)

easy mind **828** (1)

easy on **685** (2)

easy prey **544** (1)

easy ride **701** (2)

easy stages **278** (1)

easy target **661** (2), **701** (2)

easy temper **884** (1)

easy terms **812** (1)

easy thing **639** (2), **701** (2), **727** (2)

easy times **730** (2)

easy to copy **20** (4)

easy to please **837** (19)

easy virtue **951** (2)

easy win **727** (2)

easygoing **601** (3), **823** (3), **828** (2)

eat **299** (4), **301** (35), **386** (3), **634** (4), **730** (6), **786** (11), **837** (24), **947** (4)

eat away **37** (4), **306** (4), **655** (9)

eat humble pie **721** (4), **872** (5), **939** (4)

eat less **946** (4)

eat one's words **603** (7)

eat or drink one's fill **635** (8)

eat to excess **943** (3)

eat up **165** (10)

eat well **301** (35)

eatable **301** (32)

eatables **301** (9)

eaten up with **481** (6)

eater **301** (6), **837** (17), **947** (2)

eating **299** (1), **301** (1), **301** (31), **824** (3)

eating and drinking **944** (1)

eating habits **301** (1)

eating-house **192** (13)

eating meals **301** (1)

eating one's words **603** (2)

eating out **301** (2)

eats **301** (9)

eaves **226** (2), **254** (2)

eavesdrop **415** (6), **453** (4)

eavesdropper **415** (3), **453** (2), **524** (5)

eavesdropping **415** (2)

ebb **37** (1), **37** (5), **286** (2), **286** (4), **290** (3), **309** (3), **350** (9), **655** (1)

ebb and flow **141** (1), **152** (5), **317** (2), **317** (5), **350** (2)

ebb away **37** (5), **634** (4)

ebb tide **37** (1)

ebbing **37** (3), **286** (3)

ebony **428** (2)

ebullience **174** (2), **821** (1)

ebullient **176** (5), **819** (4), **821** (3), **833** (4)

eccentric **21** (3), **25** (3), **84** (5), **499** (4), **501** (1), **503** (8), **504** (2), **604** (3), **851** (3)

eccentricity **21** (1), **80** (1), **84** (1), **481** (5), **499** (2), **503** (5), **604** (2), **647** (2), **849** (1)

ecclesiarch **741** (5), **986** (4)

ecclesiastic **986** (2)

ecclesiastical **985** (6)

ecclesiastical, be **985** (8)

ecclesiastical court **956** (3)

ecclesiasticism **976** (2), **985** (1)

echelon **71** (2), **722** (7)

echo **20** (1), **20** (3), **20** (5), **20** (7), **22** (1), **24** (9), **83** (7), **91** (1), **91** (3), **106** (1), **106** (4), **280** (3), **404** (1), **404** (3), **460** (1), **460** (5), **488** (6)

echo-like **460** (4)

echoing **20** (4), **106** (3), **400** (3), **404** (2)

éclair **301** (23)

éclat **174** (1), **866** (2)

eclectic **605** (4)

eclipse **34** (7), **418** (2), **418** (6), **444** (4), **446** (1), **525** (7), **866** (11)

eclipsed **418** (4), **444** (2)

ecliptic **250** (5), **314** (3)

eclogue **593** (2)

ecological **9** (5)

ecologist **358** (2), **814** (1)

ecologists **708** (2)

ecology **9** (1), **358** (2)

economic **689** (3)

economic aid **703** (2)

economic resources **629** (1)

economic warfare **718** (6)

economical **812** (3), **814** (2), **816** (4), **942** (3)

economical, be **812** (5), **814** (3)

economically **814** (4)

economics **622** (1), **689** (1)

economies **814** (1)

economist **690** (3), **814** (1)

economize **37** (4), **632** (5), **747** (7), **814** (3), **816** (6)

economizer **814** (1)

economizing **814** (1)

economy **37** (2), **633** (1), **747** (2), **771** (3), **814** (1), **942** (1), **945** (1)

economy drive **814** (1)

economy measures **814** (1)

economy size **195** (6), **812** (3)

ecosystem **706** (2)

ecstasy **376** (1), **503** (4), **513** (1), **818** (2), **822** (2), **824** (1), **887** (1)

ecstatic **818** (4), **818** (6), **824** (4), **835** (4), **887** (10), **923** (5)

ecumenical **79** (4), **976** (8)

ecumenicalism **79** (1), **976** (1)

eczema **651** (12), **845** (1)

eddy **315** (2), **315** (5), **350** (3), **350** (9), **663** (1)

edge **34** (2), **40** (1), **69** (2), **174** (3), **200** (1), **202** (1), **220** (5), **232** (3), **233** (1), **234** (1), **234** (5), **236** (1), **236** (3), **239** (1), **239** (3),

(2), 786 (2), 963 (4), 981 (4)

ejection seat 276 (1)

ejector 298 (2), 300 (2)

ejector-seat 662 (3)

eke out 54 (6)

El Dorado 513 (3), 800 (1)

elaborate 61 (8), 574 (6), 575 (3), 575 (4), 654 (9), 669 (12), 725 (4), 725 (5), 844 (9)

elaborate style 566 (1)

elaboration 575 (1), 654 (1), 725 (1)

elan 174 (1), 571 (1), 599 (1)

elapse 69 (5), 108 (7), 111 (3), 125 (10)

elapsed 125 (6)

elapsing 111 (2)

elastic 286 (3), 325 (2), 327 (3), 328 (1), 328 (2)

elastic, be 327 (4), 328 (3)

elastic fluid 336 (2)

elasticity 160 (3), 162 (1), 280 (1), 286 (2), 327 (1), 328 (1)

elate 826 (4), 833 (8)

elated 503 (7), 822 (3), 824 (4), 833 (5), 835 (4)

elation 822 (2), 835 (1)

elbow 45 (4), 247 (1), 248 (2), 261 (1), 279 (7)

elbow aside 282 (6)

elbow grease 333 (1), 682 (1)

elbow one's way 678 (11)

elbowroom 183 (4), 744 (3)

elder 34 (3), 119 (2), 131 (7), 366 (4), 986 (4), 986 (7)

elder statesman 133 (2)

elderly 131 (6)

elderly gentleman 133 (2)

elderly lady 133 (3)

elders 131 (4)

elders first 283 (4)

eldership 127 (1), 131 (4), 985 (3)

eldest 66 (1), 119 (1), 119 (2), 131 (7)

elect 596 (6), 605 (5), 605 (6), 605 (8), 751 (4)

elect, the 80 (3)

elected 605 (5)

election 605 (2), 751 (2)

electioneer 605 (8)

electioneering 605 (4)

elective 605 (4)

electoral 605 (4)

electoral roll 87 (1), 605 (3)

electorate 480 (3), 605 (3)

electors 605 (3)

electric 160 (9), 822 (3)

electric chair 964 (3)

electric charge 160 (5)

electric current 160 (5)

electric guitar 414 (2)

electric lamp 420 (4)

electric van 274 (12)

electrical 160 (9)

electrical engineering 160 (6), 630 (3)

electrician 686 (3)

electricity 160 (5), 383 (2), 465 (3)

electrification 160 (5)

electrify 160 (11), 174 (8), 508 (5), 821 (6), 864 (7)

electrifying 374 (4)

electrocute 963 (12)

electrocution 963 (3)

electrode 160 (5)

electrolyse 51 (5)

electrolysis 51 (1), 658 (11)

electromagnetic 160 (9)

electron 196 (2), 319 (4)

electron microscope 196 (6), 442 (4)

electron physics 160 (6)

electronic 160 (9), 494 (6)

electronic data processing 86 (5)

electronic sound 398 (1)

electronics 160 (6), 630 (3)

electroplate 226 (16)

electrotherapy 658 (12)

elegance 563 (1), 566 (1), 575 (1), 694 (1), 841 (1), 846 (1), 848 (1)

elegant 24 (6), 566 (2), 575 (3), 694 (7), 841 (5), 841 (6), 846 (3), 848 (5)

elegant, be 575 (4)

elegiac 364 (8), 593 (8)

elegiac couplet 593 (5)

elegiac poet 593 (6)

elegize 593 (10)

elegy 364 (2), 593 (2), 836 (2)

element 53 (1), 58 (1), 156 (3), 208 (1), 319 (4)

elemental 5 (6), 44 (4), 68 (6), 156 (8)

elementary 44 (4), 68 (6)

elementary unit 319 (4)

elements 68 (1)

elements, the 340 (3)

elephant 195 (4), 209 (5), 365 (3)

elephantine 195 (6), 195 (9), 365 (18)

elevate 74 (11), 164 (7), 187 (5), 188 (4), 197 (5), 209 (13), 215 (4), 243 (5), 265 (5), 285 (4), 288 (3), 310 (4), 323 (5), 826 (4), 866 (14), 876 (4)

elevated 209 (8), 310 (3), 866 (8), 871 (3), 933 (3)

elevation 164 (1), 209 (1), 215 (4), 285 (1), 310 (1), 445 (6), 551 (5), 571 (1), 654 (1), 818 (2), 866 (5)

elevation, an 310 (1)

elevator 310 (2)

eleven 74 (4), 99 (2)

elevenses 301 (12)

eleventh hour 136 (1), 136 (3), 137 (3)

elf 196 (4), 970 (2)

elf-like 970 (6)

elfin 196 (8), 970 (6)

elicit 156 (9), 304 (4), 484 (4), 522 (7)

eligibility 78 (1), 894 (6)

eligible 78 (3), 894 (8)

eliminate 37 (4), 44 (7), 57 (5), 62 (6), 105 (4), 300 (8), 304 (4), 550 (3), 607 (3), 648 (10)

elimination 37 (2), 39 (1), 44 (3), 165 (1), 300 (1),

131

300 (3), 302 (3), 304 (1), 607 (1)

elite 34 (3), 638 (3), 644 (2), 722 (4), 848 (3), 855 (3)

elitism 733 (4)

elixir 658 (1)

ellipse 250 (4)

ellipsis 568 (1), 569 (1)

elliptic 250 (6), 569 (2)

elm 366 (4)

elocution 577 (2), 579 (1), 579 (3)

elocutionary 579 (6), 579 (7)

elongate 203 (8)

elongated 203 (5)

elongation 199 (1)

elope 296 (5), 620 (6), 667 (5), 894 (11)

elope with 786 (9)

elopement 296 (1), 894 (3)

eloping 667 (4)

eloquence 571 (1), 574 (2), 579 (4), 581 (1), 612 (2)

eloquent 566 (2), 571 (2), 574 (5), 579 (7)

elsewhere 190 (9)

elucidate 516 (4), 520 (8), 522 (7), 534 (7)

elucidated 520 (7)

elucidation 520 (1)

elude 477 (8), 620 (5), 667 (6)

elusive 517 (3), 620 (3), 667 (4)

elves 970 (2)

elvish 970 (6)

Elysian 971 (3)

Elysian fields 361 (3), 971 (2)

Elysium 971 (2)

emaciated 206 (5), 651 (20)

emaciation 198 (1), 206 (2)

emanate 157 (5), 298 (5)

emanating 157 (3), 298 (4)

emancipate 668 (3), 746 (3)

emancipated 744 (5), 746 (2)

emancipation 668 (1), 744 (1), 744 (2), 746 (1)

emasculate 37 (4), 161 (10)

emasculated 161 (7), 572 (2)

emasculation 163 (1)

embalm 364 (9), 666 (5)

embalmed corpse 363 (1)

embalmer 364 (1)

embalming 364 (1)

embalmment 666 (1)

embank 702 (9)

embankment 218 (2), 253 (5)

embargo 57 (1), 266 (1), 702 (1), 747 (1), 757 (1), 805 (1)

embark 269 (9), 296 (6)

embark on 68 (8), 672 (3)

embarkation 68 (3), 296 (1)

embarrass 643 (3), 702 (8), 827 (10)

embarrassing 700 (4), 827 (5)

embarrassment 700 (1), 700 (3), 827 (2), 936 (1)

embassy 529 (3), 751 (1), 754 (3)

embattled 718 (8)

embed 187 (5), 303 (6)

embedded 187 (4)

embellish 38 (3), 654 (9), 844 (12)

embellished 541 (3), 844 (10)

embellishment 574 (1), 844 (1)

ember 381 (4), 385 (3), 419 (3), 420 (3)

embers 385 (2)

embezzle 788 (8), 805 (5)

embezzlement 788 (4)

embezzler 789 (3), 805 (3)

embitter 827 (8), 829 (6), 832 (3), 888 (8), 891 (8), 891 (9)

embittered 481 (8), 829 (3), 881 (3), 891 (3)

emblazon 425 (8), 547 (19), 844 (12)

emblem 547 (1), 547 (9), 983 (3)

emblem of authority 743 (2)

emblem of royalty 743 (1)

emblematic 547 (15), 547 (16), 551 (6)

embodiment 5 (2), 50 (1), 56 (1), 78 (1), 319 (1)

embody 50 (4), 56 (4), 78 (5), 319 (7), 519 (4), 551 (8)

embolden 703 (5), 855 (8)

embolism 264 (1)

emboss 253 (9), 547 (19), 554 (3), 844 (12)

embouchure 414 (6)

embrace 45 (9), 45 (14), 48 (3), 56 (4), 78 (5), 230 (3), 235 (4), 605 (6), 778 (1), 778 (5), 880 (7), 884 (7), 889 (1), 889 (6)

embrasure 263 (5), 713 (3)

embrocation 357 (4), 658 (8)

embroider 437 (9), 541 (7), 546 (3), 844 (12)

embroidered 437 (5), 546 (2), 844 (10)

embroidery 40 (1), 546 (1), 551 (3), 574 (1), 844 (4)

embroil 63 (5), 709 (8)

embroilment 61 (2), 61 (3)

embrown 430 (4)

embryo 132 (3), 156 (3), 670 (2)

embryology 367 (1)

embryonic 68 (6), 156 (7), 196 (10), 244 (2), 670 (4)

emend 654 (10)

emendation 654 (2), 656 (2)

emender 520 (4)

emerald 434 (1), 844 (8)

emerge 68 (8), 157 (5), 269 (10), 290 (3), 296 (6), 298 (5), 305 (5), 350 (9), 667 (5), 712 (7)

emergence 68 (1), 298 (1)

emergency 8 (2), 137 (3), 154 (1), 627 (2), 661 (1), 700 (3) emergency exit **667** (2)

emergency rations **633** (1)

emergent **298** (4)

emerging **298** (1)

emeritus **915** (3)

emery board **258** (2)

emetic **300** (2), **300** (4), **391** (1), **658** (5), **658** (17)

emigrant **59** (2), **268** (2), **298** (1)

emigrate **267** (11), **290** (3), **296** (4), **298** (5)

emigration **267** (2), **290** (1), **296** (1), **298** (1)

emigré **59** (2), **268** (2), **298** (1)

eminence **32** (1), **34** (1), **209** (2), **254** (1), **310** (1), **638** (1), **644** (1), **866** (2)

eminent **32** (8), **638** (6), **866** (9)

eminently **34** (12)

emir **741** (4), **868** (5)

emirate **733** (5)

emissary **529** (5), **754** (2), **754** (3)

emission **298** (2), **300** (1)

emissive **300** (4)

emit **298** (6), **300** (9), **336** (4), **338** (4), **341** (6), **350** (11), **417** (12), **579** (8)

emit a smell **300** (9)

emit rays **300** (9)

emit sound **398** (4)

emit vapour **336** (4)

emit waves **317** (4)

emitting **300** (4)

emollient **177** (4), **327** (2), **334** (2), **658** (8), **658** (17)

emolument **804** (2), **807** (1)

emotion **818** (1), **818** (2), **821** (1)

emotional **601** (3), **609** (3), **817** (2), **818** (3), **819** (2), **822** (3)

emotional appeal **821** (1)

emotional life **817** (1)

emotionalism **612** (3), **818** (1), **819** (1), **822** (1)

emotions **817** (1)

emotive **590** (6), **818** (6), **821** (4)

empathize **513** (7)

empathy **513** (1), **818** (1), **897** (1), **905** (1)

emperor **741** (3), **868** (4)

emperor worship **982** (2)

emphasis **160** (1), **519** (2), **532** (1), **571** (1), **577** (2), **638** (1)

emphasize **162** (12), **455** (7), **475** (11), **522** (7), **528** (9), **532** (7), **547** (18), **577** (4), **638** (8), **716** (10), **740** (3), **821** (8)

emphatic **162** (6), **516** (3), **532** (4), **571** (2)

emphatic denial **533** (1)

emphatically **32** (19)

empire **184** (2), **733** (2), **733** (6)

empirical **459** (11), **461** (6)

empirical, be **461** (8)

empirical world **319** (1)

empirically **461** (9)

empiricism **449** (3), **461** (2)

empiricist **461** (3), **538** (1)

emplacement **186** (1), **187** (1)

employ **299** (3), **622** (3), **622** (6), **640** (5), **673** (3), **745** (2), **751** (4)

employ one's mind **449** (7)

employ oneself **676** (5)

employable **628** (3), **640** (2), **673** (2)

employed **622** (5), **678** (8)

employed, be **622** (7)

employee **686** (2), **742** (1)

employer **686** (1), **690** (1), **741** (1)

employment **622** (1), **622** (3), **628** (1), **640** (1), **673** (1), **676** (1), **745** (2)

employment agency **622** (3)

emporium **796** (2), **796** (3)

empower **86** (13), **160** (11), **162** (12), **469** (4), **701** (8), **751** (4), **756** (5)

empowered **160** (8), **733** (7), **751** (3)

empress **741** (3)

emptiness **2** (1), **4** (1), **183** (1), **190** (2), **201** (2), **255** (1), **325** (1), **340** (1), **515** (1)

empty **4** (3), **39** (3), **165** (9), **172** (4), **190** (5), **190** (6), **272** (7), **300** (8), **304** (4), **311** (5), **325** (2), **342** (6), **350** (11), **352** (12), **477** (4), **515** (4), **541** (4), **543** (4), **634** (4), **636** (4), **774** (3), **786** (8), **859** (9), **883** (7), **946** (3)

empty-handed **636** (4), **728** (4), **816** (4)

empty head **450** (1)

empty-headed **448** (2), **450** (2)

empty space **183** (1), **190** (2)

empty stomach **859** (2)

empty talk **4** (2), **161** (4), **477** (1), **515** (3), **541** (1), **543** (3), **560** (3), **570** (1), **574** (2), **579** (1), **581** (2), **877** (1), **877** (2)

empty threats **161** (4)

empty words **543** (2)

empurple **436** (3)

emu **365** (4)

emulate **20** (7), **83** (7), **716** (10)

emulation **83** (1), **704** (1)

emulsify **354** (6)

emulsion **226** (10), **354** (1)

emulsive **354** (4)

en avant **285** (6)

en bloc **52** (10)

en masse **52** (10), **74** (12)

en passant **137** (9), **305** (6)

en rapport **706** (3), **710** (2)

en revanche **714** (5)

en route **267** (16), **272** (9), **285** (5)

enable **160** (11), **469** (4), **701** (8), **756** (5)

enact **522** (8), **551** (8), **594** (17), **725** (6), **737** (7), **953** (7)

enacted **953** (5)

enactment **676** (1), **953** (2)

enamel **226** (16), **425** (8), **844** (12)

enamelled 844 (10)

enamelling 844 (2)

enamoured 481 (6), 499 (4), 503 (8), 887 (10)

encamp 187 (8)

encamped 187 (4)

encampment 187 (3), 192 (1), 713 (4)

encapsulate 78 (5), 226 (13), 592 (5)

encapsulation 78 (1)

encase 232 (3), 303 (4)

enchant 745 (7), 826 (4), 864 (7), 887 (15), 983 (11)

enchanted 824 (4), 887 (10), 983 (8), 983 (9)

enchanter 983 (5)

enchantess 983 (6)

enchanting 826 (2), 841 (6), 887 (11), 983 (7)

enchantment 821 (1), 824 (1), 826 (1), 887 (1), 983 (2)

enchantments 983 (1)

encircle 230 (3), 232 (3), 250 (8), 626 (3)

encircled 232 (2)

encirclement 232 (1)

enclose 45 (12), 46 (9), 56 (4), 57 (5), 74 (11), 78 (5), 218 (15), 224 (5), 226 (13), 230 (3), 232 (3), 235 (4), 261 (3), 264 (6), 369 (10), 370 (9), 660 (8), 702 (9), 712 (8), 713 (9), 747 (10), 778 (5)

enclosed 224 (3), 588 (3), 986 (12)

enclosing 194 (24), 232 (1)

enclosure 184 (1), 184 (2), 185 (1), 193 (1), 230 (1), 232 (1), 235 (1), 264 (1), 369 (3), 370 (2), 370 (3), 588 (1), 662 (2), 702 (2), 718 (6), 748 (2), 778 (1)

encode 520 (9), 525 (7)

encoder 520 (4)

encompass 78 (5), 230 (3)

encore 91 (3), 106 (1), 106 (8), 594 (2), 923 (3), 923 (14)

encounter 154 (1), 154 (7), 279 (3), 279 (8), 295 (6), 484 (4), 704 (5), 716 (7)

encounter group 74 (2)

encourage 156 (10), 612 (9), 654 (9), 703 (5), 756 (5), 821 (7), 831 (3), 833 (8), 852 (7), 855 (8)

encouragement 156 (1), 279 (1), 612 (2), 703 (1), 821 (1)

encouraging 178 (2), 612 (6), 703 (4), 852 (5)

encroach 231 (10), 306 (4), 712 (7), 738 (9), 914 (6), 916 (8)

encroachment 306 (1), 712 (1), 914 (1), 916 (2)

encrust 226 (16), 844 (12)

encumber 702 (8)

encumbrance 38 (1), 322 (1), 702 (4), 803 (1), 827 (2)

encyclical 528 (1), 737 (2)

encyclopedia 490 (2), 589 (4)

encyclopedic 78 (2), 79 (3), 490 (5)

end 54 (1), 54 (5), 65 (1), 67 (1), 69 (1), 69 (2), 69 (5), 111 (3), 125 (10), 127 (8), 145 (2), 145 (6), 154 (1), 165 (3), 165 (6), 165 (11), 213 (2), 236 (1), 361 (2), 725 (1)

end in view 617 (2)

end its run 145 (6)

end of life 361 (2)

end of one's tether 236 (1)

end of the line 69 (2)

end of time 69 (3)

end one's life 361 (7)

end-product 164 (2), 725 (1)

end result 69 (1)

end to end 202 (2), 202 (5), 203 (9)

endanger 661 (9), 727 (10)

endangered 661 (6), 700 (5)

endangered species 365 (1)

endangerment 661 (1)

endear oneself 887 (15)

endearing 826 (2), 887 (11)

endearment 612 (2), 778 (1), 889 (1), 925 (1)

endeavour 160 (1), 164 (1), 617 (6), 671 (1), 671 (4)

ended 69 (4)

endemic 224 (3), 653 (3)

ending 69 (1), 69 (4), 125 (6), 156 (7), 165 (5), 725 (3)

ending in 157 (3)

endless 107 (2), 115 (2)

endless supply 635 (2)

endless time 115 (1)

endlessly 16 (5)

endo- 224 (3)

endoderm 224 (1)

endogenous 224 (3)

endorse 153 (8), 466 (7), 473 (9), 488 (8), 547 (20), 703 (6), 758 (3), 765 (5), 767 (6), 915 (8), 923 (8), 953 (7)

endorsement 466 (3), 488 (1), 758 (1), 767 (2)

endorser 488 (3)

endow 777 (6), 781 (7)

endow with power 160 (11)

endowed 777 (5)

endowed with 5 (6), 773 (2)

endowment 160 (2), 694 (2), 781 (1)

endurance 113 (2), 115 (1), 144 (1), 160 (1), 162 (1), 600 (1), 818 (1), 823 (2), 855 (1)

endure 1 (6), 108 (7), 113 (6), 144 (3), 146 (3), 154 (7), 488 (7), 599 (3), 599 (4), 600 (4), 715 (3), 818 (7), 823 (6), 825 (7), 855 (6)

endure for ever 115 (4)

enduring 1 (4), 113 (4), 115 (2), 144 (2), 818 (3), 823 (4)

endwise 215 (5)

enema 303 (1), 658 (5)

enemy 663 (2), 705 (1), 881 (2), 888 (3), 904 (3)

energetic 160 (9), 174 (5), 571 (2), 599 (2), 678 (7), 682 (4)

energize 162 (12), 174 (8), 612 (9), 833 (8)

energizer 174 (4)

energy 26 (1), 156 (5), 160 (3), 162 (1), 174 (1), 287 (3), 465 (3), 678 (2), 682 (1), 687 (1)

energy-consuming 634 (2)

energy-saving 666 (3), 814 (1), 814 (2)

enervate 161 (10), 163 (10), 684 (6)

enervation 163 (1), 572 (1)

enfant terrible 699 (2), 827 (2)

enfeeble 163 (10)

enfilade 712 (3), 712 (11)

enfold 224 (5), 226 (13), 235 (4), 660 (8), 889 (6)

enfolded 232 (2)

enforce 740 (3)

enforce a claim 915 (5)

enforcement 740 (1)

enfranchise 744 (10), 746 (3), 919 (3)

enfranchised 605 (4), 744 (5)

enfranchised, be 605 (8)

enfranchisement 746 (1)

engage 45 (9), 45 (14), 135 (5), 532 (5), 612 (10), 617 (5), 622 (6), 716 (11), 718 (12), 751 (4), 765 (5), 771 (7), 773 (4)

engage in 622 (7), 622 (9), 672 (3)

engage in conversation 584 (6)

engage to 672 (3), 764 (4)

engaged 718 (8), 764 (3), 778 (4), 894 (8)

engaged, be 138 (5)

engagement 617 (1), 672 (1), 716 (7), 718 (7), 764 (1), 765 (1), 882 (4), 887 (3), 889 (2), 894 (3)

engagement book 87 (1)

engagement ring 889 (3)

engaging 887 (11)

engender 167 (7)

engine 156 (5), 630 (2)

engine driver 268 (5)

engine failure 702 (3)

engine power 160 (3)

engined 160 (9)

engineer 156 (9), 164 (4), 164 (7), 623 (8), 630 (5), 686 (3), 722 (5)

engineered 541 (3), 623 (6)

engineering 164 (1), 630 (3)

English 520 (9)

English rose 841 (2)

Englished 520 (7)

engrave 46 (11), 262 (3), 547 (19), 548 (7), 551 (8), 554 (3), 555 (3), 586 (8), 844 (12)

engraved 153 (6)

engraver 549 (1), 556 (3)

engraving 22 (1), 255 (1), 549 (1), 551 (1), 553 (5), 555 (1), 586 (1), 844 (2)

engross 449 (11), 455 (7), 481 (11)

engrossed 455 (3)

engulf 165 (6), 165 (10), 299 (4), 637 (5), 786 (7)

engulfing 299 (1)

enhance 36 (5), 546 (3), 638 (8), 654 (9), 832 (3), 844 (12)

enhanced 34 (4), 654 (6)

enhancement 36 (1), 654 (1), 844 (1)

enigma 459 (3), 474 (2), 491 (2), 497 (1), 515 (1), 517 (1), 518 (1), 530 (2), 700 (1), 825 (3)

enigmatic 491 (6), 496 (3), 517 (3), 568 (2), 864 (5)

enjoin 691 (4), 737 (6), 917 (11)

enjoy 376 (6), 386 (3), 673 (5), 730 (6), 773 (4), 824 (6), 828 (4)

enjoy a joke 839 (5)

enjoy good health 650 (3)

enjoy immunity 919 (4)

enjoy life 174 (7)

enjoy oneself 833 (7), 837 (21)

enjoyable 376 (3)

enjoyed 773 (3)

enjoying 824 (4)

enjoyment 376 (1), 673 (1), 824 (1), 824 (3), 837 (2), 882 (2), 944 (1)

enlace 222 (10), 251 (10), 303 (4)

enlarge 32 (15), 36 (5), 38 (3), 197 (5), 301 (39), 310 (4), 352 (12), 482 (4), 546 (3)

enlarge a hole 263 (17)

enlarge the mind 534 (6)

enlarge upon 570 (6)

enlarged 34 (4), 36 (3), 197 (3)

enlargement 36 (1), 197 (1), 546 (1)

enlighten 524 (9), 534 (6)

enlightened 498 (5), 901 (6)

enlightenment 490 (1), 524 (1), 979 (2)

enlist 78 (4), 87 (5), 299 (3), 548 (8), 612 (10), 708 (8), 718 (10)

enlist in 297 (5)

enlistment 299 (1), 548 (2)

enliven 360 (6), 821 (7), 833 (8), 837 (20)

enmesh 222 (10), 542 (10), 702 (8)

enmity 704 (1), 881 (1), 888 (1), 891 (1), 898 (1), 910 (2)

ennoble 866 (14)

ennobled 866 (8), 868 (6)

ennoblement 866 (5)

ennui 829 (1), 838 (1)

enormity 32 (1), 195 (2), 934 (1), 934 (2), 936 (2)

enormous 32 (6), 84 (6), 195 (7)

enormously 32 (17)

enormousness 195 (2)

enough 32 (17), 635 (1), 635 (3), 635 (9)

enough and to spare 637 (7)

enough, be 635 (6)

enough to go round 635 (3)

enquire 449 (8), 453 (4), 459 (13), 461 (7), 461 (8), 480 (6), 491 (8), 536 (5)

enquire for 459 (13)

enquire into 449 (8), 459 (13), 591 (5)

enquirer 453 (2), 459 (9), 461 (3), 480 (3), 484 (2), 584 (4), 671 (2)

enquiring 453 (3), 459 (11), 461 (6), 619 (4), 671 (3)

enquiring mind 453 (1), 459 (1)

enquiry 158 (1), 364 (6), 438 (4), 449 (2), 459 (1), 459 (5), 461 (1), 462 (1), 473 (1), 524 (2), 528 (2), 536 (2), 591 (1), 672 (1), 793 (1), 959 (3)

enrage 63 (3), 176 (9), 503 (12), 709 (8), 821 (6), 827 (9), 832 (3), 861 (5), 878 (6), 881 (5), 888 (8), 891 (9)

enrapture 826 (4), 887 (15)

enraptured 818 (4), 824 (4)

enrich 36 (5), 574 (6), 654 (9), 781 (7), 800 (8), 844 (12)

enrich oneself 800 (7)

enrichment 654 (1), 844 (1)

enrol 87 (5), 299 (3), 548 (8), 718 (10)

enrol oneself 78 (4), 297 (5), 708 (8)

enrolment 299 (1), 548 (2)

ensconce 187 (5)

ensconce oneself 187 (8)

ensconced 187 (4)

ensemble 52 (1), 52 (2), 228 (9), 412 (6), 413 (3)

enshrine 232 (3)

ensign 547 (12), 722 (4), 741 (8)

enslave 735 (8), 745 (7)

enslaved 745 (4)

enslavement 745 (1), 745 (3)

ensnare 291 (4), 484 (5), 508 (5), 527 (5), 542 (10), 612 (11), 619 (6), 623 (9), 702 (8), 786 (6)

ensue 65 (3), 120 (3)

ensuing 65 (2)

ensure 473 (9)

entail 156 (10), 471 (5)

entangle 63 (5), 222 (10), 542 (10), 702 (8), 709 (8)

entangled 61 (8)

entangled with, be 43 (8)

entanglement 222 (1), 887 (3)

entente 24 (1), 719 (1), 880 (2)

enter 54 (7), 78 (4), 87 (5), 263 (18), 289 (4), 293 (3), 297 (5), 305 (5), 350 (9), 548 (8), 759 (4), 808 (5)

enter a monastery or a nunnery 986 (13)

enter for 716 (10)

enter into 58 (3), 78 (4), 590 (7), 706 (4), 786 (7)

enter into detail 80 (8)

enter the church 985 (8)

enter the lists 716 (10)

enter upon 68 (8)

entered 78 (3), 87 (4), 548 (6)

entering into 58 (2)

enterprise 174 (1), 617 (1), 622 (1), 672 (1), 678 (2), 751 (2)

enterprising 174 (5), 285 (2), 618 (7), 671 (3), 672 (2), 678 (7), 855 (4), 857 (3)

entertain 781 (7), 818 (7), 837 (20), 848 (7), 849 (4), 880 (7), 882 (10)

entertained 837 (19), 882 (7)

entertainer 20 (3), 162 (4), 312 (2), 501 (1), 594 (10), 837 (14), 839 (3)

entertaining 837 (18), 882 (2)

entertainment 837 (1), 882 (3)

enthral 887 (15)

enthralled 455 (3), 818 (4)

enthralling 821 (4)

enthrone 751 (4), 866 (14), 985 (8)

enthronement 751 (2)

enthuse 818 (8), 821 (6)

enthusiasm 174 (1), 571 (1), 597 (1), 678 (2), 818 (2), 821 (1), 852 (1), 923 (3)

enthusiast 492 (3), 504 (3), 594 (14), 610 (4), 678 (5), 981 (8)

enthusiastic 482 (2), 597 (4), 678 (7), 818 (5), 819 (4), 821 (3)

entice 456 (8), 612 (11)

enticement 612 (2)

enticing 826 (2)

entire 32 (13), 44 (4), 52 (4), 54 (3), 646 (3), 646 (4)

entirely 32 (17), 52 (8), 54 (8)

entireness 54 (1)

entirety 52 (1), 54 (1)

entitle 561 (6)

entitled 561 (4), 915 (3)

entitled, be 915 (6)

entitlement 870 (1), 915 (1)

entity 1 (1), 3 (2), 52 (1), 88 (2)

entombment 364 (1)

entomological 365 (18)

entomologist 367 (2)

entomology 367 (1)

entourage 89 (2)

entrails 224 (2)

entrance 68 (5), 237 (1), 263 (6), 295 (1), 297 (1), 297 (2), 624 (2), 826 (4)

entrancing 841 (6)

entrant 459 (4), 460 (3), 705 (1), 716 (8), 763 (1)

entre-mets 301 (13)

entrée 297 (1), 299 (1), 301 (13)

entreat 761 (7), 762 (3), 981 (11)

entreating 761 (4)

entreaty 524 (2), 532 (1), 761 (2)

entrench 153 (8), 162 (12), 713 (9)
entrench oneself 187 (8)
entrench upon 306 (4)
entrenched 144 (2), 153 (5), 713 (8), 915 (2)
entrenchment 713 (2)
entrepôt 796 (2)
entrepreneur 618 (4), 671 (2), 676 (3), 794 (1)
entropy 51 (1)
entrust 272 (6), 751 (4), 780 (3), 781 (7)
entry 263 (6), 297 (1), 297 (2)
entwine 45 (14), 222 (10), 251 (10)
enumerate 80 (8), 86 (11), 87 (5)
enumerate with 78 (6)
enumeration 86 (1), 87 (1)
enumerator 86 (7)
enunciate 577 (4)
enunciation 577 (1), 577 (2), 579 (1)
envelop 78 (5), 228 (31), 232 (3)
envelope 194 (1), 226 (13), 235 (1)
enveloped 232 (2)
envelopment 232 (1)
envenom 832 (3), 888 (8), 891 (9)
enviable 859 (10), 923 (6)
envier 859 (6)
envious 829 (3), 881 (3), 888 (4), 891 (3), 898 (4), 911 (2), 912 (2), 932 (3)
envious eye 912 (1)
envious rivalry 912 (1)
enviousness 911 (1), 912 (1)
environment 8 (1), 187 (2), 230 (1)
environmental 8 (3), 9 (5)
environs 187 (2), 200 (3), 230 (1)
envisage 513 (7)
envoi 67 (1), 69 (1), 593 (4)
envoy 529 (5), 690 (4), 751 (1), 754 (3)

envy 829 (1), 829 (5), 859 (11), 881 (1), 881 (4), 888 (1), 888 (7), 891 (5), 911 (1), 912 (1), 912 (3), 923 (8)
envying 911 (2)
enzyme 143 (3), 323 (2), 358 (1)
eo- 127 (5)
epaulette 547 (9), 743 (3)
ephemeral 114 (4), 150 (4)
ephemerality 114 (1)
epic 570 (4), 590 (2), 590 (6), 593 (2)
epic poet 593 (6)
epicentre 225 (2)
epicure 301 (4), 301 (6), 846 (2), 862 (2), 944 (2), 947 (2)
epicurean 301 (34), 390 (2), 846 (2), 846 (3), 944 (2), 944 (3), 947 (3)
epicureanism 846 (1), 944 (1)
epicurism 301 (4), 846 (1), 947 (1)
epidemic 32 (5), 52 (7), 79 (1), 79 (4), 651 (4), 653 (3)
epidermis 226 (6)
epidiascope 442 (1)
epigram 496 (1), 563 (1), 569 (1), 839 (2)
epigrammatic 496 (3), 514 (3), 569 (2), 839 (4)
epigrammatize 569 (3)
epilepsy 318 (2), 503 (4), 651 (3), 651 (16)
epileptic 503 (9), 651 (22)
epilogue 67 (1), 69 (2)
epiphany 975 (1)
episcopacy 985 (1), 985 (3)
episcopal 985 (6), 986 (11)
Episcopalian 976 (4), 976 (10), 978 (6), 985 (6)
episcopalianism 985 (1)
episcopalians 978 (3)
episode 10 (2), 154 (1), 590 (2)
episodic 10 (3), 72 (2), 570 (4)
epistle 588 (1)
epistolary 588 (3)

epitaph 364 (2), 547 (1)
epithet 561 (2), 899 (2)
epitome 196 (3), 198 (1), 569 (1), 592 (1)
epitomize 204 (5), 592 (5)
epitomizer 592 (3)
epoch 110 (2), 117 (4)
epoch-making 638 (6)
epochal 110 (4)
eponym 561 (2)
eponymous 561 (4)
equability 865 (1)
equable 823 (3)
equal 13 (2), 24 (5), 24 (8), 28 (6), 28 (7), 28 (9), 86 (8), 123 (3), 219 (2), 913 (4)
equal, be 28 (9), 78 (5), 322 (5)
equal chance 159 (2), 618 (1)
equal division 28 (4)
equal rights 744 (1)
equal to 160 (8)
equal to, be 28 (9)
equalitarian 16 (1)
equality 13 (1), 18 (1), 28 (1), 153 (1), 159 (2), 219 (1), 606 (1)
equalization 28 (4), 31 (1), 31 (2), 70 (1), 322 (2)
equalize 13 (4), 16 (4), 24 (10), 28 (10), 30 (5), 31 (5), 45 (9), 153 (8)
equalized 28 (7)
equalizer 28 (4)
equally 28 (11)
equally divided 28 (7)
equanimity 823 (1)
equate 13 (4), 18 (8), 28 (10)
equation 28 (2), 28 (4), 85 (4)
equations 86 (2)
equator 28 (4), 70 (1), 92 (3), 236 (1), 250 (2)
equatorial 70 (2), 321 (15), 379 (6)
equerry 742 (3)
equestrian 268 (4)
equestrianism 267 (5)
equi- 28 (7)

equidistance 70 (1), 219 (1)

equidistant 28 (7), 70 (2), 219 (2)

equilateral 28 (7)

equilateral triangle 247 (4)

equilibrium 28 (3), 245 (1), 266 (1)

equine 273 (11), 365 (18)

equinoctial 128 (6), 129 (6)

equip 228 (31), 629 (2), 633 (5), 669 (11)

equip oneself 632 (5)

equipage 274 (6)

equipment 40 (1), 193 (1), 629 (1), 630 (4), 633 (1), 669 (2)

equipoise 28 (3), 322 (2)

equipped 669 (7)

equitable 913 (4)

equitableness 913 (2)

equitation 265 (1), 265 (2), 267 (5)

equity 913 (2)

equivalence 13 (1), 18 (1), 28 (2)

equivalent 13 (2), 18 (3), 18 (4), 28 (2), 28 (6), 28 (8), 31 (2), 31 (3), 150 (3), 150 (4), 151 (2)

equivocal 84 (5), 91 (2), 467 (2), 474 (4), 514 (4), 517 (3), 518 (2), 541 (3), 543 (4), 568 (2), 603 (4), 698 (4), 930 (4)

equivocal, be 152 (5), 467 (4), 474 (8), 477 (8), 517 (6), 518 (3), 541 (6), 570 (6), 601 (4), 603 (5), 620 (5), 769 (3), 839 (5), 930 (8)

equivocalness 14 (1), 25 (1), 474 (1), 514 (2), 517 (1), 518 (1), 519 (2), 525 (1), 541 (1), 543 (2), 559 (1), 560 (1), 568 (1), 603 (3), 620 (1), 839 (2)

equivocate 477 (8), 518 (3), 769 (3), 839 (5)

equivocating 518 (2)

equivocation 477 (1), 518 (1), 541 (1)

equivocator 477 (3)

era 108 (3), 110 (2), 117 (4), 125 (2), 127 (1)

eradicate 57 (5), 149 (4), 165 (6), 188 (4), 300 (6), 304 (4)

eradication 165 (1), 304 (1)

erase 550 (3), 648 (9)

eraser 168 (1), 333 (1), 550 (1)

erasure 333 (1), 550 (1)

ere now 119 (5)

ere then 119 (5)

erect 164 (7), 187 (5), 215 (2), 215 (4), 215 (5), 310 (3), 310 (4)

erected 310 (3)

erectile 310 (3)

erection 164 (1), 164 (3), 310 (1)

erectness 215 (1)

erector 310 (2)

erg 160 (1)

ergonomics 682 (1)

ermine 226 (6), 547 (11), 547 (16), 743 (1)

erode 37 (4), 51 (5), 306 (4), 332 (5), 333 (3), 634 (4), 655 (9)

eroded 172 (4)

erogenous 887 (12)

eros 859 (4), 887 (7), 967 (1)

erosion 37 (1), 37 (2), 51 (2), 172 (1), 332 (1), 333 (1), 655 (2)

erotic 887 (12), 944 (3), 951 (6)

erotica 951 (1)

eroticism 859 (4), 887 (1), 951 (2)

err 495 (7), 914 (5), 934 (7)

errand 529 (3), 622 (3)

errand boy 742 (1)

errant 267 (9), 282 (2)

errata 589 (5)

erratic 17 (2), 152 (4), 265 (3), 495 (6), 604 (3)

erratically 17 (3)

erratum 495 (3)

erring 495 (4), 934 (3)

erroneous 2 (4), 470 (2), 474 (5), 477 (5), 495 (4), 497 (3), 513 (6), 977 (2)

erroneousness 495 (1)

error 474 (3), 481 (1), 491 (1), 495 (1), 513 (3), 542 (1), 643 (1), 647 (1), 647 (2), 977 (1)

ersatz 150 (2), 150 (4), 542 (7)

eruct 300 (11), 302 (6)

eructation 300 (3)

erudite 490 (6), 536 (3)

erudition 490 (2), 536 (1), 589 (4)

erupt 176 (7), 298 (5), 712 (7)

erupting 379 (5)

eruption 176 (2), 300 (3), 379 (2)

eruptive 176 (5), 300 (4)

escalate 36 (4), 811 (4)

escalating 36 (3)

escalation 36 (1)

escalator 267 (6), 273 (1), 274 (15), 308 (1), 310 (2)

escalope 301 (16)

escapable 620 (4)

escapade 497 (2), 604 (2), 837 (3)

escape 46 (7), 190 (7), 290 (1), 290 (3), 296 (1), 296 (5), 298 (1), 298 (2), 298 (3), 298 (5), 298 (6), 446 (1), 446 (3), 614 (4), 620 (1), 620 (5), 620 (6), 660 (7), 660 (9), 661 (1), 667 (1), 667 (5), 668 (1), 668 (3), 744 (9), 746 (4), 918 (1), 918 (3), 919 (4)

escape attention 456 (9)

escape clause 468 (1), 667 (2), 919 (1)

escape hatch 667 (2)

escape liability 919 (4)

escape notice 444 (4), 456 (9), 506 (6), 667 (6), 874 (3)

escape one 517 (6)

escape one's memory 506 (6)

escaped 190 (4), 620 (3), 667 (4), 744 (5)

escapee 667 (3), 744 (4)

escaper 620 (2), 667 (3), 744 (4), 918 (1)

escapism 513 (3), 620 (1), 667 (1)

escapist 513 (4), 620 (2)

escapologist 667 (3)

escapology 667 (1)

escarpment 209 (2), 220 (2)

eschatology 69 (3)

eschew 620 (5)

escort 89 (2), 89 (4), 273 (12), 372 (1), 457 (6), 660 (2), 660 (8), 689 (5), 713 (6), 749 (1), 884 (7), 887 (4), 889 (7)

escritoire 194 (5)

escutcheon 547 (11)

esoteric 80 (7), 517 (2), 523 (4), 983 (7), 984 (4), 984 (6)

esotericism 523 (1), 530 (1), 984 (1)

ESP 374 (2), 984 (2)

espalier 218 (13)

especially 34 (12), 80 (9)

Esperanto 557 (1)

espionage 459 (7)

esplanade 624 (5)

espouse 605 (6), 706 (4), 894 (11)

esprit 839 (1)

esprit de corps 706 (1), 882 (1)

espy 438 (7)

esquire 372 (1)

essay 589 (2), 591 (1), 591 (2), 671 (1), 671 (4)

essayist 589 (7), 591 (3)

essence 1 (3), 5 (2), 44 (1), 164 (2), 304 (1), 514 (1), 646 (1)

essential 5 (6), 32 (14), 627 (1), 627 (3), 638 (3), 638 (5)

essential oil 357 (2)

essential part 1 (3), 3 (2), 5 (2), 89 (2), 225 (2), 447 (2), 638 (3), 817 (1)

essentiality 3 (1)

essentially 3 (4), 5 (10), 32 (16), 52 (9)

essentialness 5 (1)

establish 68 (10), 115 (3), 153 (8), 164 (7), 466 (8), 478 (4), 777 (6), 953 (7)

establish a connection 9 (8)

establish oneself 187 (8)

established 127 (6), 144 (2), 153 (5), 478 (3), 610 (6), 730 (4), 777 (5)

established order 81 (2)

establishment 68 (1), 153 (2), 164 (1), 187 (1), 478 (1), 638 (4), 708 (5), 796 (3)

establishment, the 741 (1)

estate 7 (1), 184 (2), 344 (1), 370 (2), 773 (1), 777 (2), 777 (3)

estate agent 794 (1)

estate car 274 (11)

estate duty 809 (3)

estates 800 (1)

esteem 485 (8), 638 (8), 866 (1), 866 (2), 920 (1), 920 (5), 923 (1), 923 (8)

esteemed 866 (7), 920 (4)

estimable 644 (4), 923 (6)

estimate 62 (6), 86 (12), 447 (7), 449 (8), 461 (1), 463 (1), 463 (3), 465 (1), 465 (13), 480 (2), 480 (6), 507 (1), 507 (4), 520 (1), 524 (2), 532 (1), 557 (3), 591 (2), 617 (1), 691 (1), 808 (5), 808 (3), 809 (5)

estimation 480 (2), 866 (2)

estimator 459 (9), 465 (3), 480 (3), 520 (4), 589 (6), 691 (2), 720 (2), 846 (2), 957 (2)

estrange 46 (9), 709 (8), 881 (5), 888 (8)

estranged 881 (3)

estrangement 881 (1), 883 (2), 888 (1)

estuary 263 (7), 345 (1)

et cetera 38 (5), 78 (7), 101 (3)

etcetera 562 (2)

etch 262 (3), 547 (19), 555 (3)

etched 233 (2)

etcher 556 (3)

etching 551 (1), 555 (1), 844 (2)

eternal 1 (4), 107 (2), 113 (4), 115 (2), 965 (6)

eternal, be 113 (6), 115 (4), 146 (3), 505 (11)

eternal rest 266 (2), 361 (1)

eternal triangle 911 (1), 951 (3)

eternalize 115 (3)

eternally 16 (5)

eternity 1 (1), 107 (1), 108 (1), 115 (1), 320 (1), 965 (2), 971 (1)

ether 321 (3), 323 (1), 336 (2), 340 (1), 375 (2)

ethereal 4 (3), 321 (14), 340 (5)

ethical 913 (3), 917 (7), 933 (3)

ethics 449 (3), 917 (4), 933 (1)

ethnic 11 (6), 191 (6), 371 (6)

ethnic group 11 (4)

ethnic type 371 (1)

ethnographer 371 (2)

ethnography 371 (2)

ethnology 371 (2)

ethos 5 (3), 688 (1)

etiquette 83 (1), 610 (2), 846 (1), 848 (2), 875 (2), 913 (1)

étui 194 (10)

etymological 514 (4), 557 (5), 559 (4)

etymologist 557 (4), 559 (3)

etymology 156 (3), 243 (2), 557 (2), 557 (4), 559 (3)

Eucharist 988 (4)

eucharistic 988 (8)

eugenics 167 (1)

eulogist 923 (4)

eulogize 923 (9)

eulogy 579 (2), 590 (1), 866 (4), 923 (2)

547 (1), 547 (18), 548 (4), 959 (3)

evidence against 467 (1)

evident 443 (2), 473 (4), 478 (3), 522 (4)

evidential 466 (5), 478 (2), 478 (3), 547 (15)

evidentiary 466 (5)

evil 616 (1), 616 (2), 645 (1), 645 (2), 645 (3), 659 (1), 659 (5), 675 (1), 731 (1), 825 (3), 827 (1), 827 (2), 934 (3)

evil-doing 934 (1), 934 (3)

evil eye 645 (1), 898 (1), 899 (1), 983 (2)

evil genius 645 (1)

evil hour 138 (1)

evil intent 898 (1)

evil-minded 934 (3)

evil omen 665 (1)

Evil One, the 969 (1)

evil plight 616 (1)

evil star 645 (1), 731 (2)

evildoer 904 (1), 938 (1)

evince 466 (6), 522 (7), 547 (18)

eviscerate 163 (10), 300 (8), 304 (4)

evisceration 163 (1)

evocation 505.(2), 551 (1), 590 (1)

evocative 505 (6), 514 (3), 590 (6), 821 (4)

evoke 156 (9), 590 (7), 612 (9), 821 (6)

evolution 147 (1), 285 (1), 314 (1), 316 (1), 358 (2), 654 (1)

evolutionism 316 (1)

evolve 1 (7), 157 (5), 203 (8), 285 (3), 304 (4), 316 (3), 654 (8)

evolve into 147 (6)

evolved from 157 (3)

evolving 147 (5), 316 (2)

ewe 365 (1)

ewer 194 (13)

ex- 119 (2), 125 (7)

ex cathedra 485 (6), 532 (4)

ex-convict 744 (4), 904 (3)

ex-friend 881 (2)

ex officio 733 (7), 915 (9)

exacerbate 36 (5), 176 (9), 655 (9), 827 (8), 832 (3), 888 (8)

exacerbated 655 (5), 832 (2)

exacerbation 36 (1), 655 (3), 827 (1), 832 (1)

exact 18 (5), 80 (6), 494 (6), 540 (2), 567 (2), 737 (8), 740 (3), 768 (2), 786 (8)

exact a penalty 963 (8)

exact a promise 764 (5)

exact copy 22 (1)

exact reprisals 735 (7)

exact time 117 (2)

exact tribute 786 (8)

exacting 684 (4), 700 (4), 735 (6), 859 (8), 862 (3)

exaction 737 (3), 740 (1), 786 (1), 786 (2), 916 (1)

exactly 494 (8), 540 (4)

exactness 457 (1), 494 (3), 567 (1)

exaggerate 197 (5), 306 (3), 482 (4), 513 (7), 515 (6), 541 (5), 543 (5), 546 (3), 552 (3), 594 (17), 637 (5), 638 (8), 850 (5), 877 (5), 923 (9)

exaggerated 32 (12), 84 (6), 482 (3), 497 (3), 513 (5), 515 (4), 519 (3), 541 (3), 543 (4), 546 (2), 849 (2), 850 (4), 877 (4), 925 (3)

exaggeration 32 (1), 36 (1), 197 (1), 306 (1), 482 (1), 497 (1), 513 (2), 528 (2), 541 (1), 543 (1), 543 (3), 545 (2), 546 (1), 552 (1), 574 (2), 637 (1), 849 (1), 875 (1), 877 (2)

exaggerator 546 (1)

exalt 310 (4), 638 (8), 866 (14)

exaltation 310 (1), 866 (5)

exalted 32 (4), 209 (8), 310 (3), 638 (6), 868 (6)

exam 459 (4)

examination 438 (4), 449 (2), 455 (1), 459 (1), 459 (4), 461 (1), 591 (1), 959 (3)

examination paper 459 (3)

examine 438 (9), 455 (4), 459 (13), 459 (14), 480 (6), 490 (8)

examinee 459 (4), 460 (3), 461 (5), 716 (8)

examiner 415 (3), 441 (1), 453 (2), 459 (9), 480 (3), 584 (4)

examining 459 (11)

examining board 459 (9)

example 9 (3), 18 (3), 21 (1), 22 (2), 23 (1), 53 (1), 66 (1), 81 (1), 83 (2), 520 (1), 520 (5), 664 (1)

example, be an 23 (5), 178 (3)

exasperate 832 (3), 888 (8), 891 (9)

exasperation 832 (1), 891 (2)

excavate 255 (8), 304 (4), 459 (15)

excavation 125 (2), 255 (4), 263 (8), 304 (1), 309 (1), 459 (5), 484 (1)

excavator 255 (5), 304 (2), 309 (1)

exceed 32 (15), 306 (1), 306 (5), 943 (3)

exceed one's authority 954 (8)

exceed the limit 306 (3)

exceeding 34 (4)

exceedingly 32 (18)

excel 34 (7), 644 (10), 694 (8), 866 (11)

excellence 34 (1), 638 (1), 644 (1), 741 (3), 846 (1)

excellent 32 (4), 34 (4), 34 (5), 84 (6), 605 (5), 638 (6), 644 (4), 646 (3), 694 (4), 727 (4), 826 (2), 841 (4), 846 (3), 864 (5), 866 (7), 866 (10), 933 (3)

exceller 644 (3), 646 (2), 696 (1), 727 (3), 890 (2)

excelling 638 (6)

except 8 (6), 37 (4), 39 (3), 39 (4), 46 (9), 57 (5), 57 (6), 607 (3)

excepted 46 (5)

excepting 39 (4), 57 (6), 468 (2)

exception 17 (1), 46 (2), 57 (1), 80 (1), 84 (1), 468 (1), 766 (1), 924 (1)

exception, an 57 (1)

exceptional 17 (2), 32 (8), 84 (7), 468 (2), 864 (5)

exceptionally 32 (17)

excerpt 53 (1), 592 (5), 605 (7)

excess 32 (1), 36 (1), 41 (1), 546 (1), 576 (1), 637 (1), 637 (2), 678 (4), 744 (3), 863 (1), 898 (3), 943 (1)

excessive 32 (12), 176 (5), 306 (2), 546 (2), 570 (5), 576 (2), 637 (3), 637 (4), 757 (2), 811 (2), 847 (4), 898 (7), 943 (2)

excessive charge 809 (1)

excessive interest 803 (2)

excessively 32 (18), 637 (7)

excessiveness 306 (1), 637 (1), 943 (1)

exchange 12 (1), 12 (3), 28 (2), 76 (1), 150 (1), 150 (5), 151 (1), 151 (3), 584 (1), 780 (1), 780 (3), 791 (1), 791 (4), 796 (1), 797 (3)

exchange blows 716 (11)

exchange glances 438 (8)

exchange letters 588 (4)

exchange of views 584 (3)

exchange of vows 765 (1)

exchange rate 797 (3)

exchange shots 716 (11)

exchange signals 547 (22)

exchange views 462 (3)

exchange vows 764 (4)

exchange words 584 (6)

exchangeable 12 (2), 780 (2), 791 (3)

exchanged 151 (2)

exchanging 791 (3)

exchequer 632 (2), 797 (2), 799 (1)

excisable 809 (4)

excise 39 (3), 304 (4), 809 (3)

excision 304 (1)

excitability 678 (2), 680 (1), 818 (1), 819 (1), 822 (1), 827 (1), 857 (1), 859 (1), 892 (1)

excitable 678 (7), 818 (4), 818 (5), 819 (2), 819 (3), 821 (3), 822 (3), 857 (3), 892 (3)

excitable, be 678 (12), 821 (9), 822 (4), 891 (6)

excitable state 176 (1), 818 (2), 821 (1), 822 (2), 833 (1), 887 (1), 891 (2)

excitableness 822 (1)

excitant 174 (4), 821 (2), 832 (1), 949 (4)

excitation 174 (2), 318 (3), 376 (1), 612 (2), 678 (1), 821 (1)

excite 156 (9), 162 (12), 174 (8), 176 (9), 374 (6), 378 (8), 503 (12), 612 (9), 821 (6), 826 (4), 832 (3), 859 (13), 887 (15), 949 (16)

excite attention 455 (7)

excite hate 709 (8), 861 (5), 888 (8), 891 (8)

excite love 850 (5), 859 (13), 887 (15), 889 (6), 889 (7)

excite nausea 292 (3)

excite pity 905 (8)

excited 507 (2), 612 (7), 818 (3), 818 (4), 821 (3), 822 (3), 887 (10), 887 (12), 923 (5), 949 (6)

excited, be 318 (5), 376 (6), 818 (7), 821 (9), 822 (4), 891 (7)

excitedly 821 (10)

excitement 174 (2), 821 (1)

exciting 174 (5), 374 (4), 579 (7), 590 (6), 594 (15), 612 (6), 821 (4), 826 (2), 833 (6), 949 (12)

exclaim 408 (3), 577 (4)

exclamation 408 (1), 577 (1), 864 (1)

exclamation mark 547 (14), 864 (1)

exclude 37 (4), 39 (3), 41 (6), 44 (7), 46 (9), 55 (5), 57 (5), 300 (6), 421 (4), 470 (5), 607 (3), 702 (9), 747 (7), 752 (5), 757 (4), 760 (4), 867 (11), 883 (9), 919 (3), 924 (9)

excluded 57 (3), 188 (2), 190 (4), 607 (2), 757 (3), 883 (6)

excluded, be 57 (4)

excluding 44 (5), 57 (2), 757 (2)

exclusion 44 (3), 46 (2), 57 (1), 84 (1), 145 (3), 231 (2), 300 (1), 421 (1), 481 (3), 747 (2), 883 (1), 883 (2), 924 (1), 963 (4)

exclusionary 57 (2)

exclusive 57 (2), 80 (7), 529 (1), 644 (4), 708 (7), 757 (2), 773 (2), 978 (6)

exclusive of 39 (4), 57 (6)

exclusive rights 747 (2)

exclusive sale 793 (1)

exclusively 44 (8)

exclusiveness 14 (1), 57 (1), 80 (3)

excogitate 449 (7)

excogitation 449 (2)

excommunicate 57 (5), 300 (6), 757 (4), 883 (9), 899 (6), 961 (3), 988 (10)

excommunicated 978 (7)

excommunication 57 (1), 300 (1), 961 (1), 988 (4)

excrement 302 (4), 335 (2), 341 (1), 649 (2)

excrescence 253 (2), 637 (2)

excreta 302 (4)

excrete 300 (8), 300 (9), 302 (6)

excretion 300 (1), 300 (3), 302 (1)

excretory 300 (4), 302 (5), 649 (6)

excruciating 377 (3), 827 (3)

exculpate 919 (3), 927 (6), 960 (3)

exculpated 960 (2)

exculpation 927 (1), 960 (1)

exculpatory 614 (3)

excursion 267 (1), 306 (1), 837 (1)

excursionist 268 (1), 837 (17)

excusable 909 (3), 927 (4), 935 (4)

excuse 57 (5), 156 (6), 458 (5), 468 (3), 543 (2), 614 (1), 668 (3), 698 (2), 909 (4), 919 (1), 919 (3), 927 (1), 927 (7)

excuse oneself 614 (4), 760 (4), 919 (4)

excused 909 (3), 919 (2)

excusing 468 (2), 614 (3)

execrable 645 (2), 827 (4), 888 (5)

execrate 888 (7), 924 (10)

execration 888 (1), 899 (1)

executant 676 (3), 686 (1)

execute 164 (7), 173 (3), 362 (10), 413 (9), 672 (3), 676 (5), 688 (5), 725 (6), 767 (6), 768 (3), 963 (12)

execute justice 963 (8)

execution 164 (1), 173 (1), 361 (1), 362 (1), 413 (6), 676 (1), 725 (2), 963 (3)

executioner 168 (1), 362 (6), 963 (5)

executive 164 (4), 173 (2), 676 (3), 686 (1), 689 (3), 690 (3), 955 (4)

executor 676 (3), 686 (1), 690 (3), 754 (1)

executor, be 755 (3)

exegesis 520 (1)

exegetical 520 (6)

exemplar 23 (1), 83 (2)

exemplary 23 (4), 83 (5), 520 (6), 644 (4), 664 (3), 933 (3)

exemplify 83 (9), 520 (8)

exempt 46 (5), 46 (9), 57 (5), 468 (3), 668 (3), 744

(5), 746 (3), 756 (5), 831 (3), 919 (2), 919 (3), 960 (2)

exempt, be 667 (5), 919 (4)

exempt from 44 (5), 190 (4), 831 (3)

exempted 468 (2), 919 (2)

exempting 468 (2)

exemption 46 (2), 57 (1), 84 (1), 468 (1), 668 (1), 744 (1), 756 (1), 779 (1), 915 (1), 919 (1), 960 (1)

exercise 162 (3), 173 (1), 265 (1), 534 (1), 534 (3), 534 (8), 536 (4), 622 (3), 652 (2), 669 (11), 669 (13), 672 (1), 673 (1), 673 (3), 676 (2), 676 (5), 682 (2), 682 (3), 827 (10)

exercise a pull 291 (4)

exercise a right 915 (5)

exercise authority 733 (10)

exercise power 160 (10)

exercised 162 (9)

exercising 682 (4)

exert 673 (3)

exert authority 733 (10), 735 (7)

exert energy 174 (7)

exert influence 178 (3)

exert oneself 174 (7), 455 (4), 459 (15), 599 (3), 600 (4), 671 (4), 678 (11), 682 (6)

exert weight 322 (5)

exertion 160 (1), 174 (1), 595 (0), 600 (1), 671 (1), 676 (1), 682 (1), 684 (1), 700 (1), 716 (2)

exhalation 302 (1), 336 (2), 338 (1), 352 (7), 394 (1)

exhale 298 (7), 300 (9), 338 (4), 352 (11), 394 (3)

exhaust 161 (9), 298 (3), 634 (4), 636 (9), 655 (9), 684 (6), 786 (8)

exhaust pipe 298 (3), 353 (1)

exhausted 161 (7), 163 (5), 172 (4), 634 (3), 655 (5), 684 (2)

exhausting 165 (4), 682 (5)

exhaustion 161 (2), 377 (1), 634 (1), 655 (1), 673 (1), 684 (1), 834 (1)

exhaustive 54 (3)

exhibit 445 (2), 445 (8), 466 (1), 522 (2), 522 (8), 528 (3), 547 (13), 547 (18), 632 (3), 796 (1), 875 (7)

exhibited 445 (7), 522 (6)

exhibition 445 (1), 445 (2), 522 (1), 522 (2), 632 (3), 796 (1)

exhibitionism 576 (1), 873 (1), 875 (1), 951 (1)

exhibitionist 522 (3), 873 (3), 875 (5)

exhibitor 520 (5), 522 (3)

exhilarate 821 (6), 826 (4), 833 (8)

exhilarated 824 (4)

exhilarating 821 (4), 833 (6), 949 (12)

exhilaration 821 (1), 822 (2), 824 (1), 833 (2)

exhort 612 (9), 691 (4)

exhortation 579 (2), 612 (2)

exhumation 364 (6)

exhume 125 (11), 364 (10)

exigent 627 (5), 735 (6)

exiguity 105 (1), 196 (1)

exiguous 33 (6), 196 (10), 206 (5)

exiguousness 33 (1)

exile 57 (1), 57 (5), 59 (2), 188 (1), 188 (4), 298 (1), 300 (1), 300 (6), 883 (4), 883 (9), 963 (4)

exiled 883 (6)

exist 1 (6), 121 (3), 189 (4), 360 (4)

existence 1 (1), 189 (1), 319 (1), 360 (1), 445 (1)

existent 1 (4)

existential 1 (4)

existentialism 449 (3)

existentialist 449 (4)

existing 1 (4), 121 (2), 189 (2)

exit 263 (6), 296 (1), 298 (1), 298 (3), 298 (5), 361 (2), 446 (1)

explanatory 156 (7), 520 (6), 526 (3), 547 (15)
expletive 637 (2), 899 (2)
explication 520 (1)
explicatory 516 (3), 520 (6)
explicit 80 (6), 514 (3), 516 (2), 522 (5), 522 (9), 524 (7), 567 (2)
explode 46 (13), 75 (3), 165 (7), 176 (7), 263 (17), 287 (8), 330 (3), 400 (4), 479 (3), 678 (11), 728 (8), 821 (9), 822 (4), 891 (6)
exploded 486 (5), 495 (4)
exploit 137 (7), 164 (7), 638 (2), 673 (3), 675 (2), 676 (2), 676 (5), 694 (3), 694 (8), 727 (1), 735 (8), 855 (2), 864 (2)
exploitation 673 (1), 694 (1), 771 (1)
exploitive 735 (6)
exploration 267 (1), 459 (1), 459 (5), 461 (1), 484 (1)
exploratory 66 (3), 459 (11), 461 (6), 484 (3)
explore 267 (11), 459 (15), 461 (8), 484 (4)
explored 490 (7)
explorer 66 (1), 268 (1), 453 (2), 459 (9), 461 (3), 484 (2)
exploring 837 (6)
explosion 165 (2), 176 (2), 402 (1), 822 (2), 891 (2)
explosive 168 (1), 176 (5), 287 (3), 287 (6), 298 (4), 300 (2), 300 (4), 385 (5), 661 (3), 663 (1), 723 (13), 822 (3)
explosive device 723 (14)
explosiveness 822 (1)
exponent 85 (2), 520 (4)
exponential 85 (5)
export 272 (6), 300 (6), 633 (5)
export and import 791 (4)
exportation 272 (1), 298 (1)
exporter 272 (4), 273 (1), 794 (1)

exporting 791 (2)
expose 229 (6), 340 (6), 443 (4), 479 (3), 484 (5), 522 (7), 522 (8), 526 (1), 526 (4), 551 (9), 851 (6), 867 (11), 926 (7), 928 (8)
expose itself 443 (4)
expose oneself 526 (4), 661 (8), 857 (4)
expose to view 522 (8)
exposed 161 (6), 163 (5), 229 (4), 352 (8), 374 (3), 377 (3), 443 (2), 479 (2), 526 (2), 661 (5), 670 (3)
exposed, be 867 (9)
exposed nerve 374 (1)
exposed to 180 (2)
exposed to view 263 (13), 443 (2)
exposition 478 (1), 520 (1), 520 (2), 522 (2), 591 (1)
expositor 520 (4)
expository 520 (6), 524 (7), 591 (4)
expostulate 613 (3), 762 (3)
expostulation 489 (1), 613 (1), 664 (1), 762 (1)
exposure 229 (1), 340 (1), 443 (1), 479 (1), 484 (1), 522 (1), 526 (1), 661 (2), 926 (1)
exposure meter 442 (1)
expound 520 (8), 534 (7)
expounded 520 (7)
expounder 520 (4), 973 (6)
express 80 (6), 243 (5), 277 (4), 514 (3), 514 (5), 522 (7), 526 (5), 532 (4), 532 (5), 563 (3), 577 (4)
express grief 836 (5)
express Messenger 529 (6)
express regrets 830 (4), 939 (4)
expression 85 (1), 243 (1), 243 (2), 304 (1), 413 (6), 445 (5), 514 (1), 522 (1), 532 (1), 559 (1), 563 (1), 818 (1)
Expressionism 553 (3)
expressive 514 (3), 516 (3), 566 (2), 575 (3)

expressway 624 (6)
expropriate 300 (6), 780 (3), 786 (10), 916 (9)
expropriation 46 (2), 300 (1), 752 (2), 772 (1), 786 (2), 916 (2), 916 (3), 963 (4)
expropriator 786 (4)
expulsion 39 (1), 44 (3), 46 (2), 57 (1), 160 (3), 188 (1), 272 (1), 300 (1), 786 (2), 963 (4)
expulsive 287 (6), 298 (4), 300 (4)
expunge 550 (3)
expurgate 39 (3), 57 (5), 648 (10), 655 (9)
expurgated 950 (5)
expurgation 950 (2)
exquisite 377 (3), 390 (2), 644 (4), 826 (2), 841 (3), 846 (3), 848 (5), 864 (5)
exquisitely 32 (17), 32 (20)
extant 1 (4), 121 (2), 548 (6)
extempore 116 (4), 121 (4), 609 (5)
extemporize 413 (8), 413 (9), 609 (4), 670 (7)
extemporized 670 (3)
extemporizer 609 (2)
extend 32 (15), 36 (5), 38 (3), 54 (7), 71 (6), 183 (7), 195 (10), 197 (4), 197 (5), 199 (5), 202 (3), 203 (7), 203 (8)
extend to 183 (7), 199 (5)
extended 113 (5), 203 (5)
extended family 11 (3)
extending 183 (6)
extension 36 (1), 40 (1), 113 (3), 194 (20), 195 (1), 197 (1), 203 (1), 203 (2)
extensive 32 (5), 52 (7), 78 (2), 79 (4), 183 (6), 195 (6), 203 (5)
extensive sales 528 (2)
extensively 32 (17), 183 (8)
extent 26 (1), 27 (1), 32 (1), 108 (1), 183 (1), 195 (1), 203 (1)

extenuate 163 (10), 468
(3), 614 (4), 927 (7)

extenuating 468 (2)

extenuation 927 (1)

extenuatory 927 (3)

exterior 6 (2), 59 (4), 223
(1), 223 (2), 445 (7)

exteriority 6 (1), 57 (1), 59
(1), 199 (2), 223 (1), 230
(1), 331 (2), 445 (1), 875
(1)

exterminate 165 (6), 362
(11)

extermination 165 (1), 304
(1), 362 (4)

external 6 (2), 223 (2), 445
(7)

external, the 223 (1)

externality 223 (1)

externalize 6 (4), 223 (3),
319 (7), 522 (7)

externally 223 (4)

externals 445 (1)

extinct 2 (5), 125 (6), 446
(2), 679 (7)

extinct animal 365 (2)

extinction 2 (2), 165 (1),
361 (1), 361 (2)

extinguish 2 (8), 37 (4),
165 (8), 177 (6), 418 (7)

extinguished 418 (4)

extinguisher 168 (1), 177
(2), 382 (3)

extirpate 304 (4)

extirpation 304 (1)

extol 528 (11), 923 (9), 981
(11)

extolment 981 (3)

extort 304 (4), 735 (8), 740
(3), 786 (8), 788 (9), 811
(5)

extortion 740 (1), 786 (2),
786 (3), 788 (4), 809 (1),
811 (1)

extortionate 32 (12), 735
(6), 784 (4), 786 (5), 811
(2), 816 (5), 859 (8)

extortioner 735 (3), 786
(4)

extra 29 (1), 36 (2), 38 (2),
38 (5), 40 (2), 57 (3), 58
(1), 223 (2), 528 (4), 570
(2), 594 (9), 637 (2), 662

(3), 674 (2), 807 (1), 809
(1)

extra power 160 (1)

extra time 113 (3)

extract 39 (3), 53 (1), 164
(2), 164 (7), 188 (4), 288
(3), 300 (6), 300 (8), 304
(1), 304 (4), 310 (4), 522
(7), 633 (5), 668 (3), 673
(3), 771 (7), 786 (6), 786
(8)

extract roots 86 (12)

extracted 304 (3)

extraction 169 (2), 188 (1),
272 (1), 304 (1), 668 (1)

extractor 304 (2), 310 (2)

extracts 592 (2)

extracurricular 534 (5)

extradite 57 (5)

extradition 272 (1), 300
(1)

extragalactic 321 (13)

extrajudicial 954 (5)

extramarital 894 (9), 951
(9)

extramural 223 (2), 534
(5)

extraneous 6 (2), 10 (3), 25
(4), 46 (5), 59 (4), 72 (2),
84 (5), 152 (4), 223 (2),
231 (6), 267 (9), 321 (13),
702 (6), 883 (5)

extraneousness 59 (1)

extraordinary 32 (8), 84
(6), 864 (5), 866 (9)

extrapolate 223 (3)

extrapolation 86 (2)

extras 781 (2)

extrasensory perception
374 (2), 984 (2)

extraterrestrial 59 (2), 59
(4)

extravagance 497 (2), 499
(2), 546 (1), 574 (2), 634
(1), 675 (1), 806 (1), 815
(1), 849 (1), 943 (1)

extravagant 32 (12), 497
(3), 499 (4), 513 (5), 546
(2), 634 (2), 635 (4), 806
(2), 811 (2), 815 (3), 849
(2), 943 (2)

extravagant, be 634 (4)

extravaganza 412 (4), 445
(2), 497 (2), 513 (2), 594
(3)

extreme 32 (12), 54 (3), 69
(2), 69 (4), 176 (5), 236
(1), 735 (4), 827 (7), 898
(7)

extreme penalty 963 (3)

extreme unction 361 (2),
988 (4)

extremely 32 (18), 34 (12)

extremes 546 (1), 704 (2),
898 (3)

extremism 546 (1), 654 (4)

extremist 504 (2), 654 (5),
705 (1), 738 (4)

extremity 41 (1), 69 (2),
137 (3), 213 (2), 234 (1),
236 (1), 238 (1), 295 (2)

extricable 668 (2), 746 (2)

extricate 304 (4), 668 (3),
701 (9), 746 (3)

extrication 304 (1), 667
(1), 668 (1), 746 (1)

extrinsic 6 (2), 10 (3), 38
(2), 59 (4)

extrinsic, be 6 (3)

extrinsicality 6 (1)

extrinsically 6 (5)

extrovert 882 (6)

extrude 300 (6)

extrusion 300 (1)

exuberance 171 (1), 637
(1)

exuberant 171 (4), 570 (3),
818 (5)

exudation 298 (2)

exude 298 (7), 300 (9), 302
(6), 341 (6), 350 (9)

exult 835 (6), 877 (5)

exultant 833 (5), 835 (4),
877 (4)

exultation 835 (1)

eye 225 (2), 250 (2), 263
(4), 438 (2), 438 (8)

eye-catching 443 (3), 522
(4)

eye disease 439 (1)

eye for an eye 714 (1), 910
(2)

eye of heaven 321 (8)

eye on, an 457 (2)

eye-opener **508** (1), **864** (3)
eye shade **226** (4)
eye shadow **843** (3)
eyeball **438** (2)
eyebrows **259** (2)
eyeglass **442** (2)
eyelash **206** (1), **438** (2)
eyelashes **259** (2)
eyeless **163** (7), **439** (2)
eyelet **250** (2), **263** (4)
eyelid **438** (2)
eyeliner **843** (3)
eyepiece **442** (1)
eyesight **438** (1)
eyesore **246** (2), **842** (2), **845** (1)
eyestrain **440** (1)
eyetooth **256** (4)
eyewash **515** (3), **541** (1)
eyewitness **441** (1), **443** (1), **466** (4)
eyewitness account **524** (2)
eyot **349** (1)
eyrie **192** (4)

F

Fabian **654** (5), **708** (2)
Fabian policy **136** (2)
Fabianism **654** (4)
fable **4** (2), **496** (1), **513** (3), **519** (1), **543** (3), **546** (1), **590** (2)
fabled **512** (5), **513** (6), **866** (10)
fabric **7** (2), **164** (2), **222** (4), **319** (2), **331** (1), **331** (2), **631** (1)
fabric printing **555** (2)
fabricate **56** (7), **164** (7), **513** (7), **541** (8)
fabricate evidence **466** (8)
fabricated **467** (3)
fabrication **164** (1), **541** (1), **543** (1)
fabulous **32** (7), **513** (6), **543** (4), **644** (5), **866** (9)

façade **223** (1), **237** (2), **541** (2)
face **64** (4), **68** (8), **117** (3), **155** (3), **189** (4), **223** (1), **226** (16), **227** (2), **237** (2), **237** (5), **240** (3), **281** (4), **445** (5), **445** (6), **507** (4), **599** (3), **704** (5), **855** (6)
face a **221** (4)
face about **148** (3), **282** (4)
face both ways **603** (5)
face danger **599** (3), **661** (8), **672** (3), **704** (5), **711** (3), **715** (3), **855** (6), **857** (4)
face down **216** (5), **221** (6)
face heavy odds **661** (8)
face-lift **656** (2)
face powder **843** (3)
face the music **855** (6)
face the other way **282** (4)
face the prospect **507** (4)
face to face **200** (7), **237** (6), **240** (4), **704** (3)
face value **809** (1)
faceless **16** (2), **562** (4)
facet **223** (1), **445** (1)
facetious **839** (4)
facetiousness **839** (1)
facial **843** (1)
facilitate **469** (4), **516** (4), **520** (8), **701** (8), **703** (5), **744** (10)
facilitated **701** (5)
facilitating **701** (3)
facilities **629** (1), **642** (1), **701** (1), **703** (1), **744** (3)
facility **469** (1), **597** (1), **694** (1), **701** (1), **703** (1)
facing **226** (10), **227** (1), **237** (4), **240** (2), **240** (3), **240** (4), **261** (1), **281** (3), **631** (2), **704** (3), **844** (2)
facing both ways **518** (2)
facing death **661** (6)
facsimile **22** (1), **542** (5), **551** (1)
fact **1** (2), **154** (1), **466** (1), **494** (1)
fact-finding **459** (11)
fact of life **1** (2)
faction **53** (1), **489** (1), **489** (2), **708** (1), **709** (1), **738** (2)

factional **708** (7)
factions **704** (2)
factious **709** (6)
factiousness **709** (2)
factitious **543** (4)
factor **58** (1), **85** (2), **156** (2), **178** (1), **319** (4), **690** (3)
factor, be a **9** (7)
factorization **51** (1)
factorize **46** (10), **51** (5)
factors **8** (1)
factory **164** (1), **687** (1)
factory farm **369** (2)
factory farming **370** (1)
factory ship **275** (4)
factotum **742** (1)
facts **466** (1), **524** (1)
facts and figures **808** (1)
facts of life **167** (1)
factual **1** (5), **466** (5), **473** (4), **494** (4), **540** (2), **590** (6)
factuality **1** (2)
factually **540** (4)
faculty **77** (1), **160** (2), **490** (2), **537** (1), **694** (2)
fad **481** (5), **503** (5), **604** (2), **848** (1), **850** (1), **859** (3)
faddish **481** (6), **604** (3)
faddishness **503** (5), **604** (1)
faddist **504** (2)
faddy **481** (6), **604** (3)
fade **27** (5), **37** (5), **114** (6), **127** (8), **163** (9), **418** (2), **419** (6), **426** (4), **426** (5), **427** (6), **444** (4), **446** (3), **551** (4), **655** (7), **842** (6)
fade away **69** (5), **401** (4), **446** (3), **651** (23)
fade from view **290** (3)
fade out **27** (5), **418** (5), **419** (7), **446** (3)
faded **419** (4), **425** (7), **426** (3), **655** (5), **842** (4)
faded hue **425** (3)
fading **27** (2), **37** (1), **37** (3), **114** (3), **342** (2), **426** (1), **426** (3), **655** (1)
fading out **27** (2)
faecal **302** (5), **649** (6)

faeces 302 (4)
faerie 970 (1)
fag 388 (2)
fag end 41 (1), 388 (2)
faggot 74 (6), 385 (1)
fail 35 (5), 37 (5), 138 (6), 145 (6), 161 (8), 163 (9), 307 (3), 440 (4), 509 (4), 636 (7), 641 (6), 671 (4), 684 (5), 695 (7), 695 (9), 726 (3), 728 (7), 805 (5), 867 (9), 924 (9)
fail in duty 603 (5), 620 (6), 621 (3), 769 (3), 918 (3), 919 (4)
fail one 509 (5), 728 (7)
fail-safe 660 (6)
fail to act 677 (3)
fail to catch 416 (3)
fail to interest 838 (5)
fail to succeed 728 (8)
failed 695 (3), 728 (4), 924 (7)
failing 163 (5), 307 (2), 647 (1), 934 (2)
failing sight 440 (1)
failure 35 (1), 35 (2), 161 (1), 165 (3), 167 (1), 495 (3), 641 (2), 695 (2), 697 (1), 702 (3), 726 (1), 728 (1), 728 (3), 731 (2), 769 (1), 772 (1), 867 (3)
failure to act 677 (1)
failure to agree 25 (1)
faint 33 (6), 161 (2), 163 (4), 163 (6), 163 (9), 266 (1), 375 (1), 375 (5), 399 (2), 401 (3), 419 (4), 419 (6), 426 (3), 444 (3), 684 (2), 684 (5), 721 (4), 854 (9), 887 (14)
faint heart 856 (1)
faint-hearted 601 (3), 854 (7), 856 (3)
faint praise 860 (1), 923 (2)
faintheart 601 (2), 856 (2)
faintheartedness 601 (1), 856 (1)
fainting 163 (6), 651 (2), 684 (1), 684 (2)
faintly 33 (9), 401 (6)

faintness 163 (1), 398 (1), 401 (1), 405 (1), 419 (1), 523 (1), 577 (1), 578 (1), 684 (1)
fair 33 (7), 342 (4), 379 (6), 417 (9), 426 (3), 427 (5), 475 (7), 644 (9), 730 (5), 732 (2), 796 (1), 812 (3), 837 (2), 837 (4), 841 (3), 852 (5), 913 (4), 929 (3)
fair and square 913 (4)
fair chance 137 (2), 159 (3), 469 (1), 471 (1)
fair comparison 18 (1)
fair copy 22 (1), 586 (3)
fair deal 913 (2)
fair enough 913 (4)
fair exchange 28 (2), 791 (1)
fair game 544 (1), 851 (3)
fair hair 433 (1)
fair-haired 427 (5), 433 (3)
fair hand 586 (2)
fair judgment 480 (1)
fair-minded 498 (5), 913 (4)
fair offer 759 (1)
fair play 913 (2)
fair proportions 841 (1)
fair question 459 (3)
fair sex 373 (2)
fair share 775 (2)
fair shares 783 (1)
fair-sized 32 (4), 195 (6)
fair to middling 732 (2)
fair trial 959 (3)
fair value 28 (2)
fair way 199 (1)
fair-weather 114 (3), 340 (3), 730 (2)
fair-weather friend 545 (1)
fair wind 703 (1)
fair words 764 (1)
fairground 724 (1), 837 (5)
fairly 32 (17), 33 (9)
fairmindedness 913 (2)
fairness 841 (1), 913 (2), 929 (1)
fairway 624 (4)
fairy 343 (2), 970 (1), 970 (6), 983 (6)

fairy folk 970 (1)
fairy godmother 703 (3)
fairy lights 420 (4)
fairy lore 970 (1)
fairy ring 250 (2), 970 (1)
fairy story 590 (2)
fairy tale 513 (2), 543 (3)
fairy tales 970 (1)
fairy wand 983 (4)
fairy world 970 (1)
fairyland 513 (3), 970 (1)
fairylike 970 (6), 983 (8)
fait accompli 1 (2), 725 (1)
Faith 93 (2), 485 (1), 852 (1), 929 (1), 931 (1), 933 (2), 973 (3), 979 (1)
faith healer 656 (5), 658 (14)
faith healing 658 (10)
Faith, the 976 (1)
faithful 18 (5), 83 (4), 494 (4), 494 (6), 520 (6), 739 (3), 768 (2), 880 (6), 929 (4), 931 (2), 979 (6)
faithful, the 976 (6), 976 (7), 981 (8)
faithfully 768 (5)
faithfulness 739 (2), 929 (1), 931 (1)
faithless 930 (7), 974 (5)
fake 20 (6), 466 (8), 495 (4), 541 (2), 541 (3), 541 (8), 542 (5), 542 (7), 542 (8), 545 (3), 608 (3), 623 (9), 928 (9)
fake the evidence 928 (9)
faked 542 (7), 543 (4)
faker 20 (3), 545 (1)
faking 541 (1)
fakir 945 (2), 986 (5)
falcon 365 (4)
falconer 619 (3)
falconry 619 (2)
fall 37 (1), 129 (3), 163 (9), 165 (11), 211 (1), 220 (2), 286 (1), 286 (4), 309 (1), 309 (3), 309 (4), 350 (10), 361 (8), 655 (7), 728 (1), 728 (2), 728 (7), 728 (8), 728 (9), 731 (1), 812 (1), 812 (5)
fall about 835 (7)
fall apart 46 (7), 655 (7)

fall asleep 361 (7), 679 (12)

fall astern 238 (5)

fall at one's feet 761 (7)

fall back 286 (4), 290 (3), 603 (5), 657 (2)

fall back on 673 (4)

fall behind 35 (5), 278 (4), 284 (4), 307 (3)

fall below 636 (7)

fall down 309 (3), 309 (4)

fall flat 728 (8)

fall for 487 (3), 544 (3), 612 (13), 887 (14)

fall foul of 279 (8), 716 (11), 731 (7)

fall from grace 657 (2), 934 (7)

fall guy 851 (3)

fall ill 651 (23)

fall in 16 (3), 60 (4), 71 (5), 309 (3), 313 (3)

fall in action 361 (8)

fall in love 887 (14)

fall in price 812 (5)

fall in with 293 (3), 758 (3)

fall into arrears 805 (5)

fall into disarray 61 (10)

fall into disrepute 867 (9)

fall into disuse 611 (5)

fall into line 83 (7)

fall into place 73 (3)

fall into ruin 165 (11)

fall into the trap 544 (3)

fall like rain 309 (3)

fall off 46 (7), 309 (3), 655 (7)

fall on 508 (5), 712 (7)

fall on hard times 801 (5)

fall on one's feet 730 (7)

fall on the ear 415 (7)

fall out 25 (6), 75 (3), 709 (7), 726 (3), 881 (4)

fall pat 24 (9)

fall short 29 (3), 35 (5), 55 (5), 204 (4), 307 (3), 509 (5), 636 (7), 647 (4)

fall sick 651 (23)

fall silent 582 (3)

fall through 307 (3)

fall to 301 (35), 672 (3), 917 (8)

fall to pieces 330 (3)

fall under 78 (4)

fallacious 477 (5), 495 (4)

fallacy 477 (2), 495 (1), 542 (1)

fallen 165 (5), 934 (5)

fallen angel 969 (2)

fallen, the 361 (4), 728 (3)

fallibility 474 (3), 481 (1), 495 (1), 499 (1), 647 (1)

fallible 474 (5), 477 (5), 481 (6), 495 (4)

falling 165 (5), 220 (4), 309 (1), 309 (2), 350 (7)

falling away 286 (1)

falling birthrate 172 (1)

falling off 37 (1), 655 (1), 655 (5), 657 (1)

falling short 29 (2), 55 (1)

falling star 321 (7)

falling tears 836 (1)

Fallopian tubes 167 (3)

fallout 67 (1), 160 (7), 417 (4), 653 (1), 659 (3)

fallout shelter 662 (1)

fallow 172 (4), 175 (2), 370 (2), 670 (3)

fallow mind 450 (1)

falls 350 (4)

false 2 (4), 20 (4), 467 (3), 477 (5), 495 (4), 541 (3), 542 (6), 542 (7), 543 (4), 603 (4), 916 (6), 925 (3), 930 (7)

false alarm 665 (2)

false appearance 542 (1)

false, be 535 (3), 541 (5), 543 (5), 546 (3), 552 (3), 930 (8)

false charge 928 (2)

false colours 542 (5)

false conduct 541 (2)

false creed 977 (1)

false dawn 66 (1), 481 (1), 509 (1)

false economy 816 (1)

false friend 545 (1)

false front 542 (5)

false glitter 875 (1)

false god 966 (1)

false hair 259 (2), 843 (2)

false-hearted 930 (7)

false horizon 216 (1)

false image 552 (1)

false impression 495 (1)

false light 552 (1)

false logic 497 (1), 535 (1)

false lover 952 (1)

false modesty 950 (2)

false money 797 (6)

false name 562 (1)

false note 25 (3)

false oath 543 (1)

false piety 980 (2)

false position 700 (3)

false pride 871 (1)

false reading 521 (1)

false religion 974 (1)

false report 529 (2), 926 (2)

false reputation 542 (1)

false shame 850 (1), 950 (2)

false teeth 256 (4)

false witness 545 (2)

false worship 981 (2), 982 (1)

falsehood 20 (1), 472 (1), 495 (1), 513 (2), 515 (3), 535 (1), 541 (1), 542 (1), 543 (1), 545 (2), 552 (1), 930 (1)

falsely 541 (9)

falsely accused 935 (4)

falseness 495 (1), 541 (1), 542 (1)

falsetto 407 (1), 578 (1)

falsification 20 (1), 541 (1), 543 (1)

falsified 541 (3)

falsify 495 (9), 521 (3), 541 (5)

falsity 495 (1), 541 (1)

falter 278 (4), 278 (5), 474 (8), 580 (3), 601 (4), 728 (7)

fame 32 (1), 505 (2), 528 (2), 866 (3)

familiar 224 (3), 490 (7), 610 (5), 610 (6), 707 (1), 878 (5), 921 (3), 969 (2), 970 (4), 983 (5)

familiar with 490 (5), 610 (7)

familiarity 490 (1), 610 (1), 880 (1), 882 (1), 889 (1)

149

familiarize 534 (8)

familiarize oneself 490 (8)

family 11 (1), 11 (3), 11 (5), 53 (3), 74 (3), 77 (3), 169 (1), 170 (1), 191 (5), 371 (4), 708 (4), 868 (1)

family circle 11 (3)

family likeness 18 (1)

family man 372 (1)

family tree 71 (2), 169 (2)

famine 172 (1), 636 (2), 801 (1), 859 (2)

famine-stricken 636 (5)

famish 859 (12), 946 (4)

famished 636 (5), 859 (9), 946 (3)

famous 32 (4), 490 (7), 528 (8), 644 (4), 644 (5), 866 (10)

famousness 505 (2), 528 (2), 727 (1), 866 (3)

fan 74 (6), 315 (3), 340 (1), 340 (6), 352 (6), 352 (10), 384 (1), 504 (3), 610 (4), 707 (4)

fan club 923 (4)

fan-like 205 (3)

fan out 75 (3), 197 (4), 205 (5), 263 (17), 294 (3)

fan-shaped 197 (3)

fan the flame 821 (7)

fanatic 473 (3), 481 (4), 481 (8), 504 (2), 602 (3), 678 (5), 979 (5)

fanatical 473 (5), 602 (4), 735 (4), 822 (3)

fanatically 32 (17)

fanaticism 481 (4), 487 (1), 602 (2), 735 (1), 979 (3)

fancied 512 (5), 513 (6)

fancier 504 (3), 696 (2), 859 (6)

fanciful 497 (3), 513 (6), 546 (2), 604 (3), 849 (2)

fancifulness 513 (1)

fancy 449 (7), 451 (1), 485 (8), 512 (1), 512 (6), 513 (1), 513 (2), 513 (7), 604 (2), 605 (1), 605 (6), 844 (9), 859 (3), 887 (1)

fancy dress 228 (2), 527 (3)

fancy-free 744 (5), 895 (4)

fancy-man 952 (1)

fancy, the 716 (4)

fancy woman 952 (3)

fancywork 844 (2)

fanfare 400 (1), 876 (1)

fang 256 (4), 659 (1)

fanged 256 (8)

fangs 778 (2)

fanlight 263 (5)

fanning 352 (6)

fanning out 75 (1), 294 (1)

fans 441 (2)

fantasia 412 (4)

fantastic 32 (7), 84 (6), 497 (3), 513 (5), 604 (3), 644 (5), 849 (2), 864 (5)

fantastic notion 604 (2)

fantastical 4 (3), 495 (4)

fantasy 4 (1), 4 (2), 84 (4), 440 (2), 445 (1), 481 (1), 513 (1), 513 (2), 513 (3), 590 (2), 826 (1), 852 (2), 859 (1), 864 (3), 971 (2)

far 199 (3), 199 (6)

far afield 199 (6)

far and away 34 (12)

far and near 183 (8)

far and wide 183 (8), 199 (6)

far apart 199 (6)

far away 199 (6)

far between 201 (3)

far cry 199 (1)

far distance 199 (1), 199 (2)

Far East 199 (2)

far-fetched 10 (4), 486 (5), 546 (2)

far-flung 75 (2), 183 (6), 199 (3)

far from it 15 (4), 307 (4), 533 (5)

far off 199 (6)

far-reaching 32 (5), 183 (6)

far sight 440 (1)

far-sighted 457 (4)

Far West 199 (2)

farce 497 (2), 594 (3), 835 (2), 839 (1), 849 (1)

farcical 594 (15), 835 (5), 849 (3)

fare 7 (4), 301 (12), 301 (35), 809 (1)

farewell 296 (3), 296 (7), 884 (2)

farewell address 579 (2)

farewells 296 (2)

farm 185 (1), 192 (6), 344 (3), 369 (9), 370 (2), 370 (9), 777 (3)

farm hand 370 (4)

farm manager 370 (4), 690 (3)

farm out 784 (6)

farm tool 370 (6)

farm worker 686 (2)

farmer 74 (8), 164 (4), 191 (4), 370 (4), 669 (5), 686 (2), 869 (6)

farmhand 742 (1)

farmhouse 192 (6), 370 (2)

farming 164 (1), 344 (5), 370 (1), 370 (7)

farming out 784 (1)

farmland 370 (2)

farmstead 370 (2)

farmyard 185 (1), 370 (2)

farness 59 (1), 69 (2), 199 (2), 444 (1)

farrago 43 (4), 61 (2)

farrier 369 (1)

farrow 132 (3), 167 (6)

farsighted 498 (4), 510 (2)

farther 199 (3), 199 (7)

farthest 199 (3)

farthest point 69 (2)

farthing 33 (4)

fascia 207 (2), 208 (3), 547 (13)

fascinate 178 (3), 449 (11), 455 (7), 612 (8), 887 (15), 983 (11)

fascinated 864 (4), 887 (10), 983 (9)

fascinating 178 (2), 612 (6), 983 (7)

fascination 178 (1), 612 (2), 821 (1), 826 (1), 859 (3), 864 (1), 887 (1), 887 (2), 983 (2)

Fascism 733 (4), 735 (2)

Fascist 735 (5)

fascists 708 (2)

fashion 7 (2), 18 (1), 79 (1), 83 (1), 126 (2), 164 (7), 228 (1), 243 (1), 243 (5), 610 (2), 624 (1), 688 (1), 841 (1), 848 (1), 850 (1)

fashion designer 228 (28)

fashion sense 848 (1)

fashionable 126 (6), 610 (6), 841 (6), 848 (5), 875 (5)

fashionably 848 (8)

fashioned 243 (3)

fast 45 (7), 45 (8), 45 (16), 118 (2), 153 (6), 277 (5), 495 (6), 778 (4), 880 (6), 945 (4), 946 (2), 946 (4), 951 (7), 981 (12), 988 (10)

fast asleep 679 (9)

fast, be 495 (7)

fast breeder reactor 160 (7)

fast by 200 (7)

fast colour 153 (2)

fast day 946 (2), 988 (7)

fast learner 538 (1)

fast-living 944 (3)

fast one 542 (2)

fast woman 952 (2)

fasten 45 (9), 45 (11), 45 (13), 264 (6)

fasten on 638 (8), 778 (5), 786 (6)

fastened 45 (8)

fastener 47 (5)

fastening 47 (5), 263 (12), 264 (2), 778 (2), 844 (5), 844 (7)

fastidious 455 (2), 457 (3), 463 (2), 481 (7), 604 (3), 648 (7), 654 (7), 768 (2), 829 (3), 846 (3), 862 (3)

fastidious, be 604 (4), 605 (7), 829 (5), 846 (4), 862 (4)

fastidiousness 829 (1), 862 (1)

fasting 301 (3), 636 (5), 801 (1), 859 (2), 859 (9), 941 (3), 942 (1), 945 (1), 945 (3), 946 (1), 946 (3), 988 (8)

fat 171 (4), 195 (8), 357 (3), 357 (6), 637 (1), 730 (4)

fatal 362 (8), 596 (6), 616 (2), 645 (3)

fatal accident 362 (1)

fatalism 596 (1), 721 (1)

fatalist 596 (3)

fatalistic 721 (2)

fatality 361 (2), 361 (4), 616 (1)

fate 69 (3), 124 (1), 155 (1), 156 (2), 159 (1), 178 (1), 449 (3), 473 (1), 507 (1), 596 (2), 618 (1)

fated 124 (4), 155 (2), 473 (4), 596 (6), 608 (2)

fated, be 596 (7)

fateful 638 (5)

Fates, the 93 (2), 596 (2), 966 (2)

fathead 501 (3)

father 11 (2), 167 (7), 169 (3), 372 (1), 986 (2)

Father Christmas 813 (2)

father confessor 986 (3)

father figure 150 (2), 169 (3)

father-in-law 169 (3)

Father, Son and the Holy Ghost 965 (3)

Father Time 108 (1)

fathered 360 (3)

fatherhood 11 (3), 169 (1), 169 (3)

fatherland 169 (3), 192 (5)

fatherly 169 (5), 897 (4)

fathom 203 (4), 211 (3), 313 (3), 465 (11), 498 (6), 516 (5)

fathoming 211 (1)

fathomless 211 (2)

fatigue 161 (2), 163 (1), 377 (1), 673 (3), 675 (2), 679 (3), 682 (3), 684 (1), 684 (6), 700 (1), 735 (8), 825 (1), 827 (10), 834 (1), 834 (12), 838 (1), 838 (5)

fatigue party 74 (4)

fatigued 161 (7), 163 (5), 651 (21), 655 (5), 679 (7), 679 (9), 684 (2), 702 (7), 825 (5), 838 (4)

fatigued, be 163 (9), 278 (4), 278 (5), 684 (5), 721 (4), 834 (9)

fatigues 228 (5)

fatiguing 165 (4), 645 (2), 684 (4), 700 (4), 838 (3)

fatness 195 (3)

fatten 36 (4), 197 (5), 205 (5), 369 (9)

fatten on 301 (35)

fatten up 301 (39)

fattening 301 (33)

fatty 357 (6)

fatuity 497 (1)

fatuous 497 (3), 499 (4), 515 (4)

fatuousness 499 (2)

faucet 264 (2)

fault 72 (1), 201 (2), 307 (1), 647 (2), 934 (2), 936 (2)

faultfinder 829 (2), 924 (5), 926 (3)

faultfinding 829 (3), 924 (1), 924 (2), 924 (6)

faultiness 495 (2), 645 (1), 647 (1)

faultless 646 (3), 935 (4)

faultlessness 646 (1), 950 (1)

faulty 495 (6), 565 (2), 576 (2), 645 (2), 647 (3), 695 (6)

faun 970 (5)

fauna 365 (1)

faux pas 495 (3), 728 (1)

favour 34 (2), 178 (1), 285 (4), 481 (12), 547 (9), 605 (1), 605 (6), 615 (2), 615 (4), 644 (11), 703 (6), 729 (1), 730 (1), 730 (8), 736 (1), 781 (2), 859 (3), 859 (11), 884 (2), 889 (3), 897 (2), 897 (5), 914 (2), 914 (6), 923 (1), 923 (8)

favour with 781 (7)

favourable 8 (3), 137 (5), 597 (4), 644 (8), 703 (4), 730 (5), 852 (5), 923 (5)

favourable opportunity 137 (2)

favourably 615 (6)

151

favourably situated 187 (4)

favoured 782 (3), 923 (7)

favouring 605 (4), 914 (4), 923 (5)

favourite 34 (3), 34 (4), 291 (1), 605 (5), 638 (4), 644 (3), 716 (8), 841 (2), 859 (5), 866 (6), 871 (1), 882 (5), 887 (5), 887 (11), 890 (2), 937 (1)

favourite son 890 (2)

favouritism 481 (3), 605 (1), 914 (2)

fawn 132 (3), 365 (3), 430 (3), 745 (6)

fawn on 879 (4), 889 (6), 925 (4)

fawner 879 (2), 925 (2)

fawning 879 (1), 879 (3), 925 (1), 925 (3)

fete 837 (1)

fealty 739 (2), 917 (1)

fear 507 (1), 507 (4), 612 (1), 620 (1), 821 (1), 854 (1), 854 (9), 856 (1), 861 (1), 861 (4), 864 (1), 864 (6), 920 (1), 920 (5), 981 (1)

fear God 929 (5), 979 (9)

fear of God 979 (1)

fearful 854 (7), 856 (3), 864 (5)

fearfully 32 (18), 864 (8)

fearfulness 854 (2)

fearing 854 (6)

fearless 855 (5)

fearlessness 855 (1)

fears 854 (2)

fearsome 854 (8)

feasibility 469 (1), 701 (1)

feasible 469 (2), 701 (3)

feasible, the 469 (1)

feast 301 (2), 301 (35), 376 (1), 635 (2), 837 (23), 988 (7)

feast day 837 (2), 876 (2), 988 (7)

feast one's eyes on 438 (8)

feaster 837 (17)

feasting 301 (2), 376 (1), 635 (2), 837 (2), 882 (2), 882 (3), 944 (1), 947 (1)

feat 623 (3), 676 (2), 694 (3), 727 (1), 864 (2)

feat of arms 855 (2)

feather 77 (2), 269 (11), 323 (1)

feather bed 327 (1)

feather one's nest 800 (7), 932 (4)

featherbedded 376 (4)

featherbrain 501 (1)

featherbrained 499 (4)

feathered 259 (6), 271 (6)

feathering 259 (3)

feathers 226 (6), 259 (3), 271 (5)

featherweight 323 (3), 722 (2)

feathery 259 (6), 323 (3)

feature 58 (1), 80 (1), 233 (1), 243 (1), 445 (6), 528 (11), 531 (4), 547 (2), 594 (16)

feature film 445 (4)

featured 522 (6), 594 (15)

featureless 16 (2), 190 (5), 244 (2)

features 5 (3), 233 (1), 237 (2)

febrile 379 (4)

feckless 604 (3)

fecund 167 (4), 171 (4)

fecundity 167 (1), 171 (1)

fed up 838 (4)

federal 706 (3), 708 (6)

federalism 733 (4)

federate 50 (4), 706 (4), 708 (6), 708 (8)

federation 706 (2), 708 (3), 733 (6)

federative 708 (6)

fee 804 (2), 806 (1), 809 (1), 962 (1)

feeble 35 (4), 161 (5), 161 (7), 163 (4), 401 (3), 477 (6), 572 (2), 734 (3), 934 (5)

feeble grasp 734 (1)

feeble-minded 163 (4)

feebleness 163 (1), 566 (1), 572 (1)

feebly 33 (9)

feed 197 (5), 301 (8), 301 (35), 301 (37), 301 (39),

360 (6), 369 (10), 385 (6), 633 (5), 685 (4), 851 (3), 882 (2)

feed line 839 (2)

feed on 301 (35)

feed up 197 (5)

feedback 86 (5), 460 (1)

feeder 350 (1)

feeding 301 (1), 301 (31), 301 (33), 947 (2)

feel 331 (2), 374 (5), 378 (7), 818 (7), 821 (9), 825 (7), 891 (5)

feel at home 24 (9)

feel better 831 (4)

feel cold 380 (7)

feel confident 852 (6)

feel deeply 818 (7)

feel envy 888 (7)

feel fine 650 (3)

feel for 459 (15), 897 (5), 905 (6)

feel free 744 (9)

feel giddy 684 (5)

feel in one's bones 476 (3)

feel insulted 891 (5)

feel like 597 (6)

feel no concern 454 (3)

feel no emotion 820 (6)

feel no shame 867 (10)

feel one's way 278 (4), 439 (3), 457 (5), 461 (8), 858 (3)

feel pain 377 (6), 408 (3), 825 (7)

feel pity 905 (6)

feel pleased 835 (6)

feel pride 866 (12), 871 (6), 873 (5)

feel queer 651 (23)

feel remorse 830 (4)

feel shame 939 (4)

feel shy 854 (11)

feel sick 651 (23)

feel small 872 (6)

feel sorry 939 (4)

feel sorry for 905 (6)

feel sure 473 (7)

feel the lack of 636 (8)

feel the pinch 700 (7), 731 (7), 801 (5)

feel the pulse 459 (13), 461 (8)

feel with 818 (7)

feeler 53 (2), 208 (1), 254 (3), 378 (3), 461 (2), 759 (1), 778 (2)

feeling 178 (1), 374 (2), 374 (3), 378 (1), 476 (1), 485 (3), 490 (1), 571 (1), 609 (3), 688 (1), 746 (1), 817 (1), 817 (2), 818 (1), 818 (3), 821 (1), 821 (3), 822 (2), 887 (1), 897 (1)

feeling better 831 (1)

feeling blue 834 (6)

feeling cold 380 (6)

feeling fine 650 (2)

feeling for 905 (4)

feeling for words 566 (1)

feeling pride 871 (4)

feeling the pinch 627 (4)

feelingly 818 (9)

feelings 817 (1)

feet 214 (2), 267 (6)

feet first 237 (6)

feet of clay 163 (1), 542 (1), 647 (2), 661 (2)

feign 20 (5), 541 (6), 850 (5)

feigned 541 (4), 542 (6)

feint 542 (2), 698 (2)

felicitate 835 (6), 886 (3)

felicitation 835 (1)

felicitations 886 (1)

felicitous 24 (6), 575 (3), 727 (4)

felicity 575 (1), 824 (2)

feline 365 (11), 365 (18)

fell 46 (11), 165 (7), 209 (2), 216 (7), 279 (9), 311 (6), 348 (1), 362 (8)

fell walker 306 (2)

fellow 13 (1), 18 (3), 89 (2), 371 (3), 372 (1), 537 (1), 538 (3), 707 (3), 708 (3), 869 (7), 880 (3), 880 (5)

fellow creature 371 (3)

fellow feeling 706 (1), 710 (1), 775 (2), 887 (1), 897 (1), 905 (2)

fellow student 538 (1)

fellow traveller 488 (3), 707 (2)

fellow worshipper 976 (6), 981 (8)

fellowship 74 (3), 706 (1), 706 (2), 708 (4), 880 (1), 882 (1)

felon 904 (3)

felonious 930 (5), 954 (6)

felony 930 (3), 954 (2)

felt 222 (4), 818 (6)

felucca 275 (5)

female 134 (1), 134 (2), 134 (3), 371 (3), 373 (1), 373 (5)

female sex 373 (2)

female warrior 722 (4)

feminine 77 (4), 373 (5)

feminine gender 373 (1)

feminineness 373 (1)

femininity 373 (1)

feminism 373 (1)

feminist 373 (3), 373 (5)

femme fatale 612 (5), 841 (2), 887 (5), 952 (2)

fen 347 (1)

fence 231 (2), 232 (1), 235 (2), 264 (2), 279 (8), 421 (1), 477 (8), 620 (5), 660 (2), 702 (9), 713 (9), 713 (10), 716 (11), 789 (1), 794 (1)

fence in 232 (3), 235 (4), 370 (9), 660 (8)

fencer 273 (5), 716 (8), 722 (1)

fencing 716 (6)

fend for oneself 134 (4), 744 (9)

fend off 292 (3), 713 (10)

fender 231 (3), 713 (1)

feral 365 (18)

ferment 61 (4), 147 (7), 174 (2), 318 (3), 318 (7), 323 (2), 355 (5), 393 (3), 818 (1), 821 (1), 822 (2)

fermentation 147 (1), 174 (2), 318 (3), 355 (1)

fermented 301 (32)

fermented liquor 301 (28)

fermenting 323 (3)

fern 366 (6)

ferocious 176 (6), 898 (7)

ferocity 176 (1), 898 (2)

ferret out 484 (4)

ferreting 619 (2)

ferry 269 (9), 272 (1), 272 (6), 273 (12), 275 (1), 275 (7), 624 (3)

ferry crossing 269 (1)

ferryman 270 (4)

fertile 167 (4), 171 (4), 513 (5), 635 (4), 640 (3), 771 (5)

fertile imagination 513 (1)

fertile soil 156 (4)

fertility 167 (1), 171 (1)

fertility cult 171 (2)

fertility drug 167 (1), 171 (2)

fertility god 966 (2)

fertility rite 171 (2)

fertility symbol 171 (2)

fertilization 167 (1)

fertilize 171 (5), 174 (8), 370 (9)

fertilized 167 (5)

fertilizer 167 (1), 171 (2), 370 (1)

fervent 571 (2), 678 (7), 680 (2), 818 (5), 819 (4), 821 (3), 887 (9), 979 (7), 981 (9)

fervid 818 (5)

fervour 174 (1), 379 (1), 571 (1), 818 (2), 979 (1)

fesse-wise 216 (8)

festal 837 (18), 988 (8)

festal cheer 301 (2)

fester 649 (8), 655 (7), 827 (8), 898 (8)

festering 649 (6), 651 (5), 651 (14), 651 (22)

festival 74 (2), 837 (2), 988 (7)

festive 837 (18), 837 (19), 876 (3), 882 (6)

festive board 882 (2)

festive occasion 876 (1)

festivities 837 (2)

festivity 301 (12), 835 (1), 837 (2), 875 (3), 876 (1), 882 (3), 988 (7)

festoon 248 (2), 844 (3), 844 (12)

festooned 844 (10), 844 (11)

fetch 273 (12), 809 (6)

fetch and carry 273 (12)
fetch up at 295 (4)
fetching 826 (2), 841 (6), 859 (10)
fete 61 (11), 875 (3), 876 (1), 876 (4), 886 (3)
feted 882 (7)
fetid 394 (2), 397 (2), 645 (2), 649 (6)
fetidness 397 (1)
fetish 966 (1), 982 (3), 983 (3)
fetishism 962 (1)
fetishist 973 (7), 982 (4), 983 (5)
fetishistic 982 (5)
fetlock 214 (2)
fetter 45 (12), 47 (1), 47 (5), 47 (8), 264 (2), 679 (13), 702 (4), 702 (8), 745 (1), 745 (7), 747 (1), 747 (9), 748 (4), 964 (2)
fettered 747 (6)
fettle 7 (1)
feud 709 (3), 881 (1), 910 (2)
feudal 127 (4), 733 (9), 745 (5), 777 (5)
feudalism 733 (4), 745 (2)
fever 318 (1), 318 (3), 379 (1), 651 (2), 651 (5), 651 (6), 678 (2), 822 (2)
fever heat 379 (1)
fever of excitement 822 (2)
fever pitch 821 (1)
fevered 318 (4), 379 (4), 431 (3), 503 (9), 651 (22)
feverish 318 (4), 379 (4), 651 (21), 651 (22), 678 (7), 680 (2), 818 (5), 821 (3), 822 (3)
feverish, be 379 (7)
feverishness 318 (1), 651 (2)
few 33 (7), 105 (2), 140 (2), 636 (6)
few, a 101 (1), 105 (1)
few and far between 140 (2)
few, be 105 (3)
few words 569 (1), 582 (1)
fewer 105 (2)

fewness 26 (2), 35 (1), 41 (1), 105 (1), 140 (1), 196 (1), 636 (1), 636 (2)
fey 983 (9), 984 (7)
fez 228 (23)
fiance 887 (4)
fiasco 728 (1)
fiat 737 (2)
fib 543 (1)
fibber 545 (2)
fibre 5 (2), 47 (2), 47 (4), 208 (2), 222 (4), 259 (2), 301 (10), 331 (2), 631 (1)
fibre optics 417 (7)
fibreglass 222 (4), 631 (1)
fibrositis 651 (15)
fibrous 206 (4), 208 (4), 329 (2)
fichu 228 (22)
fickle 114 (3), 152 (3), 474 (5), 603 (4), 604 (3)
fickle, be 604 (4)
fickleness 152 (1), 474 (3), 601 (1), 604 (1)
fiction 164 (2), 513 (2), 541 (1), 543 (1), 543 (3), 557 (3), 590 (2), 590 (4)
fiction writer 590 (5)
fictional 513 (5), 590 (6)
fictionalize 513 (7), 590 (7)
fictitious 2 (4), 4 (3), 513 (6), 543 (4), 590 (6), 916 (6)
fiddle 414 (3), 541 (8), 542 (2), 623 (3), 788 (4), 788 (8), 930 (3), 930 (8)
fiddle with 378 (7)
fiddled 541 (3)
fiddler 789 (3)
fiddlesticks 515 (7)
fiddling 678 (2)
fidelity 494 (3), 540 (1), 739 (2)
fidget 822 (4)
fidgetiness 822 (1)
fidgeting 152 (1)
fidgets 318 (1), 678 (2)
fidgety 152 (4), 678 (7), 822 (3)
field 183 (3), 184 (1), 185 (1), 235 (1), 348 (2), 460 (5), 619 (3), 744 (3)

field army 722 (7)
field boundary 231 (2)
field day 876 (2)
field glasses 442 (3)
field gun 723 (11)
field marshal 741 (8)
field of action 724 (1)
field of battle 716 (7), 718 (7), 724 (3)
field of study 452 (1)
field of view 443 (1)
field piece 723 (11)
field sports 837 (6)
field, the 705 (1)
field work 536 (2)
fielder 837 (16)
fields 370 (2)
fiend 904 (4), 938 (4), 969 (2)
fiendish 898 (7), 934 (3), 969 (5)
fiendishness 898 (2)
fierce 176 (6), 718 (9), 822 (3), 855 (4), 892 (3), 898 (7)
fiercely 32 (17)
fierceness 176 (1), 891 (1), 891 (2), 892 (1)
fieriness 709 (2), 857 (1)
fiery 176 (5), 379 (5), 417 (8), 571 (2), 818 (5), 822 (3), 892 (3)
fiesta 837 (2)
fife 414 (6)
fifteen 74 (4)
fifth 99 (6)
fifth and over 99 (6)
fifth column 738 (3)
fifth columnist 603 (3), 707 (2), 738 (4)
fifty 99 (3)
fifty-fifty 28 (7), 43 (6), 159 (2)
fifty p 797 (4)
fig 7 (1), 301 (19)
fig leaf 228 (14)
fight 61 (4), 279 (9), 704 (5), 709 (3), 712 (7), 716 (7), 716 (10), 716 (11), 718 (7), 718 (10), 718 (12), 891 (2)
fight against 704 (4)

fight back **713** (10), **747** (7)

fight down **747** (7)

fight for **713** (9)

fight for air **379** (7)

fight it out **716** (11), **718** (12)

fight off **713** (10), **715** (3)

fight on **599** (4)

fight shy **620** (5)

fight shy of **598** (4)

fighter **276** (1), **671** (2), **705** (1), **716** (8), **722** (1), **722** (14)

fighter pilot **712** (5)

fighting **716** (1), **718** (6)

fighting fit **162** (9), **650** (2)

figment **4** (2), **164** (2), **513** (2)

figurative **462** (2), **514** (4), **519** (3), **523** (4), **551** (6), **574** (4), **574** (5), **590** (6)

figuratively **519** (5)

figure **85** (1), **86** (12), **233** (1), **243** (1), **243** (5), **371** (3), **519** (4), **551** (2), **551** (8), **797** (2), **809** (1), **866** (6)

figure in **445** (8)

figure of eight **248** (2), **250** (3), **314** (1)

figure of fun **851** (3)

figure of speech **519** (2), **574** (1)

figure skater **315** (3)

figure to oneself **513** (7)

figure-work **86** (1), **86** (2)

figured out **86** (9)

figurehead **4** (2), **161** (4), **237** (3), **254** (3), **551** (2), **639** (4)

figures **86** (4)

figurine **551** (2), **554** (1)

figuring **86** (1)

filament **208** (1), **420** (4)

filch **788** (7)

filching **788** (1)

file **62** (1), **62** (2), **62** (6), **71** (2), **71** (3), **71** (5), **87** (1), **87** (5), **136** (7), **194** (10), **198** (7), **256** (6), **256** (11), **258** (2), **258** (4), **259** (1), **267** (4), **332** (3), **332** (5),

333 (3), **524** (1), **548** (1), **548** (7), **632** (5), **722** (8)

file down **39** (3)

file in **297** (5)

file past **267** (14)

filed **548** (6)

filial **170** (4), **739** (3)

filibuster **113** (8), **702** (5), **702** (10)

filibustering **113** (3), **788** (2)

filigree **222** (3), **844** (2)

filing **333** (1), **548** (2)

filing system **62** (2)

filings **41** (2), **332** (2)

fill **32** (15), **36** (4), **54** (5), **54** (7), **74** (11), **187** (7), **189** (5), **193** (2), **197** (5), **198** (7), **227** (2), **306** (3), **633** (6), **637** (5), **656** (12), **773** (4), **863** (3)

fill a gap **54** (6)

fill a role **622** (8)

fill a vacancy **622** (6)

fill in **54** (7), **548** (8)

fill one's lungs **352** (11)

fill one's mind **449** (11)

fill one's time **622** (6)

fill out **36** (4), **36** (5), **54** (5), **197** (4)

fill space **54** (7)

fill the air **400** (4)

fill the bill **635** (6)

fill to bursting **197** (5)

fill to capacity **54** (7)

fill up **54** (5), **54** (7), **632** (5), **633** (6), **656** (9), **863** (3)

fill with longing **859** (13)

fill with prejudice **481** (11)

filled **54** (4), **635** (5), **863** (2)

filled, be **54** (5)

filler **529** (1), **570** (2)

fillet **228** (23), **300** (8)

filling **54** (2), **193** (1), **227** (1)

filling up **54** (2)

fillip **174** (4), **821** (2)

filly **132** (3), **273** (4)

film **207** (1), **226** (1), **226** (6), **423** (1), **423** (3), **440**

(1), **442** (6), **445** (4), **548** (7), **551** (4), **551** (9)

film director **445** (3)

film fan **594** (14)

film-making **445** (3)

film production **445** (3)

film reviewer **594** (14)

film show **445** (2)

film star **445** (3), **594** (9), **890** (2)

film studio **445** (3)

filmed **548** (6)

filmgoer **441** (1)

filminess **423** (1)

films **445** (4)

filmstrip **551** (4)

filmy **207** (4), **331** (4), **422** (2), **423** (2), **424** (2)

filter **282** (3), **298** (7), **421** (1), **648** (5), **648** (10)

filter out **421** (4)

filth **645** (1), **649** (2), **951** (1)

filthiness **649** (1)

filthy **645** (2), **645** (4), **649** (7), **951** (6)

fin **53** (2), **153** (3), **239** (1), **269** (5)

fin de siècle **110** (2)

final **69** (4), **156** (7), **460** (4), **473** (5), **716** (2), **725** (3)

final attempt **671** (1)

final defeat **728** (2)

final demand **737** (3)

final judgment **480** (1)

final notice **737** (3)

final point **69** (2)

Final Solution **362** (4)

final stage **69** (1)

final terms **766** (1)

finale **69** (1), **412** (4)

finalist **716** (8)

finality **54** (1), **69** (3), **110** (1), **124** (2), **165** (3), **361** (2), **725** (1)

finalize **473** (9)

finalized **69** (4)

finally **32** (16), **32** (18), **65** (5), **69** (7)

finance **629** (2), **784** (5), **791** (4), **797** (3)

finances **797** (2)

financial 622 (5), 797 (9)

financial embarrassment 801 (1)

financier 784 (3), 794 (1), 797 (8), 798 (1)

finch 365 (4)

find 40 (2), 154 (7), 480 (5), 484 (1), 484 (4), 615 (2), 629 (2), 633 (5), 771 (1), 771 (7), 959 (8)

find a clue 484 (5)

find a formula 770 (2)

find a home 187 (8)

find a loophole 614 (4)

find a niche 73 (3)

find a way 484 (4), 623 (8), 629 (2), 727 (8)

find against 480 (5), 961 (3)

find an example 9 (8)

find credence 485 (10)

find fault 829 (5), 862 (4), 924 (10), 924 (12), 926 (6)

find favour 923 (11)

find for 480 (5)

find guilty 961 (3)

find intolerable 891 (5)

find liable 961 (3)

find means 156 (9), 629 (2)

find necessary 627 (6)

find not guilty 960 (3)

find one's feet 656 (8)

find one's match 714 (4)

find one's tongue 579 (1)

find one's way in 297 (6)

find out 484 (4)

find palatable 386 (3)

find room for 78 (5), 187 (5)

find the meaning 520 (10)

find the place 187 (5)

find time for 455 (6), 681 (3)

find useful 640 (5), 673 (3)

find willing ears 485 (10)

finder 442 (3)

finding 480 (1), 484 (1), 771 (1), 959 (3)

finding again 771 (1)

finding of guilty 961 (1)

finding reasons 158 (1)

finding the place 187 (1)

fine 195 (6), 206 (4), 325 (2), 331 (4), 342 (4), 422 (2), 494 (6), 615 (3), 644 (4), 650 (2), 730 (5), 809 (1), 809 (7), 841 (4), 963 (4), 963 (8)

fine adjustment 494 (3)

fine airs 873 (2)

fine arts 551 (3)

fine feeling 846 (1)

fine gentleman 848 (4)

fine-grained 331 (4)

fine lady 848 (4)

fine qualities 933 (2)

fine-spun 206 (4), 208 (4), 331 (4)

fine talk 877 (1)

fine touch 378 (1)

fine-tuned 24 (8)

fine weather 340 (3)

fine words 579 (1)

fine workmanship 694 (1)

fineness 206 (2), 325 (1)

finer feelings 819 (1)

finery 228 (2), 844 (6), 875 (1)

finesse 694 (1), 698 (1), 698 (5)

finger 33 (3), 53 (5), 378 (4), 378 (7), 547 (6), 778 (2)

finger painting 553 (1)

finger puppet 551 (2)

fingering 413 (6)

fingerpost 281 (1), 547 (7)

fingerprint 41 (1), 547 (2), 547 (13), 548 (4)

fingerprints 466 (1)

fingerstall 658 (9)

finickiness 829 (1)

finicky 846 (3), 862 (3)

fining 963 (4), 963 (6)

finish 54 (1), 69 (1), 69 (5), 69 (6), 145 (6), 258 (1), 575 (1), 725 (1)

finish off 725 (5)

finished 2 (5), 32 (13), 69 (4), 125 (6), 646 (3), 694 (4), 694 (7)

finished a 164 (2)

finisher 69 (1), 479 (1), 676 (3)

finishing 725 (3)

finishing off 725 (1)

finishing school 539 (1)

finishing stroke 69 (1)

finishing touch 654 (2), 725 (1)

finite 236 (2)

finite quantity 26 (2), 33 (2), 465 (1)

fir 366 (4)

fire 168 (1), 174 (1), 287 (8), 300 (7), 319 (4), 379 (2), 381 (2), 381 (9), 381 (10), 383 (1), 385 (6), 417 (1), 420 (1), 547 (5), 571 (1), 712 (3)

fire a salute 876 (4), 884 (7)

fire a volley 287 (8)

fire alarm 665 (1)

fire and water 14 (2)

fire at 165 (7), 287 (8), 712 (11), 718 (12)

fire away 68 (8)

fire brigade 382 (3)

fire-eater 176 (4), 594 (10), 722 (1), 857 (2)

fire-eating 857 (3)

fire engine 274 (1), 341 (3), 382 (3)

fire escape 667 (2)

fire extinguisher 382 (3)

fire fighter 660 (3)

fire off 287 (8)

fire on 712 (11)

fire-raiser 381 (3)

fire-raising 165 (1), 381 (3)

fire resistance 382 (2)

fire-resistant 382 (5)

fire-walker 945 (2)

fire worship 982 (1)

firearm 287 (3), 402 (1), 723 (9)

fireball 321 (7), 379 (2), 420 (1), 420 (2)

firebomb 723 (14)

firebrand 176 (4), 385 (3), 612 (5), 663 (2), 738 (5)

firebreak 201 (2)

fired 381 (6), 779 (3)

firefighter 382 (3)

firefly 365 (16), 417 (2), 419 (3), 420 (2)

firelight 419 (3)
fireman 268 (5), 381 (2)
fireman or woman 382 (3), 660 (3)
fireplace 383 (1)
fireproof 162 (7), 226 (16), 382 (5), 660 (5)
fireside 76 (1), 192 (5)
firewood 385 (1)
firework display 420 (7)
fireworks 379 (2), 420 (7), 445 (2), 694 (3), 875 (3), 876 (1)
firing 385 (1)
firing line 718 (7), 724 (2)
firing squad 963 (5)
firkin 194 (12)
firm 45 (7), 54 (4), 153 (6), 162 (6), 324 (4), 326 (4), 599 (2), 708 (5), 778 (3), 794 (1), 796 (3), 880 (6)
firm advice 693 (1)
firm belief 485 (1)
firm control 735 (1)
firm down 324 (6)
firm foundation 153 (2)
firm hold 778 (1)
firm in 485 (4)
firm opposition 704 (1)
firm principle 81 (1)
firm stand 715 (1)
firmament 321 (3)
firmly 45 (16)
firmness 144 (1), 326 (1), 599 (1)
first 34 (5), 68 (7), 68 (11), 119 (2), 156 (8), 283 (2), 727 (3)
first aid 658 (12), 703 (1)
first-aid station 658 (13)
first and foremost 68 (11)
first appearance 68 (2)
first arrival 135 (1)
first attempt 671 (1)
first, be 64 (3)
first beginnings 68 (4)
first blush 68 (1)
First Cause 965 (1)
first choice 34 (3), 605 (1), 890 (2)
first-class 34 (5)
first come 64 (2)
First Communion 988 (4)

first copy 22 (1)
first cousin 11 (2)
first cuckoo 128 (3)
first draft 55 (1), 461 (1), 623 (1)
first edition 589 (5)
first fiddle 638 (4)
first glance 68 (1)
first-hand 126 (5)
first house 594 (2)
first impression 68 (1)
first in the field 119 (2)
first lap 68 (1)
first letter 68 (1), 558 (2)
first love 887 (1)
first move 68 (2)
first name 561 (2)
first night 68 (2)
first-nighter 594 (14)
first of all 68 (11), 283 (4)
first offence 68 (2)
first offender 750 (1), 904 (3)
first payment 804 (1)
first principle 156 (3), 475 (2)
first principles 68 (1)
first prize 729 (1)
first-rate 34 (5), 638 (6), 644 (4), 644 (6), 694 (4)
first round 68 (1)
first school 539 (2)
first served 64 (2)
first sight 68 (1), 438 (4)
first step 68 (2)
first steps 536 (1)
first thing 135 (6), 156 (3)
first violin 413 (3), 690 (2)
firstborn 66 (1), 119 (1), 119 (2), 131 (7)
firsthand 466 (5)
firstly 68 (11)
firth 345 (1)
fiscal 797 (9)
fish 301 (15), 365 (2), 365 (15), 619 (6), 837 (21)
fish and chips 301 (15)
fish cakes 301 (15)
fish farm 369 (2)
fish fingers 301 (15)
fish food 301 (15)
fish for 459 (15), 619 (5)

fish out of water 25 (3), 188 (1)
fish pie 301 (15)
fish up 310 (4)
fisher 619 (3)
fisherman or woman 619 (3)
fishing 619 (2), 619 (4), 837 (6)
fishing bird 365 (4)
fishing boat 275 (4)
fishing tackle 619 (2)
fishmonger 633 (2)
fishnet 222 (3)
fishpond 346 (1)
fishwife 892 (2)
fishy 365 (18), 472 (2), 930 (4)
fissile 46 (6), 330 (2)
fissility 330 (1)
fission 46 (2), 51 (1), 51 (5), 160 (7)
fissionable 46 (6)
fissure 46 (1), 201 (2)
fist 378 (4), 586 (2)
fisticuffs 279 (2), 709 (3), 716 (4), 716 (7), 891 (2)
fit 24 (7), 24 (9), 24 (10), 28 (10), 45 (9), 48 (3), 162 (9), 176 (1), 318 (2), 503 (4), 604 (2), 642 (2), 650 (2), 650 (3), 651 (2), 678 (1), 822 (2), 913 (3)
fit closely 45 (14)
fit for 640 (2)
fit for use 669 (7)
fit in 24 (9), 83 (7), 193 (2), 303 (4)
fit like a glove 24 (0)
fit of laughter 835 (2)
fit of temper 891 (2)
fit out 228 (31), 629 (2), 633 (5), 669 (11)
fit tight 45 (14), 48 (3), 54 (7)
fit to burst 54 (4)
fit together 45 (9), 50 (4)
fitful 17 (2), 72 (2), 142 (2), 152 (4), 822 (3)
fitfully 142 (3), 152 (6), 604 (5)
fitfulness 72 (1), 142 (1), 152 (1), 604 (1)

fitness 9 (3), 24 (3), 160 (2), 179 (1), 642 (1), 650 (1), 669 (4), 694 (2), 913 (1)

fits and starts 142 (1), 318 (1)

fitter 630 (5), 686 (3)

fitting 9 (6), 24 (7), 137 (5), 642 (2), 913 (3), 915 (2)

fitting out 633 (1), 669 (2)

fittingness 137 (1), 913 (1)

fittings 630 (4)

five 99 (1), 99 (6)

five o'clock 129 (1)

five p 797 (4)

five senses 99 (1), 374 (2)

five-star 34 (5)

five-toed 214 (4)

fivefold 99 (6)

fix 45 (11), 62 (4), 153 (8), 187 (5), 700 (3)

fix in 187 (5)

fix in one's memory 505 (10)

fix on 605 (6)

fix one's gaze 438 (8)

fix the date 117 (7)

fix the time 108 (9), 117 (7)

fixation 455 (1), 481 (2), 503 (5), 702 (1)

fixative 47 (9), 425 (4)

fixed 28 (7), 45 (7), 127 (6), 144 (2), 153 (6), 162 (6), 187 (4), 473 (5), 610 (5), 809 (4)

fixed attitude 144 (1)

fixed expression 563 (1)

fixed interval 141 (2)

fixed order 60 (1)

fixed resolve 599 (1)

fixed stare 438 (3)

fixed time 110 (1)

fixed ways 81 (2), 610 (1)

fixer 545 (4)

fixity 144 (1), 153 (1), 473 (2)

fixity of purpose 599 (1)

fixture 40 (1), 45 (2), 89 (2), 153 (2)

fixtures 777 (1)

fizz 174 (1), 301 (27), 301 (29), 355 (1), 355 (5), 406 (3)

fizzle 355 (5), 402 (3), 406 (3)

fizzle out 307 (3), 728 (8)

fizzy 174 (5), 339 (2), 352 (8), 355 (3)

fjord 345 (1)

flabbergasted 854 (6), 864 (4)

flabbiness 163 (1), 327 (1)

flabby 163 (4), 327 (2), 356 (2)

flaccid 163 (4), 175 (2), 327 (2), 572 (2)

flaccidity 163 (1), 327 (1), 572 (1)

flag 163 (9), 207 (2), 278 (4), 278 (5), 547 (12), 651 (23), 684 (5), 834 (9), 963 (3)

flag-bearer 529 (5)

flag day 761 (1), 876 (2)

flag down 547 (22)

flag-lieutenant 741 (7)

flag of convenience 547 (12)

flag waving 876 (1)

flagellant 945 (2)

flagellate 963 (10)

flagellation 941 (3), 945 (1), 963 (2)

flagellum 208 (1)

flagging 163 (5), 684 (2)

flagon 194 (13)

flagpole 547 (12)

flagrancy 528 (2), 847 (1), 875 (1), 878 (1), 934 (1)

flagrant 32 (10), 522 (4), 528 (8), 875 (5), 934 (6)

flagrantly 32 (19)

flags 226 (7), 876 (1)

flagship 722 (13)

flail 279 (9), 370 (9), 712 (9)

flair 394 (1), 447 (1), 484 (1), 694 (2), 846 (1), 848 (1)

flak 712 (3), 713 (2)

flake 33 (3), 53 (5), 207 (2), 332 (2), 332 (5), 388 (2)

flake off 207 (5)

flakiness 207 (3)

flaky 207 (4), 330 (2), 332 (4)

flamboyant 417 (8), 574 (4)

flame 379 (1), 379 (2), 383 (2), 417 (1), 420 (1), 887 (5)

flame-coloured 431 (3), 432 (2)

flame up 379 (7)

flamenco 837 (14)

flameproof 382 (5)

flames 379 (3)

flamethrower 723 (11)

flaming 176 (5), 379 (4), 379 (5)

flammable 385 (5)

flan 301 (13), 301 (23)

flange 254 (2)

flank 239 (1), 239 (3), 660 (8)

flanked 239 (2)

flanking 239 (2)

flannel 222 (4), 515 (3), 925 (1)

flannels 228 (12)

flap 49 (4), 217 (2), 217 (5), 226 (1), 265 (4), 318 (1), 352 (10), 680 (1), 822 (1)

flapping 49 (2)

flaps 228 (3), 271 (5)

flare 197 (4), 205 (5), 379 (2), 379 (7), 417 (1), 420 (3), 420 (6)

flare up 36 (4), 821 (9), 822 (4), 891 (6)

flared 197 (3), 205 (3)

flaring 32 (10), 379 (5)

flash 33 (2), 116 (2), 152 (5), 277 (1), 277 (6), 318 (1), 379 (2), 417 (2), 417 (11), 419 (3), 420 (1), 542 (7), 547 (5), 547 (10), 609 (1), 839 (5)

flash a smile 835 (8)

flash back 460 (5), 839 (5)

flash by 305 (5)

flash flood 350 (4)

flash in the pan 4 (2)

flash point 379 (1)

flash pound notes 815 (4)
flash to stardom 866 (11)
flashback 505 (2)
flasher 229 (3), 952 (1)
flashgun 442 (6)
flashing 116 (3), 277 (5), 417 (8), 951 (5)
flashlight 420 (4)
flashpoint 709 (4)
flashy 425 (6), 844 (10), 847 (4), 848 (5), 875 (5)
flask 194 (13)
flat 183 (5), 192 (9), 210 (2), 210 (3), 216 (4), 216 (8), 257 (1), 257 (2), 258 (3), 348 (3), 387 (2), 391 (2), 407 (2), 410 (2), 410 (8), 411 (2), 419 (4), 552 (2), 572 (2), 655 (5), 702 (3), 834 (3), 838 (3), 840 (2)
flat-footed 214 (4)
flat-mate 775 (3)
flat on one's back 216 (5)
flat out 277 (9)
flat rate 809 (1)
flat refusal 760 (1)
flatlet 192 (9)
flatness 216 (1), 258 (1), 387 (1), 572 (1), 838 (1), 840 (1)
flats 216 (1), 348 (1)
flatten 165 (7), 165 (8), 198 (7), 216 (7), 249 (4), 258 (4), 279 (9), 311 (4), 311 (6), 727 (10)
flatten out 271 (7)
flattened 210 (2), 257 (2)
flattener 168 (1), 216 (3), 258 (2)
flattening 165 (1)
flatter 178 (3), 488 (6), 515 (6), 541 (5), 542 (9), 546 (3), 552 (2), 612 (10), 703 (7), 841 (8), 866 (13), 873 (6), 879 (4), 884 (6), 889 (5), 923 (9), 925 (4)
flatter oneself 852 (6), 871 (6), 873 (5), 925 (4)
flattered 824 (4), 828 (2)
flattered, be 871 (6)

flatterer 20 (3), 83 (3), 488 (3), 612 (5), 696 (3), 850 (3), 879 (2), 925 (2)
flattering 20 (4), 83 (4), 515 (5), 541 (4), 542 (6), 579 (7), 603 (4), 698 (4), 826 (2), 879 (3), 884 (3), 925 (3), 930 (5)
flattery 515 (1), 515 (3), 541 (1), 546 (1), 612 (2), 866 (4), 879 (1), 884 (1), 889 (1), 923 (2), 925 (1)
flatulence 336 (1), 352 (7), 574 (2), 651 (7)
flatulent 336 (3), 340 (5), 572 (2)
flaunt 522 (8), 866 (12), 875 (7), 877 (5)
flaunted 522 (6)
flaunting 522 (5), 847 (4), 875 (5), 951 (7)
flautist 413 (2)
flavour 43 (2), 301 (40), 386 (1), 388 (6)
flavoured 386 (2), 390 (2)
flavourful 386 (2)
flavouring 301 (9), 301 (10), 386 (1), 389 (1)
flavourless 387 (2)
flaw 72 (1), 163 (1), 201 (2), 477 (2), 495 (3), 645 (1), 647 (2), 845 (1), 845 (3), 934 (2)
flawed 55 (3), 645 (2), 647 (3), 845 (2)
flawless 32 (13), 575 (3), 646 (3)
flawlessness 644 (1), 646 (1)
flax 208 (2)
flaxen-haired 427 (5)
flay 229 (6), 333 (3), 963 (10)
flay alive 963 (12)
flea 33 (5), 312 (2), 365 (16), 649 (2)
flea market 796 (1)
flea pit 445 (3)
flea-ridden 649 (6), 653 (2)
fleabite 639 (2)
fleck 33 (3), 437 (4)
fled 667 (4)

fledged 669 (8)
fledgling 126 (5), 132 (3), 365 (4)
flee 290 (3), 296 (5), 620 (6)
fleece 226 (6), 259 (2), 327 (1), 369 (10), 542 (8), 786 (11), 788 (8), 801 (6), 811 (5)
fleecy 208 (4), 258 (3), 259 (5), 259 (7), 327 (2)
fleet 275 (10), 277 (5), 722 (11)
fleet air arm 722 (14)
fleet arm 722 (11)
fleet operations 269 (2)
Fleet Street 528 (4)
fleeting 114 (3)
fleetness 277 (1)
flesh 68 (10), 301 (16), 371 (1)
flesh and blood 3 (2), 319 (2)
flesh-eater 301 (6)
flesh-eating 301 (1), 301 (31)
flesh-pink 431 (3)
flesh, the 944 (1)
fleshiness 195 (3), 356 (1)
fleshings 228 (26)
fleshly 944 (3)
fleshpots 730 (1)
fleshy 195 (8), 197 (3), 204 (3), 205 (4), 246 (4), 252 (5), 253 (7), 356 (2), 357 (6), 842 (4)
fleur-de-lis 547 (11)
flex one's muscles 669 (13)
flexibility 327 (1), 694 (1)
flexible 83 (4), 327 (3), 701 (4)
flick 279 (1), 279 (2), 279 (7), 287 (7), 378 (1), 378 (7)
flicker 33 (2), 114 (6), 152 (5), 317 (4), 318 (1), 318 (5), 379 (2), 417 (2), 417 (11), 419 (3), 419 (6)
flickering 114 (3), 116 (3), 142 (2), 417 (2)
flier 271 (4)
flies 594 (7)

flight 74 (3), 271 (1), 290 (1), 296 (1), 446 (1), 620 (1), 667 (1), 722 (14), 728 (2), 854 (1)
flight bag 194 (9)
flight deck 276 (1)
flight feathers 271 (5)
flight lieutenant 741 (9)
flight of fancy 513 (2)
flight of stairs 308 (1)
flight path 271 (2)
flight recorder 549 (3)
flight sergeant 741 (9)
flight simulator 461 (4)
flightless bird 365 (4)
flighty 114 (3), 152 (3), 456 (6)
flimsiness 163 (1), 330 (1)
flimsy 4 (3), 22 (2), 163 (8), 330 (2), 477 (6), 647 (3)
flinch 280 (3), 377 (6), 620 (5), 825 (7), 854 (10)
flinching 290 (1), 377 (4)
fling 265 (5), 279 (7), 287 (1), 287 (7), 744 (3)
fling about 63 (4)
fling away 815 (4)
flinging wide 263 (1)
flint 326 (1), 344 (3)
flinty 326 (3), 344 (5), 735 (4)
flip 279 (2), 279 (7), 279 (9), 378 (1), 378 (7)
flip side 238 (1)
flippancy 456 (1), 878 (2)
flippant 456 (6), 839 (4), 851 (4), 857 (3), 878 (5)
flipper 53 (2), 269 (5), 378 (3)
flirt 603 (3), 604 (4), 850 (3), 850 (5), 887 (4), 887 (15), 889 (7), 952 (1), 952 (2)
flirtation 604 (2), 887 (3), 889 (2)
flirtatious 604 (3), 887 (9), 889 (4)
flirting 889 (2)
flit 114 (6), 152 (5), 265 (4), 271 (7), 277 (6), 296 (1), 620 (6), 667 (1), 667 (5)

flitting 114 (3), 271 (6)
float 217 (5), 258 (5), 269 (12), 271 (7), 274 (4), 274 (12), 275 (9), 323 (4), 629 (2)
float a loan 785 (2)
float down 309 (3)
float up 308 (4)
floating 152 (4), 267 (9), 269 (3), 269 (7), 308 (3), 323 (3)
floating over 209 (11)
floating pound 797 (3)
floating up 308 (1)
floating vote 606 (1), 744 (2)
floating voter 152 (2), 601 (2)
flock 74 (3), 104 (2), 365 (2), 987 (1)
flock together 74 (10)
flog 279 (9), 612 (9), 793 (4), 963 (10)
flog a dead horse 641 (8)
flogging 279 (2), 963 (2)
flood 32 (2), 36 (1), 74 (5), 74 (10), 75 (3), 104 (6), 168 (1), 176 (7), 209 (6), 226 (14), 285 (1), 297 (7), 298 (6), 303 (7), 306 (4), 341 (2), 341 (8), 350 (4), 350 (9), 637 (5)
flood level 209 (6)
flood of light 417 (1)
flood of tears 836 (1)
flood out 298 (6)
flood plain 348 (1)
flood the market 637 (5), 812 (6)
flood tide 209 (6)
flood with light 417 (13)
flooded 226 (12)
floodgate 298 (3), 351 (1)
flooding 297 (4), 350 (7)
floodlight 420 (4), 594 (7)
floodlighting 420 (5)
floodlit 417 (8)
floods 32 (2)
floor 194 (4), 207 (1), 210 (1), 214 (1), 216 (7), 218 (4), 226 (7), 226 (15), 279 (9), 311 (6), 474 (9), 479 (3), 724 (1)

floor-cover 226 (9)
floor show 445 (2), 594 (4)
floorboards 226 (7)
flooring 214 (1), 218 (4), 226 (7)
flop 309 (3), 695 (2), 728 (1), 728 (3), 728 (8)
floppiness 327 (1)
flopping 49 (2)
floppy 49 (2), 327 (2)
floppy disk 86 (5)
flora 366 (1), 967 (2)
flora and fauna 358 (1)
floral 366 (9)
floret 366 (7)
florid 425 (6), 431 (3), 437 (5), 519 (3), 574 (4), 841 (4), 875 (5)
floridness 431 (1)
floss 208 (2), 259 (2)
flotation 669 (2)
flotilla 275 (10), 722 (11)
flotsam 779 (2)
flounce 261 (1), 844 (5), 891 (7)
flounder 312 (4), 318 (5), 474 (8), 695 (9)
flour 301 (22), 332 (2)
flourish 36 (4), 171 (6), 251 (2), 317 (6), 318 (6), 410 (2), 412 (3), 519 (2), 522 (8), 615 (5), 650 (3), 730 (6), 844 (3), 875 (1), 875 (7), 877 (2), 877 (5)
flourish of rhetoric 574 (1)
flourishing 730 (4)
floury 332 (4)
flout 704 (4)
flout authority 738 (9)
flow 26 (1), 71 (1), 111 (3), 146 (1), 217 (5), 265 (1), 265 (4), 278 (4), 298 (6), 315 (5), 337 (4), 350 (2), 350 (9), 401 (4), 570 (1), 570 (6), 575 (1), 635 (7), 637 (5)
flow back 286 (4)
flow between 46 (10)
flow chart 86 (4), 623 (1)
flow from 157 (5)
flow in 297 (7)
flow into 350 (9)

flow of ideas 449 (1)
flow of time 111 (1)
flow of traffic 305 (2)
flow of words 581 (1)
flow on 285 (3)
flow out 298 (6), 300 (9), 308 (4), 341 (6), 350 (9), 634 (4), 667 (5)
flow softly 350 (9)
flower 5 (2), 36 (4), 164 (2), 167 (6), 197 (4), 366 (7), 644 (2), 646 (2), 730 (6)
flower of life 130 (3)
flowerbed 370 (3)
floweriness 574 (1)
flowering 128 (6), 130 (4), 366 (1), 669 (8)
flowery 366 (9), 519 (3), 574 (4)
flowing 115 (2), 152 (4), 217 (4), 335 (4), 350 (7), 570 (3), 571 (2), 575 (3)
flowing on 285 (2)
flown 190 (4), 667 (4)
flu 651 (5)
fluctuate 29 (3), 141 (6), 152 (5), 317 (5), 318 (5), 601 (4)
fluctuating 141 (4), 152 (4)
fluctuation 152 (1), 265 (1), 317 (2), 350 (2)
flue 263 (10), 353 (1), 383 (1)
flue pipe 414 (5)
fluency 570 (1), 575 (1), 579 (1), 579 (4), 581 (1)
fluent 335 (4), 566 (2), 570 (3), 575 (3), 579 (6), 581 (4)
fluently 581 (6)
fluff 259 (2), 327 (1), 695 (2), 695 (9)
fluff up 63 (4)
fluffy 259 (6), 259 (7)
fluid 49 (2), 152 (2), 152 (4), 244 (2), 327 (2), 335 (2), 335 (4), 337 (3), 339 (1), 339 (2), 341 (1), 341 (4), 350 (7)
fluid mechanics 335 (1)
fluidity 49 (1), 335 (1), 337 (1), 354 (1)

fluidness 152 (1), 335 (1)
fluke 159 (1), 247 (1), 256 (2), 618 (1), 727 (1)
flume 351 (1)
flummox 456 (8), 474 (9)
flummoxed 517 (5)
fluorescence 417 (3)
fluorescent 417 (8), 420 (8)
fluoridation 658 (3)
fluoride 658 (3)
flurry 63 (3), 318 (3), 350 (6), 352 (4), 456 (8), 678 (1), 680 (1)
flush 16 (1), 16 (2), 54 (4), 216 (4), 258 (3), 350 (4), 379 (1), 379 (7), 417 (3), 425 (3), 431 (1), 431 (5), 635 (5), 648 (9), 800 (4), 818 (1), 818 (8), 821 (9)
flush out 648 (9), 648 (10)
flush with anger 891 (6)
flushed 431 (3), 833 (5), 835 (4), 949 (6)
flushed with pride 871 (4)
flushing 431 (3), 648 (2), 818 (3)
flushness 16 (1)
fluster 63 (3), 456 (8)
flustered 318 (4)
flute 262 (3), 407 (1), 407 (5), 413 (9), 414 (6)
fluted 262 (2)
flutist 413 (2)
flutter 265 (4), 271 (7), 317 (1), 317 (4), 317 (6), 318 (1), 318 (5), 318 (6), 352 (10), 411 (1), 618 (2), 680 (1), 821 (9), 854 (2), 854 (9), 887 (15)
flutter down 309 (3)
fluttering 142 (2), 271 (6)
fluvial 350 (7)
flux 337 (1), 337 (2), 350 (2)
fly 111 (3), 114 (6), 265 (4), 271 (7), 272 (6), 273 (12), 277 (6), 296 (5), 308 (4), 318 (6), 323 (4), 365 (16), 620 (6), 678 (11), 837 (21)
fly a kite 461 (8), 528 (9), 529 (8), 671 (4)
fly back 280 (3)

fly down 309 (3)
fly fishing 619 (2)
fly into a rage 818 (8), 891 (6)
fly off 294 (3)
fly open 263 (17)
fly past 875 (7)
fly the flag 547 (22)
fly to arms 718 (10)
flyblown 649 (6), 845 (2)
flyby 271 (3)
flying 49 (2), 114 (3), 209 (8), 271 (1), 271 (6), 276 (5), 837 (6)
flying boat 722 (14)
flying buttress 218 (2), 990 (5)
flying carpet 983 (4)
flying colours 876 (1)
flying column 722 (7)
flying corps 722 (14)
flying fish 365 (15)
flying machine 276 (1)
flying officer 271 (4), 741 (9)
flying saucer 276 (4)
flying start 34 (2), 68 (3), 283 (1)
flying up 308 (1)
flyover 222 (1), 305 (1), 624 (3)
flypaper 47 (9)
flypast 271 (1), 875 (3)
flyweight 722 (2)
flywheel 315 (3)
foal 132 (3), 167 (6), 273 (4)
foaled 360 (3)
foam 170 (7), 227 (1), 302 (4), 318 (7), 341 (1), 355 (1), 355 (5)
foam-flecked 427 (4)
foaming 355 (3)
foamy 323 (3), 355 (3)
fob 194 (11)
fob off 769 (3)
fob off with 542 (8)
focal 225 (3)
focal distance 199 (1)
focal point 76 (1)
fo'c'sle 237 (3)
focus 24 (10), 45 (1), 74 (1), 74 (11), 76 (1), 76 (2),

185 (1), 187 (2), 192 (14), 225 (2), 225 (4), 293 (1), 293 (3), 438 (8), 617 (2), 796 (1)
focus upon 76 (2)
focused 24 (8), 293 (2)
focusing 74 (1), 293 (2)
fodder 301 (8), 366 (6), 370 (1), 631 (1)
foe 705 (1), 881 (2)
foetus 132 (3), 156 (3)
fog 341 (1), 355 (2), 421 (4), 423 (1), 444 (1)
fog over 355 (6)
fogbound 747 (5)
fogginess 419 (1)
foggy 341 (4), 355 (4), 423 (2)
foghorn 665 (1)
fogy 851 (3)
foible 5 (4), 80 (1), 934 (2)
foil 207 (2), 257 (1), 702 (10), 704 (4), 723 (8), 851 (3)
foiled 509 (2), 728 (5)
fold 63 (4), 91 (1), 198 (7), 221 (5), 228 (3), 235 (1), 247 (7), 248 (1), 248 (5), 251 (1), 251 (11), 259 (1), 259 (9), 260 (3), 261 (1), 261 (3), 262 (3), 315 (5)
fold up 145 (6), 198 (7), 261 (3), 632 (5)
folded 251 (4), 261 (2), 262 (2)
folder 62 (2), 194 (1), 632 (3)
folds of flesh 195 (3)
foliage 53 (4), 366 (5), 434 (1)
foliate 86 (11), 207 (4)
foliated 207 (4)
folk 371 (4), 412 (1)
folk dance 837 (14)
folk singer 413 (4)
folk song 412 (5)
folk tale 590 (2)
folk wisdom 490 (1)
folklore 127 (3), 490 (1), 970 (1)
follicle 194 (4)
follow 65 (3), 89 (4), 154 (6), 200 (5), 238 (5), 267

(14), 284 (4), 441 (3), 475 (9), 478 (5), 516 (5), 619 (5), 739 (4), 742 (8), 768 (3)
follow a calling 622 (9)
follow a sect 978 (8)
follow after 120 (3), 284 (4)
follow close 200 (5)
follow hard on 289 (4)
follow on 157 (5), 284 (4)
follow one's bent 744 (9)
follow one's conscience 933 (4)
follow precedent 20 (7)
follow routine 16 (3), 60 (4)
follow suit 20 (7), 83 (7)
follow that 89 (4)
follow the crowd 83 (7)
follow the fashion 848 (7)
follow the scent 619 (5)
follow the sea 269 (8)
follow the trail 459 (15)
follow through 146 (4), 725 (5)
follow-up 67 (1), 146 (4), 619 (1), 619 (5), 725 (5)
follower 35 (2), 67 (2), 83 (3), 89 (2), 284 (2), 488 (3), 538 (1), 707 (1), 742 (3), 742 (4), 978 (4), 981 (8)
followers 284 (2), 441 (2)
following 20 (1), 20 (4), 65 (1), 65 (2), 65 (5), 67 (2), 74 (4), 83 (4), 120 (1), 120 (2), 265 (1), 284 (1), 284 (2), 284 (3), 619 (1), 619 (4)
following wind 287 (3), 352 (1), 703 (1)
folly 194 (23), 491 (1), 497 (1), 499 (2), 542 (1), 833 (2), 857 (1)
foment 176 (9), 658 (20), 703 (5), 821 (7)
fomentation 658 (9)
fomenter 156 (2)
fond 499 (4), 887 (9)
fond hope 852 (2)
fond look 889 (2)
fond of 859 (7), 887 (9)

fond of, be 887 (13)
fondle 378 (7), 887 (13), 889 (6)
fondling 889 (1)
fondness 859 (3), 887 (1)
font 990 (4)
food 301 (9), 631 (1), 633 (1), 685 (1)
food and drink 301 (9)
food chain 71 (1), 301 (1)
food content 301 (10)
food plant 366 (6)
food poisoning 651 (7), 659 (4)
food preparation 301 (5)
food processing 301 (5)
food supply 633 (1)
food web 301 (1)
foodstuff 301 (7)
foodstuffs 301 (9)
fool 301 (17), 501 (1), 542 (9), 544 (1), 594 (10), 697 (1), 839 (3), 839 (5), 851 (3), 851 (5)
fool about 497 (4), 837 (21)
fool with 695 (9)
foolery 497 (2), 499 (2), 604 (2), 837 (3), 839 (1), 851 (1)
foolhardiness 857 (1)
foolhardy 499 (5), 857 (3)
fooling about 497 (2)
foolish 163 (4), 448 (2), 481 (6), 487 (2), 497 (3), 499 (4), 503 (8), 544 (2), 639 (6), 849 (2)
foolish, be 497 (4), 499 (6), 503 (10), 515 (6)
foolishness 497 (1), 499 (2)
foolproof 473 (4), 701 (3), 727 (4)
fool's errand 641 (2)
fool's paradise 4 (2), 481 (1), 509 (1)
foolscap 586 (4), 631 (3)
foot 69 (2), 203 (4), 210 (1), 214 (1), 214 (2), 378 (4), 722 (9)
foot and mouth disease 651 (7)
foot it 312 (4)
foot pace 278 (1)

foot passenger 268 (3)
foot-pound 160 (3)
foot regiment 722 (9)
foot-slogger 268 (3)
foot-slogging 267 (3)
foot soldier 722 (9)
foot the bill 804 (5)
footage 199 (1), 203 (1)
football 194 (2), 837 (7)
football pools 618 (2)
footballer 837 (16)
footed 214 (4)
footfall 265 (2)
foothill 209 (2), 254 (2)
foothills 68 (5)
foothold 218 (1), 218 (4),
778 (1)
footing 7 (1), 8 (1), 27 (1),
73 (1), 178 (1), 214 (1),
218 (1), 218 (4)
footing it 267 (3)
footings 218 (4)
footlights 420 (5), 594 (7)
footlights, the 594 (1)
footling 639 (6)
footloose 267 (9), 282 (2),
744 (5)
footman 742 (2)
footnote 520 (2)
footpad 789 (2)
footpath 624 (5)
footplate 218 (5)
footprint 547 (2), 547 (13),
548 (4)
footrest 218 (2)
footrule 465 (5)
footsore 684 (2)
footstep 548 (4)
footwear 228 (27)
footwork 265 (1)
fop 848 (4), 850 (3), 873 (3)
foppish 848 (5), 850 (4)
foppishness 228 (1), 848
(1), 850 (1)
for 158 (5), 617 (7), 755 (4)
for a lifetime 110 (5)
for a long time 113 (10)
for a purpose 617 (7)
for a song 812 (7)
for a term 110 (5)
for a time 108 (10), 114 (7)
for ages 113 (10)
for all one is worth 682 (8)

for all that 31 (7), 468 (5)
for all time 113 (10)
for aye 115 (5)
for better for worse 115
(5)
for effect 850 (4)
for ever 115 (5)
for ever and ever 115 (5)
for everybody 79 (3)
for example 83 (10)
for form's sake 83 (10)
for good 69 (7), 108 (10),
113 (10), 144 (4)
for instance 83 (10)
for keeps 115 (5)
for long 113 (10)
for nothing 781 (6), 812 (4)
for one's pains 962 (5)
for private ends 932 (5)
for profit 791 (3)
for sale 759 (2), 779 (3)
for show 875 (4)
for starters 68 (11)
for strings 412 (7)
for the asking 812 (4)
for the best 615 (6)
for the moment 114 (7)
for the nonce 121 (4)
for the occasion 121 (2)
for the present 112 (1),
114 (7)
for the time being 114 (7),
121 (4)
for want of 190 (8), 636
(10)
for years 113 (10)
forage 301 (8), 459 (15),
633 (5), 788 (7), 788 (9)
foray 712 (1), 788 (2), 788
(9)
forbear 169 (3), 620 (5),
674 (4), 736 (3), 823 (6),
905 (7), 942 (4)
forbearance 620 (1), 674
(1), 736 (1), 823 (2), 909
(1), 942 (1)
forbearing 736 (2), 823
(4), 905 (4), 909 (2), 942
(3)
forbid 757 (4)
forbid by law 954 (9)
forbidden 757 (3)

forbidden fruit 612 (4),
757 (1), 859 (5), 951 (3)
forbidding 757 (2), 834
(7), 834 (8), 842 (3), 883
(5)
force 63 (3), 74 (4), 83 (8),
156 (2), 160 (1), 160 (3),
160 (10), 162 (1), 173 (1),
174 (1), 174 (7), 176 (1),
176 (8), 178 (1), 178 (3),
279 (3), 285 (4), 297 (7),
350 (1), 514 (1), 596 (1),
612 (8), 669 (12), 675 (1),
675 (2), 676 (1), 682 (1),
686 (4), 740 (1), 740 (3)
force a passage 305 (5)
force apart 46 (10), 46
(13)
force-feed 740 (3)
force-feeding 301 (1), 740
(1)
force in 231 (8)
force of argument 475 (1)
force of gravity 160 (3),
291 (1), 322 (1)
force of habit 610 (1)
force of law 596 (1)
force one's hand 740 (3)
force one's way 682 (6)
force oneself 598 (4)
force open 46 (10), 176
(8), 263 (17)
force out 304 (4)
force to resign 734 (7)
force to withdraw 479 (3)
force upon 740 (3)
forced 10 (4), 576 (2), 598
(3), 670 (4)
forced, be 596 (7), 606 (4)
forced entry 297 (1)
forced labour 598 (2), 682
(3), 740 (1), 745 (2)
forced landing 271 (1)
forced march 267 (4)
forceful 162 (6), 174 (5),
174 (6), 516 (3), 532 (4),
566 (2), 571 (2), 579 (7),
599 (2), 678 (7), 740 (2),
821 (5)
forcefully 571 (3)
forcefulness 571 (1)
forcemeat 301 (16)
forceps 304 (2), 778 (2)

forceps delivery 167 (2), 304 (1)

forces 722 (7)

forcible 160 (8), 176 (5), 571 (2), 740 (2)

forcible demand 761 (1)

forcible seizure 786 (2)

forcibly 174 (9), 176 (10), 740 (4)

ford 212 (1), 305 (5), 341 (6)

fore 119 (2), 237 (1), 237 (4)

fore and aft 54 (9), 203 (9)

forearmed 664 (4)

forebear 66 (1)

forebode 511 (8), 547 (18)

foreboding 510 (1), 511 (1), 511 (6), 661 (3), 664 (1), 900 (2)

forecast 124 (3), 155 (1), 155 (2), 507 (1), 507 (4), 510 (3), 511 (1), 511 (8), 623 (2)

forecaster 511 (4)

forecastle 237 (3)

foreclose 786 (10)

foreclosure 786 (2), 803 (1)

forecourt 237 (1)

forefather 169 (3)

forefinger 254 (2), 378 (4)

forefoot 214 (2)

forefront 68 (1), 237 (1)

forego 779 (4)

foregoing 64 (2), 119 (2), 125 (8)

foregone conclusion 473 (1), 608 (1)

foreground 200 (1), 237 (1)

forehead 213 (3), 237 (2)

foreign 6 (2), 10 (3), 59 (4), 223 (2), 560 (4), 883 (5)

foreign accent 577 (2)

foreign body 25 (3), 59 (1)

foreign-made 59 (4)

foreign parts 59 (1), 199 (2)

foreign rule 733 (2)

foreign tongue 517 (1)

foreigner 59 (2), 191 (1), 191 (3), 191 (4), 297 (3), 298 (1), 883 (4)

foreignness 59 (1)

foreknow 510 (3)

foreknowledge 510 (1)

foreland 254 (2)

foreleg 267 (7)

forelimb 53 (2)

forelock 237 (1), 259 (2)

foreman or -woman 690 (3)

foreman or -woman of the jury 957 (3)

foremast 237 (3)

foremost 34 (5), 68 (7), 283 (2), 638 (5)

forename 561 (2)

forenoon 128 (1)

forensic pathologist 658 (14)

forensic pathology 651 (19)

foreordain 155 (4), 608 (3)

foreordained 608 (2)

forepart 237 (1)

forerunner 66 (1), 237 (1), 529 (5)

foresaken 883 (6)

foresee 124 (6), 438 (7), 498 (6), 507 (4), 510 (3)

foreseeable 124 (4), 471 (2), 507 (3)

foreseeing 449 (5), 457 (4), 498 (4), 507 (2), 510 (2), 511 (6)

foreseen 471 (2), 507 (3), 865 (3)

foreshadow 119 (3), 155 (4), 511 (8)

foreshortened 204 (3)

foresight 119 (1), 135 (3), 449 (1), 457 (1), 490 (1), 498 (2), 510 (1), 511 (1), 669 (1), 858 (1)

foresighted 510 (2)

forest 104 (1), 324 (3), 366 (2), 366 (12)

forestall 57 (5), 119 (4), 124 (6), 135 (5), 542 (8)

forestalling 135 (3)

forested 366 (10)

forester 366 (3)

forestry 366 (3), 370 (1)

foretaste 53 (1), 66 (1), 119 (1), 507 (1)

foretell 511 (8)

foretelling 511 (6)

forethought 449 (1), 457 (1), 498 (2), 510 (1), 623 (2), 669 (1), 858 (1)

forewarn 510 (3), 511 (8), 664 (5), 900 (3)

forewarned 507 (2), 664 (4), 669 (7)

forewarning 64 (2), 66 (1), 510 (1), 511 (1), 511 (3)

foreword 66 (2)

forfeit 37 (5), 42 (1), 621 (3), 769 (3), 772 (3), 772 (4), 916 (6), 916 (9)

forfeited 772 (3), 916 (6)

forfeiting 772 (2)

forfeits 837 (3)

forfeiture 769 (1), 772 (1), 916 (3), 963 (4)

forgather 74 (10)

forgathering 45 (1), 74 (2)

forge 20 (6), 164 (7), 243 (5), 383 (1), 541 (8), 687 (1), 797 (10)

forge ahead 237 (5), 285 (3)

forged note 797 (6)

forger 20 (3), 545 (1), 789 (3), 797 (8), 904 (3)

forgery 20 (1), 541 (1), 542 (5), 797 (6)

forget 456 (7), 491 (8), 506 (5), 695 (7), 719 (5), 909 (4), 918 (3), 919 (3)

forget-me-not 435 (1)

forget one's lines 506 (5), 594 (17)

forget one's manners 885 (6)

forget one's words 695 (7)

forget oneself 891 (6)

forget to thank 908 (4)

forgetful 456 (3), 458 (2), 506 (4), 908 (2)

forgetful, be 506 (5)

forgetfulness 458 (1), 506 (1), 918 (1)

forgetting 506 (4)

forgivable **639** (6), **909** (3), **927** (4), **935** (4)

forgive **458** (5), **506** (5), **736** (3), **746** (3), **872** (5), **897** (5), **905** (6), **905** (7), **909** (4), **919** (3), **960** (3)

forgive and forget **719** (5)

forgiven **506** (3), **909** (3), **960** (2)

forgiveness **506** (2), **719** (2), **736** (1), **746** (1), **897** (1), **905** (3), **909** (1), **919** (1), **960** (1)

forgiving **506** (4), **736** (2), **897** (4), **905** (4), **909** (2)

forgo **621** (3)

forgotten **506** (3), **908** (3)

forgotten, be **506** (6)

fork **92** (2), **92** (6), **247** (1), **247** (7), **256** (2), **294** (1), **294** (3), **370** (6)

fork-bending **984** (2)

fork in **301** (35)

fork out **804** (4)

forked **92** (4), **247** (5)

forked lightning **420** (1)

forking **92** (2)

forklift **310** (2)

forlorn **731** (6), **834** (6), **853** (2), **883** (6)

forlorn hope **472** (1)

form **7** (2), **18** (1), **23** (3), **56** (3), **62** (4), **77** (2), **81** (2), **83** (1), **83** (8), **143** (6), **147** (7), **164** (7), **192** (3), **194** (1), **218** (6), **233** (1), **243** (1), **243** (5), **331** (1), **445** (1), **445** (6), **534** (6), **538** (4), **548** (1), **551** (8), **554** (3), **623** (8), **624** (1), **693** (1), **841** (1), **875** (2)

form a government **733** (11)

form a head **355** (5)

form a plan **623** (8)

form an estimate **480** (6)

form an opinion **465** (13)

form ideas **449** (7)

form letters **558** (6)

formal **7** (3), **83** (6), **243** (4), **245** (2), **278** (3), **532** (3), **576** (2), **848** (6), **850** (4), **875** (6), **884** (3), **988** (8)

formal dress **228** (4), **875** (2)

formal occasion **875** (2), **876** (1)

formalism **83** (1), **988** (2)

formalist **83** (3), **735** (3), **988** (6)

formalistic **735** (4), **979** (7)

formality **228** (4), **265** (2), **848** (2), **850** (2), **870** (1), **875** (2), **876** (1), **884** (1), **953** (1), **988** (1)

format **243** (1)

formation **56** (1), **74** (3), **74** (4), **164** (1), **243** (1), **243** (2), **551** (3), **554** (1), **722** (8)

formation flying **271** (1)

formative **7** (3), **156** (7), **164** (5), **243** (4)

formed **164** (6), **192** (20), **243** (3), **817** (2)

former **64** (2), **119** (2), **125** (7), **753** (2)

former students **538** (3)

former times **125** (1)

formerly **113** (12), **119** (5), **125** (12), **127** (9)

formication **378** (2), **651** (12)

formidable **638** (6), **700** (4), **854** (8)

forming **164** (1), **243** (2)

formless **244** (2)

formula **81** (1), **85** (1), **496** (1), **496** (2), **563** (1), **623** (2), **658** (1), **693** (1), **766** (1), **770** (1)

formulate **62** (4), **243** (5), **522** (7), **532** (5), **563** (3), **586** (8)

formulated faith **976** (1)

formulation **62** (1), **243** (2), **532** (1)

fornicate **951** (10)

fornication **951** (2)

fornicator **952** (1)

forsake **603** (5), **621** (3)

forsaken **621** (2)

forswear **533** (3), **603** (7)

forswearing **603** (2)

fort **164** (3), **235** (3), **662** (1), **713** (4)

forte **412** (8), **694** (1)

forthcoming **135** (4), **155** (2), **540** (2)

forthright **516** (2), **522** (5), **540** (2)

forthwith **116** (4), **135** (8)

fortification **254** (2), **713** (3), **718** (4)

fortified **162** (6), **713** (8)

fortify **43** (7), **162** (12), **660** (8), **703** (5), **713** (9)

fortifying **162** (5)

fortissimo **400** (1), **400** (3), **400** (5), **412** (8)

fortitude **599** (1), **600** (1), **855** (1), **933** (2)

fortnight **110** (1)

fortnightly **141** (5)

fortress **164** (3), **713** (4)

fortuitous **159** (5), **618** (5)

fortuitously **159** (8)

fortuitousness **159** (1)

fortunate **137** (5), **730** (4), **824** (5)

fortune **152** (2), **159** (1), **511** (1), **596** (2), **800** (1)

fortune-teller **511** (5)

fortune-telling **511** (2), **984** (1)

fortunes **590** (3)

forty **99** (3)

forty thieves **789** (2)

forty winks **679** (4)

forum **539** (5), **584** (3), **724** (1), **956** (1)

forward **135** (4), **237** (4), **272** (8), **285** (5), **285** (6), **498** (4), **588** (4), **597** (4), **642** (3), **654** (9), **837** (16), **878** (5), **885** (4)

forward-looking **285** (2)

forward march **285** (1)

forward motion **265** (1)

forwarding **272** (2)

forwardness **498** (1), **597** (1), **670** (1)

forwards **285** (5)

fossil **41** (1), **125** (3), **127** (2), **127** (5), **358** (1), **363** (1)

fossil footprint 125 (3)
fossil fuel 385 (1)
fossilization 125 (3), 326 (2)
fossilize 127 (8), 326 (5)
fossilized 125 (6), 127 (7), 326 (3)
fossilized remains 125 (3)
foster 11 (7), 156 (10), 457 (6), 534 (8), 654 (9), 703 (6), 756 (5), 821 (7), 889 (5)
foster child 11 (3)
foster-mother 169 (4)
foster parent 150 (2), 749 (1)
fostering 169 (1)
foul 279 (8), 391 (2), 397 (2), 616 (2), 645 (2), 645 (4), 649 (6), 649 (9), 653 (2), 655 (9), 827 (4), 930 (3), 930 (4), 934 (6)
foul air 659 (3)
foul breath 397 (1)
foul-mouthed 885 (5), 899 (4)
foul play 541 (2), 542 (2), 542 (4), 616 (1), 623 (3), 676 (2), 698 (1), 712 (1), 914 (1), 914 (2), 930 (3), 934 (1), 954 (2)
foul up 649 (8)
foul weather 340 (3)
foulness 397 (1), 645 (1)
found 68 (9), 68 (10), 153 (8), 156 (9), 164 (7), 381 (8), 656 (6), 777 (6)
found at, be 186 (4)
found, be 1 (6)
found guilty 936 (3), 961 (2)
found wanting 636 (3), 924 (7)
found wanting, be 728 (7)
found with, be 89 (4)
foundation 66 (2), 68 (1), 156 (3), 214 (1), 218 (4), 669 (1)
foundational 66 (3), 68 (6), 156 (8)
foundations 153 (2), 214 (1)
founded on 214 (3)

founder 156 (2), 164 (4), 211 (3), 313 (4), 623 (5), 707 (4), 728 (7), 903 (1)
foundered 165 (5)
foundering 309 (2)
foundling 779 (2)
foundry 147 (3), 687 (1)
fount 68 (4), 156 (3), 587 (3)
fountain 156 (3), 298 (2), 308 (2), 350 (1)
four 96 (1), 96 (2)
four and twenty 99 (3)
four elements, the 319 (4)
four-in-hand 96 (1)
four-letter word 559 (1), 573 (1)
four-poster 218 (7)
four score 99 (3)
four-sided 247 (6)
four times 97 (4)
fourfold 97 (2)
foursome 96 (1)
foursquare 96 (2), 153 (6), 247 (6)
fourth 98 (1)
fourth dimension 108 (1)
fourth estate 528 (4)
fourth part 98 (1)
fourthly 97 (4)
fowl 365 (4), 365 (6)
fowl pest 651 (17)
fowler 619 (3)
fowling 619 (2)
fox 365 (3), 545 (4), 698 (3)
fox hole 263 (8)
fox hunt 619 (2)
fox hunter 619 (3)
foxed 845 (2)
foxglove 436 (1)
foxhole 662 (1)
foxhound 365 (10), 619 (3)
foxhunter 273 (5)
foxiness 698 (1)
foxtrot 837 (14)
foxy 365 (18), 397 (2), 430 (3), 498 (4), 698 (4)
foyer 194 (20), 594 (7)
fracas 61 (4), 709 (3), 716 (7)
fraction 26 (1), 33 (2), 53 (1), 85 (2), 102 (1), 639 (2)

fractional 53 (6), 85 (5), 102 (2)
fractional part 102 (1)
fractionate 46 (10)
fractious 598 (1), 892 (3)
fractiousness 598 (1)
fracture 46 (2), 46 (13), 72 (1), 201 (2), 330 (3), 655 (4)
fragile 4 (3), 163 (8), 330 (2), 330 (3), 330 (4)
fragility 114 (1), 163 (1), 330 (1)
fragment 33 (2), 33 (3), 46 (10), 46 (13), 53 (5), 53 (7), 102 (1), 330 (3)
fragmentary 53 (6), 55 (3), 102 (2), 196 (10), 647 (3), 726 (2)
fragmentation 46 (2), 332 (1)
fragmentation bomb 723 (14)
fragrance 394 (1), 396 (1)
fragrant 376 (3), 394 (2), 396 (3)
fragrant, be 396 (4)
frail 114 (4), 163 (8), 194 (6), 330 (2), 661 (4), 934 (5), 951 (7)
frailness 161 (1), 163 (1)
frailty 114 (1), 163 (1), 934 (2)
frame 7 (2), 23 (3), 77 (2), 164 (7), 194 (1), 194 (6), 214 (1), 218 (13), 218 (15), 232 (3), 233 (1), 233 (3), 234 (3), 235 (1), 235 (4), 243 (1), 243 (5), 303 (4), 319 (2), 331 (1), 370 (3), 541 (8), 551 (4), 608 (3), 623 (8), 623 (9), 928 (9)
frame a question 459 (14)
frame of mind 7 (1), 817 (1)
frame of reference 9 (4)
frame-up 542 (4), 608 (1), 623 (4), 928 (7)
framed 232 (2), 233 (2), 542 (6), 543 (4), 608 (2), 817 (2)
framework 218 (13), 233 (1), 331 (1)

framing 218 (14), **230** (2), **232** (1)

franc-tireur 722 (4)

franchise 605 (2), **744** (1), **915** (1)

francophone 579 (6)

Franglais 560 (2)

frank 522 (5), 699 (3), **885** (5), **929** (4)

frankfurter 301 (16)

frankly 540 (4)

frankness 494 (1), **540** (1), **573** (1), **699** (1)

frantic 61 (9), 176 (6), **503** (9), **678** (7), **821** (3), **822** (3)

frantically 32 (18)

frappe 301 (27), 382 (4)

fraternal 11 (5), **708** (6), **880** (6)

fraternal twin 11 (2)

fraternity 11 (3), **706** (1), **706** (2), **708** (4)

fraternize 710 (3), 880 (7)

fratricide 362 (2)

Frau 373 (4)

fraud 541 (2), 542 (2), **545** (3), **698** (3), **788** (4)

fraudulence 542 (1)

fraudulent 541 (3), **542** (6), **788** (6), **930** (4), **930** (7), **954** (6)

Fraulein 373 (4)

fray 46 (12), 333 (3), **655** (9), **682** (1), **716** (7)

fray, the 678 (1)

frayed 655 (6)

freak 15 (3), 25 (3), 84 (3), **504** (2), **504** (3), **864** (3), **949** (4)

freak out 84 (8), 949 (15)

freakish 84 (5), 84 (7)

freakishness 84 (1)

freckle 437 (4), 845 (1)

freckled 437 (8), 845 (2)

free 46 (4), 46 (8), 49 (2), **49** (3), **304** (4), **495** (6), **520** (6), **522** (5), **540** (2), **595** (1), **597** (5), **667** (4), **668** (3), **674** (2), **701** (9), **744** (5), **746** (3), **779** (4), **781** (6), **812** (4), **812** (5), **813** (3)

free agent 744 (4)

free-and-easy 734 (3), **744** (5)

free as air 744 (5)

free, be 84 (8), 595 (2), **744** (9), **895** (5)

free choice 595 (0), **597** (1)

free consent 758 (1)

free enterprise 744 (3), **791** (2)

free entry 812 (2)

free expression 746 (1)

free fall 271 (1)

free for all 61 (4), 716 (2), **716** (7), **734** (2), **744** (3), **744** (5), **744** (8)

free from 44 (5)

free from blame 923 (7)

free from guilt 935 (4)

free from pride 874 (2)

free from rain 342 (4)

free from sin 935 (3)

free hand 701 (1), 744 (3), **756** (2), **813** (1)

free-handed 813 (3)

free love 894 (2), 951 (3)

free market 744 (3)

free-minded 744 (7)

free of charge 812 (4)

free oneself 46 (7), 746 (4)

free pardon 506 (2), **909** (1)

free person 744 (4)

free play 744 (3)

free quarters 812 (2)

free range 369 (2), 744 (6)

free school 539 (2)

free souled 744 (7)

free-speaking 579 (6), 744 (5)

free speech 744 (1)

free-spending 813 (3)

free-spoken 699 (3)

free thought 744 (1), **974** (2)

free time 681 (1)

free to choose 744 (7)

free trade 744 (3), 791 (2), **812** (2)

free trade area 708 (3), **796** (1)

free-trader 744 (4)

free translation 520 (3)

free verse 593 (4)

free will 595 (0), 744 (1)

free world 733 (6)

freebooter 722 (3), 789 (2)

freeborn 744 (5)

freed 744 (5), 746 (2)

freedom 137 (2), 744 (1), **756** (1), **915** (1)

freedom fighter 722 (4)

freedom from mixture 44 (1)

freedom of action 744 (1), **744** (2)

freedom of choice 137 (2), **605** (1), **744** (2)

freehold 777 (3), 777 (5)

freeholder 776 (1)

freeing 46 (2)

freelance 589 (7), 622 (5), **686** (2), **744** (4), **744** (7)

freeloader 679 (6), 879 (2)

freely 744 (11)

freeman 744 (4)

Freemasonry 525 (2), 706 (1)

freethinker 744 (4), **974** (3)

freethinking 744 (5), 974 (5)

freewheel 258 (5), 267 (11), 267 (15), 458 (6), 677 (3), 701 (7)

freewheeling 744 (6)

freewheeler 679 (6)

freeze 145 (3), 266 (1), 266 (8), 324 (6), 326 (5), 375 (6), 380 (2), 380 (7), 382 (0), 666 (5), 747 (2), 805 (1), 805 (5), 854 (12)

freeze-dried 382 (4)

freeze-dry 342 (6), 382 (6)

freeze one's blood 854 (12)

freezer 301 (7), 384 (1), 666 (2)

freezing 198 (1), 324 (5), 380 (5), 382 (1)

freezing cold 380 (1)

freezing point 380 (1)

freezing up 382 (1)

freight 54 (7), 193 (1), 193 (2), 272 (3), 795 (1)

freight train 274 (13)
freighted 273 (10)
freighter 273 (1), 275 (3), 276 (1)
freightliner 274 (13)
French cricket 837 (7)
French fries 301 (20)
French horn 414 (7)
French leave 190 (1)
frenetic 503 (9)
frenzied 61 (9), 176 (6), 503 (9), 515 (4), 678 (7), 818 (5), 821 (3), 822 (3), 891 (4)
frenziedly 821 (10)
frenzy 61 (4), 176 (1), 318 (2), 318 (3), 503 (4), 513 (3), 515 (1), 651 (2), 678 (2), 821 (1), 822 (2), 983 (2)
frequency 27 (1), 139 (1), 141 (1), 160 (5)
frequency band 317 (1)
frequent 104 (5), 106 (3), 139 (2), 139 (3), 189 (4), 610 (6), 610 (7)
frequent change 143 (1)
frequenter 882 (5)
frequenting 139 (1), 139 (2)
frequently 106 (7), 139 (4)
fresco 553 (5)
fresco painting 553 (2)
fresh 15 (4), 21 (3), 113 (4), 126 (5), 126 (9), 312 (3), 340 (5), 341 (4), 352 (8), 380 (5), 390 (2), 505 (5), 611 (3), 648 (7), 652 (4), 878 (5)
fresh advance 727 (1)
fresh air 340 (1), 652 (1)
fresh-air fiend 652 (3)
fresh blood 67 (3)
fresh breeze 352 (3)
fresh-faced 841 (6)
fresh fish 301 (15)
fresh fruit 301 (17)
fresh spurt 656 (3)
fresh start 68 (3)
fresh troops 707 (1)
fresh water 339 (1)
fresh-water lake 346 (1)

freshen 174 (8), 340 (6), 352 (10), 648 (10), 652 (6), 656 (10), 685 (4), 844 (12)
freshen up 685 (4)
freshened up 126 (7), 685 (3)
fresher 538 (3)
freshet 350 (1)
freshly 126 (9)
freshness 21 (1), 126 (1), 130 (1), 380 (1), 648 (1)
fret 408 (3), 414 (2), 678 (2), 738 (9), 822 (4), 825 (7), 844 (12), 891 (7), 891 (9)
fretful 604 (3), 678 (7), 829 (3), 836 (4), 892 (3)
fretfulness 604 (1)
fretting 825 (3), 844 (2)
fretwork 222 (3)
Freudian slip 565 (1)
friability 49 (1), 330 (1), 332 (1)
friable 163 (8), 330 (2), 332 (4)
friar 986 (5)
friary 986 (9)
friction 182 (1), 279 (3), 332 (1), 333 (1), 378 (1), 702 (1), 704 (1), 709 (1), 827 (1)
frictional 333 (2)
frictionless 258 (3), 701 (3), 710 (2), 826 (2)
Friday 946 (2)
fridge 384 (1)
friend 89 (2), 707 (1), 707 (3), 880 (3), 882 (1), 882 (5), 897 (3), 903 (1), 976 (5)
friend at court 178 (1), 523 (1), 707 (4)
friend in need 703 (3), 707 (1), 880 (3)
friendless 46 (5), 88 (4), 161 (6), 883 (6)
friendliness 706 (1), 719 (2), 818 (1), 880 (2), 882 (2), 884 (2), 897 (1)
friendly 488 (4), 703 (4), 708 (6), 710 (2), 719 (3), 880 (6), 882 (6), 884 (4), 897 (4)

friendly, be 710 (3), 880 (7), 882 (8), 909 (4)
friendly relations 880 (1)
friendly society 708 (3)
friendly terms 9 (1)
friendly understanding 880 (2)
friendly with 880 (6)
friends with, be 880 (7)
friendship 9 (1), 74 (4), 89 (1), 710 (1), 880 (1), 882 (1), 882 (4), 887 (1), 897 (1)
frieze 844 (2), 844 (5)
frigate 275 (5), 722 (13)
fright 842 (2), 854 (1)
frighten 161 (10), 163 (10), 613 (3), 665 (3), 702 (8), 727 (10), 735 (8), 827 (11), 834 (12), 854 (12), 864 (7), 900 (3)
frighten away 613 (3)
frighten off 854 (12)
frighten to death 854 (12)
frightened 854 (6), 854 (9)
frightened to death 854 (6)
frightening 32 (7), 507 (3), 508 (2), 661 (3), 664 (3), 827 (6), 854 (8), 864 (5), 900 (2), 970 (7)
frighteningly 32 (20)
frightful 32 (7), 842 (3), 854 (8)
frightfully 32 (18)
frigid 820 (3), 823 (3), 881 (3)
frigidity 380 (1), 820 (1), 950 (1)
frill 234 (3), 259 (3), 261 (1), 261 (3), 844 (5)
frills 40 (1), 574 (1), 637 (2)
fringe 40 (1), 69 (2), 208 (1), 234 (1), 234 (3), 234 (5), 259 (2), 843 (2), 844 (5)
fringe benefits 771 (2)
fringed 259 (5)
frippery 228 (2), 639 (3), 875 (1)
frisk 312 (4), 459 (15), 833 (7), 835 (6), 837 (21)·

frisking **459** (5)
frisky **312** (3), **678** (7), **833** (4)
frisson **318** (1)
fritter away **37** (4), **634** (4), **675** (2), **815** (4)
fritter away time **108** (8)
frittering away **634** (1)
frivolity **499** (2), **833** (2)
frivolous **456** (6), **499** (4), **604** (3), **639** (6), **833** (4)
frizz **251** (11), **261** (3)
frizzle **379** (7)
frizzy **251** (7), **259** (5)
frock **228** (8)
frock coat **228** (20)
frog **47** (5), **312** (2), **365** (12)
frogman **211** (1), **313** (2)
frogmarch **279** (7)
frogspawn **365** (12)
frolic **312** (1), **824** (3), **833** (7), **835** (6), **837** (3), **837** (21)
frolicsome **833** (4)
from bad to worse **731** (8), **832** (4)
from end to end **54** (9)
from first to last **54** (9)
from hand to hand **272** (9)
from its birth **68** (11)
from memory **505** (12)
from now on **124** (8)
from outer space **59** (5)
from outside **6** (5), **59** (4)
from personal motives **932** (5)
from pole to pole **183** (8)
from scratch **68** (11)
from side to side **317** (7)
from that angle **8** (4)
from that moment **120** (4)
from the beginnings **68** (11)
from the bottom of one's heart **818** (9)
from the start **120** (4)
from time to time **139** (6)
from top to bottom **54** (9)
from top to toe **54** (9)
frond **366** (5)
front **64** (1), **64** (4), **66** (2), **68** (1), **68** (7), **223** (1), **234**

(1), **237** (1), **237** (4), **237** (5), **283** (1), **445** (1), **541** (2), **718** (7), **724** (2)
front door **263** (6)
front elevation **237** (2)
front line **237** (1), **718** (7), **722** (7), **724** (2)
front man **545** (3)
front of house **594** (7)
front-page **638** (6)
front position **64** (1)
front-rank **34** (5), **237** (1)
front runner **716** (8)
front stage **594** (6)
front view **237** (2)
frontage **186** (1), **237** (2), **240** (1)
frontal **68** (7), **237** (4), **240** (2), **704** (3)
frontier **68** (5), **69** (2), **199** (2), **202** (1), **231** (2), **234** (1), **236** (1), **236** (2)
fronting **240** (2), **704** (3)
frontispiece **66** (2), **237** (1)
frost **380** (2), **423** (1), **423** (3), **427** (6), **659** (2)
frostbite **380** (1)
frostbitten **380** (6)
frosted **259** (4), **382** (4), **423** (2), **424** (2), **427** (4)
frosted glass **424** (1)
frostiness **380** (1)
frosting **226** (1), **332** (1)
frosty **380** (5), **427** (4), **883** (5)
froth **302** (4), **318** (7), **341** (1), **355** (1), **355** (5)
frothy **323** (3), **355** (3)
frou-frou **401** (1)
frown **246** (5), **261** (1), **547** (4), **547** (21), **829** (1), **885** (2), **885** (6), **891** (7), **893** (1), **893** (3)
frown on **757** (4)
frowned on **757** (3)
frowning **731** (4), **834** (7), **891** (4)
frowst **397** (1)
frowsty **397** (2)
frozen **153** (6), **266** (6), **324** (4), **326** (4), **375** (3), **380** (6), **382** (4), **666** (4)

frozen assets **777** (2), **803** (1)
fructify **171** (6)
frugal **814** (2), **942** (3)
frugality **814** (1), **942** (1), **945** (1)
frugally **814** (4), **945** (5)
fruit **157** (2), **164** (2), **167** (6), **301** (19), **366** (6), **366** (7)
fruit farm **370** (2)
fruit grower **370** (4), **370** (5)
fruit juice **301** (27)
fruit machine **618** (2)
fruit tree **366** (4)
fruitful **164** (5), **171** (4), **727** (4), **771** (5)
fruitful, be **36** (4), **104** (6), **167** (6), **171** (6), **635** (7), **637** (5), **640** (4), **730** (6)
fruiting **669** (8)
fruition **167** (1), **669** (3), **725** (1)
fruitless **172** (4), **634** (3), **641** (5), **728** (4)
fruitlessness **172** (1)
fruity **386** (2), **396** (3), **404** (2), **579** (6), **951** (6)
frump **842** (2), **847** (1)
frumpish **840** (2), **842** (3), **847** (5)
frumpishness **847** (1)
frumpy **842** (3)
frustrate **509** (5), **702** (10)
frustrated **509** (2), **829** (3)
frustrating **829** (4)
frustration **503** (2), **509** (1), **702** (1), **728** (1)
fry **132** (3), **301** (40), **379** (7), **381** (8)
fry-up **301** (13)
frying pan **194** (14)
fuchsia **431** (3), **436** (2)
fuddle **949** (16)
fuddled **499** (4)
fuddy-duddy **127** (2)
fudge **392** (2), **518** (3), **541** (6)
fudge the issue **620** (5)
fuel **125** (3), **160** (4), **336** (2), **357** (2), **381** (9), **383**

(2), 385 (1), 385 (6), 631
(1), 632 (5), 821 (7)
fug 397 (1)
fuggy 264 (5), 397 (2)
fugitive 114 (3), 268 (2),
620 (2), 620 (3), 667 (3),
667 (4)
fugue 412 (4)
Führer 690 (2), 741 (2)
fulcrum 218 (11)
fulfil 676 (5), 725 (6), 768
(3)
fulfil one's duty 917 (10)
fulfilled 540 (2)
fulfilment 54 (1), 635 (1),
725 (1), 768 (1), 824 (3)
full 45 (7), 52 (4), 54 (3),
54 (4), 74 (9), 104 (5), 195
(8), 205 (3), 324 (4), 540
(2), 590 (6), 635 (5), 637
(3), 725 (4)
full blast 400 (1), 400 (5)
full-blooded 174 (5)
full-blown 54 (3), 134 (3),
197 (3), 725 (4)
full-bodied 386 (2), 394 (2)
full career 277 (3)
full chorus 400 (1)
full circle 149 (1), 314 (1),
315 (1), 626 (1)
full consent 758 (1)
full dress 228 (4), 875 (2),
875 (6)
full-faced 195 (8)
full-fed 947 (3)
full-fledged 54 (3), 134
(3), 669 (8)
full frontal 237 (4)
full-grown 54 (3), 134 (3),
197 (3), 669 (8)
full house 54 (3), 74 (5),
594 (14)
full-length 52 (7), 54 (2),
203 (1), 203 (5)
full-lipped 205 (4)
full load 32 (2), 54 (2)
full measure 54 (2)
full moon 321 (9)
full observance 768 (1)
full of 54 (4)
full of faults 495 (6)
full of feeling 818 (3)
full of fight 855 (4)

full of fun 837 (18)
full of grace 979 (6)
full of hate 888 (4)
full of holes 255 (6), 263
(14)
full of honours 866 (8)
full of incident 154 (5)
full of oneself 873 (4)
full of pep 174 (5)
full of pride 871 (4)
full of promise 852 (5)
full of punch 174 (5)
full of ruses 698 (4)
full of spirit 855 (4)
full of spite 898 (4)
full of surprises 508 (2)
full of tricks 833 (4)
full out 54 (8)
full play 701 (1), 744 (3)
full pressure 160 (2)
full satisfaction 804 (1)
full-scale 32 (5), 54 (3)
full-size 32 (4), 54 (2), 195
(1)
full speed 277 (1), 277 (3)
full speed ahead 277 (9)
full steam 277 (1)
full steam ahead 174 (9)
full stop 547 (14)
full-throated 400 (3), 408
(2), 409 (2)
full-time job 622 (3)
full-toned 410 (6)
full up 301 (31)
fullness 32 (1), 54 (2), 205
(1), 635 (2), 725 (1), 863
(1)
fully 32 (17), 52 (8), 54 (8)
fully developed 134 (3)
fully fashioned 228 (30)
fully furnished 54 (3)
fully trained 669 (7)
fulminate 176 (7), 532 (7),
891 (7), 899 (6), 924 (10)
fulmination 899 (1), 900
(1)
fulsome 546 (2), 847 (4),
850 (4), 923 (5), 925 (3)
fumble 378 (7), 461 (8),
695 (9)
fumbler 697 (1), 728 (1)
fumbling 695 (5)

fume 176 (7), 338 (4), 822
(4), 891 (7)
fumes 336 (2), 394 (1), 395
(1), 397 (1)
fumigate 338 (4), 394 (3),
648 (10)
fumigation 338 (1), 395
(1), 648 (2)
fumigator 385 (4), 658 (3)
fuming 176 (6), 891 (4)
fun 824 (3), 833 (2), 837
(1), 837 (2), 837 (3)
fun and games 833 (2), 837
(2)
function 85 (1), 173 (1),
173 (3), 622 (4), 622 (8),
640 (1), 673 (1), 676 (5),
755 (3), 875 (2), 876 (1)
functional 173 (2), 622 (5),
628 (3), 640 (2)
functional disease 651 (3)
functionalism 551 (3), 640
(1)
functionary 686 (1), 690
(4), 741 (6), 754 (1)
functionless 641 (4)
fund 632 (1), 799 (1)
fund of experience 498 (3)
fund-raising 771 (1)
fundamental 5 (6), 44 (4),
68 (6), 156 (8), 167 (4),
214 (3), 218 (14), 638 (5)
fundamental note 410 (2)
fundamentalism 976 (2)
fundamentalist 976 (7),
976 (8)
fundamentally 5 (10), 32
(16)
fundamentals 1 (2), 638
(3)
funds 797 (2)
funds in hand 797 (2)
funeral 364 (2), 731 (1),
836 (3)
funeral director 364 (1)
funeral parlour 364 (1)
funerary 364 (8)
funereal 364 (8), 418 (3),
428 (4), 834 (8)
funfair 837 (2), 837 (5)
fungicide 659 (3)
fungus 366 (6), 659 (2)
funicular 624 (7)

funnel 252 (3), 255 (2), 263 (10), 353 (1)

funnel-shaped 255 (6), 263 (16)

funniness 849 (1)

funny 84 (6), 503 (8), 594 (15), 835 (5), 837 (18), 839 (4), 849 (3)

funny bone 374 (1)

funny story 839 (2)

fur 226 (6), 259 (2), 547 (11), 649 (2)

Furies 93 (2)

furious 165 (4), 176 (5), 176 (6), 503 (9), 645 (3), 821 (3), 822 (3), 857 (3), 891 (4)

furiously 32 (18)

furl 261 (3), 315 (5)

furlong 203 (4)

furlough 190 (1), 756 (2)

furnace 263 (10), 300 (2), 301 (5), 379 (2), 381 (2), 383 (1), 663 (1)

furnish 629 (2), 633 (5)

furnish evidence 466 (6)

furnishing 630 (4), 669 (2)

furnishings 193 (1)

furniture 777 (1)

furniture polish 648 (4)

furore 176 (1), 318 (3), 848 (1)

furred up 649 (7)

furrow 194 (1), 201 (2), 255 (2), 259 (1), 261 (3), 262 (1), 262 (3), 548 (4)

furrowed 259 (4), 262 (2)

furrowing 255 (1)

furry 259 (5)

further 38 (2), 38 (5), 199 (7), 285 (4), 703 (5)

further education 534 (2)

further on 199 (7), 237 (6)

furtherance 285 (1), 654 (1)

furthermore 38 (5)

furthermost 199 (3)

furthest 199 (3)

furtive 525 (5), 525 (9)

furtively 525 (11)

furtiveness 525 (2)

fury 176 (4), 821 (1), 822 (2), 891 (2), 892 (2), 904 (4), 938 (4), 970 (4)

fuse 43 (7), 45 (9), 50 (4), 381 (8), 385 (3), 662 (3), 702 (3), 723 (13)

fused 43 (6), 50 (3)

fuselage 218 (13)

fusilier 722 (5)

fusillade 712 (3), 712 (11), 963 (12)

fusion 43 (1), 43 (3), 45 (1), 50 (1), 160 (7), 337 (1), 706 (2)

fuss 318 (3), 678 (1), 678 (12), 821 (1), 825 (7), 862 (4), 875 (1)

fussiness 862 (1)

fusspot 678 (6), 862 (2)

fussy 481 (7), 862 (3)

fustiness 397 (1)

fusty 127 (7), 264 (5), 397 (2), 649 (7)

futile 497 (3), 499 (4), 634 (3), 641 (4), 922 (4)

futile regret 830 (1)

futility 161 (4), 497 (1), 641 (1), 922 (2)

future 120 (2), 124 (1), 124 (4), 155 (2), 469 (2), 473 (4), 507 (3)

future plans 155 (1)

future state 67 (1), 69 (3), 124 (2), 155 (1), 361 (3), 971 (1)

future tense 124 (1)

futures 618 (2)

futurist 126 (3)

futuristic 126 (6)

futurity 108 (1), 120 (1), 122 (1), 124 (1), 469 (1)

fuzz 259 (2)

fuzziness 244 (1)

fuzzy 244 (2), 259 (5), 419 (5), 444 (3)

G

G-string 228 (14)

gabardine 222 (4), 228 (20)

gabber 581 (3)

gabble 409 (3), 515 (3), 515 (6), 579 (8), 580 (3), 581 (2), 581 (5)

gable 213 (2)

gable end 69 (2)

gable roof 226 (2)

gad about 267 (13)

gadfly 821 (2)

gadget 319 (3), 623 (3), 630 (1)

gaff 256 (2)

gaffe 495 (3)

gaffer 133 (2), 372 (1)

gag 264 (2), 300 (10), 399 (4), 578 (4), 702 (8), 747 (7), 748 (4), 839 (2), 839 (5)

gaga 131 (6)

gage 767 (1)

gagged 578 (2), 747 (5)

gaggle 74 (3)

Gaia 967 (1)

gaiety 833 (2), 882 (2)

gaily 857 (5)

gain 36 (2), 36 (4), 40 (2), 157 (2), 164 (2), 285 (1), 285 (3), 295 (4), 495 (7), 612 (4), 615 (2), 615 (5), 640 (1), 640 (5), 727 (8), 730 (6), 771 (3), 771 (7), 771 (9), 790 (1), 800 (7), 807 (1), 962 (1), 962 (4)

gain a footing 178 (4), 187 (8)

gain a hearing 178 (3), 415 (7)

gain a reputation 920 (7)

gain admittance 297 (5)

gain by 615 (5)

gain ground 36 (4), 285 (3)

gain height 285 (3), 308 (4)

gain in value 36 (4)

gain on 277 (8), 285 (3)

gain one's end 727 (6)

gain one's freedom 746 (4)

gain power 160 (10), 733 (11)

gain recognition 866 (11)

gain strength 36 (4)

gain time 113 (8), 135 (5), 136 (7), 285 (3)

gain upon 289 (4), 306 (5)

gain weight 322 (6)

gainful 615 (3), 640 (3), 771 (5), 962 (2)

gaining 118 (2), 495 (6)

gaining height 308 (1), 308 (3)

gaining time 136 (2)

gainsay 533 (3)

gainsaying 533 (1)

gait 265 (2), 267 (3), 267 (5), 278 (1), 312 (1)

gaitered 986 (11)

gaiters 228 (26), 989 (1)

gala 837 (2), 875 (3)

gala day 876 (2)

galactic 321 (13)

galantine 301 (14)

galaxy 74 (3), 104 (2), 321 (4), 866 (6)

gale 61 (4), 176 (3), 315 (2), 318 (3), 340 (3), 350 (6), 352 (4), 663 (1)

gale-force 352 (8)

gale warning 665 (1)

gales of laughter 835 (2)

gall 253 (2), 333 (3), 393 (1), 827 (8), 827 (9), 878 (2)

gallant 848 (4), 855 (4), 875 (5), 884 (3), 887 (9)

gallant act 855 (2)

gallant company 855 (3)

gallantry 855 (1), 884 (1), 887 (1), 887 (3), 889 (2)

galled 891 (3)

galleon 275 (3), 722 (13)

gallery 194 (20), 255 (4), 263 (8), 441 (2), 522 (2), 594 (7), 632 (3), 990 (4)

galley 194 (19), 275 (2), 301 (5)

galley proof 587 (2)

galley slave 270 (4), 678 (5), 742 (6), 750 (1)

galling 827 (5)

gallivant 267 (13)

gallon 465 (3)

gallons 32 (2)

gallop 114 (6), 265 (2), 267 (15), 277 (2), 277 (6)

gallows 217 (3), 964 (3)

gallows humour 839 (1)

gallstones 651 (7)

galore 32 (2), 104 (4)

galvanize 174 (8), 612 (9), 821 (6)

gambit 68 (2), 688 (2)

gamble 159 (7), 461 (2), 461 (8), 474 (1), 511 (9), 618 (2), 618 (8), 661 (8), 661 (9), 671 (4), 791 (5), 837 (21)

gamble away 815 (4)

gamble on 473 (7)

gambler 461 (3), 618 (4), 794 (1), 837 (16)

gambling 159 (2), 159 (4), 461 (2), 474 (1), 512 (2), 618 (2), 672 (1), 837 (12)

gambling den 618 (3)

gambling game 618 (2), 837 (12)

gamboge 433 (2)

gambol 312 (1), 312 (4), 824 (3), 833 (7), 837 (21)

game 163 (7), 301 (16), 365 (2), 599 (2), 600 (3), 618 (8), 619 (2), 623 (4), 671 (3), 698 (4), 716 (2), 837 (1), 837 (3), 851 (3), 855 (4)

game and match 727 (2)

game bird 365 (5)

game for 597 (4)

game of cards 837 (11)

game of chance 837 (1)

game of skill 837 (1)

game park 369 (4)

game reserve 369 (4), 666 (1)

game warden 369 (1)

gamekeeper 369 (1), 749 (1)

gameness 600 (2), 855 (1)

games 682 (2), 716 (2), 837 (6)

games-player 837 (16)

games-playing 837 (19)

gamesmanship 698 (1), 716 (1)

gaming-house 618 (3), 837 (5)

gammon 301 (16)

gamut 71 (2)

gamy 388 (3), 390 (2), 397 (2)

gander 365 (4)

gang 74 (4), 686 (4), 708 (1)

gang rule 954 (3)

gang up 74 (10)

gang up with 89 (4)

gang warfare 709 (3), 716 (7)

gangling 195 (9), 206 (4), 695 (5)

ganglion 225 (2)

gangplank 624 (3)

gangrene 51 (2), 651 (5), 651 (14)

gangrenous 51 (3), 651 (22)

gangster 362 (7), 789 (2), 869 (7), 904 (3)

gangway 263 (6), 263 (7), 624 (2), 624 (3)

gantry 218 (5)

gaol 748 (1), 883 (2), 964 (2)

gaoler 749 (2)

gap 46 (1), 55 (1), 72 (1), 190 (2), 201 (2), 211 (1), 231 (2), 255 (3), 260 (1), 262 (1), 263 (1), 627 (1), 647 (2)

gape 201 (4), 211 (3), 263 (17), 438 (8), 441 (3), 864 (6)

gaping 197 (3), 201 (3), 263 (1), 263 (13), 864 (4)

gapped 201 (3)

gappy 201 (3)

garage 192 (10), 194 (19), 632 (2), 632 (5)

garb 228 (1), 445 (1)

garbage 649 (2)

garble 521 (3)

garbled 55 (3), 495 (6), 541 (3)

garbling 543 (1)

garden 156 (4), 235 (1),
366 (2), 370 (3), 370 (8),
370 (9), 841 (2)
garden centre 370 (2)
garden city 184 (3)
Garden of Eden 971 (2)
garden party 537 (1)
garden plant 366 (6)
gardener 167 (1), 370 (5),
742 (2)
gardening 366 (7), 370 (1),
370 (8), 844 (2)
gardens 192 (15), 837 (4)
gargantuan 195 (7)
gargle 648 (4), 658 (3)
gargoyle 298 (3), 351 (2),
551 (2), 842 (2), 844 (2)
garish 417 (8), 425 (6), 842
(5), 844 (10), 847 (4), 875
(5)
garishness 847 (1)
garland 250 (3), 729 (1),
844 (12), 866 (4), 876 (4),
923 (10)
garlanded 844 (10)
garlic 389 (1)
garment 228 (3)
garments 228 (2)
garnening 632 (2)
garner 74 (11), 632 (5)
garnet 844 (8)
garnish 40 (1), 301 (9), 301
(40), 389 (1), 844 (1), 844
(12)
garret 194 (22), 213 (2)
garrison 191 (2), 660 (3),
660 (8), 713 (6), 713 (9),
722 (7), 749 (1)
garrisoned 660 (4)
garrotte 362 (10), 963 (12)
garrotter 362 (7)
garrulity 581 (1)
garrulous 526 (3), 581 (4)
garter 47 (5), 198 (3), 228
(26), 547 (9), 729 (2), 743
(3), 866 (4)
gas 160 (4), 300 (3), 336
(2), 340 (1), 362 (12), 375
(2), 375 (6), 383 (2), 397
(1), 723 (3)
gas and air 375 (2)
gas-bag 581 (3)

gas chamber 362 (5), 964
(3)
gas-fitter 686 (3)
gas jet 420 (3)
gas mantle 420 (4)
gas mask 662 (3), 713 (5)
gas oneself 362 (13)
gas plant 336 (2)
gas ring 383 (1)
gasbag 194 (2), 877 (3)
gaseous 323 (3), 325 (2),
336 (3), 340 (5), 352 (8),
355 (3)
gaseousness 325 (1), 336
(1)
gash 46 (11), 201 (2), 260
(1), 262 (1), 262 (3), 377
(1), 655 (4), 655 (10)
gasholder 336 (2), 632 (2)
gasification 336 (1), 338
(1)
gasify 323 (5), 325 (3), 336
(4), 338 (4)
gaslight 336 (2)
gasoline 385 (1)
gasp 352 (11), 407 (4), 408
(1), 408 (3), 577 (1), 684
(5), 864 (6)
gasp for 859 (11)
gasp for breath 379 (7)
gasping 684 (3)
gassy 336 (3), 338 (3), 352
(8), 581 (4)
gastroenteritis 651 (7)
gastronomic 301 (34), 947
(3)
gastronomy 301 (4), 947
(1)
gasworks 336 (2)
gate 235 (3), 263 (6), 264
(2), 441 (2), 799 (1)
gate money 807 (1)
gateau 301 (23)
gatecrash 297 (8)
gatecrasher 59 (3)
gatekeeper 264 (3)
gatepost 263 (6)
gateway 68 (5)
gather 45 (9), 74 (10), 74
(11), 197 (4), 261 (1), 261
(3), 295 (6), 370 (9), 418
(5), 471 (6), 524 (12), 632

(5), 771 (7), 786 (6), 900
(3)
gather food 633 (5)
gather in 370 (9)
gather momentum 277 (7)
gather round 74 (10)
gather together 293 (3)
gather way 265 (4)
gathered 45 (8)
gathering 74 (1), 74 (2),
584 (3), 651 (14)
gathering cloud 664 (1)
gathering clouds 511 (3)
gating 963 (4)
gauche 499 (4), 695 (5),
847 (5)
gaucherie 491 (1), 847 (2)
gaucho 268 (4), 369 (6)
gaudiness 844 (1), 847 (1),
875 (1)
gaudy 425 (6), 842 (5), 844
(10), 847 (4), 875 (5)
gauge 86 (6), 205 (1), 209
(7), 277 (1), 461 (4), 465
(5), 465 (12), 465 (13), 480
(6), 547 (6), 549 (3)
gauging 465 (1)
gaunt 206 (5), 246 (4)
gauntlet 228 (25), 711 (1),
713 (5)
Gautama 973 (6)
gauze 222 (4), 422 (1), 424
(1), 658 (9)
gauzy 422 (2), 424 (2)
gavel 743 (2)
gavotte 837 (14)
gawk 441 (3), 864 (6)
gawkish 695 (5)
gawky 499 (4)
gawp 438 (8)
gay 84 (3), 84 (7), 417 (8),
420 (8), 425 (6), 833 (4),
839 (4), 875 (5)
gay bachelor 952 (1)
gay dog 848 (4), 952 (1)
gay liberation 744 (1)
gaze 438 (3), 438 (8), 453
(4), 455 (4), 547 (21), 864
(6), 885 (6), 889 (7)
gaze at 438 (8)
gazebo 194 (23)
gazelle 365 (3)
gazette 528 (5), 548 (1)

gazetteer 87 (3), 524 (6), 589 (4)

gear 630 (4)

gear to 9 (8)

gears 630 (2)

geezer 851 (3)

Geiger counter 417 (4), 465 (6), 484 (2)

gel 354 (3)

gelatine 354 (2)

gelatinize 324 (6), 354 (6)

gelatinous 354 (4)

geld 161 (10), 172 (6)

gelded 161 (7)

gelding 161 (3), 273 (4)

gelignite 723 (13)

gem 344 (4), 644 (3), 844 (8)

gem cutting 555 (1)

gem-engraver 556 (3)

Gemini 90 (1), 321 (5)

gender 77 (1), 564 (1)

gene 5 (5), 358 (1)

genealogy 5 (5), 11 (1), 71 (2), 77 (3), 87 (1), 169 (2), 868 (1)

general 52 (7), 78 (2), 79 (3), 83 (5), 205 (3), 371 (7), 464 (2), 490 (7), 495 (6), 610 (6), 741 (8)

general, be 79 (5)

general consent 488 (2)

general election 605 (2)

general permission 756 (1)

general post 151 (1)

general poverty 801 (1)

general practitioner 658 (14)

general principle 475 (2)

general public 869 (1)

general run 79 (1)

general servant 742 (1)

general strike 145 (3)

general surgery 658 (11)

generality 30 (1), 79 (1), 83 (1), 371 (4), 464 (1), 495 (2)

generalization 79 (1)

generalize 79 (6)

generalized 495 (6)

generally 30 (6), 32 (17), 79 (7), 139 (4)

generally believed 976 (8)

generally speaking 79 (7)

generalship 718 (4)

generate 11 (7), 45 (14), 68 (9), 156 (9), 167 (7), 171 (5), 360 (6)

generation 110 (2), 156 (1), 167 (1)

generations 113 (1)

generative 166 (2), 167 (4), 171 (4), 373 (5)

generator 156 (5), 160 (4), 160 (6)

generic 77 (4), 79 (3)

generosity 781 (1), 813 (1), 897 (1), 931 (1)

generous 32 (4), 635 (4), 781 (5), 806 (2), 813 (3), 813 (4), 884 (3), 897 (4), 923 (5), 931 (2), 933 (3), 962 (2)

generous giver 813 (2)

generously 32 (17)

genesis 68 (4), 156 (3)

genetic 5 (7), 148 (2), 157 (4), 167 (4), 170 (4), 817 (2)

genetics 5 (5), 358 (2)

genial 379 (6), 826 (2), 833 (3), 897 (4)

geniality 833 (1), 882 (2)

genie 970 (5)

genital 167 (4)

genitalia 167 (3)

genitals 167 (3)

genius 447 (1), 492 (2), 498 (1), 500 (1), 644 (3), 696 (1), 864 (3)

genius for 694 (2)

genius loci 187 (2), 967 (2)

genocidal 362 (9)

genocide 165 (1), 362 (4), 898 (3)

genotype 77 (3)

genre 77 (2)

genre painting 553 (2)

genteel 848 (6), 868 (7)

gentian 435 (1)

gentian violet 436 (1)

gentile 973 (7), 974 (4), 974 (6)

gentle 177 (3), 177 (5), 220 (4), 369 (7), 401 (3), 736

(2), 823 (3), 884 (4), 897 (4), 935 (3)

gentle birth 868 (1)

gentle breeze 352 (3)

gentle curve 253 (6)

gentle handling 688 (1)

gentle slope 210 (1), 220 (2)

gentleman 372 (1)

gentlemanly 372 (2), 848 (6), 868 (6), 884 (3)

gentleness 177 (1), 736 (1), 823 (1), 884 (1), 897 (1)

gentlewoman 373 (4)

gentry 868 (2)

Gents 649 (3)

genuflect 311 (9), 981 (11), 988 (10)

genuflexion 311 (2), 879 (1), 920 (2)

genuine 21 (4), 473 (4), 494 (5)

genuine article 21 (2)

genuinely 494 (8)

genuineness 13 (1), 21 (2), 494 (2)

genus 74 (3), 77 (3)

geocentric 225 (3), 321 (14)

geographer 321 (12)

geographic 321 (17)

geographical 186 (3), 321 (17)

geography 186 (1), 321 (12), 344 (1)

geological 127 (5), 321 (17), 344 (5)

geologist 321 (12)

geology 321 (12), 344 (1), 359 (2)

geometric 844 (9)

geometric progression 71 (2), 85 (3)

geometrical 86 (9)

geometrician 86 (7)

geometry 86 (3), 465 (2)

Geordie 560 (2)

geothermal 160 (9)

geriatric 131 (6)

geriatrician 658 (14)

geriatrics 131 (5), 658 (10)

germ 68 (4), **156** (3), **196** (5), **651** (5), **653** (1), **659** (3)

germ-carrier **651** (5), **653** (1)

germ-laden 653 (4)

germ warfare **659** (4), **718** (6), **723** (3)

german 11 (5)

German measles **651** (5)

germane 24 (6)

germicide **658** (3), **659** (3)

germinal 68 (6), **156** (7), **167** (4)

germinate 68 (8), **157** (5), **167** (6), **171** (6), **366** (12)

germination **167** (1)

gerontocracy **733** (4)

gerontologic **131** (6)

gerontology **131** (5)

gerrymander **542** (8), **698** (5), **930** (8)

gerrymandering **930** (3)

gestation **167** (1), **669** (3)

gesticulate **246** (5), **524** (11), **547** (21), **737** (6)

gesticulation **265** (1), **547** (4), **688** (1)

gesticulatory **547** (15)

gesture 20 (2), **265** (1), **279** (2), **318** (1), **524** (3), **547** (4), **547** (21), **557** (1), **578** (1), **579** (1), **676** (2), **688** (1), **878** (2)

get 147 (6), **299** (3), **771** (7), **773** (4), **782** (4)

get a cheer **923** (11)

get a chill **380** (7)

get a citation **923** (11)

get a compliment **923** (11)

get a divorce **896** (5)

get a good hand **923** (11)

get a medal **962** (4)

get a shock **508** (4)

get a whiff of **394** (3)

get aboard **297** (5)

get about **528** (12)

get above oneself **873** (5), **878** (6)

get across **514** (5), **516** (4), **524** (10)

get ahead 64 (3), **285** (3)

get ahead of **283** (3)

get along **267** (17)

get angry **503** (11), **818** (8), **822** (4), **885** (6), **891** (6), **892** (4), **900** (3)

get around **267** (11), **694** (8), **882** (8)

get-at-able **289** (3)

get away **290** (3), **667** (5), **746** (4)

get away with **667** (5), **919** (4)

get back 31 (6), **771** (7)

get behindhand **805** (5)

get better **143** (5), **285** (3), **603** (5), **615** (5), **654** (8), **656** (8), **929** (5), **939** (4)

get between **231** (10)

get bogged down **307** (3), **728** (7)

get broad **205** (5)

get burnt **379** (7)

get by effort **771** (7)

get by heart **505** (10), **536** (4)

get changed **228** (32)

get cold feet **603** (5), **854** (11)

get cracking 68 (8)

get credit **785** (2), **803** (6)

get dirty **649** (8)

get down **295** (5), **309** (3), **311** (9)

get down to **682** (7)

get dressed **228** (32)

get drunk **301** (38), **943** (3), **949** (14)

get elected **708** (8)

get even with **714** (3), **963** (8)

get fat **197** (4)

get free 46 (7), **667** (5), **744** (9)

get going **267** (17)

get healthy **650** (4)

get hold of **771** (7)

get in **297** (5)

get in advance **771** (7)

get in front **283** (3)

get in the way **702** (8)

get in touch **524** (10)

get into mischief **738** (9)

get into proportion 9 (8)

get into the way of **610** (8)

get involved **672** (3), **897** (6)

get it wrong **495** (7)

get killed **361** (8)

get leave **756** (6)

get less 33 (8)

get lost **282** (5), **661** (7)

get mad **891** (6)

get married **894** (11)

get no better **655** (7)

get no results **728** (7)

get off **295** (5), **309** (3), **667** (5)

get off lightly **667** (5)

get on **285** (3), **730** (6)

get on one's nerves **827** (11), **891** (9)

get on well with **880** (7)

get on with 24 (9), **676** (5)

get one down **829** (6), **834** (12), **838** (5)

get one's breath back **685** (5)

get one's deserts **714** (4), **962** (4), **963** (13)

get one's own back **714** (3), **910** (5)

get one's second wind **685** (5)

get out **295** (5), **304** (4), **667** (5)

get out of hand **61** (10)

get out of one's depth **661** (7)

get out of order **63** (4)

get out of practise **695** (7)

get over **656** (8)

get over it **831** (4)

got past **305** (5)

get personal **878** (6)

get pleasure from **824** (6)

get possession of **771** (7)

get pregnant **167** (6)

get printed **528** (12)

get promotion **727** (6)

get religion **979** (10)

get rich **615** (5), **730** (6), **771** (9), **800** (7)

get rid of 44 (7), **165** (6), **300** (6), **362** (10), **668** (3), **779** (4)

get round **542** (9), **620** (5)

get shot of **300** (6)

get somehow 771 (7)
get stale 684 (5)
get sunburnt 379 (7)
get the better of 479 (3), 727 (10)
get the giggles 835 (7)
get the idea 516 (5)
get the worst of it 728 (9)
get there 295 (4)
get there first 135 (5)
get through 69 (6), 305 (5), 524 (10), 725 (5), 806 (4)
get to 199 (5)
get to know 490 (8), 505 (10)
get-together 74 (2), 74 (10), 882 (3), 882 (8)
get tough with 735 (7)
get under way 68 (9), 269 (10), 296 (6)
get up 308 (4), 310 (5), 352 (10), 541 (8), 656 (8)
get up steam 174 (7)
get used to 610 (8)
get warm 200 (5)
get well 656 (8)
get wet 269 (12), 341 (6)
get wild 891 (6)
get wind of 394 (3), 484 (4), 484 (5), 524 (12)
get with it 126 (8)
get worse 35 (5), 651 (23), 655 (7)
get wrong 521 (3)
getaway 296 (1), 667 (1)
getting 771 (1), 782 (1)
getting ahead 285 (1)
getting along, be 296 (4)
getting at, be 514 (5)
getting down 301 (1)
getting less 37 (1)
getting married 894 (3)
getting old 131 (6)
getting on 131 (6)
getting on for 124 (4)
getting together 74 (2)
getting warm 200 (4), 484 (3)
getting warm, be 484 (5)
getting well 650 (2)
getting worse 655 (5)
gewgaw 639 (3)

geyser 298 (2), 308 (2), 350 (1), 379 (1), 383 (2)
ghastly 426 (3), 645 (4), 827 (6), 854 (8)
ghee 357 (3)
ghetto 192 (8), 748 (2), 883 (2)
ghost 4 (2), 361 (3), 363 (1), 440 (2), 445 (1), 513 (3), 854 (4), 970 (3), 983 (11), 984 (3)
ghost-hunting 984 (3)
ghost story 590 (4)
ghost-writer 150 (2), 589 (7)
ghostliness 320 (1)
ghostly 4 (3), 320 (3), 419 (5), 970 (7)
ghoul 970 (4)
ghoulish 453 (3), 854 (8), 898 (7), 970 (7)
ghoulishness 453 (1), 970 (4)
giant 32 (6), 162 (4), 195 (4), 195 (7), 209 (5), 321 (4), 970 (4)
giant-like 195 (7)
giantess 970 (4)
gibber 515 (6), 970 (8)
gibberish 497 (1), 515 (1), 517 (1), 560 (3)
gibbet 217 (3), 964 (3)
gibbosity 253 (1)
gibbous 252 (5), 253 (7)
gibbousness 252 (1)
gibe 851 (6), 921 (2), 922 (5)
gibing 921 (3)
giddiness 499 (2), 604 (1)
giddy 456 (6), 503 (8), 604 (3), 857 (3), 949 (9)
gift 160 (2), 179 (1), 612 (4), 615 (2), 694 (2), 703 (2), 759 (1), 771 (1), 780 (1), 781 (2), 781 (7), 782 (1), 812 (2), 813 (1), 962 (1)
gift of healing 658 (10)
gift of life 360 (1)
gift of pleasing 887 (2)
gift of the gab 581 (1)
gifted 498 (4), 694 (5), 781 (6)

gifted child 538 (1)
giftedness 498 (1)
gig 274 (6)
gigantic 32 (6), 195 (7), 209 (9), 970 (6)
giggle 835 (2), 835 (7)
giggles, the 835 (2)
gigolo 952 (1)
gild 226 (16), 425 (8), 433 (4), 844 (12)
gild the lily 637 (6)
gild the pill 826 (3)
gilded 433 (3), 844 (10)
gilding 844 (2)
gill 350 (1), 465 (3)
gillie 369 (1)
gills 239 (1), 352 (7)
gilt 433 (3), 844 (1), 844 (2), 844 (10)
gilt-edged 644 (7), 767 (4)
gimcrack 330 (2), 639 (6)
gimlet 263 (12)
gimmick 542 (2), 623 (3)
gin 301 (28), 542 (4)
gin-sodden 949 (11)
ginger 389 (1), 432 (2), 821 (2), 821 (7)
ginger ale 301 (27)
ginger beer 301 (27)
ginger group 612 (5)
ginger-haired 431 (3)
ginger up 174 (8)
gingerbread 301 (23)
gingered up 174 (5)
gingerly 177 (8), 278 (7), 457 (8), 858 (4)
gingery 388 (3)
gingham 222 (4)
ginseng 658 (6)
gipsy 511 (5)
gipsy dance 837 (14)
gipsy lingo 560 (3)
giraffe 209 (5), 365 (3)
girder 47 (1), 218 (9)
girdle 47 (7), 194 (14), 198 (3), 208 (3), 228 (17), 228 (24), 230 (3), 235 (1), 250 (3), 250 (8)
girdling 232 (1)
girl 132 (2), 371 (3), 373 (3)
girl Friday 703 (3)

girlfriend **373** (3), **880** (3), **887** (4)

girlhood **130** (1)

girlish **130** (4), **132** (5), **373** (5), **670** (4)

girlishness **130** (1), **373** (1)

giro **797** (5)

girth **32** (1), **47** (7), **195** (1)

gist **5** (2), **52** (3), **514** (1), **592** (1), **638** (3)

give **220** (5), **248** (4), **327** (4), **328** (1), **328** (3), **633** (5), **758** (3), **759** (3), **777** (6), **780** (3), **781** (7), **783** (3), **804** (4), **804** (5), **806** (4), **812** (6), **813** (4), **981** (12)

give a **780** (3)

give a bad name **867** (11)

give a breather **685** (4)

give a directive **737** (6)

give a face-lift **841** (8)

give a free hand **756** (5)

give a hiding **279** (9)

give a jump **312** (4)

give a lead **612** (8), **848** (7)

give a leg-up **310** (4)

give a mandate **737** (6)

give a name **561** (6)

give a part **594** (16)

give a party **837** (20), **882** (10)

give a ruling **737** (7)

give a second chance **905** (7)

give a wide berth **620** (5)

give advice **691** (4)

give an edge to **821** (7)

give an encore **106** (4), **106** (5), **413** (9)

give an impetus **279** (7)

give an instance **83** (9)

give an order **737** (6)

give and take **12** (1), **31** (5), **151** (1), **151** (3), **460** (1), **475** (4), **475** (11), **706** (1), **765** (1), **765** (5), **766** (4), **770** (1), **770** (2), **913** (2)

give as good as one gets **714** (3)

give assurances **660** (8)

give away **526** (4), **781** (7), **812** (6), **894** (10)

give back **787** (3)

give bail **767** (5)

give battle **716** (11), **718** (12)

give benediction **988** (10)

give birth **167** (6)

give birth to **360** (6)

give by will **781** (7)

give chase **619** (5)

give clearance **756** (5)

give communion **988** (10)

give confidence **855** (8)

give consent **758** (3)

give courage **162** (12), **612** (9), **703** (5), **821** (7), **833** (8), **855** (8)

give credit **802** (3), **866** (13), **923** (8)

give dispensation **919** (3)

give ear **415** (6)

give employment **622** (6)

give evidence **466** (7)

give fair warning **664** (5)

give first aid **658** (20)

give foundations **218** (15)

give freely **781** (7)

give full credit **907** (5)

give full marks **923** (8)

give generously **813** (4)

give glory to **981** (11)

give ground **286** (4)

give grounds for **927** (6)

give heart to **703** (5)

give hope **466** (6), **471** (4), **511** (8), **831** (3), **852** (7)

give in **621** (3), **721** (3)

give in charge **747** (10)

give in marriage **894** (10)

give increase **167** (6)

give judgment **737** (7)

give lessons **534** (7)

give life to **167** (7)

give money **806** (4)

give no quarter **362** (11), **735** (7), **906** (3)

give no trouble **701** (6)

give notice **664** (5)

give off **300** (9)

give one a free hand **744** (10)

give one a fright **854** (12)

give one cause **927** (6)

give one his or her head **734** (5), **744** (10)

give one pause **613** (3)

give one the giggles **849** (4)

give one's approval **758** (3)

give one's blessing **756** (5)

give one's mind to **455** (4)

give one's word **466** (7), **764** (4)

give oneself a **850** (5)

give oneself airs **871** (5), **873** (5)

give oneself away **495** (8), **526** (4)

give oneself up **721** (3)

give oneself up to **943** (3)

give out **524** (10), **634** (4), **781** (7)

give out sound **398** (4)

give over **145** (9)

give pain **374** (6), **377** (5), **827** (8), **963** (11)

give permission **756** (5)

give pleasure **376** (6), **826** (3)

give points to **28** (10)

give quarter **905** (7)

give satisfaction **941** (5)

give scope **146** (4), **701** (8), **734** (5), **744** (10), **746** (3), **756** (5), **813** (4)

give security **764** (4), **765** (5), **767** (6), **785** (2)

give terms **719** (4), **746** (3), **705** (5), **766** (3), **791** (6), **917** (11)

give thanks **835** (6), **907** (5), **981** (11)

give the go-ahead **756** (5)

give the slip **667** (6)

give the vote **746** (3)

give three cheers **886** (3), **923** (10)

give to **673** (3)

give to drink **301** (38)

give to eat **301** (39)

give tongue **409** (3), **577** (4)

give trouble **702** (10)

give up 145 (6), 601 (4), 611 (4), 621 (3), 674 (5), 721 (3), 726 (3), 753 (3), 779 (4), 781 (7), 853 (4), 942 (4)

give up alcohol 948 (4)

give up hope 853 (4)

give up work 681 (3)

give utterance 579 (8)

give vent to 300 (9), 746 (3)

give voice 577 (4)

give way 163 (9), 286 (4), 309 (3), 601 (4), 758 (3)

give weight to 463 (3), 638 (8)

giveaway 526 (1)

giveaway price 812 (1)

given 1 (4), 512 (5), 781 (6), 782 (3), 812 (4)

given a chance 701 (5)

given away 781 (6)

given, be 299 (3), 782 (4), 786 (6)

given to 610 (7)

given to drink 949 (11)

given up 361 (5)

giver 633 (2), 781 (4), 903 (1), 981 (8)

giving 781 (1), 781 (5), 897 (2), 931 (2)

giving back 787 (1)

giving credit 907 (3)

giving form 243 (4)

giving glory 981 (10)

giving up 621 (1), 674 (1)

giving way 721 (1)

gizzard 194 (3)

glace 382 (4)

glacial 380 (5)

glacier 380 (4)

glad 597 (4), 824 (4), 824 (6)

glad eye 889 (2)

glad of, be 859 (11)

gladden 826 (3), 833 (8)

glade 263 (7), 366 (2)

gladiator 716 (8), 722 (1)

gladiatorial 716 (9)

gladiatorial combat 716 (6)

gladly 597 (7)

gladness 824 (1)

glamorize 841 (8), 844 (12)

glamorous 841 (6)

glamour 841 (1), 866 (2)

glance 282 (3), 378 (7), 417 (11), 438 (3), 438 (8), 547 (4)

glance at 438 (8)

glance off 294 (3)

glancing 239 (2)

glandular fever 651 (5)

glare 417 (1), 417 (5), 417 (11), 438 (8), 440 (5), 891 (2), 891 (7), 893 (1), 893 (3)

glaring 32 (10), 417 (8), 443 (3), 522 (4), 891 (4)

glaring error 495 (3)

glaringly 32 (19)

glass 194 (15), 258 (1), 301 (26), 330 (1), 340 (3), 422 (1), 442 (5), 631 (1)

glass engraving 555 (1)

glass eye 439 (1)

glasses 442 (2)

glassful 301 (26)

glasshouse 370 (3)

glassy 258 (3), 326 (3), 417 (9), 422 (2), 426 (3)

glassy-eyed 949 (7)

glaucoma 439 (1)

glaucous 434 (3)

glaze 226 (10), 226 (16), 258 (1), 258 (4), 354 (3)

glazed ware 381 (5)

gleam 417 (2), 417 (11)

gleam of hope 852 (1)

gleaming 417 (9)

glean 370 (9), 592 (5), 771 (7), 786 (6)

glean facts 536 (4)

gleaner 74 (8), 370 (4)

glee 412 (5), 824 (3)

glee club 413 (5)

gleeful 833 (5)

glen 255 (3)

glib 542 (6), 581 (4)

glib tongue 698 (3)

glide 111 (3), 258 (5), 265 (4), 271 (7), 323 (4), 350 (9), 525 (9)

glide along 278 (4)

glide path 271 (2)

glider 271 (4), 276 (1)

gliding 265 (1), 271 (1), 837 (6)

glimmer 417 (2), 417 (11), 419 (3), 419 (6)

glimmer of hope 852 (1)

glimmering 490 (1), 491 (3)

glimpse 438 (3), 438 (7)

glimpsing 438 (6)

glint 417 (2), 417 (11)

glissade 309 (1), 309 (3)

glisten 417 (11)

glitter 417 (2), 417 (11), 847 (1), 875 (1), 875 (7)

glittering 800 (3), 844 (10), 875 (5)

glittery 417 (8)

gloaming 129 (1), 419 (2)

gloat 835 (6), 877 (5), 898 (8), 910 (5)

gloat over 376 (6), 438 (8), 824 (6)

gloating 824 (1), 824 (4), 898 (1), 898 (4), 898 (7), 910 (4)

global 78 (2), 79 (4), 252 (5), 321 (15), 775 (4)

global war 718 (1)

globe 252 (2), 321 (2), 551 (5)

globe-trotter 268 (1)

globular 252 (5)

globule 252 (2)

globulin 358 (1)

glockenspiel 414 (8)

gloom 418 (1), 419 (1), 731 (1), 825 (2), 834 (1)

gloomily 893 (4)

gloominess 834 (1)

gloomy 418 (3), 428 (4), 834 (5), 834 (6), 834 (8), 893 (2)

glorification 866 (5), 981 (3)

glorify 36 (5), 638 (8), 730 (8), 866 (13), 866 (14), 923 (9), 981 (11)

glorify God 979 (9)

glorious 32 (4), 644 (4), 644 (5), 727 (4), 730 (5), 841 (4), 866 (8), 866 (9), 866 (10), 965 (6)

glory 727 (1), 729 (1), 730
(1), 866 (2), 866 (3), 965
(2)

glory in 871 (6), 877 (5)

gloss 258 (1), 417 (5), 520
(2), 520 (8), 542 (5), 614
(1)

gloss over 458 (4), 477 (8),
525 (7), 541 (7), 614 (4),
927 (7)

glossary 87 (2), 520 (2),
559 (2)

glossy 417 (8), 841 (4), 841
(6)

glottal stop 577 (2)

glove 228 (25)

gloved 228 (29)

glow 379 (1), 379 (7), 417
(3), 417 (11), 420 (2), 425
(3), 431 (1), 431 (5), 818
(2), 818 (8), 841 (7)

glow-worm 365 (16), 417
(2), 417 (3), 419 (3), 420
(2)

glower 438 (8), 891 (7),
893 (1), 893 (3)

glowering 891 (4), 893 (2)

glowing 379 (4), 379 (5),
417 (8), 425 (6), 431 (3),
818 (5), 821 (3)

glue 47 (9), 48 (4), 354 (3)

glue-sniffing 949 (4)

glued 45 (7)

gluey 48 (2), 354 (5)

glum 834 (6)

glumness 834 (1)

glut 171 (1), 637 (2), 812
(1), 863 (1), 863 (3)

glut oneself 947 (4)

glutinousness 354 (3)

glutted 863 (2)

glutton 168 (1), 301 (6),
859 (6), 944 (2), 947 (2)

gluttonize 301 (35), 943
(3), 947 (4)

gluttonous 301 (31), 859
(8), 947 (3)

gluttonously 947 (5)

gluttony 301 (1), 301 (4),
637 (1), 859 (1), 943 (1),
944 (1), 947 (1)

glycerine 334 (2), 357 (3)

glyptic 554 (2)

gnarled 246 (3), 259 (4),
324 (4)

gnash 333 (3)

gnash one's teeth 161 (8),
547 (21), 891 (7)

gnashing 176 (6)

gnat 33 (5), 365 (16)

gnaw 46 (12), 301 (36), 333
(3), 377 (5), 891 (9)

gnaw at 827 (8)

gnawing 827 (3)

gnome 970 (2)

gnosticism 973 (2)

go 173 (3), 174 (1), 265 (4),
267 (11), 290 (3), 446 (3),
622 (8), 678 (2)

go about 672 (3)

go about together 880 (7)

go adrift 282 (5)

go after 617 (6)

go against 182 (3), 704 (4)

go-ahead 488 (1), 672 (2),
756 (2)

go all out 277 (6), 671 (4)

go along with 181 (3), 488
(6)

go amiss 728 (8)

go and return 141 (6)

go and see 882 (9)

go another way 46 (7)

go ashore 295 (5)

go astray 282 (5), 495 (7)

go away 46 (7), 190 (7),
265 (4), 290 (3), 296 (4)

go awry 728 (8)

go back 148 (3), 282 (4),
286 (5), 290 (3)

go back on 603 (7), 769 (3)

go backwards 286 (4)

go bad 649 (8), 655 (7)

go bail 767 (5)

go bail for 703 (6), 764 (4)

go bankrupt 728 (7), 772
(4), 805 (5)

go before 283 (3)

go begging 637 (6)

go berserk 176 (7), 503
(11), 712 (9), 891 (6)

go-between 45 (2), 231 (3),
524 (4), 529 (5), 628 (2),
720 (2), 894 (5), 952 (5)

go-between, be a 720 (4)

go beyond 34 (7), 306 (3)

go blind 439 (3)

go broke 801 (5)

go bull-headed at 857 (4)

go by 111 (3)

go by instinct 450 (4)

go by sea 269 (9)

go by the name of 561 (7)

go cart 274 (4)

go climbing 308 (5)

go contemporary 126 (8)

go courting 889 (7)

go dancing 837 (22)

go different ways 46 (7)

go down 165 (11), 309 (3),
313 (4)

go down the drain 772 (5)

go down well 485 (10), 828
(5)

go down with 651 (23)

go downhill 655 (7), 728
(9), 731 (7)

go Dutch 775 (5), 804 (5)

go easy 177 (5), 736 (3)

go easy on 905 (7)

go far 730 (6)

go fifty-fifty 92 (5), 775 (5)

go first 64 (3)

go fishing 619 (6)

go flat 655 (7)

go for 617 (6), 712 (7), 809
(6)

go for a run or a jog 267
(14)

go for a walk 267 (14)

go forward 285 (3)

go free 744 (9)

go-getter 932 (2)

go-getting 174 (5), 678 (7),
932 (3)

go grey 131 (8)

go half and half 770 (2)

go halfway 625 (6)

go halves 28 (9), 92 (5),
775 (5)

go hand in hand with 89
(4)

go hard with 731 (7)

go headfirst 313 (3)

go home 296 (4)

go hunting 619 (6)

go in 297 (5)

go in for 610 (7), 622 (7)

go in front 283 (3)

go into 591 (5)
go into ecstasies 818 (8), 824 (6)
go into exile 57 (4)
go into liquidation 805 (5)
go into mourning 836 (5)
go into orbit 271 (7), 315 (5)
go into retreat 449 (8), 981 (12)
go lame 163 (9)
go like clockwork 701 (6)
go livid 818 (8)
go mad 503 (11), 822 (4)
go modern 126 (8)
go off 176 (7), 400 (4), 655 (7)
go on 113 (6), 139 (3), 144 (3), 146 (3), 154 (6), 265 (4), 285 (3), 305 (5), 600 (4), 678 (11)
go on a diet 942 (4)
go on a fool's errand 695 (8)
go on a pilgrimage 267 (11)
go on board 296 (6)
go on foot 267 (14)
go on record 528 (10)
go on safari 267 (11)
go on the rampage 176 (7)
go one better 34 (7), 306 (5), 698 (5)
go one's own way 595 (2)
go out 298 (5), 382 (6)
go out of one's mind 503 (11)
go out of one's way 282 (3), 626 (3)
go outside 290 (3)
go over 106 (4), 221 (4), 459 (15), 536 (5)
go over the top 712 (10)
go over to the attack 712 (7)
go past 305 (5)
go pit-a-pat 318 (5)
go purple 818 (8)
go red 431 (5)
go red in the face 818 (8)
go right through one 407 (5)

go round 250 (8), 267 (12), 314 (4), 626 (3)
go rusty 695 (7)
go sailing 269 (8)
go scot-free 667 (5)
go shares 775 (5), 783 (3)
go shooting 619 (6)
go shopping 792 (5)
go sightseeing 267 (11)
go-slow 278 (1), 278 (4)
go smoothly 258 (5), 265 (4), 267 (11), 701 (6), 730 (6)
go sour 655 (7)
go steady 889 (7)
go straight 249 (3), 929 (5), 933 (4)
go straight for 281 (5)
go surety for 767 (5)
go the church 976 (12)
go the rounds 314 (4), 528 (12), 780 (5)
go through 154 (7), 305 (5), 459 (15), 688 (5), 818 (7), 825 (7)
go through it 377 (6)
go through phases 152 (5)
go through the motions 541 (6)
go to 199 (5), 267 (11)
go to arbitration 770 (2)
go to bed 266 (7), 679 (12), 683 (3)
go to bed with 45 (14)
go to church 979 (9)
go to confession 939 (4), 941 (6)
go to earth 444 (4), 525 (9)
go to extremes 546 (3)
go to it 599 (3)
go to law 709 (7), 959 (7)
go to meet 295 (6)
go to one's head 503 (12), 873 (6), 949 (16)
go to pieces 51 (5), 165 (11), 655 (7)
go to rack and ruin 165 (11)
go to sea 269 (8)
go to sleep 679 (12)
go to the bad 655 (7)
go to the dogs 165 (11), 731 (7)

go to the wall 165 (11)
go to war 709 (7), 712 (7), 716 (11), 718 (10)
go together 89 (4)
go too far 306 (3), 546 (3)
go towards 281 (5)
go under 165 (11)
go underground 309 (3), 525 (9)
go up 308 (4), 811 (4)
go visiting 882 (9)
go well 841 (8)
go wide 728 (7)
go wild 822 (4)
go with 24 (9), 89 (4), 773 (5)
go without 760 (4), 946 (4)
go without saying 522 (9)
go wrong 495 (7), 728 (8), 914 (5)
goad 174 (4), 176 (9), 612 (4), 612 (9), 821 (2), 821 (7), 891 (9)
goal 69 (2), 76 (1), 145 (5), 266 (3), 271 (2), 281 (1), 295 (2), 617 (2), 671 (1), 859 (5)
goalkeeper 837 (16)
goat 365 (7)
goat-keeping 369 (1)
goatherd 369 (6)
goatish 365 (18)
goatlike 365 (18)
gobbet 33 (3)
gobble 299 (4), 409 (3), 947 (4)
gobble up 165 (10), 634 (4)
gobbledygook 515 (1), 560 (3)
goblet 194 (15)
goblin 970 (2)
God 965 (3), 966 (1)
God-fearing 979 (6)
god-making 982 (2)
god of war 718 (1)
god or goddess of love 966 (2)
god or goddess of war 966 (2)
God revealed 975 (1)
God willing 469 (5)
godchild 11 (3)
goddess 966 (1)

goddess of love 887 (7)

godforsaken 190 (5), 883 (7)

godhead 965 (1)

godless 974 (5), 980 (4)

godlessness 974 (1), 980 (1)

godlike 965 (6)

godliness 979 (2)

godly 979 (6)

godparent 169 (1)

gods 594 (7)

gods of the underworld 966 (2)

gods, the 966 (1)

God's ways 965 (1)

God's will 596 (2)

God's word 975 (1)

godsend 615 (2)

goggle 438 (8), 508 (4)

goggle at 864 (6)

going 265 (1), 296 (3), 621 (1), 678 (7)

going after 65 (1)

going against 704 (1)

going apart 294 (1)

going away 296 (1)

going back 125 (9), 296 (1)

going, be 296 (4)

going before 64 (1), 283 (1)

going begging 637 (4), 774 (3)

going beyond 306 (1)

going cheap 812 (3)

going down 37 (3)

going forward 285 (1)

going grey 131 (6)

going halves 28 (4)

going on 55 (4)

going on board 296 (1)

going on foot 267 (3)

going out 298 (1)

going over 106 (1)

going rate 809 (1)

going the rounds 529 (7)

going to law 959 (5)

going too far 32 (12), 847 (4)

going up 308 (1)

goitre 253 (2)

gold 432 (1), 432 (2), 433 (1), 433 (3), 644 (3), 797 (1)

gold bar 797 (7)

gold-digger 459 (9), 932 (2)

gold leaf 844 (2)

gold-mine 632 (1), 800 (1)

gold standard 797 (3)

golden 730 (5), 852 (5)

Golden Age 730 (2), 824 (2), 935 (1)

golden apple 612 (4)

golden calf 982 (3)

golden-haired 433 (3)

golden handshake 804 (2)

golden-hearted 897 (4)

golden mean 30 (1), 177 (1), 625 (1)

golden oldie 127 (2)

golden opportunity 137 (2)

golden rule 496 (1), 693 (1)

golden times 730 (2)

golden touch 800 (1)

golden wedding 141 (3), 876 (2)

goldfish 365 (2)

golf 837 (7)

Goliath 162 (4), 195 (4)

gondola 275 (8), 276 (2)

gondolier 270 (4)

gone 125 (6), 190 (4), 446 (2), 772 (3)

gone bad 645 (2), 653 (2), 655 (5)

gone, be 446 (3)

gone before 361 (6)

gone by 127 (7)

gone off 391 (2)

gone out of one's head 506 (3)

gone to earth 446 (2)

gone to waste 634 (3)

gong 117 (3), 400 (2), 414 (8), 547 (5)

gonorrhoea 651 (13)

goo 354 (3)

good 615 (1), 615 (3), 640 (1), 640 (2), 640 (3), 644 (4), 660 (4), 730 (1), 739 (3), 826 (2), 884 (4), 897

(4), 913 (3), 929 (3), 933 (3), 933 (4), 950 (5), 979 (6)

good age 113 (2)

good and evil 14 (2)

good as gold 933 (3)

good at 694 (4)

good at, be 694 (8)

good, be 34 (7), 644 (10), 694 (8), 866 (11)

good behaviour 884 (1), 933 (1)

good breeding 848 (2), 884 (1)

good buy 792 (1)

good case 475 (5)

good cause 901 (1)

good chance 159 (3), 469 (1), 471 (1)

good character 929 (1)

good cheer 301 (9), 824 (3), 833 (2)

good citizenship 901 (3)

good clean fun 837 (1)

good company 882 (2), 882 (5)

good conscience 933 (1)

good cry 836 (1)

good deal 32 (2)

good deed 897 (2)

good defence 927 (1)

good ear 415 (1)

good example 24 (3)

good excuse 927 (1)

good faith 768 (1), 929 (1)

good fellowship 882 (2)

good few, a 104 (4)

good fit 24 (4)

good for 640 (2), 652 (4)

good for nothing 641 (5), 934 (4)

good form 610 (2), 848 (2), 875 (2)

good fortune 159 (1), 615 (1), 727 (1), 730 (1), 824 (2)

good giver 781 (4), 813 (2)

good grammar 564 (1)

good grounds 927 (1)

good head for 694 (2)

good health 650 (1)

good hearing 415 (1)

good housekeeping 814 (1)

good housewife 814 (1)

good humour 833 (1), 884 (1)

good-humoured 897 (4)

good in parts 647 (3)

good intentions 617 (1)

good judgment 480 (1), 498 (2)

good law 953 (1)

good likeness 18 (1)

good-looking 841 (3), 887 (11)

good looks 841 (1)

good loser 929 (2)

Good luck 730 (10)

good management 814 (1)

good manners 688 (1), 848 (2), 882 (2), 884 (1)

good many, a 104 (4)

good market 793 (1)

good match 894 (6)

good memory 505 (1)

good mixer 882 (5)

good-natured 601 (3), 897 (4)

good neighbour 703 (3), 880 (3), 882 (5), 897 (3), 903 (1), 937 (1)

good news 529 (1)

good nose 394 (1)

good offices 703 (1), 710 (1), 719 (1), 720 (1), 897 (2)

good old days 125 (1)

good omen 852 (1)

good opinion 866 (1), 923 (1)

good order 60 (1)

good person 644 (3), 903 (1), 929 (2), 937 (1), 979 (4)

good points 644 (1)

good policy 24 (3), 137 (1), 605 (1), 615 (1), 640 (1), 642 (1), 673 (1)

good reason 471 (1)

good report 866 (1)

good repute 866 (1)

good riddance 831 (1)

Good Samaritan 703 (3), 897 (3), 903 (1), 937 (1)

good sense 498 (1)

good shot 619 (3)

good sight 438 (1)

good sort 929 (2), 937 (1)

good spender 813 (2)

good sport 833 (2), 890 (2), 929 (2)

good stead 640 (1)

good taste 463 (1), 575 (1), 654 (3), 841 (1), 846 (1), 848 (2), 862 (1), 884 (1), 950 (1)

good-tempered 823 (3), 884 (4)

good time 837 (2)

good-time girl 837 (17)

good to eat 390 (2)

good try 671 (1)

good turn 615 (2), 897 (2)

good usage 673 (1)

good value 812 (1)

good will 597 (1), 703 (1), 897 (1)

good wishes 886 (1)

good works 901 (1)

goodbye 296 (7)

goodbyes 296 (2)

goodly 32 (4), 615 (3), 841 (3)

goodness 34 (1), 638 (1), 640 (1), 644 (1), 694 (1), 846 (1), 929 (1), 933 (1), 965 (2), 979 (1), 979 (2)

goods 164 (2), 272 (3), 777 (1), 795 (1)

goods and chattels 777 (1)

goods train 273 (1), 274 (13)

goods yard 624 (7)

goodwill 880 (2)

goody 937 (1)

goody-goody 501 (2), 541 (4), 935 (3), 979 (7)

gooey 354 (5)

goof 501 (2)

goofy 499 (4)

googly 282 (1)

goose 365 (4), 406 (1), 501 (1)

goose pimples 380 (1)

gooseberry bush 167 (2)

gooseflesh 259 (1), 378 (2), 380 (1), 854 (2)

Gordian knot 47 (4)

gore 228 (3), 263 (18), 335 (3), 431 (1), 655 (10)

gorge 201 (2), 209 (2), 255 (3), 863 (3), 947 (4)

gorged 54 (4), 637 (3), 863 (2)

gorgeous 425 (6), 644 (5), 841 (4), 844 (10), 875 (5)

gorgeousness 841 (1)

gorging 947 (1), 947 (3)

gorgon 84 (4)

gorilla 365 (3)

gormandize 301 (35), 947 (4)

gormandizer 947 (2)

gormandizing 301 (2), 947 (1)

gormless 499 (4)

gorse 366 (6)

gory 335 (5), 362 (9), 431 (4)

gosling 132 (3), 365 (4)

gospel 975 (1), 975 (4), 976 (8)

gossamer 163 (3), 208 (1), 422 (1)

gossamery 323 (3), 331 (4)

gossip 4 (2), 453 (2), 524 (5), 524 (9), 529 (2), 529 (4), 543 (3), 579 (8), 581 (2), 581 (3), 581 (5), 584 (2), 584 (6), 904 (1), 926 (7)

gossip columnist 926 (4)

gossip writer 589 (7)

gossiper 579 (5), 926 (4)

gossiping 581 (2), 581 (4)

gossipy 524 (7), 529 (7), 581 (4), 882 (6)

got 771 (6)

got by heart 505 (5)

got it 484 (6)

got up 844 (11)

Gothic 586 (7), 587 (3)

gothic novel 590 (4)

gouache 553 (2), 553 (6)

gouge out 255 (8), 304 (4)

gourmand 301 (6), 944 (2), 947 (2)

gourmandism 301 (4)

gourmet **301** (4), **301** (6), **846** (2), **862** (2), **944** (2), **947** (2)

gout **651** (15)

gouty **163** (7), **651** (22), **892** (3)

govern **689** (4), **733** (10)

governance **178** (1), **688** (2), **689** (1), **733** (2)

governed, be **733** (13)

governess **537** (1), **742** (2), **749** (1)

governing **689** (3), **733** (8)

governing body **690** (1)

government **178** (1), **371** (5), **689** (1), **733** (4), **741** (1), **751** (1)

governmentbypriests**733** (4)

government post **733** (5)

government service **745** (2)

Government, the **733** (1)

governmental **622** (5), **689** (3), **733** (9)

governor **537** (1), **690** (1), **741** (1), **741** (5), **986** (4)

governorship **733** (5)

gown **228** (7), **228** (8)

GP **658** (14)

grab **778** (5), **786** (6)

grab at **786** (6)

grabber **786** (4)

grace **566** (1), **574** (6), **575** (1), **694** (1), **756** (1), **781** (2), **841** (1), **841** (8), **844** (12), **846** (1), **870** (1), **905** (3), **907** (2), **923** (1), **981** (4)

grace and favour **756** (1), **812** (2)

grace note **410** (2)

grace with **866** (13)

graceful **575** (3), **841** (5), **846** (3)

gracefulness **575** (1), **841** (1)

graceless **576** (2), **695** (5), **842** (5), **934** (3), **934** (4)

gracelessness **842** (1)

Graces **93** (2), **841** (1)

gracious **841** (3), **884** (3), **897** (4)

gracious living **376** (2), **846** (1)

graciousness **688** (1), **884** (1)

gradatim **278** (8)

gradation **27** (1), **60** (1), **62** (1), **71** (2), **73** (1)

gradational **27** (2)

grade **16** (4), **27** (1), **27** (4), **62** (4), **62** (6), **71** (6), **73** (1), **73** (2), **77** (2), **216** (7), **465** (12), **538** (4)

graded **27** (2), **62** (3)

gradient **220** (2), **308** (1)

grading **27** (1), **62** (1), **62** (2)

gradual **27** (2), **71** (4), **278** (3)

gradually **27** (6), **33** (9), **71** (7)

graduate **24** (10), **27** (4), **71** (6), **73** (2), **465** (12), **492** (1), **536** (4), **538** (3), **654** (8), **696** (1), **727** (6)

graduated **27** (2), **465** (10)

graduation **27** (1)

Graeco-Roman deities **967** (1)

graft **170** (2), **303** (6), **370** (9), **612** (2), **790** (1), **930** (1)

grain **5** (4), **33** (3), **179** (1), **196** (2), **322** (2), **331** (2), **332** (2), **366** (8)

grain plant **366** (8)

grained **331** (4)

grains **301** (22)

gram **33** (2), **322** (2)

grammar **67** (1), **557** (2), **559** (1), **564** (1), **589** (3)

grammar school **539** (2)

grammarian **557** (4)

grammatical **557** (5), **564** (3)

grammaticalness **564** (1)

gramophone **398** (1), **412** (4), **414** (10), **415** (4), **548** (1), **549** (3)

gran **169** (4)

granary **632** (2)

grand **32** (4), **99** (5), **192** (20), **571** (2), **644** (5), **821**

(5), **841** (4), **866** (8), **871** (3), **875** (4), **875** (6)

grand jury **957** (3)

grand opera **594** (3)

grand piano **414** (4)

grand slam **727** (2)

grand style **553** (2)

grand vizier **741** (6)

grandad **133** (2), **169** (3)

grandchildren **170** (1)

grandee **638** (4), **868** (4)

grandeur **32** (1), **571** (1), **841** (1), **875** (1)

grandfather **133** (2), **169** (3)

grandiloquent **574** (5), **579** (7), **877** (4)

grandiose **195** (7), **574** (5), **871** (3), **875** (4)

grandiosity **195** (2), **871** (1), **875** (1)

grandma **133** (3), **169** (4)

grandmother **133** (3), **169** (4)

grandness **32** (1)

grandpa **133** (2), **169** (3)

grandparents **11** (2)

grandstand **438** (5), **441** (2), **724** (1)

grange **192** (6), **370** (2)

granite **326** (1), **344** (4)

granitic **344** (5)

granny **133** (3), **169** (4)

grant **158** (3), **468** (3), **475** (9), **488** (6), **526** (6), **703** (2), **756** (2), **758** (1), **758** (3), **777** (6), **780** (3), **780** (4), **781** (2), **781** (7), **804** (2)

grant a loan **802** (3)

grant a receipt **767** (6)

grant a request **758** (3)

grant asylum **299** (3), **660** (8)

grant claims **158** (3), **768** (4), **913** (6), **915** (8), **927** (5)

grant equal rights **746** (3)

grant immunity **919** (3)

grant impunity **919** (3)

grant leave **756** (5)

grant peace **719** (4)

granted 478 (3), 488 (5), 512 (5)

granting 8 (6), 488 (4)

granting access 624 (8)

granular 196 (11), 331 (4), 332 (4)

granulate 332 (5)

granulated 332 (4)

granulation 331 (2), 332 (1)

granule 332 (2)

grape 301 (19)

grape, the 301 (29)

grapefruit 301 (19)

grapevine 524 (4), 529 (2)

graphic 516 (3), 551 (6), 553 (7), 571 (2), 590 (6)

graphic art 551 (3)

graphics 551 (1)

graphologist 459 (8), 586 (5)

graphology 586 (1)

graphs 86 (3)

grapple 45 (14), 712 (7), 716 (10), 716 (11), 778 (5)

grapple with 704 (5), 712 (9)

grappling iron 47 (6)

grasp 160 (2), 183 (3), 199 (1), 490 (1), 490 (8), 498 (6), 516 (5), 773 (1), 778 (1), 778 (5), 786 (1)

grasp at 786 (6), 859 (11)

grasp at shadows 470 (6)

grasp the nettle 672 (3)

grasping 735 (6), 786 (5), 816 (5), 859 (8)

grass 366 (8), 524 (5), 524 (9), 928 (3)

grass-green 434 (3)

grass over 370 (9)

grass roots 869 (1)

grass snake 365 (13)

grasshopper 312 (2), 365 (16)

grasshopper mind 152 (2), 456 (1)

grassland 344 (3), 348 (2), 366 (8), 370 (2)

grasslands 348 (1)

grassy 366 (9), 434 (3)

grate 301 (40), 332 (5), 333 (3), 377 (5), 383 (1), 407 (4), 411 (3), 827 (11), 888 (8)

grate against 279 (8)

grate on 827 (11)

grated 332 (4)

grateful 828 (2), 907 (3), 923 (5)

grateful, be 828 (4), 886 (3), 907 (4), 962 (3)

grateful heart 907 (1)

gratefully 907 (6)

gratefulness 907 (1)

grater 259 (1), 263 (3), 332 (3)

gratification 376 (1), 824 (3)

gratified 824 (4)

gratify 826 (3), 828 (5)

gratifying 376 (3), 826 (2)

grating 25 (4), 222 (3), 353 (1), 407 (2), 411 (2), 576 (2), 861 (3)

gratis 781 (6), 812 (4)

gratitude 886 (1), 907 (1), 923 (1), 962 (1), 981 (6)

gratuitous 512 (4), 597 (5), 781 (6), 812 (4)

gratuity 612 (4), 771 (1), 781 (2)

grave 255 (4), 364 (5), 548 (7), 555 (3), 571 (2), 638 (5), 823 (3), 834 (7), 840 (2), 934 (6), 972 (1)

grave clothes 364 (3)

grave-digger 255 (5)

grave, the 361 (1)

gravel 226 (15), 332 (2)

gravelly 332 (4), 344 (5)

graven image 982 (3)

gravestone 364 (2)

graveyard 364 (4), 990 (2)

gravitate 309 (3), 322 (5)

gravitate towards 179 (3)

gravitation 179 (1), 322 (1)

gravitational 322 (4)

gravity 26 (1), 160 (1), 160 (3), 195 (1), 195 (3), 291 (1), 319 (1), 322 (1), 571 (1), 638 (1), 823 (1), 834 (3), 950 (2)

gravy 389 (2)

gravy boat 194 (16)

graze 200 (5), 202 (3), 212 (1), 279 (3), 279 (8), 301 (37), 301 (39), 333 (1), 333 (3), 378 (1), 378 (7), 655 (10)

grazing 202 (2), 348 (2)

grazing contact 202 (1)

grease 226 (16), 258 (2), 258 (4), 334 (2), 334 (4), 357 (3), 357 (9), 401 (2), 701 (8)

grease-gun 334 (2)

grease one's palm 612 (12), 781 (7), 804 (4)

greased 357 (7)

greasepaint 594 (6), 843 (3)

greasiness 258 (1), 357 (1)

greasing 334 (1)

greasy 258 (3), 357 (7), 649 (7)

great 32 (4), 34 (4), 34 (5), 36 (3), 160 (8), 178 (2), 195 (6), 635 (4), 644 (4), 644 (5), 866 (8), 866 (10), 868 (6), 871 (3)

great, be 32 (15), 36 (4), 104 (6)

Great Bear 321 (4)

great circle 250 (2)

great company 866 (6)

great day 876 (2)

great deal 32 (2)

great deal, a 32 (17)

great fun, be 837 (20)

great gun 723 (11)

great-hearted 931 (2)

great in age 32 (4)

great in honour 32 (4)

great in number 32 (4)

great in quantity 32 (4)

great intellect 447 (1)

great majority 104 (2)

great man 866 (6)

Great Mother 966 (2)

great news 638 (2)

great panjandrum 638 (4)

great quantity 26 (2), 32 (2), 52 (3), 74 (5), 104 (1), 171 (3), 195 (3), 635 (2), 637 (1), 797 (2), 800 (1)

Great Spirit 965 (3)

great woman 866 (6)

greatcoat 228 (20)

greater 32 (4), 34 (4)

greater good 615 (1)

greater number 26 (2), 32 (3), 34 (2), 101 (1), 104 (3), 160 (1)

greater part 32 (3)

greatest 32 (4), 34 (5)

greatheart 855 (3)

greatly 32 (17), 52 (9), 54 (8), 107 (3)

greatness 32 (1), 34 (1), 36 (1), 160 (1), 178 (1), 195 (1), 195 (2), 638 (1), 866 (2)

greed 786 (3), 816 (2), 859 (1), 932 (1), 947 (1)

greedily 859 (14)

greediness 859 (1), 944 (1), 947 (1)

greedy 301 (31), 636 (4), 771 (4), 816 (5), 859 (8), 912 (2), 932 (3), 947 (3)

greedy pig 947 (2)

Greek 491 (2)

Greek to, be 515 (6)

green 126 (5), 130 (4), 269 (6), 300 (5), 348 (2), 366 (9), 393 (2), 434 (1), 434 (3), 487 (2), 491 (4), 505 (5), 544 (2), 611 (3), 670 (4), 695 (4), 724 (1), 837 (4)

green belt 184 (3)

Green Cross code 305 (3)

green-eyed 911 (2)

green fingers 370 (1), 694 (2)

green light 547 (5), 756 (2)

green pigment 434 (2)

green room 594 (7)

green vegetable 301 (20)

green with envy 912 (2)

greenery 366 (5), 434 (1)

greenfly 365 (16)

greengrocer 633 (2)

greenhorn 501 (2), 538 (2), 544 (1), 697 (1)

greenhouse 370 (3)

greenhouse effect 340 (2)

greenish 434 (3)

greenness 126 (1), 434 (1), 491 (1)

greens 301 (20), 706 (2)

greensward 348 (2)

Greenwich Mean Time 117 (2)

greenwood 366 (2)

greet 289 (4), 295 (6), 408 (3), 583 (3), 880 (7), 882 (10), 884 (7), 920 (6)

greeting 295 (1), 583 (1), 880 (2), 882 (2), 884 (2)

greetings 295 (7), 920 (2)

greetings card 588 (1)

gregarious 882 (6)

gregariousness 882 (2)

Gregorian 413 (7)

Gregorian calendar 117 (4)

gremlin 702 (5), 970 (2)

grenade 402 (1), 723 (14)

grenadier 722 (5)

grey 16 (2), 419 (4), 426 (3), 427 (5), 429 (1), 429 (2), 625 (3), 732 (2), 834 (8)

grey dawn 419 (2)

grey hairs 131 (3), 429 (1)

grey matter 498 (1)

greybeard 133 (2)

greyhound 277 (4), 365 (10)

greying 131 (6), 429 (2)

greyish 429 (2)

greyish-brown 430 (3)

greyness 16 (1), 419 (1), 429 (1)

grid 222 (3)

grid reference 465 (4)

gridiron 222 (3)

grief 616 (1), 825 (2), 829 (1)

grief-stricken 825 (6)

grievance 616 (1), 827 (2), 829 (1), 914 (1)

grieve 825 (7), 827 (8), 834 (9), 834 (11), 836 (5), 905 (6)

grieve for 836 (5)

grieving 825 (6)

grievous 827 (6)

grievously 32 (20)

griffin 84 (4)

grill 301 (40), 379 (7), 381 (8), 383 (2), 459 (14)

grill pan 194 (14)

grill room 192 (13)

grille 222 (3), 263 (5)

grilling 459 (2)

grim 599 (2), 645 (4), 827 (6), 834 (7), 854 (8), 885 (5), 898 (7)

grim determination 599 (1)

grim-faced 898 (7)

grim look 842 (1)

grim-visaged 842 (3)

grimace 246 (1), 246 (5), 318 (1), 438 (3), 547 (4), 547 (21), 835 (8), 842 (7), 861 (4), 893 (1), 893 (3)

grimacing 246 (3)

grime 649 (2)

grimness 602 (1), 827 (1), 834 (3)

grimy 649 (7)

grin 835 (2), 835 (8), 851 (1)

grin and bear it 823 (6)

grin at 851 (5)

grind 37 (4), 46 (12), 165 (7), 198 (7), 244 (3), 256 (11), 301 (36), 332 (5), 333 (3), 377 (5), 407 (4), 655 (10), 682 (3), 735 (8)

grind one's teeth 891 (7)

grinder 256 (4), 332 (3)

grinding 165 (1), 332 (1)

grinding poverty 801 (1)

grindstone 256 (6), 682 (3), 838 (2)

grinner 835 (3)

grip 45 (9), 47 (5), 48 (3), 162 (2), 174 (1), 178 (1), 194 (9), 218 (3), 694 (1), 733 (2), 747 (7), 773 (1), 778 (1), 778 (5), 821 (8)

gripe 377 (5)

gripes 651 (7)

gripped 778 (4)

gripping 178 (2), 821 (4)

grisly 842 (4), 854 (8)

grist 631 (1)

gristle 324 (3), 329 (1)

gristly 326 (3), 329 (2)

grit 162 (1), 174 (1), 332 (2), 599 (1), 600 (2)

grit one's teeth 547 (21), 599 (3)

grittiness 332 (1)

gritty 332 (4)

grizzle 427 (6), 836 (1), 836 (6)

grizzled 427 (5), 429 (2), 437 (7)

grizzly 365 (3), 429 (2)

groan 377 (6), 408 (3), 829 (1), 829 (5), 834 (9), 836 (1), 836 (6)

groaning 836 (1)

groans 762 (1)

grocer 633 (2), 794 (2)

groceries 301 (7)

grog 301 (28)

groggy 317 (3), 651 (21)

groom 369 (10), 648 (9), 669 (11), 742 (1), 742 (2)

groom one for 534 (8)

groomed 669 (7), 844 (11)

grooming 843 (1)

groove 46 (11), 81 (2), 201 (2), 255 (2), 255 (8), 261 (3), 262 (1), 262 (3), 610 (1), 844 (12)

grope 278 (4), 378 (7), 440 (4), 461 (8), 695 (9)

grope for 459 (15)

groping 278 (3), 491 (4)

gross 32 (13), 522 (4), 645 (4), 771 (7), 782 (4), 786 (6), 847 (4), 934 (6), 944 (3), 951 (3)

gross, a 99 (5)

gross amount 52 (2)

grossness 847 (1), 944 (1), 951 (1)

grotesque 84 (6), 246 (3), 497 (3), 513 (5), 576 (2), 842 (2), 842 (4), 849 (2)

grotto 194 (23), 255 (2)

grouchy 829 (3), 893 (2)

ground 156 (6), 165 (5), 184 (2), 214 (1), 218 (1), 218 (4), 269 (10), 332 (4), 344 (1), 534 (6)

ground crew 271 (4)

ground floor 214 (1)

ground plan 551 (5)

ground staff 722 (14)

ground swell 350 (5)

grounded 214 (3), 271 (6), 728 (6)

grounded on 214 (3), 466 (5)

groundless 4 (3), 159 (6), 477 (5)

grounds 41 (2), 184 (2), 192 (15), 466 (1), 475 (5), 612 (1), 649 (2), 777 (3)

groundwork 66 (2), 156 (3), 214 (1), 669 (1)

group 50 (4), 53 (1), 53 (3), 62 (1), 62 (4), 62 (6), 74 (3), 74 (11), 77 (1), 104 (2), 123 (2), 365 (2), 371 (4), 708 (1), 708 (3), 722 (8), 722 (14)

group activity 882 (2)

group captain 741 (9)

group therapy 658 (12)

groupie 132 (2), 284 (2)

grouping 62 (1)

grouse 365 (5), 829 (5), 836 (5), 893 (3)

grouser 489 (2), 763 (1), 829 (2), 836 (3), 924 (5)

grousing 885 (5)

grove 366 (2)

grovel 721 (4), 739 (4), 879 (4)

groveller 879 (2)

grovelling 879 (3)

grow 1 (7), 36 (4), 36 (5), 74 (10), 134 (4), 143 (5), 157 (5), 164 (7), 167 (6), 197 (4), 308 (4), 366 (12), 369 (9), 370 (9), 669 (12)

grow animated 833 (7)

grow blurred 440 (4)

grow cold 380 (7)

grow dark 418 (5)

grow dazzled 440 (4)

grow dim 37 (5)

grow dissipated 943 (3)

grow fat 730 (6)

grow from 157 (5)

grow heated 891 (6)

grow indifferent 860 (4)

grow into 316 (3)

grow less 37 (5)

grow nasty 900 (3)

grow old 108 (8), 113 (6), 127 (8), 131 (8), 163 (9), 655 (7), 842 (6)

grow rank 649 (8)

grow together 48 (3), 50 (4)

grow up 36 (4), 134 (4), 197 (4), 308 (4)

grow warm 891 (6)

grow weak 163 (9), 651 (23)

growing 36 (3), 130 (4)

growing pains 68 (1), 130 (1)

growing thing 366 (6)

growing together 50 (1)

growl 409 (3), 885 (6), 891 (2), 893 (3), 900 (3)

growling 407 (3), 900 (2)

grown 164 (6), 669 (8)

grown-up 134 (2), 134 (3), 669 (8)

grown up, be 134 (4)

growth 36 (1), 147 (1), 157 (2), 164 (1), 164 (2), 167 (1), 197 (1), 253 (2), 316 (1), 651 (11)

growth area 36 (1)

groyne 254 (2)

grub 132 (3), 301 (9), 365 (17)

grub up 304 (4)

grubby 649 (6)

grudge 598 (4), 636 (9), 816 (6), 829 (1), 829 (5), 881 (1), 881 (4), 888 (1), 891 (1)

grudging 598 (3), 816 (4), 829 (1), 881 (3), 891 (3), 912 (2)

grudging giver 816 (3)

grudging praise 912 (1)

grudging thanks 908 (1)

gruel 301 (22)

gruelling 682 (5), 684 (4), 827 (3)

gruesome 645 (4), 842 (4), 854 (8)

gruff 407 (3), 582 (2), 885 (5), 892 (3), 893 (2)

gruffness 407 (1), 885 (2), 892 (1), 893 (1)

grumble 403 (3), 408 (3), 829 (5), 893 (3)

grumbler 829 (2)

grumbling 403 (1), 829 (3), 885 (5), 893 (2), 900 (2)

grumpiness 892 (1), 893 (1)

grumpy 892 (3), 893 (2)

grunt 407 (4), 408 (1), 408 (3), 409 (3)

grunting 407 (3)

guano 302 (4)

guarantee 473 (9), 532 (2), 660 (1), 660 (8), 703 (6), 764 (1), 764 (4), 767 (1), 767 (6)

guaranteed 473 (4), 494 (5), 532 (3), 660 (4), 764 (3), 767 (4)

guarantor 707 (4)

guard 264 (3), 268 (5), 457 (2), 660 (2), 660 (3), 660 (8), 713 (6), 713 (9), 749 (1)

guard against 669 (10)

guard dog 660 (3)

guard of honour 920 (2)

guarded 457 (4), 858 (2)

guardhouse 748 (2)

guardian 169 (1), 660 (3), 713 (6), 749 (1)

guardian angel 660 (3), 707 (4), 903 (1), 968 (1)

guardianship 169 (1), 660 (2)

guarding 747 (3)

guardrail 662 (3)

guardroom 748 (2)

guards 722 (4), 722 (7)

guard's van 274 (13)

gudgeon 218 (11)

guerrilla 712 (5), 722 (4), 738 (4)

guerrilla warfare 718 (6)

guess 471 (6), 476 (3), 480 (6), 485 (3), 491 (8), 512 (2), 512 (6), 524 (3)

guess wrong 481 (9)

guesswork 461 (2), 474 (1), 476 (1), 512 (2)

guest 191 (2), 295 (1), 880 (3), 882 (5)

guest house 192 (2)

guest worker 59 (2)

guffaw 835 (2)

guidance 534 (1), 689 (2), 691 (1)

guide 23 (1), 64 (3), 66 (1), 81 (1), 267 (8), 283 (3), 291 (2), 520 (5), 524 (6), 534 (6), 537 (1), 547 (18), 589 (4), 689 (5), 690 (1), 691 (2)

guide dog 365 (10)

guidebook 87 (3), 524 (6), 589 (4)

guided missile 276 (3), 723 (4)

guidelines 693 (1)

guiding 64 (1), 178 (2), 281 (3), 689 (3)

guiding principle 612 (1)

guiding star 520 (5), 547 (7), 612 (1)

guild 74 (3), 622 (1), 708 (4), 708 (5), 794 (1)

guile 541 (2), 542 (1), 698 (1)

guileful 542 (6), 930 (7)

guileless 699 (3), 929 (3), 935 (3)

guillotine 69 (1), 204 (5), 963 (12), 964 (3)

guilt 617 (1), 645 (1), 914 (1), 934 (1), 936 (1), 939 (1), 954 (2)

guilt complex 936 (1)

guilt-feeling 939 (1)

guiltily 936 (5)

guiltiness 914 (1), 936 (1)

guiltless 935 (4)

guiltlessness 935 (1)

guilty 914 (3), 934 (3), 936 (3), 954 (6)

guilty act 306 (1), 738 (1), 914 (1), 934 (2), 936 (2)

guilty, be 936 (4)

guilty behaviour 936 (1)

guilty conscience 936 (1)

guilty love 951 (3)

guilty person 904 (3)

guinea 797 (4)

guinea pig 365 (2), 461 (5)

guise 7 (2), 445 (1), 614 (1), 624 (1), 688 (1)

guitar 414 (2)

guitarist 413 (2)

gulch 201 (2)

gulf 68 (5), 201 (2), 206 (1), 255 (2), 263 (7), 297 (2), 345 (1)

gull 365 (4), 542 (9), 788 (8)

gullet 194 (3), 263 (4), 353 (1)

gullibility 481 (1), 487 (1), 499 (1)

gullible 481 (6), 487 (2), 499 (4), 544 (2)

gully 201 (2), 206 (1), 255 (3), 351 (1), 351 (2)

gulp 299 (4), 301 (26), 352 (7)

gulp down 301 (35), 947 (4)

gum 47 (9), 48 (1), 48 (4), 354 (3), 357 (5)

gum tree 366 (4)

gumboots 228 (27)

gummy 48 (2), 354 (5), 357 (8)

gun 619 (3), 723 (11)

gun carriage 274 (7)

gun dog 365 (10)

gun emplacement 713 (3), 723 (11)

gun runner 789 (1)

gun-running 723 (1)

gunboat 722 (13)

gunfire 400 (1), 712 (3)

gunman 287 (4), 362 (7), 722 (1), 789 (2)

gunmetal 429 (1)

gunner 287 (4), 722 (5)

gunnery 723 (1)

gunning for, be 619 (5)

gunpowder 168 (1), 287 (3), 723 (13)

guns 723 (11)

gurgle 350 (9)

guru 500 (1), 537 (1), 973 (6)

gush 176 (2), 298 (2), 298 (6), 300 (9), 308 (4), 350 (1), 350 (9), 515 (6), 570 (1), 570 (6)

gusher 298 (2), 308 (2), 632 (1)

gushing 298 (2), 541 (4), 570 (3), 581 (4), 818 (3), 850 (4)

gusset 228 (3)

gust 352 (3), 352 (4)

gustation 386 (1)

gustative 386 (2)

gustatory 386 (2)

gusto 174 (1), 376 (1), 824 (3)

gusty 352 (8)

gut 165 (6), 165 (7), 263 (9), 300 (8), 304 (4), 381 (10), 788 (9)

gut reaction 450 (1)

gutless 163 (4)

guts 162 (2), 174 (1), 224 (2), 599 (1)

gutted 381 (6)

gutter 152 (5), 262 (1), 318 (5), 351 (1), 351 (2), 419 (6), 649 (4)

gutter press 528 (4), 847 (1), 926 (4)

guttering 142 (2)

guttersnipe 869 (7)

guttural 407 (1), 407 (3), 560 (5), 577 (3)

gutturalize 407 (4)

guy 47 (2), 47 (3), 372 (1), 497 (4), 521 (3), 551 (2), 552 (3), 851 (3), 851 (6), 921 (5), 926 (6)

guzzle 301 (35)

guzzler 947 (2)

guzzling 301 (2), 947 (3)

gym 724 (1)

gym shoes 228 (27)

gymkhana 716 (2)

gymnasium 162 (3), 539 (4), 724 (1)

gymnast 162 (4)

gymnastic 162 (9), 682 (4)

gymnastics 162 (3), 716 (2), 837 (6)

gymslip 228 (8)

gynaecologist 167 (2), 658 (14)

gynaecology 373 (1), 658 (10)

gypsy 84 (3), 268 (2)

gyrate 315 (5)

gyration 315 (1)

gyratory 315 (4)

gyroscope 315 (3)

gyroscopic 315 (4)

H

H-bomb 723 (14)

ha-ha 201 (2), 235 (2)

habeas corpus 737 (4), 959 (2)

haberdasher 228 (28)

habit 5 (4), 7 (1), 16 (1), 60 (1), 71 (1), 79 (1), 81 (2), 106 (2), 127 (3), 141 (2), 144 (1), 563 (1), 610 (1), 673 (1), 688 (1), 838 (2), 848 (1), 943 (1), 949 (4)

habit-forming 610 (5), 612 (6), 949 (12)

habit of mind 610 (1)

habitat 185 (1), 186 (1), 187 (2), 192 (1)

habitation 164 (3), 192 (1)

habitual 60 (2), 79 (3), 106 (3), 127 (6), 139 (2), 610 (5), 612 (6), 622 (5), 676 (4)

habitually 610 (9)

habitually drunk 949 (11)

habituate 83 (8), 534 (8), 610 (8), 669 (11)

habituated 83 (4), 490 (5), 602 (4), 610 (7), 865 (2)

habituation 610 (3)

habitué 610 (4), 882 (5)

hack 46 (11), 267 (15), 273 (8), 589 (7), 655 (10), 686 (2), 742 (1)

hack work 682 (3)

hackle 259 (3), 547 (10)

hackle feathers 259 (3)

hackneyed 20 (4), 490 (7), 496 (3), 572 (2), 610 (6), 673 (2)

had 771 (6)

had it 165 (5), 361 (5)

Hades 361 (3), 967 (1), 972 (1), 972 (2)

haemoglobin 335 (3)

haemophilia 302 (2), 335 (3), 651 (10)

haemophiliac 651 (18), 651 (22)

haemophilic 335 (5)

haemorrhage 298 (2), 302 (2), 651 (10)

haemorrhoids 253 (2)

haft 218 (3)

hag 133 (3), 983 (6)

hag-ridden 983 (9)

hag-ride 983 (11)

haggard 206 (5), 246 (4), 503 (9), 684 (2), 825 (5), 834 (6)

haggardness 206 (2), 842 (1)

haggle 766 (4), 791 (6), 816 (6)

haggler 792 (2)

haggling 791 (1), 792 (4)

hagiographer 590 (5), 973 (5)

hagiography 590 (3)

haiku 569 (1)

hail 74 (5), 350 (10), 380 (2), 408 (1), 408 (3), 488 (6), 547 (8), 583 (3), 884 (7), 923 (10)

hailstone 380 (2), 380 (4)

hair 208 (1), 208 (2), 217 (2), 222 (5), 256 (3), 259 (2), 327 (1), 331 (2), 843 (2)

hair brush 648 (5)

hair cut 843 (2)

hair on end 854 (1), 854 (2)

hair-raising 821 (4), 854 (8)

hair shirt 945 (1)

hair-splitting 477 (1), 862 (1)

hair style 843 (2)

hair stylist 843 (5)

hairdo 843 (2)

hairdresser 843 (5)

hairdressing 259 (2), 843 (2)

hairiness 259 (1)

hairless 229 (5), 258 (3)

hairlessness 229 (2)

hairpiece 259 (2), 843 (2)

hairpin 47 (5)

hairpin bend 248 (2)

hair's breadth 200 (2), 206 (1)

hairy 206 (4), 256 (7), 259 (5), 259 (8), 331 (4)

hajji 268 (1), 979 (4), 981 (8)

halberd 723 (6), 723 (7)

halberdier 722 (5)

halcyon 717 (3), 730 (5)

halcyon days 730 (2), 824 (1)

hale 288 (3)

hale and hearty 650 (2)

half 53 (1), 53 (6), 55 (1), 55 (3), 92 (1)

half a chance 159 (3)

half-a-dozen 99 (2), 105 (1)

half a hundred 99 (3)

half-and-half 28 (7), 43 (6), 625 (3)

half asleep 456 (3), 679 (9)

half-awake 679 (9)

half-baked 670 (4), 695 (6), 726 (2)

half-belief 486 (2)

half-believe 486 (7)

half-blind 440 (3)

half-blood 43 (5)

half-breed 43 (5)

half-caste 43 (5), 43 (6)

half-circle 250 (4)

half-cut 949 (7)

half-dead 361 (5)

half-done 55 (3), 458 (3), 726 (2)

half-educated 491 (7)

half-finished 53 (6), 55 (3), 670 (4)

half-formed 670 (4)

half-glimpsed 419 (5)

half-god 966 (1)

half-grown 132 (5), 670 (4)

half-hardy 366 (9)

half-heard 401 (3)

half-hearted 163 (4), 598 (3), 601 (3), 820 (4), 860 (2)

half-heartedness 601 (1), 860 (1)

half-hidden 419 (5)

half hitch 47 (4)

half in 57 (3)

half landing 218 (5)

half-life 417 (4)

half-light 129 (1), 417 (1), 419 (2)

half measures 55 (1), 307 (1), 601 (1), 625 (1), 636 (1), 641 (2)

half-melted 354 (4)

half-moon 248 (2), 250 (4), 321 (9)

half-nelson 778 (1)

half out 57 (3)

half-price 812 (3)

half rations 636 (1)

half-ripe 670 (4)

half-seen 419 (5), 444 (3)

half-sleep 679 (4)

half-smile 835 (2)

half sovereign 797 (4)

half-starved 636 (5), 859 (9), 946 (3)

half the battle 638 (3)

half tide 70 (1)

half-timbered 192 (20)

half-truth 543 (2)

half-vision 440 (1)

half-white 427 (5)

half-wit 501 (1)

half year 110 (1)

halftone 417 (6), 553 (5)

halfway 30 (2), 70 (3), 625 (1), 625 (4), 770 (1)

halfway, be 231 (7), 625 (6), 770 (2)

halfway house 70 (1), 192 (17)

halitosis 397 (1)

hall 164 (3), 192 (6), 194 (20)

hall of residence 192 (2)

hallelujah 835 (1), 835 (9), 876 (1), 981 (5), 981 (13)

halliard 47 (3)

hallmark 547 (13)

hallmarked 494 (5)

hallow 876 (4), 979 (12)

hallowed 965 (5)

hallowedness 979 (2)

Hallowe'en 983 (1)

hallucinating 503 (9)

hallucination 4 (1), 445 (1), 495 (1), 513 (3), 542 (1)

hallucinatory 542 (6), 949 (12)

hallucinogen 949 (4)

halo 250 (3), 417 (1), 866 (4)

haloed 979 (8)

halt 69 (1), 69 (6), 72 (3), 145 (2), 145 (5), 145 (6), 145 (7), 145 (9), 163 (7), 163 (9), 266 (1), 266 (8), 266 (11), 295 (2), 702 (10), 747 (7)

halter 47 (8), 250 (3), 748 (4)

halting 142 (2), 278 (3), 576 (2)

halve 46 (10), 92 (5), 783 (3)

halved 92 (4)

ham 267 (7), 301 (16), 594 (9), 695 (4), 850 (5)

ham-acting 594 (8)

ham-handed 695 (5)

ham it up 594 (17)

ham up 839 (5)

hamadryad 967 (3)

hamburgers 301 (16)

hamhandedness 695 (2)

hamlet 184 (3), 192 (8)

hammed up 594 (15)

hammer 174 (7), 279 (4), 279 (9), 287 (2), 400 (4), 630 (1), 712 (9), 723 (5)

hammer and tongs 176 (10)

hammer at 682 (6)

hammer blows 176 (1)

hammer in 263 (18)

hammer into 303 (4)

hammer out 243 (5), 725 (5)

hamming 594 (8)

hammock 217 (2), 218 (7)

hamper 194 (6), 655 (9), 700 (6), 702 (8), 747 (7)

hampered 700 (5)

hampering 702 (1)

hams 238 (2)

hamster 365 (2)

hamstring 161 (9), 702 (8)

happen on 484 (4)

happening 154 (1), 154 (4)

happiness 615 (1), 730 (1), 730 (2), 824 (2), 833 (1), 935 (1)

happy 24 (6), 137 (5), 376 (4), 575 (3), 597 (4), 615 (3), 710 (2), 727 (4), 730 (4), 824 (4), 824 (5), 826 (2), 828 (2), 828 (4), 833 (3), 971 (3)

happy chance 137 (1)

happy dreams 683 (1)

happy either way 606 (2)

happy ending 727 (1)

Happy Families 837 (11)

happy family 880 (4)

happy-go-lucky 618 (6), 734 (3), 833 (3)

happy medium 30 (1), 625 (1)

happy outcome 727 (1)

happy release 361 (2)

happy returns 886 (1)

hara-kiri 362 (3), 963 (1)

harangue 534 (7), 570 (1), 570 (6), 579 (2), 579 (9)

harass 735 (8), 827 (9)

harassed 825 (5)

harassment 735 (1), 827 (1)

harbinger 66 (1), 511 (3)

harbour 295 (2), 662 (2)

harbour a grudge 910 (6)

harbour doubts 486 (7)

harbour patrol 270 (3)

hard 32 (20), 162 (6), 174 (9), 301 (32), 326 (3), 517 (3), 568 (2), 599 (2), 682 (5), 700 (4), 700 (6), 702 (6), 731 (4), 735 (4), 820 (5), 827 (3), 898 (6), 906 (2), 940 (2), 949 (12)

hard and fast rule 81 (1)

hard astern 286 (7)

hard at it 682 (4)

hard at work 678 (8)

hard bargaining 766 (1), 791 (1)

hard, be 517 (6)

hard-bitten 820 (5), 896 (6)

hard-boiled 486 (4), 735 (4), 820 (5)

hard by 200 (4), 200 (7)

hard case 731 (2)

hard copy 86 (5)

hard core 324 (3), 326 (1), 600 (2), 602 (3)

hard-core pornography 951 (1)

hard drinker 944 (2), 949 (5)

hard drinking 949 (1)

hard driving 277 (3)

hard drug 949 (4)

hard fate 731 (2)

hard-featured 842 (3)

hard feelings 818 (1), 881 (1), 891 (1)

hard-fought 682 (5)

hard going 700 (1)

hard-grained 366 (11)

hard hat 228 (23)

hard-hearted 898 (7), 906 (2)

hard-hitting 924 (6)

hard labour 682 (3), 963 (4)

hard life 731 (1)

hard line 602 (1)

hard-liner 602 (3), 735 (3)

hard lot 731 (2)

hard luck 731 (2)

hard of hearing 416 (2)

hard on 735 (6), 914 (4)

hard pad 651 (17)

hard-pressed 680 (2), 700 (5), 702 (7)

hard pressed, be 731 (7)

hard sell 528 (3), 793 (1)

hard task 470 (1), 672 (1), 700 (2)

hard taskmaster 862 (2)

hard thinking 449 (1)

hard times 731 (1)

hard to believe 472 (2), 486 (5)

hard to catch 620 (3)

hard to get 636 (6)

hard to hear 416 (2)

hard to place 84 (5)

hard to please 829 (3), 862 (3)

hard to satisfy 829 (3)

hard up 636 (4), 801 (3)

hard water 339 (1)

hard way, the 682 (8), 700 (8), 735 (1), 825 (1)

hard-won 682 (5)

hard words 568 (1), 924 (3)

hard work 682 (3)

hard worker 678 (5)

hardback 589 (1), 589 (8)

hardboard 631 (3)

harden 162 (12), 324 (6), 326 (5), 610 (8), 669 (12), 811 (4), 820 (7)

harden one's heart - 760 (4), 906 (3), 940 (4), 980 (6)

harden oneself 820 (6)

hardened 326 (3), 375 (4), 610 (7), 669 (8), 934 (3), 940 (2), 980 (4)

hardened offender 904 (3)

hardened sinner 940 (1)

hardening 162 (5), 326 (2), 610 (2), 669 (3)

hardly 33 (9), 140 (3)

hardly any 105 (2)

hardly at all 33 (9)

hardly credible 486 (5)

hardly ever 140 (3)

hardly possible 864 (5)

hardness 162 (1), 266 (1), 324 (2), 326 (1), 329 (1), 599 (1), 700 (1), 820 (1), 898 (2), 906 (1), 940 (1)

hardness of heart 906 (1), 934 (1), 940 (1)

hardship 731 (1), 827 (2)

hardware 86 (5), 164 (2)

hardwood 366 (2)

hardworking 678 (9), 682 (4)

hardy 162 (8), 366 (9), 650 (2)

hare 277 (4), 277 (6), 365 (3)

harebrained 456 (6), 497 (3), 857 (3)

harelip 845 (1)

harelipped 246 (4)

harem 373 (2), 883 (2)

hark back 125 (11), 286 (5), 505 (8), 830 (4)
harking back 148 (1), 830 (2)
harlequin 437 (1)
harlequinade 594 (3)
harlot 952 (4)
harm 616 (1), 643 (3), 645 (1), 645 (6), 655 (3), 655 (9), 827 (8), 898 (8), 914 (6)
harmful 165 (4), 616 (2), 643 (2), 645 (3), 653 (2), 659 (5), 661 (3), 731 (4), 827 (3), 898 (4), 898 (5), 914 (3)
harmfulness 645 (1), 827 (1)
harmless 161 (6), 163 (4), 177 (3), 652 (4), 660 (4), 717 (3), 872 (3), 884 (4), 935 (3)
harmlessness 161 (2), 177 (1), 935 (1)
harmonic 410 (2), 410 (8)
harmonica 414 (5), 414 (8)
harmonics 410 (1)
harmonious 24 (5), 60 (2), 89 (3), 245 (2), 410 (7), 412 (7), 425 (7), 575 (3), 826 (2), 841 (3), 880 (6)
harmonium 414 (5)
harmonization 24 (4), 43 (1), 410 (1)
harmonize 24 (9), 24 (10), 43 (7), 50 (4), 60 (3), 60 (4), 123 (4), 181 (3), 410 (9), 413 (8), 413 (10), 710 (3)
harmonized 24 (5), 43 (6), 50 (3), 412 (7)
harmony 24 (1), 43 (3), 50 (1), 54 (1), 60 (1), 181 (1), 245 (1), 410 (1), 412 (1), 488 (2), 575 (1), 710 (1), 717 (1), 826 (1)
harness 296 (6), 369 (8), 630 (4), 713 (5), 748 (4)
harness together 45 (9)
harp 414 (2)
harp on 106 (5), 838 (5)
harping 106 (1), 106 (3)
harpist 413 (2)

harpoon 256 (2), 723 (4), 723 (6)
harpsichord 414 (4)
harpy 735 (3), 786 (4), 904 (4), 970 (4)
harridan 842 (2), 892 (2)
harrier 277 (4)
harrow 370 (6), 370 (9), 827 (9), 854 (12)
harrowed 258 (3)
harrowing 377 (3), 827 (6)
harry 619 (5), 898 (8)
harsh 32 (12), 388 (3), 407 (2), 411 (2), 425 (6), 576 (2), 645 (3), 735 (6), 735 (7), 827 (3), 885 (5), 906 (2)
harsh sound 407 (1)
harsh treatment 735 (1)
harshly 32 (18)
harshness 388 (1), 411 (1), 576 (1), 735 (1), 827 (1), 885 (2), 898 (2)
harum-scarum 61 (9), 456 (6)
harvest 36 (2), 74 (1), 129 (3), 157 (2), 164 (2), 171 (3), 370 (1), 370 (9), 632 (1), 632 (5), 635 (2), 771 (2), 771 (7), 786 (6)
harvest home 74 (1), 876 (1)
harvest moon 129 (3), 321 (9)
harvest supper 837 (2)
harvest-time 129 (3)
harvester 74 (8)
has-been 125 (6), 127 (2), 728 (3)
hash 43 (3), 61 (2)
hasp 47 (5)
hassock 218 (6), 218 (8)
haste 174 (1), 277 (1), 318 (3), 670 (1), 678 (1), 680 (1), 680 (3), 857 (1)
hasten 135 (5), 156 (9), 265 (5), 277 (6), 277 (7), 285 (3), 612 (9), 678 (12), 680 (3), 857 (4)
hasten away 680 (3)
hasten one's end 362 (10)
hastening 680 (1)
hastily 135 (7), 680 (4)

hastiness 670 (1), 680 (1), 857 (1)
hasty 114 (5), 277 (5), 458 (2), 499 (5), 670 (3), 680 (2), 822 (3), 857 (3), 892 (3)
hasty, be 680 (3)
hat 228 (23)
hat box 194 (7), 252 (3)
hat trick 94 (1), 694 (3)
hatch 74 (3), 164 (7), 167 (6), 167 (7), 226 (1), 263 (6), 369 (9), 418 (6), 513 (7), 541 (8), 623 (8), 669 (12)
hatch a plot 623 (9)
hatchback 274 (11)
hatched 164 (6), 360 (3)
hatchery 192 (4), 369 (2)
hatchet 256 (5), 723 (7)
hatchet-faced 206 (5)
hatchet job 165 (1)
hatchet man 168 (1), 362 (7)
hatching 418 (2); 669 (3), 669 (6)
hatchway 263 (6)
hate 861 (4), 888 (1), 888 (7), 891 (1), 898 (8), 910 (6), 911 (1)
hated 888 (6)
hateful 645 (4), 827 (4), 861 (3), 867 (4), 888 (5)
hateful object 881 (2), 888 (3)
hatefulness 827 (1), 888 (2)
hating 861 (2), 881 (3), 888 (4), 891 (3), 898 (4)
hatless 229 (4)
hatred 709 (1), 854 (3), 861 (1), 881 (1), 888 (1), 891 (1), 898 (1), 911 (1)
hatred of mankind 902 (1)
hatted 228 (29)
haughtiness 871 (1), 878 (1)
haughty 735 (5), 871 (3), 871 (4), 883 (5), 922 (3)
haul 288 (1), 288 (3), 682 (7), 786 (1), 790 (1)
haul down 311 (4)
haul in 747 (8)

haul up 310 (4)

haulage 272 (2), 288 (1)

haulier 272 (4), 273 (1), 288 (1)

haunches 238 (2)

haunt 76 (1), 106 (6), 139 (3), 146 (3), 187 (2), 189 (4), 192 (1), 192 (5), 445 (8), 449 (11), 505 (9), 505 (11), 610 (7), 827 (9), 827 (10), 854 (12), 970 (8), 983 (11)

haunted 481 (6), 505 (6), 970 (7), 983 (9)

haunted by 455 (3)

haunter 970 (3)

haunting 106 (3), 139 (1), 139 (2), 505 (5), 610 (5), 826 (2)

haute couture 228 (1), 848 (1)

haute cuisine 301 (5)

hauteur 871 (1)

have 56 (4), 78 (5), 773 (4)

have a baby 167 (6)

have a bad time 825 (7)

have a case 475 (9)

have a chance 471 (4)

have a chat 584 (6)

have a chip on one's shoulder 829 (5)

have a clear conscience 935 (5)

have a connection 9 (7)

have a fault 647 (4)

have a fever 318 (5), 379 (7)

have a fight 716 (11)

have a free hand 744 (9)

have a gift for 694 (8)

have a go 671 (4)

have a good appetite 301 (35)

have a grievance 829 (5)

have a guess 476 (3)

have a hand in 628 (4), 676 (5), 775 (5)

have a head start 283 (3)

have a heart 905 (9)

have a hold on 178 (3)

have a hunch 476 (3), 485 (8), 512 (6)

have a lover 951 (10)

have a low opinion of 922 (6)

have a market 793 (5)

have a meaning 514 (5)

have a name for 866 (11)

have a nerve 878 (6)

have a night out 837 (23)

have a party 835 (6)

have a past 867 (8)

have a perfume 396 (4)

have a point 256 (10)

have a preference 605 (6)

have a problem 700 (7)

have a relapse 657 (2)

have a reputation 505 (11), 676 (5), 730 (6), 866 (11), 920 (7), 923 (11)

have a rest 685 (5)

have a right 915 (6)

have a sale 793 (5)

have a say in 178 (3)

have a stroke 651 (23)

have a success 727 (6)

have a temper 822 (4), 892 (4)

have a turnover 786 (6)

have a voice 178 (3), 605 (6), 605 (8)

have a vote 605 (8)

have a walkover 701 (7)

have adventures 154 (7)

have an answer 479 (3)

have an axe to grind 932 (4)

have an edge 256 (10)

have an effect 156 (9)

have an eye to 617 (5)

have an impression 485 (8)

have an income 771 (7)

have an odour 394 (3)

have an outing 837 (21)

have and hold 773 (4)

have at 712 (9)

have at one's command 773 (4)

have at one's disposal 673 (5)

have authority 733 (10)

have being 1 (6)

have charge of 689 (4)

have children 11 (7), 167 (6), 171 (6)

have confidence in 485 (7)

have conveyed 272 (8)

have credit 800 (5)

have currency 79 (5)

have designs 623 (9)

have designs on 617 (6), 859 (11)

have differences 709 (7)

have done with 145 (6), 674 (5)

have effect 173 (3)

have elapsed 125 (10)

have elbowroom 744 (9)

have enough 54 (5), 635 (8), 800 (6)

have everything 54 (5), 78 (5)

have experience 694 (9)

have expired 125 (10)

have faith 852 (6), 979 (9)

have faith in 485 (7)

have feeling 374 (5)

have free will 605 (6)

have from 782 (4)

have fun 824 (6), 837 (21)

have good cause 913 (5)

have good looks 841 (7)

have gooseflesh 378 (8)

have had enough 635 (8), 721 (3), 728 (9)

have had it 165 (11)

have had its day 125 (10), 127 (8)

have hoped better of 509 (4)

have hopes 852 (6)

have hysterics 822 (4)

have in mind 455 (5), 507 (4), 514 (5), 617 (5)

have in one's power 733 (12)

have in prospect 507 (4)

have in sight 438 (7)

have in view 617 (5)

have influence 178 (3)

have insight 463 (3)

have intercourse 45 (14)

have it 484 (4)

have it easy 730 (6)

have it from 524 (12)

have it in one's power to 160 (10)

have it pat 490 (8)

have its price 809 (6)
have justice 913 (5)
have knowledge 490 (8)
have knowledge of 490 (8)
have leisure 108 (8), 677 (3), 681 (3), 683 (3), 837 (21)
have life 360 (4)
have lift-off 271 (7)
have little to say 582 (3)
have luck 730 (7)
have means 800 (5)
have mercy 905 (9)
have merit 644 (10)
have misgivings 854 (11)
have money 800 (5)
have money to burn 800 (5)
have nine lives 113 (7), 660 (7)
have no alternative 606 (4)
have no ambition 874 (3)
have no answer 474 (8), 479 (4)
have no axe to grind 931 (3)
have no bearing on 10 (5)
have no brains 499 (6)
have no choice 596 (7), 606 (4)
have no credit 867 (8)
have no doubt 485 (7)
have no end 115 (4)
have no excuse 936 (4)
have no feelings 820 (6)
have no fight 856 (4)
have no food 946 (4)
have no friends 881 (5)
have no function 677 (3)
have no grit 856 (4)
have no heart 906 (3)
have no heart for 861 (4)
have no height 33 (8)
have no idea 491 (8)
have no liking for 861 (4)
have no looks 842 (6)
have no luck 731 (7)
have no meaning 515 (6)
have no mercy 898 (8)
have no morals 930 (8), 951 (10)

have no name to lose 867 (8)
have no objection 758 (3)
have no option 596 (7)
have no power 161 (8)
have no pride 867 (10)
have no regrets 828 (4), 940 (4)
have no religion 974 (7)
have no repute 867 (8)
have no respect or regard for 921 (5)
have no reverence 980 (6)
have no roots 114 (6)
have no say 161 (8)
have no sense 499 (6)
have no smell 395 (3)
have no stomach for 856 (4)
have no success 728 (7)
have no taste for 860 (4)
have no time for 883 (9)
have no tricks 699 (4)
have no trouble 701 (7)
have no turning 249 (3)
have no use 637 (6)
have no use for 674 (4)
have no voice 606 (4)
have no vote 606 (4)
have no will of one's own 83 (7)
have nothing in common 14 (4)
have-nots, the 801 (2), 869 (3)
have occasion for 627 (6)
have offspring 167 (6)
have on 228 (32)
have one covered 281 (7), 900 (3)
have one on 542 (9), 839 (5)
have one taped 490 (8)
have one's being 1 (6)
have one's birth 167 (6)
have one's day 108 (8), 111 (3), 727 (8), 730 (6)
have one's doubts 474 (8), 486 (7)
have one's eye or hand in 694 (8)
have one's fling 678 (11), 744 (9), 943 (3)

have one's hands full 622 (7), 678 (12), 700 (7)
have one's head 744 (9)
have one's measure 490 (8)
have one's pride 871 (5)
have one's reward 962 (4)
have one's say 532 (5), 579 (8), 581 (5)
have one's turn 65 (3)
have one's way 595 (2)
have one's wish 828 (4)
have one's wits about one 457 (5)
have patience 823 (5)
have permission 756 (6)
have pity 905 (6)
have plenty of time 681 (3)
have precedence 64 (3)
have pretensions 850 (5)
have printed 548 (7)
have priority 638 (7)
have private ends 932 (4)
have progeny 167 (6)
have quality 644 (10)
have qualms 854 (11)
have rank 73 (3)
have ready 669 (11)
have recourse to 673 (4)
have reference to 9 (7)
have regard for 457 (6)
have regard to 455 (5), 768 (3)
have regrets 825 (7), 939 (4)
have repercussions 280 (3)
have reservations 486 (7)
have responsibility 689 (5)
have round 882 (10)
have run its course 125 (10)
have scope 744 (9)
have second sight 438 (7), 510 (3)
have second thoughts 601 (4)
have seen better days 731 (7)
have sense 498 (6)
have some point 9 (7)

have some use **640** (4)
have status **866** (11)
have style **848** (7)
have taped **465** (13)
have taste **575** (4), **846** (4)
have tea **301** (35)
have the advantage **29** (3), **727** (9)
have the audacity **878** (6)
have the creeps **378** (8)
have the edge on **34** (8)
have the effect **156** (10)
have the facts **524** (12)
have the knack **694** (8)
have the know-how **694** (9)
have the last word **475** (11), **532** (5)
have the means **629** (2), **635** (8)
have the means or the wherewithal **800** (6)
have the pleasure **824** (6)
have the power **733** (12)
have the property **160** (10)
have the run of **744** (9)
have the runs **302** (6)
have the upper hand **733** (12)
have the virtue **160** (10)
have the vote **605** (8)
have the whip hand **34** (8)
have time for **781** (7)
have to do with **9** (7)
have to repay **803** (6)
have to spare **673** (5)
have too much **949** (14)
have trouble **700** (7), **731** (7), **825** (7)
have trouble with **700** (7)
have two meanings **518** (3)
have views **485** (8)
have weight **322** (5)
have words with **709** (9)
have young **167** (6)
have zest **174** (7)
haven **266** (3), **295** (2), **660** (2), **662** (2)
haversack **194** (9)
haves, the **800** (2), **868** (3)

having **56** (2), **78** (2), **773** (2)
having a fit **503** (9)
having fun **837** (19)
having teeth **160** (8)
having the right **915** (3)
havoc **61** (1), **149** (1), **165** (2), **168** (1), **655** (3), **712** (2), **788** (3)
hawk **300** (11), **365** (4), **438** (2), **712** (5), **722** (3), **793** (4)
hawker **619** (3), **794** (3)
hawking **619** (2)
hawkish **712** (6), **718** (9)
hawkishness **718** (3)
hawser **47** (2)
hawthorn **366** (4)
hay **366** (8)
hay fever **302** (1)
hay wagon **274** (5)
hay wain **274** (5)
haymaking **128** (4)
haystack **370** (6)
haywire **61** (7)
hazard **159** (1), **618** (2), **618** (8), **661** (1), **661** (9), **663** (1), **702** (2)
hazard a guess **512** (6)
hazardous **618** (7), **661** (3), **854** (8)
haze **355** (2)
hazel **366** (4), **430** (3)
haziness **474** (1)
hazy **355** (4), **419** (4), **423** (2), **444** (3), **517** (3)
he **372** (1), **837** (10)
he-man **176** (4), **372** (1)
head **34** (9), **64** (3), **68** (7), **69** (2), **77** (1), **160** (3), **201** (1), **203** (4), **213** (2), **213** (3), **213** (4), **213** (5), **237** (2), **237** (5), **253** (4), **283** (3), **355** (1), **366** (7), **371** (3), **447** (1), **498** (1), **537** (1), **554** (1), **638** (3), **638** (4), **689** (5), **690** (1), **729** (1), **741** (1), **949** (4)
head-count **86** (1)
head first **176** (10), **237** (6)
head for **281** (5)
head foremost **176** (10)

head-hunter **362** (6), **619** (3), **904** (2)
head-hunting **362** (9)
head in the sand **620** (2), **677** (1)
head of hair **259** (2)
head of state **690** (1)
head off **292** (3), **293** (3), **613** (3), **702** (8)
head-on **237** (4)
head-on collision **279** (3)
head over heels **221** (3), **221** (6)
head start **34** (2)
head teacher **537** (1)
head the list **34** (9)
head the queue **283** (3)
head to foot **203** (9)
head to tail **203** (9)
head up **215** (2)
head with **64** (4)
headache **377** (2), **651** (2), **700** (1), **825** (3)
headachy **651** (21)
headdress **228** (23)
header **309** (1), **313** (1)
headgear **228** (23)
heading **68** (1), **77** (1), **283** (1), **547** (13), **561** (2)
headlamp **420** (4)
headland **209** (2), **254** (2)
headless **39** (2)
headlight **420** (4)
headline **68** (1), **528** (11), **638** (3)
headlong **176** (10), **277** (5), **277** (9), **680** (2), **857** (3), **857** (5)
headman **741** (4)
headmaster or - mistress **537** (1)
headphones **415** (4)
headpiece **213** (3)
headquarters **76** (1), **192** (1)
headrest **218** (2)
headroom **183** (4)
heads **649** (3)
heads and tails **837** (12)
heads or tails **159** (2)
heads together **691** (1)
headset **531** (1)
headship **733** (5)

headstall 748 (4)

headstone 218 (2), 364 (2)

headstrong 602 (5), 857 (3)

headway 183 (4), 269 (1), 285 (1)

headwind 14 (1), 182 (1), 240 (1), 352 (1), 702 (2), 704 (1)

heady 174 (5), 388 (3), 394 (2), 821 (4), 949 (12)

heal 656 (11), 658 (19), 719 (4)

heal-all 658 (1)

heal over 656 (11)

healer 656 (5), 658 (14)

healing 656 (4), 656 (7), 658 (10), 658 (17)

health 162 (2), 301 (26), 376 (2), 650 (1), 652 (1)

health and wealth 730 (1)

health centre 658 (13)

health food 301 (9), 652 (1)

health-giving 652 (4)

health visitor 658 (16)

healthful 650 (2), 652 (4)

healthily 652 (7)

healthiness 162 (2), 650 (1), 652 (1)

healthy 162 (6), 162 (9), 174 (5), 644 (8), 646 (4), 650 (2), 652 (4), 652 (5), 656 (6)

healthy, be 174 (7), 650 (3), 652 (5)

healthy mind 447 (1)

heap 32 (2), 52 (3), 74 (7), 74 (11), 195 (3), 632 (1)

heap abuse on 924 (10)

heap shame upon 867 (11)

heaping up 74 (7)

heaps 26 (2), 32 (2), 104 (1)

hear 374 (5), 415 (6), 453 (4), 455 (4), 459 (13), 480 (5), 488 (11), 524 (12)

hear a cause 959 (8)

hear both sides 913 (6)

hear complaints 955 (5)

hear hear 923 (14)

hear it said 415 (6)

hear Mass 981 (12)

hear no evil 933 (4)

hear nothing 416 (3)

heard 398 (3), 400 (3), 415 (5), 466 (5), 490 (7)

heard, be 398 (4), 415 (7), 528 (10)

hearer 415 (3)

hearers 583 (1)

hearing 374 (2), 398 (1), 415 (1), 415 (2), 415 (5), 459 (4), 959 (3)

hearing aid 398 (1), 400 (2), 415 (4), 528 (2), 531 (1)

hearken 415 (6), 979 (9)

hearkening 415 (2)

hearsay 466 (1), 524 (1), 529 (2)

hearse 274 (1), 364 (2)

heart 1 (3), 5 (2), 70 (1), 76 (1), 224 (2), 225 (2), 447 (2), 817 (1), 855 (1), 889 (3), 890 (1)

heart and soul 54 (8), 682 (8), 818 (9)

heart attack 651 (9)

heart-burning 891 (1), 911 (1)

heart condition 651 (9)

heart disease 651 (9)

heart failure 651 (9)

heart-melting 826 (2)

heart of gold 897 (1), 937 (1)

heart of hearts 817 (1)

heart of stone 820 (1), 898 (2)

heart of the matter 638 (3)

heart-rending 827 (6), 905 (5)

heart-shaped 248 (3), 252 (5)

heart-to-heart 584 (2)

heart trouble 651 (9)

heart-warming 818 (6), 826 (2), 833 (6)

heart-whole 744 (5)

heartache 825 (1), 834 (1)

heartbroken 509 (2), 825 (6)

heartburn 651 (7)

hearten 174 (8), 703 (5), 821 (7), 831 (3), 833 (8), 855 (8)

heartfelt 818 (6)

hearth 192 (5), 383 (1)

hearth and home 11 (3)

hearties 270 (1)

heartily 32 (17)

heartiness 818 (2), 880 (2)

heartless 820 (3), 898 (7), 906 (2), 940 (2)

heartlessness 906 (1)

heart's desire 617 (2)

heart's ease 828 (1)

hearts of oak 599 (1)

heartstrings 817 (1)

heartthrob 841 (2), 887 (5)

heartwood 224 (1), 366 (2)

hearty 174 (5), 818 (3), 818 (6), 833 (3), 847 (5), 880 (6), 882 (6)

hearty eater 947 (2)

hearty laughter 835 (2)

hearty thanks 907 (2)

heat 128 (4), 326 (5), 337 (4), 340 (3), 342 (6), 379 (1), 381 (8), 417 (3), 427 (1), 716 (2), 859 (4), 887 (15)

heat exchanger 160 (4)

heat measurement 379 (3)

heat retention 666 (1)

heat wave 340 (3), 379 (1)

heated 379 (4), 381 (6), 821 (3)

heater 160 (4), 194 (14), 381 (1), 383 (2)

heath 172 (3), 348 (1), 366 (2)

heathen 486 (3), 486 (4), 973 (7), 974 (4), 974 (6), 980 (3), 982 (4), 982 (5)

heathenish 974 (6), 982 (5)

heathenism 491 (1), 974 (1), 974 (2), 980 (1), 982 (1)

heathenize 974 (8), 982 (6)

heather 436 (1)

heating 337 (1), 342 (2), 379 (1), 381 (1), 381 (7), 383 (2)

heave 273 (12), 279 (1), 279 (7), 287 (7), 288 (3), 300 (10), 317 (4), 352 (11), 682 (1), 682 (7), 818 (8)
heave a sigh 836 (5)
heave in sight 443 (4)
heave the lead 269 (10), 313 (3)
heave to 266 (9), 269 (10)
heave up 310 (4)
heaven 124 (2), 213 (1), 971 (1)
heaven-sent 137 (5), 615 (3)
heavenly 321 (14), 644 (5), 826 (2), 841 (4), 965 (5), 971 (3)
heavenly body 321 (4)
heavenly host 968 (1)
heavens 183 (1), 321 (3)
heavenward 209 (14)
heaviness 195 (3), 322 (1), 679 (3), 834 (1), 834 (3), 838 (1)
heaving 352 (9)
heavy 162 (6), 175 (2), 322 (4), 324 (4), 394 (2), 405 (2), 576 (2), 735 (4), 823 (3), 834 (7), 838 (3)
heavy artillery 723 (11)
heavy as lead 322 (4)
heavy-eyed 679 (9)
heavy father 735 (3)
heavy-footed 695 (5), 840 (2)
heavy hand 735 (1)
heavy-handed 378 (5), 735 (6)
heavy heart 825 (2)
heavy-hearted 825 (6), 834 (6)
heavy-laden 54 (4), 702 (7), 825 (5)
heavy meal 301 (12)
heavy metal 412 (1)
heavy news 827 (1)
heavy sleep 679 (4)
heavy water 339 (1)
heavy with 155 (2), 171 (4)
heavyweight 162 (4), 638 (4), 722 (2)
hecatomb 165 (2)

heckle 459 (14), 702 (10), 921 (5), 924 (9)
heckler 459 (10), 489 (2), 702 (5), 926 (3)
hectare 183 (2)
hectic 821 (3)
hector 877 (5), 900 (3)
hectoring 854 (8), 877 (2), 900 (2)
hedge 31 (5), 231 (2), 235 (2), 366 (2), 618 (8), 620 (5)
hedge in 232 (3), 702 (9)
hedgehog 365 (3)
hedgehop 271 (7)
hedgerow 235 (2), 366 (2)
hedonism 376 (1), 824 (3), 944 (1)
hedonist 944 (2)
hedonistic 944 (3)
heed 455 (1), 455 (4), 457 (1), 457 (5), 739 (4), 768 (3)
heedful 455 (2), 457 (3), 768 (2), 858 (2)
heedfulness 858 (1)
heedless 456 (3), 458 (2), 506 (4)
heedlessness 857 (1), 860 (1)
heel 214 (2), 220 (5), 279 (10)
heel over 221 (4), 309 (4)
heeled 214 (4)
heeling 29 (2)
hefty 32 (9), 162 (8)
hegemony 733 (1)
heifer 132 (3), 365 (7)
height 26 (4), 32 (1), 183 (2), 195 (1), 195 (2), 209 (1), 209 (2), 215 (1), 465 (3)
height of fashion 848 (1)
heighten 36 (5), 197 (5), 209 (13), 310 (4), 546 (3), 832 (3)
heightening 36 (1), 832 (1)
heights 209 (2)
heinous 934 (6)
heinousness 934 (1)
heir 67 (3), 170 (2), 782 (2), 800 (2)

heir apparent 755 (1), 776 (3), 852 (3)
heir or heiress 776 (3)
heiress 170 (2), 800 (2)
heirloom 127 (2), 777 (4)
heirs 124 (1), 170 (1)
heirship 170 (3)
held 632 (4), 773 (3), 778 (4)
held in 232 (2), 778 (4)
held responsible, be 924 (14)
held up 136 (3), 702 (7), 747 (5)
helical 251 (8)
helicopter 276 (1)
heliograph 547 (5)
heliotrope 436 (1)
heliport 271 (2)
helium 310 (2)
helix 251 (2), 314 (1)
hell 124 (2), 211 (1), 825 (1), 972 (1)
hell-bent 617 (3)
hell-broth 983 (4)
hell for leather 277 (9)
hellcat 176 (4), 983 (6)
hellfire 972 (1)
hellhag 904 (4)
hellhound 904 (4)
hellish 645 (5), 898 (7), 969 (5), 972 (3)
hellishly 32 (18)
helm 269 (4), 630 (1), 689 (2), 713 (5)
helmet 228 (23), 713 (5)
helmsman 270 (2)
helmsmanship 269 (2)
help 181 (3), 615 (4), 628 (4), 640 (1), 640 (4), 642 (3), 644 (11), 648 (6), 658 (1), 658 (19), 701 (8), 703 (1), 703 (3), 703 (5), 703 (7), 742 (1)
help one out 703 (5)
help oneself 786 (6), 788 (7)
help out 703 (5)
helper 703 (3), 707 (1), 742 (1), 903 (1)
helpful 597 (4), 615 (3), 628 (4), 640 (2), 658 (17), 701 (3), 703 (4), 706 (3)

helpfulness 597 (1), 703 (1), 706 (1), 897 (1)

helping 301 (7), 301 (12), 783 (2)

helping hand 703 (1), 707 (1)

helpless 161 (6), 161 (7), 163 (4), 661 (5)

helplessness 161 (2), 163 (1), 661 (2)

helpmate 707 (1), 707 (3), 894 (4)

helter-skelter 61 (12)

hem 202 (3), 234 (3), 234 (5), 235 (4), 239 (3), 261 (1), 844 (12)

hem in 230 (3), 232 (3), 747 (7)

hemi- 53 (6), 92 (4)

hemisphere 92 (1), 184 (1), 252 (2), 253 (4)

hemispheric 253 (7)

hemispherical 252 (5)

hemline 228 (3)

hemp 208 (2)

hen 365 (6)

hen party 373 (2), 882 (3)

hence 157 (7), 158 (5)

henceforth 124 (8)

henchman 703 (3), 707 (1), 742 (3)

henna 432 (1)

henpeck 827 (9)

henpecked 745 (4)

hepatitis 651 (7)

heptagon 247 (4)

her 373 (1)

her ladyship 373 (4)

Hera 967 (1)

herald 66 (1), 119 (1), 283 (3), 511 (3), 511 (8), 524 (4), 528 (6), 528 (10), 529 (5), 547 (11)

heraldic 547 (16)

heraldic art 844 (2)

heralding 511 (6)

heraldry 547 (11), 743 (1), 844 (2), 866 (4), 868 (1)

herb 301 (21), 366 (6), 658 (2)

herbaceous 366 (9)

herbage 366 (5)

herbal 366 (9), 368 (1), 370 (8), 658 (18)

herbalist 368 (1), 658 (14)

herbivore 301 (6), 365 (2)

herbivorous 301 (31)

Herculean 32 (4), 195 (7), 682 (5)

Herculean task 700 (2)

herd 74 (3), 74 (11), 365 (2), 369 (8), 369 (10)

herd instinct 4 (5)

herding 74 (1)

herdsman 369 (6)

here 183 (8), 186 (5), 189 (6)

here and there 72 (5), 75 (5), 105 (5), 185 (2)

here below 321 (18)

Here goes 599 (6), 671 (5)

here, there and everywhere 17 (3), 183 (8)

here today and gone tomorrow 114 (7)

hereabouts 186 (5), 200 (8)

hereafter 67 (1), 124 (2), 124 (7), 155 (1)

hereditary 5 (7), 157 (4), 170 (4), 777 (5)

hereditary peeress 868 (5)

heredity 5 (5), 106 (2), 148 (1), 169 (2), 170 (3), 358 (1), 655 (1)

here's health 301 (41)

heresy 977 (1)

heresy-hunting 976 (2)

heretic 84 (3), 486 (3), 888 (3), 977 (1)

heretical 84 (5), 495 (4), 977 (2), 978 (7), 980 (4)

heretical, be 977 (4)

heretically 977 (5)

herewith 89 (5)

heritable 5 (7), 157 (4), 779 (3), 780 (2), 915 (2)

heritage 124 (1), 773 (1)

hermaphrodite 84 (3), 91 (2)

Hermes 967 (1)

hermetic 984 (6)

hermetically sealed 264 (5)

hermit 84 (3), 88 (2), 801 (2), 883 (3), 895 (2), 945 (2), 979 (4), 986 (5)

hermitage 192 (17), 662 (1), 883 (2)

hernia 655 (4)

hero 676 (3), 855 (3), 864 (3), 887 (5), 890 (2), 937 (1)

hero worship 864 (1), 887 (1), 923 (9), 982 (2)

hero-worshipping 923 (5)

heroic 127 (4), 590 (6), 593 (8), 599 (2), 682 (5), 855 (4), 866 (8), 931 (2)

heroic age 125 (2)

heroic couplet 593 (5)

heroic poem 593 (2)

heroics 855 (2), 875 (1), 877 (1)

heroin 659 (3), 949 (4)

heroine 676 (3), 855 (3), 864 (3), 890 (2), 937 (1)

heroism 855 (1), 855 (2), 931 (1)

heron 365 (4)

heronry 192 (4)

hero's welcome 876 (1), 886 (1), 923 (3)

herpes 651 (12)

Herr 372 (1)

herringbone 220 (3), 222 (6), 844 (3)

herself 80 (4)

hesitancy 474 (2)

hesitant 474 (6), 598 (3)

hesitantly 601 (5)

hesitate 145 (8), 278 (4), 474 (8), 486 (7), 580 (3), 601 (4), 679 (11), 854 (11)

hesitating 601 (3), 854 (7), 858 (2)

hesitatingly 486 (10)

hesitation 152 (1), 278 (1), 486 (2), 598 (1), 601 (1), 854 (2), 858 (1)

Hesperus 129 (1)

hessian 222 (4)

het up 891 (4)

heterodox 84 (5), 495 (4), 977 (2)

heterodoxy 84 (1), 977 (1)

heterogeneity 10 (1), 15 (1), 17 (1), 43 (4), 82 (1)
heterogeneous 15 (4), 17 (2), 43 (6), 82 (2)
heterosexual 83 (5)
hew 46 (11), 243 (5)
hew down 311 (6)
hex 983 (2)
hexagon 99 (2), 247 (4)
hexagram 99 (2)
hexameter 99 (2), 593 (5)
heyday 130 (3), 730 (2)
hi 295 (7)
hi-fi 398 (1), 398 (3), 414 (10)
hi-fi enthusiast 415 (3)
hiatus 72 (1), 201 (1), 263 (1)
hibernate 679 (12)
hibernating 175 (2), 679 (9)
hibernation 129 (4), 679 (4)
hibernator 679 (6)
hiccup 300 (11), 352 (7), 352 (11)
hidden 444 (2), 491 (6), 517 (2), 525 (3), 883 (7)
hidden depths 523 (1)
hidden hand 156 (2), 178 (1), 663 (2), 690 (1)
hidden meaning 514 (2), 523 (1)
hide 183 (2), 226 (6), 421 (4), 444 (4), 446 (3), 523 (5), 525 (7), 527 (1), 620 (5), 631 (1), 660 (8), 856 (4)
hide-and-seek 837 (10)
hide away 525 (7)
hide from 525 (9)
hide one's face 872 (6)
hide out 525 (9), 527 (1), 883 (2)
hide the truth 541 (6)
hide underground 525 (7)
hideaway 527 (1)
hidebound 481 (7), 602 (4), 747 (4)
hideous 827 (4), 842 (3), 854 (8)
hideousness 842 (1)
hider 527 (4), 620 (2)

hiding 279 (2), 444 (1), 525 (1), 620 (3), 728 (2), 963 (2)
hiding-place 192 (17), 525 (1), 527 (1), 632 (1), 662 (1), 883 (2)
hie 265 (4)
hierarchical 985 (6)
hierarchy 27 (1), 60 (1), 71 (2)
hieroglyph 558 (1), 586 (2)
hieroglyphics 530 (2), 547 (3), 551 (1), 586 (1)
higgledy-piggledy 61 (12)
high 32 (4), 32 (6), 34 (1), 51 (3), 209 (8), 213 (4), 215 (2), 310 (3), 388 (3), 390 (2), 391 (2), 397 (2), 407 (2), 649 (6), 866 (8), 871 (3), 949 (6), 949 (10)
high a 866 (2)
high altar 990 (4)
high and low 54 (9), 183 (8)
high and mighty 871 (4), 878 (4)
high, be 34 (7), 195 (10), 209 (12), 213 (5), 308 (4), 308 (5)
high birth 868 (1)
high birthrate 171 (1)
high blood pressure 651 (9)
high camp 839 (1)
high caste 868 (1)
high casualties 362 (4)
high character 929 (1)
High Church 976 (3), 976 (10), 978 (6)
high circles 848 (3)
high-class 868 (7)
high colour 431 (1)
high-coloured 425 (6)
High Command 741 (1), 741 (8)
High Commission 754 (3)
High Commissioner 741 (5)
high cost 811 (1)
High Court 956 (2)
high-density 74 (9)
high-density housing 192 (8)

high explosive 723 (13)
high fidelity 398 (1), 398 (3), 494 (3), 494 (6)
high fidelity system 414 (10)
high finance 797 (3)
high flier 538 (1)
high-flown 513 (5), 546 (2), 574 (5)
high frequency 417 (4)
high-geared 162 (6), 277 (5)
high hand 176 (1)
high-handed 735 (6), 871 (3), 878 (4)
high heels 228 (27)
high hopes 852 (1)
high ideals 931 (1)
high IQ 498 (1)
high jump 312 (1)
high-jumper 312 (2)
high kick 312 (1)
high-kicker 837 (14)
high kicks 837 (14)
high land 209 (2), 213 (2), 215 (1), 254 (1), 259 (1), 308 (1), 310 (1), 344 (1), 348 (1)
high-level 34 (4), 638 (5), 689 (3)
high-level talks 584 (3)
high life 837 (2)
high living 943 (1), 944 (1), 944 (3)
high-minded 929 (3), 931 (2)
high moral tone 850 (1)
high noon 128 (2)
high note 407 (1)
high office 733 (5)
high old time 837 (3)
high pitch 407 (1)
high-pitched 407 (2), 482 (2), 574 (5)
high-powered 34 (4), 162 (6)
high pressure 174 (1), 174 (5), 340 (3), 740 (2)
high price 811 (1)
high-priced 811 (2)
high priest 986 (8)
high-principled 929 (3)
high-priority 638 (5)

high rank 866 (2)
high rate 809 (1)
high relief 254 (1)
high-rise 192 (20)
high road 624 (6)
high school 539 (2)
high seas 343 (1)
high society 848 (3), 868 (3)
high-souled 871 (3)
high-sounding 850 (4), 875 (4)
high-speed 274 (16), 277 (5)
high-spirited 819 (4), 871 (3)
high spirits 833 (1), 833 (2)
high standards 735 (1)
high standing 638 (1), 920 (1)
high-stepper 273 (5)
high-stepping 848 (5), 871 (3)
high street 624 (6), 678 (1)
high structure 74 (7), 164 (3), 195 (3), 209 (4), 213 (2), 254 (2), 438 (5)
high summer 128 (4), 379 (1)
high tea 301 (12)
high technology 630 (3)
high temperature 379 (1)
high tension 160 (3), 160 (9), 162 (6)
high tide 209 (6)
high time 136 (1), 137 (1)
high tone 574 (2)
high-toned 407 (2), 571 (2)
high treason 738 (3)
high turnout 104 (1)
high-up 209 (8), 209 (14)
high-ups 34 (3)
high visibility 443 (1)
high voice 407 (1)
high volume 400 (1)
high water 209 (6), 339 (1)
high-water mark 465 (5)
high wind 352 (4)
high words 891 (2)
high worth 811 (1)
highbrow 490 (6), 492 (2), 500 (1)

higher 34 (4)
higher education 534 (2)
higher position 64 (1)
higher rank 34 (1)
highest 34 (5), 209 (8), 213 (4)
highest bidder 792 (2)
highland 209 (10)
Highland fling 837 (14)
highlander 191 (1)
Highlands 184 (3), 209 (2)
highlight 522 (7), 528 (9), 532 (7), 547 (18), 553 (1), 638 (3), 638 (8), 843 (7)
highlighted 443 (3)
highlights 417 (6), 843 (2)
highly commended 923 (7)
highly respectable 868 (7)
highly-strung 819 (4), 822 (3), 854 (7)
highly wrought 725 (4)
Highness 741 (3)
highway 624 (6)
highway code 305 (3)
highway robbery 788 (1)
highwayman 789 (2)
hijack 740 (3), 788 (1), 788 (7), 900 (3)
hijacker 789 (2)
hike 267 (3), 267 (11), 837 (21)
hiker 268 (1), 268 (3)
hiking 837 (6)
hilarious 833 (4), 849 (3)
hilarity 833 (2)
hill 209 (2), 220 (2), 308 (1)
hill-climbing 308 (1)
hill fort 253 (5)
hillbilly 869 (6)
hillock 209 (3), 253 (4)
hillocky 209 (10), 253 (8)
hilltop 209 (2)
hilly 209 (10)
hilt 218 (3)
him 372 (1)
himself 80 (4)
hind 238 (4)
hind limb 53 (2)
hinder 38 (3), 63 (3), 63 (4), 145 (7), 161 (9), 182 (3), 231 (10), 238 (4), 278

(6), 322 (5), 509 (5), 655 (9), 700 (6), 702 (8), 715 (3), 747 (7), 757 (4)
hindered 63 (2), 136 (3), 161 (7), 636 (4), 700 (5), 702 (7), 728 (5), 747 (5)
hinderer 168 (1), 489 (2), 613 (1), 702 (5), 904 (1), 926 (3)
hindering 489 (3), 598 (3), 643 (2), 702 (6), 704 (3), 827 (5), 829 (4)
hindermost 238 (4)
hindfoot 214 (2)
hindleg 267 (7)
hindmost 69 (4)
hindquarters 238 (2)
hindrance 35 (1), 63 (1), 145 (2), 165 (1), 182 (1), 598 (1), 662 (3), 700 (1), 702 (1), 702 (2), 702 (5), 728 (1), 747 (1), 748 (4)
hindsight 449 (1), 505 (2)
Hindu 973 (7)
Hindu triad 965 (3)
Hinduism 449 (3), 973 (3)
hinge 45 (9), 47 (1), 47 (5), 156 (5), 218 (11)
hinge-joint 45 (4)
hinge on 157 (6), 474 (8)
hint 18 (1), 43 (2), 438 (3), 438 (8), 466 (1), 505 (3), 512 (1), 512 (7), 523 (1), 523 (6), 524 (3), 524 (11), 526 (1), 526 (5), 547 (1), 547 (4), 547 (18), 579 (8), 612 (9), 664 (1), 664 (5), 691 (1), 691 (4)
hinterland 183 (1), 184 (3), 224 (1), 344 (1)
hinting 512 (4), 612 (6), 664 (3)
hip flask 194 (13)
hip pocket 194 (11)
hippie 84 (3)
Hippocratic 658 (18)
hippodrome 594 (7), 724 (1)
hippopotamus 365 (3)
hips 238 (2)
hipsters 228 (12)

hire 622 (6), 751 (4), 780
(1), 780 (3), 785 (3), 792
(5), 809 (1)
hire out 784 (6)
hire purchase 785 (1), 792
(1), 805 (1)
hired 780 (2)
hireling 35 (2), 742 (1),
930 (6)
hiring 784 (1)
hirsute 259 (5)
his lordship 372 (1)
His Nibs 848 (4)
hiss 406 (1), 406 (3), 409
(1), 409 (3), 547 (4), 921
(2), 921 (5), 922 (5), 924
(1), 924 (9)
hissed 924 (7)
hissing 406 (1), 406 (2),
924 (1)
histology 331 (1), 358 (2)
historian 125 (5), 549 (2),
589 (7), 590 (5)
historic age 125 (1)
historical 1 (5), 125 (6),
125 (9), 127 (4), 473 (4),
494 (4), 590 (6)
history 125 (1), 589 (2),
590 (2), 688 (1)
history of 651 (2)
histrionic 546 (2), 594 (15)
histrionics 546 (1), 594
(2), 594 (8), 850 (1), 875
(1)
hit 279 (2), 279 (9), 295 (6),
378 (7), 594 (2), 716 (11),
727 (1)
hit and miss 461 (2)
hit back 280 (3), 714 (3)
hit for six 727 (10)
hit it 484 (4)
hit it off 24 (9), 710 (3), 880
(8)
hit on 623 (8)
hit or miss 495 (6)
hit out at 279 (9), 924 (10)
hit the bottle 949 (14)
hit the headlines 528 (12)
hit the jackpot 727 (6), 800
(7)
hit the mark 187 (5), 281
(7)
hit upon 159 (7), 484 (4)

hit wildly 279 (9)
hitch 45 (12), 47 (4), 145
(2), 217 (5), 369 (8), 509
(1), 616 (1), 702 (3), 728
(1)
hitch-hiker 268 (3)
hitched 894 (7)
hitchhike 267 (15), 761 (6)
hither 281 (8)
hitherto 125 (13)
hive 369 (2), 632 (2)
hive of industry 678 (1),
687 (1)
hive off 786 (9)
hives 651 (12)
hiving off 786 (2)
hoard 632 (1), 632 (5), 660
(8), 771 (7), 814 (3), 816
(6)
hoarder 74 (8), 816 (3)
hoarding 528 (3), 771 (4),
816 (5)
hoarfrost 380 (2)
hoarse 405 (2), 407 (3),
577 (3), 578 (2)
hoarseness 407 (1), 578
(1)
hoary 427 (5), 429 (2)
hoary head 429 (1)
hoary-headed 131 (6)
hoax 529 (2), 542 (2), 542
(8), 665 (2), 839 (2)
hoaxer 545 (4)
hob 218 (5)
hobbit 196 (4)
hobble 267 (14), 278 (4),
702 (8), 747 (9), 748 (4)
hobbled 163 (7)
hobbledehoy 132 (2)
hobbling 163 (7), 278 (1)
hobby 622 (1), 837 (1), 859
(3)
hobbyhorse 503 (5)
hobgoblin 854 (4), 970 (2)
hobnob 880 (7)
hobo 268 (2)
Hobson's choice 606 (1),
740 (1)
hockey 837 (7)
hockey-player 837 (16)
hocus-pocus 515 (1), 542
(3), 983 (2)
hod 194 (13)

hodgepodge 43 (4)
hoe 370 (6), 370 (9)
hog 365 (9), 773 (4), 932
(4), 947 (2)
hog's back 209 (2), 253 (4)
hogshead 194 (12)
hoist 310 (1), 310 (2), 310
(4)
hoist sail 269 (10)
hokey-cokey 837 (14)
hold 48 (3), 56 (4), 78 (5),
145 (9), 153 (7), 178 (1),
178 (4), 189 (4), 194 (1),
194 (21), 214 (1), 218 (1),
218 (15), 224 (5), 485 (7),
485 (8), 494 (7), 532 (5),
632 (2), 632 (5), 716 (5),
733 (2), 747 (7), 747 (8),
747 (10), 773 (1), 773 (4),
778 (1), 778 (5), 821 (8)
hold a meeting 74 (11)
hold a place 73 (3)
hold a seance 984 (9)
hold against 928 (8)
hold aloft 310 (4)
hold aloof 620 (5)
hold an election 605 (8)
hold an opinion 485 (8)
hold apart 46 (9), 263 (17)
hold at gunpoint 900 (3)
hold back 145 (8), 486 (7),
598 (4), 620 (5), 636 (9),
702 (8), 747 (7), 778 (5)
hold by 768 (3)
hold cheap 458 (5), 483
(4), 607 (3), 860 (4), 921
(5), 922 (6), 926 (6)
hold court 480 (5), 955 (5)
hold dear 887 (13)
hold down 311 (4), 733
(12), 735 (8), 747 (7), 778
(5)
hold fast 48 (3), 599 (4),
600 (4), 778 (5)
hold for 485 (8)
hold forth 534 (7), 579 (9)
hold good 144 (3), 494 (7),
610 (7)
hold in 747 (7)
hold in abeyance 136 (7),
674 (4)
hold in check 747 (7)
hold in common 775 (6)

hold in contempt **922** (5)
hold in honour **920** (5)
hold in horror **888** (7)
hold in leash **747** (7)
hold in pledge **767** (5)
hold in solution **337** (4)
hold in trust **755** (3)
hold in view **438** (7), **438** (9)
hold no more **54** (5)
hold off **674** (4), **713** (10), **715** (3)
hold office **622** (8), **733** (10)
hold on **136** (5), **146** (3), **266** (11), **285** (3), **778** (5)
hold one back **613** (3)
hold one's breath **507** (5), **864** (6)
hold one's ground **718** (11)
hold one's hand **145** (6), **703** (5)
hold one's horses **136** (5), **145** (8)
hold one's lead **285** (3)
hold one's own **28** (9), **704** (5), **713** (10), **727** (7)
hold one's peace **582** (3)
hold one's sides **835** (7)
hold one's tongue **399** (3), **525** (8), **578** (3), **582** (3)
hold out **599** (4), **600** (4), **612** (12), **715** (3), **759** (3), **764** (4)
hold out against **704** (4)
hold out for **766** (3), **791** (6)
hold over **136** (7)
hold rank **73** (3)
hold responsible **924** (12), **928** (8)
hold straight on **625** (5)
hold sway **733** (10)
hold talks **584** (7)
hold the faith **976** (12)
hold the lead **34** (8)
hold tight **45** (14), **778** (5)
hold to blame **924** (12)
hold to ransom **740** (3), **811** (5), **900** (3)
hold together **494** (7), **706** (4)
hold true **494** (7)

hold up **136** (7), **145** (7), **218** (15), **310** (4), **702** (8), **778** (5), **788** (9)
hold water **475** (9), **478** (5), **494** (7)
hold within **224** (5)
hold your tongue **399** (5)
holdall **194** (9), **632** (2)
holder **194** (1), **218** (3), **776** (1)
holding **78** (2), **184** (2), **218** (14), **235** (1), **370** (2), **632** (1), **773** (1), **773** (2), **777** (2), **777** (3)
holding hands **45** (5), **889** (1)
holding on **778** (1)
holding out **715** (2)
holding the reins **689** (3)
holding together **48** (1)
holdup **136** (2), **702** (3), **788** (1)
hole **8** (1), **192** (3), **192** (7), **194** (1), **201** (2), **255** (2), **255** (8), **263** (1), **263** (4), **263** (18), **303** (4), **662** (1), **700** (3)
holey **263** (14), **655** (6)
holiday **145** (4), **681** (1), **683** (1), **683** (2), **837** (1), **837** (18)
holiday camp **837** (4)
holiday home **192** (1)
holidaying **837** (2)
holidaymaker **268** (1), **837** (17)
holier than thou **922** (3), **924** (6), **979** (7)
holiness **933** (1), **965** (2), **979** (2)
holism **52** (1)
holistic **52** (4)
holler **408** (4)
hollow **4** (3), **190** (5), **210** (1), **211** (1), **211** (3), **255** (2), **255** (6), **255** (7), **255** (8), **262** (1), **263** (1), **311** (4), **325** (2), **404** (2), **407** (3), **477** (4), **541** (4), **578** (2), **850** (4), **875** (4), **877** (4)
hollow mockery **542** (5)
hollow out **255** (8)

hollow pretence **541** (2)
hollowed out **255** (6)
hollowness **4** (1), **190** (2), **255** (1), **541** (2), **542** (1)
holly **366** (4)
Hollywood **445** (3), **594** (1)
holm **349** (1)
holocaust **165** (2), **362** (4), **379** (2), **981** (6)
hologram **417** (5), **551** (2), **551** (4)
holograph **586** (3)
holster **194** (10)
holy **866** (8), **933** (3), **965** (5), **965** (6), **973** (8), **975** (4), **979** (6), **979** (8), **981** (10)
Holy Bible **975** (2)
Holy Communion **988** (4)
holy day **876** (2), **988** (7)
holy ground **990** (2)
holy man or woman **979** (4)
holy matrimony **894** (1), **988** (4)
Holy of Holies **990** (2)
Holy Office **956** (3)
holy orders **985** (2), **988** (4)
holy place **990** (2)
holy poverty **945** (1)
holy relic **983** (3)
Holy Scripture **975** (2)
Holy See **985** (3)
holy terror **904** (1), **938** (1)
Holy Trinity **965** (3)
holy war **718** (1)
holy water **339** (1)
homage **721** (1), **739** (2), **920** (2), **981** (1)
home **11** (3), **68** (4), **76** (1), **156** (3), **184** (2), **185** (1), **191** (6), **192** (1), **192** (5), **192** (6), **192** (17), **200** (4), **266** (3), **295** (2), **662** (2)
home and dry **727** (4)
Home Counties **184** (3)
home economics **301** (5)
home farm **370** (2)
home from home **192** (1)
home ground **192** (5)
Home Guard **722** (4)

home help 648 (6)
home life 883 (2)
home-loving 266 (4)
home rule 733 (4)
home stretch 69 (1), 295 (1)
home town 192 (5)
home truth 494 (1), 540 (1), 924 (2)
home truths 573 (1)
home viewing 438 (4)
homecoming 286 (2), 295 (1)
homeland 184 (2), 192 (5)
homeless 152 (4), 188 (2), 267 (9), 801 (3)
homeless person 883 (4)
homeliness 842 (1)
homely 376 (4), 573 (2), 826 (2), 842 (3), 869 (8)
homemade 164 (6), 695 (6), 699 (3)
Homeric 593 (8)
homesick 830 (2)
homesick, be 830 (4)
homesickness 825 (1), 830 (1), 834 (2), 859 (1)
homespun 164 (6), 259 (1), 331 (4), 573 (2), 699 (3), 869 (8)
homestead 192 (5)
homeward 281 (8)
homeward bound 286 (3), 295 (3)
homeward journey 286 (2)
homework 534 (3), 536 (2), 669 (1), 682 (3)
homicidal 362 (9)
homicidal mania 503 (3)
homicidal maniac 176 (4), 362 (6)
homicide 362 (2), 362 (7), 659 (4), 738 (2), 898 (3)
homiletics 534 (1)
homily 534 (4), 579 (2), 591 (1)
homing 297 (4)
homoeopath 658 (14)
homoeopathic 33 (6), 658 (18)
homoeopathy 658 (10)

homogeneous 16 (2), 18 (4), 44 (4)
homogenize 16 (4)
homograph 559 (1)
homonym 13 (1), 518 (1), 559 (1)
homonymous 13 (2), 514 (4), 518 (2)
homophone 13 (1), 518 (1), 559 (1)
homosexual 84 (3), 84 (7), 372 (1), 951 (9)
homosexuality 84 (1)
hone 256 (6), 256 (11)
honest 494 (4), 494 (5), 540 (2), 699 (3), 917 (7), 929 (3), 931 (2), 933 (3)
honest money 797 (1)
honest person 929 (2)
honest truth 494 (1)
honesty 540 (1), 699 (1), 929 (1)
honey 354 (3), 392 (2)
honey bee 365 (16)
honey-coloured 433 (3)
honey pot 76 (1)
honey-tongued 925 (3)
honeycomb 222 (3), 255 (2), 255 (8), 263 (3), 263 (18), 632 (2)
honeycombed 194 (25), 222 (6), 255 (6), 263 (14)
honeyed 392 (3)
honeyed words 612 (2), 925 (1)
honeymoon 68 (3), 824 (1), 880 (2), 887 (14), 894 (11)
honeymooners 894 (4)
honeysuckle 396 (2)
honk 409 (3), 665 (1), 665 (3)
honky-tonk 192 (12)
honorarium 962 (1)
honorary 4 (3), 597 (5), 812 (4)
honorary fellow 708 (3)
honorific 866 (8), 870 (1), 886 (2)
honour 310 (4), 612 (1), 729 (2), 730 (8), 764 (1), 804 (4), 844 (12), 866 (2), 866 (4), 866 (13), 866 (14),

870 (1), 876 (4), 884 (6), 913 (1), 917 (4), 917 (10), 920 (1), 920 (5), 923 (8), 929 (1), 933 (1), 950 (1), 962 (1), 962 (3), 981 (1), 981 (11)
honour, an 866 (4)
honour and obey 981 (11)
honour for 866 (13)
honour with 781 (7), 866 (13)
honourable 540 (2), 699 (3), 848 (6), 866 (7), 866 (8), 913 (4), 917 (7), 929 (3), 931 (2), 933 (3), 950 (5)
honourable, be 768 (4), 913 (6), 929 (5), 933 (4), 935 (5)
honourable mention 923 (2)
honourable person 866 (6), 929 (2), 937 (1)
Honourable, the 870 (1)
honoured 866 (8), 920 (4)
honoured sir or madam 866 (6)
honouring 866 (5)
honours 729 (2), 866 (4), 870 (1), 962 (1)
honours list 866 (4)
hooch 790 (1)
hood 226 (4), 226 (13), 228 (23), 421 (1), 421 (4), 869 (7)
hooded 226 (12), 421 (3), 989 (4)
hoodlum 878 (3), 904 (2)
hoodoo 983 (1), 983 (2)
hoodwink 439 (4), 542 (8)
hoodwinked 491 (5)
hoodwinker 545 (1)
hoof 214 (2)
hoofed 214 (4)
hook 47 (6), 217 (3), 247 (1), 247 (7), 256 (5), 279 (2), 282 (6), 287 (7), 542 (4), 542 (10), 778 (2), 786 (6)
hook and eye 47 (5)
hook, line and sinker 52 (2), 54 (8)
hook-nosed 247 (5)

hook on 45 (11)
hook up 217 (5)
hook up with 45 (10)
hooked 247 (5), 248 (3),
887 (10), 949 (10)
hooker 952 (4)
hookup 45 (1), 706 (2)
hooligan 176 (4), 904 (2)
hooliganism 954 (3)
hoop 47 (1), 250 (2)
hooray! 835 (9)
hoot 408 (3), 409 (3), 835
(7), 921 (2), 921 (5), 924
(9)
hooted 924 (7)
hooter 117 (3), 400 (2), 547
(5)
hooting 400 (1), 547 (4)
hop 265 (2), 267 (1), 312
(1), 312 (4), 837 (13)
hop in 297 (5)
hope 124 (3), 482 (1), 485
(1), 507 (1), 600 (4), 612
(1), 831 (1), 833 (1), 833
(7), 852 (1), 852 (6), 859
(1), 859 (11), 933 (2)
hope against hope 852 (6)
Hope and Charity 93 (2)
hope eternally 487 (3)
hope for 852 (6)
hope for the best 852 (6)
hope in 852 (6)
hope on 600 (4), 852 (6)
hoped for 507 (3)
hopeful 471 (2), 507 (2),
833 (3), 852 (3), 852 (4),
852 (5)
hopeful, be 852 (6)
hopefully 852 (8)
hopefulness 833 (1), 852
(1)
hopeless 470 (2), 483 (2),
507 (2), 825 (6), 834 (5),
853 (2), 853 (3), 856 (3),
934 (3), 934 (4), 940 (2)
hopeless, be 853 (5)
hopeless situation 853 (1)
hopelessness 470 (1), 483
(1), 506 (1), 825 (2), 834
(1), 853 (1), 854 (1), 856
(1)
hoper 671 (2), 852 (3), 859
(6)

hopes 852 (1)
hoping 507 (2), 852 (4),
859 (7)
hopper 194 (12), 312 (2)
hopping 312 (3)
hopscotch 837 (10)
horde 11 (3), 104 (1), 869
(2)
horizon 199 (1), 216 (1),
236 (1), 438 (5), 443 (1)
horizontal 216 (4)
horizontal angle 216 (1)
horizontal, be 203 (8), 210
(3), 216 (6), 311 (8), 683
(3)
horizontal line 216 (1)
horizontality 210 (1), 216
(1)
horizontally 216 (8)
hormone 658 (7)
hormone therapy 658 (12)
horn 194 (15), 252 (4), 254
(3), 256 (2), 326 (1), 400
(2), 414 (7)
horn of plenty 171 (3), 635
(2)
horn player 413 (2)
horned 248 (3), 256 (9)
horned moon 321 (9)
hornet 365 (16)
hornet's nest 659 (1)
hornpipe 837 (14)
horns 969 (2)
horny 326 (3)
horological 117 (6)
horologist 117 (3)
horology 117 (1)
horoscope 155 (1), 511 (1)
horrendous 645 (4)
horrible 645 (4), 827 (4),
854 (8)
horribly 32 (18)
horrid 645 (4), 888 (5)
horrific 827 (6)
horrified 854 (6)
horrify 827 (11), 854 (12),
888 (8)
horrifying 827 (6), 854 (8)
horror 854 (1), 861 (1), 938
(4)
horror-struck 854 (6)
horrors, the 949 (3)
hors d'oeuvre 390 (1)

hors-d'oeuvres 301 (14)
horse 267 (6), 273 (4), 365
(3), 722 (10)
horse-box 274 (5)
horse doctor 369 (1)
horse-drawn 274 (16), 288
(2)
horse-drawn carriage 274
(6)
horse pistol 723 (10)
horse power 160 (3), 274
(1), 465 (3)
horse racing 267 (5), 716
(3)
horse radish 301 (21)
horse-rider 268 (4)
horse soldier 722 (10)
horse-trading 766 (1), 791
(1)
horse-trainer 537 (2)
horseflesh 273 (4)
horseman or woman 268
(4)
horsemanship 267 (5), 694
(1)
horseplay 837 (3)
horseshoe 248 (2), 963 (3)
horsewhip 963 (10), 964
(1)
horsy 273 (11), 837 (19)
hortative 534 (5)
horticultural 366 (9), 370
(8)
horticulture 366 (7), 370
(1)
horticulturist 370 (5)
hosanna 835 (1), 923 (2),
981 (5), 981 (13)
hose 228 (26), 263 (9), 339
(1), 341 (3), 351 (1)
hose down 341 (8)
hosiery 228 (26)
hospice 192 (17), 658 (13),
662 (2)
hospitable 813 (3), 880 (6),
882 (6), 897 (4)
hospitable, be 301 (39),
781 (7), 813 (4), 837 (20),
876 (4), 880 (7), 882 (10)
hospitably 882 (11)
hospital 192 (1), 652 (2),
658 (13)
hospital case 651 (18)

hospitality 813 (1), 880 (2), 882 (2), 897 (1)

hospitalize 658 (20)

hospitalized 651 (21)

host 74 (4), 104 (1), 651 (5), 722 (6), 882 (5)

hostage 31 (2), 750 (1), 767 (1), 780 (1)

hostel 187 (3), 192 (2)

hostelry 192 (11)

hostess 882 (5)

hostile 25 (4), 182 (2), 704 (3), 712 (6), 731 (4), 757 (2), 829 (3), 861 (2), 881 (3), 883 (5), 888 (4), 896 (4), 898 (6), 924 (6)

hostile critic 926 (3)

hostile evidence 928 (2)

hostile review 924 (2)

hostile witness 467 (1)

hostilities 716 (7), 718 (2), 881 (1)

hostility 702 (1), 704 (1), 709 (1), 881 (1), 888 (1)

hosts 32 (2)

hot 342 (4), 379 (4), 381 (6), 388 (3), 412 (7), 417 (10), 431 (3), 818 (5), 821 (3)

hot air 310 (2), 323 (1), 515 (3), 581 (2), 877 (2)

hot-air balloon 276 (2)

hot-air duct 383 (2)

hot and bothered 821 (3)

hot and cold 14 (2)

hot, be 298 (7), 300 (9), 302 (6), 318 (7), 379 (7), 417 (11), 821 (9)

hot blood 822 (1), 891 (1), 892 (1)

hot-blooded 176 (5), 857 (3), 892 (3)

hot coal 419 (3)

hot-gospeller 979 (5)

hot head 818 (2)

hot-headed 680 (2), 818 (5), 822 (3), 857 (3)

hot iron 381 (2)

hot-metal 587 (6)

hot money 797 (2)

hot news 529 (1)

hot-rod 274 (11)

hot spring 350 (1)

hot springs 379 (1), 652 (2)

hot taste 388 (1)

hot temper 822 (1), 892 (1)

hot up 381 (8)

hot water 827 (1)

hot-water bottle 194 (14)

hot-water pipe 383 (2)

hotbed 156 (4), 171 (3), 663 (1)

hotchpotch 43 (4), 61 (2)

hotel 192 (11)

hotel detective 459 (8)

hotelier 633 (3)

hotfoot 680 (2), 680 (4)

hothead 857 (2)

hotheadedness 857 (1)

hothouse 59 (4), 156 (4), 370 (3), 383 (2)

hotly 32 (17)

hotplate 383 (2)

hotting up 36 (1)

hound 365 (10), 881 (4), 896 (8), 924 (9), 926 (7), 938 (3)

hounding 619 (1)

hound's tooth 437 (2)

hour 8 (2), 110 (1)

hour by hour 113 (11)

hour hand 547 (6)

hour of decision 8 (2)

hourglass 117 (3), 198 (1), 206 (3)

houri 970 (5)

hourly 110 (3), 139 (2), 139 (4), 141 (5), 141 (7)

house 11 (4), 164 (3), 169 (2), 185 (1), 187 (5), 192 (6), 441 (2), 538 (4), 594 (14), 680 (8), 708 (5), 741 (3)

house agent 794 (1)

house arrest 747 (3)

house-break 788 (7)

house-breaker 297 (3), 789 (1), 904 (3)

house-breaking 788 (1)

house magazine 528 (5)

house of cards 163 (3), 330 (1)

House of Commons 692 (2)

house of God 990 (1)

House of Lords 692 (2), 956 (2)

house-owner 776 (1)

house party 882 (3)

house plant 366 (7)

house-proud 871 (4)

house-search 459 (5)

house surgeon 191 (2)

house-trained 848 (6)

houseboat 192 (7), 275 (7)

housebound 266 (4)

houseful 74 (5)

household 11 (3), 191 (5), 490 (7)

household gods 192 (5), 966 (2)

household name 866 (3)

household pet 365 (2)

household troops 722 (7)

householder 191 (2), 776 (1)

housekeeper 191 (2), 633 (3), 690 (3), 742 (2), 749 (1)

housekeeping 689 (1)

houselights 420 (5), 594 (7)

houseman 658 (14)

houses 192 (8)

housetop 213 (2), 226 (2)

housewarming 68 (3), 882 (3)

housewife 191 (2), 194 (10), 373 (3), 633 (3), 690 (3)

housework 682 (3)

housing 184 (3), 191 (5), 192 (8), 230 (1), 624 (5)

housing association 775 (3)

housing estate 192 (8)

hovel 192 (7)

hover 209 (12), 217 (5), 265 (4), 271 (7), 289 (4), 323 (4), 601 (4)

hovercraft 275 (1)

hovering 209 (11), 271 (6), 289 (2)

how 453 (5)

how things stand 8 (1)

howitzer 723 (11)

howl 352 (10), 400 (4), 408 (1), 408 (3), 409 (3), 836 (2), 836 (6)
howler 495 (3), 497 (1)
howling 32 (9), 176 (6), 409 (1)
hoyden 132 (2)
hoydenish 847 (5)
hub 70 (1), 76 (1), 225 (2), 638 (3)
hubbub 61 (4), 318 (3), 400 (1)
hubris 871 (1), 878 (1)
huckster 794 (3)
huddle 74 (5), 74 (10), 198 (7)
hue 5 (3), 43 (2), 425 (3)
hue-and-cry 547 (8), 619 (2)
huff 352 (11), 827 (8), 829 (6), 885 (6), 891 (1), 891 (8)
huff and puff 877 (5)
huffiness 891 (1)
hug 48 (3), 198 (7), 230 (3), 235 (4), 547 (4), 778 (1), 778 (5), 884 (2), 884 (7), 889 (1), 889 (6)
hug oneself 824 (6), 871 (6)
hug the coast 289 (4)
hug the shore 200 (5), 269 (9)
huge 32 (6), 195 (7), 209 (9)
hugely 32 (17)
hugeness 32 (1), 195 (2)
hugger-mugger 61 (2)
hulk 195 (3), 275 (1)
hulking 195 (9), 695 (5)
hull 226 (6), 229 (6), 275 (1)
hullabaloo 61 (4), 400 (1)
hullo 295 (7)
hum 352 (10), 397 (3), 401 (4), 403 (1), 403 (3), 404 (3), 409 (1), 409 (3), 413 (10), 577 (4), 678 (1), 678 (11)
hum and haw 580 (3), 601 (4)
human 371 (6), 897 (4), 934 (5)

human being 371 (1), 371 (3)
human interest 590 (3), 821 (1)
human life 360 (1)
human nature 371 (1)
human race 371 (1)
human rights 915 (1)
human sacrifice 982 (1)
human species 371 (1)
human weakness 934 (2)
humane 534 (5), 897 (4), 901 (6), 905 (4)
humaneness 901 (1)
humanism 449 (3), 901 (1), 917 (4)
humanist 492 (1), 901 (4)
humanistic 901 (6), 917 (7)
humanitarian 897 (4), 901 (4), 901 (6)
humanities 557 (3)
humanities, the 490 (3)
humanity 371 (1), 736 (1), 897 (1), 901 (1), 905 (1)
humanize 897 (5)
humankind 66 (1), 360 (1), 365 (3), 371 (1)
humble 33 (7), 311 (7), 483 (2), 491 (6), 509 (5), 721 (2), 821 (8), 869 (8), 872 (3), 872 (7), 874 (2), 884 (3), 920 (3), 931 (2)
humble, be 621 (3), 721 (4), 872 (5), 874 (3), 879 (4), 884 (5), 920 (6), 931 (3)
humble folk 869 (3)
humble-minded 872 (3)
humble oneself 872 (5), 920 (6), 981 (11)
humble petitioner 763 (1)
humble servant 742 (1)
humble spirit 872 (1)
humble submission 761 (2)
humbled 509 (2), 834 (5), 867 (7), 872 (4), 939 (3)
humbled, be 603 (5), 872 (6), 981 (11)
humbleness 872 (1), 920 (1), 979 (1), 981 (1)
humbling 821 (5), 872 (2)

humbly 920 (8)
humbug 515 (3), 541 (1), 542 (8), 545 (3), 850 (2), 850 (3)
humbugging 542 (6)
humbugs 301 (18)
humdinger 195 (5)
humdrum 573 (2), 838 (3)
humid 339 (2), 341 (4), 350 (8)
humidifier 340 (1)
humidify 341 (7)
humidity 341 (1)
humiliate 37 (4), 311 (7), 509 (5), 829 (6), 851 (5), 867 (11), 872 (7), 921 (5), 922 (6)
humiliated 825 (6), 867 (7), 872 (4)
humiliating 867 (6)
humiliation 37 (2), 311 (1), 509 (1), 731 (1), 867 (1), 872 (2), 921 (2), 922 (1)
humility 35 (1), 483 (1), 721 (1), 872 (1), 874 (1), 879 (1), 920 (1), 931 (1), 979 (1), 981 (1)
humming 397 (2), 678 (8)
humming with 74 (9), 104 (5)
hummock 209 (3), 253 (4)
hummocky 209 (10), 253 (8)
humorist 20 (3), 545 (1), 594 (10), 594 (13), 839 (3)
humorous 835 (5), 839 (4), 849 (3)
humour 5 (4), 179 (1), 604 (2), 703 (7), 736 (3), 756 (5), 817 (1), 835 (2), 837 (20), 839 (1), 925 (4)
humourless 834 (7), 840 (2)
humourlessness 834 (3)
hump 209 (3), 252 (2), 253 (6), 273 (12), 682 (7)
humpback 253 (6)
humpbacked 246 (4)
humped 252 (5)
humus 344 (3)
Hun 168 (1)

hunch 476 (1), 512 (1), 609 (1)
hunch-backed 845 (2)
hunch one's back 311 (9)
hunchback 253 (6)
hunchbacked 246 (4)
hundred 99 (4), 184 (3)
hundred per cent 99 (4)
hundred thousand 99 (5)
hundredth 99 (6), 100 (2)
hundredweight 99 (4), 322 (2)
hung 445 (7)
hung jury 959 (3)
hunger 301 (1), 342 (1), 786 (3), 859 (2), 859 (12), 946 (1), 947 (1)
hunger for 859 (11)
hunger strike 946 (2)
hungering 859 (9)
hungrily 859 (14), 947 (5)
hungry 342 (4), 786 (5), 801 (3), 859 (9), 946 (3), 947 (3)
hungry, be 301 (35), 636 (8), 801 (5), 859 (12), 946 (4)
hungry for 453 (3), 859 (7)
hunk 53 (5), 195 (3), 841 (2)
hunt 300 (6), 317 (4), 459 (5), 484 (5), 619 (2), 619 (5), 619 (6), 837 (21)
hunt down 735 (7)
hunt for 459 (13), 459 (15), 619 (5)
hunt out 300 (6)
hunted 620 (3)
hunter 268 (4), 273 (5), 362 (6), 619 (3)
hunter's moon 129 (3), 321 (9)
hunting 619 (1), 619 (2), 619 (4), 837 (6)
huntress 619 (3)
huntsman 268 (4), 619 (3)
huntswoman 619 (3)
hurdle 218 (7), 235 (2), 312 (4), 702 (2)
hurdler 273 (5), 312 (2)
hurdles 716 (3)
hurdy-gurdy 414 (5)
hurl 287 (7)

hurl at 712 (12)
hurl oneself 176 (7)
hurler 287 (5)
hurling 287 (1)
hurly-burly 61 (4), 318 (3)
hurrah! 835 (9)
hurricane 61 (4), 176 (3), 352 (4)
hurricane-force 352 (8)
hurricane lamp 420 (4)
hurried 114 (5), 458 (2), 680 (2)
hurriedly 680 (4)
hurry 277 (1), 277 (6), 678 (1), 678 (12), 680 (1), 680 (3)
hurry off with 786 (9)
hurry up 680 (5)
hurt 163 (10), 374 (6), 377 (1), 377 (4), 377 (5), 616 (1), 643 (3), 645 (6), 655 (5), 655 (9), 827 (8), 891 (3), 891 (8), 898 (8), 914 (6), 963 (8)
hurt, be 825 (7)
hurt one's feelings 827 (8)
hurt one's pride 872 (7)
hurt oneself 825 (7)
hurt pride 872 (2)
hurtful 645 (3), 827 (3), 898 (5)
hurtfulness 645 (1), 827 (1)
hurting 827 (3)
hurtle 176 (7), 277 (6)
husband 372 (1), 632 (5), 894 (4)
husbandless 896 (4)
husbandly 894 (9)
husbandry 370 (1)
hush 177 (7), 266 (2), 399 (1), 399 (4), 399 (5), 401 (5), 578 (4), 582 (4)
hush-hush 523 (4), 525 (3)
hush money 612 (4), 962 (1)
hush up 525 (8)
hushed 33 (6), 266 (6), 399 (2), 401 (3)
husk 41 (1), 226 (6), 366 (8)
huskiness 407 (1), 578 (1)
husks 41 (2)

husky 162 (8), 273 (3), 365 (10), 407 (3), 841 (3)
hussar 722 (10)
hussy 878 (3), 938 (1), 952 (2)
hustings 539 (5), 605 (2), 724 (1)
hustle 265 (5), 287 (7), 680 (1), 680 (3)
hustle away 680 (3)
hustle out 300 (6)
hustler 277 (4)
hustling 277 (5)
hut 192 (3), 192 (7)
hutch 192 (10), 369 (3)
hutments 192 (8)
hybrid 43 (5), 43 (6), 84 (7), 560 (1), 560 (4)
hybrid language 560 (2)
hybridization 43 (1)
hybridize 43 (7)
hydra 84 (4)
hydra-headed 82 (2)
hydrant 350 (2), 351 (1), 382 (3)
hydrate 339 (3)
hydrated 339 (2)
hydraulics 335 (1)
hydro- 339 (2)
hydroelectric 160 (9)
hydroelectricity 160 (4)
hydrofoil 275 (1)
hydrogen 310 (2)
hydrogen bomb 723 (14)
hydroplane 276 (1)
hyena 365 (3)
hygiene 648 (2), 648 (3), 652 (2), 658 (3), 660 (2), 666 (1)
hygienic 648 (7), 648 (8), 650 (2), 652 (4), 660 (4)
hygienically 652 (7)
hygienics 652 (2)
hygienist 652 (3)
hymn 412 (5), 413 (10), 593 (2), 981 (5), 981 (11), 988 (6)
hymn-singer 981 (8)
hymn-singing 412 (5), 981 (3), 981 (5), 981 (7), 981 (9)
hymn-writer 981 (8)
hymnal 981 (5)

hymning 961 (3)
hype 482 (1), 528 (3)
hype up 528 (11)
hyped-up 482 (3)
hyper- 34 (4)
hyperactive 678 (7)
hyperbola 248 (2)
hyperbole 197 (1), 519 (2), 546 (1), 574 (2)
hyperbolic 519 (3)
hypercritical 735 (4)
hypermarket 796 (3)
hypersensitive 374 (3)
hyphen 47 (1), 547 (14)
hyphenate 45 (9)
hypnosis 375 (1)
hypnotic 177 (4), 178 (2), 375 (3), 612 (6), 679 (10), 984 (7)
hypnotism 178 (1), 375 (1), 984 (1)
hypnotist 612 (5), 984 (5)
hypnotize 178 (3), 375 (6), 485 (9), 612 (8), 963 (11), 984 (9)
hypnotized 161 (7), 375 (3), 983 (9)
hypochondria 503 (2), 651 (1), 834 (2)
hypochondriac 163 (2), 503 (7), 504 (1), 651 (18), 834 (4)
hypocrisy 541 (2), 542 (1), 925 (1), 980 (2)
hypocrite 20 (3), 545 (1), 698 (3), 850 (3), 879 (2), 925 (2)
hypocritical 20 (4), 541 (4), 542 (6), 603 (4), 850 (4), 925 (3), 930 (4), 930 (7), 980 (4)
hypodermic needle 263 (12)
hypothermia 380 (1)
hypothesis 158 (1), 475 (2), 485 (3), 512 (1)
hypothetical 469 (2), 485 (5), 512 (4), 513 (6)
hysteria 503 (2), 503 (4)
hysteric 504 (1)
hysterical 176 (6), 503 (7), 503 (9), 818 (5), 821 (3), 822 (3), 854 (6)

hysterics 176 (1), 822 (2), 836 (1)

I

I 80 (4)
I-spy 837 (8)
ice 258 (1), 380 (4), 382 (1), 384 (1), 392 (4), 422 (1)
Ice Age 110 (2), 380 (1)
ice cap 380 (4)
ice-capped 380 (5)
ice-cold 380 (5)
ice-covered 226 (12)
ice cream 392 (2)
ice-cubes 384 (2)
ice field 348 (1), 380 (4)
ice floe 380 (4)
ice hockey 837 (6)
ice over 382 (6)
ice rink 724 (1)
ice sheet 380 (4)
ice skating 837 (6)
ice up 382 (6)
iceberg 349 (1), 380 (4), 820 (2)
icebox 384 (1)
icebreaker 275 (1)
iced 382 (4), 392 (3)
iced drink 301 (27)
iced up 382 (4)
icicle 217 (2), 380 (4), 820 (2)
iciness 380 (1)
icing 226 (1), 392 (2)
icon 551 (2), 553 (5)
iconic 551 (6)
iconoclast 904 (1), 979 (5)
iconoclastic 980 (4)
icy 380 (5), 820 (3), 881 (3), 883 (5)
icy blast 352 (1)
id 80 (4), 320 (2), 447 (2), 476 (1)
idea 156 (6), 164 (2), 449 (1), 451 (1), 498 (1), 512 (1), 513 (2), 551 (2), 609 (1), 623 (3)

ideal 4 (3), 23 (1), 451 (2), 513 (6), 612 (1), 646 (2), 646 (3), 859 (5)
ideal, the 54 (1)
idealism 320 (1), 449 (3), 513 (3), 654 (4), 917 (4), 931 (1), 933 (2)
idealist 149 (2), 320 (1), 513 (4), 654 (5), 671 (2), 897 (3), 901 (4)
idealistic 470 (2), 513 (5), 654 (7), 901 (6), 931 (2), 933 (3)
ideality 164 (2), 512 (1), 513 (2), 543 (3), 617 (2)
idealization 513 (2)
idealize 482 (4), 513 (7), 982 (6)
ideals 688 (1), 901 (1), 917 (4), 931 (1), 933 (2)
ideas 449 (1), 498 (1)
ideational 451 (2)
identical 13 (2), 18 (4), 28 (7), 88 (3), 514 (4)
identical, be 13 (3)
identical twin 11 (2)
identical twins 90 (1)
identically 13 (5)
identification 18 (2), 547 (2)
identify 13 (4), 18 (8), 484 (4), 547 (18)
identity 13 (1), 16 (1), 18 (1), 18 (2), 28 (2), 80 (4), 494 (2), 514 (2)
identity card 547 (13)
ideogram 558 (1), 586 (2)
ides 108 (3)
idilation 253 (1)
idiocy 499 (1), 499 (2), 503 (1)
idiom 80 (1), 514 (2), 557 (1), 560 (2), 563 (1), 566 (1)
idiomatic 80 (5), 514 (4), 557 (5), 563 (2), 566 (2), 571 (2), 575 (3)
idiosyncrasy 5 (4), 80 (1), 84 (1), 179 (1), 610 (1)
idiosyncratic 80 (5)
idiot 501 (1), 504 (1)
idiotic 499 (4), 503 (7), 503 (8)

illogicality 10 (2), 72 (1), 477 (2), 515 (1)

illogicalness 477 (1)

illuminate 417 (13), 420 (9), 425 (8), 520 (8), 522 (7), 844 (12)

illuminated 420 (8)

illuminating 520 (6)

illumination 417 (1), 420 (5), 484 (1), 490 (1), 520 (1), 551 (3), 553 (1), 844 (2), 975 (1)

illuminations 420 (7), 876 (1)

illuminator 556 (1)

illusion 4 (2), 440 (2), 445 (1), 495 (1), 542 (1), 542 (3)

illusionist 545 (5), 983 (5)

illusory 320 (3), 477 (4), 495 (4), 513 (6), 542 (6)

illustrate 83 (9), 520 (8), 551 (8), 844 (12)

illustration 83 (2), 520 (1), 551 (1), 553 (5), 589 (5), 844 (2)

illustrative 83 (5), 516 (3), 520 (6), 551 (6)

illustrator 556 (1)

illustrious 866 (9), 866 (10)

illustriousness 866 (3)

image 18 (3), 22 (1), 417 (5), 445 (1), 451 (1), 513 (2), 519 (4), 522 (4), 547 (1), 548 (3), 551 (2), 551 (8), 554 (1), 821 (1), 837 (15), 982 (3)

image-breaker 979 (5)

image worship 982 (1)

image-worshipper 981 (8), 982 (4)

imaged 551 (7)

imagery 513 (1), 519 (1)

imaginable 469 (2), 512 (5)

imaginary 2 (4), 4 (3), 320 (3), 445 (7), 451 (2), 495 (4), 512 (5), 513 (6), 590 (6), 852 (5), 864 (5), 970 (6)

imaginary number 85 (1)

imagination 21 (1), 171 (1), 449 (1), 451 (1), 513 (1), 519 (1), 541 (1), 698 (1)

imaginative 21 (3), 164 (5), 438 (6), 497 (3), 513 (5), 590 (6), 852 (4)

imaginatively 513 (8)

imaginativeness 513 (1)

imagine 164 (7), 438 (7), 447 (7), 449 (7), 456 (7), 512 (6), 513 (7), 541 (5), 543 (5), 590 (7), 623 (8), 852 (6)

imagined 513 (6), 541 (3), 543 (4)

imam 741 (5), 986 (8)

imattractive 827 (4)

imbalance 29 (1), 152 (1), 246 (1)

imbecile 499 (3), 501 (1), 503 (7)

imbecility 161 (2), 499 (1), 503 (1)

imbibe 299 (4), 301 (38), 536 (4)

imbibing 301 (25)

imbroglio 61 (2), 61 (3)

imbue 50 (4), 303 (5), 425 (8), 534 (6), 610 (8)

imbued with 817 (2)

imitable 20 (4)

imitate 18 (7), 18 (8), 20 (5), 83 (7), 541 (6), 541 (8), 547 (21), 551 (8), 594 (17), 850 (5), 851 (6)

imitated 20 (4), 541 (3)

imitation 18 (2), 20 (1), 20 (4), 22 (1), 83 (1), 106 (1), 150 (4), 542 (5), 542 (7), 551 (1), 785 (1), 788 (1), 847 (1)

imitative 18 (6), 20 (4), 83 (4), 106 (3), 157 (3), 450 (2)

imitativeness 20 (1), 20 (2)

imitator 20 (3), 83 (3), 545 (1), 594 (9)

immaculacy 646 (1)

immaculate 646 (3), 648 (7), 935 (3), 950 (5)

immanence 5 (1), 965 (2)

immanent 5 (6), 5 (9), 965 (6)

immaterial 4 (3), 10 (4), 320 (3), 447 (6), 639 (5), 970 (7)

immateriality 4 (1), 320 (1)

immature 55 (3), 68 (6), 126 (5), 130 (4), 135 (4), 244 (2), 393 (2), 499 (3), 647 (3), 670 (4), 695 (4), 726 (2)

immaturity 55 (1), 126 (1), 130 (2), 499 (1), 647 (1), 670 (1), 695 (1), 726 (1)

immeasurable 107 (2), 965 (6)

immeasurably 32 (17), 107 (3)

immediacy 116 (1), 135 (2), 680 (1)

immediate 116 (3), 277 (5), 680 (2)

immediately 116 (4)

immediateness 116 (1)

immemorial 32 (4), 113 (4), 125 (7), 127 (6), 866 (8)

immense 32 (6), 107 (2), 195 (7)

immensity 32 (1), 183 (1), 195 (2)

immerse 303 (7), 313 (3), 341 (8)

immerse oneself 303 (7)

immersed 211 (2)

immersion 297 (1), 303 (2), 313 (1), 341 (2)

immersion heater 383 (2)

immigrant 59 (2), 59 (4), 191 (4), 297 (3)

immigrate 297 (5)

immigration 267 (2), 297 (1)

imminent 124 (4), 155 (2), 289 (2)

imminent, be 124 (5)

immobile 153 (6), 266 (6), 677 (2)

immobility 144 (1), 153 (1), 175 (1), 266 (1), 677 (1), 679 (1) immobilize 266 (9), 679 (13)

immoderate 546 (2), 576 (2), 637 (3), 943 (2), 943 (3)

immoderately 32 (18), 943 (4)

immoderation 546 (1), 943 (1)

immodest 951 (7)

immodestly 951 (12)

immodesty 873 (1), 951 (1)

immolate 362 (10), 781 (7)

immolation 362 (1), 981 (6)

immoral 914 (3), 930 (4), 934 (3), 934 (4), 934 (6), 951 (6), 951 (7), 951 (10)

immoral, be 951 (10)

immorality 914 (1), 934 (1), 951 (2), 980 (1)

immortal 115 (2)

immortality 115 (1), 866 (3)

immortalize 115 (3), 866 (13)

immortals, the 966 (1)

immovability 153 (1)

immovable 45 (7), 153 (6), 266 (6), 599 (2), 602 (4)

immune 652 (4), 660 (5), 744 (5), 919 (2), 960 (2)

immunity 652 (2), 660 (1), 744 (1), 915 (1), 919 (1)

immunization 652 (2)

immunize 652 (6), 658 (20), 660 (8)

immunized 652 (4), 660 (4)

immunizing 652 (4)

immure 235 (4), 747 (10)

immure oneself 883 (8)

immured 232 (2)

immutability 153 (1), 965 (2)

immutable 115 (2), 144 (2), 153 (4), 965 (6)

imp 969 (2), 970 (2), 970 (4), 983 (5)

imp of Satan 969 (2)

impact 45 (11), 45 (13), 279 (1), 279 (3), 303 (6), 821 (1)

impair 37 (4), 39 (3), 46 (13), 63 (3), 143 (6), 163 (10), 165 (9), 244 (3), 246 (5), 297 (6), 306 (4), 634 (4), 636 (9), 641 (7), 645 (6), 649 (9), 655 (9), 675 (2), 678 (13), 695 (9), 842 (7), 845 (3)

impaired 655 (5)

impaired hearing 416 (1)

impairment 39 (1), 43 (1), 163 (1), 339 (1), 655 (3)

impale 263 (18), 963 (12)

impalement 263 (2), 963 (3)

impaling 547 (11)

impart 524 (9)

impart momentum 279 (7)

impartial 28 (7), 498 (5), 606 (2), 625 (3), 860 (2), 913 (4), 913 (6), 931 (2)

impartiality 28 (1), 177 (1), 606 (1), 860 (1), 913 (2), 929 (1), 931 (1)

impartially 913 (7)

impassable 264 (4), 470 (3), 700 (4)

impasse 264 (1), 470 (1), 700 (1), 702 (2)

impassion 821 (6)

impassioned 571 (2), 818 (5), 819 (4), 821 (3)

impassive 175 (2), 266 (6), 454 (2), 517 (2), 677 (2), 820 (3), 823 (3), 860 (2), 865 (2), 898 (6), 906 (2), 950 (5)

impassiveness 175 (1), 820 (1), 865 (1)

impassivity 679 (2)

impatience 680 (1), 818 (2), 822 (1), 857 (1), 892 (1)

impatient 499 (5), 680 (2), 819 (4), 822 (3), 857 (3), 859 (7), 891 (4), 891 (7), 892 (3)

impeach 928 (9), 959 (7)

impeachment 926 (1)

impeccability 935 (1)

impeccable 646 (3)

impecunious 801 (3)

impede 702 (8)

impediment 700 (1), 702 (1), 702 (2), 896 (1)

impedimenta 194 (7), 272 (3), 630 (4), 702 (4)

impeding 702 (6)

impel 174 (7), 265 (5), 279 (7), 287 (7), 292 (3), 303 (4), 311 (4), 311 (6), 612 (8), 678 (11), 712 (7)

impelling 156 (7), 279 (6)

impend 124 (5), 155 (3), 289 (4), 900 (3)

impending 124 (4), 135 (4), 155 (2), 289 (2), 295 (3), 471 (2), 507 (3), 669 (6), 900 (2)

impenetrability 517 (1)

impenetrable 264 (4), 324 (4), 470 (3), 499 (3), 517 (2), 523 (2), 700 (4)

impenitence 940 (1), 980 (1)

impenitent 602 (4), 940 (2)

impenitent, be 940 (4)

impenitently 940 (5)

imperative 596 (4), 627 (5), 638 (5), 737 (5), 740 (2)

imperatively 737 (9)

imperceptible 33 (7), 196 (11), 278 (3), 444 (2)

imperceptibly 33 (9)

imperceptivity 464 (1)

imperfect 35 (4), 53 (6), 55 (3), 163 (7), 246 (4), 307 (2), 576 (2), 645 (2), 647 (3), 670 (4), 695 (6), 726 (2), 845 (2), 934 (5)

imperfect, be 647 (4)

imperfect tense 111 (1)

imperfection 35 (1), 307 (1), 576 (1), 636 (1), 645 (1), 647 (1), 661 (2), 845 (1), 934 (2)

imperfectly 33 (10), 647 (5)

imperfectness 647 (1)

imperial 32 (4), 465 (9), 733 (8)

imperialism 371 (5), 733 (2)
imperil 661 (9)
imperilment 661 (1)
imperious 733 (7), 871 (3)
imperishable 115 (2), 153 (4), 866 (10)
impermanence 114 (1), 152 (1)
impermanent 114 (3), 114 (4)
impermeable 264 (4), 324 (4), 421 (3)
impersonal 820 (3), 883 (5), 913 (4)
impersonality 79 (1)
impersonate 551 (8), 594 (17)
impersonation 551 (1), 594 (8)
impersonator 20 (3), 594 (10)
imperspicuity 517 (1), 568 (1)
impertinence 878 (2), 885 (2)
impertinent 878 (3), 878 (5), 885 (4), 921 (3), 922 (3)
impertinently 878 (7)
imperturbability 823 (1)
imperturbable 820 (3), 823 (3)
impervious 264 (4), 324 (4), 421 (3), 499 (3), 602 (4)
impervious to 820 (5)
impetigo 651 (12)
impetuosity 680 (1), 822 (1), 857 (1)
impetuous 176 (6), 680 (2), 818 (5), 822 (3)
impetus 160 (3), 174 (1), 277 (2), 279 (1), 612 (1)
impiety 675 (1), 916 (1), 921 (1), 934 (1), 974 (1), 980 (1)
impinge 306 (4), 378 (7)
impious 934 (3), 974 (5), 980 (4)
impious, be 649 (9), 655 (9), 899 (7), 916 (8), 921 (5), 974 (7), 980 (6)

impious person 980 (3)
impish 970 (6)
implacability 599 (1), 898 (2), 910 (1)
implacable 599 (2), 602 (4), 735 (4), 888 (4), 898 (4), 906 (2), 910 (4)
implant 45 (11), 187 (5), 303 (6), 370 (9), 534 (6), 610 (8)
implanted 6 (2), 610 (5)
implement 164 (7), 628 (2), 630 (1), 676 (5), 725 (6)
implementation 725 (2)
implicate 928 (8)
implicated 58 (2)
implicated in, be 58 (3)
implication 9 (1), 514 (1), 523 (1)
implicit 5 (6), 514 (3), 523 (3)
implied 514 (4), 523 (3)
implore 761 (7)
imploring 761 (2)
imply 56 (4), 78 (5), 89 (4), 156 (10), 466 (6), 514 (5), 523 (6), 524 (11)
impolite 847 (5), 885 (4), 921 (3)
impolitely 885 (7)
impoliteness 847 (2), 885 (1), 921 (1)
impolitic 643 (2), 695 (3)
imponderable 320 (3)
import 9 (1), 514 (1), 633 (5), 638 (1), 638 (7)
importance 9 (1), 32 (1), 34 (1), 64 (1), 178 (1), 638 (1), 680 (1), 866 (1)
important 9 (5), 32 (4), 34 (4), 34 (5), 137 (6), 154 (5), 156 (8), 178 (2), 638 (5), 680 (2), 689 (3), 866 (9)
important, be 34 (9), 178 (3), 638 (7)
important matter 638 (2)
importantly 638 (9)
importation 272 (1), 297 (1)
imported 59 (4), 297 (4), 560 (4)

importer 272 (4), 273 (1), 794 (1)
importunate 761 (3), 827 (5)
importunate creditor 802 (2)
importune 761 (5)
importunity 761 (1)
impose 596 (8), 737 (6), 740 (3), 920 (7), 963 (8)
impose a ban 757 (4)
impose a duty 737 (6), 917 (11)
impose a tax 809 (7)
impose on 673 (4)
impose one's will 595 (2)
impose upon 542 (8)
imposed 596 (4)
imposing 638 (6), 821 (5), 866 (8), 920 (4)
imposition 38 (1), 659 (1), 737 (1), 737 (3), 809 (3), 916 (1), 963 (4)
impossibility 470 (1), 472 (1), 853 (1)
impossible 25 (5), 450 (3), 470 (2), 472 (2), 486 (5), 700 (4), 757 (2), 760 (3), 827 (7), 864 (5)
impossible, be 470 (4)
impossible task 470 (1)
impossibly 470 (7)
impostor 20 (3), 150 (2), 493 (2), 527 (2), 527 (4), 542 (5), 545 (3), 697 (1), 850 (3), 916 (4), 938 (2)
imposture 541 (2), 542 (1), 698 (1)
impotence 161 (1), 163 (1), 172 (1), 641 (1), 677 (1), 734 (2)
impotent 161 (5), 161 (7), 163 (4), 163 (7), 172 (4), 639 (5), 641 (4), 695 (3)
impotent, be 161 (8)
impounded 747 (6)
impounding 786 (2)
impoverish 634 (4), 636 (9), 779 (4), 786 (11), 801 (6)
impoverished 655 (5), 801 (3)
impoverishment 801 (1)

impracticable 25 (5), 470 (3), 470 (4), 641 (4), 700 (4)

impractical 481 (6), 513 (5)

imprecate 899 (6)

imprecation 761 (2)

imprecatory 899 (3)

imprecise 495 (6)

imprecision 79 (1), 495 (2), 568 (1)

impregnable 162 (7), 660 (5), 950 (5)

impregnate 43 (7), 50 (4), 167 (7), 171 (5), 189 (5), 303 (5)

impregnated 167 (5)

impregnation 43 (1), 167 (1)

impresario 522 (3), 594 (12)

impress 157 (1), 178 (3), 255 (8), 291 (4), 374 (6), 449 (10), 455 (7), 508 (5), 547 (19), 555 (3), 612 (8), 740 (3), 745 (7), 818 (7), 821 (8), 834 (11), 854 (12), 864 (7), 920 (7)

impress on 532 (7)

impress on one's mind 505 (10)

impressed 818 (4), 819 (2), 864 (4)

impressible 180 (2), 327 (2), 490 (5), 818 (3), 819 (2), 822 (3), 905 (4)

impression 22 (1), 255 (1), 374 (2), 445 (1), 445 (2), 451 (1), 476 (1), 485 (3), 490 (1), 547 (1), 547 (13), 551 (1), 555 (2), 587 (2), 589 (5), 818 (1), 821 (1)

impressionable 819 (2), 822 (3)

Impressionism 553 (3)

Impressionist 556 (1), 594 (10)

impressionistic 551 (6)

impressive 32 (4), 32 (7), 178 (2), 571 (2), 638 (6), 818 (6), 821 (5), 854 (8), 864 (5), 866 (8), 871 (3), 920 (4)

impressively 32 (19)

imprimatur 488 (1), 976 (2)

imprint 22 (1), 83 (8), 255 (1), 547 (2), 547 (13), 587 (2)

imprison 224 (5), 232 (3), 235 (4), 660 (8), 745 (7), 747 (10), 778 (5), 883 (10), 963 (8)

imprisoned 232 (2), 525 (3), 660 (4), 747 (6), 750 (2), 778 (4)

imprisonment 747 (3), 963 (4)

improbability 159 (3), 472 (1), 508 (1)

improbable 84 (6), 472 (2), 472 (3), 474 (4), 508 (2), 864 (5)

improbity 788 (5), 793 (1), 930 (1), 934 (1), 954 (2)

impromptu 116 (4), 412 (4), 609 (1), 609 (3), 609 (5), 670 (1), 670 (3)

improper 25 (5), 499 (5), 565 (2), 643 (2), 645 (4), 847 (4), 867 (4), 867 (5), 914 (3), 916 (5), 934 (4)

improper fraction 85 (2)

improper offer 759 (1)

impropriety 25 (2), 565 (1), 576 (1), 643 (1), 847 (1), 914 (1), 916 (1), 934 (2), 936 (2)

improvable 654 (6)

improve 615 (5), 654 (8), 654 (9), 841 (8), 897 (6)

improve on 34 (7), 640 (5)

improve upon 654 (9)

improved 34 (4), 654 (6), 656 (6), 913 (3)

improvement 36 (1), 62 (1), 143 (1), 147 (1), 285 (1), 615 (2), 654 (1), 703 (1)

improverish 163 (10)

improvidence 634 (1), 670 (1), 815 (1), 857 (1)

improvident 458 (2), 670 (3), 815 (3), 857 (3)

improving 654 (7), 933 (3)

improvisation 412 (1), 609 (1), 623 (3), 670 (1)

improvise 413 (8), 413 (9), 513 (7), 551 (8), 579 (9), 609 (4), 669 (11), 670 (7)

improvised 609 (3), 670 (3)

improviser 593 (6), 609 (2)

imprudence 499 (2), 857 (1)

imprudent 643 (2), 857 (3)

impudence 878 (2)

impudent 878 (5), 885 (4)

impugn 486 (8), 533 (3)

impulse 160 (8), 178 (1), 277 (2), 279 (1), 287 (1), 318 (1), 547 (4), 604 (2), 609 (1), 612 (1), 818 (1), 859 (1)

impulsion 156 (1), 279 (1), 287 (1)

impulsive 476 (2), 596 (5), 609 (3), 680 (2), 822 (3), 857 (3)

impulsiveness 609 (1)

impunity 960 (1)

impure 522 (5), 645 (4), 649 (6), 744 (5), 847 (4), 867 (4), 887 (12), 944 (3), 951 (6), 980 (4)

impure, be 859 (11), 943 (3), 951 (10)

impure thoughts 951 (1)

impurely 951 (12)

impurity 453 (1), 649 (1), 847 (1), 934 (1), 944 (1), 951 (1)

imputable 158 (2)

imputation 158 (1), 867 (2), 926 (1), 928 (1)

impute 158 (3), 928 (8)

imputed 158 (2)

in 186 (5), 224 (6), 848 (5)

in a bad way 651 (21), 731 (5)

in a body 74 (12)

in a circle 315 (6)

in a cleft stick 700 (5)

in a coma 651 (21)

in a crowd 74 (9)

in a decline 651 (21)

in a dilemma 700 (5)

in a ferment 61 (12)
in a fever 379 (4)
in a fix 700 (5)
in a flash 277 (9)
in a flutter 318 (4)
in a fright 854 (6)
in a fury 891 (4)
in a groove 16 (5)
in a hole 700 (5)
in a hurry 680 (2)
in a jam 700 (5)
in a lather 379 (4)
in a line 249 (2)
in a manner of speaking 33 (10)
in a mess 61 (7)
in a minority 105 (2)
in a moment 116 (4)
in a nutshell 196 (13), 496 (4), 569 (4)
in a panic 854 (6)
in a pickle 700 (5)
in a quandary 700 (5)
in a rage 891 (4)
in a rut 16 (5)
in a sense 53 (8), 514 (6)
in a small way 33 (9)
in a spot 700 (5)
in a state 825 (5)
in a state of, be 7 (4)
in a sweat 379 (4)
in a temper 891 (4)
in a trance 375 (3), 513 (5), 949 (10)
in a trice 116 (4)
in a way 519 (5)
in a whisper 401 (6), 578 (6)
in a wink 116 (4)
in a word 569 (4)
in abeyance 175 (2), 175 (4), 523 (2), 674 (2), 677 (2)
in accordance 83 (10)
in accordance with 24 (5)
in action 173 (2), 676 (4)
in action, be 173 (3), 676 (5)
in addition 38 (5), 89 (5)
in advance 64 (5), 135 (4), 135 (7), 237 (6), 283 (4)
in adversity 731 (8)

in aid of 9 (5), 703 (4), 703 (8)
in all 54 (8)
in all directions 281 (8)
in all likelihood 471 (7)
in all quarters 183 (8)
in all respects 54 (8)
in alliance 181 (2)
in ambush 525 (3)
in an aside 578 (6)
in an undertone 401 (6), 578 (6)
in ancient days 113 (12)
in and out 251 (14), 317 (7)
in anticipation 135 (7)
in any event 159 (8)
in armour 669 (7)
in arms 132 (5)
in arrears 55 (3), 307 (4), 803 (5), 805 (4)
in articles 536 (6)
in authority 34 (4), 733 (7)
in bad taste 847 (4)
in bed 651 (21)
in between 625 (4)
in bits 46 (14), 53 (6)
in black 836 (4)
in black and white 586 (7)
in bliss 824 (5)
in bonds 742 (7)
in book form 589 (8)
in bottom gear 278 (7)
in brackets 231 (6)
in brief 569 (4), 592 (6)
in broad daylight 522 (10)
in business 791 (7)
in camera 525 (10)
in captivity 742 (7), 747 (6)
in case 8 (6), 154 (8)
in chains 745 (4), 750 (2)
in character 610 (6)
in charge 689 (6)
in charge, be 689 (5)
in chorus 24 (5), 410 (7), 488 (12)
in circles 315 (6)
in circulation 528 (7)
in close contact 202 (5)
in clover 376 (7), 730 (4), 730 (9)
in cold blood 617 (7), 820 (8)

in colour 425 (5)
in comfort 376 (7)
in commerce 791 (7)
in common 775 (7)
in company with 89 (5)
in comparison 462 (4)
in compartments 53 (6)
in compensation 31 (7)
in conclusion 69 (7)
in condition 7 (3), 162 (9), 650 (2)
in conference 584 (5)
in conflict with 704 (6)
in conformity 83 (10)
in confusion 61 (12)
in conjunction with 45 (15)
in consequence 157 (7)
in consideration 31 (7)
in constant use 673 (2)
in consternation 854 (6)
in contact 202 (2), 202 (5)
in contempt of 25 (7)
in context 9 (6)
in contrast 14 (5)
in control 689 (6)
in convoy 89 (5)
in credit 800 (4)
in-crowd 708 (1)
in custody 660 (4), 747 (6), 750 (2)
in danger 661 (6)
in danger, be 661 (7)
in danger of 180 (2), 471 (2), 661 (5)
in debt 803 (4)
in debt, be 785 (2), 803 (6)
in decay 163 (5)
in decline 37 (6), 655 (5)
in deduction 39 (4)
in deep water 700 (5)
in default 55 (3)
in default of 190 (8)
in defiance of 25 (7), 704 (6), 711 (4)
in demand 627 (3), 793 (3), 793 (5), 859 (10)
in deposit 632 (4)
in despair 853 (2)
in detail 53 (9), 80 (10)
in difficulties 700 (5), 702 (7), 728 (6), 731 (5), 801 (3)

in difficulty, be **596** (7), **700** (7), **731** (7)
in digs, be **192** (21)
in dire straits **731** (5)
in disarray **61** (7)
in disorder **61** (7), **61** (12)
in disproof **479** (5)
in disrepair **655** (6)
in distress **801** (3)
in double harness **706** (3)
in doubt **474** (6)
in draft **623** (6)
in dribs and drabs **105** (5)
in due course **124** (7), **137** (8)
in due time **111** (4), **137** (8)
in dumb show **547** (23)
in duty bound **917** (12)
in earshot **415** (8)
in echelon **220** (3)
in eclipse **867** (7)
in ecstasies **824** (4)
in effect **5** (10), **52** (9)
in embryo **55** (4), **68** (11), **124** (4), **669** (6)
in equilibrium **28** (7), **28** (11)
in error **481** (6), **495** (5)
in essence **1** (8)
in every quarter **183** (8)
in every way **54** (8)
in evidence **466** (5)
in evidence, be **189** (4)
in exchange **12** (4), **151** (2), **151** (4)
in existence **1** (4)
in expectation **507** (2)
in extremis **361** (5)
in extremities **731** (5)
in fact **1** (8), **32** (16)
in fashion **848** (5)
in fashion, be **83** (7), **848** (7)
in favour **866** (7), **923** (7)
in favour of **150** (6)
in festive mood **837** (19)
in-fighting **716** (4)
in file **71** (7)
in fine fettle **162** (6), **650** (2)
in fits **318** (8)
in flames **379** (5)

in-flight **271** (6), **271** (8), **728** (5)
in flood **350** (7)
in flower **669** (8)
in focus **443** (3)
in force **160** (8), **173** (2)
in foreign parts **59** (5)
in form **7** (3)
in formation **74** (9)
in front **199** (7), **237** (6), **283** (4)
in front, be **34** (9), **64** (3), **64** (4), **237** (5), **240** (3)
in full **54** (8)
in full bloom **134** (3)
in full career **277** (9)
in full cry **400** (5), **619** (4)
in full fig **844** (11)
in full swing **678** (8)
in full view **443** (2), **522** (10)
in fun **839** (6)
in future **124** (8)
in glowing terms **571** (3)
in good form **7** (3)
in good health **650** (2)
in good heart **650** (2), **833** (3)
in good shape **650** (2)
in good taste **846** (3), **846** (5)
in good time **135** (4), **135** (6)
in good voice **577** (3)
in halves **46** (14)
in hand **55** (4), **632** (4), **669** (7), **669** (14), **674** (2)
in harmony **50** (3), **181** (4)
in harness **669** (7), **678** (8), **745** (4)
in haste **680** (2)
in health **650** (2)
in hell **825** (5)
in high spirits **833** (3)
in hock **767** (3)
in holes **655** (6)
in holiday spirit **837** (19)
in holy orders **986** (11)
in honour bound **917** (5)
in honour of **876** (6)
in hopes **852** (4)
in hospital **651** (24)
in hot pursuit **619** (4)

in hushed tones **578** (6)
in hysterics **854** (6)
in ignorance **491** (4), **491** (9)
in imagination **513** (8)
in irons **747** (6)
in its infancy **68** (11)
in jest **839** (6)
in keeping **83** (10)
in keeping with **24** (5)
in key, be **410** (9)
in kind **151** (4)
in labour **167** (5)
in-law **11** (2)
in-laws **11** (3)
in layers **207** (4)
in league **45** (15), **50** (3), **706** (3), **708** (9)
in letters **558** (5)
in lieu **31** (7), **150** (6)
in limbo **458** (3), **506** (3)
in line **16** (2)
in line ahead **71** (7), **203** (9)
in line with **83** (10)
in litigation **959** (10)
in loco **186** (5)
in loco parentis **150** (6)
in lots **53** (9)
in love **887** (10)
in love, be **859** (11), **887** (14), **889** (7)
in low gear **278** (7)
in luck's way **730** (9)
in memoriam **364** (11), **505** (12)
in memory **505** (12)
in memory of **876** (6)
in mind **449** (12)
in miniature **196** (13)
in mint condition **126** (5)
in moderation **177** (8)
in motion **265** (3)
in motion, be **152** (5), **258** (5), **265** (4), **267** (11), **267** (13), **269** (10), **271** (7), **285** (3)
in mourning **836** (4)
in mufti **17** (2)
in name only **4** (4)
in nappies **132** (5)
in need **627** (4), **627** (7), **801** (3)

in next to no time 116 (4)
in no respect 33 (13)
in no time 116 (4)
in no way 33 (13), 533 (4)
in obedience to 739 (5)
in occupation 189 (2)
in office 733 (7)
in olden times 125 (12)
in one piece 52 (4)
in one's absence 190 (9)
in one's cups 949 (6)
in one's element 24 (6), 701 (5)
in one's grasp 773 (3)
in one's hand 773 (3)
in one's hearing 415 (8)
in one's prime 134 (3)
in one's right mind 502 (2)
in one's sleeve 525 (10)
in one's teens 99 (6)
in one's teeth 711 (4)
in one's thoughts 505 (5)
in open court 528 (13)
in open order 75 (2)
in operation 173 (2), 676 (4)
in opposition 182 (4), 704 (3), 704 (6)
in opposition to 14 (5)
in orbit 271 (8)
in order 60 (5), 74 (9)
in order, be 60 (4)
in order to 617 (7)
in orders 986 (11)
in other words 520 (11)
in outline 233 (2)
in pain 825 (5)
in paint 553 (7)
in paradise 824 (5)
in parallel 219 (4)
in part 33 (10), 53 (8)
in particular 80 (9)
in partnership 50 (3), 708 (9)
in passing 114 (7)
in-patient 191 (2), 651 (18)
in pawn 767 (3)
in perpetuity 115 (5)
in person 3 (4), 189 (6)
in perspective 9 (5), 9 (9), 203 (9)
in phase 24 (5)

in pieces 46 (4), 46 (14), 53 (6)
in pitch 410 (7)
in place 24 (6), 150 (6), 186 (5), 189 (6)
in plain English 516 (6)
in plain terms 516 (6)
in plain words 514 (6), 520 (11), 573 (4)
in play 173 (2)
in play, be 173 (3)
in poor condition 651 (20)
in poor health 651 (20)
in poor shape 651 (21), 731 (5)
in possession 773 (2)
in power 178 (2)
in power, be 733 (10)
in practice 673 (2)
in preparation 55 (4), 68 (6), 669 (6), 669 (14), 726 (4)
in print 528 (7), 548 (6), 587 (6), 589 (8)
in prison 750 (2)
in process of 108 (4)
in profile 239 (4)
in progress 55 (4)
in proof 623 (6)
in proportion 86 (9)
in prose 593 (9)
in prospect 155 (2), 507 (3)
in public 522 (10)
in purdah 883 (7)
in pursuance of 619 (7)
in pursuit 619 (4)
in quarantine 747 (6)
in quest of 619 (4), 619 (7)
in question 452 (3), 459 (12)
in rags 655 (6), 801 (4)
in rapid succession 139 (4)
in raptures 824 (4)
in ratio 9 (9), 86 (9)
in readiness 669 (7), 669 (14)
in rebuttal 479 (5)
in relation to 9 (9), 9 (10)
in relays 65 (5)
in relief 254 (4), 522 (4), 554 (7)
in repose 266 (10)

in reprisal 714 (2)
in request 627 (3)
in requital 714 (5)
in reserve 175 (4), 632 (4), 669 (7)
in retaliation 714 (2)
in retreat 728 (5), 981 (9)
in return 31 (7)
in reverse 286 (6)
in rotation 141 (8)
in ruins 165 (5), 655 (6)
in safe hands 660 (4)
in safety 660 (4)
in scale 27 (3)
in search of 459 (18)
in self-defence 713 (11), 714 (2)
in sentences 563 (2)
in service 673 (2), 742 (7)
in service, be 742 (8)
in short 204 (6), 569 (4)
in short supply 636 (6)
in shreds 655 (6)
in sight of 438 (10), 852 (4)
in sign language 547 (23)
in single file 71 (7), 203 (9)
in situ 186 (5), 189 (6)
in slavery 742 (7)
in slow time 278 (7)
in small compass 196 (13)
in some degree 27 (6)
in some way 158 (6)
in spasms 318 (8)
in spate 350 (7)
in spite of 25 (7), 182 (4), 468 (5), 704 (6)
in spite of everything 599 (5)
in sport 839 (6)
in step 24 (5)
in stock 632 (4)
in store 155 (2), 632 (4), 669 (6), 773 (3)
in style 848 (8)
in succession 71 (7)
in sum 52 (10), 204 (6), 592 (6)
in suspense 175 (4), 474 (4), 474 (6), 474 (10), 507 (2), 507 (6)
in suspense, be 507 (5)
in suspension 335 (4), 337 (3)

in syllables 558 (5)
in tandem 203 (9), 706 (3)
in tatters 655 (6)
in tears 825 (6), 836 (4)
in the act 076 (4), 676 (6), 936 (5)
in the army 718 (8)
in the ascendant 160 (8), 178 (2), 308 (3), 727 (4)
in the background 523 (2)
in the beginning 68 (11)
in the best of taste 846 (5)
in the black 800 (4)
in the bud 68 (11)
in the buff 229 (4)
in the chair 689 (3), 689 (6)
in the clear 660 (4), 960 (2)
in the clouds 209 (14)
in the course of time 111 (4)
in the crowd 43 (9)
in the dark 418 (8), 439 (2), 444 (5), 474 (6)
in the days of 108 (11)
in the distance 199 (6)
in the end 65 (5), 69 (7)
in the event of 8 (6), 154 (8)
in the file 548 (6), 548 (9)
in the first place 68 (11)
in the flesh 360 (2)
in the forefront 237 (6)
in the foreground 237 (6), 522 (4)
in the fullness of time 124 (7)
in the future 124 (4), 155 (2), 155 (5)
in the gloaming 419 (8)
in the grip of 778 (4)
in the half-light 419 (8)
in the interim 108 (10)
in the know 524 (8)
in the lead 237 (6)
in the light 702 (6)
in the light of 485 (11)
in the limelight 528 (13), 594 (18), 866 (9)
in the long run 69 (7)
in the main 5 (10), 52 (9)
in the market for 792 (4)

in the meantime 108 (10)
in the middle 70 (3), 225 (5)
in the midst 225 (5)
in the midst of 43 (9)
in the mind's eye 513 (8)
in the money 800 (4)
in the mood 597 (4)
in the name of 733 (14)
in the news 528 (7), 529 (7), 866 (10)
in the nick of time 137 (8)
in the offing 124 (7), 155 (2), 199 (6)
in the open 223 (4), 340 (7), 522 (5)
in the papers 529 (7)
in the past 125 (6)
in the pay of 745 (5)
in the pink 646 (4), 650 (2)
in the pipeline 272 (9)
in the plural 101 (2)
in the possession of 773 (3)
in the post 272 (9)
in the power of 745 (5)
in the presence of 189 (6)
in the public eye 528 (13)
in the rear 238 (6), 284 (5)
in the red 772 (2), 801 (3), 803 (4)
in the right 913 (4)
in the right, be 913 (5)
in the rough 244 (2)
in the running 716 (9)
in the same breath 123 (5)
in the shadows 418 (8)
in the singular 88 (6)
in the small hours 128 (8)
in the stars 155 (2)
in the style of 18 (4)
in the teeth of 704 (6)
in the thick 70 (3)
in the trough 214 (5)
in the van 237 (6), 283 (4)
in the way 702 (6)
in the wind 124 (4), 154 (4)
in the wings 124 (7)
in the wrong 914 (3), 936 (3)
in this way 8 (4)
in threes 93 (4)

in time 111 (4), 117 (6), 123 (5), 135 (4), 135 (6), 137 (4), 155 (5)
in token of 547 (23)
in torment 825 (5)
in toto 52 (8)
in tow 284 (5)
in trade 791 (7)
in train 669 (14)
in training 162 (9)
in transit 265 (6), 267 (16), 272 (9), 305 (6)
in trepidation 854 (6)
in triumph 727 (12)
in trouble 731 (5), 731 (7)
in tune 24 (5)
in turmoil 61 (12)
in turn 60 (5), 71 (7), 80 (10), 141 (8)
in twain 46 (14)
in two minds 474 (6), 601 (3)
in two ticks 116 (4)
in twos 90 (2)
in twos and threes 75 (5)
in uniform 16 (2)
in unison 24 (5)
in unison, be 410 (9)
in use 673 (2)
in vain 634 (3), 641 (5), 728 (10)
in view 155 (2), 438 (10), 443 (2), 507 (3)
in vogue 610 (6), 848 (5)
in want 627 (4), 627 (7), 801 (3)
in waves 65 (5)
in working order 669 (7)
in writing 524 (7), 548 (6), 586 (7)
inability 161 (1), 641 (1), 695 (1)
inability to act 677 (1)
inability to pay 803 (1), 805 (2)
inaccessible 199 (4), 470 (3)
inaccuracy 495 (2)
inaccurate 458 (2), 495 (6)
inaction 161 (2), 175 (1), 620 (1), 674 (1), 677 (1), 679 (1)

inactive 136 (3), 172 (4), 175 (2), 266 (4), 375 (3), 523 (2), 620 (3), 674 (2), 677 (2), 679 (7), 739 (3), 820 (4), 834 (5), 838 (4), 860 (2)

inactive, be 106 (8), 145 (8), 172 (5), 278 (4), 456 (7), 458 (6), 679 (11), 820 (6)

inactively 175 (4)

inactivity 136 (2), 145 (3), 172 (1), 266 (1), 458 (1), 601 (1), 620 (1), 637 (2), 674 (1), 677 (1), 679 (1), 681 (1), 683 (1), 721 (1), 731 (1), 739 (1), 820 (1), 838 (1), 860 (1)

inadequacy 29 (1), 307 (1), 636 (1), 641 (1), 647 (1)

inadequate 29 (2), 55 (3), 161 (5), 307 (2), 636 (3), 636 (7), 647 (3), 695 (3)

inadmissible 25 (5), 57 (3), 59 (4), 643 (2), 760 (3), 914 (3)

inadvertence 456 (1)

inadvertent 456 (3), 618 (5)

inadvertently 456 (10)

inadvisable 643 (2)

inalienable 915 (2)

inalterable 153 (4)

inamorata 887 (5)

inane 499 (4), 515 (4)

inanimate 359 (3), 361 (6), 375 (3), 375 (5), 448 (2), 679 (7)

inanimate nature 448 (1)

inanimate object 319 (3)

inanity 4 (1), 450 (1), 515 (1)

inapplicable 10 (4), 25 (5), 641 (4)

inappreciable 33 (7)

inappropriate 10 (3), 25 (5), 188 (3), 643 (2), 849 (2), 916 (5)

inappropriately 10 (6)

inaptitude 25 (2), 643 (1)

inarticulate 578 (2), 580 (2), 582 (2)

inartistic 695 (6), 699 (3), 842 (5)

inattention 152 (2), 439 (1), 450 (1), 456 (1), 458 (1), 495 (3), 499 (2), 678 (2), 726 (1), 769 (1), 820 (1), 857 (1), 885 (2)

inattentive 416 (2), 439 (2), 450 (2), 456 (3), 458 (2), 491 (4), 508 (3), 647 (3), 857 (3), 885 (4)

inattentive, be 450 (4), 454 (3), 456 (7), 458 (4), 506 (5), 513 (7), 670 (7), 857 (4), 860 (4)

inattentive to 769 (2)

inaudibility 401 (1), 416 (1), 517 (1)

inaudible 399 (2), 401 (3), 416 (2), 517 (2), 578 (2)

inaudibly 401 (6)

inaugural 66 (3), 68 (6)

inaugurate 68 (10), 156 (9), 876 (4)

inauguration 68 (2), 751 (2)

inauspicious 138 (3), 511 (7), 616 (2), 731 (4), 853 (3)

inboard 224 (3)

inborn 5 (7), 817 (2)

inbred 5 (7), 11 (6), 50 (3)

inbreeding 11 (4)

incalculable 107 (2), 159 (5)

incalculably 32 (17)

incandesce 379 (7)

incandescence 379 (1), 417 (1)

incandescent 379 (5), 417 (8), 420 (8)

incantation 761 (2), 983 (1), 983 (2)

incantatory 983 (7)

incapability 161 (1)

incapable 25 (5), 161 (5), 695 (3)

incapacitate 161 (9)

incapacitated 161 (7), 949 (10)

incapacity 25 (2), 161 (1), 491 (1), 499 (1), 695 (1)

incarcerate 747 (10)

incarcerated 747 (6)

incarceration 747 (3)

incarnate 319 (6), 319 (7), 360 (2), 522 (7), 551 (8), 965 (6)

incarnation 5 (2), 319 (1), 965 (4), 975 (1)

incautious 499 (5), 857 (3)

incautiousness 857 (1)

incendiarism 165 (1), 168 (1), 379 (2), 381 (3)

incendiary 165 (4), 176 (4), 176 (5), 381 (3), 381 (7), 385 (5), 904 (1)

incendiary bomb 385 (3), 723 (14)

incense 385 (4), 395 (1), 396 (2), 888 (8), 891 (9), 925 (1), 981 (6)

incensed 891 (4)

incentive 174 (4), 256 (2), 279 (1), 612 (4), 612 (6), 810 (1), 821 (2), 962 (1)

inception 68 (1)

incertitude 474 (1)

incessant 71 (4), 115 (2), 139 (2), 146 (2), 678 (7)

incessantly 139 (5)

incest 951 (3)

incestuous 951 (9)

inch 33 (2), 203 (4), 204 (1)

inch along 278 (4)

inch by inch 27 (6), 53 (9), 278 (8)

incharged 781 (6)

incident 154 (1)

incidental 6 (2), 10 (2), 10 (3), 10 (4), 154 (4), 159 (5)

incidental music 412 (4)

incidentally 10 (6), 137 (9)

incinerate 165 (6), 364 (9), 381 (10)

incinerated 381 (6)

incineration 165 (1), 364 (1), 381 (2)

incinerator 383 (1)

incipience 68 (1)

incipient 68 (6)

incise 46 (11), 262 (3), 555 (3)

incision 46 (3)

incisive 174 (6), 532 (4), 569 (2), 571 (2)

incisiveness 571 (1)

incisor 256 (4)

incitation 612 (2)

incite 156 (9), 176 (9), 178 (3), 279 (7), 612 (9), 680 (3), 691 (4), 709 (8), 821 (6), 855 (8)

incited 612 (7)

incitement 612 (2), 821 (1)

inciting 612 (6)

incivility 847 (2), 878 (2), 885 (1), 921 (1)

inclemency 176 (3), 380 (2), 906 (1)

inclement 380 (5)

inclination 179 (1), 220 (1), 595 (0), 597 (1), 605 (1), 859 (3)

inclinations 817 (1)

incline 179 (3), 209 (2), 210 (1), 220 (2), 220 (5), 220 (6), 248 (5), 289 (4), 308 (1), 309 (1), 605 (6), 612 (8), 669 (10), 859 (13)

incline towards 281 (6)

inclined 220 (3), 597 (4), 617 (3), 859 (7)

include 38 (3), 45 (9), 56 (4), 78 (5), 773 (4)

included 78 (3), 83 (4), 89 (3)

included, be 38 (4), 78 (4), 708 (8), 773 (5)

included out 57 (3)

including 38 (5), 78 (2), 78 (7)

including today 121 (5)

inclusion 38 (1), 52 (1), 56 (1), 78 (1), 79 (1), 88 (2), 299 (1), 706 (2), 775 (2)

inclusive 32 (5), 52 (7), 54 (3), 56 (2), 78 (2)

inclusive of 38 (5)

inclusively 78 (7)

inclusiveness 52 (1), 78 (1), 79 (1)

incognito 525 (1), 525 (4), 525 (10), 562 (4)

incoherence 49 (1), 515 (1), 517 (1)

incoherent 61 (7), 72 (2), 503 (9), 515 (4), 570 (4)

incombustibility 382 (2)

incombustible 382 (5)

income 629 (1), 771 (2), 777 (2), 807 (1)

income tax 809 (3)

incomer 59 (3), 126 (4), 295 (1), 297 (3)

incoming 59 (4), 65 (2), 297 (1), 297 (4)

incommode 643 (3)

incommodious 643 (2)

incommunicado 525 (3)

incommunicative 582 (2)

incommunicativeness 582 (1)

incomparable 21 (4), 34 (5)

incomparably 32 (17)

incompatible 14 (3), 25 (4), 881 (3)

incompetence 25 (2), 161 (1), 499 (1), 636 (1), 641 (1), 695 (1)

incompetent 25 (5), 161 (5), 499 (3), 501 (1), 636 (3), 641 (4), 645 (2), 695 (3), 697 (1), 916 (7)

incomplete 55 (3), 244 (2), 307 (2), 636 (3), 647 (3), 726 (2)

incomplete, be 55 (5), 670 (7)

incompleteness 55 (1), 726 (1)

incomprehensibility 517 (1)

incomprehensible 517 (2)

incomprehension 491 (1)

inconceivable 450 (3), 470 (2), 472 (2), 486 (5), 517 (2)

inconclusive 477 (6)

incongruity 15 (1), 25 (1), 25 (3)

incongruous 25 (4), 84 (5), 499 (5)

incongruous, be 25 (6)

inconsequence 10 (2), 497 (1), 639 (1)

inconsequential 10 (4), 477 (5)

inconsiderable 33 (7), 35 (3), 639 (5)

inconsiderate 450 (2), 456 (3), 885 (4)

inconsiderateness 885 (1)

inconsistency 14 (1), 17 (1), 25 (1), 84 (1), 152 (1), 604 (1)

inconsistent 14 (3), 17 (2), 25 (4), 477 (5), 497 (3), 604 (3)

inconsolable 830 (2), 853 (2)

inconspicuous 444 (3)

inconstancy 152 (1), 601 (1), 604 (1)

inconstant 152 (3), 456 (6), 601 (3), 604 (3), 930 (7)

inconstant, be 152 (5)

incontestable 473 (6)

incontinence 161 (2), 302 (1), 859 (1), 943 (1), 951 (2)

incontinent 161 (7), 943 (2), 944 (3)

incontinently 943 (4)

inconvenience 377 (1), 377 (5), 641 (1), 643 (1), 700 (1), 700 (6), 702 (2), 702 (8), 825 (1)

inconvenient 138 (2), 377 (3), 643 (2), 700 (4), 702 (6)

incorporate 45 (9), 50 (4), 78 (5), 299 (4), 708 (6)

incorporating 78 (2)

incorporation 50 (1), 56 (1), 78 (1)

incorporeal 4 (3)

incorporeity 320 (1)

incorrect 477 (5), 495 (6), 576 (2)

incorrectness 565 (1), 847 (2)

incorrigible 602 (4), 602 (5), 934 (3), 940 (2)

incorruptibility 935 (1)

incorruptible 115 (2), 929 (3), 931 (2), 950 (5)

increase 26 (2), 32 (1), 36 (1), 36 (4), 36 (5), 38 (1), 40 (1), 71 (2), 74 (5), 157 (2), 167 (1), 174 (2), 197

(1), 197 (4), 306 (1), 637 (1), 771 (3)

increase the chances 471 (5)

increased 36 (3)

increasing 36 (3), 178 (2), 197 (3)

increasingly 32 (17)

incredibility 486 (1)

incredible 32 (7), 84 (6), 470 (2), 472 (2), 486 (5), 864 (5), 864 (9)

incredibly 32 (19), 486 (9)

incredulity 486 (1)

incredulous 486 (4)

incredulous, be 486 (6)

increment 36 (2), 38 (1), 40 (1), 41 (1), 74 (7), 197 (1), 771 (3)

incriminate 924 (12), 928 (8)

incriminating 928 (5)

incubate 369 (9)

incubation 669 (3)

incubator 658 (13), 666 (2)

inculcate 534 (6)

inculcated 6 (2)

inculcation 534 (1)

inculpate 924 (12)

incumbency 622 (3), 985 (3)

incumbent 191 (2), 776 (1), 917 (6)

incumbent on, be 917 (8)

incur 154 (7), 180 (3)

incur a duty 180 (3), 622 (7), 672 (3), 689 (5), 764 (4), 917 (9)

incur blame 829 (6), 867 (9), 867 (11), 888 (8), 924 (14)

incur costs 806 (4)

incur disgrace 867 (9)

incur expenses 806 (4)

incurable 5 (8), 362 (8), 645 (2), 651 (21), 853 (3)

incuriosity 454 (1), 456 (1), 508 (1), 860 (1)

incurious 454 (2), 491 (4), 820 (4), 860 (2)

incurious, be 454 (3), 491 (8), 820 (6)

incursion 297 (1), 712 (1), 718 (6)

indebted 803 (4), 805 (4), 907 (3)

indebtedness 803 (1), 915 (1)

indecency 951 (1)

indecent 645 (4), 847 (4), 934 (4), 951 (6)

indecent assault 951 (4)

indecent exposure 951 (5)

indecently assaulted 951 (11)

indecision 474 (2), 601 (1), 606 (1)

indecisive 474 (4), 601 (3)

indecorous 847 (4)

indecorum 847 (2), 916 (1), 934 (2)

indeed 32 (16), 494 (8)

indefatigability 600 (2)

indefatigable 600 (3), 678 (9)

indefensible 934 (6)

indefinable 32 (11), 517 (4)

indefinite 79 (3), 107 (2), 444 (3), 568 (2)

indefinite time 108 (1), 111 (1)

indefinitely 107 (3)

indelible 153 (6), 505 (5)

indelible ink 153 (2)

indelicacy 847 (1), 951 (1)

indelicate 847 (4), 951 (6)

indemnify 31 (4), 767 (6), 787 (3), 941 (5), 962 (3)

indemnity 31 (2), 767 (1), 787 (1), 909 (1), 941 (1)

indent 255 (8), 260 (1), 260 (3), 627 (1), 737 (8)

indentation 247 (1), 251 (1), 255 (1), 260 (1)

indented 251 (7), 260 (2)

indenture 767 (2)

independence 10 (1), 84 (1), 595 (0), 703 (1), 733 (4), 744 (2), 800 (1), 883 (2), 895 (1), 978 (1)

independent 10 (3), 21 (3), 84 (5), 595 (1), 733 (9), 744 (4), 744 (5), 744 (7), 895 (4)

independent, be 595 (2), 744 (9)

independent means 744 (2)

independent school 539 (2)

indescribable 32 (11), 864 (5)

indestructible 153 (4), 162 (7)

indeterminacy 159 (1), 474 (1), 618 (1)

indeterminate 474 (4)

index 62 (6), 85 (2), 87 (1), 87 (5), 378 (4), 547 (1), 547 (18), 548 (1), 548 (7), 559 (2), 589 (5), 976 (2)

index card 548 (1)

index-finger 547 (6)

index forefinger 254 (2)

indexed 87 (4), 547 (17), 548 (6)

indexing 548 (2)

Indian file 71 (3)

Indian summer 128 (4), 129 (3)

indicate 64 (3), 80 (8), 281 (4), 281 (6), 455 (7), 466 (6), 511 (8), 514 (5), 522 (7), 522 (8), 524 (9), 547 (18)

indicating 466 (5), 514 (3), 526 (3), 547 (15), 551 (6), 639 (6), 664 (3)

indication 89 (2), 465 (5), 466 (1), 511 (3), 522 (1), 524 (3), 547 (1), 548 (4), 551 (1), 561 (2), 651 (2), 664 (1)

indicative 466 (5), 514 (3), 526 (3), 547 (15)

indicator 27 (1), 547 (6)

indicatory 547 (15)

indict 928 (9), 959 (7)

indictable 963 (7)

indictable offence 954 (2)

indictment 928 (1)

indifference 454 (1), 456 (1), 458 (1), 598 (1), 601 (1), 606 (1), 677 (1), 734 (1), 769 (1), 820 (1), 823 (1), 838 (1), 860 (1), 865 (1), 934 (1), 974 (1) indifferent 454 (2), 456 (3), 458 (2), 491 (4), 508 (3), 601 (3), 606 (2), 625 (3), 644 (9), 677 (2), 744 (7), 769 (2), 820 (3), 820 (4), 838 (4), 860 (2), 861 (2), 865 (2), 833 (5), 885 (4), 974 (5)

indifferent, be 454 (3), 606 (3), 621 (3), 820 (6), 860 (4)

indifferently 33 (9)

indigence 616 (1)

indigenous 5 (6), 191 (6)

indigent 801 (3)

indigestibility 329 (1)

indigestible 329 (2), 653 (2), 670 (5)

indigestion 651 (7)

indignant 891 (3), 891 (4)

indignation 891 (2), 924 (1)

indignity 827 (2), 851 (1), 867 (2), 872 (2), 878 (2), 885 (2), 891 (1), 899 (2), 921 (2), 922 (1), 926 (2), 928 (1)

indigo 425 (4), 435 (2), 435 (3)

indirect 220 (3), 282 (2), 466 (5), 568 (2), 570 (4), 626 (2)

indirect descent 170 (3)

indirect hint 524 (3)

indirect taxation 809 (3)

indirectly 626 (4)

indirectness 220 (1)

indiscernible 444 (2)

indiscipline 734 (2), 738 (1), 918 (1), 943 (1)

indiscreet 499 (5), 524 (7), 526 (3), 857 (3)

indiscreet, be 524 (9)

indiscretion 499 (2), 526 (1), 695 (2), 857 (1), 936 (2)

indiscriminate 464 (2), 618 (6)

indiscriminating 464 (3)

indiscrimination 464 (1), 481 (1)

indispensable 596 (4), 627 (3), 638 (5)

indispose 613 (3)

indisposed 598 (3), 651 (21)

indisposition 598 (1), 651 (1), 651 (2)

indissoluble 45 (8), 52 (6), 88 (3), 153 (4)

indistinct 244 (2), 419 (4), 419 (5), 444 (3), 580 (2)

indistinct, be 440 (5)

indistinctness 419 (1)

indistinguishable 13 (2), 444 (2)

individual 10 (3), 17 (2), 21 (3), 80 (4), 80 (5), 88 (2), 88 (3), 371 (3), 371 (6), 547 (15)

individualism 80 (3), 744 (2), 932 (1)

individualistic 932 (3)

individuality 10 (1), 17 (1), 21 (1), 80 (1), 84 (1), 88 (1), 744 (2)

individualize 80 (8)

indivisible 44 (4), 48 (2), 52 (6), 88 (3)

indoctrinate 485 (9), 534 (6), 534 (7)

indoctrination 534 (1)

indolence 679 (1), 679 (2)

indolent 679 (8)

indomitable 162 (7), 599 (2), 600 (3), 715 (2), 855 (4)

indoor 224 (3)

indoor game 837 (8)

indoors 224 (1), 224 (6)

indubitable 473 (6)

indubitably 32 (16), 473 (10)

induce 156 (9), 178 (3), 612 (10), 703 (5), 759 (3), 761 (5)

induced 612 (7)

induced, be 612 (13), 758 (3)

inducement 156 (1), 178 (1), 291 (1), 612 (2), 612 (4), 706 (1), 759 (1), 781 (2), 792 (1), 821 (1), 859 (3)

inducing 178 (2), 291 (3), 610 (5), 612 (6), 691 (3), 703 (4)

induct 68 (10), 751 (4)

induction 160 (5), 475 (1), 751 (2)

inductive 475 (7)

indulge 388 (7), 734 (5), 736 (3), 826 (3)

indulge in 688 (4)

indulge oneself 932 (4), 943 (3), 944 (4)

indulged 944 (3)

indulgence 734 (1), 736 (1), 756 (1), 824 (3), 909 (1), 943 (1), 944 (1)

indulgent 734 (3), 736 (2), 756 (3), 897 (4), 943 (2)

industrial 164 (5), 622 (5)

industrial archaeology 125 (4)

industrial disease 651 (3)

industrialism 622 (1)

industrialist 164 (4), 686 (1)

industrialization 164 (1)

industrialize 164 (7)

industrialized 164 (5)

industrious 162 (7), 174 (5), 455 (2), 457 (3), 536 (3), 600 (3), 622 (5), 676 (4), 678 (9), 682 (4)

industry 164 (1), 622 (1), 678 (3), 682 (3)

inebriate 174 (8), 949 (5), 949 (16)

inebriated 949 (6)

inebriating 949 (12)

inebriation 949 (1)

inebriety 949 (1)

inedible 329 (2), 391 (2), 653 (2)

ineffable 517 (4), 965 (5)

ineffective 161 (5), 172 (4), 572 (2), 641 (4), 728 (4)

ineffectiveness 161 (4), 163 (1)

ineffectual 161 (5), 641 (4), 695 (3)

ineffectuality 161 (4), 163 (1), 695 (1)

inefficiency 161 (1), 641 (1), 695 (1)

inefficient 161 (5), 641 (4), 645 (2), 695 (3)

inelastic 162 (7), 324 (4), 326 (4), 329 (2), 330 (2)

inelasticity 326 (1)

inelegance 566 (1), 576 (1), 842 (1)

inelegant 576 (2), 695 (5), 840 (2), 842 (5), 847 (4)

ineligible 25 (5), 607 (2), 643 (2)

inept 25 (5), 499 (5), 695 (3), 695 (7)

ineptitude 161 (1), 497 (1), 499 (1), 641 (1)

inequality 10 (1), 15 (1), 25 (1), 29 (1), 34 (1), 246 (1)

inequitable 914 (4)

ineradicable 5 (8), 153 (6)

inert 163 (5), 175 (2), 266 (4), 375 (3), 523 (2), 677 (2), 679 (7), 820 (4), 823 (3)

inert, be 175 (3), 266 (7), 677 (3)

inertia 175 (1), 182 (1), 677 (1), 679 (1), 734 (1), 820 (1), 860 (1)

inertness 175 (1), 601 (1), 677 (1), 679 (1), 734 (1), 820 (1)

inescapable 155 (2), 596 (4)

inessential 6 (2), 10 (2), 10 (3), 10 (4), 639 (2), 639 (5)

inestimable 644 (7), 811 (3)

inevitability 473 (1), 596 (1)

inevitable 155 (2), 473 (4), 596 (4), 740 (2), 853 (3)

inevitable, the 596 (1)

inexact 79 (3), 458 (2), 495 (6), 520 (6)

inexactitude 495 (2)

inexactness 79 (1), 458 (1), 481 (1), 491 (3), 495 (2), 568 (1)

inexcitability 175 (1), 177 (1), 266 (2), 820 (1), 823 (1)

inexcitable 175 (2), 177 (3), 820 (3), 823 (3), 858 (2)

inexcusable 914 (3), 928 (7), 934 (6)

inexhaustible 54 (4), 104 (5), 107 (2), 635 (4)

inexorability 473 (1), 599 (1), 735 (1), 906 (1)

inexorable 473 (4), 596 (4), 599 (2), 735 (4), 906 (2)

inexorable fate 596 (2)

inexpectant 458 (2), 508 (3), 661 (5), 670 (3)

inexpedience 138 (1), 641 (1), 643 (1), 700 (1)

inexpedient 25 (5), 138 (2), 499 (5), 641 (4), 643 (2), 645 (3), 674 (2), 702 (6), 916 (5)

inexpedient, be 643 (3)

inexpensive 812 (3)

inexperience 491 (1), 611 (1), 695 (1), 699 (1), 935 (1)

inexperienced 491 (4), 499 (4), 611 (3), 695 (4)

inexpert 491 (4), 695 (4)

inexpertness 491 (1), 695 (1)

inexplicable 84 (6), 159 (6), 517 (2)

inexplicably 159 (8)

inexpressible 32 (11), 517 (4), 864 (5)

inextinguishable 153 (4), 162 (7)

inextricable 45 (7), 45 (8), 48 (2), 61 (8)

inextricably 45 (16)

infallibility 473 (1), 473 (2), 646 (1)

infallible 473 (4), 494 (6), 540 (2), 727 (4)

infamous 867 (4), 867 (5), 930 (5), 934 (6)

infamy 867 (1), 934 (1)

infancy 68 (1), 130 (1), 130 (2)

infant 68 (6), 130 (4), 132 (1), 170 (2)

infant prodigy 864 (3)

infanticide 362 (2)

infantile 132 (5), 499 (4)

infantine 130 (4), 132 (5)

infantry 268 (3), 722 (9)

infantryman 722 (9)

infatuated 481 (6), 487 (2), 503 (8), 887 (10)

infatuation 481 (5), 487 (1), 499 (2), 542 (1), 887 (1)

infect 43 (8), 178 (3), 272 (6), 297 (6), 649 (9), 655 (9)

infected 645 (2), 651 (22), 653 (3)

infection 178 (1), 272 (1), 302 (1), 645 (1), 649 (1), 651 (4), 651 (5), 653 (1), 655 (3), 659 (3), 659 (4), 663 (1)

infectious 178 (2), 272 (5), 645 (3), 649 (6), 651 (22), 653 (3), 661 (3)

infectious disease 651 (3)

infelicitous 643 (2), 695 (6), 825 (6)

infer 158 (4), 471 (6), 475 (10), 478 (4), 480 (5), 514 (5), 520 (8), 523 (6), 524 (12)

inferable 158 (2)

inference 65 (1), 475 (3), 478 (1), 480 (1), 524 (3)

inferential 478 (2)

inferior 19 (2), 29 (2), 33 (7), 35 (2), 35 (4), 210 (2), 636 (3), 639 (4), 639 (5), 645 (2), 647 (3), 728 (3), 728 (5), 731 (3), 732 (2), 742 (1), 742 (4), 745 (5), 869 (3), 869 (8)

inferior, be 29 (3), 35 (5), 636 (7), 745 (6), 867 (8)

inferior numbers 35 (1)

inferior rank 745 (1)

inferior status 745 (1)

inferiority 29 (1), 35 (1), 65 (1), 150 (2), 639 (1), 645 (1), 647 (1), 745 (1) inferiority complex 503 (5)

infernal 645 (5), 898 (7), 969 (5), 972 (3)

infernal regions 972 (1)

inferno 61 (4), 379 (2), 972 (1)

inferred 158 (2), 523 (3)

infertile 161 (7), 172 (4)

infertility 172 (1)

infest 104 (6), 306 (4), 712 (7)

infestation 659 (1)

infested 54 (4)

infidel 486 (3), 486 (4), 974 (4), 974 (6)

infidelity 930 (2), 951 (3)

infiltrate 43 (8), 189 (5), 231 (8), 297 (6), 303 (5), 305 (5), 309 (3), 341 (6)

infiltration 43 (1), 231 (1), 297 (1), 305 (1), 341 (2), 738 (3)

infinite 32 (14), 104 (4), 104 (5), 107 (2), 183 (6), 195 (7), 965 (6)

infinite space 107 (1)

infinite time 111 (1)

infinitely 32 (17), 107 (3), 115 (5)

infiniteness 107 (1)

infinitesimal 33 (6), 196 (11)

infinitude 107 (1)

infinity 32 (1), 107 (1), 115 (1), 183 (1)

infirm 163 (6), 651 (20)

infirmary 658 (13)

infirmity 131 (3), 163 (1), 651 (1), 651 (2), 934 (2)

inflame 174 (8), 176 (9), 378 (8), 821 (6), 832 (3), 887 (15)

inflamed 176 (5), 379 (4), 651 (22)

inflaming 612 (6)

inflammable 381 (7), 385 (5), 661 (3), 822 (3)

inflammation 379 (1), 381 (2), 651 (14), 827 (1)

inflammatory 176 (5), 381 (7)

inflatable 194 (2)

inflate 36 (5), 197 (5), 352 (12), 482 (4), 546 (3)

inflated 340 (5), 574 (5)

inflation 36 (1), 197 (2), 352 (5), 797 (3)

inflationary 797 (9), 811 (2)

inflect 564 (4), 577 (4)

inflected 557 (5)

inflection 40 (1), 67 (1), 564 (1), 577 (2)

inflectional 564 (3)

inflexibility 153 (1), 249 (1), 326 (1), 599 (1), 602 (1), 735 (1), 906 (1)

inflexible 153 (4), 249 (2), 326 (4), 599 (2), 602 (4), 735 (4), 906 (2)

inflexion 143 (1), 564 (2)

inflict 735 (7), 963 (8)

inflict on 740 (3)

inflict pain 377 (5)

infliction 963 (4)

inflow 297 (1), 350 (2)

influence 9 (7), 32 (1), 34 (1), 58 (1), 64 (3), 147 (7), 156 (1), 156 (2), 156 (9), 160 (1), 173 (1), 173 (3), 174 (7), 178 (1), 178 (3), 179 (1), 179 (3), 189 (5), 272 (1), 466 (6), 481 (11), 485 (9), 523 (1), 534 (7), 610 (8), 612 (2), 612 (5), 612 (8), 623 (9), 628 (1), 628 (4), 638 (1), 638 (4), 638 (7), 654 (9), 663 (2), 676 (1), 676 (5), 689 (4), 690 (1), 703 (1), 727 (7), 733 (1), 733 (12), 745 (7), 821 (1), 821 (6), 821 (8), 866 (2)

influenced 147 (5)

influential 32 (4), 156 (7), 160 (8), 178 (2), 466 (5), 485 (5), 612 (6), 628 (3), 638 (6), 733 (7)

influentially 178 (5)

influenza 651 (5)

influx 297 (1)

inform 520 (8), 524 (9), 526 (4), 526 (5), 528 (9), 529 (8), 534 (6), 588 (4), 664 (5), 669 (11), 928 (8)

inform against 524 (9), 928 (8), 928 (9)

informal 84 (5), 734 (3), 744 (6)

informal dress 228 (6)

informality 84 (1), 734 (1), 744 (3)

informant 74 (3), 466 (4), 520 (4), 524 (4), 529 (4), 531 (5), 584 (4), 588 (2)

information 459 (1), 460 (1), 466 (2), 490 (1), 490 (2), 524 (1), 529 (1), 529 (3), 531 (3), 547 (1), 584 (1), 588 (1), 664 (1), 691 (1)

informative 524 (7), 526 (3), 529 (7), 534 (5), 581 (4), 584 (5), 664 (3)

informed 490 (5), 490 (6), 524 (8), 669 (7)

informed against 928 (6)

informed, be 484 (4), 490 (8), 524 (12)

informer 459 (7), 459 (8), 466 (4), 524 (5), 603 (3), 856 (2), 928 (3), 938 (2)

infra 65 (5)

infraction 84 (1)

infrastructure 214 (1)

infrequency 33 (1), 84 (1), 105 (1), 140 (1), 472 (1)

infrequent 75 (2), 84 (6), 105 (2), 140 (2), 142 (2), 636 (6), 811 (3)

infrequently 72 (5), 105 (5), 140 (3)

infringe 306 (4), 738 (9), 914 (6), 916 (8)

infringe custom 84 (8)

infringe usage 84 (8)

infringement 84 (1), 306 (1), 712 (1), 769 (1), 916 (1), 954 (2)

infringing 769 (2)

infuriate 176 (9), 503 (12), 891 (9)

infuriated 176 (6), 891 (4)

infuriating 827 (5)

infuse 43 (7), 50 (4), 303 (5), 534 (6)

infuse into 612 (8)

infusion 43 (1), 43 (2), 43 (3), 299 (1), 301 (26), 303 (1), 337 (2), 658 (2)

ingenious 513 (5), 623 (7), 694 (4), 698 (4)

ingenue 699 (2), 935 (2)

ingenuity 513 (1), 694 (1), 698 (1)

ingenuous 540 (2), 699 (3)

ingenuous person 699 (2)

ingenuousness 540 (1), 699 (1)

ingest 299 (4), 301 (35)

ingestion 299 (1), 301 (1)

ingestive 299 (2)

inglenook 192 (5)

inglorious 728 (4), 731 (5), 732 (2), 867 (7), 869 (8), 930 (4)

ingoing 297 (4)

ingot 631 (1), 797 (7)

ingrained 5 (6), 50 (3), 153 (6), 610 (5)

ingratiate oneself 879 (4), 887 (15)

ingratiating 879 (3), 884 (3), 925 (3)

ingratiation 879 (1)

ingratitude 908 (1), 916 (1)

ingredient 40 (1), 43 (2), 53 (1), 58 (1), 319 (4)

ingredients 193 (1)

ingress 43 (1), 265 (1), 286 (2), 297 (1), 299 (1), 303 (1), 350 (2), 712 (1)

inhabit 189 (4), 192 (21)

inhabitant 191 (1)

inhabitants 191 (5), 371 (4)

inhabited 191 (7)

inhabiting 189 (2)

inhalation 299 (1), 352 (7)

inhale 299 (4), 352 (11), 388 (7), 394 (3)

inhaler 658 (2)

inharmonious 25 (4), 407 (2), 411 (2)

inhere 5 (9), 58 (3), 78 (4)

inhere in 1 (6)

inherence 5 (1)

inherent 5 (6), 58 (2), 78 (3)

inherit 5 (9), 65 (3), 120 (3), 166 (3), 771 (8), 773 (4), 780 (5), 782 (4), 786 (7), 800 (7)

inheritance 67 (1), 771 (1), 773 (1), 777 (4), 780 (1), 782 (1), 800 (1), 807 (1)

inherited 5 (7), 157 (4), 771 (6)

inheritor 41 (3), 67 (3), 776 (3), 782 (2)

inhibit 182 (3), 702 (9), 747 (7), 757 (4)

inhibiting 747 (4)

inhibition 503 (5), 702 (1), 757 (1)

inhibitions 747 (1)

inhospitable 883 (5), 898 (6)

inhuman 645 (3), 820 (3), 898 (6), 898 (7), 902 (3)

inhumanity 176 (1), 735 (1), 820 (1), 898 (2), 902 (1), 906 (1), 969 (3)

inimical 25 (4), 182 (2), 704 (3), 709 (6), 712 (6), 757 (2), 829 (3), 861 (2), 881 (3), 888 (4), 898 (4), 898 (6), 910 (4), 924 (6)

inimical, be 881 (4), 910 (6)

inimitable 19 (2), 21 (4), 34 (5), 80 (5)

iniquitous 914 (3), 914 (4), 934 (3)

iniquity 934 (1)

initial 68 (1), 68 (7), 547 (20), 558 (5)

initially 68 (11)

initials 547 (13), 558 (2)

initiate 64 (4), 68 (9), 68 (10), 117 (7), 156 (9), 156 (10), 164 (7), 299 (3), 534 (8), 538 (1), 612 (9), 672 (3)

initiation 68 (2), 299 (1), 536 (1), 968 (3)

initiative 68 (1), 68 (6), 174 (1), 597 (1), 678 (2), 744 (1)

initiatory 68 (6), 299 (2)

initiatory rite 968 (3)

inject 263 (18), 303 (5), 658 (20)

inject with 612 (8)

injecting 949 (4)

injection 303 (1), 658 (2)

injudicious 499 (5), 643 (2)

injunction 627 (1), 693 (1), 737 (1), 757 (1), 959 (2)

injure 163 (10), 645 (6), 655 (9), 827 (8), 914 (6)

injurious 616 (2), 645 (3), 653 (2), 878 (4), 914 (3), 921 (3), 926 (5)

injury 616 (1), 645 (1), 655 (3), 655 (4), 675 (1), 891 (1), 934 (2), 936 (2)

injustice 29 (1), 481 (1), 481 (3), 605 (1), 616 (1), 712 (1), 891 (1), 914 (1), 914 (2), 930 (1), 954 (1)

ink 428 (2), 428 (3), 553 (8)

ink in 428 (6)

inkling 490 (1), 524 (3)

inky 418 (3), 428 (4)

inlaid 844 (10)

inland 224 (1), 224 (3), 344 (1), 344 (7)

inland navigation 269 (1)

inland waterways 351 (1)

inlay 227 (2), 303 (4), 437 (2), 437 (9), 844 (12)

inlet 68 (5), 201 (2), 297 (2), 345 (1)

inmate 191 (2), 224 (1)

inn 192 (11), 266 (3)

innards 224 (2)

innate 5 (7)

innate ability 694 (2)

inner 78 (3), 224 (3)

inner cabinet 689 (1)

inner circle 708 (1)

inner city 192 (8), 192 (18)

inner coating 227 (1)

inner man or woman 447 (2)

inner self 80 (4)

inner sense 447 (2)

inner surface 224 (1)

inner voice 917 (2)

innermost 224 (3)

innermost being 817 (1)

innings 110 (1)

innkeeper 633 (3)

inside agent 459 (7), 524 (5)

inside and out 183 (8)

inside, be 224 (4)

inside information 524 (1)

inside job 623 (4)

inside out 221 (3)

inside track 34 (2)

insides 58 (1), 224 (2), 301 (16)

insidious 523 (4), 542 (6), 616 (2), 698 (4), 930 (4)

insidiousness 523 (1)

insight 447 (1), 463 (1), 476 (1), 490 (1), 513 (1), 520 (1)

insignia 547 (9)

insignificance 33 (1), 639 (1)

insignificant 33 (7), 639 (5)

insincere 477 (4), 515 (5), 541 (4), 850 (4), 925 (3), 930 (4)

insincerity 515 (1), 541 (2), 542 (1), 850 (1), 925 (1), 930 (1)

insinuate 231 (8), 523 (6), 524 (11), 612 (9), 926 (6)

insinuating 612 (6), 925 (3), 926 (5)

insinuation 178 (1), 297 (1), 303 (1), 523 (1), 524 (3), 926 (1)

insipid 163 (4), 387 (2), 572 (2), 838 (3), 840 (2)

insipidity 387 (1), 572 (1), 838 (1), 840 (1)

insist 532 (7), 596 (8), 599 (3), 602 (6), 612 (9), 716 (10), 740 (3), 761 (5)

insist on 468 (3), 766 (3)

insistence 532 (1), 599 (1), 612 (2), 638 (1), 761 (1)

insistent 532 (4), 571 (2), 599 (2), 737 (5), 761 (3)

insisting 761 (3)

insolence 711 (1), 871 (1), 878 (1), 885 (2), 921 (2), 924 (3)

insolent 711 (2), 734 (4), 735 (5), 871 (3), 873 (4),

878 (4), 885 (4), 916 (6), 921 (3), 922 (3)

insolent, be 871 (5), 878 (6), 885 (6), 916 (8), 921 (5), 928 (8)

insolent person 878 (3), 885 (3)

insolently 878 (7)

insolubility 44 (1)

insoluble 517 (3)

insolvency 636 (1), 728 (1), 769 (1), 772 (1), 801 (1), 803 (1), 805 (2)

insolvent 728 (3), 772 (2), 801 (2), 801 (3), 803 (3), 803 (4), 805 (4)

insomnia 678 (2)

insomniac 651 (18)

insouciance 454 (1), 458 (1), 820 (1), 860 (1)

insouciant 456 (6), 458 (2), 820 (4)

inspect 438 (9), 455 (4)

inspect accounts 808 (5)

inspection 438 (4), 455 (1), 457 (2), 459 (1), 459 (9), 480 (2), 484 (1)

inspection copy 22 (2)

inspector 441 (1), 459 (9), 480 (3), 690 (3)

inspiration 156 (1), 178 (1), 476 (1), 484 (1), 498 (1), 513 (1), 570 (1), 609 (1), 612 (1), 612 (2), 623 (3), 818 (2), 821 (1), 975 (1)

inspirational 975 (3)

inspire 156 (9), 178 (3), 612 (9), 821 (6), 821 (7), 833 (8), 855 (8), 979 (11)

inspire respect 920 (7)

inspire with awe 821 (8)

inspired 476 (2), 570 (3), 571 (2), 612 (7), 821 (3), 822 (3), 975 (3), 975 (4), 979 (7)

inspired, be 513 (7), 818 (7)

inspired by 818 (4)

inspirer 612 (5)

inspiring 156 (7), 178 (2), 821 (4)

instability 152 (1), 822 (1)

install 68 (10), 187 (5), 751 (4), 866 (14)

install oneself 786 (7)

installation 187 (1), 687 (1), 751 (2)

instalment 53 (1), 53 (3), 55 (1), 589 (2), 767 (1), 804 (1)

instalment plan 785 (1)

instance 83 (2), 83 (9)

instant 33 (2), 108 (3), 114 (2), 116 (2), 116 (3), 121 (2), 627 (5), 669 (9), 678 (7), 761 (3)

instant, be 761 (5)

instantaneity 114 (1), 116 (1), 121 (1), 123 (1), 277 (1)

instantaneous 114 (5), 116 (3), 135 (4), 277 (5), 508 (2)

instantaneously 114 (7), 116 (4), 123 (5), 135 (8), 277 (9)

instantly 114 (7), 116 (4)

instead 150 (6)

instep 214 (2)

instigate 612 (9), 612 (10), 703 (5)

instigation 612 (2)

instigator 612 (5)

instil 303 (5), 534 (6)

instilled 6 (2)

instinct 447 (1), 450 (1), 461 (2), 476 (1), 512 (1), 596 (1), 618 (1), 818 (1)

instinct for 179 (1)

instinctive 5 (6), 448 (2), 450 (2), 476 (2), 596 (5), 609 (3)

instinctively 476 (4)

instincts 817 (1)

institute 68 (10), 156 (9), 539 (1), 708 (5)

institute a rite 968 (11)

institution 68 (1), 539 (1), 610 (2), 953 (3), 988 (3)

institutionalize 16 (4)

instruct 524 (9), 534 (6), 737 (6)

instructed 490 (6), 498 (5), 524 (8), 669 (7), 694 (6)

instruction 490 (3), 524 (1), 534 (1), 691 (1), 693 (1)
instructions 737 (1)
instructive 524 (7), 534 (5), 664 (3)
instructor 537 (1), 537 (2)
instrument 156 (5), 544 (1), 623 (3), 628 (2), 630 (1), 639 (4), 686 (1), 707 (1), 742 (6), 767 (2), 879 (2)
instrumental 412 (7), 628 (3), 630 (6), 640 (2), 673 (2), 703 (4)
instrumental, be 156 (10), 628 (4), 703 (7), 745 (6), 879 (4)
instrumentalist 413 (2)
instrumentality 173 (1), 628 (1)
instrumentation 412 (4)
insubordinate 734 (4), 738 (7), 921 (3)
insubordination 734 (2), 738 (1)
insubstantial 2 (4), 4 (3), 33 (7), 55 (3), 114 (3), 163 (8), 212 (2), 320 (3), 325 (2), 330 (2), 340 (5), 419 (5), 513 (6), 636 (3), 639 (6)
insubstantial thing 4 (2), 114 (2), 161 (4), 163 (3), 422 (1), 639 (4)
insubstantiality 4 (1), 114 (1), 875 (1)
insufferable 827 (7), 861 (3)
insufficiency 29 (1), 42 (1), 204 (1), 301 (3), 307 (1), 627 (1), 636 (1), 641 (1), 647 (1), 801 (1)
insufficient 29 (2), 33 (6), 53 (6), 55 (3), 161 (5), 172 (4), 204 (3), 307 (2), 636 (3), 643 (2), 647 (3), 829 (4), 924 (7)
insufficient, be 636 (7)
insufficiently 636 (10)
insular 10 (3), 46 (5), 88 (4), 184 (5), 349 (2), 481 (7)

insularity 10 (1), 46 (1), 481 (4)
insulate 46 (9), 226 (13), 227 (2), 660 (8)
insulation 227 (1), 666 (1)
insulator 160 (5)
insulin 658 (7)
insult 827 (2), 851 (1), 867 (2), 878 (2), 885 (2), 885 (6), 891 (8), 899 (2), 921 (2), 921 (5), 926 (2)
insulted 829 (3)
insulting 711 (2), 878 (4), 885 (5), 921 (3), 926 (5)
insuperable 470 (3), 700 (4)
insupportable 827 (7)
insurance 159 (4), 660 (2), 764 (1), 767 (1), 858 (1)
insurance policy 767 (2)
insure 765 (5), 767 (6), 858 (3)
insure against 473 (9)
insured 660 (4), 767 (4), 858 (2)
insurer 754 (1)
insurgency 738 (2)
insurgent 738 (4)
insurmountable 470 (3)
insurrection 715 (1), 738 (2)
intact 52 (5), 646 (3), 646 (4), 660 (4)
intaglio 255 (1), 554 (1)
intake 195 (1), 297 (1), 299 (1), 627 (1)
intangibility 4 (1), 320 (1)
intangible 2 (4), 320 (3)
integer 52 (1), 85 (1), 88 (2)
integral 5 (6), 52 (4), 85 (2), 85 (5)
integral part 58 (1)
integrality 52 (1), 88 (1)
integrally 52 (8)
integrate 50 (4), 54 (6), 86 (12)
integrated 50 (3), 52 (4), 78 (3)
integrated, be 54 (5)
integration 43 (1), 50 (1), 52 (1), 78 (1), 86 (2), 88 (1), 706 (2)

integrity 52 (1), 929 (1), 933 (1)
intellect 447 (1), 449 (1), 451 (1), 490 (1), 498 (1)
intellectual 447 (5), 449 (4), 475 (6), 490 (2), 490 (6), 492 (2), 500 (1), 696 (1)
intelligence 213 (3), 447 (1), 459 (7), 463 (1), 498 (1), 524 (1), 529 (1), 839 (1)
intelligent 486 (4), 490 (5), 498 (4), 498 (6), 502 (2), 694 (4), 698 (4), 839 (4)
intelligentsai 492 (2)
intelligibility 516 (1), 520 (3), 567 (1), 573 (1)
intelligible 44 (4), 60 (2), 473 (5), 490 (7), 502 (2), 514 (4), 516 (2), 522 (4), 567 (2), 701 (3)
intelligible, be 516 (4), 520 (8), 522 (9), 573 (3), 821 (8)
intelligibly 516 (6), 573 (4)
intemperance 859 (1), 943 (1), 944 (1), 949 (1)
intemperate 176 (5), 932 (3), 943 (2), 944 (3), 949 (11)
intemperate, be 306 (3), 943 (3), 944 (4), 951 (10)
intemperately 943 (4)
intend 155 (4), 455 (5), 507 (4), 514 (5), 595 (2), 597 (6), 599 (3), 608 (3), 617 (5), 619 (5), 623 (8), 671 (4), 852 (6), 859 (11)
intended 155 (2), 507 (3), 595 (1), 617 (4), 887 (5)
intending 179 (2), 507 (3), 532 (3), 595 (1), 597 (4), 599 (2), 608 (2), 617 (3), 852 (4), 859 (7)
intense 32 (4), 174 (5), 425 (6), 818 (3), 818 (5)
intense dislike 888 (1)
intensely 32 (17)
intensification 832 (1)
intensified 832 (2)
intensify 36 (5), 174 (8), 821 (7), 832 (3)

intensity 27 (1), 174 (1), 417 (1), 425 (3)

intensive 36 (3), 559 (1)

intensive farming 370 (1)

intent 455 (2), 595 (0), 617 (1)

intent on 617 (3)

intent upon 599 (2)

intention 155 (1), 507 (1), 595 (0), 608 (1), 612 (1), 617 (1), 622 (1), 623 (1), 852 (2), 859 (3), 981 (4)

intentional 595 (1), 617 (3), 617 (4)

intentionally 617 (7)

intentness 455 (1), 678 (3)

inter 12 (2), 12 (4), 108 (5), 151 (2), 231 (6), 303 (4), 364 (9), 525 (7), 550 (3)

inter alia 43 (9)

interact 12 (3)

interacting 12 (2)

interaction 12 (1), 173 (1), 676 (1)

interbred 11 (6)

interbreed 43 (8)

interbreeding 43 (1)

intercalary 108 (5), 231 (6)

intercalate 231 (9)

intercalated 108 (5)

intercede 231 (10), 703 (6), 762 (3), 859 (11), 981 (11)

intercede for 720 (4)

interceding 981 (9)

intercept 231 (10), 293 (3), 415 (6), 453 (4), 702 (8)

interceptor 722 (14)

intercession 703 (1), 720 (1), 762 (1), 981 (4)

intercessor 231 (3), 720 (2), 981 (8)

intercessory 231 (6), 720 (3), 762 (2), 981 (10)

interchange 12 (1), 12 (3), 28 (2), 28 (4), 63 (1), 63 (4), 143 (1), 143 (6), 150 (1), 150 (5), 151 (1), 151 (3), 181 (1), 188 (4), 221 (1), 221 (5), 265 (4), 265 (5), 272 (7), 282 (6), 780

(1), 780 (3), 791 (1), 791 (4)

interchangeable 12 (2), 13 (2), 28 (8), 151 (2)

interchanged 151 (2)

intercom 531 (1)

interdepend 12 (3)

interdependence 9 (1), 12 (1)

interdependent 12 (2)

interdict 757 (4)

interdictory 57 (2)

interest 9 (1), 9 (7), 36 (2), 40 (2), 164 (2), 452 (1), 453 (1), 455 (1), 455 (7), 612 (8), 615 (2), 638 (1), 638 (7), 703 (1), 771 (3), 777 (2), 803 (2), 807 (1), 821 (1), 821 (8), 826 (1), 826 (3), 837 (1), 837 (20), 915 (1)

interested 453 (3)

interesting 821 (4), 826 (2)

interests 154 (2), 622 (1)

interface 202 (1), 231 (3)

interfere 63 (3), 72 (4), 182 (3), 231 (10), 453 (4), 678 (13)

interfere with 951 (11)

interference 628 (1), 678 (4), 702 (1), 827 (2)

interfering 678 (4), 678 (10), 702 (6)

interim 108 (2), 110 (1), 114 (1), 145 (4), 201 (1)

interior 5 (6), 78 (3), 224 (1), 224 (3), 344 (1), 553 (4)

interior decoration 844 (2)

interior decorator 656 (5)

interiority 58 (1), 70 (1), 224 (1)

interjacency 231 (1)

interjacent 70 (2), 231 (6), 303 (3), 755 (2)

interject 72 (4), 231 (9), 702 (10)

interjected 38 (2)

interjection 10 (2), 72 (1), 231 (4), 303 (1), 532 (1), 564 (2), 579 (1), 583 (1)

interjector 231 (5)

interlace 43 (7), 222 (10)

interlaced 222 (6)

interlacement 222 (1)

interlacing 43 (1)

interlard 43 (7), 227 (2)

interleave 43 (7), 231 (9)

interlock 12 (3), 45 (9), 45 (14), 222 (10)

interlocking 12 (2), 45 (1)

interlocution 460 (1), 579 (1), 584 (1)

interlocutor 529 (4), 579 (5), 581 (3), 584 (4)

interloper 59 (3), 231 (5)

interloping 59 (4)

interlude 108 (2), 145 (4)

intermarriage 43 (1), 894 (2)

intermarry 43 (8), 894 (11)

intermediacy 231 (1)

intermediary 45 (2), 231 (3), 231 (6), 524 (4), 529 (5), 579 (5), 720 (2), 754 (1), 755 (2)

intermediate 30 (4), 70 (2), 108 (5), 231 (6), 303 (3), 625 (4), 628 (3)

intermediate technology 625 (1)

interment 303 (2), 364 (1)

intermezzo 412 (4)

interminable 107 (2), 113 (5), 115 (2), 203 (5)

interminable, be 113 (9)

intermingle 43 (7)

intermittence 72 (1), 140 (1)

intermittent 72 (2), 140 (2), 141 (4), 142 (2)

intermittent, be 141 (6)

intern 658 (14), 747 (10)

internal 224 (3), 224 (4)

internal bleeding 651 (10)

internal organs 224 (2)

internalize 224 (5), 299 (4)

international 52 (7), 79 (4), 371 (7), 774 (3), 775 (4), 901 (6)

internationalist 901 (4)

internecine 165 (4), 362 (9)

interned 747 (6)

internee 224 (1)
internment 747 (3)
internment camp 748 (3)
interplay 12 (1), 151 (1)
interpolate 231 (9)
interpolation 43 (1), 86 (2), 231 (4), 303 (1)
interpolator 231 (5)
interpose 72 (4), 231 (9), 303 (4), 678 (13)
interposed 38 (2), 231 (6)
interposition 72 (1), 231 (4)
interpret 20 (6), 62 (7), 80 (8), 158 (4), 413 (9), 475 (10), 516 (4), 520 (8), 522 (7), 534 (7), 564 (4), 591 (5), 701 (8)
interpretation 514 (2), 516 (1), 520 (1)
interpreted 516 (2), 520 (7)
interpreter 20 (3), 480 (3), 520 (4), 591 (3), 973 (6)
interpretive 520 (6), 524 (7), 526 (3), 547 (15), 591 (4)
interred 364 (7)
interregnum 114 (1), 733 (4), 734 (2)
interrelate 12 (3)
interrelation 12 (1)
interrogate 415 (6), 453 (4), 459 (14)
interrogation 459 (2)
interrogative 459 (11)
interrogator 453 (2), 459 (10)
interrogatory 459 (11)
interrupt 55 (5), 63 (3), 72 (4), 145 (6), 145 (7), 231 (10), 297 (8), 456 (8), 702 (10)
interrupted 46 (4), 55 (3), 72 (2)
interrupter 702 (5)
interrupting 138 (2)
interruption 25 (2), 72 (1), 138 (1), 145 (2), 201 (1), 231 (4), 702 (1)
intersect 222 (8)
intersection 45 (4), 222 (1), 305 (1), 624 (6)

intersperse 43 (7), 231 (9)
interspersion 231 (4)
interstellar 321 (13)
interstice 201 (2)
intermittently 141 (7)
intertwine 43 (7), 50 (4), 222 (10)
interval 72 (1), 108 (2), 110 (1), 145 (4), 201 (1), 201 (4), 410 (2), 410 (3)
interval of time 201 (1)
intervene 72 (4), 108 (7), 231 (7), 231 (10), 628 (4), 678 (13), 720 (4), 757 (4)
intervening 628 (3)
intervention 72 (1), 231 (1), 628 (1), 702 (1), 718 (1), 720 (1)
interview 415 (2), 415 (6), 459 (4), 459 (14), 584 (3)
interviewer 459 (10), 584 (4)
interviewing 231 (6)
interweave 222 (10), 231 (9)
interweaving 43 (1), 222 (1)
interwoven 222 (6)
intestinal 224 (3)
intestine 351 (2)
intestines 224 (2)
intimacy 880 (1), 882 (1), 887 (1)
intimate 80 (7), 224 (3), 490 (7), 524 (9), 524 (11), 880 (4), 880 (6), 887 (5)
intimate acquaintance 880 (3)
intimate style 553 (2)
intimately 45 (16)
intimately related 11 (5)
intimation 524 (1), 524 (3)
intimidate 613 (3), 702 (8), 735 (8), 854 (12), 900 (3)
intimidated 854 (6)
intimidating 854 (8)
intimidation 613 (1), 712 (2), 718 (1), 854 (4), 900 (1)
intimidator 854 (5)
into the bargain 38 (5)
intolerable 32 (12), 827 (7), 861 (3)

intolerance 57 (1), 182 (1), 481 (4), 602 (2), 735 (1), 757 (1), 822 (1), 898 (2), 906 (1), 976 (2)
intolerant 481 (8), 499 (5), 645 (3), 735 (4), 881 (3), 898 (4), 906 (2), 976 (8)
intonation 398 (1), 577 (1)
intone 413 (10), 577 (4)
intoxicant 659 (3), 949 (4), 949 (12)
intoxicate 174 (8), 821 (6), 826 (4)
intoxicated 949 (6)
intoxicating 162 (6), 301 (32), 821 (4), 833 (6), 949 (12)
intoxication 821 (1), 822 (2), 943 (1), 949 (1)
intractable 326 (4), 602 (5), 700 (4), 738 (7)
intramural 224 (3), 534 (5)
intransigence 602 (1)
intransigent 602 (4)
intravenous 224 (3)
intrepid 855 (5)
intrepidity 855 (1)
intricacy 61 (3), 222 (1), 251 (1), 700 (1)
intricate 45 (8), 61 (8), 251 (9), 700 (4), 844 (9)
intrigue 612 (8), 623 (4), 623 (9), 678 (4), 698 (1), 696 (5), 738 (3), 821 (8), 887 (3), 951 (3)
intrigue against 542 (8)
intriguer 623 (5), 678 (6), 698 (3)
intriguing 623 (7), 678 (10), 698 (4)
intrinsic 5 (6), 44 (4), 50 (3), 58 (2), 78 (3), 156 (8), 224 (3), 610 (5), 817 (2)
intrinsic, be 5 (9), 56 (4), 58 (1), 78 (4), 89 (4), 156 (10)
intrinsic truth 494 (1)
intrinsicality 5 (1), 89 (1), 160 (2)
intrinsically 5 (10)
introduce 38 (3), 64 (3), 68 (9), 231 (8), 283 (3), 299

irresolution **152** (1), 163 (1), 474 (2), 601 (1), 606 (1), 856 (1)

irrespective 10 (3), 10 (6)

irresponsible **152** (3), 601 (3), 604 (3), 857 (3), 918 (2), 954 (7)

irretrievable 772 (3)

irreverence 865 (1), 921 (1), 980 (1)

irreverent 921 (3), 980 (4)

irreverently 921 (6)

irreversible **153** (4), **153** (5), 285 (2), 853 (3)

irrevocable **153** (5), 473 (4)

irrigate 171 (5), 174 (8), **339** (3), 341 (8), 350 (11), 370 (9)

irrigated 341 (5)

irrigation 341 (2), 370 (1)

irrigator **339** (1), 341 (3), 632 (1)

irritability 827 (1), 892 (1)

irritable 819 (3), 822 (3), 892 (3)

irritant 821 (2), 832 (1)

irritate 176 (9), 377 (5), 378 (8), 709 (8), 821 (6), 827 (9), 829 (6), 881 (5), 891 (9)

irritated 891 (4)

irritating 827 (5)

irritation 821 (1), 825 (3), 827 (1), 829 (1), 891 (2)

irrupt 297 (7)

irruptive 297 (4)

Islam 973 (3)

Islamize 979 (11)

island 184 (1), 305 (3), 344 (1), 349 (1), 883 (2), 883 (10)

islanded 349 (2)

islander 191 (1), 349 (1)

Islands of the Blest 971 (2)

isle 344 (1), 349 (1)

islet 349 (1)

ism 485 (2)

iso- 28 (7)

isobar 340 (3)

isolable 88 (4)

isolate 46 (9), 88 (5), 883 (10)

isolated 10 (3), 46 (5), 88 (4), 349 (2), 661 (5), 883 (7)

isolated instance 88 (2)

isolation 10 (1), 46 (1), 88 (1), 883 (2)

isolationism 46 (1)

isolationist 744 (7), 883 (3)

isosceles triangle 247 (4)

isothermal 379 (6)

isotope 319 (4)

issue 53 (3), 154 (6), 157 (1), 157 (5), 170 (1), 298 (2), 298 (5), 452 (1), 528 (4), 528 (9), 589 (2), 589 (5), 638 (3), 725 (1), 797 (4), 797 (10)

issue a command 737 (6)

issue a writ 737 (6)

issue out of 298 (5)

issued 797 (9)

issueless 172 (4)

issuing 298 (4)

isthmus 47 (1), 206 (1), 344 (1)

it 13 (1), 21 (2), 494 (2)

it being so 7 (5)

it follows that 157 (7)

italic 558 (5), 586 (2), 586 (7), 587 (3)

italicize 532 (7)

italics 547 (14)

itch 318 (1), 378 (2), 378 (8), 651 (12)

itch for 291 (1), 859 (1), 859 (11)

itchiness 318 (1), 378 (2)

itching palm 816 (2)

itching to, be 822 (4)

itchy 318 (4), 374 (3)

item 40 (2), 53 (1), 58 (1), 88 (2), 319 (3)

itemize 80 (8), 87 (5)

itemized 80 (6)

itemized account 87 (1)

items 80 (2), 87 (1)

iterate 106 (4)

iteration 106 (1)

itinerant 267 (9)

itinerary 267 (8), 524 (6)

itself 80 (4)

ivory 326 (1), 427 (2), 427 (5), 844 (8)

ivory tower 662 (1), 883 (2)

ivy 366 (4)

J

jab 279 (2), 658 (2), 712 (4)

jabber 515 (6), 579 (8), 581 (2), 581 (5)

jack 218 (2), 287 (2), 310 (2), 315 (3), 547 (12), 630 (1)

Jack Tar 270 (1)

jack up 218 (15), 310 (4)

jackal 365 (3)

jackboot 735 (2), 735 (3), 954 (3)

jackdaw 365 (4)

jacket 226 (6), 228 (10)

jackpot 771 (1)

jade 434 (1), 844 (8), 863 (3)

jade-green 434 (3)

jaded 684 (2), 838 (4), 863 (2)

jag 260 (3)

jagged 247 (5), 256 (7), 259 (4), 260 (2)

jaggedness 259 (1)

jaggy 260 (2)

jail 748 (1)

jailbird 904 (3)

jailed 750 (2)

jailer 749 (2)

jalopy 274 (11)

jam 8 (1), 45 (9), 45 (11), 45 (13), 74 (5), 145 (7), 266 (7), 392 (2), 700 (3), 702 (9)

jam in 54 (7), 231 (8)

jam into 303 (4)

jam-packed 54 (4)

jam session 837 (13)

jam tight 702 (9)

jam tomorrow 109 (1)

jam yesterday, and jam tomorrow 122 (1)

jamb 218 (10)

jamjar 194 (13)

jammed 45 (7), 54 (4)

jogging 682 (2), 837 (6)
joggle 318 (6)
john 649 (3)
johnny 372 (1)
joie de vivre 833 (1)
join 24 (9), 38 (3), 38 (4), 43 (7), 45 (9), 45 (14), 48 (4), 50 (4), 54 (6), 56 (5), 74 (11), 78 (4), 198 (7), 201 (2), 202 (3), 217 (5), 222 (8), 231 (8), 264 (6), 295 (6), 303 (6), 656 (12), 703 (6), 708 (8)
join a party 45 (14), 78 (4), 708 (8), 978 (8)
join battle 718 (12)
join forces 706 (4)
join in 678 (11), 706 (4), 775 (5), 882 (8)
join in marriage 894 (10)
join issue with 716 (11)
join the navy 269 (8)
join the queue 71 (5)
join together 74 (10)
join up 718 (10)
joined 43 (6), 45 (5), 50 (3), 52 (6), 58 (2), 71 (4), 78 (3), 88 (3), 89 (3), 181 (2), 200 (4), 264 (4)
joined, be 45 (14)
joiner 45 (5), 686 (3)
joinery 243 (2)
joining 45 (2), 45 (4)
joining together 45 (2), 47 (5), 50 (1), 74 (1), 198 (1)
joint 45 (4), 45 (5), 47 (1), 47 (5), 181 (2), 192 (12), 201 (2), 218 (11), 247 (1), 254 (2), 301 (16), 388 (2), 708 (6), 775 (4)
joint action 775 (2)
joint concern 708 (5)
joint effort 181 (1), 706 (1)
joint operations 718 (6)
joint ownership 775 (1)
joint possession 632 (1), 706 (2), 775 (1), 777 (3)
joint-stock 708 (6)
joint tenancy 775 (1)
jointed 45 (5), 247 (5)
jointly 45 (15), 89 (5), 706 (5), 708 (9), 775 (7)
joist 218 (9)

joke 542 (2), 639 (2), 839 (2), 839 (5)
joke-writer 594 (13)
joker 25 (3), 84 (3), 839 (3)
joking 833 (4), 839 (1), 839 (4)
joking apart 532 (8)
jollification 837 (3)
jollity 833 (2), 837 (1)
jolly 833 (4), 837 (19), 882 (6)
jolly along 925 (4)
Jolly Roger 547 (12)
jolt 259 (8), 279 (1), 279 (7), 318 (1), 318 (6), 508 (1), 821 (7)
jolting 259 (4)
joss house 990 (1)
joss stick 385 (4), 396 (2)
jostle 200 (5), 202 (3), 702 (9)
jostling 202 (2)
jot 33 (2)
jot down 548 (7), 586 (8)
jotter 586 (4)
jottings 548 (1)
joule 160 (3)
journal 528 (4), 528 (5), 548 (1), 589 (1), 589 (2), 808 (2)
journalese 560 (1)
journalism 528 (2), 586 (1)
journalist 459 (9), 528 (6), 529 (4), 549 (2), 589 (7)
journalistic 560 (5)
journals 590 (3)
journey 267 (1), 267 (11), 305 (1)
journeying 267 (9)
journeyman 686 (3)
journey's end 266 (3), 295 (2)
joust 716 (2)
joust with 716 (10)
jousting 716 (6)
Jove 967 (1)
jovial 833 (4), 837 (19), 882 (6)
joviality 833 (2), 882 (2)
jowl 239 (1)
joy 376 (1), 821 (1), 824 (1), 826 (1), 833 (1), 835 (1), 871 (1)

joy, a 826 (1)
joy rider 268 (5)
joyful 824 (5), 833 (4)
joyful, be 835 (6)
joyfulness 824 (1)
joyless 827 (4), 834 (5)
joyous 824 (5), 833 (4)
joyousness 824 (1)
joyride 785 (1), 788 (1)
joystick 276 (1), 689 (1)
JP 957 (1)
jubilant 824 (4), 833 (5), 835 (4), 876 (3)
jubilation 833 (2), 835 (1), 876 (1)
jubilee 99 (3), 110 (1), 141 (3), 835 (1), 876 (1)
Judaism 973 (3)
Judaize 979 (11)
Judas 545 (1), 938 (2)
judder 318 (1)
judge 455 (6), 463 (3), 465 (13), 473 (9), 480 (3), 480 (5), 605 (6), 720 (4), 737 (7), 741 (6), 846 (4), 858 (3), 913 (6), 955 (2), 955 (5), 957 (1), 959 (8), 963 (5)
judge and jury 956 (1)
judge beforehand 481 (10)
judge for oneself 595 (2)
judgment 447 (1), 449 (2), 452 (1), 463 (1), 473 (1), 480 (1), 485 (3), 498 (2), 532 (1), 605 (1), 617 (1), 737 (2), 858 (1), 959 (3), 961 (1), 963 (1)
judgment seat 956 (1)
judicatory 956 (5)
judicature 955 (1)
judicial 463 (2), 480 (4), 502 (2), 846 (3), 956 (5)
judicial murder 362 (1), 963 (3)
judiciary 955 (4), 957 (1)
judicious 463 (2), 480 (4), 498 (5), 642 (2)
judo 713 (1), 716 (5)
judoist 722 (1)
jug 194 (13)
juggernaut 168 (1), 274 (12)
juggle 542 (8), 698 (5)

juggler 545 (5), 594 (10), 983 (5)

jugglery 698 (1), 983 (1)

juggling 542 (3), 542 (6)

juice 335 (2), 341 (1), 354 (1)

juiciness 130 (1), 335 (1)

juicy 128 (6), 335 (4), 341 (4), 356 (2), 390 (2), 826 (2), 951 (6)

juju 983 (3)

jukebox 414 (10)

Julian calendar 117 (4)

jumble 43 (4), 43 (7), 61 (2), 63 (4), 244 (3), 464 (4)

jumble sale 793 (1)

jumbled 61 (7)

jumbo 195 (4), 195 (6)

jumbo jet 276 (1)

jump 201 (1), 265 (2), 277 (2), 285 (1), 308 (1), 312 (1), 312 (4), 318 (1), 318 (5), 508 (4), 822 (4), 837 (21), 854 (9)

jump about 318 (5)

jump at 597 (6), 758 (3), 859 (11)

jump back 290 (3)

jump bail 620 (6), 667 (5)

jump down one's throat 892 (4)

jump for joy 824 (6)

jump in 297 (5), 313 (3)

jump jet 276 (1)

jump on 312 (4), 747 (7)

jump out 298 (5)

jump over 306 (3), 312 (4)

jump the gun 119 (4)

jump the queue 64 (3), 119 (4), 283 (3)

jump to conclusions 481 (10)

jump to it 678 (11)

jump up 308 (4), 310 (4), 310 (5), 312 (4)

jumped-up 639 (5)

jumper 228 (11), 273 (5), 312 (2), 837 (14)

jumpiness 318 (1), 678 (2)

jumping 837 (10)

jumps 318 (1)

jumpsuit 228 (9)

jumpy 318 (4), 678 (7), 854 (7)

junction 45 (1), 45 (4), 47 (1), 76 (1), 624 (6)

juncture 8 (2), 27 (1), 121 (1), 137 (1), 154 (1)

jungle 61 (2), 366 (2)

junior 35 (2), 35 (4), 120 (2), 130 (4), 745 (5)

junior counsel 958 (1)

junk 275 (5), 641 (3)

junk food 301 (9)

junket 301 (24), 837 (1)

junketing 837 (3)

junkie 949 (4)

Juno 967 (1)

Junoesque 209 (9), 841 (3)

Jupiter 321 (6)

Jupiter or Jove 967 (1)

juridical 480 (4), 955 (4)

jurisdiction 733 (1), 953 (3), 955 (1), 959 (2)

jurisdictional 955 (4), 956 (5)

jurisprudence 953 (4)

jurisprudential 953 (5), 958 (6)

jurist 958 (4)

juror 480 (3), 957 (3)

juror's panel 957 (3)

jury 480 (3), 957 (3)

jury box 956 (4)

jury list 957 (3)

juryman or -woman 957 (3)

just 28 (7), 33 (7), 475 (7), 480 (4), 498 (5), 540 (2), 606 (2), 625 (3), 860 (2), 913 (4), 929 (3), 931 (2), 933 (3), 953 (5)

just a bit 27 (6), 33 (10)

just about to 200 (8)

just around the corner, be 124 (5)

just, be 913 (6), 915 (8), 929 (5), 933 (4)

just before 119 (5)

just begun 68 (6)

just caught 401 (3)

just cause 927 (1)

just deserts 962 (1), 963 (1)

just heard 401 (3)

just in case 669 (14)

just in time 137 (4), 137 (8)

just like that 701 (10)

just married 894 (7)

just now 126 (9)

just out 126 (5)

just price 28 (2)

just pride 871 (1)

just relation 9 (3)

just right 494 (8), 635 (3), 646 (3)

just short of 33 (11)

just sit there 175 (3)

just so 60 (5)

just the moment 137 (1)

just the thing 615 (2)

just the time 137 (1)

just this once 88 (6), 140 (3)

just visible 443 (2)

justiciable 959 (6)

justice 28 (1), 480 (1), 606 (1), 860 (1), 913 (2), 929 (1), 931 (1), 933 (1), 933 (2), 953 (1), 957 (1), 962 (1), 963 (1), 965 (2)

justice of the peace 741 (6), 957 (1)

justiciable 953 (5)

justiciary 955 (4), 956 (5)

justifiable 913 (4), 915 (3), 927 (4)

justification 467 (1), 614 (1), 909 (1), 915 (1), 927 (1), 960 (1)

justificatory 614 (3)

justified 913 (4), 927 (4)

justifier 927 (2)

justify 478 (4), 614 (4), 909 (4), 915 (6), 927 (6)

justify oneself 927 (6)

justifying 927 (3)

justly 913 (7)

jut 209 (12), 254 (5), 259 (8), 298 (5), 443 (4)

jute 208 (2), 222 (4)

jutting 254 (4)

juvenile 130 (4), 132 (2), 132 (5), 572 (2), 670 (4)

juvenile court 956 (2)

juvenile delinquent 904 (3)

juvenility 130 (1)

juxtapose 200 (6), 202 (4), 462 (3)

juxtaposition 74 (1), 202 (1), 462 (1)

K

kagoule 228 (10)

kaleidoscope 437 (1), 442 (1)

kaleidoscopic 43 (6), 82 (2), 143 (4), 425 (5), 437 (5)

kangaroo 365 (3)

kangaroo court 954 (3)

kapok 208 (2), 227 (1)

kaput 165 (5)

karate 716 (5)

karma 596 (2)

karmic 596 (6)

kayak 275 (8)

kebabs 301 (13)

kedgeree 301 (15)

keel 153 (3), 214 (1), 275 (1)

keel over 221 (4), 309 (4)

keelhaul 963 (8)

keen 174 (5), 174 (6), 256 (7), 374 (3), 374 (4), 380 (5), 597 (4), 716 (9), 818 (6), 836 (2), 836 (5), 839 (4), 859 (7), 905 (2)

keen appetite 859 (2)

keen-eared 415 (5)

keen-eyed 438 (6)

keen on 887 (10)

keen-scented 394 (2)

keen sight 438 (1)

keener 836 (3)

keenly contested 716 (9)

keenness 174 (3), 818 (2)

keep 136 (7), 139 (3), 192 (6), 301 (7), 457 (6), 632 (5), 633 (5), 660 (8), 662 (1), 703 (2), 703 (6), 713 (4), 713 (9), 768 (3), 778 (5), 876 (4), 988 (11)

keep a brothel 951 (10)

keep a cool head 823 (5)

keep a count 86 (11)

keep a date 295 (6)

keep a mistress 951 (10)

keep a stock 633 (5)

keep a straight face 834 (10)

keep accounts 86 (11), 808 (5)

keep afloat 730 (6)

keep alive 146 (4), 360 (6), 666 (5)

keep amused 837 (20)

keep an eye on 457 (6)

keep an eye out for 438 (9)

keep apart 46 (9), 46 (10)

keep at arm's length 292 (3), 883 (9)

keep at bay 713 (10)

keep at it 146 (3), 600 (4), 682 (7)

keep away 190 (6), 620 (5)

keep back 525 (8), 632 (5), 747 (7), 778 (5), 816 (6)

keep be 678 (12)

keep behind bars 747 (10)

keep calm 823 (5), 865 (4)

keep cheerful 833 (7)

keep clear 620 (5)

keep clear of 199 (5)

keep company with 89 (4), 880 (7)

keep cool 823 (5)

keep costs down 814 (3)

keep down 165 (8), 311 (4), 745 (7)

keep dry 342 (5)

keep faith 739 (4), 768 (4), 917 (10), 929 (5)

keep fit 652 (5)

keep for oneself 816 (6)

keep fresh 666 (5)

keep from 760 (4)

keep going 146 (3), 600 (4), 666 (5)

keep holy 876 (4), 988 (11)

keep in 230 (3), 747 (7), 747 (10), 778 (5)

keep in custody 660 (8)

keep in hand 632 (5), 778 (5)

keep in ignorance 535 (3)

keep in mind 455 (5), 505 (7)

keep in purdah 525 (7), 883 (10)

keep in sight 438 (9)

keep in spirits 855 (8)

keep in step 83 (7), 123 (4)

keep in touch 588 (4), 882 (9)

keep in view 455 (5)

keep inside 224 (5)

keep it dark 525 (8)

keep it up 146 (4)

keep late hours 136 (4)

keep Lent 946 (4)

keep moving 678 (11)

keep nothing back 540 (3)

keep off 199 (5), 421 (4), 620 (5), 713 (10)

keep on 71 (6), 139 (3), 146 (4), 285 (3), 600 (4)

keep on ice 136 (7)

keep on trying 600 (4)

keep one waiting 136 (7), 507 (5)

keep one's balance 28 (10)

keep one's cool 747 (7)

keep one's distance 199 (5), 620 (5)

keep one's head 865 (4)

keep one's mouth shut 582 (3)

keep one's place 60 (4)

keep one's promise 768 (4), 929 (5)

keep one's senses 502 (3)

keep one's spirits up 833 (7)

keep open house 813 (4), 882 (10)

keep order 60 (3), 660 (8), 689 (4), 733 (10)

keep out 57 (5), 421 (4), 702 (9), 747 (7), 760 (4)

keep pace with 28 (9)

keep posted 524 (10)

keep prisoner 747 (10)

keep quiet 266 (7)

keep Ramadan 946 (4)

keep safe 660 (8), 666 (5)

keep secret 525 (8), 582 (3), 778 (5), 858 (3)

keep something back 541 (6)

keep steady 153 (8)
keep straight 933 (4)
keep supplied 633 (5)
keep the books 808 (5)
keep the faith 979 (9)
keep the peace 177 (5), 710 (3), 717 (4), 719 (4), 823 (6)
keep the score 86 (11), 87 (5)
keep time 117 (7), 123 (4)
keep to oneself 778 (5), 883 (8)
keep track of 455 (5)
keep under 745 (7), 747 (7)
keep up 144 (3), 146 (4), 600 (4), 876 (4)
keep up appearances 850 (5)
keep up with 28 (9)
keep vigil 457 (7)
keep warm 379 (7)
keep watch 438 (9), 457 (7)
keep well 650 (3)
keeper 264 (3), 369 (1), 457 (2), 492 (3), 537 (1), 660 (3), 690 (3), 742 (1), 749 (1), 754 (1)
keeping 747 (3), 747 (4)
keeping a 46 (2)
keeping fit 652 (2), 682 (2)
keeping in 778 (1), 963 (4)
keeping Lent 946 (3)
keeping under 311 (1)
keeping warm 381 (1)
keepsake 505 (3), 781 (2)
keg 194 (12)
ken 438 (5)
kennel 74 (3), 192 (10), 747 (10)
kennel maid 369 (6)
kepi 228 (23)
kept 666 (4), 778 (4)
kept back 778 (4)
kept in 747 (6), 778 (4)
kept out 607 (2)
kept quiet 523 (4)
kept under 747 (5)
kept waiting, be 136 (5)
kept woman 887 (5), 952 (3)

kerb 234 (1)
kerb-crawler 952 (1)
kerfuffle 318 (3)
kernel 5 (2), 70 (1)
kestrel 365 (4)
ketch 275 (5)
ketchup 389 (2)
kettle 194 (14), 383 (2)
kettle drum 414 (9)
key 27 (1), 137 (6), 156 (6), 178 (2), 263 (11), 264 (2), 410 (5), 460 (1), 484 (1), 520 (1), 520 (3), 547 (1), 628 (2), 638 (5)
key moment 137 (3)
key person 638 (4), 690 (3)
keyboard 86 (5), 410 (2), 414 (4), 414 (5)
keyed 410 (8)
keyed up 507 (2), 821 (3)
keyhole 263 (5)
keynote 81 (1), 410 (2), 638 (3)
keypunch 86 (5)
keys 410 (2), 414 (4)
keystone 213 (1), 218 (2)
khaki 228 (5), 430 (3)
kibbutz 775 (1)
kick 174 (1), 176 (7), 279 (1), 279 (2), 279 (10), 280 (1), 287 (1), 287 (7), 312 (1), 318 (5), 388 (1), 524 (3), 547 (4), 704 (4), 712 (9), 738 (9), 762 (3)
kick back 280 (3), 714 (3)
kick off 64 (3), 68 (3), 68 (8)
kick one's heels 677 (3), 679 (11)
kick out 300 (6)
kick over 165 (7)
kickback 280 (1)
kicking 176 (5)
kicks 821 (1)
kid 132 (1), 132 (3), 226 (6), 542 (8), 851 (5)
kid gloves 736 (1)
kid oneself 487 (3)
kiddie 132 (1)
kidnap 542 (10), 747 (8), 786 (9), 788 (7)
kidnapper 786 (4), 789 (1)

kidnapping 786 (1), 788 (1)
kidney 77 (2)
kidney failure 651 (7)
kidneys 224 (2)
kill 161 (9), 165 (6), 362 (10), 963 (12)
kill oneself 361 (8), 362 (13)
kill time 108 (8)
killer 162 (4), 362 (6), 362 (7), 619 (3), 722 (1), 904 (2)
killing 361 (1), 362 (1), 362 (8), 682 (5), 963 (3)
killjoy 613 (1), 702 (5), 834 (4)
kiln 383 (1)
kilo 322 (2)
kilogram 322 (2)
kilometre 203 (4)
kilowatt 160 (6)
kilt 228 (13)
kimono 228 (7)
kin 11 (2), 11 (5), 77 (3), 196 (1)
kind 27 (1), 77 (2), 243 (1), 644 (8), 703 (4), 884 (3), 884 (4), 897 (4), 897 (5), 979 (6)
kind act 615 (2), 703 (1), 813 (1), 884 (2), 897 (2)
kind-hearted 897 (4)
kind heartedness 897 (1)
kind person 897 (3), 901 (4), 903 (1), 937 (1)
kind regards 920 (2)
kind to, be 703 (5), 828 (5)
kind words 884 (2)
kindergarten 130 (2), 539 (2)
kindle 156 (9), 174 (8), 176 (9), 379 (7), 381 (9), 385 (6), 417 (13), 612 (9), 818 (7), 821 (6), 822 (4)
kindled 379 (5), 381 (6)
kindliness 880 (2), 884 (1), 897 (1)
kindling 381 (2), 385 (1)
kindly 887 (16), 897 (4)
kindly disposed 897 (4)

kindness 736 (1), 880 (2), 884 (1), 884 (2), 887 (1), 897 (1), 897 (2), 931 (1)

kindred 9 (5), 11 (1), 11 (2), 11 (5)

kindred spirit 880 (4)

kinetic 160 (9), 265 (3)

kinetic art 554 (1)

kinetic energy 265 (1)

kinetics 265 (1)

king 741 (3)

king size 195 (6)

king worship 982 (2)

kingdom 77 (3), 184 (2), 733 (6)

kingdom come 971 (1)

kingdom of God 971 (1)

kingdom of heaven 971 (1)

kingfisher 365 (4)

kingfisher-blue 435 (3)

kingliness 868 (1)

kingly 733 (8), 868 (6)

kingpin 638 (4), 690 (3)

king's ransom 800 (1)

kingship 733 (4), 733 (5)

kink 84 (1), 251 (2), 503 (5), 604 (2), 647 (2)

kinky 84 (7), 251 (7)

kinsfolk 11 (2)

kinship 9 (1), 11 (1), 18 (1), 169 (1)

kinship group 371 (4)

kinsman 11 (2), 776 (3)

kinswoman 11 (2)

kiosk 192 (7), 192 (16), 796 (3)

kipper 342 (6), 388 (6)

kirk 990 (3)

kirk session 985 (5)

kirtle 228 (13)

kismet 596 (2)

kiss 202 (3), 884 (2), 884 (7), 889 (1), 889 (6)

kiss curl 259 (2)

kiss goodbye to 728 (7)

kiss the book 532 (6)

kissable 841 (6), 887 (11)

kit 52 (2), 77 (2), 630 (4)

kit out 633 (5), 669 (11)

kitbag 194 (9)

kitchen 194 (19), 301 (5), 687 (1)

kitchen cabinet 692 (1)

kitchen garden 370 (3)

kitchen-sink 590 (6)

kite-flying 461 (2), 529 (2)

kith and kin 11 (2)

kitsch 551 (3), 847 (1)

kitschy 847 (4)

kitten 132 (3), 365 (11)

kittenish 132 (5), 833 (4), 837 (19)

kitty 632 (1), 706 (2), 775 (1)

Kiwi 59 (2)

klaxon 665 (1)

kleptomania 503 (3), 788 (5)

kleptomaniac 503 (7), 504 (1), 788 (6), 789 (1)

knack 610 (1), 623 (3), 694 (2)

knacker 362 (6)

knacker's yard 362 (5)

knapsack 194 (9)

knave 545 (1), 545 (4), 603 (3), 869 (7), 904 (2), 938 (2)

knavery 698 (1), 930 (1), 934 (1)

knavish 698 (4), 930 (5), 934 (4)

knead 43 (7), 243 (5), 327 (4), 332 (5), 333 (3)

kneading 378 (1)

knee 45 (4), 247 (1), 267 (7), 279 (10)

knee-deep 211 (2), 212 (2)

knee-high 132 (5), 196 (9), 209 (8)

knee-jerk response 450 (1)

kneecap 963 (11)

kneel 311 (9), 721 (4), 879 (4), 884 (6), 920 (6), 988 (10)

kneel to 311 (9), 761 (7), 981 (11)

kneeler 218 (8)

kneeling 311 (2), 721 (2), 920 (3), 981 (9)

knees 218 (6)

knees knocking 854 (2)

knees-up 837 (3)

knell 165 (3), 361 (1), 364 (2), 413 (9), 547 (5), 665 (3), 836 (2)

knick-knack 639 (3), 837 (15)

knickerbockers 228 (12)

knickers 228 (17)

knife 46 (11), 256 (5), 362 (10), 723 (8)

knife-edge 206 (1)

knife-edged 256 (7)

knife-thrower 287 (5)

knight 722 (1), 722 (10), 855 (3), 866 (14), 868 (5)

knight errant 268 (4), 513 (4), 713 (6), 722 (1), 855 (3), 901 (4)

knight-like 855 (4)

knighthood 870 (1)

knighting 866 (5)

knightly 855 (4), 868 (6), 884 (3), 929 (3)

knit 45 (9), 45 (12), 164 (7), 222 (9)

knit together 656 (11)

knitter 222 (5)

knitting 45 (2), 222 (3), 243 (2), 844 (4)

knob 217 (3), 218 (3), 252 (2), 253 (2)

knobby 259 (4)

knock 165 (3), 279 (2), 279 (9), 287 (1), 378 (1), 402 (1), 547 (4), 616 (1), 712 (4), 926 (6), 963 (2)

knock about 267 (11), 675 (2)

knock down 165 (7), 216 (7), 279 (9), 311 (6)

knock-down price 812 (1)

knock down to 793 (4)

knock for six 727 (10)

knock in 45 (11)

knock into 303 (4)

knock into shape 243 (5)

knock it back 301 (38)

knock-kneed 163 (7), 220 (3), 246 (4), 247 (5), 845 (2)

knock off 39 (3)

knock-on effect 71 (1)

knock out 161 (9), 165 (6), 243 (5), 279 (9), 727 (10)

knock-out blow **279** (2)
knock over **165** (7)
knock together **279** (8)
knockabout **849** (1), **849** (3)
knockabout farce **594** (3)
knocked out **728** (5)
knocker **279** (4), **547** (5)
knockers **253** (3)
knockout **69** (1), **727** (2)
knockout blow **165** (3)
knoll **209** (3)
knot **45** (12), **47** (4), **61** (3), **74** (4), **74** (5), **203** (4), **222** (8), **250** (3), **253** (2), **324** (3), **700** (1), **708** (1)
knots **277** (1)
knotted **45** (8), **61** (8), **222** (6), **251** (9), **259** (4)
knotting **45** (2)
knotty **324** (4), **459** (12), **700** (4)
knotty point **530** (2)
know **374** (5), **447** (7), **463** (3), **473** (7), **484** (4), **490** (8), **498** (6), **505** (7), **505** (10), **516** (5), **524** (12), **536** (4), **694** (9)
know a little **491** (8)
know again **490** (8), **505** (7)
know-all **492** (2), **500** (2), **850** (3), **873** (3)
know backwards **490** (8), **694** (9)
know by heart **490** (8)
know by instinct **476** (3)
know for a fact **490** (8)
know for certain **473** (7), **485** (7)
know-how **624** (1), **629** (1), **694** (1)
know inside out **490** (8)
know no better **491** (8), **699** (4), **847** (6), **885** (6), **935** (5)
know no bounds **32** (15), **637** (5)
know no wrong **935** (5)
know one's duty **739** (4)
know one's own mind **595** (2)

know one's place **83** (7), **874** (3), **920** (5)
know something **490** (8)
know the feeling **818** (7)
know the ropes **694** (9)
know the value **490** (8)
know what's what **490** (8), **694** (8)
know when to stop **942** (4)
knowable **490** (7)
knowall **473** (3)
knowing **374** (3), **447** (5), **490** (1), **490** (5), **498** (4), **524** (8), **536** (3), **610** (7), **698** (4), **965** (6)
knowing no better **491** (4), **847** (4), **847** (5)
knowledge **473** (1), **490** (1), **498** (3), **524** (1), **528** (2), **629** (1), **694** (1), **698** (1), **818** (1), **880** (1), **983** (1)
knowledgeable **490** (6), **498** (5)
known **490** (7), **505** (5), **528** (7), **610** (5), **610** (6), **673** (2), **866** (10)
known as **561** (4)
known, be **490** (9), **526** (7)
known by **547** (17)
known by heart **490** (7)
knuckle **45** (4), **247** (1), **253** (2)
knuckle under **311** (9), **721** (4), **823** (6), **856** (4), **872** (5), **879** (4), **939** (4)
koala bear **365** (3)
Koran **975** (2)
Koranic **975** (4)
kosher **301** (32), **648** (7), **988** (8)
kowtow **311** (2), **721** (4), **884** (2)
kraal **192** (3), **235** (1)
kudos **866** (2), **923** (1)
kung-fu **716** (5)
kwashiorkor **651** (6)

L

L-driver **268** (5), **538** (2)
la-di-da **850** (4)
label **40** (1), **62** (6), **77** (2), **547** (13), **547** (19)
labial **234** (4)
laboratory **147** (3), **461** (4), **539** (4), **687** (1)
laborious **678** (9), **682** (4), **682** (5), **684** (4), **700** (4)
laboriously **682** (8)
laboriousness **700** (1)
labour **106** (5), **167** (2), **174** (1), **278** (4), **532** (7), **622** (3), **629** (1), **638** (8), **669** (1), **676** (1), **676** (5), **678** (3), **682** (3), **682** (7), **686** (4), **700** (2), **838** (2)
labour force **160** (1), **686** (4)
labour in vain **307** (3), **470** (6), **634** (4), **641** (8)
labour-intensive **622** (5)
labour of love **597** (2), **672** (1), **812** (2), **897** (2), **931** (1)
labour pains **167** (2)
labour-saving **630** (6), **685** (2), **814** (1), **814** (2)
labour the obvious **641** (8)
labour under **7** (4)
labour under difficulties **700** (7)
laboured **576** (2), **682** (5)
laboured breathing **684** (1)
labourer **164** (4), **686** (2), **742** (1)
labouring **678** (9), **682** (4)
labourite **708** (2)
laburnum **366** (4)
labyrinth **61** (3), **251** (3), **530** (2)
labyrinthine **61** (8), **251** (5)
lace **43** (7), **45** (9), **45** (12), **47** (4), **222** (3), **222** (4), **844** (4)
lace tight **45** (13)
lace up **45** (12)
lace-ups **228** (27)
lacerate **46** (12), **377** (5), **655** (10)
laceration **46** (3), **655** (4)

lachrymose 836 (4)
lack 35 (5), 55 (2), 55 (5), 190 (1), 307 (1), 307 (3), 627 (1), 627 (6), 636 (2), 636 (7), 801 (5)
lack beauty 842 (6)
lack caution 857 (4)
lack courage 856 (4)
lack courtesy 921 (5)
lack faith 974 (7)
lack harmony 411 (3)
lack humour 834 (10)
lack information 491 (8)
lack interest 491 (8)
lack nothing 54 (5)
lack of affectation 573 (1)
lack of appetite 301 (1)
lack of beauty 842 (1)
lack of brains 499 (1)
lack of breadth 206 (1)
lack of candour 525 (1)
lack of ceremony 734 (1)
lack of charity 898 (2)
lack of connection 10 (1)
lack of consent 489 (1)
lack of conviction 572 (1)
lack of daring 856 (1)
lack of drive 601 (1)
lack of education 491 (1)
lack of expectation 472 (1), 508 (1)
lack of faith 974 (1)
lack of feeling 820 (1), 847 (1)
lack of finish 576 (1)
lack of friction 706 (1), 710 (1)
lack of gratitude 908 (1)
lack of harmony 704 (1)
lack of height 196 (1)
lack of humour 840 (1)
lack of hygiene 653 (1)
lack of information 491 (1)
lack of inspiration 840 (1)
lack of interest 454 (1), 456 (1), 838 (1), 860 (1)
lack of judgment 464 (1)
lack of knowledge 491 (1)
lack of light 439 (1)
lack of meaning 515 (1), 517 (1), 518 (1), 983 (2)
lack of mercy 735 (1)

lack of piety 980 (1)
lack of pigment 427 (1)
lack of pity 906 (1)
lack of power 161 (1)
lack of practice 611 (1), 695 (1)
lack of preparation 670 (1)
lack of principle 930 (1)
lack of restraint 576 (1)
lack of reverence 980 (1)
lack of security 474 (3)
lack of sensation 820 (1)
lack of sensitivity 820 (1)
lack of shape or definition 244 (1)
lack of sparkle 419 (1), 572 (1), 840 (1)
lack of spirit 823 (1)
lack of strength 163 (1)
lack of substance 4 (1), 325 (1)
lack of success 728 (1)
lack of taste 847 (1)
lack of training 670 (1)
lack of unity 46 (1)
lack of vision 439 (1)
lack of warning 508 (1)
lack of willpower 601 (1)
lack of wonder 820 (1), 860 (1), 865 (1)
lack of zeal 598 (1)
lack preparation 670 (7)
lack self-control 943 (3)
lack sparkle 834 (10)
lack spirit 820 (6)
lack verve 820 (6)
lackadaisical 679 (7), 820 (4), 823 (3), 834 (5), 860 (2)
lackey 742 (2), 742 (4), 879 (2)
lacking 55 (3), 190 (4), 307 (2), 627 (3), 627 (4), 636 (3), 772 (2), 772 (3), 774 (2)
lacking authority 734 (3)
lacking beauty 842 (3)
lacking bite 257 (2)
lacking faith 974 (5)
lacking proof 467 (3)
lacking variety 16 (2)
lacking wit 840 (2)

lacklustre 163 (6), 419 (1), 419 (4), 426 (3), 834 (5)
laconic 569 (2), 582 (2)
laconicism 569 (1)
lacquer 226 (16), 357 (5), 425 (8), 844 (12)
lacrosse 837 (7)
lacuna 201 (2), 263 (1)
lacustrine 346 (2)
lad 132 (2), 372 (1)
ladder 46 (7), 71 (2), 308 (1), 667 (2)
laddie 132 (2)
lade 54 (7), 193 (2)
laden 54 (4), 322 (4)
laden weight 322 (2)
Ladies 649 (3)
lading 193 (1), 777 (1)
ladle 194 (18), 272 (7)
lady 373 (4), 741 (1), 776 (2)
Lady Bountiful 781 (4), 813 (2), 903 (1)
Lady chapel 990 (4)
lady-in-waiting 742 (3)
lady-killer 887 (4), 952 (1)
lady-love 887 (5)
lady mayor 741 (6)
Lady Muck 848 (4)
ladybird 365 (16)
ladylike 373 (5), 848 (6), 868 (6), 884 (3)
ladyship 868 (5), 870 (1)
lag 35 (5), 226 (13), 238 (5), 278 (4), 284 (4), 307 (3), 679 (11)
lag behind 136 (4)
lager 301 (28)
laggard 278 (2)
lagging 136 (1), 226 (5), 227 (1), 278 (1), 278 (3)
lagoon 345 (1), 346 (1)
laical 987 (2)
laicize 987 (3)
laicized 987 (2)
laid 360 (3)
laid bare 526 (2)
laid low 210 (2)
laid off 677 (2)
laid out 216 (5), 806 (3)
laid to rest 364 (7)
laid up 651 (21), 674 (3)

lair 192 (3), 527 (1), 662 (1)

laird 741 (1), 776 (2), 868 (4)

laisser faire 734 (1), 744 (1), 791 (2)

laity 987 (1)

lake 339 (1), 346 (1)

lake-dwelling 346 (2)

lama 986 (8)

lamasery 986 (9)

lamb 132 (3), 167 (6), 226 (6), 301 (16), 365 (8), 699 (2), 890 (1), 935 (2)

lamb-like 935 (3)

lambency 417 (3)

lambent 417 (8)

lame 163 (7), 163 (10), 572 (2), 655 (9)

lame dog 163 (2)

lame duck 163 (2), 731 (3)

lame excuse 614 (1)

lament 364 (2), 364 (9), 408 (3), 412 (5), 547 (21), 825 (7), 829 (5), 830 (4), 834 (9), 836 (2), 836 (5), 905 (2), 905 (6), 924 (9)

lamentable 645 (2), 827 (6), 836 (4)

lamentably 32 (20)

lamentation 339 (1), 364 (2), 408 (1), 836 (1), 941 (3)

lamented 361 (6), 836 (4)

lamenting 364 (8), 408 (2), 825 (6), 830 (2), 834 (6), 836 (1), 836 (4)

lamina 53 (5), 207 (2), 218 (12), 631 (1)

laminate 207 (2), 207 (5)

laminated 207 (4)

lamp 217 (2), 336 (2), 417 (2), 420 (4), 442 (6), 547 (5)

lampblack 428 (3)

lamplight 420 (4)

lampoon 593 (10), 851 (2), 851 (6), 926 (2), 926 (6)

lampooner 839 (3), 924 (5), 926 (3)

lampshade 421 (1)

lance 256 (2), 723 (6)

lance corporal 741 (8)

lance-shaped 256 (9)

lanceolate 256 (9)

lancer 722 (5), 722 (10)

lancet 256 (2), 263 (12)

land 184 (1), 184 (3), 269 (9), 269 (10), 271 (7), 289 (4), 295 (5), 299 (3), 309 (3), 321 (2), 344 (1), 771 (7), 777 (3), 786 (6)

land a blow 279 (9)

land ahoy 269 (14), 289 (5), 438 (11)

land-line 531 (1)

land-locked 346 (2)

land mine 723 (14)

land surveyor 465 (7)

land travel 265 (1), 267 (1), 305 (1), 837 (6)

landed 773 (2), 777 (5)

landed gentry 776 (2)

landed interest 868 (2)

landed property 777 (3)

landfall 295 (1)

landing 207 (1), 218 (5), 271 (1), 271 (2), 295 (1), 295 (3), 309 (1)

landing craft 722 (13)

landing gear 276 (1)

landing place 295 (2)

landing stage 218 (5), 295 (2)

landlady 633 (3), 776 (2)

landlocked 232 (2)

landlord 633 (3), 776 (2)

landlubber 270 (1), 697 (1)

landmark 236 (1), 254 (2), 281 (8), 547 (7), 638 (2)

landmass 184 (1)

landowner 776 (2)

lands 344 (1), 370 (2), 777 (3)

landscape 344 (1), 445 (2), 553 (4)

landscape gardener 370 (5)

landscape gardening 844 (2)

landscape painter 556 (1)

landscaped 841 (3)

landslide 149 (1), 165 (3), 220 (2), 309 (1), 728 (2)

landslip 220 (2)

lane 624 (4), 624 (5)

language 557 (1), 560 (2), 579 (1)

language student 557 (4)

language study 557 (2)

languid 175 (2), 278 (3), 679 (7)

languish 651 (23), 679 (11), 684 (5), 834 (9), 859 (11), 889 (7)

languishing 163 (6)

languor 175 (1), 278 (1), 679 (2), 684 (1), 838 (1)

languorous 679 (7)

lank 842 (5)

lanky 203 (5), 206 (4), 209 (9)

lanolin 357 (4)

lantern 420 (4)

lantern-jawed 206 (5)

lanyard 47 (2)

lap 53 (1), 110 (1), 218 (6), 230 (3), 235 (4), 277 (8), 283 (3), 301 (38), 306 (5), 314 (1), 314 (4), 341 (7), 378 (7)

lap dog 365 (10)

lap of luxury 376 (2), 944 (1)

lap up 299 (4), 301 (38), 390 (3), 415 (6)

lapdog 879 (2)

lapel 228 (3), 261 (1)

lapidary 556 (3)

lapidate 287 (7), 712 (12), 924 (9), 963 (12)

lapped 232 (2)

lapse 69 (1), 111 (3), 486 (6), 611 (5), 655 (7), 657 (1), 657 (2), 934 (7), 936 (2), 974 (1)

lapse of time 111 (1)

lapsed 458 (2), 486 (4), 655 (5), 769 (2), 974 (5)

lapsed believer 486 (3)

larboard 242 (1)

larceny 788 (1)

larch 366 (4)

lard 301 (40), 357 (3)

larder 194 (19), 301 (7), 632 (2)

Lares 967 (2)

large 32 (4), 32 (15), 162 (8), 183 (6), 195 (6), 558 (5)
large amount 26 (2)
large as life 195 (6)
large, be 195 (10)
large-hearted 813 (3)
large-limbed 195 (6)
large number 104 (1)
large scale 32 (1), 195 (6)
large size 195 (6)
largely 32 (17)
largeness 32 (1), 195 (2)
larger 197 (3)
largesse 781 (2), 813 (1)
largish 32 (4)
largo 278 (7), 412 (8)
lariat 47 (8), 250 (3)
lark 308 (2), 365 (4), 824 (3), 837 (3)
lark about 497 (4)
lark around 837 (21)
larva 132 (3), 365 (16)
laryngitis 651 (8)
larynx 353 (1), 577 (1)
lasciviousness 951 (2)
laser 723 (3)
lasers 160 (6)
lash 45 (12), 174 (4), 176 (9), 208 (1), 279 (2), 612 (4), 612 (9), 963 (10)
lash out 176 (7), 891 (7)
lash out at 279 (9), 712 (9)
lashing 47 (4), 350 (7)
lashings 32 (2)
lass 132 (2), 373 (3)
lassie 132 (2)
lassitude 684 (1)
lasso 47 (8), 250 (3)
last 1 (6), 23 (3), 69 (4), 108 (7), 113 (6), 125 (8), 144 (3)
last agony 361 (2)
last arrival 136 (1)
last breath 69 (1)
last but one 69 (4)
last demand 761 (1)
last for ever 115 (4)
last gasp 69 (1), 361 (2)
last hour 361 (2)
last lap 69 (1), 295 (1)
last minute 136 (1), 136 (3), 137 (3), 680 (2)

last month 125 (12)
last place 65 (1), 284 (1)
last post 129 (1), 364 (2), 547 (8)
last resort 596 (1), 629 (1), 643 (1)
last rites 364 (2), 988 (4)
last round 69 (1)
last stage 69 (1)
last straw 827 (2), 891 (1)
last thing 136 (8)
last things 69 (3)
last throw 671 (1)
last touch 54 (1)
last trump 69 (3)
last word 646 (1)
last word, the 126 (2)
last words 67 (1), 69 (1), 296 (2)
last year 125 (12)
lasting 1 (4), 113 (4), 115 (2), 127 (6), 144 (2), 153 (5), 162 (7), 360 (2), 610 (5)
lasting monument 115 (1)
lasting quality 113 (2), 144 (1)
latch 47 (5)
latchment 547 (11)
late 113 (5), 118 (2), 125 (7), 129 (5), 129 (8), 136 (3), 136 (8), 138 (2), 278 (3), 361 (6), 670 (3), 670 (4), 679 (8)
late at night 129 (8)
late, be 113 (9), 117 (7), 118 (3), 136 (4), 138 (6), 278 (4), 306 (3), 307 (3), 495 (7), 679 (11), 680 (3)
late developer 136 (1), 278 (2), 538 (1), 670 (2)
late hour 136 (1)
late in the day 136 (8)
late-lamented 361 (6)
late riser 136 (1)
latecomer 120 (1), 136 (1)
lately 125 (12), 126 (9)
latency 175 (1), 178 (1), 415 (2), 514 (2), 523 (1), 525 (1), 542 (1), 623 (4), 698 (1), 738 (3)

lateness 118 (1), 129 (1), 136 (1), 137 (1), 137 (3), 670 (1), 680 (1)
latent 80 (7), 175 (2), 444 (2), 523 (2), 525 (3), 542 (6), 568 (2), 620 (3), 883 (7), 930 (4)
later 65 (2), 65 (5), 120 (2), 120 (4), 122 (3), 124 (4)
lateral 239 (2), 281 (3)
lateral thinking 449 (2)
laterality 239 (1)
laterally 239 (1)
latest 121 (2)
latest fashion 126 (2)
latest, the 126 (2), 848 (1)
latest thing, the 126 (2)
latex 335 (2)
lath 207 (2), 208 (3)
lath and plaster 631 (2)
lathe 315 (3)
lather 302 (4), 334 (2), 334 (4), 355 (1), 648 (9)
lathery 355 (3), 427 (4)
latitude 183 (3), 184 (1), 205 (1), 744 (3)
latitude and longitude 186 (2), 465 (4)
latrine 649 (3)
latter 65 (2), 125 (8)
latter-day 121 (2)
latter days 124 (2)
latterly 126 (9)
lattice 201 (4), 222 (3), 263 (5)
latticed 201 (3), 222 (6)
laud 981 (11)
laudable 923 (6)
laudanum 375 (2)
laudatory 923 (5)
laugh 547 (4), 547 (21), 824 (6), 833 (7), 835 (2), 835 (7), 851 (1)
laugh at 835 (7), 851 (5), 921 (5), 922 (5), 922 (6)
laugh at danger 855 (6)
laugh fit to burst 835 (7)
laugh in one's face 711 (3)
laugh off 458 (5)
laugh to scorn 922 (5)
laughable 497 (3), 499 (4), 835 (5), 837 (18), 849 (2)
laugher 835 (3)

laughing 824 (5), 833 (3), 833 (4), 835 (5)

laughing matter 835 (2)

laughingstock 25 (3), 84 (3), 501 (1), 504 (2), 544 (1), 851 (3)

laughingstock, be a 497 (4), 849 (4)

laughter 547 (4), 833 (2), 835 (2), 851 (1)

laughter and joy 833 (2)

launch 68 (9), 68 (10), 156 (9), 269 (8), 269 (10), 275 (1), 287 (7), 876 (4)

launch into 672 (3)

launch out 581 (5)

launch out at 712 (7)

launched 68 (6)

launching 68 (2), 669 (2)

launching pad 271 (3)

launder 258 (4), 648 (9)

laundered 648 (7)

launderer 648 (6)

launderette 648 (3)

laundry 194 (19), 648 (3), 687 (1)

laundry basket 194 (6)

laurels 547 (9), 729 (1), 866 (4)

lava 344 (4), 381 (4)

lavatory 194 (19), 649 (3)

lavender 396 (2), 436 (1), 436 (2)

lavender bag 396 (2)

lavender water 339 (1), 396 (2)

lavish 635 (4), 813 (3), 813 (4), 815 (3), 923 (5)

lavish, be 806 (4)

lavish upon 637 (5)

lavishness 813 (1), 815 (1)

law 81 (1), 144 (1), 596 (1), 610 (1), 693 (1), 733 (1), 737 (2), 747 (1), 953 (2), 953 (3)

law-abiding 717 (3), 721 (2), 739 (3), 929 (3), 953 (5)

law agent 754 (1), 958 (2)

law and order 717 (1), 953 (1)

law-breaker 904 (3)

law-breaking 738 (8)

law consultancy 953 (4)

law-giver 690 (1), 953 (2)

law-giving 953 (2), 953 (5)

law-making 689 (1), 953 (2)

law of nature 81 (1), 596 (1), 740 (1)

law officer 529 (5), 741 (6), 955 (2), 958 (3)

law school 539 (3)

law, the 953 (3), 975 (1)

law unto oneself, a 84 (5)

lawbreaking 61 (9), 769 (2), 930 (1), 930 (3), 934 (1), 934 (6), 954 (2), 954 (6)

lawcourt 724 (1), 956 (2)

lawcourts 956 (4)

lawful 915 (2), 953 (5)

lawful authority 733 (1)

lawfulness 953 (1)

lawless 61 (9), 84 (5), 734 (4), 738 (8), 930 (5), 954 (7)

lawlessness 734 (2), 738 (1), 738 (2), 914 (1), 954 (3)

lawn 348 (2), 366 (8), 370 (3)

laws 733 (6)

laws of motion 265 (1)

lawsuit 953 (3), 959 (1)

lawyer 475 (6), 691 (2), 958 (1)

lax 458 (2), 601 (3), 734 (3), 736 (2), 769 (2), 860 (2), 897 (4), 905 (4), 934 (3)

lax, be 458 (5), 734 (5), 736 (3), 744 (10), 746 (3), 756 (5), 769 (3), 770 (2), 823 (6), 826 (3), 943 (3)

laxative 302 (5), 658 (5), 658 (17)

laxity 458 (1), 495 (2), 601 (1), 734 (1), 736 (1), 744 (3), 746 (1), 769 (1), 860 (1), 884 (1), 934 (1), 943 (1), 951 (2)

laxness 458 (1)

lay 167 (6), 187 (5), 412 (5), 491 (4), 593 (2), 618

(8), 695 (4), 986 (11), 987 (2)

lay about one 712 (9), 716 (11)

lay an ambush 525 (9)

lay aside 57 (5), 458 (6), 674 (5)

lay at the door of 158 (3)

lay bare 522 (7), 526 (4)

lay brother 986 (5)

lay-by 187 (3), 305 (3), 632 (5)

lay claim to 915 (5)

lay down 187 (5), 216 (7), 311 (5), 475 (12), 737 (6)

lay down one's arms 719 (5)

lay down one's life 361 (8)

lay down the law 473 (8), 532 (5), 733 (10)

lay eyes on 438 (7)

lay figure 23 (3), 551 (2)

lay flat 216 (7)

lay ghosts 983 (10)

lay hands upon 786 (6)

lay in 632 (5)

lay in ashes 165 (9)

lay in ruins 165 (9)

lay into 301 (35)

lay low 311 (6), 712 (9)

lay off 300 (7), 674 (5), 779 (4)

lay on hands 988 (10)

lay oneself open to 180 (3)

lay open 229 (6), 263 (17)

lay out 62 (4), 216 (7), 364 (9), 806 (4)

lay people 987 (1)

lay person 538 (2)

lay preacher 537 (3), 986 (3)

lay siege to 712 (8)

lay sister 986 (6)

lay the foundations 68 (10), 669 (10)

lay to 266 (9)

lay to rest 364 (9)

lay up 632 (5), 641 (7), 674 (5), 679 (13)

lay waste 165 (9), 172 (6), 176 (7), 634 (4), 641 (7), 655 (9), 712 (7), 718 (11), 788 (9) layabout **679** (6)

layer 71 (2), **207** (1), **207** (5), **216** (1), **218** (4), **226** (1)

layered **207** (4)

layering **207** (3)

layette **228** (2)

laying out **784** (4)

laying waste **165** (2), **712** (2)

layout **62** (1)

laze **278** (4), **679** (11), **683** (3)

laziness **458** (1), **598** (1), **679** (2)

lazy **278** (3), **458** (2), **679** (8)

lazybones **679** (6)

lea **348** (2)

leach **337** (4)

leaching **341** (2)

lead **34** (2), **34** (8), **34** (9), **47** (8), **64** (3), **68** (9), **83** (8), **119** (4), **211** (1), **269** (4), **283** (1), **283** (3), **313** (2), **465** (5), **594** (9), **612** (8), **689** (5), **727** (1), **748** (4)

lead astray **495** (9), **612** (8), **934** (8), **951** (11)

lead from behind **856** (4)

lead in prayer **981** (12)

lead into error **495** (9)

lead off **64** (3), **68** (9)

lead on **887** (15)

lead one on **584** (6)

lead pollution **659** (3)

lead, the **64** (1)

lead the way **68** (9), **283** (3)

lead to **156** (10), **179** (3)

lead up to **669** (10)

lead with **64** (4)

leaden **322** (4), **419** (4), **426** (3), **429** (2), **838** (3)

leaden skies **419** (1)

leader **23** (2), **34** (3), **66** (1), **270** (2), **413** (3), **591** (2), **612** (5), **690** (2), **741** (5)

leader page **539** (5)

leader writer **591** (3)

leadership **64** (1), **178** (1), **689** (2), **733** (1)

leading **34** (5), **64** (1), **64** (2), **68** (7), **178** (2), **283** (1), **283** (2), **638** (5), **689** (3), **727** (4), **733** (7), **866** (9)

leading article **591** (2)

leading counsel **958** (1)

leading light **500** (1), **638** (4), **866** (6)

leading man or lady **594** (9)

leading note **410** (2)

leading question **459** (2), **459** (3)

leading role **594** (8)

leading seaman **741** (7)

leading strings **130** (2), **534** (1), **745** (1)

leading to **179** (2)

leads **226** (2)

leaf **53** (4), **207** (2), **366** (5)

leaf-like **207** (4)

leaf through **438** (9)

leafage **366** (5)

leafiness **366** (5)

leafless **129** (7)

leaflet **53** (4), **366** (5), **528** (4)

leafy **171** (4), **366** (9), **434** (3)

league **203** (4), **706** (2), **706** (4), **708** (3), **708** (8), **765** (1), **765** (5)

league together **45** (14)

leagued **708** (6), **710** (2)

leak **42** (1), **201** (2), **263** (1), **290** (1), **298** (2), **298** (6), **341** (6), **350** (9), **524** (1), **526** (1), **526** (5), **634** (4), **647** (2), **667** (5), **702** (3)

leak away **667** (5)

leak into **297** (6)

leak out **526** (7)

leakage **42** (1), **298** (2), **634** (1), **667** (1), **772** (1)

leaking **54** (4), **263** (15), **655** (6)

leaky **263** (15), **298** (4), **526** (3), **647** (3), **661** (4)

lean **29** (3), **163** (4), **163** (6), **179** (3), **196** (10), **206** (5), **220** (5), **220** (6), **246** (4), **481** (12), **605** (6), **636** (5), **841** (5)

lean backwards **238** (5)

lean on **218** (16), **740** (3)

lean or bend backward **311** (9)

lean or bend forward **311** (9)

lean over **220** (5)

lean-to **192** (7), **194** (20)

lean towards **289** (4), **859** (11)

leaning **29** (2), **179** (1), **220** (1), **220** (3), **597** (1), **605** (1), **859** (3)

leap **149** (1), **201** (1), **265** (2), **265** (4), **267** (14), **277** (2), **285** (1), **298** (5), **308** (1), **308** (4), **309** (4), **312** (1), **312** (4), **317** (4), **318** (5), **716** (3), **835** (6), **837** (10), **837** (22)

leap at **597** (6)

leap-frog **306** (3)

leap in the dark **618** (2)

leap over **306** (3)

leap up **310** (5), **312** (4)

leap year **110** (1)

leapfrog **312** (1), **312** (4), **837** (10)

leaping **312** (3)

leaps and bounds **285** (1)

learn **490** (8), **505** (10), **516** (5), **524** (12), **536** (4), **669** (13), **694** (9)

learn a trade **536** (4)

learn by rote **505** (10)

learn from experience **654** (8)

learn one's lesson **490** (8), **939** (4)

learned **490** (6), **536** (3), **557** (6)

learned in the law **958** (6)

learned person **492** (1), **500** (1), **536** (1)

learner **147** (4), **415** (3), **492** (1), **538** (1), **686** (3) learning 490 (1), 490 (2), 505 (2), 534 (3), 536 (1), 669 (1), 669 (6)

lease 780 (1), 780 (3), 784 (1), 784 (6), 785 (3)

lease-holder 191 (2)

leasehold 777 (5)

leaseholder 776 (1)

leash 47 (8), 93 (2)

leasing 784 (1)

least 33 (6), 35 (3)

leather 226 (6), 329 (1), 631 (1), 963 (9)

leathery 329 (2), 391 (2)

leave 46 (7), 190 (7), 272 (6), 290 (3), 296 (4), 620 (5), 621 (3), 683 (1), 701 (1), 756 (1), 756 (2), 780 (4), 781 (7), 919 (1)

leave a fortune 780 (4)

leave a gap 190 (6)

leave a legacy 780 (4)

leave a loophole 701 (8), 766 (3)

leave a name 505 (11)

leave alone 677 (3)

leave behind 34 (7), 41 (6), 277 (8), 285 (3), 306 (3), 306 (5), 506 (5)

leave empty 190 (6)

leave fallow 370 (9)

leave half-done 458 (4)

leave hanging 55 (5)

leave hold of 779 (4)

leave home 134 (4), 296 (4)

leave in the lurch 918 (3)

leave it to 751 (4)

leave no doubt 473 (7)

leave no escape 740 (3)

leave no hope 834 (11), 853 (5)

leave no option 740 (3)

leave no trace 2 (7), 446 (3), 550 (3)

leave nothing to add 54 (6)

leave nothing to chance 858 (3)

leave of absence 190 (1), 756 (2)

leave off 145 (6), 145 (9), 674 (5)

leave out 39 (3), 41 (6), 46 (9), 57 (5), 521 (3)

leave over 41 (6)

leave standing 306 (5)

leave stranded 621 (3)

leave-taking 296 (2)

leave the ground 308 (4)

leave to rust 674 (5)

leave undone 55 (5), 458 (4), 726 (3)

leaven 143 (3), 147 (7), 174 (4), 197 (5), 310 (2), 310 (4), 323 (2), 323 (5)

leavening 143 (1), 174 (2)

leaving 296 (1), 296 (3), 621 (1)

leaving no trace unrecorded 550 (2)

leaving out 57 (1)

leavings 41 (2), 74 (7), 164 (2), 548 (4), 641 (3), 649 (2)

lecher 952 (1)

lecherous 859 (7), 887 (9), 951 (8)

lechery 951 (2)

lectern 539 (5), 990 (4)

lecture 534 (4), 534 (7), 579 (2), 579 (9), 583 (1), 591 (1), 924 (4), 924 (11)

lecture hall 539 (4)

lecture to 583 (3)

lecturer 534 (4), 537 (1), 579 (5)

ledge 216 (1), 218 (12), 234 (1), 254 (2)

ledger 87 (1), 364 (2), 548 (1), 808 (2)

lee 662 (2)

lee wall 662 (2)

leech 48 (1), 786 (4), 879 (2)

leek 301 (20), 366 (6), 547 (11)

leer 438 (3), 438 (8), 547 (21), 889 (7)

lees 41 (2), 649 (2)

leeward 239 (1)

leeway 183 (4), 282 (1), 307 (1), 744 (3)

left 41 (4), 46 (5), 242 (1), 242 (2), 708 (2)

left alone 458 (3)

left, be 41 (5), 113 (7), 637 (6), 771 (8)

left behind 41 (4)

left hand 242 (1)

left-handed 242 (2), 378 (6), 518 (2), 695 (5)

left-handed compliment 924 (2)

left hanging 726 (2)

left high and dry 728 (6)

left in the lunch 700 (5)

left of centre 708 (7)

left open 459 (12)

left out 190 (4)

left over 41 (4)

left to rot 674 (2)

left wing 242 (1), 708 (7)

left-winger 242 (1), 708 (2)

leftist 708 (2), 708 (7)

leftovers 41 (2), 301 (13)

leg 53 (1), 53 (2), 218 (5), 267 (7)

leg-pull 542 (2), 839 (2)

leg-puller 839 (3)

leg-pulling 851 (1)

leg show 594 (4)

leg support 218 (2)

leg-up 285 (1), 310 (1), 703 (1)

legacy 67 (1), 157 (1), 771 (1), 777 (4), 781 (2), 807 (1)

legal 469 (2), 693 (2), 756 (4), 913 (4), 915 (2), 953 (5)

legal administrator 955 (2)

legal advice 953 (4)

legal adviser 691 (2), 958 (2)

legal age 134 (1)

legal argument 475 (4)

legal authority 955 (1)

legal battle 709 (3)

legal, be 953 (6)

legal code 953 (3)

legal costs 809 (2)

legal dispute 959 (1)

legal expert 958 (4)

legal flaw 954 (1)

legal incapacity 161 (2)

legal limit 236 (1)

legal necessity 596 (1)
legal opinion 480 (2)
legal practitioner 958 (1)
legal process 737 (4), 953 (3), 959 (2)
legal profession 958 (5)
legal representative 958 (2)
legal restraint 747 (1)
legal right 915 (1)
legal tender 797 (1)
legal trial 459 (1), 953 (3), 959 (3)
legalistic 481 (7)
legality 733 (1), 913 (2), 953 (1)
legalization 953 (2)
legalize 756 (5), 915 (8), 953 (7)
legalized 756 (4), 915 (2), 953 (5)
legally 953 (8)
legate 529 (5), 754 (3)
legatee 782 (2)
legation 751 (1), 754 (3)
legend 547 (1), 590 (2)
legendary 513 (6), 590 (6), 866 (10)
legerdemain 542 (3)
legged 267 (10)
leggings 228 (26)
leggy 206 (4), 267 (10)
legibility 516 (1)
legible 516 (2)
legion 722 (6), 722 (8)
legionary 722 (4)
legionnaire 722 (4)
legislate 689 (4), 733 (10), 737 (7), 953 (7)
legislated 953 (5)
legislation 689 (1), 693 (1), 737 (2), 953 (2)
legislative 689 (3), 953 (5)
legislative assembly 733 (1)
legislator 690 (1), 692 (3), 953 (2)
legislatorial 953 (5)
legislature 692 (2), 953 (2)
legitimacy 733 (1), 953 (1)
legitimate 494 (5), 594 (15), 913 (4), 915 (2), 953 (5)

legitimate succession 733 (1)
legitimately 953 (8)
legitimize 915 (8), 953 (7)
legitimized 953 (5)
legroom 183 (4)
legs 267 (6), 267 (7)
legwear 228 (26)
leisure 137 (2), 145 (4), 278 (1), 677 (1), 679 (1), 681 (1), 683 (1), 826 (1), 837 (1)
leisure wear 228 (2)
leisured 677 (2), 681 (2), 683 (2)
leisureliness 278 (1)
leisurely 136 (9), 266 (5), 278 (3), 278 (7), 677 (2), 679 (7), 679 (8), 681 (2), 683 (2), 744 (5)
leit-motiv 410 (1)
lemmings 362 (3)
lemon 301 (19), 433 (1), 728 (3)
lemon yellow 433 (3)
lemonade 301 (27)
lend 703 (5), 780 (3), 781 (7), 784 (5), 802 (3)
lend a hand 703 (5)
lend an ear 415 (6)
lend colour to 466 (6), 471 (5)
lend force to 162 (12)
lend itself to 628 (4)
lend money to 703 (5)
lend on security 784 (5)
lend one's aid 703 (5)
lend support to 703 (5)
lend wings to 277 (7), 703 (5)
lender 633 (2), 784 (3), 794 (1), 802 (2), 816 (3)
lending 784 (1), 784 (4), 785 (1), 802 (1), 803 (2)
length 26 (1), 32 (1), 53 (5), 183 (2), 195 (1), 199 (1), 201 (1), 203 (1), 203 (4), 222 (4), 465 (3)
length of days 113 (1)
length of time 110 (1), 113 (1)

lengthen 36 (5), 71 (6), 113 (8), 197 (5), 203 (8), 206 (7), 570 (6)
lengthened 113 (5), 203 (5)
lengthening 36 (1), 113 (3), 203 (2)
lengthwise 203 (9)
lengthy 32 (4), 203 (5), 570 (4)
leniency 177 (1), 688 (1), 719 (2), 734 (1), 736 (1), 756 (1), 884 (1), 884 (2), 897 (1)
lenient 177 (3), 734 (3), 736 (2), 756 (3), 823 (3), 828 (2), 884 (4), 897 (4), 905 (4), 909 (2)
lenient, be 177 (5), 719 (4), 734 (5), 736 (3), 756 (5), 758 (3), 823 (6), 905 (7), 919 (3), 927 (7)
Leninism 733 (4)
lenitive 177 (4), 258 (3), 658 (17), 831 (2)
lenity 909 (1)
lens 248 (2), 253 (1), 442 (1), 551 (4)
lent 784 (4), 946 (2)
Lenten 946 (3), 988 (8)
lenten fare 946 (1)
lento 412 (8)
Leo 321 (5)
leonine 365 (18)
leopard 437 (4)
leopard's spots 153 (2)
leotard 228 (9)
leper 883 (4)
leprechaun 970 (2)
leprosy 651 (6), 651 (12)
lesbian 84 (3), 84 (7), 373 (3), 373 (5), 951 (9)
lesion 651 (14), 655 (4)
less 26 (2), 33 (6), 35 (3), 35 (6), 39 (4)
less and less 37 (6)
less sound 401 (1)
less than perfect 647 (3)
lessee 191 (2), 776 (1), 782 (2)
lessen 37 (4), 37 (5), 177 (6), 198 (7)
lessen the strain 831 (3)

lessening 37 (1), 198 (1)
lesser 35 (3)
lesser deity 966 (1), 967 (2)
lesson 534 (4), 664 (1)
lessons 536 (2)
let 196 (1), 744 (10), 756 (5), 780 (1), 780 (3), 784 (1), 784 (6)
let alone 38 (5), 57 (6), 146 (4), 620 (5), 744 (10)
let down 311 (4), 509 (2), 542 (8), 542 (9)
let down, be 509 (4)
let drop 526 (5)
let escape 37 (4)
let evaporate 37 (4)
let fall 211 (3), 265 (5), 303 (4), 311 (5), 350 (11), 524 (11), 526 (5)
let fly 176 (7), 279 (9), 287 (8), 712 (11), 891 (6), 891 (7)
let fly at 712 (7)
let go 46 (7), 311 (5), 621 (3), 746 (3), 779 (4)
let go by 677 (3)
let in 38 (3), 231 (8), 299 (3)
let it happen 488 (7)
let it rankle 891 (5), 910 (6)
let loose 746 (3)
let off 287 (8), 905 (3), 909 (3), 960 (2)
let off steam 336 (4), 837 (23)
let on 526 (5)
let one down 509 (5), 728 (7), 918 (3)
let one know 524 (9)
let one off 668 (3)
let one's hair down 837 (23)
let one's mind wander 456 (7)
let oneself go 655 (7), 744 (9), 822 (4), 833 (7), 835 (6), 837 (23)
let oneself in 297 (5)
let out 197 (5), 203 (8), 300 (9), 526 (5), 579 (8), 629

(1), 667 (2), 746 (3), 784 (6)
let pass 458 (5), 677 (3)
let slip 456 (7), 772 (4)
let the moment pass 136 (4)
let the occasion pass 138 (6)
let things go 679 (11)
let up 145 (6), 278 (5), 683 (1), 683 (3)
let well alone 677 (3), 858 (3)
letdown 509 (1)
lethal 362 (8), 653 (4)
lethal dose 659 (3)
lethargic 679 (7)
lethargy 679 (2), 684 (1), 820 (1)
Lethe 972 (2)
letter 547 (13), 547 (19), 558 (1), 586 (2), 586 (3), 586 (8), 587 (3), 588 (1)
letter for letter 558 (7)
letter of credit 802 (1)
letter writer 588 (2)
letterbox 531 (2)
lettered 490 (6), 547 (17), 557 (6), 586 (7)
lettering 558 (1), 586 (2), 844 (2)
letterpress 22 (1), 558 (1), 586 (3), 587 (2), 589 (2)
letters 490 (2), 490 (3), 524 (2), 529 (3), 531 (2), 557 (3), 586 (2), 588 (1), 590 (3)
letters patent 737 (4), 756 (2)
letting 784 (1)
letting go 779 (1)
lettuce 301 (20)
letup 145 (4)
leucorrhoea 302 (2)
leukaemia 651 (10)
levee 253 (5)
level 16 (2), 16 (4), 27 (1), 28 (7), 28 (10), 73 (1), 123 (3), 165 (7), 207 (1), 216 (1), 216 (4), 216 (7), 247 (3), 258 (3), 258 (4), 281 (7), 311 (6), 398 (1), 823 (3)

level at 281 (7), 617 (6)
level bet 28 (2)
level crossing 222 (1)
level-headed 498 (5), 823 (3), 858 (2)
level off 37 (5), 198 (6)
level out 216 (6)
level-pegging 28 (5), 28 (7)
level temper 823 (1)
level up or down 16 (4)
level with 54 (4)
levelling 165 (1)
levelness 16 (1), 28 (1), 210 (1), 258 (1)
levels 348 (1)
lever 137 (2), 156 (5), 178 (1), 218 (3), 218 (11), 287 (3), 304 (2), 310 (2), 628 (2), 630 (1)
lever out 304 (4)
leverage 34 (2), 178 (1)
leviable 809 (4)
leviathan 84 (4), 195 (4)
levitate 308 (4), 323 (4)
levitation 308 (1)
levity 456 (1), 499 (2), 604 (1), 833 (2)
levy 74 (1), 737 (3), 737 (8), 761 (5), 761 (6), 771 (7), 786 (1), 786 (8), 809 (3), 809 (7)
levy a rate 809 (7)
lewd 951 (6), 951 (8)
lewdness 951 (2)
lexical 559 (4)
lexically 559 (5)
lexicographer 559 (3)
lexicography 557 (2), 559 (3)
lexicographical 559 (4)
lexicon 87 (2), 520 (2), 559 (2), 589 (4)
liability 179 (1), 180 (1), 661 (2), 803 (1), 936 (1), 963 (4)
liable 180 (2), 469 (2), 471 (2), 661 (5), 745 (5), 803 (4), 917 (5), 963 (7)
liable, be 180 (3), 661 (7)
liable for, be 803 (6)
liaison 181 (1), 887 (3), 951 (3)

liar 541 (1), 545 (2), 546 (1), 877 (3), 938 (2)

liar, be a 543 (5)

libation 301 (25), 981 (6)

libel 926 (2), 926 (7), 928 (2)

libeller 926 (4)

libellous 926 (5)

liberal 635 (4), 654 (5), 744 (4), 781 (5), 806 (2), 813 (3), 815 (3), 897 (4), 901 (6), 931 (2), 962 (2)

liberal, be 637 (5), 781 (7), 806 (4), 813 (4), 882 (10), 962 (3)

liberal donor 813 (2)

liberal education 490 (3), 534 (2)

liberalism 654 (4), 744 (1)

liberality 781 (1), 813 (1), 882 (2), 897 (1), 931 (1)

liberalization 746 (1)

liberalize 746 (3)

liberally 744 (11), 813 (5)

liberalness 813 (1)

liberals 708 (2)

liberate 46 (8), 304 (4), 668 (3), 701 (9), 744 (10), 746 (3), 756 (5), 779 (4), 919 (3), 960 (3)

liberated 49 (2), 744 (5), 746 (2), 779 (3), 960 (2)

liberation 46 (2), 272 (1), 304 (1), 667 (1), 668 (1), 734 (1), 744 (1), 746 (1), 756 (1), 779 (1), 960 (1)

libertarian 744 (4)

libertine 372 (1), 545 (1), 837 (17), 859 (6), 887 (4), 938 (1), 944 (2), 952 (1)

liberty 744 (1), 744 (3), 756 (1), 915 (1)

liberty horse 273 (4)

libidinous 951 (8)

libido 859 (4), 887 (1), 951 (2)

Libra 321 (5)

librarian 492 (3), 589 (6), 690 (3)

library 74 (7), 194 (19), 539 (4), 589 (4), 589 (5), 632 (3), 687 (1)

librettist 413 (1), 589 (7), 593 (6), 594 (13)

libretto 589 (2), 594 (3)

licence 734 (2), 744 (1), 744 (3), 756 (1), 756 (2), 915 (1), 919 (1), 951 (2)

license 744 (10), 746 (3), 751 (4), 756 (5), 919 (3)

licensed 756 (4), 953 (5)

licensee 754 (1), 782 (2)

licensing laws 757 (1)

licentious 744 (5), 944 (3), 951 (8)

licentiousness 944 (1), 951 (2)

lichen 366 (6)

licit 915 (2)

lick 301 (35), 341 (7), 378 (7), 727 (10)

lick into shape 534 (6), 669 (11)

lick one's boots 879 (4)

lick one's fingers 386 (3)

lick one's lips 376 (6)

lick one's lips or one's chops 947 (4)

lick one's wounds 377 (6)

lick the dust 721 (4)

licked 728 (5)

licking 279 (2), 378 (5)

lid 226 (1), 264 (2)

lid off 526 (1)

lie 7 (4), 175 (3), 186 (4), 189 (4), 216 (6), 535 (3), 541 (5), 543 (1), 543 (5), 552 (3), 928 (2)

lie ahead 124 (5)

lie around 230 (3)

lie beneath 224 (4)

lie between 231 (7), 702 (9)

lie detector 484 (2)

lie doggo 525 (9)

lie down 216 (6)

lie fallow 172 (5), 677 (3)

lie flat 210 (3)

lie heavy 322 (5)

lie hidden 523 (5)

lie idle 677 (3)

lie in ambush 444 (4), 523 (5)

lie in wait 527 (5), 542 (10)

lie low 446 (3), 523 (5), 660 (9), 667 (6), 698 (5)

lie of the land 8 (1)

lie off 199 (5)

lie on 218 (16)

lie opposite 240 (3)

lie parallel 219 (3)

lie still 266 (7)

lie to 266 (7), 269 (10)

lie with 45 (14)

lie within 224 (4)

liege 741 (1), 742 (5), 745 (5)

lieutenant 270 (3), 703 (3), 707 (1), 722 (5), 741 (7), 741 (8), 755 (1)

lieutenant-colonel 741 (8)

lieutenant-commander 741 (7)

lieutenant-general 741 (8)

lieutenant-governor 741 (5)

life 1 (1), 3 (2), 154 (2), 162 (2), 335 (3), 358 (1), 360 (1), 590 (3), 678 (1), 678 (2)

life belt 662 (3)

life cycle 141 (2), 147 (2), 360 (1)

life expectancy 360 (1)

life force 360 (1)

life-giving 167 (4)

life jacket 662 (3)

life peer 692 (3)

life peerage 868 (2)

life peeress 868 (5)

life raft 275 (9), 662 (3)

life-saver 666 (2)

life-saving 668 (1)

life sentence 110 (1), 113 (1)

life-size 32 (4), 195 (1), 195 (6)

life span 131 (1), 360 (1)

life support machine 658 (13)

life to come 124 (2)

life together 894 (1)

life work 622 (2)

lifeblood 5 (2), 335 (3), 360 (1)

lifeboat 275 (7), 662 (3)

lifeboatman 270 (3)

lifeguard 660 (3), 713 (6)
lifeless 175 (2), 361 (6), 679 (7)
lifelessness 679 (2)
lifelike 18 (5)
lifeline 47 (1), 662 (3)
lifelong 113 (4)
lifelong friend 880 (3)
lifer 750 (1), 904 (3)
lifestyle 610 (1), 624 (1)
lifestyles 688 (1)
lifetime 108 (1), 110 (1), 360 (1)
lifetime, a 113 (1)
lift 188 (4), 267 (6), 273 (12), 285 (1), 288 (3), 308 (1), 310 (1), 310 (2), 310 (4), 417 (13), 654 (1), 703 (1), 788 (7), 831 (3)
lift cattle 788 (7)
lift controls 746 (3)
lift-off 271 (3), 271 (7), 308 (1)
lift oneself 308 (4), 310 (5)
lift the veil 526 (4)
lift up 310 (4)
lifter 217 (3), 218 (5), 274 (15), 288 (1), 308 (1), 310 (2), 315 (3), 323 (1)
ligament 47 (4), 778 (1)
ligature 47 (4), 61 (3)
light 4 (3), 7 (2), 33 (6), 128 (1), 263 (5), 308 (3), 323 (3), 381 (9), 385 (3), 417 (1), 417 (8), 417 (13), 419 (3), 420 (5), 420 (9), 425 (7), 445 (1), 465 (3), 701 (5), 841 (1), 965 (2), 975 (1)
light and shade 417 (6)
light artillery 723 (11)
light as a feather 323 (3)
light, be 29 (3), 198 (6), 323 (4)
light blue 435 (3)
light breeze 352 (3)
light brown 430 (3)
light candles to 981 (11)
light comedy 594 (3)
light contrast 417 (6)
light entertainment 837 (1)
light-fingered 788 (6)

light fingers 788 (5)
light fitting 420 (4)
light-footed 323 (3), 678 (7)
light-grey 429 (2)
light hand 736 (1)
light-handed 378 (5)
light-headed 456 (6)
light heart 833 (1)
light-hearted 833 (3)
light horse 722 (10)
light meal 301 (12)
light meter 442 (1)
light-minded 61 (7), 152 (3), 456 (4), 499 (4), 503 (8), 601 (3), 604 (3), 670 (3), 833 (4), 839 (4), 851 (4), 857 (3)
light music 412 (1)
light of nature 461 (2), 476 (1)
light of touch 378 (5)
light of truth 494 (1)
light on 636 (3)
light opera 412 (5), 594 (3)
light railway 624 (7)
light reading 590 (4)
light rein 736 (1)
light relief 849 (1)
light sentence 905 (3)
light-skinned 426 (3)
light sleep 679 (4)
light the way 283 (3)
light touch 378 (1)
light tread 312 (1)
light up 417 (13), 420 (9)
light upon 159 (7), 771 (7)
light verse 593 (2), 849 (1)
light work 701 (2)
light year 203 (4)
light years 199 (1)
lighten 177 (7), 198 (7), 323 (5), 417 (13), 701 (9), 786 (9), 831 (3)
lighten ship 323 (5)
lighter 275 (7), 381 (2), 383 (1), 385 (3), 420 (3)
lighter than air 323 (3)
lightheartedness 833 (1)
lighthouse 269 (4), 420 (6)
lighthouse keeper 270 (3)
lighting 417 (1), 420 (5)

lightness 26 (1), 323 (1), 325 (1), 426 (1)
lightning 160 (5), 277 (1), 420 (1)
lightning flash 417 (2)
lightning speed 277 (1)
lightning strike 145 (3)
lights 498 (1)
lights out 418 (2), 547 (8)
lightship 269 (4), 420 (6)
lightweight 33 (7), 323 (3), 639 (4), 639 (6)
likable 859 (10), 887 (11)
like 9 (5), 18 (4), 18 (9), 376 (6), 824 (6), 859 (11), 880 (7), 887 (13)
like a fish 269 (7)
like a flash 116 (3), 116 (4), 277 (5)
like a shot 116 (4), 277 (9)
like best 605 (6)
like better 605 (6)
like clockwork 16 (5), 141 (4), 701 (10)
like company 882 (8)
like for like 714 (1), 714 (2)
like gold dust 140 (2)
like ice 380 (6)
like mad 176 (3)
like magic 864 (5)
like-minded 24 (5)
like new 126 (5), 126 (9), 656 (6)
like parchment 330 (2)
like, the 18 (3)
like this 8 (4)
like wildfire 277 (9)
liked 859 (10), 887 (11)
likelihood 180 (1), 469 (1), 471 (1)
likely 471 (2), 485 (5), 852 (5)
likely, be 179 (3), 469 (3), 471 (4), 475 (9), 852 (7)
liken 9 (8), 13 (4), 16 (4), 18 (8), 462 (3), 519 (4)
likened 462 (2)
likeness 18 (1), 18 (3), 28 (2), 462 (1), 519 (1), 551 (1)
likeness, a 22 (1)
likening 18 (2), 462 (1)

liquefiable **337** (3)
liquefied **337** (3)
liquefier **337** (1)
liquefy **49** (4), **51** (5), **327** (4), **337** (4), **350** (11), **381** (8)
liquescent **335** (4), **337** (3)
liqueur **301** (28)
liquid **244** (2), **335** (2), **335** (4), **422** (2)
liquid assets **777** (2), **797** (2), **800** (1)
liquid nutriment **301** (9)
liquidate **165** (6), **362** (11), **804** (4)
liquidation **165** (1), **362** (4), **804** (1)
liquidator **798** (1)
liquidity **335** (1), **629** (1), **797** (2)
liquidization **337** (1)
liquidize **301** (40), **337** (4)
liquidizer **337** (1)
liquidness **335** (1)
liquor **174** (4), **949** (1)
liquorice **301** (18)
lisp **577** (4), **580** (1), **580** (3)
lisping **577** (2)
lissom **327** (3), **841** (5)
list **29** (3), **52** (2), **62** (1), **62** (6), **80** (8), **86** (4), **86** (11), **87** (1), **87** (5), **117** (4), **193** (1), **220** (1), **220** (5), **234** (3), **548** (1), **548** (8), **590** (1), **592** (1), **808** (1), **808** (5)
list of items **87** (1)
list of names **87** (1)
listed **78** (3), **87** (4)
listed building **666** (1)
listen **415** (6), **455** (4), **739** (4), **979** (9)
listen in **415** (6), **453** (4)
listen to **691** (5)
listen to reason **475** (9), **498** (6)
listened to **178** (2)
listened to, be **178** (3)
listener **415** (3), **453** (2), **466** (4), **583** (1)
listening **415** (2), **415** (5), **584** (3)

listening-in **415** (2)
listing **29** (2), **87** (1)
listless **163** (6), **679** (7), **834** (5), **860** (2)
listlessness **679** (2)
lists **716** (6)
lit **379** (5), **381** (6), **417** (8), **624** (8)
litany **981** (4)
literacy **490** (3)
literal **20** (4), **481** (7), **494** (4), **494** (6), **514** (4), **520** (6), **558** (5), **559** (4), **586** (7), **699** (3), **768** (2), **976** (8)
literal meaning **514** (2)
literality **494** (3), **514** (2)
literally **494** (8), **514** (6)
literalness **494** (3), **979** (3)
literary **490** (6), **520** (6), **557** (5), **557** (6), **566** (2)
literary composition **586** (1)
literary criticism **520** (1)
literary genre **557** (3)
literary output **586** (1)
literary person **589** (6)
literary style **566** (1)
literary theft **788** (1)
literate **490** (6)
literate, be **586** (8)
literati **492** (2)
literature **490** (3), **520** (1), **524** (1), **557** (3), **586** (1)
lithe **327** (3)
litheness **327** (1)
lithograph **22** (1), **551** (1), **555** (3)
lithography **555** (2), **587** (1)
litigable **959** (6)
litigant **928** (3), **959** (4), **959** (5)
litigate **709** (7), **737** (6), **928** (9), **959** (7)
litigated **959** (6)
litigating **709** (6), **959** (5)
litigation **475** (4), **709** (3), **928** (1), **953** (1), **959** (1)
litigious **709** (6), **959** (5)
litigiousness **709** (2), **959** (1)
litmus paper **461** (4)

litotes **519** (2)
litre **465** (3)
litter **41** (2), **61** (2), **63** (4), **74** (3), **75** (3), **132** (3), **170** (1), **218** (7), **274** (1), **641** (3), **649** (2)
litter bearer **273** (2)
litter lout **649** (5)
litter-strewn **842** (4)
littered **649** (7)
litterlout **61** (5)
little **33** (6), **33** (9), **132** (5), **140** (3), **196** (8), **204** (3)
little, a **33** (10)
little angel **132** (1)
little at a time, a **53** (9)
little, be **33** (8), **196** (12)
little bird **524** (4)
little by little **27** (6), **278** (8)
little chance **472** (1)
little devil **904** (1)
little finger **378** (4)
little girl **373** (3)
little green men **59** (2)
little imp **132** (1)
little learning, a **491** (3)
little man **869** (5)
little minx **132** (2)
little monkey **132** (1)
little one **132** (1)
little ones **170** (1)
little people **196** (4), **970** (1)
littleness **33** (1), **35** (1), **196** (1), **204** (1), **210** (1), **444** (1)
liturgical **988** (8)
liturgically **988** (12)
liturgy **988** (1), **988** (4), **988** (5)
live **1** (6), **108** (8), **121** (4), **160** (9), **173** (2), **192** (21), **360** (2), **360** (4), **594** (15)
live ammunition **723** (12)
live apart **896** (5)
live at **186** (4)
live cartridge **723** (12)
live for **887** (13), **931** (3)
live for ever **115** (4)
live for pleasure **944** (4)
live from hand to mouth **801** (5)

live in 192 (21), 742 (8)
live in clover 730 (6)
live in comfort 376 (6)
live in hopes 852 (6)
live in purdah 883 (8)
live in the present 121 (3)
live it up 837 (23), 882 (8), 943 (3)
live like a hermit 945 (1)
live on 301 (35), 505 (11)
live relay 531 (4)
live single 895 (5)
live through 108 (7), 656 (8), 818 (7)
live under 745 (6)
live well 944 (4)
live wire 160 (5), 174 (1), 678 (5)
live with 45 (14), 89 (4)
lived 818 (6)
lived in 191 (7)
livelihood 622 (2)
liveliness 162 (2), 174 (1), 360 (1), 571 (1), 678 (2), 819 (1), 833 (1)
livelong 113 (4)
livelong day, the 113 (11)
lively 174 (5), 277 (5), 312 (3), 360 (2), 374 (4), 571 (2), 678 (7), 678 (8), 818 (3), 819 (4), 822 (3), 833 (3), 839 (4), 871 (3), 882 (6)
lively imagination 513 (1)
lively-minded 819 (4)
liven 360 (6)
liven up 833 (7)
liver 224 (2)
liveried 16 (2), 228 (29)
liverish 892 (3)
liverishness 651 (7)
livery 228 (5), 547 (10), 743 (3)
livery company 794 (1)
livestock 365 (2), 365 (7)
livid 426 (3), 428 (5), 429 (2), 435 (3), 436 (2), 821 (3), 891 (4)
lividity 435 (1)
living 1 (4), 360 (1), 360 (2), 557 (5), 622 (2), 777 (2)

living apart 896 (1), 896 (3)
living at 186 (3)
living being 360 (1)
living death 825 (1)
living for kicks 944 (3)
living image 18 (3), 91 (1)
living matter 358 (1), 360 (1)
living model 23 (2)
living out 190 (1)
living quarters 192 (2)
living room 194 (19)
living soul 371 (3)
living space 744 (3)
living, the 360 (1), 371 (1)
living thing 365 (2)
living wage 635 (1)
lizard 365 (13)
load 26 (2), 32 (2), 38 (1), 54 (7), 74 (6), 187 (7), 193 (1), 193 (2), 272 (3), 272 (7), 303 (4), 322 (1), 322 (5), 322 (6), 324 (6), 632 (1), 632 (6), 669 (11), 702 (4), 731 (1), 825 (3)
load the dice 542 (8)
loaded 273 (10), 322 (4), 800 (4)
loaded question 459 (3)
loaded table 301 (2)
loading 187 (1)
loads 32 (2), 104 (1)
loadstone 288 (1)
loaf 301 (22), 679 (11)
loafer 679 (6)
loafing 677 (1), 679 (1), 679 (8)
loam 344 (3)
loamy 344 (5)
loan 703 (2), 784 (1), 784 (5), 785 (1), 802 (1)
loan shark 784 (3)
loan word 559 (1), 560 (1)
loaned 560 (4), 784 (4)
loath 598 (3), 861 (2)
loathe 861 (4), 888 (7)
loathed 888 (6)
loathing 838 (1), 838 (4), 861 (1), 861 (2), 881 (1), 881 (3), 888 (1), 888 (4)
loathsome 645 (4), 827 (4), 842 (3), 861 (3), 888 (5)

loathsomeness 827 (1), 888 (2)
lob 287 (7), 310 (4)
lobby 68 (5), 178 (1), 178 (3), 194 (20), 612 (5), 612 (9), 763 (1)
lobby against 762 (3)
lobbying 612 (2)
lobbyist 612 (5), 671 (2), 763 (1)
lobe 217 (2)
local 76 (1), 184 (5), 186 (3), 191 (3), 192 (12), 192 (19), 200 (4), 560 (5)
local anaesthetic 375 (2)
local authority 955 (1)
local branch 708 (3)
local colour 590 (1)
local god 967 (2)
local inhabitant 191 (3)
local time 117 (2)
locale 186 (1)
locality 184 (1), 184 (3), 185 (1), 187 (2), 192 (1), 200 (3)
localization 187 (1)
localize 187 (5)
locally 185 (2), 200 (7)
locate 80 (8), 187 (5), 281 (4), 484 (4)
locate oneself 187 (8)
located 186 (3), 187 (4), 281 (3)
located at 186 (3)
locating 187 (1)
location 62 (1), 185 (1), 186 (1), 186 (2), 187 (1)
loch 346 (1)
Loch Ness monster 84 (4)
lock 264 (2), 264 (6), 351 (1), 778 (1), 778 (5)
lock and key 47 (5)
lock horns 716 (11)
lock keeper 270 (4)
lock of hair 208 (1)
lock, stock and barrel 52 (2)
lock up 525 (7), 747 (10), 963 (8)
locked up 747 (6)
locker 194 (4), 194 (7)
locket 844 (7)
lockjaw 651 (5)

lockout 57 (1), 145 (3)
locks 259 (2)
lockup 748 (2)
locomotion 265 (1)
locomotive 160 (9), 265
(3), 267 (9), 274 (14), 274
(16), 288 (1)
locum 150 (2), 658 (14)
locus classicus 83 (2)
locust 168 (1), 365 (16),
659 (1)
locution 559 (1), 563 (1)
lode 207 (1), 632 (1)
lodestar 291 (2), 547 (7)
lodestone 291 (2)
lodge 187 (5), 187 (8), 192
(6), 192 (7), 192 (21), 266
(7), 708 (3)
lodge a complaint 928 (9)
lodged 187 (4)
lodger 191 (2), 776 (1)
lodging 192 (2)
lodging house 192 (2)
lodgings 192 (2)
loft 194 (22), 310 (4)
loftiness 34 (1), 209 (1),
571 (1), 871 (1), 878 (1),
931 (1)
lofty 32 (4), 209 (8), 310
(3), 546 (2), 571 (2), 866
(8), 871 (3), 922 (3), 931
(2)
log 269 (4), 385 (1), 548
(1), 548 (8)
log cabin 192 (7)
log-line 465 (5)
log-rolling 706 (1)
logarithm 85 (2)
logarithmic 85 (5)
logarithms 86 (3)
logbook 548 (1)
logic 24 (2), 475 (1), 596
(1)
logical 9 (6), 449 (6), 471
(3), 475 (7), 494 (4), 596
(4)
logical necessity 596 (1)
logical order 60 (1)
logicality 9 (3)
logically 475 (13)
logician 475 (6)
logistics 633 (1), 718 (4)
logjam 702 (2)

logrolling 151 (1)
loin 238 (2)
loincloth 228 (14)
loins 167 (3)
loiter 136 (4), 525 (9), 679
(11)
loiterer 278 (2)
loll 216 (6), 217 (5), 679
(11), 683 (3)
lollipop 301 (18)
lone 88 (3), 88 (4)
lone wolf 883 (3)
loneliness 883 (2)
lonely 88 (4), 190 (5), 883
(5), 883 (6), 883 (7)
lonely heart 883 (3)
lonely person 883 (3)
loner 84 (3), 883 (3)
lonesome 88 (4), 883 (6)
long 32 (4), 113 (4), 113
(10), 203 (5), 206 (4), 570
(4), 834 (9), 838 (3), 859
(11)
long ago 113 (12), 125 (12)
long arm 203 (1)
long-awaited 113 (5)
long, be 203 (7)
long-distance 199 (3)
long dozen 99 (2)
long-drawn out 203 (5),
570 (4)
long drink 301 (26)
long duration 108 (1), 110
(1), 111 (1), 113 (1), 115
(1), 131 (1)
long expected 507 (3)
long face 834 (1)
long-faced 834 (6)
long for 830 (4)
long haul 682 (3)
long innings 113 (2)
long johns 228 (17)
long jump 312 (1)
long-legged 203 (5), 206
(4), 209 (9), 267 (10)
long life 650 (1)
long-lived 113 (4), 360 (2)
long measure 203 (4), 465
(1)
long-necked 209 (9)
long odds 159 (3), 472 (1)
long-pending 113 (5)
long period 110 (1)

long-range 199 (3)
long rope 744 (3)
long run 113 (2), 124 (1),
594 (2)
long-service 113 (4)
long shot 287 (1), 472 (1)
long sight 438 (1), 440 (1)
long-sighted 440 (3)
long since 113 (12)
long standing 113 (2), 127
(6), 144 (1), 144 (2)
long suit 644 (1)
long-term 113 (4)
long time, a 113 (1)
long use 673 (1)
long wait 113 (3)
long way 199 (1)
long way round 282 (1)
long while, a 125 (12)
long-winded 570 (4), 576
(2), 581 (4), 838 (3)
long word 559 (1)
long-worded 574 (4)
long words 574 (2)
longed for 507 (3)
longevity 113 (1), 131 (3),
650 (1)
longhand 586 (1)
longing 825 (1), 825 (6),
830 (1), 859 (1), 859 (7)
longitude 203 (1)
longitudinal 203 (6)
longlasting 115 (2)
longminded 113 (5)
longmindedness 570 (1)
longship 275 (2)
longshoreman 270 (4)
longsuffering 736 (2), 823
(2)
longueurs 838 (1)
longways 203 (9)
longwise 203 (9)
loo 649 (3)
loofah 648 (5)
look 18 (1), 243 (1), 438
(3), 438 (4), 438 (8), 438
(11), 445 (1), 445 (5), 455
(1), 547 (4), 858 (3)
look a fright 842 (6)
look a mess 842 (6)
look a wreck 842 (6)
look after 455 (5), 457 (6),
660 (8), 666 (5)

look after oneself **932** (4)
look ahead **124** (6)
look as if **18** (7)
look askance **438** (8)
look askance at **861** (4)
look at **438** (8), **441** (3)
look away **438** (8)
look back **125** (11), **286** (5), **505** (8), **830** (4)
look black **818** (8), **891** (7), **924** (9)
look blank **525** (8)
look blue **818** (8)
look daggers **891** (7), **900** (3), **924** (9)
look down on **871** (5), **878** (6), **921** (5), **922** (5)
look downcast **834** (9)
look foolish **499** (6)
look for **453** (4), **459** (13), **459** (15), **471** (6), **507** (4), **510** (3), **617** (5), **619** (5), **761** (5), **859** (11)
look for trouble **709** (8)
look forward **124** (6), **852** (6)
look forward to **507** (4)
look glum **829** (5), **834** (10)
look grave **834** (10)
look-in **137** (2), **297** (5), **441** (3), **882** (9)
look in on **189** (4)
look in the face **855** (6)
look into **459** (13)
look kindly on **730** (8)
look like **18** (7)
look of things **8** (1), **445** (1)
look on **161** (8), **189** (4), **438** (7), **441** (3), **488** (7), **677** (3)
look on the bright side **833** (7)
look one up **882** (9)
look one up and down **438** (9)
look out **457** (7), **664** (7), **858** (3)
look out for **438** (9), **507** (4)
look over **438** (9)
look pale **818** (8)
look right **848** (7)
look sharp **680** (5)

look sideways **220** (5)
look silly **849** (4)
look so **445** (8)
look through **438** (9)
look to **917** (11)
look twice **858** (3)
look up to **866** (13), **920** (5)
look upon **438** (8)
look upon as **485** (8)
look volumes **547** (21)
lookalike **18** (3)
looked down on **921** (4)
looked for **124** (4)
looker **441** (1)
looking ahead **124** (3), **510** (2), **617** (1)
looking back **125** (1), **125** (9)
looking for **619** (1)
looking for kicks **822** (3)
looking glass **442** (5)
looking like new **126** (7)
looking on **189** (2)
looking one's best **844** (11)
looking round **438** (4)
looking up **654** (6)
lookout **209** (4), **270** (2), **438** (5), **441** (1), **457** (2), **507** (1), **660** (3), **664** (2)
looks **445** (5)
loom **155** (3), **222** (4), **222** (5), **222** (9), **440** (5)
loom large **195** (10)
loom up **32** (15), **443** (4)
looming **419** (5), **471** (2)
loony **503** (8), **504** (1)
loop **47** (1), **218** (3), **248** (2), **248** (4), **250** (3), **251** (12), **263** (4), **314** (1), **626** (1)
loop the loop **221** (4), **271** (7)
loophole **263** (5), **298** (3), **614** (1), **623** (3), **647** (2), **667** (2), **713** (3), **954** (1)
looping **251** (4)
looping the loop **271** (1)
loose **46** (4), **46** (8), **49** (2), **49** (3), **79** (3), **152** (4), **217** (4), **477** (6), **734** (3), **744** (5), **746** (3), **951** (7)
loose-box **274** (5)
loose ends **726** (1)

loose-fitting **49** (2)
loose-knit **570** (4)
loose-limbed **327** (3)
loose morals **934** (1)
loose off at **287** (8)
loose rendering **520** (3)
loose talk **951** (1)
loose thinking **477** (2), **481** (1), **495** (2)
loose woman **373** (3), **938** (1), **952** (2)
loosen **37** (4), **46** (8), **49** (3), **163** (10), **746** (3)
loosened **46** (4)
looseness **46** (1), **49** (1), **79** (1), **495** (2)
loosening **46** (2), **49** (1), **734** (1)
loosing **46** (2)
loot **786** (9), **788** (9), **790** (1)
looter **786** (4)
looting **788** (3)
lop **46** (11), **204** (5)
lop-eared **217** (4)
lop-sided **695** (5)
lop-sidedness **246** (1)
lope **265** (2), **267** (3), **277** (6)
lopsided **29** (2)
lopsidedness **29** (1)
loquacious **524** (7), **526** (3), **570** (3), **579** (6), **581** (4), **584** (5)
loquacious, be **515** (6), **524** (9), **528** (9), **570** (6), **579** (8), **581** (5), **584** (6), **702** (10)
loquaciously **581** (6)
loquacity **570** (1), **579** (1), **581** (1)
lord **372** (1), **741** (1), **776** (2)
Lord Chancellor **955** (2)
lord it **735** (8), **866** (12), **871** (5)
lord it over **733** (12)
lord mayor **741** (6)
lord of creation **871** (2)
lordly **733** (7), **733** (8), **813** (3), **868** (6), **871** (3), **878** (4)
lords **868** (2)

Lord's day 683 (1)
Lords Spiritual 692 (3)
Lords Temporal 692 (3)
lordship 868 (5), 870 (1)
lore 127 (3), 490 (2), 536 (1), 698 (1)
lorgnette 442 (2)
lorry 274 (12)
lorry driver 268 (5), 273 (1)
lose 37 (5), 188 (5), 277 (8), 495 (7), 621 (3), 728 (7), 728 (9), 772 (4)
lose a chance 136 (4), 138 (6), 728 (7), 772 (4)
lose an opportunity 138 (6)
lose colour 419 (6), 426 (4)
lose consciousness 375 (5)
lose control 734 (5)
lose face 35 (5), 867 (9)
lose ground 278 (5), 307 (3), 728 (9)
lose hands down 728 (9)
lose heart 834 (9), 853 (4)
lose heat 380 (7)
lose height 309 (3)
lose hope 853 (4)
lose interest 621 (3)
lose its flavour 655 (7)
lose its novelty 838 (5)
lose its savour 391 (3)
lose momentum 278 (5)
lose no time 135 (5), 680 (3)
lose one's balance 309 (4)
lose one's bearings 282 (5)
lose one's bet 772 (4)
lose one's eyes 439 (3)
lose one's faith 974 (7)
lose one's good name 867 (9)
lose one's head 503 (11)
lose one's heart 887 (14)
lose one's life 361 (8)
lose one's looks 842 (6)
lose one's memory 506 (5)
lose one's nerve 695 (7), 856 (4)
lose one's reason 503 (11)
lose one's seat 728 (9)
lose one's sight 439 (3)
lose one's stake 772 (4)

lose one's temper 885 (6), 891 (6)
lose one's tongue 578 (3), 582 (3)
lose one's voice 399 (3), 578 (3)
lose one's wits 499 (6), 503 (11)
lose out 728 (9)
lose patience 891 (6)
lose prestige 867 (9)
lose repute 35 (5), 867 (9), 924 (14), 930 (8)
lose sight of 439 (3), 456 (7), 506 (5)
lose strength 651 (23)
lose the baby 167 (6)
lose the battle 728 (9)
lose the day 728 (9)
lose the scent 395 (3), 474 (8)
lose the thread 10 (5), 456 (7), 474 (8)
lose the way 267 (13), 282 (5)
lose touch with 188 (5)
lose track of 188 (5), 456 (7)
lose weight 198 (6), 206 (7), 323 (5)
loser 697 (1), 728 (3), 731 (3), 867 (3)
losers, the 728 (3)
losing 118 (2), 161 (6), 495 (6), 641 (5), 772 (2)
losing balance 29 (2)
losing battle 728 (2)
losing ground 655 (1)
losing height 271 (6)
losing one's touch 695 (5)
losing side 728 (3)
losing weight 301 (3)
loss 37 (1), 42 (1), 55 (2), 165 (3), 172 (1), 190 (1), 307 (1), 446 (1), 616 (1), 634 (1), 641 (1), 655 (3), 772 (1), 774 (1), 803 (1), 916 (3)
loss-making 641 (5)
loss of condition 651 (1)
loss of control 161 (2)
loss of face 867 (1)
loss of faith 486 (1)

loss of freedom 745 (1)
loss of health 651 (2)
loss of honour 867 (1)
loss of hope 853 (1)
loss of innocence 934 (1)
loss of life 361 (2)
loss of memory 506 (1)
loss of nerve 601 (1), 854 (2)
loss of rank 867 (1)
loss of reason 503 (1)
loss of right 916 (3)
loss of speech 580 (1)
loss of strength 163 (1)
loss of value 37 (1)
loss of voice 578 (1)
lost 46 (5), 55 (3), 125 (6), 165 (5), 188 (3), 190 (4), 282 (2), 474 (6), 772 (3), 940 (2)
lost battle 728 (2)
lost, be 165 (11), 361 (8), 772 (5)
lost cause 607 (1), 728 (2)
lost connection 72 (1)
lost election 607 (1)
lost habit 611 (1)
lost in thought 449 (5), 456 (4)
lost in thought, be 456 (7)
lost in wonder 864 (4)
lost labour 172 (1), 497 (1), 499 (2), 641 (2), 695 (2), 728 (1)
lost sheep 938 (1)
lost skill 611 (1)
lost soul 938 (1), 969 (2)
lost to sight 446 (2)
lost to sight, be 446 (3)
lost to view 199 (3), 446 (2)
lot 7 (1), 26 (2), 32 (2), 74 (3), 74 (6), 74 (7), 77 (2), 159 (1), 184 (2), 235 (1), 596 (2), 618 (1), 783 (2)
lot, the 52 (2)
lotion 339 (1), 658 (8)
lots 32 (2), 104 (1), 635 (2)
lottery 159 (2), 618 (1), 618 (2)
lotto 837 (11)
loud 32 (4), 176 (5), 398 (3), 400 (3), 404 (2), 407 (2), 408 (2), 409 (2), 425

(6), 574 (4), 574 (5), 847
(4), 847 (5)
loud, be 398 (4), 400 (4),
402 (4), 404 (3), 407 (5),
408 (4), 415 (7), 416 (4),
528 (10), 532 (7), 577 (4),
702 (10)
loud hailer 528 (2)
loud-mouthed 400 (3)
loud noise 400 (1)
loud pedal 400 (2)
loud report 400 (1)
loud-spoken 579 (6)
loudhailer 400 (2)
loudly 32 (19), 400 (5)
loudmouth 877 (3)
loudness 61 (4), 176 (2),
318 (3), 398 (1), 400 (1),
402 (1), 404 (1), 407 (1),
408 (1), 411 (1), 577 (1),
847 (1)
loudspeaker 398 (1), 400
(2), 415 (4), 528 (2)
lough 346 (1)
lounge 194 (19), 679 (11),
683 (3)
lounge suit 228 (9)
lounger 218 (6), 679 (6)
lour 155 (3), 217 (5), 418
(5), 511 (8), 893 (1)
louring 418 (3)
louse 365 (16), 938 (3)
lousy 645 (4), 649 (6)
lout 501 (3), 697 (1), 885
(3), 904 (2)
loutish 847 (5), 885 (4)
louvre 353 (1)
lovable 821 (4), 826 (2),
841 (6), 884 (4), 887 (11)
lovable, be 887 (15)
lovableness 887 (2)
love 103 (1), 710 (1), 818
(1), 819 (1), 859 (3), 859
(11), 864 (1), 866 (13), 880
(1), 880 (7), 887 (1), 887
(4), 887 (5), 887 (13), 889
(5), 889 (6), 889 (7), 890
(1), 897 (1), 911 (1), 923
(1), 931 (1)
love affair 887 (3), 951 (3)
love all 28 (5)
love child 170 (2)
love emblem 887 (8)

love game 727 (2)
love god 887 (7)
love-hate 14 (3), 888 (1)
love letter 588 (1), 889 (2)
love-match 894 (2)
love of pleasure 944 (1)
love of truth 540 (1)
love philtre 174 (4)
love-play 889 (2)
love poem 889 (2)
love song 889 (2)
love story 590 (4)
love token 729 (1), 887 (8),
889 (3)
lovebirds 887 (6)
loved one 373 (3), 859 (5),
880 (3), 887 (5), 890 (1),
894 (4)
loveless 860 (3), 888 (6)
loveliness 826 (1), 841 (1)
lovelorn 887 (9)
lovely 376 (3), 644 (4), 644
(5), 826 (2), 841 (3), 887
(11)
lovely, a 841 (2)
lovemaking 889 (2)
lover 859 (6), 887 (4)
lovers 887 (6)
lovers' vows 889 (1)
lovesick 887 (9)
lovesickness 887 (1)
loving 457 (3), 710 (2), 880
(6), 887 (9), 889 (4), 897
(4), 965 (6)
loving couple 887 (6)
loving cup 194 (15)
loving it 824 (4)
loving-kindness 897 (1)
loving words 889 (1)
lovingly 887 (16)
low 33 (6), 35 (4), 163 (4),
204 (3), 210 (2), 214 (3),
311 (3), 401 (3), 409 (3),
410 (6), 645 (4), 834 (5),
847 (4), 867 (4)
low, be 33 (8), 210 (3), 309
(3)
low blood pressure 651 (9)
low-born 869 (8)
low-budget 812 (3)
low-caste 35 (4), 869 (8)
Low-Church 976 (10), 978
(6)

low-density 105 (2)
low-down 930 (5)
low elevation 210 (1)
low esteem 921 (1)
low fellow 869 (7), 904 (2),
938 (2)
low gear 278 (1)
low-geared 278 (3)
low-grade 35 (4)
low IQ 499 (1)
low-key 177 (3)
low-level 35 (4), 210 (2),
639 (5)
low-life 590 (6), 934 (1)
low-loader 274 (12)
low-lying 210 (2)
low mental age 499 (1)
low morale 856 (1)
low opinion 924 (1)
low-paid 801 (3)
low-pressure 175 (2), 325
(1), 325 (2), 340 (3)
low price 812 (1)
low-priced 812 (3)
low profile 525 (2)
low rainfall 342 (1)
low-ranking 35 (4)
lów rate 809 (1)
low relief 254 (1)
low-spirited 834 (5)
low spirits 834 (1)
low standard 645 (1), 647
(1)
low stature 204 (1)
low temperature 380 (1)
low tide 210 (1)
low turnout 105 (1)
low visibility 443 (1)
low voice 404 (1), 578 (1)
low-voiced 578 (2)
low volume 401 (1)
low water 210 (1), 339 (1),
801 (1)
lowbrow 491 (5), 493 (1)
lower 35 (4), 210 (2), 210
(3), 211 (3), 288 (3), 303
(7), 311 (4), 313 (3), 322
(5), 550 (3), 655 (9), 921
(5)
lower a flag 311 (4)
lower back 238 (2)
lower by degrees 27 (5)
lower case 587 (3)

lurch 220 (1), 278 (4), 309 (4), 317 (2), 317 (4), 949 (13)

lurching 142 (1)

lure 291 (1), 291 (4), 542 (4), 542 (10), 612 (4), 612 (11), 859 (5)

lurid 417 (8), 418 (3), 425 (6), 426 (3), 875 (5)

lurk 175 (3), 267 (13), 444 (4), 446 (3), 456 (9), 523 (5), 525 (9), 527 (5), 620 (5), 660 (7), 660 (9), 667 (6), 698 (5)

lurker 527 (4), 698 (3)

lurking 444 (2), 523 (2), 525 (5)

luscious 390 (2), 826 (2)

lush 171 (4), 174 (5), 366 (9), 635 (4)

lushness 366 (1), 635 (2)

lust 859 (4), 887 (1), 951 (2)

lust after 859 (11), 912 (3)

lust for 859 (1)

lustful 859 (7), 887 (9), 951 (8)

lustily 174 (9), 682 (8)

lustiness 174 (1)

lustre 417 (5), 866 (2)

lustreless 419 (4), 426 (3)

lustrous 417 (8)

lusty 162 (6), 174 (5), 195 (8), 408 (2), 650 (2), 841 (6)

lute 414 (2)

luxuriance 171 (1), 637 (1)

luxuriant 171 (4), 324 (4), 635 (4)

luxuriate in 376 (6), 824 (6)

luxuries 637 (2)

luxurious 376 (4), 637 (4), 800 (3), 826 (2), 875 (4), 943 (2)

luxuriousness 637 (2), 944 (1)

luxury 376 (2), 637 (2), 637 (4), 730 (1), 800 (1), 944 (1)

luxury-lover 944 (2)

luxury-loving 944 (3)

lychgate 990 (5)

lye 337 (2)

lying 495 (4), 541 (1), 541 (3), 542 (6), 543 (4)

lying down 216 (2), 216 (5)

lying idle 674 (2)

lying in wait 525 (3)

lymph 335 (2)

lymphatic 335 (5), 339 (2)

lynch 362 (10), 924 (9), 963 (12)

lynch law 954 (3), 963 (3)

lynch mob 362 (6)

lyncher 963 (5)

lynching 963 (3)

lynx-eyed 438 (6)

lyre 414 (2)

lyric 412 (5), 412 (7), 413 (7), 593 (8)

lyric poet 593 (6)

lyric verse 593 (2)

lyrical 593 (8), 818 (4), 821 (3), 822 (3), 835 (4), 923 (5)

lyricism 557 (3), 821 (1)

lyricist 413 (1), 593 (6)

lyrics 589 (2)

M

ma'am 373 (4), 870 (1)

mac 228 (20)

macabre 854 (8), 970 (7)

mace 279 (4), 723 (5), 743 (2)

macerate 341 (8)

mach number 277 (1)

machete 723 (8)

Machiavellian 623 (7), 698 (4)

machinate 623 (9)

machination 542 (1), 623 (4), 698 (2)

machine 58 (1), 156 (5), 160 (4), 160 (6), 164 (1), 164 (7), 628 (1), 628 (2), 629 (1), 630 (2)

machine code 86 (5)

machine gun 403 (1), 723 (11)

machine-made 164 (6)

machine-minder 630 (5)

machine tool 630 (1)

machinery 61 (3), 630 (2)

machining 164 (1)

machinist 630 (5), 686 (3)

machismo 372 (1)

macho 372 (2)

mackerel sky 355 (2)

mackintosh 228 (20)

macramé 222 (3)

macrocosm 79 (1), 321 (1)

maculation 437 (4), 844 (3), 845 (1)

mad 176 (6), 497 (3), 503 (7), 503 (10), 821 (3), 891 (4)

mad at 891 (4)

mad dog 176 (4), 904 (5)

madam 373 (4), 741 (1), 870 (1), 878 (3), 952 (5)

madame 373 (4)

madcap 499 (4), 857 (2), 857 (3)

madden 176 (9), 503 (12), 891 (9)

maddened 503 (8), 503 (9)

maddening 827 (5)

madder 431 (2)

madding crowd 678 (1)

made 164 (6)

made a member 58 (2)

made easy 516 (2), 701 (5)

made holy 979 (8)

made law 953 (5)

made liable 961 (2)

made man and wife 894 (7)

made of 56 (2)

made of money 800 (4)

made over 780 (2)

made redundant 779 (3)

made to measure 24 (8), 80 (6), 228 (30)

made to order 80 (6)

made-up 164 (6), 541 (3), 843 (6)

madeira 301 (29)

mademoiselle 373 (4)

madhouse 61 (4), 503 (6)

madly 32 (18), 887 (16)

madman 176 (4), 504 (1), 651 (18)

madness 503 (1), 822 (2)

Madonna 968 (2)
madrigal 412 (5)
madwoman 504 (1)
maelstrom 315 (2)
maestro 413 (3), 696 (1)
mafia 738 (1), 738 (4), 904 (3)
magazine 74 (7), 528 (5), 589 (1), 589 (2), 632 (2), 723 (2)
magenta 431 (3), 436 (2)
maggot 365 (17)
maggoty 649 (6)
Magi, the 983 (5)
magic 542 (3), 628 (1), 628 (3), 864 (2), 864 (5), 866 (2), 970 (6), 983 (1), 983 (8), 983 (11), 984 (1)
magic arts 983 (1)
magic away 983 (11)
magic carpet 276 (2)
magic formula 983 (2)
magic instrument 983 (4)
magic lantern 420 (4), 442 (1)
magic lore 983 (1)
magic mirror 983 (4)
magic ring 983 (4)
magic rite 983 (1)
magic sign 983 (2)
magic skill 983 (1)
magic wand 703 (1)
magic world 970 (1)
magical 59 (4), 628 (3), 864 (5), 970 (6), 983 (8)
magician 143 (3), 545 (5), 983 (5)
magisterial 694 (4), 733 (7), 733 (8)
magistracy 733 (5), 955 (1), 957 (2)
magistrate 690 (4), 741 (6), 957 (1)
magistrates' court 956 (2)
magistrature 733 (5)
magma 344 (4)
magnanimity 897 (1), 931 (1), 933 (2)
magnanimous 897 (4), 909 (2), 931 (2), 933 (3)
magnate 638 (4)
magnet 288 (1), 291 (2), 859 (5)

magnetic 160 (9), 288 (2), 291 (3), 612 (6)
magnetic field 160 (3), 291 (1)
magnetic North 281 (2)
magnetic storm 176 (3)
magnetic tape 86 (5), 415 (4)
magnetism 160 (3), 178 (1), 288 (1), 291 (1), 612 (2)
magnetization 291 (1)
magnetize 160 (11), 291 (4)
magnetized 291 (3)
magnetizer 291 (2)
magneto 160 (6)
magnification 32 (1), 36 (1), 546 (1)
magnificence 841 (1), 875 (1)
magnificent 195 (6), 644 (4), 841 (4), 875 (4)
magnificently 32 (17)
magnify 36 (5), 197 (5), 482 (4), 546 (3), 638 (8), 877 (5), 981 (11)
magnifying glass 442 (2)
magnifying power 183 (3)
magniloquence 546 (1), 571 (1), 574 (2), 576 (1), 579 (4), 875 (1)
magniloquent 574 (5), 875 (4), 877 (4)
magnitude 26 (1), 27 (1), 32 (1), 178 (1), 195 (1), 417 (1), 638 (1)
magnolia 366 (4)
magnum 194 (13)
magnum opus 589 (1)
magpie 365 (4), 816 (3)
magus 983 (5)
mah jong 837 (8)
maharajah 741 (4)
maharani 741 (4)
mahogany 366 (4), 430 (1)
maid 132 (2), 742 (2), 895 (3), 950 (3)
maiden 68 (7), 126 (5), 132 (2), 373 (3), 895 (3), 950 (3)
maiden aunt 895 (3)
maiden name 561 (2)

maiden speech 68 (2)
maiden voyage 68 (2)
maidenhood 895 (1), 950 (1)
maidenly 130 (4), 373 (5), 895 (4), 950 (5)
mail 226 (1), 272 (8), 531 (2), 588 (1), 588 (4), 662 (3), 713 (5), 723 (3)
mail-boat 275 (1)
mail-clad 713 (8)
mail coach 274 (8)
mail-order 272 (8), 792 (1)
mailed 713 (8)
mailed fist 735 (2), 954 (3)
mailing list 588 (1)
mails 272 (3)
maim 655 (9)
maimed 647 (3)
main 32 (4), 34 (5), 343 (1), 624 (8), 638 (5)
main dish 301 (13)
main feature 638 (3)
main idea 451 (1)
main line 624 (7)
main-lining 949 (4)
main part 32 (3), 53 (1), 104 (3), 638 (3)
main road 624 (6)
main thing 638 (3)
mainland 344 (1), 344 (7)
mainlander 191 (1)
mainline 949 (15)
mainly 32 (17), 52 (9), 79 (7)
mainspring 156 (2), 612 (1)
mainstay 218 (2), 638 (3), 703 (3), 852 (1)
mainstream 104 (3), 179 (1)
maintain 144 (3), 146 (4), 173 (3), 485 (7), 532 (5), 600 (4), 633 (5)
maintain progress 285 (3)
maintaining 485 (4)
maintenance 144 (1), 146 (1), 173 (1), 600 (1), 633 (1), 666 (1), 703 (2), 807 (1)
maisonette 192 (9)
maize 301 (22)

majestic 575 (3), 733 (7),
733 (8), 821 (5), 841 (3),
866 (8), 868 (6), 871 (3),
875 (6)
majesty 32 (1), 733 (1),
741 (3), 868 (1), 965 (2)
major 32 (4), 34 (4), 131
(7), 134 (3), 410 (8), 638
(5), 741 (8)
major-general 741 (8)
major in 536 (5)
major key 410 (5)
major part 52 (3)
major planet 321 (6)
major poet 593 (6)
major work 589 (1)
majority 32 (3), 34 (2), 52
(3), 53 (1), 101 (1), 104
(3), 134 (1)
majority rule 733 (4)
majority verdict 959 (3)
make 5 (3), 56 (1), 56 (3),
56 (5), 77 (2), 147 (7), 156
(9), 164 (7), 243 (5), 295
(4), 771 (7), 771 (9)
make a beeline for 281 (5)
make a beginning 68 (8)
make a bequest 780 (4)
make a bid 671 (4), 791 (6)
make a book 618 (8)
make a breakthrough 727
(6)
make a case 466 (8)
make a circuit 314 (4), 626
(3)
make a collection 761 (6)
make a comeback 656 (8)
make a compact 765 (5)
make a conquest 887 (15)
make a crowd 74 (10)
make a date 882 (8)
make a detour 282 (3), 314
(4), 626 (3)
make a diagram 551 (8)
make a distinction 15 (7),
463 (3)
make a draught 340 (6),
352 (10)
make a face 893 (3), 924
(9)
make a fool of 542 (9), 851
(5)

make a fool of oneself 695
(8)
make a fortune 730 (6),
771 (9), 800 (7)
make a getaway 667 (5)
make a grab 786 (6)
make a habit of 610 (7)
make a journey 267 (11)
make a landfall 269 (10),
289 (4), 295 (4)
make a landing 295 (5)
make a list 87 (5)
make a loss 728 (7)
make a majority 104 (6)
make a match 894 (10)
make a mess of 695 (9)
make a mistake 495 (7)
make a mixture 43 (7)
make a move 265 (4)
make a noise 398 (4)
make a pass at 889 (7)
make a plan 623 (8)
make a prediction 511 (8)
make a present of 759 (3),
781 (7)
make a profit 615 (5), 640
(4), 771 (9)
make a promise 764 (4)
make a proposition 759
(3)
make a pun 839 (5)
make a purchase 792 (5)
make a request 761 (5)
make a retreat 883 (8)
make a row 400 (4)
make a rush 712 (10)
make a sale 793 (4)
make a scene 891 (7)
make a show of 541 (6),
850 (5)
make a signal 547 (22)
make a smell 397 (3)
make a sortie 298 (5)
make a splash 875 (7)
make a spray 338 (4)
make a stand 715 (3), 718
(12)
make a stir 638 (7)
make a success of 727 (6)
make a suggestion 512 (7)
make a vacuum 325 (3)
make a whole 54 (1)
make absolute 480 (5)

make acquainted 880 (8)
make adjustments 24 (10)
make advances 759 (3),
889 (7)
make aghast 854 (12)
make allowance for 468
(3)
make allowances 909 (4),
927 (7)
make alterations 15 (6)
make amends 31 (4), 787
(3), 941 (5)
make an arrest 747 (8)
make an attempt 671 (4)
make an effort 682 (6)
make an estimate 465 (13)
make an exception 57 (5),
463 (3)
make an exhibition of on-
eself 849 (4)
make an incision 46 (11)
make an offer 759 (3)
make an opening 137 (7)
make angular 247 (7), 248
(5)
make appetizing 390 (3),
859 (13)
make application 761 (5)
make as if 20 (5)
make as one 13 (4)
make available 759 (3)
make away with 788 (7)
make bad worse 832 (3)
make-believe 20 (5), 485
(9), 513 (3), 513 (6), 513
(7), 541 (4), 542 (5), 542
(7), 543 (4), 543 (5)
make better 62 (7), 143
(6), 147 (8), 615 (4), 644
(11), 654 (9), 656 (9), 897
(5), 979 (11)
make blunt 257 (3)
make bold to 878 (6)
make both ends meet 800
(6)
make bright 417 (13), 420
(9), 422 (3), 648 (9), 841
(8)
make certain 466 (7), 466
(8), 473 (9), 478 (4), 484
(4), 660 (8), 764 (5), 767
(6), 858 (3)
make changes 143 (6)

make claims upon 737 (8)
make clear 520 (8)
make comfortable 826 (3)
make common cause 706 (4)
make complete 36 (5), 38 (3), 54 (6), 189 (5), 725 (5)
make concave 211 (3), 255 (8), 263 (18), 309 (3), 311 (4)
make conceited 873 (6), 925 (4)
make concessions 734 (5)
make conditions 747 (9)
make conform 16 (4), 83 (8), 143 (6)
make contact 45 (10), 202 (3), 378 (7)
make contented 828 (5)
make convex 253 (9)
make copies 20 (6)
make curved 247 (7), 248 (5), 311 (9)
make demands 761 (5)
make demands on 737 (8)
make disappear 446 (3)
make do with 150 (5), 673 (4)
make dutiable 809 (7)
make easy 701 (8)
make economies 814 (3)
make enemies 46 (9), 881 (5), 888 (8)
make enquiries 459 (13)
make exceptions 468 (3)
make excuses 614 (4)
make excuses for 927 (7)
make experiments 461 (7)
make extrinsic 6 (4), 223 (3)
make eye contact 438 (8)
make eyes at 438 (8), 859 (11), 889 (7)
make faces 246 (5)
make fast 45 (13), 153 (8)
make few demands 736 (3)
make fit 534 (8)
make flow 350 (11), 648 (10)
make flush 216 (7)
make for 74 (10), 269 (10), 285 (4), 703 (5)

make free 746 (3)
make free with 744 (9), 786 (7), 878 (6)
make friends 24 (9), 880 (7), 882 (8)
make friends with 880 (8)
make fruitful 171 (5)
make fun of 542 (9), 839 (5), 851 (5)
make good 31 (4), 54 (6), 633 (6), 727 (6)
make happy 826 (3), 828 (5)
make haste 680 (3)
make havoc 63 (3), 165 (9), 712 (7)
make hay 730 (6)
make headway 285 (3), 654 (8)
make heavy 322 (6)
make higher 209 (13), 310 (4)
make history 505 (11), 676 (5), 866 (11)
make holiday 876 (4)
make holy 979 (12)
make illegal 954 (9), 961 (3)
make illegible 550 (3)
make impact 279 (8)
make important 463 (3), 532 (7), 546 (3), 638 (8)
make impossible 57 (5), 470 (5), 700 (6)
make inactive 161 (9), 266 (9), 641 (7), 679 (13)
make inroads on 306 (4), 634 (4)
make insensitive 820 (7)
make insufficient 636 (9), 816 (6)
make into 147 (7)
make invisible 444 (4)
make it 727 (8), 730 (6)
make it up 719 (5), 909 (4)
make it up to 941 (5)
make land 295 (4)
make laws 953 (7)
make legal 737 (7), 756 (5), 915 (8), 953 (7)
make less 37 (4)
make light 323 (5)

make light of 701 (7), 860 (4)
make lighter 323 (5)
make likely 466 (6), 471 (5)
make little of 483 (4)
make love 45 (14), 889 (6)
make love to 887 (13)
make mad 63 (3), 176 (9), 503 (12)
make matters right 941 (5)
make merry 835 (6), 837 (23)
make merry over 835 (7)
make merry with 839 (5), 851 (5)
make mincemeat of 46 (11)
make mischief 709 (8)
make money 615 (5), 771 (9), 800 (7)
make much of 528 (11), 546 (3), 638 (8), 866 (13), 876 (4), 887 (13), 889 (5), 925 (4)
make mute 399 (4), 578 (4)
make nervous 854 (12)
make no choice 606 (3)
make no comment 525 (8)
make no demands 701 (6), 736 (3)
make no distinction 464 (4)
make no excuses 940 (4)
make no noise 399 (3)
make no profit 772 (4)
make no sense 515 (6)
make no sound 33 (8)
make nonsense of 515 (6)
make nothing of 517 (7)
make obeisance 311 (9)
make obligatory 737 (6)
make oblique 220 (6), 282 (6)
make off 620 (6)
make off with 788 (7)
make one 44 (6), 740 (3)
make one blush 867 (11), 885 (6)
make one ill 645 (6)

make one jump **508** (5), **854** (12)

make one laugh **837** (20), **849** (4)

make one look silly **851** (5)

make one of **78** (4), **708** (8)

make one promise **764** (5)

make one see **590** (7)

make one sick **861** (5)

make one swear **764** (5)

make one think **449** (10)

make one yawn **838** (5)

make one's adieus **296** (4)

make one's choice **605** (6)

make one's day **828** (5)

make one's debut **68** (8)

make one's exit **296** (4)

make one's fortune **800** (8)

make one's getaway **296** (5)

make one's heart bleed **834** (11)

make one's mark **866** (11)

make one's own **771** (7), **773** (4), **786** (7)

make one's point **532** (5)

make one's presence felt **189** (5)

make one's pretext **614** (4)

make one's quarry **619** (5)

make one's rounds **267** (12)

make one's target **617** (6)

make one's way **265** (4), **267** (11)

make one's way up **308** (5)

make oneself **598** (4)

make oneself felt **178** (3)

make oneself liable **917** (9)

make oneself sick **947** (4)

make oneself useful **703** (7)

make opaque **419** (7), **421** (4), **423** (3)

make operate **173** (3)

make or mar **178** (3)

make out **438** (7), **520** (10), **727** (6)

make out a case **478** (4), **915** (6)

make over **272** (6), **780** (3), **781** (7)

make overtures **759** (3), **761** (5), **766** (4), **880** (8)

make part of **58** (3)

make payment **804** (4)

make peace **145** (6), **717** (4), **719** (4), **719** (5), **828** (4)

make permanent **115** (3)

make pious **979** (11)

make plain **522** (7)

make play with **673** (3)

make port **269** (10), **295** (4)

make possible **469** (4), **701** (8), **756** (5), **759** (3)

make productive **171** (5)

make progress **654** (8)

make proposals **766** (4)

make provision **510** (3), **633** (5)

make public **528** (9)

make quarrels **709** (8), **711** (3), **881** (5)

make ragged **46** (12)

make ready **587** (7), **629** (2), **633** (5), **669** (10), **669** (11), **713** (9)

make real **319** (7)

make realize **485** (9)

make redundant **300** (7), **674** (5)

make reparation **787** (3), **941** (5), **962** (3)

make responsible **158** (3)

make restitution **787** (3)

make rich **800** (8)

make room **190** (7), **265** (4)

make round **248** (5), **250** (7)

make safe **660** (8)

make sane **502** (4)

make sense **516** (4)

make sense of **520** (8)

make shift to **623** (8)

make shift with **150** (5), **673** (4)

make short work of **701** (7)

make silent **399** (4)

make smaller **37** (4), **198** (7), **204** (5), **206** (7), **311** (4), **324** (6)

make spherical **252** (6)

make sterile **161** (10), **165** (9), **172** (6), **641** (7)

make straight **249** (4)

make strides **285** (3)

make sure **858** (3)

make terms **24** (9), **622** (9), **706** (4), **758** (3), **765** (5), **766** (4), **791** (6)

make the best of **770** (2)

make the effort **671** (4)

make the eyes water **388** (5)

make the grade **28** (9), **635** (6)

make the most of **673** (3), **875** (7)

make the running **277** (8), **306** (5)

make thin **37** (4), **198** (7), **203** (8), **206** (7), **207** (5)

make things worse **645** (6), **655** (7), **700** (6), **728** (8)

make tight **264** (6)

make to measure **24** (10)

make too much of **546** (3)

make trouble **709** (8), **829** (6)

make ugly **244** (3), **547** (19), **655** (9), **842** (7), **845** (3)

make unclean **419** (7), **426** (5), **547** (19), **649** (9), **655** (9), **675** (2), **845** (3), **867** (11), **926** (7), **951** (11), **980** (6)

make understood **516** (4)

make uniform **16** (4), **28** (10), **44** (6), **60** (3), **62** (5), **83** (8), **465** (12)

make unlike **19** (4)

make unproductive **172** (6)

make unwelcome **57** (5), **292** (3), **300** (6), **607** (3), **620** (5), **883** (9), **885** (6)

make-up **5** (3), **50** (2), **50** (4), **54** (6), **56** (1), **56** (3),

56 (5), 80 (1), 164 (7), 331 (1), 513 (7), 541 (5), 587 (1), 594 (6), 594 (11), 633 (6), 654 (9), 817 (1), 843 (1), 843 (3), 843 (7)
make-up artist 843 (5)
make up for 31 (4), 941 (5)
make up leeway 31 (6), 285 (3)
make up one's mind 605 (6)
make up time 285 (3)
make up to 879 (4), 925 (4)
make use of 640 (5), 673 (3)
make useless 161 (9), 641 (7), 674 (5)
make verses 593 (10)
make vertical 215 (4), 310 (4)
make violent 176 (9)
make visible 443 (4)
make vows 981 (12)
make war 718 (11), 881 (4)
make water 302 (6)
make way for 282 (3), 701 (8), 753 (3)
make welcome 880 (8), 882 (10)
make well 656 (11)
make whole 54 (6)
make whoopee 837 (23)
make wicked 535 (3), 655 (8), 934 (8)
make work 678 (12)
make worse 832 (2), 832 (3)
maker 156 (2), 164 (4)
makeshift 35 (4), 114 (1), 150 (2), 150 (4), 609 (3), 623 (3), 629 (1)
makeweight 31 (2)
making 56 (2), 164 (1), 295 (1)
making amends 941 (1), 941 (4)
making easy 701 (1)
making friends 880 (1)
making into 147 (1)
making less 37 (2)
making like new 656 (2)
making love 887 (9)

making of, be the 644 (11), 654 (9)
making ready 669 (1)
making sure 473 (1)
making terms 766 (1)
making up 78 (3)
making war 718 (6)
making worse 832 (1)
maladjusted 503 (7)
maladjustment 25 (2), 503 (2)
maladministration 675 (1), 695 (2)
maladroit 695 (5)
malady 651 (3), 659 (1)
malaise 377 (1), 616 (1), 825 (1)
malapropism 495 (2), 560 (1), 562 (1), 565 (1), 849 (1)
malapropos 138 (2)
malaria 651 (6)
malarial 653 (3)
malcontent 489 (2), 489 (3), 705 (1), 738 (4), 763 (1), 829 (2), 829 (3), 834 (4), 836 (3), 885 (3), 902 (2), 924 (5)
male 134 (1), 134 (2), 134 (3), 162 (10), 176 (4), 371 (3), 372 (1), 372 (2)
male and female 14 (2)
male chauvinism 372 (1)
male menopause 131 (2)
male nurse 658 (16)
male sex 372 (1)
malediction 559 (1), 645 (1), 829 (1), 888 (1), 899 (1), 900 (1), 961 (1), 980 (1), 980 (3)
maledictory 899 (3)
malefactor 904 (1), 904 (3)
maleficent 616 (2), 898 (5), 934 (3), 983 (7)
malevolence 645 (1), 709 (2), 824 (1), 827 (2), 881 (1), 888 (1), 891 (1), 898 (1), 910 (1), 912 (1), 926 (1), 934 (1)
malevolent 645 (3), 881 (3), 888 (4), 891 (3), 898

(4), 910 (4), 926 (5), 934 (3), 969 (5)
malevolent, be 645 (6), 645 (7), 735 (8), 881 (4), 888 (7), 891 (5), 898 (8), 899 (6), 910 (6)
malevolently 898 (9)
malformation 246 (2)
malformed 244 (2)
malfunction 728 (7)
malice 824 (1), 888 (1), 891 (1), 898 (1)
malicious 645 (3), 888 (4), 898 (4)
malicious gossip 926 (2)
malign 731 (4), 867 (11), 898 (4), 898 (8), 926 (7)
malign influence 178 (1), 731 (2)
malignancy 898 (1)
malignant 362 (8), 645 (3), 983 (7)
malignant tumour 651 (11)
malinger 541 (6)
malingerer 545 (3), 918 (1)
malingering 541 (1), 918 (1)
mallard 365 (4)
malleability 83 (1), 327 (1), 739 (1)
malleable 83 (4), 152 (4), 327 (3), 701 (4), 721 (2)
mallet 279 (4)
malnutrition 301 (3), 636 (1), 651 (3)
malodorous 394 (2), 397 (2)
malpractice 675 (1), 936 (2), 954 (2)
malt liquor 301 (28)
maltings 687 (1)
maltreat 645 (7), 675 (2), 827 (9), 898 (8)
maltreated 825 (5)
maltreatment 645 (1), 675 (1)
mamma 169 (4)
mammal 365 (2), 365 (3), 619 (3)
mammalian 365 (18)
Mammon 800 (1), 974 (2)

market trader 793 (2), 794 (3)

marketability 793 (1)

marketable 791 (3), 793 (3)

marketing 792 (4), 793 (1)

marketplace 678 (1), 724 (1), 796 (1)

marking out 15 (5)

markings 547 (2), 547 (9)

marksman 837 (16)

marksman or - woman 287 (4)

marksmanship 694 (1)

marl 344 (3)

marly 344 (5)

marmoreal 554 (2)

maroon 430 (3), 431 (3), 547 (5), 779 (4)

marooned 702 (7)

marquee 192 (16), 226 (3)

marquess 868 (5)

marquetry 437 (2), 844 (2)

marred 842 (4)

marriage 45 (1), 45 (3), 50 (1), 765 (1), 887 (3), 889 (2), 894 (1), 988 (4)

marriage broker 231 (3)

marriage bureau 894 (5)

marriage lines 767 (2)

marriage partner 894 (4)

marriage rites 894 (3)

marriage settlement 777 (4)

marriage tie 894 (1)

marriage vows 894 (3)

marriageable 134 (3), 894 (8)

marriageable age 894 (6)

married 45 (5), 706 (3), 894 (7)

married man 372 (1)

married name 561 (2)

married quarters 192 (2)

married woman 373 (3)

marrow 3 (2), 225 (2), 301 (20)

marry 45 (14), 894 (10), 894 (11)

marry beneath one 867 (10)

marry in haste 894 (11)

marry into 11 (7)

marry off 894 (10)

marry oneself to 894 (11)

Mars 321 (6), 718 (1), 967 (1)

marsh 216 (1), 341 (1), 347 (1), 348 (1), 354 (1), 649 (2)

marsh gas 336 (2)

marshal 62 (4), 690 (4), 741 (6)

marshalled 62 (3)

marshalling 62 (1), 547 (11), 669 (2)

marshalling yard 624 (7)

marshiness 341 (1)

marshland 347 (1)

marshy 341 (4), 347 (2), 354 (4), 356 (2)

marsupial 365 (3)

mart 796 (1)

martial 718 (9), 855 (4)

martial law 733 (4), 735 (2), 954 (3)

Martian 59 (2)

martinet 735 (3)

martyr 362 (10), 825 (4), 979 (4)

martyr, be a 377 (6)

martyrdom 361 (1), 362 (1), 825 (1), 931 (1), 963 (3)

martyrize 963 (11)

martyr's crown 866 (4)

marvel 864 (3), 864 (6)

marvelling 864 (4)

marvellous 32 (7), 644 (4), 826 (2), 864 (5)

marvellously 864 (8)

Marxism 449 (3)

Marxism-Leninism 733 (4)

Marxist 149 (2), 149 (3), 654 (5)

marzipan 392 (2)

mascara 843 (3)

mascot 666 (2), 983 (3)

masculine 77 (4), 162 (10), 372 (2)

masculinity 372 (1)

mash 43 (7), 327 (4), 332 (5), 354 (6)

mashed 356 (2)

mask 226 (1), 421 (1), 421 (4), 525 (7), 527 (3)

masked 525 (4)

masochism 84 (2)

masochist 84 (3), 944 (2)

mason 686 (3)

masonry 631 (2)

masque 594 (1), 594 (3)

masquerade 20 (5), 228 (2), 525 (1), 525 (7), 527 (3), 542 (5), 837 (13)

masquerader 527 (4)

mass 26 (1), 32 (2), 32 (3), 32 (5), 52 (3), 53 (5), 74 (5), 74 (7), 74 (10), 74 (11), 79 (3), 104 (3), 195 (1), 195 (3), 319 (2), 322 (1), 324 (3), 324 (6), 632 (1), 900 (3), 981 (7)

mass execution 963 (3)

mass grave 364 (5)

mass hysteria 74 (5)

mass media 524 (1), 528 (1)

mass meeting 74 (2)

mass murder 963 (3)

mass-produce 16 (4), 164 (7), 166 (3)

mass-produced 16 (2), 164 (6)

mass production 16 (1), 164 (1), 166 (1)

mass suicide 362 (3)

massacre 165 (1), 362 (4), 362 (11), 963 (12)

massage 327 (4), 333 (1), 333 (3), 378 (1), 378 (7), 658 (20), 843 (1)

masses 26 (2), 32 (2)

masses, the 74 (5), 371 (4), 869 (1)

masseur 333 (1)

masseuse 333 (1)

massing 74 (7)

massive 32 (4), 195 (6), 322 (4), 324 (4)

massiveness 195 (3)

mast 209 (4), 218 (2), 275 (6)

mastectomy 658 (11)

master 34 (3), 178 (4), 270 (1), 372 (1), 490 (8), 500 (1), 516 (5), 536 (4), 686

(3), **690** (1), **696** (1), **727** (9), **733** (1), **741** (1), **776** (2), **786** (4), **870** (1), **870** (2)

master copy **22** (2)

master key **263** (11), **628** (2)

master mariner **270** (1)

master mind **500** (1)

master of, be **490** (8)

master of ceremonies **837** (17)

master of jurisprudence **958** (4)

master or mistress **537** (1)

master or mistress of **727** (3)

master plan **23** (1), **623** (1)

masterful **694** (4), **733** (7), **735** (5)

masterly **646** (3), **694** (4), **727** (4)

mastermind **34** (3), **623** (5), **696** (1)

masterpiece **164** (2), **553** (5), **644** (3), **646** (1), **676** (2), **694** (3), **727** (1)

mastership **733** (5)

masterstroke **623** (3), **694** (3)

mastery **490** (1), **490** (3), **694** (1), **727** (2), **733** (2)

masthead **213** (2), **547** (13)

mastic **357** (5)

masticate **301** (36)

mastication **301** (1), **356** (1)

mastiff **365** (10)

mastodon **365** (2)

mat **222** (10), **226** (9)

matador **362** (6)

match **13** (1), **13** (4), **18** (3), **18** (7), **24** (9), **28** (6), **28** (9), **28** (10), **45** (9), **90** (3), **381** (2), **385** (3), **420** (3), **462** (3), **716** (2), **894** (1), **894** (10)

match a **704** (4)

match-making **894** (3)

match oneself with **716** (10)

match times **117** (7)

match with **709** (8)

matchbox **194** (8)

matched **28** (7), **45** (5), **894** (7)

matching **18** (4), **24** (4), **24** (5), **425** (7)

matchless **34** (5)

matchmaker **231** (3), **720** (2), **894** (5)

matchstick **163** (3)

matchwood **163** (3), **330** (1)

mate **18** (3), **28** (6), **45** (14), **89** (2), **90** (3), **270** (1), **372** (1), **686** (4), **707** (3), **880** (5), **894** (4), **894** (10), **894** (11)

mated **894** (7)

mater **169** (4)

material **1** (5), **3** (1), **3** (3), **222** (4), **319** (2), **319** (6), **524** (1), **631** (1), **944** (3)

material existence **1** (2)

materialism **1** (1), **319** (1), **449** (3), **944** (1), **974** (2), **980** (1)

materialist **319** (1), **974** (3), **980** (3)

materialistic **319** (6), **932** (3), **974** (5)

materiality **1** (2), **3** (1), **319** (1), **980** (1)

materialization **319** (1), **445** (1), **522** (1), **984** (3)

materialize **154** (6), **319** (7), **445** (8)

materialized **319** (6)

materially **32** (17)

materials **156** (3), **244** (1), **319** (3), **331** (1), **629** (1), **631** (1)

maternal **11** (5), **169** (5)

maternity **167** (1), **167** (5), **169** (1), **169** (4), **373** (3)

maternity wear **228** (2)

mateyness **880** (1), **880** (2)

mathematical **86** (9), **494** (6)

mathematician **86** (7)

mathematics **86** (3)

matinal **128** (5)

matinee **129** (1), **594** (2)

matinee idol **594** (9)

mating **45** (3)

mating season **859** (4)

matins **128** (1), **981** (7), **988** (5)

matriarch **169** (4)

matriarchal **733** (9)

matriarchy **11** (3), **373** (1), **733** (4)

matricide **362** (2)

matrimonial **894** (9)

matrimony **894** (1)

matrix **23** (3), **85** (1), **230** (1)

matron **169** (4), **373** (3), **658** (16), **690** (3)

matronly **131** (6), **373** (5)

matt **419** (4), **424** (2)

matt finish **419** (1)

matted **222** (6), **259** (5), **324** (4), **649** (7)

matter **3** (1), **302** (4), **319** (2), **321** (1), **324** (3), **335** (2), **452** (1), **638** (7), **649** (2), **651** (14)

matter of **26** (2)

matter of course **610** (2), **865** (1)

matter of fact **1** (2), **473** (1), **494** (1), **593** (9), **840** (1)

matter of life and death **638** (2)

matter of regret **830** (1)

matter of time **110** (1), **111** (1)

matters **154** (2)

matting **222** (3)

mattress **218** (8)

maturation **134** (1), **167** (1), **610** (3), **669** (3)

mature **36** (4), **54** (5), **131** (6), **134** (3), **134** (4), **147** (6), **167** (6), **646** (5), **669** (8), **669** (12), **725** (5)

mature student **538** (3)

mature understanding **498** (3)

matured **54** (3), **131** (6), **134** (3), **243** (3), **646** (3), **669** (8)

matureness **134** (1)

maturing **130** (4), **669** (6)

maturity **127** (1), **131** (2), **134** (1), **669** (4), **725** (1) maudlin 818 (3), **949** (7)

maul 176 (7), **279** (9), **645**
(7), **655** (10), **712** (7), **924**
(10)

maunder 499 (6), **570** (6)

maundering 570 (4)

mausoleum 164 (3), **364**
(5), **548** (3)

mauve **436** (2)

maverick 84 (3), **738** (4),
769 (2)

maw 194 (3), **224** (2), **234**
(2), **263** (4), **301** (6)

mawkish 818 (3)

maxim 81 (1), **473** (1), **475**
(2), **480** (1), **485** (2), **496**
(1), **515** (1), **563** (1), **569**
(1), **693** (1)

maximize 36 (5), **482** (4)

maximum 32 (4), 34 (1), 34
(6), 54 (2)

maximum height 213 (1)

may 366 (4), **469** (3)

may be **469** (5)

Mayday **547** (8)

mayhem 61 (1)

maying 128 (3)

mayonnaise 301 (14), **389**
(2)

mayor **690** (4), **692** (3), **741**
(6)

mayoralty **733** (5)

mayoress **741** (6)

maypole **209** (4)

maze 61 (3), 251 (3), **530**
(2), **700** (1)

mazurka **837** (14)

mazy 61 (8), **251** (5)

MC **837** (17)

me **320** (2)

métier **694** (1)

mead **392** (2)

meadow **348** (2)

meadows **370** (2)

meagre 33 (6), **55** (3), **206**
(5), **814** (2), **946** (3)

meagre diet **301** (3)

meagreness 4 (1), **33** (1),
196 (1), **636** (2)

meal 301 (12), **301** (22),
332 (2), **837** (2)

mealy **332** (4), **426** (3)

mealy-mouthed **541** (4)

mean 26 (1), **30** (1), **30** (4),
70 (1), **70** (2), **80** (8), **86** (4),
514 (5), **518** (3), **523** (6),
547 (18), **551** (8), **638** (7),
639 (5), **645** (2), **801** (4),
816 (4), **867** (4), **879** (3),
898 (6), **922** (4), **930** (4),
930 (5), **932** (3), **934** (6)

mean business **599** (3)

mean it **540** (3)

mean-minded **932** (3)

mean no good **900** (3)

mean no harm **717** (4)

mean nothing 477 (7), **497**
(4), **499** (6), **515** (6), **517**
(6), **581** (5), **877** (5)

mean something **514** (5)

mean-spirited **879** (3)

mean to 597 (6), **617** (5)

mean to say **514** (5)

mean well **897** (5)

meander 251 (3), **251** (12),
282 (3), **314** (4), **350** (9)

meandering 251 (3), **251**
(5), **350** (7)

meaning 15 (2), **514** (1),
520 (1), **532** (3), **547** (1),
557 (2), **617** (1), **638** (3)

meaning harm **898** (4)

meaningful 466 (5), **514**
(3), **516** (2), **547** (15), **638**
(5)

meaningfully **514** (6)

meaningless 497 (3), **514**
(4), **515** (4), **639** (5), **840** (2)

meaninglessness **515** (1)

meanness 33 (1), **636** (1),
639 (1), **801** (1), **816** (1),
922 (2), **932** (1)

means 137 (2), **156** (5), **623**
(3), **628** (1), **629** (1), **631**
(1), **642** (1), **777** (2), **797**
(2), **800** (1)

means of access **624** (2)

means of approach **289** (1)

means of ascent **308** (1)

means of escape 298 (3),
614 (1), **623** (3), **629** (1),
660 (1), **662** (3), **667** (2)

means of execution **964**
(3)

means of safety **662** (3)

meantime 108 (2), **108** (10)

meanwhile **108** (10)

measles **651** (5)

measurable 86 (8), **465**
(10)

measure 26 (2), **27** (4), **78**
(1), **78** (5), **86** (12), **177** (1),
183 (2), **195** (1), **313** (3),
410 (4), **412** (3), **465** (5),
465 (11), **480** (6), **593** (5),
676 (2), **783** (2), **783** (3)

measure one's words **566**
(3)

measure out **465** (14)

measure time **117** (7)

measure up to 28 (9), **160**
(10), **635** (6)

measured 16 (2), **26** (3),
141 (4), **177** (3), **465** (10),
593 (8), **635** (3), **942** (3)

measured against **462** (2)

measured time **110** (1)

measureless **107** (2)

measurement 26 (1), **27**
(1), **78** (1), **86** (1), **203** (4),
465 (1), **480** (2)

measurements **195** (1)

measures 623 (2), **629** (1),
676 (1)

measuring instrument
465 (6)

meat 3 (2), **301** (9), **301**
(16), **631** (1)

meat-eater **301** (6)

meat-eating **301** (31)

meatballs **301** (16)

meatiness 3 (1)

meatless day **946** (2)

meaty 3 (3), **195** (8), **514**
(3), **571** (2)

Mecca 76 (1), **617** (2), **990**
(2)

mechanic **630** (5), **686** (3)

mechanical 160 (9), **596**
(5), **628** (3), **630** (6)

mechanical copy **22** (1)

mechanics 86 (5), **319** (5),
630 (3)

mechanism **630** (2)

mechanistic **596** (5)
mechanization **628** (1)
mechanize **164** (7)
mechanized **164** (5), **630** (6)
medal **547** (9), **729** (2), **844** (7), **866** (4)
medallion **554** (1), **844** (7)
medallist **727** (3)
meddle **63** (3), **182** (3), **453** (4), **655** (9), **676** (5), **678** (13), **695** (9), **702** (8)
meddle with **655** (9)
meddler **453** (2), **678** (6), **691** (2)
meddlesome **678** (10)
meddling **678** (4), **678** (10), **702** (1), **702** (6)
media personality **531** (5)
media, the **528** (1), **531** (3)
mediaeval times **125** (2)
medial **70** (2)
median **30** (1), **30** (4), **70** (2), **79** (3), **83** (5), **231** (6)
mediate **70** (2), **231** (10), **628** (1), **717** (4), **719** (4), **720** (4), **762** (3)
mediation **710** (1), **719** (1), **720** (1), **762** (1)
mediator **177** (2), **231** (3), **628** (2), **717** (2), **720** (2), **765** (3), **894** (5)
mediatory **231** (6), **717** (3), **719** (3), **720** (3)
medic **658** (14)
medical **459** (1), **658** (18)
medical adviser **691** (2)
medical art **658** (10), **703** (1)
medical care **658** (12)
medical officer **652** (3)
medical practice **658** (10)
medical school **539** (3)
medical student **658** (14)
medicament **658** (2)
medicate **658** (20)
medicated **656** (7)
medication **658** (2)
medicinal **658** (17)
medicinal herb **366** (6), **658** (2)
medicine **301** (26), **658** (2), **658** (10)

medicine chest **658** (2)
medicine man **983** (5)
medieval **127** (4)
medievalism **125** (4)
medievalist **125** (5)
mediocre **30** (4), **35** (4), **639** (6), **644** (9), **732** (2)
mediocrity **33** (1), **35** (1), **639** (4), **647** (1), **732** (1)
meditate **449** (8), **459** (13), **480** (6), **512** (6), **617** (5), **981** (11), **981** (12)
meditating **981** (9)
meditation **449** (2), **455** (1), **981** (1), **981** (4)
meditative **449** (5), **979** (6)
mediterranean **70** (2), **231** (6)
medium **30** (1), **70** (1), **230** (1), **231** (3), **511** (4), **520** (4), **628** (1), **628** (2), **984** (5)
mediumship **984** (3)
medley **17** (1), **43** (4), **53** (5), **61** (2), **74** (6), **74** (7), **412** (4), **437** (2)
meek **721** (2), **739** (3), **823** (3), **823** (4), **872** (3)
meekness **739** (1), **872** (1)
meet **24** (7), **24** (9), **45** (14), **74** (2), **74** (10), **123** (4), **154** (7), **200** (5), **202** (3), **279** (8), **289** (4), **293** (3), **295** (6), **378** (7), **484** (4), **704** (5), **804** (4), **917** (10)
meet a demand **793** (5)
meet a sticky end **361** (8)
meet and right **913** (3)
meet by chance **295** (6)
meet for prayer **981** (12)
meet halfway **597** (6), **625** (6), **719** (4)
meet one **1** (6)
meet one halfway **770** (2)
meet one's end **361** (8)
meet one's Maker **361** (7)
meet one's oligations **768** (4)
meet the eye **443** (4)
meet the train **295** (6)
meet with **154** (7), **159** (7), **484** (4)

meeting **45** (1), **74** (2), **154** (1), **202** (1), **279** (3), **289** (1), **289** (2), **293** (1), **295** (1), **584** (3), **692** (1)
meeting house **192** (14), **990** (7)
meeting place **76** (1), **185** (1), **187** (2), **192** (14), **295** (2)
meeting-point **45** (1)
megalith **125** (2), **548** (3)
megalithic **195** (6)
megalomania **482** (1), **503** (3), **873** (1)
megalomaniac **504** (1)
megaphone **400** (2), **415** (4), **531** (1)
megaton **322** (2)
megawatt **160** (6)
melancholia **834** (2)
melancholic **503** (7), **504** (1), **834** (6), **838** (4), **893** (2)
melancholy **825** (1), **825** (6), **829** (1), **834** (2), **834** (6), **838** (1), **893** (1)
melange **43** (3)
mêlée **61** (4), **716** (7)
mellifluous **410** (6), **575** (3)
mellow **147** (6), **386** (2), **390** (2), **425** (7), **425** (8), **669** (8), **669** (12)
mellowness **127** (1), **669** (4)
melodic **410** (6), **412** (7), **413** (7)
melodious **376** (3), **410** (6), **412** (7), **413** (7), **577** (3), **826** (2)
melodiousness **410** (1)
melodrama **594** (3), **821** (1)
melodramatic **546** (2), **594** (15), **821** (4)
melody **24** (1), **398** (1), **410** (1), **412** (1), **412** (3), **710** (1), **826** (1)
melt **49** (4), **51** (5), **75** (3), **244** (3), **327** (4), **337** (4), **350** (11), **379** (7), **381** (8), **834** (11), **905** (6), **905** (8)

melt away 37 (5), 446 (3), 634 (4), 772 (5)

melt down 37 (4)

melt into 27 (5), 147 (6)

melted 381 (6)

melting 37 (2), 327 (2), 335 (4), 337 (1), 381 (1), 634 (1), 905 (4)

melting point 379 (1)

melting pot 43 (1), 147 (3)

member 53 (2), 58 (1), 708 (3), 754 (2), 775 (3)

member of parliament 692 (3)

membership 78 (1), 706 (2), 775 (2), 882 (1)

membrane 207 (1), 226 (6)

membranous 207 (4)

memento 505 (3)

memo 505 (3)

memoir 548 (1), 591 (1)

memoir writer 590 (5)

memoirs 505 (2), 589 (2), 590 (3)

memorabilia 505 (2), 548 (1)

memorability 638 (1)

memorable 505 (5), 638 (6)

memorandum 505 (3), 548 (1), 623 (1)

memorial 364 (5), 505 (3), 505 (6), 524 (2), 547 (7), 548 (3), 729 (1), 866 (4)

memorialize 505 (9), 761 (5)

memorization 505 (2)

memorize 490 (8), 505 (10), 536 (4)

memorized 490 (7), 505 (5)

memory 86 (5), 449 (1), 505 (1), 632 (2), 866 (3)

memsahib 373 (4)

men 722 (7)

menace 511 (8), 661 (1), 661 (9), 664 (1), 664 (5), 827 (2), 854 (12), 888 (3), 900 (1), 900 (3)

menacing 661 (3), 664 (3), 854 (8), 900 (2)

menacingly 900 (4)

menage 689 (1)

menagerie 74 (7), 369 (4), 632 (3)

mend 45 (9), 650 (4), 654 (8), 654 (9), 654 (10), 656 (12)

mend one's manners 884 (5)

mend one's ways 603 (5), 654 (8), 979 (10)

mend the fire 385 (6)

mendable 656 (6)

mendacious 541 (3), 543 (4)

mendacity 541 (1)

Mendelian 157 (4)

Mendelism 5 (5)

mender 654 (5), 656 (5)

mendicancy 761 (1)

mendicant 679 (6), 763 (2)

mendicant friar 763 (2)

mending 656 (2), 656 (4)

menfolk 372 (1)

menial 35 (2), 35 (4), 686 (2), 742 (1), 742 (7)

meningitis 651 (5)

menopause 131 (2), 172 (1)

menses 302 (2)

menstrual 141 (5), 302 (5)

menstrual cycle 141 (2)

mensurable 86 (8), 465 (10)

mensural 465 (9)

mensuration 465 (1)

mental 320 (3), 447 (5), 490 (5), 503 (7), 651 (22)

mental act 449 (1)

mental agitation 318 (1)

mental attitude 688 (1)

mental balance 502 (1)

mental block 506 (1)

mental calibre 498 (1)

mental capacity 447 (1), 498 (1)

mental case 504 (1), 651 (18)

mental creation 164 (1)

mental decay 161 (2), 503 (1)

mental dishonesty 525 (1), 543 (2)

mental fatigue 684 (1)

mental gifts 498 (1)

mental grasp 498 (1)

mental handicap 499 (1)

mental health 502 (1)

mental home 503 (6)

mental hospital 503 (6), 658 (13)

mental illness 503 (1)

mental image 451 (1), 513 (2), 551 (2)

mental inertia 454 (1)

mental inertness 175 (1)

mental instability 503 (1)

mental process 449 (1)

mental product 164 (2)

mental torment 825 (1)

mental weakness 161 (2)

mentality 447 (1), 817 (1)

mentally handicapped 499 (3)

mentally ill 503 (7)

mention 9 (4), 9 (8), 80 (8), 455 (6), 524 (1), 524 (9), 579 (8), 729 (2)

mentionable 950 (5)

mentor 500 (1), 537 (1), 691 (2)

menu 87 (1), 301 (12)

mercantile 622 (5), 791 (3)

mercenariness 816 (2)

mercenary 722 (3), 742 (1), 816 (5), 930 (6), 932 (3)

merchandise 164 (2), 630 (4), 632 (1), 777 (1), 793 (1), 795 (1)

merchandiser 794 (1)

merchant 231 (3), 272 (4), 686 (1), 794 (1), 797 (8)

merchant jack 547 (12)

merchant navy 275 (10)

merchant ship 275 (3)

merchantman 275 (3)

merciful 736 (2), 897 (4), 905 (4), 909 (2)

merciful, be 909 (4)

mercifulness 905 (3), 909 (1)

merciless 165 (4), 735 (4), 898 (4), 898 (7), 906 (2)

mercilessness 898 (2)

mercurial 152 (3), 152 (4), 265 (3), 456 (6), 601 (3), 604 (3), 822 (3)

Mercury 321 (6), 340 (3), 967 (1)

mercy 736 (1), 897 (1), 905 (3), 909 (1), 965 (2)

mercy killer 362 (6)

mercy killing 362 (1)

mere 32 (14), 33 (7), 44 (4), 346 (1)

mere idea 451 (1)

mere nothing 639 (2)

mere trickle 105 (1)

mere words 477 (1), 515 (1)

merely 33 (9), 44 (8)

meretricious 541 (3), 542 (7)

merge 13 (3), 43 (7), 45 (9), 50 (4), 706 (4), 708 (8)

merge in 58 (3), 78 (4)

merge into 147 (6)

merged 43 (6), 45 (5), 78 (3)

merger 45 (1), 50 (1), 706 (2)

meridian 128 (2), 128 (5), 184 (1), 213 (1)

meridional 281 (3)

meringue 301 (23)

merino 208 (2)

merit 638 (1), 640 (1), 644 (1), 915 (7), 933 (2)

merited 915 (2)

meriting 915 (3)

meritocracy 644 (2), 733 (4)

meritorious 644 (4), 866 (7), 915 (3), 923 (6), 933 (3)

merits 913 (1), 915 (1)

mermaid 84 (4), 343 (2), 970 (5)

merriment 824 (3), 833 (2), 835 (1), 837 (1), 837 (2), 839 (1)

merry 819 (4), 824 (4), 824 (5), 833 (4), 837 (18), 839 (4), 882 (6), 949 (6)

merry-go-round 315 (3)

merry-maker 837 (17)

merry-making 824 (3), 833 (2), 833 (4), 835 (1), 837 (2)

Merry Widow 896 (2)

mesh 45 (14), 201 (2), 201 (4), 222 (3), 222 (8)

meshed 201 (3), 222 (7)

meshes 542 (4), 702 (4)

mesmeric 375 (3), 612 (6), 984 (7)

mesmerism 984 (1)

mesmerist 984 (5)

mesmerize 178 (3), 375 (6), 485 (9), 984 (9)

mess 43 (4), 61 (2), 194 (19), 301 (35), 700 (3), 728 (1)

mess kit 228 (5)

mess tin 194 (14)

mess up 63 (4)

message 452 (1), 524 (1), 529 (3), 531 (1), 547 (5)

messenger 66 (1), 268 (1), 511 (3), 524 (4), 528 (6), 529 (5), 531 (2), 742 (1), 754 (2), 755 (1)

Messiah 973 (6)

messianic 965 (6)

messmate 301 (6)

messy 61 (7), 649 (7)

met 74 (9)

met with, be 1 (6)

metabolize 143 (6)

metal 226 (15), 359 (1), 547 (11), 631 (1)

metal detector 484 (2)

metal lining 227 (1)

metalled 226 (12), 624 (8)

metallic 359 (3), 407 (2)

metallurgical 359 (3)

metallurgy 359 (2)

metalwork 844 (2)

metalworker 686 (3)

metalworks 687 (1)

metamorphic 82 (2)

metamorphism 82 (1)

metamorphose 143 (6), 147 (8)

metamorphosis 82 (1), 143 (2)

metaphor 18 (3), 150 (2), 462 (1), 514 (2), 519 (1),

523 (1), 563 (1), 574 (1), 988 (1)

metaphorical 462 (2), 514 (4), 519 (3), 574 (5)

metaphorical meaning 514 (2)

metaphorically 18 (9), 519 (5)

metaphysical 1 (4), 4 (3), 449 (6)

metaphysician 449 (4)

metaphysics 1 (1), 449 (3)

mete out 465 (14), 783 (3)

meteor 114 (2), 321 (7), 420 (1)

meteor shower 321 (7)

meteoric 114 (5), 277 (5), 321 (14)

meteorite 321 (7)

meteoritic 321 (14)

meteoroid 321 (7)

meteorologist 340 (3)

meteorology 340 (3)

meter 465 (6), 465 (12), 484 (2)

methane 336 (2), 385 (1)

method 16 (1), 60 (1), 62 (1), 81 (2), 624 (1), 629 (1), 688 (1)

methodical 60 (2), 62 (3), 81 (3)

methodically 16 (5), 60 (5)

Methodist 976 (5), 976 (11)

methodology 60 (1)

meticulous 83 (6), 457 (3), 494 (6), 862 (3), 929 (4)

meticulous, be 457 (5)

meticulously 768 (5)

meticulousness 457 (1), 494 (3)

metier 622 (2)

metre 203 (4), 593 (5)

metre bar 465 (5)

metric 465 (9)

metric system 465 (3)

metrical 86 (8), 465 (9), 593 (8)

metrics 465 (1)

metro 624 (7)

metrological 465 (9)

metrology 465 (3)

metronome 117 (3), 465 (6)

metropolis 184 (4)

metropolitan 191 (1), 192 (18), 741 (5), 985 (6), 986 (4)

metropolitan area 184 (3)

mettle 174 (1), 855 (1)

mettlesome 174 (5), 678 (7), 822 (3), 855 (4)

mew 409 (3)

mewed up 232 (2)

mews 192 (9), 192 (10)

mezzo 70 (2)

mezzo-soprano 413 (4)

mezzotint 417 (6), 555 (1)

MI5 459 (7)

miaow 409 (3)

miasma 336 (2), 397 (1), 653 (1)

miasmic 336 (3)

Michaelmas 129 (3)

micro- 196 (11)

micro-inch 203 (4)

microbe 196 (5), 653 (1)

microbiology 358 (2)

microcomputer 86 (6)

microcosm 196 (3), 321 (1)

microelectronics 86 (6), 160 (6), 196 (7)

microfiche 22 (1), 196 (3)

microfilm 22 (1), 196 (3), 548 (1)

microfilm reader 442 (1)

micrometer 196 (6), 465 (5)

micron 203 (4)

microorganism 33 (5), 196 (5), 358 (1), 365 (2), 653 (1)

microphone 400 (2), 531 (1), 539 (5)

microprocessor 196 (7)

microscope 196 (6), 442 (4)

microscopic 33 (6), 196 (11), 444 (3)

microscopic life 358 (1)

microscopy 196 (6), 442 (4)

microwave 417 (4)

mid 70 (2), 231 (11)

mid-life crisis 131 (2)

mid point 225 (2)

mid position 225 (1)

midair 209 (8)

midday 128 (2)

middle 30 (2), 30 (4), 70 (1), 70 (2), 76 (1), 225 (2), 225 (3), 231 (1), 231 (3), 231 (6)

middle age 131 (2), 134 (1)

middle-aged 131 (6)

Middle Ages 110 (2)

middle brow 30 (4)

middle-class 869 (8)

middle classes 732 (1), 869 (4)

middle course 30 (2), 625 (1)

middle finger 378 (4)

middle life 131 (2)

middle of the road 30 (2), 625 (3)

middle point 30 (2), 625 (1)

middle position 231 (1)

middle school 539 (2)

middle term 70 (1)

middle way 30 (2), 70 (1), 177 (1), 625 (1), 770 (1), 860 (1)

middle years 131 (2)

middlebrow 732 (2)

middleman 231 (3), 720 (2), 794 (1)

middleweight 722 (2)

middling 30 (4), 33 (7), 644 (9), 647 (3), 732 (2), 869 (8)

middling, be 732 (3)

midge 365 (16)

midget 33 (5), 196 (4)

midland 344 (1), 344 (7)

Midlands 224 (1)

midmost 70 (2), 225 (3)

midnight 129 (2), 136 (1)

midnight mass 988 (5)

midpoint 30 (2), 70 (1)

midrib 70 (1)

midriff 70 (1)

midshipman 270 (3)

midships 70 (3)

midst 70 (1), 231 (11)

midstream 70 (1)

midstream, be 625 (5)

midsummer 128 (4)

Midsummer's Day 128 (4)

midway 70 (3), 625 (4)

midweek 70 (1), 108 (5)

midwife 167 (2), 628 (2), 707 (1)

midwifery 167 (2), 628 (1), 658 (10)

midwinter 129 (4)

mien 445 (5), 547 (4), 688 (1)

miff 891 (8)

might 32 (1), 160 (1), 162 (1), 469 (3)

might and main 682 (1)

might as well 605 (6)

might do worse 605 (6)

mightily 32 (17)

mightiness 32 (1), 160 (1), 178 (1)

mighty 32 (4), 160 (8), 162 (6), 162 (11), 178 (2), 195 (7), 866 (8), 871 (3)

migraine 377 (2), 651 (2)

migrant 59 (2), 191 (1), 268 (2), 297 (3), 298 (1), 365 (4)

migrant worker 59 (2)

migrate 267 (11), 267 (13)

migration 267 (2), 296 (1)

migratory 267 (9)

mike 400 (2)

milady 373 (4)

milch cow 171 (3)

mild 177 (3), 301 (28), 379 (6), 387 (2), 736 (2), 823 (3), 884 (4)

mild-mannered 717 (3)

mildew 649 (2), 649 (8), 655 (2), 659 (2)

mildewed 127 (7), 655 (6)

mildness 177 (1), 736 (1), 884 (1), 897 (1)

mile 203 (4)

mile long, a 203 (5)

mileage 199 (1), 203 (1), 640 (1)

milepost 547 (7)

miles away 456 (4)

miles per hour 277 (1)

milestone 27 (1), 73 (1),
154 (1), 236 (1), 267 (8),
465 (5), 547 (7), 638 (2)
milieu 8 (1), 9 (1), 187 (2),
230 (1)
militancy 678 (1), 678 (2),
718 (2), 718 (3)
militant 678 (5), 678 (7),
704 (3), 708 (2), 711 (2),
712 (5), 718 (8), 718 (9),
722 (3), 973 (7)
militarism 718 (3), 735 (2)
militarist 722 (3), 735 (3)
militaristic 718 (9)
militarize 718 (10)
military 718 (9)
military college 539 (3)
military duty 718 (5)
military markings 547 (9)
military police 955 (3)
military service 718 (6)
militate 676 (5)
militate a 704 (4)
militate against 182 (3)
militia 713 (6), 722 (6)
militiaman 722 (4)
milk 300 (8), 301 (30), 304
(4), 335 (2), 369 (10), 633
(5), 673 (3), 771 (7), 786
(6)
milk and honey 301 (2),
730 (1)
milk and water 387 (1)
milk drink 301 (30)
milk dry 634 (4)
milk float 274 (5)
milk pudding 301 (17)
milk shake 301 (27)
milk white 427 (4)
milkiness 424 (1)
milking 304 (1), 771 (1)
milkmaid 369 (6)
milksop 163 (2), 501 (2),
856 (2)
milky 354 (4), 423 (2), 424
(2), 427 (5)
Milky Way 321 (4); 420 (1)
mill 164 (7), 260 (3), 332
(3), 332 (5), 687 (1)
mill around 74 (10), 318
(5)
mill race 351 (1)
milled 332 (4)

millennial 110 (4)
millennium 99 (5), 110
(1), 124 (2), 513 (3)
Millennium, the 971 (1)
miller 332 (3)
millet 301 (22)
millibar 340 (3)
millimetre 33 (2), 203 (4)
milliner 228 (28)
millinery 228 (1), 228 (23)
milling 74 (9), 234 (3), 332
(1)
million 99 (5)
million million 99 (5)
million, the 869 (1)
millionaire 99 (5), 800 (2)
millionairess 800 (2)
millions 104 (1)
millionth 99 (6)
millipede 365 (17)
millpond 346 (1)
millrace 350 (2)
millstone 332 (3), 702 (4)
milometer 465 (6)
mime 20 (2), 20 (3), 20 (5),
547 (4), 547 (21), 551 (8),
594 (9), 594 (17)
mimetic 20 (4)
mimic 20 (3), 20 (4), 20
(5), 497 (4), 547 (21), 551
(8), 594 (9), 851 (6)
mimicry 18 (2), 20 (2), 527
(3), 551 (1), 594 (8), 851
(2)
miming 594 (8)
minaret 209 (4)
mince 46 (11), 46 (12), 267
(14), 301 (16), 301 (40),
332 (5)
mince matters 541 (7)
minced 53 (6)
minced meat 301 (16)
mincing 850 (2)
mind 447 (1), 447 (2), 455
(4), 457 (5), 457 (6), 485
(3), 505 (7), 595 (0), 739
(4), 825 (7), 829 (5), 859
(3), 861 (4), 891 (5)
mind-blowing 821 (4), 864
(5)
mind-boggling 821 (4), 864
(5)

mind made up 481 (2), 599
(1)
mind one's manners 884
(5)
mind one's own business
454 (3)
mind over matter 447 (1)
mind reader 984 (5)
mind-reading 984 (7)
mind your step 664 (7)
minded 595 (1), 617 (3),
859 (7)
minder 630 (5)
mindful 455 (2), 457 (3),
505 (6)
mindful, be 455 (5), 505
(7), 858 (3)
mindful of 490 (5)
mindful of, be 449 (7)
mindfulness 457 (1)
mindless 448 (2), 450 (2)
mindlessness 448 (1)
mind's eye 505 (2)
mind's eye, the 513 (1)
mine 32 (2), 156 (3), 164
(7), 165 (7), 211 (1), 255
(4), 255 (8), 263 (8), 304
(4), 632 (1), 687 (1), 712
(8), 713 (2), 723 (14), 771
(7), 786 (6)
mine of information 490
(2)
minefield 663 (1), 713 (2)
minelayer 722 (13)
miner 255 (5), 309 (1), 686
(3), 722 (5)
mineral 319 (3), 359 (1),
359 (3), 448 (2), 631 (1)
mineral deposit 359 (1),
632 (1)
mineral kingdom 359 (1)
mineral oil 357 (2)
mineral water 301 (27),
339 (1)
mineral world 359 (1)
mineralogical 359 (3)
mineralogy 344 (4), 359
(2)
minerals 301 (10)
Minerva 967 (1)
minesweeper 722 (13)
mingle 43 (7)
mingling 43 (1)

mingy 816 (4)
mini 196 (3), 196 (8)
miniature 33 (3), 33 (6), 196 (3), 196 (8), 553 (5)
miniaturist 556 (1)
minibus 274 (10), 274 (11)
minicab 274 (9)
minim 410 (3)
minimal 33 (6), 35 (3), 196 (10)
Minimalism 553 (3)
minimization 37 (2), 483 (1)
minimize 37 (4), 481 (9), 483 (4), 926 (6)
minimizer 483 (1)
minimizing 483 (2)
minimum 33 (2), 33 (6), 35 (1), 35 (3)
mining 309 (1)
mining engineer 686 (3)
minion 742 (4)
minister 537 (1), 689 (4), 690 (4), 981 (12), 986 (2), 986 (3), 986 (7), 988 (6), 988 (10)
minister to 181 (3), 457 (6), 628 (4), 658 (20), 682 (7), 703 (7), 742 (8), 897 (6)
ministerial 733 (9)
ministering 628 (3), 742 (7), 981 (9), 985 (7)
ministration 703 (1), 985 (2)
ministry 689 (1), 703 (1)
ministry, the 986 (1)
mink 226 (6)
minnow 33 (5), 365 (15)
minor 33 (7), 35 (2), 35 (3), 130 (1), 130 (4), 410 (8), 639 (5), 732 (2)
minor arts, the 551 (3)
minor key 410 (5)
minor planet 321 (6)
minor poet 593 (6)
minor road 624 (6)
minority 35 (1), 53 (1), 105 (1), 130 (2), 161 (2), 489 (2)
Minotaur 84 (4)
minster 990 (3)

minstrel 413 (1), 413 (4), 593 (6)
minstrelsy 413 (6), 593 (1)
mint 23 (3), 32 (2), 164 (7),. 243 (5), 301 (21), 687 (1), 797 (10)
mint condition 646 (1)
mint master 797 (8), 798 (1)
mint money 800 (7)
mint of money 797 (2)
minted 797 (9)
minted coinage 797 (4)
minter 797 (8), 798 (1)
minting 797 (4)
mints 301 (18)
minuet 837 (14)
minus 2 (3), 15 (1), 35 (6), 39 (2), 39 (4), 190 (8), 307 (2), 772 (2), 774 (2)
minus, a 307 (1)
minus sign 547 (14)
minuscule 558 (1)
minute 33 (6), 110 (1), 196 (11), 247 (3), 444 (3), 457 (3), 548 (7), 570 (3), 592 (1)
minutebook 548 (1)
minuteness 33 (1), 196 (2), 319 (4), 444 (1), 457 (1)
minutes 548 (1)
minutiae 33 (2), 80 (2)
minx 878 (3), 952 (2)
miracle 84 (1), 864 (3)
miracle play 594 (3)
miracle-worker 983 (5)
miracle-working 864 (2)
miraculous 84 (6), 470 (2), 864 (5)
mirage 4 (2), 440 (2), 445 (1), 509 (1), 513 (3), 542 (1)
mire 347 (1)
mirror 18 (7), 20 (1), 20 (5), 22 (1), 417 (5), 442 (5)
mirror image 14 (1)
mirthful 833 (4)
miry 347 (2)
misadventure 154 (1)
misalliance 25 (3), 894 (2)
misandry 902 (1)
misanthrope 881 (2), 892 (2), 902 (2), 924 (5)

misanthropic 883 (5), 898 (6), 902 (3)
misanthropist 881 (2), 902 (2)
misanthropy 888 (1), 898 (2), 902 (1)
misapply 477 (8), 634 (4), 675 (2), 695 (7)
misapprehend 495 (7), 495 (8), 521 (3)
misappropriate 675 (2), 788 (8)
misappropriation 788 (4), 916 (2)
misbehave 688 (4), 738 (9), 934 (7)
misbehaving 499 (4), 738 (7), 847 (5), 934 (3)
misbehaviour 688 (1), 738 (1), 847 (2), 885 (1), 934 (1), 936 (2)
miscalculate 481 (9), 499 (6)
miscalculated 495 (5)
miscalculation 481 (1), 495 (3)
miscalled 562 (3)
miscarriage 728 (1)
miscarriage of justice 914 (2), 954 (1)
miscarry 2 (7), 167 (6), 172 (5), 307 (3), 700 (7), 728 (8), 731 (7)
miscast 594 (15)
miscellaneous 17 (2), 43 (6)
miscellany 43 (4), 74 (7), 592 (2)
mischance 731 (2)
mischief 616 (1), 641 (1), 645 (1), 655 (3), 709 (2), 914 (1)
mischief maker 663 (2), 709 (5), 738 (5)
mischief-making 898 (5)
mischievous 165 (4), 604 (3), 645 (3), 738 (7), 898 (4), 914 (3)
misconceive 481 (9), 495 (7), 521 (3)
misconceived 495 (5)
misconceiving 481 (6)

misconception 481 (1), 495 (1)

misconduct 688 (1), 885 (1), 936 (2)

misconjective 481 (9)

misconstruction 481 (1), 521 (1)

misconstrue 246 (5), 491 (8), 521 (3)

misconstrued 521 (2)

miscreant 938 (2)

misdate 118 (3)

misdated 118 (2), 122 (2)

misdeed 914 (1), 936 (2)

misdemeanour 936 (2), 954 (2)

misdirect 63 (3), 282 (6), 495 (9), 535 (3), 675 (2), 695 (7)

misdirected 10 (4), 282 (2), 495 (5), 535 (2)

misdirection 282 (1), 535 (1)

miser 74 (8), 816 (3), 932 (2)

miserable 639 (5), 645 (4), 731 (6), 825 (6), 834 (6)

miserably 32 (20)

miserliness 816 (1), 932 (1)

miserly 636 (3), 816 (4), 816 (5)

misery 616 (1), 731 (1), 825 (2), 834 (1), 834 (4), 838 (2), 853 (1)

misfire 695 (2), 728 (8)

misfit 19 (1), 25 (3), 84 (3), 188 (1), 697 (1), 728 (3)

misfortune 138 (1), 154 (1), 159 (1), 165 (3), 509 (1), 616 (1), 645 (1), 728 (1), 731 (1), 731 (2)

misgiving 486 (2)

misgivings 854 (2)

misgovern 675 (2), 734 (5), 735 (8)

misgovernment 695 (2), 733 (4), 734 (2)

misguidance 535 (1)

misguide 535 (3)

misguided 481 (6), 495 (5), 695 (6)

misguided, be 495 (7)

mishandle 645 (7), 675 (2), 695 (7), 735 (7)

mishandled 695 (6)

mishandling 675 (1), 695 (2)

mishap 138 (1), 154 (1), 731 (2)

mishit 495 (3), 695 (2)

mishmash 43 (4), 61 (2)

misinform 495 (9), 535 (3)

misinformation 535 (1)

misinformed 491 (5), 495 (5)

misinforming 535 (2)

misinterpret 246 (5), 481 (9), 495 (8), 515 (6), 521 (3)

misinterpretation 481 (1), 521 (1)

misinterpreted 495 (6), 515 (5), 521 (2)

misjudge 138 (4), 481 (9), 483 (4), 491 (8), 495 (7), 499 (6), 521 (3)

misjudged 138 (2), 495 (5)

misjudging 481 (6), 487 (2), 491 (4), 495 (5), 499 (3), 499 (5), 914 (3)

misjudgment 481 (1), 482 (1), 487 (1), 495 (1), 495 (3), 499 (1), 499 (2), 914 (2), 954 (1)

mislaid 188 (3), 190 (4), 772 (3)

mislay 63 (3), 188 (5), 772 (4)

mislead 63 (3), 282 (6), 439 (4), 474 (9), 477 (8), 495 (9), 535 (3), 542 (8), 612 (8), 934 (8)

misleading 495 (4), 535 (1)

misled 491 (5), 495 (5), 535 (2)

misled, be 495 (7)

mismanage 675 (2), 695 (7), 734 (5)

mismanaged 695 (6)

mismanagement 675 (1), 695 (2)

mismatched 25 (4)

mismatched, be 29 (3)

misname 562 (5)

misnamed 562 (3)

misnaming 562 (1)

misnomer 561 (2), 562 (1)

misogynist 881 (2), 902 (2), 924 (5)

misogyny 888 (1), 902 (1)

misplace 63 (3), 188 (5), 772 (4)

misplaced 10 (4), 25 (5), 61 (7), 188 (3), 772 (3)

misplacement 188 (1)

misprint 495 (3), 495 (8)

misprinted 495 (5)

mispronounce 565 (3), 580 (3)

mispronunciation 565 (1)

misquotation 495 (2)

misquote 495 (8), 521 (3), 541 (5)

misquoted 521 (2)

misread 495 (5), 495 (8), 521 (2), 521 (3)

misreckon 495 (7)

misreport 541 (5)

misreported 495 (6)

misrepresent 19 (4), 246 (5), 477 (8), 521 (3), 535 (3), 541 (5), 552 (3), 851 (6), 926 (6)

misrepresentation 20 (2), 535 (1), 541 (1), 543 (1), 552 (1)

misrepresented 495 (5), 552 (2)

misrule 675 (2), 695 (2), 734 (2), 734 (5), 735 (8)

miss 55 (5), 132 (2), 307 (3), 373 (4), 627 (6), 636 (8), 695 (2), 728 (7), 772 (4), 830 (4), 859 (11), 870 (1)

miss a beat 318 (5)

Miss Clever 873 (3)

miss nothing 455 (4)

miss one's cue 695 (7)

miss one's footing 309 (4)

miss one's way 282 (5)

miss out 55 (5), 57 (5)

miss the boat 138 (6), 728 (7)

miss the bus 138 (6)

miss the mark 307 (3)

missal 975 (2), 981 (4)

missed **505** (5)
missed, be **190** (6)
missed chance **695** (2)
misshape **246** (5), **842** (7)
misshapen **244** (2), **246** (4), **842** (4)
missile **287** (2), **287** (6), **723** (4), **723** (12)
missile weapon **276** (3), **287** (2), **723** (4)
missing **2** (3), **55** (3), **188** (3), **190** (4), **307** (2), **627** (3), **772** (3), **830** (2), **859** (7)
missing, be **772** (5)
missing link **55** (1), **72** (1)
missing nothing **455** (2)
mission **622** (2), **622** (3), **751** (1), **751** (2), **754** (2), **754** (3), **901** (1), **985** (2)
missionary **537** (3), **901** (4), **973** (6), **979** (5), **986** (3)
missive **588** (1)
misspell **521** (3), **565** (3)
misspend **815** (4)
misstated **495** (6)
misstatement **495** (2)
missus **373** (4)
mist **4** (2), **341** (1), **355** (2), **419** (7), **421** (4), **423** (1), **444** (1)
mist up **355** (6)
mistake **495** (3), **495** (7), **497** (1), **521** (1), **565** (1), **695** (2), **728** (1), **936** (2)
mistake the date **118** (3)
mistaken **481** (6), **495** (5), **499** (5), **521** (1), **535** (2), **977** (2)
mistaken, be **495** (7)
mistaught **535** (2)
misteach **495** (9), **535** (3), **655** (8)
misteaching **535** (1), **535** (2)
misted **423** (2)
mister **372** (1), **870** (1)
misterm **562** (5)
mistime **63** (3), **118** (3), **138** (4)
mistimed **138** (2)

mistiming **118** (1), **138** (1), **495** (2)
mistiness **419** (1)
mistranslate **521** (3)
mistranslated **495** (6), **521** (2)
mistranslation **521** (1)
mistreatment **675** (1)
mistress **373** (4), **741** (1), **776** (2), **870** (1), **887** (5), **952** (3)
mistrust **486** (2), **486** (7), **854** (2), **854** (11), **911** (1), **911** (3)
mistrustful **474** (6), **486** (4)
mistrusting **911** (2)
misty **4** (3), **341** (4), **355** (4), **419** (4), **423** (2), **424** (2), **444** (3)
misunderstand **491** (8), **495** (7), **521** (3)
misunderstanding **495** (1), **521** (1), **709** (1)
misunderstood **495** (5)
misuse **176** (8), **477** (8), **634** (1), **634** (4), **645** (7), **655** (3), **655** (8), **673** (1), **675** (1), **675** (2), **695** (2), **695** (7), **735** (7), **980** (1), **980** (6)
misused **163** (5)
mite **33** (4), **132** (1), **196** (4), **365** (16)
mitigate **37** (4), **177** (6), **468** (3), **654** (9), **831** (3), **927** (7)
mitigating **927** (3)
mitigation **37** (2), **177** (1), **468** (1), **831** (1), **927** (1)
mitigatory **468** (2)
mitre **45** (9), **743** (2), **989** (2)
mitt **228** (25)
mitten **228** (25)
mix **38** (3), **43** (7), **45** (9), **50** (4), **56** (5), **63** (4), **143** (6), **163** (10), **297** (6), **303** (5), **315** (5), **318** (6), **655** (9)
mix up **43** (7), **61** (2), **63** (4)
mix well **882** (8)
mix with **38** (3), **882** (8)

mixed **11** (6), **15** (4), **43** (6), **50** (3), **58** (2), **82** (2), **84** (7), **163** (5)
mixed-ability **534** (5)
mixed bag **17** (1), **43** (4), **74** (7)
mixed, be **43** (8), **58** (3), **78** (4), **147** (6)
mixed blessing **643** (1), **731** (1)
mixed drink **301** (28)
mixed farming **370** (1)
mixed grill **301** (13)
mixed marriage **894** (2)
mixed metaphor **519** (1)
mixed number **85** (2)
mixed up **43** (6)
mixed up in **58** (2)
mixer **43** (1)
mixing **24** (5), **43** (1)
mixing bowl **194** (16)
mixture **43** (1), **45** (1), **50** (1), **56** (1), **61** (2), **163** (1), **337** (1), **647** (1), **655** (3), **658** (2)
mixture, a **43** (3), **50** (2), **164** (2), **359** (1)
mixture as before **16** (1)
mizzenmast **238** (3)
mnemonic **505** (3), **505** (6)
mnemonic device **505** (4)
mnemonics **505** (4)
moan **352** (10), **401** (1), **401** (4), **408** (3), **829** (5), **836** (1), **836** (6)
moat **235** (2), **255** (2), **351** (1), **660** (2), **713** (2), **713** (9)
moated **713** (8)
mob **61** (11), **74** (5), **104** (1), **176** (7), **637** (1), **712** (10), **869** (2), **876** (4), **886** (3), **924** (9)
mob cap **228** (23)
mob law **733** (4), **734** (2), **954** (3)
mob rule **733** (4)
mobile **152** (4), **265** (3), **554** (1), **819** (4)
mobile features **152** (2)
mobile home **192** (7)
mobility **152** (1), **265** (1), **819** (1)

mobilization 74 (1), 718 (5)

mobilize 45 (9), 74 (10), 74 (11), 669 (11), 718 (10)

mobilized 669 (7), 718 (8)

mobster 904 (3)

moccasins 228 (27)

mock 18 (6), 20 (4), 486 (6), 542 (7), 542 (9), 835 (7), 839 (5), 851 (5), 851 (6), 867 (11), 921 (5), 922 (5), 926 (6)

mock epic 593 (3)

mock-heroic 593 (8), 849 (3), 851 (4)

mock-modest 483 (2)

mock modesty 850 (1)

mock-up 23 (1), 522 (2)

mocker 20 (3), 835 (3), 839 (3), 924 (5), 926 (3)

mockery 20 (2), 486 (1), 542 (5), 851 (1), 875 (1), 921 (1), 980 (1)

mockery of 22 (1), 851 (3)

mocking 543 (4), 835 (5), 849 (3), 851 (4), 921 (3), 926 (5), 980 (4)

mocking laughter 835 (2)

mod 132 (2)

modal 7 (3), 8 (3), 410 (8)

modality 7 (2)

mode 7 (2), 86 (4), 410 (5), 624 (1), 848 (1)

mode of address 870 (1)

mode of behaviour 688 (1)

mode of use 673 (1)

mode of worship 988 (3)

model 22 (1), 23 (2), 23 (4), 23 (5), 34 (3), 83 (2), 196 (3), 196 (8), 243 (5), 512 (1), 522 (2), 522 (8), 551 (2), 551 (8), 554 (1), 554 (3), 646 (3), 837 (15), 866 (6)

model of virtue 937 (1)

modelled 20 (4)

modeller 556 (2)

modelling 554 (1)

modelling tool 554 (1)

moderate 30 (4), 33 (6), 33 (7), 37 (4), 37 (5), 177 (3), 177 (6), 278 (6), 468 (3), 613 (3), 625 (2), 625 (3), 647 (3), 654 (9), 708 (2), 736 (3), 747 (7), 812 (3), 823 (7), 831 (3), 942 (3)

moderate, be 177 (5), 942 (4)

moderate circumstances 732 (1)

moderate drinker 948 (2)

moderately 33 (9), 177 (8)

moderateness 33 (1), 177 (1), 625 (1)

moderation 30 (1), 33 (1), 37 (2), 177 (1), 468 (1), 483 (1), 620 (1), 625 (1), 719 (1), 732 (1), 823 (1), 831 (1), 942 (1)

moderator 177 (2), 375 (2), 658 (8), 717 (2), 720 (2), 986 (4)

modern 121 (2), 126 (6), 285 (2), 848 (5)

modern art 551 (3)

modern, be 121 (3)

modern dance 594 (5)

modern generation 126 (3)

modern master 556 (1)

modern maths 86 (3)

modern times 110 (2), 121 (1)

modernism 121 (1), 126 (2), 848 (1)

modernist 126 (3)

modernistic 126 (6)

modernity 126 (2)

modernization 126 (2)

modernize 121 (3), 126 (8), 143 (5), 143 (6), 285 (3), 654 (9), 656 (9)

modernized 126 (7)

modernness 126 (2)

modest 33 (6), 33 (7), 192 (20), 483 (2), 573 (2), 598 (3), 620 (3), 732 (2), 854 (7), 867 (7), 872 (3), 874 (2), 931 (2), 950 (5)

modest, be 854 (11), 872 (5), 874 (3)

modest person 874 (1)

modest request 761 (1)

modestly 33 (9), 874 (4)

modesty 483 (1), 573 (1), 598 (1), 854 (2), 872 (1), 874 (1), 950 (1), 950 (2)

modicum 33 (2)

modification 15 (1), 143 (1), 468 (1)

modifier 143 (3)

modify 15 (6), 19 (4), 143 (6), 147 (8), 178 (3), 468 (3)

modifying 8 (3), 468 (2)

modish 848 (5)

modulate 24 (10), 143 (6), 410 (9), 577 (4)

modulation 143 (1), 410 (5), 577 (1)

module 23 (1)

modus operandi 624 (1)

modus vivendi 150 (2), 770 (1)

mogul 638 (4)

mohair 208 (2)

moiety 92 (1)

moire 437 (1)

moist 339 (2), 341 (4), 341 (6)

moisten 75 (4), 300 (9), 311 (5), 339 (3), 341 (7), 350 (9), 649 (9)

moistened 341 (4)

moistening 43 (1), 75 (1), 339 (1), 341 (2), 370 (1)

moistness 341 (1)

moisture 341 (1), 350 (6)

molar 256 (4), 332 (3)

molasses 392 (2)

mole 254 (2), 365 (3), 524 (5), 547 (2), 713 (2), 845 (1)

molecular 196 (11)

molecule 196 (2), 319 (4)

molehill 209 (3), 210 (1), 253 (4)

molest 645 (6), 827 (9), 898 (8), 951 (11)

molestation 645 (1), 827 (2)

moll 952 (3)

mollification 177 (1), 719 (1)

mollify 177 (7), 719 (4)

mollusc 365 (14)

molluscan 365 (18)

mollycoddle 163 (2)
Moloch 982 (3)
molten 337 (3), 379 (5), 381 (6)
moment 8 (2), 33 (2), 108 (3), 114 (2), 116 (2), 137 (1)
momentarily 114 (7)
momentariness 114 (2), 116 (1)
momentary 114 (5)
momentous 137 (6), 154 (5), 638 (5)
momentum 160 (3), 279 (1)
monarch 741 (3)
monarchical 733 (9)
monarchy 733 (4)
monastery 192 (2), 986 (9)
monastic 895 (4), 986 (5), 986 (12), 989 (4)
monastic life 985 (1)
monasticism 883 (2), 985 (1)
monetary 797 (9)
monetary unit 797 (4)
money 629 (1), 797 (1), 800 (1), 804 (1)
money-changer 797 (8)
money coming in 807 (1)
money-conscious 814 (2), 816 (4)
money-dealer 797 (8)
money dealings 797 (3)
money-grubber 816 (3)
money-mad 816 (5)
money-making 771 (5), 800 (1)
money market 797 (3)
money order 797 (5)
money power 797 (3)
money received 807 (1)
money-saving 814 (2)
money spider 365 (17)
money-spinner 800 (2)
moneybags 797 (2), 797 (8), 800 (1), 800 (2)
moneybox 194 (7), 799 (1)
moneyed 635 (4), 730 (4), 800 (4)
moneylender 784 (3)
money's worth 809 (1), 812 (1)

Mongolian 11 (6)
mongolism 499 (1), 503 (1)
mongrel 43 (5), 43 (6), 84 (7), 365 (10)
mongrelize 43 (7)
monies 797 (2)
monitor 415 (3), 457 (6), 459 (13), 537 (1), 690 (4)
monk 895 (2), 950 (3), 979 (4), 986 (5)
monkey 365 (3), 938 (1)
monkey about with 698 (5)
monkey trick 497 (2)
monks 986 (5)
mono- 88 (3), 398 (1), 398 (3)
monochrome 16 (2), 426 (1)
monocle 442 (2)
monogamist 894 (4)
monogamous 894 (7)
monogamy 894 (2)
monogram 547 (1), 547 (13), 558 (2)
monogrammatic 558 (5)
monograph 591 (1)
monolith 16 (1), 88 (2), 548 (3)
monolithic 13 (2), 16 (2), 44 (4), 48 (2), 52 (6), 88 (3)
monologist 579 (5), 585 (2), 594 (10)
monologue 16 (1), 88 (2), 579 (2), 585 (1), 594 (3)
monomania 481 (2), 503 (3)
monomaniac 504 (1)
monophonic 398 (3)
monopolist 932 (2)
monopolistic 178 (2), 747 (4), 773 (2), 932 (3)
monopolize 178 (4), 449 (11), 773 (4), 932 (4)
monopolizer 776 (1)
monopoly 57 (1), 708 (5), 747 (2), 773 (1), 793 (1)
monorail 624 (7)
monosyllabic 569 (2), 582 (2)
monosyllable 559 (1)

monotheism 973 (2)
monotheist 973 (7)
monotheistic 973 (8)
monotone 16 (1)
monotonous 13 (2), 16 (2), 106 (3), 572 (2), 838 (3)
monotony 16 (1), 28 (1), 71 (1), 106 (2), 838 (1), 840 (1)
monotype 77 (3), 587 (1)
monsieur 372 (1)
monsoon 350 (6)
monster 84 (2), 176 (4), 735 (3), 842 (2), 854 (4), 864 (3), 904 (4), 938 (4), 970 (4)
monstrosity 84 (2), 195 (2)
monstrous 32 (12), 84 (6), 195 (7), 645 (3), 645 (4), 842 (3), 849 (2), 864 (5), 934 (6)
monstrous birth 84 (2)
monstrously 32 (18)
montage 445 (3), 553 (5)
month 110 (1)
month of Sundays 109 (1)
monthly 141 (5), 141 (7)
monument 125 (2), 164 (3), 253 (5), 364 (2), 505 (3), 547 (7), 548 (3), 729 (1), 866 (4)
monumental 32 (6), 195 (6), 209 (9)
monumental ignorance 491 (1)
monumental mason 556 (2)
mood 7 (1), 179 (1), 564 (1), 604 (2), 688 (1), 817 (1)
moodiness 893 (1)
moody 604 (3), 834 (6), 892 (3), 893 (2)
moody person 819 (1)
moon 129 (1), 152 (2), 314 (2), 321 (9), 321 (10), 420 (1), 456 (7)
moon about 679 (11)
moon after 859 (11)
moonbeam 419 (3)
mooning 456 (4)
moonless 418 (4)
moonlet 321 (10)

moonlight 321 (9), 417 (1), 419 (3), 682 (7)

moonlight flit 296 (1), 667 (1)

moonlighting 788 (4)

moonlit 417 (9)

moonrise 129 (1)

moonscape 321 (9)

moonshine 321 (9), 543 (3), 790 (1)

moor 45 (11), 172 (3), 187 (5), 209 (2), 269 (10), 295 (4), 347 (1), 348 (1)

moored 187 (4)

moorhen 365 (4)

mooring 187 (3)

moorings 47 (2)

moot 459 (12), 474 (4), 512 (7)

moot point 452 (1)

mooted 512 (5), 669 (6)

mop 259 (2), 342 (3), 342 (6), 648 (5), 648 (9)

mop and mow 970 (8)

mop up 165 (6), 299 (4)

mope 834 (9), 893 (3)

moped 274 (3)

moper 504 (1), 829 (2), 834 (4), 838 (2), 853 (1), 924 (5)

moping 834 (2)

moppet 132 (1)

mopping up 165 (1)

moraine 209 (3), 344 (3)

moral 480 (1), 496 (1), 693 (1), 866 (7), 917 (7), 933 (3), 950 (5)

moral compulsion 740 (1)

moral education 534 (2)

moral fibre 599 (1), 929 (1)

moral insensibility 820 (1), 823 (1), 865 (1)

moral necessity 596 (1)

moral power 160 (1)

moral principles 917 (4)

moral purity 950 (1)

Moral Rearmament 654 (4)

moral rectitude 933 (1)

moral science 917 (4)

moral sensibility 513 (1), 612 (3), 818 (1), 819 (1)

moral strength 933 (1)

moral support 703 (1)

moral tone 933 (1)

moral training 534 (2)

moral turpitude 930 (1)

moral weakness 163 (1)

morale 7 (1), 739 (1)

moralistic 480 (4), 917 (7)

morality 913 (1), 917 (4), 933 (1), 950 (1)

morality play 594 (3)

moralize 480 (5), 534 (7)

moralizing 480 (4), 496 (3), 534 (5), 691 (1), 691 (3), 693 (2), 917 (7)

morals 688 (1), 913 (1), 917 (4), 933 (1), 950 (1)

moratorium 136 (2), 145 (4), 805 (1)

morbid 651 (22)

morbid curiosity 453 (1)

morbidity 645 (1)

morbidly 651 (24), 653 (5)

mordancy 174 (3), 571 (1)

mordant 174 (4), 425 (4), 571 (2), 924 (6)

more 26 (2), 34 (11), 38 (2), 38 (5), 101 (2)

more and more 36 (6)

more often than not 139 (4)

more or less 26 (3), 33 (12), 200 (8)

more so 34 (4), 36 (6)

more than a match for 34 (4)

more than a match for, be 727 (9)

more than enough 32 (17), 635 (2), 635 (4), 637 (1)

more than ever 32 (17)

more than one 101 (2)

more than one needs 637 (4)

moreover 38 (5)

mores 610 (2)

morganatic 894 (9)

morgue 361 (1), 364 (1)

moribund 361 (5)

morn 128 (1)

morning 110 (1), 128 (1), 128 (5), 135 (1), 141 (2), 417 (1)

morning after 67 (1)

morning dress 228 (4)

morning, noon and night 106 (7)

morning prayer 988 (5)

morning twilight 128 (1)

morocco 226 (6)

moron 504 (1)

moronic 448 (2), 503 (7)

morose 834 (6), 883 (5), 893 (2)

moroseness 883 (1), 902 (1)

morphine 375 (2), 679 (5), 949 (4)

morphological 344 (5), 557 (5)

morphology 358 (2), 367 (1), 557 (2)

morris dance 837 (14)

morris dancer 312 (2)

morrow 124 (1)

morse 531 (1), 547 (5)

morsel 33 (2), 53 (5), 301 (11)

mortal 114 (4), 165 (4), 361 (5), 362 (8), 371 (3), 371 (6)

mortal blow 616 (1)

mortal illness 361 (2)

mortal remains 363 (1)

mortality 114 (1), 361 (1), 361 (4), 371 (1)

mortally 32 (18)

mortally ill 651 (21)

mortar 47 (9), 723 (11)

mortarboard 228 (23)

mortgage 702 (4), 767 (1), 767 (6), 784 (1), 785 (1), 785 (2), 802 (1), 803 (1)

mortgaged 767 (4), 803 (4)

mortgagee 776 (1), 802 (2)

mortgagor 803 (3)

mortician 364 (1)

mortification 51 (2), 361 (1), 825 (2), 827 (2), 829 (1), 830 (1), 872 (2), 912 (1)

mortified 825 (6)

mortify 51 (5), 827 (8), 829 (6), 872 (7)

mortifying 827 (5), 829 (4)

mortise 45 (9), 231 (8), 255 (2), 262 (1)
mortuary 361 (1), 364 (1)
mosaic 17 (1), 43 (4), 50 (1), 82 (2), 437 (2), 553 (5), 844 (10)
mosque 990 (1), 990 (3)
mosquito 365 (16)
mosquito net 226 (3)
moss 347 (1), 366 (6)
moss-green 434 (3)
moss-grown 655 (6)
moss-trooper 722 (4)
mossy 259 (6), 327 (2), 366 (9)
most 26 (2), 32 (4)
Most High, the 965 (3)
most likely 471 (7)
most, the 34 (12)
mostly 32 (17)
mot 839 (2)
motel 192 (11)
motet 981 (5)
moth 168 (1), 365 (16), 659 (2)
moth-eaten 127 (7), 655 (6)
mothball 396 (2)
mother 11 (2), 169 (4), 373 (3), 660 (8), 703 (6), 889 (5), 897 (6), 986 (6)
Mother Church 169 (4)
mother country 169 (4)
mother earth 171 (3), 321 (2)
mother figure 150 (2)
mother goddess 966 (2)
mother-in-law 169 (4)
mother of pearl 437 (1), 844 (8)
Mother Superior 986 (6)
mother-to-be 169 (4)
mother tongue 516 (1), 557 (1)
mother-wit 498 (1)
mothered 360 (3)
motherhood 11 (3), 169 (1), 169 (4)
motherland 192 (5)
motherly 169 (5), 887 (9), 897 (4)
mother's darling 890 (2)
mother's milk 301 (30)

motif 844 (3)
motion 27 (1), 188 (1), 265 (1), 269 (1), 277 (1), 285 (1), 302 (3), 452 (1), 547 (4), 547 (21), 623 (1), 676 (1), 678 (1), 688 (1), 737 (6), 759 (1)
motion after 265 (1)
motion away 265 (1)
motion from 286 (1)
motion in front 265 (1)
motion into 265 (1)
motion out of 265 (1)
motion pictures 445 (4)
motion round 265 (1)
motion towards 265 (1)
motionless 266 (6)
motivate 156 (9), 178 (3), 512 (7), 612 (8), 638 (7), 673 (5), 676 (5), 709 (8), 859 (13)
motivated 612 (7)
motivating 612 (6)
motivation 156 (1), 612 (1)
motivator 156 (2), 612 (5), 698 (3)
motive 156 (1), 156 (6), 160 (1), 178 (1), 265 (3), 612 (1), 623 (4), 678 (1)
motive power 160 (3), 265 (1)
motiveless 618 (6)
motley 43 (4), 43 (6), 82 (2), 228 (2), 437 (1), 437 (5)
motocross 716 (3)
motor 160 (4), 265 (3), 267 (15), 274 (11), 630 (2)
motor car 274 (11)
motor coach 274 (10)
motor horn 665 (1)
motor launch 275 (7)
motor race 716 (3)
motor rally 716 (3)
motor scooter 274 (3)
motor show 796 (1)
motor vessel 275 (1)
motorbike 274 (3)
motorboat 275 (7)
motorcycle 267 (15), 274 (3)
motorcyclist 268 (4)
motorist 268 (5)

motorized 274 (16), 630 (6)
motorman 268 (5)
motorway 624 (6)
mottle 437 (4), 437 (9)
mottled 437 (8), 547 (17)
motto 496 (1), 563 (1)
mould 7 (2), 16 (1), 23 (3), 51 (2), 77 (2), 194 (1), 243 (1), 243 (5), 331 (1), 366 (6), 534 (6), 551 (8), 554 (3), 649 (2), 659 (2), 844 (12)
mould oneself on 20 (7)
mould the figure 48 (3)
moulded 243 (3), 817 (2)
moulded on 20 (4)
moulder 51 (5), 127 (8), 649 (8), 655 (7)
mouldering 51 (2), 51 (3), 127 (7), 655 (6)
moulding 48 (2), 243 (2), 554 (1), 844 (2)
mouldy 649 (7)
moult 229 (7)
moulting 229 (1), 229 (4)
mound 195 (3), 209 (3), 253 (4)
mount 36 (4), 45 (14), 209 (2), 209 (12), 218 (15), 235 (4), 267 (6), 267 (15), 273 (4), 273 (8), 296 (6), 303 (4), 308 (4), 308 (5), 369 (8), 594 (16)
mount guard 457 (7), 660 (8)
mount up to 809 (6)
mountain 32 (2), 195 (3), 209 (2)
mountain nymph 967 (3)
mountain trail 624 (5)
mountaineer 268 (1), 308 (2), 308 (5)
mountaineering 308 (1), 837 (6)
mountainous 195 (6), 195 (7), 209 (10)
mountebank 545 (3)
mounted 310 (3)
mounted, be 273 (12)
mounted police 268 (4)
mounted troops 722 (10)

mounting 218 (2), 296 (1), 308 (1)

mourn 364 (9), 836 (5)

mourner 364 (2), 836 (4)

mournful 827 (6), 834 (6), 836 (4)

mournfulness 825 (2)

mourning 228 (4), 364 (2), 364 (8), 428 (2), 428 (4), 836 (1), 836 (4)

mouse 33 (5), 365 (3), 721 (1), 856 (2), 874 (1)

mouser 365 (11), 619 (3)

mousse 301 (17), 355 (1)

moustache 259 (2)

moustached 259 (5)

mousy 426 (3), 429 (2), 842 (3), 842 (5)

mouth 68 (5), 234 (2), 263 (4), 297 (2), 301 (6), 345 (1), 577 (4)

mouth organ 414 (5)

mouth wash 648 (4)

mouthful 301 (11)

mouthpiece 263 (4), 353 (1), 414 (6), 520 (4), 524 (4), 579 (5), 755 (1)

movable 265 (3), 272 (5)

move 1 (6), 63 (3), 68 (2), 173 (3), 188 (1), 188 (4), 265 (1), 265 (4), 265 (5), 272 (7), 277 (6), 291 (4), 302 (6), 318 (5), 512 (7), 547 (4), 671 (1), 676 (2), 678 (11), 688 (2), 691 (4), 698 (2), 759 (3), 821 (6)

move along there 267 (17)

move away 290 (3)

move fast 111 (3), 114 (6), 176 (7), 265 (4), 267 (11), 267 (14), 269 (10), 277 (6), 285 (3), 296 (5), 305 (5), 306 (5), 620 (6), 678 (11), 680 (3)

move house 265 (4)

move in 187 (8), 192 (21), 297 (5), 712 (7)

move off 290 (3)

move one's bowels 302 (6)

move out 621 (3)

move over 190 (7), 265 (4)

move round 250 (8)

move sideways 239 (3)

move sinuously 251 (13)

move slowly 111 (3), 113 (9), 136 (4), 145 (8), 163 (9), 265 (4), 267 (14), 278 (4), 598 (4), 679 (11), 681 (3), 838 (5)

move towards 289 (4)

move up 200 (6), 285 (4)

move with the times 126 (8), 143 (5), 285 (3)

moved 818 (4), 819 (2)

movement 147 (2), 265 (1), 410 (1), 412 (4), 676 (1), 678 (1), 708 (1)

mover 612 (5), 691 (2)

movie 551 (4)

movies 445 (4)

moving 160 (9), 178 (2), 265 (3), 267 (9), 285 (2), 590 (6), 678 (7), 821 (4), 827 (6)

moving apart 46 (1), 294 (1)

moving sideways 239 (2)

moving staircase 274 (15)

mow 46 (11), 204 (5), 370 (9)

mow down 165 (7), 362 (11)

mowing grass 366 (8)

mowing machine 370 (6)

mown 204 (3)

MP 692 (3)

Mr 372 (1)

Mr and Mrs 894 (4)

Mr Clever 873 (3)

Mr Universe 841 (2)

Mrs 373 (4)

Ms 373 (4), 589 (1), 870 (1)

much 32 (2), 32 (17), 104 (4)

much ado 678 (1)

much obliged 907 (3), 907 (7)

much regretted 830 (3)

much the same 18 (4), 28 (8)

much-travelled 267 (9)

mucilage 354 (1)

mucilaginous 354 (5)

muck 302 (4), 649 (2)

muck-raker 926 (4)

muckraker 529 (4)

mucky 649 (7)

mucous 302 (5)

mucus 302 (4), 335 (2), 354 (1), 649 (2)

mud 347 (1), 354 (1), 649 (2)

mud flat 347 (1)

mud-slinger 926 (4)

mud-slinging 926 (5)

muddiness 423 (1)

muddle 61 (1), 61 (2), 63 (3), 63 (4), 456 (8), 700 (3), 728 (1)

muddled 61 (7), 477 (6), 568 (2)

muddy 318 (6), 341 (4), 347 (2), 423 (2), 649 (7), 649 (9)

muesli 301 (22)

muezzin's cry 981 (4)

muff 228 (25), 495 (8), 695 (9)

muffin 301 (22)

muffle 163 (10), 226 (13), 399 (4), 401 (5), 405 (3), 525 (7), 578 (4)

muffled 401 (3), 405 (2), 578 (2)

muffled drum 364 (2)

muffled drums 405 (1)

muffled tones 401 (1)

muffler 228 (22), 401 (2)

mufti 228 (6), 973 (5), 986 (8)

mug 194 (15), 279 (9), 501 (2), 544 (1), 712 (9), 788 (9)

mugger 176 (4), 789 (2)

mugging 712 (1), 788 (1)

mugging up 536 (2)

muggins 501 (2)

muggy 264 (5), 341 (4)

Muhammad 973 (6)

mulatto 43 (5)

mulberry 436 (2)

mulch 171 (2), 226 (1), 370 (9)

mule 43 (5), 228 (27), 273 (3), 602 (3)

muleteer 268 (5)

mulish 273 (11), 365 (18), 602 (4)

mulishly 602 (7)

mulishness 602 (1)

mull 254 (2), 455 (4), 490 (8)

mull over 449 (7)

mullah 973 (5)

mullification 752 (1)

mullion 218 (10), 263 (5)

multi- 101 (2)

multi-coloured 437 (5)

multi-millionaire 800 (2)

multicoloured 17 (2)

multidisciplinary 534 (5)

multifarious 10 (3), 15 (4), 82 (2), 104 (4)

multifid 100 (2)

multiform 10 (3), 15 (4), 17 (2), 19 (2), 43 (6), 82 (2), 101 (2), 104 (4), 152 (3), 437 (5)

multiformity 17 (1), 19 (1), 82 (1), 101 (1)

multilateral 101 (2), 239 (2), 247 (6), 765 (4)

multilingual 557 (5)

multinational company 708 (5)

multipartite 100 (2)

multiple 82 (2), 85 (2), 85 (5), 101 (2), 104 (3), 104 (4)

multiple sclerosis 651 (16)

multiple store 796 (3)

multiple unit 274 (13)

multiplex 82 (2)

multiplication 36 (1), 86 (2), 166 (1)

multiplication table 86 (6)

multiplicity 82 (1), 101 (1), 104 (1)

multiplier 85 (2)

multiply 20 (6), 36 (4), 36 (5), 86 (12), 104 (6), 106 (4), 166 (3), 167 (6), 171 (6)

multiply by four 97 (3)

multiply by two 91 (3)

multiracial 43 (6)

multisect 100 (3)

multisection 100 (1)

multistorey 192 (20)

multitude 32 (1), 32 (2), 74 (4), 74 (5), 101 (2), 104 (1), 171 (3), 722 (6)

multitude, the 869 (1)

multitudinous 32 (4), 74 (9), 104 (5), 139 (2), 635 (5)

mum 169 (4)

mumble 580 (3)

mumbo jumbo 515 (1), 982 (1), 982 (3), 983 (2)

mummification 364 (1), 666 (1)

mummified 342 (4)

mummify 342 (6), 364 (9), 666 (5)

mummy 169 (4), 363 (1)

mummy-case 364 (1)

mummy chamber 364 (5)

mumps 651 (5)

munch 301 (36)

mundane 974 (5)

municipal 184 (5)

municipality 184 (3)

munificence 813 (1)

munificent 813 (3)

munitions 723 (1)

mural 553 (5)

mural painting 553 (2)

murder 165 (6), 362 (1), 362 (2), 362 (12), 735 (8), 898 (3), 963 (12)

murderer 168 (1), 176 (4), 362 (7), 659 (4), 904 (2), 904 (3), 963 (5)

murderous 176 (6), 362 (9), 898 (7)

murk 418 (1), 419 (1)

murky 418 (3), 423 (2), 523 (2)

murmur 401 (1), 401 (4), 403 (1), 523 (6), 665 (1), 762 (1), 762 (3), 829 (1), 829 (5)

murmuring 738 (1)

muscle 47 (4), 160 (1), 682 (1)

muscle-bound 195 (9)

muscle in 297 (8)

muscle man 195 (3)

muscle relaxant 658 (4)

muscular 162 (8)

muscular dystrophy 651 (16)

muscularity 162 (2)

muse 449 (8), 456 (7)

Muses 593 (1), 967 (2)

museum 74 (7), 125 (2), 522 (2), 632 (3)

museum piece 127 (2)

mush 356 (1)

mushroom 36 (4), 126 (5), 171 (6), 197 (4), 252 (2), 253 (4), 301 (20), 366 (6), 427 (5)

mushroom cloud 417 (4)

mushy 327 (2), 354 (4), 356 (2)

music 50 (1), 56 (1), 398 (1), 410 (1), 412 (1), 826 (1)

music centre 414 (10)

music festival 412 (1)

music hall 594 (4), 594 (7)

music lover 413 (1)

music-making 412 (1)

music, the 412 (1)

musical 410 (6), 412 (5), 412 (7), 413 (7), 445 (4), 594 (3), 826 (2)

musical ability 413 (6)

musical box 414 (10)

musical comedy 412 (5), 594 (3)

musical ear 415 (1)

musical instrument 414 (1)

musical interval 201 (1)

musical note 71 (2), 201 (1), 403 (1), 410 (2)

musical piece 410 (1), 412 (4)

musical skill 164 (1), 410 (1), 412 (1), 413 (6)

musicality 410 (1)

musician 89 (2), 164 (4), 413 (1), 520 (4), 696 (1)

musicianly 413 (7)

musicianship 164 (1), 412 (1), 413 (6)

musing 449 (1), 449 (5)

musk 396 (2)

musket 723 (9)

musketeer 722 (5)

musketry 723 (1)

musky 396 (3)

Muslim 973 (7)

muslin 222 (4), 424 (1)

must, a 596 (1), 627 (1)

must have 627 (6), 859 (11)

mustang 273 (8)

mustard 389 (1)

mustard yellow 433 (3)

muster 74 (1), 74 (11), 86 (4), 86 (11)

muster courage 855 (7)

muster roll 87 (1)

mustiness 397 (1)

musty 397 (2), 649 (7)

mutability 114 (1), 152 (1)

mutable 114 (3), 143 (4), 152 (3)

mutation 17 (1), 84 (2), 143 (1), 147 (1)

mute 163 (10), 399 (2), 401 (2), 401 (5), 405 (1), 405 (3), 414 (11), 578 (1), 578 (2), 578 (4), 582 (2)

mute, be 399 (3), 578 (3), 582 (3)

muted 33 (6), 163 (4), 399 (2), 401 (3), 405 (2), 410 (6), 416 (2), 425 (7), 517 (2), 578 (2)

muteness 399 (1), 578 (1), 582 (1)

mutilate 39 (3), 244 (3), 655 (9), 842 (7)

mutilated 55 (3), 647 (3)

mutilation 39 (1), 244 (1), 655 (3), 842 (1)

mutineer 738 (4), 918 (1)

mutineering 738 (1)

mutinous 709 (6), 711 (2), 715 (2), 738 (7), 738 (8), 918 (2)

mutinousness 738 (1)

mutiny 145 (3), 715 (3), 738 (2), 738 (10), 918 (1), 918 (3)

mutter 403 (1), 408 (3), 577 (1), 580 (3), 893 (3)

muttering 665 (1), 900 (2)

mutton 301 (16)

mutual 9 (5), 12 (2), 151 (2)

mutual abuse 899 (2)

mutual affection 887 (1)

mutual agreement 764 (1)

mutual approach 293 (1)

mutual exclusiveness 14 (1)

mutual pledge 765 (1)

mutual profit 791 (2)

mutual regard 880 (2)

mutual relation 9 (2), 12 (1)

mutual support 880 (1)

mutual transfer 188 (1), 272 (1)

mutual understanding 710 (1)

mutuality 12 (1), 151 (1)

mutualize 775 (6)

mutually 12 (4)

mutually opposed 704 (3)

muzzle 161 (9), 254 (3), 263 (4), 264 (2), 399 (4), 578 (4), 702 (8), 747 (7), 748 (4)

my dear 890 (1)

my lady 870 (1)

my lord 372 (1), 870 (1)

my lud 957 (1)

myopic 440 (3)

myriad 99 (5), 104 (4)

myriads 104 (1)

myself 80 (4), 320 (2)

mysteries 973 (1), 981 (3), 988 (3)

mysterious 84 (6), 474 (4), 491 (6), 517 (3), 523 (4), 525 (3), 568 (2), 864 (5), 984 (6)

mystery 523 (1), 525 (2), 530 (1), 530 (2), 988 (3)

mystery play 594 (3)

mystery religion 973 (1)

mystic 523 (4), 973 (8), 975 (3), 979 (4), 979 (6), 981 (8), 981 (10), 984 (4), 984 (6)

mystical 517 (4), 965 (5)

mysticism 449 (2), 523 (1), 973 (1), 975 (1), 979 (1), 984 (1)

mystification 477 (1), 515 (1), 535 (1)

mystified 517 (5)

mystify 474 (9), 477 (8)

mystique 866 (2), 981 (2)

myth 513 (3), 543 (3), 590 (2)

myth-maker 513 (4)

mythic 513 (6), 970 (6)

mythic deity 966 (2)

mythic heaven 361 (3), 971 (2)

mythic hell 361 (3), 972 (2)

mythical 343 (1), 966 (3), 970 (6)

mythical beast 84 (4)

mythical being 84 (4), 967 (3), 970 (5)

mythological 127 (4), 513 (6), 543 (4), 590 (6), 966 (3)

mythologist 590 (5)

mythology 127 (3), 543 (3)

myxomatosis 651 (17)

N

n 104 (4)

Naafi 192 (13)

nabob 800 (2)

nadir 69 (2), 73 (1), 103 (1), 211 (1), 214 (1)

nag 273 (4), 612 (9), 709 (9), 827 (9), 891 (9)

nag into 612 (10)

naiad 967 (3)

nail 45 (11), 47 (5), 217 (3), 256 (2), 263 (12), 263 (18)

nail polish 843 (3)

nail varnish 843 (3)

nails 778 (2)

naive 487 (2), 491 (4), 499 (4), 551 (6), 699 (3), 935 (3)

naive painter 556 (1)

naivety 491 (1), 499 (1), 699 (1)

naked 229 (4), 443 (2), 522 (5)

naked eye 438 (2)

naked force 735 (2)

naked light 420 (1)

naked steel 723 (8)

nakedness 229 (2), 661 (2)

namby-pamby 163 (2)

name 62 (6), 68 (10), 80 (8), 524 (9), 547 (18), 559 (1), 561 (2), 561 (6), 562 (1), 562 (5), 751 (4), 866 (1), 928 (8)

name-day 876 (2)

name names 80 (8), 526 (5), 562 (2)

named 561 (4)

named after 561 (4)

named, be 561 (7)

nameless 84 (5), 562 (4), 867 (7)

namely 80 (11), 520 (11), 561 (8)

nameplate 547 (13)

namer 561 (3)

namesake 561 (2)

naming 547 (2), 561 (5)

naming ceremony 561 (1)

nanny 742 (2), 749 (1)

nanny goat 365 (7)

nap 222 (5), 259 (2), 331 (2), 679 (4), 679 (12)

napalm bomb 723 (14)

nape 238 (1)

napless 229 (5)

napped 259 (5)

napping 679 (9)

nappy or diaper 228 (14)

narcissism 873 (1), 932 (1)

narcissist 932 (2)

narcissistic 873 (4), 932 (3)

Narcissus 873 (3)

narcotic 177 (4), 375 (2), 658 (7), 949 (4), 949 (12)

narcotize 375 (6)

nark 524 (5)

narrate 524 (10), 590 (7)

narration 524 (1), 590 (1)

narrative 496 (1), 524 (1), 524 (2), 543 (3), 548 (1), 557 (3), 590 (2), 590 (6), 594 (2), 676 (2)

narrative verse 593 (2)

narrator 524 (4), 549 (2), 579 (5), 589 (7), 590 (5), 594 (9)

narrow 33 (6), 45 (13), 196 (8), 198 (4), 198 (6), 198 (7), 206 (4), 206 (6), 208

(4), 209 (9), 212 (2), 747 (4)

narrow, be 206 (6)

narrow down 187 (5), 293 (3)

narrow escape 661 (1), 667 (1)

narrow gauge 206 (1), 624 (7)

narrow interval 201 (1)

narrow margin 15 (1), 28 (5)

narrow mind 481 (4), 493 (1), 602 (3), 881 (2)

narrow-minded 481 (7), 499 (5), 950 (6)

narrow the gap 293 (3)

narrowboat 275 (7)

narrowing 37 (1), 206 (3), 293 (1)

narrowing gap 293 (1)

narrowly 33 (9)

narrowness 198 (1), 206 (1)

narrows 206 (1)

nasal 560 (5), 580 (2)

nasal cavity 263 (4)

nasal twang 580 (1)

nasality 407 (1), 577 (2)

nasalize 580 (3)

nascent 68 (6)

nastiness 645 (1)

nasty 397 (2), 645 (4), 649 (6), 653 (2), 661 (3), 827 (4), 842 (3), 888 (5), 898 (4), 898 (6), 900 (2), 951 (6)

nasty taste 391 (1)

nasty type 938 (1)

natal 68 (7)

nation 11 (1), 11 (4), 191 (3), 371 (5), 708 (4), 744 (2)

nation state 871 (5), 733 (6)

national 11 (6), 79 (4), 184 (5), 191 (3), 191 (6), 371 (7), 742 (5)

national dress 547 (10)

national emblem 547 (11)

national grid 160 (6)

national plant 366 (6)

national service 718 (5)

nationalism 11 (4), 80 (3), 371 (5), 901 (3)

nationalist 901 (5)

nationalistic 481 (8), 708 (7), 901 (7)

nationalists 708 (2)

nationality 11 (1), 371 (5), 745 (1)

nationalization 706 (2), 775 (1)

nationalize 775 (6), 780 (3), 786 (7)

nationhood 744 (2)

nationwide 79 (4)

native 5 (6), 80 (5), 135 (1), 191 (3), 191 (6), 699 (3), 742 (5), 869 (5)

native god or goddess 966 (2)

native heath 192 (5)

native land 192 (5), 295 (2)

native soil 192 (5)

native tongue 557 (1)

nativity 68 (4), 167 (1), 360 (1), 553 (4)

natter 584 (2), 584 (6)

natty 648 (7)

natural 1 (5), 5 (6), 18 (5), 24 (5), 83 (5), 319 (6), 410 (2), 471 (2), 494 (5), 573 (2), 575 (3), 609 (3), 610 (6), 699 (3), 880 (6)

natural bent 694 (2)

natural child 954 (4)

natural colour 425 (3)

natural course 471 (1)

natural deposit 632 (1)

natural fibre 208 (2)

natural functions 302 (3)

natural gas 385 (1)

natural history 319 (5), 358 (2)

natural number 85 (1)

natural order 81 (2)

natural pride 871 (1)

natural religion 973 (1)

natural resources 629 (1)

natural science 319 (5), 490 (4)

natural selection 358 (2)

natural virtues 933 (2)

natural weapon 723 (3)

naturalism 494 (3), 557 (3), 590 (1)

naturalist 20 (3), 358 (2)

naturalistic 551 (6), 590 (6)

naturalization 83 (1), 147 (1)

naturalize 83 (8), 147 (8), 299 (3), 610 (8)

naturalized 83 (4), 147 (5), 191 (6), 610 (7)

naturally 157 (7), 865 (5)

naturally gifted 694 (5)

naturalness 573 (1), 575 (1), 699 (1)

nature 1 (3), 5 (3), 56 (1), 77 (2), 164 (4), 179 (1), 319 (2), 817 (1)

nature cure 658 (10)

nature religion 973 (1)

nature reserve 666 (1)

nature study 358 (2)

naturism 229 (1)

naturist 229 (3), 652 (3)

naturopathy 658 (10)

naught 4 (1), 103 (1)

naughtiness 738 (1), 934 (1), 936 (2)

naughty 700 (4), 738 (7), 934 (3), 951 (6)

naughty child 938 (1)

naughty word 899 (2)

nausea 651 (2), 651 (7), 827 (1), 838 (1), 861 (1), 888 (1)

nauseate 391 (3), 827 (11), 829 (6), 838 (5), 861 (5), 888 (8)

nauseated 300 (5), 651 (21), 825 (6), 838 (4), 861 (2)

nauseating 391 (2), 645 (4), 649 (6), 829 (4), 838 (3), 861 (3), 888 (5)

nauseous 827 (4)

nautical 269 (6), 270 (5), 275 (11)

nautical almanac 269 (4), 524 (6)

nautical life 269 (1)

nautical mile 203 (4)

nautical personnel 270 (3)

naval 269 (6), 270 (5), 275 (11), 718 (9)

naval cadet 270 (3)

naval engagement 718 (7)

naval exercises 269 (2)

naval man 270 (3), 722 (12)

naval officer 270 (3), 722 (12), 741 (7)

naval service 718 (6)

naval warfare 718 (6)

nave 990 (4)

navel 225 (2)

navigable 211 (2), 269 (6)

navigate 265 (4), 269 (9), 269 (10), 278 (6), 281 (4), 288 (3), 305 (5)

navigating 269 (6)

navigation 269 (1), 269 (2)

navigational 269 (6)

navigator 270 (2), 271 (4)

navy 275 (10), 435 (3), 722 (11), 722 (12)

navy-blue 435 (3)

Navy List 87 (3)

nay 533 (1), 533 (4)

Nazism 733 (4), 735 (2)

NCO 741 (8)

ne plus ultra 34 (1), 646 (1)

neap tide 350 (2)

near 11 (5), 124 (4), 135 (4), 185 (2), 200 (4), 200 (7), 202 (2), 239 (4), 289 (2), 289 (3), 289 (4), 816 (4)

near approach 200 (2), 289 (1)

near at hand 200 (4)

near, be 155 (3), 186 (4), 200 (5), 202 (3), 271 (7), 289 (4), 305 (5)

near distance 200 (1)

near enough 33 (12), 200 (8)

near future 124 (1)

near in blood 200 (4)

near place 187 (2), 200 (3), 230 (1)

near side 239 (1), 242 (1)

near-sighted 440 (3)

near-sightedness 440 (1)

near the surface 212 (2)

near thing 28 (5), 200 (2), 661 (1), 667 (1)

near vacuum 325 (1)

nearby 200 (4), 289 (3)

nearing 124 (4), 289 (2), 295 (3)

nearly 33 (11), 200 (8)

nearness 15 (1), 187 (1), 200 (1), 202 (1), 237 (1), 289 (1)

nearside 242 (2)

neat 44 (5), 60 (2), 457 (3), 648 (7), 841 (6), 949 (12)

neaten 648 (9)

neatly put 575 (3)

neatness 694 (1)

nebula 321 (4)

nebular 321 (14)

nebulous 244 (2), 355 (4), 419 (4), 517 (3)

necessaries 627 (1)

necessarily 157 (7), 596 (9)

necessary 596 (4), 606 (2), 627 (3), 740 (2)

necessitate 155 (4), 596 (8), 627 (6), 740 (3)

necessitated 596 (4), 606 (2)

necessitating 596 (4)

necessitation 596 (1)

necessities 627 (1)

necessitous 627 (4), 801 (3)

necessity 156 (2), 596 (1), 606 (1), 608 (1), 627 (1), 643 (1), 740 (1), 801 (1)

necessity, a 596 (1)

necessity for 627 (2)

neck 206 (1), 218 (10), 889 (6)

neck-and-neck 28 (7), 123 (3), 200 (4)

neck feathers 259 (3)

neck of land 344 (1)

neck or nothing 857 (3)

neckerchief 228 (22)

necking 889 (1)

necklace 228 (22), 250 (3), 844 (7)

neckwear 226 (5), 228 (22)

necromancer 983 (5)

necromancy 511 (2), 983 (1)

necromantic 983 (7), 984 (6)

necrophilia 84 (2)

nectar 301 (9), 301 (26), 392 (2)

need 55 (2), 55 (5), 307 (1), 627 (1), 627 (6), 636 (2), 636 (7), 731 (1), 761 (5), 801 (1), 859 (1)

need a break 684 (5)

need for water 342 (1)

need reminding 506 (5)

need spectacles 440 (4)

need training 670 (7)

needed 627 (3)

needful 627 (3)

needfulness 627 (2), 636 (2)

needing 55 (3), 859 (7)

needing badly 627 (4)

needle 256 (2), 263 (12), 366 (5), 547 (6), 612 (9), 827 (9), 891 (9)

needle match 716 (2)

needlecord 222 (4)

needlelike 256 (7)

needless 637 (4)

needless risk 857 (1)

needlewoman 686 (3)

needlework 222 (3), 243 (2), 844 (4)

needs 627 (1)

needs must 596 (7)

needy 801 (3)

ne'er-do-well 679 (6), 938 (1)

negate 2 (8), 14 (4), 460 (5), 470 (5), 479 (3), 486 (6), 489 (5), 532 (5), 533 (3), 603 (7), 607 (3), 704 (4), 752 (4), 760 (4), 779 (4)

negating 533 (2)

negation 460 (2), 467 (1), 479 (1), 486 (1), 486 (3), 489 (1), 533 (1), 603 (2), 607 (1), 704 (1), 752 (1), 753 (1), 760 (1), 769 (1)

negative 23 (3), 85 (5), 160 (5), 418 (1), 460 (4), 467

(2), 489 (4), 533 (1), 533 (2), 533 (3), 551 (4)

negative answer 760 (1)

negative attitude 533 (1)

negative request 761 (1), 762 (1)

negative result 728 (1)

negatively 533 (4)

neglect 55 (5), 57 (5), 138 (6), 456 (7), 458 (1), 458 (4), 598 (4), 620 (5), 655 (2), 670 (1), 674 (4), 677 (3), 726 (3), 769 (3), 918 (1), 921 (1)

neglect of time 118 (1)

neglected 55 (3), 444 (2), 458 (3), 483 (3), 491 (6), 506 (3), 639 (5), 726 (2), 860 (3), 867 (7), 921 (4)

neglectful 458 (2), 769 (2), 921 (3)

neglectful, be 458 (6), 679 (11)

negligee 228 (18)

negligence 55 (1), 456 (1), 458 (1), 495 (2), 598 (1), 620 (1), 655 (2), 670 (1), 677 (1), 734 (1), 769 (1), 860 (1), 918 (1), 936 (2)

negligent 456 (3), 458 (2), 506 (4), 598 (3), 670 (3), 679 (8), 680 (2), 695 (5), 734 (3), 769 (2), 820 (4), 857 (3), 860 (2), 921 (3)

negligently 458 (7)

negligible 33 (7), 639 (5)

negotiable 272 (5), 469 (2), 642 (2), 780 (2)

negotiate 305 (5), 584 (7), 622 (9), 706 (4), 720 (4), 755 (3), 765 (5), 766 (4), 791 (6)

negotiate with 766 (4)

negotiated 765 (4)

negotiating 24 (5)

negotiation 720 (1), 766 (1), 791 (1)

negotiations 584 (3)

negotiator 231 (3), 720 (2), 754 (1), 765 (3)

negotiatory 755 (2)

Negroid 11 (6), 428 (4)

neigh 409 (3)

neighbour 200 (5), 880 (3)

neighbourhood 187 (2), 200 (1), 200 (3), 230 (1)

neighbouring 200 (4)

neighbourliness 880 (2)

neighbourly 703 (4), 882 (6)

neither 606 (5)

neither ... nor 606 (5)

neither here nor there 10 (4)

Nemesis 714 (1), 910 (3), 963 (1)

neoclassical 192 (20)

neolithic 110 (4), 127 (5)

neological 560 (4)

neologism 560 (1)

neologize 560 (6)

neology 557 (1), 559 (1), 560 (1), 561 (2), 565 (1)

neon light 336 (2), 420 (4)

neophyte 147 (4), 538 (2)

nephew 11 (2), 372 (1)

nepotism 11 (1), 914 (2)

Neptune 321 (6), 343 (1), 967 (1)

nereid 967 (3)

nerve 153 (1), 162 (2), 162 (12), 855 (1), 855 (8), 878 (2)

nerve centre 76 (1), 225 (2)

nerve gas 659 (3), 723 (3)

nerve oneself 855 (7)

nerve-racking 854 (8)

nerve system 374 (2)

nerveless 163 (4), 572 (2), 601 (3), 855 (5)

nerves 503 (2), 651 (1), 822 (1), 854 (2)

nervous 161 (7), 318 (4), 456 (5), 486 (4), 507 (2), 601 (3), 620 (3), 819 (4), 822 (3), 825 (5), 854 (7), 856 (3), 858 (2), 874 (2)

nervous, be 486 (7), 822 (4), 854 (11), 856 (4)

nervous breakdown 503 (2)

nervous disorders 651 (16)

nervous tic 318 (2)

nervously 177 (8)

nervousness **318** (1), **486** (2), **661** (1), **854** (2), **858** (1), **874** (1), **877** (1)

nervy **822** (3), **854** (7)

nest **68** (4), **104** (2), **192** (4), **192** (21)

nest egg **632** (1), **669** (1), **800** (1)

nest of boxes **207** (3)

nestle **889** (6)

nestled **187** (4)

nestling **132** (3)

net **41** (4), **74** (11), **194** (1), **222** (3), **222** (4), **222** (8), **235** (1), **424** (1), **542** (4), **542** (10), **619** (6), **698** (2), **771** (7), **782** (4), **786** (6)

net balance **41** (1)

netball **837** (7)

nether **210** (2)

nethermost **214** (3)

netted **222** (7)

netting **222** (3)

nettle **256** (3), **827** (8), **891** (8)

nettled **891** (4)

network **47** (4), **61** (3), **201** (2), **222** (3), **243** (2), **531** (3), **706** (4), **844** (4)

networking **706** (1)

neuralgia **377** (2)

neurasthenia **503** (2)

neurological disease **651** (3)

neurologist **658** (14)

neuropath **504** (1)

neurosis **503** (2)

neurotic **503** (7), **504** (1)

neuter **77** (4), **161** (3), **161** (7), **161** (10)

neutral **30** (4), **177** (3), **426** (3), **429** (2), **606** (2), **620** (3), **625** (2), **625** (3), **677** (2), **717** (2), **717** (3), **732** (2), **744** (7), **860** (2), **913** (4)

neutral, be **606** (3), **860** (4)

neutral tint **426** (1), **429** (1)

neutrality **46** (1), **606** (1), **625** (1), **717** (1), **860** (1)

neutralize **2** (8), **31** (5), **161** (9), **163** (10), **177** (7), **182** (3)

neutralized **163** (5)

neutralizer **182** (1)

neutron **196** (2), **319** (4)

neutron bomb **723** (14)

neutron star **321** (4)

never **109** (2), **533** (5), **760** (5)

never again **69** (7), **88** (6), **109** (2)

never before **109** (2)

never cease **115** (4)

never despair **599** (4)

never end **113** (6), **113** (9), **146** (3), **570** (6)

never-ending **115** (2), **570** (4), **726** (2)

never-failing **727** (4)

never forget **505** (7)

never happen **2** (6)

never learn **499** (6)

never mind **639** (8), **860** (5)

never on time **136** (3)

never satisfied **829** (3)

never say die **146** (5), **600** (4), **600** (5), **852** (9)

never set the Thames on fire **732** (3)

never sober **949** (11)

never stop talking **581** (5)

never the same **17** (2), **152** (3)

never wrong **494** (6)

nevermore **69** (7), **109** (2)

neverness **109** (1), **122** (1)

nevertheless **31** (7), **468** (5)

new **15** (4), **19** (2), **21** (3), **52** (5), **68** (6), **68** (7), **84** (6), **113** (4), **122** (2), **125** (8), **126** (5), **126** (9), **135** (4), **149** (3), **491** (6), **611** (3)

new and strange **19** (2)

new arrival **59** (3), **120** (1), **295** (1), **297** (3)

new beginning **68** (3)

new broom **67** (3), **126** (1), **143** (3)

new departure **21** (1), **68** (3)

new edition **589** (5)

new energy **656** (3)

new face **59** (3), **297** (3)

new-fashioned **126** (6)

new-fledged **132** (5)

new high **34** (1)

New Jerusalem **971** (1)

new-laid **126** (5)

new leaf **126** (1), **654** (1)

new life **656** (3)

new look **126** (2), **656** (2), **848** (1)

new-made **126** (5)

new man or woman **147** (4)

new moon **321** (9)

new-mown hay **396** (2)

new resolve **603** (1)

new style **117** (4)

New Testament **975** (2)

new to **611** (3)

new town **184** (3)

new word **559** (1), **560** (1)

New World **184** (1), **321** (2)

newborn **126** (5), **132** (5)

newborn babe **935** (2)

newcomer **59** (3), **297** (3)

newel post **218** (10)

newfangled **84** (6), **126** (6), **560** (4)

newish **126** (5)

newly **126** (9)

newly coined **560** (4)

newly opened **68** (6)

newly-wed **894** (7)

newlyweds **894** (4)

newness **21** (1), **68** (1), **108** (1), **125** (1), **126** (1), **130** (1), **560** (1), **670** (1)

news **524** (1), **524** (2), **528** (1), **528** (2), **529** (1), **531** (4), **638** (2)

news agency **524** (4)

news blackout **757** (1)

news item **529** (1)

news reporter **459** (9), **524** (4), **528** (6), **529** (4), **549** (2), **581** (3), **584** (4), **588** (2), **589** (7)

news value **529** (1)

newsagent 529 (4)
newscast 529 (1)
newsflash 529 (1), 531 (4)
newsletter 528 (2), 528 (4)
newsmonger 529 (4)
newspaper 528 (4), 589 (2)
newspaper report 529 (1)
newspeak 518 (1), 560 (1)
newsprint 586 (3), 631 (3)
newsreader 529 (4), 531 (5)
newsreel 445 (4), 528 (2), 529 (1)
newssheet 528 (4)
newsvendor 529 (4)
newsworthiness 529 (1)
newsworthy 529 (7), 638 (6)
newsy 524 (7), 529 (7), 581 (4)
newt 365 (12)
next 65 (2), 65 (5), 120 (2), 120 (4), 202 (5)
next door 200 (3), 200 (7)
next of kin 11 (2), 11 (5), 776 (3)
next step 285 (1)
next time 120 (4)
next to 200 (4)
next to nothing 33 (2), 103 (1)
next world 361 (3)
nexus 47 (1)
nib 586 (4)
nibble 301 (11), 301 (35), 386 (3), 889 (1), 889 (6)
nibble at 37 (4)
nibbling 301 (1)
nice 376 (3), 390 (2), 455 (2), 463 (2), 644 (9), 648 (7), 826 (2), 846 (3), 862 (3), 884 (4)
nice distinction 15 (2)
niceness 862 (1)
nicety 463 (1)
niche 185 (1), 194 (4), 247 (1), 255 (2), 527 (1)
nick 33 (3), 46 (11), 260 (1), 260 (3), 547 (1), 655 (4), 655 (10)
nick of time 137 (1)
nickel 33 (4), 797 (4)

nickname 561 (2), 561 (6), 562 (1), 562 (5)
nicotine 388 (2), 658 (6), 659 (3), 949 (4)
niece 11 (2), 373 (3)
niffy 397 (2)
nifty 277 (5)
niggard 74 (8), 814 (1), 816 (3), 932 (2)
niggardly 636 (3)
niggle 829 (6)
niggling 924 (6)
night 418 (1)
night and day 71 (7), 139 (5)
night blindness 439 (1)
night club 192 (14), 594 (7), 837 (5)
night flying 271 (1)
night life 837 (2)
night mail 274 (13)
night out 837 (3)
night-owl 129 (1)
night safe 632 (2)
night school 534 (3)
night shelter 192 (11)
night sky 321 (3)
night soil 302 (4)
night-watch 129 (2), 722 (7)
nightcap 301 (26), 679 (5)
nightclothes 228 (18)
nightdress 228 (18)
nightfall 129 (1), 418 (1)
nightgown 228 (18)
nightingale 365 (4), 413 (4)
nightlight 420 (3)
nightly 129 (5), 141 (5)
nightmare 513 (3), 665 (2), 825 (1), 854 (4), 938 (4)
nightmarish 854 (8), 970 (7)
nightmarishly 970 (9)
nightshirt 228 (18)
nighttime 129 (1)
nightwear 228 (18)
nihilism 449 (3), 734 (2), 738 (3), 974 (2)
nihilist 61 (6), 168 (1), 738 (4), 904 (1), 974 (3)
nihilistic 734 (4), 974 (5)

nil 2 (1), 103 (1)
nil desperandum 852 (9)
nimble 277 (5), 678 (7), 694 (4)
nimble-witted 839 (4)
nimbus 417 (1), 866 (4)
nincompoop 501 (2)
nine 99 (2)
nine days' wonder 4 (2), 114 (2), 864 (3)
nine Muses 99 (2)
ninety 99 (3)
ninety-nine per cent 52 (3)
ninny 501 (2), 544 (1), 699 (2)
nip 198 (7), 206 (7), 277 (6), 293 (3), 301 (26), 377 (2), 377 (5), 378 (7), 388 (1), 889 (1)
nip in the bud 135 (5), 165 (8)
nipped 198 (4)
nippers 47 (5), 256 (2), 304 (2), 378 (4), 630 (1), 778 (2)
nipping 380 (5)
nipple 253 (3)
nippy 678 (7)
nirvana 971 (1)
Nissen hut 192 (7)
nit 365 (16), 649 (2)
nit-picker 829 (2), 926 (3)
nit-picking 829 (1), 862 (1)
nitrogen 340 (1)
nitwit 501 (3)
nix 103 (1)
no 489 (6), 533 (4), 639 (2), 760 (1), 760 (5)
no-account 639 (5)
no admiration for 820 (1)
no admirer 924 (5)
no admission 57 (1)
no allegiance 744 (2)
no alternative 596 (1), 606 (1)
no answer 643 (1)
no apologies 940 (1)
no appetite 860 (1), 946 (1)
no authority 161 (1), 734 (2)
no bearing 515 (1)

no beauty 842 (1)
no believer 486 (3)
no benefit 641 (1)
no better 28 (8), 655 (5)
no brain 499 (1)
no case 960 (1)
no chance 470 (1)
no change 13 (1), 144 (1)
no charge 812 (2)
no chicken 131 (6)
no choice 596 (1), 605 (1),
 606 (1), 740 (1)
no claim 916 (1)
no colour 426 (1)
no comment 582 (4)
no compromise 602 (1),
 735 (1)
no compunction 940 (1)
no concession 735 (1)
no connection 46 (1)
no context 515 (1)
no control 734 (1)
no conversation 883 (1)
no credit to 867 (5)
no decision 28 (5)
no depth 212 (1)
no desire for 860 (1)
no difference 13 (1), 18
 (1), 606 (1)
no difficulty 701 (1)
no discipline 61 (1)
no distance 200 (2)
no encouragement 613 (1)
no end of 104 (4), 107 (2)
no end to 203 (5)
no entry 57 (1)
no escape 596 (1)
no exception 78 (1)
no excess 732 (1)
no expectation 508 (1)
no expert 491 (1)
no extremist 625 (2)
no fancy for 861 (1)
no fear 472 (4)
no feelings 820 (1)
no fixed address 267 (2)
no food 946 (1)
no freedom 596 (1)
no friend 924 (5)
no fun 838 (2)
no function 641 (1)
no genius 499 (3)
no gentleman 885 (3)

no gift for 695 (1)
no go 470 (1), 641 (4)
no-go area 724 (2), 747 (2)
no good 641 (5), 645 (2)
no great matter 639 (2)
no great shakes 33 (7)
no guarantee 474 (3)
no harm done 646 (4)
no head for 499 (1)
no heart 906 (1)
no height 204 (1), 210 (1)
no hero 856 (2)
no holds barred 716 (1),
 716 (5), 744 (8)
no hope 853 (1)
no hurry 278 (1), 681 (1)
no imagination 820 (1)
no imitation 13 (1), 21 (2),
 494 (2)
no increase 37 (1)
no interest 454 (1)
no interval 202 (1)
no joke 1 (2), 638 (2)
no lady 885 (3)
no laughing matter 638
 (2)
no liar 540 (1)
no life 2 (2), 361 (1)
no love lost 709 (1), 881
 (1), 888 (1)
no luck 728 (1), 731 (2)
no manners 847 (2), 885
 (1)
no-man's-land 184 (2), 190
 (2), 231 (3), 724 (2), 774
 (1)
no matter 639 (8)
no method 61 (1)
no morals 934 (1), 951 (2)
no more 2 (5), 125 (6), 361
 (6)
no more credit 803 (1)
no more than 33 (7), 33 (9)
no name 491 (2), 523 (1),
 525 (1), 562 (2)
no obstacle 137 (2)
no oil painting 842 (1)
no omission 78 (1)
no one 2 (1), 4 (1), 190 (3)
no ornament 845 (1)
no other 13 (1), 88 (2)
no pattern 17 (1)
no permission 470 (1)

no picnic 700 (2)
no plan 61 (1)
no preference 606 (1)
no pride 879 (1)
no progress 679 (1)
no prospects 853 (1)
no purpose 641 (1)
no quarter 906 (1)
no question 473 (10)
no questions 454 (1)
no quorum 105 (1)
no recollection 506 (1)
no regrets 940 (1)
no religion 973 (1), 974 (1)
no reputation 867 (1)
no result 726 (1)
no reward 908 (1)
no right 916 (1)
no sailor 270 (1)
no saint 938 (1)
no scholar 493 (1)
no score 103 (1)
no secret 490 (1), 490 (7)
no secret, be 490 (9)
no self-respect 879 (1)
no sense 514 (2)
no signs of 523 (1)
no sinecure 678 (1)
no slave 744 (4)
no slouch 678 (5)
no sooner said than done
 116 (4)
no standing 867 (1)
no stomach for 598 (1),
 861 (1)
no stranger to 490 (5)
no strings attached 744 (8)
no success 726 (1), 731 (2)
no such thing 2 (1), 533 (5)
no surplus 635 (1)
no surrender 715 (4)
no system 17 (1)
no taste 847 (1)
no thanks to 908 (5), 916
 (1)
no title 916 (1)
no toper 948 (2)
no trouble 701 (2)
no voice 578 (1)
no way out 853 (1)
no wonder 865 (5)
no work 677 (1)
no worse 28 (8)

nob 868 (4)

nobility 32 (1), 169 (2), 335 (3), 841 (1), 866 (2), 866 (4), 868 (1), 868 (2), 929 (1), 931 (1)

noble 32 (4), 821 (5), 841 (4), 848 (6), 866 (8), 866 (10), 868 (5), 868 (6), 871 (3), 884 (3), 929 (3), 929 (5), 931 (2)

noble descent 868 (1)

noble metal 359 (1)

noble pile 209 (4)

noble savage 699 (2)

nobleman 868 (5)

nobleness 868 (1), 929 (1), 933 (2)

noblewoman 868 (5)

nobody 4 (1), 103 (1), 190 (3), 639 (4)

nobody, a 869 (5)

nobody's 774 (3)

nobody's fool 486 (3)

nocturnal 129 (5), 428 (4)

nocturne 412 (4), 553 (4)

nod 217 (5), 311 (2), 317 (2), 317 (4), 456 (7), 458 (6), 488 (6), 524 (3), 547 (4), 547 (21), 679 (12), 684 (5), 884 (2), 884 (7), 923 (1)

nod of approval 923 (1)

nod off 679 (12)

nodding 217 (4), 679 (3), 679 (9)

node 45 (4), 253 (2)

nodular 259 (4)

nodule 253 (2)

noes, the 489 (2)

noggin 194 (15)

nohow 470 (7)

noise 398 (1), 400 (1)

noise abatement 401 (1)

noise queller 401 (2)

noiseless 399 (2)

noisily 400 (5)

noisiness 400 (1)

noisome 397 (2), 645 (2), 649 (6), 659 (5)

noisy 32 (4), 400 (3), 400 (4)

nom de plume 562 (1)

nomad 84 (3), 267 (9), 268 (2)

nomadic 84 (5), 265 (3), 267 (9)

nomadism 267 (2)

nomenclator 561 (3)

nomenclature 62 (1), 547 (2), 559 (3), 561 (1)

nominal 4 (3), 561 (4), 639 (6)

nominal charge 812 (2)

nominal price 812 (1)

nominate 605 (7), 751 (4)

nomination 751 (2)

nominee 754 (1), 754 (2)

non-being 2 (1)

non-Christian 974 (4)

non-commissioned officer 741 (8)

non-ego 6 (1)

non sequitur 10 (2), 72 (1), 477 (2)

non-U 847 (5)

nonacceptance 607 (1)

nonactive 175 (2), 677 (2), 679 (7)

nonadhesive 49 (2)

nonage 130 (2)

nonagenarian 99 (3), 133 (1)

nonaggression pact 717 (1)

nonalcoholic 301 (32)

nonalignment 606 (1), 744 (1)

nonappearance 190 (1)

nonapproval 924 (1)

nonattendance 190 (1)

nonbelief 486 (1)

nonce word 88 (2), 560 (1)

nonchalance 458 (1), 820 (1), 823 (1), 860 (1)

nonchalant 820 (4), 860 (2)

noncoherence 46 (1), 49 (1)

noncombatant 717 (2), 717 (3)

noncommittal 525 (6), 620 (3), 625 (3), 858 (2), 860 (2)

noncompletion 726 (1), 769 (1)

nonconformism 84 (1), 489 (1), 978 (1)

nonconformist 15 (3), 25 (3), 84 (3), 84 (5), 372 (1), 373 (3), 489 (2), 489 (3), 504 (2), 738 (4), 738 (7), 744 (4), 769 (2), 977 (2), 978 (4), 978 (5), 978 (7)

nonconformity 17 (1), 21 (1), 59 (1), 80 (1), 84 (1), 489 (1), 611 (1), 704 (1), 744 (2), 849 (1), 978 (1)

noncooperation 489 (1)

nondescript 639 (6)

nondesign 159 (1), 618 (1)

none 103 (1)

none else 88 (2)

nonentity 35 (2), 196 (4), 639 (4), 867 (3), 869 (5)

nones 108 (3)

nonessential 6 (2)

nonessentials 637 (2)

nonexistence 2 (1), 103 (1)

nonexistent 2 (1)

nonextreme 177 (3)

nonfiction 557 (3), 590 (6)

nonflammability 382 (2)

nonfulfilment 726 (1)

noninflammable 382 (5)

nonintervention 677 (1), 717 (1), 744 (1)

nonliability 744 (1), 915 (1), 919 (1)

nonliable 468 (2), 744 (5), 919 (2)

nonliabliity 960 (1)

nonobservance 769 (1), 918 (1), 978 (2)

nonobservant 489 (3), 769 (2), 974 (5)

nonownership 774 (1)

nonpareil 644 (3)

nonpayer 805 (3)

nonpaying 805 (4)

nonpayment 803 (1), 803 (3), 805 (1)

nonperformance 918 (1)

nonplus 474 (9), 479 (3), 700 (6), 727 (10)

nonplussed 474 (6), 700 (5)

nonpractising 974 (5), 980 (4)
nonpreparation 609 (1), 670 (1)
nonreasonance 398 (1)
nonresidence 190 (1)
nonresonance 401 (1), 405 (1)
nonresonant 405 (2)
nonretention 621 (1), 779 (1)
nonsense 497 (1), 515 (2), 515 (7), 639 (2)
nonsense verse 593 (3)
nonsensical 497 (3), 514 (4), 515 (4)
nonsmoker 274 (13), 942 (2)
nonstandard 560 (5)
nonstarter 728 (3)
nonstop 71 (4), 115 (2), 139 (2), 146 (2), 274 (16), 570 (3), 581 (4)
nonstop talker 581 (3)
nonstop talking 570 (1)
nontransferable 778 (1)
nonuniform 17 (2), 72 (2), 82 (2), 84 (7), 142 (2)
nonuniformity 17 (1), 29 (1), 43 (4), 61 (1), 72 (1), 82 (1), 259 (1), 647 (1)
nonuniformly 17 (3)
nonuse 611 (1), 674 (1), 677 (1), 679 (1)
nonviolence 177 (1), 717 (1)
nonviolent 177 (3), 717 (3)
nonworshipping 974 (5), 980 (4)
noodle 501 (2)
noodles 301 (13)
nook 185 (1), 194 (4), 247 (1), 255 (2), 527 (1)
noon 128 (2), 128 (5)
noontide 128 (2)
noose 47 (8), 542 (4)
Nordic 427 (5)
norm 23 (1), 30 (1), 81 (1), 693 (1)
normal 16 (2), 30 (4), 79 (3), 81 (3), 83 (5), 502 (2)
normal sight 438 (1)
normalcy 81 (2)

normality 81 (2), 502 (1)
normalize 16 (4), 83 (8)
normative 81 (3), 83 (5)
North 281 (2)
north and south 14 (2), 184 (1)
north pole 213 (1), 380 (1)
North Star 321 (4)
northbound 281 (3)
northerly 281 (3)
northern 240 (2), 281 (3)
northern lights 420 (1)
Northerner 59 (2), 191 (3)
nose 237 (2), 247 (1), 254 (3), 353 (1), 394 (1), 394 (3), 484 (1), 484 (5)
nose around 459 (13)
nose cone 276 (3)
nose dive 271 (1), 271 (7)
nose-in-the-air 871 (4)
nose into 453 (4)
nose out 484 (4)
nose to tail 71 (7)
nosegay 74 (6), 396 (1), 844 (1)
nosiness 453 (1)
nostalgia 505 (2), 825 (1), 830 (1), 834 (2), 859 (1)
nostalgic 505 (6), 825 (6), 830 (2), 859 (7)
nostril 263 (4), 353 (1), 394 (1)
nostrum 658 (1)
nosy 453 (3), 459 (11)
nosy, be 453 (4)
nosy parker 453 (2)
not a bit 33 (13)
not a dream 1 (2)
not a fake 494 (2)
not a few 32 (2), 104 (4)
not a hope 470 (1), 472 (4)
not a jot 33 (13)
not a scrap 4 (1)
not a soul 4 (1), 190 (3)
not a true picture 552 (1)
not a whit 33 (13)
not able 161 (5)
not absolute 468 (2)
not accept 607 (3)
not acknowledge 883 (9)
not act 136 (5), 175 (3), 458 (6), 677 (3), 679 (11)
not adhere 769 (3)

not admire 924 (9)
not admitted 57 (3)
not all there 503 (8)
not allow 533 (3), 760 (4)
not allowed 57 (3), 470 (2), 757 (3)
not amused 891 (4), 924 (6)
not an inch to spare 54 (4)
not answer 643 (1)
not answerable 919 (2)
not any 103 (2)
not at all 33 (13), 533 (4)
not at home 190 (4)
not at war 717 (3)
not attend 456 (7)
not available 674 (2)
not bad 644 (9)
not balance 29 (3)
not bargain for 508 (4)
not be 2 (6)
not be beaten 704 (5)
not be done 611 (5)
not be drawn 582 (3)
not be hurried 278 (4)
not be moved 599 (4), 711 (3), 906 (4)
not be tempted 715 (3)
not before time 113 (13), 137 (4)
not believe 865 (4)
not belong 6 (3), 57 (4)
not belonging 72 (2), 774 (3)
not big 204 (3)
not blush for 871 (6)
not bother 458 (6)
not breathe a word 525 (8)
not bright 499 (3)
not broken in 126 (5), 611 (3)
not brook 757 (4)
not budge 266 (7), 599 (4), 602 (6), 677 (3)
not care 606 (3), 857 (4)
not care for 861 (4)
not catch 175 (3)
not catch on 611 (5)
not cater for 607 (3)
not certifiable 502 (2)
not charge 781 (7)
not charged for 812 (4)
not clear 423 (2)

not combining 25 (4)
not come off 2 (6)
not come up to 35 (5)
not comparable 10 (3), 19 (2)
not complete 55 (5), 458 (4), 636 (7), 726 (3)
not comply with 738 (9), 760 (4), 769 (3)
not compromise 599 (4)
not concentrate 456 (7)
not concentrating 456 (3)
not concern 10 (5)
not conduce to 182 (3)
not conform 769 (3)
not consent 760 (4)
not consenting 489 (3)
not consider 607 (3)
not contemporary 122 (2)
not contest 721 (3)
not conversant 491 (4)
not count 639 (7)
not count the cost 815 (4)
not countenance 757 (4)
not counting 57 (6)
not cricket 914 (2)
not culpable 935 (4)
not current 611 (2)
not customary 611 (2)
not cut 257 (3)
not dare 854 (11), 856 (4)
not dead 360 (2)
not deep 212 (2)
not defend 489 (5), 860 (4)
not deny 488 (6)
not derivative 21 (3)
not despair 600 (4), 852 (6)
not deviate 249 (3)
not die 360 (4)
not discriminate 13 (4), 464 (4)
not dispose of 778 (5)
not distinguish 13 (4)
not do badly 730 (6)
not do justice to 483 (4)
not doing well 731 (5)
not done 84 (5), 611 (2), 757 (3)
not drink 948 (4)
not drinking 948 (3)
not eating 946 (3)
not endure 861 (4)

not enforce 734 (5)
not enough 105 (1), 307 (4), 636 (1), 636 (3), 636 (10)
not enough work 681 (1)
not ever 109 (2)
not exist 2 (6)
not expect 458 (6), 508 (4), 864 (6)
not face 598 (4)
not far 200 (4), 200 (7)
not far from 200 (7)
not feel well 651 (23)
not finalized 726 (2)
not find 772 (4)
not fit in 84 (8)
not follow 769 (3)
not follow up or through 726 (3)
not for long 114 (7)
not for sale 778 (4)
not foresee 508 (4)
not forget 505 (7)
not forgetting 38 (5)
not forgotten 505 (5)
not found 190 (4)
not free 879 (3)
not function 641 (6)
not gaseous 335 (4)
not genuine 495 (4)
not give 760 (4)
not give way 715 (3)
not go near 620 (5)
not go well 728 (8)
not good enough 647 (3), 924 (8)
not granted 760 (3)
not grow 33 (8), 37 (5)
not guilty 927 (4), 935 (4), 960 (2)
not hard 701 (3)
not have 627 (6)
not hear 416 (3)
not hear of 760 (4)
not help 161 (8), 643 (3)
not here 190 (9)
not hesitate 597 (6)
not hide 526 (4)
not hide one's feelings 818 (8)
not high 204 (3), 210 (2)
not hold 286 (4)
not hold water 543 (5)

not hold with 489 (5), 924 (9)
not hope for 508 (4)
not hurt 644 (11)
not ideal 647 (3)
not imagined 1 (5)
not imitated 21 (4)
not immune 661 (5)
not impossible 469 (2)
not improve 655 (7), 655 (9)
not improve matters 832 (3)
not improved 655 (5)
not in sight 444 (2)
not in the habit of 611 (3)
not in the least or the slightest 33 (13)
not in time 138 (2)
not in use 679 (7)
not include 57 (5)
not included 57 (3)
not independent 745 (5)
not indigenous 59 (4)
not infrequently 139 (4)
not insist 721 (3), 770 (2)
not interfere 744 (10)
not involved 620 (3)
not kept 779 (3)
not know 439 (3), 491 (8), 695 (7), 847 (6)
not know how 695 (7)
not know one's own mind 601 (4)
not know oneself 147 (6)
not know where to turn 700 (7)
not last 114 (6)
not let go 600 (4), 778 (5)
not likely 472 (4)
not liking 861 (2)
not listen 416 (3), 456 (7), 602 (6), 760 (4)
not listening 416 (2)
not literal 495 (6)
not literally 519 (5)
not local 199 (3)
not long ago 126 (9)
not looking 857 (3)
not lose sight of 455 (5)
not lying 540 (2)
not make out 517 (7)
not many 33 (7), 105 (2)

not matter **639** (7)
not mean it **515** (6)
not meant **618** (5)
not mention **458** (4), **525** (7), **582** (3)
not mince words **573** (3)
not mind **597** (6), **860** (4)
not missed **506** (3)
not mix **46** (7)
not mixing **25** (4)
not much **33** (6)
not much of a **33** (7)
not much to look at **842** (3)
not natural **542** (7)
not negative **532** (3)
not neurotic **502** (2)
not nice **645** (4), **649** (6), **827** (4), **842** (3), **867** (4), **867** (5), **888** (5)
not notice **456** (7)
not now **122** (1), **122** (3)
not obey **738** (9)
not observe **738** (9), **760** (4), **769** (3)
not observed **611** (2)
not of this world **59** (4)
not omit **78** (6)
not on speaking terms **881** (3)
not one **103** (2)
not one of us **59** (3)
not one's type **861** (1)
not oneself **834** (5)
not oppose **488** (7)
not out **146** (2), **146** (5)
not owing **916** (5)
not owned **774** (3)
not owning **774** (2)
not part with **778** (5)
not pass **35** (5), **924** (9)
not pass muster **647** (4)
not pay **728** (7), **772** (4), **801** (5), **805** (5)
not paying **641** (5)
not perfect **934** (5)
not permitted **760** (3)
not persevere **601** (4)
not please **827** (11)
not plural **88** (3)
not possible **470** (2)
not practise **769** (3)
not prepared to **598** (3)
not present **190** (4)

not press **177** (5), **736** (3)
not press charges **960** (3)
not proceed with **621** (3), **752** (4)
not prosecute **960** (3)
not proud **872** (3)
not proud of **872** (4)
not proved **467** (3)
not provided **636** (4)
not punish **909** (4)
not quite **33** (11), **647** (5)
not quite recall **506** (5)
not rare **139** (2)
not reach **204** (4)
not reach to **307** (3)
not react **375** (5)
not ready **55** (3), **670** (3)
not really **4** (4)
not recommended **643** (2)
not reflect **450** (4)
not register **456** (7)
not remember **456** (7), **506** (5), **918** (3)
not required **674** (2)
not resident **190** (4)
not resist **721** (3)
not respect **827** (8), **851** (6), **891** (8), **921** (5), **922** (5), **922** (6), **926** (6), **980** (6)
not respectable **847** (4), **867** (4)
not responsible **919** (2), **935** (4)
not retain **46** (7), **300** (6), **300** (7), **311** (5), **621** (3), **674** (5), **746** (3), **779** (4), **787** (3)
not retained **41** (4), **621** (2), **774** (3), **779** (3)
not retract **532** (5)
not retreat **532** (5)
not reverence **921** (5)
not right **643** (2), **914** (3)
not ring true **543** (5)
not rusty **334** (3)
not satisfying **636** (3)
not say no **758** (3)
not scruple **597** (6)
not see **439** (3)
not see the joke **840** (3)
not serious **639** (6)
not show up **190** (6)

not singular **101** (2)
not smell **395** (3)
not so **15** (8)
not so much **26** (2)
not solid **335** (4)
not sorry **824** (4)
not speak **399** (3)
not stay **114** (6)
not stay the course **726** (3)
not sticky **49** (2)
not stir **266** (7), **677** (3)
not stomach **598** (4)
not stop **305** (5)
not straight **246** (3), **930** (4)
not stretch **307** (3)
not strict **495** (6)
not succeed **728** (7)
not suffice **29** (3), **35** (5), **37** (5), **145** (6), **307** (3), **634** (4), **636** (7), **647** (4), **726** (3), **728** (7), **829** (6)
not support **704** (4)
not take into account **481** (9)
not take no for an answer **599** (3)
not take seriously **458** (4)
not talk **525** (8), **582** (3), **858** (3)
not talking **582** (2)
not thank **908** (4)
not the answer **643** (1)
not the same **15** (4)
not the whole **53** (1)
not there **190** (9)
not thick **206** (4)
not think **450** (4)
not think about **454** (3)
not think much of **924** (9)
not think of **450** (4)
not thinking **450** (2), **456** (3)
not to be endured **827** (7)
not to mention **38** (5)
not today **122** (1)
not told **491** (5)
not tolerate **757** (4), **906** (3)
not too difficult **469** (2)
not touch **10** (5), **674** (4)
not tough **327** (2)
not true **246** (3), **541** (3)

not trust 486 (7)
not trying 598 (3)
not unanimous 25 (4)
not understand 491 (8), 495 (7), 517 (7)
not unhopeful 852 (4)
not up to expectation 509 (3)
not use 634 (4), 674 (4), 677 (3)
not use one's eyes 439 (3)
not used 674 (2)
not used to 611 (3)
not utilize 674 (4)
not verse 593 (7)
not vibrate 405 (3)
not vital 639 (5)
not vote 606 (3)
not voting 606 (2)
not want 607 (3)
not wanted 702 (6)
not well 651 (21)
not well off 731 (5), 801 (3)
not whole 53 (6)
not wholly 33 (10)
not wide 206 (4)
not wonder 820 (6), 860 (4), 865 (4)
not work 161 (8), 641 (6)
not worked out 726 (2)
not working 61 (7), 161 (5), 679 (7)
not worry 823 (5)
not worthwhile 641 (5)
not yield 599 (4)
notability 638 (1), 638 (4), 866 (3)
notable 32 (8), 638 (4), 638 (6), 866 (6), 866 (9)
notably 32 (19)
notary 958 (3)
notation 86 (2), 410 (3)
notch 27 (1), 46 (11), 201 (2), 234 (3), 247 (1), 251 (1), 251 (11), 255 (1), 255 (8), 256 (1), 256 (4), 259 (1), 259 (9), 260 (1), 260 (3), 547 (1), 655 (10), 844 (12)
notch up 86 (11), 548 (8)

notched 247 (5), 251 (7), 256 (7), 256 (8), 259 (4), 260 (2)
note 409 (1), 410 (2), 447 (7), 455 (6), 547 (19), 548 (7), 586 (8), 592 (1), 797 (5)
note down 548 (7)
notebook 505 (3), 592 (2)
notecase 194 (10)
noted 490 (7)
notes 548 (1)
noteworthy 32 (8), 34 (4), 80 (5), 84 (6), 638 (6), 866 (9)
nothing 2 (1), 4 (1), 103 (1), 639 (2)
nothing at all 4 (1)
nothing but 44 (4)
nothing daunted 599 (2)
nothing in common 19 (1)
nothing in excess 942 (1)
nothing in it 865 (1)
nothing inside 190 (2)
nothing lacking 54 (1)
nothing of the kind 533 (5)
nothing omitted 78 (1)
nothing special 35 (4)
nothing to add 54 (1)
nothing to choose between 18 (4)
nothing to do with 10 (4)
nothing to it 701 (2)
nothing to spare 636 (1)
nothing venture, nothing win 671 (1)
nothingness 2 (1), 103 (1)
notice 110 (1), 438 (7), 438 (8), 447 (7), 455 (1), 455 (6), 480 (2), 484 (5), 511 (1), 524 (1), 528 (3), 591 (2), 591 (5), 664 (1), 737 (3), 884 (7)
notice board 528 (3)
noticeable 32 (8), 522 (4)
noticeably 32 (19)
notification 524 (1), 528 (1), 547 (1)
notifier 524 (4)
notify 524 (10), 528 (10), 664 (1)
notion 451 (1), 512 (1), 513 (2), 623 (3)

notional 451 (2), 512 (4), 513 (6)
notoriety 505 (2), 528 (2), 866 (3), 867 (1)
notorious 490 (7), 522 (4), 528 (8), 866 (10), 867 (4)
nougat 301 (18)
nought 103 (1)
noun 561 (2), 564 (2)
nourish 301 (39), 703 (5)
nourishing 301 (33), 652 (4)
nourishment 301 (9)
nous 498 (1)
nouveau riche 126 (4), 730 (3), 800 (2), 847 (3)
nova 321 (4)
novel 19 (2), 21 (3), 126 (5), 491 (6), 589 (2), 590 (4)
novelette 590 (4)
novelist 589 (7), 590 (5)
novella 590 (4)
novelty 21 (1), 126 (1), 639 (3)
novice 493 (1), 538 (2), 697 (1), 699 (2), 986 (5), 986 (6)
novitiate 536 (1), 669 (1)
now 121 (4)
now and again 139 (6), 201 (5)
now and then 72 (5), 139 (6), 142 (3), 201 (5)
now as always 121 (4)
now, be 121 (3)
now or never 121 (4), 137 (8)
now that 604 (5)
now this 604 (5)
now this now that 152 (6)
nowadays 121 (1), 121 (4)
nowhere 2 (3), 190 (9)
nowhere to be found 190 (4)
noxious 397 (2), 645 (3), 653 (2)
noxious animal 904 (5), 938 (2)
noxiousness 645 (1)
nozzle 254 (2), 263 (4), 298 (3), 353 (1)

nuance 15 (2), 27 (1), 33 (2), 425 (3), 463 (1)

nub 5 (2), 76 (1), 225 (2), 253.(2)

nub core 638 (3)

nubile 134 (3), 894 (8)

nubility 134 (1), 669 (4), 894 (6)

nuclear 160 (9), 225 (3)

nuclear blast 165 (2)

nuclear bomb 723 (14)

nuclear family 11 (3)

nuclear fission 46 (2)

nuclear fuel 385 (1)

nuclear physics 160 (7), 319 (5)

nuclear power 160 (4)

nuclear reactor 160 (7)

nuclear submarine 722 (13)

nuclear war 718 (1)

nucleic acid 358 (1)

nucleonics 160 (7), 319 (5), 417 (4)

nucleus 70 (1), 156 (3), 196 (2), 225 (2), 319 (4), 324 (3), 358 (1)

nude 229 (3), 229 (4), 553 (4)

nudge 279 (2), 318 (1), 318 (6), 524 (3), 524 (11), 547 (4), 547 (21)

nudism 229 (1)

nudist 229 (3), 652 (3)

nudity 229 (2)

nugget 324 (3), 797 (7)

nuisance 616 (1), 678 (6), 702 (2), 827 (2)

null 2 (3), 103 (2), 515 (4)

null and void 161 (5), 752 (3)

nullify 2 (8), 31 (5), 165 (6), 752 (4)

nullity 103 (1), 515 (1)

numb 266 (6), 375 (3), 820 (4)

number 53 (3), 80 (8), 85 (1), 86 (11), 87 (5), 192 (1), 228 (8), 465 (11), 547 (13), 547 (19), 564 (1), 589 (2)

number, a 101 (1)

number one 80 (4)

number with 78 (6)

numberable 86 (8)

numbered 86 (9), 547 (17)

numbering 86 (1)

numberless 107 (2)

numbers 26 (1), 32 (2), 104 (1), 593 (5)

numbness 266 (1), 375 (1), 679 (2), 820 (1)

numerable 86 (8)

numeracy 86 (1), 490 (3)

numeral 85 (1), 85 (5)

numerals 85 (1)

numerate 490 (6)

numeration 38 (1), 86 (1), 87 (1), 465 (1), 808 (1)

numerator 85 (2)

numerical 85 (5)

numerical element 85 (2)

numerical operation 86 (2)

numerical result 85 (4)

numerous 104 (4)

numerousness 32 (1), 104 (1)

numinous 965 (5)

numismatic 797 (9)

numismatics 797 (4)

numismatist 492 (3)

numskull 501 (3)

nun 895 (3), 979 (4), 986 (6)

nuncio 754 (3)

nunnery 986 (9)

nuptial 894 (9)

nuptial bond 894 (1)

nuptial vows 894 (3)

nuptials 894 (3)

nurse 167 (2), 301 (39), 457 (6), 534 (6), 534 (8), 656 (11), 658 (16), 658 (20), 660 (8), 666 (5), 669 (12), 703 (6), 703 (7), 742 (2), 831 (3), 889 (5), 897 (6)

nursemaid 742 (1), 742 (2)

nursery 130 (2), 156 (4), 171 (3), 194 (19), 370 (2)

nursery education 534 (2)

nursery rhyme 593 (3)

nursery school 539 (2)

nurseryman or - woman 370 (5)

nursing 658 (12), 669 (3), 703 (1)

nursing home 658 (13)

nursling 132 (1)

nurture 301 (9), 301 (39), 369 (9), 534 (6), 669 (3), 669 (12)

nut 47 (5), 301 (19), 366 (7), 504 (2), 504 (3)

nut-brown 430 (3)

nut tree 366 (4)

nutcase 504 (1)

nutcrackers 222 (2)

nutmeg 389 (1)

nutriment 301 (9)

nutrition 301 (1), 301 (9)

nutritional 301 (33), 658 (17)

nutritionist 301 (3)

nutritious 301 (33), 652 (4)

nutritive 301 (33), 658 (17)

nuts and bolts 58 (1), 629 (1), 630 (2)

nutshell 33 (2)

nutty 503 (8)

nuzzle 378 (7), 889 (6)

nylon 208 (2), 222 (4)

nylons 228 (26)

nymph 366 (1), 967 (3), 970 (5)

nymphomaniac 952 (2)

O

oaf 501 (3), 697 (1)

oafish 499 (3)

oak 162 (1), 326 (1), 366 (4)

oakum 208 (2)

oar 269 (5), 287 (3), 547 (9), 729 (2)

oarsman 270 (4)

oarswoman 270 (4)

oasthouse 383 (1)

oath 466 (2), 532 (2), 764 (1), 899 (2)

oath-breaker 545 (2)

oath-taking 532 (2)

oatmeal 430 (3)

oats 301 (22)

obbligato 89 (2), 89 (3)

obduracy 602 (1), 898 (2), 940 (1)

obdurate 602 (4), 735 (4), 940 (2)

obdurateness 602 (1)

obeah 983 (1), 983 (3)

obedience 60 (1), 597 (1), 721 (1), 739 (1), 768 (1), 879 (1), 917 (1)

obedient 60 (2), 721 (2), 739 (3), 745 (5), 747 (5), 768 (2), 823 (3), 879 (3), 884 (4), 917 (5), 929 (4), 933 (3), 953 (5), 976 (8), 979 (6)

obediently 739 (5)

obeisance 311 (2), 721 (1), 879 (1), 884 (2), 920 (2)

obelisk 209 (4), 548 (3)

obese 195 (8), 197 (3)

obesity 195 (3), 637 (1), 651 (3)

obey 488 (7), 739 (4), 742 (8), 745 (6), 768 (3), 879 (4), 917 (10), 979 (9)

obey an impulse 609 (4)

obey orders 739 (4)

obeyed 178 (2)

obeyed, be 178 (3)

obfuscation 535 (1)

obituary 296 (2), 361 (4), 364 (2), 590 (1)

object 3 (2), 164 (2), 319 (3), 468 (3), 486 (7), 489 (5), 533 (3), 564 (2), 598 (4), 617 (2), 704 (4), 715 (3), 762 (3), 829 (5), 861 (4), 924 (9)

object lesson 83 (2), 461 (1)

object of charity 782 (2)

object of dislike 861 (1)

object of pity 827 (1)

object of pride 871 (1)

object of ridicule 851 (3)

object of scorn 639 (4), 867 (3), 922 (2), 938 (1)

object of terror 854 (4)

object of worship 966 (1)

objecting 760 (2), 924 (6)

objection 468 (1), 486 (2), 489 (1), 598 (1), 702 (1), 715 (1), 760 (1), 924 (1)

objectionable 643 (2), 827 (4), 867 (4), 914 (3)

objective 3 (3), 69 (2), 76 (1), 295 (2), 319 (6), 494 (4), 612 (1), 617 (2), 671 (1), 852 (2), 859 (5), 913 (4)

objectivity 6 (1), 498 (3), 913 (2)

objector 489 (2), 705 (1), 959 (4)

objet d'art 694 (3), 844 (1)

oblation 301 (25), 781 (3), 941 (2), 981 (6)

obligated 764 (3), 917 (5)

obligation 596 (1), 627 (2), 672 (1), 803 (1), 913 (1), 915 (1), 917 (1)

obligatory 596 (4), 737 (5), 740 (2), 766 (2), 917 (6)

oblige 596 (8), 627 (6), 703 (5), 703 (7), 740 (3), 884 (5), 897 (5), 917 (11)

obliged 180 (2), 596 (6), 739 (3), 745 (5), 747 (5), 764 (3), 803 (4), 907 (3), 917 (5)

obliging 703 (4), 884 (3), 897 (4)

oblique 29 (2), 220 (3), 222 (6), 246 (3), 247 (5), 248 (3), 281 (3), 282 (2), 523 (4)

oblique angle 220 (1)

oblique, be 29 (3), 220 (5), 221 (4), 222 (8), 238 (5), 247 (7), 282 (3), 308 (4), 309 (4)

oblique figure 220 (1)

oblique line 220 (1)

oblique motion 220 (1)

obliquely 220 (7), 239 (4), 282 (7)

obliqueness 220 (1)

obliquity 220 (1), 246 (1), 247 (1), 844 (3)

obliterate 2 (8), 39 (3), 149 (4), 165 (6), 333 (3), 446 (3), 506 (5), 525 (7), 550

(3), 648 (9), 752 (4), 757 (4), 909 (4), 924 (9)

obliterated 2 (3), 57 (3), 525 (4), 550 (2), 924 (7)

obliteration 2 (2), 39 (1), 149 (1), 165 (1), 168 (1), 333 (1), 506 (1), 550 (1), 747 (1), 845 (1), 950 (2)

oblivion 2 (2), 458 (1), 506 (1), 550 (1)

oblivious 375 (3), 456 (3), 458 (2), 491 (4), 506 (4)

oblivious, be 506 (5)

obliviousness 506 (1)

oblong 203 (6)

obnoxious 827 (4), 888 (5)

oboe 414 (6)

oboist 413 (2)

obscene 645 (4), 649 (6), 847 (4), 934 (6), 951 (6)

obscenity 649 (1), 847 (1), 951 (1)

obscurantism 535 (1)

obscurantist 491 (4), 535 (2)

obscuration 418 (2), 446 (1)

obscure 418 (3), 418 (6), 419 (5), 419 (7), 439 (4), 474 (4), 491 (6), 514 (4), 517 (2), 517 (3), 523 (2), 525 (7), 568 (2), 639 (5), 700 (4), 728 (4), 867 (7), 869 (8)

obscured 444 (2)

obscurity 35 (1), 418 (1), 444 (1), 517 (1), 568 (1), 639 (4), 700 (1), 867 (1)

obsequies 296 (2), 361 (2), 364 (2), 379 (2), 548 (3), 590 (1), 836 (1)

obsequious 597 (4), 739 (3), 879 (3), 884 (3), 920 (3), 925 (3)

obsequiousness 597 (1), 879 (1)

observable 443 (2)

observance 610 (2), 739 (1), 758 (1), 768 (1), 876 (1), 917 (1), 976 (2), 979 (1), 988 (3) observant **83** (4), **455** (2), **457** (4), **739** (3), **768** (2), **917** (5), **929** (4), **979** (6)

observation **438** (3), **438** (4), **451** (1), **455** (1), **496** (1), **532** (1), **579** (1)

observations **480** (2)

observatory **321** (11), **438** (5)

observe **83** (7), **438** (7), **438** (9), **441** (3), **532** (5), **676** (5), **739** (4), **768** (3), **876** (4), **917** (10), **988** (11)

observe decorum **920** (6)

observer **441** (1), **480** (3)

obsess **106** (6), **139** (3), **146** (3), **449** (10), **449** (11), **455** (7), **481** (11), **503** (12), **505** (9), **827** (9), **827** (10), **854** (12)

obsessed **455** (3), **481** (6)

obsessed with **817** (2)

obsession **473** (2), **481** (5), **499** (2), **503** (2), **503** (5), **602** (2)

obsessive **504** (1), **610** (2)

obsolescence **2** (2), **674** (1)

obsolescent **127** (7)

obsolete **2** (2), **125** (6), **127** (7), **161** (5), **560** (4), **641** (4), **674** (3)

obstacle **182** (1), **218** (2), **235** (3), **264** (1), **470** (1), **641** (2), **643** (1), **647** (2), **663** (1), **700** (1), **702** (2), **704** (1)

obstacle race **716** (3)

obstetrician **167** (2), **658** (14)

obstetrics **167** (2), **658** (10)

obstinacy **153** (1), **595** (0), **600** (1), **602** (1), **704** (1), **934** (1), **940** (1)

obstinate **84** (5), **153** (4), **162** (7), **481** (7), **481** (8), **595** (1), **599** (2), **600** (3), **602** (4), **700** (4), **704** (3), **715** (2), **735** (4), **738** (7), **871** (3), **940** (2)

obstinate, be **595** (2), **600** (4), **602** (6), **760** (4), **940** (4)

obstinate person **473** (3), **600** (2), **602** (3), **678** (5)

obstinately **602** (7)

obstreperous **176** (5)

obstruct **145** (7), **163** (10), **165** (6), **200** (5), **264** (6), **305** (5), **350** (12), **533** (3), **641** (7), **643** (3), **700** (6), **702** (8), **702** (9), **713** (9), **713** (10), **715** (3), **778** (5), **827** (10)

obstruction **63** (1), **264** (1), **702** (1)

obstructive **489** (3), **702** (6), **829** (4)

obstructive, be **702** (10), **704** (4)

obstructor **702** (5)

obtain **1** (6), **79** (5), **610** (7), **771** (7)

obtain relief **831** (4)

obtainable **289** (3), **469** (2)

obtrusive **847** (4)

obtuse **257** (2), **499** (3), **820** (5)

obtuse angle **247** (2)

obtuseness **464** (1), **499** (1), **820** (1)

obverse **237** (2), **237** (4)

obviate **182** (3), **620** (5)

obvious **189** (2), **443** (3), **443** (4), **473** (4), **516** (2), **522** (4), **866** (9)

obvious, be **522** (9)

occasion **8** (2), **24** (3), **121** (1), **135** (2), **137** (1), **154** (1), **154** (6), **156** (1), **156** (6), **156** (9), **628** (1), **642** (1), **837** (1), **876** (1)

occasional **38** (2), **140** (2), **142** (2), **154** (4), **876** (3)

occasionally **72** (5), **139** (6)

Occident **239** (1)

occidental **239** (2), **281** (3)

occult **84** (6), **517** (2), **517** (3), **523** (4), **525** (3), **983** (7), **984** (6)

occult influence **178** (1)

occult lore **490** (1), **984** (1)

occultation **418** (2)

occultism **320** (1), **447** (2), **511** (2), **983** (1), **984** (1)

occultist **511** (4), **983** (5), **984** (4)

occupancy **189** (1), **773** (1)

occupant **191** (2), **776** (1)

occupation **189** (1), **622** (1), **622** (3), **672** (1), **676** (1)

occupational **610** (5), **622** (5), **676** (4)

occupational disease **651** (3)

occupational therapy **658** (12)

occupied **191** (7), **678** (8)

occupied, be **138** (5)

occupier **191** (2), **776** (1)

occupy **54** (7), **189** (4), **192** (21), **622** (6), **773** (4), **786** (7)

occupy a position **73** (3)

occupy one's mind **449** (11)

occupy the centre ground **625** (6)

occupying **186** (3), **189** (2)

occupying force **722** (7)

occur **154** (6), **189** (4)

occur to **449** (9)

occurrence **154** (1)

ocean **184** (1), **211** (1), **321** (2), **339** (1), **343** (1)

ocean floor **343** (1)

ocean-going **269** (6), **275** (11), **343** (3)

oceanic **343** (3)

oceanographer **343** (1), **465** (7)

oceanographic **321** (17)

oceanography **321** (12), **343** (1)

oceans **32** (2)

ochre **430** (2), **432** (1)

o'clock **117** (8)

octagon **99** (2), **247** (4)

octave **99** (2), **110** (1), **410** (2)

octet **99** (2), **412** (6)

octogenarian **99** (3), **133** (1)

octopus **365** (14)

ocular **438** (6)

ocular proof **443** (1)

oculist 438 (1), 442 (2), 658
(14)
odd 15 (4), 25 (4), 29 (2),
84 (6), 85 (5), 503 (8), 517
(3), 864 (5), 914 (3)
odd customer 84 (3)
odd jobs 622 (3)
odd man out 25 (3)
odd number 85 (1)
odd one out 19 (1), 84 (3),
489 (2)
odd type 84 (3)
oddball 84 (3)
oddity 25 (3), 84 (1), 84
(3), 504 (2), 864 (3)
oddment 40 (2)
oddments 43 (4)
oddness 29 (1), 503 (5),
849 (1)
odds 29 (1), 34 (2), 709 (1)
odds and ends 17 (1), 41
(2), 43 (4), 53 (5), 641 (3)
odds on 159 (3)
ode 593 (2)
odious 827 (4), 888 (5)
odiousness 888 (2)
odium 867 (1), 888 (2)
odoriferous 394 (2), 396
(3)
odorous 394 (2), 396 (3)
odorousness 394 (1)
odour 394 (1), 396 (1)
odourless 395 (2)
odyssey 267 (1)
Oedipus complex 503 (5)
of a day 114 (4)
of a piece 18 (4)
of age 134 (3), 894 (8)
of all sorts 15 (4), 17 (2)
of beauty 841 (3)
of concern 9 (5)
of consequence 638 (5)
of course 83 (10), 157 (7),
473 (10), 478 (6), 865 (5)
of double meaning 91 (2)
of easy virtue 951 (7)
of genius 498 (4)
of good breeding 868 (7)
of good family 868 (6)
of help 703 (4)
of high birth 868 (6)
of historical interest 127
(4)

of honour 929 (3)
of importance 638 (5)
of integrity 929 (3)
of late 126 (9)
of low origin 869 (8)
of lowly birth 872 (3)
of many kinds 17 (2)
of many parts 694 (5)
of many words 570 (4)
of mean parentage 869 (8)
of necessity 596 (9), 627
(7)
of no account 921 (4), 922
(4)
of no consequence 639 (5)
of note 866 (10)
of old 125 (12)
of one mind 181 (2), 710
(2)
of other times 127 (7)
of power 160 (8)
of price 644 (7), 811 (3)
of recent date 126 (5)
of right 153 (5), 915 (2)
of royal blood 868 (6)
of sainted memory 361 (6)
of service 640 (2), 703 (4)
of size 195 (6)
of sound mind 502 (2)
of sound reputation 866
(7)
of the senses 376 (5)
of this date 121 (2)
of today's date 121 (2)
of unsound mind 503 (7)
of use 640 (2)
of use, be 628 (4)
of value 644 (7)
of value, be 640 (4)
of yore 125 (12)
off 51 (3), 69 (4), 190 (4),
388 (3)
off and on 141 (8), 152 (6),
201 (5)
off balance 29 (2)
off, be 190 (7), 296 (5), 620
(6)
off-beam 282 (2)
off-centre 199 (3)
off-chance 472 (1)
off-colour 647 (3), 651
(21)
off-course 282 (2)

off day 138 (1)
off duty 681 (2)
off form 647 (3), 695 (5)
off guard 458 (2), 508 (3)
off key 411 (2)
off-line 86 (10)
off-load 188 (4)
off one's food 651 (21), 946
(3)
off one's guard 456 (7),
661 (5)
off one's head 503 (8)
off pitch 411 (2)
off-putting 292 (2), 702 (6)
off-season 138 (2)
off-shore 199 (3)
off-target 10 (4), 282 (2),
495 (5)
off the beam 10 (4)
off the bottle 948 (3)
off the cuff 609 (5), 670 (8)
off the mark 282 (2), 282
(7)
off the menu 190 (4)
off-the-peg 228 (30), 669
(9)
off the point 10 (4), 639 (5)
off the rails 84 (5)
off the record 80 (7), 525
(3)
off the scent 495 (5)
off-the-shoulder 229 (4)
off-white 427 (5)
offal 301 (16), 649 (2)
offbeat 84 (5)
offence 827 (2), 891 (1),
914 (1), 934 (2), 936 (2),
954 (2)
offend 827 (8), 827 (11),
829 (6), 861 (5), 891 (8),
934 (7)
offend custom 611 (5)
offended 825 (6), 891 (3)
offended dignity 872 (2)
offender 84 (3), 603 (3),
676 (3), 750 (1), 869 (7),
904 (3), 938 (2), 954 (2),
980 (3)
offending 954 (6)
offensive 397 (2), 649 (6),
712 (1), 718 (7), 827 (4),
878 (5), 885 (5), 888 (5),
951 (6)

offensive remark **926** (2)
offensive weapon **723** (3)
offensiveness **397** (1)
offer **289** (1), **299** (1), **299**
(3), **605** (1), **612** (4), **612**
(12), **633** (5), **671** (4), **759**
(1), **759** (3), **761** (1), **761**
(5), **764** (1), **764** (4), **766**
(4), **781** (7), **791** (6), **792**
(1), **792** (5), **813** (1)
offer a discount **810** (2)
offer a reward **962** (3)
offer apologies **909** (5)
offer battle **718** (12)
offer collateral **767** (6)
offer food **685** (4)
offer for sale **759** (3), **793**
(4)
offer no apologies **940** (4)
offer no hope **853** (5)
offer odds **618** (8)
offer one's apologies **941**
(5)
offer one's heart or one's
hand **889** (7)
offer oneself **597** (6), **759**
(4)
offer prayers **988** (10)
offer resistance **715** (3)
offer sacrifice **988** (10)
offer up **781** (7), **981** (12)
offer worship **761** (7), **981**
(12), **988** (10)
offered **597** (5), **759** (2)
offering **597** (5), **759** (1),
759 (2), **761** (3), **781** (3),
804 (1), **941** (2), **941** (4),
981 (3), **981** (6), **981** (10)
offertory **781** (3), **981** (6)
offhand **456** (3), **458** (2),
609 (3), **670** (8), **878** (5)
offhanded **885** (4), **921** (3)
offhandedness **458** (1),
885 (2)
office **173** (1), **194** (19),
622 (3), **622** (4), **673** (1),
687 (1), **733** (5), **751** (2),
917 (1), **988** (5)
office-bearer **690** (4)
office-holder **690** (4)
office worker **686** (2)
officer **686** (1), **690** (4),
741 (6), **755** (1)

officer of state **690** (4)
offices **194** (19), **687** (1)
official **473** (4), **494** (5),
622 (5), **689** (3), **690** (4),
692 (3), **733** (7), **733** (9),
741 (2), **741** (6), **742** (1),
754 (1), **875** (6)
official reception **876** (1)
officialese **557** (1), **560** (1)
officiant **981** (8)
officiate **622** (8), **676** (5),
981 (12), **988** (10)
officiating **981** (9)
officious **678** (10)
officious person **678** (6)
officiousness **678** (4)
offprint **22** (1), **587** (2)
offset **28** (4), **29** (1), **31** (2),
31 (5), **40** (2), **41** (1), **150**
(3), **153** (3), **170** (2), **182**
(1)
offset press **587** (4)
offset process **587** (1)
offsetting **182** (2)
offshoot **40** (1), **53** (4), **170**
(2), **978** (3)
offside **239** (1), **241** (1)
offspring **11** (2), **157** (1),
164 (2), **170** (1)
offstage **594** (18)
oft **139** (4)
often **106** (7), **139** (4)
ogee **251** (1)
ogle **438** (3), **438** (8), **547**
(21), **889** (7)
ogre **735** (3), **854** (4), **904**
(4), **938** (4), **970** (4)
ogreish **735** (6), **970** (6)
ogress **904** (4), **970** (4)
ohm **160** (6), **465** (3)
oil **160** (4), **258** (2), **334** (2),
334 (4), **357** (2), **357** (9),
631 (1), **701** (8)
oil-can **334** (2)
oil-fired **381** (7)
oil magnate **800** (2)
oil-painter **556** (1)
oil painting **553** (2), **553**
(5)
oil slick **354** (1)
oil well **632** (1)
oiled **357** (7)
oiliness **258** (1), **357** (1)

oils **553** (6)
oilskins **228** (20), **662** (2)
oily **258** (3), **357** (7), **541**
(4), **542** (6), **649** (7), **879**
(3), **925** (3)
oily fish **301** (15)
ointment **334** (2), **357** (4),
658 (8)
OK **60** (5), **644** (9), **732** (2)
okay **644** (9)
old **127** (4), **127** (7), **131**
(6), **163** (4)
old age **113** (1), **127** (1),
131 (3), **163** (1), **499** (2),
655 (2)
old as Methuselah **131** (6)
old as the hills **127** (6)
old as time **127** (6)
Old Bailey **956** (2)
old, be **127** (8)
old body **133** (1)
old boy **133** (2), **538** (1)
old campaigner **722** (4)
old clothes **228** (2), **641** (3)
old codger **133** (2)
old couple **133** (4)
old dear **133** (1)
old dutch **133** (3)
old-fashioned **118** (2), **127**
(7), **491** (4), **611** (2)
old flame **887** (5)
old fogy **127** (2), **133** (2),
501 (1), **602** (3)
old folks, the **133** (4)
old geezer **133** (2)
old gentleman **133** (2)
old girl **133** (3), **538** (1)
old gold **432** (1)
old guard **600** (2)
old hand **696** (2)
old hat **127** (7)
old joke **839** (2)
old lady **133** (3)
old maid **895** (3), **950** (3)
old-maidish **895** (4), **950**
(6)
old man **133** (2), **372** (1)
old master **553** (5), **556** (1)
old person **131** (3), **133** (1)
old salt **270** (1)
old-school **127** (7), **602** (2)
old school tie **547** (10)
old story **106** (1)

old style 117 (4)
Old Testament 975 (2)
old-time 127 (7)
old-time dancing 837 (13)
old-timer 127 (2), 133 (2)
old trout 133 (3)
old wives' tale 543 (3)
old woman 133 (3), 163 (2), 373 (3)
old-world 127 (7), 184 (1), 321 (2), 884 (3)
olde worlde 127 (7)
olden 32 (4), 125 (6), 127 (4)
olden days 125 (1)
olden times 127 (1)
older 131 (7)
oldness 68 (1), 108 (1), 113 (2), 125 (1), 127 (1), 144 (1), 165 (3)
oleaginous 357 (7)
olfaction 394 (1)
olfactory 394 (2)
oligarchic 733 (9)
oligarchy 733 (4)
olive 434 (3)
olive branch 719 (2)
olive-green 434 (3)
ologies and isms 490 (4)
Olympiad 110 (1)
Olympian 868 (7), 971 (3)
Olympian deity 967 (1)
Olympic games 716 (2)
Olympics 716 (2)
ombudsman 480 (3), 720 (2), 957 (2)
omelette 301 (13)
omen 66 (1), 510 (1), 511 (3), 522 (1), 547 (1), 665 (1), 852 (1), 864 (3), 900 (1)
ominous 511 (7), 547 (15), 645 (3), 661 (3), 664 (3), 731 (4), 853 (3), 900 (2)
omission 55 (2), 57 (1), 458 (1), 769 (1), 936 (2)
omit 55 (5), 57 (5), 458 (4), 582 (3), 769 (3)
omit to thank 908 (4)
omitted 55 (3), 190 (4), 458 (3)
omnibus 52 (7), 274 (8), 274 (10)

omnibus edition 589 (5)
omnipotence 160 (1), 965 (2)
omnipotent 160 (8), 162 (6), 965 (6)
omnipresence 189 (1), 965 (2)
omnipresent 189 (3), 965 (6)
omniscience 490 (1), 965 (2)
omniscient 490 (5), 965 (6)
omniscient, be 490 (8)
omnivore 301 (6), 365 (2)
omnivorous 301 (31), 859 (8), 947 (3)
on 9 (10), 186 (5), 189 (2), 285 (5), 310 (6)
on a lead 739 (3), 747 (5)
on a level 28 (7)
on a par 28 (7)
on a shoestring 816 (7)
on a small scale 196 (13)
on account of 158 (5)
on active service 718 (8)
on advance 784 (7)
on all sides 230 (4)
on an average 30 (6), 33 (12), 79 (7)
on and on 115 (5), 570 (7)
on approval 461 (9)
on auction 793 (3)
on bad terms 709 (6), 881 (3)
on bail 767 (3), 928 (6)
on behalf of 703 (8), 755 (4)
on bended knees 721 (2), 761 (4)
on board 189 (6), 269 (6)
on board ship 275 (12)
on call 189 (2), 669 (7)
on call, be 507 (5)
on consideration 449 (12)
on credit 764 (2), 784 (4), 784 (7), 803 (5)
on deck 269 (13)
on demand 635 (9), 804 (6)
on deposit 767 (3), 803 (5)
on display 522 (6)
on duty 917 (12)

on duty, be 917 (10)
on earth 321 (18)
on edge 259 (10), 507 (6), 822 (3)
on edge, be 822 (4), 854 (11)
on end 215 (2), 215 (5)
on equal terms 28 (7), 28 (11)
on every side 230 (4)
on everyone's lips 529 (7)
on faith 485 (11)
on familiar terms 880 (6)
on fire 379 (5)
on foot 108 (4), 154 (4), 267 (16), 669 (6)
on foot, be 154 (6)
on form, be 694 (8)
on furlough 190 (4)
on good terms 710 (2)
on guard 457 (4)
on hand 773 (3)
on hand, be 742 (8)
on-hander 585 (1)
on heat 859 (7), 951 (8)
on high 209 (14), 310 (3)
on hire 759 (2)
on holiday 681 (2), 683 (4)
on horseback 267 (16)
on impulse 604 (5)
on intimate terms 880 (6)
on its merits 913 (7)
on land 344 (8)
on leave 190 (4)
on-line 86 (10)
on loan 784 (7)
on location 189 (6), 190 (4)
on no account 760 (5)
on no occasion 109 (2)
on oath 532 (3), 532 (8), 764 (2)
on-off 72 (2), 142 (2)
on offer 759 (2)
on one's back 216 (8), 651 (21)
on one's beam-ends 728 (6)
on one's dignity 871 (4)
on one's doorstep 200 (7)
on one's feet 920 (3)
on one's feet or legs 215 (2)
on one's guard 858 (2)

on one's guard, be 457 (5), 858 (3)

on one's hands 637 (4)

on one's head 221 (3)

on one's high horse 871 (4)

on one's hind legs 215 (5), 310 (6)

on one's honour 764 (6)

on one's knees 920 (3), 981 (9)

on one's legs 650 (2)

on one's mind 449 (12)

on one's own 88 (4), 88 (6), 883 (6)

on one's tail 619 (4)

on one's tod 88 (4)

on one's toes 678 (7), 678 (14), 819 (4)

on one's way 265 (6), 285 (5)

on one's word 764 (6)

on pain of 900 (4)

on parole 747 (5), 764 (2)

on probation 461 (9)

on purpose 617 (7)

on rails 274 (16)

on recognizance 767 (3)

on record 548 (6), 548 (9)

on reflection 449 (12)

on remand 747 (6)

on runners 274 (16)

on sale 793 (3)

on sale, be 793 (5)

on second thoughts 449 (12)

on security 784 (7)

on-shore 344 (6), 344 (8)

on short commons 636 (5)

on show 443 (5), 522 (6)

on show, be 445 (8)

on side 239 (1), 242 (1)

on sleds 274 (16)

on stage 594 (18)

on stilts 209 (14), 310 (6)

on stream 160 (9)

on strike 679 (7)

on tap 189 (2), 633 (4), 635 (9)

on television 528 (7)

on terms 766 (5)

on test 461 (9)

on the agenda 154 (4), 452 (3)

on the air 528 (7)

on the alert 457 (4)

on the beam 271 (8)

on the beat 123 (5), 267 (16)

on the bias 220 (7)

on the Bible 532 (8)

on the boil 379 (4)

on the books 548 (9)

on the bottle 949 (11)

on the bottom 214 (3)

on the brain 449 (12)

on the breadline 801 (3)

on the bridge 269 (13)

on the brink or the verge of 33 (11)

on the cards 155 (2), 180 (2), 469 (2), 471 (2)

on the cheap 812 (7)

on the contrary 14 (5), 489 (6)

on the crest 213 (6)

on the cross 220 (7)

on the defensive 713 (7), 713 (11), 854 (7)

on the dot 116 (4), 804 (6)

on the face of it 445 (9)

on the fiddle 788 (6), 930 (4)

on the game 951 (7)

on the go 678 (8), 678 (14)

on the heels of 238 (6), 284 (5)

on the high seas 269 (6), 343 (4)

on the hook 700 (5)

on the horizon 124 (4), 155 (2), 199 (3), 199 (6)

on the horns of a dilemma 474 (10)

on the increase 36 (3), 36 (6)

on the instant 116 (4)

on the level 699 (3)

on the lookout 507 (2)

on the loose 744 (5)

on the make 730 (4), 771 (4), 932 (3)

on the march 265 (6)

on the market 759 (2), 793 (3)

on the mend 650 (2), 654 (6), 656 (6)

on the move 265 (6), 678 (8)

on the nail 121 (4), 804 (6)

on the occasion of 876 (6)

on the off-chance 618 (9)

on the offensive 712 (6), 712 (13), 718 (8)

on the other hand 14 (5), 31 (7), 467 (5)

on the payroll 742 (7)

on the pill 172 (4)

on the plea of 614 (5)

on the plump side 195 (8)

on the point of 124 (7), 155 (2)

on the present occasion 121 (4)

on the quiet 525 (11)

on the rack 825 (5)

on the rampage 61 (12)

on the raw 374 (7), 819 (6)

on the record 466 (5)

on the road 267 (9)

on the rocks 382 (4), 661 (6)

on the run 265 (6), 661 (6)

on the scent 484 (3), 619 (4), 619 (7)

on the shelf 41 (4), 161 (5), 674 (3), 860 (3), 895 (4)

on the sly 525 (11), 698 (6)

on the spot 116 (4), 121 (4), 189 (2), 189 (6), 200 (4), 289 (3)

on the spur of the moment 116 (4), 609 (5)

on the staff 58 (2), 742 (7)

on the stocks 55 (4), 669 (6), 726 (4)

on the surface 223 (4)

on the throne 733 (8)

on the track 484 (3), 619 (7)

on the track of 459 (18)

on the trail 619 (4)

on the trot 71 (7), 678 (8)

on the verge or the brink of 200 (8)

on the wane 37 (6), 731 (5)

on the warpath 712 (6), 712 (13), 718 (8), 718 (11)

on the way **272** (9), **289** (2), **305** (6)

on the whole **30** (6), **52** (9), **54** (8)

on the wing **265** (6), **271** (6), **271** (8)

on the wrong tack **495** (5)

on thin ice **661** (6)

on time **116** (3), **135** (4), **137** (4)

on tiptoe **209** (14), **310** (6), **525** (5)

on top **34** (4), **34** (5), **209** (14), **213** (6), **727** (4)

on top of the world **824** (4)

on tour **190** (4)

on trial **459** (17), **461** (9), **959** (6)

on trust **485** (11)

on vacation **683** (4)

on velvet **730** (4)

on view **443** (5), **445** (7)

on wheels **274** (16)

once **88** (6), **140** (3)

once bitten **664** (4)

once for all **69** (7)

once in a while **139** (6), **140** (3)

once more **91** (4), **106** (8)

once only **88** (3), **88** (6)

once-over **438** (4)

once removed **11** (5)

once upon a time **108** (11), **125** (12)

oncoming **237** (4), **289** (2)

one **13** (2), **21** (4), **44** (4), **50** (3), **52** (4), **88** (2), **88** (3), **371** (3)

one after another **71** (7), **284** (5)

one and all **52** (2), **52** (10), **79** (2)

one and only **21** (4), **88** (3)

one and the same **13** (2), **88** (3)

one another **12** (1), **12** (4)

one-armed **55** (3)

one at a time **88** (6), **278** (8)

one, be **88** (5)

one by one **46** (14), **80** (10), **88** (6)

one day **108** (11), **122** (3)

one-dimensional **203** (6)

one-eyed **55** (3), **440** (3)

one-horse **639** (6)

one hundred per cent **52** (8)

one in possession **776** (1)

one-legged **55** (3)

one-liner **839** (2)

one of **58** (1), **58** (2)

one of, be **56** (3), **58** (3), **78** (4), **297** (5)

one of the best **644** (3), **890** (2)

one of these days **122** (3)

one-off **88** (3)

one or two **105** (1)

one p **797** (4)

one-piece **228** (30)

one-sided **481** (8), **914** (4)

one-sided, be **481** (12)

one-sidedness **481** (4), **914** (2)

one step at a time **858** (1)

one thing after another **71** (1)

one-time **753** (2)

one-track mind **481** (4)

one up **34** (2), **34** (4)

one up, be **34** (8)

one up on **306** (2)

one-upmanship **34** (1), **688** (2)

one-way street **305** (3)

one with, be **13** (3)

onerous **645** (2), **700** (4), **702** (6), **827** (5)

one's age **131** (1)

one's age, be **121** (3)

one's all **890** (1)

one's authorities **466** (1)

one's background **200** (3)

one's betrothed **894** (4)

one's betters **34** (3)

one's born days **110** (1)

one's case **466** (2)

one's chance **137** (2)

one's contemporaries **123** (2)

one's conviction **485** (3)

one's country **192** (5)

one's cut **810** (1)

one's despair **700** (1)

one's devotions **981** (1)

one's due **913** (1)

one's due, be **915** (4)

one's duty **917** (1)

one's duty, be **915** (4), **917** (8)

one's fault **936** (1)

one's fill **54** (2), **635** (1), **861** (1)

one's flesh and blood **11** (2)

one's folks **11** (3)

one's good **615** (1)

one's head **744** (3)

one's honour **950** (1)

one's level best **671** (1)

one's middle name **80** (1)

one's money back **31** (2)

one's money's worth **792** (1)

one's own **773** (3), **887** (5), **890** (1)

one's own devices **744** (3)

one's own master **744** (7)

one's own way **744** (3)

one's people **11** (3)

one's persuasion **485** (3)

one's piece **579** (2)

one's position **532** (1)

one's prayers **981** (1)

one's preference **605** (1)

one's prospects **507** (1)

one's right **913** (1)

one's say **579** (2)

one's shell **883** (2)

one's solemn word **764** (1)

one's stand **532** (1)

one's stars **155** (1)

one's teens **130** (1)

one's undoing **165** (3)

one's undoing, be **165** (6)

one's word **532** (1)

oneself again **656** (6)

oneself again, be **831** (4)

oneself, be **24** (9), **744** (9)

onetime **119** (2)

ongoing **71** (4), **146** (2)

onion **301** (20)

onlooker **441** (1)

onlookers **189** (1), **438** (5), **441** (2)

only **33** (7), **33** (9), **44** (8), **88** (3), **88** (6)

only a step **200** (7)

only-begotten 88 (3)
only exception 88 (2)
only half awake 456 (3)
only human 934 (5)
only just 33 (9)
only just enough 635 (3)
only possible 2 (4)
only supposed 2 (4)
only yesterday 125 (1), 126 (9)
onomatopoeia 20 (2)
onomatopoeic 20 (4)
onset 68 (1), 289 (1), 295 (1), 712 (1)
onside 242 (2)
onslaught 712 (1)
ontology 1 (1)
onus 917 (1)
onward 285 (5)
oodles 32 (2)
oomph 174 (1)
ooze 278 (4), 298 (7), 300 (9), 341 (1), 341 (6), 347 (1), 350 (9), 354 (1)
oozing 54 (4), 298 (2)
oozy 298 (4), 341 (4)
opacity 419 (1), 421 (1), 423 (1)
opal 437 (1), 844 (8)
opalescence 424 (1)
opalescent 424 (2), 437 (6)
opaque 418 (4), 419 (4), 423 (2)
opaque, be 423 (3)
opaqueness 423 (1)
open 46 (7), 46 (8), 46 (10), 46 (11), 46 (13), 46 (15), 64 (3), 68 (8), 68 (9), 68 (10), 156 (9), 176 (8), 197 (3), 197 (4), 197 (5), 201 (3), 201 (4), 205 (3), 229 (6), 263 (13), 263 (17), 297 (5), 299 (3), 316 (3), 348 (3), 350 (11), 443 (2), 474 (4), 522 (4), 522 (5), 522 (7), 526 (4), 528 (7), 540 (2), 744 (8), 746 (3), 759 (2), 779 (4), 929 (4)
open a discussion 475 (11)
open a way 305 (5)
open air 223 (1), 340 (1)
open an account 802 (3)
open arms 299 (1)

open country 183 (1), 263 (7), 348 (1)
open court 956 (2)
open discussion 528 (2)
open door 297 (2)
open drain 351 (2)
open-ended 217 (4)
open fire 287 (8), 383 (1), 712 (11), 718 (12)
open hand 813 (1)
open-handed 813 (3), 962 (2)
open-handed, be 779 (4)
open heart 813 (1)
open-heart surgery 658 (11)
open-hearted 929 (4)
open hostilities 718 (10)
open house 813 (1), 882 (2)
open letter 79 (1), 528 (2), 588 (1), 762 (1)
open market 744 (3), 791 (2), 796 (1)
open marriage 894 (2)
open mind 474 (2), 606 (1)
open-minded 474 (6), 606 (2), 913 (4)
open mouth 864 (1)
open-mouthed 263 (13), 864 (4)
open one's eyes 524 (12)
open one's heart 540 (3)
open out 263 (17)
open prison 748 (1)
open purse 813 (1)
open question 474 (1)
open sesame 263 (11), 628 (2), 983 (2)
open space 183 (1), 183 (4), 185 (1), 263 (7)
open the door 263 (17), 299 (3)
open the door to 180 (3)
open the eyes 534 (6)
open to 180 (2), 661 (5)
open to, be 469 (3)
open to bid 759 (2)
open to criticism 924 (8)
open to doubt 486 (5)
open to question 474 (4)
open to suspicion 486 (5)

Open University 531 (3), 539 (1)
open up 68 (9), 156 (9), 526 (4), 654 (9)
open verdict 474 (2)
open vote 605 (2)
open wound 655 (4)
opencast mining 255 (4)
opener 263 (11), 304 (2), 484 (1), 628 (2)
openhanded 635 (4)
opening 66 (2), 68 (2), 68 (5), 137 (2), 183 (4), 194 (1), 263 (1), 263 (7), 297 (2), 622 (3)
openly 522 (10), 528 (13)
openness 522 (1), 528 (2)
opera 412 (5)
opera buff 504 (3)
opera glasses 442 (3)
opera house 594 (7)
opera singer 413 (4), 594 (9)
operable 656 (6), 658 (18)
operagoer 594 (14)
operate 86 (13), 164 (7), 173 (3), 265 (5), 279 (7), 622 (8), 628 (4), 640 (4), 658 (20), 673 (3), 676 (5), 688 (5), 727 (7)
operate upon 612 (8)
operatic 412 (7), 594 (15)
operating theatre 658 (13)
operation 173 (1), 624 (1), 628 (1), 658 (11), 672 (1), 676 (1), 676 (2)
operational 173 (2), 669 (7), 718 (9)
operations 718 (6)
operative 173 (2), 628 (3), 630 (5), 676 (3), 676 (4), 686 (2)
operator 85 (1), 630 (5), 676 (3), 686 (1)
operetta 412 (5)
ophthalmic 438 (6)
ophthalmologist 438 (1)
opiate 177 (2), 949 (12)
opine 485 (8), 512 (6), 532 (5)
opinion 449 (3), 451 (1), 480 (2), 481 (5), 485 (3),

512 (1), 605 (2), 688 (1), 866 (1)

opinion poll 605 (2)

opinionated 473 (5), 481 (7), 485 (4), 602 (4)

opinionatedness 481 (4), 602 (2), 735 (1)

opium 375 (2), 949 (4)

opponent 702 (5), 705 (1), 738 (4), 881 (2), 924 (5)

opportune 8 (3), 24 (6), 137 (5), 642 (2)

opportunely 137 (8), 642 (4)

opportuneness 137 (1)

opportunism 642 (1)

opportunist 603 (3), 672 (2), 930 (4), 932 (2), 932 (3)

opportunity 8 (2), 137 (2), 156 (1), 159 (3), 469 (1), 642 (1), 744 (3)

oppose 14 (4), 182 (3), 467 (4), 489 (5), 533 (3), 598 (4), 702 (10), 704 (4), 711 (3), 715 (3), 716 (10), 738 (9), 747 (7), 762 (3), 924 (10)

opposed 598 (3), 704 (3), 731 (4)

opposer 705 (1), 924 (5)

opposing 14 (3), 489 (3), 598 (3), 702 (6), 704 (3), 709 (6), 715 (2), 731 (4), 738 (7), 881 (3), 888 (4), 980 (4)

opposing causes 182 (1)

opposite 12 (2), 14 (3), 221 (3), 237 (4), 238 (4), 240 (2), 281 (3), 704 (3)

opposite, be 237 (5), 240 (3), 281 (4)

opposite camp 705 (1)

opposite extreme 14 (1)

opposite meaning 514 (2)

opposite parties 704 (2)

opposite pole 14 (1)

opposite poles 240 (1), 704 (2)

opposite side 14 (1), 240 (1)

oppositeness 14 (1)

opposites 14 (2), 704 (2)

opposition 240 (1), 468 (1), 486 (2), 489 (1), 489 (2), 598 (1), 702 (1), 704 (1), 709 (1), 715 (1), 738 (1), 762 (1), 881 (1), 924 (2)

opposition party 705 (1)

Opposition, the 704 (1), 705 (1)

oppositional 704 (3)

oppress 165 (8), 176 (7), 619 (5), 645 (7), 675 (2), 733 (10), 735 (8), 740 (3), 745 (7), 786 (8), 788 (9), 827 (9), 854 (12), 881 (4), 898 (8)

oppressed 745 (4)

oppression 645 (1), 735 (1), 745 (1)

oppressive 32 (12), 176 (5), 645 (3), 735 (6), 740 (2), 854 (8), 859 (8), 871 (3), 878 (4), 881 (3), 898 (4), 898 (7), 954 (7)

oppressor 659 (1), 735 (3)

opprobrious 867 (6)

opt for 605 (6)

optic nerve 438 (2)

optical 417 (8), 438 (6)

optical device 417 (7), 442 (1)

optical illusion 440 (2)

optician 438 (1), 442 (2), 658 (14)

optics 160 (6), 183 (3), 417 (7)

optimism 507 (1), 833 (1), 852 (1)

optimist 482 (1), 833 (1), 852 (3)

optimistic 482 (2), 507 (2), 833 (3), 833 (6), 852 (4)

optimum 644 (6)

option 605 (1)

optional 595 (1), 597 (5), 605 (4)

optionally 605 (9)

opulence 800 (1)

opulent 635 (4), 800 (3)

opus 164 (2), 412 (4)

or 547 (11), 547 (16)

oracle 500 (1), 511 (4), 523 (1), 537 (3), 691 (2), 984 (5), 986 (8), 990 (2)

oracular 473 (5), 496 (3), 511 (6), 517 (3), 518 (2), 965 (6)

oral 524 (7), 577 (3), 579 (6)

oral cavity 263 (4)

oral evidence 466 (2)

oral examination 459 (4)

oral hygiene 648 (3)

oral message 529 (3)

orange 301 (19), 432 (1), 432 (2)

orate 570 (6), 579 (9)

oration 534 (4), 570 (1), 579 (2), 583 (1)

orator 537 (3), 574 (3), 579 (5), 612 (5)

oratorical 519 (3), 574 (5), 579 (7)

oratorio 412 (5)

oratory 566 (1), 579 (3), 990 (1), 990 (3)

orb 184 (1), 743 (1)

orb of day 321 (8)

orb of night 420 (1)

orbit 178 (1), 250 (5), 250 (8), 271 (3), 271 (7), 305 (1), 314 (1), 314 (4), 315 (5), 622 (4), 624 (4)

orbital 314 (3)

orbital motion 315 (1)

orbiting 315 (1)

orchard 366 (2), 370 (2), 370 (3)

orchestra 74 (4), 413 (3), 414 (1), 594 (7)

orchestra player 413 (3)

orchestral 412 (7)

orchestrate 56 (5), 62 (4), 410 (9), 413 (8)

orchestrated 412 (7)

orchestration 412 (4)

ordain 737 (7), 751 (4), 953 (7), 985 (8), 988 (10)

ordained 953 (5), 986 (11), 988 (8)

ordained, be 986 (13)

ordeal 700 (1), 825 (1), 827 (1)

order 16 (1), 24 (10), 60 (1), 60 (3), 62 (1), 73 (1), 77 (2), 77 (3), 81 (1), 81 (2), 87 (1), 272 (8), 457

(1), 480 (1), 547 (9), 610 (1), 623 (1), 623 (8), 627 (1), 627 (6), 693 (1), 718 (6), 729 (2), 737 (1), 737 (6), 737 (8), 740 (3), 743 (3), 797 (5), 866 (4), 917 (11), 953 (2), 978 (3)

order away 300 (7)

order in council 737 (2)

order of battle 718 (7)

order of service 988 (4)

ordered 60 (2), 62 (3)

ordering 62 (1)

orderless 17 (2), 43 (6), 61 (7), 63 (2), 75 (2), 734 (3)

orderliness 60 (1), 457 (1)

orderly 16 (2), 24 (8), 60 (2), 62 (3), 81 (3), 83 (6), 457 (3), 622 (5), 623 (6), 648 (7), 742 (1)

orderly officer 741 (8)

ordinal 85 (5)

ordinal number 85 (1)

ordinance 693 (1), 737 (1), 737 (2), 953 (2)

ordinand 986 (2)

ordinariness 79 (1), 83 (1)

ordinary 30 (4), 79 (3), 83 (5), 610 (6), 647 (3), 732 (2)

ordinary run 30 (1)

ordination 751 (2), 985 (2), 988 (4)

ordnance 723 (11)

ordure 302 (4)

ore 156 (3), 344 (4), 359 (1), 631 (1)

oread 967 (3)

organ 53 (2), 414 (5), 528 (4), 628 (2)

organ loft 990 (4)

organ of touch 378 (3)

organ pipe 414 (5)

organic 5 (6), 7 (3), 331 (3), 358 (3)

organic chemistry 319 (5)

organic disease 651 (3)

organic matter 319 (2), 358 (1)

organic remains 358 (1), 363 (1)

organism 23 (1), 68 (4), 125 (3), 224 (2), 319 (2), 331 (1), 358 (1), 360 (1)

organist 413 (2)

organization 56 (1), 60 (1), 62 (1), 164 (1), 331 (1), 623 (1), 689 (1), 708 (5)

organize 56 (5), 60 (3), 62 (5), 164 (7), 623 (8)

organized 358 (3), 623 (6)

organizer 623 (5)

orgasm 318 (2)

orgiastic 61 (9), 944 (3)

orgy 301 (2), 635 (2), 837 (2), 944 (1)

oriel window 263 (5)

Orient 239 (1)

oriental 239 (2), 281 (3)

orientate 281 (4)

orientate oneself 281 (4)

orientated 281 (3)

orientation 186 (1), 239 (1), 281 (1)

orienteering 281 (1), 837 (6)

orifice 68 (5), 194 (3), 201 (2), 250 (2), 255 (2), 263 (4), 297 (2), 298 (3), 353 (1)

origami 554 (1)

origin 23 (1), 68 (4), 156 (3), 156 (4), 167 (1), 169 (2), 319 (4), 360 (1)

original 5 (6), 10 (3), 15 (4), 21 (3), 23 (1), 68 (7), 80 (5), 84 (3), 84 (5), 126 (5), 156 (8), 513 (5), 586 (3), 611 (2), 851 (3)

original sin 936 (1)

originality 15 (1), 21 (1), 68 (1), 80 (1), 84 (1), 126 (1), 156 (1), 164 (1), 513 (1)

originally 68 (11)

originate 68 (9), 156 (9), 164 (7), 595 (2)

origination 68 (1), 68 (4), 156 (1), 164 (1)

originator 156 (2), 164 (4), 623 (5)

ormolu 844 (2)

ornament 38 (3), 410 (2), 519 (2), 566 (1), 568 (1),

574 (1), 574 (6), 575 (1), 841 (1), 843 (7), 844 (12)

ornamental 17 (2), 437 (5), 553 (7), 841 (3), 844 (9)

ornamental art 222 (3), 243 (2), 437 (2), 551 (3), 844 (2)

ornamentation 40 (1), 574 (1), 841 (1), 843 (1), 844 (1), 875 (1)

ornamented 574 (4), 841 (4), 844 (10)

ornate 519 (3), 574 (4), 841 (4), 844 (10)

ornateness 844 (1)

ornithological 367 (3)

ornithologist 367 (2)

ornithology 367 (1)

orotund 574 (5)

orotundity 574 (2)

orphan 41 (3), 161 (6), 779 (2), 786 (10), 834 (11)

orphanage 192 (17)

orphaned 41 (4), 88 (4)

orrery 551 (5)

orthodontist 658 (14)

orthodox 83 (4), 83 (6), 466 (5), 473 (5), 485 (4), 485 (6), 610 (5), 976 (4), 976 (8), 979 (6), 981 (9)

orthodox, be 485 (7), 976 (12)

orthodox, the 83 (3), 973 (7), 976 (7)

orthodoxism 976 (2)

orthodoxy 79 (1), 83 (1), 473 (1), 473 (2), 485 (2), 976 (1), 976 (3)

orthographic 558 (5)

orthography 558 (4)

orthopaedic 658 (18)

orthopaedics 658 (10), 658 (12)

Oscar 729 (1)

oscillate 12 (3), 141 (6), 163 (9), 267 (14), 269 (9), 282 (3), 312 (4), 317 (4), 318 (5), 601 (4), 949 (13)

oscillating 141 (4), 152 (4), 317 (3), 318 (4), 949 (7)

oscillation 141 (1), 142 (1), 148 (1), 152 (1), 160 (5),

217 (2), 239 (1), 265 (1), 280 (1), 317 (1), 318 (1), 318 (2), 404 (1), 949 (1)
oscillator 160 (6), 317 (1)
ossification 326 (2)
ossify 326 (5)
ostensible 445 (7), 471 (3), 614 (2)
ostensibly 445 (9), 614 (5)
ostentation 271 (1), 445 (2), 522 (1), 528 (2), 541 (2), 546 (1), 574 (2), 576 (1), 676 (2), 711 (1), 815 (1), 844 (1), 850 (1), 871 (1), 873 (1), 873 (2), 875 (1), 877 (1)
ostentatious 800 (3), 850 (4), 866 (9), 873 (4), 875 (4), 877 (4)
ostentatious, be 455 (7), 522 (8), 850 (5), 866 (12), 871 (5), 873 (5), 875 (7), 877 (5), 920 (7)
ostentatiousness 875 (1)
osteoarthritis 651 (15)
osteopath 658 (14)
osteopathy 658 (12)
ostler 742 (1)
ostracism 57 (1), 883 (1), 924 (1)
ostracize 300 (6), 883 (9), 924 (9)
ostracized 883 (6)
ostrich 365 (4), 620 (2)
ostrich-like 677 (2)
other 15 (4)
other extreme 14 (1)
other half 18 (3)
other man, the 911 (1)
other ranks 35 (2), 639 (4), 722 (5)
other self 13 (1), 18 (3), 880 (4)
other side 14 (1), 238 (1), 240 (1)
other side, the 704 (1)
other, the 6 (1)
other time 122 (1)
other way round 221 (6)
other woman 952 (2)
other woman, the 911 (1)
other world 320 (1)
otherwise 14 (5), 15 (8)

otherworldly 320 (3), 447 (6), 513 (5), 983 (8)
otiose 172 (4)
otter 365 (3)
ought to be 915 (4)
ounce 33 (2), 322 (2)
Our Lady 968 (2)
ourselves 80 (4)
oust 150 (5), 300 (6), 752 (5), 786 (10)
ousting 752 (2)
out 190 (4), 223 (4), 263 (13), 282 (7), 495 (6), 669 (8), 949 (8)
out and out 32 (13), 54 (8)
out, be 197 (4), 263 (17)
out cold 375 (3)
out loud 577 (3)
out of 11 (5), 157 (3), 360 (3)
out of bounds 199 (8), 306 (2), 757 (3)
out of breath 578 (2), 684 (3)
out of character 25 (4), 25 (5)
out of commission 674 (3)
out of control 821 (3)
out of court 914 (3)
out of danger 660 (4)
out of date 118 (2), 127 (7)
out of debt 804 (3)
out of doors 223 (1), 223 (4), 340 (7)
out of earshot 199 (8), 416 (2)
out of fashion 611 (2)
out of favour 731 (6), 861 (3), 867 (7), 888 (6), 924 (7)
out of focus 444 (3)
out of gear 495 (6)
out of hand 700 (4)
out of harm's way 660 (4)
out of hearing 199 (8)
out of humour 893 (2)
out of keeping 25 (5)
out of kindness 897 (7)
out of line 61 (9), 84 (5)
out of love 860 (2), 888 (4)
out of luck 731 (6)
out of mind 506 (3)

out of one's depth 211 (4), 700 (5)
out of one's mind 503 (7)
out of orbit 282 (2)
out of order 10 (4), 17 (2), 61 (7), 641 (4), 674 (2)
out of phase 25 (5)
out of place 25 (5), 61 (7), 84 (5), 188 (3), 643 (2)
out of pocket 772 (2), 801 (3), 806 (2)
out of pocket, be 772 (4)
out of practice 695 (5)
out of print 550 (2), 589 (8)
out of proportion 10 (3)
out of range 199 (3), 199 (8)
out of reach 21 (4), 199 (8), 306 (2), 470 (3)
out of season 118 (2), 636 (6)
out of shape 246 (3)
out of sight 199 (3), 199 (6), 199 (8), 444 (2)
out of sorts 651 (21), 834 (5), 893 (2)
out of spirits 834 (5)
out of spite 898 (9)
out of step 17 (2), 25 (5), 61 (9), 84 (5)
out of stock 636 (6)
out of sympathy with 861 (2)
out of temper 893 (2)
out of the ordinary 84 (6)
out of the question 470 (2), 760 (3)
out of the running 728 (5)
out of the way 199 (4), 626 (2)
out of time 17 (2)
out of touch 199 (4), 491 (4)
out of training 695 (5)
out of true 220 (3)
out of tune 411 (2), 495 (6)
out of tune, be 411 (3)
out-of-turn 138 (2)
out of uniform 17 (2)
out of work 674 (2), 677 (2)
out-patient 651 (18)
outback 183 (1), 184 (3)

outbid **306** (5), **791** (6)
outboard **223** (2)
outbreak **68** (1), **149** (1),
 165 (2), **176** (2), **300** (3),
 738 (2), **822** (2)
outbuilding **192** (7)
outburst **176** (2), **822** (2),
 891 (2)
outcast **41** (4), **57** (3), **84**
 (3), **300** (1), **779** (2), **883**
 (4), **938** (1)
outclass **34** (7), **306** (5),
 727 (10)
outclassed **728** (5)
outcome **157** (1)
outcrop **254** (2)
outcropping **443** (2)
outcry **400** (1), **924** (1)
outdated **127** (7)
outdistance **199** (5), **277**
 (8), **285** (3), **306** (5)
outdo **34** (7), **199** (5), **277**
 (8), **306** (5), **542** (8), **698**
 (5), **727** (9), **727** (10), **872**
 (7)
outdoing **716** (9)
outdoor **223** (2)
outdoor life **837** (6)
outdoors **652** (1)
outer **223** (2)
outer darkness **57** (1)
outer edge **199** (2)
outer side **223** (1), **237** (2)
outer skin **226** (6)
outer space **183** (1), **321**
 (1)
outermost **223** (2)
outface **715** (3), **855** (6),
 878 (6)
outfall **298** (2)
outfit **52** (2), **58** (1), **88** (2),
 228 (2), **228** (9), **630** (4),
 708 (1)
outfitter **228** (28)
outflank **306** (5), **727** (10)
outflow **42** (1), **290** (1), **298**
 (2), **300** (1), **302** (1), **350**
 (2), **350** (4), **634** (1), **637**
 (1)
outgoing **64** (2), **125** (7),
 298 (4), **753** (2), **882** (6)
outgoings **806** (1)
outgrow **611** (4), **674** (5)

outgrowth **157** (2)
outhouse **40** (1), **192** (7),
 194 (19)
outing **267** (1), **824** (3), **837**
 (1)
outlandish **59** (4), **84** (5),
 864 (5)
outlast **108** (7), **113** (7), **144**
 (3), **153** (7)
outlaw **57** (5), **84** (3), **757**
 (4), **789** (2), **881** (2), **883**
 (4), **883** (9), **904** (3), **954**
 (9), **961** (3)
outlawed **757** (3), **954** (5),
 961 (2)
outlawing **963** (4)
outlawry **788** (2), **954** (3)
outlay **634** (1), **806** (1)
outlet **201** (2), **263** (4), **298**
 (3), **345** (1), **351** (2)
outline **23** (1), **55** (1), **68**
 (1), **230** (1), **233** (1), **233**
 (3), **234** (3), **235** (1), **243**
 (1), **243** (5), **250** (2), **250**
 (8), **445** (1), **445** (6), **551**
 (1), **551** (5), **551** (8), **569**
 (3), **590** (7), **592** (1), **623**
 (1), **669** (1), **669** (10)
outlined **232** (2), **233** (2)
outlive **113** (7), **144** (3)
outlook **124** (1), **124** (3),
 155 (1), **438** (5), **507** (1),
 688 (1), **817** (1)
outlook on life **485** (3)
outlying **199** (3), **223** (2)
outmanoeuvre **34** (7), **306**
 (5), **542** (8), **727** (10)
outmanoeuvred **728** (5)
outmatched **728** (5)
outmoded **127** (7), **641** (4)
outnumber **104** (6), **637**
 (5)
outplay **34** (7), **727** (10)
outplayed **728** (5)
outpoint **34** (7), **727** (10)
outpost **199** (2), **237** (1)
outpouring **298** (2), **570** (1)
output **86** (5), **164** (1), **164**
 (2), **771** (2)
outrage **176** (1), **616** (1),
 645 (7), **675** (1), **891** (8),
 898 (3), **934** (2)

outrageous **32** (12), **546**
 (2), **867** (5), **898** (7), **934**
 (6)
outrageously **32** (18)
outrank **34** (7), **64** (3)
outre **84** (6)
outride **306** (5)
outrider **66** (1)
outrigger **254** (2)
outright **54** (8)
outright win **727** (2)
outrival **306** (5)
outrun **277** (8), **306** (5)
outset **68** (3)
outshine **34** (7), **727** (10),
 866 (11)
outshone **35** (4), **728** (5)
outside **223** (1), **223** (2),
 223 (4), **445** (1), **541** (2)
outside chance **472** (1)
outside the law **954** (5)
outsider **25** (3), **59** (3), **84**
 (3), **883** (4)
outsize **84** (6), **195** (7)
outskirts **68** (5), **199** (2),
 230 (1)
outsmart **542** (8), **698** (5)
outspoken **522** (5), **532** (4),
 540 (2), **579** (6), **699** (3)
outspokenness **699** (1)
outstanding **32** (8), **34** (4),
 41 (4), **638** (6), **803** (5)
outstandingly **32** (19), **34**
 (12)
outstare **878** (6)
outstay **113** (7)
outstretch **203** (7)
outstretched **203** (5), **205**
 (3)
outstrip **34** (7), **277** (8), **285**
 (3), **289** (4), **306** (5)
outvote **607** (3)
outvoted **728** (5)
outvoted, be **728** (9)
outward **6** (2), **223** (2), **445**
 (7)
outward bound **296** (3)
outward curve **248** (1)
outward self **80** (4)
outward show **542** (1)
outwardly **6** (5), **223** (4)
outwardness **223** (1)
outwards **223** (4)

outweigh 31 (4), 178 (4)

outwit 34 (7), 306 (5), 542 (8), 542 (9), 698 (5)

outwork 254 (2), 682 (3)

oval 250 (4), 250 (6), 250 (7)

ovary 167 (3)

ovation 727 (2), 729 (1), 876 (1), 923 (3)

oven 301 (5), 383 (1)

oven-ready 669 (9)

over- 34 (4), 34 (11), 41 (4), 69 (4), 125 (6), 186 (5)

over again 91 (4), 106 (8)

over against 240 (4)

over ambitious, be 671 (4)

over and above 34 (11), 38 (5), 637 (7)

over and done with 69 (4), 125 (6), 506 (3)

over and over 106 (7)

over-complicated 61 (8)

over-cooked 301 (34)

over five 99 (2)

over one hundred 99 (5), 104 (1)

over one's dead body 602 (7)

over one's head 209 (11), 211 (4), 517 (3)

over-populated 74 (9), 104 (5)

over-refine 862 (4)

over the average 34 (11)

over the moon 824 (4)

overact 546 (3), 850 (5)

overacted 546 (2)

overacting 546 (1), 594 (8)

overactivity 678 (4)

overall 78 (2), 203 (9), 228 (15)

overalls 228 (9), 662 (2)

overawe 178 (4), 733 (12), 735 (8), 854 (12), 920 (7)

overawed 854 (6)

overbalance 29 (3), 309 (4)

overbalanced 29 (2)

overbear 178 (4)

overbearing 735 (6), 871 (3), 878 (4)

overbid 306 (5), 791 (6)

overblown 131 (6)

overburden 193 (2), 645 (7), 684 (6)

overburdened 702 (7)

overcall 306 (5)

overcast 355 (4), 418 (4), 419 (5), 419 (7), 834 (8)

overcharge 808 (5), 809 (1), 811 (5)

overcharged 637 (3), 811 (2)

overclouded 355 (4), 419 (5)

overcoat 228 (20)

overcome 178 (4), 727 (9)

overcome, be 949 (13)

overcompensate 29 (3), 31 (4)

overcomplimentary 925 (3)

overconfident 482 (2), 857 (3)

overcrowded 74 (9)

overdo 306 (3), 546 (3), 637 (5)

overdo it 678 (12), 684 (5), 925 (4)

overdoing it 306 (1), 546 (1)

overdone 391 (2), 844 (10)

overdose 659 (3), 863 (1), 863 (3)

overdraft 772 (1), 803 (1), 805 (2)

overdraw 552 (3), 772 (4), 803 (6), 815 (4)

overdrawn 772 (2), 803 (4)

overdrawn, be 772 (4), 803 (6)

overdressed 847 (4)

overdrive 160 (1), 684 (6)

overdue 118 (2), 136 (3), 803 (5)

overdue, be 118 (3)

overdue payment 803 (1)

overeating 301 (1), 943 (1), 947 (1)

overeconomical 816 (4)

overemphasize 482 (4)

overenthusiastic 482 (2)

overestimate 306 (3), 481 (9), 482 (1), 482 (4), 638 (8), 923 (9)

overestimated 482 (3)

overestimation 481 (1), 482 (1)

overexcited 821 (3)

overexposed 426 (3)

overfill 306 (3)

overfish 634 (4)

overflow 54 (5), 104 (6), 297 (7), 298 (2), 298 (6), 341 (2), 350 (4), 350 (9), 351 (2), 635 (7), 637 (1), 637 (5)

overflowing 32 (4), 54 (4), 635 (4), 637 (3), 813 (3)

overgraze 634 (4)

overgrow 306 (3)

overgrown 366 (9)

overgrowth 197 (1)

overhang 209 (12), 217 (5), 226 (14), 254 (2), 254 (5)

overhanging 209 (11), 217 (4), 289 (2)

overhaul 277 (8), 306 (5), 459 (13), 656 (9), 656 (12)

overhead 209 (14)

overheads 806 (1), 809 (2)

overhear 415 (6), 524 (12)

overhearing 415 (2)

overheated 653 (2)

overhung 254 (4)

overindulge 306 (3)

overindulgence 637 (1), 943 (1)

overindulgent 734 (3)

overjoyed 824 (4), 833 (5)

overkill 546 (1), 637 (2)

overland 344 (8)

overlap 71 (1), 71 (5), 202 (3), 207 (3), 207 (5), 226 (1), 226 (14), 306 (3), 306 (4), 378 (7), 637 (2)

overlapping 71 (4), 207 (3), 207 (4), 226 (11), 289 (1)

overlay 207 (5), 226 (13), 226 (15), 574 (6)

overlaying 226 (11)

overleaf 238 (6)

overlie 205 (5), 226 (14)

overloaded 29 (2), 273 (10), 322 (4), 637 (3)

overlong 306 (2), 838 (3)

overlook 209 (12), 456 (7), 458 (4), 458 (5), 506 (5), 674 (4), 823 (6), 909 (4)

overlooked 458 (3), 639 (5)

overlooked, be 456 (9), 506 (6)

overlord 34 (3), 741 (1)

overlordship 733 (2), 733 (5)

overly 32 (18)

overlying 209 (11), 226 (11)

overmanning 637 (2)

overmaster 162 (11), 178 (4), 712 (7), 727 (9), 733 (12), 745 (7), 786 (6), 854 (12), 872 (7)

overmuch 637 (3)

overnight 116 (4), 125 (8), 126 (5), 126 (9)

overnight bag 194 (9)

overoptimism 482 (1)

overpass 306 (3)

overpay 813 (4)

overpower 162 (11), 727 (9)

overpowered 306 (2)

overpowering 821 (5)

overprint 550 (3)

overprinting 550 (1)

overrate 36 (5), 306 (3), 481 (9), 482 (4), 487 (3), 495 (7), 528 (11), 546 (3), 638 (8), 923 (9), 925 (4)

overrated 482 (3), 639 (5)

overreach 306 (5), 542 (8)

overreach oneself 728 (7)

overreligious 979 (7)

override 34 (8), 178 (4), 306 (3), 479 (3), 727 (9), 733 (12)

overriding 34 (5), 596 (4), 638 (5), 740 (2)

overripe 131 (6)

overrule 733 (12), 752 (4)

overruling 34 (5), 638 (5), 733 (7)

overrun 54 (4), 54 (7), 104 (6), 189 (5), 197 (4), 306 (3), 306 (4), 712 (7)

overrunning 712 (1)

overseas 59 (4), 59 (5), 199 (4)

oversee 689 (4)

overseer 690 (3)

oversell 546 (3), 637 (5)

oversensitive 822 (3)

oversexed 859 (7), 951 (8)

overshadow 34 (7), 37 (4), 209 (12), 226 (14), 418 (6), 419 (7), 866 (11)

overshadowed 418 (4), 419 (5)

overshadowing 209 (11)

overshoot 306 (3)

oversight 438 (4), 456 (1), 458 (1), 495 (3), 689 (1)

oversleep 138 (6), 306 (3)

overspend 815 (4)

overspill 637 (1)

overspill estate 192 (8)

overstate 541 (5)

overstated 543 (4), 546 (2)

overstatement 482 (1), 532 (1), 541 (1), 543 (1), 574 (2)

overstep 32 (15), 34 (7), 305 (5), 306 (3), 546 (3), 637 (5), 769 (3), 943 (3)

overstepping 306 (1), 712 (1), 769 (1), 916 (1), 954 (2)

overt 522 (5)

overtake 34 (7), 277 (8), 306 (5)

overtaking 277 (2), 285 (1), 289 (1)

overtax 675 (2), 684 (6), 786 (8)

overthrow 149 (1), 165 (1), 165 (7), 311 (1), 311 (6), 479 (3), 727 (9), 734 (7), 738 (10)

overtime 113 (3), 682 (1)

overtired 655 (5)

overtone 410 (2)

overtop 32 (15), 34 (7), 209 (12), 213 (5)

overtopping 34 (4)

overtrump 34 (7)

overture 66 (2), 289 (1), 412 (4), 719 (2), 759 (1), 761 (1)

overtures 880 (1)

overturn 63 (3), 149 (4), 165 (7), 221 (5), 269 (10), 311 (1)

overturning 149 (1), 221 (2), 311 (1)

overvaluation 481 (1)

overweening 857 (3), 871 (3), 873 (4), 878 (4)

overweight 29 (2), 195 (8), 195 (9)

overwhelm 32 (15), 54 (7), 104 (6), 162 (11), 165 (6), 176 (7), 637 (5), 821 (8), 834 (11)

overwhelmed 728 (5), 745 (4), 818 (4)

overwhelmed, be 864 (6)

overwhelming 32 (7), 165 (4), 176 (5), 818 (6), 821 (5), 864 (5)

overwork 634 (4), 636 (9), 673 (3), 675 (2), 678 (12), 682 (1), 684 (5), 684 (6)

overworked 684 (2)

overwrought 818 (5), 821 (3)

ovine 365 (18)

ovoid 250 (6), 252 (5)

ovum 167 (3)

owe 803 (6)

owe everything to 157 (5)

owe money 803 (6)

owe obedience to 733 (13)

owe service to 773 (5)

owed 803 (5), 915 (2)

owing 642 (2), 803 (4), 803 (5), 915 (2), 915 (4)

owing nothing to 10 (3)

owing service 745 (5)

owing to 157 (3), 158 (2), 158 (5)

owing to, be 157 (5)

owl 365 (4)

owlish 365 (18), 499 (3)

own 488 (6), 526 (6), 773 (4)

own goal 695 (2)

own up 526 (6)

owner 741 (1), 776 (2)

ownerless 774 (3)

ownership 773 (1)

owning 773 (2)

ox 273 (3), 365 (7)

oxbow 248 (2)
Oxbridge 539 (1)
oxen 365 (7)
Oxford-blue 435 (3)
oxidize 381 (10)
oxygen 340 (1)
oxygen tent 658 (13)
oxygenate 336 (4), 340 (6)
oxygenated 340 (5)
oxymoron 25 (3)
oyster 429 (1)
ozone 340 (1), 652 (1)
ozone layer 340 (2)

P

pace 123 (4), 203 (4), 265
  (1), 265 (2), 267 (14), 277
  (1)
pace out 465 (11)
pacemaker 23 (2), 150 (2),
  690 (2)
pacer 23 (2), 273 (5)
pachyderm 365 (3)
pacific 177 (3), 717 (3)
pacific, be 717 (4)
pacification 161 (1), 177
  (1), 710 (1), 717 (1), 719
  (1), 765 (2), 828 (1), 909
  (1), 941 (5), 981 (12)
pacificatory 710 (2), 719
  (3), 720 (3), 828 (3)
pacifier 720 (2)
pacifism 717 (1)
pacifist 717 (2), 717 (3)
pacify 177 (7), 612 (10),
  719 (4), 720 (4), 770 (2),
  823 (7), 828 (5), 905 (8),
  941 (5), 981 (12)
pacifying 719 (1), 828 (3)
pack 52 (2), 54 (7), 74 (3),
  74 (6), 74 (11), 187 (7),
  193 (2), 226 (13), 227 (2),
  365 (2), 541 (8), 619 (3),
  632 (5), 669 (11), 702 (4),
  837 (15)
pack a punch 162 (11)
pack in 54 (7), 193 (2)
pack into 303 (4)
pack of lies 543 (1)

pack the jury 914 (6)
pack them in 74 (11)
pack tight 193 (2), 198 (7)
pack up 296 (5)
package 74 (6), 74 (11), 78
  (1), 88 (2)
package deal 78 (1)
packaging 194 (1), 226 (5),
  227 (1)
packed 45 (7), 54 (4), 74
  (9)
packed house 594 (14)
packed lunch 301 (12)
packet 74 (6), 194 (8), 275
  (1), 632 (1), 797 (2), 800
  (1)
packhorse 273 (3)
packing 227 (1), 666 (1)
packing case 194 (7)
pact 24 (1), 765 (1)
pad 162 (12), 192 (1), 193
  (2), 197 (5), 214 (2), 227
  (2), 267 (14), 401 (1), 586
  (4), 713 (9)
pad out 36 (5), 570 (6)
padded 327 (2)
padded cell 503 (6)
padded out 197 (3), 570 (5)
padding 36 (2), 40 (1), 227
  (1), 264 (2), 570 (2), 637
  (2)
paddle 265 (4), 267 (14),
  269 (5), 269 (11), 269 (12),
  341 (6)
paddle steamer 275 (1)
paddle wheel 269 (5)
paddler 270 (4)
paddling 269 (3)
paddock 185 (1), 235 (1)
padlock 47 (5)
padre 986 (2)
paean 876 (1)
paediatrician 658 (14)
paediatrics 658 (10)
pagan 973 (7), 974 (4), 974
  (6), 982 (4), 982 (5)
pagan god 966 (1)
paganism 491 (1), 973 (1),
  974 (2), 980 (1), 982 (1)
paganize 974 (8), 982 (6)
paganized 974 (5)
page 529 (1), 742 (2)
page boy 742 (1)

pageant 875 (3)
pageantry 875 (1)
paginate 86 (11)
pagination 86 (1)
pagoda 209 (4), 990 (1)
paid 771 (5), 782 (3), 806
  (3), 807 (2)
paid, be 782 (4)
paid for 792 (3)
paid out 806 (3)
paid servant 742 (1)
paid-up member 708 (3)
pail 194 (13)
pain 377 (1), 377 (5), 616
  (1), 645 (1), 645 (6), 651
  (2), 825 (1), 827 (1), 827
  (8), 834 (11), 963 (2)
pain-killing 177 (4), 831
  (2)
pained 377 (4), 825 (5),
  825 (6), 891 (3)
painful 374 (3), 377 (3),
  827 (3), 963 (6)
painfully 32 (20), 645 (8),
  836 (7)
painfully slow 278 (3)
painfulness 377 (1), 825
  (1), 827 (1)
paining 377 (3), 827 (3)
painkiller 375 (2), 658 (4),
  831 (1)
painless 376 (4), 701 (3),
  826 (2)
pains 455 (1), 457 (1), 682
  (1)
painstaking 278 (3), 457
  (3), 678 (3), 682 (4), 682
  (5), 862 (3)
paint 56 (5), 226 (10), 226
  (16), 425 (4), 425 (8), 513
  (7), 541 (7), 548 (7), 551
  (8), 553 (8), 590 (7), 666
  (5), 843 (3), 843 (7), 844
  (12)
paint a picture 553 (8)
paint in words 513 (7)
paint on 553 (8)
paintbox 553 (6)
paintbrush 553 (6)
painted 425 (5), 425 (6),
  551 (7), 553 (7), 843 (6)

painter 47 (2), 164 (4), 520 (4), 556 (1), 656 (5), 686 (3)

painting 20 (2), 56 (1), 164 (1), 425 (1), 551 (1), 551 (3), 553 (1), 553 (5)

paints 553 (6)

pair 13 (1), 13 (4), 18 (3), 18 (8), 45 (9), 74 (3), 90 (1), 90 (3), 462 (3)

pair of lovers 887 (6)

pair off 90 (3), 894 (11)

paired 45 (5), 89 (3), 90 (2), 894 (7)

pairing 45 (2), 45 (3)

pal 372 (1), 880 (5)

palace 192 (6)

palaeographer 125 (5)

palaeography 125 (4), 586 (2)

palaeolithic 127 (5)

palaeology 125 (4)

palaeontology 125 (4)

Palaeozoic 110 (4), 127 (5)

palatability 390 (1)

palatable 301 (32), 376 (3), 386 (2), 390 (2)

palate 386 (1), 846 (1)

palatial 192 (20)

palatinate 733 (6)

pale 163 (4), 235 (2), 419 (4), 419 (6), 425 (7), 426 (3), 426 (4), 427 (5), 427 (6), 444 (4), 651 (20), 854 (10)

pale as death 426 (3)

pale blue 435 (3)

pale with anger 891 (4)

pale yellow 433 (3)

paleface 59 (2), 427 (1)

paleness 419 (1), 426 (1)

palette 194 (17), 425 (1), 553 (6)

palette knife 553 (6)

palindrome 221 (1)

palindromic 221 (3)

paling 235 (2)

palisade 235 (3), 660 (2), 713 (2), 713 (9)

palisaded 713 (8)

pall 391 (3), 838 (5), 863 (3)

pall on 861 (5)

Palladian 192 (20)

pallbearer 364 (2)

pallet 218 (4), 218 (7), 273 (1)

palliasse 218 (8)

palliate 468 (3), 614 (4), 654 (9), 658 (19), 831 (3)

palliation 831 (1)

palliative 177 (2), 468 (2), 658 (17)

pallid 426 (3)

pallor 425 (3), 426 (1)

palm 203 (4), 366 (4), 378 (3), 378 (7), 729 (1)

palm of victory 729 (1)

palm off 542 (8)

palm off with 150 (5)

palmer 268 (1), 979 (4), 981 (8)

palmist 511 (5), 984 (4)

palmistry 511 (2)

palmy 730 (5)

palmy days 717 (1), 730 (2), 824 (1)

palomino 273 (4)

palpability 319 (1)

palpable 3 (3), 319 (6), 378 (5), 522 (4)

palpate 378 (7)

palpation 378 (1)

palpitate 317 (4), 318 (5), 818 (8), 821 (9)

palpitating 317 (3), 854 (7)

palpitation 317 (1), 318 (1), 818 (1), 854 (2)

palpitations 684 (1)

palsy 651 (16)

paltriness 639 (1), 922 (2)

paltry 33 (7), 639 (5), 922 (4), 932 (3)

paltry sum 639 (2)

pampas 348 (1)

pamper 889 (5)

pamper oneself 944 (4)

pampered 376 (4), 944 (3), 947 (3)

pamphlet 528 (4), 589 (1)

pamphleteer 475 (11), 528 (6), 528 (9), 537 (3), 591 (3)

pan- 79 (3), 194 (14), 194 (17), 322 (3), 551 (4), 967 (2)

pan out 157 (5)

panacea 658 (1)

panache 571 (1), 855 (1)

panama 228 (23)

pandemic 79 (4), 651 (4)

pandemonium 61 (4), 400 (1)

pander 938 (3), 951 (10)

pander to 628 (4), 703 (7), 826 (3), 879 (4), 925 (4)

pandering 951 (5)

pane 207 (2), 422 (1)

panegyric 579 (2), 923 (2)

panel 74 (4), 87 (1), 207 (2), 231 (2), 692 (1), 754 (1)

panel game 837 (8)

panel of judges 956 (1)

panelling 227 (1)

pang 318 (2), 377 (2), 645 (1), 825 (1)

pangs 939 (1)

pangs of jealousy 911 (1)

panic 854 (1), 854 (9), 854 (12), 856 (4)

panic-striken 854 (6)

panicky 854 (6)

pannier 194 (6), 194 (9)

panoply 228 (1), 660 (2)

panorama 52 (1), 79 (1), 438 (5), 445 (2), 553 (4)

panoramic 79 (3), 438 (6), 443 (2)

pansy 366 (6)

pant 317 (4), 318 (5), 352 (11), 379 (7), 684 (5), 818 (8)

pant for 859 (11)

pantaloons 228 (12)

pantheism 973 (2)

pantheist 973 (7)

pantheistic 973 (8)

pantheon 364 (5), 990 (1)

panties 228 (17)

panting 318 (4), 352 (7), 352 (9), 684 (3), 818 (5)

pantomime 20 (2), 445 (2), 547 (4), 547 (21), 594 (3), 594 (8), 594 (17)

pantomime dame 594 (8)

pantomimic 547 (15)

pantry 194 (19), 632 (2)

pants 228 (17)

pap 253 (3), 387 (1)
papa 169 (3)
papacy 985 (1), 985 (3)
papal 985 (6)
papal decree 737 (2)
papal nuncio 754 (3)
paper 4 (3), 207 (2), 226
(15), 528 (4), 553 (6), 579
(2), 586 (4), 591 (1), 631
(3)
paper bag 194 (9)
paper mill 687 (1)
paper modelling 554 (1)
paper money 797 (5)
paper over 656 (12)
paper over the cracks 875
(7)
paper tiger 542 (5)
paperback 589 (1), 589 (8)
papering 227 (1)
papers 548 (1)
papers, the 528 (4)
paperwork 586 (1)
papery 330 (2)
papier mâché 356 (1), 631
(3)
paprika 389 (1)
papyrus 586 (4)
par 28 (2), 28 (7), 30 (1),
30 (4)
par excellence 34 (12)
parable 18 (2), 519 (1), 534
(4), 590 (2)
parabola 248 (2)
parachute 276 (1), 276 (2),
309 (3), 662 (3)
parachute troops 722 (14)
parachuting 271 (1)
parachutist 271 (4), 309
(1)
parade 74 (1), 192 (15),
267 (4), 445 (2), 522 (8),
875 (1), 875 (3), 875 (7),
877 (5), 884 (7)
parade ground 724 (1)
paradigm 23 (1)
Paradise 824 (2), 971 (1)
paradisiac 971 (3)
paradox 14 (1), 25 (3), 475
(3), 497 (1), 508 (1), 517
(1)
paradoxical 497 (3), 517
(3)

paraffin 385 (1)
paragon 34 (3), 646 (2),
696 (1), 841 (2), 864 (3),
866 (6), 937 (1)
paragraph 53 (3), 563 (1)
parallel 12 (2), 18 (3), 18
(4), 28 (7), 28 (8), 28 (9),
89 (3), 181 (2), 184 (1),
219 (1), 219 (2), 219 (3),
239 (2), 281 (3), 462 (1)
parallel bars 219 (1)
parallel, be 219 (3)
parallel lines 219 (1)
parallelism 9 (2), 24 (2),
219 (1), 245 (1)
parallelogram 219 (1), 247
(4)
paralyse 161 (9), 161 (10),
375 (6), 679 (13), 854 (12)
paralysed 161 (7), 266 (6),
375 (3), 651 (22), 677 (2)
paralysis 161 (2), 175 (1),
375 (1), 677 (1)
paralytic 651 (18), 651
(22), 949 (8)
paramedic 658 (14)
parameter 85 (2)
paramilitary 718 (9)
paramount 34 (5), 638 (5),
733 (7)
paranoia 503 (2)
paranoiac 503 (7), 504 (1)
paranoid 503 (7)
paranormal 984 (8)
parapet 213 (1), 235 (3),
713 (3)
paraphernalia 43 (4), 228
(1), 630 (4), 777 (1)
paraphrase 20 (1), 20 (6),
22 (1), 516 (1), 520 (3),
520 (9), 563 (1)
paraphraser 20 (3), 520
(4)
paraphrasing 516 (3)
paraplegia 161 (2), 651
(16)
paraplegic 651 (18)
parasite 89 (2), 191 (2),
651 (5), 659 (1), 679 (6),
742 (4), 763 (2), 786 (4),
879 (2)
parasites 365 (16)

parasitical 679 (8), 745
(5), 879 (3)
parasol 226 (4), 421 (1)
paratrooper 271 (4), 309
(1)
paratroopers 722 (14)
paratroops 722 (7)
parboil 301 (40)
parcel 53 (5), 74 (6), 74
(11)
parcel out 46 (10), 783 (3)
parcel post 531 (2)
parch 342 (6), 381 (8), 859
(13)
parched 342 (4), 379 (4),
859 (9)
parchment 586 (4)
pardon 506 (2), 736 (1),
736 (3), 746 (3), 905 (7),
909 (1), 909 (4), 919 (1),
919 (3), 960 (1), 960 (3)
pardonable 909 (3), 927
(4), 935 (4)
pardoned 909 (3)
pare 27 (5), 37 (4), 39 (3),
46 (11), 207 (5)
parent 169 (1)
parentage 11 (1), 11 (2),
66 (1), 68 (4), 156 (2), 156
(3), 158 (1), 167 (1), 169
(1)
parental 11 (5), 169 (5)
parentheses 547 (14)
parenthesis 72 (1), 231 (4)
parenthetic 10 (1), 72 (2)
parenthetical 231 (6)
parenthood 169 (1), 360
(1)
pariah 84 (3), 779 (2), 883
(4)
paring 33 (3), 37 (2)
parish 53 (3), 184 (3), 985
(4), 987 (1)
parish church 990 (3)
parish clerk 986 (7)
parish priest 986 (3)
parish-pump 639 (6)
parishioner 191 (3)
parishioners 987 (1)
parity 18 (1), 28 (1), 797
(3)
park 184 (2), 187 (5), 187
(8), 192 (15), 235 (1), 295

(4), 348 (2), 366 (2), 837 (4)
park oneself 311 (8)
parka 228 (10)
parking meter 117 (3), 305 (3), 465 (6)
parking place 187 (3)
Parkinson's law 197 (1), 678 (4)
parkland 192 (15)
parlance 557 (1), 566 (1), 579 (1)
parley 584 (1), 584 (3), 584 (7), 691 (5), 720 (1), 766 (4)
parliament 692 (2), 733 (1)
parliamentary 692 (4)
parliamentary government 733 (4)
parlour 194 (19)
parlour game 837 (8)
parochial 184 (5), 192 (19), 481 (7), 985 (6), 987 (2)
parochialism 481 (4)
parodist 20 (3), 839 (3)
parody 20 (2), 20 (5), 22 (1), 497 (2), 497 (4), 521 (1), 521 (3), 552 (1), 552 (3), 590 (1), 851 (2), 851 (6)
parole 746 (1), 746 (3), 756 (2), 767 (1)
paroled 746 (2)
paroxysm 176 (1), 318 (2), 503 (4)
parquet 226 (7)
parricide 362 (2), 362 (7)
parrot 20 (3), 20 (5), 106 (1), 106 (4), 365 (4)
parrot fashion 106 (7)
parroting 20 (4)
parry 282 (6), 292 (3), 460 (5), 477 (8), 479 (3), 620 (5), 702 (9), 713 (1), 713 (10), 714 (3), 715 (3)
parse 51 (5), 564 (4)
parsimonious 457 (3), 636 (3), 778 (3), 814 (2), 816 (4), 932 (3)
parsimonious, be 636 (9), 814 (3), 816 (6)

parsimoniously 816 (7)
parsimoniousness 816 (1)
parsimony 636 (1), 816 (1), 932 (1)
parsing 51 (1), 564 (1)
parsley 301 (21)
parsnip 301 (20)
parson 986 (2)
parsonage 192 (6), 986 (10)
part 27 (1), 46 (7), 46 (8), 53 (1), 53 (3), 53 (7), 55 (1), 58 (1), 92 (1), 102 (1), 294 (3), 296 (4), 594 (3), 594 (8), 622 (4), 639 (2), 783 (2)
part and parcel 58 (1)
part and parcel of 5 (6)
part by part 53 (9)
part company 46 (7), 294 (3), 296 (4), 709 (7)
part of 58 (2)
part of speech 559 (1), 564 (2)
part song 412 (5)
part-time job 622 (3)
part wanting 55 (2)
part with 779 (4)
partake 301 (35)
partake of 775 (5)
partaker 301 (6)
partaking 301 (1), 775 (4)
partial 29 (2), 53 (6), 55 (3), 102 (2), 726 (2), 914 (4)
partial change 143 (1)
partial consent 758 (1)
partial eclipse 419 (2)
partial excuse 927 (1)
partial likeness 18 (1)
partial to 859 (7)
partial to, be 887 (13)
partial truth 977 (1)
partial vision 440 (1)
partiality 29 (1), 481 (3), 605 (1), 859 (3), 914 (2), 930 (1)
partially 33 (10), 53 (8)
participate 28 (9), 58 (3), 628 (4), 676 (5), 678 (11), 688 (4), 706 (4), 775 (5), 783 (3), 804 (5), 882 (8)
participating 775 (4)

participation 28 (4), 78 (1), 678 (1), 706 (1), 706 (2), 771 (3), 775 (2), 905 (2)
participator 686 (2), 707 (3), 775 (3)
participatory 775 (4)
participial 564 (3)
particle 33 (3), 196 (2), 564 (2)
particle counter 417 (4)
particular 80 (5), 455 (2), 457 (3), 463 (2), 540 (2), 604 (3), 862 (3)
particularism 80 (3)
particularity 80 (1), 463 (1), 862 (1)
particularize 15 (7), 80 (8), 570 (6), 590 (7)
particularly 32 (17), 34 (12)
particulars 33 (2), 53 (1), 80 (2), 590 (1)
parting 46 (2), 92 (3), 225 (1), 231 (2), 296 (1), 296 (3)
parting shot 296 (2)
parting with 779 (1)
partisan 481 (8), 705 (1), 707 (4), 708 (7), 722 (4), 738 (4), 880 (3), 914 (4)
partisanship 481 (3), 706 (1), 914 (2)
partition 46 (2), 46 (3), 46 (10), 51 (1), 53 (7), 70 (1), 92 (3), 201 (2), 225 (1), 231 (2), 235 (3), 236 (1), 421 (1), 783 (1), 783 (3)
partitioned 46 (4)
partly 33 (10), 53 (8)
partly-seen 444 (3)
partner 45 (14), 50 (4), 89 (2), 89 (4), 584 (4), 686 (4), 707 (3), 775 (3), 894 (4)
partner in crime 707 (3)
partnered 45 (5), 708 (6)
partnering 89 (3)
partnership 89 (1), 181 (1), 706 (2), 708 (3), 708 (5), 775 (2), 894 (1)
partridge 365 (5)
parts 184 (1), 187 (2)

party 53 (1), 74 (1), 74 (2), 74 (3), 74 (4), 284 (2), 371 (3), 488 (3), 489 (1), 489 (2), 584 (3), 706 (2), 708 (1), 722 (7), 722 (8), 764 (1), 837 (2), 882 (3), 978 (3)

party game 837 (8)

party-goer 837 (17)

party line 81 (1), 623 (2), 688 (2)

party manager 690 (3)

party member 708 (2), 708 (3)

party rule 733 (4)

party system 733 (4)

party to 488 (4)

party wall 92 (3)

party worker 708 (2)

parvenu 126 (4), 730 (3), 847 (3), 871 (2)

pas de deux 594 (5)

paschal 988 (8)

pass 34 (7), 45 (10), 68 (5), 83 (7), 108 (7), 111 (3), 125 (10), 154 (1), 201 (2), 206 (1), 222 (8), 263 (11), 265 (4), 267 (12), 297 (1), 300 (9), 302 (6), 305 (5), 306 (3), 350 (9), 605 (7), 660 (2), 700 (3), 712 (4), 727 (1), 727 (6), 756 (2), 756 (5), 758 (3), 848 (7), 923 (8), 953 (7)

pass a law 737 (7)

pass along 305 (5)

pass away 2 (7), 37 (5), 69 (5), 114 (6), 361 (7), 361 (8), 446 (3)

pass belief 486 (8)

pass beyond 305 (5)

pass by 111 (3), 305 (5)

pass current 485 (10)

pass for 18 (7)

pass for truth 485 (10)

pass in 299 (3)

pass into 27 (5), 305 (5)

pass judgment 480 (5), 737 (7)

pass laws 689 (4)

pass muster 28 (9), 83 (7), 635 (6), 644 (10), 732 (3)

pass off 154 (6)

pass on 272 (6), 285 (3), 361 (7), 524 (10)

pass out 161 (8), 305 (5), 375 (5), 949 (13)

pass over 57 (5), 458 (4), 458 (5), 582 (3), 607 (3), 909 (4), 919 (3)

pass round 528 (9)

pass sentence 480 (5)

pass the buck 620 (5), 677 (3), 919 (4)

pass the hat 761 (6)

pass the time 1 (6), 837 (21)

pass through 154 (7), 265 (4), 267 (12), 305 (5)

pass time 108 (8), 111 (3)

pass to 272 (6), 305 (5), 780 (3)

pass to another 780 (5)

pass under review 480 (6)

passable 33 (7), 644 (9), 732 (2), 828 (3), 841 (6)

passage 47 (1), 53 (1), 68 (5), 143 (1), 147 (2), 194 (20), 201 (2), 212 (1), 263 (7), 265 (1), 269 (1), 272 (1), 282 (3), 305 (1), 305 (2), 306 (1), 410 (1), 412 (3), 624 (3)

passage into 305 (1)

passage of time 108 (1)

passant 547 (16)

passbook 756 (2)

passe-partout 263 (11)

passé 125 (6), 127 (7)

passed 756 (4), 923 (7)

passed away 125 (6), 361 (6)

passenger 268 (4), 272 (3), 679 (6)

passenger ship 275 (1)

passerby 305 (2), 441 (1)

passim 72 (5), 75 (5), 185 (2)

passing 111 (2), 114 (3), 265 (3), 305 (4), 361 (2)

passing along 265 (1), 267 (6), 305 (2)

passing away 361 (2)

passing bell 361 (2), 547 (5)

passing fancy 604 (2)

passing through 267 (9), 305 (1)

passion 571 (1), 817 (1), 818 (2), 821 (1), 859 (1), 859 (4), 887 (1)

passion play 594 (3)

passionate 818 (3), 818 (5), 822 (3), 887 (9), 892 (3)

passionate friendship 880 (1)

passions 817 (1)

passive 175 (2), 523 (2), 620 (3), 677 (2), 739 (3), 820 (4), 823 (3)

passive resistance 715 (1)

passiveness 721 (1), 739 (1)

passivity 175 (1), 266 (2), 601 (1), 739 (1)

passkey 628 (2)

passport 263 (11), 466 (3), 547 (13), 628 (2), 737 (4), 756 (2)

password 263 (11), 460 (1), 547 (2), 628 (2), 718 (6), 756 (2)

past 2 (5), 125 (6), 127 (4), 127 (7), 611 (2), 867 (1)

past, be 64 (3), 111 (3), 125 (10), 145 (6), 154 (6)

past behaviour 688 (1)

past enduring 827 (7)

past history 64 (1)

past it 131 (6)

past its best 647 (3)

past master 696 (1)

past midnight 128 (8)

past one's best 655 (5)

past one's prime 131 (6)

past recall 853 (3)

past tense 108 (1), 125 (1)

past, the 119 (1), 125 (1)

past time 64 (1), 108 (1), 113 (1), 119 (1), 122 (1), 125 (1)

past times 125 (1)

pasta 301 (13)

paste 47 (9), 48 (4), 327 (1), 354 (3), 356 (1), 542 (5), 847 (1)

pasteboard 542 (7), 631 (3)

pastel 425 (7), 553 (5), 553 (6), 553 (7)
pastellist 556 (1)
pastern 214 (2)
pasteurization 652 (2)
pasteurize 172 (6), 652 (6)
pasteurized 652 (4)
pastiche 43 (3), 553 (2), 553 (5)
pasties 392 (2)
pastille 392 (2)
pastime 622 (1), 826 (1), 837 (1)
pasting 279 (2)
pastor 537 (1), 537 (3), 986 (3)
pastoral 370 (7), 553 (4), 826 (2), 985 (7)
pastoral staff 743 (2)
pastorate 985 (2), 985 (3)
pastorship 985 (2), 985 (3)
pastries 301 (23)
pastry 301 (23)
pastry cook 633 (3)
pasturage 301 (8), 348 (2)
pasture 301 (8), 301 (37), 301 (39), 344 (3), 348 (2), 366 (8), 370 (2)
pasturing 301 (1)
pasty 301 (13), 301 (23), 426 (3)
pat 24 (6), 45 (7), 279 (2), 279 (9), 378 (1), 378 (7), 547 (21), 826 (3), 889 (1), 889 (6)
pat down 216 (7)
pat on the back 923 (3)
patch 40 (1), 53 (5), 370 (3), 437 (4), 649 (2), 656 (2), 656 (12), 842 (2)
patch up 656 (12), 770 (2)
patched 801 (4)
patchiness 17 (1), 437 (4), 647 (1)
patching 656 (2)
patchwork 17 (1), 43 (4), 437 (1), 844 (4)
patchy 17 (2), 29 (2), 35 (4), 43 (6), 72 (2), 437 (7), 647 (3)
pate 213 (3)
pâté 301 (14)

patent 522 (4), 756 (2), 777 (2), 915 (1), 915 (5)
patent medicine 658 (2)
patented 80 (7), 777 (5)
pater 169 (3)
paterfamilias 169 (3), 372 (1)
paternal 11 (5), 169 (5)
paternalism 733 (3), 733 (4)
paternity 167 (1), 169 (1), 169 (3), 372 (1)
path 305 (1), 624 (5)
pathetic 639 (5), 818 (6), 827 (6), 836 (4), 905 (5)
pathfinder 66 (1), 268 (1)
pathogen 651 (5)
pathogenic 651 (22), 653 (3)
pathological 651 (22), 658 (18)
pathologist 658 (14)
pathology 651 (19), 658 (10)
pathos 818 (1), 821 (1), 827 (1)
pathway 624 (5)
patience 736 (1), 818 (1), 820 (1), 823 (2), 837 (11), 858 (1), 909 (1)
patient 278 (3), 461 (5), 600 (3), 651 (18), 736 (2), 823 (4), 825 (4), 858 (2), 905 (4), 909 (2)
patient, be 736 (3), 756 (5), 823 (6), 884 (5), 909 (4)
patina 207 (1), 425 (3), 434 (1)
patio 194 (20)
patois 560 (2)
patrial 191 (3)
patriality 915 (1)
patriarch 133 (2), 169 (3), 372 (1), 741 (5), 986 (4)
patriarchal 127 (4), 131 (6), 733 (9), 985 (6)
patriarchy 11 (3), 372 (1), 733 (4)
patrician 868 (4), 868 (7)
patrician order 868 (2)
patricide 362 (2)
patrimonial 771 (6), 777 (5)

patrimony 771 (1), 773 (1), 777 (4), 915 (1)
patriot 713 (6), 901 (5), 903 (1)
patriotic 901 (7)
patriotism 901 (3)
patrol 267 (1), 267 (12), 305 (5), 314 (2), 660 (8), 713 (6), 722 (7)
patrol boat 722 (13)
patrol car 274 (11)
patrol plane 722 (14)
patron 231 (3), 441 (2), 466 (4), 488 (3), 504 (3), 660 (3), 703 (3), 707 (4), 713 (6), 741 (1), 755 (1), 767 (1), 775 (3), 792 (2), 859 (6), 880 (3), 897 (3), 903 (1), 923 (4)
patron saint 968 (2)
patronage 178 (1), 660 (2), 689 (1), 703 (1), 733 (1), 767 (1), 792 (1), 923 (1)
patronize 488 (3), 605 (6), 605 (7), 628 (4), 660 (8), 703 (6), 706 (4), 713 (9), 871 (5), 880 (8), 897 (5), 914 (6), 923 (8), 927 (5)
patronizing 871 (4)
patronymic 561 (2)
patter 265 (4), 267 (14), 350 (6), 350 (10), 401 (1), 515 (3), 557 (1), 560 (3), 581 (1)
pattern 12 (1), 16 (1), 16 (4), 23 (1), 56 (1), 56 (5), 60 (1), 62 (1), 83 (2), 222 (1), 243 (1), 243 (5), 248 (2), 260 (1), 331 (1), 437 (9), 462 (1), 553 (5), 646 (2), 844 (3), 844 (12)
patterned 16 (2), 437 (5), 844 (10)
patterning 243 (2)
patty 301 (23)
paucity 105 (1), 196 (1), 636 (2)
paunch 253 (2)
paunchy 195 (8)
pauper 801 (2)
pauperism 774 (1), 801 (1)
pause 72 (1), 72 (3), 110 (1), 136 (2), 136 (5), 145

(4), 145 (8), 201 (1), 266 (1), 410 (3), 474 (8), 677 (3), 683 (1)
pavane 837 (14)
pave 226 (15)
pave the way 669 (10), 701 (8)
paved 226 (12), 624 (8)
pavement 218 (4), 226 (7), 624 (5)
pavilion 192 (16), 194 (23), 226 (3)
paving 214 (1), 218 (4), 226 (7), 631 (2)
paving stone 226 (7)
paw 214 (2), 378 (3), 378 (7), 778 (2), 889 (6)
paw the ground 312 (4), 547 (21)
pawky 839 (4)
pawn 544 (1), 628 (2), 639 (4), 767 (1), 767 (6), 780 (1), 780 (3), 785 (2), 837 (15)
pawnbroker 784 (3)
pawnbroker's 784 (2)
pawnbroking 784 (1)
pawned 767 (3)
pawnshop 784 (2)
pay 31 (4), 615 (4), 640 (4), 771 (2), 771 (10), 797 (12), 804 (2), 804 (4), 806 (4), 807 (1), 962 (1), 962 (3)
pay a dividend 771 (10)
pay a visit 882 (2)
pay attention 455 (4)
pay back 31 (4), 804 (4)
pay cash down 804 (4)
pay cash for 792 (5)
pay compensation 787 (3), 941 (5)
pay compliments 884 (6)
pay court to 879 (4), 925 (4)
pay damages 787 (3)
pay dearly 811 (6)
pay dividends 727 (7)
pay for 703 (6), 792 (5), 804 (5)
pay for it 963 (13)
pay homage 884 (6), 920 (6)
pay homage to 981 (11)

pay in advance 804 (4)
pay in kind 804 (4)
pay increase 771 (3)
pay interest 803 (6)
pay no attention 456 (7)
pay no heed 456 (7)
pay no regard to 458 (5)
pay off 679 (13), 727 (7)
pay on demand 804 (4)
pay on the dot 804 (4)
pay on the nail 804 (4)
pay one out 714 (3), 963 (8)
pay one's debt 768 (4)
pay one's dues 915 (8)
pay one's last respects 364 (9)
pay one's respects 311 (9), 876 (4), 884 (6), 886 (3), 920 (6)
pay one's way 804 (5)
pay out 203 (8), 772 (4), 804 (4), 806 (4)
pay packet 771 (2), 804 (2)
pay respect 866 (13)
pay rise 36 (2)
pay scale 771 (2)
pay the penalty 941 (5)
pay through the nose 811 (6)
pay too much 811 (6)
pay towards 781 (7)
pay tribute 739 (4), 745 (6), 962 (3)
pay tribute to 923 (9)
pay up 804 (4)
pay wages 804 (4)
pay well 771 (10), 813 (4)
payable 803 (5)
payday 108 (3)
payee 782 (2)
payer 804 (2)
paying 164 (5), 171 (4), 640 (3), 771 (5), 804 (3)
paying attention 455 (2)
paying for 804 (1)
paying guest 191 (2)
paying in full 804 (3)
paying off 804 (1)
payload 193 (1), 272 (3)
paymaster 798 (1), 804 (2)

payment 53 (1), 612 (4), 797 (2), 804 (1), 806 (1), 809 (3), 915 (1), 963 (4)
payment in kind 791 (1)
payoff 69 (1), 725 (1)
payroll 87 (1), 686 (4)
pea 252 (2)
pea-green 434 (3)
pea-shooter 287 (3)
peace 266 (2), 376 (2), 399 (1), 717 (1), 719 (2), 826 (1)
peace and quiet 683 (1), 717 (1), 826 (1)
peace-lover 717 (2)
peace-loving 717 (3)
peace of mind 823 (1), 828 (1)
peace offering 719 (2), 781 (3)
peace party 717 (2), 720 (2)
peace treaty 765 (2)
peaceable 177 (3), 710 (2), 717 (3), 884 (4)
peaceableness 717 (1)
peaceably 717 (5)
peacede treaty 719 (1)
peaceful 177 (3), 266 (5), 376 (4), 399 (2), 683 (2), 710 (2), 717 (3), 721 (2), 739 (3), 826 (2), 884 (4)
peacefully 717 (5)
peacefulness 266 (2), 717 (1)
peacemaker 177 (2), 717 (2), 720 (2)
peacemaking 719 (1), 719 (3)
peacetime 717 (1), 717 (3)
peacock-blue 435 (3)
peak 34 (1), 54 (1), 69 (2), 209 (2), 213 (1), 256 (2), 646 (1)
peaky 206 (5), 651 (20)
peal 400 (1), 400 (4), 402 (1), 403 (1), 403 (3), 404 (1), 412 (2), 414 (8)
peal of laughter 835 (2)
peal the bells 413 (9)
pealing 400 (3)
peanuts 33 (2), 639 (2)
pear 301 (19)

pear shape 252 (4)
pear-shaped 248 (3), 250 (6), 252 (5)
pearl 427 (2), 644 (3), 841 (2), 844 (8)
pearl-grey 429 (2)
pearly 424 (2), 425 (7), 427 (5), 429 (2), 437 (6)
peas 301 (20)
peasant 370 (4), 370 (7), 869 (6)
peashooter 353 (1)
peat 385 (1)
peat-brown 430 (3)
pebble 344 (3)
pebbly 344 (5)
peccadillo 639 (2), 934 (2), 936 (2)
peck 104 (2), 301 (35), 465 (3)
peck at 301 (35)
pecking 301 (1)
peckish 859 (9)
pectoral 222 (2), 989 (2)
peculate 788 (8)
peculation 675 (1), 788 (4)
peculator 789 (3)
peculiar 15 (4), 80 (5), 84 (6), 503 (8)
peculiarity 5 (4), 80 (1), 84 (1)
peculiarly 32 (19)
pecuniary 797 (9)
pedagogic 537 (4)
pedagogue 537 (1)
pedagogy 534 (1)
pedal 287 (3), 287 (7), 630 (1)
pedal cycle 274 (3)
pedal-driven 274 (16)
pedal power 160 (3), 274 (1)
pedant 83 (3), 475 (6), 492 (1), 537 (1), 602 (3), 735 (3), 850 (3), 862 (2)
pedantic 455 (2), 457 (3), 481 (7), 490 (6), 574 (4), 735 (4), 768 (2), 862 (3), 976 (8)
pedantry 457 (1), 481 (4), 490 (2), 491 (3), 494 (3), 850 (2), 862 (1)
peddle 793 (4)

peddler 794 (3)
pederast 952 (1)
pederasty 951 (3)
pedestal 214 (1), 218 (5)
pedestrian 267 (9), 268 (3), 305 (2), 572 (2), 593 (9), 840 (2)
pedestrian traffic 305 (2)
pedestrianism 265 (1), 267 (3)
pedicure 658 (11), 843 (1)
pedigree 71 (2), 87 (1), 169 (2), 868 (1)
pediment 213 (1)
pedlar 793 (2), 794 (3)
pee 302 (6)
peek 438 (3), 438 (8)
peel 41 (2), 46 (8), 207 (5), 226 (6), 229 (6)
peel off 49 (3), 49 (4), 229 (7)
peeled 229 (4)
peeling 229 (1)
peelings 41 (2)
peep 409 (3), 438 (3), 438 (8), 453 (4)
peep of day 128 (1)
peep out 298 (5)
peep show 445 (2), 837 (15)
peephole 263 (5), 438 (5)
peeping 438 (4), 453 (3)
Peeping Tom 438 (4), 441 (1)
peer 28 (6), 438 (8), 438 (9), 440 (4), 459 (13), 692 (3), 866 (6)
peer group 123 (2)
peer or peeress 868 (5)
peer out 298 (5)
peerage 866 (4), 868 (2)
peerdom 962 (1)
peerless 34 (5), 644 (6)
peeve 827 (9), 891 (9)
peeved 891 (4)
peevish 829 (3), 885 (5), 892 (3), 893 (2)
peevishness 892 (1), 893 (1)
peg 27 (1), 47 (5), 217 (3), 264 (2), 301 (26)
peg away 146 (3), 600 (4)
peg top 252 (4)

pejorative 483 (2), 559 (1), 921 (3), 926 (5)
pelican 365 (4)
pell-mell 61 (12), 680 (4)
pellet 252 (2), 723 (4), 723 (12)
pellucid 422 (2)
pellucidity 422 (1)
pelt 226 (6), 277 (6), 279 (9), 287 (7), 350 (10)
pelt with 712 (12)
pelting 287 (1)
pen 185 (1), 235 (1), 235 (4), 549 (3), 586 (4), 586 (8), 747 (10)
pen and ink 586 (4)
pen-and-ink drawing 553 (5)
pen and paper 586 (4)
pen friend 880 (5)
pen name 561 (2), 562 (1)
pen-pusher 586 (5), 589 (7)
penal 757 (2), 963 (6)
penal code 953 (3), 963 (4)
penal judgment 480 (1)
penal servitude 963 (4)
penal settlement 748 (3)
penalize 643 (3), 954 (9), 963 (8)
penalizing 963 (6)
penalty 42 (1), 682 (3), 740 (1), 747 (1), 769 (1), 772 (1), 787 (1), 805 (1), 809 (1), 809 (2), 809 (3), 963 (4)
penalty clause 468 (1)
penance 31 (2), 939 (1), 941 (3), 945 (1), 963 (1)
Penates 967 (2)
penchant 179 (1), 859 (3)
pencil 549 (3), 553 (8), 586 (4), 586 (8)
pencil sharpener 256 (6)
pencilled 586 (7)
pendant 217 (2), 844 (7)
pendency 217 (1)
pendent 217 (4)
pending 108 (4), 108 (10)
pending, be 108 (7), 136 (6)
pendulous 49 (2), 217 (4), 317 (3)

pendulum 117 (3), 217 (2), 317 (1)

penetrate 79 (5), 263 (18), 297 (6), 305 (5), 449 (10), 516 (5), 821 (8)

penetrating 79 (4), 297 (4), 388 (3), 407 (2), 498 (4), 818 (6)

penetration 43 (1), 231 (1), 297 (1), 305 (1), 498 (2)

penfriend 588 (2)

penguin 365 (4)

penicillin 658 (7)

peninsula 184 (1), 254 (2), 344 (1)

penis 167 (3)

penitence 603 (1), 830 (1), 936 (1), 939 (1), 941 (3), 981 (3)

penitent 830 (2), 939 (2), 939 (3), 945 (2)

penitent, be 603 (5), 654 (8), 830 (4), 939 (4), 979 (10)

penitential 941 (4)

penitentiary 748 (1), 941 (4)

penitently 939 (5)

penknife 256 (5)

pennant 547 (12)

penned 586 (7), 778 (4)

penned up 747 (6)

penniless 774 (2), 801 (3)

penny pincher 816 (3)

penny-pinching 816 (1)

penological 963 (6)

penologist 747 (3), 963 (1)

penology 747 (3), 963 (1), 963 (4)

pension 192 (2), 753 (1), 771 (2), 804 (2), 807 (1)

pension off 779 (4)

pensionable age 131 (3)

pensioned 782 (3)

pensioned off, be 753 (3)

pensioner 133 (1), 753 (1), 782 (2)

pensive 449 (5), 456 (4), 834 (6)

pent up 747 (5)

pentagon 99 (1), 247 (4)

pentagram 99 (1)

pentameter 99 (1), 593 (5)

Pentateuch 99 (1), 975 (2)

pentathlon 99 (1), 716 (2)

penthouse 192 (9), 194 (22)

penultimate 69 (4)

penumbra 418 (1), 419 (2)

penurious 801 (3), 816 (4)

penury 801 (1)

people 11 (4), 191 (5), 192 (21), 371 (4), 371 (5), 786 (7)

people of taste 492 (3), 504 (3), 846 (2)

people, the 869 (1)

peopled 104 (5)

pep 174 (1)

pep pill 821 (2), 949 (4)

pep talk 174 (4), 583 (1), 612 (2)

pep up 174 (8), 390 (3)

pepper 263 (18), 287 (8), 388 (1), 388 (6), 389 (1), 655 (10), 712 (11)

peppercorn rent 812 (1)

peppered 263 (14)

peppery 388 (3), 892 (3)

peptic 658 (17)

per 628 (5)

per annum 141 (7)

per cent 85 (3)

per diem 141 (7)

per head 783 (4)

per se 5 (10), 88 (6)

perambulation 267 (3)

perambulator 274 (4)

perambulatory 267 (9)

perceive 374 (5), 438 (7), 447 (7), 484 (5), 490 (8)

perceived 490 (7)

percentage 36 (2), 53 (1), 85 (3)

percentile 85 (3), 86 (9)

perceptible 438 (6)

perception 438 (1), 447 (1), 463 (1), 490 (1), 498 (2)

perceptive 447 (5)

perceptivity 374 (1)

perceptual 374 (3), 447 (5)

perch 187 (8), 192 (4), 192 (21), 203 (4), 218 (4), 309

(3), 311 (8), 365 (15), 679 (12)

perchance 159 (8)

percolate 297 (6), 298 (7), 341 (6), 350 (9)

percolating 263 (15), 341 (4)

percolation 341 (2)

percolator 194 (14)

percussion 279 (1), 413 (3), 414 (1)

percussionist 413 (2)

perdition 165 (3), 728 (2)

peregrination 267 (1)

peremptory 532 (4), 733 (7), 737 (5), 740 (2)

peremptory, be 740 (3)

perennial 113 (4), 115 (2), 366 (7)

perennial optimist 833 (1)

perfect 32 (13), 34 (5), 44 (5), 52 (4), 54 (3), 125 (1), 575 (3), 575 (4), 644 (4), 644 (6), 646 (3), 646 (5), 648 (7), 669 (12), 694 (4), 725 (4), 725 (5), 841 (3), 923 (6), 933 (3), 935 (3), 950 (5)

perfect being 965 (2)

perfect fit 24 (4)

perfect fool 501 (1)

perfect gentleman 929 (2)

perfect picture 841 (2)

perfected 646 (3), 669 (8)

perfectible 654 (6)

perfection 23 (1), 34 (1), 54 (1), 213 (1), 644 (1), 646 (1), 669 (4), 694 (1), 725 (1), 841 (1), 859 (5), 935 (1), 950 (1), 965 (1), 965 (2)

perfectionism 457 (1), 654 (4), 829 (1), 862 (1)

perfectionist 457 (3), 654 (7), 671 (2), 862 (2)

perfectly 646 (6)

perfectly dreadful 645 (4)

perfectness 646 (1)

perfidious 541 (3), 541 (4), 542 (6), 543 (4), 698 (4), 769 (2), 881 (3), 898 (4), 918 (2), 930 (7) perfidy 523 (1), 541 (1), 542 (1), 543 (1), 603 (1), 738 (3), 769 (1), 881 (1), 918 (1), 930 (2)

perforate 263 (18)

perforated 255 (6), 263 (14)

perforation 263 (2), 655 (4)

perforator 256 (2), 263 (12), 630 (1)

perforce 596 (9)

perform 164 (7), 173 (3), 413 (9), 551 (8), 594 (17), 628 (4), 640 (4), 676 (5), 768 (3), 876 (4), 917 (10)

perform ritual 981 (12), 988 (10)

perform the rites 988 (10)

performable 469 (2)

performance 157 (1), 164 (1), 412 (1), 413 (6), 551 (1), 676 (1), 725 (2), 768 (1), 876 (1), 917 (1)

performer 413 (1), 520 (4), 594 (10), 676 (3), 686 (1)

performing 676 (4)

perfume 300 (9), 394 (1), 394 (3), 396 (2), 396 (4), 843 (3)

perfumed 376 (3), 394 (2), 396 (3)

perfumer 396 (1)

perfumery 396 (1)

perfunctoriness 726 (1)

perfunctory 55 (3), 307 (2), 458 (2), 458 (3), 598 (3), 647 (3), 695 (6), 726 (2), 860 (2)

pergola 194 (23)

perhaps 159 (8), 469 (5)

perigee 200 (2)

perihelion 200 (2)

peril 661 (1)

perilous 661 (3)

perimeter 233 (1), 235 (1), 236 (1)

period 53 (1), 69 (1), 108 (1), 110 (1), 110 (2), 141 (1), 141 (2), 302 (2), 547 (14), 563 (1), 682 (3)

periodic 71 (4), 110 (3), 141 (4), 142 (2)

periodic, be 65 (3), 141 (6)

periodical 72 (2), 81 (3), 106 (3), 108 (4), 139 (2), 141 (4), 152 (4), 317 (3), 528 (5), 589 (1)

periodically 110 (5), 141 (7), 610 (9)

periodicity 16 (1), 71 (1), 72 (1), 106 (2), 139 (1), 141 (1), 143 (1), 265 (1), 317 (1)

peripatetic 267 (9), 314 (3)

peripheral 10 (4), 57 (3), 199 (3), 223 (2), 230 (2), 233 (2), 639 (5)

periphery 199 (1), 223 (1), 230 (1), 233 (1)

periphrasis 570 (2)

periphrastic 570 (4)

periscope 442 (3)

perish 2 (7), 51 (5), 165 (11), 361 (8), 362 (13), 655 (7)

perishability 114 (1)

perishable 114 (4)

perishable goods 795 (1)

perishing 380 (6)

perjure oneself 541 (5)

perjured 541 (3), 541 (5), 543 (4)

perjurer 545 (2)

perjury 541 (1), 543 (1)

perk up 310 (4), 685 (5), 833 (7)

perks 771 (2), 781 (2)

perky 833 (3), 878 (5)

perm 843 (2)

permafrost 380 (1)

permanence 113 (2), 115 (1), 144 (1), 153 (1), 666 (1)

permanency 144 (1), 622 (3)

permanent 108 (4), 113 (4), 115 (2), 144 (2), 153 (4), 965 (6)

permanent wave 843 (2)

permanent way 624 (7)

permanently 144 (4)

permeable 263 (15)

permeate 43 (8), 178 (4), 189 (5), 231 (7), 297 (6)

permeating 189 (3)

permeation 43 (1), 189 (1), 224 (1), 231 (1), 305 (1)

permissible 469 (2), 756 (4)

permission 160 (2), 297 (1), 488 (1), 701 (1), 734 (1), 736 (1), 756 (1), 758 (1), 919 (1), 923 (1)

permissive 734 (3), 756 (3)

permissiveness 734 (1), 951 (2)

permit 263 (11), 297 (1), 466 (3), 469 (3), 469 (4), 488 (6), 488 (7), 547 (13), 628 (2), 660 (2), 734 (5), 736 (3), 737 (4), 744 (10), 751 (2), 751 (4), 756 (2), 756 (5), 758 (3), 781 (7), 823 (6), 915 (1), 915 (8), 919 (3), 923 (8)

permit oneself 756 (5)

permitted 469 (2), 488 (5), 756 (4), 781 (6), 915 (2), 927 (4), 953 (5)

permitting 488 (4), 756 (3)

permutation 86 (2), 143 (1), 151 (1)

permute 151 (3)

pernicious 165 (4), 645 (3)

pernickety 862 (3)

perorate 570 (6), 579 (9)

peroration 67 (1), 69 (1), 579 (2), 579 (4)

peroxide 426 (2)

perpendicular 215 (1), 215 (2), 249 (2)

perpendicularity 249 (1)

perpetrate 676 (5), 914 (6)

perpetration 676 (1)

perpetrator 676 (3), 686 (1)

perpetual 1 (4), 71 (4), 107 (2), 108 (4), 113 (4), 115 (2), 115 (4), 139 (2), 144 (2), 146 (2), 153 (4), 866 (10), 965 (6)

perpetually 108 (10), 139 (5)

perpetuate 115 (3), 146 (4), 153 (8)

perpetuation 115 (1), 146 (1), 666 (1)

perpetuity 1 (1), 71 (1), 107 (1), 108 (1), 113 (1), 115 (1), 146 (1), 320 (1), 965 (2)

perplex 63 (5), 474 (9), 517 (6), 700 (6), 827 (10)

perplexed 474 (6), 517 (5)

perplexing 474 (4), 700 (4)

perplexity 474 (2)

perquisite 771 (2)

perquisites 781 (2)

persecute 619 (5), 645 (7), 735 (7), 735 (8), 827 (9), 881 (4), 898 (8), 906 (3), 963 (8), 963 (11)

persecuting 735 (6), 881 (3), 898 (4)

persecution 182 (1), 619 (1), 645 (1), 735 (1), 827 (1), 827 (2), 898 (2), 976 (2), 979 (3)

persecution mania 503 (3)

persecutor 735 (3), 963 (5)

perseverance 144 (1), 599 (1), 600 (1), 602 (1), 619 (1), 678 (3), 855 (1)

persevere 71 (6), 146 (3), 599 (4), 600 (4), 602 (6), 619 (5), 678 (11), 682 (6), 682 (7), 852 (6)

persevering 146 (2), 162 (7), 599 (2), 600 (3), 602 (4), 678 (9), 682 (4), 855 (4)

persiflage 839 (2), 851 (1)

persist 144 (3), 146 (3), 600 (4), 602 (6), 619 (5), 678 (11)

persistence 144 (1), 146 (1), 600 (1), 619 (1)

persistent 113 (4), 146 (2), 162 (7), 600 (3)

persistently 599 (5), 600 (5)

persisting 144 (2), 146 (2)

person 3 (2), 80 (4), 88 (2), 319 (3), 371 (3)

person in authority 741 (6)

person in charge 690 (3)

person of few words 582 (1)

person of mark 866 (6)

person of rank 866 (6), 868 (5)

person of repute 531 (5), 638 (4), 730 (3), 741 (6), 866 (6), 890 (2)

person on the spot 754 (2)

persona grata 880 (3), 890 (2)

persona non grata 881 (2)

personable 841 (6)

personage 371 (3), 594 (8), 638 (4)

personal 5 (8), 21 (3), 80 (5), 80 (7), 320 (3), 371 (6), 773 (3)

personal account 590 (3)

personal attendance 189 (1)

personal column 528 (3), 894 (5)

personal effects 777 (1)

personal enemy 881 (2)

personal estate 777 (1)

personal motives 932 (1)

personal property 777 (1)

personal remark 926 (2)

personal remarks 851 (1), 899 (2)

personal servant 742 (2)

personal style 566 (1)

personal world 321 (2)

personality 5 (1), 5 (3), 80 (1), 80 (4), 178 (1), 320 (2), 447 (2), 638 (4), 817 (1)

personality disorder 503 (2)

personalize 80 (8)

personalized 80 (6)

personally 80 (9)

personification 519 (1)

personify 319 (7), 519 (4), 522 (7), 551 (8), 594 (17)

personnel 58 (1), 74 (4), 160 (1), 629 (1), 686 (4), 708 (1), 722 (7), 742 (2)

persons 371 (4)

perspective 9 (2), 183 (3), 203 (1), 293 (1), 438 (5), 553 (1)

perspicacious 438 (6), 498 (4)

perspicacity 498 (2), 862 (1)

perspicuity 516 (1), 567 (1), 575 (1)

perspicuous 516 (2), 567 (2), 575 (3)

perspiration 298 (2), 302 (1)

perspiratory 302 (5)

perspire 298 (7), 300 (9), 302 (6), 379 (7)

perspiring 379 (4)

persuadability 601 (1), 612 (3)

persuadable 487 (2)

persuade 178 (3), 473 (9), 485 (9), 612 (10), 761 (5)

persuade against 613 (3)

persuade oneself 512 (6)

persuaded 473 (5), 485 (4)

persuaded, be 758 (3)

persuader 612 (5)

persuasion 77 (1), 178 (1), 473 (2), 485 (1), 534 (1), 612 (2)

persuasive 178 (2), 471 (3), 485 (5), 612 (6)

pert 833 (3), 878 (5)

pertain 9 (7), 78 (4)

pertinacity 600 (1), 602 (1)

pertinence 9 (3), 24 (3)

pertinent 9 (6), 24 (6), 78 (3)

pertinently 24 (11)

pertness 878 (2)

perturb 63 (3), 318 (6), 821 (8)

perturbation 174 (2), 318 (1), 822 (2), 854 (2)

perusal 536 (2)

peruse 536 (5)

pervade 43 (8), 54 (7), 79 (5), 178 (4), 189 (5), 231 (7), 305 (5)

pervading 189 (3)

pervasion 43 (1), 189 (1), 224 (1)

pervasive 79 (4), 178 (2), 189 (3)

pervasiveness 79 (1)

perverse 602 (4), 602 (5), 604 (3), 700 (4), 738 (7)

perversion 521 (1), 535 (1), 541 (1), 543 (1), 675 (1), 951 (3)

perversity 602 (1)

pervert 84 (3), 246 (5), 477 (8), 495 (9), 521 (3), 535 (3), 645 (6), 655 (8), 675 (2), 820 (7), 934 (8), 938 (3), 952 (1)

pervert the law 914 (6)

perverted 495 (5), 934 (4), 951 (8), 980 (4)

pessary 658 (9)

pessimism 483 (1), 507 (1), 834 (1), 853 (1)

pessimist 483 (1), 834 (4), 853 (1), 854 (5)

pessimistic 483 (2), 507 (2), 834 (5), 853 (2)

pest 616 (1), 651 (4), 659 (1), 825 (3), 827 (2), 888 (3)

pester 139 (3), 678 (13), 827 (9), 891 (9)

pestering 827 (5)

pesticide 659 (3)

pestiferous 653 (3)

pestilence 645 (1), 651 (4)

pestilent 653 (3), 659 (5)

pestle 279 (4)

pestle and mortar 332 (3)

pet 612 (11), 703 (6), 736 (3), 826 (3), 887 (13), 889 (5), 889 (6), 890 (1), 897 (6)

pet aversion 861 (1), 888 (3)

pet name 561 (2)

petal 366 (7)

peter out 37 (5), 69 (5)

Peter Pan 130 (1)

petite 196 (8), 841 (5)

petition 524 (2), 756 (6), 761 (1), 761 (5), 959 (1), 959 (7), 981 (4), 981 (11)

petition against 762 (3)

petitionary 961 (10)

petitioner 763 (1), 859 (6), 915 (1), 928 (3), 959 (4), 981 (8)

petrifaction 326 (2)

petrified 854 (6)

petrify 326 (5), 821 (8), 854 (12), 864 (7)

petrol 385 (1)

petroleum 357 (2), 385 (1)

petrological 359 (3)

petrology 359 (2)

petticoat 228 (17)

pettifogger 545 (4), 958 (1)

pettifoggery 542 (2)

pettifogging 477 (4), 639 (6)

pettiness 33 (1), 639 (1), 922 (2), 932 (1)

petting 889 (1)

petty 33 (7), 639 (5), 867 (4), 922 (4), 932 (3)

petty cash 797 (1)

petty detail 33 (2)

petty larceny 788 (1)

petty-minded 481 (7)

petty officer 270 (3), 741 (7)

petty sessions 956 (2)

petty thief 789 (1)

petty tyrant 735 (3), 741 (2)

petulance 892 (1)

petulant 829 (3), 892 (3), 893 (2)

pew 194 (4), 218 (6), 990 (4)

pewter 43 (3), 427 (2), 429 (1)

phalanx 48 (1), 324 (3), 722 (6), 722 (8)

phallic 167 (4)

phallus 171 (2)

phantasm 440 (2), 970 (3)

phantom 4 (2), 440 (2), 513 (3), 970 (2)

pharisaical 541 (4), 980 (4)

Pharisaism 980 (2)

pharmaceutics 658 (10)

pharmacist 658 (15)

pharmacologist 658 (15)

pharmacology 658 (10)

pharmacopoeia 658 (2)

pharmacy 658 (15)

phase 7 (2), 62 (5), 117 (7), 123 (4), 445 (1), 623 (8)

phased 123 (3)

phasing 123 (1), 141 (1)

pheasant 301 (16), 365 (5)

phenomenal 3 (3), 84 (6), 864 (5)

phenomenon 154 (1), 864 (3)

phial 194 (13)

philander 887 (15), 889 (7)

philanderer 887 (4), 952 (1)

philandering 887 (3), 889 (2)

philanthropic 897 (4), 901 (6), 931 (2), 933 (3)

philanthropist 513 (4), 597 (3), 897 (3), 901 (4), 903 (1)

philanthropize 813 (4), 897 (6), 901 (8)

philanthropy 597 (2), 703 (2), 781 (1), 781 (2), 897 (1), 901 (1), 979 (1)

philatelist 492 (3)

philharmonic 412 (7)

philippic 579 (2)

Philistine 491 (1), 491 (5), 493 (1), 699 (3), 847 (3), 847 (4)

Philistinism 699 (1), 820 (1), 847 (1)

philological 557 (5), 559 (4)

philologist 557 (4), 559 (3)

philology 557 (2), 559 (3), 564 (1)

philosopher 449 (4), 459 (9), 475 (6), 492 (2), 500 (1), 512 (3)

philosophic 449 (6)

philosophical 823 (3), 823 (4)

philosophize 449 (8), 475 (10)

philosophy 447 (1), 449 (3), 459 (1), 475 (1), 485 (2), 485 (1), 973 (1), 974 (2)

philtre 174 (4), 983 (4)

phlebotomize 658 (20)

phlegm 302 (4), 354 (1), 679 (2), 820 (1)

phlegmatic 677 (2), 820 (3), 860 (2), 865 (2)

phlegmy 302 (5), 335 (4)

phobia 503 (2), 825 (3), 854 (3), 861 (1), 888 (1)

Phoebe 321 (9)

Phoebus 321 (8), 967 (1)

phoenix 84 (4), 166 (1), 970 (5)

phon 398 (1)

phone 524 (10), 558 (3)

phone book 524 (6)

phone call 529 (3)

phone-in 531 (4)

phoneme 558 (3), 559 (1), 577 (1)

phonetic 398 (3), 558 (5)

phonetician 398 (2), 557 (4)

phoneticize 398 (4)

phonetics 398 (2), 557 (2)

phoney 541 (3), 542 (7), 543 (4), 545 (3), 850 (4)

phonic 398 (3)

phonics 398 (2)

phonology 398 (2), 559 (3)

phosphorescence 417 (3)

phosphorescent 417 (8), 420 (8)

photo 551 (4), 551 (9)

photo finish 28 (5), 200 (2), 716 (2)

photocomposition 587 (1)

photocopier 20 (3), 549 (3)

photocopy 20 (6), 22 (1), 551 (4)

photoelectric cell 160 (6)

photogenic 551 (6), 841 (3)

photograph 548 (1), 548 (7), 551 (4), 551 (9)

photograph well 841 (7)

photographer 549 (1), 551 (4)

photographic 18 (5), 494 (6), 551 (6), 590 (6)

photographic memory 505 (1)

photography 22 (1), 321 (11), 442 (1), 442 (6), 445 (3), 549 (1), 551 (4)

photosensitive 417 (8)

photostat 22 (1)

phrase 410 (1), 410 (2), 412 (3), 520 (2), 559 (1), 563 (1), 563 (3), 574 (1)

phrasemonger 563 (1), 574 (3)

phraseological 563 (2)

phraseology 563 (1), 566 (1)

phrasing 410 (1), 413 (6), 563 (1), 566 (1)

phrenology 213 (3)

phylum 77 (3)

physical 1 (5), 3 (3), 319 (6), 376 (5), 447 (6)

physical beauty 841 (1)

physical being 319 (1)

physical chemistry 319 (5)

physical education 682 (2)

physical element 319 (4)

physical energy 174 (1)

physical fatigue 684 (1)

physical force 162 (1), 740 (1)

physical insensibility 375 (1)

physical necessity 596 (1)

physical pain 377 (1)

physical pleasure 376 (1)

physical power 160 (1)

physical science 319 (5)

physical wreck 655 (2)

physically 3 (4)

physician 658 (14)

physicist 319 (5)

physics 319 (5)

physiognomy 237 (2), 445 (6)

physiological 358 (4)

physiology 331 (1), 358 (2)

physiotherapist 658 (14)

physiotherapy 658 (12)

physique 162 (2), 331 (1)

pianissimo 401 (6), 412 (8)

pianist 413 (2)

piano 401 (3), 401 (6), 412 (8), 414 (4)

pianola 414 (4)

picador 362 (6)

picaresque 590 (6)

piccolo 407 (1), 414 (6)

pick 256 (2), 304 (2), 370 (9), 605 (1), 605 (7), 638 (3), 644 (2), 771 (7), 786 (6)

pick-a-back 218 (17), 273 (10)

pick a fight 709 (8)

pick and choose 604 (4), 605 (7), 862 (4)

pick clean 648 (9)

pick holes 924 (10)

pick holes in 924 (12), 926 (6)

pick locks 788 (7)

pick-me-up 388 (1), 658 (6)

pick off 362 (10), 712 (11)

pick on 928 (8)

pick one's brains 459 (14)

pick one's way 267 (11), 700 (7)

pick oneself up 310 (5)

pick out 39 (3), 46 (9), 304 (4), 438 (7), 463 (3), 605 (7), 844 (12)

pick out a tune 413 (9)

pick over 459 (15)

pick pockets 788 (7)

pick quarrels 709 (8)

pick the best 605 (7)

pick up 310 (4), 484 (5), 654 (1), 656 (8), 747 (8), 771 (7), 786 (6), 952 (2), 952 (4)

pick up the bill 804 (5)

pickaxe 304 (2)

picked 605 (5), 644 (4)

picked out 46 (5), 844 (10)

picked troops 722 (4), 722 (7)

picker 370 (4)

picket 45 (11), 187 (5), 664 (2), 702 (10), 713 (6), 722 (7), 747 (9)

picket line 57 (1)

picketing 702 (1)

picking out 46 (2), 605 (1)

picking up 310 (1), 771 (1)

pilot vessel 275 (1)
pilotage 269 (2), 689 (2)
piloting 269 (2)
pimp 938 (3), 951 (10), 952 (5)
pimping 951 (5)
pimple 210 (1), 253 (2), 651 (12), 845 (1)
pimply 253 (7), 651 (22)
pin 47 (5), 256 (2), 263 (12), 844 (7)
pin down 740 (3), 778 (5)
pin money 797 (1)
pin on 928 (8)
pin-stripe 844 (3)
pin together 45 (10)
pin-up 553 (5), 841 (2)
pinafore 228 (15)
pinafore dress 228 (8)
pince-nez 442 (2)
pincer movement 293 (1), 712 (1), 778 (1)
pincers 304 (2), 778 (2)
pinch 33 (2), 104 (2), 137 (3), 198 (7), 206 (7), 260 (3), 293 (3), 377 (2), 377 (5), 378 (7), 627 (2), 700 (3), 731 (1), 747 (8), 788 (7), 814 (3), 816 (6), 889 (1)
pinch out 418 (7)
pinched 198 (4), 206 (4), 206 (5)
pinching 816 (1), 816 (4), 816 (5)
pine 366 (4), 651 (23), 859 (11), 889 (7)
pine for 830 (4)
pineapple 301 (19)
ping 403 (1), 403 (3), 404 (1), 404 (3)
pinhead 196 (2)
pinion 259 (3), 271 (5), 747 (9)
pinioned 778 (4)
pink 260 (3), 263 (18), 431 (3), 655 (10), 708 (7)
pinkie 378 (4)
pinnace 275 (5), 275 (7)
pinnacle 34 (1), 213 (1), 646 (1)
pinnate 271 (6)
pinned 778 (4)

pinned down 747 (5)
pinny 228 (15)
pinpoint 33 (3), 80 (8), 185 (1), 187 (5), 196 (2), 281 (4)
pinpointing 187 (1)
pinprick 33 (3), 212 (1), 639 (2), 827 (2), 891 (9)
pins 267 (7)
pins and needles 377 (2), 378 (2)
pinstripes 228 (12)
pint 465 (3)
pint-size 196 (8)
pioneer 64 (3), 66 (1), 68 (9), 191 (4), 237 (1), 268 (1). 283 (1), 537 (3), 669 (5), 669 (10), 672 (3), 701 (8)
pioneering 64 (1), 64 (2), 68 (7), 672 (2)
pious 485 (4), 929 (3), 979 (6), 981 (9)
pious, be 929 (5), 979 (9), 981 (11), 981 (12)
pious hope 852 (2)
pious person 979 (4)
piousness 979 (1)
pip 117 (3), 366 (7)
pipe 252 (3), 263 (9), 351 (1), 353 (1), 407 (1), 407 (5), 413 (9), 414 (6)
pipe band 413 (3)
pipe down 266 (7), 399 (3)
pipe dream 4 (2), 513 (3), 852 (2)
pipe of peace 719 (2)
pipe up 579 (8)
piped 263 (16)
pipedream 826 (1)
pipeline 263 (9), 272 (2), 351 (1), 632 (1), 633 (1)
piper 413 (2)
pipette 263 (9)
piping 234 (3), 263 (9), 407 (1), 407 (2), 844 (5)
piping hot 379 (4)
pips 743 (3)
piquancy 388 (1), 571 (1)
piquant 388 (3), 390 (2), 821 (4), 839 (4)
pique 821 (6), 827 (8), 829 (1), 891 (1), 891 (8)

piqued 825 (6), 891 (3)
piracy 786 (1), 788 (2)
piranha 365 (15)
pirate 270 (1), 722 (3), 786 (7), 788 (7), 789 (1), 789 (2), 881 (2), 938 (2)
pirate ship 275 (2), 722 (13)
piratical 788 (6)
pirating 788 (1)
pirouette 315 (1), 315 (5), 594 (5)
piscatorial 619 (4)
Pisces 321 (5)
pistol 723 (10)
pistol case 194 (10)
pistol-shot 402 (1)
piston 264 (2)
pit 211 (1), 255 (2), 255 (4), 255 (8), 441 (2), 594 (7), 687 (1), 845 (3)
pit against 704 (4)
pit pony 273 (6)
pitch 27 (1), 73 (1), 184 (2), 185 (1), 209 (1), 220 (1), 269 (9), 287 (7), 309 (4), 317 (2), 317 (4), 357 (5), 398 (1), 410 (2), 410 (9), 428 (2), 577 (1), 724 (1), 793 (1)
pitch and toss 313 (3)
pitch-black 428 (4)
pitch-dark 418 (3)
pitch into 712 (7), 716 (11), 924 (10)
pitch one's tent 187 (8), 192 (21)
pitched 24 (8)
pitched battle 716 (7), 718 (7)
pitcher 194 (13), 287 (5)
pitchfork 287 (7), 370 (6)
pitching 269 (6), 287 (1)
piteous 905 (5)
pitfall 527 (2), 542 (4), 659 (1), 661 (1), 663 (1), 698 (2)
pith 3 (2), 225 (2), 356 (1), 514 (1)
pith helmet 228 (23)
pithiness 3 (1)
pithy 3 (1), 496 (3), 514 (3), 569 (2), 592 (4)

pitiable **639** (5), **645** (2), **825** (6), **827** (6), **836** (4), **905** (5)

pitiably **32** (20)

pitiful **639** (5), **645** (2), **827** (6), **836** (4), **905** (5)

pitifulness **827** (1)

pitiless **165** (4), **599** (2), **602** (4), **735** (4), **898** (4), **898** (7), **906** (2), **910** (4)

pitiless, be **362** (11), **735** (7), **820** (6), **898** (8), **906** (3), **940** (4)

pitilessness **176** (1), **599** (1), **735** (1), **898** (2), **906** (1), **910** (1), **940** (1)

pittance **26** (2), **33** (2), **636** (1), **807** (1)

pitted **259** (4), **845** (2)

pitter-patter **317** (1), **401** (1)

pity **736** (1), **736** (3), **819** (5), **836** (5), **897** (1), **905** (1), **905** (6), **909** (1), **931** (1)

pity of it **830** (1)

pity oneself **825** (7)

pitying **736** (2), **819** (2), **897** (4), **905** (4)

pivot **156** (5), **218** (11), **225** (2), **304** (2), **310** (2), **315** (3), **630** (1), **638** (3)

pivot on **157** (6)

pivotal **156** (7), **225** (3), **638** (5)

pixie **970** (2)

pizza **301** (13)

pizzicato **412** (8)

placard **522** (2), **528** (3), **528** (11)

placate **719** (4), **909** (5)

placatory **719** (3)

place **62** (4), **64** (4), **73** (1), **73** (2), **184** (1), **185** (1), **186** (1), **187** (2), **187** (5), **192** (6), **235** (1), **263** (7), **281** (4), **301** (12), **733** (5)

place after **65** (4)

place at one's disposal **759** (3)

place in history **866** (3)

place of amusement **192** (14), **837** (5)

place of business **796** (3)

place of pilgrimage **990** (2)

place of residence **185** (1)

place of torment **972** (1)

place on record **548** (7)

place oneself **60** (4), **187** (8), **266** (7), **297** (5), **786** (7)

place under **78** (6)

placebo **658** (2)

placed **8** (3), **187** (4)

placement **187** (1)

placenta **167** (2)

placid **823** (3)

placidity **266** (2), **823** (1)

placing **187** (1)

placket **228** (3)

plagiarism **20** (1), **22** (1), **106** (1), **785** (1), **788** (1)

plagiarist **20** (3), **789** (1)

plagiarize **20** (6), **541** (8), **785** (2), **786** (7), **788** (7)

plagiarized **106** (3)

plague **139** (3), **616** (1), **645** (1), **645** (6), **651** (4), **659** (1), **659** (2), **731** (1), **827** (2), **827** (9)

plague on, a **899** (8)

plague pit **364** (5)

plague-spot **663** (1)

plague with doubt **474** (9)

plagued **505** (6)

plaid **228** (21), **437** (2), **437** (5)

plain **16** (2), **44** (4), **54** (3), **183** (1), **210** (1), **216** (1), **263** (7), **344** (1), **348** (1), **398** (3), **425** (7), **443** (3), **514** (3), **514** (4), **516** (2), **519** (3), **522** (4), **522** (5), **524** (7), **532** (4), **540** (2), **566** (2), **567** (2), **572** (2), **573** (2), **575** (3), **576** (2), **593** (9), **699** (3), **744** (5), **838** (3), **842** (3), **846** (3), **869** (8), **926** (5), **942** (3), **945** (3)

plain, be **443** (4), **522** (9), **526** (7)

plain-clothes police **955** (3)

plain cooking **391** (1)

plain-dealing **540** (1)

plain English **516** (1), **573** (1)

plain living **732** (1), **942** (1), **945** (1)

plain Mr or Mrs **869** (5)

plain sailing **701** (2)

plain speaking **516** (1), **522** (1), **540** (1)

plain-spoken **516** (2), **744** (5)

plain to see **443** (3)

plain truth **494** (1)

plain words **516** (1)

plainly **522** (10), **573** (4), **945** (5)

plainness **44** (1), **514** (2), **516** (1), **519** (2), **540** (1), **559** (1), **566** (1), **567** (1), **572** (1), **573** (1), **575** (1), **593** (7), **699** (1), **840** (1), **842** (1), **846** (1)

plainsong **412** (5), **981** (3), **981** (5)

plaint **836** (2)

plaintiff **915** (1), **928** (3), **959** (4)

plaintive **836** (4)

plait **45** (12), **47** (4), **222** (1), **222** (9), **259** (2)

plaited **222** (6)

plan **23** (1), **55** (1), **62** (1), **86** (4), **155** (4), **156** (9), **164** (1), **164** (7), **233** (1), **267** (8), **331** (1), **449** (7), **510** (3), **512** (6), **524** (6), **551** (1), **551** (5), **551** (8), **592** (1), **608** (3), **617** (1), **617** (5), **623** (1), **623** (8), **629** (2), **669** (1), **669** (10), **672** (1), **688** (2), **688** (5), **718** (4), **718** (6), **859** (11)

plan ahead **510** (3)

plan for **617** (5), **859** (11)

plan of attack **623** (2)

plan of campaign **718** (6)

plan out **623** (8)

plane **216** (1), **216** (4), **216** (7), **256** (5), **258** (2), **258** (4), **271** (7), **276** (1)

plane geometry **465** (2)

planet **314** (2), **315** (3), **321** (6)

planet earth 321 (2)
planetarium 321 (11)
planetary 321 (14)
planetary orbit 321 (6)
planets 596 (2)
plangency 404 (1)
plangent 400 (3), 404 (2)
planing 271 (1)
plank 207 (2), 218 (12), 623 (2), 631 (1)
planking 207 (1)
plankton 196 (5)
planned 608 (2), 623 (6), 669 (6)
planner 86 (7), 164 (4), 512 (3), 545 (1), 612 (5), 623 (5), 678 (6), 698 (3)
planning 62 (1), 164 (1), 623 (1), 623 (7), 669 (1), 698 (4), 718 (4), 930 (7)
plant 132 (4), 156 (3), 187 (5), 196 (5), 218 (2), 301 (20), 303 (6), 366 (6), 366 (12), 370 (9), 542 (4), 630 (4), 687 (1), 777 (1), 928 (2)
plant a blow 279 (9)
plant ecology 368 (1)
plant life 360 (1)
plant physiology 368 (1)
plantation 366 (2)
planted 45 (7), 366 (10)
planter 191 (4), 370 (4)
plaque 207 (2), 649 (2), 866 (4)
plash 350 (6), 401 (1), 401 (4)
plasma 335 (2)
plasmatic 335 (5)
plaster 48 (1), 226 (10), 226 (16), 658 (9)
plaster down 216 (7), 258 (4)
plasterboard 631 (3)
plastered 226 (12), 949 (7)
plasterer 686 (3)
plastic 243 (3), 243 (4), 327 (3), 631 (1)
plastic art 551 (3), 554 (1)
plastic bag 194 (9)
plastic surgeon 843 (5)
plastic surgery 658 (11), 843 (1)

plasticity 327 (1)
plastics 357 (5)
plat du jour 301 (13)
plate 23 (3), 194 (17), 207 (2), 207 (5), 216 (1), 226 (1), 226 (16), 250 (2), 256 (4), 553 (5), 589 (5), 723 (3), 729 (1)
plate engraving 555 (1)
plate printing 587 (1)
plateau 209 (2), 213 (2), 216 (1), 348 (1)
platform 207 (1), 216 (1), 218 (5), 528 (1), 528 (2), 539 (5), 623 (2), 724 (1)
platinum 427 (2)
platinum blond 426 (1)
platitude 496 (1), 515 (1)
platitudinous 572 (2)
Platonic 950 (5)
Platonic idea 1 (1)
Platonic love 887 (1)
platoon 74 (4), 722 (8)
platter 194 (17), 207 (2), 216 (1), 414 (10)
plaudits 923 (3)
plausibility 471 (1)
plausible 471 (3), 477 (4), 485 (5), 541 (4), 614 (2), 852 (5), 927 (4)
play 173 (1), 173 (3), 183 (3), 317 (4), 350 (9), 413 (9), 417 (11), 594 (3), 594 (17), 618 (8), 716 (10), 744 (3), 837 (1), 837 (3), 837 (21), 889 (6)
play a part 178 (3), 541 (6), 594 (17)
play-act 541 (6)
play-acting 541 (2), 541 (4), 594 (8), 594 (15), 850 (1)
play-actor 594 (9)
play against 716 (10)
play at 837 (21)
play back 106 (4)
play cards 837 (21)
play down 177 (6), 483 (4)
play fair 929 (5)
play false 541 (5), 542 (8), 603 (5), 930 (8)
play first fiddle 34 (9)
play flat 411 (3)

play for time 698 (5), 702 (10)
play games 837 (21)
play havoc with 63 (4), 645 (6), 655 (9)
play it by ear 476 (3)
play music 413 (9)
play of colour 437 (1)
play of light 417 (2)
play off against 673 (3)
play on 673 (3)
play on words 18 (2), 518 (1), 518 (3), 839 (5)
play one's part 622 (8), 688 (4), 917 (10)
play out 69 (6)
play pranks 837 (21)
play safe 660 (9), 858 (3)
play sharp 411 (3)
play the fool 497 (4), 499 (6), 837 (21), 849 (4)
play the fop 873 (5)
play the fox 698 (5)
play the game 913 (6), 929 (5)
play the lead 34 (9)
play the market 618 (8), 791 (5)
play the piano 413 (9)
play the tyrant 735 (8)
play to the gallery 594 (17), 875 (7)
play tricks 604 (4), 837 (21)
play tricks or a joke on 542 (9)
play truant 190 (6), 620 (6), 621 (3), 918 (3)
play up 702 (10), 738 (9)
play upon 612 (8)
play upon words 839 (2)
play with 458 (4), 839 (5), 889 (6)
play with fire 661 (7), 857 (4)
playact 594 (17)
playback 106 (1), 414 (10)
playboy 837 (17), 848 (3)
played down 573 (2)
player 413 (1), 413 (2), 594 (9), 618 (4), 676 (3), 686 (1), 837 (16)
player piano 414 (4)

playful 604 (3), 833 (4), 837 (19), 839 (4)

playfulness 604 (1), 935 (1)

playgoer 441 (1), 594 (14)

playground 724 (1), 837 (4)

playgroup 539 (2)

playhouse 594 (7), 837 (5)

playing 412 (1), 837 (19)

playing card 207 (2)

playing field 724 (1), 837 (4)

playing fields 539 (4)

playing for time 688 (2)

playing the fool 499 (4)

playing the game 929 (3)

playmate 837 (16), 880 (5)

plays 557 (3)

plaything 639 (3), 837 (15)

plaything of fate 731 (3)

playtime 837 (2)

playwright 589 (7), 594 (13)

plea 466 (2), 475 (4), 614 (1), 761 (1), 927 (1), 959 (1)

plead 466 (7), 475 (11), 614 (4), 927 (6), 958 (7), 959 (7)

plead for 762 (3)

plead for mercy 905 (8)

plead guilty 526 (6), 928 (8), 936 (4), 959 (9), 961 (3)

plead not guilty 959 (9)

pleader 231 (3), 475 (6), 579 (5), 612 (5), 720 (2)

play sharp 411 (3)

play the fool 497 (4), 499 (6), 837 (21), 849 (4)

play the fop 873 (5)

play the fox 698 (5)

play the game 913 (6), 929 (5)

play the lead 34 (9)

play the market 618 (8), 791 (5)

play the piano 413 (9)

play the tyrant 735 (8)

play to the gallery 594 (17), 875 (7)

play tricks 604 (4), 837 (21)

play tricks or a joke on 542 (9)

play truant 190 (6), 620 (6), 621 (3), 918 (3)

play up 702 (10), 738 (9)

play upon 612 (8)

play upon words 839 (2)

play with 458 (4), 839 (5), 889 (6)

play with fire 661 (7), 857 (4)

playact 594 (17)

playback 106 (1), 414 (10)

playboy 837 (17), 848 (3)

played down 573 (2)

player 413 (1), 413 (2), 594 (9), 618 (4), 676 (3), 686 (1), 837 (16)

player piano 414 (4)

playful 604 (3), 833 (4), 837 (19), 839 (4)

playfulness 604 (1), 935 (1)

playgoer 441 (1), 594 (14)

playground 724 (1), 837 (4)

playgroup 539 (2)

playhouse 594 (7), 837 (5)

playing 412 (1), 837 (19)

playing card 207 (2)

playing field 724 (1), 837 (4)

playing fields 539 (4)

playing for time 688 (2)

playing the fool 499 (4)

playing the game 929 (3)

playmate 837 (16), 880 (5)

plays 557 (3)

plaything 639 (3), 837 (15)

plaything of fate 731 (3)

playtime 837 (2)

playwright 589 (7), 594 (13)

plea 466 (2), 475 (4), 614 (1), 761 (1), 927 (1), 959 (1)

plead 466 (7), 475 (11), 614 (4), 927 (6), 958 (7), 959 (7)

plead for 762 (3)

plead for mercy 905 (8)

plead guilty 526 (6), 928 (8), 936 (4), 959 (9), 961 (3)

plead not guilty 959 (9)

pleader 231 (3), 475 (6), 579 (5), 612 (5), 720 (2)

pleading 612 (2)

pleadings 959 (3)

pleasance 192 (15)

pleasant 376 (3), 396 (3), 826 (2), 837 (18)

pleasantness 826 (1)

pleasantry 839 (1)

please 376 (6), 826 (3), 828 (5), 833 (8), 837 (20)

please oneself 595 (2), 602 (6), 734 (6), 735 (8), 738 (9), 744 (9), 756 (5), 943 (3), 954 (8)

pleased 488 (4), 597 (4), 824 (4), 828 (2), 833 (5), 837 (19)

pleased as Punch 824 (4)

pleased, be 376 (6), 818 (8), 824 (6), 828 (4), 835 (6), 871 (6), 877 (5)

pleased with oneself 871 (4)

pleasing 376 (3), 826 (2)

pleasurable 376 (3), 615 (3), 644 (5), 818 (6), 826 (2), 837 (18), 841 (6), 859 (10), 944 (3)

pleasurableness 824 (1), 826 (1)

pleasure 376 (1), 824 (1), 837 (1), 944 (1)

pleasure, a 701 (2)

pleasure gardens 837 (4)

pleasure-giving 615 (3), 944 (3)

pleasure ground 192 (15), 724 (1), 837 (4)

pleasure-lover 944 (2)

pleasure-loving 376 (5)

pleasure-seeking 944 (3)

pleasure trip 837 (1)

pleasures of 826 (1)

pleat 228 (3), 261 (1), 261 (3)

plebeian 35 (4), 79 (3), 847 (5), 869 (5), 869 (8), 872 (3)

plebeians 869 (1)

plebiscite 605 (2), 737 (2), 953 (2)

plectrum 414 (2)

pledge 532 (2), 532 (5), 764 (1), 764 (4), 767 (1), 767 (6), 780 (1), 780 (3), 876 (5)

pledge one's word 764 (4)

pledged 532 (3), 764 (3), 767 (3), 917 (5)

Pleistocene 110 (4)

plenary 54 (3)

plenitude 54 (2), 341 (1), 633 (1), 635 (2), 637 (1), 863 (1)

plenteous 32 (4), 104 (4), 146 (2), 171 (4), 635 (4), 813 (3)

plentiful 32 (4), 635 (4)

plentiful, be 635 (7)

plenty 32 (1), 32 (2), 171 (1), 301 (2), 632 (1), 635 (2), 637 (1), 730 (1), 800 (1), 813 (1)

plenty to do 678 (1)

pleonasm 559 (1), 570 (2), 637 (2)

pleonastic 559 (4), 570 (5)

plethora 637 (1)

pleurisy 651 (8)

pliability 327 (1)

pliable 327 (3)

pliancy 83 (1), 152 (1), 327 (1), 597 (1), 601 (1), 612 (3)

pliant 83 (4), 327 (3), 701 (4), 721 (2), 879 (3)

pliers 304 (2), 630 (1), 778 (2)

plight 7 (1), 731 (1)

Plimsoll line 465 (5), 547 (6)

plimsolls 228 (27)

plinth 214 (1), 218 (5)

plod 267 (14), 278 (4), 600 (4)

plod on 146 (3)

plodding 600 (1), 678 (9), 682 (4)

plonk 301 (29), 402 (3), 405 (1)

plop 309 (3), 309 (4), 402 (1), 402 (3), 405 (1)

plop in 313 (3)

plot 50 (4), 53 (5), 181 (1), 181 (3), 185 (1), 370 (3), 452 (1), 523 (1), 525 (2), 525 (9), 541 (8), 542 (1), 542 (8), 551 (8), 590 (2), 594 (2), 608 (1), 623 (4), 623 (9), 669 (10), 678 (4), 698 (1), 698 (2), 698 (5), 706 (1), 706 (4), 738 (3), 765 (1), 777 (3)

plot one's course 281 (4)

plotted 465 (10), 623 (6)

plotter 545 (1), 623 (5), 698 (3)

plotting 542 (6), 623 (7), 930 (7)

plough 262 (3), 321 (4), 370 (6), 370 (9)

ploughed 370 (7)

ploughed land 370 (2)

ploughing 255 (1), 370 (1)

ploughman 370 (4)

ploughman's lunch 301 (12)

ploughshare 256 (5)

ploy 623 (3), 698 (2)

pluck 46 (8), 229 (6), 288 (3), 304 (4), 318 (6), 370 (9), 599 (1), 600 (2), 786 (6), 855 (1)

pluck at 288 (3)

pluck the strings 413 (9)

pluck to pieces 46 (12)

pluck up courage 855 (7)

plucked 229 (4)

plucking 843 (2)

plucky 600 (3), 855 (4)

plug 106 (5), 264 (2), 264 (6), 350 (12), 388 (2), 528 (3), 528 (11), 532 (7), 656 (12), 778 (1)

plug in 45 (10), 160 (11), 173 (3)

plum 301 (19), 436 (1), 644 (2), 859 (5)

plum-coloured 436 (2)

plumage 226 (6), 259 (3), 271 (5)

plumb 32 (16), 54 (3), 215 (2), 465 (11)

plumb the depths 211 (3), 313 (3)

plumber 656 (5), 686 (3)

plumbing 351 (1), 648 (2)

plumbline 215 (1)

plume 259 (3), 844 (5)

plume oneself 873 (5)

plume oneself on 877 (5)

plummet 211 (1), 269 (4), 313 (2), 313 (4)

plummy 579 (6)

plump 116 (4), 195 (8), 309 (4), 405 (1)

plump down 309 (4)

plump up 197 (5)

plumpish 195 (8)

plumpness 195 (3)

plunder 771 (1), 786 (9), 788 (9), 790 (1)

plunderer 789 (2)

plundering 788 (3)

plunge 37 (1), 149 (1), 165 (8), 165 (11), 211 (3), 265 (1), 265 (4), 269 (3), 269 (10), 269 (12), 271 (7), 277 (6), 297 (5), 303 (2), 303 (7), 309 (1), 309 (3), 309 (4), 311 (1), 311 (4), 312 (4), 313 (1), 313 (3), 318 (5), 341 (6), 341 (8), 465 (11), 648 (3), 812 (5)

plunger 309 (1), 313 (2)

plunging 211 (2)

pluperfect 125 (1)

plural 101 (2), 564 (3)

plural, the 101 (1)

plurality 26 (1), 82 (1), 101 (1), 104 (3)

plus 15 (1), 38 (5)

plus fours 228 (12)

plus sign 547 (14)

plush 844 (10)

plushy 800 (3)

Pluto 321 (6), 967 (1)

plutocracy 733 (4), 800 (1)

plutocrat 800 (2)

plutocratic 733 (9)

plutonium 385 (1), 659 (3)

ply 141 (6), 207 (1), 269 (9), 378 (7), 673 (3), 676 (5), 761 (5)

ply a trade 622 (9)

ply the oar 269 (11)

plywood 207 (2)

p.m. 117 (8), 129 (1)

pneumatic 336 (3), 340 (5)

pneumatics 336 (1), 340 (4), 352 (2)

pneumonia 651 (8)

poach 301 (40), 306 (4), 619 (6), 788 (7)

poacher 619 (3), 789 (1)

pocket 77 (1), 187 (7), 194 (11), 228 (3), 255 (2), 303 (4), 782 (4), 786 (6), 788 (7), 823 (6), 872 (5), 909 (4)

pocket calculator 86 (6)

pocket money 797 (1), 807 (1)

pocket-size 196 (8)

pockmark 255 (2), 255 (8), 651 (12), 845 (1), 845 (3)

pockmarked 255 (6), 437 (8), 845 (2)

pod 226 (6), 366 (7)

podgy 195 (8), 327 (2)

podium 218 (5), 539 (5)

poem 557 (3), 589 (2), 590 (2), 593 (2), 841 (2)

poesy 593 (1)

poet 520 (4), 589 (7), 593 (6), 594 (13)

poet laureate 593 (6)

poetic 513 (5), 593 (8)

poetic art 593 (1)

poetic composition 593 (2)

poetic drama 594 (3)

poetic fire 593 (1)

poetic justice 714 (1), 963 (1)

poetic licence 513 (2), 593 (1)

poetic vein 593 (1)

poetical 593 (8)

poetical works 589 (2)

poetics 593 (1)

poetize 586 (8), 593 (10)

poetry 56 (1), 513 (2), 557 (3), 589 (2), 593 (1)

pogrom 362 (4)

poignancy 174 (3), 388 (1), 571 (1)

poignant 174 (6), 374 (4), 818 (6)

point 8 (2), 9 (3), 27 (1), 33 (3), 69 (2), 73 (1), 116 (2), 174 (3), 185 (1), 186 (1), 196 (2), 254 (2), 256 (2), 256 (11), 281 (7), 452 (1), 475 (5), 547 (18), 547 (21), 673 (1)

point a moral 534 (7)

point at issue 452 (1), 459 (3), 709 (4)

point-blank 573 (4)

point-blank refusal 760 (1)

point duty 305 (3)

point of departure 68 (3)

point of etiquette 848 (2)

point of honour 929 (1)

point of time 116 (2)

point of view 438 (5), 451 (1), 481 (5), 485 (3)

point out 80 (8), 281 (6), 455 (7), 522 (8), 524 (9)

point the way 547 (18)

point to 76 (2), 158 (3), 179 (3), 281 (6), 471 (5), 511 (8), 514 (5), 547 (18)

point-to-point 716 (3)

point towards 281 (6)

point well taken 475 (5)

pointed 9 (6), 174 (6), 256 (7), 293 (2), 514 (3), 532 (4), 569 (2), 571 (2), 839 (4)

pointedly 32 (19)

pointedness 256 (1), 839 (1)

pointer 365 (10), 547 (1), 547 (6)

pointing 547 (4)

pointing out 547 (1)

pointing to 179 (2), 928 (5)

pointing towards 281 (3)

pointless 10 (4), 641 (4), 840 (2)

pointlessness 10 (2), 499 (2)

points 34 (2), 86 (1)

poise 28 (1), 28 (3), 28 (10), 445 (5), 688 (1), 823 (1), 848 (2)

poised 848 (6)

poison 160 (7), 165 (6), 168 (1), 301 (28), 336 (2), 362

(12), 391 (1), 417 (4), 616 (1), 645 (1), 651 (5), 655 (9), 658 (3), 659 (3), 723 (3), 888 (8), 891 (9), 898 (8)

poison gas 659 (3)

poison pen 588 (2)

poisoned 645 (2), 653 (4)

poisoner 362 (7), 659 (4), 904 (3)

poisoning 362 (1), 651 (2), 655 (3), 659 (4)

poisonous 165 (4), 362 (8), 391 (2), 645 (3), 651 (22), 653 (4), 659 (5), 661 (3), 827 (3), 898 (5)

poisonously 653 (5)

poisonousness 653 (1)

poke 263 (18), 547 (21)

poke at 279 (9)

poke fun at 839 (5), 849 (4), 851 (5)

poke into 303 (4)

poke out 254 (5)

poker 837 (11)

poker face 834 (3)

poker-faced 266 (6), 517 (2), 525 (6), 820 (3), 834 (7)

poking fun 851 (1)

poky 196 (8), 747 (4), 842 (5)

polar 69 (4), 213 (4), 240 (2), 321 (15), 380 (5)

polarity 14 (2), 90 (1), 182 (1), 240 (1)

polarization 240 (1), 417 (5)

polarized 240 (2), 704 (3)

polder 344 (1)

pole 69 (2), 199 (2), 203 (4), 209 (4), 213 (1), 218 (10), 218 (11), 225 (2), 236 (1), 269 (5), 279 (7), 630 (1)

pole position 34 (2)

Pole Star 321 (4), 547 (7)

pole vault 308 (1), 312 (4)

pole-vaulter 312 (2)

poleaxe 362 (10), 723 (7)

polecat 397 (1)

polemic 475 (4), 709 (3)

polemical 475 (8), 709 (6)

polemicist 475 (6)
polemics 475 (4), 584 (3),
716 (1)
poles asunder 14 (3), 15
(4), 240 (4)
police 660 (3), 660 (8), 689
(4), 733 (10), 955 (3)
police car 274 (11)
police enquiry 459 (6)
police force 955 (3)
police inspector 955 (3)
police officer 955 (3)
police sergeant 955 (3)
police state 733 (3)
police station 748 (2)
policeman or policewo-
man 660 (3), 955 (3)
policy 86 (3), 623 (2), 676
(1), 676 (2), 688 (2), 689
(1), 698 (1), 767 (2)
polio 651 (16)
poliomyelitis 651 (16)
polish 226 (10), 258 (1),
258 (2), 258 (4), 333 (1),
333 (3), 417 (5), 417 (13),
575 (1), 575 (4), 648 (1),
648 (4), 648 (9), 654 (2),
654 (9), 846 (1)
polish off 678 (11), 725 (5)
polished 258 (3), 417 (9),
557 (6), 575 (3), 648 (7),
848 (6)
polite 848 (6), 884 (3), 920
(3)
polite regard 920 (1)
politely 884 (8)
politeness 884 (1)
politic 498 (5), 642 (2), 694
(4)
political 688 (3), 689 (3),
733 (9)
political economist 690
(3)
political organization 184
(2), 733 (6)
political party 706 (2), 708
(2), 733 (4)
political prisoner 750 (1)
politician 623 (5), 690 (3),
696 (2), 708 (2)
politics 688 (2), 733 (4)
polka 837 (14)
polka dot 437 (4), 844 (3)

poll 86 (1), 86 (4), 86 (11),
459 (1), 605 (2)
poll tax 809 (3)
pollard 198 (7), 366 (4)
pollen 167 (3), 332 (2)
pollinate 167 (7)
pollination 167 (1)
pollinator 167 (1)
polling 605 (2)
polls 605 (2)
pollster 86 (7), 459 (9)
pollute 641 (7), 645 (6),
649 (9), 655 (9), 675 (2)
polluted 649 (7), 653 (2)
polluting 645 (3)
pollution 649 (1), 653 (1),
655 (3), 659 (3), 675 (1)
Pollyanna 833 (1)
polo 837 (7)
polo neck 228 (11)
polonaise 837 (14)
poltergeist 702 (5), 970 (3)
poltergeists 984 (3)
poly- 101 (2), 539 (1)
polyandrous 894 (7)
polyandry 894 (2)
polyester 222 (4)
polygamist 894 (4)
polygamous 894 (7)
polygamy 894 (2)
polyglot 557 (4), 557 (5),
579 (6)
polygon 101 (1), 247 (4)
polygonal 247 (6)
polyhedral 247 (6)
polyhedron 101 (1)
polymath 492 (1), 696 (2)
polymorphic 82 (2), 101
(2)
polymorphism 82 (1)
polymorphous 82 (2)
polyp 253 (2)
polyphony 410 (1)
polystyrene 631 (1)
polysyllable 559 (1)
polytechnic 539 (1)
polytheism 101 (1), 973
(2)
polytheist 973 (7)
polythene 631 (1)
polythene bag 194 (9)
polyurethane 357 (5)
pomander 396 (2)

pommel 218 (3), 252 (2)
pommie 59 (2)
pomp 871 (1), 875 (1)
pompom 844 (5)
pomposity 574 (2), 576 (1),
871 (1), 875 (1)
pompous 574 (5), 576 (2),
871 (4), 873 (4), 875 (4)
pompous twit 873 (3)
pompousness 873 (2)
ponce 952 (5)
poncho 228 (21)
pond 212 (1), 346 (1)
ponder 449 (8), 480 (6)
pondering 449 (2)
ponderous 322 (4), 576
(2), 695 (5), 840 (2)
ponderousness 322 (1)
pong 397 (1), 397 (3)
poniard 723 (8)
pontifical 473 (5), 985 (6),
989 (3)
pontificate 473 (8), 532 (5)
pontification 473 (2), 532
(1)
pontoon 275 (9), 837 (11)
pony 273 (9)
pony-trekking 837 (6)
ponytail 259 (2), 843 (2)
poodle 365 (10), 879 (2)
pooh-pooh 922 (6)
pooh-poohing 922 (3)
pool 50 (4), 346 (1), 632
(1), 632 (5), 706 (2), 771
(1), 775 (1), 775 (6), 837
(7)
pool room 837 (5)
pooling 706 (2)
poop 238 (3)
poor 172 (4), 627 (4), 636
(4), 639 (5), 645 (2), 647
(3), 655 (5), 655 (6), 731
(5), 731 (6), 774 (2), 801
(3), 805 (4), 825 (6), 946
(3)
poor, be 731 (7), 801 (5),
805 (5), 946 (4)
poor head 499 (1)
poor health 651 (1)
poor judgment 481 (1)
poor lookout 731 (1), 853
(1)

poor person 61 (5), 731 (3), 801 (2), 869 (7)

poor quality 35 (1)

poor relation 35 (2), 639 (4), 867 (3)

poor return 172 (1)

poor risk 731 (3)

poor second 35 (2)

poor shot 697 (1)

poor taste 847 (1)

poor, the 801 (2)

poor unfortunate 731 (3)

poor value 811 (1)

poor visibility 419 (1), 444 (1)

poor wretch 731 (3), 825 (4)

poorhouse 192 (17), 801 (1)

poorly 33 (9), 163 (6), 651 (21)

poorly reasoned 477 (6)

poorness 801 (1)

pop 301 (27), 401 (1), 402 (1), 402 (4), 412 (1)

pop-eyed 254 (4)

pop group 74 (4), 413 (3)

pop gun 287 (3)

pop out 254 (5)

pop singer 413 (4), 594 (10)

pop up 106 (6)

pope 986 (4)

popgun 837 (15)

popish 976 (9)

poplar 366 (4)

poplin 222 (4)

popper 47 (5)

poppet 890 (1)

popping eyes 864 (1)

poppycock 515 (3)

populace 191 (5), 371 (4), 869 (1)

popular 79 (3), 191 (6), 733 (9), 882 (7), 923 (7)

popular belief 488 (2)

popular front 708 (2)

popular hero 866 (6)

popular music 412 (1)

popularity 882 (2), 887 (2), 923 (1)

popularize 847 (6)

popularizing 516 (3)

populate 171 (6), 192 (21), 786 (7)

populated 74 (9), 191 (7)

population 187 (1), 191 (5), 371 (4)

populous 74 (9), 104 (5)

populousness 74 (5)

porcelain 330 (1), 381 (5)

porch 68 (5), 194 (20), 263 (6), 990 (5)

porcine 365 (18)

pore 255 (2), 263 (4), 298 (3), 455 (4)

pore over 438 (9), 536 (5)

pork 301 (16)

pork barrel 612 (4)

porker 365 (9)

pornographic 887 (12), 951 (6)

pornography 951 (1)

porosity 62 (2), 255 (2), 263 (3)

porous 255 (6), 263 (15)

porousness 263 (3)

porpoise 365 (3)

porridge 301 (22)

porringer 194 (16)

port 242 (1), 295 (2), 301 (29), 662 (2)

port of call 145 (5)

portability 323 (1)

portable 196 (8), 272 (5), 323 (3), 531 (3)

portage 272 (2)

portal 263 (6)

portcullis 235 (3), 702 (2), 713 (4)

portend 511 (8)

portent 511 (3), 864 (3)

portentous 511 (7)

porter 264 (3), 273 (2), 742 (1)

porterage 272 (2)

portfolio 87 (1), 194 (10), 632 (3), 733 (1), 767 (2), 777 (2), 955 (1)

porthole 263 (5)

portion 26 (2), 27 (1), 53 (1), 53 (5), 301 (7), 301 (12), 596 (2), 775 (2), 783 (2)

portion out 783 (3)

portly 195 (8)

portmanteau 194 (7), 632 (2)

portmanteau word 50 (2)

portrait 548 (1), 553 (5), 590 (1)

portrait painter 556 (1)

portraitist 20 (3)

portraiture 18 (2), 20 (2), 551 (1), 553 (2)

portray 18 (8), 20 (5), 551 (8), 553 (8)

portrayal 18 (2), 20 (2), 551 (1), 590 (1)

portrayer 20 (3)

pose 23 (5), 445 (1), 551 (8), 688 (1), 688 (4), 759 (3), 850 (1), 850 (5)

pose a question 459 (14)

pose as 20 (5), 551 (8)

Poseidon 343 (1), 967 (1)

poser 23 (2), 459 (3), 530 (2), 850 (3)

poseur 850 (3)

posing 20 (4), 850 (1), 850 (4)

posit 475 (12), 512 (6)

position 7 (1), 62 (4), 73 (1), 185 (1), 186 (1), 187 (3), 187 (5), 485 (3), 512 (1), 622 (3)

position of authority 733 (5)

position of power 160 (1)

positive 1 (5), 32 (14), 85 (5), 160 (5), 473 (5), 481 (7), 485 (4), 532 (3), 532 (4), 602 (4)

positively 1 (8), 32 (16), 532 (8)

positiveness 473 (2), 532 (1), 602 (2)

positivism 319 (1), 449 (3), 974 (2)

positivist 319 (1), 974 (3)

posse 74 (4)

possess 189 (4), 503 (12), 673 (5), 773 (4), 786 (7), 969 (6)

possess with 777 (6)

possessed 187 (4), 503 (8), 503 (9), 773 (3), 821 (3), 969 (5)

possessed of 773 (2)

possessed of, be 773 (4)
possessed with 817 (2)
possessing 773 (2)
possession 189 (1), 673 (1), 773 (1), 777 (1), 821 (1), 983 (2)
possession, a 773 (1)
possessions 777 (1), 800 (1)
possessive 773 (2), 816 (5), 859 (8), 887 (9), 911 (2), 932 (3)
possessiveness 911 (1), 932 (1)
possessor 741 (1), 775 (3), 776 (1), 915 (1)
possibility 137 (2), 159 (3), 160 (2), 180 (1), 469 (1), 471 (1), 507 (1), 523 (1), 701 (1), 852 (1)
possibility, be a 469 (3)
possible 124 (4), 180 (2), 289 (3), 469 (2), 475 (7), 485 (5), 523 (2), 701 (3)
possible, be 469 (3), 471 (4)
possible choice 605 (1)
possible need 633 (1)
possible, the 469 (1)
possibly 159 (8), 469 (5)
post- 120 (2), 186 (1), 187 (5), 188 (4), 218 (10), 272 (4), 272 (8), 524 (10), 531 (2), 548 (8), 588 (1), 622 (3), 733 (5), 751 (4), 808 (5), 917 (11)
post chaise 274 (8)
post-dated 118 (2)
post-horse 273 (6)
post meridiem 129 (8)
post mortem 361 (1), 364 (6)
post-obit 120 (2), 361 (9)
post off 588 (4)
post office 272 (4), 531 (2)
post-paid 812 (4)
post sentries 457 (7)
postage 809 (1)
postal 588 (3)
postal communications 531 (2), 588 (1)
postal order 797 (5)
postal services 531 (2)

postbag 588 (1)
postbox 531 (2)
postcard 529 (3), 588 (1)
postdate 118 (3)
posted 186 (3), 187 (4), 524 (8)
posted, be 186 (4)
poster 528 (3), 553 (5)
posterior 120 (2), 238 (2), 238 (4)
posteriority 120 (1), 124 (1)
posterity 11 (2), 41 (3), 65 (1), 67 (3), 120 (1), 124 (1), 157 (1), 170 (1)
postern 238 (1), 263 (6)
postgraduate 538 (3)
postgraduate studies 534 (2)
posthaste 277 (9), 680 (4)
posthumous 120 (2), 136 (3)
posthumously 361 (9)
postilion 268 (4)
posting 187 (1), 272 (1), 751 (2)
postman or -woman 273 (2), 529 (6), 531 (2)
postmarital 894 (9)
postnatal 167 (5)
postpone 136 (7), 620 (5), 726 (3)
postponement 136 (2), 598 (1)
postpositive 65 (2)
postprandial 120 (2), 301 (34)
postscript 40 (1), 67 (1), 69 (2)
postulant 763 (1), 986 (6)
postulate 475 (2), 475 (12), 496 (2), 512 (6)
postulated 512 (5)
posture 8 (1), 445 (5), 688 (1), 688 (4), 850 (5)
posturing 850 (1), 850 (4)
postwar 108 (6), 120 (2), 717 (3)
posy 74 (6)
pot 194 (13), 287 (1), 303 (4), 381 (5)
pot at 287 (8)

pot-bellied 195 (8), 197 (3), 252 (5)
pot plant 366 (7)
pot shot 287 (1)
potable 301 (32)
potato 301 (20)
potbellied 253 (7)
potbelly 253 (2)
potboiler 590 (4)
potency 160 (1), 162 (1), 640 (1)
potent 160 (8), 162 (6), 173 (2), 174 (5), 178 (2), 949 (12)
potentate 741 (4), 868 (5)
potential 2 (4), 5 (6), 26 (1), 124 (4), 160 (3), 469 (2), 523 (2)
potentiality 5 (1), 160 (2), 178 (1), 180 (1), 469 (1), 523 (1)
pother 61 (4), 822 (2)
potherb 301 (21), 389 (1)
pothole 255 (2)
potholed 259 (4)
potholer 309 (1), 484 (2)
potholing 211 (1), 309 (1)
potion 301 (26), 658 (2), 983 (4)
potluck 159 (1), 618 (2), 670 (1)
potpourri 43 (4), 396 (2), 412 (4)
pots 32 (2)
potsherd 53 (5)
potted 204 (3), 592 (4)
potter 267 (13), 686 (3)
pottering 678 (2)
potter's wheel 315 (3)
pottery 164 (2), 243 (2), 330 (1), 381 (5), 551 (3), 554 (1)
potty 503 (8)
pouch 194 (9), 194 (11)
poulterer 633 (2)
poultice 356 (1), 658 (9), 658 (20)
poultry 301 (16), 365 (6)
poultry farm 369 (2)
poultry farming 369 (1)
pounce 277 (2), 309 (3), 312 (4), 313 (1), 786 (6)
pounce on 508 (5)

pound 235 (1), 279 (9), 322 (2), 332 (5), 748 (2)

pound coin 797 (4)

pound of flesh 735 (1), 906 (1)

pound sterling 797 (1)

pounds, shillings and pence 797 (1)

pour 300 (9), 341 (6), 350 (9), 350 (10), 635 (7)

pour balm 177 (7), 334 (4)

pour in 293 (3), 297 (7), 303 (5)

pour out 298 (6), 300 (8), 311 (5), 350 (11), 570 (6)

pour scorn on 851 (5)

pour water on 747 (7)

pour with rain 350 (10)

pouring 171 (4), 350 (7)

pouring rain 350 (6)

pout 254 (5), 547 (4), 547 (21), 850 (5), 893 (1), 893 (3)

poverty 33 (1), 35 (1), 616 (1), 627 (2), 636 (2), 649 (1), 655 (2), 731 (1), 774 (1), 801 (1), 945 (1)

poverty-stricken 801 (3), 801 (4)

pow-wow 584 (3)

powder 226 (15), 332 (2), 841 (8), 843 (3), 843 (7)

powder and shot 723 (12)

powder barrel 723 (2)

powder-blue 435 (3)

powder keg 663 (1)

powder puff 843 (3)

powdered 843 (6)

powderiness 332 (1)

powdering 332 (1)

powdery 196 (11), 330 (2), 332 (4), 342 (4)

power 32 (1), 85 (2), 160 (1), 160 (11), 162 (1), 162 (12), 173 (1), 173 (3), 178 (1), 265 (5), 571 (1), 579 (4), 628 (1), 629 (1), 640 (1), 733 (1), 735 (2), 965 (2)

power dive 313 (1)

power-driven 630 (6)

power line 160 (6)

power of 32 (2)

power of attorney 751 (2)

power of judgment 480 (1)

power of sight 438 (1)

power pack 160 (6)

power politics 932 (1)

power station 160 (4), 687 (1)

power vacuum 161 (1), 734 (2)

powered 160 (9), 630 (6)

powerful 32 (4), 160 (8), 160 (10), 162 (6), 174 (5), 178 (2), 400 (3), 571 (2), 628 (3), 638 (6), 640 (2), 733 (7), 740 (2), 965 (6)

powerful voice 577 (1)

powerfully 32 (17), 160 (12), 162 (13)

powerhouse 160 (4), 678 (5), 687 (1)

powerless 161 (5), 161 (7), 163 (4), 639 (5)

powerlessness 161 (2), 734 (2)

powers of darkness 969 (2)

powers that be 178 (1), 733 (1)

pox 651 (13)

PR 528 (2)

practicable 469 (2), 640 (2), 642 (2)

practical 173 (2), 469 (2), 498 (4), 534 (5), 628 (3), 640 (2), 642 (2), 673 (2)

practical ability 694 (1)

practical experience 490 (1)

practical joke 497 (2), 542 (2), 839 (2), 851 (1)

practical joker 545 (1)

practical joking 839 (1)

practical person 676 (3)

practical test 461 (1)

practicality 498 (2), 673 (1)

practically 200 (8)

practice 83 (1), 86 (2), 106 (1), 461 (2), 514 (2), 610 (2), 622 (1), 624 (1), 669 (1), 673 (1), 676 (1), 682 (2), 688 (1), 693 (1), 768

(1), 848 (2), 976 (2), 988 (3)

practise 106 (4), 413 (0), 534 (8), 536 (4), 610 (8), 669 (13), 673 (3), 676 (5), 768 (3)

practise birth control 172 (5)

practise law 958 (7)

practise occultism 984 (9)

practise sorcery 983 (10)

practise tax evasion 805 (5)

practise upon 461 (7)

practised 490 (5), 610 (6), 610 (7), 669 (7), 694 (6)

practised eye 696 (2)

practised hand 696 (2)

practising 768 (2), 973 (8), 976 (8), 979 (6)

practitioner 676 (3), 686 (1)

praetor 741 (6)

pragmatic 640 (2)

pragmatism 449 (3), 642 (1)

prairie 348 (1)

praise 482 (4), 590 (1), 835 (1), 835 (6), 866 (4), 866 (13), 907 (2), 907 (5), 923 (2), 923 (9), 925 (4), 962 (1), 979 (9), 981 (3), 981 (11), 981 (12), 982 (6)

praise oneself 923 (9)

praised 923 (7)

praised, be 828 (5), 866 (11), 920 (7), 923 (11)

praiser 923 (4)

praises 907 (2)

praiseworthy 615 (3), 644 (4), 923 (6), 933 (3)

praising 907 (3), 981 (10)

pram 274 (4)

prance 267 (14), 312 (1), 312 (4), 875 (7), 877 (5)

prancer 312 (2)

prank 604 (2), 837 (3), 843 (7)

prate 515 (6), 581 (5), 877 (5)

pratical joker 839 (3)

prattle 515 (3), 515 (6), 579 (8), 581 (2)

pray 761 (7), 762 (3), 859 (11), 979 (9), 981 (11)
pray aloud 585 (4)
pray for 703 (6), 859 (11), 897 (5)
pray to 583 (3), 761 (7)
prayer 761 (1), 761 (2), 981 (1), 981 (4)
prayer book 981 (4)
prayer-cap 989 (1)
prayer meeting 981 (7)
prayer-wheel 981 (4)
prayerful 761 (4), 979 (6), 981 (9)
prayers 703 (1), 761 (2), 762 (1), 897 (2), 981 (4)
praying 761 (4), 979 (6), 981 (3), 981 (9)
praying mantis 365 (16)
pre- 119 (2), 119 (5), 123 (1)
Pre-Cambrian 110 (4)
pre-Christian 108 (6), 119 (2)
Pre-Raphelite 556 (1)
pre-school 130 (4)
preach 534 (7), 579 (9)
preacher 528 (6), 537 (3), 579 (5), 979 (5), 986 (3)
preaching 534 (1), 985 (2)
preamble 64 (3), 66 (2), 579 (2)
prearrange 119 (4), 608 (3), 623 (8), 669 (10)
prearranged 608 (2)
prebendal 986 (11)
prebendary 986 (4)
precarious 114 (3), 474 (5), 661 (4)
precariously 112 (1)
precaution 660 (2), 767 (1), 858 (1)
precautionary 669 (6)
precautions 662 (3), 669 (1)
precede 64 (3), 119 (3), 237 (5), 267 (14), 283 (3), 612 (8)
precedence 34 (1), 64 (1), 119 (1), 131 (4), 135 (3), 283 (1), 638 (1), 733 (1), 866 (2)

precedent 21 (1), 23 (1), 64 (1), 66 (1), 66 (3), 68 (1), 68 (3), 81 (1), 83 (2), 119 (1), 119 (2), 520 (5), 610 (1), 959 (3)
preceding 64 (1), 64 (2), 66 (3), 119 (2), 125 (8), 265 (1), 283 (1), 285 (1), 669 (6)
precentor 690 (2)
precept 23 (1), 81 (1), 496 (1), 691 (1), 693 (1), 737 (2), 913 (1), 917 (3), 953 (2)
preceptive 496 (3), 693 (2)
preceptor 537 (1)
precepts 485 (2)
precinct 185 (1), 235 (1)
precincts 184 (1), 230 (1), 986 (10)
precious 32 (4), 574 (4), 644 (7), 811 (3), 850 (4), 890 (1)
precious few 105 (2)
precious metal 359 (1)
precious stone 344 (4), 844 (8)
preciousness 574 (1)
precipice 209 (2), 215 (1), 309 (1)
precipitate 41 (2), 156 (9), 277 (5), 300 (6), 309 (3), 324 (3), 324 (6), 649 (2), 670 (3), 680 (2), 857 (3)
precipitately 135 (7), 176 (10), 680 (4)
precipitation 165 (1), 287 (1), 300 (1), 350 (6)
precipitous 215 (2), 220 (4)
precipitousness 215 (1)
précis 204 (2), 520 (3), 569 (1), 592 (1)
précis-writer 592 (3)
precise 62 (3), 80 (6), 83 (6), 494 (6), 516 (2), 862 (3), 875 (6)
precise time 116 (1)
precisely 494 (8)
preciseness 494 (3), 862 (1), 875 (2)
precision 494 (3), 516 (1)
precision tool 630 (1)

preclude 57 (5)
preclusive 57 (2)
precocious 135 (4), 670 (4)
precociously 135 (7)
precocity 135 (3), 670 (1)
precognition 490 (1), 510 (1), 984 (2)
preconceive 481 (10)
preconceived idea 481 (2)
preconsultation 669 (1)
precursor 64 (1), 66 (1), 68 (1), 83 (2), 119 (1), 128 (1), 135 (1), 169 (3), 191 (4), 237 (1), 268 (1), 283 (1), 361 (3), 529 (5), 537 (3), 669 (5)
precursory 66 (3), 68 (6), 119 (2)
predator 735 (3), 786 (4), 904 (5)
predatory 735 (6), 786 (5)
predecease 119 (4), 361 (7)
predecessor 66 (1)
predestinate 608 (3)
predestination 155 (1), 608 (1)
predestine 155 (4), 596 (8), 608 (3), 612 (8), 617 (5)
predestined 155 (2), 596 (6), 608 (2)
predetermination 596 (1), 608 (1), 669 (1)
predetermine 155 (4), 481 (10), 608 (3), 612 (8), 617 (5), 623 (8), 669 (10), 737 (7)
predetermined 155 (2), 481 (8), 595 (1), 596 (6), 608 (2), 617 (4)
predicament 8 (1), 61 (3), 137 (3), 497 (2), 596 (1), 616 (1), 661 (1), 700 (3), 731 (1), 827 (1), 853 (1)
predicate 158 (3), 475 (3)
predicative 564 (3)
predict 124 (6), 155 (4), 507 (4), 510 (3), 511 (8), 540 (3), 547 (18), 664 (5), 852 (7), 900 (3), 984 (9)
predictable 124 (4), 153 (4)

predicted 124 (4), 155 (2), 507 (3)

predicting 155 (2), 507 (2), 510 (2), 511 (6), 965 (6), 984 (7)

prediction 124 (3), 155 (1), 507 (1), 510 (1), 511 (1), 623 (2), 664 (1)

predigested 301 (32), 669 (9)

predilection 179 (1), 481 (3), 605 (1), 817 (1), 859 (3)

predispose 481 (11), 612 (8), 669 (10)

predisposed 481 (8), 597 (4)

predisposition 179 (1)

predominance 160 (1), 178 (1)

predominant 160 (8), 178 ·(2)

predominate 29 (3), 34 (8), 178 (4), 638 (7), 727 (9), 733 (12)

preeminence 34 (1), 64 (1)

preeminent 34 (5), 866 (9)

preeminently 34 (12)

preempt 57 (5), 119 (4), 135 (5), 791 (6), 792 (5)

preemption 283 (1), 773 (1), 792 (1)

preemptive 57 (2), 792 (4)

preen 843 (7)

preen oneself 871 (6), 873 (5)

preexist 1 (6), 119 (3)

preexistence 1 (1), 119 (1)

preexistent 119 (2)

preexiting 119 (2)

prefab 192 (6)

prefabricate 119 (4), 164 (7)

prefabricated 669 (9)

preface 64 (3), 64 (4), 66 (2)

prefatory 64 (2), 66 (3)

prefect 537 (1), 690 (4), 741 (6)

prefer 285 (4), 605 (6), 859 (11)

prefer not to 861 (4)

preferable 34 (4), 605 (5)

preferably 605 (9)

preference 64 (1), 595 (0), 605 (1), 887 (1)

preferment 285 (1), 654 (1)

preferred 34 (4), 605 (5)

prefiguration 511 (1)

prefigure 511 (8), 547 (18)

prefigurement 66 (1)

prefiguring 511 (6)

prefix 38 (3), 40 (1), 45 (11), 64 (4), 66 (1), 237 (1), 564 (2)

prefixed 38 (2), 64 (2)

pregnancy 167 (1)

pregnant 167 (5), 171 (4), 514 (3), 569 (2)

pregnant with 155 (2)

prehensile 378 (5), 778 (3)

prehensility 778 (1)

prehistorian 125 (5)

prehistoric 119 (2), 125 (6), 125 (7), 127 (4)

prehistoric age 125 (2)

prehistory 125 (2)

prejudge 119 (4), 481 (10)

prejudging 481 (8)

prejudgment 481 (2)

prejudice 11 (4), 57 (1), 178 (3), 179 (1), 481 (3), 481 (11), 485 (1), 495 (1), 608 (1), 612 (8), 718 (3), 861 (1), 888 (1), 914 (2), 979 (3)

prejudiced 481 (8), 499 (5), 914 (4)

prejudicial 616 (2), 645 (3)

prelacy 985 (1), 985 (3)

prelate 986 (4)

preliminaries 68 (1), 669 (1)

preliminary 64 (2), 66 (2), 66 (3), 669 (6)

prelims 68 (1)

prelude 64 (3), 64 (4), 66 (2), 68 (1), 412 (4)

premarital 894 (9)

premature 135 (4), 138 (2), 670 (4), 728 (4)

premature, be 670 (7)

prematurely 135 (7)

prematurity 135 (3)

premeditate 608 (3)

premeditation 608 (1), 669 (1)

premier 690 (1)

premiere 68 (2), 594 (2)

premiership 689 (2), 733 (5)

premise 466 (1), 475 (2), 475 (12), 481 (10), 485 (3), 485 (7), 507 (1), 512 (1), 512 (6)

premised 119 (2)

premises 66 (2), 185 (1), 466 (1), 796 (3)

premium 803 (2), 807 (1)

premium bond 797 (5)

premonition 66 (1), 119 (1), 510 (1), 664 (1)

premonitory 64 (2), 511 (6)

prenatal 119 (2)

preoccupation 455 (1), 456 (2)

preoccupied 455 (3), 456 (5)

preoccupy 449 (11)

preordain 155 (4)

preordained 596 (6)

preordination 596 (2), 608 (1)

prep 534 (3)

prep school 539 (2)

preparation 62 (1), 66 (2), 68 (1), 124 (3), 135 (3), 164 (1), 510 (1), 534 (1), 536 (1), 536 (2), 633 (1), 658 (2), 669 (1), 858 (1)

preparative 669 (6)

preparatory 64 (2), 66 (3), 124 (4), 155 (2), 669 (6)

preparatory to 64 (5)

prepare 68 (8), 68 (10), 510 (3), 534 (6), 534 (8), 623 (8), 664 (5), 669 (10), 858 (3)

prepare a budget 808 (5)

prepare a meal 301 (40)

prepare for 669 (10)

prepare oneself 507 (4), 536 (4), 632 (5), 669 (13)

prepare the ground 669 (10)

presumptuous 857 (3), 878 (4), 916 (6)

presuppose 119 (4), 481 (10), 512 (6)

pretence 4 (2), 20 (2), 497 (2), 541 (2), 542 (5), 543 (2), 614 (1)

pretend 20 (5), 512 (6), 513 (7), 543 (5), 614 (4), 850 (5)

pretended 486 (5), 512 (5), 513 (6), 542 (6), 614 (2)

pretender 545 (3), 763 (1), 859 (6), 916 (4)

pretension 541 (2), 695 (1), 850 (2), 875 (1)

pretensions 850 (2), 873 (2), 875 (1)

pretentious 497 (3), 572 (2), 574 (4), 850 (4), 871 (4), 873 (4), 875 (4), 877 (4)

pretentiousness 850 (1)

preterite 125 (1)

preternatural 84 (6), 984 (8)

pretext 156 (6), 466 (2), 475 (5), 477 (1), 543 (2), 614 (1), 698 (2), 927 (1)

prettify 843 (7), 844 (12)

prettiness 841 (1)

pretty 32 (17), 841 (3)

pretty big 32 (4)

pretty face 841 (1)

pretty near 33 (11)

pretty pass 700 (3)

pretty well 32 (17)

prevail 1 (6), 34 (8), 79 (5), 156 (9), 160 (10), 178 (4), 610 (7), 612 (8), 727 (9)

prevail upon 178 (3), 612 (10)

prevailing 178 (2)

prevailing wind 352 (1)

prevalence 34 (1), 79 (1), 178 (1)

prevalent 32 (5), 79 (3), 79 (4), 178 (2), 490 (7)

prevaricate 518 (3), 541 (6), 930 (8)

prevaricating 518 (2), 930 (4)

prevarication 518 (1), 541 (1)

prevent 182 (3), 757 (4)

prevent disease 652 (5)

preventable 620 (4)

preventative 182 (1), 182 (2)

prevented 702 (7)

preventive 57 (2), 182 (2), 658 (3), 666 (3), 702 (6)

preventive detention 747 (3)

preventive medicine 658 (10)

preview 66 (1), 119 (1), 119 (4), 438 (4), 522 (1), 594 (2)

previous 64 (2), 118 (2), 119 (2), 135 (4)

previous, be 119 (4)

previously 119 (5)

previousness 118 (1), 119 (1)

prevision 510 (1)

prewar 119 (2), 127 (7), 717 (3)

prey 365 (2), 617 (2), 619 (2), 728 (3), 731 (3), 790 (1), 825 (4)

prey on 301 (35)

prey on one's mind 449 (11)

prey to 180 (2)

prey upon 645 (7)

price 87 (1), 150 (3), 465 (13), 644 (1), 808 (5), 809 (1), 809 (5), 963 (4)

price control 747 (2), 809 (1)

price index 86 (4)

price list 87 (1), 809 (1)

price ring 747 (2)

priced 28 (8), 809 (4)

priced at, be 809 (6)

priceless 644 (7), 811 (3), 849 (3)

prick 33 (3), 46 (11), 256 (2), 256 (10), 263 (18), 377 (5), 378 (8), 547 (19), 612 (9), 655 (4), 655 (10), 821 (2)

prick up 254 (5), 310 (4)

prick up one's ears 455 (4)

prickle 256 (3), 259 (1), 366 (5), 378 (8)

prickliness 256 (1), 709 (2), 819 (1), 871 (1), 892 (1)

prickly 84 (5), 256 (7), 892 (3)

pricy 811 (2)

pride 74 (3), 482 (1), 871 (1), 873 (1), 878 (1), 883 (1), 922 (1)

pride and joy 871 (1), 890 (2)

pride of place 34 (1), 64 (1), 283 (1)

pride oneself 871 (6)

prideful 871 (4), 873 (4), 883 (5)

priest 986 (2), 986 (7), 986 (8), 988 (6)

priestess 986 (8)

priesthole 527 (1)

priesthood 985 (1), 985 (3), 986 (1)

priestliness 985 (1)

priestly 985 (7), 985 (8)

prig 850 (3), 950 (4)

priggish 850 (4), 950 (6)

priggishness 950 (2)

prim 834 (7), 840 (2), 850 (4), 862 (3), 950 (6)

prima ballerina 594 (9)

prima donna 413 (4), 594 (9), 638 (4), 696 (1)

prima facie 466 (5)

primacy 34 (1), 638 (1), 866 (2)

primal 68 (6), 110 (4), 125 (6), 127 (5)

primarily 68 (11), 283 (4), 638 (9)

primary 21 (3), 44 (4), 68 (7), 156 (8), 534 (5)

primary colour 425 (1)

primary education 534 (2)

primary school 539 (2)

primate 365 (3), 986 (4)

primateship 985 (3)

prime 85 (5), 127 (5), 128 (1), 134 (1), 135 (1), 534 (6), 638 (5), 644 (2), 644 (4), 669 (11), 730 (2) prime minister 690 (1), 741 (6)

prime mover 156 (2), 612 (5)

prime number 85 (1)

prime of life 130 (3), 131 (2), 134 (1)

primed 490 (6), 524 (8), 669 (7)

primer 68 (1), 589 (3)

primeval 68 (6), 127 (5)

primeval deities 967 (1)

primeval forest 366 (2)

primeval soup 68 (4)

priming 669 (1)

primitive 125 (6), 127 (5), 551 (6), 556 (1), 699 (3), 869 (9)

primitive form 23 (1)

primitiveness 68 (1), 127 (1), 699 (1)

primness 834 (3), 840 (1), 862 (1), 950 (2)

primogeniture 119 (1), 170 (3)

primordial 21 (3), 68 (6)

primp 228 (31), 431 (5), 654 (9), 841 (8), 843 (7), 844 (12), 873 (5), 875 (7)

primped 843 (6)

primrose 433 (1)

prince 741 (3), 741 (4)

princeliness 868 (1)

princely 733 (8), 813 (3), 866 (8), 868 (6)

princess 741 (3)

principal 34 (5), 68 (7), 537 (1), 690 (1), 741 (1)

principal boy 594 (8)

principal part 32 (3), 52 (3)

principality 733 (6)

principally 34 (12)

principle 5 (2), 81 (1), 156 (3), 451 (1), 475 (2), 496 (2), 693 (1)

principle of evil 934 (1)

principled 929 (3), 933 (3)

principles 485 (2), 688 (1), 929 (1)

prink 843 (7)

print 20 (6), 22 (1), 56 (1), 56 (5), 157 (1), 166 (1),

243 (1), 528 (9), 547 (1), 547 (19), 548 (7), 551 (4), 551 (9), 553 (5), 555 (2), 555 (3), 586 (1), 586 (8), 587 (1), 587 (2), 587 (7), 589 (5), 844 (3)

print off 587 (7)

print-type 547 (14), 558 (1), 587 (3)

printable 950 (5)

printed 528 (7), 548 (6), 587 (6)

printed matter 586 (3), 587 (2)

printed word 589 (2)

printer 20 (3), 528 (6), 556 (3), 587 (5), 589 (6)

printers 587 (4)

printer's devil 587 (5)

printer's ink 428 (3)

printer's reader 587 (5)

printing 166 (1), 551 (1), 555 (2), 586 (2), 587 (1)

printing press 587 (4)

printing works 587 (4)

printout 86 (5), 587 (2)

prior 21 (3), 64 (2), 108 (6), 119 (2), 125 (7), 127 (7), 131 (7), 135 (4), 986 (5)

prior to 119 (5)

prioress 986 (6)

priority 23 (1), 66 (1), 108 (1), 119 (1), 125 (1), 170 (3), 283 (1), 638 (1), 638 (3), 733 (1)

priory 192 (6), 986 (9)

prism 247 (4), 425 (1), 425 (2), 437 (1), 442 (1)

prison 194 (1), 235 (1), 748 (1), 883 (2), 964 (2)

prison camp 748 (3)

prison fare 391 (1)

prison guard 749 (2)

prison officer 749 (2)

prison ship 748 (1)

prisoner 742 (6), 750 (1), 928 (4)

prisoner of state 750 (1)

prisoner of war 750 (1)

privacy 444 (1), 662 (1), 883 (2)

private 10 (3), 35 (2), 80 (5), 80 (7), 517 (2), 525 (3), 722 (5), 773 (3), 883 (7)

private detective 459 (8)

private devotion 981 (4)

private ends 932 (1)

private eye 459 (8)

private parts 167 (3)

private school 539 (2)

private sector 791 (2)

private society 708 (3)

private soldier 722 (5)

private teaching 534 (1)

private world 883 (2)

privateer 275 (2), 722 (3), 722 (13), 789 (2)

privateering 788 (2)

privately 525 (10)

privation 801 (1)

privatize 786 (7)

privet 366 (4)

privilege 34 (2), 744 (1), 915 (1), 915 (8), 919 (1)

privy 525 (3), 649 (1)

privy councillor 692 (3)

privy seal 743 (2)

privy to 490 (5)

prize 615 (2), 617 (2), 644 (2), 729 (1), 771 (1), 781 (2), 786 (1), 790 (1), 807 (1), 859 (5), 866 (13), 887 (13), 923 (8), 962 (1)

prize fellowship 962 (1)

prize fighter 716 (8)

prize fighting 716 (4)

prize-giver 781 (4)

prize-giving 781 (1), 962 (1)

prize open 176 (8)

prize-winner 696 (1), 782 (2)

PRO 528 (6), 696 (2), 755 (1), 755 (2), 755 (4)

pro rata 783 (4)

probability 159 (3), 180 (1), 469 (1), 471 (1), 485 (1), 507 (1)

probable 155 (2), 179 (2), 466 (5), 469 (2), 471 (2), 485 (5), 507 (3), 852 (5)

probably 471 (7)

probation 461 (1), 671 (1)

probationary 461 (6), 671 (3)

probationer 461 (5), 538 (2), 904 (3)

probationer nurse 658 (16)

probe 211 (1), 263 (12), 263 (18), 459 (1), 459 (5), 459 (13), 459 (14), 459 (15), 461 (1), 461 (8), 465 (11), 484 (2)

prober 459 (9)

probing 459 (11)

probity 457 (1), 494 (1), 540 (1), 699 (1), 739 (2), 768 (1), 802 (1), 855 (1), 913 (1), 917 (4), 929 (1), 931 (1), 933 (1), 935 (1)

problem 452 (1), 459 (3), 475 (3), 530 (2), 700 (1), 825 (3)

problematic 459 (12), 700 (4)

proboscis 254 (3), 378 (3)

procedural 988 (8)

procedure 610 (2), 623 (2), 624 (1), 676 (1), 688 (1)

proceed 146 (3), 157 (5), 265 (4), 267 (11), 285 (3), 676 (5)

proceed to 672 (3)

proceed with 676 (5)

proceeding 154 (1), 676 (2)

proceedings 959 (2)

proceeds 36 (2), 771 (2), 782 (1), 807 (1)

process 62 (6), 86 (13), 143 (1), 143 (6), 147 (7), 164 (1), 164 (7), 173 (1), 173 (3), 551 (9)

process of law 913 (2)

process of time 111 (1)

processable 86 (10)

processed 164 (6), 669 (9)

processing 147 (1), 164 (1), 173 (1)

procession 67 (2), 71 (3), 285 (1), 875 (3)

processional 988 (8)

processor 86 (5)

proclaim 522 (7), 528 (10), 532 (5), 638 (8), 665 (3), 737 (7), 866 (13), 875 (7)

proclamation 522 (1), 528 (1), 547 (8)

proconsul 741 (5), 741 (6)

procrastinate 136 (7), 458 (6), 677 (3)

procrastination 136 (2), 458 (1), 679 (1)

procreate 167 (7), 171 (5)

procreation 164 (1), 166 (1), 167 (1), 171 (1)

procreative 167 (4)

procreator 167 (1), 169 (3)

proctor 537 (1), 958 (2)

procurator 958 (2)

procure 156 (9), 612 (10), 771 (7), 951 (10)

procurement 173 (1), 771 (1)

prod 279 (7), 547 (21), 612 (4), 612 (9)

prodigal 634 (2), 635 (4), 772 (2), 806 (2), 813 (3), 815 (2), 815 (3), 857 (3), 943 (2)

prodigal, be 634 (4), 779 (4), 806 (4), 813 (4), 815 (4), 943 (3)

prodigal son 815 (2), 938 (1), 939 (2)

prodigality 634 (1), 635 (2), 806 (1), 813 (1), 815 (1), 943 (1)

prodigally 815 (5)

prodigious 32 (7), 195 (7), 644 (5), 864 (5)

prodigy 34 (3), 84 (1), 492 (2), 644 (3), 646 (2), 696 (1), 864 (3)

produce 56 (5), 156 (9), 157 (2), 157 (5), 164 (2), 164 (7), 167 (7), 171 (5), 203 (8), 243 (5), 513 (7), 522 (7), 594 (16), 633 (5), 771 (2), 771 (10)

produce evidence 466 (8)

produce results 642 (3)

produce sound 398 (4)

produced 164 (6), 522 (6)

producer 156 (2), 164 (4), 556 (1), 594 (12), 686 (1)

producing 164 (1)

product 36 (2), 41 (1), 85 (4), 154 (1), 157 (1), 164 (2), 771 (2)

production 1 (1), 21 (1), 36 (1), 56 (1), 68 (1), 147 (1), 156 (1), 164 (1), 164 (2), 166 (1), 171 (1), 203 (2), 243 (2), 594 (2), 622 (1), 676 (1)

production line 164 (1), 687 (1)

productive 36 (3), 156 (7), 164 (5), 167 (4), 640 (3), 771 (5)

productiveness 164 (1), 167 (1), 171 (1), 635 (2)

productivity 164 (1), 171 (1), 640 (1)

profanation 675 (1), 916 (1), 980 (1)

profane 649 (9), 655 (9), 675 (2), 899 (4), 916 (8), 921 (3), 934 (3), 974 (5), 974 (6), 980 (5), 980 (6)

profaneness 974 (1)

profaner 980 (3)

profaning 980 (4)

profanity 899 (2), 980 (1)

profess 485 (7), 532 (5), 614 (4)

profession 488 (1), 532 (1), 543 (2), 614 (1), 622 (2), 875 (1)

professional 490 (6), 492 (1), 622 (5), 694 (6), 696 (2)

professional classes 869 (4)

professional code 917 (3)

professional soldier 722 (4)

professional standards 917 (4)

professionalism 694 (1)

professions 764 (1)

professor 492 (1), 537 (1), 870 (2)

proffer 759 (3), 764 (4), 766 (4)

proficiency 490 (3), 694 (1)

proficient 490 (5), 694 (6)

proficient person 492 (1), 500 (1), 686 (3), 696 (1)

profile 233 (1), 233 (3), 239 (1), 243 (1), 445 (6), 553 (5), 590 (1)

profit 36 (2), 157 (2), 612 (4), 615 (2), 615 (4), 640 (1), 640 (4), 642 (1), 642 (3), 730 (8), 771 (3), 771 (9), 771 (10), 962 (1)

profit and loss account 808 (1)

profit by 108 (8), 137 (7), 614 (4), 615 (5), 640 (5), 654 (8), 673 (3), 678 (11), 694 (8)

profit-making 791 (2)

profit-sharing 775 (2)

profitability 640 (1)

profitable 164 (5), 171 (4), 615 (3), 640 (3), 642 (2), 644 (8), 727 (4), 771 (5), 962 (2)

profitable, be 615 (4), 640 (4), 771 (10)

profitably 615 (6), 962 (5)

profiteer 730 (3), 730 (6), 791 (5), 811 (5)

profiteering 730 (4), 771 (1)

profitless 172 (4), 634 (3), 641 (5), 641 (6), 728 (4), 772 (2)

profits 807 (1)

profligacy 815 (1), 934 (1)

profligate 815 (2), 815 (3), 934 (4), 938 (1), 943 (2), 944 (2), 951 (8), 952 (1)

profound 32 (4), 211 (2), 498 (4), 517 (4), 568 (2), 818 (6)

profoundly 211 (4), 224 (6)

profundity 211 (1), 449 (1)

profuse 104 (4), 570 (3), 635 (4), 813 (3), 815 (3)

profusely 815 (5)

profuseness 570 (1)

profusion 32 (2), 171 (3), 635 (2), 637 (1), 815 (1)

progenitor 169 (3)

progenitrix 169 (4)

progeny 170 (1)

prognosis 510 (1), 511 (1), 651 (19), 658 (10)

prognostic 66 (1)

prognostication 511 (1)

program 62 (6), 86 (5), 86 (13)

programmable 86 (10)

programme 87 (1), 510 (1), 528 (1), 531 (4), 623 (1), 623 (2), 623 (8), 672 (1)

programmer 86 (7)

progress 36 (4), 111 (3), 126 (8), 146 (1), 146 (3), 265 (4), 267 (11), 285 (1), 285 (3), 289 (4), 305 (1), 654 (1), 654 (8), 727 (1), 727 (6)

progress of time 111 (1)

progression 60 (1), 71 (1), 71 (2), 85 (3), 146 (1), 265 (1), 285 (1), 289 (1), 624 (1), 654 (1), 727 (1)

progressive 36 (3), 71 (4), 174 (5), 285 (2), 654 (5), 654 (7), 672 (2)

progressively 71 (7)

progressivism 654 (4)

prohibit 46 (9), 57 (5), 182 (3), 300 (7), 470 (5), 489 (5), 533 (3), 702 (9), 737 (6), 747 (7), 757 (4), 760 (4), 916 (9), 924 (9), 954 (9)

prohibited 57 (3), 470 (2), 489 (4), 702 (7), 757 (3), 760 (3)

prohibiting 57 (2), 702 (6), 747 (4), 757 (2)

prohibition 57 (1), 182 (1), 266 (1), 470 (1), 702 (1), 737 (1), 747 (1), 757 (1)

prohibitive 702 (6), 757 (2), 811 (2)

prohibitory 757 (2)

project 6 (4), 223 (3), 254 (5), 287 (7), 298 (5), 443 (4), 534 (3), 551 (8), 617 (1), 623 (1), 623 (8), 672 (1)

projectile 287 (2), 287 (6), 723 (12)

projecting 209 (11), 217 (4), 253 (7), 254 (4), 554 (2)

projecting edge 234 (1)

projection 6 (1), 209 (2), 218 (2), 218 (12), 234 (1), 253 (1), 254 (2), 287 (1), 445 (3), 513 (2), 551 (2), 551 (5)

projector 420 (4), 442 (1)

proletarian 847 (3), 869 (5), 869 (8)

proletariat 686 (4), 869 (1), 869 (3)

proliferate 36 (4), 171 (6), 635 (7)

proliferation 36 (1), 167 (1)

prolific 36 (3), 104 (5), 164 (5), 167 (4), 171 (4), 174 (5), 570 (3), 635 (4), 640 (3)

prolix 113 (5), 570 (4), 570 (6), 572 (2), 581 (4), 838 (3)

prolixity 570 (1), 581 (1), 838 (1)

prologue 66 (2), 579 (2), 579 (5), 594 (9)

prolong 36 (5), 71 (6), 113 (8), 146 (4), 203 (8), 666 (5)

prolong the agony 377 (5)

prolongation 36 (1), 65 (1), 113 (3), 146 (1), 203 (2), 666 (1)

prolonged 113 (5)

prolonged noise 400 (1)

promenade 192 (15), 267 (3), 624 (5), 875 (7)

promenader 268 (2)

prominence 34 (1), 253 (1), 254 (1), 443 (1), 522 (1), 638 (1), 866 (2)

prominent 209 (11), 254 (4), 443 (1), 522 (4), 638 (6), 866 (9)

prominently 32 (19), 34 (12)

promiscuity 464 (1), 951 (1)

promiscuous 464 (2), 951 (7)

promiscuous, be **951** (10)

promise **471** (4), **511** (8), **532** (2), **532** (5), **617** (1), **617** (5), **672** (1), **672** (3), **764** (1), **764** (4), **765** (1), **765** (5), **767** (1), **767** (6), **852** (1), **852** (7), **917** (1), **917** (9)

promise-maker **764** (1)

promise oneself **507** (4), **617** (6), **852** (6), **859** (11)

promise trouble **900** (3)

promise well **730** (8), **852** (7)

promised **124** (4), **507** (3), **764** (3), **767** (4), **894** (8)

promised land **76** (1), **513** (3), **852** (2)

promises **612** (2)

promising **124** (4), **471** (2), **511** (7), **730** (5), **764** (2), **852** (5)

promissory **532** (3), **764** (2)

promissory note **797** (5)

promontory **254** (2), **344** (1)

promote **68** (9), **156** (10), **179** (3), **181** (3), **285** (4), **471** (5), **528** (11), **628** (4), **629** (2), **640** (4), **642** (3), **654** (9), **703** (5), **791** (4), **866** (14)

promoter **528** (6), **623** (5), **703** (3), **707** (4)

promoting **703** (4)

promotion **285** (1), **654** (1), **669** (2), **703** (1), **866** (5)

prompt **68** (9), **135** (4), **178** (3), **277** (5), **505** (3), **505** (9), **524** (3), **524** (11), **597** (4), **612** (9), **678** (7), **680** (2), **691** (4)

prompt book **594** (3)

prompter **594** (11), **612** (5)

prompting **612** (2), **612** (6)

promptitude **135** (2)

promptly **116** (4)

promptness **277** (1), **597** (1)

promulgate **528** (10), **737** (7)

prone **216** (5)

prone to **179** (2)

proneness **179** (1), **216** (2)

prong **92** (2), **256** (2)

pronoun **564** (2)

pronounce **480** (5), **528** (10), **532** (5), **577** (4), **579** (8)

pronounce guilty **961** (3)

pronounce sentence **959** (8)

pronounced **443** (3), **522** (4), **577** (3)

pronouncement **480** (1), **528** (1)

pronouncing **532** (3)

pronto **116** (4)

pronunciation **557** (2), **559** (3), **560** (2), **577** (2), **579** (1), **580** (1)

proof **162** (7), **326** (3), **461** (1), **466** (1), **473** (1), **478** (1), **522** (1), **587** (2), **589** (2), **596** (1), **660** (5), **713** (8), **959** (3)

proof against **820** (3)

proof against, be **715** (3)

proof copy **623** (1)

proof-read **654** (10)

proof reader **587** (5)

proofed **715** (2)

proofread **587** (7)

prop **153** (3), **162** (12), **194** (1), **217** (3), **218** (2), **218** (15), **254** (2), **267** (7), **275** (6), **310** (4), **662** (1)

prop man **594** (11)

prop up **666** (5), **703** (5)

propaganda **475** (4), **528** (2), **534** (1), **535** (1), **612** (2), **718** (6)

propagandist **528** (6), **535** (2), **537** (3), **612** (5)

propagandize **475** (11), **485** (9), **528** (9), **534** (7), **535** (3), **655** (8)

propagate **167** (7), **171** (5), **528** (9)

propagation **45** (3), **156** (4), **164** (1), **166** (1), **167** (1), **169** (4), **171** (1), **171** (2), **360** (1), **669** (3)

propagator **167** (1), **370** (3)

propane **385** (1)

propel **265** (5), **279** (7), **279** (9), **287** (7), **300** (6), **310** (4), **311** (5), **352** (10), **712** (12)

propellant **269** (5), **279** (5), **287** (3), **287** (6), **300** (2), **353** (1), **723** (13)

propeller **269** (5), **287** (3), **315** (3)

propelling **160** (9), **287** (6)

propensity **179** (1), **597** (1), **859** (3)

proper **9** (6), **24** (7), **58** (2), **80** (5), **83** (6), **642** (2), **773** (3), **846** (3), **848** (6), **913** (3), **915** (2), **933** (3)

proper fraction **85** (2)

proper mind **502** (1)

proper noun **561** (2)

proper pride **871** (1)

proper thing, the **917** (1)

proper time **137** (1)

proper to **5** (8)

properly **644** (12)

propertied **773** (2), **777** (5), **800** (4)

properties **594** (6)

property **5** (2), **160** (2), **272** (3), **629** (1), **632** (1), **773** (1), **777** (1), **777** (3), **800** (1)

prophecy **511** (1), **975** (1)

prophesy **510** (3), **511** (8)

prophet **500** (1), **511** (4), **537** (3), **664** (2), **973** (6), **984** (5), **986** (8)

Prophet of God **973** (6)

prophetess **511** (4), **986** (8)

prophetic **510** (2), **511** (6), **540** (2), **547** (15), **975** (3), **975** (4), **984** (7)

prophetic, be **540** (3)

prophylactic **652** (2), **652** (4), **658** (3), **658** (17)

prophylaxis **652** (2)

propinquity **200** (1)

propitiate **719** (4), **720** (4), **828** (5), **905** (8), **909** (5), **941** (5), **981** (12) propitiation 719 (2), 941 (2), 981 (6)

propitiator 720 (2)

propitiatory 719 (3), 720 (3), 941 (4)

propitious 137 (5), 644 (8), 703 (4), 730 (5), 852 (5)

proponent 475 (6)

proportion 9 (2), 12 (1), 24 (10), 27 (1), 53 (1), 60 (1), 85 (3), 86 (2), 245 (1), 575 (1), 783 (2)

proportional 9 (5), 12 (2), 24 (5), 27 (3), 85 (5)

proportional representation 605 (2)

proportionate 9 (5), 12 (2), 24 (5), 86 (8)

proportionate, be 9 (7)

proportionately 783 (4)

proportioned 245 (2)

proportions 183 (2), 195 (1)

proposal 512 (1), 617 (1), 623 (1), 759 (1), 889 (2)

propose 512 (7), 605 (7), 691 (4), 703 (6), 759 (3), 889 (7)

propose a motion 512 (7)

propose conditions 766 (3)

proposed 512 (5)

proposed action 623 (2)

proposer 623 (5), 707 (4)

proposition 452 (1), 475 (3), 512 (1), 532 (1), 623 (1), 759 (1), 951 (11)

propositional 512 (4)

propound 512 (7), 532 (5), 691 (4), 759 (3)

proprietary 777 (5)

proprieties 848 (2)

proprietor 776 (2)

proprietorial 773 (2)

proprietress 776 (2)

propriety 575 (1), 642 (1), 846 (1), 848 (2), 913 (1), 950 (1)

props 594 (6)

propulsion 160 (3), 279 (1), 287 (1), 300 (1), 630 (1)

propulsive 160 (9), 287 (6)

pros and cons 475 (5)

prosaic 83 (5), 572 (2), 573 (2), 593 (9), 699 (3), 823 (3), 838 (3), 840 (2)

proscenium 594 (6)

proscribe 737 (6), 757 (4), 961 (3)

proscribed 961 (2)

proscription 737 (1), 757 (1), 899 (1), 963 (4)

prose 581 (5), 589 (2), 593 (7)

prose writer 589 (7), 593 (7)

prose-writing 593 (7)

prosecute 928 (9), 959 (7)

prosecution 928 (1), 959 (1), 959 (3)

prosecutor 928 (3), 959 (4)

proselyte 147 (4), 538 (1)

proselytize 147 (7), 485 (9), 534 (7), 979 (11)

proselytized 147 (5)

prosing 570 (4), 581 (4)

prosodist 593 (6)

prosody 106 (2), 593 (5)

prospect 124 (1), 124 (3), 155 (1), 183 (3), 438 (5), 459 (15), 461 (8), 471 (1), 507 (1), 511 (1), 617 (1)

prospective 124 (4), 507 (3), 617 (3)

prospective time 108 (1)

prospectively 124 (7)

prospector 459 (9), 461 (3), 484 (2)

prospectus 87 (1), 510 (1), 592 (1), 623 (2)

prosper 36 (4), 285 (3), 376 (6), 615 (5), 644 (11), 654 (8), 678 (11), 727 (6), 730 (6), 730 (8), 771 (9), 771 (10), 800 (7), 828 (4), 866 (11), 944 (4)

prosperity 124 (2), 154 (2), 159 (1), 171 (1), 285 (1), 301 (9), 615 (1), 656 (3), 727 (1), 730 (1), 793 (1), 800 (1), 824 (2), 828 (1)

prosperous 511 (7), 644 (8), 727 (4), 730 (4), 771 (4), 800 (3), 824 (5), 852 (5)

prosperous person 727 (3), 730 (3), 800 (2)

prosperously 730 (9)

prosthesis 150 (2), 658 (11)

prostitute 655 (8), 675 (2), 951 (11), 952 (4)

prostituted 951 (7)

prostitution 675 (1), 951 (5)

prostrate 161 (9), 210 (2), 216 (5), 216 (7), 311 (3), 311 (6), 651 (21), 684 (2), 684 (6), 834 (11), 920 (3)

prostrated 161 (7)

prostration 161 (2), 163 (1), 165 (1), 216 (2), 311 (1), 651 (2), 684 (1), 721 (1), 825 (2), 879 (1), 979 (1)

prosy 570 (4), 572 (2)

protagonist 594 (9)

protean 82 (2), 152 (3)

protect 421 (4), 660 (8), 666 (5), 703 (6), 713 (9), 880 (8)

protected 666 (4), 747 (5)

protecting 660 (6)

protection 169 (1), 299 (1), 421 (1), 457 (2), 632 (2), 652 (2), 660 (2), 662 (3), 666 (1), 689 (1), 703 (1), 713 (1), 747 (3), 767 (1), 791 (2)

protection money 962 (1)

protection racket 788 (4)

protectionism 747 (2)

protectionist 747 (4)

protective 660 (6), 666 (3), 713 (7)

protective clothing 662 (2)

protector 89 (2), 264 (3), 270 (3), 660 (3), 664 (2), 690 (3), 703 (6), 707 (4), 713 (6), 722 (4), 722 (7), 741 (1), 749 (1), 903 (1)

protectorate 733 (6)

protectorship 733 (5)

protectress 660 (3)

protege 742 (4), 880 (3)

protein 301 (10), 358 (1)

protest 489 (1), 489 (5), 532 (1), 532 (5), 533 (1), 598 (1), 598 (4), 664 (1), 678 (11), 704 (4), 715 (1), 715 (3), 738 (10), 760 (1), 762 (1), 769 (1), 829 (5), 924 (1), 924 (9)

protest against 762 (3)

protestant 489 (2), 976 (5), 976 (11), 978 (4), 978 (6)

protestantism 489 (1), 976 (3)

protester 489 (2), 738 (5)

protesting 489 (3), 533 (2), 598 (3), 664 (3), 715 (2), 762 (2), 829 (3), 924 (6)

proto- 125 (6), 127 (5)

protocol 610 (2), 848 (2), 875 (2)

proton 196 (2), 319 (4)

protoplasm 23 (1), 358 (1), 360 (1)

protoplasmic 358 (3), 360 (2)

prototypal 21 (3), 23 (4)

prototype 21 (1), 23 (1), 81 (1), 83 (2), 243 (1), 462 (1), 465 (5), 623 (1)

protozoan 196 (5)

protozoon 365 (2)

protract 113 (8), 136 (7), 146 (4), 203 (8)

protracted 113 (5), 203 (5), 570 (4)

protraction 36 (1), 113 (3), 136 (2), 146 (1), 203 (2)

protractor 247 (3), 465 (5)

protrude 254 (5)

protruding 253 (7), 254 (4)

protrusion 253 (1)

protuberance 237 (2), 247 (1), 253 (1), 254 (3)

protuberant 254 (4)

proud 481 (7), 711 (2), 871 (3), 873 (4), 878 (4), 922 (3)

proud, be 267 (14), 871 (5), 877 (5), 878 (6), 922 (5), 980 (6)

proud-hearted 871 (3)

proud of 871 (4)

proud person 871 (2)

provactiveness 709 (2)

prove 154 (6), 461 (7), 478 (4), 494 (7), 927 (5)

prove a fiasco 728 (8)

prove acceptable 635 (6)

prove expensive 811 (4)

prove guilty 961 (3)

prove helpful 640 (4)

prove innocent 960 (3)

prove one's case 475 (11)

prove one's point 478 (4)

prove to be 154 (6)

proved 540 (2)

proved, be 478 (5), 522 (9)

provenance 68 (4)

provender 301 (8), 366 (6), 370 (1), 633 (1)

proverb 496 (1)

proverbial 490 (7), 496 (3)

proverbially 496 (4)

provide 54 (7), 301 (39), 629 (2), 632 (5), 633 (5), 635 (6), 666 (5), 669 (11), 759 (3), 781 (7), 793 (4), 882 (10)

provide a living 360 (6)

provide against 510 (3)

provide for 360 (6), 635 (6)

provide the answer 460 (5)

provide with arms 713 (9)

provided 468 (4), 633 (4)

provided that 8 (6)

providence 510 (1), 965 (1)

provident 457 (4), 510 (2)

providential 137 (5), 730 (5), 965 (5)

provider 633 (2), 669 (5)

providing 633 (4)

province 77 (1), 184 (3), 622 (4), 733 (6)

provinces 184 (3)

provincial 184 (5), 191 (1), 192 (19), 481 (7), 560 (5), 847 (5), 869 (6), 869 (8)

provincialism 481 (4)

provinciality 847 (2)

proving 466 (5), 478 (2)

proving ground 461 (4)

provision 74 (7), 193 (1), 301 (5), 301 (7), 510 (1), 629 (1), 632 (1), 633 (1),

633 (5), 656 (1), 666 (1), 669 (2), 703 (2), 766 (1), 797 (2), 808 (1)

provision for 701 (1)

provisional 8 (3), 35 (4), 114 (4), 143 (4), 150 (4), 461 (6), 468 (2), 474 (4), 647 (3), 766 (2)

provisionally 8 (6), 112 (1), 114 (7), 766 (5)

provisioner 669 (5)

provisioning 633 (4), 635 (5), 669 (2), 669 (7)

provisions 301 (7), 633 (1)

proviso 468 (1), 614 (1), 766 (1)

provisory 766 (2)

provocation 532 (1), 612 (2), 821 (1), 827 (2), 891 (1)

provocative 532 (4), 612 (6), 711 (2), 821 (4), 878 (5), 951 (6)

provoke 156 (9), 612 (9), 709 (8), 827 (9), 878 (6)

provoked 891 (4)

provoking 827 (5)

provost 741 (6)

prow 237 (3), 254 (3)

prowess 676 (2), 694 (1), 855 (2), 866 (2)

prowl 267 (13), 525 (9)

prowling 525 (5)

proximal 200 (4)

proximate 200 (4)

proximity 200 (1)

proxy 150 (2), 686 (1), 751 (1), 754 (1), 755 (1)

prude 850 (3), 924 (5), 950 (4)

prudence 449 (1), 457 (1), 498 (2), 510 (1), 814 (1), 858 (1), 933 (2)

prudent 449 (5), 457 (4), 510 (2), 642 (2), 814 (2), 856 (3), 858 (2)

prudent, be 498 (6)

prudery 483 (1), 850 (2), 862 (1), 874 (1), 950 (2)

prudish 735 (4), 850 (4), 862 (3), 950 (6)

prudishness 874 (1), 950 (2)

prune 39 (3), 46 (11), 198 (7), 204 (5), 304 (4), 370 (9)

pruning 37 (2)

prurience 859 (4), 951 (1)

prurient 453 (3), 951 (6)

prussic acid 659 (3)

pry 438 (9), 453 (4), 459 (13)

prying 438 (4), 453 (3), 459 (11)

P.S. 40 (1)

psalm 412 (5), 981 (5)

psalm-book 988 (6)

psalm-singer 981 (8)

psalm-singing 981 (5), 981 (7), 981 (9)

psalmody 412 (5)

psalter 975 (2), 981 (5)

psephologist 605 (2)

psephology 605 (2)

pseud 545 (3)

pseudo 18 (6), 541 (3), 542 (7)

pseudonym 4 (2), 561 (2), 562 (1)

pseudonymous 562 (3)

psittacosis 651 (17)

psyche 80 (4), 320 (2), 447 (1), 447 (2)

psychedelic 949 (12)

psychiatric hospital 503 (6)

psychiatrist 447 (4), 503 (1), 656 (5), 658 (14)

psychiatry 447 (3), 503 (1)

psychic 320 (3), 447 (6), 476 (2), 984 (5), 984 (7)

psychic science 984 (2)

psychical 320 (3), 970 (7), 984 (7)

psychics 374 (2), 449 (1), 476 (1), 505 (2), 984 (2)

psycho 504 (1)

psychoanalysis 447 (3)

psychoanalyst 447 (4), 503 (1), 658 (14)

psychokinesis 984 (2)

psychological 447 (6), 688 (3)

psychological warfare 718 (6)

psychologist 447 (4)

psychology 447 (3), 658 (12), 817 (1)

psychopath 362 (6), 504 (1)

psychopathic 503 (7)

psychopathy 82 (1), 447 (1), 447 (2), 503 (2), 651 (1), 651 (16)

psychosis 503 (2)

psychosomatic 447 (6), 651 (22)

psychotherapist 447 (4)

psychotherapy 447 (3), 503 (1), 658 (12)

psychotic 503 (7), 504 (1)

pterodactyl 365 (2)

pub 76 (1), 192 (12)

pub-crawling 949 (11)

puberty 130 (1), 167 (1), 669 (4)

pubescent 130 (4), 259 (6)

public 371 (4), 371 (7), 490 (7), 522 (4), 522 (5), 528 (7), 528 (8), 875 (5), 875 (6)

public address system 400 (2)

public attorney 958 (2)

public convenience 649 (3)

public enemy 881 (2)

public enquiry 459 (1)

public entertainer 594 (10)

public eye 528 (2)

public figure 866 (6)

public footpath 624 (5)

public good 640 (1)

public health inspector 652 (3)

public house 192 (12)

public knowledge 490 (1)

public life 622 (2)

public opinion 488 (2)

public ownership 775 (1)

public property 775 (1)

public prosecutor 928 (3), 955 (2)

public purse 799 (1)

public record 548 (1)

public relations 528 (2)

public relations officer 520 (4), 528 (6)

public sale 793 (1)

public school 539 (2)

public sector 791 (2)

public servant 741 (6), 742 (1)

public service 622 (2), 751 (1)

public speaker 579 (5)

public speaking 579 (3)

public spirit 901 (3)

public-spirited 901 (7)

public squalor 801 (1)

public transport 274 (1)

public worship 981 (7)

publican 633 (3)

publication 511 (1), 522 (1), 526 (1), 528 (1), 531 (4), 547 (8), 589 (1), 875 (1)

publicist 522 (3), 528 (6), 591 (3)

publicity 79 (1), 482 (1), 522 (1), 524 (1), 528 (2), 529 (1), 531 (3), 534 (1), 539 (5), 588 (1), 875 (1)

publicity agent 528 (6)

publicize 522 (7), 524 (10), 526 (5), 528 (11)

publicized 522 (6)

publicizer 522 (3), 524 (4), 528 (6), 529 (5), 537 (3), 589 (7), 923 (4)

publicizing 528 (2)

publicly 32 (19), 522 (10), 528 (13)

publish 455 (7), 522 (7), 524 (10), 526 (5), 528 (9), 529 (8), 587 (7)

published 522 (6), 528 (7), 587 (6)

published, be 490 (9), 528 (12)

publisher 528 (6), 589 (6)

publishing 528 (1), 532 (3)

puce 436 (2)

puck 287 (2), 970 (2)

pucker 198 (6), 261 (1), 261 (3)

Puckish 970 (6)

pudding 301 (17)

pudding basin 194 (16)

puddle 212 (1), 318 (6), 346 (1)

puddled 423 (2)
pudgy 195 (8)
puerile 499 (4), 639 (6)
puerility 499 (2)
puerperal 167 (5)
puff 300 (9), 301 (23), 352 (3), 352 (10), 352 (11), 388 (7), 528 (3), 528 (11), 684 (5), 923 (9)
puff away 287 (7)
puff up 197 (5), 310 (4), 873 (6)
puffed-up 482 (3), 871 (4)
puffed-up chest 873 (1)
puffiness 197 (2)
puffing 352 (9), 684 (3)
puffy 195 (8), 197 (3)
pugilism 716 (4), 722 (2), 837 (6)
pugilist 162 (4), 716 (8), 722 (2)
pugilistic 716 (9)
pugnacious 709 (6), 712 (6), 716 (9), 718 (9)
pugnacity 709 (2), 712 (1), 892 (1)
puissant 160 (8), 162 (6)
pule 408 (3), 836 (6)
pull 34 (2), 176 (8), 178 (1), 265 (5), 269 (11), 282 (6), 287 (1), 287 (7), 288 (1), 288 (3), 291 (1), 291 (4), 304 (1), 304 (4), 388 (7), 587 (2), 612 (8), 682 (7)
pull back 288 (3), 747 (7)
pull down 165 (7), 311 (6)
pull-in 192 (13), 295 (4)
pull it off 727 (6)
pull its weight 727 (7)
pull one's leg 542 (9), 839 (5), 851 (5)
pull oneself together 831 (4)
pull oneself up 310 (5)
pull out 39 (3), 188 (4), 197 (5), 203 (8), 271 (7), 288 (3), 296 (5), 296 (6), 300 (6), 304 (4)
pull strings 178 (3), 623 (9), 628 (4)
pull the strings 689 (4)
pull the trigger 287 (8)

pull through 656 (8)
pull tight 45 (13)
pull to pieces 165 (7), 475 (11), 926 (6)
pull together 24 (9), 181 (3), 706 (4)
pull towards 288 (3), 291 (4)
pull-up 145 (5), 145 (6), 266 (8), 295 (4), 304 (4), 310 (4)
pulled muscle 651 (15)
pullet 365 (6)
pulley 630 (1)
pulling out 296 (1)
pulling together 198 (1)
pulling towards 291 (1)
pullover 228 (11)
pullulate 104 (6), 171 (6)
pulp 165 (7), 244 (3), 327 (4), 354 (6), 356 (1)
pulped 165 (5), 356 (2)
pulpiness 327 (1), 335 (1), 354 (1), 356 (1)
pulping 356 (1)
pulpit 528 (2), 539 (5), 990 (4)
pulpy 327 (2), 354 (4), 356 (2)
pulsar 321 (4)
pulsate 141 (6), 317 (4)
pulsating 141 (4)
pulsation 160 (5), 317 (1)
pulsatory 317 (3)
pulse 141 (1), 141 (6), 160 (5), 317 (1), 317 (4), 318 (2)
pulses 301 (20)
pulverization 165 (1), 332 (1)
pulverize 46 (12), 165 (7), 176 (8), 198 (7), 244 (3), 279 (9), 301 (36), 327 (4), 332 (5), 333 (3), 354 (6), 655 (9), 655 (10)
pulverizer 332 (3)
pumice stone 333 (1)
pummel 279 (9), 716 (11)
pump 304 (4), 341 (3), 352 (5), 459 (14)
pump out 300 (8), 342 (6), 350 (11), 352 (12)
pump room 837 (5)

pump rooms 192 (14)
pump up 197 (5), 310 (4), 352 (12)
pumping 304 (1)
pumping up 352 (5)
pumpkin 301 (20)
pumps 228 (27)
pun 18 (2), 518 (1), 518 (3), 559 (1), 839 (2), 839 (5)
punch 23 (3), 174 (1), 263 (12), 273 (6), 279 (2), 279 (4), 279 (9), 301 (28), 547 (19), 555 (2), 571 (1), 712 (4)
punch bowl 194 (16)
punch-drunk 375 (3)
punch holes in 263 (18)
punch in 255 (8)
punch line 839 (2)
punch out 243 (5)
punched cards 86 (5)
puncher 279 (4)
punctilio 875 (2)
punctilious 455 (2), 494 (6), 768 (2), 848 (6), 862 (3), 875 (6)
punctual 116 (3), 123 (3), 135 (4), 137 (4), 141 (4), 494 (6)
punctuality 116 (1), 135 (2), 141 (1), 678 (1)
punctually 116 (4), 135 (6)
punctuate 72 (4), 547 (19), 564 (4)
punctuation 547 (14), 564 (1)
punctuation mark 547 (14)
puncture 37 (4), 198 (7), 263 (2), 263 (18), 311 (4), 311 (7), 479 (3), 655 (4), 702 (3), 926 (6)
pundit 500 (1), 591 (3), 696 (2), 958 (4)
pungency 174 (3), 388 (1), 393 (1), 571 (1)
pungent 174 (6), 386 (2), 388 (3), 390 (2), 393 (2), 394 (2), 397 (2), 571 (2), 818 (6), 885 (5)
pungent, be 388 (5)
puniness 163 (1)

punish 57 (5), 279 (9), 300 (6), 714 (3), 735 (7), 809 (7), 867 (11), 883 (9), 924 (11), 954 (9), 963 (8)

punishable 963 (7)

punished, be 714 (4), 769 (3), 867 (9), 941 (5), 941 (6), 963 (13)

punisher 168 (1), 910 (3), 963 (5)

punishing 682 (5), 684 (4), 827 (3)

punishment 480 (1), 714 (1), 752 (2), 910 (2), 924 (4), 961 (1), 963 (1)

punitive 735 (4), 757 (2), 963 (6)

punitive tax 809 (3)

punk 84 (3), 132 (2), 412 (1), 847 (3), 904 (2)

punnet 194 (6)

punning 839 (1)

punt 269 (11), 275 (8), 279 (7), 618 (8)

punt pole 269 (5)

punter 618 (4)

puny 33 (6), 163 (4), 196 (8), 639 (5)

pup 132 (3), 167 (6), 365 (10), 878 (3)

pupa 132 (3), 365 (16)

pupil 225 (2), 438 (2), 538 (1)

puppet 196 (4), 551 (2), 628 (2), 707 (1)

puppet show 837 (15)

puppy 132 (3), 365 (10), 878 (3)

puppy fat 130 (1)

puppy love 887 (1)

purblind 440 (3)

purblindness 440 (1)

purchasable 792 (3), 930 (6)

purchase 178 (1), 218 (11), 668 (1), 668 (3), 771 (1), 771 (7), 785 (2), 791 (2), 792 (1), 792 (5), 806 (4)

purchase, a 792 (1)

purchase price 809 (2)

purchase tax 809 (3)

purchased 792 (3)

purchaser 610 (4), 707 (4), 776 (2), 782 (2), 792 (2)

purchasing 792 (4)

purdah 373 (2), 883 (2)

pure 32 (14), 44 (5), 52 (4), 427 (4), 494 (5), 573 (2), 646 (3), 648 (7), 652 (4), 846 (3), 895 (4), 929 (3), 931 (2), 933 (3), 935 (3), 942 (3), 950 (5)

pure and simple 44 (5)

pure heart 699 (2)

pure in heart 979 (6)

pure mathematics 86 (3)

pure motives 935 (1)

pure soul 935 (2)

pure white 427 (4)

purebred 44 (5), 273 (5), 369 (7)

puree 356 (1)

pureed 356 (2)

purgation 941 (3)

purgative 263 (11), 300 (2), 302 (5), 648 (4), 648 (8), 658 (5)

purgatorial 941 (4)

purgatory 825 (1), 941 (3), 972 (1)

purge 44 (7), 362 (4), 362 (11), 648 (10), 963 (3), 963 (12)

purging 648 (2), 658 (17)

purification 44 (2), 395 (1), 648 (2), 654 (2)

purifier 648 (4)

purify 44 (7), 57 (5), 172 (6), 300 (8), 395 (3), 648 (10), 652 (6), 654 (9), 979 (11), 988 (10)

purist 575 (2), 862 (2)

Puritan 834 (7), 924 (5), 945 (2), 950 (4), 950 (6), 978 (4), 978 (6), 979 (5)

puritanical 735 (4), 834 (7), 862 (3), 945 (3)

puritanism 950 (2)

puritans 978 (3)

purity 44 (1), 648 (1), 846 (1), 874 (1), 895 (1), 933 (1), 942 (1), 950 (1), 979 (2)

purlieus 187 (2), 199 (2), 230 (1)

purloin 788 (7), 788 (8)

purple 431 (3), 436 (1), 436 (2), 436 (3)

purple passage 579 (4)

purple-red 436 (2)

purpled 436 (2)

purpleness 436 (1)

purplish 436 (2)

purport 514 (1), 514 (5)

purporting 514 (3)

purpose 595 (0), 595 (2), 599 (3), 617 (1), 617 (5), 673 (1), 852 (2)

purposed 617 (4)

purposeful 599 (2), 617 (4), 623 (7)

purposeless 618 (6), 641 (4)

purposely 617 (7)

purposive 599 (2)

purr 401 (1), 401 (4), 409 (3), 824 (6)

purr with content 828 (4)

purse 194 (11), 198 (6), 261 (3), 799 (1)

purse-proud 871 (4)

purse-seine 222 (3)

purse-seiner 275 (4)

purse strings 797 (3)

purser 633 (2), 798 (1), 804 (2)

pursuance 619 (1)

pursuant to 619 (7)

pursue 89 (4), 238 (5), 284 (4), 455 (5), 459 (13), 459 (15), 617 (6), 619 (5), 676 (5), 588 (4), 735 (7), 859 (11), 887 (14), 889 (7), 926 (7)

pursue a hobby 622 (7)

pursue no further 69 (6)

pursue one's ends 619 (5)

pursue one's hobby 837 (21)

pursuer 619 (3)

pursuing 619 (4)

pursuit 284 (1), 289 (1), 459 (5), 484 (1), 617 (1), 619 (1), 622 (1)

purulence 651 (5), 651 (14)

purulent 651 (22)

purvey 633 (5)

purveyance 633 (1)
purveyor 633 (3)
purview 438 (5)
pus 302 (4), 335 (2), 354 (1), 649 (2), 651 (14)
push 174 (1), 174 (7), 265 (5), 279 (1), 279 (7), 285 (4), 287 (1), 287 (7), 300 (1), 532 (1), 547 (4), 612 (8), 678 (2), 678 (11), 712 (1), 712 (7), 712 (9), 793 (4)
push around 279 (7)
push aside 282 (6)
push away 292 (3)
push bike 274 (3)
push button 628 (2), 628 (3)
push-button war 718 (1)
push down 311 (4)
push forward 285 (3)
push in 255 (8), 297 (8)
push into 303 (4)
push off 269 (10), 279 (7), 296 (5), 296 (6)
push on 285 (3)
push one's luck 618 (8), 857 (4)
push to extremes 599 (3)
push up 791 (6)
pushcart 274 (4)
pushchair 274 (4)
pusher 287 (3)
pushing 678 (7)
pushing down 311 (1)
pushing power 160 (3)
pusillanimity 856 (1)
puss 365 (11)
pussy 365 (11)
pussycat 365 (11)
pussyfoot 525 (9), 620 (5)
pustule 651 (12)
put 45 (7), 187 (5)
put a brave face on it 823 (6)
put a case 512 (7)
put a curse on 983 (11)
put a match to 385 (6)
put a price on 809 (5)
put a question 459 (14)
put a stop to 69 (6), 145 (7)
put about 269 (10), 528 (9)
put across 485 (9)

put ahead 285 (4)
put aside 46 (9), 57 (5), 458 (3), 458 (6), 632 (5)
put at ease 826 (3)
put away 165 (6), 187 (7), 632 (5), 896 (5)
put back 187 (6)
put between 38 (3), 72 (4), 231 (9), 303 (4)
put by 187 (7), 632 (5)
put down 165 (6), 165 (8), 187 (5), 311 (5), 362 (10), 727 (9)
put down roots 187 (8)
put down to 158 (3)
put faith in 485 (7)
put forward 285 (4), 759 (3)
put heart into 855 (8)
put in 54 (7), 78 (6), 231 (10), 295 (4)
put in an appearance 189 (4)
put in check 727 (10)
put in commission 669 (11)
put in context 9 (8)
put in for 759 (4), 761 (5)
put in front 64 (4), 285 (4)
put in good humour 833 (8)
put in irons 747 (9)
put in jeopardy 661 (9)
put in lights 528 (11)
put in motion 265 (5)
put in order 62 (4)
put in perspective 9 (8)
put in possession of 777 (6), 780 (3)
put in quarantine 652 (6)
put in readiness 669 (11)
put in splints 658 (20)
put in touch 45 (10)
put in words 563 (3)
put in writing 586 (8)
put into 303 (4)
put into practice 673 (3), 676 (5)
put into rhyme 593 (10)
put into shape 62 (4)
put into words 577 (4)
put it over 524 (10)
put itself right 656 (11)

put nothing by 815 (4)
put off 113 (8), 136 (7), 292 (3), 601 (4), 613 (3), 620 (5), 677 (3), 679 (11), 702 (10), 726 (3), 861 (5)
put off one's stroke 456 (5), 456 (8)
put off the scent 282 (6)
put on 20 (5), 228 (32), 522 (8), 541 (4), 541 (6), 553 (8), 594 (16), 850 (4), 850 (5)
put on a front 875 (7)
put on a pedestal 982 (6)
put on airs 850 (5), 873 (5), 878 (6)
put on black 836 (5)
put on board 187 (7)
put on oath 764 (5)
put on sale 793 (4)
put on show 522 (8)
put on speed 277 (7)
put on the brake 145 (7)
put on top 310 (4)
put on trial 928 (9), 959 (7)
put on weight 36 (4), 197 (4), 322 (6)
put one in a bad light 867 (11)
put one in mind of 18 (7), 505 (9)
put one's back into 682 (6)
put one's back up 861 (5), 891 (8)
put one's case 475 (11), 532 (5)
put one's feet up 683 (3)
put one's foot in it 695 (9)
put one's mark 547 (20)
put oneself first 932 (4)
put oneself forward 875 (7)
put oneself last 931 (3)
put oneself out 682 (6), 884 (5)
put others first 872 (5)
put out 382 (6), 456 (5), 524 (10), 528 (9)
put out of action 161 (9)
put out of one's head 456 (8)
put out of one's mind 450 (4)

347

put out one's eyes 439 (4)
put over 485 (9)
put paid to 69 (6)
put pressure on 178 (3)
put right 524 (9), 654 (10), 656 (12), 658 (19), 913 (3)
put space between 290 (3)
put teeth into 160 (11)
put the boot in 279 (10)
put the clock back or forward 117 (7)
put the finishing touch 54 (6), 646 (5)
put through to 45 (10)
put to bed 679 (13)
put to death 362 (10), 963 (12)
put to death, be 361 (8)
put to flight 727 (10), 728 (5)
put to good use 673 (3)
put to rights 62 (5)
put to sea 269 (9), 269 (10)
put to shame 867 (11), 872 (7)
put to sleep 362 (10), 831 (3)
put to the sword 362 (10)
put to the test 461 (7)
put to the torture 963 (11)
put to the vote 605 (8)
put together 45 (5), 45 (9), 50 (4), 56 (5), 164 (7)
put two and two together 475 (10)
put under arrest 747 (8)
put up 187 (5), 187 (8), 310 (4), 605 (7), 608 (2), 608 (3)
put up a fight 716 (10)
put up at 192 (21)
put up for 703 (6)
put up for sale 793 (4)
put-up job 541 (2), 608 (1), 928 (2)
put up posters 528 (11)
put up prices 811 (5)
put up to 612 (9)
put up with 488 (7), 721 (4), 734 (5), 756 (5), 823 (6), 825 (7), 909 (4)
put upon 645 (7), 735 (8)
putative 485 (5), 512 (5)

putrefaction 51 (2), 397 (1)
putrefy 51 (5)
putrid 51 (3), 391 (2), 397 (2), 645 (4)
putridness 51 (2)
putsch 738 (2)
putt 287 (7)
putting aside 46 (2)
putting away 896 (1)
putting between 231 (4)
putting in 187 (1)
putting in order 60 (1)
putting off 136 (2)
putting on airs 873 (4)
putting on sale 793 (1)
putty 47 (9), 327 (1), 356 (1)
puzzle 61 (3), 456 (8), 474 (9), 515 (6), 517 (6), 530 (2), 700 (1), 700 (6), 727 (10), 827 (10), 864 (7)
puzzle out 520 (10)
puzzle over 449 (7), 517 (7)
puzzled 474 (6), 517 (5), 700 (5)
puzzlement 728 (2)
puzzling 61 (8), 159 (6), 459 (12), 474 (4), 496 (3), 508 (2), 517 (3), 517 (6), 864 (5)
pyjamas 228 (18)
pylon 160 (6), 209 (4)
pyramid 71 (2), 74 (7), 164 (3), 195 (3), 209 (4), 247 (4), 364 (5)
pyramidal 247 (6), 256 (9), 293 (2)
pyre 364 (1), 379 (2)
pyrexia 379 (1)
pyromania 381 (3)
pyromaniac 168 (1), 504 (1)
pyrotechnics 379 (2), 420 (7), 445 (2), 875 (3)
Pyrrhic victory 727 (2)
python 365 (13)

Q

QC 958 (1) ;
QED 475 (3), 478 (6)
quack 409 (1), 409 (3), 493 (2), 541 (3), 545 (3), 581 (5), 658 (14), 695 (4), 697 (1), 850 (3)
quackery 491 (3), 535 (1), 541 (2), 542 (1), 850 (2)
quad 76 (1), 96 (1), 185 (1), 192 (14)
quadrangle 96 (1), 185 (1)
quadrangular 247 (6)
quadrant 247 (3), 269 (4), 465 (5)
quadraphonic 398 (3)
quadratic 96 (2)
quadratic equations 86 (3)
quadratics 85 (1)
quadri 96 (2)
quadrilateral 96 (1), 96 (2), 239 (2), 247 (4), 247 (6)
quadrille 837 (14)
quadrillion 99 (5)
quadrisect 98 (2)
quadrisection 98 (1)
quadruped 96 (1), 365 (2)
quadruple 36 (5), 97 (2), 97 (3)
quadruplet 96 (1)
quadruplicate 97 (2), 97 (3)
quadruplication 97 (1)
quaff 301 (38), 949 (14)
quagmire 347 (1)
quail 365 (5), 854 (10), 854 (11), 856 (4)
quaint 841 (3), 844 (9), 849 (2)
quaintness 849 (1)
quake 176 (2), 818 (8), 854 (10)
Quaker 976 (5), 976 (11)
quaking 854 (2)
qualification 40 (1), 143 (1), 160 (2), 468 (1), 486 (2), 489 (1), 543 (2), 598 (1), 614 (1), 715 (1), 727

(1), 766 (1), 915 (1), 919 (1), 924 (1), 927 (1)

qualified 24 (7), 43 (6), 468 (2), 642 (2), 669 (7), 694 (6)

qualify 143 (6), 177 (6), 463 (3), 468 (3), 486 (7), 489 (5), 533 (3), 534 (8), 715 (3), 727 (6), 766 (3)

qualify oneself 669 (13), 694 (9)

qualifying 8 (3), 467 (2), 468 (2), 766 (2)

qualitative 5 (8)

qualities 817 (1), 933 (2)

quality 5 (3), 34 (1), 77 (2), 644 (1), 644 (4)

quality daily 528 (4)

quality of sound 398 (1)

qualm 486 (2)

qualmish 861 (2), 862 (3)

qualms 830 (1), 854 (2), 939 (1)

quandary 474 (2), 700 (3)

quango 692 (1), 754 (1)

quantify 26 (4), 80 (8), 465 (11)

quantitative 26 (3)

quantities 32 (2)

quantity 26 (1), 32 (1), 32 (2), 85 (1), 632 (1)

quantity, a 104 (1)

quantity surveyor 465 (7)

quantum 26 (2)

quantum mechanics 319 (5)

quarantine 46 (1), 46 (9), 652 (2), 658 (3), 660 (2), 747 (3), 747 (10), 883 (2)

quark 196 (2), 319 (4)

quarrel 25 (1), 25 (6), 61 (4), 489 (5), 584 (1), 709 (3), 709 (7), 716 (1), 716 (7), 716 (11), 829 (1), 881 (1), 881 (4), 891 (2), 891 (5), 959 (1), 978 (2)

quarreller 704 (2), 705 (1), 709 (5), 716 (8), 722 (1)

quarrelling 25 (4), 489 (3), 704 (3), 709 (6), 716 (9), 718 (8), 881 (3), 892 (3), 893 (2), 959 (5)

quarrelsome 709 (6), 716 (9)

quarrelsomeness 709 (2), 718 (3), 892 (1)

quarrier 255 (5)

quarry 156 (3), 164 (7), 255 (4), 304 (4), 617 (2), 619 (2), 632 (1), 687 (1), 790 (1)

quart 98 (1), 465 (3)

quarter 46 (10), 46 (11), 53 (1), 55 (1), 74 (3), 96 (1), 98 (1), 98 (2), 110 (1), 184 (3), 185 (1), 187 (5), 238 (3), 239 (1), 465 (3), 524 (4), 797 (4), 905 (3)

quarter day 108 (3)

quarter sessions 956 (2)

quarter upon 187 (5)

quartercentenary 97 (1)

quarterdeck 207 (1)

quartered 46 (4)

quarterfinal 716 (2)

quartering 98 (1), 547 (11)

quarterly 93 (3), 98 (1)

quartermaster 633 (2), 741 (8)

quarters 185 (1), 187 (2), 192 (2), 266 (3)

quartet 96 (1), 412 (6)

quarto 98 (1)

quasar 321 (4)

quash 165 (8), 752 (4), 960 (3)

quashed 165 (5), 752 (3)

quasi 18 (9), 512 (5), 562 (3)

quaternity 96 (1)

quatrain 96 (1), 593 (4)

quaver 318 (1), 403 (3), 410 (3), 580 (3), 854 (10)

quay 192 (10), 796 (2)

queasiness 651 (2), 861 (1)

queasy 651 (21), 861 (2)

queen 741 (3)

queen bee 365 (16)

queen cat 365 (11)

queen it 866 (12), 871 (5)

queenliness 868 (1)

queenly 733 (8), 868 (6)

Queen's counsel 958 (1)

Queen's English 557 (1)

Queen's Messenger 529 (6)

queer 84 (3), 84 (6), 84 (7), 503 (8), 651 (21), 849 (2), 914 (3)

queer fish 84 (3), 851 (3)

Queer Street 801 (1)

queerness 503 (5), 849 (1)

quell 37 (4), 165 (8), 177 (6), 266 (9), 727 (9), 745 (7)

quench 165 (8), 382 (6), 418 (7), 613 (3), 863 (3)

quenchless 859 (8)

querulous 829 (3), 836 (4), 892 (3)

querulousness 829 (1)

query 459 (3), 459 (13), 474 (1)

quest 267 (1), 459 (5), 619 (1), 671 (1), 672 (1)

questing 619 (4)

question 452 (1), 453 (1), 453 (4), 459 (3), 459 (14), 461 (2), 474 (1), 486 (7), 533 (3), 584 (6)

question mark 474 (1), 547 (14)

question paper 459 (3)

question time 459 (2)

questionable 459 (12), 474 (4), 486 (5), 867 (4), 930 (4)

questionable, be 459 (16)

questioner 415 (3), 453 (2), 459 (10)

questioning 453 (3), 459 (2)

questionnaire 87 (1), 459 (3)

queue 67 (2), 71 (3), 203 (3), 305 (2)

queue-jumping 64 (1), 283 (1)

queue up 71 (5), 507 (5)

quibble 475 (11), 477 (1), 477 (8), 614 (1)

quibbler 475 (6), 477 (3)

quibbling 475 (8), 477 (1), 477 (4)

quick 114 (5), 277 (5), 360 (2), 498 (4), 597 (4), 694 (4), 839 (4), 892 (3) quick as thought 116 (3), 277 (5)

quick, be 680 (5)

quick-change 152 (3)

quick-change artist 594 (10)

quick-footed 277 (5)

quick march 265 (2), 267 (4), 277 (3), 680 (5)

quick one 301 (26)

quick-tempered 892 (3)

quick thinking 498 (1)

quick-witted 498 (4)

quicken 277 (7), 360 (4), 821 (7)

quicken the pulse 821 (6)

quickening power 173 (1)

quickness 277 (1), 498 (1), 678 (1)

quicksand 347 (1)

quicksilver 152 (2), 174 (1)

quickstep 837 (14)

quid 388 (2)

quid pro quo 31 (2), 150 (3), 151 (1)

quiescence 153 (1), 175 (1), 266 (1), 295 (1), 399 (1), 677 (1), 679 (1), 683 (1), 820 (1)

quiescent 175 (2), 187 (4), 266 (4), 375 (3), 399 (2), 523 (2), 677 (2), 679 (7)

quiescent, be 136 (6), 175 (3), 177 (5), 266 (7), 523 (5)

quiet 33 (6), 177 (1), 177 (3), 177 (7), 258 (3), 266 (2), 266 (4), 266 (6), 266 (9), 376 (2), 399 (1), 399 (2), 399 (4), 399 (5), 425 (7), 429 (2), 613 (3), 683 (2), 717 (3), 721 (2), 732 (2), 823 (3), 826 (2), 874 (2), 883 (5), 883 (7)

quiet, be 399 (3)

quiet tone 401 (1)

quieten 266 (9), 399 (4)

quietly 717 (5), 874 (4)

quietness 266 (2)

quietude 177 (1), 266 (2), 361 (1), 823 (1), 826 (1), 828 (1), 883 (2)

quietus 69 (1), 362 (1), 728 (2)

quiff 259 (2)

quill 256 (3), 586 (4)

quilt 226 (8)

quin 99 (1)

quintessence 5 (2), 646 (1)

quintet 99 (1), 412 (6)

quintuplet 99 (1)

quip 839 (2), 839 (5), 921 (2)

quire 631 (3)

quirk 80 (1), 84 (1), 604 (2)

quisling 603 (3), 738 (4), 938 (2)

quit 46 (7), 296 (4), 621 (3), 918 (3)

quit of 772 (2)

quite 32 (17), 33 (9), 54 (8)

quite a few 32 (2), 104 (4)

quite so 865 (5)

quite something 864 (3)

quite the reverse/the contrary 14 (1)

quits 28 (2), 28 (7), 941 (1)

quits, be 714 (3)

quittance 941 (1)

quitter 620 (2), 721 (1), 753 (1), 856 (2)

quitting 856 (1)

quiver 194 (10), 317 (4), 318 (1), 318 (5), 818 (1), 818 (8), 821 (9), 854 (10)

quiver with rage 891 (7)

quivering 377 (4)

quixotic 513 (5), 931 (2)

quiz 438 (8), 453 (4), 459 (2), 459 (14), 837 (8)

quizzical 459 (11), 851 (4)

quizzing 453 (1), 459 (11)

quoit 250 (2), 287 (2)

quorum 26 (2), 605 (3), 635 (1), 692 (2)

quota 26 (2), 53 (1), 783 (2)

quotable 9 (6), 950 (5)

quotation 9 (4), 53 (1), 466 (1), 522 (2), 809 (1)

quotation marks 547 (14)

quote 83 (9), 106 (4)

quoted 106 (3)

quoted price 809 (1)

quotient 85 (2)

R

rabbi 973 (5), 986 (8)

rabbit 365 (3)

rabbit hole 263 (8)

rabbit on 570 (6), 581 (5)

rabbit punch 279 (2)

rabbit warren 171 (3)

rabbiting 619 (2)

rabble 74 (5), 869 (2)

rabble-rouser 612 (5), 738 (5), 821 (2)

Rabelaisian 951 (6)

rabid 176 (6), 503 (9), 822 (3)

rabies 651 (5), 651 (17)

race 11 (4), 77 (3), 169 (2), 267 (11), 277 (3), 306 (5), 350 (2), 371 (1), 680 (3), 716 (3), 716 (10), 837 (21)

race course 277 (3)

racecourse 618 (3), 716 (3), 724 (1)

racehorse 273 (5), 277 (4)

racer 274 (3), 277 (4), 716 (8)

races 716 (3)

racial 11 (6)

racialism 11 (4), 481 (3), 888 (1)

racialist 481 (4), 481 (8)

raciness 388 (1), 566 (1), 571 (1)

racing 267 (3), 277 (3), 619 (2), 716 (3), 837 (6)

racing car 274 (11)

racing driver 277 (4)

racism 481 (3), 888 (1)

racist 481 (4), 481 (8)

rack 194 (4), 217 (3), 218 (12), 355 (2), 648 (10), 735 (8), 827 (9), 963 (11)

rack and pinion 624 (7)

rack one's brains 449 (7)

rack rents 811 (1)

racket 61 (4), 318 (3), 400 (1), 403 (1), 411 (1), 542 (2), 623 (4), 930 (3)

racketeer 791 (5), 904 (3), 930 (8)

racketeering 930 (1)

racking 377 (3), 827 (3)

raconteur 590 (5), 839 (3)

racy 174 (5), 390 (2), 566 (2), 571 (2), 839 (4)

radar 187 (1), 269 (4), 484 (2), 531 (1), 547 (6)

radially 203 (9)

radiance 417 (1), 417 (3), 841 (1)

radiant 294 (2), 417 (8), 417 (10), 420 (8), 824 (5), 833 (3), 841 (3), 841 (4)

radiant heat 379 (1)

radiate 46 (7), 75 (3), 294 (3), 300 (9), 317 (4), 417 (12)

radiating 75 (2), 294 (2), 300 (4), 417 (10), 420 (8), 841 (4)

radiation 75 (1), 160 (6), 160 (7), 294 (1), 300 (1), 317 (1), 321 (4), 398 (1), 417 (4), 531 (3), 659 (3)

radiator 383 (2)

radical 54 (3), 85 (5), 149 (2), 149 (3), 156 (8), 654 (5), 654 (7), 708 (7)

radical change 149 (1)

radicalism 654 (4)

radically 32 (16)

radicals 708 (2)

radio 160 (6), 398 (1), 524 (10), 528 (2), 531 (3)

radio astronomer 321 (11)

radio astronomy 321 (11)

radio drama 594 (3)

radio ham 415 (3), 504 (3), 531 (1)

radio listener 415 (3)

radio mast 209 (4)

radio star 321 (4)

radio station 531 (3)

radio telephone 531 (1)

radio telescope 321 (11)

radio wave 317 (1), 417 (4)

radio waves 531 (3)

radioactive 417 (10), 645 (3), 653 (2), 661 (3)

radioactive, be 417 (12)

radioactivity 160 (7), 417 (4), 653 (1), 659 (3)

radiocarbon dating 117 (4)

radiograph 551 (4), 551 (9)

radiographer 551 (4), 658 (14)

radioisotope 417 (4)

radiology 417 (7)

radiophonic 398 (3)

radiotherapy 658 (12)

radius 183 (3), 203 (3), 205 (1), 249 (1)

raffia 47 (4), 208 (2)

raffish 847 (4)

raffle 159 (2), 618 (2), 618 (8), 837 (12)

raft 218 (4), 275 (9)

rafter 218 (9)

rafters 226 (2)

rag 528 (4), 542 (9), 827 (9), 837 (3), 839 (5), 851 (5)

rag-and-bone man 794 (3)

rag-picker 801 (2)

rag trade, the 228 (1)

raga 412 (4)

ragamuffin 61 (5), 869 (7)

ragbag 43 (4)

rage 176 (1), 176 (7), 352 (10), 821 (1), 822 (2), 822 (4), 891 (2), 891 (7)

rage against 924 (10)

ragged edge 260 (1)

raggedness 17 (1), 801 (1)

raging 165 (4), 176 (5), 891 (4)

raglan 228 (20)

rags 53 (5), 228 (2)

rags and bones 641 (3)

ragtime 412 (1)

raid 165 (2), 165 (9), 297 (1), 297 (7), 712 (1), 712 (7), 718 (6), 786 (1), 786 (9), 788 (2), 788 (9)

raider 168 (1), 297 (3), 712 (5), 722 (4), 722 (13), 786 (4), 789 (2)

raiding 718 (6), 788 (2), 788 (6)

raiding party 722 (7)

rail 218 (3), 272 (2), 273 (12), 579 (9), 899 (6)

rail at 899 (7), 924 (13)

rail in 232 (3)

railing 218 (3), 235 (2), 662 (3)

raillery 851 (1), 878 (2)

railroad 624 (7), 740 (3)

railroaded 680 (2)

rails 219 (1), 235 (2)

railway 274 (13), 624 (7)

railway lines 219 (1), 624 (7)

railway station 295 (2)

railway terminus 295 (2)

rain 176 (3), 309 (1), 309 (3), 339 (1), 340 (3), 341 (1), 341 (2), 341 (6), 350 (6), 350 (10), 635 (7)

rain and rain 350 (10)

rain cloud 355 (2)

rain forest 366 (2)

rain gauge 340 (3)

rain hard 350 (10)

rain in torrents 350 (10)

rain-making 350 (6)

rain of blows 279 (2)

rain water 339 (1)

rainbow 71 (2), 248 (2), 250 (4), 253 (6), 425 (1), 437 (1)

rainbow-coloured 437 (5)

raincoat 228 (20)

rainfall 341 (1), 350 (6)

rainless 342 (4)

rainproof 342 (4)

rains, the 350 (6)

rainy 176 (5), 341 (4), 350 (8)

rainy day 731 (1)

rainy season 350 (6)

raise 36 (5), 68 (9), 164 (7), 167 (7), 188 (4), 209 (13), 215 (4), 265 (5), 285 (1), 310 (4), 323 (5), 369 (9), 771 (3), 771 (7), 786 (8)

raise a cry 408 (3)

raise a laugh 839 (5), 849 (4)

raise a loan 785 (2)

raise a smile 837 (20)

raise a storm 176 (7)

raise a thirst 859 (13)

raise aloft 310 (4)

raise by degrees 27 (5)

raise from seed 167 (7)

raise objections **489** (5), **702** (10)

raise one's banner **718** (10)

raise one's expectations **852** (7)

raise one's glass **301** (38)

raise one's hat **229** (7), **884** (7)

raise one's hopes **852** (7)

raise one's voice **400** (4), **408** (4), **532** (7), **579** (8)

raise questions **486** (8)

raise spirits **983** (10)

raise steam **669** (11)

raise the alarm **455** (7), **547** (22), **664** (5), **665** (3), **854** (12)

raise the bid **791** (6)

raise the dust **678** (11)

raise the roof **400** (4), **923** (10)

raise the spirits **833** (8)

raise the subject **68** (9)

raise the voice **577** (4)

raise to the peerage **866** (14)

raise up **215** (4), **310** (4)

raised **254** (4), **369** (7)

raised voice **408** (1)

raised voices **709** (3)

raiser **310** (2)

raising **36** (1)

raising agent **310** (2), **323** (2)

raison d'être **156** (6)

rajah **741** (4), **868** (5)

rake **206** (2), **220** (1), **220** (6), **254** (2), **258** (4), **370** (6), **370** (9), **372** (1), **712** (11), **938** (1), **944** (2), **952** (1)

rake in **74** (11)

rake-off **42** (1), **771** (2), **807** (1), **809** (1)

rake out **382** (6)

rake over **459** (15)

rake through **459** (15)

rake together **771** (7)

raked **258** (3)

rakish **220** (3), **848** (5), **875** (5)

rakish angle **220** (1)

rakishly **220** (7)

rallentando **410** (4), **412** (8)

rally **50** (4), **71** (2), **74** (1), **74** (10), **74** (11), **146** (1), **162** (11), **287** (1), **612** (9), **654** (8), **656** (3), **656** (8), **703** (5), **716** (2), **718** (12), **851** (5), **855** (7), **855** (8), **878** (6)

rally round **706** (4)

rallying cry **528** (1), **547** (8), **612** (2), **665** (1)

rallying point **76** (1)

ram **165** (7), **279** (5), **279** (8), **287** (3), **332** (3), **365** (8), **630** (1), **712** (9), **712** (10), **723** (5)

ram down **54** (7), **279** (7), **324** (6)

ram in **54** (7)

ram into **303** (4)

Ramadan **946** (2)

ramble **10** (5), **267** (3), **267** (13), **282** (5), **503** (10), **570** (6), **837** (21)

ramble on **581** (5)

rambler **268** (1), **268** (2)

rambling **10** (4), **61** (7), **267** (2), **503** (9), **570** (4), **572** (2), **837** (6)

ramekin **194** (16)

ramification **53** (4), **170** (2), **245** (1), **294** (1)

ramify **183** (7), **294** (3)

rammer **264** (2), **279** (5)

ramp **215** (3), **220** (1), **220** (2), **308** (1), **312** (4), **542** (2), **822** (4), **891** (7)

rampage **61** (11), **176** (7), **318** (5), **400** (4), **678** (11), **709** (9), **822** (4), **891** (2), **891** (7), **924** (10)

rampaging **891** (4)

rampant **176** (6), **215** (2), **308** (3), **547** (16)

rampart **713** (1), **713** (3)

ramrod **264** (2), **279** (5)

ramshackle **163** (8), **655** (6)

ranch **369** (2), **369** (9), **370** (2), **370** (9), **777** (3)

rancher **369** (6)

rancid **51** (3), **391** (2), **397** (2)

rancorous **888** (4), **898** (4), **910** (4)

rancour **891** (1), **898** (1)

random **17** (2), **43** (6), **61** (7), **159** (5), **464** (2), **474** (4), **618** (6)

random order **61** (1)

random sample **159** (2), **461** (2)

randomness **10** (1), **72** (1), **159** (1)

randy **951** (8)

range **27** (1), **62** (4), **71** (2), **74** (7), **77** (1), **160** (2), **183** (3), **183** (7), **186** (1), **199** (1), **199** (5), **205** (1), **207** (1), **267** (12), **348** (1), **383** (1), **443** (1), **622** (4), **724** (1), **744** (3), **795** (1)

range finder **281** (1)

range of choice **605** (1)

range of colour **425** (1)

range of view **438** (5)

range oneself **60** (4), **605** (6)

range together **202** (4)

ranger **268** (2), **749** (1)

ranging **32** (5), **744** (5)

rani **741** (4)

rank **7** (1), **9** (2), **27** (1), **27** (4), **32** (13), **62** (4), **62** (6), **71** (2), **73** (1), **73** (2), **77** (1), **366** (9), **391** (2), **397** (2), **480** (6), **635** (4), **638** (1), **722** (8), **866** (2), **868** (1), **934** (6)

rank and file **869** (1), **869** (8)

rank correlation test **86** (4)

rank heresy **977** (1)

rank high **920** (5), **920** (7)

rank low **867** (8)

ranked **74** (9)

ranking **27** (1), **73** (1), **866** (9)

rankle **827** (8), **891** (8), **898** (8)

ranks, the **722** (5)

ransack **165** (9), **459** (15), **788** (9)

rave 482 (4), 497 (4), 503 (10), 515 (6)

rave about 824 (6)

ravel 63 (5)

raven 301 (35), 428 (2)

raven-haired 428 (4)

ravening 176 (6), 786 (5)

ravenous 859 (9)

ravenously 947 (5)

ravine 201 (2), 206 (1), 209 (2), 255 (3), 262 (1), 351 (1)

raving 503 (4), 503 (9), 515 (1), 515 (4), 818 (4), 821 (3)

raving beauty 841 (2)

raving lunatic 504 (1)

raving mad 503 (7)

ravish 176 (8), 826 (4), 951 (11)

ravishing 826 (2), 841 (4)

ravishment 821 (1)

raw 55 (3), 68 (6), 126 (5), 244 (2), 301 (34), 374 (3), 377 (3), 380 (5), 391 (2), 425 (6), 491 (4), 611 (3), 647 (3), 670 (5), 695 (4), 819 (3)

raw deal 731 (2)

raw feelings 819 (1)

raw material 156 (3), 244 (1), 319 (3), 629 (1), 631 (1), 670 (2)

raw recruit 493 (1)

raw sienna 430 (2)

raw, the 229 (2)

raw umber 430 (2)

raw wind 352 (1)

rawness 126 (1), 244 (1), 491 (1), 670 (1)

ray 417 (2)

ray of comfort 831 (1)

ray of hope 852 (1)

ray of sunshine 831 (1)

rayon 208 (2), 222 (4)

rays 294 (1)

raze 165 (7), 550 (3)

raze to the ground 165 (7)

razing 165 (1)

razor 256 (5), 843 (3)

razor-edged 256 (7)

razor-sharp 256 (7)

razor's edge 206 (1)

re 9 (10), 106 (8)

re-sell 793 (4)

reach 27 (1), 28 (9), 160 (2), 183 (3), 199 (1), 203 (1), 203 (7), 249 (1), 295 (4), 305 (5), 345 (1)

reach a new high 34 (10)

reach an end 54 (5)

reach its peak 725 (7)

reach maturity 54 (5)

reach one's goal 295 (4), 727 (6)

reach out for 786 (6)

reach safety 660 (7)

reach the depths 309 (3)

reach the ear 415 (7)

reach the top 308 (4)

reach the zenith 308 (4)

reach to 54 (7), 183 (7), 199 (5), 202 (3)

reaching 295 (1)

react 12 (3), 182 (3), 280 (3), 374 (5), 460 (5), 714 (3), 818 (7)

react against 861 (4)

reacting 12 (2), 818 (3)

reaction 148 (1), 157 (1), 182 (1), 280 (1), 374 (2), 460 (1), 714 (1), 762 (1), 818 (1)

reactionary 144 (1), 144 (2), 148 (2), 286 (3), 705 (1), 738 (4)

reactivation 656 (3)

reactive 182 (2), 280 (2)

read 455 (4), 520 (10), 536 (4), 536 (5), 558 (6), 579 (8), 688 (5)

read aloud 577 (3)

read easily 516 (4)

read into 521 (3)

read off 465 (12)

read one's hand 511 (9)

read out 577 (3)

read the future 511 (9)

read the stars 511 (9)

read through 438 (9)

readability 516 (1)

readable 516 (2)

reader· 537 (1), 589 (3), 589 (6)

readership 528 (2)

readily 116 (4), 597 (7)

readiness 137 (1), 179 (1), 455 (1), 457 (1), 498 (1), 510 (1), 575 (1), 597 (1), 640 (1), 669 (4), 678 (1), 725 (1), 739 (1)

reading 465 (1), 490 (2), 520 (1), 534 (4), 536 (2), 579 (2)

reading list 589 (4)

reading matter 87 (1), 524 (1), 557 (3), 586 (1), 589 (2), 590 (4)

reading off 465 (1)

ready 189 (2), 455 (2), 457 (4), 498 (4), 507 (2), 581 (4), 597 (4), 597 (6), 628 (3), 640 (2), 669 (7), 669 (11), 678 (7), 694 (4), 739 (3), 758 (2)

ready and willing 597 (4)

ready for 859 (9)

ready for anything 855 (4)

ready for, be 507 (4)

ready for bed 684 (2)

ready for more 685 (3)

ready for use 669 (7)

ready-formed 669 (9)

ready-made 164 (6), 669 (9)

ready money 797 (1), 797 (2)

ready reckoner 86 (6)

ready speech 579 (1)

ready to 124 (4), 179 (2)

ready to burst 822 (3)

ready to cry 836 (4)

ready to drop 684 (2)

ready to go 669 (7)

ready to hand 669 (7)

ready to use 669 (9)

ready-to-wear 228 (30), 669 (9)

ready wit 839 (1)

ready wits 498 (1)

reaffirm 532 (7)

reafforest 656 (6)

real 1 (5), 3 (3), 319 (6)

real ale 301 (28)

real-life 590 (6)

real-life story 590 (3)

real number 85 (1)

real risk 471 (1)

real self 80 (4)

real thing 1 (2), 21 (2), 887 (1)

real thing, the 13 (1), 494 (2)

real world 319 (2)

realism 1 (1), 20 (2), 449 (3), 494 (3), 540 (1), 551 (3), 553 (3), 557 (3), 590 (1)

realist 20 (3), 319 (1), 676 (3)

realistic 18 (5), 494 (4), 498 (5), 551 (6), 590 (6)

realities 1 (2)

reality 1 (2), 3 (1), 154 (1), 494 (1), 638 (3)

realization 1 (1), 319 (1), 445 (1), 484 (1), 488 (1), 490 (1), 551 (1), 725 (2), 818 (1)

realize 6 (4), 154 (7), 319 (7), 374 (5), 447 (7), 484 (4), 490 (8), 513 (7), 516 (5), 524 (12), 551 (8), 725 (6), 771 (7), 797 (12), 809 (6)

realized 490 (7)

realized, be 154 (6)

really 1 (8), 3 (4), 494 (8)

really mean 514 (5)

realm 184 (2), 622 (4), 733 (6)

realm of Pluto 972 (2)

realness 494 (2)

realpolitik 688 (2), 698 (1)

ream 197 (5), 263 (17), 631 (3)

reams 32 (2)

reanimate 656 (10)

reanimation 656 (3)

reap 370 (9), 771 (7), 786 (6)

reap the benefit 640 (5)

reap the fruits 962 (4)

reap the fruits of 727 (8)

reaper 74 (8), 370 (4)

reaping 74 (1), 370 (1)

reappear 106 (6)

reappearance 106 (2)

rear 36 (5), 65 (1), 67 (1), 69 (2), 69 (4), 164 (7), 167 (7), 199 (1), 215 (3), 215 (4), 238 (1), 238 (2), 238 (4), 284 (1), 312 (4), 318 (5), 369 (9), 534 (6), 722 (7)

rear-admiral 741 (7)

rear up 308 (4), 310 (4)

reared 369 (7)

rearguard 238 (1), 664 (2), 713 (6), 722 (7)

rearing 215 (2), 308 (3), 369 (1)

rearmost 238 (4)

rearrange 62 (4), 143 (6)

rearward 65 (5), 238 (6), 284 (5)

reason 156 (6), 447 (1), 447 (7), 449 (1), 449 (7), 463 (3), 471 (6), 475 (1), 475 (10), 478 (4), 480 (5), 502 (1), 512 (6), 520 (8)

reason badly 477 (7), 481 (9), 487 (3)

reason, be the 156 (9)

reason out 449 (7)

reason why 156 (6), 158 (1), 612 (1)

reasonable 177 (3), 469 (2), 471 (3), 475 (7), 485 (5), 494 (4), 498 (5), 502 (2), 812 (3), 913 (4)

reasonable, be 24 (9), 473 (7), 475 (9), 478 (5), 488 (6), 498 (6)

reasonableness 177 (1)

reasonably 475 (13), 502 (5)

reasoner 475 (6)

reasoning 9 (3), 24 (2), 65 (1), 86 (3), 447 (1), 447 (5), 449 (1), 475 (1), 475 (7), 478 (1), 480 (1)

reasons 466 (1), 471 (1), 475 (4), 475 (5), 612 (1)

reassemble 74 (10), 656 (12)

reassert 532 (7)

reassurance 852 (1)

reassure 855 (8)

rebate 42 (1), 810 (1), 810 (2)

rebel 84 (3), 489 (2), 718 (10), 738 (4), 738 (10), 918 (1), 918 (3), 978 (5)

rebel against God 980 (6)

rebellion 149 (1), 738 (2)

rebellious 709 (6), 711 (2), 734 (4), 738 (7), 738 (8), 878 (4), 918 (2), 978 (7)

rebirth 106 (2), 124 (2), 147 (1), 656 (3), 979 (2)

reborn 147 (5), 656 (6), 979 (8)

rebound 280 (1), 280 (3), 312 (4)

rebuff 292 (1), 292 (3), 607 (1), 607 (3), 613 (1), 702 (3), 702 (8), 704 (4), 715 (1), 715 (3), 727 (10), 728 (2), 731 (1), 760 (1), 760 (4), 883 (9), 885_(2), 922 (1)

rebuffed 760 (3)

rebuild 656 (9)

rebuilding 656 (1)

rebuke 872 (2), 924 (4), 924 (11), 963 (8)

rebuked 872 (4)

rebus 530 (2), 547 (11)

rebut 460 (5), 467 (4), 533 (3)

rebut the charge 927 (6), 928 (8)

rebuttal 460 (2), 467 (1), 479 (1), 533 (1), 927 (1)

rebutting 467 (2)

recalcitrance 182 (1), 598 (1), 715 (1), 760 (1)

recalcitrant 84 (5), 182 (2), 598 (3), 704 (3), 715 (2), 738 (7)

recall 272 (1), 505 (2), 505 (7), 505 (8), 752 (1), 752 (2), 752 (4), 752 (5)

recalled 752 (3)

recant 148 (3), 486 (6), 489 (5), 533 (3), 603 (7), 607 (3), 752 (4), 939 (4), 979 (10)

recantation 486 (1), 489 (1), 533 (1), 603 (2), 607 (1)

recanting 603 (4)

recapitulate 106 (4), 480 (5), 505 (9)

recapitulation 106 (1), 480 (2)

recapture 505 (8), 513 (7), 656 (13), 771 (7), 786 (7)

recast 143 (6), 623 (8)

recede 286 (4), 290 (3), 620 (5), 728 (9)

receding 286 (3), 290 (2)

receipt 629 (1), 767 (2), 771 (2), 777 (2), 782 (1), 782 (4), 804 (1), 807 (1)

receipted 807 (2)

receipts 36 (2), 782 (1), 807 (1)

receivable 299 (2)

receive 78 (5), 295 (6), 299 (3), 771 (7), 782 (4), 786 (6), 807 (3), 882 (10), 884 (7), 962 (4)

receive a legacy 771 (8)

receive a tribute 923 (11)

receive notice 664 (6)

receive one's due 915 (7), 962 (4)

receive respect 920 (7)

received 807 (2)

received, be 782 (5), 807 (3)

received meaning 514 (2)

receiver 415 (4), 782 (2), 786 (4), 798 (1)

receiving 782 (1), 782 (3)

receiving form 243 (3)

recency 126 (1)

recent 125 (8), 126 (5)

recent arrival 295 (1)

recent date 126 (1)

recent past 125 (1), 126 (1)

recent time 108 (1)

recently 126 (9)

recentness 126 (1)

receptacle 194 (1), 226 (1), 226 (5), 235 (1), 632 (2)

reception 50 (1), 78 (1), 160 (3), 295 (1), 297 (1), 299 (1), 301 (2), 398 (1), 415 (1), 584 (3), 782 (1), 876 (1), 882 (3), 923 (1)

reception class 538 (4)

reception room 194 (19)

receptionist 549 (1)

receptive 299 (2), 498 (4), 536 (3), 597 (4), 612 (7), 782 (3)

receptivity 299 (1)

recess 194 (4), 255 (2), 685 (1)

recesses 224 (1)

recession 37 (1), 265 (1), 286 (1), 290 (1), 296 (1), 655 (1), 679 (1), 731 (1), 801 (1)

recessional 981 (5), 988 (8)

recessive 148 (2)

recherche 84 (6), 605 (5)

recidivism 148 (1), 603 (1), 657 (1), 934 (1), 974 (1)

recidivist 603 (3), 603 (4), 655 (5), 904 (3), 980 (3)

recipe 301 (5), 623 (3), 658 (1), 693 (1)

recipient 194 (24), 588 (2), 776 (3), 782 (2), 782 (3)

reciprocal 9 (5), 12 (2), 85 (5), 151 (2), 714 (2)

reciprocally 12 (4)

reciprocate 9 (7), 12 (3), 151 (3), 706 (4), 710 (3), 714 (3)

reciprocating 12 (2), 151 (2)

reciprocation 12 (1), 28 (2), 151 (1), 714 (1)

reciprocity 12 (1), 28 (4), 31 (1), 151 (1), 706 (1)

recital 106 (1), 579 (2), 590 (1)

recitation 579 (2)

recitative 412 (5), 412 (7)

recite 106 (4), 579 (8), 590 (7)

recite a spell or an incantation 983 (10)

recite the creeds 976 (12)

reciter 593 (6)

reckless 458 (2), 499 (5), 711 (2), 815 (3), 857 (3), 857 (4)

reckless speed 277 (1)

recklessly 815 (5), 857 (5)

recklessness 458 (1), 499 (2), 822 (1), 857 (1), 860 (1)

reckon 86 (12), 507 (4)

reckon among 78 (6)

reckon on 617 (5)

reckon without 481 (9)

reckoning 86 (1), 465 (1), 507 (1), 808 (1), 808 (4), 809 (1), 963 (1)

reclaim 654 (9), 656 (9), 656 (13), 771 (7), 786 (7), 915 (5)

reclaimed 656 (6)

reclaimed land 344 (1)

reclamation 656 (1), 941 (2)

recline 216 (6), 311 (8), 683 (3)

recluse 883 (3), 945 (2), 986 (6)

recognition 438 (1), 488 (1), 490 (1), 884 (2), 907 (2), 915 (1), 923 (1), 962 (1)

recognizable 443 (2)

recognize 455 (6), 484 (4), 490 (8), 505 (7), 516 (5), 756 (5), 758 (3), 884 (7), 915 (8), 962 (3)

recognized 178 (2), 547 (17)

recoil 46 (7), 148 (1), 182 (1), 182 (3), 280 (1), 280 (3), 286 (2), 286 (4), 290 (1), 290 (3), 292 (1), 308 (4), 328 (3), 598 (4), 620 (1), 714 (1), 714 (3), 861 (4)

recoiling 182 (2), 280 (2), 286 (3)

recollect 505 (7), 505 (8)

recollected 505 (5)

recollecting 505 (6)

recollection 505 (2)

recommend 605 (7), 691 (4), 703 (6), 923 (2)

recommendation 691 (1)

recommendatory 691 (3)

recommended 615 (3)

recommender 691 (2)

recompense 31 (1), 714 (1), 962 (1), 962 (2)

reconcilable 24 (5)

reconcile 719 (4)

reconciled, be 828 (4), 909 (4)

reconcilement 24 (4)

reconciliation 710 (1), 719 (1), 828 (1), 880 (1), 909 (1)

recondite 517 (3), 525 (3)

reconditioned 656 (6)

reconditioning 656 (2)

reconnaissance 459 (1)

reconnoitre 267 (12), 438 (4), 438 (9), 459 (13)

reconsider 449 (8)

reconstitute 656 (9)

reconstruct 166 (3)

reconstruction 166 (1)

record 22 (1), 32 (6), 34 (1), 34 (4), 34 (6), 62 (1), 62 (6), 87 (1), 117 (4), 117 (7), 125 (3), 315 (3), 414 (10), 460 (1), 466 (1), 466 (2), 524 (1), 547 (18), 548 (1), 548 (7), 551 (8), 563 (1), 586 (1), 586 (3), 586 (8), 590 (1), 590 (2), 590 (7), 592 (1), 632 (3), 688 (1), 767 (2), 808 (2)

record-breaking 34 (6)

record for, a 34 (4)

record-holder 34 (3)

record-keeper 549 (1), 749 (1)

record low 35 (1)

record-making 548 (5)

record-player 398 (1), 414 (10)

record size 195 (7)

recordable 548 (5)

recorded 78 (3), 466 (5), 548 (6), 586 (7)

recorded sound 398 (1)

recorder 117 (5), 414 (6), 549 (1), 549 (3), 586 (5), 590 (5), 749 (1), 957 (1)

recording 412 (4), 414 (10), 531 (4), 548 (1), 548 (2), 548 (5)

recording instrument 531 (3), 549 (3)

records 548 (1)

recount 86 (1), 505 (9), 524 (10), 590 (7)

recoup 31 (6), 285 (3), 656 (13), 771 (7), 787 (3)

recourse 623 (3), 673 (1)

recover 31 (6), 148 (3), 182 (3), 654 (8), 656 (8), 656 (12), 656 (13), 668 (3), 771 (7), 773 (4), 786 (7), 787 (3)

recover one's mind 502 (3)

recoverable 656 (6)

recovered 148 (2), 656 (6), 685 (3)

recovery 148 (1), 272 (1), 654 (1), 656 (1), 656 (3), 656 (4), 771 (1), 786 (1), 787 (1)

recreant 938 (2)

recreate 837 (20)

recreation 685 (1), 837 (1)

recreational 837 (18)

recriminate 709 (7), 714 (3), 924 (12), 928 (8)

recrimination 709 (1), 714 (1), 927 (1), 928 (1)

recriminations 924 (3)

recriminatory 714 (2)

recrudescence 657 (1)

recruit 538 (2), 622 (6), 707 (1), 718 (10), 722 (4)

recruitment 36 (1), 718 (5)

recruits 703 (3)

rectangle 247 (4)

rectangular 247 (6)

rectification 31 (1), 654 (2), 656 (2)

rectified 656 (6)

rectify 24 (10), 62 (5), 143 (6), 623 (8), 646 (5), 654 (10), 656 (12), 913 (6)

rectilinear 71 (4), 249 (2)

rectitude 913 (1), 929 (1), 933 (1)

recto 237 (2), 241 (1)

rector 690 (1), 986 (2), 986 (3)

rectorship 985 (3)

rectory 986 (10)

rectum 224 (2)

recumbency 216 (2)

recumbent 210 (2), 216 (5), 220 (3)

recuperate 650 (4), 656 (8), 685 (4)

recuperation 656 (4), 658 (1), 658 (10), 685 (1), 787 (1)

recuperative 656 (7)

recur 106 (6), 139 (3), 141 (6), 146 (3)

recurrence 71 (1), 106 (2), 141 (1), 146 (1), 166 (1), 657 (1)

recurrent 71 (4), 106 (3), 108 (4), 139 (2), 141 (4), 146 (2)

recurrently 106 (7)

recurring 106 (3), 141 (4)

recurring decimal 85 (2)

recurved 248 (3)

recusancy 978 (2)

recusant 978 (5), 978 (7), 980 (4)

recyclable 51 (4)

recycle 106 (4), 656 (9), 673 (3), 814 (3)

recycled 148 (2)

recycling 656 (1)

red 149 (2), 149 (3), 301 (34), 379 (5), 425 (6), 431 (3), 670 (5), 708 (7), 841 (6)

red alert 665 (1)

red and yellow 432 (1)

red blood 335 (3)

red-blooded 162 (10), 855 (4)

red carpet 876 (1), 920 (2)

red-cheeked 431 (3)

red cheeks 431 (1)

red colour 431 (1)

red corpuscle 335 (3)

Red Cross 658 (14)

red dye 431 (2)

red ensign 547 (12)

red-eyed 836 (4)

red eyes 836 (1)

red flag 547 (5), 547 (12)

red-haired 431 (3)

red-handed 362 (9), 676 (4), 676 (6), 936 (3), 936 (5)

red herring 10 (2), 542 (2), 702 (5)

red-hot 176 (5), 379 (4), 431 (3)

red lead 431 (2)

red-letter day 638 (2), 876 (2)

red light 547 (5), 665 (1)

red light district 951 (5)

red meat 301 (16)

red ochre 431 (2)

red pigment 431 (2)

red roses 889 (3)

red tape 136 (2), 702 (2)

red wine 301 (29)

red with anger 891 (4)

redbrick University 539 (1)

redcoat 722 (4)

redden 425 (8), 431 (5), 818 (8), 874 (3), 891 (6)

reddened 431 (3)

reddening 431 (1)

reddish 431 (3)

reddish-brown 430 (3)

redeem 31 (4), 668 (3), 771 (7), 787 (3), 792 (5), 804 (4)

redeemable 668 (2)

redeemed 792 (3), 979 (8)

redeemer 903 (1)

redeeming 31 (3)

redemption 31 (1), 668 (1), 746 (1), 787 (1), 792 (1), 941 (2)

redhead 373 (3), 431 (1), 841 (2)

redirect 272 (8)

redness 431 (1)

redo 656 (9)

redolence 394 (1)

redolent 394 (2), 396 (3)

redouble 36 (5), 91 (3), 106 (4), 174 (8), 197 (5)

redoubling 36 (1), 139 (1)

redoubt 713 (2)

redoubtable 854 (8)

redound to 179 (3)

redress 31 (1), 658 (1), 913 (2), 913 (6)

redress the balance 28 (10)

redskin 431 (1)

reduce 37 (4), 46 (10), 51 (5), 86 (12), 105 (4), 147 (7), 163 (10), 198 (7), 204 (5), 206 (7), 592 (5)

reduce speed 278 (5)

reduce the pressure 325 (3)

reduce to 147 (7)

reduce to chaos 734 (5)

reduce to order 60 (3)

reduce to poverty 801 (6)

reduce to powder 332 (5)

reduce to the ranks 752 (5)

reduce weight 323 (5)

reduced 33 (6), 51 (3), 812 (3)

reduced circumstances 801 (1)

reduced payment 805 (1)

reducing 301 (3)

reduction 37 (2), 44 (2), 86 (2), 147 (1), 198 (1), 810 (1)

redundance 32 (1), 171 (1), 635 (2), 637 (1), 812 (1), 815 (1), 863 (1)

redundancy 637 (2)

redundancy pay 804 (2)

redundant 32 (4), 41 (4), 54 (4), 635 (4), 637 (3), 641 (4), 674 (2), 813 (3)

redundantly 637 (7)

reduplicate 20 (6), 91 (3)

reduplication 91 (1), 106 (1), 166 (1)

reecho 106 (5), 404 (3), 460 (5)

reed 366 (8)

reedy 407 (2)

reef 261 (3), 278 (6), 349 (1), 663 (1)

reefer 388 (2)

reek 336 (2), 338 (4), 341 (6), 394 (1), 397 (1), 397 (3)

reek of 394 (3)

reeking 338 (3), 341 (4), 394 (2), 397 (2)

reel 312 (1), 315 (3), 315 (5), 317 (2), 317 (4), 818 (8), 837 (14), 949 (13)

reel in 288 (3)

reel off 20 (6), 579 (8), 581 (5)

reeling 317 (3), 949 (7)

reentry 271 (3), 286 (2), 297 (1)

refectory 194 (19)

refer 519 (4), 547 (18)

refer to 9 (7), 9 (8), 158 (3), 514 (5), 524 (9)

referable 9 (5)

referee 9 (4), 466 (4), 480 (3), 480 (5), 691 (2), 720 (2), 957 (2)

reference 9 (1), 9 (4), 466 (1), 514 (2), 923 (1)

reference book 87 (3), 524 (6), 589 (4)

reference system 62 (2)

referenced 547 (17)

references 466 (3)

referendum 605 (2)

referent 9 (4)

referential 9 (5)

referral 9 (4), 23 (1)

referred to 158 (2)

refill 54 (2), 632 (5), 633 (1), 633 (6), 635 (6)

refine 15 (7), 325 (3), 374 (6), 575 (4), 648 (10), 654 (9), 862 (4)

refine upon 463 (3), 654 (9)

refined 425 (7), 575 (3), 648 (7), 841 (6), 846 (3), 950 (5)

refined gold 644 (3)

refined palate 301 (4)

refinement 463 (1), 575 (1), 654 (3), 841 (1), 846 (1), 862 (1)

refiner 648 (6)

refinery 687 (1)

refining 648 (2), 654 (2)

refit 656 (9)

reflate 197 (5)

reflation 797 (3)

reflect 18 (7), 20 (5), 417 (11), 417 (12), 449 (8), 505 (8), 551 (8)

reflect honour 866 (13)

reflect upon 867 (11)

reflected 551 (7)

reflecting 18 (4), 417 (8), 498 (5)

reflection 18 (3), 20 (1), 292 (1), 417 (5), 449 (2), 451 (1), 551 (2), 867 (2)

reflective 449 (5)

reflector 417 (5), 442 (5)

reflex 280 (1), 286 (2), 374 (2), 450 (1), 596 (5), 609 (1)

reform 143 (6), 147 (8), 603 (5), 654 (2), 654 (8), 654 (9), 656 (9), 897 (5), 897 (6), 913 (2), 929 (5), 939 (4), 979 (10)

reformation 654 (2), 656 (1)

Reformation, the 976 (3)

reformative 654 (7)

reformatory 748 (1)

reformed 34 (4), 654 (6), 913 (3), 939 (3), 976 (11)

reformed, be 939 (4)

reformed character 939 (2)

reformer 654 (5), 901 (4)

reforming 654 (7)

reformism 654 (4)

refract 417 (12)

refraction 282 (1), 417 (5)

refractive 417 (8)

refractory 602 (5), 604 (3), 700 (4), 704 (3), 738 (7), 893 (2)

refrain 106 (1), 141 (1), 145 (6), 412 (1), 412 (5), 593 (4), 620 (5), 736 (3), 942 (4)

refraining 677 (1)

refresh 162 (12), 174 (8), 382 (6), 654 (9), 656 (10), 685 (4), 703 (5), 826 (4), 831 (3), 837 (20)

refresh one's memory 505 (9)

refresh oneself 685 (5)

refreshed 376 (4), 656 (6), 685 (3)

refreshed, be 656 (8), 683 (3), 685 (5)

refresher 685 (1)

refresher course 534 (2), 536 (2)

refreshing 177 (4), 376 (3), 644 (8), 652 (4), 685 (2), 826 (2), 831 (2), 837 (18)

refreshment 145 (4), 162 (5), 301 (12), 376 (1), 656

(3), 683 (1), 685 (1), 703 (1), 826 (1), 831 (1), 837 (1)

refreshment room 192 (13)

refreshments 685 (1)

refrigerate 382 (6), 666 (5), 685 (4)

refrigeration 382 (1), 384 (1), 666 (1)

refrigerator 382 (1), 384 (1), 632 (2), 666 (2)

refuel 633 (6)

refuge 192 (17), 266 (3), 305 (3), 527 (1), 660 (2), 662 (1), 713 (4)

refugee 59 (2), 188 (1), 268 (2), 300 (1), 667 (3), 883 (4)

refugee camp 192 (1)

refund 31 (2), 42 (1), 787 (1), 787 (3)

refunding 787 (2)

refurbish 654 (9), 656 (9)

refurbished 126 (7)

refusal 292 (1), 489 (1), 533 (1), 598 (1), 607 (1), 620 (1), 702 (3), 715 (1), 757 (1), 760 (1), 924 (1)

refusal to pay 805 (1)

refuse 41 (2), 292 (3), 489 (5), 533 (3), 598 (4), 607 (3), 634 (1), 641 (3), 649 (2), 702 (8), 704 (4), 715 (3), 757 (4), 760 (4), 778 (5), 816 (6)

refuse a hearing 702 (10)

refuse bail 747 (10)

refuse collector 648 (6)

refuse comment 582 (3)

refuse credence 533 (3)

refuse lorry 274 (12)

refuse marriage 895 (5)

refuse one's food 946 (4)

refuse permission 757 (4), 760 (4)

refuse to act 677 (3)

refuse to answer 460 (5)

refuse to hear 416 (3)

refuse to recant 940 (4)

refused 760 (3), 778 (4)

refused bail 747 (6)

refusing 489 (3), 598 (3), 760 (2)

refutable 479 (2)

refutation 460 (2), 467 (1), 479 (1), 533 (1)

refute 479 (3), 533 (3)

regain 656 (13)

regal 733 (8), 821 (5), 866 (8), 868 (6)

regale 826 (4), 837 (20), 882 (10)

regalia 547 (9), 743 (1), 844 (7), 875 (2), 989 (2)

regard 9 (1), 9 (7), 438 (3), 438 (8), 455 (1), 866 (1), 866 (13), 880 (2), 887 (1), 920 (1), 920 (5), 923 (1)

regard as 150 (5), 485 (8)

regardful 457 (3)

regarding 9 (10)

regardless 10 (3), 10 (6), 456 (3), 857 (3)

regards 920 (2)

regatta 716 (3)

regency 733 (2), 733 (4), 733 (5), 751 (1)

regenerate 147 (5), 147 (7), 166 (3), 654 (9), 656 (10), 939 (3)

regeneration 147 (1), 166 (1), 654 (1), 656 (3)

regent 741 (4)

reggae 412 (1)

regicide 362 (2), 362 (7), 738 (2), 738 (4)

regime 8 (1), 301 (3), 689 (1), 733 (2)

regimen 301 (3), 658 (12), 689 (1)

regiment 16 (4), 74 (4), 722 (8), 740 (3)

regimental badge 547 (10)

regimental colours 547 (12)

regimentals 228 (5)

regimentation 16 (1), 740 (1)

regimented 739 (3)

regina 741 (3)

region 183 (1), 183 (3), 184 (1), 186 (1), 321 (2), 344 (1), 733 (6)

regional 184 (5)

register 27 (1), 62 (1); 62 (6), 87 (1), 87 (5), 410 (2), 455 (6), 516 (5), 547 (18), 548 (1), 548 (8), 808 (2), 808 (5)

register one's vote 605 (8)

registered 548 (6)

registrar 549 (1), 658 (14)

registration 548 (2)

registry 87 (1), 548 (2)

regress 148 (1), 148 (3), 221 (4), 278 (6), 286 (1), 286 (4), 290 (3), 295 (4), 655 (7), 657 (2)

regression 37 (1), 148 (1), 265 (1), 286 (1), 290 (1), 309 (1), 350 (2), 620 (1), 655 (1), 657 (1), 667 (1)

regressive 148 (2), 286 (3), 290 (2), 655 (5)

regret 148 (1), 505 (2), 509 (1), 509 (4), 825 (2), 825 (7), 829 (5), 830 (1), 830 (4), 834 (9), 836 (5), 859 (1), 859 (11), 905 (1), 924 (9), 939 (1), 939 (4)

regret it 963 (13)

regretful 825 (6), 830 (2), 939 (3)

regretfully 939 (5)

regretfulness 830 (1)

regrets 505 (2), 509 (1), 830 (1)

regrettable 830 (3)

regretted 505 (5), 830 (3), 836 (4)

regretting 825 (6), 829 (3), 830 (1), 830 (2), 834 (5), 834 (6), 859 (7), 939 (3)

regular 16 (2), 28 (7), 32 (13), 60 (2), 81 (3), 83 (6), 139 (2), 141 (4), 153 (4), 245 (2), 494 (6), 610 (4), 610 (5), 722 (4), 841 (5), 986 (5)

regular army 722 (6)

regular buying 792 (1)

regular features 245 (1), 841 (1)

regular motion 265 (1)

regular return 106 (2), 141 (2)

regularity 16 (1), 81 (2), 139 (1), 141 (1), 144 (1), 245 (1), 610 (1)

regularize 16 (4), 60 (3), 62 (5), 83 (8)

regularly 81 (4), 139 (4),ₗ 141 (7), 610 (9)

regulate 24 (10), 60 (3), 62 (5), 689 (4)

regulated 62 (3), 81 (3), 83 (6)

regulation 81 (1), 693 (1), 953 (2)

regulations 702 (2), 737 (1)

regulative 81 (3)

regurgitate 286 (4)

regurgitation 286 (1), 300 (3)

rehabilitate 656 (9), 787 (3), 927 (5)

rehabilitation 656 (1), 866 (5), 927 (1)

rehash 106 (1), 520 (9)

rehearsal 106 (1), 505 (2), 590 (1), 594 (2), 669 (1)

rehearse 106 (4), 590 (7), 594 (16), 669 (11), 669 (13)

reify 319 (7)

reign 108 (3), 733 (2), 733 (10)

reign of terror 734 (2), 854 (4)

reign supreme 733 (10)

reigning 178 (2), 733 (8)

reimburse 31 (4), 787 (3), 804 (4)

reimbursement 787 (1)

rein 177 (2), 748 (4)

rein in 278 (6), 747 (7)

reincarnated 319 (6)

reincarnation 106 (2), 124 (2), 143 (2), 166 (1), 319 (1)

reinfection 657 (1)

reinforce 36 (5), 38 (4), 162 (12), 197 (5), 218 (15), 656 (9), 703 (5), 713 (9)

reinforced 162 (6), 326 (4)

reinforced concrete 326 (1), 631 (2)

reinforcement 38 (1), 40 (2), 162 (5), 197 (1), 633 (1), 656 (1), 656 (2), 703 (1), 707 (1)

reinforcements 703 (3)

reins 47 (8)

reinstate 148 (3), 187 (6), 787 (3)

reinstatement 148 (1), 787 (1)

reinvigorate 162 (12), 685 (4)

reissue 22 (2), 106 (1), 106 (4), 589 (5)

reiterate 106 (4)

reiteration 106 (1), 532 (1), 571 (1)

reiterative 571 (2)

reject 35 (2), 41 (6), 57 (5), 292 (3), 300 (6), 509 (5), 533 (3), 598 (4), 605 (8), 607 (1), 607 (3), 636 (8), 641 (3), 704 (4), 760 (4), 769 (3), 861 (4), 867 (3), 921 (5), 922 (5), 924 (9)

rejected 35 (4), 41 (4), 57 (3), 509 (2), 607 (2), 888 (6), 922 (4), 924 (7)

rejection 35 (2), 57 (1), 292 (1), 300 (1), 489 (1), 533 (1), 598 (1), 607 (1), 620 (1), 757 (1), 760 (1), 769 (1)

rejects 41 (2), 812 (1)

rejoice 824 (6), 826 (3), 826 (4), 833 (7), 833 (8), 835 (6), 837 (23), 876 (4)

rejoice in 824 (6)

rejoicer 835 (3)

rejoicing 408 (1), 824 (1), 824 (4), 835 (1), 835 (4), 837 (19), 876 (1), 876 (3)

rejoin 74 (10), 295 (6), 460 (5)

rejoinder 151 (1), 460 (2), 479 (1), 533 (1), 714 (1), 878 (2), 928 (1)

rejuvenate 656 (10)

rejuvenated 126 (7)

rejuvenation 656 (3)

rekindle 821 (7)

relapse 148 (1), 148 (3), 286 (2), 486 (6), 603 (1),

603 (5), 655 (1), 655 (7), 657 (1), 657 (2), 934 (7)

relapsed 603 (4)

relate 9 (8), 45 (10), 158 (3), 505 (9), 590 (7)

related 9 (5), 11 (5), 200 (4)

related, be 9 (7), 11 (7), 58 (3), 78 (4), 89 (4), 157 (5)

relatedness 9 (1)

relater 590 (5)

relation 8 (1), 9 (1), 18 (1), 47 (1), 590 (1), 706 (2)

relational 9 (5)

relations 9 (1), 11 (2)

relationship 9 (1), 11 (1)

relative 8 (3), 9 (5), 11 (2), 12 (2), 27 (3), 78 (3), 86 (8), 158 (2)

relative density 324 (1)

relative quantity 27 (1)

relative to 9 (10)

relatively 9 (9), 33 (9), 462 (4)

relativeness 9 (2), 27 (1)

relativism 449 (3)

relativity 9 (2), 449 (3)

relax 37 (4), 46 (8), 266 (8), 677 (3), 683 (3), 734 (5), 736 (3), 746 (3), 823 (5), 831 (3), 882 (8)

relax one's grip 779 (4)

relaxation 49 (1), 177 (1), 681 (1), 683 (1), 734 (1), 837 (1)

relaxed 266 (5), 683 (2), 734 (3)

relaxing 683 (2)

relay 141 (1), 528 (9), 531 (4), 706 (1), 707 (1)

relay race 706 (1), 716 (3)

release 46 (8), 272 (1), 361 (2), 528 (9), 668 (1), 668 (3), 744 (10), 746 (1), 746 (3), 756 (1), 779 (1), 779 (4), 919 (3)

release on bail 767 (5)

released 594 (15), 744 (5), 746 (2), 779 (3)

relegate 57 (5), 188 (4)

relegation 300 (1)

relent 177 (5), 905 (6), 905 (7), 909 (4)

relenting 939 (3)

relentless 599 (2), 735 (4), 906 (2), 910 (4)

relevance 9 (3), 24 (3), 514 (1)

relevancy 24 (3)

relevant 9 (6), 24 (6), 475 (7), 478 (2)

relevant, be 9 (7)

relevant fact 466 (1)

reliability 473 (1), 768 (1), 802 (1)

reliable 153 (4), 466 (5), 471 (2), 473 (4), 485 (5), 494 (5), 540 (2), 599 (2), 660 (4), 768 (2), 929 (4)

reliance 485 (1), 852 (1)

relic 41 (1), 505 (3), 548 (4), 983 (3)

relics 125 (2), 363 (1)

relict 896 (2)

relief 14 (1), 150 (2), 177 (1), 188 (1), 243 (1), 254 (1), 445 (6), 554 (1), 656 (4), 668 (1), 685 (1), 703 (1), 746 (1), 831 (1), 852 (1), 897 (2), 905 (2)

relief map 551 (5)

relieve 37 (4), 65 (3), 177 (7), 658 (19), 668 (3), 685 (4), 701 (9), 703 (5), 823 (7), 826 (3), 828 (5), 831 (3), 833 (8)

relieve of 780 (3), 786 (9), 788 (7)

relieve oneself 302 (6)

relieved 376 (4), 667 (4), 746 (2)

relieved, be 828 (4), 831 (4), 833 (7), 852 (6)

relieving 685 (2), 831 (2)

religion 449 (3), 973 (1), 979 (1), 981 (7)

religionist 973 (7)

religiosity 979 (3)

religious 320 (3), 768 (2), 965 (5), 973 (8), 979 (6), 979 (9), 986 (5)

religious belief 485 (1)

religious cult 973 (1)

religious doctrine 973 (4)

religious faith 485 (1), 973 (3)

religious feeling 818 (1), 973 (1)

religious order 978 (3), 986 (5)

religious quest 973 (1)

religious song 981 (5)

religious teacher 973 (6)

religious truth 976 (1)

religiously 768 (5)

religiousness 979 (1)

relinquish 46 (7), 145 (6), 296 (4), 458 (5), 489 (5), 533 (3), 601 (4), 603 (5), 621 (3), 674 (4), 674 (5), 753 (3), 779 (4), 781 (7), 896 (5), 918 (3)

relinquished 190 (5), 621 (2), 779 (3)

relinquishment 621 (1), 753 (1), 779 (1), 916 (3)

relish 174 (1), 376 (6), 386 (1), 389 (1), 390 (1), 390 (3), 824 (3), 824 (6), 826 (1), 859 (3)

reload 633 (6)

reluctance 278 (1), 598 (1), 715 (1), 861 (1)

reluctant 598 (3), 613 (2), 620 (3), 715 (2)

reluctantly 598 (5), 924 (15)

rely 471 (6)

rely on 218 (16), 473 (7), 485 (7), 507 (4), 852 (6)

rely on intuition 476 (3)

rem 417 (4)

remade 656 (6)

remain 41 (5), 108 (7), 113 (6), 113 (7), 144 (3), 146 (3), 192 (21)

remain hopeful 852 (6)

remain the same 144 (3)

remainder 15 (1), 41 (1), 53 (1), 53 (5), 85 (4), 637 (2), 793 (4)

remaining 41 (4), 46 (5), 548 (6), 637 (4)

remains 41 (1)

remake 106 (1), 106 (4), 166 (3), 656 (9)

remaking 166 (1)

remand 136 (7), 747 (3), 747 (10)

remand home 748 (1)
remanded 928 (6)
remark 532 (1), 579 (1)
remark on 455 (6)
remarkable 32 (8), 84 (6),
638 (6), 866 (9)
remarkably 32 (19)
remedial 177 (4), 182 (2),
652 (4), 654 (7), 656 (7),
658 (17), 727 (4), 831 (2)
remedy 177 (2), 182 (3),
460 (1), 623 (3), 629 (1),
656 (4), 658 (1), 658 (19),
693 (1), 913 (6)
remember 106 (5), 449
(7), 455 (5), 505 (7), 516
(5), 548 (8), 866 (13), 876
(4)
remember nothing 506
(5)
remembered 106 (3), 490
(7), 505 (5), 638 (6)
remembered, be 106 (6),
505 (11), 866 (11)
remembering 125 (9), 505
(6), 548 (5), 876 (3)
remembrance 125 (1), 505
(2), 590 (2), 590 (3)
remind 505 (9), 524 (11)
remind oneself 505 (7)
reminder 87 (1), 115 (1),
505 (3), 524 (3), 547 (7),
548 (1), 548 (3), 691 (2),
729 (1), 866 (4)
reminding 505 (6)
reminisce 505 (7), 590 (7)
reminiscence 505 (2), 590
(2)
reminiscent 505 (6)
remiss 458 (2), 734 (3)
remission 42 (1), 142 (1),
145 (4), 909 (1)
remissness 458 (1), 598
(1)
remit 145 (8), 272 (8), 909
(4)
remittance 272 (1), 797
(2), 804 (1)
remitted 909 (3)
remitter 272 (4)
remnant 41 (1), 105 (1)
remnants 41 (2)
remodel 149 (4), 654 (10)

remodelling 656 (1)
remonstrance 613 (1), 762
(1), 924 (4)
remonstrate 613 (3), 762
(3), 924 (9), 924 (11)
remorse 825 (2), 830 (1),
905 (1), 936 (1), 939 (1)
remorseful 825 (6), 830
(2), 905 (4), 939 (3)
remorseless 906 (2), 910
(4)
remorselessness 906 (1)
remote 199 (3), 883 (7)
remote control 689 (2)
remoteness 199 (2), 444
(1)
remount 150 (2), 273 (7)
removal 39 (1), 46 (2), 188
(1), 199 (2), 304 (1), 786
(1), 788 (1)
removal man 272 (4)
remove 27 (1), 39 (3), 46
(8), 57 (5), 73 (1), 165 (6),
188 (4), 272 (7), 304 (4),
752 (5), 786 (6), 786 (9)
remove bodily 786 (9)
remove doubt 473 (9)
remove friction 258 (4)
remove the spell 148 (3)
remove the traces 550 (3)
removed 188 (2), 199 (4),
304 (3)
remover 786 (4)
remunerate 804 (4), 962
(3)
remuneration 771 (2), 804
(2), 807 (1), 962 (1)
remunerative 640 (3), 771
(5), 962 (2)
renaissance 656 (3)
renascent 166 (2), 656 (6)
rend 46 (12), 165 (7), 176
(8), 301 (36)
render 147 (7), 226 (16),
337 (4), 520 (9), 781 (7),
787 (3)
render callous 820 (7)
render few 105 (4), 163
(10), 300 (8)
render gaseous 338 (4)
render insensible 375 (6),
679 (13), 820 (7), 831 (3)
render liquid 337 (4)

render necessary 627 (6)
render simple 44 (6)
render soft 327 (4)
render suspect 486 (8)
rendered 520 (7)
rendering 226 (10), 520
(3), 631 (2)
rendezvous 74 (10), 76 (1),
295 (2), 295 (6), 882 (4)
rending 46 (3)
renegade 603 (3), 603 (4),
938 (2)
renege on 769 (3)
renew 166 (3), 654 (9), 656
(9)
renewable energy 160 (4)
renewal 106 (1), 126 (1),
656 (2), 656 (3), 685 (1)
renewed 126 (7), 166 (2),
600 (3), 656 (6)
renewing 166 (2)
renounce 533 (3), 603 (7),
621 (3), 753 (3)
renovate 166 (3), 654 (9),
656 (9)
renovated 126 (7)
renovation 126 (1), 166
(1), 654 (2), 656 (2)
renovator 656 (5)
renown 32 (1), 730 (1), 866
(3)
renowned 32 (4), 490 (7),
727 (4), 866 (10)
rent 46 (1), 46 (4), 201 (2),
780 (3), 785 (3), 792 (5),
809 (1)
rental 780 (1), 809 (1)
renter 191 (2)
rents 807 (1)
renunciation 603 (2), 621
(1), 753 (1), 779 (1), 883
(2), 942 (1)
renunciatory 533 (2)
reoccur 106 (6), 139 (3),
141 (6)
reopen 68 (8)
reopening 68 (3)
reorganization 62 (1)
reorganize 147 (8)
rep player 594 (9)
repair 45 (9), 654 (2), 654
(9), 654 (10), 656 (2), 656
(12), 666 (5)

repair to 267 (11)

repairer 656 (5)

repairs 656 (2)

reparation 31 (1), 787 (1), 941 (1), 962 (1)

reparations 31 (2)

repartee 151 (1), 460 (1), 479 (1), 584 (1), 839 (2)

repast 301 (12)

repatriate 187 (6), 300 (6)

repatriation 300 (1)

repay 31 (4), 615 (4), 771 (10), 787 (3), 804 (4), 907 (5), 910 (5), 962 (3)

repayable 803 (5)

repayment 31 (1), 787 (1), 804 (1), 941 (1), 963 (1)

repeal 752 (1), 752 (4)

repeat 20 (7), 24 (9), 83 (7), 91 (1), 91 (3), 106 (1), 106 (4), 166 (3), 460 (5), 505 (9), 528 (11), 531 (4), 532 (7), 570 (6), 610 (8)

repeat oneself 106 (5), 139 (3), 570 (6), 838 (5)

repeatable 950 (5)

repeated 16 (2), 18 (4), 20 (4), 71 (4), 106 (3), 108 (4), 139 (2), 141 (4), 146 (2), 514 (4), 570 (5), 600 (3), 838 (3)

repeated efforts 600 (1)

repeatedly 106 (7), 139 (4)

repeater 106 (1), 117 (3), 723 (10)

repel 292 (3), 300 (7), 391 (3), 713 (10), 715 (3), 727 (10), 760 (4), 827 (11), 861 (5), 883 (9), 888 (8)

repelled 861 (2)

repellent 292 (2), 715 (2), 827 (4), 842 (3), 861 (3), 888 (5)

repelling 715 (2)

repent 603 (5), 939 (4), 979 (10)

repentance 603 (1), 830 (1), 939 (1)

repentant 830 (2), 872 (4), 939 (3), 941 (4)

repercussion 157 (1), 182 (1), 280 (1)

repercussive 280 (2)

repertoire 87 (1), 632 (3)

repertory 87 (1), 594 (1), 632 (3)

repertory company 594 (9)

repetition 13 (1), 16 (1), 20 (2), 22 (1), 71 (1), 91 (1), 106 (1), 124 (2), 139 (1), 146 (1), 166 (1), 403 (1), 505 (2), 532 (1), 570 (1), 571 (1), 600 (1), 610 (3)

repetition, a 106 (1)

repetitional 106 (3)

repetitious 106 (3), 570 (5), 838 (3)

repetitive 13 (2), 16 (2), 71 (4), 106 (3), 108 (4), 570 (5), 838 (3)

repetitiveness 106 (2), 570 (1)

rephrase 106 (4), 520 (9), 563 (3)

repine 829 (5), 830 (4), 834 (9)

repining 829 (3), 830 (1), 830 (2)

replace 148 (3), 150 (5), 187 (6), 674 (5), 752 (5), 755 (3), 779 (4)

replacement 67 (3), 150 (1), 150 (2), 150 (3), 188 (1), 752 (2)

replant 366 (12), 656 (9)

replanting 656 (1)

replay 106 (1), 106 (4)

replenish 54 (7), 632 (5), 633 (6), 635 (6), 656 (9)

replenished 54 (4)

replenishment 54 (2), 633 (1), 656 (1)

replete 54 (4), 635 (5), 637 (3), 863 (2)

repletion 54 (2), 635 (1), 863 (1)

replica 22 (1)

replier 460 (3)

reply 460 (1), 460 (2), 460 (5), 588 (4), 927 (1)

replying 460 (4)

report 400 (1), 402 (1), 466 (1), 480 (2), 524 (1), 524 (2), 524 (10), 526 (5), 528 (2), 528 (9), 529 (1), 531

(4), 548 (1), 579 (1), 588 (4), 590 (1), 590 (7), 866 (1)

report on 480 (6)

reported 529 (7)

reporter 480 (3), 524 (4), 528 (6), 529 (4), 590 (5)

reporting 528 (2)

reports 548 (1)

repose 145 (6), 145 (8), 266 (2), 266 (7), 266 (8), 376 (2), 677 (1), 677 (3), 679 (4), 679 (11), 681 (1), 681 (3), 683 (1), 683 (3), 685 (1), 685 (5), 823 (5), 837 (1), 882 (8)

repose on 218 (16)

reposeful 266 (5), 376 (4), 681 (2), 683 (2), 685 (2), 826 (2), 828 (2)

repossess 786 (7)

reprehensible 914 (3), 924 (8), 934 (6)

represent 6 (4), 18 (7), 20 (5), 233 (3), 243 (5), 465 (12), 466 (6), 513 (7), 514 (5), 519 (4), 522 (8), 547 (18), 548 (7), 551 (8), 553 (8), 590 (7), 594 (17), 755 (3)

representation 20 (1), 22 (1), 522 (1), 547 (1), 548 (1), 551 (1), 553 (1), 553 (5), 605 (2), 751 (1)

representational 551 (6), 751 (3)

representative 83 (5), 686 (1), 692 (3), 754 (2)

represented 551 (7)

representing 18 (4), 547 (15), 551 (6), 571 (2), 590 (6), 594 (15), 755 (2), 988 (8)

repress 165 (8), 182 (3), 702 (8), 745 (7), 747 (7), 757 (4), 823 (7)

repress a smile 834 (10)

repression 182 (1), 503 (5), 747 (1), 757 (1), 820 (1)

repressive 747 (4), 757 (2)

reprieve 667 (1), 668 (1), 752 (1), 909 (1), 909 (4), 960 (1), 960 (3)

reprieved 909 (3), 960 (2)

reprimand 664 (1), 872 (2), 924 (4), 924 (11), 963 (1), 963 (8)

reprimanded 924 (7)

reprimanding 924 (6)

reprint 20 (6), 22 (2), 106 (1), 106 (4), 589 (5)

reprisal 714 (1), 963 (1), 963 (4)

reprisals 910 (2)

reprise 106 (1), 412 (3)

reproach 867 (2), 867 (3), 899 (2), 924 (3), 924 (11), 924 (13), 928 (1), 928 (8), 936 (1)

reproach oneself 830 (4), 939 (4)

reproached 867 (4)

reproachful 891 (3), 924 (6)

reprobate 899 (6), 899 (7), 921 (5), 922 (5), 924 (13), 934 (3), 980 (3), 980 (4)

reproduce 36 (5), 106 (4), 164 (7), 166 (3)

reproduce itself 36 (4), 164 (7), 166 (3), 167 (6), 171 (6)

reproduced 166 (2)

reproducing 18 (4)

reproduction 22 (1), 166 (1), 167 (1), 551 (1), 553 (5)

reproductive 166 (2), 167 (4)

reproof 613 (1), 924 (4)

reproofed 656 (6)

reprove 613 (3), 664 (5), 762 (3), 899 (6), 924 (11), 928 (8), 963 (8)

reprove oneself 939 (4)

reptile 365 (2), 365 (13), 938 (2)

reptilian 365 (18)

republic 371 (5), 733 (6)

republican 733 (9)

republicanism 733 (4)

republicans 706 (2)

repudiate 489 (5), 532 (5), 533 (3), 603 (7), 607 (3), 752 (4), 760 (4)

repudiation 489 (1), 533 (1), 607 (1), 752 (1), 769 (1), 896 (1)

repugnance 598 (1), 704 (1), 715 (1), 861 (1), 888 (1)

repugnant 861 (3)

repulse 292 (1), 292 (3), 607 (1), 607 (3), 713 (10), 715 (1), 727 (10), 728 (2), 760 (1), 760 (4)

repulsion 292 (1), 715 (1), 760 (1), 861 (1)

repulsive 292 (2), 842 (3), 888 (5)

repulsive force 292 (1)

repulsiveness 292 (1), 842 (1)

reputability 866 (1)

reputable 866 (7), 920 (4), 923 (7), 929 (3)

reputation 802 (1), 866 (1)

repute 32 (1), 178 (1), 638 (1), 729 (1), 802 (1), 866 (1), 920 (1), 929 (1)

request 452 (1), 459 (13), 512 (7), 532 (5), 612 (2), 627 (1), 627 (6), 737 (3), 737 (8), 756 (6), 759 (1), 759 (4), 761 (1), 761 (5), 762 (1), 785 (2), 915 (5), 959 (1), 959 (7), 981 (4)

requesting 761 (3)

requiem 364 (2), 412 (5), 836 (2)

requiem mass 988 (4)

require 55 (5), 307 (3), 468 (3), 596 (8), 627 (6), 636 (7), 636 (8), 737 (3), 761 (5), 761 (6), 766 (3), 792 (5), 801 (5), 859 (11), 917 (11)

require an explanation 459 (16)

require no effort 701 (6)

required 596 (4), 627 (3), 638 (5), 774 (2)

requirement 55 (2), 307 (1), 596 (2), 627 (1), 638 (3), 647 (1), 761 (1), 766

(1), 792 (1), 801 (1), 859 (1), 859 (5)

requirements 792 (1)

requiring 55 (3)

requisite 627 (3)

requisition 627 (1), 627 (6), 673 (5), 737 (3), 737 (8), 740 (3), 761 (1), 761 (5), 786 (1), 786 (7)

requital 714 (1)

requite 151 (3), 714 (3), 962 (3)

requited 12 (2), 151 (2)

rerun 106 (4)

rescind 603 (7), 752 (4)

rescue 656 (1), 656 (9), 667 (1), 668 (1), 668 (3), 703 (1), 713 (9), 746 (1), 746 (3), 787 (1)

rescued 746 (2)

rescuer 903 (1)

research 453 (4), 459 (1), 459 (13), 461 (7), 536 (2)

research into 536 (5)

research laboratory 687 (1)

research worker 459 (9), 461 (3), 512 (3), 538 (3)

researcher 459 (9), 461 (3), 538 (3)

resemblance 18 (1), 22 (1)

resemble 18 (7), 20 (5), 24 (9), 28 (9), 166 (3), 445 (8)

resembling 18 (4)

resent 829 (5), 830 (4), 861 (4), 881 (4), 891 (5), 910 (6), 912 (3)

resentful 709 (6), 825 (6), 829 (3), 830 (2), 881 (3), 888 (4), 891 (3), 898 (4), 910 (4), 912 (2)

resentment 709 (1), 818 (1), 819 (1), 827 (2), 829 (1), 830 (1), 861 (1), 872 (2), 881 (1), 888 (1), 891 (1), 898 (1), 910 (1), 911 (1), 914 (1)

reservation 468 (1), 486 (2), 489 (1), 548 (2), 766 (1), 883 (2)

reserve 135 (5), 136 (7), 150 (2), 525 (1), 525 (8), 582 (1), 605 (7), 627 (6),

632 (5), 666 (5), 674 (4), 747 (1), 748 (2), 771 (7), 773 (4), 874 (1), 883 (2)

reserved 525 (6), 582 (2), 627 (3), 674 (2), 747 (5), 764 (3), 778 (4), 820 (3), 823 (3), 874 (2)

reserves 34 (2), 40 (2), 629 (1), 632 (1), 633 (1), 722 (7), 797 (2), 799 (1)

reservist 150 (2), 722 (4)

reservoir 341 (3), 346 (1), 632 (2)

reset 187 (6)

resettle 187 (6)

resettlement 187 (1)

reside 192 (21)

reside in 1 (6)

residence 189 (1), 192 (1), 192 (6)

residency 192 (1)

resident 189 (2), 191 (2), 191 (6), 754 (3)

resident alien 59 (2), 191 (4)

residential 192 (18)

residential area 192 (8)

residing 187 (4), 189 (2)

residual 41 (4), 85 (4)

residuary 41 (4)

residue 41 (1)

resign 145 (6), 286 (4), 603 (5), 621 (3), 734 (5), 753 (3)

resign oneself 721 (3), 823 (5), 823 (6)

resignation 145 (1), 508 (1), 621 (1), 721 (1), 753 (1), 823 (2), 828 (1), 872 (1)

resigned 721 (2), 739 (3), 823 (3), 828 (2)

resigned, be 721 (3), 823 (5)

resigning 533 (2), 753 (2)

resilience 162 (1), 286 (2), 328 (1)

resilient 286 (3), 328 (2), 833 (3)

resin 354 (3), 357 (5)

resinous 357 (8)

resist 145 (6), 176 (7), 182 (3), 489 (5), 598 (4), 704

(4), 704 (5), 713 (10), 714 (3), 715 (3), 716 (10), 718 (12), 727 (8), 738 (10), 747 (7), 760 (4)

resist change 144 (3)

resist control 734 (6)

resist temptation 933 (4)

resistance 113 (3), 145 (3), 160 (5), 182 (1), 326 (1), 602 (1), 613 (1), 704 (1), 713 (1), 715 (1), 738 (1), 738 (2), 738 (4)

resistance movement 738 (2)

resistant 182 (2), 326 (4), 489 (3), 704 (3), 715 (2)

resisting 182 (2), 329 (2), 713 (7), 715 (2), 738 (7), 738 (8)

resolute 153 (4), 162 (7), 595 (1), 599 (2), 600 (3), 602 (4), 617 (3), 671 (3), 727 (5), 855 (4)

resolute, be 547 (21), 595 (2), 599 (3), 605 (6), 617 (5), 671 (4), 833 (7), 855 (7)

resolutely 599 (5), 600 (5)

resoluteness 599 (1)

resolution 153 (1), 162 (2), 174 (1), 452 (1), 455 (1), 520 (1), 595 (0), 599 (1), 600 (1), 602 (1), 617 (1), 678 (3), 725 (1), 855 (1)

resolve 51 (5), 520 (10), 599 (1), 599 (3), 617 (1), 617 (5), 623 (8)

resolve into 147 (7)

resolved 51 (3), 599 (2)

resonance 106 (1), 280 (1), 398 (1), 400 (1), 403 (1), 404 (1)

resonant 398 (3), 400 (3), 403 (2), 404 (2), 410 (6), 574 (5), 579 (6)

resort 76 (1), 623 (3), 629 (1), 673 (1), 698 (2)

resort to 74 (10), 189 (4), 673 (4)

resort to arms 718 (2), 718 (10)

resort to violence 176 (7)

resound 106 (5), 280 (3), 315 (5), 400 (4), 404 (3)

resounding 398 (3), 400 (3)

resource 623 (3), 698 (2)

resourceful 171 (4), 513 (5), 623 (7), 694 (4), 698 (4)

resourcefulness 694 (1)

resources 629 (1), 631 (1), 777 (2), 800 (1)

respect 9 (1), 9 (7), 311 (2), 457 (6), 488 (6), 638 (8), 768 (3), 854 (1), 854 (9), 866 (1), 866 (13), 880 (2), 884 (1), 884 (5), 887 (1), 887 (13), 920 (1), 920 (5), 923 (1), 923 (8), 979 (1), 981 (1), 981 (11), 982 (2)

respect for law 953 (1)

respectability 929 (1)

respectable 32 (4), 644 (9), 866 (7), 920 (4), 929 (3)

respected 866 (7), 920 (4), 981 (10)

respectful 739 (3), 854 (6), 884 (3), 920 (3), 979 (6), 981 (9)

respectfully 920 (8)

respective 9 (5), 80 (5)

respectively 80 (10), 783 (4)

respects 884 (2), 920 (2)

respiration 299 (1), 317 (1), 352 (7), 360 (1), 408 (1)

respirator 352 (7), 658 (13), 662 (3), 666 (2)

respiratory disease 651 (8)

respire 352 (11)

respite 108 (2), 136 (2), 145 (4), 668 (1), 683 (1)

resplendence 417 (1)

resplendent 417 (8), 841 (4)

respond 460 (5), 706 (4), 710 (3), 818 (7)

respondent 460 (3), 460 (4), 461 (5), 584 (4), 928 (4), 959 (4) responder 460 (3)

response 157 (1), 374 (2), 460 (1), 818 (1), 981 (5)

responsibility 622 (4), 689 (2), 917 (1)

responsible 134 (3), 156 (7), 180 (2), 768 (2), 858 (2), 917 (5), 929 (4), 936 (3)

responsible, be 156 (9), 180 (3)

responsive 374 (3), 460 (4), 818 (3), 819 (2)

responsive, be 460 (5)

rest 41 (5), 72 (3), 144 (3), 145 (4), 145 (6), 145 (8), 218 (2), 266 (1), 266 (2), 266 (7), 266 (8), 376 (1), 376 (2), 410 (3), 677 (1), 681 (1), 683 (1), 683 (3), 831 (1)

rest assured 485 (7), 852 (6)

rest content 828 (4)

rest home 192 (17)

rest in the belief 485 (7)

rest on 218 (16)

rest with 917 (8)

restate 106 (4)

restaurant 192 (13), 301 (5)

restaurateur 633 (3)

restful 266 (5), 376 (4), 683 (2)

restfulness 683 (1)

resting 266 (4)

resting place 266 (3)

restitute 31 (4), 148 (3), 787 (3), 804 (4), 927 (5), 941 (5), 962 (3)

restitution 658 (1), 719 (2), 787 (1), 804 (1), 915 (1), 927 (1), 941 (1), 962 (1), 963 (1), 963 (4)

restive 598 (3), 602 (5), 738 (7), 821 (3), 822 (3), 829 (3)

restiveness 738 (2), 829 (1)

restless 152 (4), 265 (3), 318 (4), 601 (3), 678 (7), 821 (3), 822 (3), 829 (3)

restlessness 152 (1), 318 (1), 318 (3), 678 (2), 738 (1), 738 (2), 822 (1), 829 (1)

restorable 656 (6)

restoration 106 (1), 126 (1), 166 (1), 654 (1), 656 (1), 656 (2), 668 (1), 685 (1), 787 (1), 866 (5), 927 (1), 963 (4)

restorative 174 (4), 652 (4), 654 (7), 656 (7), 658 (6), 658 (17), 685 (2), 831 (2)

restore 31 (4), 54 (6), 106 (4), 148 (3), 166 (3), 187 (6), 654 (9), 656 (9), 658 (19), 668 (3), 685 (4), 787 (3), 821 (7), 831 (3)

restore harmony 719 (4)

restore to health 656 (11)

restore to sanity 502 (4)

restored 51 (4), 126 (7), 147 (5), 148 (2), 360 (2), 650 (2), 656 (6), 685 (3), 979 (8)

restored, be 162 (11), 360 (4), 654 (8), 656 (8), 685 (5), 831 (4)

restorer 654 (5), 656 (5)

restoring 787 (2), 941 (4), 962 (2)

restrain 145 (7), 177 (6), 236 (3), 278 (6), 468 (3), 613 (3), 636 (7), 702 (8), 747 (7), 757 (4), 778 (5), 823 (7)

restrain oneself 747 (7)

restrained 177 (3), 232 (2), 266 (4), 573 (2), 575 (3), 745 (4), 747 (5), 942 (3)

restraining 182 (2), 702 (6), 747 (4), 757 (2), 778 (3)

restraining hand 177 (2)

restraint 136 (2), 145 (1), 161 (2), 172 (2), 177 (1), 177 (2), 182 (1), 278 (1), 575 (1), 660 (2), 702 (1), 735 (1), 745 (1), 747 (1), 757 (1), 809 (1), 846 (1), 942 (1), 959 (1), 963 (4)

restrict 236 (3), 468 (3), 747 (7), 757 (4)

restrict access 747 (7)

restricted 232 (2), 525 (3), 747 (5)

restricted area 747 (2)

restricting 468 (2)

restriction 232 (1), 236 (1), 468 (1), 702 (1), 747 (2), 757 (1), 791 (2), 814 (1)

restrictive 57 (2), 702 (6), 747 (4)

restrictive practice 747 (2)

result 41 (1), 41 (5), 67 (1), 69 (1), 120 (3), 154 (1), 154 (6), 157 (1), 157 (5), 164 (2), 480 (1), 725 (1)

result, be the 157 (5)

result in 157 (5)

resultant 41 (4), 154 (3), 157 (3)

resulting 65 (2), 154 (3)

resulting from 157 (3)

results 460 (1)

resume 68 (8), 106 (4), 148 (3), 656 (8), 786 (7)

resumé 592 (1), 592 (5)

resumption 68 (3), 106 (1)

resurface 656 (12)

resurgence 166 (1), 656 (3)

resurgent 166 (2), 656 (6)

resurrect 166 (3), 656 (10)

resurrection 166 (1), 656 (3)

resuscitate 656 (10)

resuscitation 166 (1), 656 (3)

retail 524 (10), 528 (9), 791 (3), 793 (4)

retail trade 791 (2)

retailer 633 (2), 793 (2), 794 (2)

retailer's 796 (3)

retain 45 (9), 48 (3), 178 (4), 505 (7), 516 (5), 600 (4), 632 (5), 747 (7), 760 (4), 773 (4), 778 (5), 786 (6), 889 (6), 932 (4)

retained 760 (3), 778 (4)

retainer 35 (2), 89 (2), 742 (3), 879 (2), 962 (1)
retaining 778 (3)
retaining wall 218 (2)
retaliate 151 (3), 460 (5), 709 (7), 712 (7), 714 (3), 735 (7), 910 (5), 913 (6), 924 (12), 962 (3), 963 (8)
retaliation 151 (1), 460 (1), 709 (1), 712 (1), 714 (1), 910 (2), 913 (2), 963 (1), 963 (4)
retaliative 714 (2), 910 (4)
retaliatory 714 (2), 910 (4), 962 (2), 963 (6)
retard 37 (4), 136 (7), 145 (7), 266 (9), 278 (6), 702 (8), 747 (7)
retardation 136 (2), 499 (1)
retarded 499 (3)
retarding 182 (2)
retch 300 (10)
retching 651 (7)
retell 106 (4)
retention 48 (1), 162 (2), 218 (1), 505 (1), 760 (1), 773 (1), 778 (1), 786 (1)
retentive 378 (5), 778 (3), 816 (4)
retentiveness 505 (1), 778 (1)
reticence 525 (1), 582 (1), 858 (1)
reticent 525 (6), 582 (2), 698 (4), 858 (2)
reticular 222 (7)
reticulate 222 (8)
reticulated 222 (7), 437 (8)
reticulation 222 (3)
reticule 194 (9)
retina 438 (2)
retinue 67 (2), 71 (3), 74 (4), 89 (2), 284 (2), 742 (3)
retire 145 (6), 266 (7), 286 (4), 290 (3), 296 (4), 620 (6), 621 (3), 681 (3), 753 (3), 779 (4), 874 (3)
retired 119 (2), 125 (7), 131 (6), 674 (3), 681 (2), 744 (5), 753 (2)
retired person 133 (1)

retirement 286 (1), 290 (1), 621 (1), 681 (1), 753 (1), 883 (2)
retirement age 131 (3)
retiring 874 (2), 883 (5)
retold 106 (3)
retort 151 (1), 194 (13), 338 (2), 460 (1), 460 (5), 479 (1), 479 (3), 714 (1), 714 (3), 839 (2), 839 (5), 878 (6)
retouch 553 (8), 656 (12)
retrace 505 (8)
retrace one's steps 286 (5)
retract 148 (3), 288 (3), 486 (6), 489 (5), 603 (7), 752 (4)
retractable 288 (2)
retractile 288 (2)
retraction 148 (1), 486 (1), 489 (1), 603 (2)
retreat 37 (1), 76 (1), 148 (1), 192 (17), 286 (1), 286 (4), 290 (1), 290 (3), 527 (1), 620 (1), 620 (6), 662 (1), 667 (1), 728 (2), 728 (9), 883 (2), 981 (1)
retreating 290 (2)
retrench 37 (4), 747 (7), 814 (3)
retrenchment 37 (2), 747 (2), 814 (1)
retrial 959 (3)
retribution 714 (1), 913 (2), 963 (1)
retributive 714 (2), 962 (2), 963 (6)
retrievable 656 (6)
retrieval 86 (5), 148 (1), 272 (1), 668 (1), 771 (1), 786 (1)
retrieve 31 (6), 148 (3), 182 (3), 656 (13), 668 (3), 771 (7), 773 (4), 786 (7), 787 (3), 915 (5)
retriever 365 (10)
retro- 238 (6)
retroactive 125 (9), 280 (2), 286 (3)
retroactively 125 (13)
retroflex 248 (3)
retroflexion 248 (1), 286 (1)

retrograde 148 (2), 286 (3), 286 (4), 655 (5)
retrogress 286 (4), 657 (2)
retrogression 286 (1), 655 (1), 657 (1)
retrogressive 148 (2), 286 (3)
retrospect 125 (11), 286 (5), 505 (2), 505 (8), 590 (7), 830 (4)
retrospection 125 (1), 449 (1), 505 (2)
retrospective 125 (9), 127 (7), 148 (2), 286 (3), 491 (4), 522 (2), 830 (2)
retrospectively 125 (13)
retroussé 204 (3), 248 (3)
retroversion 221 (1)
return 106 (2), 106 (6), 141 (6), 148 (1), 148 (3), 164 (2), 280 (3), 282 (4), 286 (2), 286 (5), 295 (1), 296 (1), 297 (1), 314 (1), 460 (1), 524 (2), 603 (1), 605 (8), 607 (3), 714 (3), 751 (2), 751 (4), 787 (1), 787 (3), 807 (1), 962 (1)
return a favour 907 (5)
return action 182 (1)
return an answer 460 (5)
return empty-handed 728 (7)
return fire 280 (1)
return home 295 (4)
return match 106 (1)
return to 106 (5)
return to health 650 (4)
returned 148 (2), 605 (5), 607 (2)
returning 286 (3)
returns 460 (1), 548 (1), 807 (1)
reunion 45 (1), 74 (2), 710 (1), 882 (3)
reusable 640 (2)
reuse 673 (3), 814 (3)
rev up 403 (3), 669 (11)
reveal 522 (7), 524 (9), 526 (4), 528 (9), 547 (18)
revealed 445 (7), 526 (2), 975 (3), 975 (4)
revealing 422 (2), 526 (3), 547 (15), 951 (7)

revealment 526 (1)
reveille 547 (8)
revel 301 (35), 497 (2), 835 (1), 835 (6), 837 (3), 837 (23), 876 (4), 882 (2), 882 (8), 882 (10), 943 (3), 944 (1), 949 (1), 949 (14)
revel in 376 (6)
revelation 445 (1), 484 (1), 490 (1), 494 (1), 508 (1), 511 (1), 522 (1), 526 (1), 975 (1)
revelational 975 (3)
revelatory 526 (3)
reveller 835 (3), 837 (17), 949 (5)
revelling 835 (1), 835 (4)
revels 835 (1), 837 (2)
revenge 106 (1), 709 (3), 714 (1), 891 (1), 910 (2), 963 (1)
revenge oneself 910 (5), 963 (8)
revengeful 888 (4), 891 (3), 906 (2), 910 (4)
revengeful, be 888 (7), 900 (3), 910 (6)
revengefulness 910 (1)
revenue 629 (1), 771 (2), 777 (2), 807 (1)
reverberant 403 (2), 404 (2)
reverberate 106 (5), 280 (3), 400 (4), 403 (3), 404 (3)
reverberation 280 (1), 400 (1), 403 (1), 404 (1)
reverberative 404 (2)
revere 866 (13), 920 (5), 981 (11)
revered 920 (4), 981 (10)
reverence 311 (2), 920 (1), 920 (2), 920 (5), 979 (1), 981 (1)
reverend 866 (8), 920 (4), 979 (8), 986 (2)
reverent 920 (3), 979 (6), 981 (9)
reverential 981 (9)
reverie 449 (1), 456 (2), 513 (3)
revers 261 (1)

reversal 148 (1), 221 (1), 508 (1), 752 (1)
reverse 14 (1), 14 (3), 143 (6), 148 (3), 221 (4), 221 (5), 238 (1), 238 (4), 240 (2), 282 (4), 286 (3), 286 (4), 728 (2), 731 (1), 752 (4), 772 (1)
reverse image 14 (1)
reverse side 238 (1)
reversed 148 (2), 221 (3)
reversibly 148 (4)
reversing 286 (1)
reversion 68 (3), 148 (1), 165 (1), 221 (1), 280 (1), 286 (1), 286 (2), 657 (1), 780 (1), 787 (1)
revert 68 (8), 106 (6), 143 (6), 148 (3), 165 (6), 280 (3), 282 (4), 286 (5), 655 (7), 657 (2)
reverted 148 (2), 280 (2), 286 (3)
reverting 148 (1)
review 74 (1), 438 (4), 455 (4), 459 (1), 459 (13), 480 (2), 480 (6), 505 (2), 505 (8), 520 (1), 524 (2), 528 (5), 591 (2), 592 (1), 875 (3)
reviewer 480 (3), 520 (4), 589 (6), 591 (3)
revile 899 (6), 924 (10), 924 (13)
revise 143 (6), 536 (5), 623 (8), 654 (10)
revised 34 (4), 126 (7), 654 (6)
revised edition 589 (5)
reviser 143 (3), 589 (7), 654 (5)
revision 438 (4), 536 (2), 654 (2)
revitalize 656 (10)
revival 106 (1), 126 (1), 162 (5), 166 (1), 594 (2), 654 (1), 656 (3), 831 (1)
revival meeting 981 (7)
revivalism 981 (7)
revivalist 978 (6), 979 (5), 981 (8), 986 (3)
revive 147 (7), 148 (3), 162 (11), 166 (3), 174 (8), 360

(4), 360 (6), 650 (4), 654 (8), 654 (9), 656 (8), 656 (10), 658 (20), 685 (4), 685 (5), 821 (7)
revived 656 (6), 685 (3)
revived corpse 970 (3)
reviver 685 (1)
reviving 685 (2)
revocation 533 (1), 603 (2), 752 (1)
revoke 165 (6), 533 (3), 603 (7), 607 (3), 752 (4), 757 (4), 779 (4)
revoked 752 (3)
revolt 61 (11), 149 (1), 176 (7), 704 (5), 715 (1), 715 (3), 718 (10), 738 (2), 738 (10), 746 (4), 827 (11), 829 (6), 861 (5), 918 (3), 954 (3)
revolt from 888 (7)
revolter 84 (3), 149 (2), 489 (2), 705 (1), 708 (2), 738 (4), 829 (2), 904 (1), 918 (1)
revolting 391 (2), 854 (8), 861 (3), 888 (5)
revolution 141 (2), 143 (1), 148 (1), 149 (1), 165 (1), 165 (3), 176 (2), 221 (2), 315 (1), 550 (1), 654 (4), 738 (2)
revolutionary 126 (6), 149 (2), 149 (3), 165 (4), 176 (5), 654 (5), 738 (7)
revolutionist 149 (2), 168 (1), 489 (2), 738 (4)
revolutionize 63 (3), 143 (6), 147 (8), 149 (4), 738 (10)
revolve 141 (6), 314 (4), 315 (5), 449 (8)
revolver 723 (10)
revolving 141 (4), 315 (1)
revue 445 (2), 594 (4)
revulsion 148 (1), 149 (1), 280 (1), 290 (1), 620 (1)
reward 31 (1), 31 (4), 40 (2), 612 (2), 612 (4), 612 (12), 703 (2), 714 (3), 729 (1), 753 (1), 771 (1), 771 (2), 781 (1), 781 (2), 781 (7), 804 (2), 804 (4), 807

(1), 866 (4), 876 (4), 907 (2), 907 (5), 913 (2), 962 (1), 962 (3)

reward of conduct 688 (1)

rewarded, be 962 (4)

rewarder 781 (4)

rewarding 771 (5), 962 (2)

rewardingly 962 (5)

rewardless 908 (3)

reword 106 (4), 520 (9), 563 (3)

rewording 520 (3)

rewrite 654 (10)

rex 741 (3)

rhapsodic 513 (5), 593 (8)

rhapsodist 513 (4)

rhapsodize 513 (7)

rhapsody 412 (4)

Rhea 967 (1)

Rhesus factor 335 (3)

rhetoric 571 (1), 574 (1), 579 (3), 875 (1)

rhetorical 519 (3), 546 (2), 566 (2), 570 (3), 574 (5), 576 (2), 579 (7), 875 (4)

rhetorical question 459 (3)

rhetorician 574 (3), 579 (5), 612 (5)

rheum 335 (2)

rheumatic 163 (7), 651 (22)

rheumatic fever 651 (15)

rheumaticky 651 (22)

rheumatics 651 (15)

rheumatism 651 (15)

rheumatoid 651 (22)

rheumatoid arthritis 651 (15)

rheumy 302 (5), 335 (4)

rheumy-eyed 131 (6)

rhinoceros 365 (3)

rhizome 366 (6)

rhododendron 366 (4)

rhomboid 220 (1), 247 (4)

rhombus 247 (4)

rhubarb 301 (19)

rhyme 106 (2), 593 (1), 593 (5), 593 (10)

rhyme scheme 593 (5)

rhymer 593 (6)

rhymester 593 (6)

rhyming 18 (4), 106 (3), 593 (8)

rhyming slang 560 (3)

rhythm 16 (1), 106 (2), 141 (1), 265 (1), 317 (1), 410 (4), 575 (1), 593 (5)

rhythm 'n' blues 412 (1)

rhythmic 16 (2), 71 (4), 317 (3), 575 (3), 593 (8)

rhythmical 106 (3), 141 (4)

rib 851 (5)

rib-tickling 839 (4)

ribald 851 (4), 867 (4), 951 (6)

ribaldry 847 (2), 851 (1), 899 (2), 951 (1)

ribbed 222 (6)

ribbing 851 (1)

ribbon 47 (4), 208 (3), 547 (9), 729 (2), 844 (5), 866 (4)

ribbons 47 (8)

ribs 218 (13), 239 (1)

rice 301 (22), 366 (8)

rich 160 (8), 171 (4), 301 (33), 357 (6), 386 (2), 390 (2), 425 (6), 797 (9), 800 (3), 841 (4), 844 (10)

rich, be 635 (7), 780 (4), 800 (5)

rich harvest 635 (2)

rich in 635 (5)

rich person 730 (3), 797 (8), 800 (2), 868 (3)

rich uncle 707 (4)

rich vein 632 (1)

riches 615 (1)

richly deserved 915 (2)

richly furnished 800 (3)

richly ornamented 844 (10)

richness 390 (1), 570 (1), 635 (2), 637 (1), 844 (1)

rick 63 (3)

rickets 246 (2), 651 (3)

rickety 163 (4), 163 (8), 647 (3), 655 (6), 661 (4)

rickshaw 274 (4), 274 (9)

ricochet 280 (1), 280 (3)

rid of 746 (2), 772 (2)

rid oneself of 300 (6), 668 (3)

riddance 44 (3), 668 (1), 746 (1)

riddle 263 (3), 263 (18), 479 (3), 517 (1), 518 (1), 530 (2)

riddled 263 (14)

riddles 837 (8)

ride 267 (1), 267 (15), 296 (6), 369 (8), 624 (5), 837 (21)

ride at anchor 266 (7)

ride down 619 (5), 712 (10)

ride it out 660 (7)

ride roughshod over 176 (7), 735 (8)

ride to hounds 619 (6)

rider 40 (1), 268 (4)

ridge 47 (1), 206 (1), 209 (2)

ridged 259 (4)

ridicule 20 (5), 22 (1), 483 (4), 486 (1), 486 (6), 497 (2), 497 (4), 521 (1), 521 (3), 542 (9), 552 (1), 835 (2), 835 (7), 839 (1), 839 (5), 849 (4), 851 (1), 851 (5), 867 (11), 878 (2), 878 (6), 885 (2), 921 (1), 921 (2), 921 (5), 922 (1), 922 (5), 924 (1), 924 (3), 926 (2), 926 (6)

ridiculing 851 (4), 878 (5)

ridiculous 84 (6), 497 (3), 499 (4), 835 (5), 849 (2)

ridiculous, be 497 (4), 499 (6), 837 (20), 849 (4)

ridiculousness 497 (1), 499 (2), 849 (1)

riding 265 (1), 267 (5), 837 (6)

riding habit 228 (10)

riding horse 273 (8)

rife 79 (4), 529 (7)

rife, be 178 (4)

riffle through 438 (9)

riffraff 869 (2), 938 (1)

rifle 287 (3), 723 (9), 788 (7), 788 (9)

rifle range 724 (1)

rifle through 459 (15)

rifleman 722 (5)

rift 46 (1), 201 (2), 709 (1)

rig 47 (3), 228 (1), 274 (6), 275 (6), 541 (8)
rig-out 228 (1), 228 (31), 669 (11)
rig the jury 914 (6)
rig the market 791 (5)
rigged 541 (3)
rigged out 228 (29), 669 (7)
rigging 47 (3), 275 (6)
right 24 (5), 24 (6), 24 (7), 241 (1), 249 (2), 494 (4), 494 (6), 642 (2), 708 (2), 733 (1), 777 (2), 913 (1), 913 (3), 915 (1), 915 (2), 929 (1), 933 (3)
right a wrong 913 (6)
right amount 635 (1)
right and left 239 (4)
right and proper 913 (3)
right angle 215 (1), 247 (2)
right-angled 247 (6)
right, be 913 (5)
right behind 200 (7)
right hand 241 (1), 241 (2)
right-hand man 703 (3), 707 (1)
right-hand page 241 (1)
right-handed 241 (2), 378 (6)
Right Honourable 870 (1)
right itself 656 (11)
right line 203 (3)
right-minded 913 (4), 933 (3)
right mood 597 (1)
right now 121 (4)
right number 635 (1)
right of centre 708 (7)
right of choice 605 (1)
right of entry 297 (1)
right of way 305 (1), 624 (2), 624 (5)
right oneself 28 (10)
right people 848 (3)
right royal 813 (3)
right side 237 (2)
right thing, the 917 (1)
right time 8 (2), 117 (2), 137 (1)
right wing 241 (1), 708 (7)
right-winger 241 (1), 708 (2)

righteous 913 (4), 933 (3)
righteously 933 (5)
righteousness 913 (1), 933 (1)
rightful 494 (5), 913 (3), 915 (2)
rightfulness 913 (1)
righting wrong 913 (2)
rightist 708 (7)
rightly 644 (12), 913 (7)
rightly served 714 (2)
rightly served, be 714 (4), 962 (4)
rightness 494 (1), 913 (1)
rights 744 (1)
rigid 83 (6), 162 (7), 249 (2), 266 (6), 324 (4), 326 (4), 329 (2), 330 (2), 735 (4), 747 (4)
rigidity 249 (1), 326 (1)
rigmarole 515 (1), 570 (1)
rigor mortis 361 (2)
rigorous 735 (4), 862 (3), 906 (2), 945 (3)
rigorous proof 478 (1)
rigour 735 (1)
rile 891 (9)
rill 350 (1)
rim 233 (1), 234 (1)
rime 380 (2)
rind 226 (6)
ring 74 (4), 232 (1), 233 (1), 235 (1), 235 (4), 250 (2), 400 (4), 403 (3), 404 (1), 404 (3), 413 (9), 524 (10), 529 (3), 706 (2), 708 (1), 724 (1), 773 (1), 844 (7), 889 (3)
ring a bell 505 (11)
ring finger 378 (4)
ring in 64 (3), 68 (9), 117 (7)
ring off 145 (6), 578 (3)
ring out 117 (7)
ring road 624 (6)
ring round 232 (3)
ring, the 716 (1)
ring the changes 143 (6), 152 (5)
ring true 494 (7)
ring up 524 (10)
ringed 250 (6)
ringer 18 (3), 150 (2)

ringing 400 (3), 404 (1), 404 (2), 410 (6), 412 (2)
ringing tones 400 (1)
ringleader 612 (5), 690 (2), 738 (5)
ringlet 251 (2), 259 (2)
ringlike 250 (6)
ringmaster 690 (3)
ringside seat 200 (3)
ringworm 651 (12)
rink 724 (1)
rinse 648 (9)
riot 61 (4), 61 (10), 61 (11), 171 (3), 176 (1), 176 (7), 635 (2), 635 (7), 637 (1), 637 (5), 709 (3), 716 (7), 738 (2), 954 (3)
riot of colour 437 (1)
riot shield 713 (5)
rioter 61 (6), 738 (6)
rioting 738 (2), 738 (8), 954 (3)
riotous 61 (9), 176 (5), 635 (4), 734 (4), 738 (8), 822 (3), 943 (2), 944 (3)
rip 46 (12), 350 (5), 364 (11), 655 (10)
rip-off 786 (2), 788 (8), 811 (5)
rip open 263 (17)
rip out 304 (4)
rip-roaring 833 (4)
rip tide 350 (2)
riparian 234 (4), 344 (6)
ripe 131 (6), 390 (2), 669 (8)
ripe old age 131 (3)
ripen 646 (5), 669 (12), 725 (5)
ripened 646 (3), 669 (8)
ripeness 137 (1), 669 (4)
ripening 669 (3)
riper years 131 (2)
riposte 280 (1), 460 (1), 460 (5), 713 (10), 714 (1), 714 (3)
ripping out 304 (1)
ripple 217 (5), 251 (1), 251 (11), 259 (1), 262 (1), 318 (5), 318 (6), 350 (5), 350 (9), 401 (4)
rippling 259 (4), 262 (2)

rise 36 (1), 36 (4), 68 (1), 68 (4), 68 (8), 197 (4), 209 (2), 209 (12), 215 (1), 215 (3), 220 (2), 220 (5), 285 (1), 285 (3), 298 (6), 308 (1), 308 (4), 310 (5), 417 (13), 445 (1), 654 (1), 654 (8), 715 (3), 718 (10), 727 (6), 738 (10), 771 (3), 920 (6)
rise above 34 (7), 306 (5)
rise against 704 (5)
rise and fall 309 (4)
rise in price 811 (4)
rise late 136 (4)
rise to fame 866 (11)
rise to the bait 487 (3)
rise to the occasion 727 (7)
rise up 308 (4), 738 (10)
risibility 835 (2)
risible 835 (5), 849 (2)
rising 124 (4), 131 (6), 178 (2), ·220 (4), 308 (1), 715 (1), 730 (4), 738 (2), 811 (2), 920 (3)
rising air 308 (1)
rising damp 341 (1)
rising generation 130 (1)
rising ground 209 (2), 220 (2), 308 (1)
rising prices 811 (1)
rising star 727 (3), 866 (6)
rising tide 36 (1)
risk 618 (2), 618 (8), 661 (1), 791 (5)
risk it 159 (7), 661 (8)
risk of 469 (1)
risk one's money 784 (5)
risk-taker 618 (4), 855 (3)
risk-taking 159 (4), 618 (2), 618 (7), 857 (3)
risky 474 (4), 618 (7), 645 (3), 661 (3)
risky venture 661 (1)
risque 839 (4), 847 (4), 867 (4), 951 (6)
rissoles 301 (16)
rite 60 (1), 610 (2), 981 (3), 981 (6), 983 (1), 988 (3)
rite of passage 988 (3)
rites 981 (3), 988 (3)

ritual 60 (1), 610 (2), 875 (2), 875 (6), 876 (1), 988 (1), 988 (8)
ritual killing 362 (1)
ritual object 339 (1)
ritualism 988 (2)
ritualist 988 (6)
ritualistic 979 (7), 981 (9), 988 (9)
ritualize 988 (11)
ritually 988 (12)
ritually clean 648 (7)
ritually pure 301 (32)
ritzy 848 (5), 875 (4)
rival 28 (6), 702 (5), 704 (3), 704 (4), 705 (1), 709 (5), 716 (8), 716 (9), 716 (10), 881 (2), 911 (1), 911 (2)
rivalry 704 (1), 709 (2), 716 (1), 911 (1), 912 (1)
rivals 704 (2)
river 350 (1)
river bank 344 (2)
river basin 348 (1)
river god 966 (2)
river of hell 972 (2)
river police 270 (3)
river travel 269 (1)
riverbed 351 (1)
riverside 234 (4), 344 (2), 344 (6)
rivet 45 (11), 47 (5)
rivet one's eyes 438 (8)
riveter 45 (2)
Riviera 837 (4)
rivulet 350 (1)
RNA 358 (1)
roach 365 (15)
road 192 (8), 226 (7), 272 (2), 305 (3), 624 (6), 628 (2)
road block 264 (1), 702 (2)
road building 624 (6)
road junction 222 (1)
road patrol 305 (3)
road race 716 (3)
road to ruin 165 (3)
road user 305 (2)
roadhouse 192 (11)
roadside 234 (1), 234 (4), 289 (3)

roadster 273 (8), 274 (3), 274 (11)
roadway 624 (6)
roadworthy 272 (5)
roam 267 (13), 744 (9)
roan 273 (11)
roar 176 (7), 352 (10), 400 (4), 403 (3), 408 (4), 409 (3), 594 (17), 822 (4), 891 (2), 891 (7), 900 (3)
roar of laughter 835 (2)
roar with laughter 835 (7)
roaring 176 (6), 400 (1), 409 (2)
roaring drunk 949 (6)
roaring trade 730 (1)
roast 301 (40), 379 (7), 381 (8)
roast meat 301 (16)
roasted 301 (34), 381 (6)
roaster 365 (6)
rob 163 (10), 165 (9), 786 (9), 788 (7), 788 (9), 801 (6)
rob of freedom 745 (7)
rob with violence 788 (9)
robbed 772 (2), 801 (3)
robber 168 (1), 270 (1), 738 (4), 786 (4), 789 (2), 881 (2), 938 (2)
robber band 789 (2)
robbery 788 (1)
robe 228 (7), 228 (31), 743 (2), 989 (1)
Robe, the 958 (5)
robed 989 (4)
robes 228 (5), 228 (7), 875 (2)
robin 365 (4)
robot 551 (2), 628 (2), 630 (2), 742 (6)
robotics 630 (3)
robust 162 (8), 650 (2)
rock 29 (3), 144 (1), 153 (2), 266 (9), 317 (4), 324 (3), 326 (1), 344 (4), 359 (1), 662 (1), 663 (1), 679 (13), 703 (3), 889 (5)
rock bottom 35 (1), 214 (1)
rock-climbing 837 (6)
rock-hard 326 (3)
rock 'n roll 318 (1), 412 (1), 837 (14), 837 (22)

rose-coloured spectacles 852 (1)
rose-pink 431 (3)
rose-scented 396 (3)
roseate 431 (3)
rosette 547 (9), 547 (10), 729 (2), 844 (5)
rosin 357 (5)
rosiness 431 (1)
roster 87 (1)
rostrum 218 (5), 528 (2), 539 (5), 579 (3)
rosy 431 (3), 730 (5), 841 (6), 852 (5)
rosy-cheeked 431 (3), 650 (2)
rosy cheeks 650 (1)
rot 51 (2), 51 (5), 515 (2), 649 (2), 649 (8), 655 (2), 655 (7), 659 (2)
rota 65 (1), 87 (1), 141 (2)
rotary 141 (4), 315 (4)
rotary press 587 (4)
rotate 141 (6), 251 (10), 252 (6), 287 (7), 314 (4), 315 (5), 318 (5), 318 (6), 350 (9), 837 (22)
rotating 315 (4)
rotation 141 (2), 149 (1), 265 (1), 314 (1), 315 (1), 321 (6), 594 (5)
rotator 250 (2), 315 (3)
rotatory 315 (4)
rotisserie 192 (13), 301 (5)
rotor 269 (5), 315 (3)
rotten 51 (3), 163 (5), 391 (2), 645 (4), 649 (7), 655 (5), 655 (6), 934 (4)
rotten hand 731 (2)
rotter 888 (3)
rotting 51 (2), 649 (6)
rotund 195 (8), 250 (6), 252 (5), 253 (7), 263 (16)
rotunda 192 (16)
rotundity 250 (1), 252 (1), 253 (1)
roue 952 (1)
rouge 425 (4), 425 (8), 431 (2), 431 (5), 841 (8), 843 (3), 843 (7)
rouged 431 (3), 843 (6)
rough 17 (2), 61 (9), 176 (4), 176 (5), 253 (7), 259

(4), 331 (4), 350 (7), 388 (3), 407 (3), 645 (3), 700 (4), 735 (6), 827 (3), 898 (7)
rough air 259 (1)
rough and ready 647 (3), 695 (6)
rough and tumble 61 (4), 716 (7)
rough, be 259 (8)
rough behaviour 847 (2)
rough diamond 670 (2), 699 (2)
rough draft 55 (1)
rough-edged 259 (4)
rough going 259 (1)
rough guess 512 (2)
rough handling 176 (1)
rough-hew 243 (5), 259 (9), 554 (3), 669 (10)
rough-hewn 55 (3), 670 (4)
rough plan 23 (1)
rough sketch 233 (1)
rough skin 259 (1)
rough surface 259 (1)
rough type 869 (7)
rough water 259 (1)
rough weather 176 (3), 340 (3)
roughage 301 (10)
roughcast 226 (16), 259 (4), 259 (9)
roughen 259 (9), 260 (3)
roughened 259 (4)
roughhouse 61 (4), 176 (1), 716 (7)
roughly 200 (8)
roughneck 938 (1)
roughness 17 (1), 176 (1), 259 (1), 318 (1), 388 (1), 407 (1), 827 (1), 885 (2)
roulette 618 (2), 837 (12)
round 16 (1), 53 (1), 71 (1), 73 (1), 85 (5), 106 (2), 110 (1), 195 (8), 243 (5), 248 (3), 248 (5), 250 (6), 250 (7), 252 (3), 252 (5), 252 (6), 257 (2), 267 (1), 269 (10), 314 (4), 412 (2), 412 (5), 610 (1), 622 (4), 716 (4), 723 (1)
round a corner 314 (4)

round about 230 (4), 251 (14), 626 (4)
round and round 141 (8), 315 (6)
round-eyed 864 (4)
round head 252 (2)
round-headed 252 (5)
round number 85 (1)
round of pleasure 837 (2)
round off 28 (10), 54 (6)
round on 712 (7), 714 (3), 924 (12)
round robin 588 (1), 762 (1)
round-shouldered 246 (4)
round the clock 113 (11)
round trip 148 (1), 267 (1), 314 (1)
round up 74 (1), , 74 (11), 369 (8)
round upon 899 (6)
roundabout 223 (2), 230 (2), 250 (2), 282 (2), 305 (3), 314 (3), 315 (3), 570 (4), 624 (6), 626 (2), 837 (4)
roundabout way 314 (1), 626 (1)
rounded 220 (4), 243 (3), 245 (2), 248 (3), 250 (6), 253 (8), 257 (2), 258 (3)
roundel 547 (9)
roundelay 412 (5)
rounders 837 (7)
rounding off 725 (1)
roundness 16 (1), 250 (1), 252 (1)
roundsman 268 (1), 314 (2)
rouse 174 (8), 612 (9), 821 (6), 887 (15)
rouse curiosity 821 (8)
rouse oneself 678 (11)
rousing 174 (5), 579 (7), 612 (6), 821 (1), 821 (4)
rousing cheers 835 (1)
rout 75 (4), 727 (10), 728 (2), 869 (2)
route 267 (8), 269 (1), 281 (1), 305 (1), 624 (1), 624 (4)
route map 524 (6)
route march 267 (4)

rule out 57 (5), 470 (5), 919 (3)

rule the roost 733 (12)

ruled, be 733 (13)

ruled line 216 (1)

ruled out 470 (2)

ruler 465 (5), 741 (4)

rulership 733 (5)

rules 737 (1), 913 (1)

rules and regulations 610 (2)

ruling 34 (4), 162 (6), 178 (2), 480 (1), 733 (8), 959 (3)

ruling class 741 (1), 868 (3)

ruling party 741 (1)

ruling passion 503 (5), 602 (2)

rum 84 (6), 301 (28), 849 (2)

rumba 837 (14)

rumble 403 (3), 516 (5)

rumbling 403 (1)

rumbustious 61 (9), 822 (3)

ruminant 365 (2)

ruminate 301 (37), 449 (8)

rumination 301 (1), 449 (2)

ruminative 449 (5)

rummage 459 (15)

rummaging 459 (5)

rummy 837 (11)

rumour 4 (2), 529 (2), 529 (8), 543 (3), 584 (2)

rumoured 529 (7)

rump 238 (2)

rumple 63 (4), 259 (9), 261 (1), 261 (3), 318 (6)

rumpus 61 (4), 176 (1)

run 46 (7), 49 (4), 71 (1), 71 (2), 79 (1), 106 (2), 111 (3), 146 (1), 173 (3), 265 (1), 265 (2), 265 (4), 267 (3), 269 (1), 269 (9), 277 (6), 279 (7), 284 (1), 298 (6), 298 (7), 337 (4), 350 (9), 425 (8), 589 (5), 620 (6), 678 (11), 680 (3), 688 (5), 689 (4), 837 (21)

run a race 716 (10)

run a risk 618 (8)

run a temperature 379 (7)

run abreast 219 (3)

run after 619 (5), 859 (11), 889 (7)

run against 279 (8)

run aground 269 (10), 295 (5), 728 (7)

run ahead 64 (3)

run amok 176 (7), 503 (11), 712 (9), 822 (4)

run at 712 (1)

run away 277 (6), 286 (4), 290 (3), 296 (5), 446 (3), 620 (6), 660 (9), 667 (5), 728 (9), 854 (9), 856 (4)

run-away match 894 (3)

run away with 786 (9)

run back 286 (4)

run before the wind 269 (10)

run counter 467 (4)

run counter to 14 (4), 182 (3)

run down 37 (5), 163 (6), 279 (8), 289 (4), 619 (5), 636 (9), 651 (21), 655 (6), 674 (3), 712 (10), 898 (8), 921 (5), 924 (7), 924 (10), 926 (6)

run for 759 (4)

run for cover 856 (4)

run for port 269 (10), 660 (9)

run high 176 (7)

run in 68 (8), 68 (9), 297 (5), 747 (8)

run in the blood/the family 5 (9)

run into 279 (8), 295 (6)

run into debt 785 (2), 803 (6)

run into trouble 700 (7)

run its course 111 (3)

run low 37 (5), 634 (4)

run of luck 727 (1), 730 (1)

run of, the 744 (3)

run of the mill 30 (4)

run off 298 (6), 300 (8), 350 (9), 587 (2), 587 (7), 716 (2)

run-on 71 (4), 71 (5), 71 (6), 141 (6), 146 (3), 285 (3), 581 (5), 627 (1)

run out 69 (5), 111 (3), 125 (6), 145 (6), 300 (7), 634 (4), 636 (7)

run over 54 (5), 279 (8), 449 (8)

run riot 176 (7), 546 (3), 637 (5), 678 (11), 822 (4), 943 (3)

run short 307 (3)

run smoothly 730 (6)

run the gauntlet 661 (8), 711 (3)

run the risk of 180 (3), 661 (7)

run through 16 (4), 43 (8), 165 (10), 189 (5), 263 (18), 279 (9), 362 (10), 634 (4), 655 (10), 712 (9), 806 (4)

run to 761 (5)

run to seed 131 (6), 634 (4)

run to waste 634 (4)

run together 219 (3)

run up 164 (7), 310 (4)

run up an account 803 (6)

run up to 289 (4)

run well 701 (6)

run wild 176 (7)

runabout 274 (11)

runaway 268 (2), 620 (2), 620 (3), 667 (3), 667 (4), 856 (2)

runaway tongue 581 (1)

runaway victory 727 (2)

rune 983 (2)

runes 586 (2)

rung 27 (1), 73 (1), 252 (3), 308 (1)

runic 586 (7), 983 (7)

runnel 351 (1)

runner 217 (3), 268 (3), 277 (4), 529 (6), 716 (8), 789 (1)

runner-up 716 (8)

running 71 (4), 71 (7), 265 (1), 298 (4), 335 (4), 689 (1), 716 (9), 837 (6)

running amok 503 (9), 821 (3)

running battle 716 (1)

running costs 809 (2)

running down 266 (1), 926 (1)

running fight 716 (7)

running jump 312 (1)
running over 54 (4), 637 (3)
running repairs 656 (2)
running shoes 228 (27)
running short 307 (2)
running sore 655 (4), 659 (1), 827 (1)
running through 16 (2)
running water 339 (1), 350 (1)
runny 49 (2), 335 (4), 337 (3), 350 (7)
runs 86 (1)
runs, the 651 (7)
runt 196 (4)
runty 196 (8)
runway 271 (2)
rupture 46 (2), 46 (13), 201 (2), 655 (4), 709 (1)
rural 184 (5), 192 (19), 348 (3), 370 (7)
rural economy 370 (1)
rural population 191 (5)
ruse 542 (2), 698 (2)
rush 61 (11), 176 (2), 176 (7), 277 (2), 277 (6), 318 (3), 318 (5), 350 (9), 366 (8), 670 (1), 670 (3), 680 (1), 680 (2), 680 (3), 712 (1), 712 (10), 876 (4)
rush at 857 (4)
rush for 786 (6)
rush headlong 176 (7)
rush hour 74 (5)
rush in 297 (2)
rush into 857 (4)
rush job 680 (1)
rush one's fences 680 (3)
rushed 680 (2)
rushed into 680 (2)
rushlight 420 (3)
rusk 301 (22)
russet 430 (3), 431 (3)
rust 51 (2), 51 (5), 168 (1), 172 (5), 257 (3), 611 (1), 649 (2), 649 (8), 655 (2), 655 (7), 659 (2), 674 (5)
rust-coloured 431 (3)
rustic 191 (3), 192 (19), 370 (7), 699 (2), 847 (5), 869 (6), 869 (8)
rustication 883 (2), 963 (4)

rusticity 847 (2)
rustiness 611 (1), 655 (2), 679 (1), 695 (1)
rusting 163 (5)
rustle 401 (1), 401 (4), 406 (1), 406 (3), 788 (7)
rustle up 669 (11)
rustler 789 (1)
rusty 127 (7), 257 (2), 407 (2), 611 (3), 655 (6), 679 (7), 695 (5)
rut 81 (2), 259 (1), 262 (1), 610 (1), 859 (4)
ruthless 898 (7), 906 (2)
ruthlessness 599 (1), 906 (1), 910 (1)
rutted 259 (4)
rye 301 (22)
rythmically 141 (7)

S

S-shape 248 (2)
S-shaped 251 (6)
Sabbatarian 945 (3), 988 (6), 988 (9)
Sabbath 683 (1), 988 (7)
sabbatical year 99 (2)
sable 226 (6), 428 (1), 428 (4), 547 (16)
sabotage 63 (3), 161 (9), 165 (1), 165 (6), 634 (1), 634 (4), 641 (7), 655 (3), 702 (1), 702 (10), 738 (2)
sabotaged 63 (2)
saboteur 168 (1), 702 (5), 738 (6), 904 (1)
sabre 723 (8)
sabre-rattling 854 (4)
sabres 722 (10)
saccharin 392 (2)
saccharine 925 (3)
sacerdotal 985 (7), 986 (11)
sack 194 (9), 300 (1), 300 (7), 788 (7), 788 (9)
sack cloth and ashes 939 (1), 941 (3)
sackcloth 259 (1), 945 (1)
sacked 674 (3)

sacker 789 (2)
sackful 26 (2)
sacking 222 (4), 788 (3)
sacrament 988 (3), 988 (4)
sacramental 973 (8), 961 (10), 985 (7), 988 (8)
sacred 866 (8), 965 (5), 973 (8), 975 (4), 979 (8), 981 (10)
sacred edifice 990 (1)
sacred music 412 (1)
sacred tomb 990 (2)
sacred writings 975 (2)
sacredness 979 (2)
sacrifice 37 (5), 150 (2), 362 (1), 362 (10), 597 (1), 772 (1), 772 (4), 781 (3), 781 (7), 825 (4), 941 (2), 979 (9), 981 (3), 981 (6), 981 (12), 982 (1), 988 (10)
sacrifice oneself 759 (4), 931 (3)
sacrifice to 759 (3)
sacrificed 772 (3), 825 (5)
sacrificer 981 (8)
sacrificial 165 (4), 941 (4), 981 (10), 988 (8)
sacrificing 772 (2), 781 (5)
sacrilege 980 (1)
sacrilegious 921 (3), 980 (4)
sacrilegiousness 980 (1)
sacristan 986 (7)
sacristy 990 (4)
sacrosanct 485 (6), 660 (5), 866 (8), 915 (2), 965 (5), 979 (8)
sad 364 (8), 825 (6), 827 (6), 834 (6)
sad ending 616 (1)
sad spectacle 827 (1)
sad world 616 (1)
sadden 821 (6), 827 (8), 834 (11)
saddened 834 (6)
sadder and wiser 830 (2)
saddle 209 (2), 218 (6), 296 (6), 369 (8)
saddle horse 273 (8)
saddle with 38 (3), 917 (11)
saddlebag 194 (9)
saddled with 702 (7)

salubrious 301 (33), 644 (8), 648 (7), 650 (2), 652 (4), 658 (17), 660 (4), 660 (6), 666 (3), 833 (6), 945 (3)
salubrious, be 652 (5)
salubrity 652 (1)
salutary 652 (4)
salutation 583 (1), 884 (2), 920 (2)
salutatory 583 (2)
salute 547 (22), 583 (3), 876 (1), 884 (2), 884 (7), 886 (1), 920 (2), 920 (6), 923 (8), 923 (9)
salvage 656 (1), 656 (9), 668 (1), 668 (3), 771 (7)
salvaged 656 (6)
salvation 666 (1), 668 (1)
salvationist 979 (5), 986 (3)
salve 334 (2), 357 (4), 658 (8), 831 (1)
salver 194 (17)
salvo 402 (1), 712 (3), 876 (1)
samba 837 (14)
same 13 (3), 16 (2), 28 (7), 838 (3)
same all through 16 (2)
same date 123 (1)
same day 123 (1)
same degree 28 (1)
same generation 123 (2)
same meaning 514 (2)
same mind 488 (2)
same name 561 (2)
same old story 16 (1)
same quantity 28 (1)
same, the 13 (1), 13 (2)
same time 123 (1)
same wavelength 488 (2)
sameness 13 (1), 16 (1)
samovar 194 (14)
sampan 275 (5)
sample 23 (1), 53 (1), 83 (2), 386 (3), 459 (13), 461 (7), 522 (2)
sampler 844 (4)
sampling 461 (2)
Samurai 722 (3)
sanatorium 192 (1), 652 (2), 658 (13)

sanctification 979 (2)
sanctified 656 (6), 933 (3), 965 (6), 979 (8)
sanctify 866 (14), 876 (4), 968 (4), 979 (12), 981 (12), 982 (6), 985 (8)
sanctimonious 541 (4), 850 (4), 950 (6), 979 (7)
sanctimoniousness 850 (2), 979 (3), 980 (2)
sanction 488 (1), 488 (6), 488 (8), 751 (4), 756 (1), 756 (5), 758 (1), 758 (3), 923 (1), 923 (8)
sanctioned 915 (2)
sanctioned by law 953 (5)
sanctioning 488 (4)
sanctions 740 (1)
sanctity 965 (2), 979 (2)
sanctuary 192 (17), 299 (1), 660 (2), 662 (1), 990 (2), 990 (4)
sanctum 192 (17), 194 (19), 883 (2), 990 (2)
sand 332 (2)
sand dune 209 (3)
sand dunes 172 (3)
sandals 228 (27)
sandbag 723 (5)
sandbank 349 (1)
sandblast 648 (9)
sandiness 332 (1)
sandpaper 258 (2), 259 (1)
sands 342 (1), 344 (2)
sands of time 108'(1)
sandstone 344 (4)
sandstorm 176 (3)
sandwich 207 (3), 207 (5), 231 (9), 301 (11), 301 (12)
sandwich board 528 (3)
sandwich course 534 (2)
sandwiched 231 (6)
sandwiching 231 (4)
sandy 332 (4), 342 (4), 344 (5), 431 (3), 433 (3)
sane 498 (5), 502 (2)
sane, be 502 (3)
sanely 502 (5)
saneness 502 (1)
sangfroid 820 (1), 823 (1)
sanguinary 335 (5), 362 (9), 431 (4)

sanguine 431 (3), 482 (2), 507 (2), 833 (3), 852 (4)
sanguineous 335 (5)
sanitarian 652 (3)
sanitary 648 (8), 650 (2), 652 (4)
sanitate 648 (10), 652 (6), 658 (20), 660 (8)
sanitation 648 (2), 652 (2), 658 (3)
sanity 177 (1), 447 (1), 498 (2), 502 (1)
sans 190 (8)
Santa Claus 781 (4), 813 (2), 903 (1)
sap 5 (2), 161 (9), 163 (10), 165 (7), 255 (8), 335 (2), 341 (1), 354 (1), 655 (9), 712 (8)
sap-green 434 (3)
sapling 132 (4), 366 (4)
sapped 163 (5), 655 (5)
sapper 255 (5), 722 (5)
sapphire 435 (1), 844 (8)
sappiness 130 (1)
sapping 309 (1), 309 (2)
sappy 128 (6), 335 (4), 354 (4), 356 (2)
sapwood 224 (1), 366 (2)
sarcasm 839 (1), 839 (2), 851 (1), 885 (2), 921 (2), 924 (3), 926 (2)
sarcastic 174 (6), 839 (4), 851 (4), 885 (5), 921 (3), 924 (6), 926 (5)
sarcophagus 364 (1)
sardonic 851 (4)
sari 228 (7)
sarong 228 (13), 228 (14)
sartorial 228 (30)
sash 47 (7), 218 (13), 228 (24), 250 (3), 263 (5), 547 (9), 729 (2), 743 (3)
Satan 934 (1), 969 (1)
satanic 898 (7), 934 (3), 969 (5)
Satanism 969 (3), 974 (2)
Satanist 969 (4)
satchel 194 (9)
sate 301 (35), 637 (5), 820 (7), 838 (5), 861 (5), 863 (3)

sated 54 (4), 301 (31), 635 (5), 684 (2), 820 (4), 838 (4), 861 (2), 863 (2)

sated, be 635 (8)

satellite 89 (2), 276 (4), 314 (2), 315 (3), 321 (10), 707 (1), 742 (4), 742 (5), 745 (5)

satiate 637 (5), 820 (7), 863 (3)

satiated 838 (4), 863 (2)

satiating 637 (3), 838 (3)

satiety 54 (2), 635 (1), 637 (1), 637 (2), 861 (1), 863 (1)

satin 222 (4)

satin-smooth 258 (3)

satiny 258 (3)

satire 20 (2), 519 (2), 546 (1), 590 (1), 839 (1), 839 (2), 851 (2), 926 (2)

satirical 519 (3), 849 (3), 851 (4), 921 (3)

satirical verse 593 (3)

satirist 926 (3)

satirize 546 (3), 593 (10), 839 (5), 851 (6), 926 (6)

satisfaction 635 (1), 768 (1), 804 (1), 824 (3), 828 (1), 923 (1), 941 (1), 941 (2)

satisfactory 635 (3), 644 (9), 828 (3)

satisfied 485 (4), 635 (5), 824 (4), 828 (2), 863 (2), 923 (5)

satisfied, be 635 (8)

satisfy 54 (7), 478 (4), 485 (9), 635 (6), 719 (4), 768 (3), 804 (4), 826 (3), 828 (5), 863 (3)

satisfy oneself 473 (7)

satisfying 376 (3), 635 (3), 828 (3)

saturate 341 (8), 637 (5), 863 (3)

saturated 54 (4), 341 (5), 863 (2)

saturation 54 (2), 341 (2), 637 (1), 863 (1)

saturation bombing 712 (3)

saturation point 54 (2), 236 (1), 341 (1), 863 (1)

Saturn 321 (6), 967 (1)

Saturnalia 61 (4), 837 (2), 944 (1)

Saturnalian 61 (9)

saturnine 834 (7), 893 (2)

satyr 970 (1)

sauce 174 (4), 301 (14), 389 (2), 878 (6), 899 (2)

saucepan 194 (14)

saucer 194 (17), 250 (2), 255 (2)

saucer-shaped 255 (6)

sauciness 547 (4), 878 (2), 899 (2), 921 (2)

saucy 711 (2), 878 (5), 921 (3)

sauna 383 (2), 648 (3)

saunter 136 (4), 267 (3), 267 (13), 278 (4)

sausage 301 (16)

saute 301 (40)

savage 176 (4), 176 (5), 176 (6), 176 (7), 491 (4), 645 (7), 655 (10), 699 (2), 699 (3), 712 (7), 735 (4), 738 (7), 822 (3), 847 (3), 869 (7), 869 (9), 885 (3), 898 (7), 904 (2), 924 (10), 938 (4)

savagely 32 (20)

savagery 176 (1), 491 (1), 699 (1), 847 (2), 898 (2)

savanna 348 (1)

savant 696 (2)

save 39 (4), 57 (6), 632 (5), 666 (5), 668 (3), 674 (4), 746 (3), 771 (7), 778 (5), 814 (3)

save from 668 (3)

save nothing 815 (4)

save oneself 668 (3)

save up 632 (5), 771 (7)

saved 746 (2), 778 (4), 979 (8)

saving 468 (2), 666 (1), 771 (4), 814 (1), 814 (2), 816 (5)

saving grace 933 (2)

saving quality 933 (2)

saving up 666 (1)

savings 632 (1), 674 (1), 771 (3), 814 (1)

savings bank 799 (1)

saviour 903 (1)

savoir faire 490 (1), 694 (1), 848 (2)

savoir vivre 882 (2)

savour 386 (1), 386 (3), 390 (3), 824 (6)

savour of 18 (7), 386 (3)

savouriness 390 (1)

savoury 301 (13), 301 (32), 357 (6), 386 (2), 388 (3), 390 (1), 390 (2), 392 (3), 826 (2)

savoury, be 390 (3)

saw 46 (11), 256 (4), 260 (1), 411 (3), 496 (1)

saw edge 260 (1)

saw the air 547 (21)

saw-toothed 260 (2)

sawdust 332 (2)

sawmill 687 (1)

sawn-off 204 (3)

sawn-off shotgun 723 (9)

sawyer 686 (3)

saxophone 414 (6)

saxophonist 413 (2)

say 532 (5), 579 (8)

say a prayer 981 (11)

say after 106 (4)

say again 106 (4)

say aye 488 (6)

say goodbye 296 (4)

say in defence 927 (6)

say in reply 460 (5)

say no 533 (3), 760 (4)

say nothing 582 (3)

say one will 764 (4)

say one's lines 594 (17)

say one's piece 106 (4)

say one's prayers 979 (9), 981 (11)

say outright 532 (5), 573 (3)

say so 737 (7)

say the magic word 983 (10)

say together 123 (4)

say truly 540 (3)

say yes 488 (6), 758 (3)

saying 496 (1), 532 (4), 563 (1)

saying again 106 (1)
sayings 975 (2)
scab 84 (3), 603 (3), 738 (4), 888 (3)
scabbard 194 (10)
scabbing over 656 (4)
scabby 259 (4)
scabrous 259 (4)
scaffold 964 (3)
scaffolding 218 (13), 310 (2)
scald 381 (10), 651 (14), 655 (4)
scalded 379 (4)
scalding 379 (4)
scale 9 (2), 27 (1), 27 (4), 53 (5), 71 (2), 207 (1), 226 (6), 308 (5), 322 (3), 410 (2), 410 (5), 423 (1), 465 (5)
scale down 37 (4), 105 (4)
scale drawing 623 (1)
scale the heights 308 (5)
scalene triangle 247 (4)
scales 194 (17), 322 (3), 465 (5)
scaliness 207 (3)
scallop 251 (2), 251 (11), 260 (1), 260 (3)
scalp 213 (3), 229 (6), 729 (1)
scalpel 256 (5)
scaly 207 (4), 259 (4)
scamp 458 (4), 598 (4), 726 (3), 738 (4), 938 (1)
scamped 680 (2)
scamper 277 (6)
scamping 458 (1)
scan 267 (12), 438 (9), 441 (3), 453 (4), 455 (4), 459 (13), 480 (6), 490 (8), 593 (10), 858 (3)
scandal 529 (2), 645 (1), 867 (2), 914 (1), 926 (2), 934 (1)
scandalize 827 (11), 829 (6), 861 (5), 924 (14)
scandalized 924 (6)
scandalmonger 529 (4), 821 (2)
scandalous 645 (2), 847 (4), 867 (5), 914 (3), 926 (5), 934 (6)

scanner 658 (13)
scanning 593 (8)
scansion 593 (5)
scant 105 (2), 196 (10), 636 (3), 747 (5)
scant courtesy 885 (1)
scantiness 33 (1), 105 (1), 196 (1), 636 (2)
scanty 33 (6), 105 (2), 196 (10), 204 (3), 636 (3), 946 (3)
scapegoat 150 (2), 731 (3), 755 (1), 825 (4), 941 (2)
scapegrace 738 (4), 938 (1)
scar 209 (2), 547 (1), 547 (2), 547 (19), 548 (4), 655 (4), 655 (9), 845 (1), 845 (3)
scarce 105 (2), 140 (2), 172 (4), 307 (2), 636 (6), 946 (3)
scarcely 33 (9), 140 (3)
scarcely ever 140 (3)
scarceness 636 (2)
scarcity 37 (1), 105 (1), 172 (1), 190 (1), 636 (2), 811 (1), 946 (1)
scarcity value 809 (1)
scare 665 (2), 854 (1), 854 (12)
scare stiff 854 (12)
scarecrow 206 (2), 542 (5), 551 (2), 842 (2), 854 (4)
scared 854 (6)
scaremonger 665 (2), 854 (5)
scarf 226 (5), 228 (22), 228 (23)
scarify 655 (10)
scarlet 431 (1), 431 (3), 934 (6)
scarlet fever 651 (5)
scarmongering 854 (4)
scarp slope 220 (2)
scarred 547 (17)
scars 729 (1)
scary 854 (8)
scatology 649 (1)
scatter 46 (7), 46 (8), 61 (10), 63 (4), 75 (1), 75 (3), 75 (4), 188 (4), 265 (5), 294 (3), 311 (5), 634 (4)

scatter diagram 86 (4)
scatterbrain 456 (1)
scatterbrained 499 (4)
scatterbrains 501 (1)
scattered 46 (4), 75 (2), 105 (2), 728 (5)
scattering 37 (2), 46 (1), 46 (2), 49 (1), 75 (1)
scatty 456 (6)
scavenger 648 (6), 649 (5)
scavenging bird 365 (4)
scenario 445 (3), 589 (2), 590 (2), 594 (3), 623 (2)
scene 186 (1), 230 (1), 438 (5), 443 (1), 445 (2), 594 (2), 594 (6), 724 (1), 822 (2)
scene-painter 556 (1), 594 (11)
scene painting 553 (2)
scene shifter 594 (11)
scenery 344 (1), 445 (2), 594 (6), 841 (1)
scenic 821 (5), 826 (2), 841 (3), 844 (9), 875 (5)
scenic beauty 841 (1)
scent 300 (9), 394 (1), 394 (3), 396 (2), 396 (4), 484 (5), 510 (3), 548 (4), 843 (3)
scent a rival 911 (3)
scent bottle 396 (2)
scent out 619 (5)
scented 394 (2), 396 (3), 843 (6)
scentless 395 (2)
sceptic 486 (3), 974 (3), 980 (3)
sceptical 474 (6), 486 (4), 489 (3), 974 (5)
sceptical, be 486 (7)
scepticism 449 (3), 486 (2), 974 (1)
sceptre 547 (9), 743 (1)
schedule 87 (1), 87 (5), 623 (2), 623 (8)
scheduled flight 271 (2)
schematic 60 (2), 62 (3), 623 (6)
schematize 60 (3), 62 (5), 623 (8)
scheme 62 (1), 623 (1), 623 (4), 623 (9), 698 (5)

sea foam **355** (1)
sea-girt **349** (2)
sea god **966** (2)
sea-going **269** (6), **275** (11), **343** (3)
sea-green **434** (3)
sea lane **269** (1), **343** (1)
sea legs **28** (3), **269** (2)
sea level **210** (1)
sea line **236** (1)
sea lion **365** (3)
Sea Lord **722** (12), **741** (7)
sea mail **531** (2)
sea mark **269** (4)
sea nymph **343** (2), **967** (3)
sea of, a **104** (1)
sea of faces **74** (5)
sea room **183** (4)
sea rover **789** (2)
sea scout **270** (1)
sea serpent **84** (4), **365** (13)
sea travel **269** (1)
sea water **339** (1)
sea-worthy **275** (11)
seabird **365** (4)
seaboard **344** (2)
seafarer **270** (1)
seafaring **269** (1), **269** (6), **275** (11), **343** (3)
seafood **301** (15)
seal **22** (1), **23** (3), **264** (2), **264** (6), **365** (3), **466** (3), **488** (1), **488** (8), **547** (13), **547** (19), **656** (12), **743** (2), **765** (1), **767** (2), **767** (6)
seal of approval **923** (1)
seal off **264** (6)
seal up **45** (9), **747** (10)
sealed **264** (5), **488** (5)
sealed book **491** (2), **530** (1)
sealed lips **523** (1)
sealed off **264** (5), **653** (2)
sealing off **264** (1)
sealing wax **47** (9)
seam **45** (4), **92** (3), **201** (2), **207** (1), **632** (1)
seaman **270** (1)
seamanlike **270** (5)
seamanship **269** (2), **694** (1), **718** (4)
seamed **207** (4)

seamless **52** (4)
seamstress **228** (28)
seance **984** (3)
search **453** (4), **459** (5), **459** (15), **484** (1), **484** (4), **619** (1), **619** (5), **671** (4), **672** (1), **761** (5)
search for **459** (15)
search for truth **973** (1)
search party **459** (9), **619** (3)
search through **459** (15)
search warrant **459** (5), **737** (4), **959** (2)
searcher **453** (2), **459** (9), **619** (3), **671** (2)
searching **453** (3), **459** (11), **671** (3), **827** (3)
searchlight **417** (2), **420** (4)
searing **379** (4), **827** (3)
seascape **445** (2), **553** (4)
seashore **344** (2)
seasick **269** (6)
seaside **344** (2), **344** (6), **837** (4)
seaside resort **192** (1)
season **43** (7), **108** (1), **110** (1), **301** (40), **388** (6), **390** (3), **468** (3), **610** (8), **666** (5), **669** (12)
seasonable **24** (6), **137** (4)
seasonably **137** (8)
seasonal **110** (3), **141** (5)
seasonally **110** (5), **141** (7)
seasoned **390** (2), **610** (7), **669** (8), **694** (6)
seasoning **43** (2), **174** (4), **389** (1), **610** (3), **669** (3)
seasons **141** (2)
seat **28** (3), **186** (1), **187** (2), **187** (3), **187** (5), **192** (1), **192** (6), **218** (6), **238** (2)
seat belt **666** (2)
seat of justice **956** (1)
seat oneself **311** (8)
seated **311** (3)
seated, be **311** (8)
seating **183** (4), **594** (7)
seating capacity **183** (4)
seaward **281** (8)

seaway **183** (4), **269** (1), **624** (4)
seaweed **366** (6)
seaworthy **269** (6), **272** (5), **646** (3), **660** (5)
sebaceous **357** (6)
secateurs **256** (5)
secede **489** (5), **738** (10), **918** (3), **978** (9)
seceder **489** (2), **738** (4), **978** (5)
seceding **978** (7)
secession **489** (1), **603** (1), **738** (2), **978** (2)
secessionist **738** (4), **978** (5), **978** (7)
seclude **46** (9), **300** (6), **525** (7), **652** (6), **883** (10)
secluded **264** (5), **266** (5), **523** (2), **525** (3), **883** (7)
seclusion **46** (1), **46** (2), **57** (1), **188** (1), **192** (17), **199** (2), **298** (1), **444** (1), **883** (2)
second **33** (2), **35** (2), **35** (4), **65** (2), **91** (2), **91** (3), **110** (1), **116** (2), **247** (3), **488** (8), **605** (7), **703** (6), **707** (1), **755** (1)
second best **35** (1), **35** (2), **35** (4), **150** (2), **647** (1), **647** (3), **770** (1)
second chance **905** (3)
second childhood **131** (3), **499** (2)
second-class **35** (4)
second-class citizens **869** (3)
second cousin **11** (2)
second echelon **722** (7)
second fiddle **35** (2), **639** (4)
second glance **438** (4)
second-hand **20** (4), **673** (2)
second helping **106** (1)
second home **192** (1)
second house **594** (2)
second-in-command **755** (1)
second lieutenant **741** (8)
second nature **610** (1)
second part **40** (1)

second place 65 (1)
second rank 35 (1)
second-rate 35 (4), 639 (6), 647 (3), 732 (2)
second-rater 35 (2)
second self 707 (3)
second sight 476 (1), 510 (1), 984 (2)
second string 35 (2)
second thoughts 67 (1), 603 (1), 654 (2), 830 (1), 858 (1)
second to none 34 (5), 644 (6)
secondariness 35 (1)
secondary 35 (4), 157 (3), 466 (5), 534 (5), 639 (5)
secondary education 534 (2)
secondary school 539 (2)
seconder 488 (3), 707 (4)
secondhand 127 (7)
seconding 703 (4)
secondly 91 (4)
seconds 812 (1)
secrecy 525 (2), 547 (3), 582 (1), 858 (1)
secret 80 (7), 491 (2), 523 (1), 523 (4), 524 (1), 525 (2), 525 (3), 530 (1), 586 (1)
secret agent 459 (7)
secret ballot 605 (2)
secret influence 178 (1), 623 (4)
secret lore 530 (1)
secret pact 765 (1)
secret passage 527 (1), 667 (2)
secret place 527 (1), 662 (1)
secret police 459 (6)
secret service 459 (7)
secret sign 547 (2)
secret society 523 (1), 525 (2), 708 (3)
secret weapon 723 (3)
secretariat 687 (1)
secretary 549 (1), 690 (4), 707 (1), 742 (1), 755 (1)
secrete 300 (9), 302 (6), 525 (7)
secretion 300 (1), 302 (1)

secretive 525 (6)
secretiveness 525 (2)
secretly 525 (10)
secretory 300 (4), 302 (5)
sect 77 (1), 708 (1), 978 (3)
sectarian 84 (3), 481 (8), 489 (2), 489 (3), 707 (1), 708 (7), 978 (4), 978 (6), 979 (5), 979 (7)
sectarianism 978 (1)
sectarianize 978 (8)
section 53 (1), 53 (3), 53 (5), 77 (1), 722 (8)
sectional 53 (6), 57 (2), 77 (5), 481 (8), 708 (7), 978 (6)
sectionalism 481 (3)
sectionalize 46 (10)
sector 53 (1), 53 (3), 724 (2)
secular 99 (6), 110 (4), 127 (5), 974 (5), 987 (2)
secularism 974 (2)
secularize 786 (7), 974 (8), 987 (3)
secularized 980 (5), 987 (2)
secure 45 (7), 45 (8), 45 (13), 135 (5), 153 (6), 660 (4), 660 (7), 660 (8), 764 (4), 767 (6), 828 (2)
secured 725 (4), 764 (3), 767 (4)
securely 45 (16)
securities 777 (2)
security 466 (2), 466 (3), 660 (1), 764 (1), 765 (1), 767 (1), 797 (5), 803 (1), 852 (1), 915 (1)
security guard 660 (3)
security risk 661 (2)
sedan chair 274 (1)
sedate 278 (3), 823 (3), 834 (7)
sedation 177 (1)
sedative 177 (2), 177 (4), 658 (4), 658 (7), 679 (5), 679 (10), 831 (1)
sedentary 266 (4)
sedge 366 (8)
sediment 41 (2), 324 (3), 649 (2)

sedition 654 (4), 738 (3), 930 (2)
seditious 149 (3), 738 (7)
seditiousness 738 (1), 738 (3)
seduce 612 (10), 826 (4), 859 (13), 887 (15), 934 (8), 951 (11)
seduced 951 (7)
seducer 545 (1), 612 (5), 859 (6), 887 (4), 952 (1)
seduction 291 (1), 612 (2), 887 (3), 951 (2)
seductive 291 (3), 826 (2), 887 (11)
seductiveness 291 (1), 612 (2)
sedulous 536 (3), 678 (9)
see 374 (5), 438 (7), 438 (9), 441 (3), 447 (7), 484 (5), 490 (8), 498 (6), 513 (7), 985 (4)
see ahead 510 (3)
see coming 510 (3)
see double 440 (4)
see eye to eye 710 (3)
see fair play 913 (6)
see fit 595 (2)
see it coming 124 (6), 865 (4)
see it out 69 (6)
see it through 599 (3), 600 (4)
see justice done 913 (6)
see no difference 464 (4)
see no evil 933 (4)
see off 296 (6), 300 (7)
see one through 703 (5)
see red 176 (7), 503 (11), 822 (4), 891 (6)
see sense 502 (3)
see the catch 698 (5)
see the light 939 (4), 979 (10)
see the point 839 (5)
see-through 422 (2), 490 (8), 516 (5), 725 (6), 865 (4)
see to 455 (5), 457 (6), 688 (5)
see visions 513 (7)

seed 62 (6), 68 (4), 156 (3), 167 (3), 167 (6), 171 (2), 196 (2), 370 (9)
seed itself 167 (6)
seed-time 128 (3)
seed vessel 366 (7)
seedbed 68 (4), 156 (4), 171 (3), 370 (3)
seeded 62 (3)
seediness 801 (1)
seeding 62 (2)
seedling 132 (4)
seedsman 370 (5)
seedy 163 (6), 651 (21), 655 (6), 801 (4)
seeing 438 (1), 438 (6), 457 (4)
seeing double 949 (7)
seeing the world 267 (1)
seek 453 (4), 459 (13), 459 (15), 619 (5), 671 (4), 756 (6), 761 (5)
seek a clue 459 (15)
seek accord 24 (9)
seek advice 691 (5)
seek an answer 459 (13)
seek refuge 269 (10), 660 (9), 662 (4)
seek repute 866 (12), 923 (11)
seek safety 618 (8), 660 (9), 662 (4), 669 (10), 858 (3)
seek to 671 (4)
seeker 453 (2), 619 (3), 763 (1)
seeking 453 (3), 619 (1), 619 (4)
seem 18 (7), 445 (8)
seem like 18 (7)
seeming 18 (1), 18 (6), 445 (1), 445 (7), 541 (4)
seemingly 471 (7)
seemliness 846 (1)
seemly 24 (7), 642 (2), 846 (3)
seen 466 (5)
seep 297 (6), 298 (7), 341 (6)
seep down 309 (3)
seepage 298 (2)
seeping 341 (4)

seer 500 (1), 504 (2), 511 (4), 513 (4), 537 (3), 983 (5), 984 (5)
seersucker 222 (4)
seesaw 12 (2), 317 (2), 317 (4), 601 (4), 837 (4)
seethe 74 (10), 301 (40), 318 (7), 379 (7), 821 (9)
seething 74 (9), 822 (3)
seething mass 61 (2)
segment 46 (10), 53 (1), 53 (3), 53 (7), 58 (1)
segmental 53 (6)
segmentation 46 (3)
segregate 46 (9), 57 (5), 883 (10)
segregation 46 (1), 46 (2), 57 (1), 481 (3), 883 (2)
seine 222 (3)
seismic 176 (5), 317 (3)
seismograph 317 (1), 465 (6), 549 (3)
seismology 317 (1)
seize 145 (7), 516 (5), 747 (8), 786 (6)
seize on 638 (8)
seize power 733 (11)
seize the chance 137 (7)
seize the crown 734 (7)
seize up 145 (7), 728 (7)
seized 651 (21)
seizure 318 (2), 651 (2), 651 (16), 786 (1)
seizure of power 733 (1)
seldom 140 (3)
seldom occur 105 (3)
select 39 (3), 46 (9), 304 (4), 463 (3), 592 (5), 605 (5), 605 (7), 644 (4), 859 (11)
select few 34 (3)
selected 605 (5)
selection 46 (2), 74 (7), 463 (1), 605 (1)
selections 589 (2), 592 (2)
selective 46 (5), 463 (2), 605 (4)
selective killing 362 (1)
self 5 (1), 80 (4), 320 (2), 447 (2)
self-abasing 872 (3)
self-absorbed 932 (3)
self-absorption 932 (1)

self-accusing 939 (3)
self-admirer 873 (3)
self-admiring 873 (4), 932 (3)
self-advertisement 877 (1)
self-assurance 873 (1), 878 (1)
self-assured 473 (5), 532 (4)
self-betrayal 526 (1)
self-centred 873 (4), 932 (3)
self-centredness 873 (1)
self-command 823 (1)
self-conceit 873 (1)
self-confidence 473 (2)
self-confident 599 (2)
self-congratulation 873 (1)
self-conscious 447 (5)
self-consciousness 447 (1)
self-consistency 494 (1)
self-consistent 16 (2), 494 (4)
self-contained 54 (3)
self-contradictory 477 (5)
self-control 177 (1), 595 (0), 599 (1), 747 (1), 823 (1), 942 (1)
self-controlled 747 (5)
self-deception 495 (1), 542 (1)
self-defence 713 (1), 715 (1), 927 (1)
self-deluding 852 (5)
self-delusion 487 (1)
self-denial 931 (1), 942 (1), 945 (1), 981 (3)
self-denying 931 (2), 942 (3)
self-deprecating 872 (3), 874 (2)
self-depreciation 874 (1)
self-destruction 362 (3)
self-determination 744 (2)
self-discipline 942 (1)
self-disciplined 942 (3)
self-effacement 872 (1)
self-effacing 872 (3), 874 (2), 931 (2)
self-employed 622 (5), 744 (7)

self-esteem 871 (1), 873 (1)

self-evident 473 (4), 522 (4)

self-evident truth 496 (2)

self-examination 981 (3)

self-excusing 614 (3), 713 (7)

self-exile 883 (2)

self-existent 10 (3)

self-explanatory 516 (2)

self-glorification 877 (1)

self-governing 733 (9), 744 (7)

self-government 733 (4)

self-help 703 (1)

self-importance 873 (1), 875 (1)

self-important 873 (4)

self-imposed 597 (5)

self-imposed task 622 (2)

self-improvement 536 (1)

self-indulgence 376 (1), 932 (1), 943 (1), 944 (1)

self-indulgent 932 (3), 943 (2)

self-interest 932 (1)

self-love 873 (1), 932 (1)

self-loving 932 (3)

self-made man or woman 800 (2)

self-mastery 599 (1)

self-mortification 945 (1), 963 (1)

self-opinionated 473 (5)

self-opinioned 481 (7)

self-pity 932 (1)

self-pitying 834 (6)

self-praise 871 (1), 873 (1), 923 (2)

self-preservation 932 (1)

self-protection 713 (1)

self-reliance 855 (1)

self-reliant 599 (2), 744 (7), 855 (5)

self-reproach 830 (1), 939 (1)

self-reproachful 939 (3)

self-respect 871 (1)

self-restraint 747 (1)

self-righteous 979 (7)

self-rule 744 (2)

self-sacrifice 931 (1)

self-sacrificing 931 (2)

self-satisfaction 873 (1)

self-seeker 932 (2)

self-seeking 932 (1), 932 (3)

self-service 633 (1), 633 (4)

self-serving 932 (1), 932 (3)

self-starter 68 (3)

self-styled 562 (3)

self-sufficiency 54 (1), 635 (1), 800 (1)

self-sufficient 54 (3), 744 (7)

self-supporting 744 (7)

self-will 595 (0), 602 (1)

self-willed 595 (1), 602 (5), 738 (7)

self-willed, be 595 (2)

selfish 450 (2), 816 (5), 859 (8), 873 (4), 932 (3)

selfish, be 816 (6), 932 (4)

selfishly 932 (5)

selfishness 456 (1), 482 (1), 612 (1), 816 (1), 873 (1), 932 (1)

selfless 931 (2)

selflessness 931 (1)

selfsame 13 (2)

sell 528 (11), 759 (3), 779 (4), 791 (4), 793 (4), 793 (5), 811 (5)

sell again 793 (4)

sell at a loss 772 (4)

sell by auction 793 (4)

sell for 809 (6)

sell forward 793 (4)

sell off 779 (4), 793 (4)

sell-out 594 (2), 793 (1), 793 (4), 793 (5), 930 (8)

sell short 926 (6)

sell up 793 (4)

sell well 793 (5)

seller 268 (1), 579 (5), 686 (2), 793 (1), 793 (2), 794 (2), 794 (3)

seller's market 796 (1), 811 (1)

selling 793 (1)

selling off 779 (1)

selvage 234 (3)

semantic 514 (4), 557 (5), 559 (4)

semanticist 557 (4)

semantics 514 (1), 557 (2)

semaphore 547 (5)

semblance 18 (1), 20 (2), 445 (1)

semen 167 (3), 171 (2)

semester 110 (1)

semi- 53 (6), 55 (3), 92 (4), 192 (6)

semi darkness 419 (2)

semi-detached 192 (20)

semi-skilled 695 (4)

semi-skilled worker 686 (3)

semicircle 250 (4)

semicircular 248 (3), 250 (6)

semicolon 547 (14)

semiconscious 375 (3)

semidetached 49 (2)

semidetached house 192 (6)

semifinal 716 (2)

semiliquid 347 (2), 354 (4), 356 (2)

semiliquidity 327 (1), 335 (1), 354 (1)

semiliterate 491 (7)

seminal 156 (7), 167 (4)

seminal fluid 167 (3)

seminar 534 (1), 538 (4), 584 (3)

seminarist 538 (3), 986 (2)

seminary 539 (3), 986 (9)

semiological 547 (15)

semiology 547 (3)

semiotic 547 (15)

semiotics 547 (3)

semiprecious stone 844 (8)

semiquaver 410 (3)

semitone 201 (1), 410 (2)

semitransparency 421 (1), 424 (1)

semitransparent 424 (2), 427 (5)

senate 131 (4), 692 (2)

senator 692 (3), 868 (4)

senatorial 692 (4), 868 (7)

send 75 (4), 188 (4), 265 (5), 272 (8), 299 (3), 300 (9), 305 (5), 786 (9)

send a letter **588** (4)
send a message **524** (10)
send ahead **64** (4)
send away **272** (8), **300** (6), **786** (9)
send back **136** (7), **607** (3)
send down **37** (4), **300** (6)
send flying **188** (4)
send for **272** (8), **737** (6)
send haywire **63** (5)
send in **299** (3)
send mad **503** (12)
send-off **68** (3), **296** (2)
send one's apologies **760** (4)
send one's regards **884** (6)
send out **300** (9)
send packing **292** (3), **300** (7)
send to Coventry **46** (9), **57** (5), **883** (9)
send to prison **747** (10)
send to sleep **375** (6), **679** (13), **684** (6)
send to the bottom **313** (3)
send to the chair **963** (12)
send to the stake **362** (10)
send up **310** (4), **594** (17), **851** (2), **851** (6)
send word **524** (10)
sender **272** (4)
sending **272** (1)
sending flying **287** (7)
senescence **131** (3)
senescent **655** (5)
senile **131** (6), **161** (7), **499** (4)
senile decay **503** (1)
senility **127** (1), **131** (3), **161** (2), **655** (2)
senior **34** (3), **34** (4), **131** (7), **741** (1)
senior citizen **133** (1)
senior service **722** (12)
seniority **34** (1), **127** (1), **131** (4), **733** (1)
señor **372** (1)
señora **373** (4)
señorita **373** (4)
sensation **374** (2), **529** (1), **818** (1), **864** (3)
sensation of cold **380** (1)

sensational **528** (8), **594** (15), **644** (4), **821** (4), **864** (5), **875** (5)
sensationalism **821** (1)
sensationalist **821** (2)
sensationalize **875** (7)
sense **374** (2), **374** (5), **447** (1), **447** (7), **476** (1), **476** (3), **484** (5), **498** (1), **514** (1), **818** (7)
sense of danger **661** (1)
sense of hearing **415** (1)
sense of humour **835** (2), **839** (1)
sense of injury **616** (1)
sense of occasion **463** (1)
sense of smell **394** (1)
sense of touch **378** (1)
sense organ **374** (2), **628** (2)
senseless **375** (3), **497** (3), **499** (4), **515** (4)
senselessness **375** (1), **497** (1)
senses **447** (1), **502** (1)
sensibility **180** (1), **374** (1)
sensible **319** (6), **374** (3), **475** (7), **498** (5), **818** (3), **819** (2)
sensible of **490** (5)
sensible of, be **374** (5)
sensibly **32** (19)
sensitive **374** (3), **494** (6), **818** (3), **819** (3), **822** (3), **846** (3), **892** (3)
sensitive, be **818** (7), **819** (5)
sensitive plant **819** (1)
sensitiveness **374** (1), **819** (1)
sensitivity **374** (1), **494** (3), **612** (3), **819** (1), **892** (1)
sensitize **374** (6)
sensitized **374** (3)
sensor **484** (2)
sensory **374** (3)
sensory apparatus **374** (2)
sensual **319** (6), **376** (5), **818** (3), **943** (2), **944** (3), **951** (8), **974** (5)
sensual, be **944** (4)
sensual pleasure **376** (1)

sensualism **301** (4), **376** (1), **824** (3), **943** (1), **944** (1), **951** (2)
sensualist **944** (2), **952** (1), **980** (3)
sensuality **376** (1), **944** (1)
sensually **944** (5)
sensuous **374** (3), **376** (5), **818** (3), **826** (2)
sensuous pleasure **376** (1)
sensuousness **374** (1), **376** (1)
sent after **619** (4)
sent back **607** (2)
sent to Coventry **883** (6)
sentence **110** (1), **480** (1), **480** (5), **563** (1), **747** (3), **961** (1), **961** (3), **963** (1), **963** (4), **963** (8)
sentence of death **361** (1)
sentenced **961** (2)
sententious **480** (4), **496** (3), **571** (2), **574** (5)
sentient **374** (3), **818** (3), **819** (2), **819** (3)
sentiment **485** (3), **818** (1), **887** (1)
sentimental **499** (4), **572** (2), **818** (3), **819** (2), **887** (9)
sentimentality **818** (1), **819** (1)
sentiments **819** (1)
sentinel **264** (3), **441** (1), **457** (2), **660** (3), **664** (2), **713** (6), **722** (7)
sentry **264** (3), **457** (2), **660** (3), **664** (2), **713** (6), **722** (7)
sepal **366** (7)
separability **46** (1), **49** (1)
separable **46** (5), **46** (6)
separate **10** (3), **15** (4), **46** (5), **46** (7), **46** (8), **49** (2), **51** (5), **53** (6), **59** (4), **72** (2), **75** (2), **75** (3), **75** (4), **92** (6), **294** (3), **463** (3), **605** (7), **896** (5), **978** (7), **978** (9)
separate out **51** (5)
separated **46** (4), **75** (2), **199** (4), **294** (3), **896** (3)
separately **46** (14)

separateness 10 (1), 46 (1)
separates 228 (9)
separation 10 (1), 46 (2),
49 (1), 51 (1), 63 (1), 72
(1), 75 (1), 88 (1), 165 (1),
199 (2), 201 (2), 294 (1),
463 (1), 709 (1), 746 (1),
883 (2), 896 (1), 978 (2)
separatism 46 (1), 978 (1)
separatist 978 (5)
separative 46 (5)
sepia 430 (2)
sepsis 651 (5)
septet 99 (2), 412 (6)
septic 645 (2), 649 (6), 653
(4)
septic tank 649 (4)
septuagenarian 99 (3), 133
(1)
sepulchral 364 (8), 404
(2), 407 (3), 578 (2)
sepulchre 364 (5), 990 (2)
sequel 41 (1), 65 (1), 67
(1), 69 (1), 69 (2), 71 (1),
120 (1), 157 (1), 238 (1),
589 (2), 603 (1), 654 (2)
sequence 9 (2), 38 (1), 60
(1), 65 (1), 71 (1), 120 (1),
157 (1), 203 (1), 284 (1),
619 (1)
sequence dancing 837
(13)
sequential 9 (5), 65 (2), 71
(4), 120 (2), 157 (3), 284
(3)
sequester 46 (9), 883 (10)
sequestered 266 (5), 523
(2), 883 (7)
sequestrate 786 (8), 786
(10)
sequestration 786 (2), 883
(2), 963 (4)
sequin 844 (6)
seraph 968 (1)
seraphic 933 (3), 968 (3)
seraphim 968 (1)
serenade 412 (4), 412 (5),
413 (10), 889 (2), 889 (7)
serendipity 159 (1), 484
(1)
serene 266 (5), 823 (3)
Serene Highness 870 (1)

serenity 823 (1), 828 (1),
865 (1)
serf 370 (4), 742 (6), 869
(5)
serge 222 (4)
sergeant 741 (8)
sergeant major 735 (3),
741 (8)
serial 9 (5), 71 (4), 106 (2),
589 (2)
serial order 9 (2)
serial place 8 (1), 27 (1),
60 (1), 73 (1), 866 (2)
serialization 62 (1), 65 (1),
71 (1)
serialize 71 (6), 141 (6),
528 (9)
serialized 71 (4)
serially 71 (7)
seriatim 60 (5), 71 (7), 80
(10)
series 48 (1), 52 (2), 60 (1),
62 (1), 65 (1), 71 (2), 74
(7), 77 (2), 85 (1), 106 (2),
146 (1), 284 (1), 410 (5),
589 (5)
series of tests 459 (4)
serious 455 (2), 498 (5),
571 (2), 573 (2), 599 (2),
638 (5), 651 (21), 823 (3),
834 (7), 840 (2), 885 (5),
891 (4), 893 (2), 934 (6)
serious, be 540 (3), 834
(10)
serious press 528 (4)
seriously 32 (16), 32 (20),
532 (8)
seriousness 455 (1), 599
(1), 638 (1), 820 (1), 823
(1), 834 (3), 840 (1), 950
(2)
sermon 534 (4), 579 (2),
591 (1)
sermonize 534 (7), 579 (9)
sermonizer 979 (5)
serpent 365 (13), 406 (1),
698 (3)
serpentine 251 (5), 251 (6)
serrate 259 (9)
serrated 247 (5), 256 (8),
260 (2)
serration 256 (1), 259 (1),
260 (1)

serried 74 (9), 324 (4)
serried ranks 48 (1), 324
(3)
serum 335 (2)
servant 35 (2), 628 (2), 639
(4), 686 (2), 690 (4), 707
(1), 742 (1), 981 (8)
servant-class 869 (8)
serve 35 (5), 45 (14), 173
(3), 284 (4), 457 (6), 615
(4), 622 (7), 628 (4), 640
(4), 642 (3), 682 (7), 703
(7), 739 (4), 742 (8), 745
(6), 783 (3), 879 (4)
serve as 622 (8)
serve notice on 959 (7)
serve one right 714 (4),
913 (6)
serve one's turn 640 (4)
serve rightly 714 (3)
serve the community 897
(6)
serve the times 879 (4)
serve up 633 (5)
server 707 (1), 986 (7), 988
(6)
service 173 (1), 615 (2),
622 (3), 633 (1), 640 (1),
656 (9), 666 (5), 673 (1),
703 (1), 739 (2), 745 (2),
781 (2), 897 (2), 981 (2),
981 (7)
service stripe 729 (2)
serviceable 173 (2), 628
(3), 640 (2)
serviceman or -woman
722 (4)
services 628 (1)
services, the 722 (6)
servicing 666 (1)
servile 83 (4), 597 (4), 739
(3), 745 (4), 745 (5), 879
(3), 884 (3), 920 (3), 925
(3)
servile, be 739 (4), 745 (6),
879 (4), 925 (4)
servilely 879 (5)
servility 597 (1), 739 (1),
879 (1), 925 (1)
serving 35 (4), 703 (4), 742
(7), 745 (4)
servitude 721 (1), 740 (1),
745 (3), 747 (3), 879 (1)

servomotor 630 (2)

session 692 (1)

sessions 956 (2), 959 (3)

sessions judge 957 (1)

set 16 (1), 45 (7), 45 (9), 52 (2), 58 (1), 62 (4), 71 (2), 74 (3), 74 (4), 74 (7), 77 (1), 77 (2), 78 (1), 88 (2), 153 (8), 179 (1), 187 (5), 217 (1), 217 (5), 235 (4), 243 (1), 281 (1), 324 (6), 326 (4), 445 (1), 473 (5), 534 (5), 538 (4), 587 (6), 589 (5), 594 (6), 602 (4), 632 (3), 656 (11), 658 (20), 669 (11), 706 (2), 708 (1), 716 (2), 843 (2)

set a bad example 934 (8)

set a trap 527 (5)

set about 68 (8), 682 (7)

set against 46 (9), 462 (2), 613 (3), 704 (4), 709 (8), 888 (4)

set an ambush 527 (5)

set an example 23 (5), 612 (8), 688 (4)

set apart 15 (7), 46 (5), 46 (9), 57 (5), 88 (5), 201 (4), 463 (3), 605 (7), 919 (3)

set aside 188 (4), 632 (5), 752 (3), 752 (4), 769 (3)

set at ease 828 (5)

set at liberty 746 (3), 919 (3)

set at naught 483 (4)

set at odds 709 (8), 861 (5), 881 (5)

set at rest 69 (4), 828 (5)

set back 136 (7), 772 (2)

set books 534 (3)

set down 187 (5), 311 (5), 532 (5), 586 (8)

set down as 485 (8)

set down to 158 (3)

set fair 379 (6), 730 (5)

set fire to 381 (9), 381 (10)

set foot in 297 (5)

set forth 296 (6)

set free 668 (3), 744 (10), 746 (2), 746 (3)

set going 68 (9), 156 (9), 265 (5), 672 (3), 673 (5)

set in 68 (8), 144 (3), 153 (7), 179 (3), 350 (10)

set in motion 68 (9), 673 (5)

set in order 56 (5)

set no store by 922 (6)

set of rules 693 (1)

set off 12 (3), 28 (9), 28 (10), 31 (5), 39 (3), 68 (9), 182 (3), 287 (8), 522 (8), 841 (8), 844 (12)

set on 612 (9), 712 (7)

set on edge 377 (5)

set on fire 381 (10), 821 (6)

set on foot 68 (9)

set one back 702 (8)

set one's face 599 (3)

set one's face against 760 (4)

set one's hand to 672 (3)

set one's heart on 859 (11)

set one's mind at rest 823 (7)

set one's teeth on edge 393 (3)

set or lay a trap 542 (10)

set out 62 (4), 267 (11), 296 (6), 522 (8), 591 (5)

set phrase 563 (1)

set piece 594 (4), 875 (3)

set right 654 (10)

set sail 269 (10), 296 (6)

set side by side 202 (4)

set snares 619 (6)

set speech 579 (2)

set square 247 (3)

set store by 638 (8), 923 (8)

set the alarm 117 (7)

set the fashion 64 (3), 178 (3), 612 (8), 848 (7)

set theory 86 (3)

set to 68 (8), 301 (35), 599 (3), 672 (3), 709 (3), 716 (7), 716 (11)

set to music 412 (7), 413 (8)

set to work 68 (8)

set too high a value on 482 (4)

set towards 179 (3)

set-up 8 (1), 20 (6), 56 (5), 62 (4), 68 (10), 156 (9),

164 (7), 215 (4), 310 (3), 310 (4), 331 (1), 587 (7), 656 (11)

set upon 859 (7)

setback 509 (1), 616 (1), 655 (1), 702 (3), 731 (1), 772 (1)

sett 192 (3), 226 (7)

settee 218 (6)

setter 365 (10)

setting 186 (1), 230 (1), 412 (4), 438 (5), 594 (6), 844 (1)

setting apart 46 (2)

setting free 667 (1), 744 (1), 746 (1)

setting out 68 (3), 296 (1)

setting sun 129 (1)

setting-up 56 (1)

settle 62 (4), 69 (6), 153 (7), 187 (8), 192 (21), 309 (3), 473 (9), 480 (5), 610 (7), 758 (3), 765 (5), 786 (7), 804 (4)

settle accounts 808 (5)

settle differences 719 (4)

settle down 153 (7), 266 (7), 313 (4)

settle for 791 (6)

settle in 297 (5)

settle on 605 (6)

settle with 963 (8)

settled 69 (4), 153 (5), 186 (3), 187 (4), 191 (6), 266 (4), 473 (5), 610 (6)

settlement 184 (2), 187 (1), 187 (3), 191 (5), 765 (1), 781 (1), 804 (1)

settler 59 (2), 191 (4), 297 (3)

settling 187 (1)

seven 99 (2)

Seven Deadly Sins 99 (2)

seven seas, the 343 (1)

seventh heaven 824 (2), 971 (1)

seventy 99 (3)

sever 46 (8)

severable 46 (6), 330 (2)

several 101 (1), 104 (4)

severally 46 (14), 80 (10)

severance 39 (1), 46 (2)

severe 32 (12), 83 (6), 174
(5), 573 (2), 735 (4), 747
(4), 827 (3), 834 (7), 862
(3), 885 (5), 898 (6), 906
(2), 914 (4), 945 (3)

severe, be 735 (7), 747 (7),
757 (4), 906 (3), 963 (8)

severe style 566 (1)

severed 46 (4)

severely 735 (9)

severity 83 (1), 176 (1),
182 (1), 481 (4), 573 (1),
602 (2), 645 (1), 688 (1),
735 (1), 745 (1), 757 (1),
827 (1), 854 (4), 885 (2),
898 (2), 898 (3), 906 (1),
916 (1), 950 (2)

sew 45 (9), 45 (12), 164 (7)

sewer 263 (8), 351 (2), 648
(4), 649 (4), 653 (1)

sewerage 648 (2), 649 (2)

sewing 45 (2)

sewn 45 (8)

sex 45 (3), 77 (1), 167 (1)

sex appeal 291 (1), 612
(2), 841 (1), 887 (2)

sex-conscious 951 (8)

sex crime 951 (4)

sex-mad 951 (8)

sex maniac 952 (1)

sexagenarian 99 (3), 133
(1)

sexiness 951 (2)

sexism 481 (3)

sexist 481 (8)

sexless 161 (7)

sextant 247 (3), 269 (4),
465 (5)

sextet 99 (2), 412 (6)

sexton 741 (6), 986 (7)

sexual 77 (1), 167 (4), 944
(3)

sexual desire 859 (4)

sexual intercourse 45 (3)

sexual jealousy 911 (1)

sexual pleasure 376 (1)

sexual urge 859 (4)

sexuality 944 (1)

sexy 841 (6), 887 (12), 951
(6)

sh! 399 (5)

shabbiness 35 (1), 801 (1),
930 (1)

shabby 645 (2), 655 (6),
801 (4), 867 (4), 930 (4),
930 (5), 934 (6)

shack 192 (7)

shackle 45 (12), 47 (1), 47
(8), 702 (4), 747 (9), 748
(4)

shackled 747 (6)

shade 27·(1), 33 (2), 226
(4), 418 (1), 418 (6), 419
(7), 421 (1), 421 (2), 421
(4), 425 (3), 425 (8), 685
(4), 831 (3)

shade of difference 15 (2),
463 (1)

shade off 27 (5)

shaded 418 (3), 419 (5)

shades 361 (3), 970 (3)

shadiness 930 (1), 954 (2)

shading 418 (2), 553 (1)

shading off 27 (2)

shadow 4 (2), 18 (3), 20
(1), 22 (1), 28 (6), 89 (2),
89 (4), 200 (5), 206 (2),
238 (5), 284 (4), 418 (1),
419 (7), 421 (4), 619 (3),
619 (5), 707 (1), 843 (7)

shadow cabinet 669 (1)

shadow of death 361 (1)

shadowiness 320 (1), 523
(1)

shadowing 459 (6)

shadows 418 (1)

shadowy 4 (3), 244 (2), 320
(3), 418 (3), 419 (5), 421
(3), 513 (6)

shady 380 (5), 418 (3), 419
(5), 421 (3), 867 (4), 930
(4), 954 (6)

shaft 211 (1), 218 (3), 218
(10), 255 (4), 256 (2), 263
(8), 417 (2)

shag 388 (2)

shagginess 259 (1)

shaggy 259 (5)

shaggy-dog story 839 (2)

shake 43 (7), 49 (4), 63 (3),
163 (9), 176 (8), 251 (13),
279 (1), 279 (7), 317 (2),
317 (4), 317 (6), 318 (1),
318 (5), 318 (6), 380 (7),
818 (8), 821 (8), 854 (10),
854 (12)

shake hands 295 (6), 719
(5), 884 (7)

shake hands on 765 (5),
791 (6)

shake off 49 (3), 277 (8),
300 (6), 667 (6)

shake one's fist 711 (3)

shake one's head 533 (3),
547 (21), 760 (4), 762 (3)

shake-up 149 (1), 318 (6),
821 (7)

shaken 601 (3), 655 (5)

shakes, the 318 (1)

shakiness 163 (1)

shaking 318 (4)

shaky 163 (4), 163 (8), 318
(4), 655 (6), 661 (4), 854
(7)

shallots 301 (20)

shallow 4 (3), 33 (7), 172
(4), 212 (2), 223 (2), 456
(3), 491 (7), 499 (4), 850
(4)

shallowness 212 (1), 499
(1), 850 (2)

shallows 212 (1)

shalom 295 (7)

shaly 207 (4), 344 (5)

sham 20 (2), 20 (4), 20 (5),
22 (1), 527 (3), 541 (2),
541 (3), 541 (6), 542 (5),
542 (7), 543 (2), 543 (5),
698 (2), 836 (2), 850 (2),
925 (1), 979 (3)

sham courage 855 (1)

shaman 983 (5), 986 (8)

shamanism 983 (1)

shamble 267 (14), 278 (4)

shambles 61 (2), 61 (4),
362 (5), 649 (4), 695 (2)

shambling 695 (5)

shame 612 (1), 616 (1), 867
(1), 867 (2), 867 (11), 872
(2), 872 (7), 885 (6), 914
(1), 921 (5), 922 (5), 926
(7), 930 (1), 934 (1), 936
(1), 950 (1), 951 (11), 963
(8)

shame, a 830 (3)

shamefaced 936 (3)

shamefaced look 872 (2)

shameful 616 (2), 645 (2),
867 (5), 934 (6)

shamefulness **930** (1)
shameless **522** (5), **820** (5), **847** (4), **878** (4), **930** (4), **934** (3), **951** (7)
shamelessly **930** (9), **951** (12)
shamelessness **878** (1), **934** (1), **951** (1)
shamming **20** (4)
shampoo **333** (1), **333** (3), **648** (3), **648** (4), **648** (9), **843** (2)
shamrock **366** (6), **547** (11)
shandy **301** (28)
shanghai **542** (10)
shank **218** (5), **267** (7)
Shanks's pony **267** (6)
shanty **192** (7), **412** (13)
shanty town **192** (8)
shape **7** (2), **77** (2), **83** (8), **164** (7), **233** (1), **243** (1), **243** (5), **331** (1), **445** (1), **445** (6), **534** (6), **551** (8), **623** (8), **844** (12), **970** (3)
shape one's course **267** (11)
shaped **243** (3)
shapeless **244** (2), **842** (4)
shapelessness **244** (1)
shapeliness **245** (1), **841** (1)
shapely **245** (2), **841** (5)
shaping **164** (1), **164** (5), **243** (2)
shard **53** (5)
share **53** (1), **92** (5), **767** (2), **775** (2), **775** (5), **783** (2), **783** (3)
share-buyer **792** (2)
share expenses **775** (5), **804** (5)
share in **775** (5)
share out **53** (7), **465** (14), **771** (3), **775** (2), **783** (2), **783** (3)
share-seller **793** (2)
shareholder **775** (3), **776** (2)
sharer **707** (3), **775** (3)
shares **783** (1)
sharing **45** (5), **708** (6), **775** (2), **775** (4)

sharing out **783** (1)
shark **365** (15), **545** (4), **786** (4), **789** (3)
sharp **174** (6), **176** (5), **256** (7), **259** (5), **260** (2), **374** (3), **374** (4), **388** (3), **393** (2), **407** (2), **410** (2), **410** (8), **411** (2), **498** (4), **571** (2), **590** (6), **698** (4), **818** (6), **827** (3), **827** (4), **839** (4), **885** (5), **892** (3), **924** (6)
sharp appetite **859** (2)
sharp, be **256** (10)
sharp bend **248** (2)
sharp ear **415** (1)
sharp edge **256** (5), **259** (1), **370** (6), **630** (1), **723** (7), **723** (8)
sharp-edged **256** (7)
sharp-eyed **455** (2), **457** (4)
sharp-nosed **394** (2)
sharp note **407** (1)
sharp point **47** (5), **69** (2), **247** (1), **254** (3), **256** (2), **263** (12), **659** (1), **723** (3), **723** (6), **723** (8), **778** (2)
sharp practice **541** (2), **542** (2), **698** (1), **930** (3)
sharp sight **438** (1)
sharp-sighted **438** (6)
sharp taste **388** (1)
sharp temper **892** (1)
sharp-tempered **892** (3)
sharp tongue **709** (2)
sharp wits **498** (1)
sharp-witted **498** (4)
sharpen **176** (9), **256** (11), **374** (6), **821** (7)
sharpen the wits **534** (6)
sharpened **256** (7)
sharpener **256** (6), **333** (1)
sharper **696** (2), **789** (3)
sharply **32** (17)
sharpness **174** (3), **256** (1), **260** (1), **388** (1), **393** (1), **498** (2), **694** (1), **827** (1), **885** (2), **892** (1)
sharpshooter **287** (4), **712** (5), **722** (4)
sharpshooting **712** (3)

shatter **46** (13), **165** (7), **330** (3)
shatter-proof **329** (2)
shattered **161** (7)
shattered silence **400** (1)
shattering **638** (6), **864** (5)
shave **46** (11), **200** (5), **204** (5), **207** (5), **378** (7), **843** (2), **843** (7)
shave off **39** (3)
shaved **229** (5)
shaven **648** (7)
shaver **843** (3)
shaving **33** (3), **206** (2), **229** (1), **843** (2)
shavings **41** (2), **641** (3)
shawl **228** (21)
she **373** (1), **373** (3)
she-demon **970** (4)
she-devil **904** (4)
she wolf **176** (4)
sheaf **74** (6)
shear **204** (5), **246** (1), **369** (10)
shears **256** (5)
sheath **194** (1), **194** (10), **226** (1)
sheathe **187** (6), **231** (8), **288** (3), **303** (4)
shebeen **192** (12)
shed **37** (5), **49** (3), **192** (7), **229** (7), **300** (9), **311** (5)
shed blood **362** (10), **718** (11), **735** (8)
shed tears **836** (6)
shedding **229** (1)
sheen **417** (1), **417** (5)
sheep **20** (3), **365** (8)
sheep farmer **369** (5)
sheep farming **369** (1)
sheepdog **365** (10)
sheepfold **369** (3)
sheepish **872** (4), **936** (3)
sheeplike **365** (18)
sheep's eyes **889** (2)
sheepskin **226** (6)
sheer **32** (14), **44** (4), **215** (2), **220** (4), **422** (2)
sheer drop **309** (1)
sheer face **215** (1)
sheer lunacy **499** (2)
sheer off **282** (3), **290** (3)
sheer perfection **646** (1)

sheet 32 (2), 207 (2), 226 (8), 528 (4), 631 (3)

sheet anchor 47 (6), 660 (2)

sheet iron 207 (2)

sheet lightning 420 (1)

sheet music 410 (3)

sheet of flame 379 (2)

sheet of light 417 (1)

sheet of water 346 (1)

sheeting 350 (7)

sheets 47 (3)

sheikh 741 (4)

sheikhdom 733 (5)

shelf 194 (4), 218 (12), 254 (2), 632 (2)

shelf-room 632 (2)

shell 41 (1), 190 (2), 226 (1), 226 (6), 229 (6), 275 (8), 287 (2), 326 (1), 331 (1), 712 (11), 723 (4), 723 (12), 723 (14)

shell burst 400 (1)

shell-pink 431 (3)

shell-shocked 161 (7), 503 (7)

shellac 357 (5)

shellfish 301 (15), 365 (14)

shellshock 503 (2)

shelter 187 (3), 192 (3), 192 (7), 192 (17), 254 (2), 266 (3), 295 (2), 299 (1), 299 (3), 421 (4), 527 (1), 660 (2), 660 (8), 662 (1), 662 (2), 713 (2)

shelter under 614 (4)

sheltered 421 (3), 660 (4)

shelve 136 (7), 220 (5), 458 (6), 620 (5)

shelved 458 (3)

shelving 194 (4), 220 (4)

shepherd 74 (8), 74 (11), 369 (6), 369 (10), 660 (8), 689 (5)

shepherding 74 (1)

sherbet 301 (27)

sherd 53 (5)

sheriff 660 (3), 741 (6), 955 (2)

sherry 301 (29)

Shetland pony 273 (9)

shibboleth 547 (8)

shield 421 (1), 421 (4), 547 (11), 660 (2), 660 (8), 662 (2), 713 (5), 713 (9), 729 (1)

shielded 660 (4)

shift 108 (1), 110 (1), 141 (1), 143 (1), 143 (5), 143 (6), 147 (2), 149 (1), 188 (1), 188 (4), 228 (8), 265 (4), 265 (5), 272 (1), 272 (7), 277 (6), 282 (1), 282 (6), 542 (2), 623 (3), 682 (3), 688 (2), 698 (2), 698 (5), 780 (5)

shift for oneself 688 (4), 744 (9)

shift one's ground 603 (5)

shift the blame 919 (4)

shiftiness 698 (1)

shifting 114 (3), 152 (3), 152 (4), 265 (3)

shifting sands 152 (2)

shiftless 670 (3)

shifty 152 (3), 541 (4), 698 (4), 867 (4), 930 (4)

shifty, be 152 (5)

shimmer 417 (2), 417 (11)

shin 267 (7)

shin up 308 (5)

shindig 61 (4), 709 (3), 716 (7)

shine 34 (7), 152 (5), 258 (1), 258 (4), 317 (4), 318 (5), 417 (1), 417 (5), 417 (11), 420 (9), 440 (5), 648 (1), 648 (9), 694 (8), 841 (7), 866 (11), 875 (7)

shine on 703 (6), 730 (8)

shine through 422 (3), 443 (4)

shine upon 417 (13)

shingle 207 (2), 332 (2), 344 (2)

shingles 651 (12)

shining 417 (8), 420 (8), 648 (7)

shining example 646 (2)

shining light 937 (1)

Shintoism 973 (3)

shiny 258 (3), 417 (8)

ship 193 (2), 238 (3), 269 (1), 272 (2), 272 (6), 273

(1), 273 (12), 275 (1), 722 (13)

ship ahoy 269 (14)

ship master 270 (1)

ship oars 269 (11)

shipmates 270 (1)

shipment 193 (1), 272 (2), 272 (3)

shipper 272 (4), 273 (1)

shipping 272 (2), 275 (10)

shipping agent 272 (4)

shipping lane 343 (1)

shipping line 275 (10)

ship's boat 275 (7)

ship's colours 547 (12)

ship's company 74 (4)

ship's steward 270 (1)

shipshape 60 (2), 83 (6), 275 (11), 694 (7)

shipwreck 165 (3), 165 (6)

shipwright 686 (3)

shire 184 (3)

shire-horse 273 (6)

shirk 620 (5), 769 (3), 918 (3)

shirker 458 (1), 598 (2), 620 (2), 856 (2)

shirking 598 (3), 620 (1), 856 (1)

shirr 261 (3)

shirt 228 (16)

shirtfront 228 (3)

shirtwaister 228 (8)

shiver 318 (1), 318 (5), 330 (3), 380 (7), 854 (10)

shivering 318 (2), 380 (1), 380 (6), 651 (22)

shivers 318 (1), 651 (2)

shivery 330 (2)

shoal 74 (3), 104 (2)

shoals 212 (1)

shock 74 (6), 160 (5), 176 (1), 279 (1), 279 (3), 318 (1), 508 (1), 508 (5), 509 (1), 651 (2), 712 (10), 821 (1), 825 (1), 827 (11), 829 (6), 854 (1), 861 (5), 864 (1), 888 (8), 924 (14)

shock absorber 177 (2)

shock-headed 259 (5)

shock of hair 259 (2)

shock tactics 712 (1)

shock troops **712** (5), **722** (1), **722** (7)

shockable **950** (6)

shocked **508** (3), **854** (6), **924** (6)

shocker **938** (4)

shocking **32** (10), **84** (6), **508** (2), **645** (4), **827** (6), **842** (3), **867** (5), **934** (6)

shocking-pink **431** (3)

shockingly **32** (20)

shockproof **329** (2)

shod **214** (4), **228** (29)

shoddiness **645** (1)

shoddy **35** (4), **163** (8), **208** (2), **645** (2)

shoe **228** (27)

shoe-repairer **656** (5)

shoed **214** (4)

shoemaker **228** (28)

shoo away **300** (7)

shoot **53** (4), **132** (4), **170** (2), **197** (4), **277** (6), **279** (10), **287** (8), **311** (6), **362** (10), **366** (4), **366** (5), **377** (5), **551** (9), **712** (11), **837** (21), **949** (15), **963** (12)

shoot ahead **285** (3), **306** (5)

shoot at **712** (11), **924** (10)

shoot down **311** (6), **362** (10), **362** (11), **712** (11)

shoot oneself **362** (13)

shoot-out **716** (7)

shoot out rays **417** (12)

shoot the rapids **269** (11)

shoot through **305** (5)

shoot up **36** (4), **254** (5), **308** (4), **310** (4)

shooter **287** (4), **619** (3), **722** (4), **837** (16)

shooting **377** (3), **445** (4), **619** (2), **619** (4), **837** (6)

shooting pain **377** (2)

shooting range **724** (1)

shooting script **445** (3)

shooting star **321** (7)

shop **524** (9), **687** (1), **792** (5), **796** (3)

shop around **605** (6)

shop assistant **686** (2), **793** (2)

shop goods **795** (1)

shop-soiled **647** (3), **812** (3), **845** (2)

shop steward **690** (4), **754** (2)

shop walker **793** (2)

shop window **796** (1)

shopfloor **687** (1)

shopkeeper **633** (2), **793** (2), **794** (2)

shoplift **788** (7)

shoplifter **789** (1)

shoplifting **788** (1)

shopper **792** (2)

shopping **792** (1), **792** (4)

shopping bag **194** (9)

shopping centre **76** (1), **192** (14), **796** (2)

shopping list **627** (1), **792** (1)

shopping spree **792** (1)

shore **218** (2), **234** (1), **239** (1), **344** (2), **344** (6)

shore up **218** (15)

shorn **204** (3), **648** (7)

shorn of **772** (2)

short **33** (6), **55** (3), **114** (5), **196** (9), **204** (3), **205** (4), **210** (2), **246** (4), **307** (2), **330** (2), **445** (4), **569** (2), **582** (2), **592** (4), **772** (3)

short and sweet **114** (5), **569** (2)

short, be **204** (4)

short circuit **160** (5), **702** (3)

short commons **636** (1)

short cut **200** (2), **249** (1), **624** (4), **625** (1)

short distance **200** (2), **201** (1), **204** (1), **206** (1)

short drink **301** (26)

short list **87** (1), **605** (1)

short-lived **114** (4)

short measure **307** (1)

short memory **506** (1)

short of **35** (6), **39** (4), **55** (3), **307** (2)

short of breath **684** (3)

short of cash **801** (3)

short period **110** (1)

short run **114** (2)

short shrift **906** (1)

short sight **438** (1), **440** (1)

short-sighted **440** (3), **481** (6)

short span **200** (2)

short step **200** (2)

short story **590** (4)

short supply **636** (2)

short temper **892** (1)

short-tempered **892** (3)

short-term **114** (5)

short while **114** (2)

short word **559** (1)

short work **701** (2)

shortage **37** (1), **42** (1), **307** (1), **636** (2)

shortbread **301** (23)

shortchange **542** (8), **811** (5)

shortcoming **29** (1), **307** (1), **769** (1), **934** (2)

shorten **27** (5), **37** (4), **39** (3), **46** (10), **46** (11), **198** (7), **204** (5), **370** (9), **569** (3), **592** (5), **655** (9)

shorten sail **278** (6)

shortened **55** (3), **204** (3)

shortening **37** (2), **39** (1), **46** (3), **198** (1), **204** (2), **569** (1), **592** (1)

shortfall **55** (1), **55** (2), **307** (1), **636** (1), **636** (2), **647** (1), **647** (2), **726** (1), **803** (1)

shorthand **586** (1)

shorthand typist **586** (6)

shorthanded **636** (4)

shortly **204** (6)

shortness **33** (1), **114** (2), **196** (1), **204** (1)

shorts **228** (12)

shot **252** (2), **287** (1), **287** (2), **287** (4), **402** (1), **551** (4), **619** (3), **658** (2), **723** (4), **723** (12)

shot across the bows **712** (2)

shot at **671** (1)

shot colours **437** (1)

shot in the arm **174** (4)

shot in the dark **461** (2), **512** (2)

shot-putter **837** (16)

shot silk **437** (1)

shot through 263 (14)
shot through with 437 (6)
shotgun 723 (9)
shotgun wedding 894 (2)
should be 915 (4)
shoulder 218 (2), 218 (15), 273 (12), 279 (7), 310 (4), 617 (5)
shoulder bag 194 (9)
shoulder belt 47 (7)
shoulder-high 209 (8)
shoulder length 203 (5)
shoulder the blame 150 (5)
shoulder to shoulder 708 (9)
shouldering 273 (10)
shoulders 253 (6)
shout 400 (4), 408 (1), 408 (4), 532 (5), 547 (8), 577 (4), 835 (6), 891 (2), 891 (6)
shout down 532 (5), 578 (4), 702 (10), 878 (6), 924 (9), 924 (10)
shout for joy 835 (6)
shout hallelujah 981 (12)
shout of laughter 835 (2)
shout of praise 923 (2)
shouting 400 (1), 400 (3), 408 (1), 824 (4), 833 (4)
shove 265 (5), 279 (1), 279 (7), 287 (7), 547 (4), 678 (11)
shove off 279 (7)
shovel 194 (18), 272 (7), 304 (2)
shovel hat 989 (1)
shovel in 301 (35)
shover 287 (3)
show 263 (17), 443 (4), 445 (1), 445 (2), 445 (8), 466 (6), 478 (4), 484 (5), 520 (8), 522 (2), 522 (8), 526 (7), 540 (3), 541 (2), 542 (1), 547 (18), 594 (4), 594 (16), 837 (1), 875 (1), 875 (3), 875 (7)
show a profit 771 (10)
show an effect 157 (5)
show bad taste 847 (6)
show business 594 (1)
show compassion 905 (6)

show concern 897 (5)
show consideration 736 (3)
show courtesy 884 (5)
show disapproval 924 (9)
show discourtesy 885 (6)
show disrespect 921 (5)
show dog 365 (10)
show energy 174 (7)
show enterprise 672 (3)
show favouritism 481 (12), 914 (6)
show fear 856 (4)
show feeling 818 (8), 821 (9), 822 (4), 824 (6)
show fight 678 (11), 711 (3), 712 (7), 713 (10), 855 (6), 855 (7)
show flair 848 (7)
show foresight 498 (6)
show girl 594 (10)
show good taste 846 (4)
show honour 866 (13)
show hostility 881 (4)
show impatience 822 (4)
show in 299 (3)
show ingratitude 908 (4)
show interest 678 (11)
show its face 443 (4)
show jumper 268 (4)
show jumping 267 (5)
show little hope 472 (3)
show mercy 177 (5), 719 (4), 736 (3), 905 (7), 909 (4), 919 (3)
show no fight 721 (4)
show no mercy 735 (7), 906 (3)
show no pity 906 (3)
show no respect for 769 (3)
show of grief 836 (2)
show of hands 605 (2)
show off 522 (8), 866 (12), 871 (5), 873 (3), 873 (5), 875 (7), 877 (3), 877 (5)
show one off 841 (8)
show one's age 842 (6)
show one's face 189 (4), 522 (9)
show one's fangs 893 (3)
show one's paces 875 (7)
show one's power 174 (7)

show one's years 131 (8)
show out 300 (7)
show over 522 (8)
show piece 522 (2)
show promise 852 (7)
show respect 311 (9), 638 (8), 866 (13), 884 (6), 884 (7), 920 (6), 979 (9)
show restraint 823 (6)
show results 727 (7)
show reverence 979 (9)
show round 522 (8)
show signs 471 (4)
show signs of 466 (6), 547 (18), 852 (7)
show signs of emotion 818 (8)
show spirit 855 (6)
show style 566 (3)
show taste 575 (4)
show the door 300 (7)
show the way 64 (3), 281 (4)
show through 224 (4), 422 (3), 443 (4)
show up 189 (4), 295 (4), 479 (3), 484 (5), 522 (8), 522 (9), 851 (6), 867 (11)
show up again 106 (6)
show valour 855 (6)
show variety 15 (6)
show willing 597 (6), 706 (4)
showcase 522 (2)
showdown 526 (1)
shower 74 (5), 287 (7), 309 (1), 309 (3), 311 (5), 341 (7), 350 (6), 350 (10), 648 (3)
shower upon 813 (4)
showers of 635 (2)
showery 350 (8)
showiness 875 (1)
showing 229 (4), 443 (2), 443 (3), 445 (7), 466 (5), 522 (4), 522 (6), 526 (2), 547 (1), 594 (15)
showing itself 445 (7)
showing off 522 (1), 850 (4), 873 (1), 873 (4), 875 (1), 875 (4)
showing respect 920 (3)
showing the way 281 (3)

showing up 526 (1)

showman 522 (3), 594 (12)

showmanship 528 (2), 875 (1)

shown 443 (3), 445 (7), 522 (6), 526 (2), 594 (15)

shown off 522 (6)

showplace 522 (2)

showroom 522 (2)

showy 425 (6), 445 (7), 522 (4), 574 (4), 841 (4), 844 (10), 847 (4), 848 (5), 871 (4), 875 (4), 875 (5), 875 (7)

shrapnel 723 (4), 723 (12)

shred 33 (3), 46 (11), 53 (5), 102 (1), 206 (3), 301 (40)

shred of wool 208 (1)

shredded 53 (6)

shrew 176 (4), 373 (3), 709 (5), 892 (2), 904 (4), 926 (4)

shrewd 480 (4), 490 (5), 498 (4), 694 (4), 698 (4)

shrewd idea 512 (2)

shrewdness 498 (2)

shrewish 892 (3), 893 (2), 926 (5)

shrewishness 709 (2)

shriek 377 (6), 407 (1), 408 (1), 836 (2), 836 (6)

shriek with laughter 835 (7)

shrieking 425 (6)

shrieks of laughter 835 (2)

shrift 941 (3)

shrill 352 (10), 400 (3), 400 (4), 407 (2), 407 (5), 577 (3)

shrillness 407 (1)

shrimp 33 (5), 196 (4), 365 (14), 619 (6)

shrine 364 (5), 990 (1)

shrink 33 (8), 37 (4), 37 (5), 198 (6), 198 (7), 280 (3), 286 (5), 290 (3), 620 (5), 655 (7), 854 (11), 874 (3)

shrink from 861 (4), 888 (7)

shrinkage 37 (1), 42 (1), 198 (1), 204 (1)

shrinking 37 (1), 290 (1), 598 (3), 620 (1), 620 (3), 854 (7), 874 (2)

shrinking violet 874 (1)

shrive 909 (4), 988 (10)

shrivel 198 (6), 342 (6), 381 (8), 655 (7)

shrivel up 37 (5)

shrivelled 131 (6), 172 (4), 198 (4), 206 (5), 342 (4)

shroud 47 (3), 226 (5), 226 (13), 364 (3), 421 (4), 525 (7)

shrub 366 (4)

shrubbery 366 (2), 370 (3)

shrubby 366 (10)

shrug 161 (8), 547 (4), 547 (21)

shrug away 922 (6)

shrug off 483 (4), 639 (7), 860 (4)

shrunk 196 (9)

shrunken 198 (4)

shudder 318 (1), 854 (10)

shudder at 861 (4)

shuddering 861 (1)

shuffle 43 (7), 63 (4), 151 (1), 151 (3), 265 (2), 265 (4), 267 (14), 278 (4), 477 (8), 541 (6), 547 (21), 603 (5), 822 (4), 930 (8)

shuffled 61 (7)

shuffling 63 (1), 541 (3), 543 (4), 603 (4)

shun 525 (9), 620 (5), 861 (4)

shunning 620 (1), 620 (3)

shunt 282 (6)

shunter 274 (14)

shut 264 (4), 264 (6)

shut down 145 (6), 264 (6)

shut fast 778 (3)

shut in 224 (3), 230 (3), 264 (6), 747 (10)

shut one up 578 (4)

shut one's eyes 820 (7)

shut out 57 (3), 57 (5)

shut up 145 (6), 145 (9), 399 (5), 578 (3), 582 (4), 747 (10), 883 (10)

shut up shop 69 (6)

shutdown 145 (2), 679 (1)

shutter 226 (1), 421 (2), 442 (6)

shutters 226 (4)

shutting in 230 (2)

shuttle 222 (5), 267 (11), 317 (2), 317 (5)

shuttle service 317 (2)

shuttlecock 317 (2), 601 (2)

shy 280 (3), 282 (3), 287 (1), 620 (3), 620 (5), 712 (12), 747 (5), 854 (7), 861 (2), 874 (2), 883 (5), 950 (5)

shy from 856 (4)

shy thing 874 (1)

shyness 854 (2), 874 (1), 883 (1)

Siamese twins 90 (1)

sib 11 (2)

sibilance 406 (1)

sibilant 406 (1), 406 (2), 577 (3)

sibilation 398 (1), 406 (1)

sibling 11 (2), 11 (5)

Sibyl 983 (6)

sibylline 511 (6)

sic 494 (8)

sick 206 (5), 300 (5), 361 (5), 503 (7), 503 (9), 651 (21), 651 (23), 825 (5), 934 (4), 949 (9)

sick and tired 838 (4)

sick at heart 825 (6), 834 (6)

sick bay 658 (13)

sick, be 300 (10)

sick fancy 513 (3)

sick headache 949 (2)

sick joke 839 (2)

sick list 87 (1), 651 (18)

sick mind 503 (1)

sick of 838 (4), 861 (2), 863 (2)

sick person 163 (2), 272 (4), 651 (18), 825 (4)

sick with disappointment, be 509 (4)

sick with worry 825 (5)

sickbed 651 (2), 658 (13)

sicken 163 (9), 391 (3), 637 (5), 651 (23), 655 (7), 827

(11), 829 (6), 838 (5), 861 (5), 863 (3)

sickened 300 (5), 825 (6)

sickening 300 (4), 391 (2), 645 (4), 829 (4), 861 (3)

sickening for 651 (21)

sickle 256 (5)

sickly 163 (6), 391 (2), 426 (3), 651 (20)

sickly hue 425 (3)

sickness 645 (1), 651 (2)

side 11 (4), 186 (1), 234 (1), 239 (1), 239 (2), 445 (1), 605 (6), 708 (1)

side arms 256 (2), 256 (5)

side by side 89 (5), 200 (7), 219 (4)

side drum 414 (9)

side-effect 157 (1)

side elevation 239 (1), 551 (5)

side-face 239 (1)

side glance 438 (3)

side movement 239 (1)

side road 624 (6)

side saddle 218 (6)

side-show 639 (2)

side with 703 (6), 708 (8)

sidearms 723 (8)

sideboard 194 (5), 218 (5)

sideboards 259 (2)

sided 239 (2)

sidedness 239 (1)

sidekick 707 (1)

sideline 234 (1), 239 (1), 622 (1)

sidelines 223 (1)

sidelong 220 (7), 239 (2)

sideslip 282 (1), 282 (3)

sidesman or - woman 986 (7)

sidestep 220 (5), 239 (1), 239 (3), 282 (1), 282 (3), 620 (1), 620 (5)

sidetrack 282 (6)

sidewalk 624 (5)

sideways 205 (6), 220 (7), 239 (4), 281 (3), 282 (7)

siding 239 (1), 624 (7)

siding against 704 (1)

sidle 220 (5), 239 (3), 282 (3)

sidle in 297 (5)

sidle up to 289 (4)

sidling 239 (2)

siege 232 (1), 702 (1), 712 (4)

siege gun 723 (11)

sieges 718 (6)

sierra 209 (2)

sieve 44 (7), 263 (3), 648 (10)

sieved 332 (4)

sift 44 (7), 62 (6), 463 (3), 605 (7), 648 (10)

sift out 62 (6)

sifted 332 (4)

sifter 263 (3)

sifting 44 (3), 463 (1)

sigh 352 (7), 352 (10), 352 (11), 401 (1), 401 (4), 408 (1), 834 (2), 834 (9), 836 (1), 836 (5), 836 (6), 887 (14), 889 (2), 889 (7)

sigh after 859 (11)

sigh for 836 (5)

sigh for pleasure 835 (6)

sigher 836 (3)

sighing 834 (2)

sight 374 (2), 438 (1), 438 (7), 442 (3), 443 (1), 445 (2), 842 (2), 864 (3)

sight-impaired 440 (3)

sight of 32 (2)

sight of, a 104 (1)

sight-read 413 (9)

sight-seeing 438 (4)

sighted 443 (2)

sightless 439 (2)

sightlessness 439 (1)

sightly 841 (6)

sights 281 (1)

sightseer 441 (1)

sign 85 (1), 466 (1), 466 (7), 488 (8), 511 (3), 522 (1), 547 (1), 547 (4), 547 (5), 547 (9), 547 (13), 547 (20), 547 (21), 558 (1), 586 (8), 737 (6), 765 (5), 767 (6), 864 (3)

sign away 753 (3), 780 (3)

sign language 20 (2), 547 (4), 557 (1), 578 (1), 579 (1)

sign of illness 651 (2)

sign of success 729 (1)

sign off 753 (3)

sign on 708 (8)

sign one's death warrant 362 (10)

sign oneself 988 (10)

sign-painter 556 (1)

sign painting 553 (2)

sign the pledge 948 (4)

sign-writer 586 (5)

signal 420 (6), 522 (4), 524 (10), 529 (3), 531 (1), 547 (4), 547 (5), 547 (22), 638 (6), 664 (1), 665 (1), 737 (1), 737 (6)

signal honour 866 (4)

signal lamp 547 (5)

signal light 420 (6)

signalize 547 (18), 866 (14)

signalling 547 (5), 547 (15)

signally 32 (19)

signalman 722 (5)

signatory 466 (4), 488 (3), 764 (1), 765 (3)

signature 21 (2), 410 (3), 410 (5), 466 (3), 488 (1), 547 (2), 547 (13), 765 (1), 767 (2)

signature tune 412 (3)

signboard 547 (13)

signed 488 (5), 765 (4)

signer 765 (3)

signet 547 (13), 743 (2)

significance 32 (1), 86 (4), 514 (2), 638 (1)

significant 466 (5), 511 (7), 514 (3), 638 (5)

significantly 514 (6), 638 (9)

signification 514 (2), 547 (1)

signify 80 (8), 514 (5), 547 (18), 638 (7)

signify assent 488 (6)

signify little 639 (7)

signor 372 (1)

signora 373 (4)

signorina 373 (4)

signpost 267 (8), 269 (4), 281 (1), 281 (4), 281 (6), 465 (5), 547 (7), 547 (18)

signposted 281 (3), 624 (8)

signs of the zodiac 321 (5)

Sikhism 973 (3)

silage 370 (1)

silence 161 (9), 266 (2), 266 (9), 399 (1), 399 (4), 399 (5), 401 (5), 416 (1), 479 (3), 525 (2), 578 (1), 578 (4), 582 (1), 727 (10), 747 (7), 820 (7)

silenced 578 (2), 864 (4)

silencer 401 (2), 405 (1)

silencing 165 (1)

silent 266 (6), 334 (3), 399 (2), 405 (2), 525 (5), 525 (6), 578 (2), 582 (2), 864 (4)

silent, be 266 (7), 399 (3), 864 (6)

silent film 445 (4)

silent majority 869 (1)

silently 444 (5)

silhouette 22 (1), 233 (1), 233 (3), 243 (1), 243 (5), 418 (1), 445 (6), 551 (2), 553 (5)

silicon chip 196 (7)

silk 208 (2), 222 (4), 958 (1)

silk-screen printing 555 (2)

silken 258 (3)

silkiness 258 (1)

silky 208 (4), 258 (3)

sill 234 (2), 254 (2)

silliness 497 (1), 497 (2), 499 (2)

silly 497 (3), 499 (4), 501 (1), 544 (2), 849 (2)

silly fool 501 (1)

silly talk 497 (1), 515 (2)

silo 271 (3), 370 (6), 632 (2)

silt 324 (3), 344 (3)

silty 344 (5)

silver 226 (16), 425 (8), 427 (2), 427 (4), 427 (6), 797 (1), 844 (12)

silver jubilee 141 (3)

silver lining 831 (1), 852 (1)

silver-tongued 579 (7)

silver wedding 141 (3), 876 (2)

silvered 427 (4)

silvery 410 (6), 427 (4), 429 (2)

similar 9 (5), 12 (2), 16 (2), 18 (4), 24 (5), 28 (8), 78 (3), 106 (3), 219 (2), 245 (2)

similar to, be 18 (7)

similarity 9 (2), 12 (1), 16 (1), 18 (1), 20 (2), 22 (1), 24 (2), 462 (1), 551 (1)

similarly 18 (9)

simile 18 (3), 462 (1), 519 (1), 574 (1)

similitude 18 (1)

simmer 301 (40), 318 (7), 355 (5), 891 (5)

simmering 822 (3)

simony 793 (1)

simper 835 (2), 835 (8), 850 (5)

simpering 850 (4)

simple 44 (4), 425 (7), 487 (2), 491 (4), 499 (4), 516 (2), 573 (2), 575 (3), 658 (2), 699 (3), 701 (6), 846 (3)

simple fare 945 (1)

simple interest 803 (2)

simple life 942 (1)

simple-minded 699 (3)

simple soul 699 (2)

simple truth 494 (1)

simpleness 44 (1), 88 (1)

simpleton 487 (1), 493 (1), 501 (2), 699 (2)

simplicity 44 (1), 487 (1), 499 (1), 516 (1), 573 (1), 575 (1), 699 (1), 701 (1), 846 (1)

simplification 44 (2), 701 (1)

simplified 44 (4), 701 (5)

simplify 44 (6), 51 (5), 516 (4), 520 (8), 701 (8)

simply 44 (8), 88 (6), 516 (6), 573 (4)

simply and solely 44 (8)

simulacrum 18 (1)

simulate 20 (5), 541 (6)

simulating 18 (6), 20 (4)

simulation 18 (2), 20 (2), 541 (2)

simulation exercise 20 (2)

simulator 20 (2), 20 (3), 461 (4)

simultaneity 89 (1), 116 (1), 123 (1)

simultaneous 89 (3), 116 (3), 123 (3)

simultaneously 123 (5)

sin 645 (1), 738 (1), 914 (1), 934 (1), 934 (2), 934 (7), 936 (2), 936 (4), 980 (1), 980 (6)

since 120 (4), 158 (5)

sincere 540 (2), 699 (3), 818 (6)

sincerely 540 (4), 818 (9)

sincerity 540 (1), 699 (1), 818 (1), 929 (1)

sine 85 (3)

sine qua non 5 (2), 80 (1), 89 (2), 627 (1), 766 (1)

sinecure 677 (1), 681 (1), 701 (2)

sinews 162 (2)

sinewy 162 (8), 329 (2)

sinful 934 (3), 934 (6), 936 (3), 980 (4)

sinfulness 936 (1)

sing 404 (3), 408 (4), 409 (3), 410 (9), 413 (10), 526 (6), 577 (4), 593 (10), 833 (7), 835 (6), 981 (11)

sing for joy 835 (6)

sing in unison 16 (3)

sing low 401 (4)

sing one's praises 923 (9)

sing out 408 (4)

sing paeans 835 (6)

sing small 872 (5)

sing-song 16 (1), 16 (2)

sing to 413 (10)

singable 410 (6), 412 (7)

singe 381 (10), 428 (6)

singed 428 (4)

singeing 381 (2)

singer 413 (4)

singing 404 (1), 412 (5), 833 (4)

singing voice 577 (1)

single 44 (4), 52 (4), 88 (3), 744 (7), 895 (4)

single combat 716 (6)

single-decker 274 (10)

single file 71 (3), 203 (3)

single-handed 88 (4)

single man 895 (2)

single-minded 455 (3), 599 (2)

single out 15 (7), 46 (9), 532 (7), 605 (7)

single parent 169 (1), 896 (1)

single person 88 (2)

single piece 88 (2)

single-sex 534 (5)

single state 895 (1)

single-storey 192 (20), 210 (2)

single voice 488 (2)

singlemindedness 599 (1)

singleness 88 (1), 895 (1)

singlet 228 (17)

singleton 88 (2)

singly 46 (14), 88 (6)

singsong 106 (3), 411 (2), 882 (3)

singular 80 (5), 84 (6), 88 (3), 564 (3)

singularity 80 (1), 84 (1)

singularly 32 (19)

sinister 242 (2), 511 (7), 616 (2), 645 (2), 645 (3), 731 (4), 854 (8), 930 (4)

sinistral 242 (2)

sinistrality 239 (1), 242 (1)

sink 35 (5), 37 (5), 165 (6), 165 (8), 165 (11), 194 (1), 265 (4), 309 (3), 311 (4), 311 (8), 313 (3), 313 (4), 322 (5), 351 (2), 632 (2), 649 (4), 651 (23), 712 (11), 728 (7), 784 (5), 834 (9)

sink back 657 (2)

sink from view 446 (3)

sink in 297 (6), 309 (3), 449 (10), 516 (4), 821 (8)

sink into 297 (5)

sink into oblivion 506 (6)

sink into silence 401 (4)

sink like a stone 313 (4)

sink money in 806 (4)

sink or swim 600 (5)

sinkable 309 (2)

sinker 313 (2), 322 (1)

sinking 37 (1), 37 (3), 165 (3), 309 (2), 313 (1), 361 (5)

sinking heart 834 (1)

sinless 935 (3), 950 (5)

sinlessness 950 (1)

sinner 938 (1), 969 (2), 980 (3)

sinning 980 (4)

sinuosity 248 (1), 251 (1)

sinuous 251 (4)

sinusitis 651 (8)

sip 33 (2), 301 (11), 301 (26), 301 (38), 386 (3)

siphon 304 (2), 351 (1)

siphon off 272 (7), 300 (8)

sipping 301 (25)

sir 372 (1), 741 (1), 870 (1)

sir or madam 562 (2)

sire 167 (7), 741 (1), 870 (1)

sired 360 (7)

siren 84 (4), 117 (3), 291 (1), 291 (3), 343 (2), 400 (1), 400 (2), 547 (5), 612 (5), 664 (1), 665 (1), 841 (2), 967 (3), 970 (5)

siren song 612 (2)

sirloin 301 (16)

sisal 208 (2)

sissy 163 (2), 372 (1)

sister 11 (2), 18 (3), 373 (3), 658 (16), 707 (3), 880 (3), 986 (6)

sisterhood 11 (3), 74 (3), 708 (4), 880 (1), 986 (6)

sisterly 11 (5), 880 (6), 887 (9), 897 (4)

sisterly love 887 (1)

sit 187 (8), 311 (8)

sit about 136 (5)

sit back 677 (3), 683 (3)

sit down 216 (6), 311 (8)

sit for 23 (5), 551 (8)

sit-in 189 (1), 773 (4)

sit in council 691 (5)

sit in judgment 480 (5), 959 (8)

sit on 165 (8), 187 (8), 218 (16), 745 (7), 747 (7), 773 (4), 816 (6), 872 (7)

sit on the fence 606 (3), 625 (6)

sit tight 266 (7), 677 (3)

sit up 215 (3), 455 (4)

sit up late 136 (4)

sit up with 457 (6)

sitar 414 (2)

site 185 (1), 186 (1), 187 (2), 187 (3), 187 (5)

sitter 23 (2)

sitting 311 (3), 692 (1)

sitting duck 544 (1), 661 (2), 701 (2)

sitting pretty 828 (1), 828 (4)

sitting room 194 (19)

situate 186 (3), 187 (5)

situated 8 (3), 186 (3), 187 (4)

situated, be 73 (3), 186 (4), 189 (4)

situation 8 (1), 154 (2), 185 (1), 186 (1), 187 (3), 189 (1), 192 (1), 230 (1), 281 (1), 622 (3)

situational 8 (3)

six 99 (2)

six-footer 209 (5)

six-shooter 723 (10)

sixth-former 538 (1)

sixth sense 374 (2), 476 (1), 984 (1)

sixty 99 (3)

sizable 32 (4), 195 (6)

size 16 (4), 26 (1), 32 (1), 47 (9), 62 (4), 162 (2), 183 (2), 195 (1), 226 (16), 465 (3), 638 (1)

size up 465 (11), 465 (13), 480 (6)

sizzle 318 (7), 379 (7), 402 (3), 406 (3)

sjambok 964 (1)

ska 412 (1)

skate 258 (5), 274 (2), 837 (21)

skate over 458 (4)

skateboard 274 (2), 837 (15)

skating 265 (1), 837 (6)

skating rink 724 (1)

skein 74 (3), 74 (6)

skeletal 218 (14), 331 (3)

skeleton 206 (2), 218 (13), 233 (1), 331 (1), 363 (1), 592 (1)

skeleton in the cupboard 530 (1)

skeleton key 263 (11), 628 (2)

skelter 277 (6)

skep 192 (4), 253 (4)

sketch 23 (1), 55 (1), 233 (1), 233 (3), 243 (5), 512 (6), 551 (1), 551 (8), 553 (5), 553 (8), 569 (3), 590 (1), 590 (7), 592 (1), 594 (3), 623 (1), 669 (10)

sketch map 551 (5)

sketch out 233 (3), 623 (8)

sketchbook 553 (6), 592 (2)

sketchiness 55 (1)

sketching 553 (1)

sketchy 55 (3)

skew 86 (4), 220 (3), 220 (6), 246 (5), 282 (6)

skewbald 273 (4), 437 (7)

skewer 47 (5), 256 (2), 263 (12), 263 (18)

skewness 29 (1), 220 (1), 246 (1)

ski 258 (5), 837 (21)

ski lift 310 (2)

skibob 274 (2)

skid 258 (5), 265 (2), 282 (3)

skiddy 258 (3)

skiff 275 (7), 275 (8)

skiing 837 (6)

skilful 24 (7), 152 (3), 241 (2), 498 (4), 513 (5), 622 (5), 646 (3), 694 (4), 698 (4), 727 (4)

skilful, be 694 (8)

skilfully 694 (10)

skill 80 (1), 160 (2), 243 (2), 267 (5), 269 (2), 319 (5), 378 (1), 413 (6), 490 (1), 498 (2), 513 (1), 622 (1), 623 (3), 624 (1), 629 (1), 644 (2), 688 (2), 689 (1), 694 (1), 698 (1), 718 (4), 837 (6), 846 (1), 983 (1)

skilled 694 (4), 694 (6)

skilled worker 686 (3), 696 (2)

skillet 194 (14)

skills 694 (1)

skim 200 (5), 202 (3), 269 (12), 277 (6), 458 (4), 648 (10)

skim off 605 (7)

skim through 438 (9)

skimmer 194 (18)

skimmings 41 (2)

skimp 204 (5), 458 (4), 598 (4), 636 (9), 816 (6)

skimped 636 (4)

skimpy 204 (3), 636 (3)

skin 207 (1), 212 (1), 223 (1), 226 (6), 229 (6), 259 (2), 333 (3), 631 (1)

skin and bone 206 (2), 206 (5)

skin-deep 33 (7), 212 (2), 223 (2)

skin disease 378 (2), 651 (12), 845 (1)

skin diver 313 (2)

skin diving 837 (6)

skin game 788 (4)

skin over 656 (11)

skinflint 816 (3)

skinful 54 (2)

skinhead 132 (2)

skinny 163 (6), 196 (10), 206 (5), 636 (5)

skintight 48 (2)

skip 190 (6), 194 (13), 265 (2), 267 (14), 312 (1), 312 (4), 458 (4), 536 (5), 726 (3), 769 (3), 835 (6)

skipper 270 (1), 312 (2), 689 (5), 690 (1)

skipping 312 (3), 837 (10)

skipping rope 837 (15)

skirl 407 (1), 407 (5)

skirmish 716 (7), 716 (11), 718 (7), 718 (12)

skirmisher 66 (1)

skirmishers 722 (4)

skirt 200 (5), 202 (3), 217 (2), 228 (13), 234 (1), 239 (3), 305 (5), 314 (4), 626 (3)

skirt round 620 (5)

skirting 234 (4), 239 (2)

skirting board 214 (1)

skirts 68 (5)

skis 274 (2)

skit 594 (3), 851 (2)

skitter 265 (4)

skittish 312 (3), 604 (3), 819 (4), 822 (3)

skittle 311 (6)

skittle alley 837 (5)

skittles 837 (7)

skive 679 (11)

skiver 679 (6)

skivvy 742 (2)

skulduggery 930 (1)

skulk 267 (13), 525 (9), 854 (10), 856 (4)

skulker 527 (4), 620 (2)

skulking 523 (2), 525 (5), 856 (1)

skull 213 (3), 253 (4), 363 (1)

skull and crossbones 222 (2), 547 (12)

skullcap 989 (1)

skunk 397 (1)

sky 213 (1), 310 (4), 321 (3)

sky-blue 435 (3)

sky diver 271 (4)

sky-high 32 (6), 209 (8)

skydiving 271 (1)

skylark 308 (2), 837 (21)

skylarking 497 (2), 837 (3)

skylight 263 (5)

skyline 199 (1), 233 (1)

skyscraper 164 (3), 209 (4)

skywriting 271 (1)

slab 53 (5), 207 (2), 218 (12)

slack 49 (2), 61 (7), 175 (2), 458 (2), 679 (8), 679 (11), 734 (3)

slack-jawed 263 (13)

slack market 172 (1)

slack off 683 (3)

slack period 679 (1)

slacken 37 (5), 46 (8), 49 (3), 163 (10), 177 (6), 679 (11)

slacken one's pace 278 (5)

slacken speed 278 (5)

slackening 37 (1)

slacker 278 (2), 458 (1), 598 (2), 679 (6), 918 (1)

slackness 458 (1), 734 (1)

slacks 228 (6), 228 (12)

slag 41 (2), 164 (2), 649 (2)

slag heap 641 (3)

slake 177 (7), 339 (3), 863 (3)

slake one's thirst 301 (38)

slalom 716 (3)

slalom course 282 (1)

slam 174 (7), 264 (6), 279 (1), 279 (7), 279 (9), 287 (7), 400 (4), 402 (1), 402 (4), 926 (6)

slamming 400 (1)

slander 867 (2), 899 (2), 926 (2), 926 (7), 928 (2)

slandered 924 (7), 928 (6)

slanderer 904 (1), 926 (4)

slanderous 926 (5)

slang 560 (3)

slanging match 584 (1), 709 (3), 899 (2)

slangy 560 (5)

slant 220 (1), 220 (3), 220 (5), 220 (6), 438 (5), 445 (1), 481 (5)

slantwise 220 (7)

slap 116 (4), 279 (2), 279 (9), 402 (1), 402 (3), 963 (2), 963 (9)

slap-bang 116 (4), 176 (10)

slap on paint 553 (8)

slap-up 813 (3)

slapdash 458 (2), 680 (2), 695 (5), 857 (3)

slaphappy 458 (2), 857 (3)

slapping 963 (2)

slapstick 594 (3), 839 (1), 849 (1), 849 (3)

slash 37 (4), 46 (11), 46 (12), 204 (5), 260 (3), 262 (1), 810 (2), 812 (6)

slash one's wrists 362 (13)

slat 207 (2), 208 (3)

slate 207 (2), 429 (1), 586 (4), 605 (3), 623 (2)

slates 226 (2)

slats 226 (4)

slattern 61 (5), 649 (5)

slatternly 61 (7), 649 (7)

slaty 207 (4), 344 (5)

slaughter 165 (1), 165 (6), 165 (7), 362 (4), 362 (11), 712 (2), 718 (11), 735 (7),

898 (3), 898 (8), 963 (3), 963 (12)

slaughterer 362 (6)

slaughterhouse 362 (5)

slave 35 (2), 678 (5), 678 (12), 686 (2), 742 (1), 742 (6), 750 (1), 869 (5)

slave away 682 (7)

slave-driver 735 (3)

slave for 703 (7)

slave trade 791 (2)

slaver 298 (7), 302 (4)

slavery 682 (3), 745 (3), 747 (3), 879 (1)

slavish 20 (4), 83 (4), 739 (3), 879 (3)

slavishly 879 (5)

slavishness 20 (1), 721 (1), 739 (1), 879 (1)

slay 362 (10)

slayer 362 (6)

slaying 362 (1)

sleazy 649 (7)

sled 274 (2)

sledge 274 (2)

sledge dog 273 (3), 365 (10)

sledge hammer 279 (4)

sleek 258 (3), 730 (4), 841 (6)

sleekness 258 (1)

sleep 129 (1), 175 (3), 266 (2), 266 (7), 375 (1), 456 (7), 458 (6), 679 (4), 679 (12), 683 (1), 683 (3), 684 (5), 831 (3)

sleep around 951 (10)

sleep it off 685 (5)

sleep off 656 (8), 831 (4)

sleep on it 136 (5)

sleep with 45 (14), 951 (11)

sleeper 218 (4), 274 (13), 679 (6)

sleepiness 679 (3)

sleeping 523 (2)

sleeping around 951 (7)

sleeping bag 194 (9)

sleeping car 274 (13)

sleeping draught 679 (5)

sleeping giant 523 (1)

sleeping partner 679 (6)

sleeping pill 658 (7), 679 (5), 831 (1)

sleeping suit 228 (18)

sleeping tablets 375 (2)

sleepless 600 (3), 678 (7)

sleeplessness 678 (2)

sleepwalker 268 (3)

sleepwalking 267 (3), 679 (4)

sleepy 266 (4), 679 (9), 684 (2)

sleepyhead 679 (6)

sleet 350 (6), 350 (10), 380 (2)

sleety 380 (5)

sleigh 274 (2)

sleight 542 (3), 698 (1), 983 (1)

sleight of hand 542 (3), 694 (1)

slender 206 (4), 636 (3), 841 (5)

slender means 801 (1)

slenderness 206 (2)

sleuth 459 (8), 524 (5)

slew 282 (1), 282 (3)

slew round 315 (5)

slice 46 (11), 53 (5), 207 (2), 207 (5), 282 (6), 287 (1), 287 (7), 695 (2)

sliced 53 (6)

slick 542 (6), 694 (4)

slick down 258 (4)

slicker 545 (4)

slide 111 (3), 207 (2), 220 (1), 258 (1), 258 (5), 265 (2), 265 (4), 282 (3), 309 (1), 350 (9), 551 (4), 677 (3), 837 (4)

slide back 148 (3), 657 (2)

slide down 309 (3)

slide in 231 (8), 303 (4)

slide rule 86 (6), 465 (5)

slide show 445 (2)

slide viewer 442 (1)

sliding 265 (1), 934 (5)

sliding down 309 (1)

slight 33 (6), 33 (7), 163 (4), 196 (10), 206 (4), 212 (2), 458 (5), 639 (6), 867 (2), 872 (7), 921 (2), 921 (5), 922 (1), 922 (6)

slight curve 248 (2)

slight gradient 210 (1)

slighting 483 (2), 921 (3), 922 (3)

slightly 33 (9)

slightly built 163 (4), 206 (4)

slightness 163 (1)

slim 33 (6), 198 (7), 206 (4), 206 (7), 841 (5)

slime 341 (1), 354 (1), 649 (2)

slimming 301 (3)

slimy 354 (5), 879 (3)

sling 194 (9), 217 (5), 287 (1), 287 (3), 287 (7), 658 (9), 712 (12), 723 (4)

slinger 287 (5)

slinging 287 (1)

slink 523 (5), 525 (9)

slink in 297 (5)

slip 33 (3), 49 (4), 53 (4), 111 (3), 132 (4), 196 (4), 206 (2), 228 (17), 258 (5), 309 (3), 309 (4), 354 (3), 495 (3), 495 (8), 565 (1), 728 (1), 936 (2)

slip away 190 (7), 296 (5)

slip back 148 (3), 286 (4), 307 (3), 655 (7), 657 (2)

slip by 111 (3)

slip in 297 (5)

slip of the pen 495 (3)

slip of the tongue 495 (3)

slip off 229 (7)

slip on 228 (32)

slip one's collar 746 (4)

slip one's lead 667 (5)

slip one's memory 456 (9), 506 (6)

slip-ons 228 (27)

slip out 190 (7)

slip stream 352 (1)

slip through 667 (5)

slip up 309 (4), 495 (3), 495 (8)

slipped disc 651 (15)

slipper 228 (27), 963 (9)

slippered 683 (2)

slipperiness 49 (1), 152 (1), 258 (1), 603 (1), 698 (1)

slippers 228 (6)

slippery 49 (2), 258 (3), 357 (7), 542 (6), 603 (4), 620 (3), 661 (4), 667 (4), 698 (4), 930 (4)

slippery slope 165 (3)

slipping 114 (3), 655 (5), 695 (5), 934 (5)

slipping back 655 (1)

slips 687 (1)

slipshod 61 (7), 458 (2), 734 (3)

slipway 258 (1)

slit 46 (1), 46 (10), 46 (11), 46 (12), 201 (2), 262 (1)

slither 265 (4)

slithery 258 (3)

sliver 33 (3), 53 (5)

slobber 298 (7), 302 (4), 302 (6), 341 (1), 341 (6)

sloe 366 (4)

sloe-eyed 428 (4)

slog 279 (9), 287 (7), 678 (12), 682 (7)

slog away 600 (4)

slog on 285 (3)

slogan 496 (1), 528 (3), 547 (8), 563 (1), 718 (6)

slogging 682 (4)

sloop 275 (5)

slop 311 (5), 341 (7), 634 (4), 695 (9)

slop a 317 (5)

slop over 54 (5), 298 (6)

slope 209 (2), 220 (1), 220 (2), 220 (5), 220 (6), 308 (1), 309 (1)

slope off 267 (11)

slope upwards 308 (4)

sloping 220 (4), 309 (2)

sloping edge 220 (1)

sloping face 220 (1)

sloppiness 458 (1), 495 (2)

slopping over 54 (4)

sloppy 61 (7), 387 (2), 458 (2), 572 (2)

sloppy thinking 477 (2)

slops 387 (1)

slosh 350 (9)

slosh about 317 (5)

sloshed 949 (7)

slot 46 (1), 62 (2), 73 (1), 194 (1), 201 (2), 262 (1), 262 (3), 548 (4)

slot in 187 (5)

slot machine 796 (3), 799 (1)

sloth 175 (1), 679 (2)

slouch 210 (3), 278 (4), 679 (6)

slouched 246 (3)

sloucher 278 (2)

slough 49 (3), 229 (7), 347 (1), 779 (2)

sloven 61 (5), 649 (5)

slovenliness 458 (1), 649 (1)

slovenly 61 (7), 458 (2), 572 (2), 649 (7)

slow 113 (5), 118 (2), 136 (3), 175 (2), 278 (3), 350 (7), 495 (6), 499 (3), 598 (3), 679 (8), 681 (2), 820 (3), 823 (3), 838 (3), 840 (2), 858 (2)

slow, be 495 (7)

slow death 377 (1)

slow down 37 (4), 266 (8), 278 (1), 278 (5), 679 (11), 683 (3), 702 (8)

slow handclap 924 (1)

slow learner 538 (1)

slow march 265 (2), 267 (4), 278 (1)

slow motion 265 (1), 278 (1), 278 (3)

slow-moving 278 (3)

slow pace 278 (1)

slow-paced 278 (3)

slow progress 679 (2)

slow start 278 (1)

slow starter 136 (1), 278 (2)

slow time 278 (1)

slow to believe 486 (4)

slow train 274 (13)

slow up 278 (5)

slowcoach 278 (2), 679 (6)

slowing down 37 (2), 278 (1)

slowly 136 (9), 278 (7)

slowness 136 (1), 136 (2), 265 (1), 278 (1), 333 (1), 499 (1), 598 (1), 679 (2), 702 (1), 820 (1)

sludge 41 (2), 354 (1), 649 (2)

slug 279 (9), 301 (26), 365 (17), 723 (12)

sluggish 175 (2), 278 (3), 350 (7), 677 (2), 679 (7), 834 (5), 840 (2)

sluggishness 136 (2), 175 (1), 278 (1), 598 (1), 679 (2)

sluice 298 (3), 341 (3), 341 (8), 350 (4), 351 (1), 648 (9)

slum 192 (8), 649 (4), 653 (1), 655 (2), 801 (1)

slum dweller 191 (1), 801 (2), 869 (7)

slumber 175 (3), 266 (2), 679 (4), 679 (12)

slumberer 679 (6)

slummy 655 (6), 801 (4)

slump 35 (5), 37 (1), 37 (5), 172 (1), 286 (1), 286 (4), 309 (1), 309 (3), 309 (4), 655 (1), 655 (7), 679 (1), 731 (1), 801 (1), 812 (1), 812 (5)

slumped 246 (3)

slur 458 (4), 580 (1), 580 (3), 645 (1), 867 (2), 914 (1), 926 (2)

slur over 525 (7)

slush 354 (1)

slush fund 612 (4)

slushy 347 (2), 354 (4), 380 (5)

slut 61 (5), 649 (5), 952 (2)

sluttish 61 (7), 458 (2), 649 (7)

sluttishness 649 (1)

sly 541 (4), 698 (4), 698 (5), 839 (4), 850 (4)

slyboots 545 (4), 696 (2), 698 (3)

slyness 698 (1), 839 (1)

smack 33 (2), 43 (2), 275 (5), 279 (2), 279 (9), 386 (1), 402 (3), 963 (2), 963 (9)

smack of 18 (7), 386 (3), 547 (18)

smack one's lips 386 (3), 824 (6)

smacking 963 (2)

small 33 (6), 35 (3), 53 (6), 102 (2), 132 (5), 163 (4), 196 (8), 196 (10), 198 (4), 636 (3), 639 (5), 639 (6), 922 (4)

small ad 528 (3)

small amount 26 (2)

small animal 33 (5), 196 (4)

small arms 723 (9)

small, be 33 (8)

small beer 639 (2)

small box 194 (8)

small chance 159 (3)

small change 33 (4), 797 (1), 797 (4)

small coin 33 (4)

small crowd 74 (5)

small door 263 (6)

small fault 934 (2)

small fry 35 (2), 132 (1), 639 (4), 869 (3)

small game 639 (4)

small hill 209 (3), 253 (4)

small hours 128 (1), 129 (2), 136 (1)

small house 192 (7)

small letter 558 (1)

small means 33 (1)

small mind 481 (4)

small number 105 (1)

small of the back 238 (2)

small orifice 263 (4)

small potatoes 639 (2)

small print 766 (1)

small quantity 26 (2), 33 (2), 43 (2), 53 (1), 53 (5), 102 (1), 105 (1), 301 (11), 636 (1), 639 (2)

small risk 159 (3)

small screen 531 (3)

small shot 287 (2)

small size 33 (1), 196 (1)

small-sized 33 (6)

small talk 581 (2), 584 (2)

small thing 33 (3), 53 (5), 196 (2), 332 (2)

small-time 35 (3), 639 (6)

small voice 578 (1)

small-wheeler 274 (3)

smaller 33 (6), 35 (3), 198 (4)

smallest 35 (3)

smallholder 370 (4)

smallholding 370 (2)

smallness 33 (1), 35 (1), 196 (1), 639 (1)

smallpox 651 (5)

smalls 228 (17)

smarm down 258 (4)

smarmy 925 (3)

smart 277 (5), 377 (2), 377 (6), 498 (4), 698 (4), 825 (1), 825 (7), 839 (4), 841 (6), 848 (5), 891 (8)

smart aleck 500 (2), 873 (3)

smart customer 696 (2)

smart for it 963 (13)

smart pace 277 (3)

smart set 848 (3)

smart under 818 (7), 891 (5)

smarten 844 (12)

smarten up 841 (8)

smarting 377 (1), 377 (3), 829 (3), 891 (3)

smartness 839 (1)

smash 46 (13), 165 (3), 165 (7), 176 (8), 279 (3), 287 (1), 332 (5), 655 (10)

smash hit 594 (2), 644 (3), 727 (1)

smash in 297 (7)

smash into 279 (8)

smash up 165 (7)

smashing 644 (5)

smattering 490 (2), 491 (3)

smear 226 (15), 419 (7), 649 (9), 845 (1), 845 (3), 926 (2), 926 (7)

smear campaign 867 (1), 926 (1)

smell 299 (4), 300 (9), 374 (2), 374 (5), 394 (1), 394 (3), 397 (3), 548 (4), 649 (8)

smell a rat 484 (5), 486 (7)

smell bad 397 (3)

smell good 390 (3)

smell of 394 (3), 547 (18)

smell offensive 397 (3)

smell out 394 (3), 484 (4)

smell sweet 396 (4)

smelling 394 (2)

smelling bottle 396 (2)

smelling salts 388 (1), 658 (6)

smelly 394 (2), 397 (2)

smelt 337 (4), 381 (8)

smelter 687 (1)

smelting 381 (1)

smile 547 (4), 547 (21), 824 (6), 833 (7), 835 (2), 835 (8), 884 (2), 884 (7)

smile at 851 (5)

smile on 644 (11), 703 (6), 730 (8)

smiles 833 (1)

smiles of fortune 730 (1)

smiling 824 (5), 828 (2), 833 (3)

smirch 419 (7), 926 (7)

smirk 835 (2), 835 (8)

smite 279 (9), 362 (10)

smith 243 (5), 686 (3)

smithereens 33 (3)

smithy 687 (1)

smitten 887 (10)

smock 228 (16), 261 (3)

smocking 844 (4)

smog 423 (1), 653 (1)

smoke 300 (9), 336 (2), 338 (4), 342 (6), 379 (7), 381 (4), 388 (2), 388 (6), 388 (7), 394 (1), 423 (3), 666 (5), 949 (15)

smoke-filled 653 (2)

smoke haze 653 (1)

smoke out 300 (6), 304 (4)

smoke ring 250 (2)

smoke screen 421 (1), 423 (1), 525 (1), 527 (3), 614 (1), 713 (2)

smoke signal 547 (5)

smoked 424 (2)

smoked fish 301 (15)

smoked glass 421 (1), 424 (1)

smokeless fuel 385 (2)

smoker 274 (13), 388 (2)

smoker's cough 388 (2), 651 (8)

smokestack 263 (10)

smoking 379 (4), 379 (5), 949 (4)

smoking hot 379 (4)

smoking mixture 388 (2)

smoking room 194 (19)

smoky 332 (4), 338 (3), 397 (2), 423 (2), 429 (2), 649 (7)

smooth 16 (2), 28 (7), 49 (2), 62 (7), 71 (4), 81 (3), 216 (4), 216 (7), 229 (5), 245 (2), 258 (3), 258 (4), 259 (6), 327 (2), 331 (4), 333 (3), 378 (7), 541 (4), 542 (6), 701 (3), 701 (8), 848 (6), 884 (3), 889 (6), 925 (3)

smooth down 216 (7), 258 (4)

smooth hair 258 (1)

smooth one's brow 831 (3)

smooth-running 334 (3), 701 (4)

smooth snake 365 (13)

smooth-spoken 541 (4)

smooth surface 258 (1)

smooth texture 258 (1)

smooth the way 469 (4)

smooth tongue 884 (1)

smooth-tongued 579 (7)

smooth water 258 (1)

smoother 216 (3), 258 (2)

smoothing 701 (1)

smoothness 16 (1), 28 (1), 49 (1), 216 (1), 257 (1), 258 (1), 266 (2), 575 (1)

smother 165 (8), 177 (6), 226 (13), 362 (10), 362 (12), 382 (6), 525 (7), 889 (5)

smoulder 175 (3), 379 (7), 822 (4), 891 (5), 893 (3)

smouldering 175 (2), 379 (5)

smudge 428 (6), 647 (2), 649 (2), 649 (9), 845 (1), 845 (3)

smug 850 (4), 873 (4)

smuggle 788 (7)

smuggle in 231 (8)

smuggler 789 (1)

smuggling 791 (2)

smugness 828 (1), 873 (1)

smut 332 (2), 381 (4), 649 (2), 845 (1)

smutty 951 (6)

snack 33 (2), 301 (11), 301 (12), 390 (1)

snack bar 192 (13)

snaffle 748 (4)

snag 333 (3), 647 (2), 663 (1), 702 (2), 702 (3)

snail 278 (2), 365 (17)

snail-like 278 (3)

snail's pace 278 (1)

snake 251 (12), 365 (13), 698 (3)

snake-charmer 983 (5)

snake in one's bosom 545 (1)

snake in the grass 659 (1)

snaky 251 (6), 365 (18)

snap 46 (13), 116 (3), 330 (3), 402 (1), 402 (3), 409 (3), 551 (4), 551 (9), 609 (3), 837 (11), 891 (7), 892 (4), 893 (1), 893 (3)

snap answer 670 (1)

snap at 827 (9)

snap decision 609 (1)

snap fastener 47 (5)

snap off 330 (3)

snap one's fingers at 738 (9)

snap shut 264 (6)

snap to 264 (6)

snap up 301 (35), 786 (6)

snappish 893 (2)

snappy 174 (4), 277 (5), 496 (3), 841 (6), 892 (3)

snapshot 551 (4), 551 (9)

snare 542 (4), 542 (10), 786 (6)

snare drum 414 (9)

snarl 61 (3), 246 (1), 246 (5), 409 (3), 885 (6), 888 (1), 891 (2), 893 (1), 893 (3), 900 (3)

snarl-up 61 (3)

snarled 61 (8)

snarling 246 (3), 893 (2), 900 (2)

snatch 786 (6)

snatch at 288 (3), 786 (6)

snatch up 786 (6)

snatcher 786 (4)

snatching 786 (1)

sneak 524 (5), 525 (9), 856 (2), 938 (2)

sneak in 297 (5)

sneak off 620 (6), 667 (5)

sneak off with 788 (7)
sneak out 298 (5)
sneak thief 789 (1)
sneakers 228 (27)
sneaking 525 (5), 930 (4)
sneaky 541 (3)
sneer 878 (1), 922 (1), 924 (3)
sneer at 878 (6), 926 (6)
sneering 878 (1), 878 (4), 926 (5)
sneeze 352 (11)
sneezing 352 (7)
sneezy 352 (9)
snick 33 (3), 46 (11)
snide 541 (3)
sniff 299 (4), 352 (11), 394 (3), 922 (1), 949 (15)
sniffle 352 (11)
sniffling 352 (9)
snifter 301 (26)
snigger 835 (2), 835 (7), 851 (1), 851 (5)
sniggering 851 (1)
snip 46 (11), 53 (5), 260 (1), 812 (1)
snipe 287 (8), 712 (11)
sniper 287 (4), 712 (5), 722 (4)
sniping 712 (3)
snippet 33 (3), 53 (5)
snivel 302 (6), 836 (6)
sniveller 836 (3)
snob 847 (3), 871 (2)
snob value 866 (2)
snobbery 871 (1)
snobbish 481 (8), 847 (5), 848 (5), 850 (4), 871 (4), 922 (3)
snobbishness 922 (1)
snood 228 (23)
snooker 702 (9), 837 (7)
snoop 438 (9), 441 (1), 453 (4), 524 (5), 525 (9)
snooper 453 (2), 459 (8)
snootiness 922 (1)
snooty 922 (3)
snooze 679 (4), 679 (12)
snore 407 (4), 408 (3), 679 (12)
snoring 679 (9)

snort 352 (11), 406 (3), 407 (4), 408 (3), 409 (3), 922 (1)
snorter 301 (26)
snorting 352 (9), 684 (3)
snot 649 (2)
snout 254 (3)
snow 350 (10), 380 (3), 427 (2)
snow blindness 439 (1)
snow-capped 226 (12)
snow-covered 380 (5)
snow crystal 380 (3)
snow under 104 (6)
snow-white 427 (4)
snowball 36 (1), 36 (4), 74 (7), 197 (4), 287 (2)
snowbound 129 (7), 747 (5)
snowdrift 74 (7), 380 (3)
snowed under 637 (3)
snowfall 380 (3)
snowflake 380 (3)
snowman 551 (2)
snowshoes 274 (2)
snowstorm 176 (3), 380 (2)
snowy 380 (5), 427 (4), 648 (7), 950 (5)
snub 204 (3), 257 (2), 292 (1), 292 (3), 702 (8), 867 (11), 872 (7), 885 (6), 921 (2), 921 (5), 922 (1), 922 (5), 924 (4)
snub-nosed 246 (4)
snuff 299 (4), 382 (6), 388 (2)
snuff out 2 (8), 165 (8), 382 (6), 418 (7), 419 (7)
snuff up 394 (3)
snuffle 352 (11), 406 (3), 580 (3)
snuffly 352 (9)
snug 24 (8), 194 (19), 196 (8), 275 (11), 376 (4), 379 (6), 660 (4), 660 (5), 828 (2)
snuggle 889 (6)
snugness 376 (2), 828 (1)
so 8 (4), 18 (9), 158 (5), 494 (4)
so and so 371 (3), 562 (2)
so, be 7 (4), 494 (7)

so-called 486 (5), 512 (5), 542 (7), 561 (4), 562 (3)
so far 236 (4)
so happen 159 (7)
so long as 108 (10)
so many 26 (3)
so minded 595 (1)
so much 26 (3)
so-so 33 (7), 647 (3), 732 (2)
so to speak 18 (9), 519 (5)
soak 189 (5), 303 (7), 339 (3), 341 (8), 637 (5), 786 (11), 811 (5), 863 (3)
soak in 309 (3)
soak into 297 (6)
soak through 297 (6), 305 (5)
soak up 299 (4), 301 (38)
soaked 341 (5)
soaking 301 (25), 341 (5)
soap 334 (2), 334 (4), 357 (3), 648 (4), 648 (9)
soap and water 648 (4)
soap opera 531 (4)
soapbox 539 (5), 579 (3)
soapy 258 (3), 355 (3), 357 (6), 427 (4), 925 (3)
soar 32 (15), 195 (10), 209 (12), 271 (7), 308 (4), 323 (4)
soaring 32 (4), 209 (8), 271 (6), 308 (1), 811 (2)
sob 352 (7), 352 (11), 407 (4), 408 (1), 836 (1), 836 (6)
sob-story 836 (2)
sobbing 408 (2), 836 (1)
sober 177 (3), 177 (6), 425 (7), 498 (5), 502 (2), 502 (4), 573 (2), 823 (3), 834 (7), 834 (12), 933 (3), 942 (3), 948 (3)
sober approval 923 (1)
sober, be 948 (4)
sober down 177 (5), 177 (6), 502 (3), 823 (7)
sober person 942 (2), 948 (2)
sober truth 540 (1)
sober up 502 (3), 834 (10), 948 (4)
sobered 834 (5), 939 (3)

sobered up 948 (3)
sobering 834 (7)
soberly 502 (5), 948 (5)
soberness 177 (1), 942 (1), 948 (1)
sobriety 498 (3), 502 (1), 823 (1), 834 (3), 858 (1), 942 (1), 948 (1)
sobriquet 561 (2)
soccer 837 (7)
sociability 301 (1), 813 (1), 833 (1), 875 (1), 880 (2), 882 (2), 884 (1), 897 (1)
sociable 708 (6), 813 (3), 833 (3), 880 (6), 882 (6), 884 (4), 897 (4)
sociable, be 45 (14), 295 (6), 835 (6), 848 (7), 880 (7), 882 (8), 884 (7)
sociable person 837 (17), 848 (3), 882 (5)
sociableness 882 (2)
sociably 882 (11)
social 371 (7), 708 (6), 882 (3)
social activity 882 (2)
social butterfly 882 (5)
social calls 882 (4)
social circle 882 (1)
social class 708 (4)
social climber 847 (3), 882 (5)
social demands 882 (4)
social democrats 708 (2)
social evil 951 (5)
social gathering 74 (2), 584 (3), 837 (2), 882 (3)
social graces 846 (1), 882 (2)
social group 74 (3), 371 (4), 708 (4)
social intercourse 584 (1), 882 (1)
social planning 901 (2)
social round 882 (4)
social science 371 (2), 901 (2)
social security 703 (2)
social services 901 (2)
social success 882 (2)
social tact 882 (2)
social usage 610 (2)

social whirl 837 (2), 882 (4)
social work 901 (2)
social worker 654 (5), 703 (3), 901 (4)
socialism 654 (4), 733 (4), 775 (1), 901 (1)
socialist 654 (5), 775 (3)
socialists 708 (2)
socialite 848 (3), 882 (5)
sociality 584 (1), 880 (1), 882 (1)
socialize 654 (9), 775 (6), 882 (8)
society 74 (3), 89 (1), 371 (4), 708 (3), 848 (3), 882 (1)
sociological 901 (6)
sociologist 654 (5)
sociology 371 (2), 901 (2)
sociopath 504 (1)
sock 228 (27)
socket 194 (1), 255 (2)
socketed 255 (6)
sod 53 (5), 344 (3)
soda 648 (4)
soda water 301 (27), 339 (1)
sodden 341 (5), 949 (11)
sodomite 952 (1)
sodomy 951 (3)
sofa 218 (6)
soft 33 (6), 152 (4), 163 (4), 258 (3), 301 (32), 327 (2), 347 (2), 356 (2), 376 (4), 391 (2), 399 (2), 401 (3), 410 (6), 417 (8), 425 (7), 499 (4), 721 (2), 734 (3), 736 (2), 905 (4)
soft answer 736 (1), 884 (2)
soft drink 301 (27), 339 (1)
soft drug 949 (4)
soft focus 419 (1)
soft footfall 401 (1)
soft fruit 301 (19), 356 (1)
soft furnishings 226 (1)
soft-grained 366 (11)
soft heart 905 (1)
soft-hearted 819 (2), 897 (4), 905 (4)
soft-hued 425 (7)
soft landing 271 (3)

soft nothings 889 (1)
soft-pedal 177 (6), 278 (4), 401 (2), 414 (11)
soft porn 951 (1)
soft sell 528 (3), 793 (1)
soft soap 541 (1), 925 (4)
soft-spoken 579 (6), 884 (4)
soft spot 647 (2), 819 (1), 827 (1)
soft touch 544 (1)
soft underbelly 661 (2)
soft voice 401 (1)
soft water 339 (1)
softback 589 (1)
softball 837 (7)
soften 177 (7), 327 (4), 401 (5), 405 (3), 831 (3), 905 (8), 927 (7)
soften one's heart 819 (5)
soften up 178 (3), 612 (10), 669 (10), 712 (11)
softening 327 (2)
softly softly 177 (8), 858 (4)
softness 83 (1), 163 (1), 177 (2), 258 (1), 325 (1), 327 (1), 356 (1), 398 (1), 401 (1), 612 (3), 736 (1), 739 (1)
software 86 (5)
softwood 366 (2)
sogginess 327 (1), 341 (1)
soggy 327 (2), 341 (5), 356 (2), 391 (2)
soi-disant 561 (4), 562 (3)
soigné 575 (3), 841 (6)
soignée 228 (29)
soil 344 (3), 631 (1), 649 (9)
soiled 649 (7), 845 (2)
soirée 129 (1), 882 (3)
sojourn 189 (4), 192 (21)
sojourner 191 (1)
sol-fa 410 (3)
solace 831 (1), 831 (3), 837 (1), 837 (20)
solar 321 (14)
solar energy 160 (4), 383 (2)
solar flare 321 (8)
solar panel 160 (4), 383 (2)

solar plexus 224 (2)
solar-powered 160 (9)
solar system 321 (8)
solar wind 321 (8)
sold 793 (3)
sold, be 793 (5)
sold off 779 (3)
sold out 793 (3)
solder 45 (9), 47 (9)
solderly conduct 855 (2)
soldier 271 (4), 362 (6), 713 (6), 718 (11), 722 (4), 855 (3)
soldier ant 365 (16)
soldier on 599 (4)
soldiering 718 (6)
soldierly 718 (9), 855 (4)
soldiership 718 (4)
soldiery 287 (4), 660 (3), 707 (1), 713 (6), 722 (4), 722 (5)
sole 88 (3), 214 (2)
solecism 477 (2), 495 (2), 495 (3), 560 (1), 562 (1), 564 (1), 565 (1), 576 (1)
solecistic 565 (2)
soled 214 (4)
solely 88 (6)
solemn 32 (4), 532 (3), 638 (5), 834 (7), 875 (6), 981 (10), 988 (8)
solemn declaration 764 (1)
solemn entreaty 761 (2)
solemn observance 876 (1)
solemnity 571 (1), 638 (1), 834 (3), 875 (1), 875 (2), 988 (3)
solemnization 876 (1)
solemnize 676 (5), 876 (4)
solemnly affirm 532 (6)
solicit 761 (5)
solicitation 612 (2), 759 (1), 761 (1)
soliciting 761 (1)
solicitor 958 (2)
solicitous 457 (3)
solicitude 457 (1), 825 (3)
solid 1 (5), 3 (2), 3 (3), 16 (2), 45 (7), 48 (2), 162 (6), 162 (7), 319 (6), 324 (3),

324 (4), 326 (4), 473 (4), 494 (5), 571 (2), 834 (7)
solid body 3 (2), 48 (1), 195 (3), 322 (1), 324 (3)
solid foundation 218 (4)
solid-fuel 381 (7)
solid geometry 465 (2)
solid-state 160 (9)
solid substance 319 (2)
solid vote 488 (2)
solidarity 24 (1), 54 (1), 88 (1), 706 (1), 706 (2), 710 (1), 880 (1)
solidification 324 (2)
solidify 324 (6)
solidifying 324 (5)
solidity 3 (1), 54 (1), 319 (1), 324 (1), 800 (1)
solidly 16 (5), 48 (5)
solidly built 205 (4)
solidness 324 (1)
soliloquist 579 (5), 585 (2)
soliloquize 579 (9), 585 (4)
soliloquizing 585 (3)
soliloquy 579 (2), 585 (1)
solitaire 837 (11)
solitariness 883 (2)
solitary 84 (3), 84 (5), 88 (2), 88 (3), 88 (4), 883 (3), 883 (5), 883 (6), 902 (2), 945 (2), 979 (4), 986 (5)
solitary confinement 747 (3)
solitude 883 (2)
solo 88 (2), 412 (3), 412 (6), 594 (5), 837 (11)
soloist 413 (1)
solubility 337 (1)
soluble 335 (4), 337 (3)
solubleness 335 (1)
solution 43 (3), 337 (2), 460 (1), 484 (1), 520 (1), 658 (1), 725 (1)
solve 520 (10), 522 (7)
solvency 800 (1)
solvent 337 (1), 337 (3), 797 (9), 800 (4)
solver 520 (4)
somatic 319 (6)
sombre 364 (8), 418 (3), 425 (7), 428 (4), 834 (8)
sombrero 228 (23)

some 26 (3), 101 (1), 101 (2), 562 (2)
some day 124 (7)
some other time 122 (1)
some other way 15 (8)
some time ago 125 (12)
some time back 125 (12)
somebody 3 (2), 371 (3), 638 (4), 866 (6)
somebody, be 638 (7), 866 (11)
someday 122 (3)
somehow 33 (10), 158 (6)
somehow feel 476 (3)
somehow or other 158 (6)
someone 371 (3)
somersault 221 (2)
something 3 (2), 319 (3)
something added 40 (1)
something in hand 34 (2), 632 (1)
something like 18 (4)
something new 21 (1)
something off 810 (1)
something over 637 (2)
something owing 803 (1)
sometime 119 (2), 122 (3), 125 (7)
sometimes 139 (6)
somewhat 33 (10)
somewhere 185 (2)
somewhere about 33 (12)
somewhere else 190 (9)
somnambulism 267 (3), 679 (4)
somnambulist 268 (3)
somnolence 679 (3)
somnolent 679 (9)
son 170 (2), 372 (1)
son and heir 119 (1)
son et lumière 875 (3)
son or daughter of the soil 869 (6)
sonar 211 (1), 484 (2)
sonata 412 (4)
song 412 (5), 593 (1), 593 (2), 981 (5)
song and dance 678 (4), 822 (2)
song writer 413 (1), 593 (6)
songbird 365 (4), 413 (4)
songster 365 (4), 413 (4)

sonic 398 (3)

sonic boom 400 (1), 402 (1)

sonnet 593 (4), 889 (2)

sonny 132 (2)

sonority 400 (1), 404 (1)

sonorous 398 (3), 400 (3), 404 (2), 574 (4), 574 (5)

sonorousness 398 (1), 404 (1)

sonship 170 (3)

soon 116 (4), 122 (3), 124 (7), 135 (6), 155 (5)

soon after 120 (4)

soon counted 33 (7), 105 (2)

sooner or later 122 (3)

soot 332 (2), 381 (4), 428 (2)

soothe 177 (7), 266 (9), 541 (5), 658 (19), 679 (13), 719 (4), 826 (3), 831 (3), 925 (4)

soothing 177 (4), 258 (3), 542 (6), 658 (17), 719 (3), 831 (2)

soothsay 511 (9)

soothsayer 511 (4), 983 (5)

soothsaying 511 (2)

sophism 10 (2), 477 (2), 495 (1), 614 (1)

sophist 475 (6), 477 (3)

sophistical 475 (8), 477 (4)

sophisticate 477 (8), 541 (7), 696 (2), 846 (2)

sophisticated 61 (8), 490 (6), 498 (4), 694 (7), 698 (4), 848 (6)

sophistication 490 (3), 694 (1), 846 (1)

sophistry 475 (4), 477 (1), 495 (2), 497 (1), 515 (1), 535 (1), 541 (1), 542 (1)

sophomore 538 (3)

soporific 177 (2), 177 (4), 375 (2), 375 (3), 658 (7), 679 (5), 679 (10), 831 (1), 838 (3)

sopping 341 (5)

sopping wet 341 (5)

soprano 407 (1), 413 (4)

sorbet 301 (17)

sorcerer 143 (3), 500 (1), 511 (4), 545 (5), 658 (14), 864 (3), 983 (5), 984 (4)

sorceress 983 (6)

sorcerous 983 (7), 984 (6)

sorcerously 983 (12)

sorcery 147 (1), 160 (1), 178 (1), 490 (1), 542 (3), 628 (1), 645 (1), 821 (1), 864 (2), 969 (1), 982 (1), 983 (1), 984 (1)

sordid 645 (4), 649 (6), 816 (5)

sore 374 (3), 377 (3), 651 (14), 651 (22), 684 (2), 709 (6), 819 (3), 827 (1), 827 (3), 829 (3), 891 (3)

sore point 709 (4), 819 (1), 827 (1), 891 (1)

sore throat 651 (8)

sorely 32 (20)

soreness 374 (1), 377 (1), 709 (1), 827 (1)

sorghum 301 (22)

sorority 11 (3), 708 (4)

sorrow 616 (1), 731 (1), 825 (2), 825 (7), 827 (1), 829 (1), 834 (1), 836 (5), 905 (1), 905 (6)

sorrowful 825 (6)

sorrowing 825 (6)

sorry 639 (5), 825 (6), 830 (2), 834 (6), 939 (3)

sorry, be 830 (4)

sorry for 905 (4)

sorry for oneself 834 (6)

sorry sight 827 (1)

sort 5 (3), 27 (1), 62 (6), 74 (3), 77 (2), 463 (3)

sort of 33 (10)

sort out 57 (5), 105 (4), 463 (3), 607 (3)

sorted 16 (2), 62 (3), 605 (5)

sortie 298 (1), 712 (1), 714 (1)

sorting 39 (1), 44 (3), 62 (2), 263 (3), 463 (1)

sorting office 531 (2)

SOS 547 (8), 665 (1)

sot 501 (1)

sotto voce 401 (6), 578 (6)

souffle 301 (13), 355 (1)

sough 352 (10), 401 (1)

sought after 793 (3), 882 (7)

soul 1 (3), 4 (2), 5 (2), 80 (4), 360 (1), 371 (3), 447 (2), 817 (1), 819 (1)

soul mate 880 (4), 887 (5)

soul music 412 (1)

soul-searching 830 (1)

soul-stirring 818 (6), 821 (4)

soulful 818 (3)

soulless 838 (3)

souls 361 (3)

sound 32 (13), 52 (4), 83 (6), 162 (7), 211 (3), 313 (3), 345 (1), 398 (1), 398 (4), 400 (1), 415 (1), 461 (8), 465 (3), 465 (11), 494 (5), 498 (5), 644 (8), 646 (3), 650 (2), 694 (4), 797 (9), 800 (4)

sound a warning 665 (3)

sound argument 475 (5)

sound asleep 679 (9)

sound barrier 236 (1), 398 (1)

sound box 414 (1)

sound character 929 (2)

sound dead 405 (3)

sound effect 398 (1)

sound effects 445 (3)

sound engineer 398 (2)

sound faint 33 (8), 352 (10), 401 (4), 408 (3), 578 (5)

sound film 445 (4)

sound like 18 (7)

sound-making 398 (1)

sound of mind 502 (1)

sound out 459 (14)

sound-proofing 401 (1)

sound proposition 802 (1)

sound recorder 415 (4)

sound recording 548 (2)

sound sleep 679 (4)

sound the alarm 547 (22), 664 (5), 665 (3)

sound the charge 712 (10), 718 (12)

sound the horn 413 (9)

sound theology 976 (1)

sound track 398 (1)

sound wave 317 (1)

sound waves 398 (1)

sounding 398 (1), 398 (3), 415 (5), 577 (3)

sounding board 414 (1), 528 (2)

soundings 211 (1), 459 (1)

soundless 266 (6), 399 (2)

soundness 498 (3), 644 (1), 650 (1), 800 (1), 929 (1)

soundproof 399 (2), 405 (2)

soundproofing 227 (1), 235 (3)

soundtrack 445 (3)

soup 301 (14)

soupçon 33 (2), 43 (2)

souped-up 160 (9), 174 (5), 277 (5)

sour 51 (3), 172 (4), 174 (6), 377 (3), 388 (3), 391 (2), 393 (2), 393 (3), 509 (5), 616 (3), 827 (4), 829 (3), 829 (6), 832 (3), 834 (7), 892 (3)

sour, be 393 (3)

sour grapes 614 (1)

source 68 (4), 132 (3), 156 (3), 158 (1), 167 (1), 167 (3), 169 (1), 298 (2), 366 (7), 524 (4), 632 (1), 965 (1)

source of light 420 (1)

sources of energy 160 (4), 630 (2)

soured 509 (2), 829 (3)

sourness 388 (1), 391 (1), 393 (1), 645 (1), 659 (1), 827 (1), 861 (1), 898 (1)

sourpuss 834 (4), 885 (3)

souse 303 (7), 313 (3), 341 (8), 388 (6)

sousing 311 (1)

South 281 (2)

south pole 213 (1), 380 (1)

southbound 281 (3)

southerly 281 (3)

southern 240 (2), 281 (3)

Southern Cross 321 (4)

Southerner 59 (2), 191 (3)

southpaw 242 (1)

souvenir 505 (3)

sou'wester 228 (23), 352 (4)

sovereign 34 (5), 727 (4), 733 (8), 741 (3), 797 (4), 868 (4), 965 (6)

sovereign remedy 658 (1)

sovereignty 733 (2), 965 (2)

sow 75 (4), 164 (7), 311 (5), 365 (9), 370 (9)

sow dissension 709 (8), 888 (8)

sow the seed 669 (10)

sow the seeds of 156 (9)

sower 370 (4)

sowing 370 (1)

sown 164 (6)

spa 192 (1), 658 (13)

space 26 (1), 32 (1), 62 (4), 73 (2), 78 (1), 107 (1), 108 (1), 183 (1), 183 (4), 183 (5), 195 (1), 199 (1), 201 (1), 201 (4), 263 (1), 263 (7), 348 (1)

space flight 271 (3)

space heating 381 (1)

space out 73 (2), 201 (4)

space probe 276 (4), 484 (2)

space shuttle 276 (4)

space station 276 (4), 321 (10)

space suit 228 (9)

space-time 108 (1), 183 (1)

space travel 271 (3)

space walk 271 (3)

spacecraft 276 (4)

spaced 201 (3), 222 (7)

spaced out 201 (3), 949 (10)

spaceman 271 (4)

spaceship 271 (3), 276 (4), 321 (10), 484 (2)

spaceship earth 321 (2)

spacewoman 271 (4)

spacious 32 (4), 32 (5), 75 (2), 183 (6), 194 (24), 195 (6), 197 (3), 205 (3), 321 (15)

spaciousness 32 (1)

spade 194 (18), 370 (6)

spadework 669 (1), 682 (3)

span 45 (10), 47 (1), 90 (1), 110 (1), 183 (3), 183 (7), 199 (1), 203 (1), 203 (4), 205 (1), 205 (5), 226 (14), 624 (3)

spangle 417 (2), 437 (9), 844 (6), 844 (12)

spaniel 365 (10)

spank 279 (9), 963 (9)

spanking 32 (9), 195 (6), 279 (2)

spanner 630 (1)

spar 218 (2), 279 (9), 716 (11)

spar with 709 (9)

spare 38 (2), 41 (4), 206 (5), 573 (2), 620 (5), 632 (4), 637 (4), 668 (3), 673 (5), 674 (2), 674 (4), 736 (3), 779 (4), 781 (7), 814 (3), 831 (3), 905 (7), 919 (3)

spare for 781 (7)

spare no effort 682 (6)

spare no expense 806 (4), 813 (4)

spare no pains 600 (4)

spare none 906 (3)

spare part 58 (1)

spare parts 40 (2), 662 (3)

spare time 137 (2), 681 (1)

spare tyre 195 (3)

spared 190 (4)

spared, be 360 (4)

spareness 573 (1)

spares 40 (2)

sparing 814 (2), 816 (4)

sparing of words 204 (3)

sparingly 814 (4)

spark 33 (2), 156 (5), 174 (1), 379 (2), 417 (2), 420 (1)

spark off 68 (9), 156 (9)

sparkle 355 (5), 417 (2), 417 (11), 571 (1), 833 (1), 833 (7), 839 (1), 839 (5)

sparkler 420 (7), 844 (8)

sparkling 355 (3), 417 (8), 571 (2), 824 (5), 833 (3), 833 (4), 839 (4)

sparkling wine 301 (29)

sparring 716 (4)

sparring partner 722 (2)

sparrow **33** (5), **365** (4)
sparse **75** (2), **105** (2), **172** (4), **636** (6)
sparsely **75** (5), **105** (5)
sparseness **33** (1), **105** (1)
sparsity **105** (1)
Spartan **814** (2), **942** (2), **942** (3), **945** (3), **946** (3)
spasm **114** (2), **142** (1), **176** (1), **318** (2), **377** (2), **503** (4), **547** (4), **651** (2), **651** (16), **678** (1), **818** (1), **821** (1)
spasmodic **17** (2), **72** (2), **142** (2), **152** (4), **176** (5), **318** (4)
spasmodically **318** (8)
spastic **651** (18), **651** (22)
spasticity **651** (16)
spat on **922** (4)
spate **32** (2), **350** (4), **637** (1)
spate of words **581** (1)
spatial **183** (5)
spats **228** (26)
spatter **75** (4), **300** (9), **341** (7), **649** (9)
spatula **194** (18), **553** (6)
spavin **651** (17)
spavined **651** (22)
spawn **132** (3), **167** (6), **167** (7)
spawned **360** (3)
spawning **171** (4)
spay **161** (10)
speak **408** (3), **524** (9), **526** (5), **528** (9), **532** (5), **577** (4), **579** (8), **584** (6)
speak at **583** (3)
speak badly **517** (6)
speak for **520** (8), **755** (3)
speak for itself **466** (6), **522** (9)
speak highly of **923** (9)
speak ill of **926** (7)
speak in earnest **540** (3)
speak low **401** (4), **578** (5)
speak no evil **933** (4)
speak of **514** (5), **528** (9)
speak on oath **466** (7)
speak one's mind **540** (3), **579** (8)

speak out **522** (9), **532** (5), **855** (6)
speak plainly **522** (9), **532** (5), **573** (3), **699** (4)
speak slowly **278** (4)
speak softly **578** (5)
speak the truth **494** (7)
speak to **466** (7), **579** (9), **583** (3), **761** (7), **884** (7)
speak up **400** (4), **532** (5), **532** (7), **579** (8), **855** (6)
speak up for **923** (8), **927** (5)
speak volumes **514** (5)
speak well of **923** (9)
speak with an accent **560** (6)
speakeasy **192** (12)
speaker **400** (2), **414** (10), **537** (3), **574** (3), **579** (5), **612** (5), **690** (1)
speaking **524** (7), **579** (6)
speaking of 9 (10)
speaking part **594** (8)
speaking voice **577** (1)
spear **256** (2), **263** (18), **723** (6)
spear side **11** (4), **372** (1)
spearhead **237** (1), **283** (3), **638** (3), **712** (5), **722** (7)
special 5 (8), **15** (4), **17** (2), **21** (3), **80** (5), **84** (5), **84** (6), **88** (3), **514** (4), **547** (15), **773** (3)
special case **15** (3), **17** (1), **57** (1), **80** (1), **84** (1)
special constable **955** (3)
special correspondent **524** (4)
special day **141** (3), **837** (2), **876** (2)
special education **534** (2)
special effects **445** (3), **594** (11)
special pleading **477** (1), **614** (1)
special points **80** (2)
special prayer **981** (4)
special repute **866** (1)
special school **539** (2)
special treatment **919** (1)
specialism **490** (1), **694** (1)

specialist **34** (3), **492** (1), **538** (3), **658** (14), **696** (2)
speciality 5 (4), **10** (1), **15** (3), **17** (1), **80** (1), **84** (1), **88** (1), **179** (1), **301** (13), **514** (2), **566** (1), **744** (2)
specialization **80** (1)
specialize **80** (8), **536** (5)
specialized **490** (6), **694** (6)
specially **32** (17), **80** (9)
species **53** (3), **74** (3), **77** (2), **77** (3)
specific **80** (5), **658** (1)
specific, be **80** (8), **524** (9)
specific gravity **322** (1), **324** (1)
specific quality **80** (1)
specifically **32** (16), **80** (9)
specification **77** (1), **80** (2), **524** (2), **590** (1)
specify **62** (6), **80** (8), **524** (9), **547** (18), **561** (6), **590** (7)
specimen **23** (1), **83** (2), **522** (2)
specious **445** (7), **471** (3), **477** (4), **542** (6), **614** (2), **850** (4), **875** (4), **927** (4)
specious argument **477** (2)
speciousness **542** (1)
speck **33** (3), **437** (4), **845** (1)
speckle **437** (4), **437** (9)
speckled **437** (8)
specs **442** (2)
spectacle **445** (2), **522** (2), **551** (2), **594** (4), **594** (6), **841** (1), **864** (3), **875** (3)
spectacle case **194** (10)
spectacles **442** (2)
spectacular **443** (3), **445** (7), **875** (5)
spectator **189** (1), **268** (1), **415** (3), **441** (1), **466** (4), **594** (14)
spectral 4 (3), **970** (7)
spectrally **970** (9)
spectre **440** (2), **854** (4), **970** (3)
spectroscope **321** (11), **425** (2), **442** (1)
spectroscopy **417** (7)

spectrum 71 (2), 417 (1), 425 (1), 437 (1)

speculate 449 (8), 461 (8), 512 (6), 618 (8), 671 (4), 784 (5), 791 (5), 792 (5)

speculation 159 (4), 449 (2), 459 (1), 461 (2), 512 (2), 618 (2), 672 (1)

speculative 449 (6), 461 (6), 474 (4), 512 (4), 618 (7), 661 (3), 791 (3)

speculator 461 (3), 618 (4), 794 (1)

speech 408 (1), 532 (1), 557 (1), 577 (1), 579 (1), 579 (2)

speech defect 517 (1), 565 (1), 577 (2), 580 (1)

speech impediment 580 (1)

speech-maker 579 (5)

speech-making 579 (3)

speech sound 559 (1)

speech therapy 580 (1)

speech-writer 579 (5)

speechifier 579 (5)

speechify 579 (9)

speechifying 579 (3)

speechless 399 (2), 578 (2), 864 (4), 891 (4)

speed 27 (1), 265 (1), 277 (1), 277 (6), 701 (8), 703 (5)

speed contest 716 (3)

speed gauge 465 (6)

speed limit 236 (1)

speed maniac 277 (4)

speed of light 277 (1)

speed of sound 277 (1)

speed rate 265 (1), 277 (1)

speed track 277 (3)

speed trap 305 (3)

speed up 36 (5), 277 (2), 277 (7), 285 (4)

speedboat 275 (7)

speeder 268 (5), 273 (5), 277 (4)

speeding 277 (3), 277 (5), 716 (3)

speedometer 277 (1), 465 (6), 549 (3)

speedway 716 (3)

speedy 114 (3), 114 (5), 116 (3), 277 (5), 678 (7), 680 (2)

speleologist 309 (1), 484 (2)

speleology 309 (1), 837 (6)

spell 108 (1), 110 (1), 511 (8), 514 (5), 523 (6), 547 (18), 558 (6), 612 (4), 898 (1), 899 (1), 983 (2)

spell danger 661 (9), 900 (3)

spell it out 573 (3)

spell-like 983 (7)

spell out 80 (8), 520 (10), 558 (6)

spellbinder 579 (5), 983 (5)

spellbinding 579 (7), 864 (2), 983 (1), 983 (7)

spellbound 455 (3), 612 (7), 864 (4), 983 (9)

spelling 558 (4)

spelt 558 (5)

spend 634 (4), 806 (4)

spend a penny 302 (6)

spend freely 813 (4)

spend money like water 815 (4)

spend on 673 (3)

spend time 108 (8), 111 (3)

spender 815 (2)

spending 634 (1), 792 (1), 806 (1), 806 (2)

spending money 807 (1)

spending spree 806 (1), 815 (1)

spendthrift 815 (2), 815 (3)

spent 163 (5), 684 (2), 772 (3), 806 (3)

sperm 156 (3), 167 (3), 171 (2)

sperm bank 632 (2)

spermaceti 357 (3)

spermatozoa 167 (3)

spew 300 (10), 350 (9)

spew out 300 (6)

sphere 8 (1), 27 (1), 74 (3), 77 (1), 92 (1), 183 (3), 184 (1), 184 (2), 252 (2), 253 (2), 321 (2), 622 (4), 837 (15)

sphere of influence 178 (1)

spherical 250 (6), 252 (5)

sphericity 253 (1)

spheroid 252 (2)

spheroidal 252 (5)

sphinx 84 (4)

spice 43 (2), 43 (7), 174 (4), 388 (1), 388 (6), 390 (3), 826 (1)

spiced 386 (2)

spices 389 (1)

spiciness 388 (1)

spick and span 60 (2), 126 (5), 648 (7)

spicy 386 (2), 388 (3), 390 (2), 396 (3), 821 (4), 951 (6)

spider 222 (5), 365 (17)

spider's web 61 (3), 527 (2)

spidery 206 (5)

spiel 515 (3), 581 (1), 793 (1)

spigot 264 (2)

spike 43 (7), 157 (2), 213 (2), 256 (2), 263 (18), 366 (7)

spike the guns 161 (9)

spiked 256 (7)

spikes 228 (27)

spiky 256 (7)

spill 221 (2), 221 (5), 264 (2), 298 (2), 298 (6), 300 (9), 309 (1), 311 (5), 341 (7), 350 (4), 350 (11), 385 (3), 420 (3), 634 (4), 695 (9), 772 (4)

spill into 350 (9)

spill over 298 (6)

spill the beans 526 (5)

spillway 350 (4), 351 (1)

spin 164 (7), 222 (9), 267 (1), 315 (1), 315 (5)

spin a yarn 543 (5), 546 (3), 590 (7)

spin-dry 342 (6)

spin dryer 342 (3)

spin-off 67 (1), 157 (1)

spin out 71 (6), 113 (8), 136 (7), 146 (4), 203 (8), 206 (7), 570 (6), 702 (10)

spina bifida 651 (16)

spinal 218 (14), 225 (3), 238 (4)

spinal column 218 (10)

spindle 218 (11), 315 (3)

spindly 206 (5), 267 (10)

spine 218 (10), 225 (2), 256 (3)

spine-chiller 445 (4)

spine-chilling 821 (4)

spineless 161 (7), 163 (4), 601 (3)

spinet 414 (4)

spinner 222 (5), 315 (3)

spinney 366 (2)

spinning jenny 315 (3)

spinning out 113 (3), 203 (2)

spinning top 252 (4)

spinning wheel 222 (5), 315 (3)

spinster 373 (3), 895 (3)

spinsterhood 895 (1)

spinsterish 895 (4)

spiny 256 (7)

spiral 36 (1), 36 (4), 251 (2), 251 (8), 251 (10), 308 (1), 308 (4), 309 (1), 309 (4), 315 (1)

spiral nebula 321 (4)

spiral staircase 308 (1)

spiralling 308 (1), 315 (1)

spire 209 (4), 213 (2), 990 (5)

spired 256 (9)

spirit 4 (2), 5 (2), 80 (4), 174 (1), 320 (2), 360 (1), 447 (2), 476 (1), 514 (1), 571 (1), 599 (1), 678 (2), 817 (1), 819 (1), 855 (1), 970 (3)

spirit away 788 (7)

spirit communication 984 (3)

spirit-laying 983 (1)

spirit of evil 969 (1)

spirit of place 187 (2)

spirit of the age 179 (1)

spirit-raiser 983 (5)

spirit-raising 983 (1)

spirited 571 (2), 678 (7), 818 (3), 819 (4), 833 (3), 855 (4)

spiritedness 819 (1)

spiritless 820 (4), 823 (3), 834 (5), 856 (3)

spirits 7 (1), 301 (28), 361 (3)

spiritual 320 (3), 412 (5), 447 (6), 965 (5), 973 (8), 979 (6), 981 (5), 985 (7)

spiritual power 160 (1)

spiritualism 320 (1), 447 (2), 520 (4), 984 (1), 984 (3)

spiritualist 320 (1), 984 (4)

spiritualistic 984 (7)

spirituality 320 (1), 979 (2)

spiritualize 979 (11), 979 (12)

spirituous 301 (32)

spirt 298 (6), 308 (4), 350 (9)

spiry 209 (8), 256 (9)

spit 47 (5), 254 (2), 256 (2), 263 (12), 263 (18), 300 (9), 300 (11), 302 (4), 302 (6), 315 (3), 318 (7), 334 (2), 406 (3), 409 (3), 891 (7), 893 (3), 900 (3)

spit and polish 648 (1), 875 (2)

spit on 921 (5)

spit out 300 (6)

spite 645 (6), 645 (7), 709 (2), 735 (8), 881 (1), 888 (1), 891 (1), 898 (1), 898 (8), 910 (1), 912 (1)

spiteful 645 (3), 881 (3), 888 (4), 891 (3), 898 (4), 910 (4), 926 (5)

spitefulness 898 (1)

spitfire 176 (4), 892 (2)

spitting 302 (1), 350 (8)

spitting image 18 (3)

spittle 302 (4), 334 (2), 341 (1)

splash 33 (2), 341 (7), 346 (1), 350 (9), 406 (1), 406 (3), 437 (4), 528 (11), 552 (3), 638 (8), 649 (9)

splash about 269 (12)

splash down 309 (3)

splash money around 815 (4)

splash out 806 (4)

splashdown 271 (3), 309 (1)

splashing out 806 (2)

splatter 341 (7)

splay 75 (4), 197 (4), 205 (5), 220 (1), 220 (6), 294 (3)

splay apart 294 (3)

splay-footed 246 (4)

splayed out 205 (3)

spleen 224 (2), 912 (1)

splendid 417 (8), 644 (4), 813 (3), 826 (2), 841 (4), 841 (7), 866 (9), 875 (4)

splendid isolation 883 (2)

splendidly 32 (17)

splendour 841 (1), 866 (2), 875 (1)

splice 45 (12), 222 (8), 231 (8), 656 (12)

spliced 894 (7)

spliced joint 45 (4)

splint 218 (2), 658 (9)

splinter 33 (3), 46 (13), 53 (5), 208 (3), 330 (3)

splinter group 489 (2), 708 (1), 738 (4)

splintery 330 (2)

split 46 (1), 46 (7), 46 (10), 46 (13), 51 (5), 72 (1), 92 (4), 92 (5), 163 (9), 201 (2), 201 (3), 201 (4), 207 (5), 263 (1), 263 (17), 330 (3), 709 (1), 709 (7), 783 (2), 783 (3)

split hairs 463 (3), 475 (11), 477 (8), 862 (4)

split off 46 (7), 294 (3)

split one's sides 835 (7)

split personality 82 (1), 447 (2), 503 (2)

split second 116 (2)

split the difference 30 (5), 770 (2)

split the eardrum 416 (4)

split up 896 (5)

splitting 46 (2)

splitting head 377 (2)

splotch 437 (4)

splurge 815 (1), 875 (7)

splutter 300 (9), 350 (9), 406 (1), 406 (3), 580 (3)

spoil 63 (3), 655 (7), 655 (9), 695 (9), 734 (5), 736 (3), 842 (7), 845 (3), 863 (3), 887 (13), 889 (5)

spoil for one 829 (6)

spoil one's chances 695 (8)

spoil one's record 867 (9)

spoil oneself 824 (6)

spoil the look of 845 (3)

spoilage 42 (1), 641 (3)

spoiled 645 (2)

spoiled child 890 (2)

spoiling 655 (3)

spoiling for 669 (7)

spoils 729 (1), 790 (1)

spoils of war 790 (1)

spoilsport 613 (1), 678 (6), 702 (5), 834 (4)

spoilt 655 (5)

spoke 203 (3)

spoken 557 (5), 577 (3), 579 (6)

spoken judgment 480 (1)

spoken letter 558 (3)

spokes 294 (1)

spokesperson 524 (4), 579 (5), 686 (1), 755 (1)

spoliation 165 (2), 786 (1), 788 (3)

sponge 125 (3), 255 (2), 263 (3), 299 (4), 342 (3), 342 (6), 356 (1), 648 (5), 761 (6)

sponge bag 194 (9)

sponge on 879 (4)

sponger 679 (6)

sponginess 325 (1), 327 (1), 356 (1)

spongy 263 (15), 325 (2), 327 (2), 347 (2), 356 (2)

sponsor 466 (4), 594 (12), 703 (3), 703 (6), 707 (4), 767 (1)

sponsorship 703 (1), 767 (1)

spontaneity 595 (0), 597 (1), 604 (2), 609 (1), 612 (1), 618 (1), 623 (3), 670 (1), 818 (1)

spontaneous 114 (5), 476 (2), 595 (1), 596 (5), 597

(5), 609 (3), 618 (5), 670 (3), 699 (3), 744 (7)

spontaneously 595 (3), 597 (7)

spoof 542 (2)

spook 854 (4), 970 (3)

spookish 970 (7)

spookishly 970 (9)

spooky 970 (7)

spool 315 (5)

spoon 194 (18), 304 (2), 889 (6)

spoon in 301 (35)

spoon out 272 (7)

spoonerism 221 (1), 560 (1), 849 (1)

spoonfeed 534 (6)

spoonful 26 (2)

spoor 547 (2), 548 (4)

sporadic 17 (2), 140 (2)

sporadically 75 (5)

spore 156 (3), 332 (2), 366 (7)

sporran 194 (11)

sport 15 (3), 17 (1), 84 (3), 162 (3), 228 (32), 269 (3), 380 (3), 522 (8), 542 (2), 619 (2), 682 (2), 716 (1), 716 (3), 833 (2), 837 (1), 837 (6), 837 (21), 851 (3), 864 (3), 875 (7), 890 (2), 929 (2), 937 (1)

sport, be a 837 (20)

sport of fortune 731 (3)

sport with 542 (9)

sported 522 (6)

sporting 716 (9), 837 (19), 844 (11), 855 (4), 913 (4), 929 (3)

sporting chance 159 (3), 471 (1)

sportive 833 (4), 837 (18), 837 (19), 839 (4)

sports 682 (2), 716 (1), 837 (6)

sports car 274 (11)

sports centre 192 (14)

sports jacket 228 (10)

sports model 274 (3)

sports trophy 729 (1)

sportsman 929 (2)

sportsman or - woman 837 (16)

sportsmanlike 913 (4), 929 (3)

sportsmanship 837 (6), 929 (1)

sportswoman 929 (2)

sporty 837 (19), 875 (5)

spot 33 (3), 185 (1), 437 (4), 437 (9), 438 (7), 455 (6), 484 (5), 844 (3), 845 (1)

spot check 459 (1)

spot of trouble 702 (3)

spot on 494 (6)

spotless 646 (3), 648 (7), 935 (3), 950 (5)

spotlight 420 (5), 522 (7), 528 (2), 528 (9), 594 (7)

spots 651 (12)

spotted 437 (8), 547 (17), 845 (2)

spotter 484 (2)

spottiness 437 (4)

spotting 350 (8), 484 (1)

spotty 651 (22), 845 (2)

spouse 89 (2), 133 (3), 372 (1), 373 (3), 707 (3), 887 (5), 894 (4)

spout 254 (2), 263 (4), 298 (3), 298 (6), 308 (4), 350 (1), 350 (9), 351 (1)

sprain 63 (3), 161 (9), 163 (1), 163 (10), 176 (8), 246 (5), 377 (1)

sprat 33 (5)

sprawl 75 (1), 197 (4), 203 (8), 216 (6), 683 (3)

sprawl over 54 (7), 75 (3)

sprawling 75 (2), 216 (5)

spray 53 (4), 74 (6), 75 (4), 287 (3), 300 (9), 338 (2), 338 (4), 341 (1), 341 (3), 341 (7), 355 (1), 366 (5), 658 (2)

spraying 75 (1)

spread 36 (1), 36 (4), 75 (1), 75 (2), 75 (3), 75 (4), 79 (6), 178 (4), 183 (3), 183 (7), 189 (5), 197 (1), 197 (4), 216 (7), 226 (13), 226 (15), 294 (1), 294 (3), 301 (2), 301 (12), 528 (9)

spread a rumour 528 (9)

spread around 783 (3)

spread canvas **269** (10)

spread-eagle **294** (3), **311** (6)

spread fast **75** (3)

spread like wildfire **528** (12)

spread out **75** (3), **75** (4), **183** (7), **203** (8)

spread over **54** (7), **75** (3), **197** (4)

spread rumours **524** (9)

spread to **199** (5)

spreading **36** (3), **178** (2), **183** (6), **197** (3)

spreading abroad **528** (1)

spreading out **203** (2)

spree **837** (3), **949** (1)

sprig **53** (4), **132** (4), **366** (5)

sprightly **678** (7), **833** (3)

spring **110** (1), **128** (3), **128** (6), **156** (3), **160** (3), **251** (2), **277** (2), **277** (6), **280** (1), **298** (2), **308** (4), **310** (2), **312** (1), **312** (4), **328** (1), **328** (3), **350** (1), **630** (2), **786** (6)

spring apart **46** (7)

spring back **280** (3), **328** (3)

spring balance **322** (3)

spring-clean **648** (2), **648** (9)

spring from **68** (8), **157** (5)

spring greens **301** (20)

spring something on **508** (5)

spring tide **209** (6), **350** (2)

spring up **36** (4), **68** (8), **197** (4), **310** (5), **312** (4)

springboard **310** (2)

springer **218** (2)

springiness **327** (1), **328** (1)

springlike **128** (6)

springtide **128** (3)

springtime **128** (3)

springy **327** (2), **328** (2)

springy step **312** (1)

sprinkle **33** (2), **75** (4), **300** (9), **311** (5), **341** (2), **341** (7)

sprinkled **341** (4)

sprinkler **341** (3), **382** (3)

sprinkling **43** (2), **75** (1)

sprint **277** (2), **277** (7), **716** (3)

sprinter **268** (3), **277** (4), **716** (8)

sprite **970** (2)

sprocket **260** (1)

sprout **36** (4), **68** (8), **132** (4), **157** (5), **167** (6), **197** (4), **366** (12)

sprouts **301** (20)

spruce **366** (4), **648** (7), **841** (6)

spruce up **648** (9), **654** (9), **844** (12)

sprung **328** (2)

spry **678** (7), **833** (3)

spume **318** (7), **350** (5), **355** (1), **355** (5)

spun **206** (4)

spun out **113** (5)

spun yarn **208** (2)

spunk **174** (1)

spur **53** (4), **174** (4), **209** (2), **254** (2), **256** (2), **256** (11), **277** (7), **279** (7), **279** (10), **612** (4), **612** (9), **680** (3), **821** (2), **821** (7)

spur of necessity **740** (1)

spur on **612** (9)

spurious **18** (6), **150** (4), **495** (4), **541** (3), **542** (7), **543** (4), **875** (4), **877** (4), **930** (4), **930** (7)

spuriousness **541** (1)

spurn **279** (10), **607** (3), **704** (4), **760** (4), **888** (7), **922** (5)

spurn an offer **636** (8)

spurned **888** (6), **922** (4)

spurred **256** (7)

spurred on **612** (7)

spurs **743** (3), **866** (4)

spurt **176** (2), **277** (2), **277** (7), **285** (1), **300** (9), **678** (1), **680** (1), **680** (3)

sputter **300** (9), **406** (1), **406** (3), **419** (6)

sputum **302** (4)

spy **438** (7), **438** (9), **441** (1), **453** (2), **453** (4), **459** (7), **459** (9), **524** (5), **664** (2)

spy out **441** (3)

spy ring **459** (7)

spyglass **442** (3)

spying **438** (4), **453** (3), **459** (7)

squab **218** (8)

squabble **709** (3), **709** (9)

squad **74** (4), **686** (4), **722** (8)

squadron **74** (4), **722** (8), **722** (11), **722** (14)

squadron leader **741** (9)

squalid **649** (6), **801** (4)

squall **176** (3), **318** (3), **352** (4), **663** (1), **709** (3)

squally **352** (8)

squalor **649** (1), **801** (1), **842** (1)

squander **165** (10), **634** (4), **636** (9), **675** (2), **772** (4), **815** (4)

squandered **772** (3)

squandering **772** (2), **815** (1), **815** (3)

square **28** (10), **31** (4), **36** (5), **81** (3), **83** (8), **86** (12), **91** (3), **96** (1), **96** (2), **97** (3), **127** (2), **185** (1), **192** (8), **243** (5), **247** (4), **247** (6), **257** (2), **722** (8), **792** (5)

square accounts **808** (5)

square dance **837** (13), **837** (14)

square meal **301** (12)

square peg in a round hole **25** (3)

square root **85** (2)

square up to **716** (11)

square with **24** (9)

squared **97** (2), **243** (3), **245** (2)

squared with **24** (5)

squaring **36** (1), **97** (1)

squash **74** (5), **165** (8), **198** (7), **216** (7), **279** (9), **301** (20), **301** (27), **311** (4), **311** (7), **327** (4), **479** (3), **837** (7), **872** (7)

squashed **165** (5), **872** (4)

squashy 327 (2), 335 (4), 347 (2), 354 (4), 356 (2)

squat 33 (6), 187 (8), 192 (2), 192 (21), 204 (3), 205 (4), 210 (2), 306 (4), 311 (8), 773 (4), 786 (7), 842 (4), 916 (8)

squat, dumpy 196 (9)

squatter 59 (3), 191 (2), 776 (1), 916 (4)

squatting 773 (1)

squaw 373 (3)

squawk 407 (1), 407 (5), 409 (1), 409 (3)

squeak 401 (1), 407 (1), 407 (4), 409 (1), 409 (3), 829 (1)

squeaky 407 (2)

squeal 407 (5), 408 (1), 409 (3), 526 (5)

squealer 603 (3)

squeamish 598 (3), 861 (2), 862 (3), 950 (6)

squeeze 33 (2), 37 (2), 37 (4), 74 (5), 198 (2), 198 (7), 324 (6), 378 (1), 702 (9), 740 (3), 747 (2), 778 (1), 786 (8), 788 (9), 884 (2), 889 (1), 889 (6)

squeeze from 304 (4)

squeeze in 54 (7), 187 (7), 193 (2), 198 (7), 324 (6)

squeeze into 297 (5)

squeeze out 304 (4)

squeeze through 305 (5)

squeezer 198 (3), 304 (2)

squeezing 198 (2)

squeezing out 304 (1)

squelch 165 (8), 341 (6), 406 (1), 406 (3)

squelchy 347 (2), 354 (4)

squib 402 (1), 851 (2)

squid 365 (14)

squidgy 354 (4)

squiggle 251 (2)

squiggly 251 (6)

squint 220 (1), 220 (5), 263 (5), 438 (3), 438 (8), 439 (3), 440 (1), 440 (4), 845 (1)

squint at 438 (9)

squinting 220 (3), 440 (3), 845 (2)

squire 89 (4), 741 (1), 742 (2), 742 (3), 776 (2), 868 (4)

squirearchy 733 (4), 868 (2)

squirm 251 (13), 318 (5), 377 (6), 821 (9), 825 (7)

squirming 251 (6)

squirrel 74 (8), 365 (3), 816 (3)

squirrel away 632 (5)

squirt 33 (2), 196 (4), 298 (2), 300 (9), 350 (9), 639 (4)

squirt in 303 (5)

stab 46 (11), 263 (18), 362 (10), 377 (2), 377 (5), 645 (7), 655 (4), 655 (10), 712 (4), 712 (9), 825 (1)

stab at 671 (1)

stab in the back 712 (1), 930 (8)

stabbing 377 (3)

stability 28 (3), 113 (2), 144 (1), 153 (1), 160 (1), 266 (1), 599 (1), 965 (2)

stabilization 153 (1)

stabilize 28 (10), 153 (8), 187 (5), 218 (15)

stabilizer 28 (3), 153 (3)

stable 74 (3), 113 (4), 153 (6), 192 (10), 369 (3), 369 (10), 632 (5), 823 (3)

stable, be 144 (3), 153 (7)

stable state 28 (3)

stabling 192 (10), 632 (2)

staccato 412 (8)

stack 32 (2), 74 (11), 344 (4), 632 (1)

stack the cards 608 (3)

stack the deck 542 (8)

stacked 608 (2)

stacks 32 (2)

stadium 162 (3), 594 (7), 716 (3), 724 (1)

staff 58 (1), 74 (4), 218 (2), 410 (3), 686 (4), 690 (1), 722 (7), 723 (5), 741 (1), 741 (8), 742 (2), 743 (2), 989 (2)

staff car 274 (7)

staff college 539 (3)

staff nurse 658 (16)

staff of life 301 (9)

staff with 622 (6)

staffed 191 (7)

stag 365 (3), 792 (2)

stag hunt 619 (2)

stag party 372 (1), 882 (3)

stage 8 (2), 9 (2), 27 (1), 73 (1), 186 (1), 207 (1), 218 (5), 274 (8), 295 (2), 438 (5), 522 (8), 539 (5), 594 (6), 594 (7), 594 (16), 724 (1)

stage a revolt 738 (10)

stage a sit-in 711 (3)

stage a strike 145 (7)

stage business 547 (4)

stage directions 594 (2)

stage door 594 (7)

stage fever 594 (8)

stage fright 594 (8), 854 (1)

stage-manage 156 (9), 523 (5), 594 (16), 875 (7)

stage management 594 (2)

stage manager 522 (3), 594 (12)

stage play 412 (5), 590 (2), 594 (3)

stage set 445 (2), 594 (6), 875 (3)

stage show 445 (2), 594 (4)

stage, the 594 (1)

stage villain 594 (8)

stagecoach 274 (8)

stagehand 594 (11)

stagestruck 594 (15)

stagger 73 (2), 267 (14), 278 (4), 309 (4), 317 (2), 317 (4), 684 (5), 818 (8), 821 (8), 864 (7), 949 (13)

staggered 247 (5)

staggering 949 (7)

staginess 594 (2), 594 (8), 850 (1)

staging 218 (13), 445 (2), 594 (2)

stagnant 175 (2), 266 (4)

stagnate 172 (5), 175 (3), 266 (7), 679 (11), 820 (6)

stagnating 172 (4)

stagnation 175 (1), 266 (1), 674 (1), 677 (1), 679 (1), 820 (1)

stagy 594 (15), 875 (5)

staid 823 (3), 834 (7)

staidness 823 (1), 834 (3)

stain 43 (8), 226 (10), 425 (4), 425 (8), 437 (9), 547 (19), 548 (4), 647 (2), 649 (2), 649 (9), 655 (9), 845 (1), 845 (3), 867 (2), 867 (11)

stain with blood 431 (5)

stained 647 (3), 649 (7), 842 (4), 845 (2)

stained glass 437 (1), 844 (2)

stainless 648 (7), 933 (3), 935 (3)

stainlessness 933 (1)

stair 27 (1), 218 (5), 308 (1)

staircase 308 (1)

stairs 71 (2), 308 (1)

stairwell 263 (6)

stake 218 (10), 618 (2), 618 (8), 661 (9), 716 (10), 764 (4), 767 (1), 777 (1), 777 (2), 964 (3)

stake a claim 915 (5)

stake one's claim 786 (7)

stake one's credit 764 (4)

stake out 236 (3)

stake, the 362 (1), 383 (1), 963 (3)

stalactite 217 (2)

stalagmite 215 (1)

stale 127 (7), 387 (2), 391 (2), 397 (2), 490 (7), 572 (2), 653 (2), 655 (5), 655 (7), 684 (2), 820 (7), 838 (3), 838 (4), 840 (2)

stalemate 28 (3), 28 (5), 145 (2), 677 (1), 702 (2), 726 (1)

staleness 387 (1), 397 (1), 572 (1), 684 (1), 838 (1), 840 (1)

stalk 218 (2), 252 (3), 265 (2), 267 (14), 366 (5), 619 (5)

stalking 267 (3), 619 (2)

stall 136 (7), 145 (2), 145 (7), 192 (7), 192 (10), 194 (4), 271 (7), 438 (5), 518 (3), 702 (10), 713 (10), 728 (7), 796 (3), 990 (4)

stall-keeper 794 (3)

stalling 702 (1), 702 (6)

stallion 273 (4)

stalls 441 (2), 594 (7)

stalwart 162 (8), 195 (8), 205 (3), 650 (2), 707 (3)

stamina 113 (2), 162 (1), 174 (1), 599 (1), 600 (2), 602 (3)

stammer 106 (5), 203 (8), 278 (4), 517 (6), 565 (3), 577 (2), 577 (4), 578 (3), 580 (1), 580 (3), 695 (9), 818 (8), 936 (1)

stammering 517 (1), 580 (1), 580 (2), 695 (5)

stamp 5 (3), 7 (2), 16 (1), 16 (4), 22 (1), 23 (3), 47 (9), 77 (2), 83 (8), 243 (1), 243 (5), 255 (1), 255 (8), 265 (2), 267 (14), 279 (2), 400 (4), 488 (1), 488 (8), 547 (1), 547 (13), 547 (19), 547 (21), 555 (2), 555 (3), 587 (7), 767 (2), 767 (6), 797 (10), 822 (4), 891 (6), 891 (7), 923 (10)

stamp down 216 (7)

stamp on 165 (8), 279 (10), 735 (7)

stamp one's feet 381 (8)

stamp out 165 (8), 382 (6)

stamped 797 (9)

stamped coinage 797 (4)

stampede 176 (7), 277 (6), 854 (1), 854 (9), 854 (12), 856 (4)

stampeding 854 (6)

stamping 923 (3)

stamping ground 76 (1), 192 (5)

stanchion 218 (10)

stand 7 (4), 113 (6), 153 (7), 186 (4), 187 (5), 187 (8), 189 (4), 194 (5), 214 (1), 215 (3), 215 (4), 218 (5), 310 (2), 478 (5), 485 (3), 512 (1), 704 (1), 715 (1), 718 (7), 724 (1), 759 (4), 781 (7), 796 (3), 823 (6)

stand a chance 469 (3), 471 (4)

stand about 136 (5)

stand accused 924 (14)

stand alone 88 (5)

stand aloof 883 (8)

stand and stare 453 (4)

stand apart 46 (7), 620 (5)

stand as example 23 (5)

stand aside 753 (3)

stand be 238 (5)

stand between 46 (10), 231 (7)

stand by 161 (8), 189 (4), 507 (5), 629 (1), 669 (13), 677 (3), 703 (3), 703 (5), 703 (6)

stand clear 620 (5)

stand condemned 936 (4)

stand corrected 924 (14)

stand down 621 (3), 734 (5), 753 (3)

stand fast 144 (3), 599 (4)

stand firm 144 (3), 153 (7), 532 (5), 599 (4), 600 (4), 602 (6), 704 (5), 713 (9), 718 (11), 727 (7), 852 (6), 855 (6), 855 (7)

stand first 34 (9)

stand for 514 (5), 547 (18), 551 (8)

stand high 866 (11)

stand-in 150 (2), 594 (9), 594 (17), 755 (1)

stand in for 150 (5), 622 (8), 755 (3)

stand in the need of 627 (6)

stand next to 200 (5)

stand no nonsense 599 (3), 735 (7)

stand off 199 (5), 779 (4)

stand-offish 883 (5)

stand on 218 (16)

stand on ceremony 920 (6)

stand on end 215 (3), 310 (4)

stand on one's dignity 871 (5)

stand on tiptoe 209 (12), 310 (5), 438 (9)

stand one's ground 144 (3), 599 (4), 715 (3)

stand opposite 240 (3)

stand out 14 (4), 19 (3), 254 (5), 443 (4), 522 (9)

stand out against 602 (6), 715 (3)

stand over 136 (6)

stand ready 669 (13)

stand revealed 526 (7)

stand sentinel 457 (7)

stand still 266 (7)

stand the test 494 (7)

stand to 266 (7), 457 (7)

stand to gain or to lose 180 (3)

stand to reason 473 (7), 475 (9), 478 (5), 522 (9)

stand together 181 (3)

stand treat 804 (5)

stand trial 959 (9)

stand up 215 (3), 310 (5)

stand-up comic 594 (10)

stand-up fight 716 (7)

stand up for 660 (8), 927 (5)

stand up in law 953 (6)

stand up to 635 (6), 704 (4), 704 (5), 711 (3)

standard 16 (2), 23 (1), 23 (4), 27 (1), 30 (1), 30 (4), 76 (1), 79 (3), 81 (1), 83 (5), 461 (4), 465 (5), 547 (12), 644 (9)

standard-bearer 722 (4)

standard dress 16 (1)

standard error 86 (4)

standard gauge 624 (7)

standard work 589 (1)

standardization 16 (1)

standardize 16 (4), 60 (3), 62 (5), 83 (8), 465 (12)

standardized 16 (2), 81 (3)

standards 917 (4)

standby 707 (3)

standfirm 715 (3)

standing 7 (1), 8 (1), 27 (1), 73 (1), 215 (2), 215 (5), 866 (2)

standing army 722 (6)

standing by 189 (2), 669 (7)

standing-in for 755 (2)

standing joke 839 (2)

standing order 81 (1), 610 (2), 804 (1), 953 (2)

standing ovation 923 (3)

standing room 183 (4)

standing start 68 (3), 278 (1)

standing still 266 (6)

standing up 215 (2)

standing water 339 (1)

standoffish 84 (5), 871 (4)

standpipe 351 (1)

standpoint 186 (1), 438 (5)

standstill 145 (2), 145 (4), 266 (1), 668 (1), 700 (1)

stanza 593 (4)

stanzas 593 (2)

staple 45 (10), 47 (5), 52 (3), 208 (2), 331 (2), 631 (1), 638 (5), 795 (1)

staple food 301 (9)

star 34 (9), 294 (1), 321 (4), 547 (14), 594 (9), 594 (16), 594 (17), 638 (4), 644 (3), 729 (2), 859 (5), 866 (4), 866 (6), 890 (2)

Star Chamber 956 (2)

star cluster 321 (4)

star-crossed 731 (6)

star in 445 (8)

star lore 321 (11)

star-spangled 321 (14)

star turn 594 (4)

star-watcher 321 (11)

star-watching 321 (16)

starboard 241 (1)

starch 258 (4), 301 (10), 326 (5), 354 (2), 354 (6), 648 (9)

starched 326 (4), 648 (7)

starchiness 850 (2), 875 (2)

starching 326 (2)

starchy 326 (4), 354 (4), 850 (4), 875 (6)

stardom 866 (3)

stardust 513 (3)

stare 438 (3), 438 (8), 441 (3), 453 (4), 508 (4), 864 (6), 885 (4)

stare one in the face 155 (3), 522 (9)

stargazer 321 (11), 441 (1)

stargazing 321 (11), 321 (16)

staring 32 (10)

stark 32 (10), 32 (14), 129 (7), 425 (6), 573 (2)

stark naked 229 (4)

stark staring mad 503 (7)

starless 418 (4)

starlet 594 (9)

starred 594 (15)

starring 866 (9)

starry 321 (14), 417 (9)

starry-eyed 824 (5), 852 (4)

stars 156 (2), 596 (2)

Stars and Stripes 547 (12)

start 68 (3), 68 (8), 68 (9), 201 (4), 279 (7), 296 (1), 312 (4), 318 (1), 318 (5), 321 (1), 445 (8), 508 (1), 508 (4), 822 (4), 854 (9)

start afresh 68 (8)

start again 148 (3)

start an action 959 (7)

start an argument 475 (11)

start back 286 (5)

start it 709 (8)

start laughing 835 (7)

start out 68 (8), 254 (5), 269 (9), 296 (6)

start talking 581 (5)

start up 68 (9), 173 (3)

start work 68 (8)

starter 68 (1), 68 (3), 301 (14), 716 (8)

starting 68 (7), 152 (1), 277 (5)

starting out 296 (1)

starting pistol 68 (3)

starting point 68 (3), 296 (1), 475 (2)

starting post 296 (1)

startle 508 (5), 821 (6), 854 (12), 864 (7)

startled 508 (3), 854 (6)

startling 508 (2), 854 (8)

starvation 636 (2), 946 (1)

starvation diet 946 (1)

starve 163 (10), 206 (7), 801 (5), 816 (6), 859 (12), 945 (4), 946 (4)

starved 206 (5), 636 (5), 946 (3)

starved of 636 (4)

starveling 801 (4)

starving 627 (4), 636 (5), 859 (9), 946 (3)

starving out 747 (2)

state 7 (1), 89 (2), 184 (3), 184 (5), 186 (1), 371 (5), 371 (7), 524 (9), 532 (5), 563 (3), 708 (4), 733 (6)

state control 733 (2)

state occasion 875 (2)

state of affairs 8 (1), 154 (2)

state of being 7 (1)

state of belief 485 (1)

state of disorder 63 (1)

state of doubt 474 (2)

state of expectation 507 (1)

state of grace 935 (1), 979 (2)

state of health 7 (1)

state of mind 7 (1), 817 (1)

state of nature 229 (2), 670 (2)

state of order 60 (1)

state of peace 717 (1)

state of siege 718 (2)

state of war 718 (2)

state of wonder 864 (1)

state one's case 466 (7)

state one's terms 761 (5), 791 (6)

state religion 973 (1), 981 (7)

state school 539 (2)

statecraft 689 (1)

stated time 141 (2)

statehood 371 (5)

stateless person 883 (4)

stateliness 871 (1), 875 (1), 875 (2)

stately 574 (5), 575 (3), 821 (5), 841 (3), 848 (6), 866 (8), 871 (3), 875 (6)

stately home 192 (6)

statement 87 (1), 466 (2), 475 (3), 524 (2), 532 (1), 808 (1)

statement on oath 532 (2)

statements 548 (1)

stateroom 194 (19)

statesman or woman 690 (3)

statesmanlike 688 (3), 694 (4)

statesmanship 688 (2), 689 (1), 720 (1)

static 127 (7), 266 (4)

station 27 (1), 73 (1), 145 (5), 185 (1), 186 (1), 187 (3), 187 (5), 192 (1), 624 (7)

station before 64 (4)

station oneself 60 (4)

stationary 266 (4), 677 (2)

stationed 186 (3), 187 (4)

stationed, be 186 (4)

stationery 549 (3), 586 (4), 631 (3)

stationing 187 (1)

statistical 86 (9)

statistical list 87 (1)

statistician 86 (7), 808 (3)

statistics 86 (4), 162 (5), 524 (2), 623 (1)

statuary 551 (2), 554 (1), 844 (2)

statue 505 (3), 551 (2), 554 (1), 866 (4)

statuesque 209 (9), 554 (2), 841 (3)

statuette 551 (2), 554 (1)

stature 209 (1)

status 7 (1), 8 (1), 9 (2), 27 (1), 73 (1), 866 (2)

status quo 8 (1), 144 (1), 148 (1)

statute 81 (1), 693 (1), 953 (2)

statute book 953 (3)

statute law 953 (3)

statutory 693 (2), 953 (5)

staunch 162 (7), 264 (6), 342 (6), 350 (12), 599 (2), 658 (20), 702 (9), 880 (6), 929 (4)

staunchness 599 (1), 600 (1)

stave 208 (3), 410 (3), 723 (5)

stave in 255 (8)

stave off 702 (9), 713 (10)

stay 47 (1), 108 (7), 113 (6), 144 (3), 145 (6), 146 (3), 153 (7), 187 (8), 189 (1), 189 (4), 192 (21), 218 (2), 218 (15), 266 (7), 882 (4), 882 (9)

stay-at-home 266 (4), 883 (3)

stay at one's post 917 (10)

stay away 190 (6)

stay in sight 443 (4)

stay of execution 136 (2)

stay one's hand 145 (8)

stay outside 57 (4)

stay put 266 (7), 599 (4)

stay small 33 (8)

stay the course 600 (4)

stay unmarried 895 (5)

stayer 600 (2), 602 (3)

staying power 113 (2), 160 (1), 162 (1), 600 (2)

stays 228 (17)

steadfast 153 (6), 599 (2), 739 (3)

steadfastness 600 (1)

steadiness 28 (3), 153 (1), 266 (1), 599 (1), 820 (1), 823 (1)

steady 16 (2), 60 (2), 81 (3), 141 (4), 146 (2), 153 (4), 153 (6), 218 (15), 599 (2), 600 (3), 778 (5), 820 (3), 823 (3), 823 (7), 887 (4)

steady advance 727 (1)

steady beam 417 (3)

steady flame 417 (3)

steady progress 285 (1)

steady state theory 321 (1)

steak 53 (5), 301 (16)

steal 20 (6), 306 (4), 525 (9), 542 (10), 786 (6), 786 (9), 788 (7), 916 (8)

steal a glance 438 (8)

steal a march on 119 (4)

steal away 620 (6), 667 (5)

steal every heart 887 (15)

steal in 297 (5)

steal one's heart 887 (15)

steal the show 34 (7), 594 (17)

steal upon 508 (5)

stealer 789 (1)

stealing 771 (1), 785 (1), 786 (1), 788 (1)

stealth 698 (1)

stealthily 444 (5), 525 (11)

stealthiness 525 (2)

stealthy 278 (3), 401 (3), 523 (4), 525 (5), 698 (4)

stealthy, be 523 (5), 525 (9)

steam 160 (3), 265 (4), 269 (9), 287 (3), 298 (7), 300 (9), 301 (40), 336 (2), 336 (4), 338 (4), 339 (1), 341 (6), 355 (2), 355 (5), 379 (1)

steam engine 274 (14)

steam roller 274 (14)

steam up 160 (3)

steamed pudding 301 (17)

steamer 194 (14), 275 (1)

steamer route 269 (1)

steaming 338 (1), 341 (4), 379 (4)

steamroller 165 (7), 216 (3), 740 (3)

steamship 275 (1)

steamy 338 (3)

steed 273 (4), 273 (7)

steel 43 (3), 162 (1), 162 (12), 256 (5), 326 (1), 326 (3), 326 (5), 820 (7)

steel band 413 (3)

steel-clad 660 (5)

steel engraving 555 (1)

steel oneself 599 (3), 820 (6)

steeled 326 (3)

steeled against 820 (3)

steeliness 599 (1)

steeling 326 (2)

steelworker 686 (3)

steelworks 687 (1)

steely 162 (6), 326 (3), 429 (2), 599 (2), 898 (7)

steely-eyed 898 (7)

steep 209 (8), 211 (2), 215 (2), 220 (4), 303 (7), 308 (3), 339 (3), 341 (8), 700 (4), 811 (2)

steepen 308 (4)

steeple 209 (4), 990 (5)

steeplechase 312 (4), 619 (2), 716 (3)

steeplechaser 268 (4), 273 (5), 312 (2)

steeplechasing 267 (5)

steeplejack 308 (2)

steepness 209 (1), 209 (2), 215 (1)

steeps 209 (2)

steer 161 (3), 269 (10), 365 (7), 689 (5)

steer a middle course 625 (5)

steer away from 613 (3)

steer clear of 282 (3)

steer for 269 (10), 281 (5)

steer straight 249 (3)

steerage 281 (1)

steering 269 (2), 281 (1), 689 (2), 689 (3)

steering committee 754 (1)

stein 194 (15)

stellar 321 (14)

stem 11 (4), 145 (7), 169 (2), 218 (2), 237 (5), 350 (12), 366 (5)

stem the course of 350 (12)

stem the tide 704 (5)

stem to stern 203 (9)

stench 394 (1), 397 (1), 649 (1)

stencil 22 (2), 23 (3), 553 (8), 586 (3)

stenographer 586 (6)

stenographic 586 (7)

stenography 586 (1)

stentorian 398 (3), 400 (3), 408 (2)

stentorian voice 400 (2)

step 27 (1), 73 (1), 170 (4), 200 (2), 203 (4), 218 (5), 265 (2), 267 (14), 308 (1), 671 (1), 676 (2)

step aside 282 (3)

step by step 27 (6), 60 (5), 71 (7), 278 (8)

step down 309 (3)

step in 231 (10), 297 (5), 720 (4)

step on 218 (16)

step out of 229 (7)

step over 305 (5), 306 (3)

step-relation 11 (2)

step up 36 (5), 174 (8), 277 (7), 285 (4)

step up to 289 (4)

stepchild 11 (3)

stepfather 169 (3)

stepmother 169 (4)

steppe 210 (1), 216 (1), 344 (1), 348 (1)

stepped 220 (3)

stepping stones 71 (2), 624 (3)

stepping up 36 (1)

steps 71 (2), 308 (1), 623 (2), 629 (1), 676 (1)

stereo 398 (1), 398 (3), 414 (10)

stereophonic 398 (3)

stereoscope 442 (1)

stereoscopic 438 (6), 443 (2)

stereotype 16 (1), 16 (4), 22 (1), 555 (2), 587 (1)

stereotyped 16 (2)

sterile 161 (7), 172 (4), 641 (5), 648 (7), 652 (4)

sterility 161 (1), 172 (1)

sterilization 161 (1), 172 (2), 648 (2), 652 (2), 666 (1)

sterilize 172 (6), 648 (10), 652 (6)

sterilized 161 (7), 172 (4), 652 (4)

sterling 494 (5), 644 (7), 797 (1), 797 (9), 933 (3)

stern 238 (1), 238 (2), 238 (3), 599 (2), 735 (4), 834 (7), 891 (4), 898 (6)

stern-sheets 238 (3)

stern wheel 269 (5)

stern-wheeler 275 (1)

sternly 735 (9)

sternmost 238 (6)

sternness 599 (1), 834 (3)

steroid 658 (7)

stethoscope 415 (4)

stetson 228 (23)

stevedore 270 (4)

stew 43 (3), 301 (13), 301
(40), 381 (8), 821 (1), 822
(2)
steward 633 (2), 690 (3),
690 (4), 742 (1), 742 (2),
742 (3), 754 (1), 798 (1)
stewardess 742 (1)
stewardship 689 (1)
stewed 949 (7)
stewed fruit 301 (17), 356
(1)
stick 48 (3), 145 (7), 146
(3), 202 (3), 218 (2), 263
(18), 333 (3), 723 (5), 964
(1)
stick at nothing 599 (3)
stick close 48 (3)
stick fast 266 (7)
stick in one's throat 578
(4)
stick in the mind 505 (11)
stick-in-the-mud 144 (1)
stick insect 365 (16)
stick into 303 (4)
stick it out 599 (4), 600 (4)
stick on 38 (3), 45 (11)
stick on to 48 (3)
stick one's neck out 857
(4)
stick out 254 (5), 443 (4)
stick out for 716 (10)
stick to 48 (3), 48 (4), 778
(5)
stick to one's fingers 782
(5)
stick to one's guns 600 (4)
stick together 45 (14)
stick up 215 (3), 215 (4),
788 (9)
stick up for 703 (6)
stick with it 600 (4)
sticker 47 (9), 547 (13),
602 (3)
stickiness 48 (1), 354 (3),
778 (1)
sticking plaster 47 (9), 150
(2), 658 (9)
stickler 602 (3), 735 (3),
862 (2)
sticky 48 (2), 354 (5), 700
(4), 778 (3)
sticky tape 47 (9)
sticky wicket 700 (3)

stiff 249 (2), 266 (6), 326
(4), 361 (6), 363 (2), 574
(4), 576 (2), 602 (4), 679
(7), 684 (2), 695 (5), 747
(4), 811 (2), 850 (4), 875
(6), 949 (12)
stiff breeze 352 (3)
stiff neck 602 (1)
stiff-necked 602 (4), 711
(2), 871 (3)
stiff upper lip 599 (1), 818
(1), 855 (1)
stiffen 162 (12), 326 (5)
stiffening 326 (2)
stiffness 153 (1), 266 (1),
326 (1), 576 (1), 850 (2),
875 (2)
stifle 161 (9), 165 (8), 362
(10), 379 (7), 381 (8), 382
(6), 399 (4), 401 (5), 525
(7), 578 (4), 702 (8), 757
(4)
stifled 401 (3), 525 (3)
stifling 165 (1), 362 (8),
379 (6)
stigma 547 (1), 547 (13),
867 (2), 924 (2), 926 (1)
stigmata 547 (1)
stigmatize 867 (11), 924
(10)
stigmatized 547 (17)
stiletto 723 (8)
still 31 (7), 153 (6), 177 (3),
177 (7), 258 (3), 266 (4),
266 (6), 338 (2), 339 (2),
361 (6), 399 (3), 399 (4),
468 (5), 551 (4), 578 (4),
679 (7)
still, be 399 (3)
still in 146 (2)
still life 319 (3), 553 (4)
still there 189 (2)
stillbirth 167 (1)
stillborn 361 (6)
stillborn, be 728 (8)
stillness 266 (1), 266 (2),
399 (1)
stilt 218 (5)
stilted 574 (4), 576 (2), 849
(2), 850 (4)
stiltedness 576 (1)
stilts 267 (7), 310 (2), 837
(15)

stimulant 156 (2), 174 (4),
279 (1), 388 (1), 612 (4),
658 (6), 685 (1), 821 (2),
949 (12)
stimulate 156 (9), 174 (8),
612 (9), 685 (4), 821 (7),
859 (13)
stimulated 821 (3)
stimulating 174 (5), 512
(4), 612 (6), 821 (4)
stimulation 36 (1), 156 (1),
162 (5), 173 (1), 174 (2),
678 (1), 685 (1), 821 (1)
stimulative 658 (17)
stimulus 156 (2), 174 (4),
612 (4)
sting 256 (2), 256 (10), 377
(2), 377 (5), 388 (1), 388
(5), 645 (1), 655 (10), 659
(1), 786 (11), 821 (6), 825
(1), 827 (9), 891 (8), 891
(9)
stinginess 636 (1), 816 (1)
stinging 256 (7), 388 (3),
827 (5)
stingray 365 (15)
stingy 636 (3), 816 (4)
stink 397 (1), 397 (3), 649
(1), 649 (8), 655 (7)
stink out 397 (3)
stinker 938 (3)
stinking 397 (2), 645 (4),
649 (6)
stint 27 (1), 110 (1), 636
(9), 682 (3), 816 (6)
stinted 636 (4)
stipend 703 (2)
stipendiary 771 (5), 782
(3)
stipple 437 (9), 555 (3)
stippling 437 (4)
stipulate 475 (12), 627 (6),
765 (5), 766 (3)
stipulation 468 (1), 475
(2), 627 (1), 766 (1)
stir 43 (7), 174 (2), 176 (9),
265 (1), 265 (4), 265 (5),
301 (40), 318 (3), 318 (5),
678 (1), 678 (11), 821 (6),
887 (15)
stir one's feelings 821 (6)
stir the blood 374 (6)
stir the senses 374 (6)

stir up 176 (9), 318 (6)
stir up strife 709 (8)
stir up trouble 829 (6)
stirred 43 (6), 818 (4)
stirrer 663 (2), 678 (6)
stirring 43 (1), 154 (5), 638
(6), 678 (7), 678 (8), 818
(6), 821 (4)
stirring up 821 (1)
stitch 45 (9), 45 (12), 47
(5), 58 (1), 377 (2)
stitch in time, a 135 (3)
stitched 45 (8)
stitched up 45 (5)
stoat 365 (3)
stock 11 (4), 83 (5), 156
(3), 169 (2), 228 (22), 389
(2), 610 (6), 631 (1), 632
(1), 633 (5), 777 (1), 795
(1), 820 (2)
stock breeder 164 (4)
stock-breeding 369 (1)
stock car 274 (11)
stock example 83 (2)
Stock Exchange 796 (1)
stock farm 365 (2), 369
(2), 370 (2), 687 (1)
stock in trade 630 (4), 795
(1)
stock list 87 (1)
stock part 594 (8)
stock-still 266 (6)
stock up 632 (5), 633 (5)
stockade 235 (1), 235 (3),
660 (2), 662 (2), 713 (2)
stockbroker 794 (1)
stockinette 222 (4)
stockings 228 (26)
stockman 369 (6)
stockpile 632 (1), 632 (5)
stocks 748 (2), 964 (2)
stocks and shares 629 (1),
777 (2)
stocks and stones 319 (3),
448 (1)
stocky 162 (8), 195 (8), 204
(3)
stodge 301 (9)
stodginess 354 (1), 838 (1),
840 (1)
stodgy 354 (4), 573 (2), 838
(3), 840 (2)
stoical 820 (3), 823 (4)

stoicism 818 (1), 820 (1),
823 (1), 823 (2), 931 (1),
942 (1)
stoke 36 (5), 381 (9), 385
(6)
stoke up 381 (8)
stoker 268 (5), 381 (2)
stole 228 (22)
stolen away 667 (4)
stolen goods 790 (1)
stolid 499 (3), 820 (3), 834
(7)
stolidity 175 (1)
stolidness 820 (1)
stomach 194 (3), 224 (2),
301 (6), 721 (4), 823 (6),
859 (3), 872 (5), 909 (4)
stomach-ache 377 (2), 651
(7)
stomach upset 651 (7)
stomach wind 352 (7)
stone 279 (9), 287 (2), 287
(7), 324 (3), 344 (3), 344
(4), 631 (2), 712 (12), 820
(2)
Stone Age 110 (2)
Stone-Age humanity 371
(1)
stone-cold sober 948 (3)
stone cutting 554 (1)
stone dead 361 (6)
stone-deaf 416 (2)
stone fruit 301 (19)
stone-thrower 287 (5)
stone to death 362 (10),
963 (12)
stoned 375 (3), 949 (8), 949
(10)
stone's throw 200 (2)
stonewall 292 (3), 702
(10), 713 (10)
stoneware 164 (2), 381 (5)
stonework 164 (3)
stony 172 (4), 259 (4), 326
(3), 344 (5), 820 (3)
stony-hearted 898 (7)
stooge 501 (1), 544 (1), 628
(2), 707 (1), 851 (3)
stool 218 (6), 302 (4)
stool pigeon 524 (5), 545
(4)
stoop 210 (3), 220 (5), 248
(5), 309 (3), 311 (9), 313

(1), 721 (4), 867 (10), 879
(4), 920 (6)
stoop to 930 (8)
stoop to anything 879 (4)
stooping 210 (2), 220 (3),
248 (1), 248 (3), 309 (2),
872 (1), 879 (3)
stop 69 (1), 69 (5), 69 (6),
145 (2), 145 (5), 145 (6),
145 (7), 145 (9), 266 (1),
266 (8), 266 (11), 295 (4),
399 (4), 405 (3), 414 (5),
442 (6), 547 (14), 656 (12),
677 (1), 700 (1), 702 (3),
747 (7), 757 (4), 778 (1)
stop a leak 350 (12)
stop at 187 (8), 295 (4)
stop breathing 361 (7)
stop burning 382 (6)
stop dead 145 (7)
stop fighting 719 (5), 721
(3)
stop for breath 145 (8)
stop-go 72 (2)
stop growing 198 (6)
stop off 295 (4)
stop one's ears 416 (3), 456
(7), 820 (7)
stop over 295 (4)
stop payment 805 (5)
stop-press news 529 (1)
stop short 145 (7), 266 (8),
307 (3)
stop the bleeding 658 (20)
stop the flow 342 (6), 350
(12)
stop up 702 (9)
stop using 161 (9), 300 (7),
607 (1), 621 (3), 674 (5),
679 (13), 779 (4)
stop work 145 (6)
stop worrying 823 (5)
stopcock 264 (2), 630 (1)
stopgap 150 (2), 150 (4)
stopover 267 (8), 295 (2)
stoppage 145 (2), 145 (3),
266 (1), 702 (3), 805 (1),
810 (1)
stopper 226 (1), 264 (2),
264 (6), 778 (1)
stopping 72 (2)
stopping over 267 (9)

stopping place 145 (5), 187 (3), 267 (8), 295 (2), 624 (7)

stopping train 274 (13), 278 (2)

stopping work 145 (3)

stopwatch 117 (3), 549 (3)

storage 46 (2), 74 (1), 74 (7), 86 (5), 183 (4), 187 (1), 301 (7), 336 (2), 346 (1), 370 (1), 370 (6), 527 (1), 632 (2), 666 (1), 723 (2), 796 (2), 799 (1)

storage space 183 (4), 632 (2)

store 32 (2), 45 (9), 46 (9), 74 (7), 74 (11), 156 (3), 187 (7), 194 (1), 194 (12), 255 (4), 339 (1), 341 (3), 359 (1), 370 (1), 370 (9), 505 (4), 525 (7), 632 (1), 632 (5), 633 (1), 633 (5), 635 (2), 637 (1), 660 (8), 666 (5), 669 (1), 669 (11), 674 (1), 674 (4), 687 (1), 771 (7), 775 (1), 778 (5), 792 (5), 795 (1), 796 (3), 799 (1), 800 (1), 814 (1), 814 (3)

store detective 459 (8)

stored 632 (4), 666 (4), 669 (7), 674 (2)

storehouse 632 (2)

storekeeper 633 (2), 794 (2), 808 (3)

storeroom 194 (19), 632 (2)

stores 301 (7), 633 (1)

storey 71 (2), 73 (1), 194 (4), 207 (1)

storeyed 207 (4)

storied 590 (6)

stork 167 (2), 365 (4)

storm 61 (4), 61 (11), 176 (3), 176 (7), 297 (7), 318 (3), 340 (3), 350 (6), 352 (10), 663 (1), 712 (7), 822 (2), 822 (4), 891 (7)

storm brewing 661 (1)

storm cloud 74 (7), 355 (2)

storm in a teacup 546 (1)

storm-tossed 259 (4), 352 (8), 655 (6)

storm troops 712 (5), 722 (7)

storminess 176 (1), 352 (1)

stormy 176 (5), 352 (8), 822 (3)

stormy exchange 709 (3)

stormy weather 352 (4)

story 529 (1), 543 (3), 590 (2), 839 (2)

story-teller 545 (2)

storyline 590 (2)

storyteller 590 (5)

stoup 194 (15)

stout 162 (6), 162 (8), 195 (8), 205 (4), 301 (28), 855 (4)

stout-hearted 855 (4)

stoutness 195 (3), 205 (2)

stove 383 (1)

stove in 255 (6)

stow 54 (7), 187 (7), 193 (2), 303 (4), 632 (5), 669 (11)

stow away 525 (7), 632 (5)

stowage 183 (4)

stowaway 59 (3), 297 (3), 527 (4)

straddle 183 (7), 197 (4), 205 (5), 226 (14), 294 (3), 305 (5)

strafe 712 (3), 712 (11)

straggle 75 (3), 267 (13)

straggling 61 (7), 75 (2)

straight 16 (2), 71 (4), 83 (5), 215 (2), 249 (1), 249 (2), 281 (3), 281 (8), 625 (4), 929 (3)

straight, be 249 (3), 281 (5)

straight-down 215 (5)

straight drama 594 (1)

straight-edge 465 (5)

straight face 834 (3)

straight-faced 834 (7)

straight from the shoulder 174 (9)

straight left 279 (2)

straight-limbed 841 (5)

straight line 203 (3), 249 (1), 625 (1)

straight man 851 (3)

straight on 249 (5)

straight stretch 249 (1)

straight up 209 (14)

straighten 249 (4)

straighten out 62 (5), 62 (7), 216 (6), 654 (10)

straighten up 215 (3)

straightened 249 (2)

straightened out 62 (3)

straightforward 516 (2), 540 (2)

straightness 203 (3), 249 (1), 281 (1)

strain 5 (4), 11 (4), 33 (2), 43 (2), 63 (3), 77 (3), 160 (1), 163 (1), 163 (10), 169 (2), 176 (8), 246 (1), 246 (5), 298 (7), 306 (3), 377 (1), 412 (3), 546 (3), 566 (1), 648 (10), 659 (1), 671 (1), 671 (4), 682 (1), 682 (3), 682 (6), 684 (1), 684 (6), 825 (3), 829 (1), 834 (12)

strain of, a 179 (1)

strain off 272 (7)

strain one's eyes 438 (9)

strain out 298 (7)

strain the sense 521 (3)

strained 10 (4), 684 (2)

strained sense 521 (1)

strainer 263 (3)

straining 44 (3)

strains 593 (2)

strait 206 (1), 345 (1)

straitjacket 198 (3), 748 (4)

straitlaced 735 (4), 747 (4), 950 (6)

straits 700 (3), 801 (1)

strand 208 (2), 344 (2)

stranded 702 (7), 728 (6)

strange 10 (3), 59 (4), 84 (6), 491 (6), 517 (3), 864 (5)

strange to say 864 (8)

stranger 59 (2)

stranger to, a 491 (4)

strangle 161 (9), 165 (8), 198 (7), 264 (6), 362 (10), 362 (12), 778 (5), 963 (12)

strangled 198 (4)

stranglehold 778 (1)

strangler 362 (7)

strangling 778 (3)

strangulate 198 (7)

strangulated 198 (4)

strangulation 198 (2), 264 (1), 362 (1), 963 (3)

strap 45 (12), 47 (7), 208 (3), 963 (9), 964 (1)

strap-shaped 208 (4)

strapping 32 (9), 162 (8), 195 (8), 650 (2)

stratagem 542 (2), 614 (1), 623 (3), 623 (4), 688 (2), 698 (2)

strategic 623 (6), 688 (3), 698 (4), 718 (9)

strategic bombing 712 (3)

strategist 612 (5), 623 (5), 696 (2), 698 (3)

strategy 623 (2), 688 (2), 718 (4)

stratification 207 (3)

stratify 207 (5)

stratosphere 209 (1), 340 (2)

stratum 207 (1), 216 (1)

straw 366 (8)

straw-coloured 433 (3)

straw hat 228 (23)

straw in the wind 547 (1)

straw vote 461 (2), 605 (2)

strawberry roan 273 (4)

stray 75 (3), 84 (5), 159 (5), 267 (13), 268 (2), 282 (2), 282 (5), 290 (3), 495 (7), 661 (7), 744 (9), 779 (2), 883 (4), 934 (7)

streak 5 (4), 33 (2), 43 (2), 203 (3), 206 (1), 208 (3), 277 (1), 277 (6), 417 (2), 437 (3), 437 (9), 649 (9)

streaked 437 (8)

streaker 229 (3)

streaky 437 (8)

stream 74 (10), 77 (1), 176 (2), 179 (1), 217 (5), 265 (1), 265 (4), 298 (2), 339 (1), 341 (6), 350 (1), 350 (9), 350 (10), 417 (2), 538 (4), 632 (1), 635 (2), 635 (7)

stream out 298 (6)

streamed 62 (3), 534 (5)

streamer 547 (12), 844 (5)

streamers 876 (1)

streaming 49 (2), 171 (4), 298 (2), 341 (5), 350 (7)

streamline 258 (4)

streamlined 258 (3), 277 (5)

streamlining 62 (1)

streams 32 (2)

street 187 (2), 192 (8), 624 (6)

street fight 716 (7)

street fighting 709 (3)

street light 420 (4)

street market 796 (1)

street musician 594 (10)

street riot 738 (2)

street rioter 738 (6)

street seller 794 (3)

street-walk 951 (10)

streets ahead 34 (4)

streetwalker 952 (4)

streetwalking 951 (5)

strength 113 (2), 160 (1), 162 (1), 174 (1), 329 (1), 571 (1), 600 (2)

strength of will 595 (0)

strengthen 36 (5), 160 (11), 162 (12), 174 (8), 326 (5), 329 (3), 656 (9), 660 (8), 703 (5), 713 (9), 821 (7), 832 (3)

strengthened 162 (6)

strengthening 36 (1), 162 (5), 656 (1), 703 (1)

strenuous 174 (5), 682 (4)

strenuously 32 (17)

stress 160 (1), 162 (12), 246 (1), 455 (7), 475 (11), 519 (2), 532 (1), 532 (7), 571 (1), 577 (2), 577 (4), 593 (5), 638 (1), 638 (8), 659 (1), 682 (1), 700 (1)

stretch 32 (15), 110 (1), 183 (3), 197 (5), 203 (1), 203 (7), 203 (8), 306 (3), 328 (1), 328 (3), 546 (3)

stretch, a 747 (3)

stretch a point 306 (3), 734 (5), 736 (3), 766 (4), 769 (3), 770 (2), 919 (3)

stretch away to 199 (5)

stretch one's legs 685 (5)

stretch out 203 (7), 203 (8)

stretch the truth 541 (5)

stretch to 199 (5), 203 (7)

stretchable 327 (3), 328 (2)

stretched 197 (3)

stretched out 216 (5)

stretcher 218 (7), 274 (1)

stretcher bearer 273 (2)

stretcher case 651 (18)

stretching 197 (1), 203 (2)

stretchy 328 (2)

strew 75 (4)

stricken 731 (6), 825 (5)

strict 60 (2), 83 (6), 520 (6), 735 (4), 747 (4), 917 (6), 929 (3), 976 (8)

strict control 747 (1)

strict order 60 (1)

strictly 60 (5)

strictness 83 (1), 735 (1)

stricture 924 (2), 924 (4), 928 (1)

stride 199 (1), 265 (2), 267 (14), 285 (1)

stridency 400 (1), 407 (1)

strident 400 (3), 407 (2), 411 (2), 577 (3)

stridor 398 (1), 407 (1)

stridulatory 407 (2)

strife 709 (3), 716 (1)

strike 145 (3), 145 (6), 165 (7), 173 (3), 174 (7), 263 (18), 279 (9), 287 (7), 311 (4), 333 (3), 362 (10), 484 (1), 484 (4), 489 (1), 621 (3), 632 (1), 645 (7), 655 (10), 679 (11), 702 (10), 712 (9), 716 (11), 738 (2), 738 (10), 762 (3), 821 (8), 946 (2), 963 (9), 963 (10)

strike a balance 28 (10), 30 (5)

strike a ball 279 (9)

strike a bargain 765 (5)

strike a light 381 (9)

strike a pose 850 (5)

strike at 279 (8), 712 (9), 716 (10), 716 (11)

strike attitudes 850 (5)

strike dumb 578 (4), 864 (7)

strike force 712 (5)

strike hard 174 (7)

strike home 712 (9)

strike it rich 730 (6), 800 (7)
strike lucky 730 (7)
strike off 57 (5), 300 (6), 752 (5)
strike oil 730 (7)
strike one 443 (4), 449 (9)
strike out 269 (12), 550 (3)
strike root 153 (7), 187 (8)
strike the flag 547 (22)
strike up 68 (8), 413 (9)
striker 738 (4), 837 (16)
striking 374 (4), 443 (3), 516 (3), 522 (4), 590 (6), 821 (5), 864 (5)
striking distance 200 (2)
striking likeness 18 (1)
strikingly 32 (19)
Strine 560 (2)
string 45 (12), 47 (2), 71 (2), 74 (3), 74 (4), 208 (2), 410 (9), 413 (9), 414 (3)
string along 542 (9)
string along with 89 (4)
string course 207 (1)
string out 75 (4), 203 (8)
string together 45 (10), 71 (6)
string up 362 (10), 963 (12)
stringency 735 (1)
stringent 32 (12), 174 (5), 735 (4)
stringing out 203 (2)
strings 178 (1), 413 (3), 414 (1), 523 (1), 766 (1)
stringy 208 (4), 329 (2)
strip 46 (8), 53 (5), 203 (3), 206 (1), 207 (2), 207 (5), 208 (3), 229 (6), 229 (7), 648 (9), 786 (10), 788 (9), 801 (6), 867 (11)
strip bare 165 (7)
strip light 420 (4)
strip off 229 (7)
strip show 594 (4)
stripe 77 (2), 203 (3), 206 (1), 437 (3), 437 (9), 743 (3), 844 (3)
striped 437 (8)
stripes 547 (9)
stripling 132 (2)
stripped 229 (4)
stripped of 772 (2)

stripper 229 (3)
striptease 229 (1)
striptease artist 594 (10)
strive 671 (4), 682 (6), 716 (10)
strive after 617 (6)
strive for effect 875 (7)
strive in vain 161 (8)
striving for effect 875 (4)
stroboscope 420 (4), 442 (1)
stroke 23 (2), 116 (2), 161 (2), 269 (10), 269 (11), 279 (1), 279 (2), 287 (1), 318 (2), 333 (3), 378 (1), 378 (7), 547 (21), 623 (3), 651 (2), 651 (9), 651 (16), 676 (2), 689 (5), 690 (1), 826 (3), 831 (3), 855 (2), 889 (1), 889 (6)
stroke of genius 727 (1)
stroke of policy 623 (2)
stroke of, the 116 (2)
stroke of wit 839 (2)
stroll 267 (3), 267 (13), 278 (4)
stroller 268 (2)
strolling 267 (9)
strolling player 594 (9)
strong 32 (4), 44 (5), 113 (4), 160 (8), 162 (6), 174 (5), 176 (5), 178 (2), 205 (4), 326 (3), 329 (2), 386 (2), 388 (3), 394 (2), 425 (6), 532 (4), 571 (2), 650 (2), 660 (5), 678 (7), 733 (7), 951 (6)
strong arm 740 (1)
strong as an ox 162 (6)
strong, be 36 (4), 162 (11), 174 (7)
strong drink 301 (28)
strong hand 629 (1), 735 (1)
strong language 899 (2)
strong man 162 (4)
strong-minded 599 (2)
strong point 694 (1), 713 (4)
strong pound 797 (3)
strong pulse 360 (1)
strong smell 394 (1)
strong-smelling 397 (2)

strong taste 388 (1)
strong-willed 599 (2)
strong wind 352 (4)
strongarm 162 (6), 740 (2)
strongarm man 162 (4), 660 (3), 722 (1)
strongbox 799 (1)
stronghold 191 (5), 662 (1), 713 (4)
strongly 162 (13)
strongly worded 516 (3), 532 (4), 924 (6)
strongroom 799 (1)
strop 256 (6), 256 (11)
struck 818 (4)
struck down 728 (5)
struck dumb, be 578 (3)
struck off 57 (3)
structural 7 (3), 45 (5), 164 (5), 218 (14), 243 (4), 331 (3)
structure 7 (2), 43 (3), 56 (1), 62 (1), 164 (1), 164 (3), 218 (13), 233 (1), 243 (1), 319 (2), 331 (1), 631 (2), 844 (3)
struggle 176 (7), 278 (4), 671 (1), 671 (4), 672 (1), 682 (1), 682 (6), 700 (7), 716 (2), 716 (7), 716 (10)
struggle against 704 (5), 715 (3)
struggle up 308 (5)
struggler 716 (8)
struggling 176 (5), 716 (9)
strum 413 (9)
strumming 412 (1)
strung 24 (8)
strung out 75 (2), 203 (5)
strut 218 (2), 265 (2), 267 (14), 871 (5), 873 (5), 875 (7), 877 (5)
strutting 871 (4)
stub 41 (1), 388 (2), 547 (13)
stub one's toe 279 (8)
stub out 382 (6)
stubble 259 (1), 259 (2), 366 (8)
stubborn 162 (7), 326 (4), 600 (3), 602 (4), 602 (6), 700 (4), 715 (2), 940 (2)
stubborn person 602 (3)

stubbornness 600 (1), 602 (1), 934 (1), 940 (1), 980 (1)

stubby 204 (3), 205 (4), 257 (2)

stucco 226 (10)

stuck 45 (7), 266 (6)

stuck fast 700 (5), 778 (4)

stuck-out tongue 547 (4)

stud 47 (5), 218 (10), 259 (9), 369 (2), 437 (9), 844 (7), 844 (12)

stud farm 369 (2)

stud horse 273 (4)

studded 259 (4), 437 (8), 844 (11)

studded with 104 (5)

student 492 (1), 538 (3)

student days 130 (3)

student nurse 658 (16)

studied 617 (4), 850 (4)

studies 536 (2)

studio 194 (19), 687 (1)

studious 449 (5), 455 (2), 490 (6), 536 (3), 669 (6), 678 (9)

studious, be 536 (5)

studiously 536 (6)

studiously vague 525 (6)

studiousness 536 (2)

study 22 (1), 194 (19), 438 (9), 449 (2), 449 (8), 452 (1), 453 (1), 455 (1), 455 (4), 459 (1), 459 (13), 490 (8), 536 (2), 536 (5), 539 (4), 553 (5), 591 (1), 617 (1), 669 (1), 669 (13), 687 (1), 688 (5), 883 (2)

study group 538 (4)

study law 958 (7)

study of handwriting 586 (1)

study of religion 973 (4)

studying 449 (5), 536 (2)

stuff 3 (1), 52 (3), 54 (7), 162 (12), 197 (5), 222 (4), 227 (2), 301 (40), 319 (2), 331 (2), 515 (2), 631 (1), 637 (5), 666 (5), 795 (1), 863 (3), 947 (4)

stuff into 303 (4)

stuff oneself 301 (35)

stuffed 54 (4), 197 (3), 637 (3)

stuffed shirt 873 (3)

stuffed up 264 (4)

stuffiness 838 (1), 840 (1)

stuffing 36 (2), 40 (1), 193 (1), 227 (1), 301 (16), 303 (1), 631 (1), 863 (1)

stuffy 264 (5), 324 (4), 379 (6), 397 (2), 653 (2), 838 (3), 840 (2)

stumble 267 (14), 309 (4), 495 (3), 495 (8), 695 (9)

stumble on 484 (4)

stumble upon 159 (7)

stumbling 695 (5)

stumbling block 702 (2)

stump 41 (1), 53 (5), 254 (2), 267 (7), 267 (14), 474 (9), 700 (6)

stump along 278 (4)

stumped 474 (6), 517 (5)

stumping 267 (3)

stumpy 204 (3), 246 (4)

stun 279 (9), 375 (6), 400 (4), 416 (4), 821 (8), 864 (7)

stung 891 (3), 891 (4)

stunned 416 (2), 854 (6)

stunning 644 (5), 821 (4)

stunt 198 (7), 204 (5), 676 (2), 875 (3)

stunt flying 271 (1)

stunted 196 (9), 198 (4), 204 (3), 246 (4), 636 (5)

stuntedness 196 (1)

stupefaction 864 (1)

stupefy 375 (6), 821 (8), 864 (7), 949 (16)

stupendous 32 (7), 864 (5)

stupid 450 (2), 487 (2), 499 (3), 501 (1)

stupidity 499 (1), 820 (1)

stupor 375 (1), 679 (2), 864 (1)

sturdy 162 (8)

stutter 106 (5), 580 (1), 580 (3), 695 (9), 818 (8), 854 (10)

stuttering 580 (2), 695 (5), 891 (4)

sty 192 (10)

stye 253 (2)

Stygian 972 (3)

style 7 (2), 18 (1), 77 (2), 243 (1), 514 (1), 561 (2), 561 (6), 566 (1), 575 (1), 579 (4), 624 (1), 688 (1), 694 (1), 841 (1), 848 (1)

style of painting 553 (2)

styled 243 (3)

styling 843 (2)

stylish 575 (3), 694 (7), 841 (6), 848 (5)

stylishness 848 (1)

stylist 563 (1), 574 (3), 575 (2)

stylistic 566 (2)

stylized 243 (3)

stylus 256 (2), 555 (1), 586 (4)

stymie 702 (9), 702 (10)

styptic 324 (5)

Styx 972 (2)

suave 884 (3)

suavity 884 (1)

sub- 35 (4), 528 (9)

sub-branch 53 (4)

sub judice 459 (17), 480 (7), 959 (6), 959 (10)

sub-lieutenant 741 (7)

sub-species 74 (3)

subaltern 741 (8)

subconscious 447 (6), 476 (1), 476 (2)

subconscious, the 447 (2)

subcutaneous 224 (3)

subdivide 46 (10)

subdivided 46 (4)

subdivision 46 (3), 53 (3), 77 (1), 231 (2)

subdue 37 (4), 177 (6), 178 (4), 727 (9), 745 (7), 747 (7), 854 (12)

subdued 177 (3), 401 (3), 834 (5)

subedit 528 (9)

subeditor 589 (7)

subhuman 371 (6), 898 (7)

subject 23 (2), 35 (2), 35 (4), 180 (2), 452 (1), 461 (5), 564 (2), 596 (6), 727 (9), 742 (5), 742 (7), 745 (5), 745 (7), 774 (2), 781 (4), 879 (3)

substitution 150 (1), 188 (1), 752 (2), 755 (1)

substitutive 150 (4)

substratum 207 (1), 214 (1), 218 (4)

substructure 214 (1), 331 (1)

subsume 56 (4), 62 (6), 78 (6)

subterfuge 477 (1), 525 (1), 543 (2), 614 (1), 698 (2)

subterranean 210 (2), 211 (2)

subtle 498 (4), 698 (4)

subtle distinction 15 (2)

subtleness 498 (2)

subtlety 477 (1), 498 (2), 698 (1)

subtract 37 (4), 39 (3), 46 (8), 86 (12), 786 (6), 810 (2)

subtracted 39 (2)

subtraction 37 (2), 39 (1), 46 (2), 86 (2)

suburb 184 (3), 192 (8)

suburban 184 (5), 192 (18), 869 (8)

suburbanite 191 (1), 191 (3)

suburbanize 192 (22)

suburbanized 192 (18)

suburbia 75 (1), 191 (5), 192 (8)

suburbs 68 (5), 200 (3)

subvention 633 (1), 703 (2), 781 (1), 781 (2), 804 (2), 962 (1)

subversion 165 (1), 221 (2), 738 (2), 738 (3)

subversionary 165 (4)

subversive 149 (3), 165 (4), 738 (7)

subvert 149 (4), 467 (4), 655 (9)

subway 263 (8), 624 (7)

succeed 65 (3), 71 (5), 120 (3), 150 (5), 154 (6), 156 (9), 284 (4), 615 (5), 642 (3), 654 (8), 725 (6), 727 (6), 730 (6), 773 (4), 786 (7), 866 (11)

succeed in 727 (6)

succeed to 771 (8), 780 (5), 782 (4)

succeeding 65 (2), 120 (2)

success 34 (1), 725 (2), 727 (1), 730 (1), 866 (3)

success, a 727 (1), 727 (3)

success, be a 727 (6)

successful 34 (4), 156 (7), 160 (8), 173 (2), 725 (4), 727 (4), 730 (4), 833 (5), 877 (4)

successful, be 173 (3), 635 (6), 678 (11), 727 (6), 727 (7)

successfully 727 (12), 730 (9)

succession 65 (1), 71 (1), 71 (2), 120 (1), 170 (1), 170 (3), 284 (1), 733 (1), 780 (1), 782 (1)

successional 65 (2)

successive 65 (2), 71 (4), 141 (4)

successively 65 (5), 71 (7)

successor 41 (3), 67 (3), 776 (3)

successor designate 755 (1)

succinct 569 (2)

succinctness 569 (1)

succour 703 (1), 703 (5)

succulent 301 (32), 335 (4), 356 (2), 366 (6), 390 (2)

succumb 165 (11), 612 (13), 684 (5), 721 (4), 728 (9), 949 (13)

such 7 (3), 8 (3)

such a one 371 (3)

such as 18 (4)

such, be 7 (4)

suchlike 18 (3)

suck 299 (4), 304 (4), 341 (6), 388 (7), 406 (3)

suck dry 634 (4), 786 (11)

suck in 288 (3), 299 (4)

suck out 300 (8)

suck up to 703 (7), 879 (4)

sucker 53 (4), 132 (4), 263 (4), 366 (4), 501 (2), 544 (1)

sucker for 859 (6)

sucking 299 (1)

sucking noise 406 (1)

sucking out 304 (1)

sucking pig 365 (9)

suckling 132 (1)

suction 160 (3), 299 (1), 304 (1)

suction pump 304 (2)

sudden 114 (5), 116 (3), 135 (4), 508 (2), 609 (3)

sudden death 361 (2)

sudden motion 318 (1)

sudden progress 285 (1)

suddenly 116 (4), 135 (8), 508 (6)

suddenness 114 (1), 116 (1)

suds 355 (1)

sue 915 (5), 928 (9), 959 (7)

sue for 761 (5)

sue for divorce 896 (5)

suede 226 (6)

suet 357 (3)

suffer 154 (7), 377 (6), 488 (7), 599 (3), 599 (4), 600 (4), 651 (23), 700 (7), 715 (3), 721 (4), 731 (7), 734 (5), 756 (5), 818 (7), 823 (6), 825 (7), 834 (9), 836 (5), 836 (6), 855 (6)

suffer defeat 728 (9)

suffer execution 361 (8)

suffer pain 377 (6), 825 (7)

suffer torments 825 (7)

suffer with 818 (7)

sufferance 736 (1), 756 (1)

sufferer 651 (18), 731 (3), 825 (4)

suffering 377 (1), 377 (4), 503 (9), 600 (1), 616 (1), 645 (1), 700 (1), 731 (1), 801 (1), 818 (1), 818 (3), 825 (1), 825 (5), 827 (1), 834 (2), 834 (5)

suffice 28 (9), 54 (7), 160 (10), 635 (6), 640 (4), 642 (3), 644 (10), 732 (3), 768 (3), 863 (3)

sufficiency 54 (2), 635 (1), 640 (1), 725 (1), 744 (2), 800 (1)

sun-tanned 381 (6), 428 (5)

sun-tanning 843 (1)

sun trap 383 (2)

sun-up 128 (1), 308 (1)

sun worship 982 (1)

sunbathe 379 (7)

sunblind 226 (3), 421 (2)

sunburn 381 (2)

sunburnt 381 (6), 430 (3)

sundae 301 (17)

Sunday best 228 (2), 844 (6)

Sunday joint 301 (16)

Sunday roast 301 (16)

Sunday school 539 (2)

Sunday school treat 837 (1)

sunder 46 (8), 46 (10), 51 (5), 53 (7), 75 (4), 86 (12), 92 (5), 165 (7), 176 (8), 204 (5), 709 (8)

sundial 117 (3)

sundown 129 (1), 418 (2)

sundowner 129 (1)

sundries 795 (1)

sundry 82 (2), 104 (4)

sung 866 (10)

sunglasses 442 (2)

sunk 165 (5), 211 (2), 255 (6)

sunk low 867 (7)

sunken 210 (2), 255 (6)

sunken cheeks 206 (2)

sunless 418 (4)

sunlight 383 (2), 417 (1)

sunned 342 (4)

sunniness 833 (1)

sunning 342 (2), 381 (1)

sunny 342 (4), 379 (6), 417 (9), 823 (3), 826 (2), 833 (3)

sunny side 826 (1)

sunrise 128 (1), 308 (1)

sunset 129 (1), 417 (3), 418 (2)

sunshade 226 (4), 421 (1)

sunshine 379 (1), 652 (1), 730 (2)

sunshine roof 263 (5)

sunshine yellow 433 (3)

suntan 430 (1)

sup 301 (35)

super- 34 (4), 34 (5), 594 (9), 644 (5)

superabound 54 (5), 104 (6), 306 (3), 635 (7), 637 (5)

superabundance 32 (2), 637 (1)

superabundant 32 (4)

superannuated 127 (7), 131 (6), 674 (3)

superb 644 (4), 841 (4), 875 (4)

supercharged 160 (9)

supercilious 871 (4), 878 (4), 922 (3)

superego 320 (2), 447 (2)

superficial 4 (3), 33 (7), 55 (3), 212 (2), 223 (2), 445 (7), 456 (3), 458 (2), 491 (7), 499 (4), 639 (6), 726 (2), 840 (2)

superficiality 850 (2)

superficially 6 (5), 223 (4)

superficies 223 (1)

superfine 644 (4)

superfluity 32 (1), 32 (2), 40 (2), 41 (1), 197 (1), 576 (1), 637 (2), 641 (1), 800 (1), 863 (1), 943 (1)

superfluous 38 (2), 546 (2), 570 (5), 634 (2), 635 (4), 637 (4), 641 (4), 943 (2)

superfluous, be 637 (6), 641 (8)

superhuman 965 (5), 965 (6)

superhuman task 700 (2)

superimpose 38 (3), 226 (13)

superimposing 38 (1)

superintend 689 (4)

superintendent 34 (3), 690 (3), 955 (3)

superior 19 (2), 21 (4), 29 (2), 32 (4), 34 (3), 34 (4), 131 (7), 162 (6), 306 (2), 596 (4), 638 (4), 638 (5), 638 (6), 644 (4), 654 (6), 690 (1), 727 (4), 741 (1), 847 (5), 866 (9), 868 (7), 871 (4)

superior airs 922 (1)

superior, be 32 (15), 34 (7), 37 (4), 64 (3), 178 (3), 306 (5), 644 (10), 694 (8), 727 (6), 727 (9), 727 (10), 727 (11), 866 (11)

superior force 596 (1)

superior person 34 (3)

superiority 29 (1), 32 (1), 34 (1), 64 (1), 160 (1), 178 (1), 306 (1), 638 (1), 644 (1), 646 (1), 689 (2), 733 (1), 733 (2), 866 (2)

superlative 34 (4), 34 (5), 564 (3), 644 (4)

superlatively 32 (17), 34 (12)

superman 34 (3), 644 (3)

supermarket 796 (3)

supernatural 59 (4), 84 (6), 84 (7), 965 (5), 983 (8), 984 (6), 984 (8)

supernova 321 (4)

supernumerary 40 (2)

superpower 638 (4), 733 (6)

supersede 150 (5), 300 (6)

superseded 127 (7), 674 (3)

supersession 150 (1), 752 (2)

supersonic 276 (5), 277 (5)

supersonic flight 271 (1)

supersonic speed 277 (1)

superstition 487 (1), 491 (1), 495 (1), 977 (1), 982 (1), 983 (1)

superstitious 481 (6), 487 (2), 491 (4), 495 (4)

superstitious, be 487 (3)

superstore 796 (3)

superstructure 331 (1)

supertanker 275 (3)

supertax 809 (3)

supervene 6 (3), 38 (4), 120 (3), 154 (6)

supervenient 6 (2)

supervention 120 (1)

supervise 689 (4)

supervision 438 (4)

supervisor 690 (3)

supervisory 689 (3)

superwoman 34 (3), 644 (3), 864 (3)

supine 210 (2), 216 (5), 311 (3), 458 (2), 820 (4)

supineness 216 (2), 721 (1)

supper 301 (12)

supplant 65 (3), 150 (5), 300 (6)

supplanter 67 (3)

supple 327 (3), 603 (4), 879 (3)

supplement 36 (2), 36 (5), 38 (1), 38 (3), 40 (1), 54 (2), 54 (6), 67 (1), 197 (5), 528 (4), 589 (5), 809 (1)

supplementary 36 (3), 38 (2), 54 (3)

supplemented 197 (3)

suppleness 327 (1), 603 (1), 698 (1)

suppliant 761 (4), 763 (1)

supplicant 763 (1), 981 (8)

supplicate 761 (7), 981 (11)

supplication 761 (2), 981 (4)

supplicatory 761 (4), 981 (9), 981 (10)

supplier 633 (2)

supplies 629 (1), 633 (1), 795 (1)

supply 54 (6), 632 (1), 633 (1), 633 (5)

supply base 632 (2)

support 146 (4), 153 (8), 162 (12), 173 (1), 173 (3), 177 (6), 218 (1), 218 (2), 218 (15), 273 (12), 310 (4), 466 (8), 488 (1), 488 (8), 605 (6), 612 (2), 628 (1), 660 (8), 666 (1), 666 (5), 703 (1), 703 (2), 703 (3), 703 (5), 778 (1), 778 (5), 823 (6), 852 (1), 880 (1), 880 (2), 923 (8), 927 (5)

support life 360 (6)

supported, be 218 (16)

supporter 218 (2), 284 (2), 488 (3), 504 (3), 707 (4), 903 (1), 923 (4)

supporters 441 (2)

supporting 214 (3), 218 (14), 466 (5), 703 (4), 923 (5)

supporting film 445 (4)

supporting part 594 (8)

supporting role 35 (1)

supportive 703 (4)

suppose 64 (4), 119 (4), 158 (4), 471 (6), 475 (12), 480 (6), 485 (8), 512 (6)

supposed 119 (2), 158 (2), 512 (5)

supposedly 485 (11)

supposing 8 (6)

supposition 66 (2), 158 (1), 451 (1), 452 (1), 475 (2), 485 (3), 512 (1), 532 (1)

suppositional 447 (5), 451 (2), 466 (5), 474 (4), 512 (4), 513 (6)

suppository 658 (9)

suppress 165 (8), 182 (3), 311 (4), 311 (7), 382 (6), 521 (3), 525 (7), 525 (8), 578 (4), 702 (8), 727 (9), 727 (10), 735 (7), 735 (8), 745 (7), 747 (7), 757 (4)

suppressed 165 (5), 525 (3)

suppression 165 (1), 182 (1), 525 (1), 735 (1), 747 (1), 757 (1)

suppurate 655 (7)

suppurating 335 (4), 653 (4)

suppuration 302 (1), 651 (5)

supra- 34 (4)

supremacy 34 (1), 638 (1), 733 (1), 733 (2)

supreme 32 (4), 34 (5), 68 (7), 69 (4), 160 (8), 162 (6), 178 (2), 213 (4), 638 (5), 644 (6), 646 (3), 733 (7), 965 (6)

Supreme Being 965 (3)

supreme control 733 (2)

supremely 32 (17), 34 (12)

surcharge 808 (5), 809 (1)

surd 85 (1), 85 (5)

sure 473 (4), 473 (5), 473 (7), 485 (4), 660 (4), 929 (4)

sure of oneself 855 (5)

surefire 727 (4)

surefooted 694 (4), 727 (4)

sureness 473 (1)

surety 660 (2), 767 (1), 959 (2)

surf 269 (12), 350 (5), 355 (1)

surf riding 269 (3), 837 (6)

surface 183 (1), 212 (2), 223 (1), 223 (2), 269 (10), 298 (5), 308 (4), 323 (4), 331 (2)

surface mail 531 (2)

surfacing 298 (1), 308 (1)

surfboard 274 (2), 837 (15)

surfeit 637 (2), 863 (1), 863 (3)

surfeited 863 (2)

surfing 269 (3)

surge 36 (1), 36 (4), 74 (10), 298 (6), 350 (3), 350 (9)

surge forward 176 (7)

surgeon 658 (14)

surgery 46 (3), 658 (11), 658 (13), 843 (1)

surgical 658 (18)

surgical dressing 226 (5), 658 (9)

surliness 893 (1)

surly 885 (5), 893 (2)

surmise 485 (3), 485 (8), 512 (2), 512 (6)

surmount 209 (12), 213 (5), 306 (3), 308 (5), 727 (8)

surmountable 469 (2)

surname 561 (2), 561 (6)

surpass 34 (7), 306 (5)

surpass belief 864 (7)

surpassing 32 (4), 32 (6), 32 (12), 34 (4), 34 (5), 306 (2), 716 (9)

surpassingly 34 (12)

surplice 989 (2)

surplus 40 (2), 41 (1), 41 (4), 53 (1), 637 (2), 637 (4)

surprise 508 (1), 508 (5), 670 (1), 670 (7), 712 (7), 821 (8), 864 (1), 864 (7)

surprised 508 (3), 864 (4), 891 (3)

surprising 84 (6), 508 (2), 864 (5)

surprisingly 32 (19)

surreal 551 (6)

surrealism 551 (3), 553 (3)

Surrealist 556 (1)

surrealistic 551 (6)

surrender 621 (3), 674 (1), 721 (1), 721 (3), 753 (1)

surreptitious 525 (5)

surrogate 755 (1)

surround 230 (3), 232 (3), 233 (1), 233 (3), 235 (1), 235 (4), 250 (8), 626 (3), 712 (8), 718 (11)

surrounded 232 (2), 661 (6)

surrounding 8 (3), 230 (1), 230 (2), 232 (1)

surroundings 8 (1), 68 (5), 187 (2), 200 (1), 223 (1), 230 (1)

surtax 809 (3)

surveillance 455 (1), 457 (2), 660 (2), 660 (3), 664 (2), 689 (1)

survey 438 (4), 438 (9), 459 (1), 459 (13), 465 (11), 480 (2), 480 (6), 551 (8), 591 (1), 591 (5), 592 (1)

survey map 551 (5)

surveyed 465 (10)

surveying 465 (1)

surveyor 86 (7), 459 (9), 465 (7), 465 (8), 480 (3)

survival 1 (1), 113 (2)

survive 41 (5), 113 (7), 144 (3), 360 (4), 656 (8), 667 (5)

surviving 1 (4), 41 (4), 360 (2)

survivor 41 (3)

susceptibility 180 (1), 819 (1)

susceptible 180 (2), 374 (3), 819 (2), 822 (3), 951 (7)

susceptive 819 (2)

susceptivity 180 (1), 374 (1), 612 (3)

suspect 474 (8), 485 (8), 486 (5), 486 (7), 491 (8), 854 (11), 904 (3), 911 (3), 914 (3), 928 (4), 928 (6)

suspect evidence 928 (2)

suspected 936 (3)

suspend 72 (4), 136 (7), 145 (8), 217 (5), 674 (5), 752 (4), 752 (5), 757 (4), 954 (9), 963 (8)

suspend hostilities 719 (5)

suspended 175 (2), 217 (4), 674 (2), 677 (2), 679 (7), 954 (5)

suspended animation 375 (1)

suspended judgment 487 (3)

suspender 47 (5), 217 (3), 228 (26)

suspender belt 228 (17)

suspense 474 (2), 507 (1)

suspenseful 821 (4)

suspension 57 (1), 136 (2), 145 (4), 217 (1), 327 (1), 328 (1), 337 (2), 674 (1), 677 (1), 752 (1), 963 (4)

suspicion 33 (2), 486 (2), 490 (1), 512 (1), 524 (3)

suspicions 854 (2)

suspicious 474 (4), 486 (4), 486 (5), 854 (7), 858 (2), 911 (2), 928 (5), 930 (4)

sustain 108 (7), 144 (3), 146 (4), 173 (3), 218 (15), 301 (39), 466 (8), 600 (4), 666 (5), 703 (5)

sustained 146 (2)

sustained action 146 (1)

sustaining 218 (14), 301 (33)

sustenance 301 (7), 301 (9)

suttee 362 (3)

suture 45 (4)

svelte 206 (4), 841 (5)

swab 342 (3), 342 (6), 648 (9), 658 (9)

swabber 648 (6)

swaddle 45 (12)

swag 194 (9), 248 (2), 248 (4), 790 (1), 844 (3)

swagger 265 (2), 871 (5), 875 (1), 877 (1), 877 (5), 878 (6)

swaggerer 871 (2), 877 (3), 878 (3)

swaggering 871 (4), 873 (4), 877 (1), 877 (4)

swallow 299 (4), 301 (11), 301 (35), 365 (4), 634 (4), 786 (7), 823 (6)

swallow insults 879 (4)

swallow one's words 580 (3)

swallow the bait 544 (3)

swallow up 165 (6), 165 (10), 299 (4)

swallow whole 485 (7)

swallowing 299 (1), 301 (1)

swallowtail 92 (2)

swami 500 (1)

swamp 32 (15), 54 (7), 104 (6), 165 (6), 341 (8), 347 (1)

swamped 54 (4), 341 (5), 728 (5)

swampy 347 (2)

swan 365 (4), 427 (2)

swan off 267 (11)

swan song 69 (1), 361 (2)

swank 871 (5), 873 (2), 873 (5), 875 (7), 877 (1), 877 (3), 877 (5), 878 (6)

swanking 871 (4)

swansong 836 (2)

swap 12 (3), 151 (1), 151 (3), 791 (1), 791 (4)

swapped 151 (2)

swapping 791 (3)

swarm 36 (4), 61 (2), 74 (3), 74 (5), 74 (10), 104 (2), 104 (6), 171 (6), 635 (7)

swarm in 297 (7)

swarm over 189 (5)

swarm up 308 (5)

swarm with 104 (6)

swarming 32 (4), 36 (1), 74 (9)

swarms 32 (2)

swarthiness 428 (1)

swarthy 428 (5)

swashbuckler 722 (1), 877 (3)

swashbuckling 877 (1)

swastika 96 (1), 222 (2)

swat 279 (2), 279 (9)

swatch 53 (5)

swathe 45 (12), 74 (6), **226 (13), 228 (31),** 548 (4), 747 (7)

sway 29 (3), 178 (1), 178 (3), 217 (5), 317 (4), 612 (8), **733 (2)**

swayed 481 (8)

swaying 29 (2), 317 (3)

swear 466 (7), 532 (6), 540 (3), 764 (4), 899 (7), 980 (6)

swear an oath 532 (6)

swear by 473 (7), 485 (7), 923 (9)

swear falsely 541 (5)

swear off 533 (3), 603 (7), 942 (4)

swear on the Bible 532 (6)

swear to 466 (7)

swear true 540 (3)

swearer 765 (3), 980 (3)

swearing 532 (2), 829 (3), 885 (5), 899 (2), 899 (4)

swearing off 533 (1)

swearword 559 (1), 899 (2)

sweat 298 (2), 298 (7), 300 (9), 302 (4), 302 (6), 339 (1), 341 (6), 379 (1), 379 (7), 671 (4), 682 (3), 682 (7)

sweat it out 600 (4)

sweated labour 742 (6)

sweater 228 (11)

sweating 298 (2), 302 (1), 379 (4), 682 (4)

sweatshirt 228 (16)

sweatshop 687 (1)

sweep 183 (3), 248 (4), 438 (4), 648 (9)

sweep along 277 (6)

sweep aside 479 (3)

sweep away 300 (8)

sweep before one 287 (7)

sweep through 267 (12)

sweep up 188 (4)

sweeper 648 (6)

sweeping 32 (5), 52 (7), 54 (3), 78 (2)

sweeping across the board 79 (3)

sweepings 641 (3)

sweepstake 618 (2)

sweet 301 (17), 376 (3), 390 (2), 392 (3), 410 (6), 823 (3), 826 (2), 841 (3), 884 (4), 887 (11), 897 (4)

sweet drink 392 (2)

sweet herb 301 (21)

sweet nothings 515 (3), 925 (1)

sweet on 887 (10)

sweet on, be 889 (7)

sweet sauce 392 (2)

sweet-scented 396 (3)

sweet smell 394 (1), 396 (1)

sweet talk 925 (1), 925 (4)

sweet-tempered 884 (4)

sweet thing 301 (10), 301 (17), 301 (18), 301 (19), 392 (2)

sweet tooth 386 (1), 392 (1)

sweet will 604 (2)

sweet wine 301 (29)

sweeten 392 (4), 826 (3)

sweetened 392 (3)

sweetening 392 (1), 392 (2)

sweetheart 373 (3), 887 (4), 887 (5), 890 (1)

sweetmeat 301 (18)

sweetness 392 (1), 826 (1), 884 (1)

sweets 301 (18), 392 (2)

swell 36 (1), 36 (4), 197 (4), 253 (2), 253 (9), 310 (4), 350 (5), 350 (9), 400 (1), 400 (4), 848 (4), 868 (4)

swell the ranks 38 (4), 74 (10), 708 (8)

swell up 254 (5)

swell with pride 871 (6)

swelling 194 (2), 195 (3), 197 (2), 252 (2), 253 (1), 253 (2), 253 (7), 254 (3), 400 (3), 651 (12), 651 (14), 845 (1), 871 (4)

swelling heart 818 (1)

swelling up 197 (2)

swelter 379 (1), 379 (7)

sweltering 379 (4)

swept away 161 (5)

swerve 220 (1), 220 (5), 248 (1), 282 (1), 282 (3)

swift 277 (5)

swift-moving 277 (5)

swiftly 116 (4), 277 (9), 680 (4)

swiftness 277 (1)

swig 301 (26), 301 (38), 949 (14)

swigging 949 (11)

swill 301 (38), 949 (14)

swilling 301 (25)

swim 269 (12), 323 (4), 440 (4), 837 (21)

swimming 269 (3), 269 (7), 440 (1), 837 (6)

swimming costume 228 (19)

swimmingly 730 (9)

swimsuit 228 (19)

swindle 542 (2), 542 (8), 786 (2), 786 (11), 788 (4), 788 (8), 805 (5), 930 (8)

swindler 545 (4), 789 (3)

swindling 542 (2)

swine 365 (9), 938 (2), 938 (3)

swine fever 651 (17)

swing 141 (1), 148 (1), 149 (1), 152 (5), 173 (1), 183 (3), 217 (2), 217 (5), 279 (9), 282 (1), 282 (3), 317 (2), 317 (4), 412 (1), 744 (3), 837 (4), 963 (13)

swing-back 280 (1), 280 (3)

swing from 217 (5)

swing round 315 (5)

swinging 412 (7)

swipe 279 (2), 279 (9), 287 (1), 712 (4)

swirl 315 (2), 315 (5), 350 (3), 350 (9)

swish 401 (1), 401 (4), 406 (1), 406 (3)

switch 53 (4), 149 (1), 150 (1), 150 (5), 151 (3), 259 (2), 272 (7), 294 (3), 628 (2), 630 (1), 843 (2)

switch off 69 (6), 418 (7)

switch on 160 (11), 173 (3), 415 (6), 417 (13)

switch over 603 (6)

switchback 251 (3), 251 (7)

switchblade 723 (8)

switchboard 76 (1), 531 (1)

switched 151 (2)

switched off 418 (4)

swivel 218 (11)

swivel round 315 (5)

swollen 32 (4), 197 (3), 253 (7), 574 (5), 651 (22), 871 (4)

swollen eyes 836 (1)

swollen head 871 (1)

swollenheaded 873 (4)

swoon 161 (2), 375 (1), 375 (5), 684 (1), 684 (5)

swooning 684 (2)

swoop 277 (2), 277 (6), 309 (1), 309 (3), 313 (1)

swooping 309 (2)

sword 168 (1), 256 (5), 723 (8)

sword in hand 718 (8)

sword of state 743 (1)

sword, the 718 (1)

swordfish 365 (15)

swordplay 716 (6)

swordsman 716 (8), 722 (1)

sworn 532 (3), 739 (3), 765 (4), 917 (5)

sworn, be 532 (6)

sworn enemy 881 (2)

sworn evidence 466 (2)

sworn to 466 (5)

swung 412 (7)

swung dash 547 (14)

sybarite 944 (2)

sycophancy 879 (1), 925 (1)

sycophant 879 (2), 925 (2)

sycophantic 879 (3), 925 (3)

syllabic 558 (5)

syllable 558 (3), 559 (1), 577 (1)

syllabus 87 (1), 592 (1)

sylph-like 206 (4)

sylvan 366 (10)

symbiotic 24 (5), 360 (2), 706 (3)

symbol 4 (2), 85 (1), 150 (2), 519 (1), 547 (1), 547 (9), 551 (2), 558 (1)

symbolic 519 (3), 523 (4), 547 (15), 551 (6), 639 (6), 988 (8)

symbolically 547 (23), 988 (12)

symbolism 519 (1), 523 (1), 547 (1), 557 (3), 988 (1)

symbolization 522 (1), 523 (1), 547 (1), 547 (3), 551 (1)

symbolize 514 (5), 519 (4), 522 (7), 547 (18), 551 (8)

symbolizing 551 (6)

symbology 547 (3)

symmetrical 16 (2), 28 (7), 81 (3), 245 (2), 841 (5)

symmetry 12 (1), 16 (1), 28 (1), 60 (1), 245 (1), 575 (1), 841 (1)

sympathetic 24 (5), 488 (4), 775 (4), 818 (3), 880 (6), 887 (11), 897 (4), 905 (4)

sympathize 513 (7), 818 (7), 880 (7), 897 (5), 905 (6)

sympathizer 707 (2), 707 (4), 775 (3), 859 (6), 897 (3)

sympathy 291 (1), 513 (1), 703 (1), 706 (1), 710 (1), 775 (2), 818 (1), 859 (3), 880 (2), 887 (1), 897 (1), 905 (1)

symphonic 412 (7)

symphony 412 (4)

symphony orchestra 413 (3)

symposium 74 (2), 475 (4), 584 (3)

symptom 89 (2), 511 (3), 522 (1), 524 (3), 547 (1), 547 (5), 651 (2)

symptomatic 466 (5), 547 (15), 664 (3)

synagogue 990 (3)

sync 123 (1), 123 (4)

synchronism 123 (1)

synchronization 123 (1)

synchronize 24 (10), 50 (4), 60 (3), 117 (7), 123 (4)

synchronized 24 (5), 24 (8), 50 (3), 123 (3)

synchronous 123 (3)

synchronously 123 (5)

syncopated 412 (7)

syncopation 410 (4), 412 (1)

syndicalism 733 (4)

syndicalist 708 (2), 708 (6)

syndicate 528 (9), 706 (2), 708 (5)

syndrome 331 (1)

synod 74 (2), 692 (1), 985 (5)

synonym 13 (1), 28 (2), 559 (1)

synonym for 866 (3)

synonymity 28 (2)

synonymous 13 (2), 28 (8), 514 (4), 559 (4)

synonymousness 514 (2)

synopsis 50 (1), 62 (1), 79 (1), 87 (1), 592 (1)

synoptic 79 (3)

syntactic 564 (3)

syntax 557 (2), 564 (1)

synthesis 45 (1)

synthesize 56 (5), 164 (7)

synthesizer 414 (1)

synthetic 18 (6), 20 (4), 164 (6), 543 (4)

syphilis 651 (13)

syphilitic 651 (22)

syphon off 304 (4)

syringe 304 (2), 341 (3), 341 (7)

syrinx 577 (1)

syrup 301 (27), 354 (3), 392 (2), 658 (8)

syrupy 354 (5)

system 52 (1), 60 (1), 62 (1), 81 (2), 485 (2), 610 (1)

systematic 60 (2), 62 (3), 81 (3), 449 (6), 475 (7), 622 (5)

systematically 60 (5)

systematize 60 (3), 62 (5), 83 (8), 623 (8)

systematized 623 (6)

systematizer 623 (5)

systems analysis 86 (3)

systems analyst 86 (7), 623 (5)

T

T-square 465 (5)
tabby 365 (11), 437 (8)
tabernacle 990 (1), 990 (3)
tabla 414 (9)
table 62 (1), 87 (1), 136 (7), 218 (5), 301 (1), 548 (8)
table bird 301 (16), 365 (5)
table d'hôte 301 (12)
table manners 301 (1), 610 (2)
table mat 218 (5)
table of contents 87 (1)
table-tapping 984 (3)
table tennis 837 (7)
table-turning 984 (3)
table water 301 (27)
table wine 301 (29)
tableau 553 (5), 594 (1), 594 (4), 875 (3)
tableland 209 (2), 213 (2), 216 (1), 348 (1)
tables 86 (4)
tablet 207 (2), 548 (3), 658 (2)
tabloid 528 (4)
taboo 46 (9), 57 (1), 757 (1), 757 (3), 757 (4)
tabor 414 (9)
tabular 62 (3), 207 (4)
tabular statement 87 (1)
tabulate 62 (6), 87 (5), 548 (8)
tabulated 62 (3), 87 (4)
tacit 514 (4), 523 (3)
taciturn 525 (6), 569 (2), 578 (2), 582 (2), 620 (3), 883 (5)
taciturn, be 399 (3), 525 (8), 569 (3), 578 (3), 582 (3)
taciturnity 523 (1), 525 (1), 569 (1), 582 (1), 883 (1)

tack 45 (12), 47 (5), 256 (2), 269 (10), 281 (1), 282 (1), 282 (3), 624 (4)
tack on 38 (3)
tackle 47 (3), 68 (8), 639 (4), 671 (4), 672 (3), 676 (5)
tackling 47 (3), 218 (2), 275 (6)
tacky 48 (2), 354 (5), 645 (2)
tact 498 (2), 689 (1), 694 (1), 846 (1)
tactful 498 (5), 848 (6)
tactfulness 884 (1)
tactical 623 (6), 688 (3), 698 (4), 718 (9)
tactical bombing 712 (3)
tactician 612 (5), 623 (5), 696 (2), 698 (3)
tactics 182 (1), 498 (2), 623 (2), 624 (1), 676 (2), 688 (2), 694 (1), 698 (1), 698 (2), 712 (1), 718 (4)
tactile 378 (5)
tactless 456 (3), 499 (4), 695 (5), 847 (5), 885 (4)
tactlessness 695 (2), 847 (1), 885 (1)
tactual 378 (5)
tadpole 365 (12)
taffeta 222 (4)
taffrail 235 (2)
tag 40 (1), 69 (2), 217 (2), 496 (1), 547 (13), 547 (19), 837 (10)
tag after 284 (4)
tag along 284 (4)
tail 40 (1), 67 (2), 69 (2), 71 (3), 217 (2), 238 (1), 238 (2), 238 (5), 284 (2), 284 (4), 619 (5)
tail end 69 (2), 238 (1), 238 (4)
tail off 37 (5), 69 (5)
tail wind 287 (3)
tailback 67 (2)
tailed 217 (4)
tailor 24 (10), 228 (28), 243 (5), 686 (3)
tailor-made 24 (8), 228 (30)
tailored 228 (30)

tailoring 228 (1), 243 (2)
tailor's dummy 23 (3)
tailpiece 67 (1), 238 (1)
tails 228 (4)
tailwind 352 (1)
taint 297 (6), 645 (1), 649 (9), 655 (9), 867 (2), 867 (11)
tainted 397 (2), 649 (6)
take 31 (6), 38 (3), 39 (3), 78 (5), 299 (3), 551 (4), 551 (9), 627 (6), 634 (4), 727 (9), 740 (3), 745 (7), 747 (8), 761 (5), 771 (7), 773 (4), 782 (4), 786 (1), 786 (6), 788 (7), 791 (6), 807 (3), 823 (6), 859 (11)
take a back seat 874 (3)
take a beating 728 (9)
take a breather 683 (3), 685 (5)
take a census 86 (11)
take a chance 671 (4)
take a class 534 (7)
take a direction 281 (4)
take a dislike to 861 (4)
take a fall 309 (4)
take a header 309 (4), 313 (3)
take a hold on 178 (4)
take a holiday 681 (3), 683 (3), 837 (21)
take a loan 785 (2)
take a look 438 (9)
take a peep 438 (8)
take a photograph 551 (9)
take a pledge 764 (5), 767 (5)
take a poll 86 (11)
take a position 718 (12)
take a potshot 712 (11)
take a pride in 457 (5)
take a reading 465 (12)
take a resolution 599 (3)
take a rest 683 (3)
take a seat 311 (8)
take a shine 417 (11)
take a toll 809 (7)
take a trip 949 (15)
take account of 455 (6)
take action 173 (3), 676 (5), 682 (6)

take advantage of 542 (9), 673 (3), 675 (2), 694 (8), 951 (11)

take advice 691 (5)

take after 5 (9), 18 (7), 166 (3)

take aim 281 (7), 617 (6)

take amiss 891 (5)

take an interest 453 (4)

take an overdose 362 (13)

take apart 46 (10)

take as a model 20 (7)

take as one's due 908 (4)

take aside 583 (3)

take authority 733 (11)

take away 37 (4), 39 (3), 86 (12), 163 (10), 188 (4), 192 (13), 786 (9), 963 (8)

take back 31 (6), 148 (3), 603 (7), 771 (7), 786 (7)

take bets 618 (8)

take by force 740 (3)

take by storm 712 (7), 727 (9), 786 (6)

take by surprise 508 (5), 712 (7)

take captive 745 (7)

take care of 455 (5), 457 (6)

take charge of 457 (6), 660 (8), 672 (3)

take comfort 828 (4), 831 (4)

take command 733 (11)

take communion 988 (10)

take control 733 (11)

take counsel 449 (8), 584 (7)

take courage 855 (7)

take cover 525 (9)

take credit 802 (3)

take cuttings 167 (7)

take dictation 586 (8)

take down 311 (4), 548 (7), 586 (8)

take down a peg 872 (7)

take effect 173 (3), 727 (7)

take exception to 762 (3), 891 (5), 924 (9)

take flight 296 (5)

take for granted 475 (12), 485 (7), 487 (3), 512 (6), 865 (4), 908 (4)

take for oneself 786 (7)

take French leave 620 (6)

take fright 854 (9)

take from 782 (4)

take heart 833 (7), 852 (6)

take heed 664 (6)

take hold 786 (6)

take hold of 48 (3)

take hope 852 (6)

take hostage 747 (8)

take in 38 (3), 56 (4), 78 (5), 198 (7), 299 (3), 299 (4), 438 (9), 490 (8), 498 (6), 516 (5), 542 (9), 632 (5), 660 (8), 782 (4), 786 (6), 882 (10)

take in hand 534 (8), 672 (3)

take in one's stride 701 (7)

take in sail 278 (6)

take in tow 288 (3), 703 (5)

take into account 78 (6), 449 (8), 463 (3), 468 (3)

take into custody 747 (8), 786 (6)

take it 721 (4)

take it badly 825 (7), 836 (5)

take it easy 278 (4), 679 (11), 683 (3)

take it that 485 (8)

take it to heart 819 (5), 825 (7)

take its course 146 (3), 154 (6)

take its source 157 (5)

take its time 108 (7)

take its turn 141 (6)

take liberties 735 (8), 744 (9), 885 (6)

take life 362 (10)

take lightly 458 (5)

take measurements 465 (11)

take measures 669 (10)

take neither side 860 (4)

take no advice 602 (6)

take no chances 660 (9)

take no interest 454 (3), 820 (6), 860 (4)

take no notice 458 (5)

take no offence 884 (5), 909 (4)

take no precautions 670 (7)

take no risks 858 (3)

take no sides 606 (3)

take note 455 (6)

take off 20 (5), 39 (3), 229 (7), 271 (7), 296 (6), 308 (4), 594 (17), 851 (2), 851 (6)

take offence 829 (5), 881 (4), 891 (5)

take office 733 (11)

take on 299 (3), 534 (8), 632 (5), 671 (4), 672 (3), 676 (5), 704 (5), 712 (7), 716 (10), 716 (11), 836 (5)

take on board 193 (2)

take on credit 764 (5)

take on oneself 599 (3), 622 (7), 734 (6), 764 (4), 878 (6), 917 (9)

take on supplies 633 (5)

take a resolution 599 (3)

take a rest 683 (3)

take a seat 311 (8)

take a shine 417 (11)

take a toll 809 (7)

take a trip 949 (15)

take account of 455 (6)

take action 173 (3), 676 (5), 682 (6)

take advantage of 542 (9), 673 (3), 675 (2), 694 (8), 951 (11)

take advice 691 (5)

take after 5 (9), 18 (7), 166 (3)

take aim 281 (7), 617 (6)

take amiss 891 (5)

take an interest 453 (4)

take an overdose 362 (13)

take apart 46 (10)

take as a model 20 (7)

take as one's due 908 (4)

take aside 583 (3)

take authority 733 (11)

take away 37 (4), 39 (3), 86 (12), 163 (10), 188 (4), 192 (13), 786 (9), 963 (8)

take back 31 (6), 148 (3), 603 (7), 771 (7), 786 (7)

take bets 618 (8)

take by force 740 (3)

take by storm 712 (7), 727 (9), 786 (6)

take by surprise 508 (5), 712 (7)

take captive 745 (7)

take care of 455 (5), 457 (6)

take charge of 457 (6), 660 (8), 672 (3)

take comfort 828 (4), 831 (4)

take command 733 (11)

take communion 988 (10)

take control 733 (11)

take counsel 449 (8), 584 (7)

take courage 855 (7)

take cover 525 (9)

take credit 802 (3)

take cuttings 167 (7)

take dictation 586 (8)

take down 311 (4), 548 (7), 586 (8)

take down a peg 872 (7)

take effect 173 (3), 727 (7)

take exception to 762 (3), 891 (5), 924 (9)

take flight 296 (5)

take for granted 475 (12), 485 (7), 487 (3), 512 (6), 865 (4), 908 (4)

take for oneself 786 (7)

take French leave 620 (6)

take fright 854 (9)

take from 782 (4)

take heart 833 (7), 852 (6)

take heed 664 (6)

take hold 786 (6)

take hold of 48 (3)

take hope 852 (6)

take hostage 747 (8)

take in 38 (3), 56 (4), 78 (5), 198 (7), 299 (3), 299 (4), 438 (9), 490 (8), 498 (6), 516 (5), 542 (9), 632 (5), 660 (8), 782 (4), 786 (6), 882 (10)

take in hand 534 (8), 672 (3)

take in one's stride 701 (7)

take in sail 278 (6)

take in tow 288 (3), 703 (5)

take into account 78 (6), 449 (8), 463 (3), 468 (3)

take into custody 747 (8), 786 (6)

take it 721 (4)

take it badly 825 (7), 836 (5)

take it easy 278 (4), 679 (11), 683 (3)

take it that 485 (8)

take it to heart 819 (5), 825 (7)

take its course 146 (3), 154 (6)

take its source 157 (5)

take its time 108 (7)

take its turn 141 (6)

take liberties 735 (8), 744 (9), 885 (6)

take life 362 (10)

take lightly 458 (5)

take measurements 465 (11)

take measures 669 (10)

take neither side 860 (4)

take no advice 602 (6)

take no chances 660 (9)

take no interest 454 (3), 820 (6), 860 (4)

take no notice 458 (5)

take no offence 884 (5), 909 (4)

take no precautions 670 (7)

take no risks 858 (3)

take no sides 606 (3)

take note 455 (6)

take off 20 (5), 39 (3), 229 (7), 271 (7), 296 (6), 308 (4), 594 (17), 851 (2), 851 (6)

take offence 829 (5), 881 (4), 891 (5)

take office 733 (11)

take on 299 (3), 534 (8), 632 (5), 671 (4), 672 (3), 676 (5), 704 (5), 712 (7), 716 (10), 716 (11), 836 (5)

take on board 193 (2)

take on credit 764 (5)

take on oneself 599 (3), 622 (7), 734 (6), 764 (4), 878 (6), 917 (9)

take on supplies 633 (5)

take on trust 485 (7), 487 (3)

take one back 505 (9)

take one to court 959 (7)

take one's all 786 (11)

take one's bearings 281 (4)

take one's breath away 821 (8)

take one's chance 678 (11)

take one's ease 681 (3), 683 (3)

take one's fancy 826 (4), 887 (15)

take one's fences 312 (4)

take one's leave 296 (4)

take one's oath 466 (7), 532 (6)

take one's part 703 (6)

take one's place 60 (4), 187 (8)

take one's revenge 898 (8), 906 (3), 910 (5)

take one's stand 187 (8)

take one's time 136 (4), 136 (5), 278 (4), 681 (3), 858 (3)

take one's wicket 300 (7)

take one's word 764 (5)

take oneself off 267 (11)

take oneself too seriously 834 (10)

take orders 895 (5), 979 (10), 985 (8), 986 (13)

take out 304 (4), 550 (3), 837 (20), 889 (7)

take over 65 (3), 733 (11); 786 (6), 786 (7)

take-over bid 792 (1)

take pains 455 (4), 457 (5), 678 (11)

take part 189 (4), 706 (4)

take pity on 905 (6)

take place 1 (6), 154 (6)

take pleasure in 376 (6), 824 (6), 887 (13)

take poison 362 (13)

take possession of 773 (4), 786 (7)

take precautions 457 (5), 510 (3), 660 (9), 669 (10), 858 (3) take precedence 34 (9), 64 (3)

take precedence over 283 (3)

take pride in 871 (6)

take prisoner 747 (8)

take refuge 660 (9), 662 (4)

take reprisals 714 (3)

take risks 618 (8)

take roll call 86 (11)

take rooms 192 (21)

take root 153 (7), 178 (4), 187 (8), 610 (7)

take seriously 455 (4), 638 (8)

take shape 1 (7)

take ship 269 (9), 296 (6)

take sides 481 (12), 605 (6)

take silk 958 (7)

take snuff 388 (7)

take soundings 211 (3), 269 (10), 459 (13)

take steps 669 (10), 676 (5)

take stock 86 (11), 480 (6), 808 (5)

take stock of 438 (9), 449 (8)

take the air 267 (14), 340 (6)

take the auspices 511 (9)

take the blame 924 (14)

take the chair 689 (5)

take the consequences 963 (13)

take the count 728 (9)

take the field 718 (11)

take the first step 68 (9)

take the floor 579 (9)

take the initiative 68 (9)

take the lead 34 (9), 64 (3), 68 (9), 237 (5), 283 (3), 638 (7)

take the liberty 756 (5)

take the mean 30 (5)

take the offensive 712 (7)

take the opportunity 137 (7)

take the part 594 (17)

take the place of 150 (5)

take the plunge 68 (9), 599 (3), 605 (6), 855 (6)

take the service 988 (10)

take the shape of 147 (6)

take the stand 466 (7)

take the sting out of 177 (7)

take the strain 635 (6)

take the veil 883 (8), 895 (5)

take things as they come 823 (5)

take time 108 (7)

take to 610 (8), 880 (8), 887 (14)

take to flight 620 (6), 728 (9)

take to heart 818 (7), 829 (5), 834 (9), 891 (5)

take to pieces 46 (10), 51 (5), 641 (7)

take umbrage 891 (5)

take up 310 (4), 536 (5), 610 (7), 622 (7), 672 (3), 673 (4), 782 (7), 786 (6), 880 (8)

take up residence 192 (21)

take up space 189 (4)

take up time 108 (7)

take upon oneself 672 (3)

take vengeance 910 (5)

take vows 979 (10), 986 (13)

take wing 271 (7), 296 (5)

taken 512 (5)

taken aback 508 (3)

taken aback, be 508 (4)

taken by surprise 508 (3)

taken by surprise, be 508 (4)

taken ill 651 (21)

taken in 544 (2)

taken in, be 544 (3)

taken off 679 (7)

taken off guard 670 (3)

taken prisoner 745 (4)

taken short, be 302 (6)

taken with 887 (10)

taken with, be 887 (14)

takeoff 271 (2), 296 (1), 308 (1)

takeover 272 (1), 786 (2), 792 (1)

takeover bid 759 (1)

taker 776 (1), 782 (2), 786 (4), 789 (1)

taking 39 (1), 46 (2), 740 (1), 771 (1), 773 (1), 786 (1), 786 (5), 788 (1), 963 (6)

taking a chance 618 (2)

taking away 46 (2), 188 (1), 786 (1)

taking back 786 (1)

taking by storm 727 (2)

taking care 457 (3)

taking counsel 691 (1)

taking exercise 682 (4)

taking food 301 (1)

taking hold 786 (1)

taking it that 8 (6)

taking life 362 (1)

taking no risks 858 (2)

taking off 308 (1), 594 (8)

taking one thing with another 30 (6)

taking one's time 278 (3)

taking pains 682 (1)

taking pride in 871 (4)

taking the waters 339 (1)

takings 36 (2), 771 (2), 782 (1), 786 (1), 807 (1)

talcum powder 843 (3)

tale 543 (3), 590 (2), 590 (4)

tale-bearing 526 (3)

tale of woe 836 (2)

talebearer 524 (5)

talent 498 (1), 694 (2)

talent scout 459 (9), 484 (2)

talented 498 (4), 694 (5)

talisman 511 (3), 666 (2), 844 (7), 983 (3)

talismanic 983 (8)

talk 524 (9), 526 (6), 529 (2), 534 (4), 557 (1), 579 (1), 579 (2), 579 (8), 581 (5), 584 (1), 584 (2)

talk about 926 (7)

talk at length 581 (5)

talk at random 477 (7)

talk big 546 (3), 850 (5), 877 (5), 878 (6), 900 (3)

talk down 581 (5)

talk for effect 873 (5), 875 (7)

talk gibberish 497 (4), 515 (6), 517 (6)

tartan 437 (2), 437 (5), 547 (10)

tartar 649 (2)

tarted up 844 (11)

tartness 393 (1), 885 (2), 892 (1)

tarty 951 (7)

task 622 (3), 672 (1), 673 (3), 676 (2), 682 (3), 684 (6), 700 (2), 735 (8), 751 (2), 917 (1), 963 (4)

task force 722 (7)

taskmaster 735 (4)

tassel 217 (2), 844 (5)

taste 43 (2), 301 (35), 374 (2), 374 (5), 386 (1), 386 (3), 390 (3), 459 (13), 461 (7), 575 (1), 605 (1), 818 (7), 824 (6), 846 (1), 859 (3)

taste good 386 (3), 390 (3)

taste horrid 391 (3)

taste of 386 (3)

tasteful 24 (5), 575 (3), 841 (3), 841 (6), 846 (3), 848 (5), 950 (5)

tastefully 846 (5)

tastefulness 846 (1)

tasteless 163 (4), 387 (2), 391 (2), 572 (2), 576 (2), 838 (3), 840 (2), 847 (4)

tastiness 390 (1), 826 (1)

tasting 301 (1), 301 (25), 386 (1)

tasty 301 (32), 376 (3), 386 (2), 390 (2), 826 (2)

tattered 801 (4)

tatters 53 (5), 228 (2)

tatting 222 (3), 844 (4)

tattler 529 (4)

tattoo 263 (18), 403 (1), 403 (3), 425 (8), 547 (8), 547 (19), 665 (1), 841 (8), 875 (3), 876 (1), 889 (3)

tattooer 843 (5)

tattooing 844 (2)

tatty 655 (6)

taught 485 (6), 490 (6)

taunt 878 (2), 878 (6), 891 (9), 921 (2), 921 (5), 924 (3), 926 (2), 928 (1), 928 (8)

Taurus 321 (5)

taut 45 (8), 326 (4)

tautological 106 (3), 570 (5)

tautologous 13 (2), 514 (4), 570 (5)

tautology 13 (1), 106 (1), 570 (2)

tavern 192 (12)

tawdry 639 (6), 847 (4)

tawny 430 (3), 433 (3)

tawse 964 (1)

tax 42 (1), 57 (1), 673 (3), 684 (6), 735 (8), 737 (3), 737 (8), 761 (5), 786 (1), 786 (8), 804 (1), 806 (1), 807 (1), 809 (3), 809 (7)

tax avoidance 805 (1)

tax demand 809 (3)

tax dodger 805 (3)

tax evader 620 (2)

tax evasion 788 (4), 805 (1)

tax-free 812 (4)

taxable 809 (4)

taxation 786 (1), 809 (3)

taxed 809 (4)

taxi 265 (4), 271 (7), 274 (9)

taxi driver 268 (5)

taxicab 274 (9)

taxidermy 367 (1), 666 (1)

taxonomic 77 (5)

taxonomy 62 (1), 77 (1), 368 (1)

tea 301 (12), 301 (27)

tea chest 194 (7)

tea estate 370 (2)

tea leaves 511 (4)

tea party 882 (3)

tea planter 370 (4)

tea service 194 (15)

tea set 194 (15)

tea urn 194 (14)

teach 147 (7), 369 (8), 475 (11), 480 (5), 485 (9), 522 (8), 524 (9), 528 (9), 534 (6), 534 (7), 579 (9), 610 (8), 834 (12)

teach-in 534 (1), 584 (3)

teach manners 654 (9)

teacher 492 (1), 500 (1), 520 (4), 534 (4), 537 (1), 691 (2), 696 (2)

teacher, be a 534 (7)

teacher's pet 890 (2)

teaching 147 (1), 443 (1), 475 (4), 490 (3), 519 (1), 524 (1), 534 (1), 538 (4), 610 (3), 669 (1), 718 (4), 973 (4), 985 (2)

teaching staff 537 (1)

teahouse 192 (13)

teak 326 (1), 366 (4)

team 74 (3), 74 (4), 708 (1)

team-mate 707 (2)

team race 706 (1), 716 (3)

team spirit 706 (1), 882 (1)

team up 706 (4)

team up with 50 (4)

team work 706 (1)

teamster 268 (5)

teapot 194 (14)

tear 46 (12), 176 (7), 176 (8), 201 (2), 277 (6), 301 (36), 655 (10)

tear along 277 (6)

tear down 165 (7), 311 (6)

tear gas 659 (3)

tear-jerking 827 (6), 836 (4)

tear off 229 (6)

tear one's hair 836 (5)

tear oneself away 296 (4)

tear open 263 (17)

tear out 304 (4)

tear to bits 165 (7)

tear to pieces or to shreds 46 (12)

tear up 165 (6), 165 (7), 752 (4)

teardrop 341 (1)

tearful 825 (6), 834 (6), 836 (4), 949 (7)

tearfully 836 (7)

tearfulness 836 (1)

tearing 46 (3)

tearing down 165 (1)

tearing one's hair 836 (1)

tearing out 304 (1)

tearoom 192 (13)

tears 339 (1), 341 (1), 836 (1)

tears of grief 836 (2)

tears of rage 836 (2)

tease 612 (11), 821 (6), 826 (4), 827 (9), 839 (5), 851

tempestuous 61 (9), 176 (5), 352 (8), 822 (3)

template 23 (1)

temple 164 (3), 662 (1), 990 (1), 990 (3)

temples 213 (3), 239 (1)

tempo 265 (1), 277 (1), 410 (4)

temporal 108 (4), 114 (3), 117 (6), 987 (2)

temporarily 114 (7)

temporariness 114 (1)

temporary 8 (3), 35 (4), 114 (4), 150 (4), 474 (4)

temporary abode 192 (1)

temporary expedient 150 (2)

temporary funds 797 (2)

temporary job 622 (3)

temporary lease 774 (1)

temporize 113 (8), 136 (7), 698 (5)

temporizing 698 (4)

tempt 178 (3), 291 (4), 456 (8), 542 (10), 612 (11), 859 (13), 887 (15), 934 (8)

tempt Providence 618 (8), 661 (8), 857 (4)

temptation 156 (1), 291 (1), 612 (2), 761 (1), 859 (3), 859 (5)

tempted 859 (7)

tempter 612 (5)

tempting 178 (2), 386 (2), 390 (2), 612 (6)

tempting offer 612 (4)

temptress 291 (1), 612 (5), 952 (2)

ten 99 (2)

Ten Commandments 99 (2), 975 (1)

ten million 99 (5)

ten p 797 (4)

ten thousand 99 (5)

ten to one 471 (7)

tenable 475 (7), 485 (5)

tenacious 48 (2), 599 (2), 600 (3), 602 (4), 778 (3)

tenacious of life 360 (2)

tenaciousness 778 (1)

tenacity 329 (1), 599 (1), 600 (1), 778 (1), 855 (1)

tenancy 773 (1), 774 (1)

tenant 191 (2), 192 (21), 776 (1)

tenant farmer 370 (4)

tenanted 191 (7)

tenantry 191 (5), 776 (1)

tend 156 (10), 179 (3), 281 (6), 289 (4), 369 (10), 457 (6), 471 (4), 605 (6), 640 (4), 658 (20), 666 (5), 742 (8), 859 (11)

tend to 156 (10)

tendency 5 (4), 7 (2), 179 (1), 180 (1), 281 (1), 471 (1), 481 (5), 597 (1), 605 (1), 694 (2), 817 (1), 859 (3)

tender 274 (14), 275 (1), 275 (7), 327 (2), 374 (3), 377 (3), 425 (7), 457 (3), 651 (22), 736 (2), 759 (1), 759 (3), 819 (2), 819 (3), 827 (3), 887 (9), 897 (4), 905 (4)

tender age 130 (1), 130 (2)

tender conscience 917 (2)

tender feelings 818 (1)

tender heart 905 (1)

tender-hearted 905 (4)

tender mercies 735 (1)

tender one's resignation 753 (3)

tender passion 887 (1)

tender spot 661 (2)

tenderfoot 538 (2)

tenderhearted 818 (3)

tenderize 327 (4)

tenderly 887 (16)

tenderness 374 (1), 377 (1), 819 (1), 827 (1), 887 (1)

tending 71 (4), 179 (2), 180 (2), 469 (2)

tendon 47 (4)

tendril 47 (4), 53 (4), 208 (1), 251 (2), 366 (5), 778 (2)

tenements 192 (8), 192 (9)

tenet 973 (4)

tenets 485 (2)

tenfold 99 (6)

tenner 99 (2)

tennis 837 (7)

tennis elbow 651 (15)

tenon 254 (2)

tenor 7 (2), 179 (1), 281 (1), 407 (1), 413 (4), 514 (1)

tenor bell 412 (2)

tenor clef 410 (3)

tense 45 (8), 326 (4), 507 (2), 564 (1), 821 (3), 822 (3), 854 (7)

tensile 328 (2), 328 (3)

tension 160 (3), 203 (2), 709 (1), 821 (1), 825 (3), 829 (1)

tent 192 (3), 192 (7), 192 (16), 226 (3)

tentacle 378 (3), 778 (2)

tentacular 378 (5)

tentative 278 (3), 459 (11), 461 (6), 491 (4), 671 (3), 695 (5), 858 (2)

tentative, be 278 (4), 378 (7), 439 (3), 457 (5), 459 (13), 459 (15), 461 (8), 474 (8), 671 (4), 695 (9), 700 (7), 766 (4), 858 (3)

tenth 100 (2)

tenuity 4 (1), 206 (2), 325 (1)

tenuous 4 (3), 163 (8), 325 (2)

tenure 773 (1), 777 (3), 985 (3)

tepee 192 (3), 226 (3)

tepid 379 (6)

tepidity 379 (1)

tercentenary 94 (1), 141 (3)

tergiversate 152 (5), 526 (6), 603 (5), 769 (3), 879 (4), 918 (3)

tergiversating 152 (3), 603 (4), 930 (7)

tergiversation 143 (1), 148 (1), 603 (1), 657 (1)

tergiversator 147 (4), 486 (3), 545 (1), 601 (2), 603 (3), 888 (3), 918 (1), 978 (5)

term 69 (1), 73 (1), 108 (1), 108 (3), 110 (1), 559 (1), 561 (6)

termagant 176 (4), 892 (2)

terminal 69 (2), 69 (4), 145 (5), 199 (3), 236 (1), 236 (2)
terminal disease 651 (2)
terminal point 69 (2)
terminate 54 (6), 69 (6), 117 (7), 145 (6), 165 (6), 725 (5)
terminated 69 (4)
termination 69 (1), 725 (1)
terminological 561 (5)
terminologist 561 (3)
terminology 559 (3), 561 (1)
terminus 69 (2), 145 (5), 236 (1), 267 (8), 295 (2)
termite 365 (16)
terms 766 (1)
terms of reference 751 (2), 766 (1)
Terpsichorean 594 (15)
terra firma 218 (1), 344 (1)
terrace 192 (8), 216 (1)
terraced house 192 (6)
terraces 441 (2)
terracotta 381 (5)
terrain 184 (1), 344 (1)
terrapin 365 (13)
terrestrial 191 (3), 191 (6), 321 (15)
terrible 645 (4), 854 (8)
terribly 32 (18)
terrier 365 (10)
terrific 32 (7), 644 (4)
terrify 854 (12)
terrifyingly 32 (20)
territorial 184 (5), 344 (5), 722 (4)
territorial waters 184 (2)
territory 184 (2), 235 (1), 271 (2), 344 (1), 733 (6), 777 (3)
terror 176 (4), 854 (1), 854 (4), 904 (2), 920 (1), 938 (4)
terror-crazed 854 (6)
terror tactics 712 (2)
terrorism 176 (1), 738 (2), 738 (3), 854 (4)
terrorist 176 (4), 362 (7), 705 (1), 712 (5), 738 (4), 854 (5), 904 (1)

terrorization 854 (4)
terrorize 735 (8), 854 (12)
terrorized 854 (6)
terry towelling 222 (4)
terse 204 (3), 496 (3), 569 (2)
terseness 569 (1)
tertiary 94 (2)
test 453 (4), 459 (1), 459 (4), 459 (13), 461 (1), 461 (7), 671 (4), 700 (2)
test case 23 (1), 461 (1), 959 (1)
test driver 461 (3)
test flight 461 (1)
test match 716 (2)
test of endurance 716 (2)
test pilot 459 (9), 461 (3)
test tube 147 (3)
test-tube baby 167 (1)
testable 461 (6)
testament 466 (2), 767 (2)
tested 473 (4), 923 (7), 929 (4)
testee 461 (5)
tester 459 (9), 461 (3), 671 (2)
testicles 167 (3)
testified 466 (5)
testifier 466 (4), 524 (4)
testify 466 (7), 532 (5), 532 (6), 547 (18), 764 (5)
testimonial 466 (3), 505 (3), 923 (1)
testimony 466 (2), 473 (1), 532 (1), 532 (2), 959 (3)
testiness 892 (1)
testing 459 (11), 671 (3)
testing agent 461 (4)
testy 829 (3), 885 (5), 892 (3)
tetanus 651 (5)
tête-à-tête 90 (2), 200 (7), 584 (1), 584 (2)
tether 45 (11), 47 (8), 187 (5), 702 (2), 747 (9), 748 (4)
tetra 96 (2)
text 23 (1), 53 (1), 452 (1), 496 (1), 589 (2)
textbook 534 (3), 589 (3)

textile 53 (5), 164 (2), 208 (2), 222 (4), 259 (1), 331 (2), 331 (4), 631 (1)
textural 163 (8), 331 (4)
texture 222 (5), 331 (2), 844 (3)
thank 835 (6), 866 (13), 907 (5), 915 (8), 923 (9), 962 (3), 981 (11)
thank Heaven 886 (3)
thank offering 781 (3), 907 (2), 981 (6)
thank you 907 (2), 907 (7)
thank you for nothing 908 (5)
thankful 828 (2), 907 (3)
thankful, be 828 (4)
thankfulness 907 (1)
thanking 907 (3)
thankless 641 (5), 827 (4), 908 (3)
thankless task 700 (2), 908 (1)
thanks 835 (1), 876 (1), 886 (1), 907 (2), 907 (7), 915 (1), 923 (2), 962 (1), 981 (3), 981 (4)
thanks to 158 (5), 628 (5), 703 (8)
thanksgiving 835 (1), 876 (1), 907 (2), 981 (3)
that is 520 (11)
thatch 226 (2), 226 (15), 259 (2), 631 (2)
thatched 192 (20)
that's why 158 (5)
thaumaturgy 864 (2)
thaw 49 (4), 327 (4), 337 (4), 379 (7), 381 (8), 905 (6), 905 (8)
thaw out 381 (8)
thawing 354 (4)
theatre 184 (1), 594 (7), 724 (1), 837 (5)
theatre of war 718 (7), 724 (2)
theatre, the 594 (1)
theatregoer 441 (1), 594 (14)
theatrical 594 (15), 850 (4), 875 (5)
theatricality 594 (2), 594 (8), 850 (1), 875 (1)

theatricals 594 (1), 594 (2)
theft 771 (1), 788 (1)
theism 973 (2)
theist 973 (7)
theistic 973 (8)
'them' 741 (1)
theme 410 (1), 412 (4), 452 (1), 591 (1)
theme song 412 (3)
themselves 80 (4)
then 122 (3)
theocracy 733 (4), 985 (1)
theocratic 965 (5)
theodolite 247 (3), 465 (5)
theologian 475 (6), 973 (5), 976 (7)
theological 973 (9)
theology 485 (2), 973 (4)
theopany 975 (1)
theophany 965 (4)
theorem 452 (1), 475 (3), 496 (2)
theoretical 447 (5), 451 (2), 512 (4)
theoretician 512 (3)
theorist 512 (3)
theorize 158 (4), 449 (8), 512 (6)
theorizer 512 (3)
theory 158 (1), 451 (1), 485 (3), 512 (1)
theosophical 984 (6)
theosophist 984 (4)
theosophy 449 (3), 973 (1), 984 (1)
therapeutic 658 (17)
therapeutics 658 (12)
therapy 74 (2), 301 (3), 339 (1), 447 (3), 551 (1), 651 (19), 652 (2), 658 (12), 691 (1)
there 186 (5), 189 (6)
there and back 148 (1)
thereabouts 33 (12), 200 (8)
thereafter 120 (4)
therefore 158 (5)
thereupon 120 (4)
therm 379 (3)
thermal 308 (1), 352 (1), 379 (6)
thermal springs 379 (1)
thermal unit 379 (3)

thermodynamics 379 (3)
thermometer 379 (3), 465 (6)
thermometry 379 (3)
thermonuclear 160 (9)
thermoplastic 327 (3)
thermostat 379 (3)
thesaurus 87 (2), 559 (2), 632 (3)
these days 121 (1)
thesis 452 (1), 475 (3), 475 (4), 512 (1), 532 (1), 591 (1)
Thespian 594 (9), 594 (15)
'they' 733 (1)
thick 70 (1), 195 (8), 204 (3), 205 (4), 205 (5), 208 (4), 324 (4), 354 (4), 580 (2)
thick and fast 139 (4)
thick as flies 74 (9), 104 (5)
thick-growing 324 (4)
thick head 949 (2)
thick-lipped 205 (4)
thick-necked 205 (4)
thick of things 70 (1), 678 (1)
thick on the ground 139 (2)
thick-ribbed 162 (6), 205 (4)
thick skin 820 (1)
thick-skinned 205 (4), 375 (4), 820 (5)
thick speech 578 (1), 580 (1)
thick-witted 499 (3)
thicken 36 (4), 36 (5), 197 (5), 205 (5), 324 (6), 354 (6)
thickener 354 (2)
thickening 324 (2), 354 (2)
thicket 104 (1), 324 (3), 366 (2)
thickhead 501 (3)
thickness 205 (2), 207 (1), 324 (1), 354 (1), 465 (3)
thickset 162 (8), 205 (4), 324 (4)
thief 297 (3), 789 (1), 904 (3), 938 (2)
thieve 788 (7)

thievery 788 (1), 788 (5)
thieving 786 (5), 788 (1), 788 (6)
thievish 788 (6)
thievishness 788 (5)
thigh 267 (7)
thimbleful 26 (2), 33 (2)
thin 4 (3), 37 (4), 105 (2), 105 (4), 196 (10), 206 (4), 206 (5), 206 (6), 212 (2), 325 (2), 325 (3), 422 (2), 572 (2), 636 (3), 636 (5), 946 (3)
thin air 4 (2), 340 (1), 446 (1)
thin as a rake 206 (5)
thin coat 212 (1)
thin excuse 614 (1)
thin on the ground 105 (2)
thin on top 229 (5)
thin out 37 (4), 37 (5), 75 (4), 304 (1)
thin skin 819 (1)
thin-skinned 819 (3)
thing 3 (2), 319 (3)
thing acquired 771 (1)
thing chosen 605 (1)
thing extracted 304 (1)
thing inserted 303 (1)
thing of beauty 841 (2)
thing of the past 127 (2)
thing said 579 (1)
thing taken 786 (1)
thing transferred 272 (3)
thingamajig 630 (1)
things 777 (1)
things for sale 795 (1)
think 447 (7), 449 (7), 455 (4), 475 (10), 485 (8), 512 (6), 513 (7), 834 (9)
think about 449 (7), 449 (8)
think again 603 (5)
think ahead 623 (8)
think alike 706 (4)
think aloud 585 (4)
think back upon 505 (8)
think best 595 (2)
think better of 449 (8), 603 (5)
think better of it 854 (11)
think desirable 923 (8)
think hard 449 (7)

think highly of **923** (8)

think likely **471** (6), **507** (4)

think of **68** (9), **505** (7), **513** (7)

think of others **931** (3)

think out **449** (7)

think over **449** (8)

think tank **692** (1)

think through **449** (7)

think too much of **482** (4)

think too much of oneself **873** (5)

think twice **457** (5), **858** (3)

think up **164** (7), **449** (7), **513** (7), **623** (8)

think well of **920** (5), **923** (8)

thinker **449** (4), **459** (9), **500** (1), **512** (3)

thinking **447** (5), **449** (1), **498** (5)

thinking alike **488** (2)

thinking aloud **585** (3)

thinking of, be **455** (5)

thinking out **449** (2)

thinking power **498** (1)

thinly spread **212** (2)

thinness **33** (1), **105** (1), **196** (1), **206** (2), **301** (3), **323** (1), **325** (1), **572** (1)

third **65** (2), **94** (2), **95** (1)

third degree **459** (2), **963** (2)

third estate **869** (1)

third force **177** (2)

third part **95** (1)

third power **93** (2)

third-rate **35** (4), **639** (6)

Third World **184** (1), **733** (6)

thirdly **94** (4)

thirst **342** (1), **379** (7), **786** (3), **859** (2), **859** (12)

thirst for **859** (11)

thirst for blood **898** (8)

thirst for knowledge **453** (1)

thirst-quenching **685** (2)

thirstily **859** (14)

thirstiness **859** (2)

thirsty **342** (4), **379** (4), **859** (9)

thirteen **99** (2)

this date **121** (1)

this day and age **121** (1)

this instant **121** (1)

this life **1** (1)

this way **289** (5)

thistle **256** (3), **366** (6), **547** (11)

thistledown **323** (1)

thither **281** (8)

tholepin **218** (11)

thong **47** (4)

thorax **253** (3)

thorn **256** (3), **366** (5), **825** (1)

thorn in the flesh **659** (1)

thorniness **256** (1)

thorny **256** (7), **700** (4)

thorough **32** (13), **54** (3), **457** (3), **599** (2), **682** (4)

thorough, be **174** (7)

thoroughbred **44** (5), **273** (5), **369** (7), **848** (6), **868** (4)

thoroughfare **263** (7), **305** (2), **624** (6)

thoroughgoing **32** (13), **54** (3), **149** (3)

thoroughly **32** (17), **54** (8)

thoroughness **457** (1), **725** (1)

though **31** (7), **468** (4)

thought **164** (1), **447** (1), **449** (1), **451** (1), **455** (1), **513** (2), **825** (3)

thought, a **451** (1)

thought about **452** (2)

thought of **164** (6)

thought-provoking **452** (2), **512** (4)

thought reader **984** (5)

thought-reading **984** (2)

thought well of **923** (7)

thoughtful **449** (5), **451** (2), **455** (2), **457** (3), **498** (5), **834** (6), **931** (2)

thoughtfulness **449** (2)

thoughtless **450** (2), **456** (3), **458** (2), **499** (5)

thoughtlessness **456** (1)

thoughts **449** (1)

thousand **99** (5)

thousand and one, a **104** (4)

thousand million **99** (5)

thousandth **99** (6)

thraldom **745** (3)

thrash **279** (9), **727** (10), **963** (10)

thrashed **728** (5)

thrashing **279** (2), **728** (2), **963** (2)

thrashing about **176** (5)

thread **33** (3), **47** (4), **71** (2), **71** (6), **206** (2), **208** (2)

thread-like **206** (4)

thread one's way **267** (11)

thread through **305** (5)

thread together **45** (10), **62** (4)

threadbare **229** (5), **673** (2), **801** (4)

threadlike **208** (4)

threat **155** (1), **236** (1), **612** (4), **661** (1), **664** (1), **711** (1), **731** (1), **737** (3), **740** (1), **761** (1), **766** (1), **854** (4), **878** (1), **900** (1)

threaten **124** (5), **155** (3), **511** (8), **613** (3), **617** (5), **661** (9), **664** (5), **711** (3), **737** (8), **740** (3), **761** (5), **854** (12), **900** (3)

threaten danger **661** (9)

threaten reprisals **900** (3)

threaten to **617** (5)

threatening **124** (4), **155** (2), **176** (6), **661** (3), **664** (3), **853** (3), **854** (8), **900** (2)

threateningly **900** (4)

three **93** (2), **93** (3)

three by three **93** (4)

three-card trick **542** (3)

three cheers **835** (1), **835** (9), **923** (3), **923** (14)

three-cornered **93** (3)

three-decker **93** (2)

three-dimensional **183** (5), **243** (3)

three-hander **93** (2)

three in one **93** (3)

three-line whip **737** (1)

three-monthly **93** (3)

three-ply 94 (2)
three-pointed 93 (3)
three-pronged 93 (3)
three Rs, the 534 (3)
three score 99 (3)
three-sided 93 (3)
three times 94 (4)
three times three 99 (2)
three-wheeler 93 (2), 274 (11)
threefold 94 (2), 94 (4)
threnody 412 (5)
thresh 279 (9), 370 (9)
thresh about 318 (5)
threshold 68 (5), 234 (2), 236 (1), 263 (6)
thrice 94 (4)
thrift 771 (3), 814 (1)
thriftiness 814 (1)
thriftless 815 (3), 857 (3)
thrifty 457 (3), 814 (2), 814 (3)
thrill 318 (5), 376 (1), 377 (2), 378 (8), 818 (1), 818 (8), 821 (1), 821 (6), 822 (2), 824 (1), 826 (4)
thrill-loving 822 (3)
thrill-seeker 944 (2)
thrill to 376 (6), 821 (9)
thriller 445 (4), 590 (4)
thrilling 818 (6), 821 (4), 826 (2)
thrive 36 (4), 174 (7), 615 (5), 650 (3), 678 (11), 730 (6)
thriving 174 (5), 730 (4)
throat 263 (4), 353 (1)
throaty 407 (3)
throb 141 (1), 141 (6), 317 (1), 317 (4), 318 (2), 318 (5), 377 (5), 818 (8)
throbbing 141 (4), 317 (1), 377 (3), 818 (1), 818 (3), 818 (5), 827 (3)
throe 318 (2)
throes 377 (2)
thrombosis 324 (2), 651 (9)
throne 218 (6), 743 (1), 956 (1)
throng 74 (5), 74 (10), 104 (1), 104 (6)
throng in 297 (7)
thronged 104 (5)

thronged 104 (5)
throttle 161 (9), 264 (6), 778 (5)
throttle down 278 (6)
throttling 778 (3)
through 121 (5), 281 (8), 624 (8), 628 (5), 629 (3)
through and through 54 (8)
through road 624 (6)
through the post 588 (5)
through thick and thin 600 (5)
through train 274 (13)
throughout 54 (9), 183 (8)
throughput 86 (5), 164 (1), 272 (1)
throw 243 (5), 265 (5), 279 (1), 279 (7), 287 (1), 287 (7), 618 (2), 618 (8)
throw a fit 318 (5)
throw a lifeline 668 (3)
throw a stone 712 (12)
throw a tantrum 891 (6)
throw aside 607 (3)
throw away 300 (6), 594 (17), 607 (3), 634 (4), 674 (5), 772 (4)
throw cold water on 834 (12)
throw down 165 (7), 311 (5), 311 (6)
throw down one's arms 721 (3)
throw down the gauntlet 711 (3)
throw fits 822 (4)
throw in 231 (8), 287 (1)
throw in the towel 721 (3)
throw into confusion 63 (3)
throw into prison 747 (10)
throw into relief 522 (7)
throw light on 417 (13), 520 (8)
throw off balance 29 (3)
throw off one's bearings 63 (3)
throw off the scent 456 (8)
throw one's weight about 174 (7)

throw open 263 (17), 522 (7)
throw out 300 (6), 607 (3), 641 (3)
throw over 542 (9), 603 (5), 621 (3)
throw overboard 779 (4)
throw things 924 (9)
throw up 300 (6), 300 (10), 310 (4)
throwaway 114 (4), 634 (2)
throwaway line 839 (2)
throwback 106 (2), 148 (1), 655 (1)
thrower 287 (5), 837 (16)
throwing 243 (2), 287 (1)
throwing out 300 (1)
thrown 243 (3), 728 (6)
thrown, be 309 (4)
thrum 234 (3), 403 (3), 404 (3), 413 (9)
thrumming 412 (1)
thrush 365 (4), 651 (12), 651 (17)
thrust 160 (3), 174 (1), 246 (1), 277 (2), 279 (1), 279 (7), 287 (3), 532 (1), 712 (1), 712 (4), 712 (7)
thrust at 712 (9)
thrust down 311 (4)
thrust into 303 (4)
thrust out 57 (5)
thruster 678 (5)
thrusting 174 (5), 279 (6)
thud 401 (1), 405 (1), 405 (3)
thug 176 (4), 789 (2), 904 (2), 938 (1)
thumb 378 (4), 378 (7), 536 (5), 547 (21), 547 (22)
thumb a lift 267 (15), 761 (6)
thumbnail 33 (6)
thumbnail sketch 196 (3), 590 (1), 592 (1)
thumbs down 757 (1), 760 (1)
thumbs up 923 (1)
thumbscrew 198 (3), 963 (11)
thump 279 (2), 279 (9), 405 (1), 405 (3)
thumping 32 (9)

thunder 176 (3), 400 (4), 532 (7), 891 (7), 900 (3), 924 (10)
thunder against 899 (6)
thunderandlightning176 (3)
thunderclap 400 (1), 402 (1)
thunderer 176 (4)
thundering 32 (9), 400 (3)
thunderous 400 (3), 923 (5)
thunderstorm 350 (6), 352 (4)
thunderstruck 508 (3), 864 (4)
thus 8 (4), 158 (5)
thus far 236 (4)
thwack 279 (2), 279 (9)
thwart 145 (7), 509 (5), 533 (3), 702 (10), 704 (4), 827 (10)
thwarted 161 (7), 509 (2), 728 (5)
thwarting 702 (1), 704 (3)
thyme 301 (21)
tiara 228 (23), 844 (7)
tic 318 (2), 547 (4), 651 (16)
tick 116 (2), 141 (1), 317 (4), 365 (16), 401 (1), 403 (3), 547 (13), 547 (19)
tick off 86 (11), 547 (19), 548 (8), 924 (11)
tick over 173 (3)
tick-tock 403 (1)
ticker 117 (3)
ticket 297 (1), 547 (13), 547 (19), 605 (3), 623 (2), 756 (2)
ticket collector 268 (5)
ticket holder 297 (3)
tickle 378 (7), 378 (8), 826 (4), 837 (20), 849 (4), 889 (1)
tickle the palate 390 (3)
tickled 837 (19)
tickled pink 824 (4)
ticklish 374 (3), 661 (4), 700 (4)
tidal 141 (4), 350 (7)
tidal barrage 160 (4)
tidal wave 209 (6), 350 (5)

tiddly-wink 837 (15)
tiddly-winks 837 (8)
tide 36 (1), 108 (1), 141 (1), 285 (1), 343 (1), 350 (2)
tide of time 111 (1)
tide one over 703 (5)
tide over 136 (7)
tide-table 117 (4)
tidemark 236 (1), 465 (5), 547 (7), 548 (4)
tideway 350 (2), 351 (1)
tidiness 60 (1), 457 (1)
tidings 529 (1)
tidy 60 (2), 62 (4), 457 (3), 648 (7), 841 (6)
tidy sum 800 (1)
tidy up 62 (4), 654 (9)
tie 9 (8), 28 (5), 28 (9), 45 (12), 47 (1), 47 (4), 50 (4), 74 (11), 153 (8), 164 (7), 187 (5), 228 (22), 228 (32), 547 (10), 656 (12), 747 (7), 747 (9), 917 (1)
tie-beam 47 (1), 218 (9)
tie down 740 (3), 766 (3)
tie-dyeing 844 (2)
tie in with 9 (7)
tie-on label 547 (13)
tie one's hands 161 (9), 702 (8)
tie the knot 894 (10)
tie-up 9 (1), 45 (11), 269 (10), 295 (4), 706 (2), 747 (9)
tie up with 9 (8), 45 (10)
tied 28 (7), 45 (8), 61 (8), 153 (6), 747 (5), 778 (3), 894 (7)
tiepin 47 (5)
tier 71 (2), 77 (1), 207 (1)
tiff 891 (1)
tiger 176 (4), 365 (11), 437 (3)
tigerish 176 (6), 365 (18)
tight 24 (8), 45 (7), 45 (8), 45 (16), 54 (4), 197 (2), 206 (4), 264 (5), 269 (6), 275 (11), 326 (4), 660 (5), 747 (4), 747 (5), 778 (3), 949 (7)
tight corner 700 (3)
tight-curled 259 (5)

tight-drawn 206 (4)
tight-fisted 778 (3), 816 (4)
tight-fitting 24 (8)
tight grasp 735 (1)
tight-lipped 525 (6), 582 (2)
tight squeeze 206 (1)
tighten 45 (13), 198 (7), 218 (15), 264 (6), 747 (7)
tighten one's belt 814 (3), 946 (4)
tighten one's grip 778 (5)
tightener 198 (3)
tightening 45 (2)
tightfistedness 816 (1)
tightrope 206 (1)
tightrope walker 28 (3)
tights 228 (26)
tilde 547 (14)
tile 207 (2), 226 (15), 381 (5), 631 (2)
tiled 192 (20)
tiler 686 (3)
tiles 226 (2), 226 (7), 226 (9)
till 108 (10), 370 (9), 549 (3), 632 (2), 799 (1)
till all hours 136 (8)
till it hurts 32 (20)
till now 125 (13)
tiller 218 (3), 269 (4), 630 (1), 689 (2)
tilt 220 (1), 220 (5), 220 (6), 309 (1), 309 (4), 712 (1), 716 (2)
tilt at 712 (10), 924 (10)
tilt at windmills 641 (8)
tilt over 221 (4)
tilt with 716 (10)
tilted 220 (3)
tilting 309 (2), 716 (6)
timber 366 (2), 631 (1)
timber-framed 192 (20)
timber tree 366 (4)
timbered 366 (10)
timbering 164 (3)
timbre 577 (1)
time 69 (3), 108 (1), 108 (9), 110 (2), 111 (1), 117 (1), 117 (7), 410 (4), 465 (11), 747 (3)
time after time 106 (7)
time ahead 124 (1)

time and again 106 (7), 139 (4)

time and place 186 (1)

time being 121 (1)

time bomb 117 (3), 663 (1), 723 (14)

time-bound 114 (3)

time-chart 117 (4)

time-clock 117 (3)

time-consuming 634 (2)

time fuse 117 (3)

time-honoured 127 (6), 610 (5), 866 (8), 920 (4)

time immemorial 125 (2)

time it badly 138 (4)

time lag 72 (1), 278 (1)

time-lapse 278 (3)

time limit 236 (1), 766 (1)

time of day 108 (3), 110 (1), 117 (3)

time of life 131 (1)

time of night 117 (2)

time of war 718 (2)

time of year 110 (1)

time off 145 (4), 681 (1)

time-saving 814 (1), 814 (2)

time-server 879 (2), 932 (2)

time-serving 603 (4), 879 (1), 879 (3), 930 (5), 930 (7), 932 (3)

time-sharing 86 (5)

time signal 117 (3)

time switch 117 (3), 465 (6)

time to come 124 (1)

time to kill 681 (1), 838 (1)

time to spare 278 (1), 681 (1)

time up 69 (3), 110 (1), 136 (3)

time was 125 (12)

time without end 115 (5)

time-worn 127 (4)

timed 123 (3)

timekeeper 117 (3), 465 (6), 547 (6), 549 (3)

timekeeping 117 (1), 117 (6)

timeless 115 (2), 965 (6)

timelessness 115 (1), 965 (2)

timeliness 24 (3), 135 (2), 137 (1)

timely 24 (6), 135 (4), 137 (4), 642 (2)

timepiece 117 (3)

timer 117 (3)

times, the 8 (1), 121 (1)

timeserver 603 (3)

timetable 87 (3), 117 (4), 117 (7), 267 (8), 524 (6)

timetabling 117 (1)

timid 601 (3), 854 (7), 856 (3), 858 (2), 874 (2)

timidity 854 (2), 856 (1), 874 (1)

timing 117 (1), 141 (1), 410 (4), 463 (1)

timorous 856 (3)

timorousness 854 (2)

timpani 414 (9)

timpanist 413 (2)

tin 194 (8), 666 (5)

tin god 741 (2)

tin hat 228 (23)

tin opener 263 (11)

tincture 43 (2), 58 (1), 179 (1)

tine 256 (2)

tinge 33 (2), 43 (2), 43 (7), 425 (3)

tinged 425 (5)

tingle 374 (5), 378 (2), 378 (8), 818 (8), 819 (5), 821 (9)

tingle with 822 (4)

tingling 377 (3), 378 (2), 818 (3), 818 (6), 821 (3)

tinker 636 (7), 656 (5), 678 (13), 698 (5), 726 (3)

tinker with 542 (8)

tinkering 636 (1), 641 (2)

tinkle 401 (1), 401 (4), 404 (1)

tinkling 410 (6)

tinning 666 (1)

tinplate 207 (2)

tinsel 417 (2), 542 (5), 542 (7), 844 (6), 847 (1)

tint 425 (3), 425 (8), 553 (8)

tinted 425 (5)

tinting 553 (1), 843 (2)

tiny 33 (6), 196 (8), 196 (12)

tiny tot 132 (1)

tip 40 (2), 64 (4), 69 (2), 213 (2), 213 (5), 220 (1), 220 (5), 220 (6), 226 (13), 234 (1), 524 (3), 612 (4), 691 (1), 781 (2), 781 (7), 804 (4), 907 (2), 907 (5), 962 (1), 962 (3)

tip-and-run raider 722 (4)

tip off 524 (11), 664 (1)

tip over 221 (5)

tip the scale 34 (8)

tip the scales 29 (3)

tip the scales at 322 (5)

tip-tilted 248 (3)

tip well 813 (4)

tipple 301 (28), 301 (38), 949 (14)

tippler 949 (5)

tippling 301 (31), 949 (11)

tipsily 220 (7)

tipsiness 949 (1)

tipstaff 741 (6), 955 (2)

tipster 524 (4), 618 (4)

tipsy 220 (3), 949 (7), 949 (14)

tiptoe 267 (14), 525 (9)

tirade 546 (1), 570 (1), 579 (2)

tire 684 (6), 827 (10)

tire oneself out 684 (5)

tire out 684 (6), 838 (5)

tired 679 (9), 684 (2)

tired-looking 684 (2)

tired of 684 (2)

tired out 684 (2)

tired to death 684 (2)

tiredness 679 (3), 684 (1)

tireless 162 (7), 678 (9)

tirelessness 600 (1), 678 (3)

tiresome 684 (4), 827 (5), 838 (3)

tisane 658 (6)

tissue 52 (3), 222 (4), 331 (2), 360 (1)

tissue paper 424 (1), 631 (3)

tit 365 (4)

tit for tat 12 (1), 28 (4), 151 (1), 714 (1)

Titan 195 (4)
titanic 195 (7)
titbit 301 (11), 390 (1)
titbits 301 (9)
tithe 100 (2), 639 (2), 809 (3)
tithing 184 (3)
titillate 826 (4), 837 (20)
titillating 376 (3), 951 (6)
titivate 843 (7)
title 547 (13), 561 (2), 561 (6), 729 (2), 741 (1), 777 (2), 866 (4), 870 (1), 915 (1), 962 (1)
title deed 548 (1), 765 (1), 767 (2), 915 (1)
title-holder 696 (1), 915 (1)
title of honour 866 (4)
title page 68 (1)
title to fame 866 (1), 866 (3), 870 (1)
titled 561 (4), 866 (8), 868 (6)
titled person 868 (5)
titles 445 (3)
tits 253 (3)
titter 835 (2), 835 (7)
tittle-tattle 581 (2), 584 (2)
titular 561 (4)
TNT 723 (13)
to a certain extent 33 (10)
to a fault 32 (18)
to a man 79 (7), 488 (10)
to all appearances 445 (9)
to all intents and purposes 28 (11), 52 (9)
to and fro 141 (8), 151 (4), 317 (7)
to be 120 (2), 124 (4)
to be expected 471 (2)
to be sure 473 (10)
to bits 46 (15)
to blame 924 (8), 936 (3)
to blame, be 156 (9), 628 (4)
to capacity 54 (8)
to come 124 (4), 155 (2)
to come, be 124 (5), 155 (3)
to date 121 (5)
to death 838 (6)
to-do 61 (4), 678 (1)

to extremes 32 (18)
to general approval 923 (13)
to good effect 178 (5)
to infinity 107 (3), 115 (5)
to leeward 239 (4)
to let 759 (2)
to no avail 641 (9)
to no purpose 641 (9), 728 (10)
to oblige 897 (7)
to one's advantage 615 (6)
to one's cost 616 (3), 645 (8)
to one's credit 773 (3)
to one's credit, be 923 (11)
to one's discredit 934 (9)
to one's face 711 (4)
to one's heart's content 828 (6)
to one's liking 826 (2), 887 (11)
to one's name 773 (3)
to one's taste 390 (2), 826 (2)
to oneself 525 (10)
to order 80 (9), 739 (5)
to perfection 646 (6)
to pieces 46 (15)
to rule 60 (5), 81 (4), 83 (10)
to scale 9 (5), 9 (9)
to shreds 46 (15)
to some degree 33 (10)
to some extent 27 (6)
to spare 637 (4)
to tatters 46 (15)
to the amount of 26 (5)
to the bitter end 54 (9)
to the effect that 514 (6)
to the end 54 (8)
to the end of time 115 (5)
to the full 54 (8), 768 (5)
to the heart 819 (6)
to the limit 32 (18)
to the minute 135 (6), 137 (4)
to the outsider 223 (4)
to the point 9 (6), 24 (6), 475 (7), 569 (2)
to the purpose 9 (6), 24 (6), 642 (2)

to the quick 374 (7), 819 (6)
to the rear 238 (6)
to the tune of 26 (5), 809 (4)
to the utmost 54 (8)
to this day 121 (5)
to windward 239 (4)
to wit 80 (11), 520 (11)
toad 365 (12)
toadstool 366 (6)
toady 703 (7), 763 (2), 879 (2), 925 (2)
toady to 879 (4), 925 (4)
toadying 879 (3)
toadyism 879 (1)
toast 301 (22), 301 (26), 301 (38), 379 (7), 381 (8), 430 (4), 505 (9), 579 (2), 876 (5), 884 (6), 886 (1), 920 (6), 923 (10)
toasted 430 (3)
toaster 383 (2)
toasting 379 (4)
toastmaster 579 (5), 837 (17)
tobacco 353 (1), 388 (2), 659 (3), 949 (4)
tobacco pipe 388 (2)
tobacconist 388 (2)
toboggan 274 (2), 309 (3), 837 (21)
tobogganning 837 (6)
toby 194 (15)
toccata 412 (4)
tocsin 414 (8), 665 (1)
today 121 (1), 121 (4)
toddle 265 (4), 267 (14), 278 (4)
toddler 132 (1)
toe 214 (1), 214 (2)
toe dance 837 (14)
toe-hold 218 (1)
toe the line 83 (7), 488 (7), 739 (4)
toed 214 (4)
toehold 778 (1)
toff 848 (4)
toffee 48 (1), 301 (18), 430 (1)
toffee apple 301 (18)
toga 228 (7), 743 (2)

together 71 (7), 74 (11), 74 (12)

together with 38 (5), 89 (5)

togetherness 89 (1), 880 (1), 882 (1)

togged up 844 (11)

toil 278 (4), 682 (3), 682 (7)

toiler 686 (2)

toilet 228 (1), 649 (3), 843 (1)

toilet water 396 (2), 843 (3)

toiletries 843 (3)

toils 702 (4)

toilsome 682 (5), 700 (4)

token 4 (2), 4 (3), 522 (1), 547 (1), 547 (9), 547 (15), 639 (6), 767 (1), 781 (2)

token of gratitude 907 (2)

told 524 (8)

told, be 524 (12)

tolerable 644 (9), 647 (3), 732 (2), 828 (3)

tolerably 33 (9)

tolerance 236 (1), 498 (3), 823 (2)

tolerant 498 (5), 734 (3), 736 (2), 756 (3), 823 (4), 897 (4)

tolerant, be 823 (6)

tolerate 488 (7), 677 (3), 734 (5), 736 (3), 756 (5), 758 (3), 823 (6)

toleration 734 (1), 736 (1), 756 (1), 823 (2)

toll 42 (1), 403 (3), 413 (9), 665 (3), 782 (1), 809 (3)

toll road 624 (6)

tollgate 702 (2)

tom 365 (11)

tom cat 365 (11)

Tom, Dick and Harry 79 (2), 869 (1)

Tom Thumb 196 (4)

tomahawk 723 (7)

tomato 301 (20)

tomato sauce 389 (2)

tomb 164 (3), 194 (7), 255 (4), 361 (1), 364 (5), 548 (3)

tombola 618 (2), 837 (12)

tomboy 132 (2)

tomboyish 61 (9)

tombstone 364 (2)

tome 589 (1)

tomfoolery 497 (2)

tommy gun 723 (11)

tomorrow 124 (1), 124 (7)

tomtom 414 (9)

ton 322 (2)

tonal 410 (8), 557 (5), 577 (3)

tonality 410 (1), 410 (2), 417 (6)

tone 7 (2), 201 (1), 398 (1), 410 (1), 410 (2), 553 (1), 566 (1), 577 (1)

tone colour 410 (1)

tone-deaf 416 (2), 464 (3)

tone down 37 (4), 177 (6), 418 (6), 426 (5), 552 (3)

tone in with 24 (9)

tone of voice 577 (1), 688 (1)

tone row 410 (5)

tone up 162 (12)

tones 579 (1)

tongs 778 (2)

tongue 254 (2), 378 (3), 378 (7), 386 (1), 557 (1), 577 (1), 579 (1)

tongue in cheek 541 (2), 542 (11), 543 (2)

tongue-lash 924 (13)

tongue of flame 379 (2)

tongue of land 254 (2)

tongue-tied 578 (2), 580 (2), 582 (2)

tongue-wagging 581 (2)

tonic 174 (4), 174 (5), 301 (27), 410 (2), 652 (4), 658 (6), 658 (17), 821 (2), 833 (6)

tonic effect 174 (2)

tonic water 301 (27)

toning 425 (7)

tonnage 195 (1)

tonsilitis 651 (8)

tonsillectomy 658 (11)

tonsured 229 (5), 986 (12)

too 38 (5)

too bad 616 (2), 639 (8), 645 (2), 731 (4), 830 (3), 867 (5)

too big 195 (9)

too careful 816 (4)

too early 135 (4)

too familiar 490 (7)

too far 199 (8)

too few 105 (1), 105 (2), 636 (1)

too late 136 (3), 136 (8)

too little 636 (3)

too many 637 (3)

too many cooks 695 (2)

too much 32 (2), 637 (1), 637 (7), 838 (3)

too much for 470 (3)

too old 131 (6)

too small 636 (3)

too soon 135 (7)

too weak 163 (4)

tool 156 (5), 178 (1), 218 (3), 623 (3), 628 (2), 629 (1), 630 (1), 686 (1)

tool, be a 745 (6)

tool-kit 630 (1)

tool-user 630 (5)

tool-using 630 (6)

tools 629 (1)

tools of the trade 630 (1)

toot 404 (3), 413 (9), 665 (1), 665 (3)

tooth 256 (4), 260 (1), 260 (3), 332 (3), 386 (1), 778 (2)

tooth and nail 176 (10)

toothache 377 (2)

toothbrush 648 (5)

toothed 256 (8), 260 (2)

toothless 131 (6), 257 (2)

toothpaste 648 (4)

toothpick 304 (2)

toothsome 390 (2)

toothy 254 (4), 256 (8)

tootle 413 (9)

top 34 (1), 34 (5), 69 (2), 213 (1), 213 (4), 213 (5), 226 (1), 228 (3), 228 (16), 236 (3), 264 (2), 308 (5), 315 (1), 355 (1), 837 (15)

top brass 638 (4)

top drawer 644 (2), 868 (3)

top-dressing 171 (2), 226 (1)

top-flight 694 (4)

top hat 228 (23)

top-heavy 29 (2), 322 (4), 661 (4), 695 (5)

top-level 34 (4), 638 (5), 689 (3)

top people 34 (3), 638 (4), 644 (2)

top-rank 638 (6)

top-secret 523 (4), 525 (3)

top seed 716 (8), 890 (2)

top to toe 203 (9)

top up 54 (7), 632 (5), 633 (6)

topaz 433 (1), 844 (8)

topcoat 228 (20)

tope 949 (14)

toper 301 (25), 949 (5)

topiary 844 (2)

topic 452 (1), 459 (3), 512 (1), 514 (1), 638 (3)

topical 121 (2), 126 (6), 452 (2), 512 (5)

topicality 121 (1), 126 (2)

toping 949 (11)

topknot 259 (2)

topless 204 (3), 229 (4)

topmast 209 (4)

topmost 32 (4), 34 (5), 209 (8), 213 (4), 638 (5), 725 (3)

topographer 465 (7)

topographical 186 (3), 465 (9)

topography 186 (1), 344 (1)

topology 86 (3)

topped up 54 (4)

topper 228 (23)

topping 226 (1)

topple 309 (4), 311 (6)

topple over 221 (4), 309 (4)

topside 213 (2)

topsoil 344 (3)

topsy-turvy 14 (5), 61 (7), 61 (12), 221 (3), 221 (6)

toque 228 (23)

tor 209 (2)

Torah 975 (2)

torch 379 (2), 385 (3), 420 (3), 420 (4)

torchlight 420 (3)

toreador 162 (4), 362 (6)

torment 377 (1), 377 (5), 645 (6), 645 (7), 735 (8), 821 (6), 825 (1), 827 (9), 854 (12), 891 (9), 963 (11)

tormenting 377 (3)

torn 46 (4)

tornado 61 (4), 315 (2), 352 (4)

torpedo 712 (11), 723 (14)

torpedoed 165 (5)

torpid 175 (2), 679 (7), 820 (4), 823 (3)

torpor 161 (2), 175 (1), 679 (1), 679 (2)

torrent 32 (2), 277 (1), 350 (1)

torrential 176 (5)

torrential rain 350 (6)

torrid 379 (4), 379 (6)

torrid heat 379 (1)

torso 52 (3), 53 (5), 554 (1)

tortoise 278 (2), 365 (2), 365 (13)

tortuosity 251 (1)

tortuous 251 (4), 568 (2), 576 (2), 930 (4)

torture 176 (1), 176 (8), 246 (5), 377 (1), 377 (5), 645 (7), 735 (8), 740 (3), 825 (1), 827 (9), 898 (3), 898 (8), 963 (2), 963 (11)

torture chamber 748 (2)

tortured 377 (4)

torturer 963 (5)

toss 63 (4), 269 (9), 287 (1), 287 (7), 309 (4), 317 (4), 318 (1), 318 (5)

toss about 318 (5)

toss and turn 821 (9)

toss aside 921 (5)

toss one's head 871 (5), 922 (5)

toss-up 159 (2), 310 (4), 474 (1), 618 (8)

tossing 269 (6), 287 (1), 312 (3), 318 (1), 678 (7)

tot 196 (4), 301 (26), 388 (1)

tot up 86 (12)

tot up to 86 (11)

total 26 (1), 32 (13), 38 (1), 38 (3), 52 (2), 52 (4), 54 (3), 78 (2), 85 (4), 86 (11)

total blank 506 (1)

total change 143 (1)

total loss 165 (3)

total recall 505 (2)

total war 718 (1)

totalitarian 733 (7), 735 (5)

totalitarianism 733 (3)

totality 52 (1), 54 (1)

totally 52 (8), 54 (8)

tote 273 (12)

totem 966 (1), 982 (3)

totem pole 982 (3)

totter 49 (4), 163 (9), 267 (14), 309 (4), 317 (4)

tottering 152 (4), 163 (4), 309 (2)

tottery 163 (4), 163 (8), 655 (6)

touch 9 (7), 28 (9), 33 (2), 43 (2), 45 (10), 186 (4), 202 (3), 279 (1), 279 (8), 331 (2), 374 (2), 374 (5), 378 (1), 378 (7), 413 (6), 547 (4), 694 (1), 821 (6), 834 (11), 837 (10), 889 (1)

touch and go 474 (3), 474 (5), 661 (4)

touch bottom 211 (3), 309 (3)

touch down 271 (7), 295 (5), 309 (3)

touch for 785 (2)

touch lightly 378 (7)

touch off 68 (9), 156 (9), 381 (9)

touch on 9 (8)

touch one's goal 725 (7)

touch roughly 378 (7)

touch the quick 377 (5)

touch up 425 (8), 546 (3), 553 (8), 654 (9), 656 (12)

touch wood 487 (3)

touchable 378 (5)

touchdown 271 (2), 295 (1)

touched 818 (4), 819 (2)

touched up 541 (3), 654 (6)

touchiness 819 (1), 871 (1), 892 (1)

touching 9 (10), 202 (1), 202 (2), 378 (5), 827 (6)

touching bottom 214 (3)

touching up 553 (1)

touchpaper 385 (3)
touchstone 23 (1), 461 (4)
touchy 819 (3), 892 (3)
touchy person 819 (1)
tough 162 (6), 176 (4), 326 (3), 329 (2), 391 (2), 700 (4), 715 (2), 820 (5), 855 (4), 898 (6), 904 (2), 906 (2)
tough assignment 700 (2)
tough, be 329 (3)
tough guy 162 (4)
tough time 731 (1)
toughen 162 (12), 326 (5), 329 (3), 820 (7)
toughened 329 (2), 375 (4)
toughening 162 (5), 326 (2)
toughness 162 (1), 324 (3), 326 (1), 329 (1)
toupee 259 (2), 843 (2)
tour 110 (1), 267 (1), 267 (11), 314 (1), 314 (4)
tour de force 623 (3), 694 (3)
touring 267 (9), 837 (6)
touring company 268 (2)
tourism 267 (1), 837 (6)
tourist 268 (1), 274 (3), 837 (17)
tournament 716 (2), 875 (3)
tourney 716 (2)
tourniquet 198 (3), 264 (2), 658 (9)
tousle 63 (4), 259 (9)
tousled 61 (7)
tout 528 (6), 618 (4), 763 (1), 793 (2), 793 (4)
tow 208 (2), 288 (1), 288 (3)
tow-headed 427 (5)
towards 281 (8)
towel 333 (3), 342 (3)
towelling 222 (4)
tower 32 (15), 153 (2), 192 (6), 195 (10), 209 (4), 209 (12), 308 (4), 662 (1), 713 (4), 748 (1), 990 (5)
tower block 192 (9)
tower of strength 660 (2), 703 (3)
tower over 34 (7)

towering 32 (6), 195 (6), 209 (8)
towering over 209 (11), 310 (3)
towline 47 (2), 288 (1)
town 184 (3), 184 (5), 192 (1), 192 (8), 848 (3)
town crier 400 (2), 528 (6), 529 (5)
town-dweller 191 (1), 869 (5)
town house 192 (6)
townscape 445 (2)
townsfolk 869 (1)
township 184 (3)
townspeople 191 (5)
townsperson 191 (3)
towpath 624 (5)
towrope 47 (2), 288 (1)
toxic 165 (4), 335 (4), 362 (8), 391 (2), 645 (3), 649 (6), 651 (22), 653 (4), 659 (5), 661 (3)
toxicity 651 (5), 659 (3)
toxicology 659 (3)
toxin 659 (3)
toy 196 (8), 639 (3), 837 (15), 837 (21), 889 (6)
toy dog 365 (10)
trace 20 (6), 33 (2), 41 (1), 157 (1), 233 (3), 255 (1), 394 (1), 484 (5), 547 (2), 547 (13), 548 (4)
trace back 125 (11)
trace to 158 (3)
traceable 158 (2), 548 (6)
tracer 20 (3)
tracery 222 (3), 248 (2), 844 (2), 844 (3)
traces 748 (4)
tracing 20 (1), 22 (1), 233 (1), 551 (1)
track 41 (1), 89 (4), 269 (1), 284 (4), 548 (4), 619 (5), 624 (4), 624 (5), 624 (7), 716 (3), 724 (1)
track down 484 (5)
track events 837 (6)
track record 688 (1)
tracked vehicle 274 (1)
tracker 619 (3)
tracking 619 (1)
tracking station 321 (11)

tracks 548 (4)
tracksuit 228 (9)
tract 184 (1), 344 (1), 589 (2), 591 (1)
tractability 327 (1), 597 (1), 612 (3), 739 (1)
tractable 327 (3), 701 (4)
traction 160 (3), 272 (2), 288 (1), 304 (1)
traction engine 274 (14), 288 (1)
tractional 288 (2)
tractive 160 (9), 288 (2)
tractor 274 (1), 288 (1), 370 (6)
tractor driver 370 (4)
trad 412 (1)
trade 151 (3), 272 (1), 622 (1), 622 (2), 622 (9), 633 (5), 780 (1), 780 (3), 791 (2), 791 (4), 793 (4), 796 (1), 804 (4)
trade fair 796 (1)
trade in 791 (4)
trade journal 528 (5)
trade on 673 (3)
trade route 624 (4)
trade sign 547 (13)
trade supplement 528 (4)
trade union 706 (2), 708 (3)
trade unionist 686 (2), 708 (3), 775 (3)
trade wind 352 (1)
trade with 791 (4)
trademark 80 (1), 547 (2), 547 (13)
trader 275 (3)
tradesman 794 (2)
tradespeople 793 (2), 794 (2)
trading 791 (1), 791 (2), 791 (3)
trading centre 796 (2)
trading post 796 (2)
tradition 127 (3), 144 (1), 524 (1), 590 (2), 610 (1), 973 (4)
traditional 83 (4), 127 (6), 590 (6), 610 (5), 610 (6), 976 (8), 979 (6)
traditionalism 83 (1)

traditionalist **83** (3), 144 (1), 610 (4), **976** (7)

traduce **926** (7)

traffic **265** (1), **267** (6), 305 (2), 791 (1), 791 (2)

traffic control **305** (3), 547 (6), 624 (4), 624 (6)

traffic density **305** (2)

traffic engineering **624** (6)

traffic in 791 (4)

traffic jam 71 (3), 305 (2), 702 (2)

traffic lane 305 (3), 624 (4)

traffic light 117 (3), 420 (6)

traffic lights **305** (3)

traffic load 305 (2)

traffic movement **305** (2)

traffic police **305** (3)

traffic rules **305** (3)

traffic warden **305** (3)

trafficator 547 (6)

trafficker 794 (1)

tragedian **594** (9)

tragedienne **594** (9)

tragedy **594** (3), **616** (1)

tragic **594** (15), **616** (2), **827** (6)

Tragic Muse **594** (1)

tragic poet **594** (13)

tragicomedy **594** (3)

tragicomic **594** (15), 849 (3)

trail 35 (5), 71 (1), 75 (3), 203 (7), 217 (5), 238 (5), 265 (4), 267 (13), 278 (4), 284 (4), 288 (3), 394 (1), 548 (4), 619 (5), 624 (5)

trail around 267 (13)

trail bike 274 (3)

trail-blazer 66 (1), **669** (5)

trail one's coat 709 (8)

trailer 66 (1), 67 (2), 83 (2), 192 (7), 274 (5), 445 (4), 528 (3), 619 (3)

trailing 619 (1)

train 67 (2), 71 (3), 83 (8), 164 (7), 217 (2), 228 (3), 238 (1), 274 (13), 284 (2), 369 (8), 534 (8), 536 (4),

610 (8), 624 (7), **669** (11), **669** (13), 742 (3)

train driver 268 (5)

train one's sights on 281 (7), 617 (6)

train spotter 441 (1)

trained 490 (6), 610 (7), **669** (7), 694 (6), 739 (3)

trainee **538** (2)

trainer 369 (5), 537 (2), **669** (5)

training 369 (1), 534 (1), 610 (3), 654 (3), **669** (1), 682 (2), 718 (4)

training college 539 (3)

training ground 724 (1)

training school 539 (3)

traipse 267 (13)

trait 5 (4), 80 (1), 445 (6), 547 (2), 610 (1), 817 (1)

traitor 545 (1), 603 (3), 738 (4), 881 (2), 904 (1), 918 (1), 938 (2)

traitorous 738 (7), 930 (7)

trajectory 248 (2), 624 (4)

tram 274 (10)

tramlines 219 (1), 624 (7)

trammel 747 (9), 748 (4)

tramp 84 (3), 265 (2), 265 (4), 267 (3), 267 (14), 268 (2), 269 (9), 273 (1), 275 (3), 278 (4), 679 (6), 763 (2), 801 (2), 869 (7)

tramper 268 (3)

tramping 267 (3)

trample 279 (10)

trample down 216 (7)

trample on 645 (7), 735 (8), 745 (7)

trample out 165 (8)

trample upon 727 (10)

trampoline 310 (2)

tramway 624 (7)

trance 266 (1), 375 (1), 513 (3), 679 (4)

tranquil 177 (3), 266 (5), 376 (4), 683 (2), 717 (3), 820 (3), 823 (3), 826 (2)

tranquillity 266 (2), 683 (1), 823 (1), 826 (1), 828 (1)

tranquillize 177 (7), 719 (4), 823 (7)

tranquillizer 177 (2), 658 (7)

tranquilly 717 (5)

trans-Pacific 199 (4)

transact 622 (9), 676 (5), 688 (5)

transaction 154 (1), 676 (1), 676 (2), 791 (2)

transactions 154 (2), 548 (1)

transatlantic 59 (4), 199 (4)

transcend 32 (15), 34 (7), 306 (5), 644 (10)

transcendence 6 (1), 306 (1), 646 (1), 965 (2)

transcendent 21 (4), 320 (3), 965 (5), 965 (6)

transcribe 20 (6), 520 (9), 586 (8)

transcriber 586 (5)

transcribing 20 (1), 586 (1)

transcript 22 (1)

transcription 20 (1), 22 (1), 586 (1)

transect 220 (5)

transept 990 (4)

transexual 84 (3)

transfer 22 (2), 46 (2), 150 (1), 187 (5), 188 (1), 188 (4), 265 (5), 272 (1), 272 (6), 272 (7), 273 (12), 284 (1), 299 (3), 300 (6), 305 (5), 621 (1), 621 (3), 751 (2), 752 (2), 752 (5), 779 (1), 779 (4), 780 (1), 780 (3), 781 (1), 781 (2), 786 (2)

transfer by deed 780 (3)

transferable 188 (2), 272 (5), 779 (3), 780 (2)

transference 46 (2), 63 (1), 147 (2), 150 (1), 151 (1), 188 (1), 265 (1), 272 (1), 297 (1), 298 (1), 305 (1), 633 (1), 780 (1), 791 (2)

transferred 187 (4), 780 (2)

transferred, be 780 (5)

transferred to 187 (4)

transferrer 272 (4), 273 (1), 351 (1)

transfiguration 147 (1), 965 (4)

transfigure 143 (6), 147 (8), 841 (8)

transfigured 147 (5), 843 (6), 965 (6)

transfix 263 (18), 303 (4)

transfixed 153 (6), 266 (6), 864 (4)

transform 143 (6), 147 (8), 149 (4), 178 (3), 654 (9), 655 (8)

transformation 143 (2), 147 (1)

transformed 147 (5), 843 (6)

transformed, be 147 (6)

transformer 143 (3), 160 (6)

transfuse 272 (7), 303 (5)

transfusion 43 (1)

transgress 306 (4), 914 (6), 934 (7), 936 (4)

tranship 188 (4), 272 (7)

transience 33 (1), 110 (1), 114 (1), 116 (1), 152 (1), 204 (1), 361 (1)

transient 8 (3), 114 (3), 191 (1), 204 (3), 446 (2), 474 (4)

transient, be 114 (6), 305 (5), 446 (3)

transiently 114 (7)

transistor 160 (6), 531 (3)

transit 147 (2), 265 (1), 305 (1), 305 (5)

transition 143 (1), 147 (2)

transitional 143 (4), 147 (5), 265 (3), 305 (4)

transitory 114 (3), 114 (6)

translate 20 (6), 520 (9)

translated 520 (7)

translation 20 (1), 22 (1), 520 (3), 563 (1)

translator 20 (3), 520 (4), 589 (7)

transliterate 20 (6), 520 (9), 558 (6)

transliteration 520 (3)

translucence 422 (1)

translucent 417 (9), 422 (2), 424 (2)

transmissible 272 (5)

transmission 272 (1), 305 (1), 531 (4)

transmit 272 (6), 272 (8), 305 (5), 524 (10), 780 (3)

transmit light 422 (3)

transmittal 272 (1)

transmitter 272 (4), 531 (3)

transmutation 143 (2), 147 (1)

transmute 143 (6), 147 (7)

transom 218 (9), 222 (2), 263 (5)

transparency 263 (5), 422 (1), 551 (4), 631 (1)

transparent 417 (9), 422 (2), 526 (3), 567 (2), 699 (3)

transparent, be 422 (3), 443 (4), 526 (4)

transpire 154 (6), 298 (5), 298 (7), 338 (4), 526 (7)

transplant 150 (2), 303 (6), 658 (11)

transport 188 (4), 265 (1), 265 (5), 271 (2), 272 (2), 272 (6), 273 (12), 274 (1), 275 (1), 276 (1), 300 (6), 722 (13)

transport cafe 192 (13)

transport plane 722 (14)

transport police 955 (3)

transportable 272 (5)

transportation 272 (2)

transported 188 (2), 824 (4)

transporter 272 (4), 273 (1)

transports 818 (2)

transpose 143 (6), 151 (3), 187 (6), 188 (4), 221 (5), 265 (5), 272 (7), 300 (8), 303 (5), 410 (9)

transposition 221 (1)

transverse 220 (3), 222 (6)

transversely 222 (11)

transvestism 84 (1)

transvestite 84 (3)

trap 47 (9), 194 (1), 235 (1), 274 (6), 484 (5), 508

(5), 527 (2), 542 (4), 542 (9), 542 (10), 612 (4), 619 (2), 661 (1), 663 (1), 698 (2), 713 (2), 723 (14), 747 (10), 786 (6)

trapdoor 226 (1), 263 (6), 542 (4)

trapeze artist 162 (4)

trapezium 247 (4)

trapezoid 247 (4), 247 (6)

trapezoidal 247 (6)

trapped 661 (6), 747 (6)

trapper 362 (6), 619 (3)

trapping 619 (2)

trappings 40 (1), 228 (1), 630 (4)

trash 639 (3), 639 (4), 641 (3), 938 (1)

trashy 639 (6)

trauma 655 (4)

travail 682 (3)

travel 265 (1), 265 (4), 267 (1), 267 (11), 277 (6), 298 (5), 589 (2)

travel-stained 267 (9)

travelled 267 (9)

traveller 59 (2), 66 (1), 268 (1), 271 (4), 272 (3), 441 (1), 459 (9), 484 (2), 793 (2), 837 (17)

traveller's tale 472 (1), 543 (3)

travelling 59 (4), 84 (5), 152 (4), 265 (3), 267 (1), 267 (9), 282 (2), 314 (3), 744 (5), 837 (6)

travelling bag 194 (9)

travelogue 445 (4), 524 (6)

traverse 218 (9), 267 (12), 305 (1), 305 (5)

traversing 305 (1)

travestied 552 (2)

travesty 20 (2), 521 (1), 521 (3), 552 (1), 552 (3), 851 (2), 851 (3), 851 (6)

trawl 222 (3), 235 (1), 288 (1), 288 (3), 619 (6)

trawler 275 (4), 619 (3)

tray 194 (4), 194 (17)

treacherous 474 (5), 541 (3), 541 (4), 542 (6), 603 (4), 661 (3), 661 (4), 898 (4), 918 (2), 930 (7)

trick of light 440 (2)

trick out 843 (7), 844 (12)

trickery 525 (1), 541 (2), 542 (2), 545 (4), 698 (2), 930 (3)

trickle 33 (2), 105 (1), 278 (4), 298 (6), 350 (9), 639 (2)

trickster 545 (4), 620 (2), 696 (2), 698 (3), 789 (3), 938 (2)

tricky 542 (6), 698 (4), 700 (4), 930 (4)

tricolour 93 (3), 437 (1), 547 (12)

tricycle 93 (2), 274 (3), 837 (15)

trident 93 (2)

tried 473 (4), 669 (8), 694 (6), 923 (7), 929 (4)

triennial 141 (5)

trier 600 (2), 671 (2)

trifid 95 (2)

trifle 4 (2), 33 (2), 196 (2), 301 (17), 458 (4), 639 (2), 889 (6)

trifle with 542 (9), 921 (5)

trifles 639 (2)

trifling 33 (7), 456 (6), 458 (1), 499 (2), 639 (5), 639 (6)

trifling amount 33 (2)

trigger 218 (3), 723 (9)

trigger-happy 362 (9), 711 (2), 822 (3), 857 (3), 892 (3)

trigger off 68 (9), 156 (9)

trigonometric 86 (9)

trigonometry 86 (3), 247 (3), 465 (1)

trilateral 93 (3), 94 (2), 239 (2), 247 (6)

trilby 228 (23)

trill 403 (1), 403 (3), 410 (2), 413 (10), 577 (4)

trillion 99 (5)

trillions 104 (1)

trilobite 125 (3)

trilogy 93 (2)

trim 7 (1), 24 (10), 28 (10), 37 (4), 46 (11), 83 (8), 198 (7), 204 (5), 234 (5), 243

(1), 541 (6), 603 (5), 841 (6), 843 (2), 844 (12)

trimaran 275 (9)

trimester 93 (2), 110 (1)

trimestrial 93 (3)

trimmed 24 (8), 234 (4), 648 (7), 844 (10)

trimmer 545 (1), 603 (3)

trimming 217 (2), 234 (3), 603 (4), 843 (2), 844 (5)

trimmings 40 (1)

trinity 93 (1)

trinket 639 (3), 837 (15)

trio 93 (2), 412 (6)

trip 267 (1), 267 (14), 309 (4), 311 (6), 312 (4), 495 (3), 495 (8)

trip over 695 (9)

trip up 542 (10), 702 (8)

tripartite 93 (3), 95 (2)

tripartition 95 (1)

tripe 301 (16)

triple 36 (5), 94 (2), 94 (3)

triple crown 743 (2)

triple jump 312 (1)

triplet 93 (2), 593 (4)

triplex 94 (2)

triplicate 94 (2), 94 (3)

triplication 36 (1), 93 (1), 94 (1)

triply 94 (4)

tripod 93 (2), 218 (5)

tripper 268 (1)

tripping 575 (3)

triptych 93 (2), 553 (5)

tripwire 542 (4)

trireme 275 (2), 722 (13)

trisect 95 (3)

trisected 95 (2)

trisection 95 (1)

trite 490 (7), 496 (3), 515 (4), 610 (6), 840 (2)

triteness 515 (1), 840 (1)

triumph 727 (1), 727 (2), 727 (8), 729 (1), 745 (7), 835 (1), 876 (1), 876 (4), 877 (5), 923 (11)

triumph over 872 (7)

triumphal 727 (4), 876 (3), 886 (2)

triumphal arch 729 (1), 876 (1)

triumphant 727 (4), 833 (5), 876 (3), 877 (4)

triumphing 833 (5)

triumvirate 93 (2)

trivet 93 (2), 218 (5)

trivia 33 (2), 639 (2)

trivial 10 (4), 33 (7), 515 (4), 639 (6)

triviality 639 (1), 639 (2)

trodden 216 (4)

troglodyte 191 (1)

troika 93 (2)

Trojan 678 (5)

Trojan horse 527 (2)

troll 970 (2), 970 (4)

trolley 218 (5), 274 (4)

trolleybus 274 (10)

trollop 952 (2), 952 (4)

trombone 414 (7)

troop 74 (3), 74 (4), 267 (14), 722 (8)

troop-carrier 722 (14)

troop up 74 (10)

trooper 722 (10)

troops 722 (4), 722 (7)

troopship 722 (13)

trope 519 (2), 546 (1), 563 (1), 574 (1)

trophy 505 (3), 547 (9), 617 (2), 644 (2), 729 (1), 771 (1), 781 (2), 790 (1), 807 (1), 859 (5), 866 (4), 876 (1), 962 (1)

tropical 379 (4), 379 (6), 519 (3)

tropical disease 651 (6)

tropical heat 379 (1)

tropics 379 (1)

trot 265 (2), 267 (3), 267 (15), 277 (6)

trot out 106 (4), 579 (8)

trotter 214 (2)

troubadour 413 (1), 413 (4), 593 (6)

trouble 61 (4), 63 (3), 139 (3), 318 (6), 377 (5), 455 (1), 616 (1), 643 (3), 645 (6), 678 (13), 682 (1), 684 (6), 700 (1), 700 (3), 700 (6), 702 (8), 821 (8), 825 (3), 827 (1), 827 (10), 834 (1), 854 (12), 891 (9)

trouble ahead 731 (1)

trouble in store 155 (1)
trouble-making 616 (2)
trouble one for 761 (5)
trouble oneself 682 (6), 825 (7)
trouble-spot 663 (1)
troubled 318 (4), 825 (5), 834 (5)
troubled brain 503 (1)
troublemaker 545 (1), 659 (1), 663 (2), 698 (3), 702 (5), 709 (5), 738 (5), 904 (1), 938 (1)
troubles 616 (1), 731 (1), 827 (2)
troubleshooter 720 (2)
troublesome 682 (5), 827 (5)
troublous 176 (5), 616 (2)
trough 194 (16), 255 (2), 262 (1), 731 (1)
trounce 165 (6), 279 (9), 727 (10)
trouncing 727 (2), 728 (2)
troupe 74 (4), 594 (9), 708 (1)
trouper 594 (9)
trouser suit 228 (9)
trousers 228 (12)
trousseau 228 (2), 632 (1)
trout 365 (15)
trout-tickler 619 (3)
trowel 194 (18), 370 (6)
truancy 190 (1), 621 (1), 667 (1), 918 (1)
truant 190 (1), 190 (4), 620 (2), 667 (3), 667 (4), 918 (1), 918 (2)
truce 136 (2), 145 (4), 201 (1), 266 (1), 668 (1), 717 (1), 719 (1)
truck 273 (1), 273 (12), 274 (4), 274 (12), 274 (13), 791 (4)
truck driver 268 (5)
truckle 879 (4)
truculent 885 (5), 898 (7)
trudge 267 (14), 278 (4)
true 1 (5), 249 (2), 466 (5), 471 (3), 473 (4), 494 (4), 494 (6), 540 (2), 699 (3), 768 (2), 929 (4)
true, be 478 (5), 494 (7)

true believer 976 (7)
true blue 708 (2), 708 (7), 739 (3), 901 (7)
true-born 494 (5)
true faith, the 976 (1)
true feeling 818 (1)
true grit 600 (2)
true lady 929 (2)
true love 887 (1), 887 (4), 887 (5)
true-love knot 47 (4)
true lover's knot 889 (3)
true picture 590 (1)
true skin 226 (6)
true to life 18 (5), 494 (4), 551 (6), 590 (6)
true to nature 18 (5)
true to type 18 (5), 83 (5)
truelove 890 (1)
trug 194 (6)
truism 494 (1), 496 (1), 496 (2), 515 (1)
truly 32 (16), 494 (8), 540 (4), 764 (6)
truly spoken 540 (2)
trump 34 (7), 727 (1), 727 (9), 929 (2), 937 (1)
trump card 34 (2), 623 (3), 727 (1)
trump up 541 (8)
trumped-up 467 (3), 541 (3), 542 (6), 543 (4)
trumped-up charge 928 (2)
trumpery 639 (3)
trumpet 404 (3), 409 (3), 414 (7), 528 (10), 529 (5), 718 (1), 875 (7), 877 (5)
trumpet blast 400 (1)
trumpet-call 665 (1)
trumpeter 413 (2), 877 (3)
trumps 629 (1)
truncate 204 (5), 244 (3)
truncated 55 (3), 204 (3)
truncheon 723 (5), 743 (2)
trundle 265 (5), 315 (5)
trunk 52 (3), 53 (5), 194 (7), 218 (2), 252 (3), 254 (3), 366 (4), 624 (8)
trunk road 624 (6)
trunks 228 (19), 228 (26)
trunpet 400 (2)

truss 45 (12), 74 (6), 74 (11), 218 (2), 218 (9), 218 (15)
trust 485 (1), 485 (7), 507 (1), 706 (2), 708 (5), 751 (2), 852 (1), 852 (6), 979 (1)
trust in 473 (7)
trust with 751 (4)
trusted 485 (5)
trustee 754 (1), 776 (1), 782 (2), 798 (1)
trusteeship 751 (1)
trustful 487 (2)
trusting 485 (4)
trustworthiness 929 (1)
trustworthy 473 (4), 485 (5), 494 (5), 540 (2), 660 (4), 768 (2), 858 (2), 866 (7), 880 (6), 929 (4)
trusty 485 (5), 929 (4)
trusty blade 723 (8)
truth 1 (2), 160 (1), 473 (1), 494 (1), 496 (1), 524 (1), 526 (1), 540 (1), 699 (1), 927 (1), 929 (1), 965 (2)
truth-speaker 540 (1)
truth-telling 540 (1)
truthful 494 (4), 540 (2), 929 (4)
truthful, be 494 (7), 526 (6), 540 (3), 699 (4), 929 (5)
truthfully 494 (8), 532 (8), 540 (4), 764 (6)
truthfulness 494 (1), 540 (1), 929 (1)
try 386 (3), 459 (13), 461 (7), 480 (5), 597 (6), 600 (4), 612 (11), 671 (1), 671 (4), 673 (4), 676 (5), 838 (5)
try a case 459 (13), 955 (5), 959 (8)
try a change 143 (6)
try for 617 (6)
try for effect 850 (5)
try in vain 509 (4)
try on 228 (32)
try one's best 682 (6)
try one's luck 618 (8), 671 (4)

try one's patience 838 (5), 891 (9)
try-out 461 (1), 461 (7)
try to stop 747 (7)
trying 671 (3), 684 (4)
trying hard 600 (3)
tu-whit tu-whoo 409 (1)
tub 194 (12), 194 (13), 275 (1), 648 (3)
tub-thumper 738 (5)
tuba 414 (7)
tubby 195 (8), 205 (4)
tube 160 (6), 252 (3), 255 (2), 255 (4), 263 (8), 263 (9), 351 (1), 624 (7)
tuber 301 (20), 366 (6)
tubercular 651 (22)
tuberculosis 651 (8)
tubing 263 (9)
tubular 252 (5), 263 (16)
tubular bell 414 (8)
tuck 261 (1), 261 (3)
tuck in 301 (35)
tuck into 303 (4)
tuck up 204 (5), 261 (3)
tucked away 883 (7)
tuft 74 (6), 105 (1), 259 (2)
tufty 259 (5)
tug 265 (5), 275 (1), 275 (7), 288 (1), 288 (3), 291 (1), 291 (4), 304 (1), 682 (1)
tug of war 288 (1), 704 (1), 716 (2)
tug towards 291 (4)
tugboat 288 (1)
tuition 534 (1)
tulle 222 (4)
tumble 49 (4), 63 (4), 163 (9), 165 (11), 221 (4), 271 (7), 309 (1), 309 (4), 311 (6), 330 (3), 655 (7), 728 (7), 728 (8)
tumble down 309 (4)
tumble-dry 342 (6)
tumble dryer 342 (3)
tumble to 484 (4), 516 (5)
tumbledown 163 (5), 309 (2), 655 (6)
tumbler 194 (15), 309 (1)
tumbril 274 (1)
tumescence 197 (2)
tumescent 197 (3)

tumid 197 (3)
tummy 194 (3)
tumour 253 (2), 651 (11)
tumult 61 (4), 318 (3), 400 (1), 738 (2)
tumultuous 61 (9), 176 (5)
tumulus 253 (5)
tun 194 (12)
tundra 348 (1)
tune 24 (10), 123 (4), 398 (1), 410 (2), 410 (9), 412 (3), 413 (9)
tune in 415 (6)
tune one's lyre 593 (10)
tune up 24 (10), 410 (9), 669 (11)
tuned 24 (8)
tuned in 415 (5)
tuneful 376 (3), 410 (6), 593 (8)
tuneful Nine 967 (2)
tuneless 411 (2)
tunic 228 (10)
tuning 669 (1)
tuning fork 414 (8)
tuning-in 415 (2)
tunnel 255 (2), 255 (4), 255 (8), 263 (8), 263 (18), 309 (3), 624 (3)
tunnel vision 439 (1)
tunnelling 309 (1)
tup 365 (8)
turban 228 (23)
turbid 423 (2)
turbidity 423 (1)
turbine 160 (4), 315 (3)
turbojet 276 (1)
turboprop 276 (1)
turbulence 61 (4), 176 (1), 176 (3), 259 (1), 318 (3), 822 (1)
turbulent 61 (9), 176 (5), 822 (3)
tureen 194 (16)
turf 53 (5), 344 (3), 348 (2), 366 (8), 385 (1), 618 (3), 724 (1)
turfy 366 (9)
turgescence 197 (2)
turgescent 197 (3)
turgid 570 (3), 574 (5), 576 (2)
turgidity 574 (2), 576 (1)

Turkish bath 648 (3)
turmoil 61 (4), 165 (2), 176 (1), 176 (3), 279 (2), 318 (3), 400 (1), 411 (1), 678 (1), 709 (3), 716 (7), 734 (2), 738 (2)
turn 110 (1), 143 (1), 148 (1), 243 (1), 243 (5), 248 (2), 250 (7), 267 (1), 282 (3), 286 (2), 314 (1), 314 (4), 315 (1), 315 (5), 318 (5), 508 (1), 520 (1), 594 (4), 655 (7), 694 (2), 713 (10), 861 (1)
turn a blind eye to 458 (5)
turn a deaf ear 416 (3), 906 (3)
turn a deaf ear to 458 (5)
turn a sentence 563 (3)
turn about 148 (3), 221 (4), 282 (4)
turn adrift 300 (6), 746 (3)
turn against 603 (5), 613 (3)
turn and turn about 12 (4), 141 (8)
turn aside 282 (3), 620 (5)
turn away 248 (5), 292 (3), 300 (7), 509 (5), 760 (4)
turn back 148 (3), 221 (4), 282 (4), 286 (5), 290 (4), 296 (4), 314 (4)
turn blue 435 (4)
turn down 221 (5), 261 (3), 760 (4)
turn from 760 (4)
turn in 679 (12)
turn inside out 221 (5), 459 (15)
turn into 147 (7), 297 (5)
turn into cash 797 (12)
turn into money 771 (7)
turn nasty 891 (7)
turn of events 154 (1)
turn of the tide 148 (1), 286 (2)
turn on 157 (6), 173 (3), 949 (15)
turn on one's heel 314 (4)
turn one aside 613 (3)
turn one's back 286 (5)
turn one's back on 883 (9)
turn one's brain 503 (12)

turn one's hand to 622 (7)
turn one's head 873 (6), 887 (15), 925 (4)
turn one's stomach 861 (5)
turn out 154 (6), 157 (5), 164 (7), 188 (4), 228 (1), 300 (6), 883 (9), 884 (7)
turn out well 615 (4), 727 (7), 730 (8)
turn over 221 (4), 248 (5), 261 (3), 272 (6), 449 (8), 459 (15), 791 (4)
turn over a new leaf 147 (6)
turn over to 751 (4)
turn pale 426 (4)
turn Queen's evidence 526 (6)
turn restive 738 (9)
turn right round 315 (5)
turn round 221 (4), 269 (10), 282 (4), 314 (4), 620 (6)
turn sour 393 (3)
turn tail 286 (4), 620 (6), 856 (4)
turn the edge 257 (3)
turn the scale 156 (9), 178 (3), 178 (4), 467 (4)
turn the stomach 391 (3)
turn the tables 221 (5), 467 (4)
turn the tables on 714 (3)
turn to 147 (6), 583 (3)
turn to account 673 (3)
turn to good account 137 (7), 640 (5)
turn topsy-turvy 63 (5)
turn turtle 221 (4), 269 (10)
turn under 261 (3)
turn up 154 (6), 159 (7), 189 (4), 204 (5), 228 (3), 261 (3), 295 (4)
turn up one's nose at 862 (4), 922 (6)
turn up trumps 727 (7), 730 (8)
turn upside down 63 (5), 143 (6)
turn white 131 (8)
turncoat 147 (4), 545 (1), 601 (2), 603 (3)

turned 131 (6), 243 (3)
turned away 509 (2)
turned down 760 (3)
turned into 147 (5)
turned on 949 (10)
turned right up 400 (3)
turned to, be l (1), 147 (6), 316 (3)
turned-up 248 (3)
turner 686 (3)
turning 152 (1), 243 (2), 251 (5), 314 (1), 318 (1)
turning away 248 (1)
turning down 760 (1)
turning into 147 (1)
turning inward 221 (1)
turning over 459 (5)
turning point 8 (2), 27 (1), 137 (3), 236 (1), 286 (2)
turnip head 252 (2)
turnip-shaped 252 (5)
turnkey 749 (2)
turnout 164 (2), 274 (6)
turnover 301 (23), 771 (2), 807 (1)
turnpike 624 (6)
turnstile 235 (3), 549 (3), 702 (2), 799 (1)
turntable 315 (3), 414 (10)
turpitude 934 (1)
turquoise 435 (1), 435 (3), 844 (8)
turret 209 (4), 713 (4)
turtle 365 (13)
turtledoves 887 (6)
tusk 256 (4)
tusker 365 (9)
tussle 716 (1), 716 (2), 716 (7), 716 (10)
tussock 74 (6)
tut-tut 762 (3)
tutelage 534 (1), 660 (2)
tutelary 660 (6), 713 (7), 983 (8)
tutor 534 (6), 534 (7), 537 (1), 690 (3), 742 (2), 749 (1)
tutor group 538 (4)
tutorial 534 (1)
tutoring 534 (1)
tutti 400 (1)
tutu 228 (13)
tuxedo 228 (10)

TV 531 (3)
TV addict 441 (1)
twaddle 515 (2)
twain 90 (1)
twang 386 (1), 388 (1), 404 (1), 404 (3), 407 (1), 407 (4), 413 (9), 577 (2), 580 (1)
twanging 404 (1)
tweak 288 (3)
twee 850 (4)
tweed 222 (4), 259 (1)
tweeds 228 (9)
tweedy 222 (6), 331 (4)
tweet 409 (3)
tweezers 304 (2), 778 (2)
twelve 99 (2)
twelve month 110 (1)
twelve o'clock 128 (2)
twelve-toned 410 (8)
twentieth century 121 (1)
twenty 99 (3)
twenty and over 99 (3)
twice 91 (2), 91 (4)
twice as much 91 (4)
twice over 91 (4)
twice removed 11 (5)
twice-told 106 (3)
twiddle 315 (5), 378 (7)
twiddling one's thumbs 838 (4)
twig 53 (4), 366 (4)
twilight 129 (1), 417 (1), 419 (2), 419 (4), 655 (1)
twill 222 (6)
twin 11 (2), 13 (1), 18 (3), 18 (4), 18 (8), 28 (6), 45 (9), 89 (2), 90 (2), 91 (2), 123 (2), 123 (3)
twin set 228 (11)
twine 45 (12), 47 (2), 208 (2), 222 (10), 248 (5), 251 (10), 315 (5), 844 (12)
twine around 230 (3)
twine round 48 (3)
twiner 366 (6)
twinge 377 (2), 377 (5), 825 (1), 939 (1)
twining 251 (4)
twinkle 152 (5), 318 (1), 417 (2), 417 (11), 547 (4), 547 (21), 835 (2), 835 (8)
twins 18 (3), 90 (1)

twirl 251 (2), 251 (10), 315 (1), 315 (5)

twist 45 (12), 61 (3), 63 (3), 83 (8), 143 (6), 176 (8), 208 (2), 222 (10), 244 (3), 246 (1), 246 (5), 251 (1), 251 (2), 251 (10), 265 (4), 282 (3), 388 (2), 481 (11), 520 (1), 655 (8), 698 (5), 837 (22), 842 (7)

twist and turn 251 (12)

twist one's arm 612 (10), 740 (3)

twist the argument 477 (8)

twist the words 521 (3)

twisted 246 (3), 251 (4), 481 (8), 842 (4)

twister 352 (4), 938 (2)

twisting 246 (1), 251 (5)

twists and turns 251 (3)

twit 839 (5), 851 (5), 921 (5)

twitch 288 (3), 318 (1), 318 (2), 318 (5), 318 (6), 377 (6), 547 (4)

twitching 318 (4)

twitchy 318 (4)

twitter 318 (1), 318 (5), 409 (1), 409 (3), 413 (10), 581 (5)

two 90 (1)

two abreast 90 (2)

two by two 90 (2)

two cheers 860 (1), 923 (2)

two-dimensional 183 (5), 216 (4), 243 (3)

two dozen 99 (3)

two-edged 91 (2), 518 (2)

two-edged sword 723 (8)

two-faced 90 (2), 541 (4), 930 (4)

two-hander 90 (1)

two-headed 91 (2)

two of a kind 18 (3)

two or three 101 (1), 105 (1)

two p 797 (4)

two-piece 228 (30)

two score 99 (3)

two-seater 90 (1)

two-sided 91 (2)

two-step 837 (14)

two-timer 545 (1)

two times 91 (4)

two-up two-down 192 (7)

two voices 14 (1), 25 (1), 518 (1)

two-way 12 (2), 91 (2), 151 (2)

two-way traffic 151 (1)

twofold 91 (2), 91 (4)

twosome 90 (1)

tycoon 638 (4), 741 (2), 800 (2)

type 5 (3), 16 (1), 18 (3), 23 (1), 77 (2), 83 (2), 243 (1), 551 (2), 555 (2), 586 (8), 587 (3)

type-cutter 556 (3)

type of marriage 894 (2), 951 (3)

type of worship 981 (2)

type out 20 (6), 586 (8)

type-setter 587 (5)

typecast 594 (16)

typeface 587 (3)

types of sound 398 (1)

typescript 586 (3), 589 (1)

typeset 587 (7)

typesetting 587 (1)

typewriter 586 (4)

typewriting 586 (1)

typhoid 651 (7)

typhoon 352 (4)

typhus 651 (5)

typical 16 (2), 18 (4), 18 (5), 77 (4), 79 (3), 80 (5), 81 (3), 83 (5), 547 (15), 610 (6), 732 (2)

typification 551 (1)

typify 16 (3), 18 (7), 519 (4), 522 (7), 547 (18), 551 (8)

typing 586 (1), 587 (1)

typist 586 (6)

typist's error 495 (3)

typographer 587 (5)

typographic 587 (6)

typography 587 (1)

tyrannical 176 (5), 733 (7), 735 (6), 898 (7), 954 (7)

tyrannically 735 (9)

tyrannicide 738 (2), 738 (4), 903 (1)

tyrannize 176 (7), 645 (7), 733 (10), 735 (8), 898 (8)

tyrannous 735 (6)

tyranny 645 (1), 733 (3), 735 (2)

tyrant 176 (4), 659 (1), 735 (3), 741 (2), 916 (4), 938 (4), 963 (5)

tyro 538 (2)

U

U-turn 148 (1), 248 (2), 314 (1), 603 (1)

ubiquitous 79 (3), 79 (4), 178 (2), 189 (3), 965 (6)

ubiquity 79 (1), 189 (1)

uboastful 874 (2)

udder 194 (2), 253 (3)

UFO 276 (4)

uglify 842 (7)

ugliness 246 (2), 292 (1), 827 (1), 842 (1)

ugly 246 (4), 576 (2), 661 (3), 827 (4), 842 (3)

ugly, be 842 (6)

ugly customer 663 (2), 904 (2), 938 (1)

ugly duckling 84 (3), 842 (2)

ugly person 842 (2)

ugly weather 352 (4)

ulcer 651 (7), 651 (14), 655 (4), 659 (1)

ulcerated 651 (22)

ulceration 651 (14)

ulcerous 651 (22)

ulterior 199 (3)

ulterior motive 525 (1), 612 (1)

ultimate 34 (5), 69 (4), 156 (8), 199 (3), 473 (5)

ultimately 124 (7), 154 (8)

ultimatum 236 (1), 664 (1), 709 (1), 737 (3), 761 (1), 766 (1)

ultra 32 (18)

ultramarine 59 (4), 435 (2), 435 (3)

ululant 409 (2)

ululate 400 (4), 409 (3), 413 (10), 836 (6)

ululation **398** (1), **407** (1), **409** (1), **836** (2)

umbilical **225** (3)

umbilical cord **47** (1), **167** (2)

umbrage **891** (1)

umbrella **226** (4), **660** (2), **662** (2)

umpire **480** (3), **720** (2), **720** (4)

umpteen **104** (4)

un-American **59** (4)

un-British **59** (4)

unabashed **855** (5), **871** (3), **878** (4)

unable **161** (5)

unable to forget **505** (6)

unable to hear **416** (2)

unable to make ends meet **801** (3)

unable to move **266** (6)

unable to pay **803** (4)

unable to pay, be **805** (5)

unabridged **52** (5), **203** (5)

unaccompanied **88** (4)

unaccountable **84** (6), **159** (6), **508** (2), **517** (2), **864** (5), **919** (2), **954** (7)

unaccountably **159** (8)

unaccustomed **611** (3), **695** (5)

unacknowledged **489** (4), **908** (3)

unadmiring **924** (6)

unadmitted **489** (4)

unadulterated **44** (5), **494** (5), **573** (2)

unadventurous **858** (2)

unaffected **573** (2), **575** (3), **820** (3)

unaffiliated **744** (7)

unafraid **855** (5)

unaggressive **175** (2), **717** (3)

unaided eye **438** (2)

unamazement **865** (1)

unambiguity **516** (1)

unambiguous **514** (4), **567** (2)

unambitious **860** (2), **867** (7)

unamusing **840** (2)

unanimity **488** (2), **706** (1), **710** (1)

unanimous **24** (5), **488** (4), **488** (5), **710** (2)

unanimously **488** (10)

unanswerable **478** (3), **596** (4), **725** (3), **954** (7)

unanticipated **508** (2)

unappetizing **387** (2), **391** (2), **391** (3)

unappreciated **483** (3), **908** (3)

unapt **25** (5), **497** (3)

unarmed **161** (6), **717** (3)

unasked **595** (1), **597** (5)

unaspiring **860** (2)

unassailable **153** (6), **660** (5)

unassembled **46** (4), **61** (7), **75** (2)

unassertive **734** (3), **874** (2)

unassimilated **49** (2)

unassuming **573** (2), **872** (3), **874** (2)

unastonished **860** (2), **865** (2)

unastonishing **865** (3)

unastonishment **865** (1)

unattached **46** (5), **152** (4), **744** (7)

unattended **458** (3)

unattested **467** (3), **474** (7)

unattractive **842** (5)

unauthorized **161** (5), **916** (6), **954** (5)

unauthorized information **524** (1)

unavailable **636** (4)

unavailing **641** (5)

unavoidable **596** (4)

unaware **491** (4)

unawareness **491** (1)

unawares **491** (9)

unbalance **29** (3), **63** (3), **503** (12)

unbalanced **29** (2), **503** (7), **822** (3)

unbaptised **974** (6)

unbar **668** (3)

unbarred **263** (13)

unbearable **32** (12), **827** (7)

unbearably **32** (20)

unbeaten **715** (2), **727** (5), **744** (7)

unbecoming **25** (5), **842** (5), **867** (5)

unbelief **486** (1), **533** (1), **865** (1), **974** (1)

unbelievable **486** (5), **864** (5)

unbelievably **486** (9)

unbelieved **486** (5)

unbeliever **486** (3), **974** (3), **980** (3)

unbelieving **474** (6), **486** (4), **489** (3), **865** (2), **974** (5), **980** (4)

unbend **249** (4), **872** (5), **882** (8), **905** (7), **909** (4)

unbending **83** (6), **481** (7), **599** (2), **602** (4), **735** (4), **883** (5)

unbent **249** (2)

unbiased **480** (4), **494** (4), **913** (4)

unbidden **595** (1), **597** (5), **860** (3)

unbind **668** (3), **746** (3)

unblemished **44** (5)

unblushing **820** (5), **871** (3), **878** (4), **934** (3), **940** (2), **951** (7)

unblushingly **940** (5)

unborn, the **67** (3)

unbosom oneself **526** (5)

unbound **744** (6), **746** (2)

unbounded **107** (2)

unbowed **215** (2), **727** (5), **855** (4)

unbridled **176** (5), **734** (4), **744** (6)

unbroken **52** (5), **71** (4)

unburden **701** (9), **831** (3)

unburden oneself **526** (5)

uncalled for **637** (4), **916** (5)

uncannily **970** (9)

uncanny **970** (7), **983** (8)

uncared for **458** (3), **860** (3)

uncaring **860** (2)

unceasing **111** (2), **113** (4), **115** (2), **144** (2), **146** (2), **600** (3), **678** (7) uncensored 951 (6)

unceremonious 885 (4)

uncertain 152 (3), 159 (5), 159 (6), 459 (12), 467 (3), 472 (2), 474 (4), 474 (6), 475 (8), 491 (4), 491 (5), 495 (5), 517 (3), 517 (5), 568 (2), 618 (7)

uncertain, be 136 (6), 474 (8), 486 (7), 491 (8), 517 (7), 601 (4), 661 (7), 679 (11), 700 (7)

uncertain temper 892 (1)

uncertainty 159 (1), 472 (1), 474 (1), 486 (2), 491 (1), 507 (1), 518 (1), 568 (1), 601 (1), 618 (2), 661 (1)

uncertified 474 (7)

unchangeable 113 (4), 153 (4), 823 (3)

unchanging 13 (2), 16 (2), 144 (2), 153 (4)

uncharacteristic 84 (7)

uncharged 812 (4)

uncharitable 816 (4), 932 (3)

uncharted 491 (6)

unchaste 934 (4), 943 (2), 951 (7)

unchastity 859 (4), 951 (2)

unchecked 744 (6), 857 (3)

unchivalrous 885 (4)

unchristian 974 (6)

uncircumcised 974 (6)

uncivil 847 (5), 885 (4)

uncivilized 491 (4), 847 (5), 869 (9)

unclaimed 774 (3)

unclassified 61 (7)

uncle 11 (2), 372 (1), 784 (3)

unclean 649 (6), 653 (2), 842 (3), 867 (4), 951 (6)

unclean, be 51 (5), 649 (8)

uncleaned 423 (2), 649 (7)

uncleanliness 649 (1)

uncleanness 51 (2), 61 (1), 645 (1), 649 (1), 653 (1), 655 (3), 675 (1), 842 (1), 951 (1)

unclear 514 (4), 517 (3), 568 (2), 576 (2)

unclothed 229 (4)

uncluttered 60 (2)

uncoil 249 (4), 316 (3)

uncomfortable 377 (3), 825 (5), 827 (4)

uncomforted 829 (3)

uncommitted 601 (3), 620 (3), 625 (3), 744 (7)

uncommon 80 (5), 140 (2)

uncommonly 32 (19)

uncommunicative 525 (6), 883 (5)

uncompetitive 717 (3)

uncomplaining 823 (4)

uncompleted 55 (3), 68 (6), 458 (3), 695 (6), 726 (2)

uncomplicated 44 (4)

uncomplimentary 885 (5), 924 (6)

uncompromising 83 (6), 599 (2), 602 (4), 735 (4)

unconcealed 522 (4)

unconcern 454 (1), 860 (1)

unconcerned 454 (2), 820 (3), 860 (2), 860 (4)

unconditional 54 (3), 744 (8), 756 (4), 917 (6)

unconfined 744 (6), 746 (2)

unconfirmed 474 (7)

unconformable 84 (5), 489 (3), 769 (2)

unconformable, be 84 (8), 769 (3)

unconformity 25 (2)

uncongealed 335 (4)

uncongenial 834 (8)

unconnected 10 (3)

unconquerable 727 (5)

unconquered 744 (7)

unconscious 161 (7), 320 (2), 375 (3), 491 (4), 596 (5), 820 (3)

unconscious, the 447 (2)

unconsciousness 375 (1), 491 (1)

unconsidered 450 (3), 458 (3)

unconstitutional 916 (6), 954 (5)

uncontentions 717 (3)

uncontrived 699 (3)

uncontrollable 176 (5), 818 (5)

uncontroversial 488 (5)

unconventional 17 (2), 84 (5), 84 (8), 744 (7)

unconventionality 84 (1), 611 (1)

unconvincing 472 (2), 572 (2)

uncooked 391 (2), 670 (5)

uncooperative 709 (6)

uncoordinated 61 (7)

uncork 263 (17), 746 (3)

uncouple 46 (8)

uncoupling 46 (2)

uncouth 244 (2), 576 (2), 695 (5), 699 (3), 842 (5), 847 (5), 869 (8), 885 (4)

uncouthness 576 (1), 699 (1)

uncover 46 (8), 165 (7), 207 (5), 229 (6), 229 (7), 263 (17), 300 (8), 304 (4), 484 (4), 522 (7), 526 (4), 786 (10), 920 (6)

uncovered 163 (5), 229 (4), 522 (5), 526 (2), 661 (5)

uncovering 229 (1), 263 (1), 526 (1)

uncritical 464 (3), 923 (5)

unction 357 (1), 357 (4), 979 (3)

unctuous 357 (7), 818 (3), 879 (3), 925 (3)

unctuousness 357 (1), 925 (1), 979 (3)

uncultivated 172 (4), 491 (5)

uncurl 249 (4), 316 (3)

uncut 52 (5)

undamaged 52 (5), 646 (4), 660 (4)

undaughterly 918 (2)

undaunted 599 (2), 600 (3), 855 (5)

undeceive 524 (9), 526 (4)

undeceived 830 (2)

undeceived, be 516 (5)

undecided 459 (12), 474 (4), 474 (6), 486 (4), 601 (3), 606 (2)

undecipherable 517 (2)

undeclared 523 (3)
undefeated 715 (2), 727 (5)
undefended 661 (5)
undefiled 950 (5)
undemanding 701 (3), 736 (2)
undemocratic 735 (5)
undemonstrative 820 (3)
undeniable 473 (6), 478 (3)
undeniably 478 (6)
undependable 474 (5)
under 9 (10), 35 (4), 186 (5), 210 (2), 210 (4), 214 (5), 745 (5)
under a ban 899 (5)
under a charm 983 (9)
under a cloud 731 (5), 731 (6), 924 (7), 928 (6)
under a curse 983 (9)
under a spell 596 (5), 899 (5), 983 (9)
under-age 130 (4)
under arms 718 (8)
under arrest 747 (6), 750 (2)
under canvas 226 (12), 269 (13), 275 (12)
under consideration 452 (3)
under control 60 (2), 739 (3), 747 (5)
under cover 226 (12), 660 (10)
under cover, be 660 (7)
under cover of 542 (11)
under detention 747 (6), 750 (2)
under duress 740 (4)
under false pretences 541 (9)
under fire 661 (6), 700 (5)
under investigation 459 (17)
under licence 756 (7)
under lock and key 750 (2)
under oath 764 (2)
under obligation 917 (5)
under one's belt 725 (4)
under one's breath 401 (6), 578 (6)

under one's nose 189 (2), 200 (7), 443 (2)
under one's thumb 745 (5)
under orders 739 (5)
under pressure 598 (5), 700 (5)
under protest 489 (6), 598 (5), 740 (4), 924 (15)
under-ripe 670 (4)
under sail 269 (13), 275 (12)
under-secretary 690 (4)
under sedation 266 (5)
under sentence 114 (4), 480 (7)
under sentence of death 361 (5)
under shelter 660 (10)
under shelter, be 660 (7)
under steam 269 (13), 275 (12)
under strength 636 (4)
under suspicion 928 (6)
under the eyes or the nose of 189 (6)
under the hammer 793 (3)
under the influence 949 (6)
under the sun 1 (4), 321 (18)
under the table 949 (8)
under the weather 651 (21)
under the yoke 745 (4)
under training 536 (6)
under treatment 651 (24)
under trial 480 (7)
under way 265 (3), 265 (6), 269 (13), 285 (5), 669 (14)
underachieve 307 (3)
underachiever 538 (1)
underact 594 (17)
underbelly 210 (1)
undercarriage 218 (13), 276 (1)
undercharge 808 (5), 812 (6)
underclothes 228 (17)
undercover 523 (2), 525 (3)
undercover agent 459 (7)
undercurrent 350 (2)

undercurrents 156 (2)
undercut 793 (4), 812 (6)
underdog 35 (2), 728 (3), 731 (3), 801 (2)
underdone 301 (34), 670 (5)
underestimate 37 (4), 458 (5), 481 (9), 483 (1), 483 (4), 495 (7), 921 (5), 922 (6), 926 (6)
underestimation 37 (2), 483 (1)
underfed 636 (5), 801 (3), 859 (9), 946 (3)
underfoot 210 (4), 745 (4)
undergo 154 (7), 818 (7), 825 (7)
undergo penance 941 (6)
undergraduate 538 (3), 670 (4)
underground 210 (2), 210 (4), 211 (2), 525 (3), 527 (1), 704 (1), 738 (4)
underground passage 527 (1)
underground railway 624 (7)
undergrowth 366 (2)
underhand 523 (4), 525 (5), 930 (4)
underhung 254 (4)
underlay 207 (1)
underlie 210 (3), 523 (5)
underline 162 (12), 455 (7), 532 (7), 547 (19), 638 (8)
underling 35 (2), 639 (4), 742 (1)
underlining 547 (14)
underlying 214 (3)
undermanned 307 (2)
undermine 161 (9), 163 (10), 165 (7), 255 (8), 311 (6), 467 (4), 623 (9), 655 (9), 702 (8), 712 (8)
undermined 163 (5), 655 (5)
undermining 221 (2)
undermost 214 (3)
underneath 210 (4)
undernourished 636 (5), 651 (20)
underpaid 801 (3)

underpants 228 (17)

underpass 263 (8), 305 (1), 624 (3)

underpin 218 (15)

underpinning 218 (1), 218 (2)

underprivileged, the 801 (2)

underproof 163 (4), 387 (2)

underrate 483 (4), 921 (5), 922 (6)

underrated 483 (3), 921 (4)

undersea 211 (2)

undersell 812 (6)

underside 210 (1)

undersigned, the 765 (3)

undersized 33 (6), 196 (9), 206 (5)

understaffed 307 (2), 636 (4)

understand 447 (7), 484 (4), 490 (8), 498 (6), 514 (5), 516 (5), 520 (8), 523 (6), 524 (12), 865 (4), 880 (7), 897 (5)

understand by 514 (5)

understandable 516 (2)

understanding 24 (1), 447 (1), 488 (2), 490 (1), 498 (1), 513 (1), 710 (1), 719 (1), 765 (1), 818 (1), 880 (2), 880 (6), 887 (1), 897 (1), 905 (1), 905 (4)

understate 483 (4), 541 (5)

understatement 483 (1)

understood 490 (7), 523 (3)

understood, be 516 (4)

understrength 163 (4)

understudy 150 (2), 594 (9), 594 (17), 755 (1)

undertake 68 (8), 461 (8), 617 (5), 671 (4), 672 (3), 676 (5), 765 (5), 855 (6)

undertake to 764 (4)

undertaker 364 (1)

undertaking 159 (4), 164 (1), 617 (1), 618 (4), 622 (1), 661 (1), 671 (1), 672 (1), 676 (2), 751 (2), 764 (1), 791 (2)

undertone 401 (1), 410 (2), 523 (1), 578 (1)

undertow 14 (1), 350 (2), 663 (1)

undervaluation 481 (1)

undervalue 483 (4)

undervalued 483 (3), 921 (4)

underwater 211 (2), 343 (3)

underwear 198 (3), 228 (17)

underweight 29 (2), 163 (6), 323 (3)

underweight, be 29 (3)

underworld 211 (1), 361 (3), 869 (3), 904 (3), 934 (1), 972 (1)

underwrite 765 (5), 767 (6)

underwriter 754 (1), 767 (1)

underwriting 159 (4), 767 (1)

undesirable 643 (2), 663 (2), 827 (4), 860 (3), 861 (3), 938 (1)

undeveloped 499 (3), 523 (2), 670 (4)

undevelopment 647 (1), 670 (2), 726 (1)

undeviating 249 (2), 625 (4)

undies 228 (17)

undifferentiated 16 (2), 464 (2)

undignified 847 (4)

undiluted 44 (5)

undiminished 52 (5)

undimmed 417 (9)

undiplomatic 695 (3)

undiscerning 464 (3)

undisciplined 61 (9), 738 (7), 943 (2)

undisclosed 525 (3)

undiscouraged 852 (4)

undiscovered 491 (6)

undisguised 522 (5), 540 (2), 699 (3)

undismayed 855 (5)

undisputed 473 (6), 488 (5), 494 (4)

undistinguished 464 (2), 732 (2)

undisturbed 266 (5)

undivided 52 (5)

undo 46 (8), 148 (3), 165 (6), 182 (3), 263 (17), 641 (7)

undoing 46 (2), 165 (1)

undomesticated 611 (3)

undone 165 (5), 458 (3), 726 (2)

undoubted 473 (6)

undreamt of 450 (3)

undress 228 (6), 229 (1), 229 (6), 229 (7)

undressed 229 (4), 670 (5)

undrinkable 653 (2)

undue 25 (5), 643 (2), 916 (5)

undue, be 734 (6), 735 (8), 786 (7), 916 (8)

undueness 916 (1)

undulate 251 (11), 317 (4)

undulating 251 (7)

undulation 251 (1), 317 (1)

undulatory 248 (3), 251 (7)

unduly 32 (18)

undutiful 458 (2), 603 (4), 769 (2), 918 (2)

undutifulness 603 (1), 620 (2), 621 (1), 738 (1), 918 (1), 930 (2)

undying 115 (2), 146 (2)

unearth 304 (4), 364 (10), 484 (4)

unearthly 59 (4), 320 (3), 970 (7)

unease 616 (1), 825 (3)

uneasiness 825 (3), 829 (1), 854 (2)

uneasy 854 (7)

uneatable 391 (2)

uneconomic 634 (2)

uneconomical 815 (3)

unedifying 934 (4), 934 (6)

uneducated 491 (5)

unemotional 820 (3)

unemphatic 573 (2)

unemployable 641 (4)

unemployed 674 (2), 677 (2)

unemployment 637 (2), 674 (1), 679 (1)

unending 115 (2)

unenlightened 491 (4)

unenthusiastic 598 (3), 820 (4)

unentitled 916 (7)

unequal 10 (3), 15 (4), 17 (2), 19 (2), 29 (2), 322 (4)

unequal, be 29 (3), 34 (8)

unequal to 636 (3)

unequalled 29 (2), 34 (5), 644 (6)

unequally 29 (4)

unequipped 161 (6), 670 (6)

unequivocal 32 (14), 473 (4), 473 (5), 516 (2)

unequivocally 32 (16)

unerring 473 (4), 727 (4)

uneven 17 (2), 29 (2), 72 (2), 142 (2), 259 (4), 647 (3)

unevenly 17 (3), 29 (4), 142 (3)

unevenness 17 (1), 29 (1), 72 (1), 259 (1), 647 (1)

uneventful 266 (5), 838 (3)

unexaggerated 540 (2)

unexamined 458 (3)

unexciting 838 (3)

unexpected 135 (4), 152 (3), 472 (2), 508 (2), 604 (3), 864 (5), 916 (5)

unexpected, the 508 (1)

unexpectedly 135 (8), 508 (6)

unexpurgated 52 (5), 951 (6)

unfailing 146 (2), 600 (3)

unfair 29 (2), 914 (4)

unfair, be 481 (12)

unfairness 914 (2)

unfaithful 486 (4), 603 (4), 769 (2), 881 (3), 930 (7), 951 (9)

unfaithful, be 951 (10)

unfaithfulness 930 (2), 951 (3)

unfaltering 600 (3)

unfamiliar 84 (6), 611 (3)

unfamiliar with 491 (4)

unfamiliarity 491 (1), 611 (1)

unfashionable 611 (5), 847 (5)

unfashionableness 847 (1)

unfasten 49 (3)

unfathomable 517 (2)

unfavourable 138 (3), 702 (6), 704 (3), 731 (4), 924 (6)

unfearing 599 (2), 855 (5), 980 (4)

unfeasible 470 (3)

unfed 946 (3)

unfeeling 375 (4), 820 (3), 906 (2), 950 (5)

unfeeling person 820 (2)

unfeigned 540 (2)

unfetter 46 (8), 746 (3)

unfettered 744 (6)

unfilial 918 (2)

unfinished 55 (4), 726 (2)

unfit 161 (9), 641 (7), 643 (2), 647 (3), 695 (3)

unfit for 25 (5)

unfitness 25 (2), 161 (1), 641 (1), 643 (1), 670 (1)

unfitted 161 (5), 670 (6)

unfitting 25 (5), 914 (3)

unflagging 162 (7), 600 (3), 678 (9)

unflappable 498 (5), 823 (3)

unflattering 842 (5), 921 (3), 924 (6)

unflinching 599 (2), 855 (4)

unfold 1 (7), 157 (5), 203 (8), 229 (6), 249 (4), 263 (17), 304 (4), 316 (3), 520 (8)

unfold a tale 590 (7)

unfolding 316 (1)

unforeseeable 474 (4), 508 (2)

unforeseen 472 (2), 508 (2)

unforeseen, the 508 (1)

unforgettable 505 (5)

unforgivable 934 (6)

unforgiving 898 (6), 906 (2), 910 (4)

unformed 670 (4)

unfortified 163 (4)

unfortunate 25 (5), 616 (2), 728 (4), 731 (6), 825 (6), 827 (5), 853 (2)

unfortunately 731 (8)

unfounded 4 (3), 477 (5), 495 (4), 543 (4)

unfrequented 883 (7)

unfriendliness 881 (1)

unfriendly 881 (3), 883 (5), 885 (5), 898 (6)

unfrock 752 (5), 786 (10), 963 (8), 988 (10)

unfrocking 752 (2)

unfurl 203 (8), 249 (4), 316 (3), 526 (4)

unfurling 316 (1)

ungainly 695 (5), 842 (5)

ungenerous 816 (4), 898 (6), 932 (3)

ungentlemanly 847 (5)

ungifted 499 (3), 695 (3)

ungodliness 934 (1), 974 (1)

ungodly 934 (3), 974 (5), 980 (4)

ungovernable 738 (7), 744 (7), 954 (7)

ungraceful 842 (5)

ungracious 569 (2), 871 (4), 885 (5), 898 (6)

ungraciousness 885 (2)

ungraded 61 (7)

ungrammatical 560 (4), 565 (2)

ungrammatical, be 565 (3)

ungrateful 506 (4), 908 (2)

ungrateful, be 908 (4)

ungratefulness 908 (1)

ungrudging 597 (4), 813 (3)

ungrudgingly 813 (5)

unguarded 458 (2), 458 (3), 609 (3), 670 (3)

unguent 334 (2), 357 (4), 843 (3)

unhabituated 611 (3)

unhappily 731 (8)

unhappiness 825 (2), 834 (1)

unhappy 138 (3), 643 (2), 695 (6), 731 (6), 825 (6),

829 (3), 834 (5), 834 (6), 836 (4), 854 (7)

unhappy times 825 (1)

unhealthily 651 (24), 653 (5)

unhealthiness 651 (1), 653 (1)

unhealthy 163 (6), 362 (8), 426 (3), 643 (2), 645 (3), 647 (3), 651 (20), 653 (2)

unheard 491 (6)

unheard of 126 (5), 470 (2), 472 (2), 491 (6), 867 (7)

unhearing 375 (3), 456 (3), 820 (3)

unheeding 456 (3)

unhelpful 598 (3), 643 (2), 702 (6), 898 (6)

unhelpfulness 598 (1)

unheralded 508 (2)

unheroic 856 (3)

unhinge 63 (3), 503 (12)

unhinged 161 (7), 503 (8)

unhistorical 513 (6)

unholy 974 (6), 980 (5)

unholy joy 824 (1), 898 (1)

unhook 46 (8)

unhoped for 508 (2)

unhopeful 853 (2)

unhorsed 728 (6)

unhurried 278 (3), 681 (2), 823 (3)

unhurt 646 (4)

unhygienic 653 (2)

unicorn 84 (4), 547 (11)

unidentified 10 (3), 491 (6)

unidiomatic 515 (4), 560 (4)

unification 44 (2), 45 (1), 45 (2), 50 (1), 88 (1), 706 (2)

uniform 13 (2), 16 (1), 16 (2), 18 (4), 24 (5), 28 (7), 44 (4), 48 (2), 52 (6), 60 (2), 81 (3), 88 (3), 106 (3), 153 (4), 228 (5), 228 (31), 245 (2), 258 (3), 494 (6), 547 (10), 743 (3), 823 (3), 838 (3)

uniform, be 16 (3)

uniformed 16 (2), 228 (29), 718 (8)

uniformity 13 (1), 16 (1), 24 (1), 24 (2), 28 (1), 44 (1), 60 (1), 71 (1), 81 (2), 141 (1), 153 (1), 245 (1), 265 (1), 610 (1), 838 (1)

uniformly 16 (5)

uniformness 16 (1)

unify 44 (6), 45 (9), 50 (4)

unilateral 10 (3), 88 (3), 744 (7)

unimaginable 472 (2)

unimaginative 450 (2), 481 (7), 499 (3), 573 (2), 820 (3), 840 (2), 865 (2)

unimpaired 52 (5)

unimpeachable 473 (6), 915 (2), 935 (4)

unimpeded 701 (5)

unimportance 33 (1), 35 (1), 639 (1), 922 (2)

unimportant 33 (7), 35 (3), 491 (6), 639 (5), 867 (4), 922 (4)

unimportant, be 161 (8), 639 (7)

unimpressed 860 (2), 865 (2), 924 (6)

unimpressive 647 (3)

uninformed 491 (5)

uninhabitable 190 (5)

uninhabited 190 (5), 883 (7)

uninhibited 699 (3), 744 (6)

uninquisitive 454 (2)

uninspired 572 (2), 820 (4), 838 (3)

uninspiring 572 (2)

uninstructed 491 (5), 495 (5), 670 (3), 695 (4)

unintegrated 59 (4)

unintelligence 464 (1), 491 (1), 499 (1), 820 (1)

unintelligent 448 (2), 450 (2), 491 (4), 499 (3), 503 (7), 820 (3)

unintelligibility 515 (1), 517 (1), 518 (1), 530 (2), 568 (1), 700 (1)

unintelligible 491 (6), 517 (2), 523 (2), 525 (3), 568 (2), 700 (4)

unintelligible, be 515 (6), 517 (6)

unintended 159 (6), 515 (5)

unintentional 159 (6), 596 (5), 618 (5)

unintentionally 159 (8)

uninterested 454 (2), 456 (3), 606 (2), 820 (4), 838 (4), 860 (2)

uninteresting 838 (3)

uninterrupted 71 (4), 115 (2), 146 (2)

uninvited 860 (3)

uninvited guest 59 (3)

uninviting 391 (2), 827 (4), 834 (8)

uninvolved 10 (3)

union 24 (1), 38 (1), 43 (1), 45 (1), 45 (3), 48 (1), 50 (1), 74 (3), 88 (1), 181 (1), 202 (1), 293 (1), 622 (1), 708 (3), 894 (1)

Union Jack 547 (12)

unionists 708 (2)

unique 17 (2), 19 (2), 21 (4), 80 (5), 84 (5), 84 (6), 88 (3), 644 (7)

uniqueness 17 (1), 21 (1), 80 (1), 84 (1), 88 (1)

unirrigated 342 (4)

unisex 13 (2), 16 (2), 228 (30)

unison 16 (1), 24 (1), 410 (1), 488 (2), 710 (1)

unit 23 (1), 52 (1), 52 (2), 58 (1), 74 (3), 74 (4), 88 (2), 194 (5), 371 (3), 722 (8)

unit of energy 465 (3)

unit of length 203 (4)

unit of sound 398 (1)

unit of work 160 (3)

unite 45 (9), 50 (4), 74 (11), 88 (5), 181 (3), 293 (3), 706 (4)

unite with 45 (14), 167 (7), 887 (13), 894 (11), 951 (11)

united **24** (5), **48** (2), **50** (3), **710** (2), **894** (7)
united front **706** (2)
United Reformed **976** (11)
unitedly **48** (5), **74** (12)
unity **13** (1), **24** (1), **44** (1), **48** (1), **50** (1), **52** (1), **88** (1), **706** (2), **710** (1)
universal **1** (1), **32** (5), **52** (4), **52** (7), **78** (2), **79** (1), **79** (4), **189** (3), **321** (13), **321** (15), **610** (6)
universal suffrage **605** (2)
universality **79** (1), **464** (1)
universalize **79** (6)
universally **32** (17)
universe **3** (1), **52** (1), **79** (1), **321** (1)
university **539** (1)
university education **534** (2)
unjust **29** (2), **735** (6), **914** (4), **914** (5), **934** (3)
unjustifiable **916** (6)
unkempt **61** (7), **259** (4), **458** (3), **649** (7)
unkind **645** (3), **898** (6), **932** (3)
unkind, be **645** (6)
unkindly **898** (6)
unkindness **645** (1), **898** (2), **898** (3)
unknowing **491** (1), **491** (4)
unknown **84** (5), **84** (6), **126** (5), **491** (6), **523** (2), **525** (4), **562** (4), **867** (7), **883** (7)
unknown person **491** (2)
unknown quantity **85** (1), **491** (2), **530** (1)
unknown thing **491** (2), **530** (1)
unladylike **847** (5)
unlamented **888** (6), **924** (7)
unlawful **757** (3), **769** (2), **951** (9), **954** (5)
unlawful desires **951** (3)
unlawfully **954** (10)
unlawfulness **914** (2), **954** (1)
unlearn **491** (8), **506** (5)
unlearned **491** (5), **699** (3)

unleash **746** (3)
unleavened **988** (8)
unless **8** (6), **468** (4)
unlettered **491** (5), **847** (5)
unlike **15** (4), **19** (2)
unlike, be **19** (3)
unlikelihood **472** (1)
unlikely **472** (2)
unlikely, be **472** (3), **486** (8), **508** (4), **543** (5)
unlikeness **15** (1), **19** (1), **21** (1), **29** (1)
unlimited **107** (2)
unlit **418** (4), **419** (5), **444** (2)
unliterary **560** (5)
unload **188** (4), **272** (7), **295** (5), **300** (8), **304** (4), **812** (6)
unloaded **701** (5)
unloading **39** (1), **188** (1), **272** (1)
unlock **263** (17), **668** (3), **746** (3), **779** (4)
unlock the door **297** (5)
unlooked for **508** (2), **916** (5)
unloose **46** (8), **668** (3), **746** (3)
unlovable **861** (3), **888** (5)
unloved **888** (5), **888** (6)
unlovely **842** (3), **861** (3)
unluckily **159** (8)
unlucky **616** (2), **728** (4), **731** (6), **825** (6), **827** (5)
unlucky person **728** (3), **731** (3), **825** (4)
unmake **148** (3), **165** (6)
unman **161** (10), **172** (6), **655** (9), **854** (12)
unmanageable **700** (4), **738** (7)
unmanliness **856** (1)
unmanly **373** (5)
unmannerly **847** (5), **885** (4)
unmarked **646** (4)
unmarried **895** (4)
unmarried man **895** (2)
unmarried mother **373** (3)
unmarried state **744** (2)
unmarried woman **373** (3), **895** (3)

unmask **526** (4)
unmeant **515** (5)
unmentionable **757** (3), **951** (6)
unmethodical **61** (7)
unmindful **456** (3), **506** (4), **908** (2)
unmistakable **443** (2), **473** (4), **522** (4)
unmitigated **32** (13), **54** (3), **832** (2)
unmixed **44** (5), **52** (4), **54** (3)
unmotivated **609** (3)
unmoved **820** (4), **860** (2), **898** (6), **906** (2)
unmoving **266** (6)
unmusical **411** (2), **416** (2)
unnamed **562** (4)
unnatural **25** (4), **59** (4), **84** (6), **84** (7), **470** (2), **850** (4), **898** (6), **898** (7)
unnaturalness **543** (2)
unnecessarily **637** (7)
unnecessary **634** (2), **637** (4), **639** (5), **641** (4), **674** (2)
unnerve **161** (10), **163** (10), **834** (12), **854** (12)
unnerved **161** (7), **834** (5)
unnoticed **444** (2)
unnumbered **104** (4), **107** (2)
unobservant **456** (3)
unobtainable **636** (6)
unobtrusive **874** (2)
unoccupied **190** (5)
unofficial **474** (7), **744** (7), **954** (5), **954** (7)
unopposed **488** (5)
unoriginal **20** (4), **840** (2)
unorthodox **84** (5), **495** (4), **977** (2), **977** (4)
unorthodoxly **977** (5)
unorthodoxy **84** (1), **977** (1)
unpack **229** (6), **263** (17), **300** (8), **304** (4)
unpacking **188** (1), **272** (1)
unpaid **803** (5)
unpaid worker **597** (3)
unpalatable **391** (2), **827** (4)

465

unpalatable, be 391 (3), 655 (7)

unparalleled 34 (5), 84 (6), 644 (6)

unpardonable 914 (3)

unpeopled 190 (5)

unperfumed 395 (2)

unpick 46 (8)

unplaced 188 (2), 728 (4), 728 (5)

unpleasant 377 (3), 391 (2), 397 (2), 827 (4), 885 (4)

unpleasantness 827 (1)

unpleasing 827 (4)

unplumbed 211 (2), 491 (6)

unpoetical 593 (9)

unpointed 257 (2)

unpolished 576 (2)

unpopular 861 (3), 867 (4), 883 (6), 888 (6)

unpopularity 888 (2), 924 (1)

unpossessed 774 (3)

unpracticable 674 (2)

unpractised, be 611 (5)

unprecedented 19 (2), 21 (3), 68 (7), 126 (5), 140 (2), 491 (6), 508 (2), 611 (2), 864 (5)

unpredictability 17 (1), 142 (1), 618 (1)

unpredictable 17 (2), 152 (3), 159 (6), 474 (4), 604 (3)

unprejudiced 498 (5), 744 (5), 913 (4)

unpremediated 596 (5), 609 (3)

unpremeditation 609 (1)

unprepared 458 (2), 508 (3), 609 (3), 670 (3), 680 (2), 695 (6)

unprepared, be 670 (7)

unprepossessing 842 (3)

unpresentable 847 (5)

unpretentious 573 (2), 872 (3), 874 (2)

unpretentiousness 872 (1)

unprincipled 930 (4), 934 (3)

unprintable 757 (3), 951 (6)

unproductive 172 (4), 641 (5)

unproductive, be 172 (5)

unproductiveness 172 (1), 636 (2)

unprofessional 769 (2)

unprofitable 643 (2), 772 (2)

unprolific 172 (5)

unpromising 853 (3)

unprosperous 731 (5)

unproved 477 (6)

unproven 467 (3)

unprovided 636 (4)

unprovided for 801 (3)

unprovoked 609 (3), 860 (3)

unprovoked attack 712 (1)

unpunctual 136 (3)

unpunctuality 118 (1)

unqualified 54 (3), 161 (5), 473 (5), 491 (4), 491 (7), 641 (4), 670 (6), 695 (4), 916 (7)

unquestionable 473 (6), 494 (4)

unquestioned 485 (6)

unquestioning 485 (4)

unquiet 318 (4)

unquiet conscience 939 (1)

unravel 44 (6), 46 (7), 46 (8), 62 (7), 249 (4), 258 (4), 304 (4), 316 (3), 701 (9), 746 (3)

unravelled 44 (4), 62 (3)

unravelling 46 (2)

unread 458 (3)

unreadable 517 (2), 840 (2)

unreadily 670 (8)

unreadiness 670 (1)

unreal 2 (4), 512 (5), 513 (6)

unrealistic 470 (2), 481 (6)

unreasonable 470 (2), 477 (5), 481 (8), 499 (5), 604 (3), 914 (3)

unreasoning 448 (2), 481 (8), 499 (5)

unrecognizable 525 (4)

unrecognized 525 (4)

unrefined 699 (3), 847 (4)

unreflecting 450 (2), 454 (2)

unregretted 888 (6), 924 (7), 940 (3)

unregretting 940 (2)

unrehearsed 618 (5)

unrelated 10 (3)

unrelated, be 10 (5)

unrelatedly 10 (6)

unrelatedness 10 (1)

unrelenting 906 (2), 910 (4), 940 (2)

unreliability 474 (3)

unreliable 152 (3), 474 (5), 486 (5), 604 (3), 918 (2), 930 (4)

unrelieved 16 (2), 829 (3), 832 (2), 834 (8)

unremarked 867 (7)

unremitting 71 (4), 600 (3)

unrenowned 867 (7)

unrepentant 940 (2)

unrepented 940 (3)

unreserved 473 (5), 522 (5), 540 (2), 699 (3), 744 (5)

unreservedly 32 (16)

unresisting 721 (2), 739 (3)

unrespected 921 (4), 922 (4)

unresponsive 820 (3), 906 (2)

unrest 829 (1)

unrestrained 576 (2), 701 (5), 744 (6)

unrestricted 744 (8)

unretentive 491 (4)

unrewarded 908 (3)

unrewarding 641 (5), 908 (3)

unrighteous 934 (3)

unripe 393 (2), 670 (4)

unrivalled 34 (5)

unroll 203 (8), 249 (4), 316 (3)

unruffled 258 (3), 266 (5), 820 (3), 823 (3)

unruffled state 823 (1)

unruliness 61 (1)

unruly 61 (9), 176 (5), 602 (5), 734 (4), 738 (7), 738 (8)
unsafe 474 (4), 661 (4)
unsaid 523 (3)
unsatisfactory 55 (3), 636 (3), 643 (2)
unsatisfied 636 (4), 859 (7), 912 (2)
unsatisfied, be 636 (8), 859 (11)
unsatisfying 829 (4)
unsavouriness 301 (9), 391 (1)
unsavoury 387 (2), 391 (2), 393 (2), 827 (4), 860 (3), 861 (3)
unscathed 646 (4)
unschooled 491 (5)
unscientific 695 (4)
unscramble 44 (6), 51 (5), 62 (7)
unscriptural 977 (2)
unscrupulous 930 (4), 934 (3)
unseasonable 25 (5), 138 (2)
unseasoned 387 (2)
unseat 188 (4), 734 (7), 752 (5)
unseated 46 (4)
unseeing 375 (3), 439 (2), 456 (3), 499 (5), 820 (3)
unseemliness 847 (1)
unseemly 499 (5), 914 (3), 934 (4)
unseen 444 (2), 491 (6), 523 (2)
unseen, be 444 (4), 446 (3), 523 (5)
unselfish 897 (4), 931 (2), 931 (3), 933 (3)
unselfishness 931 (1)
unserviceable 641 (4)
unsettle 63 (3), 821 (8)
unsettled 114 (3), 152 (4), 188 (2), 190 (5)
unshackle 746 (3)
unshakable 45 (7), 153 (6), 473 (4), 485 (6), 599 (2)
unsharpened 257 (2)
unshockable 820 (3)
unshriven 940 (2)

unsightly 246 (4), 842 (4)
unsigned 562 (4)
unskilful 161 (5), 491 (4), 611 (3), 641 (4), 695 (3)
unskilful, be 695 (7)
unskilfulness 25 (2), 161 (1), 499 (1), 641 (1), 695 (1)
unskilled 670 (4), 695 (4), 699 (3)
unsleeping 678 (9)
unsmiling 834 (7), 885 (5), 893 (2)
unsociability 883 (1), 892 (1), 893 (1), 902 (1)
unsociable 84 (5), 88 (4), 525 (6), 744 (7), 881 (3), 883 (5), 885 (5), 893 (2), 898 (6), 902 (3)
unsociable, be 881 (5), 883 (8), 893 (3)
unsocial 883 (5)
unsocial person 883 (3)
unsolicited 597 (5)
unsophisticated 699 (3)
unsought 597 (5)
unsound 35 (4), 152 (4), 477 (5), 495 (4), 647 (3), 651 (20), 661 (4)
unsound mind 448 (1), 503 (1)
unsounded 211 (2)
unsoundness 495 (1), 645 (1), 647 (1)
unsparing 635 (4), 735 (4), 735 (6), 813 (3), 931 (2)
unsparingly 32 (20)
unspeakable 32 (11), 517 (4)
unspeakably 32 (17)
unspoken 523 (3)
unsportsmanlike 914 (4)
unspotted 935 (3)
unstable 152 (4), 163 (4), 604 (3), 822 (3), 822 (4)
unsteadiness 152 (1), 163 (1)
unsteady 142 (2), 152 (4), 661 (4)
unsterilized 649 (6)
unstick 46 (8), 49 (3)
unstimulating 840 (2)
unstinting 813 (3)

unstop 263 (17), 746 (3)
unstoppable 146 (2)
unstopped 263 (13)
unstopping 263 (1)
unstuck 46 (4)
unstudied 670 (3), 699 (3)
unsubstantially 4 (4)
unsuccessful 172 (4), 509 (3), 670 (4), 695 (3), 728 (4), 731 (5), 829 (3), 924 (7)
unsuccessfully 728 (10)
unsuitable 25 (5), 607 (2), 643 (2)
unsuited to 25 (5)
unsung 523 (3), 867 (7)
unsupplied 636 (4)
unsure 474 (4)
unsurpassed 34 (5)
unsurprised 865 (2)
unsuspecting 487 (2), 508 (3)
unsweetened 393 (2)
unswerving 249 (2)
unsymmetrical 246 (3)
unsympathetic 898 (6), 906 (2)
unsystematic 17 (2), 61 (7)
unsystematically 17 (3)
untalented 695 (3)
untamed 738 (7)
untangle 62 (7)
untapped 674 (2)
untaught 491 (5)
untempting 860 (3)
untenable 477 (5), 486 (5)
untested 126 (5)
unthanked 908 (3)
unthankful 908 (2)
unthinkable 470 (2)
unthinking 448 (2), 450 (2), 454 (2), 456 (3), 458 (2), 499 (5), 596 (5)
unthought 450 (3)
unthought of 450 (3)
unthrone 734 (7)
untidiness 61 (1)
untidy 61 (7), 649 (7), 649 (9)
untie 46 (8), 701 (9), 746 (3), 779 (4)
untied 46 (4)

until 108 (10)
until now 121 (5)
untilled 172 (4), 674 (2)
untimeliness 25 (2), 118 (1), 138 (1), 695 (2)
untimely 10 (3), 138 (2), 643 (2)
untimely end 361 (2)
untiring 600 (3)
untitled 869 (8)
untold 104 (4), 107 (2), 491 (6), 525 (3)
untold of 523 (3)
untouchable 757 (3), 883 (4)
untouched 52 (5)
untoward 138 (3), 643 (2)
untraceable 772 (3)
untried 126 (5)
untrodden 126 (5)
untroubled 828 (2)
untrue 4 (3), 470 (2), 495 (4), 512 (5), 513 (6), 541 (3), 542 (6), 543 (4), 930 (4)
untrue, be 543 (5)
untrustworthy 930 (4)
untruth 495 (1), 518 (1), 525 (1), 541 (1), 543 (1), 614 (1), 665 (2), 926 (1), 926 (2), 930 (2)
untruthful 495 (4), 541 (3), 930 (4)
untruthfulness 495 (1), 541 (1)
untuned 411 (2)
untuneful 411 (2)
untutored 491 (5), 670 (3), 699 (3)
untypical 84 (7)
unusable 641 (4), 674 (2)
unused 126 (5), 266 (4), 458 (3), 670 (3), 674 (2), 677 (2), 695 (5), 752 (3)
unused, be 674 (5)
unusual 15 (4), 32 (8), 80 (5), 84 (6), 140 (2), 508 (2), 849 (2), 864 (5), 866 (9)
unusually 32 (19)
unutterable 32 (11), 517 (4), 864 (5)

unvarnished 540 (2), 573 (2), 699 (3)
unvarying 153 (4)
unveil 229 (6), 522 (9), 526 (4)
unveiling 68 (2)
unventilated 653 (2)
unvirtuous 934 (3), 934 (4)
unvoiced 398 (3), 523 (3)
unwanted 607 (2), 637 (4), 641 (4), 674 (2), 774 (3), 827 (4), 860 (3), 861 (3)
unwarlike 717 (3)
unwarranted 916 (6), 934 (6)
unwary 857 (3)
unwavering 153 (4), 599 (2), 600 (3)
unwedded 895 (4), 950 (5)
unwelcome 827 (4), 860 (3)
unwell 651 (21), 731 (5)
unwholesome 653 (2), 951 (6)
unwholesomely 653 (5)
unwholesomeness 391 (1)
unwieldy 32 (9), 195 (9), 322 (4), 695 (5), 842 (5)
unwilling 489 (3), 598 (3), 601 (3), 620 (3), 760 (2), 861 (2)
unwilling, be 486 (7), 598 (4), 620 (5), 677 (3), 760 (4), 861 (4)
unwillingly 598 (5)
unwillingness 598 (1), 861 (1)
unwind 316 (3), 683 (3)
unwinding 314 (1), 316 (2)
unwisdom 491 (1), 499 (2)
unwise 499 (5), 643 (2), 695 (3), 857 (3)
unwitting 491 (4), 596 (5)
unwonted 84 (6), 611 (2)
unwontedness 611 (1)
unwordly 487 (2)
unworkable 470 (3)
unworldliness 699 (1), 935 (1)
unworldly 491 (4), 699 (3)
unworthy 867 (5), 930 (4), 934 (3)

unwrap 229 (6), 263 (17), 304 (4), 526 (4)
unwritten 523 (3)
unwritten code 917 (3)
unwritten law 610 (2)
unyielding 113 (4), 162 (7), 326 (4), 329 (2), 599 (2), 602 (4), 715 (2)
unzip 46 (8)
up 209 (14), 215 (5), 308 (6)
up against it 700 (5), 731 (5)
up anchor 269 (9)
up and about 650 (2)
up and coming 730 (4)
up and doing 678 (8)
up-and-down 251 (7), 317 (7)
up-country 184 (5), 192 (19), 224 (1), 224 (3)
up-end 215 (4)
up for auction 759 (2)
up for sale 793 (3)
up for trial 959 (6)
up in arms 704 (3), 709 (6), 712 (6), 718 (8), 738 (8)
up on end 215 (5)
up one's street 24 (7)
up to 108 (10)
up-to-date 121 (2), 126 (6), 285 (2)
up to everything 698 (4)
up to now 121 (5)
up to one 917 (6)
up to something 623 (7), 930 (4)
up-to-the-minute 126 (6)
up to this time 125 (13)
upbeat 410 (4), 482 (2), 833 (3)
upbraid 924 (13)
upbraiding 924 (4), 924 (6)
upbringing 534 (1), 654 (3)
update 126 (8)
upend 221 (5)
upgrade 285 (4)
upheaval 61 (1), 149 (1), 165 (2), 310 (1)
uphill 220 (4), 308 (3), 308 (6), 682 (5), 700 (4)
uphill struggle 700 (2)
uphold 146 (4), 218 (15)

upholstered 800 (3)
upholstery 227 (1), 630 (4)
upkeep 666 (1), 703 (2)
upland 209 (10)
uplands 209 (2)
uplift 310 (1), 310 (4), 654 (1), 654 (9), 826 (4), 979 (11)
uplifted 310 (3)
upon one's honour 532 (8)
upon one's word 532 (8)
upper 34 (4)
upper case 587 (3)
upper class 34 (3), 371 (4), 644 (2), 868 (3), 868 (7)
upper crust 848 (3), 868 (3)
upper deck 213 (2)
upper hand 34 (2), 727 (2)
Upper House 692 (2)
upper limit 236 (1)
uppercut 279 (2)
uppermost 34 (5), 213 (4), 638 (5)
uppish 871 (4)
uppity 847 (5), 871 (4)
upright 215 (1), 215 (2), 215 (5), 310 (3), 913 (4), 929 (3), 933 (3)
upright carriage 215 (1)
uprightness 28 (3), 215 (1), 913 (1), 929 (1), 933 (1)
uprising 308 (1), 310 (1), 738 (2)
uproar 61 (4), 176 (1), 400 (1)
uproarious 176 (5), 400 (3), 822 (3), 833 (4)
uproot 57 (5), 149 (4), 165 (6), 188 (4), 300 (6), 304 (4)
uprooting 165 (1)
ups and downs 317 (2), 731 (1), 732 (1)
upset 63 (3), 149 (1), 165 (7), 221 (2), 221 (5), 311 (1), 456 (8), 702 (8), 738 (10), 821 (8), 827 (10), 829 (6), 861 (5), 891 (9)
upsetting 63 (1), 702 (6), 829 (4)

upshot 157 (1), 480 (1), 725 (1)
upside down 14 (5), 61 (7), 221 (3), 221 (6)
upstage 594 (6), 594 (17), 594 (18)
upstairs 308 (6)
upstanding 215 (2), 310 (3)
upstart 59 (3), 67 (3), 126 (4), 126 (5), 730 (3), 878 (3)
upstream 281 (8)
upsurge 36 (1), 308 (1), 637 (1)
upswing 36 (1), 310 (1), 654 (1)
uptight 892 (3)
uptown 184 (4)
upturn 221 (5), 308 (1)
upward motion 265 (1), 308 (1)
upward trend 36 (1)
upwards 209 (14), 308 (6)
upwards of 34 (11), 101 (2)
upwind 281 (8)
uranium 385 (1), 659 (3)
Uranus 321 (6), 967 (1)
urban 184 (5), 192 (18)
urban population 191 (5)
urban sprawl 192 (8)
urbane 698 (4), 848 (6), 882 (6), 884 (3)
urbanity 846 (1), 882 (2), 884 (1)
urbanization 192 (8)
urbanize 192 (22)
urbanized 192 (18)
urge 178 (3), 279 (7), 512 (7), 532 (5), 532 (7), 612 (9), 680 (3), 691 (4), 761 (5), 859 (1)
urge on 277 (7)
urgency 612 (2), 627 (2), 638 (1), 680 (1)
urgent 599 (2), 627 (5), 638 (5), 680 (2), 740 (2), 761 (3)
urging 612 (2)
urinal 649 (3)
urinary 302 (5)
urinate 302 (6)
urination 302 (1)

urine 302 (4)
urn 194 (13), 364 (1), 381 (5)
us 80 (4)
usable 640 (2), 673 (2)
usage 514 (2), 610 (1)
use 137 (7), 173 (1), 173 (3), 627 (6), 628 (1), 640 (1), 640 (5), 673 (1), 673 (3), 675 (2), 676 (1), 676 (5), 694 (1), 694 (8), 773 (4)
use few words 582 (3)
use force 176 (8)
use one's authority 733 (10)
use one's brain 449 (7)
use one's ears 524 (12)
use one's eyes 438 (7)
use one's head 447 (7), 498 (6)
use one's imagination 513 (7)
use skilfully 694 (8)
use the press 528 (9)
use threats 900 (3)
use time 108 (8)
use tobacco 388 (7)
use up 37 (4), 634 (4), 673 (3), 673 (5), 806 (4)
use wrongly 675 (2)
used 163 (5), 173 (2), 673 (2)
used to 610 (7)
used to, be 610 (7)
used up 163 (5), 673 (2), 674 (3)
useful 173 (2), 628 (3), 640 (2), 642 (2), 644 (8), 673 (2), 703 (4)
useful, be 615 (4), 628 (4), 640 (4), 642 (3), 703 (7), 742 (8), 771 (10)
usefulness 640 (1), 673 (1)
useless 61 (7), 161 (5), 163 (8), 497 (4), 637 (4), 639 (6), 641 (4), 643 (2), 645 (2), 655 (5), 655 (6), 674 (2), 811 (2), 812 (3)
useless, be 161 (8), 637 (6), 641 (6), 643 (3), 677 (3), 728 (8)
uselessly 641 (9)

uselessness **639** (1), **641** (1), **674** (1)

usher **89** (4), **537** (1), **742** (3)

usher in **64** (3), **68** (9), **283** (3), **299** (3), **884** (7)

using up **634** (1)

usual **20** (4), **79** (3), **81** (3), **83** (5), **490** (7), **496** (3), **573** (2), **610** (6), **639** (6), **693** (2), **840** (2), **848** (5), **865** (3)

usual custom **610** (2)

usual policy **610** (2)

usual way **624** (1)

usurer **784** (3), **816** (3)

usurious **784** (4), **816** (5)

usurp **306** (4), **734** (7), **786** (7), **786** (10), **916** (8)

usurp authority **734** (6)

usurp power **733** (11)

usurpation **306** (1), **733** (1), **954** (3)

usurped **916** (6)

usurper **545** (3), **786** (4), **916** (4)

usury **771** (3), **784** (1), **803** (2)

utensil **630** (1)

utensils **630** (4)

uterus **167** (3), **224** (2)

utilitarian **534** (5), **640** (2), **673** (2), **901** (4), **901** (6)

utilitarianism **901** (1)

utility **615** (2), **628** (1), **640** (1), **642** (1), **673** (1)

utility room **194** (19)

utilizable **673** (2)

utilization **640** (1), **673** (1)

utilize **640** (5), **673** (3)

utmost **32** (12), **236** (1)

Utopia **513** (3), **852** (2)

Utopian **513** (4), **513** (5), **654** (5), **654** (7), **852** (3), **852** (5), **901** (4)

Utopianism **513** (3)

utter **32** (13), **44** (4), **54** (3), **577** (4), **579** (8)

utter bore **838** (2)

utter contempt **922** (1)

utterance **577** (1), **579** (1)

utterances **408** (1)

uttered **577** (3)

utterly **32** (17), **54** (8)

utterly bad **645** (2)

V

V-shape **247** (1)

V-shaped **247** (5)

v-sign **878** (2), **921** (2)

vacancy **190** (2), **450** (1), **622** (3), **774** (1)

vacant **190** (5), **450** (2), **636** (4), **674** (2), **774** (3)

vacant, be **450** (4)

vacant lot **190** (2)

vacate **190** (6), **190** (7), **621** (3)

vacate office **753** (3)

vacation **681** (1), **683** (1)

vaccinate **303** (6), **652** (6), **658** (20), **660** (8)

vaccinated **660** (4)

vaccination **652** (2)

vaccine **658** (3)

vacillate **143** (5), **152** (5), **474** (8), **601** (4), **604** (4)

vacillating **152** (3), **603** (4)

vacillation **152** (1), **474** (2), **601** (1)

vacuity **190** (2), **448** (1)

vacuousness **499** (1)

vacuum **190** (2), **325** (1), **648** (9)

vacuum cleaner **304** (2), **648** (5)

vacuum flask **194** (14)

vacuum-pack **226** (13)

vacuuming **304** (1)

vade mecum **524** (6)

vagabond **268** (2), **869** (7), **883** (4), **938** (2)

vagabondage **267** (2)

vagabondism **267** (2)

vagary **513** (2), **604** (2)

vagina **167** (3)

vaginal **167** (4)

vagrancy **267** (2), **282** (1)

vagrant **152** (4), **267** (9), **268** (2), **801** (2)

vague **79** (3), **244** (2), **419** (5), **444** (3), **474** (4), **518** (2), **525** (6), **568** (2)

vague about **491** (5)

vaguely **419** (8)

vagueness **244** (1), **419** (1), **444** (1), **474** (1), **491** (3), **518** (1), **525** (1), **568** (1)

vain **4** (3), **641** (5), **728** (4), **850** (4), **871** (4), **873** (4), **875** (4), **877** (4), **878** (4), **932** (3)

vain attempt **728** (1)

vain, be **850** (5), **871** (6), **873** (5), **875** (7), **877** (5), **878** (6), **925** (4)

vain hope **853** (1)

vain person **500** (2), **522** (3), **850** (3), **871** (2), **873** (3), **877** (3), **932** (2)

vain pride **873** (1)

vainglorious **871** (4), **877** (4)

vainglory **871** (1)

vale **255** (3)

vale of sorrows **731** (1)

vale of tears **616** (1)

valediction **296** (2), **884** (2)

valedictory **296** (2), **296** (3), **579** (2)

Valentine **588** (1), **887** (5), **889** (3), **890** (1)

valet **742** (2)

valeting **666** (1)

Valhalla **971** (2)

valiance **855** (1)

valiant **855** (4)

valiant effort **671** (1)

valid **153** (5), **160** (8), **494** (5), **640** (2)

valid point **475** (5)

validate **153** (8), **466** (8), **915** (8)

validation **473** (1), **488** (1), **953** (2)

validity **160** (1), **494** (2)

valley **206** (1), **210** (1), **255** (3), **262** (1), **348** (1), **351** (1)

valorous **855** (4)

valour **855** (1)

valuable **32** (4), **615** (3), **638** (5), **640** (3), **644** (7), **792** (3), **811** (3)

valuables **777** (2)

valuation **27** (1), **465** (1), **480** (2)

value **28** (2), **150** (3), **465** (13), **480** (6), **514** (1), **638** (1), **638** (8), **640** (1), **644** (1), **808** (5), **809** (1), **809** (5), **809** (7), **811** (1), **846** (4), **866** (13), **887** (13), **920** (5), **923** (8)

value-added tax **809** (3)

value for money **812** (1)

value judgment **476** (1), **480** (1)

valued at, be **809** (6)

valuer **465** (8), **480** (3)

values **553** (1)

valve **160** (6), **264** (2), **351** (1)

vamp **612** (5), **952** (2)

vampire **786** (4), **904** (4), **970** (4)

van **68** (1), **237** (1), **274** (12), **283** (1), **722** (7)

Vandal **168** (1), **869** (7), **904** (1)

vandalism **165** (1), **176** (1), **634** (1), **847** (1)

vandalize **634** (4), **655** (9), **842** (7)

vandalized **842** (4)

vanguard **66** (1), **283** (1), **722** (7)

vanish **2** (7), **114** (6), **190** (7), **444** (4), **446** (3)

vanished **2** (5), **446** (2), **772** (3)

vanishing **444** (1), **446** (1), **446** (2)

vanishing point **196** (2), **293** (1), **446** (1)

vanity **482** (1), **499** (2), **828** (1), **850** (1), **871** (1), **873** (1), **875** (1), **877** (1), **932** (1)

Vanity Fair **848** (1)

vanquish **727** (9)

vanquished, the **728** (3)

vanquisher **727** (3)

vantage **34** (2)

vantage ground **160** (1), **178** (1)

vantage point **438** (5)

vapid **387** (2), **572** (2), **840** (2)

vapidity **387** (1), **572** (1)

vaporific **338** (3)

vaporizable **338** (3)

vaporization **304** (1), **323** (1), **336** (1), **338** (1), **340** (1), **342** (2), **355** (2), **446** (1), **648** (2)

vaporize **300** (9), **304** (4), **323** (5), **325** (3), **336** (4), **338** (4), **446** (3)

vaporizer **338** (2)

vaporous **4** (3), **336** (3), **338** (3), **513** (6)

vapour **4** (2), **336** (2), **336** (4), **355** (2), **877** (5)

vapour trail **271** (1), **548** (4)

vapouring **579** (3)

vapourousness **336** (1)

variability **17** (1), **82** (1), **142** (1), **143** (1), **152** (1), **604** (1)

variable **8** (3), **17** (2), **29** (2), **82** (2), **85** (1), **142** (2), **143** (4), **152** (2), **152** (3), **474** (5), **601** (3), **604** (3)

variably **152** (6)

variance **15** (1), **25** (1), **709** (1)

variant **15** (3), **84** (2), **152** (3)

variation **15** (1), **19** (1), **143** (1), **412** (4)

variations **412** (4)

varicose **197** (3)

varicose veins **651** (9)

variegate **43** (7), **143** (6), **425** (8), **437** (9), **844** (12)

variegated **29** (2), **43** (6), **82** (2), **143** (4), **222** (6), **425** (5), **437** (5), **844** (10)

variegated light **417** (1)

variegation **17** (1), **43** (4), **82** (1), **417** (1), **425** (1), **437** (1), **844** (2)

variety **15** (1), **17** (1), **43** (4), **77** (2), **82** (1), **437** (1), **594** (4)

variform **15** (4), **82** (2)

various **15** (4), **17** (2), **19** (2), **104** (4)

variously **15** (8)

varlet **869** (7), **938** (2)

varnish **226** (10), **226** (16), **258** (1), **258** (2), **258** (4), **357** (5), **477** (8), **541** (7), **553** (6), **648** (4), **844** (12)

varnished **258** (3)

varnishing **844** (2)

varsity **539** (1)

vary **15** (6), **25** (6), **29** (3), **143** (5), **143** (6), **152** (5), **603** (5), **604** (4)

vary as **9** (7), **12** (3)

vary from **15** (6)

varying **152** (3)

vascular **263** (16)

vase **194** (13)

vasectomize **172** (6)

vasectomy **172** (2), **658** (11)

vassal **742** (5), **745** (5)

vast **32** (6), **183** (6), **195** (6), **195** (7)

vastly **32** (17)

vastness **32** (1), **183** (1), **195** (2)

vat **194** (12), **809** (3)

vaudeville **594** (4)

vault **194** (21), **211** (1), **226** (2), **226** (15), **248** (2), **253** (4), **308** (1), **308** (4), **312** (1), **312** (4), **364** (5), **632** (2), **990** (4)

vault of heaven **321** (3)

vaulted **226** (12), **248** (3), **255** (6)

vaulting **226** (2), **546** (2)

vaunt **877** (2), **877** (5)

vaunter **877** (3)

vaunting **877** (4)

VDU **86** (5)

veal **301** (16)

vector **85** (1), **272** (4), **651** (5), **653** (1)

Vedas **975** (2)

veer **152** (5), **282** (1), **282** (3), **352** (10)

veer away **290** (3)

veer round **286** (5)

veering **152** (1), **152** (4)

vegan **301** (6), **301** (31), **942** (2)

veganism **301** (1), **942** (1)

vegetable **175** (1), **301** (20), **366** (6), **366** (9), **448** (2)

vegetable fibre **208** (2)

vegetable kingdom **366** (1)

vegetable life **360** (1), **366** (1), **448** (1)

vegetable oil **357** (2)

vegetal **366** (9)

vegetarian **301** (6), **301** (31), **942** (2)

vegetarianism **301** (1), **942** (1)

vegetate **1** (6), **108** (8), **175** (3), **266** (7), **366** (12), **679** (11), **820** (6)

vegetating **175** (2), **266** (4)

vegetation **175** (1), **366** (1), **448** (1), **677** (1), **820** (1)

vehemence **174** (1), **176** (1), **532** (1), **571** (1), **818** (2), **822** (1)

vehement **174** (5), **176** (5), **532** (4), **571** (2), **818** (5)

vehemently **571** (3)

vehicle **67** (2), **267** (6), **272** (2), **273** (1), **274** (1), **594** (3), **628** (2)

vehicular **274** (16)

vehicular traffic **305** (2)

veil **226** (4), **226** (13), **228** (23), **418** (6), **419** (7), **421** (1), **421** (4), **440** (1), **444** (1), **444** (4), **525** (7), **527** (3)

veiled **226** (12), **491** (6), **523** (4), **525** (3), **883** (7), **986** (12), **989** (4)

vein **5** (4), **7** (1), **179** (1), **207** (1), **208** (1), **351** (1), **437** (9), **566** (1), **570** (1), **632** (1)

veined **437** (8)

veinlet **351** (1)

veld **348** (1)

vellum **586** (4)

velocity **265** (1), **271** (1), **277** (1), **465** (6), **678** (1), **680** (1)

velour **222** (4)

velvet **222** (4), **327** (1), **410** (6), **730** (2)

velvet glove **736** (1)

velvety **258** (3), **259** (6), **327** (2), **390** (2)

venal **816** (5), **930** (6), **932** (3)

venality **816** (2), **930** (1)

vend **793** (4)

vendetta **709** (3), **881** (1), **910** (2)

vending machine **796** (3)

vendor **793** (2)

veneer **207** (1), **207** (5), **212** (1), **226** (10), **445** (1), **527** (3), **542** (5), **875** (1)

venerable **32** (4), **127** (4), **127** (6), **131** (6), **920** (4)

venerate **920** (5), **981** (11)

veneration **920** (1), **979** (1), **981** (1)

venereal **651** (22)

venereal disease **651** (13)

vengeance **910** (2)

vengeful **910** (4)

venial **639** (6), **909** (3)

venial sin **639** (2), **934** (2)

venison **301** (16)

venom **659** (3), **898** (1)

venomous **653** (4), **659** (5), **898** (4), **898** (5), **926** (5)

venomousness **659** (3)

vent **263** (4), **298** (3), **300** (8), **353** (1), **526** (5), **667** (2)

vent itself **298** (6)

ventilate **340** (6), **352** (10), **382** (6), **395** (3), **459** (13), **528** (9), **648** (10), **652** (6), **685** (4)

ventilated **352** (8), **528** (7), **652** (4)

ventilation **340** (1), **352** (6), **382** (1), **395** (1), **528** (2), **648** (2)

ventilator **340** (1), **352** (6), **353** (1), **384** (1)

ventral **194** (25)

ventricle **194** (4)

ventriloquism **20** (2), **542** (3), **579** (1)

ventriloquist **20** (3), **545** (5), **594** (10)

venture **461** (8), **618** (2), **618** (8), **622** (1), **661** (1), **661** (8), **671** (1), **671** (4), **672** (3), **777** (1), **791** (2), **791** (5), **855** (6)

venture in **297** (5)

venture on **672** (3)

venture to say **512** (7)

venturesome **618** (7), **671** (3), **672** (2), **855** (4), **857** (3)

venue **76** (1), **187** (2)

Venus **321** (6), **887** (7), **967** (1)

veracious **473** (4), **494** (4), **522** (5), **540** (2), **573** (2), **699** (3), **818** (6), **929** (1)

veraciousness **540** (1)

veracity **494** (1), **494** (3), **540** (1), **573** (1), **699** (1), **818** (1), **929** (1)

verandah **194** (20)

verb **564** (2)

verbal **514** (4), **524** (7), **559** (4), **564** (3), **579** (6)

verbalize **577** (4)

verbally **514** (6), **559** (5)

verbatim **559** (5)

verbiage **515** (3), **559** (1), **568** (1), **570** (1)

verbose **559** (4), **570** (3), **581** (4)

verbosity **559** (1), **570** (1), **581** (1)

verdancy **434** (1)

verdant **171** (4), **366** (9), **434** (3)

verdict **480** (1), **959** (3)

verdigris **434** (1)

verdure **366** (5), **366** (8), **434** (1)

verge **69** (2), **179** (3), **200** (1), **234** (1)

verger **741** (6), **986** (7)

verging on **200** (4)

verifiable **461** (6), **466** (5)

verification **461** (1), **466** (1), **473** (1), **478** (1), **488** (1) verify 461 (7), 466 (8), 473 (9), 478 (4), 484 (4), 767 (6)

veritable 494 (4), 494 (5)

veritably 494 (8)

verity 494 (1)

vermiform 251 (6)

vermilion 431 (2), 431 (3)

vermin 365 (16), 649 (2), 938 (2)

verminous 365 (18), 653 (2)

vermouth 301 (29)

vernacular 191 (6), 192 (19), 557 (1), 557 (5), 560 (2), 560 (5), 573 (1), 573 (2)

vernal 126 (5), 128 (6), 130 (4)

vernal equinox 128 (3)

verruca 253 (2), 651 (12)

versatile 152 (3), 640 (2), 694 (4)

versatility 152 (1), 603 (1), 694 (1)

verse 53 (3), 593 (1), 593 (4)

verse drama 593 (2)

verse form 243 (1), 593 (4)

verse writer 589 (7)

versed in 490 (5), 694 (6)

verses 593 (2)

versification 593 (1), 593 (5)

versifier 593 (6)

versify 593 (10)

version 77 (2), 143 (2), 520 (3), 590 (1)

verso 238 (1), 242 (1)

versus 704 (6)

vertebrae 218 (10)

vertebral 225 (3), 238 (4)

vertebrate 365 (2), 365 (18)

vertex 69 (2), 213 (2)

vertical 215 (2), 249 (2), 308 (3), 310 (3)

vertical, be 215 (3), 308 (4), 310 (4), 310 (5)

vertical height 215 (1)

vertical line 215 (1)

vertical, the 215 (1)

verticality 215 (1), 220 (2), 249 (1), 309 (1)

vertically 209 (14), 215 (5)

vertiginous 209 (8), 220 (4), 315 (4)

vertigo 315 (1), 651 (2)

verve 174 (1), 571 (1), 819 (1)

very 32 (17)

very good 644 (4)

Very light flag 665 (1)

very likely 471 (7)

very many 104 (4)

very moment, the 116 (2)

very much 32 (17)

very near 200 (4)

very odd 864 (5)

very one, the 13 (1)

very same, the 13 (1)

very thing, the 21 (2), 24 (3), 615 (2)

very words, the 494 (3)

vesicle 253 (2)

vesicular 253 (7)

Vesper 129 (1)

vespers 129 (1)

vespertine 129 (5)

vessel 194 (13), 275 (1), 381 (5)

vest 228 (17)

Vestal 986 (8)

Vestal Virgin 895 (3), 950 (3)

vested 153 (5), 915 (2)

vested in 187 (4)

vested in, be 773 (5)

vested interest 915 (1)

vestibule 194 (20)

vestige 33 (2), 41 (1), 548 (4)

vestigial 41 (4)

vestmental 989 (3)

vestments 228 (5), 989 (2)

vestry 990 (4)

vesture 228 (1)

vestured 986 (11), 989 (4)

vet 369 (1), 455 (4), 480 (6), 658 (14)

veteran 127 (4), 133 (2), 669 (8), 694 (6), 696 (2), 722 (4)

veteran car 274 (11)

veterinary disease 651 (17)

veterinary medicine 658 (10)

veterinary surgeon 369 (1)

veto 747 (1), 747 (7), 757 (1), 757 (4)

vex 645 (6), 827 (9), 891 (9)

vexation 825 (2), 827 (2), 891 (2)

vexatious 827 (5)

vexed 825 (6), 834 (5), 891 (4)

vexed question 530 (2)

via 281 (8), 624 (9)

viable 360 (2), 469 (2)

viaduct 222 (1), 624 (3)

vial 194 (13)

vibrant 174 (5), 404 (2), 818 (3)

vibraphone 414 (8)

vibrate 317 (4), 318 (5), 403 (3), 404 (3), 818 (8)

vibrating 318 (4)

vibration 317 (1), 404 (1)

vibrations 398 (1)

vibrato 403 (1), 410 (2), 412 (8)

vibratory 317 (3)

vicar 986 (3)

vicarage 192 (6), 986 (10)

vicarious 751 (3)

vicarship 985 (3)

vice 645 (1), 659 (1), 755 (1), 755 (2), 778 (2), 914 (1), 934 (1), 934 (2), 936 (2), 951 (2)

vice-admiral 741 (7)

vice-chancellor 741 (6)

vice-like 778 (3)

vice-like grip 778 (1)

vice-president 690 (1)

vice-regency 751 (1)

vice versa 14 (5), 151 (4), 221 (6)

vicereine 741 (5)

viceroy 741 (5)

viceroyalty 733 (5)

vicinity 187 (2), 200 (3), 230 (1)

vicious 176 (6), 616 (2), 645 (2), 655 (5), 738 (7), 898 (14), 914 (3), 934 (4), 934 (7), 951 (8)

vicious circle 71 (1), 702 (2)

viciousness 898 (1), 934 (1)

vicissitude 152 (2)

vicissitudes 154 (2)

victim 163 (2), 363 (1), 544 (1), 619 (2), 728 (3), 731 (3), 790 (1), 825 (4), 851 (3), 928 (4)

victimization 735 (1), 898 (3), 910 (2)

victimize 542 (9), 645 (7), 735 (8), 788 (9), 898 (8), 963 (8)

victimized 825 (5)

victor 34 (3), 644 (3), 727 (3)

Victoria Cross 729 (2)

Victorian 127 (7), 950 (4), 950 (6)

victorious 34 (4), 162 (6), 727 (4)

victorious, be 727 (11)

victory 34 (1), 701 (2), 727 (2)

victualler 633 (2)

victuals 301 (9)

videlicet 80 (11)

video 445 (2), 445 (7)

videorecorder 531 (3)

videotape 548 (7)

videotape recorder 549 (3)

vie with 716 (10)

view 183 (3), 263 (7), 438 (4), 438 (5), 438 (7), 438 (9), 441 (3), 443 (1), 445 (1), 445 (2), 480 (2), 485 (3), 553 (4), 841 (1)

view halloo 438 (11)

viewer 441 (1)

viewfinder 442 (3)

viewing 438 (4)

viewpoint 438 (5), 485 (3)

vigil 110 (1), 119 (1), 457 (2), 988 (5)

vigilance 455 (1), 457 (1), 457 (2), 498 (2)

vigilant 438 (6), 455 (2), 457 (4), 507 (2), 600 (3), 660 (6), 669 (7), 678 (7)

vigilante 660 (3)

vigils 981 (4)

vignette 553 (5), 590 (1)

vigorous 32 (4), 160 (9), 162 (6), 162 (8), 173 (2), 174 (5), 176 (5), 277 (5), 571 (2), 599 (2), 650 (2), 678 (7)

vigorous, be 174 (7), 678 (11)

vigorously 32 (17), 174 (9), 571 (3)

vigorousness 130 (1), 160 (3), 162 (1), 174 (1), 176 (1), 532 (1), 599 (1), 678 (2), 818 (2), 855 (1)

vigour 160 (3), 162 (2), 174 (1), 532 (1), 566 (1), 571 (1), 574 (2), 579 (4), 599 (1), 678 (2), 818 (2), 819 (1)

vigourousness 571 (1)

Viking 270 (1)

Viking ship 275 (2)

vile 645 (2), 930 (5), 934 (6)

vileness 934 (1)

vilification 899 (2), 926 (1)

vilify 867 (11), 924 (10), 926 (7)

villa 192 (6)

village 184 (3), 192 (8)

village commune 191 (5)

village green 76 (1), 192 (14), 837 (4)

village hall 76 (1), 192 (14)

villager 191 (1), 191 (3)

villain 904 (1), 904 (3), 938 (1), 938 (2)

villainous 645 (2), 842 (3), 930 (5), 934 (4)

villainy 930 (1), 934 (1)

villas 192 (8)

villein 742 (6)

vim 162 (2), 571 (1)

vinaigrette 389 (2), 396 (2)

vindicable 927 (4)

vindicate 466 (8), 478 (4), 713 (9), 915 (6), 927 (5), 960 (3)

vindicated 927 (4), 960 (2)

vindicating 614 (3), 713 (7), 927 (3)

vindication 466 (3), 467 (1), 614 (1), 909 (1), 915 (1), 927 (1), 960 (1)

vindicator 713 (6), 910 (3), 927 (2), 963 (5)

vindictive 888 (4), 891 (3), 898 (4), 906 (2), 910 (4), 910 (6), 963 (6)

vindictiveness 891 (1), 910 (1)

vine 366 (6)

vine-dressing 370 (1)

vine-grower 370 (5)

vinegariness 393 (1)

vinegary 393 (2)

vineyard 370 (2)

vino 301 (29)

vinous 949 (12)

vintage 108 (3), 127 (4), 164 (2), 370 (1), 386 (2), 632 (1), 644 (4)

vintage car 274 (11)

vintner 633 (2)

vinyl 226 (9)

viol 414 (3)

viola 414 (3)

violate 176 (8), 645 (7), 675 (2), 738 (9), 769 (3), 916 (8), 951 (11), 980 (6)

violating 980 (4)

violation 45 (3), 306 (1), 675 (1), 769 (1), 916 (1), 951 (4), 980 (1)

violence 61 (4), 63 (1), 165 (1), 174 (1), 176 (1), 675 (1), 712 (1), 718 (6), 735 (2), 822 (2), 898 (3)

violent 61 (9), 149 (3), 160 (8), 165 (4), 174 (5), 176 (5), 503 (9), 532 (4), 546 (2), 645 (3), 735 (6), 738 (7), 818 (5), 821 (3), 822 (3), 891 (4), 898 (7), 954 (7)

violent, be 61 (11), 165 (9), 176 (7), 318 (5), 645 (7),

655 (10), 678 (11), 712 (9), 716 (11), 822 (4), 891 (7)

violent change 143 (1), 149 (1)

violent creature 176 (4)

violent death 361 (2), 362 (1)

violently 32 (18), 176 (10)

violet 436 (1), 436 (2)

violin 414 (3)

violinist 413 (2)

VIP 638 (4), 866 (6)

viper 365 (13)

virago 162 (4), 176 (4), 373 (3), 892 (2), 904 (4)

virgin 52 (5), 126 (5), 132 (2), 373 (3), 491 (6), 950 (3), 950 (5)

virgin forest 366 (2)

virgin soil 670 (2)

virgin territory 190 (2)

virginal 126 (5), 130 (4), 895 (4), 933 (3), 950 (5)

virginity 172 (1), 895 (1), 950 (1)

Virgo 321 (5)

virile 134 (3), 162 (10), 174 (5), 372 (2)

virility 134 (1), 162 (2), 174 (1), 372 (1)

virtual 28 (8)

virtually 1 (8), 5 (10), 33 (11), 52 (9)

virtue 5 (2), 160 (2), 644 (1), 901 (1), 913 (1), 917 (4), 929 (1), 933 (1), 935 (1), 950 (1), 979 (1), 979 (2)

virtues 933 (2)

virtuosity 413 (6), 694 (1)

virtuoso 34 (3), 413 (1), 696 (1)

virtuous 866 (7), 913 (4), 917 (7), 929 (3), 933 (3), 950 (5), 979 (6), 979 (7)

virtuous, be 688 (4), 929 (5), 933 (4), 935 (5)

virtuous conduct 933 (1)

virtuously 933 (5)

virtuousness 933 (1)

virulence 891 (1), 898 (1)

virulent 174 (6), 659 (5), 898 (5)

virus 196 (5), 651 (5), 659 (3)

virus disease 651 (3)

vis-à-vis 9 (10), 237 (6)

visa 466 (3), 756 (2)

visage 237 (2), 445 (6)

viscera 224 (2)

visceral 224 (3), 818 (6)

viscid 48 (2), 205 (4), 335 (4), 354 (5), 357 (8)

viscidity 48 (1), 354 (1), 354 (3), 778 (1)

viscosity 335 (1), 354 (3)

viscount 868 (5)

viscountcy 868 (2)

viscountess 868 (5)

viscous 335 (4), 354 (5)

visibility 443 (1), 445 (1), 522 (1)

visible 438 (6), 443 (2), 445 (7), 522 (4), 522 (6), 526 (2)

visible, be 254 (5), 443 (4), 445 (8), 455 (7), 522 (9), 526 (7)

visible effect 157 (1)

visible evidence 443 (1)

visible trade 791 (2)

visibly 438 (10), 443 (5)

vision 4 (2), 438 (1), 440 (2), 445 (1), 445 (2), 510 (1), 513 (3), 617 (2), 841 (2), 852 (2)

visionary 438 (6), 445 (7), 504 (2), 513 (4), 513 (5), 513 (6), 620 (2), 654 (5), 852 (2), 901 (4), 901 (6), 981 (8)

visionless 439 (2)

visit 139 (3), 189 (1), 189 (4), 267 (1), 267 (11), 295 (4), 297 (5), 882 (4), 882 (9), 897 (6), 970 (8)

visitant 191 (1), 295 (1), 970 (3)

visitation 651 (2), 659 (2)

visiting card 547 (13)

visiting terms 882 (4)

visitor 191 (2), 268 (1), 295 (1), 297 (3), 882 (5)

visor 226 (4), 421 (1), 713 (5)

vista 263 (7), 438 (5)

visual 438 (6), 445 (7), 551 (2)

visual aid 443 (1), 551 (2)

visual display unit 86 (5)

visual fallacy 4 (2), 440 (2), 445 (1), 495 (1), 513 (3), 542 (1), 970 (3)

visual impact 445 (1)

visual organ 438 (2)

visualization 438 (1), 513 (1)

visualize 438 (7), 513 (7)

vital 627 (3), 638 (5), 819 (4)

vital role 178 (1)

vital spark 360 (1)

vital statistics 86 (4)

vitality 162 (2), 174 (1), 335 (3), 360 (1), 571 (1), 650 (1), 678 (2), 833 (1)

vitalization 360 (1)

vitalize 360 (6), 821 (7)

vitals 224 (2)

vitamin tablet 658 (6)

vitamins 301 (10)

vitreous 326 (3), 422 (2)

vitrification 326 (2)

vitrify 326 (5)

vitriol 659 (3)

vitriolic 827 (3), 899 (4)

vituperation 579 (3)

vituperative 899 (4)

viva 459 (4)

viva voce examination 459 (4)

vivacious 571 (2), 678 (7), 818 (3), 819 (4), 833 (3)

vivacity 571 (1), 678 (2), 819 (1), 833 (1)

vivarium 369 (4)

vivid 174 (5), 374 (4), 417 (8), 425 (6), 516 (3), 551 (6), 571 (2), 590 (6)

vividness 417 (1), 571 (1)

vivisect 377 (5), 461 (7)

vivisection 362 (1), 377 (1)

vivisector 461 (3)

vixen 365 (3), 892 (2)

vixenish 892 (3)

viz 80 (11), 520 (11)

vizier 741 (6)

vocabulary 87 (2), 559 (2), 566 (1)

vocal 398 (3), 408 (2), 412 (7), 413 (7), 558 (5), 577 (3), 579 (6), 762 (2)

vocal cords 577 (1)

vocal music 106 (1), 408 (1), 412 (5), 577 (1), 593 (2), 594 (3), 981 (3), 981 (5)

vocal organs 577 (1)

vocalist 413 (4), 594 (10)

vocalization 412 (5), 577 (1)

vocalize 398 (4), 413 (10), 577 (4)

vocation 612 (1), 622 (2), 688 (1), 985 (2)

vocational 534 (5), 622 (5)

vocational training 534 (2)

vocative 583 (2)

vociferate 400 (4), 408 (4), 577 (4), 835 (6), 884 (7), 900 (3)

vociferation 400 (1), 408 (1), 577 (1)

vociferous 408 (2)

vogue 610 (2), 848 (1)

vogue word 559 (1)

voguish 848 (5)

voice 398 (1), 398 (4), 408 (1), 528 (9), 532 (5), 558 (3), 560 (6), 564 (1), 577 (1), 577 (4), 579 (1), 579 (8), 605 (2)

voice box 577 (1)

voice-over 398 (1)

voice production 579 (1)

voice test 461 (1)

voiced 398 (3), 577 (3)

voiceless 399 (2), 578 (2), 580 (2), 582 (2)

voicelessly 578 (6)

voicelessness 399 (1), 401 (1), 578 (1), 580 (1), 582 (1)

void 4 (1), 190 (2), 190 (5), 201 (2), 300 (8), 304 (4), 752 (3), 752 (4)

voidance 300 (3), 634 (1)

volatile 114 (3), 152 (3), 338 (3), 456 (6), 604 (3), 822 (3)

volatile oil 357 (2)

volatility 114 (1), 323 (1), 336 (1), 338 (1)

volcanic 176 (5), 298 (4), 379 (5), 822 (3)

volcanic ash 381 (4)

volcano 176 (2), 263 (10), 300 (2), 379 (2), 383 (1), 663 (1)

volition 595 (0)

volitional 595 (1), 605 (4)

volley 74 (5), 280 (1), 287 (1), 287 (8), 402 (1), 712 (3), 712 (11)

volleyball 837 (7)

volt 160 (6)

voltage 160 (6)

volte face 148 (1), 286 (2), 603 (1)

volubility 579 (1), 581 (1)

voluble 581 (4)

volume 26 (1), 32 (1), 53 (3), 78 (1), 183 (1), 183 (2), 195 (1), 465 (3), 589 (1)

volumes 32 (2)

voluminous 32 (4), 183 (6), 194 (24), 195 (6)

volumptuous 944 (4)

volumptuousness 944 (1)

voluntarily 595 (3), 597 (7)

voluntariness 595 (0), 597 (1)

voluntary 595 (1), 597 (5), 812 (4), 859 (10)

voluntary agency 901 (1)

voluntary poverty 801 (1)

voluntary work 595 (0), 597 (2), 622 (2), 672 (1), 781 (2), 812 (2), 897 (2)

voluntary worker 686 (2)

volunteer 595 (2), 597 (3), 597 (6), 672 (3), 686 (2), 722 (4), 759 (4), 901 (4)

volunteering 597 (5)

voluptuous 376 (5), 826 (2), 944 (3), 951 (8)

voluptuously 944 (5)

volute 251 (2)

vomit 300 (3), 300 (10), 651 (23)

vomiting 300 (3), 300 (5), 651 (2), 651 (7), 861 (2)

voodoo 983 (1)

voodooism 983 (1)

voracious 786 (5), 859 (8), 947 (3)

voracious appetite 859 (2)

voracity 859 (1), 947 (1)

vortex 251 (2), 315 (2), 318 (3), 350 (3)

vortical 315 (4)

votary 707 (1), 707 (4), 764 (1), 859 (6), 979 (4), 981 (8)

vote 86 (4), 459 (1), 480 (1), 532 (1), 605 (2), 605 (8), 703 (6), 733 (4), 737 (2), 744 (1), 751 (2), 751 (4), 953 (2)

vote against 704 (4)

vote-catcher 612 (5)

vote-catching 605 (4)

vote down 605 (8), 704 (4)

vote for 488 (8), 605 (8), 703 (6)

vote in 605 (8)

vote of thanks 579 (2), 907 (2)

vote-snatcher 612 (5)

voted 488 (5)

voteless 916 (7)

voter 480 (3), 707 (4), 744 (4)

voters 605 (3)

voting 605 (4)

voting a 704 (1)

voting age 134 (1)

voting list 87 (1), 605 (3)

votive 764 (2), 981 (10)

votive offering 781 (3), 981 (6)

vouch for 466 (7), 764 (4), 767 (6)

voucher 466 (3), 548 (1), 767 (2), 807 (1)

vouchsafe 758 (3)

vow 532 (5), 764 (1), 764 (4), 981 (12)

vow to 781 (7)

vowed to silence 582 (2)

vowel 558 (3), 577 (1)

vox populi 480 (1), 605 (2), 733 (4)

voyage 267 (1), 269 (1), 269 (9)

voyager 268 (1)

voyaging 269 (1)

voyeur 441 (1), 952 (1)

voyeurism 438 (4), 453 (1), 951 (1)

vulcanization 326 (2)

vulcanize 326 (5), 329 (3)

vulcanized 329 (2)

vulgar 35 (4), 464 (3), 557 (5), 576 (2), 611 (2), 645 (4), 699 (3), 842 (5), 844 (10), 847 (4), 851 (4), 867 (4), 869 (8), 875 (5), 899 (4), 914 (3), 934 (4), 951 (6)

vulgar herd 869 (1)

vulgarian 126 (4), 493 (1), 847 (3)

vulgarism 560 (3), 576 (1), 847 (1)

vulgarity 464 (1), 576 (1), 839 (1), 847 (1), 847 (2), 899 (2)

vulgarize 655 (9), 820 (7), 847 (6), 921 (5)

vulnerability 161 (2), 180 (1), 647 (1), 647 (2), 661 (2)

vulnerable 161 (6), 180 (2), 471 (2), 647 (3), 661 (5), 670 (3), 928 (7), 934 (5)

vulnerable point 661 (2)

vulpine 365 (18)

vulture 365 (4), 648 (6), 786 (4)

vulva 167 (3)

W

wad 53 (5), 74 (6), 193 (2), 227 (2), 264 (2), 797 (5)

wadding 227 (1), 264 (2)

waddle 265 (2), 267 (14), 278 (4)

wade 267 (14), 269 (12), 341 (6)

wade across 305 (5)

wade into 68 (8), 634 (4)

wade through 265 (4), 536 (5), 682 (6)

wader 365 (4)

waders 228 (27)

wading 269 (3)

wads 32 (2)

wafer 207 (2)

wafer-thin 206 (4)

waffle 515 (6), 518 (3), 570 (1), 570 (6), 581 (2), 581 (5)

waft 323 (4), 352 (3), 352 (10), 394 (1)

wafted, be 271 (7)

wag 317 (2), 317 (4), 317 (6), 839 (3)

wag on 285 (3)

wage 771 (2)

wage bill 809 (2)

wage-earner 782 (2)

wage war 716 (11), 718 (11), 881 (4)

wager 618 (2), 618 (8), 716 (2), 716 (10)

wages 804 (2), 807 (1), 809 (2)

waggish 833 (4), 837 (19), 839 (4)

waggishness 839 (1), 849 (1)

waggle 317 (4), 317 (6)

waging war 718 (6)

wagon 274 (5), 274 (13)

waif 268 (2), 779 (2), 883 (4)

waifs and strays 75 (1)

wail 352 (10), 408 (1), 408 (3), 409 (3), 829 (5), 836 (1), 836 (5), 836 (6)

wailer 836 (3)

wailing 836 (1)

wainscot 214 (1), 227 (1)

waistband 47 (7), 228 (24)

waistcoat 228 (10)

waistline 206 (3)

wait 108 (8), 113 (3), 136 (5), 145 (8), 266 (7), 507 (5), 677 (3), 679 (11)

wait and see 136 (5), 461 (8), 474 (8), 677 (3), 858 (3)

wait on 89 (4), 284 (4), 703 (7)

wait upon 739 (4), 742 (8)

waiter 742 (1)

waiting 189 (2), 474 (2), 507 (1), 507 (2)

waiting list 87 (1), 852 (3)

waiting room 194 (20)

waitress 742 (1)

waits 413 (5)

waive 621 (3), 674 (4), 779 (4)

waive the rules 734 (5)

waived 621 (2), 674 (2)

waiver 674 (1), 753 (1), 916 (3)

wake 41 (1), 67 (2), 71 (1), 157 (1), 238 (1), 262 (1), 269 (1), 284 (2), 364 (2), 548 (4), 836 (2), 905 (2)

wake up 374 (5)

wakeful 455 (2), 678 (7)

walk 7 (1), 265 (2), 265 (4), 267 (3), 267 (14), 278 (1), 278 (4), 445 (8), 624 (5), 970 (8), 983 (11)

walk about 267 (13)

walk behind 267 (14)

walk in 297 (5)

walk in front 267 (14)

walk of life 7 (1), 622 (2), 688 (1)

walk-off 298 (1), 298 (5)

walk off with 727 (11)

walk on 594 (17)

walk-on part 594 (8)

walk-out 296 (1), 621 (1), 621 (3), 918 (3)

walk out on 603 (5)

walk out with 889 (7)

walk sideways 220 (5)

walk the plank 313 (3)

walk up 308 (5)

walkabout 267 (2), 267 (3)

walker 268 (1), 268 (3)

walkie-talkie 531 (1)

walking 265 (1), 267 (3), 267 (9), 305 (2)

walking distance 200 (2)

walking on air 824 (4)

walking tour 267 (3)

walkout 145 (2), 145 (3), 298 (1), 489 (1), 704 (1)

walkover 701 (2), 727 (2)

wall 57 (1), 218 (2), 231 (2), 235 (2), 235 (3), 235 (4), 324 (3), 702 (2), 713 (3)
wall-eye 440 (1)
wall-eyed 440 (3)
wall in 232 (3)
wall into a trap 661 (7)
wall of flame 379 (2)
wall off 57 (5)
wall up 362 (10), 747 (10)
walled 713 (8)
walled in 232 (2)
wallet 194 (10), 799 (1)
wallflower 607 (1)
wallop 279 (9), 301 (28)
walloper 195 (5)
walloping 32 (9)
wallow 269 (9), 313 (3), 318 (5), 341 (6), 346 (1)
wallow in 376 (6), 635 (7), 943 (3)
wallow in luxury 944 (4)
wallowing 824 (3)
wallpaper 227 (1)
wallpapered 226 (12)
walnut 366 (4), 430 (1)
walrus 365 (3)
waltz 315 (5), 412 (4), 837 (14), 837 (22)
wan 163 (6), 419 (4), 426 (3), 834 (6)
wand 743 (2), 983 (4)
wander 10 (5), 75 (3), 265 (4), 267 (13), 282 (5), 503 (10), 744 (9)
wanderer 59 (2), 84 (3), 188 (1), 268 (2), 679 (6), 763 (2), 869 (7), 883 (4)
wandering 10 (4), 59 (4), 84 (5), 267 (2), 267 (9), 282 (1), 282 (2), 456 (6), 744 (6), 981 (3)
wandering wits 456 (1)
wanderlust 267 (2)
wane 37 (5), 419 (6)
wangle 541 (8), 542 (2), 930 (3), 930 (8)
waning 37 (1), 37 (3), 198 (4), 419 (4)
waning moon 321 (9)
want 35 (5), 55 (2), 307 (1), 307 (3), 627 (1), 627 (2),

627 (6), 636 (2), 636 (7), 636 (8), 731 (1), 761 (1), 801 (1), 801 (5), 859 (1), 859 (11)
want back 830 (4)
want judgment 857 (4)
want nothing 54 (5)
want of chivalry 885 (1)
want of courage 854 (2), 856 (1)
want of faith 974 (1)
want of habit 611 (1)
want of intellect 499 (1)
want of practice 670 (1)
want of principle 934 (1)
want of respect 921 (1)
want of symmetry 246 (1), 842 (1)
want of thought 450 (1), 456 (1)
want one's own way 602 (6)
want practice 670 (7)
want to know 453 (4), 459 (13), 491 (8)
wanted 190 (4), 627 (3), 859 (10)
'wanted' column 761 (1)
wanting 55 (3), 190 (4), 307 (2), 448 (2), 772 (3), 859 (7)
wanting, be 55 (5)
wanting to know 453 (3)
wanton 604 (3), 837 (21), 889 (6), 938 (1), 951 (7), 952 (2)
wanton damage 165 (1)
wantonness 951 (2)
war 168 (1), 362 (4), 709 (1), 709 (3), 716 (1), 718 (1), 718 (6), 718 (11), 738 (2)
war against 718 (11)
war chariot 274 (7)
war cry 547 (8), 665 (1)
war dance 711 (1)
war drum 414 (9)
war effort 718 (5)
war fever 718 (3)
war footing 718 (5)
war galley 722 (13)
war-loving 718 (9)

war measures 718 (5), 745 (2)
war memorial 729 (1)
war of attrition 718 (1)
war of nerves 712 (2), 718 (1), 854 (4), 900 (1)
war on 676 (1)
war preparations 718 (5)
war trophy 729 (1)
war upon 718 (11)
war vessel 722 (13)
war whoop 718 (1), 900 (1)
war work 718 (5)
warble 409 (1), 409 (3), 413 (10)
warbler 365 (4), 413 (4)
warbling 413 (7)
ward 53 (3), 130 (1), 184 (3), 658 (13), 713 (4), 742 (4), 751 (2)
ward off 421 (4), 620 (5), 713 (10)
warden 264 (3), 660 (3), 690 (3), 713 (6), 741 (6), 749 (1)
wardenship 660 (2)
warder 660 (3), 749 (2)
warding off 713 (1)
wardress 749 (2)
wardrobe 194 (5), 228 (2)
wardrobe mistress 594 (11)
wardroom 194 (19)
warehouse 632 (2), 632 (5), 796 (2)
warehousing 632 (2)
wares 164 (2), 630 (4), 777 (1), 795 (1)
warfare 362 (4), 659 (4), 709 (3), 716 (1), 716 (7), 718 (6)
warhead 276 (3), 723 (13)
warhorse 273 (7), 722 (10)
wariness 455 (1), 457 (1), 858 (1)
warlike 176 (5), 678 (7), 709 (6), 711 (2), 712 (6), 716 (9), 718 (9), 855 (4), 877 (4)
warlock 983 (5)
warm 128 (7), 200 (4), 376 (4), 379 (6), 381 (8), 425 (6), 484 (3), 818 (5), 818

(3), 438 (7), 438 (9), 441 (1), 441 (3), 455 (4), 457 (2), 457 (7), 488 (7), 660 (3), 677 (3), 678 (11), 713 (6), 749 (1)

watch and ward 660 (2)

watch committee 955 (1)

watch dog 365 (10)

watch expenses 814 (3)

watch fire 379 (2)

watch-making 117 (1)

watch one's step 457 (5), 858 (3)

watch out 664 (7)

watch out for 438 (9), 457 (7)

watch over 660 (8), 713 (9)

watch the clock 117 (7)

watchdog 664 (2)

watcher 441 (1)

watchful 455 (2), 457 (4), 660 (6), 768 (2), 858 (2)

watchful eye 457 (2)

watchfulness 455 (1), 457 (1)

watching 457 (2)

watchmaker 117 (3)

watchman 664 (2)

watchtower 209 (4)

watchword 496 (1), 547 (2), 547 (8), 628 (2), 718 (6)

water 43 (7), 171 (5), 301 (27), 301 (38), 302 (4), 319 (4), 335 (1), 335 (2), 339 (1), 339 (3), 341 (8), 350 (11), 369 (10), 370 (9), 422 (1), 648 (4)

water channel 351 (1)

water closet 649 (3)

water cure 339 (1)

water diviner 459 (9), 484 (2), 511 (5)

water divining 484 (1)

water down 37 (4), 163 (10), 339 (3)

water-driven 160 (9)

water jump 201 (2)

water level 207 (1)

water line 465 (5)

water main 351 (1)

water nymph 967 (3)

water pipe 351 (1)

water pistol 287 (3), 837 (15)

water polo 837 (7)

water-ski 269 (12)

water skiing 269 (3), 837 (6)

water snake 365 (13)

water spirit 970 (5)

water sports 837 (6)

water supply 339 (1), 633 (1)

water table 207 (1)

water travel 265 (1), 269 (1)

water vapour 336 (2), 339 (1)

waterborne 269 (6)

waterborne disease 651 (3)

watercolour 553 (2), 553 (5)

watercolourist 556 (1)

watercolours 425 (4), 553 (6)

watercourse 350 (1), 351 (1)

watered 341 (5), 437 (6)

watered down 43 (6), 163 (5)

waterfall 209 (6), 309 (1), 341 (2), 350 (4), 351 (1)

waterfowl 365 (4)

waterfront 234 (1)

waterhole 346 (1)

wateriness 49 (1), 335 (1), 339 (1)

watering 163 (1), 339 (1)

watering can 194 (13), 341 (3)

watering down 43 (1), 655 (3)

waterless 342 (4)

waterline 234 (1)

waterlogged 341 (5), 347 (2), 661 (4)

Waterloo 165 (3), 728 (2)

waterman 270 (4)

watermark 547 (13), 844 (3)

waterproof 162 (7), 226 (16), 228 (20), 264 (5), 342 (4), 660 (5), 666 (5)

waters 343 (1)

watershed 213 (1)

waterside 234 (1)

watersports 269 (3)

waterspout 315 (2), 351 (2)

watertight 264 (5), 342 (4), 646 (3)

waterway 305 (1), 350 (1), 624 (4)

waterworks 302 (1), 339 (1), 648 (4)

watery 49 (2), 163 (4), 302 (5), 335 (4), 339 (2), 341 (4), 387 (2), 572 (2), 636 (3)

watt 160 (6), 465 (3)

wattle 222 (3)

wattle and daub 631 (2)

wave 217 (5), 248 (5), 251 (11), 253 (2), 259 (1), 262 (1), 265 (4), 317 (1), 317 (4), 317 (6), 339 (1), 343 (1), 350 (5), 352 (10), 522 (8), 547 (4), 547 (21), 843 (2), 843 (7), 875 (7), 877 (5), 884 (7)

wave banners 875 (7)

wave frequency 141 (1)

wave goodbye 296 (6)

wave on 547 (22)

wave one's hands 547 (21)

wave one's wand 983 (10)

wave power 160 (4)

wave through 547 (22)

waveband 417 (4)

wavelength 203 (4), 317 (1), 417 (4)

waver 152 (5), 474 (8), 486 (7), 601 (4)

waverer 601 (2)

wavering 142 (2), 152 (1), 152 (3), 152 (4), 486 (2)

wavery 318 (4)

waviness 251 (1)

wavy 248 (3), 251 (7), 262 (2)

wavy edge 234 (3)

wax 36 (4), 152 (2), 197 (4), 258 (4), 327 (1), 333 (3), 334 (2), 334 (4), 354 (3), 357 (3), 417 (13), 648 (4)

wax and wane 143 (5)

wax figure 551 (2)
wax lyrical 923 (9)
waxed 258 (3)
waxen 357 (6), 427 (5)
waxing 36 (3)
waxing moon 321 (9)
waxwork 551 (2)
waxworks 632 (3)
waxy 327 (2), 357 (6)
way 7 (1), 267 (8), 269 (1), 281 (1), 285 (1), 297 (2), 623 (2), 624 (1), 628 (2), 629 (1), 688 (1), 770 (1)
way behind 199 (6)
way forward 624 (1)
way in 68 (5), 263 (6), 297 (2)
way in front 199 (6)
way of 624 (1)
way of life 610 (1), 624 (1), 688 (1)
way of thinking 485 (3)
way-out 84 (6), 263 (6), 298 (3), 623 (3), 644 (5), 668 (1)
way over 624 (3)
way through 624 (2)
way to 624 (2)
way up 624 (2)
way with 689 (1)
way with words 579 (4)
wayfarer 268 (1)
waylay 289 (4), 527 (5), 542 (10), 698 (5)
waymarked 624 (8)
ways 610 (1)
ways and means 629 (1)
wayside 234 (1), 234 (4), 289 (3)
wayward 152 (3), 602 (5), 604 (3), 738 (7)
waywardness 934 (1)
WC 649 (3)
we 80 (4)
weak 33 (6), 35 (4), 114 (4), 161 (5), 161 (6), 161 (7), 163 (4), 175 (2), 196 (8), 330 (2), 339 (2), 401 (3), 477 (6), 572 (2), 601 (3), 636 (3), 639 (5), 651 (20), 734 (3), 856 (3), 905 (4), 934 (3), 934 (5)
weak as a kitten 163 (4)

weak, be 161 (8), 163 (9), 684 (5), 934 (7)
weak case 477 (2)
weak-eyed 440 (3)
weak eyes 440 (1)
weak foundation 163 (1)
weak in numbers 105 (2)
weak-kneed 163 (4), 601 (3), 721 (2), 734 (3)
weak-minded 856 (3)
weak point 163 (1), 647 (2), 934 (2)
weak sight 440 (1)
weak style 566 (1), 572 (1)
weak thing 4 (2), 163 (3), 330 (1)
weak will 601 (1), 734 (1)
weak-willed 163 (4), 601 (3), 734 (3)
weaken 37 (4), 43 (7), 161 (9), 163 (9), 163 (10), 165 (7), 177 (6), 325 (3), 339 (3), 426 (5), 467 (4), 655 (9)
weakened 43 (6), 163 (5), 387 (2), 647 (3), 655 (5), 655 (6)
weakening 37 (1)
weakling 161 (2), 163 (2), 372 (1), 501 (2), 731 (3), 856 (2)
weakly 163 (6), 651 (20)
weakness 37 (1), 131 (3), 161 (1), 163 (1), 179 (1), 180 (1), 330 (1), 572 (1), 601 (1), 647 (1), 647 (2), 651 (1), 651 (2), 655 (3), 659 (1), 661 (2), 734 (1), 859 (3), 934 (2)
weal 253 (2), 548 (4), 845 (1)
wealth 171 (3), 376 (2), 615 (1), 635 (2), 730 (1), 744 (2), 777 (2), 797 (1), 800 (1)
wealthy 800 (3), 800 (5)
wealthy person 800 (2)
wean away from 613 (3)
wean from 485 (9), 611 (4)
weapon 628 (2), 630 (1), 660 (2), 662 (3), 713 (1), 723 (3), 854 (4), 900 (1)

wear 113 (6), 228 (2), 228 (32), 522 (8), 673 (1), 850 (5), 875 (7)
wear and tear 37 (1), 51 (2), 634 (1), 655 (2), 673 (1)
wear away 37 (5), 333 (3)
wear blinkers 439 (3)
wear down 332 (5), 612 (10)
wear on 111 (3)
wear out 634 (4), 655 (7), 655 (9), 673 (3), 675 (2), 684 (6), 838 (5)
wear the crown 34 (7), 727 (11), 733 (10)
wear the trousers 178 (3), 689 (5), 733 (12)
wear thin 163 (9), 330 (3)
wear uniform 16 (3)
wear well 113 (6)
weariness 377 (1), 679 (3), 684 (1), 825 (1), 829 (1), 834 (1), 838 (1)
wearing 111 (2), 684 (4), 838 (3), 844 (11)
wearing away 333 (1)
wearisome 682 (5), 684 (4), 827 (5), 838 (3)
wearisomeness 838 (1)
weary 163 (5), 684 (6), 827 (10), 829 (3), 834 (12), 838 (4), 838 (5), 863 (3)
weasel 365 (3)
weasel word 518 (1)
weather 269 (10), 332 (5), 340 (3), 352 (1), 425 (8), 547 (6)
weather eye 269 (2), 457 (2)
weather forecast 340 (3), 511 (1)
weather ship 340 (3)
weather station 340 (3)
weather the storm 153 (7), 660 (7), 727 (8)
weather-wise 340 (5)
weatherbeaten 655 (6)
weatherboard 207 (2)
weathercock 152 (2), 340 (3), 352 (2)
weathered 425 (7), 669 (8)
weathering 655 (3)

weatherman or - woman 340 (3)

weatherproof 660 (5)

weathervane 340 (3)

weave 43 (7), 45 (12), 50 (4), 56 (5), 164 (7), 222 (4), 222 (9), 305 (5), 331 (2), 844 (3)

weave into 303 (4)

weave spells 983 (10)

weaver 222 (5)

weaving 45 (2), 222 (5), 243 (2), 331 (2), 551 (3)

web 61 (3), 222 (3), 222 (4), 222 (5), 542 (4), 698 (2)

web-footed 214 (4)

web of intrigue 623 (4)

web offset 587 (1)

webbing 222 (3)

wed 11 (7), 45 (14), 764 (4), 887 (14), 894 (11)

wedded 45 (5), 894 (7)

wedded bliss 894 (1)

wedded state 894 (1)

wedded to 485 (4), 602 (4), 610 (7)

wedding 894 (3)

wedding anniversary 876 (2)

wedding ring 889 (3)

wedge 45 (9), 45 (11), 53 (5), 218 (2), 231 (4), 247 (4), 264 (2)

wedge apart 46 (10), 46 (13)

wedge in 231 (8), 303 (6)

wedge oneself into 297 (5)

wedge-shaped 247 (6)

wedged 45 (7)

wedlock 45 (1), 894 (1)

wee 33 (6), 196 (8)

weed 105 (4), 163 (2), 366 (6), 370 (9), 501 (2)

weed-killer 659 (3)

weed out 37 (4), 44 (7), 57 (5), 300 (6), 304 (4), 648 (10)

weed-ridden 366 (9)

weeding out 37 (2)

weedy 206 (5), 366 (9)

week 99 (2), 110 (1)

weekday 110 (1)

weekend 108 (8), 882 (9)

weekend cottage 192 (1)

weekender 191 (3)

weekly 141 (5), 141 (7)

weekly market 796 (1)

weeny 33 (6)

weep 298 (6), 302 (6), 341 (6), 408 (3), 825 (7), 834 (9), 836 (6)

weep for 819 (5)

weep over 836 (5)

weep with rage 891 (7)

weeper 836 (3)

weeping 298 (2), 339 (1), 825 (6), 836 (1)

weepy 825 (6)

weevil 365 (16)

weft 222 (5)

weigh 29 (3), 36 (4), 310 (4), 313 (4), 322 (5), 449 (8), 455 (6), 463 (3), 465 (11), 480 (6), 612 (8), 638 (7), 702 (8)

weigh against 467 (4)

weigh anchor 269 (10), 296 (6)

weigh heavy 322 (5)

weigh heavy on 834 (12)

weigh in 924 (10)

weigh on 311 (4), 322 (5)

weigh one down 322 (5)

weigh out 465 (14)

weigh the pros and cons 480 (6)

weigh upon one 827 (10)

weighbridge 322 (3)

weighed 608 (2)

weighed against 31 (3)

weighing 28 (4), 322 (2), 322 (4), 465 (3)

weighing machine 322 (3)

weight 3 (1), 26 (1), 160 (1), 178 (1), 195 (1), 195 (3), 319 (1), 322 (1), 322 (6), 571 (1), 638 (1)

weight-lifter 162 (4)

weight of numbers 104 (3), 160 (1)

weighted 246 (3), 322 (4)

weightiness 322 (1)

weighting 31 (1), 31 (2)

weightless 33 (6), 323 (3)

weightlessness 323 (1)

weights 322 (2)

weights and measures 465 (3)

weighty 3 (3), 32 (4), 162 (6), 178 (2), 195 (6), 319 (6), 322 (4), 324 (4), 466 (5), 571 (2), 638 (5), 702 (6)

weir 350 (4), 351 (1)

weird 596 (2), 854 (8), 864 (5), 970 (7), 983 (8)

weirdie 84 (3)

weirdness 503 (5)

weirdo 84 (3)

welcome 137 (4), 295 (1), 295 (6), 295 (7), 299 (1), 299 (3), 376 (3), 488 (6), 826 (2), 859 (10), 859 (11), 876 (1), 876 (4), 880 (7), 882 (2), 882 (7), 882 (10), 884 (2), 884 (7), 886 (1), 923 (1), 923 (10)

welcome home 295 (7)

welcomed 882 (7)

welcoming 289 (3), 299 (2), 782 (3), 824 (4), 876 (3), 880 (6), 882 (6)

weld 45 (9), 48 (4), 381 (8)

welded joint 45 (4)

welder 45 (2), 686 (3)

welfare 615 (1), 730 (1)

Welfare State 901 (2)

well 32 (17), 194 (1), 211 (1), 255 (4), 339 (1), 350 (1), 453 (5), 615 (6), 632 (1), 642 (4), 644 (12), 650 (2), 694 (10)

well-adapted 24 (7)

well-adjusted 24 (8), 494 (6)

well-advised 498 (5)

well-aimed 24 (6), 281 (3), 494 (6)

well-argued 475 (7)

well-balanced 502 (2)

well-behaved 60 (2), 739 (3), 884 (4)

well-being 376 (2), 615 (1), 650 (1), 652 (1), 730 (1), 824 (2)

well-born 868 (6)

well-bred 60 (2), 846 (3), 848 (6), 868 (7), 884 (3)

well brought up 848 (6)
well-built 162 (6), 841 (3)
well-calved 267 (10)
well-chosen moment 137 (1)
well-cooked 390 (2)
well-crafted 694 (7)
well-cut 24 (8), 228 (30)
well-defended 660 (4)
well-defined 443 (3)
well-deserved 913 (4)
well-directed 9 (6), 281 (3)
well-disposed 597 (4), 703 (4)
well-documented 466 (5)
well-done 301 (34), 725 (4), 923 (14)
well-drawn 590 (6)
well-dressed 228 (29), 390 (2), 841 (6), 848 (5)
well-drilled 60 (2)
well-earned 915 (2)
well-educated 490 (6)
well-endowed 694 (5), 800 (3)
well-established 153 (5)
well-fed 195 (8), 301 (31)
well-filled 54 (4), 635 (5)
well-fitting 24 (8)
well-formed 841 (5)
well-fought 716 (9)
well-founded 153 (6), 471 (3), 473 (4), 494 (4)
well-groomed 648 (7), 848 (5)
well-grounded 471 (3), 473 (4), 475 (7), 494 (4)
well-grown 195 (6), 195 (8)
well-heeled 800 (4)
well-hocked 267 (10)
well-housed 800 (3)
well-inclined 923 (5)
well-informed 490 (6), 524 (8)
well-intentioned 897 (4)
well-judged 498 (5)
well-kept 60 (2)
well-knit 48 (2)
well-known 490 (7), 522 (4), 528 (8), 610 (6), 866 (10)

well laid-out 841 (3)
well-liked 826 (2)
well-lined 54 (4)
well-lined purse 800 (1)
well-lit 417 (8), 420 (8), 624 (8)
well-made 575 (3), 694 (7), 841 (3)
well-mannered 848 (6), 884 (3)
well-marked 443 (3)
well-matured 386 (2)
well-meaning 880 (6)
well-meant 703 (4), 897 (4)
well-merited 913 (4), 915 (2)
well-met 74 (9)
well-off 730 (4), 800 (3)
well-oiled 334 (3)
well out 298 (6)
well over 298 (6)
well-paid 800 (3)
well-pitched 410 (6)
well-placed 187 (4), 281 (3)
well-planned 698 (4)
well-pleased 824 (4)
well-prepared 669 (7)
well-preserved 131 (6), 666 (4)
well-principled 933 (3)
well-proportioned 245 (2), 575 (3), 841 (5)
well-provided 635 (5)
well-qualified 490 (6)
well-read 490 (6), 536 (3)
well-regarded 866 (7)
well-regulated 60 (2)
well rid of 667 (4)
well said 488 (11)
well-satisfied 828 (2)
well-seasoned 386 (2)
well set-up 162 (8), 841 (3)
well-situated 800 (3)
well-spent 727 (4)
well-spoken 516 (2), 577 (3), 579 (6), 848 (6)
well-sprung 328 (2)
well-stocked 635 (5)
well-sung 577 (3)
well thought of 866 (7)
well-thumbed 673 (2)

well-timed 137 (4)
well-to-do 730 (4), 800 (3)
well-to-do person 800 (2)
well-trodden 624 (8), 673 (2)
well-turned 575 (3), 841 (5)
well turned out 841 (6)
well up 298 (6), 350 (9)
well-used 673 (2)
well-ventilated 340 (5), 528 (7), 652 (4)
well-wisher 707 (4), 859 (6), 880 (3), 897 (3)
well-wishing 880 (6)
well-worn 610 (6), 655 (6), 673 (2)
well-worn phrase 563 (1)
wellingtons 228 (27)
wellspring 156 (3)
welsh 620 (6), 805 (5)
Welsh rarebit 301 (13)
welsher 789 (3), 805 (3)
welt 253 (2), 548 (4), 845 (1)
welter 61 (2), 313 (3)
welterweight 722 (2)
wen 253 (2)
wench 132 (2), 373 (3)
wend 265 (4)
wend one's way 267 (11)
werewolf 904 (4), 970 (4)
Wesleyan 976 (11)
west 239 (1), 239 (2), 281 (2)
West End 184 (4), 594 (1)
West Side 184 (4)
westerly 239 (2), 352 (1)
western 239 (2), 281 (3), 445 (4), 590 (4)
Westerner 59 (2)
westernize 147 (8)
westward 239 (2)
wet 163 (2), 339 (1), 339 (2), 341 (1), 341 (4), 341 (7), 350 (8), 499 (4), 501 (2)
wet, be 298 (7), 313 (3), 341 (6), 350 (10)
wet blanket 177 (2), 613 (1), 702 (5), 834 (4), 838 (2), 924 (5)
wet-eyed 825 (6), 836 (4)

wet eyes 836 (1)
wet oneself 302 (6)
wet rot 649 (2)
wet spell 350 (6)
wet suit 228 (9)
wet through 341 (5), 341 (8)
wether 365 (8)
wetlands 347 (1)
wetness 341 (1)
wetted 341 (4)
wetting 341 (2)
whack 53 (1), 279 (9), 963 (9)
whacked 728 (5)
whacker 195 (5)
whacking 32 (9), 195 (6)
whale 195 (4), 365 (3)
whaler 275 (4), 619 (3)
whaling 619 (3)
wham 176 (10), 279 (9), 287 (7), 402 (4)
wharf 632 (2), 796 (2)
what 453 (5)
what fate holds in store 124 (2)
what have you 79 (2)
what is due 915 (1)
what matters 638 (3)
what may be 469 (1)
what must be 596 (1)
what news 453 (5)
what one believes 485 (2)
what should be 913 (1)
what time 108 (11)
what you will 79 (2), 562 (2)
whatever comes 159 (1)
whatever happens 159 (8)
whatever next 864 (9)
whatnot 194 (5)
what's going on 453 (5)
what's his or her name 562 (2)
what's to come 155 (1)
whatsit 630 (1)
whatsoever 79 (2)
wheat 301 (22)
wheat germ 301 (22)
wheedle 612 (11), 761 (5), 879 (4), 889 (5), 925 (4)
wheedling 612 (2), 925 (1), 925 (3)

wheel 250 (2), 265 (5), 269 (4), 282 (4), 287 (7), 314 (4), 315 (3), 315 (5), 630 (1), 689 (2)
wheel about 282 (4)
wheel and deal 623 (9)
wheel of Fortune 618 (1)
wheel round 286 (5), 314 (4)
wheelbarrow 274 (4)
wheelchair 274 (4)
wheeled 274 (16)
wheeled traffic 305 (2)
wheeler-dealer 623 (5)
wheeling 314 (1)
wheelwright 686 (3)
wheeze 352 (7), 352 (11), 406 (3), 451 (1)
wheezing 352 (9)
wheezy 352 (9), 406 (2), 577 (3)
whelp 132 (3), 167 (6), 365 (10)
when 108 (11), 453 (5)
when and where 186 (1)
where 189 (6), 453 (5)
whereabouts 186 (1), 189 (1)
wherefore 158 (5)
wherever 183 (8)
wherewithal 629 (1), 797 (2)
wherry 275 (5)
whet 176 (9), 256 (11), 821 (7)
whet the appetite 859 (13)
whetstone 256 (6), 333 (1)
whey 301 (24), 335 (2)
whey-faced 426 (3)
which way 281 (8)
whiff 352 (3), 352 (11), 394 (1)
while 108 (2), 108 (10), 123 (5)
while, a 108 (1)
while away 681 (3)
while away time 108 (8), 837 (21)
whilst 108 (10), 123 (5)
whim 481 (5), 503 (5), 513 (2), 604 (2), 839 (1), 859 (3)

whimper 408 (3), 836 (1), 836 (6)
whimsical 82 (2), 84 (5), 152 (3), 513 (5), 601 (3), 604 (3), 604 (4), 839 (4), 849 (2)
whimsicality 595 (0), 604 (1), 839 (1)
whimsy 497 (2), 513 (2), 604 (2)
whine 407 (5), 408 (1), 408 (3), 409 (3), 829 (5), 836 (1), 836 (6), 879 (4)
whiner 829 (2), 836 (3)
whinge 836 (6)
whining 829 (3), 836 (4), 879 (3)
whinny 409 (3)
whip 74 (8), 176 (9), 268 (5), 301 (40), 318 (6), 612 (4), 612 (9), 619 (3), 680 (3), 690 (3), 737 (1), 963 (10), 964 (1)
whip hand 34 (2), 178 (1), 727 (2), 733 (2)
whip in 74 (11)
whip on 279 (7)
whip out 304 (4)
whip-round 781 (2)
whip up 354 (6), 821 (6)
whipcord 47 (2)
whipped 323 (3)
whipper-in 74 (8), 619 (3)
whippet 365 (10)
whipping 279 (2), 963 (2)
whipping boy 941 (2)
whipping in 74 (1)
whipping post 964 (2)
whipping up 821 (1)
whippy 327 (3)
whirl 315 (1), 315 (5), 318 (5), 678 (1), 680 (1), 837 (22)
whirligig 315 (3)
whirling dervish 315 (3)
whirlpool 251 (2), 315 (2), 318 (3), 350 (3), 663 (1)
whirlwind 61 (4), 315 (2), 318 (3), 352 (4)
whirr 315 (5), 318 (5), 403 (1), 403 (3), 404 (3)
whisk 277 (6), 301 (40), 315 (3), 315 (5), 318 (6)

whisker **208** (1), **378** (3)
whiskers **259** (2)
whiskery **208** (4)
whisky **301** (28)
whisper **33** (2), **401** (1),
401 (4), **523** (6), **524** (3),
524 (11), **529** (2), **577** (1),
577 (4), **578** (5), **579** (8),
926 (6)
whispered **401** (3), **578** (2)
whispering **926** (5)
whist or bridge **837** (11)
whistle **352** (10), **400** (2),
400 (4), **406** (3), **407** (5),
408 (3), **409** (3), **413** (9),
413 (10), **414** (6), **547** (5),
665 (1), **833** (7), **864** (1),
864 (6), **923** (10), **924** (1),
924 (9)
whistle for **761** (6)
whistling **407** (1), **923** (3)
white **417** (1), **426** (3), **427**
(4), **427** (6), **438** (2), **648**
(7)
white as a sheet **854** (6)
white-collar worker **686**
(2)
white-collar workers **869**
(4)
white corpuscle **335** (3)
white ensign **547** (12)
white feather **856** (1)
white fish **301** (15)
white flag **547** (12), **719** (2)
white goods **795** (1)
white-haired **131** (6)
white hairs **131** (3)
white heat **427** (1)
white horses **350** (5)
white-hot **379** (4), **427** (4)
white lie **518** (1), **543** (2),
698 (2)
white lines **305** (3)
white magic **983** (1)
white meat **301** (16)
white notes **410** (2)
white paint **427** (3)
white patch **427** (2)
white person **427** (1)
white sauce **389** (2)
white-skinned **427** (4)
white supremacist **481** (4)
white thing **427** (2)

white-tie **875** (6)
white wine **301** (29)
Whitehall **733** (1)
whiten **425** (8), **426** (5),
427 (6), **648** (9), **818** (8)
whitened **427** (4)
whiteness **417** (1), **426** (1),
427 (1), **648** (1)
whitewash **226** (10), **226**
(16), **425** (8), **427** (3), **427**
(6), **495** (9), **525** (7), **542**
(5), **542** (8), **648** (9)
whitewashed **427** (4)
whitewashing **541** (1), **960**
(1)
whither **281** (8)
whiting **427** (3)
whitish **425** (7), **426** (3),
427 (5), **429** (2), **433** (3)
Whitsuntide **128** (4)
whittle **37** (4), **46** (11), **243**
(5), **554** (3)
whittle away **198** (7)
whittle down **27** (5)
whittling **844** (2)
whiz kid **678** (5), **864** (3)
whizz **277** (2), **277** (6), **406**
(3)
who **453** (5)
whoa **145** (9), **266** (11)
whodunit **590** (4)
whole **26** (1), **32** (13), **44**
(4), **52** (1), **52** (4), **54** (1),
54 (3), **78** (1), **79** (1), **79**
(4), **85** (4), **85** (5), **88** (1),
183 (6), **331** (1), **646** (3),
646 (4), **706** (2)
whole, a **52** (1)
whole amount **26** (2)
whole food **652** (1)
whole-hearted **599** (2)
whole-hogging **54** (3)
whole number **85** (1)
whole skin **650** (1)
whole, the **52** (2)
whole time, the **108** (1),
108 (10)
whole truth **526** (1)
wholefood **301** (9)
wholemeal **301** (22)
wholeness **52** (1), **54** (1),
88 (1)

wholesale **32** (5), **32** (17),
52 (7), **54** (3), **78** (2), **791**
(3)
wholesale murder **362** (4)
wholesaler **793** (2), **794** (1)
wholesome **301** (33), **644**
(8), **652** (4), **841** (6), **945**
(3)
wholesomely **652** (7)
wholesomeness **652** (1)
wholly **52** (8), **54** (8), **79**
(7)
whoop **408** (1), **408** (3), **833**
(7), **835** (6)
whoopee **837** (9)
whooping **400** (3)
whooping cough **651** (8)
whop **279** (2)
whopper **195** (5), **543** (1)
whopping **32** (9), **195** (6)
whore **952** (4)
whorehouse **951** (5)
whoring **951** (2)
whorl **251** (2)
whorled **251** (8)
Who's Who **87** (3)
whosoever **79** (2)
why **453** (5)
why on earth **453** (5)
wick **208** (1), **385** (3), **420**
(3)
wicked **616** (2), **645** (2),
700 (4), **914** (3), **930** (4),
934 (3), **936** (3), **940** (2),
974 (5), **980** (4)
wicked, be **655** (7), **688**
(4), **934** (7), **936** (4), **980**
(6)
wicked fairy **983** (6)
wicked ways **934** (1)
wickedly **934** (9)
wickedness **645** (1), **655**
(1), **688** (1), **738** (1), **898**
(2), **904** (1), **914** (1), **930**
(1), **934** (1), **936** (1), **980**
(1)
wickerwork **194** (6), **222**
(3)
wicket **263** (6)
wicket-keeper **837** (16)
wide **32** (4), **183** (6), **199**
(3), **205** (3), **282** (2)
wide apart **15** (4)

wide-awake 455 (2)
wide berth 620 (1), 660 (1)
wide-bodied 205 (3)
wide-cut 205 (3)
wide-eyed 864 (4), 935 (3)
wide-hipped 205 (3)
wide horizons 183 (1)
wide margin 15 (1)
wide-mouthed 205 (3)
wide of 199 (7)
wide open 197 (3), 263 (13), 661 (5)
wide open spaces 183 (1)
wide-ranging 32 (5), 205 (3)
wide world 183 (1), 321 (2)
widely 32 (17), 54 (9), 183 (8), 199 (6), 281 (8)
widely believed, be 485 (10)
widely-read 490 (6)
widen 36 (5), 79 (6), 197 (4), 197 (5), 205 (5)
widen the breach 709 (8)
widen the gap 290 (3)
wideness 205 (1)
widening 36 (1)
widespread 32 (5), 52 (7), 75 (2), 79 (4), 183 (6), 197 (3), 610 (6)
widow 41 (3), 373 (3), 786 (10), 896 (2), 896 (5)
widowed 41 (4), 896 (4)
widowed, be 896 (5)
widower 41 (3), 372 (1), 896 (2)
widowhood 169 (1), 896 (2)
widow's weeds 228 (4)
width 205 (1)
widthways 205 (6)
wield 173 (3), 378 (7), 673 (3)
wield authority 733 (10)
wife 373 (3), 894 (4)
wifeless 896 (4)
wifely 887 (9), 894 (9)
wig 259 (2), 843 (2)
wiggle 317 (4)
wigwam 192 (3)
wild 61 (9), 172 (3), 176 (5), 176 (6), 183 (1), 456

(6), 495 (4), 495 (6), 497 (3), 499 (4), 503 (9), 699 (3), 738 (7), 738 (8), 821 (3), 857 (3), 869 (9), 891 (4), 898 (7)
wild animal 365 (2)
wild beast 176 (4), 904 (5)
wild blow 279 (2)
wild-eyed 825 (5), 836 (4)
wild-goose chase 641 (2), 695 (2), 728 (1)
wild life 365 (1)
wild plant 366 (6)
wildcat 744 (7)
wilderness 61 (2), 165 (2), 172 (3), 183 (1), 344 (1), 883 (2)
wildlife park 369 (4)
wildness 499 (2), 738 (1)
wile 698 (2)
wiles 542 (2)
wilful 595 (1), 602 (5), 604 (3), 857 (3), 898 (4)
wilfulness 595 (0), 934 (1)
wiliness 698 (1)
will 447 (1), 595 (2), 597 (6), 599 (1), 599 (3), 602 (1), 605 (6), 608 (1), 767 (2), 780 (4), 859 (1)
will and pleasure 737 (1), 859 (1)
will of Allah 596 (2)
will of heaven 596 (2)
willed 595 (1), 608 (2)
willing 174 (5), 488 (4), 595 (1), 597 (4), 599 (2), 612 (7), 617 (3), 628 (3), 671 (3), 678 (7), 701 (4), 739 (3), 758 (2), 855 (4)
willing, be 595 (2), 597 (6), 672 (3), 678 (11), 758 (3), 759 (4)
willing consent 758 (1)
willing to forget 506 (4)
willingly 488 (9), 597 (7), 833 (9)
willingness 174 (3), 488 (1), 595 (0), 597 (1), 612 (3), 678 (1), 706 (1), 739 (1), 758 (1), 833 (1), 859 (1), 917 (1)
willow 366 (4)

willowy 206 (4), 327 (3), 841 (5)
willpower 595 (0), 599 (1)
willy-nilly 596 (9)
wilt 163 (9), 655 (7), 834 (9)
wily 498 (4), 542 (6), 698 (4)
wily person 698 (3)
wimple 228 (23)
win 34 (1), 701 (7), 727 (2), 727 (11), 771 (7), 771 (9), 786 (7)
win a prize 962 (4)
win friends 880 (7)
win glory 730 (6)
win hands down 727 (11)
win honour 866 (11)
win no glory 867 (9)
win on points 727 (11)
win one's spurs 727 (6), 855 (6), 866 (11)
win over 147 (7), 485 (9), 612 (10), 962 (3)
win praise 923 (11)
win the battle 727 (11)
win the jackpot 771 (9)
win the match 727 (11)
win the pools 800 (7)
win through 727 (8)
win to 295 (4)
wince 280 (3), 377 (6), 818 (8), 825 (7), 854 (10)
winch 288 (3), 310 (2)
wincing 377 (4)
wind 152 (2), 300 (3), 314 (4), 315 (5), 340 (1), 350 (9), 352 (1), 394 (3), 413 (9), 414 (1), 651 (7), 684 (6)
wind-dried 342 (4)
wind-driven 160 (9)
wind ensemble 413 (3)
wind gauge 352 (2)
wind in 288 (3)
wind power 160 (4)
wind rose 352 (2)
wind sock 547 (6)
wind surfing 269 (3), 837 (6)
wind the clock 117 (7)
wind tunnel 353 (1), 461 (4)

wind-up 69 (3), 69 (6), 173 (3), 174 (8), 310 (4), 669 (11)
wind upwards 308 (4)
windbag 352 (5), 581 (3)
windbreak 366 (2), 662 (2)
winded 684 (3)
winder 218 (3)
windfall 40 (2), 508 (1), 615 (2), 771 (1), 782 (1)
windiness 325 (1), 336 (1), 352 (1), 352 (7)
winding 61 (8), 282 (2), 350 (7)
winding course 251 (3)
winding sheet 364 (3)
windjammer 275 (5)
windlass 288 (1), 310 (2)
windless 266 (5)
windlessness 266 (2), 352 (1)
windmill 315 (3)
window 263 (5), 330 (1), 353 (1), 438 (5)
window cleaner 648 (6)
window display 796 (3)
window-dress 875 (7)
window dressing 528 (2)
window frame 218 (13), 263 (5)
window pane 263 (5), 422 (1)
window-shop 792 (5)
window shopper 441 (1), 792 (2)
window shopping 792 (1)
window sill 218 (12)
windowed 263 (14)
windowless 423 (2)
windpipe 352 (7), 353 (1)
winds of change 143 (1)
windscreen 263 (5)
windshield 263 (5)
windsock 352 (2)
windswept 61 (7), 352 (8)
windward 239 (1)
windy 176 (5), 336 (3), 340 (5), 352 (8), 515 (4), 570 (3), 581 (4)
wine 301 (29), 944 (1), 949 (1)
wine and dine 301 (39)
wine bar 192 (12)

wine cask 194 (12)
wine-coloured 431 (3)
wine-grower 370 (4)
wine-growing 370 (1)
wine merchant 633 (2)
wine-tasting 301 (25)
wineglass 194 (15)
wing 40 (1), 53 (2), 239 (1), 271 (5), 271 (7), 277 (6), 311 (6), 655 (10), 662 (2), 702 (8), 722 (7), 722 (14)
wing commander 741 (9)
wing coverts 259 (3)
wing one's way 271 (7)
winged 271 (6)
winged insect 365 (16)
wings 594 (7)
wingspan 205 (1)
wink 438 (3), 438 (8), 440 (1), 524 (3), 524 (11), 547 (1), 547 (4), 547 (21), 889 (2)
wink at 458 (5), 756 (5), 914 (6)
winker 547 (6)
winkle out 304 (4)
winner 34 (3), 727 (3), 782 (2)
winners, the 727 (3)
winning 34 (4), 727 (4), 771 (1), 826 (2), 884 (4), 887 (11)
winning card 727 (1)
winning side 727 (3)
winning ways 612 (2), 887 (2), 925 (1)
winnings 771 (3), 782 (1), 807 (1)
winnow 44 (7), 340 (6), 370 (9), 605 (7)
wino 949 (5)
winsome 841 (6), 887 (11)
winsomeness 826 (1), 887 (2)
winter 108 (8), 110 (1), 129 (4), 129 (7), 380 (2), 731 (1)
winter feed 370 (1)
winter solstice 129 (4)
winter sports 380 (3), 837 (6)
wintertime 129 (4)

wintriness 129 (4), 176 (3), 340 (3), 350 (6), 380 (2)
wintry 129 (7), 380 (5)
wintry weather 380 (2)
wipe 342 (6), 648 (9)
wipe off 550 (3)
wipe out 2 (8), 165 (6), 362 (11), 550 (3), 727 (10)
wiped out 2 (3), 550 (3)
wiping out 165 (1)
wiping up 648 (2)
wire 47 (2), 206 (1), 208 (1), 524 (1), 524 (10), 529 (3), 531 (1)
wire-puller 523 (1), 612 (5)
wire-pulling 623 (4)
wire-tapping 415 (2)
wireless 531 (3)
wireless message 529 (3)
wiry 162 (8), 206 (5), 208 (4)
wisdom 449 (1), 480 (1), 490 (1), 490 (2), 498 (3), 623 (2), 691 (1), 858 (1)
wise 480 (4), 490 (5), 496 (3), 498 (5), 510 (2), 624 (1), 642 (2), 654 (6), 694 (4), 698 (4), 858 (2)
wise, be 447 (7), 490 (8), 498 (6), 623 (8), 694 (8), 858 (3)
wise guy 500 (2), 850 (3)
wise judgment 480 (1)
wise man 983 (5)
wise man or woman 500 (1)
wise to 490 (5)
wise woman 983 (6)
wiseacre 473 (3), 500 (2)
wisecrack 839 (2), 839 (5)
wisecracker 839 (3)
wish 595 (2), 761 (1), 859 (1), 859 (5), 859 (11)
wish for oneself 859 (11)
wish Godspeed 296 (6)
wish ill 899 (6)
wish on 859 (11), 899 (6)
wish one joy 886 (3)
wish one well 859 (11)
wish otherwise 859 (11)
wish undone 830 (4)
wish well 897 (5)

within limits 177 (8)
within one's means 812 (3)
within reach 189 (2), 200 (7), 289 (3)
within reason 177 (8)
within sight of 33 (11)
without 8 (6), 39 (2), 39 (4), 55 (3), 190 (8), 772 (2), 774 (2)
without a care 833 (9)
without a hitch 701 (10)
without a name 867 (7)
without a pang 940 (2)
without a scratch 52 (5)
without a vote 606 (2)
without affectation 699 (5)
without airs 872 (3)
without alloy 44 (5)
without appeal 473 (5)
without art 699 (3), 699 (5)
without artifice 699 (3)
without authority 161 (5)
without, be 307 (3), 627 (6)
without being 2 (3)
without ceremony 874 (4)
without colour 426 (3)
without compunction 940 (5)
without context 10 (3)
without contrast 16 (2)
without credit 908 (3)
without defence 928 (7)
without delay 116 (4), 135 (8), 680 (2)
without depth 4 (3)
without emotion 820 (8)
without end 107 (2), 107 (3), 115 (2)
without enemies 717 (3)
without exception 79 (7)
without excuse 928 (7), 936 (5)
without food 946 (3)
without force 163 (4)
without fuss 874 (4)
without grit 856 (3)
without guts 856 (3)
without incident 266 (5)
without interest 454 (2)
without law 954 (7)
without limit 107 (2)

without lumps 258 (3)
without mass 320 (3)
without meaning 514 (4), 515 (4)
without measure 107 (2)
without morals 934 (4)
without nerves 820 (3)
without notice 116 (4), 135 (8), 508 (6)
without number 107 (2)
without prestige 867 (7)
without rank 869 (8)
without regrets 940 (2)
without religion 974 (5)
without repute 867 (7)
without resource 161 (6)
without rights 916 (7)
without risk 660 (4)
without smell 395 (2)
without stopping 71 (7)
without strings 756 (4)
without substance 4 (3)
without taste 387 (2)
without tricks 699 (3)
without truth 541 (3)
without vanity 874 (2)
without violence 717 (5)
without war 717 (3)
without warmth 820 (3)
without warning 116 (4), 508 (2), 508 (6)
withstand 704 (5), 713 (10), 715 (3)
withy 47 (4)
witness 189 (4), 438 (7), 441 (1), 441 (3), 466 (2), 466 (4), 466 (7), 524 (4), 765 (3), 927 (2)
witness box 956 (4)
witness to 547 (18)
witnessed 466 (5)
wits 447 (1), 498 (1)
witticism 496 (1), 518 (1), 542 (2), 560 (1), 839 (2), 849 (1), 851 (1)
wittiness 839 (1)
witty 496 (3), 514 (3), 571 (2), 833 (4), 839 (4), 849 (3), 851 (4), 882 (6)
witty, be 569 (3), 837 (21), 839 (5)
witty remark 839 (2)

wizard 500 (1), 694 (4), 864 (3), 983 (5)
wizardly 983 (7)
wizardry 694 (1), 983 (1)
wizard's cap 983 (4)
wizened 131 (6), 196 (9), 198 (4), 206 (5)
woad 425 (4), 435 (2)
wobble 143 (5), 282 (3), 317 (4), 601 (4)
wobbling 142 (1), 142 (2), 152 (4)
wobbly 163 (4), 647 (3)
woe 616 (1), 825 (2)
woe to 899 (8)
woebegone 825 (5), 825 (6), 834 (6), 836 (4)
woeful 825 (5), 827 (6), 834 (6), 836 (4)
wold 209 (2), 348 (1)
wolf 176 (4), 301 (35), 365 (10), 947 (4), 952 (1)
wolf in sheep's clothing 545 (3)
wolfish 365 (18), 947 (3)
woman 134 (2), 371 (3), 373 (3)
woman-chaser 952 (1)
woman-hater 902 (2)
woman-hours 682 (3)
womanhood 134 (1), 373 (1)
womanish 373 (5)
womanishness 373 (1)
womanize 951 (10)
womanizer 952 (1)
womanizing 951 (2)
womankind 371 (1), 373 (2)
womanliness 373 (1)
womanly 134 (3), 373 (5)
womb 68 (4), 156 (4), 167 (3), 169 (1), 224 (2)
womb of time 124 (1)
women 373 (2)
women and song 944 (1)
womenfolk 373 (2)
women's libber 373 (3)
women's liberation 373 (1), 744 (1)
women's quarters 373 (2)
women's rights 373 (1), 915 (1)

wonder 84 (1), 474 (8), 491
(8), 508 (1), 821 (1), 864
(1), 864 (3), 864 (6), 887
(1), 920 (1), 920 (5)

wonder about 449 (8)

wonder boy 864 (3)

wonder-worker 983 (5)

wonderful 32 (7), 84 (6),
470 (2), 486 (5), 508 (2),
644 (4), 826 (2), 864 (5),
866 (8), 866 (9), 983 (7)

wonderful, be 508 (5), 821
(8), 864 (7)

wonderfully 32 (19), 864
(8)

wondering 507 (2), 508
(3), 864 (4), 920 (3)

wonderland 513 (3), 864
(3)

wonderment 864 (1)

wondrous 864 (5)

wont 673 (1)

wont, be 16 (3), 60 (4), 79
(5), 141 (6), 536 (4), 848
(7), 943 (3)

won't do 643 (3)

wonted 610 (6)

woo 619 (5), 761 (5), 859
(11), 887 (14), 889 (7)

wood 252 (2), 287 (2), 326
(1), 366 (2), 366 (11), 383
(2), 385 (1), 631 (1)

wood carving 554 (1)

wood engraving 555 (1)

wood nymph 366 (1), 967
(3)

wood pulp 356 (1)

woodcock 365 (5)

woodcut 553 (5), 555 (1)

woodcutter 366 (3)

wooded 366 (10)

wooden 366 (11), 576 (2),
820 (3)

wooden spoon 695 (1), 729
(1)

woodenness 820 (1)

woodland 366 (2), 366 (10)

woodlouse 365 (17)

woodwind 352 (5), 413 (3),
414 (1), 414 (6)

woodworker 686 (3)

woodworm 168 (1), 365
(16), 659 (2)

woody 329 (2), 366 (10),
366 (11)

wooer 763 (1), 859 (6), 887
(4)

woof 222 (5), 409 (3)

wooing 438 (3), 887 (3),
887 (9), 889 (2)

wool 208 (2), 222 (4), 259
(2)

woolgathering 456 (2), 456
(4)

woolly 208 (4), 228 (11),
259 (5), 259 (7), 477 (6)

woolsack 743 (2), 956 (1),
956 (4)

word 524 (1), 524 (3), 547
(8), 559 (1), 560 (1), 664
(1), 737 (1), 764 (1)

word fencing 477 (1)

word for word 494 (6), 494
(8), 520 (6), 559 (5)

word form 243 (1)

word game 837 (8)

word list 87 (2), 559 (2)

word magic 566 (1)

word of advice 691 (1)

word of command 718 (6),
737 (1)

word of God 975 (2)

word of honour 532 (2),
764 (1), 767 (1)

word of mouth 127 (3), 466
(2), 529 (3), 579 (1)

word order 564 (1)

word-painting 513 (1), 590
(1)

word-perfect 669 (7)

word play 519 (2)

word processor 86 (5)

word-puzzle 530 (2)

word-smith 589 (7)

word-spinner 574 (3), 579
(5)

word-spinning 566 (1), 579
(4), 579 (7)

wordiness 559 (1), 570 (1),
581 (1)

wording 563 (1)

wordless 578 (2)

wordplay 560 (1), 839 (1)

words 716 (1)

wordy 559 (4), 570 (4)

work 160 (3), 164 (2), 173
(3), 243 (5), 318 (7), 355
(5), 412 (4), 589 (1), 594
(3), 600 (4), 622 (1), 622
(3), 622 (7), 622 (8), 628
(4), 640 (4), 642 (3), 671
(4), 673 (3), 676 (1), 676
(2), 676 (5), 678 (12), 682
(3), 682 (7), 684 (6), 688
(5), 703 (7), 727 (7), 844
(12)

work a ship 269 (10)

work against 182 (3), 623
(9), 643 (3), 704 (4)

work as a team 706 (4)

work at 600 (4), 622 (7),
688 (5)

work for 622 (7), 628 (4),
682 (7), 742 (8)

work for peace 717 (4)

work hard 682 (7)

work in 231 (8)

work like magic 727 (7)

work miracles 864 (7)

work of art 56 (1), 551 (1),
694 (3), 841 (2)

work of fiction 589 (2)

work of reference 589 (4)

work on 178 (3), 821 (6)

work one's passage 269
(9)

work out 86 (12), 154 (6),
157 (5), 520 (10), 623 (8),
669 (12), 682 (2), 688 (5),
725 (5)

work party 74 (4)

work-shy 679 (8)

work study 689 (1)

work to rule 145 (3)

work together 706 (4)

work up 821 (6)

work up into 243 (5)

work upon 612 (8)

workable 160 (8), 173 (2),
469 (2), 642 (2)

workaday 573 (2), 622 (5)

workaholic 678 (5)

workbasket 194 (6)

worked 437 (5), 844 (10)

worked out 623 (6)

worked up 891 (4)

worked upon 173 (2)

worker 164 (4), 600 (2), 676 (3), 678 (5), 686 (2), 742 (1), 742 (6), 869 (5)
worker ant 365 (16)
worker bee 365 (16)
workers' cooperative 706 (2)
workhouse 192 (17), 801 (1)
working 173 (1), 173 (2), 628 (3), 676 (1), 676 (4), 678 (7), 682 (4), 742 (7)
working arrangement 770 (1)
working class 869 (3), 869 (8)
working day 110 (1), 682 (3)
working life 682 (3)
working model 551 (2)
working party 754 (1)
working to rule 278 (1)
working together 706 (1)
working towards 179 (2)
working up 821 (1)
workings 331 (1)
workman 686 (2)
workmanlike 678 (9), 694 (7)
workmanship 164 (1)
workpeople 686 (4)
workroom 194 (19), 687 (1)
works 58 (1), 331 (1), 586 (1), 630 (2), 687 (1)
works, the 52 (2)
workshop 164 (1), 534 (1), 538 (4), 539 (4), 630 (4), 678 (1), 687 (1), 796 (3)
world 3 (1), 52 (1), 154 (2), 183 (1), 321 (1), 321 (2), 321 (15)
world-beater 34 (3), 727 (3)
world-beating 34 (5), 727 (4)
world of 32 (2)
world of finance 797 (3)
world of learning 492 (1)
world of nature 3 (1), 319 (1), 319 (2)
world-shaking 149 (3)
world, the 371 (1)

world-view 79 (1)
world war 718 (1)
world-weary 838 (4)
world without end 115 (5)
worldliness 932 (1), 974 (2), 980 (1)
worldly 321 (15), 932 (3), 974 (5)
worldly wisdom 498 (2)
worldly-wise 498 (4), 932 (3)
world's end 69 (2), 199 (2)
worldwide 32 (5), 57 (2), 78 (2), 79 (4), 183 (6)
worm 251 (13), 365 (17), 938 (3)
worm-eaten 655 (6)
worm in 231 (8)
worm into 297 (5)
worm one's way 265 (4), 305 (5)
worm one's way in 297 (6)
worm out 484 (4)
wormlike 251 (6)
worms 651 (17)
wormwood 393 (1)
wormy 365 (18)
worn 163 (5), 522 (6), 655 (6), 673 (2), 684 (2), 842 (4)
worn out 161 (7), 641 (4), 655 (5), 655 (6), 674 (3)
worried 825 (5), 834 (5)
worries 731 (1), 825 (3)
worry 301 (36), 318 (1), 318 (6), 507 (1), 616 (1), 659 (1), 731 (1), 821 (8), 825 (3), 825 (7), 827 (1), 827 (2), 827 (9), 827 (10), 829 (1), 834 (1), 854 (2)
worrying 825 (3), 827 (5)
worse 655 (5)
worse and worse 832 (4)
worse for, the 655 (5), 949 (6)
worse for wear, the 655 (6)
worsen 655 (9), 832 (3)
worsening 35 (1)
worship 866 (13), 887 (1), 887 (13), 920 (1), 920 (5),

979 (1), 979 (9), 981 (1), 981 (11)
worship idols 982 (6)
worship of wealth 982 (1)
worshipful 32 (4), 127 (6), 866 (8), 920 (4), 965 (6), 979 (8), 981 (10)
worshipped 965 (6), 981 (10)
worshipper 859 (6), 976 (6), 979 (4), 981 (8), 982 (4)
worshipping 781 (5), 920 (3), 973 (8), 979 (6), 981 (9)
worst 727 (10)
worst intentions 898 (1)
worst, the 731 (2)
worsted 35 (4), 208 (2), 222 (4), 728 (5)
wort 366 (6)
worth 28 (8), 150 (3), 640 (1), 644 (1), 809 (1), 933 (2)
worth a fortune 811 (3)
worth, be 809 (6)
worth buying 792 (3)
worth choosing 605 (5)
worth eating 301 (32), 390 (2)
worth having 859 (10)
worth looking at 32 (8)
worth millions 800 (4)
worth one's keep 640 (3)
worth the money 812 (3)
worthless 639 (6), 641 (5), 645 (2), 655 (5), 922 (4), 934 (4)
worthlessness 639 (1), 641 (1), 645 (1)
worthwhile 615 (3), 638 (5), 640 (3), 642 (2), 644 (8), 923 (6)
worthwhile, be 771 (10)
worthy 638 (4), 644 (4), 866 (6), 866 (7), 923 (6), 933 (3)
worthy, be 915 (7)
worthy of 915 (3)
would-be 562 (3), 597 (4), 852 (4), 859 (7)
wound 46 (11), 163 (10), 176 (7), 251 (8), 263 (18), 279 (9), 333 (3), 377 (1), 616 (1), 645 (7), 651 (14),

655 (4), 655 (10), 702 (8), 712 (7), 827 (8), 845 (1), 891 (8)
wound up 251 (8), 821 (3)
wounded 825 (5)
wounds 729 (1)
woven 222 (6), 331 (4)
woven stuff 222 (4)
wow 411 (1)
wrack 366 (6)
wraith 970 (3)
wraith-like 206 (5), 970 (7)
wrangle 25 (1), 475 (11), 489 (5), 709 (3), 709 (9)
wrangler 86 (7), 475 (6), 705 (1), 709 (5)
wrangling 475 (4), 709 (6)
wrap 45 (12), 226 (13), 235 (4), 261 (3)
wrap round 226 (13)
wrap up 228 (31), 379 (7)
wrapped in thought 456 (4)
wrapped up in 455 (3)
wrapper 194 (1), 226 (5), 228 (6), 235 (1)
wrapping 194 (1), 226 (5), 227 (1), 235 (1)
wrath 888 (1), 891 (2)
wrathful 891 (4)
wreak vengeance 735 (7), 910 (5)
wreath 222 (1), 250 (3), 729 (1)
wreathe 222 (10), 251 (10), 844 (12), 876 (4)
wreathe around 230 (3)
wreathed 844 (10)
wreck 165 (3), 165 (6), 165 (7), 655 (2), 655 (9), 728 (2)
wreckage 41 (1), 165 (3)
wrecked 728 (6)
wrecker 168 (1), 663 (2), 738 (6), 789 (2), 904 (1)
wren 365 (4)
wrench 174 (7), 176 (8), 304 (1), 304 (2), 630 (1), 778 (2)
wrench out 304 (4)
wrest 246 (5)
wrest from 786 (8)

wrestle 716 (5), 716 (10)
wrestle with 704 (5)
wrestler 162 (4), 722 (1)
wrestling 162 (4), 713 (1), 716 (5), 722 (1), 837 (6)
wrestling match 716 (5)
wretch 731 (3), 825 (4), 938 (2)
wretched 639 (5), 645 (2), 645 (4), 731 (6), 825 (6), 834 (6), 930 (5)
wretchedly 32 (20)
wretchedness 731 (1), 825 (2), 834 (1)
wriggle 251 (13), 265 (4), 312 (4), 318 (5), 698 (5), 821 (9), 825 (7)
wriggle out of 614 (4), 667 (5), 918 (3)
wriggling 251 (6)
wright 686 (3)
wring 786 (8)
wring from 304 (4), 740 (3), 786 (8)
wring one's hands 161 (8), 547 (21), 830 (4), 836 (5)
wring one's neck 362 (10)
wring out 304 (4), 342 (6)
wringer 342 (3)
wringing wet 341 (5)
wrinkle 247 (7), 251 (1), 251 (11), 259 (9), 261 (1), 262 (3)
wrinkled 131 (6), 251 (7), 259 (4), 262 (2), 842 (4)
wrinkles 261 (1), 842 (1)
wrinkly 261 (2)
wristwatch 117 (3)
writ 693 (1), 737 (4), 751 (2), 959 (2)
write 56 (5), 164 (7), 547 (19), 548 (7), 558 (6), 586 (8), 590 (7)
write a cheque 797 (12)
write about 591 (5)
write an IOU 767 (6)
write back 460 (5), 588 (4)
write badly 517 (6)
write books 586 (8)
write down 548 (7), 586 (8)
write in 54 (7)
write letters 586 (8)

write-off 674 (1), 674 (5), 803 (1)
write one's name 547 (20), 586 (8)
write out 586 (8)
write plays 594 (16)
write poetry 586 (8)
write to 588 (4), 882 (8)
write-up 528 (2), 528 (9), 528 (11), 591 (2), 591 (5)
write well 575 (4)
writer 164 (4), 549 (1), 586 (5), 589 (7), 591 (3)
writhe 251 (13), 312 (4), 318 (5), 377 (6), 821 (9), 825 (7)
writhing 377 (4), 825 (5)
writing 56 (1), 164 (1), 551 (1), 558 (1), 586 (1), 586 (3), 587 (1), 589 (2)
writing desk 194 (5)
writing materials 586 (4)
writing music 412 (1)
writing on the wall 511 (3), 664 (1), 900 (1)
writings 586 (1), 589 (2)
written 524 (7), 548 (6), 557 (5), 557 (6), 558 (5), 586 (7)
written law 953 (3)
written matter 586 (3)
written music 410 (3)
written off 674 (3)
written speech 579 (2)
written word 589 (2)
wrong 25 (5), 481 (6), 495 (4), 616 (1), 616 (2), 643 (1), 643 (2), 645 (2), 645 (7), 645 (8), 891 (1), 914 (1), 914 (3), 914 (6), 916 (6), 930 (3), 930 (4), 934 (1), 934 (2), 934 (6), 936 (2), 954 (5)
wrong, a 914 (1)
wrong, be 914 (5)
wrong course 282 (1)
wrong date 118 (1)
wrong day 118 (1)
wrong-doer 914 (1)
wrong-headed 481 (6), 495 (4), 499 (3)
wrong impression 481 (1)
wrong moment 118 (1)

wrong place **188** (1)
wrong side **238** (1)
wrong side out **221** (3)
wrong time **138** (1)
wrong turning **282** (1)
wrong use **675** (1)
wrong verdict **481** (1), **914** (2), **954** (1)
wrongdoer **904** (1). **904** (3)
wrongdoing **934** (1), **954** (2)
wrongful **645** (2), **914** (3), **954** (5)
wrongfully **914** (7)
wrongheaded **914** (3)
wrongly **914** (7), **934** (9)
wrongness **495** (1), **643** (1), **914** (1)
wrought **575** (3)
wrought iron **844** (2)
wrought up **821** (3)
wry **220** (3)
wry humour **839** (1)

X

X **85** (1)
X-ray **417** (4), **417** (12), **459** (13), **551** (4), **551** (9)
X-shape **222** (1)
X-shaped **222** (6)
xenophobe **881** (2)
xenophobia **481** (3), **854** (3), **888** (1)
xenophobic **481** (8)
Xerox **22** (1)
xylophone **414** (8)

Y

Y-shape **294** (1)
yacht **269** (8), **275** (5), **837** (21)
yacht race **716** (3)
yachting **269** (3)
yachtsman **270** (4)
yachtswoman **270** (4)
yahoo **869** (7)

yammer **408** (3)
Yank **59** (2), **288** (3)
Yankee **59** (2)
yap **409** (3)
yard **185** (1), **203** (4), **235** (1), **263** (7), **687** (1)
yardarm **218** (2)
yardstick **86** (6), **461** (4), **465** (5)
yarn **206** (2), **543** (3), **570** (6), **590** (2), **590** (7), **631** (1)
yarn-spinner **545** (2), **590** (5)
yashmak **228** (23)
yaw **282** (1), **282** (3)
yawing **269** (6)
yawl **275** (5)
yawn **211** (3), **263** (1), **263** (17), **352** (7), **352** (11), **679** (12), **684** (5)
yawning **211** (2), **263** (1), **263** (13), **679** (3), **679** (9)
yaws **651** (6), **651** (12)
yea **488** (1)
year **108** (3), **110** (1), **123** (2)
year group **74** (3)
year in year out **106** (7), **113** (11)
year tutor **537** (1)
yearbook **589** (4)
yearling **132** (3), **365** (7)
yearly **141** (5), **141** (7)
yearly cycle **141** (2)
yearn **834** (9), **859** (11)
yearn to **597** (6)
yearning **859** (1), **859** (7), **887** (9)
years **108** (1), **113** (1), **131** (1)
years ago **125** (12)
years on end **113** (1)
yeast **174** (4), **323** (2)
yeastiness **355** (1)
yeasty **323** (3), **355** (3)
yell **408** (1), **408** (4)
yellow **425** (8), **426** (3), **433** (1), **433** (3), **433** (4), **856** (3)
yellow-eyed **911** (2)
yellow fever **651** (6)
yellow lines **305** (3)

yellow ochre **433** (2)
yellow pigment **433** (2)
yellow streak **856** (1)
yellowish **433** (3)
Yellowness **433** (1)
yellowy **433** (3)
yelp **407** (5), **409** (3)
yen **859** (1)
yeoman **722** (10), **869** (6)
yeomanry **191** (5), **722** (4), **722** (6)
yes **488** (1)
yes and no **474** (1)
yes indeed **488** (11)
yes-man **20** (3), **83** (3), **488** (3), **879** (2), **925** (2)
yesterday **125** (1), **125** (12)
yesteryear **125** (1), **125** (12)
yet **468** (5)
yet to come **124** (4)
yew **366** (4)
yield **83** (7), **163** (9), **164** (2), **167** (6), **327** (4), **488** (7), **601** (4), **621** (3), **633** (5), **721** (3), **739** (4), **758** (3), **771** (10), **779** (4), **781** (7)
yield a point **766** (4)
yield precedence **874** (3)
yield results **164** (7)
yield the palm **721** (3)
yielding **327** (2), **621** (1), **701** (4), **721** (1), **758** (2)
yin and yang **14** (2)
yo-heave-ho **269** (14), **288** (4)
yo-yo **317** (1), **837** (15)
yob **132** (2), **847** (3), **904** (2)
yobbish **847** (5)
yodel **408** (1), **413** (10)
yoga **682** (2), **973** (1)
yoghourt **301** (24)
yogi **500** (1), **945** (2), **984** (4)
yogic **945** (3)
yoke **45** (9), **47** (1), **47** (6), **90** (1), **90** (3), **369** (8), **745** (1), **745** (3), **748** (4)
yoke-fellow **707** (2)
yokel **699** (2), **869** (6)

yoking 45 (2)
yonder 199 (3), 199 (6)
you and me 371 (4)
young 126 (5), 128 (6), 130 (4), 132 (5), 162 (6), 164 (2), 170 (1), 670 (4)
young adult 132 (2)
young animal 132 (3), 365 (2)
young at heart 130 (4)
young blood 130 (1)
young creature 132 (3), 156 (3), 164 (2), 170 (1), 365 (2)
young friend 880 (3)
young hopeful 852 (3)
young man 132 (2)
young people 132 (2)
young person 132 (2)
young plant 132 (4), 366 (6)
young woman 132 (2)
younger 35 (2), 120 (2), 130 (4)
younger generation 130 (1)
youngest 120 (2), 130 (4)
youngness 130 (1)
youngster 130 (1), 132 (2), 372 (1), 373 (3)
your honour 870 (1)
your Lordship 957 (1)
your reverence 870 (1)
your worship 870 (1)
yours truly 320 (2)

yourself 80 (4)
youth 68 (1), 126 (1), 130 (1), 132 (2), 161 (2)
youth hostel 192 (11)
youth hosteller 268 (1)
youthful 130 (4), 162 (6)
youthfulness 130 (1)
yowl 408 (3), 409 (3)
Yule log 385 (1)
yuletide 129 (4)

Z

zeal 174 (3), 597 (1), 818 (2), 979 (1)
zealot 473 (3), 481 (4), 504 (3), 602 (3), 678 (5), 973 (7), 979 (5)
zealotry 602 (2)
zealous 597 (4), 599 (2), 678 (7), 818 (5)
zealously 32 (17)
zebra 365 (3), 437 (3)
Zen 973 (3)
Zen Buddhist 973 (7)
zenith 34 (1), 213 (1)
zephyr 352 (3)
zero 4 (1), 103 (1), 103 (2), 380 (1)
zero hour 68 (3), 108 (3)
zero level 103 (1)
zero-rated 812 (4)

zero temperature 380 (1)
zest 174 (1), 376 (1), 824 (3), 826 (1), 859 (3)
zestful 174 (5)
zesty 388 (3)
Zeus 967 (1)
ziggurat 990 (1)
zigzag 220 (1), 220 (3), 220 (5), 247 (1), 247 (5), 247 (7), 251 (3), 251 (12), 282 (1), 282 (2), 282 (3), 844 (3)
Zionist 901 (5)
zip 47 (5)
zip fastener 47 (5)
zip up 264 (6)
zippy 277 (5)
zither 414 (2)
zodiac 321 (5)
zodiacal 321 (14)
zombie 363 (1), 970 (3)
zone 46 (1), 46 (9), 184 (1), 184 (2), 207 (1), 207 (5), 344 (1), 783 (3)
zoned 207 (4)
zoo 74 (7), 369 (4), 632 (3)
zoological 358 (4), 365 (18), 367 (3)
zoological gardens 369 (4)
zoologist 358 (2), 367 (2)
zoology 358 (2), 367 (1)
zoom 277 (2), 277 (6), 308 (4), 551 (4)
zoom lens 442 (1)

Text

Class one

Abstract Relationships

1
Existence

Noun

(1) *existence,* being, entity; a being, an entity, Platonic idea, universal; subsistence 360 *life*; survival, eternity 115 *perpetuity*; preexistence, coexistence; this life 121 *present time*; realization, becoming 147 *conversion*; creation 164 *production*; ontology, metaphysics; realism, materialism.

(2) *reality,* actuality, material existence 319 *materiality*; factuality 494 *truth*; fact, fact of life, matter of f.; fait accompli 154 *event*; real thing, not a dream, no joke; realities, basics, fundamentals, bedrock, brass tacks.

(3) *essence,* nature 3 *substance*; sum and substance 5 *essential part*; soul, heart, core, centre.

Adjective

(4) *existing,* existent; absolute, given, being, in existence, under the sun 121 *present*; living 360 *alive*; eternal, enduring 115 *perpetual*; extant, surviving 113 *lasting*; afloat, afoot; existential, metaphysical.

(5) *real,* substantive 3 *substantial*; not imagined, actual, positive, factual, historical 494 *true*; natural, physical 319 *material*; solid, tangible.

Verb

(6) *be,* exist, have being; consist in, inhere in, reside in, preexist, coexist; subsist, abide, endure 113 *last*; vegetate, pass the time; be alive, breathe, live, move, have one's being 360 *live*; be found, be met with; meet one 189 *be present*; obtain, prevail; take place, come about 154 *happen*.

(7) *become,* come to be 360 *be born*; arise, unfold, develop, grow, take shape, evolve 147 *be turned to*.

Adverb

(8) *actually,* really, ipso facto; in essence, virtually, positively, in fact.

2
Nonexistence

Noun

(1) *nonexistence,* non-being, nothingness; absence, blank 190 *emptiness*; nothing, nil, no such thing no one.

(2) *extinction,* oblivion; no life 361 *death*; dying out, obsolescence; annihilation 165 *destruction*; cancellation, obliteration.

Adjective

(3) *nonexistent,* without being; nowhere, minus; missing 190 *absent*; null, cancelled, wiped out 550 *obliterated*.

(4) *unreal,* fictitious 513 *imaginary*; false 495 *erroneous*; intangible 4 *insubstantial*; potential, only possible, only supposed.

(5) *extinct,* died out, vanished, no more; defunct 361 *dead*; obsolete, finished, past.

Verb

(6) *not be,* not exist, never happen, not come off.

(7) *pass away,* cease to exist, become extinct, die out 361 *die*;

perish, come to nothing 728 *miscarry*; vanish, evaporate, leave no trace 446 *disappear*.

(8) *nullify,* annihilate, extinguish, snuff out; neutralize, negate, cancel 550 *obliterate*; abolish, wipe out 165 *destroy*.

3
Substantiality

Noun
(1) *substantiality,* essentiality 1 *reality*; corporeality, tangibility, solidity 319 *materiality*; weight, pithiness, meatiness; stuff, material 319 *matter*; world, world of nature 321 *universe*.

(2) *substance,* core 5 *essential part*; entity, thing, something, somebody 319 *object*; person, creature; body, flesh and blood 360 *life*; solid 324 *solid body*; pith, marrow, meat.

Adjective
(3) *substantial,* real, objective, phenomenal, physical 319 *material*; solid, tangible, palpable, considerable; bulky, weighty; pithy, meaty.

Adverb
(4) *substantially,* bodily, physically; in person; really, essentially 1 *actually*.

4
Insubstantiality

Noun
(1) *insubstantiality,* naught, nothing, nothing at all, not a scrap 103 *zero*; no one, not a soul 190 *nobody*; abstraction 320 *immateriality*; lack of substance, meagreness, tenuity; intangibility, invisibility; void, hollowness 190 *emptiness*; inanity 497 *absurdity*; hallucination, fantasy 542 *deception*.

(2) *insubstantial thing,* token, symbol; soul 447 *spirit*; abstraction, shadow, ghost, phantom; vision, dream, mirage, illusion 440 *visual fallacy*; thin air, vapour, mist; bubble 163 *weak thing*; trifle, bauble; fool's paradise; figment, pipe dream 513 *fantasy*; gossip, rumour 515 *empty talk*; tall story 543 *fable*; pretence, pseudonym; flash in the pan, nine days' wonder; cipher, figurehead, man of straw.

Adjective
(3) *insubstantial,* abstract, metaphysical, ideal; ethereal 320 *immaterial*; bloodless, incorporeal; airy 323 *light*; thin, tenuous; vaporous, misty; fragile 163 *flimsy*; ghostly, spectral, shadowy 419 *dim*; hollow 190 *empty*; vain, honorary, nominal, paper, token; fictitious 543 *untrue*; without substance, groundless, unfounded; chimerical, fantastical 513 *imaginary*; without depth, superficial, shallow.

(4) *unsubstantially,* not really, in name only.

5
Intrinsicality

Noun
(1) *intrinsicality,* inherence, immanence; essentialness; potentiality 160 *ability*; subjectivity, ego, personality 80 *self*;

(2) *essential part,* sine qua non; substance 1 *essence*; principle, property, mark, attribute; virtue, capacity; quintessence, flower, distillation; incarnation, embodiment; lifeblood, sap; heart, soul 447 *spirit*; backbone, fibre; core, kernel 225 *centre*; gist, nub 638 *chief thing*.

(3) *character,* nature, quality; make-up, personality, type, make, stamp, breed 77 *sort*;

constitution, ethos; cast, colour, hue, complexion; aspects, features.

(4) *temperament,* temper, humour, disposition 817 *affections*; grain, vein, streak, strain, trait 179 *tendency*; foible, habit, peculiarity, idiosyncrasy, characteristic 80 *speciality*.

(5) *heredity,* chromosome, gene, DNA, ancestry 169 *genealogy*; atavism; Mendelism, genetics.

Adjective
(6) *intrinsic,* immanent, deep-seated, deep-rooted, ingrained; inherent, integral, 224 *interior*; implicit, part and parcel of; indigenous, native, endowed with; natural, instinctive; organic 156 *fundamental*; a priori, original, elemental, cardinal, essential, potential.

(7) *genetic,* inherited, hereditary, atavistic, heritable; inborn, innate, congenital, inbred.

(8) *characteristic,* personal, qualitative 80 *special*; diagnostic, proper to; ineradicable, incurable, constitutional,

Verb
(9) *be intrinsic,* - immanent etc. adj. inhere; inherit, take after; run in the blood/the family.

Adverb
(10) *intrinsically,* fundamentally, essentially, substantially, virtually; per se, as such; in effect, in the main.

6
Extrinsicality

Noun
(1) *extrinsicality,* objectivity; transcendence; the other, nonego; projection 223 *exteriority*; accident, contingency 159 *chance*.

Adjective
(2) *extrinsic,* alien, foreign 59 *extraneous*; outward, external, 223 *exterior*, acquired, implanted, instilled, inculcated; supervenient, accessory, adventitious 38 *additional*; incidental, accidental 159 *casual*; inessential, nonessential.

Verb
(3) *be extrinsic,* not belong; supervene 38 *accrue*.

(4) *make extrinsic,* realize, project 223 *externalize*; body forth 551 *represent*.

Adverb
(5) *extrinsically,* superficially, outwardly; from outside.

7
State: Absolute condition

Noun
(1) *state,* state of being, condition; estate, lot, walk, walk of life; case, way, plight 8 *circumstance*; position, category, status, footing, standing, rank; habit, disposition, complexion 5 *temperament*; attitude, frame of mind, vein, temper, mood 817 *affections*; state of mind, spirits, morale; state of health, trim, fettle, fig.

(2) *modality,* mode, manner, fashion, style; stamp, mould 243 *form*; shape, frame, fabric 331 *structure*; aspect, phase, light, complexion, character, guise 445 *appearance*; tenor, tone 179 *tendency*.

Adjective
(3) *such;* modal, conditional, formal 243 *formative*; organic 331 *structural*; in condition, in form, in good f.

Verb
(4) *be in a state of,* be such, be so; stand, lie, labour under; do, fare.

Adverb

(5) *conditionally,* it being so, as it is, as things are,

8
Circumstance:
Relative condition

Noun

(1) *circumstance,* situation, circumstances, conditions, factors, the times; sphere, background, environment, milieu 230 *surroundings*; context 9 *relation*; status quo, state of affairs, how things stand; regime, set-up; posture, attitude; aspect, look of things 445 *appearance*; lie of the land 186 *situation*; footing, standing, status 73 *serial place*; corner, hole, jam 700 *predicament.*

(2) *juncture,* conjuncture, stage, point 154 *event*; contingency, eventuality; crossroads, turning point; moment, hour, right time, opportunity 137 *occasion*; critical moment, crucial m., hour of decision, emergency 137 *crisis.*

Adjective

(3) *circumstantial,* modal 7 *such*; situated, placed, circumstanced; surrounding, environmental, situational, contextual limiting 232 *circumscribed*; modifying 468 *qualifying*; provisional, temporary 114 *transient*; variable 152 *changeful*; relative, contingent 154 *eventual*; critical, crucial; favourable 137 *opportune*; suitable 24 *agreeing*; appropriate, convenient 642 *advisable.*

Adverb

(4) *thus,* so; like this, in this way; from that angle.

(5) *accordingly,* and so, according as, depending on; as the case may be.

(6) *if,* if so be, in the event of, in case; provisionally, provided that 7 *conditionally*; supposing, assuming, granting, allowing, taking it that; if not, unless, except, without.

9
Relation

Noun

(1) *relation,* relatedness, connectedness; reference, respect, regard; bearing, direction; concern, interest, import 638 *importance*; involvement, implication; relationship, rapport, affinity; kinship 11 *consanguinity*; classification 62 *arrangement*; alliance 706 *association*; relations, amicable r., friendly terms 880 *friendship*; linkage, connection, link, tie-up 47 *bond*; common reference, common source; interdependence, ecology; context, milieu 8 *circumstance.*

(2) *relativeness,* relativity, mutual relation 12 *correlation*; correspondence 18 *similarity*; analogy 462 *comparison*; close relation, approximation. collaterality 219 *parallelism*; perspective, proportion, ratio, scale; causal relation, cause and effect 156 *cause*; dependence 157 *effect*; stage, status, rank 27 *degree*; serial order 65 *sequence.*

(3) *relevance,* logicality, chain of reasoning 475 *reasoning*; just relation, due proportion; suitability, point, applicability, appositeness, pertinence 24 *fitness*; case in point, 83 *example.*

(4) *referral,* reference, cross-r.; application, allusion, mention; citation, quotation; frame of reference, referent; referee.

Adjective

(5) *relative,* relational, referen-

tial, respective; referable; related, connected, associated, linked; bearing upon, concerning, in aid of; of concern 638 *important*; appertaining to, appurtenant; mutual, reciprocal, corresponding to, answering to 12 *correlative*; classifiable 62 *arranged*; serial, consecutive 65 *sequential*; kindred 11 *akin*; analogous, like 18 *similar*; comparable, collateral 462 *compared*; approximating, approaching; commensurate, proportional, proportionate, to scale; in perspective; contextual, environmental, ecological.

(6) *relevant,* logical, in context; apposite, pertinent, applicable; pointed, to the point, to the purpose, well-directed; proper, appropriate, suitable, fitting 24 *apt*; alluding, allusive; quotable.

Verb
(7) *be related,* have reference to, have to do with, refer to, regard, respect, bear upon; be a factor 178 *influence*; touch, concern, deal with, interest, affect; belong, pertain, appertain to; answer to, correspond, reciprocate 12 *correlate*; have a connection, tie in with; be proportionate, vary as; be relevant, have some point; come to the point

(8) *relate,* put in perspective, get into proportion; connect with, gear to, apply, link, connect, bracket together, tie up with 45 *tie*; put in context; compare 18 *liken*; draw a parallel, establish a connection, find an example; refer to, touch on, allude to, mention.

Adverb
(9) *relatively,* in relation to, contextually; in ratio, to scale, in perspective.

(10) *concerning,* touching, regarding; as to, as regards, with regard to, with respect to; relative to, vis-à-vis, with reference to, about, re, on, under; in relation to, bearing on; speaking of, apropos, by the way.

10
Unrelatedness:
Absence of relation

Noun
(1) *unrelatedness,* absoluteness, independence; arbitrariness; separateness, insularity, isolation 46 *separation*; individuality 80 *speciality*; randomness, lack of connection 61 *disorder*; disconnection, dissociation 46 *disunion*, 72 *discontinuity*; disproportion, disparity 29 *inequality*; diversity, heterogeneity 15 *difference*; alien element 59 *intruder*.

(2) *irrelevance,* irrelevancy; illogicality 477 *sophism*; pointlessness, bad example; inconsequence, non sequitur 231 *interjection*; diversion, red herring 282 *deviation*; episode, incidental; inessential.

Adjective
(3) *unrelated,* absolute, self-existent; independent; owing nothing to 21 *original*; irrespective, regardless, unilateral, arbitrary; unidentified; rootless, adrift, astray 282 *deviating*; isolated, insular 88 *alone*; uninvolved, detached, without context; disconnected, 46 *disunited*; digressive, parenthetic, anecdotal; episodic, incidental, unconnected 72 *discontinuous*; separate, individual, private; inessential 6 *extrinsic*; foreign, alien, strange, 59 *extraneous*; intrusive, untimely 138 *illtimed*; inappropriate 25 *disagreeing*; not comparable, disparate 29 *unequal*; out of proportion, disproportionate

246 *distorted*; multifarious 82 *multiform*.

(4) *irrelevant*, illogical; inapplicable, pointless; out of order, misplaced, misdirected, off-target, off the beam; rambling, wandering 570 *diffuse*; beside the point, off the point, nothing to do with, neither here nor there; trivial, incidental, inessential inconsequential, peripheral; far-fetched, forced, strained; academic, immaterial.

Verb
(5) *be unrelated*, not concern, not touch; be irrelevant, have no bearing on; ramble, wander, lose the thread 570 *be diffuse*.

Adverb
(6) *unrelatedly*, irrespective, regardless; irrelevantly, incidentally, inappropriately, by the way.

11
Consanguinity: Relations of kindred

Noun
(1) *consanguinity*, kinship, kindred, blood relationship 169 *parentage*; affiliation, relationship, affinity; ancestry, lineage, descent 169 *genealogy*; connection, alliance, family, tribalism, nationality 371 *nation*; nepotism.

(2) *kinsman*, kinswoman; kin, kindred, kith and kin, next of kin, one's flesh and blood; kinsfolk, relations; blood relation, relative; in-law, step-relation; grandparents, father, mother 169 *parentage*; children, offspring 170 *posterity*; twin, identical t., fraternal t.; sibling, sib; sister, brother, cousin, first c., second c., uncle, aunt, nephew, niece; clansman, tribesman, compatriot.

(3) *family*, matriarchy, patriarchy; motherhood, fatherhood, brotherhood, sisterhood; fraternity, sorority; foster child, adopted child, godchild, stepchild; in-laws; one's people, one's folks; family circle, household, hearth and home 192 *home*; nuclear family, extended f.; tribe, horde.

(4) *race*, stock, stem, breed, strain, line, side, spear s., distaff s.; house, tribe, clan, ethnic group; nation, people; nationalism, racialism 481 *prejudice*; inbreeding.

Adjective
(5) *akin*, kindred, kin; out of; by; maternal, paternal 169 *parental*; sibling, fraternal, brotherly, sisterly, avuncular; related, family, consanguineous, collateral, lineal, cognate, german; near, related, intimately r; once removed, twice r.; next-of-kin.

(6) *ethnic*, racial, tribal, clannish 371 *national*; interbred, inbred 43 *mixed*; Caucasian, Mongolian, Negroid.

Verb
(7) *be akin*, be related; marry into 894 *wed*; have children 167 *generate*; be brother or sister to; adopt, foster.

12
Correlation: Double or reciprocal relation

Noun
(1) *correlation*, mutual relation; proportion 245 *symmetry*; pattern 62 *arrangement*; correspondence 18 *similarity*; mutuality, interdependence, interrelation, interaction, interplay; alternation, reciprocity, reciprocation 151 *interchange*; each, each other, one another; give and take 770

compromise; exchange, *barter*, tit for tat.

Adjective

(2) *correlative*, reciprocal 9 *relative*; corresponding, opposite, answering to, analogous, parallel 18 *similar*; proportional, proportionate; complementary, interdependent; interlocking; mutual, requited; reciprocating, reacting; alternating, alternate, seesaw; interlocking, interacting; exchangeable, interchangeable; inter -, two-way, bilateral.

Verb

(3) *correlate*, interrelate, interlock, interact; interdepend; vary as, correspond, answer to; react, reciprocate; alternate 317 *oscillate*; exchange, swap, barter 151 *interchange*; balance, set off 31 *compensate*.

Adverb

(4) *correlatively,* mutually, reciprocally, inter, between; each other, one another 151 *in exchange*; alternately, by turns, turn and turn about.

13
Identity

Noun

(1) *identity,* sameness, 88 *unity*; the same, no other, the very same, the very one; genuineness 494 *authenticity*; the real thing, it 21 *no imitation*; tautology 106 *repetition*; other self, alter ego, double; coincidence, 24 *agreement*; coalescence, absorption; equivalence 28 *equality*; no difference 16 *uniformity*; no change, constant; counterpart, duplicate 22 *copy*; fellow, pair, match, twin 18 *analogue*; homonym, homophone, synonym.

Adjective

(2) *identical,* the same, indistinguishable, selfsame, one and the same 88 *one*; interchangeable, unisex, convertible, equivalent 28 *equal*; homonymous, synonymous; coincident, congruent 24 *agreeing*; always the same, invariable, constant; monotonous, unchanging; monolithic 16 *uniform*; tautologous, repetitive.

Verb

(3) *be identical,* the same, etc. adj.; coincide, coalesce, merge, be one with; be congruent, agree 24 *accord*.

(4) *identify,* make as one; not distinguish 464 *not discriminate*; equate 28 *equalize*; match, pair 18 *liken*.

Adverb

(5) *identically,* ditto.

14
Contrariety

Noun

(1) *contrariety,* absolute difference 15 *difference*; exclusiveness, mutual e., irreconcilability; antidote 182 *counteraction*; conflict, clash, discord 25 *disagreement*; contradistinction, contrast, relief, counterpoint; contradiction, antonym; inconsistency, two voices, paradox 518 *equivocalness*; oppositeness, antithesis, direct opposite, antipodes, opposite pole; other extreme, opposite e., quite the reverse/the contrary; other side, opposite s. reverse; inverse, converse, reverse image, mirror image; headwind, undertow.

(2) *polarity,* contraries 704 *opposites*; north and south; east and west; day and night; hot and cold; fire and water; black and white; good and evil; yin and yang, male and female.

Adjective

(3) *contrary,* as different as chalk from cheese 15 *different*;

contrasting, contrasted, incompatible, clashing, discordant 25 *disagreeing*; inconsistent, ambivalent, bittersweet, love-hate; contradictory, antithetical; antonymous; poles asunder, diametrically opposite; antipodal, antipodean 240 *opposite*; reverse, converse, inverse; adverse 704 *opposing*; counteractive, antidotal; counter-, contra-, anti-.

Verb
(4) *be contrary,* have nothing in common 15 *differ*; contrast, stand out 25 *disagree*; clash, conflict with; run counter to 704 *oppose*; contradict, 533 *negate*; cancel out 182 *counteract*.

Adverb
(5) *contrarily,* conversely, on the other hand; contrariwise; vice versa, topsy-turvy, upside down; on the contrary; otherwise, in contrast, in opposition to.

15
Difference

Noun
(1) *difference,* unlikeness 19 *dissimilarity*; disparity 29 *inequality*; margin, differential, minus, plus 41 *remainder*; wide margin 199 *distance*; narrow margin 200 *nearness*; heterogeneity, variety, diverseness, diversity divergence, departure from 282 *deviation*; distinctness 21 *originality*; variance, discrepancy, incongruity 25 *disagreement*; disharmony, discord; contrast 14 *contrariety*; variation, modification, alteration 143 *change*, 147 *conversion*.

(2) *differentiation* distinction, nice d., delicate d., subtle d. 463 *discrimination*; nuance, shade of difference 514 *meaning*.

(3) *variant,* different thing, different kettle of fish; another story, another version, another light on, special case 80 *speciality*; freak, sport 84 *nonconformist*.

Adjective
(4) *different,* differing, unlike 19 *dissimilar*; original, fresh 126 *new*; various, variform, diverse, heterogeneous multifarious 82 *multiform*; assorted, of all sorts, all manner of, divers 43 *mixed*; distinct, distinguished, discriminated 46 *separate*; divergent, departing from 282 *deviating*; odd 84 *unusual*; discrepant, discordant 25 *disagreeing*; disparate 29 *unequal*; contrasting, contrasted; far from it, anything but; wide apart, poles asunder 14 *contrary*; other, another, not the same, peculiar 80 *special*; changed, altered 147 *converted*.

(5) *distinctive,* diagnostic, characteristic, marking out; differentiating, distinguishing.

Verb
(6) *differ,* be different etc. adj.; show variety; vary from, diverge f., depart f., deviate; contrast, conflict 25 *disagree*; change one's tune, modify, vary, make alterations 143 *change*.

(7) *differentiate,* distinguish, make a distinction; mark out, single o. 463 *discriminate*; refine, particularize 46 *set apart*.

Adverb
(8) *differently,* variously; otherwise, not so, some other way, with a difference.

16
Uniformity

Noun
(1) *uniformity,* uniformness, consistency 71 *continuity;* regularity 14↓ *periodicity;* method 60 *order;* unison, accordance 24 *agreement;* evenness, levelness, flushness 258 *smoothness;* roundness 245 *symmetry;* 18 *similarity,* sameness, 13 *identity;* invariability, monotony, even tenor; mixture as before, same old story; even pace, jog trot, rhythm; round, daily r., routine, drill, treadmill 610 *habit;* monotone, greyness; drone, sing-song, monologue; monolith; pattern, mould; type, stereotype 22 *copy;* stamp, common s. set, assortment; suit, flush; standard dress 228 *uniform;* standardization, mass production 83 *conformity;* cliche 106 *repetition;* regimentation 740 *compulsion;* equalitarian, egalitarian.

Adjective
(2) *uniform,* all of a piece, same all through, solid, monolithic; homogeneous 18 *similar;* same, consistent, self-c., constant, steady, unchanging, invariable; rhythmic, measured, even-paced 258 *smooth;* unrelieved 573 *plain;* without contrast, undifferentiated, lacking variety; in uniform, uniformed, liveried; characterless, featureless, faceless, blank; monotonous, droning, sing-song; monochrome, drab, grey; repetitive, running through 106 *repeated;* standard, normal 83 *typical;* patterned, standardized, stereotyped, mass-produced, unisex; sorted, aligned, in line; orderly, regular 245 *symmetrical;* straight, even, flush, level.

Verb
(3) *be uniform,* follow routine

610 *be wont;* sing in unison, chorus 24 *accord;* typify 83 *conform;* fall in, wear uniform.

(4) *make uniform,* homogenize; stamp, characterize, run through 547 *mark;* level, level up *or* down 28 *equalize;* assimilate 18 *liken;* size, grade; drill, align; regiment, standardize, stereotype, pattern; mass-produce; institutionalize, normalize, regularize 83 *make conform.*

Adverb
(5) *uniformly,* solidly etc. adj.; like clockwork, methodically, invariably, eternally, endlessly; in a rut, in a groove.

17
Nonuniformity

Noun
(1) *nonuniformity,* variability, patchiness, unpredictability, inconsistency 152 *changeableness;* irregularity, no system, no pattern 61 *disorder;* asymmetry raggedness, unevenness 259 *roughness;* heterogeneity 15 *difference;* contrast 14 *contrariety,* 19 *dissimilarity;* divergence, deviation; diversity, variety, all shapes and sizes 82 *multiformity;* mixed bag, odds and ends 43 *medley;* patchwork, crazy paving, mosaic 437 *variegation;* abnormality, exception, special case, sport, mutation 84 *nonconformity;* uniqueness, individuality 80 *speciality.*

Adjective
(2) *nonuniform,* variable, unpredictable, never the same 152 *changeful;* spasmodic, sporadic 142 *fitful;* inconsistent 604 *capricious;* patchy 29 *unequal;* random, irregular, unsystematic; asymmetrical 244 *amorphous;* out of order 61 *orderless;* uneven 259 *rough;* erratic, out of step, out of time; heterogeneous, various, diverse 15

different, 19 dissimilar; miscellaneous, of many kinds, of all sorts 82 multiform; multicoloured, decorated 844 ornamental; divergent, dissenting 25 disagreeing; unconventional, atypical, exceptional 84 abnormal; unique 80 special; individual, hand-made; out of uniform, in mufti.

Adverb
(3) nonuniformly, irregularly, unevenly, erratically, unsystematically 61 confusedly; chaotically; here, there and everywhere

18
Similarity

Noun
(1) similarity, resemblance, likeness, similitude; simulacrum, semblance, seeming, look 445 appearance; fashion, style 243 form; common feature 9 relation; congruity 24 agreement; affinity, kinship; comparability, analogy, correspondence 12 correlation; equivalence, parity 28 equality; no difference 13 identity; family likeness; good likeness, striking l.; approximation, partial likeness; suggestion, hint; fair comparison, about the size of it.

(2) assimilation, likening 462 comparison; identification 13 identity; simulation, mimicry 20 imitation; parable, allegory; portrayal 590 description; portraiture 553 picture; alliteration, assonance; pun, play on words.

(3) analogue, the like, suchlike, the likes of; type 83 example; correlate, correlative 12 correlation; simile, parallel, metaphor; equivalent 150 substitute; brother, sister, twin; match, fellow, mate, companion; complement, counterpart, other half 89 concomitant; alter

ego, other self, double, ringer, lookalike, likeness reflection, shadow, the picture of it; image; spitting image, living l., chip off the old block; twins, two of a kind, couple, pair 90 duality; copy, clone 22 duplicate.

Adjective
(4) similar, resembling, like, alike, twin, matching, nothing to choose between 13 identical; of a piece, homogeneous 16 uniform; parallel 28 equivalent; corresponding to, bracketed with; close, approximate; typical 551 representing; reproducing, reflecting; à la, in the style of; much the same, something like, such as; rhyming, alliterative 106 repeated.

(5) lifelike, realistic, photographic, exact, faithful, natural, typical; true to life, true to nature, true to type.

(6) simulating 20 imitative; seeming 542 deceiving; mock, pseudo 542 spurious; synthetic, artificial 150 substituted.

Verb
(7) resemble, be similar to, pass for, mirror, reflect 20 imitate; seem, seem like, sound l., look as if; look like, take after, put one in mind of; savour of, smack of; bear a resemblance, compare with, approximate to; match, correspond to; typify 551 represent.

(8) liken, assimilate to 462 compare; equate 13 identify; pair, twin, bracket with; portray 20 imitate.

Adverb
(9) similarly, as, like, as if, quasi, so to speak 519 metaphorically; as it were; likewise, so, correspondingly.

19
Dissimilarity

Noun

(1) *dissimilarity,* unlikeness; disparity, divergence 15 *difference;* variation 82 *multiformity;* contrast 14 *contrariety;* nothing in common 25 *disagreement;* camouflage 527 *disguise;* caricature, bad likeness; odd one out 25 *misfit.*

Adjective

(2) *dissimilar,* unlike, distinct 15 *different;* various 82 *multiform;* disparate 29 *unequal;* not comparable 34 *superior,* 35 *inferior;* unique 21 *inimitable;* atypical, unprecedented, new and strange, novel 126 *new.*

Verb

(3) *be unlike,* dissimilar etc. adj.; bear no resemblance 15 *differ;* stand out.

(4) *make unlike,* distinguish 15 *differentiate;* modify 143 *change;* caricature 552 *misrepresent;* disguise, camouflage 525 *conceal.*

20
Imitation

Noun

(1) *imitation* 551 *representation;* following, slavishness 83 *conformity;* imitativeness, affectedness 850 *affectation;* reflection, mirror, echo, shadow; paraphrase, translation; cribbing, plagiarism; forgery, falsification 541 *falsehood;* copying, transcribing, transcription, tracing, duplication 22 *copy.*

(2) *mimicry,* onomatopoeia; mime, pantomime 594 *dramaturgy;* sign language 547 *gesture;* ventriloquism; portrayal, portraiture 553 *painting,* 590

description; realism 494 *accuracy;* mockery, caricature, parody 851 *satire;* travesty 552 *misrepresentation;* imitativeness 106 *repetition.* simulator, simulation exercise, role play; simulation, semblance, disguise, camouflage 18 *similarity;* pretence 542 *sham.*

(3) *imitator,* copycat, ape; parrot, echo; sheep 83 *conformist;* yes-man 925 *flatterer;* mocker, parodist, caricaturist 839 *humorist;* mime, ventriloquist, mimic, impersonator, drag artiste 594 *entertainer;* actor, portrayer, portraitist 556 *artist;* copyist, printer, tracer 586 *calligrapher;* translator, paraphraser 520 *interpreter;* realist, naturalist; simulator, hypocrite 545 *impostor;* borrower, plagiarist; counterfeiter, forger, faker; duplicator, copier, photocopier.

Adjective

(4) *imitative,* mimetic; onomatopoeic, aping, parroting, following; echoing, flattering; posing 850 *affected;* disguised, camouflaged; mock, mimic; simulating, shamming 541 *hypocritical;* sham, imitation 541 *false;* synthetic 150 *substituted;* hackneyed 610 *usual;* derivative, unoriginal, imitated, second-hand 106 *repeated;* conventional 83 *conformable;* modelled, moulded on; slavish, literal; copied etc. verb; easy to copy, imitable.

Verb

(5) *imitate,* ape, parrot, echo; mirror, reflect 18 *resemble;* pose as; pretend, masquerade; make-believe, make as if; act, mimic, mime, portray 551 *represent;* parody, take off, caricature 851 *ridicule;* sham, simulate, put on, feign 541 *dissemble;* disguise, camouflage 525 *conceal.*

(6) *copy,* draw, trace; catch a likeness; set up 587 *print*; reprint, duplicate, cyclostyle, photocopy; make copies, reduplicate, multiply, reel off; copy out, transcribe, transliterate, type out; paraphrase, translate 520 *interpret*; copy from, crib, plagiarize, borrow 788 *steal*; counterfeit, forge 541 *fake.*

(7) *do likewise,* mould oneself on, emulate, take as a model; follow suit, echo, ditto; chorus 106 *repeat*; follow precedent 83 *conform.*

21
Originality

Noun
(1) *originality,* creativeness, inventiveness 513 *imagination*; creation, invention, 164 *production*; uniqueness; precedent, example 23 *prototype*; new departure 68 *beginning*; something new, novelty, innovation, freshness 126 *newness*; eccentricity, individuality 84 *nonconformity*; unlikeness 16 *dissimilarity.*

(2) *no imitation,* genuineness 494 *authenticity*; real thing, genuine article; the very thing, it, absolutely it; autograph signature.

Adjective
(3) *original,* creative, inventive 513 *imaginative*; not derivative; prototypal, archetypal; primordial, primary 119 *prior*; unprecedented, fresh, novel 126 *new*; individual, personal 80 *special*; independent, eccentric.

(4) *inimitable,* transcendent, incomparable, out of reach 34 *superior*; not imitated, atypical 15 *different*; unique, one and only 88 *one*; authentic 494 *genuine.*

22
Copy

Noun
(1) *copy,* exact c., clone 166 *reproduction*; replica, facsimile, tracing; fair copy, transcript, transcription 18 *analogue*; cast, death mask; stamp, seal, impression, imprint; mechanical copy, stereotype, lithograph, print, offprint 587 *letterpress,* 555 *engraving*; photocopy, photostat, Xerox (tdmk); contact print 551 *photography*; microfilm, microfiche 548 *record*; dummy, counterfeit 542 *sham*; plagiarism, crib 20 *imitation*; a likeness, resemblance, 18 *similarity*; study, picture, image, model, effigy 551 *representation*; echo, mirror 106 *repetition*; apology for, mockery of, parody 851 *ridicule*; shadow, silhouette; first copy, draft; paraphrase 520 *translation.*

(2) *duplicate,* flimsy, carbon copy; stencil, master copy; transfer, rubbing; reprint, reissue; inspection copy 83 *example.*

23
Prototype

Noun
(1) *prototype,* archetype, type, norm 30 *average*; primitive form, protoplasm 358 *organism*; original 68 *origin*; precedent, test case 119 *priority*; guide, rule 693 *precept*; standard, criterion, touchstone 9 *referral*; ideal 646 *perfection*; module, unit; specimen, sample 83 *example*; exemplar, pattern, template, paradigm; dummy, mockup; copybook, copy; text, manuscript; blueprint, design, master plan 623 *plan*; rough plan, outline, draft, sketch.

(2) *living model* model, poser, sitter, subject; stroke, pacer, pacemaker; conductor 690 *leader*.

(3) *mould,* matrix, mint; plate, stencil, negative; frame 243 *form*; lay figure, tailor's dummy; last; die, stamp, punch, seal.

Adjective
(4) *prototypal,* exemplary, model, standard, classic, copybook.

Verb
(5) *be an example,* set an e.; stand as e.; model, sit for, pose.

24
Agreement

Noun
(1) *agreement,* consent 488 *assent*; accord; unison 16 *uniformity*; harmony 410 *melody*; understanding, entente, pact 765 *compact*; unity, solidarity 706 *cooperation*; union 50 *combination*.

(2) *conformance* 83 *conformity*; consistency 16 *uniformity*; coherence, consequence, logic 475 *reasoning*; parallelism 18 *similarity*.

(3) *fitness,* aptness; capability 694 *aptitude*; suitability 642 *good policy*; the very thing; relevancy, pertinence, admissibility, appositeness, case in point, good example 9 *relevance*; timeliness 137 *occasion*.

(4) *adaptation,* conformation, harmonization, matching 18 *assimilation*; reconcilement, accommodation 770 *compromise*; attunement, adjustment 62 *arrangement*; compatibility, congeniality; good fit, perfect f.

Adjective
(5) *agreeing,* right, in accordance with, in keeping with; corresponding, answering; proportional, proportionate,

commensurate, according to 12 *correlative*; coinciding, congruous 28 *equal*; squared with, consistent w., conforming to 83 *conformable*; in step, in phase, in tune, synchronized consistent 16 *uniform*; consonant, harmonized 410 *harmonious*; combining, mixing; suiting, matching 18 *similar*; becoming 846 *tasteful*; natural, congenial, sympathetic; reconcilable, compatible; coexisting, symbiotic; agreeable, acquiescent 488 *assenting*; concurrent, agreed, at one; in unison, in chorus, unanimous; united, concerted; like-minded; bipartisan 706 *cooperative*; negotiating 765 *contractual*.

(6) *apt,* applicable, admissible, germane, appropriate, pertinent, to the point, well-aimed 9 *relevant*; to the purpose, bearing on; pat, in place, apropos; right, happy, felicitous 575 *elegant*; at home, in one's element; seasonable, opportune 137 *timely*.

(7) *fit,* fitting, befitting, seemly, decorous; suited, well-adapted, adaptable; capable, qualified, cut out for 694 *skilful*; suitable, up one's street 642 *advisable*; meet, proper 913 *right*.

(8) *adjusted,* well-a. 60 *orderly*; synchronized; focused, tuned, fine-t. 494 *accurate*; strung, pitched, attuned to; trimmed, balanced 28 *equal*; well-cut, well-fitting, tight-fitting, tight; made to measure, tailormade, snug, comfortable.

Verb
(9) *accord,* agree 488 *assent*; concur 758 *consent*; echo, chorus, chime in 106 *repeat*; coincide, square with, dovetail 45 *join*; fit, fit like a glove; tally, correspond, match 18 *resemble*; go with, tone in w., harmonize;

come naturally to; fit in, belong, feel at home; answer, do, meet, suit 642 *be expedient*; fall pat, come apropos, befit; pull together 706 *cooperate*; be consistent, hang together 475 *be reasonable*; seek accord, come to terms 766 *make terms*; get on with, hit it off make friends 880 *befriend*; behave naturally, be oneself.

(10) *adjust,* make adjustments 654 *rectify*; fit, suit, adapt, accommodate, conform; attune, tune, tune up 410 *harmonize*; modulate, regulate 60 *order*; graduate, proportion 12 *correlate*; align 62 *arrange*; balance 28 *equalize*; trim 31 *compensate*; tailor, make to measure; focus, synchronize.

Adverb
(11) *pertinently,* aptly etc. adj.; apropos of.

25
Disagreement

Noun
(1) *disagreement,* failure to agree, 489 *dissent*; controversy 475 *argument*; wrangle 709 *quarrel*; disunion, disunity, dissension, dissidence; jarring, clash 279 *collision*; variance, divergence, discrepancy 15 *difference*; two voices, ambiguity 518 *equivocalness*; credibility gap; inconsistency contradiction, conflict 14 *contrariety*; dissonance, disharmony, 411 *discord*; incongruity disparity 29 *inequality*; disproportion, distortion.

(2) *inaptitude,* unfitness, incapacity, incompetence 695 *unskilfulness*; impropriety 847 *bad taste*; irrelevancy 10 *irrelevance*; intrusion, interruption 138 *untimeliness*; maladjustment 84 *unconformity*.

(3) *misfit,* bad fit; bad match, misalliance; oxymoron, paradox; incongruity, false note 411 *discord*; outsider, foreign body 59 *intruder*; dissident, dissenter 84 *nonconformist*; joker, odd man out, freak, eccentric, oddity 851 *laughingstock*; fish out of water, square peg in a round hole.

Adjective
(4) *disagreeing,* not unanimous 489 *dissenting*; at odds, at cross purposes, at variance; at loggerheads 718 *warring*; bickering 709 *quarrelling*; hostile, antagonistic 881 *inimical*; antipathetic 861 *disliked*; conflicting, clashing, contradictory 14 *contrary*; unnatural, out of character; inconsistent incompatible; odd 59 *extraneous*; not combining, not mixing; inharmonious, grating 411 *discordant*; mismatched, ill-assorted, discrepant 15 *different*; incongruous 497 *absurd*.

(5) *unapt,* incapable, incompetent inept 695 *clumsy*; wrong, unfitting, unfortunate, improper, unbecoming, undue, inappropriate, unsuitable 643 *inexpedient*; impracticable 470 *impossible*; unfit for, unsuited to, ineligible; intrusive, unseasonable 138 *inopportune*; inapplicable, inadmissible 10 *irrelevant*; out of character, out of keeping; misplaced, out of place, out of step, out of phase.

Verb
(6) *disagree* 489 *dissent*; differ 475 *argue*; fall out 709 *quarrel*; clash, conflict, collide, contradict 14 *be contrary*; be discrepant, vary, diverge 15 *differ*; come amiss, be incongruous, jar.

Adverb
(7) *in defiance of,* in contempt of, despite, in spite of.

26
Quantity

Noun
(1) *quantity*, amount, sum, total 52 *whole*; magnitude, extent 465 *measurement*; mass, substance, body, bulk 195 *size*; dimensions 203 *length*, 205 *breadth*, 209 *height*, 211 *depth*; area, volume 183 *space*; weight 322 *gravity*, 323 *lightness*; flow, potential 160 *energy*; numbers 101 *plurality*, 102 *fraction*; mean 30 *average*.

(2) *finite quantity*, matter of, limited amount, ceiling 236 *limit*; definite amount, quantum, quota, quorum; measure, dose, dosage, ration, piece 783 *portion*; pittance, spoonful, thimbleful, cupful; bagful, sackful; whole amount, lot, batch 52 *all*; load 193 *contents*; large amount, masses, heaps 32 *great quantity*; small amount, bit 33 *small quantity*; more, most 36 *increase*, 104 *greater number*; less, not so much 37 *decrease*, 105 *fewness*.

Adjective
(3) *quantitative*, some, certain, any, more or less; so many, so much; measured.

Verb
(4) *quantify*, allot, rate, ration 783 *apportion*.

Adverb
(5) *to the amount of*, to the tune of.

magnitude; level, pitch, key, register; reach, compass, scope 183 *range*; rate, speed 265 *motion*; gradation, graduation, calibration; differential, shade, nuance; grade, remove, step, rung, tread, stair 308 *ascent*; point, stage, milestone, turning point 8 *juncture*; mark, peg, notch, score 547 *indicator*; valuation 465 *measurement*; ranking, grading, class, kind 77 *sort*; standard, rank, grade 73 *serial place*; hierarchy 733 *authority*; sphere, station, status, standing, footing 8 *circumstance*.

Adjective
(2) *gradational*, graduated, calibrated, graded; gradual, shading off, tapering; fading, fading out.

(3) *comparative*, relative, proportional, in scale 9 *relative*.

Verb
(4) *graduate*, rate, class, rank 73 *grade*; scale, calibrate; compare, measure.

(5) *shade off*, taper, die away, pass into, melt into, dissolve, fade, fade out; raise by degrees 36 *augment*; lower by degrees 37 *abate*; whittle down, pare 204 *shorten*.

Adverb
(6) *by degrees*, gradually, little by little, step by step, drop by drop, bit by bit, inch by inch; in some degree, to some extent, just a bit.

27
Degree: Relative quantity

Noun
(1) *degree*, relative quantity; proportion, ratio, scale 9 *relativeness*, 462 *comparison*; ration, stint 783 *portion*, 53 *part*; extent, intensity, frequency,

28
Equality: Sameness of quantity or degree

Noun
(1) *equality*, same quantity, same degree; parity, coincidence 24 *agreement*; symmetry, balance, poise; evenness, levelness 258 *smoothness*; monotony

16 *uniformity*; impartiality 913 *justice*.

(2) *equivalence,* likeness 13 *identity*; equation 151 *interchange*; synonymity, synonym; reciprocation, exchange, fair e. 791 *barter*; par, quits; equivalent, value, fair v., just price; level bet, even money.

(3) *equilibrium,* equipoise, balance, poise; even keel, steadiness, uprightness; balance of forces, balance of nature, balance of power, stable state, stability; deadlock, stalemate; sea legs, seat; stabilizer; tightrope walker.

(4) *equalization,* equation, balancing 322 *weighing*; coordination, adjustment 31 *compensation*; equal division 92 *bisection*; going halves 775 *participation*; reciprocity 12 *correlation*; tit for tat 151 *interchange*; equalizer, counterpoise 31 *offset*; equator 92 *dividing line*.

(5) *draw,* drawn game; level-pegging; tie, dead heat; no decision, stalemate; love all, deuce; photo finish; near thing, narrow margin.

(6) *compeer,* peer, equal, match, mate, twin 18 *analogue*; equivalent, counterpart, shadow, rival.

Adjective

(7) *equal,* equi-, iso-, co-; same 13 *identical*; coordinate, coextensive, coincident, congruent 24 *agreeing*; equidistant; balanced, in equilibrium 153 *fixed*; even, level 258 *smooth*; even-sided, equilateral, ʼregular 16 *uniform,* 245 *symmetrical*; dingdong, matched, drawn, tied; parallel, level-pegging, neck-and-neck; equalized, bracketed; equally divided, half-and-half, fifty-fifty; impartial 913

just; on equal terms, on a par, on a level; par, quits.

(8) *equivalent,* comparable, interchangeable; parallel, synonymous, virtual; corresponding; 12 *correlative*; as good as, no better, no worse; tantamount to, much the same, all one 18 *similar*; worth, priced.

Verb

(9) *be equal,* equal; compensate 31 *set off*; coincide with 24 *accord*; be equal to, measure up to, reach, touch; cope with 160 *be able*; make the grade, pass muster 635 *suffice*; hold one's own, keep up with, keep pace w.; parallel match 18 *resemble*; tie, draw; break even; go halves 775 *participate*.

(10) *equalize,* equate; bracket, match 462 *compare*; balance, strike a b., poise, stabilize; trim, dress, square, round off, level 16 *make uniform*; fit, accommodate, 24 *adjust*; counterpoise, even up, set off; give points to, handicap, redress the balance, compensate; right oneself, keep one's balance.

Adverb

(11) *equally,* evenly etc. adj.; as good as, to all intents and purposes; on equal terms; in equilibrium.

29
Inequality: Difference of quantity or degree

Noun

(1) *inequality,* 34 *superiority,* 35 *inferiority*; unevenness 17 *non-uniformity*; disproportion, distortion, oddness, skewness, lopsidedness; disparity 15 *difference*; unlikeness 19 *dissimilarity*; imbalance, preponderance; shortcoming, inadequacy 636 *insufficiency*; odds 15

difference; counterpoise 31 *off-set*; bonus 40 *extra*; casting vote; partiality, discrimination 481 *bias*, 914 *injustice*.

Adjective
(2) *unequal*, disparate 19 *dissimilar*; unequalled, at an advantage 34 *superior*; at a disadvantage, below par 35 *inferior*; irregular, lopsided askew; odd, uneven; variable, patchy 437 *variegated*; falling short inadequate 636 *insufficient*; underweight; overweight; unbalanced, swaying, rocking overloaded, top-heavy; listing, leaning, canting, heeling 220 *oblique*; off balance, overbalanced, losing balance; unfair 914 *unjust*; partial 481 *biased*.

Verb
(3) *be unequal*, be mismatched, not balance; fall short 35 *be inferior*; have the advantage 34 *predominate*; be deficient 636 *not suffice*; overcompensate, tip the scales 322 *weigh*; be underweight, 323 *be light*; unbalance, throw off balance; overbalance, capsize; list, lean 220 *be oblique*; rock, sway 317 *fluctuate*; vary 143 *change*.

Adverb
(4) *unevenly*, unequally etc. adj.

30
Mean

Noun
(1) *average*, medium, mean, median; balance, happy medium, golden mean 177 *moderation*; standard 79 *generality*; ruck, ordinary run 732 *averageness*; norm, par.

(2) *middle point*, midpoint, halfway 70 *middle*; middle course 625 *middle way*; middle of the road 770 *compromise*; central position 225 *centre*.

(3) *common man*, man or woman in the street 79 *everyman*; average specimen 732 *averageness*.

Adjective
(4) *median*, mean, average, intermediate 70 *middle* normal, standard, par; ordinary, commonplace, run of the mill, mediocre 732 *middling*; moderate 625 *neutral*; middle brow.

Verb
(5) *average out*, average, take the mean; split the difference, 770 *compromise*; strike a balance 28 *equalize*.

Adverb
(6) *on an average*, on the whole 79 *generally*; taking one thing with another, all in all.

31
Compensation

Noun
(1) *compensation*, weighting 28 *equalization*; rectification 654 *amendment*; redemption, reparation, redress, amends; recompense, repayment 962 *reward*; reciprocity, 12 *correlation*.

(2) *offset*, allowance, balance, weighting, counterpoise, makeweight, ballast 28 *equalization*; indemnity, reparations, compensation, costs, damages; refund, one's money back; penance 941 *atonement*; equivalent, quid pro quo 150 *substitute*; cover, collateral, hostage; concession 770 *compromise*.

Adjective
(3) *compensatory*, compensating, redeeming, balancing 28 *equivalent*; weighed against 462 *compared*.

Verb
(4) *compensate*, make amends, indemnify, restore, repay, pay back 787 *restitute*; make good,

make up for 150 *substitute*; bribe, square 962 *reward*; reimburse, pay; redeem, outweigh; overcompensate.

(5) *set off*, offset, allow for; counterpoise, balance, ballast 28 *equalize*; neutralize, nullify 182 *counteract*; cover, hedge; give and take, concede 770 *compromise*.

(6) *recoup*, recover 656 *retrieve*; make up leeway, take back, get back 786 *take*.

Adverb
(7) *in return*, in consideration, in compensation, in lieu; though, although; on the other hand; nevertheless, despite, for all that, but, still, even so, after all, allowing for.

32
Greatness

Noun
(1) *greatness*, largeness, bigness, girth 195 *size*; large scale, vastness 195 *hugeness*; abundance 635 *plenty*; amplitude, fullness 54 *completeness*; superfluity 637 *redundance*; excess 546 *exaggeration*; enormity, immensity, boundlessness 107 *infinity*; numerousness, 104 *multitude*; magnitude 26 *quantity*, 27 *degree*; extent 203 *length*, 205 *breadth*, 209 *height*, 211 *depth*; expanse, area, volume, capacity 183 *space*; spaciousness 183 *room*; mightiness, might 160 *power*, 178 *influence*; magnification 36 *increase*; significance 638 *importance*; eminence 34 *superiority*; grandeur, grandness 868 *nobility*; majesty 733 *authority*; fame, renown 866 *repute*.

(2) *great quantity*, galore 635 *plenty*; profusion, abundance, superabundance, superfluity, too much; flood, spate, torrent; expanse, sheet, sea; sight of, world of, power of; much, lot, deal, good d., great d.; mint, mine 632 *store*; quantity, bushels, gallons; heap, mass, stack, mountain 74 *accumulation*; load (of), full l. 193 *contents*; quantities, lots, lashings, oodles, wads, pots, bags; heaps, loads, masses, stacks; oceans, floods, streams; volumes, reams; numbers, not a few, quite a f.; crowds, masses, hosts, swarms 104 *multitude*.

(3) *main part*, almost all, principal part, best part of, 52 *chief part*; greater part, majority 104 *greater number*; body, bulk, mass, substance.

Adjective
(4) *great*, greater, main, most, major 34 *superior*; maximum, greatest 34 *supreme*; grand, big 195 *large*; fair-sized, largish, biggish, pretty big; substantial, considerable, respectable, sizable. full-size, life-s.; bulky, massive 322 *weighty*; lengthy 203 *long*; wide 205 *broad*; swollen 197 *expanded*; ample, generous, voluminous, capacious 183 *spacious*; profound 211 *deep*; tall, lofty 209 *high*; Herculean 162 *strong*; mighty 160 *powerful*, 178 *influential*; intense 174 *vigorous*; noisy 400 *loud*; soaring 308 *ascending*; culminating, at its maximum, at its peak, at its height 213 *topmost*; great in quantity, plentiful, abundant, overflowing 635 *plenteous*; superabundant 637 *redundant*; great in number, many, swarming 104 *multitudinous*; great in age, antique, ancient, venerable, immemorial 127 *olden*, 131 *ageing*; great in honour, imperial, august 868 *noble*; goodly, precious 644 *valuable*, sublime, exalted 821 *impressive*; glorious, famous 866 *renowned, worshipful*; solemn 638 *important*; excellent 306 *surpassing*, 644 *best*.

(5) *extensive,* ranging, wide-ranging, far-reaching, 183 *spacious*; widespread, prevalent, epidemic; worldwide, universal, cosmic; mass, wholesale, full-scale, all-embracing, sweeping, comprehensive 78 *inclusive.*

(6) *enormous,* immense, vast, colossal, giant, gigantic, monumental 195 *huge*; towering, sky-high 209 *high*; record 306 *surpassing.*

(7) *prodigious,* marvellous, astounding, amazing, astonishing 864 *wonderful*; fantastic, fabulous, incredible, stupendous, tremendous, terrific; dreadful, frightful 854 *frightening*; breathtaking, overwhelming 821 *impressive.*

(8) *remarkable,* noticeable, worth looking at 866 *noteworthy*; outstanding, extraordinary, exceptional 84 *unusual*; eminent, distinguished, marked 638 *notable.*

(9) *whopping,* walloping, whacking, spanking, thumping, thundering, rattling, howling; hefty, strapping 195 *unwieldy.*

(10) *flagrant,* flaring, glaring, stark, staring; blatant, shocking 867 *discreditable.*

(11) *unspeakable,* unutterable, indescribable, indefinable 517 *inexpressible.*

(12) *exorbitant,* extortionate, harsh, stringent, severe 735 *oppressive*; excessive, extreme, utmost 306 *surpassing*; monstrous, outrageous, unbearable 827 *intolerable*; inordinate, preposterous, extravagant, astronomical 546 *exaggerated*; going too far.

(13) *consummate* finished, flawless 646 *perfect*; entire, sound 52 *whole*; thorough, thoroughgoing; utter, total, out and out,

double-dyed, arch, crass, gross, arrant, rank, regular, downright, desperate, unmitigated.

(14) *absolute,* essential, positive, unequivocal; stark, pure, sheer, mere 107 *infinite.*

Verb

(15) *be great* - large etc. adj.; bulk large, loom up; stretch 183 *extend*; tower, soar 308 *ascend*; transcend 34 *be superior*; clear, overtop; exceed, know no bounds 306 *overstep*; enlarge 36 *augment,* 197 *expand*; swamp, overwhelm 54 *fill.*

Adverb

(16) *positively,* indeed, in fact 494 *truly*; seriously, indubitably 473 *certainly*; decidedly, absolutely, definitely, finally, unequivocally, directly, specifically, unreservedly; essentially, fundamentally, radically; downright, plumb.

(17) *greatly,* much, well; very, very much, ever so; fully, quite, entirely, utterly 54 *completely*; thoroughly, wholesale; widely, extensively, universally 79 *generally*; largely, mainly, mostly, considerably, fairly, pretty, pretty well; a great deal, ever so much; materially, substantially; increasingly, more than ever, doubly, trebly; specially, particularly; dearly, deeply; exceptionally; vastly, hugely, enormously; powerfully, mightily; actively, strenuously, vigorously, heartily, intensely; zealously, fanatically, hotly, bitterly, fiercely; acutely, sharply, exquisitely; enough, more than e., abundantly, generously; magnificently, splendidly; supremely, superlatively; incomparably, immeasurably, incalculably, infinitely, unspeakably.

(18) *extremely,* ultra, to extremes, to the limit; beyond measure, beyond compare;

overly, unduly, to a fault; bitterly, harshly, drastically, with a vengeance; immoderately, desperately, madly, frantically, furiously 176 *violently*; exceedingly, excessively, inordinately, outrageously, abominably, monstrously, horribly; devilishly, damnably, hellishly; tremendously, terribly, fearfully, dreadfully, awfully, frightfully, horribly; finally, mortally.

(19) *remarkably*, noticeably, sensibly, markedly, pointedly; notably, strikingly, conspicuously, signally, emphatically, prominently, glaringly, flagrantly, blatantly; publicly 400 *loudly*; outstandingly, singularly, peculiarly, curiously, uncommonly, unusually surprisingly, astonishingly, impressively, incredibly, amazingly 864 *wonderfully*.

(20) *painfully*, unsparingly, till it hurts; badly, bitterly, hard; seriously, sorely, grievously; sadly, miserably, wretchedly; pitiably, lamentably; cruelly, savagely; unbearably, exquisitely; shockingly, frighteningly, terrifyingly.

33
Smallness

Noun

(1) *smallness*, small size, minuteness 196 *littleness*; brevity 204 *shortness*; meagreness 206 *thinness*; briefness 114 *transience*; sparseness 140 *infrequency*; exiguousness, scantiness; moderateness, moderation; small means 801 *poverty*; pettiness, meanness, insignificance 639 *unimportance*; mediocrity 732 *averageness*; compression, abbreviation 198 *contraction*; diminution 37 *decrease*.

(2) *small quantity*, fraction, modicum, minimum 26 *finite quantity*; minutiae, trivia; peanuts 639 *trifle*; detail, petty detail 80 *particulars*; nutshell 592 *compendium*; trifling amount, drop in the ocean; thimbleful, cupful; trickle, dribble; sprinkle, dash, splash, squirt, squeeze; tinge, trace, smack, breath, whisper, suspicion, vestige, soupçon, suggestion; nuance, shade, touch; strain, streak; spark, scintilla, flash, flicker; pinch, handful; snack, sip, bite, scrap, morsel; pittance, iron ration; fragment bit, iota, jot; ounce, gram; inch, millimetre; second, moment 116 *instant*; next to nothing.

(3) *small thing* 196 *miniature*; particle, atom; dot, point, pinpoint; dab, spot, fleck, speck, grain, crumb; drop, droplet; thread, wisp, shred, fragment 53 *piece*; smithereens, confetti; flake, snippet, gobbet, finger; splinter, chip, clipping, paring, shaving; sliver, slip; pinprick, snick, prick, nick.

(4) *small coin*, farthing, mite, cent, nickel, dime; bean, small change 797 *coinage*.

(5) *small animal*, amoeba 196 *microorganism*; gnat, flea, ant; minnow, shrimp, sprat; sparrow, mouse; bantam; midget 196 *dwarf*.

Adjective

(6) *small*, exiguous, not much, moderate, modest, homoeopathic, minimal, infinitesimal; microscopic 444 *invisible*; tiny, weeny, wee, minute, diminutive, miniature 196 *little*; least, minimum; small-sized, undersized 196 *dwarfish*; slim, meagre 206 *narrow*; slight, puny 163 *weak*; weightless 323 *light*; quiet, soft, low, faint, hushed 401 *muted*; squat 210 *low*; brief 204 *short*; smaller cut, compact, thumbnail 198 *contracted*;

scanty 636 *insufficient*; reduced, limited; less 37 *decreasing.*

(7) *inconsiderable,* minor, lightweight, trifling, trivial, petty, paltry, insignificant 639 *unimportant*; not many, soon counted 105 *few*; imperceptible, inappreciable 444 *invisible*; marginal, negligible, slight; superficial, cursory 4 *insubstantial*; skin-deep 212 *shallow*; fair, so-so 732 *middling*; moderate, modest, humble; passable no great shakes, not much of a 35 *inferior*; no more than, just, only, mere.

Verb

(8) *be small,* stay small, not grow 196 *be little*; have no height 210 *be low*; make no sound 401 *sound faint*; get less 37 *decrease*; shrink 198 *become small.*

Adverb

(9) *slightly,* little; faintly, feebly; gradually, imperceptibly, insensibly; modestly, in a small way; fairly, moderately, tolerably, quite; comparatively, relatively, rather; indifferently, poorly, badly, dismally; hardly, scarcely, barely, only just, by the skin of one's teeth; narrowly, hardly at all, no more than; only, merely; at least,

(10) *partially,* to some degree, to a certain extent; somehow, after a fashion, sort of, in a manner of speaking; somewhat, a little, a bit, just a bit; not wholly, in part, partly 647 *imperfectly.*

(11) *almost,* all but, within an ace *or* an inch of; within sight of, on the brink *or* the verge of; approximately 200 *nearly*; pretty near, just short of, not quite, virtually.

(12) *about,* somewhere about, thereabouts; on an average,

more or less; near enough, at a guess.

(13) *in no way,* by no means, in no respect, not at all, not a bit, not a whit, not a jot, not in the least *or* the slightest.

34
Superiority

Noun

(1) *superiority,* loftiness, sublimity 32 *greatness*; quality, excellence 644 *goodness*; ne plus ultra 646 *perfection*; primacy, pride of place, seniority, precedence, eminence, preeminence 866 *prestige*; higher rank 868 *aristocracy*; supremacy 733 *authority*; ascendancy, domination, 178 *influence*; directorship 689 *management*; preponderance, prevalence 29 *inequality*; win, championship 727 *victory*; prominence 638 *importance*; one-upmanship 698 *cunning,* 727 *success*; climax, zenith; maximum, top, peak, pinnacle, crest, record, high, new h. 213 *summit.*

(2) *advantage,* privilege, prerogative, handicap, favour 615 *benefit*; head start, flying s., lead, pole position, inside track; odds, points, vantage, pull, edge; command, upper hand, whip h.; one up, something in hand, reserves; trump card; majority, 104 *greater number*; lion's share; leverage, scope 183 *room.*

(3) *superior,* superior person, superman, superwoman 864 *prodigy*; first choice 890 *favourite*; select few 644 *elite*; high-ups, one's betters; top people, 638 *bigwig*; aristocracy 868 *upper class*; overlord, boss 741 *master*; commander, chief 690 *leader*; superintendent 690 *manager*; model 646 *paragon*; virtuoso, specialist 696 *expert*; mastermind 500 *sage*; world-

beater, winner, champion, cup-holder, record-h. 727 *victor*; elder, senior.

Adjective

(4) *superior,* more so; comparative, superlative; major, greater 32 *great*; upper, higher, senior, over-, super-, supra-, hyper-; above average, 15 *different*; better, a cut above, 644 *excellent*; competitive, one up, more than a match for; ahead, streets a.; preferable, preferred, favourite 605 *chosen*; record, a record for, exceeding, overtopping 306 *surpassing*; on top, winning, victorious 727 *successful*; outstanding, distinguished 866 *noteworthy*; top-level, high-l., high-powered 689 *directing*, 638 *important*; commanding, in authority 733 *ruling*; revised, reformed 654 *improved*; enlarged, enhanced 197 *expanded*.

(5) *supreme,* arch-, greatest 32 *great*; uppermost, highest 213 *topmost*; first, chief, foremost; main, principal, leading, over-ruling, overriding, cardinal, capital 638 *important*; excellent, classic, superlative, super, champion, first-rate, first-class, A1, 5-star, front-rank, world-beating 644 *best*; top, on top, second to none; dominant, paramount, preeminent, sovereign, royal; incomparable, un-rivalled, matchless, peerless, unparalleled, unequalled, unsurpassed 21 *inimitable*; ultimate 306 *surpassing*; beyond compare 646 *perfect*.

(6) *crowning,* capping, culminating 725 *completive*; climactic, maximum; record, record-breaking, best ever 644 *best*.

Verb

(7) *be superior,* transcend, rise above, overtop, tower over 209 *be high*; go beyond, 306 *overstep*; wear the crown; pass,
surpass, beat the record; improve on, better, go one b., cap, trump, overtrump; shine, excel 644 *be good*; steal the show outshine, eclipse, overshadow, score off; best, outclass, outrank 306 *outdo*; outplay, out-point, outmanoeuvre, outwit; overtake, leave behind 277 *outstrip*; beat 727 *defeat*;

(8) *predominate,* preponderate, have the edge on, tip the scale 29 *be unequal*; override, have the whip hand 178 *prevail*; lead, hold the l., be one up.

(9) *come first,* stand f., head the list, take precedence; play first fiddle; 638 *be important*; take the lead 237 *be in front*; lead, play the l., star; head, captain 689 *direct*.

(10) *culminate,* come to a head; crown all 213 *crown*; reach a new high 725 *climax*.

Adverb

(11) *beyond,* more, over; above par, over the average; upwards of, over and above; at its height, at the peak.

(12) *eminently,* preeminently, outstandingly, surpassingly, prominently, superlatively, supremely, above all; the most, par excellence; principally, especially, particularly; all the more; far and away, by far 32 *extremely*.

35
Inferiority

Noun

(1) *inferiority,* minority, inferior numbers 105 *fewness*; littleness 33 *smallness*; subordination, dependence 745 *subjection*; secondariness, supporting role 639 *unimportance*; lowliness 872 *humility*; second rank, back seat; obscurity, commonness 869 *commonalty*; disadvantage, handicap 702 *hindrance*; blemish, defect 647 *imperfection*; failure 728 *defeat*; poor quality, second best 645 *badness*; shabbiness 801 *poverty*; worsening, decline 655 *deterioration*; record low, minimum, the bottom, rock b. 214 *base*; mediocrity 732 *averageness*.

(2) *inferior*, subordinate, underling, assistant, subsidiary 707 *auxiliary*, 755 *deputy*; follower, retainer 742 *dependant*; menial, hireling 742 *servant*; poor relation, small fry 639 *nonentity*; subject, underdog 742 *slave*; private, other ranks, backbencher; second, second best, second string, second fiddle, second-rater; poor second, also-ran; failure, reject, dregs 607 *rejection*; younger, junior, minor.

Adjective
(3) *lesser*, less, minor 33 *inconsiderable*; small-time 639 *unimportant*; small, smaller, diminished 37 *decreasing*; smallest, least, minimal, minimum, lowest, bottommost.

(4) *inferior*, lower, junior, under-, sub-; subordinate 742 *serving*; dependent 745 *subject*; secondary, tributary, ancillary, subsidiary, auxiliary 703 *aiding*; second, second-best, second-class, second-rate, mediocre; third-rate 922 *contemptible*; lowly, low-level, menial; low-ranking; substandard, low-grade 607 *rejected*; unsound, defective 655 *deteriorated*; patchy 647 *imperfect*; shoddy 645 *bad*; low, common 847 *vulgar*; low-caste 869 *plebeian*; scratch, makeshift temporary, provisional; feeble 163 *weak*; outshone, worsted, beaten 728 *defeated*; nothing special.

Verb
(5) *be inferior*, come short of, not come up to 307 *fall short*; lag, trail fall behind; want, lack 636 *not suffice*; not pass 728 *fail*; bow to 742 *serve*; lose face 867 *lose repute*; get worse 655 *deteriorate*; slump, sink 309 *descend*.

Adverb
(6) *less*, minus, short of; below average, below par, at the bottom.

36
Increase

Noun
(1) *increase*, augmentation, crescendo; advance, growth, growth area, boom town; buildup, development 164 *production*; extension, prolongation, protraction 203 *lengthening*; widening, broadening; spread, escalation, inflation, 197 *expansion*; proliferation, multiplication, swarming 171 *abundance*; squaring, cubing; adding 38 *addition*; enlargement, magnification 32 *greatness*; excess 546 *exaggeration*; enhancement, appreciation, heightening, raising; recruitment 162 *strengthening*; stepping up, doubling, redoubling, trebling 91 *duplication*, 94 *triplication*; acceleration, hotting up 174 *stimulation*; exacerbation 832 *aggravation*; advancement, boost 654 *improvement*; rise, spiral, upward trend, upswing 308 *ascent*; upsurge, flood, tide, rising t., swell, surge; snowball 74 *accumulation*.

(2) *increment*, augmentation, bulge; contribution 38 *addition*; supplement, pay rise 40 *extra*; padding, stuffing 303 *insertion*; percentage, commission, interest, profit 771 *gain*; harvest 164 *product*; takings, receipts, proceeds.

Adjective
(3) *increasing*, spreading,

progressive, escalating 32 *great*; growing, waxing, crescent; on the increase; supplementary 38 *additional*; cumulative 71 *continuous*; intensive; productive 171 *prolific*; increased, enlarged 197 *expanded*.

Verb
(4) *grow,* increase, gain, develop, escalate; dilate, swell, bulge, wax, fill 197 *expand*; fill out, fatten, thicken 205 *be broad*; put on weight 322 *weigh*; sprout, bud, burgeon, flower, blossom 167 *reproduce itself*; breed, spread, swarm, proliferate, mushroom, multiply 104 *be many*, 171 *be fruitful*; grow up 669 *mature*; spring up, shoot up, spiral, climb, mount, rise 308 *ascend*; flare up, gain strength 162 *be strong*; flourish, thrive, prosper; gain ground, advance, snowball, accumulate 285 *progress*; earn interest, gain in value, appreciate; boom, surge 32 *be great*.

(5) *augment,* increase, bump up, double, triple 94 *treble*, 97 *quadruple*; redouble, square, cube; duplicate, multiply 166 *reproduce*; grow, breed, raise, rear 369 *breed stock*, 370 *cultivate*; enlarge, magnify, inflate, blow up 197 *expand*; amplify, develop, build up, fill out, pad out 54 *make complete*; condense, concentrate 324 *be dense*; supplement, enrich, bring to, contribute to 38 *add*; extend, prolong 203 *lengthen*; broaden, widen, thicken, deepen; heighten, enhance; speed up 277 *accelerate*; intensify, redouble, step up 174 *invigorate*; reinforce, boost 162 *strengthen*; glorify 482 *overrate*; stoke, exacerbate 832 *aggravate*; maximize, bring to a head.

Adverb
(6) *crescendo,* more so, with a vengeance; on the increase, more and more, all the more.

37
Decrease: No increase

Noun
(1) *decrease,* getting less, lessening, dwindling, falling off; waning, fading, contraction; shrinking 206 *narrowing*; ebb, retreat, withdrawal 286 *regression*; ebb tide; sinking, decline, downward trend, fall, drop, plunge 309 *descent*; deflation, recession, slump 655 *deterioration*; loss of value, depreciation 812 *cheapness*; weakening 163 *weakness*; shortage 636 *scarcity*; shrinkage, evaporation, erosion, crumbling 655 *dilapidation*; wear and tear, consumption 634 *waste*; no increase, slackening; damage, loss 52 *decrement*;

(2) *diminution,* making less; deduction 39 *subtraction*; reduction, slowing down, deceleration; retrenchment, cut 814 *economy*; cutting back, pruning, paring, abridgment 204 *shortening*; compression, squeeze 198 *contraction*; abrasion, erosion; melting, dissolution; scattering, dispersal; weeding out, elimination 300 *ejection*; alleviation, mitigation, minimization 177 *moderation*; belittlement 483 *underestimation*; demotion 872 *humiliation*.

Adjective
(3) *decreasing,* dwindling; waning, fading, evaporating; decreased, declining, going down, ebbing, sinking.

Verb
(4) *abate,* make less, diminish, decrease, lessen, take away, detract from 39 *subtract*; except 57 *exclude*; reduce, scale down,

whittle, pare 206 *make thin*; clip, trim, slash 46 *cut*; shrink, abridge, boil down 204 *shorten*; squeeze, compress, contract 198 *make smaller*; cut back, retrench 814 *economize*; slow down, decelerate 278 *retard*; depress, send down; tone down, minimize, mitigate 177 *moderate*; allay, alleviate 831 *relieve*; deflate, puncture; disparage, belittle 483 *underestimate*; dwarf, overshadow 34 *be superior*; degrade, demote 872 *humiliate*; loosen, ease, relax; use up, fritter away 634 *waste*; let escape, let evaporate, melt down; grind, crumble, rub away; nibble at, eat away, erode 655 *impair*; emasculate 161 *disable*; dilute, water down 163 *weaken* thin, thin out, weed o., eliminate 300 *eject*; damp down, cool, quell, subdue, extinguish.

(5) *decrease*, grow less, lessen, abate, dwindle; slacken, ease, moderate, subside, die down; shrink, shrivel up, contract 198 *become small*; wane, waste, wear away; fade, die away, grow dim; withdraw, ebb, run low, run down, ebb away, drain away, dry up, fail 636 *not suffice*; tail off, taper off, peter out; subside, sink, decline, drop, slump 309 *descend*; not grow, level off; melt away, evaporate; thin out, become scarce 75 *disperse*; die out, become extinct 2 *pass away*; lose, shed, cast off; forfeit, sacrifice 772 *lose*.

Adverb
(6) *diminuendo,* decreasingly; less and less; in decline, on the wane, at a low ebb.

38
Addition

Noun
(1) *addition,* adding to, annexation 45 *union*; superimposing, affixture 65 *sequence*; contribution 703 *aid*; imposition, load 702 *encumbrance*; accession, accretion 78 *inclusion*; reinforcement 36 *increase*; increment, supplement 40 *adjunct*; adding up, total 86 *numeration*.

Adjective
(2) *additional,* additive; added; adventitious, adopted, occasional 6 *extrinsic*; supplementary, 725 *completive*; subsidiary, auxiliary, contributory; another, further, more; extra, spare 637 *superfluous*; interjected, interposed, prefixed.

Verb
(3) *add,* add up, sum, total 86 *do sums*; add to, annex, append, subjoin; attach, tack on; conjoin, stick on 45 *join*; add on, prefix, affix, suffix, introduce 231 *put between*; let in 303 *insert*; bring to, contribute to 36 *augment*; extend 197 *enlarge*; supplement 54 *make complete*; saddle with 702 *hinder*; superimpose, pile on 74 *bring together*; ornament, embellish 844 *decorate*; mix with 43 *mix*; annex 786 *take*; take in, include 299 *admit*

(4) *accrue,* be added 78 *be included*; supervene 295 *arrive*; adhere, join 50 *combine*; reinforce, swell the ranks.

Adverb
(5) *in addition,* additionally, more, plus, extra; with interest; and, too, also, furthermore, further; likewise, and also, besides; et cetera; and so on, and so forth; moreover, into the bargain, over and above, including, inclusive of, with, as well as, not to mention, let alone, not forgetting; together with, along w.

39
Subtraction

Noun

(1) *subtraction,* deduction diminution 37 *decrease*; abstraction, removal, withdrawal 786 *taking*; elimination 62 *sorting*; expulsion 300 *ejection*; unloading 188 *displacement*; curtailment 204 *shortening*; severance, amputation 46 *scission*; mutilation 655 *impairment*; deletion 550 *obliteration*; discount 42 *decrement.*

Adjective

(2) *subtracted,* deducted; curtailed, docked; headless, decapitated; minus, without 307 *deficient.*

Verb

(3) *subtract,* take away, deduct, do subtraction; detract from, diminish, decrease 37 *abate*; cut 810 *discount*; take off, knock o., allow, set off; except, leave out 57 *exclude*; abstract, withdraw, remove 786 *take*; draw off 300 *empty*; file down 333 *rub*; pull out 304 *extract*; pick out 605 *select*; cross out, delete, censor, expurgate 550 *obliterate*; mutilate 655 *impair*; amputate, excise; shave off, clip 46 *cut*; cut back, cut down, prune, pare, curtail, abridge, abbreviate 204 *shorten.*

Adverb

(4) *in deduction,* at a discount; less; short of; minus, without, except, excepting, with the exception of; bar, save, exclusive of.

40
Adjunct: Thing added

Noun

(1) *adjunct,* something added 38 *addition*; addendum, carry-over; supplement, annex; attachment, fixture; inflection, affix, suffix, prefix; tag 547 *label*; appendage, tail; appendix, postscript, P.S., coda, rider, codicil 468 *qualification*; corollary, complement; accessory 89 *concomitant*; extension, continuation, second part; outhouse, wing; offshoot, arm, limb; accretion increment 36 *increase*; patch, padding, stuffing; ingredient 58 *component*; fringe, edging 234 *edge*; embroidery, garnish, frills, trimmings 844 *ornamentation*; trappings, equipment.

(2) *extra,* additive; by-product, interest 771 *gain*; bonus, tip 962 *reward*; windfall, find; allowance 31 *offset*; oddment, item; supernumerary, extra; reserves, spare parts, spares; reinforcement 707 *auxiliary*; surplus 637 *superfluity.*

41
Remainder: Thing remaining

Noun

(1) *remainder,* residue; result 164 *product*; margin 15 *difference*; balance, net b. 31 *offset*; surplus, carry-over 36 *increment*; excess 637 *superfluity*; remnant 105 *fewness*; stump, stub, fag end, 69 *extremity*; fossil, bones; husk, shell; wreckage, debris 165 *ruin*; ashes; track, fingerprint 548 *trace*; wake, afterglow 67 *sequel*; vestige, relic, remains.

(2) *leavings,* leftovers; precipitate, deposit, sediment; grounds, lees, dregs; scum, skimmings, dross, slag, sludge; shavings, filings, crumbs; husks, peel, peelings; remnants, scraps, odds and ends 641 *rubbish*; rejects, waste; refuse, litter 649 *dirt.*

(3) *survivor*, inheritor, successor; widower, widow, orphan 779 *derelict*; descendant 170 *posterity*.

Adjective
(4) *remaining,* surviving, left, vestigial, resultant; residual, residuary; left behind, deposited; abandoned, discarded 779 *not retained*; on the shelf over, left over; net, surplus; outstanding, spare 637 *redundant*; cast-off, outcast 607 *rejected*; orphaned, widowed.

Verb
(5) *be left,* remain, rest, result, survive.

(6) *leave over,* leave out, leave behind 57 *exclude*; discard, abandon 607 *reject.*

42
Decrement: Thing deducted

Noun
(1) *decrement,* deduction, depreciation, cut 37 *diminution*; allowance; remission, rebate, refund 810 *discount*; shortage 636 *insufficiency*; loss, forfeit 963 *penalty*; leak, leakage 298 *outflow*; shrinkage, spoilage, wastage; rake-off, toll 809 *tax.*

43
Mixture

Noun
(1) *mixture,* mingling, mixing, stirring; blending, harmonization 45 *union*; admixture 38 *addition*; interpolation 303 *insertion*; interweaving, interlacing 222 *crossing*; integration 50 *combination*; fusion, infusion, suffusion, transfusion; impregnation 341 *moistening*; adulteration, contamination, watering down 655 *impairment*; infiltration, penetration, pervasion, permeation

297 *ingress*; interbreeding, intermarriage; cross-fertilization, hybridization; melting pot; mixer, blender.

(2) *tincture,* admixture; ingredient 58 *component*; strain, streak; sprinkling, infusion; tinge, touch, drop, dash, soupçon 33 *small quantity*; smack, hint, flavour 386 *taste*; seasoning, spice; colour, dye 425 *hue.*

(3) *a mixture,* melange; blend, harmony; composition 331 *structure*; amalgam, fusion, compound, confection, concoction 50 *combination*; pastiche, cocktail; alloy, bronze, brass, pewter, steel; stew, hash 301 *dish*; solution, infusion.

(4) *medley,* heterogeneity, complexity, variety 17 *nonuniformity*; motley, patchwork, mosaic 437 *variegation*; assortment, miscellany, mixed bag, job lot, ragbag, lucky dip; farrago, hotchpotch, hodgepodge, mishmash, potpourri; jumble, mess 74 *accumulation*; tangle 61 *confusion*; clatter 411 *discord*; all sorts, odds and ends, bits and pieces, paraphernalia, oddments.

(5) *hybrid,* cross, cross-breed, mongrel; mule; half-blood, half-breed, half-caste; mulatto.

Adjective
(6) *mixed,* mixed up, stirred; blended, harmonized, fused 50 *combined*; tempered, qualified, adulterated, watered down 163 *weakened*; merged, amalgamated 45 *joined*; composite, half-and-half, fifty-fifty; complex, tangled, confused 61 *orderless*; heterogeneous, kaleidoscopic, 82 *multiform*; patchy, motley 437 *variegated*; miscellaneous, random; hybrid, mongrel; cross-bred, half-caste; multiracial.

Verb
(7) *mix,* make a mixture, mix up,
stir, shake; shuffle, scramble 63
jumble; knead, mash; compound 56 *compose*; fuse, merge,
amalgamate 45 *join*; blend, harmonize 50 *combine*; mingle, intermingle, intersperse 437 *variegate*; interlard, interleave 303
insert; intertwine, interlace
222 *weave*; tinge, dye 425
colour; impregnate 303 *infuse*;
water, adulterate 163 *weaken*;
season, spice, fortify, lace,
spike; hybridize, mongrelize,
cross, cross-breed.

(8) *be mixed,* be entangled with,
pervade, permeate, run
through 297 *infiltrate*; infect,
contaminate; stain 425 *colour*;
intermarry, interbreed.

Adverb
(9) *among,* amid, in the midst of;
with; in the crowd; inter alia.

44
Simpleness:
Freedom from
mixture

Noun
(1) *simpleness,* freedom from
mixture 16 *uniformity*; purity
648 *cleanness*; absoluteness 1
essence; insolubility 88 *unity*;
simplicity 573 *plainness*.

(2) *simplification,* purification,
distillation 648 *cleansing*; reduction 51 *decomposition*; unification, assimilation.

(3) *elimination,* riddance, clearance 300 *ejection*; sifting,
straining 62 *sorting*; expulsion
57 *exclusion*.

Adjective
(4) *simple,* homogeneous, monolithic 16 *uniform*; sheer, bare,
mere, utter, nothing but; single
88 *one*; elemental, indivisible,

entire 52 *whole*; primary, fundamental 5 *intrinsic*; elementary, uncomplicated; unravelled, disentangled; simplified
516 *intelligible*; direct 573
plain.

(5) *unmixed,* pure and simple,
without alloy; clear, pure 648
clean; purebred, thoroughbred; free from, exempt f., excluding; unblemished 646 *perfect*; unadulterated, undiluted,
neat 162 *strong*.

Verb
(6) *simplify,* render simple 16
make uniform; break down 51
decompose; disentangle, unscramble 62 *unravel*; unify,
make one.

(7) *eliminate,* sift 62 *class*; winnow, sieve; purge 648 *purify*;
clear, clarify, cleanse, distil;
get rid of, weed out 57 *exclude*;
expel 300 *eject*.

Adverb
(8) *simply,* simply and solely;
only, merely, exclusively.

45
Union

Noun
(1) *union,* junction, coming together, meeting, concurrence,
conjunction; clash 279 *collision*; contact 202 *contiguity*;
forgathering, reunion 74 *assembly*; confluence, meeting-
point 76 *focus*; coalescence, fusion, merger 43 *mixture*;
unification, synthesis 50 *combination*; cohesion 48 *coherence*;
coagulation, consolidation,
condensation; coalition, alliance 706 *association*; connection, hookup, linkup 47 *bond*;
wedlock 894 *marriage*; interlocking 222 *crossing*.

(2) *joining together,* bringing
together 74 *assemblage*; unification 50 *combination*; joining,
etc. vb.; knitting, sewing,

weaving 222 *crossing*; tightening, drawing together 264 *closure*; knotting, binding, etc. vb.; attachment, annexation 38 *addition*; fixture 48 *coherence*; coupling, yoking, pairing; joiner, riveter, welder; go-between 231 *intermediary*.

(3) *coition,* copulation, sex, sexual intercourse 167 *propagation*; pairing, mating, union 894 *marriage*; violation 951 *rape*.

(4) *joint,* joining, suture, seam 47 *bond*; bonding, welded joint, spliced joint; hinge-joint 247 *angularity*; ankle, knuckle, knee, elbow; node; junction, intersection 222 *crossing*.

Adjective
(5) *joined,* connected, etc. vb.; coupled, matched, paired; partnered 775 *sharing*; rolled into one, merged; joint, allied, associated 706 *cooperative*; wedded 894 *married*; holding hands, hand in hand, arm in arm; coalescent, adhesive 48 *cohesive*; composite 50 *combined*; put together 74 *assembled*; articulated, jointed 331 *structural*; stitched up.

(6) *conjunctive,* adhesive 48 *cohesive*; copulatory, coital.

(7) *firm,* fast, secure 153 *fixed*; solid, set 324 *dense*; glued, cemented 48 *cohesive*; put, pat; planted, rooted; close-set, crowded, tight, wedged, jammed, stuck; inextricable, inseparable, immovable, unshakable; packed 54 *full*.

(8) *tied,* bound, knotted, etc. vb.; stitched, sewn, gathered; attached, fastened 48 *cohesive*; tight, taut, tense, fast, secure; intricate, involved, tangled, inextricable, indissoluble.

Verb
(9) *join,* conjoin, couple, yoke, hyphenate, harness together;

pair, match, bracket 28 *equalize*; put together, fit t., piece t., assemble, unite 50 *combine*; collect, gather, mobilize 74 *bring together*; add to, amass, accumulate 632 *store*; associate, ally, twin (town); merge 43 *mix*; incorporate, unify, lump together, roll into one; include, embrace 78 *comprise*; grip 778 *retain*; hinge, articulate, dovetail, mortise, mitre; fit, set, interlock, engage; wedge, jam 303 *insert*; weld, solder, fuse, cement 48 *agglutinate*; draw together, lace, knit, sew, stitch; do up, fasten 264 *close*; close a gap, seal up; darn, mend 656 *repair*.

(10) *connect,* attach, annex (see *affix*); staple, clip, pin together; thread t., string t., link t.; contact 378 *touch*; make contact, plug in; link, bridge, span 305 *pass*; communicate, put through to, put in touch; hook up with, tie up w. 9 *relate*.

(11) *affix,* attach, fix, fasten; tie up, moor, anchor; tether, picket; hang on, hook on stick on 48 *agglutinate*; suffix, prefix 38 *add*; implant 303 *insert*; impact, drive in, knock in; wedge, jam; screw, nail, rivet, bolt, clamp, clinch.

(12) *tie,* knot, hitch, lash, belay; knit, sew, stitch; tack, baste; plait, twine, twist, lace 222 *weave*; truss, string, rope, strap, lace up; handcuff, shackle 747 *fetter*; bind, splice, bandage, swathe, swaddle, wrap 235 *enclose*.

(13) *tighten,* jam, impact; constrict, compress, narrow; fasten, make fast, secure; draw tight, pull t., lace t.; brace, trice up.

(14) *unite with,* be joined, join, meet 293 *converge*; fit tight, hold t., fit closely, hang together, stick t. 48 *cohere*; mesh,

interlock, engage (gear); grapple, clinch; embrace, entwine; link up with, partner, 882 *be sociable*; league together 708 *join a party*; marry 894 *wed*; live with, cohabit; lie with, sleep w., go to bed with; make love, have intercourse; copulate, couple, mate 167 *generate*; mount, cover, serve; cross with, breed w.

Adverb

(15) *conjointly,* jointly, with, in conjunction with 708 *in league*; all together, as one.

(16) *inseparably,* inextricably, intimately; securely, firmly, fast, tight.

46
Disunion

Noun

(1) *disunion,* being separated; disconnection, disconnectedness, break 72 *discontinuity*; looseness, separability 49 *noncoherence*; diffusion, dispersal, scattering 75 *dispersion*; breakup, dissolution 51 *decomposition*; abstraction, dissociation, withdrawal, disengagement; moving apart 294 *divergence*; split, detachment, schism; isolation, quarantine, segregation 883 *seclusion*; zone, compartment; insularity, neutrality; lack of unity 709 *dissension*; separateness; isolationism, separatism; no connection 15 *difference*; breach, rent, rift, split; fissure, crack, cleft, chasm; slit, slot 201 *gap*.

(2) *separation,* severance, parting; uncoupling, 896 *divorce*; undoing, unravelling, loosening, loosing, freeing 746 *liberation*; setting apart, segregation, apartheid 883 *seclusion*; exception, exemption 57 *exclusion*; expulsion 300 *ejection*; picking out, selection 605 *choice*; putting aside, keeping

a. 632 *storage*; taking away 39 *subtraction*; deprivation, expropriation 786 *taking*; detachment, withdrawal, removal, transfer 272 *transference*; dislocation, scattering, dispersal 75 *dispersion*; dissolution, disintegration 51 *decomposition*; dissection, analysis, breakdown; disruption, fragmentation 165 *destruction*; splitting, fission, nuclear f. breaking, cracking, rupture, fracture; dividing line 231 *partition*; boundary 236 *limit*.

(3) *scission,* cutting, tearing; division, dichotomy 92 *bisection*; subdivision, segmentation; partition 783 *apportionment*; cutting off, decapitation, curtailment 204 *shortening*; cutting away, cutting open, incision 658 *surgery*; dissection; rending, clawing, etc. vb.; laceration.

Adjective

(4) *disunited,* separated, divorced; disconnected, unstuck; unseated, dismounted; broken, interrupted 72 *discontinuous*; divided, subdivided, partitioned, in pieces, quartered, dismembered; severed, cut; torn, rent, cleft, cloven; divergent 282 *deviating*; scattered, dispersed 75 *unassembled*; untied, loosened, loose, free.

(5) *separate,* apart, asunder; adrift, lost; unattached, distinct, discrete, separable, 15 *different*; exempt, excepted, abstracted; alien 59 *extraneous*; insular, isolated 88 *alone,* 883 *friendless*; picked out, set apart 605 *chosen*; abandoned, left, remaining; disjunctive, separative, dividing, selective, 15 *distinctive*.

(6) *severable,* separable, detachable; divisible, fissionable,

fissile, dissoluble, dissolvable; biodegradable 51 *decomposable*.

Verb

(7) *separate,* stand apart, not mix 620 *avoid*; go away 296 *depart*; go different ways, radiate 294 *diverge*; go another way 282 *deviate*; part, part company, cut adrift, cut loose, divorce; split off, get free 667 *escape*; disengage, free oneself, break away; cast off, let go 779 *not retain*; leave, quit 621 *relinquish*; scatter, break up 75 *disperse*; spring apart 280 *recoil*; come apart, fall a., break, disintegrate 51 *decompose*; come undone, unravel, ladder, run; fall off 49 *come unstuck*; split, crack 263 *open*.

(8) *disunite,* dissociate, divorce; part, separate, sunder, sever; uncouple, disconnect, disengage, dislocate; detach 49 *unstick*; remove, deduct 39 *subtract*; strip, peel, pluck 229 *uncover*; undo, unhook, unzip 263 *open*; untie, unpick, disentangle 62 *unravel*; loosen, relax, slacken, unfetter, unloose, loose, free, release 746 *liberate*; expel 300 *eject*; dispel, scatter, break up, disband, demobilize 75 *disperse*; disintegrate, break down 51 *decompose*, 165 *destroy*.

(9) *set apart,* put aside 632 *store*; conserve 666 *preserve*; mark out, distinguish 15 *differentiate*; single out, pick o. 605 *select*; except, exempt, leave out 57 *exclude*; boycott, send to Coventry 620 *avoid*; taboo, black, blacklist 757 *prohibit*; insulate, isolate, cut off 235 *enclose*; zone, screen off 232 *circumscribe*; segregate, sequester, quarantine 883 *seclude*; keep apart, hold a., drive a.; estrange, alienate, set against 881 *make enemies*.

(10) *sunder* (see *disunite*); divide, keep apart, flow between, stand b.; subdivide, fragment, fractionate, segment, sectionalize, reduce, factorize, analyse; dissect 51 *decompose*; halve 92 *bisect*; divide up, split, partition, parcel out 783 *apportion*; dismember, quarter, carve (see *cut*); behead, decapitate, amputate 204 *shorten*; take apart, take to pieces, cannibalize, dismantle, break up; force open, force apart, wedge a. 263 *open*; slit, split, cleave.

(11) *cut,* hew, hack, slash, gash 655 *wound*; prick, stab, knife 263 *pierce*; cut through, cleave, saw, chop; cut open, slit 263 *open*; cut into, make an incision; incise 555 *engrave*; cut deep, carve, slice; cut round, pare, whittle, chisel, chip, trim, bevel; clip, snick, snip; cut short, shave 204 *shorten*; cut down, fell, scythe, mow; cut off, lop, prune, dock; cut up, chop up, quarter, dismember; dice, shred, mince, make mincemeat of; bite, scratch; score 262 *groove*; nick 260 *notch*.

(12) *rend,* tear, scratch, claw; gnaw, fray, make ragged; rip, slash, slit (see *cut*); lacerate, tear to pieces or to shreds 165 *destroy*; pluck to pieces; mince, grind, crunch, scrunch 301 *chew*, 332 *pulverize*.

(13) *break,* fracture, rupture, bust; split, burst, blow up, explode; break in pieces, smash, shatter, splinter 165 *demolish*; fragment, crumble, disintegrate, cave in 51 *decompose*; break up, chip, crack 655 *impair*; bend, buckle 246 *distort*; break in two, snap, cleave, force apart, wedge a. 263 *open*.

Adverb

(14) *separately,* severally, singly, one by one, bit by bit,

piecemeal, in bits, in pieces, in halves, in twain; disjointedly.

(15) *apart,* open, asunder, adrift; to pieces, to bits, to tatters, to shreds; limb from limb.

47
Bond: Connecting medium

Noun
(1) *bond,* chain, shackle, fetter, tie, band, hoop, yoke; nexus, connection, link 9 *relation;* junction, hinge 45 *joint;* connective, copula; hyphen, dash, bracket; tie-beam, girder 218 *beam;* passage 624 *bridge;* span, arch; isthmus, col, ridge; lifeline; umbilical cord.

(2) *cable,* line, guy, hawser, painter, moorings; towline, towrope; lanyard, rope, cord, whipcord, string, twine 208 *fibre;* chain, wire.

(3) *tackling,* tackle, cordage; rig, rigging, shroud, ratline; sheets, guy, stay; halliard, bowline.

(4) *ligature,* ligament, tendon, muscle; tendril, withy, raffia 208 *fibre;* lashing, binding; cord, thread, tape, band, ribbon, bandage; drawstring, thong, lace, bootlace; braid, plait 222 *network;* tie, cravat; knot, hitch, bend; half hitch, clove h.; true-love knot, Gordian k.

(5) *fastening* 45 *joining together;* fastener, snap f., press-stud, popper, zip fastener, zip; drawstring, stitch, basting; button, frog, hook and eye; stud, cuff link; garter, suspender, braces; tiepin, brooch 844 *jewellery;* clip, grip, hairpin; skewer, spit; pin, drawing p., safety p.; peg, nail, tack 256 *sharp point;* staple, clamp, brace 778 *nippers;* nut, bolt,

screw, rivet; buckle, clasp; hasp, hinge 45 *joint;* catch, click, latch, bolt; lock and key 264 *closure;* combination lock, padlock; handcuffs 748 *fetter.*

(6) *coupling,* yoke; grappling iron, hook, claw; anchor, sheet a. 662 *safeguard.*

(7) *girdle,* band, strap 228 *belt;* waistband, girth, cinch, sash, shoulder belt, bandolier, collar, bandeau.

(8) *halter,* collar, noose; tether, lead, leash, reins, ribbons; lasso, lariat 250 *loop;* shackle 748 *fetter.*

(9) *adhesive,* glue, birdlime, gum, fixative, solder; paste, size, cement, putty, mortar; sealing wax; sticker, stamp, adhesive tape, sticky t.; flypaper 542 *trap;* sticking plaster 48 *coherence.*

48
Coherence

Noun
(1) *coherence,* connection, connectedness 71 *continuity;* chain 71 *series;* holding together, cohesion, cohesiveness 778 *retention;* adherence, adhesion, adhesiveness; stickiness 354 *viscidity;* cementing, union, consolidation 45 *union;* congealment 324 *condensation;* 88 *unity;* phalanx, serried ranks; agglomerate, concrete 324 *solid body;* leech, limpet, clinging vine; gum, toffee, plaster 47 *adhesive.*

Adjective
(2) *cohesive,* coherent, adhesive, adherent; clinging, tenacious; sticky, tacky, gummy, gluey 354 *viscid;* compact, well-knit, solid 324 *dense;* monolithic 16 *uniform;* united, indivisible, inseparable, inextricable; closefitting, skintight, clinging, moulding.

Verb

(3) *cohere,* hang together, grow together 50 *combine;* hold, stick close, hold fast; bunch, close the ranks 74 *congregate;* grip, take hold of 778 *retain;* hug, clasp, embrace, twine round; close with, clinch; fit, fit tight, mould the figure; adhere, cling, stick; stick to, cleave to, come off on, rub off on, stick on to; cake, coagulate 324 *be dense.*

(4) *agglutinate,* glue, gum, paste, cement, weld 45 *join;* stick to, affix 38 *add.*

Adverb

(5) *cohesively,* unitedly, solidly, compactly.

49
Noncoherence

Noun

(1) *noncoherence,* incoherence 72 *discontinuity;* scattering 75 *dispersion;* separability, looseness, bagginess; loosening, relaxation 46 *separation;* wateriness 335 *fluidity;* slipperiness 258 *smoothness;* friability 330 *brittleness.*

Adjective

(2) *nonadhesive,* slippery 258 *smooth;* not sticky, dry; detached, semidetached 46 *separate;* loose, free 746 *liberated;* slack, baggy, loose-fitting, flopping, floppy, flapping, flying, streaming; watery, runny 335 *fluid;* pendulous, dangling; unassimilated, aloof 620 *avoiding.*

Verb

(3) *unstick,* peel off; detach, free, unfasten, loosen, loose, slacken 46 *disunite;* shake off, shed, slough 229 *doff.*

(4) *come unstuck,* peel off; melt, thaw, run 337 *liquefy;* totter, slip 309 *tumble;* dangle, flap 217 *hang;* rattle, shake, flap.

50
Combination

Noun

(1) *combination,* composition 45 *joining together;* growing together, coalescence, 45 *union;* fusion, blending 43 *mixture;* merger, amalgamation, assimilation, absorption 299 *reception;* unification, integration, 88 *unity;* incorporation, embodiment; marriage, union, alliance 706 *association;* chord 412 *music;* chorus 24 *agreement;* harmony 710 *concord;* assembly 74 *assemblage;* synopsis, conspectus 592 *compendium;* mosaic, jigsaw, collage.

(2) *compound,* alloy, amalgam, blend, composite 43 *a mixture;* portmanteau word; make-up 56 *composition.*

Adjective

(3) *combined,* united 88 *one;* integrated, centralized; inbred, ingrained, absorbed 5 *intrinsic;* fused 43 *mixed;* blended, harmonized 24 *adjusted;* connected 45 *joined;* congregated 74 *assembled;* coalescent, synchronized, in harmony, in partnership, in league; associated, allied 706 *cooperative.*

Verb

(4) *combine,* put together, fit t.; make up 56 *compose;* intertwine 222 *weave;* harmonize, synchronize 24 *accord;* bind, tie 45 *join;* unite, unify, centralize; incorporate, embody, integrate, absorb, assimilate; merge, amalgamate, pool; blend, fuse 43 *mix;* impregnate, imbue 303 *infuse;* lump together 38 *add;* group, rally 74 *bring together;* band together, associate; federate, partner, team up with 706 *cooperate;* conspire 623 *plot;* coalesce, grow together, combine with.

51
Decomposition

Noun

(1) *decomposition* 46 *disunion*; division, partition 46 *separation*; dissection, dismemberment; analysis, breakdown; factorization, parsing; electrolysis, catalysis; atomization; dissolving, dissolution 337 *liquefaction*; fission; devolution, delegation; collapse, breakup, entropy 165 *destruction*; disintegration, chaos.

(2) *decay* 655 *dilapidation*; erosion, wear and tear 37 *diminution*; corruption 361 *death*; mouldering, rotting, putridness, putrefaction, mortification; gangrene, caries 649 *uncleanness*; rot, rust, mould 659 *blight*; carrion 363 *corpse*.

Adjective

(3) *decomposed,* resolved, reduced, disintegrated 46 *disunited*; corrupted, mouldering 655 *dilapidated*; putrid, gangrenous, rotten, bad, off, high, rancid, sour.

(4) *decomposable,* disposable, biodegradable, recyclable 656 *restored*.

Verb

(5) *decompose,* resolve, reduce, factorize 44 *simplify*; separate, separate out; parse dissect; break down, analyse, unscramble; take to pieces 46 *sunder*; electrolyse, split, fission 46 *disunite*; atomize 165 *demolish*; disband, break up 75 *disperse*; decentralize; disorder, disturb 63 *derange*; dissolve, melt 337 *liquefy*; erode 37 *abate*; rot, rust, moulder, decay, consume, waste away, crumble, perish 655 *deteriorate*; corrupt, putrefy, mortify 649 *be unclean*; disintegrate, go to pieces 165 *be destroyed*.

52
Whole. Principal part

Noun

(1) *whole,* wholeness, integrality 54 *completeness*; integration, integrity 88 *unity*; a whole, integer, entity 88 *unit*; entirety, ensemble, corpus, complex, totality; summation, sum 38 *addition*; panorama, conspectus, inclusiveness 78 *inclusion*; system, world, cosmos 321 *universe*; holism.

(2) *all,* one and all, everybody, everyone 79 *everyman*; all the world, 74 *crowd*; the whole, total, aggregate, ensemble; gross amount, sum, sum total; lock, stock and barrel; hook, line and sinker; unit, set, complete s. 71 *series*; outfit, pack, kit; inventory 87 *list*; the lot, the works.

(3) *chief part,* best part, principal p., major p. 638 *chief thing*; bulk, mass, substance; heap, lump 32 *great quantity*; tissue, staple, stuff; body, torso, trunk; lion's share, biggest slice of the cake; gist, sum and substance; ninety-nine per cent, majority.

Adjective

(4) *whole,* total, universal, holistic; integral, pure 44 *unmixed*; entire, sound 646 *perfect*; full 54 *complete*; single, integrated 88 *one*; in one piece, seamless.

(5) *intact,* untouched, virgin 126 *new*; undivided, undiminished; unbroken, unimpaired; without a scratch 646 *undamaged*; uncut, unabridged, unexpurgated.

(6) *indivisible,* indissoluble; inseparable 45 *joined*; monolithic 16 *uniform*.

(7) *comprehensive,* omnibus, all-embracing, full-length 78 *inclusive*; wholesale, sweeping 32

extensive; widespread, epidemic 79 *general*; international, world-wide 79 *universal*.

Adverb

(8) *wholly*, integrally, body and soul, as a whole; entirely, totally, fully, every inch, one hundred per cent; in toto 54 *completely*.

(9) *on the whole*, by and large, altogether, all in all, all things considered; substantially, essentially, virtually, to all intents and purposes; in effect; as good as; mainly, in the main 32 *greatly*.

(10) *collectively*, one and all, all together; in sum; bodily, en masse, en bloc.

53
Part

Noun

(1) *part*, not the whole, portion; proportion, certain p.; majority 32 *main part*; minority 33 *small quantity*; fraction, half, quarter, percentage; balance, surplus 41 *remainder*; quota, contingent; dividend, share, whack 783 *portion*; item, detail 80 *particulars*; ingredient, constituent, element 58 *component*; faction 708 *party*; leg, lap, round 110 *period*; group, detachment; attachment 40 *adjunct*; excerpt, extract, passage, quotation, text; segment, sector, section; instalment, advance, deposit 804 *payment*; sample, foretaste 83 *example*.

(2) *limb*, member, organ, appendage; hind limb 267 *leg*; forelimb 271 *wing*; flipper, fin; arm, hand 378 *feeler*.

(3) *subdivision*, segment, sector, section, division, compartment; species, family 74 *group*; ward, parish, department 184 *district*; chapter, paragraph,

verse; part, number, issue, instalment, volume 589 *edition*.

(4) *branch*, sub-b., ramification, offshoot 40 *adjunct*; bough, limb, spur, twig, tendril, leaf, leaflet; switch, shoot, scion, sucker, slip, sprig, spray 366 *foliage*.

(5) *piece*, torso, trunk, stump 41 *remainder*; limb, section (see *part*); patch, insertion 40 *adjunct*; length, roll 222 *textile*; strip, swatch; fragment, bit, scrap, shred 33 *small thing*; morsel, bite, crust, crumb 33 *small quantity*; splinter, sliver, chip, snip, snippet; wedge, finger, slice, rasher; cutlet, chop, steak; hunk, chunk, wad, slab, lump mass 195 *bulk*; clod, turf, divot, sod; sherd, shard, potsherd; flake, scale 207 *lamina*; dollop, dose 783 *portion*; bits and pieces, odds and ends 43 *medley*; rubble, debris 641 *rubbish*; rags, tatters; piece of land, parcel, plot, allotment.

Adjective

(6) *fragmentary*, broken, crumbly 330 *brittle*; in bits, in pieces 46 *disunited*; not whole 647 *imperfect*; partial, bitty, scrappy, half-finished 636 *insufficient*; fractional, half, semi-, hemi-; segmental, sectional, divided, in compartments 46 *separate*; shredded, sliced, minced 33 *small*.

Verb

(7) *part*, divide, partition, segment 46 *sunder*; share out 783 *apportion*; fragment 46 *disunite*.

Adverb

(8) *partly*, in part, partially; in a sense.

(9) *piecemeal*, a little at a time; part by part, limb from limb; bit by bit, inch by inch, drop by drop, by degrees; in detail, in lots.

54
Completeness

Noun

(1) *completeness,* nothing lacking, nothing to add, entireness, wholeness 52 *whole;* solidity, solidarity 706 *cooperation;* harmony, balance 710 *concord;* self-sufficiency; entirety, totality 52 *all;* the ideal 646 *perfection;* peak, culmination, crown 213 *summit;* finish 69 *end;* last touch 725 *completion;* fulfilment, consummation 69 *finality.*

(2) *plenitude,* fullness, amplitude, capacity, maximum, one's fill, saturation 635 *sufficiency;* saturation point 863 *satiety;* completion, filling, replenishment, refill; filling up, brimming full house, complement, full load; full measure, bumper; bellyful, skinful, repletion; full size, full length; complement, supplement.

Adjective

(3) *complete,* plenary, full; utter, total 52 *whole;* entire 646 *perfect;* full-blown, full-grown, full-fledged 669 *matured;* self-contained, self-sufficient 635 *sufficient;* fully furnished; comprehensive, full-scale 78 *inclusive;* exhaustive, detailed 570 *diffuse;* absolute, extreme, radical; thorough, thoroughgoing, whole-hogging, sweeping, wholesale 32 *consummate;* unmitigated, downright, plumb, plain 44 *unmixed;* crowning, completing, supplementary, complementary 725 *completive;* unqualified, unconditional.

(4) *full,* replete, filled, replenished, topped up; well-filled, well-lined, bulging, bursting at the seams; brimful, brimming; level with, flush; overflowing, running over, slopping o., swamped, drowned; saturated, oozing, leaking 637 *redundant;* crop-full, gorged, fit to burst, 863 *sated;* chock-full, chock-a-block, not an inch to spare; crammed, stuffed, packed, jam-p., jammed, tight 45 *firm;* laden, heavy-l.; infested, overrun, crawling with, full of; ever-full, inexhaustible.

Verb

(5) *be complete,* be integrated, make a whole; have everything; culminate 725 *climax;* reach an end 69 *end;* want nothing, lack n. 635 *have enough;* become complete, fill out, reach maturity 669 *mature;* be filled, fill, fill up, brim, hold no more, run over, slop o., overflow 637 *superabound.*

(6) *make complete,* complete, complement, integrate 45 *join;* make whole 656 *restore;* build up, make up, piece together 56 *compose;* eke out, supplement, supply, fill a gap 38 *add;* make good 31 *compensate;* do thoroughly, leave nothing to add 725 *carry through;* put the finishing touch, round off 69 *terminate.*

(7) *fill,* fill up, top up, swamp, drown, overwhelm; replenish 633 *provide;* satisfy 635 *suffice;* fill to capacity, cram, pack, stuff, line, pack in, pile in, squeeze in, ram in, jam in 303 *insert;* load, charge, lade, freight, ram down 187 *stow;* fill space, occupy, reach to 183 *extend;* spread over, sprawl o., overrun 189 *pervade;* fit tight, be chock-a-block; fill in, put in, write in, enter 38 *add.*

Adverb

(8) *completely,* fully, wholly, totally, entirely, utterly 32 *greatly;* all told, in all 52 *on the whole;* in all respects, in every way; quite, altogether; outright, downright, thoroughly; to the utmost, to the end, to the

full; out and out, through and through, heart and soul; hook, line and sinker; root and branch; every whit, every inch; full out, in full; as ... as can be, to capacity.

(9) *throughout,* from first to last, from top to bottom; all round, from end to end 183 *widely*; fore and aft; from top to toe, high and low; to the bitter end.

(4) *unfinished,* in progress, in hand, going on; in embryo 68 *beginning*; in preparation, on the stocks.

Verb
(5) *be incomplete,* miss, lack, need 627 *require,* 307 *fall short*; be wanting 190 *be absent*; default, leave undone 458 *neglect*; omit, miss out 57 *exclude*; break off, interrupt 72 *discontinue*; leave hanging 726 *not complete.*

55
Incompleteness

Noun
(1) *incompleteness,* immaturity 68 *debut*; sketch, outline, first draft, rough d. 623 *plan*; half measures, sketchiness 458 *negligence*; deficiency, falling short 307 *shortfall*; break, gap, missing link 72 *discontinuity*; half, quarter; instalment 53 *part.*

(2) *deficit,* part wanting, screw loose, omission 647 *defect*; shortfall 772 *loss*; want, lack, need 627 *requirement.*

Adjective
(3) *incomplete,* inadequate, unsatisfactory, defective 307 *deficient*; short of 636 *insufficient*; wanting, lacking, needing, requiring 627 *demanding*; garbled, mutilated; without, -less; one-armed, one-legged, one-eyed 163 *crippled*; truncated, shortened 204 *short*; blemished, flawed 647 *imperfect*; half, semi-, partial 53 *fragmentary*; half-finished, neglected 726 *uncompleted*; not ready 670 *immature*; raw, crude, rough-hewn 244 *amorphous*; sketchy, scrappy, bitty, superficial, meagre 4 *insubstantial*; perfunctory, half-done 458 *neglected*; omitted, missing, lost 190 *absent*; interrupted 72 *discontinuous*; in default, in arrears.

56
Composition

Noun
(1) *composition,* constitution, make-up; make, formation, construction, build-up, build 331 *structure*; organization 62 *arrangement*; nature, character 5 *temperament*; embodiment, incorporation 78 *inclusion*; combination 43 *mixture*; artistic composition, work of art 412 *music,* 551 *art,* 553 *painting,* 554 *sculpture*; 586 *writing,* 593 *poetry,* 594 *drama*; choreography 594 *ballet*; composing, setting-up 587 *print*; compilation 74 *assemblage*; construction 164 *production*; pattern, design 12 *correlation.*

Adjective
(2) *composing,* constituting, making; composed of, made of; containing, having 78 *inclusive.*

Verb
(3) *constitute,* compose, form, make; make up, build up to; belong to 58 *be one of.*

(4) *contain,* subsume, include, consist of 78 *comprise*; hold, have, take in 299 *admit*; comprehend, embrace, embody 235 *enclose*; involve, imply 5 *be intrinsic.*

(5) *compose,* compound 43 *mix,* 50 *combine*; organize, set in order 62 *arrange*; synthesize,

put together, make up 45 *join*; compile, assemble 74 *bring together*; compose, set up 587 *print*; draft, draw up 586 *write*; orchestrate, score 413 *compose music*; draw 553 *paint*; construct, build, make, fabricate 164 *produce*; pattern, design 222 *weave*.

57
Exclusion

Noun
(1) *exclusion*, exclusiveness, monopoly, closed shop; an exception, special case; exemption, exception, dispensation; leaving out, omission, deliberate o. 607 *rejection*; no entry, no admission; closed door, lockout; picket line; embargo, ban, bar, taboo 757 *prohibition*; ostracism, boycott 620 *avoidance*; segregation, colour bar, apartheid 883 *seclusion*; intolerance 481 *prejudice*; expulsion, eviction; dismissal, suspension, excommunication; deportation, exile, expatriation 188 *displacement*; wall, barricade 235 *barrier*; tariff 809 *tax*; outer darkness 223 *exteriority*.

Adjective
(2) *excluding*, exclusive, exclusionary, restrictive 708 *sectional*; preventive, interdictory 757 *prohibiting*; preclusive, preemptive.

(3) *excluded*, barred, etc. vb.; extra-, not included, not admitted; peripheral, half in, half out; included out, counted o.; not allowed, banned 757 *prohibited*; disbarred, struck off 550 *obliterated*; shut out, outcast 607 *rejected*; inadmissible, beyond the pale.

Verb
(4) *be excluded*, not belong, stay outside; go into exile 190 *be absent*.

(5) *exclude*, preclude 470 *make impossible*; preempt, forestall 64 *come before*; keep out, warn off ; blackball, deny entry, shut out, debar 607 *reject*; bar, ban, black, disallow 757 *prohibit*; cold-shoulder 883 *make unwelcome*; boycott, send to Coventry 620 *avoid*; not include, leave out, count o.; exempt, excuse, except, make an exception, treat as a special case; omit, miss out, pass over, disregard 458 *neglect*; lay aside, put a., relegate 46 *set apart*; disbar, strike off, remove, disqualify 963 *punish*; rule out, draw the line; wall off, curtain off, segregate 235 *enclose*; excommunicate, thrust out, dismiss, deport, extradite, exile, banish, outlaw, expatriate; weed out, sort out 44 *eliminate*; eradicate, uproot 300 *eject*; expurgate, censor 648 *purify*.

Adverb
(6) *exclusive of*, with the exception of; excepting, barring, bar, not counting, except, save; let alone, apart from.

58
Component

Noun
(1) *component*, component part, integral p., element, item; piece, bit, segment; link, stitch; constituent, part and parcel 53 *part*; factor 178 *influence*; feature 40 *adjunct*; one of, member; staff, crew, complement 686 *personnel*; ingredient 43 *tincture*; works, insides 224 *interiority*; nuts and bolts 630 *machine*; spare part 40 *extra*; components, set, outfit 88 *unit*.

Adjective
(2) *component*, constituent 56 *composing*; entering into, belonging, proper, inherent 5 *intrinsic*; built-in 45 *joined*; admitted, made a member, part of,

one of, on the staff; involved, implicated, mixed up in 43 *mixed*.

Verb
(3) *be one of,* make part of, inhere, belong 5 *be intrinsic*; enter into 56 *constitute*; be implicated in 775 *participate*; merge in 43 *be mixed*; belong to, appertain to 9 *be related*.

59
Extraneousness

Noun
(1) *extraneousness,* foreignness 223 *exteriority*; foreign parts 199 *farness*; foreign body, accretion 38 *addition*; alien element 84 *nonconformity*.

(2) *foreigner,* alien, stranger 268 *traveller*; continental, Southerner, Northerner, Easterner, Westerner; Martian, extraterrestrial, little green men; pommie, limey, Yank, Yankee, Aussie, Kiwi; paleface; colonial, Creole 191 *settler*; resident alien, expatriate; immigrant, migrant, migrant worker, guest w., emigrant, émigré, exile; refugee 268 *wanderer*.

(3) *intruder,* interloper, cuckoo in the nest; trespasser, squatter; uninvited guest, gatecrasher; stowaway; outsider, not one of us 126 *upstart*; new arrival, new face, newcomer 297 *incomer*; invader 712 *attacker*.

Adjective
(4) *extraneous,* from outside 223 *exterior*, 6 *extrinsic*; not indigenous, imported, foreign-made; foreign, alien, unearthly, extraterrestrial, strange, outlandish, barbarian; overseas, ultramarine, transatlantic 199 *distant*; continental, exotic, hothouse; wandering 267 *travelling*; unintegrated 46

separate; immigrant 297 *incoming*; intrusive, interloping, invading 712 *attacking*; un-British, un-American 15 *different*; unnatural, supernatural, not of this world 983 *magical,* inadmissible

Adverb
(5) *abroad,* in foreign parts, beyond seas, overseas; from outer space.

60
Order

Noun
(1) *order,* state of order, orderliness, tidiness 648 *cleanness*; harmony, proportion 245 *symmetry*; good order, system, method, methodology; fixed order, pattern, rule 16 *uniformity*; custom, routine 610 *habit*; rite 988 *ritual*; strict order, discipline 739 *obedience*; due order, hierarchy, gradation 73 *serial place*; even tenor, progression, series 71 *continuity*; logical order, alphabetical o. 65 *sequence*; organization, putting in order, disposition, array 62 *arrangement*.

Adjective
(2) *orderly,* harmonious 710 *concordant*; well-behaved, decorous 848 *well-bred*; well-drilled, disciplined 739 *obedient*; under control, well-regulated 81 *regular*; ordered, classified, schematic 62 *arranged*; methodical, systematic, businesslike; strict, invariable 16 *uniform*; routine, steady 610 *habitual*; correct, shipshape, neat, tidy, spick and span 648 *clean*; well-kept, uncluttered 62 *arranged*; clear, lucid 516 *intelligible*.

Verb
(3) *order,* reduce to order, dispose 62 *arrange*; schematize,

systematize, organize 62 *regularize*; harmonize, synchronize, regulate 24 *adjust*; standardize 16 *make uniform*; keep order, call to order, control 733 *rule*.

(4) *be in order,* harmonize 24 *accord*; fall in, range oneself, line up; take one's place, station oneself 187 *place oneself*; keep one's place; follow routine 610 *be wont*.

Adverb
(5) *in order,* strictly, just so, by the book, as directed 81 *to rule*; in turn, seriatim; step by step, methodically, systematically; all correct, OK.

61
Disorder

Noun
(1) *disorder,* random order, muddle, no plan, no method, chaos (**see** *confusion*); mayhem 734 *anarchy*; irregularity, anomalousness, anomaly 17 *nonuniformity*; disunion, disharmony 411 *discord*; disorderliness, unruliness, no discipline 738 *disobedience*; untidiness 649 *uncleanness*; discomposure, disarray 63 *derangement*; upheaval, convulsion 165 *havoc*.

(2) *confusion* (**see** *disorder*); welter, jumble, shambles, hugger-mugger, mix-up, medley, embroilment, imbroglio 43 *mixture*; wilderness, jungle; chaos; swarm, seething mass, scramble 74 *crowd*; muddle, litter, clutter 641 *rubbish*; farrago, mess, mishmash, hash, hotchpotch, lucky dip 43 *medley*; Babel, bedlam (**see** *turmoil*).

(3) *complexity,* complication, snarl-up 700 *difficulty*; imbroglio, embroilment; intricacy 251 *convolution*; maze, labyrinth, warren; web, spider's w. 222 *network*; coil, tangle, twist,

snarl, knot 47 *ligature*; clockwork, machinery; puzzle pickle 700 *predicament*.

(4) *turmoil,* turbulence, tumult, frenzy, ferment, storm, convulsion 176 *violence*; pandemonium, inferno; hullabaloo, hubbub, racket, row, riot, uproar 400 *loudness*; affray, fracas, brawl, mêlée 716 *fight*; hurlyburly, to-do, rumpus, ruction, pother, trouble, disturbance 318 *commotion*; whirlwind, tornado, hurricane 352 *gale*; shambles, madhouse, Bedlam; Saturnalia, Bacchanalia; shindig, roughhouse, rough and tumble, free for all 709 *quarrel*; breach of the peace.

(5) *slut,* sloven, slattern, litterlout 649 *dirty person*; ragamuffin 801 *poor person*.

(6) *anarchist,* nihilist 738 *rioter*.

Adjective
(7) *orderless,* in disorder, in disarray, disordered, disorganized, jumbled, shuffled 63 *disarranged*; unclassified, ungraded; out of order, not working 641 *useless*; out of place, misplaced 188 *displaced*; askew, awry, topsy-turvy, upside down 221 *inverted*; straggling, dispersed 75 *unassembled*; random, uncoordinated, incoherent, rambling; irregular, anomalous; unsystematic, unmethodical; desultory, aimless, casual; confused, muddled, chaotic, in a mess, messy, haywire; untidy, unkempt, windswept, tousled, dishevelled; slatternly, slovenly, sluttish, bedraggled, messy 649 *dirty*; sloppy, slipshod, slack, careless 456 *light-minded*.

(8) *complex,* intricate, involved, elaborate, sophisticated, complicated, over-c., 251 *coiled*, 517

puzzling; mazy, winding, inextricable 251 *labyrinthine*; entangled, balled up, snarled, knotted 45 *tied*.

(9) *disorderly*, undisciplined, unruly; out of step, out of line; rumbustious, tumultuous 738 *riotous*; frantic 503 *frenzied*; orgiastic, Saturnalian, 949 *drunken*; rough, tempestuous, turbulent 176 *violent*; lawless, anarchic 954 *lawbreaking*; wild, harum-scarum, tomboyish, boisterous.

Verb
(10) *be disordered*, fall into disarray, scatter 75 *disperse*; riot, get out of hand 738 *disobey*; disorder 63 *derange*.

(11) *rampage*, storm 176 *be violent*; rush, mob, riot 738 *revolt*; romp 837 *amuse oneself*; fete 876 *celebrate*.

Adverb
(12) *confusedly*, in confusion, in disorder, anyhow, all a.; pellmell; in turmoil, in a ferment; on the rampage; at cross purposes; at sixes and sevens; topsy-turvy 221 *inversely*; helter-skelter, higgledy-piggledy.

62
Arrangement:
Reduction to order

Noun
(1) *arrangement*, ordering, disposal, disposition, marshalling, arraying 187 *location*; collocation, grouping 74 *assemblage*; division, distribution 783 *apportionment*; method, organization, reorganization, rationalization, streamlining 654 *improvement*; administration 689 *management*; planning 669 *preparation*; taxonomy 561 *nomenclature*; analysis 51 *decomposition*; codification, digestion; grading, gradation 71

series; continuation, serialization 71 *continuity*; formulation, construction 56 *composition*; array, system 60 *order*; layout, pattern, architecture 331 *structure*; collection, assortment 74 *accumulation*; register, file 548 *record*; inventory, catalogue, table 87 *list*; code, digest, synopsis 592 *compendium*; scheme 623 *plan*; class, group 77 *classification*.

(2) *sorting*, grading, seeding; reference system, cross-reference 12 *correlation*; file, folder, filing system, card index, pigeonhole, slot. 263 *porosity*.

Adjective
(3) *arranged*, disposed, marshalled, ordered, etc. vb.; schematic, tabulated, tabular; methodical, systematic, precise, definite, cut and dried; analysed, classified, sorted; unravelled, disentangled, straightened out; regulated 60 *orderly*; seeded, graded, streamed, banded.

Verb
(4) *arrange*, set, dispose, set up, set out, lay out; formulate, form, put into shape; orchestrate, score 56 *compose*; range, rank, align, line up, position 187 *place*; marshal, array; put in order, grade, size; group, space; collocate, thread together 45 *connect*; settle, fix, determine, define; allot, assign 783 *apportion*; rearrange, tidy up, tidy.

(5) *regularize*, bring order into, straighten out, put to rights 654 *rectify*, 24 *adjust*; regulate, coordinate, phase; organize, systematize, schematize; standardize, centralize 16 *make uniform*.

(6) *class*, classify, subsume, group; specify 561 *name*; process, analyse; divide, dissect 51 *decompose*; rate, rank, grade,

evaluate 480 *estimate*; sort, sift, seed; sift out 44 *eliminate*; label 547 *mark*; file, pigeonhole; index, cross-reference, tabulate, catalogue, inventory 87 *list*; register 548 *record*; codify, program.

(7) *unravel,* untangle, disentangle, disembroil; comb out, iron, press, iron out 258 *smooth*; debug 654 *make better*; unscramble; straighten out, clean up, 648 *clean*; explain 520 *interpret.*

63
Derangement

Noun

(1) *derangement,* disarrangement; shuffling 151 *interchange*; displacement, disturbance 272 *transference*; obstruction 702 *hindrance*; dislocation, disruption 46 *separation*; upsetting 221 *inversion*; convulsion 176 *violence*; state of disorder 61 *disorder.*

Adjective

(2) *disarranged,* deranged, disordered 61 *orderless*; demented 503 *insane*; sabotaged 702 *hindered.*

Verb

(3) *derange,* disarrange, disorder, disturb 265 *move*; meddle, interfere 702 *hinder*; mislay 188 *misplace*; disorganize, muddle, scramble, confound, confuse, convulse, make havoc, throw into confusion; tamper with, spoil, damage, sabotage 655 *impair*; strain, bend, twist 176 *force*; unhinge, dislocate, sprain, rick 188 *displace*; dislodge, derail, unbalance, upset, overturn 221 *invert,* 149 *revolutionize*; shake, jiggle 318 *agitate*; trouble, perturb, unsettle, discompose, disconcert, ruffle, rattle, flurry, fluster 456 *distract*; interrupt, break in on 138

mistime; misdirect, disorientate, throw off one's bearings 495 *mislead*; unhinge, drive mad 503 *make mad,* 891 *enrage.*

(4) *jumble,* shuffle, get out of order 151 *interchange*; mix up 43 *mix*; toss, tumble 318 *agitate*; ruffle, dishevel, tousle, fluff up; rumple, crumple 261 *fold*; muddle, mess up, litter, clutter; scatter, fling about 75 *disperse*; play havoc with 702 *hinder.*

(5) *bedevil,* confuse, confound, complicate, perplex, involve, ravel, ball up, entangle, tangle, embroil; turn topsy-turvy, turn upside down 221 *invert*; send haywire.

64
Precedence

Noun

(1) *precedence,* going before, coming b., queue-jumping 283 *preceding*; front position 237 *front*; higher position, pride of place 34 *superiority*; preference 605 *choice*; preeminence 638 *importance*; captaincy, leadership 733 *authority*; the lead, leading, guiding, pioneering; precedent 66 *precursor*; past history 125 *past time.*

Adjective

(2) *preceding,* antecedent; foregoing, outgoing; anterior, former, previous 119 *prior*; abovementioned; aforesaid, said; leading, pioneering, avantgarde; forewarning, premonitory; anticipatory preliminary, prefatory, preparatory, introductory; prefixed, prepositional; first come, first served.

Verb

(3) *come before,* be first 283 *precede*; go first, run ahead, jump the queue; lead, guide, conduct, show the way 547 *indicate*; pioneer, clear the

way, blaze the trail 484 *discover*; head, take the lead 237 *be in front*; have precedence, take p., outrank 34 *be superior*; set the fashion 178 *influence*; open, lead off, kick off 68 *begin*; preamble, prelude, preface, introduce, usher in, ring in; get ahead 119 *be before*; antedate 125 *be past*.

(4) *put in front,* lead with, head w.; advance, send ahead, station before 187 *place*; prefix 38 *add*; front, face, tip 237 *be in front*; 512 *suppose*, preface, prelude 68 *initiate*.

Adverb
(5) *before,* in advance 283 *ahead*; preparatory to, as a preliminary; earlier 119 *before* (in time); ante, above.

65
Sequence

Noun
(1) *sequence,* coming after; descent, line, lineage 170 *posterity*; going after 284 *following*; inference 475 *reasoning*; succession, rota, series 71 *continuity*; alternation, serialization; continuation, prolongation 146 *continuance*; subordination, second place, 35 *inferiority*; last place 238 *rear*; consequence 67 *sequel*; conclusion 69 *end*.

Adjective
(2) *sequential,* following, succeeding, successional; next, incoming, ensuing; later, latter, 120 *subsequent*; another, second, third 38 *additional*; successive, consecutive 71 *continuous*; alternating, alternate, every other; postpositive 238 *back*; consequent, resulting 157 *caused*.

Verb
(3) *come after,* have one's turn, come next, ensue 284 *follow*; succeed, inherit, supplant 150

substitute; alternate 141 *be periodic*; relieve, take over.

(4) *place after,* suffix, append; subscribe, subjoin 38 *add*.

Adverb
(5) *after,* following; afterwards 120 *subsequently*, 238 *rearward*; in relays, in waves, successively; in the end 69 *finally*; next, later, infra, below.

66
Precursor

Noun
(1) *precursor,* predecessor, ancestor, forebear 169 *parentage*; early man, Adam and Eve 371 *humankind*; the ancients 125 *antiquity*; eldest, firstborn; discoverer, inventor 461 *experimenter*; pioneer, pathfinder, explorer 268 *traveller*; guide, pilot 690 *leader*; scout, skirmisher; vanguard, avant-garde, innovator, trail-blazer; trend-setter; forerunner, outrider; herald, harbinger 529 *messenger*; dawn, false d.; anticipation, prefiguration, foretaste, prognostic, preview, premonition, forewarning 664 *warning*, 511 *omen*; trailer; precedent 83 *example*; antecedent, prefix, preposition 40 *adjunct*; eve, day before 119 *priority*.

(2) *prelude,* preliminary, preamble, preface, prologue, foreword, avant-propos; opening, introduction, overture 68 *beginning*; frontispiece 237 *front*; groundwork, foundation 218 *basis*, 669 *preparation*; aperitif, appetizer; premises 512 *supposition*.

Adjective
(3) *precursory,* preliminary, exploratory 669 *preparatory*; introductory, prefatory 68 *beginning*; inaugural, foundational; precedent 64 *preceding*.

67
Sequel

Noun

(1) *sequel,* consequence, result, aftermath, by-product, spin-off 157 *effect;* conclusion 69 *end;* aftereffect, hangover, morning after; aftertaste; afterglow, fallout; inheritance, legacy 777 *dower;* afterthought, second thoughts; epilogue, postscript; peroration, envoi, last words; follow-up 725 *completion;* continuation, sequel; tailpiece, coda 238 *rear;* codicil, supplement 40 *adjunct;* suffix, affix, inflection 564 *grammar;* afters, dessert; afterlife, hereafter 124 *future state.*

(2) *retinue,* following 284 *follower;* queue 71 *procession;* suite, train 71 *procession;* tail, tailback, wake 89 *concomitant;* trailer 274 *vehicle.*

(3) *successor,* descendant, the unborn 170 *posterity;* heir, inheritor 776 *beneficiary;* replacement, supplanter 150 *substitute;* fresh blood, new broom 126 *upstart.*

68
Beginning

Noun

(1) *beginning,* birth, rise (see *origin*); infancy babyhood 130 *youth;* dawn 126 *newness;* primitiveness 127 *oldness;* commencement, outbreak, onset 295 *arrival;* emergence 445 *appearance;* incipience, inception, institution, constitution, foundation, establishment 156 *causation;* origination, invention 484 *discovery;* creation 164 *production;* initiative, innovation 21 *originality;* introduction 66 *prelude;* first letter, initial; heading, headline title page, prelims; van, forefront 237 *front;* growing pains; first blush, first glance, first sight, first impression; first lap, first round; early stages, early days; primer, outline; rudiments, elements, first principles, alphabet, ABC; debutante, starter 538 *beginner;* precedent 66 *precursor;* preliminaries 669 *preparation.*

(2) *debut,* coming out, presentation, initiation, launching; inauguration, opening, unveiling; first night, premiere; first appearance, first offence; first step, first move, move, gambit; maiden voyage, maiden speech; baptism of fire.

(3) *start,* outset; starting point, point of departure; zero hour, D-day; send-off, setting out, embarkation, countdown 296 *departure;* starting pistol, kick-off; house-warming, honeymoon; fresh start, new beginning, resumption, reopening 148 *reversion;* new departure, precedent; standing start, flying s.; starter, self-s.

(4) *origin,* origination, derivation, conception, genesis, birth, nativity; provenance, ancestry 169 *parentage;* fount, rise 156 *source;* nest, womb 156 *seedbed;* bud, germ, egg, seed; primeval soup 358 *organism;* first beginnings, cradle 192 *home.*

(5) *entrance* 297 *way in;* inlet 345 *gulf;* mouth, opening 263 *orifice;* threshold 624 *access;* porch 194 *lobby;* gateway 263 *doorway;* frontier, border 236 *limit;* outskirts, skirts, suburbs 230 *surroundings;* foothills, pass, corridor 289 *approach,* 305 *passage.*

Adjective

(6) *beginning,* initiatory, initiative, introductory 66 *precursory;* inaugural, foundational;

elemental, rudimental 156 *fundamental*; aboriginal, primeval, primordial 127 *primal*; rudimentary, elementary 670 *immature*; embryonic, germinal, nascent, budding, incipient; raw, begun, in preparation 726 *uncompleted*; early, infant 126 *new*; just begun, newly opened, launched.

(7) *first,* initial, primary, maiden, starting, natal; pioneering 21 *original*; unprecedented 126 *new*; foremost, front 237 *frontal*; leading, principal, head, chief 34 *supreme*.

Verb
(8) *begin,* make a beginning, commence; set in, open, dawn, break out, burst forth, spring up, crop up; arise, emerge, appear; rise, spring from; sprout, germinate; come into existence 360 *be born*; make one's debut, come out; start, enter upon, embark on 296 *start out*; fire away, kick off, strike up; start work, clock in; limber up 669 *prepare*; run in; resume, begin again 148 *revert*; start afresh, resume, reopen; set to, set about, set to work, get cracking; attack, wade into, tackle, face, address oneself to 672 *undertake.*

(9) *initiate,* found, launch; originate, invent, think of 484 *discover*; call into being 167 *generate*; usher in, ring in, introduce; start, start up, prompt, promote, set going, set in motion, get under way; raise, set on foot; run in; lead, lead off, lead the way, take the lead, pioneer, open up, break new ground 64 *come before*; broach, open, raise the subject; break the ice; take the initiative, take the first step, take the plunge, cross the Rubicon, burn one's boats; trigger off, touch off, spark off, set off.

(10) *auspicate,* inaugurate, open; institute, install, induct 751 *commission*; found, set up, establish 156 *cause*; baptize, christen, launch 561 *name*; initiate, blood, flesh; lay the foundations 669 *prepare.*

Adverb
(11) *initially,* originally, at the beginning, in the b.; in the bud, in embryo, in its infancy; from the beginnings, from its birth; first, firstly, in the first place; primarily, first of all, first and foremost; as a start, for starters; from scratch.

69
End

Noun
(1) *end,* close, conclusion, consummation 725 *completion*; payoff, result, end r. 157 *effect*; expiration, lapse; termination, closure, guillotine; finishing stroke, death blow, quietus, coup de grace; knockout, finisher, clincher; catastrophe, denouement; ending, finish, finale, curtain;. term, period, stop, halt 145 *cessation*; final stage 129 *evening*; peroration, last words, swan song, envoi, coda 67 *sequel*; last stage, last round, last lap, home stretch; last breath, last gasp 361 *decease*. (See *finality*).

(2) *extremity,* final point, extreme; pole, antipodes; farthest point, world's end 199 *farness*; fringe, verge, brink 234 *edge*; frontier, boundary 236 *limit*; terminal point, end of the line, terminus, terminal 295 *goal*, 617 *objective*; foot, bottom nadir 214 *base*; tip, cusp, point 256 *sharp point*; vertex, peak, head, top 213 *summit*; tail, tail end 67 *sequel*; end, butt end, gable e. 238 *rear*; tag, epilogue, postscript, appendix 40 *adjunct*.

(3) *finality,* bitter end; time, time up, deadline; conclusion 54 *completeness*; breakup, wind-up 145 *cessation*; dissolution 165 *destruction*; eschatology, last things, doom, destiny 596 *fate*; last trump, crack of doom, Day of Judgment, end of time, 124 *future state*.

Adjective
(4) *ending,* final, terminal, last, ultimate, supreme, closing; extreme, polar; definitive, conclusive, crowning, completing 725 *completive*; coterminous; ended, at an end; settled, terminated, finalized, decided, set at rest; finished, over, over and done with; off, all off, cancelled; penultimate, last but one; hindmost, rear 238 *back*; caudal.

Verb
(5) *end,* come to an end, expire, run out 111 *elapse*; close, draw to a close, finish, conclude, be all over; become extinct, die out 2 *pass away*; fade away, peter out, tail off; stop 145 *cease*.

(6) *terminate,* conclude, close, determine, decide, settle; apply the closure, bring to an end, put a stop to, put paid to; discontinue, drop, pursue no further; finish, achieve, consummate, get through, play out, act o., see it o. 725 *carry through*; shut up shop, wind up, close down, switch off, stop 145 *halt*.

Adverb
(7) *finally,* in conclusion; at last, at long last; once for all, for good, never again, nevermore; in the end, in the long run.

70
Middle

Noun
(1) *middle,* midst, midpoint; mean 30 *average*; medium, middle term; thick, thick of things; heart, kernel, hub 225 *centre*; nucleus 224 *interiority*; midweek; half tide; midstream 625 *middle way*; equator, the Line 28 *equalization*; midriff, midrib 231 *partition*; distance, middle, equidistance, halfway house.

Adjective
(2) *middle,* medial, mean, mezzo, mid 30 *median*; mediate, midmost 225 *central*; intermediate 231 *interjacent*; equidistant; mediterranean, equatorial.

Adverb
(3) *midway,* in the middle, in the thick; at the midpoint, halfway; midships.

71
Continuity: Uninterrupted sequence

Noun
(1) *continuity,* monotony 16 *uniformity*; continuation, overlap; one thing after another, succession; line, lineage, descent, dynasty; serialization 65 *sequence*; continuous time, continuum 115 *perpetuity*; assembly line 146 *continuance*; recurrence, cycle 106 *repetition*, 141 *periodicity*; course, run, career, flow, trend 285 *progression*; circuit, round 314 *circuition*; daily round 610 *habit*; trail, wake 67 *sequel*; concatenation, chain, food c.; chain reaction, knock-on effect, domino theory; circle, vicious c. 250 *circularity*.

(2) *series,* gradation 27 *degree*; succession, run, rally, break; progression, arithmetic p., geometric p.; ascending order 36 *increase*; descending order 37 *decrease*; pedigree, family tree 169 *genealogy*; chain, line, string, thread; line ahead, line abreast; rank, file, echelon;

array 62 *arrangement*; row, range, colonnade; ladder, steps, stairs 308 *ascent*; range, tier, storey 207 *layer*; set, suite, suit (of cards); assortment, spectrum, rainbow; gamut, scale 410 *musical note*; stepping stones; hierarchy, pyramid.

(3) *procession* 267 *marching*; crocodile, queue, traffic jam; tail, train, suite 67 *retinue*; file, single f., Indian f.; cortege; cavalcade.

Adjective

(4) *continuous,* continued, run-on 45 *joined*; consecutive, running, successive 65 *sequential*; serial, serialized; progressive, gradual 179 *tending*; overlapping, unbroken, smooth, uninterrupted, circular; continuing, ongoing; continual, incessant, ceaseless, unremitting, nonstop 115 *perpetual*; rhythmic 110 *periodic*; repetitive, recurrent 106 *repeated*; linear, lineal, rectilinear 249 *straight.*

Verb

(5) *run on,* continue; line up, fall in, queue up, join the queue; succeed, overlap 65 *come after*; file, defile; circle 626 *circuit.*

(6) *continue,* run on, extend, prolong 113 *spin out*, 203 *lengthen*; serialize, thread, string together 45 *connect*; grade 27 *graduate*; keep on 600 *persevere.*

Adverb

(7) *continuously,* serially, seriatim; successively, in succession, in turn; one after another; at a stretch, together, running; without stopping, on the trot; around the clock, night and day; cumulatively, progressively; gradually, step by step 27 *by degrees*; in file, in single f., in line ahead, nose to tail.

72
Discontinuity:
Interrupted sequence

Noun

(1) *discontinuity,* intermittence; discontinuation 145 *cessation*; interval, hiatus, pause, time lag 145 *lull*; disconnection, randomness 61 *disorder*; unevenness 17 *nonuniformity*; jerkiness dotted line, broken ranks; disruption, interruption, intervention, interposition; parenthesis 231 *interjection*; break, fracture, flaw, fault 46 *separation*; split, crack 201 *gap*; missing link, lost connection; illogicality, non sequitur; alternation 141 *periodicity*; irregularity 142 *fitfulness.*

Adjective

(2) *discontinuous,* discontinued; interrupted, broken, stopping; disconnected 46 *disunited*; discrete 46 *separate*; patchy, bitty 17 *nonuniform*; irregular, intermittent 142 *fitful*; alternating, stop-go, on-off 141 *periodical*; spasmodic, jerky, uneven; incoherent, 477 *illogical*; parenthetic, episodic, not belonging 59 *extraneous.*

Verb

(3) *be discontinuous,* halt, rest 145 *pause*; alternate.

(4) *discontinue,* suspend, break off, desist; interrupt, intervene, break, break in upon, interfere; interpose, interject, punctuate 231 *put between*; disconnect 46 *disunite.*

Adverb

(5) *discontinuously,* at intervals, occasionally, infrequently, irregularly, now and then, here and there, passim.

73
Term: Serial position

Noun

(1) *serial place,* term, order, remove 27 *degree*; rank, ranking, grade, gradation; station, place, position, slot; status, standing, footing; point, mark, pitch, level, storey; step, tread, round, rung; stage, milestone; climax 213 *summit*; bottom rung, nadir 214 *base.*

Verb

(2) *grade,* rank, rate, place; stagger, space out 201 *space,* 27 *graduate.*

(3) *have rank,* hold r., hold a place, occupy a position 186 *be situated*; fall into place, drop into p., find a niche.

74
Assemblage

Noun

(1) *assemblage,* bringing together, collection 50 *combination,* 62 *arrangement*; collocation, juxtaposition 45 *joining together*; compilation, anthology 56 *composition*; gathering, reaping, harvest 771 *acquisition*; harvest home 632 *storage*; concentration, centering, focusing 76 *focus*; mobilization, muster, levy, call-up; review, parade, march, demonstration, rally; whipping in, roundup, lineup; herding, shepherding; caucus 708 *party*; collective noun.

(2) *assembly,* getting together, forgathering, congregation, concourse, concurrence 293 *convergence*; gathering, meeting, mass m., meet; coven; conventicle; business meeting, board m.; convention, convocation, synod; conclave 692 *council*; eisteddfod, festival 876 *celebration*; reunion, get-together,

company, party 882 *social gathering*; circle, encounter group 658 *therapy*; discussion group, symposium 584 *conference.*

(3) *group,* constellation, cluster, galaxy; pride (lions), troop, bevy, swarm, flock, herd; drove, team; pack, kennel; stable, string; brood, hatch, litter; gaggle, flight, skein, covey; shoal, school; unit, brigade 722 *formation*; batch, lot, clutch; brace, pair 90 *duality*; set, class, genus, species, sub-s. 77 *sort*; breed, tribe 11 *family*; brotherhood, sisterhood, fellowship, guild, union 706 *association*; club 708 *society*; sphere, quarter, circle 524 *informant*; charmed circle, coterie 708 *party*; social group 869 *commonalty*; age group, year g. 538 *class*; hand (at cards), set.

(4) *band,* company, troupe; brass band, pop group 413 *orchestra*; team, string, fifteen, eleven, eight; knot, bunch; set, coterie, clique, ring; gang, squad, party, work p., fatigue p.; ship's company, crew, complement, staff 686 *personnel*; following 67 *retinue*; squadron, troop, platoon; unit, regiment, corps 722 *formation*; squad, posse; force, body, host 104 *multitude*; brothers and sisters 880 *friendship*; committee, commission, panel.

(5) *crowd,* throng 104 *multitude*; huddle, cluster, swarm, colony; small crowd, knot, bunch; the masses, mass, mob 869 *rabble*; sea of faces, full house, houseful 54 *completeness*; congestion, press, squash, squeeze, jam, scrum, crush; rush hour; flood 32 *great quantity*; volley, shower, hail; populousness 36 *increase*; herd instinct, crowd psychology, mass hysteria.

(6) *bunch,* assortment, lot 43 *medley*; clump, tuft, wisp,

handful; bag, bundle, packet, wad; batch, pack, package, parcel; bale, roll, bolt; load, pack 193 *contents*; tussock, shock; faggot, sheaf, truss, swathe, fan; bouquet, nosegay, posy, spray; skein, hank.

(7) *accumulation,* heaping up, aggregation; concentration, massing; pileup; mass, pile, pyramid 209 *high structure*; heap, drift, snowdrift; snowball 36 *increment*; debris, detritus, dump 41 *leavings*; cumulus, storm cloud; store, storage 633 *provision*; magazine, battery 723 *arsenal*; set, lot 71 *series*; mixed bag 43 *medley*; range, selection, assortment; museum, library 632 *collection*; menagerie 369 *zoo*; miscellany, compilation 56 *composition*.

(8) *accumulator,* squirrel, miser, hoarder 816 *niggard*; connoisseur 492 *collector*; reaper, harvester, gleaner 370 *farmer*; whip, whipper-in; shepherd.

Adjective
(9) *assembled,* met, well-met, ill-m.; convened, summoned, called-up; collectivized; crowded, packed, serried, high-density 324 *dense*; populated, over-p., overcrowded 54 *full*; humming with, populous, teeming, swarming, thick as flies 104 *multitudinous*; in a crowd, seething, milling; in formation, ranked, in order 62 *arranged*.

Verb
(10) *congregate,* meet, forgather, rendezvous; assemble, reassemble, rejoin; associate, come together, get t., join t., flock t., make a crowd, gather, gather round, collect, rally, roll up, troop up, swell the ranks; resort to, make for 293 *converge*; band together, gang up; mass, concentrate, mobilize; conglomerate, huddle, cluster, bunch, crowd; throng, swarm,

seethe, mill around; surge, stream, flood 36 *grow*.

(11) *bring together,* assemble, together draw 45 *join*; draw, pack them in 291 *attract*; gather, collect, rally, muster, call up, mobilize; concentrate, consolidate; collocate, lump together, group, unite; compile 56 *compose*; focus, centre; convene, convoke, summon, hold a meeting; herd, shepherd, whip in, call in, round up, corral 235 *enclose*; mass, aggregate, accumulate, conglomerate, heap, pile, amass; catch, rake in, net 771 *acquire*; scrape together, garner 632 *store*; truss, bundle, parcel, package; bunch, bind 45 *tie*; pack, cram 54 *fill*; build up, pile up, stack 310 *elevate*.

Adverb
(12) *together,* unitedly, as one; collectively, all together, en masse, in a body.

75
Nonassembly.
Dispersion

Noun
(1) *dispersion,* scattering, breakup 46 *separation*; branching out, fanning o., spread, scatter, radiation 294 *divergence*; sprawl, suburbia; distribution 783 *apportionment*; delegation, decentralization; evaporation, dissipation 634 *waste*; circulation, diffusion; dissemination, broadcasting; spraying, sprinkling 341 *moistening*; dispersal, disbandment, demobilization sea drift, driftwood; waifs and strays, diaspora.

Adjective
(2) *unassembled,* dispersed, etc. vb.; scattered, dotted about, strung out, sparse 140 *infrequent*; broadcast, diffused; widespread, far-flung 183 *spacious*; spread, separated, in

open order 46 *separate*; sprawling, decentralized; branching, radiating, centrifugal 294 *divergent*; adrift, astray; straggling 61 *orderless*.

Verb

(3) *be dispersed*, disperse, scatter, spread, spread out, fan o.; spread fast, flood; radiate, branch 294 *diverge*; break up, break ranks, fall out 46 *separate*; break away 49 *come unstuck*; drift away, drift apart 267 *wander*; straggle, trail 282 *stray*; spread over, sprawl over, cover, litter; explode, blow up, burst; evaporate, melt, disintegrate, dissolve; decay 51 *decompose*.

(4) *disperse*, scatter, spread out, splay 294 *diverge*; separate 46 *sunder*; thin out, string o.; circulate, disseminate, diffuse, broadcast, sow, strew, bestrew, spread; dissipate, dispel 51 *decompose*; dispense, deal, deal out 783 *apportion*; decentralize; break up, disband, demobilize, dismiss 46 *disunite*; draft, draft off, detach 272 *send*; sprinkle, spray, spatter 341 *moisten*; disorder 63 *derange*; rout 727 *defeat*.

Adverb

(5) *sporadically*, here and there, in twos and threes; sparsely, passim.

76
Focus: Place of meeting

Noun

(1) *focus*, focal point, junction, crossroads 293 *convergence*; switchboard, exchange, nerve centre; hub, nub, core, heart, middle 225 *centre*; civic centre, community c., village hall, village green; campus, quad; shopping centre, market place; resort, retreat, haunt, stamping ground; club, pub, local 192 *meeting place*; headquarters, depot; rallying point, standard; venue, rendezvous; fireside 192 *home*; honey pot, centre of attraction 291 *attraction*; Mecca, promised land 295 *goal*, 617 *objective*.

Verb

(2) *focus*, centre on 293 *converge*; centralize, concentrate, focus upon; point to.

77
Class

Noun

(1) *classification*, categorization 62 *arrangement*; taxonomy; diagnosis, specification, designation; category, class, bracket; set, subset, head, heading, section, subsection 53 *subdivision*; division, branch, department, faculty; pocket, pigeonhole 194 *compartment*; tier, rank, caste 27 *degree*; province, domain, sphere, range; sex, gender; blood group, age g., stream 74 *group*; coterie 74 *band*; persuasion, school of thought, denomination 978 *sect*.

(2) *sort*, order, type, version, variety, kind, species; manner, genre, style; nature, quality, grade, calibre 5 *character*; mark, brand 547 *label*; ilk, stripe, kidney, feather, colour; stamp, mould, shape, frame, make 243 *form*; assortment, kit, set, suit, lot 71 *series*.

(3) *breed*, strain, blood, family, kin, tribe, clan, caste, line 11 *race*, 169 *genealogy*; kingdom, phylum, class, order, genus, species, subspecies genotype, monotype.

Adjective

(4) *generic*, typical; sexual; masculine, feminine, neuter.

(5) *classificatory*, taxonomic; sectional, denominational.

78
Inclusion

Noun

(1) *inclusion,* comprising; incorporation, embodiment, assimilation, encapsulation; comprehension, admission, integration 299 *reception*; admissibility, eligibility; membership 775 *participation*; inclusiveness, comprehensiveness, coverage; no exception, no omission, nothing omitted; set, complement, package 52 *whole*; package deal 765 *compact*; constitution 56 *composition*; capacity, volume, measure 183 *space*, 465 *measurement*; accommodation 183 *room*.

Adjective

(2) *inclusive,* including, comprising, counting, containing, having; holding, consisting of 56 *composing*; incorporating; all-inclusive, all-in; accommodating; overall, all-embracing 52 *comprehensive*; wholesale, blanket, sweeping 32 *extensive*; total, global, worldwide, universal; encyclopedic, expansive, broad-based 79 *general.*

(3) *included,* admitted, counted; admissible, eligible; integrated, constituent, making up 56 *composing*; inherent 5 *intrinsic*; belonging, pertinent 9 *relative*; classified with 18 *similar*; entered, recorded 87 *listed*; merged 45 *joined*; inner 224 *interior.*

Verb

(4) *be included,* be contained in, be comprised in, make one of 58 *be one of*; enlist, enrol oneself, join 708 *join a party*; come under, fall u.; merge in 43 *be mixed*; appertain to, pertain 9 *be related*; come in, enter into 297 *enter*; constitute 56 *compose*; inhere, belong 5 *be intrinsic.*

(5) *comprise,* include, involve, imply, consist of, hold, have, count, boast 56 *contain*; take, measure 28 *be equal*; receive, take in 299 *admit*; accommodate, find room for; comprehend, encapsulate, cover; embody, incorporate; encompass, embrace, envelop 235 *enclose*; have everything, 54 *be complete.*

(6) *number with,* count w., reckon among, enumerate with; subsume, place under, classify as; put in 62 *class*; not omit, take into account.

Adverb

(7) *including,* inclusively; et cetera.

79
Generality

Noun

(1) *generality,* universality, catholicity, ecumenicalism 976 *orthodoxy*; generalization, universal; macrocosm 321 *universe*; world-view; panorama, synopsis, 52 *whole*; inclusiveness 78 *inclusion*; currency, prevalence, custom 610 *habit,* 848 *fashion*; pervasiveness, ubiquity 189 *presence*; epidemic 651 *disease*; looseness, imprecision 495 *inexactness*; open letter, circular 528 *publicity*; commonness, ruck, run, general r., 30 *average*; ordinariness 732 *averageness*; impersonality.

(2) *everyman,* everywoman; man *or* woman in the street 869 *commoner*; everybody, every one, each one, one and all, every man Jack, all hands, all and sundry 52 *all*; Tom, Dick and Harry; all sorts, whosoever, anyone, what have you, what you will, whatsoever.

Adjective

(3) *general,* generic, typical, standard; encyclopedic, broad-

based; collective, all-embracing, pan-, blanket 52 *comprehensive*; broad, sweeping across the board; panoramic, synoptic; current, prevalent 189 *ubiquitous*; usual, normal, customary 610 *habitual*; vague, loose, indefinite 495 *inexact*; common, ordinary, average 30 *median*; commonplace 83 *typical*; popular, mass 869 *plebeian*; for everybody.

(4) *universal,* catholic, ecumenical; national, international, cosmopolitan, global, worldwide, nationwide; widespread 32 *extensive*; pervasive, penetrating, besetting, prevalent, rife, epidemic, pandemic 189 *ubiquitous*; every, each, any, all 52 *whole*.

Verb

(5) *be general,* cover all cases 78 *comprise*; prevail, obtain, be the rule, have currency 610 *be wont*; penetrate 189 *pervade*.

(6) *generalize,* broaden, widen, universalize, spread, broadcast, diffuse 75 *disperse*.

Adverb

(7) *generally,* mainly 52 *wholly*; to a man, without exception; always; by and large, generally speaking 30 *on an average*.

80
Speciality

Noun

(1) *speciality,* specific quality, personality, uniqueness; originality, individuality, particularity; personality, make-up 5 *character*; characteristic, one's middle name; idiosyncrasy, eccentricity, peculiarity, singularity; trademark, mannerism, quirk, foible; trait, mark, feature, attribute; sine qua non 89 *accompaniment*; distinction, distinctive feature 15 *difference*; idiom, jargon 560 *dialect*;

exception, special case 84 *nonconformity*; specialization, speciality 694 *skill*.

(2) *particulars,* details, minutiae, items, counts; special points, specification; circumstances.

(3) *particularism,* chosen race, chosen few, the elect; exclusiveness, caste; chauvinism, nationalism, individualism, egoism.

(4) *self,* ego, id, identity, personality 320 *subjectivity*; psyche, soul 447 *spirit*; I, myself, number one; we, us, ourselves; yourself, himself, herself, itself, themselves; real self, inner s.; outward s.; character, individual, being 371 *person*.

Adjective

(5) *special,* specific, respective, particular; peculiar, singular, unique 15 *different*; individual, idiosyncratic, idiomatic, original 21 *inimitable*; native, proper, personal, private; appropriate 24 *apt*; typical, diagnostic 5 *characteristic*; distinctive, uncommon, marked, noteworthy 84 *unusual*.

(6) *definite,* definitive, defining; distinct, concrete, express, explicit, clear-cut, cut and dried; certain, exact, precise 494 *accurate*; itemized, detailed, bespoke, made to order, made to measure, personalized.

(7) *private,* intimate, esoteric, personal, exclusive; patented; off the record, secret 523 *latent*.

Verb

(8) *specify,* be specific, enumerate, quantify 86 *number*; particularize, itemize, detail 87 *list*; cite, mention, name names 561 *name*; enter into detail, spell out 570 *be diffuse*; define, determine 236 *limit*; pinpoint, locate,

designate, point out 547 *indicate*; explain 520 *interpret*; signify, denote 514 *mean*; individualize, personalize 15 *differentiate*; specialize.

Adverb

(9) *specially,* especially, in particular; personally, specifically; ad hoc, to order; with respect to.

(10) *severally,* each, apiece, one by one; respectively, in turn, seriatim; in detail, bit by bit.

(11) *namely, viz,.* videlicet, to wit, i.e., e.g.

81
Rule

Noun

(1) *rule,* norm, formula, canon, code; maxim, principle 693 *precept*; law of nature; firm principle, hard and fast rule; statute, by-law 953 *law*; regulation, order, standing o., party line; guide, precedent 23 *prototype*; standard, keynote 83 *example.*

(2) *regularity,* consistency 16 *uniformity*; natural order, established o. 60 *order*; normality, normalcy; form, routine, drill 610 *habit*; fixed ways, rut, groove; method, system 62 *arrangement*; convention 83 *conformity.*

Adjective

(3) *regular,* constant, steady 141 *periodical*; even 258 *smooth*; circular, square 245 *symmetrical*; standardized 16 *uniform*; regulated, according to rule, methodical, systematic 60 *orderly*; regulative, normative; normal 83 *typical*; customary 610 *usual*; conforming, conventional 83 *conformable.*

Adverb

(4) *to rule,* by the book, by the clock; regularly.

82
Multiformity

Noun

(1) *multiformity,* multiplicity, heterogeneity, variety, diversity 17 *nonuniformity*; polymorphism 101 *plurality*; split personality 503 *psychopathy*; metamorphism, metamorphosis; variability 152 *changeableness,* 437 *variegation.*

Adjective

(2) *multiform,* multifarious, polymorphous, polymorphic; multiple, multiplex, manifold, many-headed, many-sided, hydra-headed; protean, metamorphic; variform, heterogeneous, diverse 17 *nonuniform*, motley, mosaic, kaleidoscopic 43 *mixed*; many-coloured 437 *variegated*; divers, sundry; all manner of, 15 *different*; variable, changeable 152 *changeful*; whimsical 604 *capricious.*

83
Conformity

Noun

(1) *conformity,* conformation, accommodation, adjustment 24 *agreement, adaptation*; pliancy, malleability 327 *softness*; acquiescence 721 *submission*; assimilation, naturalization bourgeois ethic, conventionalism, traditionalism, orthodoxy; formalism strictness 735 *severity*; convention, etiquette, form 848 *fashion,* 610 *practice*; emulation 20 *imitation*; ordinariness 79 *generality.*

(2) *example,* exemplar, type, pattern, model 23 *prototype*; stock example, locus classicus; case, case in point, instance, illustration, object lesson; sample, specimen, trailer; precedent 66 *precursor.*

(3) *conformist,* conventionalist, traditionalist; formalist, pedant; copycat, yes-man 20 *imitator,* 925 *flatterer*; follower, loyalist 976 *the orthodox.*

Adjective

(4) *conformable,* adaptable, adjustable, consistent with; malleable, pliant, flexible; agreeable, complaisant, accommodating 24 *agreeing*; conforming, following, faithful, loyal 768 *observant*; conventional, traditional, orthodox; slavish, servile 20 *imitative,* 925 *flattering*; adjusted, adapted 610 *habituated*; assimilated, naturalized 78 *included.*

(5) *typical,* normal, natural, everyday, ordinary, common, common or garden 79 *general*; average 30 *median*; representative, true to type; commonplace, prosaic; conventional 610 *usual*; heterosexual, straight; stock, standard; normative, exemplary, illustrative.

(6) *regulated,* according to rule, regular; shipshape, copybook 60 *orderly*; correct, sound, proper; canonical 976 *orthodox*; precise, scrupulous, meticulous 875 *formal*; rigid, strict, unbending, uncompromising 735 *severe.*

Verb

(7) *conform,* correspond, conform to, tally with; adapt oneself, accommodate o., adjust o. 24 *accord*; fit in, know one's place; pass, pass muster; bend, yield, fall into line, toe the l. 721 *submit*; comply with 768 *observe*; echo 106 *repeat*; keep in step, follow the crowd, do as others do 848 *be in fashion*; emulate, follow suit 20 *imitate*; have no will of one's own.

(8) *make conform,* assimilate, naturalize 610 *habituate*; systematize 62 *regularize*; normalize, standardize, conventionalize 16 *make uniform*; shape, press 243 *form*; stamp, imprint 547 *mark*; train, lead 689 *direct*; bend, twist, force 740 *compel*; square, trim 24 *adjust.*

(9) *exemplify,* illustrate, cite, quote, instance; give an instance.

Adjective

(10) *conformably,* to rule; by the book; in conformity, in line with, in accordance, in keeping; according to; according to plan; as usual, of course, for form's sake; for example, for instance.

84
Nonconformity

Noun

(1) *nonconformity,* inconsistency 25 *disagreement*; contrast 14 *contrariety*; nonconformism, unorthodoxy 977 *heterodoxy*; dissidence 489 *dissent*; deviationism 744 *independence*; anomalousness, eccentricity, irregularity 282 *deviation*; androgyny; bisexuality, homosexuality transvestism; informality, unconventionality; freakishness, oddity; rarity 140 *infrequency*; infringement, infraction 954 *illegality*; wonder, miracle 864 *prodigy*; anomaly, exception 57 *exclusion*; exemption, special case 80 *speciality*; individuality, idiosyncrasy, quirk, kink, peculiarity, singularity, mannerism; uniqueness 21 *originality.*

(2) *abnormality,* aberration 282 *deviation*; mutation 15 *variant*; abortion, monstrous birth, monstrosity, monster; necrophilia, sadism, masochism.

(3) *nonconformist,* dissident, deviationist, dissenter, maverick 489 *dissentient*; heretic, 978 *sectarian*; blackleg, scab; Bohemian, hippie, weirdie, dropout, rebel, punk 738 *revolter*; outsider, outlaw, criminal 904 *offender*; pariah 883 *outcast*; hermit, loner 883 *solitary*; gypsy, nomad, tramp 268 *wanderer*; odd one out, joker, ugly duckling 25 *misfit*; deviant, odd type, albino, sport, freak, oddity, original, character, card, caution, odd customer, oddball, weirdo 504 *crank*; queer fish 851 *laughingstock*; curiosity, rarity; hermaphrodite; invert, transexual, transvestite; homosexual, lesbian, gay; queer; pervert, sadist, masochist.

(4) *rara avis,* mythical beast, unicorn, phoenix, griffin, sphinx, centaur, Minotaur; dragon, basilisk, salamander, hydra; sea serpent, leviathan, Loch Ness monster; mermaid, siren, gorgon, 970 *mythical being*, 513 *fantasy*.

Adjective

(5) *unconformable,* antipathetic 14 *contrary*; obstinate, recalcitrant 711 *defiant*; crotchety, prickly, awkward, eccentric, whimsical 604 *capricious*, 893 *sullen*; arbitrary, a law unto oneself 744 *independent*; freakish, outlandish; original, unique 80 *special*; solitary, standoffish 883 *unsociable*; nonconformist, dissident 489 *dissenting*; unorthodox, heretical 977 *heterodox*; offbeat, Bohemian, unconventional; informal, irregular, against the rules, not done 924 *disapproved*; lawless, criminal 954 *illegal*; aberrant, astray, off the rails 282 *deviating*; out of place, incongruous 188 *displaced*; out of step, out of line 25 *disagreeing*; alien, exotic 59 *extraneous*; hard to place, nameless 491

unknown; stray, nomadic, wandering 267 *travelling*; amphibious, ambiguous 518 *equivocal*.

(6) *unusual,* unwonted, unfamiliar, out of the ordinary 491 *unknown*; newfangled 126 *new*; exotic, extraordinary, wayout; phenomenal, unparalleled, singular, unique 80 *special*, 140 *infrequent*; rare, choice, recherche 644 *excellent*; strange, bizarre, curious, odd, queer, rum, funny, peculiar, fantastic; grotesque 849 *ridiculous*; noteworthy, remarkable, surprising, astonishing, miraculous 864 *wonderful*; mysterious, inexplicable, unaccountable 523 *occult*; incredible 472 *improbable*; monstrous, unnatural, preternatural, supernatural; outsize 32 *enormous*; outre 546 *exaggerated*; shocking 924 *disapproved*.

(7) *abnormal,* unnatural, supernatural, untypical, uncharacteristic, freakish; atypical, exceptional; anomalous, anomalistic; kinky, deviant; homosexual, lesbian, gay, bent, queer; bisexual, androgynous; mongrel, hybrid 43 *mixed*; irregular 17 *nonuniform*; substandard, subnormal; deformed 246 *distorted*.

Verb

(8) *be unconformable,* unconventional etc. adj.; not fit in; infringe usage, infringe custom; break a law, break with custom; drop out, freak o., do one's own thing 744 *be free*; be ahead of one's time.

85
Number

Noun

(1) *number,* any n., real number, imaginary n.; natural n., cardinal n., ordinal n.; round n., complex n.; prime number, odd n., even n., whole n., integer;

numeral, cipher, digit, figure, character; numerals, Arabic n., Roman n., decimal system, binary s.; quantity, unknown q., X, symbol, constant; mapping; operator, sign; function, variable; vector, matrix, surd; expression, quadratics; formula, series.

(2) *numerical element,* multiplier, coefficient, multiple, dividend, divisor, quotient, factor, fraction, proper f., improper f.; mixed number; numerator, denominator; decimal, recurring d.; common factor, common denominator; parameter; power, root, square r., cube r.; exponent, index, logarithm, antilogarithm; differential, derivative, integral, determinant.

(3) *ratio,* proportion; progression, arithmetic p., geometric p., sine, tangent, cosine, cotangent; percentage, per cent, percentile.

(4) *numerical result,* answer, product, equation; sum, total 52 *whole*; difference, residual 41 *remainder*; score, tally 38 *addition.*

Adjective
(5) *numerical,* numeral, digital; arithmetical; cardinal, ordinal; round, whole; even, odd; prime; positive, negative, surd, radical; divisible, multiple; reciprocal, complementary; fractional, decimal; commensurable, proportional; exponential, logarithmic, differential, .integral; algebraic, rational, irrational.

86
Numeration

Noun
(1) *numeration,* numbering, enumeration, census, counting, figuring, reckoning, dead r.; sum, tally, score, runs,

points; count, recount, countdown; figure-work, summation, calculation, computation 465 *measurement*; pagination; algorithm, decimal system; accountancy 808 *accounts*; counting heads, poll, head-count, capitation; numeracy.

(2) *numerical operation,* figurework, notation; addition, subtraction, multiplication, division, proportion, rule of three, practice, equations, analysis, reduction, approximation, extrapolation, interpolation; integration, permutation, combination.

(3) *mathematics,* pure m., applied m., arithmetic, algebra; quadratic equations, set theory, modern maths; differential calculus; geometry, trigonometry; topology; graphs, logarithms; algorithm; systems analysis 623 *policy*; axiomatics 475 *reasoning.*

(4) *statistics,* figures, tables, averages; mode, mean 30 *average*; significance, deviation, standard error; skew; correlation, rank c. test; poll 605 *vote*; census, capitation; roll call, muster 87 *list*; demography, birth rate, death r.; vital statistics; price index, cost of living; bar graph, scatter diagram, pie chart, flow c. 623 *plan.*

(5) *data processing,* electronic d.p., computing, computation; cybernetics 630 *mechanics*; hardware, software; program, computer p.; input, output, throughput, feedback; storage, retrieval; batch processing, time-sharing; machine code, BASIC; card punch, keypunch, keyboard; data, bit, byte; punched cards, magnetic tape, floppy disk; processor, word processor; data bank, memory; visual display unit, VDU; hard copy, printout.

(6) *counting instrument,* abacus, ready reckoner, multiplication table; yardstick 465 *gauge*; slide rule; tallies, counters; Comptometer (tdmk), calculator, pocket c.; cash register; computer, digital c., analogue c; microcomputer 196 *microelectronics.*

(7) *enumerator,* census-taker; calculator, counter, teller, pollster; mathematician, wrangler; arithmetician, geometrician, algebraist; programmer, computer p.; systems analyst 623 *planner*; statistician, actuary, bookkeeper 808 *accountant*; surveyor.

Adjective
(8) *numerable,* numberable, countable; calculable, computable, measurable, mensurable 465 *metrical*; commensurable, commensurate 28 *equal*; proportionate 9 *relative.*

(9) *statistical,* digital, ciphered, numbered, figured out; mathematical, arithmetical, geometrical, algebraic, trigonometric; in ratio, in proportion, percentile.

(10) *computerized,* automatic, on-line, off-line; programmable, processable; analogue, digital, binary,

Verb
(11) *number,* cast, count, tell; score, keep the s., keep a count, notch up; tell off, tick off, count down; foliate, paginate; enumerate, poll, count heads; take a poll, take a census; muster, call over, take roll call; take stock, inventory 87 *list*; check, audit, balance, keep accounts 808 *account*; amount to, add up to, total, tot up to, come to.

(12) *do sums,* count up, carry over, tot up 38 *add*; take away 39 *subtract*; multiply 36 *augment*; divide 46 *sunder*; cast up,

square, cube, extract roots; integrate, differentiate; figure, cipher; work out, reduce; compute, calculate, reckon, estimate 465 *measure.*

(13) *computerize,* automate 160 *empower*; program, process; debug; compute 173 *operate.*

87
List

Noun
(1) *list,* enumeration, items; list of items, inventory, stock list; chart, table, catalogue, listing; portfolio; statement, tabular s., schedule, manifest, bill of lading; checklist; invoice; price list, tariff, bill, account, itemized a. 809 *price*; registry, Domesday Book; file, register 548 *record*; ledger, books 808 *account book*; table of contents, index; bill of fare, menu; programme, prospectus, synopsis, syllabus 592 *compendium*; roll, electoral r., voting list; muster roll, payroll; statistical list, census 86 *numeration*; book list, bibliography 589 *reading matter*; list of names, rota, roster, panel; waiting list, short l.; pedigree 169 *genealogy*; scroll, roll of honour; blacklist, sick list; calendar, engagement book 505 *reminder*; questionnaire; alphabet 60 *order*; repertory, repertoire.

(2) *word list,* vocabulary, glossary, lexicon, thesaurus 559 *dictionary.*

(3) *directory,* gazetteer, atlas; almanac, calendar, timetable 117 *chronology*; ABC 524 *guidebook*; Army List, Navy L., Who's Who 589 *reference book.*

Adjective
(4) *listed,* entered, catalogued, tabulated, indexed.

Verb
(5) *list,* make a l., enumerate; itemize, inventory, catalogue;

index, tabulate; file, docket, schedule, enter, book 548 *register*; enlist, enrol, inscribe; score, keep the s. 86 *number*.

time; once, once only, just this once; never again, only, solely, simply; alone, on one's own, by oneself, per se; in the singular.

88
Unity

Noun

(1) *unity,* absoluteness 44 *simpleness*; integrality, integration, wholeness 52 *whole*; uniqueness, individuality 80 *speciality*; singleness 895 *celibacy*; isolation 46 *separation*; union, solidarity 48 *coherence*, 706 *association*; unification 50 *combination*.

(2) *unit,* integer, one, ace, item, piece; individual, atom, entity 371 *person*; single piece, monolith; singleton, nonce word; none else, no other; isolated instance, only exception; solo, monologue; single person 895 *celibate*; hermit 883 *solitary*; set, outfit, package 78 *inclusion*.

Adjective

(3) *one,* not plural, singular, sole, single, solitary; unique, only, lone, one and only; one and the same 13 *identical*; only-begotten; once only, one-off; a, an, a certain 562 *anonymous*; individual 80 *special*; unilateral, mono-; monolithic 16 *uniform*; rolled into one 45 *joined*; indivisible, indissoluble.

(4) *alone,* lonely, orphaned, deserted 883 *friendless*; lonesome, solitary, lone 883 *unsociable*; isolable, isolated 46 *disunited*; insular 199 *distant*; single-handed, on one's own; unaccompanied, by oneself, on one's tod; celibate.

Verb

(5) *be one,* stand alone; unite 50 *combine*; isolate 46 *set apart*.

Adverb

(6) *singly,* one by one, one at a

89
Accompaniment

Noun

(1) *accompaniment,* concomitance 5 *intrinsicality*; companionship, togetherness 880 *friendship*; partnership 706 *association*; coexistence; 181 *concurrence*; coincidence, simultaneity; attendance, society, company.

(2) *concomitant,* attribute, sine qua non 5 *essential part*; complement 54 *completeness*; accessory, appendage, fixture 40 *adjunct*; by-product, corollary; symptom 547 *indication*; coincidence 159 *chance*; context, circumstance 7 *state*; accompaniment, obbligato; accompanist 413 *musician*; entourage, court 742 *retainer*; attendant, suite 67 *retinue*; convoy, escort, chaperon, bodyguard 660 *protector*; inseparable, shadow 284 *follower*; consort 894 *spouse*; companion 880 *friend*; mate, co-worker, partner, associate 707 *colleague*; accomplice 707 *collaborator*; twin, fellow 18 *analogue*; satellite, parasite, hanger-on 742 *dependant*.

Adjective

(3) *accompanying,* with, concomitant, attendant; always with, inseparable, built-in 45 *joined*; partnering, associated, coupled, paired; hand-in-glove 706 *cooperative*; obbligato 410 *harmonious*; belonging 78 *included*, 58 *component*; parallel, collateral; coincidental contemporary, simultaneous.

Verb

(4) *accompany,* be found with, coexist; cohabit, live with;

keep company with, consort w., string along with; attend, wait on 284 *follow*; bear one company, squire, chaperon 660 *safeguard*; convoy, escort, conduct, usher; track, dog, shadow 619 *pursue*; associate with, partner 706 *cooperate*; gang up with 880 *befriend*; coincide 181 *concur*; imply 5 *be intrinsic*; be inseparable, go hand in hand with, follow that 157 *depend*; belong, go with, go together 9 *be related*.

Adverb
(5) *with,* herewith 38 *in addition*; together with, along w., in company w.; in convoy, hand in hand, arm in arm, side by side; cheek by jowl; jointly, collectively.

90
Duality

Noun
(1) *duality,* double life, dual personality, Jekyll and Hyde 14 *polarity*; two, deuce, duo, twain, couple, Darby and Joan; brace, pair; doublets, twins, Gemini, Siamese twins, identical t. 18 *analogue*; yoke, span, double file; couplet; twosome, two-hander; duel; duet; tandem, two-seater; biped; bivalve.

Adjective
(2) *dual,* binary, binomial; bilateral, bipartisan; bicameral; twin 91 *double*; paired, conjugate, two abreast, two by two; in twos, both; tête à tête; amphibious; ambidextrous 91 *double*; bifocal; two-faced; di-, bi-.

Verb
(3) *pair,* couple, match, bracket, yoke; mate, pair off.

91
Duplication

Noun
(1) *duplication,* doubleness; doubling 261 *fold*; reduplication, repeat, echo 106 *repetition*; copy 22 *duplicate*; double exposure; living image 18 *analogue*.

Adjective
(2) *double,* doubled, twice; duplex, twofold, two-sided, two-headed, two-edged; amphibious, ambidextrous; dual-purpose, two-way; of double meaning 518 *equivocal*; bisexual, hermaphrodite; twin, duplicate, second; 90 *dual*.

Verb
(3) *double,* multiply by two; redouble, square; encore, echo, second 106 *repeat*; duplicate, reduplicate 20 *copy*.

Adverb
(4) *twice,* two times, once more; over again 106 *again*; as much again, twofold; secondly, again; twice as much, twice over; doubly.

92
Bisection

Noun
(1) *bisection,* bipartition, dichotomy; dividing by two, half, moiety 53 *part*; hemisphere 252 *sphere*.

(2) *bifurcation,* forking, branching 294 *divergence*; swallowtail, fork, prong 222 *cross*.

(3) *dividing line,* diameter, diagonal, equator; parting, seam; date line; party wall 231 *partition*.

Adjective
(4) *bisected,* halved; bipartite; bifurcate, forked; semi-, demi-,

hemi-; split, cloven, cleft 46
disunited.

Verb
(5) *bisect,* divide, split, cleave 46
sunder; cut in two, share, go
halves, go fifty-fifty 783 *appor-*
tion; halve, divide by two.

(6) *bifurcate,* separate, fork;
branch off 294 *diverge.*

93
Triality

Noun
(1) *triality,* trinity ·94
triplication.

(2) *three,* triad, Fates, Furies,
Graces; Faith, Hope and Charity; triumvirate; leash; troika;
triplet, trio, trimester, trefoil,
triangle, trident, tripod, trivet,
three-wheeler, tricycle; three-
decker, three-hander; triptych,
trilogy; third power, cube.

Adjective
(3) *three,* triadic, three in one,
tripartite; tricolour; three-sided, three-cornered, triangular,
trilateral;   three-pointed,
three-pronged; three-monthly,
trimestrial, quarterly; tri-.

Adverb
(4) *in threes,* three by three.

94
Triplication

Noun
(1) *triplication,* hat trick,
tercentenary.

Adjective
(2) *treble,* triple triplex, triplicate,   threefold,   three-ply;
third, tertiary; trilateral.

Verb
(3) *treble,* triple, triplicate, cube.

Adverb
(4) *trebly,* triply, threefold;
three times, thrice; thirdly.

95
Trisection

Noun
(1) *trisection,* tripartition;
third, third part.

Adjective
(2) *trifid,* trisected; tripartite.

Verb
(3) *trisect,* divide by three.

96
Quaternity

Noun
(1) *quaternity,* four, square, quadrilateral, quadrangle, quad;
quarter; swastika 222 *cross*;
quatrain; quartet, foursome;
four-in-hand;   quadruplet,
quad; quadruped.

Adjective
(2) *four,* quadratic; square, quadrilateral, foursquare; quadri-,
tetra-.

97
Quadruplication

Noun
(1) *quadruplication,* squaring;
quartercentenary.

Adjective
(2) *fourfold,* quadruple, quadruplicate, squared.

Verb
(3) *quadruple,* quadruplicate,
multiply by four; square.

Adverb
(4) *four times;* fourthly.

98
Quadrisection

Noun
(1) *quadrisection,* quartering,
fourth, fourth part; quarterly;·
quart, quarter; quarto.

Verb
(2) *quadrisect,* quarter, divide by four.

99
Five and over

Noun
(1) *five,* quintuplet, quin; quintet; pentagon, pentagram, pentameter; Pentateuch; pentathlon; five senses.

(2) *over five,* six, half-a-dozen, sextet, hexagon, hexagram, hexameter; seven, week, sabbatical year, septet, Seven Deadly Sins; eight, octave, octet, octagon; nine, three times three, nine Muses; ten, tenner, decade, decagon, Decalogue, Ten Commandments; eleven, twelve, dozen; thirteen, baker's dozen, long d.; double figures, teens.

(3) *twenty and over,* twenty, a score; four and twenty, two dozen; forty, two score; fifty, half a hundred, jubilee; sixty, three score, sexagenarian; seventy, septuagenarian; eighty, four score, octogenarian; ninety, nonagenarian.

(4) *hundred,* century, centenary; hundredweight; centurion; centenarian; centipede; hundred per cent; treble figures.

(5) *over one hundred,* a gross; thousand, grand; millennium; ten thousand, myriad; hundred thousand, million; ten million, crore; thousand million, billion; million million; trillion, quadrillion, trillion; millionaire.

Adjective
(6) *fifth and over,* five, fifth etc. n., fivefold; tenfold; decimal, duodecimal; in one's teens;

centennial, centenary, centenarian, secular, hundredth; bicentenary, thousandth, millionth, billionth.

100
Multisection

Noun
(1) *multisection,* decimation.

Adjective
(2) *multifid,* multipartite; decimal, tenth, tithe; duodecimal, hundredth.

Verb
(3) *multisect,* decimate, decimalize.

101
Plurality

Noun
(1) *plurality,* the plural; multiplicity 104 *multitude*; polygon, polyhedron 82 *multiformity*; polytheism; a number, some, two or three; a few, several; majority 104 *greater number*.

Adjective
(2) *plural,* in the p., not singular; composite, multiple; polymorphic, multiform; many-sided; multilateral, multi-, poly-; more than one, some, certain; upwards of, more 104 *many*.

Adverb
(3) *et cetera.*

102
Fraction: Less than one

Noun
(1) *fraction,* decimal f., fractional part, fragment 53 *part*; shred 33 *small quantity.*

Adjective
(2) *fractional,* partial 53 *fragmentary,* 33 *small.*

103
Zero

Noun
(1) *zero,* nil, nothing, next to nothing, naught, nought, nix; no score, love, duck; blank, cipher; nullity, nothingness 2 *nonexistence*; none, nobody 190 *absence*; zero level, nadir.

Adjective
(2) *not one,* not any, zero; invisible, null.

104
Multitude

Noun
(1) *multitude,* numerousness, multiplicity; large number, millions 99 *over one hundred*; a quantity, lots, loads, heaps 32 *great quantity*; numbers, scores, myriads, millions, trillions; a sea of, a sight of; forest, thicket; host, array 722 *army*; throng, mob, high turnout 74 *crowd*; tribe, horde.

(2) *certain quantity,* peck, bushel, pinch; galaxy, bevy, cloud, flock, shoal, swarm 74 *group.* nest,

(3) *greater number,* weight of numbers, majority, great m., mass, bulk, mainstream 32 *main part*; multiple 101 *plurality.*

Adjective
(4) *many,* myriad, several, sundry, divers, various, quite a few, not a f., a good f.; considerable, numerous, very many, a good many, ever so m., many more, no end of, umpteen, n, a thousand and one; untold, unnumbered 107 *infinite*; multifarious, manifold 82 *multiform*; much, ample, multiple, profuse, abundant, galore 635 *plenteous.*

(5) *multitudinous,* crowded, thronged, studded with 54 *full*;

populous, peopled, over-populated, teeming, crawling, humming with, alive with 171 *prolific*; thick as flies 139 *frequent*; inexhaustible, countless 107 *infinite*;

Verb
(6) *be many,* swarm with, crawl w., bristle w., teem w. 637 *superabound*; pullulate, multiply 171 *be fruitful*; clutter, crowd, throng, swarm 74 *congregate*; flood, overflow, snow under, swamp, overwhelm, infest, overrun; outnumber, make a majority 32 *be great.*

105
Fewness

Noun
(1) *fewness,* paucity, exiguity, thinness, sparsity, sparseness, rarity 140 *infrequency*; scantiness 636 *scarcity*; a few, a handful; wisps, tuft; small number, low turnout; trickle, mere t. 33 *small quantity*; almost none; limited number, too few, not enough, no quorum; minority, one or two, two or three, half a dozen, remnant.

Adjective
(2) *few,* precious few, weak in numbers; scant, scanty 636 *scarce*; thin, thin on the ground sparse, rare, scattered, low-density 140 *infrequent*; not many, hardly any; soon counted; fewer, diminishing 37 *decreasing*; too few, in a minority.

Verb
(3) *be few,* seldom occur.

(4) *render few,* reduce, diminish, scale down 37 *abate*; eliminate, decimate; weed, thin sort out 300 *eject.*

Adverb
(5) *here and there,* in dribs and drabs; sparsely, rarely, infrequently.

106
Repetition

Noun

(1) *repetition,* doing again, iteration, reiteration; doubling, reduplication 20 *imitation*; going over, recital, practice, rehearsal; beginning again, renewal, resumption, reprise, recapitulation; saying again, harping, tautology; a repetition, repeat, encore; second helping; playback, replay, return match, revenge; chorus, refrain 412 *vocal music*; echo 404 *resonance*; cliche, plagiarism; old story 838 *tedium*; reprint, reissue, remake, rehash; revival 656 *restoration*; repeater, cuckoo, parrot.

(2) *recurrence,* cycle, round, return, rebirth, reincarnation 141 *regular return*; run, series, serial 71 *continuity*; throwback, atavism 5 *heredity*; reappearance, curtain call; rhythm 141 *periodicity*; alliteration, assonance, rhyme 593 *prosody*; repetitiveness, monotony 838 *tedium*; busman's holiday, routine 610 *habit.*

Adjective

(3) *repeated,* repetitional; recurrent, recurring, ever-r. 141 *periodical*; haunting 505 *remembered*; tautological, repetitive, repetitious, harping; echoing, rhyming, chiming, alliterative, assonant 18 *similar*; monotonous, singsong, dingdong 16 *uniform*, rhythmical, drumming; habitual 139 *frequent*; twicetold, retold, quoted, cited, plagiarized 20 *imitative.*

Verb

(4) *repeat,* do again, iterate, duplicate, redouble 91 *double*; multiply 166 *reproduce*; reiterate, say again, recapitulate, go over, restate, rephrase, reword; retell, trot out; say

one's piece, recite, say after; echo, ditto, parrot 20 *copy*; quote, cite; practise, rehearse; play back, rerun, recycle, resume 68 *begin*; replay, give an encore; reprint, reissue; remake 656 *restore.*

(5) *repeat oneself,* give an encore; reverberate, reecho 404 *resound*; stutter 580 *stammer*; plug, labour, harp on 570 *be diffuse*; return to 505 *remember.*

(6) *reoccur,* recur; return, revert, happen again; reappear, pop up, show up again; haunt, obsess 505 *be remembered.*

Adverb

(7) *repeatedly,* recurrently, frequently 139 *often*; by rote, parrot fashion; again and again, over and over, time and again; time after time, day after day, year in year out; day by day, morning, noon and night; ad nauseam.

(8) *again,* afresh, anew, over again, once more; ditto; encore, re-.

107
Infinity

Noun

(1) *infinity,* infinitude, infiniteness, boundlessness, limitlessness, infinite space 183 *space*; eternity 115 *perpetuity.*

Adjective

(2) *infinite,* indefinite; immense, measureless; eternal 115 *perpetual*; numberless, countless, innumerable, immeasurable, interminable; incalculable, beyond reckoning, inexhaustible, without number, without limit, without end, no end of; without measure, limitless, endless, boundless, untold, unnumbered 104 *many*; unbounded, unlimited.

Adverb
(3) *infinitely*, to infinity, ad infinitum; without end, indefinitely; immeasurably 32 *greatly*.

108
Time

Noun
(1) *time*, tide; duration, extent 113 *long duration*; limited time, season, term; shift, spell, space 110 *period*; a bit, a while; the whole time, lifetime; eternity 115 *perpetuity*; passage of time 111 *course of time*; years, days; Time, Father Time; sands of time; fourth dimension, space-time; indefinite time; past tense 125 *past time*, 119 *priority*; prospective time 124 *futurity*; the present 121 *present time*; recent time 126 *newness*; distant time 127 *oldness*.

(2) *interim*, meantime, while; interval, interlude 145 *lull*, 72 *discontinuity*; close season, respite, adjournment 136 *delay*.

(3) *date*, day, age, day and a., reign 110 *era*; vintage, year 117 *chronology*; birthday 141 *anniversary*; calends, ides, nones; time of day 117 *clock time*; moment 116 *instant*; zero hour, D-day; term, quarter day, payday.

Adjective
(4) *continuing*, permanent 115 *perpetual*, on foot, in process of, pending; repetitive, recurrent 106 *repeated*; temporal 141 *periodical*.

(5) *intermediate*, midweek; intercalary, intercalated, inter-.

(6) *dated*, calendared; pre-Christian 119 *prior*; postwar 120 *subsequent*.

Verb
(7) *continue*, endure, drag on 113 *last*; roll on, intervene, pass 111

elapse; take time, take up t.; live through, sustain; stay, remain, abide 113 *outlast*; take its time 136 *be pending*.

(8) *pass time*, vegetate, subsist 360 *live*; age 131 *grow old*; spend time, consume t., use t. 137 *profit by*; while away time, kill t.; summer, winter, weekend 681 *have leisure*; waste time, fritter away t. 679 *be inactive*; mark time 136 *wait*; have one's day.

(9) *fix the time*, calendar, date 117 *time*.

Adverb
(10) *while*, whilst, during, pending; day by day 113 *all along*; so long as; meantime, meanwhile; between whiles, in the meantime, in the interim; for a time, till, until, up to; always, the whole time 139 *perpetually*; all along, for good.

(11) *when*, what time; in the days of; one day, once upon a time.

(12) *anno domini*, AD; before Christ, BC.

109
Neverness

Noun
(1) *neverness*, month of Sundays, blue moon; jam tomorrow, mañana.

Adverb
(2) *never*, not ever, at no time, on no occasion; nevermore, never again; never before.

110
Period

Noun
(1) *period*, matter of time; long period 113 *long duration*; short period 114 *transience*; season; time of day, morning, evening; time of year, spring, summer,

autumn, winter 128 *morning*, 129 *evening*; fixed time, term, notice 766 *conditions*; time up 69 *finality*; measured time, spell, tour, stint, shift, span, stretch, sentence; innings, turn; round, bout, lap; vigil, watch; length of time, second, minute, hour; pause, interval 108 *interim*; day, weekday, working day; week, octave, fortnight, month, calendar m., lunar m.; quarter, trimester; half year, semester; twelve month, year, leap y.; Olympiad, decade; jubilee 141 *anniversary*; century, millennium; one's born days; lifetime, life sentence.

(2) *era*, time, period, generation, age, days; epoch; aeon; cycle; Ice Age; Stone A., Iron A., Dark Ages, Middle A.; fin de siècle; modern times.

Adjective
(3) *periodic* 141 *seasonal*; hourly, annual, biennial, centennial.

(4) *secular,* epochal, millennial; Pre-Cambrian, Palaeozoic, Pleistocene, neolithic 127 *primal.*

Adverb
(5) *periodically,* seasonally; for a term, for a lifetime.

111
Course: Indefinite duration

Noun
(1) *course of time,* matter of t., progress of t., process of t., lapse of t., flow of t., tide of t., march of t., 108 *time*; duration 146 *continuance*; continuous tense, imperfect t.; indefinite time, infinite t. 113 *long duration.*

Adjective
(2) *elapsing,* wearing, passing, rolling 146 *unceasing*;

Verb
(3) *elapse,* pass, lapse, flow, run, roll 285 *progress*; wear on, drag on, crawl 278 *move slowly*; fly, slip, slide, glide 277 *move fast*; run its course, run out, expire 69 *end*; go by, pass by, slip by 125 *be past*; have one's day, spend time 108 *pass time.*

Adverb
(4) *in time,* in due time, in the course of time, with the years.

112
Contingent duration

Adverb
(1) *provisionally,* precariously, by favour; for the present; as *or* so long as.

113
Long duration

Noun
(1) *long duration,* length of time, a long t., years, donkey's years, years on end; a lifetime, life sentence; generations, a century, an age, ages 115 *perpetuity*; length of days, longevity 131 *old age*; distance of time, corridor of t. 125 *past time.*

(2) *durability,* lasting quality, endurance, defiance of time; stamina, staying power 162 *strength*; survival 146 *continuance*; permanence 153 *stability*; long standing, good age 127 *oldness*; long run, long innings.

(3) *protraction,* prolongation, extension 203 *lengthening*; dragging out, spinning o., filibustering; 715 *resistance*; wait, long w. 136 *delay*; extra time, overtime.

Adjective
(4) *lasting,* abiding 146 *unceasing*; lifelong, livelong; inveterate, deep-seated, deep-rooted;

long-term, long-service; marathon 203 *long*; durable, enduring 162 *strong*; long-lived 127 *immemorial*; evergreen, fresh 126 *new*; eternal, perennial 115 *perpetual*; persistent, chronic 162 *unyielding*; constant, stable, permanent 153 *unchangeable*.

(5) *protracted,* prolonged, lengthened, extended, spun out 197 *expanded*; lingering, tarrying 278 *slow*; long-pending, long-awaited 136 *late*; interminable, longminded 570 *prolix*.

Verb
(6) *last,* endure, stand, stay, remain, abide, continue 146 *go on*; defy time, never end 115 *be eternal*; carry one's years 131 *grow old*; wear, wear well.

(7) *outlast,* outlive, outstay, survive; remain 41 *be left*; have nine lives.

(8) *spin out,* draw o., drag o.; protract, prolong 203 *lengthen*; temporize, gain time 136 *put off*; talk out, filibuster.

(9) *drag on,* be interminable, never end; creep, linger, dawdle 278 *move slowly*; tarry, delay, waste time 136 *be late*.

Adverb
(10) *for a long time,* long, for long, for ages, for years; for good, for all time, all one's life.

(11) *all along,* all day, all day long, the livelong day, round the clock, hour by hour, day by day; year in year out; before and since; ever since.

(12) *long ago,* long since, in ancient days 125 *formerly*.

(13) *at last,* at long last, not before time.

114
Transience

Noun
(1) *transience,* ephemerality, impermanence; evanescence 446 *disappearance*; volatility, fragility, frailty 4 *insubstantiality*; mortality, perishability 361 *death*; mutability 152 *changeableness*; suddenness 116 *instantaneity*; temporariness, makeshift; interregnum 108 *interim*.

(2) *brief span,* short while; briefness, momentariness, brevity 204 *shortness*; meteor, nine days' wonder 4 *insubstantial thing*; April shower, summer cloud; bird of passage, brief encounter; short run spasm, moment 116 *instant*.

Adjective
(3) *transient,* time-bound, temporal, impermanent, transitory, fading, passing 4 *insubstantial*; fair-weather, summer; cursory, flying, fleeting, flitting, fugitive, 277 *speedy*; shifting, slipping; precarious, volatile, evanescent 446 *disappearing*; unsettled, rootless; flickering, mutable 152 *changeful*; fickle, flighty 604 *capricious*.

(4) *ephemeral,* of a day, short-lived, throwaway, disposable, biodegradable; perishable, mortal 361 *dying*; annual, deciduous; frail 163 *weak*; impermanent, temporary, acting, provisional, doomed, under sentence.

(5) *brief,* short-term 204 *short*; summary, short and sweet 569 *concise*; quick, brisk 277 *speedy*; sudden, momentary, meteoric 116 *instantaneous*; hurried 680 *hasty*; at short notice 609 *spontaneous*.

Verb
(6) *be transient,* - transitory etc.
adj.; not stay, not last; flit, fly,
gallop 277 *move fast*; fade,
flicker, vanish, evaporate 446
disappear; have no roots 2 *pass
away.*

Adverb
(7) *transiently,* briefly, momentarily; in passing; temporarily,
provisionally; for the present,
for the moment, for the time
being; for a time, not for long;
instantly 116 *instantaneously*;
easy come, easy go; here today
and gone tomorrow.

115
Perpetuity: Endless duration

Noun
(1) *perpetuity,* endless time, 107
infinity; eternity, timelessness
113 *long duration*; endurance
144 *permanence*; immortality,
deathlessness 146 *continuance*;
perpetuation, lasting monument 505 *reminder.*

Adjective
(2) *perpetual,* perennial, longlasting, enduring 113 *lasting*;
nonstop, constant, continual,
ceaseless, incessant 146 *unceasing*; flowing, uninterrupted 71
continuous; dateless, ageless,
immutable 144 *permanent*; evergreen; everlasting, incorruptible; imperishable, undying,
deathless, immortal; never-
ending, interminable; endless,
without end, timeless, eternal,
unending.

Verb
(3) *perpetuate,* make permanent,
establish; immortalize, eternalize.

(4) *be eternal,* - perpetual etc.
adj.; last for ever, endure for e.,
live for e.; have no end, never
cease.

Adverb
(5) *for ever,* for ever and ever; in
perpetuity, on and on 71 *continuously*; ever and always, for
better for worse; for aye, ever-
more, time without end, world
without e.; for keeps, to the end
of time, to infinity 107
infinitely.

116
Instantaneity: Point of time

Noun
(1) *instantaneity,* immediateness, immediacy; simultaneity
121 *present time*; suddenness,
abruptness; precise time 135
punctuality; momentariness
114 *transience.*

(2) *instant,* moment, point, point
of time; second, split s., tick,
trice, jiffy; stroke, flash; the
very moment, the stroke of.

Adjective
(3) *instantaneous,* simultaneous, immediate, instant, sudden, abrupt, snap; flickering,
flashing; quick as thought, like
a flash 277 *speedy*; on time,
punctual 135 *early.*

Adverb
(4) *instantaneously,* instantly,
on the instant, at once, immediately, directly; punctually,
without delay, forthwith; in no
time, in next to no time, soon;
promptly, readily, presto, pronto; without warning, without
notice, abruptly; overnight, all
at once 135 *suddenly*; plump,
slap, slap-bang; at a stroke, at
one jump, in a trice, in a
moment, in a wink, in two
ticks; on the spot, on the dot;
extempore, impromptu, on the
spur of the moment; like a
flash, like a shot, no sooner said
than done 277 *swiftly.*

117
Chronometry

Noun
(1) *chronometry,* horology; watch-making; timetabling; timing, dating; timekeeping 108 *time.*

(2) *clock time,* right time, exact t., correct t., Greenwich Mean Time; date, date line; time of day, time of night; summer time, local t.

(3) *timekeeper,* chronometer, timepiece, clock; dial, face; hand; bob, pendulum; watch, ticker; repeater; wristwatch, digital watch; sundial, hourglass, egg timer; chronograph, time signal, pip, siren, hooter; gong, bell; time-clock, timer, stopwatch; parking meter; traffic light, time fuse, time switch, time bomb; metronome, conductor; watchmaker, horologist.

(4) *chronology,* dating, radiocarbon d., date, age, epoch 110 *era*; old style, new style; almanac, calendar, Gregorian c., Julian c.; chronicle, annals, diary 548 *record*; date list, time-chart 87 *list*; tide-table, timetable.

(5) *chronologist,* chronologer, chronicler, diarist 549 *recorder.*

Adjective
(6) *chronological,* horological, timekeeping; chronographic; in time, temporal.

Verb
(7) *time,* clock; fix the time, fix the date; timetable; match times 123 *synchronize*; phase 24 *adjust*; put the clock back *or* forward 135 *be early,* 136 *be late*; wind the clock, set the alarm; calendar, chronologize, chronicle 548 *record*; date, be dated; measure time, mark t., beat t., keep t.; count the minutes, watch the clock; clock in,

clock out; ring in 68 *initiate*; ring out 69 *terminate.*

Adverb
(8) *o'clock,* a.m., p.m.

118
Anachronism

Noun
(1) *anachronism,* chronological error; wrong date, wrong day; mistiming, previousness 135 *anticipation*; unpunctuality 136 *lateness*; neglect of time; wrong moment 138 *untimeliness.*

Adjective
(2) *anachronistic,* misdated, antedated, previous, before time 135 *early*; post-dated 136 *late*; overdue, behind time; slow, losing; fast, gaining; out of season, out of date, behind the times, old-fashioned 127 *antiquated.*

Verb
(3) *misdate,* mistake the date 138 *mistime*; antedate, anticipate 135 *be early*; be overdue, be behind time, postdate 136 *be late.*

119
Priority

Noun
(1) *priority,* previousness, preexistence; primogeniture, birthright; eldest, firstborn, son and heir 64 *precedence*; the past 125 *past time*; eve, vigil, day before; precedent, antecedent; foretaste, preview, premonition, presentiment 510 *foresight*; herald 66 *precursor.*

Adjective
(2) *prior,* pre-, fore-; earliest, first, first in the field; precedent 64 *preceding*; previous, earlier, anterior, antecedent; antediluvian, prehistoric; pre-

Christian, BC, prewar; preexiting, preexistent; prenatal, antenatal; elder, eldest, firstborn; former, ci-devant, onetime, sometime, ex-, retired; foregoing, aforesaid, above-mentioned; introductory 66 *precursory*; premised 512 *supposed*.

Verb

(3) *be before* 135 *be early*; come before 283 *precede*; foreshadow, preexist.

(4) *do before*, presuppose 512 *suppose*; predecease; prefabricate, prearrange, preempt, prejudge, preview; be previous, anticipate, forestall, jump the gun, jump the queue, steal a march on; lead 64 *come before*.

Adverb

(5) *before*, pre-, prior to, beforehand, by; just before, earlier, previously, formerly; ere now, before n.; ere then, before t., already.

120
Posteriority

Noun

(1) *posteriority*, supervention; succession 65 *sequence*, 284 *following*; days to come 124 *futurity*; line, lineage, descent 170 *posterity*; new arrival, latecomer, aftermath 67 *sequel*.

Adjective

(2) *subsequent*, later, post-, posterior, following, next, after; junior, cadet, younger, youngest; succeeding, designate, to be 124 *future*; posthumous, post-obit; postwar; after Christ, AD; postprandial, after-dinner 65 *sequential*.

Verb

(3) *ensue*, supervene, follow after 65 *come after*, 157 *result*; succeed 771 *inherit*.

Adverb

(4) *subsequently*, later, after, afterwards; next, next time; thereafter, thereupon; since, from that moment; from the start; after a while, after a time; soon after, close upon.

121
The present time

Noun

(1) *present time*, topicality 126 *modernism*; time being, the present, present time, present day; this instant 116 *instantaneity*; juncture 137 *occasion*; the times, modern t., these days, this day and age; today, nowadays; twentieth century, present generation; this date, current d.

Adjective

(2) *present*, actual, instant, current, extant 1 *existing*; of this date, of today's d.; topical, contemporary, present-day, latter-day; latest, up-to-date 126 *modern*; for the occasion.

Verb

(3) *be now*, exist 1 *be*; live in the present; be modern 126 *modernize*; be one's age, admit one's a.

Adverb

(4) *at present*, now, right now, at this time, at this moment; on the present occasion; live; today, nowadays; for the nonce; for the time being; on the nail, on the spot 609 *extempore*; now or never; now as always.

(5) *until now*, to this day, up to now, to date; including today, through.

122
Different time

Noun

(1) *different time*, other time 124 *futurity*, 125 *past time*; another

time, some other t., not now, not today; jam yesterday, and jam tomorrow 109 *neverness*.

Adjective
(2) *not contemporary,* behind the times 127 *antiquated*; before the times 126 *new*; misdated 118 *anachronistic*.

Adverb
(3) *not now,* later; ago, earlier, then; one day, one of these days, someday, sometime, any time; any time now, soon, sooner or later.

123
Synchronism

Noun
(1) *synchronism,* coincidence, concurrence, concomitance 89 *accompaniment*; simultaneity, same time 116 *instantaneity*; same date, same day 121 *pre* dead heat 28 *draw*; synchronization; sync, phasing.

(2) *contemporary,* one's contemporaries, same generation; coeval, twin 28 *compeer*; age group, peer g., class, year 74 *group*.

Adjective
(3) *synchronous,* contemporary 121 *present*; simultaneous, coincident, coexistent 24 *agreeing*; level, neck and neck 28 *equal*; coeval, twin; synchronized, timed, phased, punctual.

Verb
(4) *synchronize,* sync; concur, coexist 89 *accompany*; coincide 295 *meet*; keep time 410 *harmonize*; say together, chorus; tune, phase 24 *adjust*; pace, keep in step.

Adverb
(5) *synchronously,* at the same time; concurrently, along with, in time, on the beat, simultaneously, with one voice; in the same breath 116

instantaneously; while, whilst 89 *with*.

124
Futurity:
Prospective time

Noun
(1) *futurity,* future tense; womb of time, time to come, morrow 120 *posteriority*; future, time ahead, prospect, outlook 507 *expectation*; coming events, fate 155 *destiny*; near future, tomorrow; advent 289 *approach*; long run, distant future; descendants, heirs, heritage 170 *posterity*.

(2) *future state,* what fate holds in store; 155 *destiny*; latter days, doomsday 69 *finality*; afterlife, life to come, hereafter 971 *heaven*, 972 *hell*; millennium 730 *prosperity*; rebirth, reincarnation 106 *repetition*.

(3) *looking ahead,* anticipation 669 *preparation*; prospect, outlook 507 *expectation*; expectancy 852 *hope*; forecast 511 *prediction*.

Adjective
(4) *future,* to be, to come; coming, nearing 289 *approaching*; close at hand 200 *near*; on the horizon, in the wind; due, destined, fated, threatening, imminent 155 *impending*; in the future, ahead, yet to come 154 *eventual*; in embryo 669 *preparatory*; prospective, designate 605 *chosen*; promised, looked for 507 *expected*; predicted, predictable, foreseeable 473 *certain*; ready to, rising, getting on for; potential, promising 469 *possible*; later 120 *subsequent*.

Verb
(5) *be to come,* lie ahead, be just around the corner; threaten 155 *impend*; be imminent 289 *approach*.

(6) *look ahead,* look forward, see it coming, await 507 *expect;* foresee 511 *predict;* anticipate, forestall 135 *be early.*

Adverb

(7) *prospectively,* eventually, ultimately, in due course, in the fullness of time, by and by; tomorrow, soon, some day; on the point of, about to; in the wings, in the offing; hereafter.

(8) *henceforth,* in future, from now on.

125
Past time:
Retrospective time

Noun

(1) *past time* 119 *priority;* retrospection, looking back 505 *remembrance;* past tense, historic age, preterite, perfect, pluperfect; the past, recent p., only yesterday 126 *newness;* distant past, history, antiquity 127 *oldness;* past times, days of yore, olden days, good old d., bygone d.; yesterday, yesteryear, former times.

(2) *antiquity,* time immemorial; prehistory, ancient world; mediaeval times; prehistoric age, heroic a., Classical Age 110 *era;* the ancients; antiquities, relics 127 *archaism;* ruin, ancient monument, megalith 548 *monument,* 253 *earthwork;* excavation 484 *discovery;* museum.

(3) *fossil,* fossilized remains; trilobite, ammonite; fossil footprint 548 *record;* coal forest 385 *fuel;* sponge, coral 358 *organism;* dinosaur 365 *animal;* fossilization.

(4) *palaeology,* palaeontology, palaeography; archaeology, industrial a., medievalism; antiquarianism.

(5) *antiquarian,* archaeologist; palaeographer; antiquary 492 scholar; historian, prehistorian; medievalist, classicist.

Adjective

(6) *past,* in the p., historical; ancient, prehistoric 127 *olden;* early, primitive, proto- 127 *primal;* gone, bygone, lost, irrecoverable, passed away, no more 2 *extinct,* 361 *dead;* passé, has-been, obsolete, fossilized 127 *antiquated;* over, over and done with, behind one; elapsed, expired, run out, finished 69 *ending.*

(7) *former,* late, sometime, ex-119 *prior;* retired, outgoing; ancestral, ancient, prehistoric 127 *immemorial.*

(8) *foregoing,* last, latter 64 *preceding;* recent, overnight 126 *new.*

(9) *retrospective,* backward-looking; looking back 505 *remembering;* historical; retroactive, going back; with hindsight.

Verb

(10) *be past,* have elapsed, have expired; pass, elapse, 69 *end;* have run its course, have had its day.

(11) *look back,* trace back; dig up the past, exhume; archaize, hark back 505 *retrospect.*

Adverb

(12) *formerly,* of old, of yore; time was, once upon a time, ago, in olden times; long ago, a long while, years ago; lately, some ago, some time back; yesterday, yesteryear; last year, last month.

(13) *retrospectively,* retroactively; hitherto; till now, up to this time.

126
Newness

Noun
(1) *newness,* recency, recent-ness; recent date, recent past; innovation, novelty, 21 *originality*; freshness, dewiness 648 *cleanness*; greenness, immaturity, rawness 130 *youth*; renovation, restoration, renewal 656 *revival*; new leaf, new broom.

(2) *modernism,* modernity, modernness, modernization; topicality 121 *present time*; the latest, the latest thing, latest fashion; the last word, new look 848 *fashion*.

(3) *modernist,* futurist; advanced thinker, avant-garde; .bright young thing, trendy; modern generation.

(4) *upstart,* parvenu 297 *incomer*; nouveau riche 847 *vulgarian*.

Adjective
(5) *new,* newish, recent, of recent date, overnight; upstart, mushroom; novel, unprecedented, unheard of 21 *original*; brand-new, spick and span, like new, in mint condition 648 *clean*; green, evergreen, dewy, fresh 128 *vernal*; maiden, virgin, virginal; newborn 130 *young*; raw 670 *immature*; just out, new-made, new-laid; unused, first-hand; untried, untrodden 491 *unknown*; untested 461 *experimental*; not broken in, budding, fledgling 68 *beginning*.

(6) *modern,* contemporary, topical 121 *present*; up-to-date, up-to-the-minute; trendy 848 *fashionable*; modernistic, advanced, avant-garde, futuristic, revolutionary; innovating, newfangled, new-fashioned.

(7) *modernized,* renewed, renovated, rejuvenated, refurbished 656 *restored*; brought up to date, freshened up, revised; looking like new.

Verb
(8) *modernize,* do up; update, bring up to date; go modern, go contemporary, get with it; move with the times 285 *progress*.

Adverb
(9) *newly,* freshly, afresh, anew, like new; fresh-, new-; recently, overnight, just now, only yesterday; not long ago, lately, latterly, of late.

127
Oldness

Noun
(1) *oldness,* primitiveness 68 *beginning*; olden times 110 *era*; age, dust of ages, ruins 125 *antiquity*; maturity, mellowness 129 *autumn*; decline 51 *decay*; senility 131 *old age*; eldership 131 *seniority*.

(2) *archaism,* antiquities 125 *antiquity*; museum piece, thing of the past; antique, heirloom, bygone, golden oldie; dodo, dinosaur, fossil; old fogy, fuddy-duddy, square; old-timer, has-been, back number.

(3) *tradition,* lore, folklore, mythology; inveteracy, custom, prescription 610 *habit*; common law; ancient wisdom, word of mouth.

Adjective
(4) *olden,* old, ancient, antique, antiquarian, of historical interest; veteran, vintage; venerable, patriarchal; archaic, ancient; time-worn, ruined; prehistoric, mythological, heroic, classic, feudal, medieval historical 125 *past*.

(5) *primal,* prime, primitive, primeval, aboriginal 68 *beginning*; geological, fossil, palaeozoic 110 *secular*; palaeolithic, neolithic; early, proto-, dawn-, eo-; antediluvian.

(6) *immemorial,* ancestral, traditional, time-honoured 610 *habitual*; venerable 866 *worshipful*; inveterate, rooted, established, long-standing 153 *fixed*; old as time, old as the hills; age-old 113 *lasting.*

(7) *antiquated,* of other times, archaic; old-world, olde worlde, old-time; prewar 119 *prior*; anachronistic 125 *retrospective*; fossilized, static; out of date; behind the times, dated, antediluvian conservative, Victorian, old-fashioned, old-school; outdated, outmoded; passé, démodé, old hat; gone by 125 *past*; rusty, motheaten, crumbling 655 *dilapidated*; mildewed, mouldering, fusty; stale, secondhand; obsolete, obsolescent; superseded, superannuated 674 *disused*; old 131 *ageing.*

Verb
(8) *be old,* - anticipated etc. vb., have had its day 69 *end*; age 131 *grow old*; fade, wither 655 *deteriorate*; fossilize; moulder, decay 51 *decompose.*

Adverb
(9) *anciently,* before the Flood 125 *formerly.*

128
Morning. Spring. Summer

Noun
(1) *morning,* morn, forenoon, a.m., small hours 135 *earliness*; matins, prime; aurora, dawn, dawning, morning twilight, cockcrow, dawn chorus 66 *precursor*; sunrise, sun-up, daybreak 417 *light*; peep of day, break of d.; daylight, daytime.

(2) *noon,* high noon, meridian, midday, noontide; eight bells, twelve o'clock.

(3) *spring,* springtime, springtide, Eastertide; seed-time, blossom-time, maying; first cuckoo; vernal equinox.

(4) *summer* summertime, summertide, Whitsuntide; midsummer, summer solstice, Midsummer's Day, high summer, dog days 379 *heat*; haymaking; Indian summer.

Adjective
(5) *matinal,* morning; diurnal, daytime, auroral, dawning, dewy 135 *early*; noon, meridian.

(6) *vernal,* springlike, spring; equinoctial; sappy, juicy, flowering, 130 *young.*

(7) *summery,* summer 379 *warm.*

Adverb
(8) *at sunrise,* at first light, at crack of dawn, with the lark; past midnight, in the small hours.

129
Evening. Autumn. Winter

Noun
(1) *evening,* p.m., eventide, even, eve; evensong, vespers; afternoon, matinee; afternoon tea, five o'clock; sundowner, soirée; dog-watches; sunset, sundown, setting sun, evening star, Hesperus, Vesper; dusk, twilight, gloaming 419 *half-light*; moonrise 321 *moon*; close of day, nightfall, nighttime; dark 418 *darkness*; bedtime 679 *sleep*; curfew, last post; night-owl 136 *lateness.*

(2) *midnight,* dead of night, witching time; night-watch, small hours.

(3) *autumn,* back-end, fall, harvest, harvest-time; harvest moon, hunter's m.; Michaelmas; Indian summer; autumnal equinox.

(4) *winter* 380 wintriness; wintertime, yuletide, Christmas; midwinter, winter solstice; hibernation.

Adjective
(5) *vespertine,* afternoon, evening; dusky, crepuscular 418 *dark*; nightly, nocturnal, benighted, late.

(6) *autumnal,* equinoctial.

(7) *wintry,* winter, snowbound 380 *cold*; leafless, stark, bleak.

Adverb
(8) *post meridiem,* late, late at night; at night, by n.

130
Youth

Noun
(1) *youth,* freshness, juiciness, sappiness 126 *newness*, 174 *vigorousness*; young blood, youthfulness, youngness, juvenility; babyhood, infancy, childhood, tender age 68 *beginning*; puppy fat; boyhood, girlhood; one's teens, adolescence, puberty; boyishness, girlishness; awkward age, growing pains; younger generation, rising g. 132 *youngster*; minor, ward; Peter Pan.

(2) *nonage,* tender age, immaturity, minority, infancy, leading strings; cradle, nursery, kindergarten.

(3) *salad days,* school d., student d., heyday, prime of life, flower of l., bloom.

Adjective
(4) *young,* youthful, boyish, gir-

lish; virginal, maidenly; adolescent, pubescent; teenage, juvenile; maturing, developing, growing; budding, burgeoning, blooming, flowering 128 *vernal*; beardless, green, callow 670 *immature*; school-age, under-age, minor, infant, pre-school; younger, minor, junior, cadet; youngest; childish 132 *infantine*; young at heart, ever-young, evergreen, ageless.

131
Age

Noun
(1) *age,* one's age, time of life, years, lifespan 113 *long duration*.

(2) *middle age,* middle years, middle life; riper years 134 *adultness*; maturity, prime of life; a certain age, climacteric, change of life, menopause, male m., mid-life crisis.

(3) *old age,* anno domini; pensionable age, retirement age; advanced years, grey hairs, white hairs 133 *old person*; senescence, declining years, infirmity, debility 163 *weakness*; second childhood, dotage, senility 655 *deterioration*; longevity, ripe old age.

(4) *seniority* 64 *precedence*; eldership, deanship; doyen; elders, senate.

(5) *gerontology,* geriatrics.

Adjective
(6) *ageing,* aged, old, elderly; matronly, middle-aged, ripe, mature 669 *matured*; overblown, overripe, run to seed; past one's prime, no chicken; getting on, getting old, going grey, greying; white-haired, hoary-headed, declining 361 *dying*; wrinkled, lined, rheumy-eyed, toothless, shrivelled, wizened, decrepit 655

deteriorated; drivelling, doddering, senile, gaga; advanced in years, old as Methuselah; well-preserved; venerable, patriarchal; turned, rising; too old, past it; retired, superannuated; gerontologic, geriatric.

(7) *older,* major; elder, senior 34 *superior*; firstborn, eldest 119 *prior*.

Verb
(8) *grow old,* age; show one's years, go grey, turn white.

132
Young person. Young animal. Young plant

Noun
(1) *child,* children, small fry; babe, baby, bundle of joy; infant, nursling, suckling, bairn, little one, tiny tot, mite, moppet, toddler; brat, kid, kiddie; little angel, little monkey, little imp, cherub.

(2) *youngster,* juvenile, young person, young adult, young people 130 *youth*; teenager, adolescent; boy, schoolboy, stripling, youth, young man, lad, laddie, sonny; hobbledehoy, yob, mod, rocker, punk, skinhead; girl, schoolgirl, young woman, miss, lass, lassie, wench, maid, maiden, virgin; groupie, tomboy, hoyden; little minx.

(3) *young creature,* young animal, yearling, lamb, kid, calf, heifer; piglet; fawn, colt, foal, filly; kitten; puppy, pup, whelp, cub; chick, chicken, duckling, gosling, cygnet 365 *animal,* bird; fledgling, nestling; fry, litter, farrow, clutch, spawn, brood; larva, pupa, caterpillar, grub; chrysalis, cocoon; embryo, foetus 156 *source*.

(4) *young plant,* seedling; sucker, shoot, sprout, slip; sprig, sapling 366 *plant*.

Adjective
(5) *infantine,* baby, infantile, babyish, childish, childlike; juvenile, boyish, girlish 130 *young*; kittenish, coltish; newborn, new-fledged; in arms, in nappies, at the breast; small, knee-high, half-grown 196 *little*.

133
Old person

Noun
(1) *old person,* retired p., pensioner, senior citizen; old dear, old body; sexagenarian, septuagenarian, octogenarian, nonagenarian, centenarian.

(2) *old man,* old gentleman, elderly g., patriarch, elder statesman 500 *sage*; grandad, grandfather, grandpa; veteran, old-timer 696 *expert*; old boy, gaffer, greybeard; old geezer, o. codger, o. fogy 127 *archaism*.

(3) *old woman,* old lady, elderly l., dowager; grandmother, grandma, granny; old girl, old trout; old dutch 894 *spouse*; crone, hag, witch.

(4) *old couple,* Darby and Joan, the old folks.

134
Adultness

Noun
(1) *adultness,* adulthood, maturation, development, maturity, matureness; legal age, voting a., majority; manhood, womanhood, virility, nubility 372 *male*, 373 *female*; prime, prime of life 131 *middle age*.

(2) *adult,* grown-up; man 372 *male* woman, 373 *female*.

Adjective

(3) *grown-up,* adult, major, of age, responsible; mature, full-grown, fully developed 669 *matured*; virile, nubile 894 *marriageable*; manly 372 *male*; womanly 373 *female*; blooming, full-blown, in full bloom, full-fledged; in one's prime.

Verb

(4) *come of age,* attain one's majority; grow up, mature 36 *grow*; be grown up, leave home, fend for oneself.

135
Earliness

Noun

(1) *earliness,* early hour prime 128 *morning*; early stage 68 *beginning*; early riser, early bird; early comer, first arrival 66 *precursor*; aborigine, native.

(2) *punctuality,* timeliness 137 *occasion*; dispatch, promptitude, immediacy.

(3) *anticipation,* a stitch in time 510 *foresight,* 669 *preparation*; prematurity, precocity; forestalling 64 *precedence*.

Adjective

(4) *early,* bright and e.; previous 119 *prior*; timely, in time, on t., in good t., punctual, prompt; forward, in advance; advanced, precocious, ahead of its time 126 *new*; summary, sudden 116 *instantaneous,* 508 *unexpected*; forthcoming, impending, at hand 200 *near*; too early, premature 670 *immature*.

Verb

(5) *be early,* anticipate, forestall, nip in the bud, get there first, corner the market 64 *come before*; engage, book, preempt, reserve, secure, bespeak; expedite 277 *accelerate*; lose no time 680 *hasten*; gain time.

Adverb

(6) *betimes,* early, soon, before long; first thing; punctually, to the minute, in time, in good time.

(7) *beforehand,* in advance, in anticipation; precipitately 680 *hastily*; precociously, prematurely, too soon, before one's time.

(8) *suddenly,* without notice 508 *unexpectedly*; without delay 116 *instantaneously*; forthwith, directly; at short notice.

136
Lateness

Noun

(1) *lateness,* late hour, small hours 129 *midnight*; high time, eleventh hour, last minute; tardiness, lagging 278 *slowness*; afterthought, delayed reaction; latecomer, last arrival; late developer, slow starter; late riser 679 *idler*.

(2) *delay,* Fabian policy, 858 *caution*; delaying tactics, gaining time, dragging out 113 *protraction*; deceleration, retardation, check 278 *slowness*; detention, holdup 747 *restraint*; postponement, adjournment, pause, truce 145 *lull*; deferment, moratorium, respite, days of grace; suspension, stay of execution; putting off, procrastination 679 *sluggishness*; red tape, pigeonholing, cold storage 679 *inactivity*.

Adjective

(3) *late,* eleventh-hour, last-minute, deathbed; too late, time up; overdue, delayed, belated, tardy; held up, bogged down 702 *hindered*; behindhand, behind time, behind schedule; backward 278 *slow*; unpunctual, never on time; dilatory 679 *inactive*; posthumous 120 *subsequent*.

Verb

(4) *be late,* sit up late, burn the midnight oil; rise late, keep late hours; lag behind; tarry, take one's time, linger, dally, dawdle, saunter, loiter 278 *move slowly;* let the moment pass 138 *lose a chance;* be behindhand.

(5) *wait* 507 *await;* bide one's time, hold one's horses, take one's time, wait and see 145 *pause;* sleep on it 677 *not act;* hang on, hold on; stand about, sit a.; be kept waiting, cool one's heels.

(6) *be pending,* drag 113 *drag on;* hang fire 474 *be uncertain;* stand over 266 *be quiescent.*

(7) *put off,* defer, postpone, adjourn; keep, reserve, hold over; file, pigeonhole; table, shelve, keep on ice; remand, send back; suspend, hold in abeyance; procrastinate, protract, delay, retard, set back, hold up, gain time 113 *spin out;* temporize, tide over; stall, keep one waiting.

Adverb

(8) *late,* after time, behind t.; late in the day, at the eleventh hour; last thing; at length, at last, at long l.; till all hours; too late.

(9) *tardily,* slowly, leisurely, deliberately, at one's leisure.

137
Occasion: Timeliness

Noun

(1) *occasion,* happy chance, juncture 154 *event;* timeliness, opportuneness, readiness, ripeness; fittingness 642 *good policy;* just the time, just the moment; right time, proper t., auspicious hour, moment, well-chosen m.; high time, nick of t. 136 *lateness.*

(2) *opportunity,* golden o., favourable o., 469 *possibility;* one's chance, break, piece of luck 159 *chance;* opening, look-in 744 *scope;* freedom of choice 744 *freedom;* convenience, spare time 681 *leisure;* no obstacle, clear field 159 *fair chance;* handle, lever 629 *means.*

(3) *crisis,* critical time, key moment, crucial m., turning point; emergency, extremity, pinch 700 *predicament;* eleventh hour, last minute 136 *lateness.*

Adjective

(4) *timely,* in time, on time, to the minute, punctual 135 *early;* seasonable, welcome, well-timed; just in time, not before time.

(5) *opportune,* favourable, providential, heaven-sent, auspicious, propitious, fortunate, lucky, happy; fitting 642 *advisable.*

(6) *crucial,* critical, key, momentous, decisive 638 *important.*

Verb

(7) *profit by,* seize the chance, take the opportunity; make an opening, create an o.; capitalize on, exploit, turn to good account 673 *use.*

Adverb

(8) *opportunely,* seasonably, in due time, in due course; all in good time; just in time, in the nick of time; now or never.

(9) *incidentally,* by the way, en passant, apropos.

138
Untimeliness

Noun

(1) *untimeliness,* wrong time, inopportuneness 643 *inexpedi-*

ence; mishap, contretemps; evil hour 731 *misfortune*; off day; intrusion, interruption 72 *discontinuity*; mistiming 118 *anachronism*.

Adjective
(2) *ill-timed,* mistimed, misjudged, ill-judged, ill-advised; out-of-turn, untimely, interrupting, intrusive; inconvenient, malapropos 643 *inexpedient*; unseasonable, off-season; not in time 136 *late*; premature 135 *early*.

(3) *inopportune,* untoward, inauspicious, unfavourable, ill-omened, ill-starred, unhappy 731 *adverse*.

Verb
(4) *mistime,* time it badly 481 *misjudge*; intrude, disturb.

(5) *be engaged,* be occupied 678 be busy.

(6) *lose a chance,* lose an opportunity, let the occasion pass; miss the bus, miss the boat 728 *fail*; bungle, 695 *act foolishly*; oversleep 136 *be late*; allow to lapse 458 *neglect*.

139
Frequency

Noun
(1) *frequency,* rapid succession rapid fire 71 *continuity*; regularity 141 *periodicity*; redoubling 106 *repetition*; frequenting, haunting.

Adjective
(2) *frequent,* recurrent 106 *repeated*; common, not rare 104 *many*; thick on the ground 104 *multitudinous*; incessant, perpetual, continual, nonstop, constant, regular, hourly 141 *periodical*; haunting, frequenting, assiduous 610 *habitual*.

Verb
(3) *recur 106 reoccur;* do nothing but; keep, keep on 146 *go on*, 106

repeat oneself; frequent, haunt 882 *visit*; obsess; plague, pester 827 *trouble*.

Adverb
(4) *often,* oft, many a time, time and again; frequently, commonly, generally; not infrequently, more often than not; again and again 106 *repeatedly*; in rapid succession, thick and fast; regularly, daily, hourly.

(5) *perpetually,* continually, constantly, incessantly 71 *continuously*; at all times, night and day, day after day.

(6) *sometimes,* occasionally, once in a while, every so often, at times, from time to time, now and then, now and again.

140
Infrequency

Noun
(1) *infrequency,* rareness, rarity 105 *fewness*; intermittence 72 *discontinuity*.

Adjective
(2) *infrequent,* uncommon, sporadic, occasional; intermittent, 72 *discontinuous*; scarce, rare, few and far between 105 *few*; like gold dust; almost unheard of, unprecedented 84 *unusual*.

Adverb
(3) *seldom,* little, rarely, scarcely, hardly, infrequently; scarcely ever, hardly e., once in a while; once, just this once.

141
Periodicity: Regularity of recurrence

Noun
(1) *periodicity,* regularity, punctuality, rhythm, evenness 16 *uniformity*; timing, phasing, alternation 12 *correlation*; ebb

and flow, tide; pulse, tick, beat, throb, rhythm, swing 317 *oscillation*; chorus, refrain 106 *recurrence*; frequency, wave f.; shift, relay 110 *period*.

(2) *regular return,* rota, cycle, revolution 315 *rotation*; life cycle, menstrual cycle; yearly cycle, seasons 128 *morning,* 129 *evening*; fixed interval, stated time 110 *period*; routine, daily round 610 *habit*.

(3) *anniversary,* birthday, jubilee, diamond j., silver j., silver wedding, ruby w., golden w.; centenary, bicentenary, tercentenary; saint's day 876 *special day*.

Adjective
(4) *periodical,* periodic, cyclic, circling, revolving 315 *rotary*; tidal, fluctuating 317 *oscillating*; measured, rhythmical, steady, even, punctual, like clockwork 81 *regular*; pulsating, throbbing, beating; recurrent, recurring, intermittent 106 *repeated*; alternating 12 *correlative*; successive 71 *continuous*.

(5) *seasonal,* anniversary; hourly, daily, nightly; weekly, fortnightly, monthly; menstrual; yearly, annual, biennial, triennial, centennial.

Verb
(6) *be periodic,* recur 106 *reoccur*; serialize 71 *run on*; revolve 315 *rotate*; return, come round again; take its turn, alternate; be intermittent, fluctuate 317 *oscillate*; beat, pulse, pulsate, throb 318 *be agitated*; ply, go and return, commute 610 *be wont*.

Adverb
(7) *periodically,* rythmically etc. adj.; regularly, at regular intervals; seasonally, hourly, daily, weekly, monthly, yearly;

per diem, per annum; at intervals, every so often, intermittently.

(8) *by turns,* in turn, in rotation, turn and turn about; alternately, every other day, off and on; round and round 317 *to and fro*.

142
Fitfulness: Irregularity of recurrence

Noun
(1) *fitfulness,* irregularity 61 *disorder*; jerkiness, fits and starts 318 *spasm*; remission 72 *discontinuity*; variability, unpredictability 143 *change*; wobbling, lurching 317 *oscillation*.

Adjective
(2) *fitful,* periodic, intermittent, on-off 72 *discontinuous*; irregular uneven 17 *nonuniform*; occasional 140 *infrequent*; fluttering, unsteady, variable; jerky, spasmodic 318 *agitated*; *wobbling, halting,* wavering, flickering, guttering.

Adverb
(3) *fitfully,* unevenly, now and then 72 *discontinuously*.

143
Change: Difference at different times

Noun
(1) *change,* alteration, variation 15 *difference*; mutation, permutation, modulation, inflexion, declension; frequent change, variability 152 *changeableness*; partial change, modification, adjustment, process, treatment, qualification; total change 147 *conversion*; violent change 149 *revolution*; winds of change 654 *improvement*; change for the worse 655 *deterioration*; change of direction

shift, turn 282 *deviation*; transition 305 *passage*; change of position 151 *interchange*; alternation 141 *periodicity*; catalysis, leavening; change of heart 603 *tergiversation*.

(2) *transformation*, metamorphosis, transmutation 147 *conversion*; reincarnation; version, adaptation.

(3) *alterer*, activator, converter, transformer; catalyst, enzyme, leaven; adapter, modifier, reviser; alchemist, chemist; decorator, dyer; magician 983 *sorcerer*; new broom; bad apple.

Adjective
(4) *changeable*, variable, mutable 152 *changeful*; transitional, provisional; kaleidoscopic 437 *variegated*.

Verb
(5) *change*, be changed, alter 152 *vary*; wax and wane 36 *grow*, 37 *decrease*; vacillate, wobble; chop and change 604 *be capricious*; shift, change course 282 *deviate*; be converted 654 *get better*; move with the times 126 *modernize*.

(6) *modify*, alter, vary, modulate, diversify, shift 437 *variegate*; innovate 126 *modernize*; turn upside down, 149 *revolutionize*; reverse 148 *revert*; make changes, rearrange 62 *arrange*; adapt 24 *adjust*; conform 83 *make conform*; recast 243 *form*; process, treat; revise, correct 654 *rectify*; reform 654 *make better*; tamper with 655 *impair*; bend, twist 246 *distort*; adulterate, doctor, qualify 43 *mix*; disguise 525 *conceal*; change round, ring the changes, interchange, transpose; try a change 461 *experiment*; effect a change 156 *cause*; transform, transfigure, metamorphose, transmute 147 *convert*; metabolize, digest.

144
Permanence:
Absence of change

Noun
(1) *permanence,* permanency, no change, status quo; 153 *stability*; lasting quality, persistence 600 *perseverance*; endurance, duration 113 *durability*; fixity, immobility, firmness, rock, bedrock; maintenance, conservation 666 *preservation*, 146 *continuance*; law, rule 81 *regularity*; long standing, 127 *oldness*; tradition, custom 610 *habit*; fixed attitude, conservatism; conservative, traditionalist, reactionary, stick-in-the-mud.

Adjective
(2) *permanent,* enduring, durable 113 *lasting*; persisting, continuing 146 *unceasing*, 115 *perpetual*; inveterate, longstanding; entrenched, fixed, immutable, unchanging 153 *established*; conservative, reactionary.

Verb
(3) *stay,* come to stay, set in 153 *be stable*; abide, endure, subsist, outlive, survive, outlast 113 *last*; persist, hold good; maintain, sustain, keep up 146 *go on*; rest, remain 192 *dwell*; stand fast, stand one's ground 599 *stand firm*; resist change, remain the same.

Adverb
(4) *as before,* at a standstill; permanently, for good.

145
Cessation: Change
from action to rest

Noun
(1) *cessation,* ceasing, discontinuation 72 *discontinuity*; arrest

747 *restraint*; withdrawal 753 *resignation*.

(2) *stop,* halt, standstill; deadlock, stalemate, checkmate; breakdown; stoppage, stall; shutdown, closing down, walkout 69 *end*; hitch, check 702 *hindrance*; blockage 264 *closure*; interruption 72 *discontinuity*.

(3) *strike,* stopping work 679 *inactivity*; general strike, work to rule 715 *resistance* stoppage, walkout, lightning strike; mutiny; lockout 57 *exclusion*.

(4) *lull,* interval, pause, remission, letup; break, breather, rest 685 *refreshment*; holiday, time off 681 *leisure*; interlude, breathing space 108 *interim*; abeyance, suspension; close season, respite, moratorium, truce, armistice, cease-fire, standstill 136 *delay*.

(5) *stopping place,* port of call; stop, halt, pull-up, station; bus stop; terminus, terminal; dead end, blind alley, cul-de-sac; destination 295 *goal*.

Verb
(6) *cease,* stay, desist, refrain, hold one's hand; stop, halt, pull up, draw up; rest 683 *repose*; have done with, 69 *end*, finish interrupt, leave off, break o., let up 72 *discontinue*; ring off, hang up; stop work, down tools, strike, come out 715 *resist*; dry up, run out, come to an end 636 *not suffice*; come off, end its run; fold up, collapse 728 *fail*; blow over, clear up 125 *be past*; retire 753 *resign*; leave off, give up 621 *relinquish*; shut up, shut down, close 69 *terminate*; cease fire 719 *make peace*.

(7) *halt,* stop, put a stop to; check, stem 702 *obstruct*; hold up, bring to a stand still; cut short, call a halt, interrupt 747 *restrain*; call out, stage a

strike; checkmate, thwart 702 *hinder*; check oneself, stop short, stop dead; seize, freeze; seize up, stall, jam, stick, catch; brake, put on the b. 278 *retard*.

(8) *pause,* stop for breath; hold back, hang fire 278 *move slowly*; stay one's hand, hold one's horses, hesitate 679 *be inactive*; suspend, adjourn, remit 136 *wait*; rest 683 *repose*.

Interjection
(9) *halt!* hold! stop! whoa! leave off! shut up! give over!

146
Continuance in action

Noun
(1) *continuance,* continuation 71 *continuity*; course, flow; prolongation 113 *protraction*; maintenance, perpetuation 115 *perpetuity*; sustained action, persistence, progress 285 *progression*; break, run, rally 71 *series*; recurrence 106 *repetition*.

Adjective
(2) *unceasing,* continual, steady, sustained; nonstop, uninterrupted, incessant, invariable 71 *continuous*; undying 115 *perpetual*; unfailing, ever-running 635 *plenteous*; not out, still in; persistent, persisting, unstoppable 600 *persevering*; recurrent, ongoing 106 *repeated*.

Verb
(3) *go on,* continue; keep going, march on, drive on, proceed 285 *progress*; run on, never end 115 *be eternal*; roll on, take its course; endure, stick, remain, linger 144 *stay*; obsess, haunt 139 *recur*; keep at it, persist, hold on, carry on, jog on, plod on, peg away 600 *persevere*.

(4) *sustain,* maintain, uphold, support; follow up, follow

through 71 *continue*; keep up, keep alive 666 *preserve*; keep on, keep it up, prolong, protract 113 *spin out*, 115 *perpetuate*; let alone 744 *give scope*.

Interjection
(5) *carry on!* drive on! never say die! not out!

147
Conversion: Change to something different

Noun
(1) *conversion,* turning into, making i.; processing 164 *production*; reduction, fermentation, crystallization; chemistry, alchemy; mutation, transmutation, bewitchment 143 *transformation*; transfiguration 983 *sorcery*; evolution, development 157 *growth*; degeneration 655 *deterioration*; regeneration, rebirth 654 *improvement*; assimilation, naturalization; evangelization 534 *teaching*.

(2) *transition,* transit 305 *passage*; movement, shift 272 *transference*; alteration 143 *change*; life cycle.

(3) *crucible,* melting pot, test tube, laboratory, foundry.

(4) *changed person,* new man *or* woman; convert, neophyte, proselyte 538 *learner*; apostate, turncoat 603 *tergiversator*; degenerate 938 *bad person*.

Adjective
(5) *converted,* influenced, affected; turned into, assimilated, naturalized; reborn, regenerate 656 *restored*; proselytized, brainwashed; becoming, transitional; evolving, transformed, transfigured 15 *different*.

Verb
(6) *be turned to,* become, get; turn to, develop into, evolve i.; melt into, merge i. 43 *be mixed*; mellow 669 *mature*; degenerate 655 *deteriorate*; be transformed, not know oneself; take the shape of 143 *change*; turn over a new leaf.

(7) *convert,* reduce, process, ferment, leaven; make into, reduce to, resolve into, turn i. 983 *bewitch*; transmute, render, make 243 *form*; brainwash 178 *influence*; proselytize, evangelize 534 *teach*; win over 485 *convince*; regenerate 656 *revive*.

(8) *transform,* transfigure; disguise 844 *decorate*, 525 *conceal*; deform 246 *distort*; change out of recognition 149 *revolutionize*; metamorphose 143 *modify*; reform, reorganize 654 *make better*; assimilate, naturalize, Americanize, Anglicize, Europeanize, westernize.

148
Reversion

Noun
(1) *reversion,* reverting, changing back; return, regress, retreat, withdrawal 286 *regression*; harking back 127 *archaism*; atavism, throwback 5 *heredity*; reaction, backlash, recoil; revulsion, disenchantment 830 *regret*; reversal, counter-revolution 149 *revolution*; retraction, volte face, about-turn, U-t. 603 *tergiversation*; backsliding, recidivism 657 *relapse*; reinstatement, recovery, retrieval; turn, turn of the tide; swing 317 *oscillation*; round trip, there and back; status quo; back where one started.

Adjective
(2) *reverted,* reversed, retrograde, retrogressive, recessive

286 *regressive*; reactionary 125 *retrospective*; atavistic 5 *genetic*; recycled, returned; recovered, disenchanted 656 *restored*.

Verb
(3) *revert,* go back, turn b., return 286 *regress*; reverse, face about, turn a.; slip back, slide b., backslide 657 *relapse*; retract, back down 603 *recant*; start again, unmake, undo 68 *begin*; revive 656 *restore*; disenchant, remove the spell 613 *dissuade*; take back, recover 656 *retrieve*; resume 771 *acquire*; reinstate, replace 787 *restitute*.

Adverb
(4) *reversibly,* back to the beginning, as you were.

149
Revolution: Sudden or violent change

Noun
(1) *revolution,* radical change; full circle 315 *rotation*; clean slate, clean sweep 550 *obliteration*; catastrophe, coup d'état; leap, plunge; shift, swing, switch, landslide; violent change, upset, overthrow 221 *overturning*; convulsion, shake-up, upheaval 176 *outbreak*; avalanche, crash, debacle 165 *havoc*; revulsion, rebellion 738 *revolt*.

(2) *revolutionist,* radical, revolutionary, Marxist, Red 738 *revolter*; anarchist, idealist.

Adjective
(3) *revolutionary 126 new;* radical, thoroughgoing, root and branch 54 *complete*; cataclysmic, catastrophic, world-shaking 176 *violent*; seditious, subversive, Marxist, red 738 *disobedient*; anarchistic 165 *destructive*.

Verb
(4) *revolutionize,* subvert, overturn 221 *invert*; uproot, eradicate 550 *obliterate*, 165 *demolish*; break up with the past; change the face of, remodel 147 *transform*.

150
Substitution: Change of one thing for another

Noun
(1) *substitution,* commutation, exchange, switch 151 *interchange*; supersession, replacement, transfer 272 *transference*; compensation.

(2) *substitute,* proxy, agent 755 *deputy*; understudy, stand-in 594 *actor*; ghost-writer 589 *author*; locum 658 *doctor*; reserve, reservist 707 *auxiliary*; replacement, relief, remount; double, ringer, changeling 545 *impostor*; mother figure, father f., foster parent; metaphor, symbol; prosthesis, artificial limb, pacemaker; transplant; alternative, second best, ersatz 35 *inferiority*; scapegoat, sacrifice makeshift, stopgap; expedient, temporary e.; sticking plaster; modus vivendi 770 *compromise*.

(3) *quid pro quo,* equivalent, compensation 31 *offset*; value, worth 809 *price*; replacement.

Adjective
(4) *substituted,* substitutive; substitutable, commutable 28 *equivalent*; imitation, ersatz, counterfeit 542 *spurious*; makeshift, stopgap, provisional, acting, temporary 114 *ephemeral*.

Verb
(5) *substitute,* change for, commute; exchange, switch 151 *interchange*; palm off with 542

deceive; make do with, make shift w.; count as, treat as, regard as; replace, take the place of; succeed; supersede, supplant, displace, oust 300 *eject*; replace, be substitute for, stand in f. 755 *deputize*; cover up for, shoulder the blame.

Adverb
(6) *instead,* in place, in lieu; in favour of; in loco parentis; by proxy; alternatively.

151
Interchange: Double or mutual change

Noun
(1) *interchange,* swap, exchange 791 *barter*; commutation, permutation, anagram; all change, general post; shuffle 272 *transference*; reciprocity, mutuality; interplay, two-way traffic, reciprocation 12 *correlation*; quid pro quo; give and take; retort, repartee 460 *rejoinder*; tit for tat 714 *retaliation*; logrolling 706 *cooperation*.

Adjective
(2) *interchanged,* switched, exchanged, bartered, swapped; in exchange, reciprocating, mutual, two-way 12 *correlative*; reciprocal, requited; inter-; interchangeable, substitutable 28 *equivalent*.

Verb
(3) *interchange,* exchange, change money, convert; swap, barter 791 *trade*; permute, commute; switch, shuffle 272 *transpose*; give and take 770 *compromise*; reciprocate 12 *correlate*; requite 714 *retaliate*; bandy words 460 *answer*.

Adverb
(4) *in exchange,* vice versa; to and fro, by turns, in kind; au pair; conversely.

152
Changeableness

Noun
(1) *changeableness,* changeability, mutability, changefulness 143 *change*; variability, inconsistency, inconstancy, irregularity; instability, imbalance, unsteadiness; pliancy, fluidness, slipperiness; mobility, restlessness, darting, starting, fidgeting 318 *agitation*; fluctuation, alternation 317 *oscillation*; turning, veering 142 *fitfulness*; impermanence 114 *transience*; vacillation, hesitation, wavering 601 *irresolution*; fickleness 604 *caprice*; versatility 694 *aptitude*.

(2) *changeable thing,* variable; moon, chameleon; shifting sands; wax, clay; quicksilver 335 *fluid*; wind, weathercock, April showers; fortune, vicissitude 159 *chance*; mobile features; grasshopper mind 456 *inattention*; floating voter.

Adjective
(3) *changeful,* changing, mutable, alterable 143 *changeable*; shifting, varying, variant, variable; protean 82 *multiform*; quick-change, versatile 694 *skilful*; uncertain, vacillating, wavering 601 *irresolute*; unpredictable 508 *unexpected*; unreliable, never the same, volatile, mercurial; wayward, fickle, whimsical 604 *capricious*; flighty, irresponsible 456 *lightminded*; shifty, inconstant 603 *tergiversating*.

(4) *unstable,* unsound, built on sand; unsteady, wavering, wobbling, tottering 317 *oscillating*; mobile, restless, fidgety 318 *agitated*; desultory, spasmodic 142 *fitful*; shifting, veering 282 *deviating*; unsettled, loose, unattached, floating; erratic, mercurial; rootless, homeless

59 *extraneous*; vagrant 267 *travelling*; fluctuating 141 *periodical*; malleable, alterable 327 *soft*; flowing 335 *fluid*.

Verb
(5) *vary,* be changeful, ring the changes, go through phases, chop and change 143 *change*; be shifty 518 *be equivocal*; dart, flit 265 *be in motion*; flicker, gutter 417 *shine*; twinkle, flash; swing, alternate, ebb and flow 317 *fluctuate*; veer 282 *deviate*; vacillate, waver, change one's mind 601 *be irresolute*; blow hot and cold 603 *tergiversate*; be inconstant 604 *be capricious*.

Adverb
(6) *changeably,* variably; fitfully, off and on, now this now that.

153
Stability: Lack of change

Noun
(1) *stability,* immutability; invariability 16 *uniformity*; fixity, rootedness 144 *permanence*; immobility, immovability 266 *quiescence*; stabilization, steadiness, balance 28 *equality*; nerve, aplomb 599 *resolution*; stiffness, inflexibility 602 *obstinacy*.

(2) *fixture,* establishment, firm foundation; foundations, rock, bedrock; pillar, tower; constant; fast colour, indelible ink; leopard's spots.

(3) *stabilizer,* fin, centreboard, keel; ballast 31 *offset*; buttress 218 *prop*.

Adjective
(4) *unchangeable,* inflexible 602 *obstinate*; unwavering 599 *resolute*; predictable, reliable 473 *certain*; immutable, irreducible, indissoluble; unchanging;

inalterable, changeless, irreversible; invariable, constant 16 *uniform*; steady, unvarying 81 *regular*; durable 144 *permanent*; indestructible 115 *perpetual*; imperishable, inextinguishable.

(5) *established,* well-e., entrenched, vested, settled; inveterate, prescriptive 113 *lasting*; irrevocable, irreversible; of right; valid, ratified *confirmed*, 488 *assented*.

(6) *fixed,* steadfast, firm, fast, secure, immovable, unassailable, unshakable, steady, stable; ingrained, indelible; engraved; ineradicable, deeprooted; deep-seated; foursquare, well-founded, anchored 45 *tied*; transfixed, immobile, frozen 266 *still*.

Verb
(7) *be stable,* stand, hold 599 *stand firm*; weather the storm 113 *outlast*; set in, come to stay 144 *stay*; settle, settle down 192 *dwell*; strike root, take r.

(8) *stabilize,* entrench, found, establish 115 *perpetuate*; 218 *support*; fix, set; validate, confirm, ratify 488 *endorse*; bind, make fast 45 *tie*; keep steady, balance 28 *equalize*.

154
Present events

Noun
(1) *event,* phenomenon; fact 1 *reality*; case, circumstance, occurrence, eventuality, happening, turn of events; incident, episode, adventure, occasion; milestone 8 *juncture*; accident, contingency 159 *chance*; misadventure, mishap 731 *misfortune*; emergency, pass 137 *crisis*; coincidence 181 *concurrence*; encounter, meeting; transaction, proceeding

676 *action*; result, product, consequence 157 *effect*; denouement, catastrophe 69 *end*.

(2) *affairs,* matters, doings, transactions 676 *deed*; agenda, concerns, interests 622 *business*; world, life, situation 8 *circumstance*; current affairs, state of affairs; course of events 111 *course of time*; vicissitudes 730 *prosperity,* 731 *adversity*.

Adjective
(3) *eventual,* consequential, resulting, resultant 157 *caused*; contingent.

(4) *happening,* incidental, accidental, occasional; current, on foot, in the wind, on the agenda.

(5) *eventful,* stirring, bustling, busy, full of incident 678 *active*; momentous, critical 638 *important.*

Verb
(6) *happen,* become, come into existence; materialize, be realized, come off 727 *succeed*; take place, occur, come about, come to pass 159 *chance*; turn up, crop up, arise 295 *arrive*; present itself, announce i. 189 *be present*; supervene 284 *follow*; issue, transpire 157 *result*; turn out, work o.; be on foot, take its course; continue 146 *go on*; pass off 125 *be past*; prove, prove to be; bring about, occasion 156 *cause*.

(7) *meet with,* incur, encounter 295 *meet*; realize, find 484 *discover*; experience, pass through, go t.; have adventures; endure, undergo 825 *suffer*.

Adverb
(8) *eventually,* ultimately, in the event of, in case; as things go.

155
Destiny: Future events

Noun
(1) *destiny,* what's to come, one's stars 596 *fate*; horoscope, forecast 511 *prediction*; prospect, outlook 507 *expectation*; coming events, future plans 617 *intention*; trouble in store 900 *threat*; hereafter 124 *future state*; predestination.

Adjective
(2) *impending,* hanging over, imminent 900 *threatening*; preparing, brewing, cooking 669 *preparatory*; destined, predestined, in the stars, 596 *fated*; predicted, forthcoming, forecast 511 *predicting*; inescapable, inevitable, bound to happen 473 *certain*; on the cards 471 *probable*; intended 608 *predetermined*; in prospect, in view, in the offing, on the horizon; in the future, to come, 124 *future*; at hand 289 *approaching*; about to be, on the point of; pregnant with, heavy w. 511 *presageful*; in store 669 *prepared*.

Verb
(3) *impend* 124 *be to come*; hang over, lour, loom 900 *threaten*; come on 289 *approach*; face, stare one in the f. 200 *be near*.

(4) *predestine,* destine, doom, preordain, foreordain 596 *necessitate*; foreshadow, adumbrate, presage 511 *predict*; plan, intend 608 *predetermine*.

Adverb
(5) *in the future,* in time; soon, at any moment.

156
Cause: Constant antecedent

Noun

(1) *causation,* causality, cause and effect, aetiology 158 *attribution;* authorship; origination, creation 21 *originality;* invention 484 *discovery;* inspiration 178 *influence;* generation 164 *production;* impulsion, stimulation, encouragement, motivation 612 *motive;* cultivation; abetment 706 *cooperation;* temptation 612 *inducement;* opportunity 137 *occasion.*

(2) *cause,* prime mover 965 *the Deity;* creator, maker 164 *producer;* begetter 169 *parentage;* causer, author, inventor, originator, founder; agent, stimulus 174 *stimulant;* contributor, factor, decisive f.; determinant; mainspring 612 *motivator;* fomenter, aider, abettor; hidden hand, undercurrents 178 *influence;* stars 155 *destiny;* fate 596 *necessity;* force 740 *compulsion.*

(3) *source,* fountain, fount 68 *origin;* spring, wellspring; mine, quarry 632 *store;* birthplace 192 *home;* genesis 169 *parentage;* rudiment, element, principle, first p., first thing; nucleus, germ, seed, sperm, spore; egg, foetus, embryo 132 *young creature;* bud, stock, rootstock 366 *plant;* derivation, etymology 557 *linguistics;* foundation, bedrock 214 *base;* groundwork, beginnings 68 *beginning;* raw material, ore 631 *materials.*

(4) *seedbed,* hotbed; cradle, nursery, womb 68 *origin;* breeding ground, fertile soil 167 *propagation;* hothouse 370 *garden.*

(5) *causal means,* appliance 629 *means;* pivot, hinge, lever, instrument 630 *tool;* dynamo, generator, spark 160 *energy;* engine 630 *machine;*

(6) *reason why,* reason, cause, explanation, key 460 *answer;* excuse 614 *pretext;* ground, basis, rationale, motive, idea, occasion, raison d'etre.

Adjective

(7) *causal,* causative, formative, effective, effectual 727 *successful;* pivotal, decisive final 69 *ending;* seminal, germinal 164 *productive;* embryonic 68 *beginning;* inspiring 178 *influential;* impelling 740 *compelling;* answerable, responsible; aetiological, explanatory 158 *attributed;* creative, inventive.

(8) *fundamental,* primary, elemental, ultimate; foundational, radical, basic 5 *intrinsic;* crucial, central 638 *important;* original 68 *first.*

Verb

(9) *cause,* originate, create, make 164 *produce;* beget 167 *generate;* invent 484 *discover;* be the reason, be at the bottom *or* the root of 158 *account for;* be answerable, be responsible, be to blame; institute, found, inaugurate 68 *auspicate;* set up, launch, set going; trigger off, spark off, touch o. 68 *begin;* open, open up, broach 68 *initiate;* sow the seeds of 370 *cultivate;* contrive, effect, effectuate, bring about, bring off 727 *succeed;* procure 629 *find means;* stage-manage, engineer 623 *plan;* bring on, induce, precipitate 680 *hasten;* evoke, elicit 291 *attract;* provoke, arouse 821 *excite;* stimulate 174 *invigorate;* kindle, inspire, incite 612 *induce;* occasion 612 *motivate;* have an effect 178 *influence;* be the agent 676 *do;* determine, turn the scale 178

prevail.

(10) *conduce,* tend to 179 *tend;* lead to 64 *come before;* contribute to 628 *be instrumental;* involve, imply 5 *be intrinsic;* have the effect, entail 68 *initiate;* promote, advance, encourage, foster 703 *aid.*

Adverb

(11) *causally,* because, by reason of.

157
Effect: Constant sequel

Noun

(1) *effect,* consequent, consequence, corollary 65 *sequence;* result, upshot, outcome, issue 154 *event,* 725 *completion;* visible effect, mark, print, impress 548 *trace;* by-product, side-effect, spin-off; aftermath, legacy, wake, repercussion 67 *sequel;* response 460 *answer;* performance 676 *deed;* reaction, backlash 182 *counteraction;* offspring 170 *posterity;* handiwork 164 *product.*

(2) *growth,* outgrowth, development 36 *increase;* blossom, fruit; ear, spike; produce, crop, harvest; profit 771 *gain.*

Adjective

(3) *caused,* owing to, due to, attributed to; consequential, resulting from, consequent upon 65 *sequential;* contingent, depending, dependent on; resultant, derivable, derivative, descended; secondary 20 *imitative;* arising, born of, emanating, developed from, evolved f.; out of ending in 154 *eventual;* effected, done.

(4) *inherited,* heritable, hereditary, Mendelian 5 *genetic.*

Verb

(5) *result,* be the r., come of; follow on, accrue; be owing to, be due to; owe everything to 9 *be related;* take its source, derive from, descend f., issue, proceed, emanate 298 *emerge;* begin from, grow f., spring f., arise f., flow f.; develop, unfold 316 *evolve;* sprout, germinate 36 *grow;* show an effect, bear the stamp; turn out, pan o., work o. 154 *happen;* result in 164 *produce.*

(6) *depend,* hang upon, hinge on, pivot on, turn on, be subject to 12 *correlate.*

Adverb

(7) *consequently,* as a consequence, in consequence; because of, as a result; of course, naturally, necessarily; it follows that, and so 158 *hence.*

158
Attribution: Assignment of cause

Noun

(1) *attribution,* imputation, ascription; theory, hypothesis, assumption 512 *supposition;* explanation finding reasons, accounting for 459 *enquiry;* rationale 156 *reason why;* affiliation 169 *parentage;* derivation 156 *source;* credit, acknowledgement 915 *dueness.*

Adjective

(2) *attributed,* assigned etc. vb.; attributable, assignable, imputable, referred to 9 *relative;* credited, imputed 512 *supposed;* inferred, inferable, derivable, traceable; owing to, explained by 157 *caused.*

Verb

(3) *attribute,* ascribe, impute; predicate 532 *affirm;* accord, grant, allow; put down to, set down to; refer to, point to, trace to, derive from 9 *relate;* charge with, lay at the door of, make responsible, blame for 928 *accuse;* credit with, acknowledge 915 *grant claims.*

(4) *account for,* explain 520 *interpret*; theorize, assume, infer 512 *suppose*.

(5) *hence,* therefore, wherefore; for, since, on account of, because, owing to, thanks to, thus, so; that's why.

(6) *somehow,* in some way, somehow or other.

159
Chance: No assignable cause

Noun
(1) *chance,* blind c., indeterminacy; randomness, fortuitousness 474 *uncertainty*; lot, fortune 596 *fate*; whatever comes, potluck; good fortune, luck 730 *prosperity*; bad luck 731 *misfortune*; hazard, accident, casualty, contingency, coincidence; lucky shot, fluke 618 *nondesign*; chance discovery, serendipity.

(2) *equal chance,* even c., fifty-fifty 28 *equality*; toss-up, heads or tails, lucky dip, random sample; lottery, raffle 618 *gambling*.

(3) *fair chance,* sporting c. 469 *possibility*; half a chance, small c. 472 *improbability*; good chance 137 *opportunity*; long odds, odds on 34 *advantage*; small risk, safe bet 471 *probability*.

(4) *calculation of chance,* risk-taking, assurance, insurance, underwriting 672 *undertaking*; speculation 461 *experiment*; bookmaking 618 *gambling*.

Adjective
(5) *casual,* fortuitous, chance, haphazard, random, stray, adventitious; accidental, incidental, coincidental 618 *designless*; chancy, incalculable 474 *uncertain*.

(6) *causeless,* groundless; unpredictable 474 *uncertain*; unintended 618 *unintentional*; unaccountable, inexplicable 517 *puzzling*.

Verb
(7) *chance,* turn up, crop up, so happen 154 *happen*; chance upon, light u., hit u., stumble u. 154 *meet with,* 484 *discover*; risk it, chance it 618 *gamble*.

Adverb
(8) *by chance,* by accident, unintentionally, accidentally, fortuitously at random; perchance, perhaps 469 *possibly*; luckily, unluckily; whatever happens, in any event; unaccountably, inexplicably.

160
Power

Noun
(1) *power,* potency, mightiness 32 *greatness*; predominance 34 *superiority*; omnipotence 733 *authority*; moral power, ascendancy 178 *influence*; spiritual power, charisma, witchcraft 983 *sorcery*; staying power, endurance 153 *stability*; driving force 612 *motive*; physical power, might, muscle 162 *strength*; effort, endeavour 682 *exertion*; force 740 *compulsion*; stress, strain; weight 322 *gravity*; weight of numbers 104 *greater number*; labour force 686 *personnel*; position of power, vantage ground 34 *advantage*; validity 494 *truth*; cogency, emphasis 532 *affirmation*; extra power, overdrive.

(2) *ability,* capability, potentiality 469 *possibility*; competence, efficiency, efficacy, effectuality 694 *skill*; capacity, faculty, virtue, property 5 *intrinsicality*;

qualification 24 *fitness*; attribute 89 *concomitant*; endowment, gift 694 *aptitude*; compass, reach, grasp 183 *range*; authorization 756 *permission*.

(3) *energy*, vigour, drive, dynamism 174 *vigorousness*; pedal power, engine power, horsepower; force, force of gravity 322 *gravity*; compression, spring 328 *elasticity*; pressure, head, charge, steam; full pressure, steam up; tension, high t.; motive power 288 *traction*; pushing power, thrust 287 *propulsion*; momentum, impetus 279 *impulse*; magnetism, magnetic field 291 *attraction*; suction 299 *reception*; expulsion 300 *ejection*; potential; work, unit of work, erg, joule; foot-pound, calorie.

(4) *sources of energy*, coal, gas, oil 385 *fuel*; nuclear power (see *nucleonics*); wind power, wave p., solar energy, renewable e.; powerhouse, power station; hydroelectricity, tidal barrage; solar panel, heat exchanger 383 *heater*; generator, turbine, motor 630 *machine*.

(5) *electricity*, electrification; lightning; induction, resistance, conduction; oscillation, pulsation, frequency; electric charge, pulse, shock; electric current, direct c., alternating c.; circuit, short c.; electrode, anode, cathode; positive, negative; conductor, insulator; earth; live wire 661 *danger*.

(6) *electronics*, electrical engineering; electron physics, optics 417 *optics*; lasers 417 *radiation*; microelectronics 86 *data processing*; automation 630 *machine*; telegraph, telephone, television, radio 531 *telecommunication*; power line, pylon,

national grid; generator, magneto, dynamo; oscillator, alternator; transformer, commutator, power pack; battery, accumulator; cell, photoelectric c.; valve, tube, transistor; voltage, volt, watt, megawatt, kilowatt, ohm; ampere, amp.

(7) *nucléonics*, nuclear physics; fission, fusion; atomic pile, nuclear reactor, fast breeder r.; radioactivity, fallout 417 *radiation*, 659 *poison*; atomic bomb 723 *bomb*.

Adjective

(8) *powerful*, potent 162 *strong*; puissant, mighty 32 *great*; in the ascendant, predominant 178 *influential*; almighty, omnipotent 34 *supreme*; empowered 733 *authoritative*; competent, capable, able 694 *expert*; equal to 635 *sufficient*; with resources 800 *rich*; effective 727 *successful*; of power, workable, having teeth; in force, valid; cogent 740 *compelling*; forcible 176 *violent*.

(9) *dynamic*, energetic 174 *vigorous*; high-tension, supercharged, souped-up; magnetic 291 *attracting*; tractive 288 *drawing*; propelling 287 *propulsive*; locomotive, kinetic 265 *moving*; powered, engined, automated 630 *mechanical*; electric, electrical, electromagnetic, electronic; solid-state; live, charged; on stream; atomic, nuclear, thermonuclear; hydroelectric, geothermal; solar-powered, wind-driven, water-d.

Verb

(10) *be able*, - powerful etc. adj.; be capable of, have it in one's power to; have the virtue *or* the property; compass, manage 676 *do*; measure up to 635 *suffice*; exercise power, control 733 *dominate*; force 740 *compel*; gain power, come to p. 178 *prevail*.

(11) *empower,* enable, authorize; endow with power, invest with p.; put teeth into, arm 162 *strengthen*; electrify, charge, magnetize; plug in, switch on; automate; power, drive.

Adverb
(12) *powerfully,* by virtue of, by dint of,

161
Impotence

Noun
(1) *impotence,* lack of power, no authority, power vacuum; inability, incapacity; incapability, incompetence, inefficiency 728 *failure*; ineptitude, unfitness 695 *unskilfulness*; frailness 163 *weakness*; invalidation 752 *abrogation*; sterility, sterilization 172 *contraception*; disarmament 719 *pacification*.

(2) *helplessness,* defencelessness 661 *vulnerability*; harmlessness 935 *innocence*; powerlessness 745 *subjection,* 747 *restraint*; prostration, exhaustion 684 *fatigue*; collapse, breakdown; faint, swoon 375 *insensibility*; stroke, apoplexy, paralysis, paraplegia 651 *disease*; torpor 677 *inaction*; atrophy 655 *deterioration*; senility 131 *age*; loss of control, incontinence; mental decay 503 *insanity*; mental weakness, imbecility; legal incapacity, minority 130 *youth*; invalid 163 *weakling*.

(3) *eunuch,* gelding, capon, bullock, steer, neuter.

(4) *ineffectuality,* ineffectiveness; futility 497 *absurdity*; dead letter 752 *abrogation*; figurehead, dummy, man of straw, broken reed 4 *insubstantial thing*, empty threats, bluster 515 *empty talk*.

Adjective
(5) *powerless,* impotent, not able, unable; invalid, null and void; unauthorized, without authority 954 *illegal*; inoperative, not working 752 *abrogated*; abolished, swept away 165 *destroyed*; obsolete, on the shelf 674 *disused*; disqualified, deposed; unqualified, unfitted, dud 641 *useless*; inadequate 636 *insufficient*; ineffective, ineffectual, feeble 163 *weak*; incapable, incompetent, inefficient 695 *unskilful*.

(6) *defenceless,* helpless, without resource; bereaved, bereft 772 *losing*; orphan 883 *friendless*; weak, harmless 935 *innocent*; unarmed, disarmed 670 *unequipped*; exposed 661 *vulnerable*.

(7) *impotent,* powerless, feeble 163 *weak*; emasculated, castrated, gelded, sterilized; sexless, neuter; sterile, barren, infertile; senile 131 *ageing*; unconscious, drugged, hypnotized 375 *insensible*; incapacitated, disabled, paralysed 163 *crippled*; incontinent; worn out, exhausted 684 *fatigued*; prostrated, helpless; spineless, boneless 601 *irresolute*; shattered, unhinged, unnerved, demoralized, shell-shocked 854 *nervous*; drifting, rudderless; baffled, thwarted 702 *hindered*.

Verb
(8) *be impotent,* - defenceless etc. adj.; not work, not help 641 *be useless*; strive in vain 728 *fail*; have no power 745 *be subject*; have no say 639 *be unimportant*; shrug, wring one's hands, gnash one's teeth; look on, stand by 441 *watch*; pass out 375 *be insensible*; drop, collapse 163 *be weak*.

(9) *disable,* incapacitate, unfit 641 *make useless*; disqualify 916 *disentitle*; deprive of power, invalidate 752 *abrogate*; disarm, demilitarize 163 *weaken*;

neutralize 182 *counteract*; undermine, sap, exhaust 634 *waste*; prostrate, bowl over, knock out, paralyse 679 *make inactive*; sprain, dislocate; cripple, hamstring 702 *hinder*; stifle, throttle, strangle 362 *kill*; muzzle 399 *silence*; spike the guns, draw the teeth, clip the wings; tie one's hands, cramp one's style; sabotage, put out of action 674 *stop using*.

(10) *unman*, unnerve, enervate, paralyse 854 *frighten*; emasculate, castrate, neuter, spay, geld 172 *make sterile*.

162
Strength

Noun
(1) *strength*, might, potency 160 *power*; energy 174 *vigorousness*; force, physical f. 735 *brute force*; resilience 328 *elasticity*; iron, steel 326 *hardness*; oak 329 *toughness*; staying power, endurance, grit 600 *stamina*.

(2) *vitality*, healthiness 650 *health*; vim, vigour, liveliness 360 *life*; animal spirits 833 *cheerfulness*; virility 855 *manliness*; guts, nerve, backbone 599 *resolution*; physique, muscularity, biceps, sinews, brawn 195 *size*; grip, iron g. 778 *retention*.

(3) *athletics* 837 sport, 716 *contest*; athleticism, gymnastics, acrobatics; body-building 682 *exercise*; stadium, gymnasium 724 *arena*.

(4) *athlete*, gymnast, acrobat, contortionist, trapeze artist, circus rider 594 *entertainer*; Blue, all-rounder 716 *contender*; wrestler 716 *wrestling*; heavyweight 722 *pugilist*; weight-lifter, strong man; strongarm man, tough guy 857 *desperado*; amazon, virago; toreador 362 *killer*; Goliath 195 *giant*.

(5) *strengthening*, fortifying etc. vb., reinforcement 703 *aid*; toughening 326 *hardening*; invigoration 174 *stimulation*; revival 685 *refreshment*; dynamics, statistics.

Adjective
(6) *strong*, lusty, vigorous, youthful 130 *young*; mighty, puissant, potent, armed 160 *powerful*; high-powered, high-geared, high-tension; all-powerful, omnipotent 34 *superior*; irresistible, victorious; supreme 733 *ruling*; in fine fettle, 650 *healthy*; heavy 322 *weighty*; strongarm, forceful 740 *compelling*; emphatic 532 *assertive*; tempered, steely 326 *hard*; case-hardened, reinforced 329 *tough*; deep-rooted 45 *firm*; solid, substantial 153 *fixed*; thick-ribbed, well-built, stout; strong as an ox; alcoholic 949 *intoxicating*; strengthened, fortified 660 *invulnerable*.

(7) *unyielding*, staunch 599 *resolute*; stubborn 602 *obstinate*; persistent 600 *persevering*; inelastic 326 *rigid*; solid 324 *dense*; impregnable 660 *invulnerable*; indomitable, invincible, unflagging, tireless 678 *industrious*; inextinguishable, indestructible 113 *lasting*; proof, sound; waterproof, fireproof, bulletproof.

(8) *stalwart*, stout, sturdy, hardy, rugged, robust, doughty 174 *vigorous*; able-bodied, muscular, brawny; sinewy, wiry, strapping, well set-up, thickset, stocky, burly, beefy, husky, hefty 195 *large*.

(9) *athletic*, gymnastic, acrobatic; exercised, fit, fighting f., in training, in condition 650 *healthy*.

(10) *manly,* masculine 372 *male*; virile, red-blooded, manful 855 *courageous*; amazonian.

Verb

(11) *be strong,* - mighty etc. adj., pack a punch; come in force; overpower, overwhelm 727 *overmaster*; rally, revive 656 *be restored.*

(12) *strengthen,* confirm, lend force to 36 *augment*; underline, stress 532 *emphasize*; reinforce, fortify, entrench; stuff, pad 227 *line*; buttress, prop 218 *support*; nerve, brace, steel 855 *give courage*; stiffen, toughen 326 *harden*; energize 174 *invigorate*; beef up, tone up, build up animate 821 *excite*; reinvigorate 685 *refresh*; power 160 *empower.*

Adverb

(13) *strongly,* powerfully etc. adj.; by force; by main force.

163
Weakness

Noun

(1) *weakness,* lack of strength, feebleness, puniness; helplessness 161 *impotence*; ineffectiveness 161 *ineffectuality*; slightness, flimsiness, fragility, frailness 330 *brittleness*; delicacy, effeminacy; shakiness, unsteadiness; weak foundation, feet of clay; moral weakness, frailty 601 *irresolution*; bodily weakness, debility, infirmity, decrepitude 131 *old age*; delicate health, anaemia 651 *ill health*; flaccidity, flabbiness 327 *softness*; loss of strength, enervation, faintness; prostration, collapse 684 *fatigue*; decline declension 655 *deterioration*; adulteration, watering, dilution 43 *mixture*; debilitation 655 *impairment*; emasculation, evisceration, invalidation 752 *abrogation*; crack, flaw

845 *blemish*; strain, sprain; weak point 647 *defect.*

(2) *weakling,* sissy, milksop, mollycoddle, namby-pamby; old woman, effeminate; invalid, hypochondriac 651 *sick person*; lame dog, lame duck; baby, crybaby 856 *coward*; drip, weed, wet; victim 544 *dupe.*

(3) *weak thing,* house of cards 4 *insubstantial thing*; cobweb, gossamer; matchwood, matchstick, eggshell 330 *brittleness.*

Adjective

(4) *weak,* powerless 161 *impotent*; without force, invalid 161 *powerless*; understrength, underproof; unfortified 161 *defenceless*; helpless, harmless 935 *innocent*; babyish effeminate; feeble, slight, puny 33 *small*; slightly built 206 *lean*; feeble-minded 499 *foolish*; gutless, weak-willed, half-hearted 601 *irresolute*; nerveless, spineless, weak-kneed, submissive 721 *submitting*; bloodless, anaemic, pale 426 *colourless*; limp, flaccid, flabby 327 *soft*; drooping, sagging; watery, wishy-washy, insipid 387 *tasteless*; low, faint 401 *muted*; tottering, decrepit, old 131 *ageing*; too weak, weak as a kitten rickety, tottery, shaky, wobbly 152 *unstable.*

(5) *weakened,* debilitated; diminished 37 *decreasing*; wasted, dissipated, spent, used up, burnt out 673 *used*; misused, abused; sapped, undermined; disarmed, disabled 161 *defenceless*; denuded, exposed 229 *uncovered*; flagging, failing, exhausted, weary 684 *fatigued*; worn, broken, crumbling, tumbledown 655 *dilapidated*; rotten, rusting, decaying in decay 51 *decomposed*; neutralized 175 *inert*; diluted, adulterated, watered down 43 *mixed.*

(6) *weakly,* infirm, delicate, sickly 651 *unhealthy*; run down, seedy, poorly; underweight, skinny 206 *lean*; languishing, listless; faint, fainting; wan, lacklustre 426 *colourless*.

(7) *crippled,* disabled 161 *impotent*; halt, lame, game, limping, hobbling; hamstrung, hobbled; knock-kneed 246 *deformed*; rheumatic, gouty; armless, eyeless 647 *imperfect*.

(8) *flimsy,* wispy, tenuous 4 *insubstantial*; delicate, dainty 331 *textural*; frail, fragile, friable 330 *brittle*; shoddy 641 *useless*; rickety, ramshackle, shaky, tottery, teetering 655 *dilapidated*.

Verb
(9) *be weak,* grow w., weaken; sicken 651 *be ill*; faint, fail, flag 684 *be fatigued*; drop, fall 309 *tumble*; dwindle 37 *decrease*; decline 655 *deteriorate*; droop, wilt, fade 131 *grow old*; wear thin, crumble; yield, give way, sag, split. totter, teeter 317 *oscillate*; tremble, shake 318 *be agitated*; halt, limp, go lame 278 *move slowly*.

(10) *weaken,* enfeeble, debilitate, enervate; unnerve 854 *frighten*; slacken, loosen 46 *disunite*; strain, sprain, cripple, lame 161 *disable*; hurt, injure 655 *wound*; cramp 702 *obstruct*; disarm; cushion 257 *blunt*; improverish, starve; deprive, rob 786 *take away*; reduce, extenuate 37 *abate*; dilute, water down 43 *mix*; devitalize, eviscerate; neutralize 182 *counteract*; decimate 105 *render few*; muffle 401 *mute*; invalidate 752 *abrogate*; damage 655 *impair*; sap, undermine; dismantle 165 *demolish*.

164
Production

Noun
(1) *production,* producing, creation; mental creation 449 *thought*; origination, invention 21 *originality*, 484 *discovery*; productivity 171 *productiveness*; effort, endeavour 672 *undertaking*; artistic effort, composition 551 *art*, 553 *painting*, 554 *sculpture*, 586 *writing*; musicianship 413 *musical skill*; doing, accomplishment, performance; output, throughput; execution, achievement 725 *effectuation*; concoction, brewing 669 *preparation*; shaping, forming, workmanship, craftsmanship 243 *formation*; planning, design 623 *plan*; organization 331 *structure*, 62 *arrangement*; engineering, civil e., building, architecture; construction, establishment, erection 310 *elevation*; making, fabrication, manufacture, industry 622 *business*; processing, process 147 *conversion*; machining, assembly; assembly line, production l. 71 *continuity*, 630 *machine*; factory 687 *workshop*; technology, mass production, industrialization, automation; development, growth; farming 370 *agriculture*; breeding 369 *animal husbandry*; procreation 167 *propagation*.

(2) *product,* creature, creation, result 157 *effect*; output, turnout; end-product, by-p.; waste, slag 41 *leavings*; extract, essence; confection, compound 43 *a mixture*; handiwork, artefact; article, finished a. 319 *object*; goods, wares 795 *merchandise*; earthenware 381 *pottery*; stoneware, hardware, ironware; fabric, cloth 222 *textile*; production, work, opus, piece 56 *composition*; chef d'oeuvre 694 *masterpiece*; fruit, flower, blossom, berry; produce, yield, harvest, crop, vintage 157 *growth*; interest, return 771 *gain*; mental product, brainchild, conception 451 *idea*; figment, fiction 513

ideality; offspring, young 132 *young creature*.

(3) *edifice,* building, structure, erection, pile; skyscraper 209 *high structure*; pyramid 548 *monument*; church 990 *temple*; mausoleum 364 *tomb*; habitation, mansion, hall 192 *house*; college 539 *school*; fortress 713 *fort*; stonework, timbering, brickwork, bricks and mortar 631 *building material*.

(4) *producer,* creator, maker; Nature, the Creator; originator, inventor, discoverer, founder 156 *cause*; creative worker, writer 589 *author*; composer 413 *musician*; painter, sculptor 556 *artist*; designer 623 *planner*; developer, constructor, builder, architect, engineer; manufacturer, industrialist; executive 686 *agent*; labourer 686 *worker*; craftsperson 686 *artisan*; agriculturalist 370 *farmer*; stock breeder 369 *breeder*.

Adjective
(5) *productive,* creative, inventive 513 *imaginative*; shaping, constructive 331 *structural*; manufacturing, industrial 243 *formative*; industrialized, developed, mechanized, automated; paying 640 *profitable*; fruitful 171 *prolific*.

(6) *produced,* made, made-up, cobbled together; created, artificial, man-made, synthetic, cultivated; manufactured, processed; handmade, done by hand; homemade, homespun; ready-made 243 *formed*; machine-made, mass-produced; bred, hatched; sown, grown; thought of, invented.

Verb
(7) *produce,* create, originate, make; invent 484 *discover*; think up, conceive 513 *imagine*; write, design 56 *compose*; operate 676 *do*; frame, fashion,

shape 243 *form*; knit, spin 222 *weave*; sew, run up 45 *tie*; forge, chisel, carve, sculpture, cast; coin 797 *mint*; manufacture, fabricate, prefabricate, process, turn out, mill, machine; mass-produce, churn out 166 *reproduce*; construct, build, raise, rear, erect, set up 310 *elevate*; put together, make up, assemble, compose; synthesize, blend 50 *combine*; mine, quarry 304 *extract*; establish, found 68 *initiate*; organize 62 *arrange*; develop, exploit; industrialize, mechanize, automate; engineer, contrive 623 *plan*; perform, implement, execute 725 *carry out*; bring about, yield results, effect 156 *cause*; breed, hatch, rear 369 *breed stock*; sow, grow 370 *cultivate*; bear young 167 *reproduce itself*; ring up, educate 534 *train*.

165
Destruction

Noun
(1) *destruction,* undoing 148 *reversion*; blotting out 550 *obliteration*; annihilation 2 *extinction*; abolition, suppression 752 *abrogation*; suffocation, stifling, silencing; subversion 149 *revolution*; prostration, precipitation, overthrow; levelling, razing, flattening; dissolving, dissolution 51 *decomposition*; breaking up, tearing down, demolition 655 *dilapidation*, 46 *disunion*; disruption 46 *separation*; crushing, grinding, pulverization; incineration 381 *burning*; liquidation, elimination, extermination; eradication, uprooting 300 *ejection*; wiping out, mopping up 725 *completion*; decimation, massacre, genocide 362 *slaughter*; hatchet job; wanton damage, destructiveness, vandalism 176

violence; sabotage 702 *hindrance*; fire-raising, arson 381 *incendiarism*.

(2) *havoc,* disaster area, chaos 61 *confusion, turmoil*; desolation, wilderness, scorched earth 172 *desert*; carnage, shambles; upheaval, cataclysm 176 *outbreak*; devastation, laying waste, ravages; depredation, raid 788 *spoliation*; blitz, explosion, nuclear blast 712 *bombardment*; holocaust, hecatomb.

(3) *ruin,* downfall, ruination, perdition, one's undoing; crushing blow 731 *adversity*; catastrophe, disaster, act of God 731 *misfortune*; collapse, debacle, landslide 149 *revolution*; breakdown, break-up 728 *failure*; crash, smash 279 *collision*; wreck, shipwreck, wreckage; sinking, loss, total l.; Waterloo 728 *defeat*; knockout blow 279 *knock*; slippery slope, road to ruin 655 *deterioration*; coup de grace 725 *completion*; apocalypse, doom, crack of doom, knell, end 69 *finality*; ruins 127 *oldness*.

Adjective
(4) *destructive,* destroying etc. vb.; internecine, root and branch 54 *complete*; consuming, ruinous 634 *wasteful*; sacrificial, costly 811 *dear*; exhausting, crushing 684 *fatiguing*; apocalyptic, cataclysmic, overwhelming 176 *violent*; raging 176 *furious*; merciless 906 *pitiless*; mortal, suicidal, cut-throat 362 *deadly*; subversive, subversionary 149 *revolutionary*; incendiary, mischievous, pernicious 645 *harmful*; poisonous 653 *toxic*.

(5) *destroyed,* undone, fallen, ruined, crushed, ground; pulped, broken up; suppressed, squashed, quashed 752 *abrogated*; lost, foundered, torpedoed, sunk; done for, had it, kaput; falling, crumbling, in ruins 655 *dilapidated*; doomed 69 *ending*.

Verb
(6) *destroy,* unmake, undo 148 *revert*; abolish, annihilate, liquidate, exterminate, axe 2 *nullify*; devour, consume 634 *waste*; swallow up, engulf 299 *absorb*; swamp, overwhelm, drown 341 *drench*; incinerate, burn up, gut 381 *burn*; wreck, shipwreck, sink (see *suppress*); end 69 *terminate*; put down, put away, do away with, get rid of 362 *kill*; poison 362 *murder*; decimate, exterminate 362 *slaughter*; remove, eradicate, uproot 300 *eject*; wipe out, efface, delete, blot out 550 *obliterate*; annul, revoke, tear up 752 *abrogate*; dispel, dissipate 75 *disperse,* 634 *waste*; knock out, mop up, trounce 726 *defeat*; sabotage 702 *obstruct*; ruin, be the ruin of, be one's undoing.

(7) *demolish,* dismantle, break down, knock d., pull d., tear d. 46 *disunite*; level, raze, raze to the ground 216 *flatten*; throw down, steamroller, bulldoze 311 *fell*; blow down, blow away, carry a.; cut down, mow d. 362 *slaughter*; knock over, kick o.; overthrow, overturn, upset 221 *invert*; sap 163 *weaken*; undermine, mine, dynamite, explode, blow up; bombard, bomb, blitz, blow to bits 712 *fire at*; wreck, break up, smash up; smash, shatter 46 *break*; pulp, crush, grind 332 *pulverize*; rend, tear up, tear to bits, pull to pieces 46 *sunder*; beat down, batter, ram 279 *strike*; gut, strip bare 229 *uncover*.

(8) *suppress,* quench, blow out, snuff o. 382 *extinguish*; cut short, nip in the bud 72 *discontinue*; quell, put down, stamp out, trample out, stamp on, sit on 735 *oppress*; squelch, squash, 216 *flatten*; quash 752 *abrogate*; stifle, smother, suffocate,

strangle 161 *disable*; keep down, repress 745 *subjugate*; cover 525 *conceal*; drown, sink, scuttle 313 *plunge*.

(9) *lay waste,* desolate, devastate, depopulate 300 *empty*; despoil, raid, ransack 788 *rob*; ravage, ruin 655 *impair*; make havoc 176 *be violent*; lay in ruins 311 *abase*; lay in ashes 381 *burn*; deforest, defoliate 172 *make sterile*.

(10) *consume,* devour, eat up, gobble up; swallow up, engulf 299 *absorb*; squander, run through 634 *waste*.

(11) *be destroyed,* go under, be lost 361 *perish*; sink, go down 313 *plunge*; have had it, be all over with 69 *end*; fall, bite the dust 309 *tumble*; break up, go to pieces, crumple up; fall into ruin, crumble 655 *deteriorate*; go to rack and ruin, succumb; go to the wall, go to the dogs.

166
Reproduction

Noun
(1) *reproduction,* procreation 167 *propagation*; remaking, reconstruction 164 *production*; multiplication, reduplication, mass production 106 *repetition*; printing 587 *print*; renovation 656 *restoration*; regeneration, resuscitation 656 *revival*; reincarnation, resurrection, resurgence 106 *recurrence*; Phoenix.

Adjective
(2) *reproduced,* renewed, renewing; reproductive 167 *generative*; renascent, resurgent.

Verb
(3) *reproduce,* remake, reconstruct; mass-produce, duplicate 20 *copy*, 106 *repeat*; take after, inherit 18 *resemble*; renovate, renew 656 *restore*; regenerate, resurrect 656 *revive*; breed,

multiply 167 *reproduce itself,* 104 *be many*.

167
Propagation

Noun
(1) *propagation* 166 *reproduction*; fertility, fecundity 171 *productiveness*; proliferation 36 *increase*; breeding 369 *animal husbandry*; eugenics 358 *biology*; sex, facts of life, copulation 45 *coition*; generation, procreation 156 *source*; fertilization, pollination, impregnation, insemination, artificial i., AID; test-tube baby; fertility drug 171 *fertilizer*; conception, pregnancy, germination, gestation; birth, nativity 68 *origin*; stillbirth 728 *failure*; birth rate; development 157 *growth*; fruition, puberty 669 *maturation*; maternity, paternity 169 *parentage*; procreator, inseminator, donor; fertilizer, pollinator; propagator, cultivator 370 *gardener*.

(2) *obstetrics,* midwifery; birth, childbirth, confinement; labour, labour pains, contractions; delivery, breech delivery, forceps d., Caesarian; umbilical cord; placenta, afterbirth; gynaecologist, obstetrician, midwife 658 *nurse*; stork, gooseberry bush.

(3) *genitalia,* loins, womb 156 *source*; genitals, private parts; penis, testicles, scrotum; vulva, clitoris, vagina; uterus, ovary, Fallopian tubes; ovum, egg; semen, seminal fluid, sperm, spermatozoa; seed, pollen.

Adjective
(4) *generative,* productive, reproductive, procreative; fertile, fecund 171 *prolific*; lifegiving, germinal, seminal, genetic 156 *fundamental*; sexual, bisexual; genital, vaginal, phallic.

(5) *fertilized,* impregnated; breeding, broody, pregnant, expecting, carrying, with child; in labour; puerperal, maternity; antenatal, postnatal.

Verb
(6) *reproduce itself,* yield, give increase 171 *be fruitful*; hatch, breed, spawn, multiply 104 *be many*; germinate, sprout, burgeon 36 *grow*; bloom, flower, fruit, bear fruit 669 *mature*; seed, seed itself; conceive, get pregnant; carry, bear; give birth, have a baby; abort, lose the baby 728 *miscarry*; have children, have young, have offspring, have progeny; lay (eggs), farrow, lamb, foal, calve, cub, pup, whelp; have one's birth 360 *be born*.

(7) *generate,* give life to, call into being 164 *produce*; beget, engender, spawn, father, sire; copulate 45 *unite with*; impregnate, inseminate, pollinate; procreate, propagate; breed, hatch, raise, rear 369 *breed stock*; raise from seed, take cuttings 370 *cultivate*.

168
Destroyer

Noun
(1) *destroyer,* demolisher; nihilist, anarchist 149 *revolutionist*; wrecker, arsonist, pyromaniac 381 *incendiarism*; despoiler, ravager, raider 712 *attacker*, 789 *robber*; saboteur 702 *hinderer*; defacer, eraser, extinguisher 550 *obliteration*; hatchet man, assassin 362 *murderer*; executioner 963 *punisher*; barbarian, Vandal, Hun; angel of death 361 *death*; locust 947 *glutton*; moth, woodworm, rust 51 *decay*; corrosive, acid, blight, poison 659 *bane*; earthquake, fire, flood 165 *havoc*; sword 718 *war*; bomb, gunpowder, dynamite 723 *explosive*; juggernaut, bulldozer 216 *flattener*.

169
Parentage

Noun
(1) *parentage,* paternity, maternity; parenthood, fatherhood, motherhood; womb 156 *source*; kinship 11 *family*; adoption, fostering, guardianship 660 *protection*; parent, single p. 896 *divorce*, *widowhood*; godparent, guardian.

(2) *genealogy,* family tree, lineage, 11 *consanguinity*; pedigree, heredity; line, blood, strain; blue blood 868 *nobility*; stock, stem, tribe, house, clan 11 *race*; descent, extraction, birth, ancestry 68 *origin*.

(3) *paternity,* fatherhood; father, dad, daddy, papa, pater; paterfamilias; procreator, begetter; grandfather, grandad, grandpa; ancestor, progenitor, forefather, forbear, patriarch 66 *precursor*; father figure; adoptive father, stepfather, father-in-law; fatherland.

(4) *maternity,* motherhood; expectant mother, mother-to-be 167 *propagation*; mother, mummy, mamma, mum, mater; grandmother, grandma, granny, gran; matron, matriarch; ancestress, progenitrix; foster-mother, stepmother; mother-in-law; Mother Church, mother country.

Adjective
(5) *parental,* paternal, maternal; fatherly, motherly.

170
Posterity

Noun
(1) *posterity,* progeny, issue, offspring, young, little ones 132 *child*; brood, litter 132 *young*

creature; children, grandchildren 11 *family*; succession, heirs 120 *posterity*.

(2) *descendant,* son, daughter; infant 132 *child*; scion, shoot; heir, heiress 776 *beneficiary*; love child 954 *bastardy*; branch, ramification, colony; graft, offshoot, offset.

(3) *sonship,* line, direct l., lineage, descent 11 *consanguinity*; indirect descent, collaterality; illegitimacy 954 *bastardy*; succession, heredity, heirship; primogeniture 119 *priority*.

Adjective
(4) *filial,* daughterly; descended, lineal; collateral; adopted, adoptive; step-; hereditary 5 *genetic*.

171
Productiveness

Noun
(1) *productiveness,* productivity 164 *production*; boom 730 *prosperity*; glut 637 *redundance*; fecundity, fertility, luxuriance, exuberance 635 *plenty*; high birthrate, baby boom, procreation 167 *propagation*; inventiveness 513 *imagination*.

(2) *fertilizer,* top-dressing, mulch 370 *agriculture*; semen, sperm, seed; fertility drug 167 *propagation*; fertility cult, f. rite, f. symbol, phallus; Earth Mother.

(3) *abundance,* wealth, riot, profusion, harvest 32 *great quantity*; teeming womb, mother earth; hotbed, nursery 156 *seedbed*; cornucopia, horn of plenty, milch cow; rabbit warren, ant heap 104 *multitude*.

Adjective
(4) *prolific,* fertile, fecund; teeming, spawning 167 *generative*; fruitful, pregnant, heavy with; exuberant, lush, leafy, verdant,

luxuriant, rich, fat 635 *plenteous*; copious, streaming, pouring; paying 640 *profitable*; creative, inventive, resourceful.

Verb
(5) *make fruitful,* make productive etc. adj., fertilize, water, irrigate 370 *cultivate*; impregnate, inseminate; procreate, produce, propagate 167 *generate*.

(6) *be fruitful,* fructify, flourish; burgeon, bloom, blossom; germinate; conceive, bear, have children 167 *reproduce itself*; teem, proliferate, pullulate, swarm, multiply, mushroom 104 *be many*; populate.

172
Unproductiveness

Noun
(1) *unproductiveness,* dearth, famine 636 *scarcity*; sterility, barrenness, infertility 161 *impotence*; deforestation, desertification, defoliation, erosion; dying race, falling birthrate 37 *decrease*; virginity 895 *celibacy*; change of life, menopause; poor return 772 *loss*; fruitlessness, waste of time 641 *lost labour*; slump, slack market, idleness 679 *inactivity*.

(2) *contraception,* birth control; contraceptive, pill, condom; chastity 747 *restraint*; sterilization, vasectomy.

(3) *desert,* dryness, aridity 342 *dryness*; waste, barren w., lunar landscape; heath, moor, bush, wild, wilderness; desert sands, sand dunes; dustbowl 634 *waste*.

Adjective
(4) *unproductive,* dried up, exhausted 634 *wasted*; sparse, scarce 636 *insufficient*; waste, desert, desolate; treeless, bleak, bare 190 *empty*; poor, stony,

shallow, eroded; barren, infertile, sour, sterile; withered, shrivelled, blasted; arid 342 *dry*; fallow, stagnating 674 *disused*; untilled, uncultivated impotent, sterilized, on the pill; childless, issueless; otiose 679 *inactive*; fruitless 641 *profitless*; inoperative, ineffective 161 *impotent*; abortive 728 *unsuccessful*.

Verb
(5) *be unproductive* - unprolific etc. adj.; rust, stagnate, lie fallow 679 *be inactive*; abort 728 *miscarry*; practise birth control.

(6) *make sterile*, make unproductive 634 *waste*; sterilize, vasectomize; castrate, geld 161 *unman*; deforest 165 *lay waste*; pasteurize, disinfect 648 *purify*.

173
Agency

Noun
(1) *agency*, operation, working, doing 676 *action*; job, office 622 *function*; exercise 673 *use*; force, play, swing 160 *power*; interaction 178 *influence*; procurement 689 *management*; service 628 *instrumentality*; effectiveness, efficiency 156 *causation*; quickening power 174 *stimulation*; maintenance, support 703 *aid*; co-agency 706 *cooperation*; execution 725 *effectuation*; process, processing, treatment, handling.

Adjective
(2) *operative*, effectual, efficacious 727 *successful*; executive, operational, functional; acting, working, in action, in operation, in force, in play, being exercised, at work 676 *doing*, 673 *used*; live, potent 174 *vigorous*; practical, workable 642 *advisable*; serviceable 640 *useful*; worked upon, acted u.

Verb
(3) *operate*, be in action, be in play, play; act, work, go, run 676 *do*; start up, tick over, idle; serve, execute, perform 622 *function*; do its job 727 *be successful*; take effect 156 *cause*; have effect 178 *influence*; take action, strike 678 *be active*; maintain, sustain 218 *support*; crew, man; make operate, bring into play, wind up, turn on, plug in, switch on, press the button; actuate, power, drive 265 *move*; process, treat; manipulate, handle, wield 673 *use*.

174
Vigour: Physical energy

Noun
(1) *vigorousness*, lustiness, energy, vigour 678 *activity*; dynamism, physical energy, dynamic e., impetus 160 *energy*; intensity, high pressure 162 *strength*; dash, elan 680 *haste*; exertion, effort 682 *labour*; fervour, enthusiasm 571 *vigour*; gusto, relish, zest, liveliness, spirit, éclat; fire, mettle 855 *courage*; fizz, verve, pep, drive, go, enterprise, initiative; vehemence, force 176 *violence*; oomph, thrust, push, kick, punch 712 *attack*; grip, bite, teeth, backbone, spunk 599 *resolution*; guts, grit 600 *stamina*; virility 162 *vitality*; live wire, spark, dynamo, dynamite, quicksilver.

(2) *stimulation*, activation, tonic effect; boost 36 *increase*; excitement 821 *excitation*; stir, bustle 678 *activity*; perturbation, ferment, 318 *agitation*; fermentation, leavening; ebullience, effervescence;

(3) *keenness*, acrimony, mordancy 388 *pungency*; poignancy,

point, edge 256 *sharpness*; zeal 597 *willingness*.

(4) *stimulant,* energizer, activator, booster; yeast, leaven, catalyst; stimulus, fillip, shot in the arm; spur, goad, lash 612 *incentive*; restorative 658 *tonic*; aperitif, appetizer seasoning, spice 389 *sauce*; liquor 301 *alcoholic drink*; aphrodisiac, philtre, love p.; pep talk 821 *excitant*.

Adjective
(5) *vigorous,* energetic 678 *active*; forceful, vehement 176 *violent*; vivid, vibrant 160 *dynamic*; high-pressure, intense, strenuous 678 *industrious*; enterprising, go-getting 285 *progressive*; aggressive, thrusting 712 *attacking*; keen 597 *willing*; double-edged, potent 160 *powerful*; hearty, virile, full-blooded 162 *strong*; full of punch, full of pep, zestful, lusty, mettlesome 819 *lively*; blooming, bouncing 650 *healthy*; brisk, snappy; fizzy, heady, racy; tonic, bracing, rousing, invigorating, stimulating 821 *exciting*; drastic, stringent 735 *severe*; gingered up, souped up 160 *powerful*; thriving, lush 171 *prolific*.

(6) *keen,* acute, sharp, incisive, trenchant 571 *forceful*; mordant, biting, poignant, pointed, sarcastic 851 *derisive*; virulent, corrosive, caustic 388 *pungent*; acid 393 *sour*.

Verb
(7) *be vigorous,* thrive, have zest, enjoy life 650 *be healthy*; burst with energy 162 *be strong*; show energy 678 *be active*, 682 *exert oneself*; exert energy, drive, push 279 *impel*; bang, slam, wrench 176 *force*; get up steam 277 *accelerate*; be thorough 725 *carry through*; strike hard, hammer 279 *strike*;

show one's power, throw one's weight about 178 *influence*.

(8) *invigorate,* energize, activate; galvanize, electrify, intensify, redouble; wind up, step up, pep up, ginger up, boost 162 *strengthen*; rouse, kindle, inflame, stimulate 821 *excite*; hearten, animate 833 *cheer*; intoxicate 949 *inebriate*; freshen, revive, act like a tonic 685 *refresh*; fertilize, irrigate 370 *cultivate*.

Adverb
(9) *vigorously,* forcibly, hard, straight from the shoulder; lustily, with a will; at full tilt, full steam ahead.

175
Inertness

Noun
(1) *inertness,* inertia 677 *inaction*; languor, paralysis, torpor 375 *insensibility*; vegetation, stagnation, passivity 266 *quiescence*; dormancy 523 *latency*; mental inertness, apathy, sloth 679 *sluggishness*; immobility, impassiveness, stolidity 823 *inexcitability*; vegetable, cabbage.

Adjective
(2) *inert,* passive, dead 677 *nonactive*; lifeless, languid, torpid 375 *insensible*; heavy, lumpish, sluggish 278 *slow*, 679 *inactive*; hibernating, vegetating, stagnant, fallow 266 *quiescent*; slack, low-pressure; limp, flaccid 163 *weak*; apathetic 820 *impassive*; unaggressive 823 *inexcitable*; suspended, in abeyance, smouldering, dormant 523 *latent*.

Verb
(3) *be inert,* slumber 679 *sleep*; hang fire, not catch; smoulder 523 *lurk*; lie, stagnate, vegetate 266 *be quiescent*; just sit there 677 *not act*.

Adverb

(4) *inactively,* at rest; in suspense, in abeyance, in reserve.

176
Violence

Noun

(1) *violence,* vehemence, frenzy 174 *vigorousness*; vandalism 165 *destruction*; turbulence, storminess 318 *commotion*; bluster, uproar, riot, row, roughhouse, rumpus, furore 61 *turmoil*; roughness, rough handling 735 *severity*; force, hammer blows, high hand, terrorism 735 *brute force*; atrocity, outrage torture 898 *cruel act*; barbarity, brutality, savagery, blood lust 898 *inhumanity*; fierceness, ferocity 906 *pitilessness*; rage, hysterics 822 *excitable state*; fit, paroxysm 318 *spasm*; shock, clash 279 *collision.*

(2) *outbreak,* outburst 318 *agitation*; cataclysm, convulsion, quake, tremor, eruption, volcano 149 *revolution*; explosion, blow-up, burst, blast 165 *destruction*; bursting open 46 *disunion*; detonation 400 *loudness*; rush, assault 712 *attack*; gush, spurt, jet 350 *stream.*

(3) *storm,* turmoil, turbulence, dirty weather, rough w., inclemency; squall, tempest, hurricane 352 *gale*; thunder, thunder and lightning, cloudburst 350 *rain*; snowstorm, blizzard 380 *wintriness*; sandstorm 352 *gale*; magnetic storm.

(4) *violent creature,* brute, beast, wild b.; tiger, wolf, she w., mad dog; demon, devil, hellcat 938 *monster*; savage, barbarian 168 *destroyer*; he-man 372 *male*; assassin, butcher 362 *murderer*; homicidal maniac 504 *madman*; rough, tough, rowdy, thug, mugger 904 *ruffian*; hooligan, bully, bully boy, terror

735 *tyrant*; thunderer, fire-eater 877 *boaster*; firebrand, incendiary 738 *agitator*; anarchist, terrorist 857 *desperado*; virago, termagant, Amazon; spitfire, fury 892 *shrew.*

Adjective

(5) *violent,* vehement, forcible 162 *strong*; acute 256 *sharp*; excessive 32 *exorbitant*; rude, abrupt, brusque, bluff 885 *discourteous*; extreme, tyrannical 735 *oppressive*; barbarous, savage, brutal, bloody 898 *cruel*; hot-blooded 892 *irascible*; aggressive 718 *warlike*; struggling, kicking, thrashing about 61 *disorderly*; rough, wild, furious, raging, blustery, tempestuous, stormy 352 *windy*; torrential 350 *rainy*; uproarious, obstreperous 400 *loud*; rowdy, turbulent, tumultuous, boisterous 738 *riotous*; incendiary, anarchistic 149 *revolutionary*; intemperate, unbridled, uncontrollable, unruly 738 *disobedient*; irrepressible 174 *vigorous*; ebullient, red-hot, inflamed; inflammatory, scorching, flaming 379 *fiery*; eruptive, cataclysmic, overwhelming, volcanic, seismic 165 *destructive*; explosive, bursting; convulsive, spasmodic 318 *agitated*; disturbed, troublous.

(6) *furious,* fuming, boiling, infuriated, mad 891 *angry*; impetuous, rampant, gnashing; roaring, howling; desperate 857 *rash*; savage, wild; blustering, threatening 899 *cursing*; vicious, fierce, ferocious 898 *cruel*; blood-thirsty, ravening, rabid, berserk 362 *murderous*; waspish, tigerish; frantic, hysterical 503 *frenzied.*

Verb

(7) *be violent,* break bounds, run wild, run riot, run amok 165 *lay waste*; tear, rush, dash, hurtle, hurl oneself, rush headlong 277 *move fast*; crash in, burst in;

surge forward, stampede, mob 712 *charge*; break the peace, raise a storm, riot, go on the rampage 61 *rampage*; resort to violence 738 *revolt*; see red, go berserk 891 *be angry*; storm, rage, roar, bluster 352 *blow*; foam, fume, run high, boil over 318 *effervesce*; burst its banks, flood, overwhelm; explode, go off, blow up, detonate, burst; let fly, fulminate; erupt, break out, burst o.; struggle, bite, kick, lash out 715 *resist*; savage, maul 655 *wound*; bear down on, ride roughshod over, tyrannize 735 *oppress*.

(8) *force*, use f., smash 46 *break*; tear, rend 46 *sunder*; bruise, crush 332 *pulverize*; blow up 165 *demolish*; strain, wrench, pull, dislocate, sprain; twist, warp, deform 246 *distort*; force open, prize o. 263 *open*; blow open, burst o.; shake 318 *agitate*; do violence to, abuse 675 *misuse*; violate, ravish, rape; torture 645 *ill-treat*.

(9) *make violent*, stir 821 *excite*; goad, lash, whip 612 *incite*; stir up, inflame 381 *kindle*; foment, exacerbate 832 *aggravate*; whet 256 *sharpen*; irritate, infuriate 891 *enrage*; madden 503 *make mad*.

Adverb
(10) *violently*, forcibly, bodily, by storm, by force, by main force; tooth and nail, hammer and tongs, with a vengeance, like mad; precipitately, headlong, slap bang, wham; head foremost, head first.

177
Moderation

Noun
(1) *moderation*, nonviolence; mildness, gentleness 736 *leniency*; harmlessness, innocuousness 935 *innocence*; moderateness, reasonableness 502

sanity; measure, golden mean 732 *averageness*; temperateness, restraint, self-control 942 *temperance*; soberness 823 *inexcitability*; impartiality 625 *middle way*; mitigation 831 *relief*; relaxation, easing, alleviation; mollification, appeasement, *assuagement* 770 *compromise*; détente 719 *pacification*; sedation; quiet, calm 266 *quietude*; control, check 747 *restraint*.

(2) *moderator*, palliative 658 *remedy*; alleviative 658 *balm*; sedative, tranquillizer, dummy 679 *soporific*; opiate 375 *anaesthetic*; wet blanket, damper 382 *extinguisher*; brake 747 *restraint*; cushion, shock absorber 327 *softness*; third force, peacemaker 720 *mediator*; restraining hand, rein.

Adjective
(3) *moderate*, nonviolent, reasonable; tame, gentle, harmless, mild 736 *lenient*; measured, low-key 747 *restrained*; chastened, subdued, sober; tempered 942 *temperate*; cool, calm, composed 823 *inexcitable*; still, quiet 266 *tranquil*; peaceable, pacific 717 *peaceful*; nonextreme, neutral.

(4) *lenitive*, alleviative, assuaging, pain-killing 658 *remedial*; anodyne, sedative, hypnotic, narcotic 679 *soporific*; soothing, bland, emollient 334 *lubricated*; comforting 685 *refreshing*.

Verb
(5) *be moderate*, - gentle etc. adj.; go easy, sober down 266 *be quiescent*; disarm, keep the peace 717 *be at peace*; relent 905 *show mercy*; not press 736 *be lenient*; ease off 278 *decelerate*.

(6) *moderate*, mitigate, temper; correct 24 *adjust*; tame, check, curb, control 747 *restrain*; lessen, diminish, slacken 37 *abate*; qualify 163 *weaken*; cushion

218 *support*; play down, soft-pedal, tone down; sober, sober down, dampen, cool, chill 613 *dissuade*; smother, subdue, quell 382 *extinguish*.

(7) *assuage,* ease, take the sting out of; pour balm, mollify 327 *soften*; alleviate, lighten 831 *relieve*; neutralize 182 *counteract*; allay, dull, deaden soothe, calm, tranquillize, comfort, still, quiet, hush, lull, cradle 266 *bring to rest*; appease 719 *pacify*; slake 301 *drink*.

Adverb
(8) *moderately,* in moderation, within bounds, within limits, within reason; gingerly, nervously, softly softly.

178
Influence

Noun
(1) *influence,* capability, power, potentiality 160 *ability*; prevalence, predominance 34 *superiority*; mightiness, magnitude 32 *greatness,* 638 *importance*; whip hand, casting vote; vantage ground, footing, hold, grip; leverage, purchase, clout, weight, pressure; pull, magnetism 291 *attraction*; contagion, infection; atmosphere, climate 8 *circumstance*; occult influence 983 *sorcery*; destiny 596 *fate*; fascination, hypnotism malign influence, curse, ruin 659 *bane*; impulse, feeling 817 *affections*; persuasion, insinuation, suggestion, inspiration 612 *motive*; personality, charisma, leadership; credit, repute 866 *prestige*; ascendancy, sway, control 733 *governance*; sphere of influence, orbit; factor, contributing f., vital role 156 *cause*; patronage, favour, friend at court 703 *aid*; strings, lever 630 *tool*; secret influence, hidden hand 523 *latency*; force,

lobby, pressure group 612 *inducement*; manipulator, manoeuvrer; big noise 638 *bigwig*; powers that be 733 *government*.

Adjective
(2) *influential,* dominant, predominant, prevalent, prevailing, monopolistic 34 *supreme*; in power, ruling, reigning, listened to, obeyed; recognized, with authority 733 *authoritative*; rising, in the ascendant 36 *increasing*; strong, potent, mighty 32 *great*, 160 *powerful*; leading, guiding 689 *directing*; inspiring, encouraging; contributing, effective 156 *causal*; weighty, key, decisive 638 *important*; telling, moving 821 *impressive*; appealing, attractive 291 *attracting*; gripping, fascinating, charismatic; irresistible, hypnotic 740 *compelling*; persuasive, tempting 612 *inducing*; spreading, catching, contagious 653 *infectious*; pervasive 189 *ubiquitous*.

Verb
(3) *influence,* have i., carry weight 638 *be important*; be listened to, be obeyed 737 *command*; dominate, have a hold on wear the trousers 34 *be superior*; exert influence, make oneself felt, assert oneself; put pressure on, lobby, pull strings 612 *motivate*; gain a hearing 455 *attract notice*; have a voice, have a say in; affect, sway, tell, turn the scale 821 *impress*; soften up, work on 925 *flatter*; urge, prompt, tempt, incite, inspire, persuade, prevail upon 612 *induce*; force 740 *compel*; brainwash, prejudice 481 *bias*; fascinate, hypnotize, mesmerize 291 *attract*; make or mar, change 147 *transform*; infect, colour 143 *modify*; play a part 689 *direct*; set the fashion, 23 *be an example*.

(4) *prevail,* outweigh, override, overbear, turn the scale 34

predominate; overawe, overcome, subdue, subjugate; master 727 *overmaster*; control, rule, monopolize 733 *dominate*; hold, take a hold on 778 *retain*; gain a footing, take root; permeate 189 *pervade*; catch on, spread, be rife.

Adverb

(5) *influentially,* to good effect, with telling e.;

179
Tendency

Noun

(1) *tendency,* trend, tenor; set, drift 281 *direction*; course, stream, mainstream, spirit of the age, climate 178 *influence*; gravitation, affinity 291 *attraction*; aptness 24 *fitness*; gift, instinct for 694 *aptitude*; proneness, propensity, predisposition readiness, inclination, penchant, predilection, liking, leaning, bias, prejudice; weakness 180 *liability*; cast, bent, grain; a strain of 43 *tincture*; vein, humour, mood; nature 5 *temperament*; idiosyncrasy 80 *speciality*.

Adjective

(2) *tending,* trending, conducive, leading to, pointing to; working towards, aiming at 617 *intending*; calculated to 471 *probable*; apt to, prone to; ready to, about to 669 *prepared*.

Verb

(3) *tend,* trend, verge, lean, incline; set in, set towards, gravitate t. 289 *approach*; affect, dispose, bias, bend to 178 *influence*; point to, lead to 156 *conduce*; bid fair to, be calculated to 471 *be likely*; redound to, contribute to 285 *promote*.

180
Liability

Noun

(1) *liability,* weakness 179 *tendency*; susceptibility 661 *vulnerability*; susceptivity 374 *sensibility*; potentiality 469 *possibility*; likelihood 471 *probability*; accountability 917 *duty*.

Adjective

(2) *liable,* apt to 179 *tending*; subject to, prey to, at the mercy of 745 *subject*; open to, exposed to, in danger of 661 *vulnerable*; dependent on, contingent 157 *caused*; on the cards 469 *possible*; susceptible 819 *impressible*; answerable, responsible 917 *obliged*.

Verb

(3) *be liable,* - subject to etc. adj.; be responsible, answer for 917 *incur a duty*; incur, lay oneself open to; run the risk of, stand to gain *or* to lose; open the door to 156 *conduce*.

181
Concurrence:
Combination of
causes

Noun

(1) *concurrence,* joint effort, collaboration 706 *cooperation*; coincidence 24 *conformance*; concord, harmony 24 *agreement*; compliance 758 *consent*; consensus 488 *assent*; acquiescence 721 *submission*; collusion, conspiracy 623 *plot*; alliance, partnership 706 *association*; conjunction, liaison 45 *union*.

Adjective

(2) *concurrent,* coincident, concomitant, parallel 89 *accompanying*; in alliance 706 *cooperative*; banded together 708

corporate; of one mind 488 *assenting*; joint, combined 45 *joined*; conforming 24 *agreeing*; colluding, conniving, abetting, contributing 703 *aiding*.

Verb
(3) *concur,* acquiesce 488 *assent*; collude, connive, conspire 623 *plot*; agree, harmonize 24 *accord*; pull together 706 *cooperate*; contribute, help, abet 703 *minister to*; promote 156 *conduce*; go along with, 89 *accompany*; unite, stand together 48 *cohere*.

Adverb
(4) *concurrently,* with one consent, with one accord, in harmony; hand in glove.

182
Counteraction

Noun
(1) *counteraction,* opposing causes; polarity antagonism, antipathy, clash, conflict 14 *contrariety,* 279 *collision*; return action, reaction, repercussion 280 *recoil*; recalcitrance 715 *resistance*; inertia, friction, drag, check 702 *hindrance*; repression, suppression 747 *restraint*; intolerance, persecution 735 *severity*; cancellation 165 *destruction*; crosscurrent,

headwind 702 *obstacle*; antidote, neutralizer 31 *offset*; counterblast 688 *tactics*; deterrent 713 *defence*; preventative 757 *prohibition*.

Adjective
(2) *counteracting,* counter 14 *contrary*; antipathetic, antagonistic, hostile 881 *inimical*; resistant, recalcitrant 715 *resisting*; reactive 280 *recoiling*; retarding, checking 747 *restraining*; preventive, preventative, contraceptive; antidotal, corrective 658 *remedial*; balancing, offsetting 31 *compensatory*.

Verb
(3) *counteract,* counter, run c to, cross, work against, go a., militate a.; not conduce to 702 *hinder*; react 280 *recoil*; resist 704 *oppose*; conflict with 14 *be contrary*; clash 279 *collide*; interfere 678 *meddle*; cancel out 31 *set off*; repress 165 *suppress*; undo, cancel 752 *abrogate*; neutralize, demagnetize; cure 658 *remedy*; recover 656 *retrieve*; obviate, prevent, inhibit 757 *prohibit*.

Adverb
(4) *although,* in spite of, despite, against, contrary to 704 *in opposition*.

Class two

Spatial Relationships

183
· Space: Indefinite space

Noun

(1) *space,* expanse, extent, surface, area; volume, cubic content; continuum, space-time; empty space 190 *emptiness;* depth of space 107 *infinity;* outer space 321 *heavens;* world, wide w., vastness, immensity; open space, open country; wide horizons, wide open spaces 348 *plain;* outback, hinterland 184 *region;* wild, wilderness, waste 172 *desert.*

(2) *measure,* proportions, dimension 203 *length,* 205 *breadth,* 209 *height,* 211 *depth;* area, acreage, acres; hectare, hide; volume, cubic content 195 *size.*

(3) *range,* reach, carry, compass, coverage; stretch, grasp, span; radius, latitude, amplitude; sweep, spread; play, swing 744 *scope;* sphere, field, arena 184 *region;* prospect 438 *view;* perspective 199 *distance;* magnifying power 417 *optics.*

(4) *room,* space, accommodation; capacity, stowage, storage space 632 *storage;* seating capacity, seating; standing room; margin, clearance, room to spare, r. to manoeuvre, elbowroom, legroom, headroom, headway; sea room, seaway, leeway; opening 263 *open space.*

Adjective

(5) *spatial,* space; cubic, three-dimensional; flat two-dimensional.

(6) *spacious* 32 *extensive;* expansive, roomy, commodious; ample, vast, cavernous, capacious, broad, deep, wide; voluminous, baggy 195 *large;* far-reaching, far-flung, widespread, world-wide 52 *whole;* boundless 107 *infinite;* extending, spreading, branching.

Verb

(7) *extend,* spread, spread out, range, cover; span, straddle, bestride; extend to, reach to 202 *be contiguous;* branch, ramify.

Adverb

(8) *widely,* extensively, everywhere, wherever; far and near, far and wide, all over, from pole to pole, in every quarter, in all quarters 54 *throughout;* at every turn, here, there and everywhere, high and low, inside and out.

184
Region: Definite space

Noun

(1) *region,* locality, parts 185 *place;* sphere, orb, hemisphere; zone, belt; latitude, parallel, meridian; clime, climate; tract, *terrain,* country 344 *land;* island, peninsula, continent, landmass sea 343 *ocean;* Old World, New W.; East and West, North and South; Third World; circumference, boundaries, confines 236 *limit;* precincts 235 *enclosure;* area, field, theatre 724 *arena.*

(2) *territory,* sphere, zone; catchment area; beat, pitch, ground;

lot, holding, claim 235 *enclosure*; grounds, park, domain 777 *estate*; airspace, territorial waters; defensible space; colony, settlement; homeland 192 *home*; kingdom, realm, empire 733 *political organization*; no-man's-land.

(3) *district,* quarter 187 *locality*; state, province, county, shire, hundred, tithing; diocese, bishopric, archbishopric; parish, ward, constituency; borough, township, municipality; county, district, metropolitan area; hamlet, village, town 192 *abode*; built-up area, suburb 192 *housing*; garden city, new town; green belt; Home Counties, provinces, Borders; Highlands, Lowlands; hinterland, outback, backwoods, bush, brush, countryside 344 *land*.

(4) *city,* capital c., cathedral c., metropolis, conurbation; the Big City, West End, W. Side, East End, E. side, City; uptown, downtown.

Adjective
(5) *regional,* territorial, continental, insular; national, state; local, municipal, parochial 192 *provincial*; suburban, urban, rural, up-country; district, town, country.

185
Place: Limited space

Noun
(1) *place,* site, location, position 186 *situation*; station, substation; quarter, locality 184 *district*; assigned place, pitch, beat, billet; centre, meeting place 76 *focus*; dwelling place 192 *home*; address, habitat 187 *locality,* 192 *quarters*; premises, place of residence 192 *house*; spot, plot; point, dot, pinpoint; niche, nook, corner 194 *compartment*; confines, bounds 236

limit; precinct, paddock, compound, pen 235 *enclosure*; close, quadrangle, quad, square; yard, courtyard 263 *open space*; farmyard, field 370 *farm*.

Adverb
(2) *somewhere,* here and there, passim; locally 200 *near.*

186
Situation

Noun
(1) *situation,* position, setting; scene, locale; time and place, when and where; location, address, whereabouts; point, stage 27 *degree*; site, seat, emplacement, base 185 *place*; habitat, range 184 *region*; post, station; standpoint 7 *state*; side, aspect, frontage, orientation; geography, topography 321 *earth sciences*; chart 551 *map.*

(2) *bearings,* declination, ascension; latitude and longitude 187 *location.*

Adjective
(3) *situated,* situate, located at, living at, settled, stationed, posted; occupying 187 *located*; local; topographical, geographical.

Verb
(4) *be situated,* be found at, be, lie, stand; centre on; be stationed, be posted; live at 192 *dwell*; touch 200 *be near.*

Adverb
(5) *in place,* in situ, in loco, here, there; in, on, over, under; hereabouts.

187
Location

Noun
(1) *location,* placing, placement,

emplacement, disposition 62 *arrangement*; posting, stationing; finding the place, locating, pinpointing; radar; centering, localization 200 *nearness*; settling, colonization, population; settlement, resettlement, establishment, installation; putting in 303 *insertion*; loading 632 *storage*.

(2) *locality,* quarters, purlieus, environs, environment, surroundings, milieu, neighbourhood, parts 184 *district*; vicinity 200 *near place*; address, street, habitat 192 *abode*; seat, site 185 *place*; meeting place, venue, haunt 76 *focus*; genius loci, spirit of place.

(3) *station,* seat, site, position 186 *situation*; depot, base; colony, settlement; anchorage, mooring 662 *shelter*; camp, encampment, bivouac; hostel 192 *abode*; lay-by, parking place 145 *stopping place*.

Adjective
(4) *located,* placed etc. vb., stationed, posted 186 *situated*; ensconced, embedded, cradled, nestled 232 *circumscribed*; settled, domesticated 153 *fixed*; encamped, camping, lodged 192 *residing*; moored, anchored 266 *quiescent*; vested in 773 *possessed*; transferred to 780 *transferred*; well-placed, favourably situated.

Verb
(5) *place,* assign a place 62 *arrange*; situate, position, site, locate; base, centre, localize; narrow down, pinpoint; find the place, aim well, hit the mark 281 *aim*; put, lay, set, seat; station, post, park; install, ensconce, fix 153 *stabilize*; fix in, root, plant, implant, embed, slot in 303 *insert*; accommodate, find room for, lodge, house, quarter, billet; quarter upon, billet on; moor,

tether, picket, anchor 45 *tie*; dock, berth 266 *bring to rest*; deposit, lay down, put d., set d.; stand, put up, erect 310 *elevate*; transfer 780 *assign*; array, deploy.

(6) *replace,* put back, sheathe; reinstate 656 *restore*; repatriate, resettle 272 *transpose*; reset.

(7) *stow,* put away, put by; pocket, pack, bale, store; put on board 193 *load*; squeeze in, cram in 54 *fill*.

(8) *place oneself,* stand, take one's place, take one's stand; anchor, drop a., cast a. 266 *come to rest*; settle, strike root, take r.; gain a footing, entrench oneself, dig in 144 *stay*; perch, alight, sit on, sit, squat, park; pitch one's tent, encamp, camp, bivouac; stop at, lodge, put up; ensconce oneself, locate oneself, establish o., find a home, move in, put down roots; settle, colonize 192 *dwell*.

188
Displacement

Noun
(1) *displacement,* dislocation, derailment 63 *derangement*; misplacement, wrong place 84 *abnormality*; shift, move 265 *motion*; aberration 282 *deviation*; transfer 272 *transference*; mutual transfer 151 *interchange*; relief, replacement 150 *substitution*; removal, taking away 304 *extraction*; unloading, unpacking; expulsion 300 *ejection*; exile, banishment 883 *seclusion*; refugee 268 *wanderer*; fish out of water 25 *misfit*.

Adjective
(2) *displaced,* removed etc. vb.; transported 272 *transferable*; aberrant 282 *deviating*; unplaced, rootless, unsettled, roofless, homeless 57 *excluded*.

(3) *misplaced,* out of place 84 *abnormal*; inappropriate 10 *irrelevant*; mislaid, lost, missing 190 *absent.*

Verb

(4) *displace,* disturb, disorientate, derail, dislocate; dislodge, unseat 46 *disunite*; scatter, send flying 75 *disperse*; shift, remove 265 *move*; cart away, transport 272 *transfer*; transpose 151 *interchange*; dispatch, post 272 *send*; relegate, banish, exile 300 *dismiss*; set aside 752 *depose*; turn out, evict 300 *eject*; eradicate, uproot 165 *destroy*; discharge, unload, offload, tranship; clear away, sweep up 648 *clean*; take away, cart off; lift, raise 310 *elevate*; draw, draw out, pull o. 304 *extract.*

(5) *misplace,* mislay, lose, lose touch with, lose track of.

189
Presence

Noun

(1) *presence,* existence, whereabouts 186 *situation*; being everywhere, ubiquity, omnipresence; permeation, pervasion, diffusion; availability, attendance, personal a.; residence, occupancy, occupation, sit-in 773 *possession*; visit, stay; spectator, bystander 441 *onlookers.*

Adjective

(2) *on the spot,* present 1 *existing*; occupying, in occupation; inhabiting, resident, domiciled 192 *residing*; attendant, waiting, still there; ready, on tap, available, on 669 *prepared*; at home, at hand, within reach, on call; under one's nose, before one's eyes 443 *obvious*; looking on, standing by.

(3) *ubiquitous,* omnipresent, permeating, pervading, pervasive 79 *universal.*

Verb

(4) *be present,* exist, be; take up space, occupy; colonize, inhabit 192 *dwell*; hold 773 *possess*; stand, lie 186 *be situated*; look on, stand by, witness 441 *watch*; resort to, frequent, haunt; occur 154 *happen*; stay, sojourn 882 *visit*; attend, assist at, take part; show up, turn up, present oneself, announce o. 295 *arrive*; be in evidence, show one's face, put in an appearance, look in on; face, confront.

(5) *pervade,* permeate, fill 54 *make complete*; be disseminated, impregnate, soak, run through; overrun, swarm over, spread 297 *infiltrate*; make one's presence felt 178 *influence.*

Adverb

(6) *here,* there, where, everywhere, in situ, in place; on location; aboard, on board, at home; on the spot; before, in the presence of, under the eyes *or* the nose of; in person,

190
Absence

Noun

(1) *absence* 446 *disappearance*; lack 636 *scarcity*; deprivation 772 *loss*; being elsewhere, alibi; nonresidence, living out; leave of absence, furlough; nonappearance, nonattendance, truancy, absenteeism, French leave 620 *avoidance*; absentee, truant; absentee landlord.

(2) *emptiness,* bareness, empty space, void, vacuity, vacancy; blank 201 *gap*; nothing inside, hollowness, shell; vacuum, air pocket; blank cartridge, blank paper; virgin territory, no-man's-land; waste 172 *desert*; vacant lot, bomb site 183 *room.*

(3) *nobody,* no one, not a soul.

Adjective

(4) *absent,* not present, not found, away, not resident; on tour, on location; out, not at home; gone, flown, disappeared 446 *disappearing;* lacking, wanting, missing, wanted; absent without leave, AWOL; truant, absentee 667 *escaped;* off the menu, off lost, mislaid, nowhere to be found; exempt from, spared; on leave, on furlough; omitted, left out 57 *excluded.*

(5) *empty,* void, devoid, bare; blank, clean; characterless, featureless; vacant, hollow; unoccupied, uninhabited; unpeopled, depopulated; deserted 621 *relinquished;* unsettled, godforsaken, lonely; bleak, desolate, uninhabitable.

Verb

(6) *be absent,* absent oneself, not show up, stay away, keep away, play truant; cut, skip 620 *avoid;* be missed, leave a gap, leave empty, evacuate, vacate 300 *empty.*

(7) *go away,* withdraw, leave 296 *depart;* slip out, slip away, be off 296 *decamp,* 667 *escape;* vanish 446 *disappear;* move over, make room, vacate.

Adverb

(8) *without,* minus, sans; in default of, for want of.

(9) *not here,* not there; elsewhere, somewhere else; nowhere; in one's absence, behind one's back.

191
Inhabitant

Noun

(1) *dweller,* inhabitant, denizen; sojourner, transient, visitant; migrant, expatriate 59 *foreigner;* mainlander, Continental; islander; highlander, lowlander, borderer; city-dweller, town-d., slum d.; suburbanite, commuter; metropolitan, provincial; villager, countrydweller; cave-dweller, troglodyte.

(2) *resident,* householder, ratepayer; housewife, housekeeper; cottager, crofter; addressee, occupier, occupant, incumbent; tenant, renter, lessee, lease-holder; inmate, in-patient; house surgeon; garrison, crew; lodger, boarder, au pair, paying guest; guest, visitor; squatter 59 *intruder;* parasite.

(3) *native,* aboriginal, aborigines; tribe 371 *nation;* local, local inhabitant; parishioner, villager, townsperson, city slicker, cockney, suburbanite, weekender; rustic 869 *countrydweller;* national, patrial, citizen, burgher; Northerner, Southerner 59 *foreigner;* earthdweller, terrestrial.

(4) *settler,* pioneer, Pilgrim Fathers 66 *precursor;* immigrant, colonist, colonial, creole; planter 370 *farmer;* resident alien 59 *foreigner.*

(5) *inhabitants,* population, urban p., rural p., townspeople, country folk; populace, people, citizenry, tenantry, yeomanry; suburbia 192 *housing;* household 11 *family;* settlement, stronghold; colony, commune. village c.

Adjective

(6) *native,* vernacular, popular, national, ethnic; indigenous, aboriginal; earthbound, terrestrial; home, domestic, domiciliary; settled, domiciled, naturalized; resident.

(7) *occupied,* inhabited, lived in, tenanted, populated; manned, staffed.

192
Abode: Place of habitation or resort

Noun

(1) *abode*, habitat, haunt 186 *situation*; habitation 187 *locality*; home, second h.; address, number; domicile, residence, residency; town, city 184 *district*; headquarters, base, seat; temporary abode, hangout, camp, pad, pied-a-terre, home from home; weekend cottage, country seat, holiday home, seaside resort; spa, sanatorium 658 *hospital*; cantonment, lines 187 *station*; bivouac, encampment; camp, refugee c.

(2) *quarters*, living q., married q., accommodation, lodging, billet, berth, squat; barracks, lodgings, rooms, chambers, digs; guest house, boarding h., lodging h., pension; boarding school, hostel, dormitory, hall of residence; convent 986 *monastery*.

(3) *dwelling*, cave, hut, kraal, igloo; wigwam, tepee, tent; lair, den, hole, form, burrow, warren, earth, sett 662 *shelter*.

(4) *nest*, branch 366 *tree*; eyrie, perch, roost; covert, heronry, rookery, hatchery, aviary, apiary, beehive, skep; wasp's nest, anthill.

(5) *home*, hearth, fireside, chimney corner, inglenook; roof, homestead; birthplace, native land, homeland, one's country, motherland, fatherland; native soil, native heath, home ground, home town, haunt, stamping ground; household gods.

(6) *house*, building 164 *edifice*; home, residence, dwelling; country house, town h.; villa, detached house, semidetached

h., semi, terraced house; prefab; bungalow, chalet-b.; seat, place, mansion, hall, stately home; palace, castle, keep, tower, manor house, dower h., manor, grange, lodge, priory, abbey; vicarage 986 *parsonage*; farmhouse, croft 370 *farm*.

(7) *small house*, two-up two-down, back-to-back; chalet, lodge, cottage, cabin, log c.; hut, Nissen h., shanty, hovel; dump, hole, box; shed, shack, lean-to, outhouse, outbuilding; shelter, tent; kiosk, booth, stall; houseboat, mobile home, caravan, trailer.

(8) *housing*, high-density h.; bricks and mortar built-up area, urban sprawl; urbanization, conurbation; town, suburb 184 *city*; suburbia, housing estate, overspill e., residential area 184 *district*; crescent, close, terrace, square, avenue, street, road; block, court, row, mansions, villas, buildings; houses, tenements; inner city, ghetto, slum, shanty town, hutments; hamlet, village.

(9) *flat*, flatlet, bedsitter; penthouse; apartment, suite, chambers; maisonette, duplex; apartment block, tower b.; mews, tenements.

(10) *stable*, byre, kennel, doghouse; sty, stall, cage, coop, hutch, battery; stabling, mews; garage, carport, hangar; boathouse; marina, dock; berth, quay, jetty.

(11) *inn*, hotel, hostelry, roadhouse, motel; doss-house, night shelter; youth hostel.

(12) *tavern*, pub, public house, local; saloon, speakeasy, dive, joint, honky-tonk; shebeen; wine bar, beer cellar, beer garden; bar, taproom.

(13) *café*, restaurant, cafeteria; eating-house, diner, brasserie,

bistro, grill room, rotisserie; coffee bar, snack bar; teahouse, tearoom; refreshment room, buffet, canteen, Naafi; takeaway; pull-in, transport cafe.

(14) *meeting place*, meeting house 990 *church*; day centre, community c., village hall; assembly rooms, pump r.; club, clubhouse; night club 837 *place of amusement*; sports centre, shopping c.; quad campus, village green 76 *focus*.

(15) *pleasance*, park, grounds, gardens; avenue, parade, promenade, boulevard; parkland 837 *pleasure ground*.

(16) *pavilion*, kiosk, bandstand, rotunda 194 *arbour*; tent, marquee.

(17) *retreat*, sanctuary, refuge, asylum 662 *shelter*; cubbyhole 527 *hiding-place*; den, sanctum 194 *chamber*; cell, hermitage 883 *seclusion*; almshouse, workhouse, poorhouse; orphanage, home, rest h., hospice, halfway house.

Adjective
(18) *urban*, metropolitan, cosmopolitan, inner-city, suburban; built-up, urbanized, suburbanized; residential.

(19) *provincial*, parochial, local, domestic, vernacular; up-country, countrified, rural, rustic.

(20) *architectural*, designed 243 *formed*; classical, neoclassical, Palladian; brick, concrete, cob, timber-framed, half-timbered; thatched, tiled 226 *covered*; modest, substantial, palatial, grand; detached, semi-d.; back-to-back; single-storey, multistorey, high-rise.

Verb
(21) *dwell*, dwell in, inhabit, populate, people, settle, colonize; take up residence, move in; reside, remain, abide, sojourn, live; take rooms, put up at, stay, lodge, live in, board out, be in digs; tenant, occupy, squat; perch, roost, nest; camp, bivouac, doss down, pitch one's tent; berth, dock, anchor, come to rest.

(22) *urbanize*, suburbanize, develop, build up.

193
Contents: Things contained

Noun
(1) *contents*, ingredients, constituents 58 *component*; inventory 87 *list*; furnishings, equipment 633 *provision*; load, payload, cargo, lading, freight, shipment; enclosure, stuffing, filling.

Verb
(2) *load*, lade, freight, charge, stow; containerize; take on board, ship; burden with overburden; pack, pack in, fit in 303 *insert*; pack tight, squeeze in 54 *fill*; pad, wad, line;

194
Receptacle

Noun
(1) *receptacle*, container, holder; frame 218 *prop*; cage 748 *prison*; folder, wrapper, envelope; net, trap; sheath, cocoon; packaging 226 *wrapping*; capsule, ampoule; mould 243 *form*; socket 255 *cavity*; slot 262 *furrow*; hole 263 *opening*; well, hold 632 *store*; drain 649 *sink*; crockery.

(2) *bladder*, balloon, inflatable; gasbag; football; blister, bubble 253 *swelling*; udder, teat.

(3) *maw*, stomach, tummy, abdomen, belly; gizzard, gullet, crop, jaws 263 *orifice*.

(4) *compartment,* cell, follicle, ventricle; cage, cubicle, booth, stall; box, pew; niche, nook, cranny, recess, bay; pigeonhole, cubbyhole; tray, drawer, locker; shelving, rack, shelf; storey, floor, deck.

(5) *cabinet,* closet, commode, wardrobe, chest of drawers, chiffonier, tallboy; cupboard, unit; whatnot, dresser, china cabinet; buffet, sideboard 218 *stand;* escritoire, bureau, desk, writing d.; console; bookcase.

(6) *basket,* creel; hamper, picnic basket; pannier; trug, punnet, frail; laundry basket; workbasket, wickerwork, basketwork; crate 218 *frame.*

(7) *box,* chest, coffer, locker; case, canteen; safe, moneybox; coffin 364 *tomb;* packing case, tea chest; attaché case, dispatch box; suitcase, trunk, portmanteau; bandbox, hat box; ammunition chest, canister, caisson; luggage, baggage, impedimenta; boot, luggage van.

(8) *small box,* matchbox; cardboard box, carton, packet; can, tin, caddy, canister; casket.

(9) *bag,* sack; handbag, reticule; shoulder bag, shopping b., carrier b.; polythene b., plastic b., paper b.; travelling bag, overnight b., flight b., sponge b.; sleeping bag, bedding-roll; holdall, grip; haversack, knapsack, rucksack; kitbag, duffel bag; pouch, sling; pannier, saddlebag; school bag, satchel; bundle, swag.

(10) *case,* étui, housewife; wallet, notecase; spectacle case, cigarette c., compact; briefcase, portfolio; file, box f.; scabbard, sheath; pistol case, holster; arrow case, quiver.

(11) *pocket,* hip p., breast p.; fob, pouch; purse, sporran.

(12) *vat,* butt, cask, barrel, tun, tub, keg; drum; wine cask, hogshead, firkin; hopper, cistern, tank 632 *store.*

(13) *vessel,* vase; jar, jamjar; urn, amphora, cruse, crock, pot, pitcher, ewer, jug; carafe, decanter, bottle; demijohn, magnum, jeroboam; flask, hip f., flagon, vial, phial; carboy, crucible, retort; chamber pot, bedpan; pail, bucket, churn, can, watering c.; bin, dustbin; coal scuttle, hod; skip, bath, tub.

(14) *cauldron* 383 heater; boiler, copper, kettle; skillet, pan, saucepan, billycan; steamer, double-boiler; frying pan, grill p., girdle; casserole, bain-marie; mess tin, dixie, tea urn, teapot, samovar; coffee pot, percolator; vacuum flask, hot-water bottle, warming pan.

(15) *cup,* tea service, tea set; chalice, goblet, beaker; drinking cup, loving c.; horn, drinking h., tankard, stoup, can, mug, stein, toby, noggin, schooner, tumbler, glass, wineglass.

(16) *bowl,* basin, dish; pudding basin, mixing bowl; punch bowl, drinking b.; porringer, ramekin; manger, trough; colander, tureen, gravy boat.

(17) *plate,* salver, tray, platter, dish; palette; saucer; pan, scales.

(18) *ladle,* skimmer, dipper, scoop, cupped hands; spoon, spatula; spade, trowel, shovel.

(19) *chamber,* room, apartment; cockpit, cubicle, cab; cabin, stateroom; cabinet, closet, study, sanctum; library, studio, workroom, office; nursery; reception room, drawing room, sitting r., living r., lounge, parlour, salon, boudoir; bedroom, dormitory; bathroom,

washroom; dining room, breakfast r.; mess, refectory, canteen; wardroom; smoking room, bar, snug; cookhouse, galley, kitchen; scullery, pantry, larder, dairy, laundry, utility room; offices, outhouse, garage; storeroom, box room; cloakroom, lavatory.

(20) *lobby,* vestibule, foyer, anteroom, waiting room; corridor, passage, hall; gallery, verandah, patio; porch 263 *doorway*; extension, lean-to.

(21) *cellar,* cellarage, vault, crypt, basement 214 *base*; coalhole, bunker, hold; dungeon.

(22) *attic,* loft, penthouse, garret 213 *summit.*

(23) *arbour,* alcove, bower, grotto, summerhouse, gazebo, folly, pergola, pavilion; sun lounge, conservatory.

Adjective
(24) *recipient,* capacious, voluminous 183 *spacious*; containing, enclosing; baggy.

(25) *cellular,* honeycombed 255 *concave*; abdominal, ventral.

195
Size

Noun
(1) *size,* magnitude, proportions, dimensions, measurements, measure; extent, expanse, area 183 *space*; extension 203 *length*, 209 *height*, 211 *depth*, 205 *breadth*; volume, girth, circumference; bulk, mass, weight 322 *gravity*; capacity, intake, tonnage; full size, life size 32 *greatness.*

(2) *hugeness,* largeness, bigness, grandiosity 32 *greatness*; enormity, enormousness, immensity, vastness; monstrosity 209 *height.*

(3) *bulk,* mass, weight, heaviness, avoirdupois 322 *gravity*; lump, block 324 *solid body*; hunk, chunk 53 *piece*; mound, heap 32 *great quantity*; mountain, pyramid 209 *high structure*; massiveness, bulkiness; obesity, corpulence, fatness, stoutness, chubbiness, plumpness, chunkiness, fleshiness; folds of flesh, double chin, spare tyre 253 *swelling*; muscle man, hulk.

(4) *giant,* colossus 209 *tall creature*; leviathan, whale; elephant, jumbo; mammoth, dinosaur; Titan, Goliath.

(5) *whopper,* walloper, whacker, humdinger.

Adjective
(6) *large,* of size, big 32 *great*; large size, economy s., king s., jumbo; fair-sized, considerable, sizable; bulky, massive, weighty; ample, capacious, voluminous, baggy 205 *broad*; vast, extensive 183 *spacious*; monumental, towering, mountainous 209 *tall*; fine, magnificent, spanking, whacking 32 *whopping*; life-size, large as life; well-grown, large-limbed, elephantine; large-scale, megalithic.

(7) *huge,* immense, enormous, vast; mighty, grandiose; monstrous 32 *prodigious*; record size; colossal, mammoth, gigantic, giant, giant-like, mountainous; titanic, Herculean, gargantuan; outsize 32 *exorbitant*; limitless 107 *infinite.*

(8) *fleshy,* meaty, fat, stout, obese, overweight, plump, ample, plumpish, on the plump side; chubby, podgy, pudgy 205 *thick*; dumpy, chunky, stocky 205 *broad*; tubby, portly, corpulent, paunchy, pot-bellied 253 *convex*; puffy, bloated 197 *expanded*; round, rotund, roly-poly, full, full-faced, chubby-f.;

dimpled, dimply, buxom; well-fed, well-grown, strapping, lusty, burly, beefy, brawny 162 *stalwart*.

(9) *unwieldy*, cumbersome, hulking, lumbering, gangling; lumpy, lumpish; too big, elephantine, overweight; awkward, muscle-bound 695 *clumsy*.

Verb
(10) *be large*, - big etc. adj.; become large 197 *expand*; loom large, bulk l. 183 *extend*; tower, soar 209 *be high*.

196
Littleness

Noun
(1) *littleness*, small size 33 *smallness*; lack of height 204 *shortness*; dwarfishness, stuntedness; scantiness, paucity, exiguity 105 *fewness*; meagreness 206 *thinness*; - kin, - let.

(2) *minuteness*, point, vanishing p.; pinpoint, pinhead; atom, molecule, particle, electron, neutron, proton, quark; nucleus, cell; corpuscle; drop, droplet; dust, grain, seed 33 *small thing*; button 639 *trifle*.

(3) *miniature* 553 picture; microfilm, microfiche; thumbnail sketch, epitome 592 *compendium*; model, microcosm; mini -

(4) *dwarf*, midget, pigmy, Lilliputian, hobbit little people 970 *elf*; chit, slip, mite, tot 132 *child*; bantam 33 *small animal*; squirt 639 *nonentity*; manikin, doll, puppet; Tom Thumb, shrimp, runt.

(5) *microorganism*, protozoan, plankton, amoeba; bacillus, bacteria, microbe, germ, virus; algae 366 *plant*.

(6) *microscopy*, microscope, electron m., micrometer.

(7) *microelectronics*, microprocessor, chip, silicon c. 86 *data processing*.

Adjective
(8) *little* 33 small; petite, dainty, dinky, dolly, elfin; diminutive, pigmy, Lilliputian; wee, tiny, teeny, teeny-weeny; toy, baby, pocket-size, pint-size, mini-; miniature, model; portable, handy, compact; bijou, snug, cosy; poky, cramped 206 *narrow*; runty, puny 163 *weak*.

(9) *dwarfish*, dwarf, dwarfed, pigmy, undersized, stunted, wizened, shrunk 198 *contracted*; squat, dumpy 204 *short*; knee-high.

(10) *exiguous*, minimal, slight, scant, scanty 33 *small*; thin, skinny, scraggy 206 *lean*; rudimentary, embryonic 68 *beginning*; bitty 53 *fragmentary*.

(11) *minute*, micro-, microscopic, infinitesimal; atomic, molecular, corpuscular; granular 332 *powdery*; imperceptible 444 *invisible*.

Verb
(12) *be little*, - tiny etc. adj., contract 198 *become small*; dwindle 37 *decrease*.

Adverb
(13) *in small compass*, on a small scale; in a nutshell; in miniature.

197
Expansion

Noun
(1) *expansion*, enlargement, augmentation 36 *increase*; amplification, reinforcement 38 *addition*; hyperbole 546 *exaggeration*; stretching, extension, spread 75 *dispersion*; increment 40 *adjunct*; overgrowth 637 *superfluity*; development, growth; Parkinson's law.

(2) *dilation,* distension, inflation 352 *blowing*; swelling up, turgescence, tumescence, puffiness 253 *swelling.*

Adjective
(3) *expanded,* enlarged etc. vb., larger, bigger, expanding 36 *increasing*; stuffed, padded out, supplemented; spreading, widespread; expansive 183 *spacious*; fan-shaped, flared 205 *broad*; wide open, gaping 263 *open*; tumescent, budding, bursting; full-blown, full-grown; obese, puffy, pot-bellied, bloated 195 *fleshy*; swollen, turgescent, distended, stretched, tight; tumid, dropsical, varicose 253 *convex.*

Verb
(4) *expand,* wax, increase, snowball 36 *grow*; widen, broaden, flare, splay . 205 *be broad*; spread, extend, sprawl; fan out, deploy 75 *be dispersed*; spread over, overrun, mantle, straddle 226 *cover*; rise, gather, swell, distend, dilate, fill out; mushroom, balloon 253 *be convex*; get fat, put on weight; grow up, spring up, shoot, sprout, open, blossom, flower, blow, bloom, be out.

(5) *enlarge,* expand; leaven 310 *elevate*; bore, ream; widen, broaden, let out; open, pull out; stretch, extend 203 *lengthen*; heighten, deepen, draw out; amplify, supplement, reinforce 38 *add*; double, redouble; develop, build up 36 *augment*; distend, inflate, reflate, pump up, blow up, puff up; bulk, thicken; stuff, pad 227 *line*; fill to bursting 54 *fill*; feed up, fatten, plump up 301 *feed*; blow up, magnify, aggrandize 546 *exaggerate.*

198
Contraction

Noun
(1) *contraction,* reduction, abatement, lessening, deflation 37 *diminution*; decrease, shrinkage, curtailment, abbreviation 204 *shortening*; pulling together, drawing t. 45 *joining together,* 264 *closure*; freezing, contracting; attenuation, emaciation 655 *deterioration*; bottleneck, hourglass 206 *narrowness*; epitome 592 *compendium.*

(2) *compression,* pressure, compaction, squeeze, squeezing, strangulation; constriction, astringency; contractility.

(3) *compressor,* squeezer, mangle; tightener, constrictor, astringent; bandage, tourniquet; belt, garter 47 *girdle*; corset 228 *underwear*; straitjacket, thumbscrew; bear, boa constrictor.

Adjective
(4) *contracted,* shrunken, smaller 33 *small*; waning 37 *decreasing*; constricted, strangled, strangulated; deflated, condensed, compact, compacted, compressed; pinched, nipped, drawn tight 206 *narrow,* 264 *closed*; compressible, contractile; stunted, shrivelled, wizened 196 *dwarfish*; wasting, consumptive 655 *deteriorated.*

(5) *compressive,* contractional, astringent, binding, constipating.

Verb
(6) *become small,* dwindle 37 *decrease*; shrivel, wither, waste away; lose weight 323 *be light*; stop growing, level off; contract, shrink, narrow, taper, taper off, draw in; condense, evaporate; draw together, close up 264 *close*; pucker, purse.

(7) *make smaller,* lessen, reduce 37 *abate;* contract, shrink, abridge, take in; dwarf, stunt 204 *shorten;* diet, slim 323 *lighten;* taper, narrow 206 *make thin;* puncture, deflate; boil down, evaporate, dehydrate; cramp, constrict, pinch, nip, squeeze, bind, corset; draw in 45 *tighten;* draw together 45 *join;* hug, crush, strangle, strangulate; compress, compact, condense 324 *be dense;* huddle, crowd together; squeeze in, pack tight 54 *fill;* squash 216 *flatten;* chip away, whittle away, clip, trim, prune, pollard 46 *cut;* file, grind 332 *pulverize;* fold up, crumple 261 *fold.*

199
Distance

Noun
(1) *distance,* astronomical d., light years, depths of space 183 *space;* mileage, footage 203 *length;* focal distance; elongation, apogee; far distance, horizon, skyline; background 238 *rear;* periphery, circumference; reach, grasp, compass, span, stride 183 *range;* far cry, long way, fair w., day's march, marathon.

(2) *farness,* far distance, remoteness, removal, separation; antipodes, pole, world's end; Far West, Far East; foreign parts outpost, back of beyond 883 *seclusion;* purlieus, outskirts 223 *exteriority;* outer edge, frontier 236 *limit.*

Adjective
(3) *distant,* distal, peripheral, terminal; far, farther; ulterior; ultimate, farthest, furthest, furthermost; long-distance, long-range; yonder; not local, away; outlying, peripheral; offshore, on the horizon; remote, far-flung, antipodean; out of

range, telescopic; lost to view, out of sight 444 *invisible;* off-centre, wide.

(4) *removed,* separated, inaccessible, out of the way; out of touch, beyond, overseas, transatlantic, trans-Pacific.

Verb
(5) *be distant,* stretch to, reach to, extend to, spread to, go to, get to, stretch away to, carry on to 183 *extend;* carry, range; outdistance 306 *outdo;* keep off, stand off, lie off; keep clear of, keep one's distance 620 *avoid.*

Adverb
(6) *afar,* away, far, far away, far afield, far off; way behind, way in front; yonder, in the distance, in the offing, on the horizon, at a distance, out of sight; far and wide 183 *widely;* asunder, apart, far a.; abroad, afield; at arm's length.

(7) *beyond,* further, farther; further on, ahead, in front; clear of, wide of; below the horizon.

(8) *too far,* out of reach, out of range, out of sight, out of hearing, out of earshot, out of bounds.

200
Nearness

Noun
(1) *nearness,* proximity, propinquity, closeness, near distance, foreground; neighbourhood 230 *surroundings;* brink, verge 234 *edge;* adjacency 202 *contiguity;* collision course 289 *approach.*

(2) *short distance,* no d., beeline, short cut; step, short s., walking distance; close quarters, close grips; close range, stone's throw, striking distance; short span, hair's breadth; close-up, near approach; perigee, perihelion; close finish, photo f., near thing.

(3) *near place,* vicinity, neighbourhood, environs, suburbs 187 *locality*; one's background; ringside seat, next door 202 *contiguity.*

Adjective
(4) *near,* proximate, proximal; very near, approximate; getting warm, warm 289 *approaching*; nearby 289 *accessible*; not far, hard by, inshore; near at hand, at hand, handy, present 189 *on the spot*; home, local, close to, next to, neighbouring, bordering on, verging on; adjacent, adjoining 202 *contiguous*; close 45 *joined*; at close quarters, at close grips 716 *contending*; close-run, neck-and-neck; near in blood, related 11 *akin.*

Verb
(5) *be near,* be around, be about 189 *be present*; hang around, hang about; draw near, get warm 289 *approach*; meet 293 *converge*; neighbour, stand next to, abut, adjoin, border 202 *be contiguous*; hug the shore; come close, skirt, graze, shave, brush, skim, jostle 702 *obstruct*; follow close, shadow 284 *follow*; clasp, cling to 889 *caress*; close the ranks 74 *congregate.*

(6) *bring near,* approach, approximate; move up 202 *juxtapose.*

Adverb
(7) *near,* not far, locally; hard by, fast by, close to; at close range, at close quarters; close behind, right b.; within call, within earshot, only a step, not far from; on one's doorstep, next door; at one's elbow, at one's side, at one's fingertips; under one's nose, within reach, close at hand; face to face; side by side, cheek by jowl, tête-à-

tête, arm in arm, beside, alongside.

(8) *nearly,* practically, almost, all but; more or less, near enough, as good as roughly, around, about; hereabouts, thereabouts, circa, approximately; on the verge *or* the brink of, just about to.

201
Interval

Noun
(1) *interval,* distance between, space; narrow interval 200 *short distance*; daylight, head, length; clearance, margin 183 *room*; interval of time, 108 *interim*; pause, break, truce 145 *lull*; hiatus 72 *discontinuity*; interruption, jump, leap; musical interval, tone, semitone 410 *musical note.*

(2) *gap,* interstice, mesh 222 *network*; lacuna, cavity, hole 263 *orifice*; pass, defile 305 *passage*; firebreak; ditch, dike 351 *drain*; water jump, ha-ha 231 *partition*; ravine, gorge, gully, chimney, crevasse, gulch, canyon; cleft, crevice, chink, crack, rift, cut, gash, tear, rent, slit flaw, fault, breach, break, split, fracture, rupture, fissure, chap 46 *separation*; slot, groove 262 *furrow*, 260 *notch*; seam, join 45 *joint*; leak 298 *outlet*; inlet 345 *gulf*; abyss, chasm 211 *depth*; void 190 *emptiness.*

Adjective
(3) *spaced,* spaced out, with an interval; gappy, gapped; split, cloven 46 *disunited*; gaping 263 *open*; far between; latticed, meshed.

Verb
(4) *space,* interval, space out 46 *set apart*; crack, split, start, gape 263 *open*; clear a space; lattice, mesh.

Adverb
(5) *at intervals* 72 discontinuously; now and then, now and
again, every so often, off and
on; by a head, by a length.

202
Contiguity

Noun
(1) *contiguity,* juxtaposition 200
nearness; touching, no interval
71 *continuity*; contact, abutment; meeting, interface; conjunction 45 *union*; close contact, adhesion 48 *coherence*;
grazing contact, tangent; border 234 *edge*; frontier 236 *limit*;
buffer state.

Adjective
(2) *contiguous,* touching, in contact; tangential, grazing,
brushing; abutting, end to end;
adjacent, with no interval 71
continuous; adjoining, close,
jostling 200 *near*.

Verb
(3) *be contiguous,* overlap 378
touch; make contact, come in c.,
brush, rub, skim, scrape, graze,
kiss; join, meet 293 *converge*;
stick, adhere 48 *cohere*; abut
on, adjoin, reach to 183 *extend*;
crowd, jostle, rub shoulders
with 200 *be near*; border with,
skirt 234 *hem*; coexist, coincide
89 *accompany*.

(4) *juxtapose,* range together,
set side by side.

Adverb
(5) *contiguously,* tangentially;
in contact, in close c.; next,
close; end to end; cheek by
jowl; arm in arm.

203
Length

Noun
(1) *length,* longitude; extent,
extension; reach, long arm; full
length, stretch, span; mileage,

footage 199 *distance*; perspective 211 *depth*.

(2) *lengthening,* prolongation,
extension, production, spinning out 113 *protraction*;
stretching, tension; spreading
out, stringing o.

(3) *line,* bar, rule; strip, stripe,
streak; spoke, radius; single
file, line ahead, crocodile,
queue 65 *sequence*; straight
line, right l. 249 *straightness*;
bent line 248 *curvature*.

(4) *long measure,* linear m. 465
measurement; unit of length,
hand, hand's breadth, palm,
span, arm's length, fathom;
head, length; pace, step; inch,
foot, yard; rod, pole, perch;
chain, furlong; mile, nautical
m., knot, league; millimetre,
centimetre, metre, kilometre;
micro-inch, micron, wave-
length; light year.

Adjective
(5) *long,* lengthy, extensive, a
mile long; long-drawn out 113
protracted; lengthened, elongated, outstretched, extended,
strung out; ankle-length,
shoulder length; lanky, long-
legged 209 *tall*; interminable,
no end to; unabridged, full-
length 54 *complete*.

(6) *longitudinal,* oblong, linear;
one-dimensional.

Verb
(7) *be long,* stretch, outstretch,
stretch out; reach, stretch to
183 *extend*; drag, trail 113 *drag
on.*

(8) *lengthen,* stretch, elongate,
draw out 206 *make thin*; pull
out, stretch o., expand; sprawl
216 *be horizontal*; spread out,
string o. 75 *disperse*; extend,
pay out, unfurl, unroll, unfold
316 *evolve*; let out, drop the
hem; produce, continue; prolong, protract 113 *spin out*;
drawl 580 *stammer*.

Adverb

(9) *longwise,* longways, length-wise; along, radially, in line ahead, in single file; in tandem; in perspective; at full length, end to end, overall; fore and aft; head to tail, stem to stern, top to toe, head to foot.

204
Shortness

Noun

(1) *shortness,* brevity, briefness; transience 114 *brief span*; inch, centimetre 200 *short distance*; low stature, dwarfishness 196 *littleness*; no height 210 *low-ness*; shrinkage 636 *insufficiency*; concision 569 *conciseness.*

(2) *shortening,* abridgment, abbreviation; precis 592 *compendium*; curtailment, cutback, cut 37 *diminution*; contraction 198 *compression.*

Adjective

(3) *short,* brief 114 *transient*; not big, dwarfish, stunted 196 *little*; squat, dumpy, stumpy, stocky, stubby 195 *fleshy,* 205 *thick*; not high 210 *low*; snub, retroussé, blunt; skimpy, scanty 636 *insufficient*; foreshortened 246 *distorted*; abbreviated, abridged; shortened, sawn-off; cut, curtailed, truncated; topless, shorn, mown; sparing of words, terse 569 *concise*; potted, compact 592 *compendious*; compressed 198 *contracted.*

Verb

(4) *be short,* - brief etc. adj.; not reach 307 *fall short.*

(5) *shorten,* abridge, abbreviate; epitomize, boil down 592 *abstract*; sum up 569 *be concise*; compress, contract, telescope 198 *make smaller*; reduce, diminish 37 *abate*; take up, turn up, tuck up; guillotine, axe 46

sunder; cut short, dock, curtail, truncate; cut back, cut down, slash, lop, prune; mow, shear, shave, trim, crop, clip 46 *cut*; stunt, check; scrimp, skimp.

Adverb

(6) *shortly,* in short 592 *in sum.*

205
Breadth. Thickness

Noun

(1) *breadth,* width, latitude; span, wingspan; diameter, radius, gauge; bore, calibre; expanse, amplitude 183 *range*; wideness, fullness, bagginess.

(2) *thickness,* stoutness, corpulence 195 *bulk.*

Adjective

(3) *broad,* wide, expansive 183 *spacious*; wide-cut, full, flared, ample, baggy; fan-like, outstretched, splayed out 197 *expanded*; bell-bottomed, broad-based; wide-hipped; wide-bodied; broad-brimmed; wide-mouthed 263 *open*; broad-chested 162 *stalwart*; wide-ranging 79 *general.*

(4) *thick,* stout, dumpy, squat 204 *short*; thickset, tubby, stubby 195 *fleshy*; thick-lipped, blubber-l., full-l.; thick-necked, bull-n.; thick-skinned, thick-ribbed, 162 *strong*; solidly built 324 *dense*; ropy, lumpy 354 *viscid.*

Verb

(5) *be broad,* - thick etc. adj.; get broad, broaden, widen, fatten, thicken; fan out, flare, splay 197 *expand*; straddle, bestride, span 226 *overlie.*

Adverb

(6) *broadways,* breadthways, widthways 239 *sideways.*

206
Narrowness.
Thinness

Noun

(1) *narrowness,* tight squeeze, crack, chink, hair's breadth 200 *short distance*; lack of breadth, line, strip, stripe, streak; knife-edge, razor's edge, tightrope, wire; narrow gauge; bottleneck, narrows, strait 345 *gulf*; ridge, col; ravine, gully 255 *valley*; pass, defile; neck, isthmus.

(2) *thinness,* tenuity, fineness; slenderness, emaciation, consumption; skin and bone, skeleton; scarecrow, rake, beanpole, broomstick, shadow; haggardness, sunken cheeks; thread, shaving, slip, wisp.

(3) *narrowing,* compression 198 *contraction*; tapering constriction; waistline, hourglass.

Adjective

(4) *narrow,* not wide, tight, close; pinched 198 *contracted*; not thick, fine, thin, wafer-thin; tight-drawn, attenuated, spun, fine-s. 203 *long*; thread-like 208 *fibrous*; tapering slight, wispy; slightly built, slender, slim, svelte, sylph-like; willowy, long-legged, leggy, lanky, gangling; wasp-waisted.

(5) *lean,* thin, spare, wiry; meagre, skinny, bony; cadaverous, skin-and-bone, haggard, gaunt, drawn, lantern-jawed, hatchet-faced; spindly, spidery; undersized, weedy, scrawny, scraggy 196 *exiguous*; consumptive, emaciated, wasted, shrivelled wizened, pinched, peaky 651 *sick*; starved, wraith-like, thin as a rake.

Verb

(6) *be narrow,* - thin etc. adj.; narrow, taper 293 *converge*; taper off 198 *become small.*

(7) *make thin,* contract, compress, pinch, 198 *make smaller*; nip starve, reduce, slim, lose weight; draw, spin out 203 *lengthen*; attenuate 325 *rarefy.*

207
Layer

Noun

(1) *layer,* stratum, substratum, underlay 214 *base*; bed, course, string c.; *range,* zone, vein, seam, lode; thickness, ply; storey, tier, floor, landing; stage, planking, platform; deck, quarterdeck; film, bloom, scum; patina, coating, coat, veneer 226 *covering*; scale, membrane 226 *skin*; level, water l., water table.

(2) *lamina,* sheet, slab, foil, strip; plate, tinplate, sheet iron; plank, board, weatherboard, fascia; laminate, plywood; slat, lath, leaf, tablet; plaque, panel, pane; slab, flag, slate; shingle, tile; slide, wafer, flake, slice; sheet 631 *paper*; card, playing c.; platter, disc 250 *circle.*

(3) *stratification,* bedding, layering, flakiness, scaliness, overlapping, overlap; nest of boxes; sandwich.

Adjective

(4) *layered,* laminated, flaky; shaly, slaty; foliated, foliate, leaf-like; bedded, zoned, seamed; overlapping, clinkerbuilt; tabular, decked, storeyed, in layers; scaly, membranous, filmy.

Verb

(5) *laminate,* layer, overlap 226 *overlay*; zone, stratify, sandwich; plate, veneer 226 *coat*; split; flake off, pare, peel, strip 229 *uncover*; shave, slice 206 *make thin.*

208
Filament

Noun
(1) *filament,* flagellum, lash, eyelash 259 *hair;* shred of wool, lock of hair, wisp, curl, fringe; tendril, whisker 378 *feeler;* gossamer, cobweb; capillary, vein; wire, element, wick.

(2) *fibre,* natural f., animal f., hair, mohair, wool, merino; shoddy; silk, floss; vegetable fibre, cotton, cotton wool, kapok; linen, flax; manila, hemp; jute, sisal, coir; tow, oakum; bast, raffia; worsted, yarn; spun yarn, thread, twine, twist, strand; cord, string, line 47 *cable;* artificial fibre, manmade f., acrylic f., rayon, nylon 222 *textile;* staple, denier.

(3) *strip,* fascia, band, bandage; braid, tape, strap, ribbon 47 *girdle;* lath, slat, batten, stave splinter, shred 53 *piece;* streak 203 *line.*

Adjective
(4) *fibrous,* woolly, silky; whiskery, downy, fleecy 259 *hairy;* wiry, threadlike; fine-spun 206 *narrow;* stringy, ropy 205 *thick;* strap-shaped.

209
Height

Noun
(1) *height,* altitude, elevation, ceiling, pitch; loftiness, steepness, dizzy height; tallness, stature; stratosphere 340 *atmosphere.*

(2) *high land,* height, highlands, heights, steeps, uplands, wold, moor, downs, rolling country; rising ground, rise, bank, brae, slope, climb 220 *incline;* hill, eminence, mount, mountain; fell, scar, tor, chain, sierra; ridge, hog's back, col, saddle,

spur, headland, foothill 254 *projection;* hilltop, crest, peak 213 *summit;* steepness, precipice, cliff, crag, scar, bluff, escarpment; gorge, canyon, ravine; plateau, tableland.

(3) *small hill,* knoll, hillock, hummock, hump, dune, sand d., moraine; barrow, mound 253 *earthwork;* anthill, molehill.

(4) *high structure,* column, pillar, turret, tower; pile, noble p., skyscraper; steeple, spire, minaret; obelisk; dome, pyramid, pagoda; mast, topmast; pole, maypole; pylon, radio mast; watchtower, lookout, crow's nest 213 *summit.*

(5) *tall creature,* giraffe, elephant, mammoth; six-footer, colossus 195 *giant.*

(6) *high water,* high tide, flood t., spring t.; billow, tidal wave; cataract 350 *waterfall;* flood, flood level.

(7) *altimetry,* altimeter, barograph 465 *gauge.*

Adjective
(8) *high,* high-up, sky-high; exalted, lofty 310 *elevated;* highest 213 *topmost;* aerial, midair, airborne, flying; soaring 308 *ascending;* spiry, towering, cloud-capped; steep, dizzy, vertiginous; knee-high, breast-h., shoulder-h.; altitudinal.

(9) *tall,* lanky 206 *narrow;* long-legged, long-necked, statuesque, Junoesque; colossal, gigantic, monumental 195 *huge.*

(10) *alpine,* mountainous, hilly, upland, highland; rolling, hillocky, hummocky.

(11) *overhanging,* beetling, overlying; towering over, overshadowing, dominating; hovering, floating over; over one's head, aloft; prominent 254 *projecting.*

Verb

(12) *be high*, tower, soar; surmount, clear, overtop, overlook, dominate, command a view; overhang, overshadow 254 *jut*; hover, hang over; mount, rise 308 *ascend*; stand on tiptoe.

(13) *make higher*, heighten, build up, raise 310 *elevate*.

Adverb

(14) *aloft*, up, on high, high up, in the clouds; on top, above, overhead; upwards, heavenward; straight up 215 *vertically*; on tiptoe, on stilts.

210
Lowness

Noun

(1) *lowness*, no height, sea level 216 *horizontality*; levelness, steppe 348 *plain*; low elevation, lowlands; molehill, pimple 196 *littleness*; gentle slope, slight gradient 220 *incline*; bottom, hollow, depression 255 *valley*; sea-bottom, sea-floor; depths 211 *depth*; floor, foot 214 *base*; underside, underbelly; low water, low tide.

Adjective

(2) *low*, not high, squat 204 *short*; crouching, stooping, bending; recumbent, laid low, prostrate 216 *supine*; low-lying at sea level 216 *flat*; low-level, single-storey; lower, under, nether, inferior; sunken, lowered 255 *concave*; flattened, blunt; subterranean, underground, below the surface, submarine 211 *deep*.

Verb

(3) *be low*, - flat etc. adj.; lie flat 216 *be horizontal*; be beneath, underlie; slouch; crouch 311 *stoop*; depress 311 *lower*.

Adverb

(4) *under*, beneath, underneath, below, at the foot of; downwards; down, underfoot, underground, downstairs.

211
Depth

Noun

(1) *depth*, drop, fall; deepness, profundity; lowest point, nadir; deeps 343 *ocean*; depression, bottom, hollow, pit, shaft, mine, well 255 *cavity*; abyss, chasm 201 *gap*; vault, crypt, dungeon, cellar; cave, catacomb; pot-holing 309 *descent*; underworld, bottomless pit 972 *hell*; fathoming, soundings, probe, plummet, lead, sonar; diving bell, bathysphere; submarine, submariner, frogman 313 *diver*; depth required, draught, displacement.

Adjective

(2) *deep*, steep, plunging, profound; abysmal, yawning, cavernous; deep-sea; unplumbed, unsounded, bottomless, fathomless; subterranean, underground; underwater, undersea, submarine; deep in, immersed, submerged, buried sunk, drowned; navigable; knee-deep, ankle-d.

Verb

(3) *be deep*, gape, yawn; deepen, hollow 255 *make concave*; fathom, sound, take soundings; drop, lower 311 *let fall*; plumb the depths, touch bottom; plunge 313 *founder*.

Adverb

(4) *deeply*, profoundly; deep down, out of one's depth, deep in, over one's head.

212
Shallowness

Noun

(1) *shallowness*, no depth; veneer, thin coat 226 *skin*;

scratch, pinprick, graze; shoals, shallows; ford 305 *passage*; pond, puddle.

Adjective
(2) *shallow*, slight, superficial 4 *insubstantial*; surface, skin-deep; near the surface, not deep; ankle-deep, knee-d.; thin, thinly spread 206 *narrow*.

213
Summit

Noun
(1) *summit*, sky, heaven; pole, north p., south p.; top, peak, crest, apex, pinnacle, crown; maximum height, zenith, meridian; culmination, apogee; acme 646 *perfection*; divide, watershed; coping, copingstone, keystone; lintel, pediment, capital, cornice; battlements, parapet.

(2) *vertex*, apex, crown, cap, brow, head; tip, cusp, spike, end 69 *extremity*; spire; plateau, tableland 209 *high land*; housetop, rooftop, gable 226 *roof*; garret, attic; topside, upper deck; masthead, crow's nest 209 *high structure*.

(3) *head*, headpiece; pate, brow, dome, temples, forehead; brain 498 *intelligence*; scalp, crown; skull, cranium; phrenology.

Adjective
(4) *topmost*, top, highest 209 *high*; uppermost 34 *supreme*; polar, crowning; capital, head; cephalic, cranial; culminating, etc. vb.

Verb
(5) *crown*, cap, head, top, tip, surmount, crest, overtop 209 *be high*; culminate, climax.

Adverb
(6) *atop*, on top, at the top, on the crest.

214
Base

Noun
(1) *base*, foot, toe 210 *lowness*; bottom, root; rock bottom, nadir; footing, foundation 218 *basis*; groundwork, substructure, infrastructure; chassis 218 *frame*; baseboard, plinth, pedestal 218 *stand*; substratum, floor, bed, bedrock; subsoil, ground, foundations, footing; damp course; basement, ground floor; flooring 226 *paving*; skirting board, wainscot; keel, hold.

(2) *foot*, feet, forefoot, hindfoot; sole, heel, instep, arch; toe, big toe; trotter hoof, paw, pad; ankle, fetlock, pastern.

Adjective
(3) *undermost*, lowermost, nethermost, bottom 210 *low*; basic, basal, fundamental; grounded, on the bottom, touching b.; based on, founded on, grounded on, built on, underlying 218 *supporting*.

(4) *footed*, hoofed, cloven-h.; web-footed; soled, heeled, shod, shoed; toed, five-t.; flat-footed, 845 *blemished*.

Adverb
(5) *in the trough*, at the bottom 210 *under*.

215
Verticality

Noun
(1) *verticality*, the vertical, erectness, uprightness, upright carriage; steepness, precipitousness 209 *height*; right angle, perpendicular; elevation; vertical line, plumbline; upright, stalagmite 218 *pillar*; sheer face, precipice, cliff 209 *high land*; vertical height, rise.

Adjective
(2) *vertical,* upright, erect, standing; perpendicular, sheer, abrupt, steep, precipitous 209 *high*; straight, plumb; upstanding, standing up, on one's feet *or* legs; bolt upright, unbowed, head-up; rampant, rearing; on end.

Verb
(3) *be vertical,* stick up, cock up, bristle, stand on end; sit up, stand up, straighten up; rise, stand, ramp, rear;

(4) *make vertical,* erect, rear, raise 310 *elevate*; up-end; stand, set up, stick up, raise up, cock up.

Adverb
(5) *vertically,* upright, erect; on end, up on end, endwise, up; on one's hind legs, standing; at right angles; down, straight-d.

216
Horizontality

Noun
(1) *horizontality,* horizontal angle, azimuth; horizontal line, ruled line; flatness 258 *smoothness*; level, plane, dead level; stratum 207 *layer*; steppe 348 *plain*; flats 347 *marsh*; platform, ledge, terrace; plateau, tableland; platter 194 *plate*; horizon, false h.

(2) *recumbency,* lying down, prostration; proneness, supineness.

(3) *flattener,* iron, press; rolling pin, steamroller 258 *smoother*; bulldozer 168 *destroyer*.

Adjective
(4) *flat,* horizontal, two-dimensional; level, plane, even, flush 258 *smooth*; trodden, beaten down.

(5) *supine,* flat on one's back; prone, face down, prostrate; recumbent, lying down, laid out; stretched out, sprawling; conchant.

Verb
(6) *be horizontal,* lie, lie down, recline, couch, sprawl, loll 311 *sit down*; straighten out, level out.

(7) *flatten,* lay out, roll o., lay down, spread; lay flat, beat f., tread f., stamp down, trample d., squash; make flush, align, level, even, grade, plane; iron 258 *smooth*; pat down, smooth d, plaster d.; prostrate, knock down, floor 311 *fell*.

Adverb
(8) *horizontally,* flat, on one's back; fesse-wise; at full length.

217
Pendency

Noun
(1) *pendency,* suspension, hanging, dangle; set, hang, drape.

(2) *hanging object,* pendant, dangler, drop, earring; .tassel, tag 844 *trimming*; hangings, draperies, drapes, curtains; train, skirt, coat-tails; flap; pigtail, tail 259 *hair*; dewlap, lobe; pendulum, bob; swing, hammock 317 *oscillation*; chandelier 420 *lamp*; icicle, stalactite.

(3) *hanger,* curtain rod, runner, rack; hook, peg, knob, nail 218 *prop*; suspender, braces; clothesline 47 *cable*; clotheshorse, airer davit, crane 310 *lifter*; gallows, gibbet 964 *pillory*.

Adjective
(4) *hanging,* pendent, pendulous; hanging from, dependent, suspended; hanging the head, nodding, drooping; lowering, overhanging 254 *projecting*; open-ended, dangling, loose 46 *disunited*; baggy, flowing; etc. vb., tailed, lop-eared.

Verb

(5) *hang,* drape, set; hang down, draggle, trail, flow; hang on to, swing from; swing, sway, dangle, bob; hang the head, nod, loll, droop, sag; stream, wave, float, ripple, flap; hang over, hover; overhang, lour; hang up, suspend, sling, hook up, hitch 45 *join.*

218
Support

Noun

(1) *support,* underpinning 703 *aid;* footing, ground, terra firma; hold, foothold, handhold, toe-hold 778 *retention.*

(2) *prop,* support, mounting, bearing; carriage, carrier, chassis; buttress, flying b., abutment, bulwark, embankment, wall, retaining w.; underpinning, shore, jack; rod, bar, brace, strut; stay, mainstay 47 *tackling;* boom, spar, mast, yardarm 254 *projection;* trunk, stem, stalk 366 *plant;* arch 248 *curve;* keystone, headstone, cornerstone, springer; cantilever; pier (see *pillar*); truss, splint; rest, headrest, footrest, chock, wedge 702 *obstacle;* staff, baton, stick, alpenstock, crutch, crook; leg support, irons; bracket (see *shelf*); arm, back, shoulder; supporter 707 *auxiliary.*

(3) *handle,* holder; grip, hilt, pommel, shaft, haft; knob, lug, loop; railing, handrail, rail, banisters, balustrade; handlebar, tiller; winder, crank, lever, trigger 630 *tool.*

(4) *basis,* foundation, solid f., footings, deck; raft, pallet, sleeper; substratum 207 *layer;* ground, floor, bed, bedrock 214 *base;* flooring, pavement 226 *paving;* perch, footing, foothold.

(5) *stand,* tripod, trivet, hob; table mat, coaster; anvil, block, bench; trolley; table, board; sideboard, dresser 194 *cabinet;* desk, counter; pedestal, plinth, podium; platform, gantry; footplate; landing, half l.; landing stage, pier; dais, stage 539 *rostrum;* step, stair, tread 308 *ascent;* stilt 310 *lifter;* shank 267 *leg.*

(6) *seat,* throne; bank, bench, form; pew, choirstall; chair, armchair, easy chair, lounger; chaise longue; sofa, settee, divan, couch, chesterfield; stool, hassock; saddle, side s., pillion; lap, knees.

(7) *bed,* cot, crib, cradle; bedstead, divan, couch; four-poster; camp bed, pallet, bedroll, hammock, bunk; litter, hurdle, stretcher; bier.

(8) *cushion,* pillow; bolster, mattress, palliasse; squab, hassock, kneeler.

(9) *beam,* balk, joist, girder, box g., rafter; tie beam, truss 47 *bond;* transom, crossbar, traverse; architrave, lintel.

(10) *pillar,* shaft, pier, pile, pole, stake, stud, stanchion, post; jamb, door j., doorpost; newel post, banister, baluster; mullion; pilaster, column, caryatid; spinal column, spine, backbone, vertebrae; neck, cervix.

(11) *pivot,* fulcrum, lever, purchase; hinge 45 *joint;* pole, axis; axle, swivel, spindle, bearing, gudgeon, rowlock, tholepin.

(12) *shelf,* ledge 254 *projection;* corbel, bracket, console; window sill, mantelpiece, mantelshelf, rack, dresser; counter; plank, board, slab 207 *lamina.*

(13) *frame,* skeleton, ribs; framework, staging, scaffolding 331 *structure;* trellis, espalier;

chassis, fuselage, undercarriage; trestle, easel; picture frame, window f., sash.

Adjective
(14) *supporting,* sustaining; fundamental, basal; cervical, spinal; structural, skeletal; framing, holding.

Verb
(15) *support,* sustain, bear, carry, hold, shoulder; uphold, hold up, bear up, buoy up; prop, shore up, underpin, jack up; reinforce, buttress, bolster, cushion brace, truss 45 *tighten*; steady, stay; cradle, pillow, cup; back up 703 *aid*; frame, mount 235 *enclose*; give foundations 153 *stabilize.*

(16) *be supported,* stand on, lie on, sit on, repose on, rest on; bear on, press on, step on, lean on, rely on, be based on.

Adverb
(17) *astride,* pick-a-back, piggyback.

219
Parallelism

Noun
(1) *parallelism,* equidistance, concentricity; parallel 28 *equality*; parallel lines, tramlines, rails, railway lines; parallel bars; parallelogram.

Adjective
(2) *parallel,* coextensive, collateral, concurrent, concentric; equidistant 28 *equal*; corresponding 18 *similar.*

Verb
(3) *be parallel,* run together, run abreast, lie parallel; correspond, concur; parallel, draw a p.

Adverb
(4) *in parallel,* alongside, side by side, abreast.

220
Obliquity

Noun
(1) *obliquity,* obliqueness, skewness; oblique line, diagonal; oblique figure, rhomboid; oblique angle, inclination 247 *angularity*; indirectness, squint; curvature, camber 248 *curve*; crookedness, zigzag, chevron; oblique motion, swerve, lurch 282 *deviation*; splay, bias, warp 246 *distortion*; leaning, list, tip, cant; slope, slant, tilt, pitch, rake, rakish angle; sloping face, batter; sloping edge, bevel; ramp, chute, slide.

(2) *incline,* rise, ascent; ramp, slope, gradient; hill, rising ground; fall, dip, downhill 309 *descent*; gentle slope, dip s.; scarp s., escarpment 215 *verticality*; bank, scree, landslip, landslide.

Adjective
(3) *oblique,* inclined, bevel; tipsy, tilted, rakish; biased, askew, skew, slant, aslant, out of true; leaning, recumbent, stooping; wry, awry, crooked, squinting, cock-eyed, knock-kneed 246 *distorted*; diagonal, transverse, athwart, across 222 *crossed*; indirect, zigzag, herringbone; bent 248 *curved*; stepped, in echelon; divergent 282 *deviating.*

(4) *sloping,* uphill, rising 308 *ascending*; downhill, falling, dipping 309 *descending*; steep, abrupt, sheer, precipitous, vertiginous, breakneck; easy, gentle, shelving, rounded.

Verb
(5) *be oblique,* incline, lean, tilt; slope, slant, shelve, dip, decline 309 *descend*; rise, climb 308 *ascend*; transect, cut across 222 *cross*; lean, list, tip, lean over, bank, heel, careen, cant; bend, sag, give; bend over 311 *stoop*;

walk sideways, edge, sidle, sidestep; look sideways, squint; zigzag; dodge, swerve; diverge, converge.

(6) *make oblique*, incline, lean, slant, slope, cant, tilt, tip, rake; splay 282 *deviate*; bend, crook, warp, skew 246 *distort*; bevel; divert 282 *deflect*; curve, camber.

Adverb
(7) *obliquely*, diagonally, crosswise, across; on the cross, on the bias; askew, rakishly, tipsily; aslant, slantwise, askance; edgewise, crabwise, sidelong, sideways; at an angle.

221
Inversion

Noun
(1) *inversion*, retroversion, reversal 148 *reversion*; turning inward, introversion, invagination; transposition 151 *interchange*; palindrome, spoonerism.

(2) *overturning*, capsizal, upset, spill; somersault, cartwheel; subversion, undermining 149 *revolution*.

Adjective
(3) *inverted*, inverse, back-to-front; upside down, inside out, wrong side out; capsized, bottom up; topsy-turvy, head over heels, on one's head; reversed 14 *contrary*; antipodal 240 *opposite*; palindromic.

Verb
(4) *be inverted*, turn round, turn about, face a. 286 *turn back*; turn over, heel o., keel o., capsize, turn turtle; tilt over 220 *be oblique*; go over, topple o. 309 *tumble*; do a handstand, loop the loop; reverse, back 286 *regress*.

(5) *invert*, transpose 151 *interchange*; reverse, turn the tables; turn down 261 *fold*; introvert, invaginate; turn inside out; upend, upturn, overturn, tip over, spill, upset, capsize.

Adverb
(6) *inversely*, vice versa; contrariwise, other way round; back to front, upside down; topsy-turvy, head over heels, face down, bottom side up.

222
Crossing:
Intertexture

Noun
(1) *crossing*, crisscross, intersection; X-shape; interlacement, interweaving, arabesque 844 *pattern*; braid, wreath, plait 251 *convolution*; entanglement, intricacy 61 *complexity*; crossroads, intersection, road junction; level crossing; viaduct, flyover 624 *bridge*.

(2) *cross*, crux, rood, crucifix, pectoral; saltire, swastika, crossbones, skull and c.; crossbar, transom 218 *beam*; scissors, nutcrackers.

(3) *network*, reticulation, netting, mesh, fishnet; webbing, matting, wickerwork, basketwork, trellis, wattle; honeycomb, lattice, grating, grid, grille, gridiron; tracery, fretwork, filigree 844 *ornamental art*; lace, crochet, knitting, tatting, macramé 844 *needlework*; web, cobweb; net, seine, purses., drag-net, trawl.

(4) *textile*, weave, web, loom; woven stuff, piece goods, dry g.; bolt, roll, length, piece, cloth, stuff, material; broadcloth, fabric, tissue, suiting; jute, hessian, sacking, canvas; towelling, terry t.; damask, brocade, tapestry 226 *covering*; wool, worsted 208 *fibre*; felt, baize;

tweed, serge, gabardine; flannel, stockinette, jersey; velvet, velour, corduroy, needlecord; cotton, denim, drill; poplin, calico, gingham, seersucker, cheesecloth, muslin, linen; silk, chiffon, satin, taffeta; lace, tulle, net, gauze; rayon, nylon, polyester, fibreglass.

(5) *weaving,* texture; web, warp, weft, woof, nap, pile 259 *hair;* loom, shuttle; weaver, knitter; spinning wheel, distaff; spinner, spider.

Adjective
(6) *crossed,* crossing, crisscross; diagonal, transverse 220 *oblique;* X-shaped, cross-legged, cruciform; knotted, matted 61 *complex;* plaited, interlaced, interwoven; woven, tweedy; twill, herringbone; trellised, latticed, honeycombed; corded, ribbed 437 *variegated.*

(7) *reticular,* reticulated; netted, meshed 201 *spaced.*

Verb
(8) *cross,* cross over, cross under 305 *pass;* intersect, cut 220 *be oblique;* splice, dovetail 45 *join;* reticulate, mesh, net, knot

(9) *weave,* loom; plait, braid; knit, crochet; spin;

(10) *enlace,* interlace, interlock, intertwine, interweave; enmesh, twine, entwine, twist, wreathe; mat, tangle, entangle 63 *derange.*

Adverb
(11) *across,* athwart, transversely; crosswise.

223
Exteriority

Noun
(1) *exteriority,* outwardness the external; externality 230 *surroundings;* periphery, circumference, sidelines; exterior 445

appearance; surface, superficies, crust 226 *skin;* outer side, face, facet, facade 237 *front;* outside, out of doors, open air.

Adjective
(2) *exterior,* outward, extra-; external; roundabout, peripheral; outer, outermost, outlying 199 *distant;* outside, outboard; outdoor, extramural; foreign 59 *extraneous;* centrifugal 282 *deviating;* surface, superficial, skin-deep 212 *shallow.*

Verb
(3) *externalize,* body forth 6 *make extrinsic;* project, extrapolate; expel 300 *eject.*

Adverb
(4) *externally,* outwardly, outwards, superficially, on the surface; to the outsider; outside, out, out of doors, in the open, al fresco.

224
Interiority

Noun
(1) *interiority,* interior, inside, indoors; inner surface, endoderm; sapwood, heartwood; centre 225 *centrality;* inland, Midlands, hinterland, up-country; permeation, pervasion; deepness, recesses 211 *depth;* inmate, internee.

(2) *insides* 193 contents; internal organs, viscera, vitals; heart, lungs, liver, kidneys, spleen; bowels, entrails, innards, guts, intestines, colon, rectum; abdomen, belly, stomach 194 *maw;* womb, uterus; chest, solar plexus; cell 358 *organism.*

Adjective
(3) *interior,* internal, inward 5 *intrinsic;* inside, inner, innermost 225 *central;* inland, up-country; domestic, intimate, familiar; indoor, intramural, shut in, enclosed; inboard,

built-in, endemic 5 *intrinsic*; intestinal, visceral; intravenous, subcutaneous; endo-, endogenous.

Verb
(4) *be inside,* - internal etc. adj.; lie within, lie beneath, show through.

(5) *hold within,* hold 78 *comprise*; 303 *insert*; keep inside 747 *imprison*; enfold, 235 *enclose*; internalize 299 *absorb.*

Adverb
(6) *inside,* within, in, inwardly, deep down; deeply, profoundly; indoors, at home.

225
Centrality

Noun
(1) *centrality,* concentricity; central position, mid p.; parting 231 *partition.*

(2) *centre,* dead c.; centre of gravity; nerve centre, ganglion; epicentre 76 *focus*; heart, core, nucleus 5 *essential part*; nub, hub; navel; spine, backbone; marrow, pith; pole, axis 218 *pivot*; centre point, mid p. 70 *middle*; eye, pupil; bull's-eye.

Adjective
(3) *central,* centro-, nuclear, midmost 70 *middle*; focal, pivotal; umbilical; concentric, geocentric; spinal, vertebral; centripetal.

Verb
(4) *centralize,* centre, focus, centre upon; concentrate.

Adverb
(5) *centrally,* at the core, at the heart of, in the midst, in the middle.

226
Covering

Noun
(1) *covering,* capping etc. vb.; overlap, coating 207 *layer*; top dressing, mulch; topping, icing, frosting; cover, lid; hatch, trapdoor; flap, shutter 421 *screen*; cap, top 264 *stopper*; carapace, shell; mail, plate 713 *armour*; crust, film 649 *dirt*; sheath 194 *receptacle*; soft furnishings, hangings; mask 527 *disguise.*

(2) *roof,* cupola 253 *dome*; mansard roof, gable r.; housetop, rooftop; leads, slates, tiles, thatch, eaves; ceiling, vaulting, vault; rafters 218 *beam.*

(3) *canopy,* awning, sunblind 421 *screen*; marquee, pavilion, big top; tent, tepee; canvas, tarpaulin mosquito net.

(4) *shade,* hood, blind, shutters, slats; curtain, veil; umbrella, brolly; parasol, sunshade; visor, eye shade, dark glasses 421 *screen.*

(5) *wrapping,* wrapper, lining; packaging 194 *receptacle*; bandage 658 *surgical dressing*; dust jacket, binding, boards; mantle 228 *cloak*; scarf 228 *neckwear*; lagging; cocoon, chrysalis; shroud.

(6) *skin,* outer skin, epidermis, cuticle; true skin, dermis; peel, bark, crust, rind, coat, cortex; husk, hull, shell, pod, jacket; membrane, film scale; pelt, fleece, fur; leather, hide; morocco, calf, kid, suede; sheepskin, lamb, astrakhan; mink, sable, ermine; feathers 259 *plumage.*

(7) *paving,* flooring, floorboards, floor, parquet, tiles; deck, duckboards; pavement, flags, paving stone, crazy paving;

sett, cobble, cobblestone; tarmac 624 *road*.

(8) *coverlet*, bedspread, counterpane, bedding, bedclothes, bed linen; sheet, quilt, eiderdown, duvet; blanket, rug.

(9) *floor-cover*, carpeting, carpet; mat, doormat, rug, drugget; linoleum, vinyl, tiles.

(10) *facing*, cladding; veneer, coating, varnish, glaze; stucco, plaster, rendering; wash, whitewash, emulsion, paint; stain, polish, coat of paint.

Adjective
(11) *overlying*, overlaying, overlapping etc. vb.

(12) *covered*, roofed, roofed in, vaulted; wallpapered, carpeted; under cover, under canvas; cloaked, cowled, veiled, hooded 525 *concealed*; armour-plated, iron-clad; metalled, paved; snow-capped, ice-covered; inundated, flooded; plastered etc. vb.

Verb
(13) *cover*, superimpose; roof, roof in, cap, tip; spread, overlay, smother; insulate, lag; enfold, envelope 235 *enclose*; blanket, shroud, mantle, muffle; hood, veil 525 *conceal*; bind, cover (books); box, pack, vacuum-pack; wrap, bandage, swathe, wrap round; encapsulate 303 *insert*.

(14) *overlie*, overhang, overlap, overshadow; span, bestride, straddle 205 *be broad*; flood, inundate.

(15) *overlay*, pave, floor, roof, vault, deck; tile, thatch; paper 227 *line*; spread, smear; powder, dust; gravel, tarmac, metal.

(16) *coat*, face, encrust; roughcast, plaster, render 844 *decorate*; varnish, lacquer, japan, enamel, glaze, size; paint,

whitewash 425 *colour*; creosote; daub, grease; gild, plate, silver, electroplate; waterproof, fireproof.

227
Lining

Noun
(1) *lining*, liner, coating, inner c.; stuffing, wadding, padding; kapok, foam; lagging, insulation, double glazing, soundproofing; backing, facing; upholstery; papering, wallpaper; panelling, wainscot; metal lining, bush; packing, packaging 226 *wrapping*; filling (tooth); washer.

Verb
(2) *line*, insulate 226 *cover*; interlard, inlay; back, face; stuff, pad, wad; fill, pack 303 *insert*.

228
Dressing

Noun
(1) *dressing*, *investiture*; clothing, covering, dressing up, toilet; foppishness 848 *fashion*; vesture, dress, garb, attire, rig; panoply, array; accoutrements, trappings; paraphernalia, accessories; rig-out, turn-out; tailoring, dressmaking, millinery; haute couture; the rag trade.

(2) *clothing*, wear, apparel, clothes, garments; outfit, wardrobe, trousseau; maternity wear, layette; old clothes, rags, tatters; leisure wear, casual clothes; best c., Sunday best; frippery 844 *finery*; fancy dress, masquerade; motley.

(3) *garment*, article of clothing; top, bodice, bosom; corsage, bib, shirtfront; bustle, train; crutch, codpiece; arms (see *sleeve*); flaps, coat tails; placket, pocket, gusset, gore,

pleat; lapel, turn-up 261 *fold*; cuff, hemline 234 *edging*.

(4) *formal dress,* full d. 875 *formality*; evening dress, tails; morning dress; academic dress, cap and gown, mourning, black, widow's weeds.

(5) *uniform,* regimentals 547 *livery*; dress uniform mess kit; battledress, fatigues, khaki; school uniform; robes, vestments 989 *canonicals*.

(6) *informal dress,* undress, mufti, civvies; slacks, jeans; déshabillé, dressing gown, bathrobe, wrapper, slippers.

(7) *robe,* gown, robes, drapery; sari, kimono, caftan; toga; cassock.

(8) *dress,* frock, gown; creation, number; chemise, shift; shirtwaister, pinafore dress, gymslip.

(9) *suit,* outfit, ensemble; coordinates, separates; lounge suit; costume, tweeds, trouser suit; jumpsuit, tracksuit; leotard, body stocking; overalls, boiler suit; wet suit, space suit.

(10) *jacket,* coat, dinner jacket, tuxedo; blazer, sports jacket; riding habit; donkey jacket, bomber j., parka, anorak, kagoule; jerkin, tunic, waistcoat.

(11) *jersey,* pullover, woolly, jumper, sweater, polo neck; cardigan, twin set.

(12) *trousers,* trews, cords, flannels, pinstripes; hipsters, slacks, bags, plus fours; breeches, jodhpurs, knickerbockers; dungarees, denims, jeans, blue j.; shorts, bloomers, pantaloons, rompers.

(13) *skirt,* dirndl, kilt, kirtle, sarong; divided skirt, culottes; ballet skirt, tutu; crinoline.

(14) *loincloth,* dhoti, sarong; fig leaf, G-string, jockstrap; nappy *or* diaper.

(15) *apron,* bib, pinafore, pinny, overall.

(16) *shirt,* smock; tee shirt, sweatshirt; blouse, camisole, top.

(17) *underwear,* underclothes, undies, linen; lingerie, smalls; underpants, pants, briefs, panties, camiknickers, knickers, bloomers, drawers; combinations, long johns, singlet, vest; chemise, slip, petticoat; corset, stays, girdle, roll-on; brassiere, bra; suspender belt, braces.

(18) *nightwear,* nightclothes; sleeping suit; nightdress, nightgown, negligee; nightshirt, pyjamas.

(19) *beachwear,* bikini, swimming costume, swimsuit; trunks.

(20) *overcoat,* coat (see *jacket*); topcoat, greatcoat, frock coat; raglan, duffel coat; waterproof, oilskins; mac, mackintosh, raincoat, gabardine.

(21) *cloak,* mantle; cape, cycling c.; domino 527 *disguise*; shawl, plaid, poncho.

(22) *neckwear,* scarf, stole, fichu; comforter, muffler; neckerchief, stock, cravat, tie, bow t.; necklace 844 *jewellery*; ruff, collar.

(23) *headgear,* millinery; hat, cap, beret; headdress, mantilla; coronet, tiara; fillet, snood; coif; scarf, turban, hood, cowl; wimple; veil, yashmak; fez; kepi, busby, bearskin, helmet 713 *armour*; tin hat, hard h., crash helmet; sou'wester; trilby, bowler, derby; stetson, sombrero; boater, panama, straw hat, pith helmet; bonnet, mob cap, toque, cloche, pillbox; top hat, topper; mortarboard.

(24) *belt,* waistband; cummerbund, sash, girdle.

(25) *glove,* gauntlet; mitten, mitt, muff.

(26) *legwear,* hosiery; stockings, nylons, tights, fleshings; trunks, hose; leggings, gaiters, spats; garter, suspender.

(27) *footwear,* sock; slipper, mule; clog; sandals, sneakers, plimsolls, gym shoes, pumps, ballet shoes; moccasins, slip-ons, casuals; shoe, court s., high heels, lace-ups, brogues; boots, waders, gumboots, wellingtons; running shoes, spikes.

(28) *clothier,* outfitter, costumier; tailor, couturier, fashion designer. dressmaker, seamstress; shoemaker, cobbler; milliner, draper, haberdasher.

Adjective
(29) *dressed,* clothed, clad, rigged out 844 *bedecked*; uniformed, liveried; shod, gloved, hatted; well-dressed, soignée.

(30) *tailored,* tailor-made, made-to-measure, bespoke; ready-to-wear, off-the-peg; one-piece, two-p.; unisex; well-cut, fully fashioned; classic; sartorial.

Verb
(31) *dress,* clothe, array, attire; robe, drape; invest, uniform, equip, rig out, fit o.; dress up, deck 843 *primp*; envelop, wrap up, roll up in, swathe 226 *cover.*

(32) *wear,* put on, try on, assume, don, slip on; clothe oneself, get dressed; button up 45 *tie*; change, get changed; have on, dress in, carry, sport; dress up.

229
Uncovering

Noun
(1) *uncovering,* divestment, exposure 526 *disclosure*; nudism,

naturism; striptease; undress, déshabillé; moulting, shedding, peeling, shaving.

(2) *bareness,* bare neck, décolletage; nudity, nakedness, state of nature, birthday suit, the altogether, the buff, the raw; baldness, hairlessness.

(3) *stripper,* flasher, streaker; nudist, naturist; nude.

Adjective
(4) *uncovered,* bared; exposed, showing 522 *manifest*; divested of, stripped, peeled; undressed, unclothed, off-the-shoulder, décolleté(e), bare-necked, topless; barelegged, barefoot; hatless, bareheaded; bare, naked, nude; in the buff, with nothing on, stark naked; plucked, moulting.

(5) *hairless,* bald, smooth, beardless, shaved, clean-shaven, tonsured; napless, threadbare; mangy 651 *diseased*; thin on top.

Verb
(6) *uncover,* unveil, undress, divest of; strip, skin, scalp, flay, tear off; pluck, peel, hull, shell; denude, expose, bare, lay open 526 *disclose*; unfold, unwrap, unpack 263 *open.*

(7) *doff,* uncover, raise one's hat; take off, strip off, peel off, slip off, step out of; change, shed, drop, cast, moult, slough, cast its skin; divest oneself of, undress, disrobe, strip.

230
Surroundings

Noun
(1) *surroundings* 223 exteriority; ambience, atmosphere, aura; medium, matrix; containment, surrounding 235 *enclosure*; circumference, periphery 233 *outline*; milieu,

environment, background, setting, scene 186 *situation*; neighbourhood, vicinity 200 *near place*; outskirts, environs, purlieus, precincts 192 *housing*; border, cordon 236 *limit*.

Adjective
(2) *circumjacent,* circum-; framing, peripheral; shutting in, surrounding etc. vb.; roundabout 314 *circuitous*.

Verb
(3) *surround,* lie around, compass, encompass, lap; encircle 314 *circle*; girdle 235 *enclose*; wreathe around, twine a.; embrace, hug; contain, keep in, shut in, hem in 232 *circumscribe*; beset, invest, blockade 712 *besiege*.

Adverb
(4) *around,* about, on every side, round about, all round; on all sides.

231
Interjacency

Noun
(1) *interjacency,* intermediacy, intervention, penetration, permeation, infiltration 189 *presence*; middle position 70 *middle*.

(2) *partition,* curtain, Iron C. 57 *exclusion*; wall, bulkhead 235 *fence*; divide, parting 225 *centre*; division, panel 53 *subdivision*; field boundary, hedge, ditch 201 *gap*; frontier.

(3) *intermediary,* medium, link, interface 47 *bond*; negotiator, go-between, broker 720 *mediator*; marriage broker matchmaker, agent 755 *deputy*; middleman 794 *merchant*; intercessor, pleader, advocate 707 *patron*; buffer, bumper, fender; air lock, buffer state, no-man's-land 70 *middle*.

(4) *interjection,* putting between, interposition, sandwiching; interpolation, interspersion 303 *insertion*; interruption, intrusion 72 *discontinuity*; insert, parenthesis 40 *adjunct*; wedge, washer 227 *lining*;

(5) *interjector,* interpolator; intruder, interloper.

Adjective
(6) *interjacent,* interviewing etc. vb.; interposed, sandwiched; parenthetical, in brackets; intermediary, intercessory 720 *mediatory*; intercalary 303 *inserted*; intrusive 59 *extraneous*; inter-; intermediate, median, mediterranean 70 *middle*.

Verb
(7) *lie between,* come b., stand b.; intervene 625 *be halfway*; permeate 189 *pervade*.

(8) *introduce,* let in 299 *admit*; sheathe, invaginate; throw in, work in, wedge in, edge in, jam in, force in 303 *insert*; splice, dovetail, mortise 45 *join*; smuggle in, slide in, worm in, insinuate 297 *infiltrate*.

(9) *put between,* sandwich; cushion 227 *line*; interpose, interject; interpolate, intercalate, interleave, intersperse; interweave; bracket.

(10) *interfere,* come between, get b., intercept 702 *hinder*; step in, intervene, intercede 720 *mediate*; interrupt, put in, chip in, butt in 297 *intrude*; trespass 306 *encroach*.

Adverb
(11) *between,* among, amid, mid, midst.

232
Circumscription

Noun
(1) *circumscription,* enclosing

235 *enclosure*; drawing round, circle, balloon; surrounding, framing, girdling; siege, blockade; envelopment, encirclement, containment 747 *restriction*; ring 235 *fence*.

Adjective
(2) *circumscribed,* encircled, enveloped; surrounded, lapped, enfolded, landlocked; framed, outlined; boxed up, walled in, mewed up, cloistered, immured 747 *imprisoned*; invested, beleaguered, besieged; held in, contained, confined 747 *restrained*; limited, restricted.

Verb
(3) *circumscribe,* describe a circle, ring round, encircle 230 *surround*; envelop, close in cut off, cordon off, blockade 712 *besiege*; beset, hem in, corral; rail in, hedge in, fence in; box, cage, wall in 747 *imprison*; frame, encase, enshrine 235 *enclose*; edge, border 236 *limit*.

233
Outline

Noun
(1) *outline,* circumference, perimeter, periphery; surround, frame, rim 234 *edge*; circuit 250 *circle*; delineation features 445 *feature*; profile, silhouette, skyline; sketch, rough s. 623 *plan*; figure, diagram, tracing; skeleton, framework 331 *structure*; contour, shape 243 *form*; coastline, bounds 236 *limit*; ring, cordon 235 *barrier*.

Adjective
(2) *outlined,* framed etc. vb.; in outline, etched; peripheral.

Verb
(3) *outline,* describe a circle 232 *circumscribe*; frame 230 *surround*; delineate, draw, silhouette, profile, trace 551 *represent*; map, block out, sketch o., sketch.

234
Edge

Noun
(1) *edge,* verge, brim; border, tip, brink, skirt, fringe, margin 69 *extremity*; boundary, frontier, 236 *limit*; coastline, waterline, waterside, front, waterfront 344 *shore*; sideline, side, kerb, wayside, roadside; projecting edge, lip, ledge, rim 254 *projection*.

(2) *threshold,* sill, doorstep 263 *doorway*; mouth, jaws 194 *maw*.

(3) *edging,* frame 233 *outline*; thrum, list, selvage; hem, border; binding, piping; fringe, frill 844 *trimming*; milling 260 *notch*; deckle edge, wavy edge 251 *coil*.

Adjective
(4) *marginal,* border, skirting, riparian, coastal; riverside, roadside, wayside; labial; edged, trimmed, bordered.

Verb
(5) *hem,* edge, border, trim, fringe; confine 236 *limit*.

235
Enclosure

Noun
(1) *enclosure,* envelope, case 194 *receptacle*; wrapper 226 *wrapping*; girdle, ring, perimeter 233 *outline*; surround, frame; precinct, close 185 *place*; lot, holding 184 *territory*; fold, pen 369 *cattle pen*; park, garden; compound, yard, pound, paddock, field; car park; corral, kraal, stockade 713 *defences*; net, trawl 542 *trap*; cell, box, cage 748 *prison*.

(2) *fence,* hurdle; hedge, hedgerow; rails, paling, railing, taffrail; pale, wall; moat, ha-ha, dike, ditch 713 *defences*.

(3) *barrier,* wall 231 *partition*; soundproofing; barricade, cordon; balustrade, parapet; turnstile 702 *obstacle*; palisade, stockade 713 *fort*; portcullis, gate; bolt, bar 264 *closure*.

Verb

(4) *enclose,* fence in, cordon off, surround, wall; pen, hem, ring 232 *circumscribe*; cloister, immure 747 *imprison*; wrap, lap, enfold; hug, embrace 889 *caress*; frame, set, mount, box.

236
Limit

Noun

(1) *limit,* limitation, definition, demarcation 747 *restriction*; limiting factor, upper limit, ceiling; lower limit; threshold, legal limit; saturation point 54 *completeness*; utmost, extreme, pole 69 *extremity*; terminus, terminal 69 *end*; turning point 137 *crisis*; tolerance, capacity, end of one's tether; perimeter, circumference; tidemark, sea line; landmark, boundary stone; milestone 27 *degree*; boundary, frontier, border 234 *edge*; demarcation line, 231 *partition*; horizon, equator; deadline, time limit; ultimatum 900 *threat*; speed limit, sound barrier.

Adjective

(2) *limited,* definite, limitable, finite; limitative, terminal; frontier, border, boundary.

Verb

(3) *limit,* bound, border, edge; top 213 *crown*; define, confine, restrict 747 *restrain*; draw the line 232 *circumscribe*; delimit, demarcate, stake out; mark out.

Adverb

(4) *thus far,* so far, and no further.

237
Front

Noun

(1) *front,* fore, forefront; forepart; prefix, frontispiece; forelock; forecourt, anteroom, entrance 263 *doorway*; foreground 200 *nearness*; front rank, front line; van, advance guard; spearhead, bridgehead, outpost, scout; forerunner, pioneer 66 *precursor*.

(2) *face,* frontage, façade, obverse, head; right side, outer s., recto; front view, front elevation; brow, forehead, physiognomy, features, visage, countenance; nose, chin 254 *protuberance*.

(3) *prow,* figurehead; bows; bowsprit; jib, foremast, forecastle, fo'c'sle.

Adjective

(4) *frontal,* fore, forward, front, obverse; full frontal, head-on, oncoming, facing 240 *opposite*.

Verb

(5) *be in front,* front, confront, face 240 *be opposite*; breast, stem; forge ahead, take the lead, head 283 *precede*.

Adverb

(6) *in front,* before, in advance, in the lead, in the van, ahead, further on 199 *beyond*; before one's eyes; face to face, vis-a-vis; in the foreground, in the forefront; head first, feet first.

238
Rear

Noun

(1) *rear,* back end, tail end, stern 69 *extremity*; tailpiece, coda; tail, brush, scut; wake, train 67 *sequel*; rearguard; background, backdrop; behind, backstage, back side; reverse side, wrong s., verso, reverse, other side, flip side; back door, back entrance, postern; back, backbone; nape, scruff.

(2) *buttocks*, backside, behind, posterior, bottom, seat; rear, stern, tail; hindquarters, croup, crupper; hips, hams, haunches; rump, loin; dorsal region, lumbar r., lower back, small of the b.

(3) *poop*, stern, stern-sheets, quarter, rudder, mizzenmast 275 *ship*.

Adjective
(4) *back*, rear, posterior, after, hind, hinder, hindermost, rearmost, tail-end; reverse 240 *opposite*; spinal, vertebral, dorsal, lumbar.

Verb
(5) *be behind*, stand b.; back on, back; bring up the rear 284 *follow*; lag, trail, drop behind, fall astern; tail, shadow 619 *pursue*; bend backwards, lean b. 220 *be oblique*.

Adverb
(6) *rearward*, behind, in the rear, at the back, behind the scenes; after, sternmost; aft, astern, to the rear; backward, retro-; above, overleaf; on the heels of, close behind; back to back.

239
Laterality

Noun
(1) *laterality*, sidedness; side movement 317 *oscillation*; sidestep 282 *deviation*; sideline, side, bank 234 *edge*; coast 344 *shore*; siding; broadside, beam, quarter; flank, ribs, wing, fin, cheek, jowl, chops, chaps, gills; temples, side-face, profile, side elevation; leeward, windward; orientation, east, Orient, west, Occident 281 *compass point*; off side, on s., near s. 241 *dextrality*, 242 *sinistrality*.

Adjective
(2) *lateral*, side 234 *marginal*; sidelong, glancing; flanking, skirting; flanked, sided; multilateral, bilateral, trilateral, quadrilateral; collateral 219 *parallel*; moving sideways, edging, sidling; eastern, eastward, easterly, oriental; auroral, west, western, westerly, westward, occidental.

Verb
(3) *flank*, edge, skirt, border 234 *hem*; coast, move sideways, sidle; sidestep 282 *deviate*.

Adverb
(4) *sideways*, crabwise, laterally 220 *obliquely*; in profile; broadside on; abreast, abeam, alongside; aside, beside 200 *near*; to windward, to leeward, right and left.

240
Contraposition

Noun
(1) *contraposition*, opposition, frontage 281 *direction*; opposite side, other s.; polarity, polarization; opposite poles; crosscurrent, headwind;

Adjective
(2) *opposite*, reverse, inverse, contrary, facing, fronting, confronting 237 *frontal*; antipodal, antipodean; polarized, polar; antarctic, arctic, northern, southern 281 *directed*.

Verb
(3) *be opposite*, - facing, etc. adj.; stand opposite, lie o.; face, confront 237 *be in front*.

Adverb
(4) *against*, over against; poles asunder; facing, face to face, back to back.

241
Dextrality

Noun
(1) *dextrality,* right hand, ambidexterity; right, offside, starboard; right-hand page, recto; right wing, right-winger.

Adjective
(2) *dextral,* dextro-; right-hand, right-handed, dextrous, ambidextrous 694 *skilful.*

242
Sinistrality

Noun
(1) *sinistrality,* left hand, left, near side, on s.; larboard, port; verso; left wing, left-winger. southpaw.

Adjective
(2) *sinistral,* sinister, left, left-handed; onside, nearside.

243
Form

Noun
(1) *form,* art form 551 *art,* 593 *verse form;* word form 557 *linguistics;* shape, turn, lines, architecture; formation, conformation, configuration, fashion, style, design, structure; contour, silhouette, relief, profile, frame, outline; figure, cut, set, trim, build, lineament 445 *feature;* look, expression 445 *appearance;* type, kind, pattern, stamp, cast, mould; blank 23 *prototype;* format 587 *print.*

(2) *formation,* forming, shaping, creation 164 *production;* expression, formulation 62 *arrangement;* designing, patterning 844 *ornamental art;* weaving, knitting 222 *network;* tailoring 844 *needlework;* throwing 381 *pottery;* moulding 554 *sculpture;* turning, joinery

694 *skill;* etymology 557 *linguistics.*

Adjective
(3) *formed,* created etc. vb.; receiving form, plastic, sculptured, carved, moulded, thrown, turned, rounded, squared; shaped, fashioned, styled, stylized; matured 669 *prepared;* dimensional, two-d., three-d.

(4) *formative,* giving form, formal; plastic, architectural 331 *structural.*

Verb
(5) *form,* create, make 164 *produce;* shape, fashion, figure, pattern; throw (pots), blow (glass); turn, round, square; cut, tailor; cut out, silhouette 233 *outline;* sketch, draw 551 *represent;* model, carve, whittle, chisel hew, rough-h. 46 *cut;* mould, cast; stamp, coin, mint; hammer out, block o., knock o., punch o.; forge, smith; knead, work, work up into; construct, build 310 *elevate;* frame, express, formulate; knock into shape.

244
Amorphism: Absence of form

Noun
(1) *amorphism,* shapelessness chaos 61 *disorder;* amorphousness, lack of shape *or* definition, vagueness, fuzziness; rawness, raw material 631 *materials;* mutilation, deformation 246 *distortion.*

Adjective
(2) *amorphous,* shapeless; formless, liquid 335 *fluid;* featureless, characterless; ill-defined, indistinct, nebulous, vague, fuzzy, blurred 419 *shadowy;* embryonic 68 *beginning;* raw 670 *immature;* in the rough 55 *incomplete;* uncouth, barbaric

699 *artless*; malformed, misshapen 246 *deformed*.

Verb

(3) *deform*, deprive of form, dissolve, melt; batter 46 *break*; grind, pulp 332 *pulverize*; warp, twist 246 *distort*; deface, disfigure 842 *make ugly*; mutilate, truncate 655 *impair*; jumble, disorder 63 *derange*.

245
Symmetry:
Regularity of form

Noun

(1) *symmetry*, proportion 12 *correlation*; balance 28 *equilibrium*; regularity, evenness 16 *uniformity*; branching, ramification 219 *parallelism*; shapeliness, regular features 841 *beauty*; harmony, congruity 24 *agreement*.

Adjective

(2) *symmetrical*, balanced, proportioned, well-p. 12 *correlative*; harmonious, congruous 24 *agreeing*; congruent, coextensive; analogous 18 *similar*; smooth, even 16 *uniform*; squared, rounded regular; crystalline; formal, classic 841 *shapely*.

246
Distortion:
Irregularity of form

Noun

(1) *distortion*, asymmetry, disproportion, want of symmetry, imbalance 29 *inequality*; lopsidedness, crookedness, skewness 220 *obliquity*; contortion, twisting; thrust, stress, strain, shear; bias, warp; buckle, bend, twist 251 *convolution*; grimace, snarl.

(2) *deformity*, malformation 84 *abnormality*; rickets 845 *blemish*; ugliness 842 *eyesore*.

Adjective

(3) *distorted*, irregular, asymmetric, unsymmetrical; weighted, biased; not true, not straight; grotesque, warped, out of shape 244 *amorphous*; buckled, twisted, gnarled 251 *convoluted*; awry, askew, crazy, crooked, cock-eyed 220 *oblique*; slouched, slumped; grimacing, scowling, snarling.

(4) *deformed*, ugly 842 *unsightly*; defective 647 *imperfect*; ill-made, misshapen; hunch-backed, humpbacked, round-shouldered, pigeon-chested; bandy, bandy-legged, bow-legged, knock-kneed; pigeon-toed, splay-footed, club-footed; snub-nosed, hare-lipped 845 *blemished*; stunted, stumpy 204 *short*; haggard, gaunt 206 *lean*; bloated 195 *fleshy*.

Verb

(5) *distort*, bias; contort, screw, twist, bend, warp. buckle, crumple; strain, sprain, skew, wrest, torture 63 *derange*; misshape, mangle 655 *impair*; pervert 552 *misrepresent*; misconstrue 521 *misinterpret*; grimace, make faces, snarl, scowl, frown 547 *gesticulate*.

247
Angularity

Noun

(1) *angularity*, crook, hook; bend 248 *curvature*; chevron, zigzag 220 *obliquity*; V-shape, elbow, knee; knuckle 45 *joint*; crutch, crotch, fluke 222 *cross*; fork, bifurcation; corner, nook, niche; nose 254 *protuberance*; arrowhead 256 *sharp point*; indentation 260 *notch*.

(2) *angle*, right a., acute a., obtuse a., salient a.

(3) *angular measure,* trigonometry, altimetry; second, degree, minute; altimeter; level, theodolite; sextant, quadrant; protractor, set square.

(4) *angular figure,* triangle, isosceles t., equilateral t., scalene t.; parallelogram, rectangle, square; quadrilateral, lozenge, diamond; rhombus, rhomboid; trapezium, trapezoid; polygon, pentagon, hexagon, heptagon, octagon, decagon; cube, pyramid, wedge; prism.

Adjective

(5) *angular,* hooked, hooknosed, aquiline 248 *curved;* angled, jointed, cornered; staggered, crooked, zigzag 220 *oblique;* jagged, serrated 260 *notched;* akimbo; knockkneed; forked, bifurcate, V-shaped.

(6) *angulated,* triangular, trilateral; wedge-shaped, cuneiform; rectangular, right-angled, square, foursquare; quadrangular, quadrilateral, four-sided; lozenge-shaped; trapezoid, trapezoidal; multilateral, polygonal, polyhedral; cubical, pyramidal.

Verb

(7) *make angular,* angle, corner; hook, crook 248 *make curved;* wrinkle, fold 251 *crinkle;* zigzag 220 *be oblique;* fork, bifurcate.

248
Curvature

Noun

(1) *curvature,* inward curve 255 *concavity;* outward curve 253 *convexity;* bending 261 *fold;* bowing, stooping bending down; turning away, swerve; retroflexion 221 *inversion;* sinuosity 251 *convolution.*

(2) *curve,* slight c. 253 *camber;* elbow 247 *angularity;* turn, bend, sharp b., hairpin b., U-

turn; horseshoe, oxbow, bay; figure of eight 250 *loop;* S-shape; tracery, curl 251 *convolution;* festoon, swag 844 *pattern;* bow, rainbow 250 *arc;* arch, arcade, vault 253 *dome;* crescent, half-moon; lens; trajectory, parabola, hyperbola, conic section.

Adjective

(3) *curved,* bent, bowed, stooping 220 *oblique;* rounded, curvaceous, curvy, wavy, billowy 251 *undulatory;* beaked, hooked 247 *angular;* recurved, retroflex; retroussé, turned-up, tiptilted 221 *inverted;* vaulted 253 *arched;* bow-legged 246 *deformed;* semicircular 250 *round;* crescent, lunar, horned; heart-shaped, bell-s., pear-s.

Verb

(4) *be curved,* - bent etc. adj.; curve, bend, loop, camber, arch, sweep, sag, swag, give 217 *hang.*

(5) *make curved,* bend, crook 247 *make angular;* round 250 *make round;* bend over, bend down, bow, incline 311 *stoop;* turn over 261 *fold;* turn away 282 *deflect;* arch, arch over; coil 251 *twine;* curl, wave 251 *crinkle.*

249
Straightness

Noun

(1) *straightness,* directness; perpendicularity 215 *verticality;* inflexibility, rigidity; chord, radius 203 *line;* straight line, beeline; straight stretch, straight, reach; short cut.

Adjective

(2) *straight,* direct, even, right, true; in a line, linear; rectilinear, perpendicular 215 *vertical;* unbent, stiff, inflexible 326 *rigid;* straightened, dead straight, unswerving, undeviating.

Verb

(3) *be straight,* steer straight, go straight, have no turning, not deviate,

(4) *straighten,* make straight, align; iron out 216 *flatten;* unbend (a bow); uncurl 62 *unravel;* unroll, uncoil, unfurl, unfold.

Adverb

(5) *straight on,* directly, as the crow flies.

250
Circularity: Simple circularity

Noun

(1) *circularity,* roundness 252 *rotundity.*

(2) *circle,* circumference 233 *outline;* great circle, equator; wheel 315 *rotator;* plate, saucer; disc, discus; coin, button, washer; hoop, ring, quoit; eye, iris; eyelet 263 *orifice;* circular course, circuit, circus, roundabout; fairy ring; smoke ring.

(3) *loop,* figure of eight 251 *convolution;* bow, knot; circlet, bracelet, armlet; crown, corona, aureole, halo; wreath, garland; collar, necklace; band, sash, girdle 228 *belt;* lasso, lariat 47 *halter.*

(4) *arc,* semicircle, half-circle, half-moon, crescent; rainbow 248 *curve;* ellipse, oval.

(5) *orbit,* cycle, circuit, ecliptic; circulation 314 *circuition.*

Adjective

(6) *round,* rounded, circular, ringlike, ringed, annular; semicircular; oval elliptic, ovoid, egg-shaped; crescent-s., pear-s. 248 *curved;* spherical 252 *rotund.*

Verb

(7) *make round,* - oval etc. adj.; round, turn.

(8) *go round,* girdle, encircle 230 *surround;* describe a circle 233 *outline;* move round, orbit 314 *circle.*

251
Convolution: Complex circularity

Noun

(1) *convolution,* intricacy; sinuosity, tortuosity; twist, ripple, wrinkle; corrugation 261 *fold;* indentation 260 *notch;* waviness, undulation, ogee 248 *curve.*

(2) *coil,* roll, twist; spring, spiral, helix; screw, corkscrew; whorl, ammonite; whirlpool 315 *vortex;* scallop; kink, curl; ringlet, tendril; scroll, volute, flourish, twirl, curlicue, squiggle.

(3) *meandering,* meander, winding course, twists and turns 282 *deviation;* labyrinth, maze 61 *complexity;* switchback, zigzag.

Adjective

(4) *convoluted,* twisted, contorted 246 *distorted;* cranky, looping, twining, sinuous, tortuous; crumpled, buckled 261 *folded.*

(5) *labyrinthine,* mazy, meandering, serpentine; twisting, turning, circuitous.

(6) *snaky,* serpentine, eel-like, wormlike, vermiform, squiggly, squirming, wriggling, S-shaped.

(7) *undulatory,* undulating, rolling, up-and-down, switchback; wavy, curly, frizzy, kinky, crinkly; crimped, curled; scolloped, wrinkled, corrugated, indented 260 *notched.*

(8) *coiled,* spiral, helical, whorled, scroll-like, wound, wound up.

(9) *intricate,* involved, complicated, knotted 61 *complex.*

Verb

(10) *twine,* twist, twirl, roll, coil, corkscrew, spiral 315 *rotate*; wreathe, entwine 222 *enlace.*

(11) *crinkle,* crimp, frizz, crisp, curl; wave, undulate, ripple; wrinkle 261 *fold*; scallop 260 *notch*; crumple 246 *distort.*

(12) *meander,* loop, snake, twist and turn, zigzag.

(13) *wriggle,* writhe, squirm, shake; move sinuously, worm.

Adverb

(14) *in and out,* round about.

252
Rotundity

Noun

(1) *rotundity,* roundness 250 *circularity*; gibbousness 253 *convexity.*

(2) *sphere,* globe, spheroid, bladder, balloon; bubble; ball, wood (bowls), marble, cannonball, bullet, shot, pellet; bead, pill, pea, globule; drop, droplet, blot; bulb, knob, pommel 253 *swelling*; hemisphere, hump, mushroom 253 *dome*; round head, bullet h., turnip h.

(3) *cylinder,* roll, roller, rolling pin; round, rung; column; bole, trunk, stalk; funnel, pipe, drainpipe 263 *tube*; hat box, pillbox; drum, barrel.

(4) *cone,* cornet, horn 194 *cup*; spinning top, peg t.; pear shape, bell s., egg s.

Adjective

(5) *rotund,* 250 *round*; spherical, globular, global; round-headed, bullet-headed; beadlike; hemispherical; spheroidal, ovoid, egg-shaped; cylindrical, tubular; cigar-shaped 256 *tapering*; conic, conical; bell-shaped, turnip-shaped; pear-shaped, heart-

shaped; humped, gibbous; bulbous 253 *convex*; pot-bellied 195 *fleshy*; balled, rolled up.

Verb

(6) *round,* make spherical; balloon 253 *be convex*; coil up, roll, roll up 315 *rotate.*

253
Convexity

Noun

(1) *convexity,* arching 248 *curvature*; sphericity 252 *rotundity*; gibbosity, bulge, bump; projection, protrusion, protuberance 254 *prominence*; swelling 197 *idilation* lens.

(2) *swelling,* bump, lump, bulge, growth, excrescence; gall, knot, node, nodule; knuckle; tumour; bubo, goitre; Adam's apple; bunion, corn, wart, wen, verruca; boil, carbuncle, stye, pimple, blister, vesicle; polyp, adenoids, haemorrhoids, piles; weal, welt; cauliflower ear; drop, 252 *sphere*; bubble air knob, nub, bulb, button, bud; belly, potbelly, paunch 195 *bulk*; billow, swell 350 *wave.*

(3) *bosom,* bust, breast, breasts; boobs, bristols, knockers, tits; nipple, pap, teat, udder; thorax, chest; cuirass, breastplate.

(4) *dome,* cupola, vault; beehive, skep; brow, skull, cranium, 213 *head*; hemisphere, arch of heaven; hog's back, mound; hummock, hillock, 209 *small hill*; molehill, mushroom.

(5) *earthwork,* tumulus barrow, 548 *monument*; hill fort, 713 *defences*; embankment, levee.

(6) *camber,* gentle curve 248 *curve*; arch, bow, rainbow; hump, humpback, hunchback, shoulders.

Adjective

(7) *convex,* protruding 254 *projecting*; hemispheric, gibbous

252 *rotund*; curvaceous, billowy 248 *curved*; billowing, bulging, bellying, ballooning, bouffant; swelling, swollen 197 *expanded*; bloated, potbellied, 195 *fleshy*; lumpy; 259 *rough*; warty, pimply; vesicular.

(8) *arched,* cambered, bowed 248 *curved*; rounded; hillocky, hummocky,

Verb
(9) *be convex,* camber, arch, bow; swell, belly, bulge, bag, balloon; make convex, emboss, beat out.

254
Prominence

Noun
(1) *prominence,* eminence 209 *high land*; relief, high r., low r..

(2) *projection,* salient; forefinger, index f.; bowsprit, outrigger; tongue of land, spit, point, mull, promontory, foreland, headland; peninsula; spur, foothill; jetty, mole, breakwater, groyne, pier 662 *shelter*; outwork 713 *fortification*; pilaster, buttress 218 *prop*; shelf, sill, ledge, balcony; eaves 226 *roof*; overhang, rake flange, lip 234 *edge*; nozzle, spout; tongue; tenon 45 *joint*; stump, outcrop; landmark 209 *high structure*.

(3) *protuberance,* bump 253 *swelling*; nose, snout, bill, beak, muzzle, proboscis, trunk; antenna 378 *feeler*; chin, jaw, brow; figurehead 237 *prow*; horn, antler 256 *sharp point*.

Adjective
(4) *projecting,* jutting, prominent, salient, bold; protuberant, protruding, bulging, popeyed; toothy; beetle-browed, overhung; underhung, raised, in relief.

Verb
(5) *jut,* project, protrude, pout; pop out, start o.; stand out, stick o., poke o. 443 *be visible*; bristle up, prick up, cock up; shoot up, swell up; overhang 217 *hang*.

255
Concavity

Noun
(1) *concavity,* concaveness; hollowness 190 *emptiness*; depression, dint, dent, impression, stamp, imprint 548 *trace*; intaglio 555 *engraving*; ploughing, furrowing, indentation 260 *notch*.

(2) *cavity,* hollow, niche, nook, cranny, recess, corner; hole, den, burrow; chasm, abyss 211 *depth*; cave, cavern, grotto, alcove; bowl, cup, saucer, basin, trough; cell, pore 263 *orifice*; dimple, pockmark; honeycomb, sponge 263 *porosity*; funnel, tunnel 263 *tube*; groove, mortise, socket, pocket 262 *furrow*; bay, cove 345 *gulf*; ditch, moat 351 *conduit*; dip, depression, pothole, crater, pit.

(3) *valley,* vale, dell, dingle, glen, corrie; dip, depression; ravine, gorge, canyon, gully 201 *gap*.

(4) *excavation,* dugout; grave 364 *tomb*; dig; opencast mining; shaft, borehole, well, mine, pit, colliery, quarry 632 *store*; gallery, trench, burrow, warren; tube 263 *tunnel*; cutting, cut.

(5) *excavator,* miner, coal-m., quarrier; archaeologist, digger; dredger, drag-line; sapper, burrower, grave-digger.

Adjective
(6) *concave,* hollow, cavernous; vaulted, arched 248 *curved*; hollowed out, scooped o.; dug o.; caved in, stove in; depressed, sunk, sunken; saucer-

shaped, cupped; capsular, funnel-shaped, bell-shaped; socketed, dented, dimpled, pockmarked; full of holes, honeycombed; cellular, porous 263 *perforated*.

Verb

(7) *be concave,* - hollow etc. adj.; cave in; cup.

(8) *make concave,* depress, press in, punch in, stamp, impress; dent, dint, stave in; push in, beat in; excavate, hollow, dig, delve, scrape, scratch, scrabble; trench, canalize 262 *groove*; mine, sap, undermine, burrow, tunnel, bore; honeycomb 263 *pierce*; scoop out, hollow o., dig o., gouge o., scratch o. 300 *eject*; hole, pit, pockmark; indent 260 *notch*.

256
Sharpness

Noun

(1) *sharpness,* acuteness, pointedness; serration 260 *notch*; thorniness, prickliness.

(2) *sharp point,* sting, prick, point, cusp; nail, tack; pin, needle, stylus; skewer, spit; lancet 263 *perforator*; arrow, shaft, arrowhead; barb, fluke; lance 723 *spear*; gaff, harpoon; dagger 723 *side arms*; spike 713 *defences*; spur, rowel 612 *incentive*; fork, prong, tine, pick, horn, antler; claw 778 *nippers*; peak 213 *summit*.

(3) *prickle,* thorn, brier, bramble, thistle, nettle, cactus; spine, quill, bristle 259 *hair*.

(4) *tooth,* tusk, fang; eyetooth, incisor, grinder, molar; dentures; false teeth, plate, bridge; comb, saw; cog 260 *notch*.

(5) *sharp edge,* cutting e., edge tool; cutlery, steel, razor; blade, ploughshare, coulter; scythe, sickle, hook; scissors,

shears, clippers, secateurs; scalpel; chisel, plane; knife, penknife; chopper, hatchet, axe; sword 723 *side arms*.

(6) *sharpener,* pencil s.; whetstone, grindstone; hone, file, strop.

Adjective

(7) *sharp,* stinging, keen, acute; edged, cutting; pointed, cusped, barbed, spurred; spiked, spiky, spiny, thorny; needlelike, prickly, bristly, bristling 259 *hairy*; jagged 260 *notched*; sharp-edged, knife-e., razor-e.; sharpened, razorsharp.

(8) *toothed,* toothy, fanged; dental; serrated 260 *notched*.

(9) *tapering,* conical, pyramidal; spired, spiry; horned; lanceshaped, lanceolate.

Verb

(10) *be sharp,* have a point, prick, sting; bristle with; have an edge 46 *cut*; taper 293 *converge*.

(11) *sharpen,* edge, whet, hone, grind, file, strop; barb, spur, point.

257
Bluntness

Noun

(1) *bluntness,* curves 258 *smoothness*; blunt instrument, foil; blunt edge, blade, flat.

Adjective

(2) *unsharpened,* blunt, blunted; unpointed, obtuse; rusty, lacking bite, toothless; bluntnosed, stubby, snub, square; round, rounded, curving 248 *curved*; flat, flattened, bluff.

Verb

(3) *blunt,* make blunt, turn the edge; bate (a foil); dull, rust; draw the teeth of; be blunt, not cut.

258
Smoothness

Noun

(1) *smoothness,* smooth texture, silkiness 327 *softness*; smooth hair, sleekness; smooth surface, marble, glass, ice; flatness, levelness; polish, varnish, gloss, glaze, shine, finish; slipperiness, slipway, slide; oiliness, greasiness; smooth water, calm.

(2) *smoother,* roller 216 *flattener*; iron, press; comb, brush; sandpaper, emery board; plane, file; polish, varnish; lubricator, grease, oil 334 *lubricant.*

Adjective

(3) *smooth,* frictionless, streamlined; without lumps 16 *uniform*; slithery, slippery, skiddy; oily, greasy, soapy 334 *lubricated*; polished, shiny, varnished, waxed; soft, bland, soothing 177 *lenitive*; silky, silken, satiny, velvety; downy 259 *fleecy*; marble, glassy; bald 229 *hairless*; sleek, unruffled; combed, raked, harrowed; even, level, flush 216 *flat*; glassy, quiet, calm 266 *still*; rounded, blunt 248 *curved*; satin-smooth.

Verb

(4) *smooth,* remove friction, streamline; grease 334 *lubricate*; plane, even, level; rake, comb; file 333 *rub*; roll, press, iron 216 *flatten*; smooth down, smarm d., slick d., plaster d.; iron out 62 *unravel*; starch, launder; shine, buff, polish, glaze, wax, varnish 226 *coat.*

(5) *go smoothly,* glide, float, roll, bowl along slip, slide, skid 265 *be in motion*; skate, ski; coast, freewheel.

259
Roughness

Noun

(1) *roughness,* broken ground; rough water 350 *wave*; rough air, turbulence; jaggedness, broken glass 256 *sharp edge*; serration 260 *notch*; ruggedness, cragginess 209 *high land*; rough going, unevenness, bumpiness 17 *nonuniformity*; corrugation, ripple 261 *fold*; rut 262 *furrow*; coarseness, coarse grain, rough surface; grater, file, sandpaper; sackcloth, tweed, homespun 222 *textile*; creeping flesh, gooseflesh, rough skin, chap, crack; hairiness, shagginess, stubble, bristle 256 *prickle.*

(2) *hair* head of h., shock of h., thatch, fuzz, wool; mop, mane, fleece; bristle, stubble; locks, tresses, curls; ringlet, kiss curl; plait, pigtail, ponytail, rat's tails; topknot, forelock, dreadlocks; fringe, quiff; bun, chignon 843 *hairdressing*; false hair, hairpiece, switch, wig, toupee; beard, whiskers, sideboards, moustache; eyebrows, eyelashes; down, wool, fur 226 *skin*; tuft, wisp 208 *fibre*; pile, nap; floss, fluff, fuzz.

(3) *plumage,* pinion; feathering; feathers, coverts, wing c.; neck feathers, hackle f., hackle; ruff, frill, plume, crest.

Adjective

(4) *rough,* uneven, broken; rippling, choppy, storm-tossed; rutted, pitted, potholed, bumpy, jolting, bone-breaking; chunky, crisp, roughcast; lumpy, stony, nodular, knobby, studded, roughened, frosted; crinkled · knotted, gnarled, cross-grained, coarse; cracked, chapped 845 *blemished*; wrinkled, corrugated, ridged 262 *furrowed*; rough-edged 260 *notched*; craggy, cragged, jagged; scabrous, scabby, scaly, blistered; ruffled, unkempt;

(5) *hairy,* napped, brushed; woolly, fleecy, furry; hirsute, shaggy, tufty, matted, shock-headed; bristly, bristling 256 *sharp*; wispy; fringed, bearded, moustached; curly, frizzy, fuzzy, tight-curled, woolly.

(6) *downy,* pubescent, velvety, mossy 258 *smooth*; fluffy, feathery, feathered.

(7) *fleecy,* woolly, fluffy.

Verb
(8) *be rough,* hairy etc. adj.; bristle, bristle up 254 *jut*; creep (of flesh), scratch, catch; jolt, bump, jerk.

(9) *roughen,* roughcast, rough-hew; serrate 260 *notch*; stud, corrugate, wrinkle 251 *crinkle*; ruffle, tousle 63 *derange*; rumple, crumple 261 *fold*.

Adverb
(10) *on edge,* against the grain.

260
Notch

Noun
(1) *notch,* serration, saw edge, ragged e. 256 *sharpness*; indentation, deckle edge; nick, snip, cut, gash 201 *gap*; indent 255 *concavity*; scallop, dogtooth 844 *pattern*; sprocket, cog, ratchet, cogwheel, saw 256 *tooth*.

Adjective
(2) *notched,* indented, jagged, jaggy 256 *sharp*; crenellated; toothed, saw-t., serrated.

Verb
(3) *notch,* tooth, cog; nick, blaze, score, scratch 46 *cut*; indent, scallop, jag, pink, slash; dent, mill 259 *roughen*; pinch, crimp 261 *fold*.

261
Fold

Noun

(1) *fold,* doubling; facing, revers, hem; lapel, cuff, dog's ear; pleat, tuck, gather, pucker, ruffle; flounce, frill; rumple, crease; crinkle, wrinkle, ruck; frown, lines, wrinkles; elbow 247 *angularity*;

Adjective
(2) *folded,* doubled etc. vb,; wrinkly, dog-eared; creased, crumpled 63 *disarranged*.

Verb
(3) *fold,* double, turn over, bend over, roll; crease, pleat; furrow 262 *groove*; rumple, crumple 63 *derange*; curl, frizz 251 *crinkle*; pucker, purse; ruffle, gather, frill, shirr, smock; tuck, tuck up, turn up, turn down, turn under; wrap 235 *enclose*; fold up, roll up, furl, reef.

262
Furrow

Noun
(1) *furrow,* groove, slot, slit, mortise; crack, chink 201 *gap*; trough, hollow 255 *cavity*; gash, slash, score 46 *scission*; wake, rut; gutter 351 *conduit*; ravine 255 *valley*; corrugation; ripple 350 *wave*.

Adjective
(2) *furrowed,* fluted; canalled, channelled; wrinkled 261 *folded*; rippling, wavy.

Verb
(3) *groove,* slot, flute; gash, scratch, score, incise 46 *cut*; carve, etch 555 *engrave*; furrow, plough; wrinkle, line; corrugate 261 *fold*.

263
Opening

Noun
(1) *opening,* flinging wide; unstopping, 229 *uncovering*; yawn, yawning, gaping; hiatus, lacuna, space 201 *gap*;

aperture, split, crack, leak 46
disunion; hole, hollow 255
cavity.

(2) *perforation*, piercing, impalement, puncture, acupuncture; borehole, bore.

(3) *porosity*, porousness, sponge; sieve, sifter, riddle, screen, 62 *sorting*; strainer, colander; grater; honeycomb.

(4) *orifice*, oral cavity, mouth, jaws, muzzle; throat, gullet 194 *maw*; sucker; mouthpiece, nozzle, spout, vent 298 *outlet*; blower, blowhole; air-hole, nasal cavity, nostril; small orifice, pore; hole, manhole, crater 255 *cavity*; eye, eyelet 250 *loop*.

(5) *window*, lattice, grille; embrasure, loophole; bay window, oriel w.; light, fanlight, skylight, sunshine roof; porthole; peephole, keyhole; squint; windscreen, windshield; window frame, casement, sash, mullion, transom; window pane 422 *transparency*.

(6) *doorway*, archway; doorstep, threshold 68 *entrance*; approach, drive, drive-in, entry 297 *way in*; exit, way out; gangway, drawbridge 624 *access*; gate, portal; porch, door, front d., back d., postern; small door, wicket; hatch, hatchway; trapdoor, companionway; stairwell; door jamb, gatepost, lintel.

(7) *open space* 183 space; yard, court 185 *place*; opening, clearing, glade; vista 438 *view*; rolling downs, open country 348 *plain*; alley, aisle, gangway, thoroughfare 305 *passage*; estuary 345 *gulf*.

(8) *tunnel*, boring; subway, underpass, tube; mine, shaft, gallery 255 *excavation*; cave 255 *cavity*; rabbit hole, fox h.; sewer 351 *drain*.

(9) *tube*, pipe, duct 351 *conduit*; pipette; tubing, piping, pipeline, hose; colon, gut.

(10) *chimney*, chimney stack, smokestack, funnel; flue; volcano 383 *furnace*.

(11) *opener*, key, master k., skeleton k., passe-partout; doorknob, handle; corkscrew, tin opener, can o., bottle o.; aperient, purgative; password, open sesame; passport, pass, safe conduct 756 *permit*.

(12) *perforator*, borer, corer; gimlet, corkscrew; auger, drill; probe, lancet, needle, hypodermic n.; awl 256 *sharp point*; pin, nail 47 *fastening*; skewer, spit; punch, card p.

Adjective
(13) *open*, exposed to view 522 *manifest*; unstopped, ajar; unbarred 289 *accessible*; wide-open, agape, gaping; yawning, open-mouthed, slack-jawed; aperient; blooming, out.

(14) *perforated*, drilled, bored; honeycombed, riddled; peppered, shot through; holey, full of holes; windowed,

(15) *porous*, permeable, spongy, percolating, leaky, leaking.

(16) *tubular*, piped; cylindrical 252 *rotund*; funnel-shaped; vascular, capillary.

Verb
(17) *open*, unfold, unwrap unpack, undo; unlock, open the door 299 *admit*; uncover, unstop, uncork 46 *disunite*; lay open, throw o. 522 *show*; force open, rip o., tear o., crack o.; enlarge a hole, ream; fly open, split, gape, yawn; burst, explode; open out, fan o. 75 *be dispersed*; hold apart; bloom, be out.

(18) *pierce*, transfix, impale; gore, run through, stick, pink,

spear 655 *wound*; spike, skewer, spit; prick, puncture, tattoo; probe, stab, poke; inject; perforate, hole, riddle, pepper, honeycomb; nail, drive, hammer in 279 *strike*; punch holes in; bore, drill; burrow, tunnel 255 *make concave*; cut through, penetrate 297 *enter*.

264
Closure

Noun
(1) *closure,* closing etc. vb.; contraction, strangulation 198 *compression*; sealing off, blockade 235 *enclosure*; embolism, obstruction, constipation; dead end, cul-de-sac, impasse; road block 702 *obstacle*.

(2) *stopper,* cork, plug, bung, peg, spill, spigot; ramrod, rammer, piston; valve; wedge, wad, tampon; wadding, padding 227 *lining*; dummy, gag, muzzle 748 *fetter*; tourniquet 198 *compressor*; damper, choke, cut-out; tap, faucet, stopcock; top, lid, cap, cover, seal 226 *covering*; lock, key, bolt, bar 47 *fastening*; gate 263 *doorway*; cordon 235 *fence.*

(3) *doorkeeper,* doorman, gatekeeper, porter, janitor, commissionaire, concierge; sentry, sentinel 660 *protector*; warden, guard 749 *keeper*.

Adjective
(4) *closed,* shut etc. vb.; bolted, barred; impervious, impermeable; impenetrable, impassable, dead-end, blank; clogged up, stuffed up 198 *contracted*; drawn together 45 *joined*.

(5) *sealed off,* sealed, hermetically s.; cloistered 883 *secluded*; close, stuffy, muggy, fuggy, fusty 653 *insalubrious*; tight, airtight, watertight, waterproof, 660 *invulnerable*.

Verb
(6) *close,* shut, seal; bind, make tight 45 *tighten*; slam, bang (a door); lock, fasten, snap shut, snap to; plug, caulk, cork, stopper 226 *cover*; zip up, do up 45 *join*; clench (fist); block, dam, staunch 702 *obstruct*; choke, throttle, strangle; blockade, enclose, shut in, seal off 232 *circumscribe*; bolt, bar; shut down, clamp d., batten d.

265
Motion: Successive change of place

Noun
(1) *motion,* movement 143 *change*; going, move, march; speed rate, speed, pace, tempo; locomotion, mobility, kinetic energy, motive power; forward motion, advance 285 *progression*; backward motion 286 *regression*, 290 *recession*; motion towards 289 *approach*; motion away 294 *divergence*, 282 *deviation*; motion into 297 *ingress*; motion out of 298 *egress*; upward motion 308 *ascent*; downward motion 309 *descent*, 313 *plunge*; motion round, 315 *rotation*; fluctuation 317 *oscillation*; irregular motion 318 *agitation*; stir, bustle 678 *activity*; rapid motion 277 *velocity*; slow motion 278 *slowness*; regular motion 16 *uniformity*, 71 *continuity*; rhythm 141 *periodicity*; motion in front 283 *preceding*; motion after 284 *following*; conductivity 272 *transference*; current, flow 350 *stream*; course, career, run; traffic 305 *passing along*; transit 305 *passage*, 272 *transport*; running, walking 267 *pedestrianism*; riding 267 *equitation*; travel 267 *land travel*, 269 *water travel*, 271 *air travel*; dancing, gliding, sliding, skating, rolling; manoeuvre, manoeuvring,

footwork; exercise 162 *athletics*; gesticulation 547 *gesture*; laws of motion, kinetics, dynamics.

(2) *gait,* rolling g.; walk, carriage; tread, tramp, footfall, stamp; pace, step, stride; run, lope, jog, jog trot hop, skip, jump 312 *leap*; skid, slide; waddle, shuffle; swagger, stalk, strut 875 *formality*; march, slow m., quick m., double; trot, canter, gallop 267 *equitation*.

Adjective

(3) *moving,* in motion, under way; motive, motor; movable, mobile; locomotive; transitional, shifting; passing; mercurial 152 *changeful*; restless 678 *active*; nomadic 267 *travelling*; erratic 282 *deviating*; kinetic.

Verb

(4) *be in motion,* move, go, hie, wend, trail; gather way 269 *navigate*; budge, stir; flutter, wave, flap 217 *hang*; march, tramp 267 *walk*; dance 312 *leap*; shuffle 278 *move slowly*; toddle, patter; run 277 *move fast*; roll, taxi; stream, drift 350 *flow*; paddle 269 *row*; skitter, slide, slither, glide 258 *go smoothly*; fly, flit, dart, hover 308 *ascend*; sink, plunge 309 *descend*; cruise, steam, chug proceed 146 *go on*; make one's way 285 *progress*; pass through, wade t. 305 *pass*; make a move, shift, dodge, manoeuvre 282 *deviate*; twist 251 *wriggle*; creep, crawl, worm one's way; change places 151 *interchange*; move house *move over, make room* 190 *go away*; travel 267 *wander*.

(5) *move,* put in motion; set going, power, actuate 173 *operate*; stir 318 *agitate*; budge, shift, manhandle, trundle, roll, wheel 188 *displace*; push, shove 279 *impel*; drive, hustle 680 *hasten*; tug, pull 288 *draw*; fling, throw 287 *propel*; convey, transport 272 *transfer*; dispatch 272 *send*; scatter 75 *disperse*;

raise 310 *elevate*; drop 311 *let fall*; transpose 151 *interchange*.

Adverb

(6) *on the move,* under way; on one's w., on the run; in transit; on the march, on the wing.

266
Quiescence

Noun

(1) *quiescence,* dying down, running down 145 *cessation*; rest, stillness; stagnation 679 *inactivity*; pause, truce, standstill 145 *lull*; stoppage, halt; deadlock 145 *stop*; embargo, freeze 757 *prohibition*; immobility, stiffness 326 *hardness*; steadiness, equilibrium 153 *stability*; numbness, trance, faint 375 *insensibility*.

(2) *quietude,* quiet, quietness, stillness, hush 399 *silence*; tranquillity, peacefulness 717 *peace*; rest 683 *repose*; eternal rest 361 *death*; slumber 679 *sleep*; calm, dead c. 258 *smoothness*; windlessness, dead quiet; placidity, passivity 823 *inexcitability*.

(3) *resting place,* bivouac 192 *quarters*; roof 192 *home, inn*; shelter, haven 662 *refuge*; journey's end 295 *goal*.

Adjective

(4) *quiescent,* quiet, still; asleep 679 *sleepy*; resting, at rest, at anchor, becalmed; at a standstill 679 *inactive*; dormant 674 *unused*; stagnant, vegetating, static, stationary 175 *inert*; sedentary; disabled, housebound 747 *restrained*; settled, stay-at-home, home-loving.

(5) *tranquil,* sequestered 883 *secluded*; peaceful, restful; easygoing 681 *leisurely*; uneventful, undisturbed, without incident; calm, windless, airless; relaxed 683 *reposeful*; under sedation; unruffled, serene.

(6) *still, stock-still;* unmoving, immobile, motionless; deadpan, poker-faced 820 *impassive*; standing still, rooted, trans-fixed, immovable, unable to move, stuck; stiff, frozen 326 *rigid*; numb, paralysed 375 *insensible*; quiet, hushed, soundless 399 *silent*.

Verb
(7) *be quiescent,* subside, die down 37 *decrease*; pipe down 399 *be silent*; stand still, lie s., keep quiet; stagnate, vegetate 175 *be inert*; mark time 136 *wait*; stay put, sit tight, not stir, not budge 144 *stay*; stand to, lie to, ride at anchor; rest 683 *repose*; retire, go to bed 679 *sleep*; settle down 187 *place oneself*; catch, jam, lodge, stick fast.

(8) *come to rest,* stop, stop short, freeze 145 *halt*; pull up, draw up; slow down 278 *decelerate*; anchor, cast a.; relax, calm down, rest 683 *repose*.

(9) *bring to rest,* quiet, quieten, quell 399 *silence*; lull, soothe, calm down 177 *assuage*; cradle, rock; bring to, lay to, heave to; brake 278 *retard*; immobilize 679 *make inactive*.

Adverb
(10) *at a stand,* at a halt; in repose.

Interjection
(11) stop! halt! whoa! hold on!

267
Land travel

Noun
(1) *land travel,* travel, travelling, exploration, seeing the world, tourism; journey, voyage, peregrination, odyssey; pilgrimage, quest, expedition, safari, trek; visit, trip, tour; circuit, turn, round, patrol, commuting; round trip, day t.

jaunt, hop, spin; ride, drive, excursion, outing, airing.

(2) *wandering,* wanderlust, nomadism; vagrancy, vagabondage, vagabondism; no fixed address; roving, rambling etc. vb.; walkabout, migration, emigration, immigration.

(3) *pedestrianism,* walking, going on foot, footing it; foot-slogging, stumping, tramping, marching, perambulation; walkabout, walk, promenade, stroll, saunter, amble, ramble; hike, tramp, march, walking tour; run, jog, trot, lope 265 *gait*; marathon 716 *racing*; stalking 619 *chase*; sleepwalking, somnambulism.

(4) *marching,* campaigning, manoeuvres, campaign; march, forced m., route m., quick march, slow m.; march past, parade; column, file.

(5) *equitation,* equestrianism, horsemanship, dressage 694 *skill*; show jumping 716 *contest*; steeplechasing, horse racing; riding 265 *gait*.

(6) *conveyance,* lift, escalator; feet, legs, Shanks's pony; mount 273 *horse*; bicycle, car 274 *vehicle*; traffic 305 *passing along*.

(7) *leg,* limb, foreleg, hindleg; shank, shin, calf; thigh, ham, hamstrings; knee 247 *angularity*; legs, pins 218 *prop*; stilts; stump, artificial leg

(8) *itinerary,* route 624 *way*; course 281 *direction*; plan, chart 551 *map*; guide, timetable; milestone 547 *signpost*; stopover, terminus 145 *stopping place*.

Adjective
(9) *travelling,* journeying, on the road; itinerant, vagrant; travel-stained, travelled,

much-t.; touring, rubbernecking; migratory, passing through, stopping over; nomadic, nomad, floating; homeless, rootless 59 *extraneous*; footloose, errant, roving, wandering 282 *deviating*; strolling, peripatetic; walking, pedestrian, perambulatory; locomotive 265 *moving*.

(10) *legged*, bow-l., bandy-l. 845 *blemished*; well-calved, well-hocked; long-legged, leggy, spindly. 209 *tall*.

Verb

(11) *travel*, journey, tour, visit, explore 484 *discover*; get around, knock about; go sightseeing, rubberneck; pilgrimage, go on a p.; make a journey, go on safari, trek, hike; set out 296 *depart*; migrate, emigrate; shuttle, commute; take oneself off, swan off, slope o.; go to, repair to 882 *visit*; go 265 *be in motion*; wend one's way, bend one's steps, shape one's course, make one's way, pick one's way, thread one's w.; course, race 277 *move fast*; proceed, advance 285 *progress*; coast, free-wheel 258 *go smoothly*.

(12) *traverse*, cross, range, pass through 305 *pass*; go round 314 *circle*; make one's rounds, patrol; scout, reconnoitre 438 *scan*; scour, sweep through 297 *burst in*.

(13) *wander*, migrate; rove, roam, ramble, amble, stroll, saunter, potter, dawdle, walk about, trail around; traipse, gallivant, gad about 265 *be in motion*; prowl, skulk 523 *lurk*; straggle, trail 75 *be dispersed*; lose the way 282 *stray*.

(14) *walk*, go on foot; step, tread, pace; stride 277 *move fast*; strut, stalk, prance, mince 871 *be proud*; tread lightly, tiptoe,

trip, skip 312 *leap*; tread heavily, lumber, clump, stamp, tramp; toddle, patter, pad; totter, stagger, stumble 317 *oscillate*; limp, shuffle, shamble, hobble, waddle, dawdle 278 *move slowly*; paddle, wade; plod, stump, trudge; go for a walk, take the air; go for a run or a jog; march, troop, file past, defile; walk behind 284 *follow*; walk in front 283 *precede*.

(15) *ride*, mount, hack; trot, amble, canter, gallop; cycle, bicycle, bike, motorcycle; freewheel; drive, motor; thumb a lift, hitchhike.

Adverb

(16) *on foot*, on the beat; on horseback, en route 272 *in transit*; by road, by rail.

Interjection

(17) come along! move along there! get along! get going!

268
Traveller

Noun

(1) *traveller*, wayfarer, explorer, adventurer, voyager 270 *mariner*; air traveller 271 *aeronaut*; pioneer, pathfinder 66 *precursor*; mountaineer 308 *climber*; pilgrim, palmer, hajji; walker, hiker, rambler, camper, backpacker, youth hosteller; globetrotter, tourist 441 *spectator*; tripper, excursionist; holidaymaker, visitor; roundsman 793 *seller*; messenger 529 *courier*; commuter.

(2) *wanderer*, migrant, bird of passage; nomad, bedouin; gypsy, Romany; rover, ranger, rambler, promenader, stroller; touring company; rolling stone, drifter, vagrant, vagabond, tramp, hobo; emigrant, émigré, refugee; runaway, fugitive, waif, stray.

(3) *pedestrian,* foot passenger, walker, tramper; jogger, sprinter, runner; hiker, hitch-h., foot-slogger; marcher 722 *infantry;* somnambulist, sleepwalker.

(4) *rider,* horse-rider, horseman, horsewoman, equestrian; postilion 529 *courier;* mounted police; knight errant 722 *cavalry;* huntsman 619 *hunter;* jockey, steeplechaser; show jumper 716 *contender;* cowboy, gaucho; cyclist, bicyclist, motorcyclist; back-seat driver, passenger, pillion p.

(5) *driver,* drover, carter, teamster, muleteer; charioteer, coachman, whip; car driver, chauffeur, motorist 277 *speeder;* joy rider; L-driver; taxi driver, cab d., cabby; bus driver, coach d.; lorry d., truck d.; motorman, train driver, engine d.; stoker, fireman; guard, conductor, ticket collector.

269
Water travel

Noun

(1) *water travel,* sea t., river t., inland navigation; seafaring, nautical life, navigation, voyaging, sailing, cruising (see *aquatics);* voyage, navigation, cruise, sail; run, passage, crossing, ferry c.; way, headway, seaway 265 *motion;* wake, track, wash; steamer route, sea lane 624 *route;* boat 275 *ship;* sailor 270 *mariner.*

(2) *navigation,* piloting, steering, pilotage 689 *directorship;* compass reading, dead reckoning; helmsmanship, seamanship 694 *skill;* weather eye, sea legs; naval exercises, fleet operations.

(3) *aquatics,* boating, sailing, yachting, cruising; rowing, canoeing; watersports, water skiing, surf riding, surfing, wind s. 837 *sport;* swimming, floating; breast stroke, crawl; diving 313 *plunge;* wading, paddling.

(4) *sailing aid,* sextant, quadrant; chronometer; log, line; lead, plummet; anchor; compass, binnacle; radar 484 *detector;* helm, wheel, tiller, rudder; sea mark, buoy, lighthouse, lightship 547 *signpost;* chart 551 *map;* nautical almanac.

(5) *propeller,* screw, blade, rotor 287 *propellant;* paddle wheel, stern w., oar, paddle, scull; pole, punt p., barge p.; fin, flipper; canvas 275 *sail.*

Adjective

(6) *seafaring,* sea, salty, deep-sea; nautical, naval 275 *marine;* navigational, navigating; sailing etc. vb.; sea-going, ocean-g.; at sea, on the high seas; afloat, waterborne; on board; pitching, tossing, yawing; seasick, green; seaworthy, tight; navigable.

(7) *swimming,* floating, afloat, buoyant; aquatic, like a fish; amphibian.

Verb

(8) *go to sea,* follow the s., join the navy; go sailing, boat, yacht; launch.

(9) *voyage,* sail, go by sea, take ship, book a passage, work one's p.; embark, put to sea, up anchor 296 *start out;* land, disembark 295 *arrive;* cruise, navigate, steam, ply, run, tramp, ferry; hug the shore; roll, pitch, toss, wallow 317 *oscillate.*

(10) *navigate,* man a ship, work a s., crew; put to sea, set sail; launch, push off, cast off, weigh anchor; hoist sail, spread canvas; get under way 265 *be in motion;* make for 281 *steer for;* pilot, steer 689 *direct;* stroke, cox; put about 282 *turn round;*

scud, run before the wind 277 *move fast*; luff, tack, weather; back and fill; round, circumnavigate 314 *circle*; turn turtle, capsize, overturn; run for port 662 *seek refuge*; lie to, heave to 266 *bring to rest*; take soundings, heave the lead; ground, run aground; make a landfall 289 *approach*; make port; cast anchor, drop a.; moor, tie up, dock, disembark 295 *land*; surface, break water 298 *emerge*; dive 313 *plunge*.

(11) *row,* ply the oar, pull, stroke, scull; feather; catch a crab; ship oars; punt; paddle, canoe; shoot the rapids.

(12) *swim,* float, sail, skim; surf, water-ski; strike out, breast the current, tread water; dive 313 *plunge*; bathe, dip, duck; wade, paddle, splash about, get wet.

Adverb
(13) *under way,* under sail, under canvas, under steam; before the mast; on deck, on the bridge, at the helm, at the wheel.

Interjection
(14) ship ahoy! belay there! all aboard! man overboard! yo-heave-ho! land ahoy!

270
Mariner

Noun
(1) *mariner,* sailor, seaman, seafarer; salt, old s., tar, Jack Tar; no sailor, landlubber; skipper, master mariner, master, ship m.; mate, boatswain, bosun; able seaman, A.B.; deckhand; ship's steward, cabin boy; shipmates, hearties; crew, complement, watch; Viking, pirate 789 *robber*; sea scout, sea cadet.

(2) *navigator,* pilot, helmsman, cox 690 *leader*; lookout; boatswain, bosun's mate; compass, binnacle.

(3) *nautical personnel,* marine, submariner, naval cadet, rating 722 *naval man*; petty officer, midshipman, lieutenant 741 *naval officer*; coastguard, lighthouse keeper 660 *protector*; lifeboatman; river police, harbour patrol,

(4) *boatman,* waterman; galley slave; oarsman, oarswoman, sculler, rower, paddler, canoeist; yachtsman, yachtswoman, ferryman, gondolier, bargee; stevedore, docker, longshoreman; lock keeper.

Adjective
(5) *seamanlike,* sailorly 694 *expert*; nautical, naval 275 *marine*.

271
Aeronautics

Noun
(1) *aeronautics,* aerodynamics, ballooning; aerospace, astronautics; rocketry 276 *rocket*; flight, subsonic f., supersonic f. 277 *velocity*; aviation, flying, night f., blind f.; gliding, hang-g.; parachuting, skydiving, free fall; flypast, formation flying, stunt f., aerobatics 875 *ostentation*; skywriting, vapour trail; planing, looping the loop; nose dive, crash dive 309 *descent*; landing, crash l., forced l.

(2) *air travel,* air transport, airlift 272 *transport*; airline; scheduled flight, charter f.; airway, flight path, glide p.; air space 184 *territory*; takeoff, touchdown, landing; airstrip, runway, airfield, airbase, aerodrome, airport, heliport, air terminal 295 *goal*; jetlag.

(3) *space travel,* space flight, manned s.f. 276 *spaceship*; lift-off, blast-off; orbit, flyby; docking, space walk; reentry, splashdown, soft landing; launching pad, silo.

(4) *aeronaut,* balloonist; glider, hang g., sky diver, parachutist; paratrooper 722 *soldier*; aviator, airman, airwoman; astronaut, cosmonaut spaceman, spacewoman; jet set 268 *traveller*; flier, pilot, automatic p., navigator, air crew; flying officer 741 *air officer*; aircraftman, aircraftwoman; ground crew.

(5) *wing,* pinion, feathers, flight f., 259 *plumage*; aerofoil, aileron, flaps.

Adjective

(6) *flying,* on the wing; fluttering, flitting, hovering; winged, pinnate, feathered; aerial 340 *airy*; airworthy, airborne; air-to-air; soaring, climbing 308 *ascending*; in-flight; airsick; losing height 309 *descending*; grounded; aeronautical, aerospace, aerodynamic, aerobatic.

Verb

(7) *fly,* wing, take w., wing one's way, be wafted, soar 308 *ascend*; hover, hang over; flutter, flit 265 *be in motion*; taxi, take off, clear, climb, be airborne, have lift-off; glide, plane, float, drift; loop the loop, hedgehop, buzz 200 *be near*; stall, dive, nose-d. 313 *plunge*; crash, crash-land, ditch 309 *tumble*; pull out, flatten o.; touch down 295 *land*; bale out, eject; blast off, lift o., take o.; orbit, go into o.

Adverb

(8) *in flight,* on the wing, on the beam, in orbit.

272
Transference

Noun

(1) *transference,* change of place, transfer, bussing; shift 282 *deviation*; posting 751 *mandate*; deportation, expulsion 300 *ejection*; unpacking, unloading, airdrop 188 *displacement*; exportation, importation 791 *trade*; mutual transfer 791 *barter*; transmittal, forwarding, sending, remittance, dispatch; recall, extradition 304 *extraction*; recovery, retrieval 771 *acquisition*; handing over, delivery; takeover 780 *transfer*; release 746 *liberation*; ferry 305 *passage*; transmission, throughput; communication, diffusion, dispersal 75 *dispersion*; contagion, infection, contamination 178 *influence*.

(2) *transport,* transportation; conveyance, carriage, shipping, shipment; portage, porterage, haulage 288 *traction*; carting, air freight, airlift; rail, road 274 *vehicle*; sea, canal 275 *ship*; conveyor belt, pipeline.

(3) *thing transferred,* consignment; 777 *property*; container, cargo, load, payload, freight; shipment 193 *contents*; goods, mails; luggage, baggage, impedimenta; passenger 268 *traveller*.

(4) *transferrer,* sender, remitter, dispatcher, dispatch clerk, shipper, shipping agent, transporter; exporter, importer 794 *merchant*; haulier, removal man, 273 *carrier*; post office, post; communicator, transmitter, diffuser; vector, carrier 651 *sick person*.

Adjective

(5) *transferable,* negotiable; transportable, movable, portable; roadworthy, airworthy, seaworthy; transmissible, communicable; contagious 653 *infectious*.

Verb
(6) *transfer,* hand over, deliver 780 *assign*; devise, leave 780 *bequeath*; commit, entrust 751 *commission*; transmit, hand down, hand on, pass on; make over, turn over, hand to, pass to; export, transport, convey, ship, airlift, fly, ferry 273 *carry*; infect, contaminate.

(7) *transpose,* shift, move, tranship 188 *displace*; transfer, switch 151 *interchange*; detach, detail, draft; deport, expel 300 *eject*; containerize 193 *load*; transfuse, decant, strain off, siphon off 300 *empty*; unload, remove 188 *displace*; shovel, ladle, spoon out, bail out.

(8) *send,* have conveyed, remit, transmit, dispatch; direct, consign, address; post, mail; redirect, forward; send for, order, mail-order; send away, detach, detail.

Adverb
(9) *in transit,* en route, on the way; in the post; in the pipeline; by hand; from hand to hand.

273
Carrier

Noun
(1) *carrier,* haulier, carter, shipper, transporter, exporter, importer 272 *transferrer*; lorry driver delivery van, truck, cart, goods train 274 *vehicle*; barge, cargo vessel, freighter, tramp 275 *ship*; pallet, container; carrier bag 194 *bag*; escalator 274 conveyor.

(2) *bearer,* litter b., stretcher b.; caddy, porter, coolie; carrier pigeon, postman *or* -woman, 529 *courier*.

(3) *beast of burden,* packhorse, donkey, mule; ox, bullock, draught animals 365 *cattle*; sledge dog, husky; camel, dromedary.

(4) *horse,* horseflesh; nag, mount, steed; stallion, gelding, mare, colt, filly, foal; stud horse, brood mare; circus horse, liberty h.; strawberry roan, dapple grey, bay, chestnut, piebald, skewbald, palomino.

(5) *thoroughbred,* purebred, blood-horse, bloodstock; pacer, high-stepper, racehorse 277 *speeder*; steeplechaser, hurdler, fencer, jumper, hunter, foxhunter.

(6) *draught horse,* cart h., coach-h., post-h.; shire-h., punch; pit pony.

(7) *warhorse,* remount; charger, courser, steed 722 *cavalry*.

(8) *saddle horse,* riding h., mount, hack, roadster; mustang, bronco.

(9) *pony,* cob, Shetland pony.

Adjective
(10) *bearing,* shouldering, burdened, freighted, loaded, overloaded; pick-a-back.

(11) *equine,* horsy; roan etc. n.; mulish.

Verb
(12) *carry,* bear 218 *support*; hump, heave, tote, shoulder; fetch, bring, fetch and carry; transport, cart, truck, rail, ship; lift, fly 272 *transfer*; carry through, carry over, ferry; convey, conduct, convoy, escort; be mounted; be saddled with, be burdened w.

274
Vehicle

Noun
(1) *vehicle,* conveyance, transport, public t.; pedal power, horse p.; sedan chair, litter,

stretcher; tumbril, hearse; ambulance, fire engine; tractor, tracked vehicle; amphibian.

(2) *sled,* sledge, sleigh, bobsleigh, toboggan; surfboard; skate, skateboard; snowshoes, skis, skibob.

(3) *bicycle,* cycle, pedal c., bike, push b.; sports model, racer, tourist, roadster; smallwheeler; tandem, tricycle, moped; scooter, motor s., motorcycle, motorbike, trail bike.

(4) *pushcart,* perambulator, pram, pushchair; bath chair, wheelchair; rickshaw; barrow, wheelbarrow, go cart; trolley, truck, float.

(5) *cart,* wagon, hay w., hay wain; dray, milk float; caravan, trailer, horse-box, loose-b.

(6) *carriage,* horse-drawn c., equipage, turnout, rig; chariot, coach, coach and four; trap, gig, dogcart.

(7) *war chariot,* gun carriage, caisson; tank, armoured car 722 *cavalry;* jeep, staff car.

(8) *stagecoach,* stage, mail coach; diligence, post chaise, omnibus. See *bus.*

(9) *cab,* hansom c.; minicab, taxicab, taxi; rickshaw.

(10) *bus,* omnibus, double-decker, single-d.; trolleybus, tram; motor coach, coach, minibus.

(11) *automobile,* car, motor car; motor, auto; limousine, saloon, roadster, runabout, buggy; convertible; coupe, sports car; racing car, stock c., hot-rod; hatchback, estate car; police car, patrol c.; veteran car, vintage car, banger, jalopy; invalid car, three-wheeler; minibus, camper.

(12) *lorry,* truck, pickup t., refuse lorry, dustcart; articulated lorry, juggernaut; tanker,

car transporter, low-loader; van, delivery v., electric v., float.

(13) *train,* boat t., through train, slow train, stopping t.; goods train, freight t., freightliner; night mail; rolling stock, multiple unit; coach, carriage, compartment, smoker, nonsmoker; sleeping car, sleeper; guard's van, luggage v.; truck, wagon; cable railway 624 *railway.*

(14) *locomotive,* iron horse; diesel, steam engine; tank e., shunter, cab, tender; traction engine, steam roller.

(15) *conveyor,* conveyor belt; escalator, moving staircase; crane 310 *lifter.*

Adjective
(16) *vehicular,* wheeled, on wheels; on rails, on runners, on sleds; horse-drawn, pedal-driven; motorized, automobile, locomotive; non-stop, high-speed.

275
Ship

Noun
(1) *ship,* vessel, boat, craft, barque; hull, keel; tub, hulk; steamer, steamship, motor vessel; paddle steamer, sternwheeler, passenger ship, liner; channel steamer, ferry; hovercraft, hydrofoil; mail-boat, packet; dredger, icebreaker; transport, tender, pilot vessel; tug, launch; submarine 722 *warship.*

(2) *galley, trireme;* pirate ship, privateer, corsair; Viking ship, longship.

(3) *merchant ship,* merchantman, trader; galleon, clipper; cargo boat, freighter, tramp; coaster, lugger, tanker, supertanker.

(4) *fishing boat,* inshore f. b.; drifter, trawler, purse-seiner; factory ship; whaler.

(5) *sailing ship,* sailing boat, windjammer, clipper, tall ship; barque, brig, schooner, pinnace; frigate 722 *warship*; cutter, sloop, ketch, yawl; wherry; yacht, sailing dinghy, smack; felucca, dhow, junk, sampan.

(6) *sail,* sailcloth, rig, rigging 47 *tackling*; mast 218 *prop.*

(7) *boat,* skiff, lifeboat; ship's boat, tender, dinghy; pinnace, cutter; barge, lighter; ferry; canal boat, narrowboat, houseboat; tug; motorboat, speedboat; motor launch, cabin cruiser.

(8) *rowing boat,* eight, sculler, shell, skiff, dinghy; punt, gondola; canoe, kayak.

(9) *raft,* liferaft; catamaran, trimaran; float, pontoon.

(10) *shipping,* fleet, flotilla 722 *navy*; marine, merchant navy, shipping line.

Adjective
(11) *marine,* maritime, naval, nautical, sea-going, ocean-g. 269 *seafaring*; sea-worthy, snug, tight, shipshape.

Adverb
(12) *afloat,* aboard, on board ship, under sail, under steam, under canvas.

276
Aircraft

Noun
(1) *aircraft* 271 *aeronautics*; flying machine; aeroplane, airplane, plane; biplane, hydroplane; airliner, airbus, transport, freighter; fighter, bomber 722 *air force*; jet, jumbo j., jump

j., turbojet, turboprop; helicopter, chopper; glider, sailplane; controls, joystick, rudder; aerofoil, aileron; cockpit, flight deck; undercarriage, landing gear; parachute, ejection seat; airport 271 *air travel.*

(2) *airship,* balloon, hot-air b.; barrage b.; parachute, hang glider; magic carpet; car, gondola.

(3) *rocket,* rocketry; nose cone, warhead; guided missile 723 *missile weapon.*

(4) *spaceship,* spacecraft, space probe, space shuttle; lunar module; space station 321 *satellite*; flying saucer, UFO.

Adjective
(5) *aviational,* aeronautical, aerospace; aerodynamic, airworthy 271 *flying*; supersonic; astronautical.

277
Velocity

Noun
(1) *velocity,* celerity, rapidity, speed, swiftness, fleetness, quickness, alacrity, agility; promptness, expedition, dispatch 116 *instantaneity*; speed, tempo, rate, pace 265 *motion*; speed-rate, miles per hour, knots; mach number; speed of light, speed of sound, supersonic speed; lightning s.; full s., full steam; hurry 680 *haste*; reckless speed, breakneck s. 857 *rashness*; streak, flash; lightning, tempest, torrent; speedometer 465 *gauge.*

(2) *spurt,* acceleration, speed-up, overtaking; burst of speed, burst of energy; thrust, drive, impetus 279 *impulse*; jump, spring, bound, pounce 312 *leap*; whizz, swoop, zoom; down rush, dive; rush, dash, sprint, gallop.

(3) *speeding,* driving, hard d., racing, burn-up; course, race, career, full c.; full speed, quick march, smart pace; race course, speed track 716 *racing.*

(4) *speeder,* hustler, speed maniac, racing driver; runner, harrier; racer, sprinter; courser, racehorse, greyhound, hare; arrow, bullet; jet, rocket; express.

Adjective

(5) *speedy,* swift, fast, quick, rapid, nimble, darting, dashing; lively, brisk, smart, snappy, nifty, zippy 174 *vigorous;* expeditious, hustling 680 *hasty;* double-quick, rapid-fire; prompt 135 *early;* immediate 116 *instantaneous;* high-geared, high-speed, streamlined, souped-up; speeding etc. vb.; breakneck, headlong, precipitate 857 *rash;* fleet, quick-footed; darting, starting, flashing; swift-moving, agile, nimble; like a flash, quick as thought, meteoric; jet-propelled, telegraphic. supersonic,

Verb

(6) *move fast,* move, shift, travel, speed; drive, pelt, streak, flash, shoot; scorch, scud, skim, nip, cut; bowl along, sweep along, tear a.; tear, hare, rush, dash; fly, wing, whizz, hurtle, zoom; dash forward, plunge, lunge, swoop; run, trot, lope, gallop; bolt, scamper, scurry, skelter, scuttle 620 *run away;* dart, flit whisk; spring, bound; hurry 680 *hasten;* chase, charge, stampede, career, go all out.

(7) *accelerate,* speed up, gather momentum, spurt, sprint, put on speed, quicken, step up; drive, spur, urge on; lend wings to, expedite 680 *hasten.*

(8) *outstrip,* overtake, overhaul, catch up, lap, outrun 306 *outdo;*

gain on, outdistance, leave behind; lose, shake off; make the running.

Adverb

(9) *swiftly,* rapidly etc. adj.; posthaste; at full speed, at full tilt; in full career, all out, flat out, headlong, hell for leather; like a shot, in a flash 116 *instantaneously;* full speed ahead; at the double; like wildfire.

278
Slowness

Noun

(1) *slowness,* languor 679 *sluggishness;* deliberation, reluctance, hesitation 858 *caution;* go-slow, working to rule; slowing down, slow-down, deceleration; brake, curb 747 *restraint;* leisureliness, no hurry, time to spare, easy stages 681 *leisure;* slow motion, low gear; slow march, dead m.; slow time, andante; slow pace, foot p., snail's p., crawl, creep, dawdle; walk, amble, jog trot 265 *gait;* limping, hobbling; standing start, slow s.; lagging, time lag 136 *delay.*

(2) *slowcoach,* snail, tortoise; stopping train; cortege; dawdler, loiterer, lingerer; slow starter, late developer; laggard, sloucher 598 *slacker.*

Adjective

(3) *slow,* painfully s.; slow-paced, low-geared, slow-motion, time-lapse; snail-like, creeping, crawling, dragging; slow-moving 695 *clumsy;* limping, halting; taking one's time, tardy, dilatory, lagging 136 *late;* unhurried 681 *leisurely;* sedate 875 *formal;* deliberate 823 *patient;* painstaking 457 *careful;* groping, tentative 858 *cautious;* languid, sluggish 679 *lazy;* gradual, stealthy, imperceptible.

Verb

(4) *move slowly,* go slow; amble, crawl, creep, inch along, glide a.; ooze, drip, trickle, dribble 350 *flow*; drift 282 *deviate*; shamble, slouch, shuffle, toddle, waddle; plod, trudge, tramp, lumber, stump along; stagger, lurch; struggle, toil, labour, chug; limp, hobble; flag, falter 684 *be fatigued*; trail, lag, fall behind; hang fire, drag one's feet; tarry, not be hurried, take one's time 136 *be late*; laze, idle 679 *be inactive*; take it easy, linger, stroll, saunter, dawdle 267 *walk*; grope, feel one's way 461 *be tentative*; soft-pedal, hesitate 858 *be cautious*; speak slowly, drawl 580 *stammer.*

(5) *decelerate,* slow down, slow up, ease up, let up, lose momentum; reduce speed, slacken s., slacken one's pace; lose ground, flag, falter 684 *be fatigued.*

(6) *retard,* check, curb, rein in, throttle down 177 *moderate*; reef, shorten sail, take in s. 269 *navigate*; brake 747 *restrain*; backpedal 286 *regress*; handicap, clip the wings 702 *hinder.*

Adverb

(7) *slowly,* leisurely etc. adj.; at half speed, in low gear, in bottom g.; with leaden step; gingerly; in slow time, adagio, largo.

(8) *gradatim,* by degrees, by slow d., little by little, bit by bit, inch by inch, step by step, one at a time.

279
Impulse

Noun

(1) *impulse,* impulsion, pressure; impetus, momentum; boost 174 *stimulant*; encouragement 612 *incentive*; thrust, push, shove, heave; throw 287 *propulsion*; lunge, kick 712 *attack*; percussion, beating, drumming 403 *roll*; concussion, stroke; shock, impact; slam, bang; flick, clip, tap 378 *touch*; shake, rattle, jolt, jerk 318 *agitation.*

(2) *knock,* dint, dent rap, tap, clap; dab, pat, flip, flick; nudge, dig 547 *gesture*; smack, slap; cuff, clout, blow; lash, stroke, hit, crack; cut, drive (cricket); thwack, thump, bang; punch, rabbit p., straight left, uppercut, jab, hook; body blow, knock-out b.; wild b., swipe; stamp, kick; whop, swat; spanking, hiding, dusting, pasting, licking, whipping, flogging, thrashing, beating, rain of blows; assault 712 *attack*; fisticuffs 61 *turmoil.*

(3) *collision,* head-on c.; encounter, meeting, clash; graze, scrape 333 *friction*; impact, bump, shock, crash, smash, accident, pileup; brunt, charge, force 712 *attack*; collision course.

(4) *hammer,* sledge h.; punch, puncher; mallet; knocker, door k.; cosh, cudgel, club, mace; boxing glove; pestle, anvil.

(5) *ram,* battering r., bulldozer; piledriver; ramrod; rammer, tamper 287 *propellant.*

Adjective

(6) *impelling,* dynamic, dynamical, thrusting.

Verb

(7) *impel,* fling, heave, throw 287 *propel*; give an impetus, impart momentum; slam, bang 264 *close*; press, push, thrust, shove; ram down, tamp; shove off, push off, pole, punt; prod, urge, spur 277 *accelerate*; flip, flick; jerk, shake, rattle, jog, jolt 318 *agitate*; shoulder, elbow, push around 282 *deflect*;

frogmarch 300 *eject*; drive forward, whip on 612 *incite*; drive, start, run 173 *operate*.

(8) *collide,* make impact 378 *touch*; meet, encounter, clash; cross swords, fence 712 *strike at*; ram, butt, batter, dint, dent; bulldoze 165 *demolish*; cannon into, bump into; graze 333 *rub*; drive into, crash i., smash i., run i., run down, run over; clash with, collide w., foul, fall foul of; run against, dash a. grate a.; bark one's shins, stub one's toe; knock together.

(9) *strike,* smite, hit, land a blow, plant a b.; hit out at, lunge at, poke at, lash out at, let fly; hit wildly, swing, flail, beat the air; slam, bang, knock; knock down, floor 311 *fell*; pat, flip, tap, rap, clap; slap, smack; clout, clobber, box, spar 716 *fight*; buffet, punch, thump, thwack, whack, wham, pummel, trounce, belabour, beat up; pound, batter, bludgeon 332 *pulverize*; slog, slug, cosh, cudgel, club, mug, crown; concuss, stun, knock out; spank, wallop, thrash, beat 963 *flog*; belt, give a hiding 963 *punish*; thresh, flail; hammer, drum; squash, swat 216 *flatten*; scratch, maul 655 *wound*; run through 263 *pierce*; stone, pelt; strike a ball, bat, swipe, drive, cut 287 *propel*.

(10) *kick,* spurn, boot, knee, put the boot in; trample, tread on, stamp on; spur; heel, dribble, shoot (a football).

280
Recoil

Noun

(1) *recoil,* revulsion, reaction 148 *reversion*; repercussion, reverberation 404 *resonance*; reflex, kick, kickback, backlash; ricochet, rebound; bounce, spring 328 *elasticity*; swingback, 317 *oscillation*; volley,

(tennis), boomerang; riposte, return fire.

Adjective

(2) *recoiling,* reactive, repercussive, retroactive 148 *reverted.*

Verb

(3) *recoil,* react 182 *counteract*; shrink, wince, flinch, jib, shy 620 *avoid*; kick back, hit b.; ricochet, cannon off; spring back, fly b., rebound; return, swing back 148 *revert*; reverberate, echo 404 *resound*; have repercussions, boomerang.

281
Direction

Noun

(1) *direction,* bearing, compass reading 186 *situation*; orientation, alignment; set, drift 350 *current*; tenor, trend 179 *tendency*; aim, course, tack, beam; beeline, line of sight 249 *straightness*; way 624 *route*; steering, steerage; aim, target, sights 295 *goal*; fingerpost 547 *signpost*; direction finder, range f.; orienteering.

(2) *compass point,* cardinal points, North, East, South, West; magnetic North; azimuth.

Adjective

(3) *directed,* orientated, directed towards, pointing t., signposted; aimed, well-a., well-directed, well-placed 187 *located*; bound for; aligned with 219 *parallel*; diagonal 220 *oblique*; sideways 239 *lateral*; facing 240 *opposite*; direct 249 *straight*; northbound, southbound; northern, northerly; southern, southerly, meridional; western, occidental; eastern, oriental; directive, guiding; showing the way.

Verb

(4) *orientate,* orientate oneself, take one's bearings, plot one's

course 269 *navigate*; take a direction, bear; signpost, direct, show the way 547 *indicate*; pinpoint, locate 187 *place*; face 240 *be opposite*.

(5) *steer for,* go towards, go straight for, head for, aim for, be bound for; make a beeline for 249 *be straight*.

(6) *point to,* point out, point towards, signpost 547 *indicate*; trend towards, incline t. 179 *tend*.

(7) *aim,* level, point; take aim, aim at; train one's sights on, level at; cover, have one covered; hit the mark.

Adverb
(8) *towards,* through, via, by way of; straight, direct, as the crow flies; upstream, downstream; upwind downwind; seaward, landmark, homeward; cross-country; in all directions 183 *widely*; hither, thither; whither, which way?

282
Deviation

Noun
(1) *deviation,* misdirection, disorientation; wrong course, wrong turning; aberration, deflection, refraction; diversion, digression; shift, veer, slew, swing swerve, bend 248 *curvature*; branching off 294 *divergence*; detour, long way round 626 *circuit*; vagrancy 267 *wandering*; drift, leeway; sidestep, sideslip; break, googly (cricket); yaw, tack; zigzag, slalom course.

Adjective
(2) *deviating,* aberrant, out of orbit; errant, wandering, footloose 267 *travelling*; disorientated, off-course, off-beam, lost, stray, astray; misdirected, ill-aimed, off-target, off the mark,

wide; devious, winding, roundabout 314 *circuitous*; indirect, crooked, zigzag 220 *oblique*; branching 294 *divergent*.

Verb
(3) *deviate,* digress, go out of one's way, make a detour; branch out 294 *diverge*; turn, filter, turn aside, swerve, slew; step aside, make way for; alter course, change direction, yaw, tack; veer, back (wind); bend, curve, zigzag, twist 251 *meander*; swing, wobble 317 *oscillate*; steer clear of, sheer off; sidle, passage; slide, skid, sideslip; break (cricket); glance 220 *be oblique*; shy, jib, sidestep 620 *avoid*.

(4) *turn round,* turn about, about turn, wheel, wheel about, face a., face the other way; reverse, return 148 *revert*; go back 286 *turn back*.

(5) *stray,* ramble, drift 267 *wander*; go astray, go adrift, lose one's bearings; miss one's way, lose the w., get lost 495 *blunder*.

(6) *deflect,* bend, crook 220 *make oblique*; warp, skew; misdirect, put off the scent 495 *mislead*; avert 713 *parry*; divert, sidetrack, draw aside; push a., elbow a., edge off; bias, slice, pull, hook, bowl a break (cricket); shift, shunt 151 *interchange*.

Adverb
(7) *astray,* adrift; out; off the mark; at a tangent, sideways, crabwise 220 *obliquely*.

283
Preceding: Going before

Noun
(1) *preceding* going before, leading, heading 64 *precedence*; flying start; preemption, queue-jumping 119 *priority*; pride of place, lead; pioneer 66

precursor; van, vanguard, avant-garde 237 *front*.

Adjective
(2) *foremost*, first; leading etc. vb.;

Verb
(3) *precede*, go before, herald 64 *come before*; usher in, introduce; head, spearhead, lead, head the queue; take the lead, go in front, clear the way, light the w., lead the w.; guide, conduct 689 *direct*; get in front, jump the queue; have a head start; get ahead of, lap; be beforehand 135 *be early*; take precedence over.

Adverb
(4) *ahead*, before, in advance, in the van, in front; primarily, first of all; elders first.

284
Following: Going after

Noun
(1) *following* 65 *sequence*; run, suit 71 *series*; pursuit 619 *chase*; succession 780 *transfer*; last place 238 *rear*.

(2) *follower*, attendant, hanger-on, camp follower, groupie 742 *dependant*; train, tail, wake, suite, followers 67 *retinue*; following, party, adherent, supporter 703 *aider*.

Adjective
(3) *following*, subsequent 65 *sequential*.

Verb
(4) *follow*, come behind, succeed, follow on, follow after, come to heel 65 *come after*; tag after, beset; ⁻attend, wait on 742 *serve*; tag along 89 *accompany*; dog, shadow, trail; tail, track 619 *pursue*; drop behind, fall b., lag, trail; bring up the rear 238 *be behind*.

Adverb
(5) *behind,* in the rear 238 *rearward*; in tow 65 *after*; on the heels of, one after another.

285
Progression: Motion forwards

Noun
(1) *progression,* going forward; procession, march, way, course, career; march of time 111 *course of time*; progress, steady p., forward march 265 *motion*; sudden progress, stride, leap, jump, leaps and bounds 277 *spurt*; flood, tide 350 *current*; gain, advance, headway 654 *improvement*; getting ahead, overtaking 283 *preceding*; next step, development, evolution 71 *continuity*; furtherance, promotion, advancement, preferment; rise, raise, lift, leg-up 310 *elevation*; achievement 730 *prosperity*.

Adjective
(2) *progressive*, enterprising, forward-looking; flowing on, irreversible 265 *moving*; advanced, up-to-date 126 *modern*.

Verb
(3) *progress*, proceed 265 *be in motion*; advance, go forward; come on, develop, evolve; maintain progress 654 *get better*; get on, do well 730 *prosper*; march on, run on, flow on, pass on, jog on, wag on, hold on, keep on, slog on 146 *go on*; move with the times 126 *modernize*; hold one's lead; press on, push on, drive on, push forward, press onwards 680 *hasten*; gain, gain ground, make headway, make strides 277 *move fast*; get ahead, shoot a., forge a., gain on, distance, outdistance, leave behind 277 *outstrip*; gain height, rise 308 *climb*; make up leeway 31 *recoup*; gain time, make up t.

(4) *promote,* further, contribute to, advance 703 *aid*; prefer, upgrade, move up 310 *elevate*; bring forward, push, force, develop 174 *invigorate*; step up, speed up 277 *accelerate*; put ahead, put forward 64 *put in front*; favour, make for, bring on 156 *cause.*

Adverb

(5) *forward,* forwards, onward, on, ahead; on one's way, under w., en route.

Interjection

(6) *forward!* en avant!

286
Regression: Motion backwards

Noun

(1) *regression,* regress; retroflexion, retrogression, backward step 148 *reversion*; motion from, retreat, withdrawal, retirement, disengagement 290 *recession*; regurgitation; reversing, backing; falling away, decline, drop, fall, slump.

(2) *return,* homeward journey; homecoming 295 *arrival*; reentry 297 *ingress*; ebb, turn of the tide; relapse, backsliding; volte-face, about turn 148 *reversion*; turn, turning point 137 *crisis*; resilience 328 *elasticity*; reflex 280 *recoil.*

Adjective

(3) *regressive,* receding, declining, ebbing; retrogressive, retrograde, backward; reactionary, backward-looking 125 *retrospective*; retroactive 280 *recoiling*; backing, anticlockwise, reverse 148 *reverted*; resilient 328 *elastic*; returning, homeward bound.

Verb

(4) *regress,* recede, retrogress; retreat, beat a r., *retrograde,* retire, withdraw, fall back,

draw b.; turn tail 620 *run away*; disengage, back out, back down; 753 *resign*; backtrack, backpedal; give way, give ground, reverse, back, back water, go backwards; run back, flow back, regurgitate; not hold, slip back; ebb, slump, fall, drop, decline 309 *descend*; bounce back 280 *recoil.*

(5) *turn back,* retrace one's steps; go back, return 148 *revert*; look back, hark back 505 *retrospect*; turn one's back, veer round, wheel r., about face, double back, countermarch; start back, jib, shrink 620 *avoid*; come back again, come home.

Adverb

(6) *backwards,* back, astern, in reverse.

Interjection

(7) *back!* hard astern! hands off!

287
Propulsion

Noun

(1) *propulsion,* jet p., drive; impulsion, push 279 *impulse*; projection, throwing, tossing, hurling, pelting, slinging, precipitation; cast, throw, chuck, toss, fling, sling, shy, cock-shy; pot shot, pot, shot, long s.; discharge, volley 712 *bombardment*; bowling, pitching, throw-in; kick, dribble (football); stroke, drive, swipe 279 *knock*; pull, slice (golf); rally, volley, smash (tennis); ballistics, archery.

(2) *missile,* projectile, shell, rocket, cannonball; bullet, shot, small s.; brickbat, stone, snowball; arrow, dart 723 *missile weapon*; ball, bowl, wood, jack, puck; quoit, discus; javelin; hammer, caber.

(3) *propellant,* thrust, driving force, jet, steam 160 *energy*;

spray, aerosol; pusher, shover 279 *ram*; tail wind, following w.; lever, treadle, pedal, bicycle p.; oar, blade 269 *propeller*; gunpowder, dynamite 723 *explosive*; rifle 723 *firearm*; pop gun, water pistol; blowpipe, pea-shooter; catapult, sling, bow.

(4) *shooter,* gunman, gunner, 722 *soldiery*; archer, bowman, marksman *or* - woman, sharpshooter. sniper, shot, crack s.

(5) *thrower,* hurler etc. vb.; knife-thrower, javelin-t., discus-t., stone-t., slinger; bowler, pitcher.

Adjective
(6) *propulsive,* propellant, propelling etc. vb.; expulsive, explosive, projectile, missile; ballistic.

Verb
(7) *propel,* launch, project; throw, cast, deliver, heave, pitch, toss, chuck; bowl, lob, hurl, fling, sling, catapult; dart, flick; pelt, stone, shower 712 *lapidate*; sending flying; expel, pitchfork 300 *eject*; blow away, puff a.; slam, slog, wham; drive, cut, pull, hook, slice 279 *strike*; kick, dribble, putt; push, shove 279 *impel*; wheel, pedal, roll 315 *rotate*; drive, hustle, sweep before one.

(8) *shoot,* fire, open fire, fire off; volley, fire a v.; discharge, explode, let off, set off; let fly, pull the trigger; cannonade, bombard 712 *fire at*; snipe, pot at, loose off at; pepper 263 *pierce*.

288
Traction

Noun
(1) *traction,* drawing etc. vb.; magnetism 291 *attraction*; haulage; draught, pull, haul; tug,

tow; towline, towrope; tugboat; trawl, dragnet; drawer, haulier; windlass 310 *lifter*; tractor, traction engine 274 *locomotive*; loadstone 291 *magnet*; tug of war.

Adjective
(2) *drawing,* tractional, tractive; retractile, retractable; magnetic 291 *attracting*; drawn, horse-d.

Verb
(3) *draw,* pull, haul, hale; warp 269 *navigate*; tug, tow, take in tow; lug, drag, trail, trawl; winch, reel in, wind in; lift, heave 310 *elevate*; drag down 311 *lower*; suck in 299 *absorb*; pluck, pull out 304 *extract*; yank, jerk, twitch, tweak, pluck at, snatch at; pull towards 291 *attract*; pull back, draw b.; draw in, retract, sheathe (claws).

Interjection
(4) *yo-heave-ho!*

289
Approach: Motion towards

Noun
(1) *approach,* coming towards, advance 285 *progression*; near approach, approximation 200 *nearness*; meeting, confluence 293 conveyance; accession, advent, coming 205 *arrival*; overtaking, overlapping 619 *pursuit*; onset 712 *attack*; advances, approaches, overture 759 *offer*; means of approach, accessibility 624 *access*.

Adjective
(2) *approaching,* nearing, close 200 *near*; meeting, conveying; overhanging, hovering, closing in, imminent 155 *impending*; advancing, coming, oncoming, on the way 295 *arriving*.

(3) *accessible,* approachable, get-at-able; within reach, attainable 469 *possible;* available, obtainable 189 *on the spot;* wayside, roadside, nearby 200 *near;* welcoming, inviting.

Verb
(4) *approach,* draw near 200 *be near;* approximate 200 *bring near;* come within range, come into view 295 *arrive;* be drawn to, come closer, meet 293 *converge;* run down 279 *collide;* near, draw n., come n.; run up to, step up to, sidle up to; roll up 74 *congregate;* come in 297 *enter;* waylay, buttonhole; accost 884 *greet;* lean towards, incline 179 *tend;* move towards, drift t., advance 285 *progress;* advance upon, bear down on 712 *attack;* close in on 232 *circumscribe;* hover 155 *impend;* gain upon, catch up with 277 *outstrip;* follow hard on, tread on one's heels; hug the coast, make a landfall 295 *land.*

Interjection
(5) *this way!* come closer! roll up! land ahoy!

290
Recession: Motion from

Noun
(1) *recession,* retirement, withdrawal, retreat 286 *regression;* leak 298 *outflow;* emigration, evacuation 296 *departure;* flight 667 *escape;* shrinking, flinching, revulsion 280 *recoil.*

Adjective
(2) *receding,* retreating 286 *regressive.*

Verb
(3) *recede,* retire, withdraw, fall back, draw b., retreat 286 *regress;* ebb, subside, shrink, decline 37 *decrease;* fade from view 446 *disappear;* go, go away, leave, evacuate, emigrate 296 *depart;* go outside 298 *emerge;* move away, move off, put space between, widen the gap 199 *be distant;* veer away, sheer off 282 *deviate;* drift away 282 *stray;* back away 620 *avoid;* flee 620 *run away;* get away 667 *escape;* go back 286 *turn back;* jump back 280 *recoil.*

291
Attraction

Noun
(1) *attraction,* pull, drag, draw, tug; drawing to, pulling towards; magnetization, magnetism, magnetic field; gravity, force of g.; itch for 859 *desire;* affinity, sympathy; seductiveness, allure, appeal, sex a.; allurement, seduction, temptation; lure, bait, decoy, charm 612 *inducement;* charmer, temptress, siren 890 *favourite.*

(2) *magnet,* lodestone; lodestar 520 *guide;* magnetizer.

Adjective
(3) *attracting,* attractive; magnetic, magnetized; siren, seductive, charming 612 *inducing;* centripetal.

Verb
(4) *attract,* magnetize, pull, drag, tug 288 *draw;* exercise a pull, draw towards, pull t., drag t., tug t.; appeal, charm, move 821 *impress;* lure, allure, bait 612 *tempt;* decoy 542 *ensnare.*

292
Repulsion

Noun
(1) *repulsion,* repulsive force, centrifugal f.; repulsiveness 842 *ugliness;* reflection 280 *recoil;* driving off 713 *defence;* repulse, rebuff, snub, refusal 607 *rejection;* brush-off, dismissal 300 *ejection.*

Adjective

(2) *repellent,* repulsive, off-putting, antipathetic 861 *disliked*; centrifugal.

Verb

(3) *repel,* put off, excite nausea 861 *cause dislike*; push away, butt a. 279 *impel*; drive away, chase a., repulse, beat off, fend off, keep at arm's length; stonewall 713 *parry*; dispel 75 *disperse*; head off, turn away 282 *deflect*; be deaf to 760 *refuse*; rebuff, snub, brush off 607 *reject*; cold-shoulder 883 *make unwelcome*; send packing 300 *dismiss*.

293
Convergence

Noun

(1) *convergence,* mutual approach 289 *approach*; narrowing gap, collision course 279 *collision*; concourse, confluence, meeting 45 *union*; concurrence, concentration 74 *assemblage*; closing in, pincer movement; centering 76 *focus*; narrowing, tapering; converging line, tangent; perspective, vanishing point.

Adjective

(2) *convergent,* focusing, focused; centripetal, centering; tangential; pointed, conical, pyramidal 256 *tapering*.

Verb

(3) *converge,* come closer, draw in, close in; narrow the gap; fall in with, come together 295 *meet*; unite, gather together 74 *congregate*; roll in, pour in 297 *enter*; close with, intercept, head off 232 *circumscribe*; pinch, nip; concentrate, focus, bring into f.; centre, centre on 225 *centralize*; taper, narrow down, come to a point.

294
Divergence

Noun

(1) *divergence* 15 *difference*; contradiction 14 *contrariety*; going apart, moving apart 46 *separation*; aberration 282 *deviation*; spread, fanning out, deployment 75 *dispersion*; fork, bifurcation, crossroads 222 *crossing*; radiation, ramification, branching out; Y-shape 247 *angularity*; star, rays, spokes.

Adjective

(2) *divergent,* separated; radiating, radiant, centrifugal, centrifuge; aberrant 282 *deviating*.

Verb

(3) *diverge* 15 *differ*; radiate; ramify, branch off, split off, fork, bifurcate; part, part company 46 *separate*; change direction, switch; glance off, fly off 282 *deviate*; fan out, spread, scatter 75 *be dispersed*; straddle, spread-eagle; splay, splay apart.

295
Arrival

Noun

(1) *arrival,* advent, accession, appearance, entrance 289 *approach*, 189 *presence*; onset 68 *beginning*; coming, reaching, making; landfall, landing, touchdown, docking 266 *quiescence*; meeting, greeting 884 *courteous act*; homecoming 286 *return*; reception, welcome 876 *celebration*; guest, visitor, visitant, new arrival, recent a. 297 *incomer*; last lap, home stretch.

(2) *goal,* 617 *objective*; native land 192 *home*; journey's end, terminus 69 *extremity*; stopover, stage, halt 145 *stopping place*; landing p., landing stage, pier; port, harbour, haven, anchorage 662 *shelter*; dock,

berth; airport 271 *air travel*; railway terminus, railway station, bus s., depot; rendezvous 192 *meeting place*.

Adjective

(3) *arriving,* landing etc. vb., homeward-bound; nearing 289 *approaching,* 155 *impending.*

Verb

(4) *arrive,* come, reach, fetch up at, get there 189 *be present*; make land, make a landfall, make port; dock, berth, tie up, moor, drop anchor; draw up, pull up, park; return home 286 *regress*; make, win to, gain, attain; reach one's goal; appear, show up, turn up, roll up, drop in, blow in 882 *visit*; put in, pull in, stop at, stop over, stop off, stop.

(5) *land,* unload, discharge 188 *displace*; run aground, touch down, make a landing; go ashore, disembark; get off, get out, get down, alight, dismount.

(6) *meet,* join, rejoin; receive, greet, welcome, shake hands 882 *be sociable*; go to meet, meet the train; keep a date, rendezvous; come upon, encounter, run into, meet by chance; hit, bump into, collide with 279 *collide*; gather, assemble 74 *congregate.*

Interjection

(7) *welcome!* welcome home! greetings! hullo! hi! shalom! salaam!

296
Departure

Noun

(1) *departure,* leaving, parting, going away; walk-out, exit 298 *egress*; pulling out, emigration 290 *recession*; going back 286 *return*; migration, exodus;

flight, flit, moonlight f., elopement, getaway 667 *escape*; embarkation, going on board; mounting, saddling; setting out, starting out 68 *start*; takeoff, blast-off 308 *ascent*; starting point, starting post.

(2) *valediction,* valedictory; obituary 364 *obsequies*; leave-taking, send-off, dismissal; goodbyes, farewells, adieus; last words, parting shot.

Adjective

(3) *departing,* going etc. vb.; valedictory, farewell; parting, leaving; outward bound.

Verb

(4) *depart,* quit, leave, abandon 621 *relinquish*; retire, withdraw 286 *turn back*; leave home, emigrate, go away; take one's leave, be going, be getting along; bid farewell, say goodbye, make one's adieus, tear oneself away, part, part company; clock out, go home; bow out, make one's exit; depart this life 361 *die.*

(5) *decamp,* break camp, pack up, clear off; clear out, pull out, evacuate; be off, push o.; take wing 271 *fly*; bolt, scuttle, slip away, cut and run 277 *move fast*; flee, take flight 620 *run away*; make one's getaway 446 *disappear*; elope, abscond 667 *escape.*

(6) *start out,* set out 68 *begin*; set forth, sally f. 298 *emerge*; take ship, embark, go on board; cast off, weigh anchor, push off, get under way, set sail; mount, bridle, harness, saddle 267 *ride*; pull out, drive off, take off; see off, wish Godspeed, wave goodbye.

Interjection

(7) *goodbye!* farewell! adieu! au revoir! bon voyage!

297
Ingress: Motion into

Noun

(1) *ingress,* incoming, entry, entrance; reentry 286 *return*; inflow, influx, inrush; intrusion, trespass, invasion, forced entry, inroad; raid, incursion 712 *attack*; immersion, diffusion, penetration, infiltration, insinuation 303 *insertion*; immigration, intake 299 *reception*; importation 272 *transference*; right of entry, admission, admittance, access, entree 756 *permission*; ticket, pass 756 *permit.*

(2) *way in,* way 624 *access*; entrance, entry, door 263 *doorway*; mouth, opening 263 *orifice*; inlet 345 *gulf*; channel 351 *conduit*; open door.

(3) *incomer,* newcomer, new arrival, new face 538 *beginner*; visitor, caller; immigrant, migrant, colonist, settler 59 *foreigner*; stowaway 59 *intruder*; invader, raider 712 *attacker*; house-breaker 789 *thief*; ticket holder.

Adjective

(4) *incoming,* ingoing, inward, inward bound, homing; intrusive, irruptive, invasive 712 *attacking*; penetrating, flooding; allowed in, imported.

Verb

(5) *enter,* turn into, go in, come in, move in, drive in, run in, breeze in, venture in, sidle in, step in, walk in, file in; set foot in, darken the doors; let oneself in; unlock the door 263 *open*; gain admittance, be invited; look in, drop in, call 882 *visit*; board, get aboard; get in, hop in, jump in, pile in; squeeze into, wedge oneself i.; creep in, slip in, edge in, slink in, sneak in, steal in; worm into, bore i. 263 *pierce*; sink into 313

plunge; enlist in, enroll oneself 58 *be one of*; immigrate, settle in 187 *place oneself.*

(6) *infiltrate,* percolate, seep, soak through, soak into, leak i.; sink in, penetrate, permeate 43 *mix*; taint, infect 655 *impair*; find one's way in, worm one's way in.

(7) *burst in,* irrupt, rush in, charge in, crash in, smash in, break in 176 *force*; flood, overflow, flow in, pour in; crowd in, throng in, swarm in 74 *congregate*; invade, raid, board, storm 712 *attack.*

(8) *intrude,* trespass, gatecrash; barge in, push in, muscle in; burst in upon, interrupt 63 *derange*; break in.

298
Egress: Motion out of

Noun

(1) *egress,* going out; exit, walkoff; walkout, exodus, evacuation 296 *departure*; emigration, expatriation, exile 883 *seclusion*; emergence, emerging, surfacing; sortie, breakout 667 *escape*; exportation 272 *transference*; migrant, emigrant, émigré 59 *foreigner*; expatriate, exile.

(2) *outflow,* efflux, effusion; emission 300 *ejection*; issue, outpouring, gushing, streaming; exudation, oozing, dribbling, weeping; bleeding 302 *haemorrhage*; perspiration, sweating, sweat; leak, escape, leakage, seepage 634 *waste*; drain, outfall, effluent; discharge, drainage, overflow, spill; fountain, spring 156 *source*; gush, squirt 350 *stream*; gusher, geyser 300 *ejector.*

(3) *outlet,* vent, chute; spout, nozzle, tap; pore 263 *orifice*;

sluice, floodgate 351 *conduit*; exhaust, exhaust pipe; drainpipe, gargoyle; exit, way out 263 *doorway*; escape, loophole 667 *means of escape*.

Adjective

(4) *outgoing,* emergent, issuing, emanating; oozy, running, leaky; explosive, volcanic 300 *expulsive*.

Verb

(5) *emerge,* project 254 *jut*; peep out, peer out; surface, break water 308 *ascend*; emanate, transpire; issue, debouch, sally, make a sortie; issue out of, go out, come o., creep o., sneak o.; jump out, bale o. 312 *leap*; clear out, evacuate 296 *decamp*; emigrate 267 *travel*; exit, walk off 296 *depart*; erupt, break out, break through 667 *escape*.

(6) *flow out,* flood o., pour o., stream o. 350 *flow*; gush, spirt, spout, jet 300 *emit*; drain out, run, drip, dribble, trickle; rise, surge, well out, well up, well over, boil o.; overflow, spill, spill over, slop o.; run off, escape, leak; vent itself, discharge i.; debouch; bleed, weep; flood, inundate 341 *drench*.

(7) *exude,* perspire, sweat, steam 379 *be hot*; ooze, seep, percolate; strain, strain out, filter, distil; run, dribble, drip, drop; drivel, drool, slaver, slobber, salivate 341 *be wet*; transpire, exhale 352 *breathe*.

299
Reception

Noun

(1) *reception,* admission, admittance, entree, access 297 *ingress*; introduction invitation 759 *offer*; receptivity, acceptance; open arms, welcome enlistment, enrolment 78 *inclusion*; initiation, baptism 68

debut; asylum, sanctuary, shelter 660 *protection*; inhalation 352 *respiration*; sucking, suction; assimilation, digestion, absorption, engulfing, swallowing; ingestion (of food) 301 *eating,* 301 *drinking*; intake, consumption; infusion 303 *insertion*.

Adjective

(2) *admitting,* receptive; inviting, welcoming 289 *accessible*; receivable, admissible, acceptable; absorbent, ingestive; digestive, assimilative; introductory, initiatory, baptismal.

Verb

(3) *admit,* receive, accept, take in; naturalize; grant asylum, afford sanctuary, shelter; welcome, invite, call in 759 *offer*; enlist, enrol, take on 622 *employ*; pass in, allow in, allow access, open the door 263 *open*; bring in, land 272 *transfer*; let in, show in, usher in, introduce 64 *come before*; send in 272 *send*; initiate, baptize; take, be given, get 782 *receive*.

(4) *absorb,* incorporate, assimilate, digest; suck, suck in; soak up, sponge, mop up, blot 342 *dry*; internalize, take in, ingest, imbibe; lap up, swallow, swallow up, engulf; gulp, gobble, devour 301 *eat,* drink; breathe in, inhale, sniff, snuff 394 *smell*.

300
Ejection

Noun

(1) *ejection,* ejaculation, extrusion, expulsion; throwing out, precipitation 287 *propulsion*; disqualification, excommunication 57 *exclusion*; drumming out, marching orders; dismissal, discharge, sack, boot, push

607 *rejection*; repatriation, deportation, extradition; relegation, exile, banishment; eviction **188** *displacement*; dispossession, deprivation **786** *expropriation*; clean sweep, elimination **165** *destruction*; radiation, emission, effusion **298** *outflow*; secretion, salivation **302** *excretion*; deportee, refugee **883** *outcast*.

(2) *ejector,* dispossessor, evictor, bailiff; expeller, chucker-out, bouncer; emetic, aperient **658** *purgative*; propellant **723** *explosive*; volcano **383** *furnace*.

(3) *voidance,* clearance, drainage, curettage, aspiration; eruption **176** *outbreak*; regurgitation, vomiting, vomit; eructation, gas, wind, burp, belch; breaking wind, belching; elimination, evacuation **302** *excretion.*

Adjective

(4) *expulsive,* explosive, eruptive; radiating, emitting, emissive; secretory, salivary; sickening, emetic; cathartic **302** *excretory.*

(5) *vomiting,* sick, sickened, nauseated, green, belching, airsick, carsick.

Verb

(6) *eject,* expel, send down **963** *punish*; strike off, disbar, excommunicate **57** *exclude*; export, send away **272** *transfer*; deport, expatriate, repatriate; exile, banish, transport **883** *seclude*; extrude, throw up, cast up, wash up; spit out, spew o.; throw out, **287** *propel*; kick out, boot o., bundle out, hustle o.; drum out; precipitate **287** *propel*; pull out **304** *extract*; root out, weed o., uproot, eradicate **165** *destroy*; exorcise, get rid of, rid oneself of, get shot of; shake off, brush o.; dispossess, expropriate **786** *deprive*; oust, evict, dislodge, turn out, turn adrift,

188 *displace*; hunt out, smoke o. **619** *hunt*; jettison, discard, throw away **779** *not retain*; blackball **607** *reject*; ostracize **883** *make unwelcome*; supplant, supersede **150** *substitute*.

(7) *dismiss,* discharge, lay off, make redundant **674** *stop using*; axe, sack, fire **779** *not retain*; turn away, send packing **292** *repel*; see off, shoo away; show the door, show out; bowl out, run o., catch o., take one's wicket; tell to go, order away **757** *prohibit*.

(8) *empty,* drain, void; evacuate, eliminate **302** *excrete*; vent, disgorge, discharge; pour out, decant **272** *transpose*; drink up, drain off **301** *drink*; bail out, pump o., suck o., aspirate; run off, siphon o.; draw off, tap, broach **263** *pierce*; milk, bleed **304** *extract*; clear, sweep away, clear a. **648** *clean*; clean out, clear out, curette; unload, unpack **188** *displace*; disembowel, eviscerate, gut, clean, bone, fillet **229** *uncover*; disinfest **648** *purify*; depopulate **105** *render few.*

(9) *emit,* let out, give vent to; send out **272** *send*; emit rays **417** *radiate*; emit a smell, give off, exhale, breathe out, perfume, scent **394** *smell*; smoke, steam, puff **338** *vaporize*; spit, spatter, sputter, splutter; pour, spill, shed, sprinkle, spray; spurt, squirt, jet, gush **341** *moisten*; bleed **298** *flow out*; drip, drop, ooze **298** *exude*; sweat, perspire **379** *be hot*; secrete, pass **302** *excrete*.

(10) *vomit,* be sick, bring up, throw up; retch, gag, spew, heave.

(11) *eruct,* belch, burp, break wind, blow off; hiccup, cough, hawk, clear the throat, expectorate, spit.

301
Food: Eating and drinking

Noun

(1) *eating*, taking food, ingestion; nutrition; feeding, drip-f., force-f.; consumption, devouring; swallowing, downing, getting down; biting, chewing, mastication; rumination, digestion; chewing the cud; pasturing, cropping; eating meals, table, diet, dining; dining out 882 *sociability*; partaking, tasting, nibbling, pecking; lack of appetite, anorexia; overeating 947 *gluttony*; appetite 859 *hunger*; eating habits, table manners; flesh-eating, anthropophagy, man-eating, cannibalism; vegetarianism, veganism; edibility, digestibility; food chain, food web.

(2) *feasting*, gormandizing, guzzling; banqueting, eating out; orgy, feast; reception, do 876 *celebration*; blowout, spread (see *meal*); loaded table, festal cheer; milk and honey 635 *plenty*; banqueting hall.

(3) *dieting*, dietetics 658 *therapy*; slimming 206 *thinness*; reducing, losing weight 946 *fasting*; diet, balanced d.; regimen, regime, course; meagre diet 636 *insufficiency*; malnutrition 651 *disease*; dietitian, nutritionist,

(4) *gastronomy*, epicurism 944 *sensualism*; gourmandism 947 *gluttony*; dainty palate, refined p. epicure, gourmet.

(5) *cookery*, cooking, baking, cuisine, haute c.; food preparation, dressing; domestic science, home economics, catering 633 *provision*; food processing; cook, chef, cordon bleu 633

caterer; bakery, rotisserie, restaurant 192 *café*; kitchen, cookhouse, galley; oven 383 *furnace*; recipe, cookery book.

(6) *eater*, consumer, partaker etc. vb.; boarder, messmate; diner, banqueter, picnicker; connoisseur, gourmet, epicure; gourmand, trencherman or -woman 947 *glutton*; flesh-eater, meat-e., carnivore; man-eater, cannibal; vegetarian, vegan; herbivore; omnivore; teeth, jaws, mandibles; mouth, stomach 194 *maw*.

(7) *provisions*, stores, commissariat; foodstuff, groceries; keep, board, sustenance 633 *provision*; commons, rations, iron r.; helping 783 *portion*; freezer, larder, cellar 632 *storage*.

(8) *provender*, animal food, fodder, feed, pasture, pasturage, forage; chicken feed, cattle cake.

(9) *food*, meat, bread, staff of life; nutriment, liquid n.; nutrition; nurture, sustenance, nourishment, food and drink; nectar, ambrosia, manna; daily bread, staple food; foodstuffs, comestibles, edibles, eatables, eats, victuals, grub; stodge 391 *unsavouriness*; wholefood, health food, convenience f., junk f.; cheer, good c., cakes and ale 730 *prosperity*; delicatessen, delicacies; dainties, titbits; garnish, flavouring 389 *condiment*.

(10) *food content*, vitamins; calories; roughage, bulk, fibre; minerals, salts; protein, cholesterol, carbohydrates, starch; sugar 392 *sweet thing*; additive, preservative, flavouring.

(11) *mouthful*, bite, nibble, morsel 33 *small quantity*; sip, swallow; titbit, sandwich, snack, crust.

(12) *meal,* refreshment, fare; light meal, snack, bite to eat; sandwich, packed lunch, ploughman's l.; square meal, heavy meal; repast, collation, spread, blowout 837 *festivity*; picnic, barbecue; breakfast, elevenses, luncheon, lunch, brunch; tea, high tea; dinner, supper; table d'hôte, à la carte; menu, bill of fare; cover, place; helping 783 *portion.*

(13) *dish,* course; main dish, entrée; salad, entre-mets; dessert, savoury; speciality, plat du jour; casserole, stew, curry; pasta, noodles; pizza, pasty, pie, flan; fry-up, mixed grill, kebabs; souffle, omelette; *Welsh rarebit, scrambled eggs,* bread and butter, bread and cheese; leftovers.

(14) *hors-d'oeuvres,* appetizer, starter, canapé; soup, broth, consomme; cold meats, cooked m., pâté, galantine; salad, coleslaw, mayonnaise 389 *sauce.*

(15) *fish food,* fish, fish and chips, fish pie, fish cakes, fish fingers, kedgeree; white fish, oily f., fresh f., smoked f.; seafood shellfish; caviar.

(16) *meat,* flesh; red meat, white m.; beef, mutton, lamb, veal, pork, venison; game, poultry; pheasant, chicken 365 *table bird,* roast meat, Sunday roast, S. joint; minced meat, mince; meatballs, rissoles, hamburgers; sausage, banger, frankfurter; cut, joint; baron of beef, sirloin; cutlet, chop, escalope; steak; ham, bacon, gammon; tripe, offal 224 *insides*; forcemeat, stuffing.

(17) *dessert,* pudding, sweet; milk pudding, steamed p.; stewed fruit, compote, fool; sorbet, mousse, sundae, trifle, 392 *sweet thing*; fresh fruit, cheese board.

(18) *sweets,* boiled s., confectionery; candy, chocolate, caramel, toffee; mints, humbugs, acid drops, barley sugar, butterscotch, liquorice, nougat; chewing gum, bubble g.; lollipop, toffee apple, sweetmeat 392 *sweet thing.*

(19) *fruit,* soft fruit, berry; stone fruit, plum, apple, pear; citrus fruit, orange, grapefruit, lemon; banana, pineapple, grape; rhubarb; date, fig, dried fruit; nut, coconut; bottled fruit, preserves 392 *sweet thing.*

(20) *vegetable,* greens 366 *plant*; root vegetable, tuber; parsnip, carrot, potato; French fries, chips; green vegetable, cabbage, cauliflower, sprouts, spring greens; peas, beans; leek, onion, shallots; marrow, pumpkin, squash; salads, lettuce; tomato, cucumber, cress; dried vegetables, pulses; edible fungus, mushroom; baked beans, bubble and squeak.

(21) *potherb,* herb, culinary h., sweet h., bouquet garni; mint, parsley, thyme; horse radish 389 *condiment.*

(22) *cereals,* grains, wheat, oats, rye, maize, corn; rice, millet, sorghum; cornflakes, muesli, porridge, gruel; flour, meal, wholemeal, wheat germ, bran; batter, dough; bread, crust, crumb; toast, rusk, croutons; loaf, roll, bun (see *pastries*); crumpet, muffin, scone; cracker, cream c.

(23) *pastries,* confectionery; patty, pasty, turnover, dumpling; tart, flan, puff, pie, piecrust; pastry, gateau, cake; meringue, éclair, doughnut; gingerbread, shortbread, biscuits.

(24) *dairy product* (see *milk*); cream, clotted c., curds, whey,

junket, yoghourt; cheese, cream c., cottage c.

(25) *drinking,* imbibing, sipping, tasting, wine-tasting; soaking, swilling 949 *drunkenness*; libation 981 *oblation*; drinker; toper 949 *drunkard*.

(26) *draught,* drink, beverage, dram; gulp, sip; bottle, glass, cuppa, glassful, bumper; swig, nip, tot, slug; peg, double peg, snorter, snifter, chaser; long drink, short drink, quick one, nightcap; health, toast; potion, decoction, infusion 658 *medicine*; nectar.

(27) *soft drink,* teetotal d., water, soda w.; table water, mineral w., tonic w., barley w., squash; iced drink, frappe; milk shake; ginger beer, ginger ale, fizz, pop, lemonade; cordial, fruit juice; tea, coffee 658 *tonic*; cocoa **(see** *milk*); sherbet, syrup.

(28) *alcoholic drink,* strong d., booze, wallop, tipple, poison; brew, fermented liquor, alcohol; malt liquor, beer, ale, real ale; stout, lager, bitter, mild, home brew; shandy; cider; distilled liquor, spirits, brandy, cognac, gin, whisky, rum, grog, punch; mixed drink, cocktail; aperitif; liqueur.

(29) *wine,* the grape, red wine, white w., rose; vermouth; sparkling wine, sweet w., dry w.; vino, plonk; table wine, dessert w.; sherry, port, madeira; champagne, fizz, bubbly.

(30) *milk,* cream; mare's milk, mother's milk, breast m.; milk drink, cocoa, chocolate; curdled milk, curds.

Adjective
(31) *feeding,* eating etc. vb.; flesh-eating, meat-e.; carnivorous, cannibalistic; herbivorous, vegetarian, vegan; omnivorous, greedy, 947 *gluttonous*;

teetotal 942 *temperate*; tippling 949 *drunken*; well-fed, full up 863 *sated*.

(32) *edible,* eatable; ritually pure, kosher; digestible, predigested; potable, drinkable; worth eating, palatable, succulent 386 *tasty,* 390 *savoury*; fermented, distilled, spirituous, alcoholic, hard 949 *intoxicating*; nonalcoholic, soft.

(33) *nourishing,* feeding, sustaining, nutritious, nutritive, nutritional; alimentary; dietary, dietetic; fattening, rich, calorific, body-building; wholesome 652 *salubrious*.

(34) *culinary,* cooked; well-done; underdone, red, rare, raw; over-cooked, burnt; roasted etc. vb.; gastronomic, epicurean; post-prandial, after-dinner.

Verb
(35) *eat,* feed, fare, board, mess; partake 386 *taste*; breakfast, lunch, have tea, dine, sup; dine out, feast, banquet 837 *revel*; eat well, have a good appetite; drool, raven 859 *be hungry*; fall to, set to, tuck in, lay into; fork in, spoon in, shovel in; stuff oneself 863 *sate*; guzzle, gormandize 947 *gluttonize*; swallow, gulp down, snap up, devour, dispatch, bolt, wolf; feed on, live on, fatten on, batten on, prey on; nibble, peck, lick, peck at; ingest, digest 299 *absorb*.

(36) *chew,* masticate, champ, chomp, munch, crunch, scrunch; worry, gnaw, grind 332 *pulverize*; bite, tear, rend, chew up 46 *cut*.

(37) *graze,* browse, pasture, crop, feed; ruminate, chew the cud.

(38) *drink,* imbibe 299 *absorb*; quaff, drink up, drink one's fill, slake one's thirst; lap, sip; lap up, soak up, wash down; swill, swig, tipple 949 *get drunk*; drain one's glass, knock it back; raise one's glass 876 *toast*; give to drink, water.

(39) *feed*, nourish, nurture, sustain; give to eat, cater 633 *provide*; nurse, breast-feed; pasture, graze, fatten up 197 *enlarge*; dine, wine and dine 882 *be hospitable*.

(40) *cook*, prepare a meal; bake, roast, braise; broil, grill, barbecue, saute, fry; scramble, poach; boil, parboil; seethe, simmer, steam; casserole, stew; baste, lard; whip, whisk, beat, blend, liquidize, stir; stuff, dress, garnish; dice, shred, mince, grate; flavour 388 *season*.

Interjection
(41) *bon appetit!* here's health! cheers!

302
Excretion

Noun
(1) *excretion*, discharge, secretion 300 *ejection*; exhalation, breathing out; sweating, perspiration 298 *outflow*; suppuration 651 *infection*; cold, catarrh, hay fever; salivation, expectoration, spitting; coughing, cough; urination, waterworks; incontinence.

(2) *haemorrhage*, bleeding, haemophilia 335 *blood*; menses, period, curse; leucorrhoea.

(3) *defecation*, evacuation, elimination; natural functions; bowel movement, motion; diarrhoea, constipation 651 *digestive disorders*.

(4) *excrement* waste matter; faeces, stool, excreta, ordure, night soil; dung, cowpat, manure, muck; droppings, guano; urine, water; sweat, beads of s., lather; spittle, spit, sputum;

saliva, slaver, slobber, froth, foam; phlegm, catarrh, mucus; matter, pus.

Adjective
(5) *excretory*, secretory; purgative, laxative, aperient; diuretic; menstrual; perspiratory; faecal, anal, urinary; rheumy, watery; mucous, phlegmy.

Verb
(6) *excrete*, secrete; pass, move; move one's bowels, defecate; be taken short, have the runs; relieve oneself, ease o., urinate, piddle, pee; make water, spend a penny; wet oneself; sweat, perspire 379 *be hot*; salivate, slobber, snivel; cough, spit 300 *eruct*; weep 298 *exude*.

303
Insertion: Forcible ingress

Noun
(1) *insertion*, interpolation 231 *interjection*; adding 38 *addition*; introduction, insinuation 297 *ingress*; inoculation, injection; infusion, enema; thing inserted, insert, inset; stuffing 227 *lining*.

(2) *immersion*, submersion, submergence 311 *lowering*; dip, bath 313 *plunge*; baptism 988 *Christian rite*; burial 364 *interment*.

Adjective
(3) *inserted*, added 38 *additional*; intermediate 231 *interjacent*.

Verb
(4) *insert*, introduce; weave into 222 *enlace*; put into, thrust i., intrude; poke into, stick i.; transfix 263 *pierce*; ram into, jam i., stuff i., pack i., push i., tuck i., press i. 193 *load*; pocket 187 *stow*; ease into place, slide in, fit in; knock into, hammer i. 279 *impel*; inlay, inset 227 *line*;

mount, frame 232 *circumscribe*; subjoin 38 *add*; interpose 231 *put between*; drop in 311 *let fall*; pot, hole; bury 364 *inter*; sheathe, encase 226 *cover*.

(5) *infuse,* instil, pour in 43 *mix*; imbue, impregnate 297 *infiltrate*; transfuse, decant 272 *transpose*; squirt in, inject 263 *pierce*.

(6) *implant,* plant, transplant; graft, bud; inoculate, vaccinate embed, bury; wedge in, impact 45 *join*.

(7) *immerse,* bathe, steep, souse, marinate, soak 341 *drench*; baptize, duck, dip 311 *lower*; submerge, flood; immerse oneself 313 *plunge*.

304
Extraction: Forcible egress

Noun

(1) *extraction,* withdrawal, removal 188 *displacement*; elimination, eradication 300 *ejection*; extermination, extirpation 165 *destruction*; extrication, disengagement, liberation 668 *deliverance*; tearing out, ripping o.; cutting out, excision; Caesarian birth, forceps delivery; expression, squeezing out; suction, sucking out, aspiration; vacuuming, pumping; drawing out, pull, tug, wrench 288 *traction*; digging out 255 *excavation*; distillation 338 *vaporization*; drawing off, tapping, milking; thing extracted, essence, extract.

(2) *extractor,* wrench, forceps, pincers, pliers, tweezers 778 *nippers*; mangle, squeezer 342 *dryer*; corkscrew, screwdriver 263 *opener*; lever 218 *pivot*; scoop, spoon, shovel; pick, pickaxe; toothpick 648 *cleaning*

utensil; vacuum cleaner; excavator, dredger; syringe, siphon; suction pump.

Adjective

(3) *extracted,* removed etc. vb.

Verb

(4) *extract,* remove, pull 288 *draw*; draw out, elicit, unfold 316 *evolve*; pull out, take o., get o., pluck; withdraw, excise, cut out, rip o., tear o., whip o.; excavate, mine, quarry, dig out, unearth; dredge, dredge up; lever out, winkle o., smoke o. 300 *eject*; extort, wring from; press out, squeeze o., gouge o.; force out, wring o., wrench o., drag o.; draw off, milk, tap; syphon off, aspirate, suck, void, pump; wring from, squeeze f., drag f.; pull up, dig up, grub up; eliminate, weed out, root up, uproot, eradicate, extirpate 165 *destroy*; prune, thin out; distil 338 *vaporize*; extricate, unravel, free 746 *liberate*; unpack, unload 188 *displace*; eviscerate, gut 300 *empty*; unwrap 229 *uncover*; pick out 605 *select*.

305
Passage: Motion through

Noun

(1) *passage,* transmission 272 *transference*; passing through, traversing; transit, traverse, crossing, journey 267 *land travel*; passage into, penetration, permeation, infiltration; right of way 624 *access*; flyover, underpass 624 *bridge*; route, orbit 624 *path*; intersection 222 *crossing*; waterway, channel 351 *conduit*.

(2) *passing along,* passage, thoroughfare; traffic, pedestrian t., wheeled t., vehicular t.; traffic

movement, flow of traffic, circulation; walking, crossing, cycling, driving; traffic load; traffic density; traffic jam, queue; road user 268 *pedestrian*, *driver*; passerby.

(3) *traffic control*, traffic rules, highway code, Green Cross C.; traffic lane, bus l., cycle l., one-way street, dual carriageway 624 *road*; diversion 282 *deviation*; white lines, yellow l., cat's-eyes; crossing, traffic lights, roundabout; bollard, refuge, island; car park, parking meter, lay-by; point duty, road patrol, speed trap; traffic police, traffic warden.

Adjective
(4) *passing*, crossing etc. vb.; transitional.

Verb
(5) *pass*, pass by, skirt, coast 200 *be near*; flash by 277 *move fast*, 114 *be transient*; go past, not stop 146 *go on*; pass along, circulate, weave; pass through, transit, traverse; shoot through 269 *navigate*; pass out 298 *emerge*; go through, soak t. 189 *pervade*; patrol, beat, scour; pass into, penetrate, infiltrate 297 *enter*; open a way, force a passage 297 *burst in*; thread through, worm one's way, squeeze through 285 *progress*; cross, cross over, wade across, ford; get through, get past, negotiate; pass beyond 306 *overstep*; cut across 702 *obstruct*; step over, straddle, bestride bridge, bridge over; carry over, carry across, transmit 272 *send*; pass to, hand, reach, hand over 272 *transfer*.

Adverb
(6) *en passant*, by the way; on the way, in transit.

306
Overstepping: Motion beyond

Noun
(1) *overstepping*, going beyond 305 *passage*; transcendence 34 *superiority*; excursion, digression 282 *deviation*; violation, trespass 936 *guilty act*; usurpation, encroachment 916 *arrogation*; infringement, intrusion; excessiveness, overdoing it 546 *exaggeration*.

Adjective
(2) *surpassing*, one up on 34 *superior*; overlong, overpowered; excessive 32 *exorbitant*; out of bounds, out of reach.

Verb
(3) *overstep*, overpass; pass, leave behind; go beyond, go too far, exceed, exceed the limit; overrun, override, overshoot, aim too high; overlap surmount, jump over, leap o., leapfrog; step over, cross 305 *pass*; overfill, brim over 54 *fill*; overgrow 637 *superabound*; overdo 546 *exaggerate*; strain, stretch, stretch a point; overestimate 482 *overrate*; overindulge 943 *be intemperate*; oversleep 136 *be late*.

(4) *encroach*, invade, make inroads on 712 *attack*; infringe, transgress, trespass 954 *be illegal*; poach 788 *steal*; squat, usurp 786 *appropriate*; barge in 297 *intrude*; overlap, impinge, trench on; entrench upon; eat away, erode 655 *impair*; infest, flood, overrun 297 *burst in*. 341 *drench*.

(5) *outdo*, exceed, surpass, outclass; transcend, rise above, outrival 34 *be superior*; go one better, overcall, overbid, outbid; outwit, overreach 542 *deceive*; outmanoeuvre, outflank, make the running 277 *move*

fast; outrun, outride, outdistance; overhaul, gain upon, overtake, shoot ahead; lap, leave standing 277 *outstrip*; leave behind, race, beat 727 *defeat*.

307
Shortfall

Noun

(1) *shortfall,* inadequacy 636 *insufficiency*; a minus, deficit, short measure, shortage, loss; leeway, drift 282 *deviation*; default, half measures; fault, defect, shortcoming 647 *imperfection*, 845 *blemish*; want, lack, need 627 *requirement*.

Adjective

(2) *deficient,* short, short of, minus, wanting, lacking, missing; substandard; undermanned, understaffed; perfunctory 55 *incomplete*; inadequate 636 *insufficient*; failing, running short 636 *scarce*; below par 647 *imperfect*.

Verb

(3) *fall short,* come s., underachieve; run short 636 *not suffice*; not stretch, not reach to; lack, want, be without 627 *require*; miss, miss the mark; lag 136 *be late*; stop short, break down, get bogged down; fall behind, lose ground, slip back; fall through, come to nothing, fizzle out, fail 728 *miscarry*; labour in vain 641 *waste effort*; tantalize 509 *disappoint*.

Adverb

(4) *behindhand,* in arrears; not enough; below the mark, far from it.

308
Ascent: Motion upwards

Noun

(1) *ascent,* ascension, lift, upward motion, gaining height; levitation; taking off, takeoff, lift-off 296 *departure*; flying up, soaring, spiralling, spiral 271 *aeronautics*; culmination 213 *summit*; floating up, surfacing, breaking surface; going up, rising, uprising; rise, upturn; upsurge, crescendo 36 *increase*; rising air, thermal; sunrise, sun-up; mounting, climbing; hill-climbing, mountaineering; bounce, jump, vault, pole v. 312 *leap*; rising ground, hill 209 *high land*; gradient, slope, ramp 220 *incline*; means of ascent, stairs, steps, flight of stairs, staircase, spiral s.; ladder, companionway; ratlines; stair, step, tread, rung; lift, escalator 310 *lifter*.

(2) *climber,* mountaineer, fell walker; steeplejack; lark, skylark; gusher, geyser, fountain.

Adjective

(3) *ascending,* climbing etc. vb.; rearing, rampant; buoyant, floating 323 *light*; airborne, gaining height; in the ascendant; uphill, steep 215 *vertical*; climbable.

Verb

(4) *ascend,* rise, rise up, go up, leave the ground; defy gravity, levitate; take off, become airborne 271 *fly*; gain height, mount, soar, spiral, zoom, climb; reach the top, reach the zenith; float up, bob up, surface, break water; jump up, spring, vault 312 *leap*; bounce 280 *recoil*; grow up, shoot up 36 *grow*; curl upwards; tower, aspire 209 *be high*; gush, spirt, spout, jet 298 *flow out*; rear up 215 *be vertical*; get up 310 *lift*

oneself; wind upwards, slope u., steepen 220 *be oblique.*

(5) *climb,* make one's way up, walk up, struggle up; mount; go climbing, mountaineer; clamber, scramble, swarm up, shin up; surmount, top, breast, conquer, scale, scale the heights 209 *be high.*

Adverb
(6) *up,* uphill, upstairs; upwards 209 *aloft.*

309
Descent

Noun
(1) *descent,* falling, dropping; cadence; downward trend, spiral, decline, drop, slump 37 *decrease*; comedown, demotion 286 *regression*; downfall, collapse 165 *ruin*; tumble, crash, spill, fall; swoop, dive, header 313 *plunge*; landing, splashdown 295 *arrival*; sliding down, glissade; subsidence, landslide, avalanche; downdraught; downpour, shower 350 *rain*; cascade 350 *waterfall*; slope, tilt, dip 220 *incline*; chute, slide, precipice, sheer drop 215 *verticality*; submergence 311 *lowering*; boring, tunnelling, burrowing, mining, sapping 255 *excavation*; speleology, potholing, caving; tumbler; plunger 313 *diver*; burrower, miner 255 *excavator*; parachutist, paratrooper; speleologist, pot holer, caver.

Adjective
(2) *descending,* dropping 220 *sloping*; swooping, stooping; tumbledown, falling, tottering; tilting, sinking, foundering; burrowing, sapping; drooping 311 *lowered*; submersible, sinkable.

Verb
(3) *descend,* come down, go d., dip d.; decline, abate, ebb 37

decrease; slump, fall, drop, sink; soak in, seep down 297 *infiltrate*; reach the depths, touch bottom 210 *be low*; gravitate, precipitate, settle; fall down, fall in, cave in, collapse; sink in, subside, slip, give way; hang down, droop, sag 217 *hang*; submerge, dive 313 *plunge*; go underground, dig down, burrow, bore, tunnel 255 *make concave*; parachute; swoop, stoop, pounce; fly down, flutter d., float d.; lose height, drop down; touch down, alight, perch 295 *land*; lower oneself, abseil; get down, climb d., step d., get off, fall o., dismount; slide down, glissade, toboggan; fall like rain, shower, cascade, drip 350 *rain*; duck 311 *stoop*; flop, plop, splash down.

(4) *tumble,* fall; tumble down, fall d.; topple, topple over, heel o., keel o., overbalance 221 *be inverted*; miss one's footing, slip, slip up, trip, stumble; lose one's balance, stagger, totter, lurch; tilt, droop 220 *be oblique*; rise and fall, pitch, toss, roll; take a header, dive 313 *plunge*, 312 *leap*; take a fall, be thrown, bite the dust; plop, plump, plump down; slump, spiral, crash.

Adverb
(5) *down,* downwards; downhill, downstairs, downstream.

310
Elevation

Noun
(1) *elevation,* erection, uplift, upheaval; picking up, lift; hoist, boost; leg-up 703 *aid*; exaltation, Assumption; uprising, upswing 308 *ascent*; an elevation, eminence 209 *high land.*

(2) *lifter,* erector, builder, raiser; raising agent 323 *leaven*; lever, jack 218 *pivot*; dredger

304 *extractor*; crane, derrick, hoist, windlass; winch, capstan; rope and pulley, block and tackle; forklift, elevator, dumb waiter, escalator, lift, ski l., cable railway; hot air, hydrogen, helium; spring, springboard, trampoline; stilts; scaffolding 218 *stand*.

Adjective

(3) *elevated*, exalted, uplifted; erectile; erected, set up; upright, erect, upstanding 215 *vertical*; mounted, on high; towering over, lofty, sublime 209 *high*.

Verb

(4) *elevate*, heighten 209 *make higher*; puff up, blow up, swell, leaven 197 *enlarge*; raise, erect, set up, put up, run up, rear up, build up, build; lift, lift up, raise up, heave up; uplift, jack up, prop 218 *support*; stand on end 215 *make vertical*; hold up, bear up, buoy up; raise aloft, hold a.; hoist, haul up, trice; pick up, take up; pull up, wind up, weigh (anchor); fish up, drag up, dredge up, pump up 304 *extract*; chair, shoulder, exalt 866 *honour*; put on top 213 *crown*; jump up, bounce up, give a leg-up 703 *aid*; throw up, cast up, toss up; sky, loft; send up, shoot up, lob 287 *propel*; bristle, perk up, prick up 215 *be vertical*.

(5) *lift oneself*, arise, rise 308 *ascend*; stand up, get up, pick oneself up; jump up, leap up, spring up, pull oneself up; stand on tiptoe 215 *be vertical*.

Adverb

(6) *on*, on stilts, on tiptoe; on one's hind legs.

311
Lowering

Noun

(1) *lowering*, pushing down etc. vb.; ducking, sousing 313 *plunge*; debasement, demotion 872 *humiliation*; overthrow, prostration; overturn, upset 221 *overturning*; keeping under, depression, dent, dip 255 *cavity*.

(2) *obeisance*, reverence, bow, salaam, kowtow 884 *courtesy*; curtsy, bob, duck, nod 884 *courteous act*; kneeling, genuflexion 920 *respect*.

Adjective

(3) *lowered*, dipped etc. vb.; 210 *low*; prostrate 216 *supine*; sitting, seated; submersible.

Verb

(4) *lower*, depress, push down, thrust d. 279 *impel*; hold down, keep d. 165 *suppress*; lower, let down, take d.; lower a flag, dip, haul down, strike; deflate, puncture, flatten, squash, crush 198 *make smaller*; sink, scuttle, drown; duck, douse, dip 313 *plunge*; weigh on, press on; roll over 221 *invert*; crush, dent, hollow 255 *make concave*.

(5) *let fall*, drop, shed; let go 779 *not retain*; pour out, decant 300 *empty*; spill, slop 341 *moisten*; sprinkle, shower, scatter, dust, dredge; sow, broadcast 75 *disperse*; lay down, put d., set d., throw down 287 *propel*.

(6) *fell*, trip, topple, tumble, overthrow; prostrate, spreadeagle, lay low, 216 *flatten*; knock down, bowl over, skittle; floor, drop, down 279 *impel*; throw down, cast d., pull down, tear d., level 165 *demolish*; hew down, cut d., axe 46 *cut*; blow down 352 *blow*; bring down, undermine; shoot down, wing 287 *shoot*.

(7) *abase,* demote, humble, deflate, puncture, debunk 872 *humiliate;* crush, squash 165 *suppress.*

(8) *sit down,* sit, be seated, squat, subside, sink, lower oneself; recline 216 *be horizontal;* take a seat, seat oneself, park oneself; perch, alight 309 *descend.*

(9) *stoop,* bend, bend down, get d.; bend over, lean *or* bend forward, lean *or* bend backward; cringe, crouch, cower 721 *knuckle under;* hunch one's back 248 *make curved;* bow, curtsy 884 *pay one's respects;* bow down, make obeisance 920 *show respect;* kneel, kneel to, genuflect.

312
Leap

Noun
(1) *leap,* jump, hop, skip; spring, bound, vault; high jump, long j., running j.; triple j., hop, caper, gambol, frolic; leapfrog; kick, high k.; prance, springy step, light tread 265 *gait;* dance step, dance reel, jig 837 *dancing.*

(2) *jumper,* high-j., pole-vaulter, hurdler, steeplechaser; skipper, hopper, prancer; dancer 837 *dance;* tap dancer, clog d., morris d. 594 *entertainer;* frog, grasshopper, flea; bucking bronco.

Adjective
(3) *leaping,* skittish, frisky, fresh 819 *lively;* skipping, hopping; dancing, jiving; bobbing, bucking, bouncing; tossing 318 *agitated.*

Verb
(4) *leap,* jump, spring, bound, vault, pole-v., hurdle, steeplechase, take one's fences; skip, hop, leapfrog, bob, bounce, rebound, buck 317 *oscillate;* trip, foot it 837 *dance;* cavort, caper, cut capers, gambol, frisk, romp; prance, paw the ground, ramp, rear, plunge; start, give a jump; jump on, pounce; jump up, leap up, spring up; jump over, clear; flounder, jerk 318 *be agitated;* writhe 251 *wriggle.*

313
Plunge

Noun
(1) *plunge,* swoop, pounce, stoop 309 *descent;* power dive 271 *aeronautics;* dive, header; dip, ducking; immersion, submergence; crash dive; drowning, sinking.

(2) *diver,* skin d., scuba d., frogman, aquanaut; diving bird, dipper; submariner; submarine, bathysphere; plunger, sinker, lead, plummet.

Verb
(3) *plunge,* dip, duck, bathe 341 *be wet;* walk the plank, fall in, jump in, plop in; dive, take a header, go headfirst; welter, wallow, pitch and toss; souse, douse, immerse, drown; submerge 309 *descend;* sink, scuttle, send to the bottom 311 *lower;* sound, fathom, plumb the depths, heave the lead 465 *measure.*

(4) *founder, drown,* go down 309 *descend;* settle down 211 *be deep;* plummet, sink, sink like a stone 322 *weigh.*

314
Circuition:
Curvilinear motion

Noun
(1) *circuition,* circulation, circling, wheeling 315 *rotation;* turning, cornering, turn, U-turn 286 *return;* orbit; circuit, lap; tour, round trip, full circle; figure of eight 250 *loop;* helix 251 *coil;* unwinding 316

evolution; roundabout way 626 *circuit.*

(2) *circler,* 270 *mariner*; roundsman patrol; moon, satellite 321 *planet.*

Adjective
(3) *circuitous,* orbital, ecliptic; peripatetic 267 *travelling*; circumflex 248 *curved*; devious 626 *roundabout.*

Verb
(4) *circle,* circulate, go the rounds; compass, circuit, make a c., lap; tour, go round, skirt; turn, round, round a corner, corner; revolve, orbit; wheel, come full circle 315 *rotate*; turn round, bend r.; wheel r., turn on one's heel 286 *turn back*; draw a circle 232 *circumscribe*; curve, wind 251 *meander*; make a detour 626 *circuit.*

315
Rotation: Motion in a continued circle

Noun
(1) *rotation,* orbital motion, revolving, orbiting; revolution, full circle; gyration, circling, spiralling; spin, spiral, roll; turn, twirl, whirl, pirouette 837 *dance*; dizziness, vertigo.

(2) *vortex,* whirlwind, tornado, cyclone 352 *gale*; waterspout, whirlpool, maelstrom swirl, eddy.

(3) *rotator,* rotor, spinner; whirligig, top; merry-go-round, roundabout; churn, whisk; potter's wheel, lathe, circular saw; spinning wheel, spinning jenny; wheel, catherine w., flywheel; gyroscope; turntable, record, disc; windmill, fan, sail; propeller, screw, turbine; capstan 310 *lifter*; spit, jack; spindle, axle, axis 218 *pivot*; reel, roller 252 *cylinder*;

planet, satellite; whirling dervish; dancer, figure skater.

Adjective
(4) *rotary,* rotating, rotatory, gyratory, gyroscopic, circling, cyclic; vortical, cyclonic; vertiginous, dizzy.

Verb
(5) *rotate,* revolve, orbit, go into orbit, circle; turn right round, spin, twirl, pirouette; corkscrew 251 *twine*; gyrate, waltz, wheel; whirl, whirr 404 *resound*; swirl, eddy 350 *flow*; roll, bowl, trundle; twirl, twiddle; churn, whisk 43 *mix*; turn, crank, wind, reel, spool, spin; slew round, swing round, swivel r.; roll up, furl 261 *fold*; roll itself up, curl up, scroll.

Adverb
(6) *round and round,* in a circle, in circles, clockwise, anticlockwise.

316
Evolution: Motion in a reverse circle

Noun
(1) *evolution,* unfolding, unfurling 221 *inversion*; development 157 *growth*; evolutionism 358 *biology.*

Adjective
(2) *evolving,* unwinding etc. vb.

Verb
(3) *evolve,* unfold, unfurl, unroll, unwind, uncoil, uncurl 263 *open*; disentangle 62 *unravel*; develop, grow into 147 *be turned to,* 1 *become.*

317
Oscillation: Reciprocating motion

Noun

(1) *oscillation,* vibration, tremor; pulsation, rhythm 141 *periodicity*; throbbing, drumming, pulse, beat, throb; pitter-patter, flutter, palpitation 318 *agitation*; breathing 352 *respiration*; undulation, frequency band, wavelength 417 *radiation*; sound wave, radio w.; 350 *wave*; earthquake, tremor; seismology, seismograph; oscillator, pendulum, bob; yo-yo.

(2) *fluctuation,* alternation 12 *correlation*; coming and going, shuttle service; ups and downs, boom and bust, ebb and flow 14 *contrariety*; roll, pitch, lurch, stagger, reel; shake, nod, wag, dance; swing, seesaw; rocking chair, rocking horse; shuttlecock, shuttle.

Adjective

(3) *oscillating,* swaying; vibratory, pulsatory, palpitating; earth-shaking, seismic; pendulous, dangling; reeling, groggy; rhythmic 141 *periodical.*

Verb

(4) *oscillate,* emit waves 417 *radiate*; wave, undulate; vibrate, pulsate, pulse, beat, drum; tick, throb, palpitate; pant, heave 352 *breathe*; play, sway, nod; swing, dangle 217 *hang*; seesaw, rock; hunt (trains), lurch, reel, stagger, totter, wobble; wiggle, waggle, wag; bob, bounce, dance 312 *leap*; toss, roll, pitch; rattle, shake; flutter, quiver 318 *be agitated*; flicker 417 *shine.*

(5) *fluctuate,* alternate 12 *correlate*; ebb and flow, come and go, shuttle; slosh about, slop a.

(6) *brandish,* wave, wag, waggle, shake, flourish; flutter 318 *agitate.*

Adverb

(7) *to and fro,* back and forth; in and out, up and down, from side to side.

318
Agitation: Irregular motion

Noun

(1) *agitation,* irregular motion, jerkiness, fits and starts, bumpiness, choppiness 259 *roughness*; flicker, twinkle 417 *flash*; sudden motion, start, jump; shake, jiggle; toss shock, jar, jolt, jerk, judder, bump 279 *impulse*; nudge, dig, jog 547 *gesture*; palpitation, flutter 317 *oscillation*; shudder, shiver, frisson; quiver, quaver, tremor; tremulousness, trembling; restlessness, feverishness, fever; tossing, turning; jiving, rock 'n roll 837 *dancing*; itchiness, itch, twitch, grimace; mental agitation, perturbation 825 *worry*; trepidation, jumpiness, twitter, flap, butterflies 854 *nervousness*; the shakes, shivers, jumps, jitters, fidgets; aspen leaf.

(2) *spasm,* ague, shivering, chattering; twitch, tic, nervous t.; cramp, throe 377 *pang*; convulsion, paroxysm, access, orgasm 503 *frenzy*; fit, epilepsy; pulse, throb 317 *oscillation*; attack, seizure, stroke.

(3) *commotion,* turbulence, tumult 61 *turmoil*; hurly-burly, hubbub, brouhaha; fever 503 *frenzy*; flurry, rush, bustle 680 *haste*; furore, fuss, bother, kerfuffle 678 *restlessness*; racket, din 400 *loudness*; stir, ferment 821 *excitation*; boiling, fermentation, effervescence 355 *bubble*; squall, tempest 176 *storm*;

whirlpool 315 *vortex*; whirlwind 352 *gale*; disturbance,
atmospherics.

Adjective
(4) *agitated,* shaking etc. vb.;
brandished; troubled, unquiet
678 *active*; feverish, fevered,
restless; scratchy, jittery,
jumpy, twitchy; flustered, in a
flutter 854 *nervous*; breathless,
panting; twitching, itchy; convulsive, spasmodic; doddering,
shaky, wavery, tremulous; vibrating 317 *oscillating*.

Verb
(5) *be agitated,* ripple, boil 355
bubble; stir, move, shake, tremble, quiver, shiver; have a fever, throw a fit; writhe,
squirm, twitch 251 *wriggle*;
toss, turn, toss about, thresh a.;
kick, plunge, rear 176 *be violent*; flounder, wallow 317 *fluctuate*; thrill, vibrate 317 *oscillate*; whirr, whirl 315 *rotate*; jig
around, jump about 312 *leap*;
flicker, gutter 417 *shine*; flutter, twitter, start, jump; throb,
pant, palpitate, miss a beat, go
pit-a-pat 821 *be excited*; bustle,
rush, mill around 61 *rampage*.

(6) *agitate,* disturb, rumple, ruffle 63 *derange*; discompose, perturb, worry 827 *trouble*; ripple,
puddle, muddy stir up 43 *mix*;
whisk, whip, beat, churn 315
rotate; shake up, shake; flourish 317 *brandish*; flutter, fly (a
flag); jog, joggle, jiggle, jolt,
nudge, dig; jerk, pluck, twitch.

(7) *effervesce,* froth, spume,
foam, bubble up; boil, seethe,
simmer, sizzle, spit 379 *be hot*;
ferment, work.

Adverb
(8) *jerkily,* spasmodically, in fits,
in spasms.

Class three

Material Universe

319
Materiality

Noun

(1) *materiality,* empirical world, world of nature; physical being, 1 *existence*; concreteness, tangibility, palpability; solidity 324 *density*; weight 322 *gravity*; embodiment, incarnation, reincarnation, realization, materialization; positivism, materialism; materialist, realist, positivist.

(2) *matter,* brute m., stuff; mass, material, fabric, body, frame 331 *structure*; substance, solid s.; organic matter, flesh and blood 358 *organism*; real world, world of nature, Nature.

(3) *object,* inanimate object, still life; body 371 *person*; thing, gadget, something, commodity, article, item; stocks and stones 359 *mineral*; raw material 631 *materials*.

(4) *element,* elementary unit 68 *origin*; the four elements, earth, air, fire, water; factor, ingredient 58 *component*; chemical element, basic substance; physical element, atom, isotope, nucleus, molecule; electron, neutron, proton, quark 196 *minuteness*.

(5) *physics,* physical science, natural s., science of matter; natural history 358 *biology*; chemistry, organic c., inorganic c., physical c.; mechanics, quantum m., atomic physics, nuclear physics 160 *nucleonics*; technology 694 *skill*; 490 *science*; chemist, physicist, scientist.

Adjective

(6) *material,* real, natural; solid, concrete, palpable, tangible, sensible, weighty; physical, objective 3 *substantial*; incarnate, corporal, somatic, corporeal, bodily, carnal; reincarnated, materialized; materialistic 944 *sensual*.

Verb

(7) *materialize,* substantiate, reify; realize, make real, body forth 223 *externalize*; embody, incarnate, personify.

320
Immateriality

Noun

(1) *immateriality,* incorporeity, intangibility, ghostliness, shadowiness; idealism, spirituality; animism; spiritualism 984 *occultism*; other world, eternity 115 *perpetuity*; animist, spiritualist, idealist.

(2) *subjectivity,* personality, myself, me, yours truly 80 *self*; ego, id, superego; Conscious, Unconscious; psyche 447 *spirit*.

Adjective

(3) *immaterial,* without mass; abstract 447 *mental*; disembodied; ghostly, shadowy 4 *insubstantial*; imponderable, intangible; unearthly, transcendent; psychic 984 *psychical*; spiritual, otherworldly 973 *religious*; personal, subjective; illusory 513 *imaginary*.

321
Universe

Noun
(1) *universe,* world, creation, sum of things 319 *matter;* cosmos, macrocosm, microcosm; outer space, deep s.; cosmology, cosmogony, big bang theory, steady state t. 68 *start.*

(2) *world,* wide w., earth, mother e., planet e., spaceship e.; globe, sphere, biosphere; crust 344 *land,* 343 *ocean;* atlas 551 *map;* Old World, New World 184 *region;* personal world 8 *circumstance.*

(3) *heavens,* sky, ether, firmament, vault of heaven; night sky.

(4) *star,* heavenly body, celestial b. 420 *luminary;* constellation, Great Bear, Plough, Southern Cross; giant, dwarf; radio star 417 *radiation;* quasar, pulsar, neutron star, black hole; nova, supernova; Pole Star, North Star, Milky Way; star cluster, galaxy; cosmic dust, nebula, spiral n.

(5) *zodiac,* signs of the z.; Aries (the Ram), Taurus (the Bull), Gemini (the Twins), Cancer (the Crab), Leo (the Lion), Virgo (the Virgin), Libra (the Balance), Scorpio (the Scorpion), Sagittarius (the Archer), Capricorn (the Goat), Aquarius (the Watercarrier), Pisces (the Fishes);

(6) *planet,* major p., minor p., asteroid; Mercury, Venus, Mars, Earth, Jupiter, Saturn, Uranus, Neptune, Pluto; comet; planetary orbit 315 *rotation.*

(7) *meteor,* falling star, shooting s., fireball, meteorite, meteoroid; meteor shower.

(8) *sun,* day-star, orb of day, eye of heaven; Phoebus, Apollo; sun spot, solar flare, corona; solar wind; solar system.

(9) *moon,* Phoebe, Diana; new moon, waxing moon, waning m., half-m., crescent m., horned m., full m., harvest m., hunter's m.; moonscape, crater; moonlight, moonshine.

(10) *satellite,* moon, moonlet; space station 276 *spaceship;* astronaut.

(11) *astronomy,* star lore, stargazing; radio astronomy, astrophysics; astrology 511 *divination;* observatory, planetarium; tracking station; telescope, radio t., dish; spectroscope 551 *photography;* astrophysicist, astronomer, radio a., stargazer, star-watcher; astrologer.

(12) *earth sciences,* geography, oceanography, geology; geographer, geologist.

Adjective
(13) *cosmic,* universal, cosmological, cosmogonic; interstellar, galactic, extragalactic 59 *extraneous.*

(14) *celestial,* heavenly, ethereal; starry, star-spangled; astral, stellar; solar, zodiacal; lunar, nebular; geocentric; planetary, cometary, meteoric; meteoritic.

(15) *telluric,* terrestrial; polar, equatorial; world, global, universal 183 *spacious;* worldly, earthly.

(16) *astronomic,* astronomical, astrophysical; stargazing, star-watching; astrological.

(17) *geographic,* geographical, oceanographic, geological.

Adverb
(18) *under the sun,* here below, on earth.

322
Gravity

Noun
(1) *gravity,* gravitation, force of gravity; weight, weightiness, heaviness, ponderousness 195 *bulk*; specific gravity; pressure, displacement, draught; encumbrance, load, burden; ballast, counterpoise; mass, lump 324 *solid body*; weight, bob, sinker.

(2) *weighing,* balancing, equipoise 28 *equalization*; weights, grain, carat, scruple, drachm; ounce, pound, hundredweight, ton; gram, kilogram, kilo; megaton; axle load, laden weight.

(3) *scales,* weighing machine; balance, spring b.; pan, scale weighbridge.

Adjective
(4) *weighty,* heavy, ponderous; leaden, heavy as lead; cumbersome 195 *unwieldy*; massive 324 *dense*; pressing, weighing; weighted, loaded, laden, charged, burdened; overloaded, top-heavy 29 *unequal*; gravitational.

Verb
(5) *weigh,* have weight, exert w.; tip the scales at; balance 28 *be equal*; counterpoise 31 *compensate*; sink, gravitate 309 *descend*; weigh heavy, lie h.; press, weigh on, weigh one down 311 *lower*; load, cumber 702 *hinder*.

(6) *make heavy,* weight, hang weights on; charge, burden 193 *load*; gain weight, put on w.

323
Lightness

Noun
(1) *lightness,* portability; thinness, air, ether 325 *rarity*: buoy-

ancy; volatility 338 *vaporization*; weightlessness 308 *ascent*; feather, thistledown; cork, buoy, balloon, bubble; hot air 310 *lifter*.

(2) *leaven,* raising agent; ferment, enzyme, barm, yeast, baking-powder.

Adjective
(3) *light,* underweight 307 *deficient*; lightweight, featherweight; portable, handy; light-footed; weightless, lighter than air; airy, gaseous 325 *rare*; yeasty, fermenting; aerated, frothy, foamy, whipped; floating, buoyed up, buoyant; feathery, gossamery, light as a feather.

Verb
(4) *be light,* buoyant etc. adj.; defy gravity, levitate, surface, float, swim; drift, waft, glide, be airborne 271 *fly*; soar, hover 308 *ascend.*

(5) *lighten,* make light, make lighter, reduce weight, lose w.; ease 701 *disencumber*; lighten ship, jettison; gasify, vaporize 340 *aerate*; leaven, raise 310 *elevate.*

324
Density

Noun
(1) *density,* solidity, consistency; compactness, solidness, concreteness, thickness; coalescence 48 *coherence*; relative density, specific gravity.

(2) *condensation,* concentration; constipation; concretion 326 *hardness*; coagulation, thrombosis; solidification congealment 354 *thickening.*

(3) *solid body,* solid; block, mass 319 *matter*; knot, nugget, lump; nucleus, hard core; aggregate, conglomerate, concretion;

stone, crystal 344 *rock*; precipitate, deposit, sediment, silt; cake, clod, clump; gristle, cartilage 329 *toughness*; curd, clot; phalanx, serried ranks; forest, thicket; wall.

Adjective
(4) *dense,* thick; close, heavy, stuffy (air); lumpy, ropy, clotted, curdled; caked, matted 48 *cohesive*; firm, close-textured; knotty, gnarled; massive 322 *weighty*; concrete, solid, frozen, crystallized; condensed, compact, close-packed 54 *full*; thickset, thick-growing, bushy, luxuriant; serried, densely arrayed; inelastic 326 *rigid*; impenetrable, impermeable, impervious

(5) *solidifying,* binding, constipating; freezing, congealing; styptic, astringent.

Verb
(6) *be dense,* become solid, solidify, consolidate 48 *cohere*; condense, thicken; precipitate, deposit; freeze 380 *be cold*; set, gelatinize, jell; congeal, coagulate, clot, curdle; cake, crust; crystallize 326 *harden*; compact, compress, firm down, squeeze 198 *make smaller*; squeeze in, ram down 193 *load*; mass, crowd; bind, constipate; precipitate, deposit.

325
Rarity

Noun
(1) *rarity,* low pressure, vacuum, near v. 190 *emptiness*; sponginess 327 *softness*; tenuity, fineness 206 *thinness*; lack of substance 323 *lightness*; airiness, windiness 336 *gaseousness*, 340 *air*; expansion, attenuation.

Adjective
(2) *rare,* tenuous, thin, fine 4 *insubstantial*; low-pressure;

compressible, spongy 328 *elastic*; rarefied, aerated 336 *gaseous*; hollow 190 *empty*.

Verb
(3) *rarefy,* reduce the pressure; expand, dilate; make a vacuum; attenuate, refine, thin; dilute 163 *weaken*; gasify 338 *vaporize.*

326
Hardness

Noun
(1) *hardness,* resistance 329 *toughness*; stiffness, rigidity, firmness, inflexibility; inelasticity; flint, granite, marble 344 *rock*; steel, iron; cement, concrete, reinforced c.; block, board, teak, oak 366 *wood*; bone, horn, ivory; crust, shell; callus, corn; hard core.

(2) *hardening,* toughening, stiffening, backing; starching; steeling, tempering; vulcanization; petrifaction, fossilization; crystallization, vitrification; ossification; sclerosis.

Adjective
(3) *hard,* steeled, proof 162 *strong*; iron, cast-i.; steel, steely; rock-hard; stony, rocky, flinty; crystalline, vitreous, glassy; horny, calloused; bony, gristly 329 *tough*; hardened, tempered; fossilized, frozen.

(4) *rigid,* stubborn, resistant, intractable, firm, inflexible, inelastic, stiff 162 *unyielding*; starchy, starched; boned, reinforced; braced, tense, taut, tight; set, solid; crisp 330 *brittle.*

Verb
(5) *harden,* steel 162 *strengthen*; temper, vulcanize, toughen; crisp, bake 381 *heat*; petrify, fossilize, ossify; calcify, vitrify, crystallize, freeze; stiffen, back, bone, starch.

327
Softness

Noun
(1) *softness,* pliancy, pliability, flexibility, plasticity, ductility, tractability; malleability, adaptability; suppleness, litheness; springiness,, suspension 328 *elasticity;* sponginess 356 *pulpiness;* flaccidity, flabbiness, floppiness; sogginess 354 *semiliquidity;* butter, wax, putty, paste, clay, dough; cushion, pillow, feather bed; velvet, down, fluff, fleece 259 *hair.*

Adjective
(2) *soft,* not tough, tender; melting 335 *fluid;* yielding, springy compressible; pillowed, padded, podgy; impressible, waxy, doughy, spongy; soggy, mushy, squashy 356 *pulpy;* fleecy 259 *downy;* mossy, velvety 258 *smooth;* limp, flaccid, flabby, floppy; softening, emollient.

(3) *flexible,* whippy, pliant, pliable; ductile, malleable, tractable, plastic, thermoplastic; stretchable 328 *elastic;* lithe, willowy, supple, lissom, acrobatic, athletic; loose-limbed, double-jointed.

Verb
(4) *soften,* render soft, tenderize; knead, massage, mash, pulp, squash 332 *pulverize;* melt, thaw 337 *liquefy;* cushion, pillow; yield, give, bend 328 *be elastic.*

328
Elasticity

Noun
(1) *elasticity,* give, stretch; spring, springiness; suspension; resilience, bounce, buoyancy; rubber, elastic; chewing gum.

Adjective
(2) *elastic,* stretchy, stretchable, tensile; rubbery, springy, bouncy, resilient, buoyant; sprung, well-s.

Verb
(3) *be elastic* - tensile etc. adj.; bounce, spring, spring back 280 *recoil;* stretch, give.

329
Toughness

Noun
(1) *toughness,* durability, tenacity 162 *strength;* indigestibility; leather, gristle, cartilage 326 *hardness.*

Adjective
(2) *tough,* durable, resisting; shockproof, shatter-proof; vulcanized, toughened 162 *strong;* sinewy, woody, stringy, fibrous; gristly, cartilaginous; rubbery, leathery, indigestible, inedible; inelastic, unyielding 326 *rigid.*

Verb
(3) *be tough,* - durable etc. adj.; toughen, tan, vulcanize, temper, anneal 162 *strengthen.*

330
Brittleness

Noun
(1) *brittleness,* crispness, friability, crumbliness, fissility; fragility, flimsiness 163 *weakness;* eggshell, matchwood; window, glass; porcelain 381 *pottery;* house of cards 163 *weak thing.*

Adjective
(2) *brittle,* breakable, inelastic 326 *rigid;* papery, like parchment; shivery, splintery; friable, crumbly 332 *powdery;* crisp, crispy, short, flaky, fissile 46 *severable;* fragile, frail, delicate, flimsy 163 *weak;* gimcrack, jerry-built 4 *insubstantial;* about to burst.

Verb
(3) *be brittle,* - fragile etc. adj.; fracture 46 *break*; crack, snap; chip, split, shatter, shiver, fragment; splinter, break off, snap off; burst, explode; fall to pieces crumble, 309 *tumble*; wear thin.

Interjection
(4) *fragile!* with care!

331
Structure. Texture

Noun
(1) *structure,* organization, pattern, plan; complex, syndrome 52 *whole*; mould, shape, build 243 *form*; constitution, make-up, set-up 56 *composition*; construction, architecture, works, workings; fabric 631 *materials*; substructure, superstructure skeleton, framework, chassis, shell 218 *frame*; physique, anatomy 358 *organism*; physiology, histology 358 *biology*.

(2) *texture,* tissue, fabric, stuff 222 *textile*; staple, denier 208 *fibre*; weave, 222 *weaving*; nap, pile 259 *hair*; granulation, grain; surface 223 *exteriority*; feel 378 *touch*.

Adjective
(3) *structural,* organic; skeletal; anatomical; architectural.

(4) *textural,* textile, woven 222 *crossed*; grained, granular; fine-grained 258 *smooth*; coarse-grained 259 *rough*; fine, fine-spun, delicate, gossamery, filmy; coarse, homespun, tweedy 259 *hairy*.

332
Powderiness

Noun
(1) *powderiness,* crumbliness 330 *brittleness*; dustiness 649 *dirt*; sandiness, grittiness, granulation; friability 330 *brittleness*; pulverization, attrition, erosion 51 *decomposition*; grinding, milling; abrasion 333 *friction*; fragmentation 46 *disunion*; dusting, powdering, frosting.

(2) *powder,* pollen, spore; dust, soot, smut, ash; flour, meal; sawdust, filings; sand, grit, gravel, shingle; grain, flake 53 *piece*; granule 33 *small thing*.

(3) *pulverizer,* miller, grinder; mill, millstone, pestle and mortar; grater, file; molar 256 *tooth*; bulldozer 279 *ram*.

Adjective
(4) *powdery,* chalky, dusty, smoky 649 *dirty*; sandy 342 *dry*; floury, mealy, flaky, granulated, granular; gritty, gravelly; grated, milled, ground, sifted, sieved; crumbly, friable.

Verb
(5) *pulverize,* reduce to powder, granulate; crush, mash, smash 46 *break*; grind, mill, mince, beat, pound; knead; crumble, crumb, rub in (pastry); crunch, scrunch 301 *chew*; chip, flake, grate, scrape, file 333 *rub*; weather, wear down, erode.

333
Friction

Noun
(1) *friction,* rubbing etc. vb.; drag 278 *slowness*; attrition, rubbing against rubbing out, erasure 550 *obliteration*; abrasion, scraping, filing; wearing away, erosion 165 *destruction*; scrape, graze, scratch; brushing, rub; polish, elbow grease; shampoo, massage; pumice stone; eraser, rubber, whetstone 256 *sharpener*; masseur, masseuse 843 *beautician*.

Adjective
(2) *rubbing,* frictional, abrasive.

Verb
(3) *rub,* rub against, strike (a match); gnash, grind; fray, chafe, gall; graze, scratch, bark 655 *wound*; rub off, abrade; skin, flay; scuff, scrape, scrub, scour, burnish; brush, rub down, towel, currycomb 648 *clean*; polish, buff 258 *smooth*; rub out 550 *obliterate*; gnaw, erode, wear away 165 *consume*; rasp, file, grind 332 *pulverize*; knead, shampoo, massage; rub in; anoint 334 *lubricate*; wax, chalk (one's cue); grate, catch, stick, snag; rub gently, stroke 889 *caress*.

334
Lubrication

Noun
(1) *lubrication,* greasing; anointment.

(2) *lubricant,* glycerine, wax, grease, axle g. 357 *oil*; soap, lather 648 *cleanser*; saliva, spit, spittle; ointment, salve 658 *balm*; emollient 357 *unguent*; lubricator, oil-can, grease-gun.

Adjective
(3) *lubricated,* well-oiled; not rusty; smooth-running, silent.

Verb
(4) *lubricate,* oil, grease, wax, soap, lather; butter 357 *grease*; anoint, pour balm.

335
Fluidity

Noun
(1) *fluidity,* fluidness, liquidity, liquidness; wateriness 339 *water*; juiciness 356 *pulpiness*; solubleness 337 *liquefaction*; viscosity 354 *semiliquidity*; hydraulics, fluid mechanics.

(2) *fluid,* liquid 339 *water*; drink 301 *draught*; milk, whey; juice,

sap, latex; rheum, mucus, saliva 302 *excrement*; serum, lymph, plasma; pus, matter.

(3) *blood,* gore; lifeblood 360 *life*; bloodstream, circulation; red blood 162 *vitality*; blue blood 868 *nobility*; clot, blood c.; corpuscle, red c., white c., haemoglobin; blood group, Rhesus factor; haemophilia, blood count;

Adjective
(4) *fluid* 244 *amorphous*; liquid, not solid, not gaseous; in suspension; uncongealed clear, clarified; soluble, liquescent, melting; viscous 354 *viscid*; fluent, running 350 *flowing*; runny, rheumy, phlegmy 339 *watery*; succulent, juicy, sappy, squashy; suppurating 653 *toxic*.

(5) *sanguineous,* lymphatic, plasmatic; bloody, sanguinary 431 *bloodstained*; gory, bleeding; haemophilic.

336
Gaseousness

Noun
(1) *gaseousness,* vapourousness; windiness, flatulence; aeration, gasification; volatility 338 *vaporization*; aerodynamics 340 *pneumatics*.

(2) *gas,* vapour, elastic fluid; ether 340 *air*; exhalation, miasma 298 *egress*; fumes, reek, smoke; steam, water vapour 355 *cloud*; methane 385 *fuel*; marsh gas 659 *poison*; gasworks, gas plant; gasholder 632 *storage*; gaslight, neon light 420 *lamp*.

Adjective
(3) *gaseous,* vaporous 340 *airy*; carbonated, effervescent 355 *bubbly*; gassy, windy, flatulent; miasmic 659 *baneful*; pneumatic, aerodynamic.

Verb
(4) *gasify,* vapour, steam, emit

vapour 338 *vaporize*; let off steam, blow off s. 300 *emit*; aerate, oxygenate carbonate.

337
Liquefaction

Noun
(1) *liquefaction,* liquidization; solubility, deliquescence 335 *fluidity*; fusion 43 *mixture*; melting 381 *heating*; solvent, flux; liquefier, liquidizer.

(2) *solution,* decoction, infusion; suspension; flux, lye.

Adjective
(3) *liquefied,* molten; runny, liquescent, deliquescent; solvent; soluble, dissoluble, liquefiable 335 *fluid*; in suspension.

Verb
(4) *liquefy,* liquidize, render liquid; dissolve, deliquesce, run 350 *flow*; thaw, melt, smelt 381 *heat*; render, clarify; leach, hold in solution.

338
Vaporization

Noun
(1) *vaporization,* gasification; exhalation 355 *cloud*; evaporation, distillation; steaming, fumigation; volatility; atomization.

(2) *vaporizer,* atomizer, spray, aerosol; retort, still, distillery,

Adjective
(3) *vaporific,* vaporous, steamy, gassy, smoky, reeking; vaporizable, volatile.

Verb
(4) *vaporize,* evaporate; render gaseous 336 *gasify*; distil, sublimate; exhale, transpire 300 *emit*; smoke, fume, reek, steam; fumigate, spray; make a spray, atomize.

339
Water

Noun
(1) *water,* H_2O; heavy water; D_2O; hard water, soft w.; drinking water, tap w.; mineral w., soda w. 301 *soft drink*; water vapour, steam 355 *cloud*; rain water 350 *rain*; running water, fresh w. 350 *stream*; holy water 988 *ritual object*; weeping, tears 836 *lamentation*; sweat, saliva 335 *fluid*; high water, low w. 350 *wave*; standing water 346 *lake*; sea water, salt w., brine 343 *ocean*; water cure, taking the waters 658 *therapy*; bath water 648 *ablutions*; lotion, lavender water 843 *cosmetic*; adulteration, dilution 655 *impairment*; wateriness, damp, wet; watering 341 *moistening*; tap 351 *conduit*; hose 341 *irrigator*; water supply, waterworks; well, borehole 632 *store*.

Adjective
(2) *watery,* aqueous, aquatic; lymphatic 335 *fluid*; hydro-, hydrated; diluted 163 *weak*; still, fizzy, effervescent; wet, moist 341 *humid*.

Verb
(3) *add water,* water, water down, dilute 163 *weaken*; steep, soak, irrigate, drench 341 *moisten*; hydrate; slake.

340
Air

Noun
(1) *air,* oxygen, nitrogen, argon 336 *gas*; thin air, ether 325 *rarity*; cushion of air, air pocket 190 *emptiness*; blast 352 *wind*; open air, fresh a., exposure; sea air, ozone; airing 342 *desiccation*; aeration 338 *vaporization*; air-conditioning 352

ventilation; ventilator, blower, fan; air-filter, humidifier.

(2) *atmosphere,* stratosphere, ionosphere; ozone layer; aerospace; greenhouse effect.

(3) *weather,* the elements; fair weather, fine w., dry spell, heat wave 379 *heat*; anticyclone, high pressure; cyclone, depression, low pressure; rough weather 176 *storm,* 352 *gale*; bad weather, foul w. 350 *rain*; cold weather 380 *wintriness*; meteorology, weather forecast; isobar, millibar; glass, mercury, barometer; weathervane, weathercock; weather ship, weather station, rain gauge; weatherman *or* - woman, meteorologist; clime, climate, climatology.

(4) *pneumatics,* aerodynamics, barometry 352 *anemometry*; barometer, barograph.

Adjective
(5) *airy,* ethereal 4 *insubstantial*; aerial; pneumatic, containing air, aerated, oxygenated; inflated, blown up 197 *expanded*; flatulent 336 *gaseous*; breezy 352 *windy*; well-ventilated fresh, 382 *cooled*; weather-wise; atmospheric, barometric; cyclonic, anticyclonic; climatic.

Verb
(6) *aerate,* oxygenate; air, expose 342 *dry*; ventilate, freshen 648 *clean*; fan, winnow, make a draught 352 *blow*; take the air 352 *breathe*.

Adverb
(7) *alfresco,* out of doors, in the open.

341
Moisture

Noun
(1) *moisture,* humidity, sap, juice 335 *fluid*; dampness, wetness, moistness, dewiness; dew point; dankness, condensation, rising damp; sogginess, marshiness; saturation point 54 *plenitude*; rainfall 350 *rain*; damp, wet; spray, froth, foam 355 *bubble*; mist, fog 355 *cloud*; drizzle, drip, dew, drop, teardrop, tears; saliva, slobber, spittle 302 *excrement*; ooze, slime 347 *marsh*.

(2) *moistening,* damping, wetting etc. vb.; saturation, deluge 350 *rain*; sprinkle, aspersion, baptism; ducking, submersion 303 *immersion*; overflow, flood 350 *waterfall*; wash, bath 648 *ablutions*; infiltration, percolation, leaching; irrigation.

(3) *irrigator,* sprinkler, watering can; spray, hose, syringe; pump, fire engine; dam, reservoir 632 *store*; sluice 351 *conduit*.

Adjective
(4) *humid,* moistened, wet 339 *watery*; drizzling 350 *rainy*; damp, moist, dripping; dank, muggy, foggy, misty 355 *cloudy*; steaming, reeking; oozy, muddy 347 *marshy*; dewy, fresh, juicy 335 *fluid*; seeping, percolating; wetted, sprinkled, dabbled.

(5) *drenched,* saturated; watered, irrigated; soaking, sopping, streaming, soggy, sodden, soaked; wet through, wringing wet, dripping w., sopping wet; waterlogged, awash, swamped, drowned.

Verb
(6) *be wet,* - moist etc. adj.; squelch, suck; slobber, salivate, sweat 298 *exude*; steam, reek

300 *emit*; percolate, seep 297 *infiltrate*; weep, bleed, stream; ooze, drip, leak 298 *flow out*; drizzle, pour 350 *rain*; get wet, dive 313 *plunge*; bathe, wash; wallow; paddle, wade, ford.

(7) *moisten,* humidify, wet, dampen; dilute 339 *add water*; lick, lap, wash; splash, splatter; spill, slop; spray, shower, spatter, bespatter, dabble, sprinkle, syringe.

(8) *drench,* saturate, soak, deluge, wet through; wash, bathe; hose down, sluice 648 *clean*; plunge, dip, duck, submerge 303 *immerse*; swamp, flood, inundate; irrigate, water; dunk, douse, souse, steep; macerate, marinate 666 *preserve*.

342
Dryness

Noun
(1) *dryness,* aridity; need for water, thirst 859 *hunger*; drought, low rainfall; sands 172 *desert*; dry climate, dry season.

(2) *desiccation,* drying, drying up; evaporation 338 *vaporization*; draining, drainage; dehydration; sunning 381 *heating*; bleaching, fading, withering.

(3) *dryer,* spin d., tumble d.; absorbent, blotting paper, blotter; mop, swab, sponge, towel; wringer, mangle.

Adjective
(4) *dry,* thirsty 859 *hungry*; arid, waterless, unirrigated; sandy, dusty 332 *powdery*; bare, desert, rainless; dehydrated, desiccated; shrivelled, withered, dried up, mummified; sunned, aired; sun-dried, wind-d., bleached; baked, parched 379 *hot*; free from rain, sunny, fine, cloudless, fair; dried out, drained, evaporated; waterproof, rainproof, watertight.

Verb
(5) *be dry,* - and etc. adj.; keep dry; dry up, evaporate; dry off, dry out.

(6) *dry,* desiccate, freeze-dry; dehydrate; drain, pump out 300 *empty*; wring out, mangle; spin-dry, tumble-d., drip-d.; hang out, air; sun, sun-dry; smoke, kipper, cure; parch, bake 381 *heat*; shrivel, bleach; mummify 666 *preserve*; stop the flow 350 *staunch*; blot, mop, sponge 299 *absorb*; swab, wipe.

343
Ocean

Noun
(1) *ocean,* sea, salt water, brine, briny; waters, billows, tide 350 *wave*; main, deep, deep sea; high seas sea lane, shipping lane; ocean floor, sea bed; the seven seas; oceanography, oceanographer; Neptune, Poseidon. 970 *mythical*.

(2) *sea nymph,* siren, mermaid 970 *fairy*.

Adjective
(3) *oceanic,* sea, marine, maritime; ocean-going, sea-g. 269 *seafaring*; submarine, underwater; 211 *deep*.

Adverb
(4) *at sea,* on the high seas, afloat.

344
Land

Noun
(1) *land,* dry l., terra firma; earth, ground, crust, earth's c.; continent, mainland; hinterland; midland, inland, interior; delta, promontory, peninsula; neck of land, isthmus; terrain 209 *high land,* 210 *lowness*; reclaimed land, polder; steppe 348 *plain*; wilderness 172 *desert*; isle 349 *island*; zone,

clime; country, district, tract 184 *region*; territory, estate 777 *lands*; landscape, scenery; topography, geography, geology 321 *earth sciences.*

(2) *shore,* coastline, coast 234 *edge*; strand, beach sands, shingle; seaboard, seashore, seaside; bank, river bank, riverside.

(3) *soil,* arable land 370 *farm*; pasture 348 *grassland*; deposit, moraine, silt, alluvium; topsoil, subsoil; humus, loam, clay, marl; stone, pebble, flint; turf, sod, clod.

(4) *rock, stack,* cliff, crag; stone, boulder; granite, basalt; magma, lava; sandstone, limestone, chalk; ore 359 *mineralogy*; precious stone 844 *gem.*

Adjective
(5) *territorial,* earthy; farming, agricultural 370 *agrarian*; alluvial, silty, sandy, loamy; clayey, marly; chalky; flinty, pebbly, gravelly, stony, rocky; granitic, slaty, shaly; geological, morphological.

(6) *coastal,* riparian, riverside; seaside; shore, on-shore.

(7) *inland,* continental, midland, mainland.

Adverb
(8) *on land,* overland; ashore, on shore.

345
Gulf: Inlet

Noun
(1) *gulf,* bay, bight; cove, creek, reach, lagoon; inlet, outlet, fjord, mouth, estuary; firth, sound, strait, belt, channel.

346
Lake

Noun
(1) *lake,* lagoon, loch, lough, fresh-water lake, Dead Sea; broad, sheet of water; pool, tarn, mere, pond, millpond, fishpond, dewpond, artificial lake, reservoir 632 *storage*; ditch 351 *drain*; puddle, splash, wallow, waterhole.

Adjective
(2) *lacustrine,* lake-dwelling, land-locked.

347
Marsh

Noun
(1) *marsh,* marshland, wetlands; washlands, mud flat, salt marsh; fen, moor; moss, bog, quagmire, quicksand; slough, mire, mud, ooze; swamp.

Adjective
(2) *marshy,* swampy, boggy; squashy, squelchy, spongy 327 *soft*, 354 *semiliquid*; slushy muddy, miry; waterlogged 341 *drenched.*

348
Plain

Noun
(1) *plain,* flood plain, levels; river basin, lowlands 255 *valley*; flats 347 *marsh*; delta, alluvial plain; tundra, ice field; grasslands, steppe, prairie, pampas, savanna; heath, wold, downs, moor, fell; plateau, tableland 209 *high land*; bush, veld, range, open country 183 *space.*

(2) *grassland,* pasture, pasturage, grazing 369 *animal husbandry*; field, meadow, lea; chase, park; green, greensward, lawn, turf.

Adjective
(3) *campestral,* rural; flat, open, rolling.

349
Island

Noun
(1) *island,* isle, islet, eyot, holm; atoll, reef, coral r.; sandbank, bar; iceberg; archipelago; islander.

Adjective
(2) *insular,* sea-girt; islanded, isolated; archipelagic.

350
Stream: Water in motion

Noun
(1) *stream,* running water, watercourse, river, waterway; tributary, branch, feeder; rivulet, brook, bourne, burn, rill, beck, gill; freshet, torrent, force; spring, fountain; jet, spout, gush; geyser, hot spring, well.

(2) *current,* flow, flux; confluence; inflow 297 *ingress;* outflow 286 *regression;* undercurrent, undertow, crosscurrent, rip tide; tide, spring t., neap t.; ebb and flow 317 *fluctuation;* tideway, bore, race, millrace; hydrant 351 *conduit.*

(3) *eddy,* swirl, whirlpool 315 *vortex;* surge, wash, backwash.

(4) *waterfall,* falls, cataract, cascade, rapids, weir; flush, chute, spillway, sluice; overflow, spill; flood, flash f., spate, deluge 298 *outflow.*

(5) *wave,* bow w.; wash, backwash; ripple, cat's-paw; swell, ground s.; billow, roller, comber, breaker; surf, spume, white horses; tidal wave, bore, rip.

(6) *rain,* rainfall 341 *moisture;* precipitation, drizzle; sleet 380 *wintriness;* shower, downpour, deluge, cloudburst, thunderstorm 176 *storm;* flurry 352 *gale;* pouring rain, teeming r., driving r., torrential r.; wet spell, rainy season, the rains, monsoon; plash, patter; rainmaking, cloud-seeding.

Adjective
(7) *flowing,* falling etc. vb.; runny 335 *fluid;* fluvial, tidal; streaming, in flood, in spate; flooding, cataclysmic; choppy 259 *rough;* winding, meandering; sluggish 278 *slow;* pouring, sheeting, lashing, driving.

(8) *rainy,* showery, drizzly; spitting, spotting; wet 341 *humid.*

Verb
(9) *flow,* run, course, pour; ebb; swirl, eddy 315 *rotate;* surge, break, dash ripple, roll, swell; gush, rush, spirt, spout, spew, jet, play, squirt, splutter; well up, bubble up 298 *emerge;* pour, stream; trickle, dribble 298 *exude;* drip, drop 309 *descend;* slosh, splash 341 *moisten;* flow softly, babble, bubble, gurgle, glide, slide; overflow, cascade, flood 341 *drench;* flow into, drain i., spill i. 297 *enter;* run off, discharge itself 298 *flow out;* leak, ooze, percolate 305 *pass;* wind 251 *meander.*

(10) *rain,* shower, stream, pour, pelt; snow, sleet, hail; fall, come down, bucket down, rain hard, pour with rain, rain in torrents; patter, drizzle, drip, drop; be wet, rain and rain, set in.

(11) *make flow* 300 *emit;* broach, tap 263 *open;* decant, pour out, spill 311 *let fall;* pump out 300 *empty;* water, irrigate; melt 337 *liquefy.*

(12) *staunch,* stop the flow, stem the course of 342 *dry;* stop a leak, plug 264 *close;* stem, dam up 702 *obstruct.*

351
Conduit

Noun

(1) *conduit,* water channel, riverbed, tideway; ravine, gully 255 *valley*; inland waterways, canal system; canal, channel, watercourse; ditch, dike; trench, moat, runnel, gutter, mill race; duct, aqueduct; plumbing, water pipe, water main; pipe, hose; standpipe, hydrant, siphon, tap, spout 263 *tube*; valve, flume, sluice, weir, lock, floodgate, spillway; chute 350 *waterfall*; pipeline 272 *transferrer*; blood vessel, vein, artery, veinlet, capillary.

(2) *drain,* gully, gutter, gargoyle, waterspout; scupper, overflow, drainpipe 298 *outlet*; covered drain, culvert; open drain, ditch; sewer 649 *sink*; intestine, colon, catheter.

352
Wind: Air in motion

Noun

(1) *wind* 340 *air*; draught, thermal; breeziness, windiness etc. adj.; storminess weather; blast, blow (see *breeze, gale*); air stream, current, air c., crosswind, headwind; following wind, tailwind; air flow, slip stream; windlessness; cold wind, raw w., icy blast; prevailing wind, trade w., westerly.

(2) *anemometry,* aerodynamics 340 *pneumatics*; wind rose; anemometer, wind gauge; windsock, weathercock.

(3) *breeze,* zephyr; breath of air, waft, whiff, puff, gust; light breeze, gentle b., fresh b., stiff b.

(4) *gale,* strong wind, high w.; blow, blast, gust, flurry, squall;

sou'wester; hurricane, whirlwind, cyclone, tornado, twister, typhoon; thunderstorm, dust storm, blizzard; dirty weather, ugly w., stormy w.

(5) *blowing,* inflation, blowing up, pumping up; pump, bellows, windbag; bagpipe; woodwind, brass; blowpipe.

(6) *ventilation,* airing 340 *air*; draught; fanning, cooling; ventilator 353 *air pipe*; blower, fan.

(7) *respiration,* breathing, inhalation, exhalation; stomach wind, windiness, flatulence, belch; gills, lungs; respirator, windpipe 353 *air pipe*; sneezing, coughing, cough; sigh, sob, gulp; hiccup, yawn; panting, wheeze, rattle, death r.

Adjective

(8) *windy,* airy, exposed, draughty, breezy, blowy; ventilated, fresh; blowing, gusty, squally; blustery, stormy, tempestuous; windswept, storm-tossed; fizzy, gassy 336 *gaseous*; gale-force, hurricane-f.

(9) *puffing,* snorting, wheezing; wheezy, asthmatic; panting, heaving; sniffling, snuffly, sneezy; coughing, chesty.

Verb

(10) *blow,* puff, blast; freshen, blow up, get up, blow hard, rage, storm; wail, howl, roar; scream, whistle 407 *shrill*; hum, moan, sough, sigh 401 *sound faint*; wave, flap, flutter 318 *agitate*; draw, make a draught, ventilate, fan; blow along, waft 287 *propel*; veer, back, die down, drop, abate.

(11) *breathe,* respire, breathe in, inhale, fill one's lungs; breathe out, exhale; aspirate, puff, huff, whiff; sniff, sniffle, snuffle, snort; breathe hard, breathe heavily, gasp, pant, heave; wheeze, sneeze, cough; sigh,

sob, catch one's breath, hiccup, yawn; belch, burp.

(12) *blow up*, pump up, inflate, dilate 197 *enlarge*; pump out 300 *empty*.

353
Air pipe

Noun
(1) *air pipe*, airway, air-passage, air shaft; wind tunnel; blowpipe, peashooter 287 *propellant*; windpipe, larynx; throat, gullet; nose, nostril, blowhole, nozzle, vent, mouthpiece 263 *orifice*; pipe 388 *tobacco*; funnel, flue, exhaust pipe 263 *chimney*; air duct, ventilator, grating, louvre, air hole 263 *window*.

354
Semiliquidity

Noun
(1) *semiliquidity*, viscidity; thickness, stodginess; colloid, emulsion; pus, mucus, mucilage, phlegm, clot; juice, sap 335 *fluidity*; cream, curds 356 *pulpiness*; oil slick; mud, slush, sludge, ooze, slime 347 *marsh*.

(2) *thickening*, coagulation, clotting 324 *condensation*; thickener, starch, gelatine.

(3) *viscidity*, viscosity, glutinousness, stickiness, adhesiveness 48 *coherence*; glue, gum 47 *adhesive*; paste, glaze, slip; gel, jelly; treacle, syrup, honey, goo; wax 357 *resin*.

Adjective
(4) *semiliquid*, stodgy, starchy, thick, lumpy, ropy 324 *dense*; curdled, clotted, coagulated, gelatinous, pulpy, sappy, milky, creamy, emulsive; thawing, half-melted, mushy, slushy; squashy, squidgy, squelchy 347 *marshy*.

(5) *viscid*, viscous, gummy, gooey 48 *cohesive*; slimy, clammy, sticky, tacky; treacly, syrupy, gluey; mucilaginous.

Verb
(6) *thicken*, congeal 324 *be dense*; coagulate 48 *cohere*; emulsify; gelatinize, jelly, jell; starch; curdle, clot; whip up, beat up; mash, pulp 332 *pulverize*.

355
Bubble. Cloud: Air and water mixed

Noun
(1) *bubble*, bubbles, suds, lather, foam, froth; head, top; sea foam, spume, surf, spray; candyfloss, mousse, souffle; bubbling, boiling, effervescence; fermentation, yeastiness, fizz.

(2) *cloud*, cloudlet, scud, rack; cloudbank, cloudscape; rain cloud, storm c.; cumulus, cirrus, mackerel sky vapour, steam 338 *vaporization*; haze, mist, fog; cloudiness.

Adjective
(3) *bubbly*, effervescent, fizzy, sparkling 336 *gaseous*; foaming, foamy; frothy, soapy, lathery; yeasty, aerated.

(4) *cloudy*, clouded, overcast, overclouded; nebulous; foggy, hazy, misty 419 *dim*.

Verb
(5) *bubble*, spume, foam, froth, form a head; boil, simmer, fizzle 318 *effervesce*; work, ferment, fizz, sparkle; aerate, carbonate; steam.

(6) *cloud*, cloud over, become overcast, cloudy etc. adj.; fog over, mist up.

356
Pulpiness

Noun
(1) *pulpiness,* sponginess; fleshiness 327 *softness*; poultice, pulp, pith, paste, putty, puree, mush; dough, batter, sponge; soft fruit, stewed f.; papier mâché, wood pulp; pulping, mastication.

Adjective
(2) *pulpy,* pulped, mashed, crushed, pureed 354 *semiliquid*; mushy 327 *soft*; succulent, juicy, sappy, squashy; doughy, flabby 195 *fleshy*; soggy, spongy 347 *marshy*.

357
Unctuousness

Noun
(1) *unctuousness,* oiliness, greasiness 334 *lubrication*; anointment, unction.

(2) *oil,* volatile o., essential o.; cod-liver o.; vegetable oil; mineral oil, petroleum 385 *fuel*; lubricating oil 334 *lubricant*.

(3) *fat,* animal f., grease, blubber, tallow, spermaceti; wax, beeswax; suet, lard, dripping 301 *cookery*; glycerine, margarine, butter, ghee; soap.

(4) *unguent,* salve, unction, ointment, liniment, embrocation; lanolin, cream 843 *cosmetic*.

(5) *resin,* rosin, gum, camphor, amber, ambergris; pitch, tar, bitumen, asphalt; varnish, mastic, shellac, lacquer; polyurethane, plastics.

Adjective
(6) *fatty,* fat, blubbery 195 *fleshy*; sebaceous, waxy, waxen; soapy; buttery, creamy, rich 390 *savoury*.

(7) *unctuous,* greasy, oily, oleaginous; anointed, basted; slippery, greased, oiled 334 *lubricated*.

(8) *resinous,* gummy, tarry 354 *viscid*.

Verb
(9) *grease,* oil, anoint 334 *lubricate*; baste; butter.

358
Organisms: Living matter

Noun
(1) *organism,* organic matter, animate m.; flora and fauna, living matter 360 *life*; microscopic life 196 *microorganism*; cell, protoplasm, cytoplasm, nucleus, nucleic acid, RNA, DNA; chromosome, gene 5 *heredity*; albumen, protein; enzyme, globulin; organic remains 125 *fossil*.

(2) *biology,* microbiology; natural history, nature study; biotechnology; biochemistry, cytology, histology; morphology, anatomy, physiology 367 *zoology,* 368 *botany*; ecology; genetics, evolution, natural selection; naturalist, biologist, zoologist, ecologist.

Adjective
(3) *organic,* organized; cellular, protoplasmic, cytoplasmic.

(4) *biological,* physiological, zoological.

359
Mineral: Inorganic matter

Noun
(1) *mineral,* mineral world, mineral kingdom; inorganic matter, earth's crust 344 *rock*; mineral deposit, ore, metal, noble m., precious m., base m.; alloy

43 *a mixture*; coal measures 632 *store*.

(2) *mineralogy*, geology, petrology, metallurgy.

Adjective
(3) *inorganic*, inanimate; mineral, mineralogical, petrological; metallurgical, metallic.

360
Life

Noun
(1) *life*, living, being alive 1 *existence*; the living, living being; plant life 366 *vegetable life*; animal life 365 *animality*; human life 371 *humankind*; gift of life, birth, nativity 68 *origin*; vitalization, animation; vitality, life force; soul 447 *spirit*; beating heart, strong pulse; animal spirits, liveliness, animation; breathing 352 *respiration*; breath of life, lifeblood, vital spark; parenthood 167 *propagation*; living matter, protoplasm, tissue, cell 358 *organism*; lifetime, life expectancy, life span, life cycle.

Adjective
(2) *alive*, living, quick, live; breathing, alive and kicking; animated 819 *lively*; incarnate, in the flesh; not dead, surviving, long-lived tenacious of life 113 *lasting*; capable of life, viable 656 *restored*; symbiotic, biological; protoplasmic.

(3) *born*, born alive; conceived, begotten; fathered, sired; mothered, dammed; foaled, dropped; out of, by 11 *akin*; spawned, laid, hatched.

Verb
(4) *live*, be alive, have life; draw breath 352 *breathe*; exist, subsist 1 *be*; come to life, quicken, revive 656 *be restored*; not die, be spared, survive.

(5) *be born*, come into the world 68 *begin*; draw breath.

(6) *vitalize*, give birth to, beget, conceive 167 *generate*; liven, enliven, breathe life into, bring to life 656 *revive*; support life, provide a living; provide for, keep alive 301 *feed*.

361
Death

Noun
(1) *death*, no life 2 *extinction*; dying (see *decease*); mortality 114 *transience*; sentence of death, doom, knell, death k.; execution, martyrdom; deathblow 362 *killing*; mortification 51 *decay*; the beyond, eternal rest, 266 *quietude*; the grave 364 *tomb*; jaws of death, shadow of d.; Death, Angel of Death; autopsy, post mortem; mortuary, morgue 364 *cemetery*.

(2) *decease*, clinical death, brain d.; end of life, extinction, exit, demise, curtains 69 *end*; passing, passing away; release, happy r.; loss of life, fatality; sudden death, violent d., untimely end; mortal illness 651 *disease*; dying day, last hour; deathbed, deathwatch, last agony, last gasp, dying breath; swan song, death rattle, rigor mortis 69 *finality*; extreme unction; passing bell 364 *obsequies*.

(3) *the dead*, ancestors 66 *precursor*; saints, souls 968 *saint*; shades, spirits 970 *ghost*; dead body 363 *corpse*; next world 124 *future state*; underworld, Hades 972 *mythic hell*; Elysian fields 971 *mythic heaven*.

(4) *death roll*, mortality, fatality, death toll, death rate; death certificate obituary, the fallen, death notice; casualties.

Adjective
(5) *dying*, mortal; moribund,

half-dead, deathly; given up, despaired of, all over with, done for, had it; sinking 651 *sick*; at death's door; in extremis; under sentence of death, doomed.

(6) *dead,* deceased, no more; passed away, departed, gone before, dead and gone; born dead, stillborn; lifeless, inanimate, still; stone dead, cold, stiff; defunct, late, lamented, late-lamented, of sainted memory.

Verb

(7) *die* (see *perish*); be dead, cease to be; die a natural death, die in one's sleep; end one's life, decease, predecease; expire, stop breathing, breathe one's last; fall asleep, pass away, pass on, depart this life; meet one's Maker.

(8) *perish,* die out, become extinct 2 *pass away,* 165 *be destroyed*; wither, come to dust 51 *decompose*; meet one's end, die hard, die fighting; get killed, fall, fall in action, lose one's life, be lost; lay down one's life, become a martyr; meet a sticky end, die untimely, drop down dead, break one's neck, bleed to death, drown; suffer execution, be put to death; commit suicide 362 *kill oneself.*

Adverb

(9) *post-obit,* posthumously.

362
Killing: Destruction of life

Noun

(1) *killing,* slaying, taking life 165 *destruction*; blood sports 619 *chase*; bloodshed, bloodletting; vivisection; selective killing, cull; mercy killing, euthanasia; murder (see *homicide*); poisoning, drowning, suffocation, strangulation, hanging; ritual killing, immolation,

sacrifice; crucifixion, martyrdom; judicial murder, execution 963 *capital punishment*; burning alive, the stake; dispatch, deathblow, coup de grace, quietus; violent death, fatal accident.

(2) *homicide,* manslaughter; murder, capital m.; assassination; regicide, parricide, patricide, matricide, fratricide; infanticide.

(3) *suicide,* self-destruction; suttee, hara-kiri; mass suicide, lemmings.

(4) *slaughter,* bloodshed, high casualties, butchery, carnage; wholesale murder, bloodbath, massacre, holocaust; pogrom, purge, liquidation, decimation, extermination 165 *destruction*; genocide, Final Solution; war, battle 718 *warfare.*

(5) *slaughterhouse,* abattoir, knacker's yard, shambles; bullring 724 *arena*; battlefield 724 *battleground*; gas chamber.

(6) *killer,* slayer, man of blood; mercy killer; soldier 722 *combatant*; slaughterer, butcher, knacker; trapper 619 *hunter*; rat catcher, rodent officer; toreador, picador, matador; executioner, hangman, lynch mob; homicidal maniac, psychopath; head-hunter, cannibal; beast of prey, man-eater.

(7) *murderer,* homicide, killer, assassin, terrorist; poisoner, strangler, garrotter; hatchet man, gangster, gunman; desperado, cutthroat 904 *ruffian*; parricide, regicide, suicide.

Adjective

(8) *deadly,* killing, lethal; fell, mortal, fatal, capital; malignant, poisonous 653 *toxic*; suffocating, stifling; unhealthy 653 *insalubrious*; inoperable, incurable.

(9) *murderous,* homicidal, genocidal; suicidal, internecine; death-dealing, trigger-happy; sanguinary, bloody, gory, bloodstained, red-handed; head hunting, bloodthirsty 898 *cruel.*

Verb
(10) *kill,* slay, take life 165 *destroy;* put down, put to sleep; hasten one's end, drive to one's death, put to death, hang, behead 963 *execute;* stone to death string up, lynch; do away with, dispatch, get rid of; shed blood, put to the sword, knife, stab, run through 263 *pierce;* shoot down, pick off 287 *shoot;* wring one's neck, strangle, garrotte, choke, suffocate, smother, stifle, drown; wall up, bury alive; smite, brain, poleaxe 279 *strike;* send to the stake, burn alive, immolate, sacrifice, martyr; sign one's death warrant 961 *condemn.*

(11) *slaughter,* butcher, cut one's throat; massacre, decimate, wipe out; cut to pieces, cut down, shoot d., mow d.; give no quarter 906 *be pitiless;* annihilate, exterminate, liquidate, purge 165 *destroy.*

(12) *murder,* commit m., assassinate, smother, suffocate, strangle, poison, gas. See *kill.*

(13) *kill oneself,* do away with oneself, commit suicide, commit hara-kiri, commit suttee; hang oneself, shoot o., slash one's wrists; gas oneself; take poison, take an overdose; drown oneself 361 *perish.*

363
Corpse

Noun
(1) *corpse,* dead body, body; victim; cadaver, carcass, skeleton, bones; death's-head, skull, embalmed corpse, mummy; mortal remains, relics, ashes;

carrion; organic remains 125 *fossil;* zombie 970 *ghost.*

Adjective
(2) *cadaverous,* deathly; stiff, carrion.

364
Interment

Noun
(1) *interment,* burial, entombment; cremation, incineration; embalming, mummification; coffin, casket, urn, sarcophagus, mummy-case; pyre, crematorium; mortuary, morgue, charnel house; funeral parlour; undertaker, funeral director; mortician; embalmer.

(2) *obsequies,* mourning, wake 836 *lamentation;* last rites, burial service, funeral; hearse, bier, cortege, knell, dead march, muffled drum, last post, taps; requiem, elegy, dirge 836 *lament;* inscription, epitaph, obituary; tombstone, gravestone, headstone, ledger; cross 548 *monument;* pallbearer, mourner.

(3) *grave clothes,* shroud, winding sheet.

(4) *cemetery,* burial place, churchyard, graveyard.

(5) *tomb,* vault, crypt; burial chamber, mummy c.; pyramid, mausoleum, sepulchre; pantheon; grave, mass g., plague pit; barrow 253 *earthwork;* shrine, memorial, cenotaph.

(6) *inquest* 459 *enquiry;* autopsy, post-mortem; exhumation, disinterment.

Adjective
(7) *buried,* interred, coffined, laid to rest.

(8) *funereal,* funerary, sombre, sad 428 *black;* elegiac; sepulchral; mourning 836 *lamenting.*

Verb
(9) *inter,* bury; lay out, close one's eyes; embalm, mummify; consign to earth, lay to rest; cremate, incinerate 381 *burn*; pay one's last respects, mourn 836 *lament.*

(10) *exhume,* disinter, unearth, dig up.

Adverb
(11) *in memoriam,* RIP.

365
Animality. Animal

Noun
(1) *animality,* animal life, bird life, wild life; animal kingdom, fauna; endangered species.

(2) *animal,* created being, living thing; birds, beasts and fishes; creature, brute, beast, dumb animal; protozoon, zoophyte 196 *microorganism*; mammal, amphibian, fish, bird, reptile; arthropod; crustacean, insect, arachnid; invertebrate, vertebrate; biped, quadruped; carnivore, herbivore, insectivore, omnivore, ruminant, man-eater; wild animal, game, big game; prey, beast of prey; pack, flock, herd 74 *group*; livestock 369 *stock farm*; tame animal, domestic a.; household pet, goldfish, hamster, guinea pig, tortoise; young animal 132 *young creature*; draught animal 273 *beast of burden*; extinct animal, dodo, pterodactyl, dinosaur, mammoth, mastodon.

(3) *mammal,* man 371 *humankind*; primate, ape, anthropoid ape, gorilla, chimpanzee, baboon, monkey; marsupial, kangaroo, koala bear; rodent, rat, mouse; squirrel, mole, hare, rabbit, bunny; badger, hedgehog; stoat, weasel, fox, dog f., vixen; jackal, hyena, lion (see *cat*); aquatic mammal, otter,

beaver; marine mammal, walrus, seal, sea lion; cetacean, dolphin, porpoise, whale; pachyderm, elephant, rhinoceros, hippopotamus; bear, grizzly giraffe, zebra (see *cattle*); deer, stag, doe, fawn; gazelle, antelope; horse, donkey, camel 273 *beast of burden.*

(4) *bird,* fowl; fledgling; cagebird, canary, budgerigar, parrot; songbird, songster, warbler, nightingale, lark, thrush, blackbird; dove, pigeon; magpie, jackdaw, crow; finch, tit, wren, robin, sparrow; bird of passage, summer visitor, migrant, cuckoo, swallow; flightless bird, emu, ostrich, penguin; scavenging bird, vulture; bird of prey, owl, eagle, kestrel, hawk, falcon; fishing bird, pelican, kingfisher; seabird, gull, albatross; wader, stork, crane, heron; waterfowl, swan, cygnet; duck, drake, duckling; goose, gander, gosling; mallard, moorhen, coot.

(5) *table bird,* game b., woodcock, grouse, pheasant, partridge, quail.

(6) *poultry,* fowl, hen, cock, cockerel, rooster; chicken, pullet; boiler, broiler, roaster, capon; bantam.

(7) *cattle,* livestock; bull, cow, calf, heifer, yearling; bullock, steer; beef cattle, dairy cattle; ox, oxen; goat. billy g., nanny g.,

(8) *sheep,* ram, tup, wether, bell w., ewe, lamb.

(9) *pig,* swine, boar, tusker; hog, sow, piglet, sucking pig, porker.

(10) *dog,* canine; bitch, whelp, pup, puppy; cur, hound, mongrel; guide dog, watch d., bloodhound, mastiff; sheepdog, collie; bulldog, boxer; greyhound, courser, whippet; foxhound,

beagle; gun dog, retriever, pointer, setter; terrier, spaniel, poodle; show dog, toy d., lap d., husky, sledge dog; wolf, coyote.

(11) *cat,* feline; puss, pussy, kitten, pussycat; tom, tom cat, queen c., tabby; mouser; big cat, lion, tiger.

(12) *amphibian,* frog, frogspawn, tadpole; toad, newt.

(13) *reptile,* serpent, sea s.; snake, water s.; grass s., smooth s., viper, adder; cobra, rattlesnake; boa constrictor, python; crocodile, alligator; lizard; turtle, tortoise, terrapin.

(14) *marine life,* marine organisms, coral, jellyfish; shellfish, mollusc, bivalve; squid, octopus; crustacean, crab, shrimp.

(15) *fish,* flying f., swordfish, shark; piranha, stingray; pike, roach, perch, dace, bream, carp; trout, salmon, eel; minnow.

(16) *insect,* larva, pupa, winged insect, fly, gnat, midge, mosquito; greenfly, aphid; ladybird, firefly, glow-worm; dragonfly, crane fly, daddy longlegs; butterfly, moth; bee, bumble b., honey b., queen b., worker b., drone; wasp, hornet; beetle, cockroach; insect pests, vermin, parasites, bug, flea, louse, nit, mite, tick; woodworm, weevil; ant, soldier a., worker a., termite; stick insect, praying mantis; locust, grasshopper, cicada, cricket.

(17) *creepy-crawly,* grub, maggot, caterpillar, worm, centipede, millipede; slug, snail; earwig, woodlouse; spider, money s.

Adjective
(18) *animal,* brutish, bestial; feral, domestic; entomological, zoological; vertebrate, invertebrate; mammalian, warmblooded; anthropoid; equine,

asinine, mulish; bovine, ovine, sheeplike, goatlike, goatish; porcine, piggy; bearish, elephantine; canine, doggy; wolfish, lupine; feline, catlike, tigerish, leonine; vulpine, foxy; avian, birdlike, aquiline, owlish; cold-blooded, fishy, molluscan, amphibian, amphibious, reptilian, snaky, wormy; verminous.

366
Vegetable life

Noun
(1) *vegetable life,* vegetable kingdom; flora, vegetation; flowering, blooming, lushness, wood nymph 967 *nymph.*

(2) *wood,* timber, lumber, softwood, hardwood, heartwood, sapwood; forest, virgin f., primeval f.; rain f., jungle; bush, heath, scrub, maquis; greenwood, woodland, copse, coppice, spinney; thicket, brake, covert; park, plantation, arboretum, orchard 370 *garden;* grove, clump; clearing, glade; brushwood, undergrowth; shrubbery, windbreak, hedge, hedgerow.

(3) *forestry,* tree-planting, afforestation, conservation; forester, woodcutter, lumberjack.

(4) *tree,* shrub, bush, sapling, pollard; bonsai; shoot, sucker, trunk, bole; limb, branch, bough, twig; conifer, evergreen tree, deciduous t.; fruit tree, nut t., timber t.; mahogany, teak, walnut; oak, elm, ash, beech; larch, fir, spruce, pine; poplar, willow, birch, rowan; hazel, elder, hawthorn, may, blackthorn, sloe; privet, yew, holly, ivy; rhododendron, magnolia, laburnum, lilac; palm, gum tree 370 *agriculture.*

(5) *foliage,* greenery, verdure; leafiness, leafage; herbage;

shoot; spray, sprig; leaf, frond, blade; leaflet, needle; stalk, stem; tendril, prickle, thorn.

(6) *plant,* growing thing, herb, wort, weed; root, tuber, rhizome, bulb, corm; rootstock, cutting 132 *young plant*; culinary herb, medicinal h.; food plant, fodder 301 *vegetable, fruit, provender*; national plant, rose, leek, daffodil, thistle, shamrock; garden plant, pansy, carnation, lily; wild plant, daisy, dandelion, buttercup; cactus, succulent; bramble, gorse; creeper, climber, twiner, vine; fern, bracken; moss, lichen, mould; fungus, mushroom, toadstool; seaweed, wrack; algae.

(7) *flower,* floret, blossom, bloom, bud; head, spike; petal, sepal; corolla, calyx; fruit, berry, nut, drupe; seed vessel, pod, capsule, cone; pip, spore 156 *source*; annual, biennial, perennial; house plant, pot p.; gardening, horticulture.

(8) *grass,* mowing g., hay; pasture 348 *grassland*; verdure, turf, lawn; sedge, rush, reed, bamboo, sugar cane; grain plant, rice 301 *cereals*; grain, husk, chaff, stubble, straw.

Adjective
(9) *vegetal,* vegetable, botanical; evergreen, deciduous; hardy, half-hardy; horticultural; floral, flowery, blooming; rank, lush, overgrown; weedy, weed-ridden; leafy, verdant 434 *green*; grassy, mossy, turfy; herbaceous, herbal.

(10) *arboreal,* treelike; forested, timbered; woodland, woody, wooded, sylvan; bushy, shrubby; afforested, planted.

(11) *wooden,* wood, woody, hard-grained, soft-grained.

Verb
(12) *vegetate,* germinate, sprout

36 *grow*; plant 370 *cultivate*; forest, afforest, replant.

367
Zoology: The science of animals

Noun
(1) *zoology,* animal physiology, morphology; embryology, anatomy 358 *biology*; ornithology, bird lore, bird watching; entomology; taxidermy.

(2) *zoologist,* ornithologist, entomologist, anatomist.

Adjective
(3) *zoological,* ornithological.

368
Botany: The science of plants

Noun
(1) *botany,* taxonomy; plant physiology; plant ecology; botanical garden; herbal; botanist, herbalist.

369
Animal husbandry

Noun
(1) *animal husbandry,* breeding, stock-b., rearing; training, domestication; dairy farming, beef f.; sheep f., poultry f., pig-keeping, goat-k., bee-k.; veterinary surgeon, vet, horse doctor; farrier, blacksmith; keeper, gamekeeper, gillie; game warden.

(2) *stock farm,* stud f., stud; dairy farm, cattle f., ranch; fish farm, hatchery; pig farm, piggery; beehive, hive, apiary; poultry farm, chicken run, free range; broiler house, battery; deep litter; factory farm.

(3) *cattle pen,* cow shed, byre, stable; sheepfold 235 *enclosure*;

hutch, coop, pigsty; bird cage, aviary.

(4) *zoo,* zoological gardens; menagerie, circus; aviary, vivarium, aquarium; wildlife park, safari p.; game park, game reserve.

(5) *breeder,* trainer; cattle farmer, sheep f., pig-keeper, bee-k.; bird-fancier,

(6) *herdsman,* cowherd; stockman, rancher; cowgirl, cowboy, gaucho; shepherd, goatherd, milkmaid, kennel maid.

Adjective
(7) *tamed,* broken, broken in; gentle, docile; domestic, domesticated; reared, raised, bred; purebred, thoroughbred.

Verb
(8) *break in,* tame, domesticate, train 534 *teach;* mount 267 *ride;* yoke, harness, hitch, bridle, saddle; round up, herd, corral 235 *enclose.*

(9) *breed stock,* breed, rear, raise, grow, hatch, culture, incubate, nurture, fatten; ranch, farm.

(10) *groom,* currycomb, rub down, stable, bed down; tend, herd, shepherd; shear, fleece; milk; water 301 *feed.*

370
Agriculture

Noun
(1) *agriculture,* agronomics, rural economy; agribusiness cultivation, ploughing, sowing, reaping; harvest, crop, vintage 632 *store;* husbandry, farming, mixed f., factory f., intensive f., subsistence f.; cattle farming 369 *animal husbandry;* arable farming, irrigation 341 *moistening;* green fingers; horticulture, gardening, market g.; wine-growing, vine-dressing;

afforestation 366 *forestry;* manure 171 *fertilizer;* fodder, winter feed 301 *provender;* silage 632 *storage.*

(2) *farm,* home f., grange; arable farm, dairy f., ranch 369 *stock farm;* farmhouse, farmstead; farmyard 235 *enclosure;* farmland, arable land, ploughed land, fallow; pasture, fields, meadows 348 *grassland;* estate, holding, smallholding, croft 777 *lands;* market garden, nursery, garden centre; vineyard; fruit farm, orchard; tea estate, coffee e., sugar plantation.

(3) *garden,* kitchen g., allotment; orchard, arboretum; patch, plot 235 *enclosure;* lawn, shrubbery, border, flowerbed; seedbed, frame, cloche, propagator; conservatory, hothouse, greenhouse, glasshouse.

(4) *farmer,* farm manager, bailiff; cultivator, planter, tea p.; agronomist, agriculturist; peasant, serf; tenant farmer; smallholder, crofter, fruit grower, wine-grower; farm hand, agricultural worker 869 *country-dweller;* ploughman, tractor driver, sower, reaper, gleaner; picker.

(5) *gardener,* horticulturist; landscape gardener; seedsman, nurseryman *or* - woman; market gardener; fruit-grower, vine-grower.

(6) *farm tool,* plough, harrow, spade, fork, hoe, rake, trowel; pitchfork; scythe 256 *sharp edge;* tractor; mowing machine, combine harvester; haystack, barn, silo 632 *storage.*

Adjective
(7) *agrarian,* peasant, farming; bucolic, pastoral, rural, rustic; agricultural, agronomic; arable, ploughed etc. vb.

(8) *horticultural,* garden, gardening, herbal.

Verb

(9) *cultivate*, farm, ranch, garden, grow; till, dig, delve; seed, sow, plant; plough, harrow, rake, hoe; weed, prune 204 *shorten*; graft 303 *implant*; fertilize, mulch, manure; grass over, leave fallow; harvest, gather in 632 *store*; glean, reap, mow, cut, bind, bale; flail, thresh, winnow; pluck, pick, gather; fence in 235 *enclose*; ditch, drain; water 341 *irrigate*.

371
Humankind

Noun

(1) *humankind*, mankind, womankind; humanity, human nature; flesh, mortality; the world, everyone, everybody, the living, human race, human species, human being, man; earthling; early humanity, Stone-Age h.; ethnic type 11 *race*.

(2) *anthropology*, ethnology, ethnography; demography; social science 901 *sociology*; ethnographer, demographer.

(3) *person*, individual, human being, creature, fellow c., mortal, body; soul, living s.; one, somebody, someone, so and so, such a one; party, customer, character; chap, fellow 372 *male*; girl, female 373 *woman*; personage, figure 638 *bigwig*; unit, head.

(4) *social group*, society, community 74 *group*; kinship group 11 *family*; tribalism; people, persons, folk; public, you and me 79 *generality*; population, populace, citizenry 191 *inhabitants*; the masses 869 *commonalty*; aristocracy 868 *upper class*.

(5) *nation*, nationality, statehood, nationalism; chauvinism, jingoism, imperialism, colonialism; body politic, people;

state, nation s.; democracy, republic 733 *government*.

Adjective

(6) *human*, creaturely, mortal; anthropoid, subhuman; anthropological 11 *ethnic*; personal, individual.

(7) *national*, international; state, civic, civil, public, general, communal, tribal, social.

372
Male

Noun

(1) *male*, male sex, man, he, him; masculinity, manliness, manhood, virility; machismo, male chauvinism; patriarchy; *mannishness*, esquire, gentleman, sir, master; lord, my l., his lordship; Mr, mister, monsieur, Herr, senor, signor, sahib; mate, buddy, pal 880 *chum*; gaffer 133 *old man*; fellow, guy, bloke, chap, johnny; rake 952 *libertine*; he-man, caveman; sissy 163 *weakling*; homosexual, eunuch 84 *nonconformist*; escort, beau, boy friend; bachelor, widower; bridegroom, married man, husband 894 *spouse*; family man, paterfamilias, patriarch; father, son 169 *paternity*; uncle, brother, nephew; lad, boy 132 *youngster*; spear side; stag party, menfolk.

Adjective

(2) *male*, masculine, manly, gentlemanly, chivalrous; virile; macho; mannish, manlike, butch.

373
Female

Noun

(1) *female*, feminine gender, she, her, -ess; femininity, feminineness, womanhood 134 *adultness*; womanliness, girlishness;

feminism, women's rights, women's liberation; matriarchy; womanishness; gynaecology.

(2) *womankind,* female sex, fair s., distaff side, womenfolk, women; hen party; women's quarters, purdah, harem.

(3) *woman,* Eve, she; girl, little g. 132 *youngster;* virgin, maiden; unmarried woman 895 *spinster;* bachelor girl, career woman, housewife; feminist, sister, women's libber; suffragette; bride, married woman, wife, squaw, widow, matron 894 *spouse;* dowager 133 *old woman;* mother, unmarried m. 169 *maternity;* aunt, niece, sister, daughter; wench, lass, damsel; brunette, blonde, redhead; girlfriend, sweetheart 887 *loved one;* courtesan 952 *loose woman;* lesbian 84 *nonconformist;* shrew, virago, Amazon.

(4) *lady,* gentlewoman; dame; milady, her ladyship; madam, ma'am, mistress, Mrs, missus, Ms, miss, madame, mademoiselle, Frau, Fraulein; signora, signorina, señora, señorita, memsahib.

Adjective
(5) *female,* feminine, girlish, womanly, ladylike, maidenly, matronly; child-bearing 167 *generative;* feminist, lesbian; womanish, effeminate, unmanly; androgynous.

374
Physical sensibility

Noun
(1) *sensibility,* sensitivity, sensitiveness, soreness, tenderness, exposed nerve; perceptivity, awareness, consciousness; susceptivity, allergy; funny bone; sensuousness, aesthetics.

(2) *sense,* sensory apparatus, sense organ, nerve system, five senses; touch, hearing, taste,

smell, sight; sensation, impression 818 *feeling;* effect, response, reaction, reflex; sixth sense, extrasensory perception, ESP 984 *psychics.*

Adjective
(3) *sentient,* sensitive, sensitized; sensible, susceptible, sensory, perceptual; sensuous, aesthetic 818 *feeling;* aware, conscious 490 *knowing;* acute, sharp, keen 377 *painful;* ticklish, itchy; tender, raw, sore, exposed; alive to, responsive; hypersensitive, allergic.

(4) *striking,* keen, sharp, poignant, acute, vivid, clear, lively; electrifying 821 *exciting.*

Verb
(5) *have feeling,* sense, become aware; wake up, come to one's senses; perceive, realize 490 *know;* be sensible of, react, tingle 818 *feel;* hear, see, touch, taste, smell.

(6) *cause feeling,* stir the senses, stir the blood; disturb 318 *agitate;* arouse, excite 821 *impress;* sharpen, refine, sensitize; hurt 377 *give pain.*

Adverb
(7) *to the quick,* on the raw.

375
Physical insensibility

Noun
(1) *insensibility,* physical i., anaesthesia; analgesia; hypnosis, autohypnosis, hypnotism; paralysis, numbness; catalepsy, stupor, coma, trance, faint, swoon, blackout, unconsciousness, senselessness; suspended animation 679 *sleep.*

(2) *anaesthetic,* local a., ether, chloroform, morphine, cocaine, gas, gas and air; narcotic, sleeping tablets 679 *soporific;* opium, laudanum 658 *drug;* painkiller,

analgesic 177 *moderator*; acupuncture.

Adjective
(3) *insensible,* insentient, insensate; unhearing, oblivious 416 *deaf*; unseeing 439 *blind*; senseless, unconscious; inert, 679 *inactive*; inanimate, out cold 266 *quiescent*; numb, benumbed, frozen; paralysed; doped, drugged; stoned 949 *dead drunk*; anaesthetized, hypnotized; punch-drunk, dazed; semiconscious, in a trance; cataleptic, comatose; anaesthetic, analgesic; hypnotic, mesmeric 679 *soporific.*

(4) *unfeeling,* cold; inured, toughened, hardened, thick-skinned.

Verb
(5) *be insensible,* inanimate etc. adj.; not react, cease to feel; pass out, black o., faint, swoon; lose consciousness.

(6) *render insensible,* blunt, deaden; freeze, paralyse, benumb; send to sleep, hypnotize, mesmerize, anaesthetize, gas; narcotize, drug, dope; dull, stupefy; stun, concuss.

376
Physical pleasure

Noun
(1) *pleasure,* physical p., sensual p., sensuous p., sexual p.; thrill 821 *excitation*; enjoyment, gratification, sensuousness, sensuality; self-indulgence hedonism 944 *sensualism*; rest 685 *refreshment*; feast 301 *feasting*; gusto, zest; ecstasy 824 *joy.*

(2) *euphoria,* well-being 828 *content*, 650 *health*; gracious living; ease, convenience, comfort, snugness; luxury, lap of luxury 800 *wealth*; peace, quiet, rest 683 *repose.*

Adjective
(3) *pleasant,* pleasing, titillating 826 *pleasurable*; delightful, welcome, gratifying, satisfying 685 *refreshing*; congenial, nice, agreeable, enjoyable; palatable, delicious 386 *tasty*, 392 *sweet*; perfumed 396 *fragrant*; tuneful 410 *melodious*; lovely 841 *beautiful.*

(4) *comfortable,* homely, snug, cosy, warm, comforting; restful 683 *reposeful*; painless, peaceful 266 *tranquil*; convenient, easy, easeful; downy 327 *soft*; luxurious, de luxe; happy, euphoric, at one's ease 828 *content*; pampered, featherbedded; relieved 685 *refreshed.*

(5) *sensuous,* of the senses, bodily, physical; voluptuous, pleasure-loving 944 *sensual.*

Verb
(6) *enjoy,* relish, like, take pleasure in 824 *be pleased*; thrill to 821 *be excited*; luxuriate in, revel in, bask in, wallow in; gloat over, lick one's lips; live in comfort 730 *prosper*; give pleasure 826 *please.*

Adverb
(7) *in comfort,* at one's ease; in clover.

377
Physical pain

Noun
(1) *pain,* physical p., bodily p.; distress, discomfort, malaise, inconvenience; exhaustion, weariness, strain 684 *fatigue*; hurt, bruise, sprain; cut, gash 655 *wound*; aching, smarting; anguish, agony 825 *suffering*; slow death, torment, torture; vivisection; painfulness, soreness, tenderness; hangover.

(2) *pang,* thrill, throes; stab, twinge, nip, pinch; pins and needles, stitch, crick; cramp, convulsion 318 *spasm*; smart,

sting, shooting pain, ache, headache, splitting head, migraine; toothache, earache; stomach-ache, colic; backache; neuralgia 651 *ill health.*

Adjective

(3) *painful,* paining, aching, agonizing, excruciating, exquisite; harrowing, racking, tormenting; burning, biting, stabbing, shooting; tingling, smarting, throbbing, sore, raw, tender, exposed; bitter, bittersweet 393 *sour;* disagreeable, uncomfortable, inconvenient 827 *unpleasant.*

(4) *pained,* hurt, tortured, suffering, aching, flinching, wincing, quivering, writhing.

Verb

(5) *give pain,* ache, hurt, pain, sting; inflict pain, torment 963 *torture;* crucify, vivisect; lacerate 46 *cut;* touch the quick; prick, stab 263 *pierce;* gripe, nip, pinch, twinge, shoot, throb; bite, gnaw; grind, grate, jar, set on edge; chafe, irritate 333 *rub;* prolong the agony; inconvenience, annoy, distress 827 *trouble.*

(6) *feel pain,* suffer p. 825 *suffer;* agonize, ache, smart, chafe; twitch, wince, flinch, writhe, squirm 318 *be agitated;* be a martyr, go through it; shriek, scream, groan 408 *cry;* lick one's wounds.

378
Touch: Sensation of touch

Noun

(1) *touch,* handling, feeling, palpation, manipulation; massage, kneading, squeeze, pressure 333 *friction;* graze, contact, light touch; stroke, pat, caress; flick, flip 279 *knock;* sense of touch, fine t., delicacy, artistry 694 *skill.*

(2) *formication,* creeps, gooseflesh; tingle, tingling, pins and needles; scratchiness, itchiness, itch, rash 651 *skin disease.*

(3) *feeler,* organ of touch, antenna, whisker, tentacle; proboscis, tongue; digit (see *finger*); hand, paw, palm, flipper.

(4) *finger,* forefinger, index, middle finger, ring f., little f., pinkie; thumb, big toe 214 *foot;* hand, fist 778 *nippers.*

Adjective

(5) *tactual,* tactile; tentacular; prehensile 778 *retentive;* touching, licking; touchable, tangible, palpable; light of touch, light-handed, heavy-h.

(6) *handed,* with hands; right-handed, left-handed; digital, manual.

Verb

(7) *touch,* make contact, come into c.; graze, scrape, shave, brush, glance 202 *be contiguous;* impinge, overlap; hit, meet 279 *collide;* feel, palpate; finger, thumb, pinch, nip; massage 333 *rub;* palm, stroke, smooth; touch lightly, tap, pat, dab, flick, flip; tickle, scratch; lip, lap, lick, tongue; nuzzle, rub noses; paw, fondle 889 *caress;* handle, twiddle, fiddle with; manipulate, wield, ply, manhandle; touch roughly, bruise, crush; fumble, grope, scrabble 461 *be tentative.*

(8) *itch,* tickle, tingle, creep, crawl, have gooseflesh, have the creeps; prick, prickle; scratch; thrill, excite, irritate, inflame 374 *cause feeling.*

379
Heat

Noun

(1) *heat,* radiant heat; conveeted h. 381 *heating;* incandescence, flame, glow, flush, blush;

warmth, fervour, ardour; tepidity, lukewarmness; sweat, swelter; fever heat, pyrexia, fever; inflammation 651 *disease*; high temperature, boiling point, flash p., melting p.; torrid heat, tropical h., high summer, heat wave, 128 *summer*; hot springs, thermal s., geyser, steam; tropics, sun, sunshine.

(2) *fire,* flames; bonfire, watch fire, beacon f.; pyre 364 *obsequies*; coal fire 383 *furnace*; inferno, conflagration, holocaust; fireball, blaze, flame, tongue of f., sheet of f., wall of f.; spark, flicker 417 *flash*; flare 420 *torch*; eruption, volcano; pyrotechnics 420 *fireworks*; arson 381 *incendiarism.*

(3) *thermometry,* heat measurement, thermometer, thermostat; thermal unit, therm, calorie; thermodynamics.

Adjective

(4) *hot,* heated, inflamed, flaming, glowing, red-hot, white-h.; piping hot, smoking h.; feverish, febrile, fevered; sweltering, sweating, perspiring; steaming, smoking; on the boil, boiling, scalding; tropical, torrid, scorching, broiling, searing, blistering, baking, toasting, scorched, scalded 381 *heated*; thirsty, burning, parched 342 *dry*; in a fever, in a lather, in a sweat.

(5) *fiery,* ardent, burning, blazing, flaming, flaring; smoking, smouldering; ablaze, afire, on fire, in flames; incandescent, molten, glowing, aglow 431 *red*; igneous, ignited, lit, alight, kindled; volcanic, erupting.

(6) *warm,* tepid, lukewarm; temperate, mild, genial, balmy; fair, set f., sunny, summery, tropical, equatorial; torrid, sultry; stuffy, close, suffocating, stifling 653 *insalubrious*;

warm, snug; at blood heat; calorific, thermal, isothermal.

Verb

(7) *be hot,* be warm, incandesce; burn, kindle, catch fire, draw; blaze, flare, flame up, burst into flame; glow, flush; smoke, smoulder; boil, seethe 318 *effervesce*; toast, grill, roast, sizzle, crackle, frizzle, fry, bake 381 *burn*; get burnt, scorch; bask, sun oneself, sunbathe; get sunburnt, tan; swelter, sweat, perspire, glow; melt, thaw; thirst 342 *be dry*; stifle, pant, gasp for breath, fight for air; be feverish, have a fever, run a temperature; keep warm, wrap up.

380
Cold

Noun

(1) *coldness,* low temperature, drop in t.; cool, coolness, freshness; cold, freezing c., zero temperature, zero, freezing point; frigidity, iciness, frostiness; sensation of cold, chilliness, hypothermia, shivering, gooseflesh, goose pimples, frostbite, chilblains; chill, catching cold; cold climate, North Pole, South P.; Arctic, Antarctic; permafrost; Ice Age.

(2) *wintriness,* winter, cold snap; cold weather, cold front; inclemency, wintry weather, snowstorm, blizzard; frost, rime, hoarfrost; sleet, hail, hailstone, black ice, freeze.

(3) *snow,* snowfall, snowflake, snow crystal; avalanche, snowdrift; winter sports 837 *sport.*

(4) *ice,* hailstone, icicle; ice cap, ice field, ice sheet, ice floe, iceberg, glacier.

Adjective

(5) *cold,* cool, shady, temperate; chill, chilly, fresh, raw, keen, bitter, nipping, biting, piercing; inclement, freezing, ice-

cold, below zero; frosty, snowy, snow-covered 129 *wintry*; slushy, sleety, icy; glacial, ice-capped, polar, arctic.

(6) *chilly,* feeling cold, shivering, chattering, blue with cold; perishing, frozen, frostbitten, like ice.

Verb
(7) *be cold,* chilly etc. vb.; grow cold, lose heat, feel cold, chatter, shiver, shake; freeze, catch cold, get a chill.

381
Heating

Noun
(1) *heating,* warming, keeping warm; space heating, central h. 383 *heater*; sunning 342 *desiccation*; melting, smelting 337 *liquefaction*; boiling, baking 301 *cookery.*

(2) *burning,* combustion; inflammation, kindling, ignition; conflagration 379 *fire*; incineration, cremation; cauterization, branding; scorching, singeing, charring, carbonization; burner 383 *furnace*; hot iron, brand; match 385 *lighter*; stoker, fireman; burn mark, burn, brand; sunburn, tan.

(3) *incendiarism,* arson, fire-raising, pyromania; incendiary, arsonist, fire-raiser.

(4) *ash,* ashes, volcanic ash, lava, carbon, soot, smut, smoke; ember, cinder.

(5) *pottery,* ceramics; earthenware, stoneware, glazed ware; chinaware, porcelain; crockery, china, bone c.; terracotta; tile, brick; pot, urn 194 *vessel.*

Adjective
(6) *heated,* 379 *hot*; lit, kindled, fired; incinerated, burnt, burnt out, burnt down, gutted; cooked, roasted etc. vb.; warmed up; melted, molten;

bronzed, tanned, sun-t., sunburnt.

(7) *heating,* warming etc. vb.; calorific; solid-fuel, coal-burning, oil-fired; incendiary, inflammatory; inflammable 385 *combustible.*

Verb
(8) *heat,* warm; hot up, warm up, stoke up; rub one's hands, stamp one's feet; thaw, thaw out; stew, stifle, suffocate; parch, shrivel 342 *dry*; toast, bake, grill, fry, roast 301 *cook*; melt, defrost 337 *liquefy*; smelt, fuse, weld, cast, found.

(9) *kindle,* ignite, light, strike a l.; apply a match, set fire to, touch off 385 *fire*; fuel, stoke.

(10) *burn,* burn up, burn out, gut; fire, set fire to, set on fire; commit to the flames, cremate, incinerate; carbonize, oxidize, corrode; char, singe, scorch, tan; cauterize, brand, burn in; scald.

382
Refrigeration

Noun
(1) *refrigeration,* cooling, freezing, freezing up 380 *ice*; ventilation, air-conditioning; cold storage 384 *refrigerator.*

(2) *incombustibility,* fire resistance; nonflammability.

(3) *extinguisher,* fire e.; sprinkler, hydrant; fire engine, fire brigade, fireman *or* - woman, firefighter.

Adjective
(4) *cooled,* chilled etc. vb.; iced up; frozen, deep-frozen, freeze-dried; frosted, iced, glacé, frappe on the rocks 380 *cold.*

(5) *incombustible,* fireproof, flameproof, noninflammable, fire-resistant.

Verb
(6) *refrigerate,* cool 685 *refresh*; ventilate, air-condition, air 340 *aerate*; freeze, congeal, deep-freeze, freeze-dry; ice up, ice over; chill, benumb, pierce, chill to the marrow. quench, snuff, put out, blow o., snuff o.; stifle, smother 165 *suppress*; damp, douse, rake out, stamp o., stub o.; stop burning, go out, die down.

383
Furnace

Noun
(1) *furnace,* the stake; volcano; forge, blast furnace, kiln, oasthouse; incinerator, crematorium; brazier, stove; oven, range, cooker, gas ring, burner, bunsen b., blowlamp; open fire 379 *fire*; brand 385 *lighter*; fireplace, grate, hearth; flue 263 *chimney*.

(2) *heater,* radiator, solar panel; hot-air duct, hot-water pipe, immersion heater, geyser, boiler; copper, kettle 194 *cauldron*; hotplate; sauna 648 *ablutions*; hothouse, sun trap; grill, toaster; flame, sunlight 381 *heating*; gas, electricity, solar energy; wood, coal 385 *fuel*.

384
Refrigerator

Noun
(1) *refrigerator,* cooler; ventilator, fan; fridge, cooler; coolant, ice; icebox, ice-cubes; cold storage, freezer, deep-freeze 382 *refrigeration*.

385
Fuel

Noun
(1) *fuel,* firing, kindling; wood, brushwood, firewood, faggot, log, Yule l.; turf, peat; charcoal; fossil fuel, coal, natural gas, petroleum; nuclear fuel, uranium, plutonium; petrol, gasoline; diesel oil, derv; paraffin; propane, butane, methane.

(2) *coal,* coke, anthracite; smokeless fuel; coal seam, coal deposit, coal measure, coalfield; cinders, embers, ash.

(3) *lighter,* igniter, light, pilot l., taper, spill, touchpaper; candle 420 *torch*; coal, ember, firebrand, incendiary bomb; wick, fuse, match, flint, detonator.

(4) *fumigator,* incense, joss stick, sulphur, brimstone.

Adjective
(5) *combustible,* burnable, flammable, inflammable, incendiary, explosive; carboniferous, coal-bearing.

Verb
(6) *fire,* stoke, feed, fuel, mend the fire; put a match to 381 *kindle*.

386
Taste

Noun
(1) *taste,* savour; flavour, flavouring; smack, tang, twang, aftertaste; relish, appetite 859 *liking*; tasting, gustation; palate, tongue, tooth, sweet t.

Adjective
(2) *tasty,* palatable, flavourful, tempting, appetizing, 390 *savoury*; well-seasoned, tangy 388 *pungent*; flavoured, spiced, spicy, rich, strong, full-bodied, fruity; well-matured, mellow, vintage; gustatory, gustative.

Verb
(3) *taste,* find palatable, roll on the tongue, smack one's lips, lick one's fingers 376 *enjoy*; savour, sample, try; sip, nibble 301 *eat*; taste of, savour of, smack of; taste good.

387
Insipidity

Noun
(1) *insipidity,* vapidity, jejuneness, flatness, staleness; milk and water, pap, slops.

Adjective
(2) *tasteless,* without taste, devoid of taste; jejune, vapid, insipid, watery, mild, underproof; diluted 163 *weakened*; wishy-washy, sloppy; unappetizing, unseasoned 391 *unsavoury*; flat, stale; flavourless.

388
Pungency

Noun
(1) *pungency,* piquancy, poignancy, sting, kick, bite, edge; burning taste, causticity; hot taste, spiciness; sharp taste, acridity, sharpness, acerbity, acidity 393 *sourness*; roughness, harshness; strong taste, tang, twang, raciness; salt, pepper, spice 389 *condiment*; sal volatile, smelling salts; cordial, pick-me-up 174 *stimulant*; nip, tot 301 *draught.*

(2) *tobacco,* nicotine; blend, smoking mixture; snuff; plug, quid, twist; flake, shag; cigar, cheroot; smoke, cigarette, fag, coffin-nail; reefer, joint 949 *drug-taking*; butt, stub, fagend, dog-end; tobacco pipe, briar; smoker's cough; smoker, chain s.; tobacconist.

Adjective
(3) *pungent,* penetrating, strong; stinging, biting 256 *sharp*; caustic, burning; harsh 259 *rough*; bitter, acrid, tart, astringent 393 *sour*; heady, high, gamy, off; spicy, curried; hot, gingery, peppery; zesty, tangy, piquant, aromatic 390 *savoury.*

(4) *salty,* salt, brackish, briny, saline, pickled.

Verb
(5) *be pungent,* sting, make the eyes water.

(6) *season,* salt, marinade, souse, pickle; flavour, spice, pepper; devil, curry; smoke, kipper 666 *preserve.*

(7) *smoke,* use tobacco, indulge; puff, pull, draw, suck, inhale; chain-smoke; take snuff.

389
Condiment

Noun
(1) *condiment,* seasoning, flavouring, dressing, relish, garnish; aspic; salt, mustard, pepper, cayenne, paprika; curry powder; garlic 301 *potherb*; spices, cinnamon, ginger, nutmeg, clove.

(2) *sauce,* roux; gravy, stock; brown sauce, white s.; tomato sauce, ketchup; chutney, pickles, salad dressing, mayonnaise, vinaigrette.

390
Savouriness

Noun
(1) *savouriness,* tastiness, palatability; richness; body, bouquet; savoury, relish, appetizer; delicacy, dainty, titbit, snack, hors d'oeuvre.

Adjective
(2) *savoury,* nice, good to eat, worth eating; seasoned, flavoured, spicy 386 *tasty*; welldressed, well-cooked, tempting, appetizing, aromatic, piquant 388 *pungent*; to one's taste, palatable, toothsome, dainty, sweet; delectable, delicious, exquisite, choice, epicurean, ambrosial; fresh, crisp; ripe, mellow, luscious, juicy, succulent;

creamy, rich, velvety; gamy, racy, high.

Verb
(3) *make appetizing,* spice, pep up 388 *season*; be savoury, tickle the palate, smell good, taste good; relish, savour, lap up 386 *taste.*

391
Unsavouriness

Noun
(1) *unsavouriness,* nasty taste; unwholesomeness 653 *insalubrity*; coarseness, plain cooking; acerbity, acridity 393 *sourness*; austerity, prison fare, bread and water; emetic 659 *poison.*

Adjective
(2) *unsavoury,* unpalatable, unappetizing, uninviting flat 387 *tasteless*; coarse, raw 670 *uncooked*; burnt, overdone, uneatable, inedible; stale, leathery 329 *tough*; soggy 327 *soft*; bitter, acrid, acid 393 *sour*; rank, rancid, putrid, rotten, gone off, high; foul, revolting, disgusting 827 *unpleasant*; sickly, cloying, sickening, nauseating 861 *disliked*; poisonous 653 *toxic.*

Verb
(3) *be unpalatable,* unappetizing etc. adj.; taste horrid; repel, sicken, nauseate, turn the stomach 861 *cause dislike*; lose its savour, pall.

392
Sweetness

Noun
(1) *sweetness,* sweetening; sugariness; sweet tooth.

(2) *sweet thing,* sweetening, honey, saccharin, sugar, molasses, syrup, treacle; sweet sauce, custard; sweet drink, nectar, mead; jam, jelly; marzipan, icing, fudge, candy 301 *sweets*; cachou, lozenge, pastille; ice cream, confectionery, cake 301 *pasties, dessert.*

Adjective
(3) *sweet,* sweetened, honeyed, candied, crystallized; iced, sugared, sugary; delicious 390 *savoury.*

Verb
(4) *sweeten,* sugar, candy, crystallize, ice; sugar the pill.

393
Sourness

Noun
(1) *sourness,* vinegariness, acerbity, astringency; tartness, bitterness, sharpness 388 *pungency*; acidity, acid; bitters; gall, wormwood.

Adjective
(2) *sour,* acid, acidulous; acetic, acid-forming; acerbic, tart, bitter, sharp, astringent 388 *pungent*; vinegary 391 *unsavoury*; unripe, green 670 *immature*; unsweetened, dry.

Verb
(3) *be sour,* acid etc. adj.; sour, turn sour; ferment; set one's teeth on edge.

394
Odour

Noun
(1) *odour,* smell, aroma, bouquet, nose; sweet smell, perfume 396 *fragrance*; bad smell 397 *stench*; exhalation, smoke, fumes, reek; breath, whiff, waft; strong smell, odorousness, redolence; tang, scent, trail 548 *trace*; olfaction, sense of smell; nostril, nose, good n., flair.

Adjective
(2) *odorous,* odoriferous, smell-

ing; scented, perfumed 396 *fragrant*; strong, heady, heavy, full-bodied 388 *pungent*; smelly, redolent, reeking; malodorous 397 *fetid*; olfactory; keen-scented, sharp-nosed.

Verb
(3) *smell,* have an odour, smell of, reek of; exhale; smell out, scent, nose, wind, get wind of, get a whiff of 484 *detect*; snuff up, sniff, inhale 352 *breathe*; cause to smell, scent, perfume, fumigate.

395
Inodorousness

Noun
(1) *inodorousness,* absence of smell, deodorant, deodorizer; fumes, incense; deodorization, fumigation, ventilation, purification 648 *cleansing.*

Adjective
(2) *odourless,* scentless, unperfumed, without smell; deodorized.

Verb
(3) *have no smell,* not smell; deodorize, ventilate, clear the air 648 *purify*; lose the scent.

396
Fragrance

Noun
(1) *fragrance,* sweet smell, balminess; aroma, bouquet 394 *odour*; buttonhole, nosegay; perfumery, perfumer.

(2) *scent,* perfume, incense; breath-sweetener, cachou; musk, lavender, honeysuckle; new-mown hay; toilet water, lavender w. 843 *cosmetic*; camphor, mothball, lavender bag, pomander, potpourri; scent bottle, smelling b., vinaigrette; joss stick.

Adjective
(3) *fragrant,* redolent, odorous, odoriferous, aromatic, scented, perfumed 376 *pleasant*; sweet-scented, musky, spicy, fruity; rose-scented.

Verb
(4) *be fragrant,* smell sweet, have a perfume, scent, perfume.

397
Stench

Noun
(1) *stench,* fetidness, offensiveness; bad smell, bad odour, body o., BO; foul breath, halitosis; stink, pong, reek; fumes, miasma 336 *gas*; putrefaction 51 *decay*; foulness 649 *dirt*; mustiness, fustiness, staleness, frowst, fug; skunk, polecat.

Adjective
(2) *fetid,* strong-smelling reeking, malodorous; smelly, niffy, humming; stinking, rank, foxy; gamy, high; tainted, rancid; putrid 51 *decomposed*; stale, airless, musty, fusty, frowsty, fuggy, smoky, stuffy, suffocating; foul, noisome, noxious, sulphurous; acrid, burning 388 *pungent*; nasty, disagreeable, offensive 827 *unpleasant.*

Verb
(3) *stink,* smell, reek, pong, hum; make a smell, smell offensive; smell bad 51 *decompose*; stink out.

398
Sound

Noun
(1) *sound,* sounding, sound-making; distinctness, audibility, reception 415 *hearing*; audio, mono, stereo; sound waves, vibrations 417 *radiation*; electronic sound, sound effect; sound track, voice-over;

sonorousness 404 *resonance*; noise 400 *loudness*; softness 401 *faintness*; quality of sound, tone, pitch, level, cadence; accent, intonation 577 *voice*; tune 410 *melody*, 412 *music*; types of sound 402 *bang*, 403 *roll*, 404 *resonance*, 405 *nonreasonance*, 406 *sibilation*, 407 *stridor*, 408 *cry*, 409 *ululation*, 411 *discord*; telephone, radio 531 *telecommunication*; recorded sound, high fidelity, hi-fi; record-player 414 *gramophone*; loudspeaker 415 *hearing aid*; unit of sound, decibel, phon, sound barrier.

(2) *acoustics,* phonics; phonology, phonetics; acoustician, sound engineer; phonetician; audiometer.

Adjective
(3) *sounding,* sonic; plain, audible, distinct, heard; resounding, sonorous 404 *resonant*; stentorian 400 *loud*; auditory, acoustic; monophonic, mono; stereophonic, stereo; quadraphonic; high fidelity, hi-fi; audio, audiovisual; radiophonic; phonic, phonetic; unvoiced, voiced 577 *vocal.*

Verb
(4) *sound,* produce s., give out s., emit s. 415 *be heard*; make a noise 400 *be loud*; vocalize, phoneticize 577 *voice.*

399
Silence

Noun
(1) *silence,* stillness, hush, lull, peace, quiet 266 *quiescence*; muteness 578 *voicelessness*; dead silence, deathly hush.

Adjective
(2) *silent,* still, hushed; calm, peaceful, quiet 266 *quiescent*; soft, faint 401 *muted*; noiseless,

soundless, inaudible; sound-proof; speechless, mute 578 *voiceless.*

Verb
(3) *be silent,* hold one's tongue 582 *be taciturn*; not speak 578 *be mute*; be still, make no noise, pipe down, be quiet, lose one's voice.

(4) *silence,* still, lull, hush, quiet, quieten, make silent; stifle, muffle, gag, stop, muzzle 578 *make mute.*

Interjection
(5) *hush!* sh! silence! quiet! hold your tongue! shut up!

400
Loudness

Noun
(1) *loudness,* distinctness, audibility 398 *sound*; noise, loud n., high volume; broken silence, shattered s., burst of sound, report, loud r., sonic boom, thunderclap, shell burst, 402 *bang*; siren, alarm 665 *danger signal*; prolonged noise, reverberation, boom 403 *roll*; gunfire, artillery 712 *bombardment*; stridency, blast, blare, bray, fanfare, trumpet blast; clarion call 547 *call*; sonority, clangour 404 *resonance*; ringing tones; peal, chimes 412 *campanology*; swell, crescendo, fortissimo, tutti, full blast, full chorus; vociferation, clamour, outcry; roaring, shouting, bawling 408 *cry*; noisiness, din, row, racket, crash, clatter, hubbub, hullabaloo, slamming, banging, chanting, hooting, uproar, tumult, bedlam, pandemonium 61 *turmoil.*

(2) *megaphone,* amplifier, loud pedal; loudspeaker, loudhailer, public address system; speaker, microphone, mike; ear trumpet 415 *hearing aid*; whistle, siren, hooter, horn, gong; trumpet,

brass; stentorian voice; town crier.

Adjective
(3) *loud,* distinct, audible, heard; turned right up, at full volume; noisy, uproarious 61 *disorderly*; many-tongued 411 *discordant*; clamorous, shouting, whooping, bellowing 408 *crying*; big-mouthed, loud-m.; sonorous, booming, deep, powerful; full-throated, stentorian, ringing, carrying; deafening, piercing, ear-splitting; thundering, thunderous, rattling, crashing; pealing, clangorous, plangent; shrill 407 *strident*; blaring, brassy; echoing, resounding 404 *resonant*; swelling, crescendo; fortissimo.

Verb
(4) *be loud,* noisy etc. adj.; break the silence, speak up, raise one's voice; call, catcall, caterwaul; scream, whistle 407 *shrill*; shout 408 *vociferate*; clap, stamp, raise the roof; roar, bellow, howl 409 *ululate*; boom, reverberate 404 *resound*; rattle, thunder, clash; ring, peal, clang, crash; bray, blare; slam 402 *bang*; explode, go off; hammer, drill; deafen, stun; swell, fill the air; make a row 61 *rampage*.

Adverb
(5) *loudly,* noisily etc. adj.; aloud; at the top of one's voice; in full cry, full blast, fortissimo, crescendo.

401
Faintness

Noun
(1) *faintness,* softness, inaudibility; less sound, low volume, sound-proofing, noise abatement; dull sound, thud 405 *nonresonance*; whisper, breath, muffled tones 578 *voicelessness*; undertone, murmur 403 *roll*; sigh, sough, moan; squeak,

creak, pop; tick, click; tinkle, clink, chink; purr; plash, swish; rustle, frou-frou; patter, pitter-p.; soft footfall, pad; soft voice, quiet tone.

(2) *silencer,* noise queller, mute, damper, muffler, soft pedal; rubber soles; grease 334 *lubricant*; double glazing, ear plugs.

Adjective
(3) *muted,* distant, faint, inaudible, barely audible, just caught, just heard, half-h.; dying away; weak, feeble, soft, low, gentle; piano, subdued, hushed, stealthy, whispered; dull, dead, muffled, stifled.

Verb
(4) *sound faint,* drop one's voice, whisper, murmur 578 *speak low*; sing low, hum, croon, purr; buzz, drone; babble, ripple, plash 350 *flow*; tinkle, chime; moan, sigh 352 *blow*; rustle, swish etc. n.; fade away, sink into silence.

(5) *mute,* soften, dull, deaden, dampen, hush, muffle, stifle 399 *silence*.

Adverb
(6) *faintly,* inaudibly; in a whisper, under one's breath, sotto voce, aside, in an undertone; piano, pianissimo.

402
Bang: Sudden and violent noise

Noun
(1) *bang,* report, explosion, detonation, blast, blowout, backfire, sonic boom; peal, thunderclap, crash 400 *loudness*; crackle, crack, snap; slap, clap, tap, rap, rat-tat-tat; knock, slam; pop, plop, burst of fire, volley, salvo; shot, pistol-s.; cracker, banger, squib; bomb, grenade 723 *firearm*.

Adjective
(2) *rapping,* banging etc. vb.;

Verb
(3) *crackle,* sizzle, fizzle 318 *effervesce*; crack, click, rattle; snap, clap, rap, tap, slap, smack; plop, plonk.

(4) *bang,* slam, wham, clash, crash, boom; blast, pop, burst 400 *be loud.*

403
Roll: Repeated and protracted sounds

Noun
(1) *roll,* rumbling, grumbling; mutter, murmur; rattle, racket, clack, clatter, chatter; booming, clang, ping, reverberation 404 *resonance*; drumming, tattoo, rat-a-tat; peal, carillon 412 *campanology*; ticktock 106 *repetition*; trill, tremolo, vibrato 410 *musical note*; hum, whirr, buzz, drone; barrage, cannonade, machine gun.

Adjective
(2) *rolling,* booming etc. vb.; reverberant 404 *resonant.*

Verb
(3) *roll,* drum, tattoo, beat a t.; tap, thrum; chug, rev up; boom, roar, grumble, rumble, drone, hum, whirr, trill, chime, peal, toll; tick, beat; rattle, chatter, clatter, clack; reverberate, clang, ping, ring; quaver, vibrate.

404
Resonance

Noun
(1) *resonance,* sonorousness; vibration, reverberation 317 *oscillation*; lingering note, echo; twang, twanging; ringing; singing, peal; sonority, boom; clang, clangour, plangency; brass 400 *loudness*; peal, blare;

tinkle, jingle; chink, clink; ping, ring, chime; low voice, bass, baritone, contralto.

Adjective
(2) *resonant,* vibrant, reverberant, reverberative; fruity, carrying 400 *loud*; booming, echoing, lingering; sonorous, plangent; ringing, deep-toned; booming, hollow, sepulchral.

Verb
(3) *resound,* vibrate, reverberate, echo, reecho 403 *roll*; whirr, buzz; hum, sing; ping, ring, ding; jingle, jangle etc. n.; twang, thrum; toot, trumpet, blare, bray 400 *be loud.*

405
Non resonance

Noun
(1) *nonresonance,* dead sound, dull s.; thud, thump, bump; plump, plop, plonk; muffled drums 401 *faintness*; mute, damper 401 *silencer.*

Adjective
(2) *nonresonant,* muffled, damped 401 *muted*; dead, dull, heavy; cracked 407 *hoarse*; soundproof 399 *silent.*

Verb
(3) *sound dead,* not vibrate, arouse no echoes, click, thump, thud, bump muffle, damp, stop, soften, deaden 401 *mute.*

406
Sibilation: Hissing sound

Noun
(1) *sibilation,* sibilance, hissing, hiss; sibilant; sputter, splutter, splash, rustle, swish; sucking noise, squelch; goose, serpent.

Adjective
(2) *sibilant,* hissing etc. vb.; wheezy, asthmatic.

Verb
(3) *hiss*, snort, wheeze, snuffle, whistle; buzz, fizz, fizzle, sizzle, sputter, splutter, splash, spit; swish, whizz; squelch, suck; rustle 407 *rasp*.

407
Stridor: Harsh sound

Noun
(1) *stridor*, stridency, cacophony 411 *discord*; roughness, raucousness, hoarseness, huskiness, gruffness; harsh sound, aspirate, guttural; scrape, scratch, creak, squeak; shriek, screech, squawk 409 *ululation*; high pitch, shrillness, piping, whistling, bleep; piercing note, high n., sharp n.; high voice, soprano, treble, falsetto, tenor, countertenor; nasality, twang; skirl, brassiness 400 *loudness*; pipe, piccolo 414 *flute*.

Adjective
(2) *strident*, stridulatory; grating, rusty, creaking, jarring harsh, brassy, brazen, metallic; high, high-pitched, high-toned, acute, shrill, piping, penetrating, piercing; ear-splitting 400 *loud*; blaring, braying; dry, reedy, squeaky, scratchy; cracked sharp, flat, inharmonious 411 *discordant*.

(3) *hoarse*, husky, throaty, guttural, raucous, rough, rasping, gruff; grunting, growling; hollow, deep, sepulchral.

Verb
(4) *rasp*, grate, crunch, scrunch, grind, scrape, scratch, squeak; snore, snort; cough, choke, gasp, sob; bray, croak, caw, grunt; burr, aspirate, gutturalize; jar, clash, jangle, twang 411 *discord*.

(5) *shrill*, drone, skirl; blare 400 *be loud*; pipe, flute, whistle; caterwaul 408 *cry*; scream, squeal, screech, squawk; whine, yelp; go right through one.

408
Human cry

Noun
(1) *cry*, exclamation, ejaculation 577 *voice*; utterances 579 *speech*; raised voice, vociferation, shouting 400 *loudness*; yodel, chant 412 *vocal music*; shout, yell, whoop, bawl; howl, scream, shriek; hail 547 *call*; cheer 835 *rejoicing*; sob, sigh 836 *lamentation*; squeal, wail, whine; grunt, gasp 352 *respiration*.

Adjective
(2) *crying*, bawling, clamorous; loud, vocal, vociferous; stentorian, full-throated, lusty; sobbing 836 *lamenting*.

Verb
(3) *cry*, cry out, exclaim, ejaculate 579 *speak*; call, hail 884 *greet*; raise a cry, cheer, whoop; hoot, boo, whistle 924 *disapprove*; scream, screech, yowl, howl, groan 377 *feel pain*; caterwaul, whine, whimper, wail, fret, pule 836 *weep*; yammer, moan 836 *lament*; mutter, grumble 401 *sound faint*; gasp, grunt, snort, snore.

(4) *vociferate*, clamour, shout, bawl, yell, holler; chant, chorus 413 *sing*; cheer, boo; roar, bellow yell, cry out, sing o.; raise one's voice, 400 *be loud*.

409
Ululation: Animal sounds

Noun
(1) *ululation*, animal noise, howling, barking etc. vb.; birdsong, warble, call, cry, note, squeak, cheep, twitter; buzz, drone, hum; hiss, quack, cluck,

squawk etc. vb.; cuckoo, tu-whit tu-whoo.

Adjective
(2) *ululant,* full-throated 400 *loud*; roaring, lowing etc. vb.

Verb
(3) *ululate,* cry, call, give tongue; squawk, screech, caterwaul, yowl, howl, wail; roar, bellow; hum, drone, buzz; spit 406 *hiss*; woof, bark, bay, yelp, yap; snap, snarl, growl, whine; trumpet, bray, neigh, whinny, bleat, low; miaow, mew, purr; quack, cackle, gobble, gabble, cluck; grunt, snort, squeal; chatter, sing, chirp, chirrup, cheep, peep, tweet, twitter; coo, caw, croak; hoot, honk; squeak 407 *rasp*; warble, whistle 413 *sing*.

410
Melody: Concord

Noun
(1) *melody,* musicality 412 *music*; melodiousness, tonality, euphony, harmony, concord; unison; cadence; harmonics, harmonization, counterpoint, polyphony; continuo; tone, tone colour; phrasing 413 *musical skill*; phrase, passage, theme, leit-motiv, coda; movement 412 *musical piece*.

(2) *musical note,* note, keys, keyboard, manual; black notes, white n., sharp, flat, accidental, natural, tone, semitone; keynote, fundamental note; tonic, dominant, leading note; interval, octave; scale (**see** *key*); chord, arpeggio; grace note, ornament; trill, tremolo, vibrato, cadenza; tonality, register, pitch; undertone, overtone, harmonic; phrase, flourish 412 *tune*.

(3) *notation,* sol-fa; written music, sheet m., score; signature, clef, treble c., bass c., tenor c.,

alto c.; bar, stave, staff; rest, pause, interval; breve, minim, crotchet, quaver, semiquaver.

(4) *tempo,* time, beat, rhythm; measure, timing; syncopation; upbeat, downbeat; rallentando, andante, adagio.

(5) *key,* signature, clef, modulation, major key, minor k.; scale; series, tone row; mode.

Adjective
(6) *melodious,* melodic, musical, lilting, tuneful, singable, catchy; tinkling, low, soft 401 *muted*; sweet, dulcet, velvet, mellifluous; clear, ringing, silvery; full-toned 404 *resonant*; euphonious, euphonic; well-pitched.

(7) *harmonious,* concordant 24 *agreeing*; in pitch; in chorus.

(8) *harmonic,* diatonic, chromatic; tonal, atonal, sharp, flat, twelve-toned, keyed, modal, minor, major.

Verb
(9) *harmonize,* concert, blend 24 *accord*; chorus 413 *sing*; attune, tune, tune up, pitch, string 24 *adjust*; be in key, be in unison; orchestrate 413 *compose music*; modulate, transpose.

411
Discord

Noun
(1) *discord,* discordance, dissonance, disharmony 25 *disagreement*; atonality; harshness, cacophony, Babel, caterwauling 400 *loudness*; row, din, racket 61 *turmoil*; atmospherics, wow, flutter.

Adjective
(2) *discordant,* dissonant, jangling 25 *disagreeing*; jarring, grating, scraping, rasping,

harsh, cacophonous 407 *strident*; inharmonious, unmusical, untuneful, untuned, off pitch, off key, out of tune, sharp, flat; tuneless, singsong.

Verb
(3) *discord,* lack harmony 25 *disagree*; jangle, jar, grate, saw, scrape 407 *rasp*; be out of tune, play sharp, play flat.

412
Music

Noun
(1) *music,* harmony 410 *melody*; musicianship 413 *musical skill*; music-making, playing; strumming, thrumming, improvisation; writing music, composition; classical music, chamber m.; sacred m., soul m.; light music, popular m., pop; syncopation, jazz, blues, trad, Dixieland, ragtime, swing; jive, rock 'n' roll, heavy metal, punk; ska, reggae; rhythm 'n' blues, country and western, folk; the music, score; performance, concert; music festival, eisteddfod.

(2) *campanology,* bell ringing, hand r.; ringing, chiming; carillon, chime, peal; round; changes; bell, treble b., tenor b.; bell ringer, campanologist.

(3) *tune,* melody, strain; theme song, signature tune; descant; reprise, refrain; air, aria, solo; flourish, phrase, passage, measure.

(4) *musical piece,* piece, composition, opus, work; recording 414 *gramophone*; orchestration, instrumentation; arrangement, setting; prelude, overture, intermezzo, finale; incidental music, background m.; romance, rhapsody, extravaganza, impromptu, fantasia, caprice, divertimento, variations, raga; medley,

potpourri; suite, fugue, canon, toccata; sonata, concerto, symphony; scherzo, rondo; waltz 837 *dance*; march; dirge; nocturne, serenade; theme, variation; movement; cadenza, coda.

(5) *vocal music,* singing, vocalization; opera, operetta, light opera, comic o., musical comedy, musical 594 *stage play*; choir-singing, oratorio, cantata, chorale; hymn-singing, psalmody, chant, plainsong; recitative; anthem, canticle psalm 981 *hymn*; song, lay, roundelay, carol, lyric, ballad, folk song, ditty, shanty, calypso; spiritual, blues; part song, glee, madrigal, round, catch, canon; chorus, refrain lullaby, cradle song, serenade; requiem, dirge, threnody, 836 *lament.*

(6) *duet,* duo, trio, quartet, quintet, sextet, septet, octet; concerto, solo, ensemble.

Adjective
(7) *musical* 410 melodious; philharmonic, symphonic; melodic, vocal, singable; operatic, recitative; lyric, choral; harmonized 410 *harmonious*; contrapuntal; orchestrated, scored; set to music, arranged; instrumental, orchestral, for strings; blue, cool; hot, jazzy, syncopated, swinging, swung.

Adverb
(8) *adagio,* lento, largo, andante, allegro, allegretto; presto, piano, pianissimo, forte, fortissimo, staccato; crescendo, diminuendo, rallentando; pizzicato, vibrato.

413
Musician

Noun

(1) *musician,* artiste, virtuoso, soloist; player, performer; bard, minstrel, troubadour; busker; composer etc. vb.; librettist, song writer, lyricist; concert goer, music lover.

(2) *instrumentalist,* player; pianist, accompanist; organist; violinist, cellist; harpist, guitarist, banjoist; piper, flautist, flutist, clarinettist, oboist, bassoonist; saxophonist, horn player, trumpeter, bugler; cornetist; drummer, percussionist, timpanist.

(3) *orchestra,* symphony o., chamber o.; ensemble, wind e.; strings, brass, woodwind, percussion, drums; band, jazz b.; brass b., pipe b.; pop group, steel band; conductor, maestro, bandmaster; leader, first violin; orchestra player, bandsman.

(4) *vocalist,* singer, songster, warbler, chanter; minstrel, troubadour, folk singer, pop s., crooner, chanteuse; opera singer, prima donna; treble, soprano, mezzo-s., contralto, alto, tenor, countertenor, baritone, bass b., bass; songbird, nightingale.

(5) *choir,* chorus, waits, wassailers, carol singers, glee club; chorister, choirboy.

(6) *musical skill,* musical ability, musicianship, minstrelsy; performance, execution, fingering, touch, phrasing, expression; virtuosity, bravura 694 *skill.*

Adjective

(7) *musicianly,* musical; vocal, lyric, choral; Gregorian, melodic, warbling, 410 *melodious.*

Verb

(8) *compose music,* compose, set to music, score, arrange, orchestrate; harmonize, improvise, extemporize.

(9) *play music,* play, perform, execute, interpret; sight-read; pick out a tune; conduct, beat time; play the piano, accompany; pluck the strings, strum, thrum, twang; wind, blow, sound the horn; toot, tootle; pipe, flute, whistle; clash the cymbals; drum, beat, tap, ruffle 403 *roll;* peal the bells, ring, toll, knell; tune, string; practise, do scales; improvise, extemporize; strike up; give an encore.

(10) *sing,* vocalize, chant, hymn; intone, descant; warble, carol, lilt, trill, croon, hum, whistle, yodel; harmonize, chorus; sing to, serenade; chirp, twitter 409 *ululate.*

414
Musical instruments

Noun

(1) *musical instrument,* strings, brass, wind, woodwind, percussion 413 *orchestra;* sounding board, sound box; synthesizer.

(2) *harp,* lyre, lute, sitar; guitar, electric g., mandolin, banjo, zither; plectrum, fret.

(3) *viol,* violin, fiddle; viola, cello, double bass; bow, string.

(4) *piano,* grand piano; harpsichord, spinet; player piano, pianola; keyboard, manual, keys.

(5) *organ,* harmonium; mouth organ, harmonica; accordion, concertina; barrel organ, hurdy-gurdy; organ pipe, flue p.; stop, manual, keyboard.

(6) *flute,* fife, piccolo, recorder; woodwind, clarinet, saxophone, oboe, cor Anglais; bassoon; pipe, whistle; bagpipes; mouthpiece, embouchure.

(7) *horn,* brass; bugle, trumpet, clarion; French horn; cornet, trombone, tuba.

(8) *gong,* bell, church bell, alarm bell, tocsin 665 *danger signal;* peal, carillon, chimes, bells; bones, rattle, clappers, castanets, maracas; cymbals; xylophone, vibraphone; harmonica; tubular bell, glockenspiel; triangle; tuning fork.

(9) *drum,* big d., side d., snare d., kettle d., timpani; war drum, tomtom; tabor, tambourine; tabla.

(10) *gramophone,* record player, tape recorder, cassette r.; high fidelity system, hi-fi, stereo, music centre; playback; recording, tape r., tape, cassette; record, disc, platter; musical box, jukebox; deck, turntable; amplifier, speaker.

(11) *mute,* damper, soft pedal.

415
Hearing

Noun
(1) *hearing,* acoustics 398 *sound;* sense of hearing, good h.; good ear, sharp e., acute e., musical e.; audibility, reception, earshot.

(2) *listening,* hearkening 455 *attention;* listening-in, tuning-in; lip-reading eavesdropping, overhearing, wire-tapping, bugging 523 *latency;* audition, interview; audience, hearing 584 *conference.*

(3) *listener,* hearer, audience 441 *spectator;* radio listener, radio ham; hi-fi enthusiast, audiophile; disciple 538 *learner;* monitor, examiner 459 *questioner;*

eavesdropper 453 *inquisitive person.*

(4) *hearing aid,* ear; deaf-aid, ear trumpet; stethoscope; loudspeaker, amplifier 400 *megaphone;* telephone, receiver; headphones, earphones 531 *telecommunication;* sound recorder, magnetic tape 414 *gramophone.*

Adjective
(5) *auditory,* hearing, aural; audiovisual 398 *sounding;* acoustic; keen-eared, listening, tuned in; all ears 455 *attentive;* within earshot, audible, heard.

Verb
(6) *hear,* catch; listen, listen in, switch on, tune in; overhear, eavesdrop; intercept, bug, tap; hearken, give ear, lend an e.; interview 459 *interrogate;* be all ears, lap up 455 *be attentive;* hear it said, come to one's ears.

(7) *be heard,* become audible, reach the ear, fall on the e. 400 *be loud;* gain a hearing.

Adverb
(8) *in earshot,* in one's hearing.

416
Deafness

Noun
(1) *deafness,* impaired hearing; deaf-mutism, deaf-mute; inaudibility 399 *silence.*

Adjective
(2) *deaf,* hard of hearing; stonedeaf, deaf and dumb, deaf-mute; deafened, stunned, unable to hear; deaf to, not listening 456 *inattentive;* unmusical, tonedeaf; hard to hear 401 *muted;* inaudible, out of earshot.

Verb
(3) *be deaf,* not hear, hear nothing, fail to catch; not listen, refuse to hear, stop one's ears, turn a deaf ear 458 *disregard;* lip-read.

(4) *deafen*, stun, split the eardrum, drown one's voice 400 *be loud*.

417
Light

Noun

(1) *light*, daylight, broad day 128 *morning*; sunlight, sun 420 *luminary*; moonlight, twilight 419 *half-light*; artificial light 420 *lighting*; illumination, resplendence, intensity, brightness, vividness, brilliance; luminosity, candle power, magnitude; incandescence, radiance (**see** *glow*); sheen, shine (**see** *reflection*); blaze of light, sheet of l., flood of l.; glare, dazzle, flare, flame 379 *fire*; halo, nimbus, aureole, corona; variegated light, spectrum 437 *variegation*; coloration 425 *colour*; white 427 *whiteness*.

(2) *flash*, lightning flash; beam, stream, shaft, ray, streak; sparkle, spark; glint, glitter, play of light; twinkle, flicker, *flickering*, glimmer, gleam, shimmer; spangle, tinsel; searchlight 420 *lamp*; firefly 420 *glow-worm*.

(3) *glow*, flush, dawn, sunset; steady flame, steady beam; lambency; radiance 379 *heat*; luminescence, fluorescence, phosphorescence 420 *glow-worm*.

(4) *radiation*, background r.; radioactivity 160 *nucleonics*; radioisotope; particle counter, Geiger c.; fallout, mushroom cloud 659 *poison*; radio wave, waveband, wavelength, high frequency; microwave; X-ray; röntgen, rem; half-life.

(5) *reflection*, refraction, diffraction; polarization; polish, gloss, sheen, shine, lustre; glare, dazzle; reflector 442 *mirror*; hologram 551 *image*.

(6) *light contrast*, tonality, chiaroscuro; light and shade, black and white, half-tone, mezzotint; highlights.

(7) *optics*, fibre optics; spectroscopy 442 *optical device*; radiology.

Adjective

(8) *luminous*, light, lit, well-lit, floodlit; bright, gay, shining, resplendent, splendid, brilliant, flamboyant, vivid; colourful 425 *coloured*; radiant, dazzling, blinding, glaring, lurid, garish; incandescent, glowing, aflame, aglow, ablaze 379 *fiery*; luminescent, fluorescent, phosphorescent; soft, lambent; beaming etc. vb.; glittery, flashing, scintillating, sparkling; lustrous, shiny, glossy; reflecting, refractive; optical; photosensitive.

(9) *undimmed*, clear, bright, fair, cloudless, sunny; moonlit, starry; burnished, polished, glassy, gleaming; translucent 422 *transparent*.

(10) *radiating*, radiant; cosmic, radioactive, irradiated, hot.

Verb

(11) *shine*, be bright, glow, burn, blaze 379 *be hot*; glare, dazzle, blind; play, dance; flash, coruscate; glisten, glimmer, flicker, twinkle; glitter, shimmer, glance; scintillate, sparkle; reflect; take a shine, come up, gleam, glint.

(12) *radiate*, beam, shoot out rays 300 *emit*; reflect, refract; be radioactive; X-ray.

(13) *make bright*, lighten; dawn, rise, wax (moon); clear, clear up, lift, brighten; light, ignite 381 *kindle*; light up, switch on, throw light on; shine upon, flood with light, irradiate, illuminate; polish, burnish.

418
Darkness

Noun

(1) *darkness*, dark; black 428 *blackness*; night, nightfall; obscurity, murk, gloom, dusk, shadows 419 *dimness*; shade, shadow, penumbra; silhouette, negative; cavern, dungeon.

(2) *obscuration*, darkening 419 *dimness*; blackout, fade; occultation, eclipse; lights out; sunset, sundown 129 *evening*; blackening, shading, hatching, cross-h.

Adjective

(3) *dark*, sombre, dark-coloured 428 *black*; obscure, pitch-dark, inky; murky, funereal, gloomy, dreary, dismal; louring, lurid 419 *dim*; shady 419 *shadowy*; shaded, darkened 421 *screened*.

(4) *unlit*, sunless, moonless, starless; eclipsed, overshadowed; overcast, cloudy 423 *opaque*; switched off, extinguished; dipped, dimmed, blacked out.

Verb

(5) *be dark*, grow d., lour, gather; fade out 419 *be dim*.

(6) *darken*, black, brown; black out, dim the light, eclipse 226 *cover*; obscure veil 421 *screen*; dim, tone down; overshadow, cast a shadow; shade, hatch, cross-h. 428 *blacken*.

(7) *snuff out*, extinguish, quench, pinch out, blow o., switch off, dip, douse.

Adverb

(8) *darkling*, in the dark, in the shadows; by night.

419
Dimness

Noun

(1) *dimness*, vagueness, indistinctness, blur, soft focus; faintness, paleness 429 *greyness*; lacklustre, lack of sparkle, matt finish; leaden skies; cloudiness, dullness, poor visibility 423 *opacity*; mistiness, fogginess, murk, gloom 418 *darkness*.

(2) *half-light*, bad light; semidarkness, gloaming 129 *evening*; twilight; dusk; grey dawn; penumbra, partial eclipse.

(3) *glimmer*, flicker 417 *flash*; firefly 420 *glow-worm*; firelight, candlelight 417 *light*; ember, hot coal; moonbeam, moonlight.

Adjective

(4) *dim*, dusky, dusk, twilight; wan, grey, pale, faint, faded, waning; indistinct, blurred; dull, lustreless, lacklustre, leaden; flat, matt; hazy, misty nebulous, cloudy 423 *opaque*.

(5) *shadowy*, shady, shaded, overshadowed, overcast, overclouded 418 *unlit*; vague, indistinct, obscure, fuzzy, blurry, looming; half-seen, half-glimpsed, half-hidden 444 *invisible*; dreamlike, ghostly 4 *insubstantial*.

Verb

(6) *be dim*, faint etc. adj.; fade, wane, pale 426 *lose colour*; glimmer, flicker, gutter, sputter.

(7) *bedim*, dim, dip; lower the lights, fade out 418 *snuff out*; obscure 440 *blur*; smirch, smear, dirty 649 *make unclean*; mist 423 *make opaque*; overshadow, overcast; shade, shadow, veil 418 *darken*.

Adverb
(8) *dimly,* vaguely, in the half-light, in the gloaming.

420
Luminary: Source of light

Noun
(1) *luminary,* naked light, flame 379 *fire*; source of light 321 *sun,* orb of night 321 *moon*; fireball 321 *meteor*; Milky Way, northern lights; lightning, sheet l., forked l.; scintilla, spark 417 *flash.*

(2) *glow-worm,* firefly 417 *glow*; fireball; dragon.

(3) *torch,* brand, coal, ember; match 385 *lighter*; candle, taper, spill, wick, dip, rushlight; flare, gas jet, burner; torchlight, nightlight.

(4) *lamp,* lantern, safety lamp, hurricane l.; gas mantle, electric lamp; torch, flashlight, searchlight, arc light, floodlight; headlight, headlamp; bulb, filament; stroboscope; neon light, strip l.; street l., lamplight; Chinese lantern, fairy lights; magic lantern, projector; light fitting, chandelier; candelabra, candlestick.

(5) *lighting,* illumination 417 *light*; floodlighting, limelight, footlights, spotlight, houselights.

(6) *signal light,* traffic light 665 *danger signal*; rocket, flare; beacon 547 *signal*; lighthouse, lightship.

(7) *fireworks,* illuminations, firework display, pyrotechnics; rocket, Catherine wheel, sparkler; banger.

Adjective
(8) *luminescent,* luminous, incandescent, shining; phosphorescent, fluorescent; radiant

417 *radiating*; illuminated, well-lit; bright, gay.

Verb
(9) *illuminate,* light up, light 417 *shine, make bright.*

421
Screen

Noun
(1) *screen,* shield 660 *protection*; bower 194 *arbour*; sunshade, parasol; sun hat 226 *shade*; awning, visor, lampshade, blinkers; dark glasses, sun g.; smoked glass 424 *semitransparency*; smoke screen 423 *opacity*; partition 235 *fence*; filter 57 *exclusion*; mask 527 *disguise*; hood, veil, mantle 228 *cloak.*

(2) *curtain* 226 shade; blind, sunblind, shutter.

Adjective
(3) *screened,* sheltered; shady, bowery 419 *shadowy*; blindfolded, hooded 439 *blind*; screening, impervious, impermeable.

Verb
(4) *screen,* shield, shelter, protect; ward off, keep off, keep out, filter out 57 *exclude*; veil, hood 226 *cover*; mask, hide, shroud 525 *conceal*; blinker, blindfold 439 *blind*; shade, shadow, darken; curtain off 264 *close*; cloud, fog, mist 423 *make opaque.*

422
Transparency

Noun
(1) *transparency,* translucence; lucidity, pellucidity, limpidity; clearness, clarity; water, ice, crystal, glass; pane, window p.; gossamer, gauze 4 *insubstantial thing.*

Adjective
(2) *transparent,* diaphanous, re-

vealing, sheer, see-through; thin, fine, filmy, gauzy, pellucid, translucent; liquid, limpid; crystal, crystalline, vitreous, glassy; clear, lucid; crystal-clear.

Verb
(3) *be transparent,* transmit light, show through; shine through 417 *make bright.*

423
Opacity

Noun
(1) *opacity,* opaqueness; filminess, frost; turbidity, muddiness 649 *dirt;* fog, mist, smog 355 *cloud;* film, scale 421 *screen;* smoke screen.

Adjective
(2) *opaque,* blank, windowless; not clear, cloudy, milky, filmy; turbid, muddy, puddled; foggy, hazy, misty, murky, smoky 419 *dim;* uncleaned 649 *dirty;* coated, frosted, misted, clouded.

Verb
(3) *make opaque,* cloud, cloud over; frost, film, smoke 226 *coat;* be opaque 421 *screen.*

424
Semi transparency

Noun
(1) *semitransparency,* milkiness, opalescence; smoked glass, frosted g., dark glasses; gauze, muslin, net; tissue paper.

Adjective
(2) *semitransparent,* gauzy, filmy; translucent, opalescent, milky, pearly; frosted, matt, misty, smoked 419 *dim.*

425
Colour

Noun
(1) *colour,* primary c.; range of colour, chromatic scale; prism, spectrum, rainbow 437 *variegation;* colour scheme, palette; coloration 553 *painting.*

(2) *chromatics,* science of colour; spectroscope, prism.

(3) *hue,* brilliance, intensity, warmth; coloration, pigmentation, colouring, complexion, natural colour; flush, blush; glow; sickly hue, pallor; faded hue, discoloration; tint, shade, nuance; tinge, patina.

(4) *pigment,* colouring matter, rouge, warpaint 843 *cosmetic;* dyestuff, dye, cochineal, indigo, woad; stain, fixative, mordant; wash, colourwash, paint; watercolours 553 *art equipment.*

Adjective
(5) *coloured,* tinted etc. vb.; in colour, painted, tinged, dyed; colourful, chromatic; kaleidoscopic, many-coloured 437 *variegated.*

(6) *florid,* colourful, high-coloured, bright-hued; ruddy 431 *red;* intense, deep, strong, vivid, brilliant 417 *luminous;* warm, glowing, rich, gorgeous; painted, gay, bright; gaudy, garish, showy, flashy; harsh, stark, raw, crude; lurid, loud, screaming, shrieking; clashing, discordant.

(7) *soft-hued,* soft, quiet, tender, delicate, refined; pearly, creamy 427 *whitish;* light, pale, pastel, muted; dull; simple, sober, plain; sombre, dark 428 *black;* drab, dingy, faded; weathered, mellow; matching, toning, harmonious 24 *agreeing.*

Verb
(8) *colour,* colour in, crayon, daub 553 *paint*; rouge 431 *redden*; pigment, tattoo; dye, dip, imbue; tint, touch up; shade, 428 *blacken*; wash, lacquer 226 *coat*; stain, run, discolour; tan, weather, mellow; illuminate, emblazon; whitewash, silver 427 *whiten*; yellow 433 *gild*; enamel 437 *variegate.*

426
Achromatism:
Absence of colour

Noun
(1) *achromatism,* fading, bleaching 427 *whiteness*; pallor, paleness, lightness, no colour, anaemia, bloodlessness; neutral tint; monochrome, black and white; albino, blond(e), platinum b.

(2) *bleacher,* peroxide, bleach, lime.

Adjective
(3) *colourless,* neutral; discoloured; bleached, faint, faded; overexposed; fading; albino, light-skinned, fair, blond 433 *yellow,* 427 *whitish*; lustreless, mousy; bloodless, anaemic; without colour, drained of colour, washed out, washy; pale, pallid 427 *white*; ashy, ashen, livid, whey-faced, pasty, doughy, mealy, sallow, sickly 651 *unhealthy*; dingy, dull, leaden 429 *grey*; blank, glassy, lacklustre; lurid, ghastly, wan 419 *dim*; deathly, cadaverous, pale as death.

Verb
(4) *lose colour* 419 *be dim*; pale, fade, bleach, blanch, turn pale.

(5) *decolorize,* fade, blanch, bleach 427 *whiten*; tone down, weaken; dim dull, tarnish, discolour 649 *make unclean.*

427
Whiteness

Noun
(1) *whiteness,* lack of pigment; white heat 379 *heat*; white person, paleface; albino.

(2) *white thing,* alabaster, snow, ivory, lily, swan; silver, pewter, platinum; pearl, teeth; white patch, blaze.

(3) *whiting,* whitewash, white paint.

Adjective
(4) *white,* pure, dazzling 417 *luminous*; silvered, silvery, silver; chalky, snowy, frosty, frosted; foam-flecked; soapy, lathery; white hot; pure white, lily-white, milk-w., snow-w.; white-skinned, Caucasian; whitened, whitewashed, bleached.

(5) *whitish,* pearly, milky 424 *semitransparent*; creamy ivory, waxen; sallow, pale 426 *colourless*; off-white, half-w.; mushroom, hoary, grizzled 429 *grey*; blond, fair, Nordic; ash-blond(e), fair-haired, flaxen-h., tow-headed.

Verb
(6) *whiten,* white, whitewash; blanch, bleach; pale, fade 426 *decolorize*; frost, silver, grizzle.

428
Blackness

Noun
(1) *blackness,* black, sable; swarthiness, duskiness, pigmentation, dark colouring; blackening, darkening 418 *darkness*; black person, coloured p.

(2) *black thing,* coal, charcoal, soot, pitch, tar; ebony, jet, ink crow, raven; crepe, mourning.

(3) *black pigment*, blacking, lampblack, ink, printer's i.

Adjective
(4) *black*, sable; jetty, inky; nocturnal 418 *dark*; blackened, singed, charred; black-haired, raven-haired; black-eyed, sloe-e.; dark, brunette; black-skinned, Negroid, pigmented, coloured; sombre, gloomy, mourning 364 *funereal*; coal-black, jet-b., pitch-b.; blue-b.

(5) *blackish*, rather black, swarthy, dusky, dark, dark-skinned, tanned, sun-t.; livid, black and blue.

Verb
(6) *blacken*, black, japan, ink in; blot, smudge; deepen 418 *darken*; singe, char 381 *burn*.

429
Greyness

Noun
(1) *greyness*, grey, neutral tint; grey hairs, hoary head; pewter, gunmetal, ashes, slate; oyster.

Adjective
(2) *grey*, neutral; leaden, livid; cool, quiet; greying, grizzled, grizzly, hoary, silvery, pearly 427 *whitish*; light-grey, ash-g., dove-g., pearl-g.; mousy, donkey-grey; steely, bluish-grey, greyish, ashy, smoky, dapple-grey.

430
Brownness

Noun
(1) *brownness*, brown, bronze, copper, amber; autumn colours; cinnamon, coffee, chocolate; butterscotch, caramel, toffee; walnut, mahogany; suntan; brunette.

(2) *brown pigment*, ochre, sepia, raw sienna, burnt s., raw umber, burnt u.

Adjective
(3) *brown*, bronze etc. n.; browned, toasted; bronzed, tanned, sunburnt; dark, brunette; nut-brown, hazel; light brown, oatmeal, beige, buff, fawn, biscuit; brownish, greyish-brown, dun, drab, khaki; tawny, tan, foxy; reddish-brown, chestnut, auburn, russet, maroon; dark brown, peat-b.; coffee-coloured. n.

Verb
(4) *embrown*, brown, bronze, tan; toast 381 *burn*.

431
Redness

Noun
(1) *redness*, blush, flush 417 *glow*; reddening, warmth; rosiness, ruddiness, red cheeks; high colour, floridness; red colour, crimson, scarlet etc. adj.; burgundy, claret; gore 335 *blood*; ruby; redskin, redhead.

(2) *red pigment*, red dye, cochineal, carmine, vermilion; madder, crimson lake, red ochre, red lead; rouge, lipstick 843 *cosmetic*.

Adjective
(3) *red*, reddish; ruddy, sanguine, florid; glowing, red-hot 379 *hot*; flushed, fevered; flushing, blushing; red-cheeked, rosy-c.; bright red, beetroot-red; flame-coloured, red-haired, ginger-h.; carroty, sandy, auburn; russet, rust-coloured 430 *brown*; pink, rose-p., roseate, rosy, rose-coloured, flesh-pink, shell-p., salmon-p., shocking-p.; coral, crimson, cherry-red, cerise, carmine; fuchsia, magenta, maroon 436 *purple*; wine-coloured; scarlet, cardinal-red, vermilion; reddened, rouged.

(4) *bloodstained,* bloodshot; blood-red; sanguinary, bloody, gory.

Verb
(5) *redden,* rouge 843 *primp*; dye red, stain with blood; flush, blush, glow; mantle, colour, colour up, crimson, go red.

432
Orange

Noun
(1) *orange,* red and yellow, gold, old gold; copper, amber; apricot, tangerine; ochre, henna.

Adjective
(2) *orange,* gold etc. n.; coppery, ginger, tan; flame-coloured, copper-c., brassy.

433
Yellowness

Noun
(1) *Yellowness,* yellow etc. adj.; brass, gold, topaz, amber; sulphur, brimstone; buttercup, primrose; lemon, saffron; biliousness, jaundice, sallow skin; fair hair; blond(e).

(2) *yellow pigment,* gamboge, cadmium yellow, chrome y., yellow ochre.

Adjective
(3) *yellow,* gold etc. n.; tawny, sandy; fair-haired, golden-h. 427 *whitish*; creamy, creamcoloured; honey-c., straw-c.; pale yellow, acid y., lemon y.; canary yellow, sunshine y., mustard y.; gilt, gilded; yellowy, yellowish, jaundiced, bilious.

(4) *gild,* yellow.

434
Greenness

Noun
(1) *greenness,* green etc. adj.; verdancy, greenery, verdure 366 *foliage*; jade, emerald; verdigris, patina.

(2) *green pigment,* chlorophyll.

Adjective
(3) *green,* verdant; grassy, leafy; grass-green, moss-g.; sea-green 435 *blue*; jade-green, sap-g., bottle-g.; sage-g., pea-g., apple-g., lime-g.; avocado, olive, olivegreen, glaucous, greenish.

435
Blueness

Noun
(1) *blueness,* blue, azure; blue sky, blue sea; cornflower, gentian, forget-me-not; sapphire, aquamarine, turquoise etc. adj.; bluishness, lividity.

(2) *blue pigment,* indigo, woad; ultramarine, cobalt.

Adjective
(3) *blue,* azure, sky-blue; turquoise; light blue, pale blue, powder-b., Cambridge-b.; aquamarine, peacock-blue, kingfisher-b.; royal-b., ultramarine, deep blue, dark b., Oxford-b., navy-b., navy; indigo; blueblack, black and blue, livid.

Verb
(4) *blue,* turn blue; dye blue.

436
Purpleness

Noun
(1) *purpleness,* purple, blue and red; amethyst; lavender, violet, heliotrope, heather, foxglove; plum, aubergine; gentian violet.

Adjective

(2) *purple,* purplish, purpled; violet, mauve, lavender, lilac; purple-red, fuchsia, magenta; plum-coloured, puce; dark purple, mulberry, livid, black and blue.

Verb

(3) *empurple,* purple.

437
Variegation

Noun

(1) *variegation,* variety, play of colour, shot colours, iridescence, opal, mother of pearl; shot silk, moire; tricolour 425 *colour*; motley, harlequin, patchwork; riot of colour; stained glass, kaleidoscope; rainbow, spectrum, prism.

(2) *chequer,* check, hound's tooth, plaid, tartan; chessboard; marquetry, inlay 844 *ornamental art*; mosaic, crazy paving 43 *medley*.

(3) *stripe,* line, streak, band, bar; agate; zebra, tiger; crack, craze.

(4) *maculation,* mottle, dappling, stippling, marbling; spottiness, patchiness; patch, speck, speckle; spot, freckle, fleck, dot, polka d.; blotch, splotch, splash; leopard, Dalmatian.

Adjective

(5) *variegated,* patterned etc. vb.; embroidered, worked 844 *ornamental*; colourful 425 *florid*; multi-coloured, rainbow-c.; motley; kaleidoscopic 82 *multiform*; plaid, tartan.

(6) *iridescent,* opalescent, pearly; shot through with, watered.

(7) *pied,* grizzled, piebald, skewbald; chequered, dappled, patchy.

(8) *mottled,* marbled, veined, reticulated; studded, spotted, speckled, freckled; streaky, streaked, barred, banded, striped 222 *crossed*; brindled, tabby; pockmarked 845 *blemished*.

Verb

(9) *variegate,* pattern, chequer; embroider 844 *decorate*; damascene, inlay; stud, dot with, mottle, speckle, spangle, spot; stipple, dapple; streak, stripe, marble, vein; stain, discolour.

438
Vision

Noun

(1) *vision,* sight, power of s., eyesight; seeing, visualization, perception, recognition; good sight, keen s., sharp s., long s., normal s.; defective vision, short sight 440 *dim sight*; oculist, optician, ophthalmologist.

(2) *eye,* visual organ; eyeball, iris, pupil, white, cornea, retina, optic nerve; eyelid, eyelash, naked eye, unaided e., hawk, eagle.

(3) *look,* regard, glance, side g., squint, blink; gaze, observation, contemplation, watch; stare, fixed s.; come-hither look, ogle, leer 889 *wooing*; wink 524 *hint*; grimace, dirty look, scowl; peep, peek, glimpse.

(4) *inspection,* examination 459 *enquiry*; view, preview 522 *manifestation*; oversight, supervision 689 *management*; survey, sweep, reconnoitre; sight-seeing, rubbernecking; look, once-over; second glance, double take; review, revision; viewing, home v. 531 *broadcasting*; discernment, catching sight, first sight; looking round, observation, prying, spying; peeping, voyeurism, Peeping Tom.

(5) *view,* vista, prospect, outlook, perspective; aspect 445 *appearance*; panorama, bird's-eye view; horizon; line of sight, line of vision; range of view, purview, ken; scene, setting, stage; angle of vision, slant; point of view, viewpoint, standpoint; vantage point, lookout 209 *high structure*; observatory; grandstand, stall 441 *onlookers*; peephole 263 *window.*

Adjective

(6) *seeing,* glimpsing etc. vb.; visual, perceptible 443 *visible*; panoramic; ocular, ophthalmic, optical; stereoscopic, binocular; perspicacious, clear-sighted, sharp-s., keen-eyed, lynx-e.; vigilant, all eyes; visionary 513 *imaginative.*

Verb

(7) *see,* behold, use one's eyes; perceive, discern, distinguish, make out, pick o.; descry, discover 484 *detect*; sight, espy, spy, spot, observe 455 *notice*; lay eyes on, catch sight of, sight, glimpse; view, hold in view, have in sight; witness, look on 441 *watch*; visualize 513 *imagine*; have second sight 510 *foresee.*

(8) *gaze,* regard, quiz, gaze at, look, look at; eye, stare, peer; goggle, gape, gawp; focus, rivet one's eyes, fix one's gaze; glare, glower 891 *be angry*; glance, glance at; squint, look askance; wink, blink 524 *hint*; make eyes at, ogle, leer 889 *court*; gloat over, feast one's eyes on; steal a glance, peep, peek, take a peep; direct one's gaze, notice, look upon 455 *be attentive*; look away, avert one's eyes; exchange glances, make eye contact.

(9) *scan,* scrutinize, inspect, examine, look one up and down; take stock of, contemplate, pore over 536 *study*; look over, look through, read t., riffle t., leaf t., skim t.; take a look, see, take in; view, survey, reconnoitre; scout, spy, pry, snoop; observe, watch 457 *invigilate*; hold in view, keep in sight; watch out for, look out f., keep an eye out for, keep watch; strain one's eyes, peer; squint at, crane one's neck, stand on tiptoe.

Adverb

(10) *at sight,* at first sight; in view 443 *visibly*; in sight of.

Interjection

(11) *look!* view halloo! land ahoy!

439
Blindness

Noun

(1) *blindness,* lack of vision; lack of light 418 *darkness*; sightlessness, eye disease, glaucoma, cataract; night blindness, snow b., colour b. 440 *dim sight*; blind side, blind spot; tunnel vision; blind eye 456 *inattention*; glass eye, artificial e.; blind person.

Adjective

(2) *blind,* sightless, eyeless, visionless; unseeing 456 *inattentive*; blinded, blindfold, blinkered 440 *dim-sighted*; in the dark, benighted; blind as a bat.

Verb

(3) *be blind,* go blind, lose one's sight, lose one's eyes; not use one's eyes, not see; lose sight of; feel one's way 461 *be tentative*; wear blinkers; be blind to 491 *not know*; avert one's eyes 458 *disregard*; blink, squint 440 *be dim-sighted.*

(4) *blind,* put out one's eyes, deprive of sight; dazzle, darken, obscure 419 *bedim*; blinker, blindfold, bandage; hoodwink 495 *mislead.*

440
Dim-sightedness: Imperfect vision

Noun

(1) *dim sight,* weak s., failing s., purblindness 439 *blindness;* half-vision, partial v., defective v.; weak eyes, eyestrain, bleariness; short-sight, near-sightedness; long sight, far s.; double vision; astigmatism, cataract, film; dizziness, swimming; cast, squint, cross-eye; wall-eye, cock-e., wink, blink; blinker, veil, curtain, blind side, blind spot 444 *invisibility.*

(2) *visual fallacy,* illusion, optical i., trick of light, phantasm, mirage 542 *deception;* phantom, spectre, apparition 970 *ghost;* vision, dream 513 *fantasy.*

Adjective

(3) *dim-sighted,* one-eyed; sight-impaired, purblind, half-blind; weak-eyed, bespectacled; myopic, short-sighted, near-s.; long-sighted; astigmatic; colour-blind; cross-eyed, wall-eyed, squinting 845 *blemished;* bleary-eyed, blinking, dazzled, blinded 439 *blind.*

Verb

(4) *be dim-sighted,* need spectacles, grope, peer, squint; blink, screw up one's eyes, see double, grow dazzled; swim, grow blurred, dim, fail.

(5) *blur,* confuse; glare, dazzle 417 *shine;* darken, be indistinct, loom 419 *be dim.*

441
Spectator

Noun

(1) *spectator,* beholder; looker, viewer, observer, watcher; inspector, examiner, scrutinizer; witness, eyewitness; passerby, bystander, onlooker; voyeur, peeping Tom; window shopper; sightseer 268 *traveller;* stargazer, astronomer; bird watcher, train spotter; lookout, watch, sentinel 664 *warner;* scout, spy, snoop 459 *detective;* filmgoer, theatregoer 594 *playgoer;* viewer, TV addict.

(2) *onlookers,* audience, auditorium, gate; house, gallery, circle, dress c., pit, stalls; grandstand, terraces; crowd, supporters, followers, fans 707 *patron.*

Verb

(3) *watch,* look on, look at, look in, view 438 *see;* witness 189 *be present;* follow, observe 455 *be attentive;* gape, gawk, stare; spy out 438 *scan.*

442
Optical instrument

Noun

(1) *optical device,* lens, eyepiece; prism, spectroscope, kaleidoscope; stroboscope; stereoscope; light meter, exposure m.; telephoto lens, zoom l.; projector, epidiascope, magic lantern 445 *cinema;* microfilm reader, slide viewer 551 *photography.*

(2) *eyeglass,* spectacles, specs, glasses, pince-nez, sunglasses, dark glasses, bifocals; contact lens; lorgnette, monocle; magnifying glass, hand lens; oculist, optician.

(3) *telescope* 321 *astronomy;* sight, finder, viewfinder; periscope; spyglass, binoculars, field glasses, opera g.

(4) *microscope,* electron m. 196 *microscopy.*

(5) *mirror,* reflector; glass, looking g.

(6) *camera,* cinecamera; shutter, aperture, stop; flashgun 420 *lamp;* film 551 *photography.*

443
Visibility

Noun
(1) *visibility,* sight, exposure 445 *appearance*; distinctness, clearness, clarity, definition, conspicuousness, prominence; eyewitness, ocular proof, visible evidence 522 *manifestation*; visual aid 534 *teaching*; scene, field of view 438 *view*; high visibility, low v.; ceiling, horizon 183 *range*.

Adjective
(2) *visible,* discernible, observable, detectable; recognizable, unmistakable, apparent 445 *appearing*; evident, showing 522 *manifest*; exposed, open, naked, outcropping, exposed to view; sighted, in view, in full v.; before one's eyes, under one's nose; telescopic, just visible, panoramic, stereoscopic.

(3) *obvious,* showing 522 *shown*; plain, clear, clear-cut, crystal-clear, well-defined, well-marked; distinct, in focus; spectacular, conspicuous, prominent, salient; eye-catching, striking, glaring, pronounced, highlighted; plain to see.

Verb
(4) *be visible,* obvious etc. adj.; become visible, show; show through, shine t. 422 *be transparent*; meet the eye 455 *attract notice*; strike one, catch the eye, stand out; loom up, heave in sight, come into view, show its face 445 *appear*; stick out, project 254 *jut*; manifest itself, expose i., betray i. 522 *be plain*; stay in sight; make visible, expose 522 *manifest*.

Adverb
(5) *visibly,* clearly etc. adj.; before one's eyes; on show, on view.

444
Invisibility

Noun
(1) *invisibility,* vanishing 446 *disappearance*; vagueness, poor visibility, obscurity 419 *dimness*; remoteness 199 *farness*; littleness 196 *minuteness*; privacy 883 *seclusion*; hiding 525 *concealment*; mist, fog, veil, curtain 421 *screen*; blind spot, blind corner 439 *blindness*.

Adjective
(2) *invisible,* indistinguishable, imperceptible, indiscernible; unseen, unnoticed 458 *neglected*; out of sight 446 *disappearing*; not in sight 199 *distant*; hidden, lurking 523 *latent*; disguised, camouflaged 525 *concealed*; obscured, eclipsed, darkened 418 *unlit*.

(3) *indistinct,* partly-seen, half-s.; ill-defined, indefinite, indistinct 419 *dim*; faint, inconspicuous, microscopic 196 *minute*; confused, vague, blurred, out of focus; fuzzy, misty, hazy.

Verb
(4) *be unseen,* hide, go to earth, lie in ambush 523 *lurk*; escape notice, blush unseen; become invisible, pale, fade 419 *be dim*; vanish 446 *disappear*; make invisible 525 *conceal*; veil 421 *screen*; darken, eclipse.

Adverb
(5) *invisibly,* silently 525 *stealthily*; behind the scenes; in the dark.

445
Appearance

Noun
(1) *appearance* 443 *visibility*; rise 68 *beginning*; becoming, realization, materialization, presence 1 *existence*; exhibition, display 522 *manifestation*;

revelation 484 *discovery*; externals, outside 223 *exteriority*; appearances, look of things; visual impact, impression, effect; image, pose, front 541 *duplicity*; veneer, show, seeming, semblance; side, aspect, facet; phase, guise, garb; colour, light; outline, shape 243 *form*; set, hang, look; angle, slant 438 *view*; vision 513 *fantasy*; mirage, hallucination, illusion 440 *visual fallacy*; apparition 970 *ghost*.

(2) *spectacle,* impression, effect; vision, sight, scene; scenery, landscape, seascape, townscape; panorama 438 *view*; display, parade 875 *ostentation*; revue, extravaganza, pantomime, floor show 594 *stage show*; television, video 531 *broadcasting*; pyrotechnics 420 *fireworks*; presentation, show, exhibition 522 *exhibit*; peep show, slide s., film s.; staging, decor 594 *stage set*.

(3) *cinema,* big screen, Hollywood; film studio, film production, film-making, shooting 551 *photography*; direction, continuity, cutting, montage, projection; screenplay, scenario, script, shooting s.; credits, titles; special effects, animation; sound effects, soundtrack; picture house, flea pit; film director, film star 594 *actor*.

(4) *film,* films, pictures, motion p., movies; silent film, sound f., talkie; big picture, supporting film, short, newsreel, trailer; cartoon, animated c., travelogue, documentary, feature film; thriller, spine-chiller, Western, musical.

(5) *mien,* look, face, expression; countenance, looks; complexion, colour; air, demeanour, carriage, bearing, deportment, poise, presence; posture, behaviour 688 *conduct*.

(6) *feature,* trait, mark, lineament; lines, cut, shape 243 *form*; outline, contour, relief, elevation, profile, silhouette; visage, physiognomy 237 *face*.

Adjective
(7) *appearing,* apparent, seeming, specious, ostensible; deceptive 542 *deceiving*; outward, external, superficial 223 *exterior*; showing, on view 443 *visible*; visual, video-; exhibited, hung 522 *shown*; spectacular 875 *showy*; showing itself, revealed 522 *manifest*; visionary, dreamlike 513 *imaginary*.

Verb
(8) *appear,* show 443 *be visible*; seem, look so 18 *resemble*; be on show, figure in, star in; exhibit 522 *manifest*; start 68 *begin*; materialize 295 *arrive*; walk 970 *haunt*.

Adverb
(9) *apparently,* ostensibly, to all appearances; on the face of it, at first sight.

446
Disappearance

Noun
(1) *disappearance,* loss, vanishing; flight 667 *escape*; exit 296 *departure*; evanescence, evaporation 338 *vaporization*; eclipse 418 *obscuration*; vanishing point, thin air 444 *invisibility*.

Adjective
(2) *disappearing,* vanishing; evanescent 114 *transient*; vanished 190 *absent*; lost to sight, lost to view 444 *invisible*; gone to earth 525 *concealed*; gone 2 *extinct*.

Verb
(3) *disappear,* vanish, evanesce, evaporate 338 *vaporize*; dissolve, melt away, dwindle a.; fade, fade out, fade away 114 *be transient*; disperse, dissipate; absent oneself 190 *be absent*; go,

be gone, depart 296 *decamp*; run away 667 *escape*; hide, lie low 523 *lurk*; leave no trace 525 *conceal*; sink from view, be lost to sight 444 *be unseen*, 2 *pass away*; make disappear 550 *obliterate*.

Class four

Human Beings

447
Intellect

Noun

(1) *intellect,* mind, psyche, mentality; understanding, conception; rationality, reason 475 *reasoning*; philosophy 449 *thought*; awareness, sense, consciousness, self-c.; cognition, perception, insight; instinct 476 *intuition*; flair, judgment 463 *discrimination*; mental capacity, brains, wits, senses 498 *intelligence*; great intellect, genius; brain, cortex 213 *head*; healthy mind 502 *sanity*; diseased mind 503 *psychopathy*; mind over matter 595 *will.*

(2) *spirit,* soul, mind, inner sense; heart, bosom, inner man *or* woman 5 *essential part*; psyche, id, ego, superego, animus, anima, self; the unconscious, the subconscious; personality, split p. 503 *psychopathy*; spiritualism 984 *occultism.*

(3) *psychology,* science of mind; behaviourism; psychiatry, psychoanalysis, psychotherapy 658 *therapy.*

(4) *psychologist,* psychoanalyst, psychiatrist, psychotherapist 658 *doctor.*

Adjective

(5) *mental,* thinking, reasoning 475 *rational*; cerebral, intellectual, conceptual, abstract; theoretical 512 *suppositional*; perceptual, perceptive; cognitive 490 *knowing*; conscious, self-c., subjective.

(6) *psychic,* psychological; psychosomatic; subconscious, subliminal; spiritual 984 *physical*; otherworldly 320 *immaterial.*

Verb

(7) *cognize,* perceive 490 *know*; realize, sense, become aware of; note 438 *see*, 455 *notice*; ratiocinate 475 *reason*; use one's head, understand 498 *be wise*; conceptualize 449 *think*; conceive, invent 484 *discover*, 513 *imagine*; appreciate 480 *estimate.*

448
Absence of intellect

Noun

(1) *absence of intellect,* brute creation 365 *animality*; vegetation 366 *vegetable life*; inanimate nature, stocks and stones; vacuity, brainlessness, mindlessness 450 *absence of thought*; brain damage, unsound mind 503 *insanity.*

Adjective

(2) *mindless,* unintelligent; animal, vegetable; mineral, inanimate 359 *inorganic*; unreasoning 450 *unthinking*; instinctive, brute 476 *intuitive*; brainless, empty-headed 499 *foolish*; moronic, wanting 503 *insane.*

449
Thought

Noun

(1) *thought,* mental process, thinking; mental act, cogitation 447 *intellect*; cerebration, brainwork; hard thinking, concentration 455 *attention*; deep thought, profundity 498

wisdom; abstract thought, thoughts, ideas 451 *idea*; flow of ideas, current of thought; reason 475 *reasoning*; brown study, reverie, musing; invention, inventiveness 513 *imagination*; retrospection, hindsight 505 *memory*; forethought, prudence 510 *foresight*; telepathy 984 *psychics*.

(2) *meditation,* speculation 459 *enquiry*; lateral thinking; reflection, deep r., brooding, rumination, consideration, pondering; contemplation, thoughtfulness; introspection; mysticism 979 *piety*; deliberation, excogitation, thinking out 480 *judgment*; examination, close study, concentration, application 536 *study*.

(3) *philosophy,* metaphysics, ethics; school of thought 485 *opinion*; idealism, realism, positivism, determinism, existentialism, rationalism, humanism, materialism; empiricism, pragmatism; relativism, relativity; agnosticism, scepticism 486 *doubt*; atheism 974 *irreligion*; nihilism 596 *fate*; dialectical materialism, Marxism; theosophy; Hinduism, Buddhism 973 *religion*.

(4) *philosopher,* thinker 492 *intellectual*; existentialist etc. (**see** *philosophy*); metaphysician.

Adjective

(5) *thoughtful,* cogitative, deliberative; pensive, meditative, ruminative, contemplative, reflective; introspective; absorbed, lost in thought; musing, dreaming 456 *abstracted*; concentrating 455 *attentive*; studying 536 *studious*; prudent 510 *foreseeing*.

(6) *philosophic,* metaphysical, speculative, abstract, conceptual, systematic, rational, logical.

Verb

(7) *think,* conceive, form ideas, fancy 513 *imagine*; devote thought to, think about, cogiate; employ one's mind, use one's brain, collect one's thoughts; concentrate 455 *be attentive*; bend the mind, apply the m., cerebrate, mull over, puzzle over; think hard, beat one's brains, rack one's b.; think through, reason out 475 *reason*; think out, think up, excogitate; invent 484 *discover*; devise 623 *plan*; bear in mind, be mindful of 505 *remember*.

(8) *meditate,* ruminate, chew over, digest; wonder about, debate, enquire into 459 *enquire*; reflect, contemplate, study; speculate, philosophize, theorize; think about, consider, take into account, take stock of, ponder, weigh 480 *estimate*; think over, turn o., revolve, run over; reconsider, think better of; take counsel 691 *consult*; introspect, brood, muse, go into retreat.

(9) *dawn upon,* occur to, cross the mind, come to m.; strike one; come into one's head, suggest itself.

(10) *cause thought,* make one think 821 *impress*; penetrate, sink in; obsess 481 *bias*.

(11) *engross,* absorb, preoccupy, monopolize; occupy one's mind, fill one's m., prey on one's mind, haunt, obsess 481 *bias*; fascinate 983 *bewitch*.

Adverb

(12) *in mind,* on one's mind, on the brain; on reflection, on consideration, on second thoughts.

450
Absence of thought

Noun
(1) *absence of thought,* blank mind, fallow m. 491 *ignorance*; vacancy, abstraction 456 *abstractedness*; inanity, empty head; want of thought 456 *inattention*; reflex, automatism; knee-jerk response, gut reaction; instinct 476 *intuition*.

Adjective
(2) *unthinking,* unreflecting 448 *mindless*; unimaginative 20 *imitative*; automatic, instinctive 476 *intuitive*; blank, vacant, empty-headed; not thinking 456 *inattentive*; thoughtless, inconsiderate 932 *selfish*; irrational 477 *illogical*; stupid 499 *unintelligent*.

(3) *unthought,* unthought of, inconceivable, unconsidered, undreamt of 470 *impossible*.

Verb
(4) *not think,* not reflect; be blank, be vacant; not think of, put out of one's mind 458 *disregard*; dream 456 *be inattentive*; go by instinct 476 *intuit*.

451
Idea

Noun
(1) *idea,* notion, abstraction, a thought; abstract idea, concept; mere idea, theory 512 *supposition*; image, mental i.; conception 447 *intellect*; reflection, observation 449 *thought*; impression, fancy 513 *imagination*; invention, brain-child; brain wave 484 *discovery*; wheeze, device 623 *contrivance*; point of view, attitude 485 *opinion*; principle, main idea.

Adjective
(2) *ideational,* conceptual 449

thoughtful; theoretical 512 *suppositional*; notional, ideal 513 *imaginary*.

452
Topic

Noun
(1) *topic,* subject matter, subject; argument, plot, theme, message; text, contents; concern, interest; matter, affair; business on hand, agenda; motion 761 *request*; resolution 480 *judgment*; problem 459 *question*; theorem, proposition 512 *supposition*; thesis, case, point 475 *argument*; issue, moot point, point at issue; field of study 536 *study*.

Adjective
(2) *topical,* challenging, debatable, thought about, thought-provoking.

Adverb
(3) *in question,* on the agenda; before the house, under consideration.

453
Curiosity: Desire for knowledge

Noun
(1) *curiosity,* enquiring mind, thirst for knowledge 536 *study*; interest, curiousness; nosiness, inquisitiveness; quizzing 459 *question*; morbid curiosity, ghoulishness; voyeurism 951 *impurity*.

(2) *inquisitive person,* examiner, inquisitor, interrogator, questioner 459 *enquirer*; nosy parker, busybody, gossip 678 *meddler*; seeker, searcher, explorer 461 *experimenter*; snooper, spy 459 *detective*; eavesdropper 415 *listener*.

Adjective
(3) *inquisitive,* curious, interest

ed; avid for, hungry for; searching, seeking; ghoulish, prurient; agog, all ears 455 *attentive*; wanting to know, burning with curiosity; nosy, prying, spying, peeping; questioning 459 *enquiring*.

Verb

(4) *be curious,* want to know, seek, look for 459 *search*; test, research 461 *experiment*; take an interest 455 *be attentive*; peep, spy 438 *scan*; snoop, pry, nose into 459 *enquire*; 'eavesdrop, intercept, listen in 415 *hear*; be nosy, interfere 678 *meddle*; ask questions, quiz, question 459 *interrogate*; stare, stand and stare 438 *gaze*.

Interjection

(5) well? what news? what's going on? who? what? where? when? how? why? why on earth?earth?

454
Incuriosity

Noun

(1) *incuriosity,* lack of interest, no questions, mental inertia; no interest, insouciance 860 *indifference*; apathy, unconcern.

Adjective

(2) *incurious,* unreflecting 450 *unthinking*; without interest, uninterested; aloof, distant; blase 838 *bored*; unconcerned, uninquisitive 860 *indifferent*; apathetic 820 *impassive*.

Verb

(3) *be incurious,* not think about, take no interest 456 *be inattentive*; feel no concern 860 *be indifferent*; mind one's own business 458 *disregard*.

455
Attention

Noun

(1) *attention,* notice, regard 438 *look*; consideration 449 *thought*; heed, alertness, readiness, attentiveness 457 *carefulness*; observation, watchfulness, vigilance 457 *surveillance*; wariness 858 *caution*; contemplation 449 *meditation*; intentness, earnestness, seriousness 599 *resolution*; concentration, application 536 *study*; examination, scrutiny 438 *inspection*; close attention, attention to detail 494 *accuracy*; diligence, pains, trouble 678 *assiduity*; absorption, preoccupation; interest 453 *curiosity*; fixation 503 *mania*.

Adjective

(2) *attentive,* intent, diligent, assiduous 678 *industrious*; considerate, thoughtful 884 *courteous*; heedful, mindful 457 *careful*; alert, ready, wakeful, awake, wide-a.; observant, sharp-eyed, watchful 457 *vigilant*; rapt, paying attention, missing nothing; all eyes, all ears; concentrating, deep in; serious, earnest 536 *studious*; nice, particular, punctilious 494 *accurate*; pedantic 862 *fastidious*.

(3) *obsessed,* engrossed, preoccupied, wrapped up in; single-minded; rapt, enthralled, spellbound; haunted by.

Verb

(4) *be attentive,* attend, pay attention; heed, mind 457 *be careful*; take pains, bother 682 *exert oneself*; listen, prick up one's ears, sit up, take seriously; give one's mind to 449 *think*; concentrate, miss nothing; watch 438 *gaze*; be all ears, drink in 415 *hear*; examine, inspect, scrutinize, vet, review

438 *scan*; pore, mull, read, digest 536 *study*.

(5) *be mindful*, keep in mind, bear in m., have in m., be thinking of 505 *remember*; take care of, see to 457 *look after*; have regard to, keep in view 617 *intend*; keep track of, not lose sight of 619 *pursue*.

(6) *notice*, note, take n., register; mark, recognize, spot; take account of, consider, weigh 480 *judge*; mention, remark on, comment upon, 584 *converse*; find time for

(7) *attract notice*, draw attention; arouse notice 875 *be ostentatious*; interest 821 *impress*; excite attention, invite a., claim a., demand a., catch the eye 443 *be visible*; call attention to, bring to one's notice, advertise 528 *publish*; point out 547 *indicate*; stress, underline 532 *emphasize*; fascinate, obsess 449 *engross*; alert, warn 665 *raise the alarm*.

456
Inattention

Noun

(1) *inattention,* inadvertence, oversight, aberration; lack of interest 454 *incuriosity*; aloofness, detachment 860 *indifference*; disregard 458 *negligence*; want of thought 827 *rashness*; thoughtlessness 932 *selfishness*; flippancy, levity; deaf ears 416 *deafness*; blind spot 439 *blindness*; absent-mindedness, wandering wits; daydreamer, scatterbrain, grasshopper mind, butterfly.

(2) *abstractedness*, abstraction, woolgathering, daydreaming, doodling; reverie, brown study; distraction, preoccupation.

Adjective

(3) *inattentive*, careless, unobservant 458 *negligent*; unseeing 439 *blind*; unhearing 416 *deaf*; unmindful, inadvertent, not thinking 450 *unthinking*; not concentrating, half asleep, only half awake; uninterested 860 *indifferent*; oblivious 506 *forgetful*; unheeding, inconsiderate, thoughtless, tactless; heedless, regardless 857 *rash*; cavalier, offhand; cursory, superficial, shallow.

(4) *abstracted*, absent-minded, miles away; lost in thought, wrapped in t., rapt, absorbed; bemused; pensive, dreamy, dreaming, daydreaming, mooning, woolgathering.

(5) *distracted*, preoccupied, diverted 282 *deviating*; disconcerted, put out, put off one's stroke 854 *nervous*.

(6) *light-minded*, wandering, desultory, trifling; frivolous, flippant, insouciant, light-headed; volatile, mercurial, flighty, giddy, dizzy, scatty, harebrained; wild, harum-scarum; inconstant 604 *capricious*.

Verb

(7) *be inattentive*, not attend, pay no attention, pay no heed, not listen, close one's eyes 439 *be blind*; stop one's ears 416 *be deaf*; not register, not notice; overlook 495 *blunder*; be off one's guard, let slip, be caught out; lose track of, lose sight of; not remember 506 *forget*; dream, drowse, nod 679 *sleep*; not concentrate, let one's mind wander 513 *imagine*; be lost in thought, muse, moon; idle, doodle 679 *be inactive*; be distracted, lose the thread; disregard, ignore 458 *neglect*.

(8) *distract*, divert, put out of one's head; entice 612 *tempt*; confuse, muddle 63 *derange*;

disturb, interrupt, disconcert, upset, discompose, fluster, bother, flurry, agitate; put off one's stroke; bewilder, flummox 474 *puzzle*; throw off the scent.

(9) *escape notice,* escape attention, be overlooked 523 *lurk*; slip one's memory.

Adverb
(10) *inadvertently,* by oversight.

457
Carefulness

Noun
(1) *carefulness,* mindfulness, attentiveness, solicitude; diligence, pains 678 *assiduity*; heed, care 455 *attention*; tidiness, orderliness 60 *order*; thoroughness, minuteness, meticulousness; exactness 494 *accuracy*; pedantry, perfectionism; conscience, scruples 929 *probity*; vigilance, watchfulness, alertness, readiness 669 *preparedness*; prudence, wariness 858 *caution*; forethought 510 *foresight*.

(2) *surveillance,* an eye on, watching 660 *protection*; vigilance, invigilation, inspection; baby-sitting, chaperonage 660 *protection*; lookout, weather eye; vigil, watch, guard; watchful eye, sentry, sentinel 749 *keeper*.

Adjective
(3) *careful,* thoughtful, considerate, mindful, regardful, heedful 455 *attentive*; taking care, painstaking; solicitous, anxious; cautious, afraid to touch; loving, tender; conscientious, scrupulous, diligent, assiduous 678 *industrious*; thorough, meticulous, minute, particular 494 *accurate*; pedantic, perfectionist 862 *fastidious*; tidy, neat 60 *orderly*; thrifty 816 *parsimonious*.

(4) *vigilant,* alert, ready 669 *prepared*; on the alert, on guard; watchful, observant, sharp-eyed 438 *seeing*; prudent, provident, far-sighted 510 *foreseeing*; circumspect, guarded, wary 858 *cautious*.

Verb
(5) *be careful,* mind, heed, beware 455 *be attentive*; take precautions, think twice, check 858 *be cautious*; have one's wits about one, be on one's guard, watch one's step; feel one's way 461 *be tentative*; take pains, be meticulous, take a pride in.

(6) *look after,* see to, take care of 689 *manage*; take charge of, care for, mind, tend, keep 660 *safeguard*; sit up with, babysit; nurse, foster, cherish; have regard for, treat gently 920 *respect*; keep an eye on, monitor; escort, chaperon; serve 703 *minister to*.

(7) *invigilate,* keep vigil, watch; stand sentinel; keep watch, look out, watch out for; mount guard, post sentries, stand to 660 *safeguard*.

Adverb
(8) *carefully,* attentively etc. adj.; with care, gingerly, with kid gloves.

458
Negligence

Noun
(1) *negligence,* carelessness 456 *inattention*; forgetfulness 506 *oblivion*; remissness, neglect, oversight, omission; insouciance, nonchalance, 860 *indifference*; recklessness 857 *rashness*; procrastination 136 *delay*; slackness, laziness 679 *inactivity*; slovenliness 61 *disorder*; sloppiness 495 *inexactness*; offhandedness, casualness, laxness 734 *laxity*;

trifling, scamping 695 *bungling*; slacker, shirker 679 *idler*.

Adjective

(2) *negligent,* neglectful, careless 456 *inattentive*; remiss 918 *undutiful*; thoughtless 450 *unthinking*; oblivious 506 *forgetful*; insouciant 860 *indifferent*; reckless, heedless 857 *rash*; casual, offhand 734 *lax*; sloppy, slipshod, slaphappy, slapdash, perfunctory, superficial; hurried 680 *hasty*; inaccurate 495 *inexact*; slack, supine 679 *lazy*; sluttish, slovenly 649 *dirty*; unguarded, off guard 508 *inexpectant*; improvident 670 *unprepared*; lapsed 974 *irreligious*.

(3) *neglected,* uncared for; unkempt 649 *dirty*; unguarded, deserted; left alone, unattended; disregarded, ignored, unconsidered, overlooked, omitted; in limbo; shelved, pigeonholed, put aside; unread, unexamined; undone, half-done, perfunctory 726 *uncompleted*. 674 *unused*.

Verb

(4) *neglect,* omit, pass over; overlook 456 *be inattentive*; leave undone, leave half-done 726 *not complete*; slur, skimp, scamp, skip, skim; not mention, skate over, gloss over 525 *conceal*; not take seriously, dabble in, play with, trifle.

(5) *disregard,* ignore, pass over, turn a blind eye to 439 *be blind*; let pass, pay no regard to; wink at, connive at, take no notice 734 *be lax*; excuse, overlook 909 *forgive*; discount 483 *underestimate*; slight, cold-shoulder, cut dead 885 *be rude*; turn a deaf ear to 416 *be deaf*; take lightly laugh off 922 *hold cheap*; desert, abandon 621 *relinquish*.

(6) *be neglectful,* drowse, nod 679 *sleep*; be caught napping 508 *not expect*; drift, freewheel, procrastinate 677 *not act*; not

bother 679 *be inactive*; shelve, pigeonhole, lay aside, put aside.

Adverb

(7) *negligently,* cursorily any how.

459
Enquiry

Noun

(1) *enquiry,* asking; asking about 524 *information*; witchhunt, inquisition; examination, investigation; checkup, medical; inquest, autopsy 959 *legal trial*; public enquiry; census, canvass, survey, market research; poll 605 *vote*; probe, test 461 *experiment*; check, spot c., review 438 *inspection*; research 536 *study*; analysis, dissection; exploration, reconnaissance, survey 484 *discovery*; soundings, canvassing, consultation 584 *conference*; speculation 449 *philosophy*; enquiring mind 453 *curiosity*.

(2) *interrogation,* questioning, asking questions; leading question, cross-examination; catechism; inquisition, grilling, third degree; dialogue, dialectic; quiz, question time.

(3) *question,* query; questionnaire, question paper, examination p.; challenge, fair question; loaded q., catch; leading question; rhetorical q.; point at issue 452 *topic*; crucial question, burning q.; controversy, contention 475 *argument*; problem, poser 530 *enigma*.

(4) *exam,* examination, oral e., viva voce e., viva; interview, audition 415 *hearing*; test, series of tests, battery; IQ test; examinee, entrant.

(5) *search,* probe, investigation, enquiry; quest, hunt, treasure h., witch-h. 619 *pursuit*; house-

search, search warrant; frisking; rummaging, turning over; exploration, excavation, digging, dig.

(6) *police enquiry,* investigation, criminal i., detection 484 *discovery*; detective work, shadowing; secret police.

(7) *secret service,* espionage, counter-e., spying, intelligence, MI5; informer, spy, undercover agent, secret a., double agent, inside a.; spy ring.

(8) *detective,* investigator, criminologist; private detective, private eye; hotel detective, store d.; sleuth, bloodhound, snooper 524 *informer*; graphologist.

(9) *enquirer,* investigator, prober; journalist 529 *news reporter*; thinker 449 *philosopher*; searcher, search party; water diviner 484 *detector*; prospector, gold-digger; talent scout; scout, spy; surveyor, inspector 438 *inspection*; checker, scrutineer 480 *estimator*; examiner, examining board; tester, test pilot; researcher, research worker 461 *experimenter*; pollster, canvasser; explorer 268 *traveller*.

(10) *questioner,* catechizer; interrogator, inquisitor, cross-examiner; interviewer 453 *inquisitive person*; heckler;

Adjective

(11) *enquiring,* curious, prying, nosy 453 *inquisitive*; quizzing, quizzical; interrogatory, interrogative; examining, probing, digging, investigative; testing, searching, fact-finding, exploratory, empirical, tentative 461 *experimental*; analytic, diagnostic.

(12) *moot,* in question, questionable, debatable; problematic, doubtful 474 *uncertain*; knotty, puzzling 700 *difficult*; undecided, left open.

Verb

(13) *enquire,* ask, want to know, seek an answer; demand 761 *request*; air, ventilate, discuss, query, bring in question 475 *argue*; ask for, look for, enquire for, seek (see *search*); hunt for 619 *pursue*; enquire into, make enquiries, probe, delve into, dig i., look into, investigate; try, hear 959 *try a case*; review, overhaul; audit, scrutinize, monitor, screen; analyse, dissect; research 536 *study*; consider, examine 449 *meditate*; check, check on; feel the pulse, take soundings; X-ray 438 *scan*; peer, pry, nose around 453 *be curious*; survey, reconnoitre 461 *be tentative*; test, try, sample, taste 461 *experiment*.

(14) *interrogate,* ask questions, question, cross-question, cross-examine; badger, challenge, heckle; interview, examine, sound out, probe, quiz, catechize, grill; pump, pick one's brains; put a question, frame a q., pose a q.

(15) *search,* seek, look for; rummage, ransack, scour, comb; scrabble, forage, root about; turn over, rake o., pick o., turn inside out, rake through, rifle t., go t., search t.; frisk, go over, search for, feel for, grope for, hunt for, drag for, fish for, dig for 682 *exert oneself*; cast about, seek a clue, follow the trail 619 *pursue*; probe, explore 461 *be tentative*; dig, excavate, prospect, dowse.

(16) *be questionable,* debatable etc. adj.; arouse suspicion, call for enquiry, require an explanation.

Adverb

(17) *on trial,* under investigation, sub judice.

(18) *in search of,* on the track of.

460
Answer

Noun

(1) *answer,* reply, response; re-action; acknowledgement, return; returns, results 548 *record*; feedback 524 *information*; echo, antiphon; password, countersign; answering back, backchat, repartee; retort, riposte 714 *retaliation*; give and take, dialogue 584 *interlocution*; clue, key, explanation solution 658 *remedy*.

(2) *rejoinder,* rebuttal 479 *confutation*; defence, reply; refutation, contradiction 533 *negation*.

(3) *respondent,* defendant; answerer, responder, replier, correspondent; examinee, candidate, applicant, entrant 716 *contender*.

Adjective

(4) *answering,* replying etc, vb.; respondent, responsive; echolike, antiphonal; counter (-) 182 *counteracting*; corresponding to 12 *correlative*; contradicting 533 *negative*; conclusive, final.

Verb

(5) *answer,* return an a.; write back, acknowledge, reply, respond, be responsive; echo, reecho 106 *repeat*; react, answer back, flash back, come back at, retort, riposte 714 *retaliate*; say in reply, rejoin, rebut, counter 479 *confute*; field, parry, refuse to answer 620 *avoid*; contradict 533 *negate*; provide the answer 642 *be expedient*.

461
Experiment

Noun

(1) *experiment,* experimentation, verification; exploration, probe; analysis, examination 459 *enquiry*; object lesson, proof 478 *demonstration*; assay 480 *estimate*; check, test, acid t., test case; probation; practical test, trial, try-out, trial run, dry r., test flight; audition, voice test; pilot scheme, first draft 68 *debut*.

(2) *empiricism,* speculation, guesswork 512 *conjecture*; experience, practice, rule of thumb, trial and error, hit and miss; shot in the dark, gamble 618 *gambling*; instinct, light of nature 476 *intuition*; sampling, random sample, straw vote; feeler 459 *question*; kite-flying.

(3) *experimenter,* empiricist, researcher, research worker, analyst, vivisector; assayer, chemist; tester 459 *enquirer*; test driver, test pilot; speculator, prospector; explorer, adventurer 618 *gambler*.

(4) *testing agent,* criterion, touchstone; standard, yardstick 465 *gauge*; breathalyser; control; litmus paper; proving ground, wind tunnel; simulator, flight s.; laboratory.

(5) *testee,* examinee 460 *respondent*; probationer 538 *beginner*; candidate 716 *contender*; subject, patient; guinea pig.

Adjective

(6) *experimental,* analytic; probationary, provisional; tentative 618 *speculative*; trial, exploratory 459 *enquiring*; empirical 671 *attempting*; testable, verifiable.

Verb

(7) *experiment,* make experiments; check, check on, verify; prove, assay, analyse; research; dabble; experiment upon, vivisect, practise upon; test, put to the t. 459 *enquire*; try, try out 671 *attempt*; sample 386 *taste*.

(8) *be tentative,* be empirical, feel one's way, probe, grope, fumble; fly a kite, feel the pulse; wait and see; speculate 618 *gamble*; venture, explore, prospect 672 *undertake*; probe, sound 459 *enquire*.

Adverb

(9) *experimentally,* on test, on trial, on approval, on probation; empirically, by trial and error.

462
Comparison

Noun

(1) *comparison,* comparing, likening; collation, juxtaposition; check 459 *enquiry*; comparability, analogy, parallel, likeness 18 *similarity*; contrast, antithesis 14 *contrariety*; simile, allegory 519 *metaphor*; criterion, pattern, check list, control 23 *prototype*.

Adjective

(2) *compared,* likened, set against, measured a., contrasted; comparative, comparable, analogical; allegorical, metaphorical 519 *figurative*.

Verb

(3) *compare,* collate, confront; bring together 202 *juxtapose*; draw a comparison 18 *liken*, contrast 15 *differentiate*; compare and contrast 463 *discriminate*; match, pair; check with 12 *correlate*; draw a parallel; compare to *or* with; compare notes, exchange views.

Adverb

(4) *comparatively,* relatively, in comparison.

463
Discrimination

Noun

(1) *discrimination,* distinction 15 *differentiation*; discernment 480 *judgment*; insight, perception 498 *intelligence*; appreciation, critique, 480 *estimate*; refinement 846 *good taste*; timing, sense of occasion; nicety, particularity; sifting, separation 62 *sorting*; selection 605 *choice*; shade of difference, nuance 15 *difference*.

Adjective

(2) *discriminating,* selective, judicious, discerning; nice, particular 862 *fastidious*; appraisal, critical 480 *judicial*.

Verb

(3) *discriminate,* distinguish, make a distinction 15 *differentiate*, 462 *compare*; sort, sort out, sift, separate 46 *set apart*; pick out 605 *select*; make an exception, draw the line 468 *qualify*; refine upon, split hairs 475 *reason*; criticize, appraise 480 *estimate*; weigh, consider 480 *judge*; discern, have insight 490 *know*; take into account, give weight to 638 *make important*.

464
Indiscrimination

Noun

(1) *indiscrimination,* promiscuity, universality 79 *generality*; lack of judgment 499 *unintelligence*; imperceptivity, obtuseness; coarseness, vulgarity 847 *bad taste*.

Adjective

(2) *indiscriminate,* rolled into one, undistinguished, undifferentiated; random, confused; promiscuous, haphazard, blanket 79 *general*.

(3) *indiscriminating,* uncritical, undiscerning; coarse 847 *vulgar*; tone-deaf, colour-blind.

Verb

(4) *not discriminate,* see no difference, make no distinction; jumble, confuse; average out.

465
Measurement

Noun

(1) *measurement,* mensuration, surveying; dose, dosage 26 *finite quantity*; rating, valuation, evaluation, appraisal, assessment 480 *estimate*; calculation, computation, reckoning 86 *numeration*; dead reckoning, gauging; reading, reading off; metrics 203 *long measure*; trigonometry 247 *angular measure*;

(2) *geometry,* plane g., solid geometry; altimetry.

(3) *metrology,* dimensions, length, breadth, height, depth, thickness 195 *size*; metric system, weights and measures 322 *weighing*; linear measure, volume, cubic contents; gill, pint, quart, gallon, litre; dry measure, peck, bushel, quarter; unit of energy, ohm, watt 160 *electricity*; horse power 160 *energy*; candlepower 417 *light*; decibel, 398 *sound*.

(4) *coordinate,* latitude and longitude, grid reference.

(5) *gauge,* measure, scale; balance 322 *scales*; micrometer; footrule, yardstick, metre bar; tape measure; lead, log-line; ruler, slide rule; straight-edge, T-square, dividers, callipers, compass, protractor; sextant, quadrant 269 *sailing aid*; theodolite; astrolabe; Plimsoll line, bench mark 547 *indication*; high-water mark, tidemark, water line 236 *limit*; axis, coordinate; standard, criterion 23

prototype; milestone 547 *signpost.*

(6) *meter,* measuring instrument; altimeter, thermometer, barometer, anemometer; speed gauge, speedometer, milometer 277 *velocity*; metronome, time switch, parking meter 117 *timekeeper*; Geiger counter, seismograph.

(7) *surveyor,* land s., quantity s.; topographer, cartographer, oceanographer.

(8) *appraiser,* valuer, assessor, surveyor 480 *estimator*.

Adjective

(9) *metrical,* mensural; imperial, metric; metrological; cubic, linear; topographical.

(10) *measured,* surveyed, mapped, plotted, taped; graduated, calibrated; mensurable, measurable, assessable, computable, calculable.

Verb

(11) *measure,* survey, compute, calculate 86 *number*; quantify, size up, take measurements; pace out, count one's steps; probe, sound, fathom, plumb 313 *plunge*; check the speed 117 *time*; balance 322 *weigh*.

(12) *gauge,* meter, take a reading, read off; standardize 16 *make uniform*; grade 27 *graduate*; map 551 *represent*.

(13) *appraise,* gauge, value, cost, rate 809 *price*; evaluate, estimate, make an e.; appreciate, assess 480 *estimate*; form an opinion 480 *judge*; tape, have taped, size up.

(14) *mete out,* measure out, weigh o., dole o., share o. 783 *apportion*.

466
Evidence

Noun

(1) *evidence,* facts, data, case history; grounds 475 *reasons*; premises 475 *premise*; hearsay 524 *report*; proof 478 *demonstration*; corroboration, verification, confirmation 473 *certainty*; piece of evidence, fact, relevant f.; document, exhibit, fingerprints 548 *record*; clue 524 *hint*; sign 547 *indication*; reference, quotation, 'citation, chapter and verse; one's authorities, documentation; line of evidence, authority, canonicity.

(2) *testimony,* witness; statement 524 *information*; admission, confession 526 *disclosure*; one's case, plea 614 *pretext*; assertion, allegation 532 *affirmation*; sworn evidence, deposition, affidavit, attestation 532 *oath*; word of mouth, oral evidence; case record, dossier 548 *record*; deed, testament 767 *security*.

(3) *credential,* testimonial, character, references 927 *vindication*; seal, signature, endorsement; voucher, warranty, certificate, diploma 767 *security*; passport, visa 756 *permit*; authority, scripture.

(4) *witness,* eyewitness 441 *spectator*, 415 *listener*; informant 524 *informer*; deponent, testifier 765 *signatory*; referee, sponsor 707 *patron*.

Adjective

(5) *evidential,* evidentiary; prima facie 445 *appearing*; suggesting, significant 514 *meaningful*; showing, indicative, symptomatic 547 *indicating*; indirect, secondary, circumstantial; firsthand, direct, seen, heard; deducible, verifiable 471 *probable*; constructive 512 *suppositional*; cumulative, supporting, corroborative, confirmatory; telling, damning 928 *accusing*; reliable 473 *certain*; proving, demonstrative, conclusive, decisive 478 *demonstrating*; based on, grounded on; factual, documentary, documented, well-d., authentic 494 *true*; weighty, authoritative 178 *influential*; biblical, scriptural, canonical 976 *orthodox*; attested, testified, witnessed sworn to; in evidence, on the record 548 *recorded*.

Verb

(6) *evidence,* show, evince, furnish evidence; show signs of 852 *give hope*; betoken, bespeak 551 *represent*; tell of 522 *manifest*; lend colour to 471 *make likely*; speak for itself; carry weight, 178 *influence*; suggest 547 *indicate*, 523 *imply*.

(7) *testify,* witness; take one's oath, swear, speak on oath 532 *affirm*; bear witness, take the stand, give evidence, speak to, swear to, vouch for, give one's word; authenticate, certify 473 *make certain*; attest, subscribe, countersign, endorse, sign; plead, state one's case 475 *argue*; admit, avow 526 *confess*.

(8) *corroborate,* support, sustain 927 *vindicate*; bear out, verify; validate, confirm, ratify, establish, make a case 473 *make certain*; produce evidence, document; fabricate evidence 541 *fake*; countervail 467 *tell against*; adduce, cite the evidence.

467
Counter evidence

Noun

(1) *counterevidence,* evidence against, defence, rebuttal 460 *answer*; refutation, disproof

479 *confutation*; denial 533 *negation*; justification 927 *vindication*; hostile witness.

Adjective
(2) *countervailing,* rebutting 460 *answering*; cancelling out 182 *counteracting*; ambiguous 518 *equivocal*; denying 533 *negative*; damaging, telling against 468 *qualifying.*

(3) *unattested,* lacking proof, not proved, unproven 474 *uncertain*; disproved 479 *confuted*; trumped-up, fabricated 541 *false.*

Verb
(4) *tell against,* damage the case; weigh against, run counter; contradict, rebut 479 *confute*; oppose 14 *be contrary*; cancel out 182 *counteract*; cut both ways 518 *be equivocal*; weaken, damage, undermine, subvert 165 *destroy*; turn the tables, turn the scale.

Adverb
(5) *conversely,* on the other hand.

468
Qualification

Noun
(1) *qualification,* modification, mitigation 177 *moderation*; stipulation, condition 766 *conditions*; limitation 747 *restriction*; reservation, proviso; escape clause, penalty c.; exception, exemption; demur, objection 704 *opposition*; concession, allowance.

Adjective
(2) *qualifying,* restricting, limiting; modifying, altering the case; mitigatory, extenuating, palliative, excusing; provisional 766 *conditional*; discounting, allowing for; saving, excepting, exempting; qualified, not absolute; exceptional, exempted 919 *nonliable.*

Verb
(3) *qualify,* condition, limit, restrict 747 *restrain*; colour, alter 143 *modify*; temper, season, palliate, mitigate 177 *moderate*; excuse 927 *extenuate*; grant, concede, make allowance for, take into account; make exceptions 919 *exempt*; insist on 627 *require*; object, demur 762 *deprecate.*

Adverb
(4) *provided,* subject to, conditionally; if, if not, unless; though, although, even if.

(5) *nevertheless,* even so, all the same, for all that; despite, in spite of; but, yet, still, at all events.

469
Possibility

Noun
(1) *possibility,* potentiality; capacity 160 *ability*; what may be 124 *futurity*; the possible, the feasible; contingency, eventuality, chance 159 *fair chance*; good chance 137 *opportunity*; likelihood 471 *probability*; feasibility 701 *facility*; risk of.

Adjective
(2) *possible,* potential, hypothetical; able, capable, viable; arguable, reasonable; feasible, practicable, negotiable; workable, performable, achievable; attainable, accessible, obtainable; surmountable; not too difficult, not impossible; conceivable, credible, imaginable; practical 642 *advisable*; allowable, permissible, legal 756 *permitted*; contingent 124 *future*; on the cards 471 *probable*; liable, tending.

Verb
(3) *be possible,* may, might; admit of, allow 756 *permit*; be open to, be a possibility, stand a chance 471 *be likely.*

(4) *make possible,* enable 160 *empower*; allow 756 *permit*; smooth the way 701 *facilitate.*

Adverb
(5) *possibly,* conceivably, perhaps; may be, could be; God willing.

470
Impossibility

Noun
(1) *impossibility,* no chance, not a hope 853 *hopelessness*; impasse, deadlock 702 *obstacle*; no permission 757 *prohibition*; impossible task, no go 700 *hard task.*

Adjective
(2) *impossible,* not possible; out of the question, hopeless; not allowed, ruled out 757 *prohibited*; unnatural, against nature; unreasonable 477 *illogical*; untrue 495 *erroneous*; incredible, inconceivable, unthinkable, unheard of; miraculous 864 *wonderful*; idealistic, unrealistic.

(3) *impracticable,* unfeasible, unworkable; insurmountable; insuperable, too much for, beyond one 700 *difficult*; impassable, impenetrable, inaccessible, out of reach.

Verb
(4) *be impossible,* impracticable etc. adj.; defy nature.

(5) *make impossible,* rule out, exclude, disallow 757 *prohibit*; tantalize 533 *negate.*

(6) *attempt the impossible,* labour in vain 641 *waste effort*; grasp at shadows.

Adverb
(7) *impossibly,* nohow.

471
Probability

Noun
(1) *probability,* likelihood 159 *chance*; good chance fair c., sporting c. 469 *possibility*; prospect 507 *expectation*; safe bet 473 *certainty*; real risk 661 *danger*; natural course 179 *tendency*; credibility 485 *belief*; plausibility, good reason 475 *reasons.*

Adjective
(2) *probable,* likely 180 *liable*; on the cards, natural, to be expected, foreseeable, foreseen; reliable 473 *certain*; hopeful, promising 507 *expected*; looming 155 *impending*; in danger of 661 *vulnerable.*

(3) *plausible,* specious, apparent. ostensible 445 *appearing*; logical, reasonable 475 *rational*; convincing, persuasive, believable 485 *credible*; well-grounded, well-founded 494 *true.*

Verb
(4) *be likely,* have a chance, stand a chance 469 *be possible*; bid fair to 179 *tend*; show signs, promise 852 *give hope.*

(5) *make likely,* increase the chances; entail 156 *conduce*; promote 703 *aid*; lend colour to, point to 466 *evidence.*

(6) *assume,* presume 485 *believe*; conjecture, guess 512 *suppose*; think likely, look for 507 *expect*; rely, count upon 473 *be certain*; gather, deduce, infer 475 *reason.*

Adverb
(7) *probably,* presumably; in all likelihood, very likely, most l., ten to one; seemingly, apparently.

472
Improbability

Noun
(1) *improbability,* unlikelihood, doubt 474 *uncertainty*; little chance, outside c., off-chance, long shot 470 *impossibility*; long odds, bare possibility; forlorn hope 508 *lack of expectation*; rarity 140 *infrequency*; traveller's tale 541 *falsehood.*

Adjective
(2) *improbable,* unlikely, dubious 474 *uncertain*; unforeseen 508 *unexpected*; hard to believe, fishy, unconvincing; unheard of, inconceivable 470 *impossible*; incredible, unimaginable.

Verb
(3) *be unlikely,* - improbable etc. vb.; show little hope.

Interjection
(4) *not likely!* no fear! not a hope!

473
Certainty

Noun
(1) *certainty,* certitude 490 *knowledge*; assuredness, sureness; inevitability, inexorability 596 *fate*; infallibility, reliability 494 *truth*; proof 478 *demonstration*; ratification, validation; certification, verification, authentication, confirmation; attestation 466 *testimony*; making sure, check 459 *enquiry*; dead certainty, matter of fact; foregone conclusion 480 *judgment*; dogma 976 *orthodoxy*; dictum, axiom 496 *maxim.*

(2) *positiveness,* assurance, confidence, self-c.; conviction, persuasion 485 *belief*; fixity, obsession 481 *bias*; dogmatism, orthodoxy, bigotry; infallibility, pontification.

(3) *doctrinaire,* dogmatist 602 *obstinate person*; bigot, fanatic, zealot; knowall 500 *wiseacre.*

Adjective
(4) *certain,* sure, solid, unshakable, well-founded, well-grounded 3 *substantial*; reliable 929 *trustworthy*; authoritative, official 494 *genuine*; factual, historical 494 *true*; ascertained, attested, guaranteed, certified, warranted; tested, tried, foolproof 660 *safe*; infallible, unerring 540 *veracious*; axiomatic, dogmatic 485 *creedal*; self-evident, evident, apparent; unequivocal, unmistakable, clear as day 443 *obvious*; inevitable, irrevocable, inexorable 596 *fated*; bound to be 124 *future*; inviolable 660 *invulnerable*; demonstrable 478 *demonstrated.*

(5) *positive,* confident, assured, self-assured, convinced, persuaded, sure 485 *believing*; opinionated, self-o; pontifical, oracular 532 *assertive*; dogmatic, doctrinaire 976 *orthodox*; bigoted, fanatical 481 *biased*; set, fixed, definite, unequivocal 516 *intelligible*; convincing 485 *credible*; affirmative, categorical, absolute, unqualified, unreserved; final, ultimate, conclusive, settled, without appeal.

(6) *undisputed,* beyond doubt, undoubted, indubitable, incontestable, unimpeachable, undeniable, irrefutable, unquestionable.

Verb
(7) *be certain,* sure etc. adj.; leave no doubt, stand to reason 475 *be reasonable*; satisfy oneself, convince o., feel sure 485 *believe*; know for certain 490 *know*; depend on, rely on, bank on, trust in, swear by; gamble on, bet on.

(8) *dogmatize,* pontificate, lay down the law 532 *affirm.*

(9) *make certain,* ensure; certify, authenticate, ratify 488 *endorse*; guarantee, warrant, assure; finalize, settle, decide 480 *judge*; remove doubt, persuade 485 *convince*; ascertain, check, double-check, verify, confirm 466 *corroborate*; insure against 660 *safeguard.*

Adverb
(10) *certainly,* definitely, to be sure, indubitably, of course, no question.

474
Uncertainty

Noun
(1) *uncertainty,* incertitude, doubtfulness, dubiousness; ambiguity 518 *equivocalness*; vagueness, haziness, yes and no; indeterminacy, borderline case; query, question mark 459 *question*; open question, guesswork 512 *conjecture*; contingency 159 *chance*; gamble, toss-up 618 *gambling.*

(2) *dubiety* 486 *doubt*; state of doubt, open mind, open verdict; suspense, waiting 507 *expectation*; doubt, indecision, hesitancy, vacillation 601 *irresolution*; perplexity, bewilderment, bafflement, quandary, dilemma 530 *enigma.*

(3) *unreliability,* fallibility 495 *error*; insecurity, touch and go 661 *danger*; changeability fickleness 604 *caprice*; lack of security, no guarantee.

Adjective
(4) *uncertain,* unsure; doubtful, dubious; insecure, chancy, risky 661 *unsafe*; temporary, provisional 114 *transient*; contingent, depending on 766 *conditional*; unpredictable, unforeseeable; indeterminate, random; indecisive, undecided, open, in suspense; open to question, questionable 459 *moot*; arguable, debatable, disputable, controversial; suspicious 472 *improbable*; speculative 512 *suppositional*; borderline; ambiguous 518 *equivocal*; cryptic, obscure 517 *puzzling*; vague, mysterious, perplexing, bewildering, confusing 61 *complex.*

(5) *unreliable,* treacherous 930 *dishonest*; variable, changeable 152 *changeful*; undependable, fickle 604 *capricious*; fallible 495 *erroneous*; precarious, touch and go.

(6) *doubting,* in doubt, doubtful, dubious, agnostic, sceptical 486 *unbelieving*; in two minds; in suspense, open-minded; mistrustful 858 *cautious*; uncertain, diffident; hesitant, undecided 601 *irresolute*; baffled, perplexed, bewildered 517 *puzzled*; nonplussed, stumped; lost, disorientated, in the dark, abroad, all at sea; at a loss, at one's wits' end.

(7) *uncertified,* unconfirmed; unofficial, unattested; apocryphal.

Verb
(8) *be uncertain,* be contingent, hinge on 157 *depend*; be ambiguous 518 *be equivocal*; have one's doubts 486 *doubt*; wait and see 507 *await*; suspect, wonder, dither, waver, vacillate, falter, pause, hesitate 601 *be irresolute*; flounder, cast about, experiment 461 *be tentative*; lose the thread, lose the scent, have no answer.

(9) *puzzle,* perplex, confuse, bewilder, baffle, nonplus, flummox, stump, floor 727 *defeat*; mystify 495 *mislead*; plague with doubt 486 *cause doubt.*

Adverb
(10) *in suspense,* on the horns of a dilemma.

475
Reasoning

Noun

(1) *reasoning,* ratiocination, force of argument; reason, rationality; dialectics, art of reasoning, logic; deduction, induction; rationalism, dialectic 449 *philosophy.*

(2) *premise,* postulate, principle, general p., first p.; starting point; assumption, stipulation 512 *supposition*; axiom 496 *maxim*; data; hypothesis

(3) *argumentation,* dialectic, dialogue; proposition, statement, thesis, theorem, problem; predicate; inference, corollary; conclusion, QED 478 *demonstration*; paradox 497 *absurdity.*

(4) *argument,* discussion, symposium, dialogue; give and take, cut and thrust; disputation, controversy, debate 489 *dissent*; appeal to reason, plea; thesis, case; reasons, submission; apologetics, defence; polemics, polemic; propaganda 534 *teaching*; wrangling 709 *dissension*; bad argument 477 *sophistry*; legal argument 959 *litigation.*

(5) *reasons,* basis of argument, grounds 156 *cause*; alleged reason 614 *pretext*; arguments, pros and cons; case, good c., case to answer; sound argument, point, valid p., point well taken, clincher.

(6) *reasoner,* theologian 449 *philosopher*; logician, dialectician; casuist 477 *sophist*; polemicist, apologist; debater, disputant; proponent, canvasser; pleader 958 *lawyer*; wrangler, quibbler, pedant; scholastic 492 *intellectual.*

Adjective

(7) *rational,* clear-headed, reasoning, reasonable, logical; cogent, to the point, well-grounded, well-argued 9 *relevant*; sensible, fair 913 *just*; consistent, systematic; dialectic, discursive, deductive, inductive; axiomatic 473 *certain*; tenable 469 *possible.*

(8) *arguing,* polemical; controversial, disputatious, argumentative, quibbling 477 *sophistical*; debatable, arguable 474 *uncertain.*

Verb

(9) *be reasonable* 471 be likely; stand to reason, follow, hang together, hold water; appeal to reason; listen to reason, admit, concede, grant, allow 488 *assent*; have a case.

(10) *reason,* philosophize 449 *think*; rationalize, explain away; put two and two together, infer, deduce; explain 520 *interpret.*

(11) *argue,* give and take, cut and thrust; discuss 584 *confer*; debate, dispute; quibble, split hairs; stress 532 *emphasize*; put one's case, plead; propagandize, pamphleteer 534 *teach*; defend, attack, cross swords; demur, cavil 489 *dissent*; analyse, pull to pieces; 479 *confute*; prove one's case 478 *demonstrate*; wrangle 709 *bicker*; answer back 460 *answer*; start an argument, open a discussion; have the last word.

(12) *premise,* posit, postulate, stipulate, lay down, assume 512 *suppose*; take for granted.

Adverb

(13) *reasonably,* logically; consequently.

476
Intuition: Absence of reason

Noun
(1) *intuition*, instinct, light of nature 450 *absence of thought*; sixth sense, telepathy; insight, second sight, clairvoyance 984 *psychics*; id, subconscious 447 *spirit*; divination, dowsing; inspiration, presentiment 818 *feeling*; rule of thumb; hunch, impression, sense, guesswork; value judgment 481 *bias*; wishful thinking; irrationality 503 *insanity*.

Adjective
(2) *intuitive*, instinctive, impulsive; devoid of logic 477 *illogical*; subjective; involuntary 609 *spontaneous*; subconscious 447 *psychic*; inspired, clairvoyant.

Verb
(3) *intuit*, know by instinct, sense, have a hunch; somehow feel, feel in one's bones; rely on intuition, play it by ear; guess, have a g.

Adverb
(4) *intuitively*, instinctively, by instinct.

477
Sophistry: False reasoning

Noun
(1) *sophistry*, illogicalness 476 *intuition*; double think 525 *concealment*; equivocation, mystification; word fencing, casuistry; subtlety, special pleading; mere words 515 *empty talk*; hair-splitting, quibbling, quibble; chicanery, subterfuge, evasion 614 *pretext*.

(2) *sophism*, specious argument; illogicality, fallacy, bad logic, loose thinking, sloppy t.; solecism, flaw, non sequitur; weak case, bad c.

(3) *sophist*, casuist, quibbler, equivocator; caviller, devil's advocate.

Adjective
(4) *sophistical*, specious, plausible, evasive, insincere; hollow, empty; deceptive, illusory; pettifogging, captious, quibbling; casuistical.

(5) *illogical*, irrational, unreasonable; arbitrary; fallacious, fallible; contradictory, self-c., inconsistent, inconsequential; invalid, untenable, unsound; unfounded, groundless; incorrect, false 495 *erroneous*.

(6) *poorly reasoned*, inconclusive, weak, feeble, flimsy; loose, woolly, muddled, confused; unproved.

Verb
(7) *reason badly*, beg the question, talk at random, babble 515 *mean nothing*.

(8) *sophisticate*, mislead, mystify, quibble, cavil, split hairs 475 *argue*; equivocate 518 *be equivocal*; dodge, shuffle, fence 713 *parry*; evade 667 *elude*; varnish, gloss over 541 *cant*; colour 552 *misrepresent*; pervert, misapply 675 *misuse*; twist the argument.

478
Demonstration

Noun
(1) *demonstration*, documentation 466 *evidence*; proof, rigorous p.; establishment 473 *certainty*; verification 461 *experiment*; deduction, inference 475 *reasoning*; exposition, clarification 522 *manifestation*.

Adjective
(2) *demonstrating*, demonstrative, 466 *evidential*; deducible,

inferential, consequential 9 *relevant*; convincing, proving; conclusive, categorical, decisive, crucial.

(3) *demonstrated*, evident 466 *evidential*; established, granted, allowed; unanswerable, undeniable, irrefutable, irresistible; capable of proof, demonstrable.

Verb
(4) *demonstrate*, prove, show 522 *manifest*; justify 927 *vindicate*; bear out 466 *corroborate*; document, substantiate, establish, verify 466 *evidence*; infer, deduce 475 *reason*; satisfy 473 *make certain*; prove one's point, make out a case 485 *convince*.

(5) *be proved*, be demonstrated, follow, stand to reason 475 *be reasonable*; stand, hold water 494 *be true*.

Adverb
(6) *of course*, undeniably; QED.

479
Confutation

Noun
(1) *confutation*, refutation, disproof, invalidation; exposure; rebuttal, rejoinder, complete answer 460 *answer*; clincher, finisher; retort, repartee; contradiction, denial, denunciation 533 *negation*.

Adjective
(2) *confuted*, disproved etc. vb.; exposed, convicted 961 *condemned*; disprovable, refutable.

Verb
(3) *confute*, refute, disprove, invalidate; retort, have an answer, explain away; deny, contradict 533 *negate*; force to withdraw; confound, silence; floor, nonplus; show up, expose; convict 961 *condemn*;

blow sky-high, puncture, riddle, destroy, explode 165 *demolish*; get the better of; overthrow, squash, crush 727 *defeat*; score off; parry; dismiss, override, sweep aside, brush a. 532 *affirm*.

(4) *be confuted*, have no answer.

Adverb
(5) *in rebuttal*, in disproof.

480
Judgment:
Conclusion

Noun
(1) *judgment*, good judgment 463 *discrimination*; power of judgment 733 *authority*; arbitration; verdict, finding; penal judgment, sentence 963 *punishment*; spoken judgment, pronouncement; act of judgment, adjudication, decision, award; order, ruling 737 *decree*; final judgment, conclusion, result, upshot; moral 496 *maxim*; value judgment 476 *intuition*; deduction, inference, corollary 475 *reasoning*; wise judgment 498 *wisdom*; fair judgment 913 *justice*; vox populi 605 *vote*.

(2) *estimate*, estimation, view 485 *opinion*; assessment, valuation, evaluation; calculation 465 *measurement*; consideration, comparing, contrasting 462 *comparison*; appreciation, appraisal, criticism; critique, review, notice, press n., comments, observations; summing up, recapitulation; survey 438 *inspection*, 524 *report*; legal opinion 691 *advice*.

(3) *estimator*, judge, adjudicator; arbitrator, umpire, referee; surveyor, valuer 465 *appraiser*; inspector, reporter, examiner, ombudsman 459 *enquirer*; counsellor 691 *adviser*;

censor, critic, reviewer, commentator, observer 520 *interpreter*; juror, assessor 957 *jury*; voter 605 *electorate*.

Adjective
(4) *judicial,* judicious, shrewd 498 *wise*; dispassionate, unbiased 913 *just*; juridical; moralizing, moralistic, sententious; censorious 924 *disapproving*; critical, appreciative; advisory 691 *advising*.

Verb
(5) *judge,* sit in judgment, arbitrate, referee; hear, try 955 *hold court*; rule, pronounce; find, find for, find against; decree, award, adjudge, adjudicate; decide, settle, conclude; confirm, make absolute; pass judgment, sentence, pass s. 961 *condemn*; deduce, infer 475 *reason*; sum up, recapitulate; moralize 534 *teach*.

(6) *estimate,* form an e., measure, calculate 465 *gauge*; value, evaluate, appraise; rate, rank; sum up, size up; conjecture, guess 512 *suppose*; take stock, consider, weigh, ponder, weigh the pros and cons 449 *meditate*; examine, investigate, vet 459 *enquire*; report on, comment, criticize, review; survey, pass under review 438 *scan*; censure 924 *disapprove*.

Adverb
(7) *sub judice,* under trial, under sentence.

481
Misjudgment.
Prejudice

Noun
(1) *misjudgment,* miscalculation, misconception, wrong impression 495 *error*; loose thinking 495 *inexactness*; poor

judgment 464 *indiscrimination*; fallibility, gullibility; misconstruction 521 *misinterpretation*; wrong verdict 914 *injustice*; overvaluation 482 *overestimation*; undervaluation 483 *wishful thinking* 542 *deception*; fool's paradise 513 *fantasy*; false dawn.

(2) *prejudgment,* preconceived idea, mind made up; fixation, monomania 503 *mania*.

(3) *prejudice,* predilection; partiality, favouritism 914 *injustice*; bias, biased judgment, jaundiced eye; blind spot 439 *blindness*; partisanship, sectionalism; chauvinism, xenophobia, class prejudice; sexism, ageism, anti-Semitism, racialism, racism; colour prejudice; segregation, discrimination 57 *exclusion*.

(4) *narrow mind,* small mind; insularity, parochialism, provincialism; closed mind, one-track m.; one-sidedness; pedantry, donnishness 735 *severity*; illiberality, intolerance, dogmatism; bigotry, fanaticism 602 *opinionatedness;* zealot, bigot, fanatic 473 *doctrinaire*; racialist, racist, chauvinist, white supremacist.

(5) *bias,* warp, bent, slant 179 *tendency*; angle, point of view 485 *opinion*; infatuation, obsession 503 *eccentricity*; crankiness, fad 604 *whim*.

Adjective
(6) *misjudging,* misconceiving etc. vb.; in error 495 *mistaken*; fallible, gullible 499 *foolish*; wrong, wrong-headed; shortsighted, misguided; superstitious 487 *credulous*; subjective; unrealistic, impractical; faddy, faddish 503 *crazy*; besotted, infatuated 887 *enamoured*; obsessed, haunted, eaten up with.

(7) *narrow-minded,* petty-m., hidebound; parochial, provincial, insular; legalistic, pedantic, donnish; literal, unimaginative; fussy 862 *fastidious*; unbending 602 *obstinate*; dictatorial, dogmatic 473 *positive*; self-opinioned, opinionated 871 *proud.*

(8) *biased,* warped, twisted, swayed; jaundiced, embittered; prejudiced, closed; snobbish, clannish, cliquish 708 *sectional*; partisan, one-sided 978 *sectarian*; nationalistic, chauvinistic, jingoistic, xenophobic; racist, racialist; sexist; predisposed, prejudging 608 *predetermined*; unreasoning unreasonable 477 *illogical*; illiberal, intolerant; bigoted, fanatic 602 *obstinate.*

Verb
(9) *misjudge,* miscalculate 495 *blunder*; not take into account, reckon without 477 *reason badly*; minimize 483 *underestimate*; overestimate 482 *overrate*; guess wrong, misconjective, misconceive 521 *misinterpret.*

(10) *prejudge,* judge beforehand 608 *predetermine*; preconceive, presuppose, presume 475 *premise*; jump to conclusions 857 *be rash.*

(11) *bias,* warp, twist; jaundice, prejudice, fill with p.; predispose 178 *influence*; obsess 449 *engross.*

(12) *be biased,* be one-sided, be unfair; show favouritism; discriminate against; lean, favour, take sides; blind oneself to 439 *be blind.*

482
Overestimation

Noun
(1) *overestimation,* overestimate

481 *misjudgment*; overstatement 546 *exaggeration*; boasting 877 *boast*; buildup, hype 528 *publicity*; megalomania, vanity 871 *pride*; egotism 932 *selfishness*; overoptimism, optimist 852 *hope.*

Adjective
(2) *optimistic,* upbeat, sanguine; overconfident; high-pitched, enthusiastic, overenthusiastic.

(3) *overrated,* overestimated, puffed-up, cracked-up, hyped-up 546 *exaggerated.*

Verb
(4) *overrate,* overestimate, set too high a value on; idealize, think too much of; rave 546 *exaggerate*; inflate, magnify 197 *enlarge*; boost, cry up 923 *praise*; overemphasize, maximize.

483
Underestimation

Noun
(1) *underestimation,* underestimate, minimization; conservative estimate 177 *moderation*; depreciation 926 *detraction*; understatement; euphemism 950 *prudery*; modesty 872 *humility*; pessimism 853 *hopelessness*; pessimist, minimizer; cynic 926 *detractor.*

Adjective
(2) *depreciating,* derogatory, pejorative, slighting, belittling 926 *detracting*; minimizing, conservative; modest 872 *humble*; pessimistic, despairing 853 *hopeless*; mock-modest, euphemistic 850 *affected.*

(3) *undervalued,* underrated, unappreciated 458 *neglected.*

Verb
(4) *underestimate,* underrate, undervalue 922 *hold cheap*; depreciate, disparage 926 *detract*; not do justice to 481 *misjudge*;

understate, play down, shrug off 458 *disregard*; make little of, minimize; deflate, belittle 922 *despise*; set at naught, scorn 851 *ridicule*.

484
Discovery

Noun
(1) *discovery,* breakthrough, finding, invention; exploration, excavation 459 *search*; nose, flair 619 *pursuit*; detection, spotting 438 *inspection*; dowsing, water divining; exposure, revelation 522 *manifestation*; inspiration, illumination, realization; chance discovery, serendipity; strike, find, treasure trove; solution, explanation; key 263 *opener*.

(2) *detector,* probe; space p. 276 *spaceship*; sonar, radar; lie detector; sensor; Geiger counter 465 *meter*; metal detector; divining rod, dowsing r.; water diviner; spotter, scout, talent s.; discoverer, inventor; explorer 268 *traveller*; archaeologist, speleologist, potholer, prospector 459 *enquirer*.

Adjective
(3) *discovering,* exploratory; on the track, on the scent, warm, getting w.

Verb
(4) *discover,* invent, explore, find a way 461 *experiment*; find out, hit it, have it; strike, hit upon; come upon, happen on, stumble on; meet, encounter 154 *meet with*; realize, tumble to 516 *understand*; find, locate; recognize, identify 490 *know*; verify, ascertain 473 *make certain*; unearth, uncover 522 *manifest*; elicit, worm out, ferret o., nose o., smell o. 459 *search*; get wind of 524 *be informed*.

(5) *detect,* expose, show up 522 *show*; find a clue, be getting warm; perceive, notice, spot 438 *see*; sense, trace, pick up; smell a rat; nose, scent, get wind of; track down 619 *hunt*; trap 542 *ensnare*.

Interjection
(6) *eureka!* got it!

485
Belief

Noun
(1) *belief,* act of believing, credence, credit; state of belief, assurance, conviction, persuasion; confidence, reliance, dependence on, trust, faith; religious belief 973 *religious faith*; firm belief, 473 *certainty*; blind belief 481 *prejudice*; expectation 852 *hope*; credibility 471 *probability*.

(2) *creed,* credo, what one believes; dogma 976 *orthodoxy*; precepts, principles, tenets, articles; catechism, articles of faith; canon 496 *maxim*; declaration of faith, confession, 526 *disclosure*; doctrine, system, school, ism 449 *philosophy*, 973 *theology*.

(3) *opinion,* one's conviction, one's persuasion; sentiment, mind, view; point of view, viewpoint, stand, position, attitude; impression 818 *feeling*; way of thinking, outlook on life 449 *philosophy*; assumption, presumption 475 *premise*; theory, hypothesis 512 *supposition*; surmise, guess 512 *conjecture*; conclusion 480 *judgment*.

Adjective
(4) *believing,* maintaining etc. vb.; confident, assured 473 *certain*; sure, cocksure 473 *positive*; convinced, persuaded, satisfied, converted; firm in, wedded to; trusting, unquestioning 487 *credulous*; pious

976 *orthodox*; opinionated 481 *biased*.

(5) *credible,* plausible, believable, tenable, reasonable 469 *possible*; likely 471 *probable*; reliable, trustworthy, trusty; persuasive, convincing 178 *influential*; trusted, believed etc. vb.; putative, hypothetical.

(6) *creedal,* taught, doctrinal, dogmatic, confessional; canonical, orthodox, authoritative, accredited, ex cathedra; accepted on trust; sacrosanct, unquestioned; absolute, unshakable.

Verb

(7) *believe,* be a believer 976 *be orthodox*; credit, put faith in; hold, maintain 532 *affirm*; profess, confess; accept 488 *assent*; take on trust; swallow whole 487 *be credulous*; take for granted, assume 475 *premise*; have no doubt, know for certain, be convinced 473 *be certain*; rest assured, rest in the belief; have confidence in, trust, rely on, depend on, have faith in, believe in, swear by, count on, bank on; come to believe, be converted.

(8) *opine,* think, fancy, have an impression; have a hunch, surmise, suspect 512 *suppose*; deem, esteem, assume, presume, take it that, hold; have views, regard as, consider as, look upon as, set down as, hold for, account; hold an opinion, cherish an o.

(9) *convince,* make believe, assure, persuade, satisfy; make realize, bring home to 478 *demonstrate*; convert, win over, bring round, wean from; evangelize, propagandize, indoctrinate, proselytize 534 *teach*; put over, put across 178 *influence*; mesmerize, hypnotize; come round to, convince oneself.

(10) *be believed,* be widely b.; go down well, find willing ears; carry conviction; find credence, pass current, pass for truth.

Adverb

(11) *credibly,* supposedly etc. adj.; on faith, on trust; in the light of.

486
Unbelief. Doubt

Noun

(1) *unbelief,* nonbelief; disbelief, incredulity 489 *dissent*; denial 533 *negation*; agnosticism, atheism 974 *irreligion*; scorn, mockery 851 *ridicule*; loss of faith, retraction 603 *recantation*; incredibility 472 *inprobability*.

(2) *doubt* 474 *dubiety*; half-belief, hesitation, wavering, uncertainty; misgiving, distrust, mistrust; scepticism, agnosticism; reservation 468 *qualification*; demur, objection 704 *opposition*; scruple, qualm, suspicion 854 *nervousness*; jealousness 911 *jealousy*.

(3) *unbeliever,* no believer, disbeliever; heathen, infidel 977 *heretic*; atheist 974 *irreligionist*; sceptic, agnostic; doubter, doubting Thomas; dissenter; lapsed believer 603 *tergiversator*; denier 533 *negation*; cynic, nobody's fool; scoffer 926 *detractor*.

Adjective

(4) *unbelieving,* disbelieving, incredulous, sceptical; heathen, infidel; unfaithful, lapsed; doubtful, undecided 474 *doubting*; suspicious 854 *nervous*, 911 *jealous*; slow to believe, distrustful, mistrustful; cynical, hard-boiled 498 *intelligent*.

(5) *unbelieved,* disbelieved etc. vb.; discredited, exploded; incredible, unbelievable 470 *impossible*; inconceivable 864 *wonderful*; hard to believe, hardly credible; untenable, open to suspicion, open to doubt, suspect, suspicious, questionable, disputable, farfetched, unreliable; so-called, pretended.

Verb
(6) *disbelieve,* be incredulous; explain away, discredit; disagree 489 *dissent*; mock, scoff at 851 *ridicule*; deny 533 *negate*; retract, lapse, relapse 603 *recant.*

(7) *doubt,* half-believe 474 *be uncertain*; demur, object, cavil, question, have reservations 468 *qualify*; hesitate, waver 601 *be irresolute*; distrust, mistrust, suspect 854 *be nervous*; be sceptical, not trust, have one's doubts, harbour d.; smell a rat, hold back 598 *be unwilling.*

(8) *cause doubt,* raise questions; render suspect; call in question, discredit; pass belief 472 *be unlikely*; argue against 613 *dissuade*; impugn 479 *confute.*

Adverb
(9) *incredibly,* unbelievably.

(10) *doubtfully,* hesitatingly, with a pinch of salt.

487
Credulity

Noun
(1) *credulity,* credulousness; simplicity, gullibility; rash belief 485 *belief*; blind faith, infatuation, dotage; self-delusion, wishful thinking 481 *misjudgment*; superstition, bigotry, fanaticism; credulous person, simpleton 544 *dupe.*

Adjective
(2) *credulous,* believing, persuadable, amenable; easily taken in 544 *gullible*; unwordly, naive, simple, green; stupid 499 *foolish*; doting, infatuated; superstitious 481 *misjudging*; confiding, trustful, unsuspecting.

Verb
(3) *be credulous,* kid oneself; suspended judgment 477 *reason badly*; take on trust, take for granted 485 *believe*; accept 299 *absorb*; fall for, rise to the bait 544 *be duped*; be superstitious, cross one's fingers, touch wood; hope eternally 482 *overrate*; dote 481 *be biased.*

488
Assent

Noun
(1) *assent,* yes, yea; agreement, concurrence 758 *consent*; acceptance 597 *willingness*; acquiescence 721 *submission*; recognition, realization; admission, confession, avowal 526 *disclosure*; profession 532 *affirmation*; sanction, imprimatur, go-ahead 756 *permission*; approval 923 *approbation*; accordance, corroboration 466 *evidence*; confirmation, verification 478 *demonstration*; validation, ratification; certification, endorsement, seal, signature, stamp, rubber s.; support 703 *aid.*

(2) *consensus,* same mind 24 *agreement*; concordance, harmony, unison 710 *concord*; unanimity, solid vote, general consent, common c., popular belief, public opinion; chorus, single voice; thinking alike, same wavelength; understanding, bargain 765 *compact.*

(3) *assenter,* follower 83 *conformist*; fellow traveller 707 *collaborator*; yes-man 925 *flatterer*; the ayes; seconder, supporter 707 *patron*; subscriber, endorser 765 *signatory*; party, consenting p.

Adjective

(4) *assenting* 758 *consenting*; concurring, party to 24 *agreeing*; collaborating 706 *cooperative*; sympathetic 880 *friendly*; unanimous, with one voice; acquiescent 597 *willing*; delighted 824 *pleased*; allowing, granting 756 *permitting*; sanctioning, conceding.

(5) *assented,* carried, voted, unanimous; unopposed 473 *undisputed*; admitted, granted, conceded 756 *permitted*; confirmed, signed, sealed; uncontroversial, bipartisan.

Verb

(6) *assent,* concur, agree with 24 *accord*; welcome, hail acclaim 923 *applaud*; accept 473 *be certain*; not deny, concede, admit, own, acknowledge, grant, allow 475 *be reasonable*; avow 526 *confess*; signify assent, nod, say aye, say yes, agree to, go along with 758 *consent*; sanction 756 *permit*; echo, ditto, chorus; defer to 920 *respect*; rubber-stamp 925 *flatter*; collaborate, go along with 706 *cooperate*; 765 *contract*.

(7) *acquiesce,* not oppose, accept, abide by 739 *obey*; tolerate, put up with, suffer, endure 721 *submit*; yield, defer to, allow 756 *permit*; let it happen, look on 441 *watch*; toe the line 83 *conform*.

(8) *endorse,* second, support, vote for 703 *patronize*; subscribe to, attest 547 *sign*; seal, stamp, confirm, ratify, sanction 758 *consent*; authenticate; rubberstamp, countersign.

Adverb

(9) *consentingly,* willingly, by consent.

(10) *unanimously,* with one voice, in chorus, to a man.

Interjection

(11) *amen!* amen to that! hear, hear! well said! yes indeed!

489
Dissent

Noun

(1) *dissent,* dissidence 704 *opposition*; contrary vote, disagreement, controversy 709 *dissension*; faction 708 *party*; disaffection 829 *discontent*; disapproval 924 *disapprobation*; repudiation 607 *rejection*; protestantism, nonconformism 84 *nonconformity*; withdrawal, secession; walkout 145 *strike*; noncooperation 738 *disobedience*; denial, lack of consent 760 *refusal*; contradiction 533 *negation*; recantation, retraction; doubtfulness 486 *doubt*; cavil, demur, objection, reservation 468 *qualification*; protest, expostulation 762 *deprecation*; challenge 711 *defiance*.

(2) *dissentient,* objector, critic 926 *detractor*; heckler 702 *hinderer*; dissident, dissenter, protester; protestant 978 *sectarian*; seceder 978 *schismatic*; rebel 738 *revolter*; dropout 84 *nonconformist*; grouser 829 *malcontent*; odd one out, minority; splinter group, faction 708 *party*; the noes 704 *opposition*; agitator 149 *revolutionist*.

Adjective

(3) *dissenting,* differing, dissident 709 *quarrelling*; sceptical 486 *unbelieving*; schismatic 978 *sectarian*; nonconformist 84 *unconformable;* malcontent 829 *discontented*; apostate 769 *nonobservant*; not consenting 760 *refusing*; protesting 762 deprecatory; disinclined 598 *unwilling*; obstructive 702 *hindering*; challenging 711 *defiant*; resistant 704 *opposing*.

(4) *unadmitted,* unacknowledged; denied 533 *negative*; disallowed 757 *prohibited*.

Verb

(5) *dissent,* differ 25 *disagree*; beg to differ 479 *confute*; demur, object, raise objections, cavil, scruple 468 *qualify*; protest 762 *deprecate*; resist 704 *oppose*; challenge 711 *defy*; withhold assent 760 *refuse*; disallow 757 *prohibit*; contradict 533 *negate*; repudiate, not defend; not hold with 924 *disapprove*; secede, withdraw 621 *relinquish*; recant, retract 603 *apostatize*; argue, wrangle 709 *quarrel*.

Adverb

(6) *no,* on the contrary; at issue with, at variance w.; under protest.

490
Knowledge

Noun

(1) *knowledge,* knowing, cognition, recognition, realization; comprehension, perception, understanding, grasp, mastery 447 *intellect*; conscience, consciousness, awareness; insight 476 *intuition*; precognition 510 *foresight*; illumination 975 *revelation*; enlightenment 498 *wisdom*; learning (see *erudition*); folk wisdom, folklore; occult lore 983 *sorcery*; education, background; experience, practical e.; acquaintance, familiarity; no secret, public knowledge 524 *information*; specialism; omniscience; glimmering, inkling, suspicion; impression 818 *feeling*; detection, clue 484 *discovery*; savoir faire, expertise 694 *skill*.

(2) *erudition,* lore, wisdom, scholarship, letters 536 *learning*; smattering, dilettantism; reading, book-learning; bookishness, pedantry; information, mine of i., encyclopedia; faculty 539 *academy*; scholar 492 *intellectual*.

(3) *culture,* letters 557 *literature*; the humanities, the arts; education, liberal e.; instruction 534 *teaching*; literacy, numeracy; civilization, cultivation, sophistication; accomplishments, proficiency, mastery.

(4) *science,* natural s.; applied s., technology. ologies and isms.

Adjective

(5) *knowing,* all-k., encyclopaedic, omniscient 498 *wise*; cognitive 447 *mental*; conscious, aware, mindful of 455 *attentive*; alive to, sensible of 819 *impressible*; experienced, no stranger to, at home with, acquainted, familiar with 610 *habituated*; privy to, wise to 524 *informed*; shrewd 498 *intelligent*; conversant, practised, versed in, proficient 694 *expert*.

(6) *instructed,* briefed, primed 524 *informed*; taught, trained, bred to; lettered, literate; numerate; schooled, educated, well-e.; learned, book-l., bookish, literary; erudite, scholarly 536 *studious*; well-read, widely-r., well-informed, knowledgeable; donnish, scholastic, pedantic; highbrow, intellectual, cultured, cultivated, sophisticated, blue-stocking; well-qualified, professional, specialized 694 *expert*.

(7) *known,* perceived, heard; ascertained 473 *certain*; realized, understood; discovered, explored; noted, famous 866 *renowned*; no secret, public, notorious 528 *well-known*; familiar, intimate, dear; too familiar, hackneyed, stale, trite;

proverbial, household, commonplace 610 *usual*; current, prevalent 79 *general*; memorized, known by heart 505 *remembered*; knowable, discoverable 516 *intelligible*.

Verb

(8) *know,* have knowledge, be acquainted with; apprehend, conceive, catch, grasp, take in 516 *understand*; comprehend, master; come to know, realize; get to know, acquaint oneself, familiarize o.; know again, recognize; know the value, appreciate; be conscious of, be aware 447 *cognize*; perceive 438 *see*; examine, study 438 *scan*; mull, con 455 *be attentive*; see through, have one's measure, have one taped, know inside out; know for a fact 473 *be certain*; have knowledge of, know something 524 *be informed*; know by heart 505 *memorize*; know backwards, have it pat, be master of 694 *be expert*; experience, learn one's lesson 536 *learn*; be omniscient; know what's what 498 *be wise*.

(9) *be known,* become k., come to one's knowledge; be no secret 528 *be published*.

491
Ignorance

Noun

(1) *ignorance,* unknowing; unawareness, unconsciousness; incomprehension, incapacity, backwardness 499 *unintelligence*; superstition 495 *error*; blind ignorance, monumental i.; lack of knowledge, lack of education; unfamiliarity inexperience, greenness, rawness; gaucherie, awkwardness; inexpertness, naivety 699 *artlessness*; bewilderment, lack of information 474 *uncertainty*; unwisdom 499 *folly*; savagery,

heathenism, paganism 982 *idolatry*; ignorant person, illiterate 493 *ignoramus*; amateur, no expert 697 *bungler*; Philistine.

(2) *unknown thing,* unknown quantity, sealed book, Greek; Dark Continent, dark horse, enigma 530 *secret*; unknown person, anonymity 562 *no name*.

(3) *sciolism,* smattering, glimmering, a little learning; vagueness 495 *inexactness*; dilettantism, dabbling; pedantry, quackery, charlatanism, bluff 850 *affectation*.

Adjective

(4) *ignorant,* unknowing, blank; in ignorance, unwitting; unconscious, unaware, oblivious 375 *insensible*; unfamiliar with a stranger to; bewildered, confused, clueless 474 *uncertain*; blinkered, blindfolded 439 *blind*; groping, tentative 461 *experimental*; lay, amateurish, unqualified, inexpert 695 *unskilful*; not conversant, inexperienced, green, raw; unworldly 935 *innocent*; naive, simple 699 *artless*; knowing no better, unenlightened; savage, uncivilized; backward, dull, dumb 499 *unintelligent*; obscurantist, superstitious 481 *misjudging*; old-fashioned, out of touch, behind the times 125 *retrospective*; unretentive 456 *inattentive*; indifferent 454 *incurious*.

(5) *uninstructed,* not told, uninformed; misinformed, misled, hoodwinked; vague about 474 *uncertain*; unschooled, untaught, untutored, unlettered, illiterate, inumerate, uneducated; unlearned, uncultivated, lowbrow; Philistine.

(6) *unknown,* untold, unheard; unseen, hidden, veiled 525 *concealed*; dark, enigmatic, mysterious 517 *unintelligible*; strange, new, unprecedented;

unidentified 562 *anonymous*; undiscovered 458 *neglected*; uncharted, unplumbed; virgin, novel 126 *new*; unheard of, obscure, humble 639 *unimportant*.

(7) *dabbling,* unqualified, bluffing 850 *affected*; half-educated, semiliterate; shallow, superficial, dilettante.

Verb
(8) *not know,* be ignorant, lack information; know no better; have no idea 474 *be uncertain*; misunderstand 517 *not understand*; misconstrue 481 *misjudge*; know a little, dabble in; guess, suspect, wonder 486 *doubt*; unlearn 506 *forget*; lack interest 454 *be incurious*; ignore 458 *disregard*; want to know, ask 459 *enquire*.

Adverb
(9) *ignorantly,* in ignorance, unawares.

492
Scholar

Noun
(1) *scholar,* learned person, man *or* woman of letters; don, professor 537 *teacher*; doctor, clerk; pedant, bookworm; classicist, humanist; polymath; student 538 *learner*; graduate, professional, specialist 696 *proficient person*; world of learning, academic circles.

(2) *intellectual,* academic, scholastic 449 *philosopher*; brain worker; brain, genius, prodigy 500 *sage*; know-all, highbrow, egghead, bluestocking; literati, intelligentsai; scientist, technologist; academician.

(3) *collector,* connoisseur, dilettante 846 *people of taste*; librarian, curator 749 *keeper*; antiquary 125 *antiquarian*; numismatist, philatelist, bibliophile 504 *enthusiast*.

493
Ignoramus

Noun
(1) *ignoramus,* illiterate, no scholar, lowbrow; philistine 847 *vulgarian*; duffer 501 *dunce*; novice, raw recruit 538 *beginner*; simpleton, innocent 544 *dupe*; bigot 481 *narrow mind*.

(2) *sciolist,* dilettante; quack, charlatan 545 *impostor*.

494
Truth

Noun
(1) *truth,* verity; rightness, intrinsic truth; truism 496 *axiom*; consistency, self-c., honest truth, plain t., simple t.; light of truth 975 *revelation*; fact, matter of f. 1 *reality*; home truth, candour, frankness 929 *probity*; truthfulness 540 *veracity*.

(2) *authenticity,* validity, realness, genuineness; the real thing, it 13 *identity*; not a fake 21 *no imitation*.

(3) *accuracy,* exactness, preciseness, precision; realism, naturalism; fine adjustment, sensitivity, fidelity, high f.; aptness 24 *adaptation*; meticulousness 455 *attention*; pedantry, literality, literalness; the very words 540 *veracity*.

Adjective
(4) *true,* veritable; correct, right, so; actual, factual, historical; well-grounded, well-founded 478 *demonstrated*; unquestionable 473 *undisputed*; literal, truthful 540 *veracious*; ascertained 473 *certain*; consistent, self-c., logical, reasonable 475 *rational*; true to life, faithful; realistic, objective, unbiased; candid, honest, warts and all.

(5) *genuine,* unadulterated, authentic, veritable, bona fide; valid, guaranteed, official; sound, solid, reliable, honest 929 *trustworthy*; natural, pure; sterling, hallmarked; true-born, rightful, legitimate.

(6) *accurate,* exact, precise, definite; well-adjusted, high-fidelity, dead-on 24 *adjusted*; well-aimed, direct, dead-centre 281 *directed*; constant, regular 16 *uniform*; punctual, right, correct, true, spot on; never wrong, infallible; close, faithful, photographic; fine, delicate, sensitive; mathematical, scientific, electronic; scrupulous, punctilious, meticulous 455 *attentive*; word for word, literal.

Verb
(7) *be true,* be so, be the case 1 *be*; hold, hold true, hold good, hold water, stand the test, ring true; hold together, be consistent; speak the truth 540 *be truthful*; substantiate 466 *corroborate*; prove 478 *demonstrate*.

Adverb
(8) *truly,* really, veritably, genuinely, indeed 540 *truthfully*; sic, literally, word for word; exactly, accurately, precisely, just right.

495
Error

Noun
(1) *error,* erroneousness, wrongness, unsoundness; untruth, falsity; fallacy 477 *sophism*; superstition 491 *ignorance*; fallibility 481 *misjudgment*; self-deception, wishful thinking, doublethink; misconception, misunderstanding; falseness, untruthfulness 541 *falsehood*; illusion, hallucination 440 *visual fallacy*; false impression, (see *mistake*); prejudice 481 *bias*.

(2) *inexactness,* inexactitude, inaccuracy, imprecision faultiness; looseness, laxity 79 *generality*; loose thinking 477 *sophistry*; sloppiness, carelessness 458 *negligence*; mistiming 118 *anachronism*; misstatement, misquotation; malapropism 565 *solecism*.

(3) *mistake,* miscalculation 481 *misjudgment*; blunder 695 *bungling*; glaring error, bloomer, clanger, howler, gaffe; oversight 456 *inattention*; mishit 728 *failure*; bungle, slip-up, slip, slip of the tongue, slip of the pen 565 *solecism*; clerical error, typist's e.; misprint, erratum, corrigendum; trip, stumble; faux pas 847 *bad taste*; blot, flaw 845 *blemish*.

Adjective
(4) *erroneous,* erring, wrong; aberrant 282 *deviating*; devoid of truth 543 *untrue*; unsound, ill-reasoned 477 *illogical*; unfounded, baseless; disproved 479 *confuted*; exploded, discredited 924 *disapproved*; fallacious, misleading; unorthodox, heretical 977 *heterodox*; untruthful, lying 541 *false*; not genuine, fake 542 *spurious*; illusory, deceptive 542 *deceiving*; fantastical 513 *imaginary*; wild, crackpot 497 *absurd*; fallible, wrong-headed 481 *biased*; superstitious 491 *ignorant*.

(5) *mistaken,* misunderstood, misconceived; misrepresented, perverted; misread, misprinted; miscalculated, misjudged 481 *misjudging*; in error, at fault; misled, misguided; misinformed, ill-informed 491 *uninstructed*; deluded, on the wrong tack; blundering 695 *clumsy*; misdirected, off-target 282 *deviating*; off the scent, at sea 474 *uncertain*.

(6) *inexact,* imprecise, inaccurate; not strict, not literal, free;

broad, generalized 79 *general*; incorrect, misstated, misreported, garbled; erratic, wild, hit or miss; out, badly adjusted; out of tune, out of gear; slow, losing, fast, gaining; faulty, full of faults, mangled 695 *bungled*; mistranslated 521 *misinterpreted*.

Verb
(7) *err,* commit an error, make a mistake, go wrong, mistake, be mistaken; delude oneself 481 *misjudge*; be misled, be misguided; misunderstand, misconceive, misapprehend, get it wrong 517 *not understand*; misreckon 482 *overrate*, 483 *underestimate*; go astray 282 *stray*; gain, be fast 135 *be early*; lose, be slow 136 *be late*.

(8) *blunder,* trip, stumble 695 *be clumsy*; slip, slip up, drop a brick *or* a clanger; betray oneself, give oneself away 526 *disclose*; muff, botch, bungle 695 *act foolishly*; misread, misquote, misprint, misapprehend 521 *misinterpret*.

(9) *mislead,* misdirect, misinform, lead into error, lead astray, pervert 535 *misteach*; beguile 542 *deceive*; falsify 541 *dissemble*; whitewash, cover up 525 *conceal*.

496
Maxim

Noun
(1) *maxim,* adage, saw, proverb, byword, aphorism; dictum, tag, saying, truth; epigram 839 *witticism*; truism, cliche, commonplace, platitude, banality; motto, watchword, slogan, catchword; formula, mantra; text, rule, golden r. 693 *precept*; observation 520 *commentary*; moral, fable 590 *narrative*.

(2) *axiom,* self-evident truth, truism; principle, postulate, theorem, formula.

Adjective
(3) *aphoristic,* proverbial 498 *wise*; moralizing, sententious; epigrammatic, pithy 839 *witty*; terse, snappy 569 *concise*; enigmatic, oracular 517 *puzzling*; banal, trite, corny, hackneyed, clichéd 610 *usual*; axiomatic 693 *preceptive*.

Adverb
(4) *proverbially,* as they say; in a nutshell.

497
Absurdity

Noun
(1) *absurdity,* absurdness 849 *ridiculousness*; ineptitude, inconsequence 10 *irrelevance*; false logic 477 *sophistry*; foolishness, silliness 499 *folly*; senselessness, futility, fatuity 641 *lost labour*; rubbish, nonsense, gibberish 515 *silly talk*; bombast 546 *exaggeration*; howler 495 *mistake*; paradox 530 *enigma*; anticlimax, bathos.

(2) *foolery,* antics, fooling about, silliness, tomfoolery, skylarking 837 *revel*; whimsy, extravagance, extravaganza; escapade, scrape 700 *predicament*; practical joke, monkey trick; drollery, clowning, buffoonery; burlesque, parody, caricature 851 *ridicule*; farce, pretence 850 *affectation*.

Adjective
(3) *absurd,* ludicrous, laughable, comical, grotesque 849 *ridiculous*; rash, silly 499 *foolish*; nonsensical, senseless 515 *meaningless*; preposterous 477 *illogical*; wild, extravagant 546 *exaggerated*; pretentious 850 *affected*; mad, crazy, harebrained 495 *erroneous*; fanciful,

fantastic 513 *imaginative*; futile, fatuous 641 *useless*; paradoxical, inconsistent 25 *unapt*.

Verb

(4) *be absurd,* play the fool 499 *be foolish*; fool about, lark about 837 *amuse oneself*; be a laughing stock 849 *be ridiculous*; clown, parody, mimic, guy 851 *ridicule*; talk gibberish 515 *mean nothing*; talk wildly, rant, rave 503 *be insane*.

498
Intelligence. Wisdom

Noun

(1) *intelligence,* thinking power, 447 *intellect*; brains, grey matter, head; nous, wit, mother-w., commonsense; lights, understanding, sense, good s.; wits, sharp w., ready w., quick thinking, quickness, readiness; ability, capacity, mental c., mental grasp; calibre, mental c., IQ; high IQ, forwardness, brightness, braininess; cleverness 694 *aptitude*; mental gifts, giftedness, brilliance, talent, genius; ideas, inspiration 476 *intuition*; bright idea 451 *idea*.

(2) *sagacity,* judgment, good j., discretion, discernment 463 *discrimination*; perception, perspicacity, clear thought, clear thinking; acumen, sharpness, acuteness, acuity, penetration; practicality, shrewdness; balance 502 *sanity*; prudence, forethought 510 *foresight*; subtleness, subtlety, craftiness 698 *cunning*; worldly wisdom 694 *skill*; vigilance, alertness, awareness 457 *carefulness*; tact 688 *tactics*.

(3) *wisdom,* depth of mind, breadth of m., mature understanding, experience, fund of e. 490 *knowledge*; tolerance, broadmindedness; soundness, sobriety, objectivity.

Adjective

(4) *intelligent,* brainy, clever, forward, bright, brilliant, scintillating, talented, of genius 694 *gifted*; capable, able, practical 694 *skilful*; apt, ready, quick, receptive; acute, sharp, sharp-witted, quick-w.; alive, aware 455 *attentive*; astute, shrewd, smart, canny, knowing, sophisticated, worldly-wise; sagacious, farsighted, clear-sighted 510 *foreseeing*; discerning penetrating, perspicacious, clear-headed; subtle, crafty, wily, foxy, artful 698 *cunning*.

(5) *wise,* sage; thinking, reflecting 449 *thoughtful*; knowledgeable 490 *instructed*; profound, deep; sound, sensible, reasonable 502 *sane*; sober 834 *serious*; experienced, cool, collected, unflappable; balanced, level-headed, realistic; judicious, impartial 913 *just*; tolerant, broad-minded, fair-minded, enlightened, unprejudiced; tactful, politic 698 *cunning*; well-advised, well-judged 642 *advisable*.

Verb

(6) *be wise,* intelligent etc. adj.; use one's head 490 *know*; show foresight 510 *foresee*; be prudent 858 *be cautious*; grasp, fathom, take in 516 *understand*; discern 438 *see*; distinguish 463 *discriminate*; have sense, listen to reason 475 *be reasonable*.

499
Unintelligence. Folly

Noun

(1) *unintelligence,* want of intellect 448 *absence of intellect*; lack of brains, low IQ, low mental age, immaturity; Down's syndrome, mongolism, mental handicap, retardation,

backwardness; imbecility, idiocy; stupidity, slowness, obtuseness, denseness; poor head, no head for, no brain; incapacity, ineptitude, incompetence 695 *unskilfulness*; naivety, simplicity, fallibility, gullibility 481 *misjudgment*; vacuousness, shallowness.

(2) *folly,* foolishness, extravagance, eccentricity 849 *ridiculousness*; act of folly 497 *foolery*; trifling, levity, frivolity; giddiness 456 *inattention*; unwisdom imprudence, indiscretion; fatuousness, pointlessness 641 *lost labour*; silliness, asininity; brainlessness, idiocy, lunacy, sheer l.; recklessness, wildness 857 *rashness*; obsession, infatuation 481 *misjudgment*; puerility, childishness; second childhood 131 *old age*; conceit 873 *vanity.*

Adjective

(3) *unintelligent,* ungifted, no genius; incompetent 695 *clumsy*; not bright, dull; mentally handicapped, subnormal, undeveloped, immature; backward, retarded, imbecile 503 *insane*; limited, slow, stupid, obtuse, dense; stolid, unimaginative; oafish, doltish, owlish; dumb, dim, dim-witted, thick-w., bone-headed; impenetrable, impervious; wrong-headed, pig-h. 481 *misjudging.*

(4) *foolish,* silly, idiotic, asinine, senseless, fatuous, futile, inane 497 *absurd*; ludicrous, laughable 849 *ridiculous*; simple, naive 544 *gullible*; inexperienced 491 *ignorant*; tactless, gauche, awkward; soft, wet, gormless; goofy, gawky, dopey; childish, babyish, puerile, infantile; senile 131 *ageing*; besotted, fond, doting; amorous, sentimental 887 *enamoured*; fuddled 949 *drunk*; brainless, shallow, superficial; frivolous, featherbrained, scatterbrained 456

light-minded; playing the fool, misbehaving, boyish; eccentric, extravagant, wild, madcap, daft 503 *crazy.*

(5) *unwise,* unreasoning, irrational 477 *illogical*; indiscreet, injudicious 481 *misjudging*; unseeing 439 *blind*; thoughtless 450 *unthinking*; impatient 680 *hasty*; incautious, foolhardy, reckless 857 *rash*; prejudiced, intolerant 481 *narrowminded*; unreasonable, against reason; inept, incongruous, unseemly, improper 643 *inexpedient*; ill-considered, ill-advised, ill-judged 495 *mistaken.*

Verb

(6) *be foolish,* maunder, dote, drivel 515 *mean nothing*; lose one's wits, 503 *be insane*; have no brains, have no sense; never learn; look foolish 849 *be ridiculous*; play the fool 497 *be absurd*; burn one's fingers 695 *act foolishly*; miscalculate 481 *misjudge.*

500
Sage

Noun

(1) *sage,* learned person 492 *scholar*; wise man *or* woman, counsellor, consultant, authority 691 *adviser*; expert 696 *proficient person*; genius, master mind; master, mentor, guru, pundit 537 *teacher*; seer, prophet 511 *oracle*; yogi, swami 945 *ascetic*; leading light, luminary; doctor, thinker 449 *philosopher*; highbrow 492 *intellectual*; wizard, witch doctor 983 *sorcerer.*

(2) *wiseacre,* wise guy, know-all 873 *vain person*; smart aleck, clever dick.

501
Fool

Noun

(1) *fool,* silly f., buffoon, clown, comic, jester 594 *entertainer*;

(1) *fool,* silly f., buffoon, clown, comic, jester 594 *entertainer*; perfect fool, complete idiot, ass, donkey, goose; idiot, imbecile; half-wit, sot, stupid, silly; stooge, butt 851 *laughingstock*; blunderer, incompetent 697 *bungler*; scatterbrains, bird-brain, featherbrain; eccentric, old fogy 504 *crank.*

(2) *ninny,* simpleton, noodle, nincompoop, muggins, booby; dope, jerk, goof; greenhorn 538 *beginner*; wet, weed, drip, milksop, goody-goody 163 *weakling*; sucker, mug 544 *dupe.*

(3) *dunce,* dullard; blockhead, numskull, duffer, dolt 493 *ignoramus*; fathead, thickhead, bonehead, blockhead, nitwit, dimwit; chump, clot, clod, oaf, lout.

502
Sanity

Noun
(1) *sanity,* saneness, sound of mind; sobriety, rationality, reason; balance, mental b.; common sense; coherence, lucidity; normality, proper mind, senses; mental health.

Adjective
(2) *sane,* normal, not neurotic; of sound mind, all there; in one's right mind, compos mentis, rational, reasonable 498 *intelligent*; sober, coherent 516 *intelligible*; lucid, clear-headed; balanced, well-b. 480 *judicial*; not certifiable.

Verb
(3) *be sane,* keep one's senses, recover one's mind, come to one's senses, cool down, sober down, sober up, see sense.

(4) *make sane,* restore to sanity, bring to their senses, sober, bring round.

Adverb
(5) *sanely,* soberly, reasonably.

503
Insanity

Noun
(1) *insanity,* lunacy, madness; mental instability, mental illness; loss of reason, sick mind, unsound m., troubled brain, brain damage; mental decay, senile d., dotage, dementia; idiocy, congenital i., imbecility, cretinism, mongolism, Down's syndrome; autism; psychiatry, psychotherapy; psychoanalyst, psychiatrist 658 *doctor.*

(2) *psychopathy,* maladjustment, personality disorder; neurosis, nerves, neurasthenia; hysteria; attack of nerves, nervous breakdown, brainstorm; shellshock, combat fatigue; obsession, compulsion, phobia 854 *phobia*; paranoia, delusions; split personality, schizophrenia; psychosis; confusion, frustration; hypochondria; depression, maniac d.

(3) *mania,* megalomania, kleptomania; homicidal mania; persecution m.; monomania.

(4) *frenzy,* ecstasy, delirium, raving, hysteria; delirium tremens 949 *alcoholism*; epilepsy, fit, paroxysm 318 *spasm.*

(5) *eccentricity,* craziness, crankiness, faddishness; queerness, oddness, weirdness; kink, craze, fad 84 *abnormality*; fixation, inhibition, repression; complex, inferiority c., Oedipus c.; obsession, ruling passion 481 *bias*; hobbyhorse 604 *whim.*

(6) *lunatic asylum,* mental home, mental hospital, psychiatric h.; madhouse, Bedlam; padded cell.

Adjective

(7) *insane,* mad, lunatic, of unsound mind, out of one's mind, deranged, demented; certifiable, mental; abnormal, sick, mentally ill, unbalanced, maladjusted; psychopathic; psychotic; neurotic, hysterical; paranoiac, paranoid, schizophrenic, schizoid; manic, maniacal; depressive, elated; hypochondriac 834 *melancholic*; kleptomaniac; autistic; brain-damaged, shell-shocked; imbecile, moronic, idiotic, cretinous, defective, subnormal 499 *unintelligent*; raving mad, stark staring m.; certified.

(8) *crazy,* bewildered, bemused 456 *abstracted*; off one's head, not all there; maddened; crazed, demented, unhinged; bedevilled, bewitched, deluded; infatuated, possessed; besotted 887 *enamoured*; idiotic 499 *foolish*; crackers screwy, nutty, batty, barmy, daft, loony, potty, dotty; cranky, eccentric, funny, queer, odd, peculiar 84 *abnormal*; dizzy, giddy 456 *light-minded*.

(9) *frenzied,* rabid, maddened; furious 891 *angry*; haggard, wild, distraught 825 *suffering*; possessed, frantic, frenetic, demented, beside oneself, berserk, running amok 176 *violent*; epileptic, having a fit; hysterical, delirious, hallucinating, raving, rambling, incoherent, fevered 651 *sick*.

Verb

(10) *be insane,* - mad etc. adj.; dote, drivel 499 *be foolish*; ramble, wander; babble, rave; be delirious.

(11) *go mad,* go out of one's mind, lose one's reason, lose one's wits, crack up; go berserk, run amok, see red, lose one's head 891 *get angry*.

(12) *make mad,* drive m., send m., drive insane, madden; craze, derange, turn one's brain; blow one's mind 821 *excite*; unhinge, unbalance; infuriate 891 *enrage*; possess, obsess; go to one's head.

504
Madman

Noun

(1) *madman,* madwoman, lunatic, mental case; nutcase, loony; psychopath, psycho; sociopath; hysteric, neurotic, neuropath; psychotic; obsessive, paranoiac; schizoid; maniac depressive; raving lunatic, maniac; kleptomaniac, pyromaniac, monomaniac, megalomaniac; dope addict, drug a. 949 *drug-taking*; hypochondriac, melancholic 834 *moper*; idiot, congenital i., cretin, moron.

(2) *crank,* crackpot, nut, eccentric, oddity 851 *laughingstock*; freak 84 *nonconformist*; faddist, fanatic, extremist, lunatic fringe; seer, dreamer 513 *visionary*

(3) *enthusiast,* zealot, devotee, aficionado, addict, nut, freak, buff; fan, supporter 707 *patron*; connoisseur, fancier 846 *people of taste*; radio ham, opera buff; bibliophile 492 *collector*.

505
Memory

Noun

(1) *memory,* good m., photographic m.; retentiveness, retention.

(2) *remembrance,* recollection, recall, total r.; commemoration, evocation, mind's eye; rehearsal 106 *repetition*; memorization 536 *learning*; reminiscence, retrospection, review,

retrospect, hindsight; flashback, déjà vu 984 *psychics*; nostalgia, regrets 830 *regret*; memorabilia, memoirs; fame, notoriety 866 *famousness*.

(3) *reminder,* memorial, testimonial, commemoration 876 *celebration*; souvenir, keepsake, relic, memento, autograph; trophy, bust, statue 548 *monument*; memorandum, memo; aide-memoire, notebook, diary; album, scrapbook; prompt, cue 524 *hint*; mnemonic, aid to memory.

(4) *mnemonics,* art of memory; mnemonic device; data bank 632 *store*.

Adjective
(5) *remembered,* recollected etc. vb.; not forgotten, green, fresh; in one's thoughts, missed, regretted; memorable, unforgettable, haunting, indelible; got by heart, memorized 490 *known*.

(6) *remembering,* mindful; evocative, memorial, commemorative 876 *celebratory*; reminiscent, recollecting, anecdotal; nostalgic; unable to forget, haunted, plagued; reminding, mnemonic.

Verb
(7) *remember,* mind, bring to m., call to m.; recognize, know again 490 *know*; not forget, bottle up 778 *retain*; never forget, cherish; recollect, recall, call to mind, think of; keep in mind 455 *be mindful*; reminisce, remind oneself.

(8) *retrospect,* recollect, recall, recapture; reflect, review, think back upon, retrace, hark back, conjure u. 125 *look back.*

(9) *remind,* jog one's memory, refresh one's m., put one in mind of, take one back; prompt, suggest; haunt, obsess; commemorate, memorialize, toast

876 *celebrate*; relate, recount, recapitulate 106 *repeat*, 590 *describe*.

(10) *memorize,* commit to memory, get to know, con 490 *know*; get by heart, learn by rote 536 *learn*; fix in one's memory, impress on one's mind.

(11) *be remembered,* ring a bell; stick in the mind, haunt; make history, leave a name 866 *have a reputation*; live on 115 *be eternal.*

Adverb
(12) *in memory,* in memoriam; by heart, from memory.

506
Oblivion

Noun
(1) *oblivion,* blankness, no recollection; obliviousness, forgetfulness, loss of memory, amnesia, blackout, total blank, mental block; dim memory, short memory; effacement 550 *obliteration.*

(2) *amnesty,* pardon, free p. 909 *forgiveness.*

Adjective
(3) *forgotten,* beyond recall; not missed; in limbo 458 *neglected*; out of mind, gone out of one's head; over and done with 909 *forgiven.*

(4) *forgetful,* forgetting, oblivious; amnesic; unmindful, heedless 908 *ungrateful*; absent-minded 458 *negligent*; willing to forget 909 *forgiving.*

Verb
(5) *forget,* clean f., not remember, be oblivious; bury the hatchet 909 *forgive*; unlearn, efface 550 *obliterate*; lose one's memory, remember nothing; be forgetful, need reminding; lose sight of, leave behind, overlook 456 *be inattentive*; forget one's

lines, dry; almost remember, not quite recall.

(6) *be forgotten,* slip one's memory, escape one's m.; sink into oblivion; be overlooked 456 *escape notice.*

507
Expectation

Noun

(1) *expectation,* state of e., expectancy 455 *attention;* contemplation 617 *intention;* confidence, trust 473 *certainty;* presumption 475 *premise;* foretaste 135 *anticipation;* optimism 852 *hope;* waiting, suspense 474 *uncertainty;* pessimism, dread, apprehension, 854 *fear;* anxiety 825 *worry;* one's prospects 471 *probability;* reckoning, calculation 480 *estimate;* prospect, lookout, outlook, forecast 511 *prediction;* contingency 469 *possibility;* destiny 596 *fate.*

Adjective

(2) *expectant,* expecting, in expectation, in suspense; confident 473 *certain;* anticipatory, anticipating, banking on; presuming, predicting 510 *foreseeing;* forewarned ready 669 *prepared;* waiting, awaiting; on the lookout 457 *vigilant;* tense, keyed up 821 *excited;* agog 859 *desiring;* optimistic, hopeful, sanguine 852 *hoping;* apprehensive, dreading, anxious 854 *nervous;* pessimistic 853 *hopeless;* wondering, curious 453 *inquisitive.*

(3) *expected,* long e.; anticipated, predicted, foreseen, foreseeable 471 *probable;* prospective, future 155 *impending;* promised, intended, in view, in prospect 617 *intending;* hoped for, longed for 859 *desired;* apprehended, dreaded 854 *frightening.*

Verb

(4) *expect,* look for, have in prospect, face the prospect, face; contemplate, have in mind, promise oneself 617 *intend;* reckon, calculate 480 *estimate;* predict, forecast 510 *foresee;* think likely, presume 471 *assume;* rely on, bank on 473 *be certain;* anticipate 669 *prepare oneself;* look out for, be ready f. 457 *be careful;* apprehend 854 *fear;* look forward to, 859 *desire.*

(5) *await* 136 *wait;* queue up, mark time, bide one's t.; stand by, be on call; hold one's breath, be in suspense; be expected, keep one waiting.

Adverb

(6) *expectantly,* in suspense, on edge, with bated breath.

508
Lack of expectation

Noun

(1) *lack of expectation,* no expectation 472 *improbability;* resignation 853 *hopelessness;* apathy 454 *incuriosity;* lack of warning, surprise, the unexpected, the unforeseen; windfall 615 *benefit;* shock, start, jolt, turn; blow, bombshell; revelation, eye-opener; culture shock; paradox, reversal; astonishment, amazement 864 *wonder;* anticlimax.

Adjective

(2) *unexpected,* unlooked for, unhoped for; unanticipated, unforeseen; unforeseeable 472 *improbable;* unheralded, without warning, surprising, astounding, amazing 864 *wonderful;* shocking, startling 854 *frightening;* sudden 116 *instantaneous;* unprecedented 84 *unusual;* full of surprises, unaccountable 517 *puzzling.*

(3) *inexpectant,* off guard, unsuspecting 456 *inattentive*; surprised, disconcerted; taken by surprise 670 *unprepared*; taken aback, astonished, amazed, thunderstruck, dumbfounded 864 *wondering*; startled, shocked; apathetic 860 *indifferent.*

Verb

(4) *not expect,* not foresee 472 *be unlikely*; not hope for 853 *despair*; be caught out, be taken aback, not bargain for; get a shock, be taken by surprise, start, jump; goggle, stare.

(5) *surprise,* take by s., spring something on; catch, trap, ambush 542 *ensnare*; catch napping, catch off one's guard; startle, make one jump; bowl one over, astonish, amaze, dumbfound 864 *be wonderful*; shock, electrify 821 *impress*; fall on pounce on; steal upon, creep up on.

Adverb

(6) *unexpectedly,* suddenly, abruptly, without warning, without notice.

509
Disappointment

Noun

(1) *disappointment,* regrets 830 *regret*; tantalization, frustration, bafflement; blighted hopes, bad news, disillusion 829 *discontent*; mirage, false dawn, fool's paradise; shock, blow, setback 702 *hitch*; bad luck 731 *misfortune*; anticlimax comedown, letdown 872 *humiliation*.

Adjective

(2) *disappointed,* frustrated, thwarted, baffled, foiled 728 *defeated*; disconcerted, crestfallen, chagrined 872 *humbled*; disgruntled, soured 829 *discontented*; heartbroken 834 *dejected*; badly served, let down,

betrayed, jilted; turned away 607 *rejected.*

(3) *disappointing,* not up to expectation 829 *discontenting*; abortive 728 *unsuccessful*; deceptive 542 *deceiving.*

Verb

(4) *be disappointed,* try in vain 728 *fail*; expect otherwise, be let down, have hoped better of 830 *regret*; be sick with disappointment 853 *despair*.

(5) *disappoint* 307 *fall short*; dash one's hopes, blight one's h.; disillusion; fail one, let one down; thwart, frustrate, tantalize 702 *hinder*; disconcert, humble 872 *humiliate*; betray 930 *be dishonest*; discontent, dissatisfy, sour 829 *cause discontent*; turn away 607 *reject.*

510
Foresight

Noun

(1) *foresight,* prevision; anticipation, precognition, foreknowledge, prescience, second sight, premonition, presentiment, foreboding, forewarning 511 *omen*; prognosis 511 *prediction*; programme, prospectus; forethought, vision 498 *sagacity*; prudence, providence 858 *caution*; readiness, provision 669 *preparation.*

Adjective

(2) *foreseeing,* foresighted; clairvoyant, prophetic 511 *predicting*; prescient, farsighted, sagacious 498 *wise*; looking ahead, provident, prudent 858 *cautious*; anticipatory 507 *expectant.*

Verb

(3) *foresee,* divine, prophesy, forecast 511 *predict*; forewarn 664 *warn*; foreknow, have second sight; see ahead, see coming, scent, look for 507 *expect*; anticipate, 135 *be early*; make provision 669 *prepare*; plan ahead 623 *plan*; take precautions, provide against 858 *be cautious*.

511
Prediction

Noun

(1) *prediction,* forewarning, prophecy 975 *revelation*; forecast, weather f.; prognostication, prognosis; presentiment, foreboding 510 *foresight*; presage, prefiguration; announcement, notice 528 *publication*; warning 665 *danger signal*; prospect 507 *expectation*; horoscope, fortune.

(2) *divination,* clairvoyance; augury, soothsaying; astrology; fortune-telling, palmistry, chiromancy; crystal gazing; casting lots; necromancy 984 *occultism*.

(3) *omen,* portent, symptom, sign 547 *indication*; augury, auspice; forewarning, writing on the wall 664 *warning*; harbinger, herald 529 *messenger*; gathering clouds 661 *danger*; luck-bringer 983 *talisman*.

(4) *oracle,* consultant 500 *sage*; prophet, prophetess, seer, forecaster 664 *warner*; soothsayer 983 *sorcerer*; clairvoyant, medium 984 *occultist*; tarot cards, dice; crystal ball, tea leaves.

(5) *diviner,* water d.; astrologer; fortune-teller, gipsy, palmist, crystal-gazer.

Adjective

(6) *predicting,* foretelling; clairvoyant 510 *foreseeing*; prophetic, apocalyptic; oracular, sibylline; premonitory, foreboding 664 *cautionary*; heralding, prefiguring.

(7) *presageful,* significant, ominous, portentous; auspicious, promising 730 *prosperous*; inauspicious, sinister 731 *adverse*.

Verb

(8) *predict,* forecast, make a prediction; foretell, prophesy, forebode, bode, augur, spell; presage, portend; foreshadow, prefigure, herald 64 *come before*; point to, betoken 547 *indicate*; announce 528 *advertise*; forewarn 664 *warn*; lour, menace 900 *threaten*; promise 852 *give hope*.

(9) *divine,* take the auspices; soothsay; cast a horoscope; cast lots 618 *gamble*; tell fortunes; read the future, read the stars; read one's hand.

512
Supposition

Noun

(1) *supposition,* notion 451 *idea*; fancy, conceit 513 *ideality*; presumption, assumption 475 *premise*; proposal, proposition, submission 475 *argument*; hypothesis, theory, model 452 *topic*; thesis, position, stand, attitude 485 *opinion*; suggestion 524 *hint*; clue, data 466 *evidence*; suspicion, hunch, instinct 476 *intuition*.

(2) *conjecture,* guess, surmise; rough guess, crude estimate; shrewd idea 476 *intuition*; guesswork, speculation; shot in the dark 618 *gambling*.

(3) *theorist,* theorizer, theoretician, research worker 623 *planner*; academic, thinker 449 *philosopher*.

Adjective

(4) *suppositional,* notional, conjectural, propositional, hypothetical, theoretical, armchair, speculative, academic, gratuitous; suggestive, hinting, allusive; thought-provoking, stimulating.

(5) *supposed,* assumed etc. vb.; taken, postulated; proposed, mooted 452 *topical*; given, granted, 488 *assented*; putative, presumptive; pretended, so-called, quasi; alleged, fabled 2 *unreal*; fancied 543 *untrue*; imaginable 513 *imaginary*.

Verb

(6) *suppose,* pretend, fancy 513 *imagine*; think, conceive 485 *opine*; divine, have a hunch 476 *intuit*; surmise, conjecture, guess, hazard a g.; persuade oneself 485 *believe*; presume, presuppose 475 *premise*; posit 532 *affirm*; take for granted, postulate 475 *reason*; speculate, theorize 449 *meditate*; sketch 623 *plan*.

(7) *propound,* propose, moot, move, propose a motion 761 *request*; put a case, submit 475 *argue*; make a suggestion, venture to say, suggest 524 *hint*; urge 612 *motivate*.

513
Imagination

Noun

(1) *imagination,* fertile i., lively i.; imaginativeness, creativeness; creativity, inventiveness 21 *originality*; ingenuity 694 *skill*; fancifulness, fantasy; understanding, insight, empathy, sympathy 819 *moral sensibility*; ecstasy, inspiration; fancy, the mind's eye, visualization, imagery, word-painting.

(2) *ideality,* conception 449 *thought*; idealization; mental image, projection 445 *appearance*; concept, image, conceit, fancy, notion 451 *idea*; whim, whimsy 497 *absurdity*; vagary 604 *caprice*; figment, fiction 541 *falsehood*; science fiction, fairy tale; flight of fancy, romance, fantasy, extravaganza 546 *exaggeration*; poetic licence 593 *poetry*.

(3) *fantasy,* vision, dream, bad d., nightmare; bogey, phantom 970 *ghost*; mirage 440 *visual fallacy*; delusion, hallucination, chimera 495 *error*; reverie, trance; sick fancy, delirium 503 *frenzy*; wishful thinking, make-believe, daydream, pipe dream 859 *desire*; romance, stardust; romanticism, escapism, idealism, Utopianism; Utopia, promised land, El Dorado; fairyland, wonderland; dream world, millennium; myth 543 *fable*.

(4) *visionary,* seer 511 *diviner*; dreamer, day-d.; idealist, Utopian 901 *philanthropist*; escapist; romantic, romanticist, rhapsodist, myth-maker; knight-errant 504 *crank*; creative worker 556 *artist*.

Adjective

(5) *imaginative,* creative, original, inventive, fertile, ingenious; resourceful 694 *skilful*; romancing, romantic; high-flown, rhapsodic 546 *exaggerated*; poetic, fictional; Utopian, idealistic; dreaming, in a trance; extravagant, grotesque, bizarre, fantastic, whimsical, airy-fairy, preposterous, impractical 497 *absurd*; visionary, otherworldly, quixotic.

(6) *imaginary,* ideal, visionary; unreal 4 *insubstantial*; subjective, notional; chimerical, illusory 495 *erroneous*; dreamy, vaporous 419 *shadowy*; unhistorical, fictitious, fabulous, fabled, legendary, mythic, mythological 543 *untrue*; fanciful, fancied, imagined etc. vb.; hypothetical 512 *suppositional*; pretended, make-believe.

Verb

(7) *imagine,* fancy, dream, think of, think up, dream up 449 *think*; make up, devise, invent, create, improvise; coin, hatch, concoct, fabricate 164 *produce*; visualize, envisage 438 *see*; conceive, figure to oneself, picture to o.; paint, p. in words, realize, capture, recapture 551 *represent*; use one's imagination, pretend, make-believe; daydream 456 *be inattentive*; be inspired, see visions, dream dreams; idealize, romanticize, fictionalize, rhapsodize 546 *exaggerate*; empathize, sympathize.

Adverb
(8) *imaginatively*, in imagination, in the mind's eye.

514
Meaning

Noun
(1) *meaning*, substance, essence, spirit, gist, pith; contents, subject matter 452 *topic*; sense, value, drift, tenor, purport, import, implication; force, effect; relevance, bearing, scope; expression 566 *style*; semantics 557 *linguistics*.

(2) *connotation*, denotation, signification, significance; reference, application; construction 520 *interpretation*; context; idiom 80 *speciality*; received meaning, usage 610 *practice*; ambiguity 518 *equivocalness*; same meaning, synonymousness 13 *identity*; opposite meaning, antonym 14 *contrariety*; literal meaning, literality 573 *plainness*; metaphorical meaning 519 *metaphor*; hidden meaning 523 *latency*; no sense 497 *absurdity*.

Adjective
(3) *meaningful*, significant; substantial, pithy, meaty, pregnant; purporting, indicative 547 *indicating*; telling 516 *expressive*; pointed, epigrammatic 839 *witty*; suggestive, evocative, allusive, implicit; express, explicit 573 *plain*.

(4) *semantic*, etymological 557 *linguistic*; literal, verbal 573 *plain*; metaphorical 519 *figurative*; unambiguous 516 *intelligible*; ambiguous 518 *equivocal*; implied 523 *tacit*; synonymous, homonymous 13 *identical*; tautologous 106 *repeated*; antonymous 14 *contrary*; idiomatic 80 *special*; obscure 568 *unclear*; nonsensical 497 *absurd*; without meaning 515 *meaningless*.

Verb
(5) *mean*, have a meaning, mean something; convey a meaning, get across 524 *communicate*; symbolize 547 *indicate*; signify, denote, connote, stand for 551 *represent*; purport, intend; point to, add up to, boil down to, spell, involve 523 *imply*; convey, express, declare 532 *affirm*; tell of, speak of, speak volumes 466 *evidence*; mean to say, be getting at, be driving at, really mean, have in mind; allude to, refer to; infer, understand by 516 *understand*.

Adverb
(6) *significantly*, meaningfully; to the effect that 520 *in plain words*; in a sense; literally, verbally.

515
Lack of meaning

Noun
(1) *lack of meaning*, meaninglessness 497 *absurdity*; no context; no bearing 10 *irrelevance*; 497 *absurdity*; inanity, emptiness, triteness; truism, platitude, cliche 496 *maxim*; mere words, illogicality 477 *sophistry*; invalidity, nullity; illegibility, scribble, daub; jargon, rigmarole, gobbledygook, abracadabra, hocus-pocus, mumbo jumbo; gibberish, double dutch 517 *unintelligibility*; incoherence, raving, delirium

503 *frenzy*; double-talk, mystification 530 *enigma*; insincerity 925 *flattery*.

(2) *silly talk,* nonsense 497 *absurdity*; stuff, rubbish, rot, drivel, twaddle.

(3) *empty talk,* sweet nothings; hot air, verbiage 570 *diffuseness*; rant, bombast 877 *boasting*; eyewash, claptrap, poppycock, humbug 541 *falsehood*; flannel, blarney 925 *flattery*; patter, sales p., spiel; chatter, prattle, babble, gabble 581 *chatter*.

Adjective
(4) *meaningless,* without meaning, unidiomatic; nonsensical 497 *absurd*; senseless, null; inane, empty, trivial, trite; fatuous; windy, ranting 546 *exaggerated*; incoherent, raving 503 *frenzied*.

(5) *unmeant,* unintended 521 *misinterpreted*; insincere 925 *flattering*.

Verb
(6) *mean nothing,* have no meaning, make no sense; scribble, daub; babble, prattle, prate, gabble, gibber, jabber 581 *be loquacious*; talk gibberish 517 *be unintelligible*; rant 546 *exaggerate*; gush, rave, drivel, drool, waffle 499 *be foolish*; not mean it 925 *flatter*; make nonsense of 521 *misinterpret*; be Greek to 474 *puzzle*.

Interjection
(7) *Rubbish!* nonsense! fiddlesticks!

516
Intelligibility

Noun
(1) *intelligibility,* readability, legibility, clearness, clarity, coherence, lucidity 567 *perspicuity*; precision, unambiguity 473 *certainty*; simplicity, plain speaking, plain words, plain English, mother tongue 573 *plainness*; paraphrase 520 *interpretation*.

Adjective
(2) *intelligible,* understandable, comprehensible; audible, coherent; unequivocal 514 *meaningful*; explicit, distinct, precise; well-spoken, articulate; plain-spoken, forthright 573 *plain*; simple, straightforward 701 *easy*; obvious, self-explanatory; made easy, explained 520 *interpreted*; clear, limpid, lucid 567 *perspicuous*; readable, legible, decipherable.

(3) *expressive,* telling, striking, vivid, graphic; emphatic, forceful, strongly worded; illustrative, explicatory 590 *descriptive*; amplifying, paraphrasing, popularizing.

Verb
(4) *be intelligible,* - clear etc. adj.; read easily, make sense; be understood, come over, get across, sink in; make understood, clarify, elucidate 520 *interpret*; simplify 701 *facilitate*.

(5) *understand,* comprehend, apprehend 490 *know*; master 536 *learn*; retain 505 *remember*; see through, penetrate, fathom 484 *detect*; discern, distinguish, recognize, grasp, follow, seize; take in, register; catch one's drift, get the idea; realize, tumble to, rumble; be undeceived, be disillusioned.

Adverb
(6) *intelligibly,* lucidly, simply, in plain terms, in plain English.

517
Unintelligibility

Noun
(1) *unintelligibility,* incomprehensibility; impenetrability,

difficulty, obscurity 568 *imperspicuity*; ambiguity 518 *equivocalness*; incoherence 515 *lack of meaning*; double dutch, gibberish; jargon, foreign tongue 560 *dialect*; stammering, inaudibility 580 *speech defect*; illegibility, scribble, scrawl; paradox riddle 530 *enigma*;

Adjective

(2) *unintelligible,* incomprehensible; inconceivable, inexplicable, unaccountable; unfathomable, inscrutable, impenetrable; blank, poker-faced, 820 *impassive*; inaudible 401 *muted*; unreadable, undecipherable, illegible, crabbed; hidden, arcane 523 *occult*; cryptic, obscure, esoteric 80 *private.*

(3) *puzzling,* complex 700 *difficult*; hard, beyond one, over one's head; recondite, abstruse, elusive; enigmatic, mysterious 523 *occult*; nebulous, hazy, dim, obscure 568 *unclear*; ambiguous 518 *equivocal*; oracular, paradoxical; strange, odd 84 *abnormal*; insoluble 474 *uncertain.*

(4) *inexpressible,* unspeakable, unutterable, ineffable; indefinable; profound, deep, mystical.

(5) *puzzled,* mystified, flummoxed, stumped, baffled, perplexed 474 *uncertain.*

Verb

(6) *be unintelligible,* - puzzling etc. adj.; be hard 474 *puzzle*; talk in riddles 518 *be equivocal*; talk gibberish 515 *mean nothing*; speak badly 580 *stammer*; write badly, scribble, scrawl; perplex, confuse 63 *bedevil*; escape one, baffle comphrehension.

(7) *not understand,* not make out, make nothing of, puzzle over 474 *be uncertain.*

518
Equivocalness

Noun

(1) *equivocalness,* two voices 14 *contrariety*; ambiguity, ambivalence 517 *unintelligibility*; vagueness 474 *uncertainty*; double meaning 514 *connotation*; weasel word, newspeak, doubletalk 515 *lack of meaning*; conundrum, riddle 530 *enigma*; prevarication, equivocation, white lie 543 *untruth*; play on words, pun, double entendre 839 *witticism*; anagram, acrostic; homonym, homophone 18 *analogue.*

Adjective

(2) *equivocal,* ambiguous, ambivalent, two-edged; left-handed, back-h.; equivocating, prevaricating, facing both ways; vague, evasive, oracular; homonymous.

Verb

(3) *be equivocal,* play on words, pun; have two meanings 514 *mean*; fudge, waffle, stall 620 *avoid*; equivocate, prevaricate 541 *dissemble.*

519
Metaphor: Figure of speech

Noun

(1) *metaphor,* mixed m.; allusion, application; allegory; fable, parable 534 *teaching*; symbol; symbolism, imagery 513 *imagination*; simile, likeness 462 *comparison*; personification.

(2) *trope,* figure of speech, flourish 574 *ornament*; irony 851 *satire*; litotes, hyperbole; stress, emphasis; euphemism 850 *affectation*; colloquialism

573 *plainness*; contrast, antithesis 462 *comparison*; word play 518 *equivocalness*.

Adjective
(3) *figurative,* metaphorical, tropical; allusive, symbolic, allegorical 462 *compared*; euphemistic 850 *affected*; colloquial 573 *plain*; hyperbolic 546 *exaggerated*; satirical, ironical 851 *derisive*; flowery, florid 574 *ornate*; oratorical 574 *rhetorical*.

Verb
(4) *figure,* image, embody, personify; typify, symbolize 551 *represent*; allude, refer, liken, contrast 462 *compare*.

Adverb
(5) *metaphorically,* not literally, figuratively; in a way, so to speak.

520
Interpretation

Noun
(1) *interpretation,* definition, explanation, explication, exposition, exegesis; elucidation, clarification, illumination; illustration 83 *example*; resolution, solution, key, clue 460 *answer*; decoding, cracking 484 *discovery*; application, twist, turn; construction, reading 514 *meaning*; criticism, literary c., appreciation 557 *literature*; critique, review 480 *estimate*; insight.

(2) *commentary,* comment, gloss, footnote; inscription, caption 563 *phrase*; annotation, exposition 591 *dissertation*; glossary, lexicon.

(3) *translation,* version, rendering, free translation, loose rendering; key, crib; rewording, paraphrase, précis 592 *compendium*; adaptation, amplification 516 *intelligibility*; transliteration; decoding, decipherment; lip-reading.

(4) *interpreter,* explainer, exponent, expounder, expositor 537 *teacher*, editor, emender; commentator, annotator; critic, reviewer 480 *estimator*; medium 984 *spiritualism*; translator, paraphraser 557 *linguist*; cryptographer, encoder; decoder, solver, code-breaker; lip-reader; mouthpiece, public relations officer 524 *informant*; performer 413 *musician*, 594 *actor*; poet, painter 556 *artist*.

(5) *guide,* precedent 83 *example*; guiding star; courier 690 *director*; demonstrator 522 *exhibitor*.

Adjective
(6) *interpretive,* explanatory, explicatory, expository 557 *literary*; exegetical; defining, illuminating, illustrative, exemplary; annotative, editorial; literal, faithful, strict, word-for-word 494 *accurate*; free 495 *inexact*.

(7) *interpreted,* explained, defined, expounded, elucidated etc. vb.; translated, rendered, Englished; deciphered, decoded, cracked.

Verb
(8) *interpret,* define, clarify, make clear, explain, unfold, expound, elucidate 516 *be intelligible*; illustrate 83 *exemplify*; demonstrate 522 *show*; comment on, edit, annotate, gloss; construe, make sense of 516 *understand*; illuminate, throw light on 524 *inform*; account for, deduce, infer 475 *reason*; speak for 755 *deputize*; simplify 701 *facilitate*.

(9) *translate,* render, do into, English; rehash, reword, rephrase, paraphrase; abridge, amplify, adapt; transliterate, transcribe; cipher, encode.

(10) *decipher,* crack, decode; find the meaning, read, lip read; spell out, puzzle o., make o., work o.; piece together, solve, resolve.

Adverb
(11) *in plain words,* that is, i.e.; in other words, viz, to wit, namely.

521
Misinterpretation

Noun
(1) *misinterpretation,* misunderstanding, misconstruction; crossed lines 495 *mistake;* perversion 246 *distortion;* strained sense; false reading, mistranslation; parody, travesty 851 *ridicule.*

Adjective
(2) *misinterpreted,* misconstrued etc. vb.; mistranslated 495 *mistaken;* misread, misquoted.

Verb
(3) *misinterpret,* misunderstand, misapprehend, misconceive 481 *misjudge;* get wrong 495 *blunder;* misread, misspell, mistranslate, misconstrue; pervert, strain the sense, twist the words 246 *distort;* add a meaning, read into; leave out, suppress; misrepresent, misquote; falsify, garble 552 *misrepresent;* travesty, parody, caricature, guy 851 *ridicule.*

522
Manifestation

Noun
(1) *manifestation,* revelation, exposure 526 *disclosure;* expression 532 *affirmation;* proof 466 *evidence;* presentation 551 *representation;* symbolization 547 *indication;* symptom, sign, token 511 *omen;* preview, display, demonstration, exhibition; showing off 875 *ostentation;* proclamation

528 *publication;* openness 528 *publicity;* candour, plain speaking prominence 443 *visibility;* materialization, apparition 445 *appearance.*

(2) *exhibit,* specimen, sample; quotation, citation 466 *evidence;* model, mock-up 551 *image;* show piece, collector's p., antique, curio; display, show 445 *spectacle;* showplace, showroom, showcase; placard 528 *advertisement;* museum, gallery 632 *collection;* retrospective, exhibition, exposition.

(3) *exhibitor,* advertiser, publicist 528 *publicizer;* demonstrator; showman, impresario 594 *stage manager;* exhibitionist 873 *vain person.*

Adjective
(4) *manifest,* apparent 445 *appearing;* plain, clear 516 *intelligible;* unconcealed, showing 443 *visible;* conspicuous, noticeable, prominent, pronounced; signal, marked, striking; in relief, in the foreground 443 *obvious;* open, patent, evident; gross, crass, palpable; self-evident, unmistakable 473 *certain;* public, notorious 528 *well-known;* eye-catching 875 *showy;* arrant, glaring, flagrant.

(5) *undisguised,* overt, explicit 532 *affirmative;* in the open, public; unreserved, open, candid 540 *veracious;* free, frank, forthright, outspoken, blunt 573 *plain;* bold, daring 711 *defiant;* flaunting, brazen, shameless 951 *impure;* bare, naked 229 *uncovered.*

(6) *shown,* declared, 526 *disclosed;* showing, featured, on show, on display 443 *visible;* produced, exhibited, shown off; worn, sported; flaunted, brandished; publicized 528 *published.*

Verb

(7) *manifest,* reveal 526 *disclose*; evince, betoken 466 *evidence*; bring to light 484 *discover*; explain, make plain 520 *interpret*; expose, lay bare 229 *uncover*; throw open 263 *open*; elicit, draw forth 304 *extract*; bring out 164 *produce*; incarnate, personify 223 *externalize*; typify, symbolize 547 *indicate*; highlight, spotlight 420 *illuminate*; throw into relief 532 *emphasize*; express, formulate 532 *affirm*; bring to notice, come out with, proclaim, publicize 528 *publish*; solve, elucidate 520 *decipher*.

(8) *show,* put on s., exhibit, display; set out, expose to view, wave, flourish, dangle 317 *brandish*; sport 228 *wear*; flaunt, parade 875 *be ostentatious*; affect 850 *be affected*; present, enact 551 *represent*; put on, stage 594 *dramatize*; hang (a picture); show off, set o., model (garments); demonstrate 534 *teach*; show round, show over, point out, draw attention to 547 *indicate*; show up, expose 526 *disclose*.

(9) *be plain,* explicit etc. adj.; show one's face, unveil 229 *doff*; speak out 573 *speak plainly*; speak for itself 516 *be intelligible*; be obvious, stand to reason, go without saying 478 *be proved*; be conspicuous, stand out 443 *be visible*; show up 455 *attract notice*; stare one in the face 445 *appear*.

Adverb

(10) *manifestly,* plainly etc. adv.; openly, publicly; in full view, in broad daylight, in public.

523
Latency

Noun

(1) *latency,* no signs of 525 *concealment*; insidiousness 930 *perfidy*; dormancy, potentiality 469 *possibility*; esotericism, mysticism; hidden meaning 511 *oracle*; symbolism 519 *metaphor*; implication, symbolization; mystery 530 *secret*; shadowiness 419 *dimness*; dark horse, hidden depths; sleeping giant 661 *danger*; anonymity 562 *no name*; wire-puller, strings, friend at court 178 *influence*; innuendo, insinuation 524 *hint*; sealed lips 582 *taciturnity*; undertone, aside 401 *faintness*; secret society, cabal 623 *plot*; ambushment 527 *ambush*; code, cryptography.

Adjective

(2) *latent,* lurking, skulking 525 *concealed*; dormant, sleeping 679 *inactive*; passive 266 *quiescent*; in abeyance 175 *inert*; potential, undeveloped 469 *possible*; crypto- 491 *unknown*; below the surface 211 *deep*; in the background, behind · the scenes, backroom, undercover 421 *screened*; unseen 444 *invisible*; murky, obscure 418 *dark*; arcane, impenetrable 517 *unintelligible*; sequestered 883 *secluded*.

(3) *tacit,* unsaid, unspoken, undeclared, unvoiced; untold of, unsung; unwritten, understood, inferred, implied, implicit, between the lines.

(4) *occult,* mysterious, mystic; symbolic, allegorical 519 *figurative*; cryptic, esoteric 984 *cabbalistic*; veiled, covert; crooked 220 *oblique*; clandestine, secret, kept quiet; insidious, underhand 525 *stealthy*; hush-hush, top-secret; coded, cryptographic.

Verb

(5) *lurk,* hide, lie hidden, lie in ambush; lie low 266 *be quiescent*; avoid notice 444 *be unseen*; evade detection 541 *dissemble*; creep, slink 525 *be*

stealthy; stage-manage; underlie 156 *cause*.

(6) *imply,* insinuate, whisper, murmur, suggest 524 *hint*; understand, infer, allude, be allusive; spell, connote 514 *mean*.

524
Information

Noun

(1) *information,* communication of knowledge; dissemination, diffusion; tradition, hearsay; enlightenment, instruction, briefing 534 *teaching*; communication; mass media 528 *the press*, 531 *broadcasting*; telling, narration 590 *narrative*; notification, announcement, intimation, warning, advice, notice, mention, (see *hint*); advertisement 528 *publicity*; common knowledge; background, facts, documentary 494 *truth*; material, literature 589 *reading matter*; inside information, confidence 530 *secret*; acquaintance 490 *knowledge*; file, dossier 548 *record*; word, report, intelligence 529 *news*; a communication, wire, cable 529 *message*; unauthorized information, leak 526 *disclosure*.

(2) *report,* review 459 *enquiry*; account, eyewitness a. 590 *narrative*; statement, return 86 *statistics*; specification 480 *estimate*; bulletin, communiqué, press release 529 *news*; presentation, case; memorial, petition 761 *entreaty*; dispatches, letters 588 *correspondence*.

(3) *hint,* whisper, aside; indirect hint, intimation; broad hint, nod, wink, nudge, kick 547 *gesture*; prompt, cue 505 *reminder*; suggestion 547 *indication*; caution 664 *warning*; tip, word 691 *advice*; insinuation, innuendo 926 *calumny*; clue,

symptom; inkling, adumbration; suspicion, inference, guess 512 *conjecture*.

(4) *informant,* teller 590 *narrator*; spokesperson, mouthpiece 754 *delegate*; announcer 531 *broadcaster*; notifier, advertiser 528 *publicizer*; herald 529 *messenger*; testifier 466 *witness*; authority, source; quarter, channel, circle, grapevine; go-between, contact 231 *intermediary*; news agency 528 *the press*; communicator, correspondent, special c., reporter, commentator 529 *news reporter*; tipster 691 *adviser*; little bird.

(5) *informer,* spy, snoop, sleuth 459 *detective*; inside agent, mole; stool pigeon, nark; sneak, grass, eavesdropper, telltale, talebearer 928 *accuser*; gossip 581 *chatterer*.

(6) *guidebook,* travelogue; handbook, manual, vade mecum, ABC; timetable; itinerary, route map, chart, plan 551 *map*; gazetteer 589 *reference book*; nautical almanac; phone book; catalogue 87 *directory*; courier 520 *guide*.

Adjective

(7) *informative,* communicative, newsy, chatty, gossipy; instructive, documentary 534 *educational*; expository 520 *interpretive*; in writing 586 *written*; oral, verbal 579 *speaking*; advisory 691 *advising*; explicit, clear 573 *plain*; indiscreet 581 *loquacious*.

(8) *informed,* well-i., posted, primed, briefed, instructed 490 *knowing*; told, in the know.

Verb

(9) *inform,* advise, intimate, impart, apprise, acquaint, brief, instruct 534 *teach*; let one know, enlighten 534 *educate*; point out 547 *indicate*; put

right, correct, disabuse, undeceive, disillusion; be specific, state, name 80 *specify*; mention, refer to 579 *speak*; gossip, spread rumours; be indiscreet, blurt out, talk 581 *be loquacious*; reveal 526 *disclose*; tell, grass 526 *confess*; betray one, tell tales, inform against, shop, denounce 928 *accuse*.

(10) *communicate,* transmit, pass on; dispatch news 588 *correspond*; report, cover; post, keep posted; get through, get across, put it over; contact, get in touch; convey, bring word, send w. 588 *correspond*; send a message 547 *signal*; wire, telegraph, telex, radio; telephone, phone, call, dial, ring, ring up; disseminate, broadcast, telecast, televise; announce, notify 528 *advertise*; give out, put out, publicize 528 *publish*; retail, recount, narrate 590 *describe*; commune 584 *converse*.

(11) *hint,* drop a h., suggest, insinuate; prompt 505 *remind*; caution 664 *warn*; tip off 691 *advise*; wink, nudge 547 *gesticulate*; breathe, whisper, let fall, imply, allude, intimate.

(12) *be informed,* have the facts 490 *know*; be told, have it from; use one's ears, overhear 415 *hear*; get wind of 484 *discover*; gather, infer, realize 516 *understand*; come to know 536 *learn*; open one's eyes, awaken to 455 *be attentive*.

525
Concealment

Noun
(1) *concealment,* hiding 523 *latency*; cache 527 *hiding-place*; covering up, disguise, camouflage 542 *deception*; masquerade, anonymity, incognito 562 *no name*; smoke screen 421 *screen*; reticence, reserve, discretion 582 *taciturnity*; ulterior

motive 543 *mental dishonesty*; lack of candour, vagueness, evasiveness 518 *equivocalness*; subterfuge 542 *trickery*; suppression, cover-up 543 *untruth*; deceitfulness, dissimulation 541 *duplicity*.

(2) *secrecy,* close s. 399 *silence*; mystery 530 *secret*; secret society, Freemasonry; secretiveness, furtiveness, stealthiness, low profile; conspiracy 623 *plot*; cryptography, cryptogram, cipher, code.

Adjective
(3) *concealed,* crypto-, hidden; in ambush, lying in wait 523 *latent*; incommunicado 747 *imprisoned*; mysterious, recondite, arcane 517 *unintelligible*; cryptic 523 *occult*; private 883 *secluded*; privy, confidential, off the record, secret, top secret, restricted, hush-hush; undisclosed, untold; 562 *anonymous*; covert, behind the scenes; veiled 421 *screened*; stifled, suppressed; clandestine, undercover, underground 211 *deep*.

(4) *disguised,* camouflaged; incognito 562 *anonymous*; unrecognized 491 *unknown*; disfigured, unrecognizable 246 *distorted*; masked 226 *covered*; blotted out 550 *obliterated*; coded, cryptographic.

(5) *stealthy,* silent, furtive, sneaking; treading softly, on tiptoe; prowling, skulking, lurking; clandestine, conspiratorial, cloak and dagger; underhand, surreptitious 930 *dishonest*.

(6) *reticent,* reserved, withdrawn; uncommunicative, noncommittal, evasive; vague, studiously v.; discreet, silent 582 *taciturn*; tight-lipped, poker-faced; close, secretive, buttoned-up 883 *unsociable*.

Verb

(7) *conceal,* hide, hide away, secrete; confine, keep in purdah 883 *seclude*; stow away, lock up 632 *store*; hide underground, bury 364 *inter*; cover up, whitewash 226 *cover*; blot out 550 *obliterate*; slur over, gloss over, not mention 458 *disregard*; smother, stifle 165 *suppress*; veil, muffle, mask, disguise, camouflage; shroud 421 *screen*; obscure, eclipse 418 *darken*; masquerade 541 *dissemble*; code, encode.

(8) *keep secret,* keep it dark; look blank, hold one's tongue, not talk, not breathe a word 582 *be taciturn*; be discreet, make no comment; keep back, reserve, withhold; hush up, cover up, suppress; bamboozle, 542 *deceive*.

(9) *be stealthy,* - furtive etc. adj.; conspire 623 *plot*; snoop, sneak, slink, creep; glide, steal, tiptoe, pussyfoot; prowl, skulk, loiter; assume a disguise 541 *dissemble*; lie doggo 523 *lurk*; evade, shun, hide from 620 *avoid*; take cover, go to earth; go underground, hide out 446 *disappear*; lay an ambush 527 *ambush*.

Adverb

(10) *secretly,* between ourselves; to oneself, in one's sleeve; privately, in camera, behind closed doors; anonymously, incognito,

(11) *stealthily,* furtively, by stealth 444 *invisibly*; on the sly, on the quiet.

526
Disclosure

Noun

(1) *disclosure,* revealment, revelation, discovery, uncovering; lid off, expose 528 *publication*;

exposure, showing up 522 *manifestation*; explanations, showdown; leak, indiscretion 524 *hint*; betrayal, giveaway; telltale sign, self-betrayal; admission, avowal, confession; clean breast, whole truth 494 *truth*.

Adjective

(2) *disclosed,* exposed, revealed 522 *shown*; showing 443 *visible*; confessed, avowed, acknowledged; laid bare 229 *uncovered*.

(3) *disclosing,* revelatory; revealing 422 *transparent*; explanatory 520 *interpretive*; communicative 524 *informative*; leaky, indiscreet, garrulous 581 *loquacious*; tell-tale, indicative 547 *indicating*; tale-bearing, betraying.

Verb

(4) *disclose,* reveal, expose 522 *manifest*; bare, lay b. 229 *doff*; unwrap, unfurl 229 *uncover*; unveil, lift the veil; break the seal 263 *open*; open up 484 *discover*; not hide 422 *be transparent*; give away, betray; unmask, expose oneself, declare o.; give oneself away; disabuse, disillusion, undeceive 524 *inform.*

(5) *divulge,* declare, express, vent 579 *speak*; air, publicize 528 *publish*; let on, blurt out, spill the beans; let out, leak 524 *communicate*; let drop, let fall 524 *hint*; come out with, unbosom oneself, unburden o.; confide; report, tell, name names 928 *accuse*; squeal 524 *inform.*

(6) *confess,* admit, avow, acknowledge; concede, grant, allow, own 488 *assent*; own up, plead guilty; talk, sing, come clean 540 *be truthful*; turn Queen's evidence 603 *tergiversate.*

(7) *be disclosed,* come to light 445 *appear*; stand revealed 522 *be plain*; transpire, leak out,

become known 490 *be known*;
show 443 *be visible*.

527
Hiding. Disguise

Noun

(1) *hiding-place,* hide, hideaway, hide-out, priesthole 662
refuge; lair, den 192 *retreat*;
secret place, cache; crypt 194
cellar; safe place, safe 632 *storage*; closet, corner, nook, cranny, niche; secret passage,
underground p.; cover, underground 662 *shelter*.

(2) *ambush,* ambushment 525
concealment; spider's web 542
trap; catch 663 *pitfall*; Trojan
horse, decoy; agent provocateur 545 *impostor*.

(3) *disguise,* blind, masquerade
542 *deception*; camouflage, 20
mimicry; dummy 542 *sham*; veneer 226 *covering*; mask, veil;
fancy dress; smoke screen.

(4) *hider,* lurker, skulker; stowaway;   masquerader   545
impostor.

Verb

(5) *ambush,* set an a., lie in wait
523 *lurk*; set a trap 542 *ensnare*;
waylay.

528
Publication

Noun

(1)   *publication,*   spreading
abroad, dissemination 526 *disclosure*; proclamation, edict 737
decree; call-up, summons; cry,
rallying c. 547 *call*; press conference, press release; notification, announcement, pronouncement;   manifesto,   programme, platform; the media,
mass m.; publishing, book
trade; broadcasting 531 *telecommunication*; broadcast 529
news; circulation, circular,
encyclical.

(2) *publicity,* limelight, spotlight, public eye; common
knowledge 490 *knowledge*;
open discussion, ventilation,
canvassing; openness, flagrancy, blatancy 522 *manifestation*;
notoriety, fame 866 *famousness*; currency, sale, extensive
sales; readership, audience;
public relations, PR; propaganda; display, showmanship,
window dressing 875 *ostentation*; ballyhoo 546 *exaggeration*; advertising, publicizing;
television, radio 531 *broadcasting*; loudspeaker, loud hailer
415 *hearing aid*; journalism,
reporting, coverage, report,
write-up 459 *enquiry*; newsreel,
newsletter 529 *news*; sounding
board, open letter, editorial 591
article; pulpit, platform 539
rostrum.

(3) *advertisement,* notice, insertion, advert, ad, small a., classified a.; personal column; puff,
blurb, buildup, hype; handout,
handbill; bill, poster 522 *exhibit*; hoarding, placard, sandwich board, notice b.; advertising copy, slogan, jingle; plug,
trailer, commercial 531 *broadcasting*; hard sell, soft s.

(4) *the press,* fourth estate, Fleet
Street, the papers; newspaper,
sheet, paper, rag, tabloid, comic; serious press, gutter p.;
organ, journal, daily, quality
d., broadsheet; issue, edition,
extra; supplement, colour s.,
trade s.; leaflet, handbill, pamphlet, brochure; newssheet,
newsletter.

(5) *journal,* review, magazine,
periodical; gazette, annual;
trade journal, house magazine.

(6) *publicizer,* announcer; town
crier; herald 529 *messenger*;
barker, tout; promoter, publicist, publicity agent, press a.,

advertising a.; advertiser, copywriter; public relations officer, PRO; propagandist, pamphleteer 537 *preacher*; printer, publisher; reporter, journalist 529 *news reporter*.

Adjective

(7) *published,* in print 587 *printed*; in circulation, current; in the news, public 490 *known*; open, distributed, circularized, disseminated, broadcast; ventilated, well-v.; on the air, on television.

(8) *well-known,* public, celebrated, famous, notorious; flagrant, blatant, sensational 522 *manifest*.

Verb

(9) *publish,* make public 524 *communicate*; report, write up; reveal 526 *divulge*; highlight, spotlight 532 *emphasize*; broadcast, telecast, televise, relay; diffuse, spread, circulate, distribute, disseminate, circularize 524 *inform*; canvass, ventilate, discuss 475 *argue*; pamphleteer, propagate, propagandize 534 *teach*; use the press 587 *print*; syndicate, serialize, edit, subedit, sub; issue, release, put out; spread a rumour, fly a kite; retail, pass round, put about 581 *be loquacious*; voice, broach, talk of, speak of 579 *speak*.

(10) *proclaim,* announce, herald, promulgate, notify; denounce 928 *accuse*; pronounce, declare, go on record 532 *affirm*; celebrate, trumpet, blazon 400 *be loud*; declaim 415 *be heard*.

(11) *advertise,* publicize; bill, placard, put up posters; headline, splash; put in lights; build up, promote; make much of, feature; sell, boost, puff, cry up, crack up, write up, hype up, extol 482 *overrate*; plug 106 *repeat*.

(12) *be published,* become public, come out; get printed, hit the headlines; circulate, go the rounds, get about, spread like wildfire.

Adverb

(13) *publicly,* openly, in open court; in the limelight, in the public eye.

529
News

Noun

(1) *news,* good n.; bad n., tidings; intelligence, report, dispatch 524 *information*; bulletin, communiqué, handout; newspaper report, press notice; news item, news flash 531 *broadcast*; hot news, stop-press n.; sensation, scoop, exclusive; copy, filler; story; newscast, newsreel 528 *publicity*; news value, newsworthiness.

(2) *rumour,* hearsay, gossip, talk, 584 *chat*; scandal 926 *calumny*; whisper, buzz; false report, hoax, canard; grapevine, bush telegraph; kite-flying.

(3) *message,* oral m., word of mouth 524 *information*; communication 547 *signal*; wireless message, cable, telegram, wire 531 *telecommunication*; postcard, letters 588 *correspondence*; ring, phone call; errand, embassy 751 *commission*.

(4) *news reporter,* reporter, cub r., journalist, correspondent 589 *author*; press representative 524 *informant*; newsreader 531 *broadcaster*; newsmonger, gossip, talker 584 *interlocutor*; tattler, chatterer, muckraker, scandalmonger 926 *defamer*; newsagent, newsvendor.

(5) *messenger,* forerunner 66 *precursor*; announcer, town crier 528 *publicizer*; ambassador, legate 754 *envoy*; apostle, emissary; flag-bearer, herald,

trumpet; summoner 955 *law officer*; go-between 231 *intermediary.*

(6) *courier,* runner, Queen's Messenger, express m., dispatch rider; postman *or* - woman; page, commissionaire; carrier pigeon 273 *carrier.*

Adjective
(7) *rumoured,* talked about, in the news, in the papers; reported, going the rounds, rife, on everyone's lips; newsy, gossipy, chatty 524 *informative*; newsworthy.

Verb
(8) *rumour,* fly a kite; 524 *inform,* 526 *disclose,* 528 *publish.*

530
Secret

Noun
(1) *secret,* mystery; secret lore, esotericism; confidence; skeleton in the cupboard; dark horse, unknown quantity; sealed book 491 *unknown thing.*

(2) *enigma,* mystery, puzzle, problem, poser, brain-twister, teaser; knotty point, vexed question, crux 700 *difficulty*; cipher, code, cryptogram, hieroglyphics 517 *unintelligibility*; word-puzzle, anagram, acrostic, crossword; riddle, conundrum, rebus; labyrinth, maze 61 *complexity.*

531
Communications

Noun
(1) *telecommunication,* telephony, telegraphy, morse 547 *signal*; cable, cablegram, telegram, wire 529 *message*; radar; telex, teleprinter; intercom, walkie-talkie, bleeper; microphone 400 *megaphone*; headset 415 *hearing aid*; telephone,

radio t., line, land-l., switchboard; radio ham, telegrapher, telephonist.

(2) *postal communications,* postal services; post, mail, letters 588 *correspondence*; surface mail, sea m., air m.; parcel post; postbox, pillarbox, letterbox; post office, sorting o.; postman *or* -woman 529 *messenger*; pigeon post; diplomatic bag, dispatch box.

(3) *broadcasting,* the media 528 *publicity*; transmitter, booster, aerial, antenna; radio waves 417 *radiation*; radio station, network; wireless, radio, portable, transistor; television, TV, small screen; videorecorder 549 *recording instrument*; teletext 524 *information*; Open University.

(4) *broadcast,* telecast, transmission, relay, live r. 528 *publication*; recording, repeat; programme, phone-in 837 *amusement*; newsflash 529 *news*; feature, documentary 524 *report*; soap opera 594 *drama*; commercial 528 *advertisement.*

(5) *broadcaster,* announcer, commentator, newsreader 524 *informant*; presenter, anchor, compere; disc jockey, media personality 866 *person of repute.*

532
Affirmation

Noun
(1) *affirmation,* proposition, statement; submission, thesis 512 *supposition*; conclusion 480 *judgment*; ballot 605 *vote*; expression, formulation; one's position, one's stand; declaration, profession; allegation 928 *accusation*; assertion, asseveration; admission, confession,

avowal 526 *disclosure*; corroboration, confirmation, assurance, one's word 466 *testimony*; insistence, vehemence 571 *vigour*; stress, accent, emphasis, overstatement; reiteration 106 *repetition*; provocation 711 *defiance*; protest 762 *deprecation*; appeal, adjuration 761 *entreaty*; observation, remark, interjection 579 *speech*; comment, criticism 480 *estimate*; assertiveness, push, thrust, drive 174 *vigorousness*; pontification 473 *positiveness*.

(2) *oath,* oath-taking, swearing, adjuration, statement on oath, deposition, affidavit 466 *testimony*; word of honour, pledge, warrant, guarantee 764 *promise*.

Adjective
(3) *affirmative,* affirming etc. vb.; not negative 473 *positive*; declaratory 526 *disclosing*; pronouncing 528 *publishing*; committed, pledged, guaranteed 764 *promissory*; earnest, meaning 617 *intending*; solemn, sworn, on oath, formal

(4) *assertive,* saying, telling; assured, dogmatic, confident, self-assured 473 *positive*; trenchant, incisive, pointed, decided 571 *forceful*; express, peremptory, categorical, absolute, emphatic, insistent; strongly-worded, vehement 176 *violent*; blunt, strong, outspoken 573 *plain*; ex cathedra 485 *creedal*; challenging, provocative 711 *defiant*.

Verb
(5) *affirm,* state, express, formulate, set down; declare, pronounce 528 *proclaim*, voice 579 *speak*; comment, observe, say; dare swear 485 *opine*; vow, protest; assert, maintain, hold, contend 475 *argue*; make one's point 478 *demonstrate*; urge 512

propound; put one's case, submit; appeal, adjure 761 *request*; allege, asseverate, aver; bear witness 466 *testify*; certify, confirm 466 *corroborate*; commit oneself, pledge, engage 764 *promise*; profess, avow; admit 526 *confess*; abide by, not retreat, not retract 599 *stand firm*; challenge 711 *defy*; repudiate 533 *negate*; speak up, speak out, say outright, assert roundly 573 *speak plainly*; be assertive, brook no denial; shout, shout down; lay down the law, pontificate 473 *dogmatize*; have one's say, have the last word.(6) *swear,* be sworn, swear an oath, take one's o., attest 466 *corroborate*; cross one's heart, solemnly affirm 466 *testify*; kiss the book, swear on the Bible.

(7) *emphasize,* stress, accent, accentuate; underline, italicize, raise one's voice, speak up, thunder, fulminate 400 *be loud*; be earnest, urge, insist, reaffirm, reassert; drive home, impress on, rub in; plug, dwell on, labour 106 *repeat*; single out, highlight 638 *make important*.

Adverb
(8) *affirmatively,* positively; seriously, joking apart; on oath, on the Bible; upon one's word, upon one's honour 540 *truthfully*.

Interjection
(9) *As I stand here!* As God is my witness!

533
Negation

Noun
(1) *negation,* negative, nay; denial 760 *refusal*; disbelief 486 *unbelief*; disagreement 489 *dissent*; rebuttal, appeal 460 *rejoinder*; refutation, disproof 479 *confutation*; emphatic denial, contradiction, gainsaying;

challenge 711 *defiance*; protest 762 *deprecation*; repudiation, disclaimer, disavowal, dissociation 607 *rejection*; abjuration, swearing off 603 *recantation*; negative attitude 738 *disobedience*; cancellation, invalidation, revocation 752 *abrogation*.

Adjective
(2) *negative,* denying, negating, contradictory 14 *contrary*; contravening 738 *disobedient*; protesting 762 *deprecatory*; renunciatory 753 *resigning*; disowned etc. vb.

Verb
(3) *negate,* negative; contravene 738 *disobey*; deny, gainsay, contradict; 470 *repudiate*, disavow, disclaim, disown 607 *reject*; deny in part, demur, object 468 *qualify*; disagree 489 *dissent*, 704 *oppose*; impugn, question, call in q., refute, rebut, disprove 479 *confute*; refuse credence 486 *disbelieve*; challenge 711 *defy*; thwart 702 *obstruct*; say no, shake one's head 760 *refuse*; not allow 757 *prohibit*; revoke, invalidate 752 *abrogate*; renounce 621 *relinquish*; abjure, forswear, swear off 603 *recant*.

Adverb
(4) *nay* 489 *no*; negatively; not at all 33 *in no way*.

Interjection
(5) *never!* far from it! no such thing! nothing of the kind!

534
Teaching

Noun
(1) *teaching,* pedagogy; private teaching, tutoring; education, schooling, upbringing; tutelage, leading strings; direction, guidance, instruction, edification; tuition, preparation, coaching, cramming; seminar,

teach-in, clinic, workshop, tutorial; training, discipline, drill 682 *exercise*; inculcation, indoctrination; catechization, preaching, homiletics; persuasion, conversion, conviction; conditioning, brainwashing; propaganda 528 *publicity*.

(2) *education,* liberal e. 490 *culture*; moral education, moral training; technical t., vocational t.; coeducation; nursery education, primary e., secondary e., further e., higher e., university e., adult e., special e.; day release, block r.; sandwich course, refresher c.; correspondence c., evening classes; advanced studies, postgraduate s.

(3) *curriculum,* course of study 536 *learning*; ABC, the three Rs 68 *beginning*; set books 589 *textbook*; project, exercise, homework, prep; night school 539 *school.*

(4) *lecture,* talk, reading, discourse, disquisition; sermon, homily 579 *oration*; lesson, parable; lecturer 537 *teacher.*

Adjective
(5) *educational,* scholastic, scholarly, academic; audiovisual, instructive 524 *informative*; educative, didactic, hortative; edifying, moralizing; primary, secondary etc. n.; single-sex, coeducational; comprehensive, all-ability; set, streamed, creamed, mixed-ability; extramural, intramural; extracurricular; cultural, humane, multidisciplinary; scientific, technological; practical, utilitarian; vocational.

Verb
(6) *educate,* edify (see *teach*); rear, nurse, nurture, bring up, develop, form, mould, shape, lick into shape; tutor, teach, school; ground, coach, cram, spoonfeed; prime 669 *prepare*; guide 689 *direct*; instruct 524 *inform*; enlighten, enlarge the mind, sharpen the wits,

open the eyes; inculcate, indoctrinate, imbue, infuse, instil, implant; disabuse.

(7) *teach,* be a teacher, give lessons, take a class, lecture, tutor; preach, harangue, sermonize; discourse, hold forth; moralize, point a moral; elucidate, expound 520 *interpret*; indoctrinate, propagandize, proselytize, condition, brainwash 178 *influence*.

(8) *train,* coach 669 *prepare*; take on, take in hand, initiate 369 *break in*; nurse, foster, cultivate; drill, exercise; practise, familiarize, accustom, groom one for 610 *habituate*; make fit, qualify.

535
Misteaching

Noun

(1) *misteaching,* misguidance, misleading, misdirection; quackery, mystification, obfuscation; misinformation 552 *misrepresentation*; obscurantism 491 *ignorance*; propaganda 541 *falsehood*; perversion 246 *distortion*; false logic 477 *sophistry*.

Adjective

(2) *misteaching,* misinforming etc. vb.; propagandist; obscurantist 491 *ignorant*; misled, mistaught, misdirected 495 *mistaken*.

Verb

(3) *misteach,* bring up badly; misinform, misdirect, misguide 495 *mislead*; corrupt 934 *make wicked*; pervert 552 *misrepresent*; lie 541 *be false*; keep in ignorance; propagandize, brainwash.

536
Learning

Noun

(1) *learning,* lore, scholarship, attainments 490 *erudition*; noviciate, apprenticeship, initiation 669 *preparation*; first steps 68 *beginning*; culture, cultivation; self-improvement; learned person 492 *scholar*.

(2) *study,* studying; application, studiousness; cramming, mugging up; studies, course of s., lessons, class; homework, preparation; revision, refresher course; perusal, reading, close r. 455 *attention*; research, field work, investigation 459 *enquiry*.

Adjective

(3) *studious,* academic; bookish, well-read, scholarly, erudite, learned, scholastic 490 *knowing*; sedulous, diligent 678 *industrious*; receptive 455 *attentive*.

Verb

(4) *learn,* acquire knowledge; read, glean facts, imbibe, drink in 490 *know*; learn a trade, article oneself, apprentice oneself 669 *prepare oneself*; train, practise, exercise 610 *be wont*; get by heart, master 505 *memorize*; graduate.

(5) *study,* apply oneself; take up, research into 459 *enquire*; specialize, major in; revise, go over, brush up; read, peruse, pore over, wade through; thumb, browse, skip, dip into; be studious.

Adverb

(6) *studiously,* at one's books; under training, in articles.

537
Teacher

Noun

(1) *teacher,* preceptor, mentor 520 *guide*; minister 986 *pastor*; guru 500 *sage*; instructor, educator; tutor, coach; governor, governess 749 *keeper*; educationist, pedagogue; pedant beak, schoolmarm; school teacher, master *or* mistress; year tutor; deputy head, head teacher, headmaster *or* - mistress, head, principal; usher, monitor; prefect, proctor;

dean, don, fellow; lecturer, reader, professor; catechist, catechizer; confidant, consultant 691 *adviser*; teaching staff, faculty.

(2) *trainer,* instructor, coach, athletics c.; disciplinarian; horse-trainer, breaker-in, lion-tamer 369 *breeder.*

(3) *preacher,* lay p. 986 *pastor*; orator 579 *speaker*; evangelist, apostle, missionary; pioneer 66 *precursor*; seer, prophet 511 *oracle*; pamphleteer, propagandist 528 *publicizer.*

Adjective

(4) *pedagogic* 534 *educational.*

538
Learner

Noun

(1) *learner,* disciple, follower, proselyte, convert, initiate; empiricist 461 *experimenter*; bookworm 492 *scholar*; pupil, scholar, day pupil, boarder; sixth-former; classmate, fellow student; gifted child, fast learner, high flier; slow learner, late developer, underachiever; school-leaver; old boy, old girl.

(2) *beginner,* novice, tyro, greenhorn, tenderfoot, neophyte; amateur 987 *lay person*; recruit, cadet, trainee, apprentice, articled clerk; probationer, L-driver.

(3) *student,* undergraduate, seminarist; fresher, sophomore; former students, alumni; graduate, post-g., fellow; mature student, research worker, researcher, specialist.

(4) *class,* reception c.; form, grade; set, band, stream; age group, tutor g., house; study group, workshop 584 *conference*; seminar 534 *teaching.*

539
School

Noun

(1) *academy,* institute, institution, educational i.; conservatoire, ballet school, art s., finishing s.; college. c. of further *or* higher education; university, campus; Open University; redbrick u., Oxbridge, varsity; polytechnic, poly.

(2) *school,* nursery s., creche, playgroup, kindergarten; private school, prep s., independent s., public s., state s., free s.; primary school, first s., middle s., secondary s., high s., grammar s., comprehensive s.; special school; Sunday s.

(3) *training school,* training college, agricultural c., technical c., tech; seminary; law school, medical school; military college, staff college.

(4) *classroom,* study; lecture hall, auditorium; library; workshop, laboratory; gymnasium, playing fields; campus.

(5) *rostrum,* tribune, dais, forum; platform, stage, podium; hustings, soapbox; pulpit, lectern; microphone 531 *broadcasting*; leader page, column 528 *publicity.*

Adjective

(6) *scholastic* 534 educational.

540
Veracity

Noun

(1) *veracity,* veraciousness, truthfulness, truth-telling; fidelity, realism 494 *accuracy*; frankness, candour 522 *manifestation*; love of truth, honesty, sincerity 929 *probity*; ingenuousness 699 *artlessness*; downrightness, plain speaking, plain dealing 573 *plainness*; home truth, sober t. 494 *truth*; clean breast 526 *disclosure*; truth-speaker, no liar.

Adjective

(2) *veracious,* truthful 494 *true*; telling the truth, not lying; reliable 929 *trustworthy*; fac-

tual, bald, unvarnished, unexaggerated; scrupulous, exact, just 494 *accurate*; full, particular 570 *diffuse*; ingenuous 699 *artless*; bona fide; unfeigned 522 *undisguised*; open, aboveboard candid, unreserved, forthcoming; blunt, free, downright, forthright, outspoken, straightforward 573 *plain*; honest, sincere 929 *honourable*; truly spoken, fulfilled, proved 478 *demonstrated*; infallible, prophetic 511 *presageful*.

Verb

(3) *be truthful,* tell the truth, tell no lie, swear true 532 *swear*; speak in earnest, mean it, 834 *be serious*; speak one's mind, open one's heart, keep nothing back 522 *show*; come clean, confess the truth 526 *confess*; drop the mask 526 *disclose*; be prophetic 511 *predict*; say truly 478 *demonstrate*.

Adverb

(4) *truthfully,* sincerely 494 *truly*; frankly, candidly, factually, exactly.

541
Falsehood

Noun

(1) *falsehood,* falseness, spuriousness, falsity; treachery, bad faith 930 *perfidy*; untruthfulness, mendacity, deceitfulness, malingering; lying, perjury 543 *untruth*; fabrication, fiction; faking, forgery, falsification 542 *deception*; invention 513 *imagination*; prevarication, equivocation, double-talk 518 *equivocalness*; whitewashing, cover-up; casuistry 477 *sophistry*; overstatement 546 *exaggeration*; misrepresentation, perversion 246 *distortion*; humbug 515 *empty talk*; cant, eyewash; euphemism, soft soap 925 *flattery*; liar 545 *deceiver*.

(2) *duplicity,* false conduct, double-dealing, guile 542 *trickery*; hollowness, front, facade, outside, show 875 *ostentation*; pretence, hollow p., bluff, act; fake, counterfeit, imposture 542 *sham*; hypocrisy, acting, play-a., simulation, dissimulation, dissembling, insincerity, tongue in cheek; lip service, cupboard love, crocodile tears; fraud, cheat, cheating, sharp practice; collusion, put-up job 930 *foul play*; quackery, charlatanism 850 *pretension*; artfulness 698 *cunning*.

Adjective

(3) *false,* not true, without truth; imagined, made-up; untruthful, lying, mendacious 543 *untrue*; perfidious, treacherous, perjured; sneaky 698 *cunning*; disingenuous, dishonest, ambiguous, evasive, shuffling 518 *equivocal*; falsified, garbled; meretricious, embellished, touched up 546 *exaggerated*; imitated, counterfeit, fake, phoney, sham, pseudo, snide, quack, bogus 542 *spurious*; cheating, deceptive, deceitful, fraudulent 542 *deceiving*; collusive; fiddled, engineered, rigged, trumped up.

(4) *hypocritical,* hollow, empty, insincere, diplomatic; put on, seeming, feigned; make-believe, acting, play a.; two-faced, shifty, sly, treacherous, designing 930 *perfidious*; sanctimonious, pharisaical; plausible, smooth, smooth-spoken, oily; creepy, goody-goody; mealymouthed, euphemistic 850 *affected*; canting, gushing 925 *flattering*.

Verb

(5) *be false,* - perjured etc. adj.; perjure oneself, swear falsely, tell a fib, lie, tell lies; stretch the truth 546 *exaggerate*; invent, make up 513 *imagine*; tamper with, falsify 246 *distort*; overstate, understate 552 *misrepresent*; misreport, misquote; lull, soothe 925 *flatter*; play

false 930 *be dishonest*; break faith, betray.

(6) *dissemble,* dissimulate, disguise 525 *conceal*; simulate, counterfeit 20 *imitate*; put on, assume, affect, 20 *imitate*; put on, assume, affect, go through the motions, make a show of; dress up, play-act, play a part 594 *act*; feign, sham, malinger 542 *deceive*; hide the truth, keep something back; fudge, prevaricate, shuffle, dodge, trim 518 *be equivocal*.

(7) *cant,* mince matters 850 *be affected*; varnish, paint, embroider, dress up; gloss over 477 *sophisticate*.

(8) *fake,* fabricate, coin, forge, plagiarize, counterfeit 20 *imitate*; get up, trump up, frame; manipulate, fiddle, wangle, rig, pack (a jury); cook up, concoct, hatch, invent 623 *plot*.

Adverb

(9) *falsely,* deceitfully, under false pretences.

542
Deception

Noun

(1) *deception,* self-d., wishful thinking 487 *credulity*; infatuation 499 *folly*; fallacy 477 *sophistry*; illusion, delusion, hallucination 495 *error*; deceptiveness, speciousness 523 *latency* (see *trap*); false appearance, mirage 440 *visual fallacy*; show, outward s. (see *sham*); false reputation, feet of clay; hollowness, falseness, deceit, quackery, imposture 541 *falsehood*; deceitfulness, guile, craft 698 *cunning*; hypocrisy, insincerity 541 *duplicity*; treachery, betrayal 930 *perfidy*; machination, collusion 623 *plot*; fraudulence, cheating; cheat 545 *deceiver*.

(2) *trickery,* swindling, sharp practice, chicanery, pettifoggery; swindle, ramp, racket, wangle, fiddle, fraud, cheat; cardsharping 930 *foul play*;

trick, dirty t., confidence t., fast one; wiles, ruse, shift, dodge, blind, feint 698 *stratagem*; bait, gimmick, diversion, red herring, hoax, bluff, spoof, leg-pull; sport, joke, practical j. 839 *witticism*.

(3) *sleight,* sleight of hand, legerdemain; conjuring, hocus-pocus, illusion, ventriloquism; juggling; three-card trick; magic 983 *sorcery*.

(4) *trap,* deathtrap 527 *ambush*; catch, plant, frame-up 930 *foul play*; hook, noose, snare, gin; net, meshes, web; diversion, blind, decoy, bait, lure; booby trap, tripwire, trapdoor 663 *pitfall*.

(5) *sham,* false front, veneer 541 *duplicity*; lip service, make-believe, pretence 850 *affectation*; whitewash, gloss; man of straw, paper tiger; 545 *impostor*; dummy, scarecrow; imitation, facsimile, copy; mockery, hollow m.; counterfeit, forgery, fake; masquerade, disguise, false colours 525 *concealment*; tinsel, paste.

Adjective

(6) *deceiving,* deceitful, lying 543 *untrue*; deceptive 523 *latent*; hallucinatory, delusive, illusory; specious 445 *appearing*; glib, slick, oily, slippery 258 *smooth*; fraudulent, humbugging, cheating; soothing 925 *flattering*; beguiling, treacherous, insidious 930 *perfidious*; trumped-up, framed 541 *false*; feigned, pretended 541 *hypocritical*; juggling, conjuring; tricky, crafty, wily, guileful, artful 698 *cunning*; collusive, plotting; sugared, coated.

(7) *spurious,* false, faked, fake; sham, counterfeit 541 *false*; make-believe, mock, ersatz, bogus, phoney; pseudo-, so-called; not natural, artificial, cultured, imitation; tinsel, meretricious, flash; cardboard, pasteboard 330 *brittle*.

Verb

(8) *deceive,* delude, dazzle; beguile, sugar the pill; let down 509 *disappoint*; blinker, blindfold 439 *blind*; kid, bluff, bamboozle, hoodwink, hoax, humbug 495 *mislead*; play false, betray, double-cross 930 *be dishonest*; intrigue against 623 *plot*; circumvent, overreach, outwit, outmanoeuvre 306 *outdo*; forestall 135 *be early*; outsmart 698 *be cunning*; trick, cheat (**see** *befool*); con, swindle, do down; do out of, fleece, shortchange 788 *defraud*; juggle, conjure, palm off, fob off with; gerrymander, tinker with, load the dice, stack the deck; impose upon 541 *dissemble*; whitewash 541 *cant*; counterfeit 541 *fake*.

(9) *befool,* fool, make a fool of; mock, make fun of 851 *ridicule*; rag, play tricks *or* a joke on, pull one's leg, have one on 497 *be absurd*; string along, sport with, trifle w., throw over, jilt; take in, dupe, victimize, gull, outwit; trick, trap, catch out; take advantage of, manipulate, bamboozle; cajole, get round 925 *flatter*; let down 509 *disappoint*.

(10) *ensnare,* snare, trap, set *or* lay a trap; enmesh, entangle, net; trip up, catch out; bait, hook, lure, decoy 612 *tempt*; lie in wait, waylay 527 *ambush*; kidnap, shanghai 788 *steal*.

Adverb

(11) *deceptively,* deceitfully; under cover of, disguisedly; tongue in cheek.

543
Untruth

Noun

(1) *untruth* 541 *falsehood*; overstatement 546 *exaggeration*; lie, barefaced l.; fib, whopper, broken word, breach of promise 930 *perfidy*; perjury, false oath; pack of lies, concoction, fiction, fabrication, invention (**see** *fable*); perversion 246 *distortion*; garbling, falsification, misrepresentation.

(2) *mental dishonesty,* disingenuousness; half-truth 468 *qualification*; white lie 525 *concealment*; tongue in cheek, pretence, profession, excuse 614 *pretext*; evasion, subterfuge, doublethink 518 *equivocalness*; irony 850 *affectation*; artificiality, unnaturalness; sham, empty words 541 *duplicity*.

(3) *fable,* invention, fiction 513 *ideality*; story 590 *narrative*; tall story, traveller's tale 546 *exaggeration*; fairy tale, romance, tale, yarn; cock-and-bull story, old wives' tale; 497 *absurdity*; gossip 529 *rumour*; myth, mythology; moonshine, 515 *empty talk*.

Adjective

(4) *untrue,* lying, mendacious 541 *false*; trumped-up, framed etc. vb.; unfounded, empty; mythological, fabulous; fictitious, imagined, make-believe; faked, artificial, synthetic, factitious; phoney, bogus 542 *spurious*; overstated 546 *exaggerated*; boasting 877 *boastful*; perjured 930 *perfidious*; evasive, shuffling 518 *equivocal*; ironical 850 *affected*; mocking 851 *derisive*.

Verb

(5) *be untrue,* not hold water, not ring true 472 *be unlikely*; lie, be a liar 541 *be false*; spin a yarn 546 *exaggerate*; make-believe 513 *imagine*; pretend, sham, counterfeit 541 *dissemble*.

544
Dupe

Noun

(1) *dupe,* fool, April f. 851 *laughingstock*; easy prey, sitting duck, soft touch, cinch; fair game, victim, stooge, mug, sucker 501 *ninny*; dude, greenhorn, innocent 538 *beginner*; cat's-paw, pawn 628 *instrument*; admass.

Adjective
(2) *gullible* 487 *credulous*; duped, deceived, taken in; innocent, green, silly 499 *foolish*.

Verb
(3) *be duped,* be taken in; fall for, swallow the bait; carry the can; fall into the trap.

545
Deceiver

Noun
(1) *deceiver,* practical joker 839 *humorist*; dissembler, hypocrite; false friend, fair-weather f.; turncoat, trimmer 603 *tergiversator*; two-timer, double-crosser, double agent; traitor, Judas 938 *knave*; seducer 952 *libertine*; snake in one's bosom 663 *troublemaker*; plotter, conspirator 623 *planner*; counterfeiter, forger, faker 20 *imitator*.
(2) *liar,* confirmed l.; fibber, story-teller, yarn-spinner 546 *exaggeration*; oath-breaker, perjurer, false witness 541 *falsehood*.
(3) *impostor,* malingerer usurper 59 *intruder*; wolf in sheep's clothing; boaster, bluffer; pretender, charlatan, quack, mountebank; fake, fraud, humbug; pseud, phoney 850 *affecter*; front man 525 *concealment*.
(4) *trickster,* hoaxer, hoodwinker, cheat, cardsharp 542 *trickery*; pettifogger, swindler, shark 789 *defrauder*; slicker, fixer; rogue 938 *knave*; confidence man, con man; decoy, stool pigeon; fox 698 *slyboots*.
(5) *conjuror,* illusionist, juggler, ventriloquist; magician 983 *sorcerer*.

546
Exaggeration

Noun
(1) *exaggeration,* magnification, enlargement 197 *expansion*; extravagance, extremes, immoderation, extremism; overkill; excess, exorbitance, overdoing it; overacting, histrionics 875 *ostentation*; hyperbole 519 *trope*; adulation 925 *flattery*; embroidery 38 *addition*; disproportion 246 *distortion*; caricature, burlesque 851 *satire*; big talk 877 *boasting*; ranting tirade, 574 *magniloquence*; tall story 543 *fable*; storm in a teacup 318 *commotion*; exaggerator 545 *liar*.

Adjective
(2) *exaggerated,* blown up 197 *expanded;* added to, embroidered; overstated 574 *rhetorical*; overacted, histrionic, melodramatic; bombastic 877 *boastful*; tall, fanciful, high-flown, preposterous, outrageous, far-fetched 497 *absurd*; vaulting, lofty, extravagant, excessive; violent, immoderate 32 *exorbitant*; fulsome, inordinate 637 *superfluous*.

Verb
(3) *exaggerate,* magnify, inflate 197 *enlarge*; pile it on 38 *add*; touch up, enhance, heighten, add a flourish, embroider 844 *decorate*; overdo, make too much of 638 *make important*; oversell, cry up 482 *overrate*; make much of 925 *flatter*; stretch, strain 246 *distort*; caricature 851 *satirize*; overact, dramatize, rant; talk big 877 *boast*; run riot, go to extremes, go too far 306 *overstep*; spin a yarn 541 *be false*.

547
Indication

Noun
(1) *indication,* pointing out, showing 522 *manifestation*; signification, meaning 514 *connotation*; notification 524 *information*; symbolization, symbolism 551 *representation*; symbol, image, token, emblem; symptom, sign 466 *evidence*;

blush 526 *disclosure*; wink 524 *hint* (see *gesture*); straw in the wind 511 *omen*; clue key 484 *discovery*; pointer (see *indicator*) index, 87 *directory*; mark, blaze, nick 260 *notch*; stamp, print, impression; stigma, stigmata; scar 845 *blemish*; legend, caption 590 *description*; inscription, epitaph; cipher, monogram.

(2) *identification,* naming 561 *nomenclature,* 77 *classification*; brand, earmark, trademark, imprint (see *label*); autograph, signature, hand 586 *script*; fingerprint, footprint, spoor 548 *trace*; secret sign, password, watchword; diagnostic, markings, colouring; trait 445 *feature*; mole, scar 845 *blemish*.

(3) *symbology,* symbolization; semiotics, semiology; cipher, code 525 *secrecy*; hieroglyphics 586 *script*.

(4) *gesture,* gesticulation, sign language; sign 524 *hint*; pantomime, dumb show, charade, mime; by-play, stage business; body language, demeanour 445 *mien*; motion, move; tic, twitch 318 *spasm*; shrug, nod, wink, twinkle, glance, grimace 438 *look*; smile, laugh 835 *laughter*; touch, kick, nudge 279 *knock*; hug, handshake; push, shove 279 *impulse*; pointing, signal, wave; clenched fist 711 *defiance*; clap, clapping, cheer 923 *applause*; hiss, hooting, boo, booing, catcall 924 *disapprobation*; stuck-out tongue 878 *sauciness*; frown, scowl 893 *sullenness*; pout 829 *discontent*.

(5) *signal* 529 message; sign, symptom 522 *manifestation*; flash, rocket, maroon; signalling, smoke signal, heliograph, semaphore; telegraph, morse 531 *telecommunication*; signal lamp 420 *lamp*; warning light, beacon 379 *fire*; warning signal,

red flag, red light; green light, all clear; alarm, distress signal, 665 *danger signal*; whistle, siren, hooter; bleeper; buzzer, knocker 414 *gong*; bell, passing bell, knell.

(6) *indicator,* pointer, arrow, needle, finger, index-f.; hand, hour h. 117 *timekeeper*; Plimsoll line 465 *gauge*; trafficator, winker; direction finder, radar; cat's-eyes 305 *traffic control*; wind sock 340 *weather*.

(7) *signpost,* fingerpost; milestone, milepost; buoy 662 *safeguard*; compass 269 *sailing aid*; lodestar, guiding star, pole s.; landmark, benchmark; monument, memorial 505 *reminder*; tidemark 236 *limit*.

(8) *call,* proclamation, hue-and-cry 528 *publication*; shout, hail; summons, word 737 *command*; distress call, SOS, Mayday; bugle-call, reveille; lights out, last post; drum-roll, tattoo; call to arms, battle cry, war c.; rallying c., slogan, catchword, watchword, shibboleth; challenge, countersign.

(9) *badge,* token, emblem, symbol, sign, markings, military m., roundel; sceptre, crown 743 *regalia*; insignia, mark of authority, badge of office 743 *badge of rule*; baton, stripes, epaulette 743 *badge of rank*; medal, cross, order; garter, sash, ribbon 729 *decoration*; laurels, bays 729 *trophy*; colours, blue, cap, oar; badge of loyalty, favour, rosette; badge of mourning, black, crepe.

(10) *livery,* dress, national d. 228 *uniform*; tartan; tie, old school t., regimental badge; flash, hackle, cockade, rosette.

(11) *heraldry,* blazonry; coat of arms, blazon; achievement, latchment; shield, escutcheon; crest; charge, device, bearing;

marshalling, quartering, impaling, differencing; animal charge, lion, unicorn; badge, rebus; national emblem, rose, thistle, leek, daffodil, shamrock, fleur-de-lis; metal, or, argent; fur, ermine; College of Arms, herald.

(12) *flag*, ensign, white e., blue e., red e,; jack, merchant j.; flag of convenience; colours, ship's c., regimental c., standard, banner; streamer, pennant, bunting; white flag 721 *submission*; tricolour; Union Jack; Stars and Stripes; Red Flag; Jolly Roger, skull and crossbones; flagpole.

(13) *label*, mark of identification; ticket, bill, docket, chit, counterfoil, stub, duplicate; tally, counter, chip; tick, letter, number, check, mark, sticker; tie-on label, tag; signboard, nameplate, fascia; sign 522 *exhibit*; trade sign, trademark, hallmark; brand, stigma; seal, signet, stamp, impression; masthead, caption, heading, title, rubric; imprint, watermark; card, visiting c.; identity card; passport 756 *permit*; signature, autograph, mark, cross, initials, monogram; fingerprint, footprint 548 *trace*.

(14) *punctuation*, punctuation mark, stop, full s., period; comma, colon, semicolon; inverted commas, quotation marks, apostrophe; exclamation mark, question mark; parentheses, brackets; hyphen, dash, swung d.; asterisk, star; accent, diaeresis, cedilla, tilde; plus sign, minus s., decimal point; underlining, italics 587 *print-type*.

Adjective
(15) *indicating*, indicative, indicatory, connotative, denotative 514 *meaningful*; typical, token, symbolic, emblematic, diagrammatic 551 *representing*;

telltale, revealing 526 *disclosing*; symptomatic 466 *evidential*; semiological, semiotic; diagnostic, individual 80 *special*; demonstrative, explanatory 520 *interpretive*; ominous, prophetic 511 *presageful*; gesticulatory, pantomimic; signalling etc. vb.

(16) *heraldic*, emblematic; crested, armorial, blazoned, azure, sable, or, argent, ermine; rampant, passant.

(17) *marked*, recognized, known by; scarred, branded etc. vb.; stigmatized, earmarked; spotted 437 *mottled*; numbered, lettered; referenced, indexed.

Verb
(18) *indicate*, point 281 *point to*; exhibit 522 *show*; mark out, blaze, signpost; register 548 *record*; name, identify, classify 80 *specify*; index, refer; point the way, guide 689 *direct*; signify, denote, connote, spell 514 *mean*; symbolize, typify, stand for 551 *represent*; signalize, highlight 532 *emphasize*; evince, show signs of, testify, witness to 466 *evidence*; smack of, smell of 524 *hint*; reveal 526 *disclose*; prefigure, forebode, presage 511 *predict*.

(19) *mark*, mark off, mark out, chalk o., demarcate, delimit 236 *limit*; label, ticket, docket, tag, earmark, designate; note, annotate, underline; number, letter; tick, tick off, chalk up; scribble 586 *write*; blot, stain, blacken 649 *make unclean*; scar, disfigure 842 *make ugly*; punctuate, dot, dash, cross out; blaze, brand, burn in; prick, tattoo 263 *pierce*; stamp, seal, punch, impress, emboss 587 *print*; etch 555 *engrave*; emblazon, blazon.

(20) *sign,* ratify, countersign 488 *endorse*; autograph, write one's name; initial, put one's mark.

(21) *gesticulate,* pantomime, mime, mimic 20 *imitate*; wave one's hands, saw the air; wave, 318 *agitate*; stamp 923 *applaud*; gesture, motion, sign; point, thumb, beckon 455 *attract notice*; nod, wink, shrug; jog, nudge, poke, prod, look volumes, leer, ogle 438 *gaze*; twinkle, smile 835 *laugh*; shake one's head 924 *disapprove*; wring one's hands 836 *lament*; grit one's teeth 599 *be resolute*; gnash one's teeth 891 *be angry*; grimace, pout, scowl, frown 829 *be discontented*; curl one's lip 922 *despise*; shuffle, scrape one's feet, paw the ground; pat, stroke 889 *caress.*

(22) *signal,* make a s., exchange signals 524 *communicate*; flag down, thumb; wave on, wave through; break the flag, fly the f., strike the f., dip the f., dip, salute; alert, sound the alarm. 665 *raise the alarm.*

Adverb
(23) *symbolically,* in token of; in dumb show, in sign language.

548
Record

Noun
(1) *record,* recording; memoir, chronicle, annals 590 *narrative*; case history, curriculum vitae 590 *biography*; photograph, portrait 551 *representation*; file, dossier, rogues' gallery; public record, gazette, Hansard; minutes, transactions; notes, jottings, cuttings, press c.; memorabilia, memorandum 505 *reminder*; reports, returns, statements 524 *report*; tally, scoreboard; form, document; voucher, certificate, diploma, charter 466 *credential,*

767 *title deed*; copy 22 *duplicate*; documentation, records, archives, papers; book, minutebook, register, logbook, log, diary, journal; ledger 808 *account book*; index 87 *list*; card, index c., microfilm; tape 86 *data processing,* 414 *gramophone.*

(2) *registration,* registry, recording, sound r., tape r.; inscribing, enrolment, enlistment; booking, reservation; bookkeeping 808 *accounts*; filing, indexing.

(3) *monument,* memorial 505 *reminder*; mausoleum 364 *tomb*; bust 551 *image*; brass, tablet 364 *obsequies*; obelisk, monolith; ancient monument, megalith 125 *antiquity*; cairn 253 *earthwork.*

(4) *trace,* vestige, relic 41 *leavings*; track, tracks, footstep, footprint, tread 547 *indication*; spoor, slot; scent, smell, wake, wash, trail, vapour t.; furrow, swathe fingerprint 466 *evidence*; mark, tidemark, stain, scar, weal, welt 845 *blemish.*

Adjective
(5) *recording,* record-making etc. vb,; recordable; inscriptional 505 *remembering.*

(6) *recorded,* on record, in the file, documented; filmed, taped; filed, indexed, entered, booked, registered; down, in writing 586 *written*; in print 587 *printed*; traceable, extant 41 *remaining.*

Verb
(7) *record,* tape-record, tape, videotape; film 551 *photograph*; paint 551 *represent*; place on record, document; docket, file, index, catalogue; grave 555 *engrave*; take down, note down 586 *write*; have printed 587 *print*; write down, jot d.; note, minute; chronicle 590 *describe.*

(8) *register,* mark up, chalk up, tick off, tally, notch up, score; tabulate, table; enrol, enlist 87 *list*; fill in, enter, post, book 808 *account*; log 505 *remember.*

Adverb
(9) *on record,* in the file, on the books.

549
Recorder

Noun
(1) *recorder,* registrar, record-keeper, archivist; amanuensis; secretary, receptionist; writer, clerk; book-keeper 808 *accountant*; engraver 555 *engraving*; draughtsman *or* - woman 556 *artist*; photographer 551 *photography.*

(2) *chronicler,* diarist, historian 590 *narrator*; archaeologist 125 *antiquarian*; journalist 529 *news reporter.*

(3) *recording instrument,* recorder, tape r., videotape r. 414 *gramophone*; dictaphone (tdmk); teleprinter; cash register, till, checkout; turnstile; seismograph, speedometer 465 *gauge*; flight recorder, black box; stopwatch 117 *timekeeper*; camera, photocopier; pen, pencil 586 *stationery.*

550
Obliteration

Noun
(1) *obliteration,* erasure, effacement; overprinting, defacement; deletion, blue pencil, censorship; crossing out, cancellation 752 *abrogation*; burial, oblivion 506 *amnesty*; clean sweep 149 *revolution*; rubber, eraser.

Adjective
(2) *obliterated,* wiped out, effaced; out of print, leaving no trace unrecorded.

Verb
(3) *obliterate,* remove the traces, cover up 525 *conceal*; overprint, deface, make illegible; efface, eliminate, erase, scratch out, rub o. 333 *rub*; expunge, wipe out; black out, blot o.; rub off, wipe o.; take out, cancel, delete, strike out, cross out, score through, censor, blue-pencil; raze 165 *demolish*; bury 364 *inter*; drown 311 *lower*, leave no trace 446 *disappear.*

551
Representation

Noun
(1) *representation,* typification, symbolization 547 *indication*; diagram, hieroglyphics 586 *writing*; realization, evocation 522 *manifestation*; impersonation, performance 594 *acting*; role-playing 658 *therapy*; mimicry, charade 20 *imitation*; depiction 590 *description*; delineation, drawing, illustration, graphics 553 *painting*; creation, work of art; impression, likeness 18 *similarity*; facsimile 22 *duplicate*; tracing 233 *outline*; portraiture, portrayal 553 *picture*; reproduction, lithograph 555 *printing*; etching 555 *engraving*; design, blueprint, draft, sketch 623 *plan.*

(2) *image,* mental image 451 *idea*; silhouette, projection, hologram 417 *reflection*; visual, visual aid 445 *spectacle*; idol, icon; statuary, statue, statuette 554 *sculpture*; effigy, figure, figurine, figurehead; gargoyle; wax figure, waxwork; dummy, lay figure; model, working m.; marionette, puppet, finger p.; snowman, scarecrow, guy; robot, automaton; type, symbol.

(3) *art,* architecture 243 *formation*; fine arts, beaux arts; graphic art 553 *painting*; plastic art 554 *sculpture*; art nouveau; modern art, abstract art; realism, surrealism 553 *art style*; kitsch 847 *bad taste*; functionalism; decorative art 844 *ornamental art*; the minor arts, illumination, calligraphy, weaving, tapestry, embroidery, pottery.

(4) *photography,* photograph, photo, picture, snapshot, snap; film, negative, print, slide, transparency; frame, still; filmstrip, movie 445 *film*; hologram; radiograph, X-ray; photocopy 22 *copy*; shot, take, close-up, pan, zoom, dissolve, fade; lens 442 *camera*; cameraman *or* - woman, photographer, radiographer.

(5) *map,* chart, plan, outline; sketch map, relief m., survey m.; Admiralty chart; ground plan, elevation, side-e.; projection; atlas, globe; orrery 321 *astronomy*;   map-making, cartography.

Adjective
(6) *representing,* symbolizing etc. vb.; 590 *descriptive*; iconic, pictorial, graphic, vivid; emblematic, symbolic 547 *indicating*; figurative, illustrative, diagrammatic; representational, realistic, naturalistic, true-to-life; primitive, naive; impressionistic, surrealistic, surreal; abstract; artistic; photogenic; photographic.

(7) *represented,* drawn; reflected, imaged; painted, pictured etc. vb.

Verb
(8) *represent,* stand for, denote, symbolize 514 *mean*; typify, incarnate, embody, personify; impersonate, pose as 542 *deceive*; pose, model, sit for; present, enact, perform 594 *dramatize*; project, adumbrate, suggest; reflect, image; mimic, mime 20 *imitate*; depict, characterize

590 *describe*; delineate, draw, picture, portray, figure; illustrate 553 *paint*; catch, capture, realize 548 *record*; carve, cast 554 *sculpt*; cut 555 *engrave*; mould, shape 243 *form*; design, blueprint 623 *plan*; make a diagram, 233 *outline*; sketch, scrawl, doodle, dash off 609 *improvise*; map, chart, survey, plot.

(9) *photograph,* take a p.; photo, snapshot, snap; take, shoot, film; X-ray, radiograph; expose, develop, process, print.

552
Misrepresentation

Noun
(1) *misrepresentation,* not a true picture 19 *dissimilarity*; false light 541 *falsehood*; bad likeness, travesty, parody 546 *exaggeration*; caricature 851 *ridicule*; daub, botch, scrawl; distorted image, false i. 246 *distortion*;

Adjective
(2) *misrepresented,* travestied etc. vb.; flat, cardboard.

Verb
(3) *misrepresent,* deform 246 *distort*; tone down 925 *flatter*; overdraw 546 *exaggerate*; caricature, guy, burlesque, parody, travesty; daub, botch, splash; lie 541 *be false*.

553
Painting

Noun
(1) *painting,* colouring, illumination 425 *colour*; daubing, finger painting; washing, tinting,   touching   up; depicting,
drawing, sketching 551 *representation*; artistry, composition, design; technique, draughtsmanship, brushwork; line, perspective; tone, values;

highlight, shading, chiaroscuro, contrast.

(2) *art style,* style of painting, genre p.; grand style, intimate s.; pastiche; portraiture; scene painting, sign p.; oil painting, watercolour, tempera, gouache; fresco painting, mural p.

(3) *school of painting,* Mannerism, Baroque, Rococo, Realism, Romanticism, Impressionism, Cubism, Expressionism, Surrealism, Minimalism; action painting.

(4) *art subject,* landscape, seascape, panorama 438 *view*; interior, still life; pastoral, nocturne; nude; crucifixion, nativity.

(5) *picture* 551 *representation*; tableau, mosaic, tapestry; collage, montage, brass rubbing; painting, pastiche; icon, triptych, diptych; fresco, mural; canvas; drawing, line d.; sketch, cartoon; oil painting, watercolour, pastel, wash drawing, pen-and-ink d.; design, pattern, doodle; caricature, silhouette; miniature, vignette; old master, masterpiece; study, portrait, profile; poster, pin-up; reproduction, halftone; aquatint, woodcut 555 *engraving*; illustration, print, plate.

(6) *art equipment,* palette, paintbox; palette knife, spatula, paintbrush; paints, oils, watercolours, gouache, varnish tempera; crayon, pastel, chalk, charcoal; sketchbook 631 *paper.*

Adjective
(7) *painted,* daubed etc. vb.; graphic, pictorial, decorative 844 *ornamental*; pastel, in paint 425 *coloured.*

Verb
(8) *paint,* wash 425 *colour*; tint,

touch up, retouch; daub, put on, paint on 226 *coat*; slap on paint; paint a picture, do a portrait, portray, draw, sketch 551 *represent*; ink, chalk, crayon, pencil, stencil, block in.

554
Sculpture

Noun
(1) *sculpture,* plastic art, modelling, moulding 243 *formation*; stone cutting, wood carving; paper modelling, origami; construction, mobile; kinetic art; statuary; statue, colossus; statuette, figurine, bust, torso, head; model, cast 551 *image*; ceramics 381 *pottery*; medallion, cameo, intaglio; relief, bas-relief; modelling tool, chisel.

Adjective
(2) *glyptic,* sculptured, carved; statuesque, marmoreal; in relief 254 *projecting.*

Verb
(3) *sculpt,* sculpture, block out, rough-hew 243 *form*; cut, carve, whittle, chisel, chip; chase, engrave, emboss; model, mould, cast.

555
Engraving. Printing

Noun
(1) *engraving,* etching, line engraving, plate e., steel e., copper e.; gem cutting, glass engraving; mezzotint, aquatint; wood engraving, woodcut; linocut; block, chisel, dry-point, stylus.

(2) *printing,* type 587 *print*; lithography, colour printing; fabric printing, batik; silk-screen printing; stereotype, impression; die, punch, stamp.

Verb
(3) *engrave,* grave, incise, cut,

etch, stipple; impress, stamp; lithograph 587 *print.*

556
Artist

Noun
(1) *artist,* craftsperson 686 *artisan;* architect 164 *producer;* draughtsperson, designer; delineator, copyist; caricaturist, cartoonist; illustrator, painter; dauber, amateur; scene-painter, sign-p.; oilpainter, watercolourist, pastellist; illuminator, miniaturist; portrait painter, landscape p.; old master, modern m.; naive painter, primitive; Pre-Raphelite, Impressionist, Cubist, Surrealist; art historian, aesthetician.

(2) *sculptor,* sculptress; carver, monumental mason; modeller.

(3) *engraver,* etcher; lapidary, gem-engraver; type-cutter 587 *printer.*

557
Language

Noun
(1) *language,* tongue, speech, idiom, parlance, talk; patter, lingo 560 *dialect;* mother tongue, native t.; vernacular, common speech 579 *speech;* correct speech, Queen's English; lingua franca, Esperanto, creole, pidgin; sign language 547 *gesture;* officialese 560 *neology;* Babel 61 *confusion.*

(2) *linguistics,* language study, philology, comparative p.; syntax 564 *grammar;* phonetics 577 *pronunciation;* lexicography 559 *etymology;* morphology; semantics 514 *meaning;* bilingualism.

(3) *literature,* creative writing 589 *reading matter;* letters,

classics, arts, humanities; literary genre, fiction, nonfiction 590 *narrative, description;* lyricism, poetry 593 *poem;* plays 594 *drama;* criticism 480 *estimate;* Classicism, Romanticism, Symbolism, Realism, Naturalism.

(4) *linguist,* language student, philologist, etymologist 559 *etymology;* semanticist; grammarian, phonetician; belletrist 492 *scholar;* polyglot, bilingual.

Adjective
(5) *linguistic,* lingual, philological, etymological, grammatical, morphological; semantic; tonal, inflected; written, literary; spoken, living, idiomatic; vulgar, colloquial, vernacular 560 *dialectal;* current, common, demotic; bilingual, multilingual, polyglot.

(6) *literary,* written, polished; classical, romantic, decadent; lettered, learned.

558
Letter

Noun
(1) *letter,* sign, symbol, character 586 *writing;* alphabet, ABC; ideogram, cuneiform, hieroglyph 586 *lettering;* big letter, capital l., small letter, minuscule; letterpress 587 *print-type.*

(2) *initials,* first letter; monogram, cipher; anagram, acrostic, acronym.

(3) *spoken letter,* phone, phoneme; consonant, vowel, syllable 577 *voice.*

(4) *spelling,* orthography.

Adjective
(5) *literal,* in letters, alphabetic; in syllables, syllabic; italic 586 *written;* large, capital, initial; spelt, orthographic; ciphered, monogrammatic; anagrammatic; phonetic 577 *vocal.*

Verb
(6) *spell,* spell out, read; transliterate; form letters 586 *write.*

Adverb
(7) *alphabetically,* by letters; letter for letter.

559
Word

Noun
(1) *word,* expression, locution 563 *phrase;* term 561 *name;* phoneme, syllable 398 *speech sound;* synonym, homonym, homograph, homophone; pun 518 *equivocalness;* antonym 14 *contrariety;* root, derivation; doublet; part of speech 564 *grammar;* diminutive, pejorative, intensive; contraction, abbreviation 569 *conciseness;* cliche, catchword, vogue word, buzz w.; new word, loan w. 560 *neology;* four-letter word 573 *plainness;* swearword 899 *malediction;* long word, polysyllable; short word, monosyllable; many words, verbiage, wordiness, verbosity 570 *pleonasm.*

(2) *dictionary,* lexicon, thesaurus; word list, glossary, vocabulary; concordance, index.

(3) *etymology,* philology 557 *linguistics;* phonology 577 *pronunciation;* terminology 561 *nomenclature;* lexicography; philologist, etymologist, lexicographer.

Adjective
(4) *verbal,* literal; etymological, lexical, philological, lexicographical; antonymous, synonymous 514 *semantic;* wordy, verbose 570 *pleonastic.*

Adverb
(5) *verbally,* lexically; verbatim, word for word.

560
Neology

Noun
(1) *neology,* neologism 126 *newness;* coinage, new word, nonce w. 559 *word;* catch phrase, cliché; borrowing, loan word; jargon, technical term; barbarism, hybrid; journalese, officialese, telegraphese; newspeak 518 *equivocalness;* archaism 850 *affectation;* malapropism 565 *solecism;* wordplay, spoonerism 839 *witticism.*

(2) *dialect,* idiom, lingo, patois, vernacular 557 *language;* burr, brogue, accent 577 *pronunciation;* cockney, Geordie; broken English, pidgin E., pidgin; lingua franca, hybrid language; Strine, Franglais; anglicism, Americanism.

(3) *slang,* vulgarism, colloquialism; jargon, argot, cant, patter; gipsy lingo, Romany; rhyming slang, back slang; gibberish, gobbledygook 515 *empty talk.*

Adjective
(4) *neological,* newfangled, newly coined; hybrid, corrupt, pidgin; loaned, borrowed, imported, foreign; archaic, obsolete; unidiomatic 565 *ungrammatical.*

(5) *dialectal,* vernacular; Cockney, broad; guttural, nasal, burred; provincial, local; colloquial; nonstandard, slangy; jargonistic, journalistic; unliterary, technical.

Verb
(6) *neologize,* coin words; talk slang, jargonize, cant; speak with an accent 577 *voice.*

561
Nomenclature

Noun
(1) *nomenclature,* terminology; description, designation, appellation; christening, naming ceremony.

(2) *name,* first name, forename, Christian name; surname, patronymic; maiden name, married n.; appellation, nickname, pet name, diminutive, sobriquet; epithet, description; designation, handle, style 870 *title*; heading, caption 547 *indication*; technical term, 560 *neology*; same name, namesake, eponym; pen name, pseudonym 562 *misnomer*; noun, proper n.

(3) *nomenclator,* terminologist; namer, baptizer; announcer.

Adjective
(4) *named,* called etc. vb.; titled, entitled; christened; known as, alias; so-called, soi-disant; nominal, titular; named after, eponymous.

(5) *naming,* terminological.

Verb
(6) *name,* give a name, call, christen, baptize; surname, nickname; dub, title, entitle; style, term 80 *specify*; define, characterize 463 *discriminate*; call by name, announce; blacklist.

(7) *be named,* answer to; go by the name of.

Adverb
(8) *by name;* namely.

562
Misnomer

Noun
(1) *misnomer,* misnaming, malapropism 565 *solecism*; false name, alias; nom de plume, pen name; pseudonym, nickname 561 *name.*

(2) *no name,* anonymity; anon, certain person, so-and-so, what's his *or* her name; N or M, X, sir or madam; etcetera; some, any, what you will.

Adjective
(3) *misnamed,* miscalled; self-styled, soi-disant, would-be, so-called, quasi, pseudonymous.

(4) *anonymous,* unnamed, unsigned; unknown, faceless, nameless; incognito.

Verb
(5) *misname,* misterm; nickname, dub 561 *name*; assume an alias; be anonymous.

563
Phrase

Noun
(1) *phrase,* clause, sentence, period, paragraph; expression, locution; idiom, fixed expression, formula, set phrase; euphemism, metaphor 519 *trope*; catch phrase, slogan; well-worn phrase, cliché, commonplace 610 *habit*; saying, motto, epigram 496 *maxim*; inscription, caption 548 *record*; phraseology, phrasing, diction, wording, choice of words 575 *elegance*; circumlocution 570 *diffuseness*; paraphrase 520 *translation*; phrasemonger 575 *stylist.*

Adjective
(2) *phraseological,* in sentences; idiomatic.

Verb
(3) *phrase,* articulate; reword, rephrase; express, formulate, put in words, state 532 *affirm*; turn a sentence.

564
Grammar

Noun
(1) *grammar*, comparative g.,
philology 557 *linguistics*; analysis, parsing, construing; accidence, inflection, case, declension; conjugation, mood, voice,
tense; number, gender; accentuation 547 *punctuation*; syntax, word order; bad grammar
565. *solecism*; good grammar,
grammaticalness.

(2) *part of speech*, substantive,
noun, pronoun; adjective;
verb, adverb; preposition, conjunction, interjection; subject,
object; article, particle, affix,
suffix, prefix; inflexion, case-
ending.

Adjective
(3) *grammatical*, correct; syntactic, inflectional; singular,
plural; substantival, adjectival, attributive, predicative;
verbal, adverbial; participial;
prepositional; conjunctive, copulative; comparative, superlative.

Verb
(4) *parse*, analyse, inflect, conjugate, decline; punctuate; construe 520 *interpret*.

565
Solecism

Noun
(1) *solecism*, bad grammar, incorrectness; irregularity 560
dialect; impropriety, barbarism
560 *neology*; malapropism, slip,
Freudian s. 495 *mistake*; mis-
prononciation 580 *speech
defect*.

Adjective
(2) *ungrammatical*, solecistic;
irregular, abnormal; faulty,
improper.

Verb
(3) *be ungrammatical*, commit a
solecism; mispronounce 580
stammer; misspell 495 *blunder*.

566
Style

Noun
(1) *style*, tone, manner, vein,
strain, idiom; personal style,
mannerism 80 *speciality*; diction, parlance, phrasing, phraseology; choice of words, vocabulary; literary style, raciness
571 *vigour*; feeling for words,
grace 575 *elegance*; word magic,
word-spinning 579 *oratory*;
weak style 572 *feebleness*; severe style 573 *plainness*; elaborate style 574 *ornament*; clumsy
style 576 *inelegance*.

Adjective
(2) *stylistic*, elegant, mannered,
literary; rhetorical, expressive,
eloquent, fluent; racy, idiomatic; plain, forceful.

Verb
(3) *show style*, measure one's
words.

567
Perspicuity

Noun
(1) *perspicuity*, clearness, clarity, lucidity, limpidity 516 *intelligibility*; directness 573 *plainness*; definiteness, exactness
494 *accuracy*.

Adjective
(2) *perspicuous*, lucid, limpid 422
transparent; clear, unambiguous 516 *intelligible*; explicit,
clear-cut 80 *definite*; exact 494
accurate; direct 573 *plain*.

568
Imperspicuity

Noun
(1) *imperspicuity*, obscurity 517

unintelligibility; abstraction, abstruseness; complexity 574 *ornament*; hard words 700 *difficulty*; vagueness 474 *uncertainty*; imprecision 495 *inexactness*; ambiguity 518 *equivocalness*; ellipsis 569 *conciseness*; verbiage 570 *diffuseness*.

Adjective
(2) *unclear,* obscure 517 *unintelligible*; mysterious, enigmatic; abstruse, profound; allusive, indirect 523 *latent*; vague, indefinite 474 *uncertain*; ambiguous 518 *equivocal*; muddled, confused, tortuous, involved 61 *complex*; hard 700 *difficult.*

569
Conciseness

Noun
(1) *conciseness,* concision, succinctness, brevity; aphorism 496 *maxim*; epigram, clerihew; haiku few words, terseness, laconicism 582 *taciturnity*; compression, telegraphese; ellipsis, abbreviation 204 *shortening*; epitome, precis 592 *compendium.*

Adjective
(2) *concise,* brief, short and sweet 204 *short*; laconic, monosyllabic 582 *taciturn*; succinct, crisp, brisk, to the point; trenchant, incisive; terse, curt, brusque 885 *ungracious*; condensed, compact; pithy, pregnant; pointed, aphoristic, epigrammatic; elliptic, telegraphic, contracted, summary, abbreviated.

Verb
(3) *be concise,* brief etc. adj.; telescope, compress, condense, contract, abbreviate 204 *shorten*; outline, sketch; summarize 592 *abstract*; waste few words on 582 *be taciturn*; epigrammatize 839 *be witty.*

Adverb
(4) *concisely,* briefly; in brief, in short, in a word, in a nutshell.

570
Diffuseness

Noun
(1) *diffuseness,* profuseness 197 *expansion*; inspiration, vein, flow, outpouring; abundance, richness, verbosity, wordiness, verbiage; fluency, nonstop talking 581 *loquacity*; longmindedness, prolixity; repetitiveness 106 *repetition*; gush, rigmarole, waffle 515 *empty talk*; tirade, harangue 579 *oration*; disquisition 591 *dissertation.*

(2) *pleonasm,* tautology; periphrasis; padding, filler 40 *extra.*

Adjective
(3) *diffuse,* verbose, nonstop 581 *loquacious*; profuse 171 *prolific*; inspired, flowing, fluent; expatiating, detailed, minute; exuberant, gushing, effusive; windy, turgid, bombastic 574 *rhetorical.*

(4) *prolix,* of many words, longwinded, wordy, prosy, prosing; long drawn out 113 *protracted*; boring 838 *tedious*; lengthy, epic, never-ending 203 *long*; diffusive, discursive, episodic; rambling, maundering 282 *deviating*; loose-knit, incoherent; indirect, periphrastic, roundabout.

(5) *pleonastic,* excessive 637 *superfluous*; repetitious, repetitive 106 *repeated*; tautologous, tautological; padded out.

Verb
(6) *be diffuse,* prolix etc. adj.; dilate, expatiate, amplify, particularize, detail, expand, enlarge upon; descant, discourse; repeat 106 *repeat oneself*; pad out, spin o. 203 *lengthen*; gush, pour out 350 *flow*; rant, harangue, perorate 579 *orate*, 838

be tedious; rabbit on 581 *be loquacious*; waffle, digress 282 *deviate*; ramble, maunder, drivel, yarn, never end; beat about the bush 518 *be equivocal*.

Adverb

(7) *diffusely,* at great length, on and on, ad nauseam.

571
Vigour

Noun

(1) *vigour* power, strength, vitality, drive, forcefulness 174 *vigourousness*; incisiveness, trenchancy; vim, punch; sparkle, verve, elan, panache, vivacity, liveliness, vividness, raciness; spirit, fire, ardour, warmth, fervour, vehemence, enthusiasm, passion 818 *feeling*; piquancy, poignancy, mordancy 388 *pungency*; stress, emphasis 532 *affirmation*; reiteration 106 *repetition*; solemnity, gravity, weight; loftiness, elevation, sublimity, grandeur 574 *magniloquence*; rhetoric 579 *eloquence*.

Adjective

(2) *forceful,* powerful 162 *strong*; energetic 174 *vigorous*; racy, idiomatic; bold, dashing, spirited, sparkling, vivacious 819 *lively*; fiery, ardent, impassioned 818 *fervent*; vehement, emphatic, insistent, reiterative 532 *affirmative*; cutting, incisive, trenchant 256 *sharp*; pointed, pungent, mordant 839 *witty*; grave, sententious 834 *serious*; meaty, solid; weighty, forcible, cogent 740 *compelling*; vivid, graphic 551 *representing*; flowing, inspired 579 *eloquent*; high-toned, lofty, grand, sublime 821 *impressive*.

Adverb

(3) *forcefully,* vigorously, vehemently, in glowing terms.

572
Feebleness

Noun

(1) *feebleness* weak style 163 *weakness*; flatness, staleness, vapidity 387 *insipidity*; jejuneness, thinness; enervation, flaccidity, lack of conviction, lack of sparkle; baldness 573 *plainness*; anticlimax.

Adjective

(2) *feeble,* weak, thin, flat, vapid, insipid 387 *tasteless*; wishy-washy, watery; sloppy, sentimental; colourless, bald 573 *plain*; flaccid, nerveless, emasculated; tame, conventional; uninspired, uninspiring, ineffective; prosaic, monotonous, prosy, pedestrian, dull, dry, boring 838 *tedious*; cliché-ridden, platitudinous, hackneyed, stale; pretentious, flatulent; juvenile, childish; careless, slovenly; lame, unconvincing; disjointed, rambling 570 *prolix*.

573
Plainness

Noun

(1) *plainness,* naturalness, simplicity 699 *artlessness*; severity, baldness, spareness; plain English 516 *intelligibility*; home truths 540 *veracity*; vernacular, common speech; lack of affectation 874 *modesty*; bluntness, frankness, coarseness, four-letter word.

Adjective

(2) *plain,* simple 699 *artless*; austere, severe, disciplined; bald, spare, stark; pure, unadulterated, unvarnished, 540 *veracious*; unemphatic, played down; unassuming, unpretentious 874 *modest*; chaste, restrained; unaffected, natural, homely, homespun, vernacular; prosaic, sober 834 *serious*;

dry, stodgy 838 *tedious*; humdrum, workaday 610 *usual*; unimaginative 593 *prosaic*.

Verb
(3) *speak plainly,* call a spade a spade 516 *be intelligible*; say outright, spell it out, not mince words.

Adverb
(4) *plainly,* simply 516 *intelligibly*; in plain words; directly, point-blank.

574
Ornament

Noun
(1) *ornament,* embellishment, decoration, embroidery, frills 844 *ornamentation*; floweriness, arabesques 563 *phrase*; preciousness, euphemism; rhetoric, flourish of r.; figure of speech 519 *trope*; alliteration, assonance; metaphor, simile, antithesis.

(2) *magniloquence,* high tone 579 *eloquence*; declamation, orotundity 571 *vigour*; overstatement, extravagance, hyperbole 546 *exaggeration*; turgidity, flatulence; affectation, pomposity 875 *ostentation*; bombast 877 *boasting*; rant 515 *empty talk*; long words 570 *diffuseness*.

(3) *phrasemonger,* word-spinner 575 *stylist*; rhetorician, orator 579 *speaker*.

Adjective
(4) *ornate,* florid, flowery 844 *ornamented*; precious, euphemistic; pretentious 850 *affected*; flamboyant 875 *showy*; sonorous, clanging 400 *loud*; alliterative 519 *figurative*; stiff, stilted; pedantic, long-worded.

(5) *rhetorical,* declamatory, oratorical 579 *eloquent*; resonant, sonorous 400 *loud*; ranting, orotund; high-pitched, high-

flown; grandiose, stately; bombastic, pompous, sententious, grandiloquent, magniloquent; inflated, turgid, swollen; antithetical, alliterative, metaphorical 519 *figurative*.

Verb
(6) *ornament,* grace, adorn, enrich 844 *decorate*; charge, overlay, elaborate.

575
Elegance

Noun
(1) *elegance,* style, grace, gracefulness 841 *beauty*; refinement, taste 846 *good taste*; propriety, restraint, dignity; clarity simplicity 567 *perspicuity*; naturalness 573 *plainness*; classicism, harmony, euphony, balance, proportion 245 *symmetry*; rhythm, flow, smoothness, fluency; readiness, felicity; polish, finish; elaboration, artificiality 574 *ornament*.

(2) *stylist,* classical author, classic, purist.

Adjective
(3) *elegant,* majestic, stately 841 *beautiful*; well-proportioned, graceful; stylish, refined 846 *tasteful*; distinguished, dignified; correct, idiomatic; expressive, clear 567 *perspicuous*; simple, natural, unaffected 573 *plain*; flowing, fluent, tripping, rhythmic, mellifluous, euphonious, harmonious; felicitous, happy, neatly put, well-turned 694 *well-made*; artistic, wrought; elaborate, polished, soigné; restrained, controlled; flawless 646 *perfect*; classic, classical.

Verb
(4) *be elegant,* show taste 846 *have taste*; write well; elaborate, polish, refine 646 *perfect*.

576
Inelegance

Noun
(1) *inelegance,* clumsiness, uncouthness 699 *artlessness*; coarseness, lack of finish 647 *imperfection*; harshness, cacophony 411 *discord*; stiffness, stiltedness; impropriety, barbarism 565 *solecism*; vulgarism, vulgarity 847 *bad taste*; mannerism, artificiality 850 *affectation*; exhibitionism 875 *ostentation*; lack of restraint, excess 637 *superfluity*; turgidity, pomposity 574 *magniloquence*.

Adjective
(2) *inelegant,* graceless 842 *ugly*; faulty, incorrect; crabbed, tortuous 568 *unclear*; long-winded 570 *diffuse*; unpolished 647 *imperfect*; bald 573 *plain*; coarse, crude, rude, uncouth, barbarous 699 *artless*; tasteless 847 *vulgar*; unrestrained, immoderate, excessive; turgid, pompous 574 *rhetorical*; forced, laboured, artificial, mannered, grotesque 850 *affected*; jarring, grating, heavy, ponderous, insensitive; harsh, abrupt; halting, cramped, clumsy, awkward; wooden, stiff, stilted 875 *formal*.

577
Voice

Noun
(1) *voice,* speaking v. 579 *speech*; singing voice 412 *vocal music*; powerful voice, vociferation, lung power 400 *loudness*; tongue, vocal organs, vocal cords; lungs, larynx, voice box, syrinx; vocalization, phoneme, vowel, diphthong, closed vowel, consonant, syllable; articulation, distinctness; utterance, enunciation, delivery, attack; exclamation, ejaculation, gasp 408 *cry*; mutter, whisper 401 *faintness*; tone of voice, accents, timbre, pitch, tone, intonation, modulation.

(2) *pronunciation,* articulation, elocution, enunciation, inflection, accentuation, stress, emphasis; accent, broad a.; foreign a.; burr, brogue, drawl, twang 560 *dialect*; aspiration, glottal stop; nasality, lisping, stammer 580 *speech defect*.

Adjective
(3) *vocal,* voiced, oral, aloud, out loud 398 *sounding*; well-spoken, articulate, distinct, clear; well-sung, in good voice 410 *melodious*; pronounced, uttered, spoken, dictated, read out, read aloud; aspirated 407 *hoarse*; accented, tonal, accentuated; guttural 407 *hoarse*; shrill 407 *strident*; wheezy 406 *sibilant*.

Verb
(4) *voice,* pronounce, verbalize, put into words 579 *speak*; mouth, give tongue, give voice, express, utter, enunciate, articulate; vocalize; inflect, modulate; breathe, aspirate, trill, roll, burr; accent, stress 532 *emphasize*; raise the voice, lower the v., whisper; exclaim, ejaculate, rap out 408 *cry*; drone, intone, chant, hum 413 *sing*; bellow, shout, vociferate 400 *be loud*; lisp, drawl 580 *stammer*.

578
Voicelessness

Noun
(1) *voicelessness,* no voice, loss of v.; thick speech, hoarseness, huskiness, raucousness; muteness 399 *silence*; dumbness, deaf-mutism; treble, falsetto; breaking voice, cracked v.; undertone, low voice, small v., bated breath 401 *faintness*; sign

language 547 *gesture*; mute, deaf-mute.

Adjective
(2) *voiceless,* breathed, whispered, muffled, low-voiced, inaudible 401 *muted*; mute, dumb, deaf and dumb; speechless, wordless; inarticulate, silent 582 *taciturn*; tongue-tied; silenced, gagged; hollow, sepulchral, breaking, cracked, croaking 407 *hoarse*; breathless, out of breath.

Verb
(3) *be mute,* hold one's tongue 582 *be taciturn*; check oneself, dry up, shut up, ring off, hang up; lose one's voice; be struck dumb lose one's tongue 580 *stammer.*

(4) *make mute,* strike dumb, dumbfound; stick in one's throat, choke on; muffle, hush 401 *mute*; shout down, drown one's voice; muzzle, gag, stifle 165 *suppress*; shut one up, cut one short, hang up on; still, hush 399 *silence.*

(5) *speak low,* speak softly, whisper 401 *sound faint*; lower one's voice, drop one's v.

Adverb
(6) *voicelessly,* in hushed tones, in a whisper, in an undertone, sotto voce, under one's breath, in an aside.

579
Speech

Noun
(1) *speech,* tongue, lips 577 *voice*; parlance 557 *language*; word of mouth 524 *report*; accents, tones; discourse, colloquy, conversation, talk 584 *interlocution*; address, apostrophe 583 *allocution*; ready speech, fluency, talkativeness, volubility 581 *loquacity*; effusion 570 *diffuseness*; elocution, voice production; articulation, utterance, delivery, enunciation 577 *pronunciation*; ventriloquism; sign language 547 *gesture*; thing said, speech, dictum, utterance, remark, observation, comment, interjection 532 *affirmation*; fine words 515 *empty talk.*

(2) *oration,* speech; one's say, one's piece, discourse, disquisition, address, talk; panegyric, eulogy; valedictory, farewell address; toast, vote of thanks; broadcast, commentary 534 *lecture*; recitation, recital, reading; set speech, declamation; sermon, homily, exhortation, harangue; tirade, diatribe, philippic, invective; monologue 585 *soliloquy*; written speech, paper 591 *dissertation*; preamble, prologue; peroration.

(3) *oratory,* rhetoric, public speaking, speech-making, speechifying, declamation, elocution; vapouring, ranting; vituperation, invective; soapbox 539 *rostrum.*

(4) *eloquence,* fluency, articulacy; command of words, way with w., word-spinning 566 *style*; power 571 *vigour*; peroration, purple passage 574 *magniloquence.*

(5) *speaker,* talker; gossiper 581 *chatterer*; conversationalist 584 *interlocutor*; speechifier, speech-maker, speech-writer, rhetorician, orator, public speaker, toastmaster; declaimer, ranter; demagogue 738 *agitator*; word-spinner, spellbinder; lecturer, preacher; presenter, announcer 531 *broadcaster*; prologue, narrator, chorus 594 *actor*; mouthpiece, spokesperson 754 *delegate*; advocate, pleader 231 *intermediary*; salesperson 793 *seller*; monologist 585 *soliloquist.*

Adjective

(6) *speaking*, talking; able to speak, bilingual, polyglot; anglophone, francophone; articulate, fluent, outspoken, free-speaking, talkative 581 *loquacious*; oral 577 *vocal*; well-spoken, soft-s., loud-s.; audible, spoken, verbal; plummy, fruity 404 *resonant*; elocutionary.

(7) *eloquent*, spellbinding, silver-tongued, smooth-t. 925 *flattering*; elocutionary, oratorical 574 *rhetorical*; grandiloquent 571 *forceful*; ranting, word-spinning, rousing 821 *exciting*.

Verb

(8) *speak*, mention, say; utter, articulate 577 *voice*; pronounce, declare 532 *affirm*; let out, blurt out 526 *divulge*; whisper, breathe 524 *hint*; talk 584 *converse*; emit, give utterance, break silence, find one's tongue; pipe up, speak up, raise one's voice; gossip, prattle, chatter 581 *be loquacious*; jabber, gabble; speak one's mind, have one's say, expatiate on 570 *be diffuse*; trot out, reel off; recite; read, dictate.

(9) *orate*, speechify; declaim, deliver a speech; take the floor, hold forth, preach, sermonize, harangue; lecture, address 534 *teach*; invoke, apostrophize 583 *speak to*; perorate, rant, rail; talk to oneself 585 *soliloquize*; ad-lib 609 *improvise*.

580
Speech defect

Noun

(1) *speech defect*, aphasia, loss of speech 578 *voicelessness*; speech impediment, stammering, stammer, stutter, lisp; drawl, slur; thick speech, cleft palate; burr, brogue 560 *dialect*; accent, twang, nasal t. 577 *pronunciation*; speech therapy.

Adjective

(2) *stammering*, stuttering etc. vb.; nasal, adenoidal; indistinct, thick, inarticulate; tongue-tied, aphasic; breathless 578 *voiceless*.

Verb

(3) *stammer*, stutter, drawl, hesitate, falter, quaver, hum and haw; mumble, mutter; lisp; snuffle, splutter; nasalize, drone; clip one's words, swallow one's w., gabble, slur; mispronounce.

581
Loquacity

Noun

(1) *loquacity*, garrulity, talkativeness, volubility, runaway tongue, flow of words, fluency 570 *diffuseness*; verbosity, wordiness, prolixity; spate of words, patter, spiel; gift of the gab 579 *eloquence*;

(2) *chatter*, chattering, gossiping, tongue-wagging; gabble, jabber; babble, prattle; small talk, gossip, idle g., tittle-tattle; waffle, hot air 515 *empty talk*.

(3) *chatterer*, nonstop talker, chatterbox; gossip, blabber 529 *news reporter*; talker, gabber; windbag, gas-bag; conversationalist 584 *interlocutor*.

Adjective

(4) *loquacious*, talkative, garrulous; gossiping, communicative, chatty, gossipy, newsy 524 *informative*; gassy, windy, prosing, verbose, long-winded 570 *prolix*; nonstop, voluble, fluent, glib, ready, effusive, gushing.

Verb

(5) *be loquacious*, talkative etc. adj.; chatter, run on, reel off, gossip 584 *converse*; quack, gabble, jabber 515 *mean nothing*; talk, prate, prose, waffle, twitter, ramble on, rabbit on; launch out, start talking; have

one's say, talk at length; expatiate, effuse 570 *be diffuse*; talk down; talk shop, buttonhole, bore 838 *be tedious*; never stop talking.

Adverb
(6) *loquaciously,* fluently etc. adv.

582
Taciturnity

Noun
(1) *taciturnity,* incommunicativeness 399 *silence*; reserve, reticence 525 *secrecy*; few words, brusqueness, curtness 885 *rudeness*; muteness 578 *voicelessness*; person of few words; clam.

Adjective
(2) *taciturn,* mute 399 *silent*; monosyllabic, short, curt, laconic, brusque, gruff 569 *concise*; not talking, vowed to silence; withdrawn, reserved, incommunicative 525 *reticent*; close, tight-lipped; discreet 858 *cautious*; inarticulate, tongue-tied 578 *voiceless*.

Verb
(3) *be taciturn,* brusque etc. adj.; use few words 569 *be concise*; not talk, say nothing, have little to say; not be drawn, refuse comment 525 *keep secret*; hold one's peace, hold one's tongue, keep one's mouth shut; fall silent, lose one's tongue 578 *be mute*; not mention, pass over, omit.

Interjection
(4) *hush!* shut up! no comment!

583
Allocution

Noun
(1) *allocution,* apostrophe; address, lecture, pep talk 579 *oration*; greeting, salutation; invocation, appeal, interjection,

buttonholing, aside; hearers, audience 415 *listener*.

Adjective
(2) *vocative,* salutatory, invocatory.

Verb
(3) *speak to,* speak at; address, talk to, lecture to; turn to, apostrophize; appeal to, pray to, invoke; approach, accost; hail, call to, salute 884 *greet*; take aside, buttonhole 584 *converse*.

584
Interlocution

Noun
(1) *interlocution,* parley, colloquy, conversation, talk; dialogue, exchange, repartee, banter, badinage; slanging match 709 *quarrel*; social intercourse 882 *sociality*; commerce, communion, communication 524 *information*; duologue, tête à tête.

(2) *chat,* natter; chit-chat, talk, small t.; gossip 529 *rumour*; tittle-tattle 581 *chatter*; cosy chat, tête-à-tête, heart-to-heart.

(3) *conference,* colloquy, conversations, talks; parley, powwow; discussion, debate, forum, symposium, seminar, teach-in; exchange of views, controversy, polemics 475 *argument*; high-level talks, summit meeting, summit; negotiations, bargaining 765 *treaty*; convention, meeting, gathering 74 *assembly*; reception, party 882 *social gathering*; audience, interview, audition 415 *listening*; consultation, council 691 *advice*.

(4) *interlocutor,* examiner, interviewer 459 *enquirer*; answerer 460 *respondent*; partner, conversationalist 581 *chatterer*; informant 529 *news reporter*.

Adjective

(5) *conversing,* conversational; chatty 581 *loquacious*; communicative 524 *informative*; conferring, in conference; consultative, advisory 691 *advising.*

Verb

(6) *converse,* engage in conversation; carry on a c.; lead one on, draw one out; bandy words, exchange w.; question, answer; chat, have a chat 579 *speak*; gossip, natter 581 *be loquacious*; commune with, talk tête à tête.

(7) *confer,* talk it over, take counsel 691 *consult*; canvass, discuss, debate 475 *argue*; parley, negotiate, hold talks.

585
Soliloquy

Noun

(1) *soliloquy,* monologue, apostrophe; aside; on-hander.

(2) *soliloquist,* monologist.

Adjective

(3) *soliloquizing,* thinking aloud.

Verb

(4) *soliloquize,* talk to oneself, think aloud; apostrophize, pray aloud.

586
Writing

Noun

(1) *writing,* creative w., composition, literary c., authorship, journalism; literary output 557 *literature*; script, copy, writings, works, books 589 *reading matter*; paperwork 548 *record*; copying, transcribing, transcription; handwriting, longhand, shorthand, stenography; typewriting, typing 587 *print*; braille; cipher, code 530 *secret*;

picture writing, hieroglyphics; inscribing, carving 555 *engraving*; study of handwriting; graphology.

(2) *lettering,* handwriting, hand, fist; calligraphy, fair hand; script, italic, copperplate; printing, block letters; clumsy hand, scribble, scrawl; letters, characters 558 *letter*; runes, ideogram; hieroglyph; palaeography.

(3) *script,* written matter, writing, screed, scrawl, scribble; manuscript 589 *book*; original, autograph, holograph; copy, fair copy 22 *duplicate*; typescript, stencil; newsprint; printed matter 587 *letterpress*; letter 588 *correspondence*; inscription 548 *record.*

(4) *stationery,* writing materials, pen and paper, pen and ink; stylus, quill, pen, nib; pencil, crayon, chalk; papyrus, parchment, vellum; foolscap 631 *paper*; pad, jotter; slate, blackboard; typewriter.

(5) *calligrapher,* calligraphist; scribbler, scrawler; pen-pusher, scribe, clerk 549 *recorder*; copyist, transcriber; sign-writer; writer 589 *author*; graphologist.

(6) *stenographer,* typist, shorthand t., audiotypist.

Adjective

(7) *written,* inscribed, inscriptional 548 *recorded*; in writing, in black and white; stenographic; handwritten, manuscript; penned, pencilled; scrawled etc. vb.; cursive, copybook, copperplate; italic, calligraphic; lettered, alphabetic; runic, Gothic, roman, italic 558 *literal.*

Verb

(8) *write,* be literate; engrave, inscribe; letter, block, print; scribble, scrawl; put in writing,

set down, write d., jot d., note 548 *record*; transcribe, copy out, write out; take down, take dictation; type, type out; draft, formulate, compose, concoct, pen, pencil, dash off; write letters 588 *correspond*; write one's name 547 *sign*; write books 590 *describe*; write poetry 593 *poetize*.

587
Print

Noun
(1) *print*, printing, typing 586 *writing*; typography, block printing, plate p., offset process, web offset; lithography 555 *printing*; composition, photocomposition, typesetting, make-up; monotype, linotype, stereotype.

(2) *letterpress*, printed matter, print, impression, printout, run-off; copy, pull, proof, galley p.; imprint 589 *edition*; offprint.

(3) *print-type*, type; upper case, lower c.; fount, typeface, boldface; roman, italic, Gothic 558 *letter*.

(4) *press*, printing p., printing works, printers; rotary press, offset press.

(5) *printer*, book p., jobbing p., typographer, compositor, typesetter; printer's devil, printer's reader, proof r.

Adjective
(6) *printed*, in print 528 *published*; cold-type, hot-metal; set, composed; typographic.

Verb
(7) *print*, stamp; typeset, compose, align; make ready, set up; run off, print off; proofread, correct; bring out 528 *publish*.

588
Correspondence

Noun
(1) *correspondence*, communication 524 *information*; mailing list, distribution l.; letters, mail, post, postbag 531 *postal communications*; letter, epistle, missive, dispatch, bulletin; love letter, billet doux, greetings card, Valentine; postcard, card, air letter; bill, account, enclosure; open letter 528 *publicity*; circular, round robin; answer, acknowledgement.

(2) *correspondent*, letter writer, penfriend; poison pen; recipient, addressee; contributor 529 *news reporter*; contact 524 *informant*.

Adjective
(3) *epistolary*, postal, by post; enclosed.

Verb
(4) *correspond*, correspond with, exchange letters 524 *communicate*; keep in touch, write to, send a letter; report 524 *inform*; acknowledge, reply, write back 460 *answer*; post off, forward, mail.

Adverb
(5) *by letter*, by mail, through the post.

589
Book

Noun
(1) *book*, volume, tome; manuscript, MS, script, typescript; publication, best-seller; work, standard w., classic; major work, magnum opus; magazine, periodical 528 *journal*; booklet, brochure, pamphlet; hardback, softback, paperback.

(2) *reading matter*, printed word, written w. 586 *writing*;

script, text, libretto, lyrics, scenario, screenplay; proof 587 *letterpress*; writings, 593 *prose*; 593 *poetry*; history, biography, travel 590 *description*; work of fiction 590 *novel*; memoirs 590 *biography*; essay, tract, treatise 591 *dissertation*; piece 591 *article*; poetical works 593 *poem*; selections 592 *anthology*; complete works, corpus; newspaper, magazine 528 *journal*; issue, number, instalment, serial, sequel.

(3) *textbook,* school book, reader, primer, grammar; handbook, manual.

(4) *reference book,* work of reference, encyclopedia 490 *erudition*; lexicon 559 *dictionary*; gazetteer, yearbook, annual 87 *directory*; calendar 117 *chronology*; guide 524 *guidebook*; bibliography, reading list; library.

(5) *edition,* impression, issue, run; series, set, collection, library; omnibus edition, complete works; first edition, new e., revised e.; reissue, reprint; adaptation, abridgment 592 *compendium*; errata, corrigenda, addenda; appendix, supplement, index, bibliography; plate, print, illustration.

(6) *bookperson,* literary person man *or* woman of letters; reader, bookworm 492 *scholar*; bibliophile, book lover, book collector, bibliographer; librarian, bookseller, book dealer; publisher, printer, bookbinder; editor, reviewer 480 *estimator*.

(7) *author,* writer, creative w., word-smith; novelist, historian, biographer 590 *narrator*; essayist, prose writer; verse writer 593 *poet*; playwright, librettist, script writer 594 *dramatist*; freelance; copywriter 528 *publicizer*; journalist 529

news reporter; editor, subeditor, copy editor, contributor, correspondent, columnist, gossip writer, diarist; scribbler, pen-pusher, hack; ghost writer; reviser, translator, adapter.

Adjective
(8) *bibliographical,* in book form; bound, hardback, paperback; bibliophilic, book-loving, antiquarian; in print, out of print.

590
Description

Noun
(1) *description,* account, summary 524 *report*; abstract 592 *compendium*; narration, relation, rehearsal, recital, version; specification, details, particulars 87 *list*; portrayal, delineation, depiction; portrait, sketch, profile; case history 548 *record*; evocation, word-painting, local colour; picture, true p., realism, naturalism; vignette, cameo, thumbnail sketch; eulogy 923 *praise*; parody 851 *satire*; obituary 364 *obsequies*.

(2) *narrative,* storyline, plot, subplot, scenario 594 *stage play*; episode 154 *event*; dramatic irony, comic relief; fiction, story, tale, romance, folk tale, fairy story 513 *fantasy*; tradition, legend, myth; saga, epic, ballad 593 *poem*; parable, allegory, cautionary tale; yarn 543 *fable*; anecdote, reminiscence 505 *remembrance*; chronicle, history 548 *record*.

(3) *biography,* real-life story, human interest; life, experiences, adventures, fortunes; hagiography; rogue's gallery; personal account, autobiography, confessions, memoirs 505 *remembrance*; diary, journals, letters.

(4) *novel,* fiction, tale; short story, novelette, novella; light reading, bedside r. 589 *reading matter*; romance, love story, Western, science fiction, sci-fi; gothic novel, ghost story; crime story, detective s., thriller, whodunit; potboiler, blockbuster, best-seller 589 *book*.

(5) *narrator,* reporter, relater; raconteur, anecdotist; yarn-spinner, teller of tales, storyteller; mythologist, allegorist; fiction writer, novelist 589 *author*; biographer, hagiographer, autobiographer, memoir writer, diarist; historian, chronicler 549 *recorder*.

Adjective
(6) *descriptive,* graphic, colourful, vivid; well-drawn, sharp 551 *representing*; true-to-life, naturalistic, realistic, real-life, photographic, convincing; picturesque, striking; suggestive, evocative, emotive; moving 821 *exciting*; traditional, legendary, storied, mythological 519 *figurative*; epic, heroic, romantic, picaresque, low-life, kitchen-sink; narrative, historical, biographical, autobiographical; full, detailed 570 *diffuse*; nonfiction, factual, documentary 494 *accurate*; fictitious, fictional, imaginative 513 *imaginary*.

Verb
(7) *describe,* draw, picture, depict, paint 551 *represent*; evoke, bring to life, tell vividly, make one see; characterize, particularize, detail, enter into 80 *specify*; sketch, adumbrate 233 *outline*; relate, recount, rehearse, recite, report 524 *communicate*; write 548 *record*; narrate, tell, tell a story, yarn, spin a y., unfold a tale; construct a plot, fictionalize; romance 513 *imagine*; reminisce 505 *retrospect*.

591
Dissertation

Noun
(1) *dissertation,* treatise, tract; commentary, exposition; summary 592 *compendium*; theme, thesis 475 *argument*; disquisition, essay, examination, survey 459 *enquiry*; discourse, discussion; memoir, paper, monograph, study; homily, sermon 534 *lecture*.

(2) *article,* column; leading article, leader, editorial; essay, belles-lettres; comment, review, notice, critique, criticism, write-up 480 *estimate*.

(3) *dissertator,* essayist; pamphleteer, publicist; editor, leader writer; writer, belletrist, contributor 589 *author*; reviewer, critic, commentator, pundit 520 *interpreter*.

Adjective
(4) *discursive,* expository, critical 520 *interpretive*.

Verb
(5) *dissertate,* treat, handle, write about, deal with, do justice to; descant, discourse upon 475 *argue*; go into, enquire into, survey; set out, discuss; notice, criticize, comment upon, write up; annotate, commentate 520 *interpret*.

592
Compendium

Noun
(1) *compendium,* epitome, resume, summary; gist; digest, precis; conspectus, synopsis, bird's-eye view, review, survey; minute, note 548 *record*; sketch, thumbnail s., outline, skeleton; blueprint 623 *plan*; syllabus, prospectus 87 *list*; abridgment, abbreviation 204

shortening; contraction, compression 569 *conciseness*.

(2) *anthology,* treasury; selections, extracts; collection, compilation, miscellany; album, scrapbook, sketchbook, notebook, commonplace book; anthologist.

(3) *epitomizer,* abridger, abbreviator; abstracter, summarizer, precis-writer.

Adjective
(4) *compendious,* pithy 569 *concise*; potted, abstracted, abridged 204 *short*; collected etc. vb.

Verb
(5) *abstract,* sum up, resumé, summarize reduce, abbreviate, abridge 204 *shorten*; epitomize, encapsulate; condense consolidate; compile, collect 74 *bring together*; excerpt, glean, select, anthologize.

Adverb
(6) *in sum,* in brief 569 *concisely*; at a glance.

593
Poetry. Prose

Noun
(1) *poetry,* poesy, minstrelsy, song; poetic art, poetics; versification, verse, rhyme; poetic licence; poetic fire, poetic vein, Muses.

(2) *poem,* poetic composition, lines, verses, stanzas, strains; narrative verse, heroic poem, epic; dramatic poem, verse drama 594 *drama*; light verse, lyric verse, ode, dirge, elegy; idyll, eclogue; song, hymn, lay, ballad 412 *vocal music*; collected poems 592 *anthology*.

(3) *doggerel,* jingle, ditty, nursery rhyme; nonsense verse; clerihew, limerick; mock epic, burlesque, satirical verse.

(4) *verse form,* sonnet, ballade, rondeau; burden, refrain, envoi; couplet, triplet, quatrain; verse, free v.; stanza.

(5) *prosody,* versification; metre, measure, numbers, scansion; rhyme, rhyme scheme; assonance, alliteration; cadence, rhythm; pentameter, hexameter, blank verse; heroic couplet, elegiac c.; stress, accent, accentuation; caesura, diaeresis.

(6) *poet,* major p., minor p., poet laureate; prosodist, versifier, rhymer, rhymester; bard, minstrel, troubadour; epic poet, lyric p., dramatic p., elegiac p.; song-writer, lyricist, librettist; improviser, reciter.

(7) *prose,* not verse; prose-writing 573 *plainness*; prose writer 589 *author*.

Adjective
(8) *poetic,* poetical, bardic; tuneful; heroic, Homeric, mock-heroic; lyric, elegiac; lyrical, rhapsodic; rhyming, jingling, doggerel; metrical, measured, rhythmic, scanning.

(9) *prosaic,* unpoetical, pedestrian; matter-of-fact, in prose 573 *plain*.

Verb
(10) *poetize,* sing, tune one's lyre; scan, rhyme, put into rhyme; versify, make verses, elegize; lampoon 851 *satirize*.

594
Drama. Ballet

Noun
(1) *drama,* the theatre, the stage, the boards, the footlights; Broadway, West End; Hollywood 445 *cinema*; show business; straight drama, repertory; theatricals, amateur t.; masque, charade, dumb show,

tableau; Tragic Muse, Comic Muse.

(2) *dramaturgy,* dramatization 590 *narrative*; theatricals, dramatics; histrionics; theatricality, staginess; plot, subplot 590 *narrative*; production, revival; auditions, casting; rehearsal, dress r.; direction, stage management; staging, stage directions; act, scene, coup de théâtre, curtain, blackout; curtain call, encore; premiere, preview; matinee, first house, second h.; sell-out, hit, smash h., box-office h., long run.

(3) *stage play,* play, drama, work, piece, vehicle; libretto, scenario, script, book of words, prompt book; part, lines; sketch, skit; double bill; monologue, dramatic m.; masque; mystery play, miracle p., morality p., passion p.; poetic drama, melodrama, blood and thunder; tragedy, classical t.; tragicomedy, comedy, light c., comedy of manners; black comedy, farce, knockabout f., slapstick, burlesque, extravaganza; pantomime, harlequinade; musical comedy, musical, light opera, comic o., grand o. 412 *vocal music*; radio drama, television play 531 *broadcast*; screenplay 445 *cinema*.

(4) *stage show,* show 445 spectacle; circus 837 *amusement*; variety, music hall, vaudeville; revue, leg show, strip s.; floor s., cabaret; act, turn; star turn; set piece, tableau.

(5) *ballet,* dance, ballet dancing; classical ballet, modern dance; tap d., clog d. 837 *dance*; solo, pas de deux; pirouette 315 *rotation.*

(6) *stage set,* set, setting, decor, scenery, scene 445 *spectacle*; drop curtain, drop, backdrop, backcloth; stage, boards; upstage; front stage, down stage

apron, proscenium; properties, props, costume, make-up, greasepaint.

(7) *theatre,* amphitheatre, stadium 724 *arena*; circus, hippodrome; picture house 445 *cinema*; big top; playhouse, opera house, music hall, night club, cabaret; stage, wings, flies (see *stage set*); dressing room, green r.; footlights, spotlight, limelight, floodlight, houselights; auditorium, orchestra; seating, stalls, pit, box, circle, gallery, balcony, gods; front of house, foyer, box office, stage door.

(8) *acting,* impersonation; pantomime, miming, taking off 20 *mimicry*; histrionics, play-acting; ham-acting, hamming, barnstorming; overacting, staginess, theatricality; character, personage, role, leading r.; part, supporting p., bit p., speaking p., walk-on p.; stock p., stage villain, pantomime dame, principal boy; stage fever; stage fright.

(9) *actor,* actress, Thespian; mimic, mime 20 *imitator*; play-actor, player, strolling p., trouper, barnstormer, ham; rep player, character actor; actor-manager, star, film star, starlet, matinee idol; tragedian, tragedienne; comedian, comedienne; opera singer, prima donna; ballet dancer, ballerina, prima b.; protagonist, lead, leading man *or* lady; understudy, stand-in 150 *substitute*; super, extra, bit player; chorus, corps de ballet; troupe, company, repertory c.; dramatis personae, characters, cast; presenter, narrator; prologue.

(10) *entertainer,* public e., performer; artiste, artist, quick-change a., drag a., striptease a.; monologist; impressionist, impersonator; street musician, busker; crooner, pop singer 413

vocalist; comic, stand-up c. 839 *humorist*; ventriloquist, fire-eater, juggler, conjuror; acrobat; clown 501 *fool*; pierrot, dancer, belly d., show girl, chorus g.

(11) *stagehand,* scene shifter; prop man, scene painter; wardrobe mistress, make-up, special effects; continuity girl; prompter.

(12) *stage manager,* producer, director; designer; manager, press agent; impresario, showman; backer, sponsor.

(13) *dramatist,* tragic poet, comic p. 593 *poet*; playwright, script writer, librettist; joke-writer 839 *humorist*; choreographer.

(14) *playgoer,* theatregoer, operagoer, film fan 504 *enthusiast*; first-nighter; audience, house, packed h., full h. 441 *spectator*; dramatic critic, film reviewer.

Adjective
(15) *dramatic,* theatrical, stagy 551 *representing*; operatic, balletic, Terpsichorean, choreographic; live, legitimate; Thespian, histrionic, tragic, comic, tragicomic; farcical, burlesque 849 *funny*; cathartic, melodramatic, sensational 821 *exciting*; avant-garde; released, showing 522 *shown*; dramatized, acted; badly-acted, hammed up, camped up; acting, play-a.; cast, miscast; featured, starred, billed; all-star; stagestruck.

Verb
(16) *dramatize,* write plays; do a play, stage, mount, produce, direct, stage-manage; rehearse; cast, typecast, give a part, assign a role; star, feature, bill; present, put on 522 *show*.

(17) *act,* perform, enact, play, playact, do a play 551 *represent*; ~sonify, impersonate; act the role, take the part; mime, pantomime, take off 20 *imitate*; create a role, play a part; star, co-star; steal the show, upstage ham it up, camp it up, send up 546 *exaggerate*; rant, roar, play to the gallery; underact, throw away; walk on; understudy, stand in; say one's lines; cue in; forget one's lines, dry; ad-lib.

Adverb
(18) *on stage,* upstage, downstage; offstage, backstage; in the limelight.

595
Will

Noun
volition; disposition, inclination, mind, preference 597 *willingness*; act of will, effort of w. 682 *exertion*; strength of will, willpower, determination 599 *resolution*; controlled will, self-control 942 *temperance*; intent, purpose 617 *intention*; decision 737 *command*; self-will, wilfulness 602 *obstinacy*; whimsicality 604 *caprice*; free will 744 *independence*; free choice 605 *choice*; voluntariness, spontaneity 597 *voluntary work*.

Adjective
(1) *volitional,* willing, unasked, unbidden, spontaneous 597 *voluntary*; discretionary, optional 605 *choosing*; minded, so m. 617 *intending*; self-willed, wilful 602 *obstinate*; arbitrary, autocratic, dictatorial 735 *authoritarian*; independent 744 *free*; determined 599 *resolute*; decided, intentional, willed, intended 608 *predetermined*.

Verb
(2) *will,* impose one's will, have one's way 737 *command*; do as one will 744 *be free*; see fit, think best 605 *choose*; purpose, determine 617 *intend*; wish 859

desire; be independent, go one's own way 734 *please oneself*; judge for oneself be self-willed 602 *be obstinate*; know one's own mind 599 *be resolute*; volunteer 597 *be willing*; originate 156 *cause*.

Adverb
(3) *at will,* at pleasure, ad lib, voluntarily, spontaneously.

596
Necessity

Noun
(1) *necessity,* no alternative, no escape 606 *no choice*; last resort 700 *predicament*; inevitability, the inevitable, what must be 155 *destiny*; necessitation, dictation, determinism, fatalism 608 *predetermination*; act of God 154 *event*; no freedom 745 *subjection*; physical necessity, law of nature; force, superior f. 740 *compulsion*; logical necessity, logic, proof 478 *demonstration*; legal necessity, force of law 953 *law*; moral necessity, obligation, conscience 917 *duty*;.a necessity, a must 627 *requirement*; instinct, 476 *intuition*.

(2) *fate,* inexorable f., lot, cup, portion; weird, karma, kismet; doom, preordination 155 *destiny*; book of fate, God's will, will of Allah, will of heaven; fortune 159 *chance*; stars, planets, the Fates.

(3) *fatalist,* determinist.

Adjective
(4) *necessary,* indispensable 627 *required*; logical, unanswerable; necessitating, imperative, compulsive 740 *compelling*; overriding, irresistible 34 *superior*; compulsory, mandatory, binding 917 *obligatory*; necessitated, unavoidable, inevitable,

inescapable, inexorable 473 *certain*; dictated, imposed, deterministic.

(5) *involuntary,* instinctive 476 *intuitive*; unpremeditated 618 *unintentional*; unconscious, unthinking, unwitting, blind, impulsive 609 *spontaneous*; under a spell 983 *bewitched*; conditioned, reflex, controlled, automatic, mechanistic, mechanical.

(6) *fated,* decided by fate, karmic, fatal; appointed, destined, predestined, preordained 608 *predetermined*; elect 605 *chosen*; doomed 961 *condemned*; bound, obliged 745 *subject*.

Verb
(7) *be forced,* compelled etc. adj.; 721 *submit*; be fated, bow to fate; be cornered, 700 *be in difficulty*; have no choice, have no option, needs must.

(8) *necessitate,* dictate, impose, oblige 740 *compel*; bind by fate, destine, doom 155 *predestine*; insist, demand 627 *require*.

Adverb
(9) *necessarily,* of necessity, perforce; willy-nilly.

597
Willingness

Noun
(1) *willingness,* voluntariness 609 *spontaneity*; free choice 605 *choice*; disposition, inclination, leaning, bent, propensity 179 *tendency*; facility 694 *aptitude*; readiness, right mood, cordiality, good will 897 *benevolence*; acquiescence 488 *assent*; compliance 758 *consent*; alacrity, promptness, zeal, ardour, enthusiasm; initiative, forwardness; devotion, dedication, sacrifice 931 *disinterestedness;* helpfulness 706 *cooperation*; loyalty 739 *obedience*; pliancy,

docility, tractability 721 *submission*; obsequiousness 879 *servility*.

(2) *voluntary work,* labour of love 901 *philanthropy*.

(3) *volunteer,* unpaid worker; do-gooder 901 *philanthropist*.

Adjective
(4) *willing,* ungrudging, acquiescent 488 *assenting*; compliant, agreeable, content, game for 758 *consenting*; in the mood, receptive, favourable, inclined, disposed, well-d., predisposed, amenable; happy, pleased, glad, charmed, delighted; ready 669 *prepared*; ready and willing, prompt, quick 678 *active*; forward, anticipating; zealous, eager, enthusiastic, dedicated, keen; doing one's best 671 *attempting*; helpful 706 *cooperative*; docile, biddable 24 *agreeing*; submissive 721 *submitting*; obsequious 879 *servile*; dying to 859 *desiring*; would-be 617 *intending*.

(5) *voluntary,* offered, unasked, unbidden 609 *spontaneous*; unsolicited, unsought; self-imposed; discretionary, optional 605 *chosen*; volunteering 759 *offering*; gratuitous, free, honorary.

Verb
(6) *be willing,* ready etc. adj.; not mind; feel like 595 *will*; yearn to 859 *desire*; mean to 617 *intend*; agree, acquiesce 488 *assent*; show willing, comply 758 *consent*; try, do one's best 671 *attempt*; collaborate 706 *cooperate*; anticipate, meet halfway; jump at, leap at; not scruple, not hesitate; choose freely 605 *choose*; volunteer 759 *offer oneself*.

Adverb
(7) *willingly,* with a will, readily, voluntarily, spontaneously; ~ly, with pleasure.

598
Unwillingness

Noun
(1) *unwillingness,* indisposition, disinclination, reluctance 489 *dissent*; demur, objection 468 *qualification*; protest 762 *deprecation*; recalcitrance 704 *opposition*; rejection 760 *refusal*; unhelpfulness 702 *hindrance*; abstention 190 *absence*; lack of zeal 860 *indifference*; backwardness 278 *slowness*; hesitation 858 *caution*; scruple 486 *doubt*; repugnance 861 *dislike*; aversion, no stomach for 620 *avoidance*; bashfulness 874 *modesty*; fractiousness, sulkiness 893 *sullenness*; postponement 136 *delay*; laziness 679 *sluggishness*; remissness 458 *negligence*.

(2) *slacker,* shirker 679 *idler*; forced labour.

Adjective
(3) *unwilling,* indisposed, loath, reluctant, averse to; not prepared to 760 *refusing*; opposed 704 *opposing*; demurring, protesting 762 *deprecatory*; squeamish 861 *disliking*; hesitant 858 *cautious*; shrinking, bashful 874 *modest*; shirking 620 *avoiding*; half-hearted, lukewarm, unenthusiastic; backward, dragging 278 *slow*; unhelpful 702 *hindering*; fractious, restive, recalcitrant 738 *disobedient*; not trying, perfunctory 458 *negligent*; grudging, sulky 893 *sullen*; forced, begrudged.

Verb
(4) *be unwilling,* not stomach 861 *dislike*; disagree 489 *dissent*; object, demur, protest 762 *deprecate*; resist 704 *oppose*; reject 760 *refuse*; recoil, back away, not face; fight shy of, jib at 620 *avoid*; skimp, scamp 458 *neglect*; drag one's feet, hold back, hang back 278 *move slowly*; abstain, dissociate oneself;

grudge, begrudge 893 *be sullen*; drag oneself, force o., make o.

Adverb
(5) *unwillingly,* with a bad grace; reluctantly, under protest, under pressure, against one's will, against the grain.

599
Resolution

Noun
(1) *resolution,* resoluteness, determination, grim d.; earnestness, seriousness; resolve, fixed r., mind made up, decision; drive, vigour 174 *vigorousness*; fixity of purpose, concentration, iron will, willpower 595 *will*; self-control, self-mastery; tenacity 600 *perseverance*; aplomb, dash, elan 712 *attack*; guts, pluck, grit, backbone, spirit; fortitude, stiff upper lip, moral fibre 855 *courage*; single-mindedness, devotion, dedication; staunchness, steadiness, constancy, firmness 153 *stability*; insistence, pressure; sternness, ruthlessness, inexorability implacability 906 *pitilessness*; inflexibility, steeliness 326 *hardness*; hearts of oak 600 *stamina*;

Adjective
(2) *resolute,* resolved, determined 597 *willing*; serious, earnest; intent upon 617 *intending*; insistent, pressing, urgent; forceful, energetic, heroic 174 *vigorous*; zealous, thorough 455 *attentive*; steady, firm, staunch, reliable, constant; iron-willed, strong-w., strong-minded, decisive, decided, unbending, immovable, unyielding, inflexible, uncompromising 602 *obstinate*; stern, grim, inexorable, implacable, relentless 906 *pitiless*; steely 326 *hard*; indomitable, undaunted, nothing daunted 855

unfearing; steadfast, unshakable, unflinching, unwavering; game, tenacious 600 *persevering*; 942 *temperate*; self-reliant, self-confident, purposive, purposeful; single-minded, wholehearted, devoted, dedicated.

Verb
(3) *be resolute,* determined etc. adj.; steel oneself, brace o., set one's face, clench one's teeth, grit one's t.; take a resolution, resolve, determine, purpose 617 *intend*; take on oneself 595 *will*; insist, not take no for an answer; stand no nonsense, mean business, stick at nothing, push to extremes; see it through 725 *carry through*; face 661 *face danger*; dare 711 *defy*; endure 825 *suffer*; take the plunge, burn one's boats; commit oneself, set to, buckle to, go to it 682 *exert oneself*.

(4) *stand firm,* not be moved, dig one's heels in, stand one's ground, stay put; not budge, not yield, not compromise; never despair, stand fast, hold f., hold out 600 *persevere*; fight on, soldier on, stick it out, endure 825 *suffer*.

Adverb
(5) *resolutely,* in spite of everything; at any price, at all costs; come what may 600 *persistently*.

Interjection
(6) *Here goes!*

600
Perseverance

Noun
(1) *perseverance,* persistence, tenacity, pertinacity, stubbornness 602 *obstinacy*; staunchness, constancy, steadfastness 599 *resolution*; application, tirelessness 678 *assiduity*; doggedness, plodding 682 *exertion*;

endurance, fortitude 825 *suffering*; maintenance 146 *continuance*; repeated efforts 106 *repetition*.

(2) *stamina,* staying power, indefatigability 162 *strength*; grit, true g., backbone, gameness, pluck 855 *courage*; hard core, old guard 602 *obstinate person*; trier, stayer 686 *worker*.

Adjective

(3) *persevering,* persistent, tenacious, stubborn 602 *obstinate*; game, plucky; patient, dogged, trying hard 678 *industrious*; steady, unfaltering, unwavering, untiring, unflagging, indefatigable; sleepless 457 *vigilant*; unfailing, unremitting, constant 146 *unceasing*; renewed 106 *repeated*; indomitable, undaunted 599 *resolute*.

Verb

(4) *persevere,* persist, keep at it, not despair, never say die; hope on 852 *hope*; endure 825 *suffer*; try, keep on trying 671 *attempt*; maintain, keep up 146 *sustain*; plod, slog away, peg a., work at 682 *work*; continue, go on, keep on, keep going; not let go, hold fast 778 *retain*; hang on, stick it out, sweat it out, stay the course, stick with it, see it through; stick to one's guns 602 *be obstinate*; hold out 599 *stand firm*; die in harness; spare no pains 682 *exert oneself*; complete 725 *carry through*.

Adverb

(5) *persistently,* never say die; sink or swim 599 *resolutely*; through thick and thin.

601
Irresolution

Noun
(1) *irresolution,* loss of nerve, faintheartedness 856 *cowardice*; broken resolve, broken promise; hesitation, indecision, uncertainty 474 *dubiety*; inconstancy, vacillation, fickleness 604 *caprice*; lack of willpower, lack of drive 175 *inertness*; passivity 679 *inactivity*; compromise 734 *laxity*; half measures, half-heartedness; apathy 860 *indifference*; weak will 163 *weakness*; pliancy 612 *persuadability*.

(2) *waverer,* shuttlecock, butterfly 152 *changeable thing*; floating voter; chameleon, turncoat 603 *tergiversator*; faintheart.

Adjective

(3) *irresolute,* undecided, indecisive, in two minds 474 *doubting*; hesitating 598 *unwilling*; timid, faint-hearted, nerveless 856 *cowardly*; shaken, rattled 854 *nervous*; half-hearted, lukewarm 860 *indifferent*; compromising, weak-willed, weak-kneed, spineless 163 *weak*; easygoing, good-natured 734 *lax*; inconstant, variable, temperamental 152 *changeful*; whimsical, mercurial 604 *capricious*; emotional, restless, uncommitted, irresponsible 456 *light-minded*.

Verb

(4) *be irresolute,* not know one's own mind; blow hot and cold 518 *be equivocal*; fluctuate, vacillate, seesaw, wobble, waver, hover, teeter, dither 317 *oscillate*; hum and haw 474 *be uncertain*; delay, 136 *put off*; debate, balance 475 *argue*; have second thoughts, hesitate 858 *be cautious*; falter, not persevere, give up 621 *relinquish*, 770 *compromise*; yield, give way 721 *submit*; change sides 603 *apostatize*.

Adverb

(5) *irresolutely,* hesitantly etc. adj.

602
Obstinacy

Noun

(1) *obstinacy*, determination, will 599 *resolution*; grimness, doggedness, pertinacity 600 *perseverance*; stubbornness, obduracy, obdurateness; self-will, pigheadedness; inflexibility, intransigence, hard line, no compromise; stiff neck, contumacy 715 *resistance*; mulishness, sulkiness 893 *sullenness*; perversity, cussedness.

(2) *opinionatedness*, dogmatism, bigotry, zealotry 473 *positiveness*; intolerance, fanaticism 735 *severity*; ruling passion, obsession 481 *bias*; illiberality, old school.

(3) *obstinate person*, stubborn p., mule; hard-liner, hard core; stickler, pedant, dogmatist; fanatic, zealot, bigot 481 *narrow mind*; sticker, stayer; diehard 600 *stamina*; old fogy 504 *crank*.

Adjective

(4) *obstinate*, stubborn; pigheaded, mulish; unyielding, determined 599 *resolute*; dogged, tenacious 600 *persevering*; stiff, adamant, inflexible, unbending, obdurate, uncompromising, intransigent; immovable, implacable 906 *pitiless*; set, wedded to, hidebound 610 *habituated*; impervious, blind, deaf; opinionated, dogmatic 473 *positive*; bigoted, fanatical 481 *biased*; stiff-necked, contumacious 940 *impenitent*; perverse, incorrigible, bloody-minded.

(5) *wilful*, self-willed, wayward, arbitrary; headstrong, perverse; unruly, restive, refractory; irrepressible, incorrigible, intractable 738 *disobedient*; crotchety 892 *irascible*.

Verb

(6) *be obstinate*, stubborn etc. adj.; persist 600 *persevere*; stand out against, not budge 599 *stand firm*; insist, want one's own way 734 *please oneself*; not listen, take no advice 857 *be rash*.

Adverb

(7) *obstinately*, mulishly; over one's dead body.

603
Tergiversation

Noun

(1) *tergiversation*, change of mind; second thoughts 67 *sequel*; change of allegiance, conversion; change of purpose, new resolve; repentance 939 *penitence*; backsliding, recidivism 657 *relapse*; about-face, about-turn, U-turn, volte-face 286 *return*; versatility, slipperiness, suppleness; apostasy, defection, desertion 918 *undutifulness*; treachery 930 *perfidy*; secession, withdrawal 978 *schism*; change of mood, coquetry 604 *caprice*.

(2) *recantation*, eating one's words, retraction, withdrawal, apology; renunciation, abjuration, forswearing; revocation, disavowal, disclaimer, denial 533 *negation*

(3) *tergiversator*, turncoat, rat; opportunist, timeserver, trimmer 518 *equivocalness*; doubledealer 545 *deceiver*; jilt, flirt, coquette 604 *caprice*; apostate, renegade, traitor 938 *knave*; quisling, fifth columnist 707 *collaborator*; deserter, defector; squealer 524 *informer*; blackleg, scab; recidivist, backslider 904 *offender*; convert 147 *changed person*.

Adjective

(4) *tergiversating*, trimming etc. vb.; shuffling 518 *equivocal*;

slippery, supple, treacherous 541 *hypocritical*; fickle 604 *capricious*; time-serving 925 *flattering*; vacillating 601 *irresolute*; apostate, recanting, renegade; recidivist, relapsed; false, unfaithful, disloyal 918 *undutiful*.

Verb

(5) *tergiversate,* change one's mind, think again, think better of 601 *be irresolute*; change one's tune, shift one's ground 152 *vary*; get cold feet, back out, scratch, withdraw 753 *resign*; back down, crawl 872 *be humbled*; repent 939 *be penitent*; reform, mend one's ways 654 *get better*; fall back, backslide 657 *relapse*; trim, shuffle, face both ways 518 *be equivocal*; ditch, jilt, throw over, desert, walk out on 918 *fail in duty*; forsake, abandon 621 *relinquish*; turn against, play false.

(6) *apostatize,* change sides, switch over, cross the floor; desert, defect; blackleg, rat; betray, collaborate 930 *be dishonest;*

(7) *recant,* eat one's words, apologize; take back, go back on, backpedal, backtrack; withdraw, retract, disavow, disclaim, repudiate 533 *negate*; renounce, abjure, forswear, swear off; revoke, rescind 752 *abrogate*.

604
Caprice

Noun

(1) *caprice,* arbitrariness, whimsicality, inconsistency; crankiness, faddishness 481 *bias*; fitfulness, changeability, variability, fickleness, levity, giddiness, inconstancy, playfulness; fretfulness, 892 ░░░░ility.

(2) *whim,* whimsy, caprice, fancy, fantastic notion; passing fancy, impulse 609 *spontaneity*; vagary, sweet will, humour, mood, fit; quirk, kink, fad, craze, bee in one's bonnet 503 *eccentricity*; escapade, prank 497 *foolery*; coquetry, flirtation.

Adjective

(3) *capricious,* whimsical, fanciful, fantastic; eccentric, temperamental, crotchety; mischievous, wanton, wayward, perverse; faddy, faddish, particular 862 *fastidious*; captious, arbitrary, unreasonable; fretful, moody, contrary 892 *irascible*; refractory 602 *wilful*; erratic, unpredictable 508 *unexpected*; volatile, mercurial, skittish, giddy, frivolous 456 *light-minded*; inconsistent, inconstant, variable 152 *unstable*; unreliable, irresponsible, feckless; fickle, flirtatious, coquettish, playful.

Verb

(4) *be capricious,* whimsical etc. adj.; pick and choose 862 *be fastidious*; chop and change 152 *vary*; be fickle, vacillate 601 *be irresolute*; play tricks 497 *be absurd*; flirt, coquette 837 *amuse oneself*.

Adverb

(5) *capriciously,* fitfully, now this, now that; on impulse.

605
Choice

Noun

(1) *choice,* act of choosing 463 *discrimination*; picking out, selection; co-option, co-optation, adoption; appointment 751 *commission*; right of choice, option; freedom of choice, discretion, pick; decision 480 *judgment*; preference, predilection, partiality, inclination, leaning, bias 179 *tendency*;

taste 859 *liking*; availability 759 *offer*; range of choice, selection, short list; possible choice, alternative; difficult choice, dilemma 474 *dubiety*; limited choice; 606 *no choice*; desirability 642 *good policy*; one's preference, favour, fancy, first choice; thing chosen, selection; favouritism 914 *injustice*.

(2) *vote,* voice 485 *opinion*; representation, proportional r.; ballot, secret b., open vote, card v.; show of hands, division; poll, plebiscite, referendum; franchise, suffrage, universal s., ballot box, vox populi; polling, straw vote, opinion poll; election, general e.; by-election; polls, hustings, candidature; psephology, psephologist; suffragette.

(3) *electorate,* voters, electors, quorum; electoral roll, voting list; constituency, marginal c.; slate, ticket, manifesto.

Adjective
(4) *choosing,* optional 595 *volitional*; choosy 463 *discriminating*; favouring 923 *approving*; selective, eclectic; co-optative, elective, electoral; voting, enfranchised; vote-catching; electioneering, canvassing.

(5) *chosen,* worth choosing, preferable, better 642 *advisable*; select, choice, recherche, picked, hand-p. 644 *excellent*; sorted 62 *arranged*; elect, designate; elected, returned; adopted, selected; preferred, favourite.

Verb
(6) *choose,* make one's choice; have a voice, have free will 595 *will*; shop around, be choosy; opt for, elect, co-opt, adopt 923 *approve*; favour, fancy, like best; incline, lean 179 *tend*; prefer, have a preference, like better; might as well, might do worse; decide, make up one's

mind 480 *judge*; settle on, fix on, come out for, commit oneself; take the plunge, cross the Rubicon 599 *be resolute*; range oneself, take sides, side, back, support, embrace, espouse 703 *patronize*.

(7) *select,* pick, pick out, single o.; pass 923 *approve*; nominate, appoint 751 *commission*; designate, mark down 547 *mark*; earmark, reserve 46 *set apart*; recommend, put up, propose, second 703 *patronize*; excerpt, cull 592 *abstract*; winnow, sift 463 *discriminate*; draw the line, separate; skim off, cream, pick the best; pick and choose 862 *be fastidious*.

(8) *vote,* have a v., have a voice; have the vote, be enfranchised; cast a vote, register one's v., vote for, vote in, elect, return; vote down 607 *reject*; electioneer, canvass; count heads; put to the vote, hold an election.

Adverb
(9) *optionally,* alternatively, either ... or; preferably, rather; a la carte.

606
Absence of choice

Noun
(1) *no choice,* Hobson's c., no alternative 596 *necessity*; dictation 740 *compulsion*; impartiality 913 *justice*; no preference, nonalignment, neutrality 860 *indifference*; no difference 28 *equality*; indecision, open mind 474 *dubiety*; floating vote 601 *irresolution*; abstention.

Adjective
(2) *choiceless,* necessitated 596 *necessary*; happy either way 625 *neutral*; open-minded, undecided 601 *irresolute*; uninterested, apathetic 860 *indifferent*; impartial 913 *just*; not voting.

abstaining; without a vote, disfranchised.

Verb
(3) *be neutral,* take no sides, make no choice, not vote, abstain; sit on the fence 601 *be irresolute;* not care 860 *be indifferent.*

(4) *have no choice,* have no alternative 596 *be forced;* have no voice, have no vote.

Adverb
(5) *neither,* neither ... nor.

607
Rejection

Noun
(1) *rejection,* nonacceptance; disapproval repudiation 924 *disapprobation;* 533 *negation;* apostasy 603 *recantation;* rebuff, repulse, cold shoulder 760 *refusal;* lost election 728 *defeat;* elimination 300 *ejection;* discard, reject, wallflower; lost cause.

Adjective
(2) *rejected,* declined etc. vb.; ineligible, unsuitable; returned, sent back 860 *unwanted;* kept out 57 *excluded;* discarded 674 *disused.*

Verb
(3) *reject,* not accept, decline; rebuff, repulse, spurn 760 *refuse;* return, send back 924 *disapprove;* not consider, pass over, ignore 458 *disregard;* outvote 489 *dissent;* scrap, discard, ditch, throw away, throw aside 674 *stop using;* disallow, revoke 752 *abrogate;* expel, throw out, 300 *eject;* sort out 44 *eliminate;* except 57 *exclude;* blackball, cold-shoulder 885 *be rude;* not want, not cater for 883 *make unwelcome;* disclaim, disavow 533 *negate;* repudiate 603 re-ᵖᵃⁿt; scorn, disdain 922 *hold*

608
Predetermination

Noun
(1) *predetermination,* predestination 596 *necessity;* preordination 155 *destiny;* decree 595 *will;* premeditation 617 *intention;* frame-up, put-up job 623 *plot;* closed mind 481 *prejudice;* foregone conclusion.

Adjective
(2) *predetermined,* decreed, appointed etc. vb.; predestined, foreordained 596 *fated;* deliberate, willed, aforethought 617 *intending;* designed, calculated; weighed, considered; devised, contrived 623 *planned;* put-up, framed, stacked, prearranged 669 *prepared.*

Verb
(3) *predetermine,* destine, appoint, foreordain, predestinate 155 *predestine;* premeditate 617 *intend;* contrive, arrange, prearrange 623 *plan;* frame, put up, stack the cards 541 *fake.*

609
Spontaneity

Noun
(1) *spontaneity,* unpremeditation, improvisation; ad-libbing, impromptu 670 *nonpreparation;* reflex, automatic r.; impulsiveness, impulse 476 *intuition;* snap decision; inspiration, hunch, flash 451 *idea.*

(2) *improviser,* extemporizer.

Adjective
(3) *spontaneous,* offhand, ad hoc, improvised; sudden, snap; makeshift, impromptu, unpremediated 670 *unprepared;* unmotivated, unprovoked; unguarded 857 *rash;* natural,

instinctive, involuntary 476 *intuitive*; artless; impulsive, emotional 818 *feeling*.

Verb
(4) *improvise*, extemporize, adlib; obey an impulse, 604 *be capricious*; blurt, come out with.

Adverb
(5) *extempore*, impromptu, ad hoc, off the cuff; on the spur of the moment.

610
Habit

Noun
(1) *habit*, disposition, habit of mind 5 *temperament*; force of habit; familiarity, second nature; addiction, confirmed habit; trait, idiosyncrasy; knack, trick, mannerism; usage, custom 146 *continuance*; tradition, law, precedent; ways, way of life, lifestyle; fixed ways, groove, rut; regularity round, daily r. 16 *uniformity*; routine, drill, system 60 *order*; conservatism 83 *conformity*.

(2) *practice*, common p., usual custom, usual policy, matter of course; conformism 83 *conformity*; mores, social usage; institution, ritual, observance 988 *rite*; vogue, craze 848 *fashion*; convention, protocol, unwritten law, done thing; procedure, drill; good form 848 *etiquette*; manners, table m.; standing order, rules and regulations; routine 688 *conduct*.

(3) *habituation*, training 534 *teaching*; inurement, seasoning, hardening 669 *maturation*; conditioning, conditioned reflex; drill 106 *repetition*.

(4) *habitué*, creature of habit, addict, drug a. 949 *drug-taking*; traditionalist 83 *conformist*; customer, regular, client 792

purchaser; devotee, fan 504 *enthusiast*.

Adjective
(5) *habitual*, customary, familiar 490 *known*; routine 81 *regular*; conventional, traditional 976 *orthodox*; time-honoured 113 *lasting*; occupational; haunting, besetting, obsessive; habit-forming 612 *inducing*; ingrained 5 *intrinsic*; deep-rooted, deep-seated, implanted 153 *fixed*.

(6) *usual*, accustomed, wonted, traditional; in character, natural; familiar, well-known 490 *known*; trite, well-worn, hackneyed; banal, commonplace, common, ordinary 79 *general*; stock 83 *typical*; widespread 79 *universal*; daily, everyday 139 *frequent*; practised, done; settled, established 923 *approved*; invariable 740 *compelling*; in vogue 848 *fashionable*.

(7) *habituated*, accustomed to, given to, addicted to; devoted to, wedded to; used to, familiar with, conversant w., at home in 490 *knowing*; inveterate, confirmed; practised, inured, seasoned, hardened 669 *prepared*; trained 369 *tamed*; naturalized, acclimatized.

Verb

be used to; haunt, frequent; make a habit of, take up, go in for; become a habit, catch on; settle, take root; be the rule, obtain, hold good 178 *prevail*.

(8) *habituate*, accustom oneself, get used to, get into the way of; take to, acquire the habit; practise 106 *repeat*; accustom, inure, season, harden 534 *train*; domesticate, tame 369 *break in*; naturalize, acclimatize; implant, imbue 534 *teach*; condition, brainwash 178 *influence*.

Adverb

(9) *habitually*, regularly 141 *periodically*; as usual; automatically, by force of habit.

611
Desuetude

Noun

(1) *desuetude*, disuse 674 *non-use*; rust, decay 655 *deterioration*; lost habit, lost skill, rustiness, lack of practice; unwontedness, unfamiliarity; unconventionality 84 *nonconformity*; want of habit, inexperience.

Adjective

(2) *unwonted*, not customary, not current, not observed, not done; bad form 847 *vulgar*; out of fashion, old-fashioned 125 *past*; discarded 674 *disused*; against custom, unprecedented 21 *original*.

(3) *unhabituated*, unaccustomed, not in the habit of, not used to; not broken in, undomesticated; inexperienced, new to, unfamiliar; new, raw, fresh, green; rusty 695 *unskilful*.

Verb

(4) *disaccustom*, wean from, cure of 656 *cure*; break a habit, give up, outgrow.

(5) *be unpractised*, unfashionable etc. adj.; not catch on; not be done, offend custom; lapse, fall into disuse.

612
Motive

Noun

(1) *motive*, cause of action, 156 *cause*; rationale, reasons, grounds 156 *reason why*; motivation, driving force, impetus, mainspring 156 *causation*; intention 617 *objective*; ideal, guiding star, guiding principle; aspiration 852 *hope*; ambition 859 *desire*; calling 622 *vocation*; conscience, honour 917 *duty*; shame 854 *fear*; ulterior motive 932 *selfishness*; impulse, inspiration 609 *spontaneity*.

(2) *inducement*, pressure, urgency, insistence; lobbying 178 *influence*; provocation, urging, incitement, encouragement, incitation, instigation, prompting, inspiration 821 *excitation*; support 703 *aid*; solicitation 761 *request*; temptation, enticement, allurement, seduction, seductiveness, witchery, bewitchment, fascination, charm, sex appeal, magnetism, attraction; cajolery, blandishment 925 *flattery*; coaxing, wheedling 889 *endearment*; persuasion, salesmanship, sales talk 579 *eloquence*; pep talk, rallying cry 547 *call*; exhortation, castigation; pleading, advocacy 691 *advice*; propaganda, advertising 528 *advertisement*; promises, bribery, graft 962 *reward*; honeyed words, siren song, winning ways.

(3) *persuadability*, tractability 597 *willingness*; pliancy 327 *softness*; susceptibility, sensitivity, emotionalism 819 *moral sensibility*; credulousness 487 *credulity*.

(4) *incentive*, inducement; stimulus, prod, spur, goad, lash, whip; big stick 900 *threat*; carrot 174 *stimulant*; charm 983 *spell*; attraction, lure, bait 542 *trap*; profit 771 *gain*; bonus 804 *payment*; donation, handout 781 *gift*; gratuity, tip, bribe, hush money, slush fund 962 *reward*; pork barrel; golden apple, forbidden fruit; tempting offer, 759 *offer*.

(5) *motivator*, mover, prime m. 156 *cause*; manipulator, manager, wire-puller 178 *influence*;

manoeuvrer, tactician, strategist 623 *planner*; instigator, prompter, suggester, inspirer, counsellor 691 *adviser*; abettor, aider and abettor 703 *aider*; 545 *deceiver*; tantalizer, tempter, seducer; temptress, vamp, femme fatale, siren; hypnotist; persuader, orator, rhetorician 579 *speaker*; advocate, pleader; 925 *flatterer*; vote-catcher, vote-snatcher; salesman, advertiser, propagandist ringleader 690 *leader*; firebrand rabble-rouser 738 *agitator*; lobbyist, lobby, pressure group, ginger g.

Adjective

(6) *inducing*, inciting; incentive, provocative, persuasive; motivating 178 *influential*; stimulating, challenging, encouraging, rousing, inflaming 821 *exciting*; prompting, insinuating, hinting; teasing, tantalizing; inviting, tempting, alluring 291 *attracting*; magnetic, fascinating, bewitching; hypnotic, mesmeric; habit-forming 610 *habitual*.

(7) *induced*, brought on 157 *caused*; inspired, motivated, incited, spurred on 821 *excited*; receptive 597 *willing*; spellbound 983 *bewitched*.

Verb

(8) *motivate*, actuate, work upon, play u., act u., operate u. 178 *influence*; weigh, count, sway 178 *prevail*; appeal, challenge, inject with, infuse into 534 *educate*; interest, intrigue 821 *impress*; charm, fascinate, captivate, hypnotize 983 *bewitch*; pull 291 *attract*; push 279 *impel*; force 740 *compel*; bend, incline, dispose; predispose, prejudice 481 *bias*; predestine 608 *predetermine*; lead, direct 689 *manage*; lead astray 495 *mislead*; give a lead, set the fashion, set an example 283 *precede*.

(9) *incite*, energize, galvanize, stimulate 174 *invigorate*; encourage, cheer on, root for 855 *give courage*; inspire, animate, provoke, rouse, rally 821 *excite*; evoke, call forth; exhort, invite, urge, insist, press, lobby; nag, needle, goad, prod, spur, prick; whip, lash, flog; spur on, set on; drive 680 *hasten*; instigate, prompt, put up to; aid and abet 703 *aid*; insinuate 524 *hint*; advocate 691 *advise*; kindle 68 *initiate*.

(10) *induce*, instigate, bring about 156 *cause*; persuade, carry with one 485 *convince*; prevail upon, talk into, nag i., bully i., browbeat, twist one's arm 740 *compel*; wear down, soften up; bring round, talk round, win over procure, enlist, engage; seduce, cajole 925 *flatter*; conciliate 719 *pacify*.

(11) *tempt*, try, entice, tantalize, tease; lure, inveigle 542 *ensnare*; coax, wheedle 889 *pet*.

(12) *bribe*, hold out 759 *offer*; suborn, corrupt; buy off; grease one's palm 962 *reward*.

(13) *be induced*, succumb 721 *submit*; fall for 487 *be credulous*; concede 758 *consent*.

613
Dissuasion

Noun

(1) *dissuasion*, discouragement 664 *warning*; deterrence 854 *intimidation*; expostulation, remonstrance, reproof, admonition 762 *deprecation*; rebuff 715 *resistance*; no encouragement, disincentive; damper, wet blanket; killjoy, spoilsport 702 *hinderer*.

Adjective

(2) *dissuasive*, discouraging, damping; reluctant 762 *deprecatory*; warning against 664 *cautionary*.

Verb

(3) *dissuade,* persuade against, advise a., argue a., talk out of 479 *confute*; caution 664 *warn*; remonstrate, castigate 924 *reprove*; expostulate, cry out against 762 *deprecate*; give one pause 486 *cause doubt*; intimidate 900 *threaten*; deter, frighten away 854 *frighten*; steer away from, wean away from, head off, turn one aside, deflect; hold one back 747 *restrain*; disincline, indispose; disenchant, disillusion, disaffect; set against, turn a., put off 861 *cause dislike*; dishearten, discourage, dispirit 834 *depress*; crush, quench, dampen, cool, chill, damp one's ardour; calm, quiet 177 *moderate*.

614
Pretext

Noun

(1) *pretext,* allegation, profession, claim 532 *affirmation*; plea, excuse, defence, apology, justification 927 *vindication*; loophole, alibi 667 *means of escape*; thin excuse, lame e.; special pleading, quibble 477 *sophism*; proviso 468 *qualification*; subterfuge 698 *stratagem*; pretence 543 *untruth*; blind, smoke screen, cloak, cover 421 *screen*; colour, gloss, guise 445 *appearance*; bluff, sour grapes.

Adjective

(2) *ostensible,* alleged, pretended; specious, plausible.

(3) *excusing,* self-e., apologetic; exculpatory, apologetic, justificatory 927 *vindicating*.

Verb

(4) *plead,* allege, claim, profess 532 *affirm*; make one's pretext 475 *argue*; make excuses, excuse oneself, defend o. 927 *justify*; gloss over, palliate 927 *extenuate*; shelter under 137

profit by; find a loophole, wriggle out of 667 *escape*; bluff, pretend, affect 541 *dissemble*.

Adverb

(5) *ostensibly,* as an excuse, on the plea of.

615
Good

Noun

(1) *good,* one's g.; the best; greater good 642 *good policy*; well-being, welfare 730 *prosperity*; riches 800 *wealth*; luck, good fortune; 824 *happiness*; blessing, benediction 897 *benevolence*.

(2) *benefit,* advantage, interest; service, convenience 640 *utility*; profit 771 *gain*; betterment 654 *improvement*; boon 781 *gift*; good turn 897 *kind act*; favour, blessing, godsend, windfall, piece of luck, find, prize; the very thing, just the t. 859 *desired object*.

Adjective

(3) *good,* goodly, fine; blessed, beatific 824 *happy*; advantageous, gainful 640 *profitable*; heaven-sent 644 *beneficial*; worthwhile 644 *valuable*; helpful 706 *cooperative*; praiseworthy, commendable, recommended 923 *approved*; pleasure-giving 826 *pleasurable*.

Verb

(4) *benefit,* favour, bless; do good, help 654 *make better*; serve, profit; 640 *be useful*; pay, repay 771 *be profitable*; turn out well.

(5) *flourish,* thrive, do well 730 *prosper*; arrive 727 *succeed*; benefit by, gain by, improve 654 *get better*; cash in on 137 *profit by*; make a profit 771 *gain*; make money 800 *get rich*.

Adverb

(6) *well,* favourably, profitably,

to one's advantage; for the best, all to the good.

616
Evil

Noun

(1) *evil,* disservice, injury, dirty trick 930 *foul play*; wrong, outrage 914 *injustice*; shame, abuse; curse, scourge, poison, pest, plague 659 *bane*; sad world, vale of tears; ill, trouble, troubles 731 *adversity*; affliction, misery, distress 825 *suffering*; grief, woe 825 *sorrow*; unease, malaise, discomfort 825 *worry*; nuisance 827 *annoyance*; hurt, bodily harm, wound, bruise 377 *pain*; blow, mortal b. 279 *knock*; calamity, bad luck 731 *misfortune*; accident 154 *event*; fatality 361 *death*; catastrophe 165 *ruin*; tragedy, sad ending 655 *deterioration*; mischief, harm, damage 772 *loss*; ill effect, bad result; disadvantage, drawback, 647 *defect*; setback 702 *hitch*; evil plight 700 *predicament*; indigence 801 *poverty*; sense of injury, grievance 829 *discontent*.

Adjective

(2) *evil,* wicked 934 *vicious*; black, foul, shameful 914 *wrong*; bad, too bad 645 *damnable*; unlucky, inauspicious, sinister 731 *adverse*; insidious, injurious, prejudicial 645 *harmful*; trouble-making 898 *maleficent*; troublous 827 *distressing*; fatal 362 *deadly*; ruinous, disastrous 165 *destructive*; catastrophic, calamitous, tragic 731 *unfortunate*; all wrong, awry.

Adverb

(3) *amiss,* awry; sour; to one's cost.

617
Intention

Noun

(1) *intention,* intent, meaning; calculated risk 480 *estimate*; purpose, determination, resolve 599 *resolution*; criminal intent 936 *guilt*; good intentions 897 *benevolence*; prospect, proposal 124 *looking ahead*; study, pursuit; project, design 623 *plan*; enterprise 672 *undertaking*; ambition 859 *desire*; decision 480 *judgment*; bid for 671 *attempt*; engagement 764 *promise*.

(2) *objective,* destination; object, end in view, aim; axe to grind; target 295 *goal*; Mecca 76 *focus*; quarry, prey 619 *chase*; prize, crown 729 *trophy*; dream, aspiration, vision 513 *ideality*; heart's desire 859 *desired object*.

Adjective

(3) *intending,* intent on, hellbent 599 *resolute*; intentional, deliberate; minded, disposed, inclined 597 *willing*; aspiring, prospective, ambitious 859 *desiring*.

(4) *intended,* deliberate, intentional, studied, designed, purposed, purposeful, aforethought 608 *predetermined*.

Verb

(5) *intend,* purpose, have in mind, have in view, contemplate, meditate; reckon on, look for 507 *expect*; mean to 599 *be resolute*; resolve, determine 608 *predetermine*; design, plan for 623 *plan*; shoulder 672 *undertake*; engage 764 *promise*; threaten to 900 *threaten*; destine for 155 *predestine*; mark down for, earmark 547 *mark*; have an eye to.

(6) *aim at,* make one's target, go for, go after, strive after 619

pursue; try for, bid f., endeavour 671 *attempt*; have designs on, promise oneself, aspire to, dream of 859 *desire*; train one's sights on, take aim, level at 281 *aim*.

Adverb
(7) *purposely,* on purpose, in cold blood, deliberately, intentionally; designedly, advisedly; for, for a purpose, in order to, with the object of.

618
Nondesign. Gamble

Noun
(1) *nondesign,* indeterminacy, unpredictability 159 *chance*; instinct 609 *spontaneity*; coincidence, accident, fluke, luck 154 *event*; lottery 159 *equal chance*; lot, wheel of Fortune 596 *fate*.

(2) *gambling,* taking a chance, risk-taking; risk, hazard, leap in the dark 661 *danger*; gamble, potluck 159 *chance*; venture, speculation, flutter 461 *experiment*; blind bargain 474 *uncertainty*; bid, throw; wager, bet, stake; desperate bid 857 *rashness*; dice, cards; bingo; fruit machine; roulette 837 *gambling game*; betting, football pools; draw, lottery, raffle, tombola, sweepstake; futures.

(3) *gaming-house,* gambling den; betting shop; casino, amusement arcade; racecourse, turf.

(4) *gambler,* player, better, backer, punter; bookmaker, tout, tipster; risk-taker; adventurer, entrepreneur 672 *undertaking*; speculator 461 *experimenter*.

Adjective
(5) *unintentional,* inadvertent,

not meant 596 *involuntary*; unrehearsed 609 *spontaneous*; accidental, fortuitous, coincidental 159 *casual*.

(6) *designless,* aimless, purposeless; motiveless 159 *causeless*; random, haphazard 464 *indiscriminate*; happy-go-lucky, devil-may-care.

(7) *speculative,* experimental 474 *uncertain*; hazardous, risky, chancy; risk-taking, venturesome, adventurous, enterprising.

Verb
(8) *gamble,* game, play, do the pools; throw, dice, bet, stake, wager, lay; take bets, offer odds, make a book; back, punt; hedge 660 *seek safety*; play the market, speculate 461 *experiment*; hazard, risk, run a r., take risks 857 *be rash*; push one's luck, tempt Providence; buy blind, 857 *be rash*; venture, chance it, try one's luck; raffle, draw, draw lots, toss up.

Adverb
(9) *at random,* on the off-chance.

619
Pursuit

Noun
(1) *pursuit,* pursuance, follow-up 65 *sequence*; hunting, seeking, looking for, quest 459 *search*; tracking, trailing, dogging 284 *following*; hounding, persecution, witch-hunt; persistence 600 *perseverance*.

(2) *chase,* steeplechase 716 *racing*; hunt, hue and cry, tally-ho; shooting, hunting 837 *sport*; blood sport, fox hunt, stag h.; big-game h., pigsticking; stalking, deer s.; hawking, fowling, falconry; fishing, angling, fly fishing, coarse f., sea f.; inshore f., deep-sea f., whaling; trapping, ferreting, rabbiting; fishing tackle, rod and

line; manhunt, dragnet 542 *trap*; game, quarry, prey, victim.

(3) *hunter,* seeker, searcher, search party; pursuer, tracker, trailer, shadow; huntsman, huntswoman; huntress, Diana; whip, whipper-in; beater; gun, shot, good s. 287 *shooter*; headhunter 362 *killer*; big-game hunter, fox h., deer stalker; poacher, trout-tickler; trapper, rat-catcher, rodent officer; bird catcher, fowler, falconer, hawker; fisherman *or* woman, fisher, angler, trawler, whaler; field, pack; foxhound, bloodhound 365 *dog*; man-eater 365 *mammal*; mouser 365 *cat*.

Adjective
(4) *pursuing,* seeking, questing 459 *enquiring*; in quest of, sent after; on one's tail, in pursuit, in hot p., in full cry, on the scent, on the trail 284 *following*; hunting, shooting; fishing, piscatorial.

Verb
(5) *pursue,* seek, look for, cast about for; be gunning for, hunt for, fish for, dig for 459 *search*; stalk, shadow, dog, track, trail, tail, follow the scent 284 *follow*; scent out 484 *discover*; witchhunt, harry, persecute 735 *oppress*; chase, give c., hunt, run down, ride d. 712 *charge*; make one's quarry 617 *aim at*; run after, woo 889 *court*; pursue one's ends 617 *intend*; follow up, persist 600 *persevere*.

(6) *hunt,* go hunting, go shooting, ride to hounds; go fishing, cast one's net, fish, shrimp, angle, trawl; net, catch 542 *ensnare*; set snares, poach.

Adverb
(7) *pursuant to,* in pursuance of, in quest of, after; on the track,

620
Avoidance

Noun
(1) *avoidance,* abstinence, abstention 942 *temperance*; forbearance 177 *moderation*; refusal 607 *rejection*; inaction 679 *inactivity*; evasiveness 518 *equivocalness*; evasive action, dodge, duck, sidestep; delaying action, retreat, withdrawal 286 *regression*; evasion, flight 667 *escape*; jibbing, shrinking 854 *fear*; shunning, wide berth, safe distance; shirking 458 *negligence*; revulsion 280 *recoil*; escapism 190 *absence*.

(2) *avoider,* evader, tax e. 545 *trickster*; quitter 856 *coward*; shirker 679 *idler*; skulker 527 *hider*; truant, deserter 918 *undutifulness;* runaway, fugitive 667 *escaper*; escapist 513 *visionary*; head in the sand ostrich.

Adjective
(3) *avoiding,* shunning; evasive, elusive, slippery, hard to catch; shy 874 *modest*; shrinking 854 *nervous*; backward, reluctant 598 *unwilling*; noncommittal 582 *taciturn*; passive 679 *inactive*; not involved, uncommitted 625 *neutral*; fugitive, hunted, runaway 667 *escaped*; hiding 523 *latent*.

(4) *avoidable,* escapable, preventable.

Verb
(5) *avoid,* not go near, keep off, keep away; bypass, circumvent 282 *deviate*; turn aside, coldshoulder 883 *make unwelcome*; hold aloof, stand apart, shun, eschew, leave, let alone; fight shy, back away, draw back 290 *recede*; keep clear, stand c., keep one's distance, give a wide berth; forbear, spare; refrain, abstain, do without; hold back, hang b., balk at 598 *be unwilling*; shelve, postpone 136 *put*

off; pass the buck, shirk 458 *neglect*; shrink, flinch, jib, shy; sidestep, dodge, duck; deflect, ward off 713 *parry*; avoid the issue, fudge the i., get round, obviate, skirt round, fence, hedge, pussyfoot 518 *be equivocal*; escape, evade 667 *elude*; hide 523 *lurk*.

(6) *run away*, desert, play truant, jump bail, take French leave 918 *fail in duty*; abscond, welsh, flit, elope 667 *escape*; withdraw, retire, retreat, turn tail 282 *turn round*; flee, fly, take to flight, be off, make o., bolt, run, cut and run 277 *move fast*; steal away, sneak off 296 *decamp*.

621
Relinquishment

Noun

(1) *relinquishment*, abandonment; going, leaving, evacuation 296 *departure*; desertion, truancy, defection 918 *undutifulness*; withdrawal, walk-out 620 *avoidance*; yielding, giving up, handing over 780 *transfer*; renunciation 779 *nonretention*; retirement 753 *resignation*; disuse 611 *desuetude*.

Adjective

(2) *relinquished*, forsaken, abandoned etc. vb.; waived 779 *not retained*.

Verb

(3) *relinquish*, drop, let go 779 *not retain*; surrender, resign, give up, yield; waive, forgo; lower one's sights 872 *be humble*; cede, hand over, transfer 780 *assign*; forfeit 772 *lose*; renounce, not proceed with; deny oneself, abstain 620 *avoid*; cast off, divest 229 *doff*; drop, discard 674 *stop using*; lose interest 860 *be indifferent*; abdicate, back down, stand down, withdraw, retire, drop out 753 *resign*; give in 721 *submit*;

leave, quit, move out, vacate, evacuate 296 *depart*; forsake, abandon, leave stranded; desert 918 *fail in duty*; play truant 190 *be absent*; walk out, strike 145 *cease*; throw over, jilt, break it off; cancel 752 *abrogate*.

622
Business

Noun

(1) *business*, affairs, interests, occupation, concern, care; aim, ambition 617 *intention*; case, agenda 154 *affairs*; enterprise, venture, undertaking, pursuit 678 *activity*; routine, daily round 610 *practice*; art, technology, industry, commerce, economics; business; business company 708 *corporation*; industrialism, manufacture, cottage industry 164 *production*; trade, craft, handicraft 694 *skill*; guild, union 706 *association*; employment, work; sideline, hobby, pastime 837 *amusement*.

(2) *vocation*, calling, life work, mission 751 *commission*; walk of life, career; self-imposed task 597 *voluntary work*; living, livelihood, daily bread; profession, metier, craft, trade; public service, public life.

(3) *job*, work, task, exercise 682 *labour*; chores, odd jobs 678 *activity*; duty, charge, commission, mission, errand 751 *mandate*; employ, service, employment, occupation; situation, position, berth, incumbency, appointment, post, office; full-time job, permanency; temporary job, part-time j.; opening, vacancy; employment agency, Job Centre,

(4) *function*, office, duty; area, realm, province, domain, orbit, sphere 183 *range*; beat, round; department, line; role, part;

business, job; responsibility, concern, care.

Adjective

(5) *businesslike*, efficient 694 *skilful*; industrious, busy 678 *active*; vocational, professional; industrial, technological, commercial, financial, mercantile; labour-intensive, capitali.; occupational, functional; official, governmental; routine, systematic 60 *orderly*; workaday 610 *habitual*; earning, employed, self-e., freelance.

Verb

(6) *employ*, busy, occupy, fill one's time; give employment, engage, recruit, hire, appoint 751 *commission*; fill a vacancy, staff with.

(7) *busy oneself*, work, work for 742 *serve*; be employed, do a job, earn one's living; have one's hands full 678 *be busy*; work at, turn one's hand to, engage in, take up, go in for; take on oneself 917 *incur a duty*; pursue a hobby 837 *amuse oneself*.

(8) *function*, work, go 173 *operate*; fill a role, play one's part; hold office; officiate, serve as, do duty for; stand in for 755 *deputize*.

(9) *do business*, transact, negotiate 766 *make terms*; ply a trade follow a calling, engage in, carry on; do business with, deal w. 791 *trade*.

623
Plan

Noun

(1) *plan*, scheme, design; planning, organization 60 *order*; programme, project, proposal 617 *intention*; proposition, suggestion, motion; master plan; scale drawing, blueprint 551 *map*; diagram, flow chart 86 *statistics*; sketch, outline, draft, first d., memorandum;

proof copy, pilot scheme 23 *prototype*; drawing board.

(2) *policy*, forethought 498 *wisdom*; course of action, plan of attack, procedure, strategy 688 *tactics*; approach 624 *way*; steps, measures 676 *action*; stroke of policy, coup 676 *deed*; proposed action, scenario, forecast 511 *prediction*; programme, prospectus, platform, plank, ticket, slate; line, party l.; formula 81 *rule*;. schedule, agenda 622 *business*.

(3) *contrivance*, expedient, resource, recourse, resort, trump card, 629 *means*; recipe 658 *remedy*; loophole, way out, alternative, answer 667 *means of escape*; artifice, device, gimmick, dodge, ploy, shift 698 *stratagem*; fiddle 930 *foul play*; knack, trick 694 *skill*; inspiration, bright idea 451 *idea*; notion, invention; tool, contraption, gadget 628 *instrument*; improvisation 609 *spontaneity*; makeshift 150 *substitute*; feat, tour de force; bold move, stroke, masterstroke 676 *deed*.

(4) *plot*, deep-laid p., intrigue, web of i., cabal, conspiracy; inside job; scheme, racket, game 698 *stratagem*; frame-up, machination; manipulation, wire-pulling 612 *motive*; secret influence 523 *latency*.

(5) *planner*, contriver etc. vb.; inventor, originator, proposer, promoter; founder, author, architect, designer; brains, mastermind; organizer, systematizer, systems analyst; strategist, tactician; wheeler-dealer, politician, careerist; schemer, axe-grinder; plotter, intriguer; conspirator 545 *deceiver*.

Adjective

(6) *planned*, blueprinted, schematic, worked out 669 *prepared*; organized, systematized

60 *orderly*; in draft, in proof; strategic, tactical; plotted, engineered.

(7) *planning,* contriving, resourceful, ingenious 698 *cunning*; purposeful, scheming, up to something; intriguing, plotting, conspiratorial, Machiavellian.

Verb

(8) *plan,* form a p., resolve 617 *intend*; make a plan, draw up, design, draft, blueprint; frame, shape, form; revise, recast 654 *rectify*; project, plan out, work o., sketch o., map o.; programme, organize, systematize, rationalize, schematize 60 *order*; schedule, phase, adjust; think up, hit on 484 *discover*; conceive a plan 513 *imagine*; find a way, make shift to; contrive, devise, engineer; hatch, concoct 669 *prepare*; arrange, prearrange 608 *predetermine*; calculate, think ahead 498 *be wise*.

(9) *plot,* scheme, have designs, wheel and deal; manipulate, pull strings 178 *influence*; cabal, conspire, intrigue, machinate; concoct, cook up, brew; hatch a plot 698 *be cunning*; undermine; 542 *ensnare*; work against; frame 541 *fake*.

624
Way

Noun

(1) *way,* route; manner, wise, guise; fashion, style 243 *form*; method, mode, line, approach, address, attack; procedure, way of, modus operandi 688 *tactics*; operation, treatment; usual way, routine 610 *practice*; technique, know-how 694 *skill*; way forward 285 *progression*; way of life, behaviour, lifestyle.

(2) *access,* means of a., right of way, way to 289 *approach*; entrance 263 *doorway*; drive, gangway, corridor; way through channel 351 *conduit*; way up 308 *ascent*.

(3) *bridge,* way over; flyover, aqueduct, viaduct, span; drawbridge; causeway, gangway, gangplank, catwalk, duckboards; stepping stones, ferry 305 *passage*; underpass 263 *tunnel*.

(4) *route,* direction, line, course, march, tack, track, beat; trajectory, orbit; lane, traffic l. 305 *traffic control*; seaway, fairway, waterway 351 *conduit*; trade route; short cut, bypass; detour 626 *circuit*.

(5) *path,* pathway, footpath, pavement, sidewalk; towpath, bridlepath, bridleway, ride; byway, lane, track, trail, mountain t.; right of way, public footpath; walk, promenade, esplanade; arcade, colonnade.

(6) *road,* high r., highway; main road, minor r., side r.; toll road, turnpike, thoroughfare, through road, trunk r., artery; bypass, ring road; motorway, expressway, clearway; crossroads, junction, intersection, roundabout, cloverleaf; crossing 305 *traffic control*; roadway, carriageway, dual c.; street, high s., back s.; alleyway, alley, blind a., cul de sac; avenue 192 *housing*; road building, traffic engineering.

(7) *railway,* railroad, line; permanent way, track, railway lines; main line, branch l.; tramway, tramlines; monorail; rack and-pinion, funicular; underground railway, subway, tube, metro 274 *train*; light railway, narrow gauge, standard g.; siding, marshalling yard, goods y.; station 145 *stopping place*.

Adjective

(8) *communicating,* granting access 289 *accessible*; through, main, arterial, trunk; bridged, crossed; paved, metalled, cobbled, tarmac; signposted, waymarked; lit, well-lit; well-trodden, beaten.

Adverb

(9) *via,* by way of.

625
Middleway

Noun

(1) *middle way,* middle course; golden mean, happy medium 30 *average*; intermediate technology; moderateness, central position, halfway 30 *middle point*; direct course, straight line, short cut, beeline; neutrality 177 *moderation*; lukewarmness, half measures.

(2) *moderate,* neutral, no extremist.

Adjective

(3) *neutral,* impartial 913 *just*; noncommittal uncommitted 860 *indifferent*; moderate, middle-of-the-road; half-and-half; grey.

(4) *undeviating,* direct 249 *straight*; in between, halfway, midway, intermediate.

Verb

(5) *be midstream,* hold straight on, steer a middle course.

(6) *be halfway,* go halfway, meet h., 770 *compromise*; occupy the centre ground; sit on the fence.

626
Circuit

Noun

(1) *circuit,* roundabout way, circuitous route; detour, loop, digression 282 *deviation*; circulation 314 *circuition*; full circle 250 *circle*.

Adjective

(2) *roundabout,* circuitous, indirect; out of the way.

Verb

(3) *circuit,* go round, make a circuit 314 *circle*; make a detour, go out of one's way 282 *deviate*; bypass 620 *avoid*; encircle 230 *surround*; skirt, edge round.

Adverb

(4) *round about,* circuitously, indirectly.

627
Requirement

Noun

(1) *requirement,* essential, sine qua non, a must 596 *necessity*; needs, necessities, necessaries; indent, order, requisition, shopping list; stipulation, prerequisite 766 *conditions*; want, lack, need 636 *insufficiency*; gap 190 *absence*; demand, call for, run on; consumption, input, intake; balance due 803 *debt*; claim 761 *request*; injunction 737 *command*.

(2) *needfulness,* necessity for, desirability; want, pinch 801 *poverty*; urgency, emergency 137 *crisis*; obligation 917 *duty*.

Adjective

(3) *required,* requisite, prerequisite, needful, needed; necessary, essential, vital, indispensable; called for, in request, in demand 859 *desired*; reserved, booked; wanted, lacking, missing 190 *absent*.

(4) *necessitous,* in want, in need, feeling the pinch; lacking, deprived of; needing badly, craving; starving, destitute 801 *poor*.

(5) *demanding,* crying out for, calling for, imperative, urgent, instant, exigent, pressing; compulsory 740 *compelling*.

Verb
(6) *require,* need, want, lack, stand in the need of; not have, be without, have occasion for; miss, crave 859 *desire*; call for, cry out f.; claim, apply for 761 *request*; find necessary, must have; consume, take 673 *use*; render necessary, necessitate, oblige 740 *compel*; stipulate 737 *demand*; order, requisition; reserve, book.

Adverb
(7) *in need,* in want; of necessity, at a pinch.

628
Instrumentality

Noun
(1) *instrumentality,* operation 173 *agency*; occasion 156 *cause*; pressure 178 *influence*; efficacy 160 *power*; magic 983 *sorcery*; services, assistance, midwifery 703 *aid*; support 706 *cooperation*; intervention, interference 678 *activity*; medium 629 *means*; use, employment, application 640 *utility*; mechanization, automation 630 *machine*.

(2) *instrument,* hand, organ, sense o.; handmaid, amanuensis 742 *servant*; agent, midwife, medium, assistant 703 *aider*; go-between 720 *mediator*; catalyst; vehicle; robot 630 *machine*; pawn, cat's paw, stooge, puppet, creature 707 *auxiliary*; weapon, implement, appliance, lever 630 *tool*; key, skeleton key, master k., passkey 263 *opener*; open sesame, watchword, password; passport 756 *permit*; channel, way 624 *road*; push button, switch, controls; device, expedient 623 *contrivance*.

Adjective
(3) *instrumental,* working 173 *operative*; hand-operated, manual; automatic, push-button 630 *mechanical*; effective, efficient, efficacious 160 *powerful*; telling 178 *influential*; magic 983 *magical*; conducive 156 *causal*; practical, applied; serviceable, employable, handy 640 *useful*; ready, available 597 *willing*; helpful 703. *aiding*; functional, subservient, ministering; intermediate, intervening.

Verb
(4) *be instrumental,* work, act 173 *operate*; perform 676 *do*; serve, lend itself to, work for, pander to 703 *minister to*; help, assist 703 *aid*; advance, promote 703 *patronize*; have a hand in 775 *participate*; be to blame 156 *cause*; be of use 640 *be* useful; intervene 720 *mediate*; pull strings 178 *influence*; effect 156 *cause*; achieve 725 *carry through*.

Adverb
(5) *through,* per, by means of, thanks to.

629
Means

Noun
(1) *means,* ways and m., wherewithal; power, capacity 160 *ability*; strong hand, trumps, aces; conveniences, facilities; appliances, tools 630 *tool*; technology 490 *knowledge*; technique, know-how 694 *skill*; wherewithal, equipment, supplies 633 *provision*; resources, economic r., natural r., raw material 631 *materials*; nuts and bolts 630 *machine*; labour manpower 686 *personnel*; capital, liquidity 797 *money*; assets 777 *property*; stocks and shares, investments, revenue, income 807 *receipt*; reserves, stand-by; method, measures, steps 624

way; cure 658 *remedy*; expedient, device, resort 623 *contrivance*; makeshift 150 *substitute*; let-out 667 *means of escape*; desperate remedy, last resort.

Verb

(2) *find means,* find, furnish 633 *provide*; equip, fit out 669 *make ready*; finance, promote, float; have the means 160 *be able*; contrive, find a way 623 *plan*; beg, borrow or steal, 771 *acquire*.

Adverb

(3) *by means of,* with, by, through; by dint of.

630
Tool

Noun

(1) *tool,* precision t., machine t., implement, instrument apparatus, appliance, utensil; weapon 723 *arms*; device, contraption, gadget 623 *contrivance*; thinga-majig, whatsit; screwdriver, drill 263 *perforator*; wrench, spanner; pliers 778 *nippers*; chisel, edged tool 256 *sharp edge*; lever, jack 218 *pivot*; tiller, helm 218 *handle*; pulley 250 *wheel*; switch, stopcock; pedal, pole 287 *propulsion*; ram 279 *hammer*; tool-kit, tools of the trade.

(2) *machine,* machinery, mechanism, works; clockwork, nuts and bolts 58 *component*; spring, gears; motor, engine 160 *sources of energy*; servomotor; robot, automaton; computer 86 *data processing*.

(3) *mechanics,* engineering; electrical e. 160 *electronics*; robotics, cybernetics; automation, technology, advanced t, high t.

(4) *equipment,* stock in trade; gear, tackle, harness; fittings 40 *adjunct*; outfit, kit; upholstery, furnishing; trappings 228 *dress*; utensils, impedimenta, paraphernalia; wares 795 *merchandise*; plant 687 *workshop*.

(5) *machinist,* operator, operative; driver, minder, machine-m. 686 *agent*; engineer, technician, mechanic, fitter; tool-user, craftsman *or* - woman 686 *artisan*.

Adjective

(6) *mechanical,* mechanized, motorized, powered, power-driven; labour-saving, automatic 628 *instrumental*; automated; tool-using.

631
Materials

Noun

(1) *materials,* resources 629 *means*; material, stuff, staple, stock; raw material, grist; meat, fodder 301 *food*; oil 385 *fuel*; ore, mineral, metal, pig-iron, ingot; clay, china c. 344 *soil*; glass 422 *transparency*; plastic, polythene, polystyrene, fibreglass; rope, yarn 208 *fibre*; leather, hide 226 *skin*; timber 366 *wood*, 218 *beam*; plank 207 *lamina*; stuffing 227 *lining*; cloth, fabric 222 *textile*.

(2) *building material,* building block, breeze b., bricks and mortar, lath and plaster, wattle and daub 331 *structure*; thatch, tile 226 *roof*; masonry stone, marble; rendering 226 *facing*; cement, concrete, reinforced c.; cobble 226 *paving*.

(3) *paper,* newsprint; card, cartridge paper, carbon p., tissue p., crepe p., cellophane; papier mâché, cardboard, pasteboard; chipboard, hardboard, plasterboard; sheet, foolscap, quire, ream 586 *stationery*.

632
Store

Noun

(1) *store,* mass, heap, load, stack, stockpile 74 *accumulation;* packet, bundle 26 *quantity;* harvest, crop, vintage 771 *acquisition;* stock 795 *merchandise;* assets, capital, holding, investment 777 *property;* fund, reserves, something in hand, backlog; savings, nest egg; deposit, hoard, treasure; cache 527 *hiding-place;* trousseau 633 *provision;* pool, kitty 775 *joint possession;* quarry, mine, gold-m.; natural deposit, mineral d.; seam, lode, vein, rich v.; bonanza, strike 484 *discovery;* well, oil w., gusher 156 *source;* supply, constant s., stream; tap, pipeline, artesian well 341 *irrigator;* cornucopia, abundance 635 *plenty.*

(2) *storage,* garnening 74 *accumulation;* bottling 666 *preservation;* safe deposit 660 *protection;* stabling, warehousing; storage space, shelf-room 183 *room;* hold, bunker 194 *cellar;* supply base, storehouse, store-room, warehouse, depository, depot; dock, wharf, garage; magazine, arsenal, armoury; treasure house 799 *treasury;* exchequer, vault, coffer, till, safe, night s., bank; blood b., sperm b.; data bank, memory 86 *data processing;* hive, honeycomb; granary, barn, silo; reservoir, cistern, tank; gasholder; drain, cesspool 649 *sink;* pantry, larder; cupboard, shelf 194 *cabinet;* refrigerator, deep freeze; portmanteau, holdall 194 *box;* container 194 *receptacle.*

(3) *collection,* set, complete s.; archives 548 *record;* folder, portfolio 74 *accumulation;* museum 125 *antiquity;* gallery, art

g.; library, thesaurus; menagerie 369 *zoo;* waxworks, exhibition 522 *exhibit;* repertory, repertoire.

Adjective

(4) *stored,* in store, in deposit; in hand, held; in reserve, banked, invested; available, in stock; spare.

Verb

(5) *store,* stow, pack 193 *load;* roll up, fold up; lay up, stow away, put a., garage, stable, warehouse; garner, gather, harvest 370 *cultivate;* amass, accumulate 74 *bring together;* stock up, lay in, bulk-buy; stockpile, pile up, build up 36 *augment;* take on, take in, fuel 633 *provide;* fill up, top up, refill 633 *replenish;* put by, save, keep, hold, file, hang on to 778 *retain;* pickle, conserve 666 *preserve;* set aside, put a., lay by, keep back, keep in hand, reserve; bank, deposit, invest; hoard, treasure; bury, squirrel away 525 *conceal;* husband, save up 814 *economize;* equip oneself 669 *prepare oneself;* pool 775 *communalize.*

633
Provision

Noun

(1) *provision,* logistics, equipment 669 *fitting out;* purveyance, catering; service, delivery; self-service; board and lodging, maintenance; assistance 703 *subvention;* supply, food s., water s.; pipeline 272 *transference;* commissariat, supplies, stores, rations, iron r., emergency r.; reserves 632 *store;* reinforcement, replenishment, refill 54 *plenitude;* food, provender 301 *provisions;* 814 *economy;* budgeting possible need 669 *preparation.*

(2) *provider,* donor 781 *giver;* creditor 784 *lender;* purser 798

treasurer; steward, butler; commissary, quartermaster, storekeeper; supplier, victualler, grocer, greengrocer, poulterer, fishmonger, butcher, vintner, wine merchant; retailer, shopkeeper.

(3) *caterer,* purveyor, hotelier, restaurateur; innkeeper; landlord, landlady, publican; housekeeper, housewife; cook, chef; pastry cook, baker, confectioner.

Adjective
(4) *provisioning,* providing etc. vb.; self-service; all-sufficing 635 *sufficient*; provided, all found; available, on tap.

Verb
(5) *provide,* afford, offer 781 *give*; provision, find; equip, furnish, arm, man, fit out, kit o. 669 *make ready*; supply, keep supplied; yield 164 *produce*; cater, purvey; deliver, hand out hand round, serve up, dish up; feed, cook for, board, maintain, keep, clothe; stock, keep a s.; budget, make provision, take on supplies, stock up 632 *store*; gather food, forage; tap, draw on, milk 304 *extract*; export, import 791 *trade*.

(6) *replenish,* make good, make up; fill up, top up refill 54 *fill*; refuel, reload.

634
Waste

Noun
(1) *waste,* wastage leakage 298 *outflow*; inroads, consumption; spending, outlay, expense 806 *expenditure*; using up, depletion, exhaustion 300 *voidance*; dissipation, evaporation, melting 75 *dispersion*; damage 772 *loss*; wear and tear 655 *deterioration*; wastefulness, improvidence, extravagance, 815 *prodigality*; frittering away 675

misuse; vandalism, sabotage 165 *destruction*; waste product, refuse 641 *rubbish*.

Adjective
(2) *wasteful,* extravagant, unnecessary, uneconomic 815 *prodigal*; throwaway 637 *superfluous*; time-consuming, energy-c.; damaging 165 *destructive*.

(3) *wasted,* exhausted, depleted, consumed; gone to waste, fruitless, bootless 641 *profitless*; illspent, futile, in vain.

Verb
(4) *waste,* consume, make inroads on, wade into; swallow, devour, gobble up 301 *eat*; spend 806 *expend*; take, use up, exhaust, deplete, drain, suck dry 300 *empty*; dissipate, scatter 75 *disperse*; abuse, overwork, overfish, overgraze, impoverish, milk dry 675 *misuse*; wear out, erode, damage 655 *impair*; misapply, fritter away 674 *not use*; labour in vain 641 *waste effort*; be extravagant, squander, run through, throw away, 815 *be prodigal*; be careless, slop, spill; be destructive, sabotage, vandalize 165 *lay waste*; leak, ebb away, run to waste; run low, dry up 298 *flow out*; melt away, evaporate, burn out; run out, give o. 636 *not suffice*; 381 *burn*; run to seed 655 *deteriorate*.

635
Sufficiency

Noun
(1) *sufficiency,* right amount; right number, quorum; adequacy, enough; adequate income, competence, living wage; self-sufficiency; no surplus, bare minimum; satisfaction 828 *content*; fulfilment 725 *completion*; repletion, one's fill 863 *satiety*.

(2) *plenty,* horn of p., cornucopia 171 *abundance*; showers of 350 *stream*; lots 32 *great quantity*; fullness 54 *plenitude*; affluence 800 *wealth*; feast, banquet 301 *feasting*; orgy, riot, profusion 815 *prodigality*; richness, lushness 171 *productiveness*; harvest, rich h., bumper crop; bonanza, endless supply 632 *store*; more than enough 637 *redundance*.

Adjective

(3) *sufficient,* sufficing, all-s. 54 *complete*; enough, adequate, enough to go round; satisfactory, satisfying 828 *contenting*; measured, just right; only just enough.

(4) *plenteous,* plentiful, ample, more than enough 637 *superfluous*; openhanded, generous, lavish 813 *liberal*; extravagant 815 *prodigal*; unsparing, inexhaustible 32 *great*; luxuriant, riotous, lush, rank, fertile 171 *prolific*; profuse, abundant, copious, overflowing 637 *redundant*; opulent, affluent 800 *moneyed*.

(5) *filled,* well-f., flush 54 *full*; chock-full, replete 863 *sated*; satisfied, contented 828 *content*; well-provided, wellstocked 633 *provisioning*; rich in, teeming, crawling with 104 *multitudinous*.

Verb

(6) *suffice,* be enough, answer 642 *be expedient*; pass muster, make the grade 727 *be successful*; measure up to, fill the bill; stand up to, take the strain; refill 633 *replenish*; prove acceptable, satisfy 828 *content*; provide for 633 *provide*.

(7) *abound,* be plentiful, proliferate, teem, swarm, bristle with 104 *be many*; riot 171 *be fruitful*; flow, pour, stream 350 *rain*;

brim, overflow 637 *superabound*; roll in, wallow in 800 *be rich*.

(8) *have enough,* be satisfied 828 *be content*; eat *or* drink one's fill be sated, have had enough; have the means 800 *afford*.

Adverb

(9) *enough,* sufficiently; on tap, on demand.

636
Insufficiency

Noun

(1) *insufficiency,* not enough 829 *discontent*; inadequacy, incompetence; nothing to spare, 33 *small quantity*; too few 105 *fewness*; deficiency, imperfection 647 *defect*; half measures, tinkering 307 *shortfall*; deficit 805 *insolvency*; bare subsistence, pittance, dole; stinginess, meanness 816 *parsimony*; short commons, iron rations, half r.; austerity, bread and water 945 *asceticism*; malnutrition 651 *disease*.

(2) *scarcity,* scarceness, paucity 105 *fewness*; dearth, drought 172 *unproductiveness*; famine, starvation; shortage, short supply 307 *shortfall*; scantiness, meagreness; deprivation 801 *poverty*; lack, want, need 627 *needfulness*.

Adjective

(3) *insufficient,* not satisfying, disappointing 829 *discontenting*; inadequate, not enough, too little; scant, scanty, skimpy, slender; too small, cramping 33 *small*; deficient, light on, lacking 55 *incomplete*; found wanting, unsatisfactory 35 *inferior*; incompetent, unequal to; weak, thin, watery 4 *insubstantial*; niggardly, miserly; stingy 816 *parsimonious*.

(4) *unprovided,* unsupplied; vacant, bare 190 *empty;* unsatisfied, empty-handed 829 *discontented;* insatiable 859 *greedy;* deficient in, starved of; cramped 702 *hindered;* hard up 801 *poor;* understaffed, shorthanded, under strength; stinted, rationed skimped; not provided, unavailable.

(5) *underfed,* undernourished, half-starved, on short commons; famished, starved, starving, famine-stricken 946 *fasting;* thin, skinny, stunted 206 *lean.*

(6) *scarce,* rare 140 *infrequent;* sparse 105 *few;* in short supply, at a premium, hard to get, unobtainable, out of season, out of stock.

Verb
(7) *not suffice,* be insufficient, inadequate etc. adj.; cramp one's style 747 *restrain;* want, lack, need 627 *require;* fail 509 *disappoint;* fall below 35 *be inferior;* come short 307 *fall short;* run out, dry up; tinker 726 *not complete.*

(8) *be unsatisfied,* ask for more, 859 *be hungry,* 829 *be discontented;* spurn an offer, 607 *reject;* miss, want, feel the lack of 627 *require.*

(9) *make insufficient,* expect too much; overwork, impoverish, damage 655 *impair;* exhaust, deplete, run down, squander 634 *waste;* grudge, hold back, stint, skimp 816 *be parsimonious.*

Adverb
(10) *insufficiently,* not enough; for want of.

637
Redundance

Noun
(1) *redundance,* overspill, over-

flow 298 *outflow;* abundance, superabundance, exuberance, luxuriance, riot, profusion 635 *plenty;* richness, bonanza 632 *store;* upsurge 36 *increase;* avalanche, spate 32 *great quantity;* mob 74 *crowd;* saturation 54 *plenitude;* excess 634 *waste;* excessiveness, exorbitance, too much 546 *exaggeration;* overindulgence 947 *gluttony,* 949 *drunkenness;* plethora, congestion 863 *satiety;* fat, obesity; more than enough.

(2) *superfluity,* luxury, luxuriousness; frills, luxuries, nonessentials; duplication, overkill; something over, bonus 40 *extra;* margin, overlap, excess, surplus, balance 41 *remainder;* excrescence, accessory 641 *inutility;* padding, expletive 570 *pleonasm;* redundancy, unemployment 679 *inactivity;* overmanning; glut, surfeit, 863 *satiety.*

Adjective
(3) *redundant,* too many 104 *many;* overmuch, excessive, immoderate 32 *exorbitant;* overflowing, running over 54 *full;* snowed under 341 *drenched;* cloying, satiating 838 *tedious;* replete, gorged, stuffed, bursting; overcharged, overloaded; congested, bloated 197 *expanded.*

(4) *superfluous,* needless, unnecessary, uncalled for 641 *useless;* excessive 634 *wasteful;* luxury, luxurious, surplus 41 *remaining;* more than one needs, spare, to spare 38 *additional;* on one's hands, going begging 860 *unwanted;* dispensable, expendable.

Verb
(5) *superabound,* riot, run riot 635 *abound,* 171 *be fruitful;* bristle with, outnumber 104 *be many;* overflow, brim over 54 *be complete;* flood, inundate,

deluge, overwhelm 350 *flow*; engulf 299 *absorb*; know no bounds 306 *overstep*; soak, saturate 341 *drench*; stuff, cram 54 *fill*; congest, choke, suffocate; cloy, satiate, sicken 863 *sate*; oversell, flood the market; overdo, pile it on 546 *exaggerate*; lavish upon 813 *be liberal*.

(6) *be superfluous,* go begging 41 *be left*; do twice over, duplicate; gild the lily 641 *waste effort*; have no use 641 *be useless*.

Adverb
(7) *redundantly,* over and above, enough and to spare; too much, excessively, unnecessarily.

638
Importance

Noun
(1) *importance,* primacy, priority, urgency 64 *precedence*; supremacy 34 *superiority*; import, consequence, significance, weight, gravity, seriousness, solemnity; substance, interest, consideration, concern; notability, memorability, prominence, eminence 866 *repute*; influence 866 *prestige*; size, magnitude 32 *greatness*; rank, high standing; value, excellence, merit 644 *goodness*; stress, emphasis, insistence 532 *affirmation*.

(2) *important matter,* matter of life and death 137 *crisis*; no joke, no laughing matter; great news 529 *news*; exploit 676 *deed*; landmark, milestone, red-letter day.

(3) *chief thing,* what matters, main thing; issue, crux 452 *topic*; fundamentals, essential 1 *reality*; priority 627 *requirement*; gist 514 *meaning*; substance 5 *essential part*; highlight, main feature; cream, pick 644 *elite*; keynote, cornerstone, mainstay, linchpin; head,

spearhead; nub core, heart of the matter 225 *centre*; hub 218 *pivot*; half the battle 32 *main part*.

(4) *bigwig,* personage, notable, notability, personality, heavyweight, somebody 866 *person of repute*; worthy, pillar of the community, VIP; big gun, big noise, great panjandrum; leading light, kingpin, key person 696 *expert*; first fiddle, prima donna; star, lion 890 *favourite*; head, chief 34 *superior*; grandee 868 *aristocrat*; magnate, mogul, mandarin; baron, tycoon 741 *autocrat*; big battalions, top brass, top people, establishment 733 *authority*; superpower 178 *influence*.

Adjective
(5) *important,* weighty, grave, solemn, serious; of consequence, of importance; considerable, earth-shaking, momentous, critical, fateful; chief, capital, cardinal, staple, major, main, paramount 34 *supreme*; crucial, essential, pivotal 225 *central*; basic, fundamental; prime, foremost, leading; overriding, overruling, uppermost 34 *superior*; worthwhile 644 *valuable*; vital, indispensable, irreplaceable, key 627 *required*; significant, telling 514 *meaningful*; imperative, urgent, high-priority; high-level, top-l., summit 213 *topmost*.

(6) *notable,* egregious 32 *remarkable*; memorable, signal 505 *remembered*; first-rate, outstanding, excelling 644 *excellent*; top-rank 34 *superior*; conspicuous, prominent, eminent, distinguished, exalted, august 866 *noteworthy*; imposing, commanding 821 *impressive*; formidable, powerful 178 *influential*; newsworthy, front-page; eventful, stirring, shattering, epoch-making.

Verb

(7) *be important,* matter, bulk large 612 *motivate*; weigh, carry, tell, count 178 *influence*; import, signify 514 *mean*; concern, interest, affect; have priority, come first 34 *predominate*; take the lead 64 *come before*; be somebody 920 *command respect*; make a stir, cut a dash 455 *attract notice*.

(8) *make important,* give weight to, seize on, fasten on, enhance, highlight; rub in, stress, underline, labour 532 *emphasize*; headline, splash 528 *advertise*; bring to notice, 528 *proclaim*; magnify 546 *exaggerate*; lionize, glorify, exalt 920 *show respect*; take seriously; value, esteem, make much of, set store by 920 *respect*; overestimate 482 *overrate*.

Adverb

(9) *importantly,* primarily, significantly; above all.

639
Unimportance

Noun

(1) *unimportance,* inconsequence, insignificance 35 *inferiority*; pettiness 33 *smallness*; paltriness, meanness triviality; worthlessness 812 *cheapness*; uselessness irrelevance.

(2) *trifle,* inessential, triviality, technicality; nothing, mere n., no no great matter; accessory, side-show; tithe, fraction 53 *part*; small beer, small potatoes; paltry sum, peanuts, fleabite; pinprick, scratch; child's play 701 *easy thing*; jest, joke; peccadillo, venial sin; trifles, trivia. trickle 33 *small quantity*; nonsense 497 *absurdity*.

(3) *bauble,* toy 837 *plaything*; gewgaw, knick-knack, bric-a-brac; novelty, trinket; trumpery, frippery, trash.

(4) *nonentity,* nobody, obscurity; man of straw 4 *insubstantial thing*; figurehead, cipher; mediocrity, lightweight, small fry, small game; banana republic; other ranks, lower orders 869 *commonalty*; second fiddle 35 *inferior*; underling 742 *servant*; pawn 628 *instrument*; Cinderella, poor relation; squirt, trash 867 *object of scorn*.

Adjective

(5) *unimportant,* immaterial, of no consequence, insignificant 515 *meaningless*; off the point 10 *irrelevant*; inessential, not vital; unnecessary, dispensable, expendable; small, petty, trifling, paltry 33 *inconsiderable*; negligible, weak, puny, powerless 161 *impotent*; wretched, miserable, pitiful, pitiable, pathetic; mean, sorry 801 *poor*; obscure, disregarded, overlooked 458 *neglected*; overrated, jumped-up, no-account; low-level, secondary, minor, by-, subsidiary, peripheral 35 *inferior*.

(6) *trivial,* trifling, footling, pettifogging, technical; frivolous, puerile, childish 499 *foolish*; superficial 4 *insubstantial*; slight, lightweight 33 *small*; not serious, forgivable, venial; parish-pump, small-time; one-horse, second-rate, third-r.; trashy, tawdry, gimcrack 645 *bad*; worthless 641 *useless*, 922 *contemptible*; token, nominal, symbolic 547 *indicating*; mediocre, nondescript, commonplace, 610 *usual*.

Verb

(7) *be unimportant,* not matter, carry no weight, not count, count for nothing, cut no ice, signify little; attach no importance to, shrug off 458 *disregard*.

Interjection
(8) *no matter!* never mind! too
bad!

640
Utility

Noun
(1) *utility,* use, usefulness; efficacy, efficiency 160 *ability*;
adequacy 635 *sufficiency*;
adaptability, applicability, suitability 642 *good policy*; readiness, availability 189 *presence*;
service, help, good stead 703
aid; value, worth, merit 644
goodness; function, capacity,
potency 160 *power*; advantage,
profitability, productivity,
profit; mileage 771 *gain*; convenience, benefit, public good 615
good; functionalism; employment, utilization 673 *use*.

Adjective
(2) *useful,* of use, helpful, of
service 703 *aiding*; practical,
applied, functional; versatile,
all-purpose; practicable, convenient, expedient 642 *advisable*; handy, ready, available;
serviceable, fit for, good for,
disposable, adaptable, applicable; usable, reusable, employable; good, valid, current; subservient 628 *instrumental*; able,
competent, efficacious, effective, efficient 160 *powerful*;
adequate 635 *sufficient*; pragmatic, utilitarian.
(3) *profitable,* paying, remunerative 771 *gainful*; prolific,
fertile 164 *productive*; beneficial, advantageous, worthwhile
615 *good*; worth one's keep;
invaluable 644 *valuable*.

Verb
(4) *be useful,* prove helpful, be of
value, come in handy, have
some use, work 173 *operate*;
perform 676 *do*; serve, serve
one's turn, answer 635 *suffice*;
suit one's purpose 642 *be expedient*; help, advance, promote

703 *aid*; conduce 179 *tend*; benefit, profit 644 *do good*; bear
fruit 171 *be fruitful*; pay, make a
profit 771 *be profitable*.

(5) *find useful,* employ, make use
of, utilize 673 *use*; improve on,
turn to good account, reap the
benefit 137 *profit by*, 771 *gain*.

641
Inutility

Noun
(1) *inutility,* uselessness; no
function, no purpose 637 *superfluity*; futility 497 *absurdity*;
worthlessness, inadequacy 636
insufficiency; inability 161 *impotence*; inefficiency, incompetence, ineptitude 695 *unskilfulness*; inconvenience, unfitness
643 *inexpedience*; no benefit,
disservice, mischief, damage,
detriment 772 *loss*.

(2) *lost labour,* wasted effort 728
failure; waste of time, dead
loss; wild-goose chase, fool's
errand; blind alley 702 *obstacle*; half measures, tinkering.

(3) *rubbish,* trash, waste, refuse,
lumber, junk, scrap, litter;
spoilage, wastage, waste pro-
ducts, waste paper; sweepings,
shavings 41 *leavings*; scraps,
bits, crumbs; dust, debris 649
dirt; odds and ends, bits and
pieces, rags and bones, old
clothes, cast-offs; reject, throw-
out; rubbish heap, slag heap,
dump.

Adjective
(4) *useless,* functionless, purposeless, pointless, futile 497
absurd; impracticable, no go;
redundant 637 *superfluous*; expendable, dispensable, unnecessary 860 *unwanted*; inapplicable 643 *inexpedient*; unusable,
unemployable; unqualified, inefficient, incompetent 695 *unskilful*; ineffective, ineffectual

161 *impotent*; inoperative, invalid 752 *abrogated*; unserviceable, out of order; broken down, worn out, obsolete, outmoded 127 *antiquated*.

(5) *profitless*, unavailing; loss-making, not worthwhile, wasteful, not paying 772 *losing*; idle, vain, in vain, abortive 634 *wasted*; unrewarding, thankless; fruitless, barren, sterile 172 *unproductive*; worthless, good for nothing; no good 645 *bad*.

Verb
(6) *be useless*, profitless etc. adj.; waste one's time; not work, not function 728 *fail*.

(7) *make useless*, disqualify, unfit, disarm 161 *disable*; clip the wings of 655 *impair*; dismantle, dismast, lay up 679 *make inactive*; sabotage 702 *obstruct*; undo, take to pieces, break up 46 *disunite*; deface, devalue 812 *cheapen*; pollute, contaminate, lay waste 172 *make sterile*.

(8) *waste effort*, waste one's breath, labour the obvious 637 *be superfluous*; labour in vain, flog a dead horse; tilt at windmills; cry for the moon 497 *be absurd*.

Adverb
(9) *uselessly*, to no purpose, to no avail.

642
Good policy

Noun
(1) *good policy*, expediency, advisability, desirability, suitability 640 *utility*; fitness, propriety; opportunity 137 *occasion*; convenience, pragmatism, opportunism, profit, advantage 615 *benefit*; facilities 629 *means*; an expedient, 623 *contrivance*.

Adjective
(2) *advisable*, desirable, worthwhile 644 *beneficial*; acceptable 923 *approved*; suitable 24 *fit*; fitting, seemly, proper 913 *right*; owing 915 *due*; auspicious, opportune 137 *timely*; prudent, politic, judicious 498 *wise*; expedient, advantageous, profitable 640 *useful*; convenient, workable, practical; practicable, negotiable; qualified, cut out for; to the purpose, applicable.

Verb
(3) *be expedient*, suit the occasion, befit; help 703 *aid*; forward, advance, promote 640 *be useful*; answer, produce results 156 *conduce*; work, do, serve 635 *suffice*; achieve one's aim 727 *succeed*; profit, benefit 644 *do good*.

Adverb
(4) *expediently*, conveniently, opportunely 615 *well*.

643
Inexpedience

Noun
(1) *inexpedience*, no answer, not the a., bad policy 495 *error*; unfitness 25 *inaptitude*; impropriety, wrongness 914 *wrong*; disability, handicap 702 *obstacle*; inconvenience, disadvantage, detriment; mixed blessing, last resort 596 *necessity*.

Adjective
(2) *inexpedient*, better not, inadvisable, undesirable, not recommended 924 *disapproved*; ill-advised, impolitic, imprudent, injudicious 499 *unwise*; inappropriate, unsuitable, out of place 916 *undue*; not right, improper, objectionable 914 *wrong*; unfit, ineligible, inadmissible; unhappy, infelicitous, inopportune, untimely 138 *ill-*

timed; unsatisfactory 636 *insufficient*; incommodious, inconvenient; detrimental, disadvantageous 645 *harmful*; unhealthy 653 *insalubrious*; unprofitable 641 *useless*; unhelpful 702 *hindering*; untoward 731 *adverse*; cumbersome, awkward 695 *clumsy.*

Verb
(3) *be inexpedient,* won't do, not answer; not help 641 *be useless*; incommode 827 *trouble*; penalize, hurt 645 *harm*; work against 702 *obstruct*; embarrass 700 *be difficult.*

644
Goodness

Noun
(1) *goodness,* soundness, quality; long suit, good points, merit, desert; excellence, eminence 34 *superiority*; virtue, worth, value 809 *price*; flawlessness 646 *perfection*; beneficence 897 *benevolence.*

(2) *elite,* chosen few, pick, prime, flower, cream, meritocracy; crack troops 694 *skill*; top people 638 *bigwig*; charmed circle, top drawer; aristocracy 868 *upper class*; plum, prize 729 *trophy.*

(3) *exceller,* nonpareil; prodigy, genius; superman, superwoman 864 *prodigy*; one of the best 937 *good person*; treasure 890 *favourite*; jewel, pearl 844 *gem*; gold, refined g.; chef-d'oeuvre 694 *masterpiece*; best-seller, smash hit; charmer 841 *a beauty*; star 890 *favourite*; champion 727 *victor.*

Adjective
(4) *excellent,* fine, exemplary; good, better 34 *superior*; very good, first-rate, prime, quality, superfine, superlative, all-star; rare, vintage, classic 646 *perfect*; exclusive, choice, select,

picked, handpicked, exquisite, 605 *chosen*; worthy, meritorious 915 *deserving*; admirable, estimable, praiseworthy, creditable; famous, great; lovely 841 *beautiful*; glorious, dazzling, splendid, magnificent, marvellous, wonderful, terrific, sensational, superb.

(5) *super,* fantastic, way-out, fabulous; lovely, glorious, gorgeous, heavenly 32 *prodigious*; smashing, stunning, great, grand, famous, capital; delicious, 826 *pleasurable.*

(6) *best,* optimum, A1, champion, first-rate, a cut above, second to none 34 *supreme*; unequalled, unparalleled, peerless 646 *perfect.*

(7) *valuable,* of value, invaluable, inestimable, priceless, costly, 811 *of price*; irreplaceable, unique, rare, precious sterling, gilt-edged, blue-chip.

(8) *beneficial,* wholesome, healthy, sound 652 *salubrious*; refreshing, edifying, worthwhile, advantageous, profitable 640 *useful*; favourable, kind, propitious 730 *prosperous.*

(9) *not bad,* tolerable, passable, respectable; standard, fair, satisfactory; nice, decent, all right, okay, OK; indifferent, middling, mediocre.

Verb
(10) *be good,* have quality; have merit 915 *deserve*; pass muster 635 *suffice*; excel, transcend 34 *be superior.*

(11) *do good,* be the making of 654 *make better*; help 615 *benefit*; favour, smile on 730 *prosper*; do a favour 897 *be benevolent*; not hurt, do no harm.

Adverb
(12) *aright,* well, rightly, properly.

645
Badness

Noun

(1) *badness,* bad qualities, nastiness, beastliness, foulness;
worthlessness 641 *inutility;* low
standard; shoddiness 35 *inferiority;* faultiness, flaw 647 *imperfection;* unsoundness, taint,
decay 655 *deterioration;* disruption, confusion 61 *disorder;*
morbidity 651 *disease;* harmfulness, hurtfulness, ill, harm, injury, damage, mischief 616 *evil;*
noxiousness 653 *insalubrity;*
poison, blight, cancer 659 *bane;*
pestilence, sickness 651 *plague;*
contamination, 651 *infection;*
affair, scandal 867 *slur;* filth
649 *uncleanness;* bitterness,
393 *sourness;* sting, ache, pang
377 *pain;* molestation 827 *annoyance;* anguish 825 *suffering;*
tyranny, maltreatment, oppression, persecution 735 *severity;*
unkindness, cruelty 898 *malevolence;* depravity, vice 934
wickedness; sin 936 *guilt;* bad
influence, evil genius; ill wind,
evil star 731 *misfortune;* black
magic, evil eye, 983 *sorcery;*
curse 899 *malediction.*

Adjective

(2) *bad,* vile, base, evil; utterly
bad, irredeemable; poor, mean,
wretched, execrable, awful 35
inferior; no good, worthless,
shoddy, tacky 641 *useless;*
faulty, flawed 647 *imperfect;*
bad at, incompetent, inefficient
695 *clumsy;* badly done, spoiled
695 *bungled;* scruffy, filthy 649
dirty; foul, noisome 397 *fetid;*
gone bad 655 *deteriorated;* decaying, 51 *decomposed;* infected, poisoned, septic 651 *diseased;* irremediable, incurable;
depraved, vicious, villainous
934 *wicked;* mean, shabby 930
dishonest; wrongful 914 *wrong;*
sinister 616 *evil* (see *harmful*);

contemptible, shameful, scandalous, disgraceful 867 *discreditable;* lamentable, deplorable,
pitiable, pitiful 827 *distressing;*
onerous, burdensome 684 *fatiguing;* too bad 827 *annoying.*

(3) *harmful,* hurtful, injurious,
damaging, detrimental, prejudicial 643 *inexpedient;* corrosive, 165 *destructive;* pernicious, fatal 362 *deadly;* costly
811 *dear;* disastrous, ruinous,
calamitous 731 *adverse;* noxious, malignant, unhealthy, infectious 653 *insalubrious;* polluting, poisonous, radioactive
653 *toxic;* risky 661 *dangerous;*
sinister, ominous, dire, dreadful 616 *evil;* mischievous, spiteful, malicious, malevolent, ill-
disposed   898   *unkind;*
bloodthirsty, inhuman 898 *cruel;* rough, furious 176 *violent;*
harsh, intolerant 735 *oppressive;* monstrous 32 *exorbitant.*

(4) *not nice,* nasty, beastly, horrid, horrible, terrible, gruesome, grim, ghastly, awful,
dreadful, perfectly d.; scruffy
867 *disreputable;* foul, rotten,
lousy, putrid, stinking, sickening, nauseating 861 *disliked;*
loathsome, detestable, abominable 888 *hateful;* vulgar, sordid,
low, indecent, improper, gross,
filthy, obscene 951 *impure;*
shocking, disgusting, monstrous, horrendous 924 *disapproved;* wretched, miserable
827 *annoying.*

(5) *damnable,* damned, darned,
blasted, confounded, dratted,
bothersome, cursed, hellish, infernal, devilish, diabolical.

Verb

(6) *harm* 827 *hurt;* disagree
with, make one ill; injure, damage, pollute 655 *impair;* corrupt
655 *pervert;* play havoc with 63
derange; make things worse;
do evil, 914 *do wrong;* molest,
pain 827 *torment;* plague, vex

827 *trouble*; spite, be unkind 898 *be malevolent*.

(7) *ill-treat*, maltreat, mishandle, abuse 675 *misuse*; burden, overburden, put upon, tyrannize, trample on, victimize, prey upon; persecute 735 *oppress*; wrong 914 *do wrong*; distress 827 *torment*; outrage, violate 176 *be violent*; savage, maul 655 *wound*; stab 263 *pierce*; batter, bruise, buffet 279 *strike*; crucify 963 *torture*; spite 898 *be malevolent*; crush 165 *destroy*.

Adverb

(8) *badly,* amiss, wrong, ill; to one's cost; cruelly 32 *painfully*.

646
Perfection

Noun

(1) *perfection,* sheer p.; perfectness, immaculacy, faultlessness, flawlessness, mint condition; infallibility, transcendence 34 *superiority*; quintessence, essence; peak, pinnacle 213 *summit*; ne plus ultra, last word; chef d'oeuvre 694 *masterpiece*.

(2) *paragon,* flower, a beauty, ideal 644 *exceller*; classic, pattern, shining example; demigod 864 *prodigy*.

Adjective

(3) *perfect,* perfected, finished, ripened 669 *matured*; just right, ideal, flawless, faultless, impeccable, immaculate, spotless; pure 935 *innocent*; sound, watertight, seaworthy; whole, entire, complete 52 *intact*; beyond praise 644 *excellent*; consummate 34 *supreme*; brilliant, masterly 694 *skilful*; model, classic.

(4) *undamaged,* safe and sound, unscathed, no harm done; unhurt, unmarked; whole, entire 52 *intact*; in the pink 650 *healthy*.

Verb

(5) *perfect,* consummate, ripen 669 *mature*; correct 654 *rectify*; put the finishing touch 213 *crown*; complete 725 *carry through*.

Adverb

(6) *perfectly,* to perfection.

647
Imperfection

Noun

(1) *imperfection,* imperfectness, faultiness, fallibility 495 *error*; patchiness, unevenness, curate's egg 17 *nonuniformity*; immaturity 670 *undevelopment*; bit missing 627 *requirement*; deficiency, inadequacy 636 *insufficiency*; unsoundness 661 *vulnerability*; failing, weakness 307 *shortfall*; low standard, mediocrity 35 *inferiority*; second best 150 *substitute*; adulteration 43 *mixture*.

(2) *defect,* fault 495 *error*; flaw, leak, loophole, crack 201 *gap*; deficiency, limitation 307 *shortfall*; kink 503 *eccentricity*; weak point, soft spot 661 *vulnerability*; feet of clay 163 *weakness*; scratch, stain, smudge 845 *blemish*; drawback, catch, snag 702 *obstacle*.

Adjective

(3) *imperfect,* not ideal, less than perfect, uneven, patchy, good in parts; faulty, botched 695 *bungled*; flawed, cracked; leaky, wobbly, rickety 163 *flimsy*; unsound 661 *vulnerable*; shop-soiled, stained, marked 845 *blemished*; past its best 655 *deteriorated*; below par, off form; unfit, off-colour 651 *unhealthy*; not good enough, inadequate, deficient 636 *insufficient*; defective 55 *incomplete*; broken 53 *fragmentary*; perfunctory 456 *inattentive*; warped, distorted 246 *deformed*; mutilated, maimed, 163

weakened; raw, crude, 670 *immature*; rough and ready, provisional 150 *substituted*; second-best, second-rate 35 *inferior*; unimpressive, poor 645 *bad*; ordinary, so-so, middling, average; moderate, tolerable.

Verb
(4) *be imperfect,* have a fault; be defective 307 *fall short*; not pass muster, dissatisfy 636 *not suffice.*

Adverb
(5) *imperfectly,* almost, not quite.

648
Cleanness

Noun
(1) *cleanness,* freshness, dewiness, whiteness 950 *purity*; shine, polish, spit and polish; cleanliness, daintiness,

(2) *cleansing,* clean, spring-c.; washing, washing up, wiping up; refining, clarification, purification; washing out, flushing, purging; airing, ventilation, fumigation 338 *vaporization*; deodorization; sterilization, disinfection, delousing; sanitation, drainage, sewerage, plumbing 652 *hygiene.*

(3) *ablutions,* washing; hygiene, oral h.; bathing etc. vb.; dip 313 *plunge*; bath, tub; bidet; washbasin, washstand; Turkish bath, sauna; shower, douche; shampoo wash, laundry; launderette.

(4) *cleanser,* purifier; disinfectant, carbolic, deodorant; soda, detergent, soap, water, soap and w., shampoo; mouth wash, gargle; dentifrice, toothpaste; polish, furniture p., boot p.; wax, varnish; aperient 658 *purgative*; sewer, waterworks.

(5) *cleaning utensil,* sponge, loofah; brush, toothbrush; comb, hair brush, clothes b.; broom, mop, dustpan, carpet sweeper, vacuum cleaner; duster filter, air-f.

(6) *cleaner,* refiner, distiller; dry cleaner, launderer; scrubber, swabber; washer-up, dishwasher, charwoman, cleaner, help, home help; sweeper, dustman, refuse collector; chimney sweep, window cleaner; barber 843 *beautician*; scavenger, vulture.

Adjective
(7) *clean,* dirt-free; snowy 427 *white*; polished etc. vb.; clean, bright, shining; dainty, nice 862 *fastidious*; dewy, fresh; cleaned, scrubbed etc. vb.; shaven, shorn, barbered, trimmed; laundered, starched; spruce, natty, spick and span, neat, tidy, well-groomed 60 *orderly*; aseptic, antiseptic, hygienic, sterile 652 *salubrious*; pure, refined, immaculate, spotless, stainless 646 *perfect*; ritually clean, kosher 301 *edible.*

(8) *cleansing,* disinfectant; hygienic, sanitary; purgative; detergent; ablutionary.

Verb
(9) *clean,* spring-clean, clean up; groom, spruce up, neaten 62 *arrange*; wash, wipe, dry; mop, swab, scrub, scour; flush, flush out; sandblast, scrape 333 *rub*; launder, starch, iron; bleach, dry-clean; soap, lather, shampoo; bathe, rinse, sluice 341 *drench*; dust, sweep, beat, vacuum; brush, comb; buff, polish; shine 417 *make bright*; whitewash 427 *whiten*; erase 550 *obliterate*; strip, pick clean, clear out 300 *eject.*

(10) *purify,* purge, clean up; bowdlerize, expurgate; sublimate; cleanse, freshen, ventilate, deodorize fumigate; desalinate; decontaminate, disinfect, sterilize 652 *sanitate*; refine, distil, clarify, rack, skim, strain, filter; sift, sieve 44 *eliminate*; weed out, flush o., wash o. 350 *make flow.*

649
Uncleanness

Noun
(1) *uncleanness,* dirty habits; uncleanliness scruffiness, filthiness; squalor 801 *poverty*; sluttishness, slovenliness 61 *disorder*; stink 397 *stench*; pollution, defilement; corruption 51 *decomposition*; contamination 651 *infection*; scatology, obscenity 951 *impurity.*

(2) *dirt,* filth, stain, patch, blot; muck, mud, sludge, slime; bog 347 *marsh*; dung, droppings 302 *excrement*; snot, mucus; dust, cobweb; grime, smut, smudge; grounds, dregs, lees 41 *leavings*; sediment, deposit, precipitate, fur; scum, dross; ashes, cinders, clinker, slag 381 *ash*; drainage, sewerage; scurf, dandruff; tartar, plaque; pus, matter; refuse, garbage, litter 641 *rubbish*; rot, dry r., wet r., rust, mildew, mould 51 *decay*; carrion, offal; vermin, flea, nit 365 *insect.*

(3) *latrine,* privy, heads; john, loo; water closet, WC; lavatory, toilet; urinal, public convenience, Ladies, Gents; commode, bedpan, chamber pot 302 *defecation.*

(4) *sink,* cesspit, cesspool, sump, septic tank; gutter, sewer 351 *drain*; dunghill, rubbish heap, dustbin; pigsty, slum; shambles.

(5) *dirty person,* sloven, slattern, 61 *slut*; litter lout; scavenger; beast, pig.

Adjective
(6) *unclean,* obscene, corrupt 951 *impure*; septic, festering 653 *toxic*; unsterilized 653 *infectious*; sordid, squalid, insanitary 653 *insalubrious*; foul, offensive, nasty 645 *not nice*; noisome, nauseating, stinking 397 *fetid*; grubby, scruffy, flea-ridden, lousy, crawling; faecal 302 *excretory*; rotting, tainted, high; flyblown, maggoty 51 *decomposed.*

(7) *dirty,* filthy; dusty, grimy, smoky; polluted, littered, rubbish-strewn; unkempt, untidy, slatternly, sleazy, slovenly, sluttish, bedraggled; dingy, uncleaned, tarnished, stained, soiled; greasy, oily; clotted, caked, matted; messy, mucky, muddy; furred up, dirt-encrusted; musty, fusty, cobwebby; mouldy, rotten 655 *dilapidated.*

Verb
(8) *be unclean,* dirty etc. adj.; get dirty, collect dust, foul up, clog; rust, mildew, moulder, fester, rot, go bad 51 *decompose*; grow rank, smell 397 *stink.*

(9) *make unclean,* foul, dirty, soil; stain, blot, sully, tarnish; untidy 61 *be disordered*; smudge, streak, smear; cake, clog, muddy; spatter, splash 341 *moisten*; taint, infect, corrupt, pollute, contaminate 655 *impair*; defile, profane, desecrate 980 *be impious.*

650
Health

Noun
(1) *health,* good h.; healthiness 162 *vitality*: fitness, condition;

bloom, rosy cheeks, ruddy complexion; well-being 376 *euphoria*; whole skin, soundness; long life, longevity.

Adjective
(2) *healthy,* healthful, hygienic, sanitary 652 *salubrious*; in health, in good h., blooming, ruddy, rosy-cheeked; lusty, bouncing, strapping; hale and hearty, sound, fit, well, fine, bonny 174 *vigorous*; robust, hardy, strong 162 *stalwart*; fighting fit, in condition, in the pink, in good shape, in good heart, in fine fettle, feeling fine; getting well, convalescent, on the mend, up and about, on one's legs 656 *restored.*

Verb
(3) *be healthy,* feel fine, bloom, thrive, flourish, enjoy good health; keep well, fit etc. adj.

(4) *get healthy,* recuperate, return to health, mend, convalesce 656 *revive.*

651
Ill health. Disease

Noun
(1) *ill health,* bad h., poor h., delicate h.; unhealthiness, infirmity, debility 163 *weakness*; loss of condition, indisposition, allergy; hypochondria; nerves 503 *psychopathy.*

(2) *illness,* loss of health; affliction, disability, handicap, infirmity 163 *weakness*; sickness, indisposition, ailment, complaint, complication; condition, history of; bout of sickness, visitation, attack, spasm, stroke, seizure, apoplexy, fit; shock; poisoning; nausea, queasiness, vomiting; dizziness, vertigo; headache, migraine 377 *pain*; sign of illness, symptom 547 *indication*; temperature, feverishness, fever,

shivers 318 *spasm*; delirium 503 *frenzy*; breakdown, collapse; fainting 375 *insensibility*; prostration, coma; terminal disease 361 *decease*; sickbed, deathbed.

(3) *disease,* malady, disorder; infectious disease; occupational d., industrial d.; alcoholism, drug addiction; obesity; malnutrition, rickets, scurvy; wasting disease, atrophy; organic disease, functional d., neurological d., epilepsy; diabetes; cancer; virus disease, bacterial d., waterborne d.; brain d. 503 *insanity.*

(4) *plague,* pest, scourge 659 *bane*; pestilence, infection, contagion; epidemic, pandemic; Black Death.

(5) *infection,* contagion, bug 653 *insalubrity*; suppuration, festering, purulence, gangrene; toxicity, sepsis 659 *poison*; vector, carrier, germ-c., host; parasite 659 *bane*; virus, bacillus, bacteria, germ, pathogen; cold, common c., influenza, flu; chicken pox, measles, German m., mumps; smallpox, scarlet fever; fever, typhus; glandular fever; meningitis; tetanus, lockjaw; rabies.

(6) *tropical disease,* fever, malaria; cholera, yellow fever; yaws; leprosy; beri-beri, kwashiorkor.

(7) *digestive disorders,* indigestion, dyspepsia, liverishness; biliousness, nausea, vomiting, retching; colic, gripes; stomach ache, stomach upset; diarrhoea, the runs, 302 *defecation*; gastroenteritis, dysentery, cholera, typhoid; food poisoning; flatulence, wind, belching heartburn; ulcer; appendicitis; jaundice, hepatitis, kidney failure; gallstones, piles; constipation.

(8) *respiratory disease,* cough, cold, sore throat, tonsilitis, sinusitis; catarrh, laryngitis, bronchitis; asthma; pleurisy, pneumonia; diphtheria; whooping cough; smoker's cough, lung cancer; cystic fibrosis; tuberculosis, consumption.

(9) *cardiovascular disease,* heart condition, heart trouble; heart disease, heart failure; heart attack, coronary thrombosis, coronary; stroke; blood pressure, high b. p., low b. p.; varicose veins; thrombosis, clot.

(10) *blood disease,* anaemia, leukaemia, haemophilia; bleeding, internal b., haemorrhage.

(11) *cancer,* growth, tumour, benign t.; malignant t., cancerous growth.

(12) *skin disease,* yaws; leprosy; impetigo, herpes, shingles; dermatitis, eczema; hives, thrush; ringworm, athlete's foot; rash, itch 378 *formication*; acne, spots, blackheads; pustule, pimple; wart, verruca 253 *swelling*; birthmark, pockmark 845 *blemish*.

(13) *venereal disease,* pox; syphilis, gonorrhoea, the clap.

(14) *ulcer,* ulceration, gathering, festering, purulence; inflammation, lesion 655 *wound*; scald, burn; sore, boil, abscess; cyst; chilblain, corn 253 *swelling*; gangrene 51 *decay*; discharge, pus, matter.

(15) *rheumatism,* rheumatics; rheumatic fever; fibrositis; tennis elbow, pulled muscle; arthritis, rheumatoid a.; osteoarthritis; gout; lumbago, sciatica; slipped disc.

(16) *nervous disorders,* breakdown 503 *psychopathy*; brain tumour; brain haemorrhage, stroke, seizure; paraplegia;

atrophy 375 *insensibility*; palsy, spasticity; tremor, tic 318 *spasm*; epilepsy, poliomyelitis, polio; spina bifida; multiple sclerosis; muscular dystrophy.

(17) *animal disease,* veterinary d.; distemper, foot and mouth disease, swine fever; myxomatosis; anthrax; worms; spavin, thrush; fowl pest; psittacosis; hard pad; mange; rabies.

(18) *sick person,* sufferer; patient, in-p., out-p.; case, stretcher c., hospital c.; mental case 504 *madman*; invalid, chronic i.; hypochondriac; consumptive, asthmatic, diabetic; haemophiliac; insomniac; addict, alcoholic; spastic, paralytic; paraplegic, disabled person; cripple; sick list.

(19) *pathology,* forensic p.; diagnosis, prognosis 658 *therapy*.

Adjective

(20) *unhealthy,* unsound, sickly; infirm, decrepit, weakly 163 *weak*; delicate, in poor health; in poor condition, mangy; undernourished, emaciated; sallow, pale, peaky, anaemic 426 *colourless*; bilious; jaundiced.

(21) *sick,* ill, unwell, not well, indisposed, out of sorts, under the weather, off-colour, below par; queasy, nauseated, in poor shape, in a bad way; poorly, seedy, groggy, queer, ailing; sickening for, feverish, headachy, off one's food; laid up, bedridden, on one's back, in bed; invalided, hospitalized; run down 684 *fatigued*; seized, taken ill; prostrate, collapsed; in a coma 375 *insensible*; critical, serious; comfortable; chronic, incurable, inoperable; mortally ill 361 *dying*; wasting away, in a decline.

(22) *diseased,* pathological; affected, infected, contaminated; gangrenous 51 *decomposed*;

morbid, pathogenic; psychosomatic 447 *mental*; infectious, contagious; poisonous, festering, purulent 653 *toxic*; degenerative, consumptive, tubercular; diabetic, anaemic; bloodless, haemophiliac; arthritic, rheumatic, rheumatoid, rheumaticky; paralysed, paralytic, spastic, epileptic; cancerous; syphilitic, venereal; swollen, gouty; bronchial, bronchitic, asthmatic; allergic; fevered, shivering, feverish, delirious; sore, tender; ulcerous, ulcerated, inflamed; spotty, pimply; spavined, broken-winded; mangy.

Verb
(23) *be ill,* sick etc. adj.; suffer, not feel well, complain of; feel queer, feel sick 300 *vomit*; sicken, fall sick, fall ill; catch, contract, go down with; have a stroke, collapse; languish, pine, waste away, flag, lose strength, grow weak, get worse, sink, fade away 655 *deteriorate.*

Adverb
(24) *morbidly,* unhealthily; in hospital, under treatment.

652
Salubrity

Noun
(1) *salubrity,* healthiness; well-being 650 *health*; wholesomeness; whole food, health food; fresh air, ozone 340 *air*; sunshine, outdoors; benign climate.

(2) *hygiene,* sanitation, cleanliness 648 *cleanness*; prophylaxis 658 *prophylactic*; quarantine 660 *protection*; immunity, immunization, inoculation, vaccination; pasteurization; sterilization, disinfection, chlorination; sanatorium 658 *hospital*; hot springs 658 *therapy*; keeping fit 682 *exercise*; hygienics.

(3) *sanitarian,* hygienist, public health inspector, medical officer; fresh-air fiend, naturist, nudist.

Adjective
(4) *salubrious,* healthful, healthy, wholesome; pure, fresh 648 *clean*; ventilated, well-v.; tonic, bracing, invigorating, refreshing 656 *restorative*; hygienic, sanitary, disinfected, chlorinated; pasteurized, sterilized, sterile, aseptic, antiseptic; prophylactic, immunizing 658 *remedial*; good for, salutary 644 *beneficial*; nutritious, nourishing; body-building, health-giving; harmless, benign, innocuous; immune, immunized etc. vb. 660 *invulnerable.*

Verb
(5) *be salubrious,* healthy etc. adj.; agree with one; prevent disease; keep fit 650 *be healthy.*

(6) *sanitate,* disinfect, boil, sterilize, chlorinate, pasteurize; immunize, inoculate, vaccinate; put in quarantine, 883 *seclude*; ventilate 340 *aerate*; freshen 648 *purify*; cleanse 648 *clean.*

Adverb
(7) *healthily,* wholesomely, hygienically.

653
Insalubrity

Noun
(1) *insalubrity,* unhealthiness, lack of hygiene, dirty habits 649 *uncleanness*; slum; bad air, bad climate; smoke haze, smog; bad drains, sewer; carrier, germ-c., vector; germ, microbe 196 *microorganism*; miasma, contagion 651 *infection*; pollution, radioactivity, fallout; poisonousness 659 *bane.*

Adjective
(2) *insalubrious,* unwholesome,

unhealthy; insanitary, unhygienic 649 *unclean*; bad, nasty, noxious, injurious 645 *harmful*; radioactive, carcinogenic; verminous, flea-ridden, rat-infested; foul, polluted, undrinkable, inedible; indigestible, stale, gone bad 655 *deteriorated*; unventilated, airless 264 *sealed off*; smoke-filled, stuffy; overheated.

(3) *infectious,* pathogenic; contagious, catching, communicable; pestiferous, pestilent, malarial, epidemic, endemic; infected 649 *dirty*.

(4) *toxic,* poisonous, germ-laden; venomous, poisoned; septic, suppurating; lethal 362 *deadly*.

Adverb
(5) *unwholesomely,* poisonously; unhealthily, morbidly.

654
Improvement

Noun
(1) *improvement,* change for the better, amelioration; uplift, regeneration; conversion, new leaf; revival, recovery 656 *restoration*; evolution, development; elaboration, enrichment; advance, progress 285 *progression*; furtherance, advancement, enhancement, preferment, promotion; rise, lift 308 *ascent*; upswing 310 *elevation*.

(2) *amendment,* renovation 656 *repair*; reformation, reform; purification, refining, rectification; correction, revision, emendation; second thoughts 67 *sequel*; polish, finishing touch 725 *completion*.

(3) *civilization,* culture; civility, refinement 846 *good taste*; training, upbringing 534 *education*; cultivation 490 *culture*.

(4) *reformism,* perfectionism, idealism; Moral Rearmament; liberalism, socialism, radicalism; extremism, revolution 738 *sedition*; progressivism; Fabianism.

(5) *reformer,* restorer 656 *mender*; editor, reviser; progressive, Fabian; liberal, radical, extremist, revolutionary 738 *agitator*; socialist, communist, Marxist; idealist, Utopian 513 *visionary*; sociologist, social worker.

Adjective
(6) *improved,* touched up, enhanced; reformed, revised; better 34 *superior*; looking up, on the mend; better for 498 *wise*; improvable, perfectible.

(7) *improving,* reformative, remedial 656 *restorative*; reforming, progressive, radical; civilizing, cultural; idealistic, Utopian; perfectionist 862 *fastidious*.

Verb
(8) *get better,* improve, mend, pick up, rally, revive, recover 656 *be restored*; make progress, make headway, advance, develop, evolve 285 *progress*; rise 308 *ascend*; graduate 727 *succeed*; better oneself 730 *prosper*; mend one's ways, reform 939 *be penitent*; learn from experience 137 *profit by*.

(9) *make better,* better, improve, ameliorate 644 *do good*; improve upon, refine u.; polish, elaborate, enrich, enhance; reform, transform; be the making of 178 *influence*; uplift, regenerate; refine, sublimate 648 *purify*; civilize, socialize, teach manners; mend 656 *repair*; restore 656 *cure*; revive 685 *refresh*; mitigate, palliate 177 *moderate*; forward, advance 285 *promote*; foster, encourage, bring to fruition; develop, open up, reclaim 370 *cultivate*; tidy

up, spruce up 648 *clean*; do up, renovate, refurbish, renew 126 *modernize*; touch up 841 *beautify*, make up 843 *primp*; embellish 844 *decorate*.

(10) *rectify,* put right, set right, straighten out 24 *adjust*; mend 656 *repair*; correct, debug, blue-pencil, proof-read; revise, edit, amend, emend; rewrite, remodel.

655
Deterioration

Noun

(1) *deterioration,* retrogression, slipping back, losing ground 286 *regression*; throwback 5 *heredity*; decline, ebb 37 *decrease*; twilight, fading 419 *dimness*; falling off, slump, depression, recession; exhaustion 634 *waste*; depravation, degeneration, decadence 934 *wickedness*; downward course 309 *descent*; setback 657 *relapse*.

(2) *dilapidation,* collapse, ruination 165 *destruction*; disrepair, neglect 458 *negligence*; slum, back street 801 *poverty*; erosion, wear and tear, corrosion, rustiness, rust, rot 51 *decay*; mildew 659 *blight*; decrepitude, senility 131 *old age*; ruin, wreck, physical w.,

(3) *impairment,* spoiling 675 *misuse*; detriment, damage, waste 772 *loss*; discoloration, weathering; pollution, contamination 649 *uncleanness*; poisoning, contamination 651 *infection*; adulteration, watering down 43 *mixture*; ruination, demolition 165 *destruction*; injury, mischief, harm 165 *havoc*; disablement, crippling, mutilation 163 *weakness*; sabotage 63 *derangement*; exacerbation 832 *aggravation*.

(4) *wound,* injury, trauma; open wound, running sore 651 *ulcer*; laceration, lesion; cut, gash, abrasion, nick, scratch 46 *scission*; stab, prick, puncture 263 *perforation*; contusion, bruise, bump, black eye; burn, scald; rupture, hernia; broken bones, fracture; scar 845 *blemish*.

Adjective

(5) *deteriorated,* not improved, the worse for; exacerbated 832 *aggravated*; spoilt, impaired, damaged, hurt; worn out, exhausted, worthless 641 *useless*; flat, stale, gone bad, rotten 645 *bad*; sapped, undermined, shaken 163 *weakened*; over-tired, 684 *fatigued*; no better, deteriorating, worse, getting w.; past one's best, in decline, senescent 131 *ageing*; slipping, 309 *descending*; faded, withered, decaying 51 *decomposed*; wasting away, at a low ebb; falling off 37 *decreasing*; degenerative, retrograde, backward 286 *regressive*; lapsed, recidivist; degenerate, depraved, corrupt 934 *vicious*; impoverished 801 *poor*.

(6) *dilapidated,* the worse for wear, in disrepair, in shreds, in ruins; broken, cracked, leaking; battered, storm-tossed, weatherbeaten; decrepit, ruinous, ramshackle, tottery, shaky, rickety, tumbledown 163 *weakened*; run-down, slummy, condemned; worn, well-w., frayed, shabby, tatty, dingy, holey, in holes, in tatters, in rags; worn out 641 *useless*; seedy, down at heel 801 *poor*; rusty, rotten, mildewed, mouldering, moss-grown, moth-eaten, worm-e., dog-eared 51 *decomposed*.

Verb

(7) *deteriorate,* not improve, get no better; get worse, go downhill 657 *relapse*; fall off, slump, decline 37 *decrease*; slip back,

revert 286 *regress*; lapse degenerate, let oneself go, go to pieces 165 *be destroyed*; go to the bad 934 *be wicked*; disintegrate, fall apart, collapse, fall 309 *tumble*; shrink, wear out; age 131 *grow old*; fade, wither, wilt, shrivel, perish, crumble, moulder, rust, rot, decay 51 *decompose*; spoil, stale, lose its flavour, go flat, go off, go sour, turn 391 *be unpalatable*; go bad 397 *stink*; fester, suppurate 51 *decompose*; sicken 651 *be ill*; make things worse 832 *aggravate*.

(8) *pervert*, deform, warp, twist 246 *distort*; abuse, prostitute 675 *misuse*; deprave 951 *debauch*; corrupt 934 *make wicked*; degrade, debase 311 *abase*; brutalize, dehumanize, barbarize; denature 147 *transform*; propagandize, brainwash 535 *misteach*.

(9) *impair*, damage, hurt, injure 645 *harm*; play havoc with 63 *derange*; dismantle, dismast; spoil, mar 695 *be clumsy*; tamper, meddle with 678 *meddle*; not improve, worsen, exacerbate 832 *aggravate*; lower, coarsen 847 *vulgarize*; devalue, debase 812 *cheapen*; blacken, stain 842 *make ugly*; scar 845 *blemish*; deface, disfigure, deform, warp 246 *distort*; mutilate, maim, lame, cripple 161 *disable*; cramp, hamper 702 *hinder*; castrate 161 *unman*; expurgate, bowdlerize; curtail, dock 204 *shorten*; adulterate 43 *mix*; subvert, sap, undermine, demoralize 163 *weaken*; eat away, erode, corrode 51 *decompose*; blight, blast; ravage 165 *lay waste*; vandalize, wreck, ruin 165 *destroy*; crumble 332 *pulverize*; fray, wear out; exhaust, consume, 634 *waste*; infect, contaminate, poison taint, foul, pollute 649 *make unclean*; defile, desecrate, profane 980 *be impious*.

(10) *wound*, scotch, draw blood; tear, lacerate, mangle, rip 46 *disunite*; maul, savage 176 *be violent*; black one's eye, bloody one's nose; bite, scratch, claw; gash, hack 46 *cut*; scarify, nick 260 *notch*; sting, prick, pink, stab, gore, run through 263 *pierce*; bruise 279 *strike*; crush, grind 332 *pulverize*; chafe 333 *rub*; smash 46 *break*; graze, pepper, wing.

656
Restoration

Noun
(1) *restoration*, recovery; reclamation, recycling; rescue, salvage; reformation, rehabilitation; replanting, rebuilding; remodelling 654 *amendment*; reinforcement 162 *strengthening*; replenishment 633 *provision*.

(2) *repair*, repairs, running r., renovation, reconditioning, renewal; rectification, emendation; restoration, making like new; mending, darning, patching, cobbling; patch, reinforcement; new look, face-lift.

(3) *revival*, recovery 685 *refreshment*; renewal, resurgence, rally, comeback; fresh spurt, new energy; boom 730 *prosperity*; reactivation, reanimation; resuscitation, rejuvenation; rebirth, renaissance, regeneration; new life, resurrection.

(4) *recuperation*, recovery, cure; healing, mending, scabbing over; convalescence 658 *remedy*; easing 831 *relief*; curability.

(5) *mender*, repairer, restorer, renovator, painter, decorator, interior d.; cobbler, shoe-repairer; tinker, plumber, handyman; curer, healer 658 *doctor*; faith healer; psychiatrist.

Adjective
(6) *restored*, refreshed etc. vb.;

revived, remade, reconditioned, reproofed; rectified 654 *improved*; like new, renewed; reborn 979 *sanctified*; renascent, resurgent; alive and kicking 650 *healthy*; cured, better, convalescent, on the mend; back to normal, oneself again; retrievable, restorable, recoverable; mendable, curable, operable; found, recovered, salvaged, reclaimed.

(7) *restorative,* recuperative, curative, healing, medicated 658 *remedial*.

Verb
(8) *be restored,* recover, come round, come to, revive, pick up, rally 685 *be refreshed*; pull through, get over; get up, get well, convalesce, recuperate; 654 *get better*; survive, live through; make a comeback, sleep off, bounce back, find one's feet, resume.

(9) *restore,* rehabilitate; reconstitute, rebuild, reform 654 *make better*; renovate, 648 *clean*; renew, remake, redo; overhaul, service, refit, refurbish, 126 *modernize*; replant, reafforest, reclaim, recycle; reinforce 162 *strengthen*; fill up 633 *replenish*; rescue, salvage 668 *deliver*.

(10) *revive,* revitalize, reanimate, resuscitate, regenerate; resurrect, rejuvenate; freshen 685 *refresh*.

(11) *cure,* heal, make well, cure of, break of; nurse 658 *doctor*; bind up, bandage; restore to health, set up, set (a bone); heal over, skin o., knit together; right itself, put itself right.

(12) *repair,* do repairs; put right 654 *rectify*; overhaul, mend; recover, resurface 226 *cover*; darn, patch, patch up; stop, fill (teeth); do up, touch up, retouch, paper over; seal, plug

264 *close*; splice, bind 45 *tie*; piece together, reassemble 45 *join*. See *restore*.

(13) *retrieve,* recover, regain, recapture 771 *acquire*; reclaim 31 *recoup*.

657
Relapse

Noun
(1) *relapse,* lapse 148 *reversion*; retrogression 286 *regression*; falling off 655 *deterioration*; backsliding, recidivism, apostasy 603 *tergiversation*; recrudescence, recurrence, reinfection.

Verb
(2) *relapse,* slip back, slide b., sink b., fall b.; retrogress 286 *regress*; degenerate 655 *deteriorate*; backslide, lapse, fall from grace 603 *apostatize*; have a relapse 148 *revert*.

658
Remedy

Noun
(1) *remedy,* help 703 *aid*; corrective 654 *amendment*; redress, amends 787 *restitution*; expiation 941 *atonement*; cure 656 *recuperation*; sovereign remedy, specific; answer, solution; prescription, recipe, formula, nostrum; panacea, heal-all, cure-all, elixir.

(2) *medicine,* pharmacopoeia; herb, medicinal h., simple; balm, medication, medicament, patent medicine, placebo; pill, tablet; draught, potion, decoction, infusion; dose, drops, drip; injection, jab, shot; preparation, mixture; spray, inhaler; medicine chest.

(3) *prophylactic,* preventive; sanitation, quarantine; vaccine; antiseptic, disinfectant

652 *hygiene*; germicide, fumigator 659 *poison*; gargle 648 *cleanser*; fluoridation, fluoride.

(4) *antidote,* antihistamine; antigen, antibody; antibiotic; sedative, muscle relaxant; antacid, analgesic, painkiller.

(5) *purgative,* laxative, aperient; diuretic; emetic, expectorant; douche, enema.

(6) *tonic,* restorative; cordial, tisane; pick-me-up 174 *stimulant*; caffeine, nicotine, alcohol; smelling salts, sal volatile; ginseng; vitamin tablet, iron pill.

(7) *drug,* antibiotic, sulpha drug; penicillin; insulin, cortisone; hormone, steroid; contraceptive pill 172 *contraception*; analgesic 375 *anaesthetic*; tranquillizer, sedative; barbiturate, sleeping pill 679 *soporific*; narcotic, dope 949 *drug taking*.

(8) *balm,* syrup, emollient 177 *moderator*; salve, ointment; cream, liniment, embrocation; lotion, wash.

(9) *surgical dressing,* dressing, lint, gauze; swab; bandage, sling, splint, cast; tourniquet; fingerstall; plaster, sticking p.; fomentation, poultice, compress; tampon; pessary, suppository.

(10) *medical art,* art of healing, 656 *recuperation*; medical practice; allopathy, homoeopathy, naturopathy, nature cure; acupuncture; medicine, preventive m.; diagnosis, prognosis 651 *pathology*; healing, gift of h., faith h.; gynaecology, midwifery 167 *obstetrics*; geriatrics, paediatrics; orthopaedics pharmaceutics, pharmacology; veterinary medicine.

(11) *surgery,* general s., open-heart s.; plastic s. prosthesis; chiropractice; dialysis; operation, transplant; cauterization; amputation; tonsillectomy, appendectomy, mastectomy, vasectomy; dentistry; chiropody, pedicure, manicure electrolysis.

(12) *therapy,* therapeutics, medical care; treatment; nursing, bedside manner; first aid, aftercare; course, cure, regimen, diet; bone-setting, orthopaedics, osteopathy; hormone therapy; chemotherapy; physiotherapy, occupational therapy; radiotherapy; electrotherapy; psychotherapy 447 *psychology*; group therapy, aversion t.; acupuncture.

(13) *hospital,* infirmary; mental hospital 503 *lunatic asylum*; dispensary, clinic; nursing home, convalescent h.; hospice; ward, sick bay, sickbed; oxygen tent, life support machine, respirator, incubator; scanner; dressing station, first-aid s., casualty s.; operating theatre; health centre, surgery; sanatorium, spa.

(14) *doctor,* physician, faith h., healer; quack, charlatan; vet; herbalist, homoeopath, acupuncturist; witch' doctor 983 *sorcerer*; medic, medical student; houseman, intern, registrar; general practitioner, GP; locum; surgeon, consultant, specialist; diagnostician, pathologist, forensic p.; psychiatrist, psychoanalyst, neurologist; anaesthetist, paramedic, radiographer, physiotherapist, paediatrician, geriatrician; obstetrician, gynaecologist; osteopath; chiropodist; optician, oculist; dentist, dental surgeon, orthodontist; Red Cross.

(15) *druggist,* apothecary, chemist, pharmacist; dispenser, pharmacologist; pharmacy.

(16) *nurse,* male n., probationer n., student n., staff n.; charge n., sister, matron; district nurse, health visitor.

Adjective
(17) *remedial,* corrective, curative 656 *restorative;* helpful 644 *beneficial;* therapeutic, medicinal, healing; soothing, emollient, palliative 177 *lenitive;* analgesic, anaesthetic 375 *insensible;* peptic, digestive; purging 648 *cleansing;* cathartic, emetic, laxative; antidotal 182 *counteracting;* prophylactic 652 *salubrious;* tonic, stimulative; nutritive, nutritional.

(18) *medical,* pathological, Hippocratic; allopathic, homoeopathic, herbal; surgical, orthopaedic; clinical; operable, curable.

Verb
(19) *remedy,* put right 656 *restore;* help 703 *aid;* treat, heal 656 *cure;* palliate, soothe 831 *relieve.*

(20) *doctor,* treat, prescribe, attend 703 *minister to;* tend, nurse; give first aid 656 *revive;* hospitalize; medicate, dose, inject; dress, bandage; stop the bleeding 350 *staunch;* poultice, foment; set, put in splints; drug, anaesthetize; operate, cut open, amputate; cauterize; bleed, phlebotomize; massage, manipulate; immunize, vaccinate, inoculate 652 *sanitate.*

659
Bane

Noun
(1) *bane,* cause of injury, curse, plague, infestation, pest, scourge 616 *evil;* malady 651 *disease;* weakness, bad habit 934 *vice;* affliction 731 *adversity;* cross, trial; thorn in the flesh 827 *annoyance;* burden, imposition; stress, strain 825 *worry;* running sore 651 *ulcer;* bitterness 393 *sourness;* bite, sting, fang 256 *sharp point;* hornet's nest 663 *pitfall;* snake in the grass 663 *troublemaker;* parasite 365 *creepy-crawly;* locust 168 *destroyer;* oppressor 735 *tyrant.*

(2) *blight,* rot, mildew, mould, rust, fungus 51 *decay;* moth, woodworm, canker, cancer; visitation 651 *plague;* frost, cold; drought.

(3) *poison,* venomousness, toxicity; pollution; bacteria, bacillus, germ, virus 651 *infection;* carcinogen; chemical weapon, biological w.; venom, toxin; germicide, insecticide, pesticide; fungicide, weed-killer, defoliant; acid, corrosive; arsenic, cyanide, prussic acid, vitriol; nicotine 388 *tobacco;* poison gas, nerve g., tear g.; choke damp; foul air 653 *insalubrity;* lead pollution; uranium, plutonium; radioactivity, fallout 417 *radiation;* heroin 949 *drug-taking;* intoxicant 949 *alcoholism;* lethal dose, overdose; toxicology.

(4) *poisoning* 362 *homicide;* blood poisoning 651 *infection;* food poisoning, botulism; germ warfare 718 *warfare;* poisoner 362 *murderer.*

Adjective
(5) *baneful,* pestilent, noisome 645 *harmful;* virulent, poisonous, venomous 653 *toxic;* accursed 616 *evil.*

660
Safety

Noun
(1) *safety,* safeness, security; immunity, charmed life; safe distance, wide berth 620 *avoidance;* all clear, danger past; guarantee, warrant 473 *certainty;* assurance, confidence

855 *courage*; safety valve 667 *means of escape*.

(2) *protection*, conservation 666 *preservation*; insurance, surety 858 *caution*; patronage, auspices, aegis 703 *aid*; guardianship, wardenship, tutelage, custody 747 *restraint*; safekeeping, charge, safe hands; watch and ward 457 *surveillance*; safeguard, precaution 713 *defence*; cordon sanitaire, quarantine 652 *hygiene*; cushion, buffer; umbrella 662 *shelter*; deterrent 723 *weapon*; safe-conduct, pass 756 *permit*; escort, convoy, guard 722 *armed force*; defence, tower of strength 713 *defences*; haven, sanctuary 662 *refuge*; anchor, sheet a. 662 *safeguard*; moat, ditch, palisade, stockade 235 *fence*; shield, breastplate, panoply, armour plate 713 *armour*.

(3) *protector,* protectress, guardian, guardian angel 707 *patron*; life guard, preserver 713 *defender*; bodyguard, strongarm man, bouncer, vigilante; custodian, curator, warden; warder, guard, security g.; chaperon, baby-sitter 749 *keeper*; lookout, watch 664 *warner*; fire fighter, fireman *or* woman; sheriff; policeman *or* woman 955 *police*; sentry, sentinel, garrison 722 *soldiery*; guard dog 457 *surveillance*.

Adjective
(4) *safe,* without risk, assured, secure, sure, snug; safe and sound 666 *preserved*; intact 646 *undamaged*; garrisoned, well-defended; insured, covered; immunized, vaccinated, inoculated; hygienic 652 *salubrious*; in safety, out of harm's way; out of danger, in the clear; sheltered, shielded etc. vb.; in safe hands; in custody 747 *imprisoned*; reliable, guaranteed, 929 *trustworthy*; benign, harmless 615 *good*.

(5) *invulnerable,* immune, impregnable, sacrosanct; defensible, unassailable 162 *strong*; proof, weatherproof, waterproof, fireproof, bulletproof; snug, tight, seaworthy, airworthy; armoured, steel-clad.

(6) *tutelary,* custodial; protective; watchful 457 *vigilant*; fail-safe, doubly sure; protecting 666 *preserving*; antiseptic 652 *salubrious*.

Verb
(7) *be safe,* secure etc. adj.; reach safety come through 667 *escape*; weather the storm, ride it out; have nine lives; be under shelter, be under cover 523 *lurk*.

(8) *safeguard,* keep safe, guard, protect; stand up for 713 *defend*; cover up for, shield; champion 703 *patronize*; grant asylum; keep, conserve 666 *preserve*; treasure, hoard 632 *store*; keep in custody 747 *imprison*; watch over, care for, mother, nurse, cherish; take charge of 457 *look after*; hide 525 *conceal*; cushion, cocoon, insulate, earth; cover, cloak 421 *screen*; take in, house, shelter; enfold 235 *enclose*; make safe, secure, fortify 162 *strengthen*; fence in 232 *circumscribe*; arm, armourplate; shepherd, convoy, escort; flank, support; garrison, mount guard; immunize, inoculate, vaccinate 652 *sanitate*; give assurances, guarantee 473 *make certain*; keep order, police, patrol.

(9) *seek safety,* take precautions, play safe, take no chances 858 *be cautious*; dig in, lie low 523 *lurk*; run away 667 *escape*; run for port, take refuge 662 *seek refuge*.

Adverb
(10) *under shelter,* under cover, safely, with impunity.

661
Danger

Noun
(1) *danger,* peril; desperate situation 700 *predicament*; emergency 137 *crisis*; insecurity, risk, hazard 474 *uncertainty*; black spot 663 *pitfall*; trap, death t. 527 *ambush*; endangerment, imperilment, dangerous course; daring 857 *rashness*; venture, risky v. 672 *undertaking*; menace 900 *threat*; sense of danger, apprehension 854 *nervousness*; storm brewing 665 *danger signal*; narrow escape, close shave, near thing 667 *escape.*

(2) *vulnerability,* danger of 180 *liability*; security risk; insecurity exposure, nakedness 161 *helplessness*; easy target, sitting duck; vulnerable point, Achilles' heel 163 *weakness*; tender spot, soft underbelly feet of clay 647 *imperfection*;

Adjective
(3) *dangerous,* perilous, treacherous 854 *frightening*; risky, hazardous, dicey, dodgy, chancy 618 *speculative*; ugly, nasty, critical, menacing, ominous, foreboding 900 *threatening*; toxic, poisonous 645 *harmful*; infectious 653 *insalubrious*; inflammable, explosive, radioactive.

(4) *unsafe,* slippery, treacherous, insecure, unsound, precarious; top-heavy, unsteady shaky, rickety, frail 655 *dilapidated*; leaky, waterlogged; critical, ticklish, touch and go.

(5) *vulnerable,* in danger of, not immune 180 *liable*; open to, wide open, exposed 229 *uncovered*; undefended 161 *defenceless*; isolated, helpless, at the mercy of; off one's guard 508 *inexpectant.*

(6) *endangered,* in danger, facing death; on the rocks, on thin ice; surrounded, trapped, under fire; between two fires on the run, at bay, with one's back to the wall.

Verb
(7) *be in danger,* run the risk of 180 *be liable*; wall into a trap; get out of one's depth, play with fire 474 *be uncertain*; hang by a thread, tremble in the balance; get lost 282 *stray.*

(8) *face danger,* dice with death 855 *be courageous*; expose oneself 711 *defy*; face heavy odds, tempt providence, court disaster 857 *be rash*; run the gauntlet, come under fire; venture, dare, risk it 618 *gamble.*

(9) *endanger,* be dangerous, spell danger, put in jeopardy, imperil, hazard, jeopardize, compromise; stake 618 *gamble*; drive dangerously; be dangerous; threaten danger, menace 900 *threaten.*

662
Refuge. Safeguard

Noun
(1) *refuge,* sanctuary, asylum; trench, foxhole, shelter, fallout s.; burrow, earth, hole, den, lair, covert; privacy; cloister, cell, hermitage, ivory tower 192 *retreat*; temple, citadel; keep, stronghold 713 *fort*; secret place 527 *hiding-place*; rock, pillar, tower 218 *prop.*

(2) *shelter,* cover, roof; lee, lee wall, windbreak; stockade 235 *enclosure*; shield, wing; umbrella, oilskins; protective clothing, overalls; haven, harbour, port; almshouse, home, hospice.

(3) *safeguard,* means of safety, protection 660 *safety*; precautions 702 *hindrance*; crush barrier, guardrail, railing; mail

713 *armour*; arms 723 *weapon*; respirator, gas mask; safety catch, safety valve, fuse, earth; crash helmet; ejector-seat, parachute; safety net; lifeboat, life raft, life belt, life jacket; lifeline 667 *means of escape*; spare parts 40 *extra*.

Verb
(4) *seek refuge,* take refuge 660 *seek safety.*

663
Pitfall: Source of danger

Noun
(1) *pitfall,* snag 702 *obstacle*; booby trap 542 *trap*; minefield 527 *ambush*; reef, rock; chasm, abyss; crosscurrent, undertow 350 *current*; whirlpool 350 *eddy*; storm, squall 352 *gale*; volcano 383 *furnace*; dynamite, time bomb, powder keg 723 *explosive*; trouble-spot 661 *danger*; plague-spot, hotbed 651 *infection*; hazard 659 *bane*.

(2) *troublemaker,* mischief maker; stirrer, wrecker; ill-wisher 881 *enemy*; firebrand 738 *agitator*; ugly customer, undesirable, 904 *ruffian*; hidden hand 178 *influence*.

664
Warning

Noun
(1) *warning,* caution, caveat; example, lesson; notice, advance n. 524 *information*; word, tip-off 524 *hint*; ultimatum 737 *demand*; admonishment 924 *reprimand*; protest, expostulation 762 *deprecation*; warning shot; foreboding, premonition 511 *prediction*; alarm, siren 665 *danger signal*; gathering cloud, 661 *danger*; writing on the wall 547 *indication*; beacon 547 *signal*; menace 900 *threat*.

(2) *warner,* admonisher 691 *adviser*; prophet 511 *diviner*; watchman, lookout 457 *surveillance*; scout, spy; picket, sentinel, sentry 660 *protector*; advanced guard, rearguard; watchdog.

Adjective
(3) *cautionary,* hinting, warning, admonitory; protesting 762 *deprecatory*; exemplary, instructive 524 *informative*; symptomatic 547 *indicating*; ill-omened, ominous 511 *presageful*; menacing 900 *threatening*; deterrent 854 *frightening*.

(4) *warned,* once bitten 858 *cautious*; forewarned 507 *expectant*; forearmed 669 *prepared*.

Verb
(5) *warn,* caution; give fair warning, give notice, notify 524 *inform*; blow the whistle on 524 *hint*; counsel 691 *advise*; admonish 924 *reprove*; forewarn 511 *predict*; alert 669 *prepare*; menace 900 *threaten*; advise against 613 *dissuade*; 762 *deprecate*; sound the alarm 665 *raise the alarm*.

(6) *be warned,* receive notice; beware, take heed 457 *be careful.*

Interjection
(7) *look out!* watch out! mind your step!

665
Danger signal

Noun
(1) *danger signal,* alarm 664 *warning*; murmur, muttering 829 *discontent*; evil omen 511 *omen*; gale warning; alarm clock, burglar alarm, fire a.; foghorn; motor horn, klaxon, bell, whistle; blast, honk, toot; church bell, curfew, tocsin; siren, alert, red a.; tattoo, trumpet-call 547 *call*; war cry, battle c., rallying cry; warning light,

red l., Very l. flag; beacon; distress signal, SOS 547 *signal*.

(2) *false alarm,* scare, hoax; nightmare, bad dream 543 *untruth*; scaremonger 854 *alarmist*.

Verb
(3) *raise the alarm,* sound the a., dial 999, alert, arouse 854 *frighten*; honk, toot; cry wolf, cry too soon; sound a warning, toll, knell 528 *proclaim*.

666
Preservation

Noun
(1) *preservation,* safekeeping; safe conduct 660 *protection*; saving, salvation 668 *deliverance*; conservation, conservancy; perpetuation, prolongation 144 *permanence*; upkeep, maintenance, support 633 *provision*; servicing, valeting 648 *cleansing*; insulation, heat retention; saving up 632 *storage*; bird sanctuary, game reserve, nature r.; listed building; taxidermy, mummification, embalmment; cold storage 382 *refrigeration*; drying, dehydration 342 *desiccation*; canning, tinning, packing; sterilization 652 *hygiene*.

(2) *preserver,* life-saver 668 *deliverance*; charm, mascot 983 *talisman*; preservative, pickle, brine; freezer 384 *refrigerator*; cannery, bottling plant; safety device, seat belt 662 *safeguard*; incubator, respirator; conservator, conservationist.

Adjective
(3) *preserving,* conserving etc. vb.; energy-saving; preservative, conservative; protective, preventive 652 *salubrious*.

(4) *preserved,* well-p., kept, frozen, pickled etc. vb.; treasured 632 *stored*; conserved, protected 660 *safe*.

Verb
(5) *preserve,* conserve, keep fresh, freeze 382 *refrigerate*; embalm, mummify, stuff; pickle, salt 388 *season*; cure, smoke, dehydrate 342 *dry*; bottle, tin, can; protect, paint, creosote, waterproof; service 656 *repair*; prop up 218 *support*; keep alive, sustain 633 *provide*; keep safe 660 *safeguard*; reserve 632 *store*; nurse, tend 658 *doctor*; cherish, treasure 457 *look after*; keep going, prolong; save 668 *deliver*.

667
Escape

Noun
(1) *escape,* leakage 298 *egress*; extrication, delivery, rescue 668 *deliverance*; getaway, breakout; flight, flit, moonlight f. 296 *departure*; withdrawal, retreat 286 *regression*; evasion, truancy 620 *avoidance*; narrow escape, close shave, near thing 661 *danger*; discharge, reprieve 960 *acquittal*; setting free 746 *liberation*; escapology, escapism.

(2) *means of escape,* emergency exit secret passage 298 *egress*; ladder, fire escape, escape hatch; vent, safety valve 662 *safeguard*; trick 623 *contrivance*; loophole, escape clause, let-out.

(3) *escaper,* escapee, runaway; truant; fugitive, refugee; escapologist.

Adjective
(4) *escaped,* fled, flown, stolen away; eloping, truant; fugitive, runaway; slippery, elusive 620 *avoiding*; free, at large; relieved, well rid of.

Verb
(5) *escape,* effect one's e. 746 *achieve liberty*; make a getaway, break out, abscond,

jump bail; flit, elope 620 *run away*; steal away, sneak off 296 *decamp*; slip through, break away, get free, slip one's lead; get out 298 *emerge*; get away, get away with, get off, get off lightly, go scot-free; scrape through, survive; wriggle out of 919 *be exempt*; leak, leak away 298 *flow out*.

(6) *elude*, give the slip; evade, abscond, 620 *avoid*; lie low 523 *lurk*; shake off, escape notice.

668
Deliverance

Noun
(1) *deliverance*, delivery, extrication 304 *extraction*; riddance 831 *relief*; emancipation 746 *liberation*; rescue, life-saving; salvage, retrieval 656 *restoration*; salvation, redemption 965 *divine function*; ransom, buying off 792 *purchase*; release, amnesty; discharge, reprieve 960 *acquittal*; respite 136 *delay*; truce, standstill 145 *cessation*; way out 667 *escape*; dispensation, exemption.

Adjective
(2) *extricable*, deliverable, redeemable.

Verb
(3) *deliver*, save, rescue, come to the r., throw a lifeline; extricate 304 *extract*; unloose, unbind 46 *disunite*; disburden 701 *disencumber*; save from 831 *relieve*; release, unlock, unbar; emancipate, free, set free 746 *liberate*; let one off 960 *acquit*; save oneself, 667 *escape*; rid oneself of, get rid of; redeem, ransom 792 *purchase*; salvage, retrieve, recover, bring back, restore; spare, excuse, dispense from 919 *exempt*.

669
Preparation

Noun
(1) *preparation*, preparing, making ready; preliminaries, tuning, priming; trial run, trials 461 *experiment*; practice, rehearsal; briefing; training 534 *teaching*; novitiate 68 *beginning*; study, homework 536 *learning*; spadework 682 *labour*; groundwork, foundation 218 *basis*; planning, outline, blueprint, 623 *plan*; shadow cabinet; arrangement, premeditation 608 *predetermination*; preconsultation 691 *advice*; forethought, anticipation, precautions 510 *foresight*; nest egg 632 *store*.

(2) *fitting out*, provisioning, furnishing, equipment 633 *provision*; appointment, commission; marshalling, armament; promotion, flotation, launching 68 *debut*.

(3) *maturation*, ripening, seasoning; hardening, hatching, gestation, incubation 167 *propagation*; nursing, nurture; cultivation, 370 *agriculture*; bloom, efflorescence; fruition 725 *completion*.

(4) *preparedness*, readiness, ripeness, mellowness, maturity; puberty, nubility 134 *adultness*; fitness 646 *perfection*.

(5) *preparer*, coach 537 *trainer* trail-blazer, pioneer 66 *precursor*; provisioner 633 *provider*; cultivator 370 *farmer*.

Adjective
(6) *preparatory*, preparative; precautionary, preliminary 64 *preceding*; brooding, hatching, maturing; in embryo; in preparation, on foot, on the stocks; in store 155 *impending*; mooted 623 *planned*; learning 536 *studious*.

(7) *prepared,* ready, alert 457 *vigilant*; in readiness, at the ready; mobilized, standing by, on call; all set, ready to go, spoiling for; trained, fully t., qualified; well-prepared, practised, word-perfect; primed, briefed, instructed 524 *informed*; forewarned 664 *warned*; groomed 228 *dressed*; armed, in armour; in harness; rigged out, equipped 633 *provisioning*; in hand 632 *stored*; in reserve, ready to hand, ready for use; fit for use, in working order, operational.

(8) *matured,* ripened, digested; ripe, mellow, mature, seasoned, weathered, hardened; tried, experienced, veteran 694 *expert*; adult, grown, full-g., fledged, full-f. 134 *grown-up*; out, in flower, flowering, fruiting; deep-laid; perfected 725 *completed*.

(9) *ready-made,* cut and dried, ready to use, ready-to-wear, off the peg; ready-formed, prefabricated; oven-ready; predigested, processed, instant.

Verb
(10) *prepare,* take steps, take measures; make ready, pave the way; lead up to, pioneer 64 *come before*; do the groundwork, lay the foundations; predispose, incline, soften up; sow the seed 370 *cultivate*; prepare the ground 68 *begin*; roughhew, block out; sketch, outline 623 *plan*; plot, concert, prearrange 608 *predetermine*; prepare for, guard against, take precautions 660 *seek safety*; anticipate 507 *expect*.

(11) *make ready,* ready, have´r., put in readiness; stow, pack 632 *store*; commission, put in c.; wind up, tune up, adjust 62 *arrange*; clear the decks, close the ranks; array, mobilize 74 *bring together*; set, cock, prime,

load; raise steam, warm up, crank up, rev up; equip, crew, man; fit out, kit out, rig out, dress, arm 633 *provide*; improvise, rustle up; rehearse, drill, groom, exercise, lick into shape 534 *train*; inure, acclimatize 610 *habituate*; coach, brief 524 *inform*.

(12) *mature,* mellow, ripen, bring to fruition 646 *perfect*; force, bring on; bring to a head 725 *climax*; brew 301 *cook*; hatch, breed 369 *breed stock*; grow 370 *cultivate*; nurse, nurture; elaborate, work out 725 *carry through*; season, dry, cure; temper 326 *harden*.

(13) *prepare oneself,* brace o., compose o.; qualify oneself, brief o. study; train, exercise, rehearse, practise 536 *learn*; limber up, warm up, flex one's muscles; be prepared, stand ready, stand by.

Adverb
(14) *in preparation,* in readiness, just in case; in hand, in train, under way.

670
Nonpreparation

Noun
(1) *nonpreparation,* lack of preparation, potluck; lack of training, want of practice; unreadiness, unfitness; rawness, immaturity 126 *newness*; belatedness 136 *lateness*; improvidence, neglect 458 *negligence*; hastiness, rush 680 *haste*; improvisation, impromptu, snap answer 609 *spontaneity*; surprise; forwardness, precocity 135 *earliness*.

(2) *undevelopment,* delayed maturity state of nature, virgin soil; raw material, rough diamond; late developer; embryo, abortion.

Adjective

(3) *unprepared,* not ready, behindhand 136 *late*; ad hoc, ad lib, extemporized, improvised, impromptu 609 *spontaneous*; unstudied 699 *artless*; rash, careless 458 *negligent*; rush, precipitate 680 *hasty*; unguarded, exposed 661 *vulnerable*; caught unawares, taken off guard 508 *inexpectant*; shiftless, improvident 456 *lightminded*; scratch, untutored 491 *uninstructed*; fallow 674 *unused.*

(4) *immature,* half-grown, unripe, half-ripe, under-ripe, green; callow, adolescent, juvenile, boyish, girlish 130 *young*; undeveloped, unformed, halfbaked 647 *imperfect*; backward 136 *late*; embryonic, rudimentary 68 *beginning*; half-formed, half-finished, rough-hewn; premature, abortive, at half-cock 728 *unsuccessful*; apprentice, undergraduate 695 *unskilled*; crude, coarse, rude 699 *artless*; early matured, forced, precocious.

(5) *uncooked,* raw, red, rare, underdone; cold, undressed; indigestible.

(6) *unequipped,* dismasted, dismantled; ill-provided 307 *deficient*; unfitted, unqualified.

Verb

(7) *be unprepared,* lack preparation 55 *be incomplete*; want practice, need training; extemporize 609 *improvise*; be premature 135 *be early*; take no precautions 456 *be inattentive*; catch unawares 508 *surprise.*

Adverb

(8) *unreadily,* off the cuff, offhand.

671
Attempt

Noun

(1) *attempt,* essay, bid; step, move; endeavour, struggle, strain, effort 682 *exertion*; try, good try, valiant effort; one's level best; trial, probation 461 *experiment*; shot at, stab at, crack at; first attempt 68 *debut*; final attempt, last throw; venture, quest 672 *undertaking*; goal 617 *objective.*

(2) *trier* 852 *hoper*; tester 461 *experimenter*; searcher 459 enquirer; fighter 716 *contender*; idealist 862 *perfectionist*; lobbyist, activist; contractor, entrepreneur.

Adjective

(3) *attempting,* trying etc. vb.; doing one's best 597 *willing*; game 599 *resolute*; searching 459 *enquiring*; tentative, testing, probationary 461 *experimental*; ambitious, venturesome, daring 672 *enterprising.*

Verb

(4) *attempt,* essay, try; seek to, aim 617 *intend*; seek 459 *search*; offer, bid, make a b.; make an attempt, make the effort; endeavour, struggle, strive 599 *be resolute*; do one's best, go all out 682 *exert oneself*; strain, sweat 682 *work*; tackle, take on, have a go 672 *undertake*; take a chance, try one's luck; venture, speculate 618 *gamble*; test 461 *experiment*; fly a kite 461 *be tentative*; be over ambitious 728 *fail.*

Interjection

(5) *Here goes!* nothing venture, nothing win!

672
Undertaking

Noun

(1) *undertaking,* job, task, assignment; labour of love, pilgrimage 597 *voluntary work*; contract, engagement, obligation 764 *promise*; operation, exercise; programme, project 623 *plan*; tall order 700 *hard task*; enterprise, quest, search, adventure 459 *enquiry*; speculation 618 *gambling*; occupation 622 *business*; struggle, effort, campaign 671 *attempt.*

Adjective

(2) *enterprising,* pioneering, adventurous, venturesome, daring; go-ahead, progressive; ambitious, opportunist.

Verb

(3) *undertake,* engage in, apply oneself to, address o. to, take up, set one's hand to; venture on, take on, tackle 671 *attempt*; go about, take in hand, set going 68 *initiate*; proceed to, embark on, launch into; fall to, set to, buckle to 68 *begin*; grasp the nettle 855 *be courageous*; take charge of 689 *manage*; execute 725 *carry out*; take upon oneself 917 *incur a duty*; engage to, commit oneself 764 *promise*; get involved, volunteer 597 *be willing*; show enterprise, pioneer; venture, dare 661 *face danger.*

673
Use

Noun

(1) *use,* enjoyment, disposal 773 *possession*; conversion, utilization, exploitation, employment, application, exercise 610 *practice*; resort, recourse; mode of use, treatment, good usage 457 *carefulness*; ill-treatment 675 *misuse*; effect of use,

wear, wear and tear 655 *dilapidation*; exhaustion, consumption 634 *waste*; usefulness, benefit, service 642 *good policy*; practicality, applicability 640 *utility*; office, purpose, point 622 *function*; long use, wont 610 *habit.*

Adjective

(2) *used,* applied etc. vb.; in service, in use, in constant u., in practice; used up, consumed, worn, threadbare, secondhand, well-used, well-thumbed, dog-eared, well-worn 655 *dilapidated*; hackneyed welltrodden 490 *known*; practical, utilitarian 642 *advisable*; subservient 628 *instrumental*; available, usable, employable, utilizable, convertible 640 *useful*; at one's service, consumable, disposable.

Verb

(3) *use,* employ, exercise, practise, put into practice; apply, exert, bring to bear, administer; spend on, give to, devote to, consecrate to, dedicate to; assign to, utilize, make use of, convert to use 640 *find useful*; reuse, recycle, exploit, milk, drain 304 *extract*; turn to account, capitalize on, make the most of, put to good use 137 *profit by*; make play with, play on, trade on, cash in on; take advantage of, play off against; wear out, use up, consume 634 *waste*; work, drive, manipulate 173 *operate*; wield, ply, brandish; overwork, tax, task 684 *fatigue.*

(4) *avail oneself of,* take up, adopt, try; resort to, have recourse to, fall back on, draw on; impose on, presume on; press into service; make do with, make shift w.

(5) *dispose of,* have at one's disposal, command; control, allot, assign 783 *apportion*; spare,

have to s.; requisition, call in;
set in motion, set going, deploy
612 *motivate*; enjoy 773 *possess*;
consume, expend, use up 634
waste.

674
Nonuse

Noun
(1) *nonuse,* abeyance, suspension 677 *inaction*; stagnation,
unemployment 679 *inactivity*;
forbearance, abstinence 620
avoidance; savings 632 *store*;
disuse, obsolescence 611 *desuetude*; waiver, giving up, surrender cancellation 752 *abrogation*; uselessness, write-off 641
inutility.

Adjective
(2) *unused,* not used; not available; out of order, unusable 641
useless; unpracticable 643 *inexpedient*; in hand, reserved 632
stored; pigeonholed; spare, extra; untilled, untapped, lying
idle; in abeyance, suspended;
left to rot 634 *wasted*; redundant, unnecessary, not required 860 *unwanted*; free, vacant; dispensed with, waived;
unemployed 679 *inactive*; jobless, out of work.

(3) *disused,* discarded, cast-off,
jettisoned, scrapped, written
off; sacked, discharged; laid up,
out of commission; used up, run
down, worn out; on the shelf,
retired; superseded, superannuated, obsolete 127
antiquated.

Verb
(4) *not use,* have no use for; not
utilize, hold in abeyance; not
touch, abstain, forbear, hold
off, do without 620 *avoid*; dispense with, waive 621 *relinquish*; overlook, disregard 458
neglect; spare, save, reserve 632
store.

(5) *stop using,* leave off 145
cease; outgrow 611 *disaccustom*; leave to rust, lay up,
dismantle 641 *make useless*;
have done with, lay aside, hang
up; discard, dump, ditch, scrap,
write off; jettison, throw away
300 *eject*; cast off 229 *doff*; give
up, relinquish 779 *not retain*;
suspend, withdraw, cancel 752
abrogate; discharge, lay off,
make redundant 300 *dismiss*;
drop, replace 150 *substitute*; be
unused, rust 655 *deteriorate*.

675
Misuse

Noun
(1) *misuse,* abuse, wrong use;
maladministration mismanagement, 695 *bungling*; malpractice 788 *peculation*; perversion
246 *distortion*; prostitution,
violation; profanation 980 *impiety*; pollution 649 *uncleanness*; extravagance 634 *waste*;
mishandling, maltreatment, ill-
treatment, force 176 *violence*;
mistreatment, outrage, injury
616 *evil*.

Verb
(2) *misuse,* abuse; use wrongly,
misdirect; divert, manipulate,
misappropriate 788 *defraud*;
violate, desecrate 980 *profane*;
prostitute 655 *pervert*; pollute
649 *make unclean*; do violence
to 176 *force*; take advantage of,
exploit 673 *use*; manhandle,
knock about 645 *ill-treat*; maltreat 735 *oppress*; misgovern,
misrule; mishandle, mismanage; overwork, overtax 684 *fatigue*; wear out 655 *impair*;
squander, fritter away 634
waste; misapply 641 *waste
effort*.

676
Action

Noun

(1) *action,* doing, performance; steps, measures 623 *policy*; transaction, enactment, commission, perpetration; execution, effectuation 725 *completion*; procedure, routine 610 *practice*; behaviour 688 *conduct*; movement 265 *motion*; operation, working, interaction 173 *agency*; force, pressure 178 *influence*; work, labour 682 *exertion*; activeness 678 *activity*; occupation 622 *business*; manufacture 164 *production*; employment 673 *use*; campaign, crusade, war on 671 *attempt*; handling 689 *management*.

(2) *deed,* act, action, exploit, feat, achievement 855 *prowess*; bad deed, crime 930 *foul play*; stunt 875 *ostentation*; gesture, measure, step, move 623 *policy*; manoeuvre 688 *tactics*; stroke, blow, coup; task, operation, exercise 672 *undertaking*; proceeding, transaction, deal 154 *affairs*; work, handiwork; chef d'oeuvre 694 *masterpiece*; drama 590 *narrative*.

(3) *doer,* man or woman of action 678 *busy person*; practical person, realist; achiever, finisher; hero, heroine 855 *brave person*; practitioner 696 *expert*; player 594 *actor*; executant, performer; perpetrator, offender; operator 686 *agent*; contractor, entrepreneur; campaigner, canvasser; executor, executive 690 *director*; operative 686 *worker*; craftsman, craftswoman 686 *artisan*; creative worker 556 *artist*.

Adjective

(4) *doing,* acting, performing etc. vb., in the act, red-handed; working, at work, in action, in operation 173 *operative*; industrious, busy 678 *active*; occupational 610 *habitual*.

Verb

(5) *do,* act, perform; be in action 173 *operate*; militate, act upon 178 *influence*; manipulate 612 *motivate*; manoeuvre 698 *be cunning*; proceed with, get on with; take action, take steps; try 671 *attempt*; tackle, take on 672 *undertake*; perpetrate, commit; achieve, accomplish, 725 *carry through*; execute, implement, fulfil, put into practice 725 *carry out*; solemnize, observe; make history, 866 *have a reputation*; practise, exercise, carry on, discharge, pursue, ply, employ oneself 622 *busy oneself*; officiate 622 *function*; transact, proceed 622 *do business*; administer 689 *direct*; labour, campaign, canvass 682 *work*; exploit 673 *use*; be active in 775 *participate*; have a hand in 678 *meddle*.

Adverb

(6) *in the act,* redhanded.

677
Inaction

Noun

(1) *inaction,* inertia 175 *inertness*; inability to act 161 *impotence*; failure to act 458 *negligence*; abstention, refraining 620 *avoidance*; suspension, abeyance, dormancy 674 *nonuse*; deadlock, stalemate 145 *stop*; immobility, paralysis 375 *insensibility*; stagnation, vegetation 266 *quiescence*; idle hours, 681 *leisure*; rest 683 *repose*; no work, sinecure; loafing, idleness 679 *inactivity*; nonintervention 860 *indifference*; head in the sand 856 *cowardice*.

Adjective

(2) *nonactive,* inoperative, idle,

suspended, in abeyance 679 *inactive*; passive, sluggish 175 *inert*; leisured 681 *leisurely*; do-nothing, ostrich-like; stationary, immobile 266 *quiescent*; laid off, unemployed, jobless, out of work 674 *unused*; paralysed 375 *insensible*; apathetic, phlegmatic 820 *impassive*; neutral 860 *indifferent*.

Verb

(3) *not act,* fail to a., refuse to a. 598 *be unwilling*; pass the buck 620 *avoid*; look on, stand by 441 *watch*; wait and see, bide one's time 136 *wait*; procrastinate 136 *put off*; leave alone, let well alone; do nothing, tolerate 458 *disregard*; sit tight, not budge, not stir 175 *be inert*; drift, slide, coast, free-wheel; let pass, let go by 458 *neglect*; sit back, relax 683 *repose*; have no function 641 *be useless*; kick one's heels 681 *have leisure*; pause 145 *cease*; lie idle, lie fallow 674 *not use*.

678
Activity

Noun

(1) *activity,* activeness, activism, militancy 676 *action*; active interest 775 *participation*; activation 612 *motive*; excitation 174 *stimulation*; agitation, movement, life, stir 265 *motion*; alacrity 597 *willingness*; readiness 135 *punctuality*; quickness, dispatch 277 *velocity*; spurt, burst, fit 318 *spasm*; hurry, flurry, bustle 680 *haste*; fuss, bother, ado, to-do 61 *turmoil*; whirl, scramble, rat race drama, much ado, thick of things, the fray; plenty to do 622 *business*; pressure of work, no sinecure; high street, marketplace, madding crowd; hum, hive of industry 687 *workshop*.

(2) *restlessness,* pottering, fiddling, aimless activity 456 *inattention*; fidgets 318 *agitation*; jumpiness 822 *excitability*; fever, fret 503 *frenzy*; eagerness, enthusiasm 818 *warm feeling*; vigour, energy, ceaseless e., dynamism, militancy, enterprise, initiative, push, drive, go 174 *vigorousness*; vivacity, spirit, animation, liveliness, vitality 360 *life*; sleeplessness, insomnia.

(3) *assiduity,* application, concentration, intentness 455 *attention*; industry, drudgery 682 *labour*; determination, earnestness 599 *resolution*; tirelessness 600 *perseverance*; painstaking, diligence.

(4) *overactivity,* excess, Parkinson's law; song and dance 318 *commotion*; officiousness, interference, meddling, interfering, tampering; intrigue 623 *plot*.

(5) *busy person,* enthusiast, zealot, fanatic 602 *obstinate person*; no slouch, hard worker, workaholic, demon for work 686 *worker*; drudge, dogsbody, slave, galley s., Trojan; eager beaver, busy bee; activist, militant 676 *doer*; live wire, dynamo, powerhouse, whiz kid; thruster, careerist.

(6) *meddler,* stirrer, officious person, spoilsport, busybody 453 *inquisitive person*; intriguer 623 *planner*; back-seat driver 691 *adviser*; fusspot, nuisance.

Adjective

(7) *active,* stirring 265 *moving*; going, working, incessant 146 *unceasing*; expeditious 622 *businesslike*; able-bodied 162 *strong*; brisk, nippy, spry 277 *speedy*; nimble, light-footed; energetic, forceful 174 *vigorous*; pushing, go-getting 672 *enterprising*; frisky, coltish, sprightly, spirited, mettlesome, animated, vivacious 819 *lively*; eager, 818 *fervent*; enthusiastic, zealous, prompt, instant, ready, on one's toes 597 *willing*; awake, alert, wakeful 457 *vigilant*; sleepless, restless, feverish, fretful, tossing, fidgety, jumpy 318 *agitated*; frantic, demonic 503 *frenzied*; hyperactive 822 *excitable*; aggressive, militant 718 *warlike*.

(8) *busy,* bustling, humming, lively, eventful; coming and going, up and doing, stirring, astir, afoot, on the move, on the go, on the trot, in full swing; hard at work, in harness, at work, employed, occupied.

(9) *industrious,* hardworking, studious, sedulous, assiduous 600 *persevering*; labouring, plodding 682 *laborious*; unflagging, unsleeping, tireless, indefatigable; efficient, workmanlike 622 *businesslike*.

(10) *meddling,* officious, interfering, meddlesome, intrusive, intriguing; dabbling.

Verb
(11) *be active,* show interest, join in 775 *participate*; stir, come and go 265 *move*; run riot, have one's fling 61 *rampage*; rouse oneself, bestir o.; hum, thrive 730 *prosper*; keep moving 146 *go on*; push, shove, 279 *impel*; elbow one's way 174 *be vigorous*; explode, burst 176 *be violent*; dash, fly, run 277 *move fast*; do one's best 671 *attempt*; take pains 455 *be attentive*; buckle to 682 *exert oneself*; persist, beaver away 600 *persevere*; polish off, dispatch 727 *be successful*; jump to it 676 *do*, 597 *be willing*; watch 457 *be careful*; take one's chance 137 *profit by*; assert oneself, show fight 711 *defy*; protest, agitate, demonstrate, raise the dust 762 *deprecate*.

(12) *be busy,* keep b. 622 *busy oneself*; bustle, hurry, scurry

680 *hasten*; fuss 822 *be excitable*; have one's hands full, slave, slog 682 *work*; overwork, overdo it, make work.

(13) *meddle,* interpose, intervene, interfere, butt in 297 *intrude*; pester, bother 827 *trouble*. tinker, tamper, 655 *impair*.

Adverb
(14) *actively,* on the go, on one's toes.

679
Inactivity

Noun
(1) *inactivity* 677 *inaction*; inertia, torpor 175 *inertness*; lull 145 *cessation*; slack period, immobility 266 *quiescence*; no progress, stagnation; rustiness 674 *nonuse*; slump, recession, unemployment, shutdown; procrastination 136 *delay*; idleness, indolence, loafing 681 *leisure*.

(2) *sluggishness,* lethargy, laziness, indolence, sloth; dawdling, slow progress 278 *slowness*; lifelessness languor, listlessness; stupor, torpor, numbness 375 *insensibility*; phlegm, impassivity.

(3) *sleepiness,* tiredness, weariness 684 *fatigue*; somnolence, doziness, drowsiness, heaviness, nodding, yawning.

(4) *sleep,* slumber; deep sleep, sound s., heavy s.; half-sleep, drowse; light sleep, nap, catnap, forty winks, snooze, doze 683 *repose*; hibernation, coma, trance 375 *insensibility*; sleepwalking, somnambulism; dreams, dreamland.

(5) *soporific,* sleeping draught, nightcap; sleeping pill, sedative; morphine 375 *anaesthetic*; lullaby.

(6) *idler,* drone, lazybones loafer, lounger; slouch, slacker,

skiver, clock-watcher; dawdler 278 *slowcoach*; tramp 268 *wanderer*; mendicant 763 *beggar*; parasite, cadger, scrounger, sponger, freeloader; layabout, ne'er-do-well, wastrel, drifter, free-wheeler; passenger, sleeping partner, idle rich; dreamer, sleepyhead; sleeper, slumberer, dozer, hibernator.

Adjective

(7) *inactive,* still, extinct 266 *quiescent*; suspended, taken off, not working, not in use, 674 *disused*; inanimate, lifeless 175 *inert*; torpid, benumbed, dopey, drugged 375 *insensible*; sluggish, stiff, rusty 677 *nonactive*; listless, lackadaisical 834 *dejected*; languid, languorous 684 *fatigued*; apathetic, lethargic; idle 681 *leisurely*; on strike.

(8) *lazy,* bone-l., work-shy, indolent, idle, bone-idle, parasitical; idling, loafing 681 *leisurely*; dawdling 278 *slow*; tardy, dilatory 136 *late*; slack 458 *negligent.*

(9) *sleepy,* tired 684 *fatigued*; half-awake, half-asleep; somnolent, heavy-eyed, drowsy, dozy, dopey, nodding, yawning; napping, dozing; asleep, dreaming, snoring, fast asleep, sound a.; hibernating, comatose.

(10) *soporific,* sedative, hypnotic.

Verb

(11) *be inactive,* do nothing, stagnate, vegetate, hang fire 677 *not act*; delay 136 *put off*; take it easy, let things go 458 *be neglectful*; hang about, kick one's heels 136 *wait*; lag, loiter, dawdle 278 *move slowly*; drag one's feet 136 *be late*; loll, lounge, laze 683 *repose*; slack, skive 620 *avoid*; loaf, idle, moon about, waste time 641 *waste effort*; slow down 278 *decelerate*; hesitate 474 *be uncertain*;

droop, languish, slacken 266 *come to rest*; strike, come out.

(12) *sleep,* slumber, snooze, nap, catnap; hibernate; dream; snore, go to sleep, nod off, drop off, fall asleep; yawn, nod, doze, drowse; go to bed, turn in, bed down, roost, perch.

(13) *make inactive,* put to bed, send to sleep, lull, rock, cradle; soothe 177 *assuage*; paralyse, drug 375 *render insensible*; immobilize 747 *fetter*; lay up 674 *stop using*; pay off 300 *dismiss.*

680
Haste

Noun

(1) *haste,* hurry, scurry, hustle, bustle, flurry, whirl, scramble 678 *activity*; flap, flutter 318 *agitation*; rush, rush job 136 *lateness*; immediacy, urgency 638 *importance*; expedition, dispatch 277 *velocity*; hastening, acceleration dash 277 *spurt*; impetuosity 857 *rashness*; hastiness, impatience 822 *excitability.*

Adjective

(2) *hasty,* impetuous, impulsive, hot-headed 857 *rash*; feverish, impatient 818 *fervent*; precipitate, headlong, breathless, breakneck 277 *speedy*; expeditious, prompt, without delay; in haste, hotfoot; in a hurry, hard-pressed; done in haste, hurried, scamped, slapdash, cursory 458 *negligent*; rushed, rush, last-minute 670 *unprepared*; rushed into, railroaded; urgent, immediate 638 *important.*

(3) *hasten,* expedite, dispatch; urge, drive, spur, whip 612 *incite*; bundle off, hustle away; rush, be hasty 857 *be rash*; haste, make haste; race, run 277 *move fast*; spurt, dash 277

accelerate; hurry, scurry, hustle, bustle 678 *be active*; brush aside, cut corners, rush one's fences 136 *be late*; lose no time, hasten away 296 *decamp*.

Adverb
(4) *hastily,* hurriedly, precipitately, pell-mell, post-haste, hotfoot, apace 277 *swiftly*; at short notice.

Interjection
(5) *hurry up!* be quick! look sharp! quick march! at the double!

681
Leisure

Noun
(1) *leisure,* spare time, free t., time to kill; not enough work, sinecure; time off, holiday, break, vacation; idleness 679 *inactivity*; time to spare, no hurry; rest, retirement, relaxation 683 *repose*.

Adjective
(2) *leisurely,* deliberate, unhurried 278 *slow*; leisured, at leisure, 683 *reposeful*; at ease; off duty, on holiday, retired.

Verb
(3) *have leisure,* have plenty of time, take one's ease, while away; take one's time 278 *move slowly*; take a holiday 683 *repose*; give up work, retire; find time for.

682
Exertion

Noun
(1) *exertion,* effort, struggle 671 *attempt*; strain, stress, might and main; tug, heave; force, pressure 160 *energy*; ergonomics; muscle, elbow grease; trouble, pains, taking pains 678 *assiduity*; overwork, overtime, busman's holiday; campaign, fray.

(2) *exercise,* practice, drill, training, work-out; keeping fit, jogging 162 *athletics*; yoga, eurhythmics, callisthenics; physical education, games, sports 837 *sport*.

(3) *labour,* industry, work, hard w., long haul; spadework, donkeywork; housework, chores; toil, travail, drudgery, slavery; sweat, grind, strain, treadmill, grindstone; hack work; hard labour 963 *penalty*; forced labour, fatigue 917 *duty*; piecework, homework, outwork; task, chore, job, exercise 676 *deed*; shift, stint 110 *period*; working life, working day, man-hours, woman-h.

Adjective
(4) *labouring,* working, drudging, sweating, hard at it 678 *busy*; hardworking, laborious 678 *industrious*; slogging, plodding 600 *persevering*; strenuous, energetic 678 *active*; painstaking, thorough 455 *attentive*; exercising, taking exercise; gymnastic, athletic.

(5) *laborious,* involving effort; crushing, killing, backbreaking; gruelling, punishing, exhausting; toilsome, troublesome, wearisome, burdensome; heroic, Herculean; arduous, hard, uphill 700 *difficult*; hardfought, hard-won; painstaking, laboured.

Verb
(6) *exert oneself,* apply oneself, make an effort 671 *attempt*; struggle, strain, strive; trouble oneself, put oneself out, bend over backwards, spare no effort, do one's utmost, try one's best; put one's back into 678 *be active*; force one's way, drive through, wade t.; hammer at 600 *persevere*; battle, campaign, take action 676 *do*.

(7) *work,* labour, toil, drudge, slog, sweat, slave away; pull,

haul, hump, heave; get down to set about 68 *begin*; keep at it 600 *persevere*; work hard, moonlight 678 *be busy*; work for, serve 703 *minister to*.

Adverb
(8) *laboriously*, the hard way; manually, by hand; lustily, heart and soul, for all one is worth.

683
Repose

Noun
(1) *repose*, rest 679 *inactivity*; restfulness, ease 376 *euphoria*; peace and quiet, tranquillity 266 *quiescence*; happy dreams 679 *sleep*; relaxation, breathing space 685 *refreshment*; pause, respite, let-up 145 *lull*; holiday, vacation, leave 681 *leisure*; day of rest, Sabbath, Lord's day.

Adjective
(2) *reposeful*, restful, easeful, relaxing; slippered, carefree, casual, relaxed, at ease 828 *content*; cushioned, pillowed 376 *comfortable*; peaceful, quiet 266 *tranquil*; leisured, holiday 681 *leisurely*.

Verb
(3) *repose*, rest, take a rest, take it easy, take one's ease, put one's feet up, sit back, recline, loll, lounge, laze, sprawl 216 *be horizontal*; go to bed, 679 *sleep*; relax, unwind, take a breather 685 *be refreshed*; slack off, let up, slow down; take a holiday, 681 *have leisure*.

Adverb
(4) *at rest*, on holiday, on vacation.

684
Fatigue

Noun
(1) *fatigue*, tiredness, weariness, lassitude, languor, lethargy; physical fatigue, aching muscles; mental fatigue, staleness; distress, exhaustion, collapse, prostration; strain 682 *exertion*; laboured breathing palpitations; faintness, fainting, swoon, blackout 375 *insensibility*.

Adjective
(2) *fatigued*, tired, ready for bed 679 *sleepy*; tired out, exhausted, spent; dull, stale; strained, overworked, dog-tired, bone-weary, tired to death, ready to drop, all in, dead beat; swooning, fainting, prostrate; stiff, aching, sore, footsore; tired-looking, haggard, worn; faint, drooping, flagging; tired of, jaded 863 *sated*.

(3) *panting*, out of breath, short of b.; breathless, gasping, snorting, winded, broken-w. 352 *puffing*.

(4) *fatiguing*, gruelling, punishing 682 *laborious*; tiresome, wearisome; wearing, exacting, demanding; irksome, trying 838 *tedious*.

Verb
(5) *be fatigued*, tire oneself out, overdo it; gasp, pant, puff, blow; languish, droop, flag, fail 163 *be weak*; stagger, faint, swoon, feel giddy; yawn, nod, drowse 679 *sleep*; succumb, collapse; overwork, get stale, need a break.

(6) *fatigue*, tire, tire out, wear out, exhaust, prostrate; double up, wind; demand too much, task, tax, strain, work, drive, overdrive, overwork, overtax, overburden; enervate, drain; distress 827 *trouble*; weary, bore, send to sleep 838 *be tedious*.

685
Refreshment

Noun

(1) *refreshment,* breather, breath of air 683 *repose;* break, recess 145 *lull;* renewal, recreation, recuperation 656 *restoration;* easing 831 *relief;* stimulation, refresher, reviver 174 *stimulant;* refreshments 301 *food;* wash 648 *cleansing.*

Adjective

(2) *refreshing,* cooling, thirst-quenching; cool 380 *cold;* comforting 831 *relieving;* bracing, reviving 656 *restorative;* easy on, labour-saving 683 *reposeful.*

(3) *refreshed,* freshened up, recovered, revived 656 *restored;* ready for more.

Verb

(4) *refresh,* freshen, freshen up 648 *clean;* air, ventilate 340 *aerate;* shade, cool off, cool one down 382 *refrigerate;* brace, stimulate 174 *invigorate;* reinvigorate, revive, recuperate 656 *restore;* ease 831 *relieve;* allow rest, give a breather; offer food 301 *feed.*

(5) *be refreshed,* get one's breath back, get one's second wind; perk up, come to revive 656 *be restored;* stretch one's legs, refresh oneself take a breather, sleep it off; have a rest 683 *repose.*

686
Agent

Noun

(1) *agent,* operator, performer, player, executant, practitioner; perpetrator 676 *doer;* tool 628 *instrument;* functionary 741 *officer;* representative 754 *delegate;* spokesperson 755 *deputy;* proxy 150 *substitute;* executor, executive, administrator; dealer 794 *merchant;* employer, manufacturer, industrialist 164 *producer.*

(2) *worker,* voluntary w. 597 *volunteer;* freelance; trade unionist 775 *participator;* toiler, drudge, dogsbody, hack; menial 742 *servant;* beast of burden 742 *slave;* beaver 678 *busy person;* business man *or* woman, breadwinner, earner, employee; brain worker, boffin; clerical worker, desk w., office w., white-collar w.; shop assistant 793 *seller;* labourer, casual l.; agricultural l., farm worker 370 *farmer;* piece-worker, manual w., blue-collar w.; workman, hand, operative.

(3) *artisan,* technician; skilled worker, semi-skilled w., master 696 *proficient person;* journeyman, apprentice 538 *learner;* craftsman *or* woman, potter, turner, joiner, carpenter, woodworker, sawyer, cooper; wright, wheelwright; shipwright, boat-builder; builder, mason, bricklayer, plasterer, tiler, painter, decorator; metalworker, smith; miner steelworker; mechanic, machinist, fitter; engineer, civil e., mining e.; plumber, welder, electrician, gas-fitter; tailor, needlewoman 228 *clothier.*

(4) *personnel,* staff, force, company, gang, squad, crew, 74 *band;* co-worker, mate, associate, partner 707 *colleague;* workpeople, hands, payroll; labour, casual l.; labour force, proletariat.

687
Workshop

Noun

(1) *workshop,* studio, workroom,

study, library; laboratory, research l.; plant, installation; works, factory, yard; sweatshop; mill, sawmill, paper mill; foundry, metalworks; steelworks, smelter; blast furnace, forge, smithy; powerhouse, power station 160 *energy*; quarry, mine 632 *store*; colliery, pit mint; arsenal, armoury; dockyard, slips; refinery, distillery, brewery, maltings; shop, shopfloor, production line; dairy, 369 *stock farm*; kitchen, laundry; office, offices, secretariat; hive of industry 678 *activity*.

688
Conduct

Noun
(1) *conduct,* behaviour, deportment; bearing, carriage; demeanour, attitude, posture 445 *mien*; tone of voice, delivery; motion, action, gesticulation 547 *gesture*; mode of behaviour, fashion, style; manner, guise, air; poise, dignity, presence; graciousness, good manners 884 *courtesy*; rudeness, bad manners 885 *discourtesy*; pose, role-playing 850 *affectation*; mental attitude, outlook 485 *opinion*; mood 818 *feeling*; misbehaviour, misconduct 934 *wickedness*; past behaviour, record, track r., history; reward of conduct, deserts 915 *dueness*; lifestyles, way of life, ethos, morals, principles, ideals, manners 610 *habit*; career, walk of life 622 *vocation*; routine 610 *practice*; procedure, method 624 *way*; treatment, handling, direction 689 *management*; gentle handling 736 *leniency*; iron hand 735 *severity*; deeds 676 *deed*.
(2) *tactics,* strategy, campaign 623 *plan*; line, party l. 623 *policy*; politics, realpolitik, statesmanship 733 *governance*;

one-upmanship 698 *cunning*; brinkmanship 694 *skill*; manoeuvres, manoeuvring, jockeying, 34 *advantage*; playing for time 136 *delay*; shift 623 *contrivance*; move, gambit 698 *stratagem*.

Adjective
(3) *behaving,* behavioural, psychological; tactical, strategic; political, statesmanlike 622 *businesslike*.

Verb
(4) *behave,* act 676 *do*; behave well 933 *be virtuous*; behave badly, misbehave 934 *be wicked*; posture, pose 850 *be affected*; conduct oneself, behave o., carry o., bear o., acquit o., comport o.; set an example; indulge in 678 *be active*; play one's part 775 *participate*; pursue 622 *busy oneself*; shift for oneself; manoeuvre, jockey; behave towards, treat.

(5) *deal with,* handle, manipulate 173 *operate*; conduct, carry on, run 689 *manage*; see to, cope with; transact, execute 725 *carry out*; work out 623 *plan*; work at 682 *work*; go through, read 536 *study*.

689
Management

Noun
(1) *management,* conduct, running, handling; managership, stewardship, agency 751 *commission*; charge, control 733 *authority*; oversight 457 *surveillance*; patronage 660 *protection*; art of management, tact, way with 694 *skill*; work study, organization, decision-making 623 *policy*; housekeeping, economics; statecraft, statesmanship; government 733 *governance*; menage, regimen, regime, dispensation; law-making 953 *legislation*; ministry,

cabinet, inner c.; administration; bureaucracy.

(2) *directorship,* direction, control, responsibility 737 *command*; dictatorship, leadership, premiership, chairmanship, captaincy 34 *superiority*; guidance, steering, pilotage; controls, helm, rudder, wheel, tiller, joystick; remote control.

Adjective
(3) *directing,* directorial, leading, guiding, steering, at the helm; governing, controlling, holding the reins, in the chair 733 *authoritative*; dictatorial 735 *authoritarian*; supervisory, managing, managerial; executive, administrative; legislative; high-level, top-l. 638 *important*; economic, political; official, bureaucratic 733 *governmental*.

Verb
(4) *manage,* manipulate, pull the strings 178 *influence*; handle, conduct, run, carry on; minister, administer, prescribe; supervise, superintend, oversee 457 *invigilate*; have charge of, keep order, police, regulate; legislate, pass laws; control, govern 733 *rule*;

(5) *direct,* lead 64 *come before*; dictate 737 *command*; be in charge, wear the trousers; have responsibility 917 *incur a duty*; preside, take the chair, head, captain, skipper, stroke; pilot, cox, steer; shepherd, guide, conduct escort 89 *accompany*.

Adverb
(6) *in control,* in charge, at the helm, in the chair.

690
Director

Noun
(1) *director,* governing body 741

governor; cabinet 692 *council*; board, chair; staff, management; manager, controller; legislator, law-giver; employer 741 *master*; chief, head of state 34 *superior*; principal, head, rector, dean, chancellor; president, vice-p.; chairperson, chairman, chairwoman, speaker; premier, prime minister; captain, skipper; stroke, cox, master 270 *mariner*; pilot 520 *guide*; hidden hand 178 *influence*.

(2) *leader,* pacemaker; conductor, first violin; precentor; drum major; Führer 741 *autocrat*; ringleader, demagogue 738 *agitator*.

(3) *manager,* person in charge; key person, kingpin 638 *bigwig*; administrator, executive, executor 676 *doer*; statesman *or* woman, politician; economist, political e.; housekeeper, housewife; steward, bailiff, farm manager, agent, factor 754 *consignee*; supervisor, superintendent, inspector, overseer, foreman *or* -woman; warden, matron, tutor 660 *protector*; party manager, whip; curator, librarian 749 *keeper*; circus manager, ringmaster; compere.

(4) *official,* office-holder, office-bearer; marshal, steward; shop steward; civil servant 742 *servant*; officer of state, minister, cabinet m., secretary, under-s.; bureaucrat, Eurocrat, mandarin 741 *officer*; magistrate, commissioner, prefect, consul; counsellor 754 *envoy*; alderman, mayor 692 *councillor*; functionary, clerk; school prefect, monitor.

691
Advice

Noun
(1) *advice,* word of a., piece of a.,

counsel 498 *wisdom*; counselling 658 *therapy*; criticism, constructive c. 480 *estimate*; didacticism, moralizing, 693 *precept*;
caution 664 *warning*; recommendation, suggestion, submission; tip 524 *hint*; guidance,
briefing, instruction 524 *information*; taking counsel, deliberation, consultation, heads together, 584 *conference*; advice
against 762 *deprecation*.

(2) *adviser,* counsellor, consultant 696 *expert*; referee, arbiter
480 *estimator*; advocate, mover,
recommender; medical adviser,
658 *doctor*; legal adviser, counsel 958 *lawyer*; guide, mentor
537 *teacher*; admonisher 505
reminder; oracle 500 *sage*;
busybody 678 *meddler*; consultative body 692 *council*.

Adjective
(3) *advising,* advisory, consultative, deliberative; recommendatory 612 *inducing*; advising
against admonitory 664 *cautionary*; didactic, moralizing.

Verb
(4) *advise,* counsel, give advice;
recommend, prescribe, advocate, commend; propose, move,
submit, suggest 512 *propound*;
prompt 524 *hint*; press, urge,
exhort 612 *incite*; advise
against 613 *dissuade*; admonish 664 *warn*; enjoin, charge,
dictate 737 *command*

(5) *consult,* seek advice, call in,
call on; confide in; take advice,
listen to, be advised; sit in
council, deliberate, parley,
compare notes 584 *confer*.

692
Council

Noun
(1) *council,* council chamber,
board room; court 956 *tribunal*;
cabinet, kitchen c.; quango,

panel, think tank, board, advisory b., Royal Commission; assembly, congregation 74 *assembly*; conclave, convocation 985
synod; convention, congress,
meeting, summit; sitting, session 584 *conference*.

(2) *parliament,* Upper House,
House of Lords, 'another place'; Lower House, House of
Commons; legislature; Congress, Senate; quorum,
division.

(3) *councillor,* privy councillor;
senator, peer, life peer; Lords
Spiritual, L. Temporal; representative 754 *delegate*; member
of parliament, MP; backbencher; legislator; mayor, alderman
690 *official*.

Adjective
(4) *parliamentary,* senatorial;
bicameral.

693
Precept

Noun
(1) *precept,* firm advice 691 *advice*; direction, instruction, injunction, charge 737 *command*;
commission 751 *mandate*; order, writ 737 *warrant*; prescription, ordinance, regulation 737
decree; canon, form, norm, formula, rubric; guidelines 81
rule; principle, rule, golden r.,
moral 496 *maxim*; recipe 658
remedy; commandment, statute 953 *legislation*; set of rules,
constitution; canon law, common l. 953 *law*; rule of custom,
convention 610 *practice*.

Adjective
(2) *preceptive,* prescriptive,
mandatory, binding; canonical, statutory 953 *legal*; moralizing 496 *aphoristic*; conventional 610 *usual*.

694
Skill

Noun

(1) *skill,* dexterity, handiness; grace, style 575 *elegance;* neatness, deftness, adroitness, address; ease 701 *facility;* proficiency, competence, efficiency; capability, capacity 160 *ability;* versatility, adaptability, flexibility; touch, grip, control; mastery, wizardry, virtuosity, prowess 644 *goodness;* strong point, metier, forte; acquirement, accomplishment, attainment, skills; seamanship, horsemanship, marksmanship; experience, expertise, professionalism; specialism, knowhow, technique 490 *knowledge;* practical ability, clever hands, deft fingers; craftsmanship, art, artistry, delicacy, fine workmanship 646 *perfection;* resourcefulness, ingenuity 698 *cunning;* cleverness, sharpness, sophistication, 498 *sagacity;* savoir faire, finesse, tact, discretion; sleight of hand 688 *tactics;* exploitation 673 *use.*

(2) *aptitude,* innate ability, good head for; natural bent 179 *tendency;* faculty, endowment, gift, flair; turn, knack, green fingers; talent, genius for; aptness, fitness.

(3) *masterpiece,* chef-d'oeuvre, a beauty; masterstroke, feat, exploit, hat trick 676 *deed;* tour de force, bravura, fireworks; work of art, objet d'art, curio, collector's piece.

Adjective

(4) *skilful,* good at, top-flight, first-rate 644 *excellent;* skilled, crack; apt, handy, dexterous, ambidextrous, deft, slick, adroit, agile, nimble, surefooted; cunning, clever, quick, shrewd, ingenious 498 *intelligent;* politic, diplomatic, statesmanlike 498 *wise;* adaptable, resourceful, ready; many-sided, versatile; sound, able, competent, efficient; wizard, masterful, masterly, magisterial; accomplished, finished 646 *perfect.*

(5) *gifted,* naturally g.; of many parts, talented, well-endowed; born for, cut out for.

(6) *expert,* experienced, veteran, seasoned, tried, versed in, au fait 490 *instructed;* skilled, trained practised, 669 *prepared;* specialized, proficient, qualified, competent, efficient; professional 622 *businesslike.*

(7) *well-made,* well-crafted; finished, artistic, artificial, sophisticated; stylish 575 *elegant;* shipshape, workmanlike.

Verb

(8) *be skilful,* deft etc. adj.; be good at have a gift for 644 *be good;* shine, excel 34 *be superior;* have the knack; be on form, have one's eye *or* hand in; use skilfully, exploit 673 *use;* take advantage of 137 *profit by;* get around, know what's what 498 *be wise.*

(9) *be expert,* have the knowhow; qualify oneself 536 *learn;* have experience, know the ropes, know backwards, 490 *know.*

Adverb

(10) *skilfully,* expertly etc. adj.; well, with skill.

695
Unskilfulness

Noun

(1) *unskilfulness,* no gift for; lack of practice, rustiness; immaturity, inexperience, inexpertness 491 *ignorance;* incapacity, inability, incompetence,

inefficiency 161 *ineffectuality*; charlatanism 850 *pretension*; clumsiness, awkwardness booby prize, wooden spoon.

(2) *bungling*, botching; bungle, botch, shambles; bad job, flop 728 *failure*; missed chance 138 *untimeliness*; hamhandedness, butter fingers, dropped catch, fluff, miss, mishit, slice, misfire, own goal 495 *mistake*; tactlessness, indiscretion; mishandling 675 *misuse*; too many cooks; mismanagement, misrule, misgovernment, maladministration; wild-goose chase 641 *lost labour*.

Adjective
(3) *unskilful*, untalented, ungifted; unfit, inept, incapable 161 *impotent*; incompetent, inefficient, ineffectual; impolitic, undiplomatic 499 *unwise*; failed inadequate 728 *unsuccessful*.

(4) *unskilled*, raw, green 670 *immature*; semi-skilled, unqualified, inexpert, inexperienced, ignorant 491 *uninstructed*; ham, lay, amateurish, amateur; charlatan, quack, unscientific.

(5) *clumsy*, awkward, gauche, gawkish, boorish, uncouth 885 *discourteous*; stuttering 580 *stammering*; tactless, bumbling, bungling; maladroit, all thumbs, left-handed, ham-h., heavy-footed; ungainly, lumbering, hulking, gangling, stumbling, shambling; stiff, rusty 674 *unused*; unaccustomed, out of practice, out of training, off form losing one's touch, slipping; slapdash 458 *negligent*; fumbling, tentative 461 *experimental*; graceless, clownish 576 *inelegant*; topheavy, lop-sided, cumbersome, ponderous, ungainly 195 *unwieldy*.

(6) *bungled*, badly done, botched, mismanaged, mishandled etc. vb.; faulty 647 *imperfect*; misguided, ill-advised, illjudged; ill-prepared 670 *unprepared*; unhappy, infelicitous; crude, rough and ready, inartistic, amateurish, homemade 699 *artless*; perfunctory, half-baked 726 uncompleted.

Verb
(7) *be unskilful,* - inept etc. adj.; not know how 491 *not know*; burn one's fingers; mishandle, mismanage; misapply 675 *misuse*; misdirect 495 *blunder*; forget one's words, miss one's cue 506 *forget*; get out of practise, go rusty; lose one's nerve, come unstuck 728 *fail*.

(8) *act foolishly,* make a fool of oneself 497 *be absurd*; spoil one's chances 495 *blunder*; go on a fool's errand 641 *waste effort*.

(9) *be clumsy*, lumber, bumble, trip over, stumble, blunder; stutter 580 *stammer*; fumble, grope, flounder 461 *be tentative*; muff, fluff; spill, slop, drop bungle, drop a brick, put one's foot in it 495 *blunder*; botch, spoil, mar, blot 655 *impair*; fool with 678 *meddle*; make a mess of 728 *fail*.

696
Proficient person

Noun
(1) *proficient person,* expert, adept, dab hand, all-rounder 646 *paragon*; master, past m., graduate, cordon bleu; intellectual, mastermind 500 *sage*; genius 864 *prodigy*; maestro, virtuoso, prima donna 413 *musician*; prize-winner, champion, title-holder; crack shot, black belt, ace 644 *exceller*.

(2) *expert*, professional, pro, specialist, authority, doyen 537

teacher; pundit, savant, polymath 492 *scholar*; veteran, old hand, sea dog; practised hand, practised eye; sophisticate, smart customer 698 slyboots; sharper 545 *trickster*; cosmopolitan, man *or* woman of the world; tactician, strategist, politician; diplomat, diplomatist; artist, technician, skilled worker 686 *artisan*; consultant 691 *adviser*; cognoscente, connoisseur, fancier.

697
Bungler

Noun
(1) *bungler,* failure 728 *loser*; incompetent, bumbler, blunderer, bungling idiot; fumbler, butterfingers; lump, lout, clumsy clot, duffer, clown, buffoon, booby, oaf, ass 501 *fool*; scribbler, dauber, bad hand, poor shot; amateur, novice, greenhorn 538 *beginner*; quack 545 *impostor*; landlubber 25 *misfit.*

698
Cunning

Noun
(1) *cunning,* craft 694 *skill*; lore 490 *knowledge*; inventiveness, ingenuity 513 *imagination*; guile, gamesmanship, craftiness, artfulness, subtlety, wiliness, slyness, foxiness; stealth 523 *latency*; suppleness, slipperiness, shiftiness; knavery, chicanery sharp practice 930 *foul play*; finesse, jugglery 542 *sleight*; cheating 542 *deception*; imposture 541 *duplicity*; disguise 525 *concealment*; manoeuvring, 688 *tactics*; policy, diplomacy, realpolitik; intrigue 623 *plot.*

(2) *stratagem,* ruse, wile, art, artifice, resource, resort, ploy, shift, dodge 623 *contrivance*; machination, game, 623 *plot*;

subterfuge, evasion; excuse 614 *pretext*; white lie 542 *deception*; trick, box of tricks 542 *trickery*; feint, catch, net, web, ambush, 542 *trap*, 663 *pitfall*; blind 542 *sham*; manoeuvre, move 688 *tactics.*

(3) *slyboots,* artful dodger, wily person, serpent, snake, fox; lurker 663 *troublemaker*; fraud, dissembler, hypocrite 545 *deceiver*; cheat 545 *trickster*; glib tongue 925 *flatterer*; diplomatist, intriguer, plotter, schemer 623 *plánner*; strategist, tactician 612 *motivator.*

Adjective
(4) *cunning,* crafty 498 *wise*; artful, sly, wily, subtle, foxy; full of ruses, tricky 525 *stealthy*; scheming, contriving, intriguing, Machiavellian 623 *planning*; knowing, smart, sophisticated, urbane; canny, sharp, astute, shrewd, acute; up to everything 498 *intelligent*; cagey 525 *reticent*; experienced 694 *skilful*; resourceful ingenious; tactical, strategic, deep-laid, well-planned; insidious 930 *perfidious*; shifty, slippery, temporizing 518 *equivocal*; deceitful, flattering 542 *deceiving*; knavish 930 *rascally*; crooked, devious 930 *dishonest.*

Verb
(5) *be cunning,* sly etc. adj.; play the fox, finesse, shift, dodge, juggle, manoeuvre, jockey, double-cross, twist, wriggle; lie low 523 *lurk*; intrigue, scheme 623 *plot*; monkey about with, tinker, gerrymander, trick, cheat 542 *deceive*; temporize, play for time; circumvent, outsmart, outwit, go one better 306 *outdo*; waylay 527 *ambush*; see the catch, avoid the trap.

Adverb
(6) *cunningly,* artfully, on the sly.

699
Artlessness

Noun

(1) *artlessness,* simplicity, naivety, ingenuousness 935 *innocence*; inexperience, unworldliness; naturalness 573 *plainness*; sincerity, candour, frankness, bluntness, outspokenness 540 *veracity*; truth, honesty 929 *probity*; primitiveness, savagery; barbarism Philistinism 491 *ignorance*; uncouthness, crudity.

(2) *ingenue,* ingenuous person, child of nature, savage, noble s.; enfant terrible; lamb, babe in arms 935 *innocent*; simpleton 501 *ninny*; novice 538 *beginner*; rough diamond; simple soul, pure heart; yokel, rustic.

Adjective

(3) *artless,* without art, without artifice, without tricks; unstudied, uncontrived 44 *simple*; unvarnished 573 *plain*; native, natural, homespun, homemade 695 *unskilled*; wild, savage, primitive, untutored, unlearned, backward 491 *ignorant*; Arcadian, unsophisticated, unworldly, ingenuous, naive, childlike 935 *innocent*; simple-minded, callow; guileless, confiding; unreserved, uninhibited 609 *spontaneous*; candid, frank 540 *veracious*; true, honest, sincere 929 *honourable*; above-board, on the level; blunt, outspoken, free-spoken; transparent 522 *undisguised*; prosaic, literal, 494 *accurate*; inartistic, Philistine; uncouth, unrefined 847 *vulgar*.

Verb

(4) *be artless,* know no better; have no tricks 935 *be innocent*; call a spade a spade 573 *speak plainly*; confide 540 *be truthful*.

Adverb

(5) *artlessly,* without art, without affectation.

700
Difficulty

Noun

(1) *difficulty,* hardness, arduousness, laboriousness 682 *exertion*; maze, intricacy 61 *complexity*; complication 832 *aggravation*; obscurity 517 *unintelligibility*; inconvenience, embarrassment 643 *inexpedience*; hard going, bad patch; knot, problem, puzzle, headache 530 *enigma*; impediment, handicap, obstacle 702 *hindrance*; cul-de-sac, dead end, impasse 264 *closure*; deadlock, standstill 145 *stop*; stress, brunt, burden 684 *fatigue*; trial, ordeal, tribulation 825 *suffering*; trouble 731 *adversity*; difficult person, handful, one's despair.

(2) *hard task,* test, trial of strength; Herculean task, superhuman t., thankless t.; task, job, no picnic; handful, tall order, tough assignment, uphill struggle 682 *labour*.

(3) *predicament,* embarrassment, false position; quandary, dilemma, cleft stick; borderline case 474 *dubiety*; catch-22 situation; fix, jam, hole, trouble, pickle, mess, muddle; pinch, straits, pass, pretty p.; sticky wicket, tight corner 661 *danger*; emergency 137 *crisis*.

Adjective

(4) *difficult,* hard, tough, formidable; steep, arduous, uphill; inconvenient, onerous, burdensome, irksome, toilsome, bothersome 682 *laborious*; exacting, demanding 684 *fatiguing*; insuperable, impracticable 470 *impossible*; problematic, delicate, ticklish, tricky; awkward, embarrassing; out of

hand, intractable, unmanageable, refractory 738 *disobedient*; stubborn, perverse 602 *obstinate*; ill-behaved, naughty 934 *wicked*; perplexing, obscure 517 *unintelligible*; knotty, complex, complicated 251 *intricate*; impenetrable, impassable thorny, rugged, craggy 259 *rough*; sticky, critical 661 *dangerous*.

(5) *in difficulties,* hampered 702 *hindered*; in a quandary, in a dilemma, in a cleft stick 474 *doubting*; baffled, clueless, nonplussed 517 *puzzled*; in a jam, in a fix, on the hook, in a spot, in a hole, in a pickle; out of one's depth, in deep water, under fire 661 *endangered*; hard pressed, under pressure, up against it; left in the lunch; cornered, at bay; stuck fast, aground.

Verb
(6) *be difficult,* hard etc. adj.; complicate 63 *bedevil*; inconvenience, bother 827 *trouble*; perplex, baffle, nonplus, stump 474 *puzzle*; hamper, obstruct 702 *hinder*; make things worse 832 *aggravate*; create deadlock 470 *make impossible*.

(7) *be in difficulty,* have a problem; tread carefully, pick one's way 461 *be tentative*; have one's hands full 678 *be busy*; not know where to turn 474 *be uncertain*; have trouble with; run into trouble 731 *have trouble*; feel the pinch 825 *suffer*; come unstuck 728 *miscarry*; struggle, labour under difficulties.

Adverb
(8) *with difficulty,* the hard way; at a pinch.

701
Facility

Noun
(1) *facility,* ease, convenience, comfort; capability, feasibility

469 *possibility*; easing, making easy, smoothing, simplification; free hand, full play, clean slate 744 *scope*; facilities, provision for 703 *aid*; leave 756 *permission*; simplicity, no difficulty; easy going, calm seas; downhill 309 *descent*.

(2) *easy thing,* no trouble, a pleasure, child's play; short work, light work, sinecure; picnic, piece of cake 837 *amusement*; plain sailing, easy ride, nothing to it; easy target, sitting duck; walkover 727 *victory*; cinch 473 *certainty*.

Adjective
(3) *easy,* effortless, undemanding, painless; frictionless 258 *smooth*; not hard, foolproof; easily done, feasible 469 *possible*; facilitating, helpful 703 *aiding*; downhill, downstream, with the current; convenient 376 *comfortable*; approachable, 289 *accessible*; comprehensible 516 *intelligible*.

(4) *tractable,* manageable, easygoing 597 *willing*; submissive 721 *submitting*; yielding, malleable, pliant 327 *flexible*; smooth-running, handy, manoeuvrable.

(5) *facilitated,* made easy; simplified; disencumbered, unloaded, light; unrestrained; unimpeded; aided, given a chance in one's element, at home 376 *comfortable*.

Verb
(6) *be easy,* simple etc. adj.; require no effort, give no trouble, make no demands; run well, go like clockwork 258 *go smoothly*.

(7) *do easily,* have no trouble, make light of, make short work of; take in one's stride; have a walkover 727 *win*; sail home, coast h., free-wheel.

(8) *facilitate,* ease, make easy; iron out 258 *smooth*; grease, oil 334 *lubricate*; explain, simplify 520 *interpret*; enable 160 *empower*; make way for, allow 469 *make possible*; help, speed, expedite 703 *aid*; pioneer, blaze a trail 64 *come before*; pave the way, bridge the gap; leave a loophole 744 *give scope*.

(9) *disencumber,* free, liberate 668 *deliver*; clear the ground; disentangle, extricate 62 *unravel*; untie 46 *disunite*; ease, lighten, unburden, alleviate 831 *relieve*.

Adverb
(10) *easily,* effortlessly, just like that; without a hitch; like clockwork.

702
Hindrance

Noun
(1) *hindrance,* impediment; inhibition, hangup, fixation, block; stalling, thwarting, obstruction, frustration; hampering etc. vb.; blockage 264 *closure*; blockade, siege 712 *attack*; limitation, restriction, control 747 *restraint*; arrest 747 *detention*; check, deceleration 278 *slowness*; drag 333 *friction*; interference, meddling; interruption, intervention; objection 762 *deprecation*; picketing, sabotage 704 *opposition*; discouragement, disincentive; hostility, blacking, boycott 620 *avoidance*; ban, embargo 757 *prohibition*; birth control 172 *contraception*.

(2) *obstacle,* impediment, hindrance, nuisance, drawback, inconvenience, handicap 700 *difficulty*; bunker, hazard; bottleneck, blockage, road block, traffic jam, logjam; tether 47 *bond*; red tape, regulations; snag, stumbling block, hurdle; wall, brick w.; portcullis, barbed wire 713 *defences*; blockade 235 *enclosure*; turnstile, tollgate; crosswind, headwind, crosscurrent; impasse, deadlock, stalemate, vicious circle, catch-22; cul-de-sac, blind alley, dead end.

(3) *hitch,* snag, catch; rebuff 760 *refusal*; contretemps, spot of trouble; technical hitch, breakdown, failure, engine f., puncture, flat; leak, burst pipe; fuse, short circuit; stoppage, holdup, setback 145 *stop*.

(4) *encumbrance,* handicap; drag, shackle, chain 748 *fetter*; meshes, toils; impedimenta, baggage, lumber; cross, millstone; pack, burden, load; commitments, dependants; mortgage, debts 803 *debt*.

(5) *hinderer,* hindrance; red herring 10 *irrelevance*; wet blanket, damper, spoilsport, killjoy; obstructor, filibuster, saboteur; heckler, interrupter, barracker; poltergeist, gremlin 663 *troublemaker*; challenger 705 *opponent*; rival, competitor 716 *contender*.

Adjective
(6) *hindering,* impeding, obstructive, stalling, delaying etc. vb.; contrary, unfavourable 731 *adverse*; restrictive, cramping 747 *restraining*; prohibitive, preventive 757 *prohibiting*; counteractive 182 *counteracting*; upsetting, disconcerting, off-putting; intrusive, not wanted 59 *extraneous*; interfering 678 *meddling*; blocking, in the way, in the light; inconvenient 643 *inexpedient*; hard 700 *difficult*; onerous, crushing, burdensome 322 *weighty*; disincentive, discouraging; disheartening, damping; unhelpful 704 *opposing*.

(7) *hindered,* handicapped etc. vb.; lumbered with saddled w.;

held up, delayed, becalmed; prevented 757 *prohibited*; hardpressed 700 *in difficulties*; heavy-laden, overburdened 684 *fatigued*; marooned, stranded.

Verb

(8) *hinder,* hamper, obstruct, impede; bother, inconvenience 827 *trouble*; embarrass, disconcert, upset, disorder 63 *derange*; trip up, tangle, entangle, enmesh 542 *ensnare*; get in the way 678 *meddle*; intercept, cut off, head off, undermine; stifle, choke; gag, muzzle; suffocate, repress 165 *suppress*; burden, encumber 322 *weigh*; cramp, handicap; tie one's hands 747 *fetter*; check, hold back 747 *restrain*; hold up, slow down, set one back 278 *retard*; cripple, hobble, hamstring 161 *disable*; scotch, wing 655 *wound*; clip one's wings, cramp one's style; intimidate, deter 854 *frighten*; discourage, dishearten 613 *dissuade*; snub, rebuff 760 *refuse*.

(9) *obstruct,* stymie, snooker 231 *lie between*; jostle, crowd, squeeze; stop up, block up, 264 *close*; jam, jam tight, cause a stoppage; bandage, bind 350 *staunch*; dam up, earth up, embank; stave off 713 *parry*; barricade 235 *enclose*; fence, hedge in, blockade 232 *circumscribe*; keep out 57 *exclude*; inhibit, ban, bar, debar 757 *prohibit*.

(10) *be obstructive,* give trouble, play up 700 *be difficult*; put off, stall, stonewall; baffle, foil, stymie, counter 182 *counteract*; check, thwart, frustrate; raise objections 704 *oppose*; interrupt, interject, heckle, barrack; refuse a hearing, shout down 400 *be loud*; talk out time, filibuster 581 *be loquacious*; play for time, drag out 113 *spin out*; picket, strike 145 *halt*; sabotage.

703
Aid

Noun

(1) *aid,* assistance, help, helping hand, leg-up, lift, boost; succour, rescue 668 *deliverance*; comfort, support, moral s.; backing, encouragement; reinforcement 162 *strengthening*; helpfulness 706 *cooperation*; service, ministry, ministration 897 *kind act*; interest, good offices; patronage, auspices, sponsorship 660 *protection*, 178 *influence*; good will, charity, sympathy 897 *benevolence*; intercession 981 *prayers*; advocacy, championship; promotion 654 *improvement*; nursing, first aid 658 *medical art*; relief, easing 685 *refreshment*; fair wind, following w.; facilities, magic wand 701 *facility*; self-help 744 *independence*.

(2) *subvention,* economic aid, donation 781 *gift*; charity 901 *philanthropy*; social security, benefit; loan 802 *credit*; subsidy, hand-out, bounty, grant, allowance, expense account; stipend, bursary, scholarship 962 *reward*; maintenance, support, keep, upkeep 633 *provision*.

(3) *aider,* help, helper, assistant, lieutenant, henchman, aide, right-hand man, man Friday, girl F.; stand-by, support, mainstay; tower of strength, rock 660 *protector*; social worker, counsellor 691 *adviser*; good neighbour, Good Samaritan, friend in need; ally 707 *collaborator*; reinforcements, recruits 707 *auxiliary*; fairy godmother 903 *benefactor*; promoter, sponsor 707 *patron*.

Adjective

(4) *aiding,* helpful, obliging 706

cooperative; kind, well-disposed, 897 *benevolent*; neighbourly 880 *friendly*; favourable, propitious; supporting, seconding, abetting; supportive, encouraging 612 *inducing*; of service, of help 640 *useful*; constructive, well-meant; assistant, auxiliary, subsidiary, ancillary, accessory; in aid of, contributory, promoting; subservient 742 *serving*; assisting 628 *instrumental*.

Verb
(5) *aid,* help, assist, lend a hand 706 *cooperate*; lend one's aid, take in tow, hold one's hand, be kind to 897 *be benevolent*; help one out, tide one over, see one through; oblige, accommodate, lend money to 784 *lend*; subsidize; facilitate, speed, lend wings to, further, advance, boost 285 *promote*; abet, instigate, foment, nourish 612 *induce*; make for, contribute to, be accessory to 156 *conduce*; lend support to, boost one's morale, back up, stand by, bolster, prop up 218 *support*; comfort, sustain, hearten, give heart to, encourage, rally, embolden 855 *give courage*; succour, come to the help of, bail out, help o., relieve 668 *deliver*; reinforce, fortify 162 *strengthen*; ease 685 *refresh*.

(6) *patronize,* favour, smile on, shine on 730 *be auspicious*; sponsor, back, guarantee, go bail for; recommend, put up for; propose, second; countenance, connive at, protect 660 *safeguard*; join, contribute to, subscribe to 488 *endorse*; take one's part, side with 880 *befriend*; champion, stick up for, stand by 713 *defend*; canvass for, vote f. 605 *vote*; pray for, intercede; pay for 804 *defray*; keep, cherish, foster, nurse, mother 889 *pet*.

(7) *minister to,* wait on, do for, help, oblige 742 *serve*; nurse 658 *doctor*; make oneself useful 640 *be useful*; pander to, toady, humour, suck up to 925 *flatter*; slave for 682 *work*; be assistant to, 628 *be instrumental*.

Adverb
(8) *in aid of,* on behalf of; thanks to.

704
Opposition

Noun
(1) *opposition,* antagonism, hostility 881 *enmity*; conflict, friction, lack of harmony 709 *dissension*; dissociation, repugnance 861 *dislike*; contrariness, cussedness 602 *obstinacy*; contradiction 533 *negation*; challenge 711 *defiance*; firm opposition, stand 715 *resistance*; going against, siding a., voting a. 924 *disapprobation*; withdrawal, walkout 489 *dissent*; headwind, crosscurrent 702 *obstacle*; cross purposes, tug of war, battle of wills; rivalry, emulation, competition 716 *contention*; the Opposition, the other side; underground 84 *nonconformity*.

(2) *opposites,* contraries, extremes, opposite poles 14 *contrariety*; rivals, competitors 716 *contender*; opposite parties, factions, cat and dog 709 *quarreller*.

Adjective
(3) *opposing,* oppositional, opposed; in opposition, anti, against; antagonistic, hostile, 881 *inimical*; unfavourable 731 *adverse*; cross, thwarting 702 *hindering*; contradictory 14 *contrary*; cussed, bloody-minded, bolshie 602 *obstinate*; refractory, recalcitrant 738 *disobedient*; resistant 182 *counteracting*; clashing, conflicting, at variance, at odds

with 709 *quarrelling*; militant,
up in arms 716 *contending*;
fronting, facing, face to face 237
frontal; polarized 240 *opposite*;
mutually opposed, rival, competitive 911 *jealous*.

Verb
(4) *oppose,* go against, militate a.
14 *be contrary*; hold out against
715 *resist*; fight against 607
reject; object, kick, protest 762
deprecate; vote against, vote
down 924 *disapprove*; not support, contradict, belie 533 *negate*; counter 479 *confute*; work
against 182 *counteract*; thwart,
baffle, foil 702 *be obstructive*;
stand up to, challenge, dare 711
defy; flout 738 *disobey*; rebuff,
spurn 760 *refuse*; rival, compete
with, bid against 716 *contend*;
set against, pit a., match a.

(5) *withstand,* confront, face,
stand up to 661 *face danger*; rise
against 738 *revolt*; take on,
meet, encounter, cross swords
with 716 *fight*; struggle
against, breast the tide, stem
the t., cope with, grapple w.,
wrestle w. 678 *be active*; not be
beaten 599 *stand firm*; hold
one's own 715 *resist*.

Adverb
(6) *in opposition,* against, versus, in conflict with, in defiance of, in spite of, in the teeth
of, despite.

705
Opponent

Noun
(1) *opponent,* opposer, adversary, antagonist, foe 881 *enemy*; assailant 712 *attacker*; opposition party the opposition,
opposite camp; cross benches;
partisan; reactionary, counter-
revolutionary; objector, conscientious o. dissident 829 *malcontent*; agitator, terrorist,
extremist 738 *revolter*; challenger, rival, competitor;

fighter, contestant, duellist;
entrant, the field, all comers
716 *contender*; brawler, wrangler 709 *quarreller*.

706
Cooperation

Noun
(1) *cooperation,* contribution,
helpfulness 597 *willingness*;
duet, double harness, tandem;
collaboration, joint effort, team
work, working together, concerted effort; relay, relay race,
team r.; team spirit, esprit de
corps; lack of friction, unanimity, agreement 710 *concord*;
clannishness, cliquishness, partisanship; connivance, collusion, abetment 612 *inducement*;
conspiracy 623 *plot*; complicity,
participation; sympathy 880
friendliness; fraternity, solidarity, fellowship, freemasonry, fellow feeling, comradeship,
common cause, networking,
log-rolling; reciprocity, give
and take 770 *compromise*; consultation 584 *conference*.

(2) *association,* coming together; partnership 775 *participation*; nationalization 775 *joint
possession*; pooling, pool, kitty;
membership, affiliation 78 *inclusion*; connection, hookup,
tie-up 9 *relation*; ecosystem;
combination union, integration, solidarity 52 *whole*; unification 88 *unity*; fusion, merger;
coalition, alliance, league, federation, confederation, confederacy, axis, united front 708
political party; an association,
fellowship, club, fraternity 708
community; set, clique, cell 708
party; trade union, chapel;
company, syndicate, combine,
consortium, trust, cartel, ring
708 *corporation*; cooperative,
workers' c., commune 708
community.

Adjective

(3) *cooperative,* helpful 703 *aiding;* en rapport 710 *concordant;* symbiotic, collaborating, in double harness, in tandem; married; associated, in league, bipartisan; federal 708 *corporate.*

Verb

(4) *cooperate,* collaborate, work together, pull t., work as a team, team up, join forces 775 *participate;* show willing, reciprocate, respond; espouse 703 *patronize;* join in, take part, enter into; rally round 703 *aid;* hang together, hold t., network, band together, associate, league, confederate, federate, ally; coalesce, merge, unite, combine, make common cause, club together; think alike, conspire 623 *plot;* collude, connive; negotiate 766 *make terms.*

Adverb

(5) *cooperatively,* hand in hand, jointly, as one.

Interjection

(6) *All together now!*

707
Auxiliary

Noun

(1) *auxiliary,* relay, recruit, fresh troops, reinforcement 722 *soldiery;* ally, confederate; assistant, helper, helpmate, helping hand 703 *aider;* right-hand man, second, adjutant, lieutenant, aide-de-camp; amanuensis, secretary, clerk; midwife, handmaid; dogsbody 742 *servant;* acolyte, server; best man, bridesmaid; friend in need 880 *friend;* hanger-on, satellite, henchman, sidekick, follower 742 *dependant;* disciple, adherent, votary 978 *sectarian;* stooge, cat's-paw, puppet 628 *instrument;* shadow, familiar 89 *concomitant.*

(2) *collaborator,* cooperator, co-worker, team-mate, yoke-fellow; sympathizer, fellow traveller, fifth columnist.

(3) *colleague,* associate, fellow, brother, sister; co-director, partner, sharer 775 *participator;* comrade, companion; alter ego, second self, mate, chum, crony 880 *friend;* helpmate 894 *spouse;* standby, stalwart; ally, confederate; accomplice, accessory, partner in crime.

(4) *patron,* guardian angel 660 *protector;* well-wisher, sympathizer; champion, advocate, friend at court; supporter, sponsor, backer, guarantor; proposer, seconder, voter; partisan, votary, aficionado, fan; rich uncle, sugar daddy 903 *benefactor;* promoter, founder; customer, client 792 *purchaser.*

708
Party

Noun

(1) *party,* movement; denomination, church 978 *sect;* group, faction, cabal, splinter group circle, inner c.; set, clique, in-crowd, coterie, caucus, committee, club, cell, cadre; ring, closed shop; team, crew 686 *personnel;* troupe, company 594 *actor;* gang, knot, bunch, outfit 74 *band;* side, camp.

(2) *political party,* right, left, centre; coalition, popular front, bloc; conservative, liberals, radicals; socialists, unionists social democrats; democrats, republicans; nationalists, loyalists; ecologists, greens; communists, fascists; comrade, labourite, Fabian, syndicalist; anarchist 738 *revolter;* rightwinger, true blue; left-winger, leftist moderate, centrist; party worker, party member, politician; militant, activist 676 *doer.*

(3) *society*, partnership, coalition, combination 706 *association*; league, alliance, axis; federation, confederation, confederacy; cooperative, union, free trade area; private society, club; secret society, lodge, cell; friendly society, trade union; chapel; group, division, branch, local b.; fellow, honorary f., associate, member; party member, paid-up m., card-carrying m.; comrade, trade unionist.

(4) *community*, fellowship, body, congregation, brotherhood, fraternity, confraternity, sorority, sisterhood; guild; tribe, clan 11 *family*; social class 371 *social group*; state 371 *nation*.

(5) *corporation*, body; company, multinational c.; firm, concern, joint c., partnership; house, business h.; establishment, organization, institute; trust, combine, monopoly, cartel, syndicate, conglomerate 706 *association*; guild, chamber of commerce.

Adjective
(6) *corporate*, incorporate, joint-stock; joint, partnered, bonded, banded, leagued, federal, federative; allied, federate, confederate; social, clubbable 882 *sociable*; fraternal, comradely 880 *friendly*; cooperative, syndicalist; communal 775 *sharing*.

(7) *sectional*, factional 978 *sectarian*; partisan, clannish, cliquish, cliquey, exclusive; nationalistic 481 *biased*; rightist, right-wing, conservative, true-blue; right of centre, left of c.; radical leftist, left-wing, pink, red.

Verb
(8) *join a party*, subscribe; join, swell the ranks, become a member, sign on, enlist, enrol oneself, get elected; belong to, make one of 78 *be included*;

align oneself, side with 706 *cooperate*; club together, associate, ally, league, federate; cement a union, merge.

Adverb
(9) *in league*, in partnership, hand in hand, hand in glove with; shoulder to shoulder, jointly, collectively; as one.

709
Dissension

Noun
(1) *dissension*, disagreement 489 *dissent*, 704 *opposition*; jarring note discord; recrimination 714 *retaliation*; bickering, differences, odds, variance, friction, tension; soreness 891 *resentment*; no love lost, hostility 888 *hatred*; disunity, disunion 25 *disagreement*; rift, separation, split, faction 978 *schism*; cross purposes, misunderstanding; breach, rupture, challenge 711 *defiance*; ultimatum 718 *war*.

(2) *quarrelsomeness*, factiousness, litigiousness; combativeness, pugnacity, 718 *bellicosity*; provactiveness 711 *defiance*; awkwardness, prickliness, fieriness 892 *irascibility*; shrewishness, sharp tongue 899 *scurrility*; contentiousness, rivalry 716 *contention*; mischief, spite 898 *malevolence*.

(3) *quarrel*, feud, blood f., vendetta 910 *revenge*; war 718 *warfare*; strife 716 *contention*; conflict, clash 279 *collision*; legal battle 959 *litigation*; controversy, dispute, wrangle, polemic 475 *argument*; raised voices, stormy exchange, altercation; set-to slanging match 899 *scurrility*; squabble, squall; shindig, commotion, fracas, brawl, fisticuffs 61 *turmoil*; gang warfare, street fighting, riot 716 *fight*.

(4) *casus belli,* flashpoint, breaking point; sore point; bone of contention; disputed point, point at issue.

(5) *quarreller,* disputer, wrangler; duellist, rival 716 *contender*; mischief-maker 663 *troublemaker*; scold 892 *shrew*; aggressor 712 *attacker*.

Adjective
(6) *quarrelling,* discordant, clashing 14 *contrary*; on bad terms, at odds, at loggerheads, at variance, up in arms 881 *inimical*; divided, factious, schismatic 489 *dissenting*; mutinous, rebellious 738 *disobedient*; uncooperative 704 *opposing*; sore 891 *resentful*; awkward, cantankerous 892 *irascible*; sulky 893 *sullen*; litigious 959 *litigating*; quarrelsome, bellicose 718 *warlike*; pugnacious, combative, belligerent, aggressive 712 *attacking*; abusive, scolding 899 *cursing*; argumentative, contentious, disputatious, wrangling, polemical 475 *arguing*.

Verb
(7) *quarrel,* disagree 489 *dissent*; clash, conflict 279 *collide*; cross swords with, be at variance with, have differences 15 *differ*; recriminate 714 *retaliate*; fall out, part company, break away split, break with; declare war 718 *go to war*; go to law 959 *litigate*; dispute 479 *confute*; sulk 893 *be sullen*.

(8) *make quarrels,* pick q., pick a fight, start it; look for trouble, trail one's coat, challenge 711 *defy*; irritate, provoke 891 *enrage*; embroil, entangle, estrange, set at odds, 888 *excite hate*; create discord, sow dissension, stir up strife, make mischief, make trouble, divide, come between 46 *sunder*; widen the breach 832 *aggravate*; set

against, match with; incite 612 *motivate.*

(9) *bicker,* squabble; spar with, wrangle, dispute with 475 *argue*; nag, scold 899 *cuss*; have words with, row with; brawl, disturb the peace 61 *rampage.*

710
Concord

Noun
(1) *concord,* harmony 410 *melody*; unison, unity, duet 24 *agreement*; unanimity 488 *consensus*; lack of friction, understanding, mutual u., rapport; solidarity 706 *cooperation*; sympathy, fellow feeling 887 *love*; compatibility, coexistence, amity 880 *friendship*; rapprochement, détente, reunion, reconciliation 719 *pacification*; good offices, arbitration 720 *mediation*

Adjective
(2) *concordant,* en rapport, unanimous, of one mind, bipartisan 24 *agreeing*; coexistent, compatible, united, allied, leagued; loving, amicable, on good terms 880 *friendly*; frictionless, happy, peaceable 717 *peaceful*; conciliatory 719 *pacificatory.*

Verb
(3) *concord* 410 harmonize; agree 24 *accord*; hit it off, see eye to eye 706 *cooperate*; reciprocate, respond; fraternize 880 *be friendly*; keep the peace 717 *be at peace.*

711
Defiance

Noun
(1) *defiance,* dare, challenge, gauntlet, bold front, brave face 855 *courage*; war dance, battle cry 900 *threat*; brazenness 878

insolence; bravura 875 *ostentation*.

Adjective
(2) *defiant,* defying, challenging, provocative, militant 718 *warlike*; saucy, insulting 878 *insolent*; mutinous, rebellious 738 *disobedient*; stiff-necked 871 *proud*; reckless, trigger-happy 857 *rash*.

Verb
(3) *defy,* challenge 489 *dissent*; stand up to 704 *oppose*; caution 664 *warn*; throw down the gauntlet; dare, beard brave, run the gauntlet 661 *face danger*; laugh in one's face, call one's bluff; show fight, bare one's teeth, shake one's fist 900 *threaten*; march, demonstrate, stage a sit-in, not be moved; ask for trouble 709 *make quarrels*.

Adverb
(4) *defiantly,* in defiance of, in one's teeth, to one's face.

Interjection
(5) *do your worst!*

712
Attack

Noun
(1) *attack,* pugnacity, combativeness 718 *bellicosity*; aggression, unprovoked a. 914 *injustice*; stab in the back 930 *foul play*; mugging, assault 176 *violence*; offensive, drive, push, thrust, pincer movement 688 *tactics*; run at, dead set at; onslaught, onset, rush, charge; sally, sortie, breakout, breakthrough; counterattack 714 *retaliation*; shock tactics, blitzkrieg, coup de main; encroachment, infringement 306 *overstepping*; invasion, incursion, overrunning 297 *ingress*; raid, foray 788 *brigandage*; blitz, air raid; boarding; siege, blockade; challenge, tilt.

(2) *terror tactics,* war of nerves 854 *intimidation*; shot across the bows; bloodbath 362 *slaughter*; devastation, laying waste 165 *havoc*.

(3) *bombardment,* cannonade, barrage, strafe, blitz; broadside, volley, salvo; bombing, strategic b., tactical b., saturation b.; fire, gunfire, fusillade, rapid fire, cross-f., enfilade; flak; sharpshooting, sniping.

(4) *lunge,* thrust, pass, cut, cut and thrust, stab, jab; bayonet, cold steel; punch, swipe 279 *knock*.

(5) *attacker,* assailant, aggressor; hawk, militant; spearhead, storm troops, shock t., strike force; fighter pilot 722 *armed force*; sharpshooter, sniper; terrorist, guerrilla; invader, raider; besieger, blockader.

Adjective
(6) *attacking,* assailing etc. vb.; pugnacious, combative, aggressive, on the offensive 718 *warlike*; hawkish, hostile 881 *inimical*; up in arms, on the warpath 718 *warring*.

Verb
(7) *attack,* take the offensive; declare war 718 *go to war*; assault, assail, go for, set on, fall on, pitch into, sail i.; savage, maul, draw blood 655 *wound*; launch out at, let fly at, round on; surprise, take by s.; move in, invade 306 *encroach*; raid, overrun, infest 297 *burst in*; show fight, counterattack 714 *retaliate*; thrust, push 279 *impel*; erupt, sally, break out 298 *emerge*; board, grapple; storm, take by storm 727 *overmaster*; ravage, make havoc 165 *lay waste*; take on, challenge 711 *defy*; go over to the attack 716 *fight*.

(8) *besiege,* lay siege to, invest, surround, blockade 235 *enclose;* sap, mine, undermine.

(9) *strike at,* lay about one, flail, hammer 279 *strike, kick;* go berserk, run amok 176 *be violent;* have at, lash out at; beat up, mug; ram 279 *collide;* lunge; close with, grapple w., cut and thrust; push, butt, thrust at; stab, bayonet, run through, cut down 263 *pierce;* strike home, lay low, bring down.

(10) *charge,* sound the c., go over the top; advance against, bear down on; rush, mob, make a rush, dash at, tilt at, ride down, run down; ram, shock 279 *collide.*

(11) *fire at,* shoot at, fire on; take a potshot; snipe, pick off 287 *shoot;* shoot down, bring d.; torpedo, sink; soften up, strafe, bombard, blitz, cannonade, shell, fusillade, pepper; bomb, drop bombs; open fire, let fly, volley; blast, rake, enfilade.

(12) *lapidate,* stone, throw a stone, shy, sling, pelt with, hurl at 287 *propel.*

Adverb
(13) *aggressively,* on the offensive, on the warpath.

713
Defence

Noun
(1) *defence,* the defensive, self-defence 715 *resistance;* judo 716 *wrestling;* parry, warding off 182 *counteraction;* safekeeping 666 *preservation;* self-protection 660 *protection;* a defence, rampart, bulwark, buffer, fender 662 *safeguard;* deterrent 723 *weapon.*

(2) *defences,* lines, entrenchment, redoubt, earthworks, mole, boom; barricade 235 *barrier;* palisade, stockade; moat, ditch, trench; booby trap 542 *trap;* barbed wire, mine, minefield; bunker 662 *shelter;* barrage, flak, smokescreen 421 *screen.*

(3) *fortification* (see *fort); bulwark, bastion; rampart, wall; parapet, battlement, embrasure, loophole; gun emplacement; buttress, abutment.

(4) *fort,* fortress, stronghold; citadel 662 *refuge;* castle, keep, ward, barbican, tower, turret, donjon; portcullis, drawbridge; blockhouse, strong point; encampment 253 *earthwork.*

(5) *armour,* harness; mail, chain m.; armour plate; breastplate, cuirass; helmet, helm, visor; bearskin, busby; gauntlet; shield, buckler; riot shield, gas mask 662 *safeguard.*

(6) *defender,* champion 927 *vindicator;* patron 703 *aider;* knight-errant; loyalist, patriot; bodyguard, lifeguard, 722 *soldier;* watch, sentry, sentinel; patrol, garrison, picket, guard, escort, rearguard; militia 722 *soldiery;* guardian, warden 660 *protector.*

Adjective
(7) *defending,* on the defensive 715 *resisting;* defensive, protective 660 *tutelary;* self-excusing 927 *vindicating.*

(8) *defended,* armoured, armour-plated; mailed, mail-clad, armour-c., iron-c. 669 *prepared;* moated, palisaded, barricaded, walled, fortified, castellated, battlemented; entrenched, dug in; defensible, proof, bulletproof 660 *invulnerable.*

Verb
(9) *defend,* guard, protect keep, watch over, 660 *safeguard;* fence, moat, palisade, barricade

235 *enclose*; block 702 *obstruct*; cushion, pad, shield 421 *screen*; cloak 525 *conceal*; provide with arms, arm 669 *make ready*; armour-plate, reinforce, fortify 162 *strengthen*; entrench, dig in 599 *stand firm*; garrison, man the defences, man the breach; champion 927 *vindicate*; fight for, 703 *patronize*; rescue 668 *deliver*.

(10) *parry,* counter, riposte, fence, fend off, ward o., hold o., keep o., fight o., stave o., keep at bay 620 *avoid*; turn, avert 282 *deflect*; stall, stonewall, block 702 *obstruct*; fight back, show fight 715 *resist*; repulse 292 *repel*; hold one's own 704 *withstand*.

Adverb
(11) *defensively,* on the defensive, at bay; in self-defence.

714
Retaliation

Noun
(1) *retaliation,* reprisal 910 *revenge*; requital, recompense deserts 915 *dueness*; poetic justice, retribution, Nemesis 963 *punishment*; reaction, boomerang, backlash 280 *recoil*; counterblast, counterattack, sally, sortie 712 *attack*; recrimination, answering back, riposte, retort 460 *rejoinder*; reciprocation, like for like, tit for tat, biter bit, an eye for an eye.

Adjective
(2) *retaliatory,* in retaliation, in reprisal, in self-defence; retaliative, retributive, recriminatory; like for like, reciprocal; rightly served.

Verb
(3) *retaliate,* take reprisals 963 *punish*; counter, riposte 713 *parry*; pay one out, be quits, get one's own back, get even with 910 *avenge*; requite, reward;

serve rightly, give as good as one gets, reciprocate; return, retort, cap, answer back 460 *answer*; recriminate 928 *accuse*; react, boomerang 280 *recoil*; round on, kick back, hit b. 715 *resist*; turn the tables on.

(4) *be rightly served,* serve one right, find one's match, get one's deserts 963 *be punished*.

Adverb
(5) *en revanche,* in requital.

715
Resistance

Noun
(1) *resistance,* stand, firm s. 704 *opposition*; reluctance, repugnance 861 *dislike*; objection, demur 468 *qualification*; recalcitrance, protest 762 *deprecation*; rising, insurrection, backlash 738 *revolt*; self-defence 713 *defence*; repulsion, repulse, rebuff 760 *refusal*; passive resistance, civil disobedience.

Adjective
(2) *resisting,* protesting, reluctant 704 *opposing*; recalcitrant, mutinous 738 *disobedient*; stubborn 602 *obstinate*; holding out, unyielding, indomitable, undefeated 727 *unbeaten*; resistant, tough, proofed, bulletproof; repelling 292 *repellent*.

Verb
(3) *resist,* offer resistance 704 *withstand*; obstruct 702 *hinder*; challenge, stand out against 711 *defy*; confront, outface 661 *face danger*; struggle against, contend with 704 *oppose*; protest 762 *deprecate*; demur, object 468 *qualify*; down tools, come out 145 *cease*; mutiny, rise 738 *revolt*; make a stand, fight off, hold off 713 *parry*; hold out, stand one's ground, not give way 599 *stand firm*; bear the brunt, endure 825 *suffer*; be proof against,

repel, rebuff 760 *refuse*; not be tempted.

Interjection
(4) *No surrender!*

716
Contention

Noun
(1) *contention,* strife, tussle, conflict, clash, running battle 709 *dissension*; combat, fighting, war 718 *warfare*; debate, dispute, controversy, polemics 475 *argument*; altercation, words 709 *quarrel*; bone of contention 709 *casus belli*; competition, rivalry 911 *jealousy*; gamesmanship, rat race; no holds barred; sports, athletics 837 *sport.*

(2) *contest,* trial, trial of strength, test of endurance, marathon, pentathlon, decathlon; tug-of-war 682 *exertion*; tussle, struggle 671 *attempt*; bitter struggle, needle match; close finish, photo f.; competition, free-for-all; tournament, tourney, joust, tilt; match, test m.; rally; event, handicap, run-off; heat, final, semifinal, quarterfinal; set, game, rubber; wager, bet; athletics, gymnastics 837 *sport*; gymkhana, rodeo; games, Olympic G., Olympics.

(3) *racing,* speed contest 277 *speeding*; races, race, sprint, dash; road race, marathon; hurdles 312 *leap*; relay race, team r.; obstacle race, slalom; horse racing, steeplechase, point-to-point; motor race, motor rally, motocross, speedway; cycle race, dog racing; boat race, yacht r., regatta, eights; racecourse, track, stadium 724 *arena.*

(4) *pugilism,* boxing, sparring, fisticuffs; prize fighting, boxing match; clinch, in-fighting;

round, bout; the ring, the fancy.

(5) *wrestling,* judo, karate, kung-fu; all-in wrestling, no holds barred; catch, hold; wrestle, wrestling match.

(6) *duel,* affair of honour; single combat, gladiatorial c.; jousting, tilting; fencing, swordplay; lists 724 *arena.*

(7) *fight,* hostilities, appeal to arms 718 *warfare*; battle royal, free-for-all, rough and tumble, roughhouse, shindig, scuffle, scrum, scrimmage, scramble, dogfight, mêlée, fracas 61 *turmoil*; gang warfare, street fight, riot; brawl 709 *quarrel*; fisticuffs, blows, cut and thrust; affray, set-to, tussle; running fight, close fighting, hand-to-hand f.; close grips, close quarters; combat, fray 279 *collision*; encounter, scrap, brush, skirmish; engagement, action, pitched battle, stand-up fight, shoot-out 718 *battle*; campaign, struggle; field of battle 724 *battleground*;

(8) *contender,* struggler, fighter, battler; gladiator, bullfighter 722 *combatant*; prize fighter 722 *pugilist*; duellist 709 *quarreller*; fencer, swordsman; candidate, entrant, examinee; contestant, competitor, rival, challenger, runner-up, finalist; front runner, favourite, top seed; starter, also-ran; racer, runner, sprinter 162 *athlete.*

Adjective
(9) *contending,* struggling etc. vb.; rival; outdoing 306 *surpassing*; competing, sporting; running, in the running; athletic, pugilistic, gladiatorial; contentious, quarrelsome 709 *quarrelling*; aggressive, combative, pugnacious, bellicose, warmongering 718 *warlike*; at loggerheads, at odds, at war,

belligerent 718 *warring*; competitive, keen, cutthroat; hand-to-hand, at close quarters; keenly contested, close-run; well-fought.

Verb
(10) *contend,* combat, strive, struggle, battle, fight, tussle, wrestle, grapple; oppose, put up a fight 715 *resist*; argue for, stick out for, insist 532 *emphasize*; contest, compete, challenge; stake, wager, bet; play, play against, match oneself with, vie with, race, run a race; emulate, rival 911 *be jealous*; enter for, enter the lists, tilt with, joust w.; take on, close with 712 *strike at.*

(11) *fight,* break the peace, have a fight, scuffle, scrap, set to 176 *be violent*; pitch into, 712 *attack*; lay about one 712 *strike at*; square up to, come to blows, exchange b., box, spar, pummel, hit 279 *strike*; fall foul of, join issue with 709 *quarrel*; duel, call out; exchange shots, skirmish; take on, engage 718 *give battle*; come to grips, close with, grapple, lock horns; fence, cross swords; appeal to arms 718 *go to war*; combat, campaign 718 *wage war*; fight it out.

717
Peace

Noun
(1) *peace,* state of p., peacefulness, peace and quiet, law and order; harmony 710 *concord*; peacetime 730 *palmy days*; demobilization; truce, armistice 145 *lull*; coexistence, peaceableness, nonintervention, neutrality; pacifism, nonviolence; disarmament 719 *pacification*; nonaggression pact 765 *treaty*.

(2) *pacifist,* peace-lover, dove; peace party 177 *moderator*;

neutral, civilian, noncombatant, conscientious objector; peacemaker 720 *mediator*.

Adjective
(3) *peaceful,* quiet, halcyon 266 *tranquil*; without war, bloodless; harmless, 935 *innocent*; mild-mannered, easy-going 884 *amiable*; uncompetitive, uncontentions; peaceable, law-abiding, peace-loving, unwarlike, pacific, unaggressive; pacifist, nonviolent; unarmed, noncombatant, civilian; submissive 721 *submitting*; conciliatory 720 *mediatory*; without enemies, at peace; not at war, neutral; postwar, prewar, peacetime.

Verb
(4) *be at peace,* keep the peace, avoid bloodshed; mean no harm, be pacific 935 *be innocent*; work for peace 720 *mediate*, 719 *make peace.*

Adverb
(5) *peacefully,* peaceably; without violence, bloodlessly; quietly, tranquilly, at peace.

718
War

Noun
(1) *war,* arms, the sword; cold war, armed neutrality; war of nerves 854 *intimidation*; disguised war, intervention, armed i.; civil war; holy w., crusade, jihad; war of attrition; world war global w.; total w., atomic w., nuclear w., push-button w.; drums, bugle, trumpet; call to arms 547 *call*; battle cry, war whoop 711 *defiance*; god of war, Mars.

(2) *belligerency,* state of war, state of siege; resort to arms, militancy, hostilities; wartime, time of war.

(3) *bellicosity,* war fever; aggressiveness, combativeness, hawkishness, militancy 709 *quarrelsomeness;* militarism, jingoism, chauvinism 481 *prejudice.*

(4) *art of war,* strategy 688 *tactics;* 713 *fortification;* generalship, soldiership, seamanship, airmanship 694 *skill;* drill, training 534 *teaching;* logistics, planning 623 *plan;* manoeuvres.

(5) *war measures,* war footing, war preparations; call to arms; war effort, war work, call-up, mobilization, recruitment, conscription, national service, military duty.

(6) *warfare,* war, warpath, making war, waging w.; bloodshed, battles, sieges 176 *violence;* fighting, campaigning, soldiering, active service; military service, naval s., air s.; bombing 712 *bombardment;* raiding besieging, blockading 235 *enclosure;* aerial warfare, naval w., submarine w.; germ w.; economic w., blockade, attrition, scorched earth policy; psychological warfare, propaganda; guerrilla warfare, bush-fighting campaign, expedition; operations, combined o., joint o.; incursion, invasion, raid 712 *attack;* order, word of command 737 *command;* password, watchword; battle cry, slogan 547 *call;* plan of campaign, battle orders 623 *plan.*

(7) *battle,* pitched b., battle royal 716 *fight;* line of battle, order of b.; array; line, firing l., front l., front, battle f., battle station; armed conflict, action, scrap, skirmish, clash; offensive, blitz 712 *attack;* defensive battle, stand 713 *defence;* engagement, naval e., sea fight, air f., dogfight; field of battle, theatre of war 724 *battleground.*

Adjective

(8) *warring,* on the warpath; campaigning, at war, belligerent, mobilized, uniformed, under arms, in the army, at the front, on active service; militant, up in arms; armed, sword in hand 669 *prepared;* embattled, engaged; at loggerheads 709 *quarrelling;* on the offensive 712 *attacking.*

(9) *warlike,* militaristic, bellicose, hawkish, militant, aggressive, pugnacious, combative; war-loving, bloodthirsty, fierce 898 *cruel;* military, paramilitary, martial; soldierly, military, naval; operational, strategic, tactical.

Verb

(10) *go to war,* resort to arms; declare war, open hostilities 716 *fight;* fly to arms, rise, rebel 738 *revolt;* raise one's banner, call to arms, arm, militarize, mobilize, call up, recruit, conscript; join up, enlist, enrol.

(11) *wage war,* make w., on the warpath, war, war against, war upon; campaign, soldier, take the field; invade 712 *attack;* hold one's ground 599 *stand firm;* manoeuvre, march, countermarch; blockade, beleaguer, besiege, invest 230 *surround;* shed blood 362 *slaughter;* ravage, burn, scorch 165 *lay waste;* press the button 165 *demolish, be destroyed.*

(12) *give battle,* offer b., accept b.; join battle, engage, combat, fight it out 716 *fight;* take a position, dig in; rally, close the ranks, make a stand 715 *resist;* sound the charge 712 *charge;* open fire 712 *fire at;* skirmish, brush with 716 *contend.*

719
Pacification

Noun

(1) *pacification,* peacemaking; pacifying, conciliation, appeasement, mollification 177 *moderation*; reconciliation, detente rapprochement; accommodation, adjustment 770 *compromise*; good offices 720 *mediation*; entente, understanding, peacede treaty 765 *treaty*; truce, armistice, cease-fire 145 *lull*; disarmament, demobilization, disbanding.

(2) *peace offering,* appeasement, propitiation 736 *leniency*; olive branch, overture 880 *friendliness*; white flag, pipe of peace 717 *peace*; blood money, compensation 787 *restitution*; amnesty 909 *forgiveness.*

Adjective

(3) *pacificatory,* conciliatory, placatory, propitiatory 880 *friendly*; disarming, soothing; peacemaking, mediatory.

Verb

(4) *pacify,* make peace allay, tranquillize, mollify, soothe 177 *assuage*; heal 656 *cure*; conciliate, propitiate, reconcile, placate, appease, satisfy 828 *content*; restore harmony, settle differences; meet halfway 770 *compromise*; accommodate 24 *adjust*; bridge over, bring together 720 *mediate*; show mercy 736 *be lenient*; grant peace 766 *give terms*; keep the peace 717 *be at peace.*

(5) *make peace,* stop fighting, 145 *cease*; bury the hatchet 506 *forget*; shake hands, make it up, forgive and forget, come to an understanding, agree to differ; suspend hostilities, lay down one's arms, beat swords into ploughshares, demilitarize, disarm, demobilize.

720
Mediation

Noun

(1) *mediation,* good offices, intercession; arbitration; intervention, statesmanship, diplomacy; parley, negotiation 584 *conference.*

(2) *mediator,* middleman, matchmaker, go-between, negotiator 231 *intermediary*; arbitrator, umpire, referee 480 *estimator*; diplomat, diplomatist; agent 754 *delegate*; intercessor, pleader, propitiator; peace party 177 *moderator*; pacifier, troubleshooter, ombudsman; 691 *adviser*; peacemaker, dove.

Adjective

(3) *mediatory,* intercessory, propitiatory 719 *pacificatory.*

Verb

(4) *mediate,* intervene, step in, intercede for, propitiate; be a go-between; bring together, negotiate arbitrate, umpire 480 *judge*; compose differences 719 *pacify.*

721
Submission

Noun

(1) *submission,* acquiescence, compliance 739 *obedience*; subservience, slavishness 745 *servitude*; consent 488 *assent*; supineness, passiveness, resignation, fatalism 679 *inactivity*; yielding, giving way, capitulation, surrender; deference 872 *humility*; act of submission, homage 739 *loyalty*; prostration 311 *obeisance*; defeatist, quitter; mouse, doormat 856 *coward.*

Adjective

(2) *submitting,* submissive 739

obedient; quiet, meek, law-abiding 717 *peaceful*; fatalistic, resigned, unresisting; acquiescent 488 *assenting*; weak-kneed, pliant, malleable 327 *soft*; crawling, kneeling, on bended knees 872 *humble*.

Verb

(3) *submit,* yield, give in; not resist, not insist, defer to; bow to, admit defeat, yield the palm 728 *be defeated*; resign oneself, be resigned 488 *acquiesce*; accept 488 *assent*; withdraw, not contest, throw in the towel; cease resistance, stop fighting, give up, cry quits, have had enough, surrender, ask for terms, capitulate; give oneself up, throw down one's arms.

(4) *knuckle under,* succumb; faint, drop 684 *be fatigued*; collapse, show no fight; be submissive, do homage, apologize, eat humble pie 872 *be humble*; take it, digest, stomach, put up with 825 *suffer*; bow, kneel, kowtow, cringe, crawl 311 *stoop*; grovel, lick the dust; beg for mercy 905 *ask mercy*.

722
Combatant. Army. Navy. Air Force

Noun
(1) *combatant,* fighter 716 *contender*; aggressor, assailant 712 *attacker*; besieger, shock troops; warrior, brave; bodyguard 713 *defender*; gunman, strongarm man 362 *killer*; bully, bravo 904 *ruffian*; fire-eater, swashbuckler 877 *boaster*; duellist 709 *quarreller*; swordsman, fencer; gladiator 162 *athlete*; wrestler, judoist 716 *wrestling*; competitor 716 *contender*; knight, knight-errant.

(2) *pugilist,* boxer, bruiser, sparring partner; flyweight, bantamweight, featherweight, welterweight, middleweight, heavyweight 716 *pugilism.*

(3) *militarist,* jingoist, chauvinist, militant, warmonger, hawk; Samurai; crusader; mercenary, adventurer, freebooter, marauder, pirate, privateer, buccaneer.

(4) *soldier,* professional s., regular; soldiery, troops; campaigner, old c., veteran; warrior, brave; man-at-arms, redcoat; legionary, legionnaire, centurion; standard-bearer, colour sergeant, ensign, cornet; skirmishers; sharpshooter, sniper, franc-tireur 287 *shooter*; auxiliary, territorial, Home Guard, militiaman, yeomanry; irregular troops, moss-trooper; raider, tip-and-run r.; guerrilla, partisan, freedom fighter; picked troops 644 *elite*; guards 660 *protector*; reservist, volunteer, conscript, recruit, serviceman *or* -woman; female warrior, Amazon.

(5) *soldiery,* cannon fodder; the ranks, other r.; private, private soldier, common s., man-at-arms; archer, bowman, halberdier, lancer; musketeer, fusilier, rifleman, grenadier, bombardier, gunner; sapper, miner, engineer; signalman; lieutenant 741 *army officer.*

(6) *army,* host, phalanx, legion; cohorts, big battalions; 104 *multitude*; militia, yeomanry; regular army, standing a.; conscript a., draft; the services, armed forces.

(7) *armed force,* forces, troops, men, personnel; armament, armada; guards, household troops; picked troops, crack t., shock t., storm t.; spearhead, flying column; paratroops,

commandoes, task force, raiding party; combat troops, field army; line, front l., echelon, wing, van, vanguard, rear, rearguard, centre; second echelon, base troops, reserves 707 *auxiliary*; base, staff; detachment, picket, party, detail; patrol, night watch, sentry, sentinel 660 *protector*; garrison, occupying force.

(8) *formation,* array, line; square, phalanx; legion, cohort, century; column, file, rank; unit, group, detachment, corps, army c., division, armoured d.; brigade; battery; regiment, cavalry r., squadron, troop; battalion, company, platoon, section, squad, detail, party 74 *band.*

(9) *infantry,* foot regiment, infantryman, foot soldier, foot.

(10) *cavalry,* sabres, horse, light h., cavalry regiment; mounted troops, horse soldier, cavalryman, yeoman; trooper; knight; lancer, hussar, dragoon; armoured car, tank; charger, warhorse.

(11) *navy,* admiralty; fleet arm, armada; fleet, flotilla, squadron.

(12) *naval man,* navy, senior service; admiral, Sea Lord 741 *naval officer*; sailor 270 *mariner*; able seaman, rating; marine, submariner.

(13) *warship,* war vessel, war galley, trireme, galleon 275 *ship*; raider, privateer, pirate ship; man-o'-war, battleship, ironclad; cruiser, battle c.; frigate, corvette; patrol boat, gunboat; destroyer; minelayer, minesweeper; submarine, nuclear s.; aircraft carrier, landing craft, amphibian; transport, troopship; flagship.

(14) *air force,* air arm, flying corps, fleet air arm; squadron,

flight, group, wing; bomber 276 *aircraft*; fighter, interceptor; flying boat, patrol plane; transport plane, troop-carrier; barrage balloon 276 *airship*; airborne division, parachute troops, paratroopers; aircraftman, ground staff.

723
Arms

Noun

(1) *arms* (see weapon); armament, munitions; armaments, arms race; arms traffic, gun-running; ballistics, rocketry, gunnery, musketry.

(2) *arsenal,* armoury, ammunition chest; arms depot 632 *storage*; magazine, powder barrel, ammunition box.

(3) *weapon,* arm, deterrent; armour, plate, mail 713 *defence*; offensive weapon 712 *attack*; secret weapon, death ray, laser; germ warfare, chemical w.; gas, nerve gas 659 *poison*; natural weapon, teeth, claws 256 *sharp point.*

(4) *missile weapon,* javelin, harpoon, dart; boomerang, arrow; shot, ball, bullet, pellet, shell, shrapnel; bow, crossbow; catapult, sling; blowpipe; rocket, bazooka, cruise missile, guided m., ballistic m., 287 *missile.*

(5) *club,* mace 279 *hammer*; battering ram 279 *ram*; staff, stave, stick; truncheon, cudgel; sandbag, cosh.

(6) *spear,* harpoon, lance, javelin, pike, assegai; halberd 256 *sharp point.*

(7) *axe,* tomahawk, hatchet, halberd, poleaxe, chopper 256 *sharp edge.*

(8) *sidearms,* sword; cold steel, naked s.; broadsword, two-edged sword; cutlass, sabre,

scimitar; blade, trusty b., rapier, foil; dagger, bayonet, dirk, poniard, stiletto 256 *sharp point*; machete, knife, switchblade 256 *sharp edge*.

(9) *firearm,* small arms; musket, blunderbuss; breechloader, rifle, shotgun, sawn-off s.; trigger.

(10) *pistol,* duelling p., horse p.; six-shooter, colt, revolver, repeater, automatic.

(11) *gun,* guns, ordnance, artillery, light a., heavy a.; battery, broadside; cannon, mortar; field piece, field gun, siege g.; great gun; howitzer, trench-mortar, trench gun; ack-ack, bazooka; machine gun, tommy g.; flamethrower; gun emplacement.

(12) *ammunition,* live a., round; powder and shot; shot, buckshot; cannonball, bullet, projectile 287 *missile*; slug, pellet; shell, shrapnel; cartridge, live c.

(13) *explosive,* propellant; gunpowder; high explosive, dynamite, gelignite, TNT; cap, detonator, fuse; warhead, atomic w.;

(14) *bomb,* explosive device; shell, grenade, hand g.; atom bomb, nuclear b., hydrogen b., neutron b.; A-bomb, H-bomb; cluster bomb, fragmentation b.; firebomb, incendiary bomb, napalm b.; mine, land mine; booby trap 542 *trap*; depth charge, torpedo; time bomb.

724
Arena

Noun
(1) *arena,* field of action; centre, scene, stage, theatre; hustings, platform, floor; amphitheatre, stadium, stand, grandstand; parade ground, training g.; forum, marketplace; hippodrome, circus, racecourse, turf; track, dog t.; ring, bullring; rink, skating r., ice r.; gymnasium, gym; range, shooting r., rifle r., butts; playground, fairground 837 *pleasure ground*; playing field, pitch; green, court; courtroom 956 *lawcourt*.

(2) *battleground,* battlefield, field of battle; theatre of war, combat zone, no-go area; front, front line, firing l.; no-man's-land; sector, salient, bulge, beachhead, bridgehead; Armageddon 718 *battle*.

725
Completion

Noun
(1) *completion,* finish, termination, conclusion 69 *end*; issue, upshot, result, end product 157 *effect*; fullness 54 *completeness*; fulfilment 635 *sufficiency*; maturity, fruition, readiness 669 *preparedness*; consummation, culmination 646 *perfection*; thoroughness 455 *attention*; elaboration, rounding off, finishing off, finishing touch; coup de grace; achievement, fait accompli; climax, payoff; resolution, solution, denouement 69 *finality*.

(2) *effectuation,* implementation, execution, discharge, performance 676 *action*; accomplishment, achievement, realization 727 *success*.

Adjective
(3) *completive,* completing, crowning, culminating 213 *topmost*; finishing, conclusive, final 69 *ending*; unanswerable, crushing.

(4) *completed,* full, full-blown 54 *complete*; done, well d. 646 *perfect*; achieved etc. vb.; highly

wrought, elaborate; under one's belt, secured 727 *successful.*

Verb
(5) *carry through,* follow t., follow up; drive home, clinch; finish off, polish off; dispose of, dispatch, complete 54 *make complete*; elaborate, hammer out, work o. 646 *perfect*; ripen 669 *mature*; get through 69 *terminate.*

(6) *carry out,* see through, effect, enact 676 *do*; execute, discharge, implement, effectuate, realize, bring about, accomplish, fulfil, consummate, achieve 727 *succeed.*

(7) *climax,* cap, crown all 213 *crown*; culminate, reach its peak; come to a crisis *or* a head; come to fruition, touch one's goal 295 *arrive.*

726
Noncompletion

Noun
(1) *noncompletion,* no success 728 *failure*; nonfulfilment 55 *incompleteness*; deficiency 307 *shortfall*; immaturity 670 *undevelopment*; perfunctoriness 456 *inattention*; job half-done, loose ends; no result, drawn game; stalemate, deadlock.

Adjective
(2) *uncompleted,* partial, fragmentary 55 *incomplete*; not finalized, unfinished, undone, half-done 458 *neglected*; half-baked 670 *immature*; perfunctory, superficial; left hanging, not worked out 647 *imperfect*; never-ending 71 *continuous.*

Verb
(3) *not complete,* leave undone 458 *neglect*; skip, scamp, do by halves, tinker 636 *not suffice*; give up, not follow up *or* through, not stay the course, fall out, drop o. 728 *fail*; defer, postpone 136 *put off.*

Adverb
(4) *on the stocks,* in preparation.

727
Success

Noun
(1) *success,* glory 866 *famousness*; happy outcome, happy ending; progress, steady advance, 285 *progression*; fresh advance, breakthrough; run of luck, good fortune 730 *prosperity*; lead 34 *advantage*; exploit, feat, achievement 676 *deed*; accomplishment 725 *completion*; a success, triumph, hit, smash h.; beginner's luck, lucky stroke, fluke; stroke of genius, 694 *masterpiece*; trump, trump card, winning c.; pass, qualification.

(2) *victory,* beating, trouncing 728 *defeat*; conquest 745 *subjection*; taking by storm 712 *attack*; win, game and match; outright win, complete victory, grand slam, checkmate; Pyrrhic victory; easy win, runaway victory, love game, walkover 701 *easy thing*; knockout; mastery, ascendancy, upper hand, whip h., edge 34 *advantage*; triumph, ovation 876 *celebration.*

(3) *victor,* winner, champion, world-beater, medallist, first, double f. 644 *exceller*; winning side, the winners; conquering hero, conqueror, conquistador; vanquisher, subjugator; master *or* mistress of; a success, rising star 730 *prosperous person.*

Adjective
(4) *successful,* effective, efficacious; crushing, efficient; sovereign 658 *remedial*; well-spent, fruitful 640 *profitable*; happy, lucky; felicitous, masterly 694 *skilful*; never-failing, surefire, foolproof; unerring,

infallible, surefooted 473 *certain*; home and dry 725 *completed*; victorious, world-beating 644 *excellent*; winning, leading 34 *superior*; on top, in the ascendant 730 *prosperous*; triumphant, crowning; triumphal, victorious; glorious 866 *renowned*.

(5) *unbeaten,* undefeated, unbowed 599 *resolute*; unconquerable, invincible.

Verb

(6) *succeed,* succeed in, effect, accomplish, achieve 725 *carry through*; be successful, make out, win one's spurs; make good, rise, do well, get promotion, 730 *prosper*; pass, qualify, graduate; come out on top 34 *be superior*; advance, make a breakthrough 285 *progress*; gain one's end, reach one's goal, pull it off, bring it off, have a success, make a success of; hit the jackpot; be a success, attain one's objective.

(7) *be successful,* be effective, answer, do the trick, show results, answer the purpose, turn out well; turn up trumps, rise to the occasion; do the job, do wonders, do marvels; compass, manage 676 *do*; work, act, work like magic 173 *operate*; take effect, tell, pull its weight 178 *influence*; pay off, pay dividends, bear fruit; hold one's own 599 *stand firm*.

(8) *triumph,* have one's day 876 *celebrate*; crow, crow over 877 *boast*; make it, win through; surmount, find a way; weather the storm 715 *resist*; reap the fruits of 771 *gain*.

(9) *overmaster,* be more than a match for 34 *be superior*; master, overcome, overpower, overthrow, override 306 *outdo*; have the advantage, prevail 34 *predominate*; checkmate, trump; conquer, vanquish, quell, subdue, subject, suppress, put down, crush 745 *subjugate*; capture, carry, take, take by storm 712 *attack*.

(10) *defeat* (see *overmaster*)*;* discomfit, dash; repulse, rebuff 292 *repel*; confound, dismay 854 *frighten*; best, get the better of 34 *be superior*; worst, outplay, outpoint, outflank, outmanoeuvre, outclass, outshine 306 *outdo*; baffle, nonplus 474 *puzzle*; defeat easily, beat, lick, thrash, trounce, crush, trample upon; beat hollow, rout, put to flight, 75 *disperse*; silence 165 *suppress*; flatten, knock out; knock for six, hit for s.; bowl out; corner, check, put in check 661 *endanger*; wipe out, do for 165 *destroy*; break, bankrupt.

(11) *win,* win the battle, carry the day, achieve victory, be victorious, come off best; win hands down, romp home, walk off with 701 *do easily*; win on points, scrape home; win the match, wear the crown, beat all comers 34 *be superior*.

Adverb

(12) *successfully,* with flying colours; in triumph.

728
Failure

Noun

(1) *failure,* lack of success, negative result; no luck 731 *misfortune*; frustration 702 *hindrance*; vain attempt, wild-goose chase 641 *lost labour*; mess, muddle, bungle 695 *bungling*; abortion, miscarriage; damp squib, washout, fiasco, flop; slip, faux pas 495 *mistake*; breakdown 702 *hitch*; collapse, fall 309 *descent*; bankruptcy 805 *insolvency*.

(2) *defeat,* bafflement, bewilderment, puzzlement; lost battle,

repulse, rebuff, check, reverse; checkmate; discomfiture, beating, drubbing, hiding, thrashing, trouncing; retreat, flight; rout, landslide; fall, downfall, collapse, debacle; wreck, perdition 165 *ruin*; lost cause, losing battle; deathblow, quietus; final defeat, Waterloo; conquest, subjugation 745 *subjection*.

(3) *loser,* also-ran, nonstarter; has-been; fumbler 697 *bungler*; dud, failure, flop, lemon; victim, prey 544 *dupe*; born loser 731 *unlucky person*; underdog 35 *inferior*; dropout 25 *misfit*; bankrupt, insolvent; the losers, losing side, the defeated, the conquered, the vanquished, the fallen.

Adjective
(4) *unsuccessful,* ineffective; inglorious, obscure, empty-handed; unlucky 731 *unfortunate*; vain, bootless, fruitless, profitless; aborted, abortive, premature: failed, unplaced.

(5) *defeated,* beaten, bested, worsted; baffled, thwarted, foiled 702 *hindered*; disconcerted, dashed, discomfited; outmanoeuvred, outmatched, outplayed, outvoted; outclassed outshone 35 *inferior*; thrashed, licked, whacked; unplaced, out of the running, in retreat, in flight, routed, scattered, put to flight; swamped, overwhelmed; struck down, knocked out, brought low.

(6) *grounded,* stranded, wrecked, washed up, left high and dry; on one's beam-ends 165 *destroyed*; unhorsed, dismounted, thrown; ruined, bankrupt 700 *in difficulties*.

Verb
(7) *fail,* not succeed, have no success, get no results; botch, bungle 495 *blunder*; be found wanting 636 *not suffice*; fail

one, let one down 509 *disappoint*; miss the boat 138 *lose a chance*; go wide, miss 282 *deviate*; draw a blank, return empty-handed 641 *waste effort*; kiss goodbye to 772 *lose*; overreach oneself, fall, collapse 309 *tumble*; break down, malfunction, come to pieces; falter, stall, seize up, get bogged down 145 *cease*; run aground, sink 313 *founder*; make a loss, go bankrupt 805 *not pay*.

(8) *miscarry,* be stillborn, abort; misfire, hang fire, fizzle out; fall, crash 309 *tumble*; come to nothing 641 *be useless*; fail to succeed, fall flat, come to grief; burst, explode, blow up; flop, prove a fiasco; not go well, go wrong, go amiss, go awry; do no good, make things worse 832 *aggravate*; dash one's hopes 509 *disappoint*.

(9) *be defeated,* lose, lose out, suffer defeat, take a beating, get the worst of it; lose the day, lose the battle; lose one's seat, be outvoted; lose hands down, come in last, take the count, bite the dust; fall, succumb 745 *be subject*; retreat, lose ground 290 *recede*; take to flight 620 *run away*; admit defeat, have had enough 721 *submit*; go downhill 165 *be destroyed*.

Adverb
(10) *unsuccessfully,* to no purpose, in vain.

729
Trophy

Noun
(1) *trophy,* sign of success; war trophy, spoils 790 *booty*; scalp, head; scars, wounds; memorial, war m. 505 *reminder*; triumphal arch 548 *monument*; triumph, ovation 876 *celebration*; prize, first p., consolation p., booby p., wooden spoon 962 *reward*; sports trophy, Ashes,

cup, plate, shield; award, Oscar; bays, laurels, crown; garland, wreath, palm, palm of victory; favour, love token 547 *badge*; glory 866 *repute*.

(2) *decoration,* honour 870 *title,* 866 *honours*; citation, mention rosette, ribbon, sash, cordon bleu; athletic honour, blue, oar; medal, star, cross, garter, order; service stripe; Victoria Cross.

730
Prosperity

Noun

(1) *prosperity,* health and wealth 727 *success*; well-being, welfare 824 *happiness*; booming economy, boom, roaring trade; luxury, affluence 800 *wealth*; fleshpots, milk and honey 635 *plenty*; favour, smiles of fortune, good f., blessings 615 *good*; bonanza, luck, run of l., break, lucky b. 159 *chance*; glory, renown 866 *prestige*.

(2) *palmy days,* heyday, prime; halcyon days, summer, sunshine, fair weather; easy times, clover, velvet, bed of roses 376 *euphoria*; golden times, Golden Age 824 *happiness*.

(3) *prosperous person,* man *or* woman of substance 800 *rich person*; child of fortune, lucky fellow; upstart, parvenu, nouveau riche, profiteer; celebrity 866 *person of repute*.

Adjective

(4) *prosperous,* thriving, flourishing, booming 727 *successful*; rising, up and coming; on the make, profiteering; established, well-to-do, well-off, affluent 800 *moneyed*; fortunate, lucky; in clover, on velvet; fat, sleek, euphoric 824 *happy*.

(5) *palmy,* balmy, halcyon, golden, rosy; blissful, blessed;

providential, favourable, promising, auspicious, propitious, cloudless, clear, fine, fair, set f.; glorious, expansive; euphoric, agreeable, cosy 376 *comfortable*.

Verb

(6) *prosper,* thrive, flourish, do well, have one's day; 376 *enjoy*; bask, make hay, live in clover, have it easy; grow fat 301 *eat*; blossom, bloom, flower 171 *be fruitful*; win glory 866 *have a reputation*; boom, profiteer 771 *gain*; get on, go far, make it, arrive 727 *succeed*; make a fortune, strike it rich 800 *get rich*; run smoothly 258 *go smoothly*; keep afloat, not do badly.

(7) *have luck,* strike lucky, strike oil, fall on one's feet.

(8) *be auspicious,* promise well, augur well; favour, prosper, profit 615 *benefit*; look kindly on, smile on, shine on, bless; turn out well, turn up trumps 644 *do good*; glorify 866 *honour*.

Adverb

(9) *prosperously,* swimmingly 727 *successfully*; in clover in luck's way.

Interjection

(10) *Good luck!* all the best!

731
Adversity

Noun

(1) *adversity,* misfortune, mixed blessing 700 *difficulty*; hardship, hard life, tough time 825 *suffering*; bad times, hard t., vale of sorrows 616 *evil*; burden, load, pressure; ups and downs, troubles, trials, cares, worries 825 *worry*; wretchedness, misery 834 *dejection*; bitter cup, bitter pill 872 *humiliation*; cross 825 *sorrow*; curse, blight, plague, scourge 659 *bane*; cold wind, draught, chill, winter 380 *coldness*; gloom 418

darkness; ill wind, cross w.; blow, setback, check, rebuff, reverse 728 *defeat*; rub, pinch, plight, funeral 700 *predicament*; poor lookout, trouble ahead; trough, bad patch, rainy day 655 *deterioration*; slump, recession, depression 679 *inactivity*; dark clouds 900 *threat*; decline, fall, downfall 165 *ruin*; want, need, distress 801 *poverty*.

(2) *misfortune,* bad fortune, ill f.; bad luck, hard luck; no luck, no success 728 *failure*; evil star, malign influence 645 *badness*; hard case, raw deal, rotten hand, hard lot, hard fate; mishap, mischance, accident, casualty 159 *chance*; disaster, calamity, catastrophe, the worst.

(3) *unlucky person,* poor unfortunate, constant loser, poor risk; sport of fortune, plaything of fate; down-and-out 728 *loser*; underdog 35 *inferior*, 801 *poor person*; lame duck 163 *weakling*; scapegoat, victim, wretch, poor w. 825 *sufferer*; prey 544 *dupe*.

Adjective

(4) *adverse,* hostile, frowning, ominous, sinister, inauspicious, unfavourable; bleak, cold, hard; opposed, contrary 704 *opposing*; malign 645 *harmful*; dire, dreadful, ruinous 165 *destructive*; disastrous, calamitous, catastrophic; too bad 645 *bad*.

(5) *unprosperous,* inglorious 728 *unsuccessful*; unwell, in poor shape; not doing well, badly off, not well off 801 *poor*; in trouble, up against it, under a cloud 700 *in difficulties*; declining, on the wane 655 *deteriorated*; in a bad way, in dire straits, in extremities.

(6) *unfortunate,* ill-fated, starcrossed; unlucky, luckless; hapless, poor, wretched, forlorn, miserable, unhappy; stricken, doomed, accursed; down on one's luck, out of luck, out of favour, under a cloud 924 *disapproved*; accident-prone.

Verb

(7) *have trouble,* be in t., have no luck, fall foul of 700 *be in difficulty*; be hard pressed 825 *suffer*; come to grief 728 *miscarry*; feel the pinch, have seen better days 801 *be poor*; go downhill, decline 655 *deteriorate*; go to the dogs 165 *be destroyed*; go hard with, be difficult for 700 *be difficult*.

Adverb

(8) *in adversity,* unfortunately, unhappily; from bad to worse.

732
Averageness

Noun

(1) *averageness,* mediocrity 30 *average*; common lot, ups and downs; plain living, no excess 177 *moderation*; moderate circumstances, bourgeoisie 869 *middle classes*; common man, man *or* woman in the street 869 *commoner*.

Adjective

(2) *middling,* average, mediocre; middlebrow; ordinary, commonplace 83 *typical*; decent, quiet 874 *modest*; undistinguished, inglorious, minor, second-rate 35 *inferior*; fair, fair to middling; so-so, all right, OK, adequate; tolerable, passable; grey 625 *neutral*.

Verb

(3) *be middling,* pass muster 635 *suffice*; manage, jog on, avoid excess; never set the Thames on fire.

733
Authority

Noun

(1) *authority,* power; powers that be, 'they' 741 *master*; the Government, Whitehall 690 *director*; right, divine r., prerogative, royal p.; legitimacy, law, lawful authority 953 *legality*; legislative assembly 692 *parliament*; delegated authority, committee 751 *commission*; portfolio 955 *jurisdiction*; patronage, prestige 178 *influence*; leadership, hegemony 689 *directorship*; supremacy 34 *superiority*; seniority, priority 64 *precedence*; majesty, royalty, crown; succession; legitimate s., accession; seizure of power, usurpation.

(2) *governance,* rule, sway, direction, command 689 *directorship*; control, supreme c.; hold, grip, domination, mastery, whip hand; dominion, sovereignty, overlordship, supremacy 34 *superiority*; regime, reign, regency, dynasty; foreign rule, empire 745 *subjection*; imperialism, colonialism; state control, civil service.

(3) *despotism,* benevolent d., paternalism; tyranny dictatorship; absolutism, autocracy; totalitarianism; police state 735 *brute force.*

(4) *government,* direction 689 *management*; politics; constitutional government, rule of law; misgovernment 734 *anarchy*; government by priests, theocracy; monarchy, kingship; republicanism, federalism; tribalism; patriarchy, matriarchy; feudalism, paternalism; squirearchy, aristocracy; meritocracy, oligarchy, elitism; gerontocracy; rule of wealth, plutocracy; parliamentary government, party system 708 *political party*, 605 *vote*; democracy, majority rule; demagogy, demagoguery, vox populi; collectivism, communism, Leninism, Marxism-L.; party rule, Bolshevism, Fascism, Nazism; army rule, martial law; mob rule, mob law; syndicalism, socialism; bureaucracy, technocracy; self-government, home rule 744 *independence*; regency, interregnum.

(5) *position of authority,* post, place, office, high o.; kingship, royalty; regency, protectorship; rulership, chieftainship, sheikhdom, emirate, sultanate, caliphate; governorship, viceroyalty; consulate, consulship; magistrature, magistracy; mayoralty; headship, presidency, premiership, chairmanship 689 *directorship*; overlordship, mastership; government post, Cabinet seat.

(6) *political organization,* body politic; state, nation s., commonwealth; country, realm, kingdom, republic, city state; federation, confederation; principality, duchy, archduchy, dukedom, palatinate, empire, dominion, colony, dependency, protectorate, mandate 184 *territory*; free world, communist bloc, Third World 184 *region*; superpower, banana republic; buffer state; province, county 184 *district*; body politic, laws, constitution.

Adjective

(7) *authoritative,* empowered, competent; in office, in authority; magisterial, official, ex officio; mandatory, binding 740 *compelling*; masterful, domineering; commanding, lordly, majestic; overruling, imperious, peremptory, arbitrary, absolute, autocratic, tyrannical, dictatorial, totalitarian 735 *authoritarian*; powerful 162

strong; leading 178 *influential*; dominant, paramount 34 *supreme*.

(8) *ruling,* reigning, sovereign, on the throne; royal, regal, majestic, kingly, queenly princely, lordly; dynastic; imperial; magisterial; governing, controlling etc. vb.

(9) *governmental,* political, constitutional; ministerial, official, administrative, bureaucratic, centralized; technocratic; matriarchal, patriarchal; monarchical, feudal, aristocratic, oligarchic, plutocratic, democratic, popular, republican; autonomous, self-governing 744 *independent.*

Verb
(10) *rule,* hold sway, reign, reign supreme, wear the crown; govern, control 737 *command*; manage 689 *direct*; hold office, be in power, have authority, wield a., exercise a., exert a., use one's a.; rule absolutely, tyrannize 735 *oppress*; dictate, lay down the law; legislate; keep order, police.

(11) *take authority,* accede to the throne, take office, take command, assume c., take over; form a government; gain power, take control; seize power, usurp p.

(12) *dominate,* have the power, have the upper hand 34 *predominate*; lord it over, rule the roost, wear the trousers 737 *command*; call the tune 727 *overmaster*; have in one's power 178 *influence*; dictate, coerce 740 *compel*; hold down 745 *subjugate*; override, overrule, overawe.

(13) *be governed,* be ruled, be dictated to; owe obedience to 745 *be subject.*

Adverb
(14) *by authority,* by warrant of, in the name of.

734
Laxity: Absence of authority

Noun
(1) *laxity,* slackness, indifference 458 *negligence*; laissez-faire 744 *scope*; informality, lack of ceremony; loosening, relaxation 746 *liberation*; connivance 756 *permission*; indulgence, toleration, permissiveness 736 *leniency*; weak will, feeble grasp, crumbling power 163 *weakness*; inertia 175 *inertness*; no control, abdication of authority; concession 770 *compromise.*

(2) *anarchy,* no authority, free-for-all, disorder, chaos 61 *turmoil*; insubordination, licence, indiscipline 738 *disobedience*; anarchism, nihilism; interregnum, power vacuum; powerlessness 161 *impotence*; misrule, misgovernment; mob law, reign of terror 954 *lawlessness*; dethronement, deposition.

Adjective
(3) *lax,* loose, slack; disorganized 61 *orderless*; feeble, soft 163 *weak*; slipshod, remiss 458 *negligent*; happy-go-lucky, relaxed, informal, free-and-easy, overindulgent, permissive, tolerant, indulgent 736 *lenient*; weak-willed, weak-kneed 601 *irresolute*; unassertive; lacking authority.

(4) *anarchic,* unbridled, insubordinate 878 *insolent*; rebellious 738 *disobedient*; disorderly, unruly 738 *riotous*; lawless, nihilistic, anarchistic.

Verb
(5) *be lax,* not enforce; give one his or her head 744 *give scope*; waive the rules, stretch a point,

connive at; tolerate, put up with, suffer 756 *permit*; indulge, spoil 736 *be lenient*; relax, make concessions 770 *compromise*; lose control, stand down, abdicate 753 *resign*; misrule, misgovern, mismanage, reduce to chaos 63 *derange*.

(6) *please oneself,* defy authority, resist control 738 *disobey*; take on oneself, arrogate, usurp authority 916 *be undue*.

(7) *unthrone,* dethrone, unseat, overthrow, force to resign 752 *depose*; usurp, seize the crown.

735
Severity

Noun
(1) *severity,* strictness, stringency; high standards; discipline, firm control, strong hand, tight grasp 733 *authority*; rod of iron, heavy hand, Draconian laws; harshness, rigour, inflexibility; no concession, no compromise, pound of flesh; intolerance, fanaticism, bigotry 602 *opinionatedness*; censorship, suppression 747 *restraint*; inquisition, persecution, harassment, oppression, victimization; callousness, lack of mercy, inexorability 906 *pitilessness*; harsh treatment, the hard way, tender mercies, cruelty 898 *inhumanity*.

(2) *brute force,* naked f.; rule of might, big battalions 160 *power*; coercion, bludgeoning 740 *compulsion*; bloodiness 176 *violence*; subjugation 745 *subjection*; arbitrary power, absolutism, autocracy, dictatorship 733 *despotism*; tyranny, Fascism, Nazism, militarism; martial law, iron hand, mailed fist, jackboot.

(3) *tyrant,* pedant, formalist, stickler; petty tyrant, disciplinarian, martinet, sergeant major; militarist, jackboot; hanging judge; heavy father, Dutch uncle, Big Brother; authoritarian, despot, dictator 741 *autocrat*; inquisitor, persecutor; oppressor, bully, taskmaster, slave-driver; extortioner, bloodsucker, predator, harpy; ogre, brute 938 *monster*; hardliner.

Adjective
(4) *severe,* strict, rigorous, extreme; strait-laced, puritanical, prudish; formalistic, pedantic; bigoted, fanatical; hypercritical, intolerant, censorious 924 *disapproving*; uncompromising, unbending, rigid 326 *hard*; hard-boiled, flinty, dour; inflexible, obdurate 602 *obstinate*; inexorable, relentless, merciless, unsparing, implacable 906 *pitiless*; heavy, stern; punitive, stringent, Draconian, drastic, savage.

(5) *authoritarian,* masterful, domineering, arrogant, haughty 878 *insolent*; undemocratic, despotic, absolute, arbitrary; totalitarian, Fascist; dictatorial, autocratic; coercive, compulsive 740 *compelling*.

(6) *oppressive,* hard on 914 *unjust*; tyrannical, despotic; tyrannous, harsh; exigent, exacting, grasping, extortionate, exploitive, predatory; persecuting, inquisitorial, unsparing; high-handed, overbearing, domineering; heavy-handed, rough, bloody 176 *violent*; brutal, ogreish 898 *cruel*.

Verb
(7) *be severe,* harsh etc. vb.; stand no nonsense, exert authority, discipline; bear hard on, deal hardly with, come down on, crack down on, stamp

on, clamp down on 165 *suppress*; persecute, hunt down 619 *pursue*; ill-treat, mishandle, abuse 675 *misuse*; treat rough, get tough with, inflict, chastise 963 *punish*; wreak vengeance 910 *avenge*; exact reprisals 714 *retaliate*; show no mercy 906 *be pitiless*; give no quarter 362 *slaughter*.

(8) *oppress,* tyrannize, play the tyrant, be despotic, abuse one's authority, take liberties 734 *please oneself*; assume, arrogate 916 *be undue*; domineer, lord it; overawe, intimidate, terrorize 854 *frighten*; bludgeon 740 *compel*; put upon, bully, harass 827 *torment*; persecute, spite, victimize 898 *be malevolent*; break one's spirit 369 *break in*; task, tax, drive 684 *fatigue*; exploit, extort, grind, trample on, tread underfoot, hold down 165 *suppress*; burden, enslave 745 *subjugate*; ride roughshod over 914 *do wrong*; misgovern, misrule; scourge, rack 963 *torture*; shed blood 362 *murder*.

Adverb
(9) *severely,* sternly, tyrannically, with a heavy hand.

736
Leniency

Noun
(1) *leniency,* softness 734 *laxity*; mildness, gentleness, forbearance, soft answer 823 *patience*; pardon 909 *forgiveness*; mercy, clemency 905 *pity*; humanity, kindness 897 *benevolence*; favour, concession; indulgence, toleration; sufferance, allowance 756 *permission*; connivance, complaisance; light rein, light hand, velvet glove, kid gloves.

Adjective
(2) *lenient,* soft, gentle, mild, indulgent, tolerant; conniving, complaisant; easy-going, undemanding 734 *lax*; forbearing, longsuffering 823 *patient*; merciful 909 *forgiving*; tender 905 *pitying*.

Verb
(3) *be lenient,* make no demands, make few d.; deal gently with, handle tenderly, go easy 177 *moderate*; spoil, indulge, humour 889 *pet*; tolerate, allow, connive 756 *permit*; stretch a point 734 *be lax*; concede 758 *consent*; not press, refrain, forbear 823 *be patient*; pity, spare 905 *show mercy*; pardon 909 *forgive*; relax, show consideration 897 *be benevolent*.

737
Command

Noun
(1) *command,* summons; commandment, ordinance; injunction, imposition; dictation, bidding, will and pleasure; charge, commission, instructions, rules, regulations; directive, order, marching orders; word of command, word, signal; whip, three-line w.; dictate 740 *compulsion*; proscription 757 *prohibition*; countermand, counterorder.

(2) *decree,* edict, fiat, law, canon, prescript 693 *precept*; bull, papal decree, circular, encyclical; ordinance, order in council; decree nisi, decree absolute; decision 480 *judgment*; act 953 *legislation*; plebiscite 605 *vote*; dictate, dictation.

(3) *demand,* claim, requisition 761 *request*; notice, final n., final demand, ultimatum; blackmail 900 *threat*; imposition, exaction, levy 809 *tax*.

(4) *warrant,* search w., commission, brevet, authorization, letters patent, passport 756 *permit*; writ, summons, subpoena, habeas corpus 959 *legal process.*

Adjective
(5) *commanding,* imperative, categorical, dictatorial 733 *authoritative*; mandatory, obligatory, peremptory, compulsive 740 *compelling*; demanding, insistent.

Verb
(6) *command,* bid, order, tell, issue a command, give an order; signal, call, motion, sign 547 *gesticulate*; give a directive, instruct, brief, circularize; rule, lay down, enjoin; give a mandate, charge 751 *commission*; impose, make obligatory 917 *impose a duty*; detail, tell off; call together, convene 74 *bring together*; send for, summon; subpoena, issue a writ 959 *litigate*; dictate 740 *compel*; countermand 752 *abrogate*; proscribe 757 *prohibit.*

(7) *decree,* promulgate 528 *proclaim*; declare, say so 532 *affirm*; prescribe, ordain 608 *predetermine*; enact, pass a law legislate 953 *make legal*; pass judgment, give j., rule, give a ruling 480 *judge.*

(8) *demand,* requisition 627 *require*; order, indent 761 *request*; make demands on, blackmail 900 *threaten*; make claims upon 915 *claim*; demand payment, bill, invoice; exact, levy 809 *tax.*

Adverb
(9) *commandingly,* imperatively, authoritatively.

738
Disobedience

Noun
(1) *disobedience,* indiscipline, naughtiness, misbehaviour; delinquency 934 *wickedness*; insubordination, mutinousness, mutineering 711 *defiance*; disloyalty, defection, desertion 918 *undutifulness*; crime, sin 936 *guilty act*; civil disobedience 715 *resistance*; conscientious objection 704 *opposition*; murmuring, restlessness 829 *discontent*; seditiousness, wildness 954 *lawlessness*; banditry, mafia 788 *brigandage.*

(2) *revolt,* mutiny; direct action 145 *strike*; faction 709 *dissension*; breakaway, secession 978 *schism*; restlessness, restiveness 318 *agitation*; sabotage 165 *destruction*; disturbance, disorder, riot, street r., rioting, tumult, barricades 61 *turmoil*; rebellion, insurrection, rising, uprising 176 *outbreak*; putsch, coup d'état; resistance movement, insurgency 715 *resistance*; subversion 149 *revolution*; terrorism 954 *lawlessness*; civil war 718 *war*; regicide, tyrannicide 362 *homicide.*

(3) *sedition,* seditiousness; cabal, intrigue 623 *plot*; subversion, infiltration, fifth column 523 *latency*; terrorism, anarchism, nihilism; disloyalty, treason, high t. 930 *perfidy.*

(4) *revolter,* awkward person, handful 700 *difficulty*; scamp, scapegrace 938 *bad person*; mutineer, rebel, demonstrator, striker 705 *opponent*; secessionist, seceder, splinter group 978 *schismatic*; deviationist, dissident 829 *malcontent*; blackleg, scab; maverick 84 *nonconformist*; traitor, quisling, fifth columnist; tyrannicide, regicide; insurgent; guerrilla, partisan; resistance, underground; extremist 149 *revolutionist*; reactionary, counter-revolutionary; terrorist, anarchist, nihilist; mafia, bandit 789 *robber.*

(5) *agitator,* protester, demonstrator; tub-thumper, rabble-rouser, demagogue; firebrand, mischief-maker 663 *trouble-maker*; suffragette; agent provocateur, ringleader.

(6) *rioter,* street r., brawler 904 *ruffian*; saboteur, wrecker, luddite.

Adjective

(7) *disobedient,* disobeying, naughty, mischievous, misbehaving; awkward, difficult, undisciplined, self-willed, wayward, restive vicious, unruly 176 *violent*; intractable, unmanageable ungovernable, insubordinate, mutinous, rebellious, bloody-minded; contrary 704 *opposing*; nonconformist, recalcitrant 715 *resisting*; challenging 711 *defiant*; refractory, perverse, 602 *obstinate*; subversive, revolutionary, seditious, traitorous 734 *anarchic*; wild, untamed, savage.

(8) *riotous,* rioting; anarchic, rowdy, unruly, wild 61 *disorderly*; law-breaking 954 *lawless*; mutinous, rebellious, up in arms 715 *resisting*.

Verb

(9) *disobey,* not obey 734 *please oneself*; be disobedient, misbehave, get into mischief; flout authority, not comply with 769 *not observe*; disobey orders 711 *defy*; defy the whip, cross-vote; snap one's fingers at 704 *oppose*; break the law 954 *be illegal*; violate, infringe 306 *encroach*; turn restive, kick, chafe, fret, play up.

(10) *revolt,* rebel, mutiny; down tools, strike 145 *cease*; secede, break away; agitate, demonstrate, protest 762 *deprecate*; stage a revolt 715 *resist*; rise, rise up 746 *achieve liberty*; overthrow, upset 149 *revolutionize*.

739
Obedience

Noun

(1) *obedience,* compliance 768 *observance*; meekness, tractability, malleability 327 *softness*; readiness 597 *willingness*; acquiescence, submissiveness 721 *submission*; passiveness, passivity 679 *inactivity*; dutifulness, morale, discipline 917 *duty*; deference, slavishness 879 *servility*; tameness, docility.

(2) *loyalty,* constancy, devotion, fidelity, faithfulness 929 *probity*; allegiance, fealty, homage, service, deference, submission.

Adjective

(3) *obedient,* complying, compliant, cooperating, conforming 768 *observant*; loyal, faithful, true-blue, steadfast, constant; devoted, dedicated, sworn; submissive 721 *submitting*; law-abiding 717 *peaceful*; complaisant, amenable, docile; good, well-behaved; filial, daughterly; ready 597 *willing*; acquiescent, resigned, unresisting; passive 679 *inactive*; meek, biddable, dutiful; at one's orders, on a lead, under control; disciplined, regimented 917 *obliged*; trained, manageable, tame; respectful, deferential; subservient, obsequious, slavish 879 *servile*.

Verb

(4) *obey,* comply, do to order, act upon 768 *observe*; toe the line; come to heel 83 *conform*; assent 758 *consent*; listen, heed, mind, obey orders, do as one is told do one's bidding, follow, wait upon 742 *serve*; be loyal 768 *keep faith*; pay tribute 745 *be subject*; know one's duty 917 *do one's duty*; yield, defer to 721 *submit*; grovel, cringe 879 *be servile*.

Adverb
(5) *obediently,* under orders, to order, in obedience to; at your service.

740
Compulsion

Noun
(1) *compulsion,* spur of necessity 596 *necessity*; law of nature, act of God; moral compulsion 917 *conscience*; Hobson's choice 606 *no choice*; dictation, coercion, regimentation; arm-twisting, blackmail 900 *threat*; sanctions 963 *penalty*; enforcement, duress, force, physical f.; big stick, strong arm 735 *brute force*; force-feeding; conscription, call-up; exaction, extortion 786 *taking*; forced labour 745 *servitude.*

Adjective
(2) *compelling,* compulsive, involuntary, inevitable 596 *necessary*; imperative, dictatorial, peremptory 737 *commanding*; compulsory, mandatory, binding 917 *obligatory*; urgent, pressing, overriding, constraining, coercive; irresistible 160 *powerful*; forcible, forceful, cogent; high-pressure, strong-arm 735 *oppressive.*

Verb
(3) *compel,* constrain, coerce 176 *force*; dictate, necessitate, oblige; order 737 *command*; impose, enforce; make one, leave no option; leave no escape, pin down, tie d.; impress, draft, conscript; drive, dragoon, regiment, discipline; force one's hand, bulldoze, steamroller, railroad, bully into; bludgeon 735 *oppress*; take by force, requisition, commandeer, extort, exact, wring from, drag f. 786 *take*; apply pressure, lean on, squeeze, twist one's arm 963 *torture*; blackmail, hijack, hold to ransom 900 *threaten*; be peremptory, insist 532 *emphasize*; brook no denial, compel to accept, force upon, inflict on; force-feed.

Adverb
(4) *by force,* compulsorily, under protest, under duress, forcibly, by main force; at gunpoint.

741
Master

Noun
(1) *master,* mistress; captor, possessor 776 *owner*; sire, lord, lady, dame; liege, lord, overlord; protector 707 *patron*; squire, laird 868 *aristocrat*; sir, madam 870 *title*; senior, head, principal 34 *superior*; president, chair 690 *director*; employer, capitalist, governor 690 *manager*; ruling class, ruling party, the authorities, the establishment, 'them' 733 *government*; staff, High Command 689 *directorship.*

(2) *autocrat,* absolute ruler, despot, tyrant, dictator, führer, Big Brother; tycoon 638 *bigwig*; petty tyrant, commissar, tin god, 690 *official.*

(3) *sovereign,* crowned head, Majesty, Highness, Royal H., Excellence; dynasty, house, royal line; royalty, monarch, king, queen, rex, regina; emperor, empress; prince, princess; sultan, caliph.

(4) *potentate,* ruler; chief, chieftain, headman, sheikh; prince, rajah, rani, maharajah, maharani; emir; duke, duchess; regent.

(5) *governor,* lieutenant-g., High Commissioner; viceroy, vicereine; proconsul; patriarch, metropolitan 986 *ecclesiarch*; archbishop, cardinal imam, ayatollah 690 *leader.*

(6) *officer,* person in authority; functionary, mandarin, bureaucrat 690 *official;* civil servant, public s.; prime minister, grand vizier, vizier; chancellor, vice-c.; constable, marshal, warden; mayor, lord m., lady m., mayoress, alderman, provost, councillor; dignitary 866 *person of repute;* sheriff, bailiff; justice of the peace 957 *judge;* magistrate, chief m.; consul, proconsul, praetor, prefect, district officer; commissioner; beadle, tipstaff 955 *law officer;* sexton, verger 986 *church officer.*

(7) *naval officer,* Sea Lord; admiral, vice-a., rear-a., commodore, captain, commander, lieutenant-c., lieutenant, flag-l., sub-l., petty officer, leading seaman.

(8) *army officer,* staff, High Command; field marshal; commander-in-chief; general, lieutenant-g., major-g.; brigadier, colonel, lieutenant-c., major, captain, lieutenant, second l., subaltern; ensign, cornet; warrant officer, non-commissioned officer, NCO, sergeant major, sergeant, corporal, lance corporal; adjutant, aide-de-camp, quartermaster, orderly officer; commander, commandant.

(9) *air officer,* air marshal, air commodore, group captain, wing commander, squadron leader, flight lieutenant, flying officer, pilot o., warrant o., flight sergeant 722 *air force.*

742
Servant

Noun

(1) *servant,* public s. 690 *official;* general servant, factotum 678 *busy person;* humble servant, menial, slave; orderly, attendant; subordinate, underling 35 *inferior;* helper, assistant,

secretary 703 *aider;* paid servant, mercenary, hireling; employee, hand, farmhand, labourer 686 *worker;* hack, drudge, dogsbody; steward, stewardess, waiter, waitress; bartender, barmaid; ostler, groom; errand boy, messenger 529 *courier;* concierge 264 *doorkeeper;* porter 273 *bearer;* callboy, page boy; caretaker, help, daily 648 *cleaner;* nursemaid 749 *keeper.*

(2) *domestic,* staff 686 *personnel;* domestic servant, footman, lackey; maid, chambermaid, domestic drudge, skivvy, scullion, washer-up; housekeeper, butler, cook; steward, chaplain, governess, tutor, nurse, nanny; personal servant, page, squire, valet, batman; nursemaid, au pair; gardener, groom; chauffeur 268 *driver.*

(3) *retainer,* follower, suite, train 67 *retinue;* court, courtier; attendant, usher; bodyguard, henchman, squire, armour-bearer; companion; lady-in-waiting; chamberlain, equerry, steward, bailiff.

(4) *dependant,* hanger-on, parasite, satellite, camp follower 284 *follower;* subordinate 35 *inferior;* minion, lackey; apprentice, protégé(e), ward, charge.

(5) *subject,* national, citizen 191 *native;* liege, vassal; dependency, colony, satellite.

(6) *slave,* serf, villein; galley slave, sweated labour 686 *worker;* robot 628 *instrument;* captive 750 *prisoner.*

Adjective

(7) *serving,* ministering 703 *aiding;* in service, menial; working, on the payroll, on the staff; in slavery, in captivity, in bonds 745 *subject.*

Verb

(8) *serve,* be in service, wait

upon, tend 703 *minister to*; live in, be on hand 89 *accompany*; attend upon, follow 739 *obey*; do chores, do for, work for 640 *be useful*.

743
Badge of rule

Noun

(1) *regalia,* emblem of royalty, crown, orb, sceptre; coronet, diadem; sword of state 733 *authority*; royal robe, ermine; royal seat, throne; royal standard 547 *heraldry*.

(2) *badge of rule,* emblem of authority; staff, wand, rod, baton, truncheon, gavel; signet, seal, privy s.; mace; pastoral staff, crosier; woolsack; triple crown, mitre 989 *canonicals*; robe, mantle, toga.

(3) *badge of rank,* sash, spurs, epaulette 547 *badge*; uniform 547 *livery*; pips, chevron, stripe; garter, order 729 *decoration*.

744
Freedom

Noun

(1) *freedom,* liberty; freedom of action, initiative; free will, free thought, free speech; rights, civil rights, equal r.; privilege, prerogative, exemption, immunity 919 *nonliability*; liberalism, licence, artistic l.; laisser faire, nonintervention; nonalignment, cross benches; emancipation, setting free 746 *liberation*; women's l., gay l.; franchise 605 *vote*.

(2) *independence,* freedom of action, freedom of choice 605 *choice*; no allegiance, floating vote; emancipation 84 *nonconformity*; unmarried state 895 *celibacy*; individualism, individuality 80 *speciality*; self-determination, nationhood 371 *nation*; autonomy, self-rule 635 *sufficiency*; independent means 800 *wealth*.

(3) *scope,* play, free p., full p. 183 *range*; swing, rope, long r.; field, room, living space, elbow-room, leeway 183 *room*; latitude, liberty, informality; fling, licence, excess 734 *laxity*; one's head, one's own way, one's own devices 137 *opportunity*; facilities, the run of, free hand, blank cheque, carte blanche; free-for-all, free enterprise, free trade, free market, open m.

(4) *free person,* freeman, citizen, voter; ex-convict, escapee 667 *escaper*; no slave, free agent, freelance; independent, crossbencher; free-trader; freethinker, liberal; libertarian, bohemian 84 *nonconformist*.

Adjective

(5) *free,* freeborn, enfranchised; heart-whole, fancy-free; scot-free 960 *acquitted*; on the loose, at large 667 *escaped*; released, freed 746 *liberated*; free as air, footloose, ranging 267 *travelling*; exempt, immune 919 *nonliable*; free-speaking, plain-spoken 573 *plain*; freethinking, emancipated, broadminded, unprejudiced, independent; free and easy; loose, licentious 951 *impure*; at leisure, retired 681 *leisurely*; free for all, unreserved 289 *accessible*.

(6) *unconfined,* unfettered, unbridled, unbound, unchecked, unrestrained, uninhibited; informal, casual, freewheeling; free-range, wandering.

(7) *independent,* unilateral 609 *spontaneous*; unattached, detached 860 *indifferent*; free to choose, uncommitted; unaffiliated 625 *neutral*; isolationist

883 *unsociable*; unconquered 727 *unbeaten*; autonomous, self-governing; self-sufficient, self-reliant, self-supporting; one's own master; ungovernable 734 *anarchic*; self-employed, freelance; unofficial, cowboy, wildcat; unconventional, free-minded, free-souled; single, bachelor; breakaway 489 *dissenting*.

(8) *unconditional,* no strings attached; free-for-all, no holds barred; unrestricted, absolute; open, discretionary, arbitrary.

Verb
(9) *be free,* go free, get f. 667 *escape*; have the run of, have a free hand, have scope, have elbowroom; have one's head; feel free, be oneself, let oneself go; have one's fling, cut loose, drop out 734 *please oneself*; follow one's bent, drift, wander, roam 282 *stray*; be independent, shift for oneself, fend for oneself; take liberties, make free with.

(10) *give scope,* give one his *or* her head 734 *be lax*; give one a free hand 701 *facilitate*; release, set free, enfranchise 746 *liberate*; let, license, charter 756 *permit*; let alone, not interfere.

Adverb
(11) *freely,* liberally, at will.

745
Subjection

Noun
(1) *subjection,* subordination; inferior rank, inferior status 35 *inferiority*; dependence, apron strings, leading s.; allegiance, nationality, citizenship; subjugation, conquest, colonialism; loss of freedom, enslavement 721 *submission*; constraint, discipline 747 *restraint*; oppression 735 *severity*; yoke 748 *fetter*.

(2) *service,* domestic s., government s., employ, employment; feudalism 739 *loyalty*; forced labour 740 *compulsion*; conscription 718 *war measures*.

(3) *servitude,* slavery, enslavement, captivity, thraldom, bondage, yoke.

Adjective
(4) *subjected etc. vb.;* subjugated, overwhelmed 728 *defeated*; taken prisoner, in chains 747 *restrained*; disfranchised; colonized, enslaved, in harness 742 *serving*; under the yoke, oppressed, downtrodden, underfoot; treated like dirt, henpecked, browbeaten; brought to heel, domesticated 369 *tamed*; submissive 721 *submitting*; subservient 879 *servile*.

(5) *subject,* not independent, satellite, bond, bound; owing service, liege, vassal, feudal 739 *obedient*; under, subordinate junior 35 *inferior*; dependent, subject to 180 *liable*; in the power of, at the mercy of, under one's thumb; parasitical, hanging on 879 *servile*; in the pay of 917 *obliged*.

Verb
(6) *be subject,* live under, pay tribute 739 *obey*; depend on 35 *be inferior*; serve 721 *submit*; be a tool 628 *be instrumental*; cringe, fawn 879 *be servile*.

(7) *subjugate,* subdue, subject 727 *overmaster*; colonize, annex, take captive 727 *triumph*; take, capture, enslave; fetter, bind 747 *imprison*; rob of freedom, disfranchise; trample on, treat like dirt 735 *oppress*; keep under, keep down, repress, sit on 165 *suppress*; captivate 821 *impress*; enchant 983 *bewitch*; dominate 178 *influence*; discipline, tame, quell 369 *break in*; bring to heel.

746
Liberation

Noun

(1) *liberation,* setting free, release, discharge 960 *acquittal*; free expression 818 *feeling*; extrication, 46 *separation*; riddance 831 *relief*; rescue, redemption 668 *deliverance*; emancipation, enfranchisement; parole, bail; liberalization 734 *laxity*; decontrol 752 *abrogation*; absolution 909 *forgiveness*.

Adjective

(2) *liberated,* rescued, delivered, saved 668 *extricable*; rid of, relieved; paroled, set free, freed, unbound 744 *unconfined*; released, discharged, acquitted; emancipated etc. vb.

Verb

(3) *liberate,* rescue, save 668 *deliver*; dispense 919 *exempt*; pardon 909 *forgive*; discharge, absolve 960 *acquit*; make free, emancipate, enfranchise, give the vote; grant equal rights; release, free, set free, set at liberty, let out; parole 766 *give terms*; unfetter, unshackle; unlock 263 *open*; loosen, unloose, loose, unbind, untie, disentangle, extricate, disengage 62 *unravel*; unstop, uncork, unleash, let loose, turn adrift; license, charter 744 *give scope*; let out, give vent to; let go 779 *not retain*; relax, liberalize 734 *be lax*; lift controls, decontrol; demobilize, disband.

(4) *achieve liberty,* gain one's freedom, breathe freely; assert oneself 738 *revolt*; free oneself, break loose, burst one's bonds, slip one's collar, get away 667 *escape.*

747
Restraint

Noun

(1) *restraint,* self-r , self-control 942 *temperance*; reserve, inhibitions; suppression, repression; constraint 740 *compulsion*; cramp, check 702 *hindrance*; curb, drag, brake, bridle 748 *fetter*; veto, ban, bar, embargo 757 *prohibition*; legal restraint 953 *law*; control, strict c., discipline 733 *authority*; censorship 550 *obliteration*; binding over 963 *penalty*.

(2) *restriction,* limitation, limiting factor 236 *limit*; restricted area, no-go area; curfew; constriction, squeeze 198 *compression*; duress, pressure 740 *compulsion*; control, rationing; exclusive rights, restrictive practice 57 *exclusion*; monopoly, price ring, cartel, closed shop; protectionism, tariff; retrenchment, cuts 814 *economy*; freeze, price control, credit squeeze; blockade, starving out.

(3) *detention,* preventive d., custody, arrest, house a.; custodianship, keeping, guarding 660 *protection*; quarantine, internment; remand, captivity; bondage, slavery 745 *servitude*; confinement, solitary c., incarceration, imprisonment; sentence, time, a stretch; penology, penologist.

Adjective

(4) *restraining,* with strings; limiting etc. vb. custodial, keeping; restrictive, conditional; cramping, hidebound; straitlaced, strict 735 *severe*; stiff 326 *rigid*; tight 206 *narrow*; close confined, poky; coercive 740 *compelling*; repressive, inhibiting 757 *prohibiting*; monopolistic, protectionist

(5) *restrained,* self-controlled 942 *temperate*; pent up, bottled up; reserved, shy; disciplined, under control 739 *obedient*; on a lead 232 *circumscribed*; pinned down, kept under 745 *subjected*; on parole 917 *obliged*; protected, rationed; limited, restricted, scant, tight; cramped 702 *hindered*; tied, bound, gagged; held up, fogbound, snowbound.

(6) *imprisoned,* confined, detained, kept in; confined, in quarantine; interned, under detention, under arrest, in custody; refused bail, on remand; inside, behind bars, doing time incarcerated, locked up 750 *captive*; corralled, penned up, impounded; in irons, fettered, shackled; caged, in captivity, trapped.

Verb

(7) *restrain,* hold back, pull b.; arrest, check, curb, rein in, brake 278 *retard*; cramp, clog, hamper 702 *hinder*; swathe, bind 45 *tie*; stop, call a halt 145 *halt*; inhibit, veto, ban, bar 757 *prohibit*; bridle, discipline, control 735 *be severe*; subdue 745 *subjugate*; restrain oneself, keep one's cool; grip, hold, hold in leash, hold in check 778 *retain*; hold in, keep in, fight down, fight back, bottle up; restrict, tighten, hem in, limit 232 *circumscribe*; damp down, pour water on 177 *moderate*; hold down, clamp down on, crack down on, keep under, sit on, jump on, repress 165 *suppress*; censor, muzzle, gag, silence; restrict access, debar from, rope off, keep out 57 *exclude*; withhold, keep back; ration, retrench 814 *economize*; try to stop, resist 704 *oppose*.

(8) *arrest,* make an a., apprehend, catch, collar, pinch, pick up; haul in, run in; handcuff, take, take prisoner, capture; kidnap, seize, take hostage; put under arrest, take into custody, hold.

(9) *fetter,* manacle, chain, bind, pinion, tie up, handcuff, put in irons; tether, picket 45 *tie*; shackle, trammel, hobble; make conditions, attach strings.

(10) *imprison,* confine, immure, quarantine, intern; hold, detain, keep in wall up, seal up; coop up, cage, kennel, pen, cabin, box up, shut up, shut in, trap 235 *enclose*; incarcerate, throw into prison, send to p., commit to p., remand, give in charge; lock up, keep behind bars; keep prisoner, refuse bail.

748
Prison

Noun

(1) *prison,* open p., penitentiary, reformatory, Borstal; remand home, assessment centre; prison ship; dungeon, Tower; gaol, jail.

(2) *lockup;* police station; guardroom, guardhouse; cell, condemned c., Death Row; dungeon, torture chamber; dock, bar; pound 235 *enclosure*; ghetto, reserve; stocks, pillory.

(3) *prison camp,* detention c., internment c., concentration c.; penal settlement.

(4) *fetter,* shackle, trammel, bond, chain, ball and c., irons, hobble; manacle, handcuff; straitjacket, corset; muzzle, gag, bit, bridle, snaffle, headstall, halter; rein, bearing r., traces; yoke, collar, harness; curb, brake, drag 702 *hindrance*; lead, tether 47 *halter*.

749
Keeper

Noun

(1) *keeper,* custodian, curator; archivist, record keeper 549 *recorder;* caretaker, concierge, housekeeper; warden, ranger, gamekeeper; guard, escort, convoy; garrison 713 *defender;* watch, coastguard; 660 *protector;* invigilator, tutor, chaperon, duenna, governess; nanny, baby-sitter 742 *domestic;* foster parent, guardian.

(2) *gaoler,* jailer, turnkey, warder, wardress, prison guard, prison officer.

750
Prisoner

Noun

(1) *prisoner,* captive, prisoner of war; political prisoner; detainee, prisoner of state; defendant 928 *accused person;* first offender 904 *offender;* convict, lifer; chain gang, galley slave 742 *slave;* hostage.

Adjective

(2) *captive,* imprisoned, in chains, under lock and key, behind bars, jailed, in prison, inside 747 *imprisoned;* in custody, under arrest, detained, under detention.

751
Commission: Vicarious authority

Noun

(1) *commission,* delegation; devolution, decentralization; deputation, legation, mission, embassy 754 *envoy;* regency, vice-r. 733 *authority;* representation, proxy; agency, trusteeship 689 *management;* public service, civil s. 733 *government.*

(2) *mandate,* trust, charge 737 *command;* commission, assignment, appointment, office, task, mission; enterprise 672 *undertaking;* nomination, return, election 605 *vote;* posting, transfer; investment, investiture, installation, induction, inauguration, ordination, enthronement, coronation; power of attorney, charter, writ 737 *warrant;* brevet, diploma 756 *permit;* terms of reference 766 *conditions;* care, ward, charge.

Adjective

(3) *commissioned,* empowered, deputed, delegated, accredited; vicarious, representational.

Verb

(4) *commission,* empower, authorize, charge; sanction, charter, license 756 *permit;* post, accredit, appoint, assign; name, nominate; engage, hire 622 *employ;* invest, induct, install, ordain; enthrone, crown; turn over to, leave it to; consign, entrust, trust with; delegate, depute; return, elect 605 *vote.*

752
Abrogation: Loss of authority

Noun

(1) *abrogation,* annulment, invalidation, mullification; disallowance, cancellation; recall, repeal, revocation, abolition, dissolution; repudiation 533 *negation;* suspension, discontinuance; reversal, counterorder, countermand, reprieve.

(2) *deposal,* deposition, dethronement; demotion, degradation; disendowment; discharge, dismissal 300 *ejection;* unfrocking 963 *punishment;*

ousting, deprivation 786 *expro-priation*; replacement, supersession 150 *substitution*; recall, transfer.

Adjective

(3) *abrogated,* cancelled etc. vb.; set aside, quashed, void, null and void; dormant 674 *unused*; recalled, revoked.

Verb

(4) *abrogate,* annul, cancel; scrub out, rub o. 550 *obliterate*; invalidate, abolish, dissolve, nullify, void, quash, set aside, reverse, overrule; repeal, revoke, recall; countermand, rescind, tear up; disclaim, disown, deny 533 *negate*; repudiate, retract 603 *recant*; call off, suspend, discontinue; not proceed with.

(5) *depose,* dethrone; unseat; divest 786 *deprive*; unfrock; disbar, strike off 57 *exclude*; disestablish, disendow; suspend, cashier 300 *dismiss*; oust 300 *eject*; demote, reduce to the ranks; recall, replace, remove 272 *transfer*.

753
Resignation

Noun

(1) *resignation,* retirement, withdrawal 296 *departure*; pension, compensation 962 *reward*; waiver, surrender, abdication, renunciation 621 *relinquishment*; abjuration, disclaimer 533 *negation*; acquiescence 721 *submission*; abdicator, quitter; pensioner.

Adjective

(2) *resigning,* abdicating, outgoing, former, retired, one-time.

Verb

(3) *resign,* tender one's resignation, hand over, vacate office; stand down, stand aside, make way for; sign off, declare (cricket); scratch, withdraw,

give up 721 *submit*; sign away 780 *assign*; abdicate, renounce 621 *relinquish*; retire, be pensioned off.

754
Consignee

Noun

(1) *consignee,* committee, steering c., panel, quango 692 *council*; counsellor, working party 691 *adviser*; bailee, nominee, licensee; trustee, executor 686 *agent*; steward 690 *manager*; caretaker, curator 749 *keeper*; attorney, counsel 958 *law agent*; proxy 755 *deputy*; negotiator 231 *intermediary*; underwriter, insurer; bursar 798 *treasurer*; functionary 690 *official.*

(2) *delegate,* shop steward; representative, nominee, member; commissary, commissioner; person on the spot 588 *correspondent*; emissary 529 *messenger*; delegation, mission.

(3) *envoy,* emissary, legate, nuncio, papal n.; resident, ambassador, ambassadress, charge d'affaires; diplomatic corps; diplomat, attache; embassy, legation, mission, consulate, High Commission.

755
Deputy

Noun

(1) *deputy,* surrogate, proxy; scapegoat, substitute, understudy, stand-in 150 *substitution*; pro-, vice-; second-in-command 741 *officer*; lieutenant, secretary 703 *aider*; successor designate, heir apparent 776 *beneficiary*; spokesperson, mouthpiece 529 *messenger*; second 707 *patron*; agent, attorney 754 *consignee.*

Adjective
(2) *deputizing,* representing, acting for, vice-, pro-; diplomatic, ambassadorial; standing-in for 150 *substituted*; negotiatory, intermediary 231 *interjacent.*

Verb
(3) *deputize,* act for 622 *function*; represent, appear for, speak for, answer for; hold in trust, be executor 689 *manage*; negotiate, be broker for, replace, stand in for 150 *substitute.*

Adverb
(4) *on behalf of,* for, pro; by proxy.

756
Permission

Noun
(1) *permission,* general p., liberty 744 *freedom*; leave, sanction, clearance; licence, authorization, warrant; allowance, sufferance, toleration, indulgence 736 *leniency*; acquiescence 758 *consent*; connivance 703 *aid*; blessing, approval 923 *approbation*; grace, grace and favour 897 *benevolence*; concession, dispensation, exemption; release 746 *liberation.*

(2) *permit,* authority 737 *warrant*; commission 751 *mandate*; grant, charter, patent, letters p.; pass, password, passport, passbook, visa, safe-conduct; ticket, licence; free hand 744 *scope*; leave, leave of absence, furlough, parole; clearance, all clear, green light, go-ahead.

Adjective
(3) *permitting,* permissive, indulgent, complaisant, tolerant 736 *lenient*; conniving 703 *aiding.*

(4) *permitted,* - allowed etc. vb.; legalized 953 *legal*; licensed, chartered; without strings 744

unconditional; permissible, allowable; passed.

Verb
(5) *permit,* let 469 *make possible*; give permission, grant leave 758 *consent*; give one's blessing, sanction, pass 923 *approve*; authorize, license, enable 160 *empower*; ratify, legalize 953 *make legal*; dispense 919 *exempt*; clear, give clearance, give the go-ahead 746 *liberate*; recognize, concede, allow 488 *assent*; foster, encourage 156 *conduce*; humour 823 *be patient*; suffer, tolerate, put up with 736 *be lenient*; connive, wink at 734 *be lax*; give a free hand 744 *give scope*; permit oneself, take the liberty 734 *please oneself.*

(6) *ask leave,* beg permission; apply for, seek, petition 761 *request*; get leave, have permission.

Adverb
(7) *by leave,* with permission, by favour of, under licence.

757
Prohibition

Noun
(1) *prohibition,* inhibition, injunction; countermand; veto, ban, embargo, restriction, curfew 747 *restraint*; proscription, taboo; rejection, thumbs down 760 *refusal*; licensing laws 942 *temperance*; censorship, repression, suppression, intolerance 735 *severity*; blackout, news b.; forbidden fruit.

Adjective
(2) *prohibiting,* prohibitory, forbidding, prohibitive, excessive 470 *impossible*; repressive 747 *restraining*; penal 963 *punitive*; hostile 881 *inimical*; exclusive 57 *excluding.*

(3) *prohibited,* forbidden, not allowed; barred, banned; censored, blacked-out; contraband, illicit, unlawful, outlawed, 954 *illegal*; taboo, untouchable, blacked; frowned on, not done; unmentionable, unprintable; out of bounds 57 *excluded*.

Verb

(4) *prohibit,* forbid; disallow, veto, refuse permission 760 *refuse*; cancel, countermand, revoke, suspend 752 *abrogate*; inhibit, prevent 702 *hinder*; restrict, stop 747 *restrain*; ban, interdict, taboo, proscribe, outlaw; black, declare b.; impose a ban, bar, debar 57 *exclude*; excommunicate 300 *eject*; repress, stifle 165 *suppress*; censor, blue-pencil, black out 550 *obliterate*; not tolerate 735 *be severe*; frown on, not countenance, not brook 924 *disapprove*; discourage 613 *dissuade*; draw the line at; block, intervene.

758
Consent

Noun

(1) *consent,* free c., full c., willing c. 597 *willingness*; agreement 488 *assent*; compliance 768 *observance*; concession, grant, accord; acquiescence, acceptance 756 *permission*; sanction, endorsement, ratification, confirmation; partial consent 770 *compromise*.

Adjective

(2) *consenting,* agreeable, compliant, ready 597 *willing*; conniving 703 *aiding*; yielding 721 *submitting*.

Verb

(3) *consent,* say yes, give consent, give one's approval; ratify, confirm 488 *endorse*; sanction, pass 756 *permit*; tolerate, recognize, allow, connive 736 *be lenient*; agree, fall in with,

accede 488 *assent*; not say no, have no objection 488 *acquiesce*; be persuaded, come round 612 *be induced*; yield, give way 721 *submit*; comply, grant a request, do as asked; grant, accord, concede, vouchsafe 781 *give*; deign, condescend 884 *be courteous*; accept, jump at 597 *be willing*; clinch a deal, settle 766 *make terms*.

759
Offer

Noun

(1) *offer,* fair o., improper o., bribe 612 *inducement*; tender, bid, takeover b.; motion, proposition, proposal; approach, overture, advance, invitation; feeler; present, presentation, offering 781 *gift*; dedication, consecration; candidature, application; solicitation 761 *request*.

Adjective

(2) *offering,* inviting; offered, open, available; on offer, on the market on hire, to let, for sale; open to bid, up for auction.

Verb

(3) *offer,* proffer, hold out, make an offer, bid, tender; make a present of, present 781 *give*; dedicate, consecrate sacrifice to; move, propose, put forward, suggest 512 *propound*; approach, make overtures, make advances, make a proposition; induce 612 *bribe*; invite tenders, offer for sale, auction 793 *sell*; cater for 633 *provide*; make available, place at one's disposal 469 *make possible*; pose, confront with.

(4) *offer oneself,* sacrifice o.; stand, be a candidate, compete, run for, enter 716 *contend*; volunteer, come forward 597 *be willing*; apply, put in for 761 *request*.

760
Refusal

Noun
(1) *refusal,* declining, turning down, thumbs down 607 *rejection*; denial, negative answer, no 533 *negation*; flat refusal, point-blank r.; repulse, rebuff 292 *repulsion*; withholding 778 *retention*; recalcitrance 738 *disobedience*; objection, protest 762 *deprecation*.

Adjective
(2) *refusing,* denying, withholding etc. vb.; jibbing, objecting, demurring 762 *deprecatory*; deaf to 598 *unwilling*.

(3) *refused,* not granted, turned down; rebuffed etc. vb.; disallowed, inadmissible, not permitted 757 *prohibited*; out of the question 470 *impossible*; withheld 778 *retained*.

Verb
(4) *refuse,* say no, shake one's head; excuse oneself, send one's apologies; deny, repudiate, disclaim 533 *negate*; decline, turn down, spurn 607 *reject*; deny firmly, repulse, rebuff 292 *repel*; turn away 300 *dismiss*; harden one's heart 602 *be obstinate*; not listen 416 *be deaf*; not give 598 *be unwilling*; hang fire, hang back, beg off, back down; turn from, jib at 620 *avoid*; debar, keep out 57 *exclude*; set one's face against, not hear of 924 *disapprove*; refuse permission, not allow 757 *prohibit*; not consent 715 *resist*; not comply with 769 *not observe*; withhold, keep from 778 *retain*; go without.

Adverb
(5) *denyingly,* no, never, on no account.

761
Request

Noun
(1) *request,* modest r., asking; negative request 762 *deprecation*; forcible demand, requisition 627 *requirement*; last demand, ultimatum 737 *demand*; blackmail 900 *threat*; claim, counterclaim; overture, approach 759 *offer*; bid, application, suit; petition, prayer, appeal, plea (see *entreaty*); pressure, insistence 740 *compulsion*; clamour, cry, dunning, importunity; soliciting, accosting, solicitation, invitation, temptation; mendicancy, begging; begging letter, flag day; 'wanted' column 528 *advertisement*; wish, want 859 *desire*.

(2) *entreaty,* imploring, beseeching; submission, humble s., clasped hands, bended knees; supplication, prayer 981 *prayers*; appeal, invocation; solemn entreaty, adjuration; incantation, imprecation.

Adjective
(3) *requesting,* asking, inviting etc. vb.; invitatory 759 *offering*; claiming 627 *demanding*; insisting, insistent; clamorous, importunate, pressing, urgent, instant.

(4) *supplicatory,* entreating, beseeching, suppliant, praying, prayerful; on bended knees, cap in hand.

Verb
(5) *request,* ask, invite, solicit; make overtures, approach, accost 759 *offer*; sue for, woo 889 *court*; seek, look for 459 *search*; need, call for, clamour f. 627 *require*; crave, make a request, beg a favour, ask a boon, trouble one for 859 *desire*; apply, make application, put in for, bid for; apply to, call on, appeal

to, run to; petition, memorialize; press a claim, expect 915 *claim*; make demands 737 *demand*; blackmail 900 *threaten*; be instant, insist, urge; persuade 612 *induce*; coax, wheedle, cajole; importune, ply, press, dun, besiege, beset; requisition 786 *take*; tax 786 *levy*; state one's terms.

(6) *beg,* cadge, crave, sponge, scrounge; thumb a lift, hitchhike; pass the hat, make a collection 786 *levy*; beg in vain, whistle for 627 *require*.

(7) *entreat,* supplicate, pray, implore, beseech, appeal, conjure, adjure, invoke, apostrophize, appeal to, call on 583 *speak to*; pray to 981 *offer worship*; kneel to, fall at one's feet.

762
Deprecation:
Negative request

Noun
(1) *deprecation,* negative request, contrary advice 613 *dissuasion*; intercession, mediation 981 *prayers*; counterclaim, counterpetition 761 *request*; murmur, complaint 829 *discontent*; expostulation, remonstrance, protest 704 *opposition*; reaction, backlash 182 *counteraction*; groans, jeers 924 *disapprobation*; open letter, round robin; demonstration, march.

Adjective
(2) *deprecatory* 613 dissuasive; protesting, vocal; intercessory, averting.

Verb
(3) *deprecate,* advise against 613 *dissuade*; beg off, plead for, intercede 720 *mediate*; pray, appeal 761 *entreat*; cry for mercy 905 *ask mercy*; tut-tut, shake one's head, 924 *disapprove*; remonstrate, expostulate 924 *reprove*; murmur, complain 829

be discontented; object, take exception to; demur, jib, kick, protest against, appeal a., petition a., lobby a., campaign a., cry out a. 704 *oppose*; demonstrate, strike, come out.

763
Petitioner

Noun
(1) *petitioner,* humble p., suppliant, supplicant; appealer, appellant; claimant, pretender; postulant, aspirant; asker, seeker; suitor, wooer; canvasser, tout; pressure group, lobby, lobbyist; applicant, candidate, entrant; complainer, grouser 829 *malcontent*.

(2) *beggar,* mendicant, mendicant friar; tramp 268 *wanderer*; cadger, borrower, scrounger; parasite 879 *toady*.

764
Promise

Noun
(1) *promise,* undertaking, commitment 759 *offer*; betrothal, engagement; word, one's solemn w., word of honour, vow 532 *oath*; declaration, solemn d. 532 *affirmation*; professions, fair words; assurance, pledge, credit, honour, warranty, guarantee, insurance 767 *security*; mutual agreement 765 *compact*; covenant, bond 803 *debt*; promise-maker, votary; party 765 *signatory*.

Adjective
(2) *promissory,* promising, votive; on oath, under o., on credit, on parole.

(3) *promised,* covenanted, guaranteed, secured 767 *pledged*; engaged, reserved; betrothed; committed, bound, obligated 917 *obliged*.

Verb

(4) *promise,* say one will 532 *affirm*; hold out, proffer 759 *offer*; make a promise, give one's word, pledge one's w.; vow 532 *swear*; vouch for, go bail for, guarantee, assure, confirm, secure 767 *give security*; pledge, stake; stake one's credit; engage to, undertake to; commit oneself, bind oneself 765 *contract*; take on oneself 917 *incur a duty*; exchange vows 894 *wed*.

(5) *take a pledge,* demand security 473 *make certain*; put on oath, make one swear 466 *testify*; make one promise, exact a p.; take on credit, take one's word 485 *believe*.

Adverb

(6) *as promised,* duly; truly 540 *truthfully*; on one's word, on one's honour.

765
Compact

Noun

(1) *compact,* contract, bargain, agreement; debt of honour 764 *promise*; mutual pledge, exchange of vows; engagement, betrothal 894 *marriage*; covenant, bond 767 *security*; league, alliance, cartel 706 *cooperation*; pact, convention, understanding, agreement; secret pact, conspiracy 623 *plot*; deal, give and take 770 *compromise*; arrangement, settlement; ratification, confirmation 488 *assent*; seal, signature; deed of agreement 767 *title deed*.

(2) *treaty,* peace treaty 719 *pacification*; convention, concordat.

(3) *signatory,* signer, countersigner, subscriber, the undersigned; swearer 466 *witness*; adherent, consenting party 488 *assenter*; contractor, covenanter; negotiator 720 *mediator*.

Adjective

(4) *contractual,* bilateral, multilateral; agreed to, negotiated, ratified etc. vb.; signed, countersigned, sworn, covenanted.

Verb

(5) *contract,* engage, undertake 764 *promise*; covenant, make a compact, strike a bargain, shake hands on, do a deal; league, ally 706 *cooperate*; treat, negotiate 791 *bargain*; give and take 770 *compromise*; stipulate 766 *give terms*; come to an agreement 766 *make terms*; conclude, settle; sign, ratify 488 *endorse*; insure, underwrite 767 *give security*.

766
Conditions

Noun

(1) *conditions,* making terms, treaty-making, diplomacy, negotiation, bargaining, collective b.; hard bargaining, horse-trading 791 *barter*; formula, terms; final terms, ultimatum, time limit 900 *threat*; condition, provision, clause, proviso, limitation, strings, reservation, exception, small print 468 *qualification*; stipulation, sine qua non 627 *requirement*; terms of reference 751 *mandate*.

Adjective

(2) *conditional,* provisory 468 *qualifying*; limiting, subject to terms, conditioned, contingent, provisional; with strings attached; binding 917 *obligatory*.

Verb

(3) *give terms,* propose conditions; bind, tie down; hold out for, insist on 737 *demand*; stipulate 627 *require*; insert a proviso, leave a loophole 468 *qualify*.

(4) *make terms,* negotiate, treat, parley 584 *confer;* deal with, treat w., negotiate w.; make overtures 461 *be tentative;* haggle 791 *bargain;* proffer, make proposals 759 *offer;* give and take, yield a point, stretch a p. 770 *compromise;* do a deal 765 *contract.*

Adverb
(5) *on terms,* conditionally, provisionally, subject to.

767
Security

Noun
(1) *security,* precaution 858 *caution;* guarantee 737 *warrant;* word of honour 764 *promise;* sponsorship, patronage 660 *protection;* surety, bail, caution, parole; gage, pledge, pawn, hostage; stake, deposit, earnest, token, instalment, down payment; indemnity, insurance, underwriting 660 *safety;* mortgage, collateral; sponsor, underwriter 707 *patron.*

(2) *title deed,* deed, instrument; bilateral deed, indenture; charter, covenant, bond 765 *compact;* receipt, voucher, IOU; certificate, marriage lines; seal, stamp, signature, endorsement 466 *credential;* blue chip, portfolio, share, debenture; policy, insurance p.; will, testament 548 *record.*

Adjective
(3) *pledged,* pawned, deposited; in hock, in pawn, on deposit; on bail, on recognizance.

(4) *secured,* covered, insured, mortgaged; gilt-edged, guaranteed 764 *promised.*

Verb
(5) *give bail,* go b., bail one out, go surety for; release on bail; hold in pledge 764 *take a pledge.*

(6) *give security,* offer collateral, mortgage; pledge, pawn 785 *borrow;* guarantee, warrant 473 *make certain;* authenticate, verify 466 *corroborate;* execute, seal, stamp, sign 488 *endorse;* grant a receipt, write an IOU; vouch for 764 *promise;* secure, indemnify, insure, assure, underwrite 660 *safeguard.*

768
Observance

Noun
(1) *observance,* full o., fulfilment, satisfaction 610 *practice;* diligence, adherence to, attention to; performance, discharge, acquittal 676 *action;* compliance 739 *obedience;* good faith 739 *loyalty;* dependability, reliability 929 *probity.*

Adjective
(2) *observant,* practising 676 *doing;* heedful, watchful, careful of 455 *attentive;* conscientious, diligent, earnest, religious, punctilious; literal, pedantic, exact 862 *fastidious* responsible, reliable, dependable 929 *trustworthy;* faithful, loyal, true, compliant 739 *obedient;* adhering to 83 *conformable.*

Verb
(3) *observe,* heed, respect, have regard to, acknowledge, attend to 455 *be attentive;* keep, practise, adhere to, follow, hold by, abide by, be loyal to 83 *conform;* comply 739 *obey;* fulfil, discharge, perform, execute, carry out 676 *do;* satisfy 635 *suffice.*

(4) *keep faith,* meet one's oligations 917 *do one's duty;* keep one's promise 929 *be honourable;* pay one's debt 915 *grant claims.*

Adverb
(5) *with observance,* faithfully, religiously, meticulously, to the full.

769
Nonobservance

Noun

(1) *nonobservance,* indifference 734 *laxity*; inattention, omission 458 *negligence*; abhorrence 607 *rejection*; anarchism 734 *anarchy*; shortcoming 726 *noncompletion*; infringement, violation 306 *overstepping*; disloyalty 738 *disobedience*; protest 762 *deprecation*; disregard, discourtesy 921 *disrespect*; bad faith, breach of promise 930 *perfidy*; repudiation, denial 533 *negation*; failure, bankruptcy 805 *insolvency*; forfeiture 963 *penalty*.

Adjective

(2) *nonobservant,* lapsed; blacklegging, nonconformist 84 *unconformable*; inattentive to, disregarding, neglectful 458 *negligent*; unprofessional, maverick, cowboy; indifferent 734 *lax*; anarchic infringing, unlawful 954 *lawbreaking*; disloyal 918 *undutiful*; unfaithful 930 *perfidious*.

Verb

(3) *not observe,* not practise, abhor 607 *reject*; not conform, not adhere, not follow 84 *be unconformable*; discard, set aside, omit, ignore, skip 458 *neglect*; disregard, show no respect for; stretch a point 734 *be lax*; violate, do violence to 306 *overstep*; not comply with 738 *disobey*; desert 918 *fail in duty*; break faith, break one's word *or* one's promise 930 *be dishonest*; renege on, go back on 603 *tergiversate*; shirk, dodge, evade 620 *avoid*; fob off, equivocate 518 *be equivocal*; forfeit 963 *be punished*.

770
Compromise

Noun

(1) *compromise,* concession; give and take, adjustment, formula 765 *compact*; second best; modus vivendi, working arrangement 624 *way*; halfway 625 *middle way*; balancing act.

Verb

(2) *compromise,* find a formula, give and take, meet one halfway 625 *be halfway*; not insist, stretch a point 734 *be lax*; go half and half, split the difference 30 *average out*; compose differences, arbitrate, go to arbitration; patch up, bridge over 719 *pacify*; make the best of.

771
Acquisition

Noun

(1) *acquisition,* getting, winning; breadwinning, earning; acquirement, procurement; collection 74 *assemblage*; fundraising; milking, exploitation, profiteering 816 *avarice*; pool, scoop, jackpot 74 *accumulation*; finding, picking up 484 *discovery*; finding again, recovery, retrieval; buying 792 *purchase*; appropriation 786 *taking*; theft 788 *stealing*; inheritance, patrimony; thing acquired, find, windfall, treasure trove 615 *benefit*; legacy, bequest 781 *gift*; gratuity 962 *reward*; prize 729 *trophy*; plunder 790 *booty*.

(2) *earnings,* income, earned i., wage, salary, pay packet 804 *pay*; pay scale, differential; pension, compensation, remuneration 962 *reward*; allowance, expense account; perquisite, perks, fringe benefits; commission, rake-off 810 *discount*; proceeds, turnover, takings, revenue, 807 *receipt*;

harvest, crop; output, produce 164 *product*.

(3) *gain,* thrift, savings 814 *economy*; credit side, profit, capital gain, winnings; dividend, share-out 775 *participation*; usury, interest, increment; pay increase, rise, raise 36 *increase*; advantage, benefit.

Adjective
(4) *acquiring,* acquisitive, accumulative; on the make 730 *prosperous*; hoarding, saving; greedy 816 *avaricious*.

(5) *gainful,* paying, money-making, remunerative, lucrative 962 *rewarding*; advantageous 640 *profitable*; fruitful, fertile 164 *productive*; stipendiary, paid.

(6) *acquired,* had, got; ill-gotten; inherited, patrimonial.

Verb
(7) *acquire,* get, come by; get by effort, earn, gain, obtain, procure; find, come across, come by, pick up, light upon 484 *discover*; get hold of, get possession of, make one's own, annex 786 *appropriate*; win, capture, catch, land, net, bag 786 *take*; pick, glean, gather, reap, crop, harvest; derive, draw, tap, milk, mine 304 *extract*; collect, accumulate 74 *bring together*; scrape together, rake t.; collect funds, raise, levy; save, save up, hoard 632 *store*; buy 792 *purchase*; get in advance, reserve, book, engage; get somehow, beg, borrow *or* steal; earn a living 622 *busy oneself*; draw a salary, have an income, gross, take 782 *receive*; turn into money, convert, cash, realize, clear, make; get back, recover, salvage, redeem, recapture 656 *retrieve*; take back, reclaim 31 *recoup*; break even, balance accounts.

(8) *inherit,* come into, be left, receive a legacy; succeed to

(9) *gain,* profit, make a p., earn a dividend; make, win; make money 730 *prosper*; make a fortune 800 *get rich*; scoop, win the jackpot, break the bank.

(10) *be profitable,* profit, repay, be worthwhile 640 *be useful*; pay, pay well; bring in, yield 164 *produce*; pay a dividend, show a profit 730 *prosper*.

772
Loss

Noun
(1) *loss,* deprivation, dispossession, eviction 786 *expropriation*; sacrifice, forfeiture 963 *penalty*; diminishing returns, depreciation 655 *deterioration*; setback, check, reverse; overdraft, failure, bankruptcy 805 *insolvency*; consumption 806 *expenditure*; wastage, leakage 634 *waste*; evaporation, drain 37 *decrease*.

Adjective
(2) *losing,* unprofitable 641 *profitless*; squandering 815 *prodigal*; forfeiting, sacrificing; deprived, dispossessed, robbed; denuded, stripped of, shorn of, bereft; minus, without, lacking; rid of, quit of; set back, out of pocket, down, in the red, overdrawn, broke, bankrupt, insolvent.

(3) *lost,* gone, vanished 446 *disappearing*; missing, untraceable, mislaid 188 *misplaced*; wanting, lacking, short 307 *deficient*; irrecoverable, irretrievable, irredeemable 634 *wasted*; spent, squandered 806 *expended*; forfeit, forfeited, sacrificed.

Verb
(4) *lose,* not find, mislay 188 *misplace*; miss, let slip 138 *lose a chance*; squander, throw away

634 *waste*; deserve to lose, forfeit, sacrifice; spill, allow to leak; be out of pocket, burn one's fingers, lose one's stake, lose one's bet, pay out; make no profit, sell at a loss, be down; go bankrupt 805 *not pay*; overdraw, be overdrawn.

(5) *be lost*, be missing 190 *be absent*; go down the drain; melt away 446 *disappear*.

773
Possession

Noun
(1) *possession*, ownership, occupancy, hold, grasp, grip 778 *retention*; a possession 777 *property*; tenure, tenancy, holding 777 *estate*; monopoly, corner, ring; preemption, squatting; inheritance, heritage, patrimony; appropriation 786 *taking*.

Adjective
(2) *possessing*, having, holding, owning, proprietorial, propertied, landed; possessed of, in possession; endowed with, blessed with; exclusive, monopolistic, possessive.

(3) *possessed*, enjoyed, held etc. vb.; in the possession of, in one's hand, in one's grasp; to one's name, to one's credit; at one's disposal, on hand, in store; proper, personal 80 *special*; belonging, one's own, private.

Verb
(4) *possess*, be possessed of, own, have; hold, have and hold 778 *retain*; command, have at one's c., boast of, call one's own; contain, include 78 *comprise*; fill, occupy; squat, sit in, sit on; enjoy, dispose of 673 *use*; monopolize, hog, corner the market; get, take possession of, make one's own 786 *take*; recover 656 *retrieve*; reserve, book engage; come into, succeed 771 *inherit*.

(5) *belong*, be vested in, belong to; go with, 78 *be included*; be subject to, owe service to 745 *be subject*.

774
Nonownership

Noun
(1) *nonownership*, vacancy; tenancy, temporary lease; dependence 745 *subjection*; pauperism 801 *poverty*; deprivation 772 *loss*; no-man's-land.

Adjective
(2) *not owning*, dependent 745 *subject*; dispossessed, destitute, penniless 801 *poor*; lacking, minus, without 627 *required*.

(3) *unpossessed*, not belonging; ownerless, unclaimed, anybody's, nobody's; international, common; not owned, disowned; vacant 190 *empty*; derelict, abandoned 779 *not retained*; going begging 860 *unwanted*.

775
Joint possession

Noun
(1) *joint possession*, joint tenancy, joint ownership, common o.; common land, common, public property; pool, kitty 632 *store*; cooperative 706 *cooperation*; nationalization, public ownership; socialism, communism, collectivism; collective farm, collective, commune, kibbutz.

(2) *participation*, membership 78 *inclusion*; sharing, co-sharing, partnership 706 *association*; Dutch treat; profit-sharing, dividend, share-out; share, fair s. 783 *portion*; complicity, involvement, sympathy; fellow feeling, joint action.

(3) *participator,* member, partner, co-p., sharer 707 *colleague*; shareholder, 776 *possessor*; co-tenant, flat-mate, roomm.; housing association; trade unionist; collectivist, socialist, communist; sympathizer, contributor 707 *patron.*

Adjective
(4) *sharing,* joint, cooperative; common, communal, international, global; collective, communistic; partaking, participating, participatory, involved, sympathetic.

Verb
(5) *participate,* join in, have a hand in 706 *cooperate*; partake of, share in, share, go shares, go halves, go fifty-fifty 783 *apportion*; share expenses, go Dutch 804 *defray.*

(6) *communalize,* socialize, mutualize, nationalize, pool, hold in common.

Adverb
(7) *in common,* jointly, collectively, communally.

776
Possessor

Noun
(1) *possessor,* one in possession; holder, taker, captor, conqueror; trespasser, squatter; monopolizer, occupant, lodger, occupier, incumbent; mortgagee, trustee; lessee, leaseholder, copyholder; tenantry, tenant; house-owner, householder, freeholder.

(2) *owner,* master, mistress, proprietor, proprietress; purchaser, buyer 792 *purchaser*; lord, lady, landed gentry, squire, laird 868 *aristocracy*; man or woman of property, shareholder, landowner; landlord, landlady.

(3) *beneficiary* 782 *recipient*; inheritor, successor, next of kin 11 *kinsman*; heir or heiress, heir apparent.

777
Property

Noun
(1) *property,* possession, possessions, personal property; stake, venture; personal estate, goods and chattels, appurtenances, belongings, paraphernalia, effects, personal e., baggage, things; cargo, lading 193 *contents*; goods, wares, stock 795 *merchandise*; plant, fixtures, furniture.

(2) *estate,* assets, frozen a., liquid a.; circumstances, resources, means; substance, capital 800 *wealth*; revenue, income 807 *receipt*; valuables, securities, stocks and shares, portfolio; stake, holding, investment; copyright, patent; right, title, interest; living 985 *benefice.*

(3) *lands,* land, acreage, grounds; estate, property, landed p.; holding, tenure, freehold, copyhold, manor, domain, demesne; plot 184 *territory*; farm, ranch; crown lands, common land 775 *joint possession.*

(4) *dower,* dowry, marriage settlement; allotment, allowance, alimony; patrimony, birthright; inheritance, legacy, bequest; heirloom; expectations.

Adjective
(5) *proprietary,* branded, patented; propertied, landed, feudal, freehold, leasehold, copyhold; patrimonial, hereditary; endowed, established.

Verb
(6) *dower,* endow, possess with 781 *give*; devise 780 *bequeath*; grant, allot 780 *assign*; put in possession of 751 *commission*; establish, found.

778
Retention

Noun
(1) *retention*, prehensility, tenacity; stickiness 354 *viscidity*; tenaciousness, retentiveness, holding on, hanging on, clinging to, handhold, foothold, toehold 218 *support*; bridgehead, beachhead 34 *advantage*; clutches, grip, iron g., vice-like g., grasp, hold, firm h., stranglehold, half-nelson; squeeze 198 *compression*; clinch, lock; hug, bear h., embrace, clasp 889 *endearment*; keeping in 747 *detention*; pincer movement 235 *enclosure*; plug, stop 264 *stopper*; ligament 47 *bond*.

(2) *nippers*, pincers, tweezers, pliers, wrench, tongs, forceps, vice, clamp 47 *fastening*; talon, claw, nails 256 *sharp point*; tentacle, hook, tendril 378 *feeler*; teeth, fangs 256 *tooth*; paw, hand 378 *finger*.

Adjective
(3) *retentive*, tenacious, prehensile; vice-like, retaining 747 *restraining*; clinging, adhesive, sticky 48 *cohesive*; firm 45 *tied*; tight, strangling, throttling; tight-fisted 816 *parsimonious*; shut fast 264 *closed*.

(4) *retained*, in the grip of, gripped, pinioned, pinned, clutched etc. vb.; fast, stuck f., bound, held; kept in, detained 747 *imprisoned*; penned, held in, contained 232 *circumscribed*; saved, kept 666 *preserved*; booked, reserved, engaged; nontransferable, not for sale; kept back, withheld 760 *refused*.

Verb
(5) *retain*, hold; grab, buttonhole, hold back 702 *obstruct*; hold up, catch, steady 218 *support*; hold on, hold fast, hold tight, not let go; cling to, hang

on to, stick to 48 *agglutinate*; fasten on, grip, grasp, grapple, clinch, lock; hug, clasp, clutch, embrace; pin down, hold d.; throttle, strangle, tighten one's grip 747 *restrain*; keep in, detain 747 *imprison*; contain 235 *enclose*; keep to oneself, keep back, withhold 525 *keep secret*; keep in hand, not dispose of 632 *store*; save, keep 666 *preserve*; not part with, keep back, withhold 760 *refuse*.

779
Nonretention

Noun
(1) *nonretention*, parting with, disposal 780 *transfer*; selling off 793 *sale*; letting go, release 746 *liberation*; dispensation, exemption; abandonment, renunciation 621 *relinquishment*; cancellation 752 *abrogation*; disuse 611 *desuetude*; availability, salability, disposability.

(2) *derelict*, deserted village; jetsam, flotsam 641 *rubbish*; cast-off, slough; waif, stray, foundling, orphan; outcast, pariah.

Adjective
(3) *not retained*, not kept, disposed of, sold off; dispensed with, abandoned 621 *relinquished*; released 746 *liberated*; fired, made redundant; disowned, divorced, disinherited; heritable, transferable; available, for sale 793 *salable*.

Verb
(4) *not retain*, let go, part with; transfer 780 *assign*; sell off, dispose of 793 *sell*; be open-handed 815 *be prodigal*; release, free, leave hold of, relax one's grip; unlock 263 *open*; untie 46 *disunite*; forego, dispense with, do without, spare, give up, waive, abandon, cede, yield 621 *relinquish*; cancel, revoke 752

abrogate; derestrict 746 *liberate*; replace 150 *substitute*; disown, disclaim 533 *negate*; disinherit 801 *impoverish*; get rid of, cast off, ditch, jettison, throw overboard 300 *eject*; cast away, abandon, maroon; pension off, invalid out, retire; discharge, ease out 300 *dismiss*; lay off, stand o.; drop, discard 674 *stop using*.

780
Transfer (of property)

Noun
(1) *transfer,* consignment, delivery 272 *transference*; conveyancing, conveyance; bequeathal, assignment, bequest 781 *gift*; lease, let, rental, hire; buying 793 *sale*; trade 791 *barter*; conversion, exchange 151 *interchange*; change of hands, changeover; devolution, delegation 751 *commission*; succession, reversion, inheritance; pledge, pawn, hostage.

Adjective
(2) *transferred,* made over; hired etc. vb.; heritable, transferable, exchangeable, negotiable.

Verb
(3) *assign,* convey, transfer by deed; grant, sign away, give a. 781 *give*; let, rent, hire 784 *lease*; barter 791 *trade*; exchange, convert 151 *interchange*; confer ownership on, put in possession of; invest with, devolve, delegate, entrust 751 *commission*; deliver, transmit, hand over, make o., pass to 272 *transfer*; pledge, pawn 784 *lend*; dispossess, expropriate, relieve of 786 *deprive*; nationalize 775 *communalize*.

(4) *bequeath,* will, grant, assign; leave, make a bequest, leave a legacy; leave a fortune 800 *be rich*;

(5) *change hands,* pass to another, change places, be transferred, shift; circulate, go the rounds; succeed to, inherit 771 *acquire*.

781
Giving

Noun
(1) *giving,* bestowal, donation; alms-giving, charity 901 *philanthropy*; generosity 813 *liberality*; contribution 703 *subvention*; award 962 *reward*; conveyance 780 *transfer*; endowment, settlement 777 *dower*; prize-giving, presentation.

(2) *gift,* keepsake, present; whip-round, tip, gratuity 962 *reward*; token, consideration; bribe 612 *inducement*; prize, award, presentation 729 *trophy*; benefit, benefit match; alms, charity 901 *philanthropy*; bounty, largesse, donation, hand-out; bonus, bonanza; extras, perks, perquisites; grant, allowance, subsidy 703 *subvention*; boon, grace, favour, service 597 *voluntary work*; bequest, legacy 780 *transfer*.

(3) *offering,* votive o. 979 *piety*; peace offering, thank o.; offertory, collection; sacrifice 981 *oblation*; contribution, subscription.

(4) *giver,* donor, rewarder, presenter, awarder, prize-giver; subscriber, contributor; tribute-payer 742 *subject*; blood donor 903 *benefactor*; Lady Bountiful, Santa Claus 813 *good giver*.

Adjective
(5) *giving,* subscribing, contributory 703 *aiding*; alms-giving, charitable 897 *benevolent*; sacrificing 981 *worshipping*; generous, bountiful 813 *liberal*.

(6) *given,* bestowed, gifted; given away, gratuitous, gratis, for nothing, free 812 *incharged*; allowable 756 *permitted.*

Verb

(7) *give,* bestow, lend, render; afford, provide; favour with, honour w.; grant, accord 756 *permit*; gift, donate, make a present of; give by will, leave 780 *bequeath*; dower, endow, enrich; present, award 962 *reward*; confer, bestow upon, invest with; dedicate, consecrate, vow to 759 *offer*; devote, offer up, immolate, sacrifice; spare for, have time for; tip, grease one's palm 612 *bribe*; bestow alms, give freely 813 *be liberal*; spare, give away, not charge; stand, treat, entertain 882 *be hospitable*; give out, dispense, dole out, deal out 783 *apportion*; contribute, subscribe, pay towards, subsidize 703 *aid*; give up, cede, yield 621 *relinquish*; hand over, make o., deliver 780 *assign*; commit, consign, entrust 751 *commission.*

782
Receiving

Noun

(1) *receiving,* acceptance, admittance 299 *reception*; getting 771 *acquisition*; inheritance, succession; collection, receipt; windfall 781 *gift*; toll, tribute, dues, receipts, proceeds, winnings, takings 771 *earnings.*

(2) *recipient,* receiver, taker; collector, debt c.; trustee 754 *consignee*; addressee 588 *correspondent*; buyer 792 *purchaser*; assignee, licensee, lessee; legatee, inheritor, heir 776 *beneficiary*; payee, wage-earner, pensioner, winner, prize-w.; object of charity.

Adjective

(3) *receiving,* recipient; receptive, welcoming; stipendiary, paid, pensioned; awarded, given, favoured.

Verb

(4) *receive,* be given, have from; get 771 *acquire*; collect, take up 786 *take*; gross, net, pocket; accept, take in 299 *admit*; accept from, take f., draw, be paid; inherit, succeed to, come into; receipt, acknowledge.

(5) *be received,* be credited with 38 *accrue*; come to hand, come in, roll in; stick to one's fingers.

783
Apportionment

Noun

(1) *apportionment,* assignment, allotment, allocation, appropriation; division, partition, sharing out; shares, fair s., distribution, deal; dispensing, dispensation.

(2) *portion,* share, share-out, cut, split; dividend; allocation, allotment, lot; proportion, ratio; quota 53 *part*; deal, hand (at cards); allowance, ration; dose, measure, helping, 53 *piece*; commission 810 *discount.*

Verb

(3) *apportion,* allot, allocate; appoint, assign; partition, zone; demarcate 236 *limit*; divide, carve up, split, cut; halve 92 *bisect*; go shares 775 *participate*; share, share out, distribute, spread around; dispense, administer, serve, deal, deal out, portion out, dole out, parcel out 781 *give*; mete out, measure, ration.

Adverb

(4) *pro rata,* respectively, proportionately, per head.

784
Lending

Noun
(1) *lending*, hiring, leasing, farming out; letting, subletting; usury 802 *credit*; investment; mortgage, bridging loan; advance, loan, pawnbroking; lease, let, sublet.

(2) *pawnshop*, pawnbroker's; bank, credit company, building society.

(3) *lender*, creditor; investor, financier, banker; moneylender, usurer, loan shark; pawnbroker, uncle.

Adjective
(4) *lending*, investing, laying out; usurious, extortionate; lent, loaned, on credit.

Verb
(5) *lend*, loan, advance, accommodate, allow credit 802 *credit*; lend on security; back, finance; invest, sink; risk one's money 791 *speculate*.

(6) *lease*, let, let out, hire out, farm out; sublet.

Adverb
(7) *on loan*, on credit, on advance; on security.

785
Borrowing

Noun
(1) *borrowing*, loan 784 *lending*; mortgage 803 *debt*; credit account, credit card; hire purchase, instalment plan joyride 788 *stealing*; plagiarism, copying 20 *imitation*.

Verb
(2) *borrow*, borrow from, touch for 761 *request*; mortgage, pawn 767 *give security*; take a loan, get credit; buy in instalments 792 *purchase*; run into debt 803 *be in debt*; ask for credit, raise a loan, float a loan; beg, borrow, or steal 771 *acquire*; plagiarize 20 *copy*.

(3) *hire*, rent, lease, charter.

786
Taking

Noun
(1) *taking*, snatching; seizure, capture; taking hold, grasp, apprehension 778 *retention*; appropriation 916 *arrogation*; requisition, commandeering 771 *acquisition*; exaction, taxation, levy 809 *tax*; taking back, recovery, retrieval; taking away, removal 188 *displacement*, 788 *stealing*; cadging, scrounging; bodily removal, abduction, press gang, kidnapping, piracy; raid 788 *spoliation*; thing taken, take, haul, catch, capture, prize 790 *booty*; takings 771 *earnings*.

(2) *expropriation*, dispossession, forcible seizure, distraint, foreclosure; eviction, expulsion 300 *ejection*; takeover, hiving off, asset-stripping 780 *transfer*; exaction, extortion; swindle, rip-off; impounding, confiscation, sequestration.

(3) *rapacity*, rapaciousness, avidity, thirst 859 *hunger*; greed, insatiability 816 *avarice*; bloodsucking; extortion, blackmail.

(4) *taker*, appropriator, remover; snatcher, grabber; raider, marauder, looter 789 *robber*; kidnapper, abductor, press gang; captor 741 *master*; usurper, extortioner, blackmailer; devourer 168 *destroyer*; bloodsucker, leech, parasite; vampire, harpy, vulture, shark; beast of prey, predator; confiscator 782 *receiver*; expropriator, asset-stripper.

Adjective
(5) *taking*, grasping, extortionate, rapacious, devouring, all-

engulfing, voracious, ravening 859 *hungry*; predatory 788 *thieving*; commandeering, acquisitive 771 *acquiring*.

Verb

(6) *take,* accept, be given 782 *receive*; take over, take in 299 *admit*; take up, snatch up; take hold, fasten on 778 *retain*; lay hands upon, seize, snatch, grab, pounce, spring; snatch at, reach out for, grasp at, clutch at, grab at, make a grab, scramble for, rush f.; capture, take by storm 727 *overmaster*; conquer 745 *subjugate*; apprehend, take into custody 747 *arrest*; hook, trap, snare 542 *ensnare*; net, land, bag, pocket; gross, have a turnover 771 *acquire*; gather, accumulate, collect 74 *bring together*; cull, pick, pluck; reap, harvest, glean; pick up, snap up; help oneself 788 *steal*; remove, deduct 39 *subtract*; draw off, milk, tap, mine 304 *extract*.

(7) *appropriate,* take for oneself, make one's own, annex; pirate, plagiarize 20 *copy*; take possession of, stake one's claim; take over, assume ownership 773 *possess*; enter into, come i., succeed 771 *inherit*; install oneself 187 *place oneself*; people, populate, occupy, settle, colonize; win, conquer; take back, recover, resume, repossess, reclaim, recapture 656 *retrieve*; commandeer, requisition 737 *demand*; nationalize, secularize 775 *communalize*; denationalize, privatize; usurp, arrogate, trespass, squat 916 *be undue*; make free with; engulf, devour, swallow 299 *absorb*.

(8) *levy,* raise, extort, exact, wrest from, wring f. 304 *extract*; exact tribute, collect a toll 809 *tax*; overtax, exhaust, drain 300 *empty*; wring, squeeze 735 *oppress*; sequestrate.

(9) *take away,* remove 188 *displace*; send away 272 *send*; lighten, hive off, abstract, relieve of 788 *steal*; remove bodily, kidnap, abduct, carry off, bear away; hurry off with, run away w., elope w., 296 *decamp*; raid, loot, plunder 788 *rob*.

(10) *deprive,* bereave, orphan, widow; divest, denude, strip 229 *uncover*; unfrock 752 *depose*; dispossess, usurp 916 *disentitle*; oust, evict 300 *eject*; expropriate, confiscate, sequestrate, distrain, foreclose; disinherit, cut off.

(11) *fleece,* swindle, cheat 542 *deceive*; blackmail, bleed, suck dry; soak, sting 788 *defraud*; devour 301 *eat*; take one's all 801 *impoverish*.

787
Restitution

Noun

(1) *restitution,* giving back, return, reversion; bringing back, reinstatement, restoration; redemption, ransom, rescue 668 *deliverance*; recuperation, recovery; compensation, repayment, refund, reimbursement; indemnity, damages 963 *penalty*; amends, reparation 941 *atonement*.

Adjective

(2) *restoring,* refunding; compensatory 941 *atoning*.

Verb

(3) *restitute,* make restitution, restore, return, render, give back 779 *not retain*; refund, repay, recoup, reimburse; indemnify, pay damages, compensate, pay compensation, make reparation, make amends 941 *atone*; ransom, redeem 668 *deliver*; bring back, reinstate, rehabilitate; recover 656 *retrieve*.

788
Stealing

Noun

(1) *stealing,* thieving, theft, larceny, petty l., pilfering, filching, pickpocketing, shoplifting; burglary, house-breaking, safe-blowing, s.-cracking; robbery, highway r., holdup; bag-snatching, mugging; cattle-rustling; abduction, kidnapping, hijack; abstraction, removal 786 *taking*; literary theft, plagiarism, pirating 20 *imitation*; joyride 785 *borrowing*; thievery, act of theft.

(2) *brigandage,* banditry, outlawry, piracy, buccaneering, filibustering; privateering, raiding; raid, foray 712 *attack.*

(3) *spoliation,* plundering, looting, pillage; sacking, depredations, ravaging 165 *havoc.*

(4) *peculation,* embezzlement, misappropriation, breach of trust, blackmail, extortion, protection racket; moonlighting, tax evasion, fraud, fiddle, swindle, cheating; confidence trick, skin game 542 *deception.*

(5) *thievishness,* thievery 786 *rapacity*; light fingers, kleptomania; dishonesty, crookedness 930 *improbity*; den of thieves.

Adjective

(6) *thieving,* thievish, light-fingered, kleptomaniac; piratical, buccaneering etc. vb.; raiding, marauding; fraudulent, on the fiddle 930 *dishonest.*

Verb

(7) *steal,* lift, thieve, pilfer, shoplift, help oneself; pick pockets, pick locks, blow a safe; burgle, house-break; rob, relieve of; rifle, sack, clean out; pinch, pocket 786 *take*; forage, scrounge; lift cattle, rustle,

drive off, make off with; abduct, kidnap; abstract, purloin, filch; sneak off with, make away w., spirit away; copy, plagiarize, pirate 20 *copy*; smuggle, bootleg, poach, hijack.

(8) *defraud,* embezzle, misappropriate, peculate, purloin, fiddle, cook the books, con, swindle, cheat 542 *deceive*; gull, dupe; rip off 786 *fleece.*

(9) *rob,* rob with violence, mug; hold up, stick up; buccaneer, maraud, raid; foray, forage, scrounge; strip, gut, ransack, rifle; plunder, pillage, loot, sack, despoil, ravage 165 *lay waste*; victimize, blackmail, extort, squeeze 735 *oppress.*

789
Thief

Noun

(1) *thief,* crook, kleptomaniac, stealer, pilferer, petty thief, sneak thief, shoplifter; pickpocket, bag-snatcher; cattle thief, rustler; burglar, cat b., house-breaker, safe-blower; poacher, smuggler, runner, gun r.; abductor, kidnapper 786 *taker*; fence; plagiarist, pirate.

(2) *robber,* robber band, forty thieves; brigand, bandit, outlaw; footpad, highwayman, mugger, thug 904 *ruffian*; gangster, gunman, hijacker; sea rover, pirate, buccaneer, corsair, privateer; marauder, raider, freebooter, plunderer, pillager, sacker, ravager, despoiler, wrecker.

(3) *defrauder,* embezzler, peculator, fiddler; defaulter, welsher; swindler, sharper, cheat, shark, con man 545 *trickster*; forger, counterfeiter.

790
Booty

Noun
(1) *booty,* spoils, spoils of war, 729 *trophy*; plunder, loot, pillage; prey, victim, quarry; prize, haul, catch 771 *gain*; stolen goods, swag; moonshine, hooch, contraband; illicit gains, graft, blackmail.

791
Barter

Noun
(1) *barter,* exchange, fair e., swap 151 *interchange*; payment in kind traffic, trading, dealing, jobbing; negotiation, bargaining, hard b., haggling, horse-trading.

(2) *trade,* trading, exporting 272 *transference*; visible trade, invisible t.; protection 747 *restriction*; free trade, open market 796 *market*; traffic, drug t., slave trade; smuggling, black market; retail trade 793 *sale*; capitalism, free enterprise, laisser faire 744 *scope*; profit-making, mutual profit; commerce, business affairs 622 *business*; private sector, public s.; venture, business v. 672 *undertaking*; transaction, deal, bargain 765 *compact*; clientele, custom 792 *purchase.*

Adjective
(3) *trading,* exchanging, swapping; commercial, mercantile; wholesale, retail; exchangeable, marketable 793 *salable*; for profit 618 *speculative.*

Verb
(4) *trade,* exchange 151 *interchange*; barter, truck, swap, do a s.; buy and sell, export and import 622 *do business*; traffic in, trade in, deal in, handle; turn over 793 *sell*; commercialize; trade with, do business w., deal w.; finance, back, promote.

(5) *speculate,* venture, risk 618 *gamble*; rig the market, racketeer, profiteer; deal in futures, dabble in shares, play the market, invest.

(6) *bargain,* negotiate, push up, beat down; haggle 766 *make terms*; bid for, make a bid, preempt; raise the bid, overbid outbid 759 *offer*; hold out for, state one's terms 766 *give terms*; settle for, take; drive a bargain, do a deal, shake hands on 765 *contract.*

Adverb
(7) *in trade,* in commerce, in business, across the counter.

792
Purchase

Noun
(1) *purchase,* buying; buying up, takeover, cornering, preemption; redemption, ransom; hire purchase 785 *borrowing*; shopping, window s., spending, shopping spree 806 *expenditure*; mail order; regular buying, custom, patronage; consumer demand 627 *requirement*; buying over, bribery 612 *inducement*; bid, take-over b. 759 *offer*; a purchase, buy, good b., bargain, one's money's worth; shopping list, requirements.

(2) *purchaser,* buyer, consignee; shopper, window-s.; customer, patron, client, clientele, consumer; bidder, highest b., bargainer, haggler; share-buyer, bull, stag.

Adjective
(3) *bought,* paid for, redeemed; purchased, bribed; purchasable, bribable; worth buying 644 *valuable.*

(4) *buying,* purchasing, in the market for; shopping, marketing; cash and carry, cash on delivery, COD., preemptive, bidding, bargaining, haggling; bullish.

Verb

(5) *purchase,* make a p., buy 771 *acquire;* shop, window-s., market, go shopping 627 *require;* buy outright, pay cash for; buy on credit, buy on account 785 *borrow;* buy in 632 *store;* buy up, preempt, corner; buy out, buy over, square 612 *bribe;* buy back, redeem, ransom 668 *deliver;* pay for 804 *defray;* invest in 791 *speculate;* rent 785 *hire;* bid for 759 *offer.*

793
Sale

Noun

(1) *sale,* selling, putting on sale, marketing; disposal clearance, sell-out; clearance sale, jumble s., bazaar; sale of office, simony 930 *improbity;* exclusive sale, monopoly public sale, auctioneering, auction, Dutch a.; good market, market for; sales, boom 730 *prosperity;* salesmanship, sales talk, pitch, sales patter, spiel; hard sell, soft s. 528 *advertisement;* market research 459 *enquiry;* salability, marketability; seller, best-s. 795 *merchandise.*

(2) *seller,* vendor; share-seller; bear; auctioneer; market trader, barrow boy 794 *pedlar;* shopkeeper, dealer 633 *caterer;* wholesaler, retailer 794 *tradespeople;* sales representative, traveller, commercial t.; agent, canvasser, tout; shop walker, shop assistant, salesman, saleswoman; clerk, booking c.

Adjective

(3) *salable,* marketable, on sale; sold, sold out; in demand, sought after, called for; available, on the market, up for sale; bearish; on auction, under the hammer.

Verb

(4) *sell,* make a sale; flog, dispose of; market, put on sale, offer for s., put up for s.; vend; bring to market, dump; hawk, peddle, push; canvass, tout; 633 *provide;* auction, auction off, sell by a., knock down to; retail 791 *trade;* undercut 812 *cheapen;* sell off, remainder; sell up, sell out; sell again, re-sell; sell forward.

(5) *be sold,* be on sale 780 *change hands;* sell, have a sale, have a market, meet a demand, be in d., sell well sell out.

794
Merchant

Noun

(1) *merchant,* livery company, guild, chamber of commerce; concern, firm 708 *corporation;* business person, entrepreneur, speculator 618 *gambler;* trafficker, fence; importer, exporter; wholesaler; merchandiser, dealer, chandler; middleman, broker, stockbroker; estate agent, house a.; financier, banker 784 *lender.*

(2) *tradespeople,* tradesman, retailer, shopkeeper, storekeeper 793 *seller;* grocer 633 *caterer.*

(3) *pedlar,* peddler 793 *seller;* rag-and-bone man; street seller, hawker, huckster, barrow boy; market trader, stallkeeper.

795
Merchandise

Noun

(1) *merchandise,* line, staple; article, commodity; stock, stock-in-trade, range 632 *store;*

freight, cargo 193 *contents*; stuff, things for sale, supplies, wares, goods, durables; shop goods, consumer g., perishable g., canned g., dry g., white g., sundries.

796
Market

Noun

(1) *market,* daily m., weekly m., mart; open market, free trade area 791 *trade*; black market, black economy; seller's market, buyer's m.; marketplace 76 *focus*; street market, flea m.; auction room, fair, trade f., motor show; exhibition, shop window 522 *exhibit*; corn market, corn exchange; exchange, Stock Exchange

(2) *emporium,* entrepot, depot, warehouse 632 *storage*; wharf, quay; trading centre, trading post; bazaar, arcade, shopping centre.

(3) *shop,* retailer's; store, multiple s., department s., chain s.; emporium, bazaar, boutique, bargain basement, supermarket, hypermarket, superstore cash and carry; concern, firm, establishment, corner shop, stall, booth, stand, kiosk, barrow, vending machine, slot m.; counter, window display; premises, place of business 687 *workshop.*

797
Money

Noun

(1) *money,* Lsd, pounds, shillings and pence; brass, dough, lucre 800 *wealth*; cash nexus; currency, decimal c.; honest money, legal tender; sterling, pound s.; gold, silver; ready money, cash, petty c.; change, small c., coppers; pocket money, pin m.

(2) *funds,* temporary f., hot money; liquidity, account, annuities; liquid assets; wherewithal 629 *means*; ready money, finances, exchequer, cash flow, monies 633 *provision*; remittance 804 *payment*; capital; funds in hand, reserves, balances; sum of money, amount, figure, sum, lump s.; mint of money, pile, packet 32 *great quantity*; moneybags, bottomless purse.

(3) *finance,* high f., world of finance; money power, purse strings, almighty dollar; money dealings, cash transaction; money market, exchange 796 *market*; exchange rate, parity; floating pound; devaluation, depreciation; strong pound; gold standard; deficit finance, inflation, deflation; reflation.

(4) *coinage,* minting, issue; stamped coinage, minted c.; coin, piece, monetary unit; guinea, sovereign, half s.; pound coin; decimal coinage, fifty p, ten p, five p, two p, one p; dollar, quarter, dime, nickel, cent; change, small c., cash; numismatics.

(5) *paper money,* bankroll, banknote, wad; note, bill, bill of exchange, draft, order, money o., postal o., cheque, giro; promissory note, IOU; certificate, bond, premium b. 767 *security.*

(6) *false money,* counterfeit m., forged note, forgery; dud cheque.

(7) *bullion,* bar, gold b., ingot, nugget.

(8) *minter,* mint master; forger; money-dealer, money-changer 794 *merchant*; cashier 798 *treasurer*; financier, capitalist; moneybags 800 *rich person.*

Adjective

(9) *monetary,* numismatic; pecuniary, financial, fiscal, budgetary; coined, stamped, minted, issued; sterling; sound, solvent 800 *rich*; inflationary, deflationary; devalued, depreciated; withdrawn, demonetized.

Verb

(10) *mint,* coin, stamp; issue, circulate; forge, counterfeit.

(11) *demonetize,* withdraw, devalue, depreciate.

(12) *draw money,* cash, realize, turn into cash, cash a cheque, write a c. 804 *pay.*

798
Treasurer

Noun

(1) *treasurer,* bursar, purser, cashier, teller, croupier; trustee, steward 754 *consignee*; liquidator 782 *receiver*; bookkeeper 808 *accountant*; banker, financier; paymaster, controller, Chancellor of the Exchequer; mint master 797 *minter*; bank 799 *treasury.*

799
Treasury

Noun

(1) *treasury,* exchequer, public purse; reserves, fund 632 *store*; counting house, custom house; bank, savings bank, building society; treasure chest, coffers 632 *storage*; strongroom, strongbox, safe, safe deposit; cash box, moneybox, piggybank; till, cash register, cash desk, slot machine; box office, gate, turnstile; purse, wallet.

800
Wealth

Noun

(1) *wealth,* Mammon, brass, moneybags 797 *money*; moneymaking, golden touch 635 *plenty*; luxury 637 *superfluity*; opulence, affluence 730 *prosperity*; ease, comfort 376 *euphoria*; solvency, soundness 802 *credit*; solidity, substance independence, competence, self-sufficiency 635 *sufficiency*; resources, well-lined purse, capital 629 *means*; liquid assets, bank account; bottomless purse, nest egg 632 *store*; tidy sum, pile, packet 32 *great quantity*; fortune, inheritance; estates, possessions 777 *property*; bonanza, gold mine, El Dorado, king's ransom; plutocracy, capitalism.

(2) *rich person,* wealthy p., well-to-do p., man *or* woman of means; tycoon, oil magnate, nabob, moneybags, millionaire, multi-m., millionairess; money-spinner, capitalist, plutocrat; heir heiress, 776 *beneficiary*; the haves, jet set; nouveau riche, self-made man *or* woman 730 *prosperous person.*

Adjective

(3) *rich,* richly furnished, luxurious, upholstered, plushy; glittering 875 *ostentatious*; wealthy, well-endowed, opulent, affluent 730 *prosperous*; well-off, well-to-do, well-situated, comfortably off, well-housed, well-paid 376 *comfortable.*

(4) *moneyed,* propertied, worth millions; made of money, rolling in m., loaded; in credit, in the black; well-heeled, flush, in the money; credit-worthy, solvent, sound, able to pay.

Verb

(5) *be rich,* - wealthy etc. adj.;

have money, have means; have credit, have money to burn; die rich 780 *bequeath.*

(6) *afford,* have the means *or* the wherewithal; make both ends meet 635 *have enough.*

(7) *get rich,* come into money 771 *inherit*; do well 730 *prosper*; enrich oneself, make money, mint m., coin m., make a fortune, feather one's nest, line one's pocket, strike it rich, hit the jackpot, win the pools 771 *gain.*

(8) *make rich,* enrich, make one's fortune 780 *bequeath.*

801
Poverty

Noun
(1) *poverty,* voluntary p. 945 *asceticism*; difficulties, financial embarrassment, Queer Street 805 *insolvency*; beggary, impoverishment, penury, pauperism, destitution; privation, necessity, need, want 627 *requirement*; famine 946 *fasting*; slender means, reduced circumstances; low water 636 *insufficiency*; straits, distress 825 *suffering*; grinding poverty, poorness, meanness, shabbiness, seediness, beggarliness, raggedness; general poverty, recession, slump, depression 655 *deterioration*; squalor, public s., slum 655 *dilapidation*; workhouse, poorhouse.

(2) *poor person,* bankrupt, insolvent; hermit 945 *ascetic*; pauper, rag-picker, vagrant, tramp, down-and-out 763 *beggar*; slum-dweller, underdog; the poor, the have-nots, the underprivileged.

Adjective
(3) *poor,* not well-off, low-paid, underpaid; hard up, impecunious, short of cash, out of pocket, in the red; cleaned out, broke, bankrupt, insolvent; on the breadline; impoverished, dispossessed, deprived, robbed; poverty-stricken, penurious, needy, indigent, in want, in need 627 *necessitous*; homeless, hungry 636 *underfed*; in distress, unable to make ends meet 700 *in difficulties*; unprovided for, penniless, destitute.

(4) *beggarly,* starveling, poverty-stricken, shabby, seedy, down at heel, down and out, barefoot in rags, tattered, patched, threadbare 655 *dilapidated*; scruffy, squalid, mean, slummy 649 *dirty.*

Verb
(5) *be poor,* scrape an existence, scratch a living, live from hand to mouth; feel the pinch, starve 859 *be hungry*; want, lack 627 *require*; fall on hard times, come down in the world; go broke 805 *not pay.*

(6) *impoverish,* reduce to poverty, beggar, ruin 165 *destroy*; rob, strip 786 *fleece*; dispossess, disinherit 786 *deprive.*

802
Credit

Noun
(1) *credit,* repute, reputation 866 *prestige*; creditworthiness, sound proposition, reliability 929 *probity*; letter of credit, credit card, credit note; credits, balances, the black; account, tally, bill 808 *accounts*; loan, mortgage 784 *lending.*

(2) *creditor,* importunate c., dun; mortgagee 784 *lender*; depositor, investor.

Verb
(3) *credit* give credit, grant a loan 784 *lend*; take credit, open an account, charge to one's a. 785 *borrow.*

803
Debt

Noun

(1) *debt,* indebtedness 785 *borrowing*; liability, obligation, commitment; encumbrance, mortgage 767 *security*; something owing, debit, charge; debts, bills; bad debt, write-off 772 *loss*; tally, account, account owing; deficit, overdraft, balance to pay 307 *shortfall*; inability to pay 805 *insolvency*; frozen assets 805 *nonpayment*; deferred payment 802 *credit*; overdue payment, arrears; no more credit, foreclosure.

(2) *interest,* simple i., compound i.; excessive i., usury 784 *lending*; premium, rate of interest, bank rate.

(3) *debtor,* borrower, mortgagor; defaulter, insolvent 805 *nonpayment*.

Adjective

(4) *indebted,* in debt, indebted; liable, committed, answerable, bound 917 *obliged*; owing, overdrawn, in the red; mortgaged; defaulting, unable to pay, insolvent.

(5) *owed,* owing, due, overdue, in arrears; outstanding, unpaid; chargeable, payable, debited; on credit, on deposit, repayable.

Verb

(6) *be in debt,* owe, have to repay; owe money, pay interest; be debited with, be liable for; overdraw (one's account), get credit 785 *borrow*; run into debt, be overdrawn, run up an account.

804
Payment

Noun

(1) *payment,* paying for, paying

off, discharge, satisfaction, full s., liquidation, settlement 807 *receipt*; cash payment, down p. 797 *money*; first payment, earnest, deposit; instalment, standing order; due payment, subscription, tribute 809 *tax*; contribution, collection 781 *offering*; repayment, compensation 787 *restitution*; remittance 806 *expenditure*.

(2) *pay,* pay packet, wages, salary 771 *earnings*; grant, subsidy 703 *subvention*; salary, pension, annuity, remuneration, emolument, fee; bribe 962 *reward*; cut, commission 810 *discount*; redundancy pay, golden handshake; payer, paymaster, purser, cashier 798 *treasurer*.

Adjective

(3) *paying,* disbursing 806 *expending*; paying in full, out of debt.

Verb

(4) *pay,* disburse 806 *expend*; contribute 781 *give*; pay in kind, barter 791 *trade*; make payment, pay out, fork o.; pay back, repay, reimburse, compensate 787 *restitute*; grease one's palm 612 *bribe*; pay wages, remunerate, tip 962 *reward*; pay in advance, pay on demand; pay on the nail or on the dot, pay cash down; honour (a bill), pay up, meet, satisfy, redeem, discharge, clear, liquidate, settle 808 *account*.

(5) *defray,* pay for, bear the cost; pay one's way, pick up the bill, foot the b.; buy a round, stand treat, 781 *give*; share expenses, go Dutch 775 *participate*.

Adverb

(6) *cash down,* cash on delivery; on the nail, on the dot, on demand.

805
Nonpayment

Noun
(1) *nonpayment,* default; reduced payment, stoppage, deduction 963 *penalty*; moratorium, embargo, freeze; dishonouring, refusal to pay; tax avoidance, tax evasion; deferred payment, hire purchase 785 *borrowing*; bouncing cheque; depreciation, devaluation.

(2) *insolvency,* inability to pay, bankruptcy; overdraft 803 *debt.*

(3) *nonpayer,* defaulter; embezzler, tax dodger 789 *defrauder*; bilker, welsher, absconder; bankrupt, discharged b.,

Adjective
(4) *nonpaying,* defaulting, behindhand, in arrears; insolvent, bankrupt 803 *indebted*; ruined 801 *poor.*

Verb
(5) *not pay,* default, embezzle, swindle 788 *defraud*; fall into arrears, get behindhand; stop payment, withhold p., freeze, block; practise tax evasion 930 *be dishonest*; become insolvent, go bankrupt, fail, crash, go into liquidation; welsh, bilk 542 *deceive*; abscond 296 *decamp*; be unable to pay 801 *be poor.*

806
Expenditure

Noun
(1) *expenditure,* spending, disbursement 804 *payment*; cost of living; outgoings, overheads, costs, expenses; expense, outlay, investment; fee, tax; extravagance, spending spree 815 *prodigality.*

Adjective
(2) *expending,* spending, generous 813 *liberal*; extravagant, splashing out 815 *prodigal*; out of pocket.

(3) *expended,* spent, disbursed, paid, paid out; laid out, invested; at one's expense.

Verb
(4) *expend,* spend; buy 792 *purchase*; lay out, invest, sink money in; incur costs, incur expenses; afford, bear the cost, pay out 804 *pay*; give money, donate 781 *give*; spare no expense, be lavish 813 *be liberal*; splash out 815 *be prodigal*; use up, consume, run through, get t. 634 *waste.*

807
Receipt

Noun
(1) *receipt,* voucher; money received, credits, revenue, royalty, rents, dues; customs 809 *tax*; money coming in, turnover, takings, proceeds, returns, receipts, gate money; income, emolument, pay, salary, wages 771 *earnings*; remuneration 962 *reward*; pension, annuity; allowance, pocket money, spending m.; pittance; alimony, maintenance; scholarship 771 *acquisition*; interest, return, rake-off; winnings, profits 771 *gain*; bonus, premium 40 *extra*; prize 729 *trophy*; legacy, inheritance 777 *dower.*

Adjective
(2) *received,* paid, receipted, acknowledged.

Verb
(3) *see 771 acquire, 782 receive, be received, 786 take.*

808
Accounts

Noun

(1) *accounts,* accountancy, accounting, bookkeeping; audit, account, profit and loss a., balance sheet, debit and credit; budgeting, budget 633 *provision*; account rendered, statement, bill, invoice, manifest 87 *list*; reckoning, computation, facts and figures 86 *numeration*.

(2) *account book,* cheque b.; cash b., journal, ledger, register, books 548 *record*.

(3) *accountant,* chartered a., bookkeeper, storekeeper; cashier 798 *treasurer*; auditor; actuary, statistician.

Adjective

(4) *accounting,* bookkeeping, actuarial, reckoning, computing, budgetary; accountable.

Verb

(5) *account,* keep the books, keep accounts; budget, prepare a b.; cost, value 480 *estimate*; book, enter, post, carry over, debit, credit 548 *register*; balance accounts; settle accounts, square a.; charge, bill, invoice; overcharge, surcharge, undercharge 809 *price*; cook the books 788 *defraud*; audit, inspect accounts; take stock, inventory, catalogue 87 *list*.

809
Price

Noun

(1) *price,* market p., rate, going r. flat r.; high rate 811 *dearness*; low rate 812 *cheapness*; price control, 747 *restraint*; value, face v., worth, money's w.; scarcity value; price list, tariff; quoted price, quotation; amount, figure, sum asked for;

ransom, fine 963 *penalty*; demand, dues, charge; surcharge, supplement 40 *extra*; overcharge, excessive charge, extortion; fare, hire, rental, rent, fee; commission, rake-off; charges; postage; cover charge, corkage; bill, invoice, reckoning.

(2) *cost,* buying price, purchase p.; expenses 806 *expenditure*; running costs, overheads; wages, wage bill; legal costs, damages 963 *penalty*; cost of living.

(3) *tax,* dues; taxation, tax demand 737 *demand*; rating, assessment 480 *estimate*; rate, levy, toll, duty; imposition, charge; punitive tax 963 *penalty*; blackmail, ransom 804 *payment*; tithe, poll tax, capitation t.; estate duty, death d.; direct taxation, income tax, surtax, supertax, capital gains tax; indirect taxation, excise, customs, tariff, purchase tax, value-added tax, VAT.

Adjective

(4) *priced,* charged, fixed; chargeable, leviable, taxable, assessable, ratable, dutiable, excisable; taxed, rated, assessed; to the tune of.

Verb

(5) *price,* put a price on, cost, assess, value, rate 480 *estimate*; ask a price, charge 737 *demand*.

(6) *cost,* be worth, fetch, bring in; amount to, come to, mount up to; be priced at, be valued at; have its price; sell for, go f., change hands for, realize.

(7) *tax,* impose a tax; levy a rate, assess for tax, value; make dutiable; take a toll 786 *levy*; fine 963 *punish*.

810
Discount

Noun
(1) *discount,* something off, reduction, rebate, cut; stoppage, deduction; concession, allowance, margin; cut price, cut rate 612 *incentive*; bargain price 812 *cheapness*; one's cut, commission.

Verb
(2) *discount,* deduct 39 *subtract*; depreciate, rebate, offer a discount, mark down, cut, slash 812 *cheapen.*

811
Dearness

Noun
(1) *dearness,* costliness, expensiveness; value, high worth; rarity 636 *scarcity*; exorbitance, extortion, rack rents; bad value, poor v.; bad bargain, high price, cost, high c.; rising prices, sellers' market, bull m.,

Adjective
(2) *dear,* high-priced, pricy, expensive, costly, extravagant, dearly-bought; overcharged, exorbitant, excessive, extortionate; steep, stiff; beyond one's means, prohibitive 641 *useless*; rising, soaring, inflationary; bullish.

(3) *of price* 644 *valuable*; priceless, beyond price, above p.; invaluable, inestimable, worth a fortune; precious, rare 140 *infrequent*; at a premium.

Verb
(4) *be dear,* cost a lot; rise in price, harden; go up, appreciate, escalate; prove expensive, cost one dear, cost a fortune.

(5) *overcharge,* ask too much; profiteer, soak, bleed, extort, rip off, short-change, hold to

ransom 786 *fleece*; put up prices, mark up 793 *sell.*

(6) *pay too much,* pay through the nose; pay dearly.

Adverb
(7) *dearly,* at a price, at great cost, at huge expense..

812
Cheapness

Noun
(1) *cheapness,* good value, value for money, money's worth, snip, bargain; seconds, rejects; low price, cheap rate 810 *discount*; nominal price, knockdown p., cut p., bargain p., budget p., sale p., giveaway p., peppercorn rent, easy terms; Dutch auction; depreciation, fall, slump; deflation; glut 637 *redundance.*

(2) *no charge,* nominal c. 781 *gift*; labour of love 597 *voluntary work*; free trade, free entry, free quarters, grace and favour.

Adjective
(3) *cheap,* inexpensive, moderate, reasonable, fair, worth the money; affordable, within one's means; cheap to make, low-budget; substandard, shop-soiled; economical, economy size; low-priced, going cheap; bargain-rate, cut-price, reduced, marked down, half-price; cheap and nasty 641 *useless*; bearish.

(4) *uncharged,* not charged for, gratuitous, complimentary; gratis, for nothing, for the asking; free, scot-f., free of charge 781 *given*; zero-rated, tax-free, post-paid; honorary 597 *voluntary.*

Verb
(5) *be cheap,* - free etc. adj.; cost little, be economical; cheapen,

fall in price, depreciate, come down, fall, slump, plunge.

(6) *cheapen,* lower the price, mark down, cut, slash; undercharge, give away 781 *give;* beat down, undercut, undersell, dump, unload; flood the market.

Adverb
(7) *cheaply,* on the cheap; at cost price, at a discount, for a song.

813
Liberality

Noun
(1) *liberality,* liberalness, bounteousness, bountifulness, munificence, generosity; open heart, open hand, open purse, hospitality, open house 882 *sociability;* free hand, blank cheque 744 *scope;* cornucopia 635 *plenty;* lavishness 815 *prodigality;* bounty, largesse 781 *gift;* handsome offer 759 *offer;* benefaction, charity 897 *kind act.*

(2) *good giver,* generous g., cheerful g., liberal donor, good spender, Lady Bountiful, Father Christmas, Santa Claus 903 *benefactor.*

Adjective
(3) *liberal,* free, free-spending, free-handed, open-h., lavish 815 *prodigal;* generous, large-hearted, 931 *disinterested;* munificent, bountiful, charitable 897 *benevolent;* hospitable 882 *sociable;* handsome, splendid, slap-up; lordly, princely, royal, right royal; unstinting, ungrudging, unsparing; abundant, ample, bounteous, profuse 635 *plenteous;* overflowing 637 *redundant.*

Verb
(4) *be liberal,* - generous etc. adj.; lavish, shower upon 781 *give;* give generously 897 *philanthropize;* overpay, pay well,

tip w.; keep open house 882 *be hospitable;* do one proud, spare no expense 744 *give scope;* spend freely 815 *be prodigal.*

Adverb
(5) *liberally,* ungrudgingly, with both hands.

814
Economy

Noun
(1) *economy,* thrift, thriftiness, frugality; prudence, carefulness; good housekeeping, good management; credit squeeze 747 *restriction;* economy drive, economy measures; time-saving, labour-s., economizing, saving etc. vb.; cheese-paring, retrenchment, economies, cuts; savings 632 *store;* conservation, energy-saving; economizer 816 *niggard;* economist; conservationist, ecologist; good housewife, careful steward.

Adjective
(2) *economical,* time-saving, labour-s., energy-s., money-s., cost-cutting; money-conscious 816 *parsimonious;* thrifty, careful, prudent, canny, frugal, saving, sparing; meagre, Spartan.

Verb
(3) *economize,* be economical, thrifty etc. adj.; keep costs down, waste nothing, recycle, reuse; watch expenses, out costs, make economies, retrench, tighten one's belt; pinch, scrape 816 *be parsimonious;* save, spare, hoard 632 *store.*

Adverb
(4) *sparingly,* economically, frugally.

815
Prodigality

Noun

(1) *prodigality,* lavishness, profusion 637 *redundance*; conspicuous expenditure 875 *ostentation*; extravagance, wastefulness, profligacy, dissipation, squandering, spending spree, splurge 634 *waste*; improvidence, deficit finance.

(2) *prodigal,* prodigal son, spender, big s.; waster, wastrel, profligate, spendthrift.

Adjective

(3) *prodigal,* lavish 813 *liberal*; profuse, extravagant, wasteful, squandering, profligate; uneconomical, thriftless, spendthrift, improvident, reckless.

Verb

(4) *be prodigal,* overspend, splash money around, spend money like water; blow one's money, flash pound notes; not count the cost, squander 634 *waste*; fritter away, fling a., gamble a., dissipate, misspend, overdraw; save nothing, put nothing by.

Adverb

(5) *prodigally,* profusely, recklessly

Interjection

(6) hang the expense! easy come, easy go!

816
Parsimony

Noun

(1) *parsimony,* parsimoniousness, false economy, cheeseparing, scrimping, pinching, penny-p.; tightfistedness, meanness, stinginess, miserliness; illiberality 932 *selfishness*

(2) *avarice,* cupidity, acquisitiveness, itching palm; rapacity, avidity, greed 859 *desire*; mercenariness, venality.

(3) *niggard,* skinflint, penny pincher, grudging giver; miser, hoarder, money-grubber; squirrel, magpie; usurer 784 *lender*; Scrooge.

Adjective

(4) *parsimonious,* careful 814 *economical*; too careful, overeconomical, money-conscious, miserly, mean, mingy, stingy, near, close, tight-fisted 778 *retentive*; grudging, churlish, illiberal, ungenerous, uncharitable, empty-handed; penurious, chary, sparing, pinching, scraping, scrimping.

(5) *avaricious,* grasping 932 *selfish*; possessive, acquisitive 771 *acquiring*; hoarding, saving; pinching, cadging; miserly; money-mad, covetous 859 *greedy*; usurious, rapacious, extortionate; mercenary, venal, sordid.

Verb

(6) *be parsimonious,* grudge, begrudge, withhold, keep back 760 *refuse*; stint, skimp, starve 636 *make insufficient*; scrape, scrimp, pinch 814 *economize*; beat down, haggle 791 *bargain*; cadge, beg, borrow; hoard, sit on, keep for oneself 932 *be selfish*.

Adverb

(7) *parsimoniously,* on a shoestring.

817
Affections

Noun

(1) *affections,* qualities, instincts; passions, feelings, emotions, emotional life; nature, disposition 5 *character*; spirit, temper, cast of mind, trait 5

temperament; personality, psychology, mentality, outlook, make-up; being, innermost b., breast, bosom, heart, soul, heart of hearts 5 *essential part*, 447 *spirit*; attitude, frame of mind, state of m., humour, mood; predilection, inclinations, bent 179 *tendency*; passion, heartstrings 818 *feeling*.

Adjective

(2) *with affections,* affected, characterized, formed, moulded, cast, framed; imbued with, possessed w., obsessed w.; inborn, congenital 5 *genetic*; deep-rooted, 5 *intrinsic*; emotional, demonstrative 818 *feeling*.

818
Feeling

Noun

(1) *feeling,* experience, sensation, emotion, sentiment; true feeling, sincerity 540 *veracity*; impulse 609 *spontaneity*; intuition, instinct; response, reaction, sympathy, involvement 880 *friendliness*; empathy, appreciation, realization, understanding 490 *knowledge*; impression, deep feeling, deep sense of 819 *moral sensibility*; religious feeling 979 *piety*; tender feelings 887 *love*; hard feelings 891 *resentment*; thrill 318 *spasm*; pathos 825 *suffering*; emotionalism 822 *excitability*; sentimentality, romanticism; demonstration, demonstrativeness; expression, blush, flush; tremor, quiver, palpitation, throbbing 318 *agitation*; ferment 318 *commotion*; swelling heart, lump in one's throat; stoicism, endurance, stiff upper lip 823 *patience*.

(2) *warm feeling,* glow; cordiality, effusiveness, heartiness;

hot head, impatience; eagerness, keenness, fervour, ardour, vehemence, enthusiasm 174 *vigorousness*; vigour, zeal 678 *activity*; emotion, passion, ecstasy, inspiration, elevation, transports 822 *excitable state*.

Adjective

(3) *feeling,* sensible, sentient; spirited, vivacious, lively 819 *sensitive*; sensuous 944 *sensual*; experiencing, enduring, bearing 825 *suffering*; intuitive, vibrant, responsive, reacting; involved, sympathetic, tender-hearted 819 *impressible*; emotional, passionate, full of feeling; unctuous, soulful; intense 821 *excited*; cordial, hearty; gushing, effusive; sentimental, romantic; mawkish, maudlin; tingling, throbbing; blushing, flushing.

(4) *impressed,* affected, stirred, aroused, moved, touched 821 *excited*; struck, awestruck, overwhelmed; aflame with, consumed w., devoured by, inspired by; rapt, enraptured, enthralled, ecstatic; lyrical, raving 822 *excitable*.

(5) *fervent,* fervid, passionate, ardent, intense; eager, breathless, panting, throbbing; impassioned, vehement, earnest, zealous; enthusiastic, exuberant, bubbling; hot-headed, warm-blooded, impetuous 822 *excitable*; warm, fiery, glowing 379 *hot*; hysterical, delirious, overwrought, feverish 503 *frenzied*; uncontrollable 176 *violent*.

(6) *felt,* experienced, lived; heartfelt, cordial, hearty, warm, sincere 540 *veracious*; deeply-felt, visceral, profound 211 *deep*; stirring, soul-s., heart-warming; emotive, overwhelming 821 *impressive*; keen, poignant, piercing 256 *sharp*; caustic, burning 388 *pungent*;

penetrating, absorbing thrilling, tingling, rapturous, ecstatic 826 *pleasurable*; pathetic, affecting 827 *distressing*.

Verb

(7) *feel,* sense, entertain; feel deeply, take to heart 819 *be sensitive*; know the feeling, experience, live through, go t., taste; bear, endure, undergo, smart under 825 *suffer*; suffer with, feel w., sympathize; respond, react, warm to; kindle, catch, be inspired 821 *be excited*; cause feeling 821 *impress*.

(8) *show feeling,* show signs of emotion; not hide one's feelings 522 *manifest*; enthuse, go into ecstasies 824 *be pleased*; fly into a rage 891 *get angry*; change colour, look blue, look black, go livid, go purple; look pale, blench 427 *whiten*; colour go red in the face, blush, flush, glow, mantle 431 *redden*; quiver, tremble, wince; shake, quake 318 *be agitated*; tingle, thrill, vibrate, throb, palpitate; pant, heave 352 *breathe*; reel, stagger; stutter, stammer.

Adverb

(9) *feelingly,* earnestly, heart and soul; sincerely, from the bottom of one's heart.

changeableness; touchy person, moody p., sensitive plant, bundle of nerves.

Adjective

(2) *impressible,* sensible, aware, conscious of, awake to, alive to, responsive 374 *sentient*; touched, moved 818 *impressed*; susceptive, impressionable 822 *excitable*; susceptible, romantic, sentimental; emotional, warm-hearted; soft-h., tender, compassionate 905 *pitying*.

(3) *sensitive,* sore, raw, tender 374 *sentient*; aesthetic 463 *discriminating*; all feeling 822 *excitable*; touchy, irritable, thin-skinned 892 *irascible*.

(4) *lively,* alive, vital, vivacious, spirited, high-s., animated; skittish 833 *merry*; irrepressible, ebullient, effervescent; lively-minded, alert, aware, on one's toes 455 *attentive*; impatient, nervous, highly-strung, temperamental; mobile, changeable; enthusiastic, impassioned 818 *fervent*.

Verb

(5) *be sensitive,* soften one's heart, take it to h.; weep for 905 *pity*; tingle 318 *be agitated*.

Adverb

(6) *on the raw,* to the quick, to the heart.

819
Sensibility

Noun

(1) *moral sensibility,* sensitivity, sensitiveness, soul; sentimentality, susceptibility; touchiness, prickliness 892 *irascibility*; raw feelings, thin skin, soft spot, sore point 891 *resentment*; finer feelings, sentiments; tenderness, affection 887 *love*; spirit, spiritedness, vivacity, liveliness, verve 571 *vigour*; emotionalism 822 *excitability*; temperament, mobility 152

820
Insensibility

Noun

(1) *moral insensibility,* lack of sensitivity, insensitiveness; lack of sensation, numbness 375 *insensibility*; inertia 175 *inertness*; lethargy 679 *inactivity*; stagnation, vegetation 266 *quiescence*; woodenness, obtuseness, stupidity, no imagination 499 *unintelligence*; slowness, delayed reaction 456 *inattention*; nonchalance, insouciance, detachment, apathy

860 *indifference*; phlegm, stolidness, calmness, steadiness, coolness, sangfroid 823 *inexcitability*; no feelings, aloofness, impassiveness; repression, stoicism 823 *patience*; inscrutability 834 *seriousness* thick skin, insensitivity, coarseness, Philistinism; cold heart, frigidity; dourness, cynicism; callousness 326 *hardness*; lack of feeling, dry eyes, heart of stone 898 *inhumanity*; no admiration for 865 *lack of wonder*.

(2) *unfeeling person*, iceberg, icicle, cold fish; stock, stone, block.

Adjective
(3) *impassive*, unconscious 375 *insensible*; insensitive, unimaginative, unresponsive 823 *inexcitable*; phlegmatic, stolid; wooden, dull, slow 499 *unintelligent*; proof against, steeled a.; stoical, ascetic; unemotional, undemonstrative; unconcerned, detached 860 *indifferent*; unaffected, calm 266 *tranquil*; steady, unruffled, imperturbable, unshockable, without nerves, cool; inscrutable, blank, deadpan, poker-faced; unseeing 439 *blind*; unhearing 416 *deaf*; impersonal, dispassionate, without warmth,
reserved; stony, frigid, icy, cold; cold-hearted, cynical, unfeeling, heartless, inhuman.

(4) *apathetic*, half-hearted, lukewarm, unenthusiastic 860 *indifferent*; uninterested 454 *incurious*; unmoved, uninspired; nonchalant lackadaisical, insouciant 458 *negligent*; spiritless, supine 679 *inactive*; passive 175 *inert*; cloyed 863 *sated*; torpid, numb, comatose 375 *insensible*.

(5) *thick-skinned*, impervious to; blind to, deaf to, dead to, closed to; obtuse, insensitive; callous, tough 326 *hard*; hard-bitten, hard-boiled; shameless, unblushing, amoral.

Verb
(6) *be insensitive*, have no feelings; be blind to 439 *be blind*; lack spirit, lack verve; harden oneself, steel o. 906 *be pitiless*, 860 *be indifferent*; feel no emotion 865 *not wonder*; take no interest 454 *be incurious*; ignore 458 *disregard*; stagnate, vegetate 679 *be inactive*.

(7) *make insensitive*, render callous, steel, toughen 326 *harden*; stop one's ears 399 *silence*; shut one's eyes 439 *blind*; brutalize 655 *pervert*; stale, coarsen 847 *vulgarize*; satiate, cloy 863 *sate*; deaden 375 *render insensible*.

Adverb
(8) *in cold blood*, with dry eyes, without emotion.

821
Excitation

Noun
(1) *excitation*, rousing, arousal, stirring up, working up, whipping up 174 *stimulation*; possession, inspiration, exhilaration, intoxication; encouragement, animation, incitement 612 *inducement*; provocation, irritation; impression, image, impact 178 *influence*; fascination, bewitchment, enchantment 983 *sorcery*; rapture, ravishment 824 *joy*; emotional appeal, human interest, pathos; sensationalism, melodrama; excitement, tension; effervescence, ebullience 318 *agitation*; shock, thrill, kicks 318 *spasm*; stew, ferment 318 *commotion*; fever pitch 503 *frenzy*; climax 137 *crisis*, passion, emotion, enthusiasm, lyricism 818 *feeling*; fuss, drama 822 *excitable state*; fury, rage 891 *anger*; interest 453 *curiosity*; amazement 864 *wonder*; awe 854 *fear*.

(2) *excitant,* rabble-rouser 738 *agitator*; sensationalist, scandalmonger; fillip, ginger, tonic 174 *stimulant*; pep pill 949 *drugtaking*; prick, goad, spur 612 *incentive*; irritant, gadfly.

Adjective

(3) *excited,* - stimulated etc. vb.; busy, bustling 678 *active*; ebullient, effervescent 355 *bubbly*; tense, wrought up, keyed up, wound up; feverish, hectic; delirious, frantic 503 *frenzied*; glowing 818 *fervent*; hot and bothered, heated 379 *hot*; violent 176 *furious*; wild, mad, livid 891 *angry*; avid, eager, agog 859 *desiring*; tingling 818 *feeling*; overexcited 318 *agitated*; restless, restive, overwrought, distraught, distracted, beside oneself, hysterical; out of control, running amok; inspired, possessed, carried away; impassioned, enthusiastic, lyrical, raving 822 *excitable*.

(4) *exciting,* stimulating, intoxicating, heady, exhilarating; provocative, piquant, tantalizing; salty, spicy; alluring 887 *lovable*; evocative, emotive, suggestive; thrilling, suspenseful, cliff-hanging, spine-chilling, hair-raising; moving, affecting, inspiring, rousing, stirring, soul-s.; sensational, dramatic, melodramatic; stunning, mind-boggling, mind-blowing; interesting, gripping, absorbing, enthralling.

(5) *impressive,* imposing, grand, stately; dignified, majestic, regal 868 *noble*; awe-inspiring, sublime, humbling; overwhelming, overpowering; picturesque, scenic; striking, arresting, dramatic; telling, forceful.

Verb

(6) *excite,* affect 178 *influence*; warm the heart 833 *cheer*; touch, move, draw tears 834

sadden; impassion, stir one's feelings, quicken the pulse, startle, electrify, galvanize; inflame, kindle, set on fire 381 *burn*; sting, pique, irritate 891 *enrage*; tantalize, tease 827 *torment*; work on, work up, whip up 612 *incite*; breathe into, enthuse, inspire, stir, rouse, arouse, awaken; evoke, summon up; thrill, exhilarate, intoxicate 826 *delight*.

(7) *animate,* enliven, quicken 360 *vitalize*; revive, rekindle 656 *restore*; inspire, encourage, hearten 855 *give courage*; give an edge to, whet 256 *sharpen*; spur, goad 277 *accelerate*; jolt, jog, shake up; stimulate, ginger 174 *invigorate*; cherish, foster, foment 162 *strengthen*; fuel, intensify, fan the flame.

(8) *impress,* sink in; interest, hold, grip, absorb; intrigue, rouse curiosity, strike, claim attention 455 *attract notice*; affect 178 *influence*; bring home to, drive home 532 *emphasize*; come home to, penetrate 516 *be intelligible*; arrest, shake, stun, amaze, astound, stagger 508 *surprise*; stupefy, petrify 864 *be wonderful*; dazzle, inspire with awe, humble; overwhelm take one's breath away; perturb, disquiet, upset, unsettle, distress, worry 827 *trouble*.

(9) *be excited,* flare up, burn 379 *be hot*; seethe, boil, explode 318 *effervesce*; thrill to 818 *feel*; tingle, tremble 822 *be excitable*; quiver, flutter, palpitate 318 *be agitated*; flush 818 *show feeling*; toss and turn, squirm, writhe 251 *wriggle*.

Adverb

(10) *excitedly,* frenziedly; with a beating heart.

822
Excitability

Noun

(1) *excitability*, excitableness, explosiveness, instability, temperament, emotionalism; hot blood, hot temper 892 *irascibility*; impatience, intolerance; vehemence, impetuosity, recklessness 857 *rashness*; boisterousness, turbulence; restlessness, fidgetiness, nerves, flap 318 *agitation*.

(2) *excitable state*, exhilaration, elation, intoxication, abandon, abandonment; thrill, ecstasy 818 *feeling*; fever, fever of excitement; perturbation, trepidation 318 *agitation*; ferment, pother, stew; storm, tempest, outburst, outbreak, explosion, scene, song and dance 318 *commotion*; brainstorm, hysterics, delirium, fit 503 *frenzy*; distraction, madness 503 *insanity*; rage, fury 176 *violence*; temper, tantrums 891 *anger*.

Adjective

(3) *excitable*, oversensitive 819 *sensitive*; passionate, emotional; susceptible, romantic; thrill-loving, looking for kicks; suggestible, inflammable; unstable, easily depressed; impressionable 819 *impressible*; temperamental, mercurial, volatile 152 *changeful*; fitful 604 *capricious*; restless, nervy, fidgety, edgy, on edge, ruffled 318 *agitated*; highly-strung, nervous, skittish, mettlesome 819 *lively*; easily provoked, irritable, fiery, hot-headed 892 *irascible*; impatient, triggerhappy 680 *hasty*; impetuous, impulsive 857 *rash*; savage, fierce; boisterous, rumbustious, tempestuous, turbulent, stormy, uproarious 176 *violent*; restive 738 *riotous*; effervescent, simmering, seething, boiling; volcanic, explosive, ready

to burst; fanatical, unbalanced; rabid 176 *furious*; feverish, frantic, hysterical, delirious 503 *frenzied*; tense, electric; elated, inspired, lyrical 821 *excited*.

Verb

(4) *be excitable*, - unstable etc. adj.; show impatience, fidget, fret, fume, stamp, shuffle, chafe 818 *show feeling*; tingle with, be itching to; be on edge 318 *be agitated*; start, jump 854 *be nervous*; have a temper 892 *be irascible*; throw fits, have hysterics 503 *go mad*; let oneself go, go wild, run riot, run amok, see red; storm 61 *rampage*; ramp, rage, roar 176 *be violent*; explode 891 *get angry*; kindle, smoulder, catch fire, flare up 821 *be excited*.

823
Inexcitability

Noun

(1) *inexcitability*, imperturbability, calmness, steadiness, composure; coolness, sangfroid, nonchalance 820 *moral insensibility*; unruffled state, tranquillity 266 *quietude*; serenity, placidity, peace of mind 828 *content*; equanimity, balance, poise; even temper, level t., selfcommand, self-control 942 *temperance*; stoicism 945 *asceticism*; dispassionateness, detachment 860 *indifference*; gravity, staidness, demureness, sobriety 834 *seriousness*; gentleness 884 *courtesy*; tameness, lack of spirit 177 *moderation*.

(2) *patience*, forbearance, endurance, tolerance, longsuffering, toleration, stoicism; resignation, acquiescence 721 *submission*.

Adjective

(3) *inexcitable*, dispassionate, cold, frigid, heavy, dull 820

impassive; stable 153 *unchangeable*; cool, imperturbable, unflappable; cool-headed, level-h.; steady, composed, controlled 942 *temperate*; deliberate, unhurried 278 *slow*; even, level, equable 16 *uniform*; good-tempered, even-t., easy-going, sunny; staid, sedate, sober, demure, reserved, grave 834 *serious*; quiet, placid, unruffled, calm, serene 266 *tranquil*; sweet, gentle, mild, meek 935 *innocent*; easygoing 736 *lenient*; philosophical, acquiescent, resigned; submissive 739 *obedient*; spiritless, lackadaisical, torpid, passive 175 *inert*; calmed down, tame 369 *tamed*; earthbound 593 *prosaic*.

(4) *patient,* meek, tolerant, forbearing, enduring; stoical, philosophical, uncomplaining.

Verb

(5) *keep calm,* keep a cool head, be composed, be collected; compose oneself, collect o., control one's temper, keep cool; take things as they come, relax, not worry, stop worrying 683 *repose*; resign oneself, have patience, be resigned 721 *submit*.

(6) *be patient,* grin and bear it; show restraint, forbear; put up with, stand, tolerate, bear, endure, support, suffer; resign oneself, put a brave face on it; take, swallow, digest, stomach, pocket 721 *knuckle under.* be tolerant, condone 736 *be lenient*; overlook 734 *be lax*; allow 756 *permit*; keep the peace, coexist 770 *compromise*.

(7) *tranquillize,* steady, moderate, sober down 177 *assuage*; calm, lull, cool down, compose 719 *pacify*; set one's mind at rest 831 *relieve*; control, repress 747 *restrain*.

824
Joy

Noun

(1) *joy,* 376 pleasure; enjoyment, thrill 826 *pleasurableness*; joyfulness, joyousness 835 *rejoicing*; delight, gladness, rapture, exhilaration, abandonment, ecstasy, enchantment; unholy joy, gloating, malice 898 *malevolence*; halcyon days, honeymoon 730 *palmy days*.

(2) *happiness,* felicity, good fortune; well-being, comfort, ease 376 *euphoria*; golden age 730 *prosperity*; blessedness, bliss, seventh heaven, Paradise,

(3) *enjoyment,* gratification, satisfaction, fulfilment 828 *content*; relish, zest, gusto; indulgence, wallowing; hedonism 944 *sensualism*; glee, merrymaking, lark, frolic, gambol 833 *merriment*; fun, treat, outing 837 *amusement*; good cheer 301 *eating*.

Adjective

(4) *pleased,* well-p., glad, not sorry; welcoming, satisfied, happy 828 *content* gratified, flattered, pleased as Punch; over the moon, on top of the world; enjoying, loving it, tickled pink 837 *amused*; exhilarated 833 *merry*; euphoric, walking on air; elated, overjoyed 833 *jubilant*; cheering, shouting 835 *rejoicing*; delighted, transported, enraptured, rapturous, ecstatic 923 *approving*; in raptures, in ecstasies; captivated, charmed, enchanted; gloating.

(5) *happy,* blithe, joyful, joyous 833 *merry*; beaming, smiling 835 *laughing*; radiant, sparkling, starry-eyed; lucky, fortunate 730 *prosperous*; blessed, blissful, in bliss, in paradise; at ease 376 *comfortable*.

Verb
(6) be pleased, - glad etc. adj.;
have the pleasure; hug oneself,
congratulate o., purr, jump for
joy 833 *be cheerful*; laugh, smile
835 *rejoice*; get pleasure from,
take pleasure in, delight in,
rejoice in; go into ecstasies,
rave about 818 *show feeling*;
luxuriate in, bask in, spoil oneself 376 *enjoy*; have fun 837
amuse oneself; gloat over, savour, appreciate, relish; smack
one's lips 386 *taste*; like 923
approve.

825
Suffering

Noun
(1) suffering, heartache 834 *melancholy*; longing, homesickness, nostalgia 859 *desire*; weariness 684 *fatigue*; nightmare,
affliction, distress, anguish,
angst, agony, torture, torment,
mental_t. 377 *pain*; twinge,
stab, smart, sting, thorn 377
pang; bitter cup 827 *painfulness*; crucifixion, martyrdom;
purgatory, hell; bed of nails,
bed of thorns 700 *difficulty*;
inconvenience, discomfort, malaise; the hard way, trial, ordeal; shock, blow 659 *bane*;
death's door, living death 651
illness; unhappy times 731
adversity.

(2) sorrow, grief, sadness,
mournfulness, gloom 834 *dejection*; woe, wretchedness, misery, depths of m.; prostration,
despair 853 *hopelessness*; unhappiness 731 *adversity*; heavy
heart, aching h., broken h.;
displeasure 829 *discontent*; vexation, bitterness, mortification, chagrin, remorse 830
regret.

(3) worry, worrying, unease, discomfort uneasiness, disquiet,
inquietude, fretting 318 *agitation*; discomposure, dismay,

distress 63 *derangement*; phobia, hang-up; anxiety, concern,
solicitude, thought, care; load,
burden; strain, tension; worries, cares, trouble 616 *evil*;
bother, annoyance, irritation,
pest 659 *bane*; bothersome task
838 *bore*; headache, problem
530 *enigma*.

(4) sufferer, victim, scapegoat,
sacrifice; prey 544 *dupe*; martyr; wretch, poor w. 731 *unlucky person*; patient 651 *sick
person*.

Adjective
(5) suffering, ill 651 *sick*; agonizing, writhing, aching, in pain,
on the rack, in torment, in hell
377 *pained*; uncomfortable, ill
at ease; distressed, anxious,
anguished, troubled, disquiet-
ed, apprehensive, dismayed 854
nervous; worried, sick with
worry, in a state 316 *agitated*;
discomposed, disconcerted 63
disarranged; ill-used, maltreated 745 *subjected*; victimized,
sacrificed; stricken, wounded;
heavy-laden, crushed 684 *fatigued*; careworn, harassed,
woeful, woebegone, haggard,
wild-eyed.

(6) unhappy, infelicitous, unlucky, accursed 731 *unfortunate*; despairing 853 *hopeless*;
doomed 961 *condemned*; pitiable, poor, wretched, miserable; sad, melancholy, despondent, disconsolate; heartbroken, heavy-hearted, sick at
heart; sorrowing, sorrowful,
grieving, woebegone 834 *dejected*; grief-stricken, weeping,
weepy, wet-eyed, tearful, in
tears 836 *lamenting*; nostalgic,
longing 859 *desiring*; displeased, disappointed 829 *discontented*; offended, vexed, annoyed, pained 924
disapproving; piqued, mortified, chagrined, humiliated 891
resentful; sickened, disgusted,
nauseated 861 *disliking*; sorry,

remorseful, regretful 830
regretting.

Verb
(7) *suffer,* undergo, endure, go
through, experience 818 *feel;*
bear, put up with; suffer pain,
suffer torments; hurt oneself,
be hurt, smart, ache 377 *feel
pain;* wince, flinch, writhe,
squirm 251 *wriggle;* have a bad
time 731 *have trouble;* trouble
oneself, distress o., fuss, worry,
fret, agonize 318 *be agitated;*
mind, take it badly, take it to
heart; sorrow, grieve, weep 836
lament; pity oneself, be despondent 834 *be dejected;* have regrets 830 *regret.*

826
Pleasurableness

Noun
(1) *pleasurableness,* pleasures
of, pleasantness, delightfulness, attractiveness; sunny
side, bright s.; appeal 291 *attraction;* amiability, winsomeness, charm, fascination, enchantment, witchery, loveliness 841 *beauty;* a delight, a
treat, a joy 824 *joy;* interest,
pastime 837 *amusement;* melody, harmony 412 *music;* tastiness, deliciousness 392 *sweetness;* spice, zest, relish; balm
685 *refreshment;* peace, peace
and quiet, tranquillity 266 *quietude,* 681 *leisure;* pipedream
513 *fantasy.*

Adjective
(2) *pleasurable,* pleasant, nice,
good 837 *amusing;* pleasing,
agreeable, gratifying, flattering; acceptable, welcome, well-
liked, to one's taste, to one's
liking; wonderful, marvellous,
splendid 644 *excellent;* frictionless, painless 376 *comfortable;*
refreshing 683 *reposeful;* peaceful, quiet 266 *tranquil;* luxurious, voluptuous 376 *sensuous;*

genial, warm, sunny 833 *cheering;* delightful, delectable, delicious, exquisite, choice; luscious, juicy, tasty 390 *savoury;*
sugary 392 *sweet;* dulcet, musical, harmonious 410 *melodious;*
picturesque, scenic, lovely 841
beautiful; amiable, winning,
endearing 887 *lovable;* attractive, fetching, appealing, interesting 291 *attracting;* seductive, enticing, inviting,
captivating; charming, enchanting, bewitching, ravishing, haunting, thrilling, heart-
melting, heart-warming 821
exciting; homely, cosy; pastoral, idyllic; heavenly, blissful
824 *happy.*

Verb
(3) *please,* give pleasure; lull,
soothe 177 *assuage;* comfort 833
cheer; put at ease, make comfortable 831 *relieve;* gild the pill
392 *sweeten;* stroke, pat, pet 889
caress; indulge, pander to 734
be lax; charm, interest 837
amuse; rejoice, gladden, make
happy; gratify, satisfy, 828 *content;* bless, crown one's wishes.

(4) *delight,* rejoice, exhilarate,
elate, elevate, uplift; thrill, intoxicate, ravish 821 *excite;* regale, refresh; take one's fancy,
tickle, titillate, tease, tantalize; entrance, enrapture, enchant, charm 983 *bewitch;* allure, seduce 291 *attract.*

827
Painfulness

Noun
(1) *painfulness,* harshness,
roughness, harassment, persecution 735 *severity;* hurtfulness, harmfulness 645 *badness;*
disagreeableness, unpleasantness; loathsomeness, hatefulness, beastliness 616 *evil;* grimness 842 *ugliness;* friction,
chafing, irritation, inflammation, exacerbation 832 *aggravation;* soreness, tenderness 377

pain; irritability 822 *excitability*; sore point, rub, soft spot, sore, running s. 659 *bane*; disgust, nausea, sharpness, bitterness 393 *sourness*; bitter cup, bitter pill 731 *adversity*; tribulation, ordeal 825 *suffering*; trouble, care 825 *worry*; dreariness, cheerlessness; pitifulness, pathos; sorry sight, sad spectacle, object of pity; heavy news 825 *sorrow*; disenchantment, disillusion; hot water 700 *predicament*.

(2) *annoyance*, vexation, death of, pest, curse, plague 659 *bane*; botheration, embarrassment 825 *worry*; interference, nuisance, pinprick; burden, drag 702 *encumbrance*; grievance, complaint; hardship, troubles 616 *evil*; last straw, limit; offence, affront, insult, provocation 921 *indignity*; molestation, persecution 898 *malevolence*; displeasure, mortification 891 *resentment*; menace, enfant terrible.

Adjective
(3) *paining*, hurting, aching, sore, tender; agonizing, racking 377 *painful*; searing, burning, sharp, biting, gnawing, throbbing; caustic, corrosive, vitriolic; harsh, hard, rough, cruel 735 *severe*; gruelling, punishing; searching, excruciating; hurtful, harmful, poisonous 659 *baneful*.

(4) *unpleasant* unpleasing, disagreeable; uncomfortable, comfortless, joyless, dreary, dismal, depressing 834 *cheerless*; imattractive, uninviting, hideous 842 *ugly*; unwelcome 860 *unwanted*; thankless, displeasing 924 *disapproved*; disappointing 829 *discontenting*; distasteful, unpalatable 391 *unsavoury*; foul, nasty, horrible 645 *not nice*; bitter, sharp 393 *sour*;

obnoxious, offensive, objectionable, undesirable, odious, hateful, loathsome, nauseous, disgusting, repellent 861 *disliked*; execrable, accursed 645 *damnable*.

(5) *annoying*, troublesome, embarrassing, worrying; bothersome, wearisome, irksome, tiresome, boring 838 *tedious*; burdensome, onerous; disappointing, unfortunate, unlucky 731 *adverse*; awkward 702 *hindering*; importunate, pestering; teasing, irritating, vexatious, aggravating, provoking, maddening, infuriating; galling, stinging, biting, mortifying.

(6) *distressing*, afflicting, crushing, grievous; moving, affecting, touching; harrowing, heart-rending, tear-jerking; pathetic, tragic, sad, woeful, rueful, mournful, pitiful, lamentable, deplorable 905 *pitiable*; ghastly, grim, dreadful, shocking, appalling, horrifying, horrific, 854 *frightening*.

(7) *intolerable*, insufferable, not to be endured; impossible, insupportable, unbearable 32 *exorbitant*; past enduring, extreme.

Verb
(8) *hurt*, injure 645 *harm*; pain, cause p. 377 *give pain*; hurt one's feelings 655 *wound*; gall, pique, nettle, mortify 891 *huff*; pierce the heart, draw tears, grieve, afflict, distress 834 *sadden*; embitter, exacerbate, gnaw at, chafe, rankle, fester 832 *aggravate*; offend, affront 921 *not respect*.

(9) *torment*, harrow, rack 963 *torture*; maltreat, bait, bully, rag, persecute 735 *oppress*; snap at, bark at 885 *be rude*; beset, besiege 737 *demand*; haunt, obsess; tease, pester, plague, nag, badger, worry, henpeck,

harass; annoy, molest, bother, vex, provoke, peeve, ruffle, irritate, needle, sting, gall 891 *enrage.*

(10) *trouble,* discomfort, disquiet, disturb, agitate, upset 63 *derange*; worry, embarrass, perplex 474 *puzzle*; exercise, tire 684 *fatigue*; weary, bore 838 *be tedious*; obsess, haunt, bedevil; weigh upon one, deject 834 *depress*; thwart 702 *obstruct.*

(11) *displease,* not please, grate, jar, disagree with, grate on, jar on, get on one's nerves; disenchant, disillusion 509 *disappoint*; dissatisfy, aggrieve 829 *cause discontent*; offend, shock, horrify, scandalize, disgust, revolt, repel, sicken, nauseate 861 *cause dislike*; curdle the blood, appal 854 *frighten.*

828
Content

Noun
(1) *content,* contentment, contentedness, satisfaction, complacency; smugness 873 *vanity*; serenity, easy mind, peace of m., tranquillity 266 *quietude*; heart's ease, 376 *euphoria*; reconciliation 719 *pacification*; snugness, comfort, sitting pretty 730 *prosperity*; resignation 721 *submission.*

Adjective
(2) *content,* contented, satisfied, well-s. 824 *happy*; cosy, snug 376 *comfortable*; at ease 683 *reposeful*; with no regrets, easy in mind, smiling 833 *cheerful*; flattered 824 *pleased*; resigned, acquiescent 721 *submitting*; easily pleased, easygoing 736 *lenient*; untroubled, secure 660 *safe*; thankful 907 *grateful.*

(3) *contenting,* satisfying, satisfactory 635 *sufficient*; pacifying, appeasing 719 *pacificatory*; tolerable, passable, acceptable;

desirable, wished for 859 *desired.*

Verb
(4) *be content,* - happy etc. adj.; purr with content 824 *be pleased*; count one's blessings, be thankful 907 *be grateful*; have one's wish 730 *prosper*; be at ease, sitting pretty 376 *enjoy*; be reconciled 719 *make peace*; take comfort 831 *be relieved*; rest content, have no regrets.

(5) *content,* make contented, satisfy, gratify, make happy, make one's day 826 *please*; go down well 923 *be praised*; be kind to, comfort 833 *cheer*, 831 *relieve*; lull, set at ease, set at rest; propitiate, conciliate, appease 719 *pacify.*

Adverb
(6) *contentedly,* to one's heart's content.

829
Discontent

Noun
(1) *discontent,* displeasure, dissatisfaction 924 *disapprobation*; cold comfort; irritation, chagrin, pique, mortification, bitterness 891 *resentment*; uneasiness, disquiet 825 *worry*; grief 825 *sorrow*; strain, tension; restlessness, unrest, restiveness 738 *disobedience*; finickiness, perfectionism, nitpicking 862 *fastidiousness*; querulousness 912 *envy*; grievance, grudge, complaint 709 *quarrel*; weariness, melancholy, ennui 834 *dejection*; sulkiness, sulks, scowl, frown 893 *sullenness*; groan, curse 899 *malediction*; squeak, murmur 762 *deprecation.*

(2) *malcontent,* grumbler, grouser, complainer, whiner, bleater, bellyacher 834 *moper*; faultfinder, nit-picker, critic; dissident, dropout 738 *revolter.*

Adjective

(3) *discontented,* displeased, dissatisfied 924 *disapproving*; frustrated 509 *disappointed*; defeated 728 *unsuccessful*; malcontent, dissident 489 *dissenting*; restless, restive 738 *disobedient*; disgruntled, weary, browned off 838 *bored*, 825 *unhappy*; repining 830 *regretting*; uncomforted, unrelieved, disconsolate 834 *dejected*; ill-disposed, grudging, jealous, envious; bitter, embittered, soured 393 *sour*; peevish, testy, cross, sulky 893 *sullen*; grouchy, grumbling, whining, swearing 899 *cursing*; protesting 762 *deprecatory*; smarting, sore, insulted, affronted 891 *resentful*; fretful, querulous, petulant, complaining; hard to please, hard to satisfy, never satisfied 862 *fastidious*; faultfinding critical 926 *detracting*; hostile 881 *inimical*.

(4) *discontenting,* unsatisfying 636 *insufficient*; sickening, nauseating 861 *disliked*; boring 838 *tedious*; displeasing, upsetting, mortifying 827 *annoying*; frustrating 509 *disappointing*; baffling, obstructive 702 *hindering*; discouraging, disheartening.

Verb

(5) *be discontented,* be critical, carp, criticize, find fault 862 *be fastidious*; groan, jeer 924 *disapprove*; mind, take offence, take to heart 891 *resent*; sulk 893 *be sullen*; look glum 834 *be dejected*; moan, murmur, whine, bleat, protest, complain, object 762 *deprecate*; grumble, grouse, wail 836 *lament*; have a chip on one's shoulder, have a grievance, cherish a g., grudge 912 *envy*; repine 830 *regret*.

(6) *cause discontent,* dissatisfy 636 *not suffice*, 509 *disappoint*; spoil for one, get one down 834

depress; dishearten, discourage 613 *dissuade*; sour, embitter, upset, niggle, bite, irritate 891 *huff*; mortify 872 *humiliate*; offend, cause resentment 827 *displease*; shock, scandalize 924 *incur blame*; nauseate, sicken, disgust 861 *cause dislike*; make trouble, stir up t. 738 *revolt*.

830
Regret

Noun

(1) *regret,* regretfulness, regretting, repining; mortification 891 *resentment*; futile regret, soul-searching, self-reproach, remorse, contrition, repentance, compunction, qualms, regrets, apologies 939 *penitence*; disillusion, second thoughts; longing, homesickness, nostalgia 859 *desire*; matter of regret, pity of it.

Adjective

(2) *regretting,* missing, homesick, nostalgic, wistful; harking back 125 *retrospective*; repining, bitter 891 *resentful*; inconsolable 836 *lamenting*; regretful, remorseful, rueful, conscience-stricken; sorry, apologetic, penitent 939 *repentant*; undeceived, disillusioned, sadder and wiser.

(3) *regretted,* much r., sadly missed; regrettable, deplorable, too bad, a shame.

Verb

(4) *regret,* rue, deplore, curse one's folly, bite one's tongue; blame oneself, reproach o.; wish undone, repine, wring one's hands 836 *lament*; hark back 505 *retrospect*; look back, miss, sadly m., want back; long for, pine for, hanker after, be homesick 859 *desire*; express regrets, apologize, feel remorse, be sorry 939 *be penitent*; deplore, deprecate 891 *resent*.

831
Relief

Noun

(1) *relief,* rest 685 *refreshment*; easing, alleviation, mitigation, palliation, abatement 177 *moderation*; good riddance 668 *deliverance*; solace, consolation, comfort, ray of c., silver lining 852 *hope*; feeling better 656 *revival*; salve 658 *balm*; painkiller, analgesic 375 *anaesthetic*; sedative, sleeping pill 679 *soporific*; pillow 218 *cushion*; ray of sunshine.

Adjective

(2) *relieving,* lulling, soothing 685 *refreshing*; pain-killing, analgesic, anodyne 177 *lenitive*; curative, restorative 658 *remedial*; consoling, consolatory, comforting.

Verb

(3) *relieve,* ease, soften, cushion; relax, lessen the strain; temper 177 *moderate*; lift, lighten, unburden 701 *disencumber*; spare, exempt from 919 *exempt*; console, dry one's eyes, solace, comfort, bring c., give hope; cheer up, buck up, encourage, hearten 833 *cheer*; shade, cool 685 *refresh*; restore 656 *cure*; calm, soothe, nurse; palliate, mitigate, moderate, alleviate 177 *assuage*; smooth one's brow, stroke 889 *caress*; cradle, lull, put to sleep 679 *sleep*; anaesthetize 375 *render insensible*.

(4) *be relieved,* obtain relief; breathe again; console oneself, take comfort, feel better, dry one's eyes 833 *be cheerful*; get over it, pull oneself together, be oneself again; sleep off 656 *be restored*.

832
Aggravation

Noun

(1) *aggravation,* exacerbation, exasperation; intensification, heightening, deepening, adding to, making worse 655 *deterioration*; complication 700 *difficulty*; irritant 821 *excitant*.

Adjective

(2) *aggravated,* exacerbated, complicated; unrelieved, unmitigated, intensified, make worse 655 *deteriorated*;

Verb

(3) *aggravate,* intensify 162 *strengthen*; enhance, heighten, deepen; worsen, make worse 655 *deteriorate*; not improve matters, rub it in; exacerbate, embitter, sour, envenom, inflame 821 *excite*; exasperate 891 *enrage*; complicate, make bad worse.

Adverb

(4) *aggravatedly,* worse and worse, from bad to worse.

833
Cheerfulness

Noun

(1) *cheerfulness,* alacrity 597 *willingness*; optimism, hopefulness 852 *hope*; cheeriness, happiness, lightheartedness 824 *joy*; geniality, sunniness, breeziness, smiles, good humour; vitality, animal spirits, high s., joie de vivre; light heart, carefree mind 828 *content*; liveliness, sparkle, vivacity, animation 822 *excitable state*; conviviality 882 *sociability*; optimist, perennial o., Pollyanna.

(2) *merriment,* laughter and joy; cheer, good c.; exhilaration, high spirits, abandon; jollity,

joviality, jocularity, gaiety, hilarity 835 *laughter*; levity, frivolity 499 *folly*; merry-making, fun, fun and games, sport, good s. 837 *amusement*; jubilation 876 *celebration*.

Adjective

(3) *cheerful,* cheery, blithe 824 *happy*; hearty, genial, convivial 882 *sociable*; sanguine, optimistic, rose-coloured; smiling, sunny, bright, beaming, radiant 835 *laughing*; breezy, in high spirits, in good heart, optimistic, upbeat, hopeful, buoyant, resilient, irrepressible; carefree, light-hearted, happy-go-lucky; debonair, bonny, buxom, bouncing; pert, jaunty, perky, chirpy, spry, spirited, sprightly, vivacious, animated, sparkling 819 *lively*.

(4) *merry,* joyous, joyful, ebullient, effervescent, sparkling; waggish, jocular 839 *witty*; gay, frivolous 456 *light-minded*; playful, sportive, frisky, frolicsome, kittenish 837 *amusing*; roguish, arch, full of tricks; merry-making, mirthful, jocund, jovial, jolly, joking, dancing, laughing, singing, drinking, shouting, hilarious, uproarious, rip-roaring, rollicking 837 *amused*.

(5) *jubilant,* overjoyed, gleeful, delighted 824 *pleased*; elated, flushed, exultant, triumphant, cock-a-hoop 727 *successful*; triumphing, celebrating 876 *celebratory*.

(6) *cheering,* warming, heart-w., exhilarating, intoxicating 821 *exciting*; optimistic, tonic; comforting, balmy, bracing, invigorating 652 *salubrious*.

Verb

(7) *be cheerful* keep cheerful, look on the bright side 852 *hope*; keep one's spirits up 599 *be resolute*; take heart, cheer up, perk up 831 *be relieved*;

brighten, liven up, grow animated, let oneself go; smile, beam, sparkle; dance, sing, whistle, laugh 835 *rejoice*; whoop, cheer 876 *celebrate*; frisk, frolic, gambol, enjoy oneself, 837 *amuse oneself*.

(8) *cheer,* gladden, warm the heart 828 *content*; comfort, console 831 *relieve*; rejoice 826 *please*; inspire, enliven 821 *animate*; exhilarate, elate 826 *delight*; encourage, hearten, raise the spirits, put in good humour; bolster up 855 *give courage*; energize 174 *invigorate*.

Adverb

(9) *cheerfully,* willingly etc. adj.; allegro; without a care.

834
Dejection
seriousness

Noun

(1) *dejection,* unhappiness, cheerlessness, despondency, dreariness, dejectedness, dispiritedness, low spirits, dumps, doldrums; sinking heart; disillusion 509 *disappointment*; defeatism, pessimism, cynicism, despair 853 *hopelessness*; weariness, exhaustion 684 *fatigue*; heartache, heaviness, sadness, misery, wretchedness 825 *sorrow*; gloominess, gloom, glumness, long face; trouble 825 *worry*.

(2) *melancholy,* melancholia, hypochondria; depression, black mood; blues, moping, sighing, sigh 829 *discontent*; angst, nostalgia, homesickness 825 *suffering*.

(3) *seriousness,* earnestness; gravity, solemnity, sobriety, demureness, staidness; sternness, grimness 893 *sullenness*; primness, humourlessness, heaviness, dullness; straight face, poker f.,

(4) *moper,* complainer 829 *malcontent*; sourpuss, crosspatch, bear with a sore head; pessimist, damper, wet blanket, spoilsport, killjoy, misery; hypochondriac.

Adjective
(5) *dejected,* joyless, dreary, unhappy, gloomy, despondent, downbeat, pessimistic, defeatist, despairing 853 *hopeless*; discouraged, disheartened, dismayed 728 *defeated*; dispirited, unnerved, troubled, worried 825 *suffering*; downcast, downhearted, low, down, low-spirited, depressed; out of sorts, out of spirits, not oneself; sluggish, listless, spiritless, lackadaisical 679 *inactive*; lacklustre 419 *dim*; humbled, crushed, crestfallen 509 *disappointed*; browned off 829 *discontented*; chastened, sobered, subdued 830 *regretting*; vexed, chagrined; disillusioned 509 *disappointed*.

(6) *melancholic,* blue, feeling blue; thoughtful, pensive, melancholy, sad, saddened, heavyhearted, sick at heart 825 *unhappy*; sorry, rueful 830 *regretting*; mournful, doleful, woeful, tearful 836 *lamenting*; forlorn, miserable, wretched, disconsolate; sorry for oneself, self-pitying, moody, sulking 893 *sullen*; dull, dismal, gloomy, morose, glum, long-faced, woebegone; wan, haggard, careworn.

(7) *serious,* sober, solemn, sedate, stolid, staid, demure, grave, stern, Puritanical 735 *severe*; unsmiling, sour, dour, Puritan, grim, frowning, forbidding, saturnine 893 *sullen*; inscrutable, straight-faced, poker-f., deadpan; prim, humourless; heavy, dull, solid 838 *tedious*; chastening, sobering.

(8) *cheerless,* comfortless, unrelieved, dreary, dull, flat 838 *tedious*; uncongenial, uninviting, dismal, lugubrious, funereal, gloomy, dark, forbidding; depressing, drab, grey, sombre, overcast.

Verb
(9) *be dejected,* lose heart, admit defeat 853 *despair*; languish, sink, droop, sag, wilt, flag 684 *be fatigued*; look downcast, hang one's head, mope, brood 449 *think*; take to heart, sulk 893 *be sullen*; yearn, long 859 *desire*; sigh, grieve 829 *be discontented*; groan 825 *suffer*; weep 836 *lament*; repine 830 *regret*.

(10) *be serious,* keep a straight face, repress a smile; sober up; look grave, look glum; lack sparkle, lack humour, take oneself too seriously 838 *be tedious*;

(11) *sadden,* grieve, bring sorrow; break one's heart, make one's heart bleed; draw tears, touch, melt 821 *impress*; annoy, pain 829 *cause discontent*; drive to despair 853 *leave no hope*; crush, overwhelm, prostrate; orphan, bereave 786 *deprive*.

(12) *depress,* deject, get one down; dismay, dishearten, discourage, dispirit; unnerve 854 *frighten*; cast a gloom over, cast a shadow 418 *darken*; damp, dampen, throw cold water on, 613 *dissuade*; dash one's hopes 509 *disappoint*; dull the spirits, weigh heavy on; disgust 827 *displease*; strain, weary 684 *fatigue*; bore 838 *be tedious*; chasten, sober 534 *teach*.

835
Rejoicing

Noun
(1) *rejoicing* jubilation 837 *festivity*; jubilee, triumph, exulta-

tion 876 *celebration*; felicitation, congratulations; clapping 923 *applause*; cheers, rousing c., three c., hosanna, hallelujah 923 *praise*; thanksgiving 907 *thanks*; raptures, elation 824 *joy*; revelling, revels 837 *revel*; merrymaking, abandonment 833 *merriment*.

(2) *laughter*, risibility; hearty laughter, roar of l., shout of l., peal of l., shrieks of l., gales of l.; mocking l., derision 851 *ridicule*; laugh, guffaw, chuckle, chortle, cackle, crow; giggle, snigger, titter; fit of laughter, the giggles; smile, simper, smirk, grin, broad g.; twinkle, half-smile; humour, sense of h. 839 *wit*; laughing matter, comedy, farce 497 *absurdity*.

(3) *laugher*, - grinner etc. vb.; mocker 926 *detractor*; rejoicer 837 *reveller*; Cheshire cat.

Adjective
(4) *rejoicing*, - revelling etc. vb.; exultant, flushed, elated 833 *jubilant*; lyrical, ecstatic 923 *approving*.

(5) *laughing*, - chuckling etc. vb.; creased, doubled up; mocking 851 *derisive*; laughable, risible, derisory 849 *ridiculous*; humorous, comic, comical, funny, farcical 497 *absurd*.

Verb
(6) *rejoice*, be joyful, sing for joy, shout for j., dance for j., skip 312 *leap*; clap, whoop, cheer 923 *applaud*; shout 408 *vociferate*; carol 413 *sing*; sing paeans 923 *praise*; exult, crow 876 *celebrate*; felicitate 886 *congratulate*; give thanks 907 *thank*; abandon oneself, let oneself go, make merry 833 *be cheerful*; frolic, frisk 837 *revel*; have a party celebrate 882 *be sociable*; feel pleased, congratulate oneself, rub one's hands, gloat 824 *be pleased*; sigh for pleasure, cry for joy.

(7) *laugh*, start laughing, burst out l., get the giggles, hoot, chuckle, chortle, crow, cackle; giggle, snigger, titter; make merry over, laugh ' at, mock, deride 851 *ridicule*; shriek with laughter, roar with l., fall about, roll around, hold one's sides, split one's s. laugh fit to burst.

(8) *smile*, break into a s.; grin, grimace, curl one's lips, smirk, simper; twinkle, beam, flash a smile.

Interjection
(9) cheers! three c.! hooray! hurrah! hallelujah!

836
Lamentation

Noun
(1) *lamentation*, lamenting, wail, groaning, weeping, wailing tearing one's hair; mourning, deep m. 364 *obsequies*; crying, - sobbing etc. vb.; tears, tearfulness 834 *dejection*; wet eyes, red e., swollen e.; falling tears, flood of t.; breakdown, hysterics; cry, good c.; sob, sigh, groan, moan, whimper, whine, grizzle, bawl.

(2) *lament*, plaint, complaint, dirge, knell, requiem, elegy, death song, swansong; keen, wake 905 *condolence*; howl, shriek, scream 409 *ululation*; tears of grief, tears of rage; sobstory, tale of woe; show of grief, crocodile tears 542 *sham*.

(3) *weeper*, wailer, keener, mourner 364 *funeral*; sigher, sniveller, whiner, crybaby; complainer, grouser 829 *malcontent*.

Adjective
(4) *lamenting*, - crying etc. vb.; in tears, bathed in t., tearful, lachrymose; wet-eyed, red-e.; close to tears, ready to cry; mourning, mournful, doleful,

lugubrious 825 *unhappy*; woeful, woebegone, wild-eyed 834
dejected; complaining, plaintive; in mourning, in black, at
half-mast; whining, fretful,
querulous; pathetic, pitiful, lamentable, tear-jerking 905 *pitiable*; lamented, deplorable 830
regretted.

Verb
(5) *lament,* grieve, sorrow, sigh,
heave a s. 825 *suffer*; deplore
830 *regret*; condole, commiserate 905 *pity*; grieve for, sigh for,
weep over, cry o., bewail, bemoan; mourn, wail, keen; express grief, put on black, go into
mourning; wring one's hands,
beat one's breast, tear one's
hair; take on, take it badly;
complain, grouse 829 *be
discontented*.

(6) *weep,* wail; shed tears, burst
into t., dissolve in t.; break
down, cry, bawl, howl, cry one's
eyes out; scream, shriek 409
ululate; sob, sigh, moan, groan
825 *suffer*; snivel, grizzle, blubber, pule, whine, whinge,
whimper.

Adverb
(7) *tearfully,* painfully.

837
Amusement

Noun
(1) *amusement,* pleasure, interest, delight, diversion, entertainment, light e.; pastime,
hobby; solace, recreation 685
refreshment; relaxation 683 *repose*; holiday, Bank h. 681 *leisure*; play, sport, fun, good
clean f., jollity 833 *merriment*;
occasion, do, show, junket 876
celebration; outing, excursion,
jaunt, pleasure trip; treat, Sunday school t., picnic; garden
party, fete 74 *assembly*; game,
game of chance, game of skill.

(2) *festivity,* holidaying, playtime, fun 824 *enjoyment*; social
whirl, round of pleasure, good
time, high life, night l.; festival,
fair, funfair, carnival, fiesta,
gala; festivities, fun and games,
merrymaking, revels, Saturnalia, Mardi Gras 833 *merriment*;
feast day, 876 *special day*; carousal, wassail 301 *feasting*;
conviviality, party 882 *social
gathering*; orgy, carouse 949
drunkenness; barbecue, harvest supper, dinner, banquet
301 *meal*.

(3) *revel,* knees-up, jollification,
whoopee, fun, high old time;
night out, spree, junketing,
horseplay; play, game, romp,
frolic, lark, skylarking, escapade, antic, prank, rag, trick
497 *foolery*.

(4) *pleasure ground,* park, chase,
gardens, pleasure g.; green, village g., common; arbour, seaside, Riviera, holiday camp;
playground, playing field 724
arena; circus, fair; swing,
roundabout, seesaw, slide.

(5) *place of amusement,* fairground, funfair, amusement arcade; skittle alley, billiard
room, pool r., assembly r., pump
r.; concert hall, picture house
445 *cinema*; playhouse 594
theatre; ballroom, dance hall,
discotheque, disco; cabaret,
night club; bingo hall, casino
618 *gaming-house*.

(6) *sport,* outdoor life; sportsmanship 694 *skill*; sports, field
s., track events; games, gymnastics 162 *athletics*, 716 *contest, racing, pugilism, wrestling*; cycling, hiking,
rambling, orienteering, camping, running, jogging; riding,
pony-trekking; archery, shooting, fishing, hunting 619 *chase*;
water sports, swimming, surf-
riding, wind surfing; skin diving, water skiing, aquaplaning,

boating, sailing 269 *aquatics*; rock-climbing, mountaineering 308 *ascent*; exploring, caving, speleology; winter sports, skiing, bobsleighing, tobogganning, luging, skating, ice s., ice hockey; flying, gliding, hang g. 271 *aeronautics*; tourism, touring, travelling 267 *land travel.*

(7) *ball game,* cricket, French c.; baseball, softball, rounders; tennis, table t., badminton, squash; handball, volleyball; netball, basketball; football, soccer; Rugby football, R. Union, R. League; lacrosse, hockey, polo, water polo; croquet, golf; skittles, bowls, curling; billiards, snooker, pool.

(8) *indoor game,* parlour g., panel g., party g.; forfeits, quiz, charades, I-spy; word game, riddles, crosswords, acrostics; darts, dominoes, mah jong, tiddly-winks, jigsaw puzzle.

(9) *board game,* chess, draughts, checkers, Chinese c., backgammon; ludo.

(10) *children's games,* skipping, jumping, leapfrog, hopscotch 312 *leap*; touch, tag, he; hide-and-seek, blind man's buff.

(11) *card game,* cards, game of cards, rubber; whist *or* bridge; bezique, rummy, canasta; solo, solitaire, patience; snap, Happy Families, lotto, bingo; pontoon, brag, poker, baccarat.

(12) *gambling game,* dice, dicing; roulette; coin-spinning, heads and tails; raffle, tombola 618 *gambling.*

(13) *dancing,* dance, ball, masquerade; square dance, ceilidh, hop, jam session, disco; ballet dancing, classical d. 594 *ballet*; country dancing, old-time d., sequence d., ballroom d.; eurhythmics.

(14) *dance,* clog d., tap d., toe d.; high kicks, cancan; gipsy dance, flamenco; country dance, morris d., barn d., square d.; sailor's dance, hornpipe; folk dance, polonaise, mazurka, jig, reel, Highland fling; gavotte, quadrille, minuet, pavane, polka, waltz; foxtrot, quickstep; Charleston, two-step, tango, rumba, samba, conga, cha-cha; hokey-cokey; bop, bebop, jive, rock 'n' roll; dancer 312 *jumper*; ballerina, 594 *actor*; high-kicker 594 *entertainer.* disco dancer

(15) *plaything,* bauble, knick-knack, trinket, toy 639 *bauble*; teddy bear, doll; top, yo-yo, marbles; ball, balloon 252 *sphere*; skipping rope, stilts, rocking horse, tricycle; roller skates, skateboard, surfboard; popgun, water pistol; model, bricks, clockwork; peep show, puppet show, marionettes 551 *image*; cards, pack, deck; domino, draught, counter, chip; tiddly-wink; chess piece, pawn.

(16) *player* sportsman *or* - woman; competitor 716 *contender*; games-player, all-rounder; ball-player, footballer, forward, striker, defence, goalkeeper; cricketer, batsman, fielder, wicket-keeper, bowler; hockey-player etc. n.; marksman, archer 287 *shooter*; shot-putter 287 *thrower*; dicer 618 *gambler*; card-player, chess-p.; playmate 707 *colleague.*

(17) *reveller,* merry-maker; drinker 949 *drunkard*; feaster 301 *eater*; party-goer 882 *sociable person*; playboy, good-time girl; debauchee 952 *libertine*; holidaymaker, excursionist, tourist 268 *traveller*; master of ceremonies, MC, toastmaster.

Adjective
(18) *amusing,* - entertaining etc. vb.; sportive, full of fun 833

merry; pleasant 826 *pleasurable*; laughable, clownish 849 *funny*; recreational 685 *refreshing*; festal, festive, holiday.

(19) *amused,* entertained, tickled 824 *pleased*; having fun, festive, sportive, rollicking, playful, kittenish, roguish, waggish, jolly, jovial; in festive mood, in holiday spirit 835 *rejoicing*; horsy, sporty, sporting, games-playing 162 *athletic*; disporting oneself, playing, at play; easy to please.

Verb

(20) *amuse,* interest, entertain, beguile, divert, tickle, make one laugh, titillate, please 826 *delight*; recreate 685 *refresh*; solace, enliven 833 *cheer*; treat, regale, take out; raise a smile 849 *be ridiculous*; humour, keep amused; give a party 882 *be hospitable*; be a sport, be great fun.

(21) *amuse oneself,* while away time pass the t. 681 *have leisure*; pursue one's hobby, dabble in; play, play at, have fun, enjoy oneself 833 *be cheerful*; take a holiday, have an outing; sport, disport oneself; dally, toy, wanton; frisk, frolic, romp, gambol, caper; play tricks, play pranks, lark around, skylark, fool about, play the fool 497 *be absurd*; jest, jape 839 *be witty*; play cards, dice 618 *gamble*; play games, camp, picnic; sail, yacht, fly; hunt, shoot, fish; ride, trek, hike, ramble; run, race, jump; bathe, swim, dive; skate, ski, toboggan.

(22) *dance,* go dancing; waltz, tango etc. n.; jive, twist, rock 'n' roll; whirl 315 *rotate*; cavort, caper, jig about 312 *leap*.

(23) *revel,* make merry, make whoopee, celebrate 835 *rejoice*; let oneself go, let one's hair down, let off steam; live it up

have a night out; feast, banquet, carouse 301 *drink*.

Interjection

(24) carpe diem! eat drink and be merry!

838
Tedium

Noun

(1) *tedium,* ennui 834 *melancholy*; lack of interest 860 *indifference*; weariness, languor 684 *fatigue*; wearisomeness, tediousness, irksomeness; dryness, stodginess stuffiness, heaviness 840 *dullness*; loathing, nausea 861 *dislike*; flatness, staleness 387 *insipidity*; longueurs, prolixity 570 *diffuseness*; monotony 16 *uniformity*; time to kill 679 *inactivity*.

(2) *bore,* utter b., no fun; boring thing, drag, bind, chore; dull work, boring w.; beaten track, daily round 610 *habit*; grindstone, treadmill 682 *labour*; boring person, drip, wet blanket, misery 834 *moper*.

Adjective

(3) *tedious,* uneventful, uninteresting, unexciting, slow, dragging, leaden, heavy; dry, flat, stale, insipid 387 *tasteless*; bald 573 *plain*; humdrum, soulless, dreary, stuffy 840 *dull*; stodgy, prosaic, uninspired; long, overlong, long-winded, drawn out 570 *prolix*; drowsy, 679 *soporific*; boring, wearisome, tiresome, irksome; wearing 684 *fatiguing*; repetitive, repetitious 106 *repeated*; same, invariable, monotonous 16 *uniform*; too much, cloying, satiating; disgusting, nauseating.

(4) *bored,* twiddling one's thumbs 679 *inactive*; browned off, fed up 829 *discontented*; stale, weary, jaded 684 *fatigued*; world-weary 834 *melancholic*; blasé, uninterested 860

indifferent; satiated, cloyed 863 *sated*; nauseated, sick of, sick and tired, fed up, loathing 861 *disliking*.

Verb
(5) *be tedious,* pall, lose its novelty, cloy 863 *sate*; nauseate, sicken, disgust 861 *cause dislike*; bore, irk, try, weary 684 *fatigue*; bore to tears, bore stiff; tire out, wear o.; get one down, try one's patience; fail to interest, make one yawn, drag 278 *move slowly*; harp on 106 *repeat oneself*.

Adverb
(6) *boringly,* ad nauseam, to death.

839
Wit

Noun
(1) *wit,* wittiness, pointedness, smartness; esprit, ready wit; sparkle, brightness 498 *intelligence*; humour, sense of h.; wry h., dryness, slyness; drollery, pleasantry, waggishness, facetiousness; jocularity, jocoseness 833 *merriment*; comicalness, absurdity; joking, practical j., jesting, clowning, comic turn 497 *foolery*; broad humour, vulgarity 847 *bad taste*; farce, slapstick, high camp; whimsicality 604 *whim*; cartoon, comic strip, caricature; biting wit, cruel humour, satire, sarcasm 851 *ridicule*; irony 850 *affectation*; black comedy, gallows humour; wordplay, punning.

(2) *witticism,* witty remark, stroke of wit, sally, mot, bon mot, epigram, conceit; pun, play upon words 518 *equivocalness*; feed line, punch l., throwaway l.; banter, chaff, badinage, persiflage; retort, repartee, backchat; sarcasm 851 *satire*; joke, standing j.;

jest, quip, gag, crack, wisecrack, one-liner; old joke, corny j., chestnut, bromide; practical joke, hoax, leg pull; dirty joke, blue j., sick j.; story, funny s., shaggy-dog s.; limerick, clerihew.

(3) *humorist,* wit, card, character, wag, wisecracker, joker; pratical joker, leg-puller, teaser; mocker, scoffer, lampooner 926 *detractor*; comedian, comedienne, comic 594 *entertainer*; cartoonist, caricaturist, parodist, raconteur; jester, court j., clown 501 *fool*.

Adjective
(4) *witty,* nimble-witted, quick; pointed, epigrammatic; brilliant, sparkling, smart, clever 498 *intelligent*; salty, racy, piquant, risque; biting, keen, sharp, sarcastic; ironic, dry, sly, pawky; facetious, flippant 456 *light-minded*; jocular, jocose, joking, waggish, roguish; lively, gay 833 *merry*; comic, rib-tickling 849 *funny*; comical, humorous, droll; whimsical 604 *capricious*; playful, sportive 497 *absurd*.

Verb
(5) *be witty,* scintillate, sparkle, flash; jest, joke, crack a j., quip, gag, wisecrack; raise a laugh 837 *amuse*; pun, make a p., play on words, equivocate 518 *be equivocal*; fool, jape 497 *be absurd*; play with, tease, chaff, rag, banter, twit, pull one's leg, have one on, make merry with, make fun of, poke fun at 851 *ridicule*; ham up, camp up; mock, caricature, burlesque 851 *satirize*; retort, flash back, come back at 460 *answer*; enjoy a joke, see the point.

Adverb
(6) *in jest,* in fun, in sport, with tongue in cheek.

840
Dullness

Noun

(1) *dullness,* stuffiness, dreariness, deadliness; monotony 838 *tedium*; drabness, lack of inspiration, lack of sparkle; stodginess, staleness, flatness 387 *insipidity*; banality, triteness; lack of humour, primness 834 *seriousness*; matter of fact 573 *plainness.*

Adjective

(2) *dull,* unamusing, unstimulating; deadly dull, stuffy, dreary; pointless, meaningless 838 *tedious*; colourless, drab; flat, bland, vapid, insipid 387 *tasteless*; unimaginative, unoriginal, superficial; humourless, grave, prim, frumpish 834 *serious*; lacking wit 576 *inelegant*; heavy-footed, clod-hopping, ponderous, sluggish 278 *slow*; stodgy, prosaic, pedestrian, unreadable, stale, banal, commonplace, trite 610 *usual.*

Verb

(3) *be dull,* drone on, bore 838 *be tedious*; not see the joke.

841
Beauty

Noun

(1) *beauty,* sublimity 646 *perfection*; grandeur, magnificence, nobility; splendour, gorgeousness, brilliance, brightness, radiance 417 *light*; ornament 844 *ornamentation*; scenic beauty, scenery, view 445 *spectacle*; form, fair proportions, regular features 245- *symmetry*; physical beauty, loveliness, comeliness, fairness, handsomeness, prettiness; charm, appeal, sex a., glamour; attractions, charms, graces; good looks, pretty face, shapeliness; gracefulness, elegance, grace; style,

dress sense 848 *fashion*; delicacy, refinement 846 *good taste*; aesthetics.

(2) *a beauty,* thing of beauty, work of art; garden, beauty spot; jewel, pearl 646 *paragon*; rose, lily; belle, raving beauty 890 *favourite*; beauty queen, bathing belle, cover girl, pinup; hunk, Mr Universe; blond(e), brunette, redhead; English rose; dream, vision, poem, picture, perfect p.; a lovely, charmer, dazzler, heartthrob; femme fatale, siren, witch.

Adjective

(3) *beautiful,* beauteous, of beauty; lovely, fair, bright, radiant; comely, goodly, bonny, pretty, sweet; handsome, good-looking, photogenic; well-built, well-set-up, husky, manly; tall, dark and handsome; gracious, stately, majestic, statuesque, Junoesque; adorable, divine; picturesque, scenic, ornamental; landscaped, well laid-out; artistic, harmonious; curious, quaint 694 *well-made*; aesthetic 846 *tasteful*; exquisite, choice 646 *perfect.*

(4) *splendid,* sublime, heavenly, superb, fine 644 *excellent*; grand, noble; glorious, ravishing, rich, gorgeous 425 *florid*; bright, resplendent, radiant 417 *radiating*; glossy, magnificent 875 *showy*; ornate 844 *ornamented.*

(5) *shapely,* well-proportioned, regular, classic 245 *symmetrical*; well-formed, well-turned; buxom, curvaceous 248 *curved*; clean-limbed, straight-l., slender, slim, lissom, svelte, willowy 206 *lean*; graceful, elegant, chic; petite, dainty, delicate.

(6) *personable,* prepossessing, agreeable; attractive, fetching 826 *pleasurable*; sexy, kissable;

charming, entrancing, enchanting, glamorous; winsome 887 *lovable*; fresh-faced, cleancut, wholesome; lusty, blooming, ruddy 431 *red*; rosy, bright-eyed; sightly, becoming, passable, presentable, neat, tidy, trim; spruce, snappy, dapper, glossy, sleek; well-dressed, well turned out, smart, stylish, soigne(e) 848 *fashionable*; elegant, refined 846 *tasteful*.

Verb

(7) *be beautiful* - splendid etc. adj.; photograph well, have good looks; bloom, glow, dazzle 417 *shine*.

(8) *beautify,* improve; brighten 417 *make bright*; tattoo 844 *decorate*; set off, grace, suit, become, go well, show one off, flatter; glamorize, transfigure; give a face-lift, smarten up; powder, rouge 843 *primp*.

842
Ugliness

Noun

(1) *ugliness,* hideousness, repulsiveness; lack of beauty, gracelessness, lumpishness, clumsiness 576 *inelegance*; want of symmetry 246 *distortion*; deformity, mutilation, disfigurement 845 *blemish*; squalor 649 *uncleanness*; homeliness, plainness, no beauty, no oil painting; grim look 893 *sullenness*; haggardness, wrinkles 131 *age*.

(2) *eyesore,* blot, patch 845 *blemish*; ugly person, fright, sight, frump, scarecrow; death's-head, gargoyle, grotesque, monster; harridan, witch; ugly duckling; Beast.

Adjective

(3) *ugly,* lacking beauty, unlovely; hideous 649 *unclean*; frightful, shocking, monstrous; repulsive, repellent, loathsome 861 *disliked*; beastly, nasty 645

not nice; homely, plain, unprepossessing, not much to look at; mousy, frumpish, frumpy; forbidding, ill-favoured, hard-featured, villainous, grim-visaged 893 *sullen*.

(4) *unsightly,* faded, worn, ravaged, wrinkled 131 *ageing*; marred 845 *blemished*; shapeless, irregular 244 *amorphous*; grotesque, twisted, deformed, disfigured 246 *distorted*; defaced, vandalized, litterstrewn; badly made, misshapen; dumpy, squat 196 *dwarfish*; bloated 195 *fleshy*; stained, discoloured; grisly, gruesome.

(5) *graceless,* ungraceful, inelegant; inartistic; unflattering, unbecoming; dingy, poky, dreary, drab; lank, dull, mousy; dowdy, garish, unattractive, badly dressed; gaudy; coarse 847 *vulgar*; rude, crude, uncouth 699 *artless*; clumsy, awkward, ungainly 195 *unwieldy*.

Verb

(6) *be ugly,* lack beauty, have no looks, lose one's l.; fade, wither, age, show one's a. 131 *grow old*; look a wreck, look a mess, look a fright.

(7) *make ugly,* uglify; spoil, deface, disfigure, mar, blemish, blot; misshape 244 *deform*; grimace 893 *be sullen*; twist 246 *distort*; mutilate, vandalize 655 *impair*.

843
Beautification

Noun

(1) *beautification,* beautifying 844 *ornamentation*; plastic surgery, cosmetic s. 658 *surgery*; beauty treatment, facial, massage, manicure, pedicure; suntanning, sun lamp; toilet, grooming, make-up.

(2) *hairdressing,* shaving, clipping, trimming; depilation,

plucking; shave, hair cut, clip, trim; tinting, highlights, bleaching, dyeing; hair style, coiffure, crop, bob; styling, hairdo, shampoo, set, wave, blow w., permanent w., perm; curl 251 *coil*; fringe, ponytail 259 *hair*; false hair, hairpiece, toupee, switch, wig; curlers, rollers.

(3) *cosmetic,* beautifier, aid to beauty; make-up, paint, greasepaint, rouge; cream 357 *unguent*; lipstick, lip gloss; nail polish, nail varnish, powder, face p., talcum p.; mascara, eye shadow, eyeliner; antiperspirant, deodorant; scent, perfume, toilet water, aftershave; powder puff, compact; shaver, razor, depilatory; toiletries.

(4) *beauty parlour,* beauty salon, boudoir.

(5) *beautician,* plastic surgeon; make-up artist, cosmetician; tattooer; barber, hairdresser, hair stylist, coiffeur, manicurist, chiropodist.

Adjective
(6) *beautified,* transfigured, transformed; made-up, rouged, painted, powdered, scented; curled, bouffant; primped, dolled up 841 *beautiful*.

Verb
(7) *primp,* prettify, doll up, dress up, ornament 844 *decorate*; prink, prank, trick out; preen, titivate, make up, rouge, paint, shadow, highlight; powder; shave; curl, wave 841 *beautify*.

844
Ornamentation

Noun
(1) *ornamentation,* decoration, adornment, garnish; ornateness, baroque, rococo; richness, gilt, gaudiness 875 *ostentation*;

enhancement, enrichment, embellishment; setting, background; centrepiece; nosegay, buttonhole; object d'art, bric-a-brac, curio.

(2) *ornamental art,* gardening, landscape g. topiary; architecture; interior decoration; statuary 554 *sculpture*; frieze, dado; cornice, gargoyle; moulding, beading, fretting, tracery; varnishing 226 *facing*; ormolu, gilding, gilt, gold leaf; lettering, illumination, illustration 551 *art*; stained glass; tie-dyeing, batik; heraldic art 547 *heraldry*; tattooing; etching 555 *engraving*; handiwork, handicraft, fancywork, filigree; whittling, carving; enamelling, marquetry 437 *variegation*; metalwork, cut glass, wrought iron.

(3) *pattern,* motif, print, design, composition 331 *structure*; detail, tracery, arabesque, flourish, curlicue 251 *coil*; swag, festoon; weave 331 *texture*; chevron, check 437 *chequer*; pin-stripe 437 *stripe*; spot, polka dot 437 *maculation*; herringbone, zigzag 220 *obliquity*; watermark.

(4) *needlework,* tapestry; cross-stitch, sampler; patchwork, applique; embroidery, smocking; crochet, lace, tatting, knitting 222 *network*.

(5) *trimming,* piping, border, fringe, frieze, frill, flounce 234 *edging*; binding, braid; rosette, cockade 547 *badge*; bow 47 *fastening*; tassel, pompom; plume, streamer, ribbon.

(6) *finery,* Sunday best 228 *clothing*; tinsel, spangle, sequin 639 *bauble*.

(7) *jewellery,* diadem, tiara 743 *regalia*; pendant, locket; amulet, charm 983 *talisman*; necklace, choker; armlet, anklet,

bracelet, bangle; ring, earring; brooch, stud, pin 47 *fastening*; medal, medallion.

(8) *gem,* jewel; precious stone, semiprecious s.; brilliant, sparkler, diamond; ruby, pearl, opal, sapphire, turquoise, emerald, garnet, amethyst, topaz; jet, jade, agate; coral, ivory, mother of pearl, amber.

Adjective
(9) *ornamental,* decorative, fancy, intricate, elaborate, quaint; picturesque, scenic, geometric.

(10) *ornamented,* richly o., adorned, decorated, embellished, ornate; picked out 437 *variegated*; patterned, mosaic, inlaid, enamelled, worked, embroidered, trimmed; wreathed, festooned, garlanded; overdone 847 *vulgar*; plush, gilt, gilded 800 *rich*; gorgeous, garish, glittering, flashy, gaudy 875 *showy*.

(11) *bedecked,* groomed, got up, togged up, wearing, sporting; decked out, looking one's best; in full fig, dolled up 843 *beautified*; tarted up, festooned, studded, beribboned, bemedalled.

Verb
(12) *decorate,* adorn, embellish, enhance, enrich; grace, set off, ornament; paint, glamorize, prettify 841 *beautify*; garnish, trim, shape; array, deck, bedeck 228 *dress*; deck out, trick o. 843 *primp*; freshen, smarten, spruce up 648 *clean*; garland, crown 866 *honour*; stud, spangle 437 *variegate*; varnish, lacquer 226 *coat*; enamel, gild, silver; emblazon, illuminate, illustrate 553 *paint*, 425 *colour*; border, trim 234 *hem*; work, pick out, embroider, tapestry; pattern, inlay, engrave; encrust, emboss, bead, mould; fret, carve 262 *groove*, 260 *notch*; wreathe, festoon, scroll 251 *twine*.

845
Blemish

Noun
(1) *blemish,* no ornament; scar, weal, welt, mark, pockmark; flaw, crack 647 *imperfection*; disfigurement, deformity 246 *distortion*; blot 842 *eyesore*; blotch, smudge 550 *obliteration*; smut, smear, stain 649 *dirt*; spot, speck 437 *maculation*; freckle, mole, birthmark; pimple, wart 253 *swelling*; acme, eczema 651 *skin disease*; harelip, cleft palate; cast, squint; cut, scratch, bruise, black eye 655 *wound*.

Adjective
(2) *blemished,* defective, flawed, cracked, damaged 647 *imperfect*; tarnished, stained, soiled, flyblown 649 *dirty*; shop-soiled 655 *deteriorated*; marked, foxed, spotted, pitted, pockmarked, spotty, freckled; squinting 440 *dim-sighted*; knock-kneed, hunch-backed, crooked 246 *deformed*.

Verb
(3) *blemish,* flaw, crack, damage 655 *impair*; blot, smudge, stain, smear, sully 649 *make unclean*; brand 547 *mark*; scar, pit, pockmark; mar, spoil spoil the look of 842 *make ugly*; deface, disfigure, scribble on 244 *deform*.

846
Good taste

Noun
(1) *good taste,* tastefulness, taste; restraint, simplicity 573 *plainness*; choiceness, excellence 644 *goodness*; refinement, delicacy, euphemism 950 *purity*; fine feeling, discernment, palate 463 *discrimination*; daintiness, decency, seemliness

848 *etiquette*; tact, consideration, manners, breeding, civility, urbanity, sophistication, social graces 884 *courtesy*; correctness, propriety, decorum; grace, polish, gracious living, elegance; cultivation, culture; dilettantism; epicureanism, epicurism; aesthetics, aestheticism; artistry, flair 694 *skill*.

(2) *people of taste,* sophisticate, connoisseur, cognoscente, amateur, dilettante; epicurean, gourmet, epicure; aesthete, critic 480 *estimator*; arbiter of taste 848 *beau monde*.

Adjective
(3) *tasteful,* in good taste, choice, exquisite 644 *excellent*; simple 573 *plain*; graceful, classical 575 *elegant*; chaste, refined, delicate, euphemistic 950 *pure*; aesthetic, artistic 819 *sensitive*; discerning, epicurean 463 *discriminating*; nice, dainty, choosy, finicky 862 *fastidious*; critical, appreciative 480 *judicial*; decent, seemly, becoming 24 *apt*; proper, correct, mannerly 848 *well-bred*.

Verb
(4) *have taste,* show good t., 463 *discriminate*; appreciate, value, criticize 480 *judge*, 862 *be fastidious*.

Adverb
(5) *tastefully,* in good taste, in the best of taste.

847
Bad taste

Noun
(1) *bad taste,* poor t. 645 *badness*; no taste, lack of t.; bad art, kitsch; commercialism, gutter press; coarseness, barbarism, vulgarism, vandalism, philistinism 699 *artlessness*; vulgarity, gaudiness, garishness, loudness, blatancy, flagrancy; tinsel, glitter, paste,

imitation; lack of feeling, insensitivity, crassness, grossness; tactlessness, indelicacy, unseemliness, impropriety; obscenity 951 *impurity*; dowdiness, unfashionableness, frumpishness; frump.

(2) *ill-breeding,* vulgarity, commonness; rusticity, provinciality; incivility, bad form, incorrectness; bad manners, no manners, gaucherie, rudeness, boorishness, impoliteness 885 *discourtesy*; savagery, brutishness; misbehaviour, indecorum, ribaldry; rough behaviour, rowdyism, ruffianism 61 *disorder*.

(3) *vulgarian,* snob, social climber; cad, bounder; parvenu, nouveau riche; proletarian 869 *commoner*; philistine, barbarian, savage; yob, punk.

Adjective
(4) *vulgar,* undignified, unrefined, inelegant; tasteless, in bad taste, gross, crass, coarse, commercialized; knowing no better, philistine, barbarian 699 *artless*; tawdry, cheap, cheap and nasty, kitschy, flashy 875 *showy*; obtrusive, blatant, loud, screaming, gaudy, garish, raffish overdressed 850 *affected*; flaunting, shameless; fulsome, excessive; not respectable, common, low 867 *disreputable*; improper, indelicate, indecorous; going too far, beyond the pale, scandalous, indecent, obscene, risqué 951 *impure*.

(5) *ill-bred,* badly brought up; unpresentable; ungentlemanly, unladylike, hoydenish; non-U 869 *plebeian*; loud, hearty; tactless, insensitive, blunt; impolite, uncivil, unmannerly, ill-mannered 885 *discourteous*; frumpish, dowdy, unfashionable; rustic, provincial; crude,

rude, boorish, churlish, yobbish, loutish, uncouth, uncivilized 491 *ignorant*; knowing no better 699 *artless*; unlettered, barbaric; awkward, gauche 695 *clumsy*; misbehaving, rowdy, ruffianly 61 *disorderly*; snobbish, uppity, superior 850 *affected*.

Verb

(6) *vulgarize,* cheapen, coarsen, debase, lower the tone; commercialize, popularize; show bad taste, know no better 491 *not know*.

848
Fashion. Etiquette

Noun

(1) *fashion,* style, mode, vogue, cult 610 *habit*; fad, craze, cry, furore 126 *modernism*; new look, the latest, height of fashion; stylishness, flair, chic; dress sense, fashion s.; haute couture, elegance, foppishness, dressiness 850 *affectation*; Vanity Fair.

(2) *etiquette,* point of e. 875 *formality*; protocol, convention, custom 610 *practice*; done thing, good form; proprieties, appearances, decency, decorum, propriety, correctness 846 *good taste*; breeding, good b., manners, good m., best behaviour 884 *courtesy*; poise, dignity, savoir faire 688 *conduct*.

(3) *beau monde,* society, high s.; town, court, salon; high circles, right people, smart set, upper crust 644 *elite*; beautiful people, jet set; man *or* woman about town, socialite, playboy, cosmopolitan 882 *sociable person*.

(4) *fop,* fine gentleman, fine lady, belle; debutante, deb; dandy, beau; swell, toff, His Nibs, Lady Muck; gay dog, gallant.

Adjective

(5) *fashionable,* modish, stylish, voguish; correct, comme il faut; in, in vogue, in fashion, a la mode; exquisite, chic, elegant, well-dressed, well-groomed 846 *tasteful*; clothes-conscious, foppish, dressy; high-stepping, dashing, rakish, flashy 875 *showy*; smart, classy, ritzy; all the rage 126 *modern*; trendy, with it; snobbish 850 *affected*; conventional, done 610 *usual*.

(6) *well-bred,* thoroughbred, blue-blooded 868 *noble*; cosmopolitan, sophisticated, civilized, urbane; polished, polite, well brought up, house-trained; gentlemanly, ladylike 868 *genteel*; civil, well-mannered, well-spoken 884 *courteous*; courtly, stately, dignified 875 *formal*; poised, easy, smooth; correct, decorous, proper, decent; tactful, diplomatic; considerate 884 *amiable*; punctilious 929 *honourable*.

Verb

(7) *be in fashion,* catch on 610 *be wont*; follow the fashion 83 *conform*; entertain 882 *be sociable*; cut a dash, cut a figure, set the fashion, give a lead; look right, pass; have style, show flair.

Adverb

(8) *fashionably,* in style, a la mode.

849
Ridiculousness

Noun

(1) *ridiculousness,* ludicrousness 497 *absurdity*; funniness, drollery, waggishness 839 *wit*; quaintness, oddness, queerness, eccentricity 84 *nonconformity*; bathos, anticlimax; extravagance, bombast 546 *exaggeration*; comic interlude,

light relief; light verse, comic v., doggerel, limerick 839 *witticism*; spoonerism, malapropism; comic turn, comedy, farce, burlesque, slapstick, knockabout, clowning, buffoonery.

Adjective

(2) *ridiculous,* ludicrous, preposterous, monstrous, grotesque, fantastic; inappropriate 497 *absurd*; awkward, clownish 695 *clumsy*; silly 499 *foolish*; derisory, contemptible, laughable, risible; bizarre, rum, quaint, queer 84 *unusual*; mannered, stilted 850 *affected*; bombastic, extravagant 546 *exaggerated*; crazy, crackpot, fanciful, whimsical 604 *capricious*.

(3) *funny,* comical, droll, humorous 839 *witty*; priceless, hilarious 837 *amusing*; comic, tragicomic; mocking, ironical, satirical 851 *derisive*; burlesque, mock-heroic; doggerel; farcical, slapstick, clownish, knockabout.

Verb

(4) *be ridiculous,* make one laugh, give one the giggles, raise a laugh; tickle, entertain 837 *amuse*; look silly; be a laughingstock, play the fool 497 *be absurd*; make an exhibition of oneself 695 *act foolishly*; poke fun at 851 *ridicule*.

850
Affectation

Noun

(1) *affectation,* fad 848 *fashion*; pretentiousness 875 *ostentation*; airs, posing, posturing, high moral tone; pose, artificiality, mannerism; coquetry 604 *caprice*; conceit, conceitedness, foppishness, dandyism 873 *vanity*; euphemism, mock modesty, false shame; insincerity, playacting 541 *duplicity*; staginess, theatricality, histrionics.

(2) *pretension,* pretensions; artifice, sham, humbug, quackery, charlatanism 542 *deception*; shallowness, superficiality; stiffness, starchiness 875 *formality*; pedantry, sanctimoniousness; demureness 950 *prudery.*

(3) *affecter,* humbug, quack, charlatan 545 *impostor*; hypocrite, flatterer 545 *deceiver*; bluffer 877 *boaster*; coquette, flirt; poser, poseur attitudinizer 873 *vain person*; dandy 848 *fop*; pedant, know-all 500 *wise guy*; prig 950 *prude*.

Adjective

(4) *affected,* studied, mannered, precious; artificial, unnatural, stilted, stiff, starchy 875 *formal*; prim prudish, priggish, euphemistic, sanctimonious, smug, demure; arch, sly, coquettish, coy, cute, twee; mincing, simpering; shallow, hollow, specious, pretentious, high-sounding 546 *exaggerated*; gushing, fulsome, theatrical 875 *ostentatious*; foppish, camp; conceited, la-di-da, showing off posturing, posing 873 *vain*; snobbish 847 *ill-bred*; for effect, assumed, put on, insincere, phoney, hypocritical 542 *deceiving*.

Verb

(5) *be affected,* affect, put on, wear, assume; pretend, feign, bluff 541 *dissemble*; make a show of 20 *imitate*; act a part, overact, ham, barnstorm 546 *exaggerate*; try for effect, camp it up, attitudinize, strike attitudes, posture, pose, strike a p. 875 *be ostentatious*; put on airs, give oneself a. 873 *be vain*; talk big 877 *boast*; pout, simper, coquette, flirt 887 *excite love*; keep up appearances.

851
Ridicule

Noun

(1) *ridicule,* derision, poking fun; mockery 921 *disrespect;* sniggering 835 *laughter;* raillery, teasing, ribbing, banter, persiflage, leg-pulling; practical joke 497 *foolery;* grin, snigger, laugh; irony, sarcasm; catcall 924 *censure;* personal remarks, insult 921 *indignity;* ribaldry 839 *witticism.*

(2) *satire,* parody, burlesque, travesty, caricature, cartoon, skit, send-up, take-off 20 *mimicry;* squib, lampoon 926 *detraction.*

(3) *laughingstock,* figure of fun, object of ridicule, by-word; sport, game, fair g.; Aunt Sally, April fool; buffoon, clown 501 *fool;* stooge, butt, foil, feed, straight man; guy, caricature, travesty, mockery of, apology for; original, eccentric 504 *crank;* queer fish, fogy, geezer; fall guy, victim.

Adjective

(4) *derisive,* ridiculing, mocking etc. vb.; chaffing, flippant 456 *light-minded;* sardonic, sarcastic; disparaging 926 *detracting;* ironical, quizzical; satirical 839 *witty;* ribald 847 *vulgar;* burlesque, mock-heroic.

Verb

(5) *ridicule,* deride, pour scorn on, laugh at, grin at, smile at, snigger; banter, chaff, rally, twit, rib, tease, rag, pull one's leg, poke fun at, make merry with, make fun of, make a fool of; kid, fool, mock 926 *detract;* make one look silly; deflate, debunk 872 *humiliate.*

(6) *satirize,* lampoon 921 *not respect;* mock, gibe; mimic, send up, take off 20 *imitate;* parody, travesty, burlesque,

caricature, guy 552 *misrepresent;* expose, show up, pillory.

852
Hope

Noun

(1) *hope,* hopes, expectations, assumption, presumption 507 *expectation;* high hopes, conviction 485 *belief;* reliance, trust, confidence, faith, assurance 473 *certainty;* reassurance 831 *relief;* security, anchor, mainstay 218 *support;* ray of hope, gleam of h., glimmer of h. 469 *possibility;* good omen, promise 511 *omen;* silver lining; hopefulness, buoyancy, optimism, enthusiasm 833 *cheerfulness;* wishful thinking, rose-coloured spectacles.

(2) *aspiration,* ambition, purpose 617 *intention;* pious hope, fond h.; vision, pipe dream 513 *fantasy;* promised land, utopia 617 *objective.*

(3) *hoper,* aspirant, candidate, waiting list; hopeful, young h.; heir apparent 776 *beneficiary;* optimist; utopian 513 *visionary.*

Adjective

(4) *hoping,* aspiring, starry-eyed, ambitious, would-be 617 *intending;* dreaming of 513 *imaginative;* hopeful, in hopes 507 *expectant;* in sight of, sanguine, confident 473 *certain;* buoyant, optimistic; undiscouraged, ever-hoping, not unhopeful.

(5) *promising,* full of promise, favourable, auspicious, propitious 730 *prosperous;* bright, fair, golden, rosy; hopeful, encouraging, plausible, likely 471 *probable;* utopian, wishful, self-deluding 513 *imaginary.*

Verb

(6) *hope,* trust, confide, have

faith; rest assured, feel confident, hope in, rely on, bank on, count on 485 *believe*; presume 471 *assume*; look forward 507 *expect*; hope for, dream of, aspire, promise oneself 617 *intend*; have hopes, live in hopes; take heart, take hope 831 *be relieved*; remain hopeful, not despair 599 *stand firm*; hope on, hope against hope, hope for the best 600 *persevere*; be hopeful, flatter oneself; dream 513 *imagine*.

(7) *give hope,* raise one's hopes, encourage, comfort 833 *cheer*; show signs of, promise, show p., promise well, augur w., bid fair 471 *be likely*; raise one's expectations 511 *predict*.

Adverb
(8) *hopefully,* - expectantly etc. adj.

Interjection
(9) *nil desperandum!* never say die!

853
Hopelessness

Noun
(1) *hopelessness,* no hope, loss of hope, defeatism, despondency, discouragement, dismay 834 *dejection*; pessimism, cynicism, despair, desperation, no way out; dashed hopes 509 *disappointment*; vain hope 470 *impossibility*; poor lookout, no prospects; hopeless situation 700 *predicament*; Job's comforter, misery, pessimist, defeatist 834 *moper*.

Adjective
(2) *hopeless,* bereft of hope, despairing, in despair, desperate, suicidal; unhopeful, pessimistic, cynical, defeatist; inconsolable, disconsolate 834 *dejected*; desolate, forlorn 731 *unfortunate*.

(3) *unpromising,* hopeless, comfortless 834 *cheerless*; desperate 661 *dangerous*; inauspicious 731 *adverse*; threatening, ominous 511 *presageful*; irremediable, incurable, inoperable; beyond hope, past recall, despaired of; irrecoverable, irredeemable, irreversible, inevitable.

Verb
(4) *despair,* lose heart, lose hope 834 *be dejected*; give up hope, abandon h.; give up 721 *submit*.

(5) *leave no hope,* offer no h. 509 *disappoint*; be hopeless, desperate etc. adj.

854
Fear

Noun
(1) *fear,* dread, awe 920 *respect*; abject fear 856 *cowardice*; fright, stage f.; terror, panic; trepidation, alarm, shock 318 *agitation*; scare, stampede, flight; horror, hair on end, cold sweat; consternation, dismay 853 *hopelessness*.

(2) *nervousness,* apprehensiveness; want of courage, cowardliness 856 *cowardice*; diffidence, shyness 874 *modesty*; defensiveness, blustering 877 *boasting*; timidity, timorousness, fearfulness, hesitation; loss of nerve, cold feet; fears, suspicions, misgivings, qualms; mistrust, apprehension, uneasiness, disquiet 825 *worry*; perturbation, trepidation, flutter, tremor, palpitation, blushing, trembling etc. vb.; quaking, nerves, butterflies, jitters 318 *agitation*; gooseflesh, hair on end, knees knocking.

(3) *phobia,* agoraphobia, claustrophobia; xenophobia 888 *hatred*; witch-hunting.

(4) *intimidation,* deterrence, war of nerves, sabre-rattling,

arms build up 900 *threat*; caution 664 *warning*; terror, terrorization, terrorism, reign of terror 735 *severity*; alarmism, scaremongering; deterrent 723 *weapon*; object of terror, hobgoblin 970 *demon*; spook, spectre 970 *ghost*; scarecrow, nightmare; ogre 938 *monster*.

(5) *alarmist,* scaremonger, doom merchant, defeatist, pessimist; terrorist, intimidator.

Adjective

(6) *fearing,* afraid, frightened, panicky; overawed 920 *respectful*; intimidated, terrorized, demoralized; in trepidation, in a fright, in a panic; terror-crazed, panic-striken, stampeding; scared, alarmed, startled; hysterical, in hysterics; dismayed, in consternation, flabbergasted; petrified, horrified, stunned; appalled, shocked, aghast, horror-struck, awestruck, frightened to death, ashen-faced, white as a sheet.

(7) *nervous,* defensive, on the d., tense; timid, shy 874 *modest*; wary, hesitating, shrinking 858 *cautious*; doubtful, distrustful, suspicious 474 *doubting*; fainthearted 601 *irresolute*; apprehensive, uneasy, fearful, dreading, anxious 825 *unhappy*; highly-strung, jumpy, nervy; tremulous, shaky; palpitating, breathless 318 *agitated*.

(8) *frightening,* - startling etc. vb.; formidable, redoubtable; hazardous 661 *dangerous*; tremendous, dreadful, awe-inspiring, fearsome, awesome 821 *impressive*; grim, grisly, hideous, ghastly, frightful, revolting, horrifying, horrible, terrible, awful, appalling; hair-raising, blood-curdling; weird, eerie, creepy, scary, ghoulish, nightmarish, gruesome, macabre, sinister; intimidating, bullying, hectoring 735 *oppressive*; menacing, nerve-racking 900 *threatening*.

Verb

(9) *fear,* be afraid, frightened etc. adj.; dread 920 *respect*; take fright, panic, stampede, 620 *run away*; start, jump, flutter 318 *be agitated*; faint, collapse, break down.

(10) *quake,* shake, tremble, quiver, shiver, shudder, stutter, quaver; change colour, blench, pale, wince, flinch 620 *avoid*; quail, cower, crouch, skulk.

(11) *be nervous,* feel shy 874 *be modest*; have misgivings, suspect, distrust, mistrust 486 *doubt*; shrink, quail, be anxious, dread, have qualms; hesitate, get cold feet, think better of it, not dare 858 *be cautious*; be on edge 318 *be agitated*.

(12) *frighten,* give one a fright; scare, panic, stampede; intimidate, menace 900 *threaten*; alarm, raise the a.; scare stiff, make one jump, startle 318 *agitate*; disquiet, disturb, haunt, obsess 827 *trouble*; make nervous, rattle, shake, unnerve, unman, demoralize; awe, overawe 821 *impress*; subdue, cow 727 *overmaster*; dismay, confound; frighten off, daunt, deter, discourage 613 *dissuade*; terrorize 735 *oppress*; browbeat, bully 827 *torment*; terrify, horrify, harrow, make aghast; chill, freeze, paralyse, petrify, appal, freeze one's blood, frighten to death.

855
Courage

Noun

(1) *courage,* bravery, valiance, valour; heroism, gallantry, chivalry 929 *probity*; self-reliance, fearlessness, intrepidity, daring, nerve; boldness, audacity 857 *rashness*; spirit, mettle,

panache 174 *vigorousness*; tenacity, bulldog courage 600 *perseverance*; fortitude, determination, endurance, stiff upper lip, gameness, manliness, pluck, heart, 599 *resolution*; sham courage, Dutch c.; brave face, bold front 711 *defiance*.

(2) *prowess*, chivalry, heroism, gallant act, feat of arms, exploit, stroke, bold s. 676 *deed*; solderly conduct, heroics.

(3) *brave person*, hero, heroine, knight, brave, warrior 722 *soldier*; man *or* woman of spirit, greatheart, lionheart; daredevil, risk-taker 857 *desperado*; knight-errant, band of heroes, gallant company 644 *elite*.

Adjective

(4) *courageous*, brave, valorous, valiant, gallant, heroic; chivalrous, knightly, knight-like; solderly, martial, amazonian 718 *warlike*; stout, doughty, tough, manful, manly, red-blooded; fierce, bold 711 *defiant*; dashing, audacious, daring, venturesome 857 *rash*; adventurous 672 *enterprising*; mettlesome, spirited, stouthearted, lion-hearted, full of spirit, full of fight; unbowed, indomitable 600 *persevering*; desperate, determined 599 *resolute*; game, plucky, sporting; ready for anything; unflinching 597 *willing*.

(5) *unfearing*, intrepid, nerveless, unafraid; danger-loving; sure of oneself, confident, self-reliant; fearless, dauntless, undaunted, unabashed, undismayed.

Verb

(6) *be courageous*, - bold etc. adj.; show spirit, venture, adventure, take the plunge 672 *undertake*; dare 661 *face danger*; show fight, brave, face, outface 711 *defy*; speak out, speak up 532 *affirm*; face the music, look

in the face 599 *stand firm*; laugh at danger 857 *be rash*; show valour, win one's spurs; bear up, endure 825 *suffer*.

(7) *take courage*, pluck up c., muster c., nerve oneself; show fight 599 *be resolute*; rally 599 *stand firm*.

(8) *give courage*, animate, put heart into, hearten, nerve, embolden, encourage, inspire 612 *incite*; rally 833 *cheer*; keep in spirits, preserve morale, bolster up, reassure, give confidence.

Adverb

(9) *bravely*, - courageously etc. adj.

856
Cowardice

Noun

(1) *cowardice*, abject fear 854 *fear*; cowardliness, faintheartedness 601 *irresolution*; unmanliness, pusillanimity, timidity, want of courage, lack of daring; defeatism 853 *hopelessness*; desertion, quitting, shirking; white feather, yellow streak; low morale, faint heart, chicken liver; braggadocio 877 *boasting*; cowering, skulking; discretion, safety first 858 *caution*.

(2) *coward*, no hero; craven, faintheart; sneak, rat, tell-tale 524 *informer*; coward at heart, bully, braggart 877 *boaster*; milksop, baby 163 *weakling*; quitter, shirker, deserter, runaway; mouse, doormat.

Adjective

(3) *cowardly*, coward, craven, timid, timorous, fearful 854 *nervous*; babyish 163 *weak*; spiritless, without grit, without guts; weak-minded, fainthearted, chicken-h.; yellow, abject, cowed 721 *submitting*; defeatist, 853 *hopeless*; prudent,

unheroic; easily frightened 601 *irresolute*.

Verb
(4) *be cowardly,* lack courage, have no fight, have no grit, have no stomach for; not dare 601 *be irresolute*; lose one's nerve 854 *be nervous*; shy from, back out, chicken o. 620 *avoid*; hide, skulk; quail, cower, cringe 721 *knuckle under*; show fear, turn tail, run for cover, panic, stampede, desert 620 *run away*; lead from behind 858 *be cautious*.

857
Rashness

Noun
(1) *rashness,* incautiousness, heedlessness 456 *inattention*; imprudence, improvidence, indiscretion 499 *folly*; recklessness, foolhardiness, temerity, audacity, presumption; hotheadedness, fieriness, impatience 822 *excitability*; impetuosity, hastiness 680 *haste*; needless risk 661 *danger*.

(2) *desperado,* daredevil, madcap, hothead, fire-eater; adventurer, bravo 904 *ruffian*.

Adjective
(3) *rash,* ill-advised, harebrained, foolhardy, indiscreet, imprudent 499 *unwise*; slapdash 458 *negligent*; not looking, incautious, unwary 456 *inattentive*; flippant, giddy devil-may-care, slaphappy, trigger-happy 456 *light-minded*; irresponsible, reckless, regardless, don't-care, foolhardy, lunatic, wild; bold, daring audacious, madcap, daredevil, do-or-die, neck or nothing, breakneck, suicidal; overconfident, overweening, presumptuous; precipitate, headlong, desperate 680 *hasty*; unchecked, headstrong 602 *wilful*; impulsive, impatient, hot-blooded,

hot-headed, fire-eating, furious 822 *excitable*; danger-loving venturesome, adventurous, risk-taking 672 *enterprising*; improvident, thriftless 815 *prodigal*.

Verb
(4) *be rash,* - reckless etc. adj.; lack caution, want judgment; expose oneself, stick one's neck out, drop one's guard; go bull-headed at, rush at, rush into 680 *hasten*; ignore the consequences, not care 456 *be inattentive*; play with fire, dice with death 661 *face danger*; court disaster, ask for trouble, tempt providence, push one's luck 695 *act foolishly*.

Adverb
(5) *rashly,* carelessly, gaily; headlong, recklessly.

858
Caution

Noun
(1) *caution,* cautiousness, circumspection, wariness, heedfulness 457 *carefulness*; hesitation, doubt, second thoughts 854 *nervousness*; reticence 525 *secrecy*; counting the risk, safety first 669 *preparation*; deliberation 480 *judgment*; sobriety, prudence, discretion 498 *wisdom*; insurance, precaution 662 *safeguard*; forethought 510 *foresight*; one step at a time 823 *patience*.

Adjective
(2) *cautious,* wary, watchful 455 *attentive*; heedful 457 *careful*; hesitating, doubtful, suspicious 854 *nervous*; taking no risks, insured, 669 *prepared*; guarded, noncommittal 525 *reticent*; on one's guard, circumspect; tentative 461 *experimental*; conservative 660 *safe*; responsible 929 *trustworthy*; prudent, discreet 498 *wise*; canny, counting the cost or the risk; timid,

unadventurous; slow, deliberate 823 *patient*; level-headed,
cold-blooded 823 *inexcitable*.

Verb
(3) *be cautious*, beware 457 *be
careful*; take no risks, play safe
498 *be wise*; cover one's tracks
525 *conceal*; not talk 525 *keep
secret*; look, look out 438 *scan*;
feel one's way 461 *be tentative*;
watch one's step, be on one's
guard; look twice, think t. 455
be mindful; calculate, count
the cost 480 *judge*; take one's
time, wait and see; let well
alone 620 *avoid*; take precautions, make sure 473 *make certain*; cover oneself, insure 660
seek safety; leave nothing to
chance 669 *prepare*.

Adverb
(4) *cautiously*, with caution,
gingerly, softly softly.

859
Desire

Noun
(1) *desire*, wish, will and pleasure 595 *will*; summons 737
command; claim, want, need
627 *requirement*; nostalgia,
homesickness 830 *regret*; wist-
fulness, longing, hankering,
yearning; wishing, daydream
513 *fantasy*; ambition, aspiration 852 *hope*; yen, urge 279
impulse; itch for, avidity, eagerness 597 *willingness*; passion, ardour, warmth 822 *excitability*; craving, lust for;
covetousness, cupidity 816
avarice; greediness, greed 786
rapacity; voracity, insatiability 947 *gluttony*; incontinence
923 *intemperance*.

(2) *hunger*, famine; empty stomach 946 *fasting*; appetite,
sharp a., keen a., voracious a.;
thirst, thirstiness 342 *dryness*;
dipsomania 949 *alcoholism*.

(3) *liking*, fancy, fondness 887
love; stomach, appetite, zest;
relish 386 *taste*; leaning, penchant, propensity 179 *tendency*; weakness, partiality; affinity, sympathy; inclination,
mind 617 *intention*; predilection, favour 605 *choice*; whim
604 *caprice*; hobby, craze, fad,
mania 481 *bias*; fascination,
temptation 612 *inducement*.

(4) *libido*, sexual urge; eros,
eroticism; sexual desire, passion; rut, heat, mating season;
prurience, lust 951 *unchastity*.

(5) *desired object*, wish, desire
627 *requirement*; catch, prize,
plum 729 *trophy*; lion, idol 890
favourite; forbidden fruit,
temptation; magnet, lure, draw
291 *attraction*, 887 *loved one*;
aim, goal, star, ambition, aspiration, dream 617 *objective*;
ideal 646 *perfection*.

(6) *desirer*, envier; wooer 887
lover; glutton, sucker for; fancier, amateur, dilettante 492
collector; devotee, votary 981
worshipper; well-wisher, sympathizer 707 *patron*; wisher,
aspirant 852 *hoper*; claimant,
pretender; candidate 763 *petitioner*; ambitious person, careerist; seducer 952 *libertine*.

Adjective
(7) *desiring*, desirous, wishing,
tempted; oversexed, lustful, on
heat 951 *lecherous*; covetous
(see *greedy*); craving, needing,
wanting 627 *demanding*; missing, nostalgic 830 *regretting*;
inclined, minded, set upon,
bent upon 617 *intending*; ambitious 852 *hoping*; aspiring,
would-be, wishful; wistful,
longing, yearning, hankering,
hungry for; unsatisfied, curious; eager, keen, ardent, avid,
agog, breathless, impatient, dying for; liking, fond of, partial
to.

(8) *greedy,* acquisitive, possessive 932 *selfish*; voracious, omnivorous 947 *gluttonous*; quenchless, insatiable; rapacious, grasping 816 *avaricious*; exacting, extortionate 735 *oppressive.*

(9) *hungry,* hungering; empty 946 *fasting*; half-starved, starving, famished 636 *underfed*; peckish, ready for, ravenous; thirsty, dry, parched.

(10) *desired,* wanted, liked; likable, desirable, worth having, enviable, in demand; acceptable, welcome 826 *pleasurable*; fetching, attractive, appealing 291 *attracting*; wished, invited 597 *voluntary.*

Verb

(11) *desire,* want, miss 627 *require*; ask for, cry out f., clamour f. 737 *demand*; call, summon 737 *command*; wish, pray; wish otherwise 830 *regret*; wish for oneself, covet 912 *envy*; promise oneself, have designs on set one's heart on 617 *intend*; plan for, angle f. 623 *plan*; aspire to, dream of, daydream 852 *hope*; look for, expect 915 *claim*; pray for, intercede; wish on, call down on 899 *curse*; wish one well 897 *be benevolent*; welcome, be glad of, jump at, grasp at 786 *take*; lean towards 179 *tend*; favour, prefer, select 605 *choose*; crave, itch for, long, yearn, pine, languish; hanker after 636 *be unsatisfied*; pant for, gasp f., burn f., be dying f. thirst f., hunger f., can't wait, must have; like, care for 887 *love*; moon after, sigh a., burn 887 *be in love*; make eyes at, woo 889 *court*; run after, chase 619 *pursue*; lust after 951 *be impure.*

(12) *be hungry,* hunger, famish, starve; thirst, be dry.

(13) *cause desire,* incline 612 *motivate*; arouse desire, fill

with longing 887 *excite love*; stimulate 821 *excite*; whet the appetite 390 *make appetizing*; parch, raise a thirst; tease, tantalize 612 *tempt*; allure, seduce, draw 291 *attract.*

Adverb

(14) *desirously,* eagerly, hungrily, thirstily, greedily.

860
Indifference

Noun

(1) *indifference,* unconcern 454 *incuriosity*; lack of interest, lukewarmness, half-heartedness; coolness, coldness, faint praise, two cheers 865 *lack of wonder*; no appetite, no desire for; inertia, apathy 679 *inactivity*; nonchalance, insouciance 458 *negligence*; 734 *laxity*; recklessness, heedlessness 857 *rashness*; amorality, impartiality 913 *justice*; neutrality 625 *middle way.*

Adjective

(2) *indifferent,* unconcerned, uncaring, uninterested 454 *incurious*; lukewarm, half-hearted; unimpressed 865 *unastonished*; phlegmatic, blase, calm, cool, cold 820 *impassive*; nonchalant, careless, perfunctory 458 *negligent*; unambitious, unaspiring; lackadaisical, listless 679 *inactive*; don't-care, easygoing 734 *lax*; unmoved, insensible to; disenchanted, disillusioned, out of love, cooling off; impartial 913 *just*; noncommittal, neutral; amoral, cynical.

(3) *unwanted,* unwelcome, uninvited, unbidden, unprovoked; loveless, uncared for 458 *neglected*; on the shelf; untempting 391 *unsavoury*; undesirable 861 *disliked.*

Verb

(4) *be indifferent,* - unconcerned etc. adj.; 865 *not wonder*; not mind, take no interest 456 *be inattentive*; have no taste for 861 *dislike*; couldn't care less, shrug off, dismiss, make light of 922 *hold cheap*; not defend, take neither side 606 *be neutral*; grow indifferent, cool off.

Interjection
(5) *Never mind!*

861
Dislike

Noun
(1) *dislike,* disinclination, no fancy for, no stomach for; reluctance, backwardness 598 *unwillingness*; displeasure 891 *resentment*; disagreement 489 *dissent*; aversion 620 *avoidance*; antipathy, allergy; rooted dislike, distaste, repugnance, repulsion, disgust, abomination, abhorrence, loathing; shuddering, horror, phobia 854 *fear*; prejudice 481 *bias*; animosity, ill feeling 888 *hatred*; nausea, queasiness, turn; one's fill 863 *satiety*; bitterness 393 *sourness*; object of dislike, not one's type, betenoire, pet aversion.

Adjective
(2) *disliking,* not liking, displeased 829 *discontented*; disinclined, loath 598 *unwilling*; squeamish, qualmish, queasy; allergic, antipathetic; disagreeing 489 *dissenting*; averse, hostile 881 *inimical*; shy 620 *avoiding*; repelled, abhorring, loathing 888 *hating*; out of sympathy with, disenchanted, disillusioned 860 *indifferent*; sick of 863 *sated*; nauseated 300 *vomiting*.

(3) *disliked,* undesirable 860 *unwanted*; unpopular, out of favour, avoided; grating, jarring, bitter, repugnant, antipathetic 292 *repellent*; revolting, loathsome 888 *hateful*; abominable, disgusting 924 *disapproved*;

nauseating, sickening 391 *unsavoury*; disagreeable, insufferable 827 *intolerable*; unlovable, unlovely.

Verb
(4) *dislike,* have no liking for, not care for; prefer not to 607 *reject*; object 762 *deprecate*; mind 891 *resent*; have no heart for 598 *be unwilling*; take a dislike to, react against 280 *recoil*; shun, shrink from 620 *avoid*; look askance at 924 *disapprove*; grimace 893 *be sullen*; not endure, can't stand, detest, loathe 888 *hate*; shudder at 854 *fear*.

(5) *cause dislike,* antagonize, put one's back up 891 *enrage*; set at odds 888 *excite hate*; pall on 863 *sate*; disagree with, upset; put off, revolt 292 *repel*; offend 827 *displease*; disgust, nauseate, sicken, turn one's stomach, make one sick; shock, scandalize.

862
Fastidiousness

Noun
(1) *fastidiousness,* niceness, daintiness, delicacy; discernment, perspicacity, refinement 846 *good taste*; preciseness, particularity 457 *carefulness*; perfectionism; fussiness, nit-picking, hair-splitting, pedantry; primness 950 *prudery*.

(2) *perfectionist,* purist; fusspot, pedant, stickler, hard taskmaster; gourmet, epicure.

Adjective
(3) *fastidious,* nice, dainty, delicate, discerning 463 *discriminating*; particular, demanding, choosy, finicky, scrupulous, meticulous, squeamish, qualmish 455 *attentive*; punctilious, painstaking, conscientious; critical, fussy, pernickety, hard

to please 924 *disapproving*; pedantic, precise, rigorous, exacting, difficult 735 *severe*; prim, puritanical 950 *prudish*.

Verb

(4) *be fastidious,* - choosy etc. adj.; pick and choose 605 *choose*; refine, over-refine, split hairs 463 *discriminate*; fuss, find fault, turn up one's nose at 922 *despise*.

863
Satiety

Noun

(1) *satiety,* fullness, repletion 54 *plenitude*; stuffing, saturation, saturation point; glut, surfeit 637 *redundance*; overdose, excess 637 *superfluity*.

Adjective

(2) *sated,* satiated, satisfied, replete; saturated, brimming 635 *filled*; surfeited, gorged, glutted; sick of; jaded 838 *bored*.

Verb

(3) *sate,* satiate; satisfy, quench, slake 635 *suffice*; fill up, saturate 54 *fill*; soak 341 *drench*; stuff, gorge, glut, surfeit, cloy, jade, pall; overdose, sicken 861 *cause dislike*; spoil; bore, weary 838 *be tedious*.

864
Wonder

Noun

(1) *wonder,* state of wonder, wonderment, raptness; admiration, hero worship 887 *love*; awe, fascination; whistle, exclamation, exclamation mark; open mouth, popping eyes; shock, surprise, astonishment, amazement; stupor, stupefaction; consternation 854 *fear*.

(2) *thaumaturgy,* miracle-working, spellbinding, magic 983 *sorcery*; feat, exploit coup de théâtre.

(3) *prodigy,* portent, sign, eye-opener 511 *omen*; quite something, phenomenon, miracle, marvel, wonder; sensation, cause celebre, nine-days' wonder; wonderland 513 *fantasy*; sight 445 *spectacle*; infant prodigy, genius; wizard 983 *sorcerer*; hero, heroine, wonder boy, dream girl, bionic man, superwoman, whiz kid 646 *paragon*; freak, sport, curiosity, oddity, monster 84 *rara avis*.

Adjective

(4) *wondering,* - marvelling etc. vb.; awed, awestruck, fascinated, surprised 818 *impressed*; astonished, amazed, astounded; spellbound, rapt, lost in wonder, wide-eyed, round-e., open-mouthed, gaping; dazzled, dumbfounded, speechless, breathless, silenced 399 *silent*; bowled over, thunderstruck; transfixed, dazed, bewildered, aghast, flabbergasted.

(5) *wonderful,* wondrous, marvellous, miraculous, monstrous, prodigious, phenomenal; stupendous, fearful 854 *frightening*; admirable, exquisite 644 *excellent*; striking, overwhelming, awesome, awe-inspiring, breathtaking 821 *impressive*; dramatic, sensational; rare, exceptional, extraordinary, unprecedented 84 *unusual*; strange, odd, very odd, weird, unaccountable, mysterious, enigmatic 517 *puzzling*; exotic, outlandish, fantastic 513 *imaginary*; impossible, hardly possible, 472 *improbable*; unbelievable, incredible, indescribable; unutterable 517 *inexpressible*; surprising 508 *unexpected*; mindboggling, mind-blowing, astounding, amazing, shattering, magic, like m. 983 *magical*.

Verb

(6) *wonder,* marvel, admire, whistle; hold one's breath,

gasp; stare, gaze goggle at, gawk, gape, rub one's eyes 508 *not expect*; be overwhelmed 854 *fear*, 399 *be silent*.

(7) *be wonderful,* do wonders, work miracles, achieve marvels; surpass belief 486 *cause doubt*; baffle description; enchant 983 *bewitch*; dazzle, strike dumb, awe, electrify 821 *impress*; bowl over, stagger, stun, daze, stupefy, petrify, dumbfound, confound, astound, astonish, amaze 508 *surprise*; baffle, bewilder 474 *puzzle*; startle 854 *frighten*.

Adverb
(8) *wonderfully,* marvellously, fearfully; strange to say.

Interjection
(9) *Amazing!* incredible! whatever next!

865
Lack of wonder

Noun
(1) *lack of wonder,* unastonishment, unamazement; irreverence 860 *indifference*; composure, calmness, serenity; equability, impassiveness 820 *moral insensibility*; disbelief 486 *unbelief*; matter of course, nothing in it.

Adjective
(2) *unastonished,* unsurprised; accustomed 610 *habituated*; collected, composed; phlegmatic, impassive 820 *apathetic*; blasé unimpressed 860 *indifferent*; unimaginative, blind to 439 *blind*; disbelieving 486 *unbelieving*; expecting 507 *expectant*.

(3) *unastonishing,* foreseen 507 *expected*; customary 610 *usual*.

Verb
(4) *not wonder,* be blind to 820 *be*

insensitive; not believe 486 *disbelieve*; see through 516 *understand*; take for granted, see it coming 507 *expect*; keep one's head 823 *keep calm*.

Interjection
(5) *no wonder;* of course; quite so, naturally.

866
Repute

Noun
(1) *repute,* good r., special r.; reputation, report, good r.; title to fame, name, character, reputability 802 *credit*; regard, esteem 920 *respect*; opinion, good o.; acclaim, applause, approval 923 *approbation*.

(2) *prestige,* aura, mystique, magic; glamour, dazzle, éclat, lustre, splendour; brilliance, prowess; glory, honour, kudos; esteem, estimation, account, high a. 638 *importance*; caste, degree, rank, standing, status 73 *serial place*; precedence 34 *superiority*; prominence, eminence, distinction, greatness; high rank 868 *nobility*; ascendancy 178 *influence*; primacy 733 *authority*; prestigiousness, snob value.

(3) *famousness,* title to fame, celebrity, notability, renown, stardom, fame, illustriousness; household name, synonym for; glory 727 *success*; notoriety 867 *disrepute*; place in history, immortality, deathlessness 505 *memory*.

(4) *honours,* honour, blaze of glory; crown, martyr's c.; halo, nimbus; laurels, bays, garland 729 *trophy*; order, star, garter, ribbon, medal 729 *decoration*; spurs, arms 547 *heraldry*; an honour, signal h., distinction, accolade, award 962 *reward*; compliment, flattery, eulogy 923 *praise*; memorial, statue, plaque, monument 505 *reminder*; title of honour, dignity 870 *title*; peerage 868 *nobility*; academic honour, baccalaureate, doctorate, degree, diploma, certificate; honours list, roll of honour.

(5) *dignification,* glorification, honouring, complimenting; crowning, commemoration, coronation 876 *celebration*; dedication, consecration, canonization, beatification; deification, apotheosis; promotion, advancement; exaltation 310 *elevation*; ennoblement, knighting; rehabilitation 656 *restoration.*

(6) *person of repute,* honoured sir *or* madam; worthy, pillar of society 929 *honourable person*; peer 868 *person of rank*; somebody, great man, great woman, VIP 638 *bigwig*; person of mark, notable, celebrity, figure, public f.; star, rising star; champion, popular hero; man *or* woman of the hour 890 *favourite*; cynosure, model 646 *paragon*; leading light 500 *sage*; great company, galaxy, constellation.

Adjective

(7) *reputable,* of sound reputation 929 *honourable*; worthy, creditworthy, trustworthy; creditable; meritorious, prestigious 644 *excellent*; esteemed, respectable, well-regarded, well thought of 920 *respected*; edifying, moral 933 *virtuous*; in favour 923 *approved.*

(8) *worshipful,* reverend, honourable; admirable 864 *wonderful*; heroic 855 *courageous*; imposing, dignified, august, stately, grand 821 *impressive*; lofty, high 310 *elevated*; mighty 32 *great*; princely, majestic, regal, aristocratic 868 *noble*; glorious, full of honours, honoured, titled, ennobled; time-honoured, ancient 127 *immemorial*; sacrosanct, sacred, holy; honorific, dignifying.

(9) *noteworthy,* notable, remarkable, extraordinary 84 *unusual*; fabulous 864 *wonderful*; distinguished 638 *important*; conspicuous, prominent, in the limelight 443 *obvious*; eminent, preeminent 34 *superior*; ranking, starring, leading; brilliant, illustrious, splendid, glorious 875 *ostentatious.*

(10) *renowned,* celebrated, acclaimed, sung; famous, fabled, legendary; illustrious, great, noble, glorious 644 *excellent*; notorious 867 *disreputable*; well-known, of note, talked of, in the news 490 *known*; evergreen, imperishable, 115 *perpetual.*

Verb

(11) *have a reputation,* have a name for; have status, stand high 920 *command respect*; do oneself credit, win honour, gain recognition 923 *be praised*; be somebody, make one's mark 730 *prosper*; win one's spurs 727 *succeed*; rise to fame, flash to stardom; shine, excel 644 *be good*; outshine, eclipse, overshadow 34 *be superior*; make history 505 *be remembered.*

(12) *seek repute,* show off, flaunt 871 *feel pride*; lord it, queen it 875 *be ostentatious*; brag 877 *boast.*

(13) *honour,* revere, regard, look up to 920 *respect*; bow down to 981 *worship*; prize, value, treasure 887 *love*; show honour, pay respect 920 *show respect*; compliment 925 *flatter*; grace with, honour w., dedicate to; praise, glorify, acclaim 923 *applaud*; make much of, lionize, chair; give credit, honour for 907

thank; immortalize 505 *remember*; celebrate, blazon 528 *proclaim*; reflect honour, do credit to.

(14) *dignify*, glorify, exalt; canonize, deify 979 *sanctify*; install, enthrone, crown 751 *commission*; signalize, mark out, distinguish; aggrandize, advance 285 *promote*; honour, confer an h., bemedal decorate; bestow a title, create, elevate, ennoble; dub, knight, raise to the peerage.

867
Disrepute

Noun
(1) *disrepute*, bad reputation, bad name, bad character, disreputableness, past; notoriety, infamy, ill repute, ill fame; no reputation, no standing, obscurity; bad odour, discredit, black books, bad light 888 *odium*; dishonour, disgrace, shame (**see slur**); smear campaign 926 *detraction*; ignominy, loss of honour; loss of face, loss of rank, demotion, degradation, abasement 872 *humiliation*.

(2) *slur*, reproach 924 *censure*; imputation, aspersion, reflection, slander, abuse 926 *calumny*; slight, insult 921 *indignity*; scandal, disgrace, shame; stain, stigma, brand, mark, blot, tarnish, taint 845 *blemish*.

(3) *object of scorn*, reproach, byword, discredit 938 *bad person*; reject, the dregs 645 *badness*; poor relation 639 *nonentity*; failure 728 *loser*.

Adjective
(4) *disreputable*, not respectable, shifty, shady 930 *rascally*; notorious, infamous; doubtful, dubious, questionable, objectionable 645 *not nice*; risque, ribald, improper 951 *impure*;

disgraced, despised 922 *contemptible*; characterless, petty, unimportant; degraded, base, abject, despicable 888 *hateful*; mean, low 847 *vulgar*; shabby, dirty, scruffy 649 *unclean*; discredited, reproached 924 *disapproved*; unpopular 861 *disliked*.

(5) *discreditable*, no credit to, damaging, compromising; unworthy, ignoble, improper, unbecoming; dishonourable 930 *dishonest*; despicable 922 *contemptible*; censurable 924 *blameworthy*; shameful, disgraceful, infamous, scandalous, shocking, outrageous, too bad 645 *not nice*.

(6) *degrading*, lowering, demeaning, ignominious, opprobrious, humiliating; derogatory; beneath one.

(7) *inglorious*, without repute, without prestige, without a name, nameless; unambitious 874 *modest*; unremarked 458 *neglected*; unheard of, obscure 491 *unknown*; unrenowned, unsung; deflated, humiliated 872 *humbled*; sunk low, withered, tarnished; discredited, disgraced, dishonoured, out of favour, in eclipse; degraded, demoted.

Verb
(8) *have no repute*, have no name to lose; have a past; have no credit, rank low 35 *be inferior*; blush unseen.

(9) *lose repute*, fall into disrepute; incur disgrace 924 *incur blame*; spoil one's record, disgrace oneself, lose one's good name; win no glory 728 *fail*; lose prestige, lose face; be exposed 963 *be punished*.

(10) *demean oneself*, lower o., degrade o.; condescend, stoop, marry beneath one; cheapen oneself, disgrace o., have no pride, feel no shame.

(11) *shame,* put to s., pillory, expose, show up; scorn, mock 851 *ridicule*; snub 872 *humiliate*; deflate, debunk; demote, defrock, deprive, strip 963 *punish*; blackball 57 *exclude*; vilify, malign, disparage 926 *defame*; put one in a bad light, reflect upon, taint; sully, mar, blacken, tarnish, stain 649 *make unclean*; stigmatize, brand, tar 547 *mark*; dishonour, disgrace, discredit, bring shame upon, give a bad name 924 *incur blame*; heap shame upon, bring into disrepute; make one blush.

868
Nobility

Noun
(1) *nobility,* nobleness, distinction, rank 27 *degree*; majesty, royalty, princeliness, kingliness, queenliness 733 *authority*; birth, high b., gentle b.; descent, noble d., ancestry, lineage, pedigree 169 *genealogy*; dynasty 11 *family*; blue blood, best b.; bloodstock, caste, high c.; crest 547 *heraldry*.

(2) *aristocracy,* patrician order; nobility, lords, peerage; dukedom, earldom, viscountcy, baronetcy; landed interest, squirearchy, county set, gentry; life peerage.

(3) *upper class,* upper crust, top drawer, high society; ruling class 733 *authority*; the haves 800 *rich person*.

(4) *aristocrat,* patrician; bloodstock, thoroughbred; senator, don, grandee, squire, laird; emperor 741 *sovereign*; nob, swell 638 *bigwig*.

(5) *person of rank,* titled person, noble, nobleman, noblewoman; lordship, ladyship; peer *or* peeress hereditary p., life p.; duke,

duchess; marquess, marchioness, count, countess, earl, viscount, viscountess, baron, baroness, baronet, knight; rajah, emir 741 *potentate*.

Adjective
(6) *noble,* chivalrous, knightly; gentlemanly, ladylike; majestic, royal, regal, kingly, queenly, princely, lordly; ducal, baronial; of royal blood, of high birth, of good family, well-born, blue-blooded; ennobled, titled, exalted 32 *great*.

(7) *genteel,* patrician, senatorial; aristocratic, Olympian; superior, high-class, upper-c.; of good breeding, highly respectable 848 *well-bred*.

869
Commonalty

Noun
(1) *commonalty,* commons, third estate, bourgeoisie, plebeians; citizenry, townsfolk, countryfolk; silent majority, grass roots; general public, populace, the people, the common p.; vulgar herd, the multitude, the million, the masses, proletariat; rank and file, Tom, Dick and Harry.

(2) *rabble,* mob, horde 74 *crowd*; rout, riffraff, scum, dregs of society, cattle.

(3) *lower classes,* lower orders, second-class citizens 35 *inferior*; small fry, humble folk; working class, the have-nots, proletariat; down-and-outs; underworld.

(4) *middle classes,* professional c.; white-collar workers, salariat; bourgeoisie 732 *averageness*.

(5) *commoner,* plebeian, bourgeois, citizen, plain Mr or Mrs; proletarian 686 *worker*; towndweller, country-d. 191 *native*;

little man, man or woman in the street; a nobody 639 *nonentity*; serf 742 *slave.*

(6) *country-dweller,* countryman or - woman; yeoman, rustic, peasant, son or daughter of the soil 370 *farmer*; yokel, bumpkin, country b., country cousin, provincial, hillbilly.

(7) *low fellow,* fellow, varlet 938 *cad*; slum-dweller 801 *poor person*; guttersnipe, ragamuffin, down-and-out, tramp, vagabond 268 *wanderer*, 763 *beggar*; rough type, bully 904 *ruffian*; rascal 938 *knave*; gangster, hood; criminal, delinquent 904 *offender*; barbarian, savage, vandal, yahoo.

Adjective
(8) *plebeian,* common, without rank, untitled, below the salt; below-stairs, servant-class; rank and file 732 *middling*; lowly, low-born, low-caste, of low origin, of mean parentage; humble, 35 *inferior*; middle-class, lower m.-c., working-c., proletarian; homely, homespun 573 *plain*; obscure 867 *inglorious*; vulgar, coarse, uncouth 847 *ill-bred*; bourgeois, suburban, provincial, rustic.

(9) *barbaric,* barbarous, barbarian, wild, savage, brutish, primitive, uncivilized 699 *artless.*

870
Title

Noun
(1) *title,* title to fame, entitlement; courtesy title, honorific; honour, distinction, knighthood 866 *honours*; royal we 875 *formality*; mode of address, Royal Highness, Serene H., Grace, Lordship, Ladyship, my lord, my lady; the Honourable,

Right Honourable; your reverence, your honour, your worship; sire, sir, madam, ma'am, master, mister, mistress, miss, Ms.

(2) *academic title,* bachelor master, doctor, Professor.

871
Pride

Noun
(1) *pride,* proper pride, just p., natural p., self-esteem, self-respect; swollen head, conceit 873 *vanity*; snobbery 850 *affectation*; false pride, touchiness, prickliness; dignity, stateliness, loftiness; condescension, hauteur, haughtiness 922 *contempt*; arrogance, hubris 878 *insolence*; pomp, pomposity, grandiosity 875 *ostentation*; self-praise, vainglory 877 *boasting*; object of pride, boast, joy, pride and j. 890 *favourite.*

(2) *proud person,* vain p., snob, parvenu; lord of creation 638 *bigwig*; swaggerer, bragger 877 *boaster.*

Adjective
(3) *proud,* elevated, haughty, lofty, sublime 209 *high*; grand, grandiose, dignified, stately 821 *impressive*; majestic, lordly, aristocratic 868 *noble*; proud-hearted, high-souled 855 *courageous*; high-stepping, high-spirited 819 *lively*; stiff-necked 602 *obstinate*; mighty 32 *great*; imperious, high-handed 735 *oppressive*; overweening, overbearing, arrogant 878 *insolent*; brazen, unblushing, unabashed.

(4) *prideful,* full of pride, flushed with p., puffed-up, swelling, swollen; high and mighty, nose-in-the-air; snobbish, uppish, uppity; on one's dignity, on one's high horse; haughty,

disdainful, superior, supercilious, patronizing, condescending 922 *despising*; standoffish,
aloof, distant 885 *ungracious*;
taking pride in, purse-proud,
house-p; feeling pride, proud of,
strutting, swaggering, vainglorious 877 *boastful*; pleased with
oneself; conceited, cocky 873
vain; pretentious 850 *affected*;
swanking, pompous 875 *showy*.

Verb

(5) *be proud,* have one's pride;
stand on one's dignity, give
oneself airs, toss one's head,
swank, show off, swagger, strut
875 *be ostentatious*; condescend, patronize; look down on,
disdain 922 *despise*; display
hauteur lord it, queen it 878 *be
insolent*.

(6) *feel pride,* swell with p., take
pride in, glory in, boast of, not
blush for 877 *boast*; hug oneself,
congratulate o. 824 *be pleased*;
be flattered, flatter oneself,
pride o., preen o. 873 *be vain*.

872
Humility.
Humiliation

Noun

(1) *humility,* humbleness, humble spirit 874 *modesty*; abasement, lowliness; self-effacement, unpretentiousness;
inoffensiveness, meekness, resignation 721 *submission*;
condescension, stooping 884
courtesy.

(2) *humiliation,* abasement,
humbling, comedown 921 *indignity*; rebuke 924 *reprimand*;
shame, disgrace 867 *disrepute*;
blush, confusion, shamefaced
look; mortification, hurt pride,
offended dignity 891
resentment.

Adjective

(3) *humble,* not proud, self-deprecating; humble-minded, lowly; meek, submissive 721 *submitting*; self-effacing 931
disinterested; self-abasing,
condescending 884 *courteous*;
harmless, inoffensive, unassuming, unpretentious, without airs 874 *modest*; of lowly
birth 869 *plebeian*.

(4) *humbled,* bowed down; chastened, crushed, dashed,
abashed, crestfallen, sheepish,
hangdog 834 *dejected*; humiliated, squashed, deflated; not
proud of, ashamed 939 *repentant*; scorned, rebuked 924 *disapproved*; brought low, discomfited 728 *defeated*.

Verb

(5) *be humble,* - lowly etc. adj.;
humble oneself 867 *demean oneself*; put others first 874 *be
modest*; condescend, unbend
884 *be courteous*; sing small, eat
humble pie 721 *knuckle under*;
stomach, pocket 909 *forgive*.

(6) *be humbled,* feel small, be
ashamed, hide one's face, blush,
colour up; hang one's head,
avert one's eyes.

(7) *humiliate,* humble, chasten,
abash, take down a peg; snub,
cut, crush, squash, sit on 885 *be
rude*; slight, mortify, hurt on-
e's pride, put to shame 867
shame; score off 306 *outdo*;
triumph over 727 *overmaster*.

873
Vanity

Noun

(1) *vanity,* vain pride 871 *pride*;
immodesty, conceit, conceitedness, self-importance, megalomania; puffed-up chest, cockiness, bumptiousness, assurance, self-a.; self-conceit, self-
esteem, self-satisfaction,

smugness; self-love, narcissism; self-praise, self-congratulation 877 *boasting*; self-centredness 932 *selfishness*; exhibitionism, showing off 875 *ostentation*.

(2) *airs,* fine a., airs and graces, pretensions 850 *affectation*; swank, pompousness 875 *ostentation*.

(3) *vain person,* self-admirer, Narcissus; coxcomb 848 *fop*; exhibitionist, show-off; know-all, bighead, smart aleck, Mr Clever, Miss Clever; stuffed shirt, pompous twit.

Adjective
(4) *vain,* conceited, overweening, proud 871 *prideful*; egotistic, egocentric, self-centred, full of oneself 932 *selfish*; smug, self-important, self-admiring, narcissistic; swollenheaded, bigheaded, bumptious 878 *insolent*; showing off, swaggering 877 *boastful*; pompous 875 *ostentatious*; pretentious, putting on airs 850 *affected*.

Verb
(5) *be vain,* - conceited etc. adj.; blow one's own trumpet 877 *boast*; admire oneself, flatter o., think too much of o., plume o., preen o. 871 *feel pride*; swank, strut, show off, put on airs, talk for effect 875 *be ostentatious*; get above oneself, give oneself airs 850 *be affected*; play the fop 843 *primp*.

(6) *make conceited,* puff up, go to one's head, turn one's h. 925 *flatter*.

874
Modesty

Noun
(1) *modesty,* shyness, diffidence, timidity 854 *nervousness*; prudishness 950 *prudery*; bashfulness, blushing, blush; chastity 950 *purity*; self-depreciation

872 *humility*; demureness, reserve;. modest person, shy thing, shrinking violet, mouse.

Adjective
(2) *modest,* without vanity, free from pride; self-effacing, unobtrusive 872 *humble*; self-deprecating, uboastful; quiet, unassuming, unassertive, unpretentious; shy, retiring, shrinking, timid, diffident 854 *nervous*; deprecating, demurring; bashful, blushing; reserved, demure, coy.

Verb
(3) *be modest,* have no ambition, efface oneself, yield precedence, know one's place 872 *be humble*; blush unseen 456 *escape notice*; retire, shrink, hang back, take a back seat; blush, colour 431 *redden*.

Adverb
(4) *modestly,* quietly, without fuss, without ceremony.

875
Ostentation. Formality

Noun
(1) *ostentation,* display, parade, show 522 *manifestation*; blatancy, flagrancy, brazenness, exhibitionism 528 *publicity*; showiness, magnificence, ostentatiousness, grandiosity; splendour, brilliance; pomposity, self-importance 873 *vanity*; fuss, swagger, showing off, pretension; pretensions 873 *airs*; bravado, heroics 877 *boast*; theatricality, histrionics 546 *exaggeration*; back-slapping, bonhomie 882 *sociability*; showmanship, effect; grandeur, dignity, stateliness, solemnity; rhetoric 574 *magniloquence*; flourish, big drum 528 *publication*; pageantry, pomp, finery; frippery, gaudiness, glitter 844 *ornamentation*; idle pomp, false

glitter, mockery, 4 *insubstantiality*; veneer 223 *exteriority*; profession, lip service 542 *deception*.

(2) *formality*, stateliness, dignity; ceremoniousness, stiffness, starchiness; ceremony, ceremonial 988 *ritual*; drill, spit and polish; correctness, protocol, form, good f. 848 *etiquette*; punctilio, preciseness 455 *attention*; solemnity, formal occasion, state o., function 876 *celebration*; full dress, court d., robes, regalia 228 *formal dress*.

(3) *pageant*, show, fete, gala, tournament, tattoo 876 *celebration*; son et lumière 445 *spectacle*; set piece, tableau 594 *stage set*; display, stunt; pyrotechnics 420 *fireworks*; carnival 837 *festivity*; procession, marchpast, flypast; review, parade 74 *assembly*.

Adjective
(4) *ostentatious*, showy, pompous; striving for effect, done for e.; for show, specious, hollow 542 *spurious*; pretentious 850 *affected*; showing off 873 *vain*; magniloquent, high-sounding 574 *rhetorical*; grand, grandiose, splendid, brilliant, magnificent, superb; sumptuous, luxurious, diamond-studded, de luxe, ritzy, expensive 811 *dear*.

(5) *showy*, flashy, dressy 848 *fashionable*; lurid, gaudy, gorgeous 425 *florid*; glittering, garish 847 *vulgar*; flaunting, flagrant, blatant, public; brave, dashing, gallant, gay, jaunty, rakish, sporty; spectacular, scenic, dramatic, theatrical, stagy; sensational, daring; exhibitionist.

(6) *formal*, dignified, solemn, stately, majestic, grand; ceremonious, punctilious, correct, precise, stiff, starchy; black-tie, white-tie, full-dress; public, official; ceremonial, ritual 876 *celebratory*.

Verb
(7) *be ostentatious*, - showy etc. adj.; splurge, cut a dash, make a splash; glitter, dazzle 417 *shine*; flaunt, sport 228 *wear*; dress up 843 *primp*; wave, flourish 317 *brandish*; blazon, trumpet, 528 *proclaim*; wave banners 711 *defy*; demonstrate, exhibit 522 *show*; make the most of, window-dress, stage-manage; put on a front, paper over the cracks 226 *coat*; strive for effect, talk for effect, sensationalize 877 *boast*; put oneself forward 455 *attract notice*; play to the gallery 850 *be affected*; show off, show one's paces, prance, promenade, parade, march past, fly past; strut, swank 873 *be vain*;

876
Celebration

Noun
(1) *celebration*, performance, solemnization, commemoration; observance, solemn o. 988 *ritual*; ceremony, function, occasion, formal o., coronation, presentation 751 *commission*; debut 68 *beginning*; reception, official r., red carpet 875 *formality*; welcome, hero's w. 923 *applause*; festive occasion, fete, jubilee 837 *festivity*; jubilation, cheering, ovation, triumph, salute, salvo, tattoo, roll of drums, fanfare, flying colours, flag waving 835 *rejoicing*; flags, streamers, decorations, illuminations 420 *fireworks*; triumphal arch 729 *trophy*; harvest home, thanksgiving 907 *thanks*; paean, hallelujah 866 *congratulation*.

(2) *special day*, day to remember, great day, red-letter d., gala d., flag d., field d.; Saint's day,

feast d. 988 *holy day*; birthday, name-day; wedding anniversary, silver wedding, golden w.; centenary, bicentenary 141 *anniversary*.

Adjective
(3) *celebratory*, celebrating, commemorative 505 *remembering*; occasional, anniversary, centennial, bicentennial; festive, jubilant 835 *rejoicing*; triumphant, triumphal, welcoming.

Verb
(4) *celebrate*, solemnize, perform 676 *do*; hallow, keep holy 979 *sanctify*; commemorate 505 *remember*; honour, observe, keep, keep up, mark the occasion; make much of, welcome 882 *be hospitable*; do honour to, fete; chair 310 *elevate*; mob, rush, garland, wreathe, crown 962 *reward*; fire a salute 884 *pay one's respects*; cheer, triumph 835 *rejoice*; make holiday 837 *revel*; inaugurate, launch 751 *commission*.

(5) *toast*, pledge, clink glasses; drink to, drink a health.

Adverb
(6) *in honour of*, in memory of, on the occasion of.

877
Boasting

Noun
(1) *boasting*, bragging, boastfulness 875 *ostentation*; swagger, swank, bounce 873 *vanity*; self-glorification, self-advertisement; fine talk 515 *empty talk*; swaggering, swashbuckling, heroics, bravado; chauvinism, jingoism 481 *bias*; defensiveness, blustering, bluster 854 *nervousness*.

(2) *boast*, brag, vaunt; flourish, bravado, bombast, rant, tall talk 546 *exaggeration*; hot air

515 *empty talk*; bluff 542 *deception*; bluster, hectoring, idle threat.

(3) *boaster*, vaunter, swaggerer, braggart, brag, loudmouth, gasbag; blusterer, charlatan, bluffer 545 *liar*; swank, show-off 873 *vain person*; swashbuckler, ranter, trumpeter; jingoist, chauvinist.

Adjective
(4) *boastful*, boasting, bragging, vaunting, big-mouthed; braggart, swaggering 875 *ostentatious*; vainglorious 873 *vain*; bellicose, jingoistic, chauvinistic 718 *warlike*; hollow, pretentious 542 *spurious*; bombastic, magniloquent, grandiloquent 546 *exaggerated*; exultant, triumphant, cock-a-hoop 727 *successful*.

Verb
(5) *boast*, brag, vaunt, talk big, bluff, huff and puff, bluster, hector; vapour, prate, rant 515 *mean nothing*; magnify 546 *exaggerate*; trumpet, parade, flaunt, show off 875 *be ostentatious*; blow one's own trumpet 528 *advertise*; flourish, wave 317 *brandish*; strut, swagger, prance, swank 873 *be vain*; gloat 824 *be pleased*; boast of, plume oneself on 871 *be proud*; glory in, crow over, exult 727 *triumph*.

878
Insolence

Noun
(1) *insolence*, hubris, arrogance, haughtiness, loftiness 871 *pride*; bravado 711 *defiance*; bluster 900 *threat*; disdain 922 *contempt*; sneer, sneering 926 *detraction*; assurance, self-a., bumptiousness, cockiness, brashness; presumption 916 *arrogation*; audacity, boldness, effrontery, shamelessness, brazenness, blatancy, flagrancy.

(2) *sauciness,* disrespect, impertinence, impudence, pertness; flippancy, nerve, gall, cheek, cool c.; v-sign 547 *gesture;* taunt, insult, affront 921 *indignity;* rudeness, incivility 885 *discourtesy;* answering back, backchat 460 *rejoinder;* raillery 851 *ridicule.*

(3) *insolent person,* impertinent, cheeky devil; minx, hussy, baggage, madam; pup, puppy, upstart; blusterer, swaggerer 877 *boaster;* bully, hoodlum 904 *ruffian.*

Adjective

(4) *insolent,* rebellious 711 *defiant;* sneering 926 *detracting;* insulting 921 *disrespectful;* injurious, scurrilous 899 *cursing;* supercilious, disdainful, contemptuous 922 *despising;* high and mighty 871 *proud;* arrogant, presumptuous; brash, bumptious, bouncing 873 *vain;* shameless, unblushing, unabashed, brazen, brazen-faced, bold as brass; audacious 857 *rash;* overweening, overbearing, lordly, high-handed 735 *oppressive;* blustering, bullying 877 *boastful.*

(5) *impertinent,* pert, forward, fresh; impudent, saucy, cheeky, cool, jaunty, perky, cocky, cocksure; flippant, offhand, familiar 921 *disrespectful;* rude 885 *discourteous;* defiant, answering back, provocative, offensive; ridiculing 851 *derisive.*

Verb

(6) *be insolent,* - arrogant etc. adj.; get personal 885 *be rude;* have a nerve, have the audacity; cheek, sauce; taunt, provoke 891 *enrage;* retort, answer back 460 *answer;* shout down 479 *confute;* get above oneself, presume, take on oneself, make bold to, make free with; put on airs 871 *be proud;* look down

on, sneer at 922 *despise;* rally 851 *ridicule;* cock a snook at 711 *defy;* outstare, outface, brazen it out; swank, swagger 873 *be vain;* brag, talk big 877 *boast.*

Adverb

(7) *insolently,* impertinently.

879
Servility

Noun

(1) *servility,* slavishness, no pride, no self-respect 856 *cowardice;* subservience 721 *submission;* obsequiousness 739 *obedience;* time-serving; abasement 872 *humility;* prostration, genuflexion 311 *obeisance;* cringing, crawling, fawning, toadyism, sycophancy, ingratiation 925 *flattery;* slavery 745 *servitude.*

(2) *toady,* time-server, yes-man, rubber stamp 488 *assenter;* groveller, crawler, creep; hypocrite, fawner, courtier 925 *flatterer;* sycophant, parasite, leech, freeloader; hanger-on 742 *dependant;* lackey 742 *retainer;* lapdog, poodle; creature, cat's-paw 628 *instrument.*

Adjective

(3) *servile,* not free, dependent 745 *subject;* slavish 856 *cowardly;* mean-spirited, mean, abject, base 745 *subjected;* tame, deferential subservient, submissive 721 *submitting;* pliant, compliant, supple 739 *obedient;* timeserving; stooping, grovelling, bowing, scraping, cringing, crawling, fawning, whining; toadying, sycophantic, parasitical; creepy, obsequious, unctuous, oily, slimy, ingratiating 925 *flattering.*

Verb

(4) *be servile,* stoop to anything 867 *demean oneself;* cringe, creep, crawl, grovel, truckle, lick one's boots 721 *knuckle*

under; bow, scrape, kneel 311 *stoop*; swallow insults 872 *be humble*; make up to, ingratiate oneself, curry favour, toady to, suck up to, fawn on, pay court to 925 *flatter*; dance attendance on 742 *serve*; comply 739 *obey*; pander to 628 *be instrumental*; whine, wheedle, beg for favours 761 *beg*; batten on, sponge on; serve the times 603 *tergiversate*.

Adverb
(5) *servilely,* slavishly, cap in hand.

880
Friendship

Noun
(1) *friendship,* bonds of f., amity 710 *concord*; compatibility, mateyness; friendly relations 882 *sociality*; companionship, belonging, togetherness; fellowship, comradeship, brotherhood, sisterhood 706 *association*; solidarity, support, mutual s. 706 *cooperation*; acquaintance, familiarity, intimacy 490 *knowledge*; close friendship, passionate f. 887 *love*; making friends, overtures; reconciliation.

(2) *friendliness,* amicability, kindliness, kindness, neighbourliness 884 *courtesy*; heartiness, cordiality 897 *benevolence*; camaraderie, mateyness; hospitality 882 *sociability*; greeting, handshake 884 *courteous act*; regard, mutual r. 920 *respect*; goodwill, sympathy, understanding, friendly u., entente, honeymoon 710 *concord*; support, loyal s. 703 *aid*.

(3) *friend,* girlfriend, boyfriend 887 *loved one*; acquaintance, intimate a., lifelong friend; neighbour, good n.; well-wisher, partisan 707 *patron*; fellow, sister, brother 707 *colleague*; ally 707 *auxiliary*; friend in

need 703 *aider*; guest, persona grata; young friend, protégé(e).

(4) *close friend,* best f.; soul mate, kindred spirit; intimate, bosom friend, alter ego, other self; comrade, companion; happy family, inseparables.

(5) *chum,* crony; pal, mate, buddy; fellow, comrade, room-mate 707 *colleague*; playmate, classmate; pen friend.

Adjective
(6) *friendly,* amicable, devoted 887 *loving*; loyal, faithful, staunch, fast, firm 929 *trustworthy*; fraternal, brotherly, sisterly; natural, easy, harmonious 710 *concordant*; compatible, congenial, sympathetic, understanding; well-wishing, well-meaning 897 *benevolent*; hearty, cordial, warm, welcoming, hospitable 882 *sociable*; effusive, demonstrative, back-slapping, comradely; friendly with, acquainted; on familiar terms, on intimate t., intimate, inseparable.

Verb
(7) *be friendly,* be friends with, get on well w.; fraternize, hobnob, keep company with, go about together, be inseparable 882 *be sociable*; make friends, win f.; embrace 884 *greet*; welcome, entertain 882 *be hospitable*; sympathize 516 *understand*; like, warm to 887 *love*.

(8) *befriend,* make welcome; take up, protect 703 *patronize*; break the ice, make overtures 289 *approach*; take to, warm to, hit it off, make friends with; make acquainted, introduce, present.

Adverb
(9) *amicably,* as friends, arm in arm.

881
Enmity

Noun

(1) *enmity,* hostility, antagonism 704 *opposition*; no love lost, antipathy 861 *dislike*; loathing 888 *hatred*; animosity, animus, spite, grudge, ill feeling, ill will, bad blood 898 *malevolence*; jealousy 912 *envy*; coolness, unfriendliness; estrangement, alienation 709 *dissension*; bitterness, hard feelings 891 *resentment*; disloyalty 930 *perfidy*; breach 709 *quarrel*; hostilities vendetta, feud.

(2) *enemy,* ex-friend, traitor; ill-wisher, antagonist 705 *opponent*; competitor, rival 716 *contender*; foe 722 *combatant*; aggressor 712 *attacker*; public enemy, outlaw, pirate 789 *robber*; personal enemy, sworn e., bitter e.; misanthropist, misogynist 902 *misanthrope*; xenophobe 481 *narrow mind*; persona non grata 888 *hateful object.*

Adjective

(3) *inimical,* unfriendly, ill-disposed, disaffected; disloyal, unfaithful 930 *perfidious*; aloof, distant 883 *unsociable*; frigid, icy 380 *cold*; antipathetic, incompatible 861 *disliking*; loathing 888 *hating*; hostile, warring, conflicting 704 *opposing*; estranged, alienated, embittered 891 *resentful*; jealous, grudging 912 *envious*; spiteful 898 *malevolent*; on bad terms, not on speaking t.; at enmity, at variance, at loggerheads 709 *quarrelling*; aggressive, belligerent, at war with 718 *warring*; intolerant, persecuting 735 *oppressive.*

Verb

(4) *be inimical,* show hostility bear ill will, bear malice 898 *be malevolent*; grudge 912 *envy*; hound, persecute 735 *oppress*; make war 718 *wage war*; take offence 891 *resent*; fall out, come to blows 709 *quarrel.*

(5) *make enemies,* have no friends 883 *be unsociable*; cause offence, antagonize, irritate 891 *enrage*; estrange, alienate, set at odds 709 *make quarrels.*

882
Sociality

Noun

(1) *sociality,* social intercourse; membership 706 *association*; belonging, team spirit, esprit de corps; fellowship, comradeship, companionship, society; camaraderie, familiarity, intimacy, togetherness 880 *friendship*; social circle 880 *friend.*

(2) *sociability,* social activity, group a.; compatibility 83 *conformity*; gregariousness, sociableness 880 *friendliness*; social success, popularity; social tact, common touch; social graces, savoir vivre, good manners, easy m. 884 *courtesy*; urbanity affability; welcome, greeting 884 *courteous act*; hospitality, entertaining, open house 813 *liberality*; good company, good fellowship, geniality, cordiality, bonhomie; conviviality, joviality 824 *enjoyment*; gaiety 837 *revel*; festive board, 301 *feasting.*

(3) *social gathering,* reunion, get-together, conversazione, social 74 *assembly*; reception, at home, soirée; entertainment 837 *amusement*; singsong, camp fire; party, hen p., stag p., housewarming, house party; banquet 301 *feasting*; coffee morning, tea party, drinks; picnic, barbecue 837 *festivity.*

(4) *social round,* social whirl, social calls; stay, visit, call, courtesy c.; visiting terms 880

friendship; social demands, engagement; rendezvous, assignation, date, blind d.

(5) *sociable person,* caller, visitor, frequenter, habitue; bon vivant, good mixer, good company; catch 890 *favourite*; good neighbour 880 *friend*; hostess, host, guest, diner-out; social butterfly, socialite, social climber.

Adjective
(6) *sociable,* gregarious, extrovert, outgoing, companionable, affable, chatty, gossipy; neighbourly 880 *friendly*; hospitable, welcoming, cordial, hearty, back-slapping; convivial, festive, jolly, jovial 833 *merry*; lively, witty 837 *amusing*; urbane 884 *courteous*.

(7) *welcomed,* feted, entertained; welcome, ever-w., popular, sought-after, invited.

Verb
(8) *be sociable,* like company, socialize, mix with 880 *be friendly*; mix well, get around, live it up 837 *amuse oneself*; join in, get together 775 *participate*; carouse 837 *revel*; relax, unbend 683 *repose*; chat to 584 *converse*; date, make a date; make friends 880 *befriend*; write to 588 *correspond*.

(9) *visit,* go visiting, pay a visit, stay, weekend; keep in touch, go and see, look one up, call in, look in, drop in.

(10) *be hospitable,* keep open house 813 *be liberal*; invite, have round, ask in, receive, welcome, make w, 884 *greet*; do the honours, preside; entertain, regale 301 *feed*; give a party 837 *revel*; take in, cater for 633 *provide*.

Adverb
(11) *sociably,* hospitably.

883
Unsociability. Seclusion

Noun
(1) *unsociability,* shyness 620 *avoidance*; introversion, autism; aloofness 871 *pride*; coldness, moroseness 893 *sullenness*; cut 885 *discourtesy*; no conversation 582 *taciturnity*; ostracism 57 *exclusion*.

(2) *seclusion,* privacy, private world 266 *quietude*; home life, domesticity; loneliness, solitariness, solitude; retreat, retirement, withdrawal; confinement, purdah 525 *concealment*; isolation, splendid i. 744 *independence*; division, estrangement 46 *separation*; renunciation 985 *monasticism*; self-exile, expatriation; sequestration, segregation, rustication, quarantine 57 *exclusion*; reserve, reservation, ghetto, harem; gaol 748 *prison*; back of beyond, island, desert, wilderness; hide-out 527 *hiding-place*; den, study, sanctum, cloister, cell, hermitage 192 *retreat*; ivory tower, one's shell.

(3) *solitary,* unsocial person, loner, lone wolf; lonely person, lonely heart; isolationist; introvert; recluse, stay-at-home, anchorite, hermit; castaway.

(4) *outcast,* pariah, leper, outsider, untouchable; expatriate, alien 59 *foreigner*; exile, deportee, evacuee, refugee, displaced person, homeless p., stateless p.; outlaw, bandit; vagabond 268 *wanderer*; waif, stray 779 *derelict*.

Adjective
(5) *unsociable,* unsocial, antisocial, introverted, morose; foreign 59 *extraneous*; quiet, domestic; inhospitable, unfriendly; forbidding, hostile, misanthropic; distant, aloof, unbending, stand-offish,

haughty 871 *prideful*; frosty, icy 893 *sullen*; uncommunicative 582 *taciturn*; cool, impersonal 860 *indifferent*; solitary, lonely 88 *alone*; shy, retiring, withdrawn 620 *avoiding*.

(6) *friendless,* forlorn, foresaken, desolate, lonely, lonesome, solitary; on one's own 88 *alone*; avoided, unpopular; blacklisted, ostracized, sent to Coventry 57 *excluded*; expelled, deported, exiled.

(7) *secluded,* private, sequestered, cloistered, hidden, tucked away 523 *latent*; veiled, in purdah 421 *screened*; quiet, lonely, isolated, remote, godforsaken, unfrequented 491 *unknown*; deserted, uninhabited, desolate 190 *empty*.

Verb
(8) *be unsociable,* keep to oneself; immure oneself, stand aloof 620 *avoid*; make a retreat, take the veil; live in purdah.

(9) *make unwelcome,* keep at arm's length; repel, turn one's back on, not acknowledge, ignore, cut dead 885 *be rude*; cold-shoulder, rebuff; turn out, expel 300 *eject*; ostracize, boycott, send to Coventry, blacklist, blackball 57 *exclude*; have no time for 620 *avoid*; excommunicate, banish, exile, outlaw 963 *punish*.

(10) *seclude,* sequester, island, isolate, segregate; keep in purdah; confine, shut up 747 *imprison*.

884
Courtesy

Noun
(1) *courtesy,* chivalry, gallantry; deference 920 *respect*; consideration, graciousness, politeness, civility, urbanity, mannerliness, manners, good m., good

behaviour, best b.; good breeding 846 *good taste*; tactfulness, diplomacy; courtliness, correctness, 875 *formality*; amiability, sweetness, kindness, kindliness 897 *benevolence*; gentleness, mildness 736 *leniency*; easy temper, good humour 734 *laxity*; agreeableness, affability, suavity, blandness; common touch 882 *sociability*; smooth tongue 925 *flattery*.

(2) *courteous act,* act of courtesy, courtesy, civility, favour, kindness 897 *kind act*; soft answer 736 *leniency*; compliment kind words; introduction, presentation 880 *friendliness*; welcome, invitation; recognition, nod, salutation, salute, greeting, smile, kiss, hug, squeeze, handshake 920 *respects*; salaam, kowtow, bow, curtsy 311 *obeisance*; farewell 296 *valediction*.

Adjective
(3) *courteous,* chivalrous, knightly, generous 868 *noble*; courtly, gallant, old-world, correct 875 *formal*; polite, civil, urbane; gentlemanly, ladylike, dignified, well-mannered 848 *well-bred*; gracious, condescending 872 *humble*; deferential 920 *respectful*; anxious to please 455 *attentive*; obliging, kind 897 *benevolent*; conciliatory, suave, bland, smooth, ingratiating 925 *flattering*; obsequious 879 *servile*.

(4) *amiable,* nice, sweet, winning 887 *lovable*; affable, friendly 882 *sociable*; considerate, kind 897 *benevolent*; inoffensive, harmless 935 *innocent*; gentle, mild, soft-spoken 736 *lenient*; good-tempered, sweett., well-behaved, good 739 *obedient*; peaceable 717 *peaceful*.

Verb
(5) *be courteous,* mind one's manners, display good m.; show courtesy 920 *respect*; call sir,

call madam; oblige, put oneself out 703 *aid*; condescend 872 *be humble*; take no offence 823 *be patient*; mend one's manners.

(6) *pay one's respects,* send one's regards; pay compliments 925 *flatter*; drink to 876 *toast*; pay homage, kneel 920 *show respect*; honour, crown, chair 876 *celebrate.*

(7) *greet,* accost 289 *approach*; acknowledge, recognize 455 *notice*; hail 408 *vociferate*; nod, wave, smile; bid good morning 583 *speak to*; salute, raise one's hat; bow, curtsy; shake hands 920 *show respect*; escort 89 *accompany*; fire a salute, present arms, parade, turn out 876 *celebrate*; receive, welcome 882 *be sociable*; embrace, hug, kiss 889 *caress*; usher in, present, introduce.

Adverb
(8) *courteously,* politely, with respect.

885
Discourtesy

Noun
(1) *discourtesy,* impoliteness, bad manners; no manners, want of chivalry, scant courtesy, incivility, churlishness, boorishness 847 *ill-breeding*; misbehaviour, misconduct, tactlessness, inconsiderateness.

(2) *rudeness,* ungraciousness, gruffness, bluntness; sharpness, tartness, acerbity, acrimony, asperity; roughness, harshness 735 *severity*; offhandedness 456 *inattention*; sarcasm 851 *ridicule*; bad language 899 *scurrility*; rebuff, insult 921 *indignity*; impertinence, cheek 878 *insolence*; scowl, frown 893 *sullenness.*

(3) *rude person,* no gentleman, no lady; savage, barbarian, brute, lout, boor 878 *insolent person*; curmudgeon, sourpuss, 829 *malcontent.*

Adjective
(4) *discourteous,* unchivalrous; unceremonious, uncivil, impolite, rude; mannerless, unmannerly, ill-mannered, bad-m.; boorish, loutish, uncouth 847 *ill-bred*; insolent, impudent; cheeky, forward 878 *impertinent*; unpleasant, disagreeable; offhanded, cavalier 860 *indifferent*; tactless, inconsiderate 456 *inattentive.*

(5) *ungracious,* unsmiling, grim 834 *serious*; gruff, bearish 893 *sullen*; peevish, testy 892 *irascible*; difficult, surly, churlish, unfriendly 883 *unsociable*; grousing, grumbling, swearing 829 *discontented*; harsh, brutal 735 *severe*; bluff, frank, blunt, brusque 569 *concise*; tart, sharp, biting, acrimonious 388 *pungent*; sarcastic, uncomplimentary 926 *detracting*; foul-mouthed, abusive 899 *cursing*; offensive, insulting, truculent 921 *disrespectful.*

Verb
(6) *be rude,* forget one's manners; know no better 699 *be artless*; show discourtesy 878 *be insolent*; snub, cold-shoulder, cut, ignore 883 *make unwelcome*; cause offence 891 *huff*; insult, abuse; take liberties; stare 438 *gaze*; make one blush 867 *shame*; lose one's temper 891 *get angry*; curse 899 *cuss*; snarl, growl, frown, scowl 893 *be sullen.*

Adverb
(7) *impolitely,* discourteously.

886
Congratulation

Noun
(1) *congratulation,* congratula-

tions, felicitations, compliments; good wishes, happy returns; salute, toast; welcome, hero's w. 876 *celebration*; thanks 907 *gratitude*.

Adjective
(2) *congratulatory*, complimentary; honorific, triumphal 876 *celebratory*.

Verb
(3) *congratulate*, felicitate, compliment; wish one joy 884 *pay one's respects*; accord an ovation, give three cheers, clap 923 *applaud*; fete, mob, lionize 876 *celebrate*; thank Heaven 907 *be grateful*.

887
Love

Noun
(1) *love*, affection, friendship, charity, brotherly love, sisterly l.; true love, real thing; closeness, intimacy; sentiment 818 *feeling*; kindness, tenderness 897 *benevolence*; Platonic love 880 *friendship*; mutual affection, compatibility, sympathy, fellow feeling, understanding; fondness, liking, preference 605 *choice*; fancy 604 *caprice*; attachment, devotion 739 *loyalty*; courtly love, gallantry; fascination, enchantment; lovesickness 859 *desire*; eroticism, lust 859 *libido*; regard 920 *respect*; admiration, hero-worship 864 *wonder*; first love, calf l., puppy l.; crush, infatuation; worship 982 *idolatry*; romantic love, passion, tender p.; rapture, ecstasy 822 *excitable state*.

(2) *lovableness*, amiability, popularity, gift of pleasing; attractiveness, winsomeness, charm, fascination, appeal, sex a., attractions, charms, beauties; winning ways, coquetry.

(3) *love affair*, romance, flirtation, entanglement; gallantry,

coquetry, philandering; liaison, intrigue, seduction, adultery 951 *illicit love*; courtship 889 *wooing*; engagement 894 *marriage*; broken romance, broken heart.

(4) *lover*, love, true l., sweetheart; boyfriend, girlfriend; escort, date; steady, fiance(e); wooer, suitor, admirer; ladykiller, seducer 952 *libertine*; flirt, coquette, philanderer.

(5) *loved one*, beloved, love, true love, soul mate, one's own 890 *darling*; intimate 880 *close friend*; intended, betrothed, 894 *spouse*; conquest, inamorata, lady-love; sweetheart, valentine, flame, old f.; idol, hero; heartthrob, favourite; mistress 952 *kept woman*; femme fatale.

(6) *lovers*, pair of lovers, loving couple, turtledoves, lovebirds.

(7) *love god*, goddess of love, Venus; Cupid, Eros.

(8) *love emblem*, bleeding heart 889 *love token*.

Adjective
(9) *loving*, brotherly, sisterly; wooing, courting, making love 889 *caressing*; affectionate, demonstrative; tender, motherly, wifely, conjugal; gallant, romantic, sentimental; lovesick, lovelorn 834 *dejected*; attached to, fond of; fond, doting; possessive 911 *jealous*; admiring, adoring, devoted; flirtatious, coquettish 604 *capricious*; amorous, ardent, passionate 818 *fervent*; yearning 859 *desiring*; lustful 951 *lecherous*.

(10) *enamoured*, in love, sweet on, keen on, taken with, smitten, bitten, hooked; charmed, enchanted, fascinated 983 *bewitched*; infatuated, besotted, crazy about; rapturous, ecstatic 821 *excited*.

(11) *lovable*, likable, congenial, sympathetic, to one's liking 859 *desired*; winsome 884 *amiable*; sweet, angelic, divine, adorable; lovely, good-looking 841 *beautiful*; attractive, seductive, alluring 291 *attracting*; prepossessing, appealing, engaging, winning, endearing, captivating, irresistible; cuddly, desirable, kissable; charming, enchanting, bewitching; liked, beloved, dear, darling, favourite.

(12) *erotic*, aphrodisiac, erogenous; sexy, pornographic 951 *impure*; amatory 821 *excited*.

Verb
(13) *love*, like, take pleasure in, be partial to, be fond of; hold dear, care for, cherish, cling to; appreciate, value, prize, treasure; admire 920 *respect*; adore, worship, idolize, live for; burn with love, make love to 45 *unite with*; make much of, spoil, pet; fondle 889 *caress*.

(14) *be in love*, burn, faint, dote 503 *be insane*; take to, warm to, be taken with 859 *desire*; fall for, fall in love, lose one's heart; woo, sigh 889 *court*; chase 619 *pursue*; honeymoon 894 *wed*.

(15) *excite love*, arouse desire 859 *cause desire*; warm, inflame 381 *heat*; rouse, stir, flutter, enrapture, enthral 821 *excite*; dazzle, charm, enchant, fascinate 983 *bewitch*; allure, draw 291 *attract*; seduce 612 *tempt*; lead on, flirt, coquette, philander; catch one's eye 889 *court*; take one's fancy, steal one's heart, turn one's head, make a conquest, captivate; endear oneself, ingratiate o.; be lovable, steal every heart.

Adverb
(16) *affectionately*, kindly, lovingly, tenderly; madly.

888
Hatred

Noun
(1) *hatred*, hate, no love lost; love-hate, disillusion; aversion, antipathy, allergy, nausea 861 *dislike*; intense dislike, repugnance, loathing, abhorrence, abomination; disaffection, estrangement, alienation 709 *dissension*; hostility, antagonism 881 *enmity*; animosity, ill feeling, bad blood, bitterness 891 *resentment*; malice, ill will, spite, grudge 898 *malevolence*; jealousy 912 *envy*; wrath 891 *anger*; execration 899 *malediction*; scowl, snarl 893 *sullenness*; phobia, xenophobia, anti-Semitism, racialism, racism 481 *prejudice*; misogyny 902 *misanthropy*.

(2) *odium*, disfavour, bad odour, black books 867 *disrepute*; odiousness, hatefulness, loathsomeness, unpopularity 924 *disapprobation*.

(3) *hateful object*, abomination, anathema; bitter pill; pet aversion, bête-noire, 881 *enemy*; pest, menace 659 *bane*; rotter 938 *cad*; heretic, blackleg, scab 603 *tergiversator*.

Adjective
(4) *hating*, - loathing etc. vb.; antipathetic 861 *disliking*; set against 704 *opposing*; averse, abhorrent, antagonistic, hostile 881 *inimical*; envious, spiteful, malicious 898 *malevolent*; bitter, rancorous 891 *resentful*; full of hate, implacable; 910 *revengeful*; vindictive out of love, disillusioned.

(5) *hateful*, odious, unlovable, unloved; invidious, antagonizing, obnoxious 659 *baneful*; beastly, nasty, horrid 645 *not nice*; abhorrent, loathsome, abominable; accursed, execrable; offensive, repulsive, repellent, nauseating, revolting, disgusting 861 *disliked*.

(6) *hated,* - loathed etc. vb.; out of favour, unpopular 861 *disliked*; discredited 924 *disapproved*; loveless, unloved; unregretted, unlamented; spurned, jilted, crossed in love 607 *rejected*.

Verb
(7) *hate,* loathe, abominate, detest, abhor, hold in horror; shrink from 620 *avoid*; revolt from, can't bear, can't stand 861 *dislike*; spurn 922 *despise*; execrate, denounce 899 *curse*; bear malice 898 *be malevolent*; feel envy 912 *envy*; bear a grudge, 910 *be revengeful*.

(8) *excite hate,* grate, jar 292 *repel*; cause loathing, disgust, nauseate 861 *cause dislike*; shock, horrify 924 *incur blame*; antagonize, estrange, alienate, sow dissension 881 *make enemies*; poison, envenom, embitter, exacerbate 832 *aggravate*; exasperate, incense 891 *enrage*.

889
Endearment

Noun
(1) *endearment,* blandishments, compliments 925 *flattery*; loving words, soft nothings, lovers' vows; dalliance, holding hands, fondling, cuddling, petting, necking; caress, embrace, clasp, hug, bear h., cuddle, squeeze; kiss, nibble; stroke, tickle, pat, pinch, nip 378 *touch*; familiarity, advances.

(2) *wooing,* courting, flirting; love-play, lovemaking; wink, glad eye, come hither look, amorous glance, sheep's eyes, fond look, sigh; flirtation, philandering, coquetry, gallantry,

courtship, suit, advances; serenade, love song; love letter, billet-doux; love poem, sonnet; proposal, engagement, betrothal 894 *marriage*.

(3) *love token,* true lover's knot, favour; ring, engagement r., wedding r.; valentine, red roses; arrow, heart, tattoo.

Adjective
(4) *caressing,* clinging, demonstrative, affectionate 887 *loving*; cuddlesome, flirtatious, coquettish.

Verb
(5) *pet,* pamper, spoil, mother, smother, cosset, coddle; make much of, treasure 887 *love*; cherish, foster; nurse, rock, cradle; coax, wheedle 925 *flatter*.

(6) *caress,* love, fondle, dandle, play with, stroke, smooth, pat, paw; kiss, embrace, enfold, clasp, hug, cling 778 *retain*; squeeze, cuddle; snuggle, nestle, nuzzle, nibble; play, romp, wanton, toy, trifle, dally; make love, carry on, spoon, bill and coo, pet, neck 887 *excite love*; fawn on, be all over.

(7) *court,* make advances, make eyes at ogle, leer 438 *gaze*; make a pass at, become familiar; philander, flirt, coquette 887 *excite love*; be sweet on 887 *be in love*; run after, chase 619 *pursue*; escort 89 *accompany*; date, take out; walk out with, go steady; woo, go courting; serenade, sigh, pine, languish 887 *love*; offer one's heart *or* one's hand, propose.

890
Darling. Favourite

Noun
(1) *darling,* dear, dearest, my dear; dear one, one's own, one's all; truelove, love, beloved 887 *loved one*; heart, dear h.;

sweetheart, valentine; precious, jewel, treasure; angel, cherub; poppet pet, lamb, chick, ducks, ducky.

(2) *favourite,* darling; spoiled child, mother's darling, teacher's pet, blue-eyed boy; persona grata, one of the best, brick, sport, good s.; first choice, top seed, 644 *exceller*; boast, pride and joy; favourite son 866 *person of repute*; idol, hero, heroine, star, film s.; 841 *a beauty*; cynosure 291 *attraction*; catch 859 *desired object.*

891
Resentment. Anger

Noun
(1) *resentment,* displeasure, dissatisfaction 829 *discontent*; huffiness, sulks 893 *sullenness*; heart-burning, rancour; umbrage, offence, huff, tiff, pique; acrimony, bitterness, hard feelings; virulence, hate 888 *hatred*; animosity, grudge 881 *enmity*; vindictiveness, spite 910 *revenge*; malice 898 *malevolence*; fierceness, hot blood 892 *irascibility*; sore point 827 *annoyance*; provocation, aggravation, last straw 921 *indignity*; wrong, injury 914 *injustice.*

(2) *anger,* irritation, exasperation, vexation, indignation; wrath, rage, fury 822 *excitable state*; temper, tantrum, fit of temper, outburst, explosion; rampage, shout, roar; fierceness, glare, growl, snarl; asperity 892 *irascibility*; high words 709 *quarrel*; blows, fisticuffs 716 *fight.*

Adjective
(3) *resentful,* piqued, stung, galled, sore, smarting 829 *discontented*; surprised, pained, hurt, offended; warm, indignant; reproachful 924 *disapproving*; bitter, embittered,

acrimonious 888 *hating*; spiteful 898 *malevolent*; vindictive 910 *revengeful*; grudging, jealous 912 *envious.*

(4) *angry,* not amused, stern, frowning 834 *serious*; impatient, cross, wild, mad, livid; wrathful, irate; peeved, nettled, rattled, annoyed, irritated, vexed, provoked, stung; worked up, het up, angry with, mad at; indignant, angered, incensed, infuriated, in a temper, in a rage, in a fury; fuming, boiling, burning; speechless, stuttering, beside oneself; raging, violent 176 *furious*; apoplectic, rampaging, berserk 503 *frenzied*; glaring, glowering; red with anger, pale with a.;

Verb
(5) *resent,* find intolerable, feel, mind, smart under 829 *be discontented*; take amiss, feel insulted, take offence, take umbrage, take exception to 709 *quarrel*; smoulder, simmer 898 *be malevolent*; take to heart, let it rankle, cherish a grudge, bear malice 912 *envy.*

(6) *get angry,* get wild, get mad; grow warm, grow heated, colour, redden, flush with anger, flare up; bridle, bristle; lose patience, lose one's temper, forget oneself; throw a tantrum, fly into a rage, stamp, shout; let fly, burst out, boil over, blow up, explode; see red, go berserk 822 *be excitable.*

(7) *be angry,* - impatient etc. adj.; chafe, fret, fume, flounce, ramp, stamp, champ; create, make a scene 61 *rampage*; turn nasty, rage, rant, roar, bellow, bluster, storm, thunder, fulminate; look black, look daggers, glare, glower, frown, scowl 893 *be sullen*; spit, snap, lash out; gnash one's teeth, grind one's t., weep with rage, quiver with

r., dance with fury 821 *be excited*; let fly 176 *be violent*.

(8) *huff*, miff, pique, sting, nettle, rankle, smart; wound, ruffle 827 *hurt*; antagonize, offend, cause offence, embitter 888 *excite hate*; put one's back up 861 *cause dislike*; affront, insult, outrage 921 *not respect*.

(9) *enrage*, upset, discompose, ruffle, irritate, rile, peeve; annoy, vex, pester, bother 827 *trouble*; tease, bait, pinprick, needle, get on one's nerves 827 *torment*; fret, nag, gnaw; try one's patience, exasperate; anger, incense, infuriate, madden, drive mad; goad, sting, taunt; cause resentment, embitter, envenom, poison; exasperate 832 *aggravate*.

Adverb
(10) *angrily*, - bitterly etc. adj.

892
Irascibility

Noun
(1) *irascibility*, irritability, impatience 822 *excitability*; grumpiness, gruffness 883 *unsociability*; sharpness, tartness, asperity; sensitivity, touchiness, prickliness; pugnacity, bellicosity 709 *quarrelsomeness*; testiness, peevishness, petulance; uncertain temper, sharp t., short t.; hot temper, limited patience; fierceness, dangerousness, hot blood, bad temper.

(2) *shrew*, scold, fishwife; spitfire, termagant, battle-axe, virago, vixen, harridan, fury; bear 902 *misanthrope*.

Adjective
(3) *irascible*, impatient, short-tempered; choleric, irritable, peppery, testy, crusty, peevish, crotchety, cranky; quick-tempered, sharp-t.; prickly, touchy 819 *sensitive*; hot-blooded,

fierce, fiery, passionate 822 *excitable*; quick, warm, hasty, trigger-happy 857 *rash*; easily roused 709 *quarrelling*; scolding, shrewish, vixenish 899 *cursing*; petulant, cantankerous, querulous; captious, bitter, sour; bilious, liverish, gouty; scratchy, snappy, waspish; tart, sharp; uptight, edgy; fractious, fretful, moody, temperamental; gruff, grumpy 829 *discontented*; ill-humoured, cross 893 *sullen*.

Verb
(4) *be irascible*, have a temper, snap, bite 893 *be sullen*; jump down one's throat 891 *get angry*.

893
Sullenness

Noun
(1) *sullenness*, sulkiness, ill humour, surliness, churlishness 883 *unsociability*; grumpiness, pout, grimace 829 *discontent*; gruffness 885 *discourtesy*; crossness, peevishness, bad temper 892 *irascibility*; sulks, moodiness, temperament 834 *melancholy*; black look, hangdog l.; glare, glower, lour, frown, scowl; snarl, snap, bite.

Adjective
(2) *sullen*, gloomy, saturnine, glowering, scowling; unsmiling 834 *serious*; sulky, sulking, cross, out of temper, out of humour, out of sorts 883 *unsociable*; surly, morose, dyspeptic, crabbed, crusty, difficult; snarling, snappish, shrewish, cantankerous 709 *quarrelling*; refractory 738 *disobedient*; grouchy, grumbling, grumpy 829 *discontented*; gruff, abrupt, brusque 885 *discourteous*; temperamental, moody 152 *changeful*; bilious, jaundiced, dyspeptic; down, depressed 834

melancholic; petulant, peevish, bad-tempered 892 *irascible*.

Verb
(3) *be sullen,* glower, glare, scowl, frown, bare one's teeth, show one's fangs, spit, snap, snarl, growl; make a face, grimace, pout, sulk 883 *be unsociable*; mope 834 *be dejected*; grouse, carp, complain, grumble, mutter, smoulder 829 *be discontented*.

Adverb
(4) *sullenly,* sulkily, gloomily, with a bad grace.

894
Marriage

Noun
(1) *marriage,* matrimony, holy m., wedlock, wedded state, wedded bliss; match, union, partnership; conjugality, nuptial bond, marriage tie; cohabitation, life together.

(2) *type of marriage,* monogamy, bigamy, polygamy, polyandry; arranged match, love-match; mixed marriage, intermarriage; open marriage, common-law m.; misalliance; free love; shotgun wedding.

(3) *wedding,* getting married, match-making, betrothal, engagement; nuptial vows, marriage v.; bridal, nuptials, marriage rites; run-away match, elopement.

(4) *spouse,* one's betrothed 887 *loved one*; marriage partner, husband, wife; Mr and Mrs, Darby and Joan; newlyweds, honeymooners; bride, bridegroom; consort, partner, mate, helpmate; monogamist, bigamist, polygamist.

(5) *matchmaker,* go-between; marriage bureau, personal column 720 *mediator*.

(6) *nubility,* marriageable age, eligibility, suitability, good match.

Adjective
(7) *married,* made man and wife; paired, mated, matched; tied, spliced, hitched; wedded, united; monogamous; polygamous; polyandrous; bigamous; just married, newly-wed.

(8) *marriageable,* nubile, of age, eligible, suitable; betrothed, promised, engaged.

(9) *matrimonial,* marital, premarital, postmarital, extra-marital; nuptial, bridal; conjugal, wifely, husbandly; morganatic.

Verb
(10) *marry,* marry off, match, mate; make a match, give in marriage, give away; join in marriage, tie the knot.

(11) *wed,* marry, espouse; get married, marry oneself to; pair off, mate, couple 45 *unite with*; honeymoon, cohabit; marry in haste, elope; intermarry.

895
Celibacy

Noun
(1) *celibacy,* singleness, single state 744 *independence*; bachelorhood, spinsterhood; maidenhood, virginity 950 *purity*.

(2) *celibate,* unmarried man, single m., bachelor; hermit 986 *monk*.

(3) *spinster,* unmarried woman, bachelor girl; maid, maiden, maiden aunt, old maid; Vestal Virgin 986 *nun*.

Adjective
(4) *unwedded,* unmarried; single; on the shelf; fancy-free 744 *independent*; maidenly, virginal 950 *pure*; spinsterish, old-

maidish; bachelor-like, celibate 986 *monastic.*

Verb

(5) *live single,* stay unmarried, refuse marriage 744 *be free;* take the veil 986 *take orders.*

896
Divorce. Widowhood

Noun

(1) *divorce,* putting away, repudiation; divorce decree, decree nisi, decree absolute; separation; annulment, impediment; desertion, living apart; alimony; broken marriage; divorce(e), single parent.

(2) *widowhood,* widower, widow, relict; dowager, Merry Widow.

Adjective

(3) *divorced,* deserted, separated, living apart; dissolved.

(4)   *widowed,*   wifeless, husbandless.

Verb

(5) *divorce,* separate, split up, live apart, desert 621 *relinquish;* dissolve a marriage 46 *disunite;* put away, sue for divorce; get a divorce; be widowed, widow, bereave.

897
Benevolence

Noun

(1) *benevolence,* good will, helpfulness 880 *friendliness;* benignity, heart of gold; amiability, bonhomie   882   *sociability;* warmth of heart, kind heartedness, kindliness, kindness, loving-k., charity 887 *love;* brotherly   love   880   *friendship;* consideration, understanding, caring, concern, fellow feeling, empathy, sympathy 818 *feeling;* condolence 905 *pity;* humanity 901 *philanthropy;* charitableness, hospitality, beneficence, generosity, magnanimity 813 *liberality;* gentleness, mildness, 736 *leniency;* mercy 909 *forgiveness;* blessing, benediction.

(2) *kind act,* kindness, favour, service, good deed; charity, relief, alms 781 *giving;* prayers, good offices, good turn 703 *aid;* labour of love 597 *voluntary work.*

(3) *kind person,* good neighbour, good Samaritan, well-wisher 880 *friend;* sympathizer 707 *patron;* altruist, idealist 901 *philanthropist.*

Adjective

(4) *benevolent,* well meant, well-intentioned 880 *friendly;* sympathetic, kindly disposed, benign, kindly, kind-hearted, warm-hearted, golden-h.; kind, good, human, decent; affectionate 887 *loving;* fatherly, motherly, brotherly, sisterly; good-humoured, good-natured, sweet, gentle 884 *amiable;* merciful 909 *forgiving;* tolerant, indulgent 734 *lax;* humane, considerate 736 *lenient;* softhearted, tender 905 *pitying;* genial, hospitable 882 *sociable;* bountiful 813 *liberal;* generous, magnanimous, unselfish, altruistic 931 *disinterested;* beneficent, charitable, humanitarian 901 *philanthropic;* obliging, accommodating 703 *aiding;* gracious, chivalrous 884 *courteous.*

Verb

(5) *be benevolent,* - kind etc. adj.; show concern, care for, feel for; sympathize, understand 909 *forgive;* wish well, pray for, mean well; favour 703 *patronize;* benefit 644 *do good;* oblige 703 *aid;* humanize, reform 654 *make better.*

(6) *philanthropize,* do good, serve the community, care; get

involved 678 *be active*; reform, improve; visit, nurse 703 *minister to*; mother 889 *pet*.

Adverb
(7) *benevolently,* charitably, out of kindness, to oblige.

898
Malevolence

Noun
(1) *malevolence,* ill will 881 *enmity*; evil intent, worst intentions; spite, viciousness, malignancy, malice, spitefulness 888 *hatred*; venom, virulence 659 *bane*; bitterness, acrimony 393 *sourness*; rancour 891 *resentment*; gloating, unholy joy; evil eye 983 *spell*.

(2) *inhumanity,* misanthropy; lack of charity, intolerance, persecution 735 *severity*; harshness, mercilessness, implacability, obduracy, heart of stone 906 *pitilessness*; unkindness, callousness 326 *hardness*; cruelty, barbarity, bloodthirstiness, brutality, barbarism, savagery, ferocity; sadism, fiendishness 934 *wickedness*.

(3) *cruel act,* ill-treatment, brutality; unkindness, disservice, ill turn; victimization, bullying 735 *severity*; bloodshed 176 *violence*; excess, extremes; act of inhumanity, atrocity, outrage, cruelty, torture, barbarity; murder 362 *homicide*; genocide 362 *slaughter*.

Adjective
(4) *malevolent,* ill-disposed, meaning harm 661 *dangerous*; ill-natured, churlish 893 *sullen*; nasty, bitchy, cussed 602 *wilful*; malicious, catty, spiteful 926 *detracting*; mischievous, baleful, malign 645 *harmful*; vicious, venomous 362 *deadly*; black-hearted, full of spite 888 *hating*; jealous 912 *envious*;

treacherous 930 *perfidious*; bitter, rancorous 891 *resentful*; implacable, merciless 906 *pitiless*; vindictive, gloating; hostile 881 *inimical*; intolerant, persecuting 735 *oppressive*.

(5) *maleficent,* hurtful, damaging 645 *harmful*; poisonous, venomous, virulent, caustic 659 *baneful*; mischief-making 645 *bad*.

(6) *unkind,* ill-natured 893 *sullen*; unkindly, unfriendly; hostile, misanthropic 881 *inimical*; inhospitable 883 *unsociable*; unhelpful, disobliging; ungenerous, unforgiving, mean, nasty; rude 885 *ungracious*; unsympathetic, unmoved 820 *impassive*; stern 735 *severe*; tough, hardbitten, hard, inhuman, unnatural.

(7) *cruel,* grim, steely, grim-faced, cold-eyed, steely-e., hard-hearted, stony-h.; callous, cold-blooded; heartless, ruthless, merciless 906 *pitiless*; tyrannical 735 *oppressive*; gloating, sadistic; bloodthirsty, cannibalistic 362 *murderous*; bloody 176 *violent*; excessive, extreme; atrocious, outrageous; unnatural, subhuman, brutalized, brutish; brutal, rough, truculent, fierce, ferocious; savage, barbarous, wild; inhuman, ghoulish, fiendish, devilish, diabolical, satanic, hellish, infernal.

Verb
(8) *be malevolent,* bear malice, cherish a grudge 888 *hate*; spite, do one's worst; have no mercy 906 *be pitiless*; gloat, take one's revenge; victimize, bully, maltreat 645 *ill-treat*; molest, hurt 645 *harm*; malign, run down 926 *detract*; tease, harry, hound, persecute, tyrannize, torture 735 *oppress*; thirst for blood 362 *slaughter*; rankle, fester, poison; blight, blast.

Adverb
(9) *malevolently*, out of spite.

899
Malediction

Noun
(1) *malediction*, curse; evil eye 983 *spell*; execration, denunciation, fulmination; ban, proscription, exorcism, bell, book and candle.

(2) *scurrility*, ribaldry, vulgarity; profanity, swearing, bad language, strong l.; naughty word, swearword, expletive, oath, curse, cuss; invective, abuse; mutual abuse, slanging match; vilification, slander 926 *calumny*; cheek, sauce 878 *sauciness*; personal remarks, epithet, insult 921 *indignity*; scorn 922 *contempt*; scolding 924 *reproach*.

Adjective
(3) *maledictory*, cursing, imprecatory.

(4) *cursing*, swearing, damning, blasting; profane, foulmouthed, scurrilous 847 *vulgar*; vituperative, abusive, vitriolic 924 *disapproving*; scornful 922 *despising*.

(5) *cursed*, accursed; under a ban, damned 961 *condemned*; under a spell 983 *bewitched*.

Verb
(6) *curse*, wish ill 898 *be malevolent*; wish on, call down on; anathematize, imprecate, invoke curses on; fulminate, thunder against 924 *reprove*; excommunicate, damn 961 *condemn*; round upon, abuse, revile, rail, chide 924 *reprobate*.

(7) *cuss*, curse, swear, damn, blast; blaspheme 980 *be impious*; abuse 924 *reprobate*; rail at, scold.

Interjection
(8) *curse!* a curse on! a plague on! woe to! confound it! blast! damn! darn! drat!

900
Threat

Noun
(1) *threat*, menace; fulmination 899 *malediction*; challenge, dare 711 *defiance*; blackmail 737 *demand*; war whoop, war of nerves 854 *intimidation*; deterrent, big stick 723 *weapon*; black cloud 511 *omen*; writing on the wall 664 *warning*; bluster, idle threat 877 *boast*.

Adjective
(2) *threatening*, menacing; blustering, bullying, hectoring 877 *boastful*; muttering, grumbling 893 *sullen*; ominous, foreboding 511 *presageful*; hanging over 155 *impending*; growling, snarling 891 *angry*; abusive 899 *cursing*; deterrent 854 *frightening*; nasty 661 *dangerous*.

Verb
(3) *threaten*, menace, use threats, blackmail 737 *demand*; hijack, hold to ransom; deter, intimidate, bully 854 *frighten*; roar, bellow 408 *vociferate*; thunder 899 *curse*; talk big, bluster, hector 877 *boast*; rattle the sabre, clench the fist, draw one's sword; bare the fangs, snarl, growl, bristle, spit, look daggers, grow nasty 891 *get angry*; hold at gunpoint, cover, have one covered; gather, mass, hang over 155 *impend*; presage disaster, mean no good, promise trouble, spell danger 511 *predict*; caution, forewarn 664 *warn*; threaten reprisals 910 *be revengeful*.

Adverb
(4) *threateningly*, menacingly, on pain of.

901
Philanthropy

Noun
(1) *philanthropy,* humanity, humaneness 897 *benevolence*; humanism, altruism 931 *disinterestedness*; ideals 933 *virtue*; common good, utilitarianism, socialism, communism; chivalry, dedication, crusading spirit, good works, mission; crusade, campaign, cause, good c.; voluntary agency, charity 703 *aid.*

(2) *sociology,* social science, social planning; benefit, dole; social services, Welfare State; social work, community service.

(3) *patriotism,* good citizenship, public spirit; nationalism, chauvinism.

(4) *philanthropist,* humanitarian, do-gooder, social worker 897 *kind person,* 597 *volunteer*; champion, knight errant; missionary, crusader; idealist, altruist 513 *visionary*; utilitarian, Utopian, humanist 654 *reformer*; cosmopolitan, internationalist.

(5) *patriot,* nationalist, chauvinist, Zionist.

Adjective
(6) *philanthropic,* humanitarian, humane 897 *benevolent*; charitable 703 *aiding*; enlightened, humanistic, liberal; cosmopolitan, international, idealistic, altruistic 931 *disinterested*; visionary, dedicated; sociological, utilitarian.

(7) *patriotic,* public-spirited; nationalistic, chauvinistic; loyal, true-blue.

Verb
(8) *be charitable* 897 philanthropize.

902
Misanthropy

Noun
(1) *misanthropy,* hatred of mankind 883 *unsociability*; misandry, misogyny; cynicism; moroseness 893 *sullenness*; inhumanity, egotism.

(2) *misanthrope,* misanthropist, man-hater, woman-h., misogynist; cynic, egotist 883 *solitary*; bear, crosspatch 829 *malcontent.*

Adjective
(3) *misanthropic,* inhuman, antisocial 883 *unsociable.*

903
Benefactor

Noun
(1) *benefactor,* benefactress 901 *philanthropist*; Lady Bountiful, Santa Claus 781 *giver*; guardian angel 660 *protector*; founder, supporter 707 *patron*; tyrannicide 901 *patriot*; saviour, redeemer, rescuer 668 *deliverance*; champion 703 *defender*; Good Samaritan 897 *kind person*; good neighbour 880 *friend*; helper 703 *aider*; saint 937 *good person.*

904
Evildoer

Noun
(1) *evildoer,* malefactor, wrongdoer 934 *wickedness*; villain, blackguard, bad lot 663 *troublemaker*; little devil, holy terror; gossip, slanderer 926 *detractor*; traitor 545 *deceiver*; saboteur 702 *hinderer*; wrecker, vandal, iconoclast 168 *destroyer*; terrorist, nihilist, anarchist 738 *revolter*; incendiary, arsonist.

(2) *ruffian,* blackguard, rogue, scoundrel 938 *knave*; lout, hooligan, hoodlum 869 *low fellow*; yob, punk; bully, terror, tough, rowdy, ugly customer, bruiser, thug, desperado, assassin; killer, butcher 362 *murderer*; brute, beast, savage, barbarian; cannibal, head-hunter.

(3) *offender,* black sheep 938 *bad person*; suspect, culprit, guilty person, law-breaker; criminal, villain, crook, malefactor, wrongdoer, felon; delinquent, juvenile d., first offender; recidivist, backslider, hardened offender, convict, ex-c. jailbird; lifer, probationer; mobster, gangster, racketeer; housebreaker 789 *thief*; forger 789 *defrauder*; blackmailer, bloodsucker; poisoner 362 *murderer*; outlaw 881 *enemy*; intruder, trespasser; criminal world, underworld, Mafia.

(4) *hellhag,* hellhound, fiend, devil incarnate; bitch, virago 892 *shrew*; she-devil, fury, harpy; ogre, ogress, vampire, werewolf 938 *monster*.

(5) *noxious animal,* brute, beast, wild b.; beast of prey, predator; 659 *bane*; mad dog, rogue elephant.

905
Pity

Noun
(1) *pity,* remorse, compunction 830 *regret*; charity, compassion, humanity 897 *benevolence*; soft heart, tender h. 825 *sorrow*; sympathy, empathy, understanding.

(2) *condolence,* commiseration, fellow feeling 775 *participation*; consolation, comfort 831 *relief*; keen, wake 836 *lament*.

(3) *mercy,* quarter, grace; second chance; mercifulness, clemency 909 *forgiveness*; light sentence, let-off 960 *acquittal*.

Adjective
(4) *pitying,* compassionate, sympathetic, understanding, commiserating; sorry for, feeling for; merciful 736 *lenient*; melting, tender, tender-hearted, soft-hearted 819 *impressible*; weak, soft 734 *lax*; disposed to mercy 909 *forgiving*; remorseful, compunctious; humane, charitable 897 *benevolent*; forbearing 823 *patient*.

(5) *pitiable,* pitiful, piteous, pathetic, heart-rending; deserving pity.

Verb
(6) *pity,* feel p., show compassion, take pity on; sympathize, feel for; sorrow, grieve, feel sorry for; commiserate, condole 836 *lament*; console, comfort 833 *cheer*; have pity, melt, thaw, relent 909 *forgive*.

(7) *show mercy,* spare, give quarter; pardon, amnesty 909 *forgive*; give a second chance 736 *be lenient*; relent, unbend, forbear, go easy on.

(8) *ask mercy,* plead for m., beg for m., ask for quarter; excite pity, propitiate, disarm, melt, thaw, soften 719 *pacify*.

Interjection
(9) *alas!* have mercy! have a heart!

906
Pitilessness

Noun
(1) *pitilessness,* lack of pity, heartlessness, ruthlessness, inclemency, intolerance 735 *severity*; callousness, hardness of heart 898 *inhumanity*; inflexibility 326 *hardness*; inexorability, remorselessness, pound of

flesh; no heart, short shrift, no quarter.

Adjective
(2) *pitiless*, unfeeling, unresponsive 820 *impassive*; unsympathetic, unmoved, dry-eyed; hardhearted, callous, tough 326 *hard*; harsh, rigorous, intolerant 735 *severe*; brutal, sadistic 898 *cruel*; merciless, ruthless, heartless; unrelenting, relentless, remorseless, unforgiving; inflexible, inexorable, implacable; vindictive 901 *revengeful*.

Verb
(3) *be pitiless*, have no heart, not be moved, show no pity, show no mercy, give no quarter, spare none; harden one's heart, turn a deaf ear; not tolerate, persecute 735 *be severe*; take one's revenge 910 *avenge*.

907
Gratitude

Noun
(1) *gratitude*, gratefulness, thankfulness, grateful heart, appreciation.

(2) *thanks*, hearty t.; vote of thanks, thankyou; thanksgiving, praises 876 *celebration*; grace, benediction; credit, credit title; acknowledgement, recognition, tribute 923 *praise*; thank-offering, token of gratitude, tip 962 *reward*.

Adjective
(3) *grateful*, thankful, appreciative; thanking, blessing, praising; crediting, acknowledging, giving credit; obliged, much o., beholden, indebted.

Verb
(4) *be grateful*, accept gracefully.

(5) *thank*, give thanks, praise, bless; acknowledge, credit, give full c. 158 *attribute*; appreciate, tip 962 *reward*; return a favour, repay.

Adverb
(6) *gratefully*, with gratitude, with thanks.

Interjection
(7) thanks! many t.! much obliged! thank you!

908
Ingratitude

Noun
(1) *ingratitude*, lack of gratitude, ungratefulness; grudging thanks; no reward, thankless task.

Adjective
(2) *ungrateful*, unthankful 885 *discourteous*; unmindful 506 *forgetful*.

(3) *unthanked*, thankless, unrewarding; without credit, unacknowledged, unappreciated; rewardless, unrewarded, forgotten.

Verb
(4) *be ungrateful*, show ingratitude, take for granted, take as one's due; not thank, omit to t., forget to t.

Interjection
(5) *thank you for nothing!* no thanks to.

909
Forgiveness

Noun
(1) *forgiveness*, pardon, free p., reprieve 506 *amnesty*; indemnity, indulgence 905 *mercy*; remission, absolution 960 *acquittal*; justification, exoneration 927 *vindication*; reconciliation 719 *pacification*; mercifulness, lenity 905 *pity*; forbearance 823 *patience*.

Adjective
(2) *forgiving*, merciful, condoning, conciliatory 736 *lenient*; magnanimous 897 *benevolent*; forbearing 823 *patient*.

(3) *forgiven,* pardoned, reprieved; remitted, cancelled; condoned, excused, exonerated, let off 960 *acquitted*; amnestied, absolved; pardonable, forgivable, venial, excusable.

Verb
(4) *forgive,* pardon, reprieve, amnesty 506 *forget*; remit, absolve, shrive; cancel 550 *obliterate*; relent, unbend, accept an apology; be merciful 905 *show mercy*; bear with, put up w., make allowances 823 *be patient*; take no offence, bear no malice, pocket, stomach, overlook, pass over, not punish 897 *be benevolent*; connive, condone 458 *disregard*; excuse 927 *justify*; exonerate 960 *acquit*; bury the hatchet, make it up, be reconciled 880 *be friendly*.

(5) *beg pardon,* offer apologies, beg forgiveness 905 *ask mercy*; propitiate, placate 941 *atone*.

910
Revenge

Noun
(1) *revengefulness,* vindictiveness, spite 898 *malevolence*; ruthlessness; 906 *pitilessness*; implacability 891 *resentment*.

(2) *revenge,* vengeance 963 *punishment*; victimization, reprisals 714 *retaliation*; eye for an eye; vendetta, feud 881 *enmity*.

(3) *avenger,* vindicator, punisher, Nemesis.

Adjective
(4) *revengeful,* vengeful, avenging 881 *inimical*; retaliative 714 *retaliatory*; implacable, unrelenting, unforgiving; remorseless, relentless 906 *pitiless*; vindictive, spiteful 898 *malevolent*; rancorous 891 *resentful*; gloating.

Verb
(5) *avenge,* avenge oneself, revenge o., take one's revenge, take vengeance, wreak v., repay, get one's own back 714 *retaliate*; gloat.

(6) *be revengeful,* - vindictive etc. adj.; 898 *be malevolent*; bear malice 888 *hate*; harbour a grudge 881 *be inimical*; let it rankle, brood on 891 *resent*.

911
Jealousy

Noun
(1) *jealousy,* pangs of j., jealousness; jaundiced eye, distrust, mistrust 486 *doubt*; heartburning 891 *resentment*; enviousness 912 *envy*; hate 888 *hatred*; competition, rivalry; possessiveness 887 *love*; sexual jealousy, eternal triangle. competitor, rival, the other man, the other woman.

Adjective
(2) *jealous,* green-eyed, yellow-e., jaundiced, envying 912 *envious*; possessive, suspicious, mistrusting, distrustful 474 *doubting*; rival, competing.

Verb
(3) *be jealous,* scent a rival, suspect, mistrust, distrust 486 *doubt*; brook no rival.

912
Envy

Noun
(1) *envy,* envious eye, enviousness, covetousness 859 *desire*; rivalry 716 *contention*; envious rivalry 911 *jealousy*; ill will, spite, spleen, bile 898 *malevolence*; mortification, grudging praise.

Adjective
(2) *envious,* green with envy 911 *jealous*; greedy, unsatisfied 829

discontented; covetous 859 *desiring*; grudging 891 *resentful*.

Verb
(3) *envy*, resent; covet, crave, lust after 859 *desire*.

913
Right

Noun
(1) *right*, rightfulness, rightness, fitness, what should be; obligation 917 *duty*; fittingness, propriety 848 *etiquette*; rules 693 *precept*; morality 917 *morals*; righteousness 933 *virtue*; rectitude, uprightness, honour 929 *probity*; one's right, one's due, deserts, merits 915 *dueness*.

(2) *justice*, righting wrong, reform, redress; process of law 953 *legality*; retribution 962 *reward*; give and take 714 *retaliation*; fairmindedness, objectivity, detachment, impartiality, equity, equitableness, fairness; fair deal, fair play.

Adjective
(3) *right*, rightful, proper, right and p., meet and right; fitting, suitable 24 *fit*; good 917 *ethical*; put right, reformed 654 *improved*.

(4) *just*, upright, righteous, right-minded 933 *virtuous*; fairminded, disinterested, unprejudiced, unbiased 625 *neutral*; detached, impersonal, dispassionate, objective, openminded; equal, egalitarian, impartial, even-handed; fair, fair and square, equitable, reasonable, fair enough; in the right, justifiable, justified; legitimate 953 *legal*; sporting, sportsmanlike 929 *honourable*; deserved, well-d., well-merited, 915 *due*.

Verb
(5) *be right*, behove 915 *be due*; have justice, have good cause, be in the right.

(6) *be just*, - impartial etc. adj.; play the game 929 *be honourable*; do justice, hand it to 915 *grant claims*; see justice done, see fair play, hear both sides 480 *judge*; right a wrong, redress, remedy 654 *rectify*; serve one right 714 *retaliate*.

Adverb
(7) *rightly*, justly, with justice; impartially; on its merits.

914
Wrong

Noun
(1) *wrong*, wrongness; curse, scandal 645 *badness*; disgrace, shame, dishonour 867 *slur*; impropriety 847 *bad taste*; culpability, guiltiness 936 *guilt*; immorality, vice, sin 934 *wickedness*; dishonesty, irregularity, crime, lawlessness 954 *illegality*; trespass, encroachment; misdeed, offence 936 *guilty act*; a wrong, injustice, mischief 930 *foul play*; complaint, charge 928 *accusation*; grievance 891 *resentment*; wrong-doer 938 *bad person*.

(2) *injustice*, miscarriage of justice, wrong verdict 481 *misjudgment*; unfairness, discrimination 481 *bias*; one-sidedness, partiality, favouritism, favour, nepotism; partisanship 481 *prejudice*; unlawfulness 954 *illegality*; not cricket 930 *foul play*.

Adjective
(3) *wrong*, not right 645 *bad*; odd, queer, suspect 84 *abnormal*; unfitting, unseemly, improper 847 *vulgar*; wrongheaded, unreasonable 481 *misjudging*; out of court, inadmissible; irregular, against the rules; wrongful, illegitimate 954 *illegal*; condemnable, culpable, in the wrong 936 *guilty*; unpardonable, inexcusable; objectionable, reprehensible,

scandalous 861 *disliked*; injurious, mischievous 645 *harmful*; iniquitous, vicious, immoral 934 *wicked*.

(4) *unjust*, inequitable, unfair, iniquitous, hard on 735 *severe*; unsportsmanlike, below the belt; favouring, discriminatory, one-sided, partial, partisan, prejudiced 481 *biased*.

Verb
(5) *be wrong*, - unjust etc. adj.; go wrong, err.

(6) *do wrong*, wrong, hurt, injure, do an injury 645 *harm*; break the rules, commit a foul; commit a crime, break the law, pervert the l. 954 *be illegal*; transgress, infringe 306 *encroach*; wink at, connive at; withhold justice, deny one's rights; pack the jury, rig the jury; show favouritism, discriminate 481 *be biased*; favour 703 *patronize*; commit, perpetrate.

Adverb
(7) *wrongly*, wrongfully, illegally.

915
Dueness

Noun
(1) *dueness*, what is due; obligation 917 *duty*; dues 804 *payment*; indebtedness 803 *debt*; tribute, credit 158 *attribution*; recognition 907 *thanks*; case for; qualification, merits, deserts 913 *right*; justification 927 *vindication*; entitlement, claim, title 913 *right*; birthright, patriality, patrimony 777 *dower*; interest, vested i., legal right; human rights, women's r. 744 *freedom*; civil rights, bill of r.; exemption, immunity 919 *nonliability*; prerogative, privilege; charter, warrant, licence 756 *permit*; liberty, franchise; bond, security 767 *title deed*;

patent, copyright; compensation 787 *restitution*; title-holder 776 *possessor*; claimant, plaintiff, appellant 763 *petitioner*.

Adjective
(2) *due*, owing 803 *owed*; ascribable, attributable, assignable; merited, well-m., deserved, richly-d., earned, well-e.; sanctioned, warranted, licit, lawful 756 *permitted*; entrenched, constitutional; unimpeachable, inviolable, sacrosanct; confirmed, vested, prescriptive, inalienable, legalized, legitimate, rightful, of right 953 *legal*; claimable, heritable; proper, fitting 913 *right*.

(3) *deserving*, meriting, worthy of, meritorious, emeritus; justifiable, entitled, having the right.

Verb
(4) *be due*, - owing etc. adj.; ought to be, should be; be one's due, be due to; behove, befit 917 *be one's duty*.

(5) *claim*, lay claim to, stake a c. 786 *appropriate*; claim unduly, arrogate; reclaim 656 *retrieve*; sue 761 *request*; enforce a claim, exercise a right; patent, copyright.

(6) *have a right*, expect, claim; be entitled; make out a case, justify 927 *vindicate*;

(7) *deserve*, merit, be worthy; earn, receive one's due;

(8) *grant claims*, acknowledge a claim 913 *be just*; ascribe, assign, credit 158 *attribute*; acknowledge, recognize 907 *thank*; warrant, authorize 756 *permit*; pay one's dues; privilege, confer a right, legalize, legitimize 953 *make legal*; confirm, validate 488 *endorse*.

Adverb
(9) *duly*, by right, by law, de jure, ex officio.

916
Undueness

Noun

(1) *undueness,* impropriety, indecorum 847 *bad taste*; illegitimacy 954 *illegality*; no thanks to 908 *ingratitude*; absence of right, no claim, no right, no title; imposition, exaction 735 *severity*; violation, breach, infringement 306 *overstepping*; profanation 980 *impiety*.

(2) *arrogation,* assumption, presumption; misappropriation 786 *expropriation*; encroachment, trespass.

(3) *loss of right,* disentitlement, disqualification; forfeiture 772 *loss*; dismissal, deprivation, dispossession 786 *expropriation*; cancellation 752 *abrogation*; waiver, abdication 621 *relinquishment*.

(4) *usurper,* 735 *tyrant*; pretender 545 *impostor*; trespasser, squatter.

Adjective

(5) *undue,* not owing, by favour; unlooked for, uncalled for 508 *unexpected*; inappropriate, improper 643 *inexpedient*; preposterous 497 *absurd*.

(6) *unwarranted,* unauthorized, unconstitutional; illicit, illegitimate 954 *illegal*; arrogated, usurped; presumptuous, assuming 878 *insolent*; unjustifiable 914 *wrong*; forfeited, forfeit; false, fictitious, invalid.

(7) *unentitled,* unqualified, incompetent; without rights, voteless; dethroned, deposed; disqualified, invalidated, disfranchised; deprived, dispossessed.

Verb

(8) *be undue,* presume, arrogate 878 *be insolent*; usurp, borrow 788 *steal*; trespass, squat 306

encroach; infringe, violate 954 *be illegal*; desecrate, profane 980 *be impious*.

(9) *disentitle,* dethrone 752 *depose*; disqualify, disfranchise; invalidate 752 *abrogate*; disallow 757 *prohibit*; dispossess, expropriate 786 *deprive*; forfeit, declare f.

917
Duty

Noun

(1) *duty,* the right thing, the proper t., the decent t.; one's duty, obligation; onus, responsibility 915 *dueness*; fealty, allegiance, loyalty 739 *obedience*; dutifulness 597 *willingness*; discharge of duty, performance, acquittal, discharge 768 *observance*; call of duty, bond, tie, commitment 764 *promise*; task, office, charge 751 *commission*.

(2) *conscience,* tender c.; inner voice.

(3) *code of duty,* code of honour, unwritten code, professional c. 693 *precept*.

(4) *morals,* morality 933 *virtue*; honour 929 *probity*; moral principles, ideals, standards, professional s.; ethics; moral science, idealism, humanism.

Adjective

(5) *obliged,* duty-bound, obligated, beholden, under obligation; sworn, pledged, committed; liable, answerable, responsible, accountable; in honour bound; conscientious 768 *observant*; dutiful 739 *obedient*.

(6) *obligatory,* incumbent, behoving, up to one; binding, de rigueur, compulsory, mandatory; strict, unconditional, categorical.

(7) *ethical,* moral 933 *virtuous*; honest, decent 929 *honourable*;

moralistic, moralizing; humanistic.

Verb

(8) *be one's duty,* be incumbent on, behove, befit 915 *be due*; devolve on, fall to, rest with.

(9) *incur a duty,* take on oneself, commit oneself 764 *promise*; accept responsibility, make oneself liable; accept the call,

(10) *do one's duty,* fulfil one's d. 739 *obey*; acquit, perform 676 *do*; do one's bit, play one's part; keep faith 768 *observe*; be on duty, stay at one's post; honour, meet, discharge.

(11) *impose a duty,* require, oblige, look to, call upon; post 751 *commission*; saddle with, order, enjoin 737 *command*; demand obedience; bind, condition 766 *give terms*.

Adverb

(12) *on duty,* at one's post, in duty bound.

918
Undutifulness

Noun

(1) *undutifulness,* default, dereliction of duty; neglect 458 *negligence*; malingering 620 *avoidance*; nonperformance 769 *nonobservance*; idleness, forgetfulness; truancy, absenteeism 190 *absence*; absconding 667 *escape*; indiscipline, mutiny 738 *disobedience*; desertion, defection; disloyalty, treachery 930 *perfidy*; truant, absentee, malingerer, defaulter 620 *avoider*; slacker 679 *idler*; deserter, absconder 667 *escaper*; traitor 603 *tergiversator*; mutineer, rebel 738 *revolter*.

Adjective

(2) *undutiful,* unfilial, undaughterly 921 *disrespectful*;

mutinous, rebellious 738 *disobedient*; disloyal, treacherous 930 *perfidious*; irresponsible, unreliable; truant, absconding.

Verb

(3) *fail in duty,* ignore one's obligations 458 *disregard*; let one down 509 *disappoint*; not remember 506 *forget*; shirk, evade, wriggle out of 620 *avoid*; play truant, 190 *be absent*; abscond 667 *escape*; quit 296 *decamp*; abandon, desert, leave in the lurch 621 *relinquish*; disobey orders 738 *disobey*; mutiny, rebel 738 *revolt*; be disloyal, 603 *tergiversate*; walk out, break away, secede.

919
Nonliability

Noun

(1) *nonliability,* exemption, dispensation; escape clause 468 *qualification*; special treatment; immunity, diplomatic i., privilege; licence, leave 756 *permission*; excuse 960 *acquittal*; absolution, pardon, amnesty 909 *forgiveness*.

Adjective

(2) *nonliable,* not responsible, not answerable, unaccountable; excused, exonerated 960 *acquitted*; exempted, exempt, immune.

Verb

(3) *exempt,* set apart, count out, rule o. 57 *exclude*; excuse, exonerate, exculpate 960 *acquit*; absolve, pardon 909 *forgive*; spare 905 *show mercy*; grant immunity, charter 756 *permit*; license, give dispensation, grant impunity; amnesty 506 *forget*; enfranchise, set at liberty, release 746 *liberate*; pass over, stretch a point 736 *be lenient*.

(4) *be exempt,* enjoy immunity; excuse oneself, pass the buck, shift the blame; get away with,

escape liability 667 *escape*; 918 *fail in duty*.

920
Respect

Noun
(1) *respect*, regard, consideration, esteem 923 *approbation*; high standing, honour 866 *repute*; polite regard, attentions 884 *courtesy*; due respect, deference, humbleness 872 *humility*; devotion 739 *loyalty*; admiration, awe 864 *wonder*; terror 854 *fear*; reverence, veneration 981 *worship*.

(2) *respects*, regards, kind r., greetings 884 *courteous act*; red carpet, guard of honour, salute, salutation, salaam; bow, curtsy, genuflexion 311 *obeisance*; reverence, homage.

Adjective
(3) *respectful*, deferential 872 *humble*; obsequious, boot-licking 879 *servile*; reverent 981 *worshipping*; admiring, awestruck 864 *wondering*; polite 884 *courteous*; at the salute, bare-headed; kneeling, on one's knees, prostrate; bobbing, bowing, scraping; showing respect, rising, on one's feet.

(4) *respected*, admired, honoured, esteemed, revered 866 *reputable*; respectable, reverend, venerable; time-honoured 866 *worshipful*; imposing 821 *impressive*.

Verb
(5) *respect*, hold in honour, think well of, rank high, look up to, esteem, regard, value; admire 864 *wonder*; reverence, venerate 866 *honour*; idolize, adore 981 *worship*; revere 854 *fear*; know one's place, defer to 721 *submit*; do homage to 876 *celebrate*.

(6) *show respect*, pay homage 884 *pay one's respects*; salute, present arms 884 *greet*; cheer, drink to 876 *toast*; bow and scrape, curtsy, kneel 311 *stoop*; observe decorum, stand on ceremony, rise, uncover; humble oneself 872 *be humble*.

(7) *command respect*, inspire r., awe, overawe, impose 821 *impress*; rank high 866 *have a reputation*; dazzle 875 *be ostentatious*; receive respect, gain a reputation 923 *be praised*.

Adverb
(8) *respectfully*, humbly, with all respect, with due r.

921
Disrespect

Noun
(1) *disrespect*, want of respect, irreverence, impoliteness, incivility, discourtesy 885 *rudeness*; neglect, low esteem 867 *disrepute*; disparagement 926 *detraction*; scorn 922 *contempt*; mockery 851 *ridicule*; descration 980 *impiety*.

(2) *indignity*, humiliation, affront, insult, slight, snub 878 *insolence*; V-sign 878 *sauciness*; gibe, taunt, jeer 922 *contempt*; quip, sarcasm 851 *ridicule*; hiss, hoot, boo, catcall 924 *disapprobation*.

Adjective
(3) *disrespectful*, slighting, neglectful 458 *negligent*; insubordinate 738 *disobedient*; irreverent, sacrilegious 980 *profane*; rude, impolite 885 *discourteous*; airy, breezy, offhanded, cavalier, familiar, cheeky, saucy 878 *impertinent*; insulting 878 *insolent*; jeering, gibing, mocking, satirical, sarcastic 851 *derisive*; injurious 899

cursing; denigratory, pejorative 483 *depreciating*; disdainful, scornful 922 *despising*; unflattering 924 *disapproving*.

(4) *unrespected,* disrespected, of no account 867 *disreputable*; ignored, disregarded, disobeyed 458 *neglected*; underrated, denigrated, disparaged 483 *undervalued*; looked down on 922 *contemptible*.

Verb
(5) *not respect,* be disrespectful; have no respect or regard for 924 *disapprove*; underrate 483 *underestimate*; look down on, disdain, scorn 922 *despise*; run down, denigrate, disparage 926 *defame*; spit on, toss aside 607 *reject*; show disrespect, lack courtesy 885 *be rude*; ignore 458 *disregard*; snub, slight, insult, affront 872 *humiliate*; dishonour, disgrace 867 *shame*; trifle with 922 *hold cheap*; lower, degrade 847 *vulgarize*; not reverence, desecrate 980 *be impious*; call names, abuse 899 *curse*; taunt, twit, cock a snook 878 *be insolent*; laugh at, guy, scoff, mock 851 *ridicule*; jeer, hiss, hoot, heckle, boo 924 *reprobate*.

Adverb
(6) *disrespectfully,* irreverently, derisively.

922
Contempt

Noun
(1) *contempt,* utter c., scorn, disdain 871 *pride*; snootiness, snobbishness 850 *affectation*; superior airs, scornful eye, snort, sniff; slight, humiliation 921 *indignity*; sneer, derision 851 *ridicule*; snub, rebuff 885 *discourtesy*.

(2) *contemptibility,* futility, pettiness, meanness, paltriness 639

unimportance; cause for shame 867 *object of scorn*.

Adjective
(3) *despising,* contemptuous, disdainful, holier than thou, snooty, snobbish; haughty, lofty, supercilious 871 *proud*; scornful, withering, jeering 924 *disapproving*; disrespectful, impertinent 878 *insolent*; slighting, pooh-poohing 483 *depreciating*.

(4) *contemptible,* despicable, beneath contempt; abject, worthless 645 *bad*; petty, paltry, mean 33 *small*; spurned, spat on 607 *rejected*; scorned, despised 921 *unrespected*; futile, of no account 639 *unimportant*.

Verb
(5) *despise,* hold in contempt 921 *not respect*; look down on, consider beneath one 871 *be proud*; disdain, spurn, turn up one's nose at 607 *reject*; curl one's lip, toss one's head; snub 885 *be rude*; scorn, hiss, boo 924 *reprobate*; laugh at, laugh to scorn, scoff, gibe, jeer, mock 851 *ridicule*; disgrace 867 *shame*.

(6) *hold cheap,* have a low opinion of 921 *not respect*; ignore, dismiss 458 *disregard*; belittle, disparage, underrate 483 *underestimate*; decry 926 *detract*; set no store by, laugh at, shrug away, pooh-pooh; slight, treat like dirt 872 *humiliate*.

Adverb
(7) *contemptuously,* disdainfully, with contempt.

923
Approbation

Noun
(1) *approbation,* approval, sober a., satisfaction 828 *content*; appreciation, recognition 907 *gratitude*; kudos, credit 866 *prestige*; regard, admiration,

esteem 920 *respect*; good opinion, grace, favour, popularity, affection 887 *love*; adoption, acceptance, welcome 299 *reception*; sanction 756 *permission*; nod of approval, seal of a., blessing; nod, thumbs up, consent 488 *assent*; patronage, championship 703 *aid*; testimonial, reference 466 *credential*.

(2) *praise,* compliment, eulogy, panegyric; adulation 925 *flattery*; faint praise, two cheers; shout of praise, hosanna, alleluia; tribute, credit 907 *thanks*; bouquet, accolade, citation, commendation, honourable mention; self-praise 877 *boasting*

(3) *applause,* acclaim, enthusiasm; warm reception, hero's welcome 876 *celebration*; acclamation, plaudits, clapping, stamping, whistling, cheering; clap, pat on the back, bouquet, three cheers, ovation, standing o.; encore, curtain call.

(4) *commender,* praiser, eulogist; admirer fan club; advocate, supporter 707 *patron*; advertiser, blurb-writer, agent, 528 *publicizer*.

Adjective
(5) *approving,* satisfied 828 *content*; favouring, supporting; appreciative 907 *grateful*; approbatory, favourable, well-inclined; complimentary, commendatory, laudatory, lyrical; admiring, hero-worshipping; lavish, generous, fulsome, uncritical; clapping, thunderous, ecstatic 821 *excited*.

(6) *approvable,* worthwhile, deserving, meritorious, commendable, laudable, estimable, worthy, praiseworthy, creditable, admirable; beyond praise 646 *perfect*; enviable, desirable 859 *desired*.

(7) *approved,* passed, tested, tried; praised etc. vb.; free from blame, blessed; popular, in favour, thought well of 866 *reputable*; commended, highly c.; favoured 605 *chosen*.

Verb
(8) *approve,* think highly of 920 *respect*; think well of, admire, esteem, value, prize, set store by 866 *honour*; appreciate, give credit, salute, hand it to, give full marks; think desirable 912 *envy*; accept, pass 488 *assent*; sanction, bless 756 *permit*; ratify 488 *endorse*; commend, recommend, advocate, support, back, favour, speak up for 703 *patronize*.

(9) *praise,* compliment 925 *flatter*; speak well of, speak highly of, swear by; bless 907 *thank*; salute, pay tribute to, commend; eulogize, sing one's praises, extol, glorify; wax lyrical 546 *exaggerate*; puff, overestimate 482 *overrate*; lionize, hero-worship, idolize; cry up, crack up 528 *advertise*; praise oneself 877 *boast*.

(10) *applaud,* welcome, hail, acclaim, clap, clap one's hands, stamp, whistle, raise the roof; cheer, give three cheers; clap or pat on the back; congratulate, garland, chair 876 *celebrate*; drink to 876 *toast*.

(11) *be praised,* get a citation 866 *seek repute*; find favour, win praise 866 *have a reputation*; get a compliment, receive a tribute, get a good hand, get a cheer 727 *triumph*; deserve praise, be to one's credit.

Adverb
(12) *approvingly,* admiringly, with admiration, with compliments.

(13) *commendably,* admirably, to general approval.

Interjection

(14) *bravo!* well done! hear hear! encore! three cheers!

924
Disapprobation

Noun

(1) *disapprobation,* disapproval 829 *discontent;* nonapproval 760 *refusal;* disfavour, unpopularity 861 *dislike;* low opinion 921 *disrespect;* bad books 867 *disrepute;* disparagement, faultfinding 926 *detraction;* objection, exception, cavil 468 *qualification;* complaint, clamour, outcry, protest 762 *deprecation;* indignation 891 *anger;* slow handclap, hissing, hiss, boo, whistle, catcall 851 *ridicule;* blacklist, ostracism, boycott 57 *exclusion.*

(2) *censure,* blame 928 *accusation;* home truth, left-handed compliment, back-handed c.; criticism, stricture, faultfinding, attack; bad press, hostile review; diatribe 704 *opposition;* conviction 961 *condemnation;* brand, stigma.

(3) *reproach,* recriminations; invective, calling names 899 *scurrility;* taunt, sneer 878 *insolence;* sarcasm, irony, biting tongue 851 *ridicule;* hard words, black look.

(4) *reprimand,* remonstrance, stricture 762 *deprecation;* piece of one's mind, censure, rebuke, reproof, snub; black mark; rap over the knuckles 963 *punishment;* admonition, chiding, upbraiding, scolding, dressing down, carpeting, lecture.

(5) *disapprover,* no friend, no admirer; damper, wet blanket 834 *moper;* puritan 950 *prude;* attacker, opposer 705 *opponent;* critic, faultfinder; lampooner,

mocker 926 *detractor;* misogynist 902 *misanthrope;* grouser 829 *malcontent.*

Adjective

(6) *disapproving,* not amused, shocked, scandalized; unadmiring, unimpressed; unfavourable, hostile 881 *inimical;* objecting, protesting 762 *deprecatory;* reproachful, chiding, upbraiding; unflattering, uncomplimentary; critical, withering, hard-hitting, strongly worded; captious, faultfinding, niggling, carping; disparaging, defamatory 926 *detracting;* caustic, sharp, trenchant, mordant; sarcastic 851 *derisive;* censorious, holier than thou; censuring, reprimanding, condemning 928 *accusing.*

(7) *disapproved,* blacklisted, 607 *rejected;* found wanting 636 *insufficient;* failed 728 *unsuccessful;* censored 550 *obliterated;* out of favour, under a cloud; criticized, decried; run down, slandered; reprimanded, scolded; unregretted, unlamented 861 *disliked;* hooted, hissed; discredited, disowned 867 *disreputable.*

(8) *blameworthy,* not good enough, open to criticism; censurable 645 *bad;* reprehensible, dishonourable 867 *discreditable;* culpable, to blame 928 *accusable.*

Verb

(9) *disapprove,* not admire, not think much of 922 *despise;* not pass, fail 607 *reject;* disallow 757 *prohibit;* cancel 752 *abrogate;* censor 550 *obliterate;* not hold with 489 *dissent;* lament, deplore 830 *regret;* abhor 861 *dislike;* disown, avoid, ignore; draw the line at, ostracize, bar, blacklist 57 *exclude;* protest, remonstrate, object, take exception to 762 *deprecate;* show disapproval, shout down, hoot, boo, heckle, hiss, whistle, throw things 712 *lapidate*; hound, chase, mob, lynch; make a face, look black 893 *be sullen*; look daggers 891 *be angry*.

(10) *dispraise*, damn 961 *condemn*; criticize, find fault, pick holes, run down, belittle 926 *detract*; oppose, tilt at, shoot at 712 *attack*; weigh in, pitch into, hit out at, savage, maul, scourge, thunder, fulminate, rage against 61 *rampage*; shout down, cry shame, call names; revile, abuse, heap a. on; execrate 899 *curse*; vilify, blacken 926 *defame*; stigmatize, brand, pillory; denounce 928 *accuse*.

(11) *reprove*, reproach, rebuke; caution 664 *warn*; book, censure, reprimand, tick off, tell off, remonstrate, admonish, castigate, chide, correct; lecture, browbeat, chastise 963 *punish*.

(12) *blame,* find fault, carp, pick holes in; hold to blame, hold responsible; inculpate, incriminate, charge 928 *accuse*; round on, recriminate 714 *retaliate*.

(13) *reprobate*, reproach, upbraid, berate, rail at, revile, abuse 899 *curse*; inveigh against, bawl out, scold, tongue-lash.

(14) *incur blame*, take the blame, carry the can, be held responsible 867 *lose repute*; stand accused, stand corrected; scandalize, shock 861 *cause dislike*.

Adverb

(15) *disapprovingly*, reluctantly, under protest.

925
Flattery

Noun

(1) *flattery,* cajolery, wheedling, blandishments, sweet talk; flannel, incense, adulation; honeyed words, sweet nothings 889 *endearment*; compliment, coquetry, winning ways; fawning, sycophancy 879 *servility*; unctuousness, insincerity, hypocrisy 542 *sham*.

(2) *flatterer,* adulator; coquette, charmer; courtier, yes-man 488 *assenter*; creep, fawner, sycophant, hanger-on 879 *toady*; hypocrite 545 *deceiver*.

Adjective

(3) *flattering,* overcomplimentary 546 *exaggerated*; complimentary, fulsome, adulatory; sugary, saccharine; cajoling, wheedling etc. vb.; honey-tongued, bland; smooth, oily, unctuous, soapy, smarmy; obsequious, all over one, fawning, sycophantic 879 *servile*; beguiling, ingratiating, insinuating; false, insincere 541 *hypocritical*.

Verb

(4) *flatter,* compliment 923 *praise*; overdo it 482 *overrate*; turn one's head 873 *make conceited*; butter up, soft-soap; blarney, sweet-talk, wheedle, coax, cajole; lull, soothe, beguile 542 *deceive*; humour, jolly along, pander to; press the flesh, make much of, 889 *caress*; fawn on, cultivate, court, pay court to; curry favour, make up to, toady to 879 *be servile*; flatter oneself 873 *be vain*.

926
Detraction

Noun

(1) *detraction,* criticism, bad press 924 *disapprobation*; impeachment 928 *accusation*; exposure, bad light 867 *disrepute*; disparagement, depreciation, running down; scorn 922 *contempt*; vilification, abuse, invective 899 *scurrility*; calumniation, defamation 543 *untruth*;

backbiting, cattiness 898 *malevolence*; innuendo, insinuation, imputation, smear campaign, character assassination; denigration, brand, stigma.

(2) *calumny,* slander, libel, false report 543 *untruth*; smear 867 *slur*; offensive remark, personal r., insult, taunt 921 *indignity*; sarcasm 851 *ridicule*; caricature lampoon 851 *satire*; scandal, malicious gossip.

(3) *detractor,* disparager; debunker, cynic; mocker, scoffer, satirist, lampooner; denouncer 924 *disapprover*; candid friend, hostile critic; attacker 928 *accuser*; faultfinder, nit-picker; heckler, barracker 702 *hinderer*.

(4) *defamer,* calumniator, slanderer, libeller; backbiter, gossiper, muck-raker; gossip columnist, gutter press; denigrator, mud-slinger; scold 892 *shrew*.

Adjective
(5) *detracting,* derogatory, pejorative; disparaging, decrying, contemptuous 922 *despising*; whispering, insinuating, denigratory, mud-slinging; compromising, damaging; scandalous, defamatory, slanderous, libellous; insulting 921 *disrespectful*; injurious, abusive, scurrilous 899 *cursing*; shrewish, scolding, caustic, venomous; blaming 924 *disapproving*; sarcastic, mocking, sneering, cynical 851 *derisive*; catty, spiteful 898 *malevolent*; candid 573 *plain*.

Verb
(6) *detract,* disparage, run down, sell short; debunk, deflate, puncture 921 *not respect*; minimize 483 *underestimate*; belittle 922 *hold cheap*; sneer at 922 *despise*; decry, cry down 924 *disapprove*; criticize, knock, slam, find fault, pick holes in,

pull to pieces, 924 *dispraise*; caricature, guy 552 *misrepresent*; lampoon 851 *satirize*; scoff, mock 851 *ridicule*; whisper, insinuate, cast aspersions.

(7) *defame,* dishonour, damage, compromise, destroy one's good name 867 *shame*; denounce, expose, pillory 928 *accuse*; calumniate, libel, slander, traduce, malign; vilify, denigrate, blacken, tarnish, sully; speak ill of, gossip, talk about, backbite, discredit 486 *cause doubt*; smear, smirch 649 *make unclean*; hound, witch-hunt 619 *pursue*.

927
Vindication

Noun
(1) *vindication,* restoration, rehabilitation 787 *restitution*; exoneration, exculpation, clearance 960 *acquittal*; justification, good grounds, just cause, every excuse; self-defence, defence, good d.; alibi, plea, excuse 614 *pretext*; good excuse 494 *truth*; partial excuse, extenuation, mitigation 468 *qualification*; reply, rebuttal 479 *confutation*; recrimination, countercharge.

(2) *vindicator,* apologist, advocate, champion; justifier 466 *witness*.

Adjective
(3) *vindicating,* justifying, defending; extenuatory, mitigating.

(4) *vindicable,* justifiable, defensible, arguable; specious, plausible; allowable 756 *permitted*; excusable, pardonable, forgivable; justified, vindicated, not guilty 935 *innocent*.

Verb
(5) *vindicate,* do justice to 915 *grant claims*; rehabilitate 787

restitute; speak up for, advocate 475 *argue*; bear out, confirm, prove 478 *demonstrate*; champion, stand up for 713 *defend*; support 703 *patronize*.

(6) *justify*, warrant, give grounds for, give one cause; clear, exonerate, exculpate 960 *acquit*; justify oneself 614 *plead*; say in defence, rebut the charge.

(7) *extenuate*, excuse, make excuses for, make allowances; mitigate, soften, gloss over 736 *be lenient*.

928
Accusation

Noun
(1) *accusation*, complaint, charge; censure, blame, stricture 924 *reproach*; recrimination 460 *rejoinder*; taunt 921 *indignity*; imputation, allegation, denunciation; action 959 *litigation*; prosecution, arraignment, indictment, summons; case to answer.

(2) *false charge*, trumped-up c., put-up job, frame-up; hostile evidence, suspect e., plant; lie, libel, slander 926 *calumny*.

(3) *accuser*, plaintiff, petitioner, appellant, litigant; grass 524 *informer*; prosecutor, public p.; calumniator 926 *defamer*.

(4) *accused person*, the accused, prisoner; defendant, respondent; culprit; suspect; victim.

Adjective
(5) *accusing*, alleging; suspicious incriminating, pointing to; condemnatory; defamatory 926 *detracting*.

(6) *accused*, informed against, suspect; under suspicion, under a cloud; denounced, charged etc. vb.; awaiting trial, on bail, remanded; slandered 924 *disapproved*.

(7) *accusable*, actionable, chargeable; inexcusable 924 *blameworthy*; without excuse, without defence 661 *vulnerable*.

Verb
(8) *accuse*, challenge 711 *defy*; taunt 878 *be insolent*; reproach 924 *reprove*; brand, pillory, calumniate 926 *defame*; impute, charge with, hold against, hold responsible; pick on, pin on 924 *blame*; expose, name 526 *divulge*; denounce, inform against, tell 524 *inform*; implicate, incriminate; recriminate, rebut the charge, 479 *confute*; plead guilty 526 *confess*.

(9) *indict*, impeach, arraign, inform against, lodge a complaint, charge, bring a charge 959 *litigate*; book, summon, prosecute, sue; bring an action, put on trial 712 *attack*; charge falsely, frame, fake the evidence, 541 *fake*.

929
Probity

Noun
(1) *probity*, rectitude, uprightness, goodness 933 *virtue*; good character, moral fibre, honesty, soundness, integrity; high character, nobleness, nobility; decent feelings, honour, principles; trustworthiness, truthfulness 540 *veracity*; candour, sincerity, good faith 494 *truth*; faith, faithfulness, constancy 739 *loyalty*; clean hands 935 *innocence*; impartiality, fairness, sportsmanship 913 *justice*; respectability 866 *repute*; point of honour, code 913 *right*.

(2) *honourable person*, honest p., man *or* woman of honour, sound character 937 *good person*; true lady, perfect gentleman; good loser, sportsman, sportswoman, sport, good sport, trump, brick, good sort.

Adjective

(3) *honourable,* upright, of integrity, of honour 933 *virtuous*; correct, strict; law-abiding, honest; principled, high-p., scrupulous, conscientious, incorruptible; noble, high-minded 950 *pure*; guileless 699 *artless*; good, straight, fair 913 *just*; sporting, sportsmanlike, playing the game; chivalrous, knightly; respectable 866 *reputable*; saintly 979 *pious*.

(4) *trustworthy,* reliable, dependable, tried, tested, trusty, sure, staunch, constant, faithful, loyal 739 *obedient*; responsible, dutiful 768 *observant*; conscientious, scrupulous, meticulous 457 *careful*; candid, frank, open, open-hearted, 494 *true*; truthful, as good as one's word 540 *veracious*.

Verb

(5) *be honourable,* - noble etc. adj.; behave well, 933 *be virtuous*; play fair, play the game 913 *be just*; fear God 979 *be pious*; keep faith, keep one's promise 540 *be truthful*; go straight, reform 654 *get better*.

930
Improbity

Noun

(1) *improbity,* dishonesty, lack of principle; insincerity 541 *falsehood*; partiality 914 *injustice*; artfulness; shadiness, deviousness, crookedness; corruption, venality, graft; baseness, shabbiness, shamefulness, disgrace, dishonour, shame 867 *disrepute*; villainy, knavery, roguery, skulduggery, racketeering; criminality, crime 954 *lawbreaking*; moral turpitude 934 *wickedness*.

(2) *perfidy,* infidelity, unfaithfulness, bad faith 543 *untruth*; disloyalty 738 *disobedience*;

double-dealing 541 *duplicity*; defection, desertion 918 *undutifulness*; betrayal, treachery, treason 738 *sedition*; breach of faith, broken word, broken promise, breach of p.

(3) *foul play,* dirty trick, foul 914 *wrong*; chicanery 542 *trickery*; sharp practice, dirty work, deal, racket; fiddle, wangle, manipulation, gerrymandering; crime, felony 954 *lawbreaking*.

Adjective

(4) *dishonest,* unprincipled, unscrupulous, shameless, immoral 934 *wicked*; untrustworthy, unreliable; disingenuous, untruthful 543 *untrue*; two-faced, insincere 541 *hypocritical*; tricky, artful, opportunist, slippery 698 *cunning*; shifty, prevaricating 518 *equivocal*; designing, scheming; sneaking, underhand 523 *latent*; up to something, on the fiddle; not straight, bent, crooked, devious, tortuous; insidious, dark, sinister 914 *wrong*; shady, fishy, suspicious, doubtful, questionable; fraudulent 542 *spurious*; illicit 954 *illegal*; foul 645 *bad*; mean, shabby, dishonourable, unworthy 867 *disreputable*; inglorious, ignominious 867 *degrading*.

(5) *rascally,* criminal, felonious 954 *lawless*; knavish, infamous, villainous; arrant, low-down, base, vile; mean, shabby, abject, wretched, contemptible; timeserving 925 *flattering*.

(6) *venal,* corrupt, corruptible, purchasable, bribable, hireling, mercenary 792 *bought*.

(7) *perfidious,* treacherous, unfaithful, inconstant, faithless 541 *false*; disloyal, time-serving 603 *tergiversating*; doublecrossing 541 *hypocritical*; falsehearted, guileful, traitorous, treasonous, treasonable, disloyal 738 *disobedient*; plotting, scheming 623 *planning*; cheating 542 *deceiving*; fraudulent 542 *spurious*.

Verb
(8) *be dishonest,* - dishonourable etc. adj.; have no morals; fiddle, wangle, gerrymander, racketeer 788 *defraud*; cheat, swindle 542 *deceive*; betray, play false, stab in the back, double-cross 541 *dissemble*; tell lies, break faith 541 *be false*; shuffle, prevaricate 518 *be equivocal*; sell out 603 *apostatize*; stoop to 867 *lose repute*.

Adverb
(9) *dishonestly;* shamelessly, treacherously.

931
Disinterestedness

Noun
(1) *disinterestedness,* impartiality 913 *justice*; unselfishness, selflessness 872 *humility*; self-denial, self-sacrifice, martyrdom; heroism, stoicism 855 *courage*; idealism, ideals, high i.; loftiness, nobility, magnanimity; chivalry, generosity, liberality 897 *benevolence*; dedication, labour of love; loyalty, faith, faithfulness 929 *probity*; altruism, consideration, kindness 884 *courtesy*; compassion 905 *pity*; charity 887 *love*.

Adjective
(2) *disinterested,* impartial 913 *just*; incorruptible, honest 929 *honourable*; self-effacing, modest 872 *humble*; unselfish, selfless, self-denying; devoted, dedicated, self-sacrificing; loyal, faithful; heroic 855 *courageous*; thoughtful, considerate 884 *courteous*; altruistic, philanthropic 897 *benevolent*; pure, idealistic, quixotic, highminded, lofty, sublime, noble,

great-hearted, magnanimous; generous, liberal, unsparing 781 *giving*.

Verb
(3) *be disinterested,* - unselfish etc. adj.; sacrifice oneself, devote o.; live for, die f.; think of others, put oneself last have no axe to grind. 872 *be humble*;

932
Selfishness

Noun
(1) *selfishness,* self-love, narcissism 873 *vanity*; self-indulgence, self-pity, ego trip; self-absorption, egocentricity; egoism, egotism, individualism, personal motives, private ends; self-seeking, self-serving, self-interest, self-preservation; illiberality, pettiness, meanness, miserliness 816 *parsimony*; greed, acquisitiveness 816 *avarice*; possessiveness 911 *jealousy*; worldliness, ambition, power politics.

(2) *egotist,* egoist, narcissist 873 *vain person*; self-seeker; careerist, go-getter, gold-digger; miser 816 *niggard*; monopolist, dog in the manger; opportunist, time-server.

Adjective
(3) *selfish,* egocentric, self-centred, self-absorbed; egoistic, egotistic; individualistic, self-seeking; self-indulgent 943 *intemperate*; self-loving, self-admiring, narcissistic 873 *vain*; uncharitable, cold-hearted 898 *unkind*; mean, mean-minded, petty, paltry; illiberal, ungenerous 816 *parsimonious*; acquisitive, mercenary 816 *avaricious*; venal 930 *dishonest*; covetous 912 *envious*; monopolistic 859 *greedy*; possessive 911 *jealous*; self-serving, designing, axe-grinding; go-getting, on the make, opportunist, time-

serving, careerist; materialistic, worldly, worldly-wise.

Verb
(4) *be selfish,* - egoistic etc. adj.; put oneself first; indulge oneself, look after o., feather one's nest; hog, monopolize 778 *retain*; have private ends, have an axe to grind.

Adverb
(5) *selfishly,* for private ends, from personal motives.

933
Virtue

Noun
(1) *virtue,* virtuousness, moral strength, moral tone; goodness, saintliness, holiness; righteousness 913 *justice*; uprightness, rectitude, moral r., character, integrity, honour 929 *probity*; stainlessness 935 *innocence*; morality, ethics 917 *morals*; temperance, chastity 950 *purity*; virtuous conduct, good behaviour, good conscience.

(2) *virtues,* cardinal v., faith, hope, charity; natural virtues, prudence, justice, temperance, fortitude; qualities, fine q., saving quality, saving grace; worth, merit, desert; nobleness, magnanimity, altruism, idealism, ideals.

Adjective
(3) *virtuous,* moral 917 *ethical*; good, good as gold 644 *excellent*; stainless 950 *pure*; irreproachable 646 *perfect*; seraphic, angelic, saintly, holy 979 *sanctified*; principled, well-p., right-minded 913 *right*; righteous 913 *just*; upright, sterling, honest 929 *honourable*; dutiful 739 *obedient*; unselfish 931 *disinterested*; generous, magnanimous, idealistic, philanthropic 897 *benevolent*; sober 942 *temperate*; chaste, virginal; proper, edifying, improving, exemplary; elevated, sublimated; meritorious, worthy, praiseworthy, commendable 923 *approved*.

Verb
(4) *be virtuous,* - good etc. adj.; behave, resist temptation 942 *be temperate*; follow one's conscience 917 *do one's duty*; go straight, keep s. 929 *be honourable*; hear no evil, see no evil, speak no evil; 913 *be just*.

Adverb
(5) *virtuously,* righteously, with merit.

934
Wickedness

Noun
(1) *wickedness,* principle of evil 645 *badness*; Devil 969 *Satan*; iniquity, sin 914 *wrong*; loss of innocence 936 *guilt*; ungodliness 980 *impiety*; amorality 860 *indifference*; hardness of heart 898 *malevolence*; wilfulness, stubbornness 602 *obstinacy*; waywardness, naughtiness, bad behaviour 738 *disobedience*; immorality, turpitude; loose morals, profligacy 951 *impurity*; degeneracy, degradation; recidivism, backsliding; vice, corruption, depravity 645 *badness*; heinousness, shamelessness, flagrancy; no morals; viciousness, baseness, vileness; villainy, knavery, roguery 930 *foul play*; laxity, want of principle, 930 *improbity*; dishonesty crime, criminality 954 *lawbreaking*; devil worship, devilry; shame, scandal, enormity, infamy 867 *disrepute*; misbehaviour, delinquency, wrongdoing, evil-doing, wicked ways; low life, criminal world, underworld.

(2) *vice*, fault, human weakness, infirmity, frailty, foible 163 *weakness*; imperfection, shortcoming, defect, failing, flaw, weak point; trespass, injury, outrage, enormity 914 *wrong*; sin, capital s., deadly s.; venial sin, small fault, peccadillo, scrape; impropriety, indecorum 847 *bad taste*; offence 936 *guilty act*; crime 954 *illegality*.

Adjective

(3) *wicked,* unvirtuous, immoral; amoral, lax, unprincipled; unscrupulous 930 *dishonest*; unblushing, hardened, shameless, brazen; ungodly, irreligious, profane 980 *impious*; unrighteous 914 *unjust*; iniquitous, evil 645 *bad*; evil-minded, black-hearted 898 *malevolent*; evil-doing 898 *maleficent*; misbehaving, bad, naughty 738 *disobedient*; weak (see *frail*); erring, sinful 936 *guilty*; unworthy, graceless, reprobate; hopeless, incorrigible, irredeemable; devilish, fiendish, satanic 969 *diabolic*.

(4) *vicious,* good-for-nothing, hopeless, worthless, graceless 924 *disapproved*; villainous, knavish 930 *rascally*; improper, unseemly, indecent, unedifying 847 *vulgar*; without morals, immoral; unvirtuous 951 *unchaste*; profligate, abandoned, characterless 867 *disreputable*; corrupt, degraded, demoralized, debauched, depraved, perverted, degenerate, sick, rotten; brutalized 898 *cruel*.

(5) *frail,* feeble 163 *weak*; human, only h.; suggestible, easily tempted 661 *vulnerable*; not perfect 647 *imperfect*; slipping, sliding, fallen.

(6) *heinous,* grave, serious, black, scarlet; sinful, immoral 914 *wrong*; unedifying, demoralizing; criminal 954 *lawbreaking*; monstrous, flagrant, scandalous, infamous, shameful, disgraceful, shocking, outrageous, obscene; gross, foul, rank; base, vile, abominable, accursed; mean, shabby, despicable 645 *bad*; blameworthy, reprehensible, indefensible 916 *unwarranted*; atrocious, brutal 898 *cruel*; inexcusable, unforgivable.

Verb

(7) *be wicked,* - vicious etc. adj.; fall from grace, lapse, relapse, backslide; do wrong, transgress, misbehave, offend, sin; err, stray 163 *be weak*.

(8) *make wicked,* set a bad example; corrupt, demoralize, brutalize 655 *pervert*; mislead, lead astray, seduce 612 *tempt*; dehumanize, brutalize.

Adverb

(9) *wickedly,* wrongly, to one's discredit.

935
Innocence

Noun

(1) *innocence,* clean hands, clear conscience; guiltlessness, blamelessness; unworldliness, inexperience 699 *artlessness*; playfulness, harmlessness, pure motives; state of grace 933 *virtue*; incorruptibility 929 *probity*; impeccability 646 *perfection*; golden age 824 *happiness*.

(2) *innocent,* babe, newborn babe; child, ingenue; lamb, dove; angel, pure soul; innocent party.

Adjective

(3) *innocent,* pure, unspotted, stainless, spotless, immaculate 648 *clean*; sinless, free from sin 646 *perfect*; naive 491 *ignorant*; guileless 699 *artless*; innocuous, harmless, inoffensive,

gentle, lamb-like, dove-like, child-like, angelic; wide-eyed, goody-goody; Arcadian.

(4) *guiltless,* free from guilt, not responsible, not guilty 960 *acquitted*; falsely accused, not culpable; blameless, faultless, above suspicion; irreproachable, unimpeachable; pardonable, forgivable, excusable.

Verb
(5) *be innocent,* know no wrong 929 *be honourable*; have a clear conscience 933 *be virtuous*; know no better 699 *be artless.*

Adverb
(6) *innocently,* blamelessly, with a clear conscience.

936
Guilt

Noun
(1) *guilt,* guiltiness, culpability; criminality, delinquency 954 *illegality*; sinfulness, original sin 934 *wickedness*; involvement, complicity, liability, one's fault; blame, censure 924 *reproach*; guilt complex, guilty conscience, bad c.; guilty behaviour, blush, stammer, embarrassment; confession 526 *disclosure*; remorse, shame 939 *penitence.*

(2) *guilty act,* sin 934 *vice*; misdeed, offence, crime, misdemeanour, misconduct, misbehaviour, malpractice; indiscretion, impropriety; peccadillo, naughtiness, scrape; lapse, slip 495 *mistake*; omission 458 *negligence*; fault, injury 914 *wrong*; enormity, atrocity 898 *cruel act.*

Adjective
(3) *guilty,* found g., convicted 961 *condemned*; suspected, blamed; responsible, in the wrong, at fault, to blame; culpable, blameful 924 *blameworthy*; sinful 934 *wicked*; criminal

954 *illegal*; caught in the act, red-handed, hangdog, sheepish, shamefaced, blushing, ashamed.

Verb
(4) *be guilty,* be at fault, bear the blame; plead guilty 526 *confess*; have no excuse, stand condemned; transgress, sin 934 *be wicked.*

Adverb
(5) *guiltily,* without excuse; red-handed, in the act.

937
Good person

Noun
(1) *good person,* model of virtue 929 *honourable person*; shining light 646 *paragon*; saint, angel 935 *innocent*; heart of gold, salt of the earth 897 *kind person*; good neighbour, Good Samaritan 903 *benefactor*; hero, heroine 890 *favourite*; goody, good sort, brick, trump, sport.

938
Bad person

Noun
(1) *bad person,* no saint, sinner, limb of Satan, 904 *evildoer*; lost sheep, lost soul; scamp, scapegrace, ne'er-do-well, black sheep, the despair of; rake, profligate 952 *libertine*; wanton, hussy 952 *loose woman*; wastrel, prodigal son; outcast, dregs, riffraff, trash, scum 867 *object of scorn*; nasty type, ugly customer, undesirable, thug, bully, roughneck 904 *ruffian*; bad guy, villain; bad influence, bad example; naughty child, holy terror, monkey 663 *troublemaker.*

(2) *knave,* varlet, vagabond, wretch, rascal 869 *low fellow*; rogue, criminal 904 *offender*; thief, pirate 789 *robber*; villain,

blackguard, scoundrel, miscreant; cheat, liar, crook; impostor, twister, con-man 545 *trickster*; sneak, rat 524 *informer*; renegade, recreant, betrayer, traitor, quisling, Judas; swine, reptile, vermin 904 *noxious animal*.

(3) *cad,* scoundrel, blackguard; bastard, bounder, stinker; pimp, pander, pervert, degenerate; cur, hound, swine, rat, worm; louse, beast, bitch.

(4) *monster,* shocker, horror, brute, savage, sadist; ogre 735 *tyrant*; fiend, demon 969 *devil*; fury, devil incarnate; bogy, terror, nightmare.

939
Penitence

Noun

(1) *penitence,* repentance, contrition, compunction, remorse, self-reproach 830 *regret*; confession 988 *Christian rite*; guilt-feeling, unquiet conscience, twinge, qualms, pangs 936 *guilt*; sack cloth and ashes 941 *penance*; apology 941 *atonement*.

(2) *penitent,* confessor; prodigal son, reformed character.

Adjective

(3) *repentant,* contrite, remorseful, regretful, sorry, apologetic 830 *regretting*; ashamed 872 *humbled*; conscience-stricken, relenting; self-accusing, self-reproachful; penitent, doing penance 941 *atoning*; chastened, sobered; reformed, converted, regenerate, born again.

Verb

(4) *be penitent,* repent, feel shame, feel sorry, express regrets, apologize; reproach oneself, blame o., reprove o., accuse o.; go to confession 526 *confess*; do penance 941 *atone*; eat humble pie 721 *knuckle under*; rue;

have regrets 830 *regret*; learn one's lesson, reform, be reformed 654 *get better*; see the light, be converted 603 *recant*.

Adverb

(5) *penitently,* regretfully.

940
Impenitence

Noun

(1) *impenitence,* obduracy, stubbornness 602 *obstinacy*; hardness of heart 326 *hardness*; no apologies, no regrets, no compunction 906 *pitilessness*; hardened sinner 938 *bad person*.

Adjective

(2) *impenitent,* unrepentant, unregretting, without regrets; obdurate, stubborn 602 *obstinate*; unrelenting, without a pang; heartless 898 *cruel*; hard, hardened; unblushing, brazen; incorrigible, irredeemable, hopeless, lost 934 *wicked*; unshriven.

(3) *unrepented,* unregretted.

Verb

(4) *be impenitent,* make no excuses, offer no apologies, have no regrets, refuse to recant 602 *be obstinate*; harden one's heart 906 *be pitiless*.

Adverb

(5) *impenitently,* unblushingly; without compunction, with no regrets.

941
Atonement

Noun

(1) *atonement,* making amends, amends, apology, satisfaction; reparation, compensation, indemnity, blood money 787 *restitution*; repayment, quittance, quits. 770 *compromise*.

(2) *propitiation,* expiation, satisfaction, conciliation 719 *pacification*; reclamation, redemption 965 *divine function*; sacrifice, offering 981 *oblation*; scapegoat, whipping boy 150 *substitute.*

(3) *penance,* shrift, confession 939 *penitence*; fasting, flagellation 945 *asceticism*; purgation 648 *cleansing*; purgatory; sackcloth and ashes 836 *lamentation.*

Adjective
(4) *atoning,* making amends 939 *repentant*; compensatory 787 *restoring*; conciliatory, apologetic; propitiatory, purgatorial 648 *cleansing*; sacrificial 759 *offering*; penitential, penitentiary, doing penance.

Verb
(5) *atone,* make amends, make reparation, indemnify, compensate, pay compensation, make it up to; apologize, offer one's apologies 909 *beg pardon*; give satisfaction 787 *restitute*; propitiate, conciliate 719 *pacify*; make up for, make matters right; expiate, pay the penalty 963 *be punished.*

(6) *do penance,* undergo p. 963 *be punished*; go to confession 526 *confess.*

942
Temperance

Noun
(1) *temperance,* temperateness, nothing in excess 177 *moderation*; self-denial, self-discipline, self-control, stoicism 747 *restraint*; continence, chastity 950 *purity*; soberness 948 *sobriety*; forbearance renunciation, abstinence, abstention, teetotalism; vegetarianism, veganism; dieting 946 *fasting*; frugality 814 *economy*; plain living, simple life 945 *asceticism.*

(2) *abstainer,* teetotaller 948 *sober person*; nonsmoker; vegetarian, vegan; dieter; Spartan 945 *ascetic.*

Adjective
(3) *temperate,* measured, tempered 177 *moderate*; plain, Spartan, frugal 814 *economical*; forbearing, abstemious 620 *avoiding*; dry, teetotal 948 *sober*; self-disciplined 747 *restrained*; chaste 950 *pure*; self-denying 945 *ascetic.*

Verb
(4) *be temperate,* avoid excess 177 *be moderate*; know when to stop; forbear, refrain, abstain 620 *avoid*; deny oneself 945 *be ascetic*; give up, swear off; ration oneself; diet, go on a d.

943
Intemperance

Noun
(1) *intemperance,* immoderation, abandon; excess, excessiveness 637 *superfluity*; wastefulness, extravagance, waste 815 *prodigality*; indiscipline, incontinence 734 *laxity*; indulgence, self-i., overindulgence; addiction, bad habit 610 *habit*; high living, dissipation, debauchery 944 *sensualism*; overeating 947 *gluttony*; intoxication 949 *drunkenness.*

Adjective
(2) *intemperate,* immoderate, excessive wasteful, extravagant, profligate 815 *prodigal*; luxurious 637 *superfluous*; indulgent, self-i.; undisciplined 738 *riotous*; incontinent 951 *unchaste*; animal 944 *sensual.*

Verb
(3) *be intemperate,* - immoderate etc. adj.; lack self-control 734 *be lax*; indulge oneself, give oneself up to, wallow in 734 *please oneself*; have one's fling 815 *be prodigal*; run riot, exceed 306

overstep; live it up 837 *revel*;
drink to excess 949 *get drunk*;
eat to excess 947 *gluttonize*;
grow dissipated 951 *be impure*;
become addicted 610 *be wont*.

Adverb
(4) *intemperately,* immoderately, incontinently, with
abandon.

944
Sensualism

Noun
(1) *sensualism,* earthiness, materialism, sensuality, carnality,
sexuality, the flesh; grossness,
bestiality; love of pleasure, hedonism, epicureanism 376 *pleasure*; volumptuousness, luxuriousness, luxury, lap of l.; high
living, wine, women and song
824 *enjoyment*; dissipation,
abandon 943 *intemperance*; licentiousness, debauchery 951
impurity; indulgence, self-i.,
greediness 947 *gluttony*; eating
and drinking 301 *feasting*;
orgy, saturnalia 837 *revel*.

(2) *sensualist,* hedonist, pleasure-lover, thrill-seeker; luxury-lover, sybarite epicurean,
epicure, gourmet, gourmand
947 *glutton*; hard drinker 949
drunkard; profligate, rake 952
libertine; drug addict 949 *drug-
taking*; degenerate, decadent;
sadist, masochist.

Adjective
(3) *sensual,* earthy, gross 319
material; fleshly, carnal, bodily; sexual 887 *erotic*; bestial,
beastly, brutish; pleasure-giving 826 *pleasurable*; pleasure-
seeking, voluptuous, living for
kicks; hedonistic, epicurean,
luxury-loving, pampered, indulged; high-living, fast-l., incontinent 943 *intemperate*; licentious, dissipated 951
impure; riotous, orgiastic, Bacchanalian 949 *drunken*.

Verb
(4) *be sensual,* - volumptuous
etc. adj.; live for pleasure; wallow in luxury, live well 730
prosper; indulge oneself, pamper o., do oneself proud 943 *be
intemperate*.

Adverb
(5) *sensually,* voluptuously.

945
Asceticism

Noun
(1) *asceticism,* austerity; self-
mortification, flagellation 941
penance; holy poverty 801 *poverty*; plain living, simple fare
946 *fasting*; self-denial 942 *temperance*; frugality 814 *economy*; sackcloth, hair shirt.

(2) *ascetic,* yogi, fakir, dervish,
fire-walker; hermit, anchorite,
recluse 883 *solitary*; flagellant
939 *penitent*; puritan 942
abstainer.

Adjective
(3) *ascetic,* yogic; fasting; puritanical, Sabbatarian; austere,
rigorous 735 *severe*; Spartan
942 *temperate*; plain, wholesome 652 *salubrious*.

Verb
(4) *be ascetic,* live like a hermit;
fast 946 *starve*.

Adverb
(5) *ascetically,* austerely, plainly, frugally.

946
Fasting

Noun
(1) *fasting,* no appetite, anorexia
651 *ill health*; cutting down 301
dieting; lenten fare, bread and
water, starvation diet, 945 *asceticism*; iron rations 636 *scarcity*; no food, starvation 859
hunger.

(2) *fast*, fast day, meatless day, Friday; Lent, Ramadan; day of abstinence; hunger strike 145 *strike*.

Adjective
(3) *fasting*, not eating, off one's food; abstinent, keeping Lent; without food, unfed, empty; half-starved 636 *underfed*; starved, starving, famished 859 *hungry*; scanty 636 *scarce*; meagre, thin, poor, Spartan; Lenten.

Verb
(4) *starve*, famish 859 *be hungry*; have no food 801 *be poor*; fast, go without, abstain, keep Lent, keep Ramadan; refuse one's food, eat less, diet; tighten one's belt.

947
Gluttony

Noun
(1) *gluttony*, greediness, greed, insatiability, voracity, piggishness; 859 *hunger*; overeating, gorging 301 *feasting;* gormandizing, belly worship; epicurism 301 *gastronomy*.

(2) *glutton*, guzzler, gormandizer; pig, hog; hearty eater 301 *eater*; greedy pig; gourmand, gourmet, epicure, bon vivant,

Adjective
(3) *gluttonous* 859 *greedy*; devouring, voracious, omnivorous, wolfish; insatiable 859 *hungry*; pampered, full-fed 301 *feeding*; guzzling, gorging etc. vb.; gastronomic, epicurean.

Verb
(4) *gluttonize*, gormandize; bolt, wolf, gobble, devour, gulp down; gorge, cram, stuff 301 *eat*; glut oneself, make oneself sick; lick one's lips *or* one's chops.

Adverb
(5) *gluttonously*, ravenously, hungrily; at a gulp, with one bite.

948
Sobriety

Noun
(1) *sobriety*, soberness 942 *temperance*; teetotalism; dry area.

(2) *sober person*, moderate drinker, no toper; teetotaller 942 *abstainer*.

Adjective
(3) *sober*, abstinent, abstemious 942 *temperate*; not drinking, drying out, teetotal; clearheaded, stone-cold sober; sobered up, dried out, off the bottle.

Verb
(4) *be sober*, abstemious, not drink, drink moderately 942 *be temperate*; dry out, come off (drugs); give up alcohol, become teetotal, sign the pledge; sober up.

Adverb
(5) *soberly*, abstemiously.

949
Drunkenness. Drug-taking

Noun
(1) *drunkenness*, inebriety 943 *intemperance* intemperance; intoxication, inebriation; tipsiness 317 *oscillation*; drop too much, hard drinking 301 *drinking*; liquor 301 *alcoholic drink, wine*; drinking bout, binge, spree 837 *revel*.

(2) *crapulence*, hangover, thick head, sick headache.

(3) *alcoholism*, dipsomania 503 *mania*; delirium tremens, dt's, the horrors.

drug-taking, smoking, glue-sniffing; injecting, main-lining; pill-popping; hard drug, soft d.; narcotic, dope; nicotine 388 *tobacco*; cannabis, marijuana, cocaine, heroin, morphine, opium; pep pill 821 *excitant*; intoxicant, hallucinogen, LSD, acid; drug addiction, drug abuse, drug dependence, habit; drug addict, dope fiend, freak; head, junkie.

(5) *drunkard,* inebriate, drunk; alcoholic, wino, dipsomaniac, drinker, hard d., tippler, toper, boozer; carouser 837 *reveller.*

Adjective
(6) *drunk,* inebriated, intoxicated, in one's cups; under the influence, the worse for; flushed, merry, high 821 *excited*; roaring drunk 61 *disorderly.*

(7) *tipsy,* tight, half-cut, stewed, sloshed, plastered; maudlin, tearful, drunken, boozy; glassy-eyed, seeing double; reeling, staggering 317 *oscillating.*

(8) *dead drunk,* stoned; blind drunk, paralytic; out, under the table.

(9) *crapulous,* with a hangover, dizzy, giddy, sick.

(10) *drugged,* doped, high, spaced out, in a trance; stoned, incapacitated 375 *insensible*; turned on, hooked. addicted.

(11) *drunken,* habitually drunk, never sober 943 *intemperate*; sodden, gin-s., boozy, beery; tippling, toping, swigging, pub-crawling; given to drink, on the bottle, alcoholic, dipsomaniac.

(12) *intoxicating,* inebriating, exhilarating, heady 821 *exciting*; stimulant, intoxicant; opiate, narcotic; hallucinatory, psychedelic; addictive, habit-forming; alcoholic, vinous, beery; hard, potent, stiff, neat.

Verb
(13) *be drunk,* succumb, be overcome, pass out; lurch, stagger, reel 317 *oscillate.*

(14) *get drunk,* - tipsy etc. adj.; have too much, drink hard, tipple, booze, tope, swig, swill, hit the bottle 301 *drink*; quaff, carouse, wassail 837 *revel.*

(15) *drug oneself,* smoke, sniff, shoot, mainline; turn on, take a trip; freak out.

(16) *inebriate,* go to one's head 821 *excite*; fuddle, befuddle, stupefy.

950
Purity

Noun
(1) *purity,* faultlessness 646 *perfection*; sinlessness 935 *innocence*; moral purity, morals, morality 933 *virtue*; decency, propriety, delicacy 846 *good taste*; shame, bashfulness 874 *modesty*; chastity, continence 942 *temperance*; coldness, frigidity; honour, one's h.; virginity, maidenhood 895 *celibacy.*

(2) *prudery,* prudishness, false modesty, false shame 874 *modesty*; demureness, gravity 834 *seriousness*; euphemism, priggishness, primness, coyness 850 *affectation*; puritanism 735 *severity*; censorship, expurgation 550 *obliteration.*

(3) *virgin,* maiden, vestal virgin, maid, old maid 895 *celibate*. 986 *monk,*

(4) *prude,* prig, Victorian, Puritan; censor.

Adjective
(5) *pure,* undefiled 646 *perfect*; sinless 935 *innocent*; maidenly,

virgin, virginal, 895 *unwedded*; blushful 874 *modest*; coy, shy 620 *avoiding*; chaste, continent 942 *temperate*; impregnable, incorruptible 929 *honourable*; unfeeling 820 *impassive*; immaculate, spotless, snowy; good, moral 933 *virtuous*; Platonic, sublimated; decent, decorous, delicate, refined 846 *tasteful*; printable, quotable, repeatable, mentionable, clean; censored, bowdlerized, expurgated.

(6) *prudish,* squeamish, shockable, Victorian; prim 850 *affected*; old-maidish, straitlaced, narrow-minded, puritan, priggish; sanctimonious.

951
Impurity

Noun
(1) *impurity,* impure thoughts, defilement 649 *uncleanness*; indelicacy 847 *bad taste*; shamelessness, indecency, immodesty, exhibitionism; coarseness, grossness, ribaldry, bawdiness, salaciousness; loose talk, double entendre, dirt, filth, obscenity; erotica; pornography, hard-core p., soft porn; prurience, voyeurism.

(2) *unchastity,* promiscuity, wantonness; incontinence, easy virtue, no morals, amorality; permissiveness 734 *laxity*; vice, immorality; lust 859 *libido*; eroticism 944 *sensualism*; sexiness, lasciviousness, lewdness; licentiousness, dissoluteness, dissipation, debauchery, licence; seduction, lechery, fornication; womanizing, whoring.

(3) *illicit love,* guilty l., unlawful desires, forbidden fruit; incest 84 *abnormality*; perversion, pederasty, buggery, sodomy, bestiality; adultery, infidelity,

unfaithfulness; eternal triangle, liaison, intrigue 887 *love affair*; free love 894 *type of marriage*; deceived husband, cuckold.

(4) *rape,* violation, indecent assault; sex crime.

(5) *social evil,* streetwalking, prostitution; indecent exposure, flashing; pimping, pandering; brothel, whorehouse, red light district.

Adjective
(6) *impure,* defiling, unclean, nasty 649 *dirty*; unwholesome 653 *insalubrious*; uncensored, unexpurgated; indelicate, vulgar, coarse, gross; ribald, broad, strong, bawdy, Rabelaisian; suggestive, provocative, titillating, spicy, juicy, fruity; immoral, risqué, naughty, blue; unmentionable, unprintable; smutty, filthy, offensive; indecent, obscene, lewd, pornographic; prurient, erotic, sexy.

(7) *unchaste,* susceptible 934 *frail*; seduced, prostituted; of easy virtue, amoral, immoral; wanton, loose, fast; immodest, daring, revealing; unblushing, shameless, flaunting; tarty, promiscuous, sleeping around; on the game.

(8) *lecherous,* carnal, voluptuous 944 *sensual*; libidinous, lustful 859 *desiring*; on heat, randy; sex-conscious, oversexed, sex-mad; perverted, bestial; lewd, licentious depraved, debauched, dissolute, dissipated, profligate 934 *vicious*.

(9) *extramarital,* irregular, unlawful, incestuous; homosexual, Lesbian 84 *abnormal*; adulterous, unfaithful.

Verb
(10) *be impure,* immoral etc.

be immoral, have no mor-
...s; be unfaithful, commit adultery; be dissipated 943 *be intemperate*; fornicate, womanize;
keep a mistress, have a lover;
be promiscuous, sleep around;
street-walk, pimp, pander, procure, keep a brothel.

(11) *debauch,* defile 649 *make
unclean*; proposition, seduce,
lead astray; take advantage of,
dishonour, deflower, prostitute, disgrace 867 *shame*; sleep
with 45 *unite with*; rape, commit r., ravish, violate, molest,
abuse, interfere with, assault,
indecently a.

Adverb
(12) *impurely,* immodestly,
shamelessly etc. adj.

952
Libertine

Noun
(1) *libertine,* gay bachelor, philanderer, flirt; gay dog, rake,
roue, profligate 944 *sensualist*;
lady-killer, fancy-man, gigolo;
seducer, deceiver, false lover;
adulterer; wolf, woman-chaser,
kerb-crawler; womanizer, fornicator; voyeur, lecher,
flasher; sex maniac, rapist;
pederast, sodomite, pervert.

(2) *loose woman,* fast w., wanton; flirt, hussy, minx; trollop,
drab, slut; tart, pick-up; vamp,
temptress, femme fatale; other
woman, adulteress, nymphomaniac.

(3) *kept woman,* fancy w., mistress, concubine; moll.

(4) *prostitute,* harlot, trollop,
whore; streetwalker, hooker;
pick-up, call girl; courtesan.

(5) *bawd,* go-between, pimp,
ponce; madam.

953
Legality

Noun
(1) *legality,* formality 959 *litigation*; respect for law, law and
order; good law 913 *justice*;
constitutionalism; lawfulness,
legitimacy.

(2) *legislation,* legislature, law-
giving, law-making; codification; legalization, validation,
ratification; enactment, regulation; plebiscite 605 *vote*; law,
statute, ordinance, order,
standing o. 737 *decree*; edict 693
precept; legislator, law-giver.

(3) *law,* the law; body of law,
constitution; charter, institution; statute book, legal code;
penal code, civil c.; written
law, statute l., common l.;
criminal law, civil l.; legal process 955 *jurisdiction*; lawsuit
959 *legal trial.*

(4) *jurisprudence,* science of
law; law consultancy, legal
advice.

Adjective
(5) *legal,* lawful 913 *just*; law-
abiding 739 *obedient*; legitimate, licensed 756 *permitted*;
sanctioned by law, · de jure;
statutory, constitutional; law-
giving, legislatorial, legislative; legislated, enacted, made
law; ordained, decreed, by order; legalized, legitimized; actionable, justiciable; jurisprudential.

Verb
(6) *be legal,* stand up in law.

(7) *make legal,* legalize, legitimize, establish, ratify 488 *endorse*; legislate, make laws,
pass, enact, ordain 737 *decree.*

Adverb
(8) *legally,* by law, by order;
legitimately.

954
Illegality

Noun

(1) *illegality,* bad law, legal flaw, loophole; wrong verdict, bad judgment 481 *misjudgment*; miscarriage of justice 914 *injustice*; illicitness, unlawfulness; illegitimacy.

(2) *lawbreaking,* breach of law, contravention, infringement 306 *overstepping*; trespass, offence; malpractice 930 *foul play*; shadiness, dishonesty 930 *improbity*; criminality 936 *guilt*; wrongdoing, criminal offence, indictable o., crime, misdemeanour, felony; criminology; criminal 904 *offender.*

(3) *lawlessness,* outlawry, crime wave 734 *anarchy*; summary justice, kangaroo court, gang rule, mob law, lynch l.; riot, rioting, hooliganism 738 *revolt*; coup d'etat, usurpation 916 *arrogation*; martial law, mailed fist, jackboot 735 *brute force.*

(4) *bastard,* bastard, illegitimate child, natural c.

Adjective

(5) *illegal,* illegitimate, illicit; contraband, black-market; unauthorized, unofficial; unlawful, wrongful 914 *wrong*; unconstitutional; suspended, annulled 752 *abrogated*; irregular, contrary to law; extrajudicial; outside the law, outlawed; actionable 928 *accusable.*

(6) *lawbreaking,* trespassing, offending 936 *guilty*; criminal, felonious; fraudulent, shady 930 *dishonest.*

(7) *lawless,* without law, ungovernable 734 *anarchic*; violent, summary; arbitrary, irresponsible, unanswerable, unaccountable; unofficial, illegitimate; above the law, despotic, tyrannical 735 *oppressive.*

Verb

(8) *be illegal,* break the law, defy the law 914 *do wrong*; exceed one's authority 734 *please oneself.*

(9) *make illegal,* outlaw 757 *prohibit*; forbid by law, penalize 963 *punish*; suspend, annul 752 *abrogate.*

Adverb

(10) *illegally,* unlawfully.

955
Jurisdiction

Noun

(1) *jurisdiction,* judicature, magistracy, legal authority 733 *authority*; local authority 692 *council*; watch committee 956 *tribunal*; portfolio 751 *mandate.*

(2) *law officer,* legal administrator; Lord Chancellor, Attorney General; public prosecutor 957 *judge*; sheriff; court officer, tipstaff, bailiff.

(3) *police,* police force, Scotland Yard; constabulary, military police, transport p.; police officer, policeman *or* policewoman; constable, special c., police sergeant, police inspector; superintendent, commissioner; plain-clothes police 459 *detective.*

Adjective

(4) *jurisdictional,* competent; executive, administrative 689 *directing*; justiciary, judiciary, juridical.

Verb

(5) *hold court,* administer justice 480 *judge*; hear complaints 959 *try a case.*

956
Tribunal

Noun
(1) *tribunal,* seat of justice, woolsack, throne; judgment seat, bar; forum 692 *council*; bench, board, bench of judges, panel of j., judge and jury.

(2) *lawcourt,* court, open c.; court of law, court of justice, criminal court, civil c.; High Court, County Court; Court of Appeal; Star Chamber; House of Lords; assizes; sessions, quarter s., petty s.; Old Bailey; magistrates' court, juvenile c.; coroner's court; court-martial.

(3) *ecclesiastical court,* Curia; Inquisition, Holy Office.

(4) *courtroom,* courthouse, lawcourts; bench, woolsack, jury box; dock, bar; witness box.

Adjective
(5) *judicatory,* judicial; justiciary 955 *jurisidictional.*

957
Judge

Noun
(1) *judge,* justice, your Lordship, my lud; chief justice, recorder, sessions judge, circuit j.; coroner; magistrate, justice of the peace, JP; bench, judiciary.

(2) *magistracy,* arbiter, referee, assessor, arbitrator, Ombudsman 480 *estimator.*

(3) *jury,* grand jury; juror's panel, jury list; juror, juryman *or* -woman, foreman *or* -woman of the jury.

958
Lawyer

Noun
(1) *lawyer,* legal practitioner;

barrister, advocate, counsel, junior c.; silk, leading counsel, Queen's C., QC 696 *expert*; pettifogger, crooked lawyer.

(2) *law agent,* attorney, public a., proctor, procurator; solicitor, legal adviser; legal representative, advocate; conveyancer.

(3) *notary,* commissioner for oaths; scrivener 955 *law officer*; clerk of the court.

(4) *jurist,* legal expert, master of jurisprudence, pundit.

(5) *bar,* civil b., criminal b., Inns of Chancery, Inns of Court; legal profession, the Robe; barristership, advocacy.

Adjective
(6) *jurisprudential,* learned in the law, called to the bar.

Verb
(7) *do law,* study l., take silk; advocate, plead; practise law.

959
Litigation

Noun
(1) *litigation,* litigiousness, legal dispute 709 *quarrel*; lawsuit, case, cause, action; prosecution, charge 928 *accusation*; test case 461 *experiment*; claim, plea, petition 761 *request*; affidavit 532 *affirmation.*

(2) *legal process,* proceedings, jurisdiction; citation, subpoena, summons, search warrant 737 *warrant*; arrest, apprehension, detention, committal 747 *restraint*; habeas corpus, bail, surety injunction, writ.

(3) *legal trial,* trial, fair t., trial by jury; assize, sessions; inquest 459 *enquiry*; hearing, prosecution, defence; 466 *evidence*; examination, cross-e.

466 *testimony*; pleadings, arguments, proof, disproof; summing up, ruling, finding, decision, verdict 480 *judgment*; majority verdict, hung jury; appeal, retrial; precedent, case law.

(4) *litigant,* suitor 763 *petitioner*; claimant, plaintiff, defendant, appellant, respondent, objector, accused 928 *accused person*; prosecutor 928 *accuser.*

Adjective
(5) *litigating,* litigant, suing 928 *accusing*; going to law, contesting 475 *arguing*; litigious 709 *quarrelling.*

(6) *litigated,* on trial, disputed, contested; up for trial, sub judice; litigable, actionable, justicable.

Verb
(7) *litigate,* go to law, start an action, bring a suit, petition 761 *request*; brief counsel; contest at law, take one to court; sue, arraign, impeach, accuse, charge, press charges 928 *indict*; summon, serve notice on; prosecute, put on trial, bring to justice; advocate, plead 475 *argue.*

(8) *try a case,* hear a cause; sit in judgment, find, decide 480 *judge*; sum up, pronounce sentence.

(9) *stand trial,* come before, plead guilty, plead not guilty.

Adverb
(10) *in litigation,* at law, sub judice.

960
Acquittal

Noun
(1) *acquittal,* exculpation, exoneration 935 *innocence*; absolution, discharge 746 *liberation*; whitewashing, justification 927 *vindication*; no case, case

dismissed; reprieve, pardon 909 *forgiveness*; exemption, impunity 919 *nonliablity.*

Adjective
(2) *acquitted,* not guilty, cleared, in the clear, exonerated, exculpated, vindicated; immune, exempt; let off, discharged 746 *liberated*; reprieved 909 *forgiven.*

Verb
(3) *acquit,* find not guilty; prove innocent 927 *vindicate*; clear, absolve, exonerate, exculpate; not press charges, not prosecute, discharge 746 *liberate*; reprieve, pardon 909 *forgive*; quash, allow an appeal 752 *abrogate.*

961
Condemnation

Noun
(1) *condemnation,* finding of guilty, conviction; excommunication 899 *malediction*; judgment, sentence 963 *punishment.*

Adjective
(2) *condemned,* found guilty, made liable; convicted, sentenced; proscribed, outlawed 924 *disapproved.*

Verb
(3) *condemn,* prove guilty, find liable, find against, find guilty, pronounce g., convict, sentence; proscribe, outlaw, bar 954 *make illegal*; blacklist 924 *disapprove*; damn, excommunicate 899 *curse*; plead guilty 526 *confess.*

962
Reward

Noun
(1) *reward,* remuneration, recompense; deserts, just d. 913 *justice*; recognition, thanks 907 *gratitude*; tribute 923 *praise*;

prize-giving, award, presentation, prize 729 *trophy*; honour 729 *decoration*, 866 *honours*; peerdom 870 *title*; prize fellowship, scholarship 703 *subvention*; fee, retainer, honorarium, remuneration 804 *pay*; bonus 612 *incentive*; return, profit 771 *gain*; reparation 787 *restitution*; tip 781 *gift*; hush money, protection m.

Adjective

(2) *rewarding,* generous, open-handed 813 *liberal*; profitable, remunerative 771 *gainful*; compensatory 787 *restoring*; retributive 714 *retaliatory.*

Verb

(3) *reward,* recompense 866 *honour*; award, present, offer a reward; recognize, acknowledge, pay tribute, thank 907 *be grateful*; remunerate 804 *pay*; tip 813 *be liberal*; repay, requite 714 *retaliate*; compensate, indemnify, make reparation 787 *restitute*; win over 612 *bribe.*

(4) *be rewarded,* win a prize, get a medal; accept payment 782 *receive*; have one's reward, get one's deserts, receive one's due 714 *be rightly served*; reap the fruits 771 *gain.*

Adverb

(5) *rewardingly,* profitably; as a reward, for one's pains.

963
Punishment

Noun

(1) *punishment,* sentence 961 *condemnation*; chastisement, carpeting 924 *reprimand*; just deserts; doom, judgment 913 *justice*; poetic justice, retribution, Nemesis; reckoning, repayment 787 *restitution*; reprisal 714 *retaliation*, 910 *revenge*; penance, self-mortification 941 *atonement*; hara-kiri 362 *suicide*; penology, penologist.

(2) *corporal punishment,* smacking, slapping, hiding, beating, thrashing, caning, whipping, flogging, birching; scourging, flagellation; slap, smack, rap, blow, cuff, clout 279 *knock*; third degree, torture 377 *pain.*

(3) *capital punishment,* extreme penalty, death sentence, death warrant; execution 362 *killing*; decapitation, beheading, hanging, strangulation, bow-stringing; electrocution; crucifixion, impalement; burning, the stake; mass murder, mass execution, purge 362 *slaughter*; martyrdom; lynching, lynch law; judicial murder.

(4) *penalty,* infliction, imposition, task, lines; sentence, penal code, penology; liability, damages, costs; compensation, restoration 787 *restitution*; fining, fine 804 *payment*; ransom 809 *price*; forfeiture, sequestration, confiscation, deprivation 786 *expropriation*; keeping in, gating, imprisonment 747 *detention*; suspension, rustication; binding over 747 *restraint*; penal servitude, hard labour; expulsion, deportation 300 *ejection*; banishment, exile, proscription, outlawing 57 *exclusion*; reprisal 714 *retaliation.*

(5) *punisher,* vindicator 910 *avenger*; chastiser, corrector; persecutor 735 *tyrant*; court 957 *judge*; torturer, inquisitor; executioner, hangman, firing squad; lyncher 362 *murderer.*

Adjective

(6) *punitive,* penological, penal; disciplinary, corrective; vindictive, retributive 714 *retaliatory*; penalizing, fining 786 *taking*; scourging 377 *painful.*

(7) *punishable,* liable, indictable 928 *accusable*; asking for it.

Verb

(8) *punish,* afflict 827 *hurt*; persecute, victimize 735 *be severe*; inflict, impose, chasten, discipline, correct, chastise, castigate; reprimand, rebuke 924 *reprove*; penalize, sentence 961 *condemn*; execute justice, exact a penalty; settle with, get even w., pay one out 714 *retaliate*; revenge oneself 910 *avenge*; fine, confiscate 786 *take away*; unfrock, demote, degrade, downgrade, suspend 867 *shame*; tar and feather, pillory; keelhaul; lock up 747 *imprison*.

(9) *spank,* slap, smack, slipper; cuff, clout, beat, belt, strap, leather, tan, cane, birch, whack 279 *strike*.

(10) *flog,* whip, horsewhip, thrash, belabour 279 *strike*; scourge, lash, flay, flagellate.

(11) *torture,* put to the t. 377 *give pain*; thumbscrew, rack, kneecap; persecute, martyrize 827 *torment*.

(12) *execute,* put to death 362 *kill*; lynch 362 *murder*; dismember, decimate; crucify, impale, flay alive; stone to death 712 *lapidate*; shoot, fusillade; burn at the stake; bow-string, garrotte, strangle; hang, string up, hang, draw and quarter; behead, decapitate, guillotine; electrocute, send to the chair; purge, massacre 362 *slaughter*.

(13) *be punished,* take the consequences, get one's deserts; regret it, smart for it; pay for it, swing; die the death.

964
Means of punishment

Noun

(1) *scourge,* birch, cat, sjambok, whip, horsewhip, strap, tawse; cane, stick, rod 723 *club*.

(2) *pillory,* stocks, whipping post, ducking stool, corner, dunce's cap; irons 748 *fetter*; prison 748 *gaol*.

(3) *means of execution,* scaffold, block, gallows, gibbet; cross, stake; axe, guillotine; electric chair; death chamber, gas c.

965
Divineness

Noun

(1) *divineness,* divinity, deity; godhead, divine principle, divine essence, perfection; First Cause 156 *source*; divine nature, God's ways, Providence.

(2) *divine attribute,* perfect being 646 *perfection*; immanence, omnipresence 189 *presence*; omniscience, omnipotence, almightiness 160 *power*; timelessness, eternity 115 *perpetuity*; immutability 153 *stability*; truth, sanctity, holiness, goodness, justice, mercy; transcendence, sublimity; sovereignty, majesty, glory, light.

(3) *the Deity,* God, Supreme Being, the Almighty, the Most High; the All-holy, the All-merciful; Creator, Preserver; Allah; Jehovah; Brahma, Hindu triad; Holy Trinity, Father, Son and the Holy Ghost; All-Father, Great Spirit.

(4) *theophany,* incarnation; transfiguration; avatar.

Adjective

(5) *divine,* holy, hallowed, sacred, sacrosanct, heavenly, celestial; sublime, ineffable; numinous, mystical, religious, spiritual; superhuman, supernatural, transcendent; providential; theocratic.

(6) *godlike,* divine, superhuman; transcendent, immanent; omnipresent 189 *ubiquitous*; immeasurable 107 *infinite*; absolute, timeless, eternal 115 *perpetual*; immutable, changeless 144 *permanent*; almighty, all-powerful, omnipotent 160 *powerful*; all-wise, all-seeing, all-knowing, omniscient 490 *knowing*; oracular 511 *predicting*; all-merciful 887 *loving*; holy, all-h., worshipped 979 *sanctified*; sovereign 34 *supreme*; deified, transfigured, gl rious 866 *worshipful*; incarnate, messianic, anointed.

Adverb
(7) *divinely,* by God's will.

966
Deities in general

Noun
(1) *deity,* god, goddess, the gods, the immortals; pagan god, false g., idol; demigod, half-god, divine hero, divine king 967 *lesser deity*; object of worship, fetish, totem 982 *idol*.

(2) *mythic deity,* native god *or* goddess, earth goddess, mother g., earth mother, Great Mother; fertility god; gods of the underworld; sun god, river god, sea g.; god *or* goddess of war, god *or* goddess of love; household gods; the Fates.

Adjective
(3) *mythological,* mythical; deified.

967
Pantheon

Noun
(1) *classical deities,* Graeco-Roman deities; primeval deities, Uranus, Saturn, Rhea, Gaia; Olympian deity, Zeus, Jupiter *or* Jove; Jove, Pluto, Hades; Poseidon, Neptune; Hermes, Mercury; Apollo, Phoebus; Dionysius, Bacchus; Ares, Mars; Aphrodite, Venus; Artemis, Diana; Hera, Juno; Athena, Minerva; Eros, Cupid.

(2) *lesser deity,* Pan, Flora, Aurora, Luna; Muses, tuneful Nine; Lares, Penates; local god, genius loci; demigod, divine hero.

(3) *nymph,* wood n., tree n., dryad, hamadryad; mountain nymph, oread; water nymph, naiad; sea nymph, nereid; siren 970 *mythical being*.

968
Angel. Saint.

Noun
(1) *angel,* archangel, heavenly host; seraph, seraphim, cherub, cherubim; guardian angel.

(2) *saint,* patron s., saint and martyr; Madonna, Our Lady, blessed virgin.

Adjective
(3) *angelic,* archangelic, seraphic, cherubic; saintly, celestial.

Verb
(4) *angelize,* beatify 979 *sanctify*.

969
Devil

Noun
(1) *Satan,* Lucifer, the Devil, the Evil One, spirit of evil.

(2) *devil,* fiend; familiar, imp, imp of Satan, demon; powers of darkness; fallen angel, lost soul, sinner; horns, cloven hoof.

(3) *diabolism,* devilry 898 *inhumanity*; Satanism, devil worship, witchcraft, black magic 983 *sorcery*; demonology.

(4) *diabolist,* Satanist, devil-worshipper.

Adjective
(5) *diabolic,* diabolical, satanic, fiendish, demonic, demoniacal, devilish 898 *malevolent*; infernal, hellish; demoniac, possessed.

Verb
(6) *diabolize,* demonize; possess, bedevil 983 *bewitch.*

970
Fairy

Noun
(1) *fairy,* fairy world, magic w., fairyland, faerie; fairy folk, little people; fairy ring, fairy lore, fairy tales, folklore.

(2) *elf,* elves, pixie, brownie, gnome, dwarf, troll, goblin, imp, sprite, hobgoblin; leprechaun, gremlin, Puck.

(3) *ghost,* spirit, departed s.; shades, Manes; revived corpse, zombie; visitant, haunter, poltergeist, spook. spectre, apparition, phantom, phantasm, shape, wraith 440 *visual fallacy.*

(4) *demon,* imp, familiar 969 *devil*; she-demon, banshee; troll, ogre, ogress, giant, giantess, bogy 938 *monster*; ghoul, vampire, werewolf; fury, harpy; ghoulishness.

(5) *mythical being* 968 angel, 969 *devil*; demon, genie, jinn; houri; centaur, satyr, faun; mermaid, Siren, water spirit 967 *nymph*; Phoenix 84 *rara avis.*

Adjective
(6) *fairylike,* fairy; gigantic, ogreish, devilish, demonic; elflike, elfin, elvish, impish, Puckish; magic 983 *magical*; mythical, mythic 513 *imaginary.*

(7) *spooky,* spookish, ghostly, ghoulish; haunted, nightmarish, macabre 854 *frightening*; weird, eerie, uncanny, unearthly 84 *abnormal*; spectral,

wraith-like, disembodied 320 *immaterial,* 984 *psychical.*

Verb
(8) *haunt,* visit, walk; gibber, mop and mow.

Adverb
(9) *spookishly,* spectrally, uncannily, nightmarishly.

971
Heaven

Noun
(1) *heaven,* kingdom of God, kingdom of heaven, kingdom come; Paradise, nirvana, seventh heaven; the Millennium, earthly Paradise, New Jerusalem, Celestial City; afterlife, eternity 124 *future state.*

(2) *mythic heaven,* Elysium, Elysian fields; Valhalla; Islands of the Blest; Earthly Paradise, Garden of Eden, 513 *fantasy.*

Adjective
(3) *paradisiac,* heavenly, celestial; beatific, blessed, blissful 824 *happy*; Elysian, Olympian.

972
Hell

Noun
(1) *hell,* lower world, infernal regions, underworld; grave, limbo, Hades; purgatory; abyss, bottomless pit, place of torment, inferno, everlasting fire, hellfire.

(2) *mythic hell,* realm of Pluto, Hades; river of hell, Styx, Lethe.

Adjective
(3) *infernal,* bottomless 211 *deep*; hellish, Stygian; damned 969 *diabolic.*

973
Religion

Noun

(1) *religion,* religious feeling 979 *piety*; search for truth, religious quest; natural religion, deism; paganism 982 *idolatry*; nature religion, mystery r., mysteries; mysticism, yoga, theosophy 449 *philosophy*; religious cult, state religion 981 *cult*; no religion, atheism 974 *irreligion*.

(2) *deism,* theism; animism, pantheism, polytheism, monotheism, gnosticism.

(3) *religious faith,* faith 485 *belief*; Christianity, the Cross; Judaism, Islam, the Crescent; Baha'ism; Hinduism; Sikhism; Buddhism, Zen; Shintoism; Taoism, Confucianism.

(4) *theology,* study of religion; tradition, deposit of faith; teaching, doctrine, religious d.; canon; dogma, tenet; articles of faith, credo 485 *creed*.

(5) *theologian,* divine; doctor, rabbi, scribe, mufti, mullah; scholastic, hagiographer.

(6) *religious teacher,* prophet, guru 500 *sage*; evangelist, apostle, missionary; expected leader, Messiah, Christ, Jesus Christ; Prophet of God, Muhammad; Buddha, Gautama; expounder, catechist 520 *interpreter*.

(7) *religionist,* deist, theist; monotheist, polytheist pantheist; fetishist 982 *idolater*; pagan, gentile 974 *heathen*; adherent, believer 976 *the orthodox*; militant 979 *zealot*; Christian, Jew; Muslim; Hindu, Buddhist, Zen B.

Adjective

(8) *religious,* divine, holy, sacred, spiritual, sacramental; deistic, theistic, animistic, pantheistic, monotheistic; mystic, devotional, devout, practising 981 *worshipping*.

(9) *theological,* doctrinal, dogmatic, creedal, canonical.

974
Irreligion

Noun

(1) *irreligion,* profaneness, ungodliness, godlessness 980 *impiety*; false religion, heathenism 982 *idolatry*; no religion, atheism 486 *unbelief*; agnosticism, scepticism 486 *doubt*; lack of faith; want of f., lapse, recidivism, backsliding; amoralism, apathy 860 *indifference*.

(2) *antichristianity,* paganism, heathenism; Satanism 969 *diabolism*; free thought, rationalism, positivism, nihilism 449 *philosophy*; materialism, secularism, worldliness, Mammon.

(3) *irreligionist,* antichrist; dissenter, atheist 486 *unbeliever*; rationalist, freethinker; agnostic, sceptic; nihilist, materialist, positivist.

(4) *heathen,* non-Christian, pagan, infidel, gentile; apostate, backslider.

Adjective

(5) *irreligious,* without religion, godless, profane 980 *impious*; nihilistic, atheistic; agnostic, doubting, sceptical 486 *unbelieving*; freethinking, rationalistic; nonworshipping, nonpractising 769 *nonobservant*; ungodly 934 *wicked*; amoral 860 *indifferent*; secular, mundane, worldly, materialistic 944 *sensual*; lacking faith, faithless; backsliding, lapsed; paganized; anti-Church, anticlerical.

(6) *heathenish,* unholy 980 *profane*; unchristian, gentile,

heathen, pagan, infidel; unbaptised, uncircumcised.

Verb
(7) *be irreligious,* have no religion, lack faith 486 *disbelieve*; lose one's faith 603 *apostatize*; demythologize, rationalize; deny God, blaspheme 980 *be impious.*

(8) *paganize,* heathenize, secularize.

975
Revelation

Noun
(1) *revelation,* divine r., apocalypse 526 *disclosure*; illumination 417 *light*; inspiration, divine i.; prophecy, intuition, mysticism; the Law, Ten Commandments; divine message, God's word, gospel; God revealed, theopany, epiphany, incarnation; avatar.

(2) *scripture,* word of God, sacred writings; Koran; Vedas; Holy Scripture, Bible, Holy B.; canonical books, canon; Old Testament, Pentateuch, Torah, New Testament; Apocrypha, sayings; Talmud; psalter, breviary, missal.

Adjective
(3) *revelational,* inspirational, mystic; inspired, prophetic, revealed; apocalyptic; prophetic, evangelical.

(4) *scriptural,* sacred, holy; revealed, inspired, prophetic; canonical 733 *authoritative*; biblical, gospel, apostolic; Talmudic, Koranic.

976
Orthodoxy

Noun
(1) *orthodoxy,* sound theology, religious truth, canonicity; the

Faith, the true faith; ecumenicalism, catholicity; formulated faith, credo 485 *creed*; catechism.

(2) *orthodoxism,* fundamentalism; ecclesiasticism 985 *the church*; practice 768 *observance*; intolerance, persecution; heresy-hunting, Inquisition; Index; imprimatur 923 *approbation.*

(3) *Christendom,* Christian fellowship, the Church; Church Militant, Church on earth; catholicism, Orthodoxy, Eastern O.; High Church; protestantism, the Reformation.

(4) *Catholic,* Orthodox, Coptic; Roman Catholic, Anglo-C., Episcopalian.

(5) *Protestant,* Anglican, Presbyterian, Baptist, Methodist, Quaker, Friend.

(6) *church member,* churchgoer, churchman *or - woman*; communicant 981 *worshipper*; the faithful, church people, chapel p.; congregation, co-religionist, fellow worshipper.

(7) *the orthodox,* the faithful, the converted; born-again Christian, evangelical; believer, true b.; traditionalist, fundamentalist 973 *theologian.*

Adjective
(8) *orthodox* 485 *believing*; loyal, devout 739 *obedient*; practising 83 *conformable*; strict, pedantic 979 *pietistic*; intolerant, witchhunting; doctrinal 485 *creedal*; authoritative, canonical, biblical, scriptural, evangelical, gospel; literal, fundamentalist; catholic, ecumenical; traditional, believed, generally b. 485 *credible.*

(9) *Roman Catholic,* Catholic, Roman; popish.

(10) *Anglican,* episcopalian; Anglo-Catholic, High-Church; Low-Church; Broad-C.

(11) *Protestant,* reformed; Calvinist, Presbyterian, United Reformed, Baptist, Methodist, Wesleyan, Quaker.

Verb
(12) *be orthodox,* hold the faith, go the church, recite the creeds 485 *believe.*

977
Heterodoxy

Noun
(1) *heterodoxy,* unorthodoxy; false creed, superstition 495 *error*; partial truth; heresy, rank h.; heretic.

Adjective
(2) *heterodox,* differing 489 *dissenting*; nonconformist; erroneous 495 *mistaken*; unorthodox, unscriptural; heretical, anathematized 961 *condemned.*

Verb
(3) *declare heretical,* anathematize 961 *condemn.*

(4) *be heretical,* - unorthodox etc. adj.

Adverb
(5) *heretically,* unorthodoxly.

978
Sectarianism

Noun
(1) *sectarianism,* bigotry 481 *bias*; independence, separatism 738 *disobedience*; nonconformism, nonconformity 489 *dissent.*

(2) *schism,* division, differences 709 *quarrel*; dissociation, breakaway, secession, withdrawal 46 *separation*; recusancy 769 *nonobservance.*

(3) *sect,* off-shoot 708 *party*; episcopalians, evangelicals, puritans; order, religious o., 708 *community*; chapel, conventicle.

(4) *sectarian,* follower, adherent, devotee; Nonconformist, Puritan 976 *Protestant.*

(5) *schismatic,* separatist, seceder, secessionist; rebel, recusant, dissident, dissenter; nonconformist; apostate 603 *tergiversator.*

Adjective
(6) *sectarian,* exclusive 708 *sectional*; High-Church, episcopalian 976 *Anglican*; Low-Church, evangelical 976 *Protestant*; Puritan, Covenanting; revivalist.

(7) *schismatical,* secessionist, seceding, breakaway 46 *separate*; excommunicated, heretical; nonconformist 489 *dissenting*; recusant, rebellious 738 *disobedient*; apostate.

Verb
(8) *sectarianize,* follow a sect 708 *join a party.*

(9) *schismatize,* separate, secede, break away 603 *apostatize.*

979
Piety

Noun
(1) *piety,* piousness, goodness 933 *virtue*; reverence, veneration 920 *respect*; loyalty, conformity 768 *observance*; religiousness, religion, fear of God; humbleness 872 *humility*; faith, trust 485 *belief*; devotion, dedication, devoutness; fervour, zeal; prostration adoration 981 *worship*; contemplation, mysticism; charity 901 *philanthropy.*

(2) *sanctity,* holiness, sacredness, hallowedness; goodness 933 *virtue*; state of grace 950

purity; godliness, saintliness, spirituality; sainthood, blessedness; enlightenment, conversion, rebirth; sanctification; canonization, beatification, consecration, dedication.

(3) *pietism,* sanctimoniousness, religiosity; unction, unctuousness; cant 542 *sham*; austerity 945 *asceticism*; literalness, Bible-worship; bigotry, fanaticism 481 *prejudice*; persecution, witch-hunting.

(4) *pietist,* pious person, 937 *good person*; conformist 488 *assenter*; communicant 981 *worshipper*; confessor, martyr; saint, contemplative, mystic, holy man *or* woman 945 *ascetic*; hermit, anchorite 883 *solitary*; monk, nun 986 *clergy*; convert, believer 976 *church member*; pilgrim, palmer, hajji; votary.

(5) *zealot,* fanatic, bigot; image-breaker, iconoclast; Puritan 978 *sectarian*; sermonizer 537 *preacher*; evangelical, salvationist, hot-gospeller; missionary, revivalist; crusader.

Adjective
(6) *pious,* good 933 *virtuous*; kind 897 *benevolent*; reverent 920 *respectful*; faithful, devoted 739 *obedient*; conforming, traditional 768 *observant*; practising, believing 976 *orthodox*; pure in heart, spiritual, godly, God-fearing, religious, devout; praying, prayerful 981 *worshipping*; meditative, contemplative, mystic; holy, saintly, full of grace.

(7) *pietistic,* ardent, fervent, inspired; austere 945 *ascetic*; earnest, overreligious, self-righteous, holier than thou; formalistic, ritualistic 978 *sectarian*; sanctimonious 850 *affected*; goody-goody 933 *virtuous*; crusading, evangelical.

(8) *sanctified,* made holy, consecrated, dedicated; reverend, holy, sacred, sacrosanct 866 *worshipful*; haloed, sainted, canonized, beatified; adopted, chosen; saved, redeemed, ransomed; reborn, born again 656 *restored*.

Verb
(9) *be pious,* - religious etc. adj.; fear God, have faith keep the f. 485 *believe*; go to church, pray, say one's prayers 981 *worship*; sacrifice, devote 897 *be benevolent*; glorify God 923 *praise*; show reverence 920 *show respect*; hearken, listen 739 *obey*.

(10) *become pious,* be converted, get religion; see the light 603 *recant*; mend one's ways, reform, repent 939 *be penitent*; take vows 986 *take orders*.

(11) *make pious,* bring religion to, bring to God, proselytize, convert 485 *convince*; Christianize, baptize; Islamize, Judaize; spiritualize 648 *purify*; edify, inspire, uplift 654 *make better*.

(12) *sanctify,* hallow, make holy; spiritualize, consecrate, dedicate; saint, canonize, beatify, bless.

980
Impiety

Noun
(1) *impiety,* irreverence, disregard 921 *disrespect*; lack of piety, lack of reverence; godlessness 974 *irreligion*; mockery, derision, scorn 922 *contempt*; sacrilegiousness, profanity; blasphemy 899 *malediction*; sacrilege, violation, desecration, profanation 675 *misuse*; immorality, sin 934 *wickedness*; stubbornness 940 *impenitence*; backsliding, apostasy; worldliness, materialism

319 *materiality*; paganism, heathenism.

(2) *false piety,* sanctimoniousness, Pharisaism 979 *pietism*; hypocrisy, lip service 541 *duplicity.*

(3) *impious person,* blasphemer, swearer 899 *malediction*; scorner 926 *detractor*; desecrator, profaner 904 *offender*; unbeliever 974 *heathen*; disbeliever, atheist, sceptic 974 *irreligionist*; materialist 944 *sensualist*; sinner, reprobate 938 *bad person*; recidivist, backslider, apostate.

Adjective

(4) *impious,* ungodly, anti-Christian, anticlerical 704 *opposing*; recusant, dissenting, heretical; unbelieving, godless 974 *irreligious*; nonpractising, nonworshipping; mocking, deriding 851 *derisive*; blaspheming, blasphemous, 899 *cursing*; irreligious, irreverent 921 *disrespectful*; sacrilegious, profaning, desecrating, violating, iconoclastic; brazen 855 *unfearing*; sinning, sinful, impure, hardened, perverted, reprobate 934 *wicked*; backsliding, apostate; canting, pharisaical 541 *hypocritical.*

(5) *profane,* unholy, accursed; secularized; deconsecrated.

Verb

(6) *be impious,* rebel against God 871 *be proud*; sin 934 *be wicked*; swear, blaspheme 899 *curse*; have no reverence 921 *not respect*; profane, desecrate, violate 675 *misuse*; commit sacrilege, defile, sully 649 *make unclean*; cant 541 *dissemble*; backslide 603 *apostatize*; harden one's heart 655 *deteriorate.*

981
Worship

Noun

(1) *worship,* honour, reverence, homage 920 *respect*; awe 854 *fear*; veneration, adoration, humbleness 872 *humility*; devotion 979 *piety*; prayer, one's devotions, one's prayers; retreat, meditation, contemplation, communion.

(2) *cult,* mystique; type of worship, service; false worship 982 *idolatry.*

(3) *act of worship,* rites, mysteries 988 *rite*; glorification, extolment 923 *praise*; hymning, hymn-singing, plainsong, chanting 412 *vocal music*; thanksgiving, blessing, benediction 907 *thanks*; offering, almsgiving, sacrifice; praying, self-examination 939 *penitence*; self-denial 945 *asceticism*; pilgrimage 267 *wandering.*

(4) *prayers,* devotions; private devotion, contemplation 449 *meditation*; prayer, bidding prayer; petition 761 *request*; invocation, intercession 762 *deprecation*; vigils; special prayer, intention; rogation, supplication, litany; exorcism 300 *ejection*; benediction, grace 907 *thanks*; dismissal, blessing; rosary, beads, prayer-wheel; prayer book, missal, breviary; call to prayer, muezzin's cry.

(5) *hymn,* song, psalm, religious song, spiritual; introit; recessional; plainsong, descant 412 *vocal music*; canticle, anthem, cantata, motet; antiphon, response; Hallelujah, Hosanna; hymn-singing, psalm-singing, hymnal, psalter.

(6) *oblation,* offertory, collection 781 *offering*; libation, incense 988 *rite*; dedication, consecration; votive offering;

thank-offering 907 *gratitude*; burnt offering, holocaust; sacrifice, devotion; immolation; expiation, propitiation 941 *atonement.*

(7) *public worship,* common prayer; service, divine service, divine office, mass, matins 988 *church service*; psalm-singing, hymn-singing; church, church-going, chapel-g. 979 *piety*; prayer meeting, revival m.; revivalism; state religion 973 *religion.*

(8) *worshipper,* fellow w. 976 *church member*; votary, devotee; follower 742 *servant*; image-worshipper 982 *idolater*; sacrificer 781 *giver*; supplicant 763 *petitioner*; intercessor; contemplative, mystic, visionary; enthusiast, revivalist; celebrant, officiant 986 *clergy*; communicant, congregation, the faithful; psalm-singer, hymn-s., hymn-writer; pilgrim, palmer, hajji.

Adjective

(9) *worshipping,* devout, devoted 979 *pious*; reverent, reverential 920 *respectful*; prayerful, fervent 761 *supplicatory*; meditating, praying, interceding; kneeling, on one's knees; at one's prayers, at one's devotions, in retreat; church-going, chapel-g., communicant 976 *orthodox*; hymn-singing, psalm s.; celebrating, officiating, ministering 988 *ritualistic.*

(10) *devotional,* worshipful, solemn, sacred, holy; revered, worshipped 920 *respected*; sacramental, mystic; invocatory, intercessory, petitionary 761 *supplicatory*; sacrificial; votive 759 *offering*; giving glory, praising.

Verb

(11) *worship,* honour, revere, venerate, adore 920 *respect*; honour and obey pay homage

to, acknowledge; deify 982 *idolatrize*; bow down before, kneel to, genuflect, humble oneself 872 *be humbled*; bless, give thanks 907 *thank*; extol, laud, magnify, glorify, give glory to 923 *praise*; hymn, anthem, celebrate 413 *sing*; light candles to, call on, invoke, petition, beseech, supplicate, intercede 761 *entreat*; pray, say a prayer, say one's prayers; meditate, contemplate 979 *be pious.*

(12) *offer worship,* celebrate, officiate, minister 988 *perform ritual*; lead in prayer; sacrifice offer up 781 *give*; propitiate appease 719 *pacify*; vow, make vows; dedicate, consecrate 97 *sanctify*; meet for prayer 979 *b pious*; hear Mass, communicate; fast, deny oneself 945 *b ascetic*; go into retreat 44 *meditate*; shout hallelujah 92 *praise.*

Interjection

(13) *Alleluia!* Hallelujah Hosanna!

982
Idolatry

Noun

(1) *idolatry,* idolatrousness false worship, superstition heathenism, paganism; fetish ism; idol worship, image wor ship; mumbo jumbo 983 *sorcery* sacrifice, human s.; sun wor ship, fire worship; devil wor ship 969 *diabolism*; worship of wealth, Mammonism.

(2) *deification,* god-making idolization, hero worship 92 *respect*; king worship, empero w.

(3) *idol,* image, graven i.; cul image, fetish, totem, toten pole; golden calf 966 *deity* Mumbo-Jumbo; Moloch.

(4) *idolater,* idol-worshipper, image w., fetishist 981 *worshipper;* pagan 974 *heathen;* devil-worshipper 969 *diabolist;* idolizer, deifier.

Adjective

(5) *idolatrous,* pagan, heathen 974 *heathenish;* fetishistic; devil-worshipping 969 *diabolic.*

Verb

(6) *idolatrize,* worship idols, deify 979 *sanctify;* idealize, idolize, put on a pedastal 923 *praise;* heathenize 974 *paganize.*

983
Sorcery

Noun

(1) *sorcery,* spellbinding, witchery, magic arts, enchantments; witchcraft, magic lore 490 *knowledge;* wizardry, magic skill 694 *skill;* magic, jugglery 542 *sleight;* white magic, black magic, black art, necromancy 969 *diabolism;* superstition, shamanism; obeah, voodooism, voodoo, hoodoo; spirit-raising 984 *occultism;* spirit-laying, exorcism 988 *rite;* magic rite, invocation, incantation; coven, witches' sabbath; Hallowe'en; witching hour.

(2) *spell,* charm, enchantment, hoodoo, curse; evil eye, jinx, hex; bewitchment, fascination 291 *attraction;* possession, demoniacal p. 503 *frenzy;* incantation, rune; magic sign, magic formula, open sesame, abracadabra; hocus pocus, mumbo jumbo 515 *lack of meaning.*

(3) *talisman,* charm; juju, obeah, fetish 982 *idol;* amulet, mascot, lucky charm; horseshoe, black cat; emblem, flag; relic, holy r.

(4) *magic instrument,* witches' broomstick, wizard's cap; hellbroth, philtre, potion; wand, fairy w., magic ring; magic mirror, flying carpet; wishing well, wishbone.

(5) *sorcerer,* wise man, seer, soothsayer 511 *diviner;* astrologer, alchemist; Druid, Druidess; magus, the Magi; wonderworker, miracle-w.; shaman, medicine man, witchdoctor; fetishist 982 *idolater;* spirit-raiser, exorcist 984 *occultist;* charmer, snake-c.; juggler, illusionist 545 *conjuror;* spellbinder, enchanter, wizard, warlock; magician, necromancer; familiar, imp 969 *devil.*

(6) *sorceress,* wise woman, Sibyl 511 *diviner;* enchantress, witch, hag, hellcat; wicked fairy 970 *fairy.*

Adjective

(7) *sorcerous,* witch-like, wizardly 864 *wonderful;* necromantic 969 *diabolic;* spell-like, incantatory, runic; conjuring, spellbinding, enchanting, fascinating; malignant, blighting, blasting 898 *maleficent;* occult, esoteric 984 *cabalistic.*

(8) *magical,* witching; otherworldly, supernatural, uncanny, weird 970 *fairylike;* talismanic, 660 *tutelary;* magic, charmed, enchanted.

(9) *bewitched,* witched, enchanted, charmed, fey; hypnotized, fascinated, spellbound, under a spell, under a charm; under a curse, cursed; blighted, blasted; hag-ridden, haunted.

Verb

(10) *practise sorcery,* - witchcraft etc. n.; cast horoscopes 511 *divine;* do magic, weave spells; recite a spell *or* an incantation, say the magic word; conjure, invoke, call up; raise spirits; lay ghosts, exorcize; wave one's wand.

(11) *bewitch,* charm, enchant, fascinate, hypnotize; magic, magic away; cast a spell on, put a curse on; blight, blast 899 *curse*; hag-ride, walk, ghost 970 *haunt*.

Adverb
(12) *sorcerously,* by means of a spell.

984
Occultism

Noun
(1) *occultism,* esotericism, mysticism, cabalism, theosophy; occult lore, alchemy, astrology, spiritualism, magic 983 *sorcery*; fortune-telling, crystal-gazing 511 *divination*; sixth sense 476 *intuition*; mesmerism, hypnotism.

(2) *psychics,* psychic science; extrasensory perception, ESP; clairvoyance, second sight 476 *intuition*; psychokinesis, forkbending; telepathy, thought-reading; precognition, deja vu.

(3) *spiritualism,* spirit communication; mediumship, seance; materialization; poltergeists; table-tapping, table-turning; automatism, automatic writing; control 970 *ghost*; ghost-hunting.

(4) *occultist,* mystic; esoteric, cabalist; theosophist, yogi; spiritualist; alchemist 983 *sorcerer*; astrologer, crystal-gazer, palmist 511 *diviner*.

(5) *psychic,* clairvoyant, telepathist; mind reader, thought r.; mesmerist, hypnotist; medium; seer, prophet 511 *oracle*.

Adjective
(6) *cabalistic,* esoteric, hermetic, cryptic 523 *occult*; mysterious, mystic, supernatural; theosophical; astrological, alchemic, necromantic 983 *sorcerous*.

(7) *psychical,* psychic, fey; prophetic 511 *predicting*; telepathic, clairvoyant, mind-reading; spiritualistic; mesmeric, hypnotic.

(8) *paranormal,* supernatural, preternatural.

Verb
(9) *practise occultism,* predict 511 *divine*; hypnotize, mesmerize; hold a seance.

985
The church

Noun
(1) *the church* 976 *Christendom*; theocracy 733 *authority*; papacy, prelacy; episcopacy, episcopalianism; presbyterianism; ecclesiasticism, priestliness, priesthood; monasticism, monastic life 895 *celibacy*, 945 *asceticism*.

(2) *church ministry,* call 622 *vocation*; holy orders, ordination, consecration; apostleship, mission; pastorate, pastorship; confession, absolution 988 *ministration*; preaching 534 *teaching*.

(3) *church office,* priesthood; apostleship; papacy, Holy See; cardinalship; primateship; archbishopric; bishopric, episcopacy, prelacy; archdeaconate, deanery; presbyterate, eldership; pastorship, pastorate; rectorship, vicarship, curacy; chaplaincy; incumbency, tenure, benefice.

(4) *parish,* deanery; presbytery; diocese, bishopric, see, archbishopric.

(5) *synod,* convocation 692 *council*; consistory, conclave; bench of bishops; kirk session, presbytery 956 *tribunal*.

Adjective
(6) *ecclesiastical,* churchly;

hierarchical, apostolic; pontifical, papal; patriarchal, metropolitan; episcopal 986 *clerical*; episcopalian, presbyterian; diocesan, parochial.

(7) *priestly*, sacerdotal, sacramental, spiritual; ministering, apostolic, pastoral.

Verb
(8) *be ecclesiastical*, - priestly etc. adj.; enter the church, take orders; ordain, consecrate, enthrone; canonize 979 *sanctify*.

986
Clergy

Noun
(1) *clergy*, the cloth, the ministry; priesthood.

(2) *cleric*, priest, deacon, deaconess; ecclesiastic, divine; clergyman, man *or* woman of the cloth; reverend, father, padre, minister, parson, rector; ordinand, seminarist.

(3) *pastor*, minister, parish priest, rector, vicar, curate, chaplain; confessor, father c.; lay preacher 537 *preacher*; missionary, evangelist, revivalist, salvationist.

(4) *ecclesiarch*, dignitary; 741 *governor*; pope, cardinal, patriarch, metropolitan, primate, archbishop; prelate, diocesan, bishop; suffragan, assistant bishop, archdeacon, deacon, dean, canon, prebendary; elder, presbyter, moderator.

(5) *monk*, monastic 895 *celibate*; hermit 883 *solitary*; dervish, fakir 945 *ascetic*; brother, regular; abbot, prior, novice, lay brother; friar; monks, religious; brotherhood, religious order.

(6) *nun*, anchoress, recluse; sister, mother; novice, postulant; lay sister; Mother Superior, abbess, prioress; sisterhood.

(7) *church officer*, elder, deacon; priest, chaplain; minister; acolyte, server; chorister 413 *choir*; sidesman *or* - woman, churchwarden; clerk, parish c.; verger, sacristan, sexton.

(8) *priest*, chief p., high p.; priestess, Vestal; prophetess, prophet 511 *oracle*; rabbi; imam, mufti; Brahman; lama; Druid, Druidess; shaman, witch doctor.

(9) *monastery*, lamasery; friary; priory, abbey; cloister, convent, nunnery; seminary.

(10) *parsonage*, presbytery, rectory, vicarage; manse; close, precincts.

Adjective
(11) *clerical*, in orders, in holy o.; ordained, consecrated; gaitered 989 *vestured*; prebendal, beneficed; lay; sacerdotal, episcopal.

(12) *monastic*, cloistered enclosed; celibate; contemplative; cowled, veiled, tonsured.

Verb
(13) *take orders*, be ordained; take vows, enter a monastery *or* a nunnery.

987
Laity

Noun
(1) *laity*, lay people, flock, parish; diocesans, parishioners; congregation 976 *church member*.

Adjective
(2) *laical*, parochial; lay, secular; temporal, laicized, secularized, deconsecrated.

Verb
(3) *laicize*, secularize, deconsecrate.

988
Ritual

Noun
(1) *ritual,* liturgy; symbolism 519 *metaphor*; ceremonial, ceremony 875 *formality.*

(2) *ritualism,* ceremonialism, ceremony, formalism.

(3) *rite,* mode of worship 981 *cult*; institution, observance 610 *practice*; ceremony, solemnity, sacrament, mystery 876 *celebration*; rites, mysteries; initiatory rite, rite of passage; circumcision, initiation, baptism.

(4) *Christian rite,* sacrament, baptism, christening; confirmation, First Communion; Holy Communion, Eucharist; absolution 960 *acquittal*; Holy Matrimony 894 *marriage*; Holy Orders 985 *the church*; extreme unction, last rites, requiem mass; liturgy, order of service; ordination, consecration; exorcism, excommunication; canonization, beatification dedication.

(5) *church service,* office, duty 981 *act of worship*; liturgy, celebration; morning prayer, matins; evening prayer, evensong, benediction; vigil, midnight mass.

(6) *ritualist,* ceremonialist, sabbatarian, formalist; celebrant, minister 986 *priest*: server, acolyte. psalm-book, book of psalms 981 *hymn.*

(7) *holy day,* feast, feast day, festival 837 *festivity*; fast day, day of observance, day of obligation; sabbath, day of rest; saint's day 141 *anniversary.*

Adjective
(8) *ritual,* procedural; formal, solemn, ceremonial, liturgical; processional, recessional; symbolic 551 *representing*; sacramental, eucharistic; baptismal; sacrificial, paschal; festal; fasting, lenten; prescribed, ordained; unleavened; kosher; consecrated, blessed.

(9) *ritualistic,* ceremonious; sabbatarian.

Verb
(10) *perform ritual,* perform the rites, celebrate, officiate; take the service 981 *offer worship*; baptize, christen, confirm, ordain, lay on hands; minister, give communion; sacrifice, offer s., offer prayers, bless, give benediction; anathematize, ban, excommunicate, unfrock; dedicate, consecrate, purify, burn incense; anoint, confess, absolve, shrive; take communion, bow, kneel, genuflect, sign oneself, cross o.; fast, do penance.

(11) *ritualize,* institute a rite; observe, keep, keep holy.

Adverb
(12) *ritually,* ceremonially; symbolically, liturgically.

989
Canonicals

Noun
(1) *canonicals,* clerical dress, the cloth; cassock, robe, cowl; bands, clerical collar, dog c.; apron, gaiters, shovel hat; biretta, skullcap prayer-cap.

(2) *vestments,* canonical robes; cassock, surplice, cope, chasuble; mitre 743 *regalia*; crosier, crook, staff 743 *badge of rank*; pectoral 222 *cross.*

Adjective
(3) *vestmental,* canonical, pontifical.

(4) *vestured,* robed; cowled, hooded, veiled 986 *monastic.*

990
Temple

Noun

(1) *temple,* pantheon; shrine, joss house 982 *idolatry*; house of God, tabernacle, mosque; oratory; sacred edifice, pagoda, ziggurat.

(2) *holy place,* holy ground; sanctuary, Sanctum, Holy of Holies, oracle; sacred tomb, sepulchre; graveyard 364 *cemetery*; place of pilgrimage, Jerusalem, Mecca.

(3) *church,* parish c., daughter c., chapel of ease; cathedral, minster, basilica, abbey; kirk, chapel, tabernacle, temple, conventicle, meeting house; oratory, chantry; synagogue, mosque.

(4) *church interior,* nave, aisle, apse, transept; font, baptistry; chancel, choir, sanctuary; altar, high a.; rood screen, rood loft, gallery, organ loft; stall, choirstall, pew; pulpit, lectern; chapel, Lady c.; confessional; calvary, Easter sepulchre; sacristy, vestry; crypt, vault; rood, cross, crucifix.

(5) *church exterior,* tower, steeple, spire, belfry, campanile; buttress, flying b.; porch, lychgate; churchyard, close.

Adjective

(6) *churchlike,* basilican.

VIKING

Published by the Penguin Group
Penguin Books Ltd, 27 Wrights Lane, London W8 5TZ, England
Penguin Books USA Inc., 375 Hudson Street, New York, New York 10014, USA
Penguin Books Australia Ltd, Ringwood, Victoria, Australia
Penguin Books Canada Ltd, 10 Alcorn Avenue, Toronto, Ontario, Canada M4V 3B2
Penguin Books (NZ) Ltd, 182–190 Wairau Road, Auckland 10, New Zealand

Penguin Books Ltd, Registered Offices: Harmondsworth, Middlesex, England

First published by the Longman Group UK Limited 1986
First published by Viking 1995
10 9 8 7 6 5 4 3 2 1

Printed in Great Britain by Clays Ltd, St Ives plc

A CIP catalogue record for this book is available from the British Library

ISBN 0–670–86239–8